Collins
STREET ATLAS
LONDON

Contents

Key to map pages 2-3

Key to map symbols 4-5

Central London maps 6-37

Main London maps 38-207

Theatres and cinemas map 208

Shopping map 209

Index to street names, place names,
and places of interest 210-376

Published by Collins
An imprint of HarperCollins Publishers
77-85 Fulham Palace Road, Hammersmith, London W6 8JB

www.collinsworld.com

Copyright © HarperCollins Publishers Ltd 2008

Collins® is a registered trademark of HarperCollins Publishers
Limited

Mapping generated from Collins Bartholomew digital databases

London Underground Map by permission of Transport Trading
Limited
Registered User No. 07/4668

The grid on this map is the National Grid taken from the
Ordnance Survey map with the permission of the Controller of
Her Majesty's Stationery Office.

The contents of this publication are believed correct at the time of
printing. Nevertheless, the publisher can accept no responsibility
for errors or omissions, changes in the detail given, or for any
expense or loss thereby caused.

The representation of a road, track or footpath is no evidence of a
right of way.

Printed in China by Leo Paper Products

Paperback   ISBN 978 0 00 725760 7   VM12348
Spiral   ISBN 978 0 00 725761 4   VM12349

Imp 001   NDL

e-mail: roadcheck@harpercollins.co.uk

Key to map pages

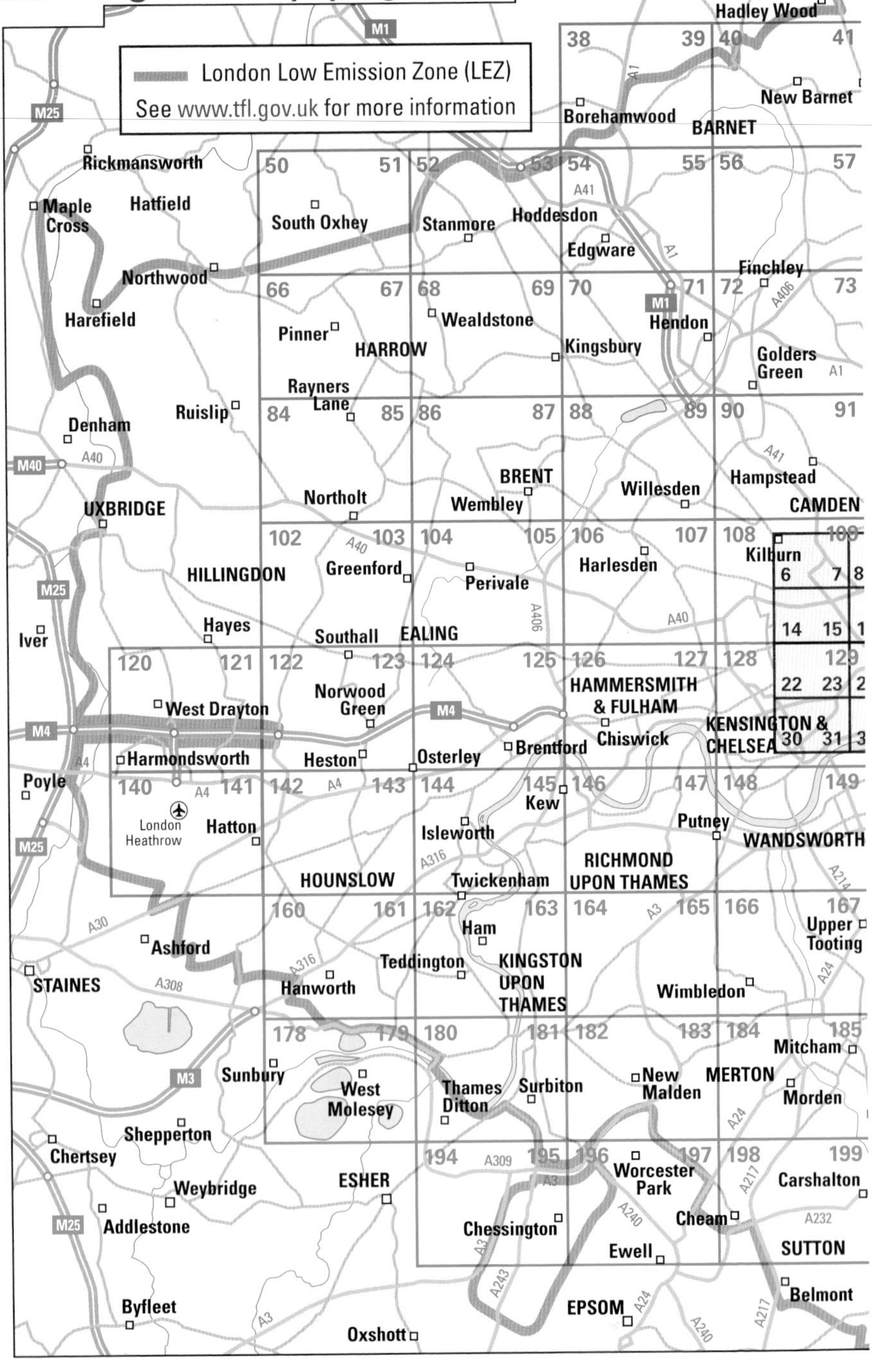

London Low Emission Zone (LEZ)
See www.tfl.gov.uk for more information

M1

Hadley Wood

38 39 40 41

New Barnet

Borehamwood BARNET

M25

Rickmansworth 50 51 52 53 54 55 56 57

Maple Cross

Hatfield

South Oxhey

Stanmore Hoddesdon

A41

Edgware

A1

Finchley

Northwood 66 67 68 69 70 71 72 73

A406

Harefield

Pinner Wealdstone

HARROW Kingsbury Hendon

M1

Golders Green

A1

Denham

Rayners Lane 84 85 86 87 88 89 90 91

Ruislip

Hampstead

A41

A40

M40

UXBRIDGE

BRENT

Willesden CAMDEN

Northolt Wembley

102 103 104 105 106 107 108 109

Kilburn

6 7 8

HILLINGDON Greenford

Perivale

Harlesden

A40

14 15 1

Hayes

Southall EALING

A406

120 121 122 123 124 125 126 127 128 129

Iver

Norwood Green

22 23 2

HAMMERSMITH & FULHAM

West Drayton

M4

Chiswick

KENSINGTON & CHELSEA

30 31 3

A4

Harmondsworth Heston Osterley Brentford

Poyle 140 141 142 143 144 145 146 147 148 149

Kew

London Heathrow

Hatton

Putney

WANDSWORTH

A214

M25

Isleworth

A316

RICHMOND UPON THAMES

Ashford

HOUNSLOW Twickenham

A30

160 161 162 163 164 165 166 167

Ham

A3

Upper Tooting

STAINES

A316

Hanworth

Teddington KINGSTON UPON THAMES

Wimbledon

A24

A308

178 179 180 181 182 183 184 185

Mitcham

M3

Sunbury

West Molesey

Thames Ditton Surbiton

New Malden

MERTON

Morden

Shepperton

194 A309 195 196 197 198 199

Chertsey

Weybridge ESHER

A3

Worcester Park

Carshalton

A232

A24

Cheam SUTTON

M25

Addlestone

Chessington

A240

Ewell

A217

Belmont

Byfleet

A3

EPSOM

A24

A243

A240

Oxshott

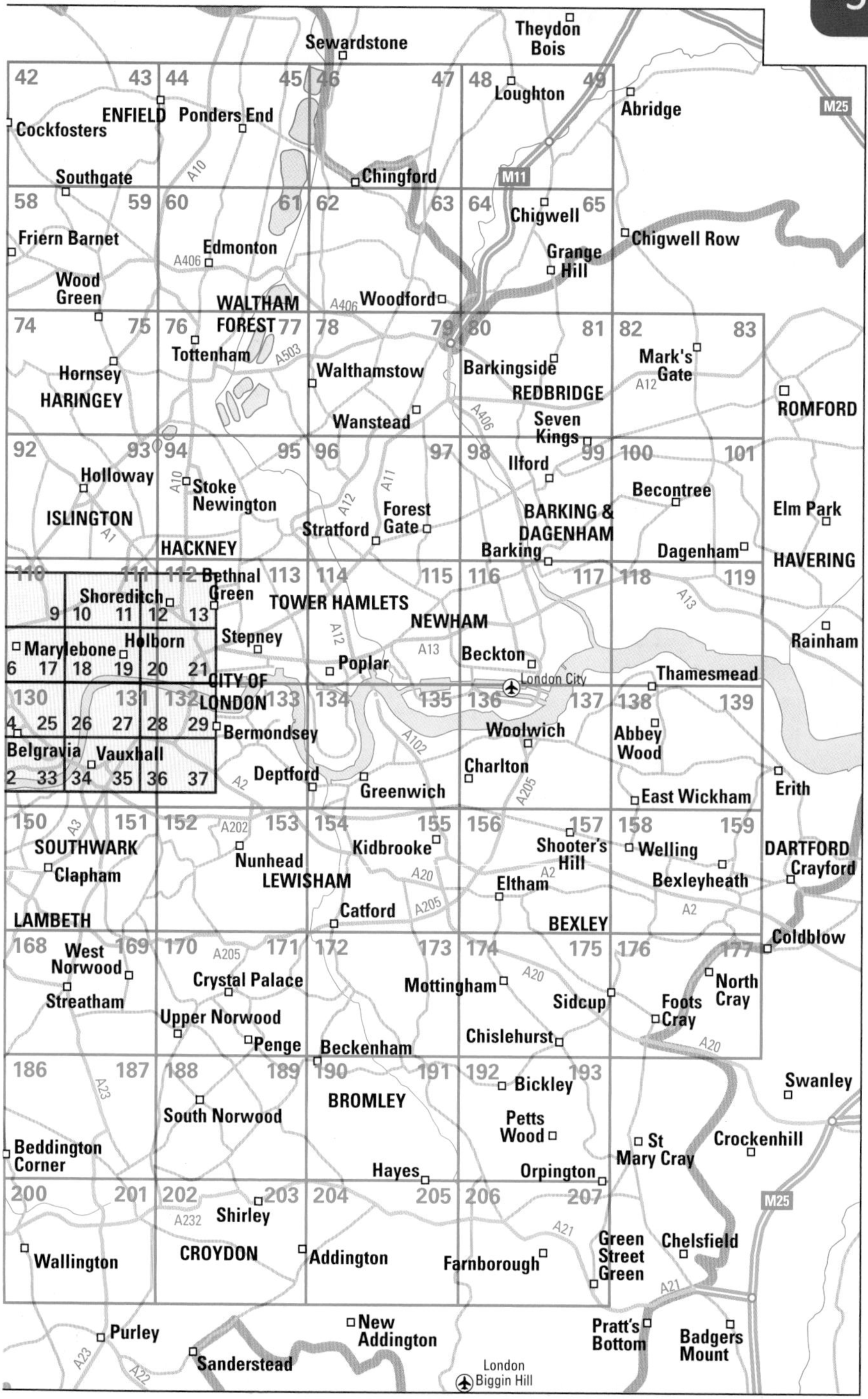

Theydon Bois

Sewardstone

| 42 | 43 | 44 | 45 | 46 | 47 | 48 | 49 |

ENFIELD Ponders End

Cockfosters

Loughton

Abridge

M25

Southgate

Chingford

A10

M11

| 58 | 59 | 60 | 61 | 62 | 63 | 64 | 65 |

Chigwell

Friern Barnet

Edmonton

Grange Hill

Chigwell Row

Wood Green

A406

Woodford

WALTHAM FOREST

A406

| 74 | 75 | 76 | 77 | 78 | 79 | 80 | 81 | 82 | 83 |

Tottenham

A503

Mark's Gate

Hornsey

Walthamstow

Barkingside

A12

HARINGEY

REDBRIDGE

ROMFORD

Wanstead

Seven Kings

A406

| 92 | 93 | 94 | 95 | 96 | 97 | 98 | 99 | 100 | 101 |

Holloway

Stoke Newington

Ilford

Becontree

A10

A11

Elm Park

ISLINGTON

A12

Forest Gate

BARKING & DAGENHAM

A1

Stratford

HACKNEY

Barking

Dagenham

HAVERING

| 118 | 111 | 112 | 113 | 114 | 115 | 116 | 117 | 118 | 119 |

Bethnal Green

Shoreditch

| 9 | 10 | 11 | 12 | 13 |

TOWER HAMLETS

A13

Rainham

Marylebone

Holborn

Stepney

NEWHAM

| 6 | 17 | 18 | 19 | 20 | 21 |

A12

Poplar

A13

Beckton

CITY OF LONDON

London City

Thamesmead

| 130 | 131 | 132 | 133 | 134 | 135 | 136 | 137 | 138 | 139 |

Bermondsey

Woolwich

Abbey Wood

| 4 | 25 | 26 | 27 | 28 | 29 |

A102

Belgravia

Vauxhall

Deptford

Charlton

A205

East Wickham

Erith

| 2 | 33 | 34 | 35 | 36 | 37 |

A2

Greenwich

| 150 | 151 | 152 | 153 | 154 | 155 | 156 | 157 | 158 | 159 |

A3

A202

SOUTHWARK

Nunhead

Kidbrooke

Shooter's Hill

Welling

DARTFORD

Clapham

LEWISHAM

A20

Eltham

A2

Bexleyheath

Crayford

LAMBETH

Catford

A205

BEXLEY

A2

| 168 | 169 | 170 | 171 | 172 | 173 | 174 | 175 | 176 | 177 |

Coldblow

West Norwood

A205

Mottingham

A20

North Cray

Streatham

Crystal Palace

Sidcup

Foots Cray

Upper Norwood

Chislehurst

A20

Penge

Beckenham

| 186 | 187 | 188 | 189 | 190 | 191 | 192 | 193 |

Swanley

A23

Bickley

BROMLEY

South Norwood

Petts Wood

Crockenhill

Beddington Corner

St Mary Cray

Hayes

Orpington

| 200 | 201 | 202 | 203 | 204 | 205 | 206 | 207 |

M25

A232

Shirley

Wallington

CROYDON

Addington

Farnborough

A21

Green Street Green

Chelsfield

A23

A22

Purley

New Addington

Pratt's Bottom

Badgers Mount

Sanderstead

London Biggin Hill

A21

4 Key to central map symbols

Dual **A4**	Primary route
Dual **A40**	'A' road
B504	'B' road
43	Address number ('A' & 'B' roads only)
	Other road
→	One way street
	Street market
	Pedestrian street
•▮	Access restriction
••••••••••••	Long distance footpath
═ ═ ═ ─ ─ ─	Track/Footpath
	Extent of London congestion charging zone See www.cclondon.com for more information
CITY	Borough boundary
NW1	Postal district boundary
⇌	Main national rail station
⇥	Other national rail station
⊖	London Overground station
⊖	London Underground station
⊖	Docklands Light Railway station
- ⊖ -	Pedestrian ferry with landing stage
●	Bus/Coach station
P	Car park
i	Information centre for visitors
i	Other information centre
�	Theatre
	Major hotel
A	Grid reference

▲	Youth hostel
m	Historic site
Pol TPol	Police station/ Transport Police station
PO PO	Post office/Postal delivery office
Lib	Library
🎥	Cinema
USA ⚑	Embassy
+	Church
☾	Mosque
✡	Synagogue
Mormon ■	Other place of worship
●	Community centre/Hall
■ Amb Sta	Ambulance station
▲	Monument/Statue
🚻	Public toilet
	Leisure & tourism
	Shopping
	Market
	Administration & law
	Health & welfare
	Education
	Industry & commerce
	Major office
	Other landmark building/ Tower block
	Public open space
	Woodland
	Park/Garden/Sports ground
	Cemetery
6	Page continuation number

SCALE
1: 10,000 6.3 inches (16 cm) to 1 mile/10 cm to 1 km

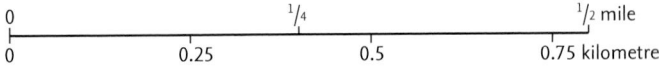

0   1/4   1/2 mile

0   0.25   0.5   0.75 kilometre

The reference grid on this atlas coincides with the Ordnance Survey National Grid system. The grid interval is 250 metres.

Key to main map symbols

M4	Motorway			Leisure & tourism
Dual A4	Primary route			Shopping
Dual A40	'A' road			Market
B504	'B' road			Administration & law
→	Other road/One way street			Health & welfare
	Toll			Education
	Street market			Industry & commerce
	Restricted access road			Major office
	Pedestrian street			Other landmark building/ Tower block
	Cycle path			Cemetery
===·----	Track/Footpath			Golf course
THAMES PATH	Long distance footpath			Public open space/Allotments
LC	Level crossing			Park/Garden/Sports ground
V P	Vehicle/Pedestrian ferry			Wood/Forest
	County/Borough boundary		USA	Embassy
	Postal district boundary		Pol	Police station
	Main national rail station		Fire Sta	Fire station
	Other national rail station		PO/Lib	Post Office/Library
	London Overground station		▲	Youth hostel
	London Underground station		i	Information centre for visitors
	Docklands Light Railway station		i	Other information centre
	Tramlink station		m	Historic site
	Pedestrian ferry landing stage		P	Car park
	Bus/Coach station			Toilets
			Ⓗ	Heliport
			+	Church
			☾	Mosque
			✡	Synagogue

Extent of London congestion charging zone
For more information see website www.cclondon.com

A Grid reference

106 Page continuation number

SCALE
1:20,000 3.2 inches (8 cm) to 1 mile/5 cm to 1 km

35 OS National Grid kilometre square

0   ¼   ½ mile

0   0.25   0.5   0.75   1 kilometre

The reference grid on this atlas coincides with the Ordnance Survey
National Grid system. The grid interval is 500 metres.

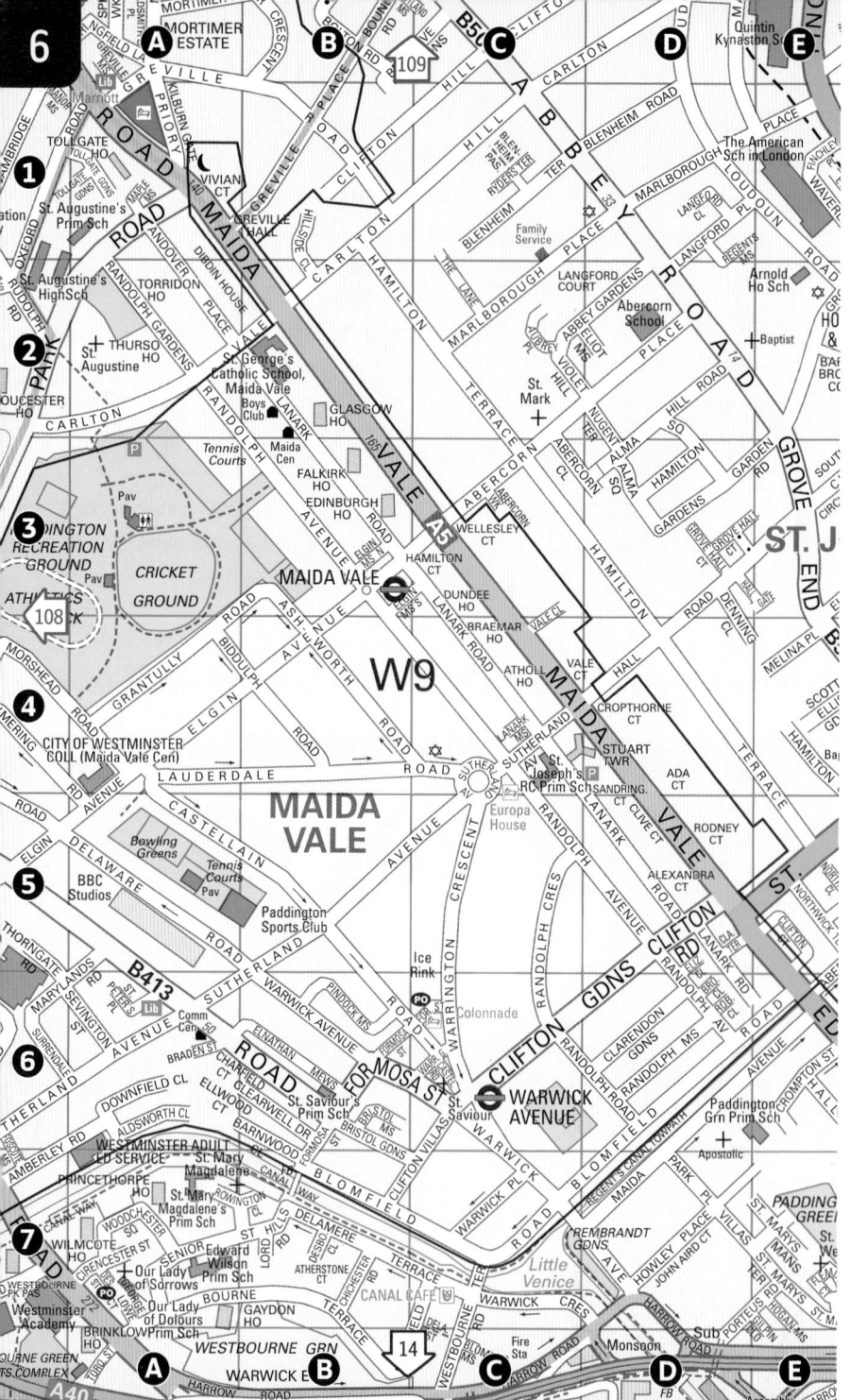

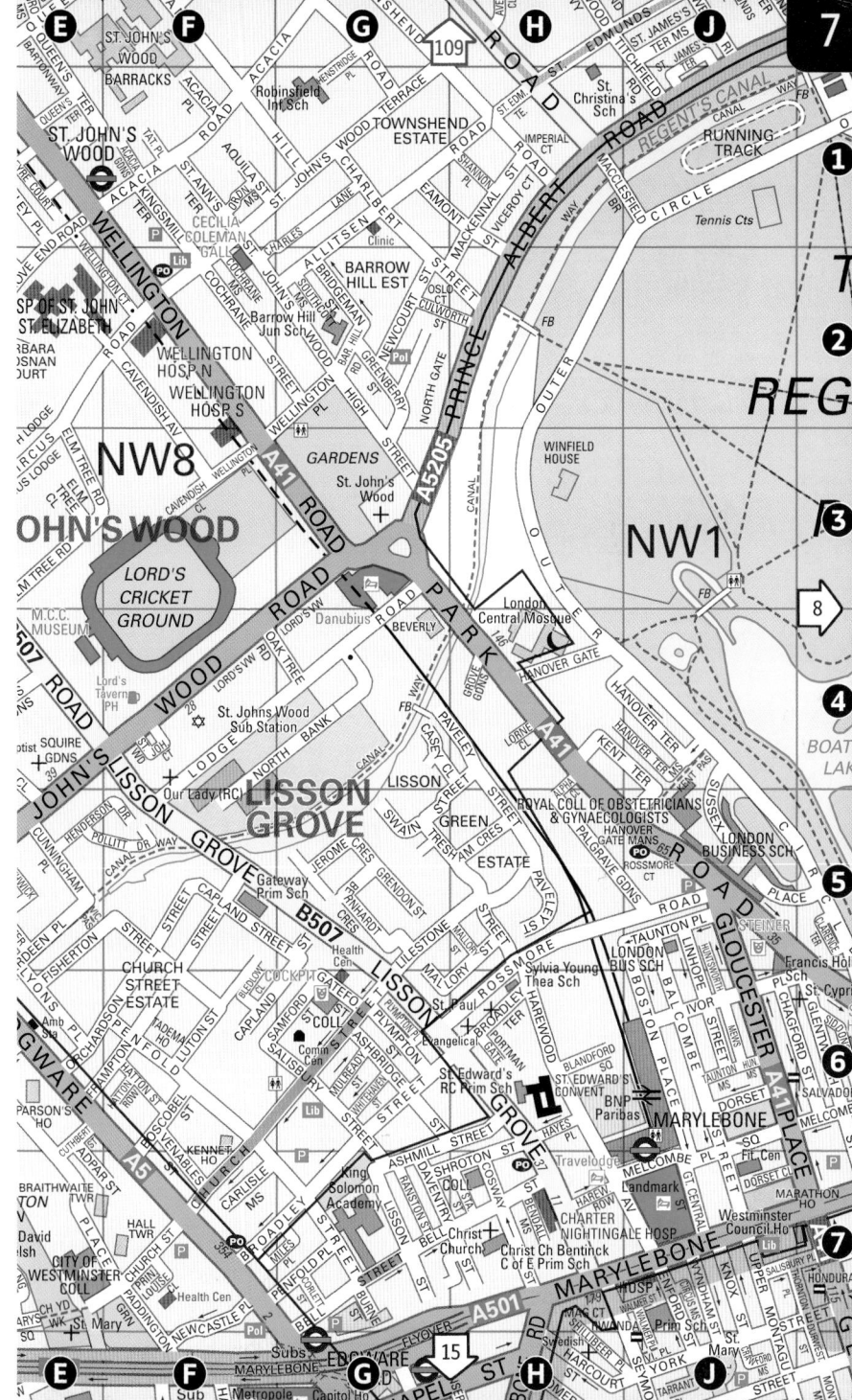

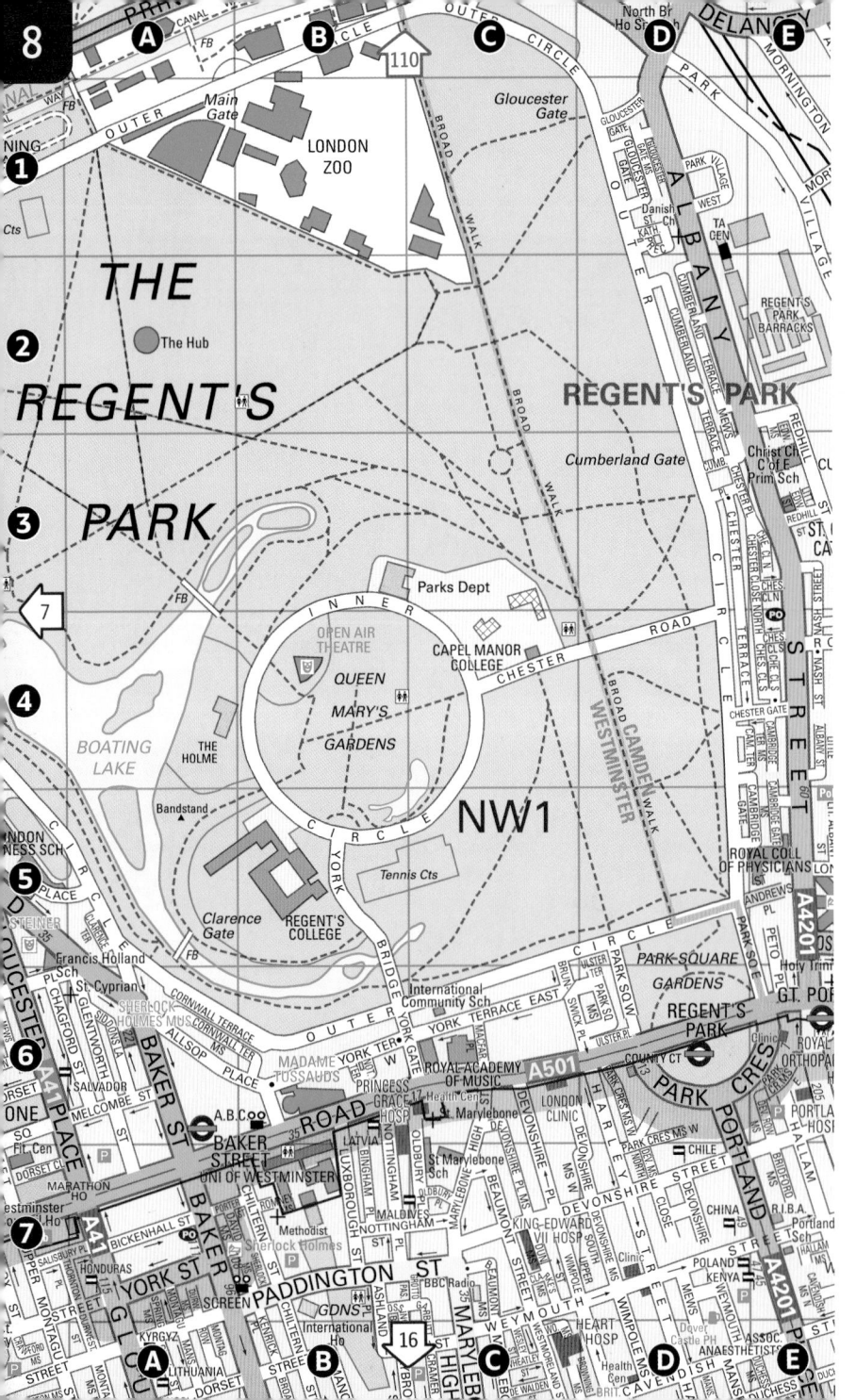

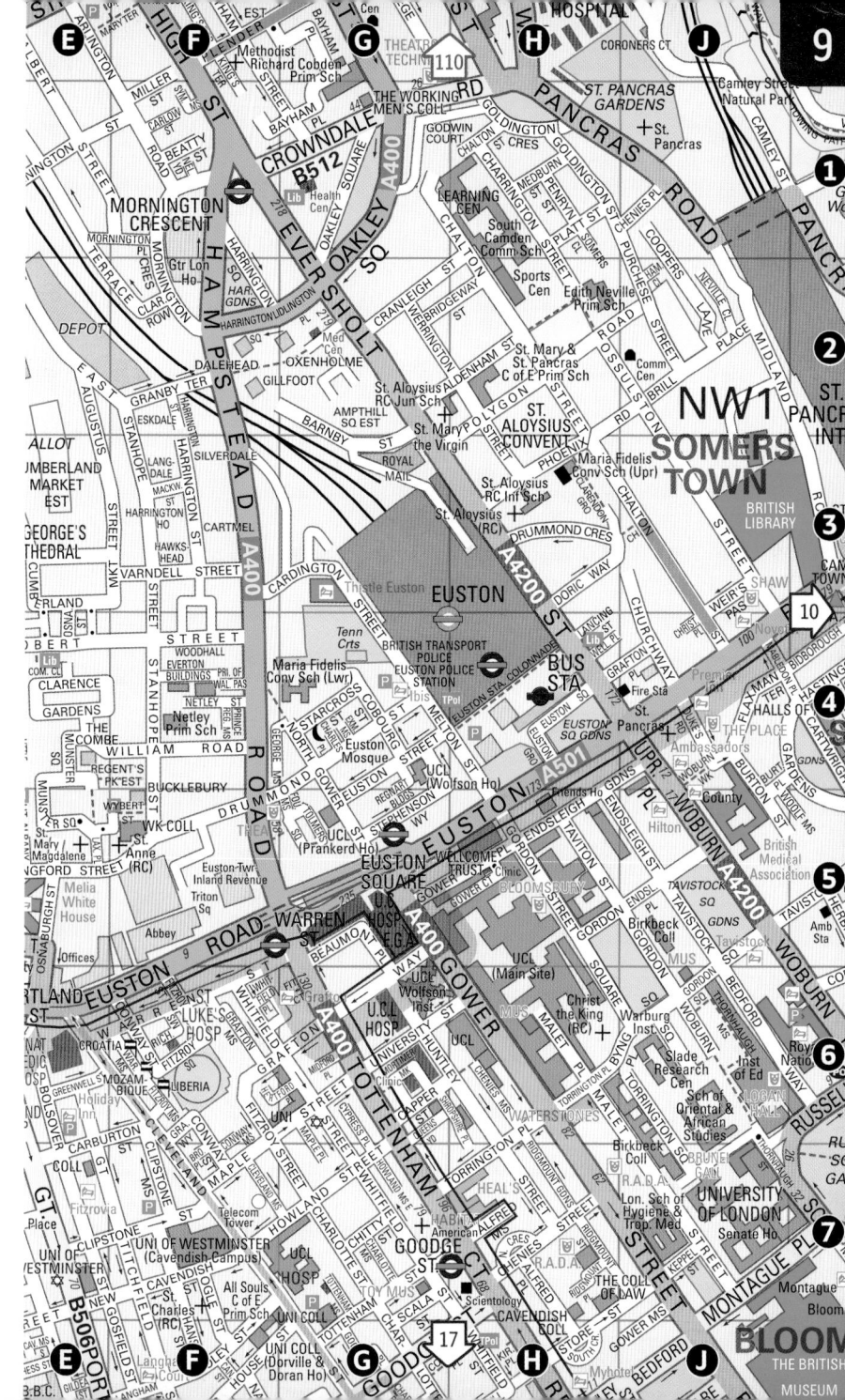

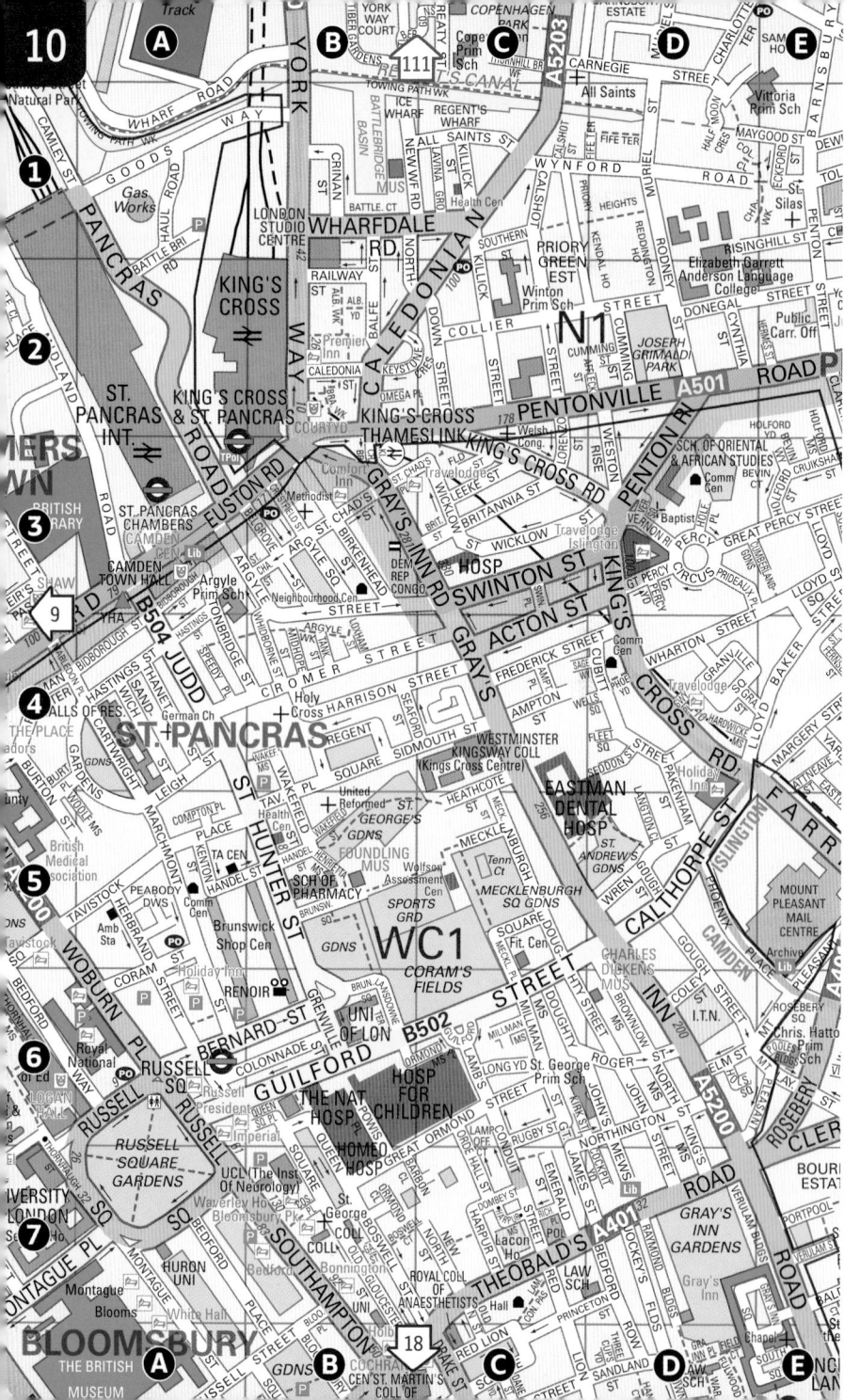

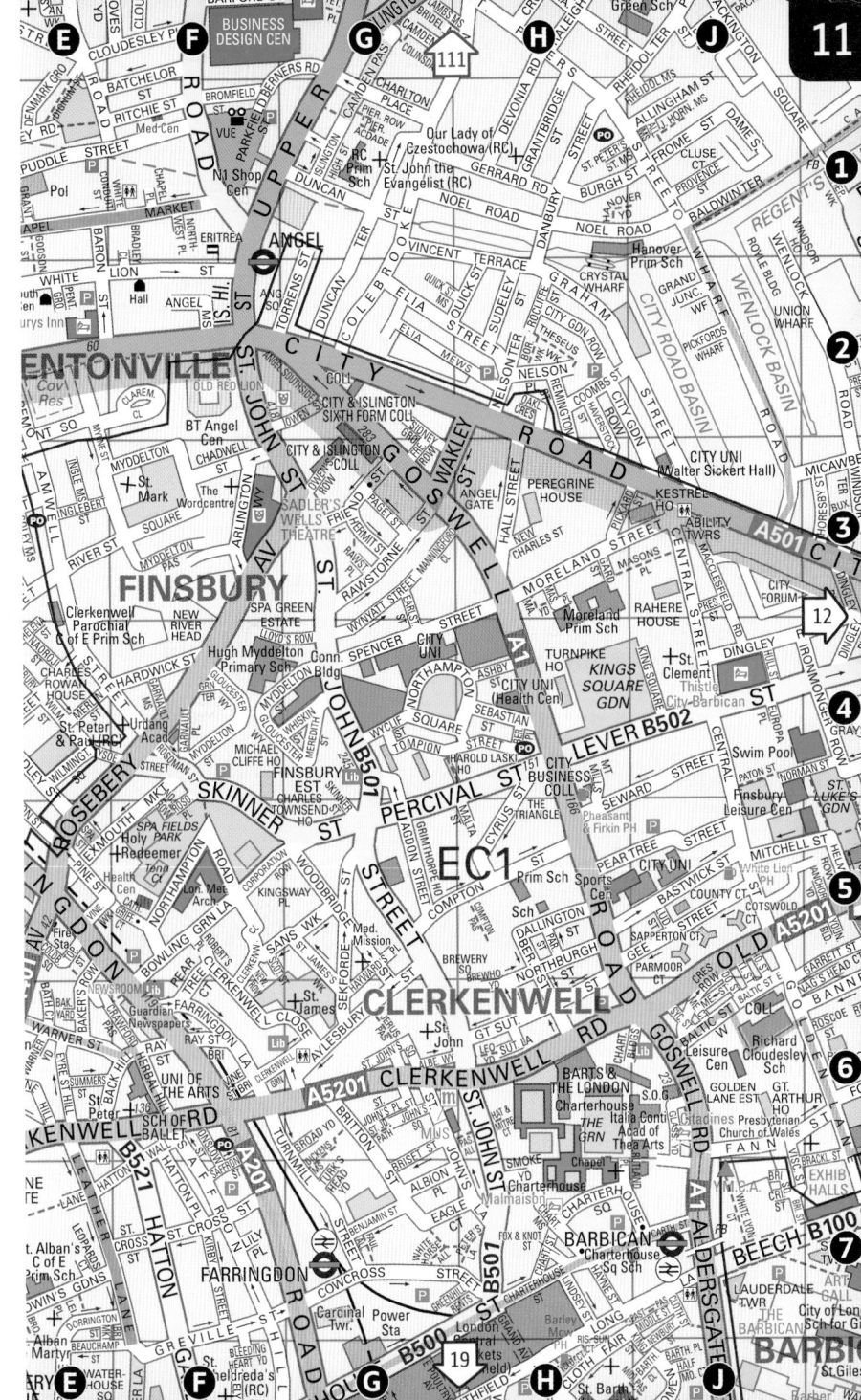

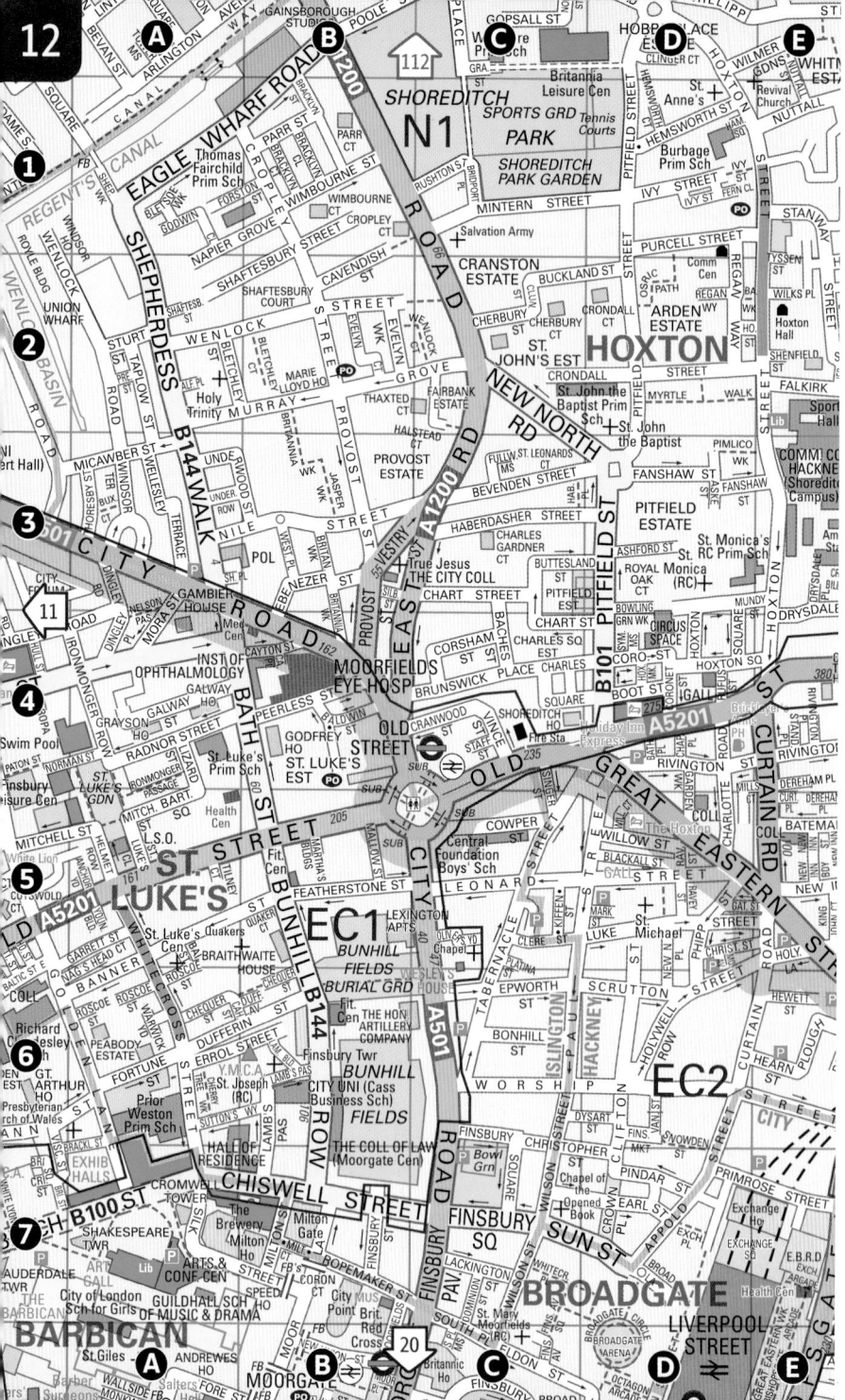

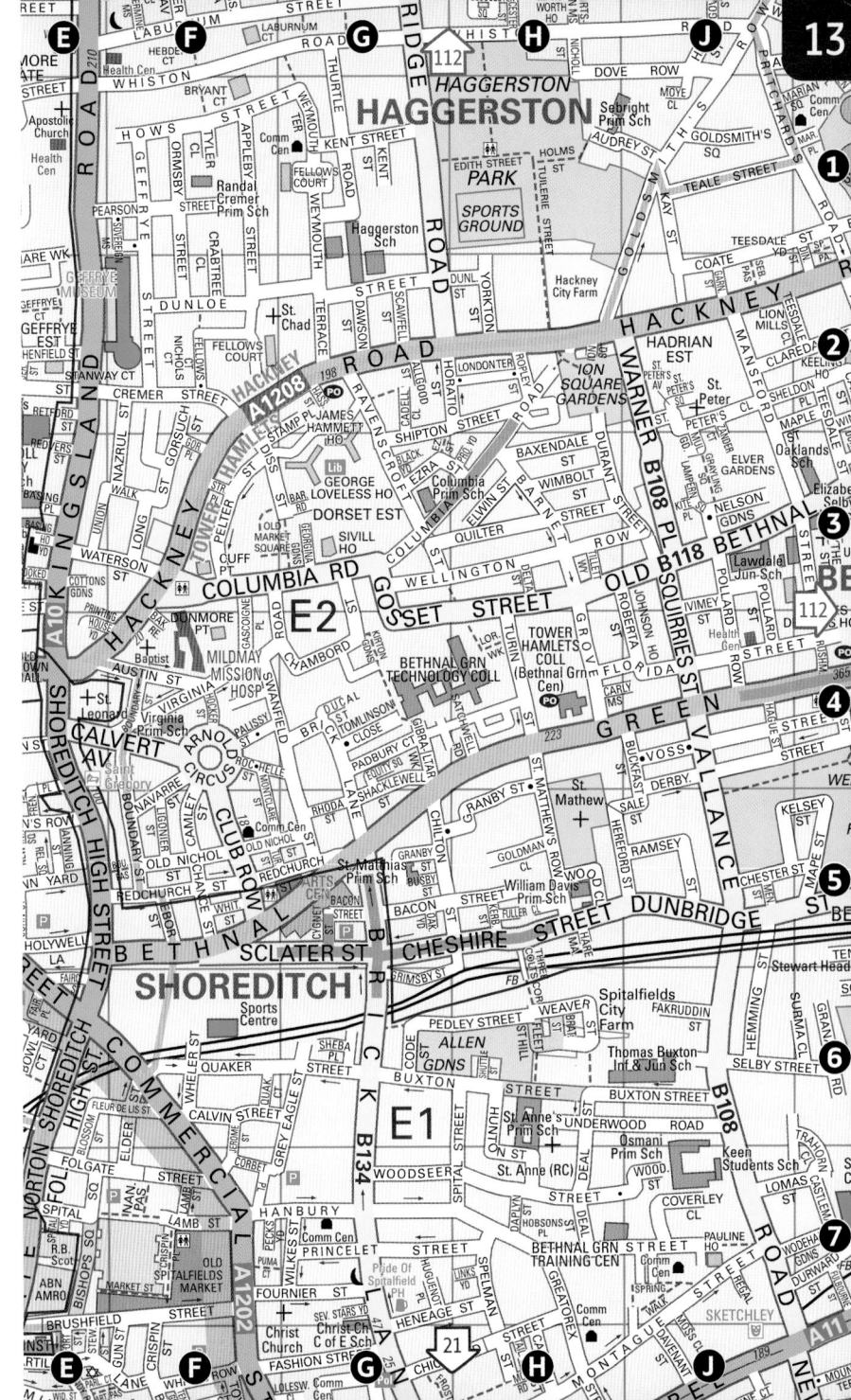

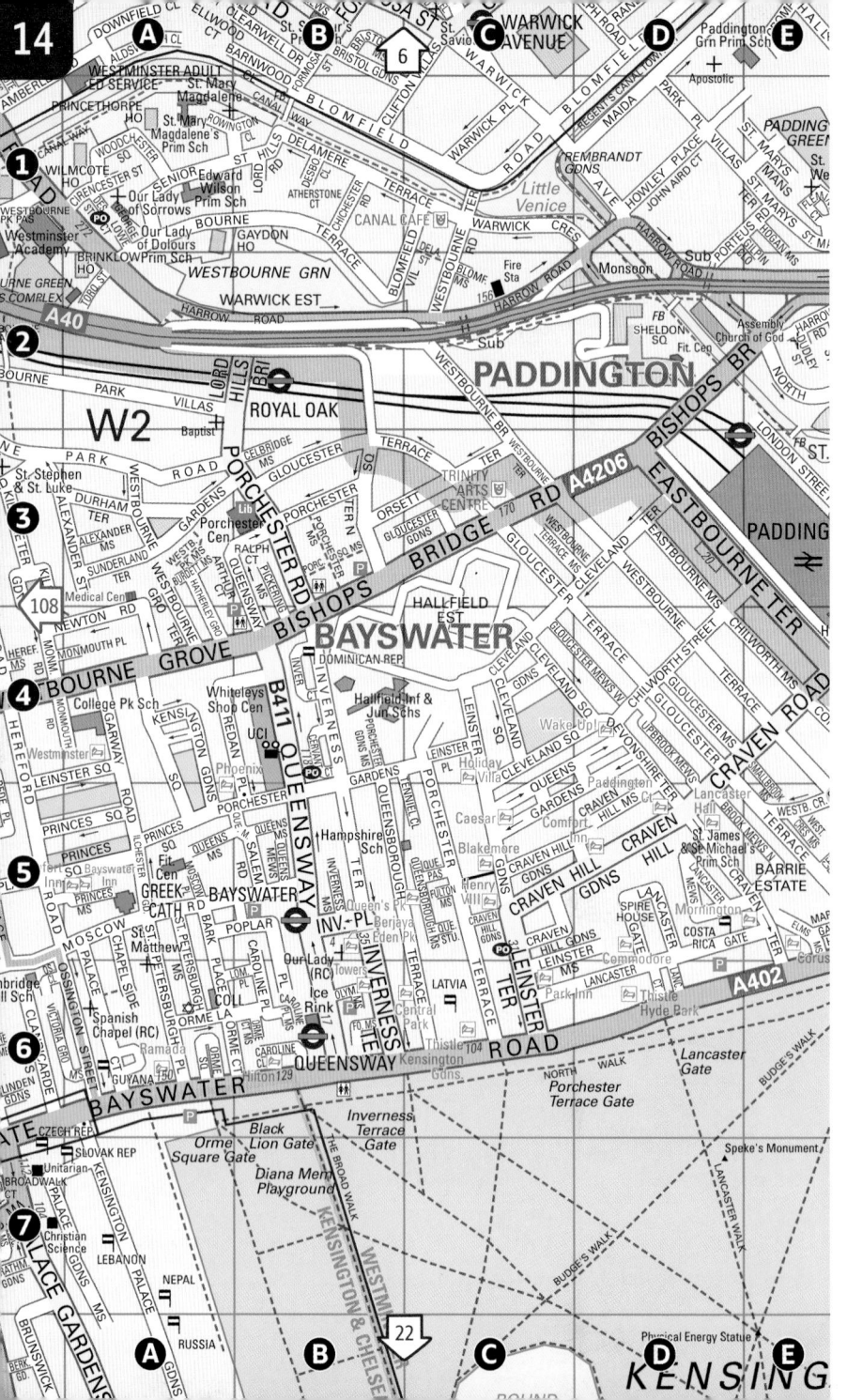

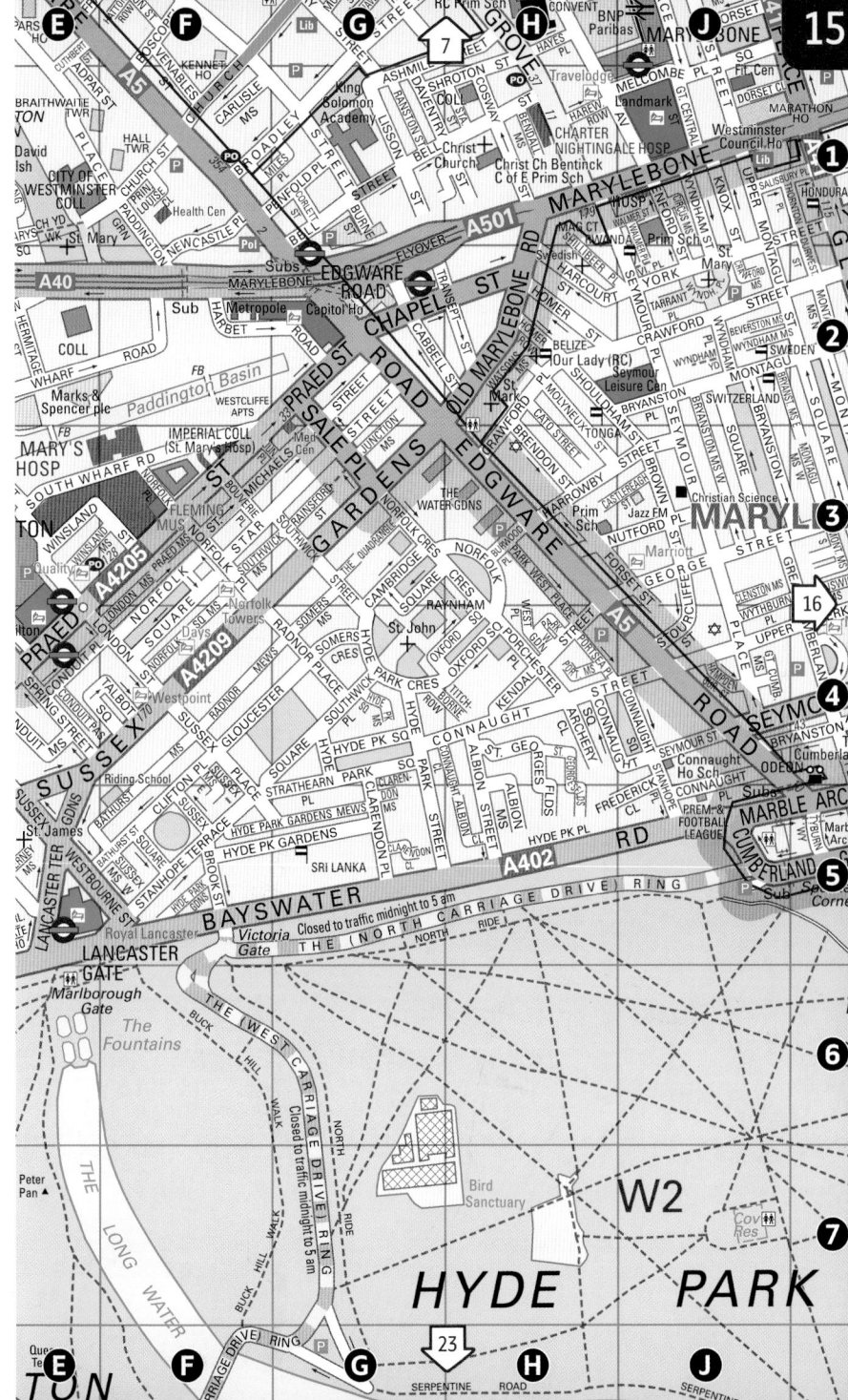

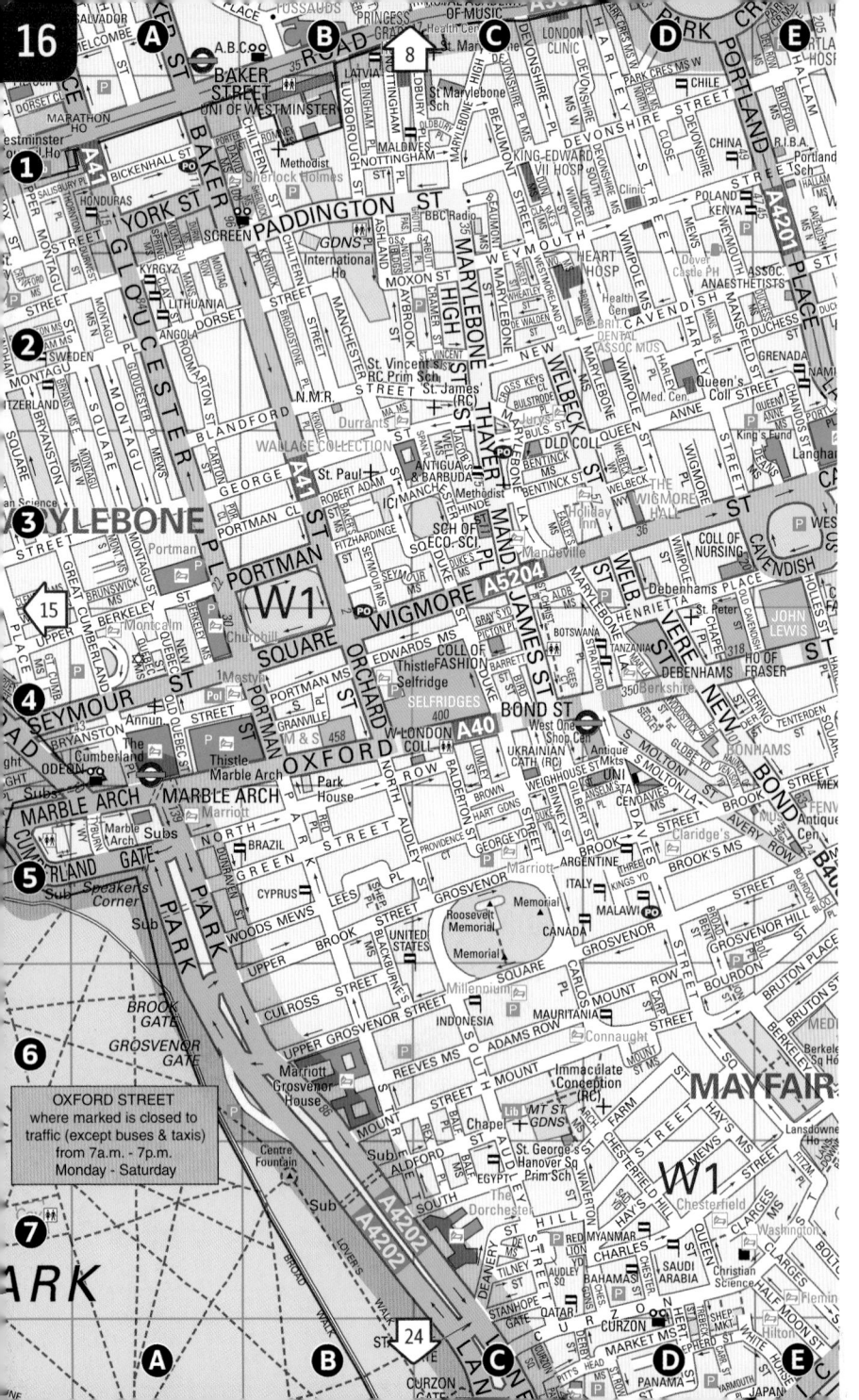

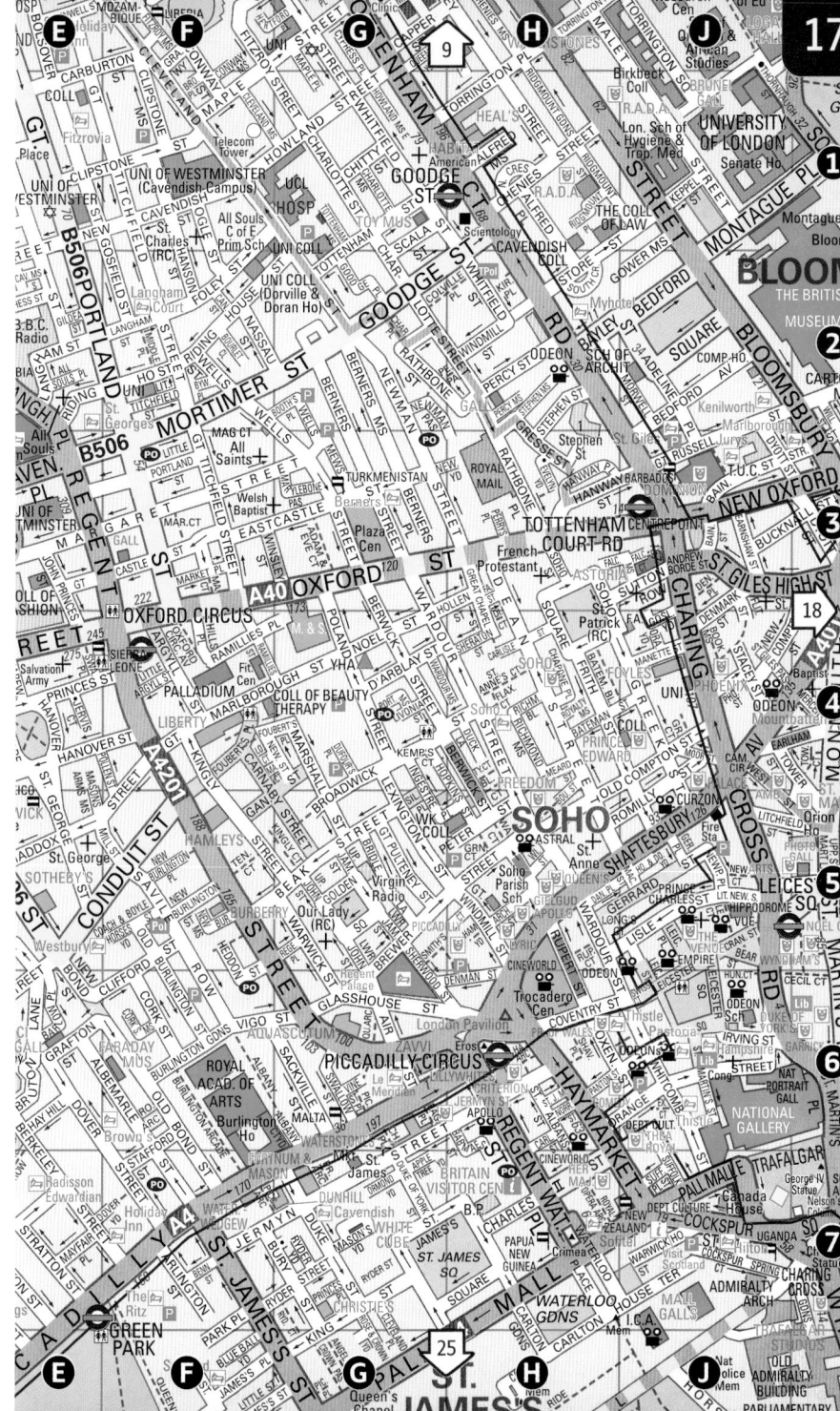

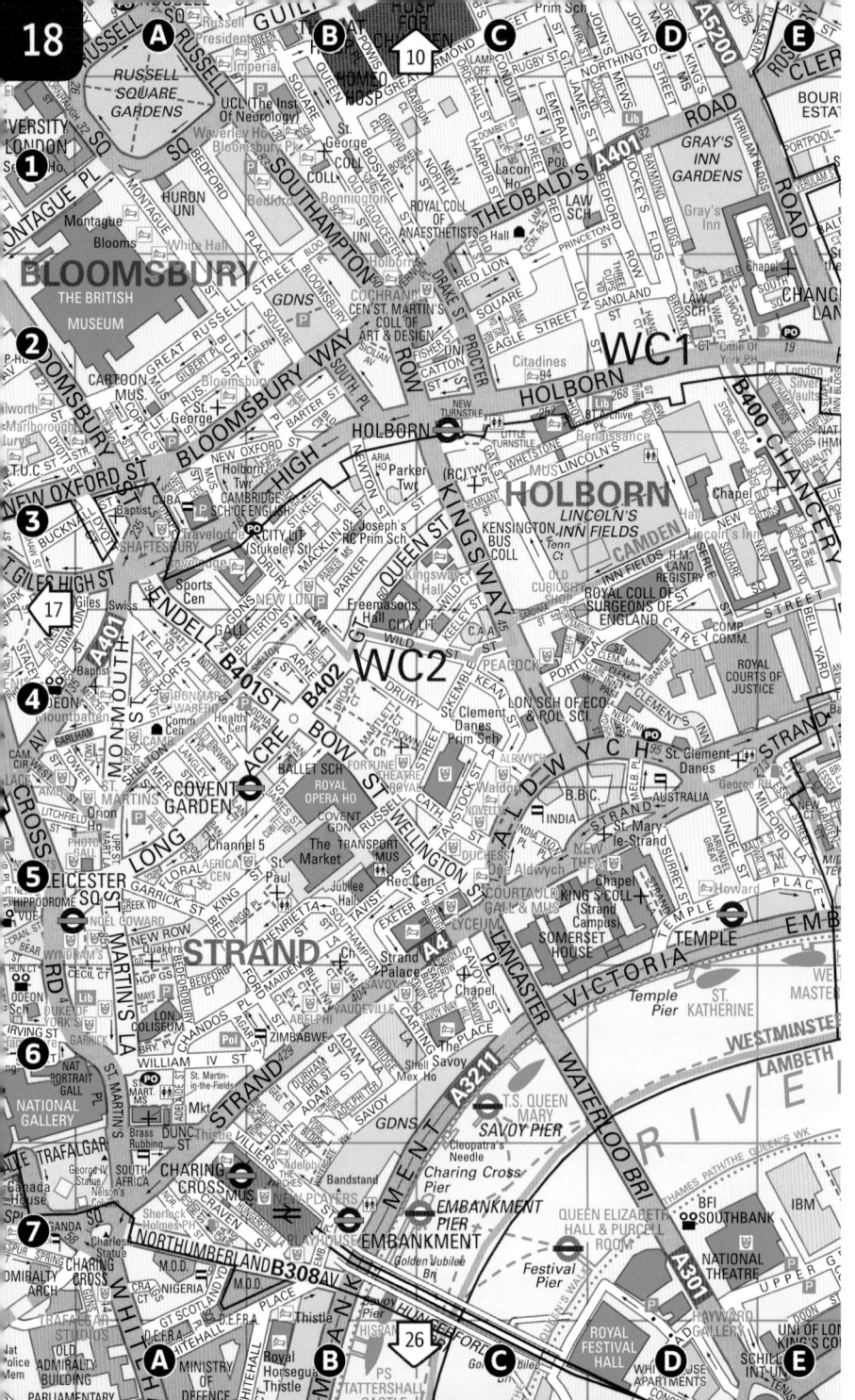

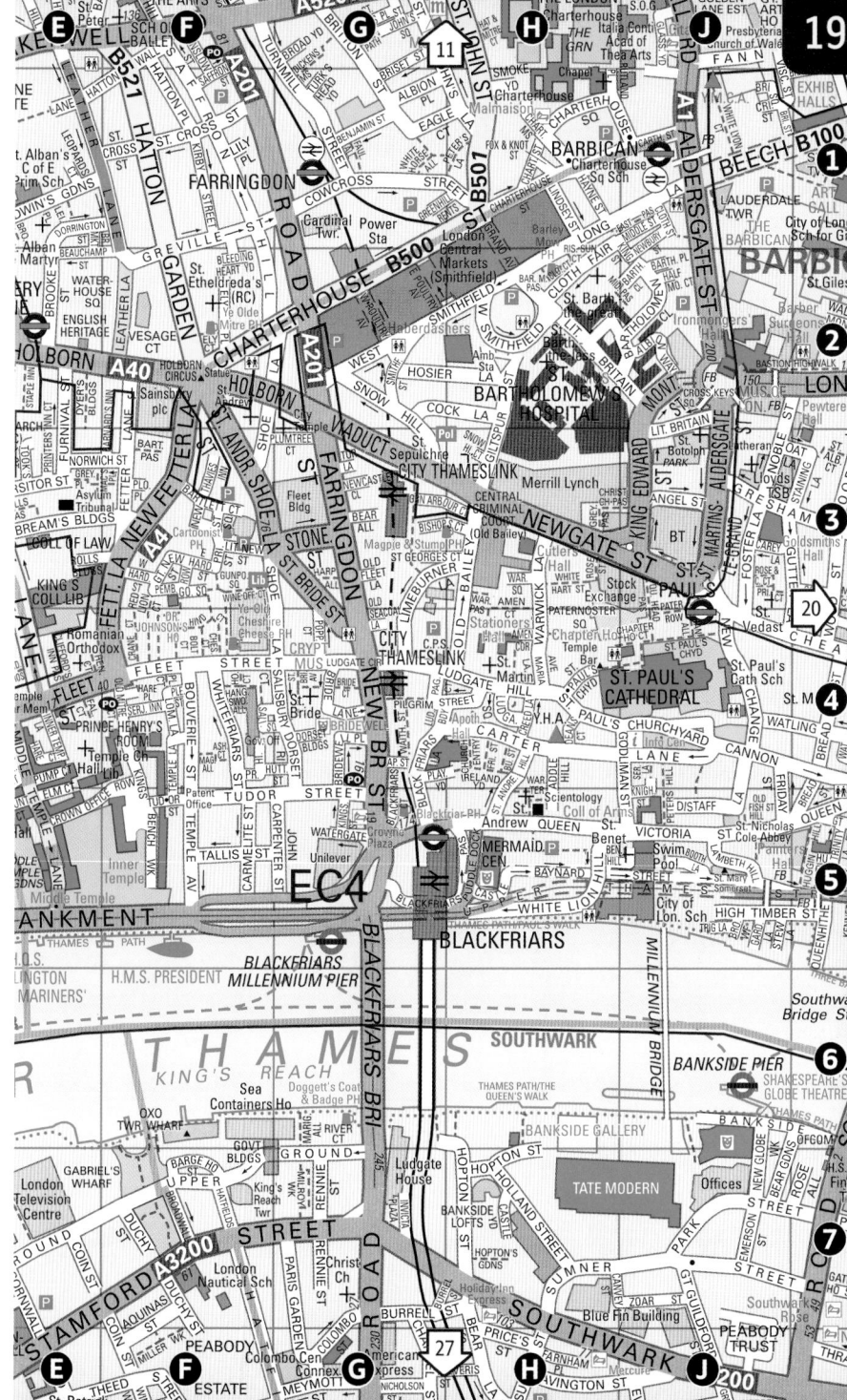

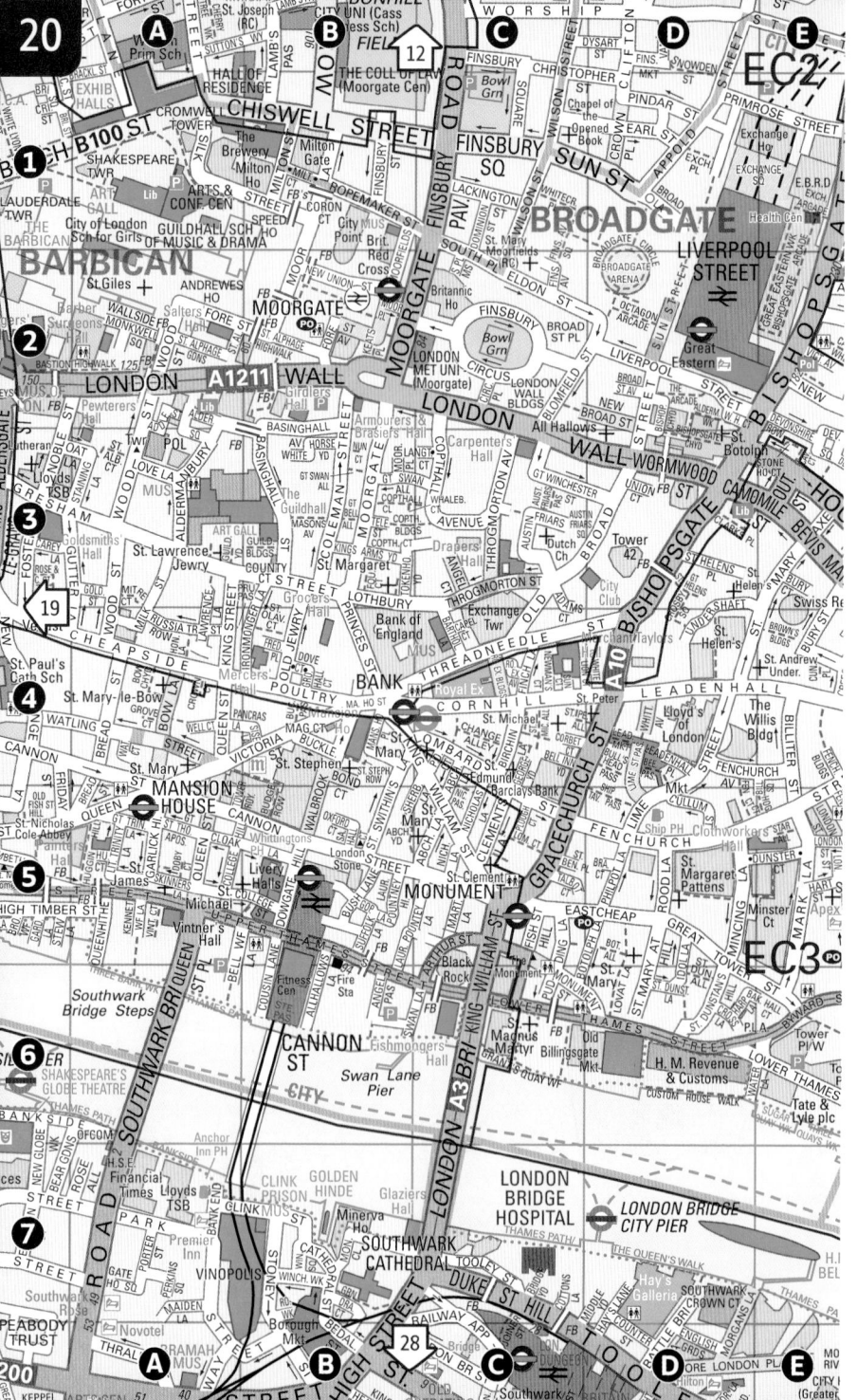

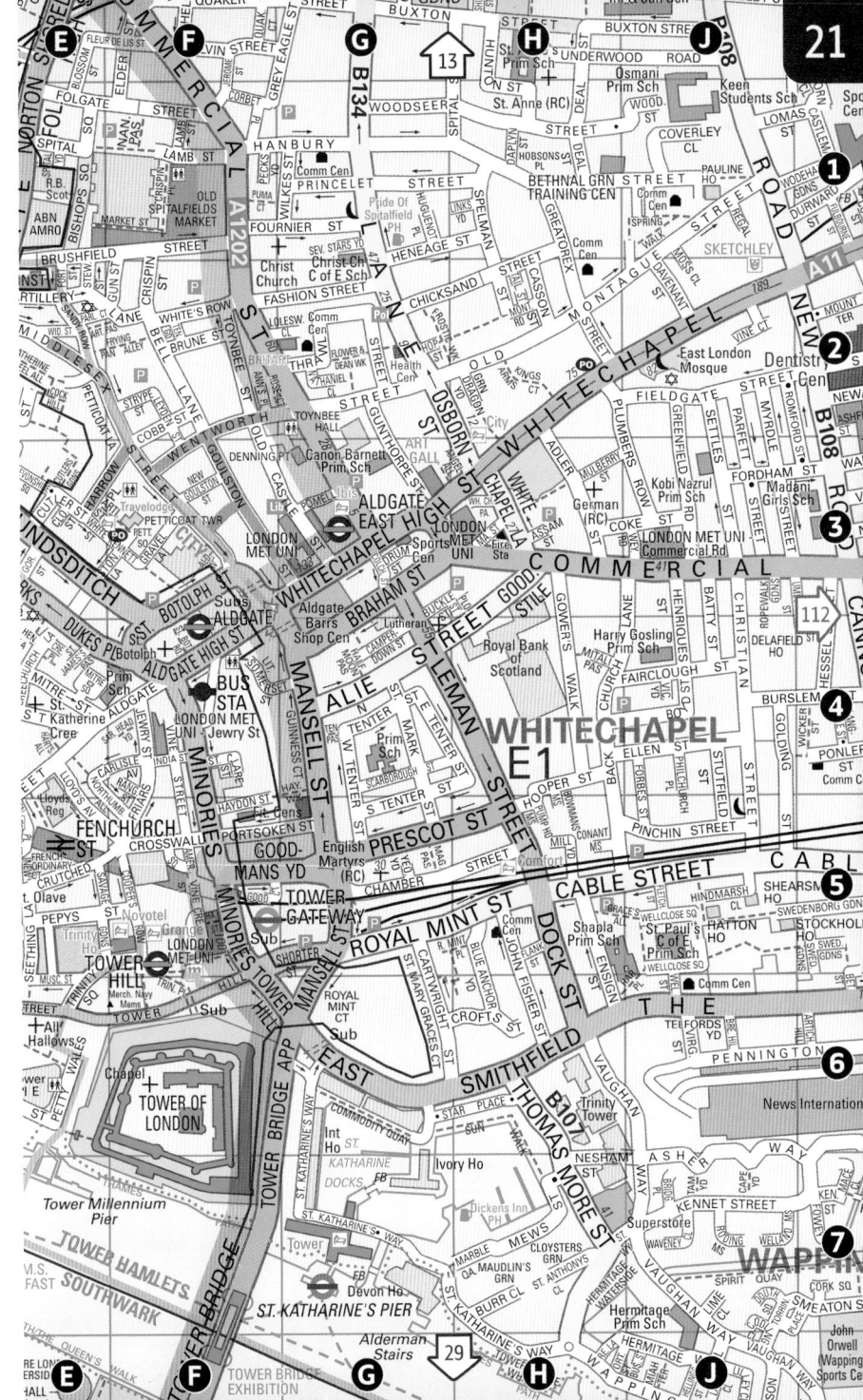

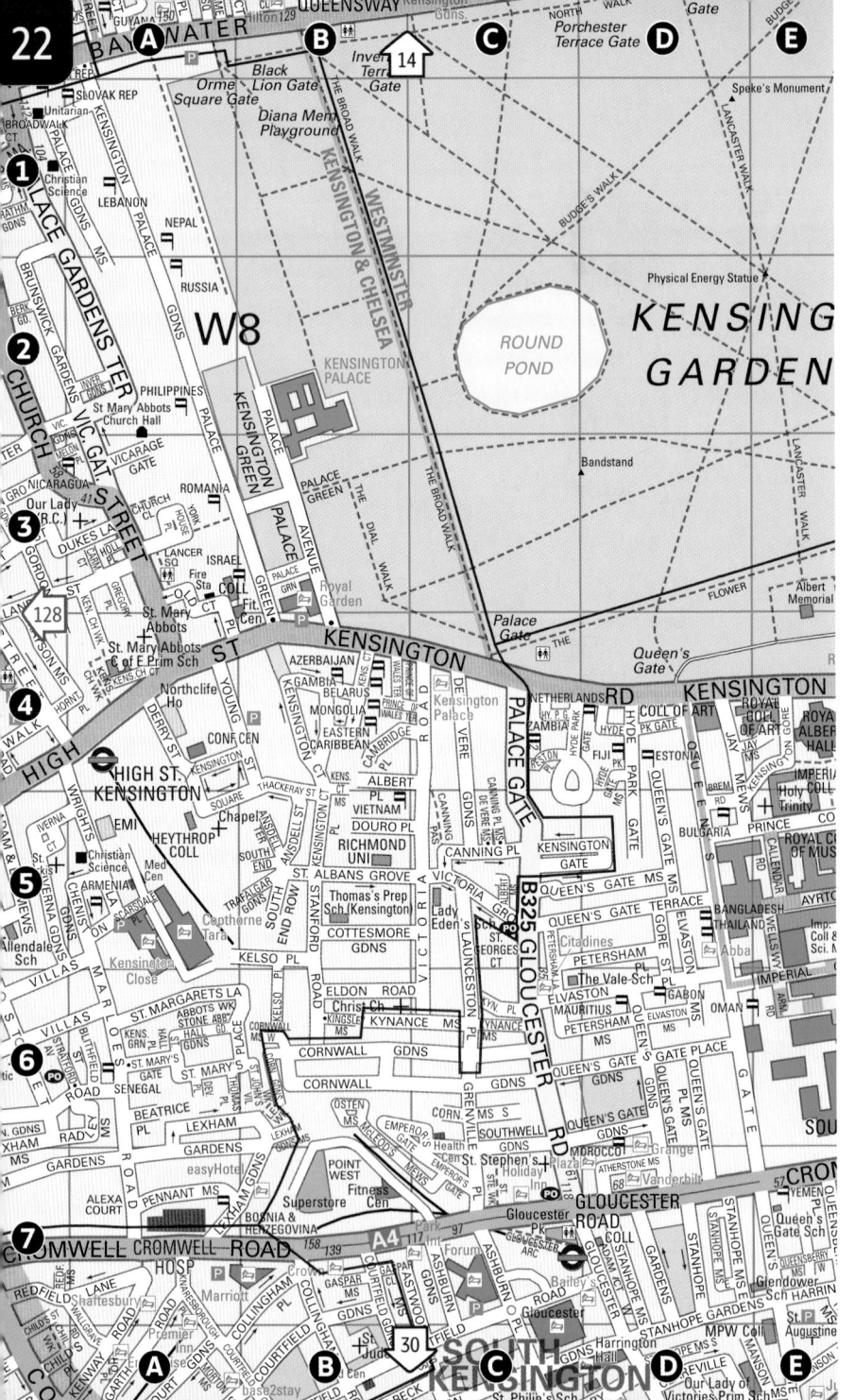

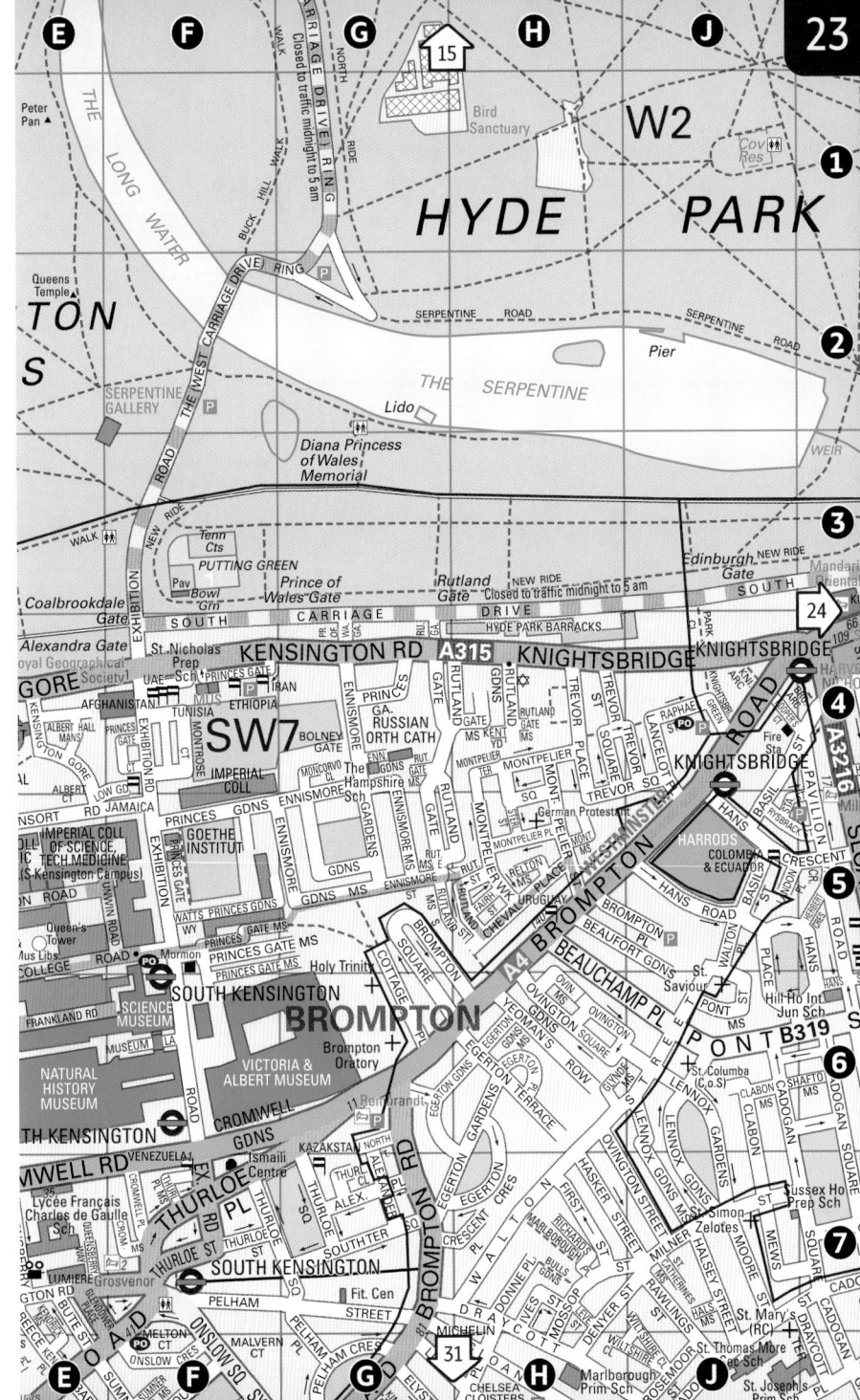

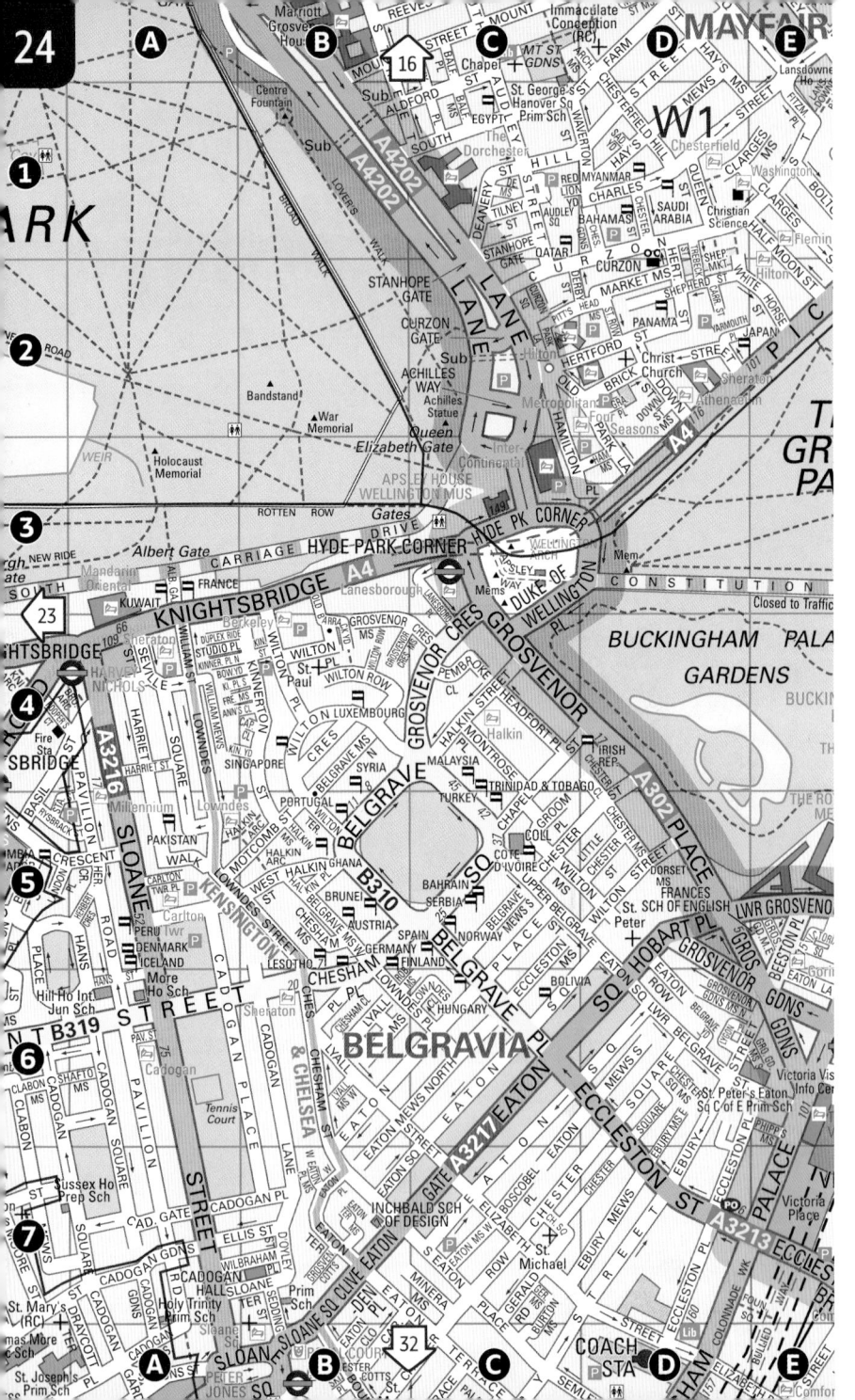

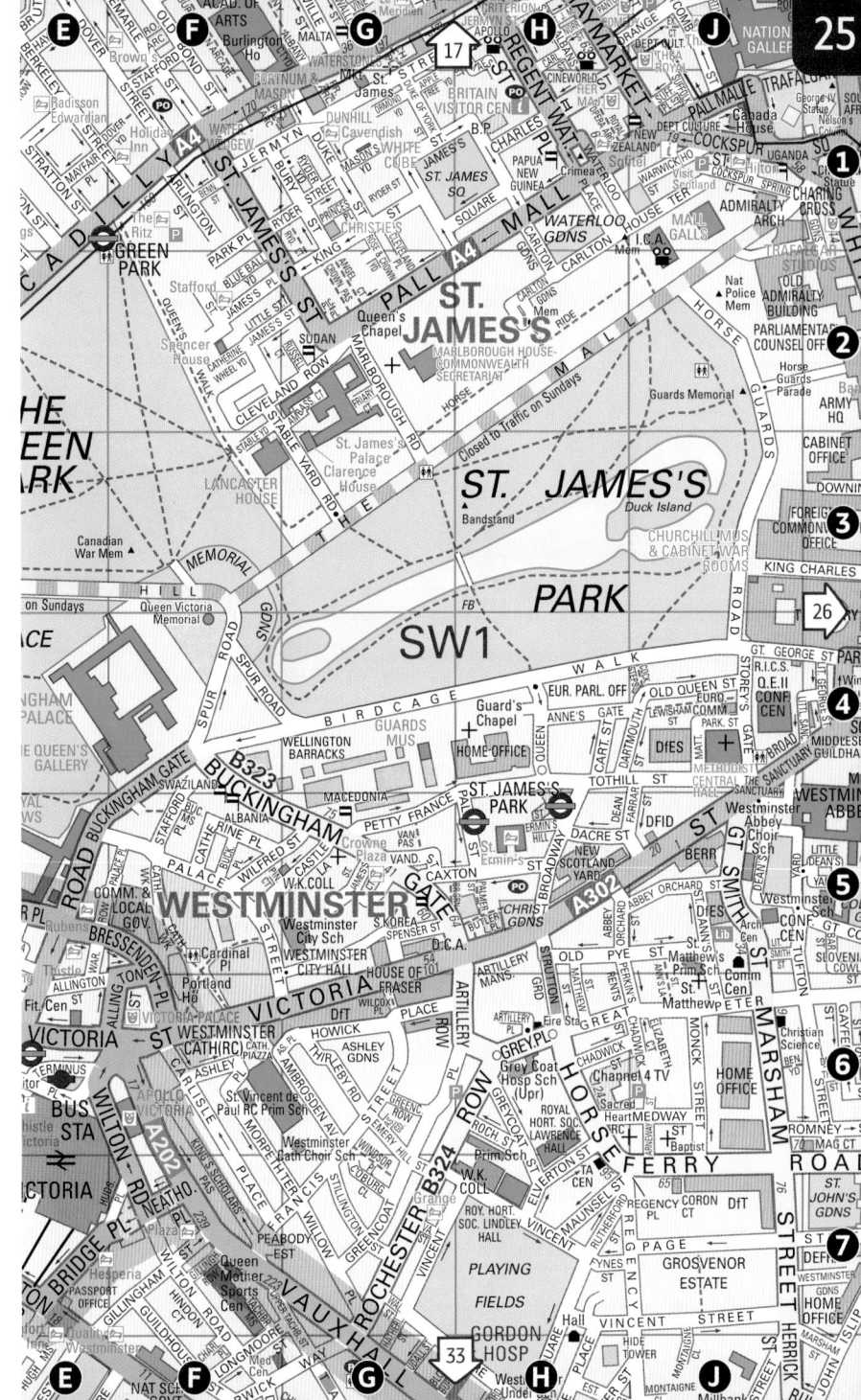

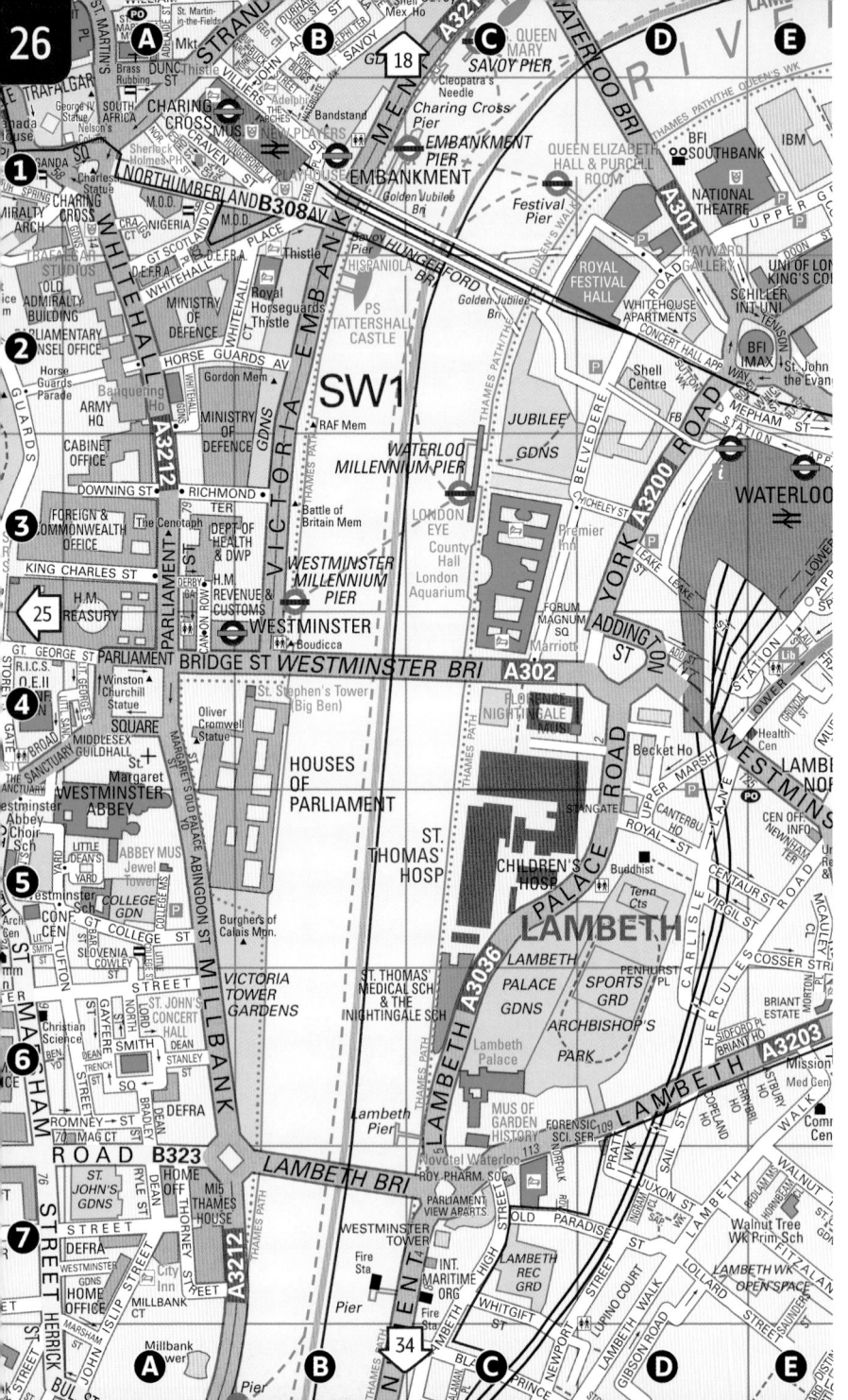

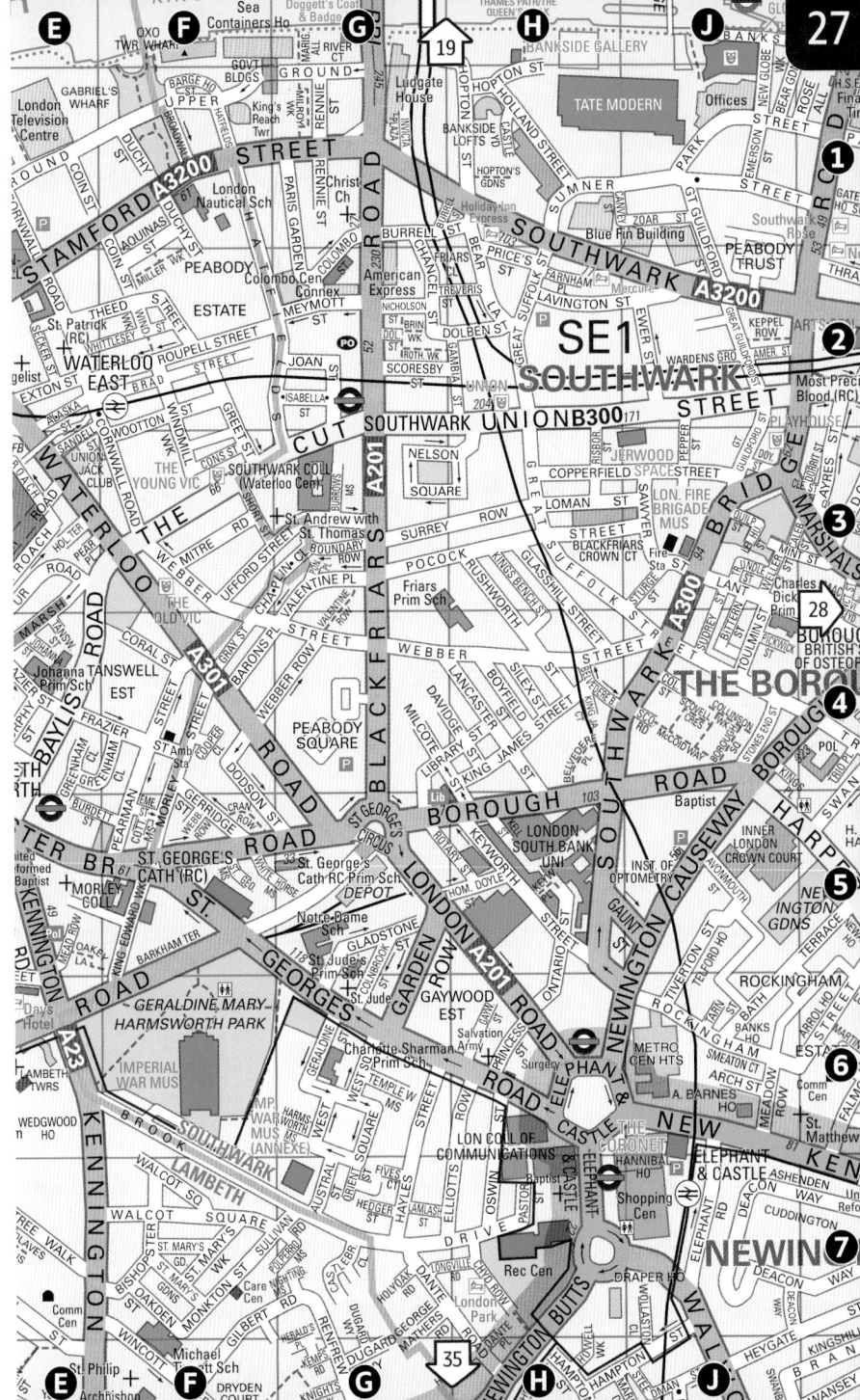

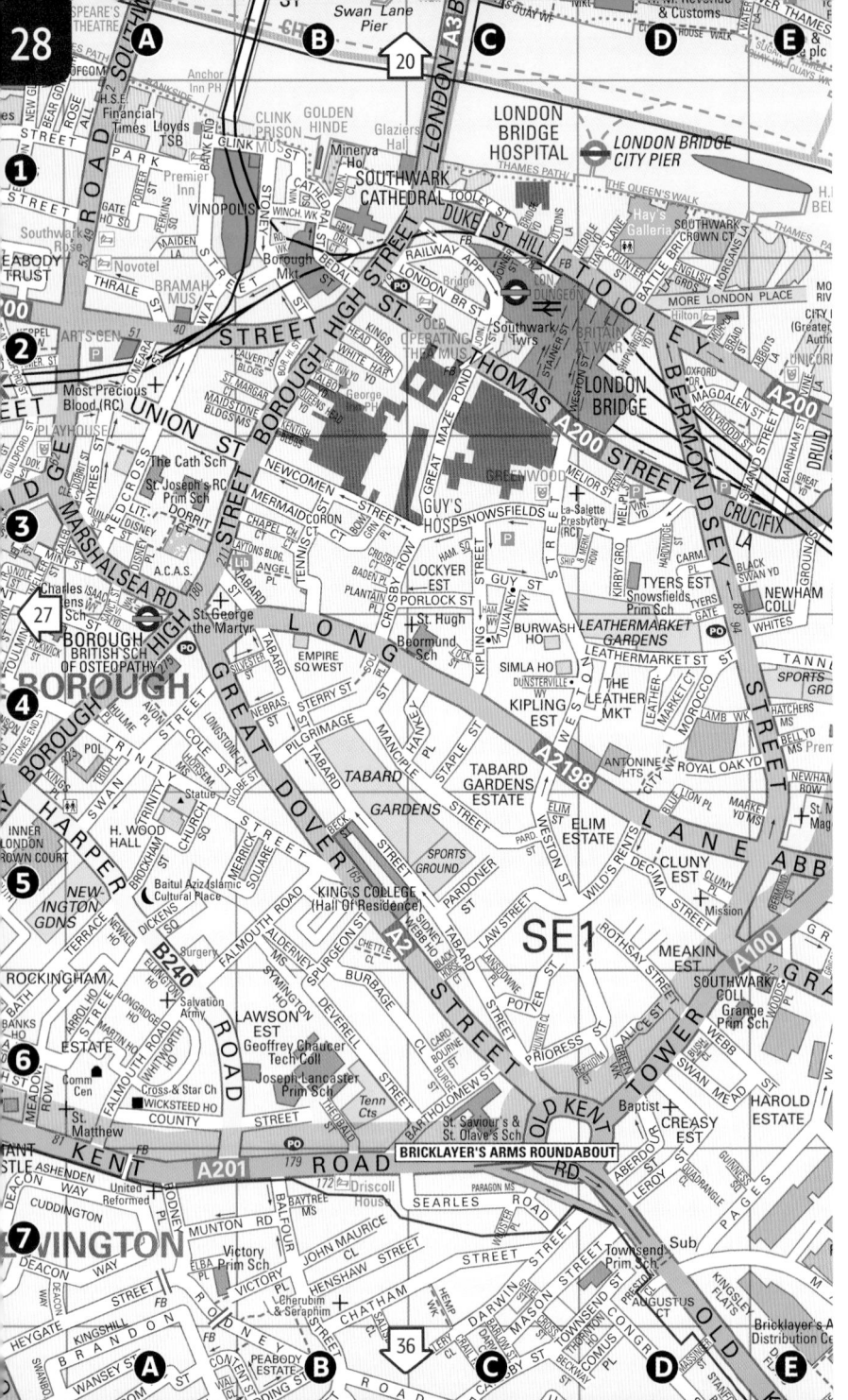

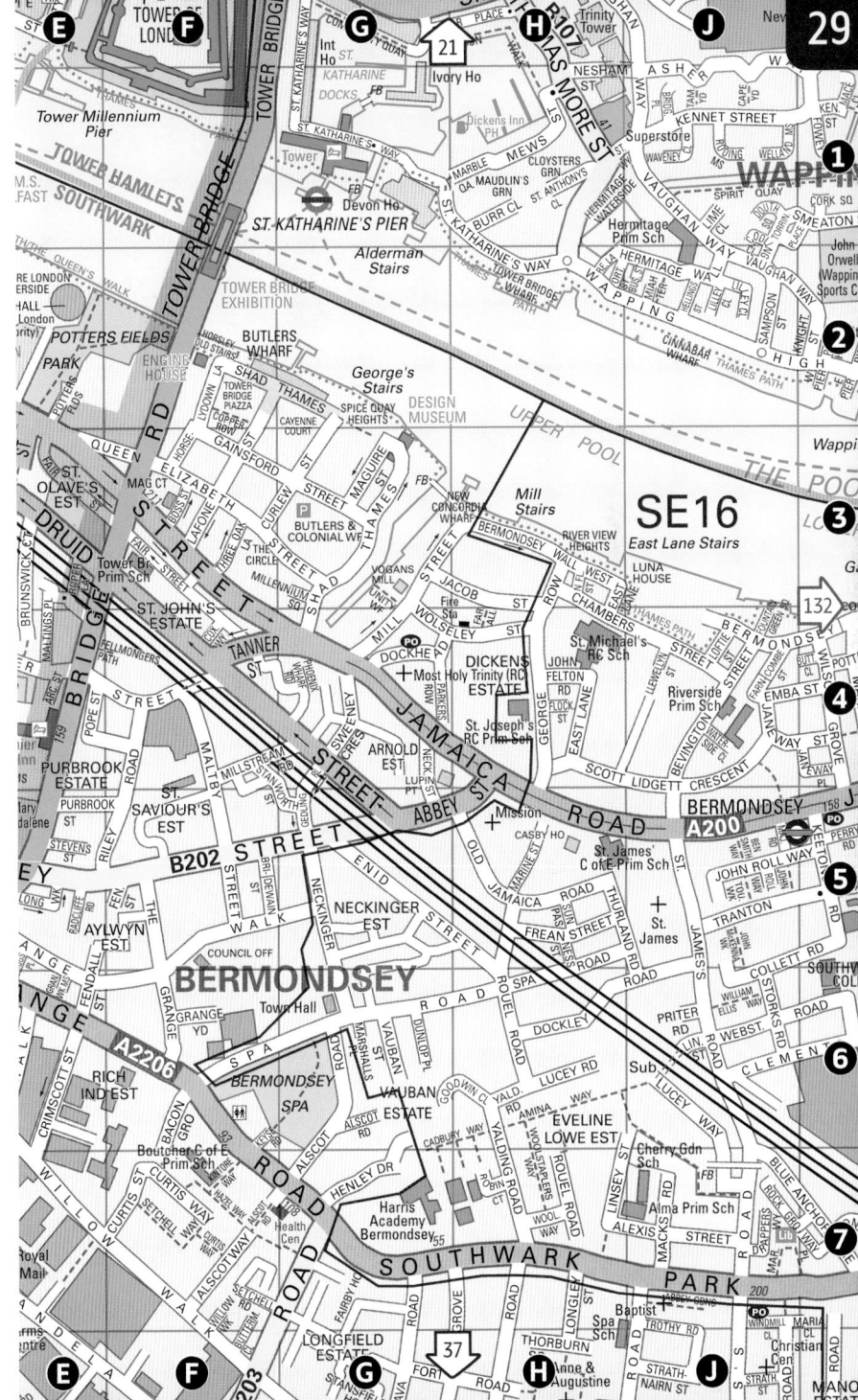

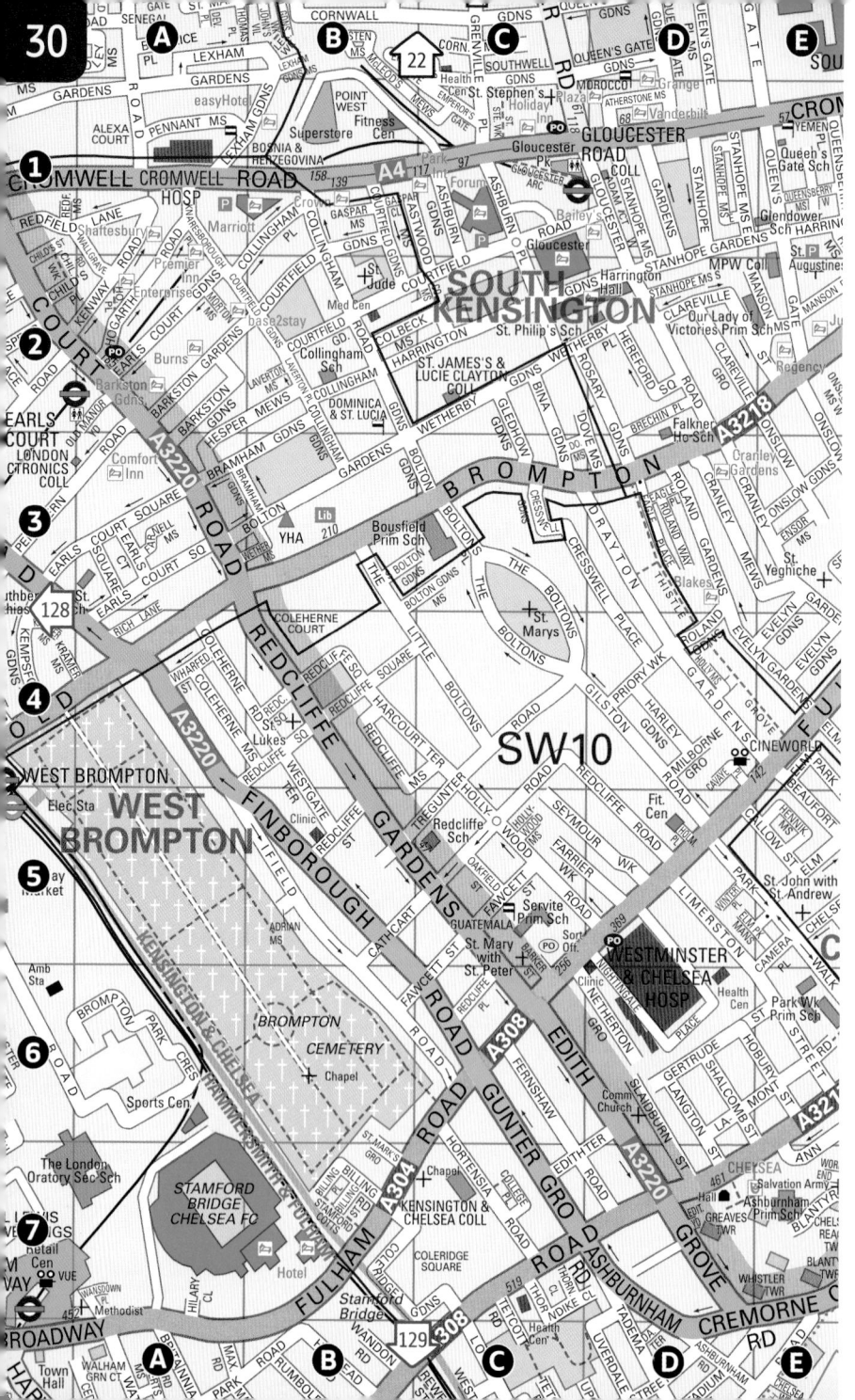

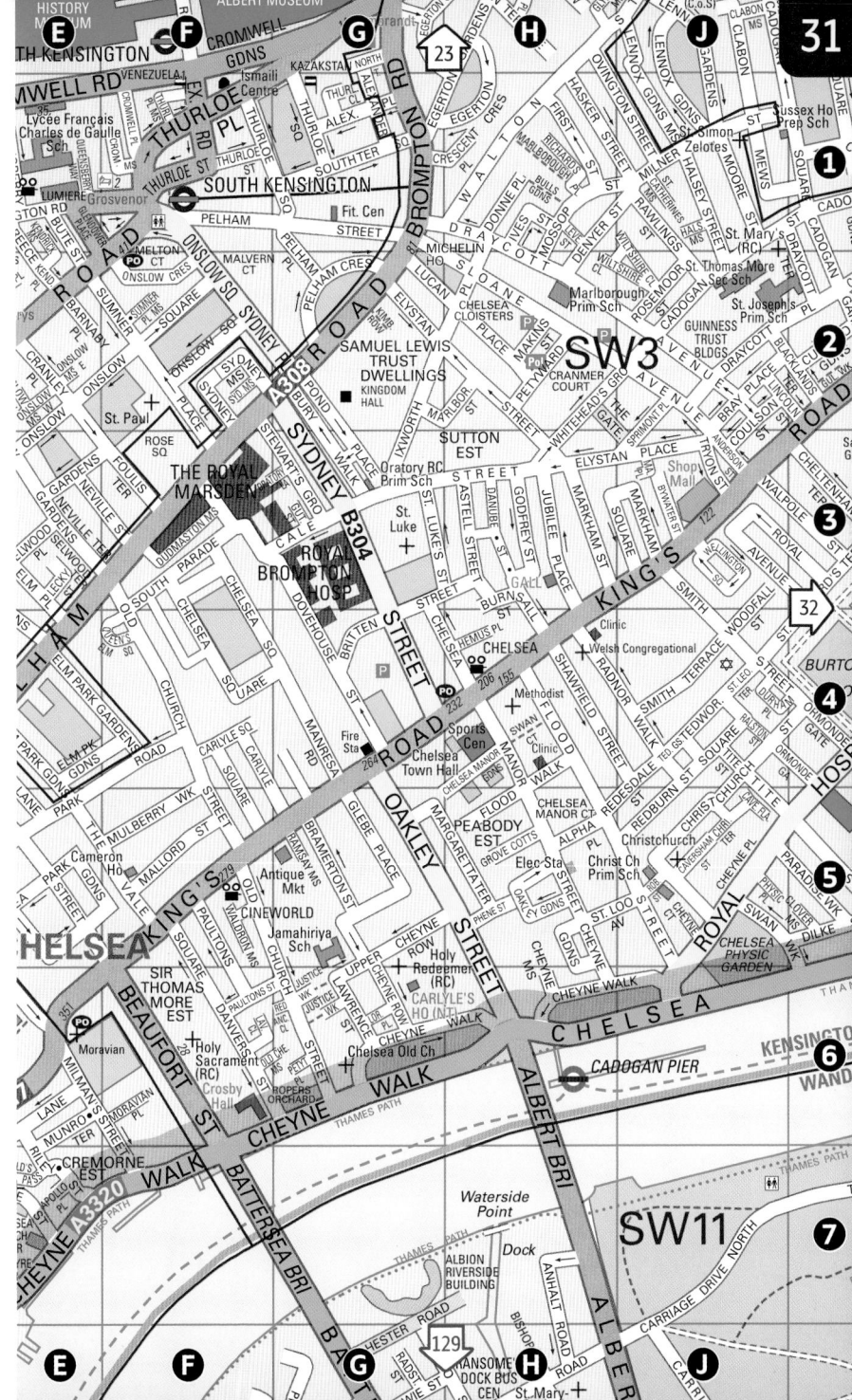

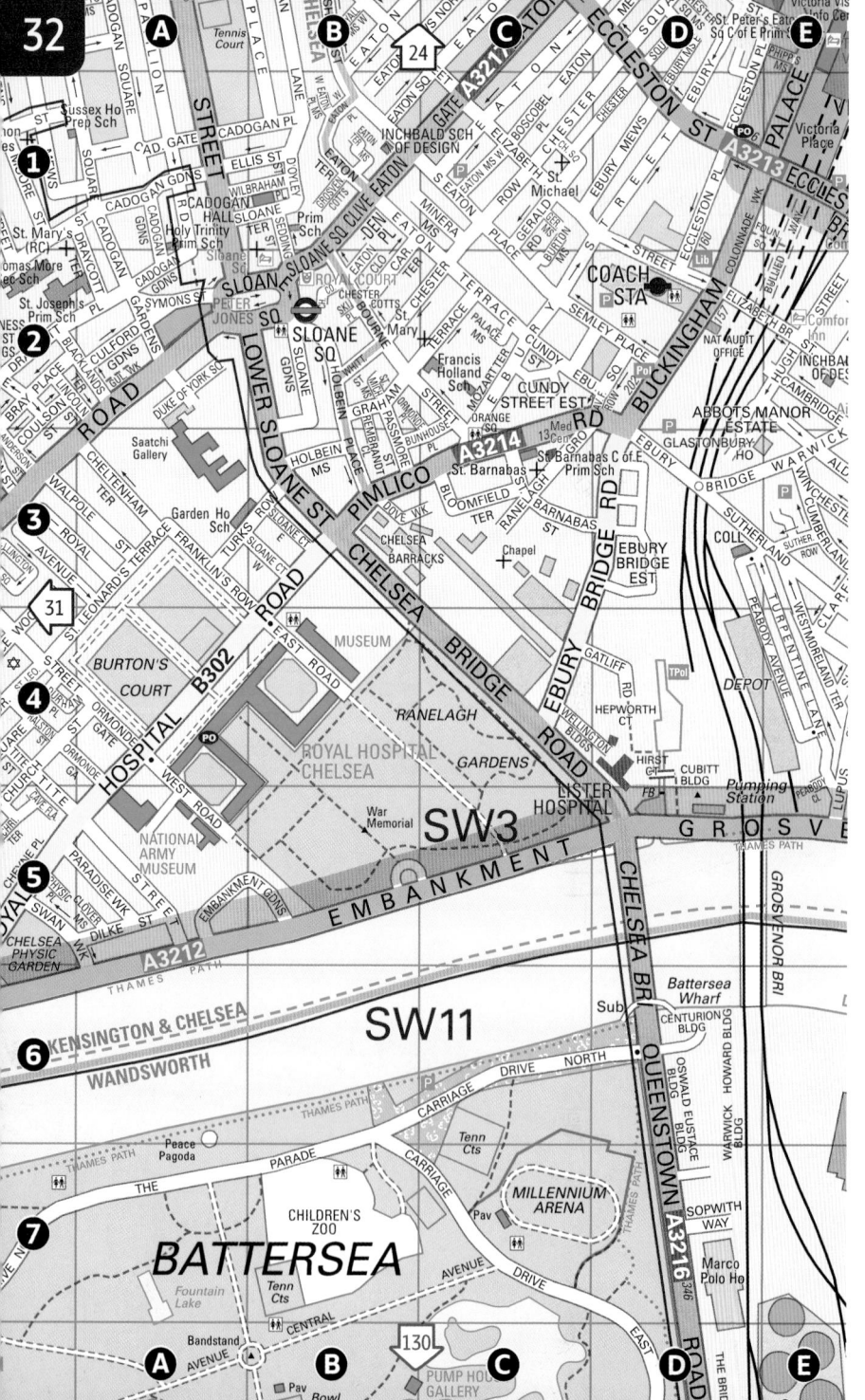

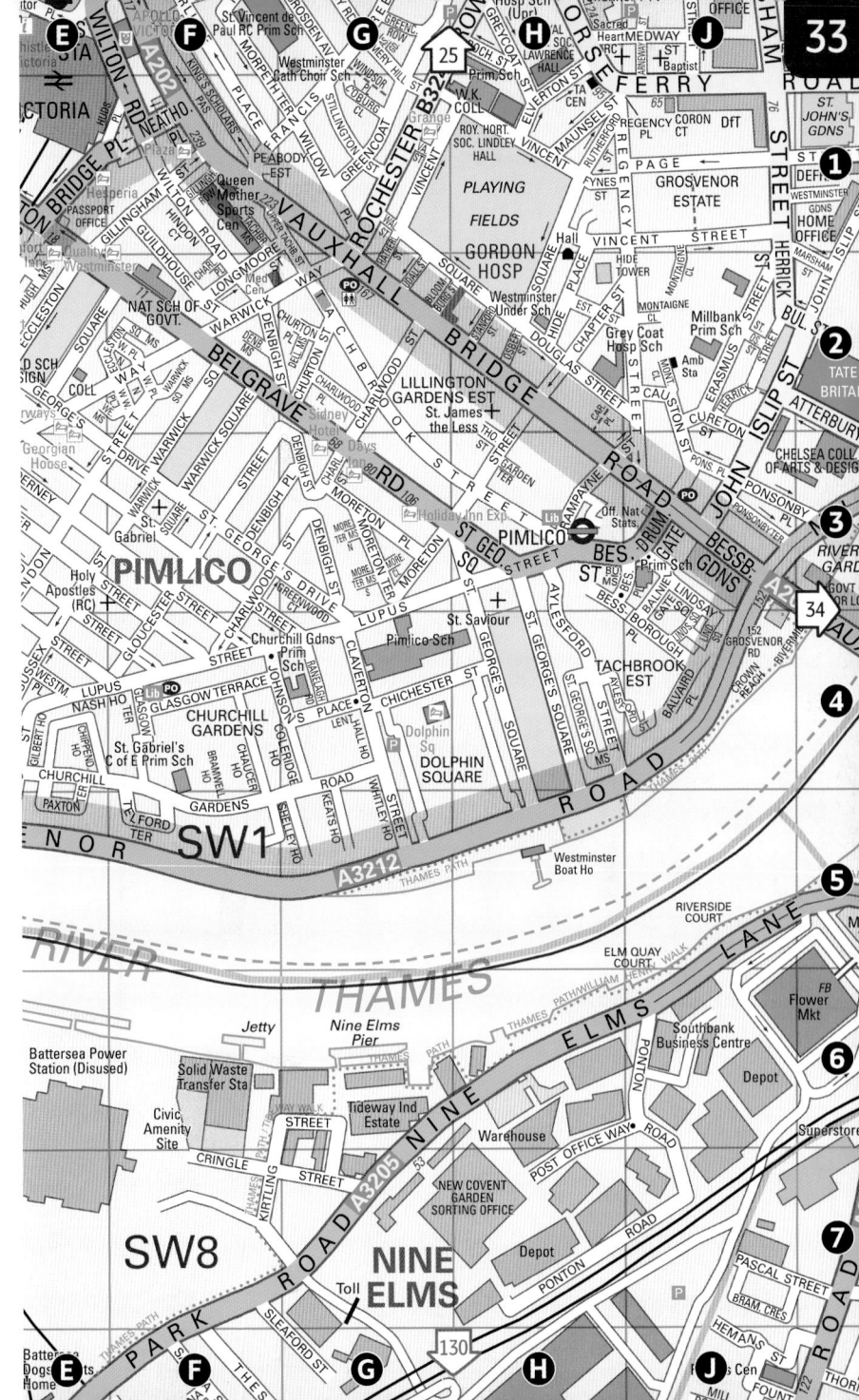

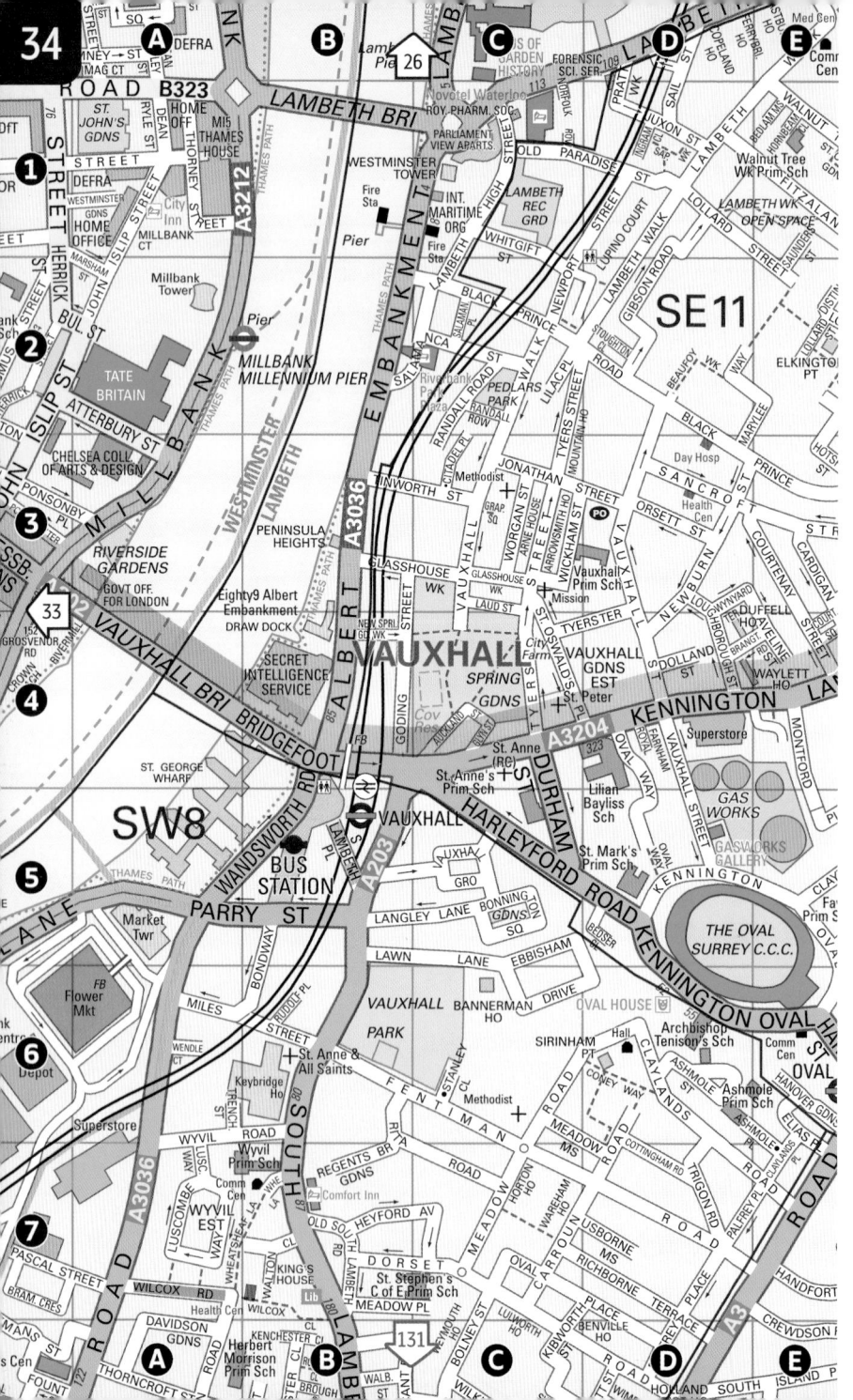

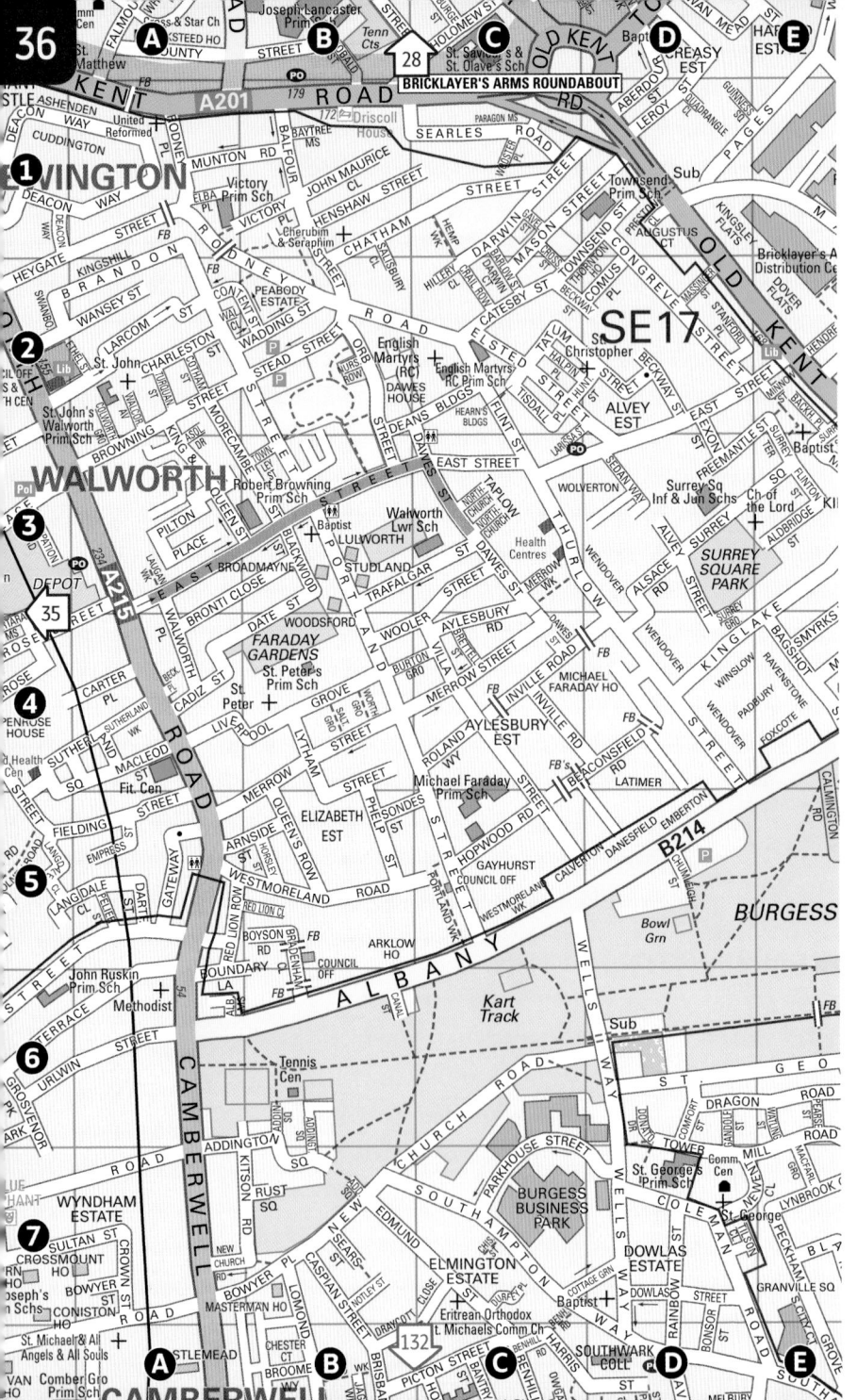

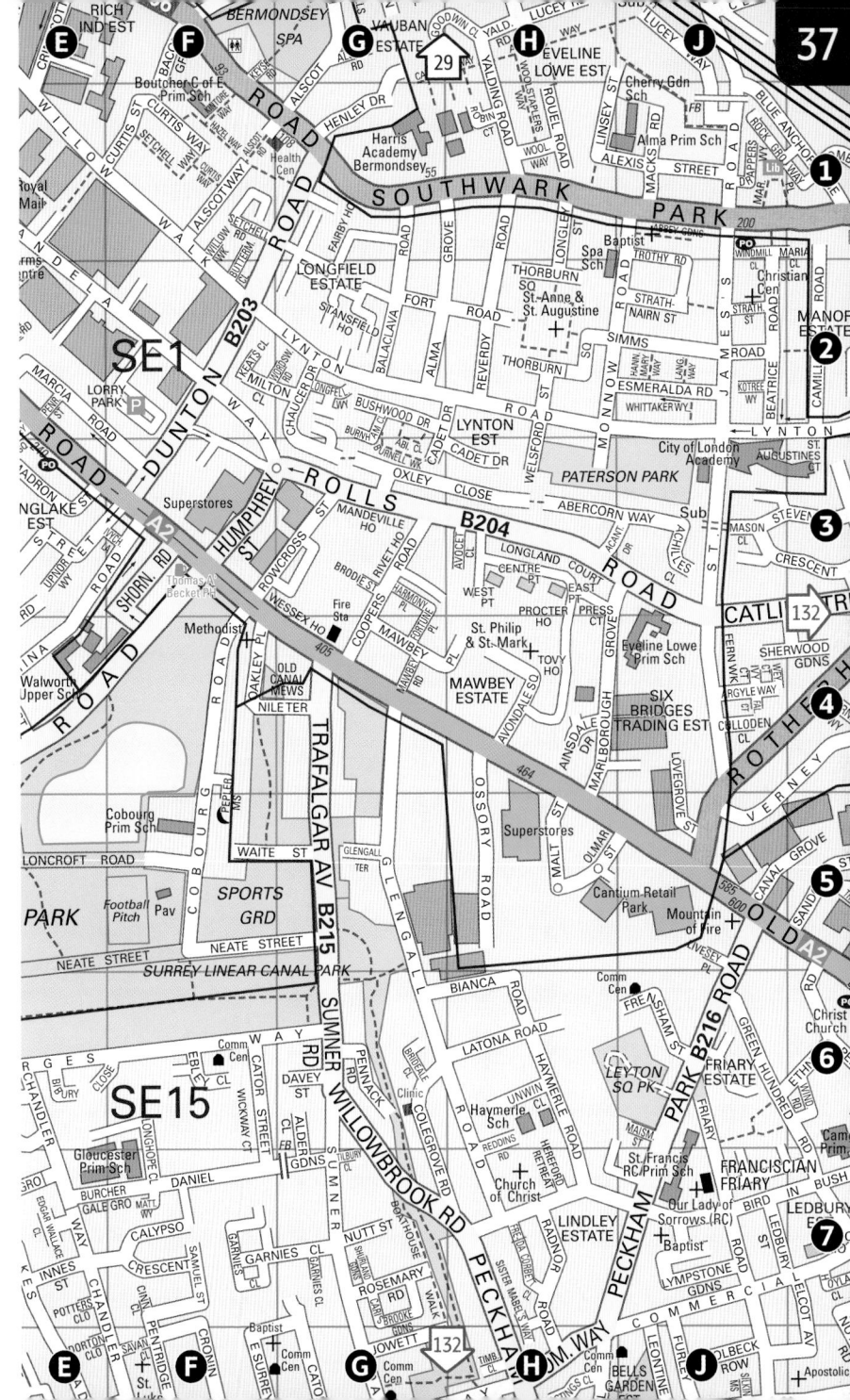

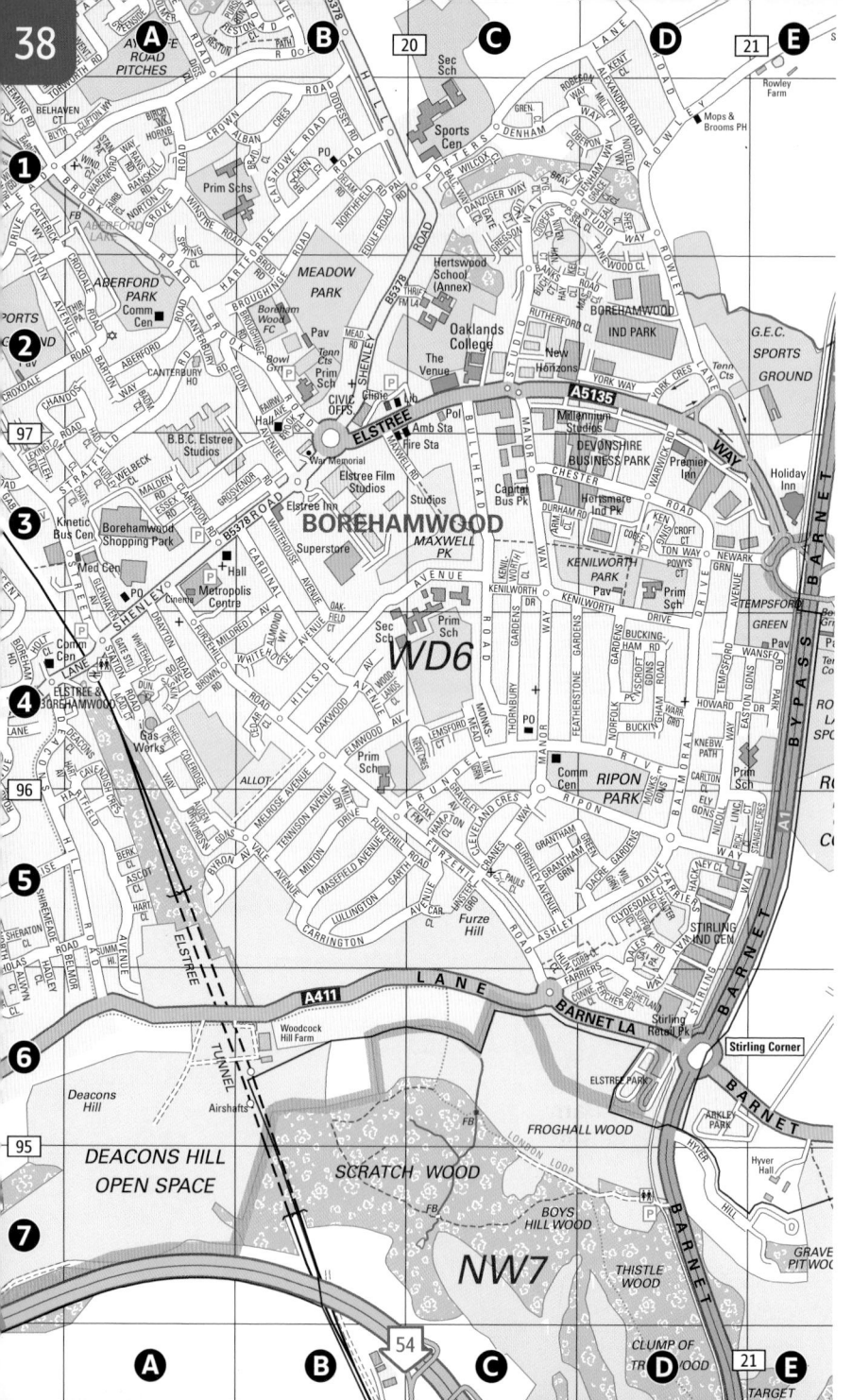

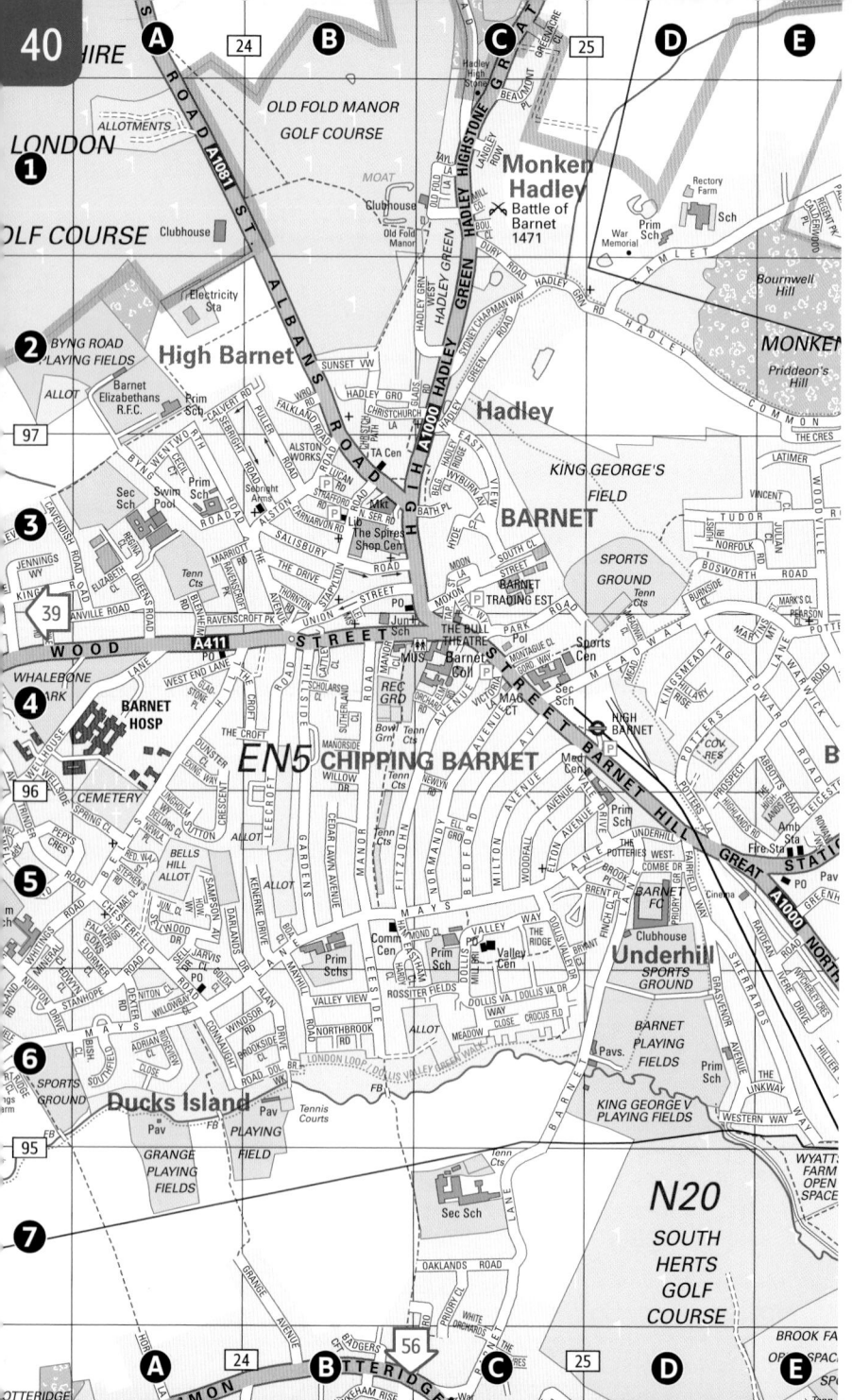

A 24 **B** **C** 25 **D** **E**

HIRE

LONDON

OLD FOLD MANOR
GOLF COURSE

1

OLF COURSE   Clubhouse

Hadley
High Stone

GREENHILL CL

Monken
Hadley
Battle of
Barnet
1471

Rectory
Farm

Prim
Sch

Sch

War
Memorial

2 BYNG ROAD
PLAYING FIELDS

ALLOTMENTS

MOAT

Clubhouse
Old Fold
Manor

High Barnet

SUNSET VW

97

Barnet
Elizabethans
R.F.C.

Prim
Sch

Bournwell
Hill

MONKEN

Priddeon's
Hill

THE CRES

HADLEY GRO

Hadley

LATIMER

3

Sec
Sch

Swim
Pool

Prim
Sch

Sebright
Alms.

The Spires
Shop Cen

BARNET

KING GEORGE'S
FIELD

TUDOR

NORFOLK

BOSWORTH

ROAD

VINCENT

JENNINGS
WY

39

SALISBURY

THE DRIVE

Tenn
Cts

STAFFORD

Mkt

SOUTH CL
STREET

SPORTS
GROUND

Tenn
Cts

MARK'S CL

BURNSIDE

4 WHALEBONE
PARK

WOOD

A411

STREET

Jun
Sch

PO

BARNET
TRADING EST

HIGH BARNET

COV
RES

B

BARNET
HOSP

WEST END LANE

THE CROFT

THE BULL
THEATRE
MUS

Barnet
Coll

P

Barnet
Pol

Sports
Cen

Sec
Sch

EN5 CHIPPING BARNET

REC
GRD

MAG
CT

96

CEMETERY

Bowl
Grn

Tenn
Cts

WILLOW
DR

Tenn
Cts

Med
Cen

Prim
Sch

UNDERHILL
WEST-
COMBE RD

Amb
Sta

PO

5

BELLS
HILL
ALLOT

ALLOT

Tenn
Cts

Comm
Cen

Prim
Sch

THE
POTTERIES

Cinema

BARNET
FC

Clubhouse

Underhill
SPORTS
GROUND

Pav

STATI

A1000

NORTH

6 SPORTS
GROUND

Ducks Island

Prim
Schs

Prim
Sch

Valley
Cen

VALLEY VIEW

ROSSITER FIELDS

NORTHBROOK
RD

ALLOT

MEADOW

DOLLIS VA. DOLLIS VA. DR.
WAY
CROCUS FLD

CLOSE

Pavs.

BARNET
PLAYING
FIELDS

Prim
Sch

THE
LINKWAY

95

Pav

PLAYING

FB

Tennis
Courts

FB

FB

LONDON LOOP DOLLIS VALLEY WAY

KING GEORGE V
PLAYING FIELDS

WESTERN WAY

WYATT'S
FARM
OPEN
SPACE

7

GRANGE
PLAYING
FIELDS

FIELD

Tenn
Cts

Sec Sch

N20
SOUTH
HERTS
GOLF
COURSE

OTTERIDGE

A 24

MON

B 56
OTTERIDGE

WHITE
ORCHARDS

OAKLANDS   ROAD

C 25

D

E

BROOK FA
OPEN SPAC
SP

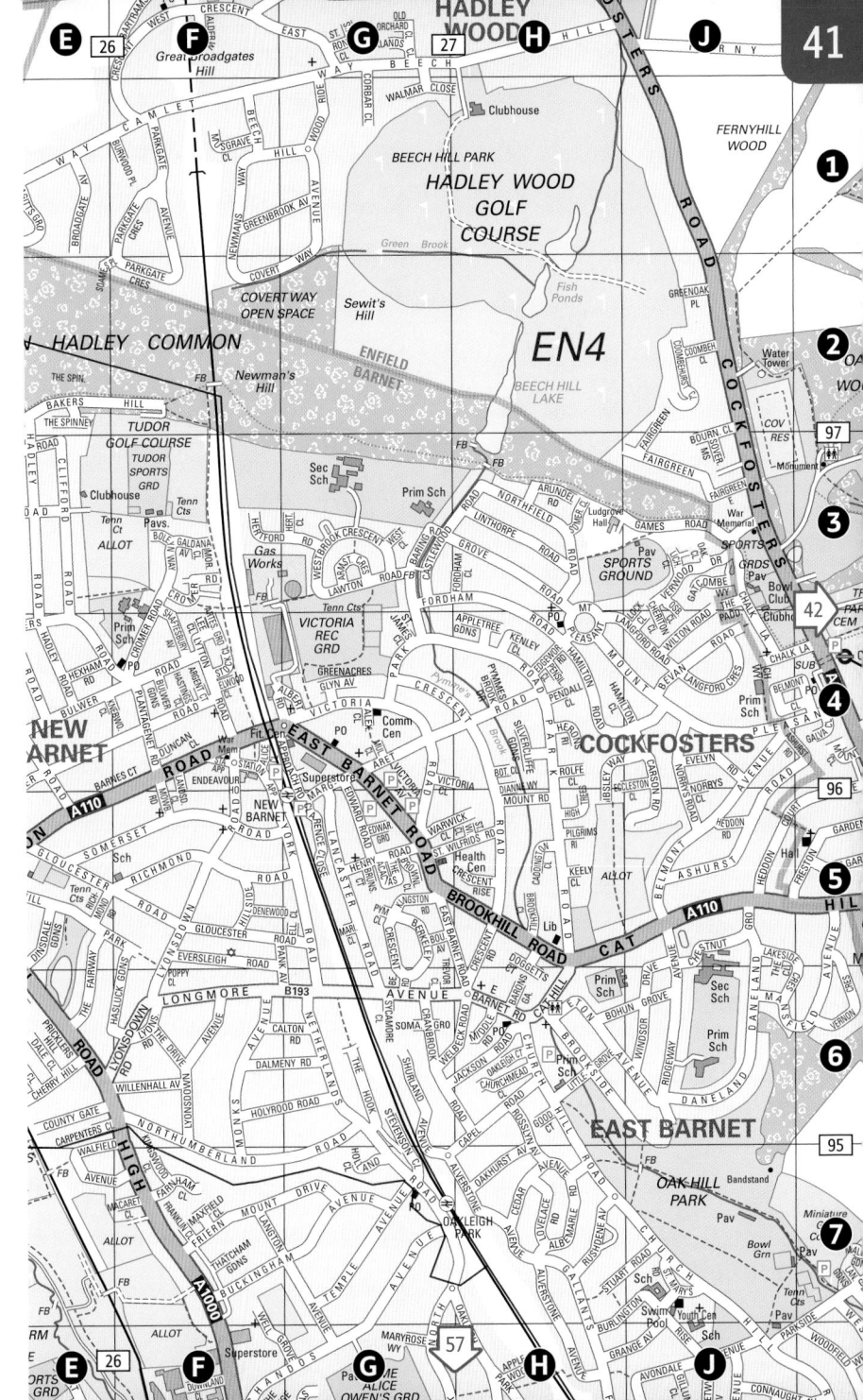

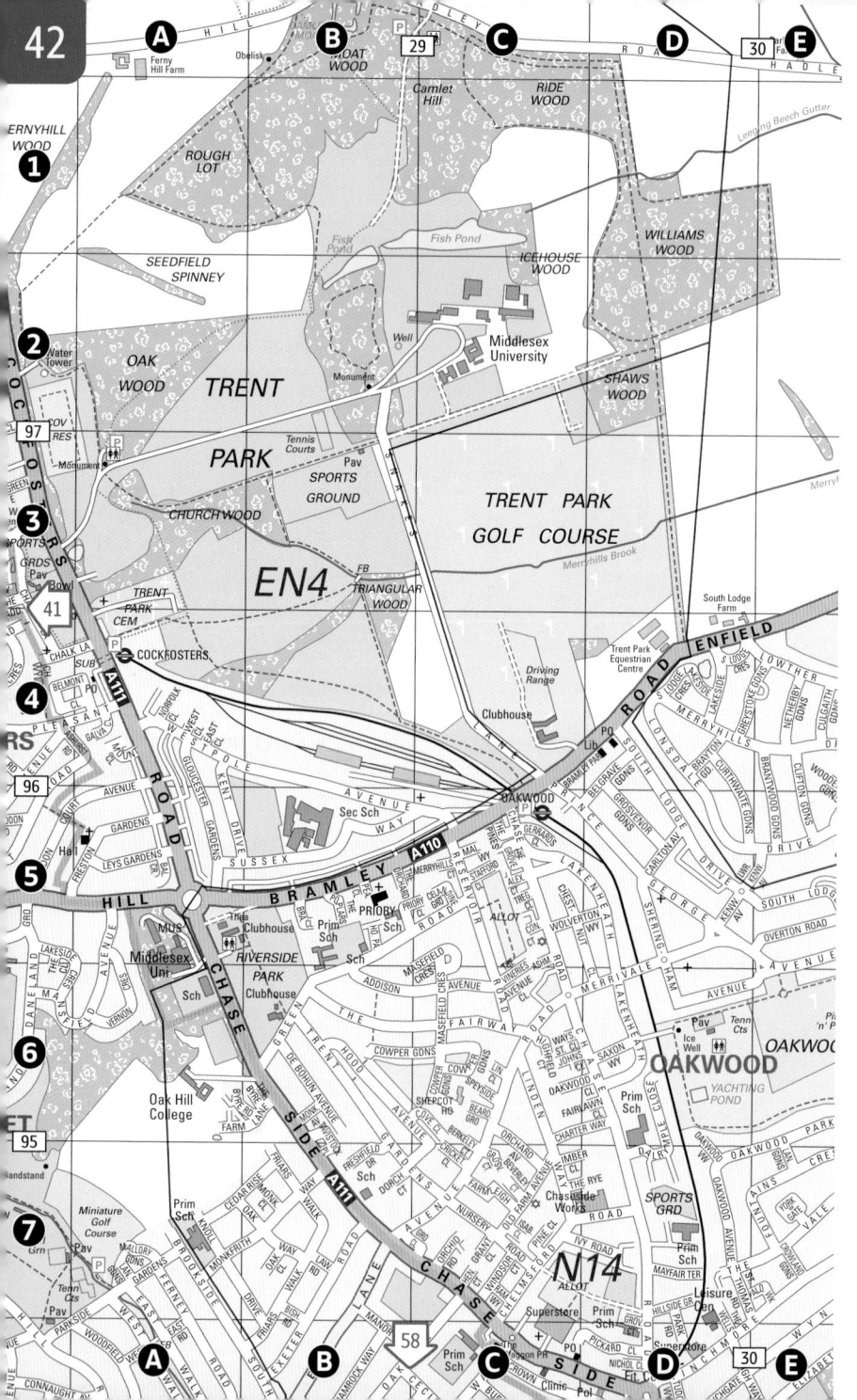

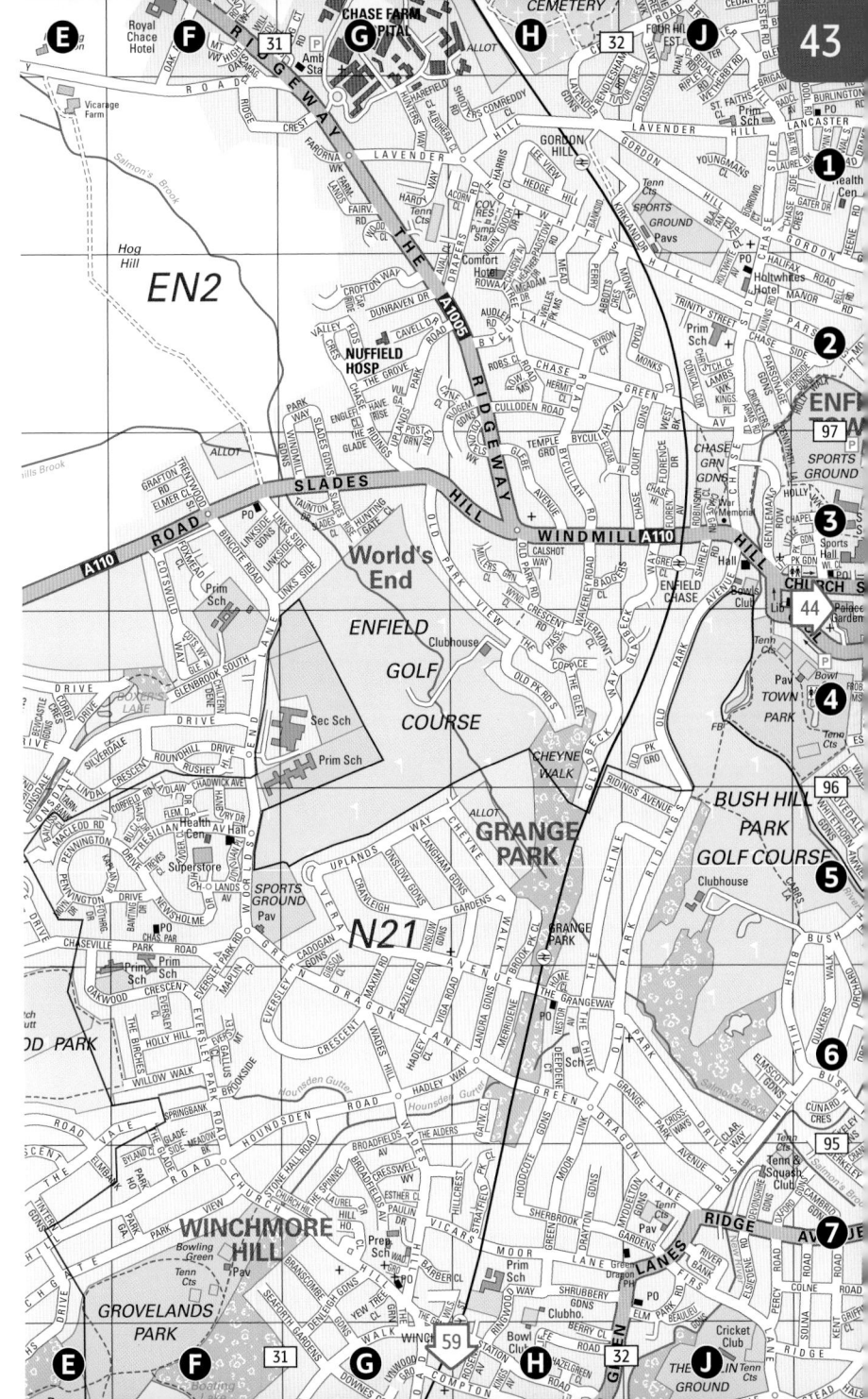

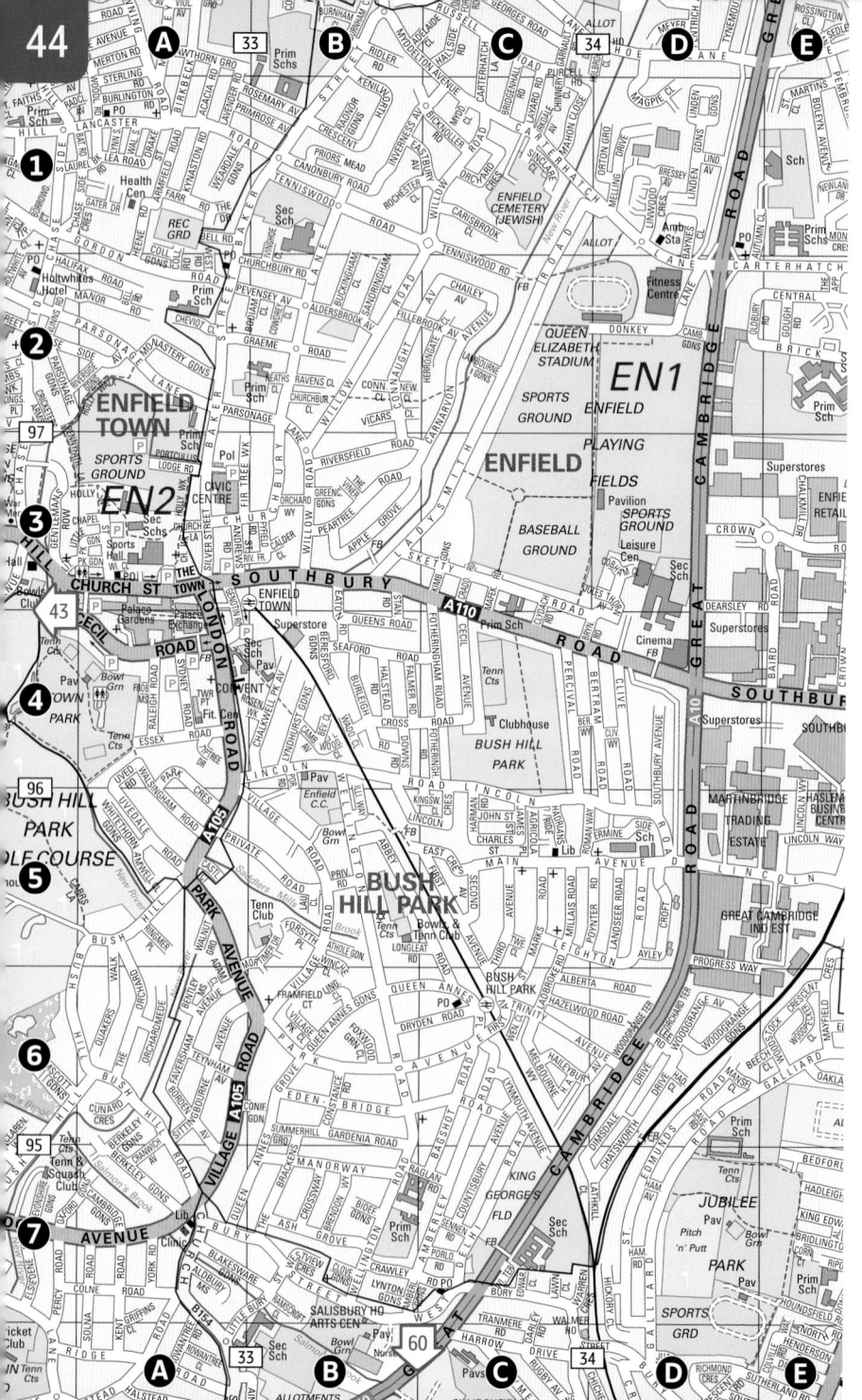

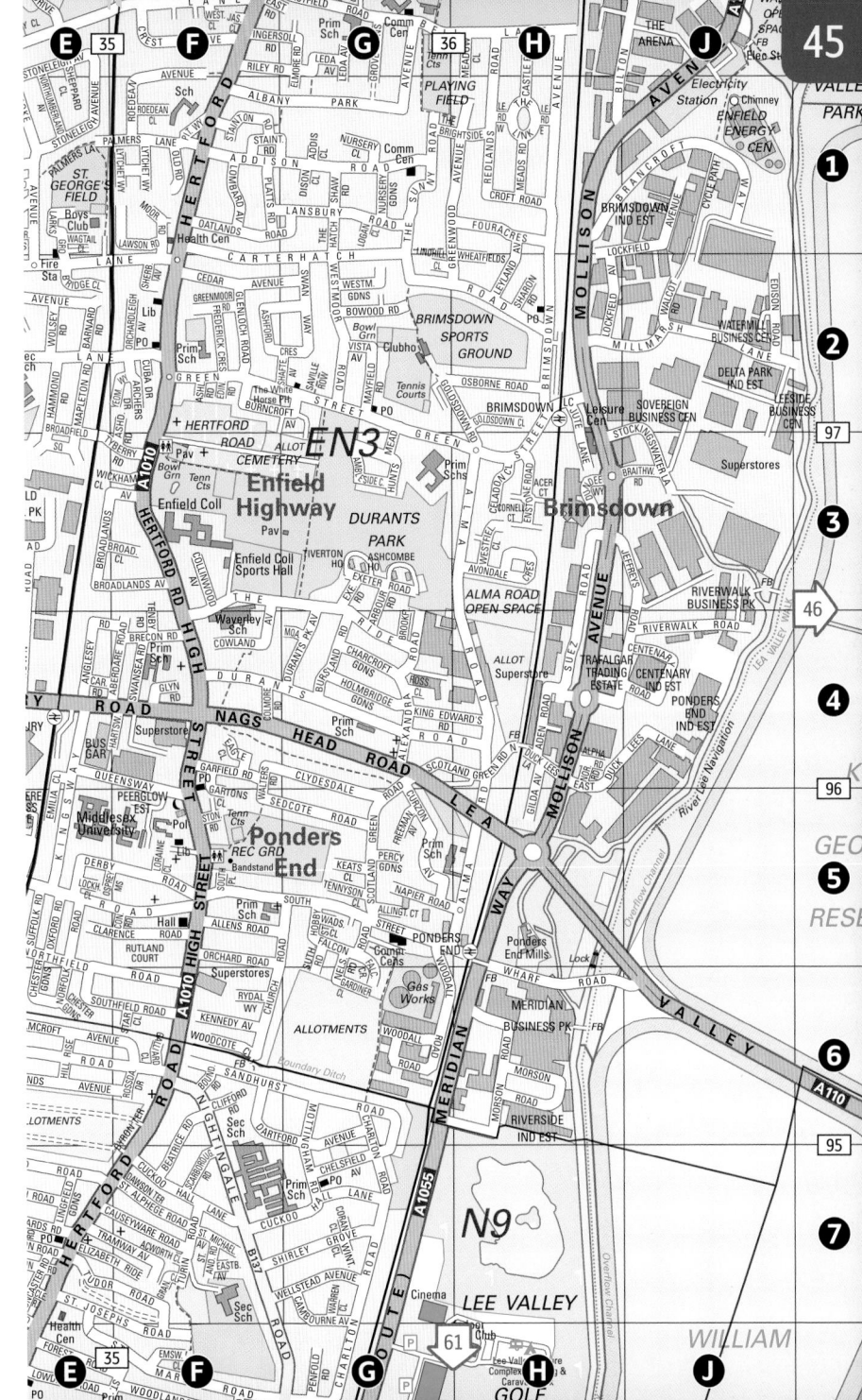

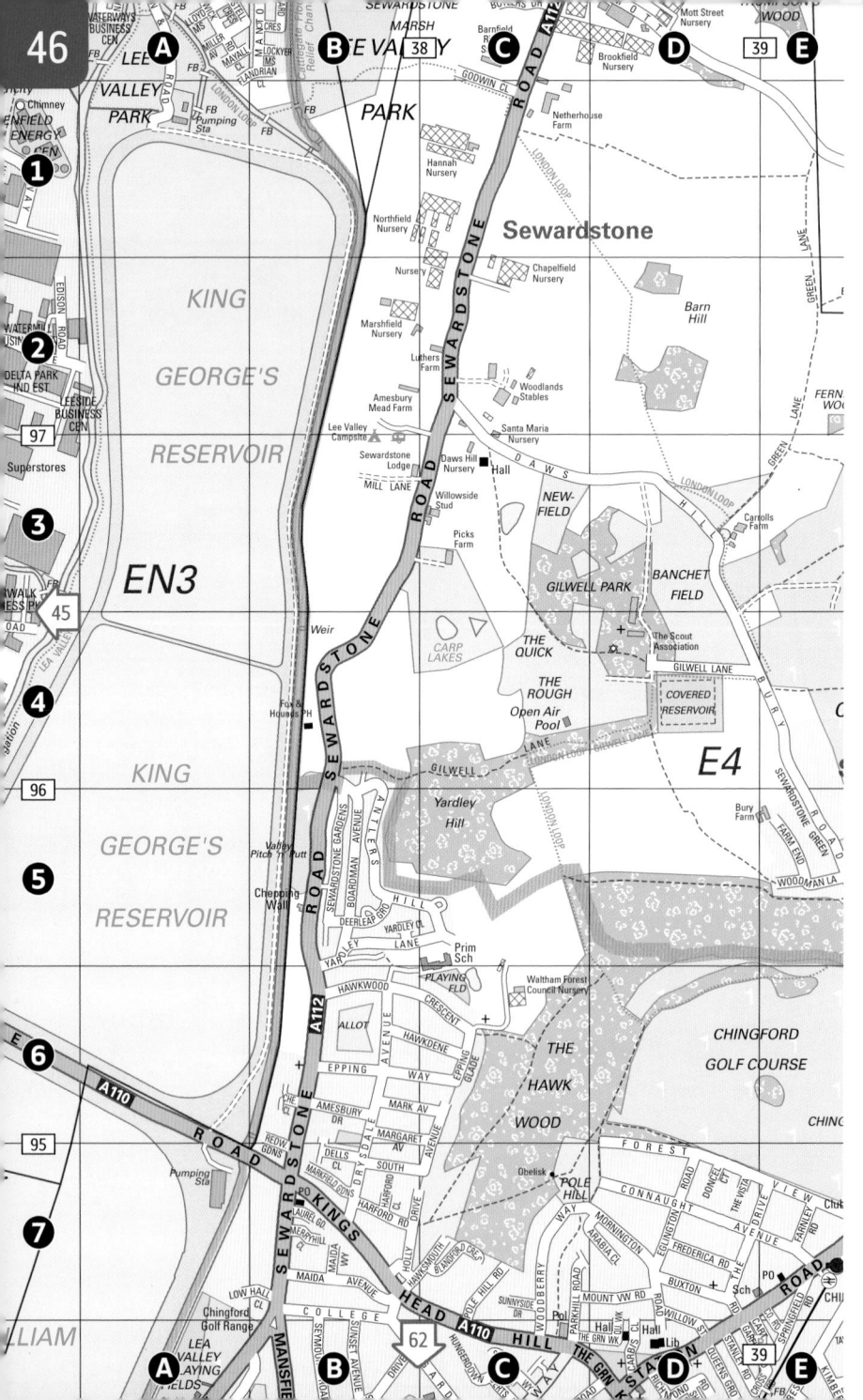

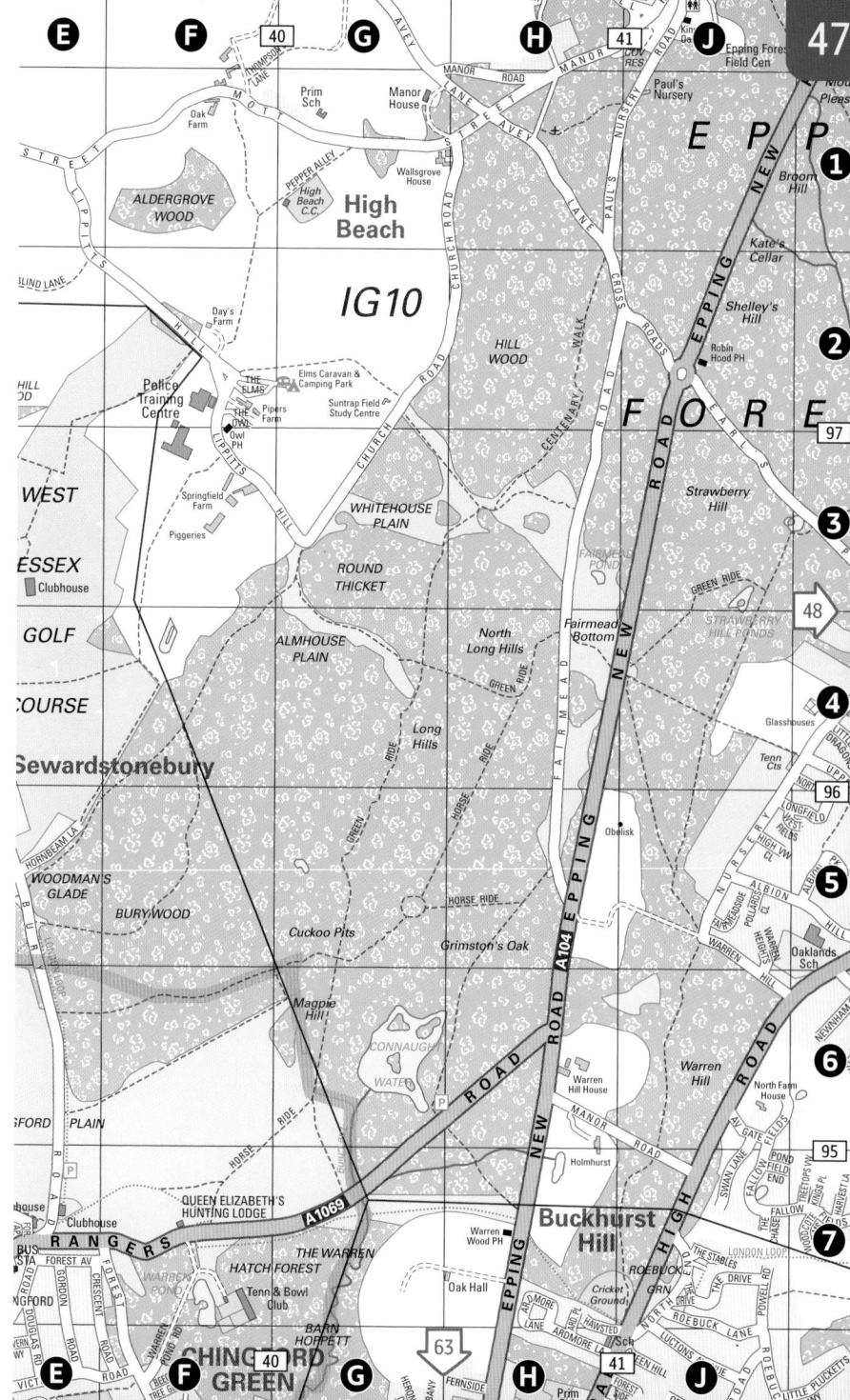

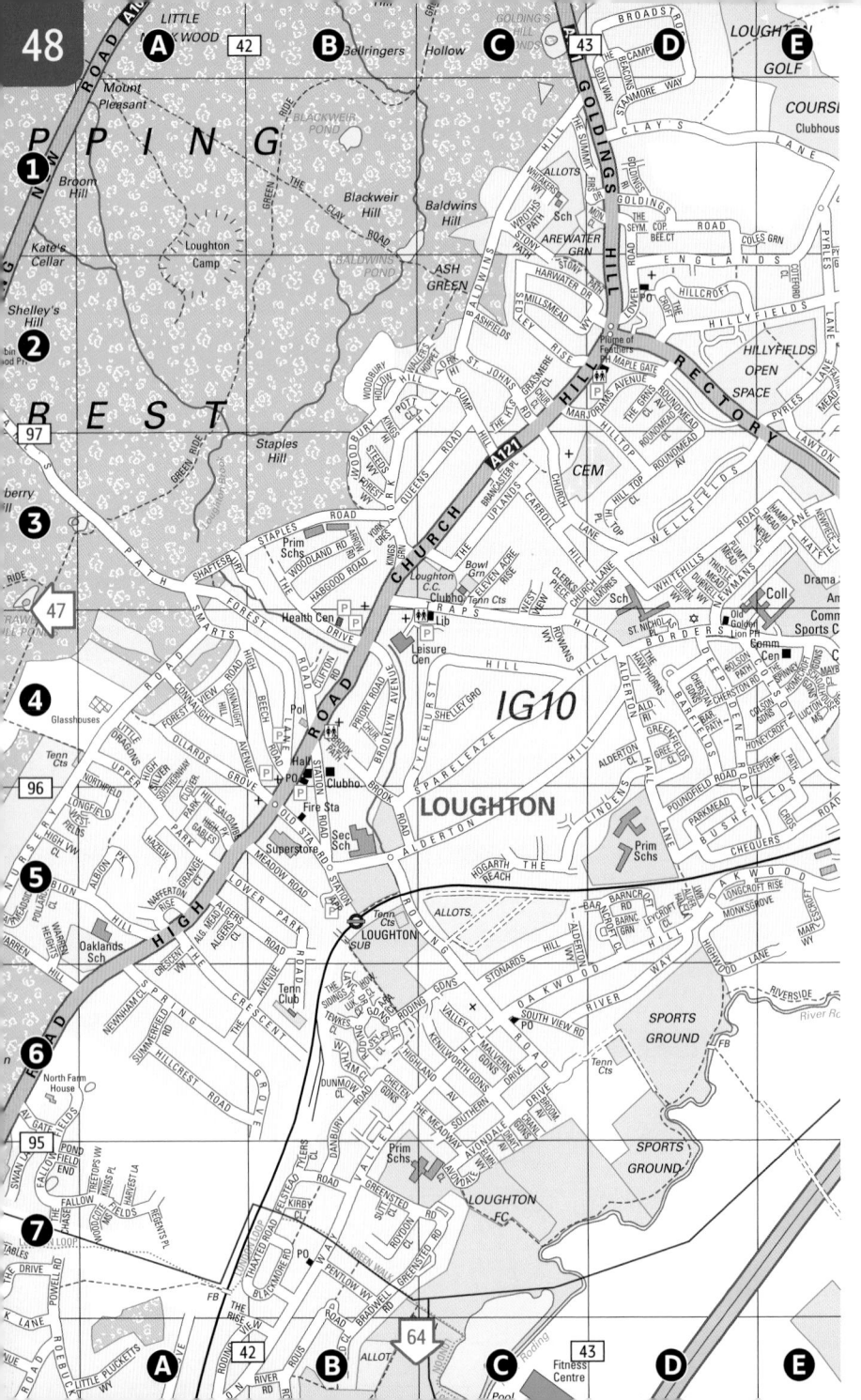

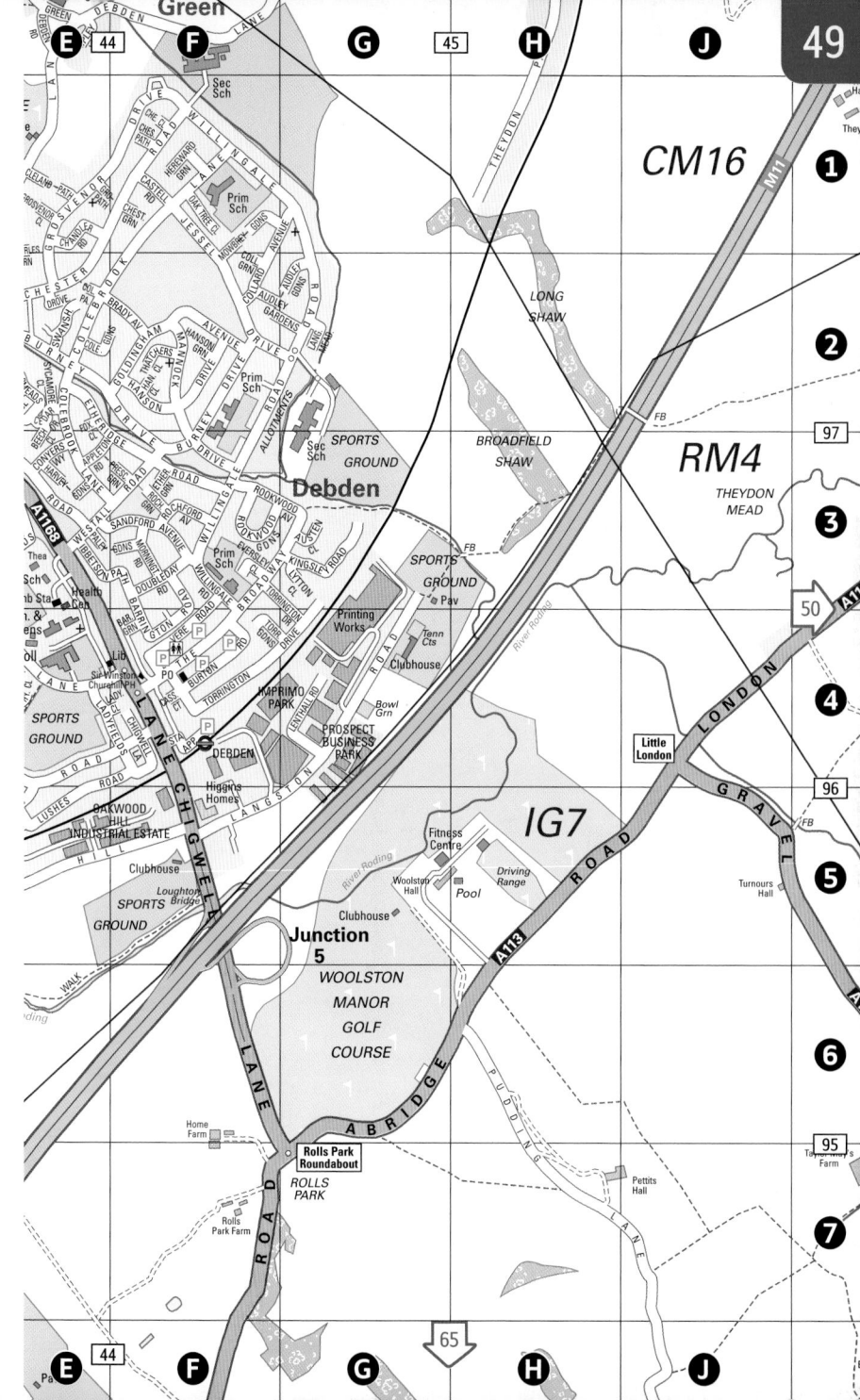

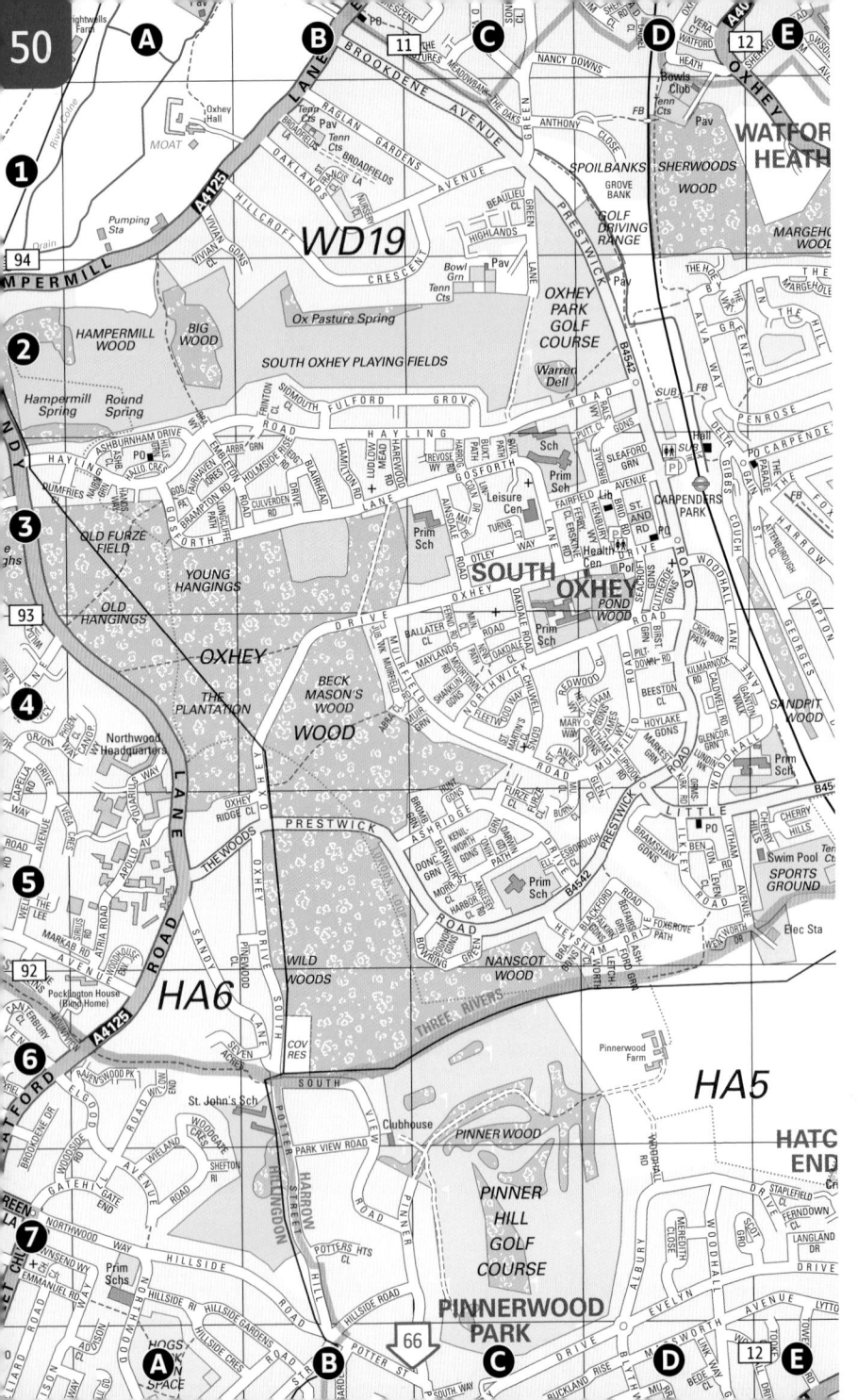

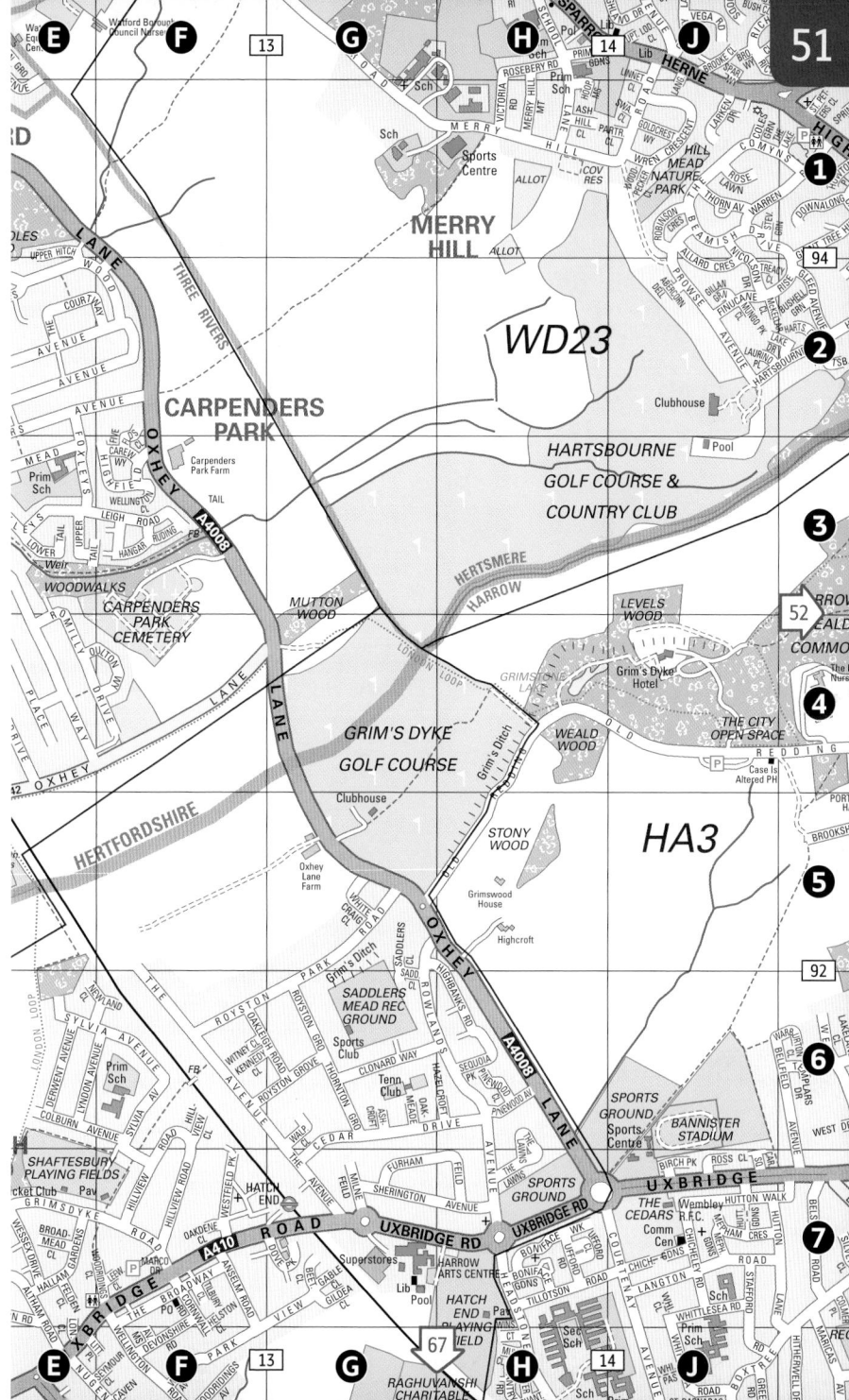

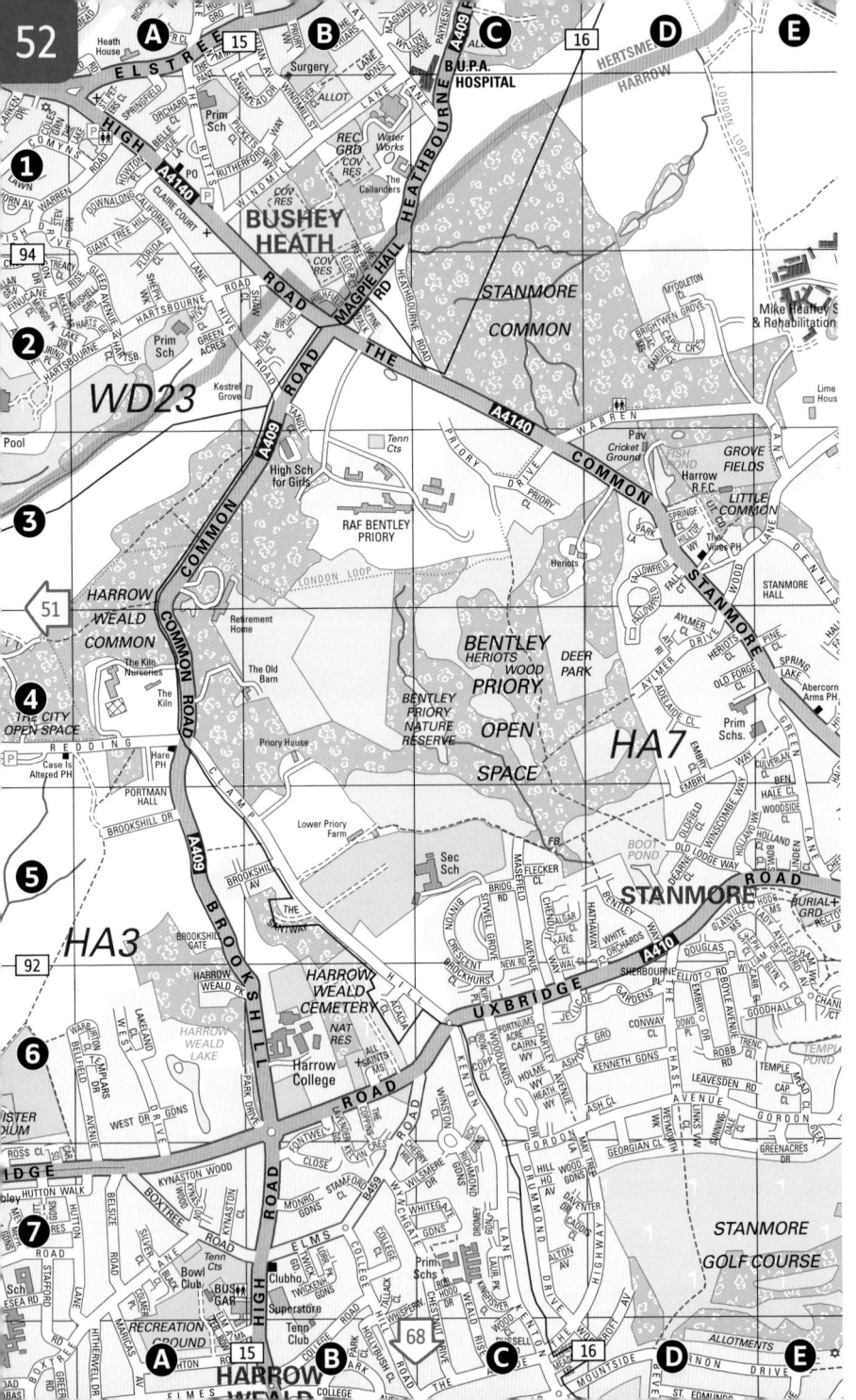

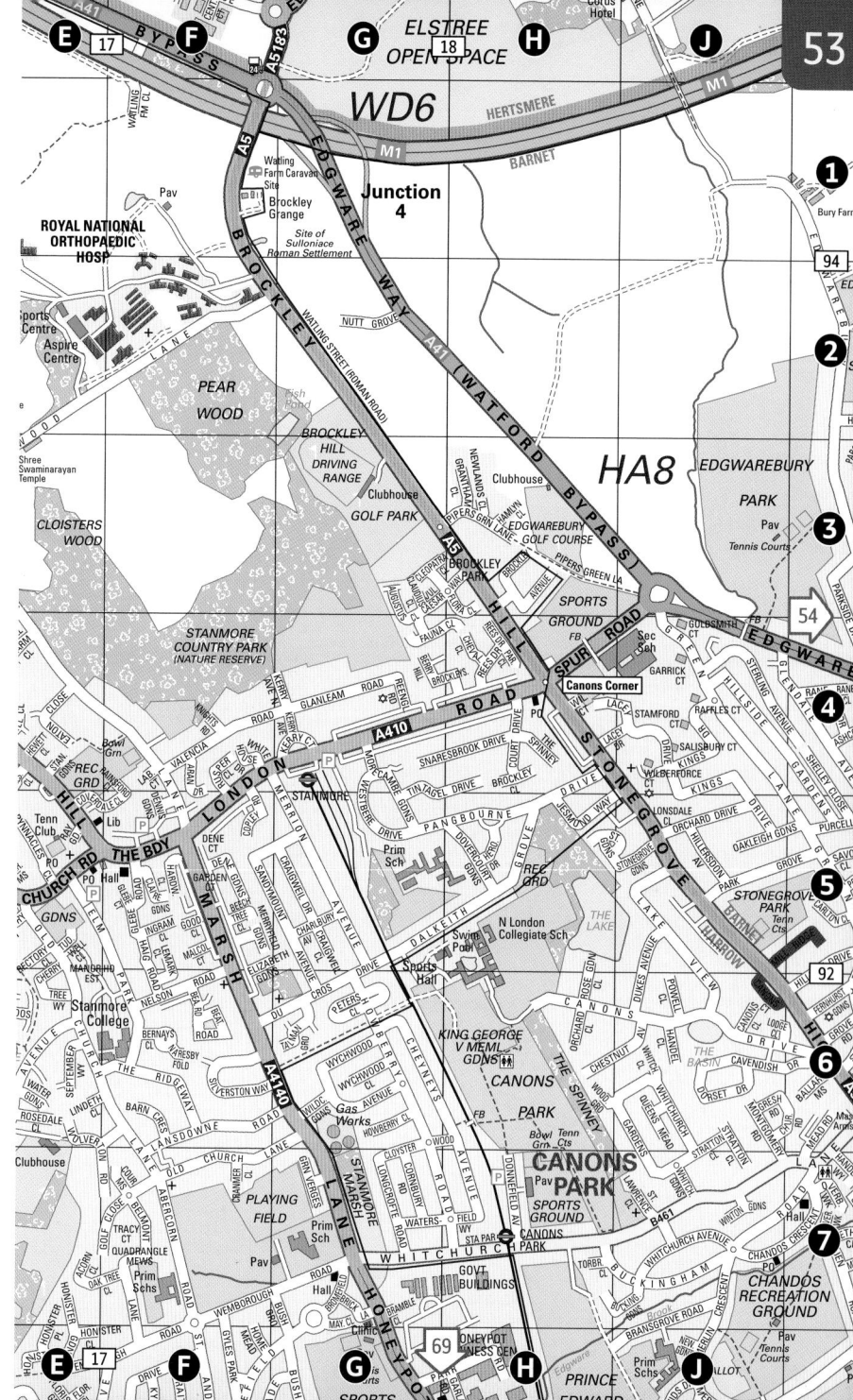

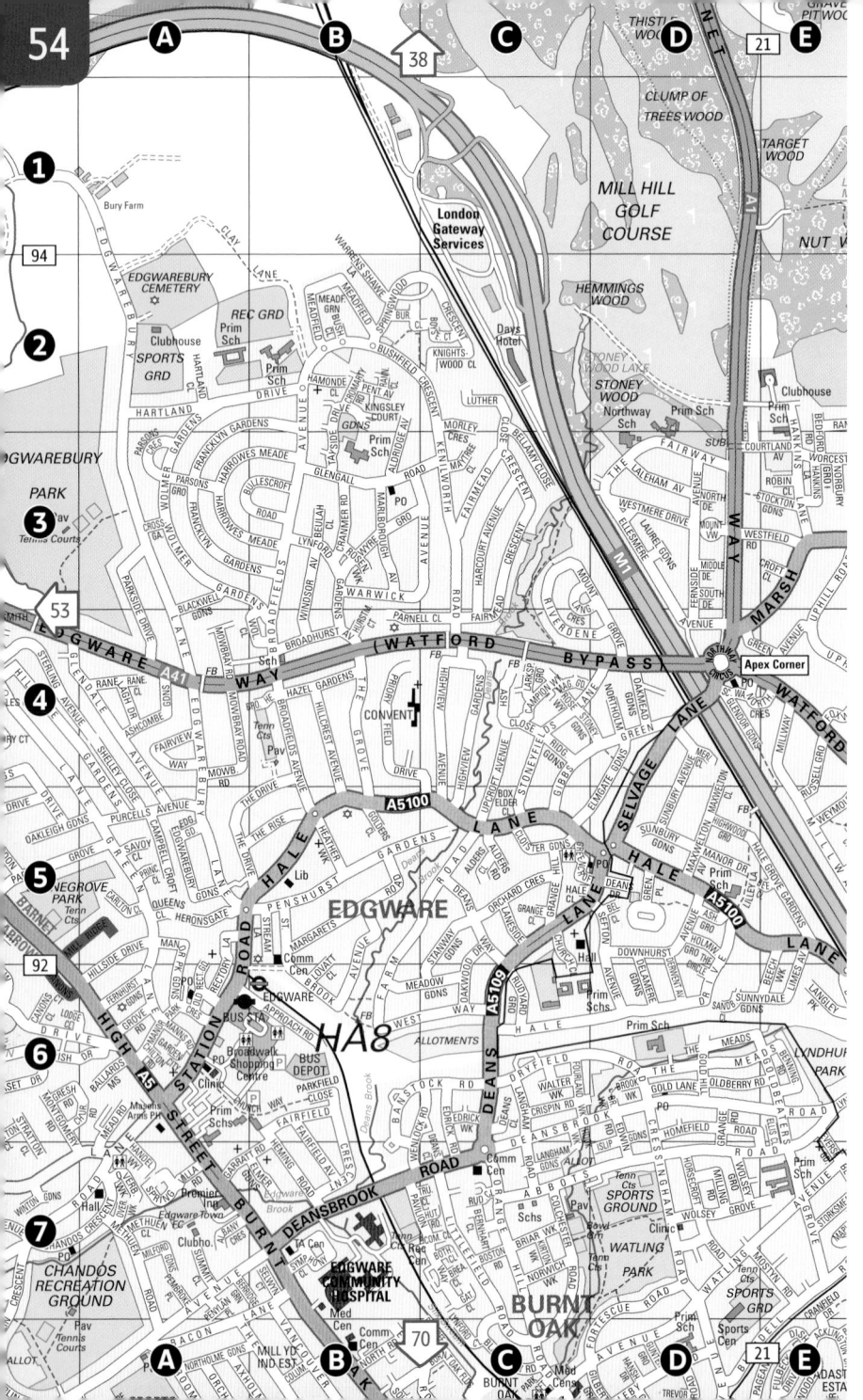

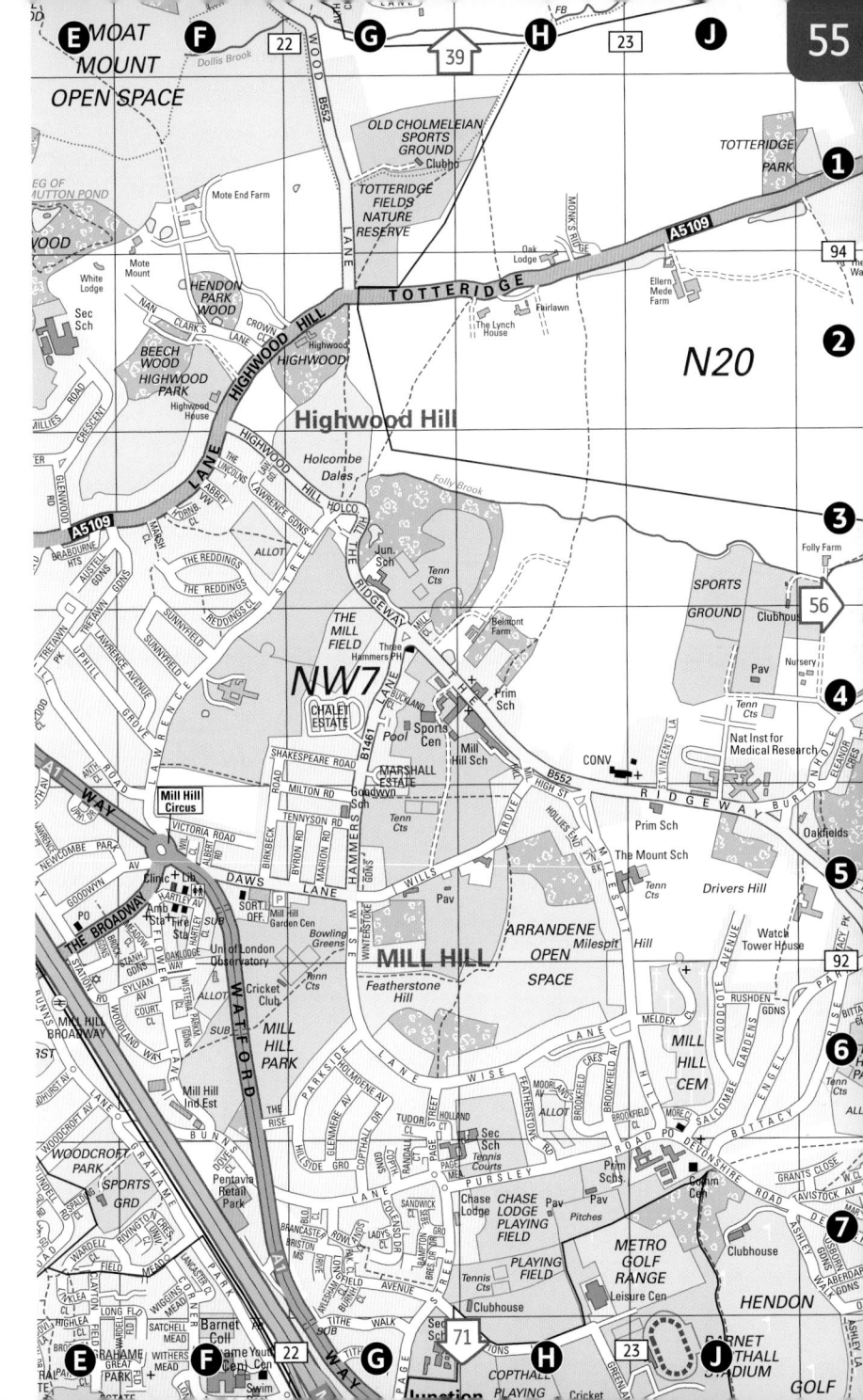

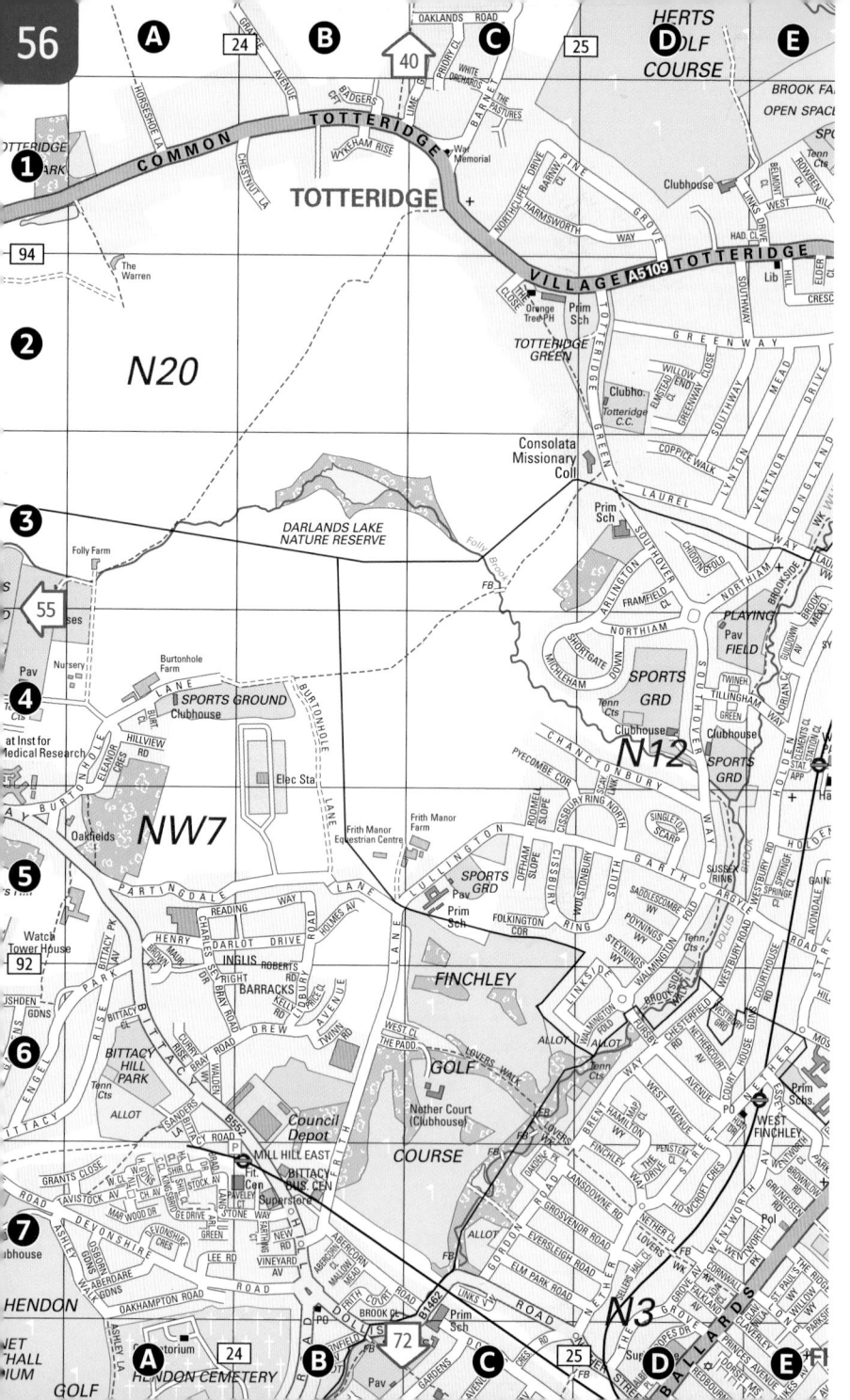

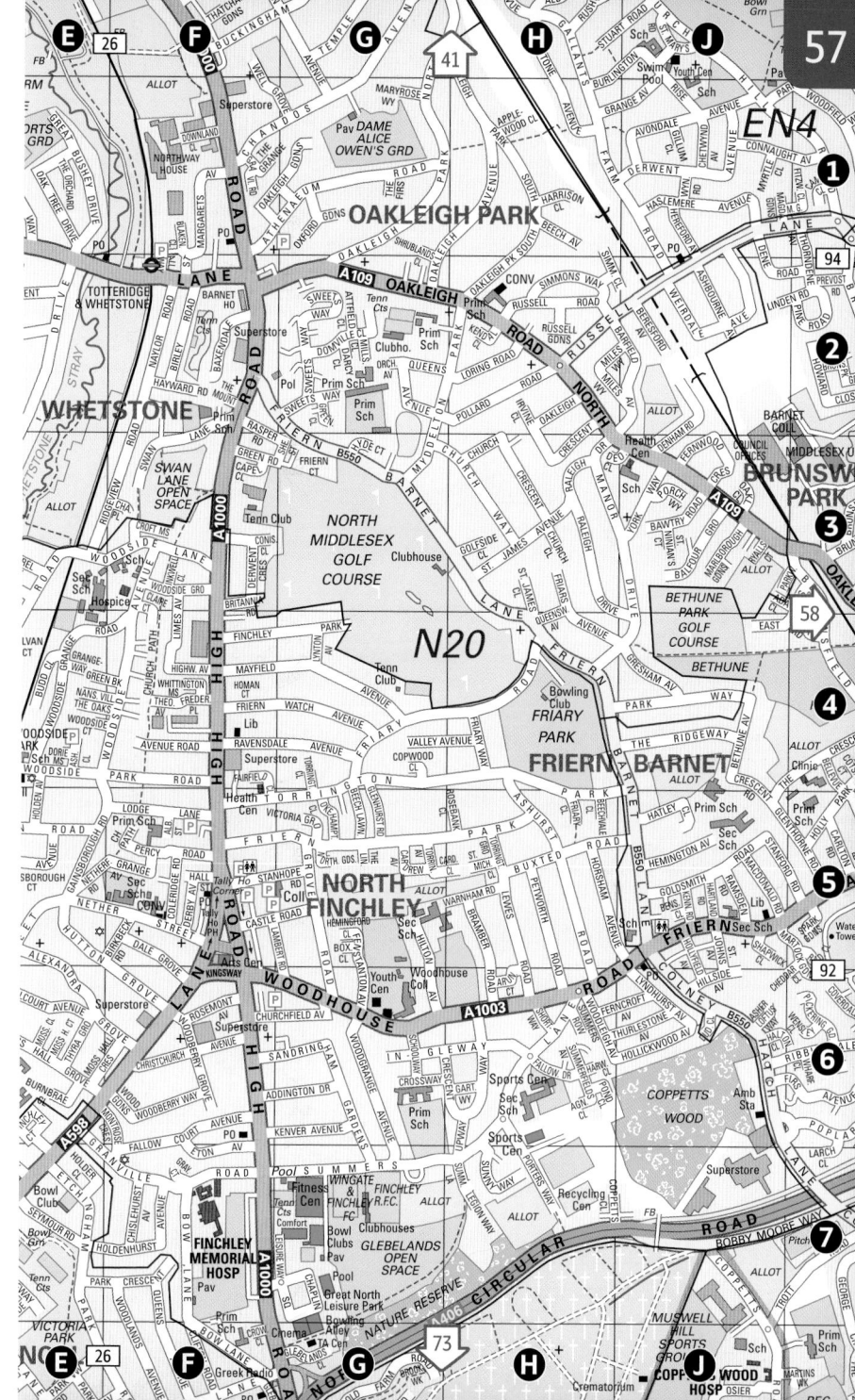

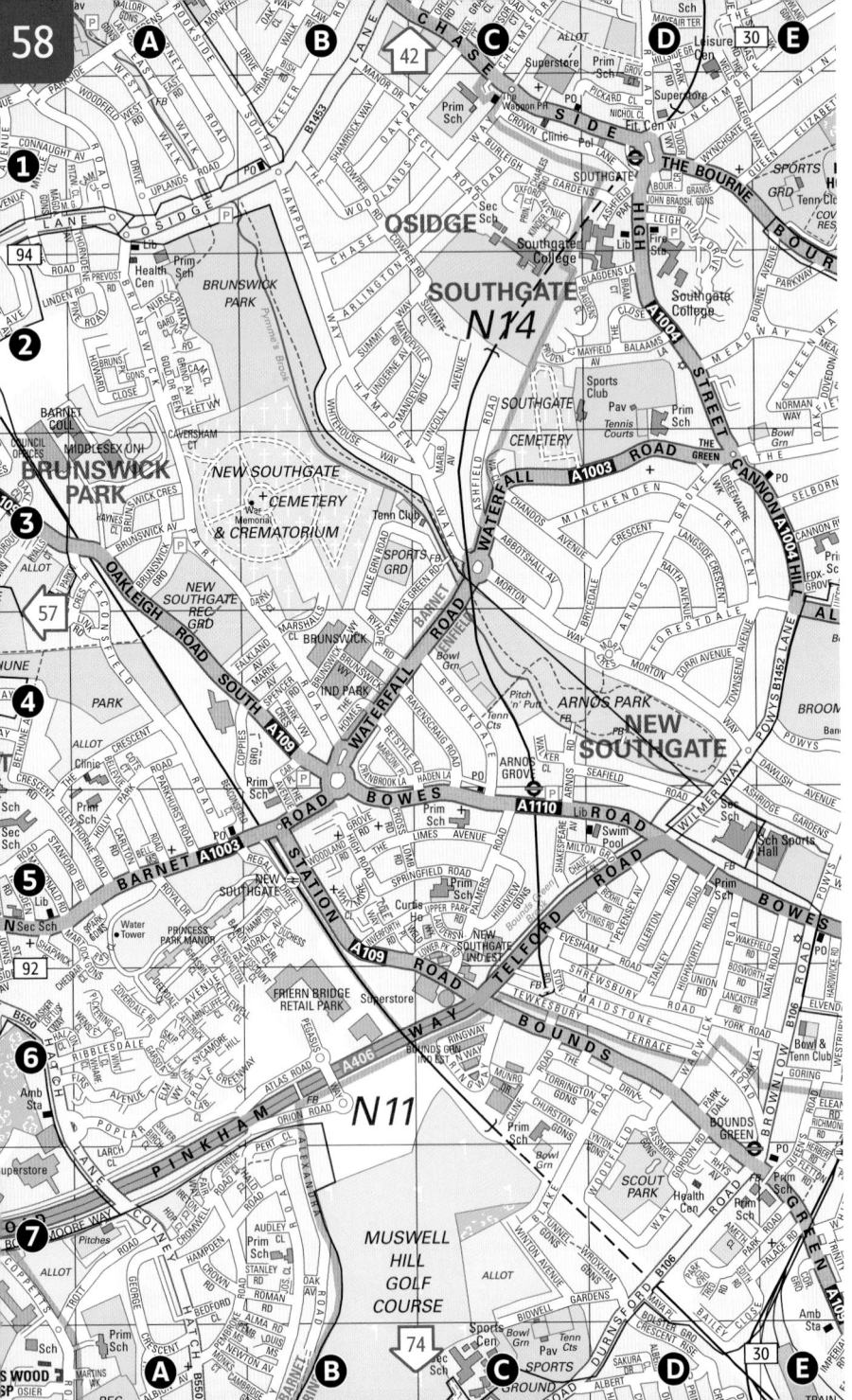

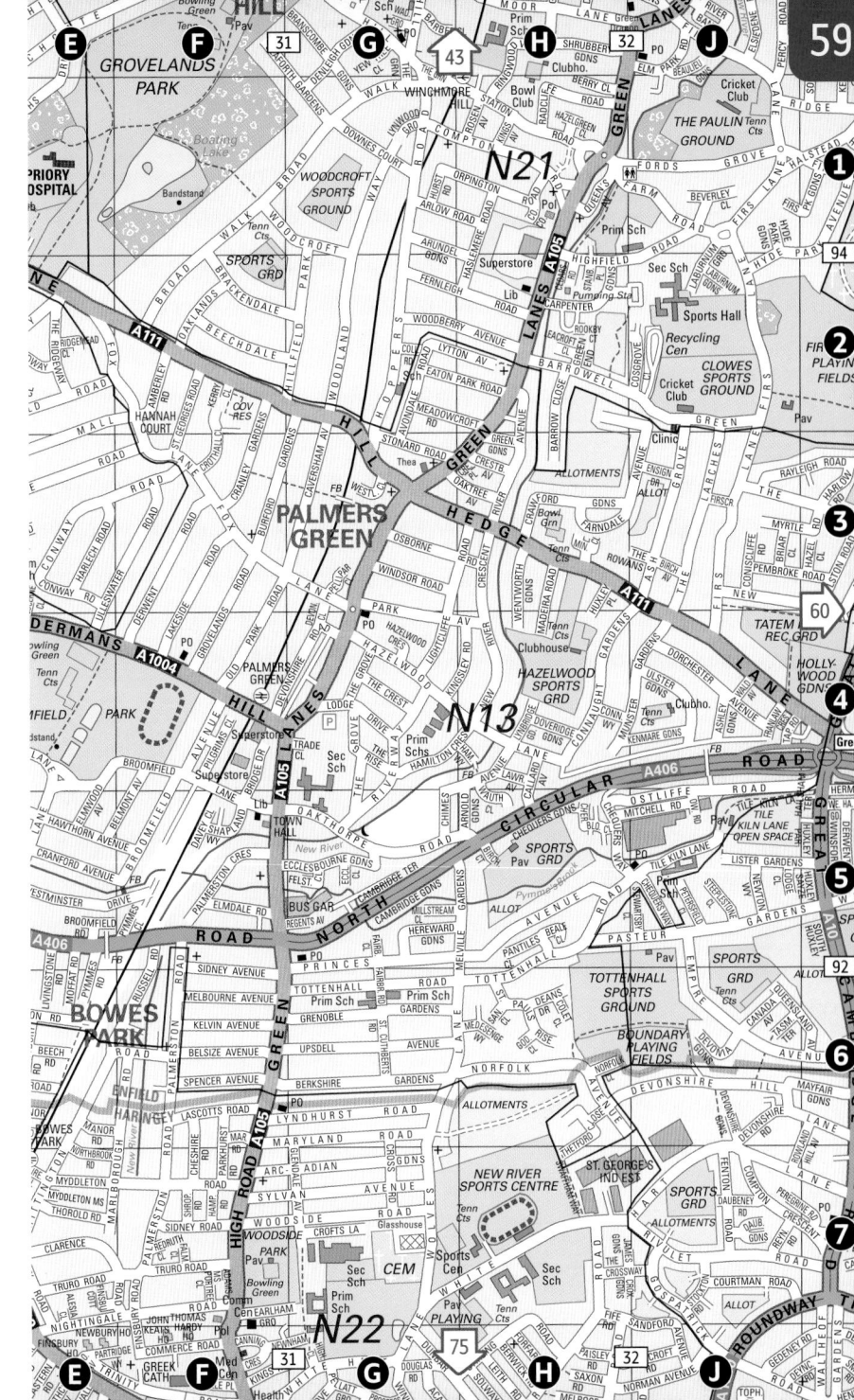

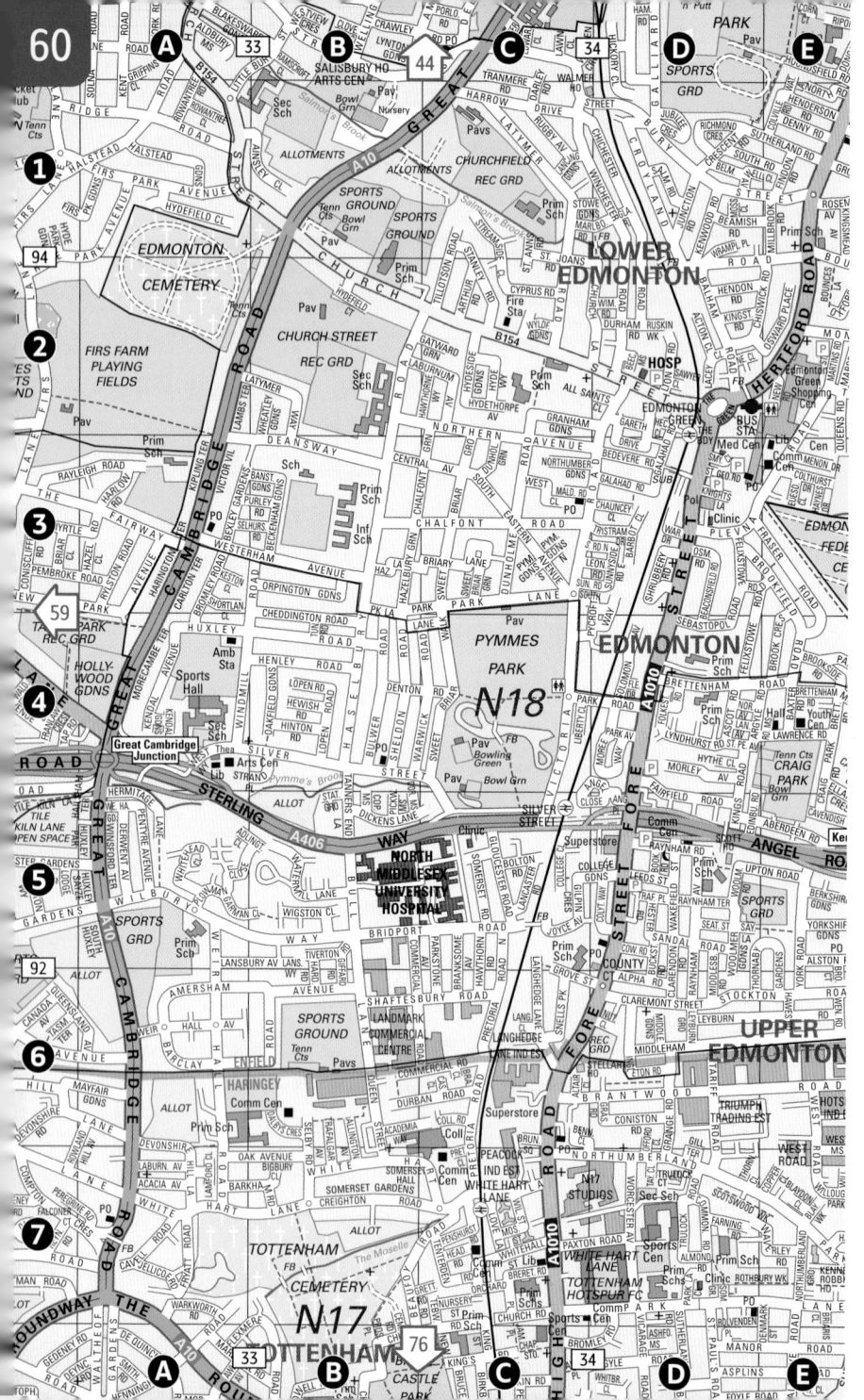

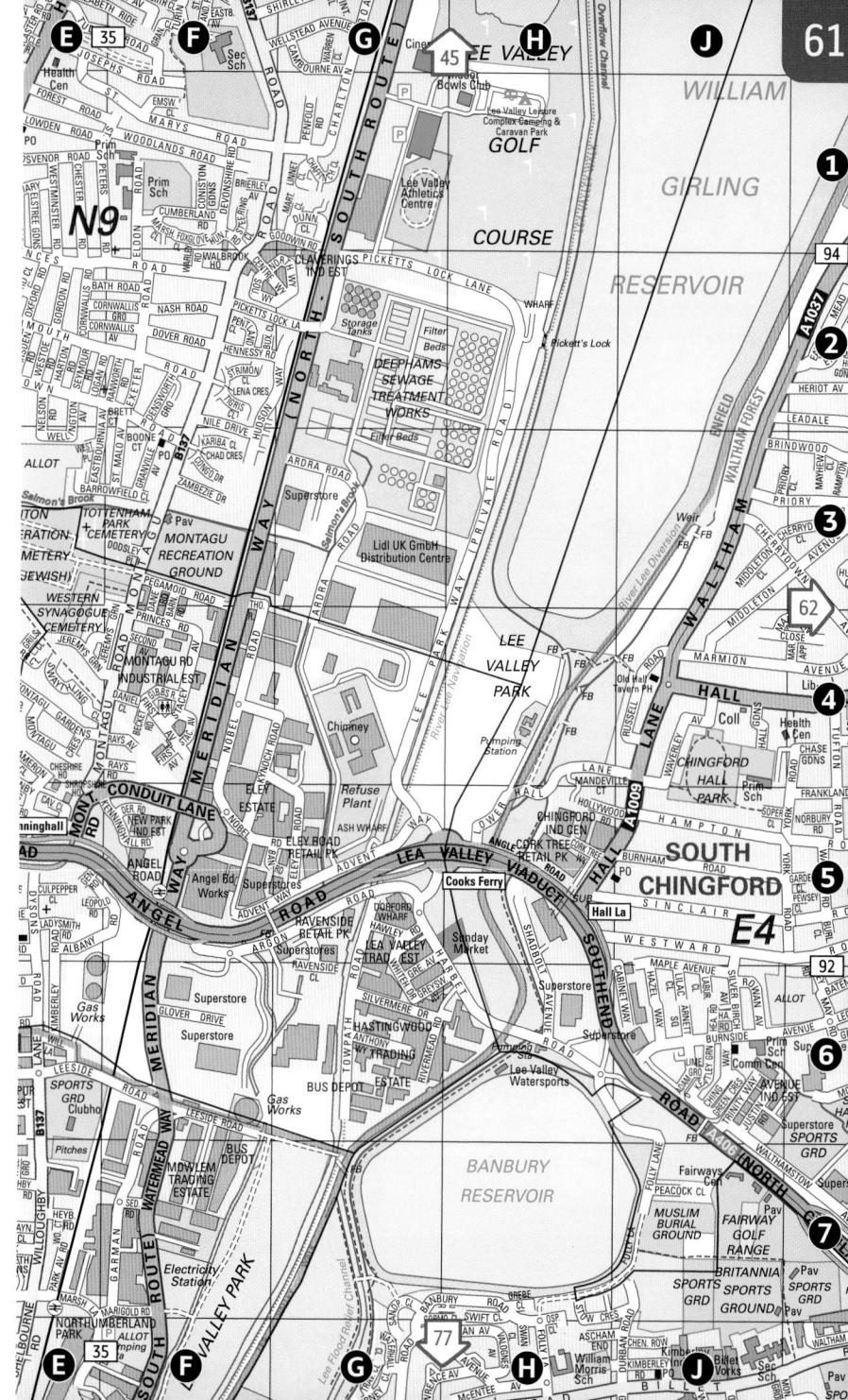

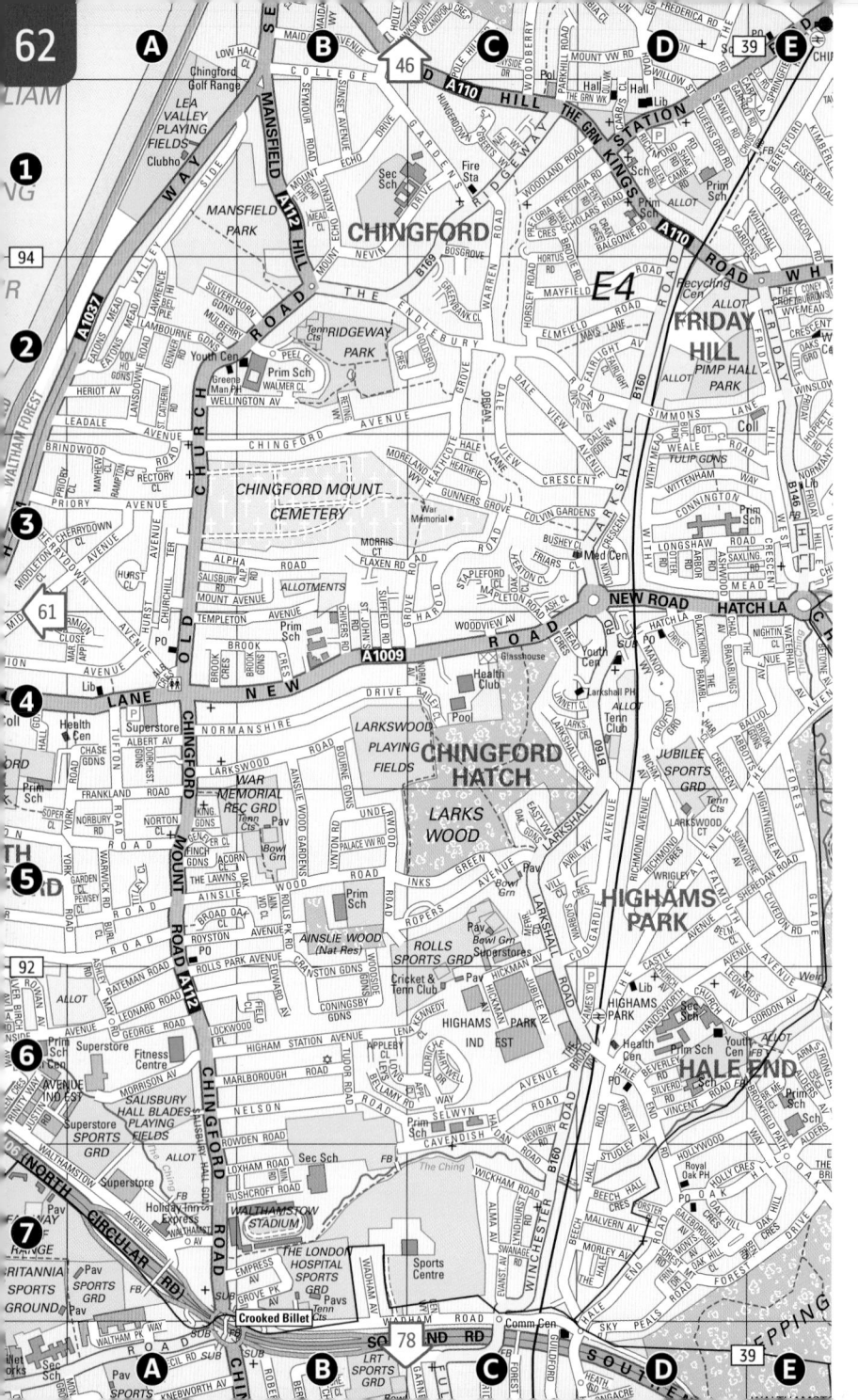

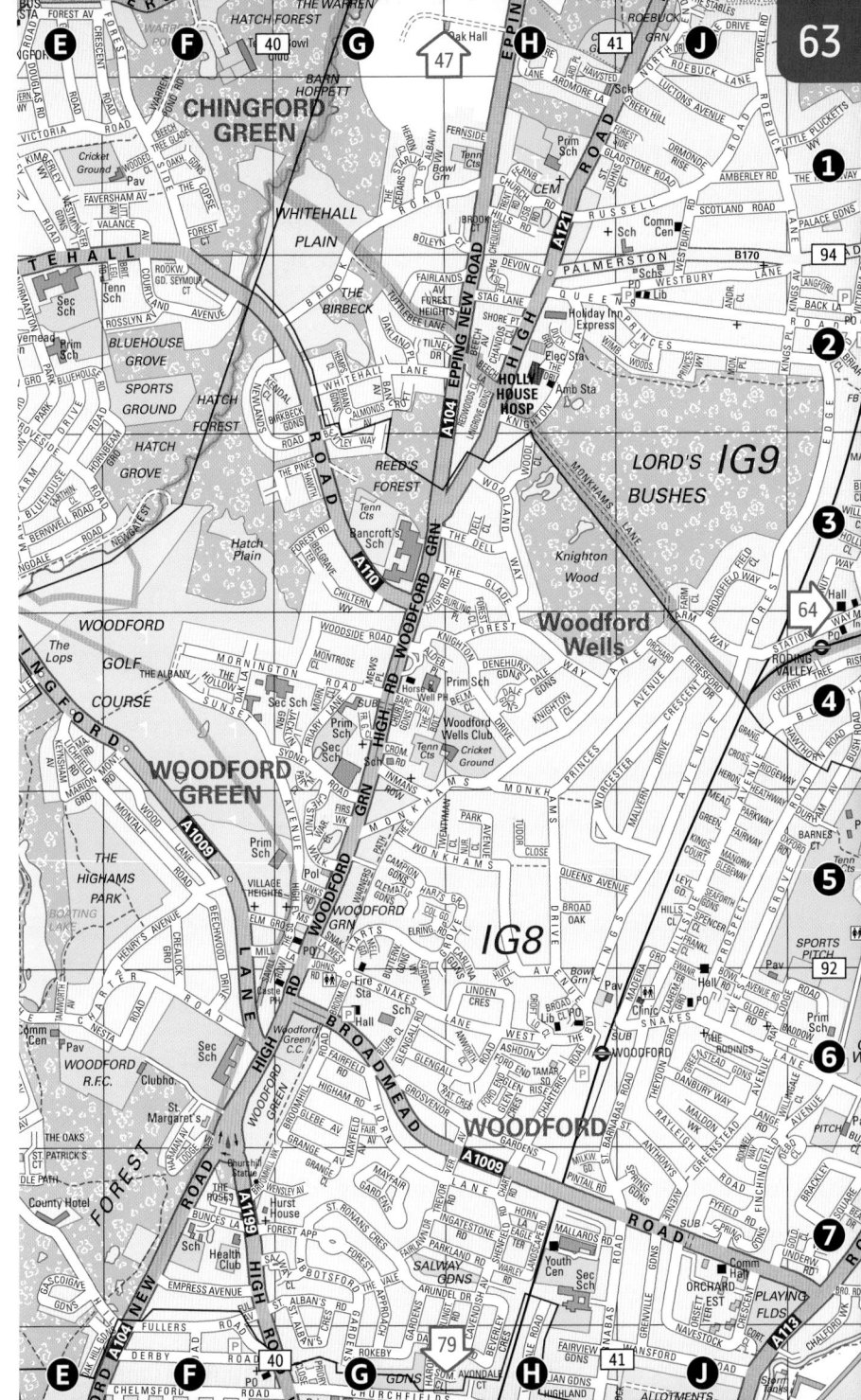

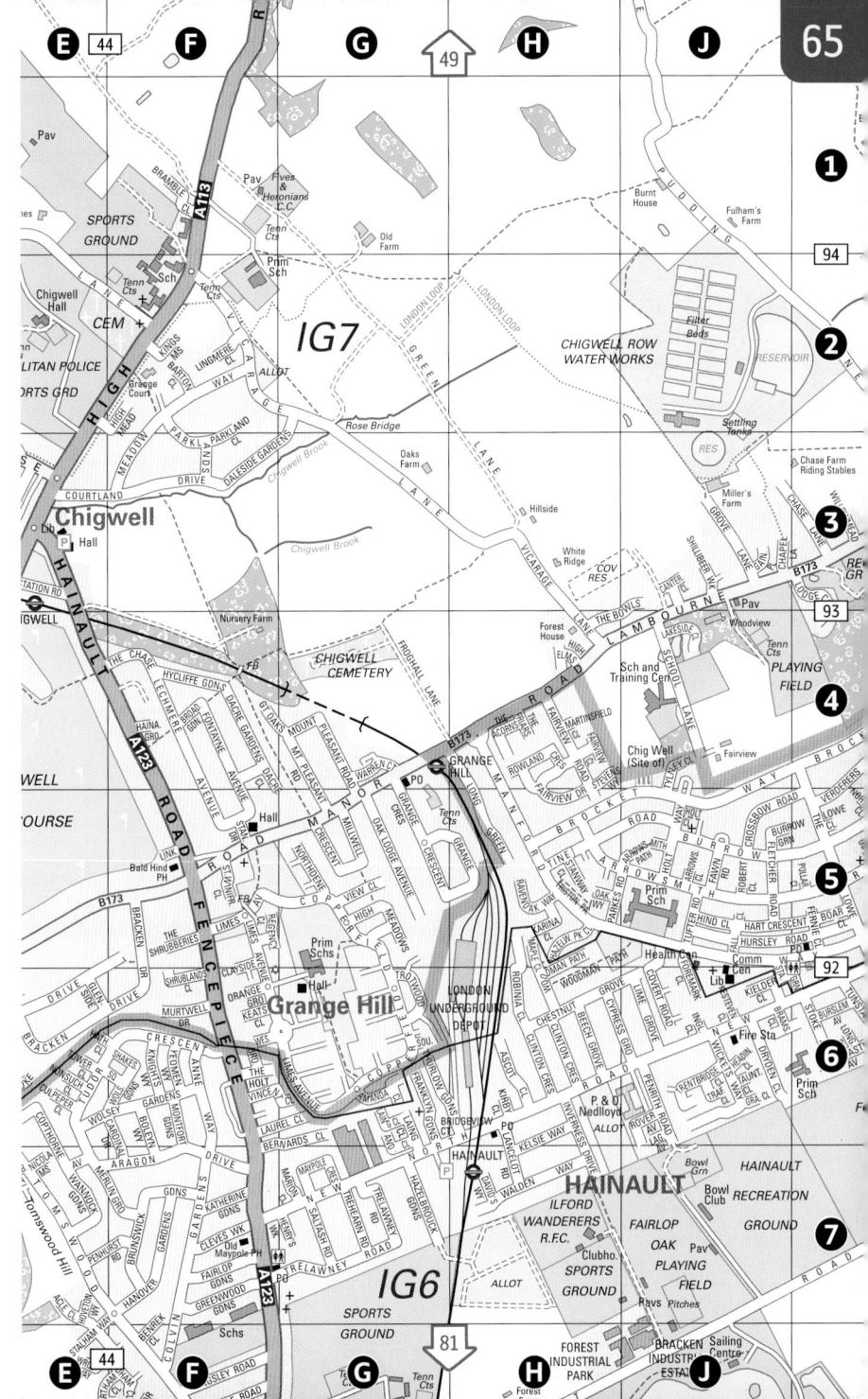

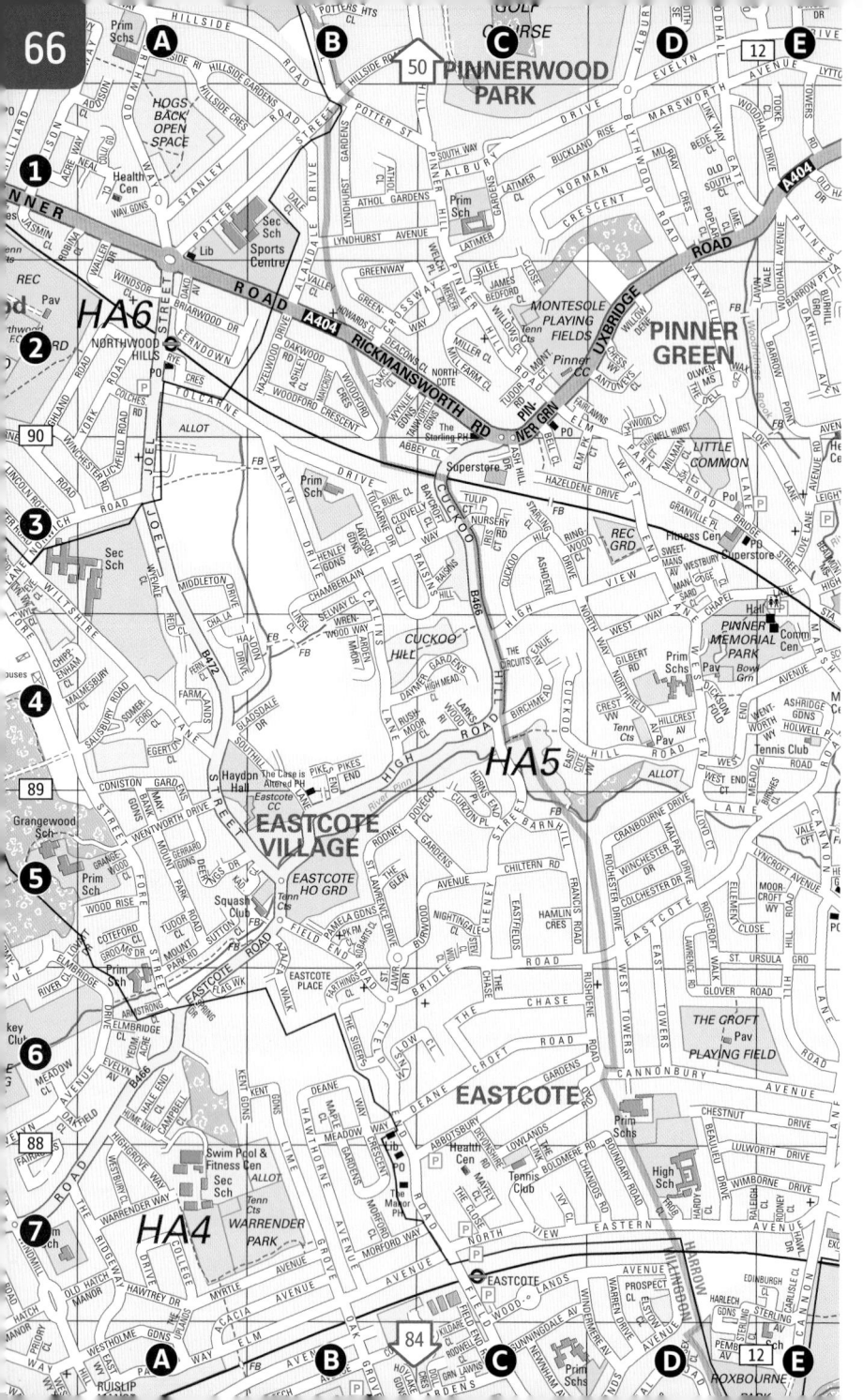

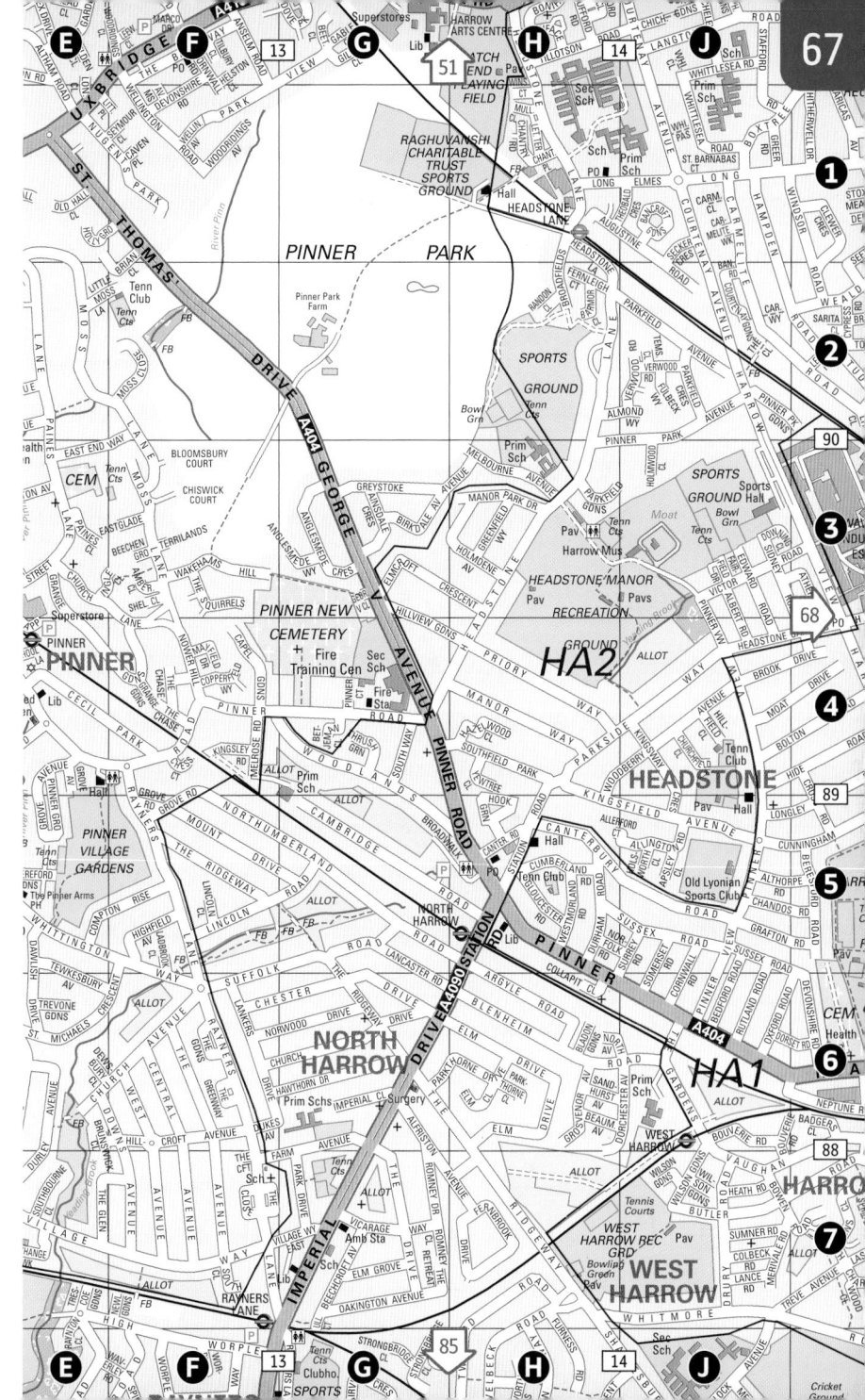

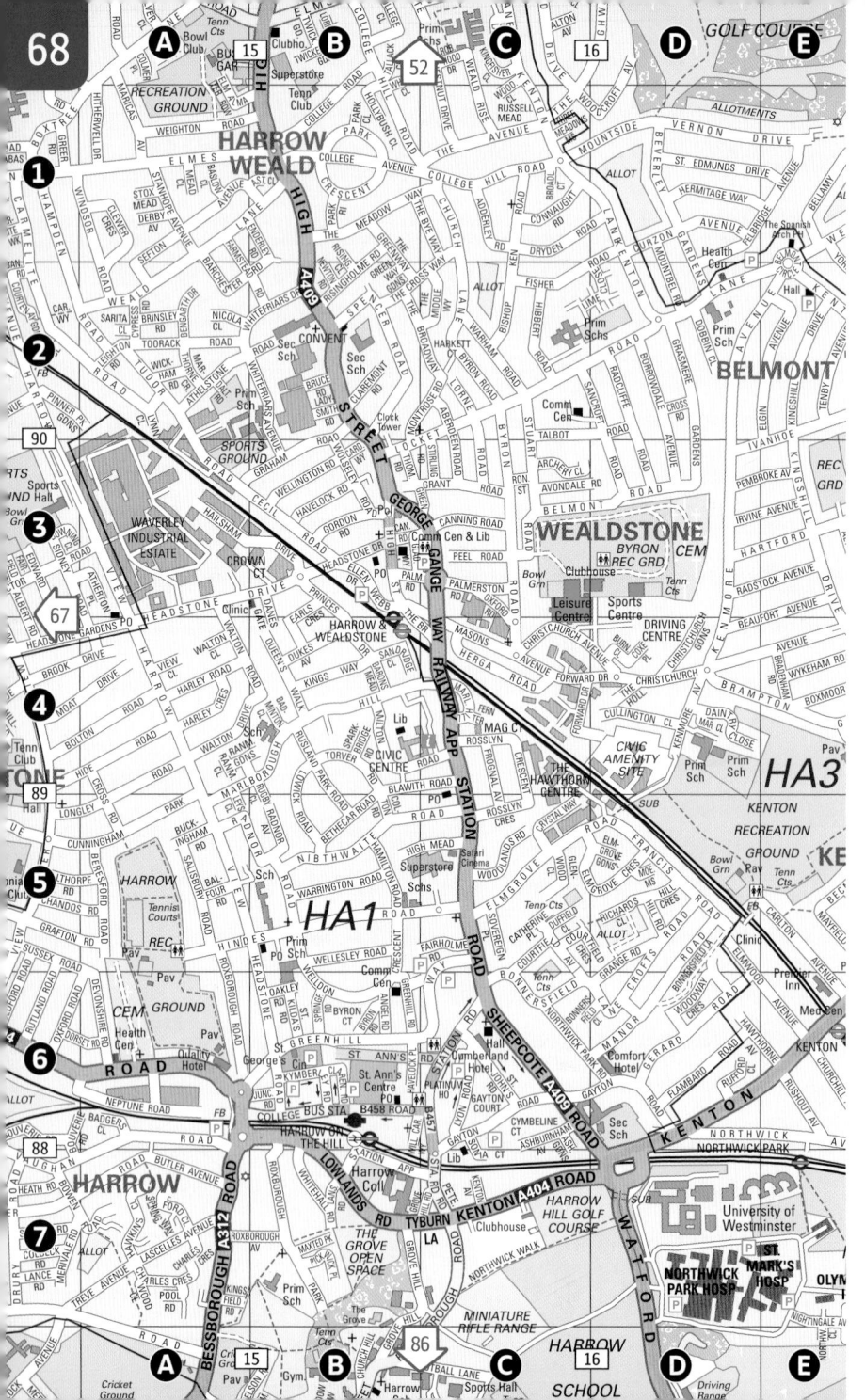

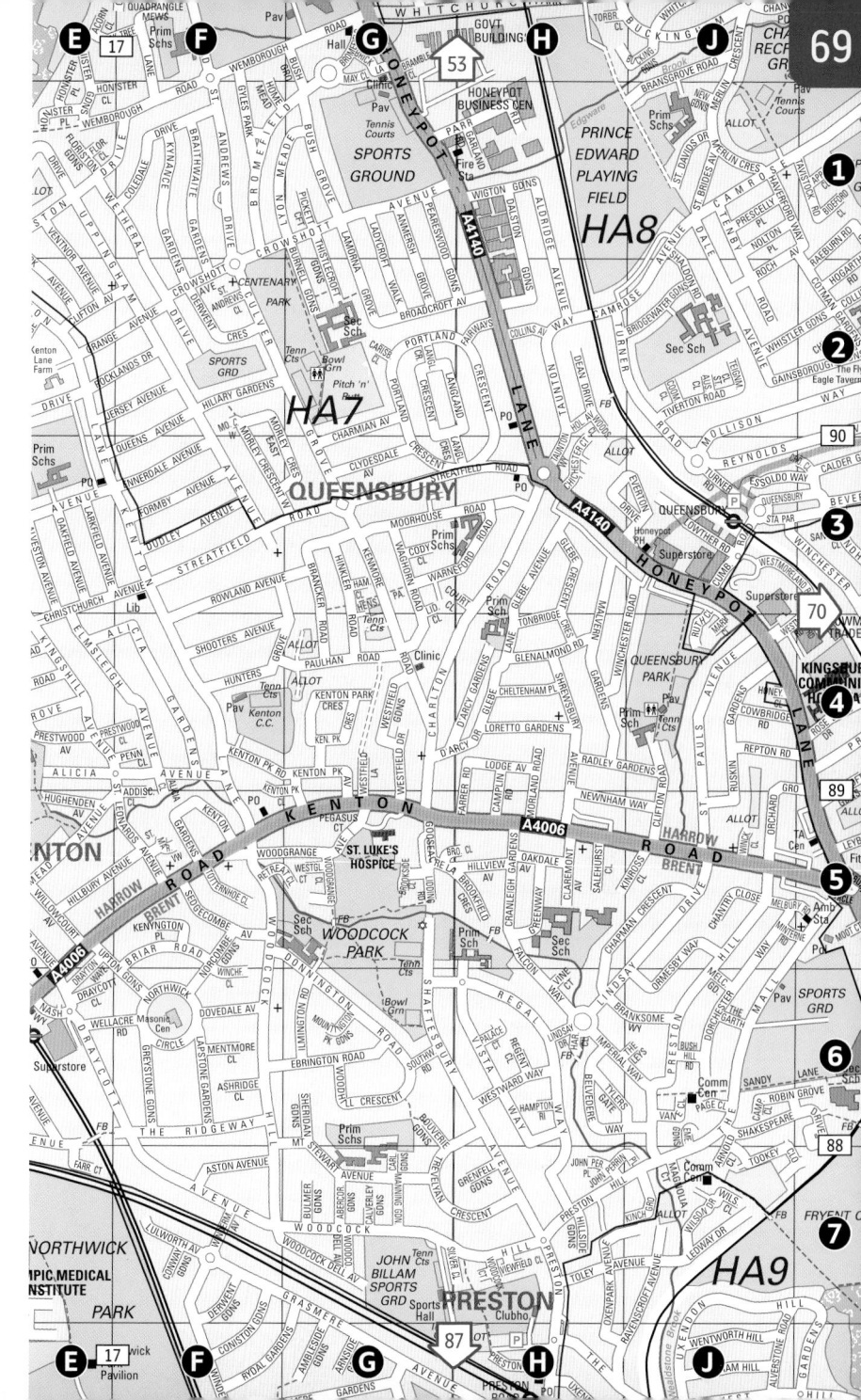

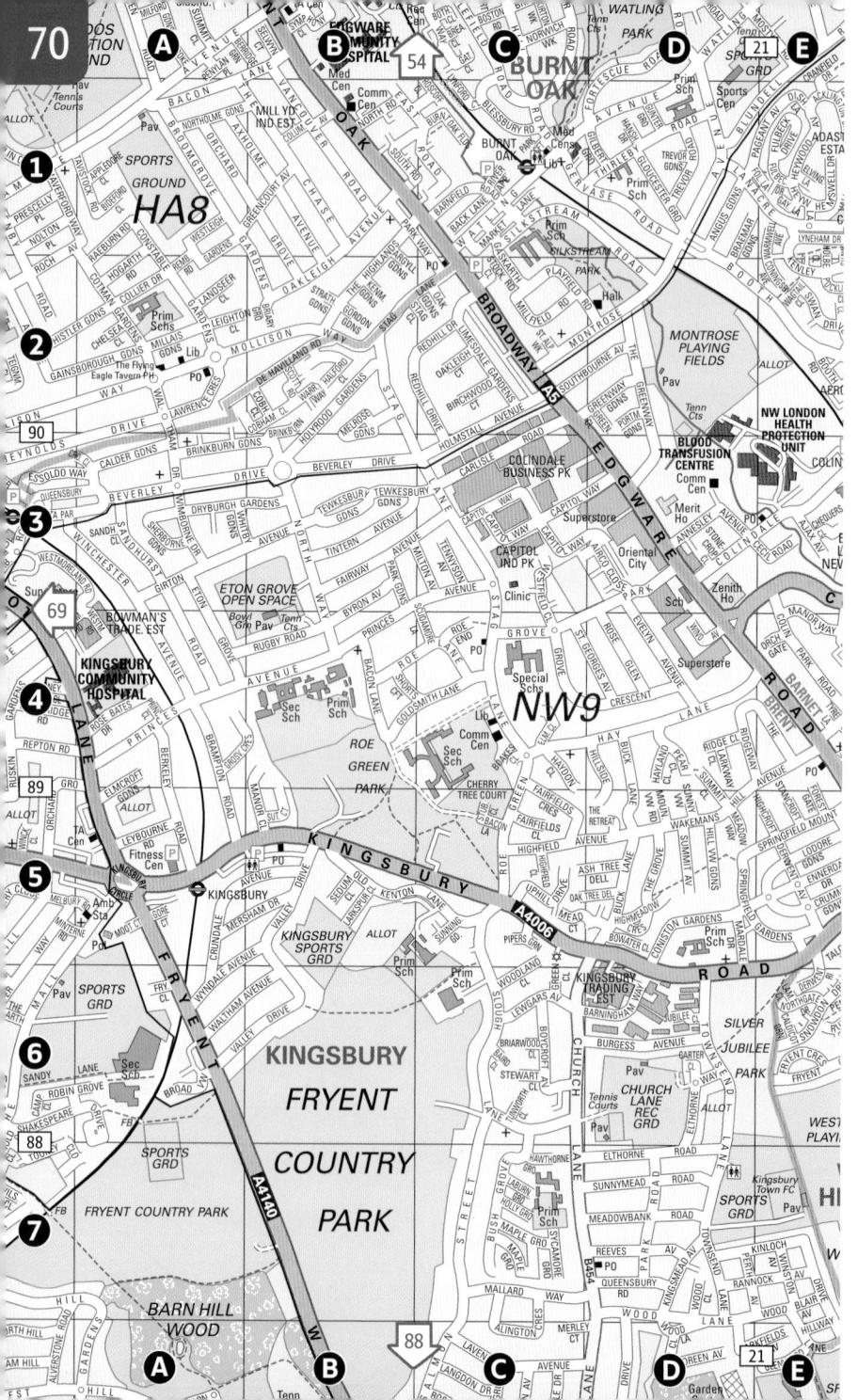

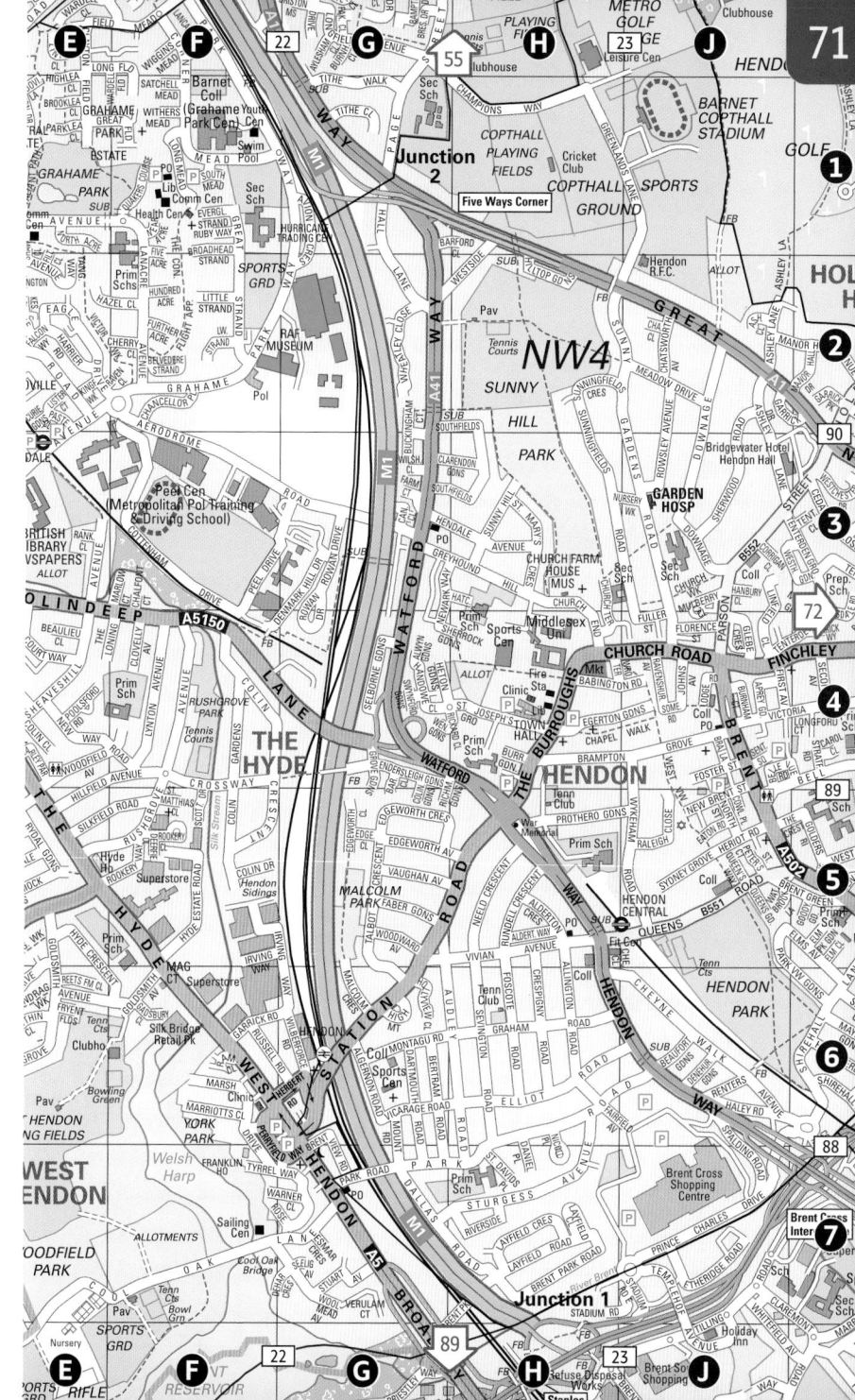

71

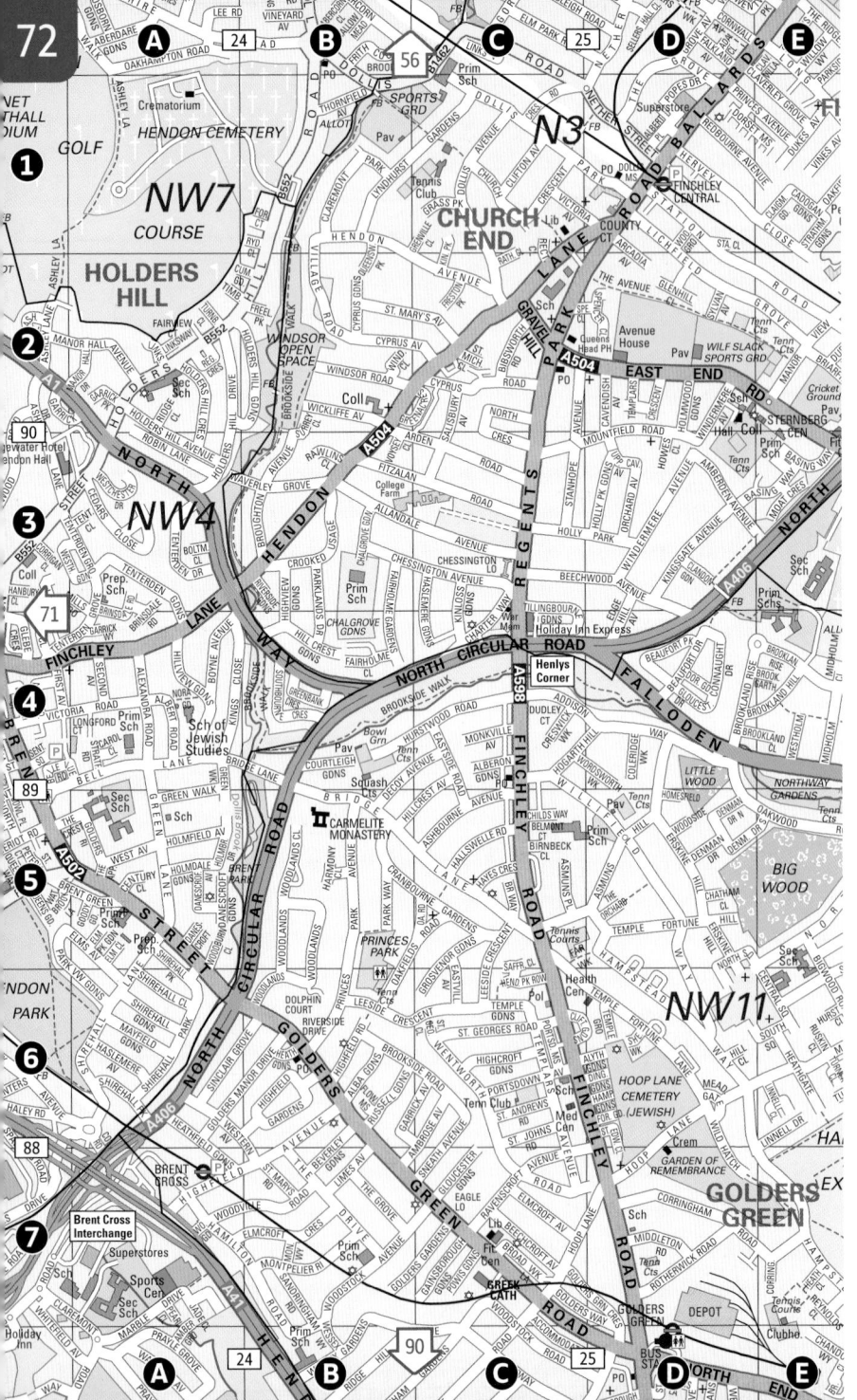

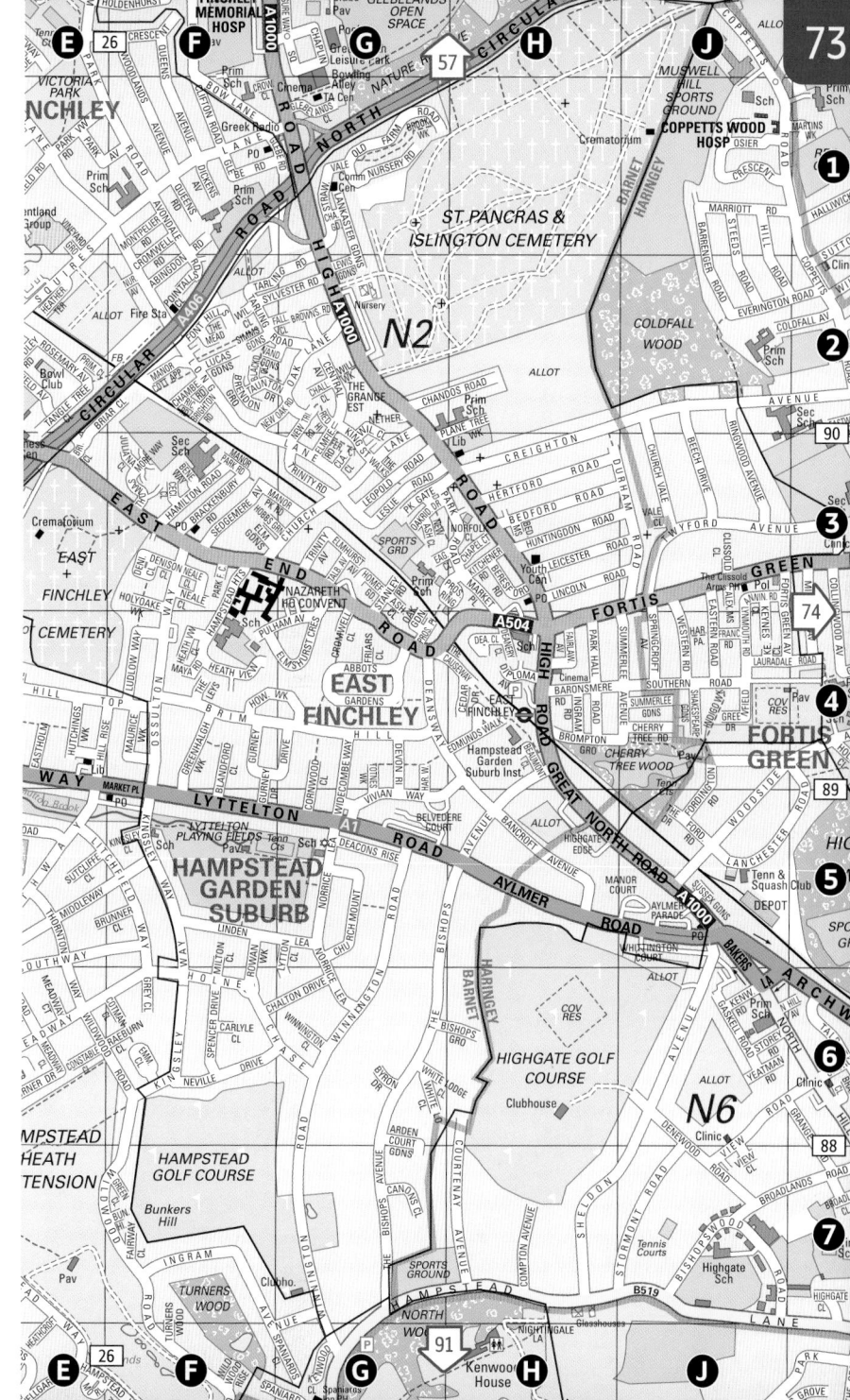

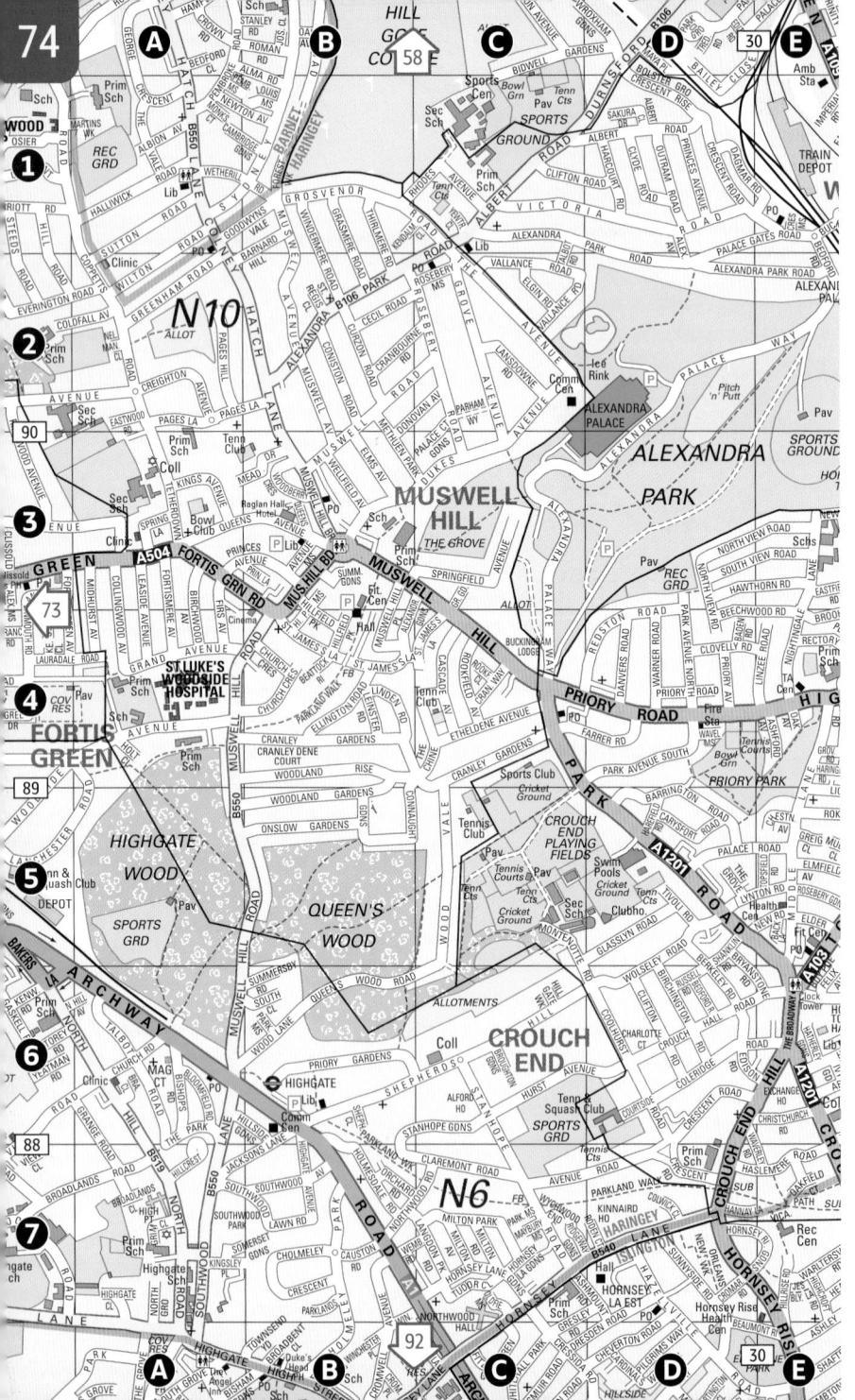

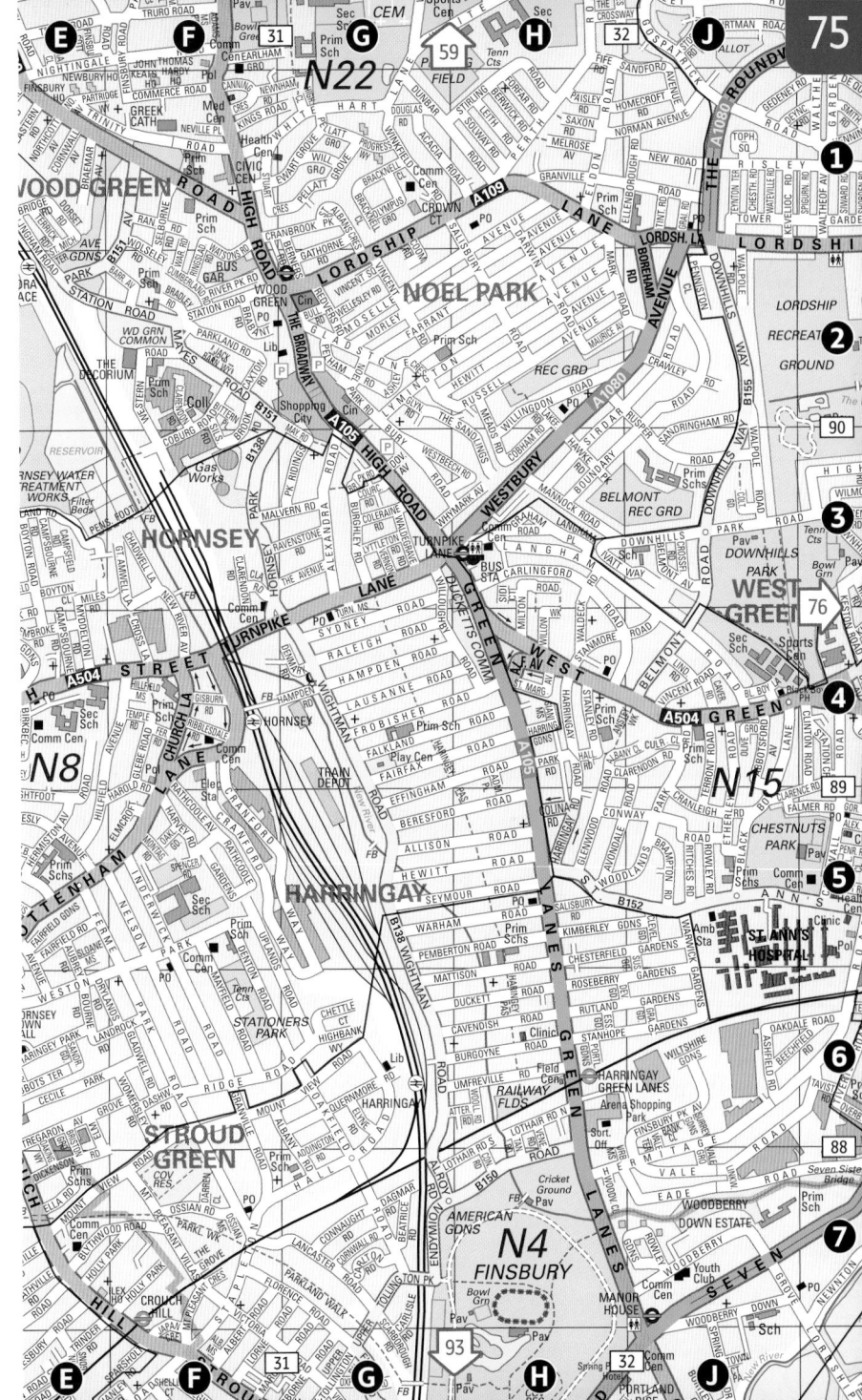

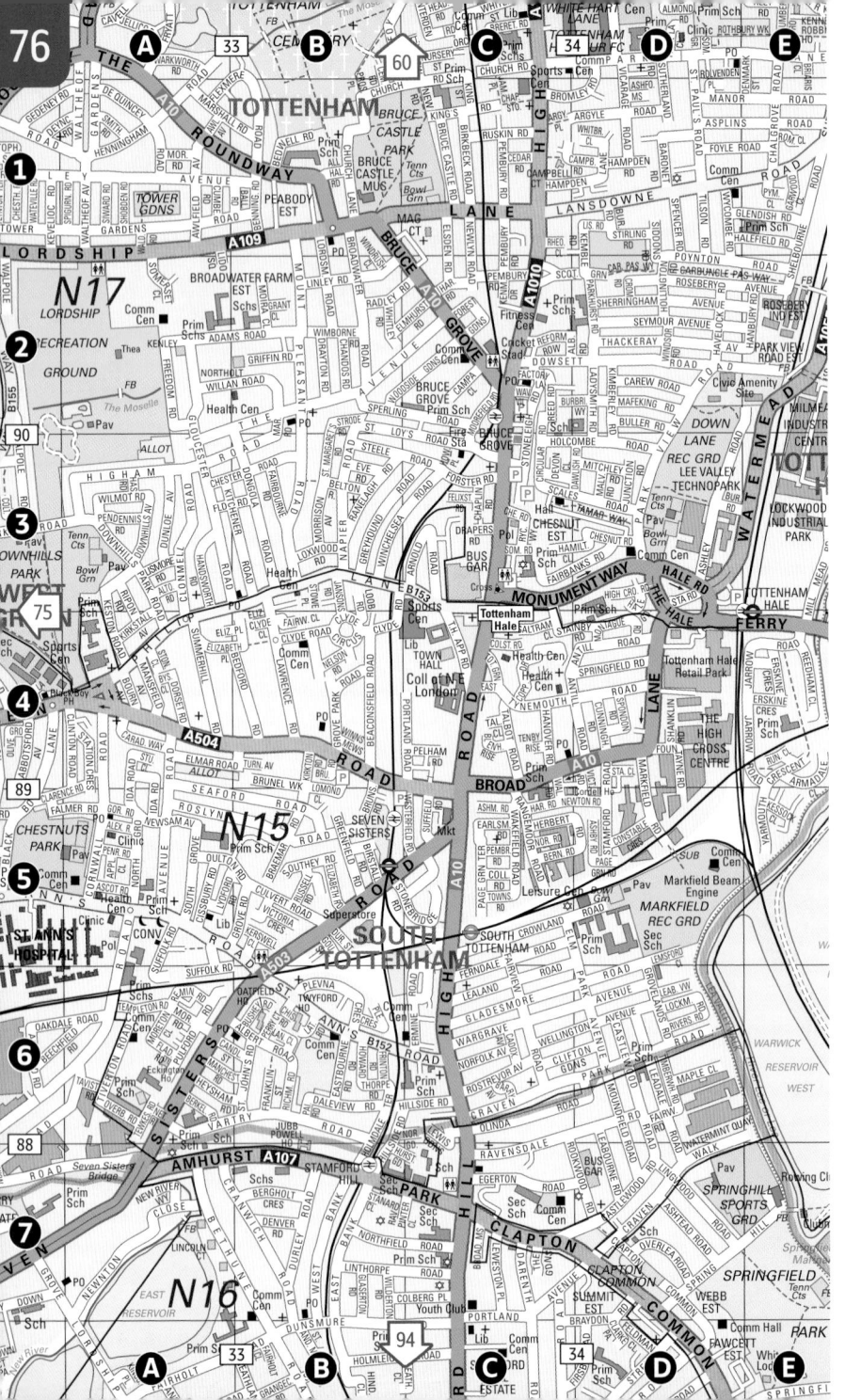

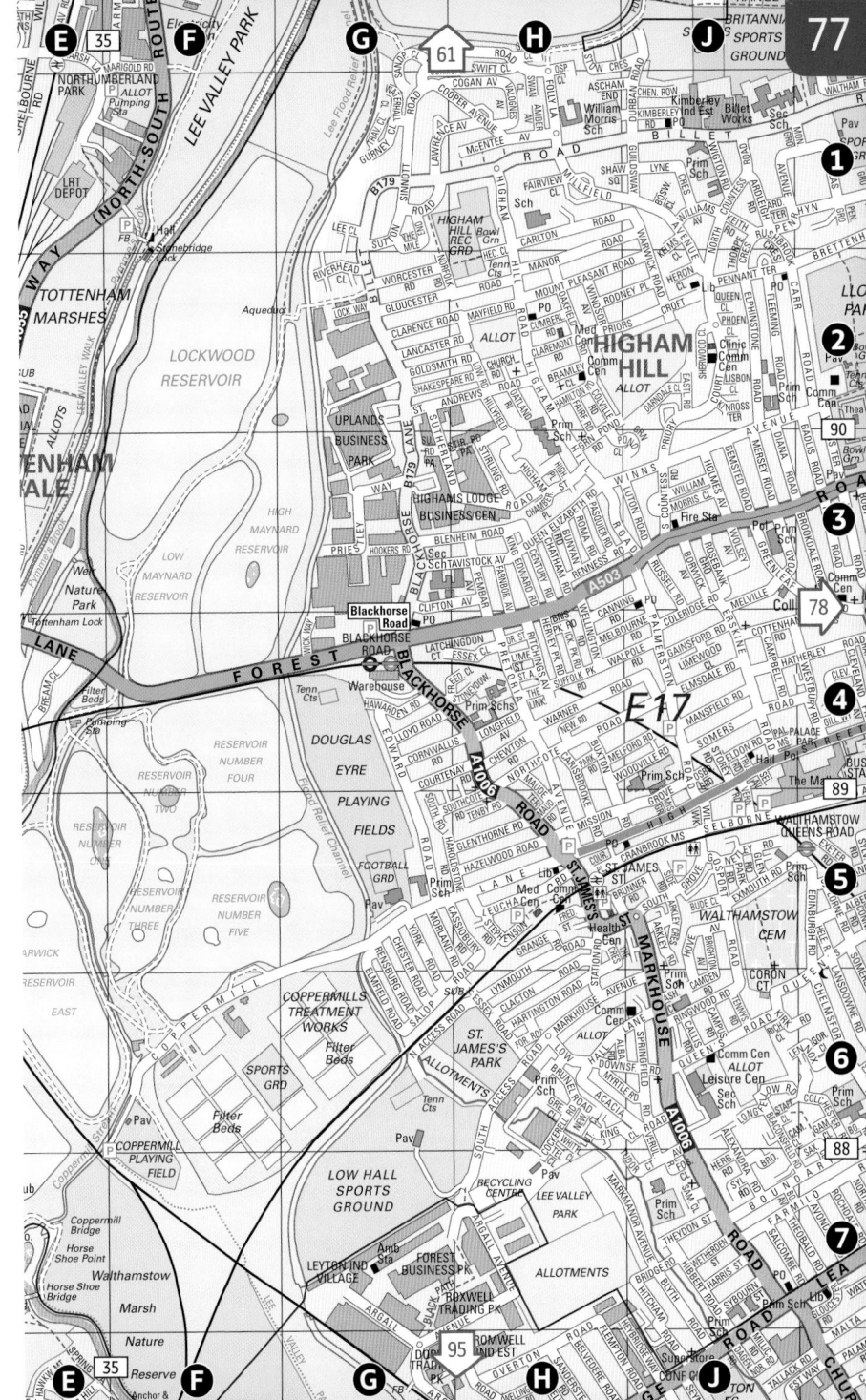

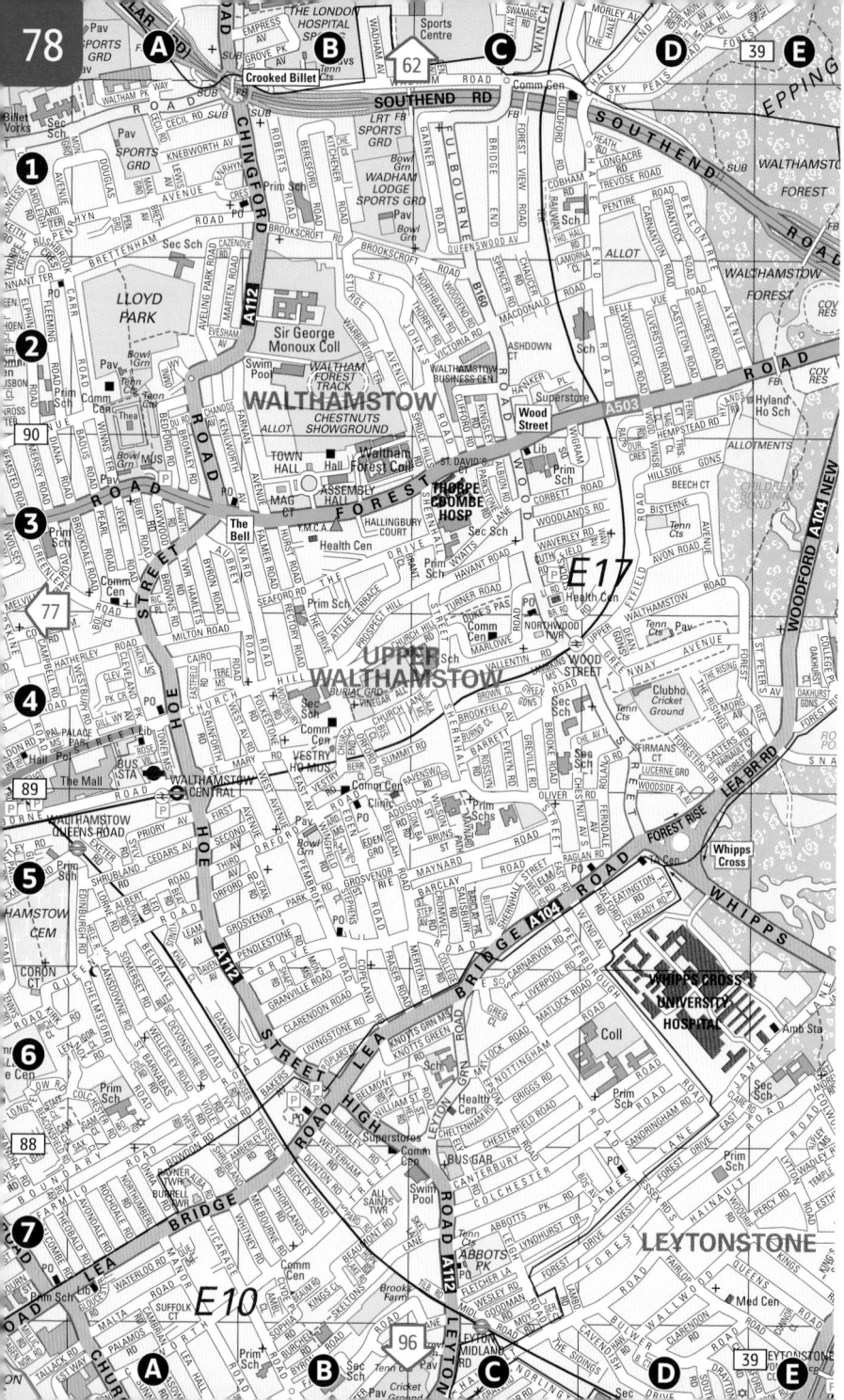

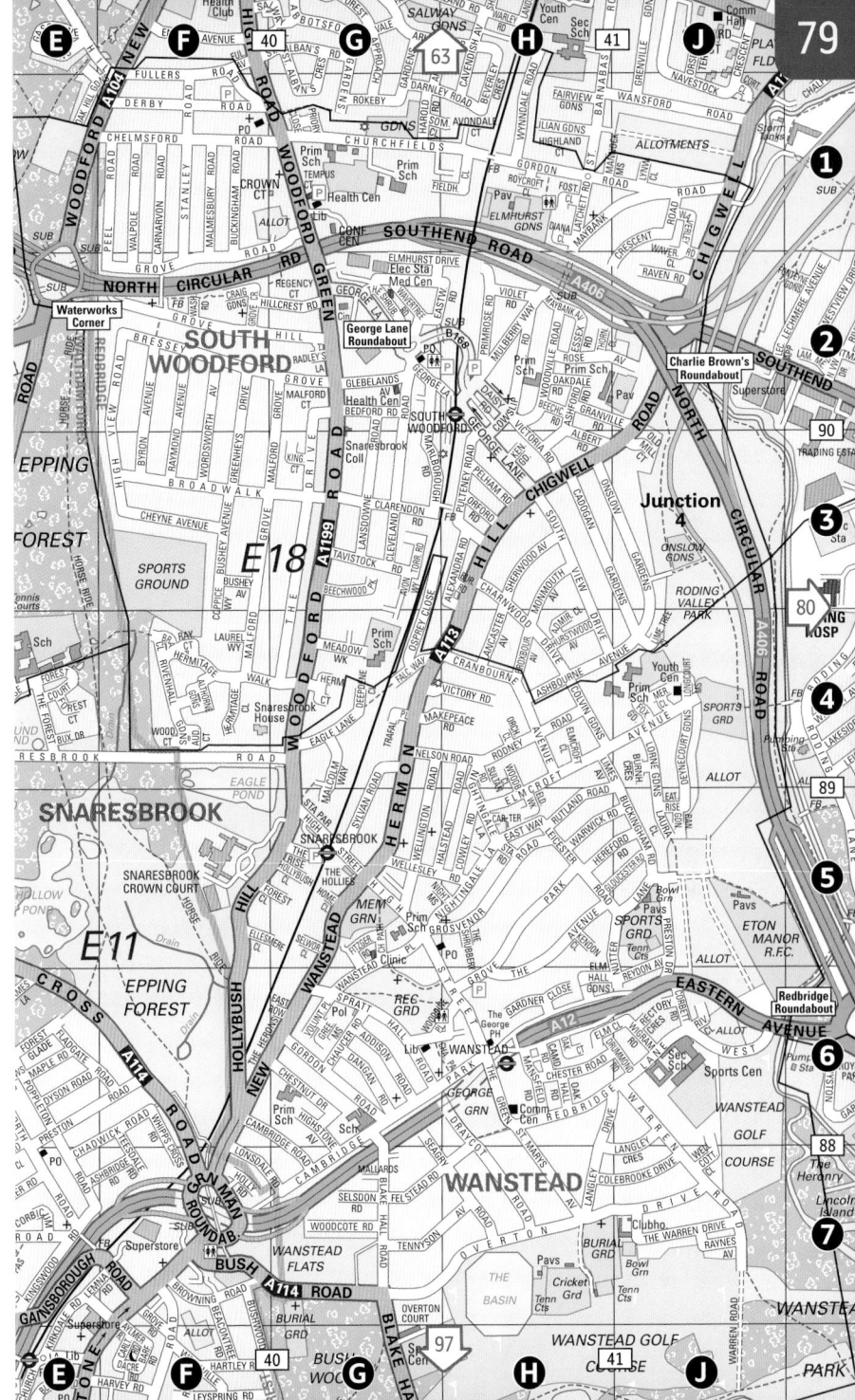

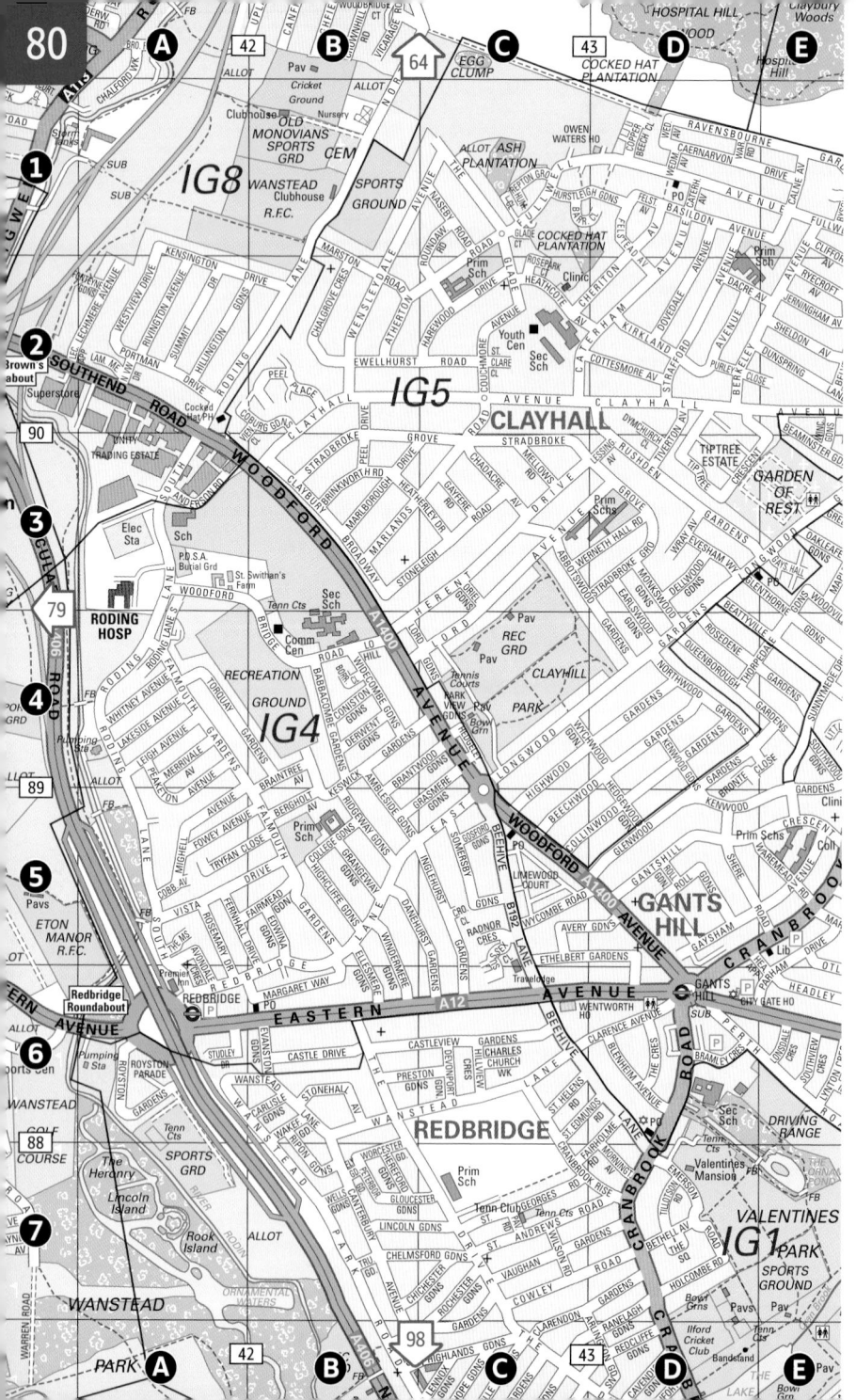

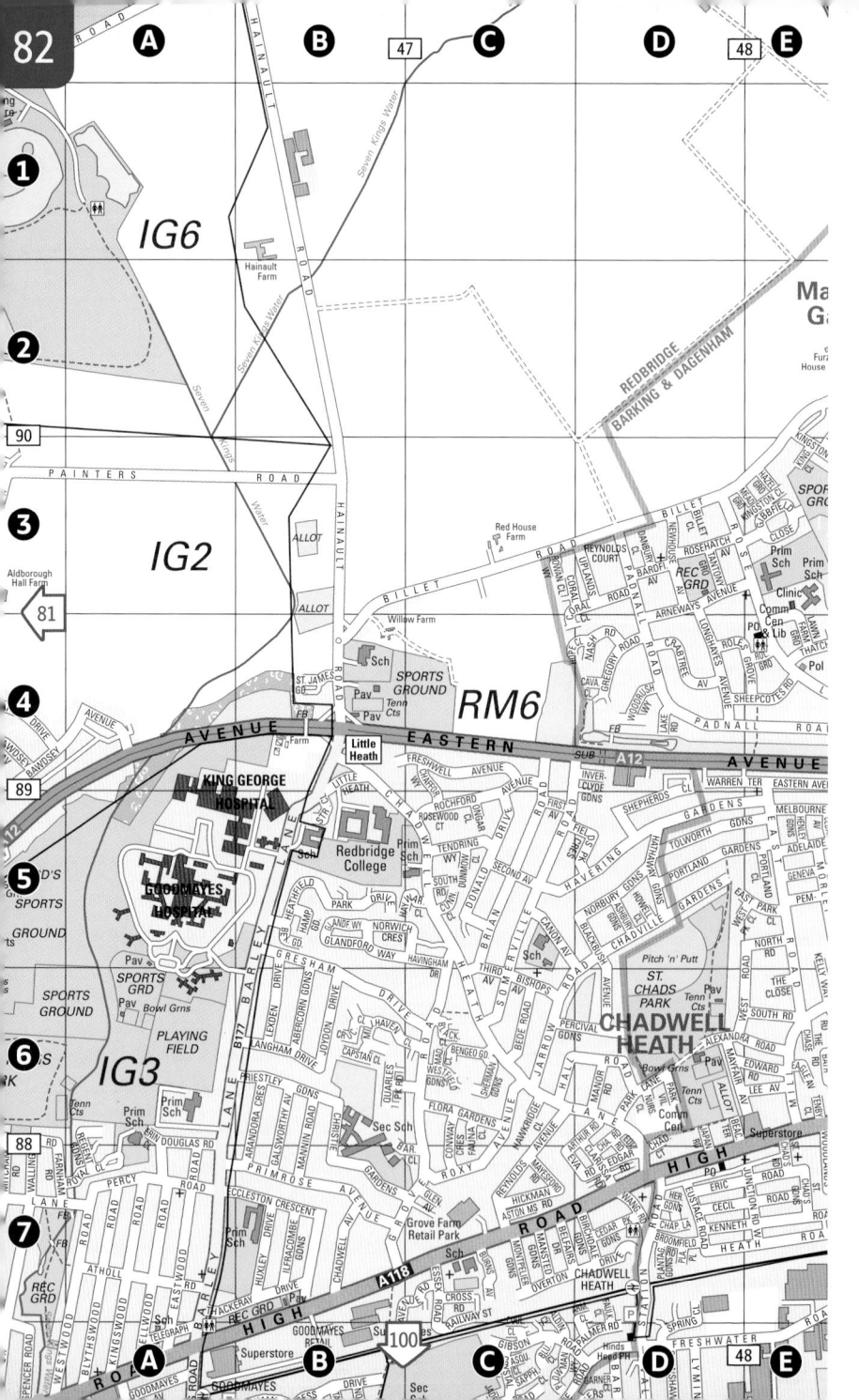

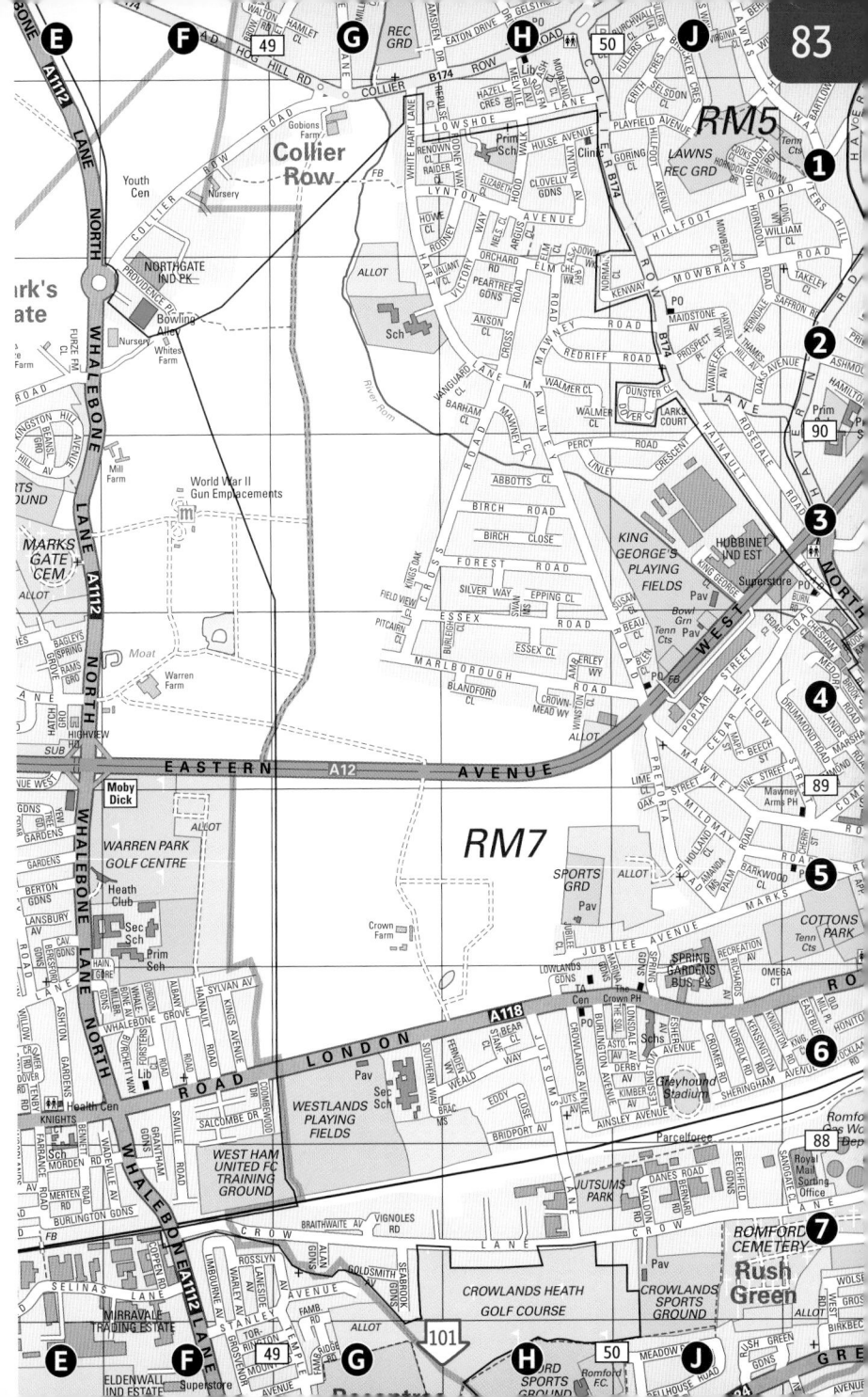

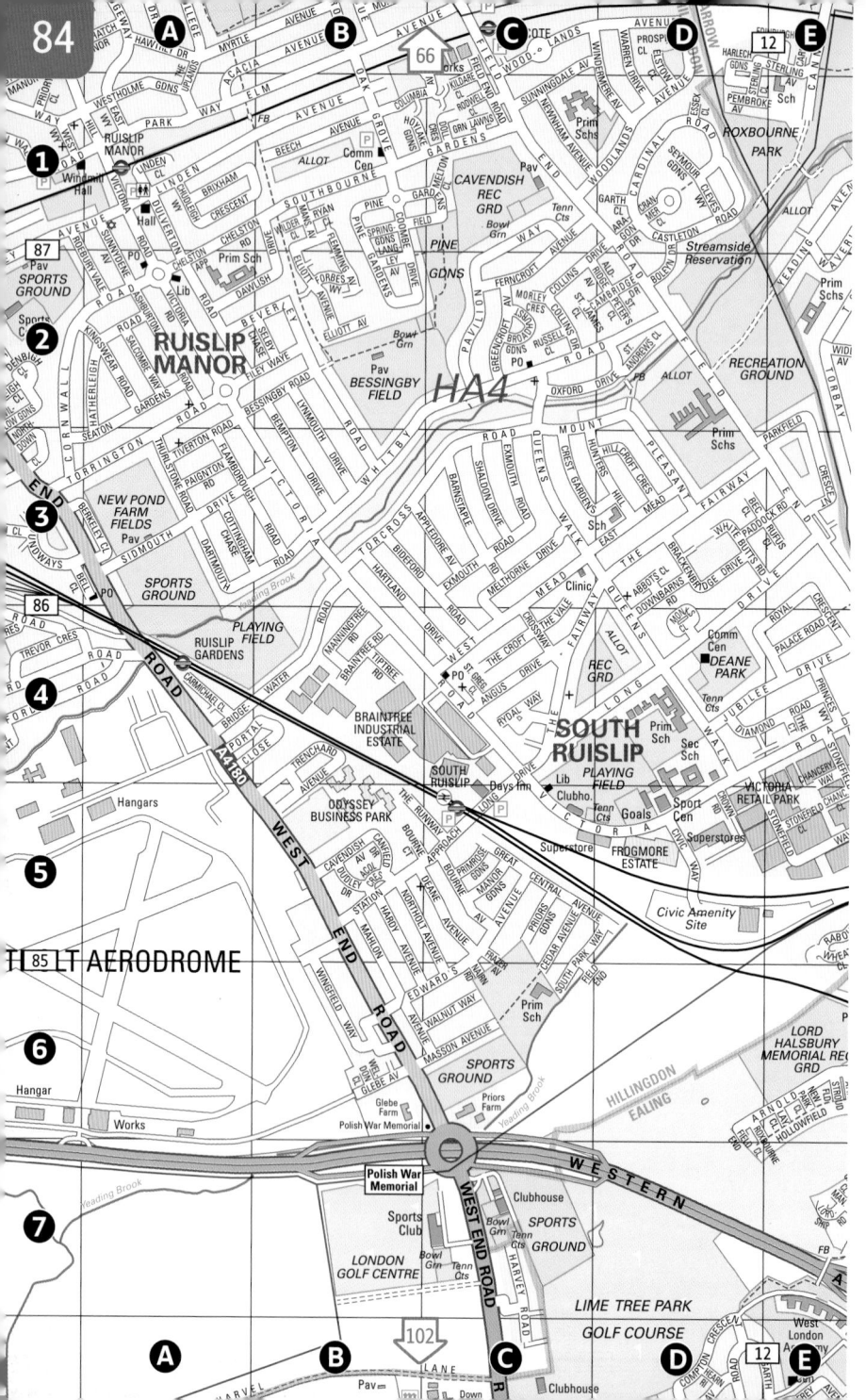

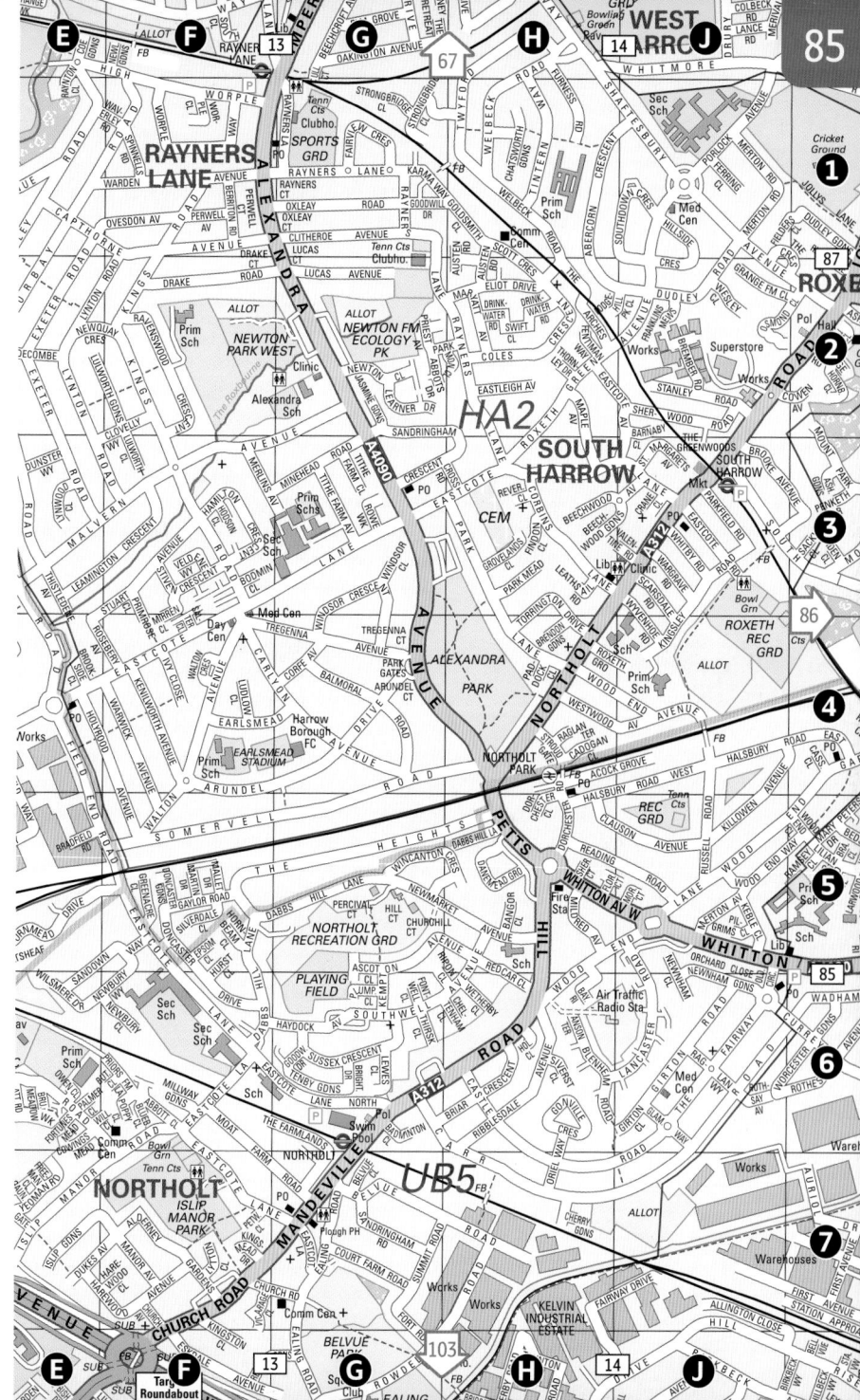

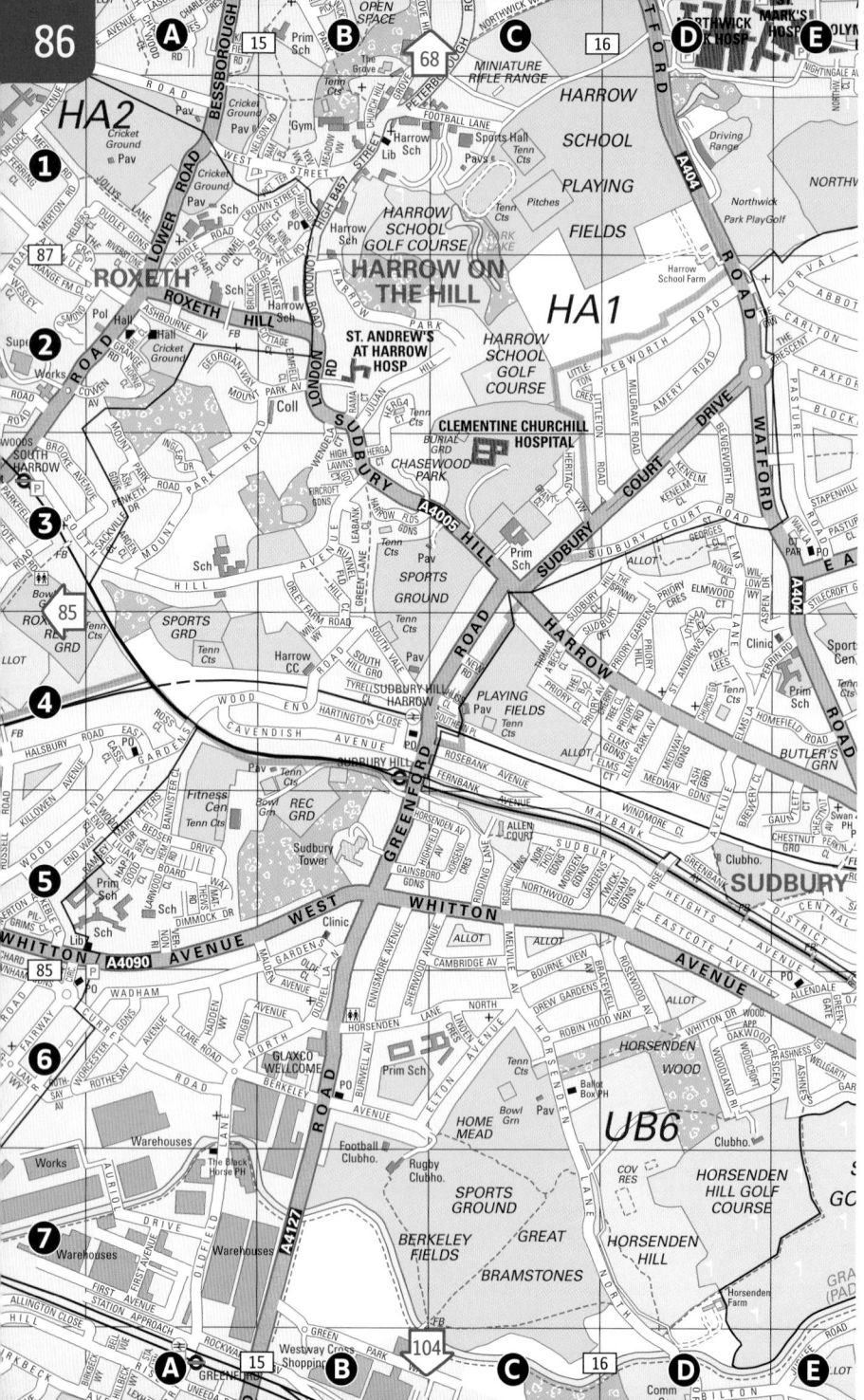

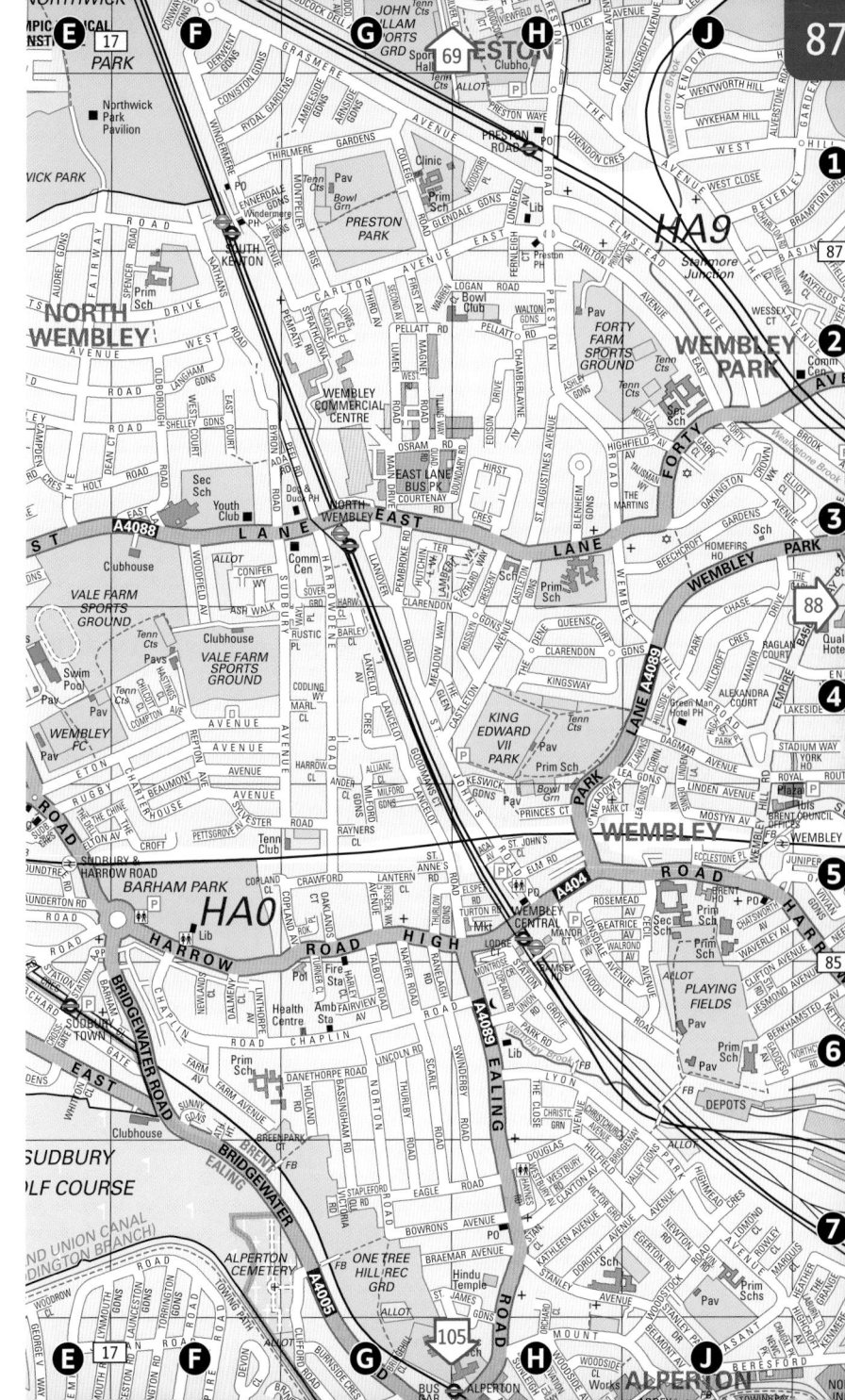

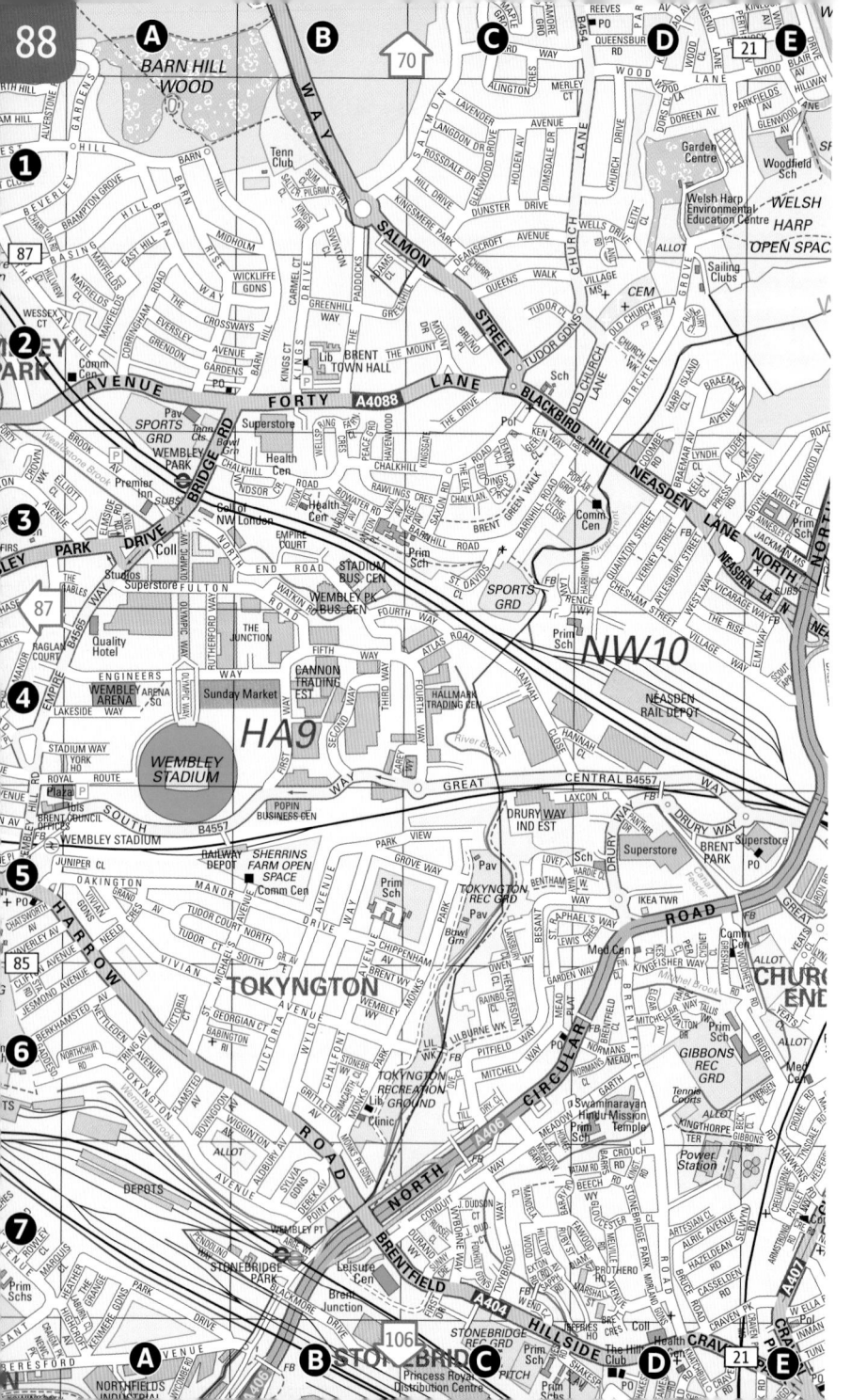

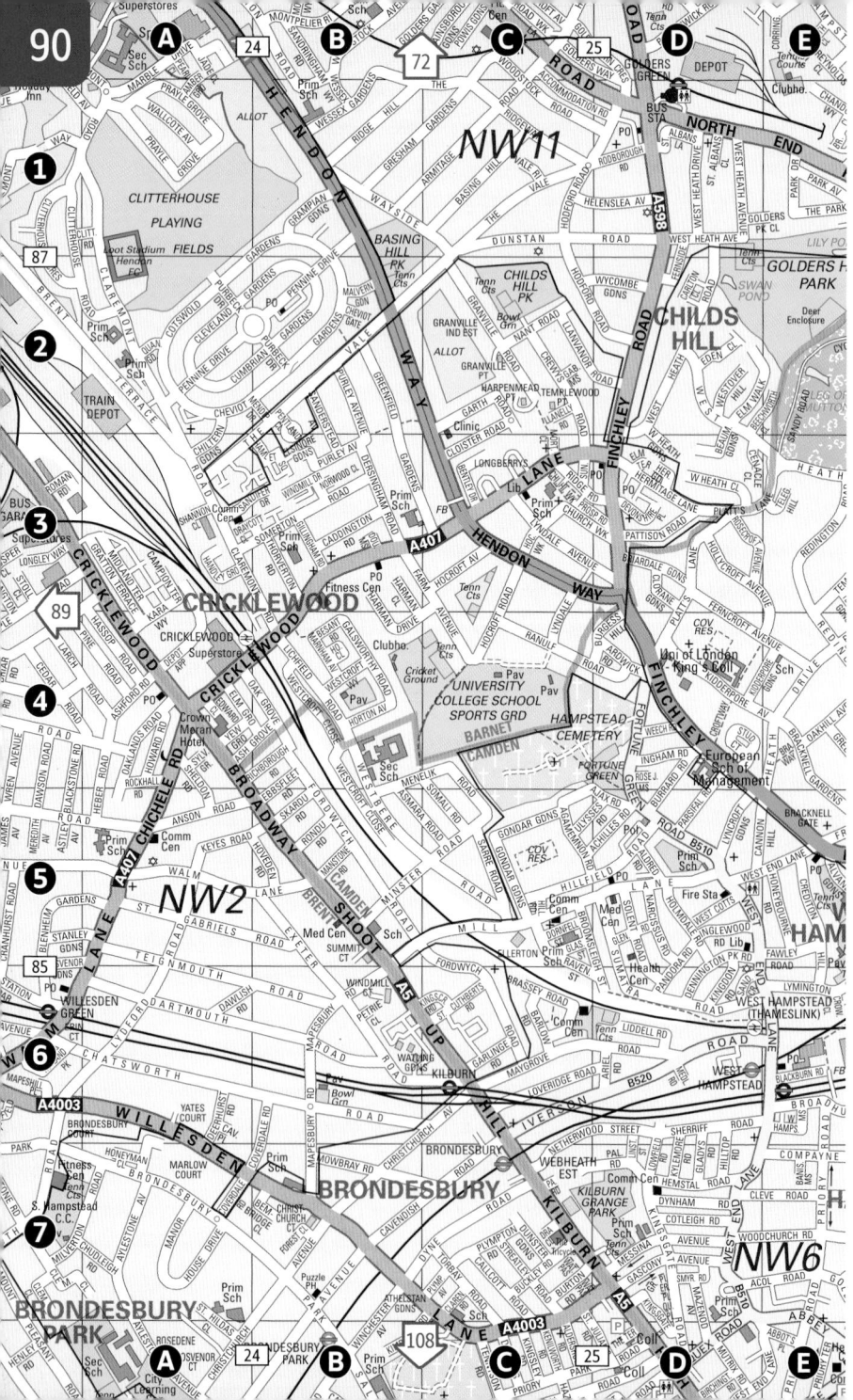

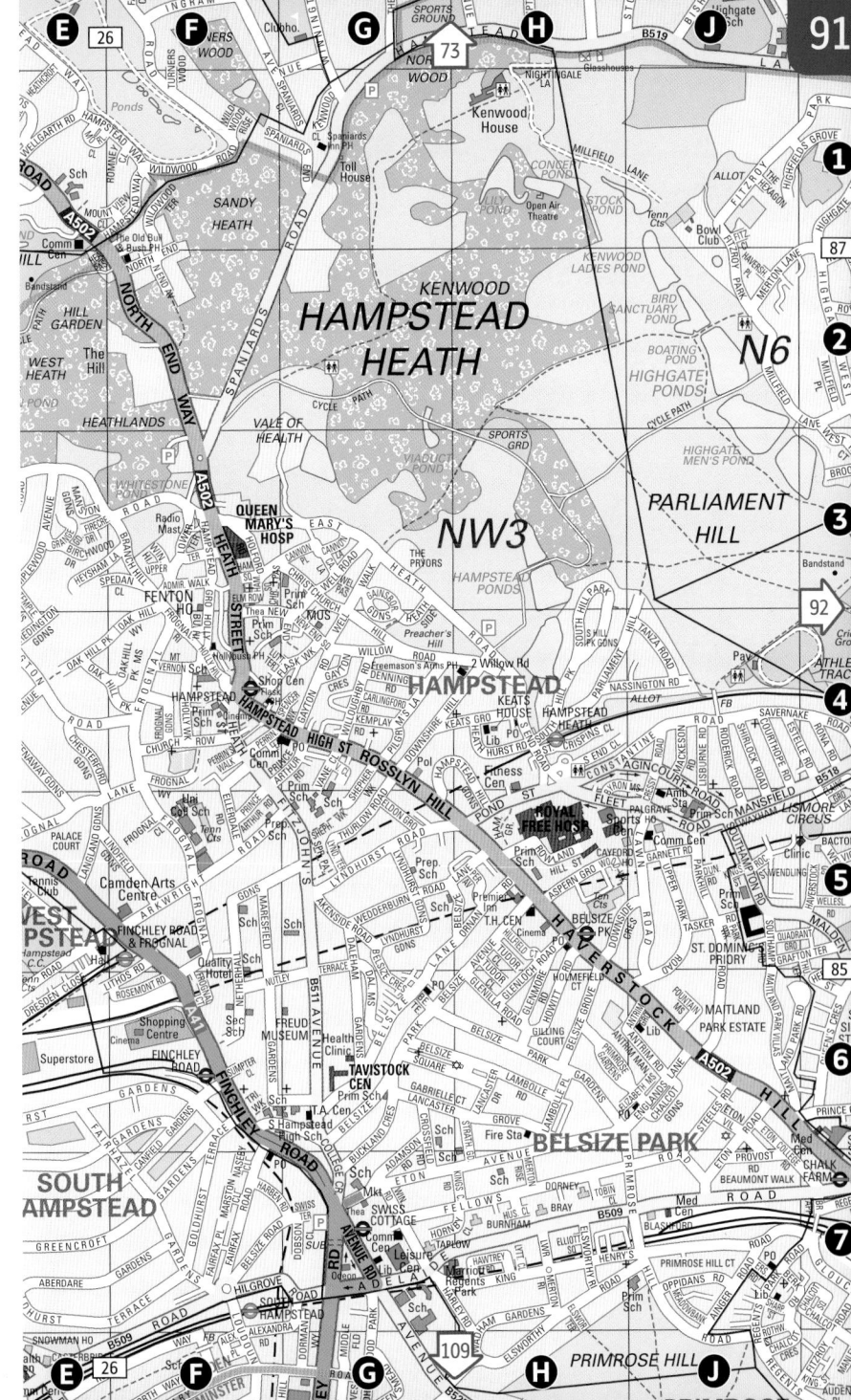

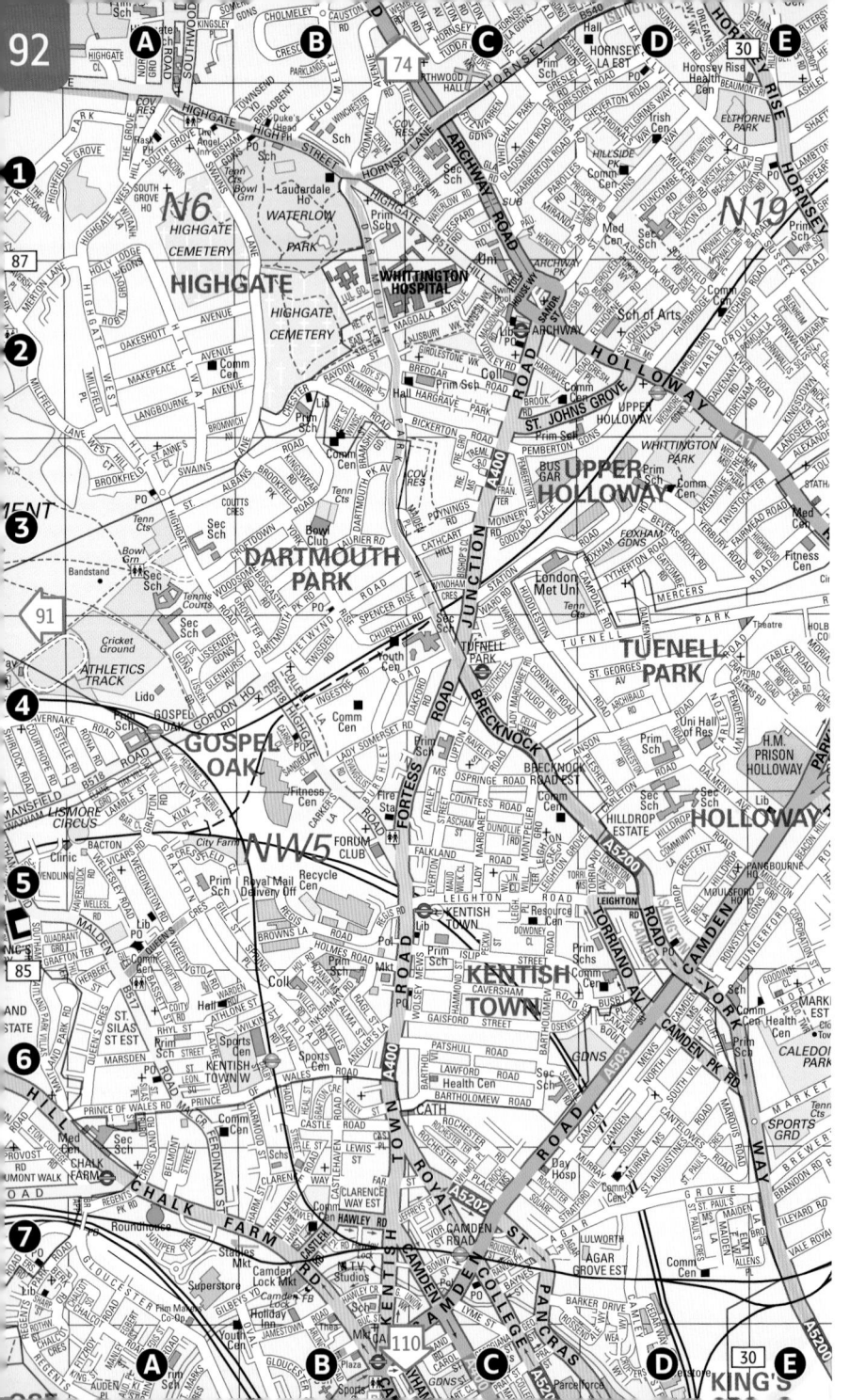

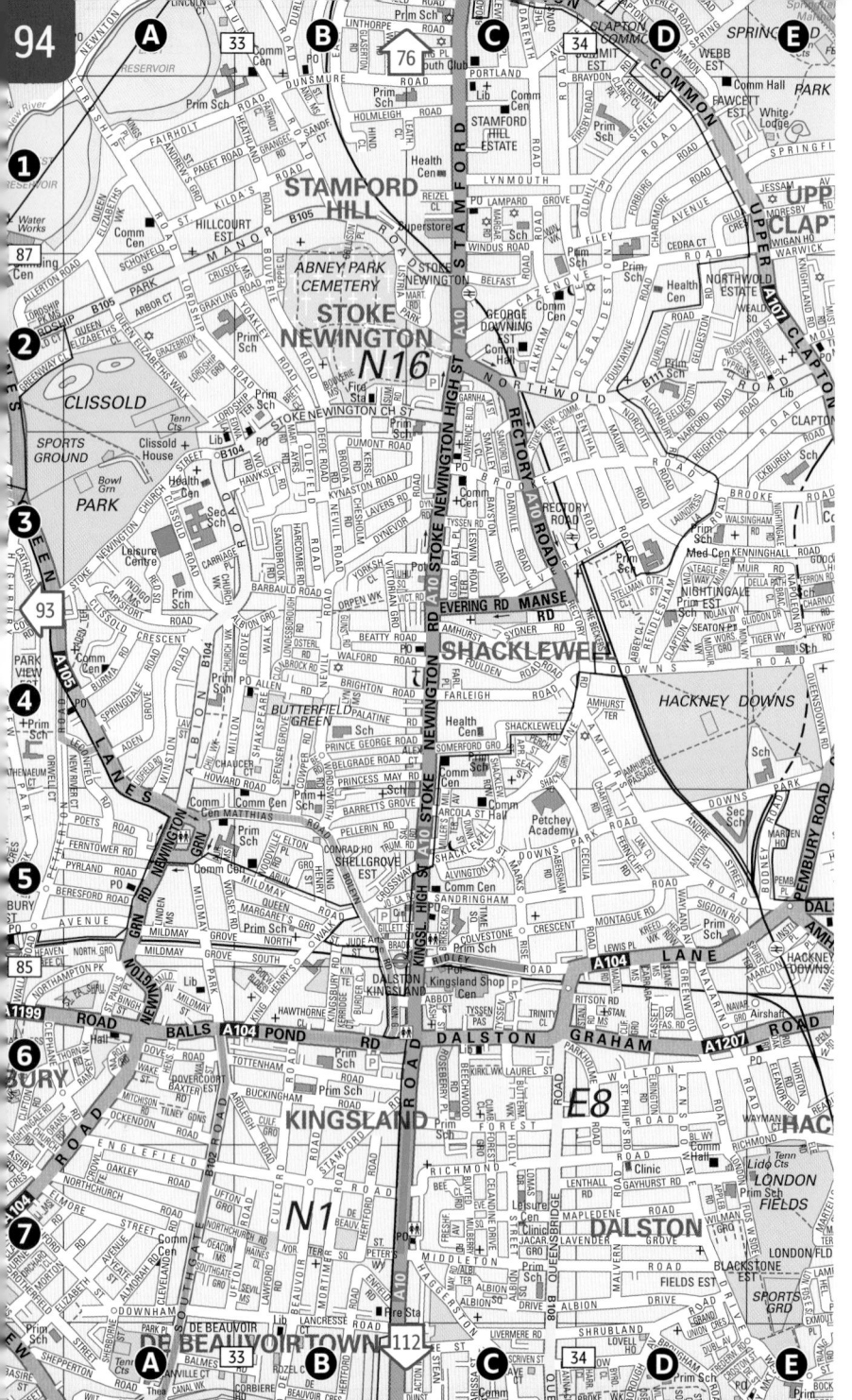

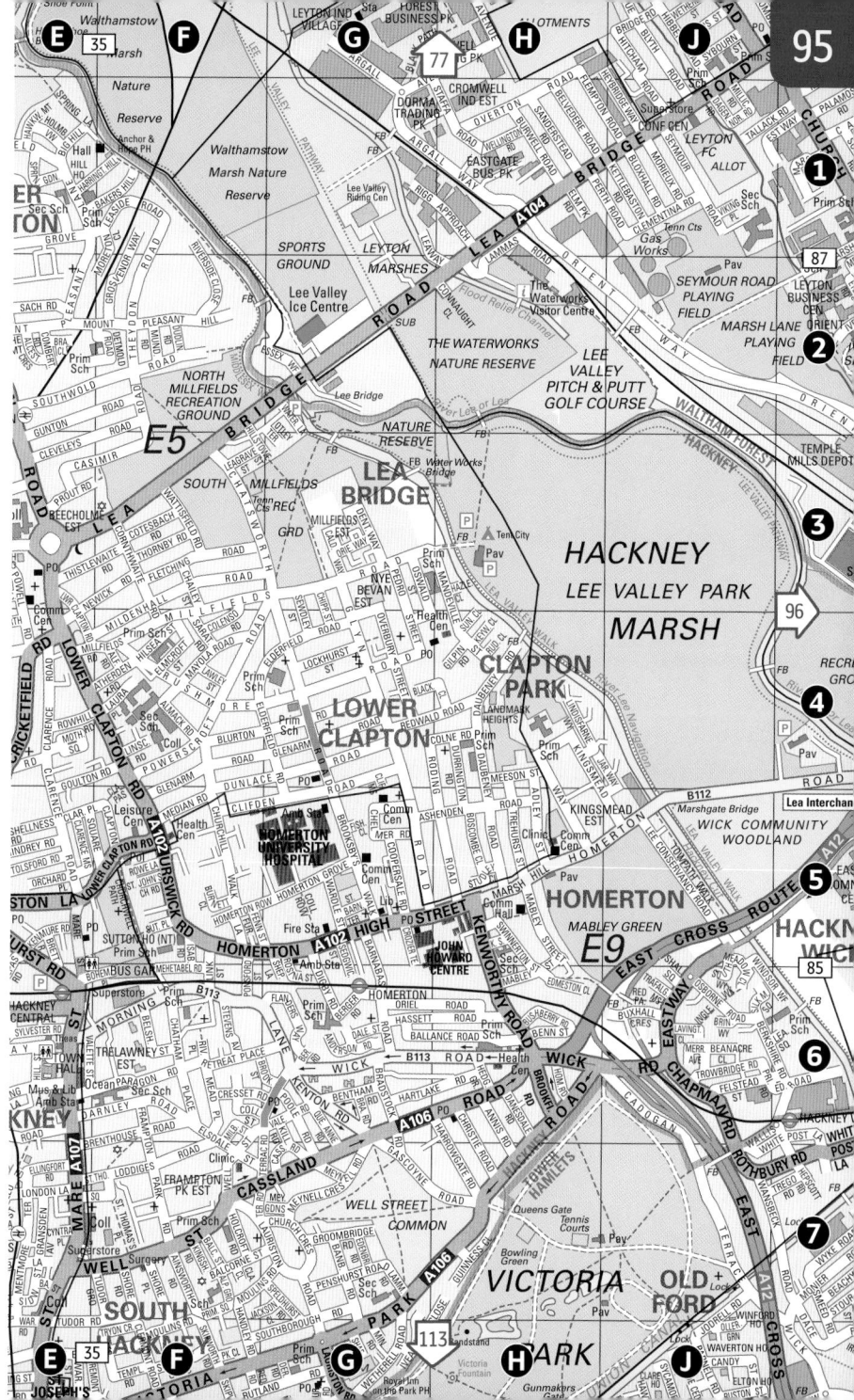

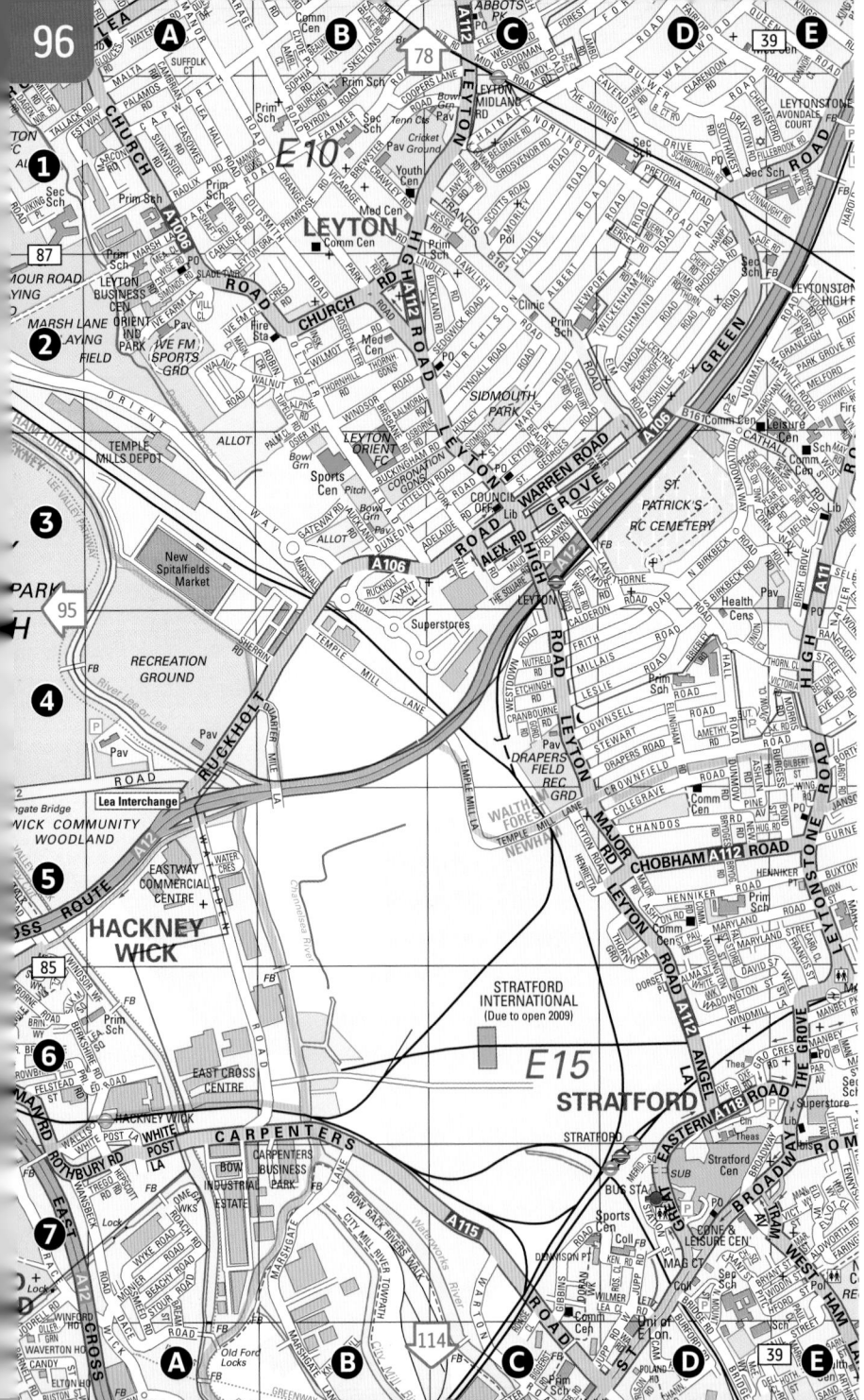

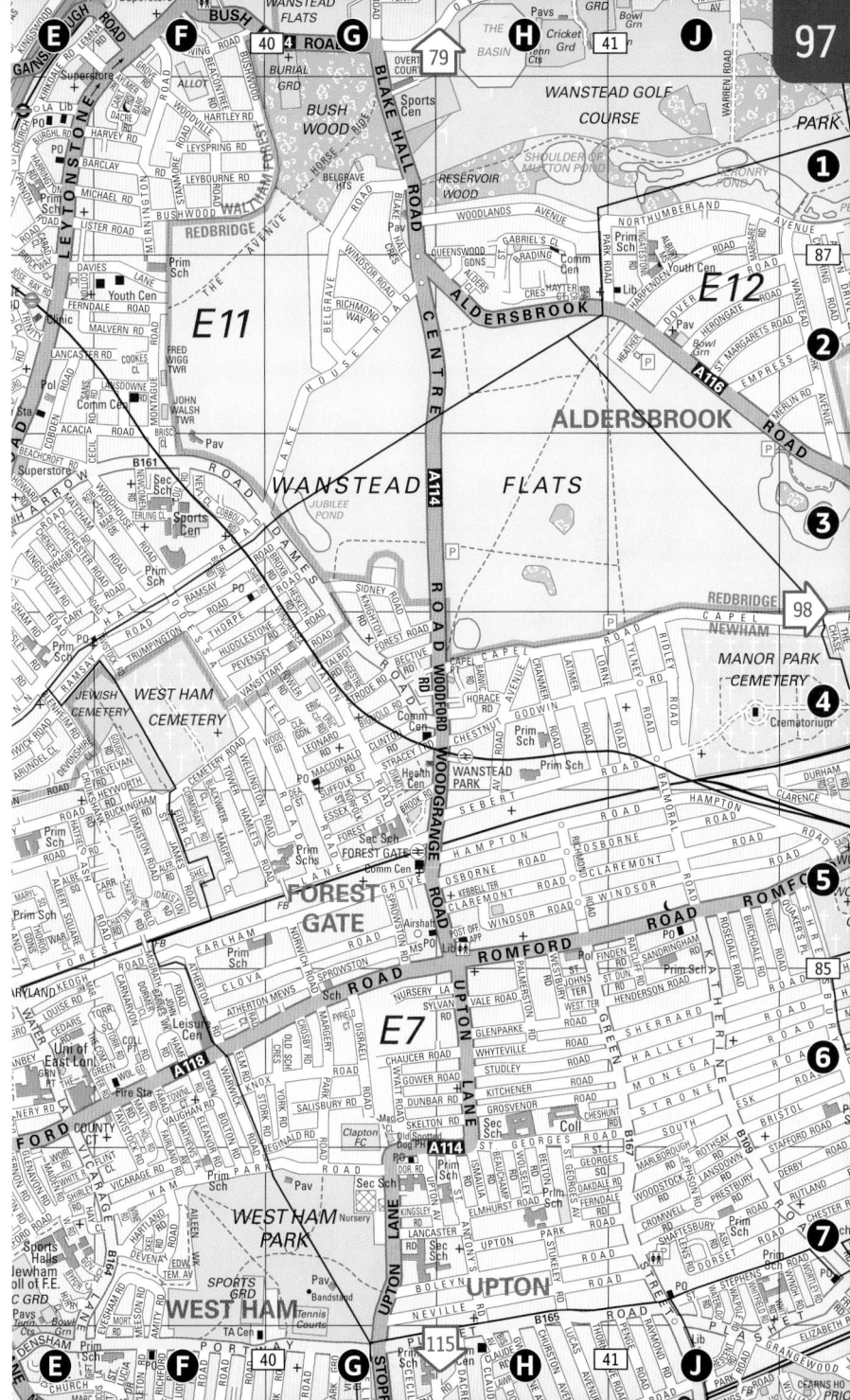

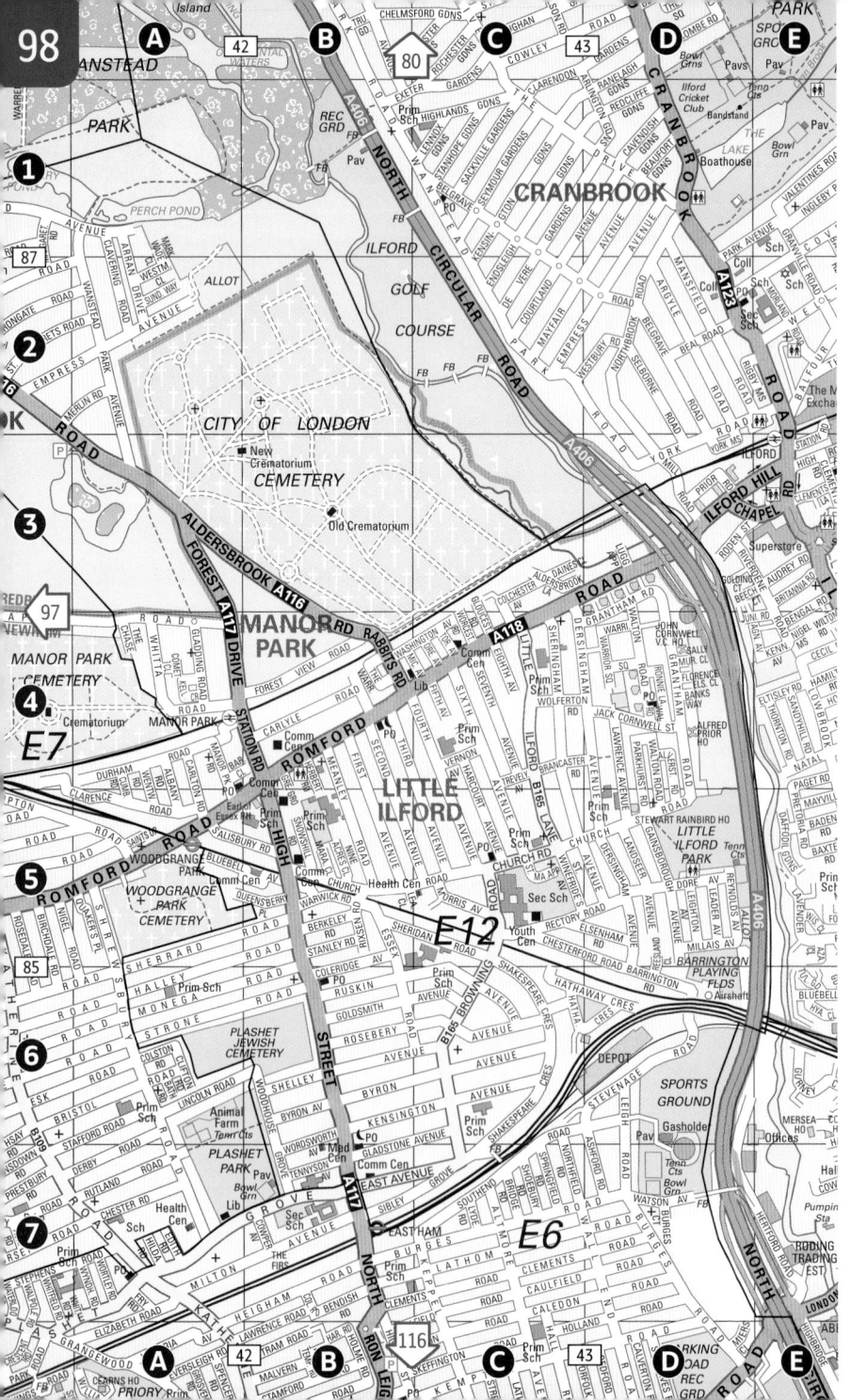

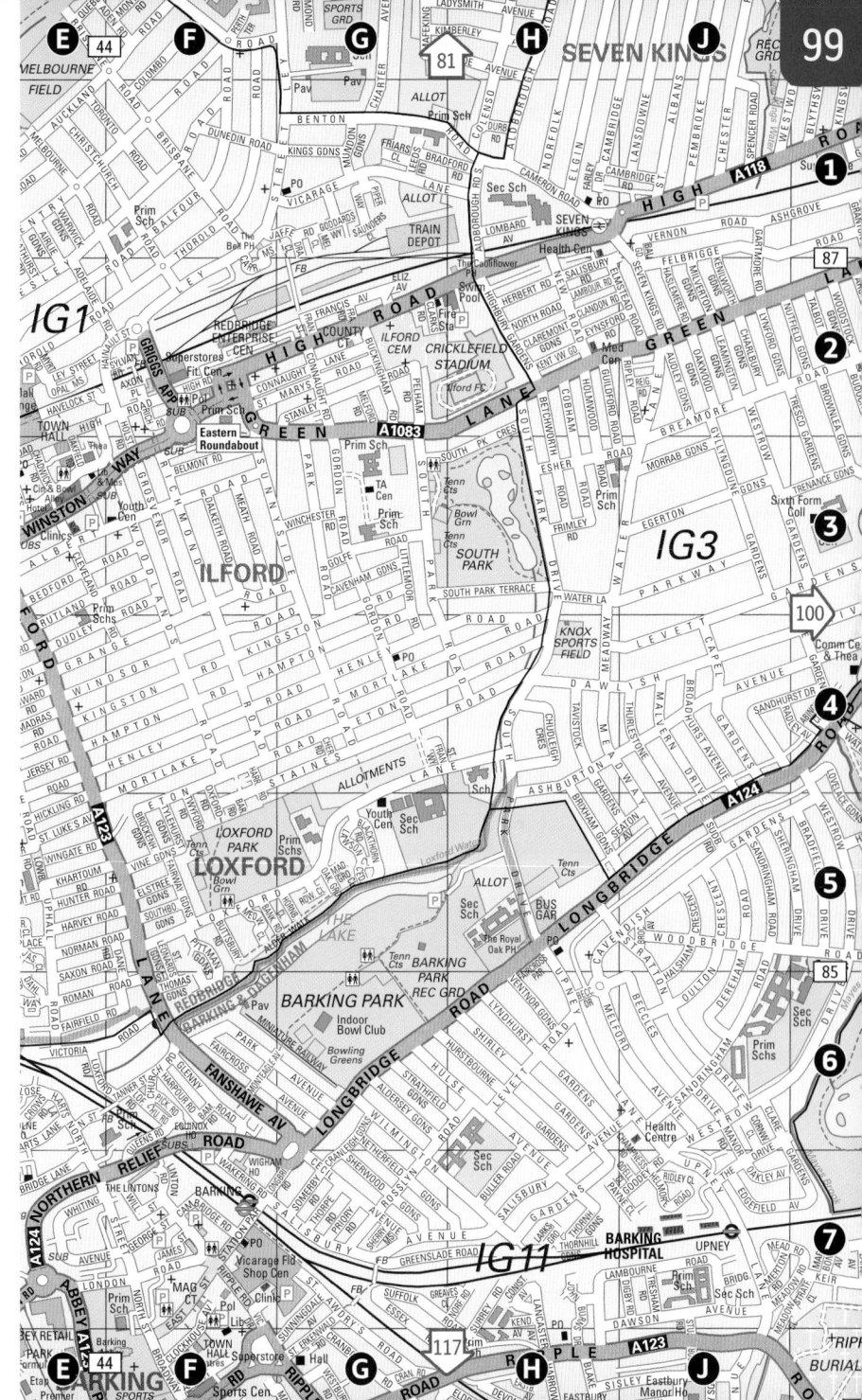

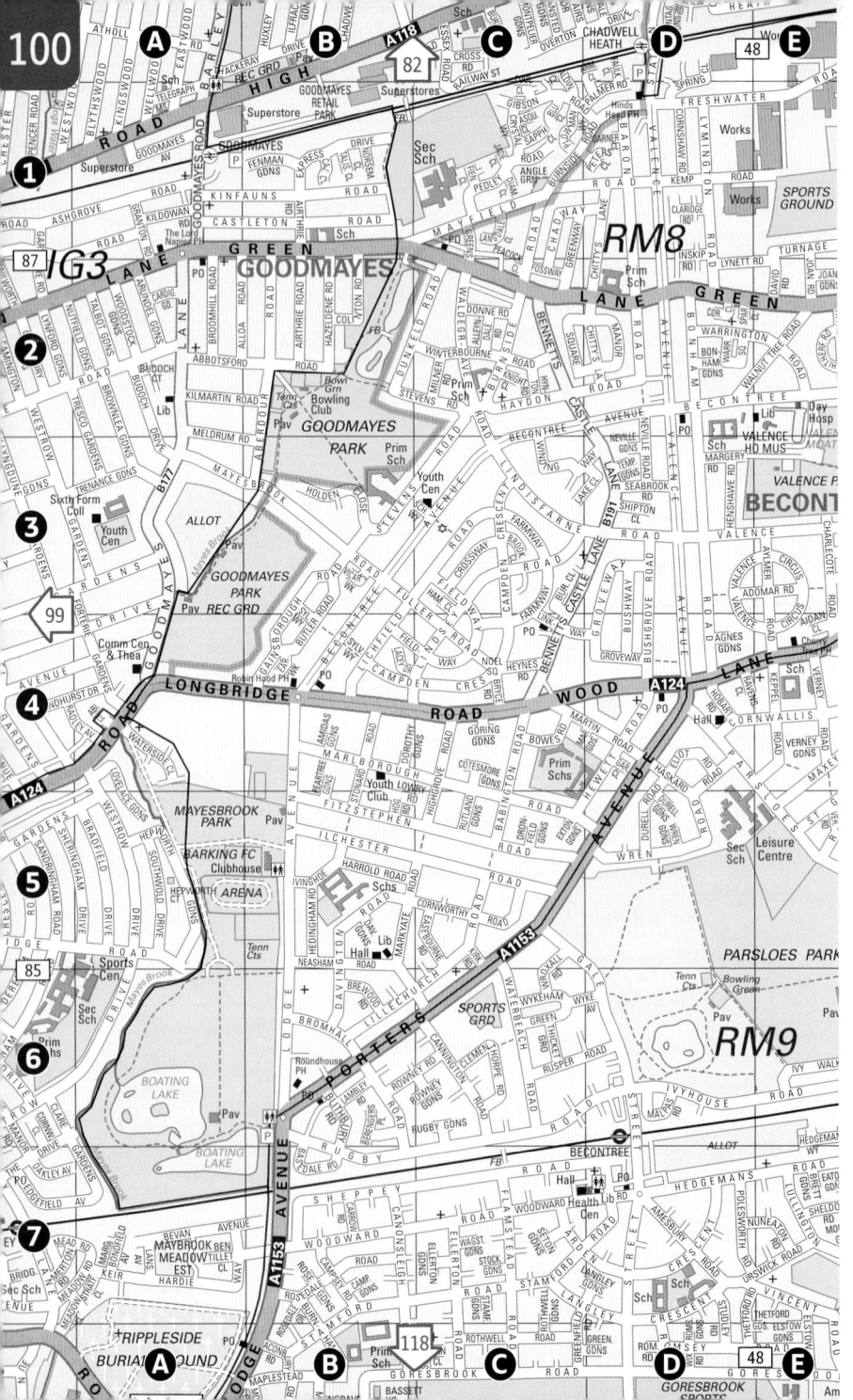

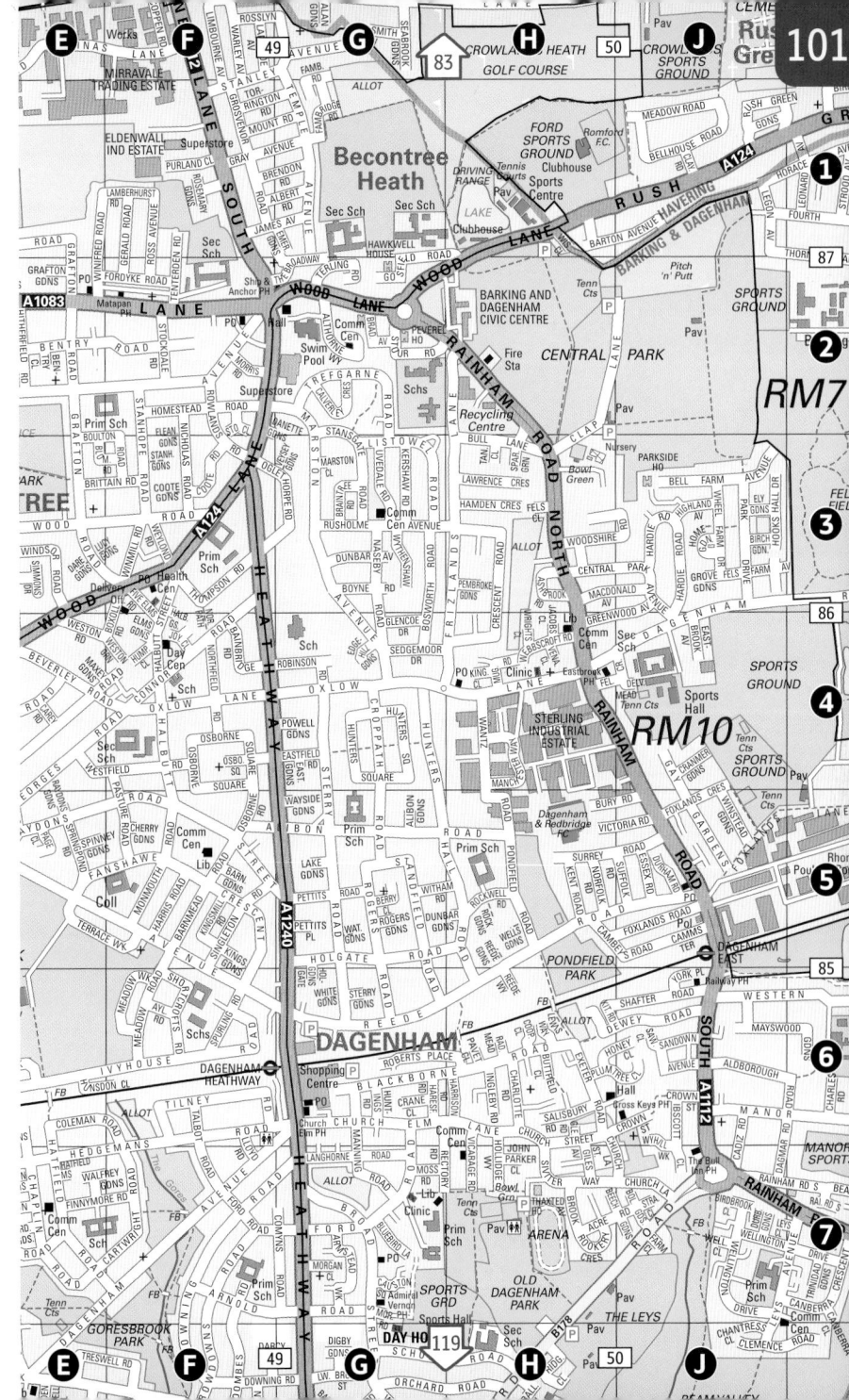

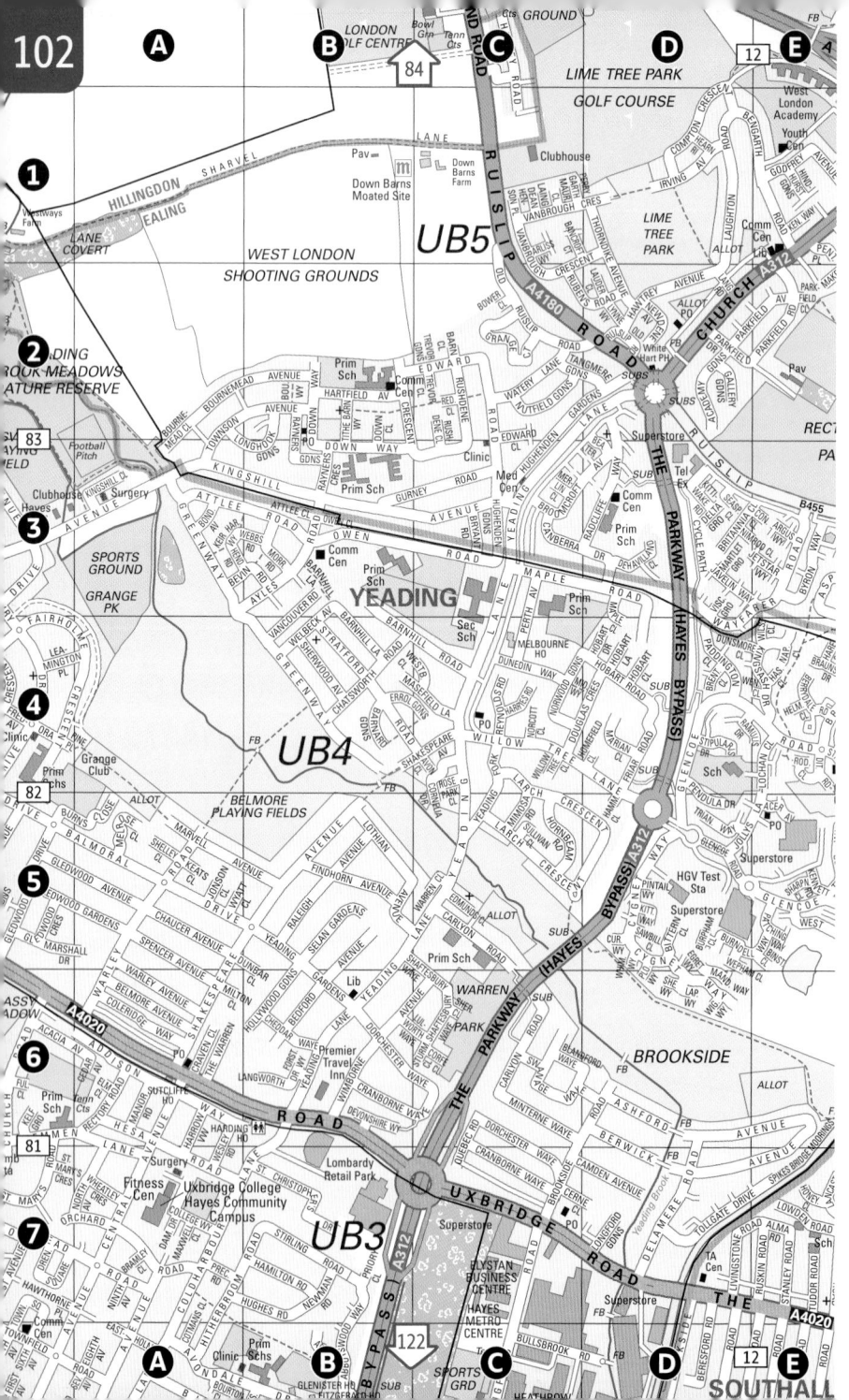

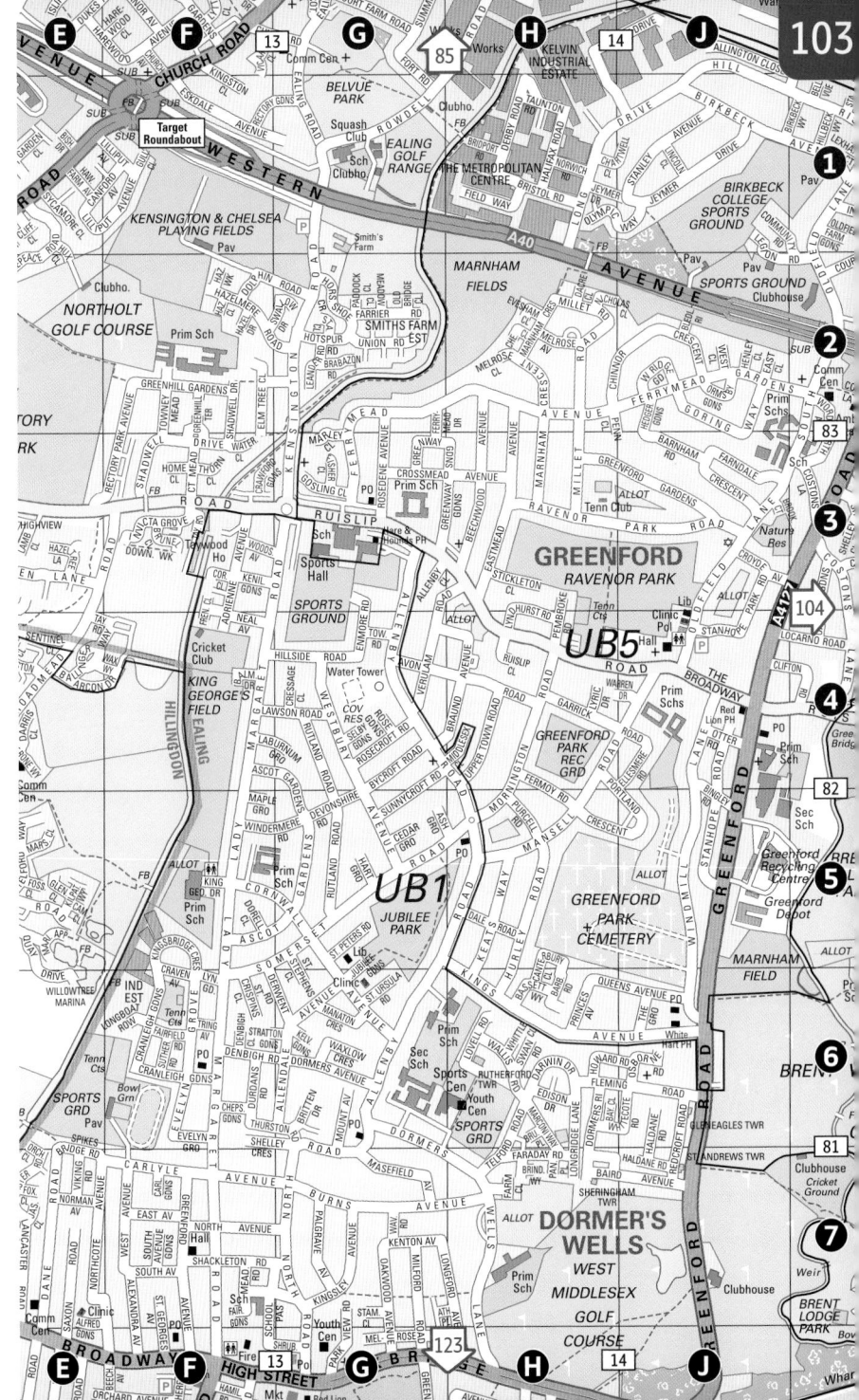

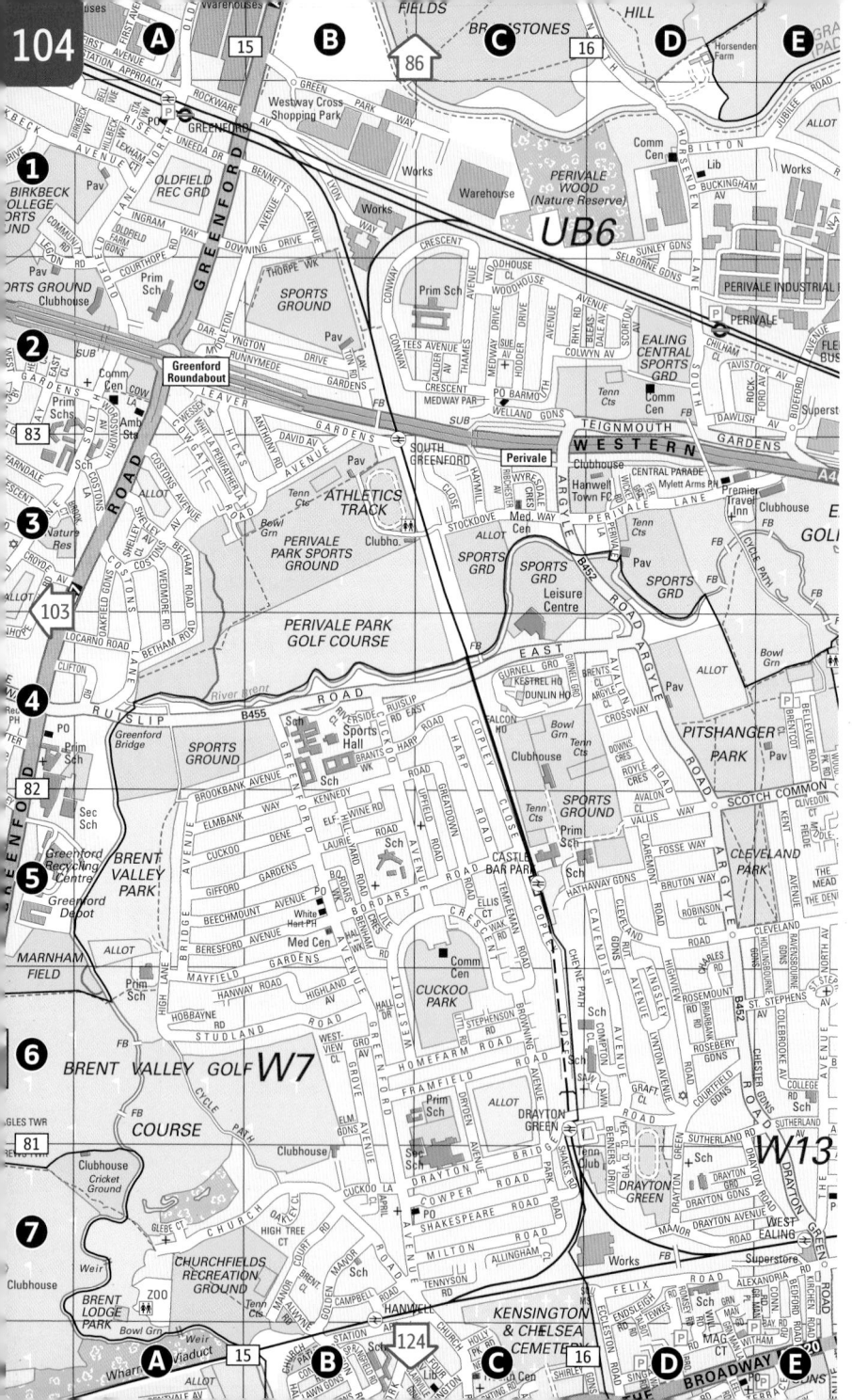

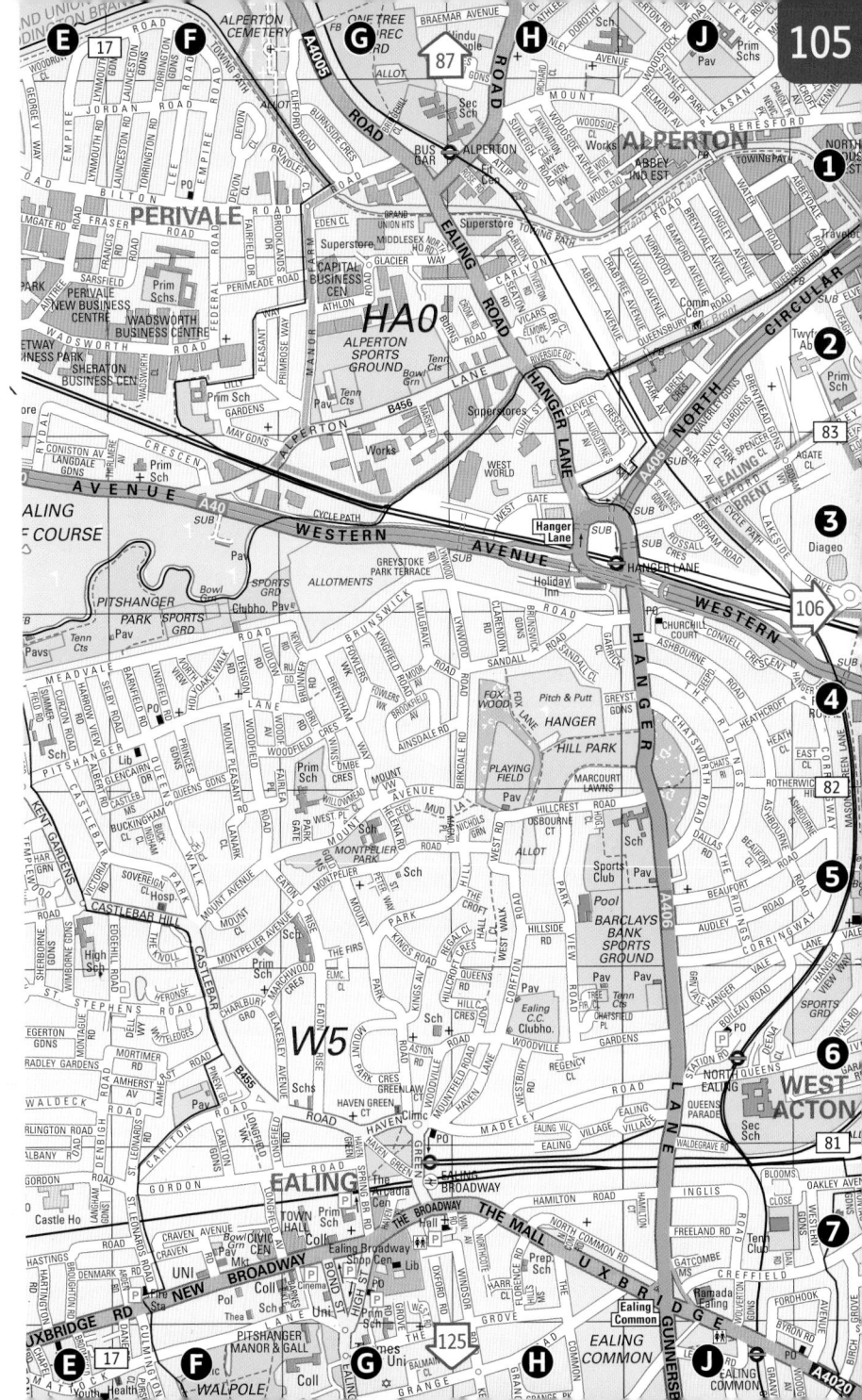

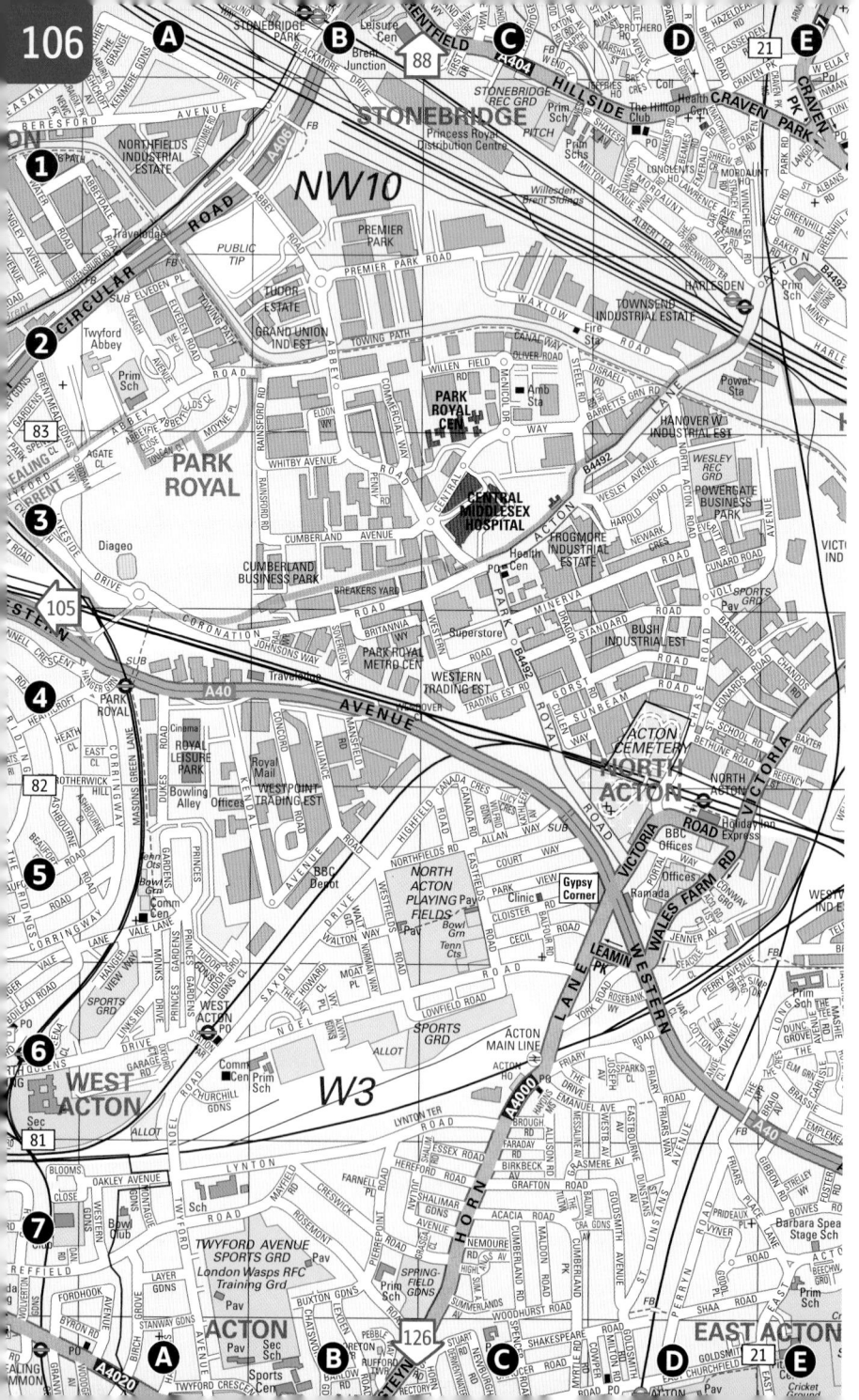

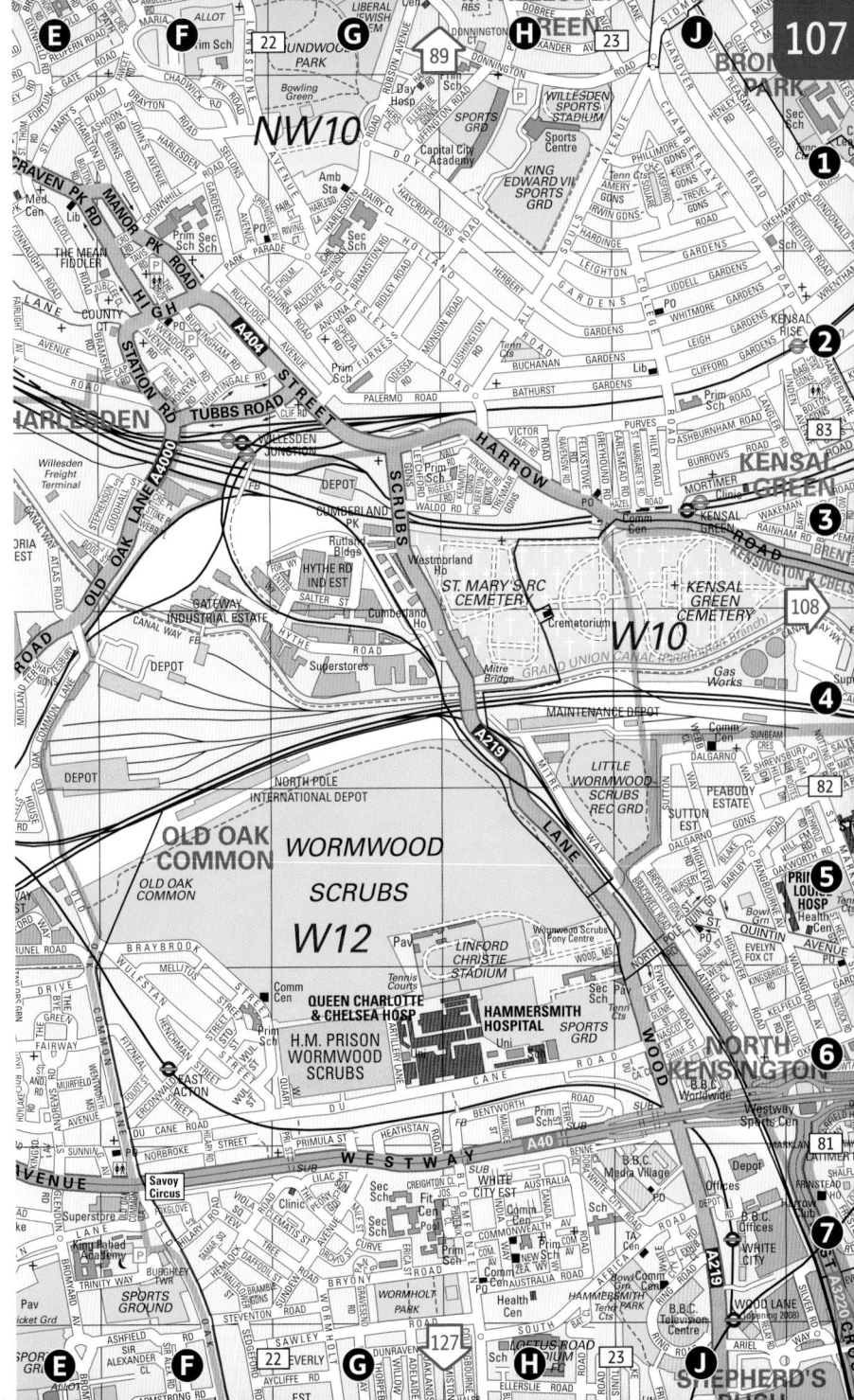

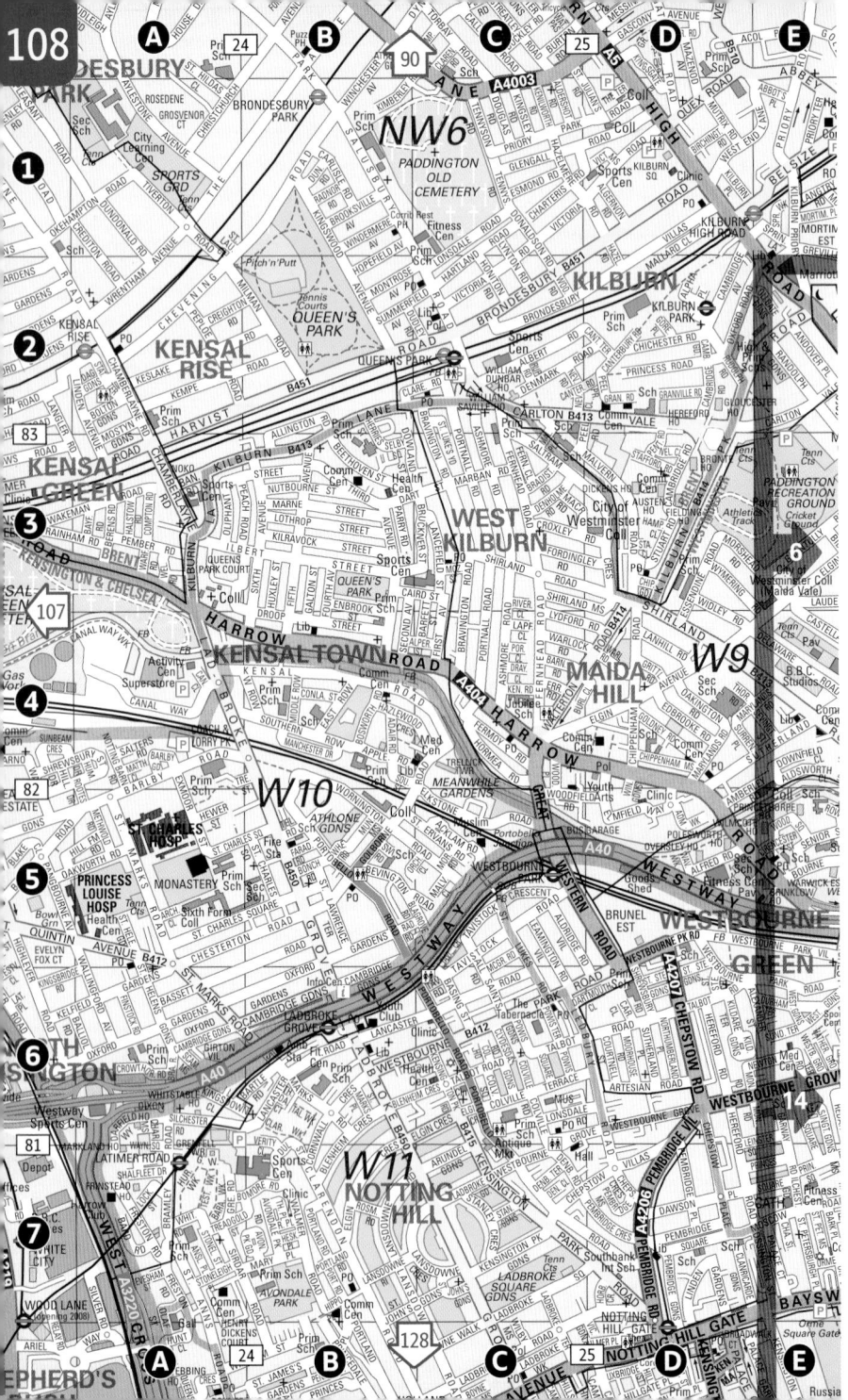

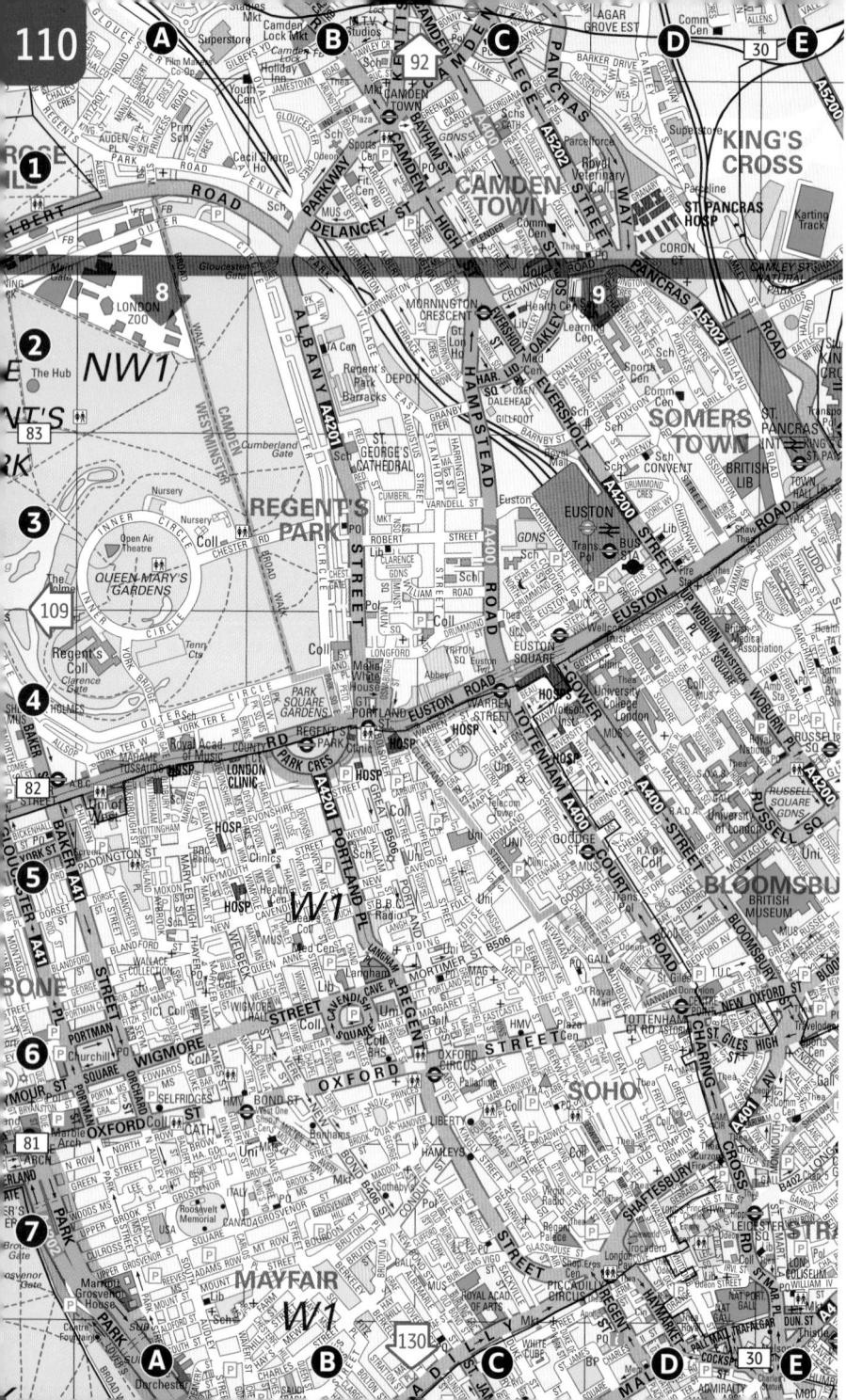

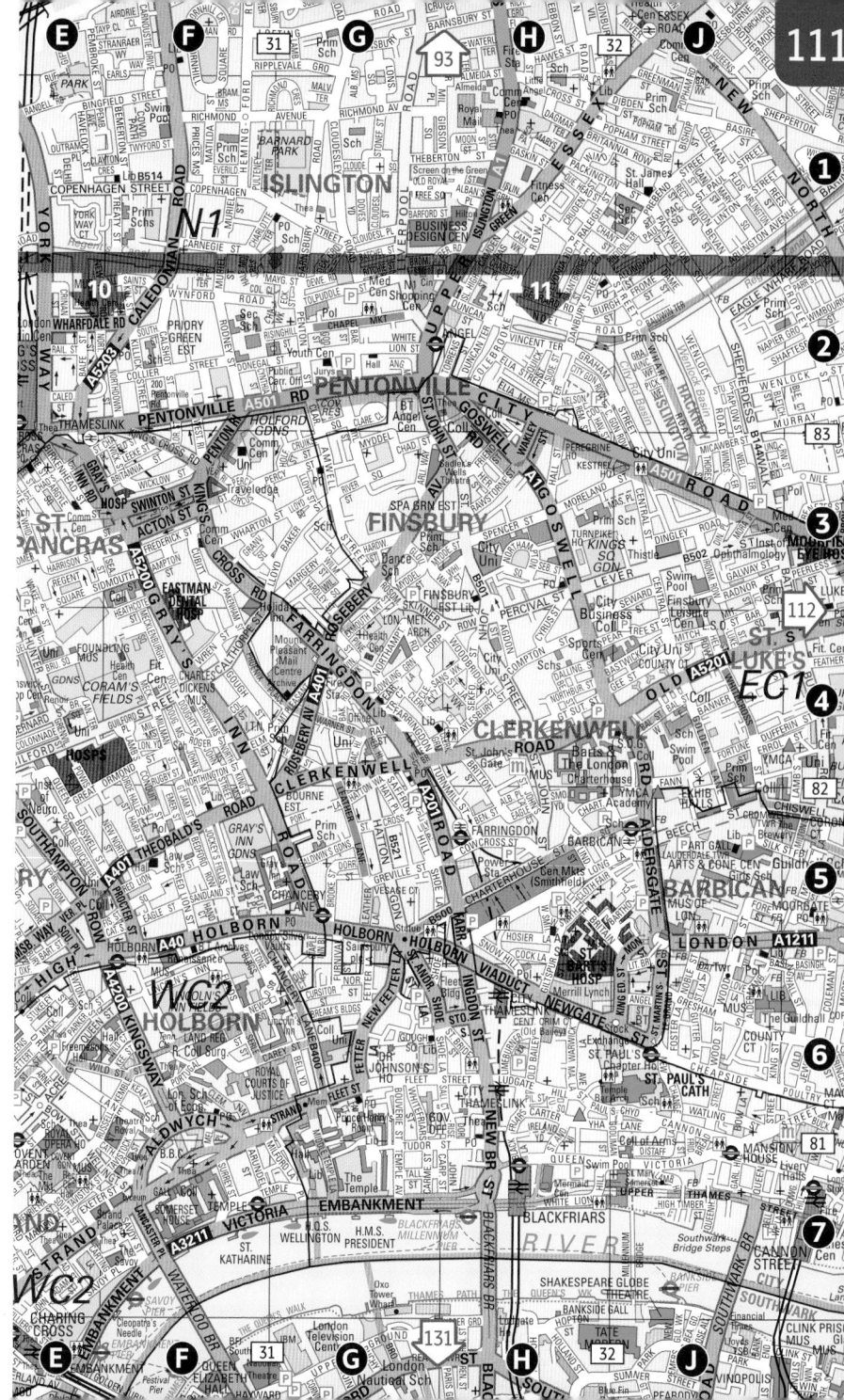

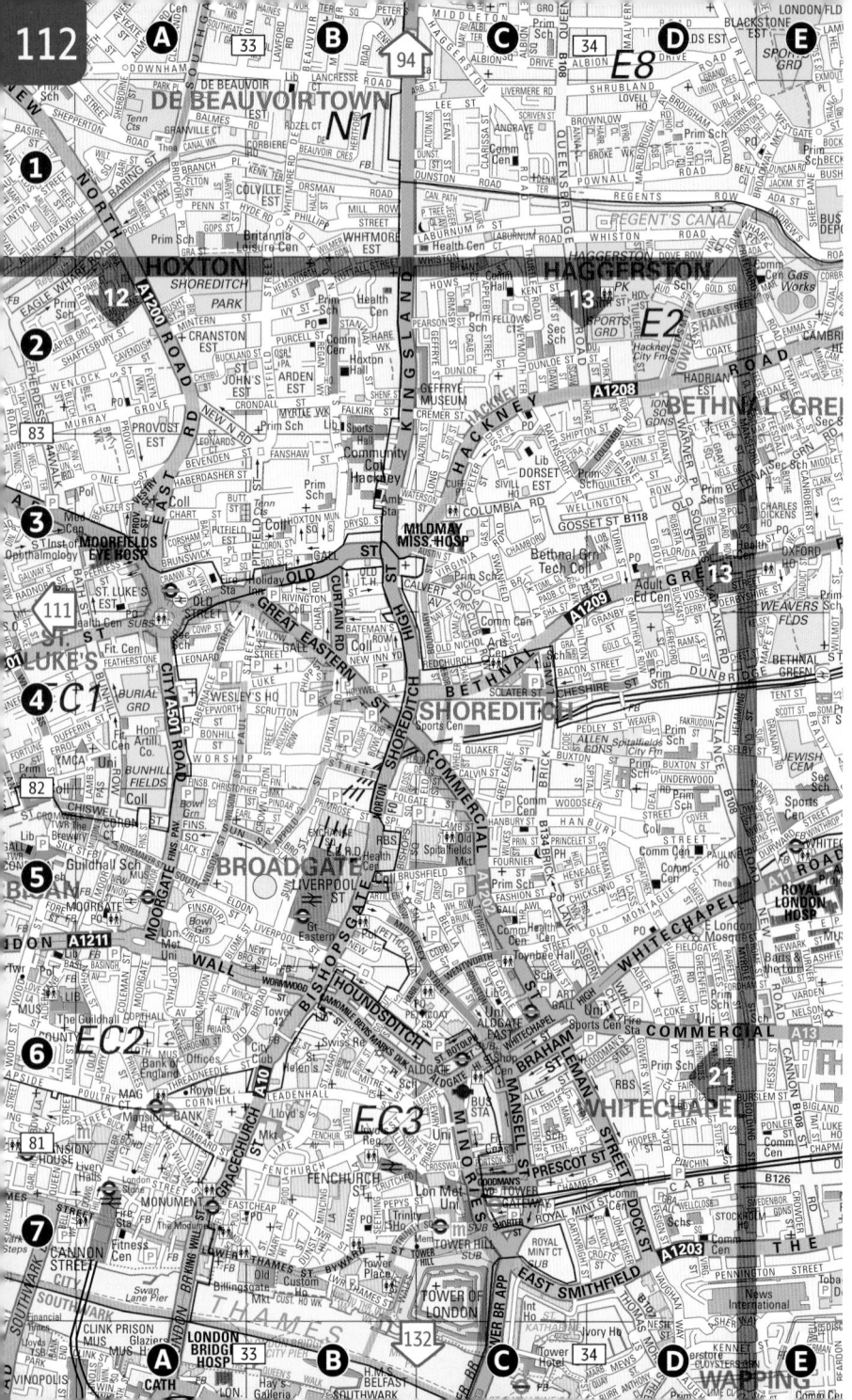

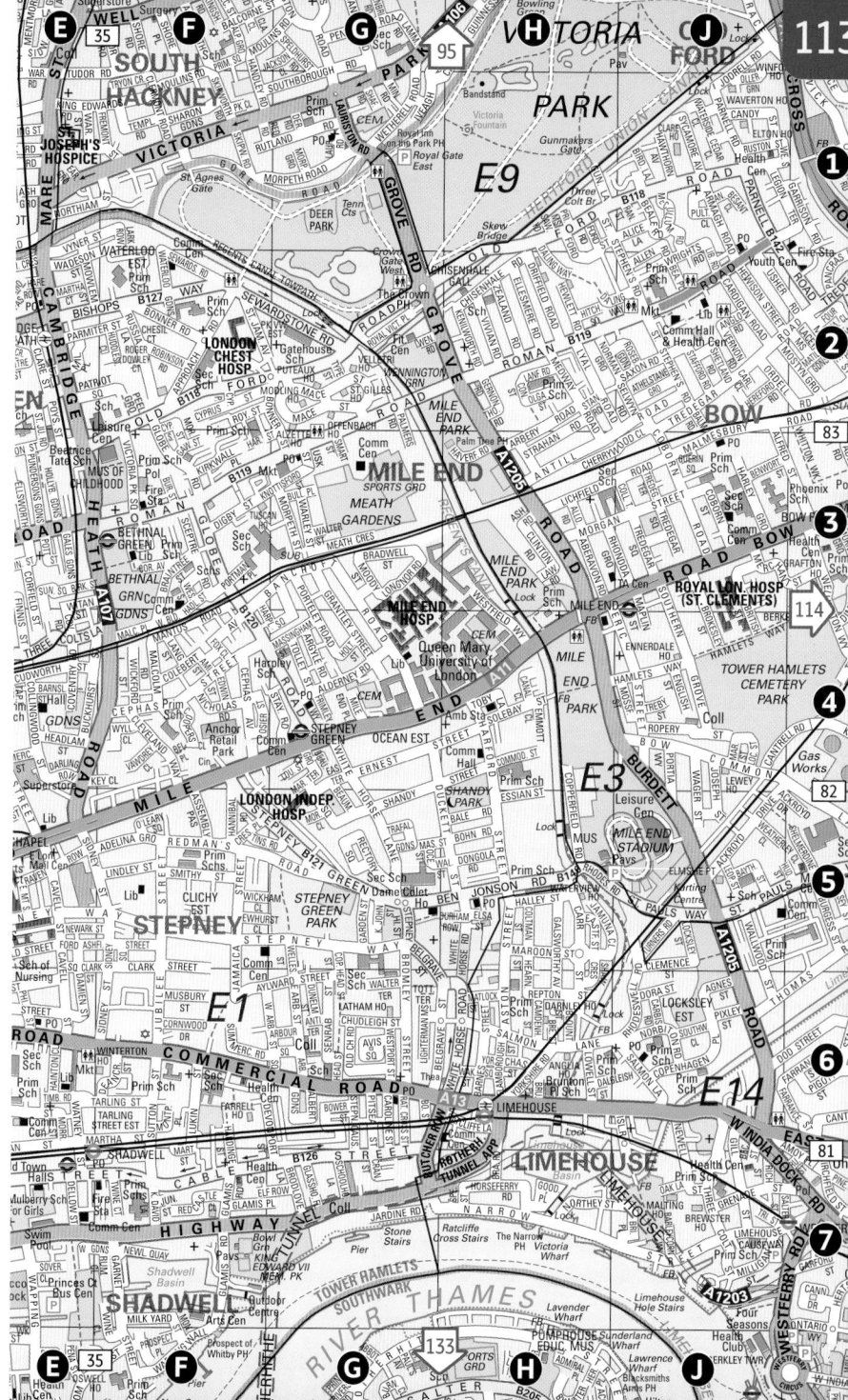

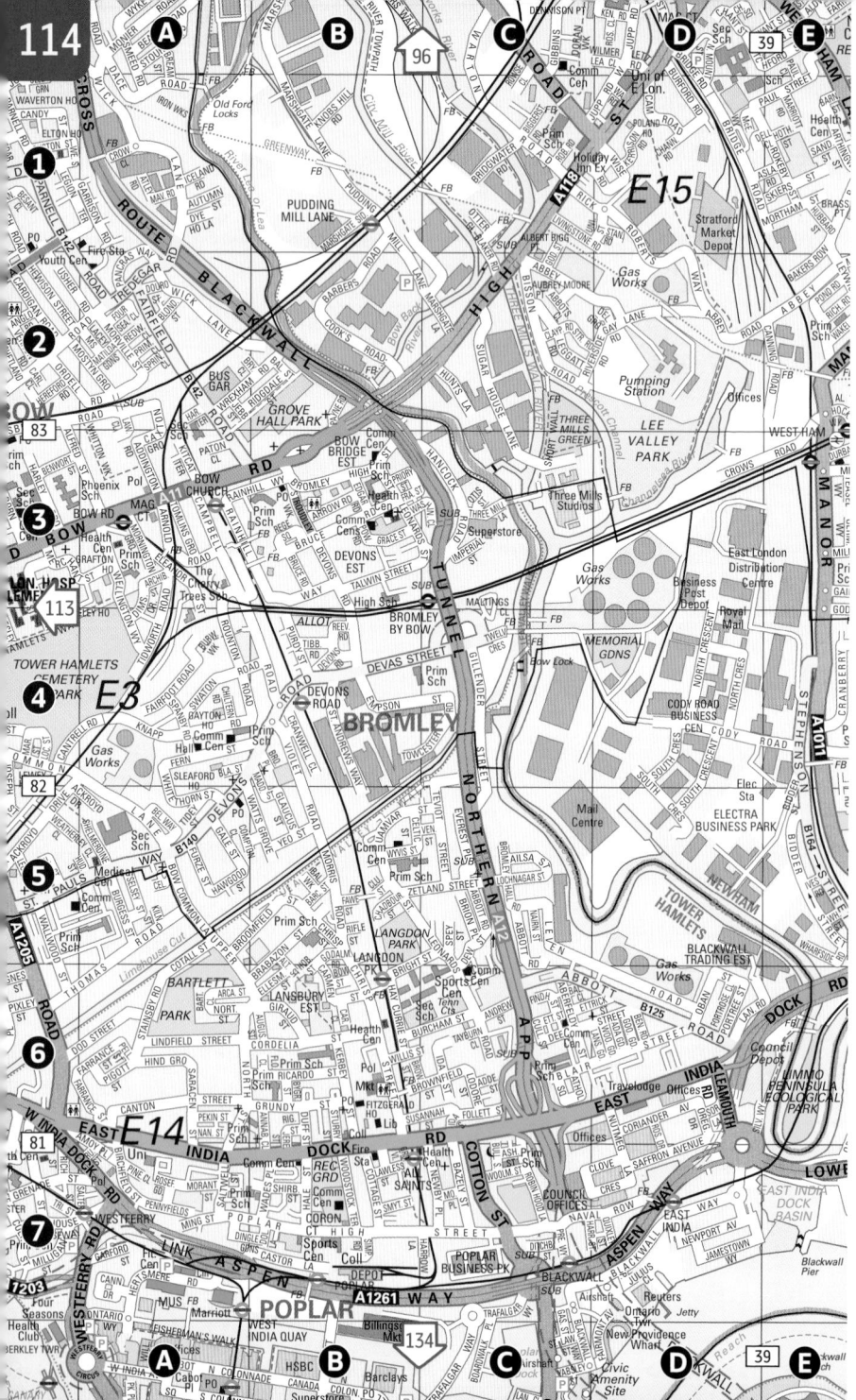

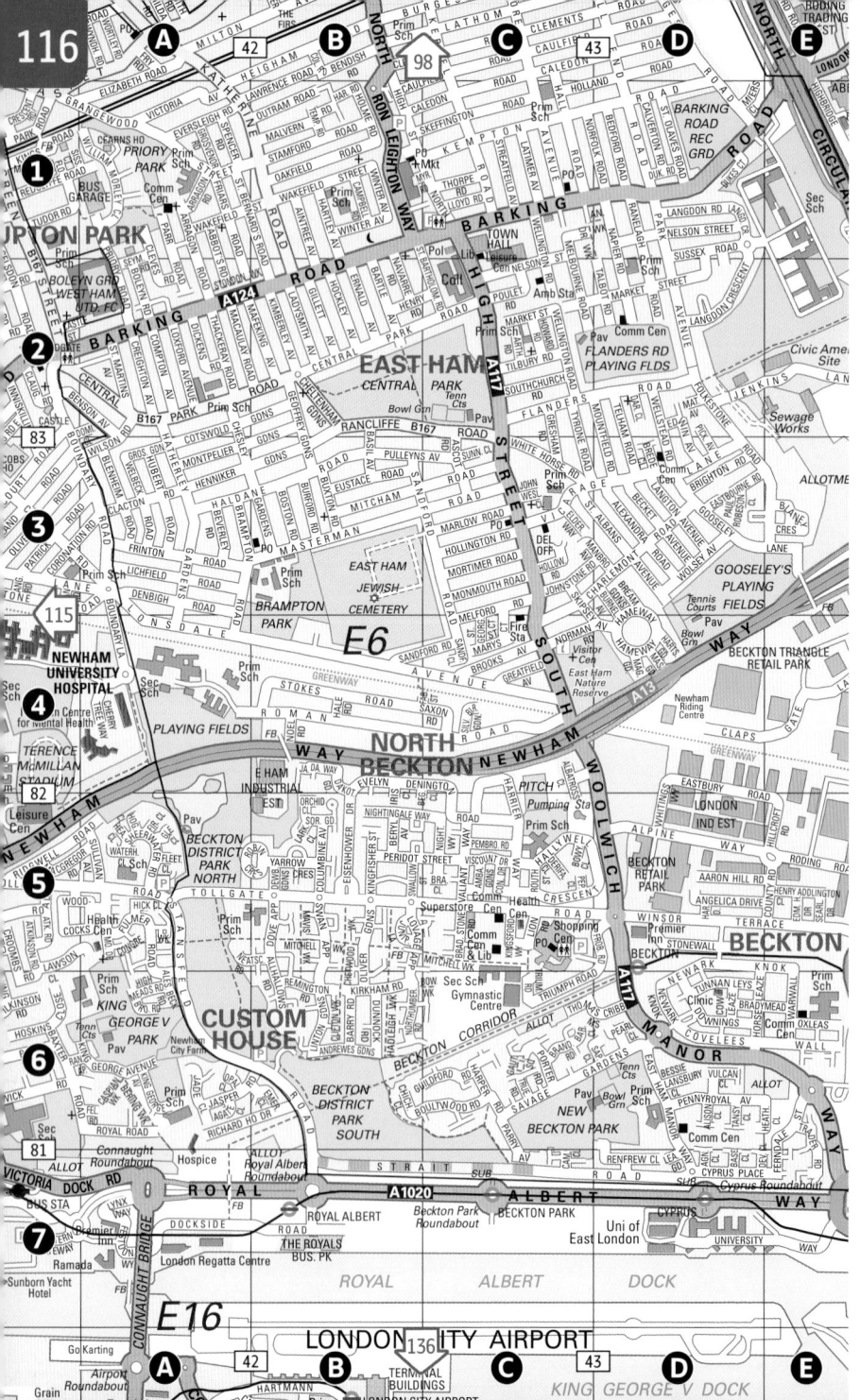

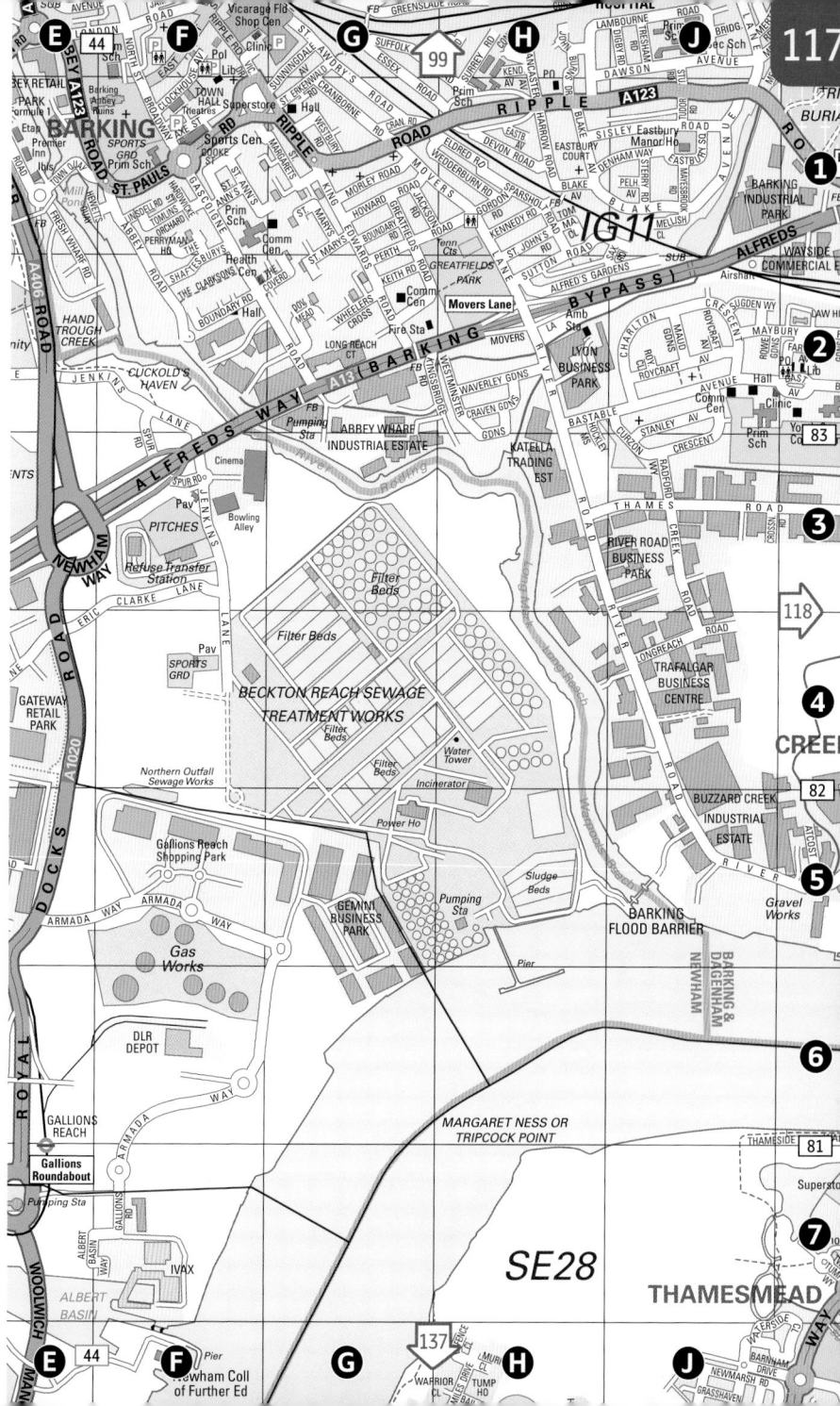

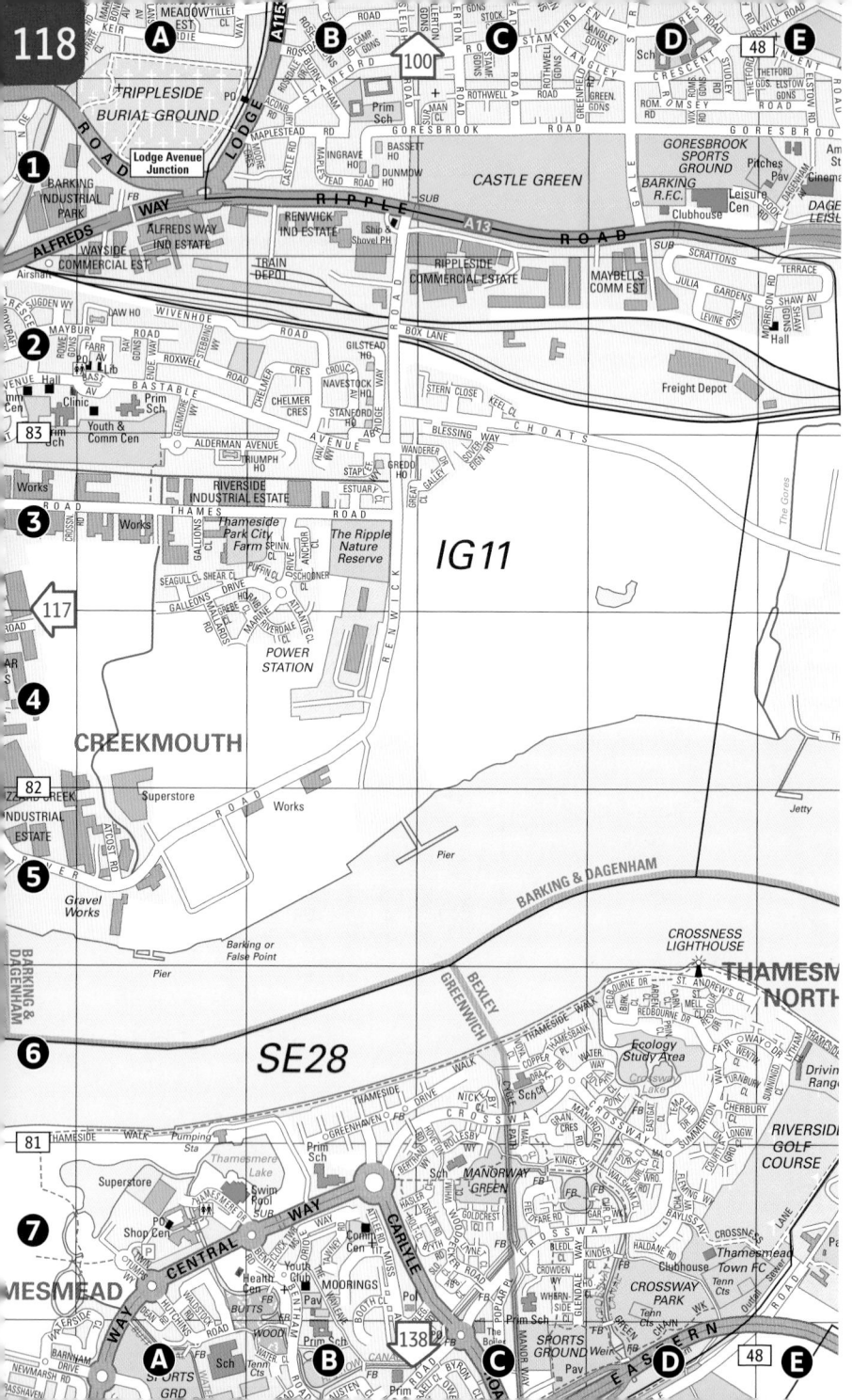

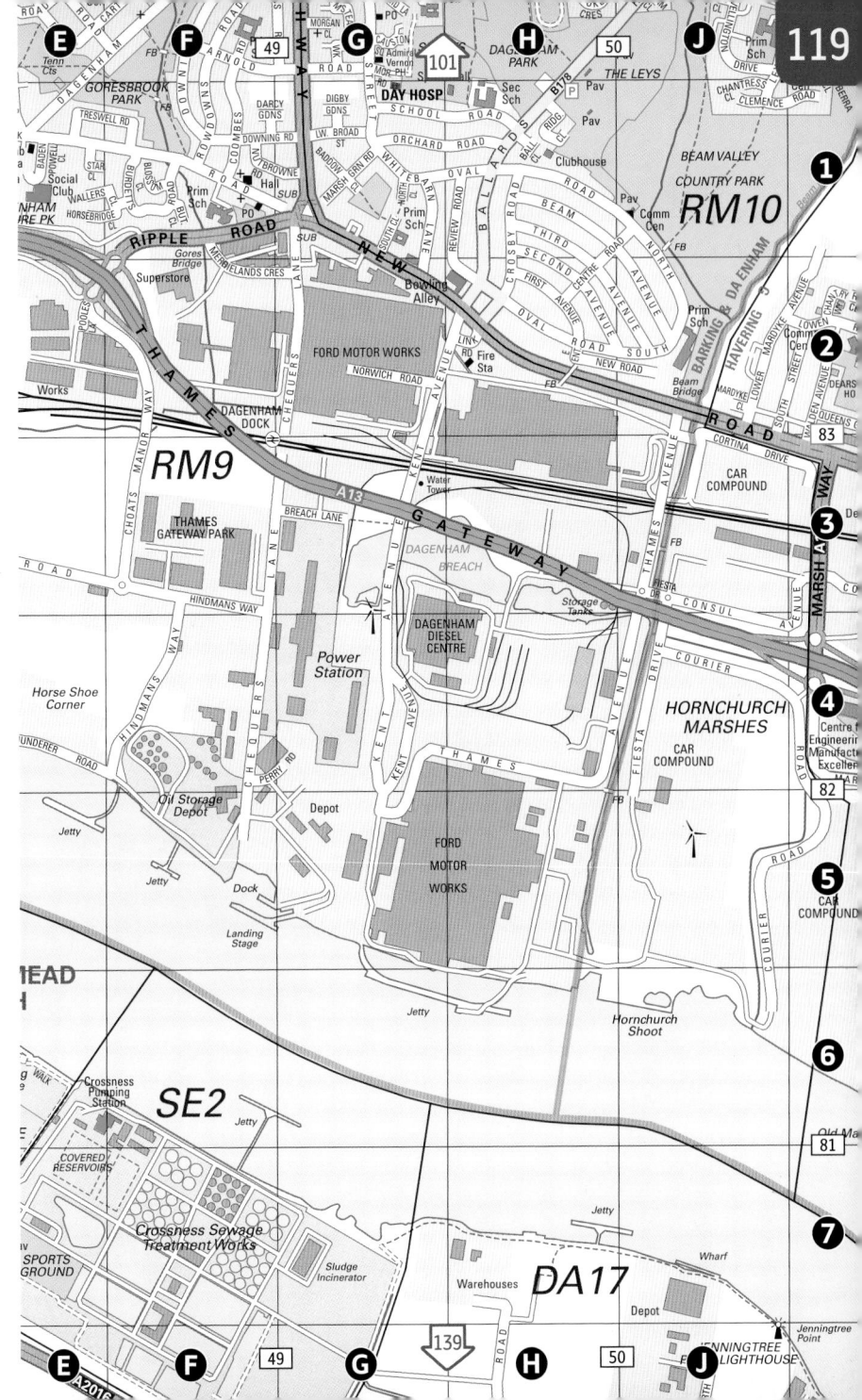

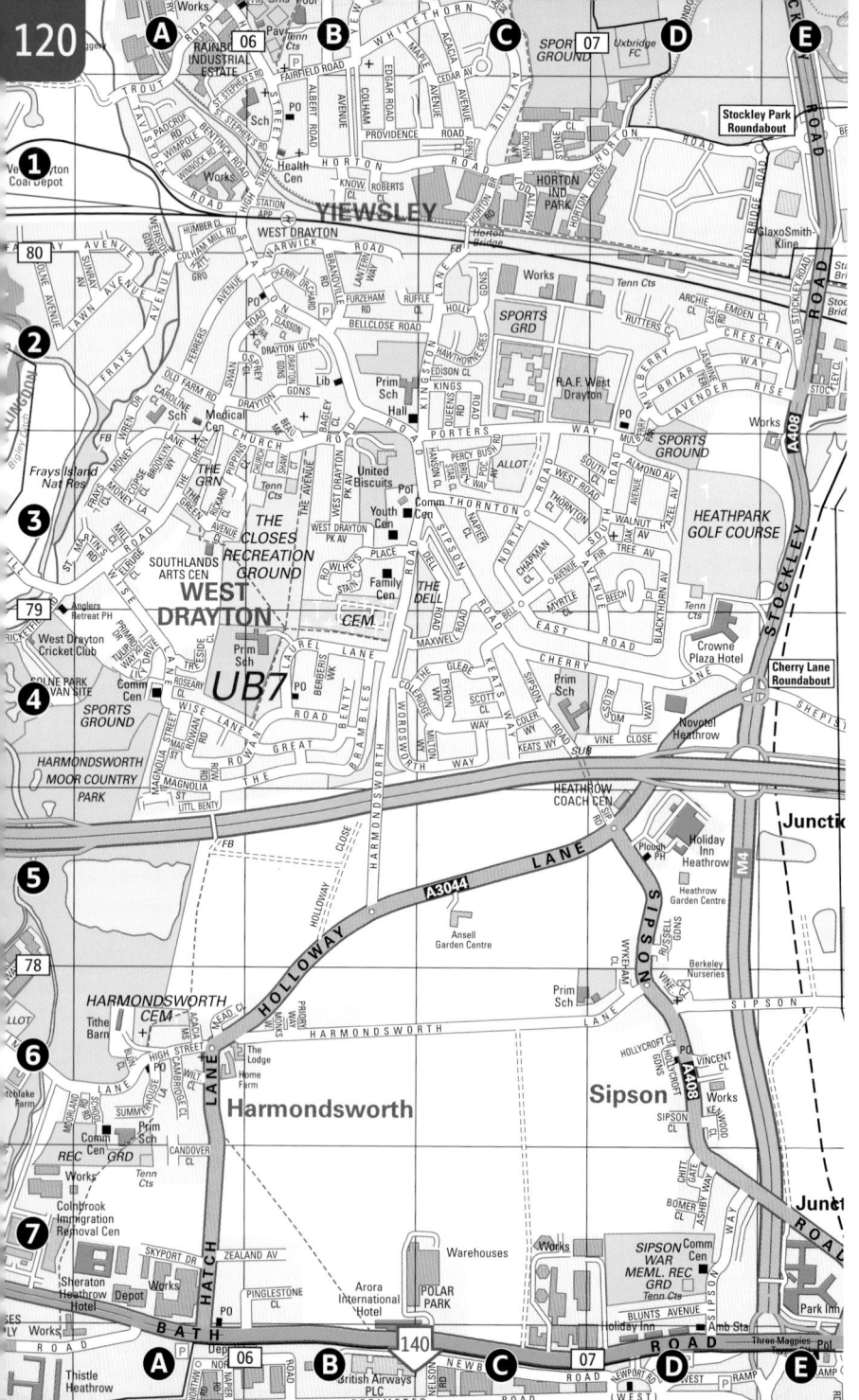

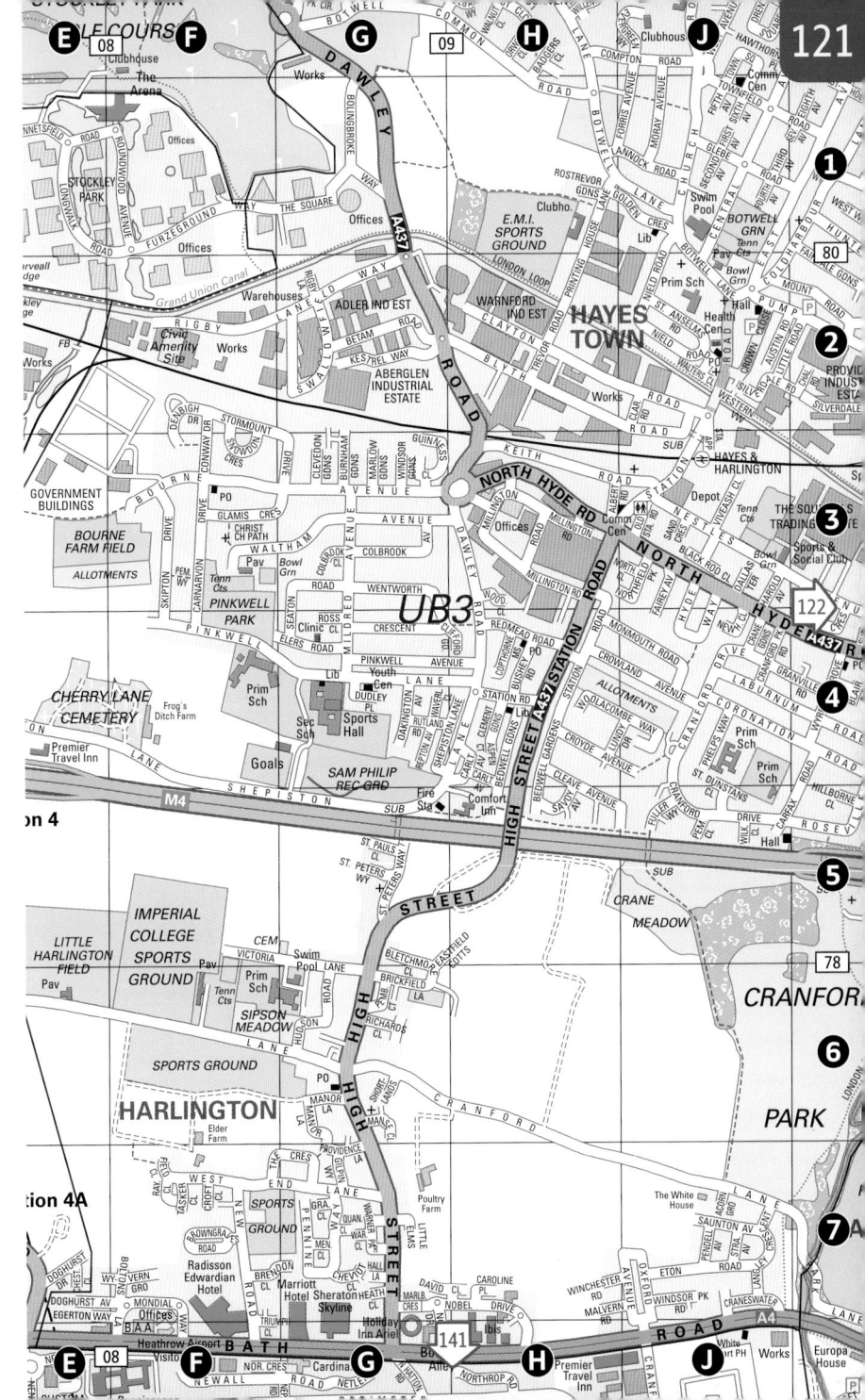

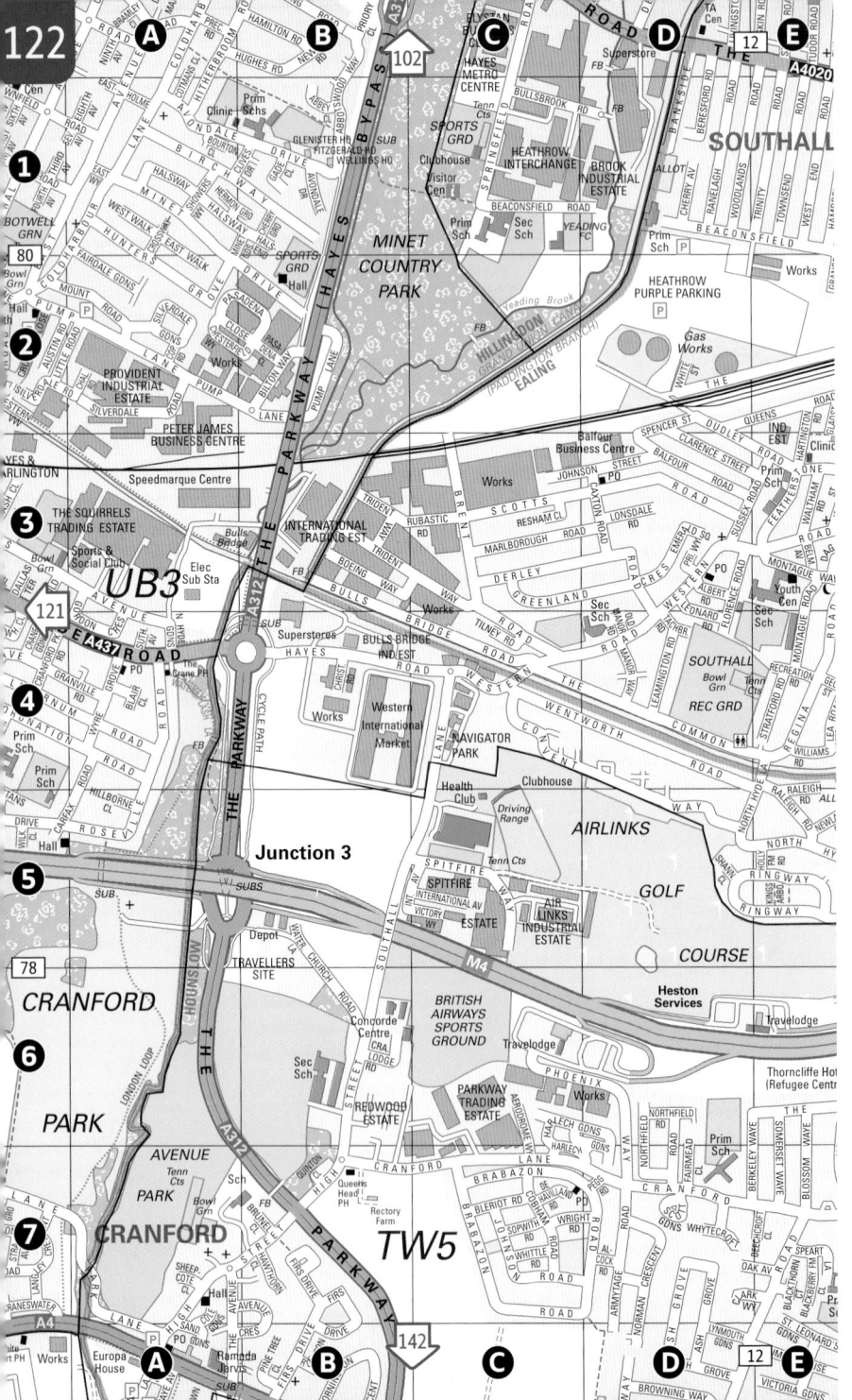

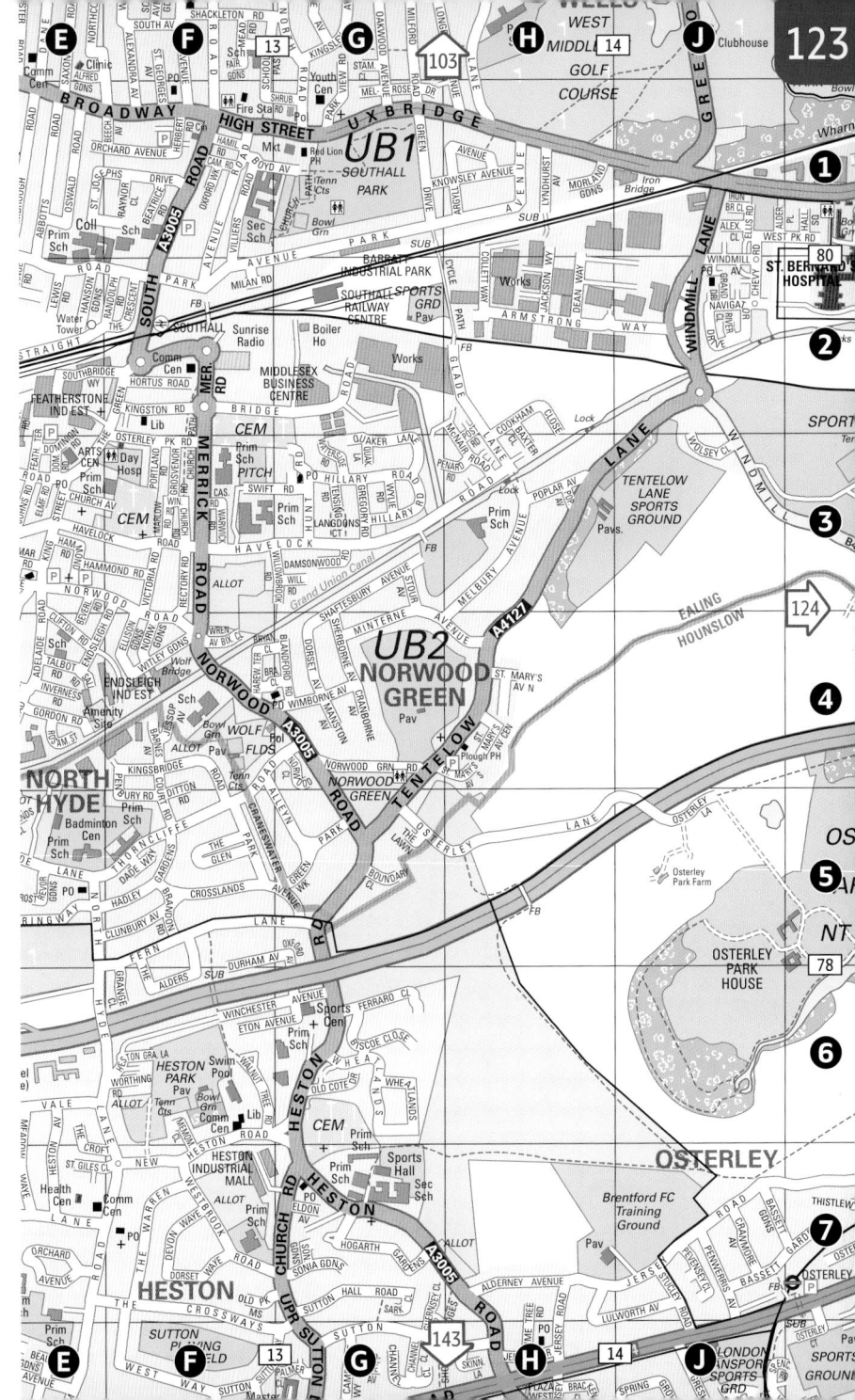

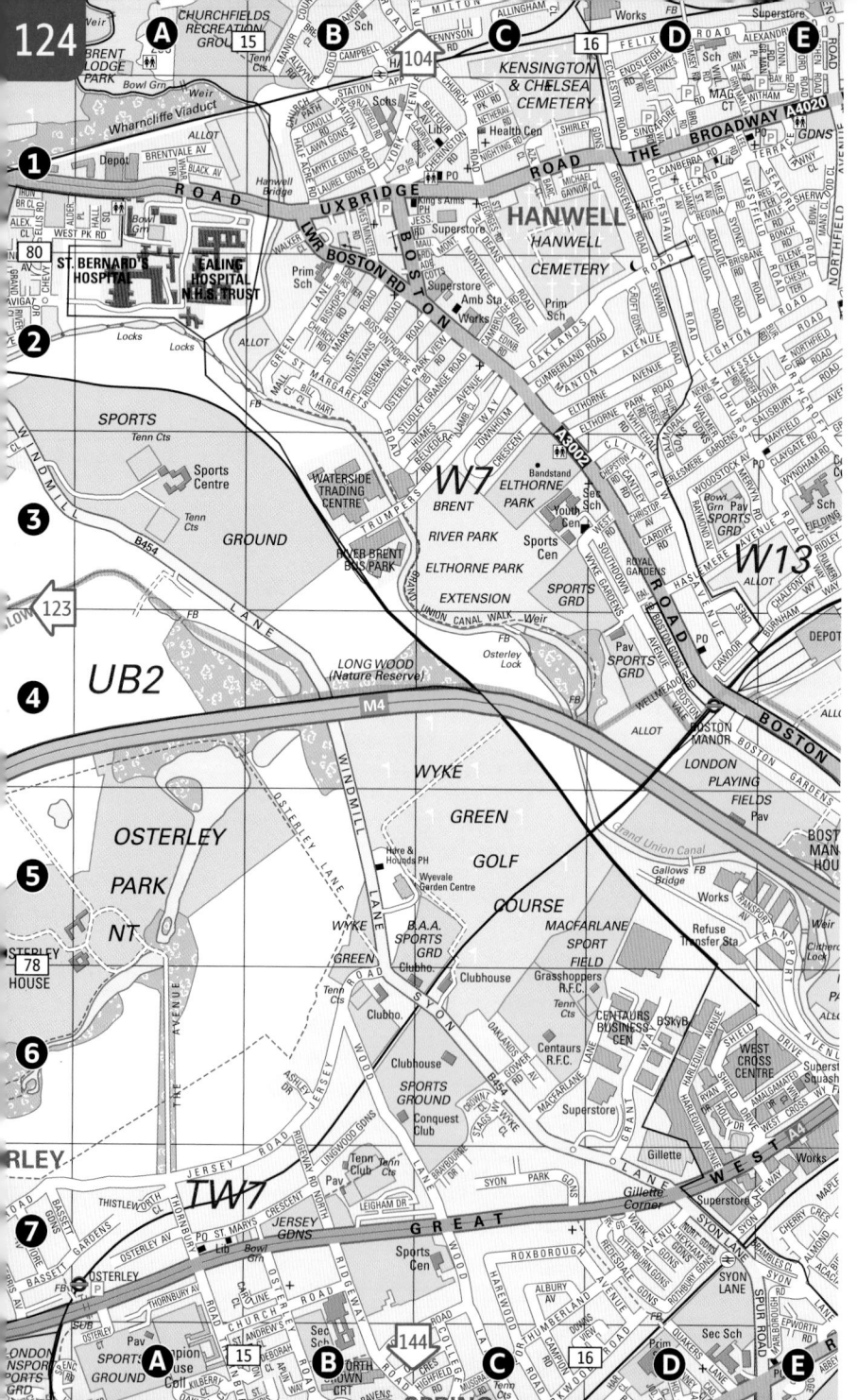

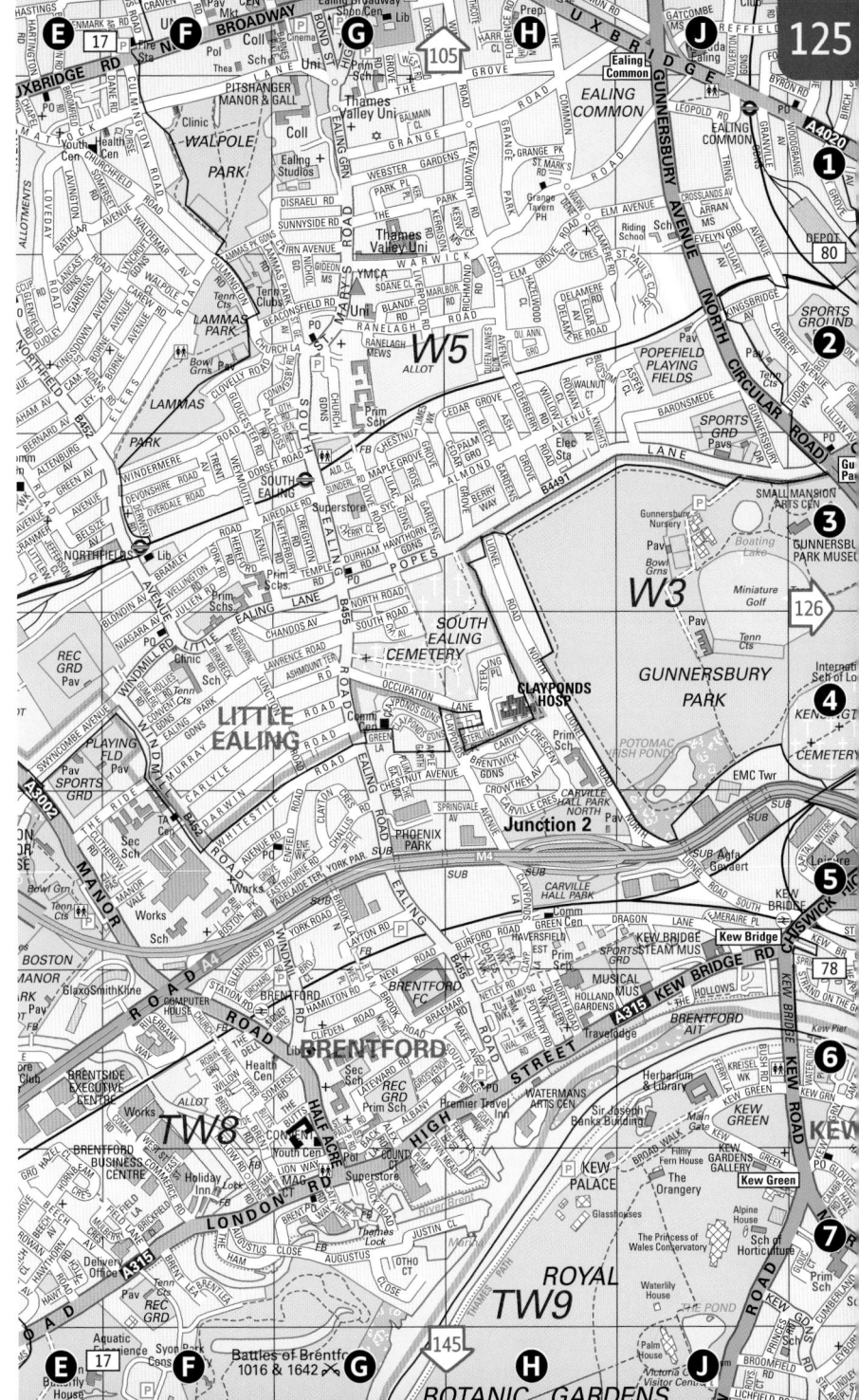

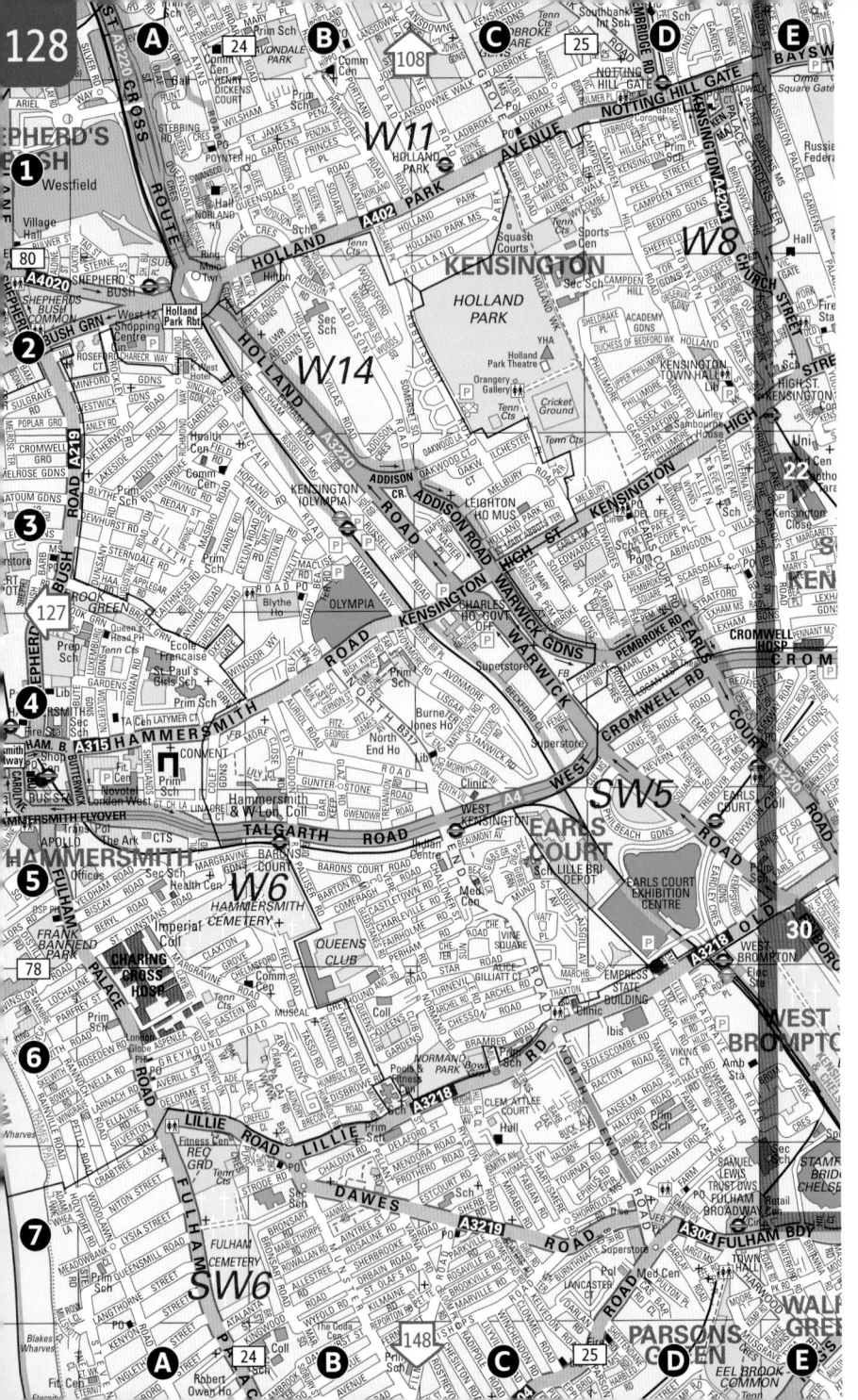

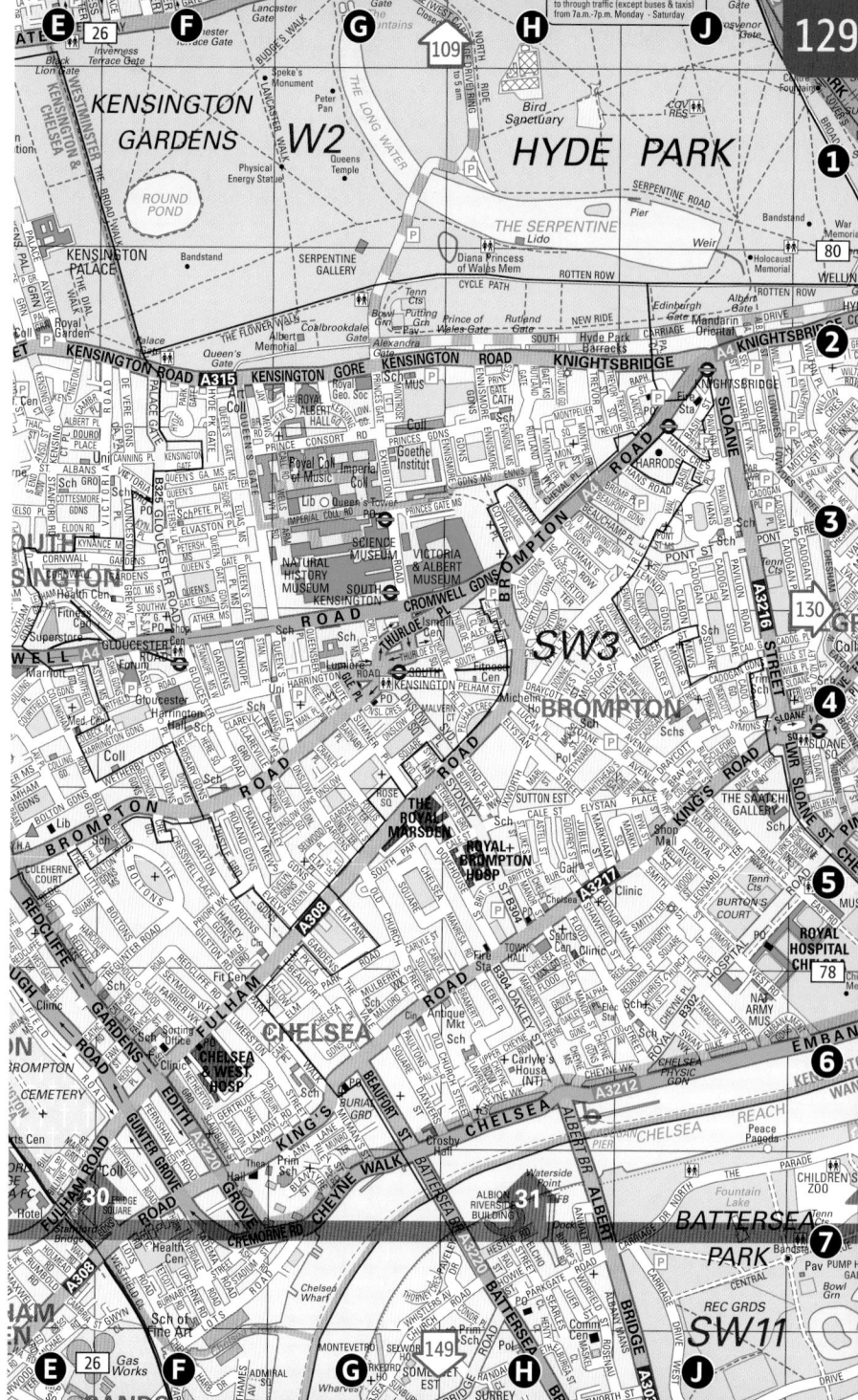

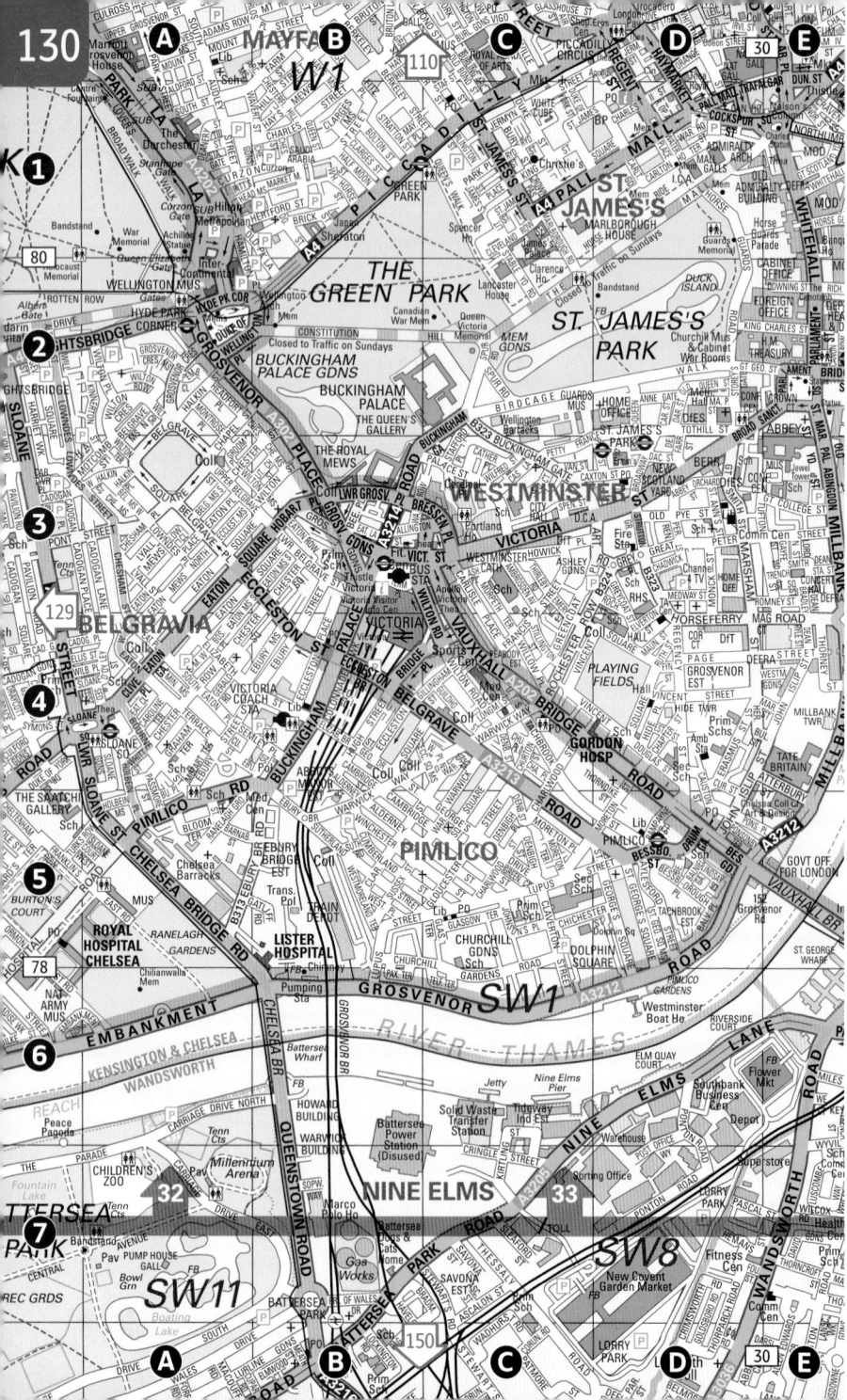

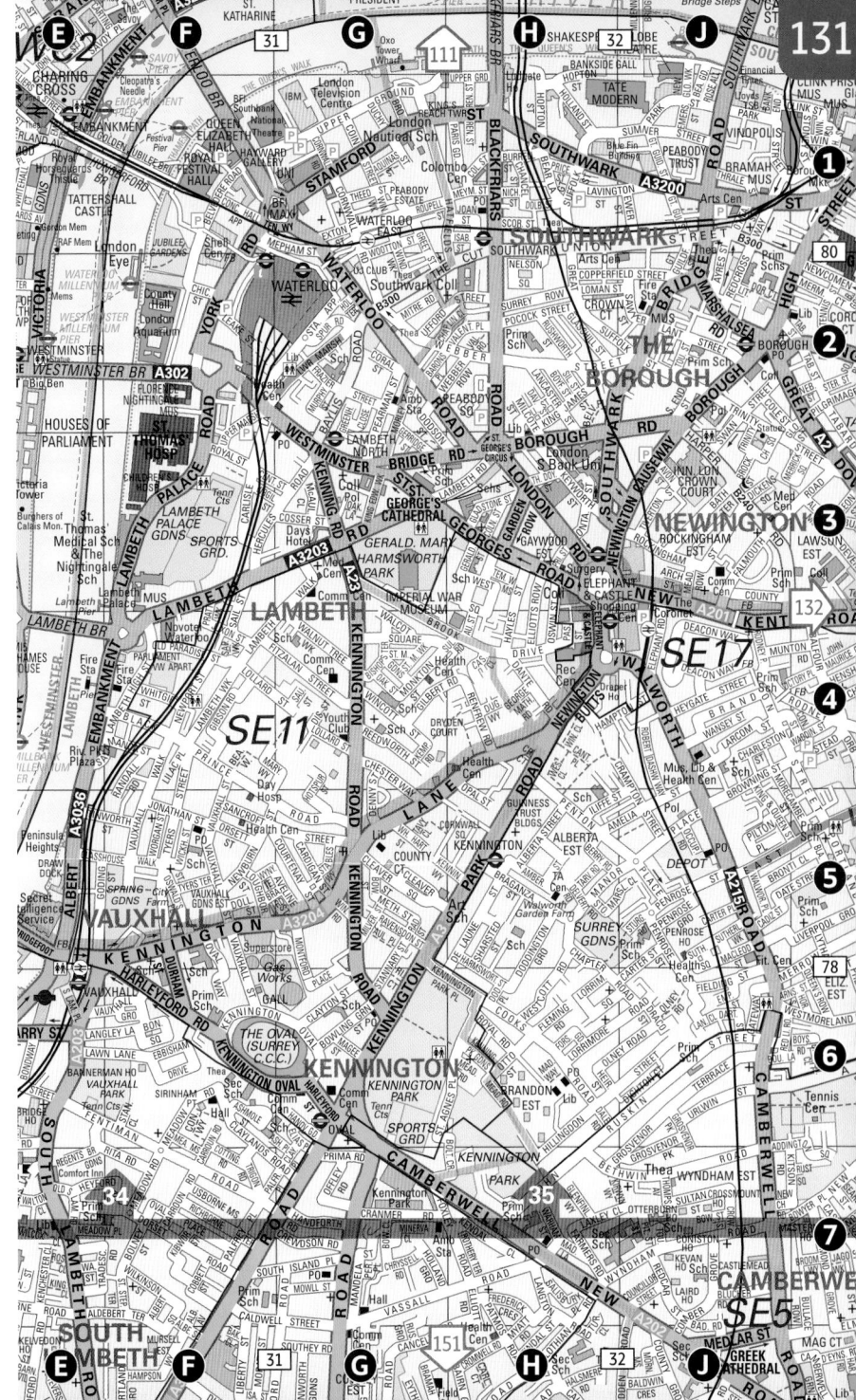

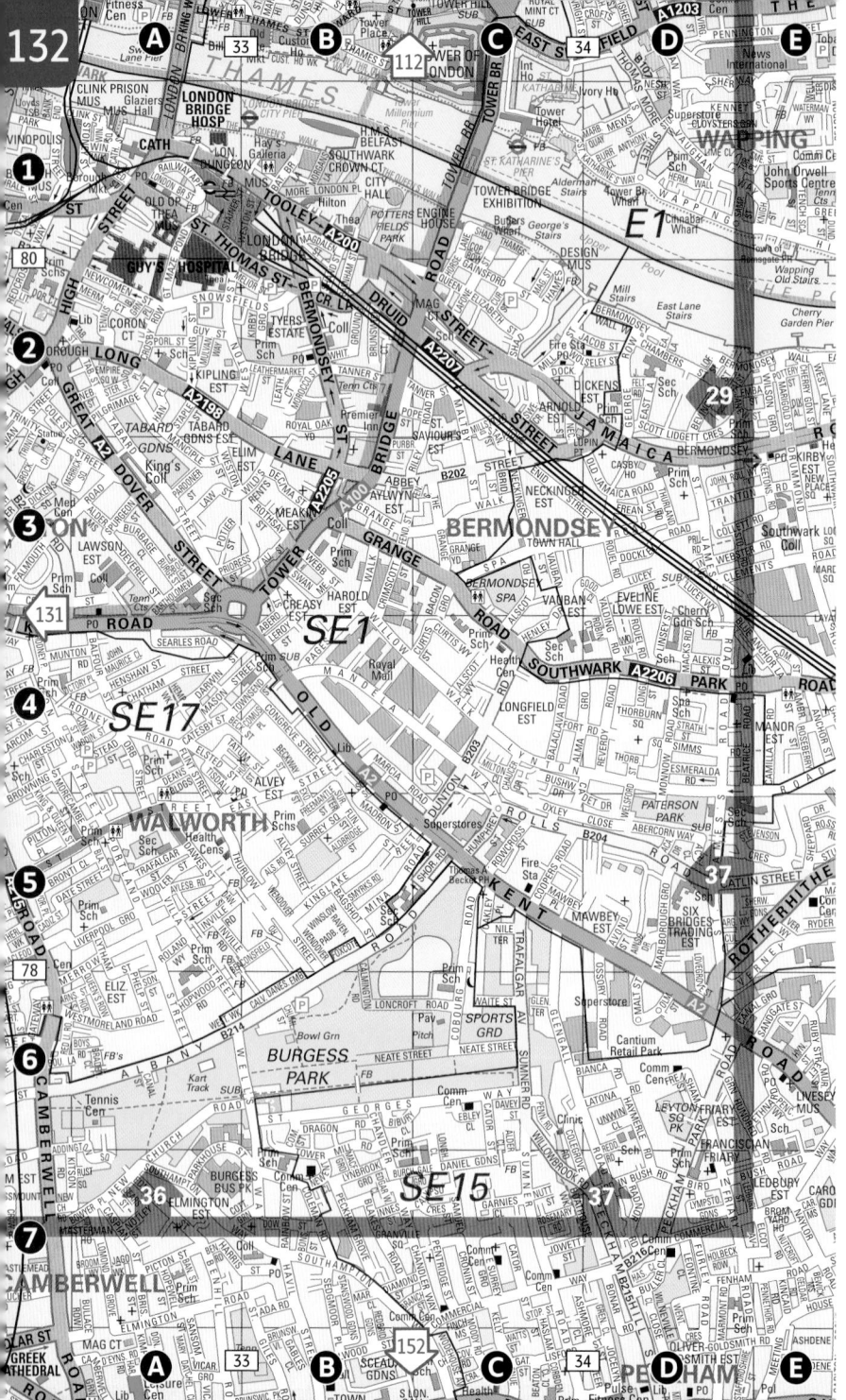

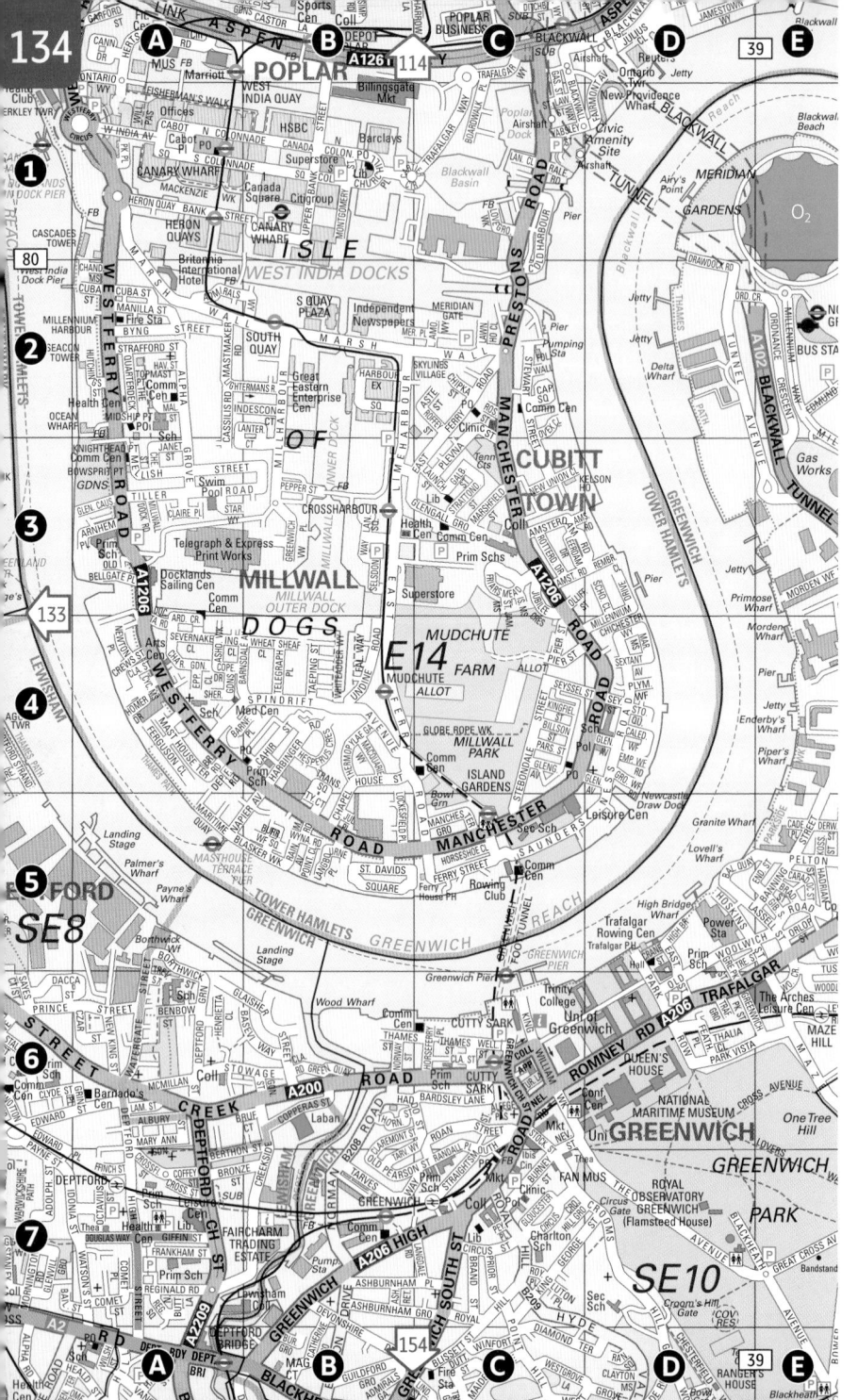

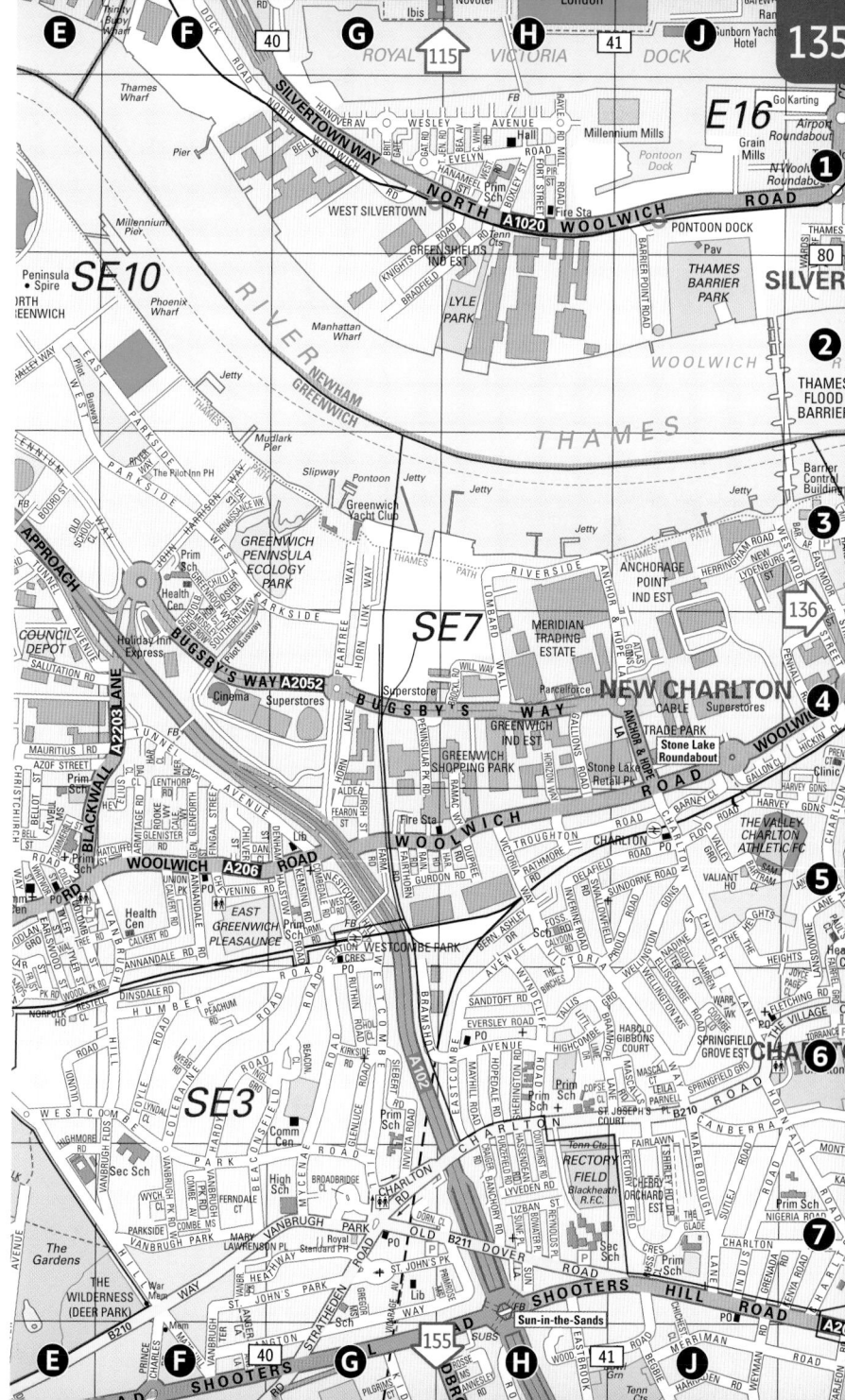

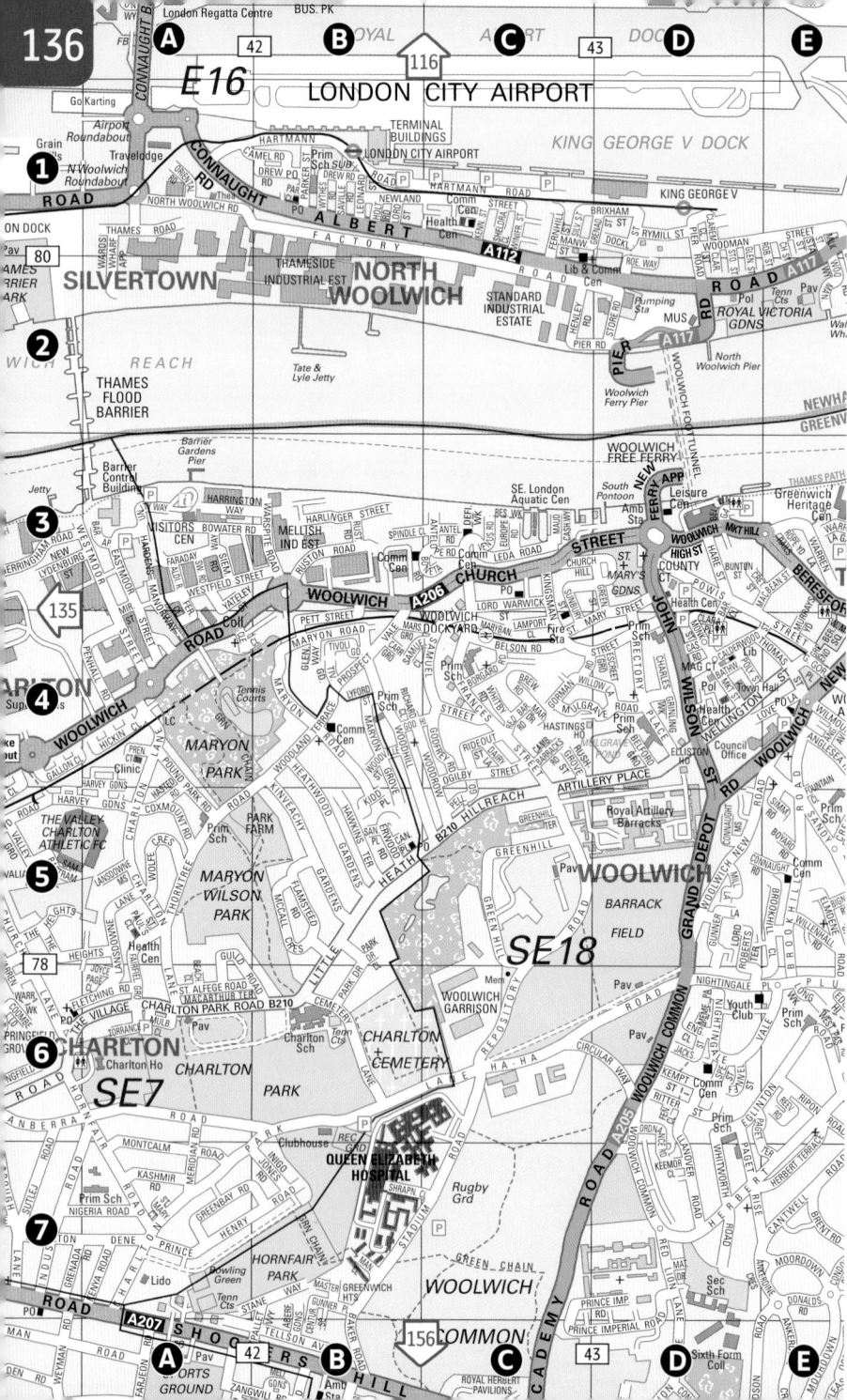

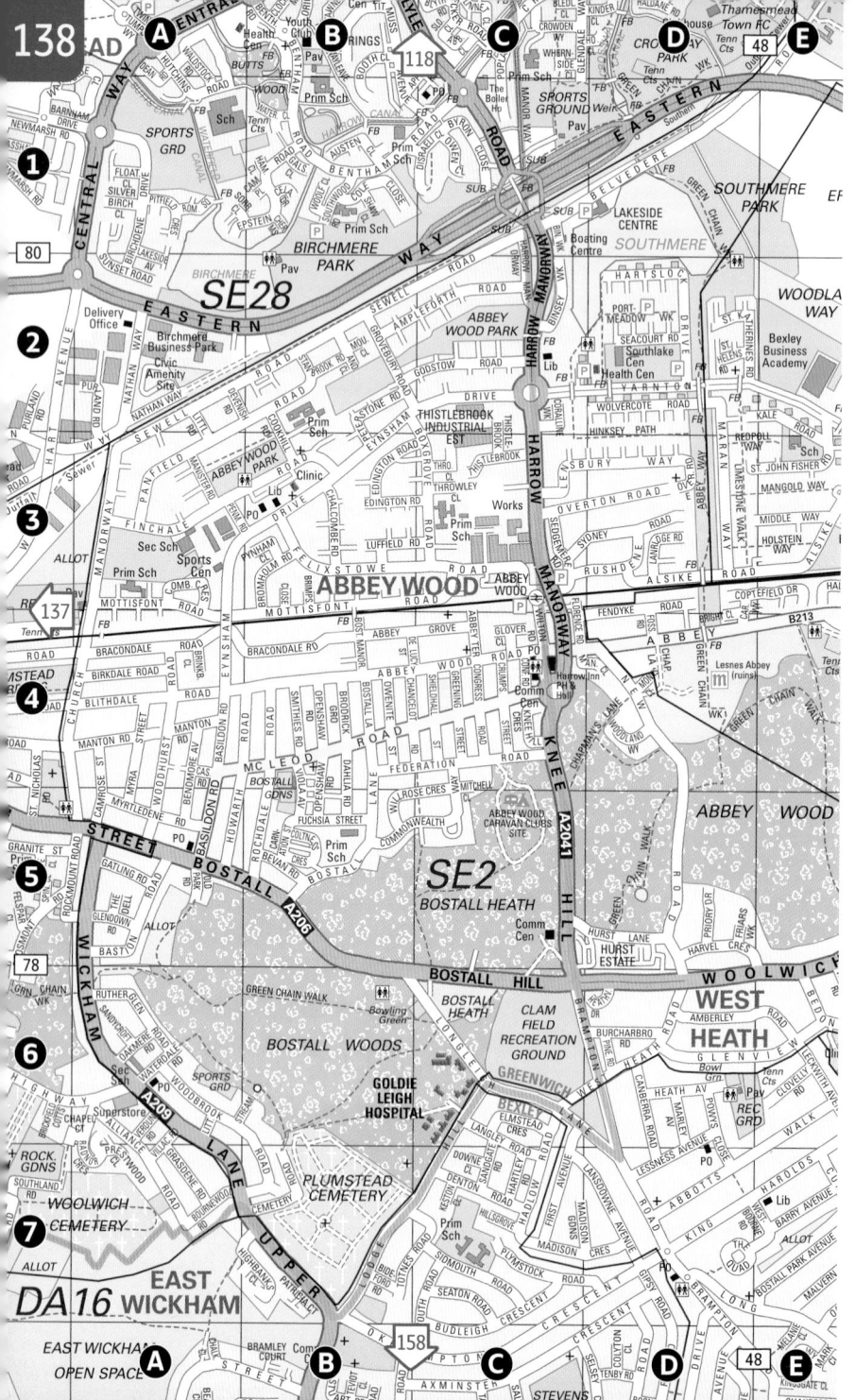

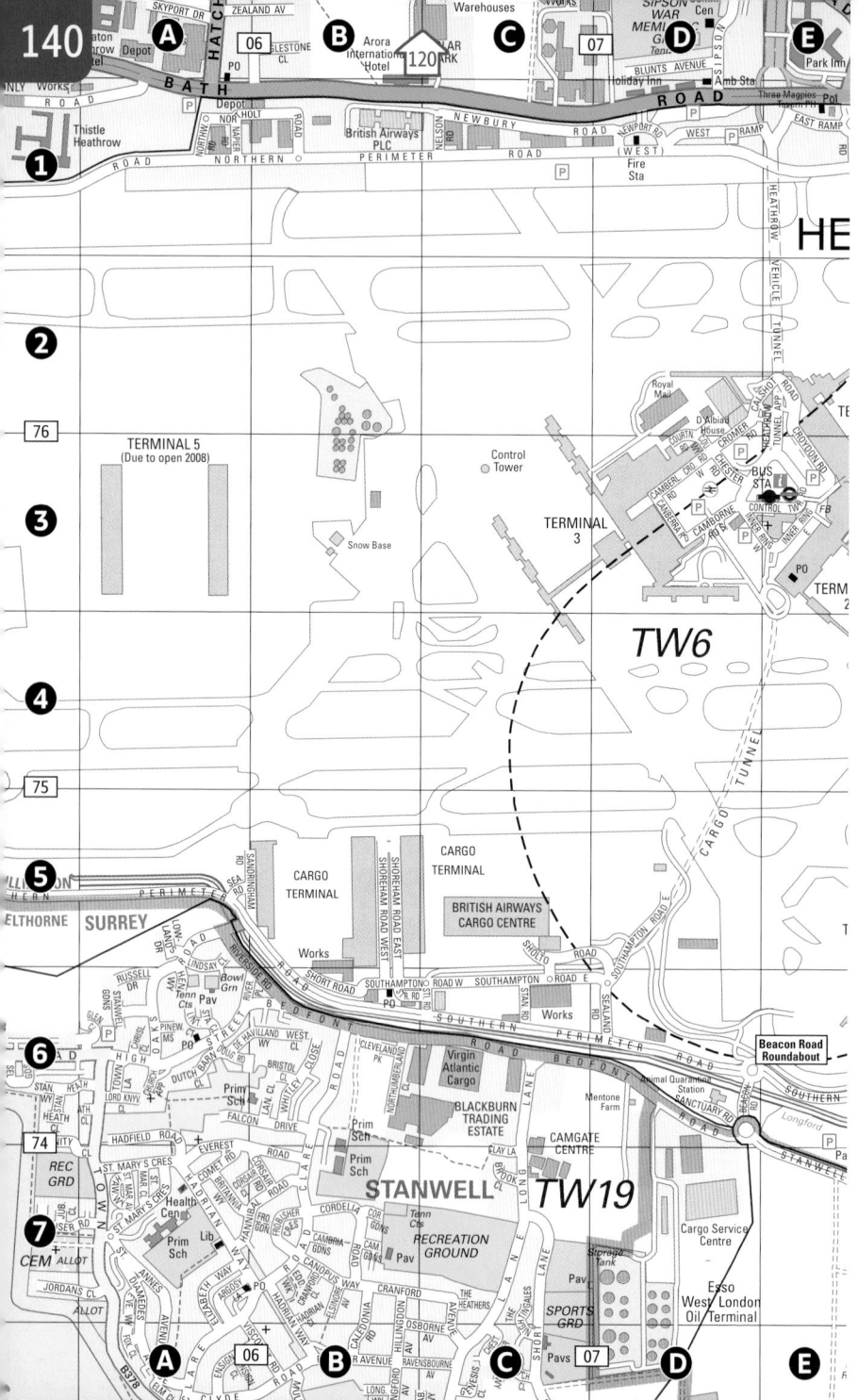

HE

TW6

TERMINAL 5
(Due to open 2008)

TERMINAL 3

Snow Base

Control Tower

TERM

SURREY

ELTHORNE

CARGO TERMINAL

CARGO TERMINAL

SHOREHAM ROAD EAST
SHOREHAM ROAD WEST

BRITISH AIRWAYS CARGO CENTRE

Works

Works

Beacon Road Roundabout

STANWELL

TW19

Virgin Atlantic Cargo

BLACKBURN TRADING ESTATE

CAMGATE CENTRE

Mentone Farm

Animal Quarantine Station

Cargo Service Centre

RECREATION GROUND

SPORTS GRD

Storage Tank

Esso West London Oil Terminal

REC GRD

Health Cen

Prim Sch

Lib

CEM ALLOT

ALLOT

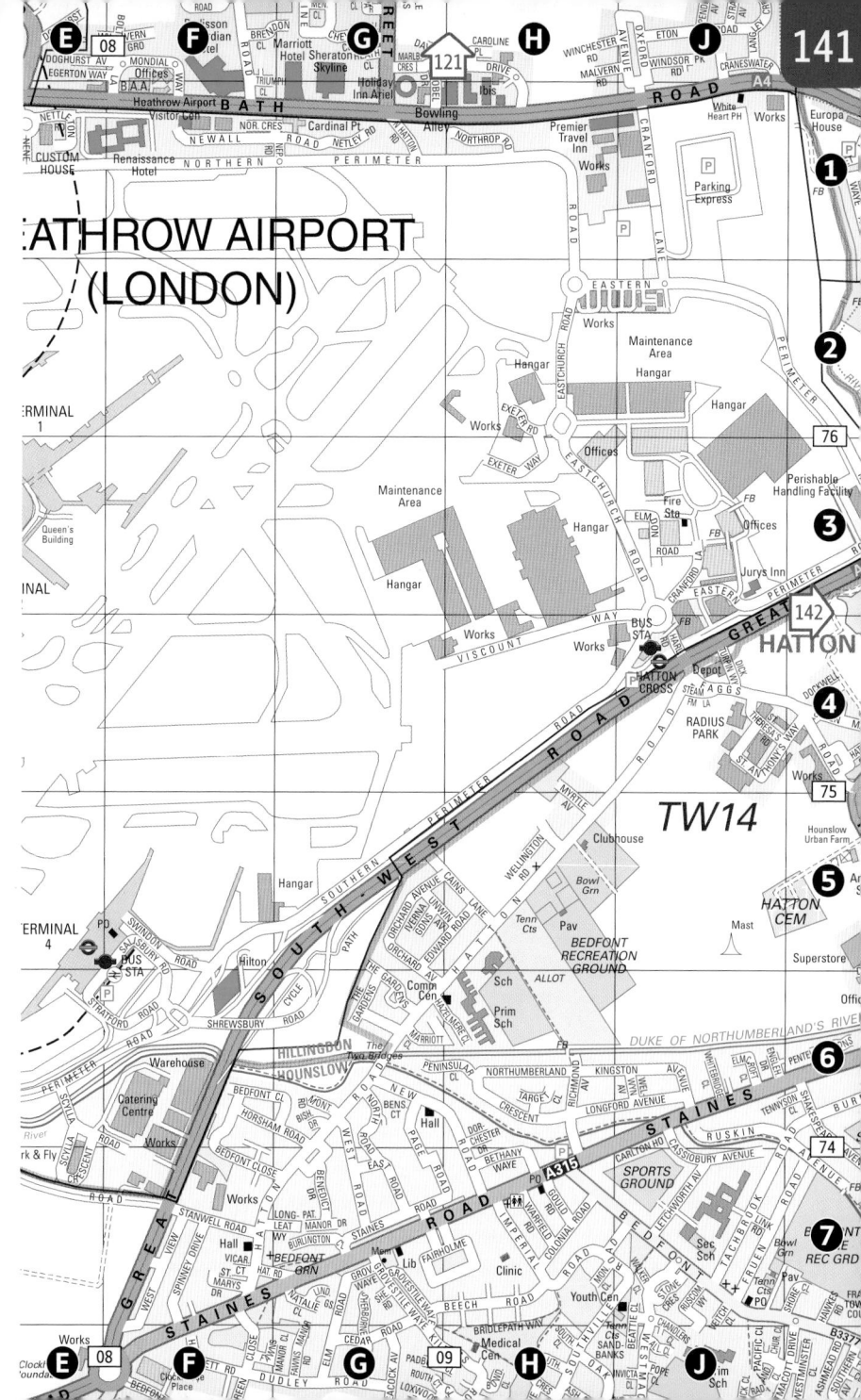

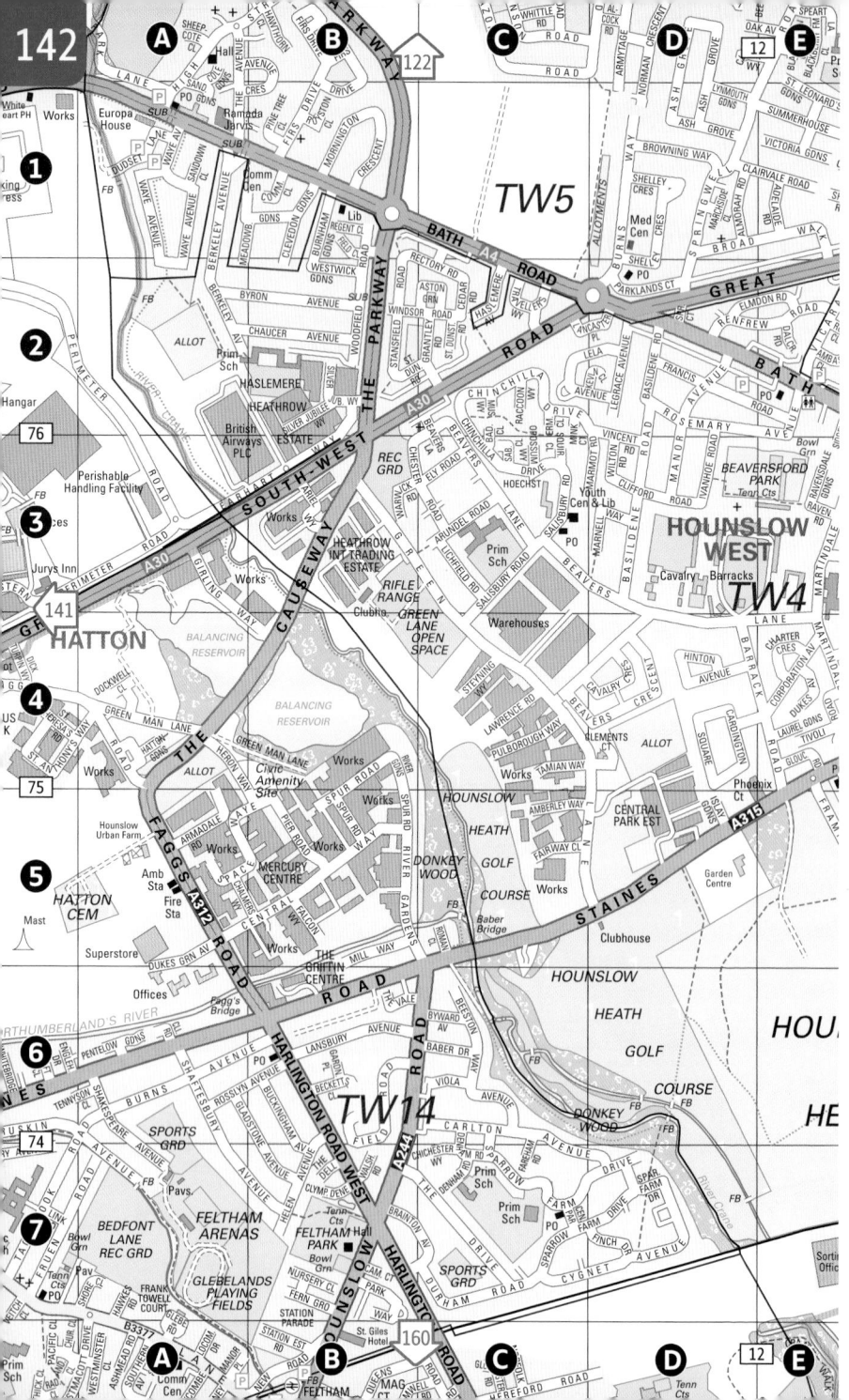

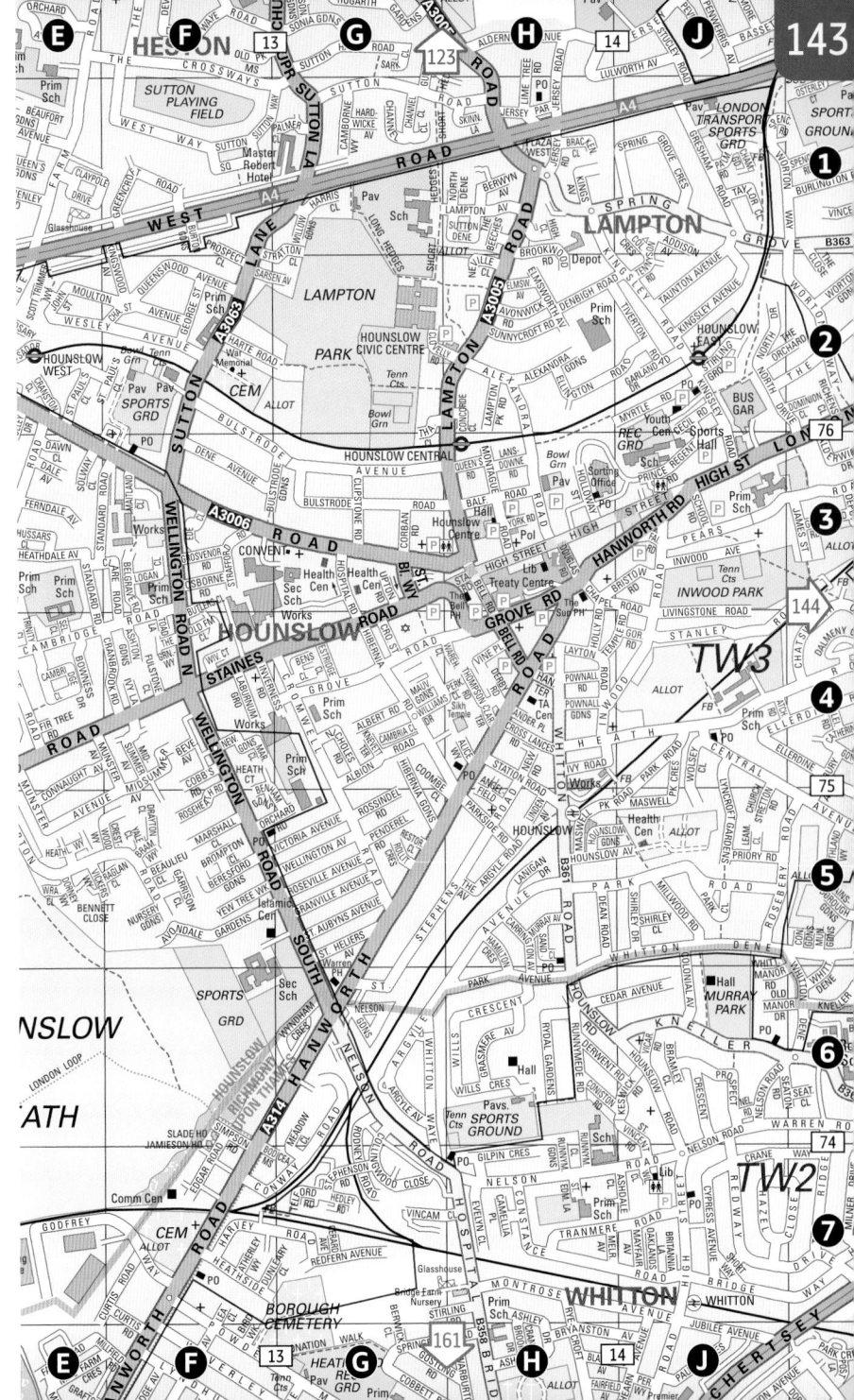

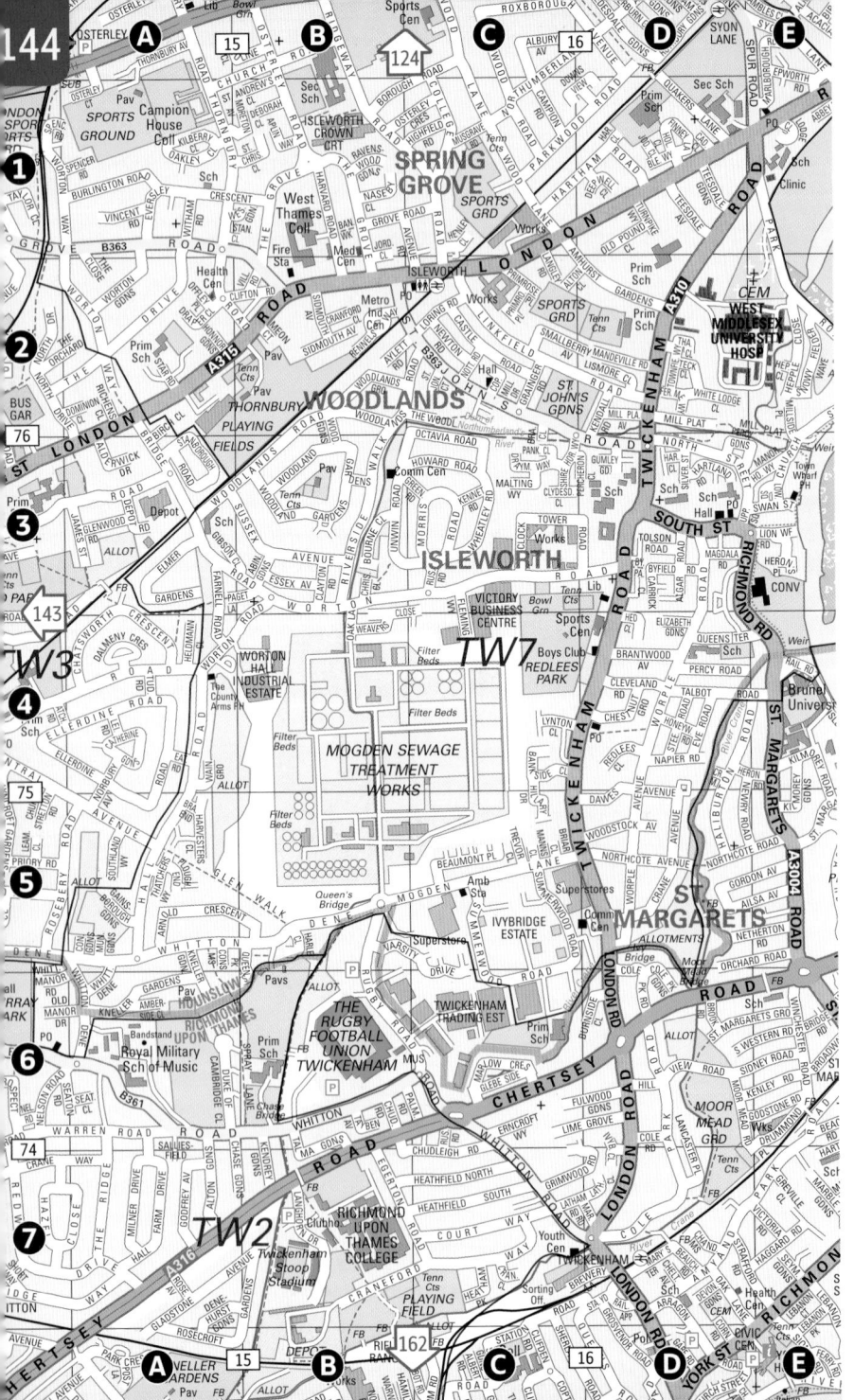

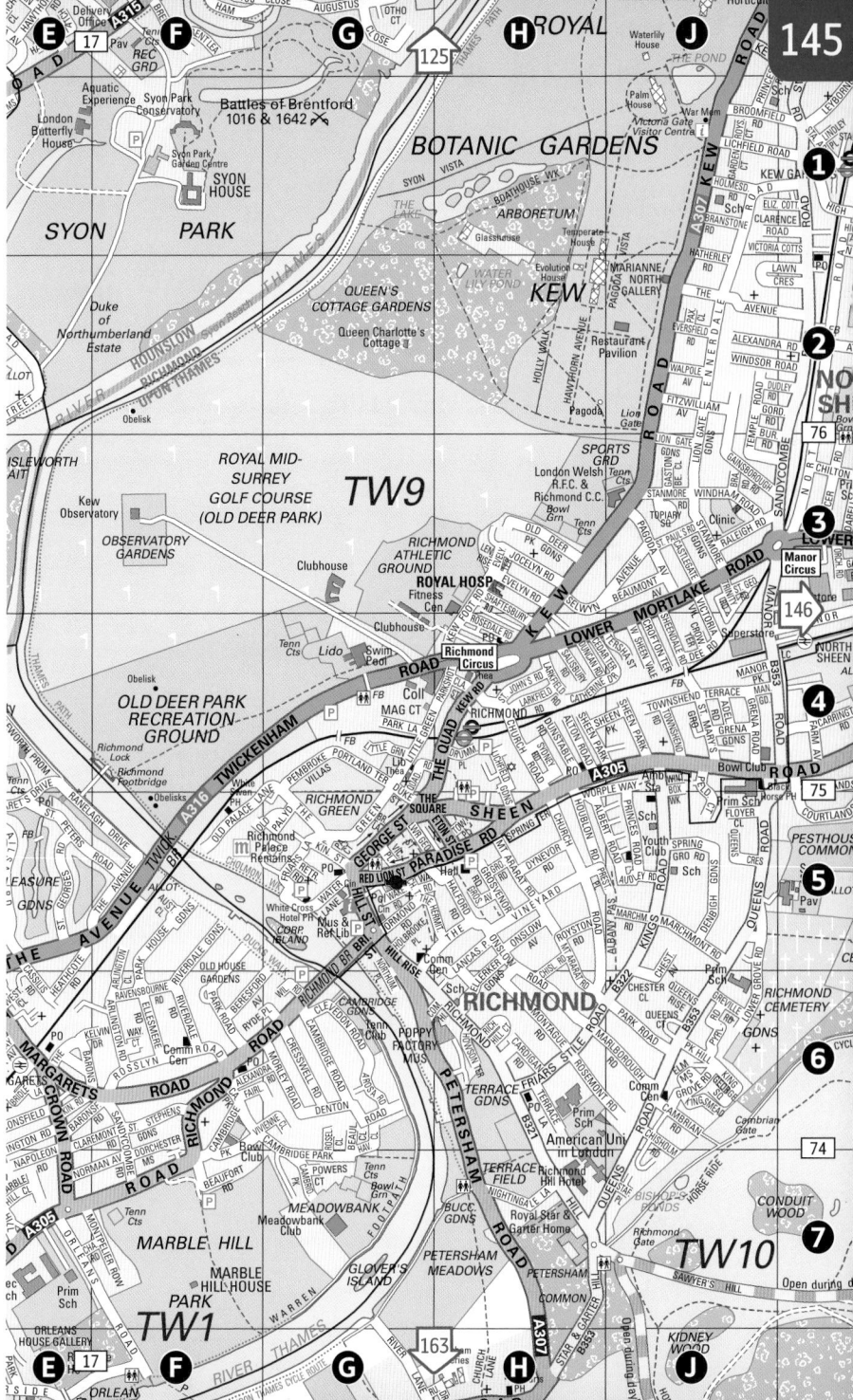

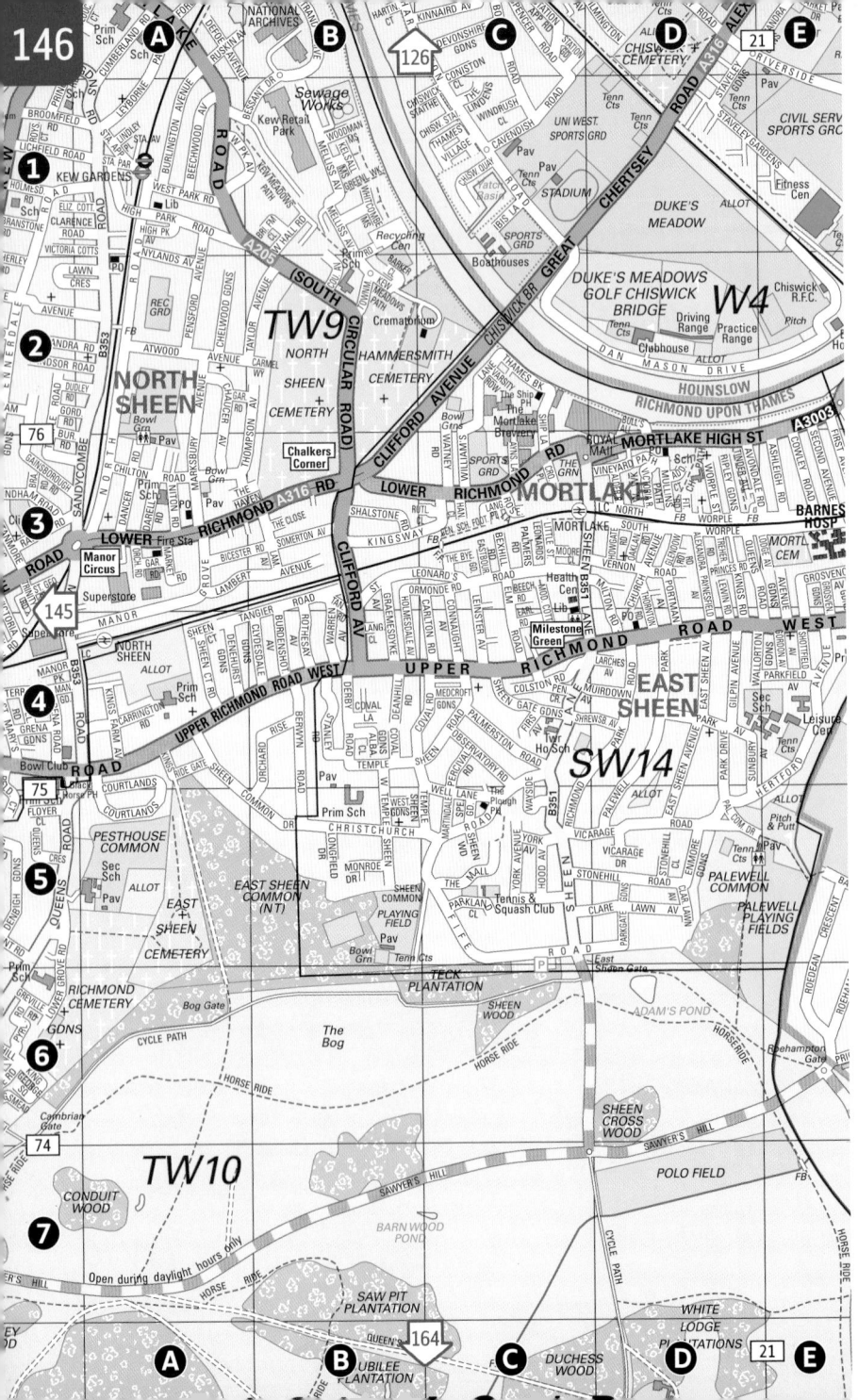

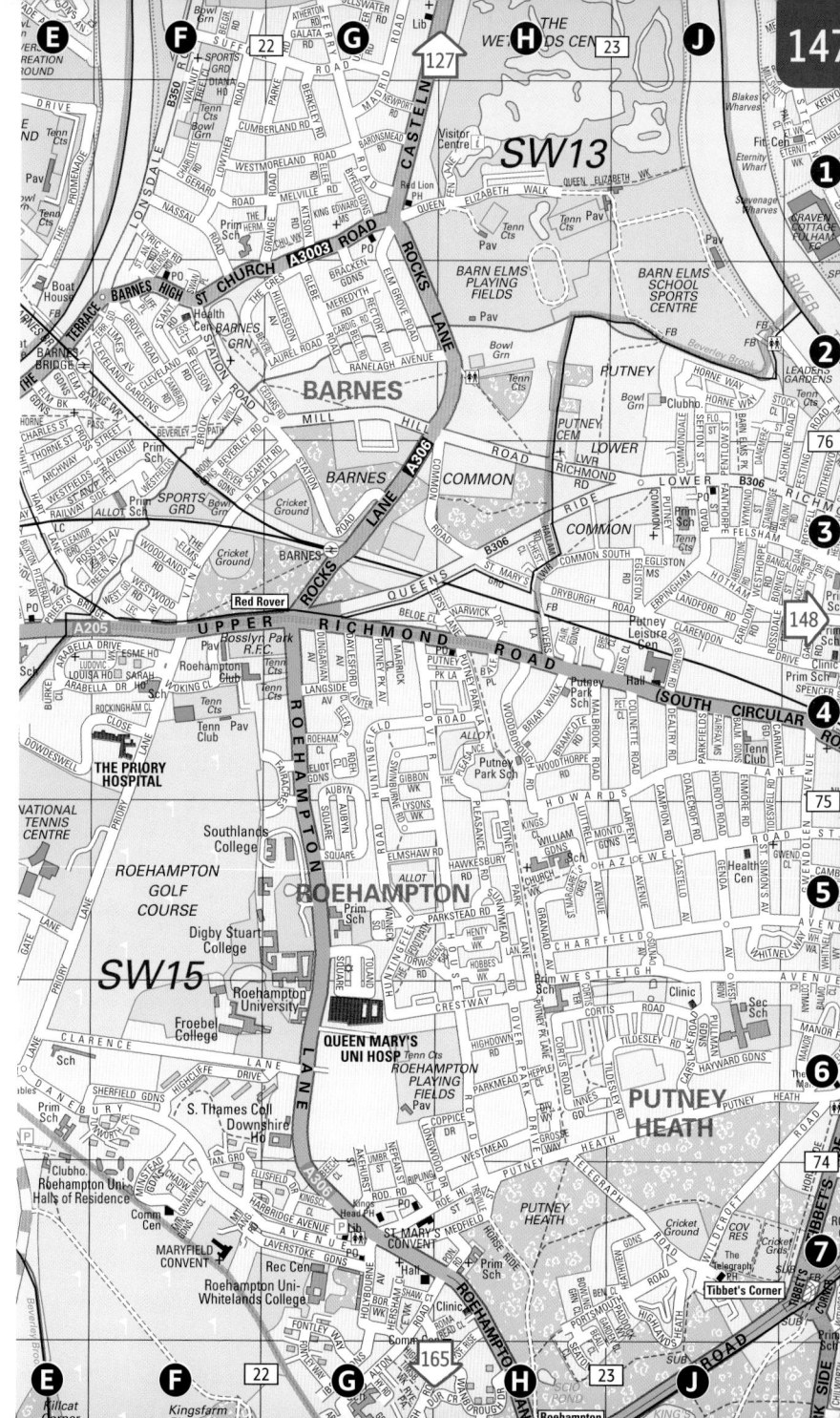

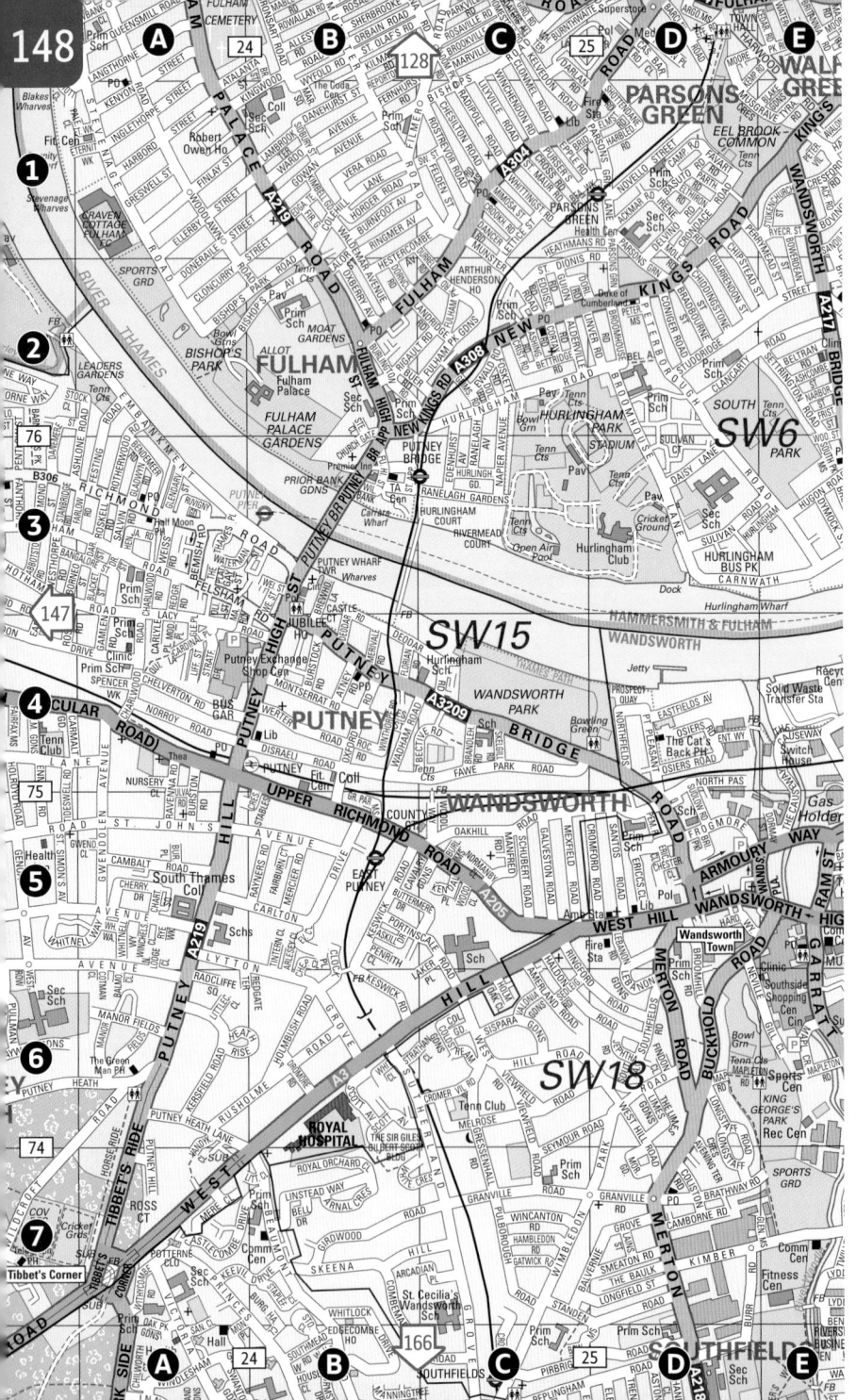

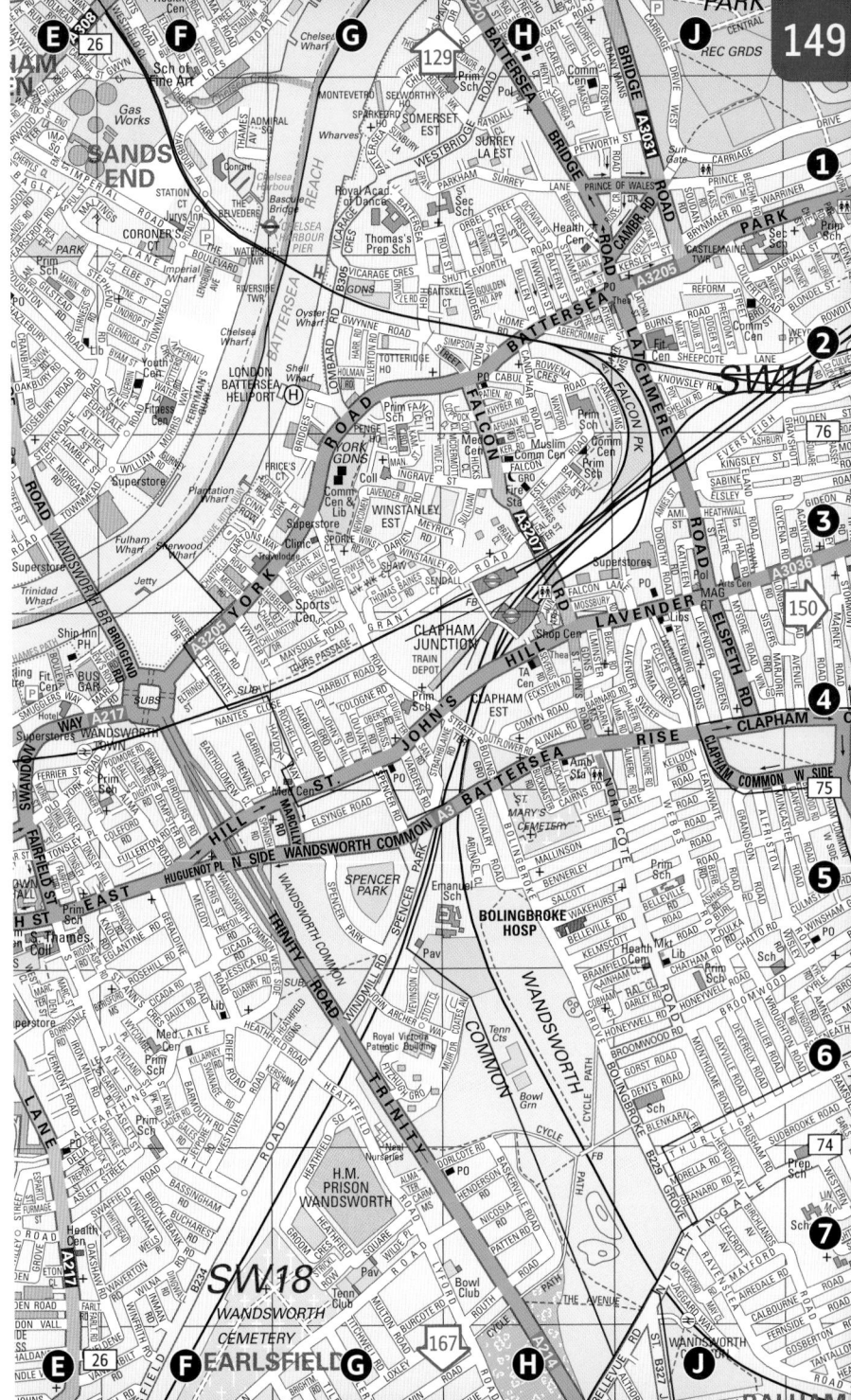

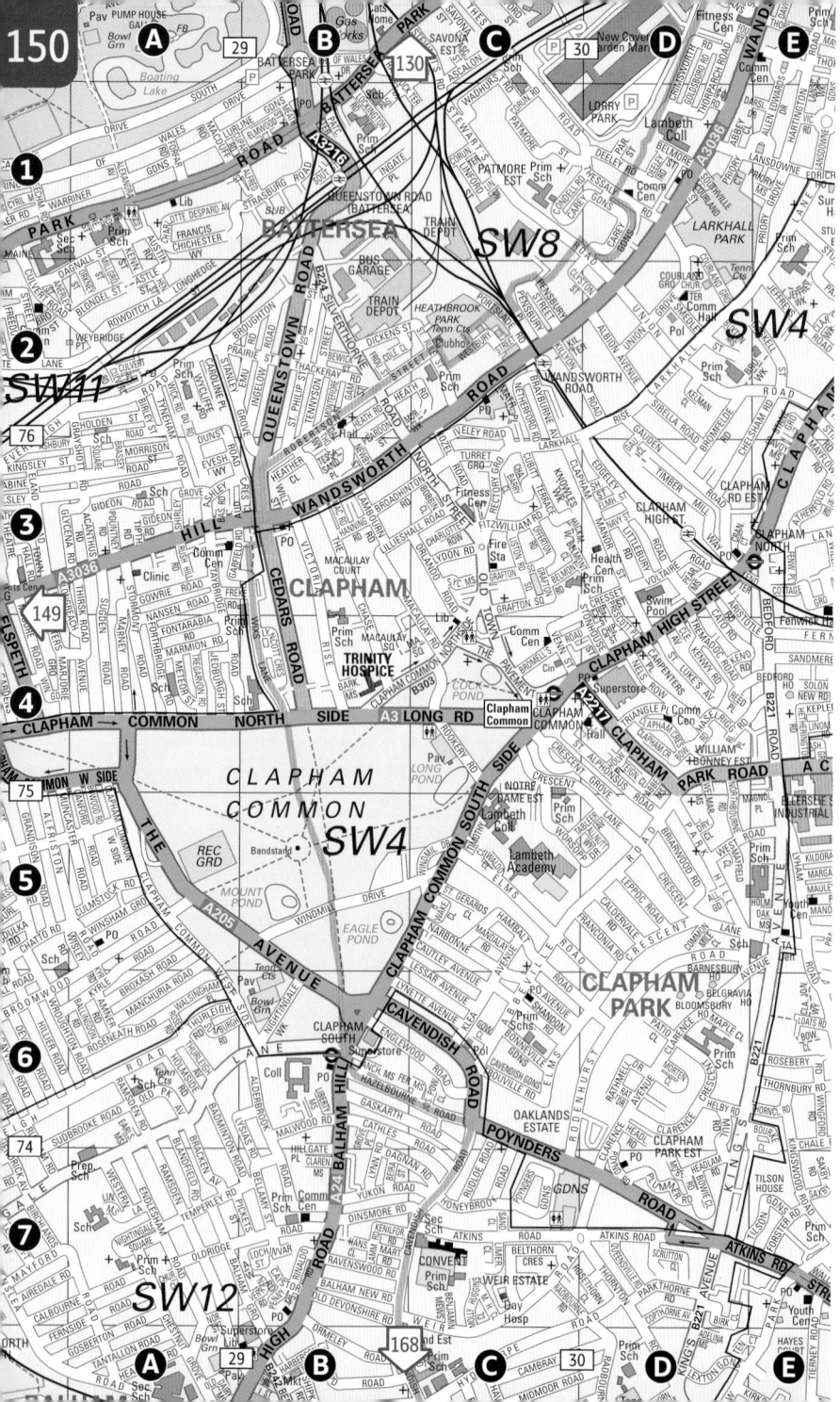

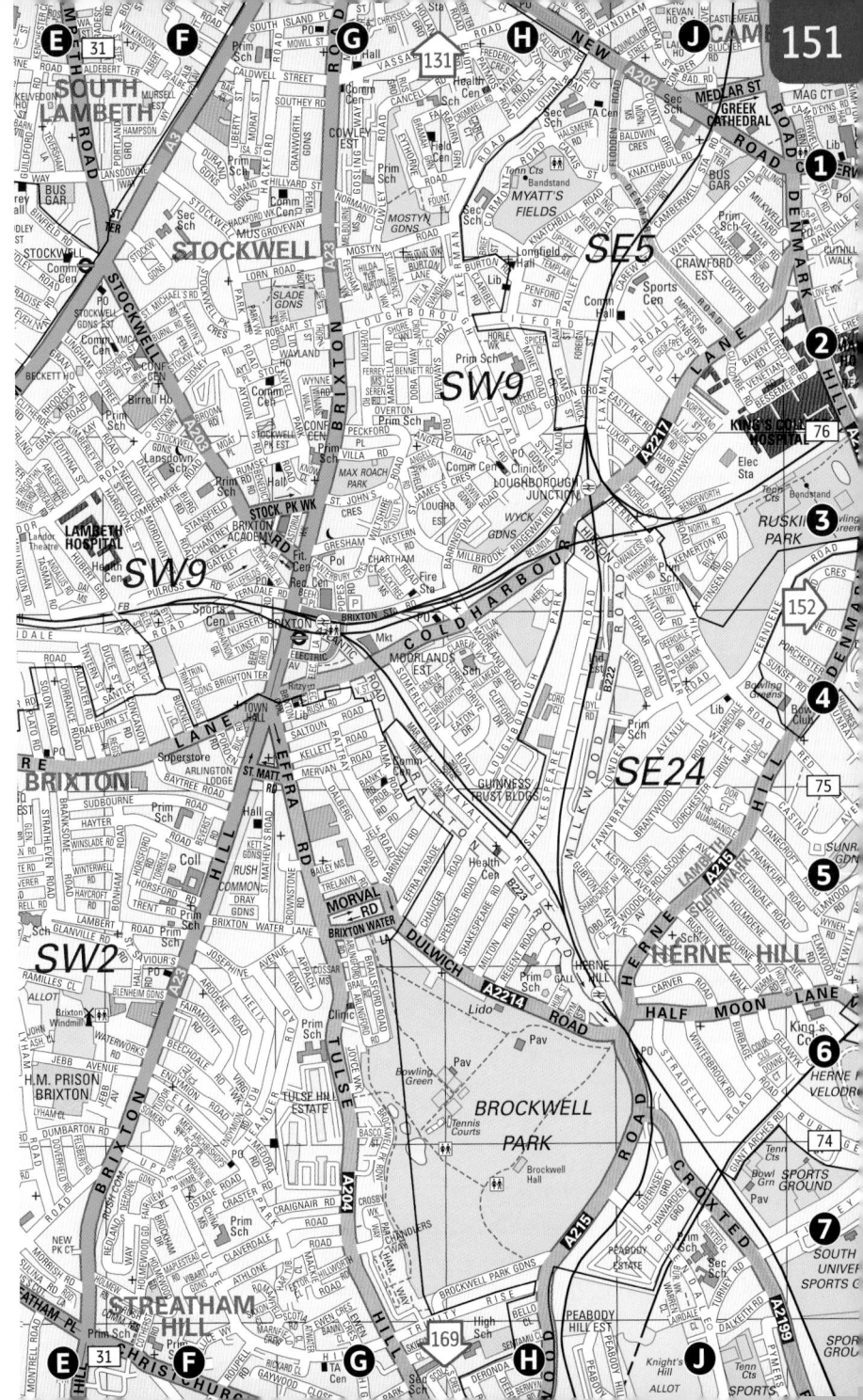

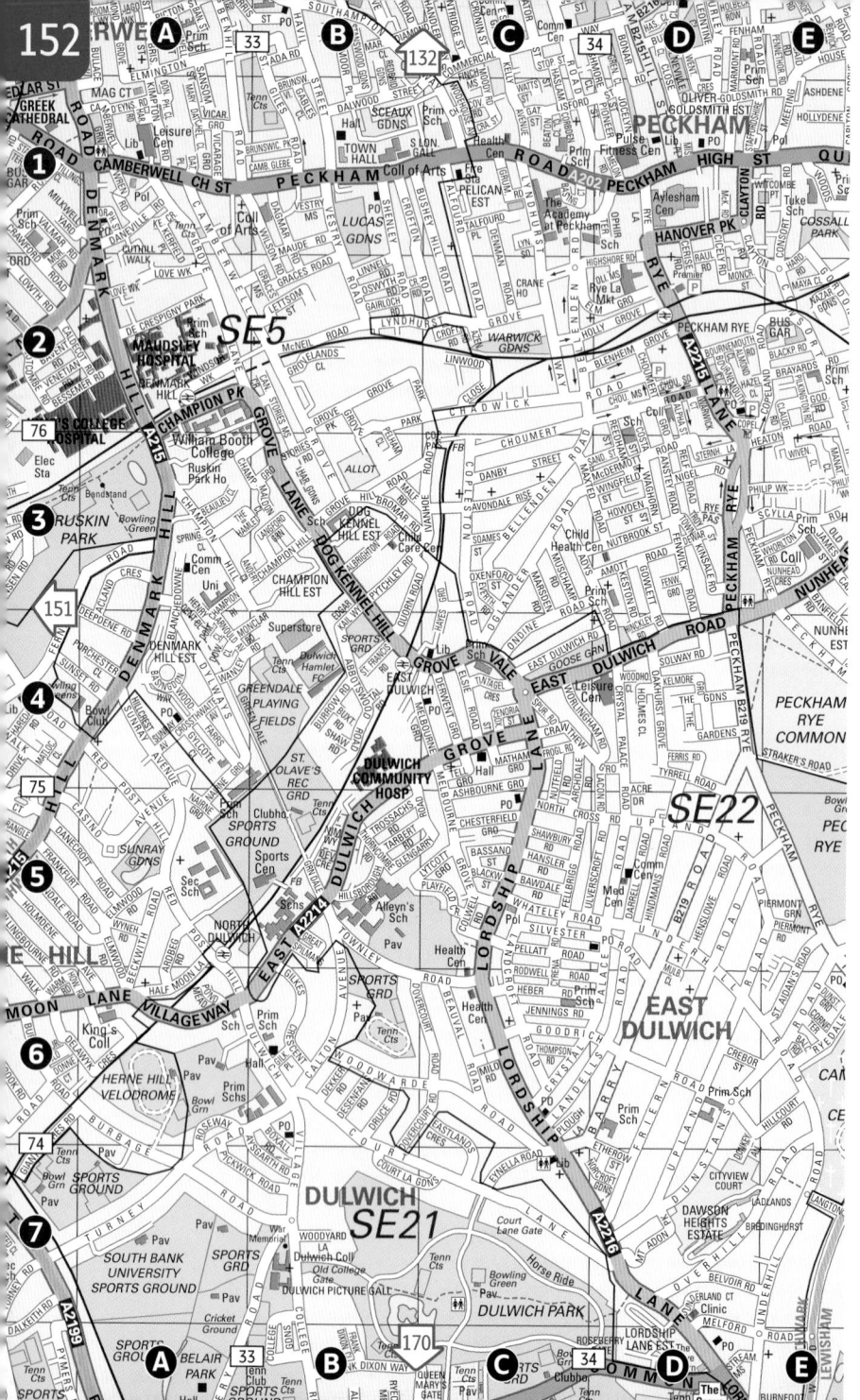

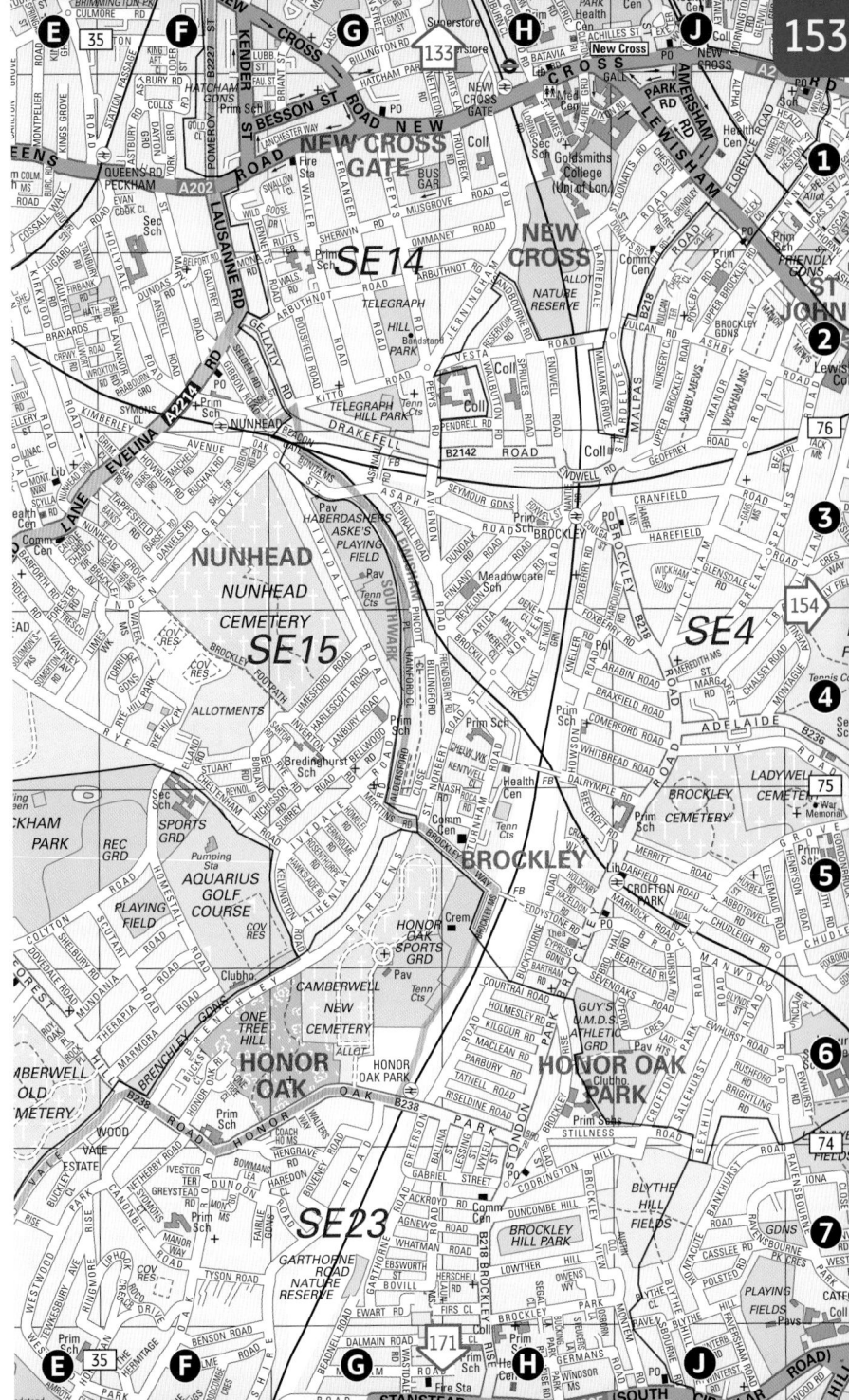

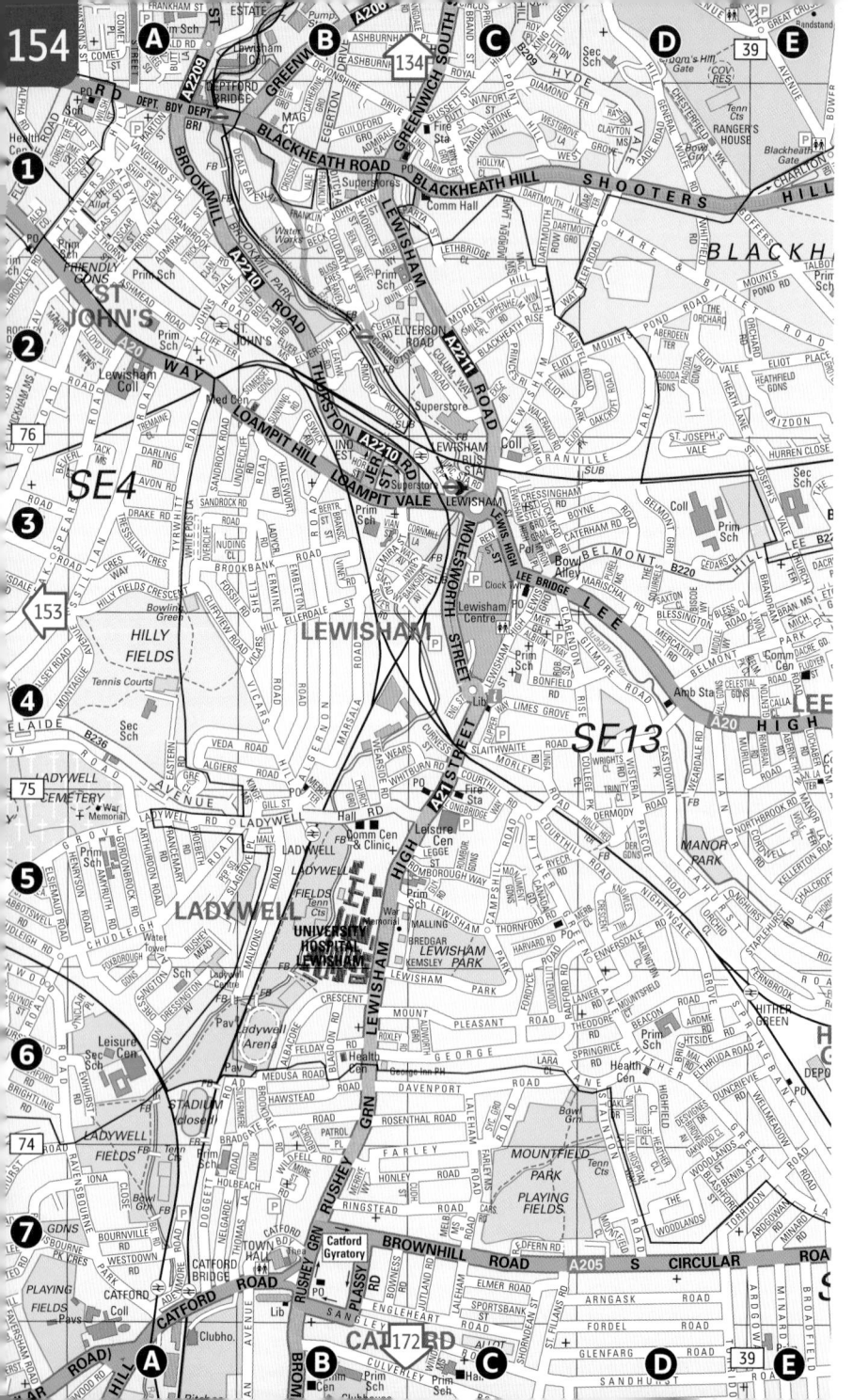

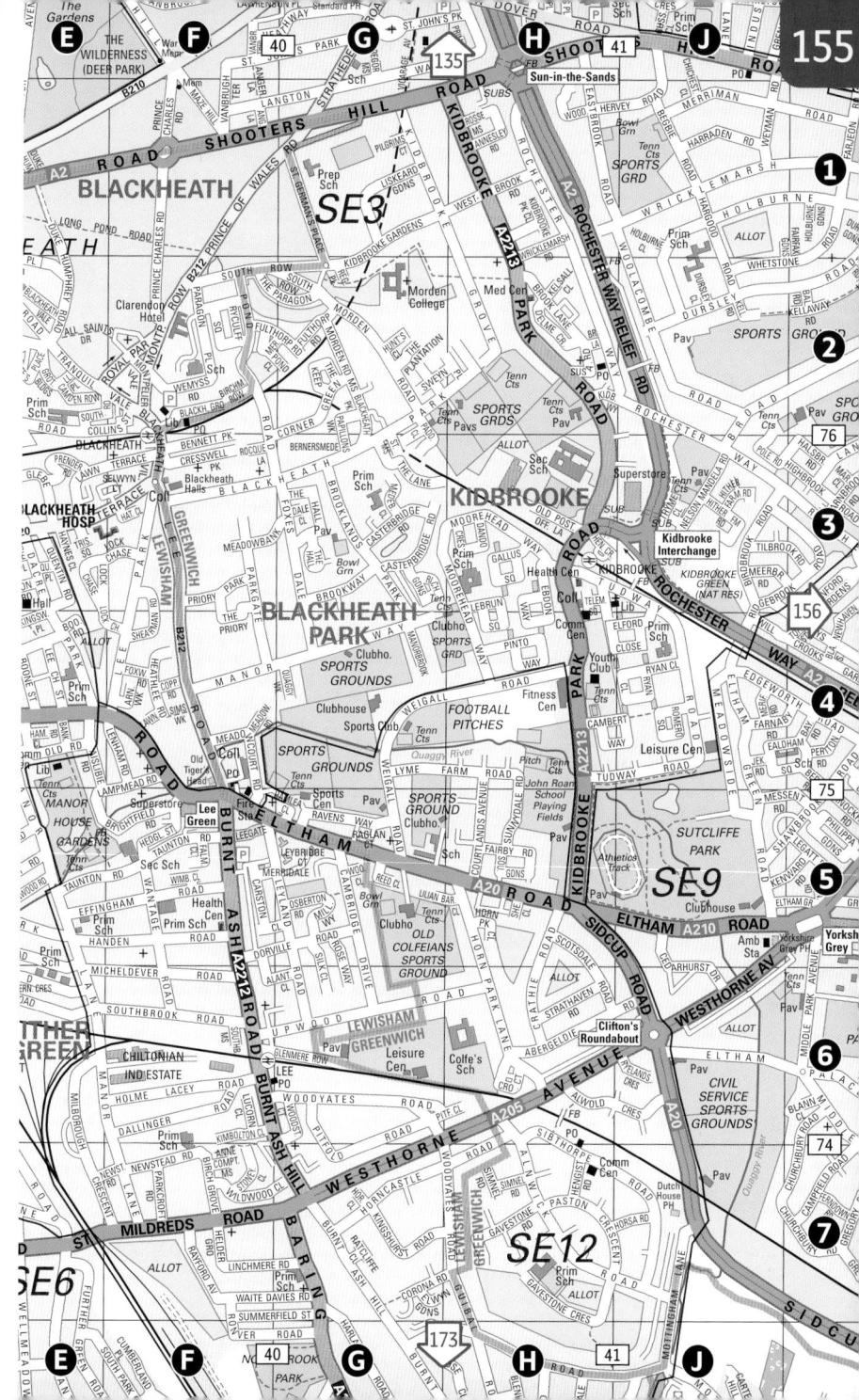

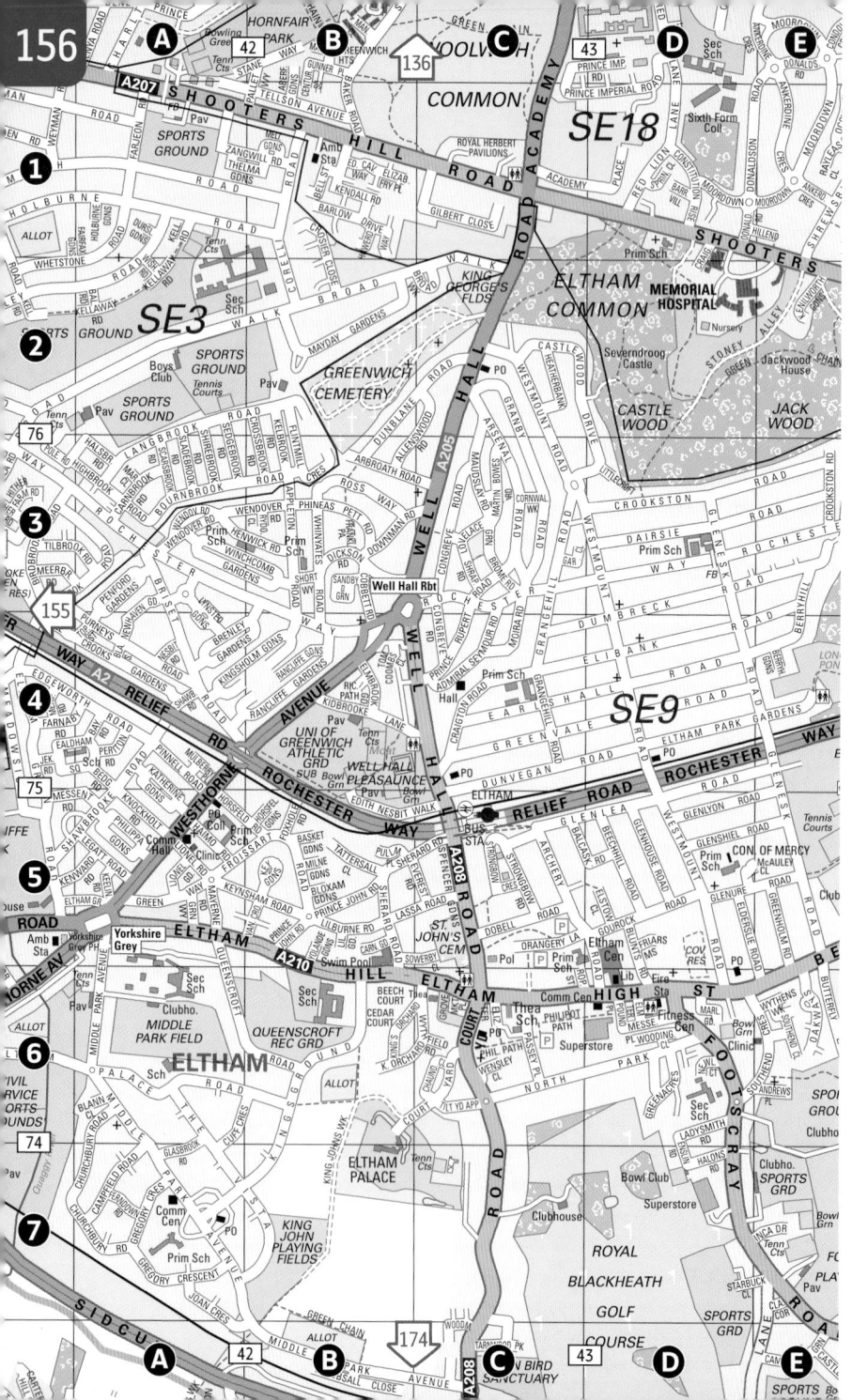

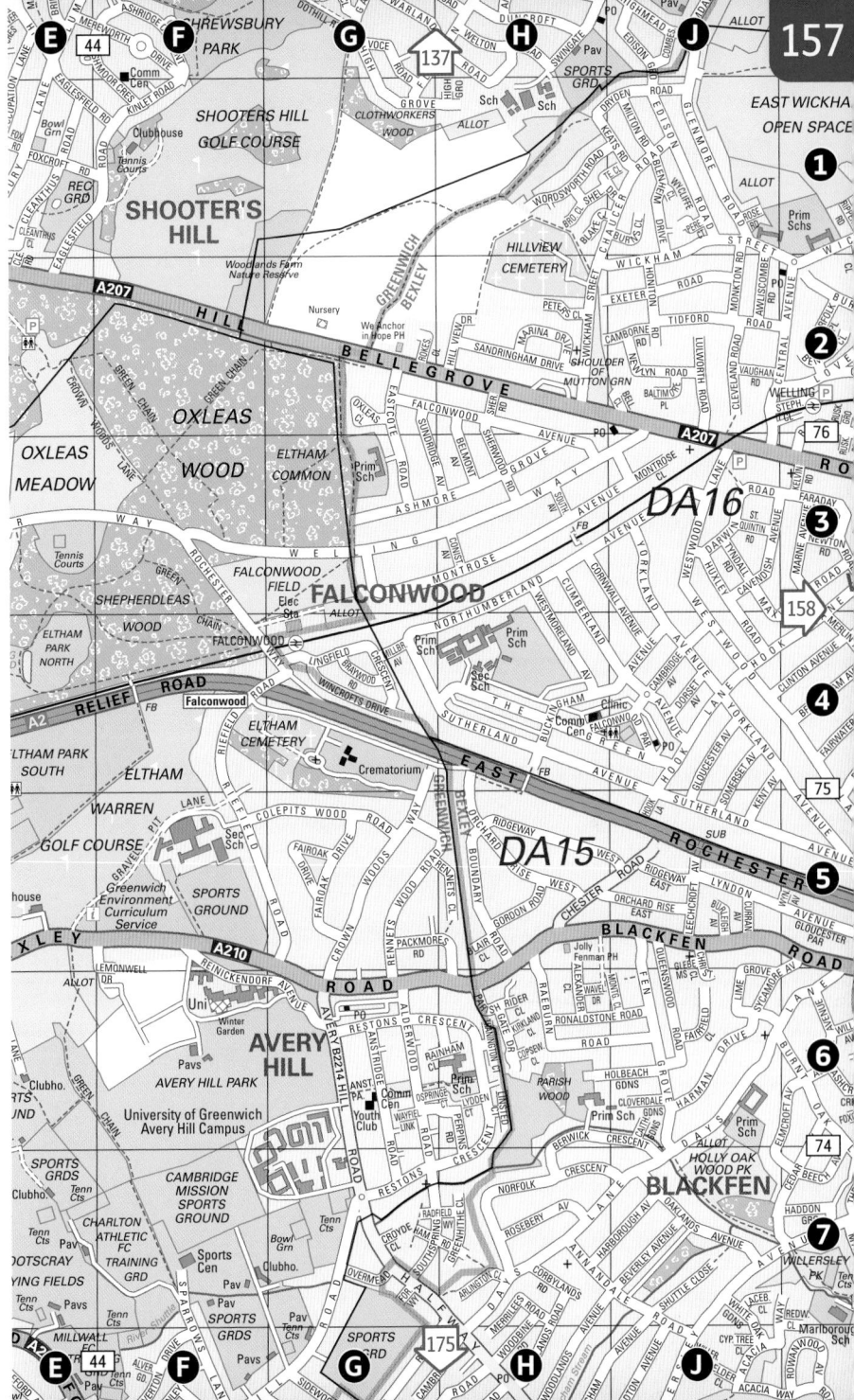

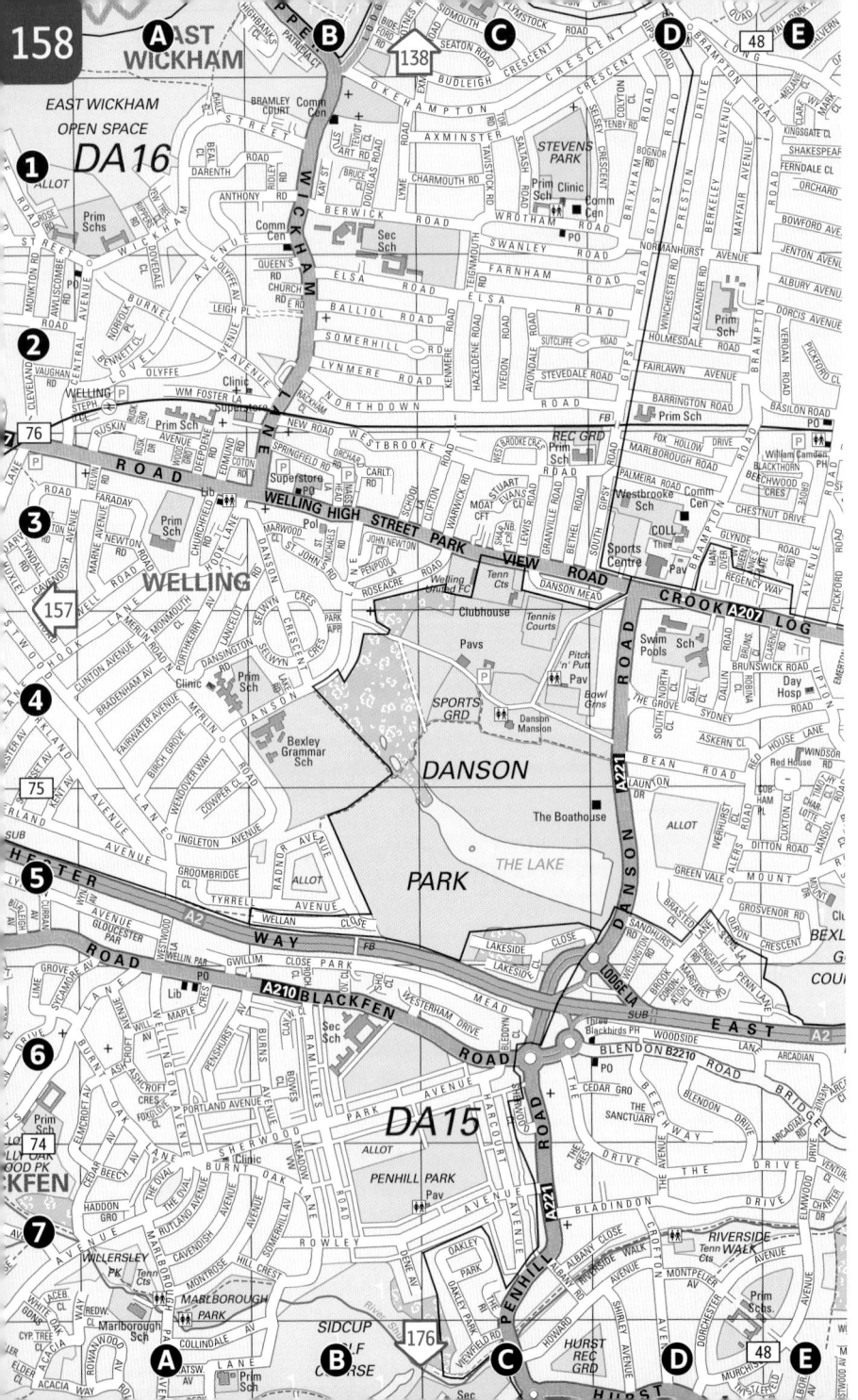

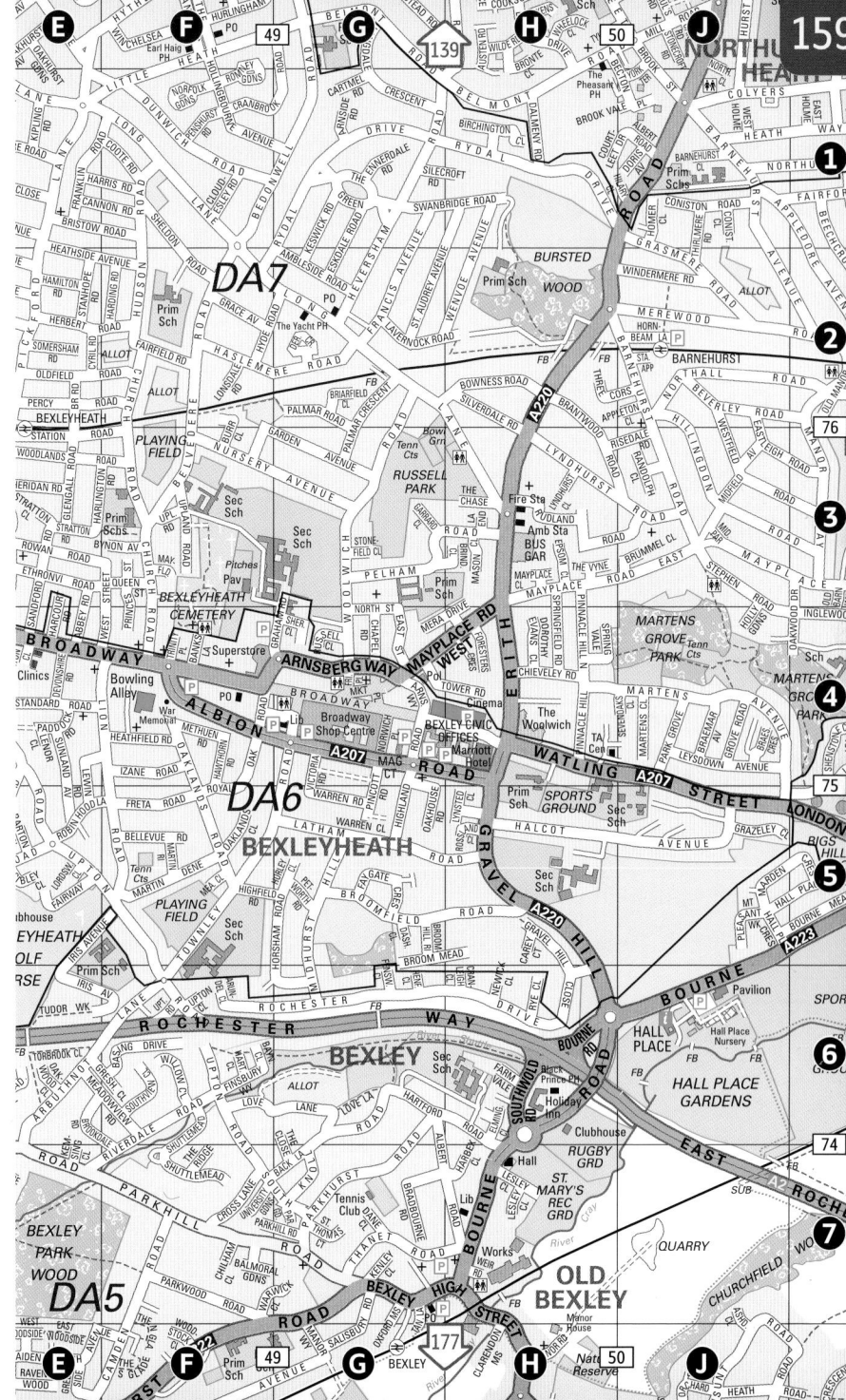

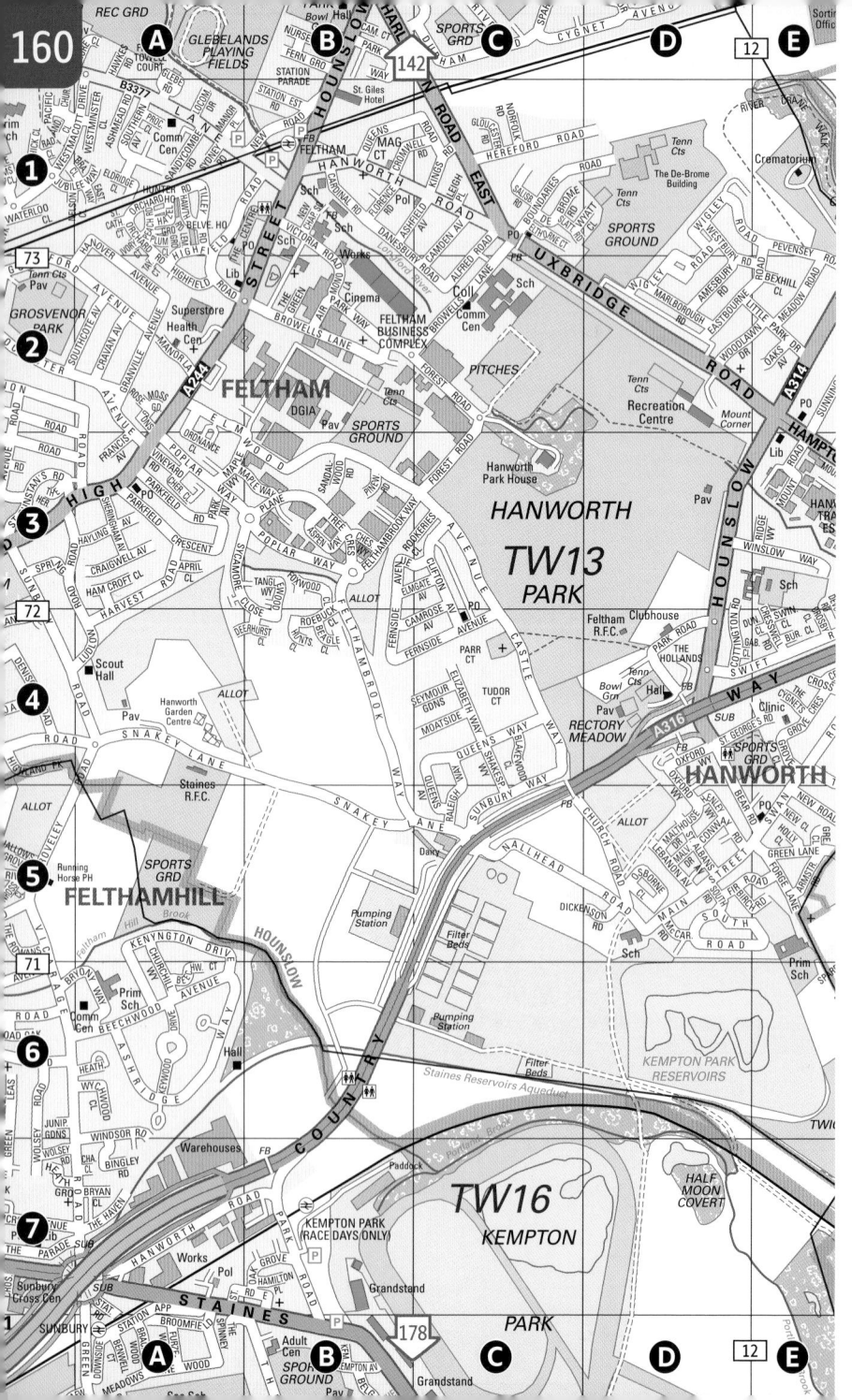

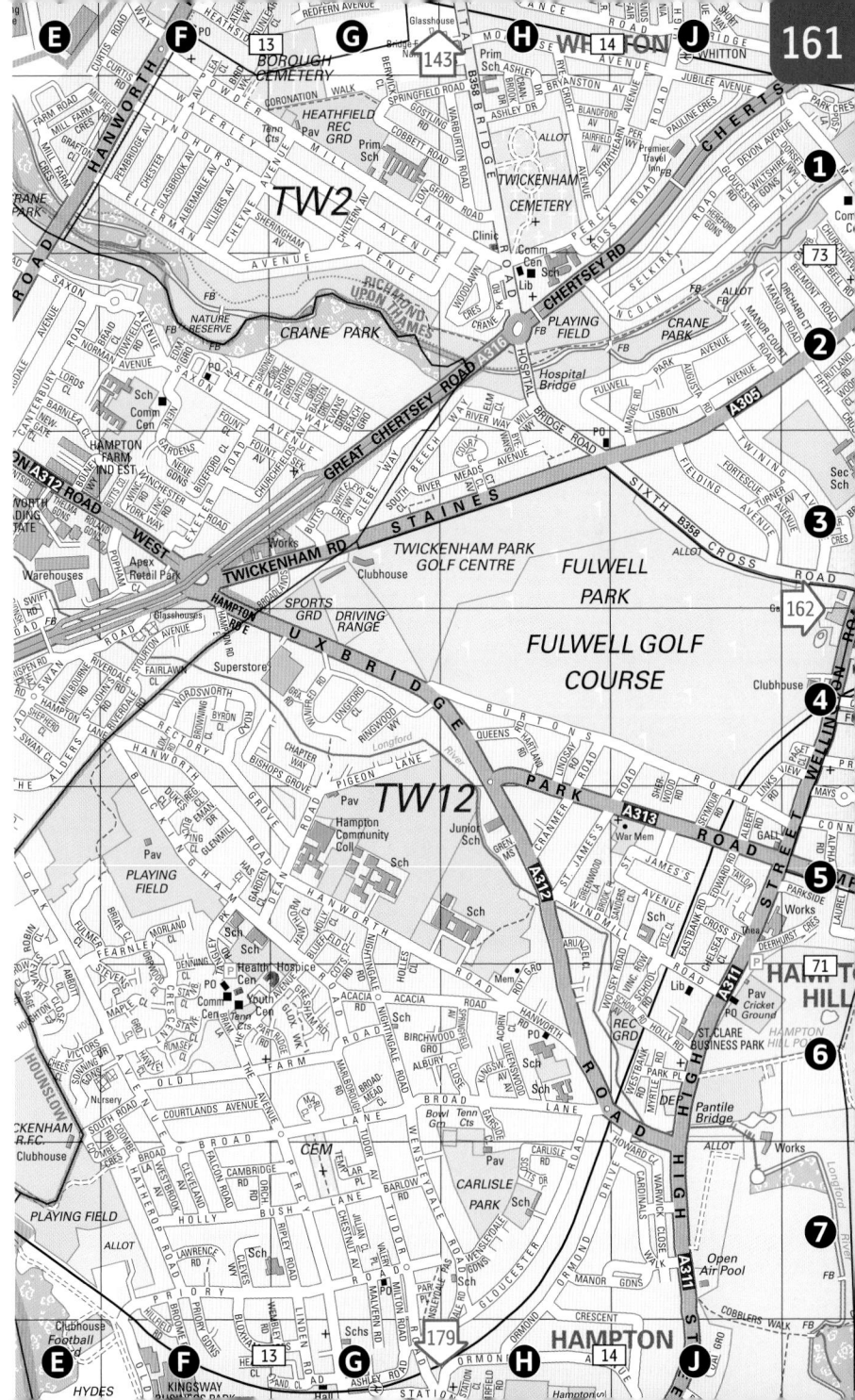

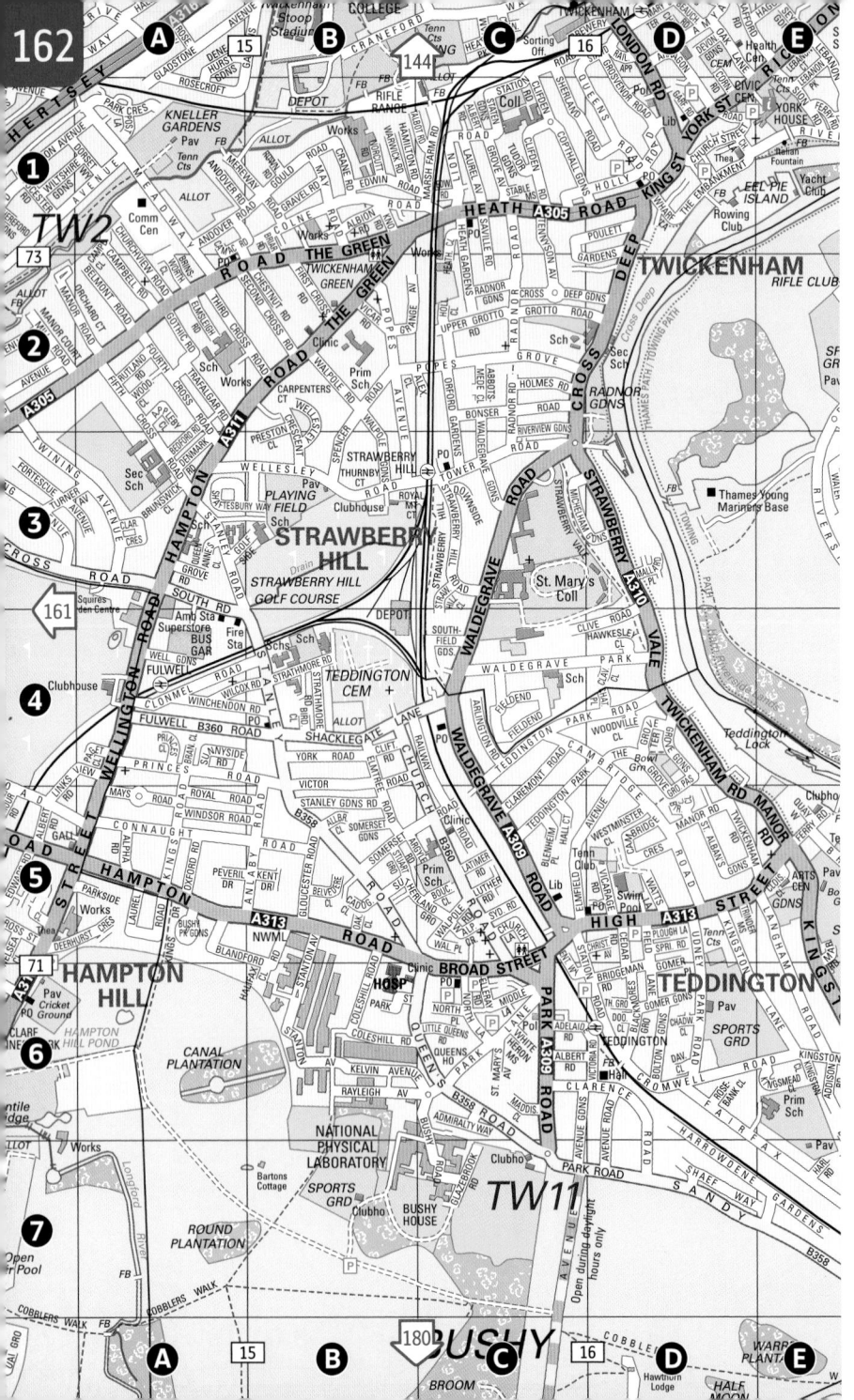

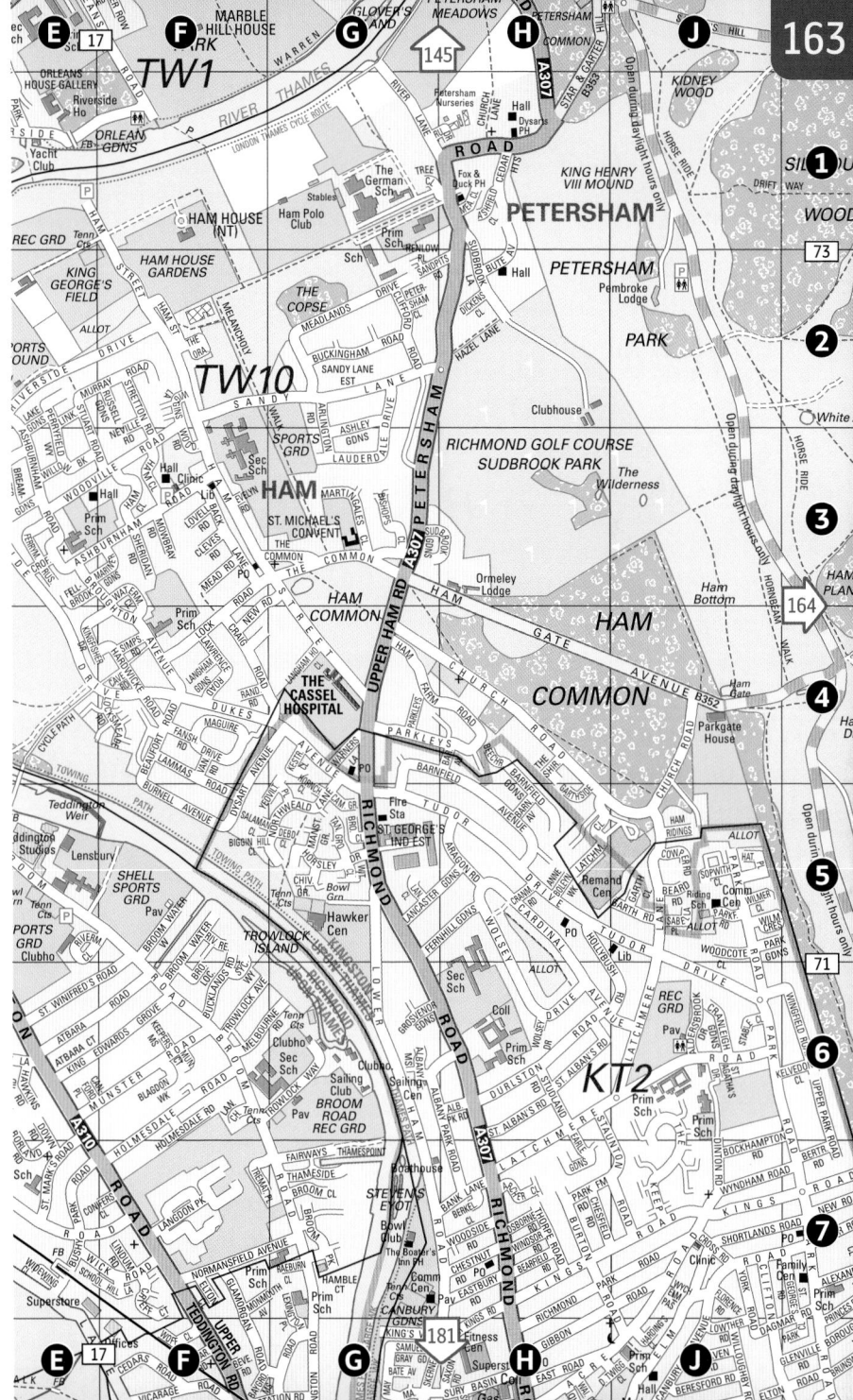

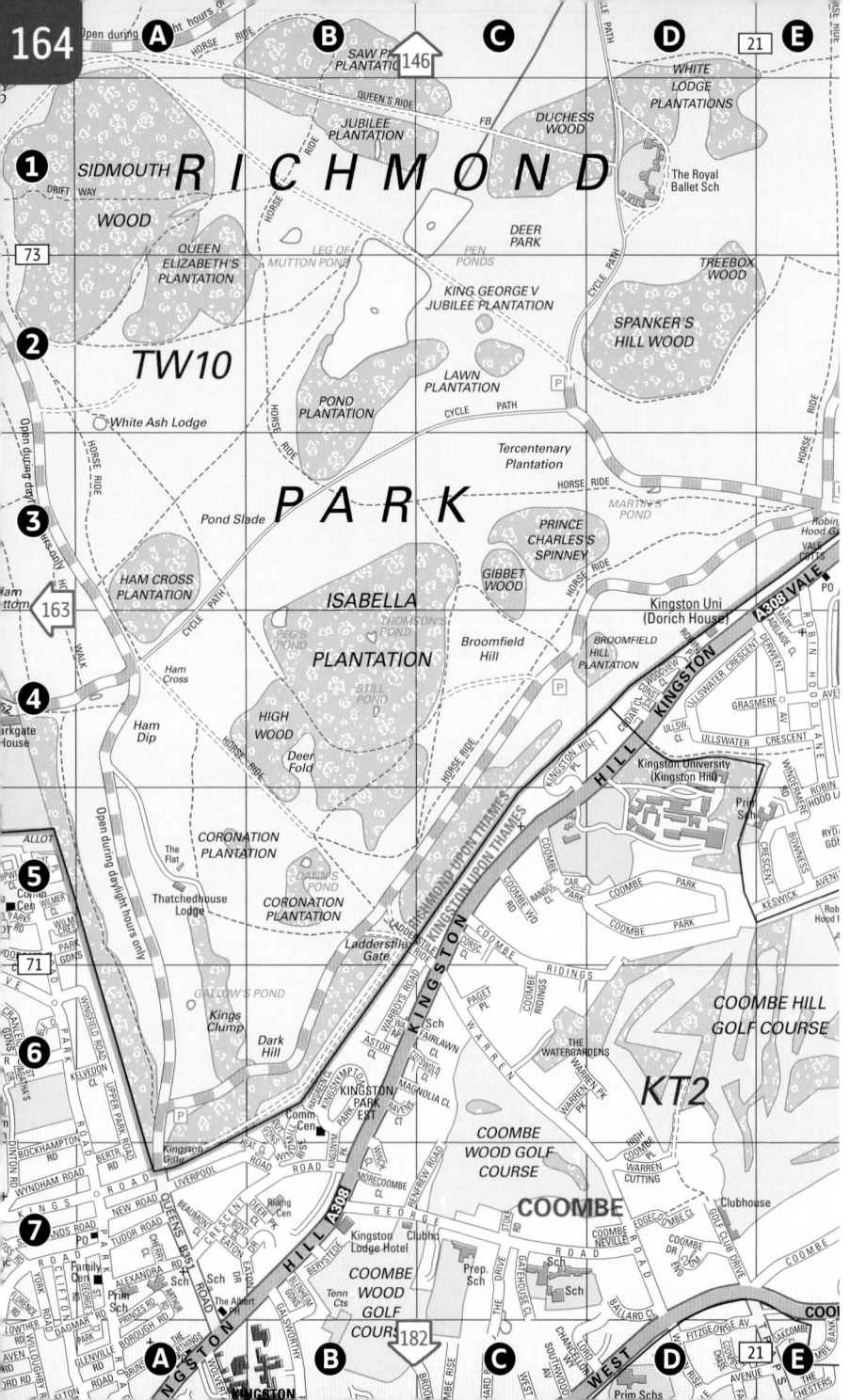

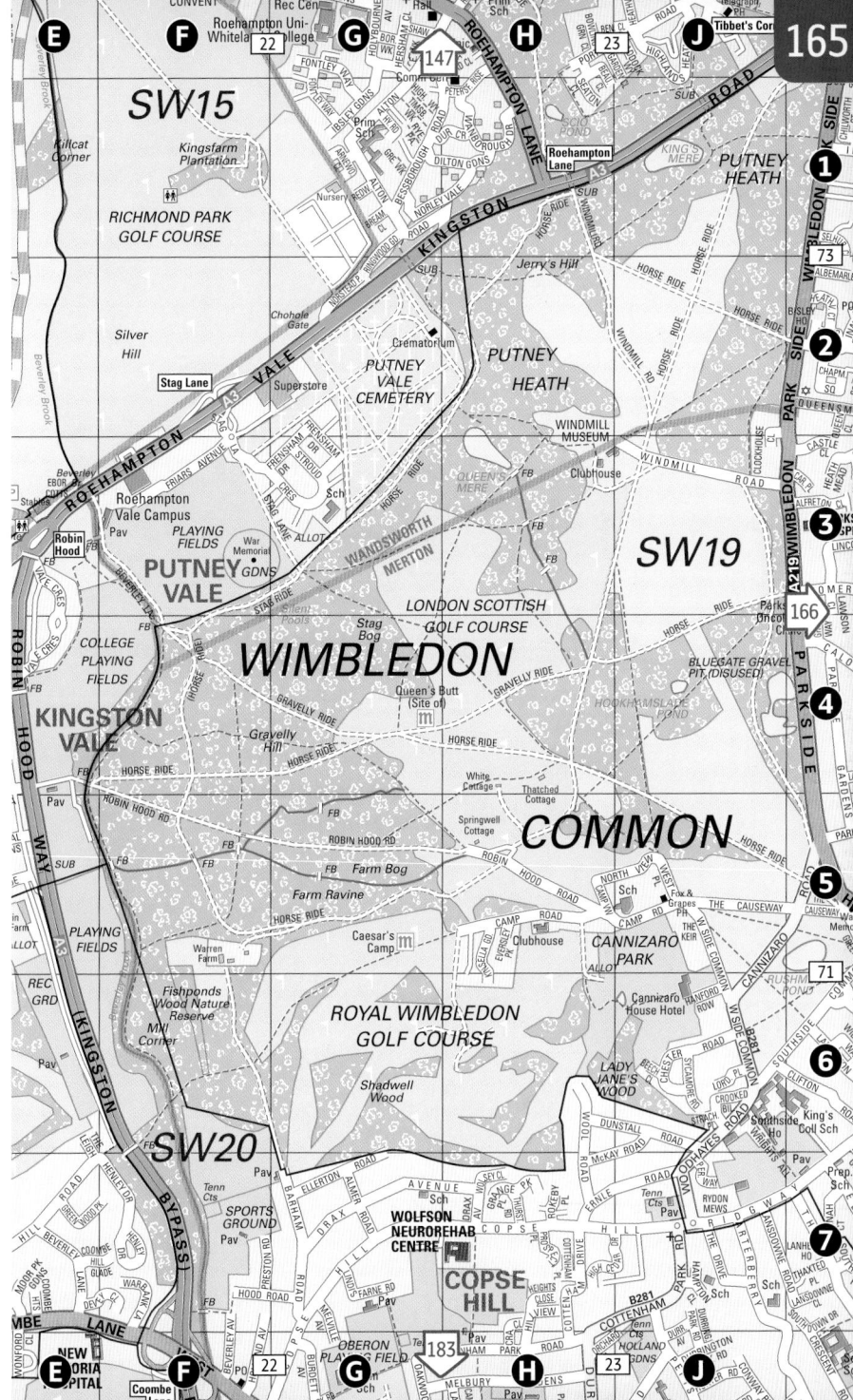

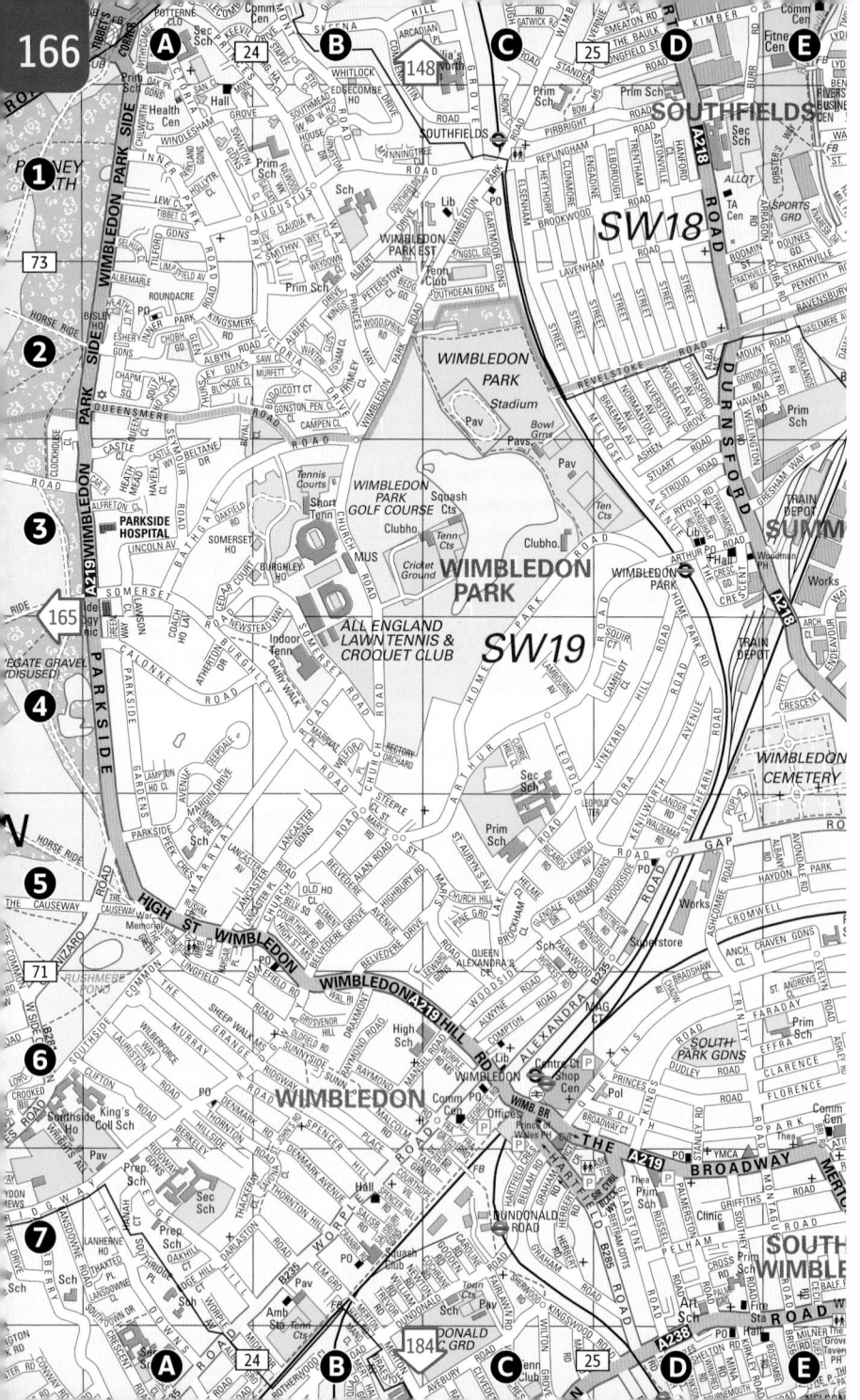

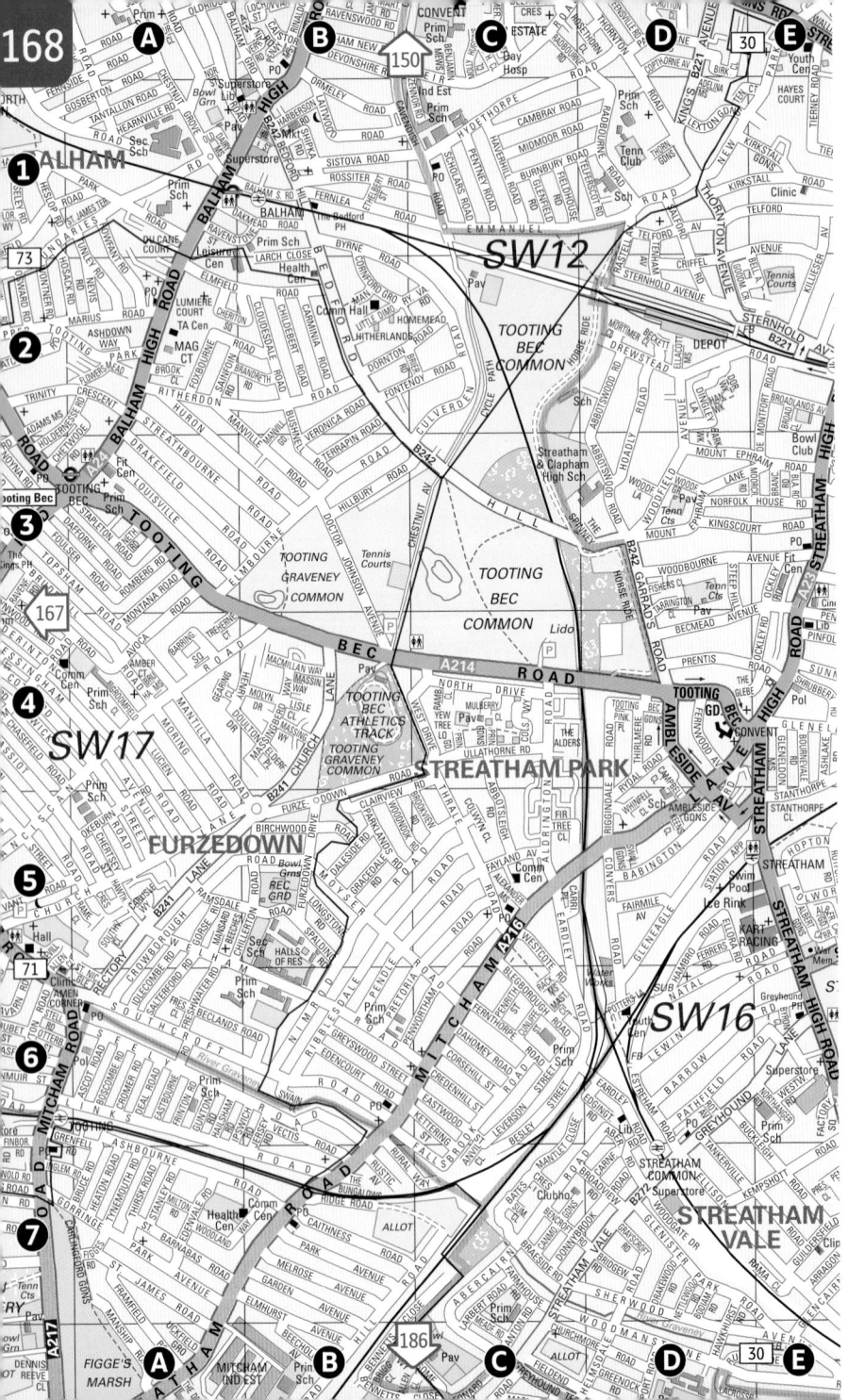

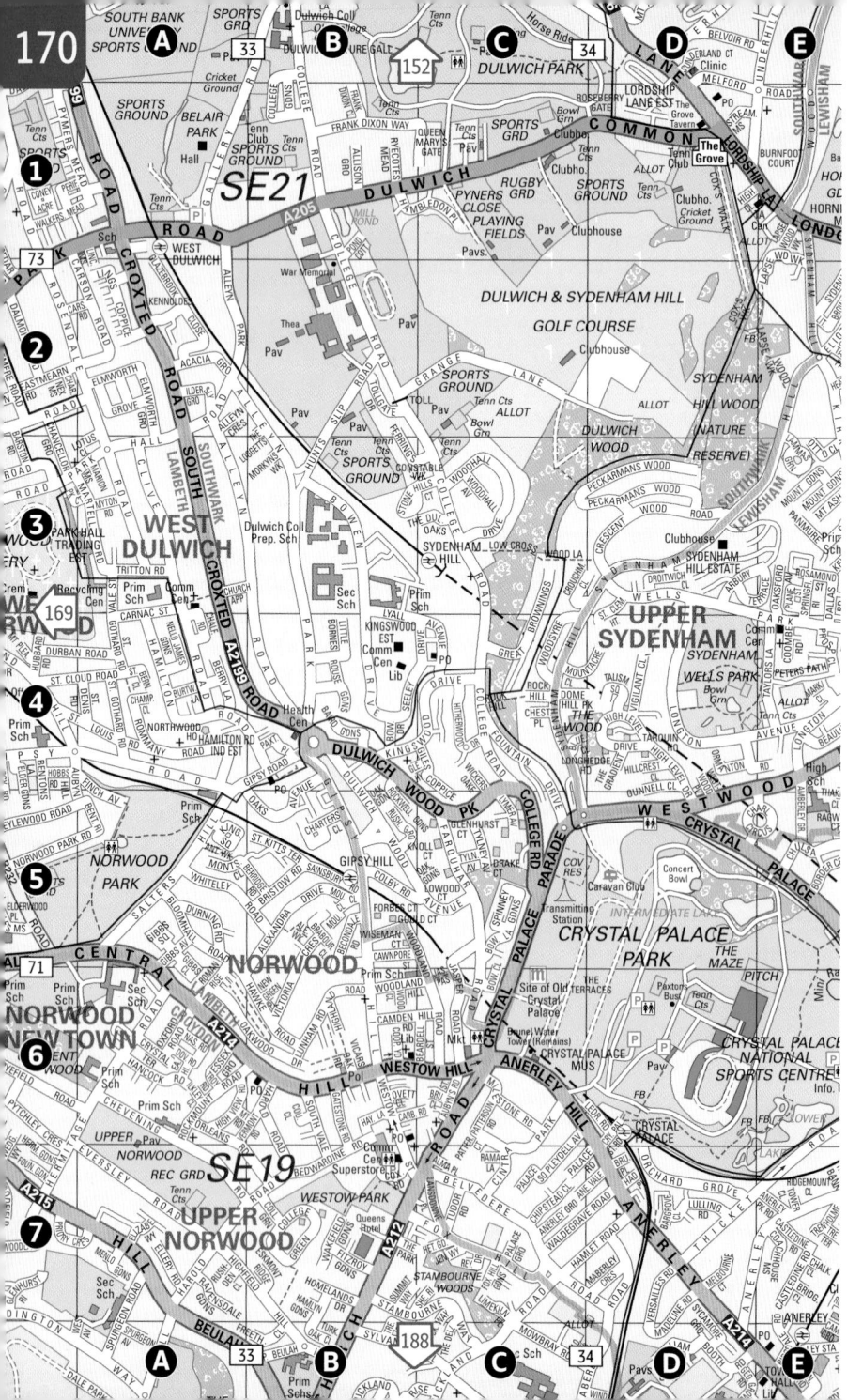

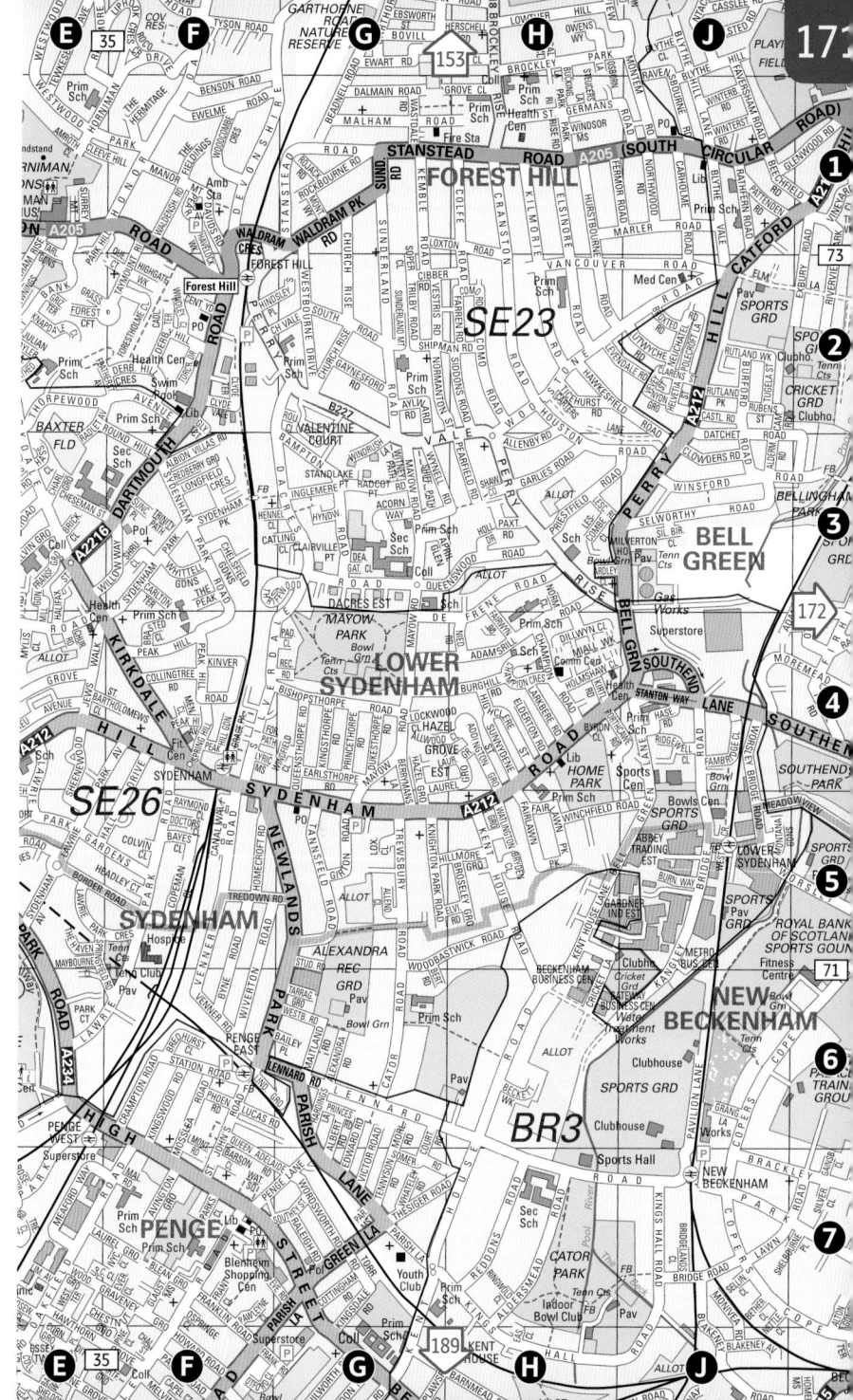

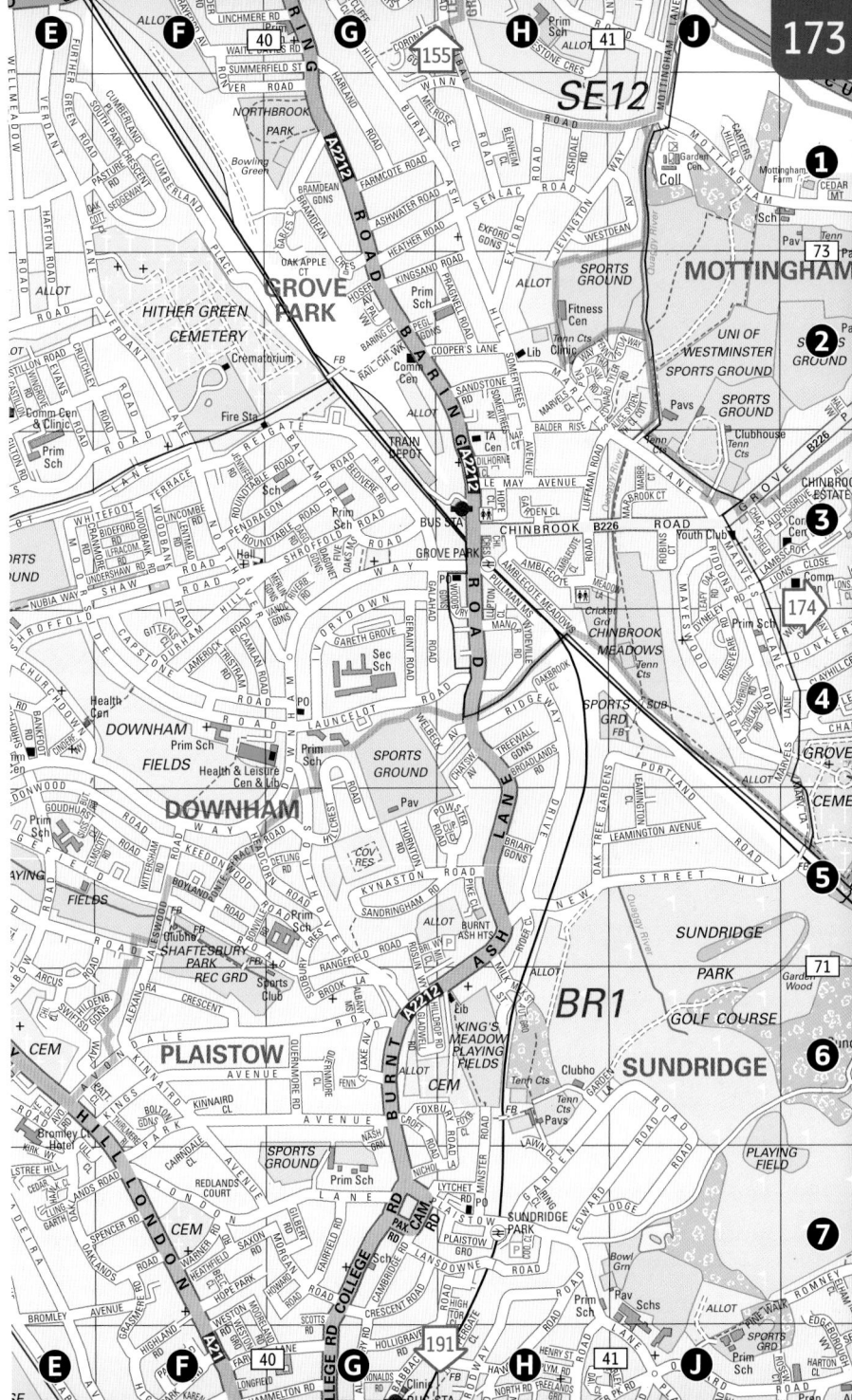

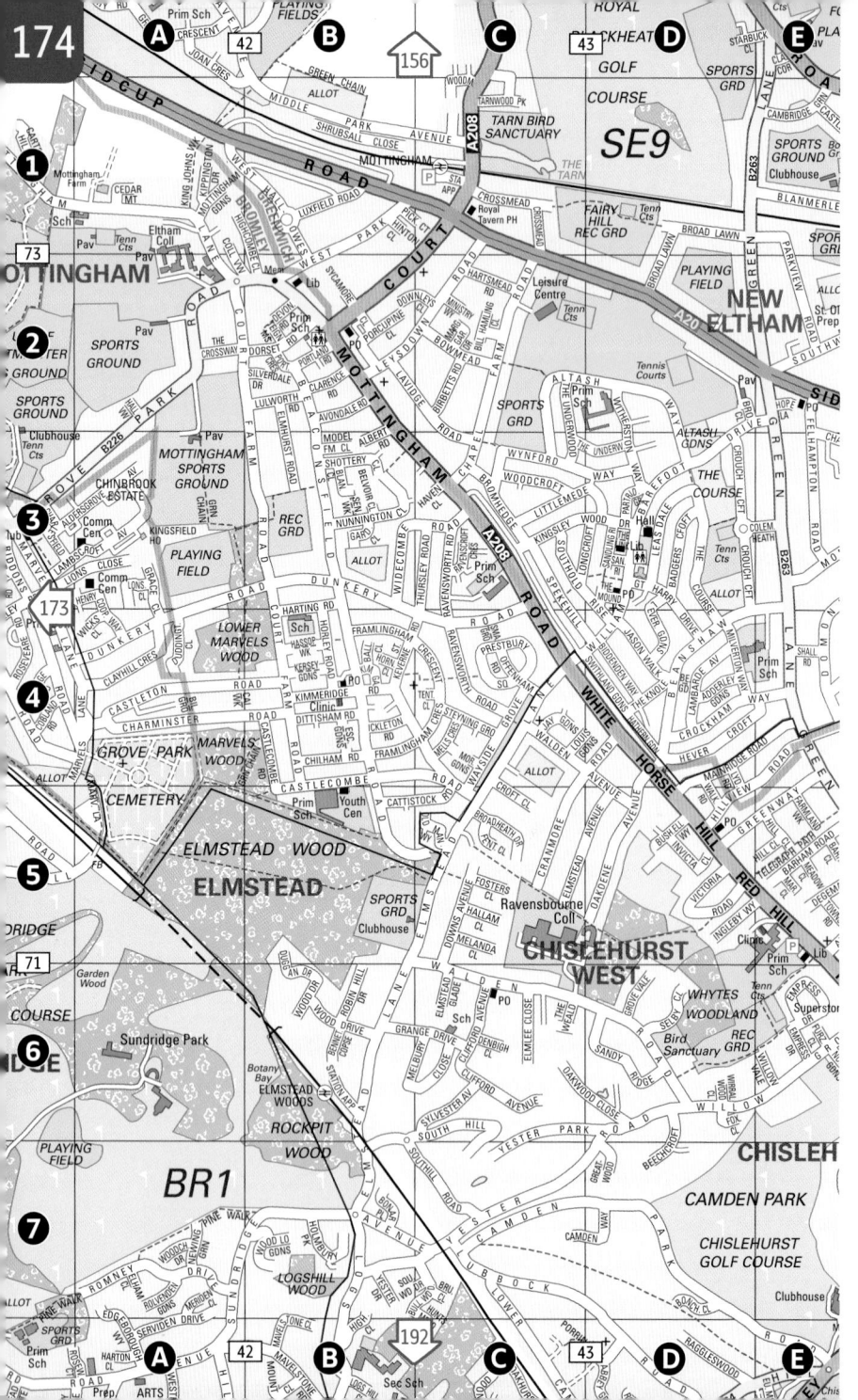

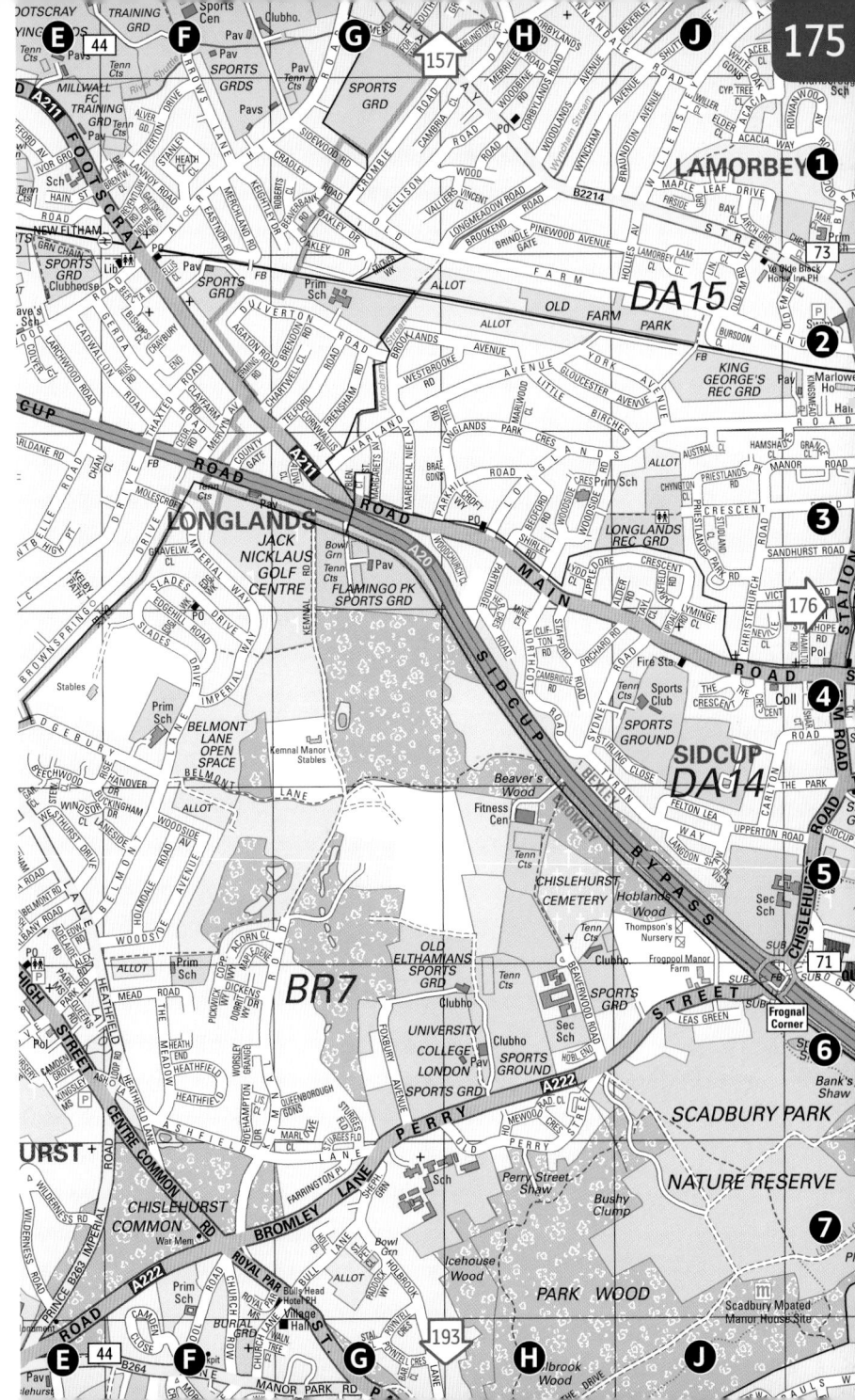

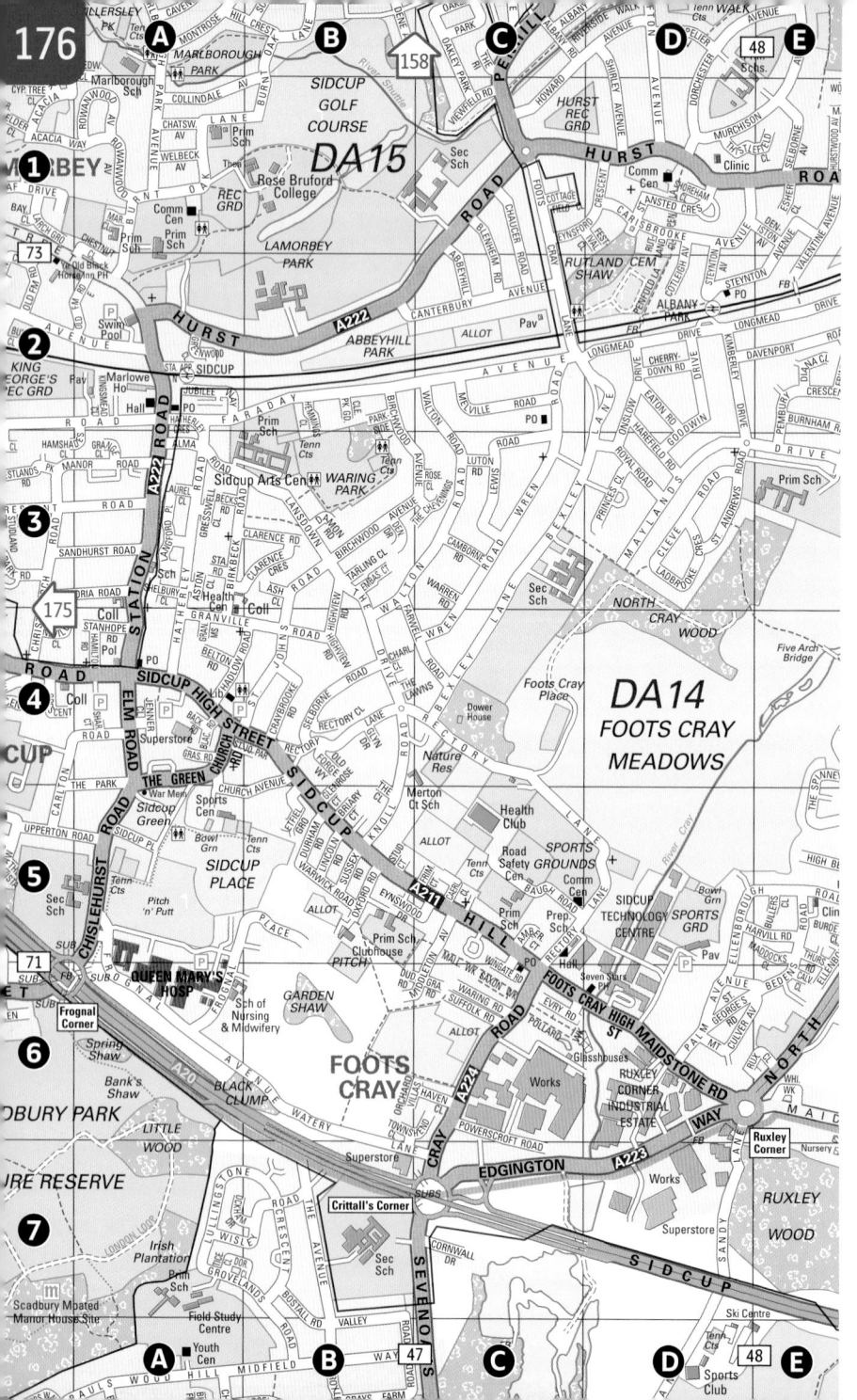

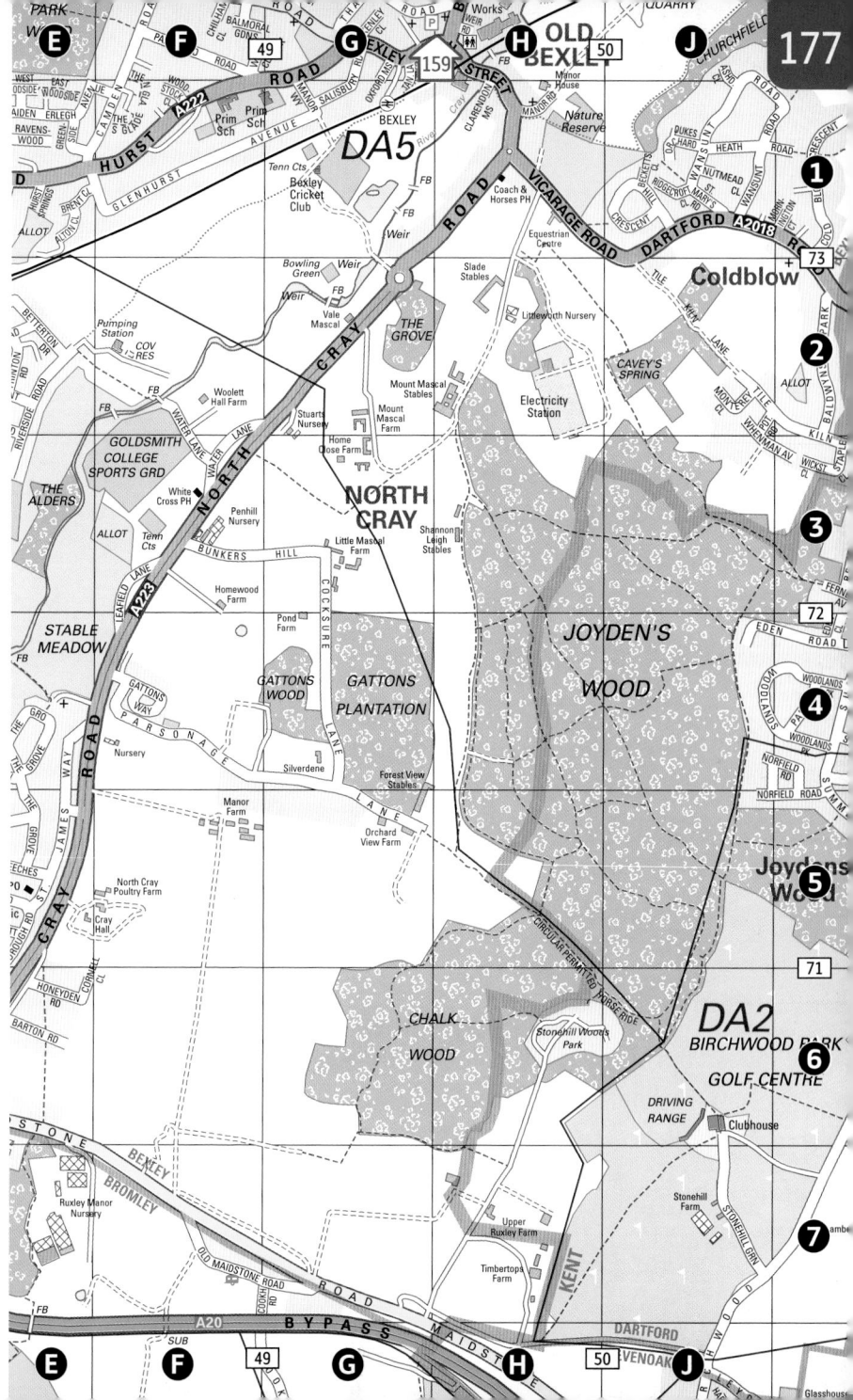

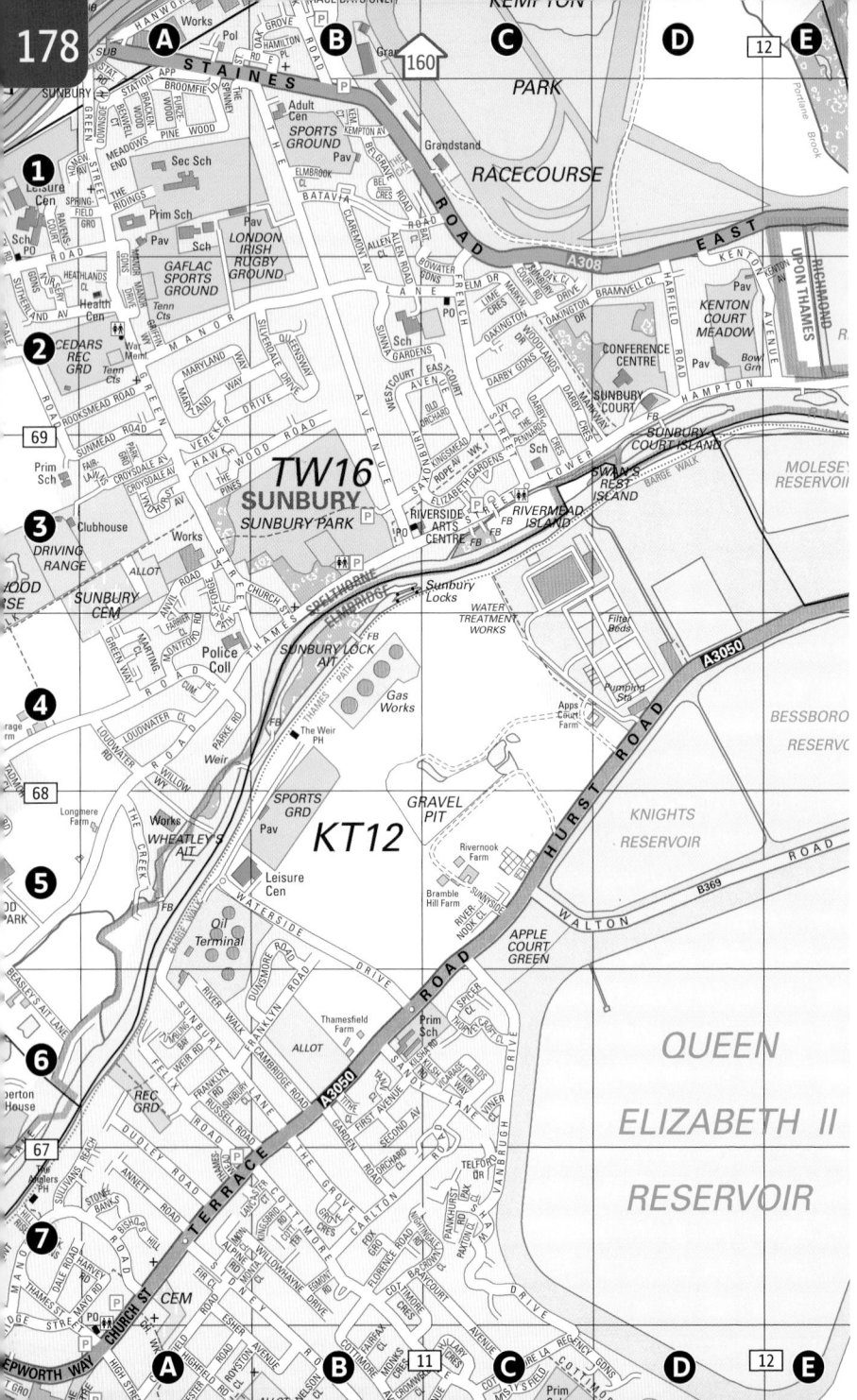

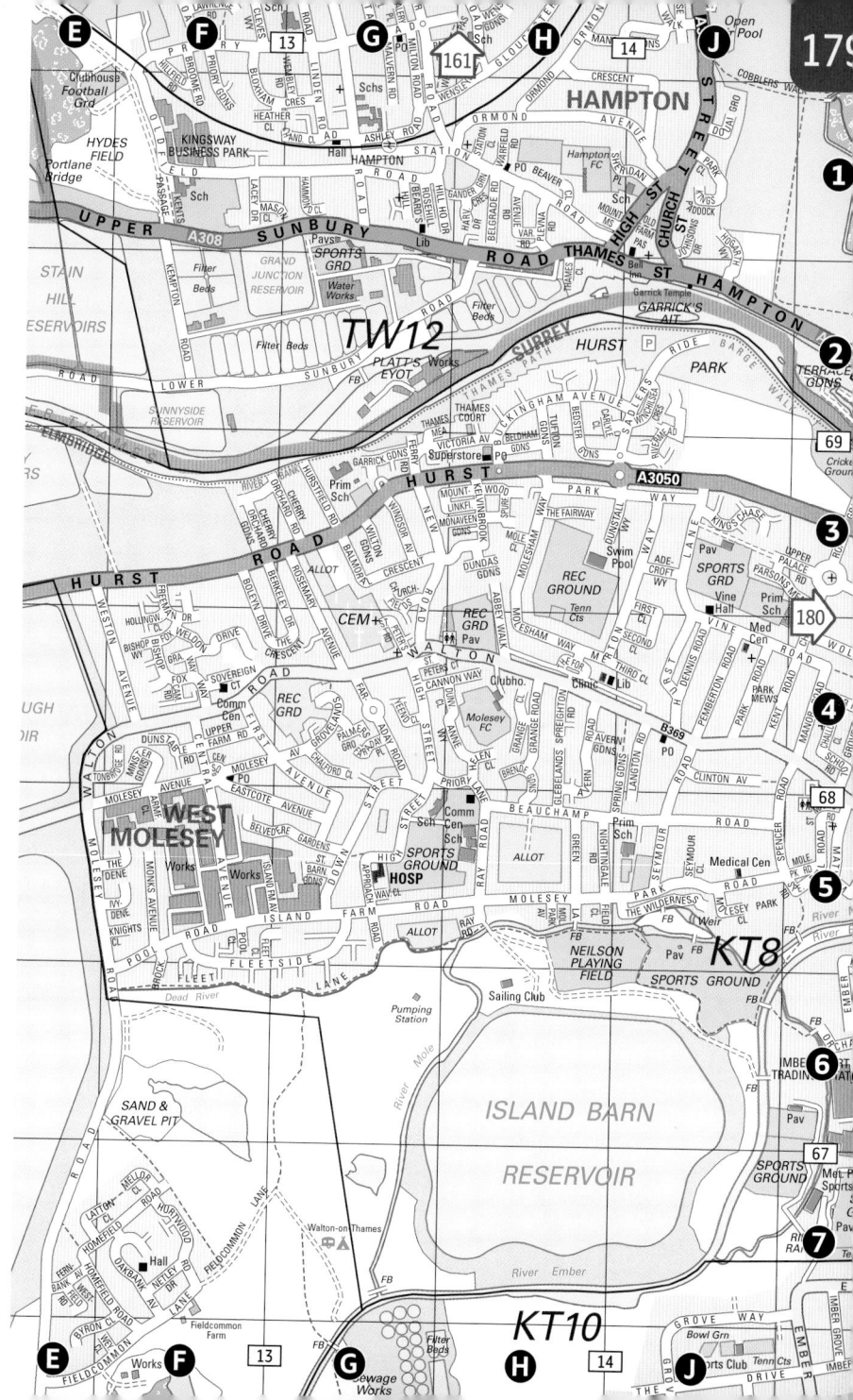

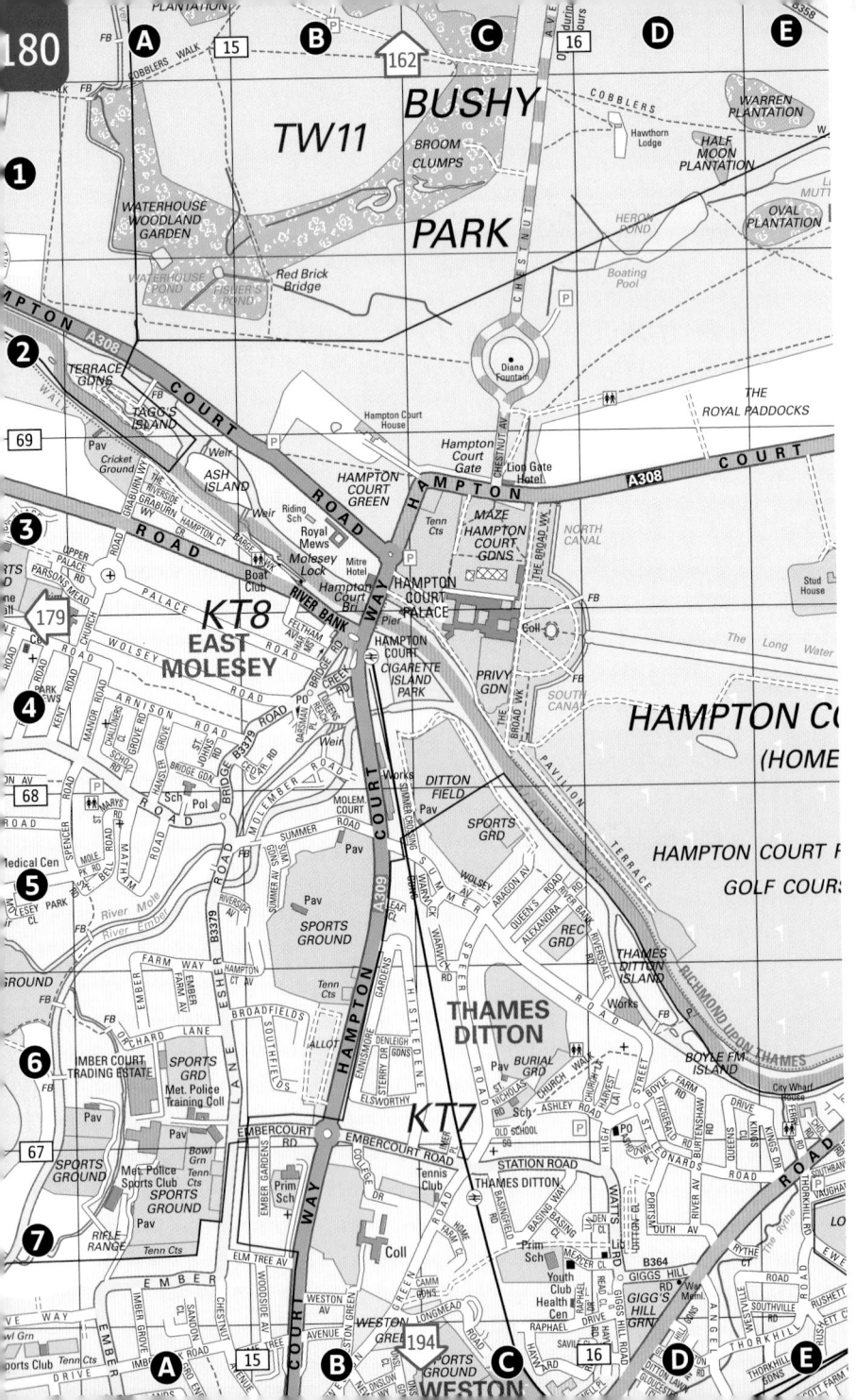

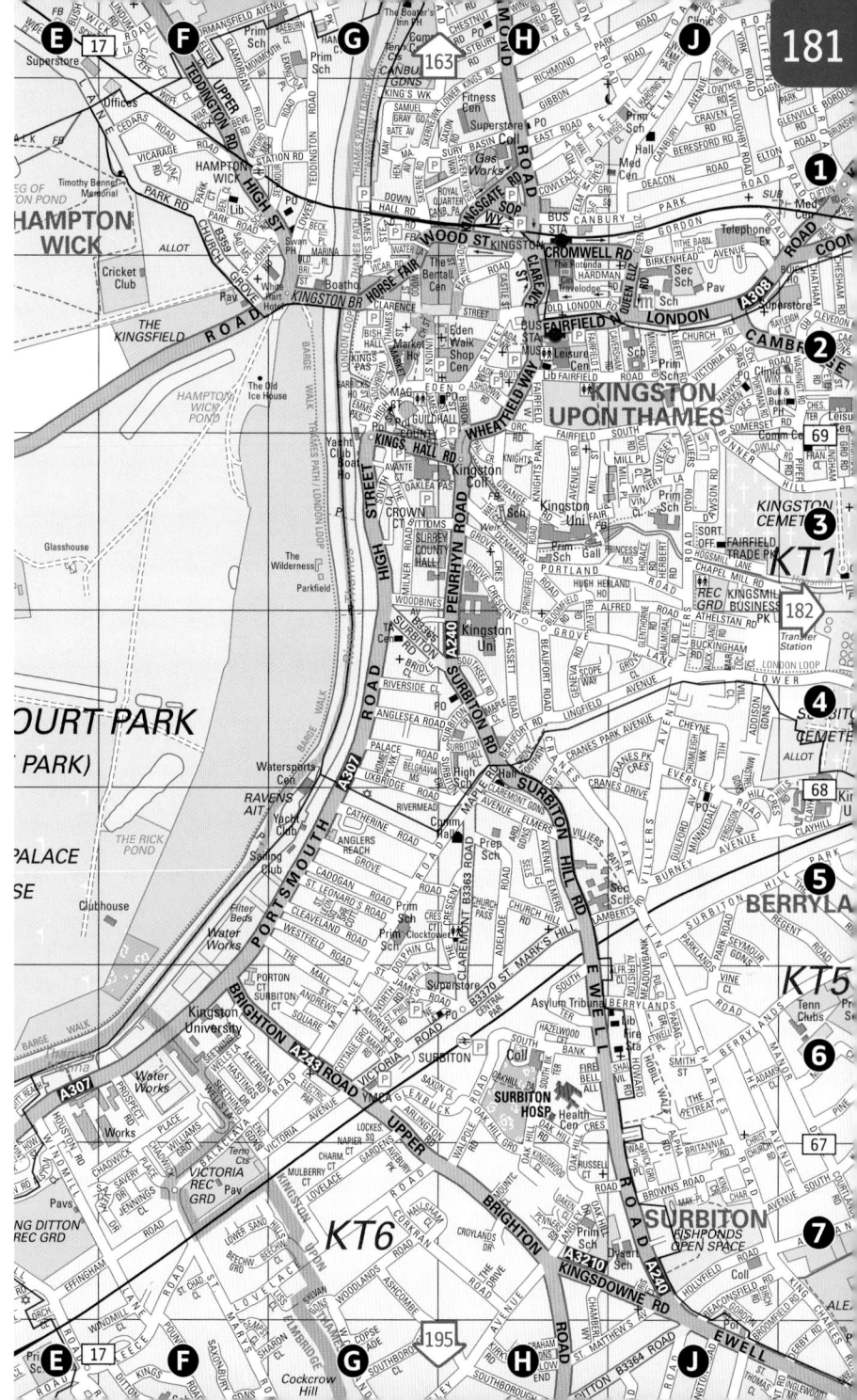

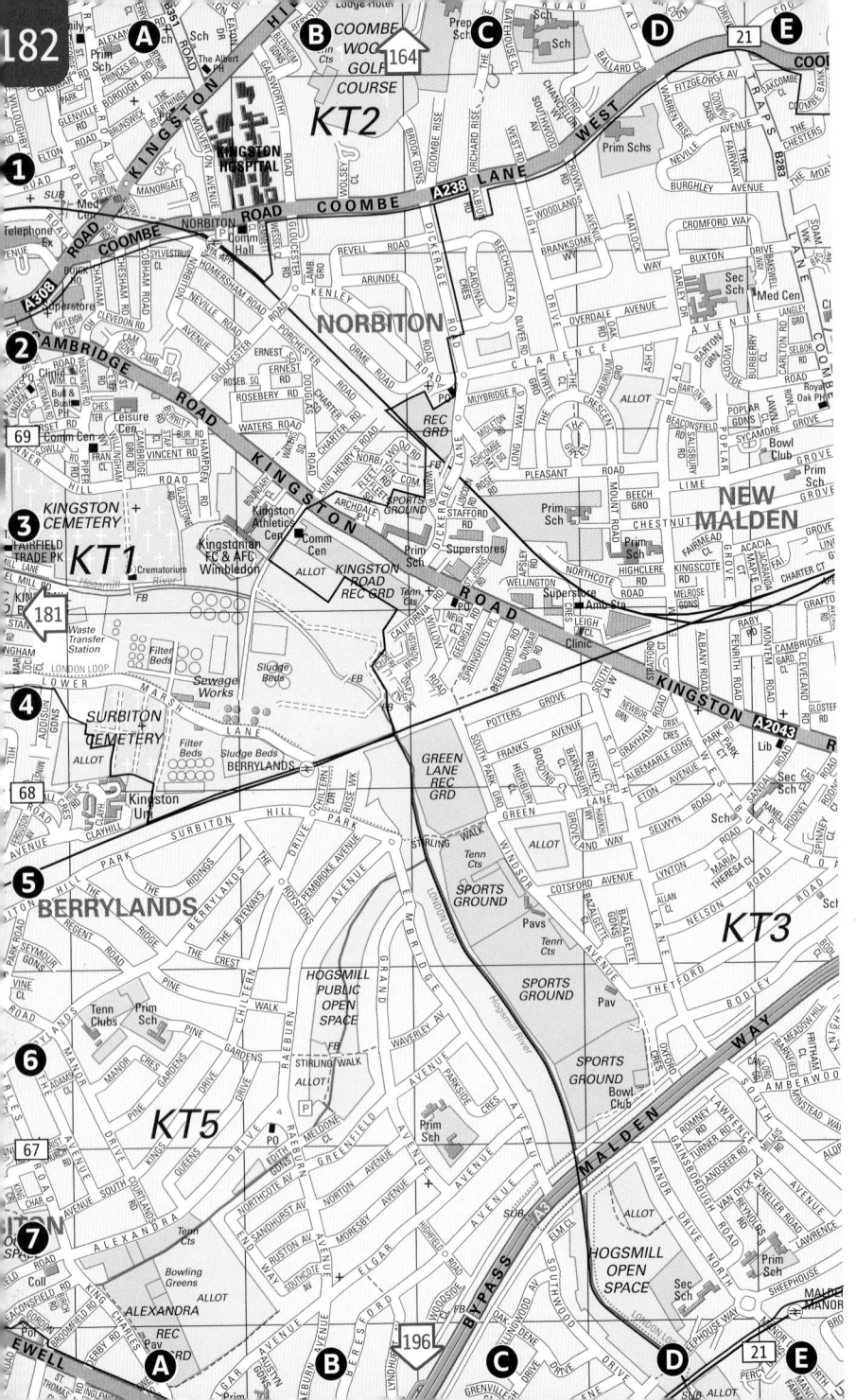

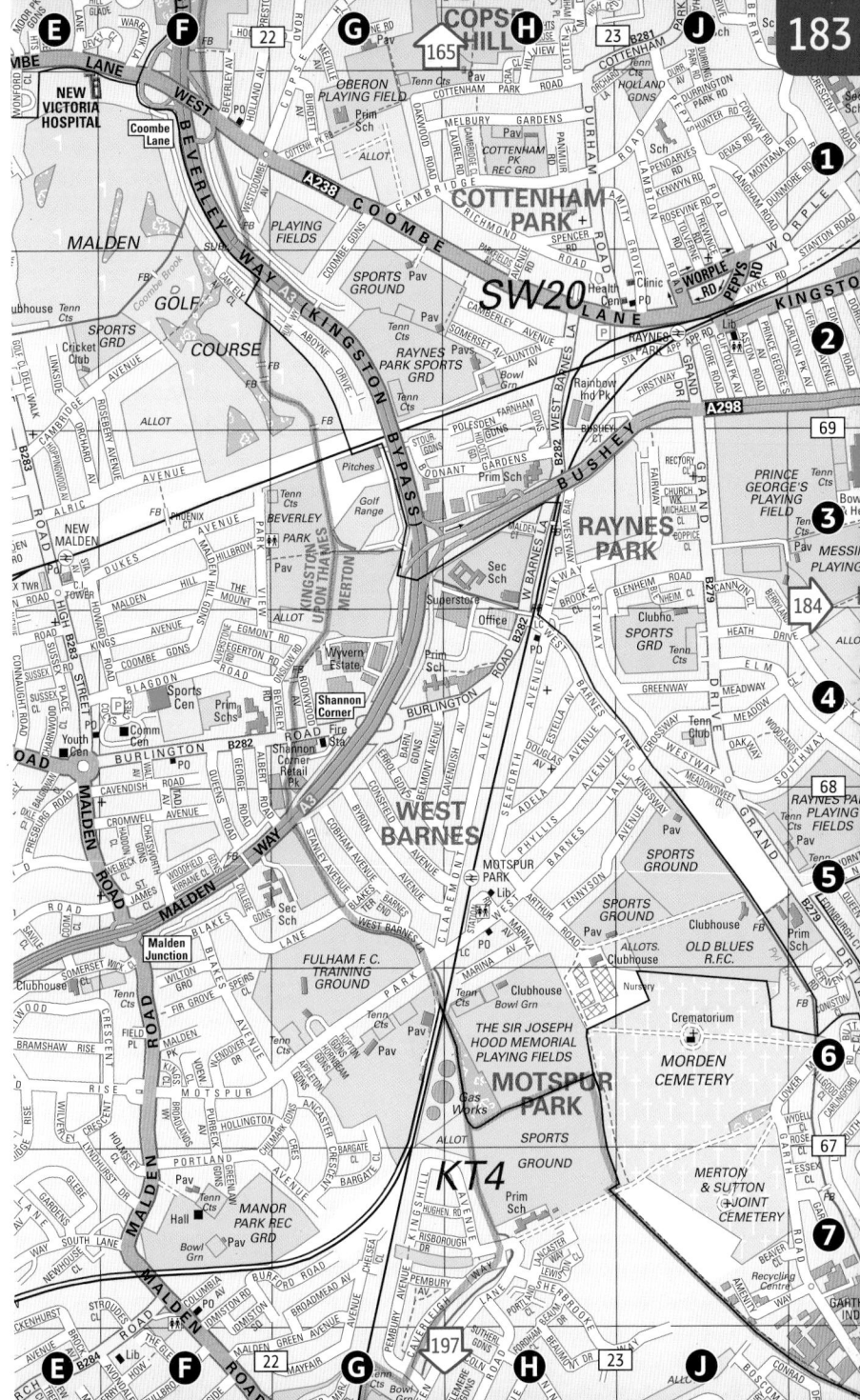

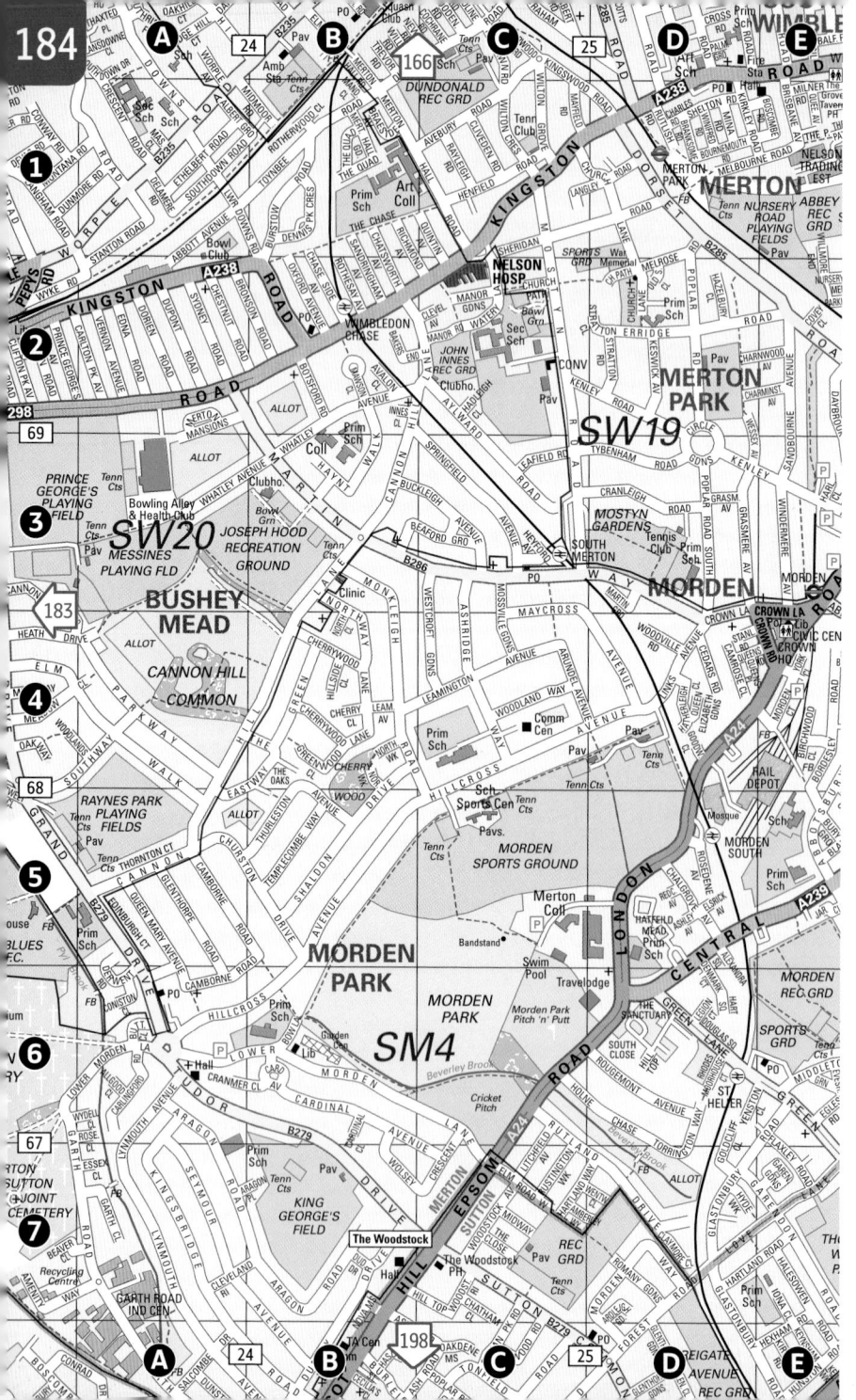

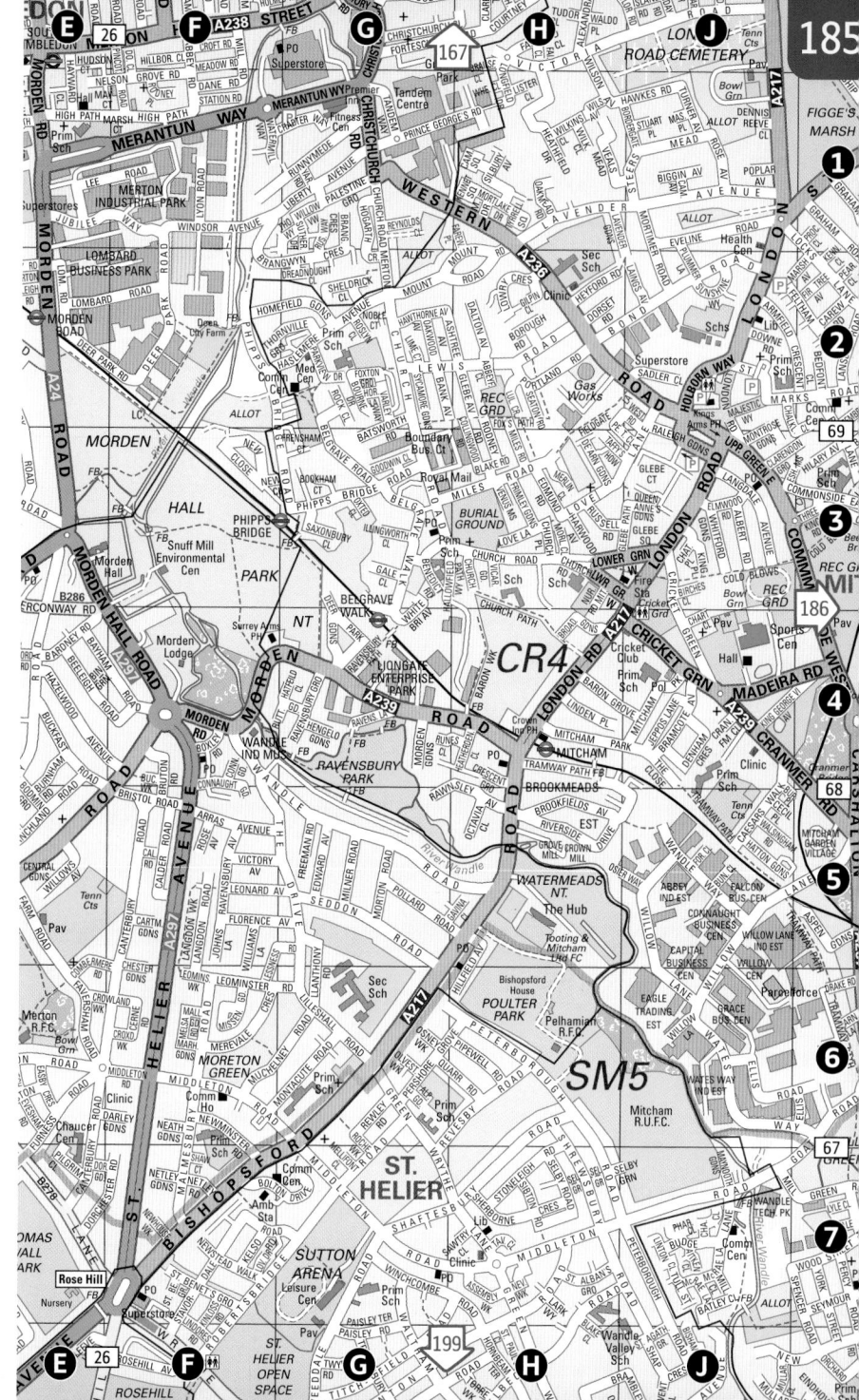

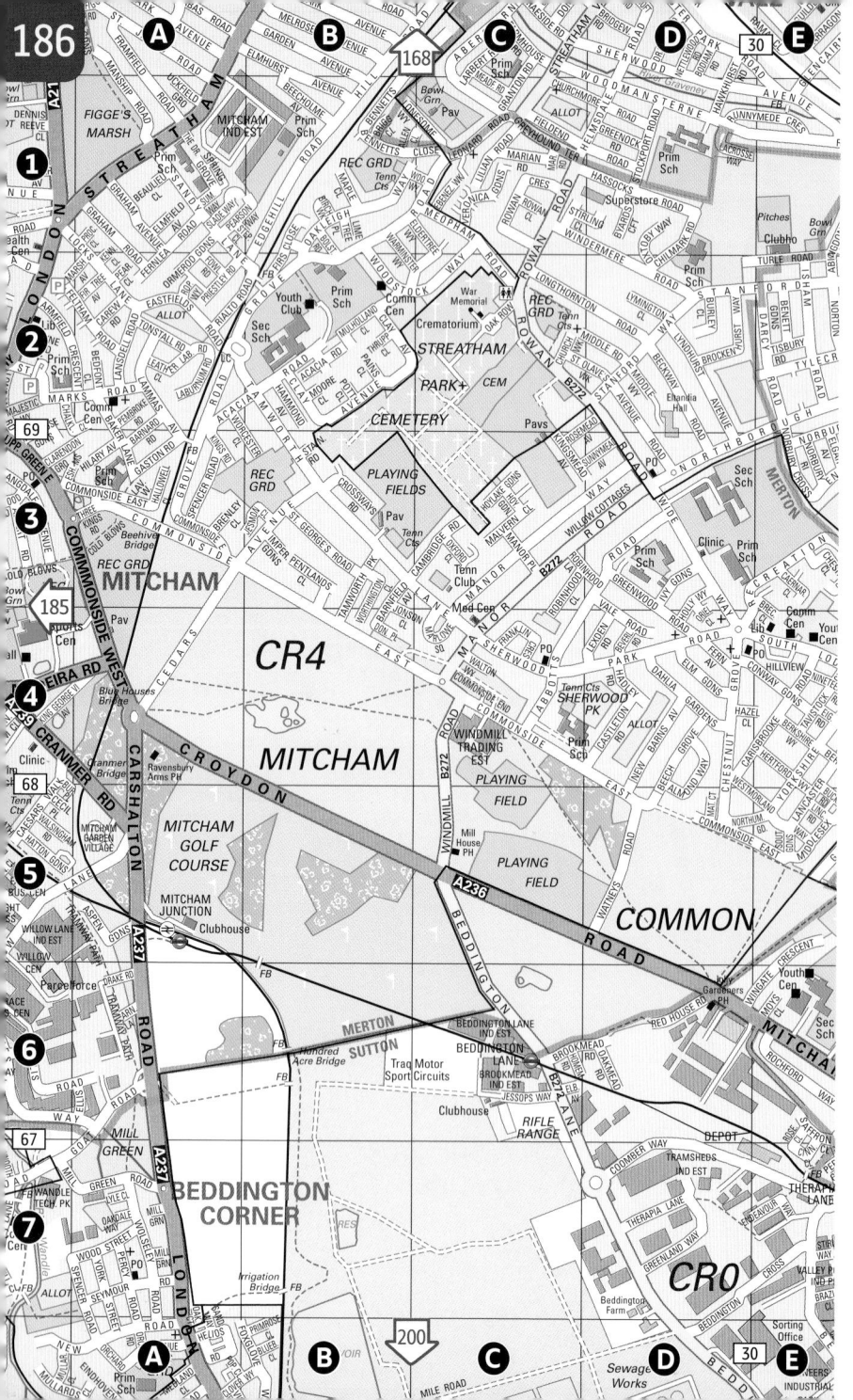

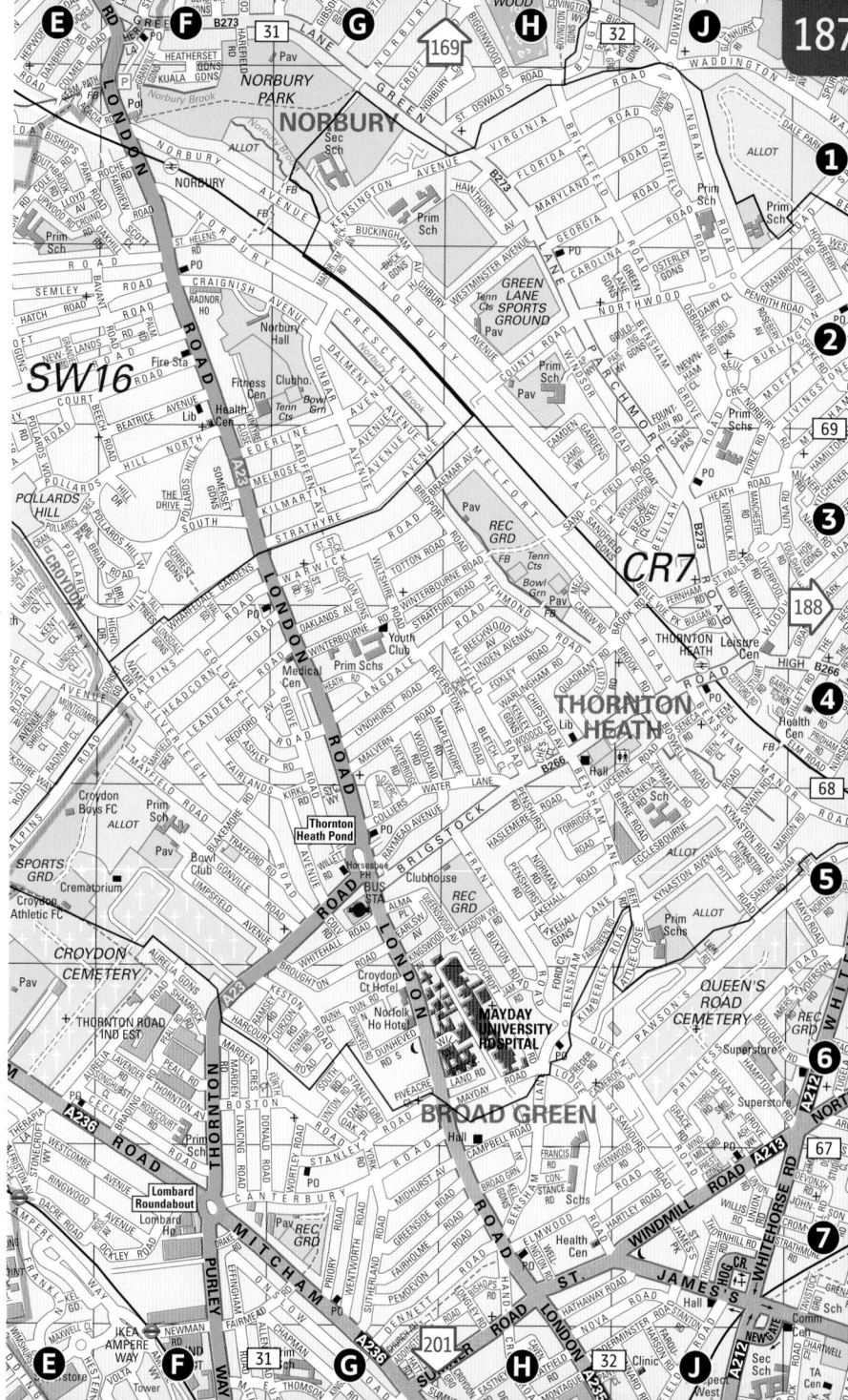

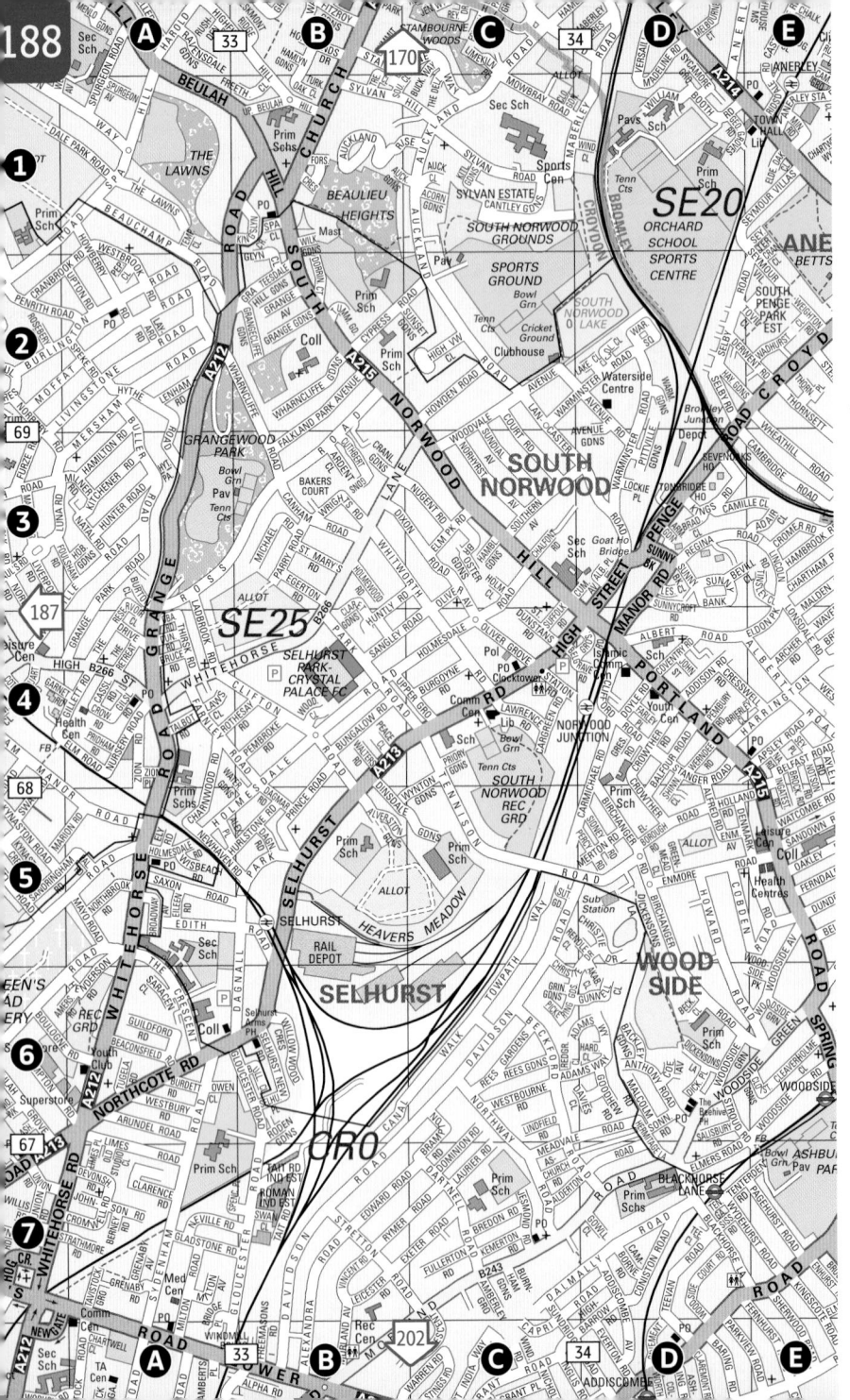

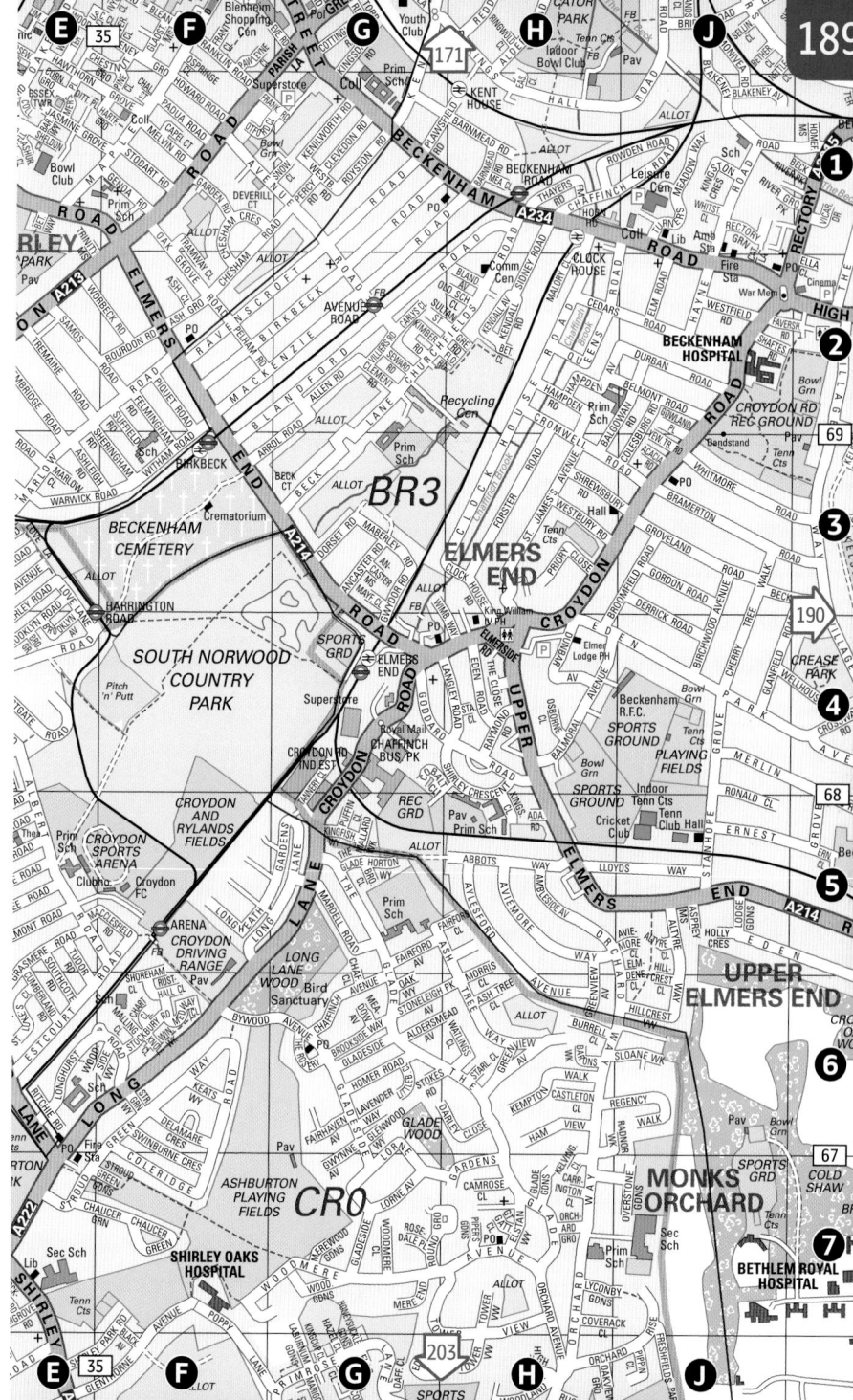

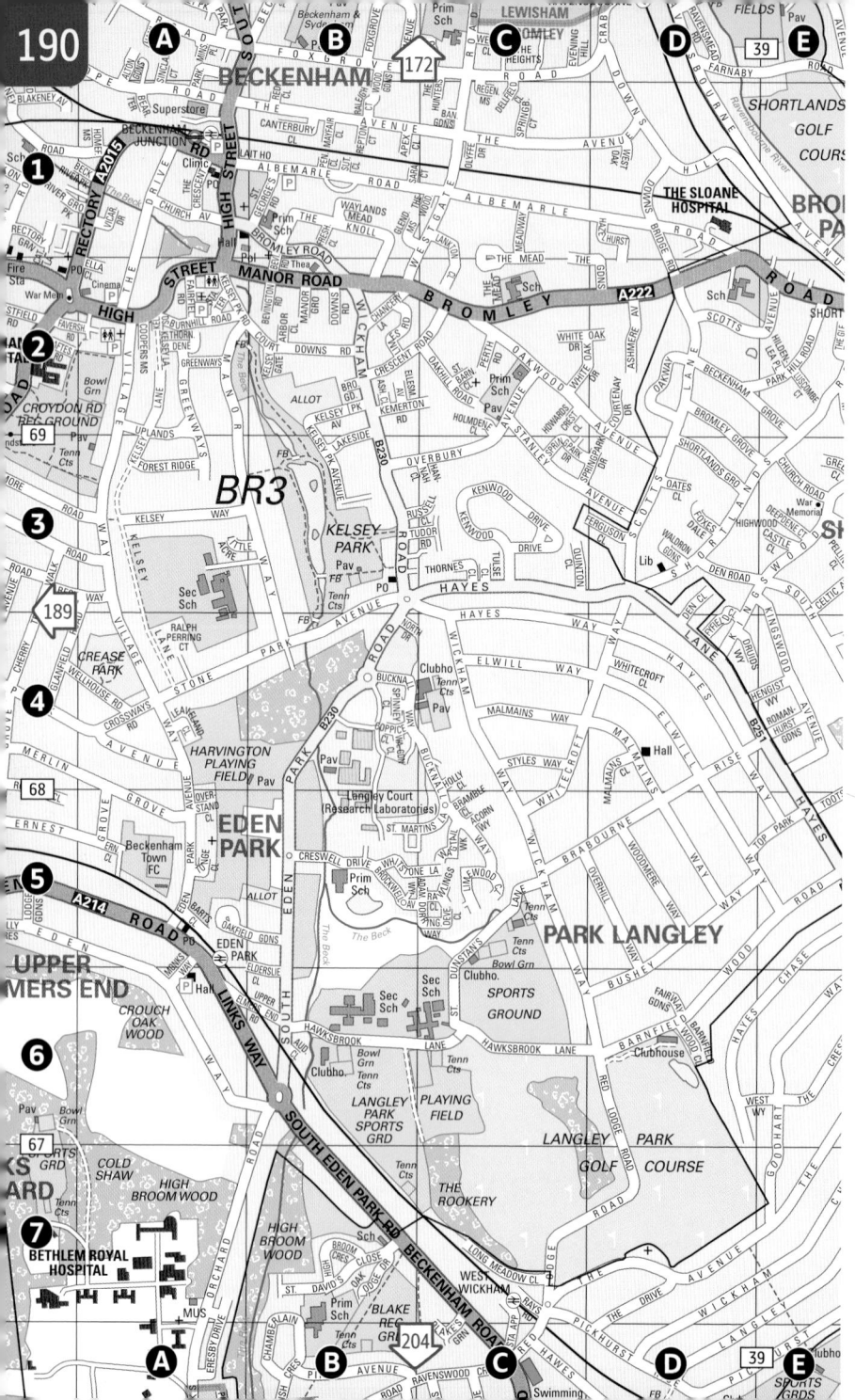

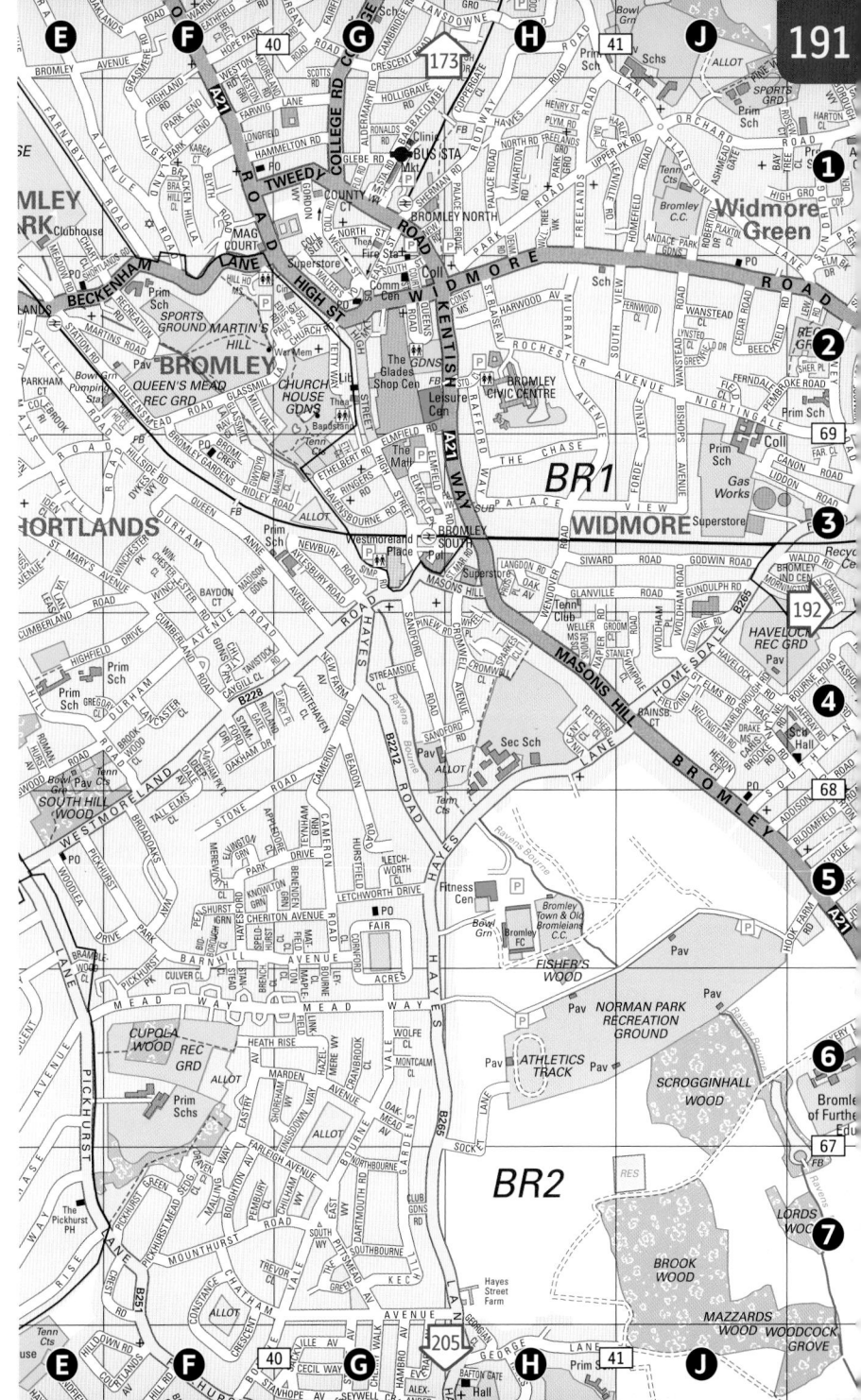

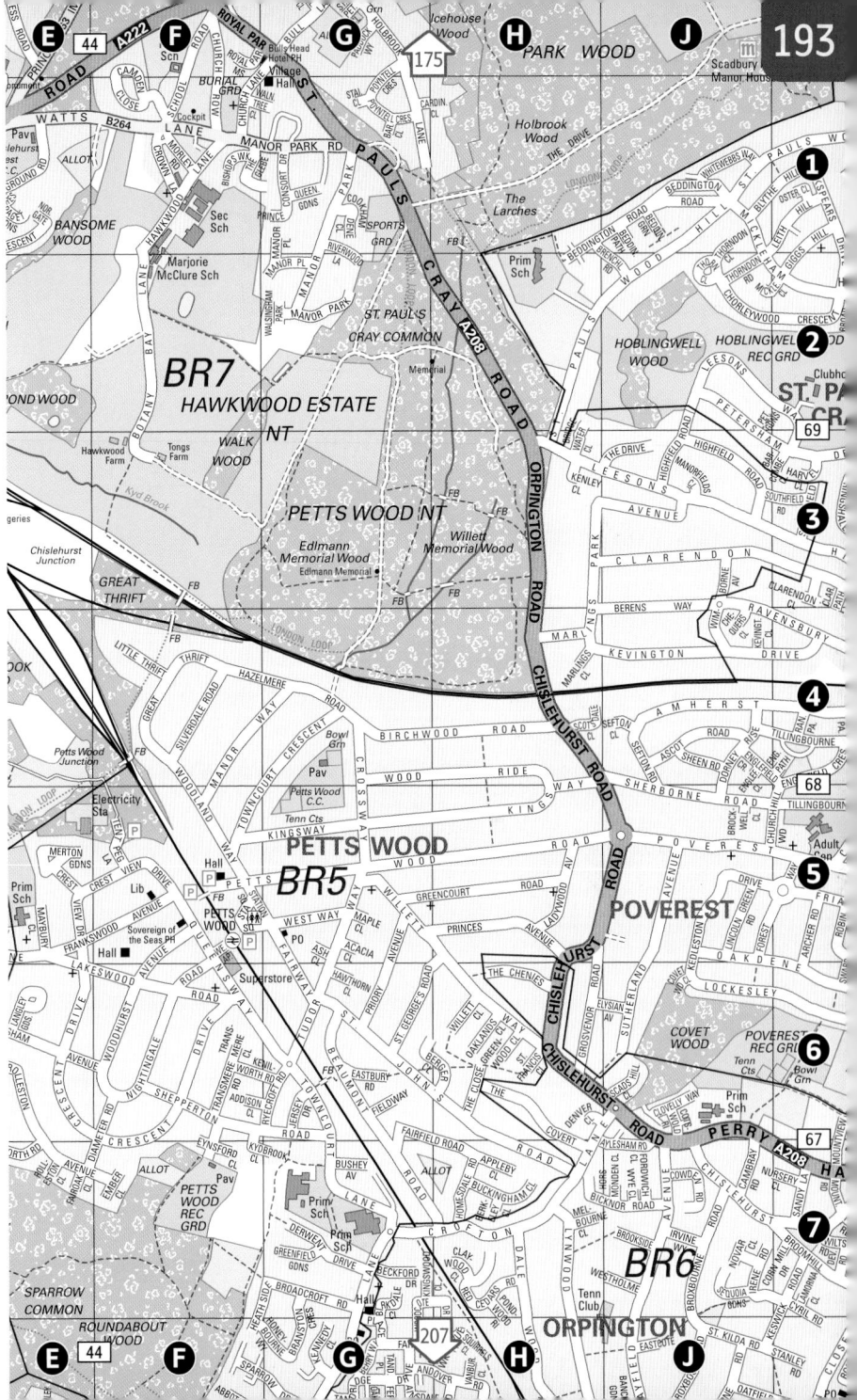

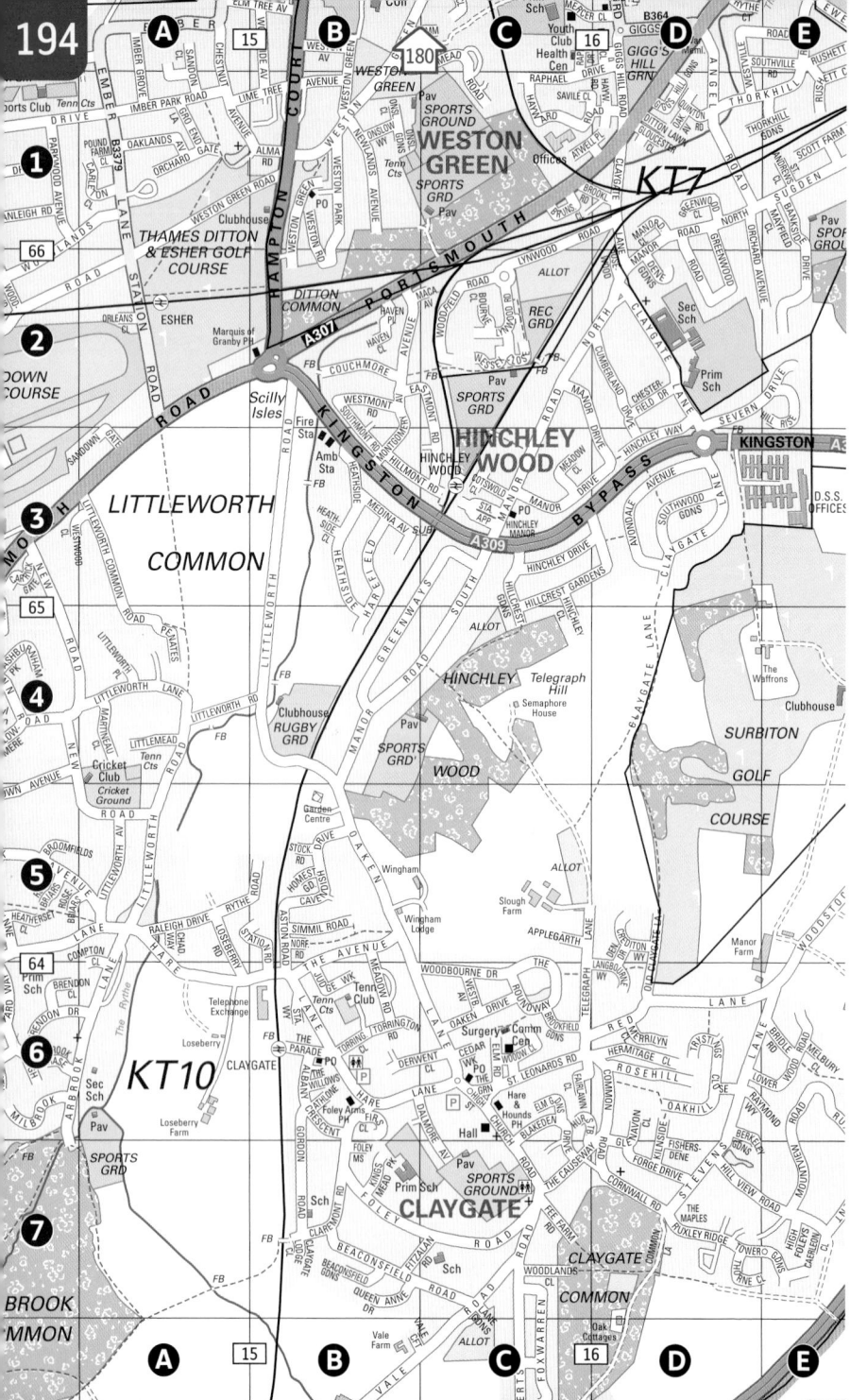

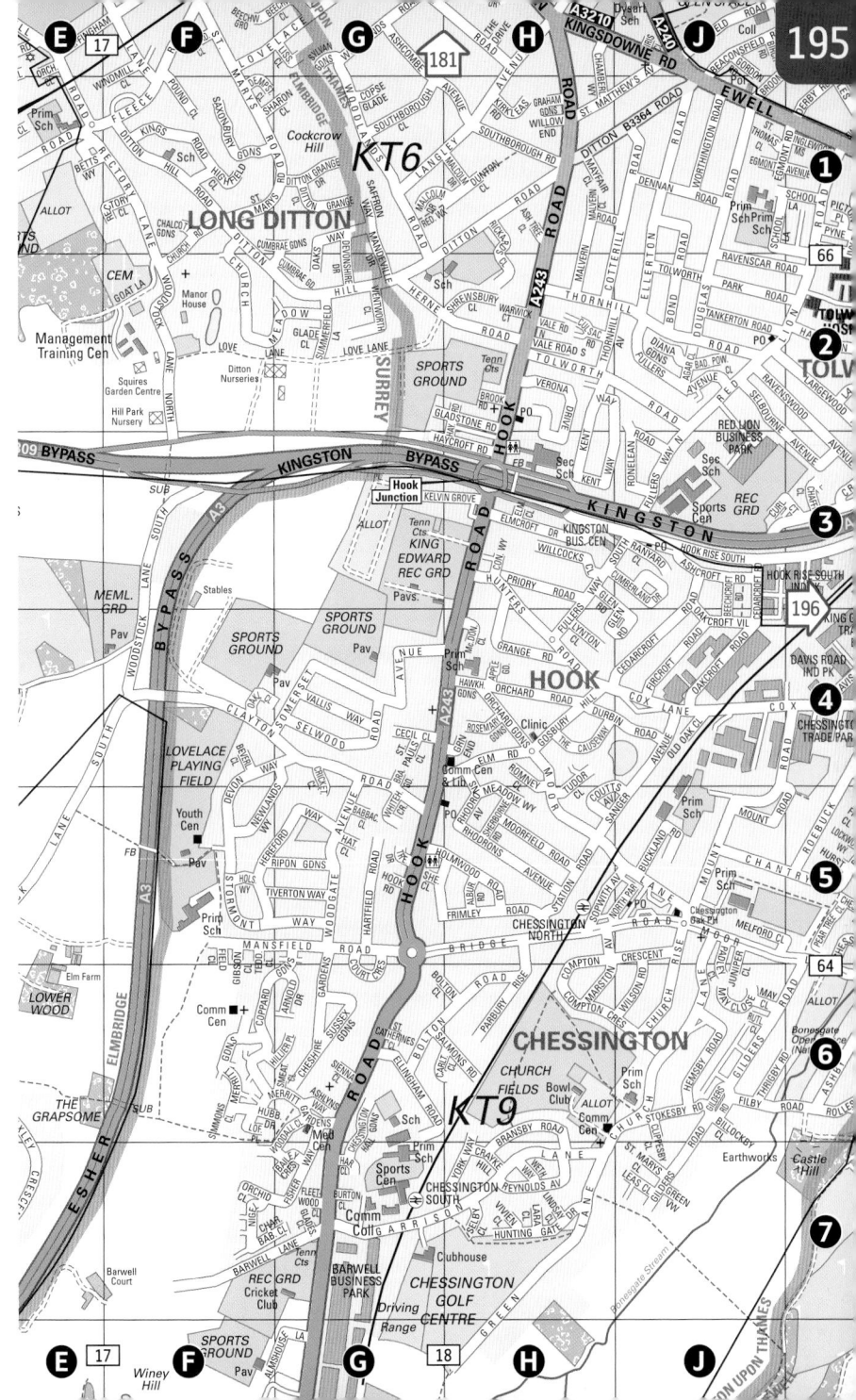

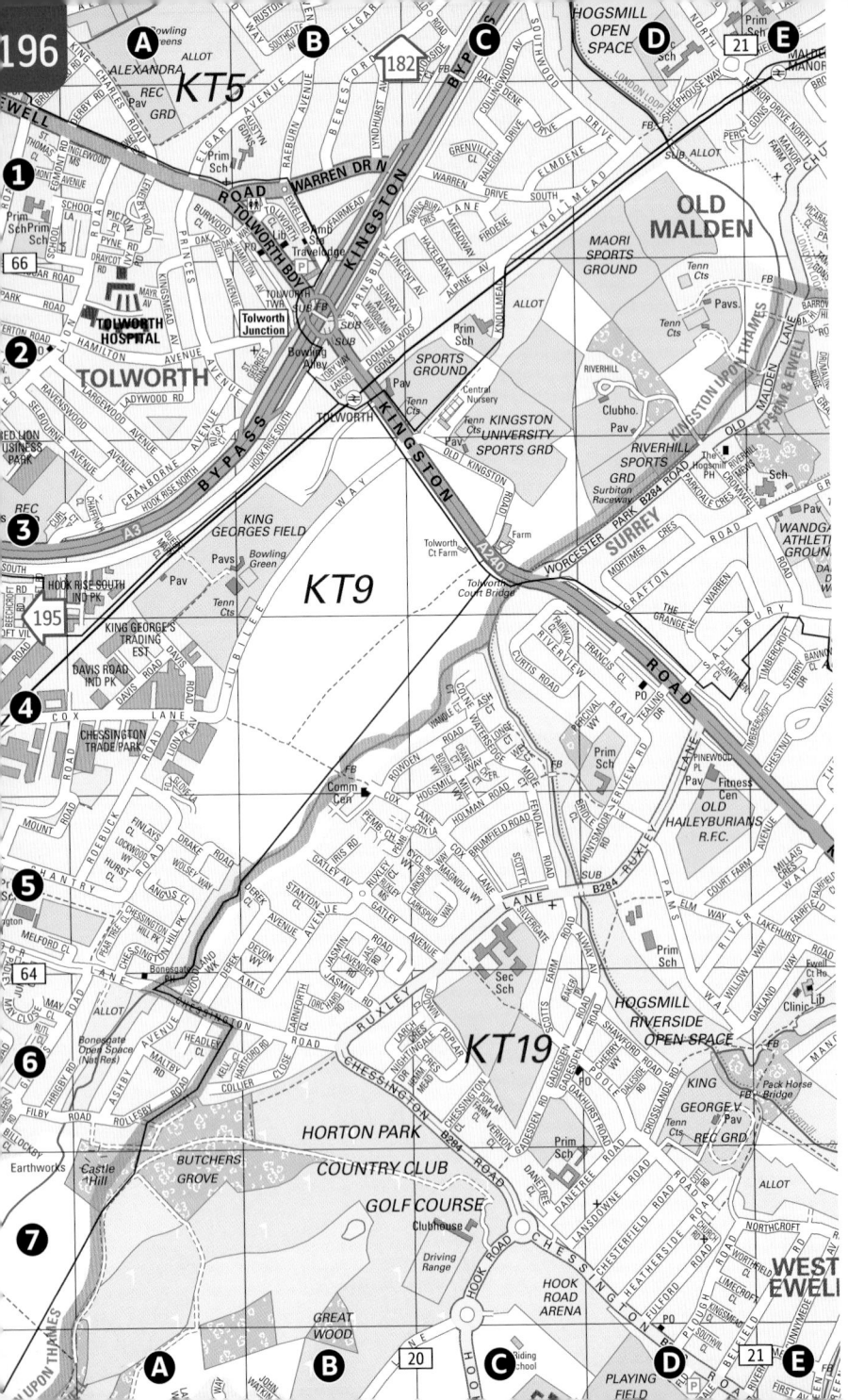

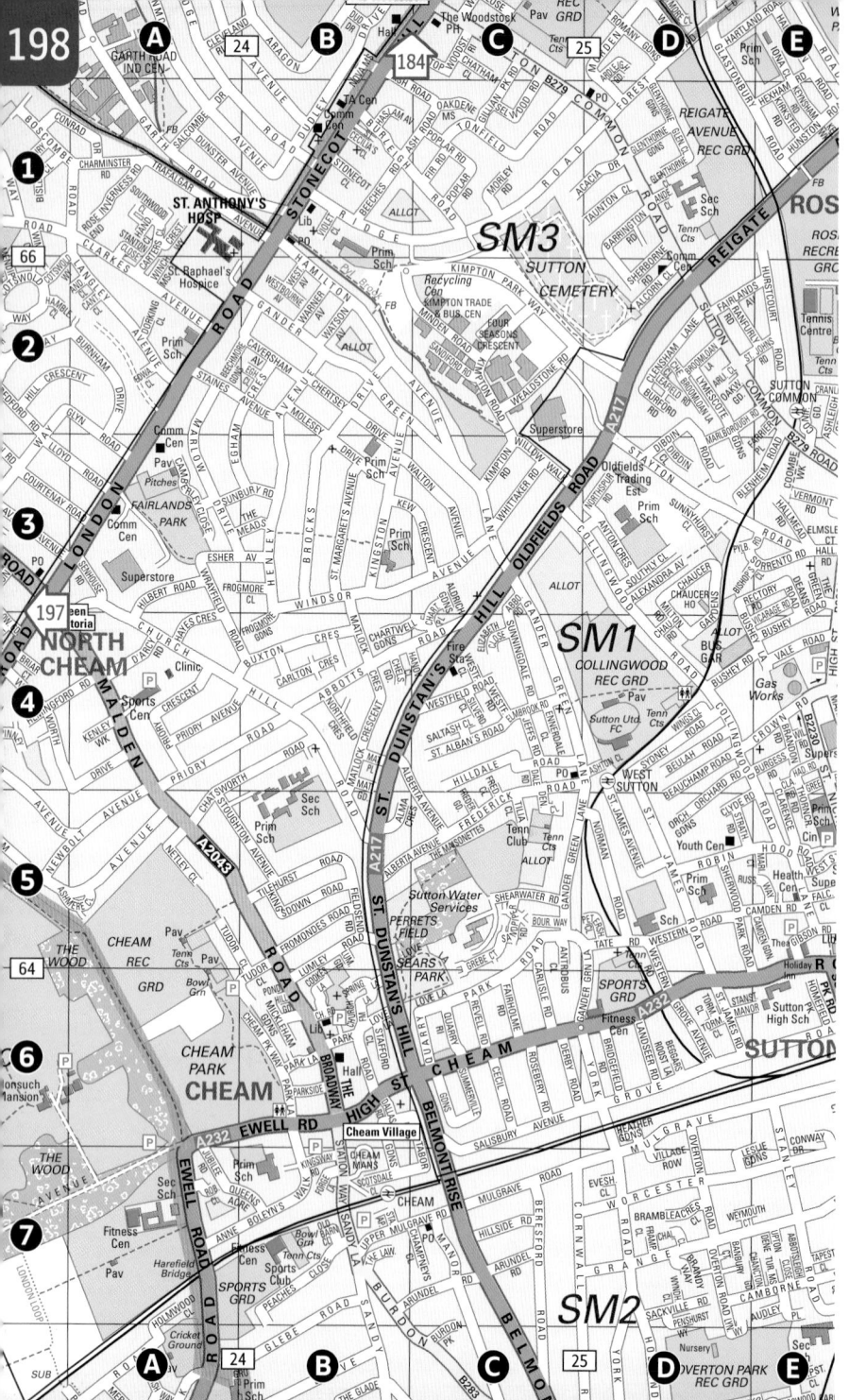

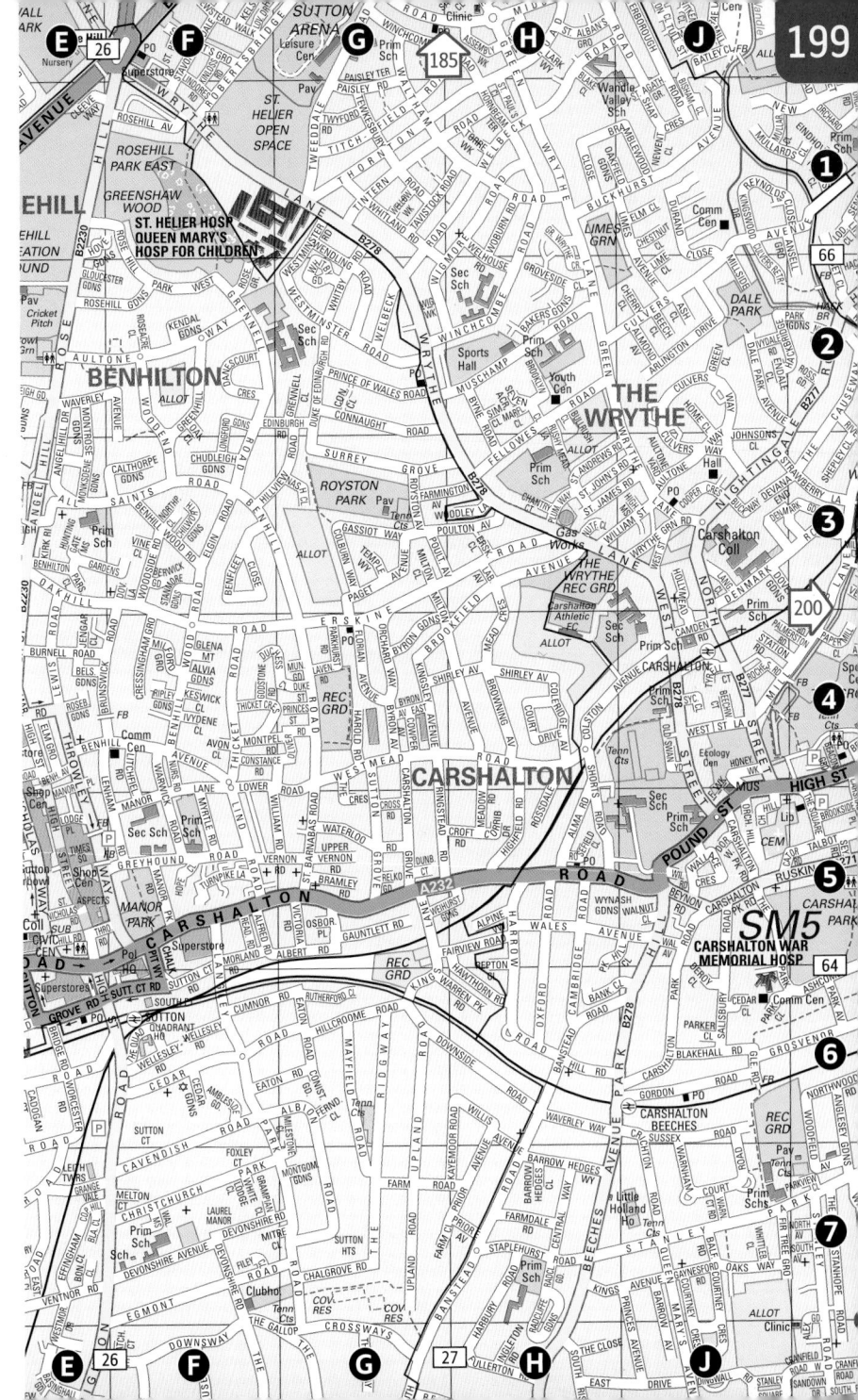

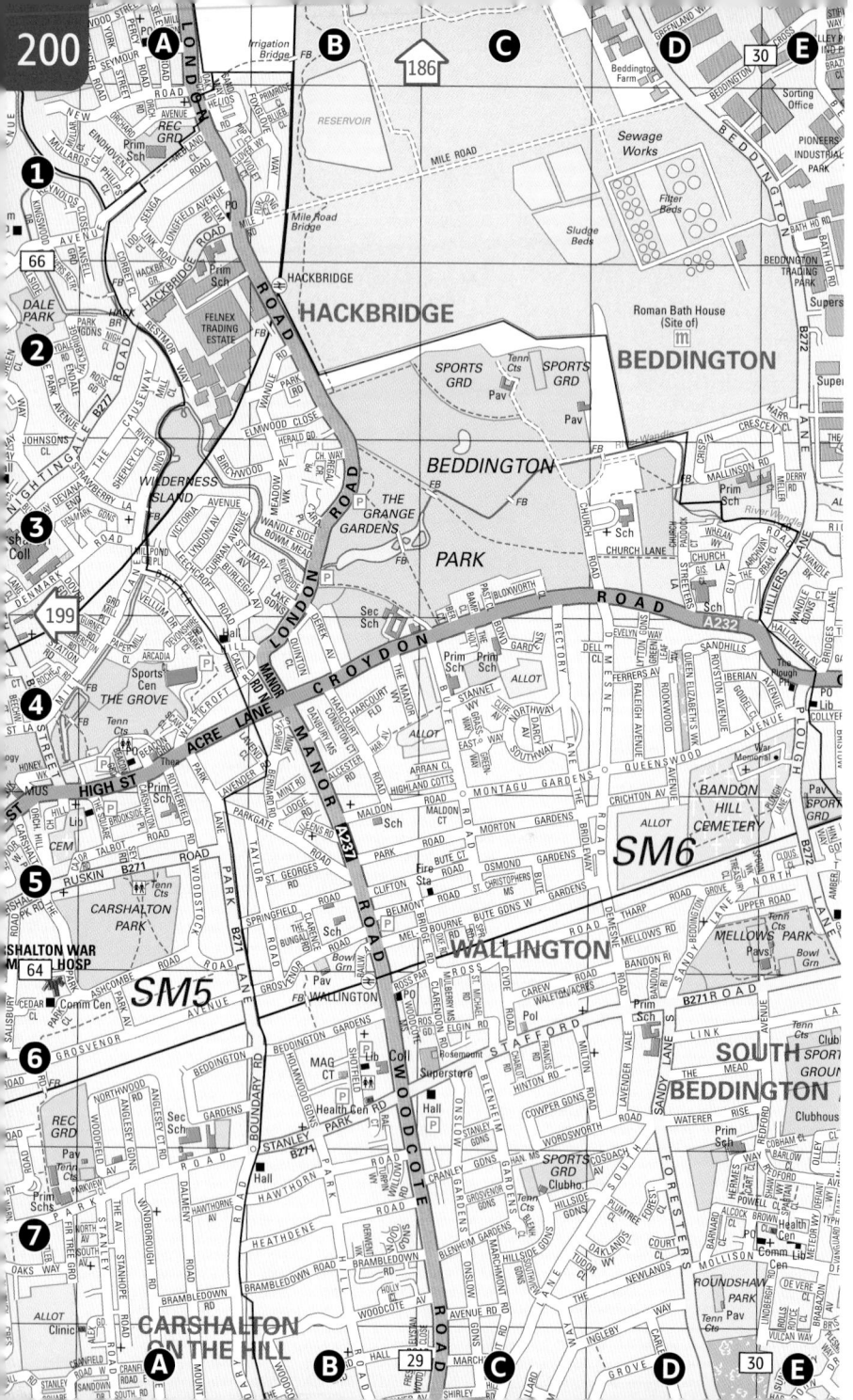

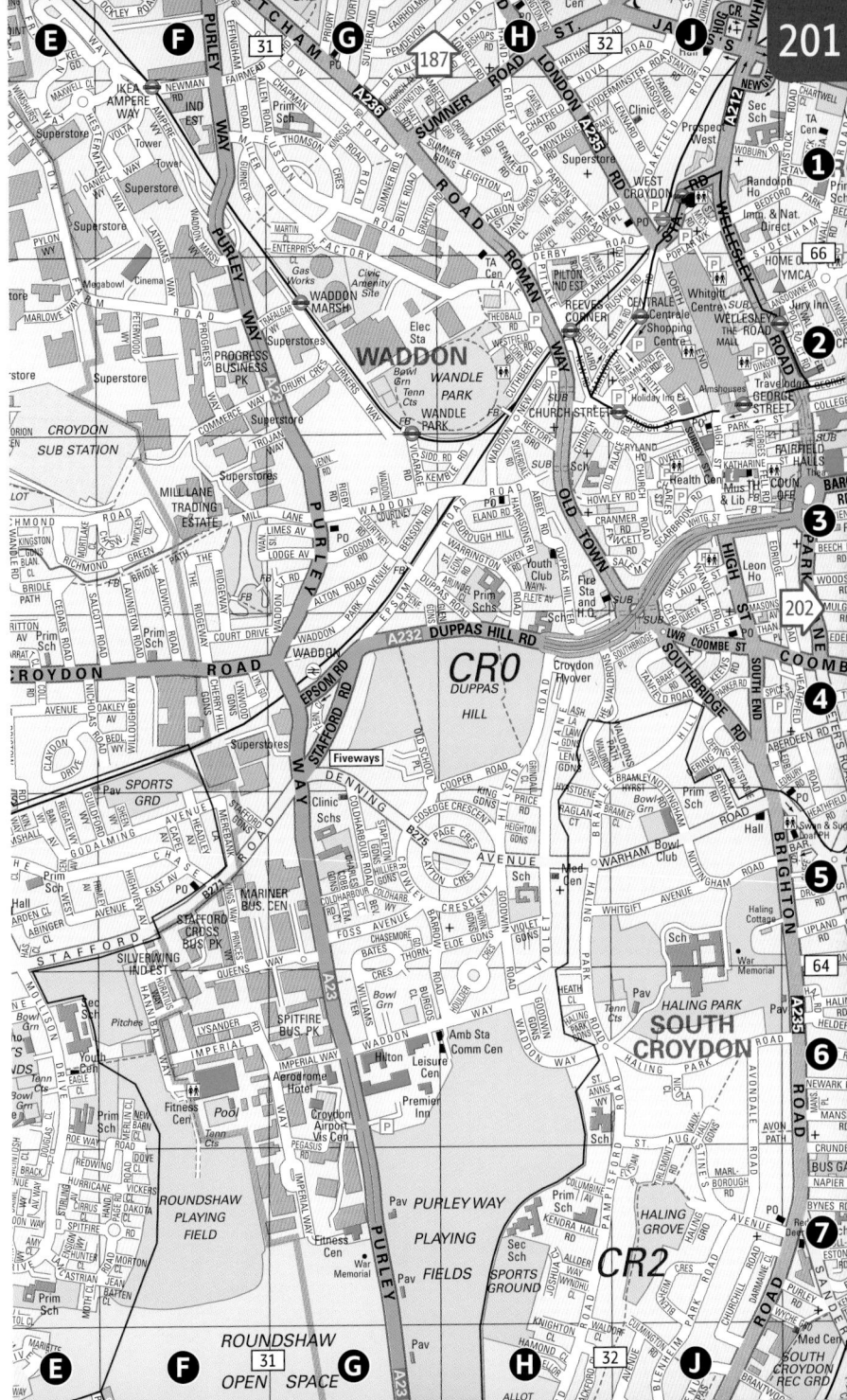

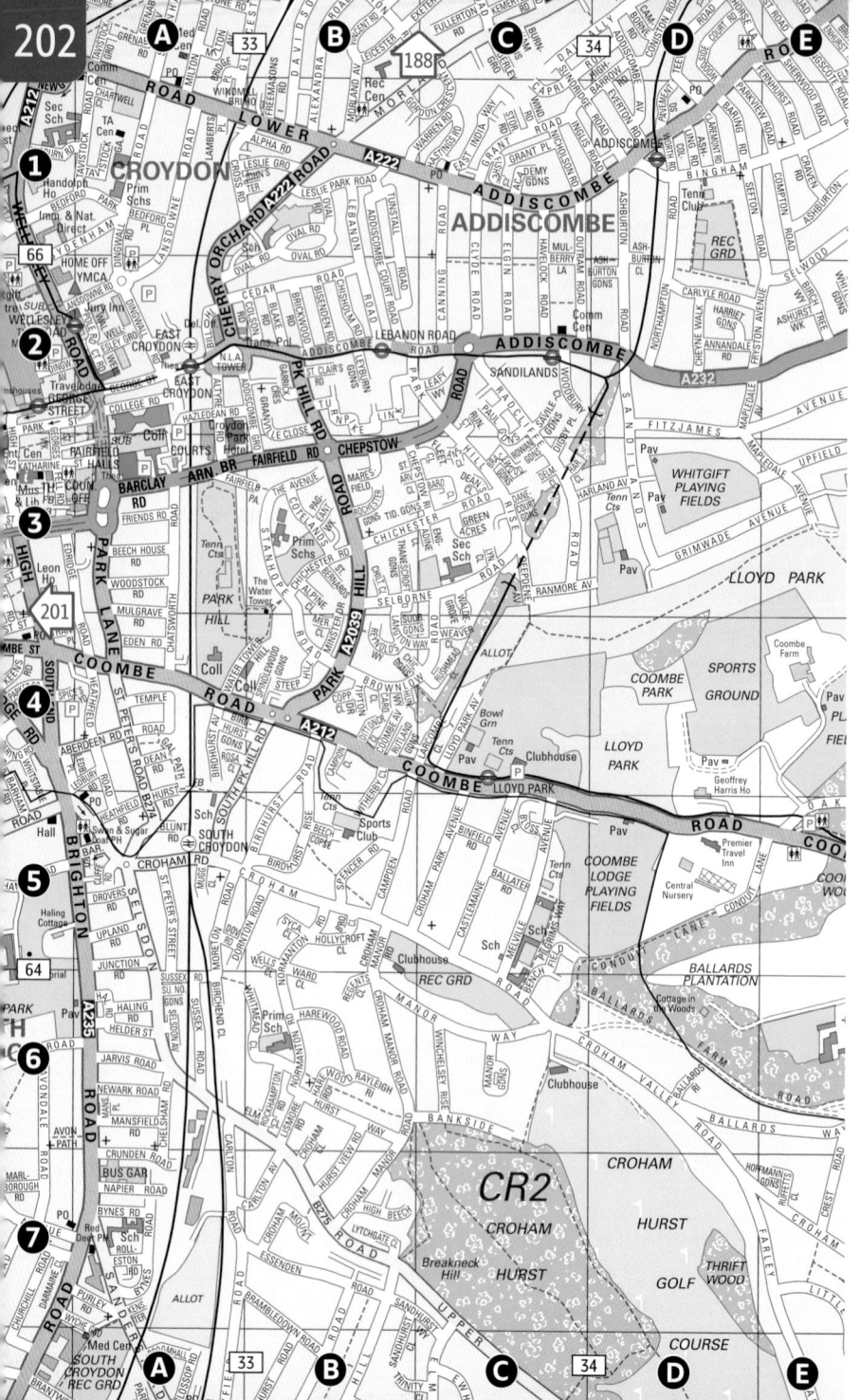

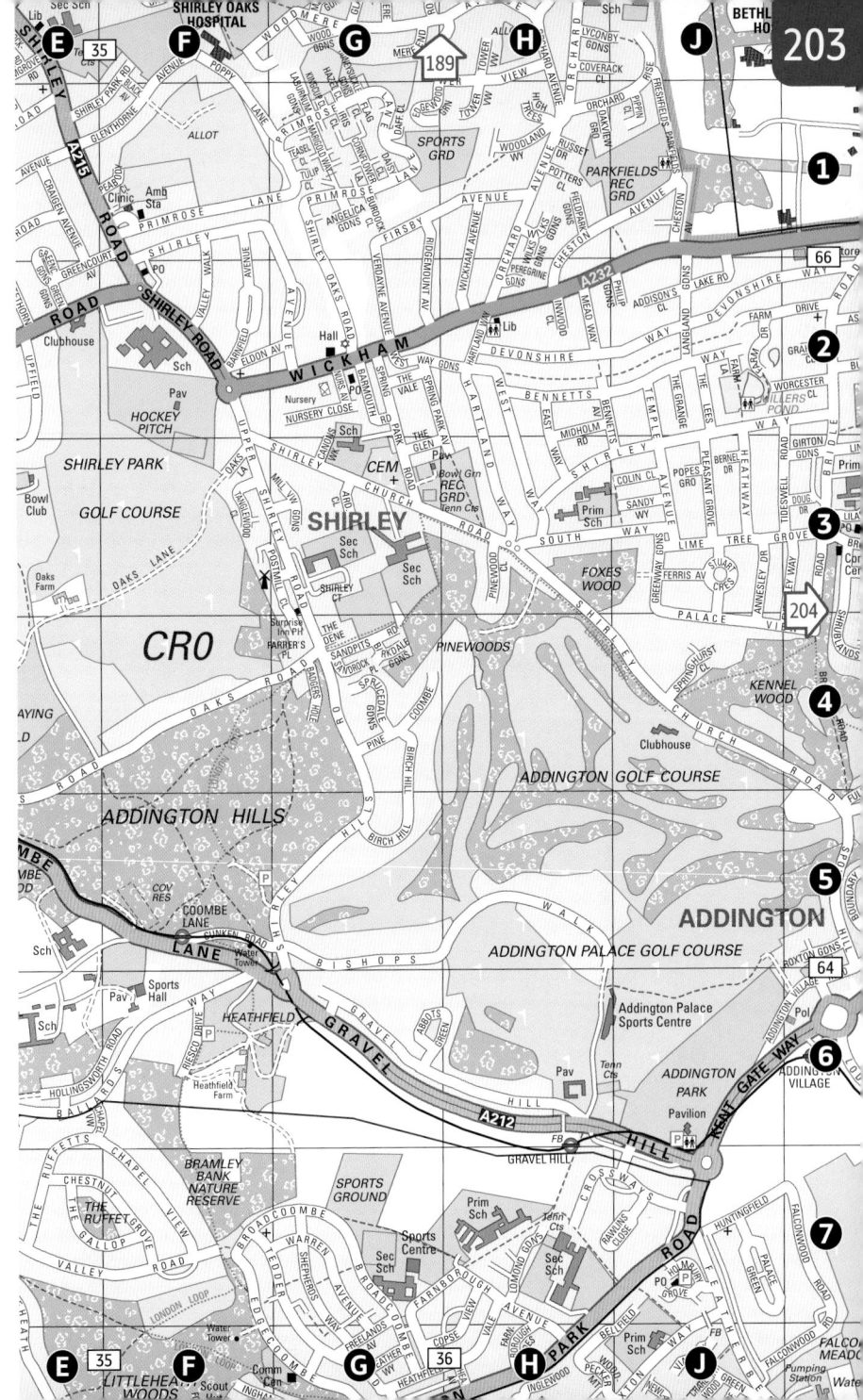

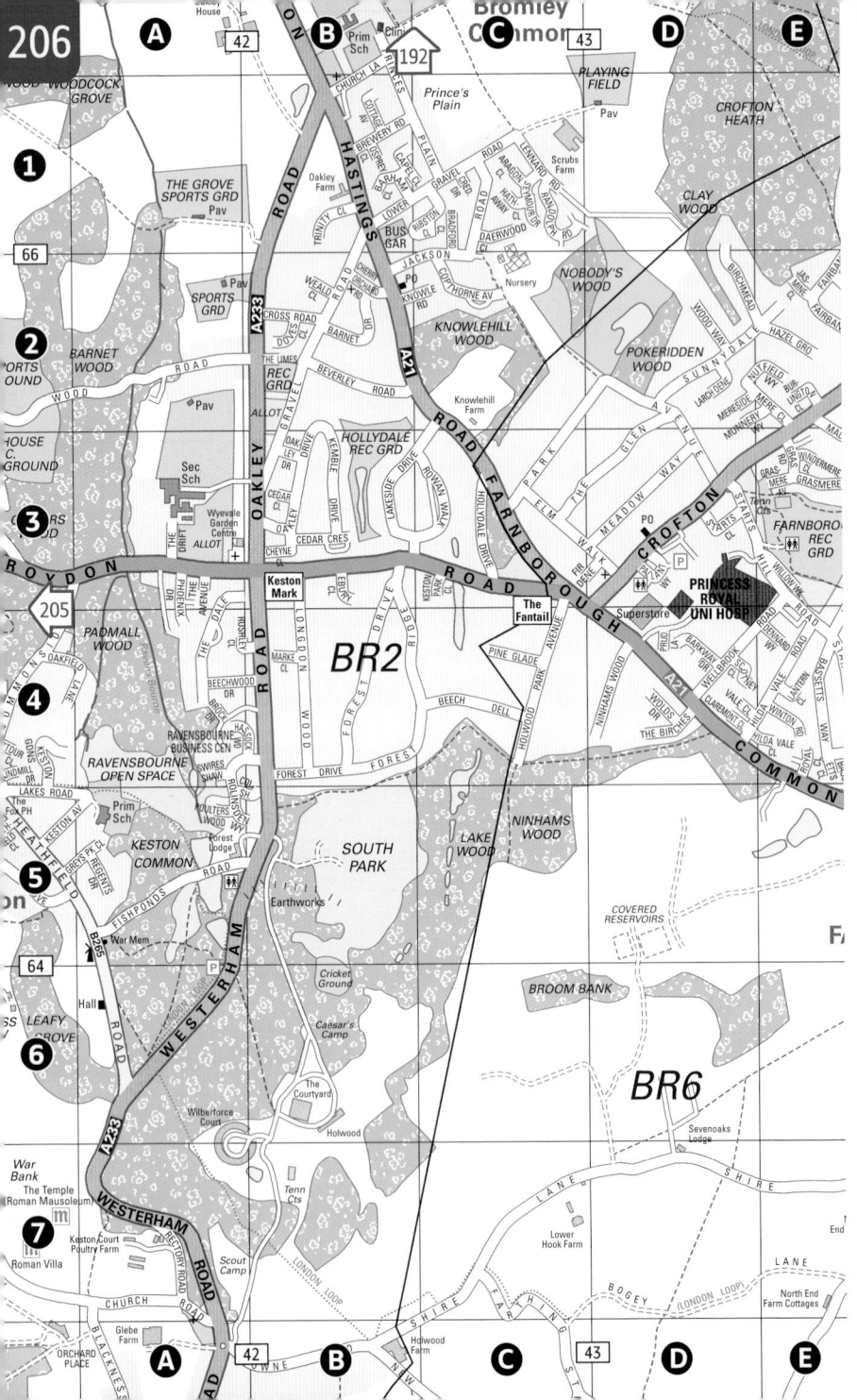

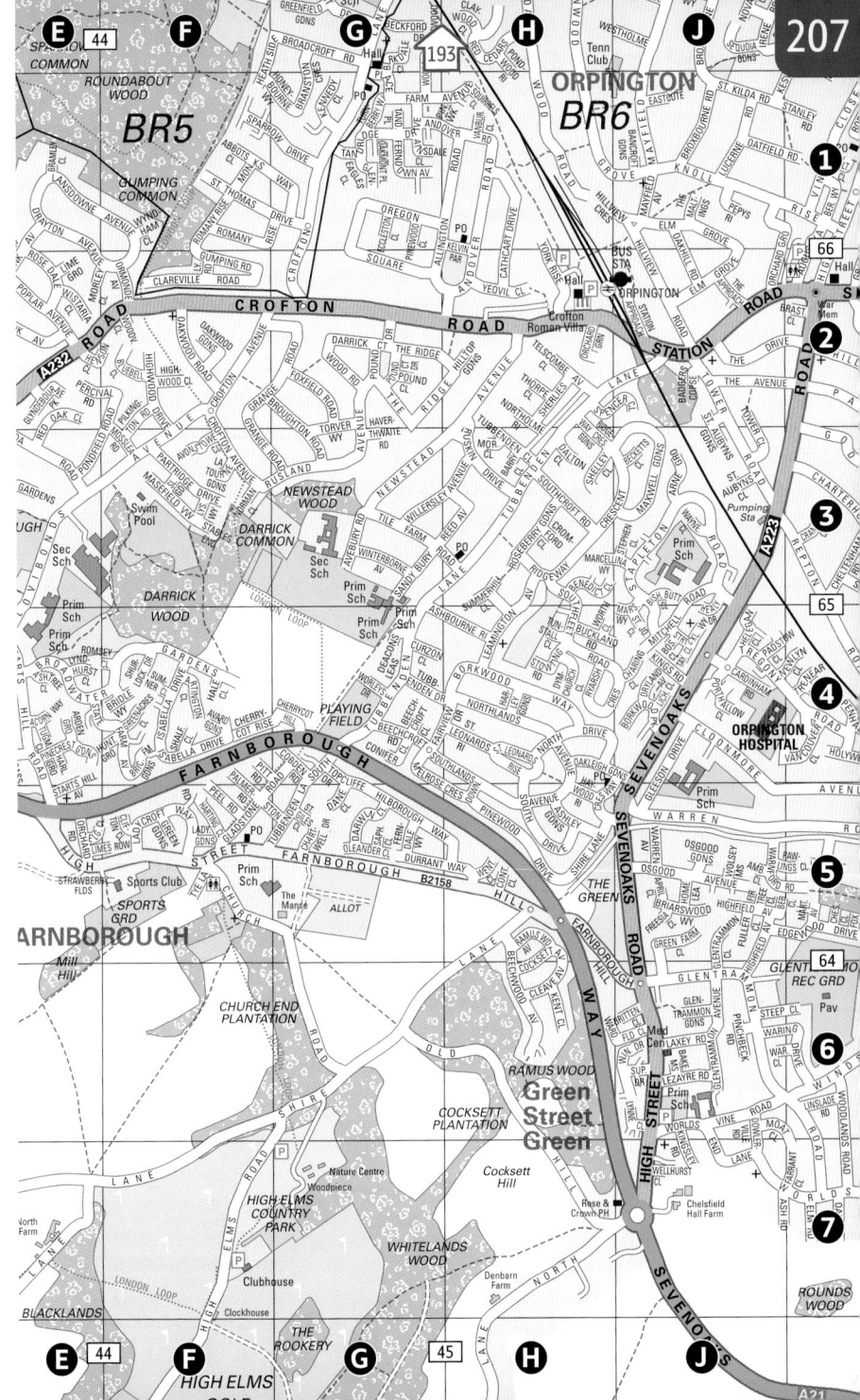

West End theatres & cinemas

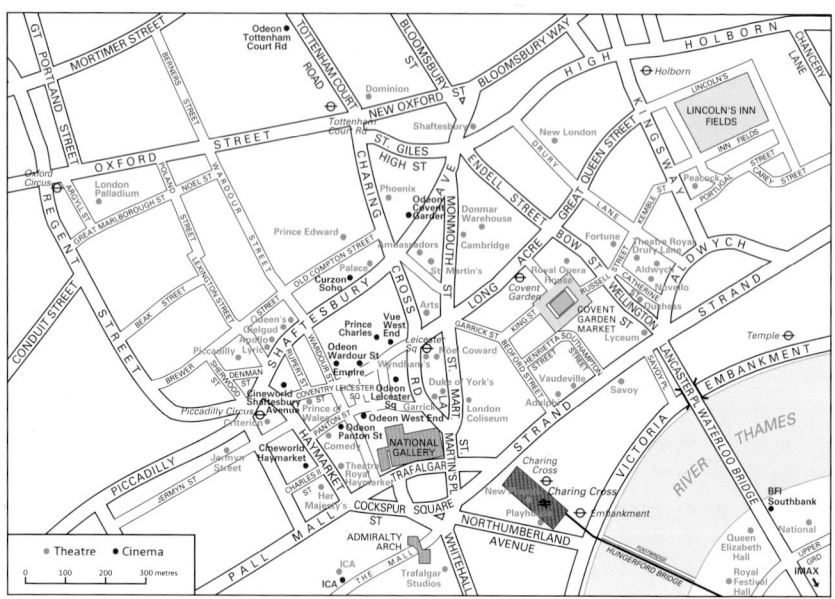

THEATRES

Adelphi *0870 895 5598*
Aldwych *020 7379 3367*
Ambassadors *0844 811 2334*
Apollo *0870 890 1101*
Arts *0844 847 1608*
Cambridge *0870 890 1102*
Comedy *0870 060 6637*
Criterion *0870 060 6663*
Dominion *0870 169 0116*
Donmar Warehouse *0870 060 6624*
Duchess *0870 040 0082*
Duke of York's *0870 060 6623*
Fortune *0870 060 6626*
Garrick *0870 890 1104*
Gielgud *0870 950 0915*
Her Majesty's *0870 890 1106*

ICA *020 7930 3647*
Jermyn Street *020 7287 2875*
London Coliseum *0871 911 0200*
London Palladium *0871 297 0748*
Lyceum *0870 243 9000*
Lyric *0870 890 1107*
New London *0870 890 0141*
New Players *0870 033 2626*
Nöel Coward *0870 950 0920*
Novello *0870 950 0935*
Palace *0870 890 0142*
Peacock *020 7863 8222*
Phoenix *0870 060 6629*
Piccadilly *0844 412 6666*
Playhouse *0870 060 6631*
Prince Edward *0870 850 9191*

Prince of Wales *0870 950 0915*
Queen's *0870 950 0931*
Royal Festival Hall *0871 663 2500*
National *020 7452 3000*
Royal Opera House *020 7304 4000*
St. Martin's *0870 162 8787*
Savoy *0870 164 8787*
Shaftesbury *020 7379 5399*
Theatre Royal, Drury Lane
    0844 412 4660
Theatre Royal Haymarket
    020 7930 8890
Trafalgar Studios *0870 060 6632*
Vaudeville *08708 900511*
Wyndham's *0870 950 0925*

CINEMAS

BFI IMAX *0870 787 2525*
BFI Southbank *020 7928 3232*
Cineworld Haymarket
    0871 200 2000
Cineworld Shaftesbury Avenue
    0871 200 2000

Curzon Soho *0871 7033 988*
ICA *020 7930 3647*
Odeon Covent Garden
    0871 224 4007
Odeon Leicester Sq *0871 224 4007*
Odeon Panton St *0871 224 4007*

Odeon Tottenham Court Rd
    0871 224 4007
Odeon West End *0871 224 4007*
Prince Charles *0870 811 2559*
Empire Leicester Sq *0871 471 4714*
Vue West End *0871 224 0240*

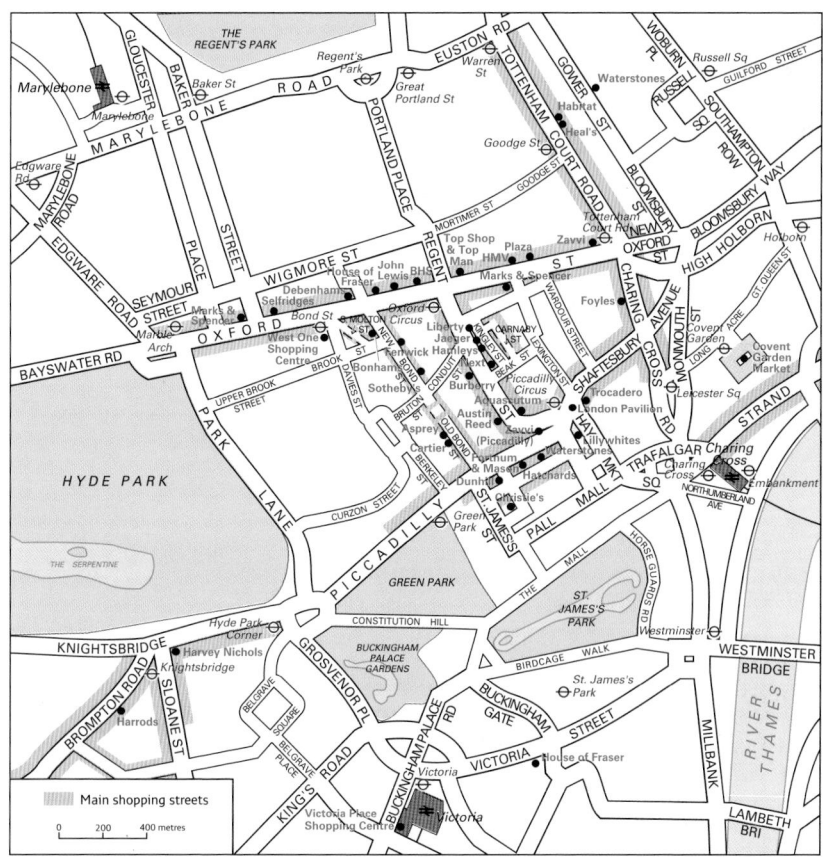

SHOPS

Aquascutum 020 7675 8200
Asprey 020 7493 6767
Austin Reed 020 7534 7777
BHS (Oxford St) 0845 841 0246
Bonhams 020 7447 7447
Burberry 020 7968 0000
Cartier 020 7408 5700
Christie's 020 7839 9060
Covent Garden Market
    020 7836 9136
Debenhams 08445 616161
Dunhill 0845 458 0779
Fenwick 020 7629 9161
Fortnum & Mason 020 7734 8040
Foyles 020 7434 1574
Habitat (Tottenham Court Rd)
    0844 499 1122

Hamleys 0800 280 2444
Harrods 020 7730 1234
Harvey Nichols 020 7235 5000
Hatchards 020 7439 9921
Heal's 020 7636 1666
HMV (Oxford Circus) 0845 602 7800
House of Fraser (Oxford St)
    0870 160 7258
House of Fraser (Victoria)
    0870 160 7268
Jaeger 020 7979 1100
John Lewis 020 7629 7711
Liberty 020 7734 1234
Lillywhites 0870 333 9600
London Pavilion 020 7439 1791
Marks & Spencer (Marble Arch)
    020 7935 7954

Marks & Spencer Pantheon (Oxford St)
    020 7437 7722
Next (Regent St) 0870 386 5283
Plaza Shopping Centre, Oxford St
    020 7637 8811
Selfridges 0800 123 400
Sotheby's 020 7293 5000
Top Shop & Top Man 020 7636 7700
Trocadero 020 7439 1791
Victoria Place Shopping Centre
    020 7931 8811
Waterstones (Gower St)
    020 7636 1577
Waterstones (Piccadilly)
    020 7851 2400
ZAVVI (Oxford St) 020 7631 1234
ZAVVI (Piccadilly) 020 7439 2500

Index

How to use this index

This index combines entries for street names, place names and places of interest.

Place names are shown in capital letters,
e.g. **ACTON**, W3 . . . .**126** A1
These include towns, villages and localities within the area covered by this atlas.

Places of interest are shown with a star symbol,
e.g. ★ **British Mus**, WC1 . . . . .**17** J2
These include parks, museums, galleries, and other important buildings or locations of tourist interest.

All other entries are for street names. When there is more than one street with exactly the same name then that name is shown only once in the index. It is then followed by a list of entries for each postal district that contains a street with that same name. For example, there are three streets called Appledore Close in this atlas and the index entry shows that one of these is in London postal district SW17, one is in Bromley, BR2 and one is in Edgware, HA8.

Appledore Cl, SW17 . . . . .**167** J2
Bromley BR2 . . . .**191** F5
Edgware HA8 . . . .**70** A1

All entries are followed by the page number and grid reference on which the name will be found. So, in the example above, **Appledore Close**, SW17 will be found on page **167** in square J2. All entries are indexed to the largest scale map on which they are shown.

The index also contains some street names which are not actually shown on the maps because there is not enough space to name them. In these cases the adjoining or nearest named thoroughfare to such streets is shown in the index in *italics*, and the reference indicates where the unnamed street is located *off* the named thoroughfare.

e.g. **Bacton St**, E2
off Roman Rd **113** F3

This means that Bacton Street is not named on the map, but it is located *off* Roman Road on page **113** in square F3.

A strict letter-by-letter alphabetical order is followed in this index. All non-alphabetic characters such as spaces, hyphens or apostrophes are not included in the index order. For example Belle Vue Road and Bellevue Road will be found listed together.

Standard terms such as Avenue, Close, Rise and Road are abbreviated in the index but are ordered alphabetically as if given in full. So, for example, **Alderton Ri** comes before **Alderton Rd**.

Names beginning with a definite article (i.e. The) are indexed from their second word onwards with the article being placed at the end of the name,
e.g. **Avenue, The**, E4 . . . .**62** D6

The alphabetical order extends to include postal information so that where two or more streets have exactly the same name, London postal district references are given first in alpha-numeric order and are followed by non-London post town references in alphabetical order, e.g. Appledore Close, SW17 is followed by Appledore Close, Bromley BR2 and then Appledore Close, Edgware HA8.

In cases where there are two or more streets of the same name in the same postal area, extra information is given in brackets to aid location. For example, High St, Orpington BR6 (Farnboro.), and High St, Orpington BR6 (Green St Grn), distinguishes between two streets called High Street which are both in the post town of Orpington, within the same postal district of BR6.

Extra locational information is also given for some localities within large post towns. This is also to aid location.
e.g. **Alford Grn**, Croy. (New Adgtn.) CR0
This street is within the locality of New Addington which is part of the post town of Croydon, and it is within postal district CR0.

A full list of locality and post town abbreviations used in this atlas is given below.

General abbreviations

Acad	Academy	BUPA	British United	Coll	College	Ctyd	Courtyard
All	Alley		Provident	Comb	Combined	Dep	Depot
Allot	Allotments		Association	Comm	Community	Dept	Department
Amb	Ambulance	C of E	Church of	Comp	Comprehensive	Dev	Development
Apts	Apartments		England	Conf	Conference	Dr	Drive
App	Approach	Cath	Cathedral	Cont	Continuing	Dws	Dwellings
Arc	Arcade	Cem	Cemetery	Conv	Convent	E	East
Assoc	Association	Cen	Central, Centre	Cor	Corner	Ed	Education,
Av	Avenue	Cft	Croft	Coron	Coroners		Educational
Bdy	Broadway	Cfts	Crofts	Cors	Corners	Elec	Electricity
Bk	Bank	Ch	Church	Cotts	Cottages	Embk	Embankment
Bldg	Building	Chyd	Churchyard	Cov	Covered	Est	Estate
Bldgs	Buildings	Cin	Cinema	Crem	Crematorium	Ex	Exchange
Boul	Boulevard	Circ	Circus	Cres	Crescent	Exhib	Exhibition
Bowl	Bowling	Cl	Close	Ct	Court	FB	Footbridge
Br	Bridge	Co	County	Cts	Courts	FC	Football Club

Abbr	Expansion	Abbr	Expansion	Abbr	Expansion	Abbr	Expansion
Fld	Field	Jun	Junior	Pol	Police	TA	Territorial Army
Flds	Fields	Junct	Junction	Poly	Polytechnic	TH	Town Hall
Fm	Farm	La	Lane	Prec	Precinct	Tech	Technical, Technology
GM	Grant Maintained	Las	Lanes	Prep	Preparatory	Tenn	Tennis
Gall	Gallery	Lib	Library	Prim	Primary	Ter	Terrace
Gar	Garage	Lit	Literary	Prom	Promenade	Thea	Theatre
Gdn	Garden	Lo	Lodge	Pt	Point	Trd	Trading
Gdns	Gardens	Lwr	Lower	Quad	Quadrant	Twr	Tower
Gen	General	Mag	Magistrates	Rbt	Roundabout	Twrs	Towers
Gra	Grange	Mans	Mansions	RC	Roman Catholic	Uni	University
Grad	Graduate	Med	Medical, Medicine	Rd	Road	Upr	Upper
Gram	Grammar	Mem	Memorial	Rds	Roads	VA	Voluntary Aided
Grd	Ground	Met	Metropolitan	Rec	Recreation	VC	Voluntary Controlled
Grds	Grounds	Mid	Middle	Rehab	Rehabilitation	Vet	Veterinary
Grn	Green	Mkt	Market	Res	Reservoir, Residence	Vil	Villa
Grns	Greens	Mkts	Markets	Ri	Rise	Vil	Villas
Gro	Grove	Ms	Mews	S	South	Vw	View
Gros	Groves	Mt	Mount	SM	Secondary Mixed	W	West
Gt	Great	Mus	Museum	Sch	School	Wd	Wood
HQ	Headquarters	N	North	Schs	Schools	Wds	Woods
Ho	House	NHS	National Health Service	Sec	Secondary	Wf	Wharf
Hos	Houses	NT	National Trust	Sen	Senior	Wk	Walk
Hosp	Hospital	Nat	National	Shop	Shop	Wks	Works
Hts	Heights	Nurs	Nursery	Spec	Special	Yd	Yard
Ind	Industrial	PH	Public House	Sq	Square		
Indep	Independent	PO	Post Office	St	Street		
Inf	Infant(s)	PRU	Pupil Referral Unit	St.	Saint		
Inst	Institute	Par	Parade	Sta	Station		
Int	International	Pas	Passage	Sts	Streets		
JM	Junior Mixed	Pav	Pavilion	Sub	Subway		
JMI	Junior Mixed & Infant(s)	Pk	Park	Swim	Swimming		
		Pl	Place				

Locality and post town abbreviations

In the list of abbreviations shown below, post towns are in **bold** type

Bark.	**Barking**	Har.Hill	Harrow on the Hill	**Rain.**	**Rainham**
Barn.	**Barnet**	Har.Wld	Harrow Weald	**Rich.**	**Richmond**
Barne.	Barnehurst	Harm.	Harmondsworth	Rod.Val.	Roding Valley
Beck.	**Beckenham**	Hatt.Cr.	Hatton Cross	**Rom.**	**Romford**
Bedd.	Beddington	High Barn.	High Barnet	**Ruis.**	**Ruislip**
Bedd.Cor.	Beddington Corner	Highams Pk	Highams Park	**S.Croy.**	**South Croydon**
Belv.	**Belvedere**	Hinch.Wd	Hinchley Wood	S.Har.	South Harrow
Bex.	**Bexley**	Hmptn H.	Hampton Hill	S.Norwood	South Norwood
Bexh.	**Bexleyheath**	Hmptn W.	Hampton Wick	S.Oxhey	South Oxhey
Borwd.	**Borehamwood**	**Hmptn.**	**Hampton**	S.Ruis.	South Ruislip
Brent.	**Brentford**	**Houns.**	**Hounslow**	Scad.Pk	Scadbury Park
Brom.	**Bromley**	Houns.W.	Hounslow West	Short.	Shortlands
Buck.H.	**Buckhurst Hill**	**Ilf.**	**Ilford**	**Sid.**	**Sidcup**
Bushey Hth	Bushey Heath	**Islw.**	**Isleworth**	St.P.Cray	St. Paul's Cray
Carp.Pk	Carpenders Park	**Kes.**	**Keston**	**Stai.**	**Staines**
Cars.	**Carshalton**	**Kings.T.**	**Kingston upon Thames**	**Stan.**	**Stanmore**
Chad.Hth	Chadwell Heath			Stanw.	Stanwell
Chess.	**Chessington**	Lon.Hthrw Air.	London Heathrow Airport	Sthl Grn	Southall Green
Chig.	**Chigwell**			**Sthl.**	**Southall**
Chis.	**Chislehurst**	Lon.Hthrw Air.N.	London Heathrow Airport North	**Sun.**	**Sunbury-on-Thames**
Clay.	Claygate			**Surb.**	**Surbiton**
Cockfos.	Cockfosters	Long Dit.	Long Ditton	**Sutt.**	**Sutton**
Coll.Row	Collier Row	**Loug.**	**Loughton**	**T.Ditt.**	**Thames Ditton**
Cran.	Cranford	Lt.Hth	Little Heath	**Tedd.**	**Teddington**
Croy.	**Croydon**	Lwr Sydenham	Lower Sydenham	**Th.Hth.**	**Thornton Heath**
Dag.	**Dagenham**	**Mitch.**	**Mitcham**	They.B.	Theydon Bois
Dart.	**Dartford**	Mitch.Com.	Mitcham Common	Tkgtn	Tokyngton
E.Barn.	East Barnet	**Mord.**	**Morden**	**Twick.**	**Twickenham**
E.Bed.	East Bedfont	Mots.Pk	Motspur Park	**Uxb.**	**Uxbridge**
E.Mol.	**East Molesey**	N.Finchley	North Finchley	W.Ealing	West Ealing
Ealing Com.	Ealing Common	N.Har.	North Harrow	W.Ewell	West Ewell
Eastcote Vill.	Eastcote Village	**N.Mal.**	**New Malden**	**W.Mol.**	**West Molesey**
Edg.	**Edgware**	New Adgtn	New Addington	**W.Wick.**	**West Wickham**
Elm.Wds	Elmstead Woods	New Barn.	New Barnet	**Wall.**	**Wallington**
Els.	Elstree	Northumb.Hth	Northumberland Heath	**Walt.**	**Walton-on-Thames**
Enf.	**Enfield**	Norwood Junct.	Norwood Junction	**Wat.**	**Watford**
Epp.	**Epping**	**Nthlt.**	**Northolt**	**Wdf.Grn.**	**Woodford Green**
Farnboro.	Farnborough	**Nthwd.**	**Northwood**	Wealds.	Wealdstone
Felt.	**Feltham**	**Orp.**	**Orpington**	**Well.**	**Welling**
Grn St Grn	Green Street Green	Petts Wd	Petts Wood	**Wem.**	**Wembley**
Grnf.	**Greenford**	**Pnr.**	**Pinner**	**West Dr.**	**West Drayton**
Hackbr.	Hackbridge	Pond.End	Ponders End	Woodside Pk	Woodside Park
Han.	Hanworth	Pr.Bot.	Pratt's Bottom	**Wor.Pk.**	**Worcester Park**
Har.	**Harrow**	**Pur.**	**Purley**	View.	Yiewsley
Harling.	Harlington				

1 Canada Sq, E14 .....134 B1
★ 2 Willow Rd, NW3 ....91 H4
30 St. Mary Axe, EC3
 off St. Mary Axe 20 E3
99 Bishopsgate, EC2
 off Bishopsgate 20 D3

A

Aaron Hill Rd, E6 ....116 D5
Abady Ho, SW1
 off Page St 33 J1
Abberley Ms, SW4
 off Cedars Rd 150 B3
Abbess CI, E6
 off Oliver Gdns 116 B5
 SW2 ....169 H1
Abbeville Ms, SW4 ......150 D4
Abbeville Rd, N8
 off Barrington Rd 74 D4
 SW4 ....150 C6
Abbey Av, Wem. HA0 ....105 H2
Abbey Business Cen, SW8
 off Ingate Pl 150 B1
Abbey CI, E5 ....94 D4
 SW8 ....150 D1
 Hayes UB3 ....122 B1
 Northolt UB5
  off Invicta Gro 103 F3
 Pinner HA5 ....66 B3
Abbey Cres, Belv. DA17 .139 G4
Abbeydale Rd, Wem. HA0 .106 A1
Abbey Dr, SW17
 off Church La 168 A5
Abbeyfield CI, Mitch. CR4 .185 H2
Abbeyfield Rd, SE16 ....133 F4
Abbeyfields CI, NW10 ...106 A2
Abbey Gdns, NW8 ....6 C2
 SE16 ....37 J1
 SW1
  off Great Coll St ...26 A5
 W6 ....128 B6
 Chislehurst BR7 ......192 D1
Abbey Gro, SE2 ....138 B4
Abbeyhill Rd, Sid. DA15 .176 C2
Abbey Ind Est, Mitch.
 CR4 ....185 J5
 Wembley HA0 ....105 J1
Abbey La, E15 ....114 C2
 Beckenham BR3 ....172 A1
Abbey Ms, E17
 off Leamington Av 78 A5
 Isleworth TW7 ....144 E1
Abbey Orchard St, SW1 ...25 J5
Abbey Par, SW19
 off Merton High St ...167 F7
 W5 off Hanger La 105 J3
Abbey Pk, Beck. BR3 ....172 A7
Abbey Retail Pk, Bark.
 IG11 ....116 E1
Abbey Rd, E15 ....114 E2
 NW6 ....90 E7
 NW8 ....109 F2
 NW10 ....106 B2
 SE2 ....138 A4
 SW19 ....167 F7
 Barking IG11 ....99 E7
 Belvedere DA17 ......138 D4
 Bexleyheath DA7 .....159 E4
 Croydon CR0 ....201 H3
 Enfield EN1 ....44 B5
 Ilford IG2 ....81 G5
Abbey Rd Est, NW8 .....108 L1
Abbey St, E13 ....115 G4
 SE1 ....28 E5
Abbey Ter, SE2 ....138 C4
Abbey Trd Est, SE26 ....171 J5
Abbey Vw, NW7 ....55 F3
Abbey Wk, W.Mol. KT8 ...179 H3
Abbey Way, SE2 ....138 D3
Abbey Wd Ind Est, Bark.
 IG11 ....117 G2
ABBEY WOOD, SE2 ....138 B3
Abbey Wd Caravan Club Site,
 SE2 ....138 C5
Abbey Wd Rd, SE2 ......138 B4
Abbot Ct, SW8
 off Hartington Rd 130 E7
Abbotsbury CI, E15 ....114 C2
 W14 ....128 C2
  off Abbotsbury Rd ..128 C2
Abbotsbury Gdns, Pnr.
 HA5 ....66 C6
Abbotsbury Ms, SE15 ...153 F3
Abbotsbury Rd, W14 ....128 B2
 Bromley BR2 ....205 F2
 Morden SM4 ....184 E5
Abbots CI, Orp. BR5 ...207 F1
 Ruislip HA4 ....84 D3
Abbots Dr, Har. HA2 ....85 G2
Abbotsford Av, N15 .....75 J4
Abbotsford Gdns, Wdf.Grn.
 IG8 ....63 G7

Abbotsford Rd, Ilf. IG3 .100 A2
Abbots Gdns, N2 ....73 G4
 W8 ....22 A6
Abbots Grn, Croy. CR0 ..203 G6
Abbotshade Rd, SE16 ...133 G1
Abbotshall Av, N14 .....58 C3
Abbotshall Rd, SE6 ....172 D1
Abbots La, SE1 ....28 E2
Abbotsleigh CI, Sutt.
 SM2 ....198 E7
Abbotsleigh Rd, SW16 ..168 C4
Abbots Manor Est, SW1 ..32 D2
Abbotsmede CI, Twick.
 TW1 ....162 C2
Abbots Pk, SW2 ....169 G1
Abbot's PI, NW6 ....108 E1
Abbot's Rd, E6 ....116 A1
Abbots Rd, Edg. HA8 ....54 C7
Abbots Ter, N8 ....74 E6
Abbotstone Rd, SW15 ...147 J3
Abbot St, E8 ....94 C6
Abbots Wk, W8 ....22 A6
Abbots Way, Beck. BR3 ..189 H5
Abbotswell Rd, SE4 ....153 J5
Abbotswood CI, Belv. DA17
 off Coptefield Dr 138 E3
Abbotswood Gdns, Ilf.
 IG5 ....80 C3
Abbotswood Rd, SE22 ...152 B4
 SW16 ....168 D3
Abbotswood Way, Hayes
 UB3 ....122 B1
Abbott Av, SW20 ....184 A2
Abbott CI, Hmptn. TW12 .161 E6
 Northolt UB5 ....85 F6
Abbott Rd, E14 ....114 C5
Abbotts CI, N1
 off Alwyne Rd 93 J6
 SE28 ....118 C7
 Romford RM7 ....83 H3
Abbotts Cres, E4 ....62 D4
 Enfield EN2 ....43 H2
Abbotts Dr, Wem. HA0 ...86 E2
Abbotts Pk Rd, E10 .....78 C7
Abbotts Rd, Barn. EN5 ..40 E4
 Mitcham CR4 ....186 C4
 Southall UB1 ....123 E1
 Sutton SM3 ....198 C3
Abbotts Wk, Bexh. DA7 ..138 D7
Abbotts Wf, E14
 off Stainsby Rd 114 A6
Abchurch La, EC4 ....20 C5
Abchurch Yd, EC4 ....20 C5
Abdale Rd, W12 ....127 H1
Aberavon Rd, E3 ....113 H3
Abercairn Rd, SW16 ....168 C7
Aberconway Rd, Mord.
 SM4 ....184 E3
Abercorn CI, NW7 ....56 B7
 NW8 ....6 C3
Abercorn Cres, Har. HA2 .85 H1
Abercorn Dell, Bushey
 WD23 ....51 J2
Abercorn Gdns, Har. HA3 .69 G7
 Romford RM6 ....82 B6
Abercorn Ms, Rich. TW10
 off Kings Rd 145 J4
Abercorn PI, NW8 ....6 C3
Abercorn Rd, NW7 ......56 B7
 Stanmore HA7 ....53 F7
Abercorn Wk, NW8 ....6 C4
Abercorn Way, SE1 .....37 H3
Abercrombie Dr, Enf. EN1
 off Linwood Cres 44 D1
Abercrombie St, SW11 ..149 H2
Aberdale CI, SE16
 off Poolmans St 133 G2
Aberdare CI, W.Wick.
 BR4 ....204 C2
Aberdare Gdns, NW6 .....91 E7
 NW7 ....56 A7
Aberdeen La, N5 ....93 H5
Aberdeen Par, N18
 off Angel Rd 61 E5
Aberdeen Pk, N5 ....93 H5
Aberdeen Pk Ms, N5 .....93 J4
Aberdeen PI, NW8 ....6 E6
Aberdeen Rd, N5 ....93 J4
 N18 ....60 E5
 NW10 ....89 F5
 Croydon CR0 ....201 J4
 Harrow HA3 ....68 C2
Aberdeen Sq, E14
 off Westferry Circ ...134 A1
Aberdeen Ter, SE3 .....154 D2
Aberdour Rd, Ilf. IG3 ..100 B3
Aberdour St, SE1 ....36 D1
Aberfeldy St, E14 .....114 C6
Aberford Gdns, SE18 ...156 B1
Aberford Rd, Borwd.
 WD6 ....38 A2
Aberfoyle Rd, SW16 ....168 D6

Abergeldie Rd, SE12 ...155 H6
Aberglen Ind Est, Hayes
 UB3 ....121 G2
Abernethy Rd, SE13 ....154 E4
Abersham Rd, E8 ....94 C5
Abery St, SE18 ....137 H4
Ability Twrs, EC1 ......11 J3
Abingdon CI, NW1
 off Camden Ms 92 D6
 SE1 ....37 G3
 SW19 ....167 F6
Abingdon Rd, N3 ....73 F2
 SW16 ....186 E2
 W8 ....128 D3
Abingdon St, SW1 ....26 A5
Abingdon Vil, W8 ......128 D3
Abinger CI, Bark. IG11 .100 A4
 Bromley BR1 ....192 B3
 Croydon (New Adgtn)
  CR0 ....204 C6
 Wallington SM6 ......201 E5
Abinger Gdns, Islw.TW7 .144 B3
Abinger Gro, SE8 ......133 J6
Abinger Ms, W9
 off Warlock Rd 108 D4
Abinger Rd, W4 ....127 E3
Ablett St, SE16 ....133 F5
Abney Gdns, N16
 off Stoke Newington
  High St 94 C2
Aboyne Dr, SW20 ......183 G2
Aboyne Est, SW17 .....167 G3
Aboyne Rd, NW10 ....88 E3
 SW17 ....167 G3
Abraham CI, Wat. WD19 ..50 B4
Abridge Rd, Chig. IG7 ..49 G6
Abridge Way, Bark. IG11 .118 B2
Abyssinia CI, SW11
 off Cairns Rd 149 H4
Abyssinia Rd, SW11
 off Auckland Rd 149 H4
Acacia Av, N17 ....60 A7
 Brentford TW8 ....124 E7
 Mitcham CR4
  off Acacia Rd 186 B2
 Ruislip HA4 ....84 A1
 Wembley HA9 ....87 H5
Acacia CI, SE8 ....133 H4
 SE20 off Selby Rd 188 D2
 Orpington BR5 ....193 G5
 Stanmore HA7 ....52 B6
Acacia Dr, Sutt. SM3 ..198 C1
Acacia Gdns, NW8 ......7 F1
 West Wickham BR4 ...204 C2
Acacia Gro, SE21 .....170 A2
 New Malden KT3 ......182 D3
Acacia Ms, West Dr. (Harm.)
 UB7 ....120 A6
Acacia PI, NW8 ....7 F1
Acacia Rd, E11 ....97 E2
 E17 ....77 H6
 N22 ....75 G1
 NW8 ....7 F1
 SW16 ....187 E1
 W3 ....106 C7
 Beckenham BR3 ......189 J3
 Enfield EN2 ....44 A1
 Hampton TW12 ....161 G6
 Mitcham CR4 ....186 B2
Acacias, The, Barn. EN4 .41 G5
Acacia Way, Sid. DA15 .175 J1
Academia Way, N17 .....60 B6
Academy Ct, Borwd. WD6 .38 A4
Academy Gdns, W8 .....128 D2
 Croydon CR0 ....202 C1
 Northolt UB5 ....102 D2
Academy PI, SE18 .....156 C1
Academy Rd, SE18 .....156 C1
Acanthus Dr, SE1 ......37 H3
Acanthus Rd, SW11 ....150 A3
Accommodation Rd,
 NW11 ....72 C7
A.C. Ct, T.Ditt. KT7
 off Harvest La 180 D6
Ace Par, Chess. KT9
 off Hook Rd 195 H3
Acer Av, Hayes UB4 ....102 E5
Acer Ct, Enf. EN3 ......45 H3
Acfold Rd, SW6 ....148 E1
Achilles CI, SE1 ....37 J3
Achilles Rd, NW6 ....90 D5
Achilles St, SE14 .....133 H7
Achilles Way, W1 ....24 C2
Acklam Rd, W10 ....108 C5
Acklington Dr, NW9 .....70 E1
Ackmar Rd, SW6 ....148 D1
Ackroyd Dr, E3 ....113 J5
Ackroyd Rd, SE23 .....153 G7
Acland CI, SE18
 off Clothworkers Rd ..137 G7
Acland Cres, SE5 .....152 A4
Acland Rd, NW2 ....89 H6
Acle CI, Ilf. IG6 ....65 E7

Acock Gro, Nthlt. UB5 ..85 H4
Acol Cres, Ruis. HA4 ...84 B5
Acol Rd, NW6 ....90 D7
Aconbury Rd, Dag. RM9 .118 B1
Acorn CI, E4 ....62 A5
 Chislehurst BR7 .....175 F5
 Enfield EN2 ....43 H1
 Hampton TW12 ....161 H6
 Stanmore HA7 ....53 E7
Acorn Ct, Ilf. IG2 .....81 H5
Acorn Gdns, SE19 .....188 C1
 W3 ....106 D5
Acorn Gro, Hayes UB3 ..121 J7
Acorn Par, SE15
 off Carlton Gro 132 E7
Acorns, The, Chig. IG7 ..65 H4
Acorn Wk, SE16 ....133 H1
Acorn Way, SE23 ......171 G3
 Beckenham BR3 ......190 C5
 Orpington BR6 ....207 E4
Acorn Dr, SE22 ....152 C4
Acre La, SW2 ....150 E4
 Carshalton SM5 ......200 A4
 Wallington SM6 ......200 A4
Acre Path, Nthlt. UB5
 off Arnold Rd 84 E6
Acre Rd, SW19 ....167 G6
 Dagenham RM10 ......101 H7
 Kingston upon Thames
  KT2 ....181 H1
Acris St, SW18 ....149 F5
ACTON, W3 ....126 A1
Acton Hill Ms, W3
 off Uxbridge Rd 126 B1
Acton Ho, W3 ....106 C6
Acton La, NW10 ....106 E2
 W3 ....126 C2
 W4 ....126 D3
Acton Ms, E8 ....112 C1
Acton Pk Est, W3 .....126 D2
Acton St, WC1 ....10 C4
Acuba Rd, SW18 ......166 E2
Acworth CI, N9 ....45 F7
Ada CI, N11 ....57 J3
Ada Ct, W9 ....6 D4
Ada Gdns, E14 ....114 D6
 E15 ....115 F1
Adair CI, SE25 ....188 E3
Adair Rd, W10 ....108 B4
Adair Twr, W10
 off Appleford Rd 108 B4
Adam & Eve Ct, W1 .....17 G3
Adam & Eve Ms, W8 ....128 D3
Adam CI, SE6 ....171 J4
 SW7 ....30 C1
Adam Meere Ho, E1
 off Tarling St 113 F6
Adam Rd, E4 ....61 J6
Adams CI, N3 ....56 D7
 NW9 ....88 B2
 Surbiton KT5 ....181 J6
Adams Ct, EC2 ....20 C3
Adams Gdns Est, SE16
 off St. Marychurch St .133 F2
Adams Ms, N22 ....59 F7
 SW17 ....167 J2
Adamson Rd, E16 ......115 G6
 NW3 ....91 G7
Adamsrill CI, Enf. EN1 ..44 A6
Adamsrill Rd, SE26 ....171 H4
Adams Rd, N17 ....76 A2
 Beckenham BR3 ......189 H5
Adams Row, W1 ....16 C5
Adams Sq, Bexh. DA6
 off Regency Way 158 E3
Adam St, WC2 ....18 B6
Adams Wk, Kings.T. KT1 .181 H2
Adams Way, Croy. CR0 ..188 C5
Ada PI, E2 ....112 D1
Ada Rd, SE5 ....132 B7
 Wembley HA0 ....87 F3
Adastral Est, NW9 .....70 E1
Ada St, E8 ....112 E1
Adcock Wk, Orp. BR6
 off Borkwood Pk 207 J4
Adderley Gdns, SE9 ...174 D4
Adderley Gro, SW11
 off Culmstock Rd 150 A5
Adderley Rd, Har. HA3 ..68 C1
Adderley St, E14 .....114 C6
ADDINGTON, Croy. CR0 ..203 J5
Addington Ct, SW14 ...146 D3
Addington Dr, N12 .....57 F6
Addington Gro, SE26 ..171 H4

Addington Rd, E3 ....114 A3
E16 ....115 E4
N4 ....75 G6
Croydon CR0 ....201 G1
West Wickham BR4 ...204 E2
Addington Sq, SE5 ....36 A7
Addington St, SE1 ....26 D4
Addington Village Rd, Croy.
CR0 ....204 A5
Addis Cl, Enf. EN3 ....45 G1
ADDISCOMBE, Croy. CR0 .202 C1
Addiscombe Av, Croy.
CR0 ....188 D7
Addiscombe Cl, Har. HA3 .69 F5
Addiscombe Ct Rd, Croy.
CR0 ....202 B1
Addiscombe Gro, Croy.
CR0 ....202 A2
Addiscombe Rd, Croy.
CR0 ....202 B2
Addison Av, N14 ......42 B6
W11 ....128 B1
Hounslow TW3 ....143 J1
Addison Br Pl, W14 ...128 C4
Addison Cl, Nthwd. HA6 ..66 A1
Orpington BR5 ......193 F6
Addison Cres, W14 ...128 B3
Addison Dr, SE12
off Eltham Rd 155 H5
Addison Gdns, W14 ...128 A3
Surbiton KT5 ....181 J4
Addison Gro, W4 .....127 E3
Addison Ind Est, Ruis. HA4
off Field End Rd 85 E4
Addison Pl, W11 ......128 B1
Southall UB1
off Longford Av 103 G7
Addison Rd, E11 ......79 G6
E17 ....78 B5
SE25 ....188 D4
W14 ....128 C3
Bromley BR2 ....191 J5
Enfield EN3 ....45 F1
Ilford IG6 ....81 F1
Teddington TW11 ....162 E6
Addison's Cl, Croy. CR0 .203 J2
Addison Way, NW11 ...72 C4
Hayes UB3 ....102 A6
Addle Hill, EC4 ......19 H5
Addle St, EC2 ....20 A2
Addy Ho, SE16
off Rotherhithe
New Rd 133 F4
Adecroft Way, W.Mol.
KT8 ....179 J3
Adela Av, N.Mal. KT3 ...183 H5
Adelaide Av, SE4 .....153 J4
Adelaide Cl, SW9
off Broughton Dr ...151 G4
Stanmore HA7 ......52 D4
Adelaide Cotts, W7 ...124 C2
Adelaide Ct, E9
off Kenworthy Rd 95 H5
Adelaide Gdns, Rom. RM6 .82 E5
Adelaide Gro, W12 ...127 G1
Adelaide Rd, E10 .....96 B3
NW3 ....91 G7
SW18
off Putney Br Rd ...148 D5
W13 ....124 D1
Chislehurst BR7 ....175 E5
Hounslow TW5 ......142 E1
Ilford IG1 ....99 E2
Richmond TW9 ......145 J4
Southall UB2 ....123 E4
Surbiton KT6 ....181 H5
Teddington TW11 ....162 C6
Adelaide St, WC2 ....18 A6
Adelaide Ter, Brent. TW8 .125 G5
Adela St, W10
off Kensal Rd 108 B4
Adelina Gro, E1 .....113 F5
Adelina Ms, SW12 ...168 D1
Adeline Pl, WC1 ......17 J2
Adeliza Cl, Bark. IG11
off North St 99 F7
Adelphi Ct, SE16
off Poolmans St 133 G2
Adelphi Ter, WC2 .....18 B6
Adeney Cl, W6 ......128 A6
Aden Gro, N16 ......94 A4
Adenmore Rd, SE6 ...154 A7
Aden Rd, Enf. EN3 ....45 H4
Ilford IG1 ....81 E7
Aden Ter, N16 ....94 A4
Adie Rd, W6 ....127 J3
Adine Rd, E13 ....115 H4
Adisham Ho, E5
off Pembury Rd 94 E5
Adler Ind Est, Hayes UB3 .121 G2
Adler St, E1 ....21 H3
Adley St, E5 ....95 H5
Adlington Cl, N18 ....60 A5

Admaston Rd, SE18 ...137 F7
Admiral Ct, NW4
off Barton Cl 71 G5
Admiral Ho, Tedd. TW11
off Twickenham Rd ..162 D4
Admiral Hyson Trd Est, SE16
off Galleywall Rd ...133 E5
SE16 ....133 H1
Admirals Cl, E18 .....79 H4
Admiral Seymour Rd,
SE9 ....156 C4
Admirals Gate, SE10 ..154 B1
Admiral Sq, SW10 ....149 F1
Admiral St, SE8 ......154 A2
Admirals Wk, NW3 ....91 F3
Admirals Way, E14 ....134 A2
Admiralty Cl, SE8
off Reginald Sq 134 A7
West Drayton UB7
off Kingston La 120 C2
Admiralty Way, Tedd.
TW11 ....162 C6
Admiral Wk, W9 ......108 D5
Adolf St, SE6 ....172 B4
Adolphus Rd, N4 .....93 H2
Adolphus St, SE8 ....133 J7
Adomar Rd, Dag. RM8 ..100 D3
Adpar St, W2 ....7 E6
Adrian Av, NW2
off North Circular Rd ..89 H1
Adrian Cl, Barn. EN5 ..40 A6
Adrian Ms, SW10 .....30 B5
Adriatic Bldg, E14
off Narrow St 113 H7
Adrienne Av, Sthl. UB1 .103 F4
Advance Rd, SE27 ....169 J4
Advent Cl, Wdf.Grn. IG8
off Wood La 63 F5
Adventurers Ct, E14
off Newport Av 114 D7
Adys Rd, SE15 ....152 C3
Aegean Apts, E16
off Western Gateway .115 G7
Aerodrome Rd, NW4 ..71 G7
NW9 ....71 F2
Aerodrome Way, Houns.
TW5 ....122 C6
Aeroville, NW9 ......70 E2
Affleck St, N1 ....10 D2
Afghan Rd, SW11 ....149 H2
★ Africa Cen, WC2 ....18 A5
Agamemnon Rd, NW6 ..90 C5
Agar Cl, Surb. KT6 ...195 J2
Agar Gro, NW1 ......92 C7
Agar Gro Est, NW1 ...92 D7
Agar Pl, NW1 ....92 C7
Agar St, WC2 ....18 A6
Agate Cl, E16 ....116 A6
NW10 ....106 A3
Agate Rd, W6 ....127 J3
Agatha Cl, E1
off Prusom St 133 F1
Agaton Rd, SE9 ......175 F2
Agave Rd, NW2 ......89 J4
Agdon St, EC1 ....11 G5
Agincourt Rd, NW3 ...91 J4
Agnes Av, Ilf. IG1 ....98 E4
Agnes Cl, E6 ....116 D7
Agnesfield Cl, N12 ...57 H6
Agnes Gdns, Dag. RM8 .100 D4
Agnes Rd, W3 ......127 F1
Agnes St, E14 ....113 J6
Agnew Rd, SE23 .....153 G7
Agricola Ct, E3
off Parnell Rd 113 J1
Agricola Pl, Enf. EN1 ..44 C5
Aidan Cl, Dag. RM8 ...100 E4
Aileen Wk, E15 ......97 F7
Ailsa Av, Twick. TW1 ..144 D5
Ailsa Rd, Twick. TW1 ..145 E5
Ailsa St, E14 ....114 C5
Ainger Ms, NW3
off Ainger Rd 91 J7
Ainger Rd, NW3 .....91 J7
Ainsdale Cl, Orp. BR6 ..207 G1
Ainsdale Cres, Pnr. HA5 .67 G3
Ainsdale Dr, SE1 .....37 H4
Ainsdale Rd, W5 .....105 G4
Watford WD19 ......50 C3
Ainsley Av, Rom. RM7 ..83 H6
Ainsley Cl, N9 ....60 B1
Ainsley St, E2 ....112 E3
Ainslie Wk, SW12 ....150 B7
Ainslie Wd Cres, E4 ..62 B5
Ainslie Wd Gdns, E4 ..62 B4
Ainslie Wd Rd, E4 ....62 A5
Ainsty Est, SE16 .....133 G2
Ainsworth Cl, NW2 ...89 G3
SE15
off Lyndhurst Gro ...152 B2

Ainsworth Rd, E9 .....95 F7
Croydon CR0 ....201 H2
Ainsworth Way, NW8 ..109 F1
Aintree Av, E6 ....116 B1
Aintree Cres, Ilf. IG6 ..81 F2
Aintree Est, SW6
off Dawes Rd 128 B7
Aintree Rd, Grnf. (Perivale)
UB6 ....105 G2
Aintree St, SW6 .....128 B7
Airco Cl, NW9 ....70 D3
Aird Ct, Hmptn. TW12
off Oldfield Rd 179 F1
Aird Ho, SE1
off Rockingham St ...27 J6
Airdrie Cl, N1 ....93 F7
Hayes UB4
off Glencoe Rd 103 E5
Airedale Av, W4 .....127 F4
Airedale Av S, W4
off Netheravon Rd S .127 F5
Airedale Rd, SW12 ...149 J7
W5 ....125 G3
Airlie Gdns, W8
off Campden Hill Rd .128 D1
Ilford IG1 ....99 E1
Air Links Ind Est, Houns.
TW5 ....122 C5
Air Pk Way, Felt. TW13 ..160 B2
Airport Rbt, E16 ......136 A1
Air St, W1 ....17 G6
Airthrie Rd, Ilf. IG3 ...100 B2
Aisgill Av, W14 ......128 C5
Aisher Rd, SE28 .....118 C7
Aislibie Rd, SE12 ....155 E4
Aiten Pl, W6
off Standish Rd 127 G4
Aitken Cl, E8
off Pownall Rd 112 D1
Mitcham CR4 ....185 J7
Aitken Rd, SE6 ......172 B2
Barnet EN5 ....39 J5
Aitman Dr, Brent. TW8
off Chiswick High Rd .126 A5
Ajax Av, NW9 ....70 E3
Ajax Rd, NW6 ....90 D5
Akabusi Cl, Croy. CR0 ..188 D6
Akehurst St, SW15 ...147 G6
Akenside Rd, NW3 ...91 G5
Akerman Rd, SW9 ...151 H2
Surbiton KT6 ....181 F6
Alabama St, SE18 ...137 G7
Alacross Rd, W5 .....125 F2
Alamaro Lo, SE10
off Renaissance Wk .135 F3
Alandale Dr, Pnr. HA5 ..66 B2
Aland Ct, SE16
off Finland St 133 H3
Alander Ms, E17 .....78 C4
Alba Cl, Hayes UB4
off Ramulis Dr 102 D4
Albacore Cres, SE13 ..154 B6
Alba Gdns, NW11 ....72 B6
Alba Ms, SW18 ......166 D2
Alban Cres, Borwd. WD6 .38 B1
Alban Highwalk, EC2
off London Wall 20 A2
Albany, W1 ....17 G6
Albany, The, Wdf.Grn.
IG8 ....63 F4
Albany Cl, N15 ......75 H4
SW14 ....146 B4
Bexley DA5 ....158 C7
Albany Ct, E4
off Chelwood Cl 46 B6
Albany Ctyd, W1 .....17 G6
Albany Cres, Edg. HA8 ..54 A7
Esher (Clay.) KT10 ..194 B6
Albany Mans, SW11 ..129 H7
Albany Ms, N1
off Barnsbury Pk 93 G7
SE5 ....36 A6
Bromley BR1 ....173 G6
Kingston upon Thames
KT2 ....163 G6
Sutton SM1
off Camden Rd 198 E5
Albany Pk Av, Enf. EN3 ..45 F1
Albany Pk Rd, Kings.T.
KT2 ....163 G6
Albany Pas, Rich. TW10 .145 J5
Albany Pl, Brent. TW8
off Albany Rd 125 H6

Albany Rd, E10 ......78 A7
E12 ....98 A4
E17 ....77 H6
N4 ....75 F6
N18 ....61 E5
SE5 ....36 B6
SE17 ....36 B6
SW19 ....166 E5
W13 ....104 E7
Belvedere DA17 ....139 F6
Bexley DA5 ....158 C7
Brentford TW8 .....125 G6
Chislehurst BR7 ....174 E5
New Malden KT3 ...182 D4
Richmond TW10
off Albert Rd 145 J5
Romford RM6 ......83 F6
Albany St, NW1 ......8 D1
Albany Vw, Buck.H. IG9 ..63 G1
Alba Pl, W11
off Portobello Rd ...108 C6
Albatross Cl, E6 .....116 C4
Albatross St, SE18 ...137 H7
Albatross Way, SE16 ..133 G2
Albemarle, SW19 ....166 A2
Albemarle App, Ilf. IG2 ..81 E6
Albemarle Av, Twick. TW2 .161 F1
Albemarle Gdns, Ilf. IG2 ..81 E6
New Malden KT3 ...182 D4
Albemarle Pk, Stan. HA7
off Marsh La 53 F5
Albemarle Rd, Barn.
(E.Barn.) EN4 ......41 H7
Beckenham BR3 ....190 B1
Albemarle St, W1 ....17 E6
Albemarle Way, EC1 ..11 G6
Alberon Gdns, NW11 ..72 C4
Alberta Av, Sutt. SM1 ..198 B4
Alberta Est, SE17 ....35 H3
Alberta Rd, Enf. EN1 ..44 C6
Erith DA8 ....159 J1
Alberta St, SE17 .....35 G3
Albert Av, E4 ....62 A4
SW8 ....131 F7
Albert Basin, E16 ....117 E7
Albert Basin Way, E16 .117 E7
Albert Bigg Pt, E15 ...114 C1
Albert Br, SW3 ......31 H6
SW11 ....31 H6
Albert Br Rd, SW11 ..31 H7
Albert Carr Gdns, SW16 .168 E5
Albert Cl, E9
off Northiam St 113 E1
N22 ....74 D1
Albert Ct, SW7 ......23 E4
Albert Cres, E4 ......62 A4
Albert Dr, SW19 .....166 B2
Albert Embk, SE1 ....34 B4
Albert Gdns, E1 .....113 G6
Albert Gate, SW1 ....24 A3
Albert Gro, SW20 ....184 A1
Albert Hall Mans, SW7 .23 E4
Albert Ho, SE28
off Erebus Dr 137 F3
Albert Mans, SW11
off Albert Br Rd 149 J1
★ Albert Mem, SW7 ...22 E3
Albert Ms, E14
off Narrow St 113 H7
N4 ....93 H1
SE4 off Arabin Rd ...153 H4
W8 ....22 C5
Albert Pl, N3 ....72 D1
N17 off High Rd 76 C3
W8 ....22 B4
Albert Rd, E10 ......96 C2
E16 ....136 B1
E17 ....78 A5
E18 ....79 H3
N4 ....93 F1
N15 ....76 B6
N22 ....74 C1
NW4 ....72 A4
NW6 ....108 C2
NW7 ....55 F5
SE9 ....174 B3
SE20 ....171 G7
SE25 ....188 D4
W5 ....105 E4
Barnet EN4 ....41 H4
Belvedere DA17 ....139 F5
Bexley DA5 ....159 G6
Bromley BR2 ....192 A4
Buckhurst Hill IG9 ...64 A2
Dagenham RM8 .....101 F1
Hampton (Hmptn H.)
TW12 ....161 J5
Harrow HA2 ....67 J3
Hayes UB3 ....121 H3
Hounslow TW3 .....143 G4

Albert Rd, Ilford IG1 . . . . . . **99** E3
Kingston upon Thames
KT1 . . . . **181** J2
Mitcham CR4 . . . . **185** J3
New Malden KT3 . . . . . **183** F4
Richmond TW10 . . . . . . **145** H5
Southall UB2 . . . . **122** D3
Sutton SM1 . . . . **199** G5
Teddington TW11 . . . . . **162** C6
Twickenham TW1 . . . . . **162** C1
West Drayton UB7 . . . . **120** B1
Albert Rd Est, Belv.
DA17 . . . . **139** F5
Albert Sleet Ct, N9
off Colthurst Dr **60** E3
Albert Sq, E15 . . . . **97** E5
SW8 . . . . **131** F7
Albert St, N12 . . . . **57** F5
NW1 . . . . **110** B1
Albert Ter, NW1 . . . . **110** A1
NW10 . . . . **106** D1
W6 *off Beavor La* **127** G5
Buckhurst Hill IG9 . . . . . . **64** A2
Albert Ter Ms, NW1
off Regents Pk Rd **110** A1
Albert Way, SE15 . . . . **132** E7
Albion Av, N10 . . . . **74** A1
SW8 . . . . **150** D2
Albion Cl, W2 . . . . **15** H5
Albion Dr, E8 . . . . **94** C7
Albion Est, SE16 . . . . **133** F2
Albion Gro, N16 . . . . **94** B4
Albion Hill, Loug. IG10 . . . . **47** J5
Albion Ms, N1 . . . . **111** G1
NW6
off Kilburn High Rd . . . **90** C7
W2 . . . . **15** H4
W6 *off Galena Rd* **127** H4
Albion Par, N16
off Albion Rd **94** A4
Albion Pk, Loug. IG10 . . . . . **48** A5
Albion Pl, EC1 . . . . **19** G1
SE25 . . . . **188** D3
W6 . . . . **127** H4
Albion Riverside Bldg,
SW11 . . . . **31** H7
Albion Rd, E17 . . . . **78** C3
N16 . . . . **94** A4
N17 . . . . **76** C2
Bexleyheath DA6 . . . . . **159** F4
Hounslow TW3 . . . . **143** G4
Kingston upon Thames
KT2 . . . . **182** C1
Sutton SM2 . . . . **199** G6
Twickenham TW2 . . . . . **162** B1
Albion Sq, E8 . . . . **94** C7
Albion St, SE16 . . . . **133** F2
W2 . . . . **15** H4
Croydon CR0 . . . . **201** H1
Albion Ter, E8 . . . . **94** C7
Albion Vil Rd, SE26 . . . . . . **171** F3
Albion Wk, N1 . . . . **10** B2
Albion Way, EC1 . . . . **19** J2
SE13 . . . . **154** C4
Wembley HA9
off North End Rd **88** B3
Albion Yd, N1 . . . . **10** B2
Albon Ho, SW18
off Neville Gill Cl **148** E6
Albrighton Rd, SE22 . . . . . **152** B3
Albuhera Cl, Enf. EN2 . . . . . **43** G1
Albury Av, Bexh. DA7 . . . . **158** E2
Isleworth TW7 . . . . **124** C7
Albury Cl, Hmptn. TW12 . . **161** G6
Albury Ct, Sutt. SM1
off Ripley Gdns **199** F4
Albury Dr, Pnr. HA5 . . . . . . **50** D7
Albury Ms, E12 . . . . **97** J1
Albury Rd, Chess. KT9 . . . **195** H5
Albury St, SE8 . . . . **134** A6
Albyfield, Brom. BR1 . . . . **192** C3
Albyn Rd, SE8 . . . . **154** A1
Alcester Cres, E5 . . . . **95** E2
Alcester Rd, Wall. SM6 . . . **200** B4
Alcock Cl, Wall. SM6 . . . . . **200** D7
Alcock Rd, Houns. TW5 . . **122** D7
Alconbury Rd, E5 . . . . **94** D2
Alcorn Cl, Sutt. SM3 . . . . . **198** D2
Alcott Cl, W7
off Westcott Cres **104** C5
Alcuin Ct, Stan. HA7
off Old Ch La **53** F7
ALDBOROUGH HATCH, Ilf.
IG2 . . . . **81** H3
Aldborough Rd, Dag.
RM10 . . . . **101** J6
Aldborough Rd N, Ilf. IG2 . **81** J5
Aldborough Rd S, Ilf. IG3 . . **99** H1
Aldbourne Rd, W12 . . . . . . **127** F1
Aldbridge St, SE17 . . . . **36** E3
Aldburgh Ms, W1 . . . . **16** C3
Aldbury Av, Wem. HA9 . . . . **88** B7
Aldbury Ms, N9 . . . . **44** A7
Aldebert Ter, SW8 . . . . **131** E7
Aldeburgh Cl, E5
off Southwold Rd **95** E2
Aldeburgh Pl, SE10
off Aldeburgh St **135** G4
Woodford Green IG8 . . . **63** G4
Aldeburgh St, SE10 . . . . . **135** G5
Alden Av, E15 . . . . **115** F3
Aldenham St, NW1 . . . . **9** G2
Aldensley Rd, W6 . . . . **127** H3
Alderbrook Rd, SW12 . . . . **150** B6
Alderbury Rd, SW13 . . . . . **127** G6
Alder Cl, SE15 . . . . **37** G6
Erith DA18
off Waldrist Way **139** F2
Alder Ct, N11
off Cline Rd **58** C6
Alder Gro, NW2 . . . . **89** H2
Aldergrove Gdns, Houns.
TW3 *off Bath Rd* **142** E2
Alder Ho, NW3
off Maitland Pk Vil **91** J6
Alderman Av, Bark. IG11 . . **118** A3
Aldermanbury, EC2 . . . . . . **20** A3
Aldermanbury Sq, EC2 . . . . **20** A2
Alderman Judge Mall,
Kings.T. KT1
off Eden St **181** H2
Aldermans Hill, N13 . . . . . . **58** E4
Alderman's Wk, EC2 . . . . . . **20** D2
Aldermary Rd, Brom.
BR1 . . . . **191** G1
Alder Ms, N19
off Bredgar Rd **92** C2
Aldermoor Rd, SE6 . . . . . . **171** J3
Alderney Av, Houns. TW5 . **123** H7
Alderney Gdns, Nthlt.
UB5 . . . . **85** F7
Alderney Ho, N1
off Arran Wk **93** J6
Alderney Ms, SE1 . . . . **28** B5
Alderney Rd, E1 . . . . **113** G4
Alderney St, SW1 . . . . **32** E3
Alder Rd, SW14 . . . . **146** D3
Sidcup DA14 . . . . **175** J3
Alders, The, N21 . . . . **43** G6
SW16 . . . . **168** C4
Feltham TW13 . . . . **160** E4
Hounslow TW5 . . . . **123** F6
West Wickham BR4 . . . . **204** B1
Alders Av, Wdf.Grn. IG8 . . . **62** E6
ALDERSBROOK, E12 . . . . . . **97** H2
Aldersbrook Av, Enf. EN1 . . **44** B2
Aldersbrook Dr, Kings.T.
KT2 . . . . **163** J6
Aldersbrook La, E12 . . . . . . **98** C3
Aldersbrook Rd, E11 . . . . . . **97** H2
E12 . . . . **98** A3
Alders Cl, E11 . . . . **97** H2
W5 . . . . **125** G3
Edgware HA8 . . . . **54** C5
Aldersey Gdns, Bark.
IG11 . . . . **99** G6
Aldersford Cl, SE4 . . . . . . **153** G5
Aldersgate St, EC1 . . . . **19** J3
Alders Gro, E.Mol. KT8
off Esher Rd **180** A5
Aldersgrove Av, SE9 . . . . . **173** J3
Aldershot Rd, NW6 . . . . . . **108** C1
Aldersmead Av, Croy.
CR0 . . . . **189** G6
Aldersmead Rd, Beck.
BR3 . . . . **171** H7
Alderson Pl, Sthl. UB2 . . . **123** J1
Alderson St, W10
off Kensal Rd **108** B4
Alders Rd, Edg. HA8 . . . . . . **54** C5
Alderton Cl, NW10 . . . . **88** D3
Loughton IG10 . . . . **48** D4
Alderton Cres, NW4 . . . . . . **71** H5
Alderton Hall La, Loug.
IG10 . . . . **48** D4
Alderton Hill, Loug. IG10 . . **48** B5
Alderton Ms, Loug. IG10
off Alderton Hall La . . . **48** D4
Alderton Ri, Loug. IG10 . . . **48** D4
Alderton Rd, SE24 . . . . . . **151** J3
Croydon CR0 . . . . **188** C7
Alderton Way, NW4 . . . . **71** H5
Loughton IG10 . . . . **48** C5
Alderville Rd, SW6 . . . . . . **148** C2
Alder Wk, Ilf. IG1 . . . . **99** F5
Alderwick Dr, Houns.
TW3 . . . . **144** A3
Alderwood Rd, SE9 . . . . . **157** G6
Aldford St, W1 . . . . **24** B1
Aldgate, EC3 . . . . **21** F4
Aldgate Av, E1 . . . . **21** F3
Aldgate Barrs Shop Cen,
E1 . . . . **21** G3
Aldgate High St, EC3 . . . . . **21** F4
Aldine Ct, W12
off Aldine St **127** J1
Aldine Pl, W12
off Uxbridge Rd **127** J2
Aldine St, W12 . . . . **127** J2
Aldington Cl, Dag. RM8 . . . **82** C7
Aldington Rd, SE18 . . . . . **136** A3
Aldis Ms, SW17 . . . . **167** H5
Aldis St, SW17 . . . . **167** H5
Aldred Rd, NW6 . . . . **90** D5
Aldren Rd, SW17 . . . . **167** F3
Aldriche Way, E4 . . . . **62** C6
Aldrich Gdns, Sutt. SM3 . . **198** C3
Aldrich Ter, SW18
off Lidiard Rd **167** F2
Aldridge Av, Edg. HA8 . . . . **54** B3
Ruislip HA4 . . . . **84** D2
Stanmore HA7 . . . . **69** H1
Aldridge Ri, N.Mal. KT3 . . **182** E7
Aldridge Rd Vil, W11 . . . . **108** C5
Aldridge Wk, N14 . . . . **42** E7
Aldrien Ct, N9
off Galahad Rd **60** D3
Aldrington Rd, SW16 . . . . **168** C5
Aldsworth Cl, W9 . . . . **6** A6
Aldwick Cl, SE9 . . . . **175** G3
Aldwick Rd, Croy. CR0 . . . **201** F3
Aldworth Gro, SE13 . . . . . **154** C6
Aldworth Rd, E15 . . . . **96** E7
Aldwych, WC2 . . . . **18** C5
Aldwych Av, Ilf. IG6 . . . . . . **81** F4
Aldwych Underpass, WC2
off Kingsway **18** C4
Alers Rd, Bexh. DA6 . . . . . **158** D5
Alesia Cl, N22 . . . . **59** E7
Alestan Beck Rd, E16 . . . . **116** A5
Alexa Ct, W8 . . . . **30** A1
Sutton SM2
off Mulgrave Rd **198** D6
Alexander Av, NW10 . . . . . . **89** H7
Alexander Cl, Barn. EN4 . . **41** G4
Bromley BR2 . . . . **205** G1
Sidcup DA15 . . . . **157** H5
Southall UB2 . . . . **123** J1
Twickenham TW2 . . . . . **162** C2
Alexander Evans Ms, SE23
off Sunderland Rd . . . **171** G1
★ **Alexander Fleming Laboratory Mus**, W2 . . **15** F3
Alexander Ho, Kings.T. KT2
off Kingsgate Rd **181** H1
Alexander Ms, SW16 . . . . **168** C5
W2 . . . . **14** A3
Alexander Pl, SW7 . . . . **31** G1
Alexander Rd, N19 . . . . **92** E3
Bexleyheath DA7 . . . . . **158** D2
Chislehurst BR7 . . . . . . **175** E5
Alexander Sq, SW3 . . . . . . **31** G1
Alexander St, W2 . . . . **108** D6
Alexandra Av, N22 . . . . **74** D1
SW11 . . . . **150** A1
W4 . . . . **126** D7
Harrow HA2 . . . . **85** F1
Southall UB1 . . . . **103** F7
Sutton SM1 . . . . **198** D3
Alexandra Cl, SE8 . . . . **133** J6
Harrow HA2
off Alexandra Av **85** G3
Alexandra Cotts, SE14 . . . . **153** J1
Alexandra Ct, N14 . . . . **42** C5
N16 . . . . **94** B4
W9 . . . . **6** D5
Wembley HA9 . . . . **87** J4
Alexandra Cres, Brom.
BR1 . . . . **173** F6
Alexandra Dr, SE19 . . . . . **170** B5
Surbiton KT5 . . . . **182** A7
Alexandra Gdns, N10 . . . . . **74** B4
W4 . . . . **126** E7
Hounslow TW3 . . . . **143** H2
Alexandra Gro, N4 . . . . **93** H1
N12 . . . . **57** E5
Alexandra Ms, N2 . . . . **73** J3
SW19
off Alexandra Rd **166** C6
★ **Alexandra Palace**,
N22 . . . . **74** D2
Alexandra Palace Way,
N22 . . . . **74** C3
Alexandra Pk Rd, N10 . . . . . **74** B2
N22 . . . . **74** D2
Alexandra Pl, NW8 . . . . . . **109** F1
SE25 . . . . **188** A5
Croydon CR0
off Alexandra Rd **202** B1
Alexandra Rd, E6 . . . . **116** D3
E10 . . . . **96** C3
E17 . . . . **77** J6
E18 . . . . **79** H3
N8 . . . . **75** G3
N9 . . . . **44** E7
N10 . . . . **58** B6
N15 . . . . **76** A5
NW4 . . . . **72** A4
NW8 . . . . **91** F7
Alexandra Rd, SE26 . . . . . **171** G6
SW14 . . . . **146** D3
SW19 . . . . **166** C6
W4 . . . . **126** D2
Brentford TW8 . . . . **125** G6
Croydon CR0 . . . . **202** B1
Enfield EN3 . . . . **45** G4
Hounslow TW3 . . . . **143** H2
Kingston upon Thames
KT2 . . . . **164** A7
Mitcham CR4 . . . . **167** H7
Richmond TW9 . . . . **145** J2
Romford (Chad.Hth)
RM6 . . . . **82** D6
Thames Ditton KT7 . . . . **180** C5
Twickenham TW1 . . . . . **145** F6
Alexandra Sq, Mord.
SM4 . . . . **184** D5
Alexandra St, E16 . . . . **115** G5
SE14 . . . . **133** H7
Alexandra Wk, SE19 . . . . . **170** B5
Alexandria Rd, W13 . . . . . **104** D7
Alexis St, SE16 . . . . **37** H1
Alfearn Rd, E5 . . . . **95** F4
Alford Grn, Croy.
(New Adgtn) CR0 . . . . . **204** D6
Alford Ho, N6 . . . . **74** C6
Alford Pl, N1 . . . . **12** A2
Alfoxton Av, N15 . . . . **75** H4
Alfreda St, SW11 . . . . **150** B1
Alfred Cl, W4
off Belmont Ter **126** D4
Alfred Gdns, Sthl. UB1 . . . **103** E7
Alfred Ms, W1 . . . . **17** H1
Alfred Pl, WC1 . . . . **17** H1
Alfred Prior Ho, E12 . . . . . . **98** D4
Alfred Rd, E15 . . . . **97** F5
SE25 . . . . **188** D5
W2 . . . . **108** D5
W3 . . . . **126** C1
Belvedere DA17 . . . . . . **139** F5
Buckhurst Hill IG9 . . . . . . **64** A2
Feltham TW13 . . . . **160** C2
Kingston upon Thames
KT1 . . . . **181** H3
Sutton SM1 . . . . **199** F5
Alfred's Gdns, Bark. IG11 . **117** H2
Alfred St, E3 . . . . **113** J3
Alfreds Way, Bark. IG11 . . . **117** F3
Alfreds Way Ind Est, Bark.
IG11 . . . . **118** A1
Alfreton Cl, SW19 . . . . **166** A3
Alfriston, Surb. KT5 . . . . . **181** J5
Alfriston Av, Croy. CR0 . . . **186** E7
Harrow HA2 . . . . **67** G6
Alfriston Cl, Surb. KT5 . . . **181** J6
Alfriston Rd, SW11 . . . . . . **149** J5
Algar Cl, Islw. TW7
off Algar Rd **144** D3
Stanmore HA7 . . . . **52** C5
Algar Rd, Islw. TW7 . . . . . . **144** D3
Algarve Rd, SW18 . . . . **167** E1
Algernon Rd, NW4 . . . . **71** G6
NW6 . . . . **108** D1
SE13 . . . . **154** B4
Algers Cl, Loug. IG10 . . . . . **48** A5
Algers Mead, Loug. IG10 . . **48** A5
Algers Rd, Loug. IG10 . . . . . **48** A5
Algiers Rd, SE13 . . . . **154** A4
Alibon Gdns, Dag. RM10 . **101** G5
Alibon Rd, Dag. RM9,
RM10 . . . . **101** F5
Alice Cl, Barn.
(New Barn.) EN5 . . . . **41** F4
Alice Ct, SW15
off Deodar Rd **148** C4
Alice Gilliatt Ct, W14 . . . . **128** C6
Alice La, E3 . . . . **113** J1
Alice Ms, Tedd. TW11
off Luther Rd **162** C5
Alice St, SE1 . . . . **28** D6
Alice Thompson Cl,
SE12 . . . . **173** J2
Alice Wk, W5
off Queens Wk **105** F5
Alice Walker Cl, SE24
off Shakespeare Rd . . **151** H4
Alice Way, Houns. TW3 . . . **143** H4
Alicia Av, Har. HA3 . . . . **69** E4
Alicia Cl, Har. HA3 . . . . **69** F4
Alicia Gdns, Har. HA3 . . . . . **69** E4
Alie St, E1 . . . . **21** G4
Alington Cres, NW9 . . . . . . **88** C1
Alison Cl, E6 . . . . **116** D6
Croydon CR0
off Shirley Oaks Rd . . **203** G1
Aliwal Rd, SW11 . . . . **149** H4
Alkerden Rd, W4 . . . . **127** E5
Alkham Rd, N16 . . . . **94** C2
Allan Barclay Cl, N15
off High Rd **76** C6
Allan Cl, N.Mal. KT3 . . . . . **182** D5
Allandale Av, N3 . . . . **72** B3

Allan Way, W3 **106** C5
Allard Cres, Bushey (Bushey Hth) WD23 **51** J1
Allard Gdns, SW4 **150** D5
Allardyce St, SW4 **151** F4
Allbrook Cl, Tedd. TW11 **162** B5
Allcroft Rd, NW5 **92** A5
Allder Way, S.Croy. CR2 **201** H7
Allenby Cl, Grnf. UB6 **103** G3
Allenby Rd, SE23 **171** H3
SE28 **137** F3
Southall UB1 **103** G6
Allen Cl, Mitch. CR4 **186** B1
Sunbury-on-Thames TW16 **178** B1
Allen Ct, Grnf. UB6 **86** C5
Allendale Av, Sthl. UB1 **103** G6
Allendale Cl, SE5 *off Daneville Rd* **152** A1
SE26 **171** G5
Allendale Rd, Grnf. UB6 **86** E6
Allen Edwards Dr, SW8 **150** E1
Allenford Ho, SW15 *off Tunworth Cres* **147** F6
Allen Pl, Twick. TW1 *off Church St* **162** D1
Allen Rd, E3 **113** J2
N16 **94** B4
Beckenham BR3 **189** G2
Croydon CR0 **187** F7
Sunbury-on-Thames TW16 **178** B1
Allensbury Pl, NW1 **92** D7
Allens Rd, Enf. EN3 **45** F5
Allen St, W8 **128** D3
Allenswood, SW19 *off Albert Dr* **166** B1
Allenswood Rd, SE9 **156** B3
Allerford Ct, Har. HA2 **67** H5
Allerford Rd, SE6 **172** B4
Allerton Ct, NW4 *off Holders Hill Rd* **72** A2
Allerton Rd, N16 **93** J2
Allerton Wk, N7 *off Durham Rd* **93** F2
Allestree Rd, SW6 **128** B7
Alleyn Cres, SE21 **170** A2
Alleyndale Rd, Dag. RM8 **100** C2
Alleyn Pk, SE21 **170** A2
Southall UB2 **123** F4
Alleyn Rd, SE21 **170** A3
Allfarthing La, SW18 **149** E6
Allgood Cl, Mord. SM4 **184** A6
Allgood St, E2 **13** G2
Allhallows La, EC4 **20** B6
★ **All Hallows-on-the-Wall C of E Ch**, EC2 **20** C2
Allhallows Rd, E6 **116** B5
All Hallows Rd, N17 **76** B1
Alliance Cl, Houns. TW4 *off Vickers Way* **143** F5
Wembley HA0 **87** G4
Alliance Ct, W3 *off Alliance Rd* **106** B5
Alliance Rd, E13 **115** J4
SE18 **138** A6
W3 **106** B4
Allied Ct, N1 *off Enfield Rd* **94** B7
Allied Way, W3 *off Larden Rd* **127** E2
Allingham Cl, W7 **104** C7
Allingham Ms, N1 **11** J1
Allingham St, N1 **11** J1
Allington Av, N17 **60** B6
Allington Cl, SW19 *off High St Wimbledon* **166** A5
Greenford UB6 **85** J7
Allington Ct, Enf. EN3 **45** G5
Allington Rd, NW4 **71** H5
W10 **108** B2
Harrow HA2 **67** J5
Orpington BR6 **207** G2
Allington St, SW1 **25** F6
Allison Cl, SE10 *off Dartmouth Hill* **154** C1
Allison Gro, SE21 **170** B1
Allison Rd, N8 **75** G5
W3 **106** C6
Allitsen Rd, NW8 **7** G2
Allnutt Way, SW4 **150** D5
Alloa Rd, SE8 **133** G5
Ilford IG3 **100** A2
Allonby Gdns, Wem. HA9 **87** F1
Allonby Ho, E14 *off Aston St* **113** H5
Allotment Way, NW2 *off Midland Ter* **90** A3
Alloway Rd, E3 **113** H3
Allport Ms, E1 *off Stepney Grn* **113** F4
All Saints Cl, N9 **60** C2
SW8 *off Lansdowne Way* **150** E1
All Saints Dr, SE3 **155** E2
All Saints Ms, Har. HA3 **52** B6
All Saints Pas, SW18 *off Wandsworth High St* **148** D5
All Saints Rd, SW19 **167** F7
W3 **126** C3
W11 **108** C5
Sutton SM1 **199** E3
All Saints St, N1 **10** C1
All Saints Twr, E10 **78** B7
Allsop Pl, NW1 **8** A6
All Souls Av, NW10 **107** H2
All Souls Pl, W1 **17** E2
Allum Way, N20 **57** F1
Allwood Cl, SE26 **171** G4
Alma Av, E4 **62** C7
Almack Rd, E5 **95** F4
Alma Cres, Sutt. SM1 **198** B5
Alma Gro, SE1 **37** G2
Alma Pl, NW10 *off Harrow Rd* **107** H3
SE19 **170** C7
Thornton Heath CR7 **187** G5
Alma Rd, N10 **58** A7
SW18 **149** F5
Carshalton SM5 **199** H5
Enfield EN3 **45** H5
Esher KT10 **194** B1
Sidcup DA14 **176** A3
Southall UB1 **102** E7
Alma Row, Har. HA3 **68** A1
Alma Sq, NW8 **6** D3
Alma St, E15 **96** D6
NW5 **92** B6
Alma Ter, SW18 **149** G7
W8 *off Allen St* **128** D3
Almeida St, N1 **93** H7
Almeric Rd, SW11 **149** J4
Almer Rd, SW20 **165** G7
Almington St, N4 **93** F1
Almond Av, W5 **125** H3
Carshalton SM5 **199** J2
West Drayton UB7 **120** D3
Almond Cl, SE15 **152** D2
Bromley BR2 **192** D7
Feltham TW13 *off Highfield Rd* **160** A1
Almond Gro, Brent. TW8 **124** E7
Almond Rd, N17 **60** D7
SE16 **133** E4
Almonds Av, Buck.H. IG9 **63** G2
Almond Way, Borwd. WD6 **38** B4
Bromley BR2 **192** D7
Harrow HA2 **67** H2
Mitcham CR4 **186** D5
Almorah Rd, N1 **94** A7
Hounslow TW5 **142** D1
Alnwick Gro, Mord. SM4 *off Bordesley Rd* **184** E4
Alnwick Rd, E16 **115** J6
SE12 **155** H7
ALPERTON, Wem. HA0 **105** J1
Alperton La, Grnf. (Perivale) UB6 **105** G3
Wembley HA0 **105** G3
Alperton St, W10 **108** B4
Alphabet Gdns, Cars. SM5 **185** G6
Alphabet Sq, E3 *off Hawgood St* **114** A5
Alpha Cl, NW1 **7** H5
Alpha Gro, E14 **134** A2
Alpha Pl, NW6 **108** D2
SW3 **31** H5
Alpha Rd, E4 **62** B3
N18 **60** D6
SE14 **153** J1
Croydon CR0 **202** B1
Enfield EN3 **45** H4
Surbiton KT5 **181** J6
Teddington TW11 **162** A5
Alpha St, SE15 **152** D2
Alphea Cl, SW19 **167** H7
Alpine Av, Surb. KT5 **196** C2
Alpine Cl, Croy. CR0 **202** B3
Alpine Copse, Brom. BR1 **192** D2
Alpine Gro, E9 **95** F7
Alpine Rd, E10 **96** B2
SE16 **133** F4
Walton-on-Thames KT12 **178** A7
Alpine Vw, Cars. SM5 **199** H5
Alpine Wk, Stan. HA7 **52** B2
Alpine Way, E6 **116** D5
Alric Av, NW10 **88** D7
New Malden KT3 **183** E3
Alroy Rd, N4 **75** G7
Alsace Rd, SE17 **36** D3
Alscot Rd, SE1 **37** G1
Alscot Way, SE1 **37** F1
Alsike Rd, SE2 **138** D3
Erith DA18 **138** E3
Alsom Av, Wor.Pk. KT4 **197** G4
Alston Cl, Surb. (Long Dit.) KT6 **181** E7
Alston Rd, N18 **60** E5
SW17 **167** G4
Barnet EN5 **40** B3
Alston Wks, Barn. EN5 **40** B3
Altair Cl, N17 **60** C6
Altash Way, SE9 **174** C2
Altenburg Av, W13 **125** E3
Altenburg Gdns, SW11 **149** J4
Alt Gro, SW19 *off St. George's Rd* **166** C7
Altham Gdns, Wat. WD19 **50** D4
Altham Rd, Pnr. HA5 **51** E7
Althea St, SW6 **149** E2
Althorne Gdns, E18 **79** F4
Althorne Way, Dag. RM10 **101** G2
Althorp Cl, Barn. EN5 **39** G7
Althorpe Gro, SW11 *off Westbridge Rd* **149** G1
Althorpe Ms, SW11 *off Battersea High St* **149** G1
Althorpe Rd, Har. HA1 **67** J5
Althorp Rd, SW17 **167** J1
Altima Ct, SE22 *off East Dulwich Rd* **152** D4
Altmore Av, E6 **98** C7
Alton Av, Stan. HA7 **52** C7
Alton Cl, Bex. DA5 **177** E1
Isleworth TW7 **144** C2
Alton Gdns, Beck. BR3 **172** A7
Twickenham TW2 **144** A7
Alton Ho, E3 *off Bromley High St* **114** B3
Alton Rd, N17 **76** A3
SW15 **165** G1
Croydon CR0 **201** G3
Richmond TW9 **145** H4
Alton St, E14 **114** B5
Altyre Cl, Beck. BR3 **189** J5
Altyre Rd, Croy. CR0 **202** A2
Altyre Way, Beck. BR3 **189** J5
Alvanley Gdns, NW6 **90** E5
Alva Way, Wat. WD19 **50** D2
Alverstone Av, SW19 **166** D2
Barnet (E.Barn.) EN4 **41** H7
Alverstone Gdns, SE9 **175** F1
Alverstone Rd, E12 **98** D4
NW2 **89** J7
New Malden KT3 **183** F4
Wembley HA9 **87** J1
Alverston Gdns, SE25 **188** B5
Alverton St, SE8 **133** J5
Alveston Av, Har. HA3 **68** E3
Alveston Sq, E18 *off Marlborough Rd* **79** G2
Alvey Est, SE17 **36** D2
Alvey St, SE17 **36** D3
Alvia Gdns, Sutt. SM1 **199** F4
Alvington Cres, E8 **94** C5
Alway Av, Epsom KT19 **196** C5
Alwold Cres, SE12 **155** H6
Alwyn Av, W4 **126** D5
Alwyn Cl, Croy. (New Adgtn) CR0 **204** B7
Alwyne La, N1 *off Alwyne Vil* **93** H7
Alwyne Pl, N1 **93** J6
Alwyne Rd, N1 **93** J7
SW19 **166** C6
W7 **104** B7
Alwyne Sq, N1 **93** J6
Alwyne Vil, N1 **93** H7
Alwyn Gdns, NW4 **71** G4
W3 **106** B6
Alyth Gdns, NW11 **72** D6
Alzette Ho, E2 **113** G3
Amalgamated Dr, Brent. TW8 **124** D6
Amanda Cl, Chig. IG7 **65** G6
Amanda Ms, Rom. RM7 **83** J5
Amazon Apts, N8 *off New River Av* **75** F4
Amazon St, E1 *off Hessel St* **112** E6
Ambassador Cl, Houns. TW3 **142** E2
Ambassador Gdns, E6 **116** C5
Ambassador's Ct, SW1 **25** G2
Ambassador Sq, E14 *off Cahir St* **134** B4
Amber Av, E17 **77** H1
Amber Ct, SW17 **168** A4
Amberden Av, N3 **72** D3
Ambergate St, SE17 **35** H3
Amber Gro, NW2 **90** A1
Amber La, Ilf. IG6 **64** E7
Amberley Cl, Orp. BR6 **207** J5
Pinner HA5 **67** F3
Amberley Ct, Sid. DA14 **176** C5
Amberley Gdns, Enf. EN1 **44** B7
Epsom KT19 **197** F4
Amberley Gro, SE26 **170** E4
Croydon CR0 **188** C7
Amberley Rd, E10 **78** A7
N13 **59** F2
SE2 **138** D6
W9 **108** D5
Buckhurst Hill IG9 **63** J1
Enfield EN1 **44** C7
Amberley Way, Houns. TW4 **142** C5
Morden SM4 **184** C7
Romford RM7 **83** H4
Amber Ms, N22 *off Brampton Pk Rd* **75** G3
Amberside Cl, Islw. TW7 **144** A6
Amber St, E15 *off Great Eastern Rd* **96** D6
Amber Wf, E2 *off Nursery La* **112** C1
Amberwood Cl, Wall. SM6 **200** E5
Amberwood Ri, N.Mal. KT3 **182** E6
Amblecote Cl, SE12 **173** H3
Amblecote Meadows, SE12 **173** H3
Amblecote Rd, SE12 **173** H3
Ambler Rd, N4 **93** H3
Ambleside, SW19 *off Albert Dr* **166** B1
Bromley BR1 **172** D6
Ambleside Av, SW16 **168** D4
Beckenham BR3 **189** H5
Ambleside Cl, E9 *off Churchill Wk* **95** F5
E10 **78** B7
N17 *off Drapers Rd* **76** C3
Ambleside Cres, Enf. EN3 **45** G3
Ambleside Gdns, SW16 **168** D5
Ilford IG4 **80** B4
Sutton SM2 **199** F6
Wembley HA9 **87** G1
Ambleside Pt, SE15 *off Ilderton Rd* **133** F7
Ambleside Rd, NW10 **89** F7
Bexleyheath DA7 **159** G2
Ambrooke Rd, Belv. DA17 **139** G3
Ambrosden Av, SW1 **25** G6
Ambrose Av, NW11 **72** B7
Ambrose Cl, E6 *off Lovage App* **116** B5
Orpington BR6 *off Stapleton Rd* **207** J3
Ambrose Ms, SW11 **149** H2
Ambrose St, SE16 **132** E4
Ambrose Wk, E3 *off Malmesbury Rd* **114** A2
Amelia Cl, W3 **126** B1
Amelia St, SE17 **35** H3
Amen Cor, EC4 **19** H4
SW17 **167** J6
Amen Ct, EC4 **19** H3
Amenity Way, Mord. SM4 **183** J7
America Sq, EC3 **21** F5
America St, SE1 **27** J2
Amerland Rd, SW18 **148** C6
Amersham Av, N18 **60** A6
Amersham Gro, SE14 **133** J7
Amersham Rd, SE14 **133** J7
Croydon CR0 **187** J6
Amersham Vale, SE14 **133** J7
Amery Gdns, NW10 **107** H1
Amery Rd, Har. HA1 **86** D2
Amesbury Av, SW2 **169** E2
Amesbury Cl, Wor.Pk. KT4 **197** J1
Amesbury Dr, E4 **46** B6
Amesbury Rd, Brom. BR1 **192** A3
Dagenham RM9 **100** D7
Feltham TW13 **160** D2
Amesbury Twr, SW8 *off Westbury St* **150** C2
Amethyst Cl, N11 **58** D7
Amethyst Ct, Enf. EN3 *off Enstone Rd* **45** H3
Amethyst Rd, E15 **96** D4
Amherst Av, W13 **105** F6
Amherst Dr, Orp. BR5 **193** J4
Amherst Rd, W13 **105** F6
Amhurst Gdns, Islw. TW7 **144** C1
Amhurst Par, N16 *off Amhurst Pk* **76** C7
Amhurst Pk, N16 **76** A7
Amhurst Pas, E8 **94** D4

Amhurst Rd, E8 ... **94** E5
N16 ... **94** C4
Amhurst Ter, E8 ... **94** D4
Amhurst Wk, SE28
off Roman Sq ... **138** A1
Amidas Gdns, Dag. RM8 ... **100** B4
Amiel St, E1 ... **113** F4
Amies St, SW11 ... **149** J3
Amina Way, SE16 ... **29** H6
Amis Av, Epsom KT19 ... **196** B6
Amity Gro, SW20 ... **183** J1
Amity Rd, E15 ... **115** F1
Ammanford Grn, NW9
off Ruthin Cl ... **70** E6
Amner Rd, SW11 ... **150** A6
Amor Rd, W6 ... **127** J3
Amott Rd, SE15 ... **152** D3
Amoy Pl, E14 ... **114** A6
Ampere Way, Croy. CR0 ... **187** E7
Ampleforth Rd, SE2 ... **138** B2
Ampthill Sq Est, NW1 ... **9** G2
Ampton Pl, WC1 ... **10** C4
Ampton St, WC1 ... **10** C4
Amroth Cl, SE23 ... **171** E1
Amroth Grn, NW9
off Fryent Gro ... **71** E6
Amsterdam Rd, E14 ... **134** C3
Amundsen Ct, E14
off Napier Av ... **134** A5
Amwell Cl, Enf. EN2 ... **44** A5
Amwell Ct Est, N4 ... **93** J1
Amwell St, EC1 ... **11** E3
Amyand Cotts, Twick. TW1
off Amyand Pk Rd ... **144** E6
Amyand La, Twick. TW1
off Marble Hill Gdns ... **145** E7
Amyand Pk Gdns, Twick. TW1
off Amyand Pk Rd ... **144** E7
Amyand Pk Rd, Twick. TW1 ... **144** D7
Amy Cl, Wall. SM6 ... **201** E7
Amyruth Rd, SE4 ... **154** A5
Amy Warne Cl, E6
off Evelyn Denington Rd ... **116** B4
Anatola Rd, N19
off Dartmouth Pk Hill ... **92** B2
Ancaster Cres, N.Mal. KT3 ... **183** G6
Ancaster Ms, Beck. BR3 ... **189** G3
Ancaster Rd, Beck. BR3 ... **189** G3
Ancaster St, SE18 ... **137** H7
Anchorage Cl, SW19 ... **166** D5
Anchorage Pt, E14
off Cuba St ... **134** A2
Anchorage Pt Ind Est, SE7 ... **135** J3
Anchor & Hope La, SE7 ... **135** H3
Anchor Cl, Bark. IG11 ... **118** B3
Anchor Ho, SW18
off Smugglers Way ... **149** E4
Anchor Ms, N1
off Balls Pond Rd ... **94** B6
SW11
off Westbridge Rd ... **149** G1
SW12 ... **150** B6
Anchor Retail Pk, E1 ... **113** F4
Anchor St, SE16 ... **132** E4
Anchor Ter, E1
off Cephas Av ... **113** F4
Anchor Wf, E3
off Watts Gro ... **114** B5
Anchor Yd, EC1 ... **12** A5
Ancill Cl, W6 ... **128** B6
Ancona Rd, NW10 ... **107** G2
SE18 ... **137** G5
Andace Pk Gdns, Brom. BR1 ... **191** J1
Andalus Rd, SW9 ... **151** E3
Ander Cl, Wem. HA0 ... **87** G4
Anderson Cl, N21 ... **43** F5
W3 ... **106** D6
Sutton SM3 ... **198** D1
Anderson Ho, Bark. IG11
off The Coverdales ... **117** G2
Anderson Pl, Houns. TW3 ... **143** H4
Anderson Rd, E9 ... **95** G6
Woodford Green IG8 ... **80** A3
Andersons Sq, N1
off Gaskin St ... **111** H1
Anderson St, SW3 ... **31** J3
Anderson Way, Belv. DA17 ... **139** H2
Anderton Cl, SE5 ... **152** A3
Andmark Ct, Sthl. UB1
off Herbert Rd ... **123** F1
Andover Av, E16
off King George Av ... **116** A6
Andover Cl, Grnf. UB6
off Ruislip Rd ... **103** H4
Andover Pl, NW6 ... **6** A1
Andover Rd, N7 ... **93** F2
Orpington BR6 ... **207** G1
Twickenham TW2 ... **162** A1
Andre St, E8 ... **94** D5
Andrew Borde St, WC2 ... **17** J3
Andrew Cl, Ilf. IG6 ... **65** G6
Andrewes Gdns, E6 ... **116** B6
Andrewes Ho, EC2 ... **20** A2
Andrew Pl, SW8
off Cowthorpe Rd ... **150** D1
Andrew Reed Ho, SW18
off Linstead Way ... **148** B7
Andrews Cl, E6
off Linton Gdns ... **116** B6
Buckhurst Hill IG9 ... **63** J2
Harrow HA1
off Bessborough Rd ... **68** A7
Worcester Park KT4 ... **198** A2
Andrews Crosse, WC2 ... **18** E4
Andrews Pl, SE9 ... **156** E6
Andrew's Rd, E8 ... **112** E1
Andrew St, E14 ... **114** C6
Andrews Wk, SE17 ... **35** H6
Andwell Cl, SE2 ... **138** B2
Anemone Ct, Enf. EN3
off Enstone Rd ... **45** H3
ANERLEY, SE20 ... **188** E1
Anerley Gro, SE19 ... **170** C7
Anerley Hill, SE19 ... **170** C6
Anerley Pk, SE20 ... **170** D7
Anerley Pk Rd, SE20 ... **170** E7
Anerley Rd, SE19 ... **170** D7
SE20 ... **170** D7
Anerley Sta Rd, SE20 ... **188** E1
Anerley St, SW11 ... **149** J2
Anerley Vale, SE19 ... **170** C7
Anfield Cl, SW12
off Belthorn Cres ... **150** C7
Angel All, E1 ... **21** G3
Angel Cl, N18 ... **60** C4
Hampton TW12
off Windmill Rd ... **161** J6
Angel Cor Par, N18
off Fore St ... **60** D5
Angel Ct, EC2 ... **20** C3
SW1 ... **25** G2
SW17 ... **167** J4
Angel Edmonton, N18
off Angel Rd ... **60** D5
Angelfield, Houns. TW3 ... **143** H4
Angel Gate, EC1 ... **11** H3
Angel Hill, Sutt. SM1 ... **199** E3
Angel Hill Dr, Sutt. SM1 ... **199** E3
Angelica Dr, E6 ... **116** D5
Angelica Gdns, Croy. CR0 ... **203** G1
Angelis Apts, N1
off Graham St ... **11** H2
Angel La, E15 ... **96** D6
Angell Pk Gdns, SW9 ... **151** G3
Angell Rd, SW9 ... **151** G3
Angell Town Est, SW9
off Overton Rd ... **151** G2
Angel Ms, E1
off Cable St ... **112** D7
N1 ... **11** F2
Angel Ms, SW15
off Roehampton High St ... **147** G7
Angel Pas, EC4 ... **20** B6
Angel Pl, N18 ... **60** D5
SE1 ... **28** B3
Angel Rd, N18 ... **60** E5
Harrow HA1 ... **68** B6
Thames Ditton KT7 ... **180** D7
Angel Rd Wks, N18 ... **61** F5
Angel Southside, EC1 ... **11** F2
Angel Sq, EC1 ... **11** F2
Angel St, EC1 ... **19** J3
Angel Wk, W6 ... **127** J4
Angerstein La, SE3 ... **135** F7
Angle Grn, Dag. RM8 ... **100** C1
Anglers Cl, Rich. TW10
off Locksmeade Rd ... **163** F4
Angler's La, NW5 ... **92** B6
Anglers Reach, Surb. KT6 ... **181** G5
Anglesea Av, SE18 ... **136** E4
Anglesea Ms, SE18
off Anglesea Av ... **136** E4
Anglesea Rd, SE18 ... **136** E4
Kingston upon Thames KT1 ... **181** G4
Anglesea Ter, W6
off Wellesley Av ... **127** H3
Anglesey Ct Rd, Cars. SM5 ... **200** A6
Anglesey Gdns, Cars. SM5 ... **200** A6
Anglesey Rd, Enf. EN3 ... **45** E4
Watford WD19 ... **50** C5
Anglesmede Cres, Pnr. HA5 ... **67** G3
Anglesmede Way, Pnr. HA5 ... **67** F3
Angles Rd, SW16 ... **169** E4
Anglia Cl, N17
off Park La ... **60** E7
Anglia Ct, Dag. RM8
off Spring Cl ... **100** D1
Anglia Ho, E14 ... **113** H6
Anglian Rd, E11 ... **96** D3
Anglia Wk, E6 ... **116** C1
Anglo Rd, E3 ... **113** J2
Angrave Ct, E8 ... **112** C1
Angrave Pas, E8
off Haggerston Rd ... **112** C1
Angus Cl, Chess. KT9 ... **196** A5
Angus Dr, Ruis. HA4 ... **84** C4
Angus Gdns, NW9 ... **70** D1
Angus Rd, E13 ... **115** J3
Angus St, SE14 ... **133** H7
Anhalt Rd, SW11 ... **31** H7
Ankerdine Cres, SE18 ... **136** D7
Anlaby Rd, Tedd. TW11 ... **162** B5
Anley Rd, W14 ... **128** A2
Anmersh Gro, Stan. HA7 ... **69** G1
Annabel Cl, E14 ... **114** B6
Anna Cl, E8 ... **112** C1
Annandale Rd, SE10 ... **135** F6
W4 ... **126** E4
Croydon CR0 ... **202** D2
Sidcup DA15 ... **157** H7
Anna Neagle Cl, E7
off Dames Rd ... **97** G4
Anne Boleyn Ct, SE9
off Avery Hill Rd ... **157** G6
Anne Boleyn's Wk, Kings.T. KT2 ... **163** H5
Sutton SM3 ... **198** A7
Anne Case Ms, N.Mal. KT3
off Sycamore Gro ... **182** D3
Anne Compton Ms, SE12 ... **155** F7
Anne Goodman Ho, E1
off Jubilee St ... **113** F6
Anne of Cleeves Ct, SE9
off Avery Hill Rd ... **157** G6
Annesley Av, NW9 ... **70** D3
Annesley Cl, NW10 ... **88** E3
Annesley Dr, Croy. CR0 ... **203** J3
Annesley Rd, SE3 ... **155** H1
Annesley Wk, N19 ... **92** C2
Annesmere Gdns, SE3
off Highbrook Rd ... **156** A3
Anne St, E13 ... **115** G4
Annette Cl, Har. HA3
off Spencer Rd ... **68** B2
Annette Cres, N1
off Essex Rd ... **93** J7
Annette Rd, N7 ... **93** F4
Annett Rd, Walt. KT12 ... **178** A7
Anne Way, Ilf. IG6 ... **65** F6
West Molesey KT8 ... **179** H4
Annie Besant Cl, E3 ... **113** J1
Annie Taylor Ho, E12
off Walton Rd ... **98** D4
Anning St, EC2 ... **13** E5
Annington Rd, N2 ... **73** J3
Annis Rd, E9 ... **95** H6
Ann La, SW10 ... **30** E7
Ann Moss Way, SE16 ... **133** F3
Ann's Cl, SW1 ... **24** A4
Ann's Pl, E1 ... **21** F2
Ann St, SE18 ... **137** G4
Annsworthy Av, Th.Hth. CR7
off Grange Pk Rd ... **188** A3
Annsworthy Cres, SE25
off Grange Rd ... **188** A2
Ansdell Rd, SE15 ... **153** F2
Ansdell St, W8 ... **22** B5
Ansdell Ter, W8 ... **22** B5
Ansell Gro, Cars. SM5 ... **200** A1
Ansell Rd, SW17 ... **167** H3
Anselm Cl, Croy. CR0 ... **202** C3
Anselm Rd, SW6 ... **128** D6
Pinner HA5 ... **51** F7
Ansford Rd, Brom. BR1 ... **172** C5
Ansleigh Pl, W11 ... **108** A7
Anson Cl, Rom. RM7 ... **83** H2
Anson Ho, E1
off Shandy St ... **113** H4
Anson Pl, SE28 ... **137** G2
Anson Rd, N7 ... **92** C4
NW2 ... **90** A5
Anson Ter, Nthlt. UB5 ... **85** H6
Anstey Rd, SE15 ... **152** D3
Anstey Wk, N15 ... **75** H4
Anstice Cl, W4 ... **127** E7
Anstridge Path, SE9 ... **157** G6
Anstridge Rd, SE9 ... **157** G6
Antelope Rd, SE18 ... **136** C3
Antelope Wk, Surb. KT6
off Maple Rd ... **181** G5
Anthony Cl, NW7 ... **55** E4
Watford WD19 ... **50** C1
Anthony Rd, SE25 ... **188** D6
Greenford UB6 ... **104** B2
Welling DA16 ... **158** A1
Anthony St, E1
off Commercial Rd ... **113** E6
Anthony Way, N18 ... **61** G6
Antigua Cl, SE19
off Salters Hill ... **170** A5
Antigua Wk, SE19 ... **170** A5
Antill Rd, E3 ... **113** H3
N15 ... **76** C4
Antill Ter, E1 ... **113** G6
Antlers Hill, E4 ... **46** B5
Anton Cres, Sutt. SM1 ... **198** D3
Antoneys Cl, Pnr. HA5 ... **66** D2
Antonine Hts, SE1 ... **28** D4
Anton Pl, Wem. HA9 ... **88** B3
Anton St, E8 ... **94** D5
Antrim Gro, NW3 ... **91** J6
Antrim Mans, NW3 ... **91** H6
Antrim Rd, NW3 ... **91** J6
Antrobus Cl, Sutt. SM1 ... **198** C5
Antrobus Rd, W4 ... **126** C4
Anvil Cl, SW16 ... **168** C7
Anvil Rd, Sun. TW16 ... **178** A3
Anworth Cl, Wdf.Grn. IG8 ... **63** H6
Apex Cl, Beck. BR3 ... **190** B1
Apex Cor, NW7 ... **54** D4
Apex Ind Est, NW10
off Hythe Rd ... **107** F4
Apex Retail Pk, Felt. TW13 ... **161** F3
Apex Twr, N.Mal. KT3 ... **182** E3
Aplin Way, Islw. TW7 ... **144** B1
Apollo, E14
off Newton Pl ... **134** A4
Apollo Av, Brom. BR1
off Rodway Rd ... **191** H1
Northwood HA6 ... **50** A5
★ **Apollo Hammersmith**, W6 ... **127** J5
Apollo Pl, E11 ... **96** E3
SW10 ... **31** E7
★ **Apollo Thea**, W1 ... **17** H5
★ **Apollo Victoria Thea**, SW1 ... **25** F6
Apollo Way, SE28
off Broadwater Rd ... **137** G3
Apostle Way, Th.Hth. CR7 ... **187** H2
Apothecary St, EC4 ... **19** G4
Appach Rd, SW2 ... **151** G5
Apple Blossom Ct, SW8
off Pascal St ... **33** J7
Appleby Cl, E4 ... **62** C6
N15 ... **76** A5
Orpington (Petts Wd) BR5 ... **193** H7
Twickenham TW2 ... **162** A2
Appleby Ct, W3
off Newport Rd ... **126** C2
Appleby Rd, E8 ... **94** D7
E16 ... **115** F6
Appleby St, E2 ... **13** F1
Appledore Av, Bexh. DA7 ... **159** J1
Ruislip HA4 ... **84** B3
Appledore Cl, SW17 ... **167** J2
Bromley BR2 ... **191** F5
Edgware HA8 ... **70** A1
Appledore Cres, Sid. DA14 ... **175** H3
Appledore Way, NW7
off Tavistock Av ... **56** A7
Appleford Rd, W10 ... **108** B4
Apple Garth, Brent. TW8 ... **125** G4
Applegarth, Croy. (New Adgtn) CR0 ... **204** B7
Esher (Clay.) KT10 ... **194** C5
Applegarth Dr, Ilf. IG2 ... **81** J4
Applegarth Rd, SE28 ... **138** B1
W14 ... **128** A3
Apple Gro, Chess. KT9 ... **195** H4
Enfield EN1 ... **44** B3
Apple Mkt, Kings.T. KT1
off Eden St ... **181** G2
Apple Rd, E11 ... **96** E3
Appleton Cl, Bexh. DA7 ... **159** H2
Appleton Gdns, N.Mal. KT3 ... **183** G6
Appleton Rd, SE9 ... **156** B3
Loughton IG10 ... **49** E3
Appleton Sq, Mitch. CR4
off Silbury Av ... **185** H1
Appletree Cl, SE20
off Jasmine Gro ... **189** E1
Appletree Gdns, Barn. EN4 ... **41** H4
Apple Tree Yd, SW1 ... **25** G1
Applewood Cl, N20 ... **57** H1
NW2 ... **89** H3
Applewood Dr, E13 ... **115** H4
Appold St, EC2 ... **20** D1

Apprentice Gdns, Nthlt.
  UB5 off Taywood Rd ...103 F3
Apprentice Way, E5
  off Clarence Rd 95 E4
Approach, The, NW4 ...72 A5
  W3 ....106 D6
  Enfield EN1 ....44 E2
  Orpington BR6 ....207 J2
Approach Cl, N16
  off Cowper Rd 94 B4
Approach Rd, E2 ......113 F2
  SW20 ....183 J2
  Barnet EN4 ....41 G4
  Edgware HA8 ....54 B6
  West Molesey KT8 ...179 G5
Aprey Gdns, NW4 ......71 J4
April Cl, W7 ....124 B7
  Feltham TW13 ......160 A3
  Orpington BR6 ....207 J5
April Glen, SE23 .....171 G3
April St, E8 ....94 C4
Apsley Cl, Har. HA2 ...67 J5
★ Apsley Ho
  (Wellington Mus), W1 ..24 B3
Apsley Rd, SE25 ......188 E4
  New Malden KT3 ......182 C3
Apsley Way, NW2 ......89 G2
  W1 ....24 C3
Aquarius Business Pk,
  NW2 ....89 F1
Aquarius Way, Nthwd.
  HA6 ....50 A5
★ Aquatic Experience,
  Brent.TW8 ....145 E1
Aquila St, NW8 ....7 F1
Aquinas St, SE1 ....27 F1
Arabella Dr, SW15 ....147 E4
Arabia Cl, E4 ....46 D7
Arabin Rd, SE4 ......153 H4
Aragon Av, T.Ditt. KT7 ..180 C5
Aragon Cl, Brom. BR2 ..206 C1
  Loughton IG10 ....48 B6
Aragon Dr, Ilf. IG6 ....65 F7
  Ruislip HA4 ....84 D1
Aragon Pl, Mord. SM4 ..184 A7
Aragon Rd, Kings.T. KT2 ..163 H5
  Morden SM4 ....184 A6
Aragon Twr, SE8 .....133 J4
Arandora Cres, Rom.
  RM6 ....82 B7
Aran Dr, Stan. HA7 ....53 F4
Aran Ms, N7
  off Barnsbury Gro 93 G7
Arbery Rd, E3 ....113 H3
Arbor Cl, Beck. BR3 ...190 B2
Arbor Ct, N16 ....94 A2
Arborfield Cl, SW2 ...169 F1
Arbor Rd, E4 ....62 D3
Arbour Rd, Enf. EN3 ...45 G4
Arbour Sq, E1 ....113 G6
Arbroath Grn, Wat. WD19 .50 A3
Arbroath Rd, SE9 .....156 B3
Arbury Ter, SE26 .....170 D3
Arbuthnot La, Bex. DA5 .159 E6
Arbuthnot Rd, SE14 ...153 G2
Arbutus St, E8 ....112 B1
Arcade, The, EC2 ......20 D2
  Croydon CR0
    off High St 201 J3
Arcadia Av, N3 ....72 D1
Arcadia Cen, The, W5 ..105 G7
Arcadia Cl, Cars. SM5 ..200 A4
Arcadian Av, Bex. DA5 .158 E6
Arcadian Cl, Bex. DA5 .158 E6
Arcadian Gdns, N22 ....59 F7
Arcadian Pl, SW18 ....148 B7
Arcadian Rd, Bex. DA5 .158 E6
Arcadia St, E14 ......114 A6
Archangel St, SE16 ...133 G2
Archbishops Pl, SW2 ..151 F6
Archdale Pl, N.Mal. KT3 .182 B3
Archdale Rd, SE22 ....152 C5
Archel Rd, W14 ......128 C6
Archer Cl, Kings.T. KT2 ..163 H7
Archer Ho, N1
  off Phillipp St 112 B1
  SW11
    off Vicarage Cres 149 G2
Archer Ms, Hmptn.
  (Hmptn H.) TW12
    off Windmill Rd 161 J6
Archer Rd, SE25 .....188 E4
Archers Dr, Enf. EN3 ...45 G2
Archer Sq, SE14
  off Knoyle St 133 H6
Archer St, W1 ....17 H5
  Harrow HA3 ....68 C3
Archery Cl, W2 ....15 H4
  Harrow HA3 ....68 C3
Archery Rd, SE9 .....156 C5
Archery Steps, W2
  off St. Georges Flds ...15 H5
Arches, SW9
  off Ridgeway Rd 151 H3

Arches, The, SW6
  off Munster Rd 148 C2
  SW8
    off New Covent
    Gdn Mkt 33 J7
  WC2 ....26 B1
  Harrow HA2 ....85 H2
Archgate Business Cen, N12
  off High Rd 57 F5
Archibald Ms, W1 ......16 C6
Archibald Rd, N7 ......92 D4
Archibald St, E3 .....114 A3
Archie Cl, West Dr. UB7 .120 D2
Archie St, SE1 ....29 E4
Arch St, SE1 ....27 J6
Archway Cl, N19
  off Archway Rd 92 C2
  SW19 ....166 E4
  W10 ....108 A5
  Wallington SM6 ......200 D3
Archway Mall, N19
  off Magdala Av 92 C2
Archway Ms, SW15
  off Putney Br Rd 148 B4
Archway Rd, N6 ....73 J6
  N19 ....92 C1
Archway St, SW13 ....147 E3
Arcola St, E8 ....94 C5
Arcon Dr, Nthlt. UB5 ..103 E4
Arctic St, NW5
  off Gillies St 92 B5
Arcus Rd, Brom. BR1 ...173 E6
Ardbeg Rd, SE24 .....152 A6
Arden Cl, SE28 ....118 D6
  Harrow HA1 ....86 A3
Arden Ct Gdns, N2 ....73 G6
Arden Cres, E14 .....134 A4
  Dagenham RM9 ......100 C7
Arden Est, N1 ....12 D2
Arden Gro, Orp. BR6 ..207 E4
Arden Ho, SW9
  off Grantham Rd 151 E2
Arden Ms, E17 ....78 B5
Arden Mhor, Pnr. HA5 ...66 B4
Arden Rd, N3 ....72 B3
  W13 ....105 F7
Ardent Cl, SE25 .....188 B3
Ardfern Av, SW16 ....187 G3
Ardfillan Rd, SE6 ....172 D1
Ardgowan Rd, SE6 ....154 E7
Ardilaun Rd, N5 ....93 J4
Ardingly Cl, Croy. CR0 .203 G3
Ardleigh Gdns, Sutt.
  SM3 ....184 D7
Ardleigh Ho, Ilf. IG1
  off Bengal Rd 98 E3
Ardleigh Rd, E17 ......77 J1
  N1 ....94 A6
Ardleigh Ter, E17 .....77 J1
Ardley Cl, NW10 ....88 E3
  SE6 ....171 H3
Ardlui Rd, SE27 .....169 J2
Ardmay Gdns, Surb. KT6 .181 H5
Ardmere Rd, SE13 ....154 D6
Ardmore La, Buck.H. IG9 .47 H7
Ardmore Pl, Buck.H. IG9 .47 H7
Ardoch Rd, SE6 ......172 D2
Ardra Rd, N9 ....61 G3
Ardrossan Gdns, Wor.Pk.
  KT4 ....197 G3
Ardshiel Cl, SW15
  off Bemish Rd 148 A3
Ardwell Av, Ilf. IG6 ....81 F5
Ardwell Rd, SW2 .....168 E2
Ardwick Rd, NW2 ......90 D4
Arena Shop Pk, N4 ....75 H6
Arena Sq, Wem. HA9 ...88 A4
Arewater Grn, Loug. IG10 .48 C1
Argali Ho, Erith DA18
  off Kale Rd 138 E3
Argall Av, E10 ....77 G7
Argall Way, E10 ....95 G1
Argenta Way, NW10 ...88 B7
Argent Cn, Barn. EN5 ...41 F4
Argon Ms, SW6 ......128 D7
Argon Rd, N18 ....61 F5
Argosy La, Stai. (Stanw.)
  TW19 ....140 A7
Argus Cl, Rom. RM7 ...83 H1
Argus Way, Nthlt. UB5 .102 E3
Argyle Cl, W13 ......104 D4
Argyle Pas, N17 ....76 C1
Argyle Pl, W6 ....127 H4
Argyle Rd, E1 ....113 G4
  E15 ....96 E4
  E16 ....115 H6
  N12 ....56 D5
  N17 ....76 D1
  N18 ....60 D4
  W13 ....104 D5
  Barnet EN5 ....39 J4
  Greenford UB6 ......104 C3

Argyle Rd, Harrow HA2 ...67 H6
  Hounslow TW3 ......143 H5
  Ilford IG1 ....98 D2
  Teddington TW11 ....162 B5
Argyle Sq, WC1 ....10 A3
Argyle St, WC1 ....10 A3
Argyle Wk, WC1 ....10 A4
Argyle Way, SE16 ......37 J4
Argyll Av, Sthl. UB1 ...123 H1
Argyll Cl, SW9
  off Dalyell Rd 151 F3
Argyll Gdns, Edg. HA8 ...70 B2
Argyll Rd, SE18 ......137 F3
  W8 ....128 D2
Argyll St, W1 ....17 F4
Aria Ho, WC2 ....18 B3
Arica Ho, SE16 ....133 E3
Arica Rd, SE4 ....153 H4
Ariel Rd, NW6 ....90 D6
Ariel Way, W12 ....127 J1
  Hounslow TW4 ......142 B3
Aristotle Rd, SW4 ....150 D3
Arizona Bldg, SE13
  off Deals Gateway ...154 B1
Arkell Gro, SE19 .....169 H7
Arkindale Rd, SE6 ....172 C3
ARKLEY, Barn. EN5 ...39 G5
Arkley Cres, E17 ......77 J5
Arkley Dr, Barn. EN5 ...39 G4
Arkley La, Barn. EN5 ...39 G3
Arkley Pk, Barn. EN5 ...38 D6
Arkley Rd, E17 ....77 J5
Arkley Vw, Barn. EN5 ...39 H4
Arklow Ms, Surb. KT6
  off Vale Rd S 195 H2
Arklow Rd, SE14 .....133 J6
Arkwright Rd, NW3 ....91 F5
Arlesey Cl, SW15 ....148 B5
Arlesford Rd, SW9 ...151 E3
Arlingford Rd, SW2 ..151 G5
Arlington, N12 ....56 A7
Arlington Av, N1 .....111 J2
Arlington Bldg, E3
  off Fairfield Rd 114 A2
Arlington Cl, SE13 ...154 D5
  Sidcup DA15 ....157 H7
  Sutton SM1 ....198 D2
  Twickenham TW1 ....145 F6
Arlington Ct, W3
  off Mill Hill Rd 126 B1
  Hayes UB3
    off Shepiston La 121 G5
Arlington Dr, Cars. SM5 .199 J2
Arlington Gdns, W4 ..126 C5
  Ilford IG1 ....98 D1
Arlington Grn, NW7 ...56 A7
Arlington Lo, SW2 ....151 F4
Arlington Ms, Twick. TW1
  off Arlington Rd 145 F6
Arlington Pl, SE10
  off Greenwich S St ..134 C7
Arlington Rd, N14 .....58 B2
  NW1 ....110 B1
  W13 ....104 E6
  Richmond TW10 ....163 G2
  Surbiton KT6 ....181 G6
  Teddington TW11 ....162 C4
  Twickenham TW1 ....145 F6
  Woodford Green IG8 ...79 G5
Arlington Sq, N1 .....111 J1
Arlington St, SW1 .....25 F1
Arlington Way, EC1 ....11 F3
Arliss Way, Nthlt. UB5 .102 C1
Arlow Rd, N21 ....59 G1
Armada Ct, SE8
  off Watergate St 134 A6
Armadale Cl, N17 ......76 E4
Armadale Rd, SW6 ...128 D7
  Feltham TW14 ......142 A5
Armagh Rd, E3 ......113 J1
Armfield Cl, W.Mol. KT8 .179 F5
Armfield Cres, Mitch.
  CR4 ....185 J2
Armfield Rd, Enf. EN2 ...44 A1
Arminger Rd, W12 ....127 H1
Armistice Gdns, SE25 .188 D3
Armitage Rd, NW11 ...90 C1
  SE10 ....135 F5
Armour Cl, N7
  off Roman Way 93 F6
Armoury Rd, SE8 .....154 B2
Armoury Way, SW18 ..148 D5
Armstead Wk, Dag.
  RM10 ....101 G7
Armstrong Av, Wdf.Grn.
  IG8 ....62 E6
Armstrong Cl, E6
  off Porter Rd 116 C6
  Borehamwood WD6 ...38 C3
  Bromley BR1 ....192 B3
  Dagenham RM8 ......82 D7

Armstrong Cl, Pinner HA5 .66 A6
  Walton-on-Thames KT12
    off Sunbury La 178 A6
Armstrong Cres, Barn.
  (Cockfos.) EN4 ....41 G3
Armstrong Rd, NW10 ...88 E7
  SE18 ....137 F3
  SW7 ....22 E6
  W3 ....127 F1
  Feltham TW13 ......160 E5
Armstrong Way, Sthl.
  UB2 ....123 H2
Armytage Rd, Houns.
  TW5 ....122 D7
Arnal Cres, SW18 ....148 B7
Arncliffe Cl, N11 ......58 A6
Arncroft Ct, Bark. IG11
  off Renwick Rd 118 B3
Arndale Wk, SW18
  off Garratt La 148 E5
Arne Gro, Orp. BR6 ...207 J3
Arne Ho, SE11 ....34 C3
Arne St, WC2 ....18 B4
Arnett Sq, E4 ....61 J6
Arne Wk, SE3 ....155 F4
Arneways Av, Rom. RM6 .82 D3
Arneway St, SW1 ......25 J6
Arnewood Cl, SW15 ..165 G1
Arney's La, Mitch. CR4 .186 A6
Arngask Rd, SE6 .....154 D7
Arnham Pl, E14 ......134 A3
Arnham Way, SE22
  off East Dulwich Gro .152 B5
Arnhem Wf, E14
  off Arnhem Pl 134 A3
Arnison Rd, E.Mol. KT8 .180 A4
Arnold Bennett Way, N8
  off Burghley Rd 75 G3
Arnold Circ, E2 ....13 F4
Arnold Cl, Har. HA3 ....69 J7
Arnold Cres, Islw. TW7 .144 A5
Arnold Dr, Chess. KT9 ..195 G6
Arnold Est, SE1 ....29 G4
Arnold Gdns, N13 .....59 H5
Arnold Rd, E3 ....114 A3
  N15 ....76 C3
  SW17 ....167 J7
  Dagenham RM9,
    RM10 ....101 F7
  Northolt UB5 ....84 D6
Arnos Gro, N14 ....58 D4
Arnos Rd, N11 ....58 C5
Arnott Cl, SE28
  off Applegarth Rd ...118 C7
  W4 ....126 D4
Arnould Av, SE5 .....152 A4
Arnsberg Way, Bexh.
  DA7 ....159 G4
Arnside Gdns, Wem.
  HA9 ....87 G1
Arnside Rd, Bexh. DA7 .159 G1
Arnside St, SE17 ......36 A5
Arnulf St, SE6 ....172 B4
Arnulls Rd, SW16 ....169 G6
Arodene Rd, SW2 ....151 F6
Arosa Rd, Twick. TW1 .145 G6
Arpley Sq, SE20
  off High St 171 F7
Arragon Gdns, SW16 .168 E7
  West Wickham BR4 ..204 B3
Arragon Rd, E6 ....116 A1
  SW18 ....166 E1
  Twickenham TW1 ....144 D7
Arran Cl, Wall. SM6 ...200 B4
Arran Dr, E12 ....98 A1
Arran Grn, Wat. WD19
  off Prestwick Rd 50 D4
Arran Ms, W5 ....125 J1
Arran Rd, SE6 ....172 B2
Arran Wk, N1 ....93 J7
Arras Av, Mord. SM4 ..185 F5
Arrol Ho, SE1 ....28 A6
Arrol Rd, Beck. BR3 ...189 F3
Arrow Rd, E3 ....114 B3
Arrowscout Wk, Nthlt. UB5
  off Wayfarer Rd 102 E3
Arrowsmith Cl, Chig. IG7 .65 J5
Arrowsmith Ho, SE11 ..34 C3
Arrowsmith Path, Chig.
  IG7 ....65 H5
Arrowsmith Rd, Chig. IG7 .65 H5
  Loughton IG10 ....48 B3
Arta Ho, E1
  off Devonport St 113 F6
Arterberry Rd, SW20 .165 J7
Artesian Cl, NW10 .....88 D7
Artesian Gro, Barn. EN5 .41 F3
Artesian Rd, W2 .....108 D6
Artesian Wk, E11 ......96 E3
Arthingworth St, E15 .114 E1

Arthur Ct, SW11
off Charlotte Despard Av 150 A1
W2 14 A3
Arthurdon Rd, SE4 154 A5
Arthur Gro, SE18 137 F4
Arthur Henderson Ho, SW6 148 C2
Arthur Horsley Wk, E7
off Magpie Cl 97 F5
Arthur Newton Ho, SW11
off Lavender Rd 149 G3
Arthur Rd, E6 116 C2
N7 93 F4
N9 60 C2
SW19 166 D3
Kingston upon Thames KT2 164 A7
New Malden KT3 183 H5
Romford RM6 82 C7
Arthur St, EC4 20 C6
Arthur Walls Ho, E12
off Grantham Rd 98 D3
Artichoke Hill, E1
off Pennington St 112 E7
Artichoke Pl, SE5
off Camberwell Ch St 152 A1
Artillery Cl, Ilf. IG2
off Horns Rd 81 F6
Artillery La, E1 20 E2
W12 107 G6
Artillery Mans, SW1 25 H5
Artillery Pas, E1 21 E2
Artillery Pl, SE18 136 C5
SW1 25 H6
Harrow HA3
off Chicheley Rd 51 J7
Artillery Row, SW1 25 H6
Artington Cl, Orp. BR6 207 F4
Artisan Cl, E6
off Ferndale St 116 E7
Artizan St, E1 21 E3
Arundel Av, Mord. SM4 184 C4
Arundel Cl, E15 97 E4
SW11 149 H5
Bexley DA5 159 F6
Croydon CR0 201 H3
Hampton (Hmptn H.) TW12 161 H5
Arundel Ct, N12 57 H6
Harrow HA2 85 G4
Arundel Dr, Borwd. WD6 38 C5
Harrow HA2 85 F4
Woodford Green IG8 63 G7
Arundel Gdns, N21 59 G1
W11 108 C7
Edgware HA8 54 D7
Ilford IG3 100 A2
Arundel Gt Ct, WC2 18 D5
Arundel Gro, N16 94 B5
Arundel Pl, N1 93 G6
Arundel Rd, Barn. (Cockfos.) EN4 41 H3
Croydon CR0 188 A6
Hounslow TW4 142 C3
Kingston upon Thames KT1 182 B2
Sutton SM2 198 C7
Arundel Sq, N7 93 G6
Arundel St, WC2 18 D5
Arundel Ter, SW13 127 H6
Arvon Rd, N5 93 G5
Asbaston Ter, Ilf. IG1
off Buttsbury Rd 99 F5
Ascalon St, SW8 130 C7
Ascham Dr, E4
off Rushcroft Rd 62 B7
Ascham End, E17 77 H1
Ascham St, NW5 92 C5
Aschurch Rd, Croy. CR0 188 C7
Ascot Cl, Borwd. (Els.) WD6 38 A5
Ilford IG6 65 H6
Northolt UB5 85 G5
Ascot Gdns, Sthl. UB1 103 F5
Ascot Rd, E6 116 C3
N15 76 A5
N18 60 D4
SW17 168 A6
Orpington BR5 193 J4
Ascott Av, W5 125 H2
Ashanti Ms, E8
off Lower Clapton Rd 95 E5
Ashbourne Av, E18 79 H4
N20 57 J2
NW11 72 C5
Bexleyheath DA7 139 E7
Harrow HA2 86 A2
Ashbourne Cl, N12 57 E4
W5 106 A5
Ashbourne Ct, E5
off Daubeney Rd 95 H4
Ashbourne Gro, NW7 54 D5
SE22 152 C5
W4 127 E5
Ashbourne Par, W5
off Ashbourne Rd 105 J4
Ashbourne Ri, Orp. BR6 207 G4
Ashbourne Rd, W5 105 J5
Mitcham CR4 168 A6
Ashbourne Ter, SW19 166 D7
Ashbourne Way, NW11
off Ashbourne Av 72 C5
Ashbridge Rd, E11 79 E7
Ashbridge St, NW8 7 G6
Ashbrook Rd, N19 92 D1
Dagenham RM10 101 H3
Ashburn Gdns, SW7 30 C1
Ashburnham Av, Har. HA1 68 C6
Ashburnham Cl, N2 73 G3
Watford WD19 50 A3
Ashburnham Dr, Wat. WD19 50 A3
Ashburnham Gdns, Har. HA1 68 C6
Ashburnham Gro, SE10 134 B7
Ashburnham Pl, SE10 134 B7
Ashburnham Retreat, SE10 134 B7
Ashburnham Rd, NW10 107 J3
SW10 129 F7
Belvedere DA17 139 J4
Richmond TW10 163 E3
Ashburnham Twr, SW10
off Blantyre St 30 E7
Ashburn Pl, SW7 30 C1
Ashburton Av, Croy. CR0 202 E1
Ilford IG3 99 H4
Ashburton Cl, Croy. CR0 202 D1
Ashburton Ct, Pnr. HA5 66 D3
Ashburton Gdns, Croy. CR0 202 D2
Ashburton Rd, E16 115 G6
Croydon CR0 202 D1
Ruislip HA4 84 A2
Ashburton Ter, E13
off Grasmere Rd 115 G2
Ashburton Triangle, N5
off Drayton Pk 93 G4
Ashbury Gdns, Rom. RM6 82 D5
Ashbury Pl, SW19 167 F6
Ashbury Rd, SW11 149 J3
Ashby Av, Chess. KT9 196 A6
Ashby Gro, N1 93 J7
Ashby Ho, N1
off Essex Rd 93 J7
Ashby Ms, SE4 153 J2
SW2 *off Prague Pl* 150 E5
Ashby Rd, N15 76 D5
SE4 153 J2
Ashby St, EC1 11 H4
Ashby Wk, Croy. CR0 187 J6
Ashby Way, West Dr. (Sipson) UB7 120 D7
Aschurch Gro, W12 127 G2
Ashchurch Pk Vil, W12 127 G3
Ashchurch Ter, W12 127 G3
Ash Cl, SE20 189 F2
Carshalton SM5 199 J2
Edgware HA8 54 C4
New Malden KT3 182 D2
Orpington BR5 193 G5
Sidcup DA14 176 B3
Stanmore HA7 52 D6
Ashcombe Av, Surb. KT6 181 G7
Ashcombe Gdns, Edg. HA8 54 A4
Ashcombe Ho, Enf. EN3 45 G3
Ashcombe Pk, NW2 89 E3
Ashcombe Rd, SW19 166 D5
Carshalton SM5 200 A6
Ashcombe Sq, N.Mal. KT3 182 C3
Ashcombe St, SW6 148 E2
Ash Ct, N11 *off Cline Rd* 58 C6
Epsom KT19 196 C4
Ashcroft, Pnr. HA5 51 G6
Ashcroft Av, Sid. DA15 158 A6
Ashcroft Ct, N20
off Oakleigh Rd N 57 G2
Ashcroft Cres, Sid. DA15 158 A6
Ashcroft Rd, E3 113 H3
Chessington KT9 195 J3
Ashcroft Sq, W6
off King St 127 J4
Ashdale Cl, Twick. TW2 143 J7
Ashdale Gro, Stan. HA7 52 C6
Ashdale Rd, SE12 173 H1
Ashdale Way, Twick. TW2
off Ashdale Cl 143 J7
Ashdene, SE15 152 E1
Pinner HA5 66 C3
Ashdon Cl, Wdf.Grn. IG8 63 H6
Ashdon Rd, NW10 107 E1
Ashdown Cl, Beck. BR3 190 B2
Bexley DA5 159 J7
Ashdown Ct, E17 78 C2
Ashdown Cres, NW5
off Queen's Cres 92 A5
Ashdown Pl, T.Ditt. KT7 180 D6
Ashdown Rd, Enf. EN3 45 F3
Kingston upon Thames KT1 181 H2
Ashdown Wk, E14 134 A4
Romford RM7 83 H2
Ashdown Way, SW17 168 A2
Ashen, E6 *off Downings* 116 D6
Ashenden, SE17 35 J1
Ashenden Rd, E5 95 G5
Ashen Gro, SW19 166 D3
Ashentree Ct, EC4 19 F4
Asher Loftus Way, N11 57 J6
Asher Way, E1 29 J1
Ashfield Av, Felt. TW13 160 B1
Ashfield Cl, Beck. BR3 172 A7
Richmond TW10 163 H1
Ashfield La, Chis. BR7 175 F6
Ashfield Par, N14 58 D1
Ashfield Rd, N4 75 J6
N14 58 C3
W3 127 F1
Ashfields, Loug. IG10 48 C2
Ashfield St, E1 112 E5
Ashfield Yd, E1
off Ashfield St 113 F5
Ashford Av, N8 74 E4
Hayes UB4 102 D6
Ashford Cl, E17 77 J6
Ashford Cres, Enf. EN3 45 F2
Ashford Grn, Wat. WD19 50 D5
Ashford Ms, N17 76 D1
Ashford Rd, E6 98 D6
E18 79 H2
NW2 90 A4
Ashford St, N1 12 D3
Ash Gro, E8 113 E1
N13 59 J3
NW2 90 A4
SE20 189 F2
W5 125 H2
Enfield EN1 44 B7
Hounslow TW5 142 D1
Southall UB1 103 G5
Wembley HA0 86 D4
West Wickham BR4 204 C2
Ashgrove Rd, Brom. BR1 172 D6
Ilford IG3 99 J1
Ash Hill Cl, Bushey WD23 51 H1
Ash Hill Dr, Pnr. HA5 66 C3
Ash Ho, SE1
off Longfield Est 37 G2
Ashingdon Cl, E4 62 C3
Ashington Ho, E1
off Barnsley St 113 E4
Ashington Rd, SW6 148 C2
Ash Island, E.Mol. KT8 180 A3
Ashlake Rd, SW16 168 E4
Ashland Pl, W1 16 B1
Ashlar Pl, SE18
off Masons Hill 137 E4
Ashleigh Gdns, Sutt. SM1 198 E2
Ashleigh Pt, SE23
off Dacres Rd 171 G3
Ashleigh Rd, SE20 189 E3
SW14 146 E3
Ashley Av, Ilf. IG6 81 E2
Morden SM4 184 D5
Ashley Cl, NW4 71 J2
Pinner HA5 66 B2
Ashley Cres, N22 75 G2
SW11 150 A3
Ashley Dr, Borwd. WD6 38 C5
Isleworth TW7 124 B6
Twickenham TW2 143 H7
Ashley Gdns, N13 59 J4
SW1 25 G6
Orpington BR6 207 H5
Richmond TW10 163 G3
Wembley HA9 87 H2
Ashley Gro, Loug. IG10
off Staples Rd 48 B3
Ashley La, NW4 71 J2
NW7 71 J2
Croydon CR0 201 H4
Ashley Pl, SW1 25 F6
Ashley Rd, E4 62 A5
E7 97 J7
N17 76 D3
N19 92 E1
SW19 166 E6
Enfield EN3 45 F2
Hampton TW12 179 G1
Richmond TW9
off Jocelyn Rd 145 H3
Thames Ditton KT7 180 C6
Thornton Heath CR7 187 F4
Ashley Wk, NW7 55 J7
Ashling Rd, Croy. CR0 202 D1
Ashlin Rd, E15 96 D4
Ashlone Rd, SW15 147 J3
Ashlyns Way, Chess. KT9 195 G6
Ashmead, N14 42 C5
Ashmead Gate, Brom. BR1 191 J1
Ashmead Ho, E9
off Kingsmead Way 95 H5
Ashmead Rd, SE8 154 A2
Feltham TW14 160 A1
Ashmere Av, Beck. BR3 190 D2
Ashmere Cl, Sutt. SM3 197 J5
Ashmere Gro, SW2 150 E4
Ashmill St, NW1 15 G1
Ashmole Pl, SW8 34 D6
Ashmole St, SW8 34 D6
Ashmore Cl, SE15 132 C7
Ashmore Ct, Houns. TW5
off Wheatlands 123 G6
Ashmore Gro, Well. DA16 157 G3
Ashmore Rd, W9 108 C4
Ashmount Rd, N15 76 C5
N19 74 C7
Ashmount Ter, W5 125 G4
Ashneal Gdns, Har. HA1 86 A3
Ashness Gdns, Grnf. UB6 86 E6
Ashness Rd, SW11 149 J5
Ashridge Cl, Har. HA3 69 F6
Ashridge Cres, SE18 137 F7
Ashridge Dr, Wat. WD19 50 C5
Ashridge Gdns, N13 58 D5
Pinner HA5 66 E4
Ashridge Way, Mord. SM4 184 C3
Sunbury-on-Thames TW16 160 A6
Ash Rd, E15 97 E5
Croydon CR0 204 A2
Orpington BR6 207 J7
Sutton SM3 184 B7
Ash Row, Brom. BR2 192 D7
Ashtead Rd, E5 76 D7
Ashton Cl, Sutt. SM1 198 D4
Ashton Ct, E4
off Connington Cres 62 E3
Ashton Gdns, Houns. TW4 143 F4
Romford RM6 83 E6
Ashton Rd, E15 96 D5
Ashton St, E14 114 C7
Ashtree Av, Mitch. CR4 185 G2
Ash Tree Cl, Croy. CR0 189 H6
Ashtree Cl, Orp. BR6 207 E4
Ash Tree Cl, Surb. KT6 195 H1
Ash Tree Dell, NW9 70 C5
Ash Tree Way, Croy. CR0 189 H5
Ashurst Cl, SE20 189 E1
Ashurst Dr, Ilf. IG2, IG6 81 E6
Ashurst Rd, N12 57 H5
Barnet EN4 41 J5
Ashurst Wk, Croy. CR0 202 E2
Ashvale Rd, SW17 167 J5
Ashville Rd, E11 96 D2
Ash Wk, SW2 169 F1
Wembley HA0 87 F4
Ashwater Rd, SE12 173 G1
Ashway Cen, The, Kings.T. KT2 *off Elm Cres* 181 H1
Ashwell Cl, E6
off Northumberland Rd 116 B6
Ashwin St, E8 94 C6
Ashwood Gdns, Croy. (New Adgtn) CR0 204 B6
Hayes UB3
off Cranford Dr 121 J4
Ashwood Rd, E4 62 D3
Ashworth Cl, SE5
off Love Wk 152 A2
Ashworth Rd, W9 6 B3
Askern Cl, Bexh. DA6 158 D4
Aske St, N1 12 D3
Askew Cres, W12 127 F2
Askew Rd, W12 127 F1
Askham Ct, W12 127 G1
Askham Rd, W12 127 G1
Askill Dr, SW15 148 B5
Asland Rd, E15 114 E1
Aslett St, SW18 149 E7
Asmara Rd, NW2 90 B5
Asmuns Hill, NW11 72 D5
Asmuns Pl, NW11 72 C5
Asolando Dr, SE17 36 A2
Aspect Ct, SW6
off Lensbury Av 149 F2
Aspects, Sutt. SM1 199 E5
Aspen Cl, N19
off Hargrave Pk 92 C2
W5 125 J2
West Drayton UB7 120 C1

Aspen Copse, Brom. BR1 **192** C2
Aspen Ct, Hayes UB3 **121** H4
Aspen Dr, Wem. HA0 **86** D4
Aspen Gdns, W6 **127** H5
Mitcham CR4 **186** A5
Aspen Grn, Erith DA18 **139** F3
Aspen Ho, NW3
off Maitland Pk Vil **91** J6
Aspen La, Nthlt. UB5 **102** E3
Aspenlea Rd, W6 **128** A6
Aspen Way, E14 **114** A7
Feltham TW13 **160** B3
Aspern Gro, NW3 **91** H5
Aspinall Rd, SE4 **153** G3
Aspinden Rd, SE16 **133** E4
Aspley Rd, SW18 **149** E5
Asplins Rd, N17 **76** D1
Asprey Ms, Beck. BR3 **189** J5
Asprey Pl, Brom. BR1
off Chislehurst Rd **192** B2
Asquith Cl, Dag. RM8 **100** C1
Assam St, E1 **21** H3
Assata Ms, N1
off St. Paul's Rd **93** H6
Assembly Pas, E1 **113** F5
Assembly Wk, Cars. SM5 **185** H7
Assurance Cotts, Belv. DA17 *off Heron Hill* **139** F5
Astall Cl, Har. HA3 **68** B1
Astbury Business Pk, SE15
off Station Pas **153** F1
Astbury Ho, SE11 **26** E6
Astbury Rd, SE15 **153** F1
Astell St, SW3 **31** H3
Aste St, E14 **134** C2
Asteys Row, N1
off River Pl **93** J7
Asthall Gdns, Ilf. IG6 **81** F4
Astle St, SW11 **150** A2
Astley Av, NW2 **89** J5
Astley Ho, SE1
off Rowcross St **37** G3
Aston Av, Har. HA3 **69** F7
Aston Cl, Sid. DA14 **176** A3
Aston Ct, N4
off Queens Dr **93** J2
Aston Grn, Houns. TW4 **142** C2
Aston Ho, SW8
off Wandsworth Rd **150** D1
Aston Ms, Rom. RM6 **82** C7
Aston Pl, SW16
off Averil Gro **169** H6
Aston Rd, SW20 **183** J2
W5 **105** G6
Esher (Clay.) KT10 **194** B5
Aston St, E14 **113** H6
Aston Ter, SW12
off Cathles Rd **150** B6
Astonville St, SW18 **166** D1
Astor Av, Rom. RM7 **83** J6
Astor Cl, Kings.T. KT2 **164** B6
Astoria Wk, SW9 **151** G3
Astrop Ms, W6 **127** J3
Astrop Ter, W6 **127** J3
Astwood Ms, SW7 **30** C1
Asylum Rd, SE15 **133** E7
Atalanta St, SW6 **148** A1
Atbara Ct, Tedd. TW11 **163** E6
Atbara Rd, Tedd. TW11 **163** E6
Atcham Rd, Houns. TW3 **143** J4
Atcost Rd, Bark. IG11 **118** A5
Atheldene Rd, SW18 **167** E1
Athelney St, SE6 **172** A3
Athelstane Gro, E3 **113** J2
Athelstane Ms, N4
off Stroud Grn Rd **93** G1
Athelstan Gdns, NW6 **90** B7
Athelstan Ho, E9
off Kingsmead Way **95** J5
Athelstan Rd, Kings.T. KT1 **181** J4
Athelstone Rd, Har. HA3 **68** A2
Athena Cl, Har. HA2
off Byron Hill Rd **86** B2
Kingston upon Thames KT1 **181** J3
Athena Ct, SE1
off Long La **28** D4
Athenaeum Ct, N5 **93** J4
Athenaeum Pl, N10
off Fortis Grn Rd **74** B3
Athenaeum Rd, N20 **57** F1
Athenlay Rd, SE15 **153** G5
Athens Gdns, W9
off Harrow Rd **108** D4
Atherden Rd, E5 **95** F4
Atherfold Rd, SW9 **150** E3
Atherley Way, Houns. TW4 **143** F7
Atherstone Ct, W2 **14** B1
Atherstone Ms, SW7 **30** D1
Atherton Cl, Stai. (Stanw.) TW19 **140** A6
Atherton Dr, SW19 **166** A4
Atherton Hts, Wem. HA0 **87** F6
Atherton Ms, E7 **97** F6
Atherton Pl, Har. HA2 **68** A3
Southall UB1 **103** G7
Atherton Rd, E7 **97** F5
SW13 **127** G7
Ilford IG5 **80** B2
Atherton St, SW11 **149** H2
Athlone, Esher (Clay.) KT10 **194** B6
Athlone Cl, E5
off Goulton Rd **95** E5
Athlone Rd, SW2 **151** F7
Athlone St, NW5 **92** A6
Athlon Rd, Wem. HA0 **105** G2
Athol Cl, Pnr. HA5 **66** B1
Athole Gdns, Enf. EN1 **44** B5
Athol Gdns, Pnr. HA5 **66** B1
Atholl Ho, W9 **6** C4
Atholl Rd, Ilf. IG3 **82** A7
Athol Rd, Erith DA8 **139** J5
Athol Sq, E14 **114** C6
Atkin Bldg, WC1
off Raymond Bldgs **18** D1
Atkins Dr, W.Wick. BR4 **204** D2
Atkinson Ho, SW11
off Austin Rd **150** A1
Atkinson Rd, E16 **115** J5
Atkins Rd, E10 **78** B6
SW12 **150** D7
Atlanta Bldg, SE13
off Deals Gateway **154** B1
Atlantic Rd, SW9 **151** G4
Atlantis Cl, Bark. IG11 **118** B3
Atlas Business Cen, NW2 **89** H2
Atlas Gdns, SE7 **135** J4
Atlas Ms, E8
off Dalston La **94** C6
N7 **93** F6
Atlas Rd, E13 **115** G2
N11 **58** B6
Atlas Rd, NW10 **107** E3
Wembley HA9 **88** C4
Atley Rd, E3 **114** A1
Atlip Cen, Wem. HA0
off Atlip Rd **105** H1
Atlip Rd, Wem. HA0 **105** H1
Atney Rd, SW15 **148** B4
Atria Rd, Nthwd. HA6 **50** A5
Attenborough Cl, Wat. WD19 **50** E3
Atterbury Rd, N4 **75** G6
Atterbury St, SW1 **33** J2
Attewood Av, NW10 **88** E3
Attewood Rd, Nthlt. UB5 **85** E6
Attfield Cl, N20 **57** G2
Attlee Cl, Hayes UB4 **102** B3
Thornton Heath CR7 **187** J6
Attlee Rd, SE28 **118** B7
Hayes UB4 **102** A3
Attlee Ter, E17 **78** B4
Attneave St, WC1 **10** E4
Atwater Cl, SW2 **169** G1
Atwell Cl, E10
off Belmont Pk Rd **78** B6
Atwell Pl, T.Ditt. KT7 **194** C1
Atwell Rd, SE15
off Rye La **152** D2
Atwood Av, Rich. TW9 **146** A2
Atwood Rd, W6 **127** H4
Atwoods All, Rich. TW9
off Leyborne Pk **146** A1
Aubert Ct, N5 **93** H4
Aubert Pk, N5 **93** H4
Aubert Rd, N5 **93** H4
Aubrey Beardsley Ho, SW1
off Vauxhall Br Rd **33** G2
Aubrey Moore Pt, E15 **114** C2
Aubrey Pl, NW8 **6** C2
Aubrey Rd, E17 **78** A3
N8 **75** E5
W8 **128** C1
Aubrey Wk, W8 **128** C1
Auburn Cl, SE14 **133** H7
Aubyn Hill, SE27 **169** J4
Aubyn Sq, SW15 **147** G4
Auckland Cl, SE19 **188** C1
Auckland Gdns, SE19 **188** B1
Auckland Hill, SE27 **169** J4
Auckland Ri, SE19 **188** B1
Auckland Rd, E10 **96** B3
SE19 **188** C1
SW11 **149** H4
Ilford IG1 **99** E1
Kingston upon Thames KT1 **181** J4
Auckland St, SE11 **34** C4
Auden Dr, Borwd. WD6 **38** A5
Auden Pl, NW1 **110** A1
Sutton SM3
off Wordsworth Dr **197** J4
Audleigh Pl, Chig. IG7 **64** D6
Audley Cl, N10 **58** B7
SW11 **150** A3
Borehamwood WD6 **38** A3
Audley Ct, E18 **79** F4
Pinner HA5
off Rickmansworth Rd **66** C2
Audley Dr, E16
off Wesley Av **135** H1
Audley Gdns, Ilf. IG3 **99** J2
Loughton IG10 **49** F2
Audley Pl, Sutt. SM2 **198** E7
Audley Rd, NW4 **71** H6
W5 **105** J5
Enfield EN2 **43** H2
Richmond TW10 **145** J5
Audley Sq, W1 **24** C1
Audrey Cl, Beck. BR3 **190** B6
Audrey Gdns, Wem. HA0 **87** E2
Audrey Rd, Ilf. IG1 **98** E3
Audrey St, E2 **13** H1
Audric Cl, Kings.T. KT2 **182** A1
Augurs La, E13 **115** H3
Augusta Cl, W.Mol. KT8
off Freeman Dr **179** F3
Augusta Rd, Twick. TW2 **161** J2
Augusta St, E14 **114** B6
Augustine Rd, W14 **128** A3
Harrow HA3 **67** H1
Augustus Cl, W12
off Goldhawk Rd **127** H2
Brentford TW8 **125** F7
Stanmore HA7 **53** G3
Augustus Ct, SE1 **36** D1
Augustus Ho, NW1
off Augustus St **9** F3
Augustus Rd, SW19 **166** B1
Augustus St, NW1 **9** E2
Aulay Lawrence Ct, N9
off Menon Dr **60** E3
Aultone Way, Cars. SM5 **199** J3
Sutton SM1 **199** E2
Aultone Yd, Cars. SM5 **199** J3
Aulton Pl, SE11 **35** F4
Aurelia Gdns, Croy. CR0 **187** F5
Aurelia Rd, Croy. CR0 **187** E6
Auriga Ms, N1 **94** A5
Auriol Cl, Wor.Pk. KT4
off Auriol Pk Rd **197** E3
Auriol Dr, Grnf. UB6 **86** A7
Auriol Pk Rd, Wor.Pk. KT4 **197** E3
Auriol Rd, W14 **128** B4
Austell Gdns, NW7 **55** E3
Austen Apts, SE20
off Croydon Rd **188** E2
Austen Cl, SE28 **138** B1
Loughton IG10 **49** G3
Austen Ho, NW6 **108** D3
Austen Rd, Erith DA8 **139** H7
Harrow HA2 **85** H2
Austin Av, Brom. BR2 **192** B5
Austin Cl, SE23 **153** J7
Twickenham TW1 **145** F5
Austin Ct, E6
off Kings Rd **115** J1
Austin Friars, EC2 **20** C3
Austin Friars Pas, EC2 **20** C3
Austin Friars Sq, EC2 **20** C3
Austin Rd, SW11 **150** A1
Hayes UB3 **121** J2
Austin St, E2 **13** F4
Austral Cl, Sid. DA15 **175** J3
Australia Rd, W12 **107** H7
Austral St, SE11 **35** G1
Austyn Gdns, Surb. KT5 **196** B1
Autumn Cl, SW19 **167** F6
Enfield EN1 **44** D1
Autumn Gro, Brom. BR1 **173** H6
Autumn St, E3 **114** A1
Avalon Cl, SW20 **184** B2
W13 **104** D5
Enfield EN2 **43** G2
Avalon Rd, SW6 **148** E1
W13 **104** D4
Avante Ct, Kings.T. KT1 **181** G3
Avard Gdns, Orp. BR6 **207** F4
Avarn Rd, SW17 **167** J6
Avebury Ct, N1
off Poole St **112** A1
Avebury Pk, Surb. KT6 **181** G7
Avebury Rd, E11
off Southwest Rd **96** D1
SW19 **184** C1
Orpington BR6 **207** G3
Avebury St, N1
off Poole St **112** A1
Aveline St, SE11 **34** E3
Aveling Pk Rd, E17 **78** A2
Ave Maria La, EC4 **19** H4
Avenell Rd, N5 **93** H3
Avening Rd, SW18
off Brathway Rd **148** D7
Avening Ter, SW18 **148** D6
Avenons Rd, E13 **115** G4
Avenue, The, E4 **62** D6
E11 (Leytonstone) **97** F2
E11 (Wanstead) **79** H6
N3 **72** D2
N8 **75** G3
N10 **74** C2
N11 **58** B4
N17 **76** B2
NW6 **108** A1
SE10 **134** D7
SW4 **150** A5
SW11 **149** H7
SW18 **149** H7
W4 **126** E3
W13 **104** E7
Barnet EN5 **40** B3
Beckenham BR3 **190** B1
Bexley DA5 **158** D7
Bromley BR1 **192** A3
Carshalton SM5 **200** A7
Croydon CR0 **202** B3
Epsom KT17 **197** H7
Esher (Clay.) KT10 **194** B6
Hampton TW12 **161** F6
Harrow HA3 **68** C1
Hounslow TW3 **143** H5
Hounslow (Cran.) TW5 **142** A1
Isleworth TW7 **124** A6
Keston BR2 **206** A3
Loughton IG10 **48** A6
Orpington BR6 **207** J2
Orpington (St.P.Cray) BR5 **176** B7
Pinner HA5 **67** F6
Pinner (Hatch End) HA5 **51** G7
Richmond TW9 **145** J2
Sunbury-on-Thames TW16 **178** B1
Surbiton KT5 **181** J6
Sutton (Cheam) SM3 **197** J7
Twickenham TW1 **145** F5
Wembley HA9 **87** J2
West Drayton UB7 **120** B3
West Wickham BR4 **190** C7
Worcester Park KT4 **197** F2
Avenue Cl, N14 **42** C6
NW8 **109** H1
Hounslow TW5
off The Avenue **142** A1
West Drayton UB7 **120** A3
Avenue Cres, W3 **126** B2
Hounslow TW5 **122** B7
Avenue Elmers, Surb. KT6 **181** H5
Avenue Gdns, SE25 **188** D3
SW14 **146** E3
W3 **126** B2
Hounslow TW5
off The Avenue **122** A7
Teddington TW11 **162** C7
Avenue Gate, Loug. IG10 **47** J6
Avenue Ind Est, E4 **61** J6
Avenue Ms, N10 **74** B3
Avenue Pk Rd, SE27 **169** H2
Avenue Rd, E7 **97** H5
N6 **74** C7
N12 **57** F4
N14 **42** B7
N15 **76** A5
NW3 **91** G7
NW8 **91** G7
NW10 **107** F2
SE20 **189** F1
SE25 **188** D2
SW16 **186** D2
SW20 **183** H2
W3 **126** B2
Beckenham BR3 **189** F1
Belvedere DA17 **139** J4
Bexleyheath DA7 **158** E3
Brentford TW8 **125** F5
Erith DA8 **139** J7
Hampton TW12 **179** H1
Isleworth TW7 **144** C1
Kingston upon Thames KT1 **181** H3
New Malden KT3 **182** E4
Pinner HA5 **66** E3
Romford (Chad.Hth) RM6 **82** B7
Southall UB1 **123** F2
Teddington TW11 **162** D7
Wallington SM6 **200** C7
Woodford Green IG8 **63** J6
Avenue Rd Est, E11
off High Rd Leytonstone **96** D4
Avenue S, Surb. KT5 **181** J7

Avenue Ter, N.Mal. KT3
off Kingston Rd 182 C3
Averil Gro, SW16 . . . . . . .169 H6
Averill St, W6 . . . . .128 A6
Avern Gdns, W.Mol. KT8 .179 H4
Avern Rd, W.Mol. KT8 . . .179 H5
Avery Fm Row, SW1 . . . . .32 D2
Avery Gdns, Ilf. IG2 . . . . . . .80 C5
AVERY HILL, SE9 . . . . . . .157 F6
★ **Avery Hill Pk**, SE9 . . . .157 F6
Avery Hill Rd, SE9 . . . . . . .157 G6
Avery Row, W1 . . . . .16 D5
Avey La, Loug.
(High Beach) IG10 . . . . . .47 H1
Aviary Cl, E16 . . . . .115 F5
Aviemore Cl, Beck. BR3 . .189 J5
Aviemore Way, Beck.
BR3 . . . . .189 H5
Avignon Rd, SE4 . . . . .153 G3
Avington Ct, SE1
off Old Kent Rd 36 E2
Avington Gro, SE20 . . . . .171 F7
Avion Cres, NW9 . . . . .71 G1
Avis Sq, E1 . . . . .113 G6
Avoca Rd, SW17 . . . . .168 A4
Avocet Cl, SE1 . . . . .37 H3
Avocet Ms, SE28 . . . . .137 G3
Avon Cl, Hayes UB4 . . . . .102 C4
Sutton SM1 . . . . .199 F4
Worcester Park KT4 . . .197 G2
Avon Ct, Buck.H. IG9
off Chequers 63 H1
Greenford UB6
off Braund Av 103 H4
Avondale Av, N12 . . . . .56 E5
NW2 . . . . .89 E3
Barnet EN4 . . . . .57 J1
Esher KT10 . . . . .194 D3
Avondale Av,
Worcester Park KT4 . . .197 F1
Avondale Cl, Loug. IG10 . . .48 C7
Avondale Ct, E11 . . . . .96 E1
E16 *off Avondale Rd* . . .115 E5
E18 . . . . .79 H1
Avondale Cres, Enf. EN3 . . .45 H3
Ilford IG4 . . . . .80 A5
Avondale Dr, Hayes UB3 .122 A1
Loughton IG10 . . . . .48 C7
Avondale Gdns, Houns.
TW4 . . . . .143 F5
Avondale Ho, SE1
off Avondale Sq 37 H4
Avondale Pk Gdns, W11 . .108 B7
Avondale Pk Rd, W11 . . . .108 B7
Avondale Ri, SE15 . . . . . .152 C3
Avondale Rd, E16 . . . . . . .115 E5
E17 . . . . .78 A7
N3 . . . . .73 F1
N13 . . . . .59 G2
N15 . . . . .75 H5
SE9 . . . . .174 B2
SW14 . . . . .146 D3
SW19 . . . . .166 E5
Bromley BR1 . . . . .173 E6
Harrow HA3 . . . . .68 C3
South Croydon CR2 . . .201 J6
Welling DA16 . . . . .158 C2
Avondale Sq, SE1 . . . . .37 H4
Avonley Rd, SE14 . . . . . . .133 F7
Avon Ms, Pnr. HA5 . . . . . . .67 F1
Avonmore Gdns, W14
off Avonmore Rd 128 C4
Avonmore Pl, W14
off Avonmore Rd 128 B4
Avonmore Rd, W14 . . . . .128 C4
Avonmouth St, SE1 . . . . . .27 J5
Avon Path, S.Croy. CR2 . .201 J6
Avon Pl, SE1 . . . . .28 A4
Avon Rd, E17 . . . . .78 D3
SE4 . . . . .154 A3
Greenford UB6 . . . . . . .103 G4
Avonstowe Cl, Orp.
BR6 . . . . .207 F3
Avon Way, E18 . . . . .79 G3
Avonwick Rd, Houns.
TW3 . . . . .143 H2
Avril Way, E4 . . . . .62 C5
Avro Way, Wall. SM6 . . . . .201 E7
Awlfield Av, N17 . . . . .76 A1
Awliscombe Rd, Well.
DA16 . . . . .157 J2
Axe St, Bark. IG11 . . . . . . .117 F1
Axholme Av, Edg. HA8 . . . .70 A1
Axis Ct, SE10
off Woodland Cres . . .134 E6
SE16 *off East La* 29 J3
Axminster Cres, Well.
DA16 . . . . .158 C1
Axminster Rd, N7 . . . . .93 E3
Axon Pl, Ilf. IG1 . . . . .99 F2
Aybrook St, W1 . . . . .16 B2
Aycliffe Cl, Brom. BR1 . . .192 C4
Aycliffe Rd, W12 . . . . .127 F1
Aylands Cl, Wem. HA9
off Preston Rd 87 H2
Aylesbury Cl, E7
off Atherton Rd 97 F6
Aylesbury Ct, Sutt. SM1
off Benhill Wd Rd 199 F3
Aylesbury Est, SE17 . . . . . .36 C4
Aylesbury Rd, SE17 . . . . . .36 C4
Bromley BR2 . . . . .191 G3
Aylesbury St, EC1 . . . . .11 G6
NW10 . . . . .88 D3
Aylesford Av, Beck. BR3 . .189 H5
Aylesford St, SW1 . . . . . . .33 H3
Aylesham Cen, SE15 . . . .152 D1
Aylesham Cl, NW7 . . . . . . .55 G7
Aylesham Rd, Orp. BR6 . .193 J7
Ayles Rd, Hayes UB4 . . . .102 B3
Aylestone Av, NW6 . . . . . .108 A1
Aylett Rd, SE25 . . . . .188 E4
Isleworth TW7 . . . . .144 B2
Ayley Cft, Enf. EN1 . . . . . .44 D5
Ayliffe Cl, Kings.T. KT1
off Cambridge Gdns . .182 A2
Aylmer Cl, Stan. HA7 . . . . .52 D4
Aylmer Dr, Stan. HA7 . . . . .52 D4
Aylmer Par, N2 . . . . .73 J5
Aylmer Rd, E11 . . . . .97 F1
N2 . . . . .73 H5
W12 . . . . .127 E2
Dagenham RM8 . . . . . .100 E3
Ayloffe Rd, Dag. RM9 . . . .101 F6
Aylton Est, SE16
off Renforth St 133 F2
Aylward Rd, SE23 . . . . . . .171 G2
SW20 . . . . .184 C2
Aylwards Ri, Stan. HA7 . . .52 D4
Aylward St, E1 . . . . .113 F6
Aylwyn Est, SE1 . . . . .29 E5
Aynhoe Rd, W14 . . . . .128 A4
Aynscombe La, SW14 . . .146 C3
Aynscombe Path, SW14
off Thames Bk 146 C2
Ayr Ct, W3 *off Monks Dr* .106 A5
Ayres Cl, E13 . . . . .115 G3
Ayres St, SE1 . . . . .28 A3
Ayrsome Rd, N16 . . . . .94 B3
Ayrton Gould Ho, E2
off Smart St 113 G3
Ayrton Rd, SW7 . . . . .22 E5
Aysgarth Ct, Sutt. SM1
off Sutton
Common Rd 198 E3
Aysgarth Rd, SE21 . . . . . .152 B6
Aytoun Pl, SW9 . . . . .151 F2
Aytoun Rd, SW9 . . . . .151 F2
Azalea Cl, W7 . . . . .124 C1
Ilford IG1 . . . . .98 E5
Azalea Ct, Wdf.Grn. IG8
off The Bridle Path 63 E7
Azalea Ho, Felt. TW13
off Bedfont La 160 B1
Azalea Wk, Pnr. HA5 . . . . . .66 B5
Southall UB2
off Navigator Dr 123 J2
Azania Ms, NW5 . . . . .92 B5
Azenby Rd, SE15 . . . . .152 C2
Azile Everitt Ho, SE18
off Blendon Ter 137 F5
Azof St, SE10 . . . . .135 E4

B

Baalbec Rd, N5 . . . . .93 H5
Babbacombe Cl, Chess.
KT9 . . . . .195 G5
Babbacombe Gdns, Ilf.
IG4 . . . . .80 B4
Babbacombe Rd, Brom.
BR1 . . . . .191 G1
Baber Dr, Felt. TW14 . . . . .142 C6
Babington Ct, WC1
off Ormond Cl 18 B1
Babington Ri, Wem. HA9 . .88 A6
Babington Rd, NW4 . . . . . .71 H4
SW16 . . . . .168 D5
Dagenham RM8 . . . . . .100 C5
Babmaes St, SW1 . . . . .17 H6
Bacchus Wk, N1 . . . . .12 D2
Baches St, N1 . . . . .12 C4
Back Ch La, E1 . . . . .21 H5
Back Hill, EC1 . . . . .11 E6
Backhouse Pl, SE17 . . . . . .36 E2
Back La, N8 . . . . .74 E5
NW3 *off Heath St* 91 F4
Bexley DA5 . . . . .159 G7
Brentford TW8 . . . . .125 G6
Buckhurst Hill IG9 . . . . . .64 A2
Edgware HA8 . . . . .70 C1
Richmond TW10 . . . . . .163 F3
Romford RM6
off St. Chad's Rd 82 E7
Backley Gdns, SE25 . . . . .188 D6
Back Rd, Sid. DA14 . . . . . .176 A4
Bacon Gro, SE1 . . . . .29 F6
Bacon La, NW9 . . . . .70 B4
Edgware HA8 . . . . .70 A1
Bacons La, N6 . . . . .92 A1
Bacon St, E1 . . . . .13 G5
E2 . . . . .13 G5
Bacon Ter, Dag. RM8
off Fitzstephen Rd . . .100 B5
Bacton, NW5 . . . . .92 A5
Bacton St, E2
off Roman Rd 113 F3
Baddow Cl, Dag. RM10 . . .119 G1
Woodford Green IG8 . . .64 A6
Baddow Wk, N1
off Popham Rd 111 J1
Baden Pl, SE1 . . . . .28 B3
Baden Powell Cl, Dag.
RM9 . . . . .119 E1
Surbiton KT6 . . . . .195 J2
Baden Rd, N8 . . . . .74 D4
Ilford IG1 . . . . .98 E5
Badger Cl, Felt. TW13
off Sycamore Cl 160 A3
Hounslow TW4 . . . . . . .142 C3
Ilford IG2 . . . . .81 F7
Badgers Cl, Enf. EN2 . . . . .43 H3
Harrow HA1 . . . . .68 A6
Badgers Copse, Orp.
BR6 . . . . .207 J2
Worcester Park KT4 . . .197 F2
Badgers Cft, N20 . . . . .56 B1
SE9 . . . . .174 D3
Badgers Hole, Croy.
CR0 . . . . .203 G4
Badgers Wk, N.Mal. KT3 .182 E2
Badlis Rd, E17 . . . . .78 A2
Badma Cl, N9
off Hudson Way 61 F3
Badminton Cl, Borwd.
WD6 . . . . .38 A2
Harrow HA1 . . . . .68 B4
Northolt UB5 . . . . .85 G6
Badminton Ms, E16
off Hanameel St 135 G1
Badminton Rd, SW12 . . . .150 A6
Badric Ct, SW11
off Yelverton Rd 149 G2
Badsworth Rd, SE5 . . . . .131 J7
Baffin Way, E14
off Prestons Rd 114 C7
Bafton Gate, Brom. BR2 . .205 H1
Bagley Cl, West Dr. UB7 . .120 B2
Bagley's La, SW6 . . . . . . .149 E1
Bagleys Spring, Rom.
RM6 . . . . .83 E4
Bagshot Ct, SE18
off Prince
Imperial Rd 156 D1
Bagshot Rd, Enf. EN1 . . . . .44 C7
Bagshot St, SE17 . . . . .36 E4
Baildon St, SE8 . . . . .133 J7
Bailey Cl, E4 . . . . .62 C4
N11 . . . . .58 D7
SE28 . . . . .137 H1
Bailey Cres, Chess. KT9 . .195 G7
Bailey Ms, SW2 . . . . .151 G5
W4 *off Herbert Gdns* . .126 B6
Bailey Pl, SE26 . . . . .171 G6
Baillies Wk, W5
off Liverpool Rd 125 G2
Bainbridge Cl, Rich.
(Ham) TW10
off Latchmere Cl 163 H5
Bainbridge Rd, Dag.
RM9 . . . . .101 F4
Bainbridge St, WC1 . . . . . . .17 J3
Baines Cl, S.Croy. CR2
off Brighton Rd 202 A5
Baird Av, Sthl. UB1 . . . . . .103 H7
Baird Cl, E10
off Marconi Rd 96 A1
NW9 . . . . .70 C6
Baird Gdns, SE19 . . . . . . .170 B4
Baird Rd, Enf. EN1 . . . . . . .44 E4
Baird St, EC1 . . . . .12 A5
Bairny Wd App, Wdf.Grn.
IG8 *off Broadway Cl* 63 H6
Baizdon Rd, SE3 . . . . .154 E2
Bakehouse Ms, Hmptn.
TW12 *off Malvern Rd* . .161 G7
Baker La, Mitch. CR4 . . . .186 A2
Baker Pas, NW10
off Baker Rd 106 E1
Baker Pl, Epsom KT19 . . .196 C6
Baker Rd, NW10 . . . . .106 E1
SE18 . . . . .136 B7
Bakers Av, E17 . . . . .78 B6
Bakers Ct, SE25 . . . . .188 B3
Bakers End, SW20 . . . . . .184 B2
Bakers Fld, N7 . . . . .92 D4
Bakers Gdns, Cars.
SM5 . . . . .199 H2
Bakers Hall Ct, EC3 . . . . . . .20 E6
Bakers Hill, E5 . . . . .95 F1
Barnet (New Barn.)
EN5 . . . . .41 E2
Bakers La, N6 . . . . .73 J5
Baker's Ms, W1 . . . . .16 B3
Bakers Ms, Orp. BR6 . . . .207 J6
Bakers Pas, NW3
off Heath St 91 F4
Baker's Rents, E2 . . . . .13 F4
Bakers Row, E15 . . . . .114 E2
Baker's Row, EC1 . . . . .11 E6
Baker St, NW1 . . . . .8 A6
W1 . . . . .16 A1
Enfield EN1 . . . . .44 A3
Baker's Yd, EC1 . . . . .11 E6
Bakery Cl, SW9 . . . . .151 F1
Bakery Path, Edg. HA8
off Station Rd 54 B6
Bakery Pl, SW11
off Altenburg Gdns . .149 J4
Bakewell Way, N.Mal.
KT3 . . . . .182 E2
Balaams La, N14 . . . . .58 D2
Balaam St, E13 . . . . .115 G3
Balaclava Rd, SE1 . . . . . . .37 G2
Surbiton KT6 . . . . .181 F7
Bala Grn, NW9
off Snowdon Dr 70 E6
Balcaskie Rd, SE9 . . . . . .156 C5
Balchen Rd, SE3 . . . . .156 A2
Balchier Rd, SE22 . . . . . . .152 E6
Balcombe Cl, Bexh.
DA6 . . . . .158 D4
Balcombe St, NW1 . . . . .7 J6
Balcon Ct, W5
off Boileau Rd 105 J6
Balcon Way, Borwd. WD6 . .38 C1
Balcorne St, E9 . . . . .95 F7
Balder Ri, SE12 . . . . .173 H2
Balderton St, W1 . . . . .16 C4
Baldock St, E3 . . . . .114 B2
Baldry Gdns, SW16 . . . . .169 E6
Baldwin Cres, SE5 . . . . . .151 J1
Baldwin Gdns, Houns.
TW3 *off Chamberlain*
Gdns 143 J1
Baldwin's Gdns, EC1 . . . . .18 E1
Baldwins Hill, Loug. IG10 . .48 C2
Baldwin St, EC1 . . . . .12 B4
Baldwin Ter, N1 . . . . .11 J1
Baldwyn Gdns, W3 . . . . . .106 C7
Balearic Apts, E16
off Western Gateway .115 G7
Bale Rd, E1 . . . . .113 H5
Balfern Gro, W4 . . . . .127 E5
Balfern St, SW11 . . . . .149 H1
Balfe St, N1 . . . . .10 B2
Balfour Av, W7 . . . . .124 C1
Balfour Business Cen,
Sthl. UB2 . . . . .122 D3
Balfour Gro, N20 . . . . .57 J3
Balfour Ho, W10
off St. Charles Sq 108 A5
Balfour Ms, N9
off Fore St 60 D3
W1 . . . . .24 C1
Balfour Pl, SW15 . . . . .147 H4
W1 . . . . .16 C6
Balfour Rd, N5 . . . . .93 J4
SE25 . . . . .188 D4
SW19 . . . . .166 E7
W3 . . . . .106 C5
W13 . . . . .124 D2
Bromley BR2 . . . . .192 A5
Carshalton SM5 . . . . . .199 J7
Harrow HA1 . . . . .68 A5
Hounslow TW3 . . . . . . .143 H3
Ilford IG1 . . . . .98 E2
Southall UB2 . . . . .122 D3
Balfour St, SE17 . . . . .36 B1
Balfron Twr, E14
off St. Leonards Rd . . .114 C6
Balgonie Rd, E4 . . . . .62 D1
Balgowan Cl, N.Mal. KT3 .183 E5
Balgowan Rd, Beck. BR3 . .189 H3
Balgowan St, SE18 . . . . . .137 J4
BALHAM, SW12 . . . . .167 J1
Balham Continental Mkt,
SW12 *off Shipka Rd* 168 B1
Balham Gro, SW12 . . . . . .150 A7
Balham High Rd, SW12 . . .168 A1
SW17 . . . . .168 A2
Balham Hill, SW12 . . . . . .150 B7
Balham New Rd, SW12 . . .150 B7
Balham Pk Rd, SW12 . . . .167 J1
Balham Rd, N9 . . . . .60 D2
Balham Sta Rd, SW12 . . .168 B1
Balkan Wk, E1
off Tobacco Dock 112 E7
Balladier Wk, E14 . . . . . . .114 B5
Ballamore Rd, Brom.
BR1 . . . . .173 G3
Ballance Rd, E9 . . . . .95 G6

Ballantine St, SW18 149 F4
Ballantyne Cl, SE9 174 B4
Ballard Cl, Kings.T. KT2 164 D7
Ballards Cl, Dag. RM10 119 H1
Ballards Fm Rd, Croy. CR0 202 D6
South Croydon CR2 202 D6
Ballards La, N3 72 D1
N12 72 D1
Ballards Ms, Edg. HA8 54 A6
Ballards Ri, S.Croy. CR2 202 D6
Ballards Rd, NW2 89 G2
Dagenham RM10 119 H1
Ballards Way, Croy. CR0 203 E6
South Croydon CR2 202 D6
Ballast Quay, SE10 134 D5
Ballater Cl, Wat. WD19 50 C4
Ballater Rd, SW2 151 E4
South Croydon CR2 202 C5
Ball Ct, EC3 *off Castle Ct* 20 C4
Ballina St, SE23 153 G7
Ballingdon Rd, SW11 150 A6
Ballinger Pt, E3 *off Bromley High St* 114 B3
Ballinger Way, Nthlt. UB5 103 E4
Balliol Av, E4 62 D4
Balliol Rd, N17 76 B1
W10 107 J6
Welling DA16 158 B2
Balloch Rd, SE6 172 D1
Ballogie Av, NW10 89 E4
Ballow Cl, SE5 *off Harris St* 132 B7
Balls Pond Pl, N1 *off Balls Pond Rd* 94 A6
Balls Pond Rd, N1 94 A6
Balmain Cl, W5 125 G1
Balmer Rd, E3 113 J2
Balmes Rd, N1 112 A1
Balmoral Apts, W2 *off Praed St* 15 G2
Balmoral Av, N11 58 A5
Beckenham BR3 189 H4
Balmoral Cl, SW15 148 A6
Balmoral Ct, Wor.Pk. KT4 197 H2
Balmoral Cres, W.Mol. KT8 179 G3
Balmoral Dr, Borwd. WD6 38 D5
Southall UB1 103 F4
Balmoral Gdns, W13 124 D3
Bexley DA5 159 F7
Ilford IG3 99 J1
Balmoral Gro, N7 93 F6
Balmoral Ms, W12 127 F3
Balmoral Rd, E7 97 J4
E10 96 B2
NW2 89 H6
Harrow HA2 85 G4
Kingston upon Thames KT1 181 J4
Worcester Park KT4 197 H3
Balmore Cl, E14 114 C6
Balmore Cres, Barn. EN4 42 A5
Balmore St, N19 92 B2
Balmuir Gdns, SW15 147 J4
Balnacraig Av, NW10 89 E4
Balniel Gate, SW1 33 J3
Baltic Apts, E16 *off Western Gateway* 115 G7
Baltic Cl, SW19 167 G7
Baltic Ct, SE16 *off Timber Pond Rd* 133 G2
Baltic Pl, N1 *off Kingsland Rd* 112 B1
Baltic Quay, SE16 *off Sweden Gate* 133 H4
Baltic St E, EC1 11 J6
Baltic St W, EC1 11 J6
Baltimore Ho, SW18 *off Juniper Dr* 149 F4
Baltimore Pl, Well. DA16 157 J2
Balvaird Pl, SW1 33 J4
Balvernie Gro, SW18 148 C7
Bamber Ho, Bark. IG11 *off St. Margarets* 117 F1
Bamber Rd, SE15 *off Moody Rd* 152 C1
Bamborough Gdns, W12 127 J2
Bamford Av, Wem. HA0 105 J1
Bamford Rd, Bark. IG11 99 F6
Bromley BR1 172 C5
Bampfylde Cl, Wall. SM6 200 C3
Bampton Dr, NW7 55 G7
Bampton Rd, SE23 171 G3
Banavie Gdns, Beck. BR3 190 C1
Banbury Cl, Enf. EN2 *off Holtwhites Hill* 43 H1
Banbury Ct, WC2 18 A5
Sutton SM2 198 D7
Banbury Enterprise Cen, Croy. CR0 *off Factory La* 201 H2
Banbury Rd, E9 95 G7
E17 61 G7
Banbury St, SW11 149 H2
Banbury Wk, Nthlt. UB5 *off Brabazon Rd* 103 G2
Banchory Rd, SE3 135 H7
Bancroft Av, N2 73 H5
Buckhurst Hill IG9 63 G2
Bancroft Ct, SW8 *off Allen Edwards Dr* 150 E1
Northolt UB5 102 C1
Bancroft Gdns, Har. HA3 67 J1
Orpington BR6 207 J1
Bancroft Rd, E1 113 F3
Harrow HA3 67 J2
Bandon Ri, Wall. SM6 200 D5
Banfield Rd, SE15 152 E3
Bangalore St, SW15 147 J3
Bangor Cl, Nthlt. UB5 85 H5
Banim St, W6 127 H3
Banister Ms, NW6 90 E7
Banister Rd, W10 108 A3
Bank, The, N6 *off Cholmeley Pk* 92 B1
Bank Av, Mitch. CR4 185 G2
Bank End, SE1 28 A1
Bankfoot Rd, Brom. BR1 173 E4
Bankhurst Rd, SE6 153 J7
Bank La, SW15 146 E5
Kingston upon Thames KT2 163 H7
Bank Ms, Sutt. SM1 *off Sutton Ct Rd* 199 F6
★ **Bank of England**, EC2 20 B4
★ **Bank of England Mus**, EC2 20 C4
Banks Ho, SE1 27 J6
Banksian Wk, Islw. TW7 144 B1
Banksia Rd, N18 61 F5
Bankside, SE1 19 J6
Enfield EN2 43 H1
South Croydon CR2 202 C6
Southall UB1 122 D1
Bankside Av, SE13 154 B3
Northolt UB5 *off Townson Av* 102 A2
Bankside Cl, N4 75 J6
Carshalton SM5 199 H6
Isleworth TW7 144 C4
Bankside Dr, T.Ditt. KT7 194 E1
★ **Bankside Gall**, SE1 19 H6
Bankside Lofts, SE1 27 H1
Bankside Rd, Ilf. IG1 99 F5
Bankside Way, SE19 *off Lunham Rd* 170 B6
Banks La, Bexh. DA6 159 F4
Banks Rd, Borwd. WD6 38 C2
Bank St, E14 134 A1
Banks Way, E12 98 D4
Bankton Rd, SW2 151 G4
Bankwell Rd, SE13 155 E4
Bannerman Ho, SW8 34 C6
Banner St, EC1 12 A6
Banning St, SE10 134 E5
Bannister Cl, SW2 169 G1
Greenford UB6 86 A5
Bannister Ho, E9 *off Homerton High St* 95 G5
Harrow HA3 *off Headstone Dr* 68 B3
Bannockburn Rd, SE18 137 H4
Bannow Cl, Epsom KT19 196 E4
★ **Banqueting Ho**, SW1 26 A2
Banstead Ct, W12 *off Hilary Rd* 107 F7
Banstead Gdns, N9 60 B3
Banstead Rd, Cars. SM5 199 H6
Banstead St, SE15 153 F3
Banstead Way, Wall. SM6 201 E5
Banstock Rd, Edg. HA8 54 B6
Banting Dr, N21 43 F5
Banton Cl, Enf. EN1 *off Central Av* 44 E2
Bantry St, SE5 132 A7
Banwell Rd, Bex. DA5 *off Woodside La* 158 D6
Banyard Rd, SE16 *off Southwark Pk Rd* 133 E3
Baptist Gdns, NW5 *off Queen's Cres* 92 A6
Barandon Wk, W11 108 A7
Barbara Brosnan Ct, NW8 6 E2
Barbara Castle Cl, SW6 128 C6
Barbara Hucklesby Cl, N22 *off The Sandlings* 75 H2
Barbauld Rd, N16 94 B3
Barber Cl, N21 43 G7
Barber's All, E13 115 H3
Barbers Rd, E15 114 B2
BARBICAN, EC2 19 J2
★ **Barbican Arts & Conf Cen**, EC2 20 A1
Barbican Rd, Grnf. UB6 103 H6
Barb Ms, W6 127 J3
Barbon Cl, WC1 18 B1
Barbot Cl, N9 60 D3
Barchard St, SW18 148 E5
Barchester Cl, W7 124 C1
Barchester Rd, Har. HA3 68 A2
Barchester St, E14 114 B5
Barclay Cl, SW6 128 D7
Barclay Oval, Wdf.Grn. IG8 63 G4
Barclay Path, E17 78 C5
Barclay Rd, E11 97 E1
E13 115 J4
E17 78 C5
N18 60 A6
SW6 128 D7
Croydon CR0 202 A3
Barcombe Av, SW2 169 E2
Barcombe Cl, Orp. BR5 193 J3
Barden St, SE18 137 H7
Bardfield Av, Rom. RM6 82 D3
Bardney Rd, Mord. SM4 185 E4
Bardolph Rd, N7 92 E4
Richmond TW9 *off St. Georges Rd* 145 J3
Bard Rd, W10 108 A7
Bardsey Pl, E1 *off Mile End Rd* 113 F5
Bardsey Wk, N1 *off Clephane Rd* 93 J6
Bardsley Cl, Croy. CR0 202 C3
Bardsley La, SE10 134 C6
Barfett St, W10 108 C4
Barfield Av, N20 57 H2
Barfield Rd, E11 97 F1
Bromley BR1 192 D3
Barfields, Loug. IG10 48 D4
Barfields Gdns, Loug. IG10 *off Barfields* 48 D4
Barfields Path, Loug. IG10 48 D4
Barfleur La, SE8 133 J4
Barford Cl, NW4 71 G1
Barford St, N1 111 G1
Barforth Rd, SE15 153 E3
Barfreston Way, SE20 189 E1
Bargate Cl, SE18 137 J5
New Malden KT3 183 G7
Barge Ho Rd, E16 136 E1
Barge Ho St, SE1 27 F1
Barge La, E3 *off Birdsfield La* 113 J1
Bargery Rd, SE6 172 B1
Barge Wk, E.Mol. KT8 180 A3
Kingston upon Thames KT1, KT2 181 G1
Walton-on-Thames KT12 178 D3
Bargrove Cl, SE20 170 D7
Bargrove Cres, SE6 *off Elm La* 171 J2
Barham Cl, Brom. BR2 206 B1
Chislehurst BR7 174 E5
Romford RM7 83 H2
Wembley HA0 87 E6
Barham Rd, SW20 165 G7
Chislehurst BR7 174 E5
South Croydon CR2 201 J4
Baring Cl, SE12 173 G2
Baring Rd, SE12 155 G7
Barnet (Cockfos.) EN4 41 G3
Croydon CR0 202 D1
Baring St, N1 112 A1
Barkantine Shop Par, The, E14 *off The Quarterdeck* 134 A2
Barker Cl, N.Mal. KT3 *off England Way* 182 B4
Richmond TW9 146 B2
Barker Dr, NW1 92 C7
Barker Ms, SW4 150 B4
Barker St, SW10 30 C5
Barker Wk, SW16 168 D3
Barkham Rd, N17 60 A7
Barkham Ter, SE1 27 F5
BARKING, IG11 117 E1
Barking & Dagenham Civic Cen, Dag. RM10 101 H2
Barking Ind Pk, Bark. IG11 117 J1
Barking Rd, E6 116 A2
E13 115 H4
E16 115 F5
BARKINGSIDE, Ilf. IG6 81 E3
Bark Pl, W2 14 A5
Barkston Gdns, SW5 30 A3
Barkway Ct, N4 *off Queens Dr* 93 J2
Barkway Dr, Orp. BR6 206 D4
Barkwood Cl, Rom. RM7 83 J5
Barkworth Rd, SE16 133 E5
Barlborough St, SE14 133 F7
Barlby Gdns, W10 108 A4
Barlby Rd, W10 108 A5
Barley Cl, Wem. HA0 87 G4
Barleycorn Way, E14 113 J7
Barleyfields Cl, Rom. RM6 82 B7
Barley La, Ilf. IG3 100 A1
Romford RM6 82 B6
Barley Mow Pas, EC1 19 H2
W4 126 D5
Barley Shotts Business Pk, W10 *off Acklam Rd* 108 C5
Barlow Cl, Wall. SM6 200 E7
Barlow Dr, SE18 156 B1
Barlow Ho, SE16 *off Rennie Est* 133 E4
Barlow Pl, W1 17 E6
Barlow Rd, NW6 90 C6
W3 126 B1
Hampton TW12 161 G7
Barlow St, SE17 36 C1
Barmeston Rd, SE6 172 B2
Barmor Cl, Har. HA2 67 H2
Barmouth Av, Grnf. (Perivale) UB6 104 C2
Barmouth Rd, SW18 149 F6
Croydon CR0 203 G2
Barnabas Ct, N21 *off Cheyne Wk* 43 G5
Barnabas Rd, E9 95 G5
Barnaby Cl, Har. HA2 85 J2
Barnaby Pl, SW7 31 E2
Barnaby Way, Chig. IG7 64 E3
Barnard Cl, SE18 136 D4
Chislehurst BR7 193 G1
Sunbury-on-Thames TW16 *off Oak Gro* 160 B7
Wallington SM6 200 D7
Barnard Gdns, Hayes UB4 102 B4
New Malden KT3 183 G4
Barnard Gro, E15 *off Vicarage La* 97 F7
Barnard Hill, N10 74 A2
Barnard Ms, SW11 149 H4
Barnardo Dr, Ilf. IG6 81 F4
Barnardo Gdns, E1 *off Devonport St* 113 G7
Barnardo St, E1 *off Devonport St* 113 G6
Barnardos Village, Ilf. IG6 81 F3
Barnard Rd, SW11 149 H4
Enfield EN1 45 E2
Mitcham CR4 186 A3
Barnard's Inn, EC1 19 F3
Barnby Sq, E15 *off Barnby St* 114 E1
Barnby St, E15 114 E1
NW1 9 G2
Barn Cl, Nthlt. UB5 102 C2
Barn Cres, Stan. HA7 53 F6
Barncroft Cl, Loug. IG10 48 D5
Barncroft Grn, Loug. IG10 48 D5
Barncroft Rd, Loug. IG10 48 D5
Barneby Cl, Twick. TW2 *off Rowntree Rd* 162 B1
Barnehurst Av, Bexh. DA7 159 J1
Erith DA8 159 J1
Barnehurst Cl, Erith DA8 159 J1
Barnehurst Rd, Bexh. DA7 159 J2
Barn Elms Pk, SW15 147 J2
BARNES, SW13 147 G2
Barnes All, Hmptn. TW12 *off Hampton Ct Rd* 179 J2
Barnes Av, SW13 127 G7
Southall UB2 123 F4
Barnes Br, SW13 147 E2
W4 147 E2
Barnesbury Ho, SW4 150 D5
Barnes Cl, E12 98 A4
★ **Barnes Common**, SW13 147 G3
Barnes Ct, E16 *off Ridgwell Rd* 115 J5
Barnet EN5 41 E4
Woodford Green IG8 64 A5
Barnes End, N.Mal. KT3 183 G5
Barnes High St, SW13 147 F2
Barnes Ho, Bark. IG11 *off St. Marys* 117 G1
Barnes Pikle, W5 105 G7
Barnes Rd, N18 61 F4
Ilford IG1 99 F5

Barnes St, E14 113 H6
Barnes Ter, SE8 133 J5
BARNET, EN4 & EN5 40 C3
Barnet Bypass, Barn. EN5 38 E3
Borehamwood WD6 38 E3
Barnet Dr, Brom. BR2 206 B2
BARNET GATE, Barn. EN5 39 F6
Barnet Gate La, Barn. EN5 39 F6
Barnet Gro, E2 13 H3
Barnet Hill, Barn. EN5 40 D4
Barnet La, N20 56 C1
Barnet EN5 40 C6
★ **Barnet Mus**, Barn. EN5 *off Wood St* 40 B4
Barnet Rd, Barn. EN5 39 H5
Barnet Trd Est, Barn. (High Barn.) EN5 40 C3
Barnett St, E1 *off Cannon St Rd* 112 E6
Barnet Way, NW7 38 D7
Barnet Wd Rd, Brom. BR2 205 J2
Barney Cl, SE7 135 J5
Barn Fld, NW3 *off Upper Pk Rd* 91 J5
Barnfield, N.Mal. KT3 182 E6
Barnfield Av, Croy. CR0 203 F2
Kingston upon Thames KT2 163 H5
Mitcham CR4 186 B4
Barnfield Cl, N4 *off Crouch Hill* 75 E7
SW17 167 F3
Barnfield Gdns, SE18 *off Barnfield Rd* 137 E6
Kingston upon Thames KT2 163 H4
Barnfield Pl, E14 134 A4
Barnfield Rd, SE18 137 E6
W5 105 F4
Belvedere DA17 139 F6
Edgware HA8 70 C1
Barnfield Wd Cl, Beck. BR3 190 D6
Barnfield Wd Rd, Beck. BR3 190 D6
Barnham Dr, SE28 137 J1
Barnham Rd, Grnf. UB6 103 J3
Barnham St, SE1 28 E3
Barnhill, Pnr. HA5 66 C5
Barn Hill, Wem. HA9 88 B2
Barnhill Av, Brom. BR2 191 F5
Barnhill La, Hayes UB4 102 B3
Barnhill Rd, Hayes UB4 102 B4
Wembley HA9 88 C3
Barnhurst Path, Wat. WD19 50 C5
Barningham Way, NW9 70 D6
Barnlea Cl, Felt. TW13 161 E2
Barnmead Gdns, Dag. RM9 101 F5
Barnmead Rd, Beck. BR3 189 H1
Dagenham RM9 101 F5
Barn Ri, Wem. HA9 88 A1
BARNSBURY, N1 93 F7
Barnsbury Cl, N.Mal. KT3 182 C4
Barnsbury Cres, Surb. KT5 196 C1
Barnsbury Est, N1 *off Barnsbury Rd* 111 F1
Barnsbury Gro, N7 93 F7
Barnsbury La, Surb. KT5 196 B2
Barnsbury Pk, N1 93 G7
Barnsbury Rd, N1 10 E1
Barnsbury Sq, N1 93 G7
Barnsbury St, N1 93 G7
Barnsbury Ter, N1 93 F7
Barnscroft, SW20 183 H3
Barnsdale Av, E14 134 A4
Barnsdale Rd, W9 108 C4
Barnsley St, E1 113 E4
Barnstaple La, SE13 *off Lewisham High St* 154 C4
Barnstaple Rd, Ruis. HA4 84 C3
Barnston Wk, N1 *off Popham St* 111 J1
Barn St, N16 *off Stoke Newington Ch St* 94 B2
Barn Way, Wem. HA9 88 A1
Barnwell Rd, SW2 151 G5
Barnwood Cl, N20 56 C1
W9 6 A6
Baron Cl, N11 58 A5
Baroness Rd, E2 13 G3
Baronet Gro, N17 *off St. Paul's Rd* 76 D1
Baronet Rd, N17 76 D1
Baron Gdns, Ilf. IG6 81 F3
Baron Gro, Mitch. CR4 185 H4
Baron Ho, SW19 *off Chapter Way* 185 G1
Baron Rd, Dag. RM8 100 D1
Barons, The, Twick. TW1 145 E6
Barons Ct, Wall. SM6 *off Whelan Way* 200 D3
Barons Ct Rd, W14 128 B5
Baronsfield Rd, Twick. TW1 145 E6
Barons Gate, Barn. EN4 41 H6
Barons Keep, W14 128 B5
Barons Mead, Har. HA1 68 B4
Baronsmead Rd, SW13 147 G1
Baronsmede, W5 125 J2
Baronsmere Rd, N2 73 H4
Barons Pl, SE1 27 F4
Baron St, N1 11 E1
Barons Wk, Croy. CR0 189 H6
Baron Wk, E16 115 F5
Mitcham CR4 185 H4
Baroque Ct, Houns. TW3 *off Prince Regent Rd* 143 J3
Barque Ms, SE8 *off Watergate St* 134 A6
Barrack Rd, Houns. TW4 142 D4
Barracks La, Barn. EN5 *off High St* 40 B3
Barratt Av, N22 75 F2
Barratt Ind Pk, Sthl. UB1 123 G2
Barratt Way, Har. HA3 *off Tudor Rd* 68 A3
Barrenger Rd, N10 73 J1
Barrett Rd, E17 78 C4
Barretts Grn Rd, NW10 106 C2
Barretts Gro, N16 94 B5
Barrett St, W1 16 C4
Barrhill Rd, SW2 169 E2
Barriedale, SE14 153 H1
Barrie Est, W2 14 E5
Barrier App, SE7 136 A3
Barrier Pt Rd, E16 135 J1
Barrier Pt Twr, E16 *off Barrier Pt Rd* 135 J2
Barringer Sq, SW17 168 A4
Barrington Cl, NW5 92 A5
Ilford IG5 80 C1
Loughton IG10 *off Barrington Rd* 49 F4
Barrington Ct, W3 *off Cheltenham Pl* 126 B2
Barrington Grn, Loug. IG10 49 F4
Barrington Rd, E12 98 D6
N8 74 D5
SW9 151 H3
Bexleyheath DA7 158 D2
Loughton IG10 49 F3
Sutton SM3 198 D1
Barrington Vil, SE18 156 D1
Barrow Av, Cars. SM5 199 J7
Barrow Cl, N21 59 H3
Barrowdene Cl, Pnr. HA5 *off Paines La* 67 E2
Barrowell Grn, N21 59 H2
Barrowfield Cl, N9 61 E3
Barrowgate Rd, W4 126 C5
Barrow Hedges Cl, Cars. SM5 199 H7
Barrow Hedges Way, Cars. SM5 199 H7
Barrow Hill, Wor.Pk. KT4 196 E2
Barrow Hill Cl, Wor.Pk. KT4 196 E2
Barrow Hill Est, NW8 7 G2
Barrow Hill Rd, NW8 7 G2
Barrow Pt Av, Pnr. HA5 66 E2
Barrow Pt La, Pnr. HA5 66 E2
Barrow Rd, SW16 168 D6
Croydon CR0 201 G5
Barrow Wk, Brent. TW8 *off Glenhurst Rd* 125 F5
Barrs Rd, NW10 88 D7
Barry Av, N15 76 C6
Bexleyheath DA7 138 E7
Barry Cl, Orp. BR6 207 H3
Barry Ho, SE16 *off Rennie Est* 133 E5
Barry Rd, E6 116 B6
NW10 88 C7
SE22 152 D6
Barset Rd, SE15 153 F3
Barson Cl, SE20 171 F7
Barston Rd, SE27 169 J2
Barstow Cres, SW2 169 F1
Barter St, WC1 18 B2
Barters Wk, Pnr. HA5 *off High St* 66 E3
Barth Ms, SE18 137 H4
Bartholomew Cl, EC1 19 J2
SW18 149 F4
Bartholomew Ct, E14 *off Newport Av* 114 D7
Bartholomew La, EC2 20 C4
Bartholomew Pl, EC1 19 J2
Bartholomew Rd, NW5 92 C6
Bartholomew Sq, E1 *off Coventry Rd* 113 E4
EC1 12 A5
Bartholomew St, SE1 28 B6
Bartholomew Vil, NW5 92 C6
Barth Rd, SE18 137 H4
Bartle Av, E6 116 B2
Bartle Rd, W11 108 B6
Bartlett Cl, E14 114 A6
Bartlett Ct, EC4 19 F3
Bartletts Pas, EC4 19 F3
Bartlett St, S.Croy. CR2 202 A5
Barton Av, Rom. RM7 101 H1
Barton Cl, E6 116 C6
E9 *off Churchill Wk* 95 F5
NW4 71 G5
SE15 *off Kirkwood Rd* 153 E3
Bexleyheath DA6 158 E5
Barton Cl, Chigwell IG7 65 F2
Barton Grn, N.Mal. KT3 182 D2
Barton Ho,
E3 *off Bow Rd* 114 B3
N1 *off Sable St* 93 H7
SW6 *off Wandsworth Br Rd* 149 E3
Barton Meadows, Ilf. IG6 81 F4
Barton Rd, W14 128 B5
Sidcup DA14 177 E6
Barton St, SW1 26 A5
Bartonway, NW8 *off Queen's Ter* 109 G1
Barton Way, Borwd. WD6 38 A2
Bartram Rd, SE4 153 H5
Barts Cl, Beck. BR3 190 A5
Barville Cl, SE4 *off St. Norbert Rd* 153 H4
Barwell Business Pk, Chess. KT9 195 G7
Barwell La, Chess. KT9 195 F7
Barwick Ho, W3 126 C2
Barwick Rd, E7 97 H4
Barwood Av, W.Wick. BR4 204 B1
Bascombe St, SW2 151 G6
Basden Gro, Felt. TW13 161 G2
Basedale Rd, Dag. RM9 100 B7
Baseing Cl, E6 116 D7
Basevi Way, SE8 134 B6
Bashley Rd, NW10 106 D4
Basil Av, E6 116 B2
Basildene Rd, Houns. TW4 142 D2
Basildon Av, Ilf. IG5 80 D1
Basildon Rd, SE2 138 A5
Basil Gdns, SE27 169 J5
Croydon CR0 *off Primrose La* 203 G1
Basilon Rd, Bexh. DA7 158 E2
Basil St, SW3 23 J5
Basin App, E14 *off Commercial Rd* 113 H6
Basing Cl, T.Ditt. KT7 180 C7
Basing Ct, SE15 152 C1
Basingdon Way, SE5 152 A4
Basing Dr, Bex. DA5 159 F6
Basingfield Rd, T.Ditt. KT7 180 C7
Basinghall Av, EC2 20 B2
Basinghall St, EC2 20 B3
Basing Hill, NW11 90 C1
Wembley HA9 87 J2
Basing Ho, Bark. IG11 *off St. Margarets* 117 G1
Basing Ho Yd, E2 13 E3
Basing Pl, E2 13 E3
Basing St, W11 108 C6
Basing Way, N3 72 D3
Thames Ditton KT7 180 C7
Basire St, N1 111 J1
Baskerville Gdns, NW10 *off Dog La* 89 E4
Baskerville Rd, SW18 149 H7
Basket Gdns, SE9 156 B5
Baslow Cl, Har. HA3 68 A1
Baslow Wk, E5 *off Overbury St* 95 G4
Basnett Rd, SW11 150 A3
Basque Ct, SE16 *off Poolmans St* 133 G2
Bassano St, SE22 152 C5
Bassant Rd, SE18 137 J6
Bassein Pk Rd, W12 127 F2
Bassett Gdns, Islw. TW7 123 J7
Bassett Ho, Dag. RM9 118 B1
Bassett Rd, W10 108 A6
Bassetts Cl, Orp. BR6 206 E4
Bassett St, NW5 92 A6
Bassetts Way, Orp. BR6 206 E4
Bassett Way, Grnf. UB6 103 H6
Bassingham Rd, SW18 149 F7
Wembley HA0 87 G6
Bassishaw Highwalk, EC2 *off Aldermanbury Sq* 20 A2
Bastable Av, Bark. IG11 117 H2
Bastion Highwalk, EC2 19 J2
Bastion Ho, EC2 *off London Wall* 19 J2
Bastion Rd, SE2 138 A5
Baston Manor Rd, Brom. BR2 205 H3
Baston Rd, Brom. BR2 205 H1
Bastwick St, EC1 11 J5
Basuto Rd, SW6 148 D1
Batavia Cl, Sun. TW16 178 C1
Batavia Ms, SE14 *off Goodwood Rd* 133 H7
Batavia Rd, SE14 133 H7
Sunbury-on-Thames TW16 178 B1
Batchelor St, N1 11 E1
Bateman Cl, Bark. IG11 *off Glenny Rd* 99 F6
Bateman Ho, SE17 35 G6
Bateman Rd, E4 62 A6
Bateman's Bldgs, W1 17 H4
Bateman's Row, EC2 12 E5
Bateman St, W1 17 H4
Bates Cres, SW16 168 C7
Croydon CR0 201 G5
Bateson St, SE18 137 H4
Bate St, E14 *off Three Colt St* 113 J7
Bath Cl, SE15 *off Asylum Rd* 133 E7
Bath Ct, EC1 11 E6
EC1 (St. Luke's Est) *off St. Luke's Est* 12 B4
Bathgate Rd, SW19 166 A3
Bath Ho, SE1 *off Bath Ter* 28 A5
Bath Ho Rd, Croy. CR0 200 E1
Bath Pas, Kings.T. KT1 *off St. James Rd* 181 G2
Bath Pl, EC2 12 D4
Barnet EN5 40 C3
Bath Rd, E7 98 A6
N9 61 E2
W4 126 E4
Hayes (Harling.) UB3 141 F1
Hounslow TW3, TW4, TW5, TW6 142 D2
Romford RM6 82 E6
West Drayton UB7 140 A1
Baths Rd, Brom. BR2 192 A4
Bath St, EC1 12 A4
Bath Ter, SE1 27 J6
Bathurst Av, SW19 *off Brisbane Av* 184 E1
Bathurst Gdns, NW10 107 H2
Bathurst Ms, W2 15 E5
Bathurst Rd, Ilf. IG1 98 E1
Bathurst St, W2 15 E5
Bathway, SE18 136 D4
Batley Cl, Mitch. CR4 185 J7
Batley Pl, N16 94 C3
Batley Rd, N16 *off Stoke Newington High St* 94 C3
Enfield EN2 43 J1
Batman Cl, W12 127 H1
Batoum Gdns, W6 127 J3
Batson Ho, E1 *off Fairclough St* 21 J4
Batson St, W12 127 G2
Batsworth Rd, Mitch. CR4 185 G3
Battenburg Wk, SE19 *off Brabourne Cl* 170 B5
Batten Cl, E6 *off Savage Gdns* 116 C6
Batten St, SW11 149 H3
Battersby Rd, SE6 172 D2
BATTERSEA, SW11 150 B1
Battersea Br, SW3 31 F7
SW11 31 F7
Battersea Br Rd, SW11 129 H7
Battersea Business Cen, SW11 *off Lavender Hill* 150 A3
Battersea Ch Rd, SW11 149 G1
★ **Battersea Dogs Home**, SW8 130 B7
Battersea High St, SW11 149 G1
★ **Battersea Park**, SW11 32 A7
Battersea Pk Rd, SW8 150 B1
SW11 149 H2
Battersea Ri, SW11 149 H5
Battersea Sq, SW11 *off Battersea High St* 149 G1
Battery Rd, SE28 137 H2

Battishill Gdns, N1 off Waterloo Ter 93 H7
Battishill St, N1 off Waterloo Ter 93 H7
Battlebridge Ct, N1 10 B1
Battle Br La, SE1 28 D2
Battle Br Rd, NW1 10 A2
Battle Cl, SW19 167 F6
Battledean Rd, N5 93 H5
Battle Rd, Belv. DA17 139 J4
Erith DA8 139 J4
Batty St, E1 21 J3
Batwa Ho, SE16 off Verney Rd 133 E5
Baudwin Rd, SE6 172 E2
Baugh Rd, Sid. DA14 176 C5
Baulk, The, SW18 148 D7
Bavant Rd, SW16 187 E2
Bavaria Rd, N19 92 E2
Bavdene Ms, NW4 off The Burroughs 71 H4
Bavent Rd, SE5 151 J2
Bawdale Rd, SE22 152 C5
Bawdsey Av, Ilf. IG2 81 J4
Bawtree Rd, SE14 133 H7
Bawtry Rd, N20 57 J3
Baxendale, N20 57 F2
Baxendale St, E2 13 H3
Baxter Cl, Brom. BR1 off Stoneleigh Rd 192 E3
Southall UB2 123 H2
Baxter Ho, E3 off Bromley High St 114 B3
Baxter Rd, E16 115 J6
N1 94 A6
N18 60 E4
NW10 106 E4
Ilford IG1 98 E5
Bay Ct, W5 off Popes La 125 H3
Baycroft Cl, Pnr. HA5 66 C3
Baydon Ct, Brom. BR2 191 F3
Bayes Cl, SE26 171 F5
Bayeux Ho, SE7 off Springfield Gro 135 J6
Bayfield Rd, SE9 156 A4
Bayford Ms, E8 off Bayford St 95 E7
Bayford Rd, NW10 108 A3
Bayford St, E8 95 E7
Baygrove Ms, Kings.T. (Hmptn W.) KT1 181 F1
Bayham Pl, NW1 9 F1
Bayham Rd, W4 126 D3
W13 104 E7
Morden SM4 185 E4
Bayham St, NW1 110 C1
Bayleaf Cl, Hmptn. TW12 off Laurel Rd 162 A5
Bayley St, WC1 17 H2
Bayley Wk, SE2 off Woolwich Rd 139 E5
Baylis Ms, Twick. TW1 off Amyand Pk Rd 144 D7
Baylis Rd, SE1 27 E4
Bayliss Av, SE28 118 D7
Bayliss Cl, N21 43 E5
Southall UB1 103 H6
Bayne Cl, E6 off Savage Gdns 116 C6
Baynes Cl, Enf. EN1 44 D2
Baynes Ms, NW3 off Belsize La 91 G6
Baynes St, NW1 92 C7
Baynham Cl, Bex. DA5 159 F6
Bayonne Rd, W6 128 B6
Bayshill Ri, Nthlt. UB5 85 H6
Bayston Rd, N16 94 C3
BAYSWATER, W2 14 B4
Bayswater Rd, W2 15 F5
Baythorne St, E3 113 J5
Bay Tree Cl, Brom. BR1 191 J1
Ilford IG6 off Hazel La 64 E7
Baytree Cl, Sid. DA15 175 J1
Baytree Ho, E4 off Dells Cl 46 B7
Baytree Ms, SE17 36 B1
Baytree Rd, SW2 151 F4
Bazalgette Cl, N.Mal. KT3 182 D5
Bazalgette Gdns, N.Mal. KT3 182 D5
Bazely St, E14 114 C7
Bazile Rd, N21 43 G6
Beacham Cl, SE7 136 A5
Beachborough Rd, Brom. BR1 172 C4
Beachcroft Rd, E11 97 E3
Beachcroft Way, N19 92 D1
Beach Gro, Felt. TW13 161 G2
Beachy Rd, E3 96 A7
Beacon Gate, SE14 153 G3
Beacon Gro, Cars. SM5 200 A4
Beacon Hill, N7 92 E5
Beacon Rd, SE13 154 D6
Hounslow (Lon.Hthrw Air.) TW6 140 D6
Beacon Rd Rbt, Houns. (Lon.Hthrw Air.) TW6 140 E6
Beacons Cl, E6 off Oliver Gdns 116 B5
Beaconsfield Cl, N11 58 A4
SE3 135 G6
W4 126 C5
Beaconsfield Gdns, Esher (Clay.) KT10 194 B7
Beaconsfield Par, SE9 off Beaconsfield Rd 174 B4
Beaconsfield Rd, E10 96 C2
E16 115 F4
E17 77 J6
N9 60 D4
N11 58 A3
N15 76 B4
NW10 89 F6
SE3 135 F7
SE9 174 B2
SE17 36 C4
W4 126 D3
W5 125 F2
Bromley BR1 192 A3
Croydon CR0 188 A6
Esher (Clay.) KT10 194 B7
Hayes UB4 122 C1
New Malden KT3 182 D2
Southall UB1 122 D1
Surbiton KT5 181 J7
Twickenham TW1 144 E6
Beaconsfield Ter, Rom. RM6 82 D6
Beaconsfield Ter Rd, W14 128 B3
Beaconsfield Wk, E6 off East Ham Manor Way 116 D6
SW6 148 C1
Beacontree Av, E17 78 D1
Beacontree Rd, E11 79 F7
Beadlow Cl, Cars. SM5 off Olveston Wk 185 G6
Beadman Pl, SE27 off Norwood High St 169 H4
Beadman St, SE27 169 H4
Beadnell Rd, SE23 171 G1
Beadon Rd, W6 127 J4
Bromley BR2 191 G4
Beaford Gro, SW20 184 B3
Beagle Cl, Felt. TW13 160 B4
Beak St, W1 17 G5
Beal Cl, Well. DA16 158 A1
Beale Cl, N13 59 H5
Beale Pl, E3 113 J2
Beale Rd, E3 113 J1
Beal Rd, Ilf. IG1 98 D2
Beam Av, Dag. RM10 119 H1
Beames Rd, NW10 106 D1
Beaminster Gdns, Ilf. IG6 80 E2
Beaminster Ho, SW8 off Dorset Rd 34 C7
Beamish Dr, Bushey (Bushey Hth) WD23 51 J1
Beamish Ho, SE16 off Rennie Est 133 F4
Beamish Rd, N9 60 D1
Beanacre Cl, E9 95 J6
Bean Rd, Bexh. DA6 158 D4
Beanshaw, SE9 174 D4
Beansland Gro, Rom. RM6 83 E2
Bear All, EC4 19 G3
Bear Cl, Rom. RM7 83 H6
Beardell St, SE19 170 C6
Beardow Gro, N14 42 C6
Beard Rd, Kings.T. KT2 163 J5
Beardsfield, E13 off Valetta Gro 115 G1
Beard's Hill, Hmptn. TW12 179 G1
Beard's Hill Cl, Hmptn. TW12 off Beard's Hill 179 G1
Beardsley Ter, Dag. RM8 off Fitzstephen Rd 100 B5
Beardsley Way, W3 126 D2
Bearfield Rd, Kings.T. KT2 163 H7
Bear Gdns, SE1 27 J1
Bear La, SE1 27 H1
Bear Rd, Felt. TW13 160 D5
Bearstead Ri, SE4 153 J5
Bearsted Ter, Beck. BR3 190 A1
Bear St, WC2 17 J5
Beaton Cl, SE15 152 C1
Beatrice Av, SW16 187 F3
Wembley HA9 87 H5
Beatrice Cl, E13 off Chargeable La 115 G4
Pinner HA5 off Reid Cl 66 A4
Beatrice Ct, Buck.H. IG9 64 A2
Beatrice Pl, W8 22 A6
Beatrice Rd, E17 78 A5
N4 75 G7
N9 45 F7
SE1 37 J2
Richmond TW10 off Albert Rd 145 J5
Southall UB1 123 F1
Beatson Wk, SE16 133 G1
Beattock Ri, N10 74 B4
Beatty Rd, N16 94 B4
Stanmore HA7 53 F6
Beatty St, NW1 9 F1
Beattyville Gdns, Ilf. IG6 80 D3
Beauchamp Cl, W4 off Beaumont Rd 126 C3
Beauchamp Ct, Stan. HA7 off Hardwick Cl 53 F5
Beauchamp Pl, SW3 23 H5
Beauchamp Rd, E7 97 H7
SE19 188 A1
SW11 149 H4
East Molesey KT8 179 H5
Sutton SM1 198 D5
Twickenham TW1 144 D7
West Molesey KT8 179 H5
Beauchamp St, EC1 19 E2
Beauchamp Ter, SW15 off Dryburgh Rd 147 H3
Beauclerc Rd, W6 127 H3
Beauclerk Cl, Felt. TW13 off Florence Rd 160 B1
Beaudesert Ms, West Dr. UB7 120 B2
Beaufort, E6 off Newark Knok 116 D5
Beaufort Av, Har. HA3 68 D4
Beaufort Cl, E4 off Higham Sta Av 62 B6
SW15 147 H7
W5 105 J5
Romford RM7 83 J4
Beaufort Ct, SW6 off Lillie Rd 128 D6
Richmond TW10 off Beaufort Rd 163 F4
Beaufort Dr, NW11 72 D4
Beaufort Gdns, NW4 71 J6
SW3 23 H5
SW16 169 F7
Hounslow TW5 143 E1
Ilford IG1 98 D1
Beaufort Ms, SW6 off Lillie Rd 128 C6
Beaufort Pk, NW11 72 D4
Beaufort Rd, W5 105 J5
Kingston upon Thames KT1 181 H4
Richmond TW10 163 F4
Twickenham TW1 145 F7
Beaufort St, SW3 31 F6
Beaufort Way, Epsom KT17 197 G7
Beaufoy Rd, N17 60 B7
Beaufoy Wk, SE11 34 D2
Beaulieu Av, E16 135 H1
SE26 170 E4
Beaulieu Cl, NW9 71 E4
SE5 152 A3
Hounslow TW4 143 F5
Mitcham CR4 186 A1
Twickenham TW1 145 G7
Watford WD19 50 C1
Beaulieu Dr, Pnr. HA5 66 D6
Beaulieu Gdns, N21 43 J7
Beaulieu Pl, W4 126 C3
Beaumanor Gdns, SE9 174 D4
Beaumaris Dr, Wdf.Grn. IG8 64 A7
Beaumaris Grn, NW9 off Goldsmith Av 71 E6
Beaumaris Twr, W3 126 B2
Beaumont Av, W14 128 C5
Harrow HA2 67 H6
Richmond TW9 145 J3
Wembley HA0 87 F5
Beaumont Cl, N2 73 H4
Kingston upon Thames KT2 164 A7
Beaumont Cres, W14 128 C5
Beaumont Dr, Wor.Pk. KT4 197 H1
Beaumont Gdns, NW3 90 D3
Beaumont Gro, E1 113 G4
Beaumont Ms, W1 16 C1
Pinner HA5 66 E3
Beaumont Pl, W1 9 G5
Barnet EN5 40 C1
Isleworth TW7 144 C5
Beaumont Ri, N19 92 D1
Beaumont Rd, E10 78 B7
E13 115 H3
SE19 169 J6
SW19 148 B7
W4 126 C3
Orpington BR5 193 G6
Beaumont Sq, E1 113 G4
Beaumont St, W1 16 C1
Beaumont Wk, NW3 91 J7
Beauvais Ter, Nthlt. UB5 102 D3
Beauval Rd, SE22 152 C6
Beaverbank Rd, SE9 175 G1
Beaver Cl, SE20 off Lullington Rd 170 D7
Hampton TW12 179 H1
Morden SM4 183 J7
Beaver Gro, Nthlt. UB5 off Jetstar Way 102 E3
Beavers Cres, Houns. TW4 142 C4
Beavers La, Houns. TW4 142 C3
Beavers La Camp, Houns. TW4 off Beavers La 142 C3
Beaverwood Rd, Chis. BR7 175 H6
Beavor Gro, W6 off Beavor La 127 G5
Beavor La, W6 127 G4
Bebbington Rd, SE18 137 H4
Beblets Cl, Orp. BR6 207 J5
Beccles Dr, Bark. IG11 99 H6
Beccles St, E14 113 J7
Bec Cl, Ruis. HA4 84 D3
Beck Cl, SE13 154 B1
Beck Ct, Beck. BR3 189 G3
BECKENHAM, BR3 190 A1
Beckenham Business Cen, Beck. BR3 171 H6
Beckenham Gdns, N9 60 B3
Beckenham Gro, Brom. BR2 190 D2
Beckenham Hill Rd, SE6 172 B5
Beckenham BR3 172 B5
Beckenham La, Brom. BR2 191 E2
Beckenham Pl Pk, Beck. BR3 172 B7
Beckenham Rd, Beck. BR3 189 G1
West Wickham BR4 190 B7
Beckers, The, N16 94 D4
Becket Av, E6 116 D3
Becket Cl, SE25 188 D6
Becket Fold, Har. HA1 off Courtfield Cres 68 C5
Becket Rd, N18 61 F4
Becket St, SE1 28 B5
Beckett Cl, NW10 88 D6
SW16 168 D2
Belvedere DA17 off Tunstock Way 139 E3
Beckett Ho, SW9 151 E2
Becketts Cl, Bex. DA5 177 J1
Feltham TW14 142 B6
Orpington BR6 207 J3
Becketts Pl, Kings.T. (Hmptn W.) KT1 181 G1
Beckett Wk, Beck. BR3 171 H6
Beckford Cl, W14 128 C4
Beckford Dr, Orp. BR5 193 G7
Beckford Pl, SE17 36 A4
Beckford Rd, Croy. CR0 188 C6
Beck La, Beck. BR3 189 G3
Becklow Gdns, W12 off Becklow Rd 127 G2
Becklow Ms, W12 off Becklow Rd 127 F2
Becklow Rd, W12 127 G2
Beck River Pk, Beck. BR3 189 J1
Beck Rd, E8 112 E1
Becks Rd, Sid. DA14 176 A3
BECKTON, E6 116 D5
Beckton Pk Rbt, E16 116 B7
Beckton Retail Pk, E6 116 D5
Beckton Rd, E16 115 F5
Beckton Triangle Retail Pk, E6 116 D4
Beck Way, Beck. BR3 189 J3
Beckway Rd, SW16 186 D2
Beckway St, SE17 36 C2
Beckwith Rd, SE24 152 A6
Beclands Rd, SW17 168 A6
Becmead Av, SW16 168 D4
Harrow HA3 68 E5
Becondale Rd, SE19 170 B5
BECONTREE, Dag. RM8 100 E3
Becontree Av, Dag. RM8 100 B4
BECONTREE HEATH, Dag. RM8 101 G1

Becquerel Ct, SE10
  off West Parkside 135 F3
Bective Pl, SW15
  off Bective Rd 148 C4
Bective Rd, E7 ....97 G4
SW15 ....148 C4
Becton Pl, Erith DA8 ....139 H7
Bedale St, SE1 ....28 B2
BEDDINGTON, Croy.
CR0 ....200 D2
BEDDINGTON CORNER,
Mitch. CR4 ....186 A7
Beddington Cross, Croy.
CR0 ....200 D1
Beddington Fm Rd, Croy.
CR0 ....200 E1
Beddington Gdns, Cars.
SM5 ....200 A6
Wallington SM6 ....200 B6
Beddington Grn, Orp.
BR5 ....193 J1
Beddington Gro, Wall.
SM6 ....200 D5
Beddington La, Croy.
CR0 ....186 C5
Beddington La Ind Est,
Croy. CR0 ....186 C6
Beddington Path, Orp.
BR5 ....193 J1
Beddington Rd, Ilf. IG3 ..81 J7
Orpington BR5 ....193 H2
CR0 ....200 E1
Beddington Trd Pk, Croy.
CR0 ....200 E1
Bede Cl, Pnr. HA5 ....66 D1
Bedens Rd, Sid. DA14 ..176 B6
Bede Rd, Rom. RM6 ......82 C6
Bedevere Rd, N9 ....60 D3
Bedfont Cl, Felt. TW14 ..141 F6
Mitcham CR4 ....186 A2
Bedfont La, Felt. TW13,
TW14 ....141 J7
Bedfont Rd, Stai. (Stanw.)
TW19 ....140 B6
Bedford Av, WC1 ....17 J2
Barnet EN5 ....40 C5
Hayes UB4 ....102 B6
Bedfordbury, WC2 ....18 A5
Bedford Cl, N10 ....58 A7
W4 ....127 E6
Bedford Cor, W4
  off The Avenue 126 E4
Bedford Ct, WC2 ....18 A6
Bedford Gdns, W8 ......128 D1
Bedford Hill, SW12 ....168 B1
SW16 ....168 B1
Bedford Ho, SW4 ....150 E4
  off Aitken Rd 73 H3
SE6 off Aitken Rd 172 B2
BEDFORD PARK, W4 ....126 D3
Bedford Pk, Croy. CR0 ..201 J1
Bedford Pk Cor, W4
  off Bath Rd 126 E4
Bedford Pas, SW6
  off Dawes Rd 128 B7
Bedford Pl, WC1 ....18 A1
Croydon CR0 ....202 A1
Bedford Rd, E6 ....116 D1
E17 ....78 A2
E18 ....79 G2
N2 ....73 H3
N8 ....74 D6
N9 ....44 E7
N15 ....76 B4
N22 ....74 E1
NW7 ....54 E3
SW4 ....150 E3
W4 ....126 D3
W13 ....104 E7
Harrow HA1 ....67 J6
Ilford IG1 ....99 E3
Sidcup DA15 ....175 H3
Twickenham TW2 ......162 A3
Worcester Park KT4 ..197 J2
Bedford Row, WC1 ....18 D1
Bedford Sq, WC1 ....17 J2
Bedford St, WC2 ....18 A5
Bedford Ter, SW2
  off Lyham Rd 150 E5
Bedford Way, WC1 ....9 J6
Bedgebury Gdns, SW19 ..166 B2
Bedgebury Rd, SE9 ......156 A4
Bedivere Rd, Brom. BR1 ..173 G3
Bedlam Ms, SE11 ....34 D1
Bedlow Way, Croy. CR0 ..201 F4
Bedonwell Rd, SE2 ......138 C6
Belvedere DA17 ....139 G6
Bexleyheath DA7 ......139 G6
Bedser Cl, SE11 ....34 D5
Thornton Heath CR7 ..187 J3
Bedser Dr, Grnf. UB6 ....86 A5
Bedster Gdns, W.Mol.
KT8 ....179 H2
Bedwardine Rd, SE19 ..170 B7

Bedwell Gdns, Hayes
UB3 ....121 H5
Bedwell Rd, N17 ....76 B1
Belvedere DA17 ....139 G5
Beeby Rd, E16 ....115 H5
Beech Av, N20 ....57 H1
W3 ....126 E1
Brentford TW8 ....125 E7
Buckhurst Hill IG9 ....63 H2
Ruislip HA4 ....84 B1
Beech Av, Sidcup
DA15 ....158 A7
Beech Cl, N9 ....44 D6
  off St. Nicholas Way
SE8 off Clyde St 133 J6
SW15 ....147 G7
SW19 ....165 J6
Carshalton SM5 ......199 J2
Loughton IG10 ....49 E3
Staines (Stanw.) TW19
  off St. Mary's Cres ..140 A7
Sunbury-on-Thames
  TW16 off Harfield Rd ..178 D2
West Drayton UB7 ....120 D3
Beech Copse, Brom.
BR1 ....192 C2
South Croydon CR2 ..202 B5
Beech Ct, E17 ....78 D3
SE9 ....156 B6
Ilford IG1 ....98 D3
Beechcroft, Chis. BR7 ..174 D7
Beechcroft Av, NW11 ....72 C7
Harrow HA2 ....67 G7
New Malden KT3 ......182 C1
Southall UB1 ....123 F1
Beechcroft Cl, Houns.
TW5 ....122 E7
Orpington BR6 ....207 G4
Beechcroft Gdns, Wem.
HA9 ....87 J3
Beechcroft Lo, Sutt. SM2
  off Devonshire Rd ..199 F7
Beechcroft Rd, E18 ......79 H2
SW14 ....146 C3
SW17 ....167 H2
Chessington KT9 ....195 J4
Orpington BR6 ......207 G4
Beechdale, N21 ....59 F2
Beechdale Rd, SW2 ....151 F6
Beech Dell, Kes. BR2 ..206 C4
Beech Dr, N2 ....73 J3
Beechen Cliff Way, Islw.
TW7 off Henley Cl ..144 C1
Beechen Gro, Pnr. HA5 ..67 F3
Beeches, The, Houns.
TW3 ....143 H1
Beeches Av, Cars. SM5 ..199 H7
Beeches Cl, SE20
  off Genoa Rd 189 F1
Beeches Rd, SW17 ......167 H3
Sutton SM3 ....198 B1
Beechfield Cotts, Brom. BR1
  off Widmore Rd 191 J2
Beechfield Gdns, Rom.
RM7 ....83 J7
Beechfield Rd, N4 ......75 J6
SE6 ....171 J1
Bromley BR1 ....191 J2
Beech Gdns, EC2
  off White Lyon Ct 19 J1
W5 ....125 H2
Dagenham RM10 ......101 H7
Beech Gro, Ilf. IG6 ......65 H6
Mitcham CR4 ....186 D4
New Malden KT3 ......182 D3
Beech Hall Cres, E4 ....62 D7
Beech Hall Rd, E4 ......62 C7
Beech Hill Av, Barn. EN4 ..41 F1
Beechhill Rd, SE9 ......156 D5
Beech Ho, NW3
  off Maitland Pk Vil ..91 J6
Croydon CR0 ....204 B6
Beech Ho Rd, Croy. CR0 ..202 A3
Beech Lawns, N12 ......57 G5
Beechmont Cl, Brom.
BR1 ....172 E5
Beechmore Gdns, Sutt.
SM3 ....198 A2
Beechmore Rd, SW11 ..149 J1
Beechmount Av, W7 ....104 A5
Beecholme Av, Mitch.
CR4 ....186 B1
Beecholme Est, E5 ......95 E3
Beech Rd, N11 ....59 G6
SW16 ....187 E2
Feltham TW14 ....141 H7
Beechrow, Rich. (Ham.)
TW10 ....163 H4
Beech St, EC2 ....19 J1
Romford RM7 ....83 J4
Beech Tree Cl, N1 ......93 G7
Stanmore HA7 ....53 F5
Beech Tree Glade, E4 ....63 F1

Beech Tree Pl, Sutt. SM1
  off St. Nicholas Way ..199 E5
Beechvale Cl, N12 ......57 H5
Beech Wk, NW7 ....54 E6
Beech Way, NW10 ....88 D7
Beechway, Bex. DA5 ....158 D6
Beech Way, Twick. TW2 ..161 G3
Beechwood Av, N3 ......72 C3
Greenford UB6 ....103 H3
Beechwood Av,
Harrow HA2 ....85 H3
Orpington BR6 ......207 H5
Richmond TW9 ......146 A1
Sunbury-on-Thames
  TW16 ....160 A6
Thornton Heath CR7 ..187 H4
Beechwood Circle, Har. HA2
  off Beechwood Gdns ..85 H3
Beechwood Cl, NW7 ....54 D5
Surbiton (Long Dit.)
  KT6 ....181 F7
Beechwood Ct, Cars.
SM5 ....199 J4
Sunbury-on-Thames
  TW16 ....160 A6
Beechwood Cres, Bexh.
DA7 ....158 D3
Beechwood Dr, Kes.
BR2 ....206 A4
Woodford Green IG8 ..63 F5
Beechwood Gdns, NW10
  off St. Annes Gdns ..105 J3
Harrow HA2 ....85 H3
Ilford IG5 ....80 C5
Beechwood Gro, W3 ..106 E7
Surbiton (Long Dit.)
  KT6 ....181 F7
Beechwood Ms, N9 ......60 D2
Beechwood Pk, E18 ......79 G3
Beechwood Ri, Chis.
BR7 ....175 E4
Beechwood Rd, E8 ......94 C6
N8 ....74 D4
Beechwoods Ct, SE19
  off Crystal Palace Par ..170 C5
Beechworth Cl, NW3 ....90 D2
Beecroft La, SE4
  off Beecroft Rd 153 H5
Beecroft Ms, SE4
  off Beecroft Rd 153 H5
Beecroft Rd, SE4 ......153 H5
Beehive Cl, E8 ....94 C7
Beehive La, Ilf. IG1, IG4 ..80 C5
Beehive Pas, EC3 ....20 D4
Beehive Pl, SW9 ......151 G3
Beeken Dene, Orp. BR6
  off Isabella Dr 207 F4
Beeleigh Rd, Mord.
SM4 ....185 E4
Beeston Cl, E8
  off Ferncliff Rd 94 D5
Watford WD19 ....50 D4
Beeston Pl, SW1 ....24 E4
Beeston Rd, Barn. EN4 ..41 G6
Beeston Way, Felt.
TW14 ....142 C6
Beethoven St, W10 ....108 B3
Beeton Cl, Pnr. HA5 ....51 G7
Begbie Rd, SE3 ....155 J1
Beggars Hill, Epsom
KT17 ....197 F7
Beggar's Hill, Epsom
(Junct) KT17 ....197 F6
Beggars Roost La, Sutt.
SM1 ....198 D6
Begonia Cl, E6 ....116 B5
Begonia Pl, Hmptn. TW12
  off Gresham Rd 161 G6
Begonia Wk, W12
  off Du Cane Rd 107 F6
Beira St, SW12 ....150 B7
Bejun Ct, Barn.
(New Barn.) EN5
  off Station App 41 F4
Bekesbourne St, E14
  off Ratcliffe La 113 H6
Belcroft Cl, Brom. BR1 ..191 F3
Beldham Gdns, W.Mol.
KT8 ....179 H3
Belfairs Dr, Rom. RM6 ..82 C7
Belfairs Grn, Wat. WD19 ..50 D5
Belfast Rd, N16 ....94 C2
SE25 ....188 E4
Belfont Wk, N7 ....93 E4
Belford Gro, SE18 ......136 D4
Belfort Rd, SE15 ......153 F2
Belfour Ter, N3
  off Squires La 73 G2
Belfry Cl, SE16
  off Masters Dr 133 E5
Bromley BR1 ....192 E4
Belgrade Rd, N16 ......94 B4
Hampton TW12 ......179 H1

Belgrave Cl, N14
  off Prince George Av ..42 C5
NW7 ....54 D5
W3 off Avenue Rd 126 B2
Belgrave Ct, E14
  off Westferry Circ ..113 J7
Belgrave Cres, Sun.
TW16 ....178 B1
Belgrave Gdns, N14 ....42 D5
Belgrave Gdns, NW8 ..109 E1
Stanmore HA7
  off Copley Rd 53 F5
Belgrave Hts, E11 ......97 G1
Belgrave Ms N, SW1 ....24 B4
Belgrave Ms S, SW1 ....24 C5
Belgrave Ms W, SW1 ....24 B5
Belgrave Pl, SW1 ......24 C5
Belgrave Rd, E10 ......96 C1
E11 ....97 G2
E13 ....115 J4
E17 ....78 A5
SE25 ....188 C4
SW1 ....33 F2
SW13 ....127 F7
Hounslow TW4 ......143 F3
Ilford IG1 ....98 C1
Mitcham CR4 ....185 G3
Sunbury-on-Thames
  TW16 ....178 B1
Belgrave Sq, SW1 ......24 B5
Belgrave St, E1 ....113 G6
Belgrave Ter, Wdf.Grn.
IG8 ....63 G3
Belgrave Wk, Mitch. CR4 ..185 G3
Belgrave Yd, SW1 ......24 D6
BELGRAVIA, SW1 ....24 B6
Belgravia Cl, Barn. EN5 ..40 C3
Belgravia Gdns, Brom.
BR1 ....172 E6
Belgravia Ho, SW4 ....150 D6
Belgravia Ms, Kings.T.
KT1 ....181 G4
Belgrove St, WC1 ....10 A3
Belham Wk, SE5
  off Datchelor Pl 152 A1
Belinda Rd, SW9 ......151 H3
Belitha Vil, N1 ....93 F7
Bell, The, E17 ....78 A3
Bellamy Cl, E14
  off Manilla St 134 A2
W14 off Aisgill Av ..128 C5
Edgware HA8 ....54 C3
Bellamy Dr, Stan. HA7 ..68 E1
Bellamy Ho, SW17
  off Garratt La 167 G4
Hounslow TW5
  off Biscoe Cl 123 G6
Bellamy Rd, E4 ....62 B6
Enfield EN2 ....44 A2
Bellamy St, SW12 ....150 B7
Bel La, Felt. TW13
  off Butts Cotts 161 F3
Bellarmine Cl, SE28 ....137 J2
Bellasis Av, SW2 ......168 E2
Bell Av, West Dr. UB7 ..120 C4
Bell Cl, Pnr. HA5 ....66 C3
Bellclose Rd, West Dr.
UB7 ....120 B2
Bell Ct, Surb. KT5
  off Barnsbury La 196 B2
Bell Dr, SW18 ....148 B7
Bellefields Rd, SW9 ..151 F3
Bellegrove Cl, Well. DA16 ..157 J2
Bellegrove Par, Well. DA16
  off Bellegrove Rd 157 J3
Bellegrove Rd, Well.
DA16 ....157 G2
Bellenden Rd, SE15 ..152 C2
Bellestaines Pleasaunce,
E4 ....62 A2
Belleville Rd, SW11 ....149 J5
Belle Vue, Grnf. UB6 ..104 A1
Belle Vue Est, NW4
  off Bell La 71 J4
Belle Vue La, Bushey
(Bushey Hth) WD23 ..52 A1
Bellevue Ms, N11 ....58 A5
Bellevue Par, SW17
  off Bellevue Rd 167 H1
Belle Vue Pk, Th.Hth.
CR7 ....187 J3
Bellevue Pl, E1 ....113 F4
Belle Vue Rd, E17 ......78 D2
Bellevue Rd, N11 ......58 A4
Belle Vue Rd, NW4 ....71 J4
Bellevue Rd, SW13 ....147 G2
SW17 ....167 H1
W13 ....104 E4
Bexleyheath DA6 ....159 F5
Kingston upon Thames
  KT1 ....181 H3
Bellew St, SW17 ......167 F3
Bell Fm Av, Dag. RM10 ..101 J3

Bellfield Av, Har. HA3 .....**51** J6
Bellfield Cl, SE3
off Charlton Rd **135** H7
Bellflower Cl, E6
off Sorrel Gdns **116** B5
Bell Gdns, E17
off Markhouse Rd **77** J5
Bellgate Ms, NW5
off York Ri **92** B3
BELL GREEN, SE6 ....**171** J3
Bell Grn, SE26 ....**171** J3
Bell Grn La, SE26 ....**171** H5
Bell Hill, Croy. CR0
off Surrey St **201** J2
Bellhouse Rd, Rom. RM7 .**101** J1
Bellina Ms, NW5
off Fortess Rd **92** C4
BELLINGHAM, SE6 ....**172** B3
Bellingham Ct, Bark. IG11
off Renwick Rd **118** B3
Bellingham Grn, SE6 ....**172** A3
Bellingham Rd, SE6 .....**172** B3
Bellingham Trd Est, SE6
off Franthorne Way ...**172** B3
Bell Inn Yd, EC3 ....**20** C4
Bell La, E1 ....**21** F2
E16 ....**135** G1
NW4 ....**72** A4
Twickenham TW1
off The Embankment .**162** D1
Wembley HA9
off Magnet Rd **87** G2
Bellmaker Ct, E3
off St. Pauls Way **114** A5
Bell Meadow, SE19
off Dulwich Wd Av ...**170** B4
Bello Cl, SE24 ....**151** H7
Bellot Gdns, SE10
off Bellot St **135** E5
Bellot St, SE10 ....**135** E5
Bellring Cl, Belv. DA17 ...**139** G6
Bell Rd, E.Mol. KT8 ......**180** A5
Enfield EN1 ....**44** A1
Hounslow TW3 ....**143** H4
Bells All, SW6 ....**148** D2
Bells Gdn Est, SE15
off Buller Cl **132** D7
Bells Hill, Barn. EN5 ......**40** A5
Bell St, NW1 ....**15** G1
SE18 ....**156** B1
Belltrees Gro, SW16 .....**169** F5
Bell Water Gate, SE18 ...**136** D3
Bell Wf La, EC4 ....**20** A6
Bellwood Rd, SE15 ......**153** G4
Bell Yd, WC2 ....**18** E3
Bell Yd Ms, SE1 ....**28** E4
Belmarsh Rd, SE28
off Western Way **137** H2
BELMONT, Har. HA3 ......**68** D2
Belmont Av, N9 ....**60** D1
N13 ....**59** E5
N17 ....**75** J3
Barnet EN4 ....**41** J5
New Malden KT3 .....**183** G5
Southall UB2 ....**122** E3
Welling DA16 ....**157** H3
Wembley HA0 ....**105** J1
Belmont Circle, Har.
HA3 ....**68** E1
Belmont Cl, E4 ....**62** D5
N20 ....**56** E1
SW4 ....**150** C3
Barnet (Cockfos.) EN4 ..**41** J4
Woodford Green IG8 ...**63** H4
Belmont Ct, NW11 ....**72** C5
Belmont Gro, SE13 ......**154** D3
W4 *off Belmont Ter* **126** D4
Belmont Hall Ct, SE13
off Belmont Gro **154** D3
Belmont Hill, SE13 ......**154** D3
Belmont La, Chis. BR7 ...**175** F5
Stanmore HA7 ....**53** F7
Belmont Ms, SW19
off Chapman Sq **166** A2
Belmont Pk, SE13 ....**154** D4
Belmont Pk Cl, SE13 ....**154** D4
Belmont Pk Rd, E10 ......**78** B6
Belmont Ri, Sutt. SM2 ...**198** C6
Belmont Rd, N15 ....**75** J4
N17 ....**75** J4
SE25 ....**188** E5
SW4 ....**150** C3
W4
off Chiswick High Rd .**126** D4
Beckenham BR3 ......**189** J2
Chislehurst BR7 ......**175** E5
Erith DA8 ....**139** G7
Harrow HA3 ....**68** C3
Ilford IG1 ....**99** F3
Twickenham TW2 .....**162** A2
Wallington SM6 ......**200** B5
Belmont St, NW1 ....**92** A7
Belmont Ter, W4 ....**126** D4
Belmor, Borwd. (Els.)
WD6 ....**38** A5
Belmore Av, Hayes UB4 ..**102** A6
Belmore La, N7 ....**92** D5
Belmore St, SW8 ....**150** D1
Beloe Cl, SW15 ....**147** G3
Belper Ct, E5
off Pedro St **95** G4
Belsham St, E9 ....**95** F6
Belsize Av, N13 ....**59** F6
NW3 ....**91** G6
W13 ....**125** E3
Belsize Ct, NW3
off Belsize La **91** H5
Belsize Cres, NW3 ....**91** G5
Belsize Gdns, Sutt. SM1 ..**199** E4
Belsize Gro, NW3 ....**91** H6
Belsize La, NW3 ....**91** G6
Belsize Ms, NW3
off Belsize La **91** G6
BELSIZE PARK, NW3 .....**91** H6
Belsize Pk, NW3 ....**91** G6
Belsize Pk Gdns, NW3 ....**91** H6
Belsize Pk Ms, NW3
off Belsize La **91** G6
Belsize Pl, NW3
off Belsize La **91** G6
Belsize Rd, NW6 ....**108** E1
Harrow HA3 ....**52** A7
Belsize Sq, NW3 ....**91** G6
Belsize Ter, NW3 ....**91** G6
Belson Rd, SE18 ....**136** C4
Beltane Dr, SW19 ....**166** A3
Belthorn Cres, SW12 ....**150** C7
Belton Rd, E7 ....**97** H7
E11 ....**96** E4
N17 ....**76** B3
NW2 ....**89** G6
Sidcup DA14 ....**176** A4
Belton Way, E3 ....**114** A5
Beltran Rd, SW6 ....**148** E2
Beltwood Rd, Belv.
DA17 ....**139** J4
BELVEDERE, DA17 ......**139** H4
Belvedere, The, SW10 ....**149** F1
Belvedere Av, SW19 .....**166** B5
Ilford IG5 ....**80** E2
Belvedere Bldgs, SE1 .....**27** H4
Belvedere Business Pk,
Belv. DA17
off Crabtree
Manorway S **139** H2
Belvedere Cl, Tedd.
TW11 ....**162** B5
Belvedere Ct, N1
off De Beauvoir Cres .**112** B1
N2 ....**73** G5
Belvedere Dr, SW19 .....**166** B5
Belvedere Gdns, W.Mol.
KT8 ....**179** F5
Belvedere Gro, SW19 ....**166** B5
Belvedere Ho, Felt.
TW13 ....**160** A1
Belvedere Ind Est, Belv.
DA17 ....**139** J3
Belvedere Ms, SE3
off Langton Way **135** H7
SE15 ....**153** F3
Belvedere Pl, SE1 ....**27** H4
SW2 *off Acre La* **151** F4
Belvedere Rd, E10 ....**95** H1
SE1 ....**26** D3
SE2 ....**138** D1
SE19 ....**170** C7
W7 ....**124** C3
Bexleyheath DA7 .....**159** F3
Belvedere Sq, SW19 .....**166** B5
Belvedere Strand, NW9 ...**71** F2
Belvedere Way, Har. HA3 ..**69** H6
Belvoir Cl, SE9 ....**174** B3
Belvoir Ho, SW1
off Vauxhall Br Rd **33** G1
Belvoir Rd, SE22 ....**152** D7
Belvue Cl, Nthlt. UB5 ....**85** G7
Belvue Rd, Nthlt. UB5 ....**85** G7
Bembridge Cl, NW6 ......**90** B7
Bemersyde Pt, E13
off Balaam St **115** H3
Bemerton Est, N1 ....**93** E7
Bemerton St, N1 ....**111** F1
Bemish Rd, SW15 ....**148** A3
Bempton Dr, Ruis. HA4 ...**84** B2
Bemsted Rd, E17 ....**77** J3
Benares Rd, SE18 ....**137** J4
Benbow Rd, W6 ....**127** H3
Benbow St, SE8 ....**134** A6
Benbury Cl, Brom. BR1 ..**172** C5
Bench Fld, S.Croy. CR2 ..**202** C6
Bencroft Rd, SW16 ......**168** C7
Bencurtis Pk, W.Wick.
BR4 ....**204** D3
Bendall Ms, NW1 ....**15** H1
Bendemeer Rd, SW15 ...**148** A3
Bendish Pt, SE28 ....**137** F2
Bendish Rd, E6 ....**98** B7
Bendmore Av, SE2 ......**138** A5
Bendon Valley, SW18 ....**148** E7
Benedict Cl, Belv. DA17
off Tunstock Way **139** E3
Orpington BR6 ....**207** H3
Benedict Dr, Felt. TW14 ..**141** G7
Benedict Rd, SW9 ....**151** F3
Mitcham CR4 ....**185** G3
Benedict Way, N2 ....**73** F3
Benenden Grn, Brom.
BR2 ....**191** G5
Benett Gdns, SW16 .....**186** E2
Benfleet Cl, Sutt. SM1 ...**199** F3
Benfleet Way, N11 ....**58** A2
Bengal Ct, EC3
off Birchin La **20** C4
Bengal Rd, Ilf. IG1 ....**98** E4
Bengarth Dr, Har. HA3 ....**68** A2
Bengarth Rd, Nthlt. UB5 ..**102** D1
Bengeo Gdns, Rom. RM6 ..**82** C6
Bengeworth Rd, SE5 ....**151** J3
Harrow HA1 ....**86** D2
Ben Hale Cl, Stan. HA7 ....**52** E4
Benham Cl, SW11 ....**149** G3
Chessington KT9
off Merritt Gdns **195** F6
Benham Gdns, Houns.
TW4 ....**143** F5
Benham Rd, W7 ....**104** B5
Benhams Pl, NW3
off Holly Wk **91** F4
Benhill Av, Sutt. SM1 ....**199** E4
Benhill Rd, SE5 ....**132** A7
Sutton SM1 ....**199** F3
Benhill Wd Rd, Sutt. SM1 .**199** F3
BENHILTON, Sutt. SM1 ..**199** E2
Benhilton Gdns, Sutt.
SM1 ....**199** E3
Benhurst Ct, SW16 ......**169** G5
Benhurst La, SW16 ......**169** G5
Benington Ct, N4
off Brownswood Rd ...**93** J2
Benin St, SE13 ....**154** D7
Benjafield Cl, N18
off Brettenham Rd **60** E4
Benjamin Cl, E8 ....**112** D1
Benjamin Ms, SW12 .....**150** C7
Benjamin St, EC1 ....**19** G1
Ben Jonson Ho, EC2
off The Barbican **20** A1
Ben Jonson Rd, E1 ......**113** H5
Benledi Rd, E14 ....**114** D6
Bennelong Cl, W12 ......**107** H7
Bennerley Rd, SW11 .....**149** H5
Bennets Ctyd, SW19
off Watermill Way **185** F1
Bennetsfield Rd, Uxb.
UB11 ....**120** E1
Bennet's Hill, EC4 ....**19** H5
Bennet St, SW1 ....**25** F1
Bennett Cl, Houns. TW4 ..**143** E5
Kingston upon Thames
(Hmptn W.) KT1 .....**181** F1
Welling DA16 ....**158** A2
Bennett Gro, SE13 ......**154** B1
Bennett Ho, SW1
off Page St **33** J1
Bennett Pk, SE3 ....**155** F3
Bennett Rd, E13 ....**115** J4
N16 ....**94** B4
SW9 ....**151** G2
Romford RM6 ....**83** E6
Bennetts Av, Croy. CR0 ..**203** H2
Greenford UB6 ....**104** B1
Bennetts Castle La, Dag.
RM8 ....**100** C4
Bennetts Cl, N17 ....**60** C6
Mitcham CR4 ....**186** B1
Bennetts Copse, Chis.
BR7 ....**174** B6
Bennett St, W4 ....**126** E6
Bennetts Way, Croy.
CR0 ....**203** H2
Bennetts Yd, SW1 ....**25** J6
Benningholme Rd, Edg.
HA8 ....**54** E6
Bennington Rd, N17 ......**76** B1
Woodford Green IG8 ...**62** E7
Benn St, E9 ....**95** H6
Benn's Wk, Rich. TW9
off Rosedale Rd **145** H4
Benrek Cl, Ilf. IG6 ....**81** F1
Bensbury Cl, SW15 ......**147** H7
Bensham Cl, Th.Hth.
CR7 ....**187** J4
Bensham Gro, Th.Hth.
CR7 ....**187** J2
Bensham La, Croy. CR0 ..**187** H7
Thornton Heath CR7 ..**187** H4
Bensham Manor Rd,
Th.Hth. CR7 ....**187** J4
Bensington Ct, Felt.
TW14 ....**141** G6
Bensley Cl, N11 ....**57** J5
Ben Smith Way, SE16 .....**29** J5
Benson Av, E6 ....**115** J2
Benson Cl, Houns. TW3 ..**143** G4
Benson Ct, SW8
off Hartington Rd **150** E1
Benson Quay, E1
off Garnet St **113** F7
Benson Rd, SE23 ....**171** F1
Croydon CR0 ....**201** G3
Bentalls Cen, Kings.T.
KT1 ....**181** G2
Bentfield Gdns, SE9
off Aldersgrove Av ...**173** J3
Benthal Rd, N16 ....**94** D2
Bentham Ct, N1
off Rotherfield St **93** J7
Bentham Ho, SE1
off Falmouth Rd **28** B5
Bentham Rd, E9 ....**95** G6
SE28 ....**118** B7
Bentham Wk, NW10 ......**88** C5
Ben Tillet Cl, Bark. IG11 ..**100** A7
Ben Tillett Cl, E16
off Newland St **136** C1
Bentinck Cl, NW8
off Prince Albert Rd **7** H2
Bentinck Ms, W1 ....**16** C3
Bentinck Rd, West Dr.
UB7 ....**120** A1
Bentinck St, W1 ....**16** C3
Bentley Ct, SE13
off Whitburn Rd **154** C4
Bentley Dr, NW2 ....**90** C3
Ilford IG2 ....**81** F6
Bentley Ms, Enf. EN1 .....**44** A6
★ **Bentley Priory Open
Space**, Stan. HA7 .....**52** C4
Bentley Rd, N1
off Tottenham Rd **94** B6
Bentley Way, Stan. HA7 ...**52** D5
Woodford Green IG8 ...**63** G3
Benton Rd, Ilf. IG1 ....**99** G1
Watford WD19 ....**50** D5
Bentons La, SE27 ....**169** J4
Bentons Ri, SE27 ....**170** A5
Bentry Cl, Dag. RM8 ....**101** E2
Bentry Rd, Dag. RM8 ....**101** E2
Bentworth Rd, W12 .....**107** H6
Benville Ho, SW8
off Oval Pl **131** F7
Benwell Ct, Sun. TW16 ...**178** A1
Benwell Rd, N7 ....**93** G4
Benwick Cl, SE16
off Aspinden Rd **133** E4
Benworth St, E3 ....**113** J3
Benyon Rd, N1
off Southgate Rd **112** A1
Benyon Wf, E8
off Kingsland Rd **112** B1
Berberis Ho, Felt. TW13
off Highfield Rd **160** A2
Berberis Wk, West Dr.
UB7 ....**120** B4
Berber Pl, E14
off Birchfield St **114** A7
Berber Rd, SW11 ....**149** J5
Berberry Cl, Edg. HA8
off Larkspur Gro **54** C4
Bercta Rd, SE9 ....**175** F2
Berengers Pl, Dag. RM9 ..**100** B6
Berenger Twr, SW10
off Blantyre St **31** E7
Berenger Wk, SW10
off Blantyre St **30** E7
Berens Rd, NW10 ....**108** A3
Berens Way, Chis. BR7 ..**193** J4
Beresford Av, N20 ....**57** J2
W7 ....**104** A5
Surbiton KT5 ....**196** B1
Twickenham TW1 .....**145** F6
Wembley HA0 ....**105** J1
Beresford Dr, Brom. BR1 .**192** B3
Woodford Green IG8 ...**63** J4
Beresford Gdns, Enf. EN1 .**44** B4
Hounslow TW4 ....**143** F5
Romford RM6 ....**83** E5
Beresford Rd, E4 ....**62** E1
E17 ....**78** B1
N2 ....**73** H3
N5 ....**93** J5
N8 ....**75** G5
Harrow HA1 ....**68** A5
Kingston upon Thames
KT2 ....**181** J1
New Malden KT3 .....**182** C4
Southall UB1 ....**122** D1
Sutton SM2 ....**198** C7
Beresford Sq, SE18 ......**136** E4
Beresford St, SE18 ......**136** E3
Beresford Ter, N5 ....**93** J5

Berestede Rd, W6 ....127 F5
Bere St, E1
  off Cranford St 113 G7
Bergenia Ho, Felt. TW13
  off Bedfont La 160 B1
Bergen Sq, SE16
  off Norway Gate 133 H3
Berger Cl, Orp. BR5 .....193 G6
Berger Rd, E9 ......95 G6
Berghem Ms, W14
  off Blythe Rd 128 A3
Bergholt Av, Ilf. IG4 ....80 B5
Bergholt Cres, N16 ......76 B7
Bergholt Ms, NW1
  off Rossendale Way ..92 C7
Berglen Ct, E14
  off Branch Rd 113 H6
Bering Sq, E14
  off Napier Av 134 A5
Bering Wk, E16 ......116 A6
Berisford Ms, SW18 ....149 E6
Berkeley Av, Bexh. DA7 .158 D1
  Greenford UB6 ......86 B6
  Hounslow TW4 ......142 A2
  Ilford IG5 ......80 D2
Berkeley Cl, Borwd.
  (Els.) WD6 ......38 A5
  Kingston upon Thames
  KT2 ......163 H7
  Orpington BR5 ......193 H7
  Ruislip HA4 ......84 A3
Berkeley Ct, N14 ......42 C6
  Wallington SM6 ......200 C3
Berkeley Cres, Barn. EN4 .41 G5
Berkeley Dr, W.Mol. KT8 .179 F3
Berkeley Gdns, N21 ......44 A7
  W8
  off Brunswick Gdns ..128 D1
  Esher (Clay.) KT10 ...194 D6
Berkeley Ho, E3 ......113 J4
Berkeley Ms, W1 ......16 A3
Berkeley Pl, SW19 ......166 A6
Berkeley Rd, E12 ......98 B5
  N8 ......74 D6
  N15 ......76 A6
  NW9 ......70 A4
  SW13 ......147 G1
Berkeley Sq, W1 ......16 E6
Berkeley St, W1 ......17 E6
Berkeley Twr, E14
  off Westferry Circ 133 J1
Berkeley Wk, N7
  off Durham Rd 93 F2
Berkeley Waye, Houns.
  TW5 ......122 D7
Berkerley Ms, Sun. TW16
  off Thames St 178 C3
Berkhampstead Rd, Belv.
  DA17 ......139 G5
Berkhamsted Av, Wem.
  HA9 ......87 J6
Berkley Gro, NW1
  off Berkley Rd 92 A7
Berkley Rd, NW1 ......91 J7
Berkshire Gdns, N13 ....59 G6
  N18 ......60 E5
Berkshire Rd, E9 ......95 J6
Berkshire Sq, Mitch. CR4
  off Berkshire Way 187 G4
Berkshire Way, Mitch.
  CR4 ......186 E4
Bermans Way, NW10 ....89 E4
BERMONDSEY, SE1 ......29 F6
Bermondsey Sq, SE1 ....28 E5
Bermondsey St, SE1 ....28 E3
Bermondsey Wall E, SE16 .29 J4
Bermondsey Wall W, SE16 .29 H3
Bernal Cl, SE28
  off Haldane Rd 118 D7
Bernard Ashley Dr, SE7 .135 H5
Bernard Av, W13 ......125 E3
Bernard Cassidy St, E16 .115 F5
Bernard Gdns, SW19 ....166 C5
Bernard Rd, N15 ......76 C5
  Romford RM7 ......83 J7
  Wallington SM6 ......200 B4
Bernards Cl, Ilf. IG6 ....65 F6
Bernard Shaw Ho, NW10
  off Knatchbull Rd 106 D1
Bernard St, WC1 ......10 A6
Bernays Cl, Stan. HA7 ...53 F6
Bernays Gro, SW9 ......151 F4
Bernel Dr, Croy. CR0 ....203 J3
Berne Rd, Th.Hth. CR7 ..187 J5
Berners Dr, W13 ......104 D6
Bernersmede, SE3 ......155 G3
Berners Ms, W1 ......17 G2
Berners Pl, W1 ......17 G3
Berners Rd, N1 ......11 F1
  N22 ......75 G1
Berners St, W1 ......17 G2
Berney Rd, Croy. CR0 ...188 A7
Bernhardt Cres, NW8 ....7 G5

Bernhart Cl, Edg. HA8 ...54 C7
Bernville Way, Har. HA3
  off Orchard Gro 69 J5
Bernwell Rd, E4 ......63 E3
Berridge Grn, Edg. HA8 ..54 A7
Berridge Ms, NW6
  off Hillfield Rd 90 D5
Berridge Rd, SE19 ......170 B5
Berriman Rd, N7 ......93 F3
Berriton Rd, Har. HA2 ...85 F1
Berrybank Cl, E4
  off Greenbank Cl 62 C2
Berry Cl, N21 ......59 H1
  Dagenham RM10 ......101 G5
Berry Ct, Houns. TW4
  off Raglan Cl 143 F5
Berrydale Rd, Hayes UB4 .102 E4
Berryfield Cl, E17 ......78 B4
  Bromley BR1 ......192 B1
Berryhill, SE9 ......156 E4
Berry Hill, Stan. HA7 ....53 G4
Berryhill Gdns, SE9 ....156 E4
BERRYLANDS, Surb. KT5 .181 J5
Berrylands, SW20 ......183 J3
  Surbiton KT5 ......182 A5
Berrylands Rd, Surb. KT5 .181 J6
Berry La, SE21 ......170 A4
Berryman Cl, Dag. RM8
  off Bennetts Castle La .100 C3
Berrymans La, SE26 ....171 G4
Berrymead Gdns, W3 ...126 C1
Berrymede Rd, W4 ......126 D3
Berry Pl, EC1 ......11 H4
Berry St, EC1 ......11 H5
Berry Way, W5 ......125 H3
Bertal Rd, SW17 ......167 G4
Berthon St, SE8 ......134 A7
Bertie Rd, NW10 ......89 G6
  SE26 ......171 G6
Bertram Cotts, SW19 ...166 D7
Bertram Rd, NW4 ......71 G6
  Enfield EN1 ......44 D4
  Kingston upon Thames
  KT2 ......164 A7
Bertram St, N19 ......92 B2
Bertram Way, Enf. EN1 ..44 C4
Bertrand St, SE13 ......154 B3
Bertrand Way, SE28 ....118 B7
Bert Rd, Th.Hth. CR7 ....187 J5
Berwick Av, Hayes UB4 .102 D6
Berwick Cl, Stan. HA7
  off Gordon Av 52 C6
  Twickenham TW2 ......143 G7
Berwick Cres, Sid. DA15 .157 H6
Berwick Gdns, Sutt. SM1 .199 F3
Berwick Rd, E16 ......115 H6
  N22 ......75 H1
  Welling DA16 ......158 B1
Berwick St, W1 ......17 H4
Berwyn Av, Houns. TW3 .143 H1
Berwyn Rd, SE24 ......169 H1
  Richmond TW10 ......146 B4
Beryl Av, E6 ......116 B5
Beryl Ho, SE18
  off Spinel Cl 137 J5
Beryl Rd, W6 ......128 A5
Berystede, Kings.T. KT2 .164 B7
Besant Ct, N1
  off Newington
  Grn Rd 94 A5
Besant Pl, SE22
  off Hayes Gro 152 C4
Besant Rd, NW2 ......90 B4
Besant Wk, N7
  off Newington
  Barrow Way 93 F2
Besant Way, NW10 ......88 C5
Besley St, SW16 ......168 C6
Bessant Dr, Rich. TW9 ..146 B1
Bessborough Gdns, SW1 .33 J3
Bessborough Pl, SW1 ....33 H3
Bessborough Rd, SW15 .165 G1
  Harrow HA1 ......86 A1
Bessborough St, SW1 ...33 H3
Bessemer Rd, SE5 ......151 J2
Bessie Lansbury Cl, E6 ..116 D6
Bessingby Rd, Ruis. HA4 .84 A2
Bessingham Wk, SE4
  off Aldersford Cl 153 G5
Besson St, SE14 ......153 F1
Bessy St, E2
  off Roman Rd 113 F3
Bestwood St, SE8 ......133 G4
Beswick Ms, NW6
  off Dresden Cl 91 E6
Betam Rd, Hayes UB3 ..121 G2
Beta Pl, SW4
  off Santley St 151 F4
Betchworth Cl, Sutt. SM1
  off St. Barnabas Rd ...199 G5
Betchworth Rd, Ilf. IG3 ..99 H2
Betham Rd, Grnf. UB6 ..104 A3

Bethany Waye, Felt.
  TW14 ......141 H7
Bethecar Rd, Har. HA1 ...68 B5
Bethell Av, E16 ......115 F4
  Ilford IG1 ......80 D7
Bethel Rd, Well. DA16 ..158 C3
Bethersden Cl, Beck.
  BR3 ......171 J7
BETHNAL GREEN, E2 ....112 D2
Bethnal Grn Est, E2
  off Roman Rd 113 F3
Bethnal Grn Rd, E1 ......13 F5
  E2 ......13 F5
Bethune Av, N11 ......57 J4
Bethune Rd, N16 ......76 A7
  NW10 ......106 D4
Bethwin Rd, SE5 ......35 H4
Betjeman Cl, Pnr. HA5 ...67 G4
Betony Cl, Croy. CR0
  off Primrose La 203 G1
Betoyne Av, E4 ......62 E4
Betstyle Rd, N11 ......58 B4
Betterton Dr, Sid. DA14 .177 E2
Betterton St, WC2 ......18 A4
Bettons Pk, E15 ......115 E1
Bettridge Rd, SW6 ......148 C2
Betts Cl, Beck. BR3 .....189 H2
Betts Ms, E17
  off Ringwood Rd 77 J6
Betts St, E1
  off The Highway 112 E7
Betts Way, SE20 ......189 E1
  Surbiton (Long Dit.)
  KT6 ......195 E1
Beulah Av, Th.Hth. CR7
  off Beulah Rd 187 J2
Beulah Cl, Edg. HA8 ....54 B3
Beulah Cres, Th.Hth. CR7 .187 J2
Beulah Gro, Croy. CR0 ..187 J6
Beulah Hill, SE19 ......169 H6
Beulah Path, E17
  off Addison Rd 78 B5
Beulah Rd, E17 ......78 B5
  SW19 ......166 C7
  Sutton SM1 ......198 D4
  Thornton Heath CR7 ..187 J3
  Wembley HA9 ......87 J5
Bevan Av, Bark. IG11 ...100 A7
Bevan Ct, Croy. CR0 ....201 G5
Bevan Rd, SE2 ......138 B5
  Barnet EN4 ......41 J4
Bevan St, N1 ......111 J1
Bev Callender Cl, SW8
  off Daley
  Thompson Way 150 B3
Bevenden St, N1 ......12 C3
Bevercote Wk, Belv. DA17
  off Osborne Rd 139 F6
Beveridge Rd, NW10 ....89 E7
Beverley Av, SW20 ......183 F1
  Hounslow TW4 ......143 F4
  Sidcup DA15 ......157 J7
Beverley Cl, N21 ......59 J1
  SW11
  off Maysoule Rd 149 G4
  SW13 ......147 F2
  Chessington KT9 ......195 F4
  Enfield EN1 ......44 B4
Beverley Cotts, SW15
  off Kingston Vale 165 E3
Beverley Cres, Wdf.Grn. .79 H1
Beverley Dr, Edg. HA8 ...70 B3
Beverley Gdns, NW11 ...72 B7
  SW13 ......147 F3
  Stanmore HA7 ......68 D1
  Wembley HA9 ......87 J1
  Worcester Park KT4
  off Green La 197 G1
Beverley La, SW15 ......165 F3
  Kingston upon Thames
  KT2 ......165 E7
Beverley Ms, E4
  off Beverley Rd 62 D6
Beverley Path, SW13 ....147 F2
Beverley Rd, E4 ......62 D6
  E6 ......116 A3
  SE20 off Wadhurst Cl .188 E2
  SW13 ......147 F3
  W4 ......127 F5
  Bexleyheath DA7 ......159 J2
  Bromley BR2 ......206 B2
  Dagenham RM9 ......101 E4
  Kingston upon Thames
  KT1 ......181 F1
Beverley Rd, Mitcham
  CR4 ......186 D4
  New Malden KT3 ......183 G4
  Ruislip HA4 ......84 A2
  Southall UB2 ......123 E3
  Worcester Park KT4 ...197 J2

Beverley Trd Est, Mord.
  SM4 off Garth Rd 184 A7
Beverley Way, SW20 ....183 F1
  New Malden KT3 ......183 F1
Beverly, NW8 ......7 G4
Beversbrook Rd, N19 ....92 D3
Beverstone Rd, SW2 ....151 F5
  Thornton Heath CR7 ..187 G4
Beverston Ms, W1 ......15 J2
Bevill Allen Cl, SW17 ...167 J5
Bevill Cl, SE25 ......188 D3
Bevin Cl, SE16
  off Stave Yd Rd 133 H1
Bevin Ct, WC1 ......10 D3
Bevington Path, SE1
  off Tanner St 29 F4
Bevington Rd, W10 ......108 B5
  Beckenham BR3 ......190 B2
Bevington St, SE16 ......29 J4
Bevin Rd, Hayes UB4 ...102 A3
Bevin Sq, SW17 ......167 J3
Bevin Way, WC1 ......10 E3
Bevis Marks, EC3 ......20 E3
Bewcastle Gdns, Enf.
  EN2 ......43 E4
Bew Ct, SE22
  off Lordship La 152 D7
Bewdley St, N1 ......93 G7
Bewick Ms, SE15 ......132 E7
Bewick St, SW8 ......150 B2
Bewley St, E1
  off Cable St 113 E7
  SW19 ......167 F6
Bewlys Rd, SE27 ......169 H5
Bexhill Cl, Felt. TW13 ...160 E2
Bexhill Rd, N11 ......58 D5
  SE4 ......153 J7
  SW14 ......146 C3
Bexhill Wk, E15
  off Mitre Rd 115 E1
BEXLEY, DA5 ......159 G6
Bexley Gdns, N9 ......60 A3
  Romford (Chad.Hth)
  RM6 ......82 B5
BEXLEYHEATH,
  DA6 & DA7 ......159 F5
Bexley High St, Bex.
  DA5 ......159 G7
Bexley La, Sid. DA14 ....176 C3
Bexley Rd, SE9 ......156 E5
  Erith DA8 ......139 J7
Beynon Rd, Cars. SM5 ..199 J5
Bianca Rd, SE15 ......37 H6
Bibsworth Rd, N3 ......72 C2
Bibury Cl, SE15 ......37 E6
Bicester Rd, Rich. TW9 .146 A3
Bickenhall St, W1 ......16 A1
Bickersteth Rd, SW17 ..167 J6
Bickerton Rd, N19 ......92 C2
BICKLEY, Brom. BR1 ....192 C3
Bickley Cres, Brom. BR1 .192 B4
Bickley Pk Rd, Brom.
  BR1 ......192 B3
Bickley Rd, E10 ......78 B7
  Bromley BR1 ......192 A2
Bickley St, SW17 ......167 H5
Bicknell Rd, SE5 ......151 J3
Bicknoller Rd, Enf. EN1 ..44 C1
Bicknor Rd, Orp. BR6 ...193 H7
Bidborough Cl, Brom.
  BR2 ......191 F5
Bidborough St, WC1 ....10 A4
Biddenden Way, SE9 ....174 D4
Bidder St, E16 ......114 E5
Biddestone Rd, N7 ......93 F4
Biddulph Rd, W9 ......6 A4
Bideford Av, Grnf. (Perivale)
  UB6 ......104 E2
Bideford Cl, Edg. HA8 ...70 A1
  Feltham TW13 ......161 F3
Bideford Gdns, Enf. EN1 .44 B7
Bideford Rd, Brom. BR1 .173 F3
  Ruislip HA4 ......84 B3
  Welling DA16 ......138 B7
Bidwell Gdns, N11 ......58 C7
Bidwell St, SE15 ......153 E1
★ Big Ben (St. Stephens Tower),
  SW1 ......26 B4
Bigbury Cl, N17 ......60 B7
Biggerstaff Rd, E15 ....114 C1
Biggerstaff St, N4 ......93 G2
Biggin Av, Mitch. CR4 ..185 J1
Biggin Hill, SE19 ......169 H7
  KT2 ......163 F5
Biggin Way, SE19 ......169 H7
Bigginwood Rd, SW16 ..169 H7
Biggs Row, SW15
  off Felsham Rd 148 A3
Big Hill, E5 ......95 E1
Bigland St, E1 ......112 E6
Bignell Rd, SE18 ......136 E5
Bignold Rd, E7 ......97 G4

Bigwood Rd, NW11 ... **72** E5
Billet Cl, Rom. RM6 ... **82** D3
Billet Rd, E17 ... **77** G2
Romford RM6 ... **82** B3
Billets Hart Cl, W7 ... **124** B2
Billet Wks, E17 ... **77** J1
Bill Faust Ho, E1 *off Tarling St* ... **113** F6
Bill Hamling Cl, SE9 ... **174** C2
Billingford Cl, SE4 ... **153** G4
Billing Pl, SW10 ... **30** B7
Billing Rd, SW10 ... **30** B7
Billings Cl, Dag. RM9 *off Ellerton Rd* ... **100** C7
★ **Billingsgate Mkt**, E14 ... **134** B1
Billing St, SW10 ... **30** B7
Billington Ms, W3 *off High St* ... **126** B1
Billington Rd, SE14 ... **133** G7
Billinton Hill, Croy. CR0 ... **202** A2
Billiter Sq, EC3 ... **20** E5
Billiter St, EC3 ... **20** E4
Bill Nicholson Way, N17 *off High Rd* ... **60** C7
Billockby Cl, Chess. KT9 ... **195** J6
Billson St, E14 ... **134** C4
Bilsby Gro, SE9 ... **174** A4
Bilton Rd, Grnf. UB6 ... **105** E1
Bilton Twrs, W1 *off Great Cumberland Pl* ... **16** A4
Bilton Way, Enf. EN3 ... **45** H1
Hayes UB3 ... **122** B2
Bina Gdns, SW5 ... **30** C2
Bincote Rd, Enf. EN2 ... **43** F3
Binden Rd, W12 ... **127** F3
Bindon Grn, Mord. SM4 ... **185** E4
Binfield Rd, SW4 ... **151** E1
South Croydon CR2 ... **202** C5
Bingfield St, N1 ... **111** E1
Bingham Ct, N1 *off Halton Rd* ... **93** H7
Bingham Pl, W1 ... **16** B1
Bingham Pt, SE18 *off Wilmount St* ... **137** E4
Bingham Rd, Croy. CR0 ... **202** D1
Bingham St, N1 ... **94** A6
Bingley Rd, E16 ... **115** J6
Greenford UB6 ... **103** J5
Sunbury-on-Thames TW16 ... **160** A7
Binley Ho, SW15 *off Highcliffe Dr* ... **147** G6
Binne Ho, SE1 *off Bath Ter* ... **27** J6
Binney St, W1 ... **16** C5
Binns Rd, W4 ... **126** E5
Binns Ter, W4 *off Binns Rd* ... **126** E5
Binsey Wk, SE2 ... **138** C1
Binstead Cl, Hayes UB4 ... **102** E5
Binyon Cres, Stan. HA7 ... **52** C5
Birbetts Rd, SE9 ... **174** C2
Bircham Path, SE4 *off Aldersford Cl* ... **153** G5
Birchanger Rd, SE25 ... **188** D5
Birch Av, N13 ... **59** J3
Birch Cl, E16 ... **115** E5
N19 *off Hargrave Pk* ... **92** C2
SE15 *off Bournemouth Rd* ... **152** D2
Brentford TW8 ... **124** E7
Buckhurst Hill IG9 ... **64** A3
Hounslow TW3 ... **144** A3
Romford RM7 ... **83** H3
Teddington TW11 ... **162** D5
Birchdale Gdns, Rom. RM6 ... **82** D7
Birchdale Rd, E7 ... **97** J5
Birchdene Dr, SE28 ... **138** A2
Birchdown Ho, E3 *off Rainhill Way* ... **114** B3
Birchen Cl, NW9 ... **88** D2
Birchend Cl, S.Croy. CR2 ... **202** A6
Birchen Gro, NW9 ... **88** D2
Birches, The, E12 *off Station Rd* ... **98** B4
N21 ... **43** F6
SE7 ... **135** H6
Orpington BR6 ... **206** D4
Birches Cl, Mitch. CR4 ... **185** J3
Pinner HA5 ... **66** E5
Birchfield St, E14 ... **114** A7
Birch Gdns, Dag. RM10 ... **101** J3
Birch Grn, NW9 *off Clayton Fld* ... **55** E7
Birch Gro, E11 ... **96** E3
SE12 ... **155** F7
W3 ... **126** A1
Welling DA16 ... **158** A4
Birchgrove Ho, Rich. TW9 *off Strand Dr* ... **126** B7
Birch Hill, Croy. CR0 ... **203** G5
Birchington Cl, Bexh. DA7 ... **159** H1
Birchington Ho, E5 *off Pembury Rd* ... **94** E5
Birchington Rd, N8 ... **74** D6
NW6 ... **108** D1
Surbiton KT5 ... **181** J7
Birchin La, EC3 ... **20** C4
Birchlands Av, SW12 ... **149** J7
Birchmead, Orp. BR6 ... **206** D2
Birchmead Av, Pnr. HA5 ... **66** C4
Birchmere Business Pk, SE28 ... **138** A2
Birchmere Row, SE3 ... **155** F2
Birchmore Wk, N5 ... **93** J3
Birch Pk, Har. HA3 ... **51** J7
Birch Rd, Felt. TW13 ... **160** D5
Romford RM7 ... **83** H3
Birch Row, Brom. BR2 ... **192** D7
Birch Tree Av, W.Wick. BR4 ... **205** F5
Birch Tree Way, Croy. CR0 ... **202** E2
Birchville Ct, Bushey (Bushey Hth) WD23 *off Heathbourne Rd* ... **52** B1
Birch Wk, Borwd. WD6 ... **38** A1
Erith DA8 ... **139** J6
Mitcham CR4 ... **186** B1
Birchway, Hayes UB3 ... **122** A1
Birchwood Av, N10 ... **74** A3
Beckenham BR3 ... **189** J4
Sidcup DA14 ... **176** B2
Wallington SM6 ... **200** A3
Birchwood Cl, Mord. SM4 ... **184** E4
Birchwood Ct, N13 ... **59** H5
Edgware HA8 ... **70** C2
Birchwood Dr, NW3 ... **91** E3
Birchwood Gro, Hmptn. TW12 ... **161** G6
Birchwood Rd, SW17 ... **168** B5
Orpington BR5 ... **193** G4
Birdbrook Cl, Dag. RM10 ... **101** J7
Birdbrook Rd, SE3 ... **155** J3
Birdcage Wk, SW1 ... **25** G4
Birdham Cl, Brom. BR1 ... **192** B5
Birdhurst Av, S.Croy. CR2 ... **202** A4
Birdhurst Gdns, S.Croy. CR2 ... **202** A4
Birdhurst Ri, S.Croy. CR2 ... **202** B5
Birdhurst Rd, SW18 ... **149** F4
SW19 ... **167** H6
South Croydon CR2 ... **202** B5
Bird in Bush Rd, SE15 ... **37** J7
Bird-in-Hand La, Brom. BR1 ... **192** A2
Bird-in-Hand Ms, SE23 *off Dartmouth Rd* ... **171** F2
Bird-in-Hand Pas, SE23 *off Dartmouth Rd* ... **171** F2
Bird in Hand Yd, NW3 *off Hampstead High St* ... **91** F4
Birds Fm Av, Rom. RM5 ... **83** H1
Birdsfield La, E3 ... **113** J1
Bird St, W1 ... **16** C4
Bird Wk, Twick. TW2 ... **161** F1
Birdwood Av, SE13 ... **154** D6
Birdwood Cl, Tedd. TW11 ... **162** B4
Birkbeck Av, W3 ... **106** C7
Greenford UB6 ... **103** J1
Birkbeck Gdns, Wdf.Grn. IG8 ... **63** F2
Birkbeck Gro, W3 ... **126** D2
Birkbeck Hill, SE21 ... **169** H2
Birkbeck Ms, E8 *off Sandringham Rd* ... **94** C5
W3 *off Birkbeck Rd* ... **126** D1
Birkbeck Pl, SE21 ... **169** J1
Birkbeck Rd, E8 ... **94** C5
N8 ... **75** E4
N12 ... **57** F5
N17 ... **76** C1
NW7 ... **55** F5
Birkbeck Rd, SW19 ... **167** E5
W3 ... **126** D1
W5 ... **125** F4
Beckenham BR3 ... **189** F2
Enfield EN2 ... **44** A1
Ilford IG2 ... **81** G5
Sidcup DA14 ... **176** A3
Birkbeck St, E2 ... **113** E3
Birkbeck Way, Grnf. UB6 ... **103** J1
Birkdale Av, Pnr. HA5 ... **67** G3
Birkdale Cl, SE16 *off Masters Dr* ... **132** E5
SE28 ... **118** D6
Orpington BR6 ... **193** G7
Birkdale Gdns, Croy. CR0 ... **203** G4
Watford WD19 ... **50** D3
Birkdale Rd, SE2 ... **138** A4
W5 ... **105** H4
Birkenhead Av, Kings.T. KT2 ... **181** J2
Birkenhead St, WC1 ... **10** B3
Birkhall Rd, SE6 ... **172** D1
Birkwood Cl, SW12 ... **150** D7
Birley Rd, N20 ... **57** F2
Birley St, SW11 ... **150** A2
Birnam Rd, N4 ... **93** F2
Birnbeck Cl, NW11 ... **72** C5
Birnbeck Ct, NW11 *off Finchley Rd* ... **72** C5
Birrell Ho, SW9 ... **151** F2
Birse Cres, NW10 ... **89** E4
Birstall Grn, Wat. WD19 ... **50** D4
Birstall Rd, N15 ... **76** B5
Biscayne Av, E14 *off Fairmont Av* ... **114** D7
Biscay Rd, W6 ... **128** A5
Biscoe Cl, Houns. TW5 ... **123** G6
Biscoe Way, SE13 ... **154** D3
Bisenden Rd, Croy. CR0 ... **202** B2
Bisham Cl, Cars. SM5 ... **199** J1
Bisham Gdns, N6 ... **92** A1
Bishop Butt Cl, Orp. BR6 ... **207** J3
Bishop Fox Way, W.Mol. KT8 ... **179** F4
Bishop Ken Rd, Har. HA3 ... **68** C2
Bishop Kings Rd, W14 ... **128** B4
Bishop Rd, N14 ... **42** B7
Bishop's Av, E13 ... **115** H1
SW6 ... **148** A2
Bishops Av, Brom. BR1 ... **191** J2
Romford RM6 ... **82** C6
Bishops Av, The, N2 ... **73** G7
Bishops Br, W2 ... **14** D3
Bishops Br Rd, W2 ... **14** B4
Bishops Cl, E17 ... **78** B4
Bishop's Cl, N19 ... **92** C3
Bishops Cl, SE9 ... **175** F2
W4 ... **126** C5
Barnet EN5 ... **40** A6
Enfield EN1 *off Central Av* ... **44** E2
Richmond TW10 ... **163** G3
Bishop's Cl, Sutt. SM1 ... **198** D3
Bishop's Ct, EC4 ... **19** G3
WC2 ... **18** E3
Bishops Dr, Felt. TW14 ... **141** G6
Northolt UB5 ... **103** E1
Bishopsford Rd, Mord. SM4 ... **185** F7
Bishopsgate, EC2 ... **20** D4
Bishopsgate Arc, EC2 ... **20** E2
Bishopsgate Chyd, EC2 ... **20** D2
Bishops Gro, N2 ... **73** G6
Hampton TW12 ... **161** F4
Bishop's Hall, Kings.T. KT1 ... **181** G2
Bishops Hill, Walt. KT12 ... **178** A7
Bishops Ho, SW8 *off South Lambeth Rd* ... **131** E7
Bishopsmead, SE5 *off Camberwell Rd* ... **131** J7
Bishop's Pk, SW6 ... **148** A2
Bishop's Pk Rd, SW6 ... **148** A2
Bishops Pk Rd, SW16 ... **187** E1
Bishops Pl, Sutt. SM1 *off Lind Rd* ... **199** F5
Bishops Rd, N6 ... **74** A6
SW6 ... **148** C1
Bishop's Rd, SW11 ... **31** H7
Bishops Rd, W7 ... **124** B2
Croydon CR0 ... **187** H7
Bishops Sq, E1 ... **21** E1
Bishops Ter, SE11 ... **35** F1
Bishopsthorpe Rd, SE26 ... **171** G4
Bishop St, N1 ... **111** J1
Bishops Wk, Chis. BR7 ... **193** F1
Croydon CR0 ... **203** G5
Bishop's Wk, Pnr. HA5 *off High St* ... **66** E3
Bishops Way, E2 ... **113** E2
Bishopswood Rd, N6 ... **73** J7
Bishop Wilfred Wd Cl, SE15 *off Moncrieff St* ... **152** D2
Bisley Cl, Wor.Pk. KT4 ... **197** J1
Bisley Ho, SW19 ... **166** A2
Bispham Rd, NW10 ... **105** J3
Bisson Rd, E15 ... **114** C2
Bisterne Av, E17 ... **78** D3
Bittacy Busines Cen, NW7 ... **56** B7
Bittacy Cl, NW7 ... **56** A6
Bittacy Ct, NW7 *off Bittacy Hill* ... **56** B7
Bittacy Hill, NW7 ... **56** A6
Bittacy Pk Av, NW7 ... **56** A6
Bittacy Ri, NW7 ... **55** J6
Bittacy Rd, NW7 ... **56** A6
Bittern Cl, Hayes UB4 ... **102** D5
Bittern Pl, N22 ... **75** F2
Bittern St, SE1 ... **27** J4
Bittoms, The, Kings.T. KT1 ... **181** G3
Bixley Cl, Sthl. UB2 ... **123** F4
Blackall St, EC2 ... **12** D5
Blackberry Fm Cl, Houns. TW5 ... **122** E7
Blackbird Hill, NW9 ... **88** C2
Blackbird Yd, E2 ... **13** G3
Blackborne Rd, Dag. RM10 ... **101** G6
Black Boy La, N15 ... **75** J5
Blackbrook La, Brom. BR1, BR2 ... **192** D3
Black Bull Yd, EC1 *off Hatton Wall* ... **19** E1
Blackburne's Ms, W1 ... **16** B5
Blackburn Rd, NW6 ... **90** E6
Blackburn Trd Est, Stai. (Stanw.) TW19 ... **140** C6
Blackburn Way, Houns. TW4 *off Vickers Way* ... **143** E5
Blackbush Av, Rom. RM6 ... **82** D5
Blackbush Cl, Sutt. SM2 ... **199** E7
Blackdown Cl, N2 ... **73** F2
Blackdown Ter, SE18 *off Prince Imperial Rd* ... **136** C7
Blackett St, SW15 ... **148** A3
Black Fan Cl, Enf. EN2 ... **43** J1
BLACKFEN, Sid. DA15 ... **157** J7
Blackfen Par, Sid. DA15 *off Blackfen Rd* ... **158** A6
Blackfen Rd, Sid. DA15 ... **157** H5
Blackford Rd, Wat. WD19 ... **50** D5
Blackford's Path, SW15 *off Roehampton High St* ... **147** G7
Blackfriars Br, EC4 ... **19** G5
SE1 ... **19** G5
Blackfriars Ct, EC4 ... **19** G5
Black Friars La, EC4 ... **19** G5
Blackfriars Pas, EC4 ... **19** G5
Blackfriars Rd, SE1 ... **27** G4
Black Gates, Pnr. HA5 *off Moss La* ... **67** F3
BLACKHEATH, SE3 ... **155** E1
★ **Blackheath**, SE3 ... **154** D1
Blackheath Av, SE10 ... **134** D7
Blackheath Gro, SE3 ... **155** F2
Blackheath Hill, SE10 ... **154** C1
BLACKHEATH PARK, SE3 ... **155** F4
Blackheath Pk, SE3 ... **155** F3
Blackheath Ri, SE13 ... **154** C2
Blackheath Rd, SE10 ... **154** B1
Blackheath Vale, SE3 ... **155** E2
Blackheath Village, SE3 ... **155** F2
Black Horse Ct, SE1 ... **28** C5
Blackhorse La, E17 ... **77** G3
Croydon CR0 ... **188** D7
Blackhorse Ms, E17 *off Blackhorse La* ... **77** G3
Blackhorse Rd, E17 ... **77** G4
SE8 ... **133** H5
Sidcup DA14 ... **176** A4
Blacklands Rd, SE6 ... **172** C4
Blacklands Ter, SW3 ... **31** J2
Black Lion La, W6 ... **127** G4
Black Lion Ms, W6 *off Black Lion La* ... **127** G4
Blackmore Av, Sthl. UB1 ... **124** A1
Blackmore Dr, NW10 ... **88** B7
Blackmore Rd, Buck.H. IG9 ... **48** B7
Blackmores Gro, Tedd. TW11 ... **162** D6
Blackmore Twr, W3 *off Stanley Rd* ... **126** C3
Black Path, E10 ... **77** G7
Blackpool Rd, SE15 ... **152** E2
Black Prince Interchange, Bex. DA5 *off East Rochester Way* ... **159** H6
Black Prince Rd, SE1 ... **34** C2
SE11 ... **34** D2
Black Rod Cl, Hayes UB3 ... **121** J3
Blackshaw Rd, SW17 ... **167** F4
Blacksmiths Cl, Rom. RM6 ... **82** C6
Blacks Rd, W6 *off Queen Caroline St* ... **127** J4

Blackstock Ms, N4 *off Blackstock Rd* 93 H2
Blackstock Rd, N4 93 H2
N5 93 H2
Blackstone Est, E8 94 D7
Blackstone Ho, SW1 *off Churchill Gdns* 33 F4
Blackstone Rd, NW2 89 J5
Black Swan Yd, SE1 28 D3
Blackthorn Av, West Dr. UB7 120 D4
Blackthorn Ct, Houns. TW5 122 E7
Blackthorne Av, Croy. CR0 189 F7
Blackthorne Dr, E4 62 D4
Blackthorn Gro, Bexh. DA7 158 D3
Blackthorn Rd, Ilf. IG1 99 G5
Blackthorn St, E3 114 A4
Blacktree Ms, SW9 151 G3
Blackwall La, SE10 135 E5
Blackwall Pier, E14 114 E7
Blackwall Trd Est, E14 114 D5
Blackwall Tunnel, E14 134 D1
Blackwall Tunnel App, SE10 134 E2
Blackwall Tunnel Northern App, E3 114 A2
E14 114 A2
Blackwall Way, E14 114 C7
Blackwater Cl, E7 97 F4
Blackwater Rd, Sutt. SM1 *off High St* 199 E4
Blackwater St, SE22 152 C5
Blackwell Cl, E5 95 G4
Harrow HA3 52 A7
Blackwell Gdns, Edg. HA8 54 A3
Blackwood Av, N18 *off Harbet Rd* 61 G5
Blackwood St, SE17 36 B3
Blade Ms, SW15 *off Deodar Rd* 148 C4
Blades Ct, SW15 *off Deodar Rd* 148 C4
Bladindon Dr, Bex. DA5 158 C7
Bladon Gdns, Har. HA2 67 H6
Blagdens Cl, N14 58 C2
Blagdens La, N14 58 D2
Blagdon Rd, SE13 154 B6
New Malden KT3 183 F4
Blagdon Wk, Tedd. TW11 163 F6
Blagrove Rd, W10 108 B5
Blair Av, NW9 70 E7
Blair Cl, N1 93 J6
Hayes UB3 122 A4
Sidcup DA15 157 H5
Blairderry Rd, SW2 169 E2
Blairhead Dr, Wat. WD19 50 B3
Blair Ho, SW9 *off Stockwell Gdns* 151 F2
Blair St, E14 114 C6
Blake Apts, N8 *off New River Av* 75 F3
Blake Av, Bark. IG11 117 H1
Blake Cl, W10 107 J5
Carshalton SM5 185 H7
Welling DA16 157 H1
Blakeden Dr, Esher (Clay.) KT10 194 C6
Blake Gdns, SW6 148 E1
Blake Hall Cres, E11 97 G1
Blake Hall Rd, E11 79 G7
Blakehall Rd, Cars. SM5 199 J6
Blake Ho, Beck. BR3 172 A6
Blake Ms, Rich. TW9 *off High Pk Rd* 146 A1
Blakemore Gdns, SW13 *off Lonsdale Rd* 127 H6
Blakemore Rd, SW16 168 E3
Thornton Heath CR7 187 F5
Blakemore Way, Belv. DA17 139 E3
Blakeney Av, Beck. BR3 189 J1
Blakeney Cl, E8 *off Ferncliff Rd* 94 D5
N20 57 F1
Blakeney Cl, NW1 *off Rossendale Way* 92 D7
Blakeney Rd, Beck. BR3 171 J7
Blakenham Rd, SW17 167 J4
Blaker Ct, SE7 *off Fairlawn* 135 J7
Blake Rd, E16 115 F4
N11 58 C7
Croydon CR0 202 B2
Mitcham CR4 185 H3
Blaker Rd, E15 114 C1
Blakes Av, N.Mal. KT3 183 F5
Blake's Grn, W.Wick. BR4 204 C1
Blakes La, N.Mal. KT3 183 F5
Blakesley Av, W5 105 F6
Blakesley Ho, E12 *off Grantham Rd* 98 D3
Blakesley Wk, SW20 *off Kingston Rd* 184 C2
Blakes Rd, SE15 36 E7
Blakes Ter, N.Mal. KT3 183 G5
Blake St, SE8 *off Watergate St* 134 A6
Blakesware Gdns, N9 44 A7
Blakewood Cl, Felt. TW13 160 C4
Blanchard Cl, SE9 174 B3
Blanchard Way, E8 94 D6
Blanch Cl, SE15 *off Culmore Rd* 133 F7
Blanchedowne, SE5 152 A4
Blanche St, E16 115 F4
Blanchland Rd, Mord. SM4 184 E5
Blandfield Rd, SW12 150 A6
Blandford Av, Beck. BR3 189 H2
Twickenham TW2 161 H1
Blandford Cl, N2 73 F4
Croydon CR0 201 E3
Romford RM7 83 H4
Blandford Cres, E4 46 C7
Blandford Rd, W4 126 E3
W5 125 G2
Beckenham BR3 189 F2
Southall UB2 123 G4
Teddington TW11 162 A5
Blandford Sq, NW1 7 H6
Blandford St, W1 16 A3
Blandford Waye, Hayes UB4 102 C6
Bland St, SE9 156 A4
Blaney Cres, E6 116 E3
Blanmerle Rd, SE9 174 E1
Blann Cl, SE9 156 A6
Blantyre St, SW10 30 E7
Blantyre Twr, SW10 30 E7
Blantyre Wk, SW10 *off Blantyre St* 30 E7
Blashford, NW3 91 J7
Blashford St, SE13 154 D7
Blasker Wk, E14 134 A5
Blawith Rd, Har. HA1 68 B4
Blaydon Cl, N17 60 E7
Blaydon Wk, N17 60 E7
Bleak Hill La, SE18 137 J6
Blean Gro, SE20 171 F7
Bleasdale Av, Grnf. (Perivale) UB6 104 D2
Blechynden St, W10 *off Bramley Rd* 108 A7
Bleddyn Cl, Sid. DA15 158 C6
Bledlow Cl, NW8 7 F6
SE28 118 C7
Bledlow Ri, Grnf. UB6 103 J2
Bleeding Heart Yd, EC1 19 F2
Blegborough Rd, SW16 168 C6
Blemundsbury, WC1 *off Dombey St* 18 C1
Blendon Dr, Bex. DA5 158 D6
Blendon Path, Brom. BR1 *off Hope Pk* 173 F7
Blendon Rd, Bex. DA5 158 D6
Blendon Ter, SE18 137 F5
Blendworth Pt, SW15 *off Wanborough Dr* 165 H1
Blenheim Av, Ilf. IG2 80 D6
Blenheim Cen, The, Houns. TW3 *off Prince Regent Rd* 143 H3
Blenheim Cl, N21 *off Elm Pk Rd* 59 J1
SE12 173 H1
SW20 183 J3
Greenford UB6 *off Leaver Gdns* 104 A2
Romford RM7 83 J4
Wallington SM6 200 C7
Blenheim Ct, N19 92 E2
Bromley BR2 *off Durham Av* 191 F4
Sidcup DA14 175 G3
Blenheim Ct, Sutton SM2 *off Wellesley Rd* 199 F6
Woodford Green IG8 *off Navestock Cres* 63 J7
Blenheim Cres, W11 108 B6
South Croydon CR2 201 J7
Blenheim Dr, Well. DA16 157 J1
Blenheim Gdns, NW2 89 J5
SW2 151 F6
Kingston upon Thames KT2 164 B7
Wallington SM6 200 C6
Wembley HA9 87 H3
Blenheim Gro, SE15 152 D2
Blenheim Pas, NW8 6 C1
Blenheim Pl, Tedd. TW11 162 C5
Blenheim Ri, N15 76 C4
Blenheim Rd, E6 116 A3
E15 97 E4
E17 77 G3
NW8 6 C1
SE20 *off Maple Rd* 171 F7
SW20 183 J3
W4 126 E3
Barnet EN5 40 A3
Bromley BR1 192 B4
Harrow HA2 67 H6
Northolt UB5 85 H6
Sidcup DA15 176 C1
Sutton SM1 198 D3
Blenheim Shop Cen, SE20 171 F7
Blenheim St, W1 16 D4
Blenheim Ter, NW8 6 C1
Blenheim Way, Islw. TW7 144 D1
Blenkarne Rd, SW11 149 J6
Bleriot Rd, Houns. TW5 122 C7
Blessbury Rd, Edg. HA8 70 C1
Blessington Cl, SE13 154 D3
Blessington Rd, SE13 154 D3
Blessing Way, Bark. IG11 118 C3
Bletchingley Cl, Th.Hth. CR7 187 H4
Bletchley Ct, N1 12 B2
Bletchley St, N1 12 A2
Bletchmore Cl, Hayes (Harling.) UB3 121 G5
Bletsoe Wk, N1 12 A1
Blewbury Ho, SE2 *off Yarnton Way* 138 D2
Blincoe Cl, SW19 166 A2
Blind La, Loug. (High Beach) IG10 46 E2
Bliss Cres, SE13 154 B2
Blissett St, SE10 154 C1
Bliss Ms, W10 *off Third Av* 108 B3
Blisworth Cl, Hayes UB4 *off Braunston Dr* 103 E4
Blithbury Rd, Dag. RM9 100 B6
Blithdale Rd, SE2 138 A4
Blithfield St, W8 22 A6
Blockley Rd, Wem. HA0 86 E2
Bloemfontein Av, W12 127 H1
Bloemfontein Rd, W12 107 H7
Bloemfontein Way, W12 *off Bloemfontein Rd* 127 H1
Blomfield Ct, SW11 *off Westbridge Rd* 149 H1
Blomfield Ms, W2 14 C2
Blomfield Rd, W9 14 C1
Blomfield St, EC2 20 C2
Blomfield Vil, W2 14 B2
Blomville Rd, Dag. RM8 101 E3
Blondell Cl, West Dr. (Harm.) UB7 120 A6
Blondel St, SW11 150 A2
Blondin Av, W5 125 F4
Blondin St, E3 114 A2
Blomburg St, SW1 33 G2
Bloomfield Ct, E10 *off Brisbane Rd* 96 B3
Bloomfield Cres, Ilf. IG2 81 E6
Bloomfield Pl, W1 16 E5
Bloomfield Rd, N6 74 A6
SE18 137 E5
Bromley BR2 192 A5
Kingston upon Thames KT1 181 H4
Bloomfield Ter, SW1 32 C3
Bloom Gro, SE27 169 H3
Bloomhall Rd, SE19 170 A5
Bloom Pk Rd, SW6 128 C7
BLOOMSBURY, WC1 17 J2
Bloomsbury Cl, NW7 55 G7
W5 105 J7
Bloomsbury Ct, WC1 18 B2
Pinner HA5 67 F3
Bloomsbury Ho, SW4 150 D6
Bloomsbury Ms, Wdf.Grn. IG8 *off Waltham Rd* 64 B6
Bloomsbury Pl, SW18 *off Fullerton Rd* 149 F5
WC1 18 B1
Bloomsbury Sq, WC1 18 B2
Bloomsbury St, WC1 17 J2
Bloomsbury Way, WC1 18 A3
Blore Cl, SW8 *off Thessaly Rd* 150 D1
Blore Ct, W1 17 H4
Blossom Cl, W5 125 H2
Dagenham RM9 119 F1
South Croydon CR2 202 C5
Blossom La, Enf. EN2 43 J1
Blossom St, E1 21 E1
Blossom Way, West Dr. UB7 120 D4
Blossom Waye, Houns. TW5 122 E7
Blount St, E14 113 H6
Bloxam Gdns, SE9 156 B5
Bloxhall Rd, E10 95 J1
Bloxham Cres, Hmptn. TW12 161 F7
Bloxworth Cl, Wall. SM6 200 C3
Blucher Rd, SE5 131 J7
Blue Anchor All, Rich. TW9 *off Kew Rd* 145 H4
Blue Anchor La, SE16 37 J1
Blue Anchor Yd, E1 21 H5
Blue Ball Yd, SW1 25 F2
Bluebell Av, E12 98 A5
Bluebell Cl, E9 *off Moulins Rd* 113 F1
SE26 170 C4
Northolt UB5 85 F6
Orpington BR6 207 F2
Wallington SM6 200 B1
Bluebell Way, Ilf. IG1 98 E6
Blueberry Cl, Wdf.Grn. IG8 63 G6
Bluebird La, Dag. RM10 101 G7
Bluebird Way, SE28 137 G2
Bluefield Cl, Hmptn. TW12 161 G5
Bluegates, Epsom (Ewell) KT17 197 G7
Bluehouse Rd, E4 63 E3
Bluelion Pl, SE1 28 D5
Blueprint Apts, SW12 *off Balham Gro* 150 B7
Bluewater Ho, SW18 *off Smugglers Way* 149 E4
Blundell Cl, E8 *off Amhurst Rd* 94 D4
Blundell Rd, Edg. HA8 70 D1
Blundell St, N7 92 E7
Blunden Cl, Dag. RM8 100 C1
Blunt Rd, S.Croy. CR2 202 A5
Blunts Av, West Dr. (Sipson) UB7 120 D7
Blunts Rd, SE9 156 D5
Blurton Rd, E5 95 F4
Blyth Cl, E14 *off Manchester Rd* 134 D4
Twickenham TW1 *off Grimwood Rd* 144 C6
Blythe Cl, SE6 153 J7
Blythe Hill, SE6 153 J7
Orpington BR5 193 J1
Blythe Hill La, SE6 153 J7
Blythe Hill Pl, SE23 *off Brockley Pk* 153 H7
Blythe Ms, W14 *off Blythe Rd* 128 A3
Blythe Rd, W14 128 A3
Blythe St, E2 112 E3
Blytheswood Pl, SW16 *off Curtis Fld Rd* 169 F4
Blythe Vale, SE6 171 J1
Blyth Rd, E17 77 J7
SE28 118 C7
Bromley BR1 191 F1
Hayes UB3 121 H2
Blyth's Wf, E14 *off Narrow St* 113 H7
Blythswood Rd, Ilf. IG3 100 A1
Blyth Wd Pk, Brom. BR1 *off Blyth Rd* 191 F1
Blythwood Rd, N4 75 E7
Pinner HA5 66 D1
Boades Ms, NW3 *off New End* 91 G4
Boadicea St, N1 *off Copenhagen St* 111 F1
Boakes Cl, NW9 70 C4
Boardman Av, E4 46 B5
Boardman Cl, Barn. EN5 40 B5
Boardwalk Pl, E14 134 C1
Boar's Head Yd, Brent. TW8 *off Brent Way* 125 G7
Boatemah Wk, SW9 *off Peckford Pl* 151 G2
Boathouse Wk, SE15 37 G7
Richmond TW9 145 H1
Boat Lifter Way, SE16 *off Sweden Gate* 133 H4
Bob Anker Cl, E13 *off Chesterton Rd* 115 G3
Bobbin Cl, SW4 150 C3
Bobby Moore Way, N10 57 J7
Bob Marley Way, SE24 *off Mayall Rd* 151 G4
Bockhampton Rd, Kings.T. KT2 163 J7
Bocking St, E8 112 E1
Boddicott Cl, SW19 166 B2
Boddington Gdns, W3 126 A2
Bodiam Cl, Enf. EN1 44 A2
Bodiam Rd, SW16 168 D7
Bodiam Way, NW10 105 J3
Bodicea Ms, Houns. TW4 143 F7

Bodley Cl, N.Mal. KT3 182 E5
Bodley Manor Way, SW2
off Hambridge Way 151 G7
Bodley Rd, N.Mal. KT3 182 D6
Bodmin Cl, Har. HA2 85 F3
Bodmin Gro, Mord. SM4 185 E5
Bodmin St, SW18 166 D1
Bodnant Gdns, SW20 183 G3
Bodney Rd, E8 94 E5
Boeing Way, Sthl. UB2 122 B3
Boevey Path, Belv. DA17 139 F6
Bogey La, Orp. BR6 206 D7
Bognor Gdns, Wat.
WD19 50 C5
Bognor Rd, Well. DA16 158 D1
Bohemia Pl, E8 95 E6
Bohn Rd, E1 113 H5
Bohun Gro, Barn. EN4 41 H6
Boileau Par, W5
off Boileau Rd 105 J6
Boileau Rd, SW13 127 G7
W5 105 J6
Bolden St, SE8 154 B2
Bolderwood Way, W.Wick.
BR4 204 B2
Boldmere Rd, Pnr. HA5 66 C7
Boleyn Av, Enf. EN1 44 E1
Boleyn Cl, E17 78 A4
Loughton IG10
off Roding Gdns 48 B6
Boleyn Ct, Buck.H. IG9 63 G1
Boleyn Dr, Ruis. HA4 84 D2
West Molesey KT8 179 F3
Boleyn Gdns, Dag. RM10 101 J7
West Wickham BR4 204 B2
Boleyn Gro, W.Wick.
BR4 204 C2
Boleyn Rd, E6 116 A2
E7 97 G7
N16 94 B5
Boleyn Way, Barn. EN5 41 F3
Ilford IG6 65 F6
Bolina Rd, SE16 133 F5
Bolingbroke Gro, SW11 149 H4
Bolingbroke Rd, W14 128 A3
Bolingbroke Wk, SW11 129 G7
Bolingbroke Way, Hayes
UB3 121 G1
Bolliger Ct, NW10
off Park Royal Rd 106 C4
Bollo Br Rd, W3 126 B3
Bollo La, W3 126 B2
W4 126 C4
Bolney Gate, SW7 23 G4
Bolney St, SW8 131 F7
Bolney Way, Felt. TW13 161 E3
Bolsover St, W1 9 E6
Bolstead Rd, Mitch. CR4 186 B1
Bolster Gro, N22 58 D7
Bolt Ct, EC4 19 F4
Boltmore Cl, NW4 72 A3
Bolton Cl, SE20
off Selby Rd 188 D2
Chessington KT9 195 G6
Bolton Cres, SE5 35 F6
Bolton Dr, Mord. SM4 185 F7
Bolton Gdns, NW10 108 A2
SW5 30 A3
Bromley BR1 173 F6
Teddington TW11 162 D6
Bolton Gdns Ms, SW10 30 C3
Bolton Rd, E15 97 F6
N18 60 C5
NW8 109 E1
NW10 107 E1
W4 126 C7
Chessington KT9 195 G6
Harrow HA1 67 J4
Boltons, The, SW10 30 C3
Wembley HA0 86 C4
Woodford Green IG8 63 G4
Boltons La, Hayes
(Harling.) UB3 121 F7
Boltons Pl, SW5 30 C3
Bolton St, W1 24 E1
Bolton Wk, N7
off Durham Rd 93 F2
Bombay St, SE16 132 E4
Bomer Cl, West Dr.
(Sipson) UB7 120 D7
Bomore Rd, W11 108 A7
Bonar Pl, Chis. BR7 174 B7
Bonar Rd, SE15 132 D7
Bonchester Cl, Chis. BR7 174 D7
Bonchurch Cl, Sutt. SM2 199 E7
Bonchurch Rd, W10 108 B5
W13 124 E1
Bond Ct, EC4 20 B4
Bondfield Av, Hayes
UB4 102 A3
Bondfield Rd, E6
off Lovage App 116 B5
Bond Gdns, Wall. SM6 200 C4
Bonding Yd Wk, SE16
off Finland St 133 H3
Bond Rd, Mitch. CR4 185 H2
Surbiton KT6 195 J2
Bond St, E15 96 E5
W4 126 E4
W5 105 G7
Bondway, SW8 34 B6
Boneta Rd, SE18 136 C3
Bonfield Rd, SE13 154 C4
Bonham Cl, Belv. DA17
off Croft Cl 139 F5
Bonham Gdns, Dag.
RM8 100 D2
Bonham Rd, SW2 151 F5
Dagenham RM8 100 D2
Bonheur Rd, W4 126 D2
Bonhill St, EC2 12 C6
Boniface Gdns, Har.
HA3 51 H7
Boniface Wk, Har. HA3 51 H7
Bonington Ho, Enf. EN1
off Ayley Cft 44 D5
Bonita Ms, SE4 153 G3
Bon Marche Ter Ms, SE27
off Gipsy Rd 170 B4
Bonner Hill Rd, Kings.T.
KT1 181 J3
Bonner Rd, E2 113 F2
Bonnersfield Cl, Har.
HA1 68 C6
Bonnersfield La, Har.
HA1 68 D6
Bonner St, E2 113 F2
Bonneville Gdns, SW4 150 C6
Bonnington Ho, N1
off Killick St 10 C2
Bonnington Sq, SW8 34 C5
Bonnington Twr, Brom.
BR2 192 B6
Bonny St, NW1 92 C7
Bonser Rd, Twick. TW1 162 C2
Bonsor St, SE5 132 B7
Bonville Gdns, NW4
off Handowe Cl 71 G4
Bonville Rd, Brom. BR1 173 F5
Bookbinders' Cotts, N20
off Manor Dr 57 J3
Booker Cl, E14
off Wallwood St 113 J5
Booker Rd, N18 60 D5
Bookham Ct, Mitch.
CR4 185 G3
Book Ms, WC2 17 J4
Boone Ct, N9 61 F3
Boones Rd, SE13 155 E4
Boone St, SE13 155 E4
Boord St, SE10 135 E3
Boothby Rd, N19 92 D2
Booth Cl, E9
off Victoria Pk Rd 113 E1
SE28 118 B7
Booth Ho, Brent. TW8
off High St 125 F7
Booth La, EC4 19 J5
Booth Rd, NW9 70 E2
Croydon CR0
off Waddon New Rd 201 H2
Booth's Pl, W1 17 G2
Boot St, N1 12 D4
Bordars Rd, W7 104 B5
Bordars Wk, W7 104 B5
Borden Av, Enf. EN1 44 A6
Border Cres, SE26 170 E5
Border Gdns, Croy. CR0 204 B4
Bordergate, Mitch. CR4 185 H1
Border Rd, SE26 171 E5
Borders La, Loug. IG10 48 D4
Bordesley Rd, Mord.
SM4 184 E4
Bordon Wk, SW15 147 G7
Boreas Wk, N1 11 H2
Boreham Av, E16 115 G6
Boreham Cl, E11
off Hainault Rd 96 C1
Boreham Rd, N22 75 J2
BOREHAMWOOD, WD6 38 B3
Borehamwood Ind Pk,
Borwd. WD6 38 D2
Borehamwood Shop Pk,
Borwd. WD6 38 A3
Borgard Rd, SE18 136 C4
Borkwood Pk, Orp. BR6 207 J4
Borkwood Way, Orp.
BR6 207 H4
Borland Rd, SE15 153 F4
Teddington TW11 162 E6
Borneo St, SW15 147 J3
BOROUGH, THE, SE1 27 J4
Borough High St, SE1 27 J4
Borough Hill, Croy.
CR0 201 H3
★ **Borough Mkt**, SE1 28 B2
Borough Rd, SE1 27 G5
Isleworth TW7 144 B1
Kingston upon Thames
KT2 182 A1
Mitcham CR4 185 H2
Borough Sq, SE1 27 J4
Borrett Cl, SE17 35 J4
Borrodaile Rd, SW18 149 E6
Borrowdale Av, Har. HA3 68 D2
Borrowdale Cl, Ilf. IG4 80 B4
Borrowdale Ct, Enf. EN2 43 J1
Borthwick Ms, E15
off Borthwick Rd 96 E4
Borthwick Rd, E15 96 E4
NW9
off West Hendon Bdy 71 F6
Borthwick St, SE8 134 A5
Borwick Av, E17 77 J3
Bosbury Rd, SE6 172 C3
Boscastle Rd, NW5 92 B3
Boscobel Cl, Brom. BR1 192 C2
Boscobel Pl, SW1 32 C1
Boscobel St, NW8 7 F6
Bosco Cl, Orp. BR6 207 J4
Boscombe Av, E10 78 D7
Boscombe Circ, NW9
off Warmwell Av 70 D2
Boscombe Cl, E5 95 H5
Boscombe Gdns, SW16 169 E6
Boscombe Rd, SW17 168 A6
SW19 184 E1
W12 127 G1
Worcester Park KT4 197 J1
Bose Cl, N3
off Claremont Pk 72 B1
Bosgrove, E4 62 C1
Boss Ho, SE1 29 F3
Boss St, SE1 29 F3
Bostall Heath, SE2 138 C5
Bostall Hill, SE2 138 A5
Bostall La, SE2 138 B5
Bostall Manorway, SE2 138 B4
Bostall Pk Av, Bexh. DA7 138 E7
Bostall Rd, Orp. BR5 176 B7
Bostal Row, Bexh. DA7
off Harlington Rd 159 F3
Bostock Ho, Houns. TW5
off Biscoe Cl 123 G6
Boston Gdns, W4 127 E6
W7 124 D4
Brentford TW8 124 D4
★ **Boston Manor Ho**,
Brent. TW8 124 E5
Boston Manor Rd, Brent.
TW8 124 E4
Boston Pk Rd, Brent.
TW8 125 F5
Boston Pl, NW1 7 J6
Boston Rd, E6 116 B3
E17 78 A6
W7 124 B1
Croydon CR0 187 F6
Edgware HA8 54 C7
Bostonthorpe Rd, W7 124 B2
Boston Vale, W7 124 D4
Bosun Cl, E14
off Byng St 134 A2
Boswell Ct, WC1 18 B1
Boswell Path, Hayes UB3
off Croyde Av 121 J4
Boswell Rd, Th.Hth. CR7 187 J4
Boswell St, WC1 18 B1
Bosworth Cl, E17 77 J1
Bosworth Rd, N11 58 D6
W10 108 B4
Barnet EN5 40 D3
Dagenham RM10 101 G4
Botany Bay La, Chis.
BR7 193 F3
Botany Cl, Barn. EN4 41 H4
Boteley Cl, E4 62 D2
Botham Cl, Edg. HA8 54 C7
Botha Rd, E13 115 H5
Bothwell Cl, E16 115 F5
Bothwell St, W6
off Delorme St 128 A6
Botolph All, EC3 20 D5
Botolph La, EC3 20 C6
Botsford Rd, SW20 184 B2
Botts Ms, W2
off Chepstow Rd 108 D6
Botts Pas, W2
off Chepstow Rd 108 D6
Botwell La, Hayes UB3 121 H1
Boucher Cl, Tedd. TW11 162 C5
Boughton Av, Brom. BR2 191 F7
Boughton Rd, SE28 137 H3
Boulcott St, E1 113 G6
Boulevard, The, SW6 149 F1
SW17
off Balham High Rd 168 A2
SW18
off Smugglers Way 149 E4
Boulevard, The,
Wembley HA9
off Engineers Way 88 A4
Woodford Green IG8 64 D6
Boulogne Rd, Croy. CR0 187 J6
Boulter Cl, Brom. BR1 192 E3
Boulton Ho, Brent. TW8
off Green Dragon La 125 H5
Boulton Rd, Dag. RM8 101 E3
Boultwood Rd, E6 116 B6
Bounces La, N9 60 E2
Bounces Rd, N9 60 E1
Boundaries Rd, SW12 167 J2
Feltham TW13 160 C1
Boundary Av, E17 77 J7
Boundary Business Ct, Mitch.
CR4 185 G3
Boundary Cl, SE20
off Haysleigh Gdns 188 D2
Barnet EN5 40 C1
Ilford IG3
off Loxford La 99 H4
Kingston upon Thames
KT1 182 B3
Southall UB2 123 G5
Boundary La, E13 116 A3
SE17 36 A6
Boundary Pas, E2 13 F5
Boundary Rd, E13 115 J2
E17 77 J7
N9 45 F6
N22 75 H3
NW8 109 E1
SW19 167 G6
Barking IG11 117 F2
Carshalton SM5 200 B6
Pinner HA5 66 D6
Sidcup DA15 157 H5
Wallington SM6 200 B6
Wembley HA9 87 H3
Boundary Row, SE1 27 G3
Boundary St, E2 13 F4
Boundary Way, Croy. CR0 204 A5
Boundfield Rd, SE6 172 E3
Bounds Grn Ind Est, N11 58 B6
Bounds Grn Rd, N11 58 C6
N22 58 C6
Bourchier St, W1 17 H5
Bourdon Pl, W1 16 E5
Bourdon Rd, SE20 189 F2
Bourdon St, W1 16 E5
Bourke Cl, NW10 89 E6
SW4 150 E6
Bourlet Cl, W1 17 F2
Bourn Av, N15 76 A4
Barnet EN4 41 G5
Bournbrook Rd, SE3 156 A3
Bourne, The, N14 58 D1
Bourne Av, N14 58 E2
Hayes UB3 121 F3
Ruislip HA4 84 C5
Bourne Cl, Islw. TW7 144 B3
Thames Ditton KT7 194 C2
Bourne Ct, Ruis. HA4 84 B5
Bourne Dr, Mitch. CR4 185 G2
Bourne Est, EC1 18 E1
Bourne Gdns, E4 62 B4
Bourne Hill, N13 58 E1
Bourne Hill Cl, N13
off Bourne Hill 59 F2
Bournemead Av, Nthlt. UB5 102 A2
Bournemead Cl, Nthlt. UB5 102 A2
Bournemead Way, Nthlt. UB5 102
B2
Bournemouth Cl, SE15 152 D2
Bournemouth Rd, SE15 152 D2
SW19 184 D1
Bourne Pl, W4
off Dukes Av 126 D5
Bourne Rd, E7 97 F3
N8 75 E6
Bexley DA5 159 H6
Bromley BR2 192 A4
Dartford DA1 159 J6
Bourneside Cres, N14 58 D1
Bourneside Gdns, SE6 172 C5
Bourne St, SW1 32 B2
Croydon CR0
off Waddon New Rd 201 H2
Bourne Ter, W2 14 A1
Bourne Vale, Brom. BR2 191 G7
Bournevale Rd, SW16 168 E4
Bourne Vw, Grnf. UB6 86 C6
Bourne Way, Brom. BR2 205 F2
Epsom KT19 196 C4
Sutton SM1 198 C5
Bournewood Rd, SE18 138 A7
Bournville Rd, SE6 154 A7
Bournwell Cl, Barn.
EN4 41 J3
Bourton Cl, Hayes UB3 122 A1
Bousfield Rd, SE14 153 G2
Boutflower Rd, SW11 149 H4

Boutique Hall, SE13
off Lewisham Cen 154 C4
Bouton Pl, N1
off Waterloo Ter 93 H7
Bouverie Gdns, Har. HA3 69 G6
Bouverie Ms, N16 94 B2
Bouverie Pl, W2 15 F3
Bouverie Rd, N16 94 B2
Harrow HA1 67 J7
Bouverie St, EC4 19 F4
Boveney Rd, SE23 153 G7
Bovill Rd, SE23 153 G7
Bovingdon Av, Wem. HA9 88 A6
Bovingdon Cl, N19
off Brookside Rd 92 C2
Bovingdon La, NW9 70 E1
Bovingdon Rd, SW6 148 E1
Bovingdon Sq, Mitch. CR4
off Leicester Av 187 E4
BOW, E3 113 J2
Bowater Cl, NW9 70 D5
SW2 150 E6
Bowater Gdns, Sun.
TW16 178 B2
Bowater Pl, SE3 135 H7
Bowater Rd, SE18 136 A3
Wembley HA9 88 B3
Bow Back Rivers Wk, E15 96 B7
Bow Br Est, E3 114 B3
Bow Chyd, EC4 20 A4
Bow Common La, E3 113 J4
Bowden St, SE11 35 F4
Bowditch, SE8 133 J5
Bowdon Rd, E17 78 A7
Bowen Dr, SE21 170 B3
Bowen Rd, Har. HA1 67 J7
Bowen St, E14 114 B6
Bower Av, SE10 154 E1
Bower Cl, Nthlt. UB5 102 C2
Bowerdean St, SW6 148 E1
Bowerman Av, SE14 133 H6
Bower St, E1 113 G6
Bowers Wk, E6 116 B6
Bowery Ct, Dag. RM10
off Reede Way 101 H6
Bowes Cl, Sid. DA15 158 B6
BOWES PARK, N22 59 E6
Bowes Rd, N11 58 B5
N13 58 E5
W3 106 E7
Dagenham RM8 100 C4
Bowfell Rd, W6 127 J6
Bowford Av, Bexh. DA7 158 E1
Bowhill Cl, SW9 35 F7
Bowie Cl, SW4 150 D7
Bow Ind Est, E15 96 A7
Bowland Rd, SW4 150 D4
Woodford Green IG8 63 J6
Bowland Yd, SW1 24 A4
Bow La, EC4 20 A4
N12 73 F1
Morden SM4 184 B6
Bowl Ct, EC2 12 E6
Bowley Cl, SE19 170 C6
Bowley La, SE19 170 C5
Bowling Grn Cl, SW15 147 H7
Bowling Grn La, EC1 11 F5
Bowling Grn Pl, SE1 28 B3
Bowling Grn Row, SE18
off Samuel St 136 C4
Bowling Grn St, SE11 35 E5
Bowling Grn Wk, N1 12 D3
Bowls, The, Chig. IG7 65 H4
Bowls Cl, Stan. HA7 52 E5
Bowman Av, E16 115 F7
Bowman Ms, SW18 166 C1
Bowmans Cl, W13 124 E1
Bowmans Lea, SE23 153 F7
Bowmans Meadow, Wall.
SM6 200 B3
Bowmans Ms, E1 21 H5
Bowman's Ms, N7
off Seven Sisters Rd 93 E3
Bowmans Pl, N7
off Holloway Rd 93 E3
Bowman Trd Est, NW9 70 A4
Bowmead, SE9 174 C2
Bowmore Wk, NW1
off St. Paul's Cres 92 D7
Bowness Cl, E8
off Beechwood Rd 94 C6
Bowness Cres, SW15 164 E5
Bowness Dr, Houns. TW4 143 E4
Bowness Rd, SE6 154 B7
Bexleyheath DA7 159 H2
Bowood Rd, SW11 150 A4
Enfield EN3 45 G2
Bowring Grn, Wat. WD19 50 C5
Bow Rd, E3 113 J3
Bowrons Av, Wem. HA0 87 G7
Bowsley Ct, Felt. TW13
off Highfield Rd 160 A2
Bowsprit Pt, E14 134 A3
Bow St, E15 96 E5
WC2 18 B4
Bow Triangle Business Cen, E3
off Eleanor St 114 A4
Bowyer Cl, E6 116 C5
Bowyer Ct, E4
off The Ridgeway 62 C1
Bowyer Pl, SE5 36 A7
Bowyer St, SE5 35 J7
Boxall Rd, SE21 152 B6
Box Elder Cl, Edg. HA8 54 C5
Boxgrove Rd, SE2 138 C3
Box La, Bark. IG11 118 B2
Boxley Rd, Mord. SM4 185 F4
Boxley St, E16 135 H1
Boxmoor Rd, Har. HA3 68 E4
Boxoll Rd, Dag. RM9 101 F4
Boxted Cl, Buck.H. IG9 64 B1
Boxtree La, Har. HA3 67 J1
Boxtree Rd, Har. HA3 52 A7
Boxwood Cl, West Dr. UB7
off Hawthorne Cres 120 C2
Boxworth Cl, N12 57 G5
Boxworth Gro, N1
off Richmond Av 111 F1
Boyard Rd, SE18 136 E5
Boyce St, SE1 26 D2
Boyce Way, E13 115 G4
Boycroft Av, NW9 70 C6
Boyd Av, Sthl. UB1 123 F1
Boyd Cl, Kings.T. KT2 164 A7
Boydell Ct, NW8
off St. John's Wd Pk 91 G7
Boyd Rd, SW19 167 G6
Boyd St, E1 21 H4
Boyfield St, SE1 27 H4
Boyland Rd, Brom. BR1 173 F5
Boyle Av, Stan. HA7 52 D6
Boyle Fm Island, T.Ditt.
KT7 180 D6
Boyle Fm Rd, T.Ditt. KT7 180 D6
Boyle St, W1 17 F5
Boyne Av, NW4 72 A4
Boyne Rd, SE13 154 C3
Dagenham RM10 101 G3
Boyne Ter Ms, W11 128 C1
Boyseland Ct, Edg. HA8 54 C2
Boyson Rd, SE17 36 B5
Boyton Cl, E1
off Stayner's Rd 113 G4
N8 75 E3
Boyton Rd, N8 75 E3
Brabant Ct, EC3 20 D5
Brabant Rd, N22 75 F2
Brabazon Av, Wall. SM6 200 E7
Brabazon Rd, Houns.
TW5 122 C7
Northolt UB5 103 G2
Brabazon St, E14 114 B6
Brabourne Cl, SE19 170 B5
Brabourne Cres, Bexh.
DA7 139 F6
Brabourne Hts, NW7 55 E3
Brabourne Ri, Beck. BR3 190 C5
Brabourn Gro, SE15 153 F2
Bracer Ho, N1
off Nuttall St 12 E1
Bracewell Av, Grnf. UB6 86 C5
Bracewell Rd, W10 107 J5
Bracewood Gdns, Croy.
CR0 202 C3
Bracey Ms, N4
off Bracey St 93 E2
Bracey St, N4 93 E2
Bracken, The, E4
off Hortus Rd 62 C2
Bracken Av, SW12 150 A6
Croydon CR0 204 B3
Brackenbridge Dr, Ruis.
HA4 84 D3
Brackenbury Gdns, W6 127 H3
Brackenbury Rd, N2 73 F3
W6 127 H3
Bracken Cl, E6 116 C5
Borehamwood WD6 38 B1
Twickenham TW2
off Hedley Rd 143 G7
Brackendale, N21 59 F2
Brackendale Cl, Houns.
TW3 143 H1
Bracken Dr, Chig. IG7 65 E6
Bracken End, Islw. TW7 144 A5
Brackenfield Cl, E5 94 E3
Bracken Gdns, SW13 147 G2
Bracken Hill Cl, Brom.
BR1 191 F1
Bracken Hill La, Brom.
BR1 191 F1
Bracken Ind Est, Ilf. IG6 65 J7
Bracken Ms, E4
off Hortus Rd 62 C2
Romford RM7 83 G6
Brackens, The, Enf. EN1 44 B7
Brackenwood, Sun.
TW16 178 A1
Brackley Av, SE15 153 E3
Brackley Cl, Wall. SM6 201 E7
Brackley Rd, W4 127 E5
Beckenham BR3 171 J7
Brackley Sq, Wdf.Grn.
IG8 64 A7
Brackley St, EC1 19 J1
Brackley Ter, W4 127 E5
Bracklyn Cl, N1 12 B1
Bracklyn Ct, N1 12 B1
Bracklyn St, N1 12 B1
Bracknell Cl, N22 75 G1
Bracknell Gdns, NW3 90 E4
Bracknell Gate, NW3 90 E5
Bracknell Way, NW3 90 E4
Bracondale Rd, SE2 138 A4
Bradbourne Rd, Bex.
DA5 159 G7
Bradbourne St, SW6 148 D2
Bradbury Cl, Borwd.
WD6 38 B1
Southall UB2 123 F4
Bradbury Ct, SW20
off Clifton Pk Av 183 J2
Bradbury Ms, N16
off Bradbury St 94 B5
Bradbury St, N16 94 B5
Braddock Cl, Islw. TW7 144 C3
Braddon Rd, Rich. TW9 145 J3
Braddyll St, SE10 134 E5
Bradenham Av, Well.
DA16 158 A4
Bradenham Cl, SE17 36 B5
Bradenham Rd, Har.
HA3 68 E4
Braden St, W9 6 A6
Bradfield Dr, Bark. IG11 100 A5
Bradfield Ho, SW8
off Wandsworth Rd 150 D2
Bradfield Rd, E16 135 G2
Ruislip HA4 85 E5
Bradford Cl, N17 60 C6
SE26 *off Coombe Rd* 170 E4
Bromley BR2 206 C1
Bradford Dr, Epsom
KT19 197 F6
Bradford Rd, W3
off Warple Way 126 E2
Ilford IG1 99 G1
Bradgate Rd, SE6 154 A6
Brading Cres, E11 97 H2
Brading Rd, SW2 151 F7
Croydon CR0 187 F6
Brading Ter, W12 127 H3
Bradiston Rd, W9 108 C3
Bradley Cl, N1 11 F1
N7 *off Sutterton St* 93 F6
Bradley Gdns, W13 104 E6
Bradley Ho, E3
off Bromley High St 114 B2
Bradley Lynch Ct, E2
off Morpeth St 113 G3
Bradley Ms, SW17
off Bellevue Rd 167 J1
Bradley Rd, N22 75 F2
SE19 169 J6
Bradley Stone Rd, E6 116 C5
Bradman Row, Edg. HA8
off Pavilion Way 54 C7
Bradmead, SW8 130 B7
Bradmore Ct, Enf. EN3
off Enstone Rd 45 H3
Bradmore Pk Rd, W6 127 H3
Bradshaw Cl, SW19 166 D6
Bradshaw Dr, NW7 56 A7
Bradshaws Cl, SE25 188 D3
Bradstock Rd, E9 95 G6
Epsom KT17 197 G5
Brad St, SE1 27 F2
Bradwell Av, Dag. RM10 101 G2
Bradwell Cl, E18 79 F4
Bradwell Ms, N18
off Lyndhurst Rd 60 D4
Bradwell Rd, Buck.H. IG9 64 B1
Bradwell St, E1 113 G3
Brady Av, Loug. IG10 49 F2
Brady Dr, Brom. BR1 192 D3
Bradymead, E6 116 D6
Brady St, E1 112 E4
Braemar Av, N22 75 E1
NW10 88 D3
SW19 166 D2
Bexleyheath DA7 159 J4
Thornton Heath CR7 187 G3
Wembley HA0 87 G7
Braemar Cl, SE16
off Masters Dr 132 E5
Braemar Gdns, NW9 70 D1
Sidcup DA15 175 G3
West Wickham BR4 204 C1
Braemar Rd, E13 115 F4
N15 76 B5
Brentford TW8 125 G6
Worcester Park KT4 197 H3
Braemer Ho, W9 6 C4
Braeside, Beck. BR3 172 A5
Braeside Av, SW19 184 B1
Braeside Cl, Pnr. HA5
off The Avenue 51 G7
Braeside Cres, Bexh.
DA7 159 J4
Braeside Rd, SW16 168 C7
Braes St, N1 93 H7
Braesyde Cl, Belv. DA17 139 F4
Brafferton Rd, Croy. CR0 201 J4
Braganza St, SE17 35 G3
Bragg Cl, Dag. RM8
off Porters Av 100 B6
Braham St, E1 21 G4
Braid Av, W3 106 E6
Braid Cl, Felt. TW13 161 F2
Braid Ct, W4
off Lawford Rd 126 C7
Braidwood Pas, EC1
off Cloth St 19 J1
Braidwood Rd, SE6 172 D1
Braidwood St, SE1 28 D2
Brailsford Cl, Mitch. CR4 167 H7
Brailsford Rd, SW2 151 G5
Brainton Av, Felt. TW14 142 B7
Braintree Av, Ilf. IG4 80 B4
Braintree Ind Est, Ruis.
HA4 84 B4
Braintree Rd, Dag. RM10 101 G3
Ruislip HA4 84 B4
Braintree St, E2 113 F3
Braithwaite Av, Rom. RM7 83 G7
Braithwaite Gdns, Stan.
HA7 69 F1
Braithwaite Ho, EC1 12 A5
Braithwaite Rd, Enf. EN3 45 J3
Braithwaite Twr, W2 15 E1
Bramah Grn, SW9 151 G1
★ **Bramah Mus**, SE1 28 A2
Bramalea Cl, N6 74 A6
Bramall Cl, E15
off Idmiston Rd 97 F5
Bramber Ct, Brent. TW8
off Sterling Pl 125 H4
Bramber Ho, Kings.T. KT2
off Kingsgate Rd 181 H1
Bramber Rd, N12 57 H5
W14 128 C6
Brambleacres Cl, Sutt.
SM2 198 D7
Bramblebury Rd, SE18 137 F5
Bramble Cl, N15
off Broad La 76 D4
Beckenham BR3 190 C5
Chigwell IG7 65 F1
Croydon CR0 204 A4
Stanmore HA7 53 G7
Bramble Cft, Erith DA8 139 J4
Brambledown Cl, W.Wick.
BR4 191 E5
Brambledown Rd, Cars.
SM5 200 A7
South Croydon CR2 202 B7
Wallington SM6 200 B7
Bramble Gdns, W12 107 F7
Bramble La, Hmptn.
TW12 161 F6
Brambles, The, Chig. IG7
off Clayside 65 F6
West Drayton UB7 120 B4
Brambles Cl, Islw. TW7 124 E7
Bramblewood Cl, Cars.
SM5 199 H1
Bramblings, The, E4 62 D4
Bramcote Av, Mitch.
CR4 185 J4
Bramcote Ct, Mitch. CR4
off Bramcote Av 185 J4
Bramcote Gro, SE16 133 F5
Bramcote Rd, SW15 147 H4
Bramdean Cres, SE12 173 G1
Bramdean Gdns, SE12 173 G1
Bramerton Rd, Beck.
BR3 189 J3
Bramerton St, SW3 31 G5
Bramfield Ct, N4
off Queens Dr 93 J2
Bramfield Rd, SW11 149 H6
Bramford Ct, N14 58 D2
Bramford Rd, SW18 149 F4
Bramham Gdns, SW5 30 A3
Chessington KT9 195 G4
Bramhope La, SE7 135 H6
Bramlands Cl, SW11 149 H3
Bramley Cl, E17 77 H2
N14 42 B5
Hayes UB3 102 A7
Orpington BR6 207 E1

Bramley Cl,
South Croydon CR2 **201** H5
Twickenham TW2 **143** J6
Woodford Green IG8
off Orsett Ter **63** J7
Bramley Ct, Well. DA16 **158** B1
Bramley Cres, SW8 **33** J7
Ilford IG2 **80** D6
Bramley Gdns, Wat.
WD19 **50** C5
Bramley Hill, S.Croy.
CR2 **201** H5
Bramley Ho, SW15
off Tunworth Cres **147** F6
W10 *off Bramley Rd* **108** A6
Bramley Hyrst, S.Croy.
CR2 **201** J4
Bramley Par, N14 **42** C4
Bramley Rd, N14 **42** B5
W5 **125** F3
W10 **108** A7
Sutton SM1 **199** G5
Bramley Way, Houns.
TW4 **143** F5
West Wickham BR4 **204** B2
Brampton Cl, E5 **95** E2
Brampton Gdns, N15
off Brampton Rd **75** J5
Brampton Gro, NW4 **71** H4
Harrow HA3 **68** D4
Wembley HA9 **88** A1
Brampton La, NW4 **71** J4
Brampton Pk Rd, N22 **75** G3
Brampton Rd, E6 **116** A3
N15 **75** J5
NW9 **70** A4
SE2 **138** C6
Bexleyheath DA7 **138** D7
Croydon CR0 **188** C7
Watford WD19 **50** A3
Bramshaw Gdns, Wat.
WD19 **50** D5
Bramshaw Ri, N.Mal.
KT3 **183** E6
Bramshaw Rd, E9 **95** G6
Bramshill Cl, Chig. IG7
off Tine Rd **65** H5
Bramshill Gdns, NW5 **92** B3
Bramshill Rd, NW10 **107** F2
Bramshot Av, SE7 **135** G6
Bramshot Way, Wat.
WD19 **50** A2
Bramston Cl, Ilf. IG6 **65** J6
Bramston Rd, NW10 **107** G2
SW17 **167** F3
Bramwell Cl, Sun. TW16 **178** D2
Bramwell Ho, SE1
off Harper Rd **28** A6
SW1 **33** F4
Bramwell Ms, N1 **111** F1
Brancaster Dr, NW7 **55** F7
Brancaster Pl, Loug.
IG10 **48** C3
Brancaster Rd, E12 **98** C4
SW16 **168** E3
Ilford IG2 **81** G6
Brancepeth Gdns, Buck.H.
IG9 **63** G2
Branch Hill, NW3 **91** F3
Branch Pl, N1 **112** A1
Branch Rd, E14 **113** H7
Branch St, SE15 **132** B7
Brancker Rd, Har. HA3 **69** G3
Brancroft Way, Enf. EN3 **45** H1
Brand Cl, N4 **93** H1
Brandesbury Sq, Wdf.Grn.
IG8 **64** D6
Brandlehow Rd, SW15 **148** C4
Brandon Est, SE17 **35** H6
Brandon Ms, EC2
off The Barbican **20** B2
Brandon Rd, E17 **78** C3
N7 **92** E7
Southall UB2 **123** F5
Sutton SM1 **198** E4
Brandon St, SE17 **35** J2
Brandram Ms, SE13 **154** E3
Brandram Rd, SE13 **154** E3
Brandreth Rd, E6 **116** C6
SW17 **168** B2
Brandries, The, Wall.
SM6 **200** D3
Brand St, SE10 **134** C7
Brandville Gdns, Ilf. IG6 **81** E4
Brandville Rd, West Dr.
UB7 **120** B2
Brandy Way, Sutt. SM2 **198** D7
Brangbourne Rd, Brom.
BR1 **172** C5
Brangton Rd, SE11 **34** D4
Brangwyn Cres, SW19 **185** G1
Branksea St, SW6 **128** B7
Branksome Av, N18 **60** C6
Branksome Cl, Tedd.
TW11 **162** A4
Branksome Rd, SW2 **151** E5
SW19 **184** D1
Branksome Way, Har.
HA3 **69** H6
New Malden KT3 **182** C1
Bransby Rd, Chess. KT9 **195** H6
Branscombe Gdns, N21 **43** G7
Branscombe St, SE13 **154** B3
Bransdale Cl, NW6
off West End La **108** E1
Bransgrove Rd, Edg. HA8 **69** J1
Branston Cres, Orp. BR5 **207** G1
Branstone Rd, Rich.
TW9 **145** J1
Brants Wk, W7 **104** B4
Brantwood Av, Erith
DA8 **139** J7
Isleworth TW7 **144** D4
Brantwood Cl, E17 **78** B3
Brantwood Gdns, Enf.
EN2 **42** E4
Ilford IG4 **80** B4
Brantwood Rd, N17 **60** C6
SE24 **151** J5
Bexleyheath DA7 **159** H2
Brasenose Dr, SW13 **127** J6
Brasher Cl, Grnf. UB6 **86** A5
Brassett Pt, E15 **114** E1
Brassey Cl, Felt. TW14 **160** A1
Brassey Rd, NW6 **90** C6
Brassey Sq, SW11 **150** A3
Brassie Av, W3 **106** E6
Brass Tally All, SE16
off Middleton Dr **133** G2
Brasted Cl, SE26 **171** F4
Bexleyheath DA6 **158** D5
Brathway Rd, SW18 **148** D7
Bratley St, E1 **13** H6
Braund Av, Grnf. UB6 **103** H4
Braundton Av, Sid.
DA15 **175** J1
Braunston Dr, Hayes
UB4 **102** E4
Bravington Pl, W9
off Bravington Rd **108** C4
Bravington Rd, W9 **108** C2
Bravingtons Wk, N1 **10** B2
Brawne Ho, SE17 **35** H6
Braxfield Rd, SE4 **153** H4
Braxted Pk, SW16 **169** F6
Bray, NW3 **91** H7
Brayards Rd, SE15 **152** E2
Braybourne Dr, Islw.
TW7 **124** C7
Braybrooke Gdns, SE19
off Fox Hill **170** B7
Braybrook St, W12 **107** F5
Brayburne Av, SW4 **150** C2
Bray Cl, Borwd. WD6 **38** C1
Braycourt Av, Walt.
KT12 **178** B7
Bray Cres, SE16
off Marlow Way **133** G2
Braydon Rd, N16 **94** C1
Bray Dr, E16 **115** F7
Brayfield Ter, N1
off Lofting Rd **93** G7
Brayford Sq, E1
off Summercourt Rd **113** F6
Bray Pas, E16 **115** G7
Bray Pl, SW3 **31** J2
Bray Rd, NW7 **56** A6
Brayton Gdns, Enf. EN2 **42** D4
Braywood Rd, SE9 **157** G4
Brazier Cres, Nthlt. UB5
off Waxlow Way **103** F4
Brazil Cl, Croy. (Bedd.)
CR0 **186** E7
Breach La, Dag. RM9 **119** G3
Bread St, EC4 **20** A4
Breakspears Ms, SE4
off Ashby Rd **154** A2
Breakspears Rd, SE4 **153** J3
Bream Cl, N17 **77** E4
Bream Gdns, E6 **116** D3
Breamore Cl, SW15 **165** G1
Breamore Rd, Ilf. IG3 **99** J2
Bream's Bldgs, EC4 **18** E3
Bream St, E3 **96** A7
Breamwater Gdns, Rich.
TW10 **163** E3
Brearley Cl, Edg. HA8 **54** C7
Breasley Cl, SW15 **147** H4
Brechin Pl, SW7 **30** D2
Brecknock Rd, N7 **92** C4
N19 **92** C4
Brecknock Rd Est, N19 **92** C4
Breckonmead, Brom. BR1
off Wanstead Rd **191** J2
Brecon Cl, Mitch. CR4 **186** E3
Worcester Park KT4 **197** J2
Brecon Grn, NW9
off Goldsmith Av **71** E6
Brecon Ms, N7
off Brecknock Rd **92** D5
Brecon Rd, W6 **128** B6
Enfield EN3 **45** F4
Brede Cl, E6 **116** D3
Bredgar, SE13 **154** C5
Bredgar Rd, N19 **92** C2
Bredhurst Cl, SE20 **171** F6
Bredinghurst, SE22 **152** D7
Bredon Rd, Croy. CR0 **188** C7
Breer St, SW6 **148** E3
Breezers Hill, E1 **21** J6
Brember Rd, Har. HA2 **85** J2
Bremer Ms, E17
off Church La **78** B4
Bremner Rd, SW7 **22** D4
Brenchley Cl, Brom. BR2 **191** F6
Chislehurst BR7 **192** D1
Brenchley Gdns, SE23 **153** F6
Brenchley Rd, Orp. BR5 **193** J1
Brenda Rd, SW17 **167** J2
Brende Gdns, W.Mol.
KT8 **179** H4
Brendon Av, NW10 **89** E4
Brendon Cl, Hayes
(Harling.) UB3 **121** F7
Brendon Gdns, Har.
HA2 **85** H4
Ilford IG2 **81** H5
Brendon Gro, N2 **73** F2
Brendon Rd, SE9 **175** G2
Dagenham RM8 **101** F1
Brendon St, W1 **15** H3
Brendon Way, Enf. EN1 **44** B7
Brenley Cl, Mitch. CR4 **186** A3
Brenley Gdns, SE9 **156** A4
Brent Cl, Bex. DA5 **177** E1
Brentcot Cl, W13 **104** E4
Brent Cres, NW10 **105** J2
Brent Cross Gdns, NW4
off Cooper Rd **72** A6
Brent Cross Interchange, The, NW2 **72** A7
Brent Cross Shop Cen,
NW4 **71** J7
Brentfield, NW10 **88** B7
Brentfield Cl, NW10 **88** D6
Brentfield Gdns, NW2
off Hendon Way **72** A7
Brentfield Ho, NW10
off Stonebridge Pk **88** D7
Brentfield Rd, NW10 **88** D6
BRENTFORD, TW8 **125** G6
Brentford Business Cen,
Brent. TW8 **125** E7
Brentford Cl, Hayes UB4 **102** D4
★ **Brentford FC**, Brent.
TW8 **125** G6
Brent Grn, NW4 **71** J5
Brent Grn Wk, Wem. HA9 **88** C3
Brentham Way, W5 **105** G4
Brenthouse Rd, E9 **95** E7
Brenthurst Rd, NW10 **89** F5
Brent Lea, Brent. TW8 **125** F7
Brentmead Cl, W7 **104** B7
Brentmead Gdns, NW10 **105** J2
Brentmead Pl, NW11
off North Circular Rd **72** A6
Brenton St, E14 **113** H6
Brent Pk, NW10 **88** D5
Brent Pk Rd, NW4 **71** H7
NW9 **89** G1
Brent Pl, Barn. EN5 **40** D5
Brent Rd, E16 **115** G5
SE18 **136** E7
Brentford TW8 **125** F6
Southall UB2 **122** C3
Brent Side, Brent. TW8 **125** F6
Brentside Cl, W13 **104** D4
Brentside Executive Cen,
Brent. TW8 **125** E6
Brent S Shop Pk, NW2 **89** J1
Brent St, NW4 **71** J4
Brent Ter, NW2 **89** J2
Brentvale Av, Sthl.
UB1 **124** A1
Wembley HA0 **105** J1
Brent Vw Rd, NW9 **71** G7
Brent Way, N3 **56** D6
Brentford TW8 **125** G7
Wembley HA9 **88** B6
Brentwick Gdns, Brent.
TW8 **125** H4
Brentwood Cl, SE9 **175** F1
Brentwood Ho, SE18
off Shooters Hill Rd **136** A7
Brereton Rd, N17 **60** C7
Bressay Dr, NW7 **55** G7
Bressenden Pl, SW1 **25** E5
Bressey Av, Enf. EN1 **44** D1
Bressey Gro, E18 **79** F2
Breton Ho, EC2
off The Barbican **20** A1
Brett Cl, N16 **94** B2
Northolt UB5
off Broomcroft Av **102** D3
Brett Ct, N9 **61** F2
Brett Cres, NW10 **88** D7
Brettell St, SE17 **36** C4
Brettenham Av, E17 **78** A1
Brettenham Rd, E17 **78** A2
N18 **60** E4
Brett Gdns, Dag. RM9 **100** E7
Brett Ho Cl, SW15
off Putney Heath La **148** A6
Brett Pas, E8
off Kenmure Rd **95** E5
Brett Rd, E8 **95** E5
Barnet EN5 **39** J5
Brewer's Grn, SW1 **25** H5
Brewers Hall Gdns, EC2 **20** A2
Brewers La, Rich. TW9 **145** G5
Brewer St, W1 **17** G5
★ **Brewery, The**, EC1 **20** A1
Brewery Cl, Wem. HA0 **86** D5
Brewery La, Twick. TW1 **144** C7
Brewery Rd, N7 **92** E7
SE18 **137** G5
Bromley BR2 **206** B1
Brewery Sq, EC1 **11** G5
SE1 **29** F2
Brewhouse La, E1 **133** E1
SW15 **148** B3
Brewhouse Rd, SE18 **136** C4
Brewhouse Wk, SE16 **133** H1
Brewhouse Yd, EC1 **11** H5
Brewood Rd, Dag. RM8 **100** B6
Brewster Gdns, W10 **107** J5
Brewster Ho, E14 **113** J7
Brewster Rd, E10 **96** B1
Brian Rd, Rom. RM6 **82** C5
Briant Est, SE1 **26** E6
Briant Ho, SE1 **26** D6
Briants Cl, Pnr. HA5 **67** F2
Briant St, SE14 **153** G1
Briar Av, SW16 **169** F7
Briarbank Rd, W13 **104** D6
Briar Cl, N2 **73** E3
N13 **59** J3
Buckhurst Hill IG9 **64** A2
Hampton TW12 **161** F5
Isleworth TW7 **144** C5
Briar Ct, Sutt. SM3 **197** J4
Briar Cres, Nthlt. UB5 **85** H6
Briardale Gdns, NW3 **90** D3
Briarfield Av, N3 **72** E2
Briarfield Cl, Bexh. DA7 **159** G2
Briar Gdns, Brom. BR2 **205** F1
Briaris Cl, N17 **60** E7
Briar La, Croy. CR0 **204** B4
Briar Pas, SW16 **187** E3
Briar Pl, SW16 **187** F3
Briar Rd, NW2 **89** J4
SW16 **187** E3
Harrow HA3 **69** F5
Twickenham TW2 **162** B1
Briarswood Way, Orp.
BR6 **207** J5
Briar Wk, SW15 **147** H4
W10 *off Droop St* **108** B4
Edgware HA8 **54** C7
Briar Way, West Dr. UB7 **120** D2
Briarwood Cl, NW9 **70** C6
Briarwood Ct, Wor.Pk. KT4
off The Avenue **197** G1
Briarwood Dr, Nthwd.
HA6 **66** A2
Briarwood Rd, SW4 **150** D5
Epsom KT17 **197** G6
Briary Cl, NW3
off Fellows Rd **91** H7
Briary Ct, E16
off Turner St **115** F6
Sidcup DA14 **176** B5
Briary Gdns, Brom. BR1 **173** H5
Briary Gro, Edg. HA8 **70** B2
Briary La, N9 **60** C3
Brick Ct, EC4 **18** E4
Brick Fm Cl, Rich. TW9 **146** B1
Brickfield Cl, Brent. TW8 **125** F7
Brickfield Cotts, SE18 **137** J6
Brickfield Fm Gdns, Orp.
BR6 **207** F4
Brickfield La, Barn. EN5 **39** F6
Hayes (Harling.) UB3 **121** G6
Brickfield Rd, SW19 **167** E4
Thornton Heath CR7 **187** H1
Brickfields, Har. HA2 **86** A2
Brickfields Way, West Dr.
UB7 **120** C3
Brickland Ct, N9
off The Broadway **60** D2
Brick La, E1 **13** G5
E2 **13** G4

Brick La, Enfield EN1, EN3 **44** E2
Stanmore HA7 **53** G7
Bricklayer's Arms Distribution Cen, SE1 **36** E2
Bricklayer's Arms Rbt, SE1 **36** B1
Brick St, W1 **24** D2
Brickwood Cl, SE26 **171** E3
Brickwood Rd, Croy. CR0 **202** B2
Brideale Cl, SE15 **37** G6
Bride Ct, EC4 **19** G4
Bride La, EC4 **19** G4
Bridel Ms, N1 *off Colebrooke Row* **111** H1
Brides Pl, N1 *off De Beauvoir Rd* **94** B7
Bride St, N7 **93** F6
Bridewain St, SE1 **29** F5
Bridewell Pl, E1 *off Brewhouse La* **133** E1
EC4 **19** G4
Bridford Ms, W1 **16** E1
Bridge, The, SW8 *off Queenstown Rd* **130** B7
Harrow HA3 **68** B3
Bridge App, NW1 **92** A7
Bridge Av, W6 **127** J5
W7 **104** A5
Bridge Cl, W10 *off Kingsdown Cl* **108** A6
Enfield EN1 **45** E2
Teddington TW11 *off Shacklegate La* **162** C4
Bridge Ct, E14 *off Newport Av* **114** D7
Bridge Dr, N13 **59** F4
Bridge End, E17 **78** C1
Bridge End Cl, Kings.T. KT2 *off Clifton Rd* **182** A1
Bridgefield Rd, Sutt. SM1 **198** D6
Bridgefoot, SE1 **34** A4
Bridge Gdns, N16 *off Green Las* **94** A4
East Molesey KT8 **180** A4
Bridge Gate, N21 *off Ridge Av* **43** J7
Bridgehill Cl, Wem. HA0 **105** G1
Bridge Ho, NW3 *off Adelaide Rd* **92** A7
SW8 *off St. George Wf* **34** A4
Bridge Ho Quay, E14 *off Prestons Rd* **134** C1
Bridgeland Rd, E16 **115** G7
Bridgelands Cl, Beck. BR3 **171** J7
Bridge La, NW11 **72** B5
SW11 **149** H1
Bridgeman Rd, N1 **93** F7
Teddington TW11 **162** D6
Bridgeman St, NW8 **7** G2
Bridge Meadows, SE14 **133** G6
Bridgend Rd, SW18 **149** F4
Bridgenhall Rd, Enf. EN1 **44** C1
Bridgen Rd, Bex. DA5 **158** E6
Bridge Pk, SW18 **148** D5
Bridge Pl, SW1 **33** E1
Croydon CR0 **188** A7
Bridgepoint Pl, N6 *off Hornsey La* **92** C1
Bridgeport Pl, E1 **29** J1
Bridge Rd, E6 **98** C7
E15 **96** D7
E17 **77** J7
N9 *off Fore St* **60** D3
N22 **74** E1
NW10 **88** E6
Beckenham BR3 **171** J7
Bexleyheath DA7 **159** E2
Chessington KT9 **195** H5
East Molesey KT8 **180** B4
Hounslow TW3 **144** A2
Isleworth TW7 **144** A3
Southall UB2 **123** F2
Sutton SM2 **199** E6
Twickenham TW1 **144** E6
Wallington SM6 **200** C5
Wembley HA9 **88** A3
Bridge Row, Croy. CR0 *off Cross Rd* **202** A1
Bridges Ct, SW11 **149** G3
Bridges La, Croy. CR0 **200** E4
Bridges Pl, SW6 **148** C1
Bridges Rd, SW19 **166** E6
Stanmore HA7 **52** C5
Bridges Rd Ms, SW19 *off Bridges Rd* **166** E6
Bridge St, SW1 **26** A4
W4 **126** D4
Pinner HA5 **66** D3
Bridge St, Richmond TW9 **145** G5
Bridge Ter, E15 *off Bridge Rd* **96** D7
SE13 *off Mercator Rd* **154** D4
Bridgetown Cl, SE19 *off St. Kitts Ter* **170** B5
Bridge Vw, W6 **127** J5
Bridgeview Ct, Ilf. IG6 **65** G6
Bridgewater Cl, Chis. BR7 **193** H3
Bridgewater Gdns, Edg. HA8 **69** J2
Bridgewater Rd, Ruis. HA4 **84** A4
Wembley HA0 **87** F7
Bridgewater Sq, EC2 **19** J1
Bridgewater St, EC2 **19** J1
Bridge Way, N11 *off Pymmes Grn Rd* **58** C3
NW11 **72** C5
Bridgeway, Bark. IG11 **99** J7
Bridge Way, Twick. TW2 **143** J7
Bridgeway, Wem. HA0 **87** H7
Bridgeway St, NW1 **9** G2
Bridge Wf Rd, Islw. TW7 *off Church St* **144** E3
Bridgewood Cl, SE20 **170** E7
Bridgewood Rd, SW16 **168** D7
Worcester Park KT4 **197** G4
Bridge Yd, SE1 **28** C1
Bridgford St, SW18 **167** F3
Bridgman Rd, W4 **126** C3
Bridgwater Rd, E15 **114** C1
Bridle Cl, Epsom KT19 **196** D5
Kingston upon Thames KT1 **181** G4
Sunbury-on-Thames TW16 *off Forge La* **178** A3
Bridle La, W1 **17** G5
Twickenham TW1 **145** E6
Bridle Ms, Barn. EN5 *off High St* **40** C4
Bridle Path, Croy. (Bedd.) CR0 **201** F3
Bridle Path, The, Wdf.Grn. IG8 **62** E7
Bridle Rd, Croy. CR0 **204** A3
Esher (Clay.) KT10 **194** E6
Pinner HA5 **66** C6
Bridle Way, Croy. CR0 **204** A5
Orpington BR6 **207** F4
Bridleway, The, Wall. SM6 **200** C4
Bridlington Rd, N9 **44** E7
Watford WD19 **50** D3
Bridport Av, Rom. RM7 **83** H6
Bridport Pl, N1 **12** C1
Bridport Rd, N18 **60** B5
Greenford UB6 **103** H1
Thornton Heath CR7 **187** G3
Bridport Ter, SW8 *off Wandsworth Rd* **150** D1
Bridstow Pl, W2 *off Talbot Rd* **108** D6
Brief St, SE5 **151** H1
Brierley, Croy. (New Adgtn) CR0 **204** B6
Brierley Av, N9 **61** F1
Brierley Cl, SE25 **188** D4
Brierley Rd, E11 **96** D4
SW12 **168** C2
Brierly Gdns, E2 *off Royston St* **113** F2
Brigade Cl, Har. HA2 **86** A2
Brigade St, SE3 *off Royal Par* **155** F2
Brigadier Av, Enf. EN2 **43** J1
Briggeford Cl, E5 *off Geldeston Rd* **94** D2
Briggs Cl, Mitch. CR4 **186** B1
Bright Cl, Belv. DA17 **138** D4
Brightfield Rd, SE12 **155** F5
Brightling Rd, SE4 **153** J6
Brightlingsea Pl, E14 **113** J7
Brightman Rd, SW18 **167** G1
Brighton Av, E17 **77** J5
Brighton Dr, Nthlt. UB5 **85** G6
Brighton Gro, SE14 *off Harts La* **153** H1
Brighton Rd, E6 **116** D3
N2 **73** F2
N16 **94** B4
South Croydon CR2 **201** J5
Surbiton KT6 **181** F6
Brighton Ter, SW9 **151** F4
Brightside, The, Enf. EN3 **45** G1
Brightside Rd, SE13 **154** D6
Bright St, E14 **114** B6
Brightwell Cl, Croy. CR0 *off Sumner Rd* **201** G1
Brightwell Cres, SW17 **167** J5
Brightwen Gro, Stan. HA7 **52** D2
Brig Ms, SE8 *off Watergate St* **134** A6
Brigstock Rd, Belv. DA17 **139** H4
Thornton Heath CR7 **187** G5
Brill Pl, NW1 **9** J2
Brim Hill, N2 **73** F4
Brimpsfield Cl, SE2 **138** B3
BRIMSDOWN, Enf. EN3 **45** H3
Brimsdown Av, Enf. EN3 **45** H2
Brimsdown Ind Est, Enf. EN3 **45** H1
Brimstone Ho, E15 *off Victoria St* **96** E7
Brindle Gate, Sid. DA15 **175** H1
Brindley Cl, Bexh. DA7 **159** H3
Wembley HA0 **105** F1
Brindley Ho, SW2 *off New Pk Rd* **150** E7
Brindley St, SE14 **153** J1
Brindley Way, Brom. BR1 **173** G5
Southall UB1 **103** H7
Brindwood Rd, E4 **61** J3
Brinkburn Cl, SE2 **138** A4
Edgware HA8 **70** B2
Brinkburn Gdns, Edg. HA8 **70** A3
Brinkley, Kings.T. KT1 *off Burritt Rd* **182** A2
Brinkley Rd, Wor.Pk. KT4 **197** H2
Brinklow Cres, SE18 **137** E7
Brinklow Ho, W2 **108** E5
Brinkworth Rd, Ilf. IG5 **80** B3
Brinkworth Way, E9 **95** J6
Brinsdale Rd, NW4 **72** A4
Brinsley Ho, E1 *off Tarling St* **113** F6
Brinsley Rd, Har. HA3 **68** A2
Brinsworth Cl, Twick. TW2 **162** A2
Brinton Wk, SE1 **27** G2
Brion Pl, E14 **114** C5
Brisbane Av, SW19 **184** E1
Brisbane Rd, E10 **96** B2
W13 **124** D2
Ilford IG1 **81** E7
Brisbane St, SE5 **132** A7
Briscoe Cl, E11 **97** F2
Briscoe Rd, SW19 **167** G6
Briset Rd, SE9 **156** A3
Briset St, EC1 **19** G1
Briset Way, N7 **93** F2
Bristol Cl, Houns. TW4 *off Harvey Rd* **143** G7
Staines (Stanw.) TW19 **140** B6
Wallington SM6 **200** E7
Bristol Gdns, SW15 *off Portsmouth Rd* **147** J7
W9 **6** B6
Bristol Ho, SE11 *off Lambeth Wk* **26** E6
Bristol Ms, W9 **6** B6
Bristol Pk Rd, E17 **77** H4
Bristol Rd, E7 **97** J6
Greenford UB6 **103** H1
Morden SM4 **185** F5
Briston Gro, N8 **75** E6
Briston Ms, NW7 **55** G7
Bristowe Cl, SW2 *off Tulse Hill* **151** G6
Bristow Rd, SE19 **170** B5
Bexleyheath DA7 **159** E1
Croydon CR0 **200** E4
Hounslow TW3 **143** J3
★ **Britain at War Experience**, SE1 **28** D2
Britannia Bldg, N1 *off Ebenezer St* **12** B3
Britannia Cl, SW4 *off Bowland Rd* **150** D4
Northolt UB5 **102** D3
Britannia Ct, Kings.T. KT2 *off Skerne Wk* **181** G1
Britannia Gate, E16 **135** G1
Britannia La, Twick. TW2 **143** J7
Britannia Rd, E14 **134** A4
N12 **57** F3
SW6 **128** E7
Ilford IG1 **98** E3
Surbiton KT5 **181** J7
Britannia Row, N1 **111** H1
Britannia St, WC1 **10** C3
Britannia Wk, N1 **12** B3
Britannia Way, NW10 **106** B4
SW6 *off Britannia Rd* **129** E7
Staines (Stanw.) TW19 **140** A7
★ **British Dental Assoc Mus**, W1 **16** D2
British Gro, W4 **127** F5
British Gro N, W4 *off Middlesex Ct* **127** F5
British Gro Pas, W4 **127** F5
British Gro S, W4 *off British Gro Pas* **127** F5
British Legion Rd, E4 **63** F2
★ **British Lib**, NW1 **9** J3
★ **British Lib Newspapers**, NW9 **70** E3
★ **British Med Assoc**, WC1 **9** J5
★ **British Mus, The**, WC1 **17** J2
★ **British Red Cross Mus & Archives**, SW1 **20** B1
British St, E3 **113** J3
Brittain Rd, Dag. RM8 **101** E3
Brittany Pt, SE11 **35** E2
Britten Cl, NW11 **90** E1
Brittenden Cl, Orp. BR6 **207** H6
Brittenden Par, Orp. (Grn St Grn) BR6 *off Glentrammon Rd* **207** J6
Britten Dr, Sthl. UB1 **103** G6
Britten St, SW3 **31** G4
Brittidge Rd, NW10 *off Paulet Way* **88** E7
Britton Cl, SE6 *off Brownhill Rd* **154** D7
Britton St, EC1 **11** G6
Brixham Cres, Ruis. HA4 **84** A1
Brixham Gdns, Ilf. IG3 **99** H5
Brixham Rd, Well. DA16 **158** D1
Brixham St, E16 **136** C1
BRIXTON, SW2 **151** E4
★ **Brixton Acad, The**, SW9 **151** F3
Brixton Hill, SW2 **151** E7
Brixton Hill Pl, SW2 *off Brixton Hill* **151** E7
Brixton Oval, SW2 **151** G4
Brixton Rd, SW9 **151** G2
Brixton Sta Rd, SW9 **151** G4
Brixton Water La, SW2 **151** F5
Broadbent Cl, N6 **92** B1
Broadbent St, W1 **16** D5
Broadberry Ct, N18 **60** E5
Broadbridge Cl, SE3 **135** G7
Broad Common Est, N16 *off Osbaldeston Rd* **94** D1
Broadcoombe, S.Croy. CR2 **203** F7
Broad Ct, WC2 **18** B4
Broadcroft Av, Stan. HA7 **69** G2
Broadcroft Rd, Orp. BR5 **193** G7
Broadeaves Cl, S.Croy. CR2 **202** B5
Broadfield Cl, NW2 **89** J3
Croydon CR0 *off Progress Way* **201** F2
Broadfield Ct, Bushey (Bushey Hth) WD23 **52** B2
Broadfield La, NW1 **92** E7
Broadfield Rd, SE6 **154** E7
Broadfields, E.Mol. KT8 **180** A6
Harrow HA2 **67** H2
Broadfields Av, N21 **43** G7
Edgware HA8 **54** B4
Broadfields Hts, Edg. HA8 **54** B4
Broadfields La, Wat. WD19 **50** B1
Broadfield Sq, Enf. EN1 **45** E2
Broadfields Way, NW10 **89** F5
Broadfield Way, Buck.H. IG9 **63** J3
BROADGATE, EC2 **20** C1
Broadgate, E13 **115** J2
Broadgate Circle, EC2 **20** D1
Broadgate Rd, E16 **116** A6
Broadgates Av, Barn. EN4 **41** E1
Broadgates Rd, SW18 *off Ellerton Rd* **167** G1
BROAD GREEN, Croy. CR0 **187** G6
Broad Grn Av, Croy. CR0 **187** H7
Broadhead Strand, NW9 **71** F1
Broadheath Dr, Chis. BR7 **174** C5
Broadhinton Rd, SW4 **150** B3
Broadhurst Av, Edg. HA8 **54** B4
Ilford IG3 **99** J4
Broadhurst Cl, NW6 *off Broadhurst Gdns* **91** F6
Richmond TW10 *off Lower Gro Rd* **145** J5
Broadhurst Gdns, NW6 **90** E6
Chigwell IG7 **65** F4
Ruislip HA4 **84** C2
Broadlands, Felt. (Han.) TW13 **161** F3
Broadlands Av, SW16 **168** E2
Enfield EN3 **45** E3
Broadlands Cl, N6 **74** A7
SW16 **168** E2
Enfield EN3 **45** E3

Broadlands Rd, N6 ... 73 J7
Bromley BR1 ... 173 H4
Broadlands Way, N.Mal. KT3 ... 183 F6
Broad La, EC2 ... 20 D1
N8 *off Tottenham La* ... 75 F5
N15 ... 76 C4
Hampton TW12 ... 161 G6
Broad Lawn, SE9 ... 174 D2
Broadlawns Ct, Har. HA3 ... 68 C1
Broadley St, NW8 ... 15 F1
Broadley Ter, NW1 ... 7 H6
Broadmayne, SE17 ... 36 A3
Broadmead, SE6 ... 172 A3
Broadmead Av, Wor.Pk. KT4 ... 183 G7
Broadmead Cl, Hmptn. TW12 ... 161 G6
Pinner HA5 ... 51 E7
Broadmead Rd, Hayes UB4 ... 102 E4
Northolt UB5 ... 102 E4
Woodford Green IG8 ... 63 G6
Broad Oak, Wdf.Grn. IG8 ... 63 H5
Broad Oak Cl, E4 ... 62 A5
Broadoak Ct, SW9 *off Gresham Rd* ... 151 G3
Broadoaks Way, Brom. BR2 ... 191 F5
Broad Sanctuary, SW1 ... 25 J4
Broadstone Pl, W1 ... 16 B2
Broad St, Dag. RM10 ... 101 G7
Teddington TW11 ... 162 C6
Broad St Av, EC2 ... 20 D2
Broad St Pl, EC2 ... 20 C2
Broad Vw, NW9 ... 70 A6
Broadview Rd, SW16 ... 168 C7
Broadwalk, E18 ... 79 F3
Broad Wk, N21 ... 59 F2
NW1 ... 8 D4
SE3 ... 155 J3
W1 ... 24 B1
Broadwalk, Har. HA2 ... 67 G5
Broad Wk, Houns. TW5 ... 142 D1
Richmond TW9 ... 125 J7
Broad Wk, The, W8 ... 14 B6
East Molesey KT8 ... 180 C3
Broadwalk Ct, W8 ... 128 D1
Broad Wk La, NW11 ... 72 C7
Broadwalk Shop Cen, Edg. HA8 ... 54 B6
Broadwall, SE1 ... 27 F1
Broadwater Fm Est, N17 ... 76 A2
Broadwater Gdns, Orp. BR6 ... 207 E4
Broadwater Rd, N17 ... 76 B1
SE28 ... 137 G3
SW17 ... 167 H4
Broadway, E15 ... 96 D7
SW1 ... 25 H5
Barking IG11 ... 117 F1
Bexleyheath DA6, DA7 ... 159 E4
Broadway, The, E4 ... 62 C6
E13 ... 115 H2
N8 ... 74 E6
N9 ... 60 D2
N14 *off Winchmore Hill Rd* ... 58 D1
N22 ... 75 G2
NW7 ... 55 E5
SW13 *off The Terrace* ... 146 E2
SW19 ... 166 C6
W5 ... 105 G7
W7 *off Cherington Rd* ... 124 B1
W7 (W.Ealing) ... 124 D1
W13 ... 124 D1
Croydon CR0 *off Croydon Rd* ... 201 E4
Dagenham RM8 ... 101 F2
Greenford UB6 ... 103 J4
Harrow (Wealds.) HA3 ... 68 B2
Loughton IG10 ... 49 F4
Pinner HA5 ... 51 F7
Southall UB1 ... 102 D7
Stanmore HA7 ... 53 F5
Sutton SM1 *off Manor La* ... 199 F5
Sutton (Cheam) SM3 ... 198 B6
Thames Ditton KT7 *off Hampton Ct Way* ... 194 B1
Wembley HA9 *off East La* ... 87 H3
Woodford Green IG8 ... 63 H6
Broadway Av, Croy. CR0 ... 188 A5
Twickenham TW1 ... 144 E6
Broadway Cl, Wdf.Grn. IG8 ... 63 H6
Broadway Ct, SW19 ... 166 C6
Broadway Gdns, Mitch. CR4 ... 185 H4
Broadway Mkt, E8 ... 112 E1
SW17 ... 167 J4
Broadway Mkt Ms, E8 *off Regents Row* ... 112 D1
Broadway Ms, E5 ... 76 C7
N13 *off Elmdale Rd* ... 59 F5
N21 *off Compton Rd* ... 59 H1
Broadway Par, N8 ... 74 E6
Hayes UB3 *off Coldharbour La* ... 122 A1
Broadway Pl, SW19 *off Hartfield Rd* ... 166 C6
Broadway Shop Cen, W6 *off Hammersmith Bdy* ... 127 J4
Bexleyheath DA6 ... 159 G4
Broadway Wk, E14 *off Alpha Gro* ... 134 A3
Broadwick St, W1 ... 17 G5
Broadwood Ter, W8 *off Pembroke Rd* ... 128 C4
Broad Yd, EC1 ... 11 G6
Brocas Cl, NW3 *off Fellows Rd* ... 91 H7
Brockbridge Ho, SW15 *off Tangley Gro* ... 147 F6
Brockdene Dr, Kes. BR2 ... 206 A4
Brockdish Av, Bark. IG11 ... 99 J5
Brockenhurst, W.Mol. KT8 ... 179 F6
Brockenhurst Av, Wor.Pk. KT4 ... 197 E1
Brockenhurst Gdns, NW7 ... 55 E5
Ilford IG1 ... 99 F5
Brockenhurst Ms, N18 *off Lyndhurst Rd* ... 60 D4
Brockenhurst Rd, Croy. CR0 ... 188 E7
Brockenhurst Way, SW16 ... 186 D2
Brocket Cl, Chig. IG7 *off Brocket Way* ... 65 J5
Brocket Way, Chig. IG7 ... 65 H5
Brockham Cl, SW19 ... 166 C5
Brockham Cres, Croy. (New Adgtn) CR0 ... 204 D7
Brockham Dr, SW2 *off Fairview Pl* ... 151 F7
Ilford IG2 ... 81 E6
Brockham St, SE1 ... 28 A5
Brockhurst Cl, Stan. HA7 ... 52 C6
Brockill Cres, SE4 ... 153 H4
Brocklebank Rd, SE7 ... 135 H4
SW18 ... 149 F7
Brocklehurst St, SE14 ... 133 G7
Brocklesby Rd, SE25 ... 188 E4
BROCKLEY, SE4 ... 153 H5
Brockley Av, Stan. HA7 ... 53 H3
Brockley Cl, Stan. HA7 ... 53 H4
Brockley Cross, SE4 *off Endwell Rd* ... 153 J3
Brockley Footpath, SE15 ... 153 F4
Brockley Gdns, SE4 ... 153 J2
Brockley Gro, SE4 ... 153 J5
Brockley Hall Rd, SE4 ... 153 H6
Brockley Hill, Stan. HA7 ... 53 F1
Brockley Ms, SE4 ... 153 H5
Brockley Pk, SE23 ... 153 H7
Stanmore HA7 ... 53 H3
Brockley Ri, SE23 ... 153 H6
Brockley Rd, SE4 ... 153 J3
Brockleyside, Stan. HA7 ... 53 G4
Brockley Vw, SE23 ... 153 H7
Brockley Way, SE4 ... 153 G5
Brockman Ri, Brom. BR1 ... 172 D4
Brock Pl, E3 ... 114 B4
Brock Rd, E13 ... 115 H5
Brocks Dr, Sutt. SM3 ... 198 B3
Brockshot Cl, Brent. TW8 ... 125 G6
Brock St, SE15 *off Evelina Rd* ... 153 F3
Brockway Cl, E11 ... 97 E1
Brockweir, E2 *off Cyprus St* ... 113 F2
Brockwell Av, Beck. BR3 ... 190 B5
Brockwell Cl, Orp. BR5 ... 193 J5
★ **Brockwell Park**, SE24 ... 151 H6
Brockwell Pk Gdns, SE24 ... 151 G7
Brockwell Pk Row, SW2 ... 151 G6
Brodewater Rd, Borwd. WD6 ... 38 B2
Brodia Rd, N16 ... 94 B3
Brodick Ho, E3 *off Saxon Rd* ... 113 J2
Brodie Ho, SE1 *off Coopers Rd* ... 37 G3
Brodie Rd, E4 ... 62 C1
Brodie St, SE1 ... 37 G3
Brodlove La, E1 ... 113 G7
Brodrick Gro, SE2 ... 138 B4
Brodrick Rd, SW17 ... 167 H2
Brograve Gdns, Beck. BR3 ... 190 B2
Broken Wf, EC4 ... 19 J5
Brokesley St, E3 ... 113 J4
Broke Wk, E8 ... 112 D1
Bromar Rd, SE5 ... 152 B3
Bromborough Grn, Wat. WD19 ... 50 C5
Bromefield, Stan. HA7 ... 69 F1
Bromehead Rd, E1 *off Commercial Rd* ... 113 F6
Bromehead St, E1 *off Commercial Rd* ... 113 F6
Bromell's Rd, SW4 ... 150 C4
Brome Rd, SE9 ... 156 C3
Bromfelde Rd, SW4 ... 150 D3
Bromfelde Wk, SW4 ... 150 D2
Bromfield St, N1 ... 11 F1
Bromhall Rd, Dag. RM8, RM9 ... 100 B6
Bromhedge, SE9 ... 174 C3
Bromholm Rd, SE2 ... 138 B3
Bromleigh Ct, SE23 *off Lapse Wd Wk* ... 170 E2
BROMLEY, E3 ... 114 B4
BROMLEY, BR1 & BR2 ... 191 F2
Bromley Av, Brom. BR1 ... 173 E7
BROMLEY COMMON, Brom. BR2 ... 192 C7
Bromley Common, Brom. BR2 ... 191 J4
Bromley Cres, Brom. BR2 ... 191 F3
Bromley Gdns, Brom. BR2 ... 191 F3
Bromley Gro, Brom. BR2 ... 190 D2
Bromley Hall Rd, E14 ... 114 C5
Bromley High St, E3 ... 114 B3
Bromley Hill, Brom. BR1 ... 172 E5
Bromley Ind Cen, Brom. BR1 ... 191 J3
Bromley La, Chis. BR7 ... 175 F7
BROMLEY PARK, Brom. BR1 ... 190 E1
Bromley Pk, Brom. BR1 *off London Rd* ... 191 F1
Bromley Pl, W1 ... 17 F1
Bromley Rd, E10 ... 78 B6
E17 ... 78 A2
N17 ... 76 C1
N18 ... 60 A3
SE6 ... 172 B1
Beckenham BR3 ... 190 B1
Bromley (Downham) BR1 ... 172 C4
Bromley (Short.) BR2 ... 190 C2
Chislehurst BR7 ... 192 E1
Bromley St, E1 ... 113 G5
BROMPTON, SW3 ... 23 G6
Brompton Arc, SW3 ... 23 J4
Brompton Cl, SE20 *off Selby Rd* ... 188 D2
Hounslow TW4 ... 143 F5
Brompton Gro, N2 ... 73 H4
★ **Brompton Oratory**, SW7 ... 23 G6
Brompton Pk Cres, SW6 ... 30 A6
Brompton Pl, SW3 ... 23 H5
Brompton Rd, SW1 ... 23 H5
SW3 ... 31 G1
SW7 ... 23 H5
Brompton Sq, SW3 ... 23 G5
Brompton Ter, SE18 *off Prince Imperial Rd* ... 156 D1
Bromwich Av, N6 ... 92 A2
Bromyard Av, W3 ... 127 E1
Bromyard Ho, SE15 ... 132 E7
W3 ... 127 E1
BRONDESBURY, NW2 ... 90 B7
Brondesbury Ct, NW2 ... 89 J6
Brondesbury Ms, NW6 *off Willesden La* ... 90 D7
BRONDESBURY PARK, NW6 ... 89 J7
Brondesbury Pk, NW2 ... 89 H6
NW6 ... 90 A7
Brondesbury Rd, NW6 ... 108 C2
Brondesbury Vil, NW6 ... 108 C2
Bronsart Rd, SW6 ... 128 B7
Bronson Rd, SW20 ... 184 A2
Bronte Cl, E7 *off Bective Rd* ... 97 G4
Erith DA8 ... 139 H7
Ilford IG2 ... 80 D5
Bronte Ho, NW6 ... 108 D3
Bronti Cl, SE17 ... 36 A4
Bronze Age Way, Belv. DA17 ... 139 J3
Erith DA8 ... 139 J3
Bronze St, SE8 ... 134 A7
Brook Av, Dag. RM10 ... 101 H7
Edgware HA8 ... 54 B6
Wembley HA9 ... 88 A3
Brookbank Av, W7 ... 104 A5
Brookbank Rd, SE13 ... 154 A3
Brook Cl, NW7 ... 56 B7
SW17 ... 168 A2
SW20 ... 183 H3
W3 *off West Lo Av* ... 126 A1
Borehamwood WD6 ... 38 B3
Staines (Stanw.) TW19 ... 140 C7
Brook Ct, Buck.H. IG9 ... 63 H1
Brook Cres, E4 ... 62 A4
N9 ... 60 E4
Brookdale, N11 ... 58 C4
Brookdale Rd, E17 ... 78 A3
SE6 ... 154 B6
Bexley DA5 ... 159 E6
Brookdene Rd, SE18 ... 137 J4
Brook Dr, SE11 ... 27 F6
Harrow HA1 ... 67 J4
Brooke Av, Har. HA2 ... 85 J3
Brooke Ct, W10 *off Kilburn La* ... 108 B2
Brookehowse Rd, SE6 ... 172 B3
Brookend Rd, Sid. DA15 ... 175 H1
Brooke Rd, E5 ... 94 D3
E17 ... 78 C4
N16 ... 94 C3
Brooke's Ct, EC1 ... 19 E1
Brookes Mkt, EC1 ... 19 F1
Brooke St, EC1 ... 19 E2
Brookfield, N6 ... 92 A3
Brookfield Av, E17 ... 78 C4
NW7 ... 55 H6
W5 ... 105 G4
Sutton SM1 ... 199 G4
Brookfield Cl, NW7 ... 55 H6
Brookfield Ct, Grnf. UB6 ... 103 J3
Harrow HA3 ... 69 G5
Brookfield Cres, NW7 ... 55 H6
Harrow HA3 ... 69 H5
Brookfield Gdns, Esher (Clay.) KT10 ... 194 C6
Brookfield Pk, NW5 ... 92 B3
Brookfield Path, Wdf.Grn. IG8 ... 62 E6
Brookfield Rd, E9 ... 95 H6
N9 ... 60 D3
W4 ... 126 D2
Brookfields, Enf. EN3 ... 45 G4
Brookfields Av, Mitch. CR4 ... 185 H5
Brook Gdns, E4 ... 62 B4
SW13 ... 147 F3
Kingston upon Thames KT2 ... 182 C1
Brook Gate, W1 ... 16 A6
Brook Grn, W6 ... 128 A4
Brookhill Cl, SE18 ... 136 E5
Barnet (E.Barn.) EN4 ... 41 H5
Brookhill Rd, SE18 ... 136 E5
Barnet EN4 ... 41 H5
Brookhouse Gdns, E4 ... 62 E4
Brook Ind Est, Hayes UB4 ... 122 D1
Brooking Cl, Dag. RM8 ... 100 C3
Brooking Rd, E7 ... 97 G5
Brookland Cl, NW11 ... 72 D4
Brookland Garth, NW11 ... 72 E4
Brookland Hill, NW11 ... 72 D4
Brookland Ri, NW11 ... 72 D4
Brooklands Av, SW19 ... 166 E2
Sidcup DA15 ... 175 G2
Brooklands Dr, Grnf. (Perivale) UB6 ... 105 G1
Brooklands Pk, SE3 ... 155 G3
Brooklands Pas, SW8 *off Belmore St* ... 150 D1
Brooklands Pl, Hmptn. TW12 ... 161 H5
Brooklands Rd, T.Ditt. KT7 ... 194 C1
Brook La, SE3 ... 155 H2
Bexley DA5 ... 158 D6
Bromley BR1 ... 173 G6
Brook La N, Brent. TW8 ... 125 G5
Brooklea Cl, NW9 ... 71 E1
Brooklyn Av, SE25 ... 189 E4
Loughton IG10 ... 48 B4
Brooklyn Cl, Cars. SM5 ... 199 H2
Brooklyn Gro, SE25 ... 189 E4
Brooklyn Pas, W12 *off Lime Gro* ... 127 J2
Brooklyn Rd, SE25 ... 188 E4
Bromley BR2 ... 192 A5
Brooklyn Way, West Dr. UB7 ... 120 A3
Brookmarsh Ind Est, SE10 *off Norman Rd* ... 134 B7
Brook Mead, Epsom KT19 ... 197 E6
Brookmead Av, Brom. BR1 ... 192 C5
Brookmead Ind Est, Croy. CR0 ... 186 C6
Brook Meadow, N12 ... 56 E4

Brook Meadow Cl, Wdf.Grn.
  IG8 ....62 E6
Brookmead Rd, Croy.
  CR0 ....186 C6
Brookmeads Est, Mitch.
  CR4 ....185 H5
Brook Ms, Chig. IG7
  off High Rd 64 E3
Brook Ms N, W2 ....14 D5
Brookmill Rd, SE8 ......154 A1
Brook Par, Chig. IG7
  off High Rd 64 E3
Brook Pk Cl, N21 ....43 H6
Brook Path, Loug. IG10 ..48 B4
Brook Pl, Barn. EN5 .....40 D5
Brook Retail Pk, Ruis. HA4
  off Victoria Rd 84 D5
Brook Ri, Chig. IG7 .....64 E4
Brook Rd, N8 ....74 E4
  N22 ....75 F3
  NW2 ....89 G2
  Borehamwood WD6 ....38 A2
  Buckhurst Hill IG9 .....63 G2
  Ilford IG2 ....81 H6
  Loughton IG10 ....48 B5
  Surbiton KT6 ....195 H2
  Thornton Heath CR7 ..187 J4
  Twickenham TW1 .....144 D6
Brook Rd S, Brent. TW8 .125 G6
Brooks Av, E6 ....116 C4
Brooksbank St, E9 ......95 F6
Brooksby Ms, N1
  off Brooksby St 93 G7
Brooksby St, N1 ....93 G7
Brooksby's Wk, E9 ......95 G5
Brooks Cl, SE9 ....174 D2
Brookscroft Rd, E17 .....78 B1
Brookshill, Har. HA3 .....52 A5
Brookshill Av, Har. HA3 ..52 A5
Brookshill Dr, Har. HA3 ..52 A5
Brookshill Gate, Har.
  (Har.Wld) HA3 ....52 A5
Brookside, N21 ....43 F6
  Barnet (E.Barn.)
  EN4 ....41 H6
  Carshalton SM5 ......200 A5
  Ilford IG6 ....65 F6
  Orpington BR6 ....193 J7
Brookside Cl, Barn. EN5 ..40 B6
  Feltham TW13
  off Sycamore Cl 160 A3
  Harrow (Kenton) HA3 ..69 G5
  Harrow (S.Har.) HA2 ...85 E4
Brookside Cres, Wor.Pk.
  KT4 off Green La 197 G1
Brookside Rd, N9 ....60 E4
  N19 ....92 C2
  NW11 ....72 B6
  Hayes UB4 ....102 C7
Brookside S, Barn.
  (E.Barn.) EN4 ....42 A7
Brookside Wk, N3 ....72 B2
  N12 ....56 D6
  NW4 ....72 B4
  NW11 ....72 B4
Brookside Way, Croy.
  CR0 ....189 G6
Brooks La, W4 ....126 A6
Brook's Ms, W1 ....16 D5
Brook Sq, SE18
  off Barlow Dr 156 B1
Brooks Rd, E13 ....115 G1
  W4 ....126 A5
Brook St, N17
  off High Rd 76 C2
  W1 ....16 C5
  W2 ....15 F5
  Belvedere DA17 ......139 H5
  Erith DA8 ....139 H6
  Kingston upon Thames
  KT1 ....181 H2
Brooksville Av, NW6 ....108 B1
Brook Vale, Erith DA8 ...159 H1
Brookview Rd, SW16 ...168 C5
Brookville Rd, SW6 .....128 C7
Brook Wk, N2 ....73 G1
  Edgware HA8 ....54 D6
Brookway, SE3 ....155 G3
Brook Way, Chig. IG7 ....64 D3
Brookwood Av, SW13 ...147 F3
Brookwood Cl, Brom.
  BR2 ....191 F4
Brookwood Rd, SW18 ..166 C1
  Hounslow TW3 ....143 H1
Broom Cl, Brom. BR2 ...192 B6
  Teddington TW11 .....163 G7
Broomcroft Av, Nthlt.
  UB5 ....102 C3
Broome Ho, E5
  off Pembury Rd 94 E5
Broome Rd, Hmptn.
  TW12 ....161 F7
Broome Way, SE5 .....132 A7

Broomfield, E17 ....77 J7
  Sunbury-on-Thames
  TW16 ....178 A1
Broomfield Av, N13 ......59 F5
  Loughton IG10 ....48 C6
Broomfield La, N13 ......59 F4
Broomfield Pl, W13
  off Broomfield Rd 125 E1
Broomfield Rd, N13 .....59 E5
  W13 ....125 E1
  Beckenham BR3 ......189 H3
  Bexleyheath DA6 .....159 G5
  Richmond TW9 ....145 J1
  Romford RM6 ....82 D7
  Surbiton KT5 ....195 J1
  Teddington TW11
  off Melbourne Rd 163 F6
Broomfield St, E14 ......114 A5
Broom Gdns, Croy. CR0 .204 A3
Broomgrove Gdns, Edg.
  HA8 ....70 A1
Broomgrove Rd, SW9 ...151 F2
Broomhill Ct, Wdf.Grn. IG8
  off Broomhill Rd 63 G6
Broomhill Ri, Bexh. DA6 .159 G5
Broomhill Rd, SW18 ....148 D5
  Ilford IG3 ....100 A2
  Woodford Green IG8 ..63 G6
Broomhill Wk, Wdf.Grn.
  IG8 ....63 F7
Broomhouse La, SW6 ..148 D2
Broomhouse Rd, SW6 ..148 D2
Broomloan La, Sutt. SM1 .198 D2
Broom Lock, Tedd. TW11 .163 F6
Broom Mead, Bexh. DA6 .159 G5
Broom Pk, Tedd. TW11 ..163 G7
Broom Rd, Croy. CR0 ...204 A3
  Teddington TW11 .....163 F6
Broomsleigh Business Pk,
  SE26
  off Worsley Br Rd 171 J5
Broomsleigh St, NW6 ...90 C5
Broom Water, Tedd.
  TW11 ....163 F6
Broom Water W, Tedd.
  TW11 ....163 F5
Broomwood Cl, Croy.
  CR0 ....189 G5
Broomwood Rd, SW11 ..149 J6
Broseley Gro, SE26 .....171 H5
Broster Gdns, SE25 ....188 C3
Brougham Rd, E8 ....112 D1
  W3 ....106 C6
Brougham St, SW11 ....149 J2
Brough Cl, SW8
  off Kenchester Cl 131 E7
  Kingston upon Thames
  KT2 ....163 G5
Broughinge Rd, Borwd.
  WD6 ....38 B2
Broughton Av, N3 ....72 B3
  Richmond TW10 .....163 E3
Broughton Dr, SW9 .....151 G4
Broughton Gdns, N6 ....74 C6
Broughton Rd, SW6 ....148 E2
  W13 ....105 E7
  Orpington BR6 ....207 G2
  Thornton Heath CR7 .187 G6
Broughton Rd App, SW6
  off Wandsworth
  Br Rd 148 E2
Broughton St, SW8 .....150 A2
Brouncker Rd, W3 ......126 C2
Browells La, Felt. TW13 .160 B2
Brown Cl, Wall. SM6 ....200 E7
Brownfield St, E14 ......114 B6
Browngraves Rd, Hayes
  (Harling.) UB3 ....121 C5
Brown Hart Gdns, W1 ...16 C5
Brownhill Rd, SE6 ......154 B7
Browning Av, W7 ....104 C6
  Sutton SM1 ....199 H4
  Worcester Park KT4 ..197 H1
Browning Cl, E17 ....78 C4
  W9 ....6 D6
  Hampton TW12 ....161 F4
  Welling DA16 ....157 H1
Browning Ms, W1 ....16 D2
Browning Rd, E11 ....79 F7
  E12 ....98 C6
Browning St, SE17 ......36 A3
Browning Way, Houns.
  TW5 ....142 D1
Brownlea Gdns, IG3 ...100 A2
Brownlow Cl, Barn. EN4 ..41 G5
Brownlow Ms, WC1 ......10 D6
Brownlow Rd, E7
  off Woodford Rd 97 G6
  E8 ....112 C1
  N3 ....56 E7
  N11 ....58 E6
  NW10 ....89 E7
  W13 ....124 D1

Brownlow Rd,
  Borehamwood WD6 ...38 A4
  Croydon CR0 ....202 B4
Brownlow St, WC1 ......18 D2
Brown's Bldgs, EC3 .....20 E4
Brownsea Wk, NW7
  off Sanders La 56 A6
Browns La, NW5 ....92 B5
Brownspring Dr, SE9 ...175 E4
Browns Rd, E17 ....78 A3
  Surbiton KT5 ....181 J7
Brown St, W1 ....15 J3
Brownswell Rd, N2 ......73 G2
Brownswood Rd, N4 ....93 H3
Broxash Rd, SW11 .....150 A6
Broxbourne Av, E18 ....79 H4
Broxbourne Rd, E7 ......97 G3
  Orpington BR6 ....193 J7
Broxholme Cl, SE25
  off Whitehorse La 188 A4
Broxholm Rd, SE27 ....169 G3
Broxted Rd, SE6 ....171 J2
Broxwood Way, NW8 ..109 H1
★ Bruce Castle Mus,
  N17 ....76 B1
Bruce Castle Rd, N17 ...76 C1
Bruce Cl, W10
  off Ladbroke Gro 108 B5
  Welling DA16 ....158 B1
Bruce Gdns, N20
  off Balfour Gro 57 J3
Bruce Gro, N17 ....76 B1
Bruce Hall Ms, SW17 ..168 A4
Bruce Rd, E3 ....114 B3
  NW10 ....88 D7
  SE25 ....188 A4
  Barnet EN5
  off St. Albans Rd 40 B3
  Harrow HA3 ....68 B2
  Mitcham CR4 ....168 A7
Bruckner St, W10 ......108 C3
Brudenell Rd, SW17 ...167 J3
Bruffs Meadow, Nthlt.
  UB5 ....85 E6
Bruford Ct, SE8 ....134 A6
Bruges Pl, NW1
  off Randolph St 92 C7
Brumfield Rd, Epsom
  KT19 ....196 C5
Brummel Cl, Bexh. DA7 .159 J3
★ Brunei Gall, WC1 .....17 J1
Brunel Cl, SE19 ....170 C6
  Hounslow TW5 ....122 B7
  Northolt UB5 ....103 F7
★ Brunel Engine Ho,
  SE16 ....133 F2
Brunel Est, W2 ....108 D5
Brunel Ms, W10
  off Kilburn La 108 B3
Brunel Rd, E17 ....77 H6
  SE16 ....133 F2
  W3 ....106 E5
  Woodford Green IG8 ..64 C5
Brunel St, E16
  off Victoria Dock Rd .115 F6
Brunel Wk, N15 ....76 B4
  Twickenham TW2
  off Stephenson Rd ...143 G7
Brune St, E1 ....21 F2
Brunlees Ho, SE1
  off Bath Ter 27 J6
Brunner Cl, NW11 ......73 E5
Brunner Rd, E17 ....77 H5
  W5 ....105 G4
Bruno Pl, NW9 ....88 C2
Brunswick Av, N11 ......58 A3
Brunswick Cl, Bexh.
  DA6 ....158 D4
  Pinner HA5 ....67 E6
  Thames Ditton KT7 ..194 C1
  Twickenham TW2 ....162 A3
Brunswick Ct, EC1
  off Tompion St 11 G4
  SE1 ....29 E4
  SW1 off Regency St ...33 J2
  Barnet EN4 ....41 G5
Brunswick Cres, N11 ....58 A3
Brunswick Gdns, W5 ...105 H3
  W8 ....128 D1
  Ilford IG6 ....65 F7
Brunswick Gro, N11 ....58 A3
Brunswick Ind Pk, N11 ..58 A4
Brunswick Ms, SW16
  off Potters La 168 D6
  W1 ....16 A3
BRUNSWICK PARK, N11 .57 J3
Brunswick Pk, SE5 .....152 A1
Brunswick Pk Gdns, N11 .58 A2
Brunswick Pk Rd, N11 ..58 A2
Brunswick Pl, N1 ....12 C4
  NW1 ....8 C5
  SE19 ....170 D7

Brunswick Quay, SE16 ..133 G3
Brunswick Rd, E10 ......96 C1
  E14 off Blackwall Tunnel
  Northern App 114 C6
  N15 ....76 B5
  W5 ....105 G4
  Bexleyheath DA6 ....158 D4
  Kingston upon Thames
  KT2 ....182 A1
  Sutton SM1 ....199 E4
Brunswick Shop Cen,
  WC1 ....10 A5
Brunswick Sq, N17 ......60 C6
  WC1 ....10 B6
Brunswick St, E17 ....78 C5
Brunswick Vil, SE5 .....152 B1
Brunswick Way, N11 ....58 B4
Brunton Pl, E14 ....113 H6
Brushfield St, E1 ....21 E1
Brushwood Cl, E14
  off Uamvar St 114 B5
Brussels Rd, SW11 ....149 G4
Bruton Cl, Chis. BR7 ...174 C7
Bruton La, W1 ....16 E6
Bruton Pl, W1 ....16 E6
Bruton Rd, Mord. SM4 ..185 F5
Bruton St, W1 ....16 E6
Bruton Way, W13 ......104 D5
Bryan Av, NW10 ....89 H7
Bryan Cl, Sun. TW16 ...160 A7
Bryan Rd, SE16 ....133 J2
Bryan's All, SW6
  off Wandsworth
  Br Rd 148 E2
Bryanston Av, Twick.
  TW2 ....161 H1
Bryanston Cl, Sthl. UB2 .123 F4
Bryanstone Ct, Sutt. SM1
  off Oakhill Rd 199 F4
Bryanstone Rd, N8 ......74 D5
Bryanston Ms E, W1 .....15 J2
Bryanston Ms W, W1 ....15 J2
Bryanston Pl, W1 ....15 J2
Bryanston Sq, W1 ....15 J3
Bryanston St, W1 ....15 J4
Bryant Cl, Barn. EN5 ....40 C5
Bryant Ct, E2 ....13 F1
Bryant Rd, Nthlt. UB5 ..102 C3
Bryant St, E15 ....96 D7
Bryantwood Rd, N7 .....93 G5
Brycedale Cres, N14 ....58 D4
Bryce Rd, Dag. RM8 ...100 C4
Brydale Ho, SE16
  off Rotherhithe
  New Rd 133 G4
Bryden Cl, SE26 ....171 H5
Brydges Pl, WC2 ....18 A6
Brydges Rd, E15 ....96 D5
Brydon Wk, N1
  off Outram Pl 111 E1
Bryer Ct, EC2
  off Bridgewater St 19 J1
Bryett Rd, N7 ....93 E3
Brymay Cl, E3 ....114 A2
Brynmaer Rd, SW11 ...149 J1
Bryn-y-Mawr Rd, Enf.
  EN1 ....44 C4
Bryony Cl, Loug. IG10 ...48 E4
Bryony Rd, W12 ....107 G7
Buchanan Cl, N21 ....43 F5
Buchanan Ct, Borwd.
  WD6 ....38 C2
Buchanan Gdns, NW10 .107 H2
Buchan Rd, SE15 ......153 F3
Bucharest Rd, SW18 ..149 F7
Buckden Cl, N2
  off Southern Rd 73 J4
  SE12 off Upwood Rd .155 F6
Buckfast Ct, W13
  off Romsey Rd 104 D7
Buckfast Rd, Mord.
  SM4 ....185 E4
Buckfast St, E2 ....13 J4
Buck Hill Wk, W2 ....15 F6
Buckhold Rd, SW18 ...148 D6
Buckhurst Av, Cars.
  SM5 ....199 H1
BUCKHURST HILL, IG9 ..47 H7
Buckhurst St, E1 ....113 E4
Buckhurst Way, Buck.H.
  IG9 ....64 A4
Buckingham Arc, WC2 ...18 B6
Buckingham Av, N20 ....41 F7
  Feltham TW14 ....142 B6
  Greenford (Perivale)
  UB6 ....104 D1
  Thornton Heath CR7 .187 G1
  Welling DA16 ....157 H4
  West Molesey KT8 ...179 H3
Buckingham Chambers,
  SW1 off Greencoat Pl .33 G1
Buckingham Cl, W5 ....105 F5
  Enfield EN1 ....44 B2

Buckingham CI,
  Hampton TW12 ....161 F5
  Orpington BR5 ....193 H7
Buckingham Ct, NW4 ....71 J2
  Loughton IG10
  off Rectory La 48 D2
Buckingham Dr, Chis.
  BR7 ....175 E5
Buckingham Gdns, Edg.
  HA8 ....53 J7
  Thornton Heath CR7 .187 G2
  West Molesey KT8
  off Buckingham Av ...179 H2
Buckingham Gate, SW1 ..25 F4
Buckingham La, SE23 ...153 H1
Buckingham Lo, N10 ....74 C4
Buckingham Ms, N1
  off Buckingham Rd ...94 B6
  NW10
  off Buckingham Rd ...107 F2
  SW1 ....25 F4
★ Buckingham Palace,
  SW1 ....24 E4
Buckingham Palace Rd,
  SW1 ....32 D2
Buckingham PI, SW1 .....25 F5
Buckingham Rd, E10 .....96 B3
  E11 ....79 J5
  E15 ....97 F5
  E18 ....79 F1
  N1 ....94 B6
  N22 ....74 E1
  NW10 ....107 F2
  Borehamwood WD6 ...38 D4
  Edgware HA8 ....53 J7
  Hampton TW12 ....161 F4
  Harrow HA1 ....68 A5
  Ilford IG1 ....99 G2
  Kingston upon Thames
  KT1 ....181 J4
  Mitcham CR4 ....186 E5
  Richmond TW10 ......163 G2
Buckingham St, WC2 .....18 B6
Buckland CI, NW7 ....55 G4
Buckland Cres, NW3 .....91 G7
Buckland Ri, Pnr. HA5 ...66 C1
Buckland Rd, E10 ....96 C2
  Chessington KT9 .....195 J5
  Orpington BR6 ....207 H4
Bucklands Rd, Tedd.
  TW11 ....163 F6
Buckland St, N1 ....12 C2
Buckland Wk, W3 ....126 C1
  Morden SM4 ....185 F4
Buckland Way, Wor.Pk.
  KT4 ....197 J1
Buck La, NW9 ....70 D5
Bucklebury, NW1 ....9 F5
Buckleigh Av, SW20 ....184 B3
Buckleigh Rd, SW16 ....168 D6
Buckleigh Way, SE19 ...188 C1
Buckler Ct, N7
  off Eden Gro 93 F5
Buckler Gdns, SE9
  off Southold Ri 174 C3
Bucklers All, SW6 ....128 C6
Bucklersbury, EC4 ....20 B4
Bucklersbury Pas, EC4 ...20 B4
Bucklers Way, Cars.
  SM5 ....199 J3
Buckles Ct, Belv. DA17
  off Fendyke Rd 138 D3
Buckle St, E1 ....21 G3
Buckley CI, SE23 ....153 E7
Buckley Rd, NW6 ....90 C7
Buckley St, SE1 ....26 E2
Buckmaster CI, SW9
  off Stockwell Pk Rd .151 F3
Buckmaster Rd, SW11 ..149 H4
Bucknall St, WC2 ....17 J3
Bucknall Way, Beck.
  BR3 ....190 B4
Bucknell CI, SW2 ....151 F4
Buckner Rd, SW2 ....151 F4
Buckrell Rd, E4 ....62 D2
Buckstone CI, SE23 ....153 F6
Buckstone Rd, N18 ....60 D6
Buck St, NW1 ....92 B7
Buckters Rents, SE16 ...133 H1
Buckthorne Rd, SE4 ....153 H6
Buck Wk, E17
  off Wood St 78 D4
Budd CI, N12 ....57 E4
Buddings Circle, Wem.
  HA9 ....88 C3
Budd's All, Twick. TW1
  off Arlington CI 145 F5
Bude CI, E17 ....79 J4
Budge La, Mitch. CR4 ..185 J7
Budge Row, EC4 ....20 B5
Budge's Wk, W2 ....22 C1
Budleigh Cres, Well.
  DA16 ....158 C1

Budoch Ct, Ilf. IG3 ....100 A2
Budoch Dr, Ilf. IG3 ....100 A2
Buer Rd, SW6 ....148 B2
Bugsby's Way, SE7 .....135 G4
  SE10 ....135 F4
Buick Ho, Kings.T. KT2 .182 A2
Building 22, SE18
  off Carriage St 137 E3
Building 36, SE18
  off Marlborough Rd .137 F3
Building 45, SE18
  off Hopton Rd 137 E3
Building 47, SE18
  off Marlborough Rd .137 F3
Building 48, SE18
  off Marlborough Rd .137 F3
Building 49, SE18
  off Argyll Rd 137 F3
Building 50, SE18
  off Argyll Rd 137 F3
Bulganak Rd, Th.Hth.
  CR7 ....187 J4
Bulinga St, SW1 ....33 J2
Bullace Row, SE5 ....132 A7
Bull All, Well. DA16
  off Welling High St ..158 B3
Bullards PI, E2 ....113 G3
Bullbanks Rd, Belv.
  DA17 ....139 J4
Bullen Ho, E1
  off Collingwood St ..113 E4
Bullen St, SW11 ....149 H2
Buller CI, SE15 ....132 D7
Buller Rd, N17 ....76 D2
  N22 ....75 G2
  NW10
  off Chamberlayne Rd .108 A3
  Barking IG11 ....99 H7
  Thornton Heath CR7 .188 A2
Bullers CI, Sid. DA14 ...176 E5
Bullers Wd Dr, Chis. BR7 .174 B7
Bullescroft Rd, Edg. HA8 .54 A3
Bullhead Rd, Borwd.
  WD6 ....38 C3
Bullied Way, SW1 ....32 E2
Bull Inn Ct, WC2 ....18 B6
Bullivant St, E14 ....114 C7
Bull La, N18 ....60 B5
  Chislehurst BR7 ......175 G7
  Dagenham RM10 .....101 H3
Bull Rd, E15 ....115 F2
Bullrush CI, Cars. SM5 .199 H2
  Croydon CR0 ....188 B6
Bull's All, SW14 ....146 D2
Bulls Br Ind Est, Sthl.
  UB2 ....122 B4
Bulls Br Rd, Sthl. UB2 .122 B3
Bullsbrook Rd, Hayes
  UB4 ....122 C1
Bulls Gdns, SW3 ....31 H1
Bull's Head Pas, EC3 ...20 D4
Bull Yd, SE15
  off Peckham High St .152 D1
Bulmer Gdns, Har. HA3 ..69 G7
Bulmer Ms, W11
  off Ladbroke Rd 108 D7
Bulmer PI, W11 ....108 D1
Bulow Est, SW6
  off Pearscroft Rd 149 E1
Bulstrode Av, Houns.
  TW3 ....143 F2
Bulstrode Gdns, Houns.
  TW3 ....143 F3
Bulstrode PI, W1 ....16 C2
Bulstrode Rd, Houns.
  TW3 ....143 G3
Bulstrode St, W1 ....16 C3
Bulwer Ct Rd, E11 ....96 D1
Bulwer Gdns, Barn. EN5 ..41 F4
Bulwer Rd, E11 ....78 D7
  N18 ....60 B4
  Barnet EN5 ....41 E4
Bulwer St, W12 ....127 J1
Bunces La, Wdf.Grn. IG8 .63 F7
Bungalow Rd, SE19 ....188 B4
Bungalows, The, SW16 ..168 B7
  Wallington SM6 ......200 B5
Bunhill Row, EC1 ....12 B5
Bunhouse PI, SW1 ....32 B3
Bunkers Hill, NW11 ....73 F7
  Belvedere DA17 ......139 G4
  Sidcup DA14 ....177 F3
Bunning Way, N7 ....93 E7
Bunns La, NW7 ....55 F6
Bunsen St, E3
  off Kenilworth Rd ...113 H2
Buntingbridge Rd, Ilf. IG2 .81 G5
Bunting CI, N9
  off Dunnock CI 61 G1
  Mitcham CR4 ....185 J5
Bunton St, SE18 ....136 D3
Bunyan Ct, EC2
  off The Barbican 19 J1

Bunyan Rd, E17 ....77 H3
Buonaparte Ms, SW1 .....33 H3
Burbage CI, SE1 ....28 B6
Burbage Rd, SE21 ......152 A6
  SE24 ....151 J6
Burberry CI, N.Mal. KT3 .183 E2
Burbridge Way, N17 ......76 C2
Burcham St, E14 ....114 B6
Burcharbro Rd, SE2 ....138 D6
Burchell Rd, E10 ....96 B1
  SE15 ....153 E1
Burcher Gale Gro, SE15 ..37 E7
Burchett Way, Rom. RM6 .83 F6
Burcote Rd, SW18 ......167 G1
Burden CI, Brent. TW8 ..125 F5
Burdenshott Av, Rich.
  TW10 ....146 B4
Burden Way, E11
  off Brading Cres 97 H2
Burder CI, N1 ....94 B6
Burder Rd, N1
  off Balls Pond Rd 94 B6
Burdett Av, SW20 ......183 G1
Burdett CI, W7
  off Cherington Rd ...124 C2
  Sidcup DA14 ....176 E5
Burdett Ms, NW3
  off Belsize Cres 91 G6
  W2 ....14 A3
Burdett Rd, E3 ....113 J4
  E14 ....113 J4
  Croydon CR0 ....188 A6
  Richmond TW9 ....145 J2
Burdetts Rd, Dag. RM9 .119 F1
Burdett St, SE1 ....27 E5
Burdock CI, Croy. CR0 .203 G1
Burdock Rd, N17 ....76 D3
Burdon La, Sutt. SM2 ..198 B7
Burfield CI, SW17 ......167 G4
Burford CI, Dag. RM8 ..100 C3
  Ilford IG6 ....81 F4
Burford Gdns, N13 ....59 F3
Burford Rd, E6 ....116 B3
  E15 ....96 D7
  SE6 ....171 J2
  Brentford TW8 ....125 H5
  Bromley BR1 ....192 B4
  Sutton SM1 ....198 D2
  Worcester Park KT4 .183 F7
Burford Wk, SW6
  off Cambria St 129 E7
Burford Way, Croy.
  (New Adgtn) CR0 ....204 C6
Burford Wf Apts, E15
  off Cam Rd 114 D1
Burges CI, E6 ....98 D7
Burges Gro, SW13 ......127 H7
Burges Rd, E6 ....98 B7
Burgess Av, NW9 ....70 D6
Burgess Business Pk,
  SE5 ....36 C7
Burgess CI, Felt. TW13 .160 E4
Burgess Hill, NW2 ....90 D4
Burgess Ms, SW19 .....167 E6
Burgess Rd, E15 ....96 E4
  Sutton SM1 ....198 E4
Burgess St, E14 ....114 A5
Burge St, SE1 ....28 C6
★ Burgh Ho
  (Hampstead Mus), NW3
  off New End Sq 91 G4
Burghill Rd, SE26 ......171 H4
Burghley Av, Borwd.
  WD6 ....38 C5
  New Malden KT3 .....182 D1
Burghley Ho, SW19 ....166 B3
Burghley PI, Mitch. CR4 .185 J5
Burghley Rd, E11 ....97 E1
  N8 ....75 G3
  NW5 ....92 B5
  SW19 ....166 A4
Burghley Twr, W3 ....107 F7
Burgh St, N1 ....11 H1
Burgon St, EC4 ....19 H4
Burgos CI, Croy. CR0 ..201 G6
Burgos Gro, SE10 ......154 B1
Burgoyne Rd, N4 ....75 H6
  SE25 ....188 C4
  SW9 ....151 F3
Burham CI, SE20
  off Maple Rd 171 F7
Burhill Gro, Pnr. HA5 ....66 E2
Burke CI, SW15 ....147 E4
Burke Ho, SW11
  off Maysoule Rd 149 G4
Burke St, E16 ....115 F6
Burket CI, Sthl. UB2
  off Kingsbridge Rd .123 F4
Burland Rd, SW11 .....149 J5
Burleigh Av, Sid. DA15 .157 J5
  Wallington SM6 .....200 A3
Burleigh CI, Rom. RM7 ..83 H4

Burleigh Gdns, N14 ......58 C7
Burleigh Ho, W10
  off St. Charles Sq ...108 A5
Burleigh PI, SW15 .....148 A5
Burleigh Rd, Enf. EN1 ....44 B4
  Sutton SM3 ....198 B1
Burleigh St, WC2 ....18 C5
Burleigh Wk, SE6
  off Muirkirk Rd 172 C1
Burleigh Way, Enf. EN2
  off Church St 44 A3
Burley CI, E4 ....62 A5
  SW16 ....186 D2
Burley Rd, E16 ....115 J6
Burlington Arc, W1 ....17 F6
Burlington Av, Rich.
  TW9 ....146 A1
  Romford RM7 ....83 H6
Burlington CI, E6
  off Northumberland
  Rd 116 B6
  W9 ....108 C4
  Feltham TW14 ....141 G7
  Orpington BR6 ......206 E2
  Pinner HA5 ....66 B3
Burlington Gdns, W1 ....17 F6
  W3 ....126 C1
  W4 ....126 C5
  Romford RM6 ....83 E7
Burlington La, W4 ......126 E7
Burlington Ms, SW15 ..148 C5
  W3 ....126 C1
Burlington PI, SW6
  off Burlington Rd 148 B2
  Woodford Green IG8 ..63 G3
Burlington Ri, Barn.
  (E.Barn.) EN4 ....57 H1
Burlington Rd, N10
  off Tetherdown 74 A3
  N17 ....76 D1
  SW6 ....148 B2
  W4 ....126 C5
  Enfield EN2 ....44 A1
  Isleworth TW7 ....144 A1
  New Malden KT3 ....183 G4
  Thornton Heath
  CR7 ....187 J2
Burma Rd, N16 ....94 A4
Burmester Rd, SW17 ...167 F3
Burnaby Cres, W4 ......126 B6
Burnaby Gdns, W4 .....126 B5
Burnaby St, SW10 ......129 F7
Burnbrae CI, N12 ....57 E6
Burnbury Rd, SW12 ....168 C1
Burncroft Av, Enf. EN3 ..45 F2
Burndell Way, Hayes
  UB4 ....102 D5
Burne Jones Ho, W14 ..128 C4
Burnell Av, Rich. TW10 .163 F5
  Welling DA16 ....158 A2
Burnell Gdns, Stan. HA7 .69 G1
Burnell Rd, Sutt. SM1 ..199 E4
Burnell Wk, SE1 ....37 G3
Burnels Av, E6 ....116 D3
Burness CI, N7
  off Roman Way 93 F6
Burne St, NW1 ....15 G1
Burnett CI, E9 ....95 F5
Burnett Ho, SE13
  off Lewisham Hill ...154 C2
Burnett Rd, Ilf. IG6 ......64 F7
Burney Av, Surb. KT5 ..181 J5
Burney Dr, Loug. IG10 ...49 E2
Burney St, SE10 ....134 C7
Burnfoot Av, SW6 ......148 B1
Burnfoot Ct, SE22 .....170 E1
Burnham, NW3 ....91 H7
Burnham Av, Uxb. UB10 .58 A1
Burnham CI, NW7 ....55 G7
  SE1 ....37 G2
  Harrow (Wealds.)
  HA3 ....68 D4
Burnham Ct, NW4 ....71 J4
Burnham Cres, E11 ......79 J4
Burnham Dr, Wor.Pk.
  KT4 ....198 A2
Burnham Gdns, Croy.
  CR0 ....188 C7
  Hayes UB3 ....121 G3
  Hounslow TW4 ....142 B1
Burnham Rd, E4 ....61 J5
  Dagenham RM9 ......100 B7
  Morden SM4 ....185 E5
  Sidcup DA14 ....176 E2
Burnham St, E2 ....113 F3
  Kingston upon Thames
  KT2 ....182 A1
Burnham Way, SE26 ...171 J4
  W13 ....124 E4
Burnhill CI, SE15
  off Gervase St 133 E7
Burnhill Rd, Beck. BR3 .190 A2
Burnley CI, Wat. WD19 ..50 C5
Burnley Rd, NW10 ....89 G5
  SW9 ....151 F2
Burnsall St, SW3 ....31 H4

Burns Av, Felt. TW14 ... 142 A6
Romford (Chad.Hth) RM6 ... 82 C7
Sidcup DA15 ... 158 B6
Southall UB1 ... 103 G7
Burns Cl, E17 ... 78 C4
SW19 ... 167 G6
Welling DA16 ... 157 J1
Burnside Av, E4 ... 61 J6
Burnside Cl, SE16 ... 133 G1
Barnet EN5 ... 40 D3
Twickenham TW1 ... 144 D6
Burnside Cres, Wem. HA0 ... 105 G1
Burnside Rd, Dag. RM8 ... 100 C2
Burns Rd, NW10 ... 107 F1
SW11 ... 149 J2
W13 ... 124 E2
Wembley HA0 ... 105 G2
Burns Way, Houns. TW5 ... 142 D2
Burnt Ash Hts, Brom. BR1 ... 173 H5
Burnt Ash Hill, SE12 ... 155 F6
Burnt Ash La, Brom. BR1 ... 173 G6
Burnt Ash Rd, SE12 ... 155 F5
Burnthwaite Rd, SW6 ... 128 D7
BURNT OAK, Edg. HA8 ... 54 C7
Burnt Oak Bdy, Edg. HA8 ... 54 A7
Burnt Oak Flds, Edg. HA8 ... 70 C1
Burnt Oak La, Sid. DA15 ... 158 A6
Burntwood Cl, SW18 ... 167 G1
Burntwood Gra Rd, SW18 ... 167 G1
Burntwood La, SW17 ... 167 H2
Burntwood Vw, SE19 off Bowley La ... 170 C5
Buross St, E1 off Commercial Rd ... 113 E6
Burpham Cl, Hayes UB4 ... 102 D5
Burrage Gro, SE18 ... 137 F4
Burrage Pl, SE18 ... 137 E5
Burrage Rd, SE18 ... 137 F6
Burrard Rd, E16 ... 115 H6
NW6 ... 90 D5
Burr Cl, E1 ... 29 H1
Bexleyheath DA7 ... 159 F3
Burrell Cl, Croy. CR0 ... 189 H6
Edgware HA8 ... 54 B2
Burrell Row, Beck. BR3 off High St ... 190 A2
Burrell St, SE1 ... 27 G1
Burrells Wf Sq, E14 ... 134 B5
Burrell Twr, E10 ... 78 A7
Burritt Rd, Kings.T. KT1 ... 182 A2
Burroughs, The, NW4 ... 71 H5
Burroughs Gdns, NW4 ... 71 H4
Burroughs Par, NW4 off The Burroughs ... 71 H4
Burrow Cl, Chig. IG7 off Burrow Rd ... 65 J5
Burrow Grn, Chig. IG7 ... 65 J5
Burrow Rd, SE22 ... 152 B4
Chigwell IG7 ... 65 J5
Burrows Ms, SE1 ... 27 G3
Burrows Rd, NW10 ... 107 J3
Burrow Wk, SE21 ... 151 J7
Burr Rd, SW18 ... 148 D7
Bursdon Cl, Sid. DA15 ... 175 J2
Bursland Rd, Enf. EN3 ... 45 G4
Burslem St, E1 ... 21 J4
Burstock Rd, SW15 ... 148 B4
Burston Rd, SW15 ... 148 A5
Burston Vil, SW15 off St. John's Av ... 148 A5
Burstow Rd, SW20 ... 184 B1
Burtenshaw Rd, T.Ditt. KT7 ... 180 D7
Burtley Cl, N4 ... 93 J1
Burton Cl, Chess. KT9 ... 195 G7
Thornton Heath CR7 ... 188 A3
Burton Ct, SW3 off Franklin's Row ... 32 A3
Burton Gdns, Houns. TW5 ... 143 F1
Burton Gro, SE17 ... 36 B4
Burtonhole Cl, NW7 ... 56 A4
Burtonhole La, NW7 ... 56 B4
Burton La, SW9 ... 151 G2
Burton Ms, SW1 ... 32 C2
Burton Pl, WC1 ... 9 J4
Burton Rd, E18 ... 79 H3
NW6 ... 90 C7
SW9 ... 151 H2
Kingston upon Thames KT2 ... 163 H7
Loughton IG10 ... 49 F4
Burtons Rd, Hmptn. (Hmptn H.) TW12 ... 161 H4
Burton St, WC1 ... 9 J4
Burtwell La, SE27 ... 170 A4
Burwash Ho, SE1 ... 28 C4
Burwash Rd, SE18 ... 137 G5
Burwell Av, Grnf. UB6 ... 86 B6
Burwell Cl, E1 off Bigland St ... 113 E6
Burwell Rd, E10 ... 95 H1
Burwell Wk, E3 ... 114 A4
Burwood Av, Brom. BR2 ... 205 H2
Pinner HA5 ... 66 C5
Burwood Cl, Surb. KT6 ... 196 A1
Burwood Pl, W2 ... 15 H3
Barnet EN4 ... 41 F1
Bury Cl, SE16 off Rotherhithe St ... 133 G1
Bury Ct, EC3 ... 20 E3
Bury Gro, Mord. SM4 ... 184 E5
Bury Pl, WC1 ... 18 A2
Bury Rd, E4 ... 47 E5
N22 ... 75 G3
Dagenham RM10 ... 101 H5
Buryside Cl, Ilf. IG2 ... 81 J4
Bury St, EC3 ... 20 E4
N9 ... 60 D1
SW1 ... 25 G1
Bury St W, N9 ... 44 A7
Bury Wk, SW3 ... 31 G2
Busbridge Ho, E14 off Brabazon St ... 114 A5
Busby Ms, NW5 off Busby Pl ... 92 D6
Busby Pl, NW5 ... 92 D6
Busby St, E2 ... 13 G5
Busch Cl, Islw. TW7 off Park Rd ... 144 E1
Bushbaby Cl, SE1 ... 28 D6
Bushberry Rd, E9 ... 95 H6
Bush Cl, Ilf. IG2 ... 81 G5
Bush Cotts, SW18 off Putney Br Rd ... 148 D5
Bush Ct, W12 off Shepherds Bush Grn ... 128 A2
Bushell Cl, SW2 ... 169 F2
Bushell Grn, Bushey (Bushey Hth) WD23 ... 52 A2
Bushell St, E1 ... 29 J2
Bushell Way, Chis. BR7 ... 174 D5
Bushey Av, E18 ... 79 F3
Orpington BR5 ... 193 G7
Bushey Cl, E4 ... 62 C3
Bushey Ct, SW20 ... 183 H2
Bushey Down, SW12 off Bedford Hill ... 168 B2
BUSHEY HEATH, Bushey WD23 ... 52 B1
Bushey Hill Rd, SE5 ... 152 B1
Bushey La, Sutt. SM1 ... 198 D4
Bushey Lees, Sid. DA15 off Fen Gro ... 157 J6
BUSHEY MEAD, SW20 ... 184 A3
Bushey Rd, E13 ... 115 J2
N15 ... 76 B6
SW20 ... 183 H3
Croydon CR0 ... 204 A2
Hayes UB3 ... 121 H4
Sutton SM1 ... 198 E4
Bushey Way, Beck. BR3 ... 190 D6
Bushfield Cl, Edg. HA8 ... 54 B2
Bushfield Cres, Edg. HA8 ... 54 B2
Bushfields, Loug. IG10 ... 48 D5
Bush Gro, NW9 ... 70 C7
Stanmore HA7 ... 69 G1
Bushgrove Rd, Dag. RM8 ... 100 D4
Bush Hill, N21 ... 43 J7
BUSH HILL PARK, Enf. EN1 ... 44 B5
Bush Hill Rd, N21 ... 44 A6
Harrow HA3 ... 69 J6
Bush Ind Est, NW10 ... 106 D4
Bush La, EC4 ... 20 B5
Bushmead Cl, N15 off Copperfield Dr ... 76 C4
Bushmoor Cres, SE18 ... 137 F7
Bushnell Rd, SW17 ... 168 B2
Bush Rd, E8 ... 112 E1
E11 ... 79 F7
SE8 ... 133 G4
Buckhurst Hill IG9 ... 64 A4
Richmond TW9 ... 125 J6
Bushway, Dag. RM8 ... 100 D4
Bushwood, E11 ... 97 F1
Bushwood Dr, SE1 ... 37 G2
Bushwood Rd, Rich. TW9 ... 126 A6
★ Bushy Park, Tedd. TW11 ... 180 C1
Bushy Pk, Hmptn. (Hmptn H.) TW12 ... 180 C1
Teddington TW11 ... 180 C1
Bushy Pk Gdns, Tedd. TW11 ... 162 A5
Bushy Pk Rd, Tedd. TW11 ... 163 E7
Bushy Rd, Tedd. TW11 ... 162 C6
★ Business Design Cen, N1 ... 111 G1
Butcher Row, E1 ... 113 G7
E14 ... 113 G7
Butchers Rd, E16 ... 115 G6
Bute Av, Rich. TW10 ... 163 H2
Bute Ct, Wall. SM6 ... 200 C5
Bute Gdns, W6 ... 128 A4
Wallington SM6 ... 200 C5
Bute Gdns W, Wall. SM6 ... 200 C5
Bute Ms, NW11 off Northway ... 73 E5
Bute Rd, Croy. CR0 ... 201 G1
Ilford IG6 ... 81 E5
Wallington SM6 ... 200 C4
Bute St, SW7 ... 31 E1
Bute Wk, N1 off Marquess Rd ... 94 A6
Butler Av, Har. HA1 ... 68 A7
Butler Cl, Edg. HA8 off Scott Rd ... 70 B2
Butler Ct, Wem. HA0 off Harrow Rd ... 86 D4
Butler Pl, SW1 ... 25 H5
Butler Rd, NW10 ... 89 F7
Dagenham RM8 ... 100 B4
Harrow HA1 ... 67 J7
Butlers & Colonial Wf, SE1 ... 29 G3
Butlers Cl, Houns. TW4 ... 143 F3
Butler St, E2 off Knottisford St ... 113 F3
Butlers Wf, SE1 ... 29 F2
Buttercup Cl, Nthlt. UB5 ... 85 E6
Butterfield Cl, N17 off Devonshire Rd ... 59 J6
SE16 off Wilson Gro ... 132 E2
Twickenham TW1 off Rugby Rd ... 144 C6
Butterfields, E17 ... 78 C5
Butterfield Sq, E6 off Harper Rd ... 116 C6
Butterfly La, SE9 ... 156 E6
Butterfly Wk, SE5 off Denmark Hill ... 152 A1
Butter Hill, Cars. SM5 ... 200 A3
Wallington SM6 ... 200 A3
Butteridges Cl, Dag. RM9 ... 119 F1
Buttermere Cl, E15 ... 96 D4
SE1 ... 37 F2
Morden SM4 ... 184 A6
Buttermere Dr, SW15 ... 148 B5
Buttermere Wk, E8 ... 94 C6
Butterwick, W6 ... 127 J4
Butterworth Gdns, Wdf.Grn. IG8 ... 63 G6
Buttesland St, N1 ... 12 C3
Buttfield Cl, Dag. RM10 ... 101 H6
Buttmarsh Cl, SE18 ... 137 E5
Butts, The, Brent. TW8 ... 125 G6
Sunbury-on-Thames TW16 off Elizabeth Gdns ... 178 C3
Buttsbury Rd, Ilf. IG1 ... 99 F5
Butts Cotts, Felt. TW13 ... 161 F3
Butts Cres, Felt. (Han.) TW13 ... 161 G3
Butts Piece, Nthlt. UB5 off Longhook Gdns ... 102 B2
Butts Rd, Brom. BR1 ... 173 E5
Buxhall Cres, E9 ... 95 J6
Buxted Rd, E8 ... 94 C7
N12 ... 57 H5
SE22 ... 152 B4
Buxton Cl, N9 ... 61 F2
Woodford Green IG8 ... 64 A6
Buxton Ct, N1 ... 12 A3
Buxton Cres, Sutt. SM3 ... 198 B4
Buxton Dr, E11 ... 79 E4
New Malden KT3 ... 182 D2
Buxton Gdns, W3 ... 106 B7
Buxton Ho, SW11 off Maysoule Rd ... 149 G4
Buxton Ms, SW4 ... 150 D2
Buxton Path, Wat. WD19 ... 50 C3
Buxton Rd, E4 ... 46 D7
E6 ... 116 B3
E15 ... 96 E5
E17 ... 77 H4
N19 ... 92 D1
NW2 ... 89 H6
SW14 ... 147 E3
Ilford IG2 ... 81 H6
Thornton Heath CR7 ... 187 H5
Buxton St, E1 ... 13 G6
Buzzard Creek Ind Est, Bark. IG11 ... 117 J5
Byam St, SW6 ... 149 F2
Byards Cft, SW16 ... 186 D1
Byatt Wk, Hmptn. TW12 off Victors Dr ... 161 E6
Bychurch End, Tedd. TW11 off Church Rd ... 162 C5
Bycroft Rd, Sthl. UB1 ... 103 G4
Bycroft St, SE20 off Penge La ... 171 G7
Bycullah Av, Enf. EN2 ... 43 H3
Bycullah Rd, Enf. EN2 ... 43 H3
Bye, The, W3 ... 107 E6
Byegrove Ct, SW19 off Byegrove Rd ... 167 G7
Byegrove Rd, SW19 ... 167 G6
Byeway, The, SW14 ... 146 C3
Bye Way, The, Har. HA3 ... 68 B1
Byeways, Twick. TW2 ... 161 H3
Byeways, The, Surb. KT5 ... 182 A5
Byfeld Gdns, SW13 ... 147 G1
Byfield Cl, SE16 ... 133 H2
Byfield Pas, Islw. TW7 ... 144 D3
Byfield Rd, Islw. TW7 ... 144 D3
Byford Cl, E15 ... 97 E7
Bygrove, Croy. (New Adgtn) CR0 ... 204 B6
Bygrove St, E14 ... 114 B6
Byland Cl, N21 ... 43 F7
Morden SM4 off Bolton Dr ... 185 G7
Bylands Cl, SE2 off Finchale Rd ... 138 B3
SE16 off Rotherhithe St ... 133 G1
Byne Rd, SE26 ... 171 F6
Carshalton SM5 ... 199 H2
Bynes Rd, S.Croy. CR2 ... 202 A7
Byng Pl, WC1 ... 9 H6
Byng Rd, Barn. EN5 ... 40 A3
Byng St, E14 ... 134 A2
Bynon Av, Bexh. DA7 ... 159 E3
Byre, The, N14 ... 42 B6
Byre Rd, N14 ... 42 A6
Byrne Rd, SW12 ... 168 B1
Byron Av, E12 ... 98 B6
E18 ... 79 F3
NW9 ... 70 B4
Borehamwood WD6 ... 38 A5
Hounslow TW4 ... 142 A2
New Malden KT3 ... 183 G5
Sutton SM1 ... 199 G4
Byron Av E, Sutt. SM1 ... 199 G4
Byron Cl, E8 ... 112 D1
SE26 ... 171 H4
SE28 ... 138 C1
SW16 ... 168 E6
Hampton TW12 ... 161 F4
Byron Ct, W9 off Lanhill Rd ... 108 D4
Enfield EN2 ... 43 H2
Harrow HA1 ... 68 B6
Byron Dr, N2 ... 73 G6
Erith DA8 ... 139 H7
Byron Gdns, Sutt. SM1 ... 199 G4
Byron Hill Rd, Har. HA2 ... 86 A1
Byron Ho, Beck. BR3 ... 172 A6
Byron Ms, NW3 ... 91 H5
W9 off Shirland Rd ... 108 D4
Byron Rd, E10 ... 96 B1
E17 ... 78 A3
NW2 ... 89 H2
NW7 ... 55 G5
W5 ... 125 J1
Harrow HA1 ... 68 B6
Harrow (Wealds.) HA3 ... 68 C2
Wembley HA0 ... 87 F3
Byron St, E14 off St. Leonards Rd ... 114 C6
Byron Ter, N9 ... 45 F6
Byron Way, Nthlt. UB5 ... 102 E3
West Drayton UB7 ... 120 C4
Bysouth Cl, N15 ... 76 A4
Ilford IG5 ... 80 E1
By the Wd, Wat. WD19 ... 50 D2
Bythorn St, SW9 ... 151 F3
Byton Rd, SW17 ... 167 J6
Byward Av, Felt. TW14 ... 142 C6
Byward St, EC3 ... 20 E6
Bywater Pl, SE16 ... 133 H1
Bywater St, SW3 ... 31 J3
Byway, The, Epsom KT19 ... 197 F4
Bywell Pl, W1 ... 17 F2
Bywood Av, Croy. CR0 ... 189 F6
Byworth Wk, N19 off Courtauld Rd ... 92 E1

C

Cabbell St, NW1 ... 15 G2
Cabinet Way, E4 ... 61 J6
Cable Pl, SE10 off Diamond Ter ... 154 C1
Cable St, E1 ... 21 H5

Cable Trade Pk, SE7 **135** J4
Cabot Pl, E14 **134** A1
Cabot Sq, E14 **134** A1
Cabot Way, E6 *off Parr Rd* **116** A1
Cabul Rd, SW11 **149** H2
Cactus Cl, SE15 *off Lyndhurst Gro* **152** B2
Cactus Wk, W12 *off Du Cane Rd* **107** F6
Cadbury Cl, Islw. TW7 **144** D1
Cadbury Way, SE16 **29** G6
Caddington Cl, Barn. EN4 **41** H5
Caddington Rd, NW2 **90** B3
Caddis Cl, Stan. HA7 **52** C7
Cadell Cl, E2 **13** G2
Cade Rd, SE10 **154** D1
Cader Rd, SW18 **149** F6
Cadet Dr, SE1 **37** G3
Cadet Pl, SE10 **134** E5
Cadiz Rd, Dag. RM10 **101** J7
Cadiz St, SE17 **36** A4
Cadley Ter, SE23 **171** F2
Cadman Cl, SW9 *off Langton Rd* **131** H7
Cadmer Cl, N.Mal. KT3 **182** E4
Cadmus Cl, SW4 *off Aristotle Rd* **150** D3
Cadnam Pt, SW15 *off Dilton Gdns* **165** H1
Cadogan Cl, E9 *off Cadogan Ter* **95** J7
Beckenham BR3 *off Albemarle Rd* **190** D1
Harrow HA2 **85** H4
Teddington TW11 **162** B5
Cadogan Ct, Sutt. SM2 **199** E6
Cadogan Gdns, E18 **79** H3
N3 **72** E1
N21 **43** G5
SW3 **32** A1
Cadogan Gate, SW1 **32** A1
Cadogan La, SW1 **24** B6
Cadogan Pl, SW1 **24** A5
Cadogan Rd, SE18 **137** F3
Surbiton KT6 **181** G5
Cadogan Sq, SW1 **24** A6
Cadogan St, SW3 **31** J2
Cadogan Ter, E9 **95** J6
Cadoxton Av, N15 **76** C6
Cadwallon Rd, SE9 **175** E2
Caedmon Rd, N7 **93** F4
Caerleon Cl, Esher (Clay.) KT10 **194** E7
Sidcup DA14 **176** C5
Caerleon Ter, SE2 *off Blithdale Rd* **138** B4
Caernarvon Cl, Mitch. CR4 **186** E3
Caernarvon Dr, Ilf. IG5 **80** D1
Caesars Wk, Mitch. CR4 **185** J5
Cahill St, EC1 **12** A6
Cahir St, E14 **134** B4
Cains La, Felt. TW14 **141** H5
Caird St, W10 **108** B3
Cairn Av, W5 **125** G1
Cairncross Ms, N8 *off Felix Av* **75** E6
Cairndale Cl, Brom. BR1 **173** F7
Cairnfield Av, NW2 **89** E3
Cairngorm Cl, Tedd. TW11 *off Vicarage Rd* **162** D5
Cairns Av, Wdf.Grn. IG8 **64** B6
Cairns Ms, SE18 *off Bell St* **156** B1
Cairns Rd, SW11 **149** H5
Cairn Way, Stan. HA7 **52** C6
Cairo New Rd, Croy. CR0 **201** H2
Cairo Rd, E17 **78** A4
Caishowe Rd, Borwd. WD6 **38** B1
Caistor Ms, SW12 *off Caistor Rd* **150** B7
Caistor Pk Rd, E15 **115** F1
Caistor Rd, SW12 **150** B7
Caithness Gdns, Sid. DA15 **157** J6
Caithness Rd, W14 **128** A4
Mitcham CR4 **168** B7
Calabria Rd, N5 **93** H6
Calais Gate, SE5 *off Calais St* **151** H1
Calais St, SE5 **151** H1
Calbourne Rd, SW12 **149** J7
Calcott Wk, SE9 **174** A4
Caldbeck Av, Wor.Pk. KT4 **197** G2
Caldecot Rd, SE5 **151** J2
Caldecott Way, E5 **95** G3
Calder Av, Grnf. (Perivale) UB6 **104** C2
Calder Cl, Enf. EN1 **44** B3
Calder Gdns, Edg. HA8 **70** A3
Calderon Pl, W10 *off St. Quintin Gdns* **107** J5
Calderon Rd, E11 **96** C4
Calder Rd, Mord. SM4 **185** F5
Caldervale Rd, SW4 **150** D5
Calderwood Pl, Barn. EN4 **40** E1
Calderwood St, SE18 **136** D4
Caldicot Grn, NW9 **70** E6
Caldwell Gdns Est, SW9 *off Caldwell St* **151** G1
Caldwell Rd, Wat. WD19 **50** D4
Caldwell St, SW9 **131** F7
Caldy Rd, Belv. DA17 **139** H3
Caldy Wk, N1 *off Clifton Rd* **93** J6
Caleb St, SE1 **27** J3
Caledonian Cl, Ilf. IG3 **100** B1
Caledonian Rd, N1 **10** B2
N7 **93** F5
Caledonian Sq, NW1 *off Canal Boul* **92** D6
Caledonian Wf, E14 **134** D4
Caledonia St, N1 **10** B2
Caledon Rd, E6 **116** B1
Wallington SM6 **200** A4
Cale St, SW3 **31** G3
Caletock Way, SE10 **135** F5
Calico Row, SW11 *off York Pl* **149** F3
Calidore Cl, SW2 **151** F6
California Bldg, SE13 *off Deals Gateway* **154** B1
California La, Bushey (Bushey Hth) WD23 **52** A1
California Rd, N.Mal. KT3 **182** B4
Callaby Ter, N1 *off Wakeham St* **94** A6
Callaghan Cl, SE13 **154** E4
Callander Rd, SE6 **172** B2
Callard Av, N13 **59** H5
Callcott Rd, NW6 **90** C7
Callcott St, W8 *off Hillgate Pl* **128** D1
Callendar Rd, SW7 **22** E5
Callingham Cl, E14 *off Wallwood St* **113** J5
Callis Fm Cl, Stai. (Stanw.) TW19 *off Bedfont Rd* **140** B6
Callisons Pl, SE10 *off Bellot St* **135** E5
Callis Rd, E17 **77** J6
Callow St, SW3 **30** D5
Calmington Rd, SE5 **36** E4
Calmont Rd, Brom. BR1 **172** D6
Calne Av, Ilf. IG5 **80** E1
Calonne Rd, SW19 **166** A4
Calshot Rd, Houns. (Lon.Hthrw Air.) TW6 **140** D2
Calshot St, N1 **10** C1
Calshot Way, Enf. EN2 **43** H3
Hounslow (Lon.Hthrw Air.) TW6 *off Calshot Rd* **140** E2
Calthorpe Gdns, Edg. HA8 *off Jesmond Way* **53** H5
Sutton SM1 **199** F3
Calthorpe St, WC1 **10** D5
Calton Av, SE21 **152** B5
Calton Rd, Barn. (New Barn.) EN5 **41** F6
Calverley Cl, Beck. BR3 **172** B6
Calverley Ct, Epsom KT19 *off Kingston Rd* **196** D4
Calverley Cres, Dag. RM10 **101** G2
Calverley Gdns, Har. HA3 **69** G7
Calverley Gro, N19 **92** D1
Calverley Rd, Epsom KT17 **197** G6
Calvert Av, E2 **13** E4
Calvert Cl, Belv. DA17 **139** G4
Sidcup DA14 **176** E6
Calverton, SE5 **36** C5
Calverton Rd, E6 **116** D1
Calvert Rd, SE10 **135** F5
Barnet EN5 **40** A2
Calvert's Bldgs, SE1 **28** B2
Calvert St, NW1 *off Chalcot Rd* **110** A1
Calvin St, E1 **13** F6
Calydon Rd, SE7 **135** H5
Calypso Cres, SE15 **37** F7
Calypso Way, SE16 **133** J3
Camac Rd, Twick. TW2 **162** A1
Camarthen Grn, NW9 *off Snowdon Dr* **70** E6
Cambalt Rd, SW15 **148** A5
Camberley Av, SW20 **183** H2
Enfield EN1 **44** B4
Camberley Cl, Sutt. SM3 **198** A3
Camberley Rd, Houns. (Lon.Hthrw Air.) TW6 **140** D3
Cambert Way, SE3 **155** H4
CAMBERWELL, SE5 **131** J7
Camberwell Business Cen, SE5 *off Lomond Gro* **132** A7
Camberwell Ch St, SE5 **152** A1
Camberwell Glebe, SE5 **152** A1
Camberwell Grn, SE5 **152** A1
Camberwell Gro, SE5 **152** A1
Camberwell New Rd, SE5 **35** E6
Camberwell Pas, SE5 *off Camberwell New Rd* **151** J1
Camberwell Rd, SE5 **36** A6
Camberwell Sta Rd, SE5 **151** J1
Cambeys Rd, Dag. RM10 **101** H5
Camborne Av, W13 **125** E2
Camborne Cl, Houns. (Lon.Hthrw Air.) TW6 *off Camborne Rd* **140** D3
Camborne Ms, SW18 *off Camborne Rd* **148** D7
W11 *off St. Marks Rd* **108** B6
Camborne Rd, SW18 **148** D7
Croydon CR0 **188** D7
Hounslow (Lon.Hthrw Air.) TW6 **140** D3
Morden SM4 **184** A5
Sidcup DA14 **176** C3
Sutton SM2 **198** D7
Welling DA16 **157** J2
Camborne Way, Houns. TW5 **143** G1
Hounslow (Lon.Hthrw Air.) TW6 *off Camborne Rd* **140** D3
Cambourne Av, N9 **45** G7
Cambray Rd, SW12 **168** C1
Orpington BR6 **193** J7
Cambria Cl, Houns. TW3 **143** G4
Sidcup DA15 **175** G1
Cambria Ct, Felt. TW14 **142** B7
Cambria Gdns, Stai. TW19 **140** B7
Cambria Ho, SE26 *off High Level Dr* **170** D4
Cambrian Av, Ilf. IG2 **81** H5
Cambrian Cl, SE27 **169** H3
Cambrian Grn, NW9 *off Snowdon Dr* **71** E5
Cambrian Rd, E10 **78** A7
Richmond TW10 **145** J6
Cambria Rd, SE5 **151** J3
Cambria St, SW6 **129** E7
Cambridge Av, NW6 **108** D2
Greenford UB6 **86** C5
New Malden KT3 **183** F2
Welling DA16 **157** J4
Cambridge Barracks Rd, SE18 **136** C4
Cambridge Circ, WC2 **17** J4
Cambridge Cl, E17 **77** J6
N22 *off Pellatt Gro* **75** G1
NW10 *off Lawrence Way* **88** C3
SW20 **183** H1
Barnet (E.Barn.) EN4 **58** A1
Hounslow TW4 **143** E4
West Drayton (Harm.) UB7 **120** A6
Cambridge Cotts, Rich. TW9 **126** A6
Cambridge Cres, E2 **112** E2
Teddington TW11 **162** D5
Cambridge Dr, SE12 **155** G5
Ruislip HA4 **84** C2
Cambridge Gdns, N10 **74** A1
N13 **59** G5
N17 *off Great Cambridge Rd* **60** A7
N21 **44** A7
NW6 **108** D2
W10 **108** B6
Enfield EN1 **44** D2
Kingston upon Thames KT1 **182** A2
Cambridge Gate, NW1 **8** E4
Cambridge Gate Ms, NW1 **8** E4
Cambridge Grn, SE9 **174** E1
Cambridge Gro, SE20 **188** E1
W6 **127** H4
Cambridge Gro Rd, Kings.T. KT1 **182** A2
Cambridge Heath Rd, E1 **113** E2
E2 **113** E2
Cambridge Mans, SW11 *off Cambridge Rd* **149** J1
Cambridge Par, Enf. EN1 *off Great Cambridge Rd* **44** D1
Cambridge Pk, E11 **79** G7
Twickenham TW1 **145** G7
Cambridge Pk Rd, E11 *off Cambridge Pk* **79** G7
Cambridge Pl, W8 **22** B4
Cambridge Rd, E4 **62** D1
E11 **79** F6
NW6 **108** D3
SE20 **188** E3
SW11 **149** J1
SW13 **147** F2
SW20 **183** G1
W7 **124** C2
Barking IG11 **99** F7
Bromley BR1 **173** G7
Carshalton SM5 **199** H6
Hampton TW12 **161** F7
Harrow HA2 **67** G5
Hounslow TW4 **143** E4
Ilford IG3 **99** H1
Kingston upon Thames KT1, KT2 **181** J2
Mitcham CR4 **186** C3
New Malden KT3 **182** E4
Richmond TW9 **126** A7
Sidcup DA14 **175** H4
Southall UB1 **123** F1
Teddington TW11 **162** C4
Twickenham TW1 **145** G6
Walton-on-Thames KT12 **178** B6
West Molesey KT8 **179** F4
Cambridge Rd N, W4 **126** B5
Cambridge Rd S, W4 **126** B5
Cambridge Row, SE18 **137** E5
Cambridge Sq, W2 **15** G3
Cambridge St, SW1 **32** E2
Cambridge Ter, N13 **59** G5
NW1 **8** E4
Cambridge Ter Ms, NW1 **8** E4
Cambstone Cl, N11 **58** A2
Cambus Cl, Hayes UB4 **103** E5
Cambus Rd, E16 **115** G5
Camdale Rd, SE18 **137** J7
★ **Camden Arts Cen**, NW3 **91** E5
Camden Av, Felt. TW13 **160** C2
Hayes UB4 **102** C7
Camden Cl, Chis. BR7 **175** F7
Camden Gdns, NW1 *off Kentish Town Rd* **92** B7
Sutton SM1 **198** E5
Thornton Heath CR7 **187** H3
Camden Gro, Chis. BR7 **175** E6
Camden High St, NW1 **110** B1
Camden Hill Rd, SE19 **170** B6
Camdenhurst St, E14 **113** H6
Camden La, N7 *off Rowstock Gdns* **92** D6
★ **Camden Lock Mkt & Waterbuses**, NW1 **92** B7
Camden Lock Pl, NW1 *off Chalk Fm Rd* **92** B7
Camden Ms, NW1 **92** D6
Camden Pk Rd, NW1 **92** D6
Chislehurst BR7 **174** C7
Camden Pas, N1 **11** G1
Camden Rd, E11 **79** H6
E17 **77** J6
N7 **92** D5
NW1 **110** C1
Bexley DA5 **177** F1
Carshalton SM5 **199** J4
Sutton SM1 **198** D5
Camden Row, SE3 **155** E2
Camden Sq, NW1 **92** D6
SE15 *off Watts St* **152** C1
Camden St, NW1 **92** B7
Camden Ter, NW1 *off North Vil* **92** D6
CAMDEN TOWN, NW1 **110** C1
Camden Wk, N1 **111** H1
Camden Way, Chis. BR7 **174** C7
Thornton Heath CR7 **187** H3
Camelford Wk, W11 *off St. Marks Rd* **108** B6
Camel Gro, Kings.T. KT2 **163** G5
Camellia Ct, Wdf.Grn. IG8 *off The Bridle Path* **63** E7
Camellia Ho, Felt. TW13 *off Tilley Rd* **160** B1
Camellia Pl, Twick. TW2 **143** H7
Camellia St, SW8 *off Hartington Rd* **130** E7
Camelot Cl, SE28 **137** G2
SW19 **166** D4
Camelot Ho, NW1 *off Camden Pk Rd* **92** D6

Camelot St, SE15
  off Bird in Bush Rd . .132 E7
Camel Rd, E16 . . . . .136 A1
Camera PI, SW10 . . . . . . .30 E6
Cameron CI, N18 . . . . . . .60 E4
  N20 off Myddelton Pk . .57 H2
Cameron Ho, SE5
  off Comber Gro 131 J7
Cameron PI, E1
  off Varden St 113 E6
  SW16 . . . . .169 G2
Cameron Rd, SE6 . . . . . .171 J2
  Bromley BR2 . . . . .191 G4
  Croydon CR0 . . . . .187 H6
  Ilford IG3 . . . . .99 H1
Cameron Sq, Mitch.
  CR4 . . . . .185 H1
Camerton CI, E8
  off Buttermere Wk 94 C6
Camgate Cen, Stai.
  (Stanw.)TW19 . . . . . . .140 C6
Camilla Rd, SE16 . . . . . .132 E4
Camille CI, SE25 . . . . . . .188 D3
Camlan Rd, Brom. BR1 . .173 F4
Camlet St, E2 . . . . .13 F5
Camlet Way, Barn. EN4 . . .40 D2
Camley St, NW1 . . . . .9 J1
★ Camley St Natural Pk,
  NW1 . . . . .9 J1
Camm Gdns, Kings.T. KT1
  off Church Rd 181 J2
  Thames Ditton KT7 . . .180 B7
Camms Ter, Dag. RM10 . .101 J5
Camomile Av, Mitch.
  CR4 . . . . .185 J1
Camomile St, EC3 . . . . . . .20 D3
Campana Rd, SW6 . . . . . .148 D1
Campbell Av, Ilf. IG6 . . . . .81 F4
Campbell CI, SE18
  off Moordown 156 D1
  SW16 . . . . .168 D4
  Ruislip HA4 . . . . .66 A6
  Twickenham TW2 . . . . .162 A2
Campbell Ct, N17 . . . . . . .76 C1
  SE22 off Lordship La . .152 D7
Campbell Cft, Edg. HA8 . . .54 A5
Campbell Gordon Way,
  NW2 . . . . .89 H4
Campbell Rd, E3 . . . . . . .114 A3
  E6 . . . . .116 B1
  E15 offTrevelyan Rd . . .97 F4
  E17 . . . . .77 J4
  N17 . . . . .76 D1
  W7 . . . . .104 B7
  Croydon CR0 . . . . .187 H7
  East Molesey KT8
    off Hampton Ct Rd . .180 A7
  Twickenham TW2 . . . . .162 A2
Campbell Wk, N1
  off Outram PI 111 E1
Campdale Rd, N7 . . . . . . .92 D3
Campden Cres, Dag.
  RM8 . . . . .100 B4
  Wembley HA0 . . . . .87 E2
Campden Gro, W8 . . . . . .128 D2
Campden Hill, W8 . . . . . .128 D2
Campden Hill Gdns, W8 . .128 D1
Campden Hill Gate, W8
  off Duchess of
    Bedford's Wk 128 D2
Campden Hill PI, W11
  off Holland Pk Av 128 C1
Campden Hill Rd, W8 . . . .128 C1
Campden Hill Sq, W8 . . . .128 C1
Campden Hill Twrs, W11
  off Notting Hill Gate . .128 D1
Campden Ho CI, W8
  off Hornton St 128 D2
Campden Ho, S.Croy.
  CR2 . . . . .202 B5
Campden St, W8 . . . . . . .128 D1
Campden Way, Dag. RM8
  off Campden Cres 100 B4
Campen CI, SW19 . . . . . .166 B2
Camperdown St, E1 . . . . . .21 G4
Campfield Rd, SE9 . . . . . .156 A7
Campion CI, E6 . . . . .116 C7
  Croydon CR0 . . . . .202 B4
  Harrow HA3 . . . . .69 J6
Campion Ct, Wem. HA0
  off Elmore St 105 H2
Campion Gdns, Wdf.Grn.
  IG8 . . . . .63 G5
Campion PI, SE28 . . . . . .138 B1
Campion Rd, SW15 . . . . .147 J4
  Isleworth TW7 . . . . . . .144 C1
Campion Ter, NW2 . . . . . .90 A3
Campion Way, Edg. HA8 . . .54 C4
Camplin Rd, Har. HA3 . . . .69 H5
Camplin St, SE14 . . . . . .133 G7
Camp Rd, SW19 . . . . . . .165 H5

Campsbourne, The, N8
  off High St 75 E4
Campsbourne Rd, N8 . . . .75 E3
Campsey Gdns, Dag.
  RM9 . . . . .100 B7
Campsey Rd, Dag. RM9 . .100 B7
Campsfield Rd, N8 . . . . . .75 E3
Campshill PI, SE13
  off Campshill Rd 154 C5
Campshill Rd, SE13 . . . . .154 C5
Campus Rd, E17 . . . . .77 J6
Campus Way, NW4
  off Greyhound Hill 71 H3
Camp Vw, SW19 . . . . . . .165 H5
Cam Rd, E15 . . . . .114 D1
Camrose Av, Edg. HA8 . . . .69 J1
  Erith DA8 . . . . .139 H6
  Feltham TW13 . . . . . . .160 B4
Camrose CI, Croy. CR0 . .189 H7
  Morden SM4 . . . . .184 D4
Camrose St, SE2 . . . . . . .138 A5
Canada Av, N18 . . . . .59 J6
Canada Cres, W3 . . . . . . .106 C5
Canada Est, SE16 . . . . . .133 F3
Canada Gdns, SE13 . . . . .154 C5
Canada Rd, W3 . . . . .106 C4
Canada Sq, E14 . . . . .134 B1
Canada St, SE16 . . . . . . .133 G2
Canada Way, W12 . . . . . .107 H7
Canadian Av, SE6 . . . . . .172 B1
Canal App, SE8 . . . . .133 H6
Canal Boul, NW1 . . . . .92 D6
Canal CI, E1 . . . . .113 H4
  W10 . . . . .108 A4
Canal Gro, SE15 . . . . .37 J5
Canal Path, E2 . . . . .112 C1
Canal St, SE5 . . . . .36 B6
Canal Wk, N1 . . . . .12 A1
  NW10 off West End CI . .88 C7
  SE26 . . . . .171 F5
  Croydon CR0 . . . . .188 B6
Canal Way, N1 . . . . .12 A1
  NW1 . . . . .7 H3
  NW8 . . . . .7 G4
  NW10 . . . . .107 H4
  W2 . . . . .14 B1
  W9
    off Great Western Rd .108 C3
  W10 . . . . .108 A4
Canal Way Wk, W10 . . . . .108 A4
Canberra CI, NW4 . . . . . . .71 G3
  Dagenham RM10 . . . . .101 J7
  Dagenham RM10 . . . . .101 J7
Canberra Dr, Hayes UB4 .102 C3
  Northolt UB5 . . . . .102 C3
Canberra Rd, E6
  off Barking Rd 116 C1
  SE7 . . . . .135 J6
  W13 . . . . .124 D1
  Bexleyheath DA7 . . . . .138 D6
  Hounslow
    (Lon.Hthrw Air.)TW6 .140 D3
Canbury Av, Kings.T.
  KT2 . . . . .181 J1
Canbury Business Pk,
  Kings.T. KT2
    off Elm Cres 181 H1
Canbury Ms, SE26
  off Wells Pk Rd 170 D3
Canbury Pk Rd, Kings.T.
  KT2 . . . . .181 H1
Canbury Pas, Kings.T.
  KT2 . . . . .181 G1
Cancell Rd, SW9 . . . . . . .151 G1
Candahar Rd, SW11 . . . . .149 H2
Candle Gro, SE15 . . . . . .153 E3
Candlemakers Apts,
  SW11 offYork Rd 149 G3
Candler St, N15 . . . . .76 A6
Candover CI, West Dr.
  (Harm.) UB7 . . . . .120 A7
Candover St, W1 . . . . .17 F2
Candy St, E3 . . . . .113 J1
Caney Ms, NW2
  off Claremont Rd 90 A2
Canfield Dr, Ruis. HA4 . . . .84 B5
Canfield Gdns, NW6 . . . . . .91 F7
Canfield PI, NW6
  off Canfield Gdns 91 H7
Canfield Rd, Wdf.Grn.
  IG8 . . . . .64 B7
Canford Av, Nthlt. UB5 . . .103 E1
Canford CI, Enf. EN2 . . . . .43 G2
Canford Gdns, N.Mal.
  KT3 . . . . .182 D6
Canford PI, Tedd. TW11 . .163 E6
Canford Rd, SW11 . . . . . .150 A5
Canham Rd, SE25 . . . . . .188 B3
  W3 . . . . .126 E2
Canmore Gdns, SW16 . . .168 C7
Cann Hall Rd, E11 . . . . . . .96 E4
Canning Cres, N22 . . . . . . .75 F1
Canning Cross, SE5 . . . . .152 B2
Canning Pas, W8 . . . . .22 C5
Canning PI, W8 . . . . .22 C5

Canning PI Ms, W8 . . . . . .22 C4
Canning Rd, E15 . . . . . . .114 E2
  E17 . . . . .77 H4
  N5 . . . . .93 H3
  Croydon CR0 . . . . .202 C2
  Harrow HA3 . . . . .68 C3
Cannington Rd, Dag.
  RM9 . . . . .100 C6
CANNING TOWN, E16 . . . .115 G6
Canning Town, E16 . . . . . .115 E5
Cannizaro Rd, SW19 . . . .165 J6
Cannonbury Av, Pnr.
  HA5 . . . . .66 D6
Cannon CI, SW20 . . . . . . .183 J3
  Hampton TW12
    off Hanworth Rd 161 H6
Cannon Ct, EC1
  off Brewhouse Yd 11 H5
Cannon Dr, E14 . . . . .114 A7
Cannon Hill, N14 . . . . .58 D3
  NW6 . . . . .90 D5
Cannon Hill La, SW20 . . .184 B3
Cannon La, NW3 . . . . .91 G3
  Pinner HA5 . . . . .84 E1
Cannon PI, NW3 . . . . .91 G3
  SE7 . . . . .136 B5
Cannon Rd, N14 . . . . .58 D3
  Bexleyheath DA7 . . . . .159 E1
Cannon St, EC4 . . . . .19 J4
Cannon St Rd, E1 . . . . . . .112 E6
Cannon Trd Est, Wem.
  HA9 . . . . .88 B4
Cannon Way, W.Mol.
  KT8 . . . . .179 G4
Cannon Wf Business Cen,
  SE8 . . . . .133 H4
Cannon Workshops, E14
  off Cannon Dr 114 A7
Canon All, EC4
  off St. Paul's Chyd 19 H4
Canon Av, Rom. RM6 . . . . .82 C5
Canon Beck Rd, SE16 . . .133 F2
Canonbie Rd, SE23 . . . . .153 F7
CANONBURY, N1 . . . . .93 J6
Canonbury Cres, N1 . . . . . .93 J7
Canonbury Gro, N1 . . . . . .93 J7
Canonbury La, N1 . . . . . . .93 H7
Canonbury Pk N, N1 . . . . . .93 J6
Canonbury Pk S, N1 . . . . . .93 J6
Canonbury PI, N1 . . . . .93 H6
Canonbury Rd, N1 . . . . . . .93 H6
  Enfield EN1 . . . . .44 B1
Canonbury Sq, N1 . . . . . . .93 H7
Canonbury St, N1 . . . . .93 J7
Canonbury Vil, N1 . . . . . . .93 H7
Canonbury Yd, N1
  off New N Rd 111 J1
Canonbury Yd W, N1
  off Compton Rd 93 H6
Canon Mohan CI, N14
  off Farm La 42 B6
Canon Rd, Brom. BR1 . . .191 J3
Canon Row, SW1 . . . . .26 A4
Canons CI, N2 . . . . .73 G7
  Edgware HA8 . . . . .53 J6
Canons Cor, Edg. HA8 . . . .53 H4
Canons Ct, Edg. HA8 . . . . .53 J6
Canons Dr, Edg. HA8 . . . . .53 H6
Canonsleigh Rd, Dag.
  RM9 . . . . .100 B7
CANONS PARK, Edg.
  HA8 . . . . .53 H7
Canons Pk CI, Edg. HA8
  off Donnefield Av 53 H7
Canon St, N1 . . . . .111 J1
Canons Wk, Croy. CR0 . .203 G3
Canopus Way, Nthwd.
  HA6 . . . . .50 A4
  Staines TW19 . . . . . . .140 B7
Canrobert St, E2 . . . . . . .112 E3
Cantelowes Rd, NW1 . . . . .92 D6
Canterbury Av, Ilf. IG1 . . . .80 B7
  Sidcup DA15 . . . . .176 C2
Canterbury CI, E6
  off Harper Rd 116 C6
  Beckenham BR3 . . . . . .190 B1
  Chigwell IG7 . . . . .65 J3
  Greenford UB6 . . . . . . .103 H6
  Worcester Park KT4 . . .198 A2
Canterbury Cres, SW9 . . .151 G3
Canterbury Gro, SE27 . . .169 H3
Canterbury Ho, E3
  off Bow Rd 114 B3
  SE1 . . . . .26 D5
  Borehamwood WD6 . . . .38 A2
Canterbury PI, SE17 . . . . . .35 H2
Canterbury Rd, E10 . . . . . .78 C7
  NW6 . . . . .108 D2
  Borehamwood WD6 . . . .38 A2
  Croydon CR0 . . . . .187 F7
  Feltham TW13 . . . . . . .161 E3
  Harrow HA1, HA2 . . . . . .67 H5
  Morden SM4 . . . . .185 F5

Canterbury Ter, NW6 . . . .108 D2
Cantium Retail Pk, SE1 . . .37 H5
Cantley Gdns, SE19 . . . . .188 C1
  Ilford IG2 . . . . .81 F6
Cantley Rd, W7 . . . . .124 D3
Canton St, E14 . . . . .114 A6
Cantrell Rd, E3 . . . . .113 J4
Cantwell Rd, SE18 . . . . . .136 E7
Canute Gdns, SE16 . . . . .133 G4
Canvey St, SE1 . . . . .27 H1
Cape CI, Bark. IG11
  off North St 99 E6
Cape Rd, N17
  off High Cross Rd 76 D3
Capel Av, Wall. SM6 . . . . .201 F5
Capel CI, N20 . . . . .57 F3
  Bromley BR2 . . . . .206 B1
Capel Ct, EC2 . . . . .20 C4
  SE20 . . . . .189 F1
Capel Cres, Stan. HA7 . . . .52 D2
Capel Gdns, Ilf. IG3 . . . . . .99 J4
  Pinner HA5 . . . . .67 F4
Capel Pt, E7 . . . . .97 H4
Capel Rd, E7 . . . . .97 H4
  E12 . . . . .97 J4
  Barnet EN4 . . . . .41 H6
Capener's CI, SW1 . . . . . . .24 B4
Capern Rd, SW18
  off Cargill Rd 167 F1
Capital Business Cen,
  Mitch. CR4 . . . . .185 J5
  Wembley HA0 . . . . .105 G2
Capital Business Pk,
  Borwd. WD6 . . . . .38 C3
Capital E Apts, E16
  off Western Gateway .115 G7
Capital Interchange Way,
  Brent. TW8 . . . . .126 A5
Capitol Ind Pk, NW9 . . . . . .70 C3
Capitol Way, NW9 . . . . . . .70 C3
Capland St, NW8 . . . . .7 F5
Caple Par, NW10
  off Harley Rd 106 E2
Caple Rd, NW10 . . . . .107 F2
Capper St, WC1 . . . . .9 G6
Caprea CI, Hayes UB4
  offTriandra Way 102 D5
Capri Rd, Croy. CR0 . . . . .202 C1
Capstan CI, Rom. RM6 . . . .82 B6
Capstan Ride, Enf. EN2 . . .43 G2
Capstan Rd, SE8 . . . . . . .133 J4
Capstan Sq, E14 . . . . . . .134 C2
Capstan Way, SE16 . . . . .133 H1
Capstone Rd, Brom. BR1 .173 F4
Capthorne Av, Har. HA2 . . .85 E1
Capuchin CI, Stan. HA7 . . .52 E6
Capulet Ms, E16
  off Hanover Av 135 G1
Capulet Sq, E3
  offTalwin St 114 B3
Capworth St, E10 . . . . .96 A1
Caradoc CI, W2 . . . . .108 D6
Caradoc St, SE10 . . . . . . .134 E5
Caradon CI, E11 . . . . .97 E1
Caradon Way, N15 . . . . . . .76 A4
Caravel CI, E14
  offTiller Rd 134 A3
Caravelle Gdns, Nthlt. UB5
  off Javelin Way 102 D3
Caravel Ms, SE8
  off Watergate St 134 A6
Caraway CI, E13 . . . . .115 H5
Caraway PI, Wall. SM6 . . .200 B3
Carberry Rd, SE19 . . . . . .170 B6
Carbery Av, W3 . . . . .125 J2
Carbis CI, E4 . . . . .62 D1
Carbis Rd, E14 . . . . .113 J6
Carbuncle Pas Way, N17 . . .76 D2
Carburton St, W1 . . . . .17 E1
Cardale St, E14
  off Plevna St 134 C3
Carden Rd, SE15 . . . . . . .152 E3
Cardiff Rd, W7 . . . . .124 D3
  Enfield EN3 . . . . .45 E4
Cardiff St, SE18 . . . . .137 H7
Cardigan Gdns, Ilf. IG3 . .100 A2
Cardigan Rd, E3 . . . . .113 J2
  SW13 . . . . .147 G2
  SW19 off Haydons Rd .167 F6
  Richmond TW10 . . . . . .145 H6
Cardigan St, SE11 . . . . . . .34 E3
Cardigan Wk, N1
  off Ashby Gro 93 J7
Cardinal Av, Borwd.
  WD6 . . . . .38 B3
  Kingston upon Thames
    KT2 . . . . .163 H5
  Morden SM4 . . . . .184 B6
Cardinal Bourne St,
  SE1 . . . . .28 C6
Cardinal Cap All, SE1
  off New Globe Wk 19 J6

Cardinal Cl, Chis. BR7 193 G1
Edgware HA8 *off Abbots Rd* 54 D7
Morden SM4 184 B7
Worcester Park KT4 197 G4
Cardinal Ct, Borwd. WD6 *off Cardinal Av* 38 B3
Cardinal Cres, N.Mal. KT3 182 C2
Cardinal Dr, Ilf. IG6 65 F6
Cardinal Hinsley Cl, NW10 107 G2
Cardinal Pl, SW15 148 A4
Cardinal Rd, Felt. TW13 160 B1
Ruislip HA4 84 D1
Cardinals Wk, Hmptn. TW12 161 J7
Cardinals Way, N19 92 D1
Cardinal Wk, SW1 *off Palace St* 25 F5
Cardinal Way, Har. HA3 68 B3
Cardine Ms, SE15 132 E7
Cardington Sq, Houns. TW4 142 D4
Cardington St, NW1 9 F3
Cardinham Rd, Orp. BR6 207 J4
Cardozo Rd, N7 93 E5
Cardrew Av, N12 57 G5
Cardrew Cl, N12 57 G5
Cardross St, W6 127 H3
Cardwell Rd, N7 92 E4
Carew Cl, N7 93 F2
Carew Rd, N17 76 D2
W13 125 F2
Mitcham CR4 186 A2
Thornton Heath CR7 187 H3
Wallington SM6 200 C6
Carew St, SE5 151 J2
Carew Way, Wat. WD19 51 F3
Carey Ct, Bexh. DA6 159 H5
Carey Gdns, SW8 150 C1
Carey La, EC2 19 J3
Carey Pl, SW1 33 H2
Carey Rd, Dag. RM9 101 E4
Carey St, WC2 18 D4
Carey Way, Wem. HA9 88 B4
Carfax Pl, SW4 *off Holwood Pl* 150 D4
Carfax Rd, Hayes UB3 121 J5
Carfree Cl, N1 *off Bewdley St* 93 G7
Cargill Rd, SW18 167 E1
Cargreen Pl, SE25 *off Cargreen Rd* 188 C4
Cargreen Rd, SE25 188 C4
Carholme Rd, SE23 171 J1
Carisbrook Cl, Enf. EN1 44 C1
Carisbrooke Av, Bex. DA5 176 D1
Carisbrooke Cl, Houns. TW4 *off Farm Rd* 161 E1
Stanmore HA7 69 G2
Carisbrooke Gdns, SE15 37 G7
Carisbrooke Ho, Kings.T. KT2 *off Kingsgate Rd* 181 H1
Carisbrooke Rd, E17 77 H4
Bromley BR2 191 J4
Mitcham CR4 186 D4
Carker's La, NW5 92 B5
Carleton Cl, Esher KT10 194 A1
Carleton Rd, N7 92 D5
Carlile Cl, E3 113 J2
Carlina Gdns, Wdf.Grn. IG8 63 H5
Carlingford Gdns, Mitch. CR4 167 J7
Carlingford Rd, N15 75 H3
NW3 91 G4
Morden SM4 184 A6
Carlisle Av, EC3 21 E4
W3 106 E6
Carlisle Cl, Kings.T. KT2 182 A1
Pinner HA5 66 E7
Carlisle Gdns, Har. HA3 69 G7
Ilford IG1 80 B6
Carlisle La, SE1 26 D6
Carlisle Ms, NW8 15 F1
Carlisle Pl, N11 58 B4
SW1 25 F6
Carlisle Rd, E10 96 A2
N4 75 G7
NW6 108 B1
NW9 70 C3
Hampton TW12 161 H7
Sutton SM1 198 C5
Carlisle St, W1 17 H4
Carlisle Wk, E8 *off Cumberland Cl* 94 C6
Carlisle Way, SW17 168 A5
Carlos Pl, W1 16 C6
Carlow St, NW1 9 F1
Carlton Av, N14 42 D5
Feltham TW14 142 C6
Harrow HA3 68 E5
Hayes UB3 121 H4
South Croydon CR2 202 B7
Carlton Av E, Wem. HA9 87 H1
Carlton Av W, Wem. HA0 86 E2
Carlton Cl, NW3 90 D2
Borehamwood WD6 38 D4
Chessington KT9 195 G6
Edgware HA8 54 A5
Northolt UB5 *off Whitton Av W* 85 J5
Carlton Ct, SW9 151 H1
Ilford IG6 81 G3
Carlton Cres, Sutt. SM3 198 B4
Carlton Dr, SW15 148 B5
Ilford IG6 81 G3
Carlton Gdns, SW1 25 H2
W5 105 F6
Carlton Gro, SE15 152 E1
Carlton Hill, NW8 109 E2
Carlton Ho, Felt. TW14 141 J7
Carlton Ho Ter, SW1 25 H2
Carlton Pk Av, SW20 183 J2
Carlton Rd, E11 97 F1
E12 98 A4
E17 77 H1
N4 75 G7
N11 58 A5
SW14 146 C3
W4 126 D2
W5 105 F7
Erith DA8 139 H6
New Malden KT3 182 E2
Sidcup DA14 175 J5
South Croydon CR2 202 A6
Walton-on-Thames KT12 178 B7
Welling DA16 158 B3
Carlton Sq, E1 *off Argyle Rd* 113 G4
Carlton St, SW1 17 H6
Carlton Ter, E11 79 H5
N18 60 A3
SE26 171 F3
Carlton Twr Pl, SW1 24 A5
Carlton Vale, NW6 108 E2
Carlton Vil, SW15 *off St. John's Av* 148 A5
Carlwell St, SW17 167 H5
Carlyle Av, Brom. BR1 192 A3
Southall UB1 103 F7
Carlyle Cl, N2 73 F6
West Molesey KT8 179 H2
Carlyle Ct, SW10 *off Chelsea Harbour* 149 F1
Carlyle Gdns, Sthl. UB1 103 F7
Carlyle Lo, Barn. (New Barn.) EN5 *off Richmond Rd* 41 F5
Carlyle Ms, E1 *off Alderney Rd* 113 G4
Carlyle Pl, SW15 148 A4
Carlyle Rd, E12 98 B4
NW10 106 D1
SE28 118 B7
W5 125 F5
Croydon CR0 202 D2
★ **Carlyle's Ho**, SW3 31 G6
Carlyle Sq, SW3 31 F4
Carly Ms, E2 13 H4
Carlyon Av, Har. HA2 85 F4
Carlyon Cl, Wem. HA0 105 H1
Carlyon Rd, Hayes UB4 102 C6
Wembley HA0 105 H2
Carlys Cl, Beck. BR3 189 G2
Carmalt Gdns, SW15 147 J4
Carmarthen Pl, SE1 28 D3
Carmel Ct, W8 22 A3
Wembley HA9 88 B2
Carmelite Cl, Har. HA3 67 J1
Carmelite Rd, Har. HA3 67 J1
Carmelite St, EC4 19 F5
Carmelite Wk, Har. HA3 67 J1
Carmelite Way, Har. HA3 67 J2
Carmel Way, Rich. TW9 146 B2
Carmen St, E14 114 B6
Carmichael Cl, SW11 *off Darien Rd* 149 G3
Ruislip HA4 84 A4
Carmichael Ms, SW18 149 G7
Carmichael Rd, SE25 188 D5
Carminia Rd, SW17 168 B2
Carnaby St, W1 17 F4
Carnac St, SE27 170 A4
Carnanton Rd, E17 78 D1
Carnarvon Av, Enf. EN1 44 C3
Carnarvon Dr, Hayes UB3 121 F3
Carnarvon Rd, E10 78 C6
E15 97 F6
E18 79 F1
Barnet EN5 40 B3
Carnation St, SE2 138 B5
Carnbrook Ms, SE3 *off Carnbrook Rd* 156 A3
Carnbrook Rd, SE3 156 A3
Carnecke Gdns, SE9 156 B5
Carnegie Cl, Surb. KT6 *off Fullers Av* 195 J2
Carnegie Pl, SW19 166 A3
Carnegie St, N1 111 F1
Carnforth Cl, Epsom KT19 196 B6
Carnforth Rd, SW16 168 D7
Carnie Lo, SW17 *off Manville Rd* 168 B3
Carnoustie Cl, SE28 118 D6
Carnoustie Dr, N1 93 F7
Carnwath Rd, SW6 148 D3
Carol Cl, NW4 72 A4
Carolina Cl, E15 96 E5
Carolina Rd, Th.Hth. CR7 187 H2
Caroline Cl, N10 *off Alexandra Pk Rd* 74 B2
SW16 169 F3
W2 14 B6
Croydon CR0 202 B4
Isleworth TW7 124 A7
West Drayton UB7 120 A2
Caroline Ct, Stan. HA7 *off The Chase* 52 D6
Caroline Gdns, SE15 132 E7
Caroline Pl, SW11 150 A2
W2 14 B5
Hayes (Harling.) UB3 121 H7
Caroline Pl Ms, W2 14 B6
Caroline Rd, SW19 166 C7
Caroline St, E1 113 G6
Caroline Ter, SW1 32 B2
Caroline Wk, W6 128 B6
Carol St, NW1 110 C1
Carolyn Ho, Croy. CR0 *off Dingwall Rd* 202 A2
Carpenders Av, Wat. WD19 50 E3
CARPENDERS PARK, Wat. WD19 51 F2
Carpenter Gdns, N21 59 H2
Carpenters Arms Path, SE9 *off Eltham High St* 156 C6
Carpenters Business Pk, E15 96 A7
Carpenters Cl, Barn. EN5 41 E6
Carpenters Ct, Twick. TW2 162 B2
Carpenters Ms, N7 *off North Rd* 93 E5
Carpenters Pl, SW4 150 D4
Carpenters Rd, E15 96 A6
Carpenter St, W1 16 D6
Carrara Cl, SW9 *off Eaton Dr* 151 H4
Carrara Ms, E8 94 D6
Carrara Wf, SW6 148 B3
Carr Cl, Stan. HA7 52 D6
Carre Ms, SE5 *off Calais St* 151 H1
Carr Gro, SE18 136 B4
Carriage Dr E, SW11 32 B7
Carriage Dr N, SW11 32 C6
Carriage Dr S, SW11 149 J1
Carriage Dr W, SW11 129 J7
Carriage Ms, Ilf. IG1 99 F2
Carriage Pl, N16 94 A3
SW16 168 C5
Carriage St, SE18 137 E3
Carrick Cl, Islw. TW7 144 D3
Carrick Dr, Ilf. IG6 81 F1
Carrick Gdns, N17 *off Flexmere Rd* 60 B7
Carrick Ms, SE8 *off Watergate St* 134 A6
Carrill Way, Belv. DA17 138 D4
Carrington Av, Borwd. WD6 38 B5
Hounslow TW3 143 H5
Carrington Cl, Barn. (Arkley) EN5 39 G5
Borehamwood WD6 38 C5
Croydon CR0 189 H7
Kingston upon Thames KT2 164 C5
Carrington Gdns, E7 *off Woodford Rd* 97 G4
Carrington Rd, Rich. TW10 146 A4
Carrington Sq, Har. HA3 51 J7
Carrington St, W1 24 D2
Carrol Cl, NW5 92 B4
Carroll Cl, E15 97 F5
Carroll Hill, Loug. IG10 48 C3
Carronade Ct, N7 *off Eden Gro* 93 F5
Carronade Pl, SE28 137 F3
Carron Cl, E14 114 B6
Carroun Rd, SW8 34 C7
Carroway La, Grnf. UB6 *off Cowgate Rd* 104 A3
Carrow Rd, Dag. RM9 100 B7
Carr Rd, E17 77 J2
Northolt UB5 85 G6
Carrs La, N21 43 J5
Carr St, E14 113 H5
CARSHALTON, SM5 199 G4
Carshalton Gro, Sutt. SM1 199 G4
Carshalton Pk Rd, Cars. SM5 199 J5
Carshalton Pl, Cars. SM5 200 A4
Carshalton Rd, Cars. SM5 199 F5
Mitcham CR4 186 A4
Sutton SM1 199 F5
Carslake Rd, SW15 147 J6
Carson Rd, E16 115 G4
SE21 169 J2
Barnet (Cockfos.) EN4 41 J4
Carstairs Rd, SE6 172 C3
Carston Cl, SE12 155 F5
Carswell Cl, Ilf. IG4 *off Roding La S* 80 A4
Carswell Rd, SE6 154 C7
Carter Cl, NW9 70 D6
Wallington SM6 200 D7
Carteret St, SW1 25 H4
Carteret Way, SE8 133 H4
Carterhatch La, Enf. EN1 44 D2
Carterhatch Rd, Enf. EN3 45 F2
Carter La, EC4 19 H4
Carter Pl, SE17 36 A4
Carter Rd, E13 115 H1
SW19 167 G6
Carters Cl, Wor.Pk. KT4 198 A2
Carters Hill Cl, SE9 173 J1
Carters La, SE23 171 H2
Carter St, SE17 35 J5
Carters Yd, SW18 *off Wandsworth High St* 148 D5
Carthew Rd, W6 127 H3
Carthew Vil, W6 127 H3
Carthusian St, EC1 19 J1
Cartier Circle, E14 134 B1
Carting La, WC2 18 B6
Cart La, E4 46 D7
Cartmel, NW1 9 F3
Cartmel Cl, N17 *off Heybourne Rd* 61 E7
Cartmel Gdns, Mord. SM4 185 F5
Cartmel Rd, Bexh. DA7 159 G1
Carton St, W1 16 A3
Cartridge Pl, SE18 137 E3
Cartwright Gdns, WC1 10 A4
Cartwright Rd, Dag. RM9 101 F7
Cartwright St, E1 21 G5
Cartwright Way, SW13 127 H7
Carver Cl, W4 126 C3
Carver Rd, SE24 151 J6
Carville Cres, Brent. TW8 125 H4
Cary Rd, E11 97 E4
Carysfort Rd, N8 74 D5
N16 94 A3
Casby Ho, SE16 29 H5
Cascade Av, N10 74 C4
Cascade Cl, Buck.H. IG9 *off Cascade Rd* 64 A2
Cascade Rd, Buck.H. IG9 64 A2
Cascades Twr, E14 133 J1
Casella Rd, SE14 133 G7
Casewick Rd, SE27 169 H4
Casey Cl, NW8 7 G4
Casimir Rd, E5 95 E3
Casino Av, SE24 151 J5
Caspian St, SE5 36 B7
Caspian Wk, E16 116 A6
Caspian Wf, E3 *off Violet Rd* 114 B5
Cassandra Cl, Nthlt. UB5 86 A4
Casselden Rd, NW10 88 D7
Cassidy Rd, SW6 128 D7
Cassilda Rd, SE2 138 A4
Cassilis Rd, E14 134 A2
Twickenham TW1 145 E5
Cassiobury Av, Felt. TW14 141 J6
Cassiobury Rd, E17 77 G5
Cassis Ct, Loug. IG10 49 F4
Cassland Rd, E9 95 F7
Thornton Heath CR7 188 A4
Casslee Rd, SE6 153 J7
Casson St, E1 21 H2
Castalia Sq, E14 *off Roserton St* 134 C2

Castalia St, E14 *off Plevna St* **134** C2
Castellain Rd, W9 **6** C6
Castellane Cl, Stan. HA7 *off Daventer Dr* **52** C7
Castello Av, SW15 **147** J5
Castell Rd, Loug. IG10 **49** F1
CASTELNAU, SW13 **127** G6
Castelnau, SW13 **127** H6
Castelnau Gdns, SW13 *off Arundel Ter* **127** H6
Castelnau Pl, SW13 *off Castelnau* **127** H6
Castelnau Row, SW13 *off Lonsdale Rd* **127** H6
Casterbridge, NW6 **109** E1
Casterbridge Rd, SE3 **155** G3
Casterton St, E8 *off Wilton Way* **95** E6
Castile Rd, SE18 **136** D4
Castillon Rd, SE6 **172** E2
Castlands Rd, SE6 **171** J2
Castle Av, E4 **62** D5
Castlebar Hill, W5 **105** E5
Castlebar Ms, W5 **105** F5
Castlebar Pk, W5 **105** E4
Castlebar Rd, W5 **105** F5
Castle Baynard St, EC4 **19** H5
Castlebrook Cl, SE11 **35** G1
Castle Cl, E9 *off Swinnerton St* **95** H5
SW19 **166** A3
W3 **126** B2
Bromley BR2 **190** E3
Castlecombe Dr, SW19 **148** A7
Castlecombe Rd, SE9 **174** B4
Castle Ct, EC3 **20** C4
SE26 *off Champion Rd* **171** H4
SW15 **148** B3
Castledine Rd, SE20 **170** E7
Castle Dr, Ilf. IG4 **80** B6
Castleford Av, SE9 **174** E1
Castleford Cl, N17 **60** C6
Castlegate, Rich. TW9 **145** J3
Castlehaven Rd, NW1 **92** B7
Castle La, SW1 **25** G5
Castleleigh Ct, Enf. EN2 **44** A5
Castlemaine Av, S.Croy. CR2 **202** C5
Castlemaine Twr, SW11 **149** J1
Castlemain St, E1 **112** E5
Castlemead, SE5 **131** J7
Castle Ms, N12 *off Castle Rd* **57** F5
NW1 *off Castle Rd* **92** B6
SW17 **167** H4
Hampton TW12 *off Station Rd* **179** H1
Castle Par, Epsom KT17 *off Ewell Bypass* **197** G7
Castle Pl, NW1 **92** B6
W4 *off Windmill Rd* **126** E4
Castle Pt, E13 **115** J2
Castlereagh St, W1 **15** H3
Castle Rd, N12 **57** F5
NW1 **92** B6
Dagenham RM9 **118** B1
Enfield EN3 **45** H1
Isleworth TW7 **144** C2
Northolt UB5 **85** H6
Southall UB2 **123** F3
Castle St, E6 **115** J2
Kingston upon Thames KT1 **181** H2
Castleton Av, Wem. HA9 **87** H4
Castleton Cl, Croy. CR0 **189** H6
Castleton Gdns, Wem. HA9 **87** H3
Castleton Rd, E17 **78** D2
SE9 **174** A4
Ilford IG3 **100** A1
Mitcham CR4 **186** D4
Ruislip HA4 **84** D1
Castletown Rd, W14 **128** B5
Castleview Cl, N4 **93** J1
Castleview Gdns, Ilf. IG1 **80** B6
Castle Wk, Sun. TW16 *off Elizabeth Gdns* **178** C3
Castle Way, SW19 **166** A3
Feltham TW13 **160** C4
Castlewood Dr, SE9 **156** C2
Castlewood Rd, N15 **76** D6
N16 **76** D7
Barnet (Cockfos.) EN4 **41** G3
Castle Yd, N6 *off North Rd* **74** A7
SE1 **27** H1
Richmond TW10 *off Hill St* **145** G5
Castor La, E14 **114** B7
Catalina Rd, Houns. (Lon.Hthrw Air.) TW6 *off Cromer Rd* **140** D2
Catalpa Ct, SE13 *off Hither Grn La* **154** D6
Caterham Av, Ilf. IG5 **80** C2
Caterham Rd, SE13 **154** C3
Catesby St, SE17 **36** C2
CATFORD, SE6 **172** B1
Catford Br, SE6 **154** A7
Catford Bdy, SE6 **154** B7
Catford Gyratory, SE6 **154** B7
Catford Hill, SE6 **171** J2
Catford Ms, SE6 *off Holbeach Rd* **154** B7
Catford Rd, SE6 **172** A1
Cathall Rd, E11 **96** D3
Cathay St, SE16 **133** E2
Cathay Wk, Nthlt. UB5 *off Brabazon Rd* **103** G2
Cathcart Dr, Orp. BR6 **207** H2
Cathcart Hill, N19 **92** C3
Cathcart Rd, SW10 **30** B5
Cathcart St, NW5 **92** B6
Cathedral Piazza, SW1 **25** F6
Cathedral St, SE1 **28** B1
Cathedral Wk, SW1 **25** F5
Catherall Rd, N5 **93** J3
Catherine Cl, Loug. IG10 *off Roding Gdns* **48** C6
Catherine Ct, N14 *off Conisbee Ct* **42** C5
Catherine Dr, Rich. TW9 **145** H4
Catherine Gdns, Houns. TW3 **144** A4
Catherine Griffiths Ct, EC1 **11** F5
Catherine Gro, SE10 **154** B1
Catherine Ho, N1 *off Phillipp St* **112** B1
Catherine Howard Ct, SE9 *off Avery Hill Rd* **157** G6
Catherine of Aragon Ct, SE9 *off Avery Hill Rd* **157** F6
Catherine Parr Ct, SE9 *off Avery Hill Rd* **157** G6
Catherine Pl, SW1 **25** F5
Harrow HA1 **68** C5
Catherine Rd, Surb. KT6 **181** G5
Catherine's Cl, West Dr. UB7 *off Money La* **120** A3
Catherine St, WC2 **18** C5
Catherine Wheel All, E1 **20** E2
Catherine Wheel Rd, Brent. TW8 **125** G7
Catherine Wheel Yd, SW1 **25** F2
Catherwood Ct, N1 *off Murray Gro* **12** B2
Cat Hill, Barn. EN4 **41** H6
Cathles Rd, SW12 **150** B6
Cathnor Rd, W12 **127** H2
Catling Cl, SE23 **171** F3
Catlins La, Pnr. HA5 **66** B3
Catlin St, SE16 **37** J4
Cator La, Beck. BR3 **189** J2
Cato Rd, SW4 **150** D3
Cator Rd, SE26 **171** G6
Carshalton SM5 **199** J5
Cator St, SE15 **37** F6
Cato St, W1 **15** H2
Catterick Cl, N11 **58** A6
Cattistock Rd, SE9 **174** B5
Cattley Cl, Barn. EN5 **40** B4
Catton St, WC1 **18** C2
Caughley Ho, SE11 *off Lambeth Wk* **26** E6
Caulfield Rd, E6 **98** C7
SE15 **153** E2
Causeway, The, N2 **73** H4
SW18 **148** E4
SW19 **166** A5
Carshalton SM5 **200** A3
Chessington KT9 **195** H4
Esher (Clay.) KT10 **194** C7
Feltham TW14 **142** A4
Hounslow TW4 **142** A4
Teddington TW11 *off Broad St* **162** C6
Causeyware Rd, N9 **45** E7
Causton Rd, N6 **74** B7
Causton Sq, Dag. RM10 **101** G7
Causton St, SW1 **33** J2
Cautley Av, SW4 **150** C5
Cavalier Cl, Rom. RM6 **82** D4
Cavalier Ho, W5 *off Uxbridge Rd* **105** F7
Cavalry Barracks, Houns. TW4 **142** D3
Cavalry Cres, Houns. TW4 **142** D4
Cavalry Gdns, SW15 **148** B5
Cavan Pl, Pnr. HA5 **67** F1
Cavaye Pl, SW10 **30** D4
Cavell Dr, Enf. EN2 **43** G2
Cavell Rd, N17 **60** A7
Cavell St, E1 **113** E5
Cavendish Av, N3 **72** D2
NW8 **7** F2
W13 **104** D5
Erith DA8 **139** J6
Harrow HA1 **86** A4
New Malden KT3 **183** H5
Ruislip HA4 **84** B5
Sidcup DA15 **158** A7
Welling DA16 **157** J3
Woodford Green IG8 **79** H1
Cavendish Cl, N18 **61** E5
NW6 *off Cavendish Rd* **90** C7
NW8 **7** F3
Cavendish Ct, EC3 **20** E3
Cavendish Cres, Borwd. (Els.) WD6 **38** A4
Cavendish Dr, E11 **96** D1
Edgware HA8 **53** J6
Esher (Clay.) KT10 **194** B5
Cavendish Gdns, SW4 **150** C6
Barking IG11 **99** H5
Ilford IG1 **98** D1
Romford RM6 **83** E5
Cavendish Ms N, W1 **16** E1
Cavendish Ms S, W1 **16** E2
Cavendish Par, SW4 *off Clapham Common S Side* **150** B6
Hounslow TW4 *off Bath Rd* **142** E2
Cavendish Pl, NW2 **90** A6
W1 **16** E3
Bromley BR1 **192** C3
Cavendish Rd, E4 **62** C6
N4 **75** G6
N18 **60** E5
NW6 **90** B7
SW12 **150** B6
SW19 **167** G7
W4 **146** C1
Barnet EN5 **39** J3
Croydon CR0 **201** H1
New Malden KT3 **183** F5
Sutton SM2 **199** F7
Cavendish Sq, W1 **16** E3
Cavendish St, N1 **12** B2
Cavendish Ter, Felt. TW13 *off High St* **160** A2
Cavendish Way, W.Wick. BR4 **204** B1
Cavenham Gdns, Ilf. IG1 **99** G3
Caverleigh Way, Wor.Pk. KT4 **197** G1
Cave Rd, E13 **115** H2
Richmond TW10 **163** F4
Caversham Av, N13 **59** G3
Sutton SM3 **198** B2
Caversham Ct, N11 **58** A3
Caversham Flats, SW3 **31** J5
Caversham Rd, N15 **75** J4
NW5 **92** C6
Kingston upon Thames KT1 **181** J2
Caversham St, SW3 **31** J5
Caverswall St, W12 **107** J6
Caveside Cl, Chis. BR7 **192** D1
Cawdor Cres, W7 **124** D4
Cawnpore St, SE19 **170** B5
Caxton Gro, E3 **114** A3
Caxton Ms, Brent. TW8 *off The Butts* **125** G6
Caxton Rd, N22 **75** F2
SW19 **167** F5
W12 **128** A2
Southall UB2 **122** D3
Caxton St, SW1 **25** G5
Caxton St N, E16 *off Victoria Dock Rd* **115** F7
Cayenne Ct, SE1 **29** G2
Cayford Ho, NW3 **91** H5
Caygill Cl, Brom. BR2 **191** F4
Cayley Rd, Sthl. UB2 *off McNair Rd* **123** H3
Cayton Pl, EC1 **12** B4
Cayton Rd, Grnf. UB6 **104** B2
Cayton St, EC1 **12** B4
Cazenove Rd, E17 **78** A1
N16 **94** C2
Cearns Ho, E6 **116** A1
Cecil Av, Bark. IG11 **99** G7
Enfield EN1 **44** C4
Wembley HA9 **87** J5
Cecil Cl, W5 **105** G5
Chessington KT9 **195** G4
Cecil Ct, WC2 **17** J6
Barnet EN5 **40** A3
Cecile Pk, N8 **75** E6
Cecilia Cl, N2 **73** F3
★ **Cecilia Coleman Gall**, NW8 **7** F1
Cecilia Rd, E8 **94** D5
Cecil Manning Cl, Grnf. UB6 *off Horsenden La S* **104** D1
Cecil Pk, Pnr. HA5 **67** E4
Cecil Pl, Mitch. CR4 **185** J5
Cecil Rd, E11 **97** E3
E13 **115** G1
E17 **78** A1
N10 **74** B2
N14 **58** C1
NW9 **70** E3
NW10 **106** E1
SW19 **166** E7
W3 **106** C5
Croydon CR0 **187** F6
Enfield EN2 **44** A4
Harrow HA3 **68** B3
Hounslow TW3 **143** J2
Ilford IG1 **98** E4
Romford RM6 **82** D7
Sutton SM1 **198** C6
★ **Cecil Sharp Ho**, NW1 **110** A1
Cecil Way, Brom. BR2 **205** G1
Cedar Av, Barn. EN4 **41** H7
Enfield EN3 **45** F2
Hayes UB3 **102** A6
Romford RM6 **82** E5
Ruislip HA4 **84** C6
Sidcup DA15 **158** A7
Twickenham TW2 **143** H6
West Drayton UB7 **120** C1
Cedar Cl, E3 **113** J1
SE21 **169** J1
SW15 **164** D4
Borehamwood WD6 **38** B4
Bromley BR2 **206** B3
Buckhurst Hill IG9 **64** A2
Carshalton SM5 **199** J6
East Molesey KT8 *off Cedar Rd* **180** B4
Ilford IG1 **99** G5
Romford RM7 **83** J4
Cedar Copse, Brom. BR1 **192** C2
Cedar Ct, E11 *off Grosvenor Rd* **79** H5
N1 *off Essex Rd* **93** J7
SE7 *off Fairlawn* **135** J6
SE9 **156** B6
SW19 **166** A3
Cedar Cres, Brom. BR2 **206** B3
Cedarcroft Rd, Chess. KT9 **195** J4
Cedar Dr, N2 **73** H4
Loughton IG10 **49** E2
Pinner HA5 **51** G6
Cedar Gdns, Sutt. SM2 **199** F6
Cedar Gro, W5 **125** H3
Bexley DA5 **158** C6
Southall UB1 **103** G5
Cedar Hts, Rich. TW10 **163** H1
Cedar Ho, Croy. CR0 **204** B6
Cedarhurst, Brom. BR1 **173** E7
Cedarhurst Dr, SE9 **155** J5
Cedar Lawn Av, Barn. EN5 **40** B5
Cedar Ms, SW15 *off Cambalt Rd* **148** A5
Cedar Mt, SE9 **174** A1
Cedarne Rd, SW6 **128** E7
Cedar Pk, Chig. IG7 *off High Rd* **65** E4
Cedar Pk Gdns, Rom. RM6 **82** D7
Cedar Pl, SE7 *off Floyd Rd* **135** J5
Cedar Ri, N14 **42** A7
Cedar Rd, N17 **76** C1
NW2 **89** J4
Bromley BR1 **191** J2
Croydon CR0 **202** B2
East Molesey KT8 **180** B4
Hounslow TW4 **142** C2
Romford RM7 **83** J4
Sutton SM2 **199** F6
Teddington TW11 **162** D5
Cedars, The, E15 *off Portway* **115** F1
W13 *off Heronsforde* **105** F6
Buckhurst Hill IG9 **63** G1
Teddington TW11 *off Adelaide Rd* **162** C6
Cedars Av, E17 **78** A5
Mitcham CR4 **186** A4
Cedars Cl, NW4 **72** A3
SE13 **154** D3
Cedars Ct, N9 *off Church St* **60** B2
Cedars Ms, SW4 *off Cedars Rd* **150** B4
Cedars Rd, E15 **97** E6
N21 **59** H2
SW4 **150** B3

Cedars Rd, SW13 ......147 F2
W4 ....126 C5
Beckenham BR3 .....189 H2
Croydon CR0 ....201 E3
Kingston upon Thames
(Hmptn W.) KT1 ....181 K1
Morden SM4 ....184 D4
Cedar Ter, Rich. TW9 ..145 H4
Cedar Tree Gro, SE27 ..169 H5
Cedarville Gdns, SW16 169 F6
Cedar Vista, Rich. (Kew)
TW9 ....145 H2
Cedar Wk, Esher (Clay.)
KT10 ....194 C6
Cedar Way, NW1 ....92 D7
Cedra Ct, N16 ....94 D1
Cedric Rd, SE9 ....175 F3
Celadon Cl, E14 ......114 A5
Celandine Cl, E14 ....114 A5
Celandine Dr, E8 ......94 C7
SE28 ....138 B1
Celandine Gro, N14 ....42 C5
Celandine Way, E15 ...115 E3
Celbridge Ms, W2 .....14 B3
Celestial Gdns, SE13 ..154 D4
Celia Rd, N19 ....64 C4
Celtic Av, Brom. BR2 ..190 E3
Celtic St, E14 ....114 B5
Cemetery La, SE7 .....136 B6
Cemetery Rd, E7 ......97 F4
N17 ....60 B7
SE2 ....138 B7
Cenacle Cl, NW3 ......90 D3
★ Cenotaph, The, SW1 .26 A3
Centaurs Business Cen,
Islw. TW7 ....124 D6
Centaur St, SE1 ......26 D5
Centenary Ind Est, Enf.
EN3 ....45 J4
Centenary Rd, Enf. EN3 ..45 J4
Centenary Wk, Loug.
IG10 ....47 H3
Central Av, E11 ....96 D2
N2 ....73 G2
N9 ....60 B7
SW11 ....129 J7
Enfield EN1 ....44 E2
Hayes UB3 ....102 A7
Hounslow TW3 .....143 J4
Pinner HA5 ....67 F6
Wallington SM6 ....201 E6
Welling DA16 ......157 J2
West Molesey KT8 ..179 F4
Central Circ, NW4 ....71 H5
off Hendon Way 71 H5
★ Central Criminal Ct
(Old Bailey), EC4 ....19 H3
Centrale Shop Cen, Croy.
CR0 ....201 J2
Central Gdns, Mord.
SM4 ....185 E6
Central Hill, SE19 ....170 A5
Central Ho, E15 ......114 C2
off High St 114 C2
Barking IG11
off Cambridge Rd 99 F7
Central Par, E17
off Hoe St 78 A4
Feltham TW14 ......142 C7
Greenford (Perivale)
UB6 ....104 D3
Hounslow TW5
off Heston Rd 123 G7
Surbiton KT6 ......181 H6
Central Pk Av, Dag.
RM10 ....101 H3
Central Pk Est, Houns.
TW4 ....142 D5
Central Pk Rd, E6 ....116 A2
Central Pl, SE25
off Portland Rd 188 E4
Central Rd, Mord. SM4 ..184 D6
Wembley HA0 ......86 E5
Worcester Park KT4 ..197 G2
Central Sch Footpath,
SW14 ....146 C3
Central Sq, NW11 ....72 E6
Wembley HA9
off Station Gro 87 H5
West Molesey KT8 ..179 F4
Central St, EC1 ....11 J4
Central Way, NW10 ...106 C3
SE28 ....138 A1
Carshalton SM5 ....199 H7
Feltham TW14 .....142 B5
Centre, The, Felt. TW13 ..160 A2
Centre Av, W3 ....126 D1
W10 off Harrow Rd ..107 J3
Centre Common Rd, Chis.
BR7 ....175 F6
Centre Ct Shop Cen,
SW19 ....166 C6
Centre Pt, SE1 ....37 H3

Centrepoint, WC1 ....17 J3
Centre Rd, E7 ....97 G2
E11 ....97 G2
Dagenham RM10 ....119 H2
Centre St, E2 ....112 E2
Centre Way, E17 ......62 C7
N9 ....61 F2
Centreway Apts, Ilf. IG1
off High Rd 99 F2
Centric Cl, NW1 ......110 B1
off Oval Rd 110 B1
Centrillion Pt, Croy. CR0
off Masons Av 201 J4
Centurion Cl, N7 ......93 F7
Centurion Ct, SE18
off Rushgrove St ...136 D4
Wallington (Hackbr.)
SM6 off Wandle Rd ..200 B3
Centurion La, E3
off Libra Rd 113 J2
Centurion Sq, SE18 ...156 B1
Centurion Way, Erith
DA18 ....139 G3
Erith DA7 ....139 H3
Century Cl, NW4 ......72 A5
Century Ms, E5
off Lower Clapton Rd ..95 F4
Century Rd, E17 ......77 H3
Century Yd, SE23 .....171 F2
Cephas Av, E1 ....113 F4
Cephas St, E1 ....113 F4
Ceres Rd, SE18 ......137 J4
Cerise Rd, SE15 ......152 D1
Cerne Cl, Hayes UB4 ..102 D7
Cerne Rd, Mord. SM4 ..185 F6
Cerney Ms, W2 ....14 E5
Cervantes Ct, W2 .....14 B4
Cester St, E2
off Whiston Rd 112 D1
Ceylon Rd, W14 ......128 A3
Chabot Dr, SE15 ......153 E3
Chadacre Av, Ilf. IG5 ...80 D3
Chadacre Rd, Epsom
KT17 ....197 H6
Chadbourn St, E14 ...114 B5
Chad Cres, N9 ....61 F3
Chadd Dr, Brom. BR1 ..192 B3
Chadd Grn, E13 ......115 G1
Chadview Ct, Rom.
(Chad.)RM6 ....82 D7
Chadville Gdns, Rom.
RM6 ....82 D5
Chadway, Dag. RM8 ..100 C1
Chadwell Av, Rom. RM6 ..82 B7
CHADWELL HEATH, Rom.
RM6 ....82 B5
Chadwell La, N8 ......75 F3
Chadwell St, EC1 ......11 F3
Chadwick Av, E4 ......62 D4
N21 ....43 F4
SW19 ....166 D6
Chadwick Cl, SW15 ...147 F7
W7 off Westcott Cres ..104 C5
Teddington TW11 ....162 D6
Chadwick Ms, W4 .....126 B6
off Thames Rd 126 B6
Chadwick Pl, Surb.
(Long Dit.) KT6 ....181 F7
Chadwick Rd, E11 .....79 E7
NW10 ....107 F1
SE15 ....152 C2
Ilford IG1 ....99 E3
Chadwick St, SW1 ....25 J6
Chadwick Way, SE28 ..118 D7
Chadwin Rd, E13 .....115 H5
Chadworth Way, Esher
(Clay.) KT10 ....194 A5
Chaffinch Av, Croy. CR0 ..189 G6
Chaffinch Business Pk,
Beck. BR3 ....189 G4
Chaffinch Cl, N9 ......61 G1
Croydon CR0 ....189 G5
Surbiton KT6 ......196 A3
Chaffinch Rd, Beck. BR3 ..189 H1
Chafford Way, Rom. RM6 ..82 C4
Chagford St, NW1 ......7 J6
Chailey Av, Enf. EN1 ...44 C2
Chailey Cl, Houns. TW5
off Springwell Rd ...142 D1
Chailey St, E5 ....95 F3
Chalbury Wk, N1 .....111 G2
Chalcombe Rd, SE2 ..138 B3
Chalcot Cl, Sutt. SM2 ..198 D7
Chalcot Cres, NW1 ...109 J1
Chalcot Gdns, NW3 ....91 J6
Chalcot Ms, SW16 ...168 E3
Chalcot Rd, NW1 ......92 A7
Chalcot Sq, NW1 ......92 A7
Chalcott Gdns, Surb.
(Long Dit.) KT6 ....195 F1
Chalcroft Rd, SE13 ...154 E5

Chaldon Path, Th.Hth.
CR7 ....187 H4
Chaldon Rd, SW6 .....128 B7
Chale Rd, SW2 ....150 E6
Chalet Est, NW7 ......55 G4
Chalfont Av, Wem. HA9 ..88 B6
Chalfont Ct, NW9 .....71 F3
Chalfont Grn, N9 ......60 B3
Chalfont Ms, SW19
off Augustus Rd ...166 C1
Chalfont Rd, N9 ......60 B3
SE25 ....188 C3
Hayes UB3 ....122 A2
Chalfont Wk, Pnr. HA5
off Willows Cl 66 C2
Chalfont Way, W13 ...124 E3
Chalford Cl, W.Mol.
KT8 ....179 G4
Chalford Rd, SE21 ....170 A4
Chalford Wk, Wdf.Grn.
IG8 ....80 A1
Chalgrove Av, Mord.
SM4 ....184 D5
Chalgrove Cres, Ilf. IG5 ..80 B2
Chalgrove Gdns, N3 ...72 B3
Chalgrove Rd, N17 ....76 E1
Sutton SM2 ....199 G7
Chalice Cl, Wall. SM6
off Lavender Vale ..200 D6
Chalkenden Cl, SE20 ..170 E7
Chalkers Cor, SW14 ..146 B3
Chalk Fm Rd, NW1 .....92 A7
Chalk Hill Rd, W6
off Shortlands 128 A4
Chalkhill Rd, Wem. HA9 ..88 B3
Chalklands, Wem. HA9 ..88 C3
Chalk La, Barn. EN4 ....41 J4
Chalkley Cl, Mitch. CR4 ..185 J2
Chalkmill Dr, Enf. EN1 ...44 E3
Chalk Pit Way, Sutt. SM1 ..199 F5
Chalk Rd, E13 ....115 H5
Chalkstone Cl, Well.
DA16 ....158 A1
Chalkwell Pk Av, Enf.
EN1 ....44 B4
Challenge Ct, Twick. TW2
off Langhorn Dr ...144 B7
Challice Way, SW2 ...169 F1
Challin St, SE20 ......189 F1
Challis Rd, Brent. TW8 ..125 G5
Challoner Cl, N2 ......73 G2
Challoner Cres, W14 ..128 C5
off Challoner St ...128 C5
Challoners Cl, E.Mol.
KT8 ....180 A4
Challoner St, W14 ....128 C5
Chalmers Ho, SW11
off York Rd 149 F3
Chalmers Wk, SE17 ....35 H6
Chalmers Way, Felt.
TW14 ....142 A5
Chaloner Ct, SE1 ......28 B3
Chalsey Rd, SE4 ......153 J4
Chalton Dr, N2 ....73 F6
Chalton St, NW1 ....9 J3
Chamberlain Cl, SE28 ..137 G3
off Broadwater Rd ..137 G3
Ilford IG1
off Richmond Rd 99 F3
Chamberlain Cotts, SE5 ..152 A1
off Camberwell Gro ..152 A1
Chamberlain Cres, W.Wick.
BR4 ....204 B1
Chamberlain Gdns, Houns.
TW3 ....143 J1
Chamberlain La, Pnr.
HA5 ....66 A4
Chamberlain Pl, E17 ...77 H3
Chamberlain Rd, N2 ...73 F2
W13 off Midhurst Rd ..124 D2
Chamberlain St, NW1
off Regents Pk Rd ...91 J7
Chamberlain Wk, Felt.
TW13 off Burgess Cl ..160 E4
Chamberlain Way, Pnr.
HA5 ....66 B3
Surbiton KT6 ......181 H7
Chamberlayne Rd, Wem.
HA9 ....87 H2
Chamberlayne Rd,
NW10 ....108 A3
Chambers Av, Sid. DA14 ..
Chambers Gdns, N2 ...73 G1
Chambers Ho, SW16
off Pringle Gdns ...168 C4
Chambers La, NW10 ...89 H7
Chambers Pl, S.Croy. CR2
off Rolleston Rd ...202 A7
Chambers Rd, N7 ......92 E4
Chambers St, SE16 ....29 H3
Chamber St, E1 ....21 G5
Chambers Wk, Stan. HA7 ..52 E5

Chambon Pl, W6
off Beavor La 127 G4
Chambord St, E2 ......13 G4
Chamers Ct, W12
off Heathstan Rd ...107 G6
Champa Cl, N17 ....76 C2
Champion Cres, SE26 ..171 H4
Champion Gro, SE5 ...152 A3
Champion Hill, SE5 ...152 A3
Champion Hill Est, SE5 ..152 B3
Champion Pk, SE5 ....152 A2
Champion Pk Est, SE5
off Denmark Hill ...152 A3
Champion Rd, SE26 ..171 H4
Champions Way, NW4 ..71 H1
NW7 ....71 H1
Champness Cl, SE27 ..170 A4
Champness Rd, Bark.
IG11 ....99 J6
Champneys Cl, Sutt.
SM2 ....198 C7
Chancellor Gro, SE21 ..169 G2
Chancellor Pas, E14
off The South
Colonnade 134 A1
Chancellor Pl, NW9 ....71 F2
Chancellors Ct, WC1
off Orde Hall St 18 C1
Chancellors Rd, W6 ...127 J5
Chancellors St, W6 ...127 J5
Chancellors Wf, W6
off Crisp Rd 127 J5
Chancelot Rd, SE2 ...138 B4
Chancel St, SE1 ....27 G1
Chancerygate Cl, Ruis.
HA4 ....84 E5
Chancerygate Way, Ruis.
HA4 ....84 E4
Chancery La, WC2 .....18 E3
Beckenham BR3 ...190 B2
Chancery Ms, SW17 ..167 H2
Chance St, E1 ....13 F5
E2 ....13 F5
Chanctonbury Cl, SE9 ..175 E3
Chanctonbury Gdns, Sutt.
SM2 ....198 E7
Chanctonbury Way, N12 ..56 C4
Chandler Av, E16 .....115 G5
Chandler Cl, Hmptn.
TW12 ....179 G1
Chandler Ct, Th.Hth. CR7
off Bensham La ...187 H5
Chandler Ms, Twick. TW1 ..144 D7
Chandler Rd, Loug. IG10 ..48 D1
Chandlers Cl, Felt. TW14 ..141 J7
Chandlers Ms, E14 ...134 A2
Chandler St, E1
off Wapping La ...133 E1
Chandlers Way, SW2 ..151 G7
Chandler Way, SE15 ...37 E6
Chandon Lo, Sutt. SM2
off Devonshire Rd ..199 F7
Chandos Av, E17 ......78 A2
N14 ....58 C3
N20 ....57 F1
W5 ....125 F4
Chandos Cl, Buck.H. IG9 ..63 H2
Chandos Ct, Stan. HA7 ..52 E6
Chandos Cres, Edg. HA8 ..53 J7
Chandos Par, Edg. HA8
off Chandos Cres ...53 J7
Chandos Pl, WC2 ......18 A6
Chandos Rd, E15 ......96 D5
N2 ....73 G2
N17 ....76 B2
NW2 ....89 J5
NW10 ....106 E4
Harrow HA1 ....67 J5
Pinner HA5 ....66 C7
Chandos St, W1 ....16 E2
Chandos Way, NW11 ...90 E1
Change All, EC3 ....20 C4
Channel Cl, Houns. TW5 ..143 G1
Channel Gate Rd, NW10
off Old Oak La 107 F3
Channel Ho, E14
off Aston St 113 H5
Channel Islands Est, N1
off Clifton Rd 93 J6
Channelsea Ho
Business Cen, E15 ..
off Canning Rd 114 D2
Channelsea Rd, E15 ..114 D1
Chantress Cl, Dag.
RM10 ....119 J1
Chantrey Rd, SW9 ....151 F3
Chantry, The, E4
off The Ridgeway ...62 C1
Chantry Cl, NW7
off Hendon Wd La ...39 F6
SE2
off Felixstowe Rd ..138 C3
W9 off Elgin Av ...108 C4

Chantry Cl, Harrow HA3 **69** J5
Sidcup DA14 *off Ellenborough Rd* **176** E5
Sunbury-on-Thames TW16 **160** A7
Chantry Ct, Cars. SM5 **199** H3
Chantry Cres, NW10 **89** F6
Chantry La, Brom. BR2 *off Bromley Common* **192** A5
Chantry Pl, Har. HA3 **67** H1
Chantry Rd, Chess. KT9 **195** J5
Harrow HA3 **67** H1
Chantry Sq, W8 *off St. Mary's Pl* **22** A6
Chantry St, N1 **111** H1
Chantry Way, Mitch. CR4 *off Church Rd* **185** G3
Chant Sq, E15 **96** D7
Chant St, E15 **96** D7
Chapel Cl, NW10 **89** F5
Chapel Ct, N2 **73** H3
SE1 **28** B3
SE18 **137** J6
Chapel Fm Rd, SE9 **174** C3
Chapel Gate Ms, SW4 *off Bedford Rd* **150** E3
Chapel Ho St, E14 **134** B5
Chapelier Ho, SW18 *off Eastfields Av* **148** D4
Chapel La, Chig. IG7 **65** J3
Pinner HA5 **66** D3
Romford RM6 **82** D7
Chapel Mkt, N1 **10** E1
Chapel Ms, Wdf.Grn. IG8 **64** D6
Chapel Mill Rd, Kings.T. KT1 **181** J3
Chapelmount Rd, Wdf.Grn. IG8 **64** C6
Chapel Path, E11 **79** G6
Chapel Pl, EC2 **12** D4
N1 **11** F1
N17 *off White Hart La* **60** C7
W1 **16** D4
Chapel Rd, SE27 **169** H4
W13 **125** E1
Bexleyheath DA7 **159** G4
Hounslow TW3 **143** H3
Ilford IG1 **98** D3
Twickenham TW1 **145** E7
Chapel Side, W2 **14** A5
Chapel Stones, N17 **76** C1
Chapel St, NW1 **15** G2
SW1 **24** C5
Enfield EN2 **43** J3
Chapel Ter, Loug. IG10 *off Forest Rd* **48** B4
Chapel Vw, S.Croy. CR2 **203** E6
Chapel Wk, NW4 **71** H4
Croydon CR0 *off Whitgift Cen* **201** J2
Chapel Way, N7 *off Sussex Way* **93** F3
Chapel Yd, SW18 *off Wandsworth High St* **148** D5
Chaplin Cl, SE1 **27** F3
Chaplin Rd, E15 **115** E2
N17 **76** C3
NW2 **89** G6
Dagenham RM9 **101** E7
Wembley HA0 **87** F6
Chaplin Sq, N12 **57** G7
Chapman Cl, West Dr. UB7 **120** C3
Chapman Cres, Har. HA3 **69** H5
Chapman Pk Ind Est, NW10 **89** F6
Chapman Pl, N4 **93** H2
Chapman Rd, E9 **95** J6
Belvedere DA17 **139** G5
Croydon CR0 **201** G1
Chapman's La, SE2 **138** C4
Belvedere DA17 **138** D4
Chapman Sq, SW19 **166** A2
Chapman St, E1 **112** E7
Chapone Pl, W1 **17** H4
Chapter Chambers, SW1 *off Chapter St* **33** H2
Chapter Cl, W4 *off Church Path* **126** C3
Chapter Ho Ct, EC4 **19** J4
Chapter Rd, NW2 **89** G5
SE17 **35** H4
Chapter St, SW1 **33** H2
Chapter Way, SW19 **185** F1
Hampton TW12 **161** G4
Chara Pl, W4 **126** D6
Charcot Ho, SW15 *off Highcliffe Dr* **147** F6
Charcroft Gdns, Enf. EN3 **45** G4
Chardin Rd, W4 *off Elliott Rd* **126** E4
Chardmore Rd, N16 **94** D1
Chard Rd, Houns. (Lon.Hthrw Air.) TW6 *off Heathrow Tunnel App* **140** E2
Chardwell Cl, E6 *off Northumberland Rd* **116** B6
Charecroft Way, W12 **128** A2
W14 **128** A2
Charfield Ct, W9 **6** A6
Charford Rd, E16 **115** G5
Chargeable La, E13 **115** F4
Chargeable St, E16 **115** F4
Chargrove Cl, SE16 *off Marlow Way* **133** G2
Charing Cl, Orp. BR6 **207** J4
Charing Cross, SW1 **25** J1
Charing Cross Rd, WC2 **17** J3
Chariot Cl, E3 *off Garrison Rd* **114** A1
Charlbert St, NW8 **7** G1
Charlbury Av, Stan. HA7 **53** G5
Charlbury Gdns, Ilf. IG3 **99** J2
Charlbury Gro, W5 **105** F6
Charlbury Ho, E12 *off Grantham Rd* **98** D3
Charldane Rd, SE9 **174** E3
Charlecote Gro, SE26 **171** E3
Charlecote Rd, Dag. RM8 **100** E3
Charlemont Rd, E6 **116** C3
Charles Babbage Cl, Chess. KT9 **195** F7
Charles Barry Cl, SW4 **150** C3
Charles Burton Ct, E5 *off Ashenden Rd* **95** H5
Charles Ch Wk, Ilf. IG1 **80** C6
Charles Cl, Sid. DA14 **176** B4
Charles Cobb Gdns, Croy. CR0 **201** G5
Charles Coveney Rd, SE15 **152** C1
Charles Cres, Har. HA1 **68** A7
Charles Dickens Ho, E2 **112** E3
★ **Charles Dickens Mus**, WC1 **10** D5
Charles Dickens Ter, SE20 *off Maple Rd* **171** F7
Charlesfield, SE9 **173** J3
Charles Flemwell Ms, E16 *off Hanameel St* **135** G1
Charles Gardner Ct, N1 **12** C3
Charles Grinling Wk, SE18 **136** D4
Charles Gro, N14 **58** C1
Charles Haller St, SW2 *off Tulse Hill* **151** G7
Charles Hocking Ho, W3 *off Bollo Br Rd* **126** C2
Charles Ho, N17 *off Love La* **60** C7
Charles La, NW8 **7** F2
Charles Mackenzie Ho, SE16 *off Linsey St* **37** H1
Charlesmere Gdns, SE28 *off Battery Rd* **137** H2
Charles Nex Ms, SE21 **169** J2
Charles Pl, NW1 **9** G4
Charles Rd, E7 *off Lens Rd* **97** J7
SW19 **184** D1
W13 **104** D6
Romford RM6 **82** D7
Charles Rowan Ho, WC1 **11** E4
Charles II Pl, SW3 *off King's Rd* **31** J4
Charles II St, SW1 **25** H1
Charles Sevright Dr, NW7 **56** A5
Charles Sq, N1 **12** C4
Charles Sq Est, N1 **12** C4
Charles St, SW13 **147** E2
W1 **24** D1
Croydon CR0 **201** J3
Enfield EN1 **44** C5
Hounslow TW3 **143** F2
Charleston Cl, Felt. TW13 *off Poplar Way* **160** A3
Charleston St, SE17 **36** A2
Charles Townsend Ho, EC1 **11** F5
Charles Whincup Rd, E16 **135** H1
Charlesworth Pl, SW13 *off Eleanor Gro* **147** F3
Charleville Circ, SE26 **170** D5
Charleville Ms, Islw. TW7 *off Railshead Rd* **144** E4
Charleville Rd, W14 **128** B5
Charlie Brown's Rbt, E18 **79** J2
Charlie Chaplin Wk, SE1 *off Waterloo Br* **26** D2
Charlieville Rd, Erith DA8 *off Northumberland Pk* **139** J7
Charlmont Rd, SW17 **167** J6
Charlotte Cl, Bexh. DA6 **158** E5
Ilford IG6 *off Connor Cl* **81** F1
Charlotte Ct, N8 **74** D6
W6 *off Invermead Cl* **127** G4
Charlotte Despard Av, SW11 **150** A1
Charlotte Ms, W1 **17** G1
W10 **108** A6
W14 *off Munden St* **128** B4
Charlotte Pk Av, Brom. BR1 **192** B3
Charlotte Pl, NW9 *off Uphill Dr* **70** C5
SW1 **33** F2
W1 **17** G2
Charlotte Rd, EC2 **12** D5
SW13 **147** F1
Dagenham RM10 **101** H6
Wallington SM6 **200** C6
Charlotte Row, SW4 **150** C3
Charlotte Sq, Rich. TW10 *off Greville Rd* **145** J6
Charlotte St, W1 **17** G1
Charlotte Ter, N1 **111** F1
Charlow Cl, SW6 *off Townmead Rd* **149** F2
CHARLTON, SE7 **135** J6
★ **Charlton Athletic FC**, SE7 **135** J5
Charlton Ch La, SE7 **135** J5
Charlton Cres, Bark. IG11 **117** J2
Charlton Dene, SE7 **135** J7
Charlton Kings Rd, NW5 **92** D5
Charlton La, SE7 **136** A5
Charlton Pk La, SE7 **136** A7
Charlton Pk Rd, SE7 **136** A6
Charlton Pl, N1 **11** G1
Charlton Rd, N9 **61** G1
NW10 **107** E1
SE3 **135** G7
SE7 **135** H7
Harrow HA3 **69** G4
Wembley HA9 **87** J1
Charlton Way, SE3 **154** E1
Charlwood Cl, Har. HA3 *off Kelvin Cres* **52** B6
Charlwood Ho, SW1 *off Vauxhall Br Rd* **33** H2
Richmond TW9 *off Strand Dr* **126** B7
Charlwood Pl, SW1 **33** G2
Charlwood Rd, SW15 **148** A3
Charlwood St, SW1 **33** G2
Charlwood Ter, SW15 *off Cardinal Pl* **148** A4
Charmian Av, Stan. HA7 **69** G3
Charminster Av, SW19 **184** D2
Charminster Ct, Surb. KT6 *off Lovelace Gdns* **181** G7
Charminster Rd, SE9 **174** A4
Worcester Park KT4 **198** A1
Charmouth Ho, SW8 *off Dorset Rd* **34** C7
Charmouth Rd, Well. DA16 **158** C1
Charnock Rd, E5 **94** E3
Charnwood Av, SW19 **184** D2
Charnwood Cl, N.Mal. KT3 **183** E4
Charnwood Dr, E18 **79** H3
Charnwood Gdns, E14 **134** A4
Charnwood Pl, N20 **57** F3
Charnwood Rd, SE25 **188** A5
Charnwood St, E5 **94** D2
Charrington Rd, Croy. CR0 *off Drayton Rd* **201** H2
Charrington St, NW1 **9** H1
Charsley Rd, SE6 **172** B2
Chart Cl, Brom. BR2 **191** E1
Croydon CR0 **189** F6
Mitcham CR4 **185** J4
Charter Av, Ilf. IG2 **99** G1
Charter Ct, N.Mal. KT3 **182** E3
Charter Cres, Houns. TW4 **142** E4
Charter Dr, Bex. DA5 **158** E7
★ **Charterhouse**, EC1 **19** H1
Charterhouse Av, Wem. HA0 **87** F4
Charterhouse Bldgs, EC1 **11** H6
Charterhouse Ms, EC1 **19** H1
Charterhouse Rd, E8 **94** D4
Charterhouse Sq, EC1 **19** H1
Charterhouse St, EC1 **19** F2
Charteris Rd, N4 **93** G1
NW6 **108** C1
Woodford Green IG8 **63** H7
Charter Rd, Kings.T. KT1 **182** B3
Charter Rd, The, Wdf.Grn. IG8 **62** E6
Charters Cl, SE19 **170** B5
Charter Sq, Kings.T. KT1 **182** B2
Charter Way, N3 **72** C4
N14 **42** C6
Chartfield Av, SW15 **147** H5
Chartfield Sq, SW15 **148** A5
Chartham Ct, SW9 **151** G3
Chartham Gro, SE27 *off Royal Circ* **169** G3
Chartham Rd, SE25 **188** E3
Chart Hills Cl, SE28 *off Fairway Dr* **118** E6
Chartley Av, NW2 **88** E3
Stanmore HA7 **52** C6
Charton Cl, Belv. DA17 *off Nuxley Rd* **139** F6
Chartridge Cl, Barn. EN5 **39** G5
Chart St, N1 **12** C3
Chartwell Cl, SE9 **175** F2
Croydon CR0 **202** A1
Greenford UB6 **103** H1
Chartwell Dr, Orp. BR6 **207** G5
Chartwell Gdns, Sutt. SM3 **198** B4
Chartwell Pl, Har. HA2 **86** A2
Sutton SM3 **198** C4
Chartwell Way, SE20 **188** E1
Charwood, SW16 **169** G4
Chase, The, E12 **98** A4
SW4 **150** B3
SW16 **169** F7
SW20 **184** B1
Bexleyheath DA7 **159** H3
Bromley BR1 **191** H3
Chigwell IG7 **65** F4
Edgware HA8 **70** B1
Loughton IG10 **47** J7
Pinner HA5 **67** F4
Pinner (Eastcote) HA5 **66** C6
Romford (Chad.Hth) RM6 **82** E6
Stanmore HA7 **52** D5
Sunbury-on-Thames TW16 **178** B1
Wallington SM6 **200** E5
Chase Ct Gdns, Enf. EN2 **43** J3
Chasefield Rd, SW17 **167** J4
Chase Gdns, E4 **62** A4
Twickenham TW2 **144** A6
Chase Grn, Enf. EN2 **43** J3
Chase Grn Av, Enf. EN2 **43** H2
Chase Hill, Enf. EN2 **43** J3
Chase La, Ilf. IG6 **81** G5
Chaseley Dr, W4 **126** B5
Chaseley St, E14 **113** H6
Chasemore Cl, Mitch. CR4 **185** J7
Chasemore Gdns, Croy. CR0 **201** G5
Chase Ridings, Enf. EN2 **43** G2
Chase Rd, N14 **42** C6
NW10 **106** D4
W3 **106** D4
Chase Side, N14 **42** A6
Enfield EN2 **43** J3
Chase Side Av, SW20 **184** B1
Enfield EN2 **43** J2
Chase Side Cres, Enf. EN2 **43** J1
Chase Side Pl, Enf. EN2 *off Chase Side* **43** J2
Chaseville Par, N21 **43** F5
Chaseville Pk Rd, N21 **43** E5
Chase Way, N14 **58** B2
Chasewood Av, Enf. EN2 **43** H2
Chasewood Pk, Har. HA1 **86** C3
Chaston Pl, NW5 *off Grafton Ter* **92** A5
Chater Ho, E2 *off Roman Rd* **113** G3
Chatfield Rd, SW11 **149** F3
Croydon CR0 **201** H1
Chatham Av, Brom. BR2 **191** F7
Chatham Cl, NW11 **72** D5
SE18 **137** E3
Sutton SM3 **184** C7
Chatham Pl, E9 **95** F6
Chatham Rd, E17 **77** H3
E18 *off Grove Hill* **79** F2
SW11 **149** J6
Kingston upon Thames KT1 **182** A2
Orpington BR6 *off Gladstone Rd* **207** F5
Chatham St, SE17 **36** B1
Chatsfield Pl, W5 **105** H6
Chatsworth Av, NW4 **71** J2
SW20 **184** B1
Bromley BR1 **173** H4
Sidcup DA15 **176** A1

Chatsworth Av, Wembley HA9 **87** J5
Chatsworth Cl, NW4 **71** J2
Borehamwood WD6 **38** A3
West Wickham BR4 **205** F2
Chatsworth Ct, W8 **128** D4
Stanmore HA7 *off Marsh La* **53** F5
Chatsworth Cres, Houns. TW3 **144** A4
Chatsworth Dr, Enf. EN1 **44** D7
Chatsworth Est, E5 *off Elderfield Rd* **95** G4
Chatsworth Gdns, W3 **106** B7
Harrow HA2 **85** H1
New Malden KT3 **183** F5
Chatsworth Par, Orp. BR5 *off Queensway* **193** F5
Chatsworth Pl, Mitch. CR4 **185** J3
Teddington TW11 **162** D4
Chatsworth Ri, W5 **105** J4
Chatsworth Rd, E5 **95** F3
E15 **97** F5
NW2 **90** A6
W4 **126** C6
W5 **105** J4
Croydon CR0 **202** A4
Hayes UB4 **102** B4
Sutton SM3 **198** A5
Chatsworth Way, SE27 **169** H3
Chatterton Ms, N4 *off Chatterton Rd* **93** H3
Chatterton Rd, N4 **93** H3
Bromley BR2 **192** A4
Chatto Rd, SW11 **149** J5
Chaucer Av, Hayes UB4 **102** A5
Hounslow TW4 **142** B2
Richmond TW9 **146** A2
Chaucer Cl, N11 **58** C5
Chaucer Ct, N16 **94** B4
Chaucer Dr, SE1 **37** G2
Chaucer Gdns, Sutt. SM1 **198** D3
Chaucer Grn, Croy. CR0 **189** E7
Chaucer Ho, SW1 **33** F4
Sutton SM1 **198** D3
Chaucer Rd, E7 **97** G6
E11 **79** G6
E17 **78** C2
SE24 **151** G5
W3 **126** C1
Sidcup DA15 **176** C1
Sutton SM1 **198** D4
Welling DA16 **157** H1
Chaucer Way, SW19 **167** G6
Chauncey Cl, N9 **60** D3
Chaundrye Cl, SE9 **156** C6
Chauntler Cl, E16 **115** H6
CHEAM, Sutt. SM3 **198** A6
Cheam Common Rd, Wor.Pk. KT4 **197** H2
Cheam Mans, Sutt. SM3 **198** B7
Cheam Pk Way, Sutt. SM3 **198** B6
Cheam Rd, Sutt. SM1 **198** C6
Cheam St, SE15 *off Nunhead La* **153** E3
Cheam Village, Sutt. SM3 **198** B6
Cheapside, EC2 **20** A4
N13 *off Taplow Rd* **59** J4
Chearsley, SE17 *off Deacon Way* **36** A1
Cheddar Cl, N11 **57** J6
Cheddar Rd, Houns. (Lon.Hthrw Air.) TW6 *off Cromer Rd* **140** D2
Cheddar Waye, Hayes UB4 **102** B6
Cheddington Rd, N18 **60** B3
Chedworth Cl, E16 *off Hallsville Rd* **115** F6
Cheeseman Cl, Hmptn. TW12 **161** E6
Cheesemans Ter, W14 **128** C5
Cheldon Av, NW7 **56** A7
Chelford Rd, Brom. BR1 **172** D5
Chelmer Cres, Bark. IG11 **118** B2
Chelmer Rd, E9 **95** G5
Chelmsford Cl, E6 *off Guildford Rd* **116** C6
W6 **128** A6
Chelmsford Gdns, Ilf. IG1 **80** B7
Chelmsford Rd, E11 **96** D1
E17 **78** A6
E18 **79** F1
N14 **42** C7
Chelmsford Sq, NW10 **107** J1
CHELSEA, SW3 **31** E5
★ **Chelsea Antique Mkt**, SW3 **31** F5
Chelsea Br, SW1 **32** D5
SW8 **32** D5
Chelsea Br Rd, SW1 **32** B3
Chelsea Cloisters, SW3 **31** H2
Chelsea Cl, NW10 *off Winchelsea Rd* **106** D1
Edgware HA8 **70** A2
Hampton (Hmptn H.) TW12 **161** J6
Worcester Park KT4 **183** G7
Chelsea Cres, SW10 *off Harbour Av* **149** F1
Chelsea Embk, SW3 **31** H6
★ **Chelsea FC**, SW6 **30** A7
Chelsea Gdns, SW1 *off Chelsea Br Rd* **32** C4
W13 *off Hathaway Gdns* **104** C5
Sutton SM3 **198** B4
Chelsea Harbour, SW10 **149** F1
Chelsea Harbour Dr, SW10 **149** F1
Chelsea Manor Ct, SW3 **31** H5
Chelsea Manor Gdns, SW3 **31** G5
Chelsea Manor St, SW3 **31** G4
Chelsea Pk Gdns, SW3 **30** E5
★ **Chelsea Physic Gdn**, SW3 **31** J5
Chelsea Reach Twr, SW10 **30** E7
Chelsea Sq, SW3 **31** F3
Chelsea Twrs, SW3 *off Chelsea Manor Gdns* **31** H4
Chelsea Village, SW6 *off Fulham Rd* **129** E7
Chelsea Vista, SW6 *off The Boulevard* **149** F1
Chelsea Wf, SW10 **129** G7
Chelsfield Av, N9 **45** G7
Chelsfield Gdns, SE26 **171** F3
Chelsfield Grn, N9 *off Chelsfield Av* **45** G7
Chelsham Rd, SW4 **150** D3
South Croydon CR2 **202** A6
Chelston App, Ruis. HA4 **84** A2
Chelston Rd, Ruis. HA4 **84** A1
Chelsworth Dr, SE18 **137** G6
Cheltenham Av, Twick. TW1 **144** D7
Cheltenham Cl, N.Mal. KT3 *off Northcote Rd* **182** C3
Northolt UB5 **85** H6
Cheltenham Gdns, E6 **116** B2
Loughton IG10 **48** B6
Cheltenham Pl, W3 **126** B1
Harrow HA3 **69** H4
Cheltenham Rd, E10 **78** C6
SE15 **153** F4
Cheltenham Ter, SW3 **32** A3
Chelverton Rd, SW15 **148** A4
Chelwood, N20 *off Oakleigh Rd N* **57** G2
Chelwood Cl, E4 **46** B6
Chelwood Gdns, Rich. TW9 **146** A2
Chelwood Gdns Pas, Rich. TW9 *off Chelwood Gdns* **146** A2
Chelwood Wk, SE4 **153** H4
Chenappa Cl, E13 **115** G3
Chenduit Way, Stan. HA7 **52** C5
Cheney Row, E17 **77** J1
Cheneys Rd, E11 **97** E3
Cheney St, Pnr. HA5 **66** C5
Chenies, The, Orp. BR6 **193** H6
Chenies Ms, WC1 **9** H6
Chenies Pl, NW1 **9** H1
Chenies St, WC1 **17** H1
Cheniston Gdns, W8 **22** A5
Chepstow Cl, SW15 **148** B6
Chepstow Cres, W11 **108** D7
Ilford IG3 **81** H6
Chepstow Gdns, Sthl. UB1 **103** F6
Chepstow Pl, W2 **108** D6
Chepstow Ri, Croy. CR0 **202** B3
Chepstow Rd, W2 **108** D6
W7 **124** D3
Croydon CR0 **202** B3
Chepstow Vil, W11 **108** C7
Chequers, Buck.H. IG9 **63** H1
Chequers Cl, NW9 **70** E3
Orpington BR5 **193** J4
Chequers Gdns, N13 **59** H5
Chequers La, Dag. RM9 **119** F4
Chequers Par, SE9 *off Eltham High St* **156** C6
Chequers Rd, Loug. IG10 **48** D5
Chequer St, EC1 **12** A6
Chequers Way, N13 **59** J5
Cherbury Cl, SE28 **118** D6
Cherbury Ct, N1 **12** C2
Cherbury St, N1 **12** C2
Cherchefelle Ms, Stan. HA7 **52** E5
Cherimoya Gdns, W.Mol. KT8 *off Kelvinbrook* **179** H3
Cherington Rd, W7 **124** C1
Cheriton Av, Brom. BR2 **191** F5
Ilford IG5 **80** C2
Cheriton Cl, W5 **105** F5
Barnet EN4 **41** J3
Cheriton Dr, SE18 **137** G7
Cheriton Ho, E5 *off Pembury Rd* **94** E5
Cheriton Sq, SW17 **168** A2
Cherry Av, Sthl. UB1 **122** D1
Cherry Blossom Cl, N13 **59** H5
Cherry Cl, E17 *off Eden Rd* **78** B5
NW9 **71** F2
SW2 *off Tulse Hill* **151** G7
W5 **125** G3
Carshalton SM5 **199** J2
Morden SM4 **184** B4
Cherrycot Hill, Orp. BR6 **207** G4
Cherrycot Ri, Orp. BR6 **207** F4
Cherry Cres, Brent. TW8 **124** E7
Cherrycroft Gdns, Pnr. HA5 *off Westfield Pk* **51** F7
Cherrydown Av, E4 **61** J3
Cherrydown Cl, E4 **61** J3
Cherrydown Rd, Sid. DA14 **176** D2
Cherrydown Wk, Rom. RM7 **83** H2
Cherry Gdns, Dag. RM9 **101** F5
Northolt UB5 **85** H7
Cherry Gdn St, SE16 **132** E2
Cherry Garth, Brent. TW8 **125** G4
Cherry Gro, Hayes UB3 **122** B1
Cherry Hill, Barn. (New Barn.) EN5 **41** E6
Harrow HA3 **52** B6
Cherry Hill Gdns, Croy. CR0 **201** F4
Cherry Hills, Wat. WD19 **50** E5
Cherrylands Cl, NW9 **88** C2
Cherry La, West Dr. UB7 **120** C4
Cherry La Rbt, West Dr. UB7 **120** E4
Cherry Laurel Wk, SW2 *off Beechdale Rd* **151** F6
Cherry Orchard, West Dr. UB7 **120** B2
Cherry Orchard Est, SE7 **135** J7
Cherry Orchard Gdns, Croy. CR0 *off Oval Rd* **202** A2
West Molesey KT8 **179** F3
Cherry Orchard Rd, Brom. BR2 **206** B2
Croydon CR0 **202** A2
West Molesey KT8 **179** G3
Cherry Tree Cl, E9 *off Moulins Rd* **113** F1
Wembley HA0 **86** C4
Cherry Tree Ct, NW9 *off Boakes Cl* **70** C4
SE7 *off Fairlawn* **135** J6
Cherry Tree Dr, SW16 **169** E3
Cherry Tree Ri, Buck.H. IG9 **63** J4
Cherry Tree Rd, E15 *off Wingfield Rd* **96** E5
N2 **73** J4
Cherry Tree Wk, EC1 **12** A6
Beckenham BR3 **189** J4
West Wickham BR4 **205** F4
Cherry Tree Way, E13 **116** A4
Stanmore HA7 **53** E6
Cherry Wk, Brom. BR2 **205** G1
Cherry Way, Epsom KT19 **196** D6
Cherrywood Cl, E3 **113** H3
Kingston upon Thames KT2 **164** A7
Cherrywood Dr, SW15 **148** A5
Cherrywood La, Mord. SM4 **184** B4
Cherrywood Lo, SE13 *off Oakwood Cl* **154** D6
Cherry Wd Way, W5 *off Hanger Vale La* **106** A5
Cherston Gdns, Loug. IG10 **48** D4
Cherston Rd, Loug. IG10 **48** D4
Chertsey Dr, Sutt. SM3 **198** B2
Chertsey Rd, E11 **96** D2
Ilford IG1 **99** G4
Twickenham TW1, TW2 **144** C6
Chertsey St, SW17 **168** A5
Chervil Cl, Felt. TW13 **160** A3
Chervil Ms, SE28 **138** B1
Cherwell Ct, Epsom KT19 **196** C4
Cherwell Ho, NW8 *off Church St Est* **7** F6
Cheryls Cl, SW6 **149** E1
Cheseman St, SE26 **171** E3
Chesfield Rd, Kings.T. KT2 **163** H7
Chesham Av, Orp. BR5 **192** E6
Chesham Cl, SW1 **24** B6
Chesham Cres, SE20 **189** F2
Chesham Ms, SW1 **24** B5
Chesham Pl, SW1 **24** B6
Chesham Rd, SE20 **189** F2
SW19 **167** G5
Kingston upon Thames KT1 **182** A1
Chesham St, NW10 **88** D3
SW1 **24** B6
Chesham Ter, W13 **124** E2
Cheshire Cl, E17 **78** B1
SE4 **153** J2
Mitcham CR4 **186** E3
Cheshire Ct, EC4 **19** F4
Cheshire Gdns, Chess. KT9 **195** G6
Cheshire Ho, N18 **61** E4
Cheshire Rd, N22 **59** F7
Cheshire St, E2 **13** G5
Chesholm Rd, N16 **94** B3
Cheshunt Rd, E7 **97** H6
Belvedere DA17 **139** G5
Chesil Ct, E2 **113** F2
Chesilton Rd, SW6 **148** C1
Chesley Gdns, E6 **116** A2
Chesney Cres, Croy. (New Adgtn) CR0 **204** C7
Chesney St, SW11 **150** A1
Chesnut Est, N17 **76** C3
Chesnut Gro, N17 *off Chesnut Rd* **76** D3
Chesnut Rd, N17 **76** C3
Chessell Cl, Th.Hth. CR7 **187** H4
CHESSINGTON, KT9 **195** H6
Chessington Av, N3 **72** B3
Bexleyheath DA7 **139** E7
Chessington Cl, Epsom KT19 **196** C6
Chessington Ct, Pnr. HA5 **67** F4
Chessington Hall Gdns, Chess. KT9 **195** G7
Chessington Hill Pk, Chess. KT9 **196** A5
Chessington Lo, N3 **72** C3
Chessington Mans, E10 *off Albany Rd* **78** A7
Chessington Trade Pk, Chess. KT9 **196** A4
Chessington Way, W.Wick. BR4 **204** B2
Chesson Rd, W14 **128** C6
Chesswood Way, Pnr. HA5 **66** D2
Chester Av, Rich. TW10 **145** J6
Twickenham TW2 **161** F1
Chester Cl, SW1 **24** C4
SW13 **147** H3
Loughton IG10 **49** F1
Richmond TW10 **145** J6
Sutton SM1 **198** D2
Chester Cl N, NW1 **8** E3
Chester Cl S, NW1 **8** E4
Chester Cotts, SW1 **32** B2
Chester Ct, NW1 *off Albany St* **8** E4
SE5 *off Lomond Gro* **132** A7
Chester Cres, E8 *off Ridley Rd* **94** C5
Chester Dr, Har. HA2 **67** F6
Chesterfield Dr, Esher KT10 **194** D2
Chesterfield Gdns, N4 **75** H5
SE10 *off Crooms Hill* **134** D7
W1 **24** D1
Chesterfield Gro, SE22 **152** C5
Chesterfield Hill, W1 **16** D6
Chesterfield Ms, N4 *off Chesterfield Gdns* **75** H5
Chesterfield Rd, E10 **78** C6
N3 **56** D6
W4 **126** C6
Barnet EN5 **40** A5
Epsom KT19 **196** D7
Chesterfield St, W1 **24** D1
Chesterfield Wk, SE10 **154** D1
Chesterfield Way, SE15 **133** F7
Hayes UB3 **122** A2
Chesterford Gdns, NW3 **91** E4
Chesterford Ho, SE18 *off Shooters Hill Rd* **156** A1
Chesterford Rd, E12 **98** C5

Chester Gdns, W13 104 D6
Enfield EN3 45 E6
Morden SM4 185 F6
Chester Gate, NW1 8 D4
Chester Grn, Loug. IG10 49 F1
Chester Ms, E17
off Chingford Rd 78 A2
SW1 24 D5
Chester Path, Loug. IG10 49 F1
Chester Pl, NW1 8 D3
Chester Rd, E7 98 A7
E11 79 H6
E16 115 E4
E17 77 G5
N9 61 E1
N17 76 A3
N19 92 B2
NW1 8 C4
SW19 165 J6
Borehamwood WD6 38 C3
Chigwell IG7 64 D3
Hounslow TW4 142 B3
Hounslow (Lon.Hthrw Air.) TW6 140 D3
Ilford IG3 99 J1
Loughton IG10 48 E2
Sidcup DA15 157 H5
Chester Row, SW1 32 B2
Chesters, The, N.Mal. KT3 182 E1
Chester Sq, SW1 32 D1
Chester Sq Ms, SW1 24 D6
Chester St, E2 13 J5
SW1 24 C5
Chester Ter, NW1 8 D3
Chesterton Cl, SW18 148 D5
Greenford UB6 103 H2
Chesterton Ho, SW11
off Ingrave St 149 G3
Chesterton Rd, E13 115 G3
W10 108 A5
Chesterton Sq, W8
off Pembroke Rd 128 C4
Chesterton Ter, E13 115 G3
Kingston upon Thames KT1 182 A2
Chester Way, SE11 35 F2
Chesthunte Rd, N17 75 J1
Chestnut All, SW6
off Lillie Rd 128 C6
Chestnut Av, E7 97 H4
N8 74 E5
SW14
off Thornton Rd 146 D3
SW17 168 C3
Brentford TW8 125 G4
Buckhurst Hill IG9 64 A3
East Molesey KT8 180 C3
Edgware HA8 53 H6
Epsom KT19 196 E4
Esher KT10 180 A7
Hampton TW12 161 G7
Teddington TW11 180 C2
Wembley HA0 86 E5
West Wickham BR4 205 E5
Chestnut Av N, E17 78 C4
Chestnut Av S, E17 78 C4
Chestnut Cl, N14 42 C5
N16
off Grazebrook Rd 94 A2
SE6 172 C5
SE14 153 J1
SW16 169 G4
Buckhurst Hill IG9 64 A3
Carshalton SM5 199 J1
Sidcup DA15 176 A1
West Drayton UB7 121 E7
Chestnut Ct, SW6
off North End Rd 128 C6
Surbiton KT6
off Penners Gdns 181 H7
Chestnut Dr, E11 79 G6
Bexleyheath DA7 158 D3
Harrow HA3 52 C7
Pinner HA5 66 D6
Chestnut Gro, SE20 171 E7
SW12 150 A7
W5 125 G3
Barnet EN4 41 J5
Ilford IG6 65 H6
Isleworth TW7 144 D4
Mitcham CR4 186 D4
New Malden KT3 182 D3
South Croydon CR2 203 E7
Wembley HA0 86 E5
Chestnut Ho, NW3
off Maitland Pk Vil 91 J6
Chestnut La, N20 56 B1
Chestnut Pl, SE26 170 C4
Chestnut Ri, SE18 137 G6
Chestnut Rd, SE27 169 H3
SW20 184 A2
Kingston upon Thames KT2 163 H7
Twickenham TW2 162 B2
Chestnut Row, N3
off Nether St 56 D7
Chestnut Wk, Wdf.Grn. IG8 63 G5
Chestnut Way, Felt. TW13 160 B3
Cheston Av, Croy. CR0 203 H2
Chettle Cl, SE1 28 B5
Chettle Ct, N8 75 G6
Chetwode Rd, SW17 167 J3
Chetwood Wk, E6 116 B6
Chetwynd Av, Barn. (E.Barn.) EN4 57 J1
Chetwynd Rd, NW5 92 B4
Chevalier Cl, Stan. HA7 53 H4
Cheval Pl, SW7 23 H5
Cheval St, E14 134 A3
Cheveney Wk, Brom. BR2
off Marina Cl 191 G3
Chevening Rd, NW6 108 A2
SE10 135 F5
SE19 170 A6
Chevenings, The, Sid. DA14 176 C3
Cheverton Rd, N19 92 D1
Chevet St, E9
off Kenworthy Rd 95 H5
Cheviot Cl, Enf. EN1 44 A2
Hayes (Harling.) UB3 121 G7
Cheviot Gdns, NW2 90 A2
SE27 169 H4
Cheviot Gate, NW2 90 B2
Cheviot Rd, SE27 169 G5
Cheviot Way, Ilf. IG2 81 H4
Chevron Cl, E16 115 G6
Chevy Rd, Sthl. UB2 123 J2
Chewton Rd, E17 77 H4
Cheyne Av, E18 79 F3
Twickenham TW2 161 F1
Cheyne Cl, NW4 71 J5
Bromley BR2 206 B3
Cheyne Ct, SW3 31 J5
Cheyne Gdns, SW3 31 H5
Cheyne Hill, Surb. KT5 181 J4
Cheyne Ms, SW3 31 H5
Cheyne Pk Dr, W.Wick. BR4 204 C3
Cheyne Path, W7 104 C5
Cheyne Pl, SW3 31 J5
Cheyne Row, SW3 31 G6
Cheyne Wk, N21 43 H5
NW4 71 J6
SW3 31 H6
SW10 30 E7
Croydon CR0 202 D2
Cheyneys Av, Edg. HA8 53 G6
Chichele Gdns, Croy. CR0 202 B4
Chichele Rd, NW2 90 A5
Chicheley Gdns, Har. HA3 51 J7
Chicheley Rd, Har. HA3 51 J7
Chicheley St, SE1 26 D3
Chichester Cl, E6 116 B6
SE3 135 J7
Hampton TW12
off Maple Cl 161 F6
Chichester Ct, NW1
off Royal Coll St 92 C7
Stanmore HA7 69 H3
Chichester Gdns, Ilf. IG1 80 B7
Chichester Ms, SE27 169 G4
Chichester Rents, WC2 18 E3
Chichester Rd, E11 97 E3
N9 60 D1
NW6 108 D2
W2 14 B1
Croydon CR0 202 B3
Chichester St, SW1 33 G4
Chichester Way, E14 134 D4
Feltham TW14 142 B7
Chicksand St, E1 21 G2
Chiddingfold, N12 56 D3
Chiddingstone Av, Bexh. DA7 139 F7
Chiddingstone St, SW6 148 D2
Chieveley Rd, Bexh. DA7 159 H4
Chignell Pl, W13
off The Broadway 124 D1
CHIGWELL, IG7 65 E3
Chigwell Hill, E1
off Pennington St 112 E7
Chigwell Hurst Ct, Pnr. HA5 66 D3
Chigwell La, Loug. IG10 49 F5
Chigwell Pk, Chig. IG7 64 E4
Chigwell Pk Dr, Chig. IG7 64 D3
Chigwell Ri, Chig. IG7 64 D2
Chigwell Rd, E18 79 H3
Woodford Green IG8 79 J2
Chilcombe Ho, SW15
off Fontley Way 147 G7
Chilcot Cl, E14
off Grundy St 114 B6
Chilcott Cl, Wem. HA0 87 F4
Childebert Rd, SW17 168 B2
Childeric Rd, SE14 133 H7
Childerley, Kings.T. KT1
off Burritt Rd 182 A3
Childerley St, SW6
off Fulham Palace Rd 148 B1
Childers, The, Wdf.Grn. IG8 64 C5
Childers St, SE8 133 H6
Child La, SE10 135 F3
CHILDS HILL, NW2 90 D2
Childs Hill Wk, NW2 90 C3
Childs La, SE19
off Westow St 170 B6
Child's Ms, SW5
off Child's Pl 30 A2
Child's Pl, SW5 128 D4
Child's St, SW5 128 D4
Child's Wk, SW5
off Child's St 128 D4
Childs Way, NW11 72 C5
Chilham Cl, Bex. DA5 159 F7
Greenford (Perivale) UB6 104 D2
Chilham Rd, SE9 174 B4
Chilham Way, Brom. BR2 191 G7
Chillerton Rd, SW17 168 A5
Chillingford Ho, SW17
off Blackshaw Rd 167 F4
Chillington Dr, SW11 149 F4
Chillingworth Gdns, Twick. TW1
off Tower Rd 162 C3
Chillingworth Rd, N7 93 F5
Chilmark Gdns, N.Mal. KT3 183 F7
Chilmark Rd, SW16 186 D2
Chiltern Av, Twick. TW2 161 G1
Chiltern Cl, Croy. CR0 202 B3
Worcester Park KT4
off Cotswold Way 197 J2
Chiltern Dene, Enf. EN2 43 F4
Chiltern Dr, Surb. KT5 182 B5
Chiltern Gdns, NW2 90 A3
Bromley BR2 191 F4
Chiltern Rd, E3 114 A4
Ilford IG2 81 H4
Pinner HA5 66 C5
Chiltern St, W1 16 B1
Chiltern Way, Wdf.Grn. IG8 63 G3
Chilthorne Cl, SE6
off Ravensbourne Pk Cres 153 J7
Chilton Av, W5 125 G4
Chilton Gro, SE8 133 G4
Chiltonian Ind Est, SE12 155 F6
Chilton Rd, Edg. HA8 54 A6
Richmond TW9 146 A3
Chiltons, The, E18
off Grove Hill 79 G2
Chilton St, E2 13 G5
Chilvers Cl, Twick. TW2
off Chestnut Rd 162 B2
Chilver St, SE10 135 F5
Chilwell Gdns, Wat. WD19 50 C4
Chilworth Ct, SW19 166 A1
Chilworth Gdns, Sutt. SM1 199 F3
Chilworth Ms, W2 14 D4
Chilworth St, W2 14 D4
Chimes Av, N13 59 G5
China Hall Ms, SE16
off Lower Rd 133 F3
China Ms, SW2 151 F7
★ **Chinatown**, W1
off Gerrard St 17 H5
Chinbrook Cres, SE12 173 H3
Chinbrook Est, SE9 174 A3
Chinbrook Rd, SE12 173 H3
Chinchilla Dr, Houns. TW4 142 C2
Chine, The, N10 74 C4
N21 43 H6
Wembley HA0 87 E5
Ching Ct, WC2 18 A4
Chingdale Rd, E4 62 E3
CHINGFORD, E4 62 B1
Chingford Av, E4 62 B3
CHINGFORD GREEN, E4 63 F1
CHINGFORD HATCH, E4 62 C4
Chingford Ind Cen, E4 61 H5
Chingford La, Wdf.Grn. IG8 62 E4
Chingford Mt Rd, E4 62 A4
Chingford Rd, E4 62 A6
E17 78 B1
Chingley Cl, Brom. BR1 173 E6
Ching Way, E4 61 J6
Chinnery Cl, Enf. EN1 44 C1
Chinnor Cres, Grnf. UB6 103 H2
Chipka St, E14 134 C2
Chipley St, SE14 133 H6
Chipmunk Gro, Nthlt. UB5
off Argus Way 102 E3
Chippendale Ho, SW1 33 E4
Chippendale St, E5 95 G3
Chippenham Av, Wem. HA9 88 B5
Chippenham Gdns, NW6 108 D3
Chippenham Ms, W9 108 D4
Chippenham Rd, W9 108 D4
CHIPPING BARNET, Barn. EN5 40 B4
Chipping Cl, Barn. EN5
off St. Albans Rd 40 B3
Chipstead Av, Th.Hth. CR7 187 H4
Chipstead Cl, SE19 170 C7
Chipstead Gdns, NW2 89 H2
Chipstead St, SW6 148 D1
Chip St, SW4 150 D3
Chirk Cl, Hayes UB4
off Braunston Dr 103 E4
Chisenhale Rd, E3 113 H2
Chisholm Rd, Croy. CR0 202 B2
Richmond TW10 145 J6
Chisledon Wk, E9
off Southmoor Way 95 J6
CHISLEHURST, BR7 174 D7
Chislehurst Av, N12 57 F7
★ **Chislehurst Caves**, Chis. BR7
off Caveside Cl 192 D1
Chislehurst Rd, Brom. BR1 192 A2
Chislehurst BR7 192 A2
Orpington BR5, BR6 193 H4
Richmond TW10 145 H6
Sidcup DA14 176 A5
CHISLEHURST WEST, Chis. BR7 174 C5
Chislet Cl, Beck. BR3 172 A7
Chisley Rd, N15 76 B6
Chiswell Sq, SE3
off Brook La 155 H2
Chiswell St, EC1 20 A1
SE5 36 C7
CHISWICK, W4 126 D6
Chiswick Br, SW14 146 C2
W4 146 C2
Chiswick Cl, Croy. CR0 201 F3
Chiswick Common Rd, W4 126 D4
Chiswick Ct, Pnr. HA5 67 F3
Chiswick Grn Studios, W4
off Evershed Wk 126 C4
Chiswick High Rd, W4 126 D4
Brentford TW8 125 J5
★ **Chiswick Ho**, W4 126 E6
Chiswick Ho Grds, W4 126 D6
Chiswick La, W4 127 E5
Chiswick La S, W4 127 F5
Chiswick Mall, W4 127 F6
W6 127 F6
Chiswick Pk, W4 126 B4
Chiswick Pier, W4 127 F7
Chiswick Quay, W4 146 C1
Chiswick Rd, N9 60 D2
W4 126 C4
Chiswick Rbt, W4 126 A5
Chiswick Sq, W4
off Hogarth Rbt 127 E6
Chiswick Staithe, W4 146 C1
Chiswick Ter, W4
off Acton La 126 C4
Chiswick Village, W4 126 B5
Chiswick Wf, W4 127 F6
Chitterfield Gate, West Dr. (Sipson) UB7 120 D7
Chitty's La, Dag. RM8 100 D2
Chitty St, W1 17 G1
Chivalry Rd, SW11 149 H5
Chivenor Gro, Kings.T. KT2 163 G5
Chivers Rd, E4 62 B3
Choats Manor Way, Dag. RM9 119 F3
Choats Rd, Bark. IG11 118 C2
Dagenham RM9 118 C2
Chobham Gdns, SW19 166 A2
Chobham Rd, E15 96 D5
Choice Vw, Ilf. IG1
off Axon Pl 99 F2

Cholmeley Cres, N6 **74** B7
Cholmeley Pk, N6 **92** B1
Cholmley Gdns, NW6
off Fortune Grn Rd **90** D5
Cholmley Rd, T.Ditt. KT7 **180** E6
Cholmondeley Av, NW10 **107** G2
Cholmondeley Wk, Rich. TW9 **145** F5
Choppins Ct, E1
off Wapping La **133** E1
Chopwell Cl, E15
off Bryant St **96** E7
Chorleywood Cres, Orp. BR5 **193** J2
Choumert Gro, SE15 **152** D2
Choumert Ms, SE15 **152** D2
Choumert Rd, SE15 **152** C3
Choumert Sq, SE15 **152** D2
Chow Sq, E8
off Arcola St **94** C5
Chrislaine Cl, Stai. (Stanw.) TW19 **140** A6
Chrisp St, E14 **114** B5
Christabel Cl, Islw. TW7 **144** B3
Christchurch Av, N12 **57** F6
NW6 **90** B7
Harrow HA3 **69** E4
Teddington TW11 **162** D5
Wembley HA0 **87** H6
Christchurch Cl, N12
off Summers La **57** G7
SW19 **167** G7
Enfield EN2 **43** J2
Christchurch Ct, NW6 **90** B7
Christchurch Gdns, Har. HA3 **68** D4
Christchurch Grn, Wem. HA0 **87** H6
Christchurch Hill, NW3 **91** G3
Christchurch La, Barn. EN5 **40** B2
Christchurch Pk, Sutt. SM2 **199** F7
Christ Ch Pas, EC1 **19** H3
Christchurch Pas, NW3 **91** F3
Barnet EN5 **40** B3
Christ Ch Path, Hayes UB3 **121** F3
Christchurch Rd, N8 **74** E6
SW2 **169** F1
SW14 **146** B5
SW19 **185** G1
Christ Ch Rd, Beck. BR3
off Fairfield Rd **190** A2
Christchurch Rd, Ilf. IG1 **99** E1
Sidcup DA15 **175** J4
Christ Ch Rd, Surb. KT5 **181** J6
Christchurch Sq, E9
off Victoria Pk Rd **113** F1
Christchurch St, SW3 **31** J5
Christchurch Ter, SW3 **31** J5
Christchurch Way, SE10 **135** E4
Christian Ct, SE16 **133** J1
Christian Flds, SW16 **169** G7
Christian St, E1 **21** J3
Christie Ct, N19
off Hornsey Rd **93** E2
Christie Dr, Croy. CR0 **188** D5
Christie Gdns, Rom. RM6 **82** B6
Christie Rd, E9 **95** H6
Christina Sq, N4 **93** H1
Christina St, EC2 **12** D5
Christine Worsley Cl, N21
off Highfield Rd **59** H2
Christopher Av, W7 **124** D3
Christopher Cl, SE16 **133** G2
Sidcup DA15 **157** J5
Christopher Gdns, Dag. RM9 *off Wren Rd* **100** D5
Christopher Pl, NW1 **9** J4
Christopher Rd, Sthl. UB2 **122** B4
Christopher's Ms, W11
off Penzance St **128** B1
Christopher St, EC2 **12** C6
Chryssell Rd, SW9 **131** G7
Chubworthy St, SE14 **133** H6
Chudleigh Cres, Ilf. IG3 **99** H4
Chudleigh Gdns, Sutt. SM1 **199** F3
Chudleigh Rd, NW6 **90** A7
SE4 **153** J5
Twickenham TW2 **144** C7
Chudleigh St, E1 **113** G6
Chudleigh Way, Ruis. HA4 **84** A1
Chulsa Rd, SE26 **170** E5
Chumleigh St, SE5 **36** D5
Chumleigh Wk, Surb. KT5 **181** J4
Church All, Croy. CR0 **201** G1
Church App, SE21 **170** A3
Staines (Stanw.) TW19 **140** A6
Church Av, E4 **62** D6
NW1
off Kentish Town Rd **92** B6
SW14 **146** D3
Beckenham BR3 **190** A1
Northolt UB5 **85** F7
Pinner HA5 **67** E6
Sidcup DA14 **176** A5
Southall UB2 **123** E3
Churchbury Cl, Enf. EN1 **44** B2
Churchbury La, Enf. EN1 **44** A3
Churchbury Rd, SE9 **156** A7
Enfield EN1 **44** A2
Church Cl, N20 **57** H3
W8 **22** A3
Edgware HA8 **54** C5
Hounslow TW3
off Bath Rd **143** F3
Loughton IG10 **48** C2
West Drayton UB7 **120** B3
Church Cor, SW17
off Mitcham Rd **167** J5
Church Ct, Rich. TW9
off George St **145** G5
Church Cres, E9 **95** G7
N3 **72** C1
N10 **74** B4
N20 **57** H3
Churchcroft Cl, SW12 **150** A7
Churchdown, Brom. BR1 **173** E4
Church Dr, NW9 **88** D1
Harrow HA2 **67** F6
West Wickham BR4 **205** E3
Church Elm La, Dag. RM10 **101** G6
CHURCH END, N3 **72** C1
CHURCH END, NW10 **88** E6
Church End, E17 **78** B4
NW4 **71** H3
Church Entry, EC4 **19** H4
Church Est Almshouses, Rich. TW9
off St. Mary's Gro **145** J4
★ **Church Farm Ho Mus**, NW4 **71** H3
Church Fm La, Sutt. SM3 **198** B6
Churchfield Av, N12 **57** F6
Churchfield Cl, Har. HA2 **67** J4
Churchfield Rd, W3 **126** C1
W7 **124** B2
W13 **125** E1
Welling DA16 **158** A3
Churchfields, E18 **79** G1
SE10 *off Roan St* **134** C6
Loughton IG10 **48** B4
West Molesey KT8 **179** G3
Churchfields Av, Felt. TW13 **161** F3
Churchfields Rd, Beck. BR3 **189** G2
Church Gdns, W5 **125** G2
Wembley HA0 **86** D4
Church Garth, N19
off Pemberton Gdns **92** D2
Church Gate, SW6 **148** B3
Church Gro, SE13 **154** B4
Kingston upon Thames KT1 **181** F1
Church Hill, E17 **78** A4
N21 **43** F7
SE18 **136** C3
SW19 **166** C5
Carshalton SM5 **199** J5
Harrow HA1 **86** B1
Loughton IG10 **48** B3
Church Hill Rd, E17 **78** B4
Barnet EN4 **41** J7
Surbiton KT6 **181** H5
Sutton SM3 **198** A4
Church Hill Wd, Orp. BR5 **193** J5
Church Hyde, SE18
off Old Mill Rd **137** H6
Churchill Av, Har. HA3 **68** E6
Churchill Ct, SE18
off Rushgrove St **136** C4
W5 **105** J4
Northolt UB5 **85** G5
Churchill Gdns, SW1 **33** F4
W3 **106** A6
Churchill Gdns Rd, SW1 **33** E4
Churchill Ms, Wdf.Grn. IG8
off High Rd Woodford Grn **63** F6
★ **Churchill Mus & Cabinet War Rooms**, SW1 **25** J3
Churchill Pl, E14 **134** B1
Harrow HA1
off Sandridge Cl **68** B4
Churchill Rd, E16 **115** J6
NW2 **89** H6
Churchill Rd, NW5 **92** B4
Edgware HA8 **53** J6
Churchill Ter, E4 **62** A4
Churchill Wk, E9 **95** F5
Churchill Way, Brom. BR1
off Ethelbert Rd **191** G3
Sunbury-on-Thames TW16 **160** A5
Church La, E11 **97** E1
E17 **78** B4
N2 **73** G3
N8 **75** F4
N9 **60** D2
N17 **76** B1
NW9 **88** C2
SW17 **168** B4
SW19 **184** C1
W5 **125** F2
Bromley BR2 **206** B1
Chessington KT9 **195** J6
Chislehurst BR7 **193** F1
Dagenham RM10 **101** H6
Enfield EN1 **44** A3
Harrow HA3 **68** C1
Loughton IG10 **48** C3
Pinner HA5 **67** E3
Richmond TW10 **163** H1
Teddington TW11 **162** C5
Thames Ditton KT7 **180** C6
Twickenham TW1 **162** D1
Wallington SM6 **200** D3
Churchley Rd, SE26 **171** E4
Church Manor Est, SW9
off Vassall Rd **131** G7
Church Manorway, SE2 **137** J4
Church Manorway Ind Est, Erith DA8 **139** J3
Churchmead, SE5
off Camberwell Rd **131** J7
Churchmead Cl, Barn. (E.Barn.) EN4 **41** H6
Church Meadow, Surb. (Long Dit.) KT6 **195** F2
Churchmead Rd, NW10 **89** G6
Churchmore Rd, SW16 **186** C1
Church Mt, N2 **73** G5
Church Paddock Ct, Wall. SM6 **200** D3
Church Pas, EC2
off Gresham St **20** A3
Barnet EN5
off Wood St **40** C4
Surbiton KT6 **181** H5
Church Path, E11 **79** G5
E17 *off St. Mary Rd* **78** B4
N5 **93** H5
N12 **57** F5
N17
off White Hart La **60** B7
N20 **57** F4
NW10 **89** E7
SW14 **146** D3
SW19 **184** D2
W4 **126** C3
W7 **124** B1
Mitcham CR4 **185** H3
Southall UB1 **123** G1
Southall (Sthl Grn) UB2 **123** F3
Church Pl, SW1 **17** G6
W5 *off Church Gdns* **125** G2
Mitcham CR4 **185** H3
Twickenham TW1
off Church St **162** D1
Church Ri, SE23 **171** G1
Chessington KT9 **195** J6
Church Rd, E10 **96** B2
E12 **98** B5
E17 **77** H2
N1 **93** J6
N6 **74** A6
N17 **76** B1
NW4 **71** H4
NW10 **89** E6
SE19 **188** B1
SW13 **147** F2
SW19 (Wimbledon) **166** B3
W3 **126** C2
W7 **124** C1
Barking IG11 **99** F6
Bexleyheath DA7 **159** F2
Bromley BR2 **191** G2
Bromley (Short.) BR2 **190** E3
Buckhurst Hill IG9 **63** H1
Croydon CR0 **201** H3
East Molesey KT8 **180** A4
Enfield EN3 **45** F6
Epsom (W.Ewell) KT19 **196** D7
Esher (Clay.) KT10 **194** C6
Feltham TW13 **160** D5
Hayes UB3 **121** J1
Church Rd, Hounslow (Cran.) TW5 **122** B5
Hounslow (Heston) TW5 **123** G7
Ilford IG2 **81** G6
Isleworth TW7 **144** A1
Keston BR2 **206** A7
Kingston upon Thames KT1 **181** J2
Loughton (High Beach) IG10 **47** H2
Mitcham CR4 **185** G2
Northolt UB5 **85** F7
Orpington (Farnboro.) BR6 **207** F5
Richmond TW9, TW10 **145** H5
Richmond (Ham) TW10 **163** J5
Sidcup DA14 **176** A4
Southall UB2 **123** F3
Stanmore HA7 **53** E5
Surbiton (Long Dit.) KT6 **195** F2
Sutton SM3 **198** B6
Teddington TW11 **162** B4
Wallington SM6 **200** C3
Welling DA16 **158** B2
West Drayton UB7 **120** A3
Worcester Park KT4 **196** E1
Church Rd Merton, SW19 **185** G1
Church Rd Twr Block, Stan. HA7 *off Church Rd* **53** F5
Church Row, NW3 **91** F4
Chislehurst BR7 **175** F7
Church St, E15 **115** E1
E16 **136** E1
N9 **60** B2
NW8 **15** F1
W2 **15** F1
W4 **127** E6
Croydon CR0 **201** J2
Dagenham RM10 **101** H6
Enfield EN2 **44** A3
Hampton TW12 **179** J1
Isleworth TW7 **144** E3
Kingston upon Thames KT1 **181** G2
Sunbury-on-Thames TW16 **178** B3
Sutton SM1
off High St **199** E5
Twickenham TW1 **162** D1
Church St Est, NW8 **7** F6
Church St N, E15 **115** E1
Church St Pas, E15
off Church St **115** E1
Church Stretton Rd, Houns. TW3 **143** J5
Church Ter, NW4 **71** H3
SE13 **154** E3
SW8 **150** D2
Richmond TW10 **145** G5
Church Vale, N2 **73** J3
SE23 **171** F2
Churchview Rd, Twick. TW2 **162** A1
Church Wk, N6
off Swains La **92** A3
N16 **94** A4
NW2 **90** C3
NW4 **71** J3
NW9 **88** D2
SW13 **147** G1
SW15 **147** H5
SW16 **186** C2
SW20 **183** J3
Brentford TW8 **125** F6
Enfield EN2 **44** A3
Richmond TW9
off Red Lion St **145** G5
Thames Ditton KT7 **180** C6
Churchward Ho, W14
off Ivatt Pl **128** C5
Church Way, N20 **57** G3
Churchway, NW1 **9** J3
Church Way, Barn. EN4 **41** J4
Edgware HA8 **54** A6
Churchwell Path, E9 **95** F5
Churchwood Gdns, Wdf.Grn. IG8 **63** G4
Churchyard Row, SE11 **35** H1
Church Yd Wk, W2 **15** E1
Churston Av, E13 **115** H1
Churston Cl, SW2
off Tulse Hill **169** H1
Churston Dr, Mord. SM4 **184** A5
Churston Gdns, N11 **58** C6
Churton Pl, SW1 **33** G2
Churton St, SW1 **33** G2
Chusan Pl, E14
off Commercial Rd **113** J6
Chyngton Cl, Sid. DA15 **175** J3

Cibber Rd, SE23 ....171 G2
Cicada Rd, SW18 ....149 F5
Cicely Rd, SE15 ....152 D1
Cinderella Path, NW11
off North End Rd 91 E1
Cinderford Way, Brom. BR1 ....173 E4
Cinnabar Wf, E1 ....29 J2
Cinnamon Cl, SE15 ....37 F7
Croydon CR0 ....186 E7
Cinnamon Row, SW11 ...149 F3
Cinnamon St, E1 ....133 E1
Cintra Pk, SE19 ....170 C7
Circle, The, NW2 ....89 E3
NW7 ....54 D5
SE1 ....29 F3
Circle Gdns, SW19 ......184 D2
Circuits, The, Pnr. HA5 ....66 C4
Circular Rd, N17 ....76 C3
Circular Way, SE18 ....136 C6
Circus Lo, NW8 ....6 E3
Circus Ms, W1 ....15 J1
Circus Pl, EC2 ....20 C2
Circus Rd, NW8 ....6 E3
Circus St, SE10 ....134 C7
Cirencester St, W2 ....14 A1
Cirrus Cl, Wall. SM6 .....201 E7
Cissbury Ring N, N12 .....56 C5
Cissbury Ring S, N12 .....56 C5
Cissbury Rd, N15 ....76 A5
Citadel Pl, SE11 ....34 C3
Citizen Ho, N7
off Harvist Est 93 G4
Citizen Rd, N7 ....93 G4
C.I. Twr, N.Mal. KT3 .....183 E3
Citron Ter, SE15
off Nunhead La 153 E3
City Business Cen, SE16
off Lower Rd 133 F2
City Cross Business Pk, SE10 *off Salutation Rd* .135 E4
City Forum, EC1 ....11 J3
City Gdn Row, N1 ....11 H2
City Gate Ho, Ilf. IG2 .....80 E6
City Mill River Towpath, E15 ....96 B7
★ **City of Westminster Archives Cen**, SW1 ....25 J5
City Pt, EC2 ....20 B1
City Rd, EC1 ....11 G2
City Twr, E14
off Limeharbour 134 B2
★ **City Uni**, EC1 ....11 G4
City Vw, Ilf. IG1
off Axon Pl 99 F2
City Vw Apts, N1
off Essex Rd 93 J7
Cityview Ct, SE22 ....152 D7
City Wk, SE1 ....28 D4
Civic Way, Ilf. IG6 ....81 F4
Ruislip HA4 ....84 D5
Clabon Ms, SW1 ....23 J6
Clack St, SE16 ....133 F2
Clacton Rd, E6 ....116 A3
E17 ....77 H6
N17 *off Sperling Rd* 76 C2
Claigmar Gdns, N3 ....72 E1
Claire Ct, N12 ....57 F3
Bushey (Bushey Hth) WD23 ....52 A1
Pinner HA5
off Westfield Pk 51 F7
Claire Gdns, Stan. HA7 ....53 F5
Claire Pl, E14 ....134 A3
Clairvale Rd, Houns. TW5 .142 D1
Clairview Rd, SW16 .....168 B5
Clairville Gdns, W7 ......124 B1
Clairville Pt, SE23 ....171 G3
Clamp Hill, Stan. HA7 .....52 A4
Clancarty Rd, SW6 ......148 D2
Clandon Cl, W3 ....126 B2
Epsom KT17 ....197 F6
Clandon Gdns, N3 ....72 D3
Clandon Rd, Ilf. IG3 ......99 H2
Clandon St, SE8 ....154 A2
Clanricarde Gdns, W2 ....108 D7
CLAPHAM, SW4 ....150 B3
★ **Clapham Common**, SW4 ....150 A4
Clapham Common, SW4 .150 C4
Clapham Common N Side, SW4 ....150 B4
Clapham Common S Side, SW4 ....150 B6
Clapham Common W Side, SW4 ....150 A4
Clapham Cres, SW4 .....150 D4
Clapham Est, SW11 .....149 H4
Clapham High St, SW4 ..150 D4
Clapham Junct Sta, SW11 ....149 G4
Clapham Manor St, SW4 .150 C3
CLAPHAM PARK, SW4 ...150 D6
Clapham Pk Est, SW4 ...150 D6
Clapham Pk Rd, SW4 ....150 D4
Clapham Rd, SW9 ....150 E3
Clapham Rd Est, SW4 ...150 D3
Clap La, Dag. RM10 ......101 H3
Claps Gate La, E6 ....116 D4
Clapton Common, E5 .....76 C7
CLAPTON PARK, E5 ......95 H4
Clapton Pk Est, E5
off Blackwell Cl 95 G4
Clapton Pas, E5 ....95 F5
Clapton Sq, E5 ....95 F5
Clapton Ter, N16
off Oldhill St 94 D1
Clapton Way, E5 ....94 D4
Clara Pl, SE18 ....136 D4
Clare Cl, N2
off Thomas More Way .73 F3
Clare Cor, SE9 ....156 E7
Claredale St, E2 ....13 J2
Clare Gdns, E7 ....97 G4
W11
off Westbourne Pk Rd .108 B6
Barking IG11 ....99 J6
Clare Ho, E3 ....113 J1
Clare La, N1 ....93 J7
Clare Lawn Av, SW14 ....146 D5
Clare Mkt, WC2 ....18 C4
Clare Ms, SW6
off Waterford Rd 128 E7
Claremont Av, Har. HA3 ...69 H5
New Malden KT3 .....183 G5
Sunbury-on-Thames TW16 ....178 B1
Claremont Cl, E16 ....136 D1
N1 ....11 F2
SW2
off Christchurch Rd ..169 F1
Orpington BR6 ....206 D4
Claremont Ct, Surb. KT6
off St. James Rd 181 G6
Claremont Gdns, Ilf. IG3 ..99 H2
Surbiton KT6 ....181 H5
Claremont Gro, W4
off Edensor Gdns 127 E7
Woodford Green IG8 ...63 J6
Claremont Pk, N3 ....72 B1
Claremont Rd, E7 ....97 H5
E11 *off Grove Grn Rd* ...96 D3
E17 ....77 H2
N6 ....74 C7
NW2 ....90 A3
W9 ....108 B2
W13 ....104 D5
Bromley BR1 ....192 B4
Croydon CR0 ....202 D1
Esher (Clay.) KT10 ....194 B7
Harrow HA3 ....68 B2
Surbiton KT6 ....181 H6
Teddington TW11 ......162 C5
Twickenham TW1 .....145 E6
Claremont Sq, N1 ....10 E2
Claremont St, E16 ......136 D1
N18 ....60 D6
SE10 ....134 B7
Claremont Way, NW2 .....89 J1
Clarence Av, SW4 ....150 D6
Bromley BR1 ....192 B4
Ilford IG2 ....80 D6
New Malden KT3 .....182 C2
Clarence Cl, Barn. EN4 ....41 G5
Clarence Cres, SW4 .....150 D6
Sidcup DA14 ....176 B3
Clarence Gdns, NW1 ......9 E4
Clarence Gate, Wdf.Grn. IG8 ....64 D6
Clarence Gate Gdns, NW1
off Glentworth St 8 A6
★ **Clarence Ho**, SW1 ....25 G3
Clarence La, SW15 ......147 E6
Clarence Ms, E5 ....95 E5
SE16 ....133 G1
SW12 ....150 B7
Clarence Pl, E5 ....95 E5
Clarence Rd, E5 ....95 E4
E12 ....98 A5
E16 ....115 E4
E17 ....77 G2
N15 ....75 J5
N22 ....59 E7
NW6 ....90 C7
SE8 ....134 B6
SE9 ....174 B2
SW19 ....166 E6
W4 ....126 A5
Bexleyheath DA6 .....158 E4
Bromley BR1 ....192 A3
Croydon CR0 ....188 A7
Enfield EN3 ....45 E5
Richmond TW9 ....145 J1
Sidcup DA14 ....176 B3
Sutton SM1 ....198 E4
Teddington TW11 .....162 C6
Clarence Rd, Wallington SM6 ....200 B5
Clarence St, Kings.T. KT1 ....181 H2
Richmond TW9 ....145 H4
Southall UB2 ....122 D3
Clarence Ter, NW1 ....8 A5
Hounslow TW3 ....143 H4
Clarence Wk, SW4 ......150 E2
Clarence Way, NW1 ......92 B7
Clarence Way Est, NW1 ...92 B7
Clarendon Cl, E9 ....95 F7
W2 ....15 G5
Clarendon Cres, Twick. TW2 ....162 A3
Clarendon Cross, W11
off Portland Rd 108 B7
Clarendon Dr, SW15 .....147 J4
Clarendon Gdns, NW4 ....71 G3
W9 ....6 D6
Ilford IG1 ....98 C1
Wembley HA9 ....87 H4
Clarendon Gro, NW1 ......9 H3
Mitcham CR4 ....185 J3
Clarendon Ms, W2 ....15 G4
Bexley DA5 ....177 H1
Borehamwood WD6
off Clarendon Rd 38 A3
Clarendon Pl, W2 ....15 G5
Clarendon Ri, SE13 ......154 C3
Clarendon Rd, E11 ....96 D1
E17 ....78 B6
E18 ....79 G3
N8 ....75 F3
N15 ....75 H4
N18 ....60 D6
N22 ....75 F2
SW19 ....167 H7
W5 ....105 H3
W11 ....108 B7
Borehamwood WD6 ....38 A3
Croydon CR0 ....201 H2
Harrow HA1 ....68 B6
Hayes UB3 ....121 J2
Wallington SM6 ......200 C6
Clarendon St, SW1 ....32 E4
Clarendon Ter, W9 ....6 D5
Clarendon Wk, W11 ......108 B6
Clarendon Way, N21 ......43 J6
Chislehurst BR7 ......193 J3
Orpington BR5 ....193 J3
Clarens St, SE6 ....171 J2
Clare Pl, SW15
off Minstead Gdns ...147 F7
Clare Pt, NW2
off Claremont Rd 90 A1
Clare Rd, E11 ....78 D6
NW10 ....89 G7
SE14 ....153 J1
Greenford UB6 ....86 A6
Hounslow TW4 ....143 F3
Staines (Stanw.) TW19 ....140 B7
Clare St, E2 ....113 E2
Claret Gdns, SE25 ....188 B4
Clareville Gro, SW7 ......30 D2
Clareville Rd, Orp. BR5 ...207 F2
Clareville St, SW7 ....30 D2
Clare Way, Bexh. DA7 ....158 E1
Clarewood Wk, SW9 .....151 H4
Clarges Ms, W1 ....24 D1
Clarges St, W1 ....24 E1
Claribel Rd, SW9 ....151 H2
Claridge Rd, Dag. RM8 ...100 D1
Clarissa Rd, Rom. RM6 ....82 D7
Clarissa St, E8 ....112 C1
Clarke Ms, N9
off Plevna Rd 60 E3
Clarke Path, N16 ....94 D1
Clarkes Av, Wor.Pk. KT4 ..198 A1
Clarke's Ms, W1 ....16 C1
Clark Lawrence Ct, SW11
off Winstanley Rd 149 G3
Clarkson Rd, E16 ....115 F6
Clarkson Row, NW1 ....9 F2
Clarksons, The, Bark. IG11 ....117 F2
Clarkson St, E2 ....112 E3
Clarks Pl, EC2 ....20 D3
Clarks Rd, Ilf. IG1 ....99 G2
Clark St, E1 ....113 E5
Clark Way, Houns. TW5 ...122 D7
Classon Cl, West Dr. UB7 ....120 B2
Claude Rd, E10 ....96 C2
E13 ....115 H1
SE15 ....152 E2
Claude St, E14 ....134 A4
Claudia Jones Way, SW2 .150 E6
Claudia Pl, SW19 ....166 B1
Claudius Cl, Stan. HA7 ....53 G3
Claughton Rd, E13 ......115 J2
Clauson Av, Nthlt. UB5 ....85 H5
Clavell St, SE10 ....134 C6
Claverdale Rd, SW2 .....151 F7
Clavering Av, SW13 .....127 H6
Clavering Cl, Twick. TW1 ..162 D4
Clavering Rd, E12 ....98 A1
Claverings Ind Est, N9 ....61 G2
Claverley Gro, N3 ....56 D7
Claverley Vil, N3 ....56 E7
Claverton St, SW1 ....33 G4
Clave St, E1
off Cinnamon St 133 F1
Claxton Gro, W6 ....128 A5
Claxton Path, SE4
off Hainford Cl 153 G4
Clay Av, Mitch. CR4 ......186 B2
Claybank Gro, SE13
off Algernon Rd 154 B3
Claybourne Ms, SE19
off Church Rd 170 B7
Claybridge Rd, SE12 .....173 J4
Claybrook Cl, N2 ....73 G3
Claybrook Rd, W6 ....128 A6
Claybury Bdy, Ilf. IG5 .....80 B3
Claybury Hall, Wdf.Grn. IG8 ....64 C7
Claybury Rd, Wdf.Grn. IG8 ....64 B7
Claydon, SE17
off Deacon Way 35 J1
Claydon Dr, Croy. CR0 ...201 E4
Claydown Ms, SE18
off Woolwich New Rd 136 D5
Clayfarm Rd, SE9 ....175 F2
CLAYGATE, Esher KT10 ..194 B7
Claygate Cres, Croy. (New Adgtn) CR0 .....204 C6
Claygate La, Esher KT10 ..194 D2
Thames Ditton KT7 ....194 D1
Claygate Lo Cl, Esher (Clay.) KT10 ....194 B7
Claygate Rd, W13 ....124 E3
CLAYHALL, Ilf. IG5 ....80 C2
Clayhall Av, Ilf. IG5 ....80 B3
Clayhill, Surb. KT5 ....182 A5
Clayhill Cres, SE9 ....174 A4
Claylands Pl, SW8 ....34 E7
Claylands Rd, SW8 ....34 D6
Clay La, Edg. HA8 ....54 A1
Staines (Stanw.) TW19 .140 C7
Claymill Ho, SE18 ....137 F5
Claymore Cl, Mord. SM4 ....184 D7
Claymore Ct, E17
off Billet Rd 77 H1
Claypole Dr, Houns. TW5 .143 E1
Claypole Rd, E15 ....114 C2
Clayponds Av, Brent. TW8 125 H4
Clayponds Gdns, W5 ....125 G4
Clayponds La, Brent. TW8 ....125 H5
Clay Rd, The, Loug. IG10 ..48 B1
Clayside, Chig. IG7 ....65 F6
Clay's La, Loug. IG10 .....48 D1
Clay St, W1 ....16 A2
Clayton Av, Wem. HA0 ....87 H7
Clayton Cl, E6
off Brandreth Rd 116 C6
Clayton Cres, N1 ....111 E1
Brentford TW8 ....125 G5
Clayton Dr, SE8
off Sapphire Rd 133 H5
Clayton Fld, NW9 ....55 E7
Clayton Ms, SE10 ....154 D1
Clayton Rd, SE15 ....152 D1
Chessington KT9 .....195 F4
Hayes UB3 ....121 H2
Isleworth TW7 ....144 B3
Romford RM7 ....101 J1
Clayton St, SE11 ....34 E5
Clayton Ter, Hayes UB4
off Jollys La 102 D5
Claywood Cl, Orp. BR6 ...193 H7
Clayworth Cl, Sid. DA15 ..158 B6
Cleanthus Cl, SE18 ......157 E1
Cleanthus Rd, SE18 .....157 E1
Clearbrook Way, E1
off West Arbour St ...113 F6
Clearwater Pl, Surb. KT6
off Portsmouth Rd ...181 F6
Clearwater Ter, W11
off Lorne Gdns 128 A2
Clearwell Dr, W9 ....6 A6
Cleave Av, Hayes UB3 ...121 H4
Orpington BR6 ....207 H6
Cleaveland Rd, Surb. KT6 ....181 G5
Cleaverholme Cl, SE25 ...188 E6
Cleaver Sq, SE11 ....35 F3
Cleaver St, SE11 ....35 F3
Cleeve Hill, SE23 ....171 E1
Cleeve Pk Gdns, Sid. DA14 ....176 B2

Cleeve Way, SW15
off Danebury Av 147 F7
Sutton SM1 199 E1
Clegg Ho, SE3
off Pinto Way 155 H4
Clegg St, E1
off Prusom St 133 E1
E13 115 G2
Cleland Path, Loug. IG10 49 E1
Clematis Gdns, Wdf.Grn. IG8 63 G5
Clematis St, W12 107 F7
Clem Attlee Ct, SW6 128 C6
Clem Attlee Par, SW6
off North End Rd 128 C6
Clemence Rd, Dag. RM10 119 J1
Clemence St, E14 113 J5
Clement Av, SW4 150 D4
Clement Cl, NW6 89 J7
W4 *off Acton La* 126 D4
Clement Gdns, Hayes UB3 121 H4
Clementhorpe Rd, Dag. RM9 100 C6
Clementina Rd, E10 95 J1
Clementine Cl, W13
off Balfour Rd 124 E2
Clementine Wk, Wdf.Grn. IG8 *off Salway Cl* 63 G7
Clement Rd, SW19 166 B5
Beckenham BR3 189 G2
Clements Av, E16 115 G7
Clements Cl, N12 56 E4
Clements Ct, Houns. TW4 142 D4
Ilford IG1
off Clements La 98 E3
Clement's Inn, WC2 18 D4
Clement's Inn Pas, WC2 18 D4
Clements La, EC4 20 C5
Ilford IG1 98 E3
Clements Pl, Brent. TW8 125 G5
Clements Rd, E6 98 C7
SE16 29 J6
Ilford IG1 98 E3
Clendon Way, SE18
off Polthorne Gro 137 G4
Clennam St, SE1 28 A3
Clensham Ct, Sutt. SM1
off Sutton Common Rd 198 D2
Clensham La, Sutt. SM1 198 D2
Clenston Ms, W1 15 J3
Cleopatra Cl, Stan. HA7 53 G3
★ **Cleopatra's Needle**, WC2 26 C1
Clephane Rd, N1 93 J6
Clere St, EC2 12 C5
CLERKENWELL, EC1 11 G6
Clerkenwell Cl, EC1 11 F5
Clerkenwell Grn, EC1 11 F6
Clerkenwell Rd, EC1 10 E6
Clerks Piece, Loug. IG10 48 C3
Clermont Rd, E9 113 F1
Clevedon Cl, N16
off Smalley Cl 94 C3
Clevedon Gdns, Hayes UB3 121 G3
Hounslow TW5 142 B1
Clevedon Rd, SE20 189 G1
Kingston upon Thames KT1 182 A2
Twickenham TW1 145 G6
Cleveland Av, SW20 184 C2
W4 127 F4
Hampton TW12 161 F7
Cleveland Cres, Borwd. WD6 38 C5
Cleveland Gdns, N4 75 J5
NW2 90 A2
SW13 147 F2
W2 14 C4
Worcester Park KT4 197 E2
Cleveland Gro, E1
off Cleveland Way 113 F4
Cleveland Ms, W1 17 F1
Cleveland Pk, Stai. TW19 140 B6
Cleveland Pk Av, E17 78 A4
Cleveland Pk Cres, E17 78 A4
Cleveland Pl, SW1 25 G1
Cleveland Ri, Mord. SM4 184 A7
Cleveland Rd, E18 79 G3
N1 94 A7
N9 45 E7
SW13 147 F2
W4 *off Antrobus Rd* 126 C3
W13 104 E5
Ilford IG1 99 E3
Isleworth TW7 144 D4
New Malden KT3 182 E4
Welling DA16 157 J2
Worcester Park KT4 197 E2
Cleveland Row, SW1 25 F2
Cleveland Sq, W2 14 C4
Cleveland St, W1 9 F6
Cleveland Ter, W2 14 D3
Cleveland Way, E1 113 F4
Cleveley Cl, SE7 136 A4
Cleveley Cres, W5 105 H2
Cleveleys Rd, E5 95 E3
Cleverly Est, W12 127 G1
Cleve Rd, NW6 90 D7
Sidcup DA14 176 D3
Cleves Cl, Loug. IG10 48 B6
Cleves Rd, E6 116 A1
Richmond TW10 163 F3
Cleves Wk, Ilf. IG6 65 F7
Cleves Way, Hmptn. TW12 161 F7
Ruislip HA4 84 D1
Clewer Cres, Har. HA3 68 A1
Clewer Ho, SE2
off Wolvercote Rd 138 D2
Clichy Est, E1 113 F5
Clifden Ms, E5
off Clifden Rd 95 G4
Clifden Rd, E5 95 F5
Brentford TW8 125 G6
Twickenham TW1 162 C1
Cliffe Rd, S.Croy. CR2 202 A5
Cliffe Wk, Sutt. SM1
off Turnpike La 199 F5
Clifford Av, SW14 146 B3
Chislehurst BR7 174 C6
Ilford IG5 80 E1
Wallington SM6 200 C4
Clifford Cl, Nthlt. UB5 103 E1
Clifford Dr, SW9 151 H4
Clifford Gdns, NW10 107 J2
Hayes UB3 121 G4
Clifford Haigh Ho, SW6
off Fulham Palace Rd 128 A7
Clifford Rd, E16 115 F4
E17 78 C2
N9 45 F6
SE25 188 D4
Barnet EN5 41 E3
Hounslow TW4 142 D3
Richmond TW10 163 G2
Wembley HA0 105 G1
Clifford's Inn Pas, EC4 19 E4
Clifford St, W1 17 F6
Clifford Way, NW10 89 F4
Cliff Rd, NW1 92 D6
Cliff Ter, SE8 154 A2
Cliffview Rd, SE13 154 A3
Cliff Vil, NW1 92 D6
Cliff Wk, E16 115 F5
Clifton Av, E17 77 G3
N3 72 C1
W12 127 F1
Feltham TW13 160 C3
Stanmore HA7 69 E2
Wembley HA9 87 J6
Clifton Cl, Orp. BR6 207 F5
Clifton Ct, N4
off Biggerstaff St 93 G2
NW8 6 E5
Woodford Green IG8
off Snakes La W 63 G6
Clifton Cres, SE15 133 E7
Clifton Est, SE15
off Consort Rd 152 E1
Clifton Gdns, N15 76 C6
NW11 72 C6
W4 *off Dolman Rd* 126 D4
W9 6 C6
Enfield EN2 42 E4
Clifton Gro, E8 94 D6
Clifton Hill, NW8 109 E2
Clifton Pk Av, SW20 183 J2
Clifton Pl, SE16
off Canon Beck Rd 133 F2
W2 15 F5
Clifton Ri, SE14 133 H7
Clifton Rd, E7 98 A6
E16 115 E5
N1 93 J6
N3 73 F1
N8 74 D6
N22 74 C1
NW10 107 G2
SE25 188 B4
SW19 166 A6
W9 6 D5
Greenford UB6 103 J4
Harrow HA3 69 J5
Hounslow (Lon.Hthrw Air.) TW6
off Inner Ring E 140 E3
Ilford IG2 81 G6
Isleworth TW7 144 A2
Kingston upon Thames KT2 163 J7
Loughton IG10 48 B4
Clifton Rd, Sidcup DA14 175 H4
Southall UB2 123 E4
Teddington TW11 162 B4
Wallington SM6 200 B5
Welling DA16 158 C3
Clifton's Rbt, SE12 155 H6
Clifton St, EC2 20 D1
Clifton Ter, N4 93 G2
Clifton Vil, W9 14 B1
Clifton Wk, E6 116 B6
W6 *off Galena Rd* 127 H4
Clifton Way, SE15 133 E7
Borehamwood WD6 38 A1
Wembley HA0 105 H1
Clinch Ct, E16 115 G5
Cline Rd, N11 58 C6
Clinger Ct, N1
off Pitfield St 112 B1
★ **Clink Prison Mus**, SE1 28 B1
Clink St, SE1 28 A1
Clinton Av, E.Mol. KT8 179 J4
Welling DA16 157 J4
Clinton Cres, Ilf. IG6 65 H6
Clinton Rd, E3 113 H3
E7 97 G4
N15 76 A4
Clinton Ter, Sutt. SM1
off Manor La 199 F4
Clipper Cl, SE16
off Kinburn St 133 G2
Clipper Way, SE13 154 C4
Clippesby Cl, Chess. KT9 195 J7
Clipstone Ms, W1 9 F6
Clipstone Rd, Houns. TW3 143 G3
Clipstone St, W1 17 E1
Clissold Cl, N2 73 J3
Clissold Ct, N4 93 J2
Clissold Cres, N16 94 A3
Clissold Rd, N16 94 A3
Clitheroe Av, Har. HA2 85 G1
Clitheroe Gdns, Wat. WD19 50 D3
Clitheroe Rd, SW9 151 E2
Clitherow Av, W7 124 D3
Clitherow Pas, Brent. TW8 125 F5
Clitherow Rd, Brent. TW8 125 E5
Clitterhouse Cres, NW2 89 J1
Clitterhouse Rd, NW2 89 J1
Clive Av, N18
off Claremont St 60 D6
Clive Ct, W9 6 D5
Cliveden Cl, N12
off Woodside Av 57 F4
Cliveden Pl, SW1 32 B1
Cliveden Rd, SW19 184 C1
Clivedon Ct, W13 104 E5
Clivedon Rd, E4 62 E5
Clive Pas, SE21
off Clive Rd 170 A3
Clive Rd, SE21 170 A3
SW19 167 H6
Belvedere DA17 139 G4
Enfield EN1 44 D4
Feltham TW14 142 A6
Twickenham TW1 162 C4
Clivesdale Dr, Hayes UB3 122 B1
Clive Way, Enf. EN1 44 D4
Cloak La, EC4 20 A5
Clockhouse Av, Bark. IG11 117 F1
Clockhouse Cl, SW19 165 J3
Clockhouse Pl, SW15 148 B5
Clock Ho Rd, Beck. BR3 189 H3
★ **Clockmakers Company Collection, The** (Guildhall Lib), EC2 20 A3
Clock Twr Ms, N1
off Arlington Av 111 J1
SE28 118 B7
W7 *off Uxbridge Rd* 124 B1
Clock Twr Pl, N7 92 E6
Clock Twr Rd, Islw. TW7 144 C3
Cloister Cl, Tedd. TW11 162 E5
Cloister Gdns, SE25 188 E6
Edgware HA8 54 C5
Cloister Rd, NW2 90 C3
W3 106 C5
Cloisters Av, Brom. BR2 192 C5
Cloisters Business Cen, SW8
off Battersea Pk Rd 130 B7
Cloisters Mall, Kings.T. KT1
off Union St 181 G2
Clonard Way, Pnr. HA5 51 G6
Clonbrock Rd, N16 94 B4
Cloncurry St, SW6 148 A2
Clonmel Cl, Har. HA2 86 A2
Clonmell Rd, N17 76 A3
Clonmel Rd, SW6 128 C7
Teddington TW11 162 A4
Clonmore St, SW18 166 C1
Cloonmore Av, Orp. BR6 207 J4
Clorane Gdns, NW3 90 D3
Close, The, E4
off Beech Hall Rd 62 C7
N14 58 D2
N20 56 C2
SE3 *off Heath La* 154 D2
Barnet (E.Barn.) EN4 41 J6
Beckenham BR3 189 H4
Bexley DA5 159 G6
Harrow HA2 67 J2
Isleworth TW7 144 A2
Mitcham CR4 185 J4
New Malden KT3 182 C2
Orpington BR5 193 H6
Pinner (Eastcote) HA5 66 C7
Pinner (Rayners La) HA5 67 F7
Richmond TW9 146 B3
Romford RM6 82 E6
Sidcup DA14 176 B4
Sutton SM3 184 C7
Wembley (Barnhill Rd) HA9 88 C3
Wembley (Lyon Pk Av) HA0 87 H6
Cloth Ct, EC1 19 H2
Cloth Fair, EC1 19 H2
Clothier St, E1 21 E3
Cloth St, EC1 19 J1
Clothworkers Rd, SE18 137 G7
Cloudesdale Rd, SW17 168 B2
Cloudesley Pl, N1 111 G1
Cloudesley Rd, N1 111 G1
Bexleyheath DA7 159 F1
Cloudesley Sq, N1 111 G1
Cloudesley St, N1 111 G1
Clouston Cl, Wall. SM6 200 E5
Clova Rd, E7 97 F6
Clove Cres, E14 114 D7
Clove Hitch Quay, SW11 149 F3
Clovelly Av, NW9 71 F4
Clovelly Cl, Pnr. HA5 66 B3
Clovelly Gdns, SE19 188 C1
Enfield EN1 44 B7
Romford RM7 83 H1
Clovelly Rd, N8 74 D4
W4 126 C2
W5 125 F2
Bexleyheath DA7 138 E6
Hounslow TW3 143 G2
Clovelly Way, E1
off Jamaica St 113 F6
Harrow HA2 85 F2
Orpington BR6 193 J6
Clover Cl, E11
off Norman Rd 96 D2
Cloverdale Gdns, Sid. DA15 157 J6
Cloverleys, Loug. IG10 48 A5
Clover Ms, SW3 31 J5
Clover Way, Wall. SM6 200 A1
Clove St, E13
off Barking Rd 115 G4
Clowders Rd, SE6 171 J3
Clowser Cl, Sutt. SM1
off Turnpike La 199 F5
Cloysters Grn, E1 29 H1
Cloyster Wd, Edg. HA8 53 G7
Club Gdns Rd, Brom. BR2 191 G7
Club Row, E1 13 F5
E2 13 F5
Clunbury Av, Sthl. UB2 123 F5
Clunbury St, N1 12 C2
Cluny Est, SE1 28 D5
Cluny Ms, SW5 128 D4
Cluny Pl, SE1 28 D5
Cluse Ct, N1 11 J1
Clutton St, E14 114 B5
Clydach Rd, Enf. EN1 44 C4
Clyde Circ, N15 76 B4
Clyde Pl, E10 78 B7
Clyde Rd, N15 76 B4
N22 74 D1
Croydon CR0 202 C1
Sutton SM1 198 D5
Wallington SM6 200 C5
Clydesdale, Enf. EN3 45 G4
Clydesdale Av, Stan. HA7 69 G3
Clydesdale Cl, Borwd. WD6 38 D5
Isleworth TW7 144 C3
Clydesdale Gdns, Rich. TW10 146 B4
Clydesdale Ho, Erith DA18
off Kale Rd 138 E2
Clydesdale Rd, W11 108 C6
Clyde St, SE8 133 J6

Clyde Ter, SE23 ... **171** F2
Clyde Vale, SE23 ... **171** F2
Clymping Dene, Felt. TW14 ... **142** B7
Clyston St, SW8 ... **150** C2
Coach & Horses Yd, W1 ... **17** E5
Coach Ho La, N5
off Highbury Hill ... **93** H4
SW19 ... **166** A4
Coach Ho Ms, SE14
off Waller Rd ... **153** G2
Coachhouse Ms, SE20 ... **170** E7
Coach Ho Ms, SE23 ... **153** G6
Coach Ho Yd, SW18
off Ebner St ... **149** E4
Coachmaker Ms, SW4
off Fenwick Pl ... **150** E3
W4 *off Berrymede Rd* ... **126** D3
Coach Yd Ms, N19
off Trinder Gdns ... **93** E1
Coaldale Wk, SE21
off Lairdale Cl ... **151** J7
Coalecroft Rd, SW15 ... **147** J4
Coalport Ho, SE11
off Walnut Tree Wk ... **34** E1
Coal Post Cl, Orp. (Grn St Grn) BR6
off Lynne Cl ... **207** J6
Coates Av, SW18 ... **149** H6
Coates Cl, Th.Hth. CR7 ... **187** J3
Coates Hill Rd, Brom. BR1 ... **192** D2
Coate St, E2 ... **13** J2
Coates Wk, Brent. TW8 ... **125** H5
Cobalt Cl, Beck. BR3 ... **189** G4
Cobb Cl, Borwd. WD6 ... **38** C5
Cobbett Rd, SE9 ... **156** B3
Twickenham TW2 ... **161** G1
Cobbetts Av, Ilf. IG4 ... **80** A5
Cobbett St, SW8 ... **131** F7
Cobble La, N1
off Edwards Ms ... **93** H7
Cobble Ms, N5 ... **93** J3
N6
off Highgate W Hill ... **92** A1
Cobblers Wk, E.Mol. KT8 ... **180** D1
Hampton TW12 ... **161** J7
Kingston upon Thames KT2 ... **180** D1
Teddington TW11 ... **180** D1
Cobblestone Pl, Croy. CR0
off Oakfield Rd ... **201** J1
Cobbold Est, NW10 ... **89** F6
Cobbold Ms, W12
off Cobbold Rd ... **127** F2
Cobbold Rd, E11 ... **97** F3
NW10 ... **89** F6
W12 ... **127** E2
Cobb's Ct, EC4
off Pilgrim St ... **19** H4
Cobb's Rd, Houns. TW4 ... **143** F4
Cobb St, E1 ... **21** F2
Cobden Rd, E11 ... **97** E3
SE25 ... **188** D5
Orpington BR6 ... **207** G4
Cobham Av, N.Mal. KT3 ... **183** G5
Cobham Cl, SW11 ... **149** H6
Bromley BR2 ... **192** B7
Edgware HA8 ... **70** B2
Enfield EN1 ... **44** D3
Sidcup DA15
off Park Mead ... **158** B6
Wallington SM6 ... **200** E6
Cobham Ho, Bark. IG11
off St. Margarets ... **117** F1
Cobham Ms, NW1
off Agar Gro ... **92** D7
Cobham Pl, Bexh. DA6 ... **158** D5
Cobham Rd, E17 ... **78** C1
N22 ... **75** H3
Hounslow TW5 ... **122** C7
Ilford IG3 ... **99** H2
Kingston upon Thames KT1 ... **182** A1
Cobland Rd, SE12 ... **173** J4
Coborn Rd, E3 ... **113** J3
Coborn St, E3 ... **113** J3
Cobourg Rd, SE5 ... **37** F5
Cobourg St, NW1 ... **9** G4
Coburg Cl, SW1 ... **33** G1
Coburg Cres, SW2 ... **169** F1
Coburg Gdns, Ilf. IG5 ... **80** A2
Coburg Rd, N22 ... **75** F3
Cochrane Ms, NW8 ... **7** F2
Cochrane Rd, SW19 ... **166** C7
Cochrane St, NW8 ... **7** F2
Cockayne Way, SE8 ... **133** H5
Cockerell Rd, E17 ... **77** H7
COCKFOSTERS, Barn. EN4 ... **41** H4
Cockfosters Par, Barn. EN4
off Cockfosters Rd ... **42** A4
Cockfosters Rd, Barn. EN4 ... **41** J2
Cock Hill, E1 ... **21** E2
Cock La, EC1 ... **19** G2
Cockpit Steps, SW1 ... **25** J4
Cockpit Yd, WC1 ... **18** D1
Cocks Cres, N.Mal. KT3 ... **183** F4
Cocksett Av, Orp. BR6 ... **207** H6
Cockspur Ct, SW1 ... **25** J1
Cockspur St, SW1 ... **25** J1
Cocksure La, Sid. DA14 ... **177** G3
Coda Cen, The, SW6 ... **148** B1
Code St, E1 ... **13** G6
Codling Cl, E1 ... **29** J1
Codling Way, Wem. HA0 ... **87** G4
Codrington Hill, SE23 ... **153** H7
Codrington Ms, W11
off Blenheim Cres ... **108** B6
Cody Cl, Har. HA3 ... **69** G3
Wallington SM6
off Alcock Cl ... **200** D7
Cody Rd, E16 ... **114** D4
Cody Rd Business Cen, E16 ... **114** D4
Coe Av, SE25 ... **188** D6
Coe's All, Barn. EN5
off Wood St ... **40** B4
Coffey St, SE8 ... **134** A7
Cogan Av, E17 ... **77** H1
Coin St, SE1 ... **27** E1
Coity Rd, NW5 ... **92** A6
Cokers La, SE21
off Perifield ... **169** J1
Coke St, E1 ... **21** H3
Colas Ms, NW6
off Birchington Rd ... **108** D1
Colbeck Ms, SW7 ... **30** B2
Colbeck Rd, Har. HA1 ... **67** J7
Colberg Pl, N16 ... **76** B7
Colborne Way, Wor.Pk. KT4 ... **197** J3
Colbrook Av, Hayes UB3 ... **121** G3
Colbrook Cl, Hayes UB3 ... **121** G3
Colburn Av, Pnr. HA5 ... **51** E6
Colburn Way, Sutt. SM1 ... **199** G3
Colby Ms, SE19
off Gipsy Hill ... **170** B5
Colby Rd, SE19 ... **170** B5
Colchester Av, E12 ... **98** C3
Colchester Dr, Pnr. HA5 ... **66** D5
Colchester Rd, E10 ... **78** C7
E17 ... **78** A6
Edgware HA8 ... **54** C7
Northwood HA6 ... **66** A2
Colchester St, E1 ... **21** G3
Coldbath Sq, EC1 ... **11** E5
Coldbath St, SE13 ... **154** B1
COLDBLOW, Bex. DA5 ... **177** J2
Cold Blow La, SE14 ... **133** G7
Cold Blows, Mitch. CR4 ... **185** J3
Coldershaw Rd, W13 ... **124** D1
Coldfall Av, N10 ... **73** J2
Cold Harbour, E14 ... **134** C2
Coldharbour Crest, SE9
off Great Harry Dr ... **174** D3
Coldharbour La, SE5 ... **151** G4
SW9 ... **151** G4
Hayes UB3 ... **102** A7
Coldharbour La Ind Est, SE5
off Coldharbour La ... **151** J2
Coldharbour Pl, SE5
off Denmark Hill ... **152** A2
Coldharbour Rd, Croy. CR0 ... **201** G5
Coldharbour Way, Croy. CR0 ... **201** G5
Coldstream Gdns, SW18 ... **148** C6
Colebeck Ms, N1 ... **93** H6
Colebert Av, E1 ... **113** F4
Colebrook Cl, NW7 ... **56** A7
SW15 *off West Hill* ... **148** A7
Colebrooke Av, W13 ... **104** E6
Colebrooke Dr, E11 ... **79** H7
Colebrooke Pl, N1
off St. Peters St ... **111** H1
Colebrooke Ri, Brom. BR2 ... **191** E2
Colebrooke Row, N1 ... **11** G2
Colebrook Gdns, Loug. IG10 ... **49** E2
Colebrook Ho, E14
off Brabazon St ... **114** B6
Colebrook La, Loug. IG10 ... **49** E2
Colebrook Path, Loug. IG10 ... **49** E2
Colebrook Rd, SW16 ... **187** E1
Colebrook Way, N11 ... **58** B5
Coleby Path, SE5
off Harris St ... **132** A7
Colechurch Ho, SE1
off Avondale Sq ... **37** H4
Cole Cl, SE28 ... **138** B1
Coledale Dr, Stan. HA7 ... **69** F1
Coleford Rd, SW18 ... **149** F5
Cole Gdns, Houns. TW5 ... **122** A7
Colegrave Rd, E15 ... **96** D5
Colegrove Rd, SE15 ... **37** G6
Coleherne Ct, SW5 ... **30** B4
Coleherne Ms, SW10 ... **30** A4
Coleherne Rd, SW10 ... **30** A4
Colehill Gdns, SW6
off Fulham Palace Rd ... **148** B1
Colehill La, SW6 ... **148** B1
Coleman Cl, SE25 ... **188** D2
Coleman Flds, N1 ... **111** J1
Coleman Rd, SE5 ... **36** D7
Belvedere DA17 ... **139** G4
Dagenham RM9 ... **101** E6
Colemans Heath, SE9 ... **174** E3
Coleman St, EC2 ... **20** B3
Colenso Dr, NW7 ... **55** G7
Colenso Rd, E5 ... **95** F4
Ilford IG2 ... **99** H1
Cole Pk Gdns, Twick. TW1 ... **144** D6
Cole Pk Rd, Twick. TW1 ... **144** D6
Cole Pk Vw, Twick. TW1
off Hill Vw Rd ... **144** D6
Colepits Wd Rd, SE9 ... **157** F5
Coleraine Rd, N8 ... **75** G3
SE3 ... **135** F6
Coleridge Av, E12 ... **98** B6
Sutton SM1 ... **199** H4
Coleridge Cl, SW8 ... **150** B2
Coleridge Gdns, NW6
off Fairhazel Gdns ... **91** F7
SW10 ... **30** B7
Coleridge Ho, SW1 ... **33** F4
Coleridge La, N8
off Coleridge Rd ... **74** E6
Coleridge Rd, E17 ... **77** J4
N4 ... **93** G2
N8 ... **74** D6
N12 ... **57** F5
Croydon CR0 ... **189** F7
Coleridge Sq, SW10 ... **30** C7
W13 *off Berners Dr* ... **104** D6
Coleridge Wk, NW11 ... **72** D4
Coleridge Way, Borwd. WD6 ... **38** A4
Hayes UB4 ... **102** A6
West Drayton UB7 ... **120** C4
Cole Rd, Twick. TW1 ... **144** D6
Colesburg Rd, Beck. BR3 ... **189** J3
Coles Cres, Har. HA2 ... **85** H2
Coles Grn, Bushey (Bushey Hth) WD23 ... **51** J1
Loughton IG10 ... **48** D1
Coles Grn Ct, NW2 ... **89** G2
Coles Grn Rd, NW2 ... **89** G1
Coleshill Flats, SW1
off Pimlico Rd ... **32** C2
Coleshill Rd, Tedd. TW11 ... **162** B6
Colestown St, SW11 ... **149** H2
Cole St, SE1 ... **28** A4
Colet Cl, N13 ... **59** H6
Colet Gdns, W14 ... **128** A4
Coley St, WC1 ... **10** D6
Colfe Rd, SE23 ... **171** H1
Colham Av, West Dr. UB7 ... **120** B1
Colham Mill Rd, West Dr. UB7 ... **120** A2
Colina Ms, N15
off Harringay Rd ... **75** H5
Colina Rd, N15 ... **75** H5
Colin Cl, NW9 ... **71** E4
Croydon CR0 ... **203** J3
West Wickham BR4 ... **205** F3
Colin Cres, NW9 ... **71** F4
Colindale Av, NW9 ... **70** D3
Colindale Business Pk, NW9 ... **70** C3
Colindeep Gdns, NW4 ... **71** G5
Colindeep La, NW4 ... **70** E3
NW9 ... **70** E3
Colin Dr, NW9 ... **71** F5
Colinette Rd, SW15 ... **147** J4
Colin Gdns, NW9 ... **71** F5
Colin Par, NW9
off Edgware Rd ... **70** E4
Colin Pk Rd, NW9 ... **70** E4
Colin Rd, NW10 ... **89** G6
Colinsdale, N1
off Camden Wk ... **111** H1
Colinton Rd, Ilf. IG3 ... **100** B2
Coliston Pas, SW18
off Coliston Rd ... **148** D7
Coliston Rd, SW18 ... **148** D7
Collamore Av, SW18 ... **167** H1
Collapit Cl, Har. HA1 ... **67** H5
Collard Av, Loug. IG10 ... **49** F2
Collard Grn, Loug. IG10 ... **49** F2
Collard Pl, NW1
off Harmood St ... **92** B7
College App, SE10 ... **134** C6
College Av, Har. HA3 ... **68** B1
College Cl, E9
off Median Rd ... **95** F5
N18 ... **60** C5
Harrow HA3 ... **52** B7
Twickenham TW2
off Meadway ... **162** A1
College Cres, NW3 ... **91** G6
College Cross, N1 ... **93** G7
College Dr, Ruis. HA4 ... **66** A7
Thames Ditton KT7 ... **180** B7
College Gdns, E4 ... **46** B7
N18 ... **60** C5
SE21 ... **170** B1
SW17 ... **167** H2
Enfield EN2 ... **44** A1
Ilford IG4 ... **80** B5
New Malden KT3 ... **183** F5
College Grn, SE19 ... **170** B7
College Gro, NW1
off St. Pancras Way ... **110** D1
College Hill, EC4 ... **20** A5
College Hill Rd, Har. HA3 ... **68** C1
College La, NW5 ... **92** B4
College Ms, SW1 ... **26** A5
SW18
off St. Ann's Hill ... **149** E5
★ **College of Arms**, EC4 ... **19** H5
College Pk Cl, SE13 ... **154** D4
College Pk Rd, N17
off College Rd ... **60** C6
College Pl, E17 ... **78** E4
NW1 ... **110** C1
SW10 ... **30** C7
College Pt, E15 ... **97** F6
College Rd, E17 ... **78** C5
N17 ... **60** C6
N21 ... **59** G2
NW10 ... **107** J2
SE19 ... **170** C5
SE21 ... **152** B7
SW19 ... **167** G6
W13 ... **104** E6
Bromley BR1 ... **173** G7
Croydon CR0 ... **202** A2
Enfield EN2 ... **44** A2
Harrow (Har.Hill) HA1 ... **68** B6
Harrow (Har.Wld) HA3 ... **68** B1
Isleworth TW7 ... **144** C1
Wembley HA9 ... **87** G1
College Row, E9 ... **95** G5
College Slip, Brom. BR1 ... **191** G1
College St, EC4 ... **20** A5
College Ter, E3 ... **113** J3
N3 *off Hendon La* ... **72** C2
College Vw, SE9 ... **174** A1
College Wk, Kings.T. KT1
off Grange Rd ... **181** H3
College Way, Hayes UB3 ... **102** A7
College Yd, NW5
off College La ... **92** B4
Collent St, E9 ... **95** F6
Colless Rd, N15 ... **76** C5
Collett Rd, SE16 ... **29** J6
Collett Way, Sthl. UB2 ... **123** H1
Collier Cl, E6
off Trader Rd ... **116** E7
Epsom KT19 ... **196** A6
Collier Dr, Edg. HA8 ... **70** A2
COLLIER ROW, Rom. RM5 ... **83** G1
Collier Row Rd, Rom. RM5 ... **83** F1
Colliers Shaw, Kes. BR2 ... **206** A4
Collier St, N1 ... **10** C2
Colliers Water La, Th.Hth. CR7 ... **187** G5
COLLIER'S WOOD, SW19 ... **167** G7
Collindale Av, Erith DA8 ... **139** H6
Sidcup DA15 ... **176** A1
Collingbourne Rd, W12 ... **127** H1
Collingham Gdns, SW5 ... **30** B2
Collingham Pl, SW5 ... **30** A2
Collingham Rd, SW5 ... **30** B1
Collings Cl, N22
off Whittington Rd ... **59** F6
Collington St, SE10
off Hoskins St ... **134** D5
Collingtree Rd, SE26 ... **171** F4
Collingwood Av, N10 ... **74** A3
Surbiton KT5 ... **196** C1
Collingwood Cl, SE20 ... **189** E1
Twickenham TW2 ... **143** G6
Collingwood Rd, E17 ... **78** A6
N15 ... **76** B4
Mitcham CR4 ... **185** H2
Sutton SM1 ... **198** D3
Collingwood St, E1 ... **113** E4
Collins Av, Stan. HA7 ... **69** H2
Collins Dr, Ruis. HA4 ... **84** C2
Collinson St, SE1 ... **27** J4

Collinson Wk, SE1 27 J4
Collins Rd, N5 93 J4
Collins Sq, SE3 *off Tranquil Vale* 155 F2
Collins St, SE3 155 E2
Collin's Yd, N1 *off Islington Grn* 111 H1
Collinwood Av, Enf. EN3 45 F3
Collinwood Gdns, Ilf. IG5 80 C5
Collis All, Twick. TW2 *off The Green* 162 B1
Collison Pl, N16 94 B2
Colls Rd, SE15 153 F1
Collyer Av, Croy. CR0 200 E4
Collyer Pl, SE15 *off Peckham High St* 152 D1
Collyer Rd, Croy. CR0 201 E4
Colman Rd, E16 115 J5
Colmar Cl, E1 *off Alderney Rd* 113 G4
Colmer Pl, Har. HA3 52 A7
Colmer Rd, SW16 187 E1
Colmore Ms, SE15 153 E1
Colmore Rd, Enf. EN3 45 F4
Colnbrook St, SE1 27 G6
Colne Ct, Epsom KT19 196 C4
Colne Ho, Bark. IG11 99 E6
Colne Rd, E5 95 H4
N21 44 A7
Twickenham TW1, TW2 162 B1
Colne St, E13 *off Grange Rd* 115 G3
Colney Hatch La, N10 58 A7
N11 57 J6
Cologne Rd, SW11 149 G4
Colombo Rd, Ilf. IG1 99 F1
Colombo St, SE1 27 G2
Colomb St, SE10 135 E5
Colonels Wk, Enf. EN2 43 H2
Colonial Av, Twick. TW2 143 J5
Colonial Dr, W4 126 C4
Colonial Rd, Felt. TW14 141 H7
Colonnade, WC1 10 A6
Colonnade Wk, SW1 32 D2
Colony Ms, N1 *off Mildmay Gro N* 94 A5
Colorado Apts, N8 *off Great Amwell La* 75 F3
Colorado Bldg, SE13 *off Deals Gateway* 154 B1
Colosseum Ter, NW1 *off Albany St* 8 E5
Colson Gdns, Loug. IG10 48 D4
Colson Grn, Loug. IG10 *off Colson Rd* 48 E4
Colson Path, Loug. IG10 48 D4
Colson Rd, Croy. CR0 202 B2
Loughton IG10 48 E4
Colson Way, SW16 168 C4
Colsterworth Rd, N15 76 C4
Colston Av, Cars. SM5 199 H4
Colston Cl, Cars. SM5 *off West St* 199 J4
Colston Rd, E7 98 A6
SW14 146 C4
Colthurst Cres, N4 93 J2
Colthurst Dr, N9 60 E3
Coltman St, E14 113 H5
Coltness Cres, SE2 138 B5
Colton Gdns, N17 75 J3
Colton Rd, Har. HA1 68 B5
Columbia Av, Edg. HA8 70 B1
Ruislip HA4 84 B1
Worcester Park KT4 183 F7
Columbia Pt, SE16 *off Moodkee St* 133 F3
Columbia Rd, E2 13 F3
E13 115 F4
Columbia Sq, SW14 *off Upper Richmond Rd W* 146 C4
Columbine Av, E6 116 B5
South Croydon CR2 201 H7
Columbine Way, SE13 154 C2
Columbus Ct, SE16 *off Rotherhithe St* 133 F1
Columbus Ctyd, E14 *off West India Av* 134 A1
Columbus Gdns, Nthwd. HA6 66 A1
Colva Wk, N19 *off Chester Rd* 92 B2
Colvestone Cres, E8 94 C5
Colview Ct, SE9 *off Mottingham La* 174 A1
Colville Est, N1 112 A1
Colville Gdns, W11 108 C6
Colville Hos, W11 108 C6
Colville Ms, W11 *off Lonsdale Rd* 108 C6
Colville Pl, W1 17 G2
Colville Rd, E11 96 C3
E17 77 H2
Colville Rd, N9 60 E1
W3 126 B3
W11 108 C6
Colville Sq, W11 108 C6
Colville Ter, W11 108 C6
Colvin Cl, SE26 171 F5
Colvin Gdns, E4 62 C3
E11 79 H4
Ilford IG6 81 F1
Colvin Rd, E6 98 B7
Thornton Heath CR7 187 G5
Colwall Gdns, Wdf.Grn. IG8 63 G5
Colwell Rd, SE22 152 C5
Colwick Cl, N6 74 D7
Colwith Rd, W6 127 J6
Colwood Gdns, SW19 167 G7
Colworth Gro, SE17 36 A2
Colworth Rd, E11 78 E6
Croydon CR0 202 D1
Colwyn Av, Grnf. (Perivale) UB6 104 C2
Colwyn Cl, SW16 168 C5
Colwyn Cres, Houns. TW3 143 J1
Colwyn Grn, NW9 *off Snowdon Dr* 70 E6
Colwyn Ho, SE1 *off Briant Est* 26 E6
Colwyn Rd, NW2 89 H3
Colyer Cl, N1 10 D1
SE9 175 E2
Colyers La, Erith DA8 159 J1
Colyton Cl, Well. DA16 158 D1
Wembley HA0 *off Bridgewater Rd* 87 F6
Colyton La, SW16 169 G5
Colyton Rd, SE22 153 E5
Colyton Way, N18 60 D5
Combe, The, NW1 9 E4
Combe Av, SE3 135 F7
Combedale Rd, SE10 135 G5
Combemartin Rd, SW18 148 B7
Combe Ms, SE3 135 F7
Comber Cl, NW2 89 H3
Comber Gro, SE5 151 J1
Comber Ho, SE5 *off Comber Gro* 131 J7
Combermere Rd, SW9 151 F3
Morden SM4 185 E6
Comberton Rd, E5 95 E2
Combeside, SE18 137 J7
Combwell Cres, SE2 138 A3
Comely Bk Rd, E17 78 C5
Comeragh Ms, W14 128 B5
Comeragh Rd, W14 128 B5
Comer Cres, Sthl. UB2 *off Windmill Av* 123 J2
Comerford Rd, SE4 153 H4
Comer Ho, Barn. EN5 *off Station Rd* 41 F4
Comet Cl, E12 98 A4
Comet Pl, SE8 134 A7
Comet Rd, Stai. (Stanw.) TW19 140 A7
Comet St, SE8 134 A7
Comfort St, SE15 36 D6
Commerce Rd, N22 75 F1
Brentford TW8 125 F7
Commerce Way, Croy. CR0 201 F2
Commercial Rd, E1 21 H3
E14 113 F6
N17 60 B6
N18 60 B5
Commercial St, E1 13 F6
Commercial Way, NW10 106 B2
SE15 132 C7
Commerell St, SE10 135 E5
Commodity Quay, E1 21 G6
Commodore Ho, SW18 *off Juniper Dr* 149 F4
Commodore St, E1 113 H4
Common, The, E15 97 E6
W5 105 H7
Richmond TW10 163 G3
Southall UB2 122 C4
Stanmore HA7 52 B2
Commondale, SW15 147 J3
Common La, Esher (Clay.) KT10 194 D7
Common Mile Cl, SW4 150 D5
Common Rd, SW13 147 G3
Esher (Clay.) KT10 194 D6
Stanmore HA7 52 A4
Commonside, Kes. BR2 205 J4
Commonside E, Mitch. CR4 185 J3
Commonside W, Mitch. CR4 185 J3
Commonwealth Av, W12 107 H7
Commonwealth Rd, N17 60 D7
Commonwealth Way, SE2 138 B5
Community Cl, Houns. TW5 142 B1
Community La, N7 92 D5
Community Rd, E15 96 D5
Greenford UB6 103 J1
Como Rd, SE23 171 H2
Compass Cl, Edg. HA8 *off Glendale Av* 53 J4
Compass Hill, Rich. TW10 145 G6
Compass Ho, SW18 *off Smugglers Way* 149 E4
Compass La, Brom. BR1 *off North St* 191 G1
Compayne Gdns, NW6 90 E7
Compton Av, E6 116 A2
N1 93 H6
N6 73 H7
Wembley HA0 87 F4
Compton Cl, E3 114 A5
NW1 9 E4
NW11 *off The Vale* 90 A3
SE15 *off Commercial Way* 132 D7
W13 104 D6
Edgware HA8 54 C7
Compton Ct, SE19 *off Victoria Cres* 170 B5
Compton Cres, N17 59 J7
W4 126 C6
Chessington KT9 195 H6
Northolt UB5 102 D1
Compton Ho, SW11 *off Parkham St* 149 H1
Compton Pas, EC1 11 H5
Compton Pl, WC1 10 A5
Watford WD19 50 E3
Compton Ri, Pnr. HA5 67 E5
Compton Rd, N1 93 H6
N21 59 G1
NW10 108 A3
SW19 166 C6
Croydon CR0 202 E1
Compton St, EC1 11 G5
Compton Ter, N1 93 H6
Computer Ho, Brent. TW8 125 F6
Comreddy Cl, Enf. EN2 43 H1
Comus Pl, SE17 36 D2
Comyn Rd, SW11 149 H4
Comyns, The, Bushey (Bushey Hth) WD23 51 J1
Comyns Cl, E16 115 F5
Comyns Rd, Dag. RM9 101 G7
Conant Ms, E1 21 H5
Concanon Rd, SW2 151 F4
Concert Hall App, SE1 26 D2
Concord Cl, Nthlt. UB5 102 E3
Concorde Cl, Houns. TW3 143 H2
Concorde Dr, E6 116 C5
Concorde Way, SE16 133 G4
Concord Rd, W3 106 B4
Enfield EN3 45 F5
Concord Ter, Har. HA2 *off Coles Cres* 85 H2
Concourse, The, N9 *off Edmonton Grn Shop Cen* 60 D2
NW9 71 F1
Condell Rd, SW8 150 C1
Conder St, E14 *off Salmon La* 113 H6
Condor Path, Nthlt. UB5 *off Brabazon Rd* 103 G2
Condover Cres, SE18 136 E7
Condray Pl, SW11 129 H7
Conduit Av, SE10 *off Crooms Hill* 134 D7
Conduit Ct, WC2 18 A5
Conduit La, N18 61 F5
Croydon CR0 202 D5
Enfield EN3 *off Morson Rd* 45 H6
South Croydon CR2 202 D5
Conduit Ms, SE18 137 E5
W2 14 E4
Conduit Pas, W2 15 E4
Conduit Pl, W2 15 E4
Conduit Rd, SE18 137 E5
Conduit St, W1 17 E5
Conduit Way, NW10 88 C7
Conewood St, N5 93 H3
Coney Acre, SE21 169 J1
Coney Burrows, E4 62 E2
Coneygrove Path, Nthlt. UB5 *off Arnold Rd* 84 E6
CONEY HALL, W.Wick. BR4 205 F3
Coney Hill Rd, W.Wick. BR4 205 E2
Coney Way, SW8 34 D6
Conference Cl, E4 *off Greenbank Cl* 62 C2
Conference Rd, SE2 138 C4
Congleton Gro, SE18 137 F5
Congo Dr, N9 61 F3
Congo Rd, SE18 137 G5
Congress Rd, SE2 138 C4
Congreve Rd, SE9 156 C3
Congreve St, SE17 36 D1
Congreve Wk, E16 116 A5
Conical Cor, Enf. EN2 43 J2
Conifer Cl, Orp. BR6 207 G4
Conifer Gdns, SW16 169 E3
Enfield EN1 44 B6
Sutton SM1 198 E2
Conifers Cl, Tedd. TW11 163 E7
Conifer Way, Wem. HA0 87 F3
Coniger Rd, SW6 148 D2
Coningham Ms, W12 *off Percy Rd* 127 G1
Coningham Rd, W12 127 H2
Coningsby Av, NW9 70 E2
Coningsby Cotts, W5 *off Coningsby Rd* 125 G2
Coningsby Gdns, E4 62 B6
Coningsby Rd, N4 75 H7
W5 125 F2
Conington Rd, SE13 154 B2
Conisbee Ct, N14 42 C5
Conisborough Cres, SE6 172 C3
Coniscliffe Cl, Chis. BR7 192 D1
Coniscliffe Rd, N13 59 J3
Coniston Av, Bark. IG11 99 H7
Greenford (Perivale) UB6 105 E3
Welling DA16 157 H3
Coniston Cl, N20 57 F3
SW13 *off Lonsdale Rd* 127 F7
SW20 184 A6
W4 146 C1
Barking IG11 *off Coniston Av* 99 H7
Bexleyheath DA7 159 J1
Coniston Ct, NW7 *off Langstone Way* 56 B7
Wallington SM6 200 B4
Conistone Way, N7 93 E7
Coniston Gdns, N9 61 F1
NW9 70 D5
Ilford IG4 80 B4
Pinner HA5 66 A4
Sutton SM2 199 G6
Wembley HA9 87 F1
Coniston Ho, SE5 35 J7
Coniston Rd, N10 74 B2
N17 60 D6
Bexleyheath DA7 159 J1
Bromley BR1 172 E6
Croydon CR0 188 D7
Twickenham TW2 143 H6
Coniston Wk, E9 *off Clifden Rd* 95 F5
Coniston Way, Chess. KT9 195 H3
Conlan St, W10 108 B4
Conley Rd, NW10 89 E6
Conley St, SE10 *off Pelton Rd* 135 E5
Connaught Av, E4 46 D7
SW14 146 C3
Barnet EN4 57 J1
Enfield EN1 44 B2
Hounslow TW4 143 E5
Loughton IG10 48 A4
Connaught Br, E16 136 A1
Connaught Business Cen, Mitch. CR4 185 J5
Connaught Cl, E10 95 H2
W2 15 G4
Enfield EN1 44 B2
Sutton SM1 199 G2
Connaught Ct, E17 *off Orford Rd* 78 B4
Buckhurst Hill IG9 *off Chequers* 63 H1
Connaught Dr, NW11 72 D4
Connaught Gdns, N10 74 B5
N13 59 H4
Morden SM4 185 F4
Connaught Hill, Loug. IG10 48 A4
Connaught La, Ilf. IG1 99 F2
Connaught Ms, NW3 *off Pond St* 91 H5
SE18 136 D5
Ilford IG1 *off Connaught Rd* 99 G2
Connaught Pl, W2 15 J5
Connaught Rd, E4 46 E7
E11 96 D1
E16 136 A1
E17 78 A5
N4 75 G7

Connaught Rd, NW10 ....107 E1
SE18 ....136 D5
W13 ....104 E7
Barnet EN5 ....40 A6
Harrow HA3 ....68 C1
Ilford IG1 ....99 G2
New Malden KT3 ....183 E4
Richmond TW10
off Albert Rd 145 J5
Sutton SM1 ....199 G2
Teddington TW11 ....162 A5
Connaught Rbt, E16 ....116 A7
Connaught Sq, W2 ....15 J4
Connaught St, W2 ....15 G4
Connaught Way, N13 ....59 H4
Connect La, Ilf.
(Barkingside) IG6 ....81 F2
Connell Cres, W5 ....105 J4
Connemara Cl, Borwd.
WD6 ....38 C6
Connington Cres, E4 ....62 D3
Connor Cl, E11 ....96 E1
Ilford IG6 ....81 E1
Connor Ct, SW11
off Alfreda St 150 B1
Connor Rd, Dag. RM9 ....101 F4
Connor St, E9
off Lauriston Rd 113 G1
Conolly Rd, W7 ....124 B1
Conrad Dr, Wor.Pk. KT4 ..197 J1
Conrad Ho, N16 ....94 B5
Consfield Av, N.Mal.
KT3 ....183 G4
Consort Ms, Islw. TW7 ...144 A5
Consort Rd, SE15 ....152 E1
Cons St, SE1 ....27 F3
Constable Av, E16
off Wesley Av 135 H1
Constable Cl, N11
off Friern Barnet La ...57 J5
NW11 ....73 E6
Constable Cres, N15 ....76 D5
Constable Gdns, Edg.
HA8 ....70 A1
Isleworth TW7 ....144 A5
Constable Ho, E14
off Cassilis Rd 134 A2
NW3 *off Adelaide Rd* ...91 J7
Constable Ms, Brom. BR1 191 H2
Dagenham RM8
off Stonard Rd 100 B4
Constable Wk, SE21 ....170 B3
Constance Cl, SW15 ....164 D4
Constance Cres, Brom.
BR2 ....191 F7
Constance Rd, Croy.
CR0 ....187 H7
Enfield EN1 ....44 B6
Sutton SM1 ....199 F4
Twickenham TW2 ....143 H7
Constance St, E16
off Albert Rd 136 B1
Constantine Rd, NW3 ....91 H4
Constitution Hill, SW1 ....24 D3
Constitution Ri, SE18 ....156 D1
Consul Av, Dag. RM9 ....119 J3
Content St, SE17 ....36 A2
Contessa Cl, Orp. BR6 ...207 H5
Control Twr Rd, Houns.
(Lon.Hthrw Air.) TW6 ..140 D3
Convair Wk, Nthlt. UB5
off Kittiwake Rd 102 D3
Convent Cl, Beck. BR3 ....172 C7
Convent Gdns, W5 ....125 F4
W11
off Kensington Pk Rd .108 C6
Convent Hill, SE19 ....169 J6
Convent Way, Sthl. UB2 ..122 C4
Conway Cl, Stan. HA7 ....52 D6
Conway Cres, Grnf.
(Perivale) UB6 ....104 B2
Romford RM6 ....82 C7
Conway Dr, Hayes UB3 ..121 F3
Sutton SM2 ....198 E6
Conway Gdns, Mitch.
CR4 ....186 D4
Wembley HA9 ....69 F7
Conway Gro, W3 ....106 D5
Conway Ms, W1 ....17 F1
Conway Rd, N14 ....59 E3
N15 ....75 H5
NW2 ....89 J2
SE18 ....137 G4
SW20 ....183 J1
Feltham TW13 ....160 D5
Hounslow TW4 ....143 F7
Hounslow
(Lon.Hthrw Air.) TW6
off Inner Ring E 140 E3
Conway St, E13 ....115 G4
W1 ....9 F6
Conway Wk, Hmptn. TW12
off Fearnley Cres 161 F6
Conybeare, NW3
off King Henry's Rd ...91 H7
Conyers Cl, Wdf.Grn. IG8 ..62 E6
Conyers Rd, SW16 ....168 D5
Conyer St, E3 ....113 H2
Conyers Way, Loug. IG10 ..49 E3
Cooden Cl, Brom. BR1 ...173 H7
Cook Ct, SE16
off Rotherhithe St 133 F1
Cookes Cl, E11 ....97 F2
Cookes La, Sutt. SM3 ....198 B6
Cooke St, Bark. IG11 ....117 F1
Cookham Cl, Sthl. UB2 ..123 H2
Cookham Cres, SE16
off Marlow Way 133 G2
Cookham Dene Cl, Chis.
BR7 ....193 G1
Cookham Rd, Sid. DA14 ..177 G7
Cookhill Rd, SE2 ....138 B2
Cook Rd, Dag. RM9 ....118 E1
Cooks Cl, E14
off Cabot Sq 134 A1
Romford RM5 ....83 J1
Cooks Ferry, N18 ....61 H5
Cooks Ferry Rbt, N18
off Advent Way 61 G5
Cookson Gro, Erith DA8 ..139 H7
Cook's Rd, E15 ....114 B2
Cooks Rd, SE17 ....35 G5
Coolfin Rd, E16 ....115 G6
Coolgardie Av, E4 ....62 C5
Chigwell IG7 ....64 D3
Coolhurst Rd, N8 ....74 D6
Cool Oak La, NW9 ....71 E7
Coomassie Rd, W9
off Bravington Rd 108 C4
COOMBE, Kings.T. KT2 ...164 C7
Coombe Av, Croy. CR0 ...202 B4
Coombe Bk, Kings.T.
KT2 ....182 E1
Coombe Cl, Edg. HA8 ....69 J2
Hounslow TW3 ....143 G4
Coombe Cor, N21 ....59 H1
Coombe Cres, Hmptn.
TW12 ....161 E7
Coombe Dr, Kings.T. KT2 .164 D7
Ruislip HA4 ....84 B1
Coombe End, Kings.T.
KT2 ....164 D7
Coombefield Cl, N.Mal.
KT3 ....183 E5
Coombe Gdns, SW20 ....183 G2
New Malden KT3 ....183 F4
Coombe Hts, Kings.T.
KT2 ....165 E7
Coombe Hill Glade,
Kings.T. KT2 ....165 E7
Coombe Hill Rd, Kings.T.
KT2 ....164 E7
Coombe Ho Chase, N.Mal.
KT3 ....182 D1
Coombehurst Cl, Barn.
EN4 ....41 J2
Coombe La, SW20 ....183 G1
Croydon CR0 ....202 E5
Coombe La W, Kings.T.
KT2 ....164 E7
Coombe Lea, Brom. BR1 .192 B3
Coombe Lo, SE7 ....135 J6
Coombe Neville, Kings.T. KT2164
D7
Coombe Pk, Kings.T. KT2 .164 D5
Coombe Ridings, Kings.T. KT2164
C5
Coombe Ri, Kings.T. KT2 .182 C1
Coombe Rd, N22 ....75 G1
NW10 ....88 D3
SE26 ....170 E4
W4 ....127 E5
W13
off Northcroft Rd 124 E3
Croydon CR0 ....202 A4
Hampton TW12 ....161 F6
Kingston upon Thames
KT2 ....182 A1
New Malden KT3 ....182 E2
Coomber Way, Croy. CR0 .186 D7
Coombes Rd, Dag. RM9 ..119 F1
Coombe Wk, Sutt. SM1 ..198 E3
Coombewood Dr, Rom.
RM6 ....83 F6
Coombe Wd Rd, Kings.T.
KT2 ....164 C5
Coombs St, N1 ....11 H2
Coomer Ms, SW6
off Coomer Pl 128 C6
Coomer Pl, SW6 ....128 C6
Coomer Rd, SW6
off Coomer Pl 128 C6
Cooms Wk, Edg. HA8
off East Rd 70 C1
Cooperage Cl, N17
off Brantwood Rd 60 C6
Cooper Av, E17 ....77 G1
Cooper Cl, SE1 ....27 F4
Cooper Cres, Cars. SM5 ..199 J3
Cooper Rd, NW4 ....72 A6
NW10 ....89 F5
Croydon CR0 ....201 G4
Coopersale Cl, Wdf.Grn. IG8
off Navestock Cres 63 J7
Coopersale Rd, E9 ....95 G5
Coopers Cl, E1 ....113 F4
Dagenham RM10 ....101 H6
Coopers Cres, Borwd.
WD6 ....38 C1
Coopers La, E10 ....96 B1
NW1 ....9 J1
Cooper's La, SE12 ....173 H2
Coopers Ms, Beck. BR3 ..190 A2
Coopers Rd, SE1 ....37 G4
Cooper's Row, EC3 ....21 F5
Cooper St, E16
off Lawrence St 115 F5
Coopers Wk, E15
off Maryland St 96 E5
Coopers Yd, N1
off Upper St 93 H7
Cooper's Yd, SE19 ....170 B6
Coote Gdns, Dag. RM8 ...101 F3
Coote Rd, Bexh. DA7 ....159 F1
Dagenham RM8 ....101 F3
Copeland Dr, E14 ....134 A4
Copeland Ho, SE11 ....26 D6
Copeland Rd, E17 ....78 B5
SE15 ....152 D2
Copeman Cl, SE26 ....171 F5
Copenhagen Gdns, W4 ...126 C2
Copenhagen Pl, E14 ....113 J6
Copenhagen St, N1 ....111 E1
Cope Pl, W8 ....128 D3
Copers Cope Rd, Beck.
BR3 ....171 J6
Cope St, SE16 ....133 G4
Copford Cl, Wdf.Grn. IG8 ..64 B6
Copford Wk, N1
off Popham St 111 J1
Copgate Path, SW16 ....169 F6
Copinger Wk, Edg. HA8
off North Rd 70 B1
Copland Av, Wem. HA0 ...87 G5
Copland Cl, Wem. HA0 ...87 F5
Copland Ms, Wem. HA0
off Copland Rd 87 H6
Copland Rd, Wem. HA0 ...87 H6
Copleston Ms, SE15
off Copleston Rd 152 C3
Copleston Pas, SE15 ....152 C3
Copleston Rd, SE15 ....152 C3
Copley Cl, SE17 ....35 H6
W7 ....104 C5
Copley Dene, Brom.
BR1 ....192 A1
Copley Pk, SW16 ....169 F6
Copley Rd, Stan. HA7 ....53 F5
Copley St, E1 ....113 G5
Coppard Gdns, Chess.
KT9 ....195 F6
Copped Hall, SE21
off Glazebrook Cl 170 A2
Coppelia Rd, SE3 ....155 F4
Coppen Rd, Dag. RM8 ....83 F7
Copperas St, SE8 ....134 B6
Copper Beech Cl, Ilf. IG5 ..80 D1
Copper Beech Ct, Loug.
IG10 ....48 D1
Copper Beeches, Islw. TW7
off Eversley Cres 144 A1
Copper Cl, N17 ....60 E7
SE19 *off Auckland Rd* ..170 C7
Copperdale Rd, Hayes
UB3 ....122 A2
Copperfield, Chig. IG7 ....65 G6
Copperfield Ct, Pnr. HA5
off Copperfield Way ...67 F4
Copperfield Dr, N15 ....76 C4
Copperfield Ms, N18 ....60 B5
Copperfield Rd, E3 ....113 H4
SE28 ....118 C6
Copperfield St, SE1 ....27 H3
Copperfield Way, Chis.
BR7 ....175 F6
Pinner HA5 ....67 F4
Coppergate Cl, Brom.
BR1 ....191 H1
Copper Mead Cl, NW2 ....89 J3
Copper Ms, W4
off Reynolds Rd 126 C3
Copper Mill Dr, Islw.
TW7 ....144 C2
Coppermill La, E17 ....77 F6
Copper Mill La, SW17 ...167 F4
Copper Row, SE1 ....29 F2
Coppetts Cl, N12 ....57 H7
Coppetts Rd, N10 ....74 A2
Coppice, The, Enf. EN2 ....43 H4
Coppice Cl, SW20 ....183 J3
Beckenham BR3 ....190 B4
Stanmore HA7 ....52 C6
Coppice Dr, SW15 ....147 H6
Coppice Wk, N20 ....56 D3
Coppice Way, E18 ....79 F4
Coppies Gro, N11 ....58 A4
Copping Cl, Croy. CR0 ...202 B4
Coppins, The, Croy.
(New Adgtn) CR0 ....204 B6
Harrow HA3 ....52 B6
Coppock Cl, SW11 ....149 H2
Coppsfield, W.Mol. KT8
off Hurst Rd 179 G3
Copse, The, E4 ....63 F1
Copse Av, W.Wick. BR4 ...204 B3
Copse Cl, SE7 ....135 H6
West Drayton UB7 ....120 A3
Copse Glade, Surb. KT6 ..195 G1
COPSE HILL, SW20 ....165 H7
Copse Hill, SW20 ....165 H7
Sutton SM2 ....199 E7
Copsewood Cl, Sid.
DA15 ....157 H6
Coptain Ho, SW18
off Eastfields Av 148 D4
Coptefield Dr, Belv.
DA17 ....138 D3
Copthall Av, EC2 ....20 C3
Copthall Bldgs, EC2 ....20 B3
Copthall Cl, EC2 ....20 B3
Copthall Ct, EC2 ....20 B3
Copthall Dr, NW7 ....55 G7
Copthall Gdns, NW7 ....55 G7
Twickenham TW1 ....162 C1
Copthorne Av, SW12 ....150 D7
Bromley BR2 ....206 C2
Ilford IG6 ....65 E6
Copthorne Ms, Hayes
UB3 ....121 H4
Coptic St, WC1 ....18 A2
Copwood Cl, N12 ....57 G4
Coral Apts, E16
off Western Gateway .115 G7
Coral Cl, Rom. RM6 ....82 C4
Coraline Cl, Sthl. UB1 ....103 F3
Coralline Wk, SE2 ....138 C2
Coral Row, SW11
off Gartons Way 149 F3
Coral St, SE1 ....27 F4
★ **Coram's Flds**, WC1 ....10 C5
Coram St, WC1 ....10 A6
Coran Cl, N9 ....45 G7
Corban Rd, Houns. TW3 ..143 G3
Corbden Cl, SE15 ....152 C1
Corbet Cl, Wall. SM6 ....200 A1
Corbet Ct, EC3 ....20 C4
Corbet Pl, E1 ....21 F1
Corbett Gro, N22 ....58 E7
Corbett Rd, E11 ....79 J6
E17 ....78 C3
Corbetts La, SE16
off Rotherhithe
New Rd 133 F4
Corbetts Pas, SE16
off Silwood St 133 F4
Corbicum, E11 ....79 E7
Corbidge Ct, SE8
off Glaisher St 134 B6
Corbiere Ct, SW19
off Thornton Rd 166 A6
Corbiere Ho, N1 ....112 B1
Corbin Ho, E3
off Bromley High St ..114 B3
Corbins La, Har. HA2 ....85 H3
Corbridge Cres, E2 ....112 E2
Corby Cres, Enf. EN2 ....43 E4
Corbylands Rd, Sid.
DA15 ....157 H7
Corbyn St, N4 ....93 E1
Corby Rd, NW10 ....106 D2
Corby Way, E3
off Knapp Rd 114 A4
Cordelia Cl, SE24 ....151 H4
Cordelia Gdns, Stai.
TW19 ....140 B7
Cordelia Rd, Stai.
TW19 ....140 B7
Cordelia St, E14 ....114 B6
Cordell Ho, N15 ....76 D5
Cording St, E14
off Chrisp St 114 B5
Cordwainers Wk, E13
off Richmond St 115 G2
Cord Way, E14
off Mellish St 134 A3
Cordwell Rd, SE13 ....154 E5
Corefield Cl, N11
off Benfleet Way 58 A2
Corelli Rd, SE3 ....156 B2
Corfe Av, Har. HA2 ....85 G4
Corfe Cl, Borwd. WD6 ....38 D3
Hayes UB4 ....102 C6

Corfe Cl, Hounslow TW4
off Farm Rd 161 E1
Corfe Ho, SW8
off Dorset Rd 34 C7
Corfe Twr, W3 126 B2
Corfield Rd, N21 43 F5
Corfield St, E2 113 E3
Corfton Rd, W5 105 H6
Coriander Av, E14 114 D6
Cories Cl, Dag. RM8 100 D2
Corinium Cl, Wem. HA9 87 J4
Corinne Rd, N19 92 C4
Corinthian Way, Stai. (Stanw.) TW19
off Clare Rd 140 A7
Corker Wk, N7 93 F2
Corkran Rd, Surb. KT6 181 G7
Corkscrew Hill, W.Wick. BR4 204 D2
Cork Sq, E1
off Smeaton St 132 E1
Cork St, W1 17 F6
Cork St Ms, W1 17 F6
Cork Tree Retail Pk, E4 61 H5
Cork Tree Way, E4 61 H5
Corlett St, NW1 15 G1
Cormont Rd, SE5 151 H1
Cormorant Cl, E17 77 G1
Cormorant Ho, Enf. EN3
off Alma Rd 45 G5
Cormorant Pl, Sutt. SM1
off Sandpiper Rd 198 C5
Cormorant Rd, E7 97 F4
Cornbury Rd, Edg. HA8 53 G7
Cornelia Dr, Hayes UB4 102 C4
Cornelia St, N7 93 F6
Cornell Cl, Sid. DA14 177 E6
Cornell Ct, Enf. EN3 45 H3
Corner Fielde, SW2
off Streatham Hill 169 E1
Corner Grn, SE3 155 G3
Corner Ho St, WC2 26 A1
Corner Mead, NW9 55 F7
Corney Reach Way, W4 127 E7
Corney Rd, W4 127 E6
Cornflower La, Croy. CR0 203 G1
Cornflower Ter, SE22 152 E6
Cornford Cl, Brom. BR2 191 G5
Cornford Gro, SW12 168 B2
Cornhill, EC3 20 C4
Cornish Ct, N9 44 E7
Cornish Gro, SE20 171 E7
Cornish Ho, SE17 35 G6
Brentford TW8
off Green Dragon La 125 J5
Corn Mill Dr, Orp. BR6 193 J7
Cornmill La, SE13 154 B3
Cornmow Dr, NW10 89 F5
Cornshaw Rd, Dag. RM8 100 D1
Cornthwaite Rd, E5 95 F3
Cornwall Av, E2 113 F3
N3 56 D7
N22 75 E1
Esher (Clay.) KT10
off The Causeway 194 C7
Southall UB1 103 F5
Welling DA16 157 H3
Cornwall Cl, Bark. IG11 99 J6
Cornwall Cres, W11 108 B7
Cornwall Dr, Orp. BR5 176 C7
Cornwall Gdns, NW10 89 H6
SW7 22 B6
Cornwall Gdns Wk, SW7 22 B6
Cornwall Gro, W4 127 E5
Cornwallis Av, N9 61 E2
SE9 175 G2
Cornwallis Ct, SW8
off Allen Edwards Dr 150 E1
Cornwallis Gro, N9 61 E2
Cornwallis Rd, E17 77 G4
N9 61 E2
N19 92 E2
SE18 137 F4
Dagenham RM9 100 D4
Cornwallis Sq, N19 92 E2
Cornwallis Wk, SE9 156 C3
Cornwall Ms S, SW7 22 C6
Cornwall Ms W, SW7 22 B6
Cornwall Rd, N4 75 G7
N15 76 A5
N18 *off Fairfield Rd* 60 D5
SE1 26 E1
Croydon CR0 201 H2
Esher (Clay.) KT10 194 D7
Harrow HA1 67 J6
Pinner HA5 51 F7
Sutton SM2 198 C7
Twickenham TW1 162 D1
Cornwall Sq, SE11 35 F3
Cornwall St, E1
off Watney St 113 E7
Cornwall Ter, NW1 8 A6
Cornwall Ter Ms, NW1 8 A6
Corn Way, E11 96 D3
Cornwood Cl, N2 73 G5
Cornwood Dr, E1 113 F6
Cornworthy Rd, Dag. RM8 100 C5
Corona Rd, SE12 155 G7
Coronation Av, N16
off Victorian Rd 94 C3
Coronation Cl, Bex. DA5 158 D6
Ilford IG6 81 F4
Coronation Rd, E13 115 J3
NW10 106 A4
Hayes UB3 121 J4
Coronation Wk, Twick. TW2 161 F1
Coronet St, N1 12 D4
Corporation Av, Houns. TW4 142 E4
Corporation Row, EC1 11 F5
Corporation St, E15 115 E2
N7 92 E5
Corrance Rd, SW2 151 E4
Corri Av, N14 58 D4
Corrib Dr, Sutt. SM1 199 H5
Corrigan Cl, NW4 71 J3
Corringham Ct, NW11
off Corringham Rd 72 D7
Corringham Rd, NW11 72 D7
Wembley HA9 88 A2
Corringway, NW11 72 E7
W5 106 A4
Corris Grn, NW9
off Snowdon Dr 70 E6
Corry Dr, SW9 151 H4
Corsair Cl, Stai. TW19 140 A7
Corsair Rd, Stai. TW19 140 B7
Corscombe Cl, Kings.T. KT2 164 C5
Corsehill St, SW16 168 C6
Corsham St, N1 12 C4
Corsica St, N5 93 H6
Cortayne Rd, SW6 148 C2
Cortina Dr, Dag. RM9 119 J3
Cortis Rd, SW15 147 H6
Cortis Ter, SW15 147 H6
Cortland Cl, Wdf.Grn. IG8 79 J1
Corunna Rd, SW8 150 C1
Corunna Ter, SW8 150 C1
Corvette Sq, SE10
off Feathers Pl 134 D6
Coryton Path, W9
off Fernhead Rd 108 C4
Cosbycote Av, SE24 151 J5
Cosdach Av, Wall. SM6 200 D7
Cosedge Cres, Croy. CR0 201 G5
Cosgrove Cl, N21 59 J2
Hayes UB4
off Kingsash Dr 102 E4
Cosmo Pl, WC1 18 B1
Cosmur Cl, W12 127 F3
Cossall Wk, SE15 153 E1
Cossar Ms, SW2 151 G6
Cosser St, SE1 26 E5
Costa St, SE15 152 D2
Costons Av, Grnf. UB6 104 A3
Costons La, Grnf. UB6 104 A3
Coston Wk, SE4
off Hainford Cl 153 G4
Cosway St, NW1 15 H1
Cotall St, E14 114 A6
Coteford Cl, Loug. IG10 48 E2
Pinner HA5 66 A5
Coteford St, SW17 167 J4
Cotelands, Croy. CR0 202 B3
Cotesbach Rd, E5 95 F3
Cotesmore Gdns, Dag. RM8 100 C4
Cotford Rd, Th.Hth. CR7 187 J4
Cotham St, SE17 36 A2
Cotherstone Rd, SW2 169 F1
Cotleigh Av, Bex. DA5 176 D2
Cotleigh Rd, NW6 90 D7
Cotman Cl, NW11 73 F6
SW15 148 A6
Cotman Gdns, Edg. HA8 70 A2
Cotman Ms, Dag. RM8
off Highgrove Rd 100 C5
Cotmans Cl, Hayes UB3 122 A1
Coton Rd, Well. DA16 158 A3
Cotsford Av, N.Mal. KT3 182 C5
Cotswold Cl, Esher (Hinch.Wd) KT10 194 C3
Kingston upon Thames KT2 164 B6
Cotswold Ct, EC1 11 J5
N11 58 A4
Cotswold Gdns, E6 116 A3
NW2 90 A2
Ilford IG2 81 G7
Cotswold Gate, NW2
off Cotswold Gdns 90 B1
Cotswold Grn, Enf. EN2
off Cotswold Way 43 F4
Cotswold Ms, SW11
off Battersea High St 149 G1
Cotswold Ri, Orp. BR6 193 J6
Cotswold Rd, Hmptn. TW12 161 G6
Cotswold St, SE27
off Norwood High St 169 H4
Cotswold Way, Enf. EN2 43 F4
Worcester Park KT4 197 J2
Cottage Av, Brom. BR2 206 B1
Cottage Cl, Har. HA2 86 B2
Cottage Fld Cl, Sid. DA14 176 C1
Cottage Grn, SE5 36 C7
Cottage Gro, SW9 150 E3
Surbiton KT6 181 G6
Cottage Pl, SW3 23 G5
Cottage Rd, N7 93 F5
Epsom KT19 196 D7
Cottage St, E14 114 B7
Cottage Wk, N16
off Brooke Rd 94 C3
Cottenham Dr, NW9 71 F3
SW20 165 H7
Cottenham Par, SW20
off Durham Rd 183 H2
COTTENHAM PARK, SW20 183 H1
Cottenham Pk Rd, SW20 165 H7
Cottenham Pl, SW20 165 H7
Cottenham Rd, E17 77 J4
Cotterill Rd, Surb. KT6 195 H2
Cottesbrook St, SE14
off Nynehead St 133 H7
Cottesloe Ms, SE1 27 F5
Cottesmore Av, Ilf. IG5 80 D2
Cottesmore Gdns, W8 22 B5
Cottimore Cres, Walt. KT12 178 B7
Cottimore La, Walt. KT12 178 B7
Cottimore Ter, Walt. KT12 178 B7
Cottingham Chase, Ruis. HA4 84 A3
Cottingham Rd, SE20 171 G7
SW8 34 D6
Cottington Rd, Felt. TW13 160 D4
Cottington St, SE11 35 F3
Cottle Way, SE16
off St. Marychurch St 133 F2
Cotton Av, W3 106 D6
Cotton Cl, E11 97 E2
Dagenham RM9
off Flamstead Rd 100 C7
Cottongrass Cl, Croy. CR0
off Cornflower La 203 G1
Cotton Hill, Brom. BR1 172 D4
Cotton Row, SW11 149 F3
Cottons Gdns, E2 13 E3
Cottons La, SE1 28 C1
Cotton St, E14 114 C7
Cottrell Ct, SE10
off Greenroof Way 135 F4
Cottrill Gdns, E8
off Marcon Pl 94 E6
Cotts Cl, W7
off Westcott Cres 104 C6
Couchmore Av, Esher KT10 194 B2
Ilford IG5 80 C2
Coulgate St, SE4 153 H3
Coulson Cl, Dag. RM8 82 C7
Coulson St, SW3 31 J3
Coulter Cl, Hayes UB4
off Berrydale Rd 102 E4
Coulter Rd, W6 127 H3
Councillor St, SE5 131 J7
Counter Ct, SE1
off Borough High St 28 B2
Counter St, SE1 28 D1
Countess Rd, NW5 92 C5
Countisbury Av, Enf. EN1 44 C7
Country Way, Felt. (Han.) TW13 160 B7
Sunbury-on-Thames TW16 160 B7
County Gate, SE9 175 F3
Barnet (New Barn.) EN5 41 E6
County Gro, SE5 151 J1
★ **County Hall**, SE1 26 C3
County Rd, E6 116 E5
Thornton Heath CR7 187 H2
County St, SE1 28 A6
Coupland Pl, SE18 137 F5
Courcy Rd, N8 75 G3
Courier Rd, Dag. RM9 119 J4
Courland Gro, SW8 150 D1
Courland Gro Hall, SW8 150 D2
Courland St, SW8 150 D1
Course, The, SE9 174 D3
Court, The, Ruis. HA4 84 E4
Courtauld Cl, SE28 138 A1
★ **Courtauld Inst of Art**, WC2 18 C5
Courtauld Rd, N19 92 D1
Court Av, Belv. DA17 139 F5
Court Cl, Har. HA3 69 H3
Twickenham TW2 161 H3
Wallington SM6 200 D7
Court Cl Av, Twick. TW2 161 H3
Court Cres, Chess. KT9 195 G5
Court Downs Rd, Beck. BR3 190 B2
Court Dr, Croy. CR0 201 F4
Stanmore HA7 53 H4
Sutton SM1 199 H4
Courtenay Av, N6 73 H6
Harrow HA3 67 J1
Courtenay Dr, Beck. BR3 190 D2
Courtenay Gdns, Har. HA3 67 J2
Courtenay Ms, E17
off Cranbrook Ms 77 H5
Courtenay Pl, E17 77 H5
Courtenay Rd, E11 97 F3
E17 77 G4
SE20 171 G7
Wembley HA9 87 G3
Worcester Park KT4 197 J3
Courtenay Sq, SE11 34 E4
Courtenay St, SE11 34 E3
Courtens Ms, Stan. HA7 53 F7
Court Fm Av, Epsom KT19 196 D5
Court Fm Rd, SE9 174 A2
Northolt UB5 85 G7
Courtfield, W5
off Castlebar Hill 105 F5
Courtfield Av, Har. HA1 68 C5
Courtfield Cres, Har. HA1 68 C5
Courtfield Gdns, SW5 30 B1
W13 104 D6
Courtfield Ms, SW5 30 C2
Courtfield Ri, W.Wick. BR4 204 D3
Courtfield Rd, SW7 30 B2
Court Gdns, N7 93 G6
Courtgate Cl, NW7 55 F6
Courthill Rd, SE13 154 C4
Courthope Rd, NW3 91 J4
SW19 166 B5
Greenford UB6 104 A2
Courthope Vil, SW19 166 B7
Court Ho Gdns, N3 56 D6
Courthouse Rd, N12 56 E6
Courtland Av, E4 63 F2
NW7 54 D3
SW16 169 F7
Ilford IG1 98 C2
Courtland Dr, Chig. IG7 65 E3
Courtland Gro, SE28 118 D7
Courtland Rd, E6
off Harrow Rd 116 B1
Courtlands, Rich. TW10 146 A4
Courtlands Av, SE12 155 H5
Bromley BR2 205 F1
Hampton TW12 161 F6
Richmond TW9 146 B2
Courtlands Dr, Epsom KT19 197 E6
Courtlands Rd, Surb. KT5 182 A7
Court La, SE21 152 B6
Court La Gdns, SE21 152 B7
Courtleet Dr, Erith DA8 159 H1
Courtleigh Gdns, NW11 72 B4
Courtman Rd, N17 59 J7
Court Mead, Nthlt. UB5 103 F3
Courtmead Cl, SE24 151 J6
Courtnell St, W2 108 D6
Courtney Cl, SE19 170 B6
Courtney Cres, Cars. SM5 199 J7
Courtney Pl, Croy. CR0 201 G3
Courtney Rd, N7
off Bryantwood Rd 93 G5
SW19 167 H7
Croydon CR0 201 G3
Hounslow (Lon.Hthrw Air.) TW6 140 D3
Courtney Way, Houns. (Lon.Hthrw Air.) TW6 140 D3
Court Par, Wem. HA0 86 E3
Courtrai Rd, SE23 153 H6
Court Rd, SE9 174 B2
SE25 188 C2
Southall UB2 123 F4
Courtside, N8 74 D6

Court St, E1
off Whitechapel Rd . . . **112** E5
Bromley BR1 . . . . **191** G2
Court Way, NW9 . . . . **71** E4
W3 . . . . **106** C5
Ilford IG6 . . . . **81** F3
Twickenham TW2 . . . . . **144** C7
Courtway, Wdf.Grn. IG8 . . . **63** J5
Courtway, The, Wat.
WD19 . . . . **51** E2
Court Yd, SE9 . . . . **156** B6
Courtyard, The, N1 . . . . **93** F7
Keston BR2 . . . . **206** B6
Courtyard Ho, SW6
off Lensbury Av **149** F2
Courtyard Ms, Orp. BR5
off Dorchester Cl **176** A7
Cousin La, EC4 . . . . **20** B6
Couthurst Rd, SE3 . . . . . . **135** H6
Coutts Av, Chess. KT9 . . . **195** H5
Coutts Cres, NW5 . . . . **92** A3
Coval Gdns, SW14 . . . . . . **146** B4
Coval La, SW14 . . . . **146** B4
Coval Pas, SW14
off Coval Rd **146** C4
Coval Rd, SW14 . . . . **146** B4
Covelees Wall, E6 . . . . **116** D6
Covell Ct, SE8
off Reginald Sq **134** A7
★ **Covent Garden**, WC2 . . **18** B5
Covent Gdn Mkt, WC2 . . . . **18** B5
Coventry Cl, E6
off Harper Rd **116** C6
NW6
off Kilburn High Rd . . **108** D1
Coventry Rd, E1 . . . . **113** E4
E2 . . . . **113** E4
SE25 . . . . **188** D4
Ilford IG1 . . . . **98** E1
Coventry St, W1 . . . . **17** H6
Coverack Cl, N14 . . . . **42** C6
Croydon CR0 . . . . **189** H7
Coverdale Cl, Stan. HA7 . . . **53** E5
Coverdale Gdns, Croy. CR0
off Park Hill Ri **202** C3
Coverdale Rd, N11 . . . . **58** A6
NW2 . . . . **90** A7
W12 . . . . **127** H1
Coverdales, The, Bark.
IG11 . . . . **117** F2
Coverley Cl, E1 . . . . **21** J1
Covert, The, Orp. BR6 . . . . **193** H6
Coverton Rd, SW17 . . . . . **167** H5
Covert Rd, Ilf. IG6 . . . . **65** J6
Covert Way, Barn. EN4 . . . . **41** F2
Covet Wd Cl, Orp. BR5 . . . **193** J6
Covey Cl, SW19 . . . . **184** E2
Covington Gdns, SW16 . . . **169** H7
Covington Way, SW16 . . . **169** F6
Cowan Cl, E6
off Oliver Gdns **116** B5
Cowbridge La, Bark. IG11 . . **98** E7
Cowbridge Rd, Har. HA3 . . **69** J4
Cowcross St, EC1 . . . . **19** G1
Cowdenbeath Path, N1 . . . **111** F1
Cowden Rd, Orp. BR6 . . . **193** J7
Cowden St, SE6 . . . . **172** A4
Cowdrey Cl, Enf. EN1 . . . . . **44** B2
Cowdrey Rd, SW19 . . . . . . **167** E5
Cowdry Rd, E9
off East Cross Route . . **95** J6
Cowen Av, Har. HA2 . . . . . . **85** J2
Cowgate Rd, Grnf. UB6 . . **104** A2
Cowick Rd, SW17 . . . . **167** J4
Cowings Mead, Nthlt.
UB5 . . . . **85** E7
Cowland Av, Enf. EN3 . . . . **45** F4
Cow La, Grnf. UB6 . . . . . . **104** A2
Cow Leaze, E6 . . . . **116** D6
Cowleaze Rd, Kings.T.
KT2 . . . . **181** H1
Cowley Est, SW9 . . . . **151** G1
Cowley Pl, NW4 . . . . **71** J5
Cowley Rd, E11 . . . . **79** H5
SW9 . . . . **151** G1
SW14 . . . . **146** E3
W3 . . . . **127** F1
Ilford IG1 . . . . **80** C7
Cowley St, SW1 . . . . **26** A5
Cowling Cl, W11
off Wilsham St **128** B1
Cowper Av, E6 . . . . **98** B7
Sutton SM1 . . . . **199** G4
Cowper Cl, Brom. BR2 . . . **192** A4
Welling DA16 . . . . **158** A5
Cowper Gdns, N14 . . . . **42** C6
Wallington SM6 . . . . **200** C6
Cowper Rd, N14 . . . . **58** B1
N16 . . . . **94** B5
N18 . . . . **60** D5
SW19 . . . . **167** F6
W3 . . . . **126** D1
W7 . . . . **104** C7
Cowper Rd, Belvedere
DA17 . . . . **139** G4
Bromley BR2 . . . . **192** A4
Kingston upon Thames
KT2 . . . . **163** J5
Cowpers Ct, EC3
off Birchin La **20** C4
Cowper St, EC2 . . . . **12** C5
Cowper Ter, W10
off St. Quintin Av **108** A5
Cowslip Rd, E18 . . . . **79** H2
Cowthorpe Rd, SW8 . . . . . **150** D1
Coxe Pl, Har. (Wealds.)
HA3 . . . . **68** D4
Cox La, Chess. KT9 . . . . . . **195** J4
Epsom KT19 . . . . **196** B5
Coxmount Rd, SE7 . . . . . . **136** A5
Coxson Way, SE1 . . . . **29** F4
Cox's Wk, SE21 . . . . **170** D1
Coxwell Rd, SE18 . . . . **137** G5
SE19 . . . . **170** B7
Coxwold Path, Chess. KT9
off Garrison La **195** H7
Crabbs Cft Cl, Orp. BR6
off Ladycroft Way **207** F5
Crab Hill, Beck. BR3 . . . . . **172** D7
Crabtree Av, Rom. RM6 . . . **82** D4
Wembley HA0 . . . . **105** H2
Crabtree Cl, E2 . . . . **13** F1
Crabtree La, SW6 . . . . **128** A7
Crabtree Manorway Ind Est,
Belv. DA17 . . . . **139** H3
Crabtree Manorway N,
Belv. DA17 . . . . **139** J2
Crabtree Manorway S,
Belv. DA17 . . . . **139** J3
Craddock Rd, Enf. EN1 . . . . **44** C3
Craddock St, NW5
off Prince of Wales Rd . **92** A6
Cradley Rd, SE9 . . . . **175** G1
Craigen Av, Croy. CR0 . . . **203** E1
Craigerne Rd, SE3 . . . . **135** H7
Craig Gdns, E18 . . . . **79** F2
Craigholm, SE18 . . . . **156** D2
Craigmuir Pk, Wem. HA0 . **105** J1
Craignair Rd, SW2 . . . . . . **151** G7
Craignish Av, SW16 . . . . . **187** F2
Craig Pk Rd, N18 . . . . **60** E5
Craig Rd, Rich. TW10 . . . . . **163** F4
Craigs Ct, SW1 . . . . **26** A1
Craigton Rd, SE9 . . . . **156** C4
Craigweil Cl, Stan. HA7 . . . **53** G5
Craigweil Dr, Stan. HA7 . . . **53** G5
Craigwell Av, Felt. TW13 . . **160** A3
Craik Ct, NW6
off Carlton Vale **108** C2
Crail Row, SE17 . . . . **36** C2
Cramer Ct, N.Mal. KT3
off Warwick Rd **182** C3
Cramer St, W1 . . . . **16** C2
Crammond Cl, W6 . . . . **128** B6
Crampton Rd, SE20 . . . . . **171** F6
Crampton St, SE17 . . . . **35** J2
Cranberry Cl, Nthlt. UB5
off Parkfield Av **102** D2
Cranberry La, E16 . . . . . . **114** E4
Cranborne Av, Sthl. UB2 . . **123** G4
Surbiton KT6 . . . . **196** A3
Cranborne Rd, Bark. IG11 . **117** G1
Cranborne Waye, Hayes
UB4 . . . . **102** C7
Cranbourn All, WC2
off Cranbourn St **17** J5
Cranbourne Av, E11 . . . . . . **79** H4
Cranbourne Cl, SW16 . . . **187** E3
Cranbourne Dr, Pnr. HA5 . . **66** D5
Cranbourne Gdns, NW11 . . **72** B5
Ilford IG6 . . . . **81** F3
Cranbourne Pas, SE16
off Marigold St **132** E2
Cranbourne Rd, E12
off High St N **98** B5
E15 . . . . **96** C4
N10 . . . . **74** B2
Cranbourn St, WC2 . . . . **17** J5
CRANBROOK, Ilf. IG1 . . . . . **98** C1
Cranbrook Cl, Brom. BR2 . **191** G6
Cranbrook Dr, Twick.
TW2 . . . . **161** H1
Cranbrook Ho, E5
off Pembury Rd **94** E5
Cranbrook La, N11 . . . . **58** B4
Cranbrook Ms, E17 . . . . **77** H5
Cranbrook Pk, N22 . . . . **75** F1
Cranbrook Ri, Ilf. IG1 . . . . . **80** C7
Cranbrook Rd, SE8 . . . . . . **154** A1
SW19 . . . . **166** B7
W4 . . . . **127** E5
Barnet EN4 . . . . **41** G6
Bexleyheath DA7 . . . . . **159** F1
Hounslow TW4 . . . . **143** F4
Ilford IG1, IG2, IG6 . . . . . **80** D7
Thornton Heath CR7 . . **187** J2
Cranbrook St, E2
off Mace St **113** G2
Cranbury Rd, SW6 . . . . . . **149** E2
Crandale Ho, E5
off Pembury Rd **94** E5
Crane Av, W3 . . . . **106** C7
Isleworth TW7 . . . . **144** D5
Cranebank Ms, Twick.
TW1 . . . . **144** D4
Cranebrook, Twick. TW2
off Manor Rd **161** J2
Crane Cl, Dag. RM10 . . . . . **101** G6
Harrow HA2 . . . . **85** J3
Crane Ct, EC4 . . . . **19** F4
Epsom KT19 . . . . **196** C4
Craneford Cl, Twick.
TW2 . . . . **144** C7
Craneford Way, Twick.
TW2 . . . . **144** B7
Crane Gdns, Hayes UB3 . . **121** J4
Crane Gro, N7 . . . . **93** G6
Crane Ho, SE15
off Talfourd Pl **152** C1
Crane Lo Rd, Houns.
TW5 . . . . **122** B6
Crane Pk Rd, Twick. TW2 . . **161** H2
Crane Rd, Twick. TW2 . . . . **162** B1
Cranesbill Cl, NW9
off Annesley Av **70** D3
Cranes Dr, Surb. KT5 . . . . **181** H4
Cranes Pk, Surb. KT5 . . . . **181** H4
Cranes Pk Av, Surb. KT5 . **181** H4
Cranes Pk Cres, Surb.
KT5 . . . . **181** J4
Crane St, SE10 . . . . **134** D5
SE15 . . . . **152** C1
Craneswater, Hayes UB3 . **121** J7
Craneswater Pk, Sthl.
UB2 . . . . **123** F5
Cranes Way, Borwd.
WD6 . . . . **38** C5
Crane Way, Twick. TW2 . . . **143** J7
Cranfield Cl, SE27
off Norwood High St . **169** J3
Cranfield Dr, NW9 . . . . **54** E7
Cranfield Rd, SE4 . . . . **153** J3
Cranfield Row, SE1 . . . . **27** F5
CRANFORD, Houns. TW5 . **122** A7
Cranford Av, N13 . . . . **59** E5
Staines TW19 . . . . **140** B7
Cranford Cl, SW20 . . . . . . **183** H1
Staines TW19 . . . . **140** B7
Cranford Cotts, E1
off Cranford St **113** G7
Cranford Dr, Hayes
UB3 . . . . **121** J4
Cranford La, Hayes
UB3 . . . . **121** G6
Hounslow (Heston)
TW5 . . . . **122** D7
Hounslow
(Lon.Hthrw Air.) TW6 . **141** J3
Hounslow
(Lon.Hthrw Air.N)
TW6 . . . . **141** J1
Cranford Pk Rd, Hayes
UB3 . . . . **121** J4
Cranford St, E1 . . . . **113** G7
Cranford Way, N8 . . . . **75** F5
Cranhurst Rd, NW2 . . . . **89** J5
Cranleigh Cl, SE20 . . . . . . **188** E2
Bexley DA5 . . . . **159** H6
Cranleigh Ct, Mitch. CR4
off Phipps Br Rd **185** G3
Cranleigh Gdns, N21 . . . . . **43** G5
SE25 . . . . **188** B3
Barking IG11 . . . . **99** G7
Harrow HA3 . . . . **69** H5
Kingston upon Thames
KT2 . . . . **163** J6
Loughton IG10 . . . . **48** C6
Southall UB1 . . . . **103** F6
Sutton SM1 . . . . **198** E2
Cranleigh Gdns Ind Est,
Sthl. UB1
off Cranleigh Gdns . . . **103** F5
Cranleigh Ms, SW11 . . . . . **149** H2
Cranleigh Rd, N15 . . . . **75** J5
SW19 . . . . **184** D3
Cranleigh St, NW1 . . . . **9** G2
Cranley Dene Ct, N10 . . . . . **74** B4
Cranley Dr, Ilf. IG2 . . . . **81** F7
Cranley Gdns, N10 . . . . **74** C4
N13 . . . . **59** F3
SW7 . . . . **30** D3
Wallington SM6 . . . . **200** C7
Cranley Ms, SW7 . . . . **30** D3
Cranley Par, SE9
off Beaconsfield Rd . . **174** B4
Cranley Pl, SW7 . . . . **31** E2
Cranley Rd, E13 . . . . **115** H5
Ilford IG2 . . . . **81** F6
Cranmer Av, W13 . . . . **124** E3
Cranmer Cl, Mord. SM4 . . **184** A6
Ruislip HA4 . . . . **84** D1
Stanmore HA7 . . . . **53** F7
Cranmer Ct, SW3 . . . . **31** H2
SW4 . . . . **150** D3
Hampton (Hmptn H.)
TW12
off Cranmer Rd **161** H5
Cranmer Fm Cl, Mitch.
CR4 . . . . **185** J4
Cranmer Gdns, Dag.
RM10 . . . . **101** J4
Cranmer Ho, SW11
off Surrey La **149** H1
Cranmer Rd, E7 . . . . **97** H4
SW9 . . . . **35** F7
Croydon CR0 . . . . **201** H3
Edgware HA8 . . . . **54** B3
Hampton (Hmptn H.)
TW12 . . . . **161** H5
Kingston upon Thames
KT2 . . . . **163** H5
Mitcham CR4 . . . . **185** J4
Cranmer Ter, SW17 . . . . . . **167** G5
Cranmore Av, Islw. TW7 . . . **123** J7
Cranmore Rd, Brom. BR1 . **173** E3
Chislehurst BR7 . . . . . . **174** C5
Cranmore Way, N10 . . . . **74** C4
Cranston Cl, Houns. TW3 . **143** E2
Cranston Est, N1 . . . . **12** C2
Cranston Gdns, E4 . . . . **62** B5
Cranston Rd, SE23 . . . . . . **171** H1
Cranswick Rd, SE16 . . . . . **133** E5
Crantock Rd, SE6 . . . . **172** B2
Cranwell Cl, E3 . . . . **114** B4
Cranwich Av, N21 . . . . **44** A7
Cranwich Rd, N16 . . . . **76** A7
Cranwood St, EC1 . . . . **12** B4
Cranworth Cres, E4 . . . . **62** D1
Cranworth Gdns, SW9 . . . **151** G1
Craster Rd, SW2 . . . . **151** F7
Crathie Rd, SE12 . . . . **155** H6
Cravan Av, Felt. TW13 . . . . **160** A2
Craven Av, W5 . . . . **105** F7
Southall UB1 . . . . **103** F5
Craven Cl, N16
off Craven Wk **76** D7
Hayes UB4 . . . . **102** A6
Craven Gdns, SW19 . . . . . **166** D5
Barking IG11 . . . . **117** H2
Ilford IG6 . . . . **81** G2
Craven Hill, W2 . . . . **14** D5
Craven Hill Gdns, W2 . . . . . **14** C5
Craven Hill Ms, W2 . . . . **14** D5
Craven Ms, SW11
off Taybridge Rd **150** A3
Craven Pk, NW10 . . . . **106** E1
Craven Pk Ms, NW10 . . . . . **88** E7
Craven Pk Rd, N15 . . . . **76** C6
NW10 . . . . **106** E1
Craven Pas, WC2 . . . . **26** A1
Craven Rd, NW10 . . . . **106** D1
W2 . . . . **14** D5
W5 . . . . **105** F7
Croydon CR0 . . . . **202** E1
Kingston upon Thames
KT2 . . . . **181** J1
Craven St, WC2 . . . . **26** A1
Craven Ter, W2 . . . . **14** D5
Craven Wk, N16 . . . . **76** D7
Crawford Av, Wem. HA0 . . . **87** G5
Crawford Cl, Islw. TW7 . . . **144** B2
Crawford Est, SE5 . . . . **151** J2
Crawford Gdns, N13 . . . . . . **59** H3
Northolt UB5 . . . . **103** F3
Crawford Ms, W1 . . . . **15** J2
Crawford Pas, EC1 . . . . **11** E6
Crawford Pl, W1 . . . . **15** H3
Crawford Rd, SE5 . . . . **151** J1
Crawford St, NW10
off Fawood Av **88** D7
W1 . . . . **15** J2
Crawley Rd, E10 . . . . **96** B1
N22 . . . . **75** J2
Enfield EN1 . . . . **44** B7
Crawshay Ct, SW9
off Eythorne Rd **151** G1
Crawthew Gro, SE22 . . . . **152** C4
Craybrooke Rd, Sid.
DA14 . . . . **176** B4
Craybury End, SE9 . . . . . . **175** F2
Crayford Cl, E6
off Neatscourt Rd **116** B5
Crayford Rd, N7 . . . . **92** D4
Crayke Hill, Chess.
KT9 . . . . **195** H7
Cray Rd, Belv. DA17 . . . . . **139** G6
Sidcup DA14 . . . . **176** C7
Crealock Gro, Wdf.Grn.
IG8 . . . . **63** F5
Crealock St, SW18 . . . . . . **149** E6
Creasy Est, SE1 . . . . **28** D6
Crebor St, SE22 . . . . **152** D6

Credenhall Dr, Brom. BR2 **206** C1
Credenhill St, SW16 **168** C6
Crediton Hill, NW6 **90** E5
Crediton Rd, E16
off Pacific Rd **115** G6
NW10 **108** A1
Crediton Way, Esher (Clay.) KT10 **194** D5
Credon Rd, E13 **115** J2
SE16 **133** E5
Creechurch La, EC3 **20** E4
Creechurch Pl, EC3 **21** E4
Creed Ct, EC4
off Ludgate Sq **19** H4
Creed La, EC4 **19** H4
Creek, The, Sun. TW16 **178** A5
CREEKMOUTH, Bark. IG11 **118** A4
Creek Rd, SE8 **134** A6
SE10 **134** A6
Barking IG11 **117** J3
East Molesey KT8 **180** B4
Creekside, SE8 **134** B7
Creeland Gro, SE6
off Catford Hill **171** J1
Crefeld Cl, W6 **128** A6
Creffield Rd, W3 **105** J7
W5 **105** J7
Creighton Av, E6 **116** A2
N2 **73** H3
N10 **74** A2
Creighton Cl, W12 **107** G7
Creighton Rd, N17 **60** B7
NW6 **108** A2
W5 **125** G3
Cremer St, E2 **13** F2
Cremorne Est, SW10 **31** E7
Cremorne Rd, SW10 **129** F7
Crescent, EC3 **21** F5
Crescent, The, E17 **77** H5
N11 **57** J4
NW2 **89** H3
SW13 **147** F2
SW19 **166** D3
W3 **106** E6
Barnet EN5 **40** E3
Beckenham BR3 **190** A1
Bexley DA5 **158** C7
Croydon CR0 **188** A5
Harrow HA2 **86** A1
Hayes (Harling.) UB3 **121** F7
Ilford IG2 **80** D6
Loughton IG10 **48** A5
New Malden KT3 **182** C2
Sidcup DA14 **175** J4
Southall UB1 **123** F2
Surbiton KT6 **181** H5
Sutton SM1 **199** G4
Wembley HA0 **86** E2
West Molesey KT8 **179** G4
West Wickham BR4 **190** E6
Crescent Arc, SE10
off Creek Rd **134** C6
Crescent Ct, Surb. KT6 **181** G5
Crescent Dr, Orp. BR5 **193** E6
Crescent Gdns, SW19 **166** D3
Ruislip HA4 **66** B6
Crescent Gro, SW4 **150** C4
Mitcham CR4 **185** H4
Crescent Ho, SE13
off Ravensbourne Pl **154** B2
Crescent La, SW4 **150** D5
Crescent Ms, N22 **74** E1
Crescent Pl, SW3 **31** G1
Crescent Ri, N22 **74** D1
Barnet EN4 **41** H5
Crescent Rd, E4 **47** E7
E6 **115** J1
E10 **96** B2
E13 **115** G1
E18 **79** J2
N3 **72** C1
N8 **74** D7
N9 **60** D1
N11 **57** J4
N15
off Carlingford Rd **75** H3
N22 **74** D1
SE18 **136** E5
SW20 **184** A1
Barnet EN4 **41** H5
Beckenham BR3 **190** B2
Bromley BR1 **173** G7
Dagenham RM10 **101** H4
Enfield EN2 **43** H3
Kingston upon Thames KT2 **164** A7
Sidcup DA15 **175** J3
Crescent Row, EC1 **11** J6
Crescent Stables, SW15 **148** B5
Crescent St, N1 **93** F7
Crescent Vw, Loug. IG10 **48** A6
Crescent Way, N12 **57** H6
SE4 **154** A3
SW16 **169** F7
Orpington BR6 **207** H5
Crescent Wd Rd, SE26 **170** D3
Cresford Rd, SW6 **148** E1
Crespigny Rd, NW4 **71** H6
Cressage Cl, Sthl. UB1 **103** G4
Cresset Rd, E9 **95** F6
Cresset St, SW4 **150** D3
Cressfield Cl, NW5 **92** A5
Cressida Rd, N19 **92** C1
Cressingham Gro, Sutt. SM1 **199** F4
Cressingham Rd, SE13 **154** C3
Edgware HA8 **54** D6
Cressington Cl, N16
off Wordsworth Rd **94** B5
Cress Ms, Brom. BR1 **172** D5
Cresswell Gdns, SW5 **30** C3
Cresswell Pk, SE3 **155** F3
Cresswell Pl, SW10 **30** C3
Cresswell Rd, SE25 **188** D4
Feltham TW13 **160** E4
Twickenham TW1 **145** G6
Cresswell Way, N21 **43** G7
Cressy Ct, E1
off Cressy Pl **113** F5
W6 **127** H3
Cressy Ho, E1
off Hannibal Rd **113** F5
Cressy Pl, E1 **113** F5
Cressy Rd, NW3 **91** J5
Crest, The, N13 **59** G4
NW4 **71** J5
Surbiton KT5 **182** A5
Crestbrook Av, N13 **59** H3
Crestbrook Pl, N13 **59** H3
Crestfield St, WC1 **10** B3
Crest Gdns, Ruis. HA4 **84** C3
Creston Way, Wor.Pk. KT4 **198** A1
Crest Rd, NW2 **89** F2
Bromley BR2 **191** F7
South Croydon CR2 **202** E7
Crest Vw, Pnr. HA5 **66** D4
Crest Vw Dr, Orp. BR5 **193** E5
Crestway, SW15 **147** H6
Crestwood Way, Houns. TW4 **143** F5
Creswell Dr, Beck. BR3 **190** B5
Creswick Rd, W3 **106** B7
Creswick Wk, E3
off Addington Rd **114** A3
NW11 **72** C4
Creton St, SE18 **136** D3
Creukhorne Rd, NW10 **88** E7
Crewdson Rd, SW9 **131** G7
Crewe Pl, NW10 **107** F3
Crews St, E14 **134** A4
Crewys Rd, NW2 **90** C2
SE15 **153** E2
Crichton Av, Wall. SM6 **200** D5
Crichton Rd, Cars. SM5 **199** J6
Crichton St, SW8
off Westbury St **150** C2
Cricketers Arms Rd, Enf. EN2 **43** J2
Cricketers Cl, N14 **42** C7
Chessington KT9 **195** G4
Cricketers Ct, SE11 **35** G2
Cricketers Ms, SW18
off East Hill **149** E5
Cricketers Ter, Cars. SM5
off Wrythe La **199** H3
Cricketers Wk, SE26
off Doctors Cl **171** F5
Cricketfield Rd, E5 **94** E4
Cricket Grn, Mitch. CR4 **185** J3
Cricket Grd Rd, Chis. BR7 **192** E1
Cricket La, Beck. BR3 **171** H6
Cricklade Av, SW2 **169** E2
CRICKLEWOOD, NW2 **90** A3
Cricklewood Bdy, NW2 **89** J3
Cricklewood La, NW2 **90** A4
Cridland St, E15
off Church St **115** F1
Crieff Ct, Tedd. TW11 **163** F7
Crieff Rd, SW18 **149** F6
Criffel Av, SW2 **168** D2
Crimscott St, SE1 **29** E6
Crimsworth Rd, SW8 **150** D1
Crinan St, N1 **10** B1
Cringle St, SW8 **33** F7
Cripplegate St, EC2 **19** J1
Cripps Grn, Hayes UB4
off Stratford Rd **102** B4
Crispe Ho, Bark. IG11
off Dovehouse Mead **117** G2
Crispen Rd, Felt. TW13 **160** E4
Crispian Cl, NW10 **89** E4
Crispin Cl, Croy. CR0
off Harrington Cl **200** E2
Crispin Cres, Croy. CR0 **200** D3
Crispin Pl, E1 **21** F1
Crispin Rd, Edg. HA8 **54** C6
Crispin St, E1 **21** F2
Crisp Rd, W6 **127** J5
Cristowe Rd, SW6 **148** C2
Criterion Ms, N19 **92** D2
Crittall's Cor, Sid. DA14 **176** B7
Crockerton Rd, SW17 **167** J2
Crockham Way, SE9 **174** D4
Crocus Cl, Croy. CR0
off Cornflower La **203** G1
Crocus Fld, Barn. EN5 **40** C6
Croft, The, E4 **62** E2
NW10 **107** F2
W5 **105** H5
Barnet EN5 **40** A4
Hounslow TW5 **123** E6
Loughton IG10 **48** D2
Pinner HA5 **67** F7
Ruislip HA4 **84** C4
Wembley HA0 **87** F5
Croft Av, W.Wick. BR4 **204** C1
Croft Cl, NW7 **54** E3
Belvedere DA17 **139** F5
Chislehurst BR7 **174** C4
Hayes (Harling.) UB3 **121** F7
Croft Ct, Borwd. WD6 **38** D3
Croftdown Rd, NW5 **92** A3
Croft End Cl, Chess. KT9
off Ashcroft Rd **195** J3
Crofters Cl, Islw. TW7
off Ploughmans End **144** A5
Crofters Ct, SE8
off Croft St **133** H4
Crofters Way, NW1 **110** D1
Croft Gdns, W7 **124** D2
Croft Lo Cl, Wdf.Grn. IG8 **63** H6
Croft Ms, N12 **57** F3
Crofton Av, W4 **126** D7
Bexley DA5 **158** D7
Orpington BR6 **207** F2
Croftongate Way, SE4 **153** H5
Crofton Gro, E4 **62** D4
Crofton La, Orp. BR5, BR6 **193** G7
Crofton Pk Rd, SE4 **153** J6
Crofton Rd, E13 **115** H4
SE5 **152** B1
Orpington BR6 **206** D3
Crofton Ter, E5
off Studley Cl **95** H5
Richmond TW9 **145** J4
Crofton Way, Barn. EN5
off Wycherley Cres **40** E6
Enfield EN2 **43** G2
Croft Rd, SW16 **187** G1
SW19 **167** F7
Bromley BR1 **173** G6
Enfield EN3 **45** H1
Sutton SM1 **199** H5
Croftside, SE25
off Sunny Bk **188** D3
Crofts La, N22 **59** G7
Crofts Rd, Har. HA1 **68** D6
Crofts St, E1 **21** H6
Croft St, SE8 **133** H4
Croftway, NW3 **90** D4
Richmond TW10 **163** E3
Croft Way, Sid. DA15 **175** H3
Crogsland Rd, NW1 **92** A7
Croham Cl, S.Croy. CR2 **202** B7
Croham Manor Rd, S.Croy. CR2 **202** B5
Croham Mt, S.Croy. CR2 **202** B7
Croham Pk Av, S.Croy. CR2 **202** C5
Croham Rd, S.Croy. CR2 **202** A5
Croham Valley Rd, S.Croy. CR2 **202** C6
Croindene Rd, SW16 **187** E1
Cromartie Rd, N19 **74** D7
Cromarty Rd, Edg. HA8 **54** B2
Crombie Cl, Ilf. IG4 **80** C5
Crombie Rd, Sid. DA15 **175** G1
Crome Rd, NW10 **88** E6
Cromer Pl, Orp. BR6
off Andover Rd **207** G1
Cromer Rd, E10
off James La **78** D6
N17 **76** D2
SE25 **188** E3
SW17 **168** A6
Barnet (New Barn.) EN5 **41** F4
Hounslow (Lon.Hthrw Air.) TW6 **140** D3
Romford RM7 **83** J6
Cromer Rd, Romford (Chad.Hth) RM6 **83** E6
Woodford Green IG8 **63** G4
Cromer St, WC1 **10** B4
Cromer Ter, E8
off Ferncliff Rd **94** D5
Cromer Vil Rd, SW18 **148** C6
Cromford Cl, Orp. BR6 **207** H3
Cromford Path, E5
off Overbury St **95** G4
Cromford Rd, SW18 **148** D5
Cromford Way, N.Mal. KT3 **182** D1
Cromlix Cl, Chis. BR7 **192** E2
Crompton St, W2 **6** E6
Cromwell Av, N6 **92** B1
W6 **127** H5
Bromley BR2 **191** H4
New Malden KT3 **183** F5
Cromwell Cl, N2 **73** G4
W3 *off High St* **126** C1
Bromley BR2 **191** H4
Cromwell Cres, SW5 **128** D4
Cromwell Gdns, SW7 **23** F6
Cromwell Gro, W6 **127** J3
Cromwell Highwalk, EC2
off Silk St **20** A1
Cromwell Ind Est, E10 **95** H1
Cromwell Ms, SW7 **31** F1
Cromwell Pl, N6 **92** B1
SW7 **31** F1
SW14 **146** C3
W3 *off Grove Pl* **126** C1
Cromwell Rd, E7 **97** J7
E17 **78** C5
N3 **73** F2
N10 **58** A7
SW5 **128** E4
SW7 **30** E1
SW9 **151** H1
SW19 **166** D5
Beckenham BR3 **189** H2
Croydon CR0 **188** A7
Feltham TW13 **160** B1
Hounslow TW3 **143** G4
Kingston upon Thames KT2 **181** H1
Teddington TW11 **162** D6
Wembley HA0 **105** H2
Worcester Park KT4 **196** D3
Cromwell St, Houns. TW3 **143** G4
Cromwell Twr, EC2 **20** A1
Crondace Rd, SW6 **148** D1
Crondall Ct, N1 **12** D2
Crondall Ho, SW15
off Fontley Way **165** G1
Crondall St, N1 **12** C2
Cronin St, SE15 **132** C7
Crooked Billet, E17 **62** B7
SW19 **165** J6
Crooked Billet Yd, E2 **12** E3
Crooked Usage, N3 **72** B3
Crooke Rd, SE8 **133** H5
Crookham Rd, SW6 **148** C1
Crook Log, Bexh. DA6 **158** D3
Crookston Rd, SE9 **156** D3
Croombs Rd, E16 **115** J5
Crooms Hill, SE10 **134** D7
Crooms Hill Gro, SE10 **134** C7
Cropley Ct, N1 **12** B1
Cropley St, N1 **12** B1
Croppath Rd, Dag. RM10 **101** G4
Cropthorne Ct, W9 **6** D4
Crosby Cl, Felt. TW13 **160** E4
Crosby Ct, SE1 **28** B3
Crosby Rd, E7 **97** G6
Dagenham RM10 **119** H2
Crosby Row, SE1 **28** B4
Crosby Sq, EC3 **20** D4
Crosby Wk, E8
off Beechwood Rd **94** C6
SW2 **151** G7
Crosier Cl, SE3 **156** B1
Crosland Pl, SW11
off Taybridge Rd **150** A3
Cross Av, SE10 **134** D6
Crossbow Rd, Chig. IG7 **65** J5
Crossbrook Rd, SE3 **156** B2
Cross Cl, SE15
off Gordon Rd **152** E2
Cross Deep, Twick. TW1 **162** C2
Cross Deep Gdns, Twick. TW1 **162** C2
Crossfield Rd, N17 **75** J3
NW3 **91** G7
Crossfields, Loug. IG10 **48** E5
Crossfield St, SE8 **134** A7
Crossford St, SW9 **151** F2
Crossgate, Edg. HA8 **54** A3
Greenford UB6 **87** E6

Cross Keys Cl, N9
off Balham Rd 60 D2
W1 16 C2
Cross Keys Sq, EC1 19 J2
Cross Lances Rd, Houns.
TW3 143 H4
Crossland Rd, Th.Hth.
CR7 187 H6
Crosslands Av, W5 125 J1
Southall UB2 123 F5
Crosslands Rd, Epsom
KT19 196 D6
Cross La, EC3 20 D6
N8 75 F4
Bexley DA5 159 F7
Crosslet St, SE17 36 C1
Crosslet Vale, SE10 154 B1
Crossley St, N7 93 G6
Crossmead, SE9 174 C1
Crossmead Av, Grnf.
UB6 103 G3
Crossmount Ho, SE5 35 J7
Crossness La, SE28 118 D7
★ **Crossness Pumping Sta**,
SE2 119 E6
Crossness Rd, Bark.
IG11 117 J3
Cross Rd, E4 62 D1
N11 58 B5
N22 59 G7
SE5 152 B2
SW19 166 D7
Bromley BR2 206 B2
Croydon CR0 202 A1
Enfield EN1 44 B4
Feltham TW13 160 E4
Harrow HA1 68 A4
Harrow (S.Har.) HA2 85 H3
Harrow (Wealds.) HA3 68 D2
Kingston upon Thames
KT2 163 J7
Romford RM7 83 G3
Romford (Chad.Hth)
RM6 82 C7
Sidcup DA14
off Sidcup Hill 176 B4
Sutton SM2 199 G5
Woodford Green IG8 64 C6
Cross Rds, Loug.
(High Beach) IG10 47 H2
Cross St, N1 111 H1
SW13 147 E2
Hampton (Hmptn H.)
TW12 161 J5
Crossthwaite Av, SE5 152 A4
Crosstrees Ho, E14
off Cassilis Rd 134 A3
Crosswall, EC3 21 F5
Crossway, N12 57 G6
N16 94 B5
NW9 71 F4
SE28 118 C6
SW20 183 J4
W13 104 D4
Dagenham RM8 100 C3
Enfield EN1 44 B7
Hayes UB3 122 A1
Orpington BR5 193 G4
Pinner HA5 66 B2
Ruislip HA4 84 C4
Woodford Green IG8 63 J4
Crossway, The, N22 59 H7
SE9 174 A2
Cross Way, The, Har. HA3 68 B2
Crossways, N21 43 J6
South Croydon CR2 203 H7
Crossways, The, Houns.
TW5 123 F7
Wembley HA9 88 A2
Crossways Rd, Beck. BR3 190 A4
Mitcham CR4 186 B3
Croston St, E8 112 D1
Crothall Cl, N13 59 F3
Crouch Av, Bark. IG11 118 B2
Crouch Cl, Beck. BR3 172 A6
Crouch Cft, SE9 174 D3
CROUCH END, N8 74 C6
Crouch End Hill, N8 74 D7
Crouch Hall Rd, N8 74 D6
Crouch Hill, N4 74 E6
N8 74 E6
Crouchman's Cl, SE26 170 C3
Crouch Rd, NW10 88 D7
Crowborough Path, Wat.
WD19 50 D4
Crowborough Rd, SW17 168 A6
Crowden Way, SE28 118 C7
Crowder Cl, N12 73 F1
Crowder St, E1 112 E7
Crowfoot Cl, E9
off Lee
Conservancy Rd 95 J5
SE28 137 H1

Crowhurst Cl, SW9 151 G2
Crowland Av, Hayes UB3 121 H4
Crowland Gdns, N14 42 E7
Crowland Rd, N15 76 C5
Thornton Heath CR7 188 A4
Crowlands Av, Rom. RM7 83 H6
Crowland Ter, N1 94 A7
Crowland Wk, Mord.
SM4 185 E6
Crow La, Rom. RM7 83 F7
Crowley Cres, Croy.
CR0 201 G5
Crowline Wk, N1
off Clephane Rd 93 J6
Crowmarsh Gdns, SE23
off Tyson Rd 153 F7
Crown Arc, Kings.T. KT1
off Union St 181 G2
Crownbourne Ct, Sutt. SM1
off St. Nicholas Way 198 E4
Crown Cl, E3 114 A1
N22 *off Winkfield Rd* 75 G1
NW6 90 E6
NW7 55 F2
Hayes UB3 121 J2
Walton-on-Thames
KT12 178 C7
Crown Ct, EC2 20 A4
SE12 155 H6
WC2 18 B4
Crown Dale, SE19 169 H6
Crowndale Rd, NW1 9 F1
Crownfield Av, Ilf. IG2 81 H5
Crownfield Rd, E15 96 D5
Crowngate Ho, E3
off Hereford Rd 113 J2
Crown Hill, Croy. CR0
off Church St 201 J2
Crownhill Rd, NW10 107 F1
Woodford Green IG8 64 B7
Crown Ho, Bark. IG11
off Linton Rd 99 F7
Crown La, N14 58 C1
SW16 169 G5
Bromley BR2 192 A5
Chislehurst BR7 193 F1
Morden SM4 184 E3
Crown La Gdns, SW16 169 G5
Crown La Spur, Brom.
BR2 192 A6
Crownmead Way, Rom.
RM7 83 H4
Crown Ms, E13
off Waghorn Rd 115 J1
W6 127 G4
Crown Mill, Mitch. CR4 185 H5
Crown Office Row, EC4 19 E5
Crown Pas, SW1 25 G2
Kingston upon Thames
KT1 *off Church St* 181 G2
Crown Pl, EC2 20 D1
NW5
off Kentish Town Rd 92 B6
SE16 *off Varcoe Rd* 133 E5
Crown Pt Par, SE19
off Beulah Hill 169 H6
Crown Reach, SW1 33 J4
Crown Rd, N10 58 A7
Borehamwood WD6 38 A1
Enfield EN1 44 E4
Ilford IG6 81 G4
Morden SM4 184 E4
New Malden KT3 182 C1
Ruislip HA4 84 D5
Sutton SM1 198 E4
Twickenham TW1 145 E6
Crownstone Rd, SW2 151 G5
Crown St, SE5 36 A7
W3 126 B1
Dagenham RM10 101 J6
Harrow HA2 86 A1
Crown Ter, Rich. TW9 145 J4
Crowntree Cl, Islw. TW7 124 C6
Crown Wk, Wem. HA9 87 J3
Crown Way, West Dr.
UB7 120 C1
Crown Wds La, SE9 157 E2
SE18 157 E2
Crown Wds Way, SE9 157 G5
Crown Wks, E2
off Temple St 112 E2
Crown Yd, Houns. TW3
off High St 143 J3
Crowshott Av, Stan. HA7 69 F1
Crows Rd, E15 114 D3
Barking IG11 99 E6
Crowther Av, Brent. TW8 125 H4
Crowther Cl, SW6
off Coomer Pl 128 C6
Crowther Rd, SE25 188 D4
Crowthorne Cl, SW18 166 C1
Crowthorne Rd, W10 108 A6
Croxden Cl, Edg. HA8 69 J3

Croxden Wk, Mord. SM4 185 F6
Croxford Gdns, N22 59 H7
Croxley Rd, W9 108 C3
Croxted Cl, SE21 151 J7
Croxted Ms, SE24
off Croxted Rd 151 J6
Croxted Rd, SE21 151 J7
SE24 151 J7
Croxteth Ho, SW8
off Wandsworth Rd 150 D2
Croyde Av, Grnf. UB6 103 J3
Hayes UB3 121 H4
Croyde Cl, Sid. DA15 157 G7
CROYDON, CR0 202 A1
Croydon Flyover, Croy.
CR0 201 H4
Croydon Gro, Croy. CR0 201 H1
Croydon Rd, E13 115 F4
SE20 188 E2
Beckenham BR3 189 H4
Bromley BR2 205 F3
Croydon (Bedd.) CR0 201 E4
Croydon (Mitch.Com.)
CR0 186 A4
Hounslow
(Lon.Hthrw Air.) TW6 140 E2
Keston BR2 205 J3
Mitcham CR4 186 A4
Wallington SM6 200 B4
West Wickham BR4 204 E3
Croydon Rd Ind Est, Beck.
BR3 189 G4
Croydon Valley Trade Pk,
Croy. CR0
off Beddington
Fm Rd 186 E7
Croyland Rd, N9 60 D1
Croylands Dr, Surb. KT6 181 H7
Croysdale Av, Sun. TW16 178 A3
Crozier Ho, SE3
off Ebdon Way 155 H3
Crozier Ter, E9 95 G5
Crucible Cl, Rom. RM6 82 B6
Crucifix La, SE1 28 D3
Cruden Ho, SE17 35 G6
Cruden St, N1 111 H1
Cruikshank Rd, E15 97 E4
Cruikshank St, WC1 10 E3
Crummock Gdns, NW9 70 E5
Crumpsall St, SE2 138 C4
Crundale Av, NW9 70 A5
Crunden Rd, S.Croy.
CR2 202 A7
Crusader Gdns, Croy.
CR0 *off Cotelands* 202 B3
Crusader Industrial Est, N4
off Hermitage Rd 75 J6
Crusoe Ms, N16 94 A2
Crusoe Rd, Mitch. CR4 167 J7
Crutched Friars, EC3 21 E5
Crutchley Rd, SE6 173 E2
Crystal Ct, SE19
off College Rd 170 C5
Crystal Ho, SE18
off Spinel Cl 137 J5
★ **Crystal Palace FC**,
SE25 188 B4
★ **Crystal Palace Nat**
Sports Cen, SE19 170 D6
Crystal Palace Par, SE19 170 C6
★ **Crystal Palace Pk**,
SE19 170 C5
Crystal Palace Pk Rd,
SE26 170 D5
Crystal Palace Rd, SE22 152 D4
Crystal Palace Sta Rd,
SE19 170 D6
Crystal Ter, SE19 170 A6
Crystal Vw Ct, Brom.
BR1 172 D4
Crystal Way, Dag. RM8 100 C1
Harrow HA1 68 C5
Crystal Wf, N1 11 H2
Cuba Dr, Enf. EN3 45 F2
Cuba St, E14 134 A2
Cubitt Bldg, SW1 32 D4
Cubitt Sq, Sthl. UB2
off Windmill Av 123 J1
Cubitt Steps, E14
off Cabot Sq 134 A1
Cubitt St, WC1 10 D4
Cubitts Yd, WC2 18 B5
Cubitt Ter, SW4 150 C3
CUBITT TOWN, E14 134 C3
Cuckoo Av, W7 104 B4
Cuckoo Dene, W7 104 A5
Cuckoo Hall La, N9 45 F7
Cuckoo Hill, Pnr. HA5 66 C3
Cuckoo Hill Dr, Pnr. HA5 66 C3
Cuckoo Hill Rd, Pnr. HA5 66 C4
Cuckoo La, W7 104 B7
Cudas Cl, Epsom KT19 197 F4
Cuddington, SE17 35 J1

Cuddington Av, Wor.Pk.
KT4 197 F3
Cudham St, SE6 154 C7
Cudworth St, E1 113 E4
Cuff Cres, SE9 156 A6
Cuff Pt, E2 13 F3
Culford Gdns, SW3 32 A2
Culford Gro, N1 94 B6
Culford Ms, N1
off Culford Rd 94 B6
Culford Rd, N1 94 B7
Culgaith Gdns, Enf. EN2 42 E4
Cullen Way, NW10 106 C4
Culling Rd, SE16
off Lower Rd 133 F3
Cullington Cl, Har. HA3 68 D4
Cullingworth Rd, NW10 89 G5
Culloden Cl, SE16 37 J4
Culloden Rd, Enf. EN2 43 H2
Culloden St, E14 114 C6
Cullum St, EC3 20 D5
Culmington Rd, W13 125 F2
Culmore Rd, SE15 133 E7
Culmstock Rd, SW11 150 A5
Culpeper Cl, Ilf. IG6 65 E6
Culpepper Cl, N18 61 E5
Culross Cl, N15 75 J4
Culross St, W1 16 B6
Culsac Rd, Surb. KT6 195 H2
Culverden Rd, SW12 168 C2
Watford WD19 50 B3
Culver Gro, Stan. HA7 69 F2
Culverhouse Gdns,
SW16 169 F3
Culverlands Cl, Stan.
HA7 52 E4
Culverley Rd, SE6 172 B1
Culvers Av, Cars. SM5 199 J2
Culvers Retreat, Cars.
SM5 199 J1
Culverstone Cl, Brom.
BR2 191 F6
Culvers Way, Cars. SM5 199 J2
Culvert Pl, SW11 150 A2
Culvert Rd, N15 76 B5
SW11 149 J2
Culworth St, NW8 7 G2
Culzean Cl, SE27
off Chatsworth Way 169 H3
Cumberland Av, NW10 106 B3
Welling DA16 157 H3
Cumberland Business Pk,
NW10 106 A3
Cumberland Cl, E8 94 C6
SW20
off Lansdowne Rd 166 A7
Ilford IG6 81 F1
Twickenham TW1
off Westmorland Cl 145 E6
Cumberland Ct, Well. DA16
off Bellegrove Rd 157 H2
Cumberland Cres, W14 128 B4
Cumberland Dr, Bexh.
DA7 138 E7
Chessington KT9 195 J3
Esher KT10 194 D2
Cumberland Gdns, NW4 72 A2
WC1 10 D3
Cumberland Gate, W1 15 J5
Cumberland Ho, SE28 137 F2
Cumberland Mkt, NW1 9 E3
Cumberland Mkt Est, NW1 8 E3
Cumberland Ms, SE11 35 F4
Cumberland Mills Sq, E14
off Saunders Ness Rd 134 D5
Cumberland Pk, NW10 107 G3
W3 106 C7
Cumberland Pl, NW1 8 D3
SE6 173 F1
Sunbury-on-Thames
TW16 178 A4
Cumberland Rd, E12 98 A4
E13 115 H5
E17 77 H2
N9 61 F1
N22 75 F2
SE25 189 E6
SW13 147 F1
W3 106 C7
W7 124 C2
Bromley BR2 190 E4
Harrow HA1 67 H5
Richmond TW9 126 A7
Stanmore HA7 69 J3
Cumberland St, SW1 32 E3
Cumberland Ter, NW1 8 D2
Cumberland Ter Ms, NW1 8 D2
Cumberland Vil, W3
off Cumberland Rd 106 C7
Cumberlow Av, SE25 188 D3
Cumberton Rd, N17 76 A1
Cumbrae Gdns, Surb.
(Long Dit.) KT6 195 G2

Cumbrian Gdns, NW2 ....**90** A2
★ **Cuming Mus**, SE17 ...**35** J2
Cumming St, N1 ....**10** C2
Cumnor Gdns, Epsom
KT17 ....**197** G6
Cumnor Rd, Sutt. SM2 ...**199** F6
Cunard Cres, N21 ....**44** A6
Cunard Pl, EC3 ....**20** E4
Cunard Rd, NW10 ....**106** D3
Cunard Wk, SE16 ....**133** H4
Cundy Rd, E16 ....**115** J6
Cundy St, SW1 ....**32** C2
Cundy St Est, SW1 ....**32** C2
Cunliffe Rd, Epsom KT19 .**197** F4
Cunliffe St, SW16 ....**168** C6
Cunningham Cl, Rom.
RM6 ....**82** C5
West Wickham BR4 ....**204** B2
Cunningham Ct, E10
off Oliver Rd **96** B3
Cunningham Pk, Har. HA1 .**67** J5
Cunningham Pl, NW8 ......**7** E5
Cunningham Rd, N15 .....**76** D4
Cunnington St, W4 ......**126** C3
Cupar Rd, SW11 ....**150** A1
Cupola Cl, Brom. BR1 ...**173** H5
Cureton St, SW1 ....**33** J2
Curie Gdns, NW9 ....**71** E2
Curlew Cl, SE28 ....**118** D7
Curlew Ct, Surb. KT6 ....**195** J3
Curlew Ho, Enf. EN3
off Allington Ct **45** G5
Curlew St, SE1 ....**29** F3
Curlew Ter, Ilf. IG5
off Tiptree Cres **80** D3
Curlew Way, Hayes UB4 ..**102** D5
Curness St, SE13 ....**154** C4
Curnick's La, SE27
off Chapel Rd **169** J4
Curnock Est, NW1
off Plender St **110** C1
Curran Av, Sid. DA15 ....**157** J5
Wallington SM6 ......**200** A3
Currey Rd, Grnf. UB6 .....**86** A6
Curricle St, W3 ....**126** E1
Currie Hill Cl, SW19 .....**166** C4
Curry Ri, NW7 ....**56** A6
Cursitor St, EC4 ....**18** E3
Curtain Pl, EC2 ....**12** E5
Curtain Rd, EC2 ....**12** D6
Curthwaite Gdns, Enf.
EN2 ....**42** D4
Curtis Dr, W3 ....**106** D6
Curtis Fld Rd, SW16 .....**169** F4
Curtis Ho, N11 ....**58** B5
Curtis La, Wem. HA0
off Montrose Cres **87** H6
Curtis Rd, Epsom KT19 ..**196** C4
Hounslow TW4 ....**143** F7
Curtis St, SE1 ....**37** F1
Curtis Way, SE1 ....**37** F1
SE28 *off Tawney Rd* ...**118** B7
Curve, The, W12 ....**107** G7
Curwen Av, E7
off Woodford Rd **97** H4
Curwen Rd, W12 ....**127** G2
Curzon Av, Enf. EN3 ......**45** G5
Stanmore HA7 ....**68** D1
Curzon Cl, Orp. BR6 .....**207** G4
Curzon Cres, NW10 ......**89** F7
Barking IG11 ....**117** J2
Curzon Gate, W1 ....**24** B2
Curzon Pl, Pnr. HA5 ......**66** C5
Curzon Rd, N10 ....**74** B2
W5 ....**105** E4
Thornton Heath CR7 ..**187** G6
Curzon Sq, W1 ....**24** C2
Curzon St, W1 ....**24** C2
Cusack Cl, Twick. TW1
off Waldegrave Rd ...**162** C4
CUSTOM HOUSE, E16 ...**116** A6
Custom Ho Reach, SE16 .**133** J2
Custom Ho Wk, EC3 ......**20** D6
Cut, The, SE1 ....**27** F3
Cutcombe Rd, SE5 ....**151** J2
Cuthberga Cl, Bark. IG11
off George St **99** F7
Cuthbert Gdns, SE25 ....**188** B3
Cuthbert Rd, E17 ....**78** C3
N18 *off Fairfield Rd* **60** D5
Croydon CR0 ....**201** H2
Cuthbert St, W2 ....**15** E1
Cuthill Wk, SE5 ....**152** A1
Cutlers Gdns, E1 ....**21** E3
Cutlers Gdns Arc, EC2
off Devonshire Sq **21** E3
Cutlers Sq, E14
off Britannia Rd **134** A4
Cutlers Ter, N1
off Balls Pond Rd **94** B6
Cutler St, E1 ....**21** E3
Cutthroat All, Rich. TW10
off Ham St **163** F2
★ **Cutty Sark**, SE10 ....**134** C6
Cutty Sark Gdns, SE10
off King William Wk ..**134** C6
Cuxton Cl, Bexh. DA6 ....**158** E5
Cyclamen Cl, Hmptn. TW12
off Gresham Rd **161** G6
Cyclamen Way, Epsom
KT19 ....**196** B5
Cyclops Ms, E14 ....**134** A4
Cygnet Av, Felt. TW14 ....**142** C7
Cygnet Cl, NW10 ....**88** D5
Borehamwood WD6 ....**38** C1
Cygnets, The, Felt. TW13 .**160** E4
Cygnet St, E1 ....**13** G5
Cygnet Way, Hayes UB4 ..**102** D5
Cygnus Business Cen,
NW10 ....**89** F6
Cymbeline Ct, Har. HA1 ...**68** C6
Cynthia St, N1 ....**10** D2
Cyntra Pl, E8 ....**95** E7
Cypress Av, Twick. TW2 ...**143** J7
Cypress Cl, E5 ....**94** D2
Cypress Gdns, SE4 ......**153** H5
Cypress Gro, Ilf. IG6 ......**65** H6
Cypress Pl, W1 ....**9** G6
Cypress Rd, SE25 ....**188** B2
Harrow HA3 ....**68** A2
Cypress Tree Cl, Sid.
DA15 ....**175** J1
Cyprus Av, N3 ....**72** B2
Cyprus Cl, N4
off Atterbury Rd **75** H6
Cyprus Gdns, N3 ....**72** B2
Cyprus Pl, E2 ....**113** F2
E6 ....**116** D7
Cyprus Rd, N3 ....**72** C2
N9 ....**60** C2
Cyprus Rbt, E16 ....**116** D7
Cyprus St, E2 ....**113** F2
Cyrena Rd, SE22 ....**152** C6
Cyril Mans, SW11 ....**149** J1
Cyril Rd, Bexh. DA7 .....**159** E2
Cyrus St, EC1 ....**11** H5
Czar St, SE8 ....**134** A6

D

Dabbs Hill La, Nthlt. UB5 ..**85** H5
Dabin Cres, SE10 ....**154** C1
Dacca St, SE8 ....**133** J6
Dace Rd, E3 ....**96** A7
Dacre Av, Ilf. IG5 ....**80** D2
Dacre Cl, Chig. IG7 ....**65** F4
Greenford UB6 ....**103** H2
Dacre Gdns, SE13 ....**154** E4
Borehamwood WD6 ....**38** D5
Chigwell IG7 ....**65** F4
Dacre Pk, SE13 ....**155** E3
Dacre Pl, SE13 ....**154** E3
Dacre Rd, E11 ....**97** F1
E13 ....**115** H1
Croydon CR0 ....**187** E7
Dacres Est, SE23 ....**171** G3
Dacres Rd, SE23 ....**171** G3
Dacre St, SW1 ....**25** H5
Dade Way, Sthl. UB2 .....**123** F5
Daerwood Cl, Brom. BR2 .**206** C1
Daffodil Cl, Croy. CR0 ....**203** G1
Daffodil Gdns, Ilf. IG1 .....**98** E5
Daffodil Pl, Hmptn. TW12
off Gresham Rd **161** G6
Daffodil St, W12 ....**107** F7
Dafforne Rd, SW17 ......**168** A3
DAGENHAM,
RM8-RM10 ....**101** G6
Dagenham Av, Dag.
RM9 ....**118** E1
Dagenham Leisure Pk, Dag.
RM9 *off Cook Rd* **118** E1
Dagenham Rd, E10 ....**95** J1
Dagenham RM10 .....**101** J4
Dagmar Av, Wem. HA9 ....**87** J4
Dagmar Gdns, NW10 ....**108** A2
Dagmar Ms, Sthl. UB2
off Dagmar Rd **123** E3
Dagmar Pas, N1
off Cross St **111** H1
Dagmar Rd, N4 ....**75** G7
N15 *off Cornwall Rd* **76** A4
N22 ....**74** D1
SE5 ....**152** B1
SE25 ....**188** B5
Dagenham RM10 .....**101** J7
Kingston upon Thames
KT2 ....**181** J1
Southall UB2 ....**122** E3
Dagmar Ter, N1 ....**111** H1
Dagnall Pk, SE25 ....**188** B6
Dagnall Rd, SE25 ....**188** B5
Dagnall St, SW11 ....**149** J2
Dagnan Rd, SW12 ....**150** B7
Dagonet Gdns, Brom.
BR1 ....**173** G3
Dagonet Rd, Brom. BR1 ..**173** G3
Dahlia Gdns, Ilf. IG1 ......**99** E6
Mitcham CR4 ....**186** D4
Dahlia Rd, SE2 ....**138** B4
Dahomey Rd, SW16 ......**168** C6
Daimler Way, Wall. SM6 ..**200** E7
Daines Cl, E12 ....**98** C3
Dainford Cl, Brom. BR1 ..**172** D5
Dainton Cl, Brom. BR1 ...**191** H1
Daintry Cl, Har. HA3 ......**68** D4
Daintry Way, E9
off Osborne Rd **95** J6
Dairsie Rd, SE9 ....**156** D3
Dairy Cl, NW10 ....**107** G1
Bromley BR1
off Plaistow La **173** H7
Thornton Heath CR7 ..**187** J2
Dairy Fm Pl, SE15
off Queens Rd **153** F1
Dairy La, SE18 ....**136** C4
Dairyman Cl, NW2
off Claremont Rd **90** B3
Dairy Ms, N2
off East End Rd **73** H4
SW9 ....**151** E3
Dairy Wk, SW19 ....**166** B4
Daisy Cl, Croy. CR0 ......**203** G1
Daisy Dobbins Wk, N19
off Hillrise Rd **74** E7
Daisy La, SW6 ....**148** D3
Daisy Rd, E16
off Cranberry La **114** E4
E18 ....**79** H2
Dakin Pl, E1
off White Horse Rd ...**113** H5
Dakota Bldg, SE13
off Deals Gateway ...**154** A1
Dakota Cl, Wall. SM6 ....**201** F7
Dakota Gdns, E6 ....**116** B4
Northolt UB5
off Argus Way **102** E3
Dalberg Rd, SW2 ....**151** G4
Dalberg Way, SE2
off Lanridge Rd **138** D3
Dalby Rd, SW18 ....**149** F4
Dalbys Cres, N17 ....**60** B6
Dalby St, NW5 ....**92** B6
Dalcross Rd, Houns.
TW4 ....**142** E2
Dale, The, Kes. BR2 ......**206** A4
Dale Av, Edg. HA8 ....**69** J1
Hounslow TW4 ....**143** E3
Dalebury Rd, SW17 .....**167** H2
Dale Cl, SE3 ....**155** G3
Barnet (New Barn.)
EN5 ....**41** E6
Pinner HA5 ....**66** B1
Dale Gdns, Wdf.Grn. IG8 ..**63** H4
Dale Grn Rd, N11 ....**58** B3
Dale Gro, N12 ....**57** F5
Daleham Gdns, NW3 .....**91** G5
Daleham Ms, NW3 ....**91** G6
Dalehead, NW1 ....**9** F2
Dalemain Ms, E16
off Hanover Av **135** G1
Dale Pk Av, Cars. SM5 ...**199** J2
Dale Pk Rd, SE19 ....**187** J1
Dale Rd, NW5
off Grafton Rd **92** A5
SE17 ....**35** H6
Greenford UB6 ....**103** H5
Sutton SM1 ....**198** C4
Dale Row, W11
off St. Marks Rd **108** B6
Daleside Gdns, Chig. IG7 ..**65** F3
Daleside Rd, SW16 ......**168** B5
Epsom KT19 ....**196** D6
Dales Path, Borwd. WD6
off Farriers Way **38** D5
Dales Rd, Borwd. WD6 ....**38** D5
Dale St, W4 ....**126** E5
Dale Vw Av, E4 ....**62** C2
Dale Vw Cres, E4 ....**62** C2
Dale Vw Gdns, E4 ....**62** D3
Daleview Rd, N15 ....**76** B6
Dalewood Gdns, Wor.Pk.
KT4 ....**197** H2
Dale Wd Rd, Orp. BR6 ....**193** H7
Daley St, E9 ....**95** G6
Daley Thompson Way,
SW8 ....**150** B2
Dalgarno Gdns, W10 .....**107** J5
Dalgarno Way, W10 ......**107** J4
Dalgleish St, E14 ....**113** H6
Daling Way, E3 ....**113** H1
Dalkeith Gro, Stan. HA7 ...**53** G5
Dalkeith Rd, SE21 ....**169** J1
Ilford IG1 ....**99** F3
Dallas Rd, NW4 ....**71** G7
SE26 ....**170** E3
W5 ....**105** J5
Sutton SM3 ....**198** B6
Dallas Ter, Hayes UB3 ....**121** J3
Dallinger Rd, SE12 ....**155** F6
Dalling Rd, W6 ....**127** H3
Dallington Sq, EC1
off Dallington St **11** H5
Dallington St, EC1 ....**11** H5
Dallin Rd, SE18 ....**137** E7
Bexleyheath DA6 .....**158** D4
Dalmain Rd, SE23 ....**171** G1
Dalmally Rd, Croy. CR0 ..**188** C7
Dalmeny Av, N7 ....**92** D4
SW16 ....**187** G2
Dalmeny Cl, Wem. HA0 ...**87** F6
Dalmeny Cres, Houns.
TW3 ....**144** A4
Dalmeny Rd, N7 ....**92** D3
Barnet (New Barn.)
EN5 ....**41** F6
Carshalton SM5 ......**200** A7
Erith DA8 ....**159** H1
Worcester Park KT4 ..**197** H3
Dalmeyer Rd, NW10 ......**89** F6
Dalmore Av, Esher (Clay.)
KT10 ....**194** C6
Dalmore Rd, SE21 ....**169** J2
Dalrymple Cl, N14 ....**42** D7
Dalrymple Rd, SE4 ......**153** H4
DALSTON, E8 ....**94** D7
Dalston Gdns, Stan. HA7 ..**69** H1
Dalston La, E8 ....**94** C6
Dalton Av, Mitch. CR4 ....**185** H2
Dalton Cl, Orp. BR6 .....**207** H3
Dalton Rd, Har. (Har.Wld)
HA3 ....**68** A2
Dalton St, SE27 ....**169** H2
Dalwood St, SE5 ....**152** B1
Daly Dr, Brom. BR1 ......**192** D3
Dalyell Rd, SW9 ....**151** F3
Damascene Wk, SE21
off Lovelace Rd **169** J1
Damask Ct, Sutt. SM1
off Cleeve Way **199** E1
Damask Cres, E16
off Cranberry La **115** E4
Damer Ter, SW10
off Tadema Rd **129** F7
Dames Rd, E7 ....**97** G3
Dame St, N1 ....**11** J1
Damien St, E1 ....**113** E6
Damon Cl, Sid. DA14 ....**176** B3
Damson Dr, Hayes UB3 ..**102** A7
Damsonwood Rd, Sthl.
UB2 ....**123** G3
Danbrook Rd, SW16 .....**187** E1
Danbury Cl, Rom. RM6 ....**82** D3
Danbury Ms, Wall. SM6 ..**200** B4
Danbury Rd, Loug. IG10 ...**48** B7
Danbury St, N1 ....**11** H1
Danbury Way, Wdf.Grn.
IG8 ....**63** J6
Danby St, SE15 ....**152** C3
Dancer Rd, SW6 ....**148** C1
Richmond TW9 ....**146** A3
Dando Cres, SE3 ....**155** H3
Dandridge Cl, SE10 ......**135** F5
Danebury, Croy.
(New Adgtn) CR0 .....**204** B6
Danebury Av, SW15 .....**147** E6
Daneby Rd, SE6 ....**172** B3
Dane Cl, Bex. DA5 ....**159** G7
Orpington BR6 ....**207** G5
Danecourt Gdns, Croy.
CR0 ....**202** C3
Danecroft Rd, SE24 ......**151** J5
Danehill Wk, Sid. DA14
off Hatherley Rd **176** A3
Danehurst Gdns, Ilf. IG4 ...**80** B5
Danehurst St, SW6 ......**148** B1
Daneland, Barn. EN4 .....**41** J6
Danemead Gro, Nthlt.
UB5 ....**85** H5
Danemere St, SW15 .....**147** J3
Dane Pl, E3
off Roman Rd **113** J2
Dane Rd, N18 ....**61** F4
SW19 ....**185** F1
W13 ....**125** F1
Ilford IG1 ....**99** F5
Southall UB1 ....**103** E7
Danesbury Rd, Felt.
TW13 ....**160** B1
Danescombe, SE12
off Winn Rd **173** G1
Danes Ct, Wem. HA9
off North End Rd **88** B3
Danescourt Cres, Sutt.
SM1 ....**199** F2
Danescroft, NW4 ....**72** A5
Danescroft Av, NW4 ......**72** A5
Danescroft Gdns, NW4 ....**72** A5
Danesdale Rd, E9 ....**95** H6
Danesfield, SE5 ....**36** D5
Danes Gate, Har. HA1 .....**68** B3
Danes Rd, Rom. RM7 .....**83** J7

Dane St, WC1 ...18 C2
Daneswood Av, SE6 ...172 C3
Danethorpe Rd, Wem.
  HA0 ...87 G6
Danetree Cl, Epsom
  KT19 ...196 C7
Danetree Rd, Epsom
  KT19 ...196 C7
Danette Gdns, Dag.
  RM10 ...101 F2
Daneville Rd, SE5 ...152 A1
Dangan Rd, E11 ...79 G6
Daniel Bolt Cl, E14
  off Uamvar St ...114 B5
Daniel Cl, N18 ...61 F4
  SW17 ...167 H6
  Hounslow TW4
  off Harvey Rd ...143 F7
Daniel Gdns, SE15 ...37 F7
Daniell Way, Croy. CR0 ...201 E1
Daniel Pl, NW4 ...71 H6
Daniel Rd, W5 ...105 J7
Daniels Rd, SE15 ...153 F3
Dan Leno Wk, SW6
  off Britannia Rd ...128 E7
Dan Mason Dr, W4 ...146 D2
Dansey Pl, W1 ...17 H5
Dansington Rd, Well.
  DA16 ...158 A4
Danson Cres, Well.
  DA16 ...158 B3
Danson Interchange,
  Sid. DA15
  off East Rochester
  Way ...158 C6
Danson La, Well. DA16 ...158 A4
Danson Mead, Well.
  DA16 ...158 C3
★ Danson Park, Well.
  DA16 ...158 C4
Danson Pk, Bexh. DA6 ...158 C5
Danson Rd, Bex. DA5 ...158 D5
  Bexleyheath DA6 ...158 D5
Danson Underpass, Sid.
  DA15 off Danson Rd ...158 C5
Dante Pl, SE11 ...35 H1
Dante Rd, SE11 ...35 G1
Danube Apts, N8
  off Great Amwell La ...75 F3
Danube St, SW3 ...31 H3
Danvers Rd, N8 ...74 D4
Danvers St, SW3 ...31 F6
Danziger Way, Borwd.
  WD6 ...38 C1
Daphne Gdns, E4
  off Gunners Gro ...62 C3
Daphne St, SW18 ...149 F6
Daplyn St, E1 ...21 H1
D'Arblay St, W1 ...17 G4
Darby Cres, Sun. TW16 ...178 C2
Darby Gdns, Sun. TW16 ...178 C2
Darcy Av, Wall. SM6 ...200 C4
Darcy Cl, N20 ...57 G2
D'Arcy Dr, Har. HA3 ...69 G4
Darcy Gdns, Dag. RM9 ...119 F1
D'Arcy Gdns, Har. HA3 ...69 H4
Darcy Ho, E8
  off Warburton Rd ...112 E1
D'Arcy Pl, Brom. BR2 ...191 G4
Darcy Rd, SW16 ...186 E2
  Isleworth TW7
  off London Rd ...144 D1
D'Arcy Rd, Sutt. SM3 ...198 A4
Dare Gdns, Dag. RM8 ...101 E3
Darell Rd, Rich. TW9 ...146 A3
Darenth Rd, N16 ...76 C7
  Welling DA16 ...158 A1
Darfield Rd, SE4 ...153 J5
Darfield Way, W10 ...108 A6
Darfur St, SW15 ...148 A3
Dargate Cl, SE19
  off Chipstead Cl ...170 C7
Darien Rd, SW11 ...149 G3
Dark Ho Wk, EC3
  off Grant's Quay Wf ...20 C6
Darlands Dr, Barn. EN5 ...40 A5
Darlan Rd, SW6 ...128 C7
Darlaston Rd, SW19 ...166 A7
Darley Cl, Croy. CR0 ...189 H6
Darley Dr, N.Mal. KT3 ...182 D2
Darley Gdns, Mord. SM4 ...185 E6
Darley Rd, N9 ...60 C1
  SW11 ...149 J6
Darling Rd, SE4 ...154 A3
Darling Row, E1 ...113 E4
Darlington Rd, SE27 ...169 H5
Darmaine Cl, S.Croy. CR2 ...201 J7
Darnaway Pl, E14
  off Abbott Rd ...114 C6
Darndale Cl, E17 ...77 J2
Darnley Ho, E14 ...113 H6
Darnley Rd, E9 ...95 E6
  Woodford Green IG8 ...79 G1

Darnley Ter, W11
  off St. James's Gdns ...128 A1
Darrell Rd, SE22 ...152 D5
Darren Cl, N4 ...75 F7
Darrick Wd Rd, Orp.
  BR6 ...207 G2
Darris Cl, Hayes UB4 ...103 E4
Darsley Dr, SW8 ...150 D1
Dartford Av, N9 ...45 F6
Dartford Gdns, Rom.
  (Chad.Hth) RM6
  off Heathfield Pk Dr ...82 B5
Dartford Ho, SE1
  off Longfield Est ...37 G2
Dartford Rd, Bex. DA5 ...177 J1
Dartford St, SE17 ...36 A5
Dartmoor Wk, E14
  off Charnwood Gdns ...134 A4
Dartmouth Cl, W11 ...108 C6
Dartmouth Gro, SE10 ...154 C1
Dartmouth Hill, SE10 ...154 C1
Dartmouth Ho, Kings.T.
  KT2 off Kingsgate Rd ...181 H1
DARTMOUTH PARK, NW5 ...92 B3
Dartmouth Pk Av, NW5 ...92 B3
Dartmouth Pk Hill, N19 ...92 B1
  NW5 ...92 B1
Dartmouth Pk Rd, NW5 ...92 B4
Dartmouth Pl, SE23
  off Dartmouth Rd ...171 F2
  W4 ...127 E6
Dartmouth Rd, E16
  off Fords Pk Rd ...115 G6
  NW2 ...90 A6
  NW4 ...71 G6
  SE23 ...171 F3
  SE26 ...171 F3
  Bromley BR2 ...191 G7
  Ruislip HA4 ...84 A3
Dartmouth Row, SE10 ...154 C2
Dartmouth St, SW1 ...25 H4
Dartmouth Ter, SE10 ...154 D1
Dartnell Rd, Croy. CR0 ...188 C7
Dartrey Twr, SW10 ...30 E7
Dartrey Wk, SW10
  off Blantyre St ...30 E7
Dart St, W10 ...108 B3
Darville Rd, N16 ...94 C3
Darwell Cl, E6 ...116 D2
Darwen Pl, E2
  off Wharf Pl ...112 E1
Darwin Cl, N11 ...58 B3
  Orpington BR6 ...207 G5
Darwin Ct, SE17 ...36 C2
Darwin Dr, Sthl. UB1 ...103 H6
Darwin Gdns, Wat. WD19 ...50 C5
Darwin Rd, N22 ...75 H1
  W5 ...125 F5
  Welling DA16 ...157 J3
Darwin St, SE17 ...36 C1
Daryngton Dr, Grnf. UB6 ...104 A2
Dashwood Cl, Bexh. DA6 ...159 G5
Dashwood Rd, N8 ...75 F6
Dassett Rd, SE27 ...169 H5
Datchelor Pl, SE5 ...152 A1
Datchet Rd, SE6 ...171 J3
Datchworth Ct, N4
  off Queens Dr ...93 J3
Date St, SE17 ...36 B4
Daubeney Gdns, N17 ...59 J7
Daubeney Pl, Hmptn. TW12
  off High St ...179 J1
Daubeney Rd, E5 ...95 H4
  N17 ...59 J7
Daubeney Twr, SE8 ...133 J5
Dault Rd, SW18 ...149 F6
Davema Cl, Chis. BR7 ...192 D1
Davenant Rd, N19 ...92 D2
  Croydon CR0
  off Duppas Hill Rd ...201 H4
Davenant St, E1 ...21 J2
Davenport Cl, Tedd. TW11 ...162 D6
Davenport Ho, SE11
  off Walnut Tree Wk ...34 E1
Davenport Rd, SE6 ...154 B6
  Sidcup DA14 ...176 D2
Daventer Dr, Stan. HA7 ...52 C7
Daventry Av, E17 ...78 A6
Daventry St, NW1 ...15 G1
Davern Cl, SE10 ...135 F4
Davey Cl, N7 ...93 F6
  N13 ...59 F5
Davey Rd, E9 ...96 A7
Davey St, SE15 ...37 G5
David Av, Grnf. UB6 ...104 B3
David Cl, Hayes (Harling.)
  UB3 ...121 G7
Davidge St, SE1 ...27 G4
David Lee Pt, E15 ...115 E1
David Ms, W1 ...16 A1
David Rd, Dag. RM8 ...100 E2
Davidson Gdns, SW8 ...130 E7

Davidson La, Har. HA1
  off Grove Hill ...68 C7
Davidson Rd, Croy. CR0 ...188 C6
Davidson Terraces, E7
  off Windsor Rd ...97 H5
Davids Rd, SE23 ...171 F1
David St, E15 ...96 D6
David's Way, Ilf. IG6 ...65 H7
David Twigg Cl, Kings.T.
  KT2 ...181 H1
Davies Cl, Croy. CR0 ...188 D6
Davies La, E11 ...97 E2
Davies Ms, W1 ...16 D5
Davies St, W1 ...16 D5
Davies Wk, Islw. TW7
  off Oakley Cl ...144 A1
Davington Gdns, Dag.
  RM8 ...100 B5
Davington Rd, Dag.
  RM8 ...100 B6
Davinia Cl, Wdf.Grn. IG8
  off Deacon Way ...64 C6
Davis Rd, W3 ...127 F1
  Chessington KT9 ...196 A4
Davis Rd Ind Pk, Chess.
  KT9 ...196 A4
Davis St, E13 ...115 H2
Davisville Rd, W12 ...127 G2
Davis Way, Sid. DA14
  off Bedens Rd ...176 E6
Dawes Av, Islw. TW7 ...144 D5
Dawes Ho, SE17 ...36 B2
Dawes Rd, SW6 ...128 B7
Dawes St, SE17 ...36 C3
Dawlish Av, N13 ...58 E4
  SW18 ...166 E2
  Greenford (Perivale)
  UB6 ...104 D2
Dawlish Dr, Ilf. IG3 ...99 H4
  Pinner HA5 ...67 E5
  Ruislip HA4 ...84 A2
Dawlish Rd, E10 ...96 C2
  N17 ...76 D3
  NW2 ...90 A6
Dawnay Gdns, SW18 ...167 G2
Dawnay Rd, SW18 ...167 F2
Dawn Cl, Houns. TW4 ...143 E3
Dawn Cres, E15
  off Bridge Rd ...114 D1
Dawpool Rd, NW2 ...89 F2
Daws Hill, E4 ...46 C3
Daws La, NW7 ...55 F5
Dawson Av, Bark. IG11 ...99 H7
Dawson Cl, SE18 ...137 F4
Dawson Gdns, Bark. IG11
  off Dawson Av ...99 J7
Dawson Hts Est, SE22 ...152 D7
Dawson Pl, W2 ...108 D7
Dawson Rd, NW2 ...89 J5
  Kingston upon Thames
  KT1 ...181 J3
Dawson St, E2 ...13 G2
Dawson Ter, N9 ...45 F7
Dax Ct, Sun. TW16
  off Thames St ...178 C3
Daybrook Rd, SW19 ...184 E2
Daylesford Av, SW15 ...147 G4
Daymer Gdns, Pnr. HA5 ...66 B4
Daysbrook Rd, SW2 ...169 F2
Days La, Sid. DA15 ...157 H7
Dayton Gro, SE15 ...153 F1
Deacon Ms, N1 ...94 A7
Deacon Rd, NW2 ...89 G5
  Kingston upon Thames
  KT2 ...181 J1
Deacons Cl, Borwd. (Els.)
  WD6 ...38 A4
  Pinner HA5 ...66 B2
Deacons Leas, Orp. BR6 ...207 G4
Deacons Ri, N2 ...73 G5
Deacons Wk, Hmptn. TW12
  off Bishops Gro ...161 F4
Deacon Trd Est, E4
  off Cabinet Way ...61 J6
Deacon Way, SE17 ...35 J1
  Woodford Green IG8 ...64 C7
Deal Ms, W5
  off Darwin Rd ...125 G4
Deal Porters Way, SE16 ...133 F3
Deal Rd, SW17 ...168 A6
Deals Gateway, SE13 ...154 A1
Deal St, E1 ...21 H1
Dealtry Rd, SW15 ...147 J4
Deal Wk, SW9
  off Mandela St ...131 G7
Dean Bradley St, SW1 ...26 A6
Dean Cl, E9
  off Churchill Wk ...95 F5
  SE16 ...133 G1
Dean Ct, SW8
  off Thorncroft St ...130 E7
  Wembley HA0 ...87 E3

Deancross St, E1 ...113 F6
Dean Dr, Stan. HA7 ...69 H2
Deane Av, Ruis. HA4 ...84 C5
Deane Cft Rd, Pnr. HA5 ...66 B6
Deanery Cl, N2 ...73 H4
Deanery Ms, W1 ...24 C1
Deanery Rd, E15 ...97 E6
Deanery St, W1 ...24 C1
Deane Way, Ruis. HA4 ...66 B6
Dean Farrar St, SW1 ...25 H5
Dean Gdns, E17 ...78 D4
  W13
  off Northfield Av ...124 E1
Deanhill Ct, SW14
  off Coval La ...146 B4
Deanhill Rd, SW14 ...146 B4
Dean Ho, E1
  off Tarling St ...113 F6
Dean Rd, NW2 ...89 J6
  SE28 ...118 A7
  Croydon CR0 ...202 A4
  Hampton TW12 ...161 G5
  Hounslow TW3 ...143 H5
Dean Ryle St, SW1 ...34 A1
Deansbrook Cl, Edg. HA8 ...54 C6
Deansbrook Rd, Edg. HA8 ...54 C7
Deans Bldgs, SE17 ...36 B2
Deans Cl, W4 ...126 B6
Deans Cl, Croy. CR0 ...202 C3
Deans Cl, Edg. HA8 ...54 C6
Deans Ct, EC4 ...19 H4
Deanscroft Av, NW9 ...88 C2
Deans Dr, N13 ...59 H6
  Edgware HA8 ...54 D5
Dean's Gate Cl, SE23 ...171 G3
Deans La, W4
  off Deans Cl ...126 B6
  Edgware HA8 ...54 C6
Deans Ms, W1 ...16 E3
Deans Rd, W7 ...124 C1
  Sutton SM1 ...198 E3
Dean Stanley St, SW1 ...26 A6
Dean St, E7 ...97 G5
  W1 ...17 H3
Deansway, N2 ...73 G4
  N9 ...60 B3
Deans Way, Edg. HA8 ...54 C5
Dean's Yd, SW1 ...25 J5
Dean Trench St, SW1 ...26 A6
Dean Wk, Edg. HA8
  off Deansbrook Rd ...54 C6
Dean Way, Sthl. UB2 ...123 H2
Dearne Cl, Stan. HA7 ...52 D5
De'Arn Gdns, Mitch. CR4 ...185 H3
Dearsley Rd, Enf. EN1 ...44 D3
Deason St, E15 ...114 C1
  off High St
DEBDEN, Loug. IG10 ...49 G3
Debden Cl, NW9 ...70 E2
  off Kenley Av
  Kingston upon Thames
  KT2 ...163 G5
  Woodford Green IG8 ...63 J7
De Beauvoir Cres, N1 ...112 B1
De Beauvoir Est, N1 ...112 A1
De Beauvoir Rd, N1 ...112 B1
De Beauvoir Sq, N1 ...94 B7
DE BEAUVOIR TOWN,
  N1 ...112 A1
Debnams Rd, SE16
  off Rotherhithe
  New Rd ...133 F4
De Bohun Av, N14 ...42 B6
Deborah Cl, Islw. TW7 ...144 B1
De Brome Rd, Felt. TW13 ...160 C1
Deburgh Rd, SW19 ...167 F7
Decima St, SE1 ...28 D5
Deck Cl, SE16
  off Thame Rd ...133 G2
Decoy Av, NW11 ...72 B5
De Crespigny Pk, SE5 ...152 A2
Deeley Rd, SW8 ...150 D1
Deena Cl, W3 ...105 J6
Deepdale, SW19 ...166 A4
Deepdale Av, Brom. BR2 ...191 F4
Deepdale Cl, N11 ...58 A6
Deepdene, W5 ...105 J4
Deepdene Av, Croy.
  CR0 ...202 C3
Deepdene Cl, E11 ...79 G4
Deepdene Ct, N21 ...43 H6
  Bromley BR2 ...190 E3
Deepdene Gdns, SW2 ...151 F7
Deepdene Path, Loug.
  IG10 ...48 D4
Deepdene Pt, SE23
  off Dacres Rd ...171 G3
Deepdene Rd, SE5 ...152 A4
  Loughton IG10 ...48 D4
  Welling DA16 ...158 A3
Deepwell Cl, Islw. TW7 ...144 D1

Deepwood La, Grnf. UB6
off Cowgate Rd **104** A3
Deerbrook Rd, SE24 **169** H1
Deerdale Rd, SE24 **151** J4
Deerfield Cl, NW9 **71** F5
Deerhurst Cl, Felt. TW13 **160** A4
Deerhurst Cres, Hmptn.
(Hmptn H.) TW12 **161** J5
Deerhurst Rd, NW2 **90** A6
SW16 **169** F5
Deerings Dr, Pnr. HA5 **66** A5
Deerleap Gro, E4 **46** B5
Dee Rd, Rich. TW9 **145** J4
Deer Pk Cl, Kings.T. KT2 **164** B7
Deer Pk Gdns, Mitch.
CR4 **185** G3
Deer Pk Rd, SW19 **185** E2
Deer Pk Way, W.Wick.
BR4 **205** F2
Deeside Rd, SW17 **167** G3
Dee St, E14 **114** C6
Defence Cl, SE28 **137** H1
Defiance Wk, SE18 **136** C3
Defiant Way, Wall. SM6 **200** E7
Defoe Av, Rich. TW9 **126** A7
Defoe Cl, SE16
off Vaughan St **133** J2
SW17 **167** H6
Defoe Ho, EC2
off The Barbican **19** J1
Defoe Pl, EC2
off The Barbican **20** A1
SW17
off Lessingham Av **167** J4
Defoe Rd, N16 **94** B2
De Frene Rd, SE26 **171** G4
De Gama Pl, E14
off Maritime Quay **134** A5
Degema Rd, Chis. BR7 **174** E5
Dehar Cres, NW9 **71** G7
Dehavilland Cl, Nthlt.
UB5 **102** D3
De Havilland Ct, Ilf. IG1
off Piper Way **99** G1
De Havilland Dr, SE18 **137** E6
De Havilland Rd, Edg.
HA8 **70** B2
Hounslow TW5 **122** C7
De Havilland Way, Stai.
(Stanw.) TW19 **140** A6
Dekker Rd, SE21 **152** B6
Delacourt Rd, SE3
off Old Dover Rd **135** H7
Delafield Ho, E1 **21** J4
Delafield Rd, SE7 **135** H5
Delaford Rd, SE16 **133** E5
Delaford St, SW6 **128** B7
Delamare Cres, Croy.
CR0 **189** F6
Delamere Ct, E17
off Hawker Pl **78** C2
Delamere Gdns, NW7 **54** D6
Delamere Rd, SW20 **184** A1
W5 **125** H1
Borehamwood WD6 **38** B1
Hayes UB4 **102** D7
Delamere St, W2 **14** C1
Delamere Ter, W2 **14** B1
Delancey Pas, NW1
off Delancey St **110** B1
Delancey St, NW1 **110** B1
De Laune St, SE17 **35** G4
Delaware Rd, W9 **6** A5
Delawyk Cres, SE24 **151** J6
Delcombe Av, Wor.Pk.
KT4 **197** J1
Delft Way, SE22
off East Dulwich Gro **152** B5
Delhi Rd, Enf. EN1 **44** C7
Delhi St, N1 **111** E1
Delia St, SW18 **149** E7
Delisle Rd, SE28 **137** H1
Delius Gro, E15 **114** D2
Dell, The, SE2 **138** A5
SE19 **188** C1
Brentford TW8 **125** F6
Feltham TW14 **142** B7
Pinner HA5 **66** D2
Wembley HA0 **87** E5
Woodford Green IG8 **63** H3
Della Path, E5 **94** E3
Dellbow Rd, Felt. TW14
off Central Way **142** B5
Dell Cl, E15 **114** D1
Wallington SM6 **200** C4
Woodford Green IG8 **63** H3
Dellfield Cl, Beck. BR3 **190** C1
Dell La, Epsom KT17 **197** G5
Dellors Cl, Barn. EN5 **40** A5
Dellow Cl, Ilf. IG2 **81** G7
Dellow St, E1 **113** E7
Dell Rd, Epsom KT17 **197** G6
West Drayton UB7 **120** C3
Dells Cl, E4 **46** B7
Teddington TW11
off Middle La **162** C6
Dell's Ms, SW1 **33** G2
Dell Wk, N.Mal. KT3 **183** E2
Dell Way, W13 **105** F6
Dellwood Gdns, Ilf. IG5 **80** D3
Delmare Cl, SW9
off Brighton Ter **151** F4
Delme Cres, SE3 **155** H2
Delmey Cl, Croy. CR0 **202** C3
Deloraine St, SE8 **154** A1
Delorme St, W6 **128** A6
Delta Cl, Wor.Pk. KT4 **197** E3
Delta Ct, NW2 **89** G2
Delta Gain, Wat. WD19 **50** D2
Delta Gro, Nthlt. UB5 **102** D3
Delta Pk Ind Est, Enf.
EN3 **45** J2
Delta Rd, Wor.Pk. KT4 **197** E3
Delta St, E2 **13** H3
De Luci Rd, Erith DA8 **139** J5
De Lucy St, SE2 **138** B4
Delvan Cl, SE18
off Ordnance Rd **136** D7
Delvers Mead, Dag.
RM10 **101** J4
Delverton Rd, SE17 **35** H4
Delvino Rd, SW6 **148** D1
De Mandeville Gate, Enf.
EN1 *off Southbury Rd* **44** D4
Demesne Rd, Wall. SM6 **200** D5
Demeta Cl, Wem. HA9 **88** C3
De Montfort Par, SW16
off Streatham
High Rd **168** E3
De Montfort Rd, SW16 **168** E3
De Morgan Rd, SW6 **149** E3
Dempster Cl, Surb.
(Long Dit.) KT6 **195** F1
Dempster Rd, SW18 **149** F5
Denbar Par, Rom. RM7
off Mawney Rd **83** J4
Denberry Dr, Sid. DA14 **176** B3
Denbigh Cl, W11 **108** C7
Chislehurst BR7 **174** C6
Southall UB1 **103** F6
Sutton SM1 **198** C5
Denbigh Dr, Hayes UB3 **121** F2
Denbigh Gdns, Rich.
TW10 **145** J5
Denbigh Ms, SW1 **33** F2
Denbigh Pl, SW1 **33** F3
Denbigh Rd, E6 **116** A3
W11 **108** C7
W13 **105** E7
Hounslow TW3 **143** H2
Southall UB1 **103** F6
Denbigh St, SW1 **33** F2
Denbigh Ter, W11 **108** C7
Denbridge Rd, Brom.
BR1 **192** C2
Den Cl, Beck. BR3 **190** D3
Dene, The, W13 **104** E5
Croydon CR0 **203** G4
Wembley HA9 **87** H4
West Molesey KT8 **179** F5
Dene Av, Houns. TW3 **143** F3
Sidcup DA15 **158** B7
Dene Cl, SE4 **153** H3
Bromley BR2 **205** F1
Worcester Park KT4 **197** F2
Dene Ct, Stan. HA7 **53** F5
Dene Gdns, Stan. HA7 **53** F5
Thames Ditton KT7 **194** D2
Denehurst Gdns, NW4 **71** J6
W3 **126** B1
Richmond TW10 **146** A4
Twickenham TW2 **144** A7
Woodford Green IG8 **63** H4
Dene Rd, N11 **57** J1
Buckhurst Hill IG9 **64** A1
Denewood, Barn.
(New Barn.) EN5 **41** F5
Denewood Rd, N6 **73** J6
Denford St, SE10
off Woolwich Rd **135** F5
Dengie Wk, N1
off Basire St **111** J1
Denham Cl, Well. DA16
off Park Vw Rd **158** C3
Denham Cres, Mitch.
CR4 **185** J4
Denham Dr, Ilf. IG2 **81** F6
Denham Rd, N20 **57** J3
Feltham TW14 **142** C6
Denham St, SE10 **135** G5
Denham Way, Bark. IG11 **117** H1
Borehamwood WD6 **38** D1
Denholme Rd, W9 **108** C3
Denison Cl, N2 **73** F3
Denison Rd, SW19 **167** G6
W5 **105** F4
Deniston Av, Bex. DA5 **176** E1
Denis Way, SW4
off Gauden Rd **150** D3
Denleigh Gdns, N21 **59** G1
Thames Ditton KT7 **180** B6
Denman Dr, NW11 **72** D5
Esher (Clay.) KT10 **194** D5
Denman Dr N, NW11 **72** D5
Denman Dr S, NW11 **72** D5
Denman Pl, W1
off Great Windmill St **17** H6
Denman Rd, SE15 **152** C1
Denman St, W1 **17** H6
Denmark Av, SW19 **166** B7
Denmark Ct, Mord. SM4 **184** D5
Denmark Gdns, Cars.
SM5 **199** J3
Denmark Gro, N1 **11** E1
Denmark Hill, SE5 **152** A1
Denmark Hill Dr, NW9 **71** F4
Denmark Hill Est, SE5 **152** A4
Denmark Pl, E3
off Kitcat Ter **114** A3
WC2 **17** J3
Denmark Rd, N8 **75** G4
NW6 **108** C2
SE5 **151** J1
SE25 **188** D5
SW19 **166** A6
W13 **105** E7
Bromley BR1 **191** H1
Carshalton SM5 **199** J3
Kingston upon Thames
KT1 **181** H3
Twickenham TW2 **162** A3
Denmark St, E11
off High Rd
Leytonstone **96** E3
E13 **115** H5
N17 **76** E1
WC2 **17** J4
Denmark Ter, N2
off Fortis Grn **73** J3
Denmark Wk, SE27 **169** J4
Denmead Ho, SW15
off Highcliffe Dr **147** F6
Denmead Rd, Croy.
CR0 **201** H1
Dennan Rd, Surb. KT6 **195** J1
Dennard Way, Orp.
(Farnboro.) BR6 **206** E4
Denner Rd, E4 **62** A2
Denne Ter, E8 **112** C1
Dennett Rd, Croy. CR0 **201** G1
Dennetts Gro, SE14
off Dennetts Rd **153** G2
Dennetts Rd, SE14 **153** F1
Denning Av, Croy. CR0 **201** G4
Denning Cl, NW8 **6** D3
Hampton TW12 **161** F6
Denning Pt, E1 **21** F3
Denning Rd, NW3 **91** G4
Dennington Cl, E5
off Detmold Rd **95** E2
Dennington Pk Rd, NW6 **90** D6
Denningtons, The, Wor.Pk.
KT4 **197** E2
Dennis Av, Wem. HA9 **87** J5
Dennis Gdns, Stan. HA7 **53** F5
Dennis La, Stan. HA7 **52** E3
Dennison Pt, E15 **96** C7
Dennis Pk Cres, SW20 **184** B1
Dennis Reeve Cl, Mitch.
CR4 **185** J1
Dennis Rd, E.Mol. KT8 **179** J4
Denny Cl, E6
off Linton Gdns **116** B5
Denny Cres, SE11 **35** F2
Denny Gdns, Dag. RM9
off Canonsleigh Rd **100** B7
Denny Rd, N9 **60** E1
Denny St, SE11 **35** F3
Den Rd, Brom. BR2 **190** D3
Densham Rd, E15 **115** E1
Densole Cl, Beck. BR3
off Kings Hall Rd **189** H1
Densworth Gro, N9 **61** F2
Denton, NW1
off Malden Cres **92** A6
Denton Cl, Barn. EN5 **39** J5
Denton Rd, N8 **75** F5
N18 **60** B4
Twickenham TW1 **145** G6
Welling DA16 **138** C7
Denton St, SW18 **149** E6
Denton Way, E5 **95** G3
Dents Rd, SW11 **149** J6
Denver Cl, Orp. BR6 **193** H6
Denver Rd, N16 **76** B7
Denyer St, SW3 **31** H2
Denzil Rd, NW10 **89** F5
Deodar Rd, SW15 **148** B4
Deodora Cl, N20 **57** H3
★ **Department for Constitutional Affairs (DCA)**, SW1 **25** G5
★ **Department for Environment, Food & Rural Affairs (D.E.F.R.A.)**, SW1 **26** A1
★ **Department for Transport (DfT)**, SW1 **33** J1
★ **Department of Health & Dept for Work & Pensions (D.W.P.)**, SW1 **26** A3
Depot App, NW2 **90** A4
Depot Rd, W12 **107** J7
Hounslow TW3 **144** A3
DEPTFORD, SE8 **133** J5
Deptford Br, SE8 **154** A1
Deptford Bdy, SE8 **154** A1
Deptford Ch St, SE8 **134** A6
Deptford Ferry Rd, E14 **134** A4
Deptford Grn, SE8 **134** A6
Deptford High St, SE8 **134** A6
Deptford Strand, SE8 **133** J4
Deptford Wf, SE8 **133** J4
De Quincey Ho, SW1
off Lupus St **33** F4
De Quincey Ms, E16
off Wesley Av **135** G1
De Quincey Rd, N17 **76** A1
Derby Av, N12 **57** F5
Harrow HA3 **68** A1
Romford RM7 **83** J6
Derby Ct, E5
off Overbury St **95** G4
Derby Gate, SW1 **26** A3
Derby Hill, SE23 **171** F2
Derby Hill Cres, SE23 **171** F2
Derby Ho, SE11
off Walnut Tree Wk **34** E1
Derby Rd, E7 **97** J7
E9 **113** G1
E18 **79** F1
N18 **61** F5
SW14 **146** B4
SW19 *off Russell Rd* **166** D7
Croydon CR0 **201** H2
Enfield EN3 **45** E5
Greenford UB6 **103** H1
Hounslow TW3 **143** H4
Surbiton KT5 **196** A1
Sutton SM1 **198** C6
Derby Rd Ind Est, Houns.
TW3 *off Derby Rd* **143** H4
Derbyshire St, E2 **13** J4
Derby St, W1 **24** C2
Dereham Pl, EC2 **12** E4
Dereham Rd, Bark. IG11 **99** J6
Derek Av, Epsom KT19 **196** A5
Wallington SM6 **200** B4
Wembley HA9 **88** B7
Derek Cl, Epsom (Ewell)
KT19 **196** B5
Derek Walcott Cl, SE24
off Shakespeare Rd **151** H5
Dericote St, E8 **112** D1
Deridene Cl, Stai. (Stanw.)
TW19 *off Bedfont Rd* **140** B6
Derifall Cl, E6 **116** C5
Dering Pl, Croy. CR0 **201** J4
Dering Rd, Croy. CR0 **201** J4
Dering St, W1 **16** D4
Derinton Rd, SW17 **167** J4
Derley Rd, Sthl. UB2 **122** C3
Dermody Gdns, SE13 **154** D5
Dermody Rd, SE13 **154** D5
Deronda Rd, SE24 **169** H1
Deroy Cl, Cars. SM5 **199** J6
Derrick Gdns, SE7
off Anchor &
Hope La **135** J4
Derrick Rd, Beck. BR3 **189** J3
Derry Rd, Croy. CR0 **200** E3
Derry St, W8 **22** A4
Dersingham Av, E12 **98** D5
Dersingham Rd, NW2 **90** B3
Derwent Av, N18 **60** A5
NW7 **54** D5
NW9 **70** E5
SW15 **164** E4
Barnet EN4 **57** J1
Pinner HA5 **51** E6
Derwent Cl, Esher (Clay.)
KT10 **194** B6
Derwent Cres, N20 **57** F3
Bexleyheath DA7 **159** G2
Stanmore HA7 **69** F2
Derwent Dr, Orp. BR5 **193** G7
Derwent Gdns, Ilf. IG4 **80** B4
Wembley HA9 **69** F7
Derwent Gro, SE22 **152** C4
Derwent Ri, NW9 **70** E6
Derwent Rd, N13 **59** F4
SE20 **188** D2
SW20 **184** A6

Derwent Rd, W5 125 F3
Southall UB1 103 G6
Twickenham TW2 143 H6
Derwent St, SE10 134 E5
Derwent Wk, Wall. SM6 200 B7
Derwentwater Rd, W3 126 C1
Derwent Yd, W5
off Northfield Av 125 F3
Desborough Cl, W2 14 B1
Desborough Ho, W14
off North End Rd 128 C6
Desborough St, W2 14 A1
Desenfans Rd, SE21 152 B6
Desford Ms, E16
off Desford Rd 115 E4
Desford Rd, E16 115 E4
★ **Design Mus**, SE1 29 G2
Desmond St, SE14 133 H6
Desmond Tutu Dr, SE23
off St. Germans Rd 171 H1
Despard Rd, N19 92 C1
Desvignes Dr, SE13 154 D6
Detling Rd, Brom. BR1 173 G5
Detmold Rd, E5 95 F2
Devalls Cl, E6 116 D7
Devana End, Cars. SM5 199 J3
Devas Rd, SW20 183 J1
Devas St, E3 114 B4
Devenay Rd, E15 97 F7
Devenish Rd, SE2 138 A2
Deventer Cres, SE22 152 B5
Deveraux Cl, Beck. BR3 190 C5
De Vere Cl, Wall. SM6 200 E7
De Vere Gdns, W8 22 C4
Ilford IG1 98 C2
Deverell St, SE1 28 B6
De Vere Ms, W8 22 C5
Devereux Ct, WC2 18 E4
Devereux La, SW13 127 H7
Devereux Rd, SW11 149 J6
Deverill Ct, SE20 189 F1
Devey Cl, Kings.T. KT2 165 E7
Devizes St, N1
off Poole St 112 A1
Devon Av, Twick. TW2 161 J1
Devon Cl, N17 76 C3
Buckhurst Hill IG9 63 H2
Greenford (Perivale)
UB6 105 F1
Devon Ct, Buck.H. IG9
off Chequers 63 H1
Devoncroft Gdns, Twick.
TW1 144 D7
Devon Gdns, N4 75 H6
Devonhurst Pl, W4
off Heathfield Ter 126 D5
Devonia Gdns, N18 59 J6
Devonia Rd, N1 11 H1
Devon Mans, SE1
off Tooley St 29 F3
Devonport Gdns, Ilf. IG1 80 C6
Devonport Ms, W12
off Devonport Rd 127 H1
Devonport Rd, W12 127 H2
Devonport St, E1 113 F6
Devon Ri, N2 73 G4
Devon Rd, Bark. IG11 117 H1
Devons Est, E3 114 B3
Devonshire Av, Sutt.
SM2 199 F7
Devonshire Business Pk,
Borwd. WD6 38 D3
Devonshire Cl, E15 97 E4
N13 59 G4
W1 16 D1
Devonshire Cres, NW7 56 A7
Devonshire Dr, SE10 134 B7
Surbiton (Long Dit.)
KT6 195 G1
Devonshire Gdns, N17 59 J6
N21 43 J7
W4 126 C7
Devonshire Gro, SE15 133 E6
Devonshire Hill La, N17 59 J6
Devonshire Ho, SE1
off Bath Ter 27 J5
Sutton SM2
off Devonshire Av 199 F7
Devonshire Ms, SW10
off Park Wk 30 E5
W4 *off Glebe St* 126 E5
Devonshire Ms N, W1 16 D1
Devonshire Ms S, W1 16 D1
Devonshire Ms W, W1 8 D6
Devonshire Pas, W4 126 E5
Devonshire Pl, NW2 90 D3
W1 8 C6
W8 22 A6
Devonshire Pl Ms, W1 8 C6
Devonshire Rd, E16 115 H6
E17 78 A6
N9 61 F1
N13 59 F4
Devonshire Rd, N17 59 J6
NW7 56 A7
SE9 174 B2
SE23 171 F1
SW19 167 H7
W4 126 E5
W5 125 F3
Bexleyheath DA6 159 E4
Carshalton SM5 200 A4
Croydon CR0 188 A7
Feltham TW13 160 E3
Harrow HA1 68 A6
Ilford IG2 81 G7
Pinner (Eastcote) HA5 66 C6
Pinner (Hatch End)
HA5 67 F1
Southall UB1 103 G5
Sutton SM2 199 F7
Devonshire Row, EC2 20 E2
Devonshire Row Ms, W1 8 E6
Devonshire Sq, EC2 20 E3
Bromley BR2 191 H4
Devonshire St, W1 16 C1
W4 126 E5
Devonshire Ter, W2 14 D4
Devonshire Way, Croy.
CR0 203 H2
Hayes UB4 102 B6
Devons Rd, E3 114 A5
Devon St, SE15 132 E6
Devon Way, Chess. KT9 195 F5
Epsom KT19 196 B5
Devon Waye, Houns.
TW5 123 F7
De Walden St, W1 16 C2
Dewar St, SE15 152 D3
Dewberry Gdns, E6 116 B5
Dewberry St, E14 114 C5
Dewey Rd, N1 10 E1
Dagenham RM10 101 H6
Dewey St, SW17 167 J5
Dewhurst Rd, W14 128 A3
Dewlands Ct, NW4
off Holders Hill Rd 72 A2
Dewsbury Cl, Pnr. HA5 67 E6
Dewsbury Ct, W4
off Chiswick Rd 126 C4
Dewsbury Gdns, Wor.Pk.
KT4 197 G3
Dewsbury Rd, NW10 89 G5
Dewsbury Ter, NW1
off Camden High St 110 B1
Dexter Ho, Erith DA18
off Kale Rd 139 E3
Dexter Rd, Barn. EN5 40 A6
Deyncourt Rd, N17 75 J1
Deynecourt Gdns, E11 79 J4
D'Eynsford Rd, SE5 152 A1
Dhonan Ho, SE1
off Longfield Est 37 G1
Diadem Ct, W1 17 H4
Dial Wk, The, W8 22 B3
Diamedes Av, Stai.
(Stanw.) TW19 140 A7
Diameter Rd, Orp. BR5 193 E7
Diamond Cl, Dag. RM8 100 C1
Diamond Rd, Ruis. HA4 84 D4
Diamond St, NW10 88 D7
SE15 132 B7
Diamond Ter, SE10 154 C1
Diamond Way, SE8
off Crossfield St 134 A7
Diana Cl, E18 79 H1
SE8 *off Staunton St* 133 J6
Sidcup DA14 176 E2
Diana Gdns, Surb. KT6 195 J2
Diana Ho, SW13 147 F1
★ **Diana Princess of
Wales Mem**, W2 23 F2
Diana Rd, E17 77 J3
Dianne Way, Barn. EN4 41 H5
Dianthus Cl, SE2
off Carnation St 138 B5
Dibden St, N1 111 H1
Dibdin Cl, Sutt. SM1 198 D3
Dibdin Ho, W9 6 A1
Dibdin Rd, Sutt. SM1 198 D3
Dicey Av, NW2 89 J5
Dickens Av, N3 73 F1
Dickens Cl, Erith DA8 139 H7
Hayes UB3
off Croyde Av 121 H4
Richmond TW10 163 H2
Dickens Dr, Chis. BR7 175 F6
Dickens Est, SE1 29 H4
SE16 29 H4
Dickens Ho, NW6 108 D3
Dickens La, N18 60 B5
Dickens Ms, EC1 19 G1
Dickenson Cl, N9
off Croyland Rd 60 D1
Dickenson Rd, N8 75 E7
Feltham TW13 160 C5
Dickensons La, SE25 188 D5
Dickensons Pl, SE25 188 D6
Dickens Ri, Chig. IG7 64 D3
Dickens Rd, E6 116 A2
Dickens Sq, SE1 28 A5
Dickens St, SW8 150 B2
Dickenswood Cl, SE19 169 H7
Dickerage La, N.Mal.
KT3 182 C3
Dickerage Rd, Kings.T.
KT1 182 C1
New Malden KT3 182 C1
Dickinson Ct, EC1
off Brewhouse Yd 11 H6
Dickson Fold, Pnr. HA5 66 D4
Dickson Rd, SE9 156 B3
Dick Turpin Way, Felt.
TW14 141 J4
Didsbury Cl, E6
off Barking Rd 116 C1
Dieppe Cl, W14 128 C5
Digby Cres, N4 93 J2
Digby Gdns, Dag. RM10 119 G1
Digby Pl, Croy. CR0 202 C3
Digby Rd, E9 95 G6
Barking IG11 99 J7
Digby St, E2 113 F3
Diggon St, E1
off Stepney Way 113 G5
Dighton Ct, SE5 35 J6
Dighton Rd, SW18 149 F5
Dignum St, N1 11 E1
Digswell St, N7
off Holloway Rd 93 G6
Dilhorne Cl, SE12 173 H3
Dilke St, SW3 32 A5
Dilloway Yd, Sthl. UB2
off The Green 123 E2
Dillwyn Cl, SE26 171 H4
Dilston Cl, Nthlt. UB5
off Yeading La 102 C3
Dilston Gro, SE16
off Abbeyfield Rd 133 F4
Dilton Gdns, SW15 165 G1
Dilwyn Ct, E17
off Hillyfield 77 H2
Dimes Pl, W6 *off King St* 127 H4
Dimmock Dr, Grnf. UB6 86 A5
Dimond Cl, E7 97 G4
Dimsdale Dr, NW9 88 C1
Enfield EN1 44 D6
Dimsdale Wk, E13
off Stratford Rd 115 G1
Dimson Cres, E3 114 A4
Dingle Cl, Barn. EN5 39 F6
Dingle Gdns, E14 114 A7
Dingley La, SW16 168 D2
Dingley Pl, EC1 12 A4
Dingley Rd, EC1 11 J4
Dingwall Av, Croy. CR0 201 J2
Dingwall Gdns, NW11 72 D6
Dingwall Rd, SW18 149 F7
Croydon CR0 202 A2
Dinmont St, E2
off Coate St 112 E2
Dinsdale Gdns, SE25 188 B4
Barnet (New Barn.)
EN5 41 E5
Dinsdale Rd, SE3 135 F6
Dinsmore Rd, SW12 150 B7
Dinton Rd, SW19 167 G6
Kingston upon Thames
KT2 163 J7
Diploma Av, N2 73 H4
Diploma Ct, N2
off Diploma Av 73 H4
Dirleton Rd, E15 115 F1
Disbrowe Rd, W6 128 B6
Discovery Business Pk, SE16
off St. James's Rd 29 J6
Discovery Wk, E1 132 E1
Dishforth La, NW9 70 E1
Disney Ms, N4
off Chesterfield Gdns 75 H5
Disney Pl, SE1 28 A3
Disney St, SE1 28 A3
Dison Cl, Enf. EN3 45 G1
Disraeli Cl, SE28 138 C1
W4 *off Acton La* 126 D3
Disraeli Gdns, SW15
off Fawe Pk Rd 148 C4
Disraeli Rd, E7 97 G6
NW10 106 C2
SW15 148 B4
W5 125 G1
Diss St, E2 13 F3
Distaff La, EC4 19 J5
Distillery La, W6
off Fulham Palace Rd 127 J5
Distillery Rd, W6 127 J5
Distillery Wk, Brent. TW8 125 H6
Distin St, SE11 34 E2
District Rd, Wem. HA0 86 E5
Ditch All, SE10 154 B1
Ditchburn St, E14 114 C7
Ditchfield Rd, Hayes
UB4 102 E4
Dittisham Rd, SE9 174 B4
Ditton Cl, T.Ditt. KT7 180 D7
Dittoncroft Cl, Croy. CR0 202 B4
Ditton Gra Cl, Surb.
(Long Dit.) KT6 195 G1
Ditton Gra Dr, Surb.
(Long Dit.) KT6 195 G1
Ditton Hill, Surb.
(Long Dit.) KT6 195 F1
Ditton Hill Rd, Surb.
(Long Dit.) KT6 195 F1
Ditton Lawn, T.Ditt. KT7 194 D1
Ditton Pl, SE20 189 E1
Ditton Reach, T.Ditt. KT7 180 E6
Ditton Rd, Bexh. DA6 158 D5
Southall UB2 123 F4
Surbiton KT6 195 H1
Divis Way, SW15 147 H6
Dixon Clark Ct, N1
off Canonbury Rd 93 H6
Dixon Cl, E6
off Brandreth Rd 116 C6
Dixon Ho, W10 108 A6
Dixon Pl, W.Wick. BR4 204 B1
Dixon Rd, SE14 153 H1
SE25 188 B3
Dixon's All, SE16 132 E2
Dobbin Cl, Har. HA3 68 D2
Dobell Path, SE9
off Dobell Rd 156 C5
Dobell Rd, SE9 156 C5
Dobree Av, NW10 89 H7
Dobson Cl, NW6 91 G7
Doby Ct, EC4 20 A5
Dockers Tanner Rd, E14 134 A3
Dockhead, SE1 29 G4
Dock Hill Av, SE16 133 G2
Dockland St, E16 136 D1
Dockley Rd, SE16 29 H6
Dock Rd, E16 115 F7
Brentford TW8 125 G7
Dockside Rd, E16 116 A7
Dock St, E1 21 H5
Dockwell Cl, Felt. TW14 142 A4
Doctor Johnson Av,
SW17 168 B3
★ **Doctor Johnson's Ho**,
EC4 19 F4
Doctors Cl, SE26 171 F5
Docwra's Bldgs, N1 94 B6
Dodbrooke Rd, SE27 169 G3
Dodd Ho, SE16
off Rennie Est 133 E4
Doddington Gro, SE17 35 G5
Doddington Pl, SE17 35 G5
Dodsley Pl, N9 61 F3
Dodson St, SE1 27 F4
Dod St, E14 113 J6
Doebury Wk, SE18
off Prestwood Cl 138 A6
Doel Cl, SW19 167 F7
Doggett Rd, SE6 154 A7
Doggetts Ct, Barn.
(E.Barn.) EN4 41 H5
Doghurst Av, Hayes
(Harling.) UB3 121 E7
Doghurst Dr, West Dr.
UB7 121 E7
Dog Kennel Hill, SE22 152 B3
Dog Kennel Hill Est,
SE22 152 B3
Dog La, NW10 89 E4
Doherty Rd, E13 115 G4
Dokal Ind Est, Sthl. UB2
off Hartington Rd 122 E3
Dolben St, SE1 27 G2
Dolby Rd, SW6 148 C2
Dolland St, SE11 34 D4
Dollis Av, N3 72 C1
Dollis Brook Wk, Barn.
EN5 40 B6
Dollis Cres, Ruis. HA4 84 C1
DOLLIS HILL, NW2 89 H3
Dollis Hill Av, NW2 89 H3
Dollis Hill La, NW2 89 H3
Dollis Ms, N3 72 D1
Dollis Pk, N3 72 C1
Dollis Rd, N3 56 B7
NW7 56 B7
Dollis Valley Dr, Barn.
EN5 40 C6
Dollis Valley Grn Wk, N20
off Totteridge La 57 F2
Barnet EN5 40 B6
Dollis Valley Way, Barn.
EN5 40 C6
Dolman Cl, N3
off Avondale Rd 73 F2
Dolman Rd, W4 126 D4

Dolman St, SW4 151 F4
Dolphin Cl, SE16
off Kinburn St 133 G2
SE28 118 D6
Surbiton KT6 181 G6
Dolphin Ct, NW11 72 B6
Dolphin Ho, SW18
off Smugglers Way 149 E4
Dolphin La, E14 114 B7
Dolphin Rd, Nthlt. UB5 103 F2
Dolphin Sq, SW1 33 G4
W4 126 E7
Dolphin St, Kings.T. KT1 181 H1
Dolphin Twr, SE8
off Abinger Gro 133 J6
Dombey St, WC1 18 C1
Dome Hill Pk, SE26 170 C4
Domett Cl, SE5 152 A4
Domfe Pl, E5
off Rushmore Rd 95 F4
Domingo St, EC1 11 J5
Dominica Cl, E13 115 J2
Dominion Business Pk,
N9 *off Goodwin Rd* 61 G2
Dominion Cl, Houns.
TW3 144 A2
Dominion Rd, Croy. CR0 188 C7
Southall UB2 123 E3
Dominion St, EC2 20 C1
★ **Dominion Thea**, W1 17 J3
Domonic Dr, SE9 174 E4
Domville Cl, N20 57 G2
Donald Dr, Rom. RM6 82 C5
Donald Rd, E13 115 H1
Croydon CR0 187 F6
Donaldson Rd, NW6 108 C1
SE18 156 D1
Donald Wds Gdns, Surb.
KT5 196 B2
Donato Dr, SE15 36 D6
Doncaster Dr, Nthlt. UB5 85 F5
Doncaster Gdns, N4
off Stanhope Gdns 75 J6
Northolt UB5 85 F5
Doncaster Grn, Wat. WD19 50 C5
Doncaster Rd, N9 44 E7
Doncel Ct, E4 46 D7
Donegal St, N1 10 D2
Doneraile St, SW6 148 A2
Dongola Rd, E1 113 H5
E13 115 H3
N17 76 B3
Dongola Rd W, E13
off Balaam St 115 H3
Donington Av, Ilf. IG6 81 F5
Donkey All, SE22 152 D7
Donkey La, Enf. EN1 44 D2
Donkin Ho, SE16
off Rennie Est 133 E4
Donne Ct, SE24 151 J6
Donnefield Av, Edg. HA8 53 H7
Donne Pl, SW3 31 H1
Mitcham CR4 186 B4
Donne Rd, Dag. RM8 100 C2
Donnington Ct, NW10 89 H7
Donnington Rd, NW10 89 H7
Harrow HA3 69 G5
Worcester Park KT4 197 G2
Donnybrook Rd, SW16 168 C7
Donovan Av, N10 74 B2
Donovan Ct, SW10
off Drayton Gdns 30 E4
Donovan Pl, N21 43 F5
Don Phelan Cl, SE5 152 A1
Doone Cl, Tedd. TW11 162 D6
Doon St, SE1 26 E2
Doral Way, Cars. SM5 199 J5
Dorando Cl, W12 107 H7
Doran Gro, SE18 137 H7
Doran Wk, E15 96 C7
Dora Rd, SW19 166 D5
Dora St, E14 113 J6
Dora Way, SW9 151 G2
Dorchester Av, N13 59 J4
Bexley DA5 176 D1
Harrow HA2 67 J6
Dorchester Cl, Nthlt. UB5 85 H5
Orpington BR5 176 A7
Dorchester Ct, N14 42 B7
SE24 151 J5
Dorchester Dr, SE24 151 J5
Feltham TW14 141 H6
Dorchester Gdns, E4 62 A4
NW11 72 D4
Dorchester Gro, W4 127 E5
Dorchester Ho, Rich. TW9
off Strand Dr 126 B7
Dorchester Ms, N.Mal. KT3
off Elm Rd 182 D4
Twickenham TW1 145 F7
Dorchester Rd, Mord.
SM4 185 E7
Northolt UB5 85 H5
Dorchester Rd,
Worcester Park KT4 197 J1
Dorchester Way, Har.
HA3 69 J6
Dorchester Waye, Hayes
UB4 102 C6
Dorcis Av, Bexh. DA7 158 E2
Dordrecht Rd, W3 127 E1
Dore Av, E12 98 D5
Doreen Av, NW9 88 D1
Dore Gdns, Mord. SM4 185 E7
Dorell Cl, Sthl. UB1 103 F5
Dorey Ho, Brent. TW8
off High St 125 F7
Doria Rd, SW6 148 C2
Doric Way, NW1 9 H3
Dorie Ms, N12 57 E4
Dorien Rd, SW20 184 A2
Doris Ashby Cl, Grnf. UB6
off Horsenden La S 104 D1
Doris Av, Erith DA8 159 J1
Doris Rd, E7 97 G7
Dorking Cl, SE8 133 J6
Worcester Park KT4 198 A2
Dorlcote Rd, SW18 149 G7
Dorman Pl, N9
off Newdales Cl 60 D2
Dorman Wk, NW10
off Garden Way 88 D5
Dorman Way, NW8 109 G1
Dorma Trd Pk, E10 95 G1
Dormay St, SW18 148 E5
Dormer Cl, E15 97 F6
Barnet EN5 40 A5
Dormers Av, Sthl. UB1 103 G6
Dormers Ri, Sthl. UB1 103 H6
DORMER'S WELLS, Sthl.
UB1 103 H7
Dormers Wells La, Sthl.
UB1 103 G6
Dornberg Cl, SE3 135 G7
Dornberg Rd, SE3
off Banchory Rd 135 H7
Dorncliffe Rd, SW6 148 B2
Dorney, NW3 91 H7
Dorney Ri, Orp. BR5 193 J4
Dorney Way, Houns.
TW4 143 E5
Dornfell St, NW6 90 C5
Dornton Rd, SW12 168 B2
South Croydon CR2 202 A5
Dorothy Av, Wem. HA0 87 H7
Dorothy Evans Cl, Bexh.
DA7 159 H4
Dorothy Gdns, Dag.
RM8 100 B4
Dorothy Rd, SW11 149 J3
Dorrell Pl, SW9
off Brixton Rd 151 G4
Dorrien Wk, SW16 168 D2
Dorrington Ct, SE25 188 B2
Dorrington Pt, E3
off Bromley High St 114 B3
Dorrington St, EC1 19 E1
Dorrington Way, Beck.
BR3 190 C5
Dorrit Ms, N18 60 B4
Dorrit St, SE1 28 A3
Dorrit Way, Chis. BR7 175 F6
Dors Cl, NW9 88 D1
Dorset Av, Sthl. UB2 123 G4
Welling DA16 157 J4
Dorset Bldgs, EC4 19 G4
Dorset Cl, NW1 15 J1
Dorset Dr, Edg. HA8 53 J6
Dorset Est, E2 13 G3
Dorset Gdns, Mitch.
CR4 187 F4
Dorset Ms, N3 72 D1
SW1 24 D5
Dorset Pl, E15 96 D6
Dorset Ri, EC4 19 G4
Dorset Rd, E7 97 J7
N15 76 A4
N22 75 E1
SE9 174 B2
SW8 34 B7
SW19 184 D1
W5 125 F3
Beckenham BR3 189 G3
Harrow HA1 67 J6
Mitcham CR4 185 H2
Dorset Sq, NW1 7 J6
Dorset St, W1 16 A2
Dorset Way, Twick. TW2 162 A1
Dorset Waye, Houns.
TW5 123 F7
Dorton Cl, SE15
off Chandler Way 132 B7
Dorville Cres, W6 127 H3
Dorville Rd, SE12 155 F5
Dothill Rd, SE18 137 G7
Douai Gro, Hmptn. TW12 179 J1
Doubleday Rd, Loug. IG10 49 F3
Doughty Ms, WC1 10 C6
Doughty St, WC1 10 C5
Douglas Av, E17 78 A1
New Malden KT3 183 H4
Wembley HA0 87 H7
Douglas Cl, Ilf. IG6 64 E7
Stanmore HA7 52 D5
Wallington SM6 201 E7
Douglas Cres, Hayes
UB4 102 C4
Douglas Dr, Croy. CR0 204 A3
Douglas Ms, NW2 90 B3
Douglas Path, E14
off Manchester Rd 134 C5
Douglas Rd, E4 47 E7
E16 115 G5
N1 93 J7
N22 75 G1
NW6 108 C1
Hounslow TW3 143 H3
Ilford IG3 82 A6
Kingston upon Thames
KT1 182 B2
Staines (Stanw.) TW19 140 A6
Surbiton KT6 195 J2
Welling DA16 158 B1
Douglas Sq, Mord. SM4 184 D6
Douglas St, SW1 33 H2
Douglas Ter, E17
off Penrhyn Av 77 J1
Douglas Way, SE8 133 J7
Doulton Ho, SE11
off Lambeth Wk 26 D6
Doulton Ms, NW6
off Dresden Cl 91 E6
Dounesforth Gdns,
SW18 166 E1
Douro Pl, W8 22 B5
Douro St, E3 114 A2
Douthwaite Sq, E1 29 J1
Dove App, E6 116 B5
Dove Cl, NW7 55 F7
Northolt UB5
off Wayfarer Rd 102 D4
Wallington SM6 201 F7
Dovecot Cl, Pnr. HA5 66 B5
Dovecote Av, N22 75 G3
Dovecote Gdns, SW14
off Avondale Rd 146 D3
Dove Ct, EC2 20 B4
Dovedale Av, Har. HA3 69 F6
Ilford IG5 80 D2
Dovedale Cl, Well. DA16 158 A1
Dovedale Ri, Mitch. CR4 167 J7
Dovedale Rd, SE22 153 E5
Dovedon Cl, N14 58 E2
Dove Ho Gdns, E4 62 A2
Dovehouse Mead, Bark.
IG11 117 G2
Dovehouse St, SW3 31 G3
Dove Ms, SW5 30 C2
Dove Pk, Pnr. HA5 51 G7
Dover Cl, NW2
off Brent Ter 90 A2
Romford RM5 83 J2
Dovercourt Av, Th.Hth.
CR7 187 G4
Dovercourt Est, N1 94 A6
Dovercourt Gdns, Stan.
HA7 53 H5
Dovercourt La, Sutt. SM1 199 F3
Dovercourt Rd, SE22 152 B6
Doverfield Rd, SW2 151 E6
Dover Flats, SE1 36 E2
Dover Gdns, Cars. SM5 199 J3
Dover Ho Rd, SW15 147 G4
Doveridge Gdns, N13 59 H4
Dove Rd, N1 94 A6
Dove Row, E2 112 D1
Dover Pk Dr, SW15 147 H6
Dover Patrol, SE3
off Kidbrooke Way 155 H2
Dover Rd, E12 97 J2
N9 61 F2
SE19 170 A6
Romford RM6 82 E6
Dover St, W1 17 E6
Dover Yd, W1 25 F1
Doves Cl, Brom. BR2 206 B2
Doves Yd, N1 111 G1
Dovet Ct, SW8
off Mursell Est 151 F1
Doveton Rd, S.Croy. CR2 202 A5
Doveton St, E1
off Malcolm Rd 113 F4
Dove Wk, SW1 32 B3
Dowanhill Rd, SE6 172 D1
Dowd Cl, N11
off Nurserymans Rd 58 A2
Dowdeswell Cl, SW15 147 E4
Dowding Pl, Stan. HA7 52 D6
Dowdney Cl, NW5 92 C5
Dowgate Hill, EC4 20 B5
Dowland St, W10 108 B2
Dowlas Est, SE5 36 D7
Dowlas St, SE5 36 D7
Dowlerville Rd, Orp.
BR6 207 J6
Dowman Cl, SW19
off Nelson Gro Rd 185 E1
Downage, NW4 71 J3
Downalong, Bushey
(Bushey Hth) WD23 52 A1
Downbarns Rd, Ruis.
HA4 84 D3
Downbury Ms, SW18
off Merton Rd 148 D6
Down Cl, Nthlt. UB5 102 B2
Downderry Rd, Brom.
BR1 172 D3
Downe Cl, Well. DA16 138 C7
Downe Ho, SE7
off Springfield Gro 135 J6
Downend, SE18
off Moordown 136 E7
Downe Rd, Mitch. CR4 185 J2
Downers Cotts, SW4
off Old Town 150 C4
Downes Cl, Twick. TW1
off St. Margarets Rd 145 E6
Downes Ct, N21 59 G1
Downfield, Wor.Pk. KT4 197 F1
Downfield Cl, W9 6 A6
Down Hall Rd, Kings.T.
KT2 181 G1
DOWNHAM, Brom. BR1 173 F5
Downham La, Brom.
BR1 172 D5
Downham Rd, N1 94 A7
Downham Way, Brom.
BR1 172 D5
Downhills Av, N17 76 A3
Downhills Pk Rd, N17 75 J3
Downhills Way, N17 75 J3
Downhurst Av, NW7 54 D5
Downing Cl, Har. HA2 67 J3
Downing Dr, Grnf. UB6 104 A1
Downing Rd, Dag. RM9 119 F1
Downings, E6 116 D6
Downing St, SW1 26 A3
Downland Cl, N20 57 F1
Downleys Cl, SE9 174 B2
Downman Rd, SE9 156 B3
Down Pl, W6 127 H4
Down Rd, Tedd. TW11 163 E6
Downs, The, SW20 166 A7
Downs Av, Chis. BR7 174 C5
Pinner HA5 67 F6
Downs Br Rd, Beck. BR3 190 D1
Downsbury Ms, SW18
off Merton Rd 148 D5
Downsell Rd, E15 96 C4
Downsfield Rd, E17 77 H6
Downshall Av, Ilf. IG3 81 H6
Downs Hill, Beck. BR3 172 D7
Downshire Hill, NW3 91 G4
Downside, Sun. TW16 178 A1
Twickenham TW1 162 C3
Downside Cl, SW19 167 F6
Downside Cres, NW3 91 H5
W13 104 D4
Downside Rd, Sutt. SM2 199 G6
Downside Wk, Brent. TW8
off Sidney Gdns 125 F6
Northolt UB5 103 F3
Downs La, E5
off Downs Rd 94 E4
Downs Pk Rd, E5 94 D5
E8 94 C5
Downs Rd, E5 94 D4
Beckenham BR3 190 B2
Enfield EN1 44 B4
Thornton Heath CR7 187 J1
Down St, W1 24 D2
West Molesey KT8 179 G5
Down St Ms, W1 24 D2
Downs Vw, Islw. TW7 144 C1
Downsview Gdns, SE19 169 H7
Downsview Rd, SE19 169 J7
Downsway, Orp. BR6 207 H5
Downton Av, SW2 169 E2
Downtown Rd, SE16 133 H2
Down Way, Nthlt. UB5 102 B3
Dowrey St, N1
off Richmond Av 111 G1
Dowsett Rd, N17 76 C2
Dowson Cl, SE5 152 A4
Doyce St, SE1 27 J3
Doyle Gdns, NW10 107 G1
Doyle Rd, SE25 188 D4
D'Oyley St, SW1 32 B1
Doynton St, N19 92 B2
Draco Gate, SW15
off Erpingham Rd 147 J3
Draco St, SE17 35 J5

Dragonfly Cl, E13 115 H3
Dragon Rd, SE15 36 D6
Dragoon Rd, SE8 133 J5
Dragor Rd, NW10 106 C4
Drake Cl, SE16
off Middleton Dr 133 G2
Drake Ct, SE19 170 C5
W12 127 J2
Harrow HA2 85 F1
Drake Cres, SE28 118 C6
Drakefell Rd, SE4 153 G2
SE14 153 G2
Drakefield Rd, SW17 168 A3
Drake Ho, SW8
off St. George Wf 34 A4
Drakeley Ct, N5 93 H4
Drake Ms, Brom. BR2 191 J4
Drake Rd, SE4 154 A3
Chessington KT9 196 A5
Croydon CR0 187 F7
Harrow HA2 85 F2
Mitcham CR4 186 A6
Drakes Ctyd, NW6 90 C7
Drake St, WC1 18 C2
Enfield EN2 44 A1
Drakes Wk, E6 116 C1
Drakewood Rd, SW16 168 D7
Draper Cl, Belv. DA17 139 F4
Isleworth TW7 144 A2
Draper Ho, SE1 35 H1
Draper Pl, N1
off Dagmar Ter 111 H1
Drapers' Ct, SW11
off Lurline Gdns 150 A1
Drapers Rd, E15 96 D4
N17 76 C3
Enfield EN2 43 H2
Drappers Way, SE16 37 J1
Draven Cl, Brom. BR2 191 F7
Drawdock Rd, SE10 134 D1
Drawell Cl, SE18 137 H5
Drax Av, SW20 165 H7
Draxmont, SW19 166 B6
Draycot Rd, E11 79 H6
Surbiton KT6 196 A1
Draycott Av, SW3 31 H1
Harrow HA3 69 E6
Draycott Cl, NW2 90 A3
SE5 *off Caspian St* 132 A7
Harrow HA3 69 E6
Draycott Ms, SW6
off New Kings Rd 148 C2
Draycott Pl, SW3 31 J2
Draycott Ter, SW3 32 A1
Drayford Cl, W9 108 C4
Dray Gdns, SW2 151 F5
Draymans Ms, SE15
off Chadwick Rd 152 C2
Draymans Way, Islw.
TW7 144 C3
Drayside Ms, Sthl. UB2
off Kingston Rd 123 F2
Drayson Ms, W8 128 D2
Drayton Av, W13 104 D7
Loughton IG10 48 C6
Orpington BR6 207 E1
Drayton Br Rd, W7 104 C7
W13 104 C7
Drayton Cl, Houns. TW4 143 F5
Ilford IG1 99 G1
Drayton Gdns, N21 43 H7
SW10 30 D3
W13 104 D7
West Drayton UB7 120 B2
Drayton Grn, W13 104 D7
Drayton Grn Rd, W13 104 E7
Drayton Gro, W13 104 D7
Drayton Pk, N5 93 G5
Drayton Pk Ms, N5
off Drayton Pk 93 G5
Drayton Rd, E11 96 D1
N17 76 B2
NW10 107 F1
W13 104 D7
Borehamwood WD6 38 A4
Croydon CR0 201 H2
Drayton Waye, Har. HA3 69 E6
Dreadnought Cl, SW19 185 G2
Dresden Cl, NW6 91 E6
Dresden Ho, SE11
off Lambeth Wk 34 D1
Dresden Rd, N19 92 C1
Dressington Av, SE4 154 A6
Drew Av, NW7 56 B6
Drew Gdns, Grnf. UB6 86 C6
Drew Rd, E16 136 B1
Drewstead Rd, SW16 168 D2
Driffield Rd, E3 113 H2
Drift, The, Brom. BR2 206 A3
Drift Way, Rich. TW10 163 J1
Driftway, The, Mitch.
CR4 186 A1
Drinkwater Rd, Har. HA2 85 H2
Drive, The, E4 46 D7
E17 78 B4
E18 79 G4
N3 56 D7
N6 73 J5
N11 58 C6
NW10
off Longstone Av 107 F1
NW11 72 B7
SW6 *off Fulham Rd* 148 B2
SW16 187 F3
SW20 165 J7
W3 106 C6
Barking IG11 99 J7
Barnet (High Barn.)
EN5 40 B3
Barnet (New Barn.)
EN5 41 F6
Beckenham BR3 190 A2
Bexley DA5 158 C6
Buckhurst Hill IG9 47 J7
Chislehurst BR7 193 J3
Chislehurst (Scad.Pk)
BR7 193 H1
Edgware HA8 54 A5
Enfield EN2 44 A1
Epsom KT19 197 F6
Erith DA8 139 H7
Feltham TW14 142 C7
Harrow HA2 67 G7
Hounslow TW3 144 A2
Ilford IG1 98 C1
Isleworth TW7 144 A2
Kingston upon Thames
KT2 164 C7
Loughton IG10 48 B3
Morden SM4 185 G5
Orpington BR6 207 J2
Romford (Coll.Row)
RM5 83 J1
Sidcup DA14 176 B3
Surbiton KT6 181 H7
Thornton Heath CR7 188 A4
Wembley HA9 88 C2
West Wickham BR4 190 D7
Driveway, The, E17
off Hoe St 78 B6
Droitwich Cl, SE26 170 D3
Dromey Gdns, Har. HA3 52 C7
Dromore Rd, SW15 148 B6
Dronfield Gdns, Dag.
RM8 100 C5
Droop St, W10 108 B4
Drovers Pl, SE15 133 E7
Drovers Rd, S.Croy.
CR2 202 A5
Droveway, Loug. IG10 49 E2
Druce Rd, SE21 152 B6
Druid St, SE1 29 E3
Druids Way, Brom. BR2 190 D4
Drumaline Ridge, Wor.Pk.
KT4 197 E2
Drummond Cres, NW1 9 H3
Drummond Dr, Stan.
HA7 52 C7
Drummond Gate, SW1 33 J3
Drummond Pl, Twick.
TW1 144 E6
Drummond Rd, E11 79 H6
SE16 132 E3
Croydon CR0 201 J2
Drummonds, The, Buck.H.
IG9 63 H2
Drummonds Pl, Rich.
TW9 145 H4
Drummond St, NW1 9 F5
Drum St, E1 21 G3
Drury Cres, Croy. CR0 201 G2
Drury La, WC2 18 B4
Drury Rd, Har. HA1 67 J7
Drury Way, NW10 88 D5
Drury Way Ind Est, NW10 88 C5
Dryad St, SW15 148 A3
Dryburgh Gdns, NW9 70 A3
Dryburgh Rd, SW15 147 H3
Dryden Av, W7 104 C6
Dryden Cl, SW4 150 D5
Ilford IG6 65 J6
Dryden Ct, SE11 35 F2
Dryden Rd, SW19 167 F6
Enfield EN1 44 B6
Harrow HA3 68 C1
Welling DA16 157 H1
Dryden St, WC2 18 B4
Dryfield Cl, NW10 88 C6
Dryfield Rd, Edg. HA8 54 C6
Dryfield Wk, SE8
off New King St 134 A6
Dryhill Rd, Belv. DA17 139 F6
Dryland Av, Orp. BR6 207 J4
Drylands Rd, N8 75 E6
Drysdale Av, E4 46 B7
Drysdale Pl, N1 12 E3
Drysdale St, N1 12 E4
Dublin Av, E8 112 D1
Du Burstow Ter, W7 124 B2
Ducal St, E2 13 G4
Du Cane Cl, W12 107 J6
Du Cane Ct, SW17 168 A1
Du Cane Rd, W12 107 F6
Duchess Cl, N11 58 B5
Sutton SM1 199 F4
Duchess Gro, Buck.H. IG9 63 H2
Duchess Ms, W1 16 E2
Duchess of Bedford's Wk,
W8 128 D2
Duchess St, W1 16 E2
Duchy St, SE1 27 F1
Ducie Ho, SE7
off Springfield Gro 135 J6
Ducie St, SW4 151 F4
Duckett Ms, N4
off Duckett Rd 75 H6
Duckett Rd, N4 75 H6
Duckett St, E1 113 G4
Duck La, W1 17 H4
Duck Lees La, Enf. EN3 45 H4
DUCKS ISLAND, Barn.
EN5 40 A6
Ducks Wk, Twick. TW1 145 F5
Du Cros Dr, Stan. HA7 53 G6
Du Cros Rd, W3
off The Vale 126 E1
Dudden Hill La, NW10 89 F4
Duddington Cl, SE9 174 A4
Dudley Av, Har. HA3 69 F3
Dudley Ct, NW11 72 C4
Dudley Dr, Mord. SM4 184 B7
Ruislip HA4 84 B5
Dudley Gdns, W13 125 E2
Harrow HA2 86 A1
Dudley Ho, W2
off North Wf Rd 14 E2
Dudley Ms, SW2
off Bascombe St 151 G6
Dudley Pl, Hayes UB3 121 G4
Dudley Rd, E17 78 A2
N3 72 E2
NW6 108 B2
SW19 166 D6
Harrow HA2 85 J2
Ilford IG1 99 E4
Kingston upon Thames
KT1 181 J3
Richmond TW9 145 J2
Southall UB2 122 D2
Walton-on-Thames
KT12 178 A6
Dudley St, W2 14 E2
Dudlington Rd, E5 95 F2
Dudmaston Ms, SW3 31 F3
Dudrich Cl, N11 57 J6
Dudrich Ms, SE22
off Melbourne Gro 152 C5
Dudsbury Rd, Sid. DA14 176 B6
Dudset La, Houns. TW5 142 A1
Duffell Ho, SE11 34 D3
Dufferin Av, EC1 12 B6
Dufferin St, EC1 12 A6
Duffield Cl, Har. HA1 68 C5
Duffield Dr, N15
off Copperfield Dr 76 C4
Duff St, E14 114 B6
Dufour's Pl, W1 17 G4
Dugard Way, SE11 35 G1
Duggan Dr, Chis. BR7 174 B5
Dugolly Av, Wem. HA9 88 B3
Duke Gdns, Ilf. IG6
off Duke Rd 81 G4
Duke Humphrey Rd, SE3 155 E1
Duke of Cambridge Cl,
Twick. TW2 144 A6
Duke of Edinburgh Rd,
Sutt. SM1 199 G2
Duke of Wellington Av,
SE18 137 E3
Duke of Wellington Pl,
SW1 24 C3
Duke of York Sq, SW3 32 A2
Duke of York St, SW1 25 G1
Duke Rd, W4 126 D5
Ilford IG6 81 G4
Dukes Av, N3 72 E1
N10 74 C3
W4 126 D5
Edgware HA8 53 J6
Harrow HA1 68 B4
Harrow (N.Har.) HA2 67 F6
Hounslow TW4 142 E4
Kingston upon Thames
KT2 163 F4
New Malden KT3 183 F3
Northolt UB5 85 E7
Richmond TW10 163 F4
Dukes Cl, Hmptn. TW12 161 F5
Dukes Ct, E6 116 D1
Dukes Gate, W4
off Acton La 126 C4
Dukes Grn Av, Felt.
TW14 142 A5
Dukes Head Yd, N6
off Highgate High St 92 B1
Duke Shore Pl, E14
off Narrow St 113 J7
Duke Shore Wf, E14
off Narrow St 113 J7
Dukes La, W8 128 D2
Duke's Meadows, W4 146 D1
Dukes Ms, N10
off Dukes Av 74 B3
Duke's Ms, W1 16 C3
Dukes Orchard, Bex. DA5 177 J1
Duke's Pas, E17 78 C4
Dukes Pl, EC3 21 E4
Dukes Rd, E6 116 D1
W3 106 A5
Duke's Rd, WC1 9 J4
Dukesthorpe Rd, SE26 171 G4
Duke St, SW1 25 G1
W1 16 C3
Richmond TW9 145 G4
Sutton SM1 199 G4
Duke St Hill, SE1 28 C1
Dukes Way, W.Wick. BR4 205 E3
Duke's Yd, W1 16 C5
Dulas St, N4 93 F1
Dulford St, W11 108 B7
Dulka Rd, SW11 149 J5
Dulverton Rd, SE9 175 F2
Ruislip HA4 84 A1
DULWICH, SE21 152 B7
★ **Dulwich Coll Picture Gall**, SE21 152 B7
Dulwich Common, SE21 170 B1
SE22 170 B1
Dulwich Lawn Cl, SE22
off Colwell Rd 152 C5
Dulwich Oaks, The,
SE21 170 B3
Dulwich Ri Gdns, SE22
off Lordship La 152 C5
Dulwich Rd, SE24 151 G5
Dulwich Village, SE21 152 B6
Dulwich Wd Av, SE19 170 B4
Dulwich Wd Pk, SE19 170 B4
Dumbarton Rd, SW2 151 E6
Dumbleton Cl, Kings.T. KT1
off Gloucester Rd 182 B1
Dumbreck Rd, SE9 156 C4
Dumont Rd, N16 94 B3
Dumpton Pl, NW1
off Gloucester Av 92 A7
Dunbar Av, SW16 187 G2
Beckenham BR3 189 H4
Dagenham RM10 101 G3
Dunbar Cl, Hayes UB4 102 A5
Dunbar Ct, Sutt. SM1 199 G5
Dunbar Gdns, Dag.
RM10 101 G5
Dunbar Rd, E7 97 G6
N22 75 G1
New Malden KT3 182 C4
Dunbar St, SE27 169 J3
Dunblane Cl, Edg. HA8
off Tayside Dr 54 B2
Dunblane Rd, SE9 156 B3
Dunboyne Rd, NW3 91 J5
Dunbridge Ho, SW15
off Highcliffe Dr 147 F6
Dunbridge St, E2 13 J5
Duncan Cl, Barn. EN5 41 F4
Duncan Gro, W3 106 E6
Duncannon St, WC2 18 A6
Duncan Rd, E8 112 E1
Richmond TW9 145 H4
Duncan St, N1 11 G1
Duncan Ter, N1 11 G2
Dunch St, E1
off Watney St 113 E6
Duncombe Hill, SE23 153 H7
Duncombe Rd, N19 92 D1
Duncrievie Rd, SE13 154 D6
Duncroft, SE18 137 H7
Dundalk Rd, SE4 153 H3
Dundas Gdns, W.Mol.
KT8 179 H3
Dundas Rd, SE15 153 F2
Dundee Ho, W9 6 C3
Dundee Rd, E13 115 H2
SE25 188 E5
Dundee St, E1 132 E1
Dundee Way, Enf. EN3 45 H3
Dundela Gdns, Wor.Pk.
KT4 197 H4
Dundonald Cl, E6
off Northumberland Rd 116 B6
Dundonald Rd, NW10 108 A1
SW19 166 B7

Dunedin Ho, E16 *off Manwood St* 136 C1
Dunedin Rd, E10 96 B3
Ilford IG1 99 F1
Dunedin Way, Hayes UB4 102 C4
Dunelm Gro, SE27 169 J4
Dunelm St, E1 113 G6
Dunfield Gdns, SE6 172 B4
Dunfield Rd, SE6 172 B5
Dunford Rd, N7 93 F4
Dungarvan Av, SW15 147 G4
Dunheved Cl, Th.Hth. CR7 187 G6
Dunheved Rd N, Th.Hth. CR7 187 G6
Dunheved Rd S, Th.Hth. CR7 187 G6
Dunheved Rd W, Th.Hth. CR7 187 G6
Dunhill Pt, SW15 *off Dilton Gdns* 165 H1
Dunholme Grn, N9 60 C3
Dunholme La, N9 *off Dunholme Rd* 60 C3
Dunholme Rd, N9 60 C3
Dunkeld Rd, SE25 188 A4
Dagenham RM8 100 B2
Dunkery Rd, SE9 174 A4
Dunkirk St, SE27 169 J4
Dunlace Rd, E5 95 F4
Dunleary Cl, Houns. TW4 143 F7
Dunley Dr, Croy. (New Adgtn) CR0 204 B7
Dunlin Ho, W13 104 C4
Dunloe Av, N17 76 A3
Dunloe St, E2 13 F2
Dunlop Pl, SE16 29 G6
Dunmore Pt, E2 13 F4
Dunmore Rd, NW6 108 B1
SW20 183 J1
Dunmow Cl, Felt. TW13 160 D4
Loughton IG10 48 B6
Romford RM6 82 C5
Dunmow Ho, Dag. RM9 118 B1
Dunmow Rd, E15 96 D4
Dunmow Wk, N1 *off Popham St* 111 J1
Dunnage Cres, SE16 *off Plough Way* 133 H4
Dunn Mead, NW9 *off Field Mead* 55 F7
Dunnock Cl, N9 61 G1
Borehamwood WD6 38 A4
Dunnock Rd, E6 116 B6
Dunns Pas, WC1 18 B3
Dunn St, E8 94 C5
Dunollie Pl, NW5 *off Dunollie Rd* 92 C5
Dunollie Rd, NW5 92 C5
Dunoon Rd, SE23 153 F7
Dunraven Dr, Enf. EN2 43 G2
Dunraven Rd, W12 127 G1
Dunraven St, W1 16 A5
Dunsany Rd, W14 128 A3
Dunsfold Way, Croy. (New Adgtn) CR0 204 B7
Dunsford Way, SW15 *off Dover Pk Dr* 147 H6
Dunsmore Cl, Hayes UB4 102 D4
Dunsmore Rd, Walt. KT12 178 B6
Dunsmure Rd, N16 94 B1
Dunspring La, Ilf. IG5 80 E2
Dunstable Ms, W1 16 C1
Dunstable Rd, Rich. TW9 145 H4
West Molesey KT8 179 F4
Dunstall Rd, SW20 165 H6
Dunstall Way, W.Mol. KT8 179 H3
Dunstall Welling Est, Well. DA16 *off Leigh Pl* 158 B2
Dunstan Cl, N2 *off Thomas More Way* 73 F3
Dunstan Ho, E1 *off Stepney Grn* 113 F5
Dunstan Rd, NW11 90 C1
Dunstans Gro, SE22 152 E6
Dunstans Rd, SE22 152 D7
Dunster Av, Mord. SM4 198 A1
Dunster Cl, Barn. EN5 40 A4
Romford RM5 83 J2
Dunster Ct, EC3 20 D5
Borehamwood WD6 *off Kensington Way* 38 D3
Dunster Dr, NW9 88 C1
Dunster Gdns, NW6 90 C7
Dunsterville Way, SE1 28 C4
Dunster Way, Har. HA2 85 E3
Wallington SM6 *off Helios Rd* 200 A1
Dunston Rd, E8 112 C1
SW11 150 A2
Dunston St, E8 112 C1
Dunton Cl, Surb. KT6 195 H1
Dunton Rd, E10 78 B7
SE1 37 F3
Duntshill Rd, SW18 167 E1
Dunvegan Cl, W.Mol. KT8 179 H4
Dunvegan Rd, SE9 156 C4
Dunwich Rd, Bexh. DA7 159 F1
Dunworth Ms, W11 *off Portobello Rd* 108 C6
Duplex Ride, SW1 24 A4
Dupont Rd, SW20 184 A2
Duppas Av, Croy. CR0 *off Violet La* 201 H4
Duppas Hill La, Croy. CR0 *off Duppas Hill Rd* 201 H4
Duppas Hill Rd, Croy. CR0 201 H4
Duppas Hill Ter, Croy. CR0 201 H3
Duppas Rd, Croy. CR0 201 G3
Dupree Rd, SE7 135 H5
Dura Den Cl, Beck. BR3 172 B7
Durand Cl, Cars. SM5 199 J1
Durand Gdns, SW9 151 F1
Durands Wk, SE16 133 J2
Durand Way, NW10 88 C7
Durants Pk Av, Enf. EN3 45 G4
Durants Rd, Enf. EN3 45 F4
Durant St, E2 13 H3
Durban Gdns, Dag. RM10 101 J7
Durban Rd, E15 114 E3
E17 77 J1
N17 60 B6
SE27 169 J4
Beckenham BR3 189 J2
Ilford IG2 99 H1
Durbin Rd, Chess. KT9 195 H4
Durdans Rd, Sthl. UB1 103 F6
Durell Gdns, Dag. RM9 100 D5
Durell Rd, Dag. RM9 100 D5
Durfey Pl, SE5 36 C7
Durford Cres, SW15 165 G1
Durham Av, Brom. BR2 191 F4
Hounslow TW5 123 F5
Woodford Green IG8 64 A5
Durham Cl, SW20 *off Durham Rd* 183 H2
Durham Hill, Brom. BR1 173 F4
Durham Ho St, WC2 18 B6
Durham Pl, SW3 31 J4
Ilford IG1 *off Eton Rd* 99 F4
Durham Ri, SE18 137 F5
Durham Rd, E12 98 A4
E16 115 E4
N2 73 H3
N7 93 F2
N9 60 D2
SW20 183 H1
W5 125 G3
Borehamwood WD6 38 C3
Bromley BR2 191 F3
Dagenham RM10 101 J5
Feltham TW14 142 C7
Harrow HA1 67 H5
Sidcup DA14 176 B5
Durham Row, E1 113 H5
Durham St, SE11 34 C4
Durham Ter, W2 14 A3
Durham Wf Dr, Brent. TW8 *off Commerce Rd* 125 F7
Durham Yd, E2 *off Teesdale St* 112 E3
Durley Av, Pnr. HA5 67 E7
Durley Rd, N16 76 B7
Durlston Rd, E5 94 D2
Kingston upon Thames KT2 163 H6
Durnell Way, Loug. IG10 48 D3
Durnford St, N15 76 B5
SE10 *off Greenwich Ch St* 134 C6
Durning Rd, SE19 170 A5
Durnsford Av, SW19 166 D2
Durnsford Ct, Enf. EN3 *off Enstone Rd* 45 H3
Durnsford Rd, N11 74 D1
SW19 166 D2
Durrant Way, Orp. BR6 207 G5
Durrell Rd, SW6 148 C1
Durrington Av, SW20 183 J1
Durrington Pk Rd, SW20 165 J7
Durrington Rd, E5 95 H4
Durrington Twr, SW8 *off Westbury St* 150 C2
Dursley Cl, SE3 155 J2
Dursley Gdns, SE3 156 A1
Dursley Rd, SE3 155 J2
Durward St, E1 112 E5
Durweston Ms, W1 16 A1
Durweston St, W1 16 A1
Dury Rd, Barn. EN5 40 C1
Dutch Barn Cl, Stai. (Stanw.) TW19 140 A6
Dutch Gdns, Kings.T. KT2 164 B6
Dutch Yd, SW18 *off Wandsworth High St* 148 D5
Dutton St, SE10 154 C1
Duxberry Cl, Brom. BR2 *off Southborough La* 192 B5
Duxford Ho, SE2 *off Wolvercote Rd* 138 D2
Dwight Ct, SW6 *off Burlington Rd* 148 B2
Dye Ho La, E3 114 A1
Dyer's Bldgs, EC1 19 E2
Dyers Hall Rd, E11 96 E1
Dyers La, SW15 147 H4
Dykes Way, Brom. BR2 191 F3
Dylan Rd, SE24 151 H4
Belvedere DA17 139 G3
Dylways, SE5 152 A4
Dymchurch Cl, Ilf. IG5 80 D2
Orpington BR6 207 H4
Dymes Path, SW19 *off Queensmere Rd* 166 A2
Dymock St, SW6 148 E3
Dymond Est, SW17 *off Glenburnie Rd* 167 H3
Dyneley Rd, SE12 173 J4
Dyne Rd, NW6 90 C7
Dynevor Rd, N16 94 B3
Richmond TW10 145 H5
Dynham Rd, NW6 90 D7
Dyott St, WC1 18 A3
Dysart Av, Kings.T. KT2 163 F5
Dysart St, EC2 12 C6
Dyson Rd, E11 79 E6
E15 97 F6
Dysons Rd, N18 61 E5

E

Eade Rd, N4 75 J7
Eagans Cl, N2 73 G3
Eagle Av, Rom. RM6 82 E6
Eagle Cl, SE16 *off Varcoe Rd* 133 F5
Enfield EN3 45 F4
Wallington SM6 201 E6
Eagle Ct, EC1 19 G1
Eagle Dr, NW9 71 E2
Eagle Hts, SW11 *off Bramlands Cl* 149 H3
Eagle Hill, SE19 170 A6
Eagle Ho Ms, SW4 *off Narbonne Av* 150 C5
Eagle La, E11 79 G4
Eagle Lo, NW11 72 C7
Eagle Ms, N1 *off Tottenham Rd* 94 B6
Eagle Pl, SW1 17 G6
SW7 30 D3
Eagle Rd, Houns. TW6 *off Elmdon Rd* 141 J3
Wembley HA0 87 G7
Eaglesfield Rd, SE18 137 E7
Eagle St, WC1 18 C2
Eagle Ter, Wdf.Grn. IG8 63 H7
Eagle Trd Est, Mitch. CR4 185 J6
Eagle Wf Rd, N1 12 A1
Eagling Cl, E3 *off Rounton Rd* 114 A3
Ealdham Sq, SE9 155 J4
EALING, W5 105 F7
Ealing Bdy Shop Cen, W5 105 G7
Ealing Cl, Borwd. WD6 38 D1
★ **Ealing Common**, W5 125 H1
Ealing Common, W5 105 J7
Ealing Downs Ct, Grnf. UB6 *off Perivale La* 104 D3
Ealing Grn, W5 125 G1
Ealing Pk Gdns, W5 125 F4
Ealing Rd, Brent. TW8 125 G5
Northolt UB5 85 G7
Wembley HA0 105 G1
Ealing Village, W5 105 H6
Eamont St, NW8 7 G1
Eardley Cres, SW5 128 D5
Eardley Pt, SE18 *off Wilmount St* 137 E4
Eardley Rd, SW16 168 C5
Belvedere DA17 139 G5
Earhart Way, Houns. TW4 142 A3
Earl Cl, N11 58 B5
Earldom Rd, SW15 147 J4
Earle Gdns, Kings.T. KT2 163 H6
Earlham Gro, E7 97 F5
N22 59 F7
Earlham St, WC2 17 J4
Earl Ri, SE18 137 G4
Earl Rd, SW14 146 C4
EARLS COURT, SW5 128 C5
★ **Earls Court Exhib Cen**, SW5 128 D5
Earls Ct Gdns, SW5 30 A2
Earls Ct Rd, SW5 128 D4
W8 128 D4
Earls Ct Sq, SW5 30 A3
Earls Cres, Har. HA1 68 B4
Earlsdown Ho, Bark. IG11 *off Wheelers Cross* 117 G2
Earlsferry Way, N1 93 F7
EARLSFIELD, SW18 167 F1
Earlsfield Ho, Kings.T. KT2 *off Kingsgate Rd* 181 G1
Earlsfield Rd, SW18 167 F1
Earlshall Rd, SE9 156 C4
Earls Ho, Rich. TW9 *off Strand Dr* 126 B7
Earlsmead, Har. HA2 85 F4
Earlsmead Rd, N15 76 C5
NW10 107 J2
Earl's Path, Loug. IG10 47 J2
Earls Ter, W8 128 C3
Earlsthorpe Ms, SW12 150 A6
Earlsthorpe Rd, SE26 171 G4
Earlstoke St, EC1 11 G3
Earlston Gro, E9 113 E1
Earl St, EC2 20 D1
Earls Wk, W8 128 D3
Dagenham RM8 100 B4
Earls Way, Orp. BR6 *off Station Rd* 207 J2
Earlswood Av, Th.Hth. CR7 187 G5
Earlswood Gdns, Ilf. IG5 80 D3
Earlswood St, SE10 135 E5
Early Ms, NW1 *off Arlington Rd* 110 B1
Earnshaw St, WC2 17 J3
Earsby St, W14 128 B4
Easby Cres, Mord. SM4 185 E6
Easebourne Rd, Dag. RM8 100 C5
Easedale Ho, Islw. TW7 *off Summerwood Rd* 144 C5
Eashing Pt, SW15 *off Wanborough Dr* 165 H1
Easley's Ms, W1 16 C3
East 10 Enterprise Pk, E10 *off Argall Way* 95 H1
EAST ACTON, W3 126 D1
East Acton La, W3 106 E7
East Arbour St, E1 113 G6
East Av, E12 98 B7
E17 78 B4
Hayes UB3 121 J2
Southall UB1 103 F7
Wallington SM6 201 F5
East Bk, N16 76 B7
Eastbank Rd, Hmptn. (Hmptn H.) TW12 161 J5
EAST BARNET, Barn. EN4 41 H6
East Barnet Rd, Barn. EN4 41 H6
Eastbourne Av, W3 106 D6
Eastbourne Gdns, SW14 146 C3
Eastbourne Ms, W2 14 D3
Eastbourne Rd, E6 116 D3
E15 115 E1
N15 76 B6
SW17 168 A6
W4 126 C6
Brentford TW8 125 F5
Feltham TW13 160 D2
Eastbourne Ter, W2 14 D3
Eastbournia Av, N9 61 E3
Eastbrook Av, N9 45 F7
Dagenham RM10 101 J4
Eastbrook Rd, SE3 135 H7
Eastbury Av, Bark. IG11 117 H1
Enfield EN1 44 B1
Eastbury Ct, Bark. IG11 117 H1
Eastbury Gro, W4 127 E5
★ **Eastbury Manor Ho**, Bark. IG11 117 J1
Eastbury Rd, E6 116 D4
Kingston upon Thames KT2 163 H7
Orpington BR5 193 G6
Eastbury Sq, Bark. IG11 117 J1
Eastbury Ter, E1 113 G4
Eastcastle St, W1 17 F3
Eastcheap, EC3 20 C5
East Churchfield Rd, W3 126 D1
Eastchurch Rd, Houns. (Lon.Hthrw Air.) TW6 141 H2
East Cl, W5 106 A4
Barnet EN4 42 A4
Greenford UB6 103 J2

Eastcombe Av, SE7 . . . . . . **135** H6
EASTCOTE, Pnr. HA5 . . . . . **66** C6
Eastcote, Orp. BR6 . . . . . . **207** J1
Eastcote Av, Grnf. UB6 . . . . **86** D5
Harrow HA2 . . . . **85** H2
West Molesey KT8 . . . . **179** F5
Eastcote La, Har. HA2 . . . . **85** G3
Northolt UB5 . . . . **85** G7
Eastcote La N, Nthlt. UB5 . **85** F6
Eastcote Pl, Pnr. HA5 . . . . . **66** B6
Eastcote Rd, Har. HA2 . . . . **85** J3
Pinner HA5 . . . . **66** D5
Pinner (Eastcote Vill.) HA5 . . . . **66** A6
Welling DA16 . . . . **157** G2
Eastcote St, SW9 . . . . **151** F2
Eastcote Vw, Pnr. HA5 . . . . **66** C4
EASTCOTE VILLAGE, Pnr. HA5 . . . . **66** B5
Eastcourt, Sun. TW16 . . . . **178** C2
East Ct, Wem. HA0 . . . . **87** F2
East Cres, N11 . . . . **57** J4
Enfield EN1 . . . . **44** C5
Eastcroft Rd, Epsom KT19 . . . . **197** E7
East Cross Cen, E15 . . . . . . **96** A6
East Cross Route, E3 . . . . . **95** J7
E9 . . . . **95** J7
Eastdown Pk, SE13 . . . . . **154** D4
East Duck Lees La, Enf. EN3 . . . . **45** H4
EAST DULWICH, SE22 . . . **152** D6
East Dulwich Gro, SE22 . . **152** B6
East Dulwich Rd, SE15 . . . **152** C4
SE22 . . . . **152** C4
East End Rd, N2 . . . . **73** F3
N3 . . . . **72** D2
East End Way, Pnr. HA5 . . . **67** E3
East Entrance, Dag. RM10 . . . . **119** H2
Eastern Av, E11 . . . . **79** J6
Ilford IG2, IG4 . . . . **80** B6
Pinner HA5 . . . . **66** D7
Romford RM6 . . . . **82** C4
Eastern Av W, Rom. RM1, RM5, RM6, RM7 . . . . . . **82** E4
Eastern Gateway, E16 . . . . **115** J7
Eastern Ind Est, Erith DA18 . . . . **139** G2
Eastern Perimeter Rd, Houns. (Lon.Hthrw Air.) TW6 . . . . **141** J3
Eastern Quay Apts, E16 *off Rayleigh Rd* **135** H1
Eastern Rd, E13 . . . . **115** H2
E17 . . . . **78** C5
N2 . . . . **73** J3
N22 . . . . **74** E1
SE4 . . . . **154** A4
Eastern Rbt, Ilf. IG1 . . . . . . **99** F2
Easternville Gdns, Ilf. IG2 . . . . **81** F6
Eastern Way, SE2 . . . . **138** D1
SE28 . . . . **138** A2
Belvedere DA17 . . . . . . **139** H2
Erith DA18 . . . . **138** D1
East Ferry Rd, E14 . . . . **134** B3
Eastfield Cotts, Hayes UB3 . . . . **121** H5
Eastfield Gdns, Dag. RM10 . . . . **101** G4
Eastfield Rd, E17 . . . . **78** A4
N8 . . . . **74** E3
Dagenham RM9, RM10 . . . . **101** G4
Eastfields, Pnr. HA5 . . . . . . **66** C5
Eastfields Av, SW18 . . . . . **148** D4
Eastfields Rd, W3 . . . . **106** C5
Mitcham CR4 . . . . **186** A2
Eastfield St, E14 . . . . **113** H5
EAST FINCHLEY, N2 . . . . . . **73** G4
East Gdns, SW17 . . . . **167** H6
Eastgate Business Pk, E10 . . . . **95** H1
Eastgate Cl, SE28 . . . . **118** D6
Eastglade, Pnr. HA5 . . . . . . **67** E3
EAST HAM, E6 . . . . **116** B2
Eastham Cl, Barn. EN5 . . . . **40** B5
East Ham Ind Est, E6 . . . . **116** B4
East Ham Manor Way, E6 . . . . **116** D6
East Ham Mkt Hall, E6 *off Myrtle Rd* **116** B1
★ **East Ham Nature Reserve & Visitor Cen**, E6 *off Norman Rd* **116** C4
East Harding St, EC4 . . . . . **19** F3
East Heath Rd, NW3 . . . . . . **91** G3
East Hill, SW18 . . . . **149** E5
Wembley HA9 . . . . **88** A2
Eastholm, NW11 . . . . **73** E4
Eastholme, Hayes UB3 . . . **122** A1
East India Dock Rd, E14 . . **114** A6
East India Way, Croy. CR0 . . . . **202** C1
Eastlake Ho, NW8 *off Frampton St* **7** F6
Eastlake Rd, SE5 . . . . **151** H2
Eastlands Cres, SE21 . . . . **152** C6
East La, SE16 . . . . **29** H4
Kingston upon Thames KT1 *off High St* **181** G3
Wembley HA0, HA9 . . . . **87** G3
East La Business Pk, Wem. HA9 . . . . **87** G3
Eastlea Ms, E16 *off Desford Rd* **115** E4
Eastleigh Av, Har. HA2 . . . . **85** H2
Eastleigh Cl, NW2 . . . . **89** E3
Sutton SM2 . . . . **199** E7
Eastleigh Rd, E17 . . . . **77** J2
Bexleyheath DA7 . . . . . **159** J2
Hounslow (Lon.Hthrw Air.) TW6 *off Cranford La* **141** J3
Eastleigh Wk, SW15 . . . . . **147** G7
Eastleigh Way, Felt. TW14 . . . . **160** A1
Eastman Rd, W3 . . . . **126** D1
East Mascalls, SE7 *off Mascalls Rd* **135** J6
East Mead, Ruis. HA4 . . . . . **84** D3
Eastmead Av, Grnf. UB6 . . **103** H3
Eastmead Cl, Brom. BR1 . **192** B2
Eastmearn Rd, SE21 . . . . . **169** J2
EAST MOLESEY, KT8 . . . . **180** A4
Eastmont Rd, Esher KT10 . . . . **194** B2
Eastmoor Pl, SE7 *off Eastmoor St* **136** A3
Eastmoor St, SE7 . . . . **136** A3
East Mt St, E1 . . . . **113** E5
Eastney Rd, Croy. CR0 . . . **201** H1
Eastney St, SE10 . . . . **134** D5
Eastnor Rd, SE9 . . . . **175** F1
Easton Gdns, Borwd. WD6 . . . . **38** D4
Easton St, WC1 . . . . **10** E4
East Pk Cl, Rom. RM6 . . . . **82** D5
East Parkside, SE10 . . . . . **135** E2
East Pas, EC1 . . . . **19** H1
East Pier, E1 *off Wapping High St* . . **132** E1
East Pl, SE27 *off Pilgrim Hill* **169** J4
East Pt, SE1 . . . . **37** H3
East Poultry Av, EC1 . . . . . . **19** G2
East Ramp, Houns. (Lon.Hthrw Air.) TW6 . . **140** E1
East Rd, E15 . . . . **115** G1
N1 . . . . **12** B4
SW3 . . . . **32** B4
SW19 . . . . **167** F6
Barnet EN4 . . . . **58** A1
Edgware HA8 . . . . **70** B1
Feltham TW14 . . . . **141** G7
Kingston upon Thames KT2 . . . . **181** H1
Romford (Chad.Hth) RM6 . . . . **82** E5
Welling DA16 . . . . **158** B2
West Drayton UB7 . . . . **120** C4
East Rochester Way, SE9 . **157** H4
Bexley DA5 . . . . **158** D6
Sidcup DA15 . . . . **157** H4
East Row, E11 . . . . **79** G6
W10 . . . . **108** B4
Eastry Av, Brom. BR2 . . . . **191** F6
Eastry Rd, Erith DA8 . . . . . **139** G7
EAST SHEEN, SW14 . . . . . **146** D4
East Sheen Av, SW14 . . . . **146** D4
Eastside Rd, NW11 . . . . **72** C4
East Smithfield, E1 . . . . **21** G6
East St, SE17 . . . . **36** A3
Barking IG11 . . . . **99** F7
Bexleyheath DA7 . . . . . **159** G4
Brentford TW8 . . . . **125** F7
Bromley BR1 . . . . **191** G2
East Surrey Gro, SE15 . . . **132** C7
East Tenter St, E1 . . . . **21** G4
East Twrs, Pnr. HA5 . . . . . . **66** D5
East Vale, W3 *off The Vale* **127** F1
East Vw, E4 . . . . **62** C5
Barnet EN5 . . . . **40** C3
Eastview Av, SE18 . . . . . . **137** H7
Eastville Av, NW11 . . . . **72** C6
East Wk, Barn. (E.Barn.) EN4 . . . . **42** A7
Hayes UB3 . . . . **122** A1
Eastway, E9 . . . . **95** J6
East Way, E11 . . . . **79** H5
Bromley BR2 . . . . **191** G7
Croydon CR0 . . . . **203** H2
Hayes UB3 . . . . **122** A1
Eastway, Mord. SM4 . . . . **184** A5
East Way, Ruis. HA4 . . . . . . **84** A1
Eastway, Wall. SM6 . . . . . **200** C4
Eastway Commercial Cen, E9 . . . . **96** A5
Eastway Cres, Har. HA2 *off Eliot Dr* **85** H2
Eastwell Cl, Beck. BR3 . . . **189** H1
Eastwick Ct, SW19 *off Victoria Dr* **166** A1
EAST WICKHAM, Well. DA16 . . . . **138** A7
Eastwood Cl, E18 *off George La* **79** G2
N7 *off Eden Gro* **93** G5
N17 *off Northumberland Gro* **60** E7
Eastwood Rd, E18 . . . . **79** G2
N10 . . . . **74** A2
Ilford IG3 . . . . **82** A7
West Drayton UB7 . . . . **120** D2
East Woodside, Bex. DA5 . **177** E1
Eastwood St, SW16 . . . . . **168** C6
Eatington Rd, E10 . . . . **78** D5
Eaton Cl, SW1 . . . . **32** B2
Stanmore HA7 . . . . **53** E4
Eaton Dr, SW9 . . . . **151** H4
Kingston upon Thames KT2 . . . . **164** A7
Eaton Gdns, Dag. RM9 . . . **100** E7
Eaton Gate, SW1 . . . . **32** B1
Eaton Ho, E14 *off Westferry Circ* **113** J7
Eaton La, SW1 . . . . **24** E6
Eaton Ms N, SW1 . . . . **32** B1
Eaton Ms S, SW1 . . . . **32** C1
Eaton Ms W, SW1 . . . . **32** C1
Eaton Pk Rd, N13 . . . . **59** G2
Eaton Pl, SW1 . . . . **24** B6
Eaton Ri, E11 . . . . **79** J5
W5 . . . . **105** G6
Eaton Rd, NW4 . . . . **71** J5
Enfield EN1 . . . . **44** B3
Hounslow TW3 . . . . **144** A4
Sidcup DA14 . . . . **176** D2
Sutton SM2 . . . . **199** G6
Eaton Row, SW1 . . . . **24** D5
Eatons Mead, E4 . . . . **62** A2
Eaton Sq, SW1 . . . . **24** D5
Eaton Ter, SW1 . . . . **32** B1
Eaton Ter Ms, SW1 . . . . **32** B1
Eatonville Rd, SW17 . . . . . **167** J2
Eatonville Vil, SW17 *off Eatonville Rd* **167** J2
Ebb Ct, E16 *off Albert Basin Way* . . **117** F7
Ebbisham Dr, SW8 . . . . **34** C5
Ebbisham Rd, Wor.Pk. KT4 . . . . **197** J2
Ebbsfleet Rd, NW2 . . . . **90** B5
Ebdon Way, SE3 . . . . **155** H3
Ebenezer Ho, SE11 . . . . **35** F2
Ebenezer St, N1 . . . . **12** B3
Ebenezer Wk, SW16 . . . . . **186** C1
Ebley Cl, SE15 . . . . **37** F6
Ebner St, SW18 . . . . **149** E5
Ebor Cotts, SW15 . . . . **165** E3
Ebor St, E1 . . . . **13** F5
Ebrington Rd, Har. HA3 . . . **69** G6
Ebsworth St, SE23 . . . . . . **153** G7
Eburne Rd, N7 . . . . **93** E3
Ebury Br, SW1 . . . . **32** D3
Ebury Br Est, SW1 . . . . **32** D3
Ebury Br Rd, SW1 . . . . **32** C4
Ebury Cl, Kes. BR2 . . . . . . **206** B3
Ebury Ms, SE27 . . . . **169** H3
SW1 . . . . **32** C1
Ebury Ms E, SW1 . . . . **32** D1
Ebury Sq, SW1 . . . . **32** C2
Ebury St, SW1 . . . . **32** D1
Ecclesbourne Cl, N13 . . . . . **59** G5
Ecclesbourne Gdns, N13 . . **59** G5
Ecclesbourne Rd, N1 . . . . . **93** J7
Thornton Heath CR7 . . **187** J5
Eccles Rd, SW11 . . . . **149** J4
Eccleston Br, SW1 . . . . **32** E1
Eccleston Cl, Barn. (Cockfos.) EN4 . . . . **41** J4
Orpington BR6 . . . . **207** G1
Eccleston Cres, Rom. RM6 . . . . **82** A7
Ecclestone Ct, Wem. HA9 *off St. John's Rd* **87** H5
Ecclestone Pl, Wem. HA9 . . **87** J5
Eccleston Ms, SW1 . . . . **24** C6
Eccleston Pl, SW1 . . . . **32** D1
Eccleston Rd, W13 . . . . . . **104** D7
Eccleston Sq, SW1 . . . . **32** E2
Eccleston Sq Ms, SW1 . . . . **33** F2
Eccleston St, SW1 . . . . **24** D6
Echo Hts, E4 . . . . **62** B1
Eckford St, N1 . . . . **10** E1
Eckington Ho, N15 *off Fladbury Rd* **76** A6
Eckstein Rd, SW11 . . . . . . **149** H4
Eclipse Ho, N22 *off Station Rd* **75** F2
Eclipse Rd, E13 . . . . **115** H5
Ector Rd, SE6 . . . . **172** E2
Edbrooke Rd, W9 . . . . **108** D4
Eddiscombe Rd, SW6 . . . . **148** C2
Eddy Cl, Rom. RM7 . . . . **83** H6
Eddystone Rd, SE4 . . . . . . **153** H5
Eddystone Twr, SE8 . . . . . **133** H4
Eddystone Wk, Stai. TW19 . . . . **140** B7
Ede Cl, Houns. TW3 . . . . . **143** F3
Edenbridge Cl, SE16 *off Masters Dr* **133** E5
Edenbridge Rd, E9 . . . . **95** G7
Enfield EN1 . . . . **44** B6
Eden Cl, NW3 . . . . **90** D2
W8 *off Adam & Eve Ms* **128** D3
Wembley HA0 . . . . **105** G1
Edencourt Rd, SW16 . . . . **168** B6
Edenfield Gdns, Wor.Pk. KT4 . . . . **197** F3
Eden Gro, E17 . . . . **78** B5
N7 . . . . **93** F5
NW10 *off St. Andrews Rd* **89** H6
Edenham Way, W10 *off Elkstone Rd* **108** C5
Edenhurst Av, SW6 . . . . . . **148** C3
Eden Ms, SW17 *off Huntspill St* **167** F3
EDEN PARK, Beck. BR3 . . . **190** A5
Eden Pk Av, Beck. BR3 . . . **189** H4
Eden Rd, E17 . . . . **78** B5
SE27 . . . . **169** H5
Beckenham BR3 . . . . . . **189** H4
Bexley DA5 . . . . **177** J4
Croydon CR0 . . . . **202** A4
Edensor Gdns, W4 . . . . **127** E7
Edensor Rd, W4 . . . . **126** E7
Eden St, Kings.T. KT1 . . . . **181** G2
Edenvale Cl, Mitch. CR4 *off Edenvale Rd* **168** A7
Edenvale Rd, Mitch. CR4 . **168** A7
Edenvale St, SW6 . . . . **149** E2
Eden Wk, Kings.T. KT1 *off Eden St* **181** H2
Eden Wk Shop Cen, Kings. T. KT1 . . . . **181** H2
Eden Way, E3 *off Old Ford Rd* **113** J1
Beckenham BR3 . . . . . . **189** J5
Ederline Av, SW16 . . . . . . **187** F3
Edgar Kail Way, SE22 . . . . **152** B4
Edgarley Ter, SW6 . . . . **148** B1
Edgar Rd, E3 . . . . **114** B3
Hounslow TW4 . . . . **143** F7
Romford RM6 . . . . **82** D7
Edgar Wallace Cl, SE15 . . . . **37** E7
Edgbaston Rd, Wat. WD19 . **50** B3
Edgeborough Way, Brom. BR1 . . . . **174** A7
Edgebury, Chis. BR7 . . . . . **175** E4
Edgebury Wk, Chis. BR7 . . . . **175** F4
Edgecombe Ho, SW19 . . . **166** B1
Edgecoombe, S.Croy. CR2 . . . . **203** F7
Edgecoombe Cl, Kings.T. KT2 . . . . **164** D7
Edgecote Cl, W3 *off Cheltenham Pl* . . . **126** C1
Edgecot Gro, N15 *off Oulton Rd* **76** B5
Edgefield Av, Bark. IG11 . . . **99** J7
Edge Hill, SE18 . . . . **136** E6
SW19 . . . . **166** A7
Edge Hill Av, N3 . . . . **72** D4
Edge Hill Ct, SW19 . . . . . . **166** A7
Edgehill Gdns, Dag. RM10 . . . . **101** G4
Edgehill Rd, W13 . . . . **105** F5
Chislehurst BR7 . . . . . **175** F3
Mitcham CR4 . . . . **186** B1
Edgeley La, SW4 *off Edgeley Rd* **150** D3
Edgeley Rd, SW4 . . . . **150** D3
Edgel St, SW18 *off Ferrier St* **149** E4
Edge Pt Cl, SE27 . . . . **169** H5
Edge St, W8 *off Kensington Ch St* . **128** D1
Edgewood Dr, Orp. BR6 . . **207** J5
Edgewood Grn, Croy. CR0 . . . . **203** G1
Edgeworth Av, NW4 . . . . . . **71** G5
Edgeworth Cl, NW4 . . . . . . **71** G5
Edgeworth Cres, NW4 . . . . **71** G5
Edgeworth Rd, SE9 . . . . . . **155** J4
Barnet (Cockfos.) EN4 . . **41** H4
Edgington Rd, SW16 . . . . **168** D6

Edgington Way, Sid. DA14 176 C7
Edgson Ho, SW1 *off Ebury Br Rd* 32 D3
EDGWARE, HA8 54 B5
Edgwarebury Gdns, Edg. HA8 54 A5
Edgwarebury La, Edg. HA8 54 A4
Edgware Ct, Edg. HA8 *off High St* 54 A6
Edgware Rd, NW2 89 H1
NW9 70 D3
W2 15 H3
Edgware Rd Sub, W2 *off Edgware Rd* 15 G2
Edgware Way, Edg. HA8 53 J4
Edinburgh Cl, E2 *off Russia La* 113 F2
Pinner HA5 66 D7
Edinburgh Ct, SW20 184 A5
Kingston upon Thames KT1 *off Watersplash Cl* 181 H3
Edinburgh Dr, Rom. RM7 *off Eastern Av W* 83 J4
Edinburgh Gate, SW1 23 J3
Edinburgh Ho, W9 6 B3
Edinburgh Rd, E13 115 H2
E17 78 A5
N18 60 D5
W7 124 C2
Sutton SM1 199 F2
Edington Rd, SE2 138 B3
Enfield EN3 45 F2
Edison Cl, E17 *off Exeter Rd* 78 A5
West Drayton UB7 120 C2
Edison Ct, SE10 *off Greenroof Way* 135 F3
Edison Dr, Sthl. UB1 103 H6
Wembley HA9 87 H3
Edison Gro, SE18 137 J7
Edison Rd, N8 74 D6
Bromley BR2 191 G2
Enfield EN3 45 J2
Welling DA16 157 J1
Edis St, NW1 110 A1
Edith Cavell Cl, N19 *off Hillrise Rd* 74 E7
Edith Cavell Way, SE18 156 B1
Edith Gdns, Surb. KT5 182 B7
Edith Gro, SW10 30 C6
Edithna St, SW9 151 E3
Edith Nesbit Wk, SE9 156 B5
Edith Rd, E6 98 A7
E15 *off Chandos Rd* 96 D5
N11 58 D7
SE25 188 A5
SW19 167 E6
W14 128 B4
Romford RM6 82 D6
Edith Row, SW6 149 E1
Edith St, E2 13 H1
Edith Summerskill Ho, SW6 *off Clem Attlee Ct* 128 C7
Edith Ter, SW10 30 C7
Edith Vil, SW15 *off Bective Rd* 148 B4
W14 128 C4
Edith Yd, SW10 30 D7
Edmansons Cl, N17 *off Bruce Gro* 76 B1
Edmeston Cl, E9 95 H6
Edmonds Ct, W.Mol. KT8 *off Avern Rd* 179 H4
EDMONTON, N9 60 D4
Edmonton Grn, N9 *off The Green* 60 D2
Edmonton Grn Mkt, N9 *off Edmonton Grn Shop Cen* 60 E2
Edmonton Grn Shop Cen, N9 60 E2
Edmonton Trade Pk, N18 *off Eley Rd* 61 F5
Edmund Gro, Felt. TW13 161 F2
Edmund Halley Way, SE10 134 E2
Edmund Hurst Dr, E6 116 E5
Edmund Rd, Mitch. CR4 185 H3
Welling DA16 158 A3
Edmunds Cl, Hayes UB4 102 C5
Edmund St, SE5 36 B7
Edmunds Wk, N2 73 H4
Edna Rd, SW20 184 A2
Edna St, SW11 149 H1
Edrich Ho, SW4 150 E1
Edric Ho, SW1 *off Page St* 33 J1
Edrick Rd, Edg. HA8 54 C6
Edrick Wk, Edg. HA8 54 C6
Edric Rd, SE14 133 G7
Edridge Rd, Croy. CR0 201 J3
Edulf Rd, Borwd. WD6 38 B1
Edward Av, E4 62 B6
Morden SM4 185 G5
Edward Cl, N9 44 C7
NW2 90 A4
Hampton (Hmptn H.) TW12 *off Edward Rd* 161 J5
Northolt UB5 102 C2
Edward Ct, E16 *off Alexandra St* 115 G5
Edwardes Pl, W8 *off Edwardes Sq* 128 C3
Edwardes Sq, W8 128 D3
Edward Gro, Barn. EN4 41 G5
Edward Ms, NW1 8 E2
Edward Pl, SE8 133 J6
Edward Rd, E17 77 G4
SE20 171 G7
Barnet EN4 41 G5
Bromley BR1 173 H7
Chislehurst BR7 175 E5
Croydon CR0 188 B7
Feltham TW14 141 G5
Hampton (Hmptn H.) TW12 161 J5
Harrow HA2 67 J3
Northolt UB5 102 C2
Romford RM6 82 E6
Edward's Av, Ruis. HA4 84 B6
Edwards Cl, Wor.Pk. KT4 198 A2
Edwards Cotts, N1 *off Compton Av* 93 H6
Edwards Dr, N11 *off Gordon Rd* 58 D7
Edwards La, N16 94 A2
Edwards Ms, N1 93 G7
W1 16 B4
Edward Sq, N1 *off Copenhagen St* 111 F1
SE16 *off Rotherhithe St* 133 H1
Edwards Rd, Belv. DA17 139 G4
Edward St, E16 115 G4
SE8 133 J6
SE14 133 H7
Edward's Way, SE4 *off Adelaide Av* 154 A5
Edwards Yd, Wem. HA0 *off Mount Pleasant* 105 H1
Edward Temme Av, E15 97 F7
Edward Tyler Rd, SE12 173 H2
Edwina Gdns, Ilf. IG4 80 B5
Edwin Av, E6 116 D2
Edwin Cl, Bexh. DA7 139 F6
Edwin Hall Pl, SE13 *off Hither Grn La* 154 D6
Edwin Pl, Croy. CR0 *off Cross Rd* 202 A1
Edwin Rd, Edg. HA8 54 D6
Twickenham TW1, TW2 162 C1
Edwin's Mead, E9 *off Lindisfarne Way* 95 H4
Edwin St, E1 113 F4
E16 115 G5
Edwyn Cl, Barn. EN5 39 J6
Edwyn Ho, SW18 *off Neville Gill Cl* 148 E6
Eel Brook Cl, SW6 *off King's Rd* 148 E1
Eel Brook Studios, SW6 *off Moore Pk Rd* 128 D7
Eel Pie Island, Twick. TW1 162 D1
Effie Pl, SW6 128 D7
Effie Rd, SW6 128 D7
Effingham Cl, Sutt. SM2 199 E7
Effingham Rd, N8 75 G5
SE12 155 E5
Croydon CR0 187 F7
Surbiton (Long Dit.) KT6 181 E7
Effort St, SW17 167 H5
Effra Par, SW2 151 G5
Effra Rd, SW2 151 G4
SW19 166 E6
Egbert St, NW1 110 A1
Egbury Ho, SW15 *off Tangley Gro* 147 F6
Egeremont Rd, SE13 154 B2
Egerton Cl, Pnr. HA5 66 A4
Egerton Cres, SW3 31 H1
Egerton Dr, SE10 154 B1
Egerton Gdns, NW4 71 H4
NW10 107 J1
SW3 23 G6
W13 105 E6
Ilford IG3 99 J3
Egerton Gdns Ms, SW3 23 H6
Egerton Pl, SW3 23 H6
Egerton Rd, N16 76 C7
SE25 188 B3
New Malden KT3 183 F4
Egerton Rd, Twickenham TW2 144 B7
Wembley HA0 87 J7
Egerton Ter, SW3 23 H6
Egerton Way, Hayes UB3 121 E7
Eggardon Ct, Nthlt. UB5 *off Lancaster Rd* 85 J6
Egham Cl, SW19 166 B2
Sutton SM3 198 B2
Egham Cres, Sutt. SM3 198 A3
Egham Rd, E13 115 H5
Eglantine Rd, SW18 149 F5
Egleston Rd, Mord. SM4 184 E6
Eglington Ct, SE17 35 J5
Eglington Rd, E4 46 D7
Eglinton Hill, SE18 137 E6
Eglinton Rd, SE18 136 D6
Egliston Ms, SW15 147 J3
Egliston Rd, SW15 147 J3
Eglon Ms, NW1 *off Berkley Rd* 91 J7
Egmont Av, Surb. KT6 195 J1
Egmont Rd, N.Mal. KT3 183 F4
Surbiton KT6 195 J1
Sutton SM2 199 F7
Walton-on-Thames KT12 178 B7
Egmont St, SE14 133 G7
Egremont Ho, SE13 *off Conington Rd* 154 B2
Egremont Rd, SE27 169 G3
Egret Way, Hayes UB4 102 D5
Eider Cl, E7 97 F5
Hayes UB4 *off Cygnet Way* 102 D5
Eighteenth Rd, Mitch. CR4 186 E4
Eighth Av, E12 98 C4
Hayes UB3 122 A1
Eileen Rd, SE25 188 A5
Eindhoven Cl, Cars. SM5 200 A1
Eisenhower Dr, E6 116 B5
Elaine Gro, NW5 92 A5
Elam Cl, SE5 151 H2
Elam St, SE5 151 H2
Eland Pl, Croy. CR0 *off Eland Rd* 201 H3
Eland Rd, SW11 149 J3
Croydon CR0 201 H3
Elba Pl, SE17 36 A1
Elberon Av, Croy. CR0 186 C6
Elbe St, SW6 149 F2
Elborough Rd, SE25 188 D5
Elborough St, SW18 166 D1
Elbury Dr, E16 115 G6
Elcho St, SW11 129 H7
Elcot Av, SE15 132 E7
Eldenwall Ind Est, Dag. RM8 *off Whalebone La S* 101 F1
Elder Av, N8 74 E5
Elderberry Cl, Ilf. IG6 *off Hazel La* 65 E7
Elderberry Gro, SE27 *off Linton Gro* 169 J4
Elderberry Rd, W5 125 H2
Elderberry Way, E6 116 C3
Elder Cl, N20 56 E2
Sidcup DA15 175 J1
Elder Ct, Bushey (Bushey Hth) WD23 52 B2
Elderfield Pl, SW17 168 B4
Elderfield Rd, E5 95 F4
Elderfield Wk, E11 79 H5
Elderflower Way, E15 96 E7
Elder Gdns, SE27 169 J4
Elder Oak Cl, SE20 188 E1
Elder Rd, SE27 169 J5
Elderslie Cl, Beck. BR3 190 B5
Elderslie Rd, SE9 156 D5
Elder St, E1 21 F1
Elderton Rd, SE26 171 H4
Eldertree Pl, Mitch. CR4 *off Eldertree Way* 186 C1
Eldertree Way, Mitch. CR4 186 B1
Elder Wk, N1 *off Essex Rd* 111 H1
SE13 *off Bankside Av* 154 C3
Elderwood Pl, SE27 169 J5
Eldon Av, Borwd. WD6 38 A2
Croydon CR0 203 F2
Hounslow TW5 123 G7
Eldon Gro, NW3 91 G5
Eldon Pk, SE25 188 E4
Eldon Rd, E17 77 J4
N9 61 F2
N22 75 H1
W8 22 B6
Eldon St, EC2 20 C2
Eldon Way, NW10 106 B2
Eldred Rd, Bark. IG11 117 H1
Eldridge Cl, Felt. TW14 160 A1
Eldridge Ct, Dag. RM10 *off Reede Way* 101 H6
Eleanor Cl, N15 *off Arnold Rd* 76 C3
SE16 133 G2
Eleanor Cres, NW7 56 A4
Eleanor Gdns, Barn. EN5 40 A5
Dagenham RM8 101 F3
Eleanor Gro, SW13 147 E3
Eleanor Rd, E8 94 E6
E15 97 F6
N11 58 E6
Eleanor St, E3 114 A3
Eleanor Wk, SE18 *off Samuel St* 136 C4
Electra Av, Houns. TW6 *off Eastchurch Rd* 141 J3
Electra Business Pk, E16 114 D5
Electric Av, SW9 151 G4
Electric La, SW9 151 G4
Electric Par, E18 *off George La* 79 G2
Surbiton KT6 181 G6
Elektron Ho, E14 *off Blackwall Way* 114 D7
Elephant & Castle, SE1 27 H6
Elephant & Castle Shop Cen, SE1 *off Elephant & Castle* 35 J1
Elephant La, SE16 133 F2
Elephant Rd, SE17 35 J1
Elers Rd, W13 125 F2
Hayes UB3 121 G4
Eleven Acre Ri, Loug. IG10 48 C3
Eley Est, N18 61 F5
Eley Rd, N18 61 G5
Eley Rd Retail Pk, N18 61 G5
Elfindale Rd, SE24 151 J5
Elfin Gro, Tedd. TW11 *off Broad St* 162 C5
Elford Cl, SE3 155 H4
Elfort Rd, N5 93 G4
Elfrida Cres, SE6 172 A4
Elf Row, E1 113 F7
Elfwine Rd, W7 104 B5
Elgal Cl, Orp. BR6 207 E5
Elgar Av, NW10 88 D6
SW16 186 E3
W5 125 H2
Surbiton KT5 182 B7
Elgar Cl, E13 *off Bushey Rd* 115 J2
SE8 *off Comet St* 134 A7
Buckhurst Hill IG9 64 A2
Elgar St, SE16 133 H3
Elgin Av, W9 6 A4
W12 127 G2
Harrow HA3 68 E2
Elgin Cl, W12 127 H2
Elgin Cres, W11 108 C6
Hounslow (Lon.Hthrw Air.) TW6 *off Eastern Perimeter Rd* 141 H2
Elgin Ms, W11 *off Ladbroke Gro* 108 B6
Elgin Ms N, W9 6 B3
Elgin Ms S, W9 6 B3
Elgin Rd, N22 74 C2
Croydon CR0 202 C1
Ilford IG3 99 H1
Sutton SM1 199 F3
Wallington SM6 200 C6
Elgood Av, Nthwd. HA6 50 A6
Elgood Cl, W11 *off Avondale Pk Rd* 108 B7
Elham Cl, Brom. BR1 174 A7
Elham Ho, E5 *off Pembury Rd* 94 E5
Elia Ms, N1 11 G2
Elias Pl, SW8 34 E6
Elia St, N1 11 G2
Elibank Rd, SE9 156 D4
Elim Est, SE1 28 D5
Elim St, SE1 28 C5
Elim Way, E13 115 F3
Eliot Bk, SE23 170 E2
Eliot Cotts, SE3 *off Eliot Pl* 155 E2
Eliot Ct, N15 *off Tynemouth Rd* 76 C4
Eliot Dr, Har. HA2 85 H2
Eliot Gdns, SW15 147 G4
Eliot Hill, SE13 154 C2
Eliot Ms, NW8 6 D2
Eliot Pk, SE13 154 C3
Eliot Pl, SE3 154 E2
Eliot Rd, Dag. RM9 100 D4
Eliot Vale, SE3 154 D2
Elizabethan Cl, Stai. (Stanw.) TW19 *off Elizabethan Way* 140 A7

Elizabethan Way, Stai. (Stanw.) TW19 **140** A7
Elizabeth Av, N1 **93** J7
Enfield EN2 **43** H3
Ilford IG1 **99** G2
Elizabeth Blackwell Ho, N22 *off Progress Way* **75** G1
Elizabeth Br, SW1 **32** D2
Elizabeth Cl, E14 *off Grundy St* **114** B6
W9 **6** D5
Barnet EN5 **40** A3
Romford RM7 **83** H1
Sutton SM1 **198** C4
Elizabeth Clyde Cl, N15 **76** B4
Elizabeth Cotts, Rich. (Kew) TW9 **145** J1
Elizabeth Ct, SW1 **25** J6
Kingston upon Thames KT2 *off Lower Kings Rd* **181** H1
Woodford Green IG8 *off Navestock Cres* **63** J7
Elizabeth Est, SE17 **36** B5
Elizabeth Fry Pl, SE18 **156** B1
Elizabeth Fry Rd, E8 *off Lamb La* **95** E7
Elizabeth Gdns, W3 **127** F1
Isleworth TW7 **144** D4
Stanmore HA7 **53** F6
Sunbury-on-Thames TW16 **178** C3
Elizabeth Ms, NW3 **91** H6
Elizabeth Pl, N15 **76** A4
Elizabeth Ride, N9 **45** E7
Elizabeth Rd, E6 **116** A1
N15 **76** B5
Elizabeth Sq, SE16 *off Rotherhithe St* **113** H7
Elizabeth St, SW1 **32** C1
Elizabeth Ter, SE9 **156** C6
Elizabeth Way, SE19 **170** A7
Feltham TW13 **160** C4
Elizabeth Wheeler Ho, Brom. BR1 *off The Mall* **191** G3
Elkanette Ms, N20 *off Ridgeview Rd* **57** F2
Elkington Pt, SE11 **34** E2
Elkington Rd, E13 **115** H4
Elkstone Rd, W10 **108** C5
Ella Cl, Beck. BR3 **190** A2
Ellacott Ms, SW16 **168** D2
Ellaline Rd, W6 **128** A6
Ella Ms, NW3 *off Cressy Rd* **91** J5
Ellanby Cres, N18 **60** E4
Elland Cl, Barn. EN5 **41** G5
Elland Rd, SE15 **153** F4
Ella Rd, N8 **75** E7
Ellement Cl, Pnr. HA5 **66** D5
Ellenborough Pl, SW15 **147** G4
Ellenborough Rd, N22 **75** J1
Sidcup DA14 **176** D5
Ellen Cl, Brom. BR1 **192** A3
Ellen Ct, N9 *off Densworth Gro* **61** F2
Ellen St, E1 **21** J4
Ellen Webb Dr, Har. (Wealds.) HA3 **68** B3
Ellen Wilkinson Ho, E2 *off Usk St* **113** G3
Elleray Rd, Tedd. TW11 **162** C6
Ellerby St, SW6 **148** A1
Ellerdale Cl, NW3 *off Ellerdale Rd* **91** F4
Ellerdale Rd, NW3 **91** F5
Ellerdale St, SE13 **154** B4
Ellerdine Rd, Houns. TW3 **143** J4
Ellerker Gdns, Rich. TW10 **145** H6
Ellerman Av, Twick. TW2 **161** F1
Ellerslie Gdns, NW10 **107** G1
Ellerslie Rd, W12 **127** H1
Ellerslie Sq Ind Est, SW2 **150** E5
Ellerton, NW6 *off Mill La* **90** C5
Ellerton Gdns, Dag. RM9 **100** C7
Ellerton Rd, SW13 **147** G1
SW18 **167** G1
SW20 **165** G7
Dagenham RM9 **100** C7
Surbiton KT6 **195** J2
Ellery Rd, SE19 **170** A7
Ellery St, SE15 **152** E2
Ellesborough Cl, Wat. WD19 **50** C5
Ellesmere Av, NW7 **54** D3
Beckenham BR3 **190** B2
Ellesmere Cl, E11 **79** F5
Ellesmere Gdns, Ilf. IG4 **80** B5
Ellesmere Gro, Barn. EN5 **40** C5
Ellesmere Rd, E3 **113** H2
NW10 **89** G5
W4 **126** D6
Greenford UB6 **103** J4
Twickenham TW1 **145** F6
Ellesmere St, E14 **114** B6
Ellingfort Rd, E8 **95** E7
Ellingham Rd, E15 **96** D4
W12 **127** G2
Chessington KT9 **195** G6
Ellington Ho, SE1 **28** A5
Ellington Rd, N10 **74** B4
Hounslow TW3 **143** H2
Ellington St, N7 **93** G6
Elliot Cl, E15 **96** E7
Elliot Rd, NW4 **71** H6
Stanmore HA7 **52** D6
Elliott Av, Ruis. HA4 **84** B2
Elliott Cl, Wem. HA9 **87** J3
Elliott Rd, SW9 **131** H7
W4 **126** E4
Bromley BR2 **192** A4
Thornton Heath CR7 **187** H4
Elliott's Pl, N1 *off St. Peters St* **111** H1
Elliott Sq, NW3 **91** H7
Elliotts Row, SE11 **35** G1
Ellis Cl, NW10 *off High Rd* **89** H6
SE9 **175** F2
Edgware HA8 **54** E6
Elliscombe Rd, SE7 **135** J5
Ellis Ct, W7 **104** C5
Ellisfield Dr, SW15 **147** F7
Ellison Gdns, Sthl. UB2 **123** F4
Ellison Ho, SE13 *off Lewisham Rd* **154** C2
Ellison Rd, SW13 **147** F2
SW16 **168** D7
Sidcup DA15 **175** G1
Ellis Rd, Mitch. CR4 **185** J6
Southall UB2 **123** J1
Ellis St, SW1 **32** A1
Elliston Ho, SE18 **136** D4
Ellora Rd, SW16 **168** D5
Ellsworth St, E2 **113** E3
Ellwood Ct, W9 **6** A6
Elmar Rd, N15 **76** A4
Elm Av, W5 **125** H1
Ruislip HA4 **84** A1
Elmbank, N14 **43** E7
Elmbank Av, Barn. EN5 **39** J4
Elm Bk Dr, Brom. BR1 **192** A2
Elm Bk Gdns, SW13 **147** E2
Elmbank Way, W7 **104** A5
Elmbourne Dr, Belv. DA17 **139** H4
Elmbourne Rd, SW17 **168** A3
Elmbridge Av, Surb. KT5 **182** B5
Elmbridge Cl, Ruis. HA4 **66** A6
Elmbridge Wk, E8 *off Wilman Gro* **94** D7
Elmbrook Cl, Sun. TW16 **178** B1
Elmbrook Gdns, SE9 **156** B4
Elmbrook Rd, Sutt. SM1 **198** C4
Elm Cl, E11 **79** H6
N19 *off Hargrave Pk* **92** C2
NW4 **72** A5
SW20 *off Grand Dr* **183** J4
Buckhurst Hill IG9 **64** A2
Carshalton SM5 **199** J1
Harrow HA2 **67** H6
Hayes UB3 **102** A6
Romford RM7 **83** H2
South Croydon CR2 **202** B6
Surbiton KT5 **182** C7
Twickenham TW2 **161** H2
Elm Ct, EC4 **19** E5
Mitcham CR4 *off Armfield Cres* **185** J2
Elmcourt Rd, SE27 **169** H2
Elm Cres, W5 **125** H1
Kingston upon Thames KT2 **181** H1
Elmcroft, N8 **75** F5
Elmcroft Av, E11 **79** H5
N9 **44** E6
NW11 **72** C7
Sidcup DA15 **157** J6
Elmcroft Cl, E11 **79** H4
W5 **105** G6
Chessington KT9 **195** H3
Feltham TW14 **141** J6
Elmcroft Cres, NW11 **72** B7
Harrow HA2 **67** G3
Elmcroft Dr, Chess. KT9 **195** H3
Elmcroft Gdns, NW9 **70** A5
Elmcroft St, E5 **95** F4
Elmdale Rd, N13 **59** F5
Elmdene, Surb. KT5 **196** C1
Elmdene Cl, Beck. BR3 **189** J5
Elmdene Rd, SE18 **136** E5
Elmdon Rd, Houns. TW4 **142** D2
Hounslow (Hatt.Cr.) TW6 **141** J3
Elm Dr, Har. HA2 **67** H6
Sunbury-on-Thames TW16 **178** C2
Elmer Cl, Enf. EN2 **43** F3
Elmer Gdns, Edg. HA8 **54** B7
Isleworth TW7 **144** A3
Elmer Rd, SE6 **154** C7
Elmers Dr, Tedd. TW11 *off Kingston Rd* **163** E6
ELMERS END, Beck. BR3 **189** H3
Elmers End Rd, SE20 **189** F2
Beckenham BR3 **189** F2
Elmerside Rd, Beck. BR3 **189** H4
Elmers Rd, SE25 **188** D7
Elmfield Av, N8 **74** E5
Mitcham CR4 **186** A1
Teddington TW11 **162** C5
Elmfield Cl, Har. HA1 **86** B2
Elmfield Pk, Brom. BR1 **191** G3
Elmfield Rd, E4 **62** C2
E17 **77** G6
N2 **73** G3
SW17 **168** A2
Bromley BR1 **191** G3
Southall UB2 **123** E3
Elmfield Way, W9 **108** D5
Elm Friars Wk, NW1 **92** D7
Elm Gdns, N2 **73** F3
Esher (Clay.) KT10 **194** C6
Mitcham CR4 **186** D4
Elmgate Av, Felt. TW13 **160** B3
Elmgate Gdns, Edg. HA8 **54** D5
Elm Grn, W3 **106** E6
Elmgreen Cl, E15 *off Church St N* **115** E1
Elm Gro, N8 **75** E6
NW2 **90** A4
SE15 **152** C2
SW19 **166** B7
Harrow HA2 **67** G7
Kingston upon Thames KT2 **181** H1
Orpington BR6 **207** J1
Sutton SM1 **199** E4
Woodford Green IG8 **63** F5
Elmgrove Cres, Har. HA1 **68** C5
Elmgrove Gdns, Har. HA1 **68** D5
Elm Gro Par, Wall. SM6 *off Butter Hill* **200** A3
Elm Gro Rd, SW13 **147** G2
W5 **125** H2
Elmgrove Rd, Croy. CR0 **188** E7
Harrow HA1 **68** C5
Elm Hall Gdns, E11 **79** H6
Elmhurst, Belv. DA17 **139** E6
Elmhurst Av, N2 **73** G3
Mitcham CR4 **168** B7
Elmhurst Dr, E18 **79** G2
Elmhurst Mans, SW4 *off Edgeley Rd* **150** D3
Elmhurst Rd, E7 **97** H7
N17 **76** B2
SE9 **174** B2
Elmhurst St, SW4 **150** D3
Elmhurst Vil, SE15 *off Cheltenham Rd* **153** F4
Elmhurst Way, Loug. IG10 **48** C7
Elmington Cl, Bex. DA5 **159** H6
Elmington Est, SE5 **36** C7
Elmington Rd, SE5 **152** A1
Elmira St, SE13 **154** B3
Elm La, SE6 **171** J2
Elmlee Cl, Chis. BR7 **174** C6
Elmley Cl, E6 *off Lovage App* **116** B5
Elmley St, SE18 **137** G4
Elm Ms, Rich. TW10 **145** J6
Elmore Cl, Wem. HA0 **105** H2
Elmore Rd, E11 **96** C3
Enfield EN3 **45** G1
Elmores, Loug. IG10 **48** D3
Elmore St, N1 **93** J7
Elm Par, Sid. DA14 *off Main Rd* **176** A4
Elm Pk, SW2 **151** F6
Stanmore HA7 **53** E5
Elm Pk Av, N15 **76** C5
Elm Pk Ct, Pnr. HA5 **66** C3
Elm Pk Gdns, NW4 **72** A5
SW10 **31** E4
Elm Pk La, SW3 **30** E4
Elm Pk Mans, SW10 **30** D5
Elm Pk Rd, E10 **95** H1
N3 **56** C7
N21 **43** J7
SE25 **188** C3
SW3 **30** E5
Pinner HA5 **66** C2
Elm Pl, SW7 **31** E3
Elm Quay Ct, SW8 **33** H5
Elm Rd, E7 **97** F6
E11 **96** D2
E17 **78** C5
N22 *off Granville Rd* **75** H1
SW14 **146** C3
Barnet EN5 **40** C4
Beckenham BR3 **189** J2
Chessington KT9 **195** H4
Epsom KT17 **197** F6
Esher (Clay.) KT10 **194** C6
Kingston upon Thames KT2 **181** J1
New Malden KT3 **182** D4
Romford RM7 **83** H2
Sidcup DA14 **176** A4
Thornton Heath CR7 **188** A4
Wallington SM6 **200** A1
Wembley HA9 **87** H5
Elm Rd W, Sutt. SM3 **184** C7
Elm Row, NW3 **91** F3
Elms, The, SW13 **147** F3
Loughton IG10 **47** F2
Elms Av, N10 **74** B3
NW4 **72** A5
Elmscott Gdns, N21 **43** J6
Elmscott Rd, Brom. BR1 **173** E5
Elms Ct, Wem. HA0 **86** C4
Elms Cres, SW4 **150** C6
Elmsdale Rd, E17 **77** J4
Elms Gdns, Dag. RM9 **101** F4
Wembley HA0 **86** D4
Elmshaw Rd, SW15 **147** G5
Elmshurst Cres, N2 **73** G4
Elmside, Croy. (New Adgtn) CR0 **204** B6
Elmside Rd, Wem. HA9 **88** A3
Elms La, Wem. HA0 **86** D4
Elmsleigh Av, Har. HA3 **69** E4
Elmsleigh Ct, Sutt. SM1 **198** E3
Elmsleigh Rd, Twick. TW2 **162** A2
Elmslie Cl, Wdf.Grn. IG8 **64** C6
Elmslie Pt, E3 **113** J5
Elms Ms, W2 **14** E5
Elms Pk Av, Wem. HA0 **86** D4
Elms Rd, SW4 **150** C5
Harrow HA3 **52** B7
ELMSTEAD, Chis. BR7 **174** A5
Elmstead Av, Chis. BR7 **174** C5
Wembley HA9 **87** H1
Elmstead Cl, N20 **56** D2
Epsom KT19 **197** E5
Elmstead Cres, Well. DA16 **138** C6
Elmstead Gdns, Wor.Pk. KT4 **197** G3
Elmstead Glade, Chis. BR7 **174** C6
Elmstead La, Chis. BR7 **174** C5
Elmstead Rd, Ilf. IG3 **99** H2
Elmstone Rd, SW6 **148** D1
Elm St, WC1 **10** D6
Elmswood, Chig. IG7 *off Copperfield* **65** G6
Elmsworth Av, Houns. TW3 **143** H2
Elm Ter, NW2 **90** D3
SE9 **156** D6
Harrow HA3 **52** A7
Elm Tree Av, Esher KT10 **180** A7
Elm Tree Cl, NW8 **7** E3
Northolt UB5 **103** F2
Elm Tree Ct, SE7 *off Fairlawn* **135** J6
Elm Tree Rd, NW8 **7** E3
Elmtree Rd, Tedd. TW11 **162** B4
Elm Wk, NW3 **90** D2
SW20 **183** J4
Orpington BR6 **206** C3
Elm Way, N11 **58** A6
NW10 **88** E4
Epsom KT19 **196** D5
Worcester Park KT4 **197** J3
Elmwood Av, N13 **59** E5
Borehamwood WD6 **38** B4
Feltham TW13 **160** A2
Harrow HA3 **68** D5
Elmwood Cl, Epsom KT17 **197** G7
Wallington SM6 **200** A2
Elmwood Ct, SW11 **150** B1
Wembley HA0 **86** D3
Elmwood Cres, NW9 **70** C4
Elmwood Dr, Bex. DA5 **158** E7
Epsom KT17 **197** G6
Elmwood Gdns, W7 **104** B6
Elmwood Rd, SE24 **152** A5
W4 **126** C6
Croydon CR0 **187** H7
Mitcham CR4 **185** J3
Elmworth Gro, SE21 **170** A2
Elnathan Ms, W9 **6** B6

Elphinstone Rd, E17 ......77 J2
Elphinstone St, N5 ......93 H4
Elrington Rd, E8 ......94 D6
  Woodford Green IG8 ..63 G5
Elruge Cl, West Dr.
  UB7 ......120 A3
Elsa Rd, Well. DA16 ....158 B2
Elsa St, E1 ......113 H5
Elsdale St, E9 ......95 F6
Elsden Ms, E2
  off Old Ford Rd 113 F2
Elsden Rd, N17 ......76 C1
Elsenham Rd, E12 ......98 C5
Elsenham St, SW18 ......166 E1
Elsham Rd, E11 ......96 E3
  W14 ......128 B2
Elsham Ter, W14 ......128 B2
Elsiedene Rd, N21 ......43 J7
Elsiemaud Rd, SE4 ......153 J5
Elsie Rd, SE22 ......152 C4
Elsinore Av, Stai. TW19 ..140 B7
Elsinore Gdns, NW2 ......90 B3
Elsinore Rd, SE23 ......171 H1
Elsinore Way, Rich. TW9
  off Lower
  Richmond Rd 146 B3
Elsley Rd, SW11 ......149 J3
Elspeth Rd, SW11 ......149 J4
  Wembley HA0 ......87 H5
Elsrick Av, Mord. SM4 ..184 D5
Elstan Way, Croy. CR0 ..189 H7
Elstead Ct, Sutt. SM3
  off Stonecot Hill 198 B1
Elsted St, SE17 ......36 C2
Elstow Cl, SE9 ......156 D5
  Ruislip HA4 ......66 D7
Elstow Gdns, Dag. RM9 ..118 E1
Elstow Rd, Dag. RM9 ....100 E7
Elstree Gdns, N9 ......61 E1
  Belvedere DA17 ......139 E4
  Ilford IG1 ......99 F5
Elstree Hill, Brom. BR1 ..172 E7
Elstree Pk, Borwd. WD6 ..38 D6
Elstree Way, Borwd. WD6 ..38 B3
Elswick Rd, SE13 ......154 B2
Elswick St, SW6 ......149 F2
Elsworthy, T.Ditt. KT7 ..180 B6
Elsworthy Ri, NW3 ......91 H7
Elsworthy Rd, NW3 ......109 H1
Elsworthy Ter, NW3 ......91 H7
Elsynge Rd, SW18 ......149 G5
ELTHAM, SE9 ......156 A6
Eltham Grn, SE9 ......155 J5
Eltham Grn Rd, SE9 ......155 J4
Eltham High St, SE9 ......156 C6
Eltham Hill, SE9 ......156 A5
  SE12 ......155 F5
★ Eltham Palace, SE9 ..156 B7
Eltham Palace Rd, SE9 ..155 J6
Eltham Pk Gdns, SE9 ....156 D4
Eltham Rd, SE9 ......155 J5
  SE12 ......155 F5
Elthiron Rd, SW6 ......148 D1
Elthorne Av, W7 ......124 C2
Elthorne Ct, Felt. TW13 ..160 C1
Elthorne Pk Rd, W7 ......124 C2
Elthorne Rd, N19 ......92 D2
  NW9 ......70 D7
Elthorne Way, NW9 ......70 D6
Elthruda Rd, SE13 ......154 D6
Eltisley Rd, Ilf. IG1 ......98 E4
Elton Av, Barn. EN5 ......40 C5
  Greenford UB6 ......86 C6
  Wembley HA0 ......87 E5
Elton Cl, Kings.T. KT1 ..163 F7
Elton Ho, E3 ......113 J1
Elton Pl, N16 ......94 B5
Elton Rd, Kings.T. KT2 ..181 J1
Eltringham St, SW18 ....149 F4
Elvaston Ms, SW7 ......22 D5
Elvaston Pl, SW7 ......22 C6
Elveden Pl, NW10 ......106 A2
Elveden Rd, NW10 ......106 A2
Elvendon Rd, N13 ......58 E6
Elver Gdns, E2 ......13 J3
Everson Ms, SE8 ......154 B3
Elverson Rd, SE8 ......154 B2
Elverton St, SW1 ......33 H1
Elvington Grn, Brom.
  BR2 ......191 F5
Elvington La, NW9 ......70 E1
Elvino Rd, SE26 ......171 H5
Elvis Rd, NW2 ......89 J6
Elwill Way, Beck. BR3 ..190 C4
Elwin St, E2 ......13 H3
Elwood Cl, Barn. EN5 ....41 G4
Elwood St, N5 ......93 H3
Elwyn Gdns, SE12 ......155 G7
Ely Cl, N.Mal. KT3 ......183 F2
Ely Ct, EC1 ......19 F2
Ely Gdns, Borwd. WD6 ..38 D5
  Dagenham RM10 ......101 J3
  Ilford IG1 ......80 B7
Elyne Rd, N4 ......75 G6

Ely Pl, EC1 ......19 F2
  Woodford Green IG8 ..64 D6
Ely Rd, E10 ......78 C6
  Croydon CR0 ......188 A5
  Hounslow (Houns.W.)
  TW4 ......142 C3
  Hounslow (Lon.Hthrw Air.)
  TW6 off Eastern
  Perimeter Rd 141 J2
Elysian Av, Orp. BR5 ....193 H6
Elysian Pl, S.Croy. CR2 ..201 J7
Elysium Bldg, The, SE8
  off Thorleys Rd 133 G5
Elysium Pl, SW6
  off Fulham Pk Gdns ..148 C2
Elysium St, SW6
  off Fulham Pk Gdns ..148 C2
Elystan Business Cen,
  Hayes UB4 ......102 C7
Elystan Pl, SW3 ......31 H3
Elystan St, SW3 ......31 G2
Elystan Wk, N1
  off Cloudesley Rd 111 G1
Emanuel Av, W3 ......106 C6
Emanuel Dr, Hmptn.
  TW12 ......161 F5
Embankment, SW15 ......148 A2
Embankment, The, Twick.
  TW1 ......162 D1
Embankment Gdns, SW3 ..32 A5
Embankment Pier, WC2 ..26 C1
Embankment Pl, WC2 ....26 B1
Embassy Ct, Sid. DA14 ..176 B3
  Welling DA16
  off Welling High St ...158 B3
Embassy Gdns, Beck. BR3
  off Blakeney Rd 189 J1
Emba St, SE16 ......29 J4
Ember Cl, Orp. BR5 ......193 F7
Embercourt Rd, T.Ditt.
  KT7 ......180 B6
Ember Fm Av, E.Mol.
  KT8 ......180 A6
Ember Fm Way, E.Mol.
  KT8 ......180 A6
Ember Gdns, T.Ditt. KT7 ..180 B7
Ember La, E.Mol. KT8 ....180 A7
  Esher KT10 ......180 A7
Emberton, SE5 ......36 D5
Emberton Ct, EC1
  off Tompion St 11 G4
Embleton Rd, SE13 ......154 B3
  Watford WD19 ......50 A3
Embleton Wk, Hmptn.TW12
  off Fearnley Cres 161 F6
Embry Cl, Stan. HA7 ......52 D4
Embry Dr, Stan. HA7 ....52 D6
Embry Way, Stan. HA7 ..52 D5
Emden Cl, West Dr. UB7 ..120 D2
Emden St, SW6 ......149 E1
Emerald Cl, E16 ......116 B6
Emerald Gdns, Dag. RM8 ..101 G1
Emerald Rd, NW10 ......106 D1
Emerald Sq, Sthl. UB2 ..122 D3
Emerald St, WC1 ......18 C1
Emerson Apts, N8
  off Chadwell La 75 F3
Emerson Gdns, Har. HA3 ..69 J6
Emerson Rd, Ilf. IG1 ......80 D7
Emerson St, SE1 ......27 J1
Emerton Cl, Bexh. DA6 ..158 E4
Emery Hill St, SW1 ......25 G6
Emery St, SE1 ......27 F5
Emes Rd, Erith DA8 ......139 J7
Emilia Cl, Enf. EN3 ......45 E5
Emlyn Gdns, W12 ......127 E2
Emlyn Rd, W12 ......127 E2
Emmanuel Rd, SW12 ....168 C1
Emma Rd, E13 ......115 F2
Emma St, E2 ......112 E2
Emmaus Way, Chig. IG7 ..64 D5
Emmott Av, Ilf. IG6 ......81 F5
Emmott Cl, E1 ......113 H4
  NW11 ......91 F6
Emms Pas, Kings.T. KT1 ..181 G2
Emperor's Gate, SW7 ....22 B6
Empire Av, N18 ......59 J5
Empire Ct, Wem. HA9 ....88 B3
Empire Par, N18
  off Empire Av 60 A4
Empire Sq, N7 ......93 E3
  SE1 ......28 B4
  SE20 off High St 171 G7
Empire Sq E, SE1
  off Empire Sq 28 B4
Empire Sq S, SE1
  off Empire Sq 28 B4
Empire Sq W, SE1
  off Empire Sq 28 B4
Empire Way, Wem. HA9 ..87 J4
Empire Wf Rd, E14 ......134 D4

Empress App, SW6
  off Lillie Rd 128 D6
Empress Av, E4 ......62 B7
  E12 ......97 J2
  Ilford IG1 ......98 B6
  Woodford Green IG8 ..63 F7
Empress Dr, Chis. BR7 ..174 E6
Empress Ms, SE5 ......151 J2
Empress Pl, SW6 ......128 D5
Empress St, SE17 ......36 A5
Empson St, E3 ......114 B4
Emsworth Cl, N9 ......61 F1
Emsworth Rd, Ilf. IG6 ....81 E2
Emsworth St, SW2 ......169 F2
Emu Rd, SW8 ......150 B2
Ena Rd, SW16 ......186 E3
Enbrook St, W10 ......108 B3
Endale Cl, Cars. SM5 ....199 J2
Endeavour Way, SW19 ..166 E4
  Barking IG11 ......118 A2
  Croydon CR0 ......186 D7
Endell St, WC2 ......18 A3
Enderby St, SE10 ......134 E5
Enderley Cl, Har. HA3
  off Enderley Rd 68 B1
Enderley Rd, Har. HA3 ....68 B1
Endersby Rd, Barn. EN5 ..39 J5
Endersleigh Gdns, NW4 ..71 G4
Endlebury Rd, E4 ......62 B2
Endlesham Rd, SW12 ....150 A7
Endsleigh Gdns, WC1 ....9 H5
  Ilford IG1 ......98 C2
  Surbiton KT6 ......181 F6
Endsleigh Ind Est, Sthl.
  UB2 ......123 F4
Endsleigh Pl, WC1 ......9 J5
Endsleigh Rd, W13 ......104 D7
  Southall UB2 ......123 E4
Endsleigh St, WC1 ......9 H5
Endway, Surb. KT5 ......182 A7
Endwell Rd, SE4 ......153 H2
Endymion Rd, N4 ......75 G7
  SW2 ......151 F6
Energen Cl, NW10 ......88 E6
ENFIELD, EN1 - EN3 ....44 C3
Enfield Enterprise Cen, Enf.
  EN3 off Queensway 45 F5
ENFIELD HIGHWAY, Enf.
  EN3 ......45 F3
Enfield Retail Pk, Enf.
  EN1 ......44 E3
Enfield Rd, N1 ......94 B7
  W3 ......126 B2
  Brentford TW8 ......125 G5
  Enfield EN2 ......42 D4
  Hounslow (Lon.Hthrw Air.)
  TW6 off Eastern
  Perimeter Rd 141 H2
Enfield Rd Rbt, Houns.
  TW6 off Northern
  Perimeter Rd 141 H2
ENFIELD TOWN, Enf. EN2 ..44 A2
Enfield Wk, Brent. TW8 ..125 G5
Enford St, W1 ......15 J1
Engadine Cl, Croy. CR0 ..202 C3
Engadine St, SW18 ......166 C1
Engate St, SE13 ......154 C4
Engel Pk, NW7 ......55 J6
Engineer Cl, SE18 ......136 D6
Engineers Way, Wem.
  HA9 ......88 A4
Engineer's Wf, Nthlt. UB5
  off Taywood Rd 103 F4
Englands La, NW3 ......91 J6
  Loughton IG10 ......48 D2
England Way, N.Mal.
  KT3 ......182 B4
Englefield Cl, Croy. CR0
  off Queen's Rd 187 J6
  Enfield EN2 ......43 G2
  Orpington BR5 ......193 J5
Englefield Cres, Orp.
  BR5 ......193 J4
Englefield Path, Orp.
  BR5 ......193 J4
Englefield Rd, N1 ......94 A6
Engleheart Dr, Felt. TW14 ..141 J4
Engleheart Rd, SE6 ......154 B7
Englewood Rd, SW12 ....150 B6
Englin Grds, SE11 ......28 D2
English St, E3 ......113 J4
Enid St, SE16 ......29 G5
Enmore Av, SE25 ......188 D5
Enmore Gdns, SW14 ....146 D5
Enmore Rd, SE25 ......188 D5
  SW15 ......147 J4
  Southall UB1 ......103 G4
Ennerdale Av, Stan. HA7 ..69 F3
  Sutt. SM1 ......198 C4
Ennerdale Dr, NW9 ......70 E5
Ennerdale Gdns, Wem.
  HA9 ......87 F1
Ennerdale Ho, E3 ......113 J4

Ennerdale Rd, Bexh. DA7 .159 G1
  Richmond TW9 ......145 J2
Ennersdale Rd, SE13 ....154 D5
Ennismore Av, W4 ......127 F4
  Greenford UB6 ......86 B6
Ennismore Gdns, SW7 ....23 G4
  Thames Ditton KT7 ..180 B6
Ennismore Gdns Ms, SW7 ..23 G5
Ennismore Ms, SW7 ......23 G5
Ennismore St, SW7 ......23 G5
Ennis Rd, N4 ......93 G1
  SE18 ......137 F6
Ensign Cl, Houns. TW6
  off Exeter Way 141 H2
Ensign Dr, N13 ......59 J3
Ensign Ho, SW8
  off St. George Wf 34 A5
Ensign St, E1 ......21 H5
Ensign Way, Wall. SM6 ..201 E7
Enslin Rd, SE9 ......156 D6
Ensor Ms, SW7 ......30 E3
Enstone Rd, Enf. EN3 ....45 H3
Enterprise Cl, Croy. CR0 .201 G1
Enterprise Ind Est, SE16
  off Bolina Rd 133 F5
Enterprise Way, NW10 ..107 G3
  SW18 ......148 D4
  Teddington TW11 ....162 C5
Enterprize Way, SE8 ....133 J4
Envoy Av, Houns. TW6
  off Eastern
  Perimeter Rd 142 A3
Envoy Av Rbt, Houns. TW6
  off Cranford La 141 J3
Epirus Ms, SW6 ......128 D7
Epirus Rd, SW6 ......128 C7
Epping Cl, E14 ......134 A4
  Romford RM7 ......83 H3
★ Epping Forest, Epp. &
  Loug. 47 J1
Epping Glade, E4 ......46 C6
Epping New Rd, Buck.H.
  IG9 ......63 H2
  Loughton IG10 ......47 H5
Epping Pl, N1
  off Liverpool Rd 93 G6
Epping Way, E4 ......46 B6
Epple Rd, SW6 ......148 C1
Epsom Cl, Bexh. DA7 ....159 H3
  Northolt UB5 ......85 F5
Epsom Rd, E10 ......78 C6
  Croydon CR0 ......201 G4
  Ilford IG3 ......81 J6
  Morden SM4 ......184 C7
  Sutton SM3 ......184 C7
Epsom Sq, Houns.
  (Lon.Hthrw Air.) TW6
  off Eastern
  Perimeter Rd 141 J2
Epstein Rd, SE28 ......138 A1
Epworth Rd, Islw. TW7 ..124 E7
Epworth St, EC2 ......12 C6
Equana Apts, SE8
  off Evelyn St 133 H5
Equinox Ho, Bark. IG11 ..99 F8
Equity Sq, E2 ......13 G4
Erasmus St, SW1 ......33 J2
Erbin Ct, N9
  off Galahad Rd 60 D2
Erconwald St, W12 ......107 F6
Erebus Dr, SE28 ......137 F3
Eresby Dr, Beck. BR3 ....204 A1
Eresby Pl, NW6 ......90 D7
Erica Gdns, Croy. CR0 ..204 B4
Erica St, W12 ......107 G7
Eric Clarke La, Bark. IG11 .117 E4
Eric Cl, E7 ......97 G4
Ericcson Cl, SW18 ......148 D5
Eric Fletches Ct, N1
  off Essex Rd 93 J7
Eric Rd, E7 ......97 G4
  NW10 off Church Rd 89 F6
  Romford RM6 ......82 D7
Eric St, E3 ......113 J4
Eridge Rd, W4 ......126 D3
Erin Cl, Brom. BR1 ......172 E7
  Ilford IG3 ......82 A6
Erin Ct, NW2 ......89 J6
Erindale, SE18 ......137 G6
Erindale Ter, SE18 ......137 G6
Erith Cres, Rom. RM5 ....83 J1
Erith Rd, Belv. DA17 ....139 G5
  Bexleyheath DA7 ......159 H4
  Erith DA8 ......159 H4
Erlanger Rd, SE14 ......153 G1
Erlesmere Gdns, W13 ..124 D3
Ermine Cl, Houns. TW4 ..142 C2
Ermine Ho, N17
  off Moselle St 60 C7
Ermine Ms, E2
  off Laburnum St 112 C1
Ermine Rd, N15 ......76 C6
  SE13 ......154 B3

Ermine Side, Enf. EN1 ... 44 D5
Ermington Rd, SE9 ... 175 F2
Ernald Av, E6 ... 116 B2
Erncroft Way, Twick. TW1 . 144 C6
Ernest Av, SE27 ... 169 H4
Ernest Cl, Beck. BR3 ... 190 A5
Ernest Gdns, W4 ... 126 B6
Ernest Gro, Beck. BR3 ... 189 J5
Ernest Rd, Kings.T. KT1 .. 182 B2
Ernest Sq, Kings.T. KT1 .. 182 B2
Ernest St, E1 ... 113 G4
Ernle Rd, SW20 ... 165 H7
Ernshaw Pl, SW15
off Carlton Dr ... 148 B5
★ **Eros**, W1 ... 17 H6
Erpingham Rd, SW15 ... 147 J3
Erridge Rd, SW19 ... 184 D2
Errington Rd, W9 ... 108 C4
Errol Gdns, Hayes UB4 ... 102 B4
New Malden KT3 ... 183 G4
Errol St, EC1 ... 12 A6
Erskine Cl, Sutt. SM1 ... 199 H3
Erskine Cres, N17 ... 76 E4
Erskine Hill, NW11 ... 72 D5
Erskine Ho, SE7
off Springfield Gro ... 135 J6
Erskine Ms, NW3
off Erskine Rd ... 91 J7
Erskine Rd, E17 ... 77 J4
NW3 ... 91 J7
Sutton SM1 ... 199 G4
Watford WD19 ... 50 C3
Erwood Rd, SE7 ... 136 B5
Esam Way, SW16 ... 169 G5
Escott Gdns, SE9 ... 174 B4
Escot Way, Barn. EN5 ... 39 J5
Escreet Gro, SE18 ... 136 D4
Esher Av, Rom. RM7 ... 83 J6
Sutton SM3 ... 198 A3
Walton-on-Thames KT12 ... 178 A7
Esher Bypass, Chess. KT9 ... 195 E7
Esher KT10 ... 195 E7
Esher Cl, Bex. DA5 ... 176 E1
Esher Cres, Houns. (Lon.Hthrw Air.) TW6
off Eastern Perimeter Rd ... 141 H2
Esher Gdns, SW19 ... 166 A2
Esher Ms, Mitch. CR4 ... 185 J3
Esher Rd, E.Mol. KT8 ... 180 A6
Ilford IG3 ... 99 H3
Eskdale, NW1 ... 9 F2
Eskdale Av, Nthlt. UB5 ... 103 F1
Eskdale Cl, Wem. HA9 ... 87 G2
Eskdale Rd, Bexh. DA7 ... 159 G2
Eskmont Ridge, SE19 ... 170 B7
Esk Rd, E13 ... 115 G4
Esmar Cres, NW9 ... 71 G7
Esme Ho, SW15 ... 147 F4
Esmeralda Rd, SE1 ... 37 J2
Esmond Gdns, W4
off South Par ... 126 D4
Esmond Rd, NW6 ... 108 C1
W4 ... 126 D4
Esmond St, SW15 ... 148 B4
Esparto St, SW18 ... 149 E7
Essenden Rd, Belv. DA17 . 139 G5
South Croydon CR2 ... 202 B7
Essendine Rd, W9 ... 108 D4
Essex Av, Islw. TW7 ... 144 B3
Essex Cl, E17 ... 77 H4
Morden SM4 ... 184 A7
Romford RM7 ... 83 H4
Ruislip HA4 ... 84 D1
Essex Ct, EC4 ... 18 E4
SW13 ... 147 F2
Essex Gdns, N4 ... 75 H6
Essex Gro, SE19 ... 170 A6
Essex Ho, E14
off Giraud St ... 114 B6
Essex Pk, N3 ... 56 E6
Essex Pk Ms, W3 ... 126 E1
Essex Pl, W4 ... 126 C4
Essex Pl Sq, W4
off Chiswick High Rd . 126 D4
Essex Rd, E4 ... 62 E1
E10 ... 78 C6
E12 ... 98 B5
E17 ... 77 H6
E18 ... 79 H2
N1 ... 111 H1
NW10 ... 89 E7
W3 ... 106 C7
W4 *off Belmont Ter* ... 126 D4
Barking IG11 ... 99 G7
Borehamwood WD6 ... 38 A3
Dagenham RM10 ... 101 J5
Enfield EN2 ... 44 A4
Romford RM7 ... 83 H4
Romford (Chad.Hth) RM6 ... 82 C7
Essex Rd S, E11 ... 78 D7
Essex St, E7 ... 97 G5
WC2 ... 18 E5
Essex Twr, SE20 ... 189 E1
Essex Vil, W8 ... 128 D2
Essex Wf, E5 ... 95 F2
Essian St, E1 ... 113 H5
Essoldo Way, Edg. HA8 ... 69 J3
Estate Way, E10 ... 95 J1
Estcourt Rd, SE25 ... 189 E6
SW6 ... 128 C7
Estella Av, N.Mal. KT3 ... 183 H4
Estelle Rd, NW3 ... 91 J4
Esterbrooke St, SW1 ... 33 H2
Este Rd, SW11 ... 149 H3
Esther Cl, N21 ... 43 G7
Esther Rd, E11 ... 78 E7
Estoria Cl, SW2 ... 151 G7
★ **Estorick Collection of Modern Italian Art**, N1 . 93 H6
Estreham Rd, SW16 ... 168 D6
Estridge Cl, Houns. TW3 .. 143 G4
Estuary Cl, Bark. IG11 ... 118 B3
Eswyn Rd, SW17 ... 167 J4
Etchingham Pk Rd, N3 ... 57 E7
Etchingham Rd, E15 ... 96 C4
Eternit Wk, SW6 ... 147 J1
Etfield Gro, Sid. DA14 ... 176 B5
Ethelbert Cl, Brom. BR1 .. 191 G3
Ethelbert Gdns, Ilf. IG2 ... 80 C5
Ethelbert Rd, SW20 ... 184 A1
Bromley BR1 ... 191 G3
Erith DA8 ... 139 J7
Ethelbert St, SW12 ... 168 B1
Ethelburga St, SW11 ... 149 H1
Ethelburga Twr, SW11
off Rosenau Rd ... 149 H1
Etheldene Av, N10 ... 74 C4
Ethelden Rd, W12 ... 127 H1
Ethelred Est, SE11
off Hotspur St ... 131 G4
Ethel Rd, E16 ... 115 H6
Ethel St, SE17 ... 35 J2
Etheridge Grn, Loug. IG10 . 49 F3
Etheridge Rd, NW2 ... 71 J7
Loughton IG10 ... 49 E2
Etherley Rd, N15 ... 75 J5
Etherow St, SE22 ... 152 D6
Etherstone Grn, SW16 ... 169 G4
Etherstone Rd, SW16 ... 169 G4
Ethnard Rd, SE15 ... 132 E6
Ethronvi Rd, Bexh. DA7 .. 159 E3
Etloe Rd, E10 ... 96 A2
Eton Av, N12 ... 57 F7
NW3 ... 91 G7
Barnet EN4 ... 41 H6
Hounslow TW5 ... 123 F6
New Malden KT3 ... 182 D5
Wembley HA0 ... 87 E4
Eton Cl, SW18 ... 149 E7
Eton Coll Rd, NW3 ... 91 J6
Eton Ct, NW3 *off Eton Av* . 91 G7
Wembley HA0
off Eton Av ... 87 F4
Eton Garages, NW3
off Lambolle Pl ... 91 H6
Eton Gro, NW9 ... 70 A3
SE13 ... 154 E3
Eton Hall, NW3
off Eton Coll Rd ... 91 J6
Eton Pl, NW3
off Haverstock Hill ... 92 A7
Eton Ri, NW3
off Eton Coll Rd ... 91 J6
Eton Rd, NW3 ... 91 J7
Hayes UB3 ... 121 J7
Ilford IG1 ... 99 F5
Eton St, Rich. TW9 ... 145 H5
Eton Vil, NW3 ... 91 J6
Etta St, SE8 ... 133 H6
Ettrick St, E14 ... 114 C6
Etwell Pl, Surb. KT5 ... 181 J6
Euesden Cl, N9 ... 60 E3
Eugenia Rd, SE16 ... 133 F4
Eugenie Ms, Chis. BR7 ... 192 E1
Eureka Rd, Kings.T. KT1
off Washington Rd ... 182 A2
Euro Cl, NW10 ... 89 G6
Europa Pl, EC1 ... 11 J4
Europe Rd, SE18 ... 136 C3
Eustace Bldg, SW8 ... 32 D6
Eustace Pl, SE18
off Borgard Rd ... 136 C4
Eustace Rd, E6 ... 116 B3
SW6 ... 128 D7
Romford RM6 ... 82 D7
Euston Cen, NW1
off Triton Sq ... 9 F5
Euston Gro, NW1 ... 9 H4
Euston Rd, N1 ... 10 A3
NW1 ... 9 E6
Croydon CR0 ... 201 G1
Euston Sq, NW1 ... 9 H4
Euston Sta, NW1 ... 9 G3
Euston Sta Colonnade, NW1 ... 9 H4
Euston St, NW1 ... 9 G5
Euston Twr, NW1 ... 9 F5
Evan Cook Cl, SE15 ... 153 F1
Evandale Rd, SW9 ... 151 G2
Evangelist Rd, NW5 ... 92 B4
Evans Business Cen, NW2 ... 89 G3
Evans Cl, E8
off Buttermere Wk ... 94 C6
Evans Gro, Felt. TW13 ... 161 G2
Evans Rd, SE6 ... 173 E2
Evanston Av, E4 ... 62 C7
Evanston Gdns, Ilf. IG4 ... 80 B6
Eva Rd, Rom. RM6 ... 82 C7
Evelina Rd, SE15 ... 153 F3
SE20 ... 171 G7
Eveline Lowe Est, SE16 ... 29 H6
Eveline Rd, Mitch. CR4 ... 185 J1
Evelyn Av, NW9 ... 70 D4
Evelyn Cl, Twick. TW2 ... 143 H7
Evelyn Ct, N1 ... 12 B2
Evelyn Denington Rd, E6 . 116 B4
Evelyn Dr, Pnr. HA5 ... 50 D7
Evelyn Fox Ct, W10 ... 107 J5
Evelyn Gdns, SW7 ... 30 E4
Richmond TW9
off Kew Rd ... 145 H4
Evelyn Gro, W5 ... 125 J1
Southall UB1 ... 103 F6
Evelyn Rd, E16 ... 135 H1
E17 ... 78 C4
SW19 ... 166 E5
W4 ... 126 D3
Barnet (Cockfos.) EN4 .. 41 J4
Richmond TW9 ... 145 H3
Richmond (Ham) TW10 163 F3
Evelyn St, SE8 ... 133 H5
Evelyn Ter, Rich. TW9 ... 145 H3
Evelyn Wk, N1 ... 12 B2
Evelyn Way, Wall. SM6 ... 200 D4
Evelyn Yd, W1 ... 17 H3
Evening Hill, Beck. BR3 ... 172 C7
Evenwood Cl, SW15 ... 148 B5
Everard Av, Brom. BR2 ... 205 G1
Everard Way, Wem. HA9 ... 87 H3
Everatt Cl, SW18
off Amerland Rd ... 148 C6
Everdon Rd, SW13 ... 127 G6
Everest Pl, E14 ... 114 C5
Everest Rd, SE9 ... 156 C5
Staines (Stanw.) TW19 ... 140 A7
Everett Cl, Bushey (Bushey Hth) WD23 ... 52 B1
Everett Wk, Belv. DA17
off Osborne Rd ... 139 F5
Everglade Strand, NW9 ... 71 F1
Evergreen Cl, SE20 ... 171 F7
Evergreen Ct, Stai. (Stanw.) TW19
off Evergreen Way ... 140 A7
Evergreen Sq, E8 ... 94 C7
Evergreen Way, Stai. (Stanw.) TW19 ... 140 A7
Everilda St, N1 ... 111 F1
Evering Rd, E5 ... 94 C3
N16 ... 94 C3
Everington Rd, N10 ... 73 J2
Everington St, W6 ... 128 A6
Everitt Rd, NW10 ... 106 D3
Everleigh St, N4 ... 93 F1
Eve Rd, E11 ... 96 E4
E15 ... 115 E2
N17 ... 76 B3
Isleworth TW7 ... 144 D4
Eversfield Gdns, NW7 ... 54 E6
Eversfield Rd, Rich. TW9 . 145 J2
Evershed Wk, W4 ... 126 C3
Eversholt Ct, Barn. EN5
off Lyonsdown Rd ... 41 F5
Eversholt St, NW1 ... 9 G1
Evershot Rd, N4 ... 93 F1
Eversleigh Rd, E6 ... 116 A1
N3 ... 56 C7
SW11 ... 149 J3
Barnet EN5 ... 41 F5
Eversley Av, Wem. HA9 ... 88 A2
Eversley Cl, N21 ... 43 F6
Loughton IG10 ... 49 F3
Eversley Cres, N21 ... 43 F6
Isleworth TW7 ... 144 A1
Eversley Mt, N21 ... 43 F6
Eversley Pk, SW19 ... 165 H5
Eversley Pk Rd, N21 ... 43 F6
Eversley Rd, SE7 ... 135 H6
SE19 ... 170 A7
Surbiton KT5 ... 181 J4
Eversley Way, Croy. CR0 . 204 A4
Everthorpe Rd, SE15 ... 152 C3
Everton Bldgs, NW1 ... 9 F4
Everton Dr, Stan. HA7 ... 69 J3
Everton Rd, Croy. CR0 ... 202 D1
Evesham Av, E17 ... 78 A2
Evesham Cl, Grnf. UB6 ... 103 H2
Sutton SM2 ... 198 D7
Evesham Ct, W13
off Tewkesbury Rd ... 124 D1
Evesham Grn, Mord. SM4 ... 184 E6
Evesham Rd, E15 ... 115 F1
N11 ... 58 C5
Morden SM4 ... 185 E6
Evesham St, W11 ... 108 A7
Evesham Wk, SE5
off Love Wk ... 152 A2
SW9 ... 151 G2
Evesham Way, SW11 ... 150 A3
Ilford IG5 ... 80 D3
Evry Rd, Sid. DA14 ... 176 C6
Ewald Rd, SW6 ... 148 C2
Ewanrigg Ter, Wdf.Grn. IG8 ... 63 J5
Ewart Gro, N22 ... 75 G1
Ewart Pl, E3
off Roman Rd ... 113 J2
Ewart Rd, SE23 ... 153 G7
Ewe Cl, N7 ... 93 E6
Ewell Bypass, Epsom KT17 ... 197 G7
Ewell Ct Av, Epsom KT19 ... 197 E5
Ewellhurst Rd, Ilf. IG5 ... 80 B2
Ewell Pk Gdns, Epsom KT17 ... 197 G7
Ewell Pk Way, Epsom (Ewell) KT17 ... 197 G6
Ewell Rd, Surb. KT6 ... 181 H6
Surbiton (Long Dit.) KT6 ... 180 E7
Sutton SM3 ... 198 B6
Ewelme Rd, SE23 ... 171 F1
Ewen Cres, SW2 ... 151 G7
Ewer St, SE1 ... 27 J2
Ewhurst Cl, E1 ... 113 F5
Ewhurst Ct, Mitch. CR4
off Phipps Br Rd ... 185 G3
Ewhurst Rd, SE4 ... 153 J6
Exbury Rd, SE6 ... 172 A2
Excalibur Ct, N9
off Galahad Rd ... 60 D3
Excel Ct, WC2 ... 17 J6
★ **ExCeL London**, E16 .. 115 H7
ExCeL Marina, E16
off Western Gateway . 115 G7
Excelsior Cl, Kings.T. KT1
off Washington Rd ... 182 A2
Excelsior Gdns, SE13 ... 154 C2
ExCeL Waterfront, E16
off Western Gateway . 115 H7
Exchange, The, E1
off Commercial St ... 13 F6
Exchange Arc, EC2 ... 20 E1
Exchange Cl, N11
off Benfleet Way ... 58 A2
Exchange Ct, WC2 ... 18 B6
Exchange Ho, N8 ... 74 E6
Exchange Pl, EC2 ... 20 D1
Exchange Sq, EC2 ... 20 D1
Exchange Wk, Pnr. HA5 ... 66 E7
Exeter Cl, E6
off Harper Rd ... 116 C6
Exeter Ct, Surb. KT6
off Maple Rd ... 181 H5
Exeter Gdns, Ilf. IG1 ... 98 B1
Exeter Ho, SW15
off Putney Heath ... 147 J6
Exeter Ms, NW6
off West Hampstead Ms ... 90 E6
SW6 *off Farm La* ... 128 D7
Exeter Rd, E16 ... 115 G5
E17 ... 78 A5
N9 ... 61 F2
N14 ... 58 B1
NW2 ... 90 B5
Croydon CR0 ... 188 B7
Dagenham RM10 ... 101 H6
Enfield EN3 ... 45 G3
Feltham TW13 ... 161 F3
Harrow HA2 ... 85 E2
Hounslow (Lon.Hthrw Air.) TW6 ... 141 H2
Welling DA16 ... 157 J2
Exeter St, WC2 ... 18 B5
Exeter Way, SE14 ... 133 J7
Hounslow (Lon.Hthrw Air.) TW6 ... 141 H3
Exford Gdns, SE12 ... 173 H1
Exford Rd, SE12 ... 173 H2
Exhibition Cl, W12 ... 107 J7
Exhibition Rd, SW7 ... 23 F4
Exmoor Cl, Ilf. IG6 ... 81 F1
Exmoor St, W10 ... 108 A4

Exmouth Mkt, EC1 ... **11** E5
Exmouth Ms, NW1 ... **9** G4
Exmouth Pl, E8 ... **94** E7
Exmouth Rd, E17 ... **77** J5
Ruislip HA4 ... **84** C3
Welling DA16 ... **158** C1
Exmouth St, E1
off Commercial Rd ... **113** F6
Exning Rd, E16 ... **115** F4
Exon St, SE17 ... **36** D2
Express Dr, Ilf. IG3 ... **100** B1
Exton Gdns, Dag. RM8 ... **100** C5
Exton Rd, NW10 ... **88** C7
Exton St, SE1 ... **27** E2
Eyebright Cl, Croy. CR0
off Primrose La ... **203** G1
Eyhurst Cl, NW2 ... **89** G2
Eylewood Rd, SE27 ... **169** J5
Eynella Rd, SE22 ... **152** C7
Eynham Rd, W12 ... **107** J6
Eynsford Cl, Orp. BR5 ... **193** F7
Eynsford Cres, Bex. DA5 . **176** C1
Eynsford Rd, Ilf. IG3 ... **99** H2
Eynsham Dr, SE2 ... **138** A4
Eynswood Dr, Sid. DA14 . **176** B5
Eyot Gdns, W6 ... **127** F5
Eyot Grn, W4
off Chiswick Mall ... **127** F5
Eyre Ct, NW8 ... **6** E1
Eyre St Hill, EC1 ... **11** E6
Eythorne Rd, SW9 ... **151** G1
Ezra St, E2 ... **13** G3

F

Faber Gdns, NW4 ... **71** G5
Fabian Rd, SW6 ... **128** C7
Fabian St, E6 ... **116** C4
Factory La, N17 ... **76** C2
Croydon CR0 ... **201** G1
Factory Rd, E16 ... **136** B1
Factory Sq, SW16 ... **168** E6
Factory Yd, W7
off Uxbridge Rd ... **124** B1
Faggs Rd, Felt. TW14 ... **142** A5
Fairacre, N.Mal. KT3 ... **182** E3
Fairacres, SW15 ... **147** G4
Fair Acres, Brom. BR2 ... **191** G5
Fairbairn Grn, SW9 ... **151** G1
Fairbank Av, Orp. BR6 ... **206** E2
Fairbank Est, N1 ... **12** C2
Fairbanks Rd, N17 ... **76** C3
Fairbourne Rd, N17 ... **76** B3
Fairbridge Rd, N19 ... **92** D2
Fairbrook Cl, N13 ... **59** G5
Fairbrook Rd, N13 ... **59** G6
Fairburn Cl, Borwd. WD6 ... **38** A1
Fairburn Ct, SW15 ... **148** B5
Fairburn Ho, W14
off Ivatt Pl ... **128** C5
Fairby Ho, SE1 ... **37** G1
Fairby Rd, SE12 ... **155** H5
Faircharm Trd Est, SE8 ... **134** A7
Fairchild Cl, SW11
off Wye St ... **149** G2
Fairchild Pl, EC2 ... **13** E6
Fairchild St, EC2 ... **13** E6
Fairclough Cl, Nthlt. UB5
off Waxlow Way ... **103** F4
Fairclough St, E1 ... **21** J4
Faircross Av, Bark. IG11 ... **99** F6
Faircross Par, Bark. IG11 ... **99** H6
Fairdale Gdns, SW15 ... **147** H4
Hayes UB3 ... **122** A1
Fairey Av, Hayes UB3 ... **121** J4
Fairfax Gdns, SE3 ... **156** A1
Fairfax Ms, E16
off Wesley Av ... **135** H1
SW15 ... **147** J4
Fairfax Pl, NW6 ... **91** F7
W14 ... **128** B3
Fairfax Rd, N8 ... **75** G4
NW6 ... **91** F7
W4 ... **127** E3
Teddington TW11 ... **162** D6
Fairfax Way, N10 ... **58** A7
Fairfield Av, NW4 ... **71** H6
Edgware HA8 ... **54** B6
Twickenham TW2 ... **161** H1
Watford WD19 ... **50** C3
Fairfield Cl, N12 ... **57** F4
Enfield EN3
off Scotland Grn Rd N . **45** H4
Epsom (Ewell) KT19 ... **196** E5
Mitcham CR4 ... **167** H7
Sidcup DA15 ... **157** J6
Fairfield Ct, NW10 ... **107** G1
Northwood HA6
off Windsor Cl ... **66** A2
Fairfield Cres, Edg. HA8 ... **54** B6
Fairfield Dr, SW18 ... **149** E5
Greenford (Perivale)
UB6 ... **105** F1
Fairfield Dr, Harrow HA2 .. **67** J3
Fairfield E, Kings.T. KT1 .. **181** H2
Fairfield Gdns, N8 ... **75** E5
Fairfield Gro, SE7 ... **136** A5
★ **Fairfield Halls**, Croy.
CR0 ... **202** A3
Fairfield N, Kings.T. KT1 .. **181** H2
Fairfield Path, Croy. CR0 . **202** A3
Fairfield Pl, Kings.T. KT1 .. **181** H3
Fairfield Rd, E3 ... **114** A2
E17 ... **77** H2
N8 ... **75** E5
N18 ... **60** D4
W7 ... **124** D3
Beckenham BR3 ... **190** A2
Bexleyheath DA7 ... **159** F2
Bromley BR1 ... **173** G7
Croydon CR0 ... **202** B3
Ilford IG1 ... **99** E6
Kingston upon Thames
KT1 ... **181** H2
Orpington BR5 ... **193** G6
Southall UB1 ... **103** F6
West Drayton UB7 ... **120** B1
Woodford Green IG8 ... **63** G6
Fairfields Cl, NW9 ... **70** C5
Fairfields Cres, NW9 ... **70** C4
Fairfield S, Kings.T. KT1 .. **181** H3
Fairfields Rd, Houns.
TW3 ... **143** J3
Fairfield St, SW18 ... **149** E5
Fairfield Trade Pk, Kings.T.
KT1 ... **181** J3
Fairfield Way, Barn. EN5 ... **40** D5
Epsom KT19 ... **196** E5
Fairfield W, Kings.T. KT1 .. **181** H2
Fairfoot Rd, E3 ... **114** A4
Fairford Av, Croy. CR0 ... **189** G5
Fairford Cl, Croy. CR0 ... **189** H5
Fairford Ct, Sutt. SM2
off Grange Rd ... **198** E7
Fairford Gdns, Wor.Pk.
KT4 ... **197** F3
Fairford Ho, SE11 ... **35** F2
Fairgreen, Barn. EN4 ... **41** J3
Fairgreen E, Barn. EN4 ... **41** J3
Fairgreen Par, Mitch. CR4
off London Rd ... **185** J3
Fairgreen Rd, Th.Hth.
CR7 ... **187** H5
Fairhaven Av, Croy. CR0 .. **189** G6
Fairhaven Cres, Wat.
WD19 ... **50** A3
Fairhazel Gdns, NW6 ... **91** E6
Fairholme, Felt. TW14 ... **141** G7
Fairholme Cl, N3 ... **72** B4
Fairholme Gdns, N3 ... **72** B3
Fairholme Rd, W14 ... **128** B5
Croydon CR0 ... **187** G7
Harrow HA1 ... **68** C5
Ilford IG1 ... **80** C7
Sutton SM1 ... **198** C6
Fairholt Cl, N16 ... **94** B1
Fairholt Rd, N16 ... **94** A1
Fairholt St, SW7 ... **23** H5
Fairland Rd, E15 ... **97** F6
Fairlands Av, Buck.H. IG9 ... **63** G2
Sutton SM1 ... **198** D2
Thornton Heath CR7 .. **187** F4
Fairlands Ct, SE9
off North Pk ... **156** D6
Fairlawn, SE7 ... **135** J6
Fairlawn Av, N2 ... **73** H4
W4 ... **126** C4
Bexleyheath DA7 ... **158** D2
Fairlawn Cl, N14 ... **42** C6
Esher (Clay.) KT10 ... **194** C6
Feltham TW13 ... **161** F4
Kingston upon Thames
KT2 ... **164** C6
Fairlawn Ct, SE7
off Fairlawn ... **135** J7
Fairlawn Dr, Wdf.Grn.
IG8 ... **63** G7
Fairlawnes, Wall. SM6
off Maldon Rd ... **200** B5
Fairlawn Gdns, Sthl. UB1 . **103** F7
Fairlawn Gro, W4 ... **126** C4
Fairlawn Pk, SE26 ... **171** H5
Fairlawn Rd, SW19 ... **166** C7
Fairlawns, Pnr. HA5 ... **66** C2
Sunbury-on-Thames
TW16 ... **178** A3
Twickenham TW1 ... **145** F6
Fairlead Ho, E14
off Cassilis Rd ... **134** A3
Fairlea Pl, W5 ... **105** G4
Fairlie Ct, E3
off Stroudley Wk ... **114** B3
Fairlie Gdns, SE23 ... **153** F7
Fairlight Av, E4 ... **62** D2
NW10 ... **107** E2
Woodford Green IG8 ... **63** G6
Fairlight Cl, E4 ... **62** D2
Worcester Park KT4 ... **197** J4
Fairlight Rd, SW17 ... **167** G4
Fairlop Gdns, Ilf. IG6 ... **65** F7
Fairlop Rd, E11 ... **78** D7
Ilford IG6 ... **81** F2
Fairmead, Brom. BR1 ... **192** C4
Surbiton KT5 ... **196** B1
Fairmead Cl, Brom. BR1 .. **192** C4
Hounslow TW5 ... **122** D7
New Malden KT3 ... **182** D3
Fairmead Cres, Edg. HA8 .. **54** C3
Fairmead Gdns, Ilf. IG4 ... **80** B5
Fairmead Ho, E9
off Kingsmead Way ... **95** H4
Fairmead Rd, N19 ... **92** D3
Croydon CR0 ... **201** F1
Loughton IG10 ... **47** H4
Fairmeads, Loug. IG10 ... **48** E2
Fairmeadside, Loug. IG10 . **47** J5
Fairmile Av, SW16 ... **168** D5
Fairmile Ho, Tedd. TW11
off Twickenham Rd ... **162** D4
Fairmont Av, E14 ... **134** D1
Fairmont Cl, Belv. DA17 .. **139** F5
Fairmount Rd, SW2 ... **151** F6
Fairoak Cl, Orp. BR5 ... **193** E7
Fairoak Dr, SE9 ... **157** G5
Fair Oak Pl, Ilf. IG6 ... **81** F2
Fairseat Cl, Bushey
(Bushey Hth) WD23
off Hive Rd ... **52** B2
Fairstead Wk, N1
off Popham Rd ... **111** J1
Fair St, SE1 ... **29** E3
Hounslow TW3
off High St ... **143** J3
Fairthorn Rd, SE7 ... **135** G5
Fairview, Ruis. HA4
off The Fairway ... **84** C4
Fairview Av, Wem. HA0 ... **87** G6
Fairview Cl, E17 ... **77** H1
Chigwell IG7 ... **65** H4
Fairview Ct, NW4 ... **72** A2
Fairview Cres, Har. HA2 ... **85** G1
Fairview Dr, Chig. IG7 ... **65** H4
Orpington BR6 ... **207** G4
Fairview Gdns, Wdf.Grn.
IG8 ... **79** H1
Fairview Pl, SW2 ... **151** F7
Fairview Rd, N15 ... **76** C5
SW16 ... **187** F1
Chigwell IG7 ... **65** H4
Enfield EN2 ... **43** G1
Sutton SM1 ... **199** G5
Fairview Way, Edg. HA8 ... **54** A4
Fairwater Av, Well. DA16 . **158** A4
Fairway, SW20 ... **183** J3
Bexleyheath DA6 ... **159** E5
Orpington BR5 ... **193** G5
Woodford Green IG8 ... **63** J5
Fairway, The, N13 ... **59** J3
N14 ... **42** B6
NW7 ... **54** D3
W3 ... **106** E6
Barnet (New Barn.)
EN5 ... **41** E6
Bromley BR1 ... **192** C5
New Malden KT3 ... **182** D1
Northolt UB5 ... **85** J6
Ruislip HA4 ... **84** D3
Wembley HA0 ... **87** E3
West Molesey KT8 ... **179** H3
Fairway Av, NW9 ... **70** B3
Borehamwood WD6 ... **38** B2
Fairway Cl, NW11 ... **73** F7
Croydon CR0 ... **189** H5
Epsom KT19 ... **196** C4
Hounslow TW4 ... **142** C5
Fairway Ct, NW7
off The Fairway ... **54** D3
Fairway Dr, SE28 ... **118** D6
Greenford UB6 ... **85** H7
Fairway Gdns, Beck.
BR3 ... **190** D6
Ilford IG1 ... **99** F5
Fairways, Stan. HA7 ... **69** H2
Teddington TW11 ... **163** G7
Fairweather Cl, N15 ... **76** B4
Fairweather Rd, N16 ... **76** D6
Fairwyn Rd, SE26 ... **171** H4
Fakenham Cl, NW7 ... **55** G7
Northolt UB5
off Goodwood Dr ... **85** G6
Fakruddin St, E1 ... **13** J6
Falcon Av, Brom. BR1 ... **192** B4
Falconberg Ct, W1 ... **17** J3
Falconberg Ms, W1 ... **17** H3
Falcon Business Cen, Mitch.
CR4 ... **185** J5
Falcon Cl, W4
off Sutton La S ... **126** C6
Falcon Ct, EC4 ... **19** E4
Falcon Cres, Enf. EN3 ... **45** G5
Falcon Dr, Stai. (Stanw.)
TW19 ... **140** A6
Falconer Ct, N17
off Compton Cres ... **59** J7
Falconer Wk, N7
off Newington
Barrow Way ... **93** F2
Falcon Est, Felt. TW14
off Central Way ... **142** B5
Falcon Gro, SW11 ... **149** H3
Falcon Ho, W13 ... **104** C4
Falcon La, SW11 ... **149** H3
Falcon Pk Ind Est, NW10 .. **89** F5
Falcon Rd, SW11 ... **149** H2
Enfield EN3 ... **45** G5
Hampton TW12 ... **161** F7
Falcon St, E13 ... **115** G4
Falcon Ter, SW11 ... **149** H3
Falcon Way, E11 ... **79** G4
E14 ... **134** B4
NW9 ... **71** E2
Feltham TW14 ... **142** B5
Harrow HA3 ... **69** H5
FALCONWOOD, Well.
DA16 ... **157** G3
Falconwood, SE9 ... **157** F4
Falconwood Av, Well.
DA16 ... **157** G2
Falconwood Par, Well.
DA16 ... **157** H4
Falconwood Rd, Croy.
CR0 ... **204** A7
Falcourt Cl, Sutt. SM1 ... **198** E5
Falkirk Gdns, Wat. WD19 .. **50** D5
Falkirk Ho, W9 ... **6** B3
Falkirk St, N1 ... **12** E2
Falkland Av, N3 ... **56** D7
N11 ... **58** A4
Falkland Pk Av, SE25 ... **188** B3
Falkland Pl, NW5
off Falkland Rd ... **92** C5
Falkland Rd, N8 ... **75** G4
NW5 ... **92** C5
Barnet EN5 ... **40** B2
Fallaize Av, Ilf. IG1
off Riverdene Rd ... **98** E4
Falloden Way, NW11 ... **72** D4
Fallow Cl, Chig. IG7 ... **65** J5
Fallow Ct, SE16 ... **37** J4
Fallow Ct Av, N12 ... **57** F7
Fallowfield, N4
off Six Acres Est ... **93** F2
Stanmore HA7 ... **52** D3
Fallowfield Ct, Stan. HA7 .. **52** D3
Fallow Flds, Loug. IG10 ... **47** J7
Fallowfields Dr, N12 ... **57** H6
Fallows Cl, N2 ... **73** F2
Fallsbrook Rd, SW16 ... **168** C7
Falman Cl, N9
off Croyland Rd ... **60** D1
Falmer Rd, E17 ... **78** B3
N15 ... **75** J5
Enfield EN1 ... **44** B4
Falmouth Av, E4 ... **62** D5
Falmouth Cl, N22 ... **59** F7
SE12 ... **155** F5
Falmouth Gdns, Ilf. IG4 ... **80** B5
Falmouth Ho, Kings.T.
KT2 *off Kingsgate Rd* .. **181** G1
Falmouth Rd, SE1 ... **28** A5
Falmouth St, E15 ... **96** D5
Falmouth Way, E17
off Gosport Rd ... **77** J5
Falstaff Ms, Hmptn.
(Hmptn H.) TW12
off Hampton Rd ... **162** A5
Fambridge Cl, SE26 ... **171** J4
Fambridge Rd, Dag. RM8 . **101** G1
Fane St, W14
off North End Rd ... **128** C6
★ **Fan Mus**, SE10 ... **134** C7
Fann St, EC1 ... **11** J6
EC2 ... **11** J6
Fanshawe, The, Dag. RM9
off Gale St ... **100** D7
Fanshawe Av, Bark. IG11 .. **99** F6
Fanshawe Cres, Dag.
RM9 ... **101** E5
Fanshawe Rd, Rich.
TW10 ... **163** F4
Fanshaw St, N1 ... **12** D3
Fantail, The, Orp. BR6 ... **206** C4
Fantail Cl, SE28
off Greenhaven Dr ... **118** C6
Fanthorpe St, SW15 ... **147** J3
Faraday Av, Sid. DA14 ... **176** A2
Faraday Cl, N7
off Bride St ... **93** F6
Faraday Lo, SE10
off Renaissance Wk .. **135** F3
★ **Faraday Mus**, W1 ... **17** F6
Faraday Pl, W.Mol. KT8 ... **179** G4

Faraday Rd, E15 ... 97 F6
SW19 ... 166 D6
W3 ... 106 C7
W10 ... 108 B5
Southall UB1 ... 103 H7
Welling DA16 ... 158 A3
West Molesey KT8 ... 179 G4
Faraday Way, SE18 ... 136 A3
Croydon CR0
off Ampere Way ... 201 F1
Fareham Rd, Felt. TW14 ... 142 C7
Fareham St, W1 ... 17 H3
Farewell Pl, Mitch. CR4 ... 185 H1
Faringdon Av, Brom.
BR2 ... 192 E6
Faringford Rd, E15 ... 96 E7
Farjeon Rd, SE3 ... 156 A1
Farleigh Av, Brom. BR2 ... 191 F6
Farleigh Pl, N16 ... 94 C4
Farleigh Rd, N16 ... 94 C4
Farley Dr, Ilf. IG3 ... 99 H1
Farley Ms, SE6 ... 154 C7
Farley Pl, SE25 ... 188 D4
Farley Rd, SE6 ... 154 B7
South Croydon CR2 ... 202 E7
Farlington Pl, SW15
off Roehampton La ... 147 H7
Farlow Rd, SW15 ... 148 A3
Farlton Rd, SW18 ... 149 E7
Farman Gro, Nthlt. UB5
off Wayfarer Rd ... 102 D3
Farm Av, NW2 ... 90 B3
SW16 ... 169 E4
Harrow HA2 ... 67 F7
Wembley HA0 ... 87 F6
Farmborough Cl, Har. HA1
off Pool Rd ... 68 A7
Farm Cl, SW6
off Farm La ... 128 D7
Barnet EN5 ... 39 J5
Buckhurst Hill IG9 ... 63 J3
Dagenham RM10 ... 101 J7
Southall UB1 ... 103 H7
Sutton SM2 ... 199 G7
West Wickham BR4 ... 205 E3
Farmcote Rd, SE12 ... 173 G1
Farm Ct, NW4 ... 71 G3
Farmdale Rd, SE10 ... 135 G5
Carshalton SM5 ... 199 H7
Farm Dr, Croy. CR0 ... 203 J2
Farm End, E4 ... 46 E5
Farmer Rd, E10 ... 96 B1
Farmers Rd, SE5 ... 35 H7
Farmer St, W8
off Uxbridge St ... 128 D1
Farmfield Rd, Brom. BR1 ... 172 E5
Farmhouse Rd, SW16 ... 168 C7
Farmilo Rd, E17 ... 77 J7
Farmington Av, Sutt.
SM1 ... 199 G3
Farmlands, Enf. EN2 ... 43 G1
Pinner HA5 ... 66 A4
Farmlands, The, Nthlt.
UB5 ... 85 F6
Farmland Wk, Chis. BR7 ... 174 E5
Farm La, N14 ... 42 A6
SW6 ... 128 D6
Croydon CR0 ... 203 J2
Farm La Trd Cen, SW6
off Farm La ... 128 D6
Farmleigh, N14 ... 42 C7
Farm Pl, W8
off Uxbridge St ... 128 D1
Farm Rd, N21 ... 59 H1
NW10 ... 106 D1
Edgware HA8 ... 54 B6
Hounslow TW4 ... 161 E1
Morden SM4 ... 185 E5
Sutton SM2 ... 199 G7
Farmstead Rd, SE6 ... 172 B4
Harrow HA3 ... 68 A1
Farm St, W1 ... 16 D6
Farm Vale, Bex. DA5 ... 159 H6
Farm Wk, NW11 ... 72 C5
Farm Way, Buck.H. IG9 ... 63 J4
Farmway, Dag. RM8 ... 100 C4
Farm Way, Wor.Pk. KT4 ... 197 J3
Farnaby Rd, SE9 ... 155 J4
Bromley BR1, BR2 ... 172 D7
Farnan Av, E17 ... 78 A2
Farnan Rd, SW16 ... 169 E5
FARNBOROUGH, Orp.
BR6 ... 206 E5
Farnborough Av, E17 ... 77 H3
South Croydon CR2 ... 203 G7
Farnborough Cl, Wem.
HA9 ... 88 B2
Farnborough Common,
Orp. BR6 ... 206 C3
Farnborough Cres, Brom.
BR2 *off Saville Row* ... 205 F1
Farnborough Hill,
Orp. BR6 ... 207 G5
Farnborough Ho, SW15
off Fontley Way ... 165 G1
Farnborough Way,
Orp. BR6 ... 207 F4
Farncombe St, SE16 ... 29 J4
Farndale Av, N13 ... 59 H3
Farndale Cres, Grnf. UB6 ... 103 J3
Farnell Ms, SW5 ... 30 A3
Farnell Pl, W3 ... 106 B7
Farnell Rd, Islw. TW7 ... 144 A3
Farnham Cl, N20 ... 41 F7
Farnham Gdns, SW20 ... 183 H2
Farnham Pl, SE1 ... 27 H2
Farnham Rd, Ilf. IG3 ... 81 J7
Welling DA16 ... 158 C2
Farnham Royal, SE11 ... 34 D4
Farningham Rd, N17 ... 60 D7
Farnley Rd, E4 ... 46 E7
SE25 ... 188 A4
Farnsworth Ct, SE10
off West Parkside ... 135 F3
Faro Cl, Brom. BR1 ... 192 D2
Faroe Rd, W14 ... 128 A3
Farorna Wk, Enf. EN2 ... 43 G1
Farquhar Rd, SE19 ... 170 C5
SW19 ... 166 D3
Farquharson Rd, Croy.
CR0 ... 201 J1
Farrance Rd, Rom. RM6 ... 83 E6
Farrance St, E14 ... 113 J6
Farrans Ct, Har. HA3 ... 69 E7
Farrant Av, N22 ... 75 G2
Farr Av, Bark. IG11 ... 118 A2
Farrell Ho, E1 ... 113 F6
Farren Rd, SE23 ... 171 H2
Farrer Ms, N8
off Farrer Rd ... 74 C4
Farrer Rd, N8 ... 74 C4
Harrow HA3 ... 69 H5
Farrer's Pl, Croy. CR0 ... 203 G4
Farrier Cl, Brom. BR1 ... 192 A3
Sunbury-on-Thames
TW16 ... 178 A4
Farrier Pl, Sutt. SM1 ... 198 D3
Farrier Rd, Nthlt. UB5 ... 103 G2
Farriers Ct, Sutt. SM3
off Forge La ... 198 B7
Farriers Ms, SE15
off Machell Rd ... 153 F3
Farrier St, NW1 ... 92 B7
Farriers Way, Borwd. WD6 ... 38 C6
Farrier Wk, SW10 ... 30 C5
Farringdon Ho, Rich. TW9
off Strand Dr ... 126 B7
Farringdon La, EC1 ... 11 F6
Farringdon Rd, EC1 ... 10 E5
Farringdon St, EC4 ... 19 G3
Farrington Pl, Chis. BR7 ... 175 G7
Farrins Rents, SE16 ... 133 H1
Farrow La, SE14 ... 133 F7
Farrow Pl, SE16
off Ropemaker Rd ... 133 H3
Farr Rd, Enf. EN2 ... 44 A1
Farthingale Wk, E15 ... 96 D7
Farthing All, SE1 ... 29 H4
Farthing Ct, NW7 ... 56 B7
Farthing Flds, E1
off Raine St ... 133 E1
Farthings, The, Kings.T.
KT2 ... 182 A1
Farthings Cl, E4 ... 63 E3
Pinner HA5 ... 66 B6
Farthing St, Orp. BR6 ... 206 C7
Farwell Rd, Sid. DA14 ... 176 B3
Farwig La, Brom. BR1 ... 191 F1
Fashion St, E1 ... 21 F2
Fashoda Rd, Brom. BR2 ... 192 A4
Fassett Rd, E8 ... 94 D6
Kingston upon Thames
KT1 ... 181 H4
Fassett Sq, E8 ... 94 D6
Fauconberg Rd, W4 ... 126 C6
Faulkner Cl, Dag. RM8 ... 82 D7
Faulkner's All, EC1 ... 19 G1
Faulkner St, SE14 ... 153 F1
Fauna Cl, Rom. RM6 ... 82 C7
Stanmore HA7 ... 53 G4
Faunce St, SE17 ... 35 G5
Favart Rd, SW6 ... 148 D1
Faversham Av, E4 ... 63 E1
Enfield EN1 ... 44 A6
Faversham Rd, SE6 ... 153 J7
Beckenham BR3 ... 189 J2
Morden SM4 ... 185 E6
Fawcett Cl, SW11 ... 149 G2
SW16 ... 169 G4
Fawcett Est, E5 ... 94 D1
Fawcett Rd, NW10 ... 107 F1
Croydon CR0 ... 201 J3
Fawcett St, SW10 ... 30 C5
Fawcus Cl, Esher (Clay.)
KT10 *off Dalmore Av* ... 194 C6
Fawe Pk Rd, SW15 ... 148 C4
Fawe St, E14 ... 114 B5
Fawkham Ho, SE1
off Longfield Est ... 37 G2
Fawley Rd, NW6 ... 90 E5
Fawnbrake Av, SE24 ... 151 H5
Fawn Rd, E13 ... 115 J2
Chigwell IG7 ... 65 J5
Fawood Av, NW10 ... 88 D7
Faygate Cres, Bexh. DA6 ... 159 G5
Faygate Rd, SW2 ... 169 F2
Fayland Av, SW16 ... 168 C5
Fearnley Cres, Hmptn.
TW12 ... 161 E5
Fearon St, SE10 ... 135 G5
Featherbed La, Croy.
CR0 ... 203 J7
Feathers Pl, SE10 ... 134 D6
Featherstone Av, SE23 ... 171 E2
Featherstone Gdns,
Borwd. WD6 ... 38 C4
Featherstone Ind Est, Sthl.
UB2 ... 123 E2
Featherstone Rd, NW7 ... 55 H6
Southall UB2 ... 122 E3
Featherstone St, EC1 ... 12 B5
Featherstone Ter, Sthl.
UB2 ... 123 E3
Featley Rd, SW9 ... 151 H3
Federal Rd, Grnf.
(Perivale) UB6 ... 105 F2
Federation Rd, SE2 ... 138 B4
Fee Fm Rd, Esher (Clay.)
KT10 ... 194 C7
Feeny Cl, NW10 ... 89 F4
Felbridge Av, Stan. HA7 ... 68 D1
Felbridge Cl, SW16 ... 169 G4
Felbridge Ho, SE22
off Pytchley Rd ... 152 B3
Felbrigge Rd, Ilf. IG3 ... 99 J2
Felday Rd, SE13 ... 154 B6
Felden Cl, Pnr. HA5 ... 51 E7
Felden St, SW6 ... 148 C1
Feldman Cl, N16 ... 94 D1
Feldspar Ct, Enf. EN3
off Enstone Rd ... 45 H3
Felgate Ms, W6 ... 127 H4
Felhampton Rd, SE9 ... 174 E2
Felhurst Cres, Dag. RM10 ... 101 H4
Felix Av, N8 ... 74 E6
Felix Pl, SW2
off Talma Rd ... 151 G5
Felix Rd, W13 ... 104 D7
Walton-on-Thames
KT12 ... 178 A6
Felixstowe Ct, E16
off Fishguard Way ... 137 E1
Felixstowe Rd, N9 ... 60 D4
N17 ... 76 C3
NW10 ... 107 H3
SE2 ... 138 B3
Fellbrigg Rd, SE22 ... 152 C5
Fellbrigg St, E1
off Headlam St ... 113 E4
Fellbrook, Rich. TW10 ... 163 E3
Fellmongers Path, SE1 ... 29 E4
Fellmongers Yd, Croy. CR0
off Surrey St ... 201 J3
Fellowes Cl, Hayes UB4
off Paddington Cl ... 102 D4
Fellowes Rd, Cars. SM5 ... 199 H3
Fellows Ct, E2 ... 13 F2
Fellows Rd, NW3 ... 91 G7
Fell Rd, Croy. CR0 ... 201 J3
Felltram Ms, SE7
off Woolwich Rd ... 135 G5
Felltram Way, SE7
off Woolwich Rd ... 135 G5
Fell Wk, Edg. HA8
off East Rd ... 70 C1
Felmersham Cl, SW4
off Haselrigge Rd ... 150 D4
Felmingham Rd, SE20 ... 189 F2
Felnex Trd Est, Wall.
SM6 ... 200 A2
Felsberg Rd, SW2 ... 151 E6
Fels Cl, Dag. RM10 ... 101 H3
Fels Fm Av, Dag. RM10 ... 101 J3
Felsham Rd, SW15 ... 148 A3
Felspar Cl, SE18 ... 137 J5
Felstead Av, Ilf. IG5 ... 80 D1
Felstead Cl, N13 ... 59 G5
Felstead Gdns, E14
off Ferry St ... 134 C5
Felstead Rd, E11 ... 79 G7
Loughton IG10 ... 48 B7
Felstead St, E9 ... 95 J6
Felsted Rd, E16 ... 116 A6
FELTHAM, TW13 & TW14 ... 160 A2
Feltham Av, E.Mol. KT8 ... 180 B4
Felthambrook Way, Felt.
TW13 ... 160 B3
Feltham Business Complex,
Felt. TW13 ... 160 B2
Feltham Rd, Mitch. CR4 ... 185 J2
Felton Cl, Orp. BR5 ... 192 E6
Felton Gdns, Bark. IG11
off Sutton Rd ... 117 H1
Felton Ho, SE3
off Ryan Cl ... 155 H4
Felton Lea, Sid. DA14 ... 175 J5
Felton Rd, W13
off Camborne Av ... 125 F2
Barking IG11
off Sutton Rd ... 117 H2
Felton St, N1 ... 112 A1
Fencepiece Rd, Chig. IG7 ... 65 F5
Ilford IG6 ... 65 F5
Fenchurch Av, EC3 ... 20 D4
Fenchurch Bldgs, EC3 ... 20 E4
Fenchurch Pl, EC3 ... 20 E5
Fenchurch St, EC3 ... 20 D5
Fen Ct, EC3 ... 20 D4
Fendall Rd, Epsom KT19 ... 196 C5
Fendall St, SE1 ... 29 E6
Fendt Cl, E16
off Bowman Av ... 115 F7
Fendyke Rd, Belv. DA17 ... 138 D3
Fenelon Pl, W14 ... 128 C4
Fen Gro, Sid. DA15 ... 157 J6
Fenham Rd, SE15 ... 132 D7
Fen La, SW13 ... 147 H1
Fenman Ct, N17
off Shelbourne Rd ... 77 E1
Fenman Gdns, Ilf. IG3 ... 100 B1
Fenn Cl, Brom. BR1 ... 173 G6
Fennel Cl, E16
off Cranberry La ... 115 E4
Croydon CR0
off Primrose La ... 203 G1
Fennel St, SE18 ... 136 D6
Fenner Cl, SE16
off Layard Rd ... 133 E4
Fenner Sq, SW11
off Thomas
Baines Rd ... 149 G3
Fenning St, SE1 ... 28 D3
Fenn St, E9 ... 95 F5
Fenstanton Av, N12 ... 57 G5
Fen St, E16
off Huntingdon St ... 115 F7
Fenswood Cl, Bex. DA5 ... 159 G5
Fentiman Rd, SW8 ... 34 B6
Fentiman Way, Har. HA2 ... 85 H2
Fenton Cl, E8
off Laurel St ... 94 C6
SW9 ... 151 F2
Chislehurst BR7 ... 174 C5
★ **Fenton Ho**, NW3 ... 91 F3
Fenton Ho, Houns. TW5
off Biscoe Cl ... 123 G6
Fenton Rd, N17 ... 59 J7
Fentons Av, E13 ... 115 H2
Fenwick Cl, SE18 ... 136 D6
Fenwick Gro, SE15 ... 152 D3
Fenwick Pl, SW9 ... 150 E3
South Croydon CR2
off Columbine Av ... 201 H7
Fenwick Rd, SE15 ... 152 D3
Ferdinand Pl, NW1
off Ferdinand St ... 92 A7
Ferdinand St, NW1 ... 92 A6
Ferguson Av, Surb. KT5 ... 181 J5
Ferguson Cl, E14 ... 134 A4
Bromley BR2 ... 190 D3
Ferguson Dr, W3 ... 106 D6
Fergus Rd, N5
off Calabria Rd ... 93 H5
Ferme Pk Rd, N4 ... 75 E5
N8 ... 75 E5
Fermor Rd, SE23 ... 171 H1
Fermoy Rd, W9 ... 108 C4
Greenford UB6 ... 103 H4
Fern Av, Mitch. CR4 ... 186 D4
Fernbank, Buck.H. IG9 ... 63 H1
Fernbank Av, Walt. KT12 ... 179 E7
Wembley HA0 ... 86 C4
Fernbank Ms, SW12 ... 150 B6
Fernbrook Av, Sid. DA15
off Blackfen Rd ... 157 H5
Fernbrook Cres, SE13 ... 154 E6
Fernbrook Dr, Har. HA2 ... 67 H7
Fernbrook Rd, SE13 ... 154 E6
Ferncliff Rd, E8 ... 94 D5
Fern Cl, N1 ... 12 D1
Ferncroft Av, N12 ... 57 H6
NW3 ... 90 D3
Ruislip HA4 ... 84 C2
Ferndale, Brom. BR1 ... 191 J2
Ferndale Av, E17 ... 78 D5
Hounslow TW4 ... 143 E3
Ferndale Cl, Bexh. DA7 ... 158 E1
Ferndale Ct, SE3 ... 135 F7
Ferndale Rd, E7 ... 97 H7
E11 ... 97 E2
N15 ... 76 C6
SE25 ... 188 E5

Ferndale Rd, SW4 ....150 E4
  SW9 ....151 F3
  Romford RM5 ....83 J2
Ferndale St, E6 ....116 E7
Ferndale Ter, Har. HA1 ...68 C4
Ferndale Way, Orp. BR6 .207 G5
Fern Dene, W13
  off Templewood 105 E5
Ferndene Rd, SE24 .....151 J4
Fernden Way, Rom. RM7 .83 H6
Ferndown, Nthwd. HA6 ...66 A2
Ferndown Av, Orp. BR6 .207 G1
Ferndown Cl, Pnr. HA5 ...50 E7
  Sutton SM2 ....199 G6
Ferndown Rd, SE9 ....156 A7
  Watford WD19 ....50 C3
Ferney Meade Way, Islw.
  TW7 ....144 D2
Ferney Rd, Barn. (E.Barn.)
  EN4 ....42 A7
Fern Gro, Felt. TW14 ....142 B7
Fernhall Dr, Ilf. IG4 .....80 A5
Fernham Rd, Th.Hth. CR7 .187 J3
Fernhead Rd, W9 ....108 C4
Fernhill Ct, E17 ....78 D2
Fernhill Gdns, Kings.T.
  KT2 ....163 G5
Fernhill St, E16 ....136 C1
Fernholme Rd, SE15 .....153 G5
Fernhurst Gdns, Edg. HA8 .54 A6
Fernhurst Rd, SW6 ......148 B1
  Croydon CR0 ....188 D7
Fern La, Houns. TW5 ....123 F5
Fernlea Rd, SW12 ....168 B1
  Mitcham CR4 ....186 A2
Fernleigh Cl, W9 ....108 C3
  Croydon CR0 ....201 G4
Fernleigh Ct, Har. HA2 ...67 H2
  Wembley HA9 ....87 H2
Fernleigh Rd, N21 ....59 G2
Fernley Cl, Pnr. (Eastcote)
  HA5 ....66 A4
Fernsbury St, WC1 ......10 E4
Fernshaw Rd, SW10 .....30 C6
Fernside, NW11 ....90 D2
  Buckhurst Hill IG9 ....63 H1
Fernside Av, NW7 ....54 D3
  Feltham TW13 ....160 B4
Fernside Rd, SW12 ......167 J1
Ferns Rd, E15 ....97 F6
Fern St, E3 ....114 A4
Fernthorpe Rd, SW16 ...168 C6
Ferntower Rd, N5 ....94 A5
Fern Wk, SE16 ....37 J4
Fernways, Ilf. IG1
  off Cecil Rd 98 E4
Fernwood, SW19 ....166 C1
  off Albert Dr
Fernwood Av, SW16 .....168 D4
  Wembley HA0
  off Bridgewater Rd 87 F5
Fernwood Cl, Brom. BR1 .191 J2
Fernwood Cres, N20 .....57 J3
Ferranti Cl, SE18 ....136 A3
Ferraro Cl, Houns. TW5 .123 G6
Ferrers Av, Wall. SM6 ...200 D4
  West Drayton UB7 .....120 A2
Ferrers Rd, SW16 ....168 D5
Ferrestone Rd, N8 ......75 F4
Ferrey Ms, SW9 ....151 G2
Ferriby Cl, N1
  off Bewdley St 93 G7
Ferrier Pt, E16
  off Forty Acre La 115 G5
Ferrier St, SW18 ....149 E4
Ferring Cl, Har. HA2 ....85 J1
Ferrings, SE21 ....170 B2
Ferris Av, Croy. CR0 ....203 J3
Ferris Rd, SE22 ....152 D4
Ferron Rd, E5 ....94 E3
Ferrour Ct, N2 ....73 G3
Ferrybridge Ho, SE11 ...26 D6
Ferryhills Cl, Wat. WD19 .50 C3
Ferry Ho, E5
  off Harrington Hill 95 F1
Ferry La, N17 ....76 D4
  SW13 ....127 F6
  Brentford TW8 ....125 H6
  Richmond TW9 ....125 J6
Ferryman's Quay, SW6 ..149 F2
Ferrymead Av, Grnf. UB6 .103 G3
Ferrymead Dr, Grnf. UB6 .103 G2
Ferrymead Gdns, Grnf.
  UB6 ....103 J2
Ferrymoor, Rich. TW10 ..163 E3
Ferry Pl, SE18
  off Woolwich High St .136 D3
Ferry Rd, SW13 ....127 G7
  Teddington TW11 .....162 E5
  Thames Ditton KT7 ...180 E6
  Twickenham TW1 .....162 E1
  West Molesey KT8 ....179 G3
Ferry Sq, Brent. TW8 ...125 G6

Ferry St, E14 ....134 C5
Festing Rd, SW15 ......148 A3
Festival Cl, Bex. DA5 ...176 D1
Festival Ct, Sutt. SM1
  off Cleeve Way 185 C5
Festival Wk, Cars. SM5 .199 J5
Festoon Way, E16 ......116 A7
Fetter La, EC4 ....19 F4
Ffinch St, SE8 ....134 A7
Fidgeon Cl, Brom. BR1 .192 D3
Field Cl, E4 ....62 B6
  NW2 ....89 G2
  Bromley BR1 ....191 J2
  Buckhurst Hill IG9 ....63 J3
  Chessington KT9 .....195 F5
  Hayes (Harling.) UB3 .121 F7
  Hounslow TW4 ....142 B1
  West Molesey KT8 ...179 H5
Fieldcommon La, Walt.
  KT12 ....179 F7
Field Ct, WC1 ....18 D2
Field End, Barn. EN5 ....39 H4
  Northolt UB5 ....84 D6
  Ruislip HA4 ....84 C6
Fieldend, Twick. TW1 ...162 C4
Fieldend Rd, SW16 .....186 C1
Field End Rd, Pnr. HA5 ..66 B6
  Ruislip HA4 ....85 E4
Fielders Cl, Enf. EN1
  off Woodfield Cl 44 B4
  Harrow HA2 ....85 J1
Fieldfare Rd, SE28 ......118 C7
Fieldgate La, Mitch. CR4 .185 H3
Fieldgate St, E1 ....21 J2
Fieldhouse Cl, E18 .....79 G1
Fieldhouse Rd, SW12 ..168 C1
Fielding Av, Twick. TW2 .161 J3
Fielding Ho, NW6 ......108 D3
Fielding La, Brom. BR2 .191 J4
Fielding Ms, SW13
  off Castelnau 127 H6
Fielding Rd, W4 ....126 D3
  W14 ....128 A3
Fieldings, The, SE23 ...171 F1
Fielding St, SE17 ....35 J5
Fielding Wk, W13 ......124 E3
Field La, Brent. TW8 ....125 F7
  Teddington TW11 .....162 D5
Field Mead, NW7 ....55 E7
  NW9 ....55 E7
Fieldpark Gdns, Croy.
  CR0 ....203 H1
Field Pl, N.Mal. KT3 ...183 F6
Field Pt, E7
  off Station Rd 97 G4
Field Rd, E7 ....97 F4
  N17 ....76 A3
  W6 ....128 B5
  Feltham TW14 ....142 B6
Fieldsend Rd, Sutt. SM3 .198 B5
Fields Est, E8 ....94 D7
Fieldside Cl, Orp. BR6
  off State Fm Av 207 F4
Fieldside Rd, Brom. BR1 .172 D5
Fields Pk Cres, Rom. RM6 .82 D5
Field St, WC1 ....10 C3
Fieldview, SW18 ....167 G1
Field Vw Cl, Rom. RM7 ..83 G3
Field Way, NW10
  off Twybridge Way ...88 C7
Fieldway, Croy.
  (New Adgtn) CR0 ....204 B6
  Dagenham RM8 ......100 B4
Field Way, Grnf. UB6 ...103 H1
  Ruislip HA4 ....84 A2
Fieldway, Orp. BR5 .....193 G6
Fieldway Cres, N5 ......93 G5
Fiennes Cl, Dag. RM8 ..100 C1
Fiesta Dr, Dag. RM9 ....119 J4
Fife Rd, E16 ....115 G5
  N22 ....59 H7
  SW14 ....146 C5
  Kingston upon Thames
  KT1 ....181 H2
Fife Ter, N1 ....10 D1
Fifield Path, SE23
  off Bampton Rd 171 G3
Fifth Av, E12 ....98 C4
  W10 ....108 B3
  Hayes UB3 ....121 J1
Fifth Cross Rd, Twick.
  TW2 ....162 A2
Fifth Way, Wem. HA9 ...88 B4
Figges Rd, Mitch. CR4 ..168 A7
Fig Tree Cl, NW10
  off Craven Pk 106 E1
Filby Rd, Chess. KT9 ...195 J6
Filey Av, N16 ....94 D1
Filey Cl, Sutt. SM2 .....199 F7
Filey Waye, Ruis. HA4 ..84 A2
Filigree Ct, SE16
  off Silver Wk 133 J1
Fillebrook Av, Enf. EN1 ..44 B2
Fillebrook Rd, E11 ......96 D1

Filmer Rd, SW6 ....148 B1
Filston Rd, Erith DA8
  off Riverdale Rd 139 J5
Filton Cl, NW9 ....71 E2
Finborough Rd, SW10 ...30 A5
  SW17 ....167 J6
Finchale Rd, SE2 ....138 A3
Finch Av, SE27 ....170 A4
Finch Cl, NW10 ....88 D5
  Barnet EN5 ....40 D5
Finchdean Ho, SW15
  off Tangley Gro 147 F7
Finch Dr, Felt. TW14 ...142 D7
Finch Gdns, E4 ....62 A5
Finchingfield Av, Wdf.Grn.
  IG8 ....63 J7
Finch La, EC3 ....20 C4
FINCHLEY, N3 ....72 E1
Finchley Cl, N3 ....57 E6
Finchley La, NW4 ......71 J4
Finchley Pk, N12 ......57 F4
Finchley Pl, NW8 ......6 E1
Finchley Rd, NW2 ......91 F6
  NW3 ....91 F6
  NW8 ....109 G1
  NW11 ....72 C6
Finchley Way, N3 ......56 D7
Finch Ms, SE15 ....132 C7
Finden Rd, E7 ....97 H5
Findhorn Av, Hayes UB4 .102 B5
Findhorn St, E14 ....114 C6
Findon Cl, SW18 ....148 D6
  Harrow HA2 ....85 H3
Findon Rd, N9 ....60 E1
  W12 ....127 G2
Fingal St, SE10 ....135 F5
Finland Quay, SE16
  off Finland St 133 H3
Finland Rd, SE4 ....153 H3
Finland St, SE16 ....133 H3
Finlays Cl, Chess. KT9 .196 A5
Finlay St, SW6 ....148 A1
Finney La, Islw. TW7 ...144 D1
Finnis St, E2 ....113 E3
Finnymore Rd, Dag. RM9 .101 E7
FINSBURY, EC1 ....11 F3
Finsbury Av, EC2 ......20 C2
Finsbury Sq, EC2 ......20 C2
Finsbury Circ, EC2 .....20 C2
Finsbury Cotts, N22 ....59 E7
Finsbury Est, EC1 ......11 F4
Finsbury Ho, N22 ......75 E1
Finsbury Mkt, EC2 .....12 D6
FINSBURY PARK, N4 ...75 H7
★ Finsbury Park, N4 ...75 H7
Finsbury Pk Av, N4 ....75 J6
Finsbury Pk Rd, N4 ....93 H2
Finsbury Pavement, EC2 .20 C1
Finsbury Rd, N22 ......75 F1
Finsbury Sq, EC2 ......20 C1
Finsbury St, EC2 ......20 B1
Finsbury Twr, EC1 .....12 B6
Finsbury Way, Bex. DA5 .159 F6
Finsen Rd, SE5 ....151 J3
Finstock Rd, W10 ......108 A6
Finucane Ri, Bushey
  (Bushey Hth) WD23 ...51 J2
Firbank Cl, E16 ....116 A5
  Enfield EN2
  off Gladbeck Way 43 J4
Firbank Rd, SE15 ......153 E2
Fir Cl, Walt. KT12 ......178 A7
Fircroft Gdns, Har. HA1 .86 B3
Fircroft Rd, SW17 .....167 J2
  Chessington KT9 .....195 J4
Fir Dene, Orp. BR6 .....206 C3
Firdene, Surb. KT5 .....196 C1
Fire Bell All, Surb. KT6 .181 H6
Firecrest Dr, NW3 .....91 E3
Firefly Gdns, E6
  off Jack Dash Way ...116 B4
★ Firepower, SE18 ....137 E3
Fire Sta All, Barn. EN5
  off Christchurch La ...40 B2
Firethorn Cl, Edg. HA8
  off Larkspur Gro 54 C4
Fir Gro, N.Mal. KT3 ....183 F6
Fir Gro Rd, SW9
  off Marcella Rd 151 G2
Firhill Rd, SE6 ....172 A4
Firmans Ct, E17 ....78 D4
Fir Rd, Felt. TW13 .....160 D5
  Sutton SM3 ....198 C1
Firs, The, E6 ....98 B7
  E17 off Leucha Rd 77 H5
  N20 ....57 G1
  W5 ....105 G5
Firs Av, N10 ....74 A3
  N11 ....58 A6
  SW14 ....146 C4
Firsby Av, Croy. CR0 ...203 G1
Firsby Rd, N16 ....94 C1
Firs Cl, N10 off Firs Av .74 A3

Firs Cl, SE23 ....153 G7
  Esher (Clay.) KT10 ...194 B6
  Mitcham CR4 ....186 B2
Firscroft, N13 ....59 J3
Firs Dr, Houns. TW5 ....122 B7
  Loughton IG10 ....48 D1
Firside Gro, Sid. DA15 ..175 J1
Firs La, N13 ....59 J3
  N21 ....59 J2
Firs Pk Av, N21 ....60 A1
Firs Pk Gdns, N21 .....59 J1
First Av, E12 ....98 B4
  E13 ....115 G3
  E17 ....78 A5
  N18 ....61 F4
  NW4 ....71 J4
  SW14 ....146 E3
  W3 ....127 F1
  W10 ....108 C4
  Bexleyheath DA7 .....138 C7
  Dagenham RM10 ....119 H2
  Enfield EN1 ....44 C6
  Greenford UB6 ......86 A7
  Hayes UB3 ....121 J1
  Romford RM6 ....82 C5
  Walton-on-Thames
  KT12 ....178 B6
  Wembley HA9 ....87 G2
  West Molesey KT8 ...179 F4
First Cl, W.Mol. KT8 ...179 J3
First Cross Rd, Twick.
  TW2 ....162 B2
First Dr, NW10 ....88 C7
First St, SW3 ....31 H1
Firstway, SW20 ....183 J2
First Way, Wem. HA9 ..88 B4
Firs Wk, Wdf.Grn. IG8 ..63 G5
Firswood Av, Epsom
  KT19 ....197 F5
Firth Gdns, SW6 ....148 B1
Fir Tree Av, Mitch. CR4 .186 A2
  West Drayton UB7 ....120 D3
Fir Tree Cl, SW16 ......168 C5
  W5 ....105 H6
  Epsom (Ewell) KT19 ..197 F6
  Orpington BR6 ....207 J5
Fir Tree Gdns, Croy. CR0 .204 A4
Fir Tree Gro, Cars. SM5 .199 J7
Fir Tree Rd, Houns. TW4 .143 E4
Fir Trees Cl, SE16 ......133 H1
Fir Tree Wk, Dag. RM10
  off Wheel Fm Dr 101 J3
  Enfield EN1 ....44 A3
Fisher Cl, E9
  off Brooksby's Wk ...95 G5
  Croydon CR0 ....202 C1
  Greenford UB6 ......103 B7
Fisherman Cl, Rich. TW10
  off Locksmeade Rd ..163 F4
Fishermans Dr, SE16 ...133 G2
Fisherman's Wk, E14 ...134 A1
Fishermans Wk, SE28
  off Tugboat St 137 H2
Fisher Rd, Har. HA3 ....68 C2
Fishers Cl, SW16 ......168 D3
Fishers Ct, SE14
  off Besson St 153 G1
Fishersdene, Esher (Clay.)
  KT10 ....194 D7
Fishers La, W4 ....126 D4
Fisher St, E16 ....115 G5
  WC1 ....18 B2
Fishers Way, Belv. DA17 .139 J1
Fisherton St, NW8 .....7 E6
Fishguard Way, E16 ...137 E2
Fishponds Rd, SW17 ...167 H4
  Keston BR2 ....206 A5
Fish St Hill, EC3 ....20 C5
Fitzalan Rd, N3 ....72 B3
  Esher (Clay.) KT10 ...194 B7
Fitzalan St, SE11 ......34 E1
Fitzgeorge Av, W14 ...128 B4
  New Malden KT3 .....182 D1
Fitzgerald Av, SW14 ...147 A3
Fitzgerald Ho, E14
  off Fitzgerald Rd 79 G5
Fitzgerald Rd, E11 .....114 B6
  SW9
  off Stockwell Pk Rd ..151 G2
  Hayes UB3 ....122 B1
Fitzgerald Rd, E11 .....79 G5
  SW14 ....146 D3
  Thames Ditton KT7 ...180 D6
Fitzhardinge St, W1 ....16 B3
Fitzherbert Ho, Rich. TW10
  off Kingsmead 145 J6
Fitzhugh Gro, SW18 ...149 G6
Fitzjames Av, W14 .....128 B4
  Croydon CR0 ....202 D2
Fitzjohn Av, Barn. EN5 ..40 B5
Fitzjohn's Av, NW3 ....91 G5
Fitzmaurice Ho, SE16
  off Rennie Est 133 E4

Fitzmaurice Pl, W1 ....24 E1
Fitzneal St, W12 ....107 F6
Fitzroy Cl, N6 ....91 J1
Fitzroy Ct, W1 ....9 G6
Fitzroy Cres, W4 ....126 D7
Fitzroy Gdns, SE19 ......170 B7
Fitzroy Ms, W1 ....9 F6
Fitzroy Pk, N6 ....91 J1
Fitzroy Rd, NW1 ....110 A1
Fitzroy Sq, W1 ....9 F6
Fitzroy St, W1 ....9 F6
Fitzroy Yd, NW1
off Fitzroy Rd 110 A1
Fitzsimmons Ct, NW10
off Knatchbull Rd 106 D1
Fitzstephen Rd, Dag. RM8 ....100 B5
Fitzwarren Gdns, N19 .....92 C1
Fitzwilliam Av, Rich. TW9 .145 J2
Fitzwilliam Cl, N20 ....58 A1
Fitzwilliam Ms, E16
off Hanover Av 135 G1
Fitzwilliam Rd, SW4 .....150 C3
Fitzwygram Cl, Hmptn. (Hmptn H.) TW12 .....161 J5
Five Acre, NW9 ....71 F1
Fiveacre Cl, Th.Hth. CR7 ....187 G6
Five Bell All, E14
off Three Colt St 113 J7
Five Elms Rd, Brom. BR2 ....205 H3
Dagenham RM9 ......101 F3
Five Flds Cl, Wat. WD19 ...51 F3
Five Oaks Ms, Brom. BR1 ....173 G3
Fives Ct, SE11 ....35 G1
Fiveways, Croy. CR0 .....201 G4
Five Ways Cor, NW4 ......71 H1
Fiveways Rd, SW9 ....151 G2
Fladbury Rd, N15 ....76 A6
Fladgate Rd, E11 ....79 E6
Flag Cl, Croy. CR0 ....203 G1
Flagon Ct, Croy. CR0
off Lower Coombe St .201 J4
Flagstaff Ho, SW8
off St. George Wf 34 A5
Flag Wk, Pnr. HA5 ....66 A6
Flambard Rd, Har. HA1 ...68 D6
Flamborough Rd, Ruis. HA4 ....84 A3
Flamborough St, E14 ....113 H6
Flamborough Wk, E14
off Flamborough St ..113 H6
Flamingo Gdns, Nthlt. UB5 off Jetstar Way ...102 E3
Flamstead Gdns, Dag. RM9 off Flamstead Rd .100 C7
Flamstead Rd, Dag. RM9 .100 C7
Flamsted Av, Wem. HA9 ...88 A6
Flamsteed Rd, SE7 ......136 B5
Flanchford Rd, W12 ......127 F3
Flanders Cres, SW17 ....167 J7
Flanders Rd, E6 ....116 C2
W4 ....127 E4
Flanders Way, E9 ....95 G6
Flank St, E1 ....21 H5
Flask Cotts, NW3
off New End Sq 91 G4
Flask Wk, NW3 ....91 G4
Flather Cl, SW16
off Blegborough Rd ..168 C5
Flat Iron Sq, SE1
off Union St 28 A2
Flavell Ms, SE10 ....135 E5
Flaxen Cl, E4
off Flaxen Rd 62 B3
Flaxen Rd, E4 ....62 B3
Flaxley Rd, Mord. SM4 ...184 E6
Flaxman Ct, W1 ....17 H4
Flaxman Rd, SE5 ....151 H2
Flaxman Ter, WC1 ....9 J4
Flaxton Rd, SE18 ....157 G1
Flecker Cl, Stan. HA7 .....52 C5
Fleece Dr, N9 ....60 D4
Fleece Rd, Surb. (Long Dit.) KT6 ....195 F1
Fleece Wk, N7
off Manger Rd 93 E6
Fleeming Cl, E17
off Pennant Ter 77 J2
Fleeming Rd, E17 ....77 J2
Fleet Cl, W.Mol. KT8 .....179 F5
Fleet La, W.Mol. KT8 .....179 F6
Fleet Pl, EC4
off Limeburner La 19 G3
Fleet Rd, NW3 ....91 H5
Fleetside, W.Mol. KT8 ....179 F6
Fleet Sq, WC1 ....10 D4
Fleet St, EC4 ....19 E4
Fleet St Hill, E1 ....13 H6
Fleetway Business Pk, Grnf. (Perivale) UB6 ...105 E2
Fleetwood Cl, E16 ....116 A5
Chessington KT9 .....195 G7
Croydon CR0 ....202 C3
Fleetwood Ct, E6
off Evelyn Denington Rd 116 C5
Fleetwood Gro, W3
off East Acton La 106 E7
Fleetwood Rd, NW10 .....89 G5
Kingston upon Thames KT1 ....182 B3
Fleetwood Sq, Kings.T. KT1 ....182 B3
Fleetwood St, N16
off Stoke Newington Ch St 94 B2
Fleetwood Way, Wat. WD19 ....50 C4
Fleming Cl, W9
off Chippenham Rd ..108 D4
Fleming Ct, W2 ....14 E1
Croydon CR0 ....201 G5
Fleming Dr, N21 ....43 F5
Fleming Mead, Mitch. CR4 ....167 H7
Fleming Rd, SE17 ....35 H5
Southall UB1 ....103 H6
Fleming Wk, NW9
off Pasteur Cl 71 E2
Fleming Way, SE28 ......118 D7
Isleworth TW7 ....144 C3
Flemming Av, Ruis. HA4 ..84 B1
Flempton Rd, E10 ....77 H7
Fletcher Cl, E6
off Trader Rd 116 E6
Fletcher La, E10 ....78 C7
Fletcher Path, SE8
off New Butt La 134 A7
Fletcher Rd, W4 ....126 C3
Chigwell IG7 ....65 J5
Fletchers Cl, Brom. BR2 ..191 H4
Fletcher St, E1 ....21 J5
Fletching Rd, E5 ....95 F3
SE7 ....135 J6
Fletton Rd, N11 ....58 E7
Fleur de Lis St, E1 ....13 E6
Fleur Gates, SW19
off Princes Way 148 A7
Flexmere Gdns, N17
off Flexmere Rd 76 A1
Flexmere Rd, N17 ....76 A1
Flight App, NW9 ....71 F2
Flimwell Cl, Brom. BR1 ..172 E5
Flint Cl, E15 ....97 F7
Orpington (Grn St Grn) BR6 off Lynne Cl 207 J6
Flintmill Cres, SE3 ......156 B2
Flinton St, SE17 ....36 E3
Flint St, SE17 ....36 C2
Flitcroft St, WC2 ....17 J3
Floathaven Cl, SE28 .....138 A1
Flock Mill Pl, SW18 ......166 E1
Flockton St, SE16 ....29 H4
Flodden Rd, SE5 ....151 J1
Flood La, Twick. TW1
off Church La 162 D1
Flood Pas, SE18
off Samuel St 136 C4
Flood St, SW3 ....31 H4
Flood Wk, SW3 ....31 H5
Flora Cl, E14 ....114 B6
Stanmore HA7 ....53 H3
Flora Gdns, W6 ....127 H4
Romford RM6 ....82 C6
Flora Ho, E3
off Garrison Rd 114 A1
Floral Pl, N1
off Northampton Gro ..94 A5
Floral St, WC2 ....18 A5
Flora St, Belv. DA17
off Victoria St 139 F5
Florence Av, Enf. EN2 .....43 J3
Morden SM4 ....185 F5
Florence Cantwell Wk, N19 off Hillrise Rd 74 E7
Florence Cl, Walt. KT12
off Florence Rd 178 B7
Florence Ct, W9
off Maida Vale 6 D4
Florence Dr, Enf. EN2 .....43 J3
Florence Elson Cl, E12 ....98 D4
Florence Gdns, W4 ......126 C6
Romford RM6
off Roxy Av 82 C7
Florence Nightingale Ho, N1
off Nightingale Rd 93 J6
★ Florence Nightingale Mus, SE1 ....26 C4
Florence Rd, E6 ....115 J1
E13 ....115 F2
N4 ....93 G1
SE2 ....138 C3
SE14 ....153 J1
Florence Rd, SW19 ......166 E6
W4 ....126 D3
W5 ....105 H7
Beckenham BR3 ......189 G2
Bromley BR1 ....191 G1
Feltham TW13 ....160 B1
Kingston upon Thames KT2 ....163 J7
Southall UB2 ....122 D4
Walton-on-Thames KT12 ....178 B7
Florence St, E16 ....115 F4
N1 ....93 H7
NW4 ....71 J4
Florence Ter, SE14 ....153 J1
SW15
off Roehampton Vale .165 E3
Florence Way, SW12 .....167 J1
Florence White Ct, N9
off Colthurst Dr 60 E3
Florey Sq, N21
off Highlands Av 43 F5
Florfield Pas, E8
off Reading La 95 E6
Florfield Rd, E8
off Reading La 95 E6
Florian Av, Sutt. SM1 ....199 G4
Florian Rd, SW15 ....148 B4
Florida Cl, Bushey (Bushey Hth) WD23 ....52 A2
Florida Ct, Brom. BR2
off Westmoreland Rd .191 F4
Florida Rd, Th.Hth. CR7 ..187 H1
Florida St, E2 ....13 H4
Florin Ct, SE1
off Tanner St 29 F4
Floris Pl, SW4
off Fitzwilliam Rd 150 C3
Floriston Cl, Stan. HA7 ....69 E1
Floriston Ct, Nthlt. UB5 ...85 H5
Floriston Gdns, Stan. HA7 .69 E1
Floss St, SW15 ....147 J2
Flower & Dean Wk, E1 ....21 G2
Flower La, NW7 ....55 F5
Flower Ms, NW11 ....72 B6
Flower Pot Cl, N15
off St. Ann's Rd 76 C6
Flowers Cl, NW2 ....89 G3
Flowersmead, SW17 ....168 A2
Flowers Ms, N19
off Archway Rd 92 C2
Flower Wk, The, SW7 .....22 C4
Floyd Rd, SE7 ....135 J5
Floyer Cl, Rich. TW10 ....145 J5
Fludyer St, SE13 ....154 E4
Foley Ho, E1
off Tarling St 113 F6
Foley Ms, Esher (Clay.) KT10 ....194 B7
Foley Rd, Esher (Clay.) KT10 ....194 B7
Foley St, W1 ....17 F2
Foley Wood., Esher KT10
off Foley Rd 194 C7
Folgate St, E1 ....21 E1
Foliot Ho, N1
off Priory Grn Est 10 C1
Foliot St, W12 ....107 F6
Folkestone Rd, E6 ....116 D2
E17 ....78 B4
N18 ....60 D4
Folkingham La, NW9 .....70 D1
Folkington Cor, N12 ......56 C5
Follett St, E14 ....114 C6
Folly La, E4 ....61 J7
E17 ....77 H1
Folly Ms, W11
off Portobello Rd 108 C6
Folly Wall, E14 ....134 C2
Fontaine Rd, SW16 ......169 F7
Fontarabia Rd, SW11 ....150 A4
Fontayne Av, Chig. IG7 ....65 F4
Fontenelle, SE5
off Sceaux Gdns 152 B1
Fontenoy Rd, SW12 .....168 B2
Fonteyne Gdns, Wdf.Grn. IG8 ....79 J2
Fonthill Cl, SE20
off Selby Rd 188 D2
Fonthill Ms, N4 ....93 F2
Fonthill Rd, N4 ....93 F1
Font Hills, N2 ....73 F2
Fontley Way, SW15 .....147 G7
Fontwell Cl, Har. HA3 .....52 B7
Northolt UB5 ....85 G6
Fontwell Dr, Brom. BR2 ..192 D5
Football La, Har. HA1 .....86 B1
Footpath, The, SW15 ....147 G5
FOOTS CRAY, Sid. DA14 .176 B6
Foots Cray High St, Sid. DA14 ....176 C6
Foots Cray La, Sid. DA14 .176 C1
Footscray Rd, SE9 ....156 D6
Forbes Cl, NW2 ....89 G3
Forbes Ct, SE19 ....170 B5
Forbes St, E1 ....21 J4
Forbes Way, Ruis. HA4 ....84 B2
Forburg Rd, N16 ....94 D1
Ford Cl, E3
off Roman Rd 113 H2
Harrow HA1 ....68 A7
Thornton Heath CR7 ..187 H6
Forde Av, Brom. BR1 ....191 J3
Fordel Rd, SE6 ....172 D1
Ford End, Wdf.Grn. IG8 ...63 H6
Fordham Cl, Barn. EN4 ....41 H3
Worcester Park KT4 ..197 H1
Fordham Rd, Barn. EN4 ...41 G3
Fordham St, E1 ....21 J3
Fordhook Av, W5 ....105 J7
Fordingley Rd, W9 ....108 C3
Fordington Ho, SE26
off Sydenham Hill Est 170 E3
Fordington Rd, N6 ....73 J5
Fordmill Rd, SE6 ....172 A2
Ford Rd, E3 ....113 H1
Dagenham RM9, RM10 ....101 F7
Fords Gro, N21 ....59 J1
Fords Pk Rd, E16 ....115 G6
Ford Sq, E1 ....113 E5
Ford St, E3 ....113 H1
E16 ....115 F6
Fordwich Cl, Orp. BR6 ...193 J7
Fordwych Rd, NW2 ....90 B4
Fordyce Ho, SW16
off Colson Way 168 C4
Fordyce Rd, SE13 ....154 C6
Fordyke Rd, Dag. RM8 ...101 F2
★ Foreign & Commonwealth Office, SW1 ....25 J3
Foreign St, SE5 ....151 H2
Foreland Ct, NW4 ....72 B1
Foreland St, SE18
off Plumstead Rd 137 G4
Foremark Cl, Ilf. IG6 ......65 J5
Foreshore, SE8 ....133 J4
Forest, The, E11 ....79 E4
Forest App, E4 ....47 E7
Woodford Green IG8 ..63 F7
Forest Av, E4 ....47 E7
Chigwell IG7 ....64 D5
Forest Business Pk, E10 ...77 G7
Forest Cl, E11 ....79 F5
NW6 ....90 B7
Chislehurst BR7 ......192 D1
Woodford Green IG8 ...63 H3
Forest Ct, E4 ....63 F1
E11 ....79 E4
Forest Cft, SE23 ....171 E2
Forestdale, N14 ....58 D4
Forestdale Cen, The, Croy. CR0
off Holmbury Gro 203 J7
Forest Dr, E12 ....98 A3
Keston BR2 ....206 B4
Woodford Green IG8 ...62 D7
Forest Dr E, E11 ....78 D7
Forest Dr W, E11 ....78 C7
Forest Edge, Buck.H. IG9 ..63 J4
Forester Rd, SE15 ....153 E4
Foresters Cl, Wall. SM6 ..200 D7
Foresters Cres, Bexh. DA7 ....159 H4
Foresters Dr, E17 ....78 D4
Wallington SM6 ......200 D7
Forest Gdns, N17 ....76 C2
FOREST GATE, E7 ....97 G5
Forest Gate, NW9 ....70 E4
Forest Glade, E4 ....62 E4
E11 ....79 E6
Forest Gro, E8 ....94 C6
Forest Hts, Buck.H. IG9 ...63 G2
FOREST HILL, SE23 .....171 G1
Forest Hill, SE23 ....171 F2
Forest Hill Business Cen, SE23 off Clyde Vale ...171 F2
Forest Hill Ind Est, SE23
off Perry Vale 171 F2
Forest Hill Rd, SE22 .....152 E5
SE23 ....152 E5
Forestholme Cl, SE23 ....171 F2
Forest Ind Pk, Ilf. IG6 .....81 H1
Forest La, E7 ....97 E5
E15 ....97 E5
Chigwell IG7 ....64 D5
Forest Mt Rd, Wdf.Grn. IG8 ....62 D7
Forest Pt, E7
off Windsor Rd 97 H5
Fore St, EC2 ....20 A2
N9 ....60 D5
N18 ....60 C6
Pinner HA5 ....66 A5
Fore St Av, EC2 ....20 B2

Forest Ridge, Beck. BR3 190 A3
Keston BR2 206 B4
Forest Ri, E17 78 D5
Forest Rd, E7 97 G4
E8 94 C6
E11 78 D7
E17 77 F4
N9 61 E1
N17 77 F4
Feltham TW13 160 C2
Ilford IG6 81 H1
Loughton IG10 48 A3
Richmond TW9 126 A7
Romford RM7 83 H3
Sutton SM3 198 D1
Woodford Green IG8 63 G3
Forest Side, E4 47 F7
E7 *off Capel Rd* 97 H4
Buckhurst Hill IG9 63 J1
Worcester Park KT4 197 F1
Forest St, E7 97 G5
Forest Vw, E4 46 D7
E11 *off High Rd Leytonstone* 79 F7
Forest Vw Av, E10 78 D5
Forest Vw Rd, E12 98 B4
E17 78 C1
Loughton IG10 48 A4
Forest Wk, N10 74 B1
Forest Way, N19 *off Hargrave Pk* 92 C2
Loughton IG10 48 B3
Orpington BR5 193 J5
Sidcup DA15 157 G7
Woodford Green IG8 63 H4
Forfar Rd, N22 75 H1
SW11 150 A1
Forge Cl, Brom. BR2 205 G1
Hayes (Harling.) UB3 *off High St* 121 G6
Forge Dr, Esher (Clay.) KT10 194 D7
Forge La, Felt. TW13 160 E5
Richmond TW10 *off Petersham Rd* 163 H1
Sunbury-on-Thames TW16 178 A3
Sutton SM3 198 B7
Forge Ms, Croy. CR0 *off Addington Village Rd* 204 A5
Forge Pl, NW1 *off Malden Cres* 92 A6
Forlong Path, Nthlt. UB5 *off Cowings Mead* 85 E6
Forman Pl, N16 *off Farleigh Rd* 94 C4
Formation, The, E16 *off Woolwich Manor Way* 136 E2
Formby Av, Stan. HA7 69 F3
Formosa St, W9 6 C6
Formunt Cl, E16 *off Vincent St* 115 F5
Forres Gdns, NW11 72 D6
Forrester Path, SE26 171 F4
Forrest Gdns, SW16 187 F3
Forris Av, Hayes UB3 121 J1
Forset St, W1 15 H3
Forstal Cl, Brom. BR2 *off Ridley Rd* 191 G3
Forster Cl, Wdf.Grn. IG8 62 D7
Forster Rd, E17 77 H6
N17 76 C3
SW2 150 E7
Beckenham BR3 189 H3
Croydon CR0 *off Windmill Rd* 187 J7
Forsters Cl, Rom. RM6 83 F6
Forster's Way, SW18 166 E1
Forsters Way, Hayes UB4 102 B6
Forston St, N1 12 B1
Forsyte Cres, SE19 188 B1
Forsyth Gdns, SE17 35 H5
Forsyth Ho, SW1 *off Tachbrook St* 33 G3
Forsythia Cl, Ilf. IG1 98 E5
Forsyth Pl, Enf. EN1 44 B5
Forterie Gdns, Ilf. IG3 100 A3
Fortescue Av, E8 *off Mentmore Ter* 95 E7
Twickenham TW2 161 J3
Fortescue Rd, SW19 167 G7
Edgware HA8 70 D1
Fortess Gro, NW5 *off Fortess Rd* 92 C5
Fortess Rd, NW5 92 B5
Fortess Wk, NW5 *off Fortess Rd* 92 B5
Fortess Yd, NW5 *off Fortess Rd* 92 B4
Forthbridge Rd, SW11 150 A4
Fortis Cl, E16 115 J6
FORTIS GREEN, N2 73 J4
Fortis Grn, N2 73 H4
N10 73 H4
Fortis Grn Av, N2 73 J3
Fortis Grn Rd, N10 74 A3
Fortismere Av, N10 74 A3
Fortnam Rd, N19 92 D2
★ **Fortnum & Mason**, W1 25 F1
Fortnums Acre, Stan. HA7 52 C6
Fort Rd, SE1 37 G2
Northolt UB5 85 G7
Fortrose Cl, E14 114 D6
Fortrose Gdns, SW2 168 E1
Fort St, E1 21 E2
E16 135 H1
Fortuna Cl, N7 *off Jupiter Way* 93 F6
Fortune Gate Rd, NW10 107 E1
Fortune Grn Rd, NW6 90 D4
Fortune Pl, SE1 37 G4
Fortunes Mead, Nthlt. UB5 85 E6
Fortune St, EC1 12 A6
Fortune Wk, SE28 *off Broadwater Rd* 137 G3
Fortune Way, NW10 107 G3
Forty Acre La, E16 115 G5
Forty Av, Wem. HA9 87 J3
Forty Cl, Wem. HA9 87 J2
Forty Footpath, SW14 146 C3
Forty La, Wem. HA9 88 B2
Forum, The, W.Mol. KT8 179 H4
Forum Cl, E3 *off Garrison Rd* 114 A1
★ **Forum Club**, NW5 92 B5
Forum Magnum Sq, SE1 26 C3
Forumside, Edg. HA8 *off Station Rd* 54 A6
Forum Way, Edg. HA8 *off High St* 54 A6
Forval Cl, Mitch. CR4 185 J5
Forward Dr, Har. HA3 68 C4
Fosbury Ms, W2 14 B6
Foscote Ms, W9 *off Amberley Rd* 108 D5
Foscote Rd, NW4 71 H6
Foskett Rd, SW6 148 C2
Foss Av, Croy. CR0 201 G5
Fossdene Rd, SE7 135 H5
Fossdyke Cl, Hayes UB4 103 E5
Fosse Way, W13 104 D5
Fossil Rd, SE13 154 A3
Fossington Rd, Belv. DA17 138 D4
Foss Rd, SW17 167 G4
Fossway, Dag. RM8 100 C2
Foster La, EC2 19 J3
Foster Rd, E13 115 G4
W3 106 E7
W4 126 D5
Fosters Cl, E18 79 H1
Chislehurst BR7 174 C5
Foster St, NW4 71 J4
Foster Wk, NW4 *off Foster St* 71 J4
Fothergill Cl, E13 115 G2
Fothergill Dr, N21 43 E5
Fotheringham Rd, Enf. EN1 44 C4
Foubert's Pl, W1 17 F4
Foulden Rd, N16 94 C4
Foulden Ter, N16 *off Foulden Rd* 94 C4
Foulis Ter, SW7 31 F3
Foulser Rd, SW17 167 J3
Foulsham Rd, Th.Hth. CR7 187 J3
Founder Cl, E6 *off Trader Rd* 116 E6
Founders Cl, Nthlt. UB5 *off Taywood Rd* 103 F3
Founders Ct, EC2 20 B3
Founders Gdns, SE19 169 J7
★ **Foundling Mus**, WC1 10 B5
Foundry Cl, SE16 133 H1
Foundry Ms, NW1 9 G5
Hounslow TW3 *off New Rd* 143 H4
Foundry Pl, E1 *off Redman's Rd* 113 F5
Fountain Cl, E5 *off Lower Clapton Rd* 95 E3
SE18 136 E5
Fountain Ct, EC4 18 E5
Fountain Dr, SE19 170 C4
Fountain Grn Sq, SE16 29 J4
Fountain Ho, SW6 *off The Boulevard* 149 F2
SW8 *off St. George Wf* 34 B4
Fountain Ms, N5 *off Highbury Gra* 93 J4
NW3 91 J6
Fountain Pl, SW9 151 G1
Fountain Rd, SW17 167 G5
Thornton Heath CR7 187 J2
Fountains, The, Loug. IG10 *off Fallow Flds* 48 A7
Fountains Av, Felt. TW13 161 F3
Fountains Cl, Felt. TW13 161 F2
Fountains Cres, N14 42 E7
Fountain Sq, SW1 32 D1
Fountayne Rd, N15 76 D4
N16 94 D2
Fount St, SW8 130 D7
Fouracres, SW12 *off Little Dimocks* 168 B2
Enfield EN3 45 H1
Fourland Wk, Edg. HA8 54 C6
Fournier St, E1 21 F1
Four Seasons Cl, E3 114 A2
Four Seasons Cres, Sutt. SM3 198 C2
Fourth Av, E12 98 C4
W10 108 B4
Hayes UB3 121 J1
Fourth Cross Rd, Twick. TW2 162 A2
Fourth Way, Wem. HA9 88 C4
Four Wents, The, E4 *off Kings Rd* 62 D2
Fowey Av, Ilf. IG4 80 A5
Fowey Cl, E1 *off Kennet St* 132 E1
Fowler Cl, SW11 149 G3
Fowler Rd, E7 97 G4
N1 *off Halton Rd* 93 H7
Mitcham CR4 186 A2
Fowlers Cl, Sid. DA14 *off Thursland Rd* 176 E5
Fowlers Wk, W5 105 G4
Fownes St, SW11 149 H3
Fox & Knot St, EC1 19 H1
Foxberry Rd, SE4 153 H3
Foxborough Gdns, SE4 154 A6
Foxbourne Rd, SW17 168 A2
Foxbury Av, Chis. BR7 175 G6
Foxbury Cl, Brom. BR1 173 H6
Foxbury Rd, Brom. BR1 173 G6
Fox Cl, E1 113 F4
E16 115 G5
Foxcombe, Croy. (New Adgtn) CR0 204 B6
Foxcombe Cl, E6 *off Boleyn Rd* 116 A2
Foxcombe Rd, SW15 *off Alton Rd* 165 G1
Foxcote, SE5 36 E4
Foxcroft Rd, SE18 157 E1
Foxes Dale, SE3 155 G3
Bromley BR2 190 D3
Foxfield Rd, Orp. BR6 207 G2
Foxglove Cl, N9 61 F1
Sidcup DA15 158 A6
Southall UB1 103 E7
Foxglove Gdns, E11 79 J4
Foxglove La, Chess. KT9 196 A4
Foxglove Path, SE28 *off Crowfoot Cl* 137 H1
Foxglove St, W12 107 F7
Foxglove Way, Wall. SM6 200 B1
Foxgrove, N14 58 E3
Fox Gro, Walt. KT12 178 B7
Foxgrove Av, Beck. BR3 172 B7
Foxgrove Path, Wat. WD19 50 D5
Foxgrove Rd, Beck. BR3 172 B7
Foxham Rd, N19 92 D3
Fox Hill, SE19 170 C7
Keston BR2 205 J5
Fox Hill Gdns, SE19 170 C7
Foxhole Rd, SE9 156 B5
Fox Hollow Cl, SE18 137 H5
Fox Hollow Dr, Bexh. DA7 158 D3
Foxholt Gdns, NW10 88 C7
Foxhome Cl, Chis. BR7 174 D6
Fox Ho, SW11 *off Maysoule Rd* 149 G4
Fox Ho Rd, Belv. DA17 139 H4
Foxlands Cres, Dag. RM10 101 J5
Foxlands La, Dag. RM10 101 J5
Foxlands Rd, Dag. RM10 101 J5
Fox La, N13 59 F3
W5 105 H4
Keston BR2 205 H5
Foxlees, Wem. HA0 86 D4
Foxley Cl, E8 *off Ferncliff Rd* 94 D5
Loughton IG10 49 E2
Foxley Ct, Sutt. SM2 199 F7
Foxley Ho, E3 *off Bromley High St* 114 B3
Foxley Rd, SW9 35 F7
Thornton Heath CR7 187 H4
Foxleys, Wat. WD19 51 E3
Foxley Sq, SW9 *off Cancell Rd* 131 H7
Foxmead Cl, Enf. EN2 43 F3
Foxmore St, SW11 149 J1
Fox Rd, E16 115 F5
Fox's Path, Mitch. CR4 185 H2
Foxton Gro, Mitch. CR4 185 G2
Foxwell Ms, SE4 *off Foxwell St* 153 H3
Foxwell St, SE4 153 H3
Foxwood Cl, NW7 54 E4
Feltham TW13 160 B3
Foxwood Grn Cl, Enf. EN1 44 B6
Foxwood Rd, SE3 155 F4
Foyle Rd, N17 76 D1
SE3 135 F6
Framfield Cl, N12 56 D3
Framfield Ct, Enf. EN1 44 B6
Framfield Rd, N5 93 H5
W7 104 B6
Mitcham CR4 168 A7
Framlingham Cl, E5 *off Detmold Rd* 95 F2
Framlingham Cres, SE9 174 B4
Frampton Cl, Sutt. SM2 198 D7
Frampton Pk Est, E9 95 F7
Frampton Pk Rd, E9 95 F6
Frampton Rd, Houns. TW4 142 E5
Frampton St, NW8 7 E6
Francemary Rd, SE4 154 A5
Frances & Dick James Ct, NW7 *off Langstone Way* 56 B7
Frances Rd, E4 62 A6
Frances St, SE18 136 C4
Franche Ct Rd, SW17 167 F3
Francis Av, Bexh. DA7 159 G2
Feltham TW13 160 A3
Ilford IG1 99 G2
Francis Barber Cl, SW16 *off Well Cl* 169 F4
Franciscan Rd, SW17 167 J5
Francis Chichester Way, SW11 150 A1
Francis Cl, E14 *off Saunders Ness Rd* 134 D4
Epsom KT19 196 D4
Francis Gro, SW19 166 C6
Francis Pl, N6 *off Holmesdale Rd* 74 B7
Francis Rd, E10 96 C1
N2 73 J4
Croydon CR0 187 H7
Greenford (Perivale) UB6 105 E2
Harrow HA1 68 D5
Hounslow TW4 142 D2
Ilford IG1 99 G2
Pinner HA5 66 C5
Wallington SM6 200 C6
Francis St, E15 96 E5
SW1 33 F1
Ilford IG1 99 G2
Francis Ter, N19 92 C3
Francis Ter Ms, N19 *off Francis Ter* 92 C3
Francis Wk, N1 *off Bingfield St* 111 F1
Francklyn Gdns, Edg. HA8 54 A3
Franconia Rd, SW4 150 C5
Frank Bailey Wk, E12 *off Gainsborough Av* 98 D5
Frank Burton Cl, SE7 *off Victoria Way* 135 H5
Frank Dixon Cl, SE21 170 B1
Frank Dixon Way, SE21 170 B1
Frankfurt Rd, SE24 151 J5
Frankham St, SE8 134 A7
Frankland Cl, SE16 133 E3
Woodford Green IG8 63 J5
Frankland Rd, E4 62 A5
SW7 23 E6
Franklin Cl, N20 41 F7
SE13 154 B1
SE27 169 H3
Kingston upon Thames KT1 182 A3
Franklin Cres, Mitch. CR4 186 C4
Franklin Ho, NW9 71 F7
Franklin Pas, SE9 156 B3
Franklin Pl, SE13 154 B1
Franklin Rd, SE20 171 F7
Bexleyheath DA7 159 E1
Franklins Ms, Har. HA2 85 J2

Franklin Sq, W14
off Marchbank Rd 128 C5
Franklin's Row, SW3 32 A3
Franklin St, E3 114 B3
N15 76 B6
Franklin Way, Croy. CR0 187 E7
Franklyn Gdns, Ilf. IG6 65 G6
Franklyn Rd, NW10 89 F7
Walton-on-Thames KT12 178 A6
Franks Av, N.Mal. KT3 182 C4
Frank St, E13 115 G4
Frankswood Av, Orp. BR5 193 E5
Frank Towell Ct, Felt. TW14 142 A7
Franlaw Cres, N13 59 J4
Fransfield Gro, SE26 171 E3
Frant Cl, SE20 171 F7
Franthorne Way, SE6 172 B2
Frant Rd, Th.Hth. CR7 187 H5
Fraser Cl, E6
off Linton Gdns 116 B6
Bexley DA5
off Dartford Rd 177 J1
Fraser Ct, W12
off Heathstan Rd 107 G6
Fraser Ho, Brent. TW8
off Green Dragon La 125 J5
Fraser Rd, E17 78 B5
N9 60 E3
Erith DA8 139 J5
Greenford (Perivale) UB6 105 E1
Fraser St, W4 126 E5
Frating Cres, Wdf.Grn. IG8 63 G6
Frays Av, West Dr. UB7 120 A2
Frays Cl, West Dr. UB7 120 A3
Frazer Av, Ruis. HA4 84 C5
Frazier St, SE1 26 E4
Frean St, SE16 29 H5
Freda Corbett Cl, SE15 37 H7
Frederica Rd, E4 46 D7
Frederica St, N7
off Caledonian Rd 93 F7
Frederick Cl, W2 15 H5
Sutton SM1 198 C4
Frederick Ct, NW2
off Douglas Ms 90 B3
Frederick Cres, SW9 131 H7
Enfield EN3 45 F2
Frederick Gdns, Croy. CR0 187 H6
Sutton SM1 198 C5
Frederick Pl, SE18 137 E5
Frederick Rd, SE17 35 H5
Sutton SM1 198 C5
Frederick's Pl, EC2 20 B4
Fredericks Pl, N12 57 F4
Frederick Sq, SE16
off Rotherhithe St 113 H7
Frederick's Row, EC1 11 G3
Frederick St, WC1 10 C4
Frederick Ter, E8
off Arbutus St 112 C1
Frederick Vil, W7
off Lower Boston Rd 124 B1
Frederic Ms, SW1 24 A4
Frederic St, E17 77 H5
Fred White Wk, N7
off Market Rd 93 E6
Fred Wigg Twr, E11 97 F2
Freedom Cl, E17 77 H4
Freedom Rd, N17 76 A2
Freedom St, SW11 149 J2
Freegrove Rd, N7 93 E5
Freeland Pk, NW4 72 B2
Freeland Rd, W5 105 J7
Freelands Gro, Brom. BR1 191 H1
Freelands Rd, Brom. BR1 191 H1
Freeling St, N1
off Caledonian Rd 93 F7
Freeman Cl, Nthlt. UB5 85 E7
Freeman Ct, N7
off Tollington Way 93 E3
Freeman Dr, W.Mol. KT8 179 F3
Freeman Rd, Mord. SM4 185 G5
Freemantle Av, Enf. EN3 45 G5
Freemantle St, SE17 36 D3
★ **Freemason's Hall** (United Grand Lodge of England), WC2 18 B3
Freemasons Pl, Croy. CR0
off Freemasons Rd 202 B1
Freemasons Rd, E16 115 H5
Croydon CR0 202 B1
Freesia Cl, Orp. BR6 207 J5
Freethorpe Cl, SE19 188 A1
Free Trade Wf, E1
off The Highway 113 G7
★ **Freightliners Fm**, N7 93 F6
Freke Rd, SW11 150 A3
Fremantle Rd, Belv. DA17 139 G4
Ilford IG6 81 F2
Fremont St, E9 113 F1
French Ordinary Ct, EC3 21 E5
French Pl, E1 13 E5
French St, Sun. TW16 178 C2
Frendsbury Rd, SE4 153 H4
Frensham Cl, Sthl. UB1 103 F4
Frensham Ct, Mitch. CR4 185 G3
Frensham Dr, SW15 165 G2
Croydon (New Adgtn) CR0 204 C7
Frensham Rd, SE9 175 G2
Frensham St, SE15 37 J6
Frere St, SW11 149 H2
Freshfield Av, E8 94 C7
Freshfield Cl, SE13
off Mercator Rd 154 D4
Freshfield Dr, N14 42 B7
Freshfields, Croy. CR0 189 J7
Freshford St, SW18 167 F3
Freshwater Cl, SW17 168 A6
Freshwater Rd, SW17 168 A6
Dagenham RM8 100 D1
Freshwell Av, Rom. RM6 82 C4
Fresh Wf Est, Bark. IG11
off Fresh Wf Rd 117 E1
Fresh Wf Rd, Bark. IG11 117 E1
Freshwood Cl, Beck. BR3 190 B1
Freston Gdns, Barn. EN4 42 A5
Freston Pk, N3 72 C2
Freston Rd, W10 108 A7
W11 108 A7
Freta Rd, Bexh. DA6 159 F5
★ **Freud Mus**, NW3 91 F6
Frewin Rd, SW18 167 G1
Friar Ms, SE27 169 H3
Friar Rd, Hayes UB4 102 D4
Friars, The, Chig. IG7 65 H4
Friars Av, N20 57 H3
SW15 165 F3
Friars Cl, E4 62 C3
N2 73 G4
SE1 27 G2
Ilford IG1 99 G1
Northolt UB5
off Broomcroft Av 102 D3
Friars Gdns, W3
off St. Dunstans Av 106 D6
Friars Gate Cl, Wdf.Grn. IG8 63 G4
Friars La, Rich. TW9 145 G5
Friars Mead, E14 134 C3
Friars Ms, SE9 156 D5
Friars Pl La, W3 106 D7
Friars Rd, E6 116 A1
Friars Stile Pl, Rich. TW10
off Friars Stile Rd 145 H6
Friars Stile Rd, Rich. TW10 145 H6
Friar St, EC4 19 H4
Friars Wk, N14 58 B1
SE2 138 D5
Friars Way, W3 106 D6
Friary Cl, N12 57 H5
Friary Ct, SW1 25 G2
Friary Est, SE15 37 J6
Friary La, Wdf.Grn. IG8 63 G4
Friary Pk Est, W3
off Friary Rd 106 D6
Friary Rd, N12 57 G4
SE15 37 J6
W3 106 D6
Friary Way, N12 57 H4
FRIDAY HILL, E4 62 D2
Friday Hill, E4 62 E2
Friday Hill E, E4 62 E3
Friday Hill W, E4 62 E2
Friday Rd, Mitch. CR4 167 J7
Friday St, EC4 19 J4
Frideswide Pl, NW5
off Islip St 92 C5
Friendly Pl, SE13
off Lewisham Rd 154 B1
Friendly St, SE8 154 A1
Friendly St Ms, SE8
off Friendly St 154 A2
Friendship Wk, Nthlt. UB5
off Wayfarer Rd 102 D3
Friendship Way, E15
off Carpenters Rd 114 C1
Friends Rd, Croy. CR0 202 A3
Friend St, EC1 11 G3
FRIERN BARNET, N11 57 H4
Friern Barnet La, N11 57 H4
N20 57 H4
Friern Barnet Rd, N11 57 J5
Friern Br Retail Pk, N11 58 B6
Friern Ct, N20 57 G3
Friern Mt Dr, N20 41 F7
Friern Pk, N12 57 F5
Friern Rd, SE22 152 D6
Friern Watch Av, N12 57 F4
Frigate Ms, SE8
off Watergate St 134 A6
Frimley Av, Wall. SM6 201 E5
Frimley Cl, SW19 166 B2
Croydon (New Adgtn) CR0 204 C7
Frimley Ct, Sid. DA14 176 B5
Frimley Cres, Croy. (New Adgtn) CR0 204 C7
Frimley Gdns, Mitch. CR4 185 H3
Frimley Rd, Chess. KT9 195 H5
Ilford IG3 99 H3
Frimley Way, E1 113 G4
Frinstead Ho, W10 108 A7
Frinton Cl, Wat. WD19 50 B2
Frinton Dr, Wdf.Grn. IG8 62 D7
Frinton Ms, Ilf. IG2
off Bramley Cres 80 D6
Frinton Rd, E6 116 A3
N15 76 B6
SW17 168 A6
Sidcup DA14 176 E2
Friston Path, Chig. IG7 65 H5
Friston St, SW6 148 E2
Friswell Pl, Bexh. DA6 159 G4
Fritham Cl, N.Mal. KT3 182 E6
Frith Ct, NW7 56 B7
Frith La, NW7 56 B7
Frith Rd, E11 96 C4
Croydon CR0 201 J2
Frith St, W1 17 H4
Frithville Gdns, W12 127 J1
Frizlands La, Dag. RM10 101 H4
Frobisher Cl, Pnr. HA5 66 D7
Frobisher Cres, EC2
off The Barbican 20 A1
Staines TW19 140 B7
Frobisher Gdns, Stai. TW19 140 B7
Frobisher Ms, Enf. EN2 44 A4
Frobisher Pas, E14
off The North Colonnade 134 A1
Frobisher Pl, SE15
off St. Mary's Rd 153 F1
Frobisher Rd, E6 116 C6
N8 75 G4
Frobisher St, SE10 135 E6
Froghall La, Chig. IG7 65 G4
Frogley Rd, SE22 152 C4
Frogmore, SW18 148 D5
Frogmore Cl, Sutt. SM3 198 A3
Frogmore Est, Ruis. HA4 84 D5
Frogmore Gdns, Sutt. SM3 198 B4
Frogmore Ind Est, NW10 106 C3
Frognal, NW3 91 F5
Frognal Av, Har. HA1 68 C4
Sidcup DA14 176 A5
Frognal Cl, NW3 91 F5
Frognal Cor, Sid. DA14 175 J6
Frognal Ct, NW3 91 F6
Frognal Gdns, NW3 91 F4
Frognal La, NW3 90 E5
Frognal Par, NW3
off Frognal Ct 91 F6
Frognal Pl, Sid. DA14 176 A6
Frognal Ri, NW3 91 F4
Frognal Way, NW3 91 F4
Froissart Rd, SE9 156 A5
Frome Rd, N22
off Westbury Av 75 H3
Frome St, N1 11 J1
Fromondes Rd, Sutt. SM3 198 B5
Frostic Wk, E1 21 G2
Froude St, SW8 150 B2
Fruen Rd, Felt. TW14 141 J7
Fruiterers Pas, EC4
off Southwark Br 20 A6
Fryatt Rd, N17 60 A7
Fryday Gro Ms, SW12
off Weir Rd 150 C7
Fryent Cl, NW9 70 A6
Fryent Cres, NW9 70 E6
Fryent Flds, NW9 71 E6
Fryent Gro, NW9 70 E6
Fryent Way, NW9 70 A5
Frying Pan All, E1 21 F2
Fry Rd, E6 98 A7
NW10 107 F1
Fryston Av, Croy. CR0 202 D2
Fuchsia St, SE2 138 B5
Fulbeck Dr, NW9 70 E1
Fulbeck Wk, Edg. HA8
off Burrell Cl 54 B2
Fulbeck Way, Har. HA2 67 J2
Fulbourne Rd, E17 78 C1
Fulbourne St, E1
off Durward St 112 E5
Fulbrook Ms, N19
off Junction Rd 92 C4
Fulbrook Rd, N19
off Junction Rd 92 C4
Fulford Gro, Wat. WD19 50 B2
Fulford Rd, Epsom KT19 196 D7
Fulford St, SE16 133 E2
FULHAM, SW6 148 B2
Fulham Bdy, SW6 128 D7
Fulham Bdy Retail Cen, SW6 *off Fulham Bdy* 128 D7
Fulham Ct, SW6
off Shottendane Rd 148 D1
★ **Fulham FC**, SW6 148 A1
Fulham High St, SW6 148 B2
★ **Fulham Palace**, SW6 148 B2
Fulham Palace Rd, SW6 128 A7
W6 127 J5
Fulham Pk Gdns, SW6 148 C2
Fulham Pk Rd, SW6 148 C2
Fulham Rd, SW3 30 E4
SW6 30 B7
SW10 30 E4
Fullbrooks Av, Wor.Pk. KT4 197 F1
Fuller Cl, E2 13 H5
Orpington BR6 207 J5
Fuller Rd, Dag. RM8 100 B3
Fullers Av, Surb. KT6 195 J2
Woodford Green IG8 63 F7
★ **Fuller's Griffin Brewery**, W4 127 F6
Fullers Rd, E18 79 F1
Fuller St, NW4 71 J4
Fullers Way N, Surb. KT6 195 J3
Fullers Way S, Chess. KT9 195 H4
Fullers Wd, Croy. CR0 204 A5
Fuller Ter, Ilf. IG1
off Oaktree Gro 99 G5
Fullerton Rd, SW18 149 F5
Croydon CR0 188 C7
Fuller Way, Hayes UB3 121 J5
Fullwell Av, Ilf. IG5, IG6 80 C1
FULLWELL CROSS, Ilf. IG6 81 G1
Fullwell Cross Rbt, Ilf. IG6
off High St 81 G2
Fullwoods Ms, N1 12 C3
Fulmar Cl, Surb. KT5 181 J6
Fulmead St, SW6 149 E1
Fulmer Cl, Hmptn. TW12 161 E5
Fulmer Rd, E16 116 A5
Fulmer Way, W13 124 E3
Fulready Rd, E10 78 D5
Fulstone Cl, Houns. TW4 143 F4
Fulthorp Rd, SE3 155 F2
Fulton Ms, W2 14 C5
Fulton Rd, Wem. HA9 88 A3
Fulwell Pk Av, Twick. TW2 161 H2
Fulwell Rd, Tedd. TW11 162 A4
Fulwood Av, Wem. HA0 105 J1
Fulwood Gdns, Twick. TW1 144 C6
Fulwood Pl, WC1 18 D2
Fulwood Wk, SW19 166 B1
Furber St, W6 127 H3
Furham Feild, Pnr. HA5 51 G7
Furley Rd, SE15 132 D7
Furlong Cl, Wall. SM6 200 B1
Furlong Rd, N7 93 G6
Furmage St, SW18 149 E7
Furneaux Av, SE27 169 H5
Furness Rd, NW10 107 G2
SW6 149 E2
Harrow HA2 67 H7
Morden SM4 185 E7
Furnival St, EC4 19 E3
Furrow La, E9 95 F5
Fursby Av, N3 56 D6
Further Acre, NW9 71 F2
Furtherfield Cl, Croy. CR0 187 G6
Further Grn Rd, SE6 155 E7
Furze Cl, Wat. WD19 50 C5
FURZEDOWN, SW17 168 A5
Furzedown Dr, SW17 168 B5
Furzedown Hall, SW17
off Spalding Rd 168 B5
Furzedown Rd, SW17 168 B5
Furze Fm Cl, Rom. RM6 83 E2
Furzefield Cl, Chis. BR7 174 E6
Furzefield Rd, SE3 135 H6
Furzeground Way, Uxb. UB11 121 F1
Furzeham Rd, West Dr. UB7 120 B2
Furzehill Par, Borwd. WD6
off Shenley Rd 38 A3
Furzehill Rd, Borwd. WD6 38 A4
Furze Rd, Th.Hth. CR7 187 J3
Furze St, E3 114 A5

Furzewood, Sun.TW16 **178** A1
Fuschia Ct, Wdf.Grn. IG8
off The Bridle Path **63** E7
Fyfe Way, Brom. BR1
off Widmore Rd **191** G2
Fyfield, N4
off Six Acres Est **93** G2
Fyfield Cl, Brom. BR2 **190** D4
Fyfield Ct, E7 **97** G6
Fyfield Rd, E17 **78** D3
SW9 **151** G3
Enfield EN1 **44** B3
Woodford Green IG8 **63** J7
Fynes St, SW1 **33** H1

G

Gable Cl, Pnr. HA5 **51** G7
Gable Ct, SE26
off Lawrie Pk Av **171** E4
Gables, The, Wem. HA9 **88** A3
Gables Cl, SE5 **152** B1
SE12 **173** G1
Gabriel Cl, Felt.TW13 **160** D4
Gabrielle Cl, Wem. HA9 **87** J3
Gabrielle Ct, NW3 **91** G6
Gabriel Ms, NW2 **90** C2
Gabriel St, SE23 **153** G7
Gabriel's Wf, SE1 **27** E1
Gad Cl, E13 **115** H3
Gaddesden Av, Wem.
HA9 **87** J6
Gade Cl, Hayes UB3 **122** B1
Gadesden Rd, Epsom
KT19 **196** C6
Gadsbury Cl, NW9 **71** F6
Gadwall Cl, E16
off Freemasons Rd **115** H6
Gadwall Way, SE28 **137** G2
Gage Rd, E16
off Malmesbury Rd **115** E5
Gage St, WC1 **18** B1
Gainford St, N1
off Richmond Av **111** G1
Gainsboro Gdns, Grnf.
UB6 **86** B5
Gainsborough Av, E12 **98** D5
Gainsborough Cl, Beck.
BR3 **172** A7
Esher KT10
off Lime Tree Av **194** B1
Gainsborough Ct, N12 **56** E5
W12 *off Lime Gro* **127** J2
Bromley BR2 **191** J4
Gainsborough Gdns,
NW3 **91** G3
NW11 **72** C7
Edgware HA8 **69** J2
Isleworth TW7 **144** A5
Gainsborough Ho, E14
off Cassilis Rd **134** A2
Enfield EN1
off Ayley Cft **44** D5
Gainsborough Ms, SE26
off Panmure Rd **170** E3
Gainsborough Pl, Chig.
IG7 **65** J3
Gainsborough Rd, E11 **79** E7
E15 **114** E3
N12 **57** E5
W4 **127** F4
Dagenham RM8 **100** B4
New Malden KT3 **182** D7
Richmond TW9 **145** J3
Woodford Green IG8 **64** B6
Gainsborough Sq, Bexh.
DA6 *off Regency Way* **158** D3
Gainsborough St, E9
off Trowbridge Rd **95** J6
Gainsborough Studios, N1
off Poole St **112** A1
Gainsford Rd, E17 **77** J4
Gainsford St, SE1 **29** F3
Gairloch Rd, SE5 **152** B2
Gaisford St, NW5 **92** C6
Gaitskell Ct, SW11 **149** G2
Gaitskell Rd, SE9 **175** F1
Gaitskell Way, SE1
off Weller St **27** J3
Galahad Rd, N9 **60** D3
Bromley BR1 **173** G3
Galata Rd, SW13 **127** G7
Galatea Sq, SE15
off Scylla Rd **152** E3
Galaxy, E14
off Crews St **134** A4
Galba Ct, Brent.TW8
off Augustus Cl **125** G7
Galbraith St, E14 **134** C3
Galdana Av, Barn.
EN5 **41** F3
Galeborough Av, Wdf.Grn.
IG8 **62** D7
Gale Cl, Hmptn.TW12
off Stewart Cl **161** E6
Mitcham CR4 **185** G3
Galena Ho, SE18
off Grosmont Rd **137** J5
Galena Rd, W6 **127** H4
Galen Pl, WC1 **18** B2
Galesbury Rd, SW18 **149** F6
Gales Gdns, E2 **113** E3
Gale St, E3 **114** A5
Dagenham RM9 **118** D1
Gales Way, Wdf.Grn. IG8 **64** B7
Galgate Cl, SW19 **166** B1
Gallants Fm Rd, Barn.
(E.Barn.) EN4 **41** H7
Galleon Cl, SE16
off Kinburn St **133** G2
Galleon Ho, SW8
off St. George Wf **34** A5
Galleons Dr, Bark. IG11 **118** A3
Gallery Gdns, Nthlt. UB5 **102** D2
Gallery Rd, SE21 **170** A1
Galley La, Barn. EN5 **39** H3
Galleywall Rd, SE16 **132** E4
Galliard Cl, N9 **45** F6
Galliard Rd, N9 **60** D1
Gallia Rd, N5 **93** H5
Gallica Ct, Sutt. SM1
off Cleeve Way **199** E1
Gallions Cl, Bark. IG11 **118** A3
Gallions Reach Shop Pk,
E6 **117** F5
Gallions Rd, E16 **117** F7
SE7 **135** H4
Gallions Rbt, E16 **116** E7
Gallions Vw Rd, SE28
off Goldfinch Rd **137** H2
Gallon Cl, SE7 **135** J4
Gallop, The, S.Croy. CR2 **203** E7
Sutton SM2 **199** F7
Gallosson Rd, SE18 **137** H4
Galloway Path, Croy.
CR0 **202** A4
Galloway Rd, W12 **127** G1
Gallus Cl, N21 **43** F6
Gallus Sq, SE3 **155** H3
Galpins Rd, Th.Hth. CR7 **187** F4
Galsworthy Av, E14 **113** H5
Romford RM6 **82** B7
Galsworthy Cl, SE28 **138** B1
Galsworthy Cres, SE3
off Merriman Rd **155** J1
Galsworthy Rd, NW2 **90** B4
Kingston upon Thames
KT2 **164** B7
Galsworthy Ter, N16
off Hawksley Rd **94** B3
Galton St, W10 **108** B4
Galva Cl, Barn. EN4 **42** A4
Galvani Way, Croy. CR0
off Ampere Way **201** F1
Galveston Rd, SW15 **148** C5
Galway Cl, SE16
off Masters Dr **133** E5
Galway Ho, EC1 **12** A4
Galway St, EC1 **12** A4
Gambetta St, SW8 **150** B2
Gambia St, SE1 **27** H2
Gambier Ho, EC1 **12** A3
Gambole Rd, SW17 **167** H4
Games Ho, SE7
off Springfield Gro **135** J6
Games Rd, Barn. EN4 **41** J3
Gamlen Rd, SW15 **148** A4
Gamuel Cl, E17 **78** A6
Gander Grn Cres, Hmptn.
TW12 **179** G1
Gander Grn La, Sutt. SM1,
SM3 **198** B2
Gandhi Cl, E17 **78** A6
Gandolfi St, SE15 **36** D6
Ganton St, W1 **17** F5
Ganton Wk, Wat. WD19 **50** D4
GANTS HILL, Ilf. IG2 **80** D5
Gants Hill, Ilf. IG2
off Eastern Av **80** D6
Gantshill Cres, Ilf. IG2 **80** D5
Gap Rd, SW19 **166** D5
Garage Rd, W3 **106** A6
Garand Ct, N7
off Eden Gro **93** F5
Garbutt Pl, W1 **16** C1
Garden Av, Bexh. DA7 **159** G3
Mitcham CR4 **168** B7
Garden City, Edg. HA8 **54** A6
Garden Cl, E4 **62** A5
SE12 **173** H3
SW15 **147** H7
Barnet (Arkley) EN5 **39** J4
Hampton TW12 **161** F5
New Malden KT3 **182** E4
Northolt UB5 **103** E1
Wallington SM6 **200** E5
Garden Ct, EC4 **18** E5
N12 *off Holden Rd* **56** E5
Richmond TW9 **145** J1
Stanmore HA7 **53** F5
West Molesey KT8
off Avern Rd **179** H4
Gardeners Cl, N11 **58** A2
SE9 **174** B3
Gardeners Rd, Croy. CR0 **201** H1
Gardenia Rd, Brom. BR1 **192** D3
Enfield EN1 **44** B6
Gardenia Way, Wdf.Grn.
IG8 **63** G5
Garden La, SW2
off Christchurch Rd **169** F1
Bromley BR1 **173** H6
Garden Ms, W2
off Linden Gdns **108** D7
Garden Pl, E8
off Haggerston Rd **112** C1
Garden Rd, NW8 **6** D3
SE20 **189** F1
Bromley BR1 **173** H7
Richmond TW9 **146** A3
Walton-on-Thames
KT12 **178** B6
Garden Row, SE1 **27** G6
Gardens, The, E5 **76** C7
SE22 **152** D4
Beckenham BR3 **190** C2
Feltham TW14 **141** G5
Harrow HA1 **67** J6
Pinner HA5 **67** F6
Garden St, E1 **113** G5
Garden Ter, SW1 **33** H3
Garden Wk, EC2 **12** D4
Beckenham BR3
off Hayne Rd **189** J1
Garden Way, NW10 **88** C6
Gardiner Av, NW2 **89** J5
Gardiner Cl, Dag. RM8 **100** D4
Enfield EN3 **45** G6
Gardner Cl, E11 **79** H6
Gardner Ct, EC1
off Brewery Sq **11** G5
N5 *off Kelvin Rd* **93** J4
Gardner Gro, Felt.TW13 **161** F2
Gardner Ind Est, Beck.
BR3 **171** H5
Gardner Pl, Felt.TW14 **142** B6
Gardner Rd, E13 **115** H4
Gardners La, EC4 **19** J5
Gardnor Rd, NW3
off Flask Wk **91** G4
Gard St, EC1 **11** H3
Garendon Gdns, Mord.
SM4 **184** E7
Garendon Rd, Mord.
SM4 **184** E7
Gareth Cl, Wor.Pk. KT4
off Burnham Dr **198** A2
Gareth Dr, N9 **60** D2
Gareth Gro, Brom. BR1 **173** G4
Garfield Ms, SW11
off Garfield Rd **150** B3
Garfield Rd, E4 **62** D1
E13 **115** F4
SW11 **150** A3
SW19 **167** F5
Enfield EN3 **45** F4
Twickenham TW1 **162** D1
Garford St, E14 **114** A7
Garganey Wk, SE28 **118** D7
Garibaldi St, SE18 **137** H4
Garland Ct, SE17
off Wansey St **36** A2
Garland Dr, Houns.TW3 **143** J2
Garland Ho, Kings.T. KT2
off Kingsgate Rd **181** H1
Garland Rd, SE18 **137** G7
Bromley BR1 **192** E3
Stanmore HA7 **69** H1
Garlands Ct, Croy. CR0
off Chatsworth Rd **202** A4
Garlick Hill, EC4 **20** A5
Garlies Rd, SE23 **171** H3
Garlinge Rd, NW2 **90** C6
Garman Cl, N18 **60** A5
Garman Rd, N17 **61** F7
Garnault Ms, EC1 **11** F4
Garnault Pl, EC1 **11** F4
Garner Cl, Dag. RM8 **100** D1
Garner Rd, E17 **78** C1
Garner St, E2 **13** J2
Garnet Rd, NW10 **89** E6
Thornton Heath CR7 **188** A4
Garnet St, E1 **113** F7
Garnett Cl, SE9 **156** C3
Garnett Rd, NW3 **91** J5
Garnett Way, E17
off McEntee Av **77** H1
Garnet Wk, E6
off Kingfisher St **116** B5
Garnham Cl, N16
off Garnham St **94** C2
Garnham St, N16 **94** C2
Garnies Cl, SE15 **37** F7
Garrad's Rd, SW16 **168** D3
Garrard Cl, Bexh. DA7 **159** G3
Chislehurst BR7 **175** E5
Garrard Wk, NW10
off Garnet Rd **89** E6
Garratt Cl, Croy. CR0 **200** E4
Garratt La, SW17 **167** G4
SW18 **148** E5
Garratt Rd, Edg. HA8 **54** A7
Garratt Ter, SW17 **167** H4
Garrett Cl, W3
off Jenner Av **106** D5
Garrett St, EC1 **12** A5
Garrick Av, NW11 **72** B6
Garrick Cl, SW18 **149** F4
W5 **105** H4
Richmond TW9
off Old Palace La **145** G5
Garrick Ct, Edg. HA8 **53** J4
Garrick Cres, Croy. CR0 **202** B2
Garrick Dr, NW4 **71** J2
SE28 **137** G3
Garrick Gdns, W.Mol.
KT8 **179** G3
Garrick Pk, NW4 **72** A2
Garrick Rd, NW9 **71** F6
Greenford UB6 **103** H4
Richmond TW9 **146** A2
Garricks Ho, Kings.T.
KT1 **181** G2
Garrick St, WC2 **18** A5
Garrick Way, NW4 **72** A4
Garrison Cl, SE18
off Red Lion La **136** D7
Hounslow TW4 **143** F5
Garrison La, Chess. KT9 **195** G7
Garrison Rd, E3 **114** A1
Garsdale Cl, N11 **58** A6
Garside Cl, SE28 **137** G3
Hampton TW12 **161** H6
Garsington Ms, SE4 **153** J3
Garter Way, SE16
off Poolmans St **133** G2
Garth, The, N12
off Holden Rd **56** E5
Hampton (Hmptn H.)
TW12 *off Uxbridge Rd* **161** H6
Harrow HA3 **69** J6
Garth Cl, W4 **126** D5
Kingston upon Thames
KT2 **163** J5
Morden SM4 **184** A7
Ruislip HA4 **84** D1
Garth Ct, W4
off Garth Rd **126** D5
Garth Ho, NW2
off Granville Rd **90** C2
Garthland Dr, Barn. EN5 **39** H5
Garth Ms, W5
off Greystoke Gdns **105** H4
Garthorne Rd, SE23 **153** G7
Garth Rd, NW2 **90** C2
W4 **126** D6
Kingston upon Thames
KT2 **163** J5
Morden SM4 **183** J6
Garth Rd Ind Cen, Mord.
SM4 **184** A7
Garthside, Rich. (Ham)
TW10 **163** H5
Garthway, N12 **57** H6
Gartmoor Gdns, SW19 **166** C1
Gartmore Rd, Ilf. IG3 **99** J1
Garton Pl, SW18 **149** F6
Gartons Cl, Enf. EN3 **45** F5
Gartons Way, SW11 **149** F3
Garvary Rd, E16 **115** H6
Garway Rd, W2 **14** A4
Garwood Cl, N17 **76** E1
Gascoigne Gdns, Wdf.Grn.
IG8 **63** E7
Gascoigne Pl, E2 **13** F4
Gascoigne Rd, Bark. IG11 **117** F1
Gascony Av, NW6 **90** D7
Gascoyne Rd, E9 **95** G7
Gaselee St, E14 **114** C7
Gaskarth Rd, SW12 **150** B6
Edgware HA8 **70** C1
Gaskell Rd, N6 **73** J6
Gaskell St, SW4 **150** E2
Gaskin St, N1 **111** H1
Gaspar Cl, SW5 **30** B1
Gaspar Ms, SW5 **30** B1
Gassiot Rd, SW17 **167** J4
Gassiot Way, Sutt. SM1 **199** G3
Gastein Rd, W6 **128** A6
Gaston Bell Cl, Rich.TW9 **145** J3
Gaston Rd, Mitch. CR4 **186** A3
★ **Gasworks Gall**, SE11 **34** D5

Gataker St, SE16 ....133 E3
Gatcombe Ho, SE22
off Pytchley Rd 152 B3
Gatcombe Ms, W5 ....105 J7
Gatcombe Rd, E16 ....135 G1
N19 ....92 D3
Gatcombe Way, Barn. EN4 .41 J3
Gate Cl, Borwd. WD6 ....38 C1
Gate End, Nthwd. HA6 ....50 A7
Gateforth St, NW8 ....7 G6
Gatehouse Cl, Kings.T.
KT2 ....164 C7
Gate Ho Sq, SE1 ....28 A1
Gateley Rd, SW9 ....151 F3
Gate Ms, SW7 ....23 H4
Gater Dr, Enf. EN2 ....44 A1
Gatesborough St, EC2 ....12 D5
Gates Grn Rd, Kes. BR2 ..205 G4
West Wickham BR4 ....205 F3
Gateside Rd, SW17 ....167 J3
Gatestone Rd, SE19 ....170 B6
Gate St, WC2 ....18 C3
Gate Studios, Borwd.
WD6 ....38 A4
Gateway, SE17 ....36 A5
Gateway Business Cen,
SE26 ....171 H6
Gateway Ind Est, NW10 ..107 F3
Gateway Ms, E8
off Shacklewell La 94 C5
Gateway Retail Pk, E6 ...117 E4
Gateway Rd, E10 ....96 B3
Gateways, The, SW3 ....31 H2
Gatfield Gro, Felt. TW13 ..161 G2
Gathorne Rd, N22 ....75 G2
Gathorne St, E2
off Mace St 113 G2
Gatley Av, Epsom KT19 ..196 B5
Gatliff Cl, SW1
off Ebury Br Rd 32 D4
Gatliff Rd, SW1 ....32 C4
Gatling Rd, SE2 ....138 A5
Gatonby St, SE15 ....152 C1
Gatting Cl, Edg. HA8 ....54 C7
Gatton Rd, SW17 ....167 H4
Gattons Way, Sid. DA14 ..177 F4
Gatward Cl, N21 ....43 H6
Gatward Grn, N9 ....60 B2
Gatwick Rd, SW18 ....148 C7
Gauden Cl, SW4 ....150 D3
Gauden Rd, SW4 ....150 D2
Gaumont Ter, W12
off Lime Gro 127 J2
Gauntlet Cl, Nthlt. UB5 ...84 E7
Gauntlett Ct, Wem. HA0 ..86 E5
Gauntlett Rd, Sutt. SM1 ..199 G5
Gaunt St, SE1 ....27 H5
Gautrey Rd, SE15 ....153 F2
Gautrey Sq, E6 ....116 C6
Gavel St, SE17 ....36 C1
Gaverick Ms, E14
off Westferry Rd 134 A4
Gavestone Cres, SE12 ...155 H7
Gavestone Rd, SE12 ....155 H7
Gaviller Pl, E5
off Clarence Rd 95 E4
Gavina Cl, Mord. SM4 ...185 H5
Gavin St, SE18 ....137 H4
Gawain Wk, N9
off Galahad Rd 60 D3
Gawber St, E2 ....113 F3
Gawsworth Cl, E15
off Ash Rd 97 E5
Gawthorne Ct, E3
off Mostyn Gro 114 A2
Gay Cl, NW2 ....89 H5
Gaydon Ho, W2 ....14 B1
Gaydon La, NW9 ....70 E1
Gayfere Rd, Epsom KT17 .197 G5
Ilford IG5 ....80 C3
Gayfere St, SW1 ....26 A6
Gayford Rd, W12 ....127 F2
Gay Gdns, Dag. RM10 ...101 J4
Gayhurst, SE17 ....36 C5
Gayhurst Rd, E8 ....94 D7
Gaylor Rd, Nthlt. UB5 ....85 F5
Gaynesford Rd, SE23 ....171 G2
Carshalton SM5 ....199 J7
Gaynes Hill Rd, Wdf.Grn.
IG8 ....64 B6
Gay Rd, E15 ....114 D2
Gaysham Av, Ilf. IG2 ....80 D5
Gaysham Hall, Ilf. IG5 ....80 E3
Gay St, SW15 ....148 A3
Gayton Ct, Har. HA1 ....68 C6
Gayton Cres, NW3 ....91 G4
Gayton Ho, E3 ....114 A4
Gayton Rd, NW3 ....91 G4
SE2 *off Florence Rd* ...138 C3
Harrow HA1 ....68 C6
Gayville Rd, SW11 ....149 J6
Gaywood Cl, SW2 ....169 F1
Gaywood Est, SE1 ....27 G6
Gaywood Rd, E17 ....78 A3
Gaywood St, SE1 ....27 H6
Gaza St, SE17 ....35 G4
Gazelle Ho, E15
off Manbey Pk Rd 96 E6
Gean Ct, N11
off Cline Rd 58 C6
Geariesville Gdns, Ilf. IG6 .81 E4
Gearing Cl, SW17 ....168 A4
Geary Ct, N9
off The Broadway 60 D2
Geary Rd, NW10 ....89 G5
Geary St, N7 ....93 F5
Geddes Pl, Bexh. DA6
off Market Pl 159 G4
Gedeney Rd, N17 ....75 J1
Gedling Ho, SE22
off Quorn Rd 152 C3
Gedling Pl, SE1 ....29 G5
Geere Rd, E15 ....115 F1
Gees Ct, W1 ....16 C4
Gee St, EC1 ....11 J5
Geffrye Ct, N1 ....12 E2
Geffrye Est, N1 ....13 E2
★ **Geffrye Mus**, E2 ....13 E2
Geffrye St, E2 ....13 F1
Geldart Rd, SE15 ....132 E7
Geldeston Rd, E5 ....94 D2
Gellatly Rd, SE14 ....153 F2
Gemini Business Pk, E6 ..117 G5
Gemini Gro, Nthlt. UB5
off Javelin Way 102 E3
Gemini Ho, E3
off Garrison Rd 114 A1
Gemini Project, SE14
off Landmann Way ...133 G5
Genas Cl, Ilf. IG6 ....81 E1
General Gordon Pl, SE18 .136 E4
General Wolfe Rd, SE10 ..154 D1
Genesta Rd, SE18 ....137 E6
Geneva Dr, SW9 ....151 G4
Geneva Gdns, Rom. RM6 ..82 E5
Geneva Rd, Kings.T. KT1 .181 H4
Thornton Heath CR7 ..187 J5
Genever Cl, E4 ....62 A5
Genista Rd, N18 ....61 E5
Genoa Av, SW15 ....147 J5
Genoa Rd, SE20 ....189 F1
Genotin Rd, Enf. EN1 ....44 A3
Genotin Ter, Enf. EN1
off Genotin Rd 44 A3
Gentian Row, SE13
off Sparta St 154 C1
Gentlemans Row, Enf.
EN2 ....43 J3
Gentry Gdns, E13
off Whitwell Rd 115 G4
Geoffrey Cl, SE5 ....151 J2
Geoffrey Gdns, E6 ....116 B2
Geoffrey Rd, SE4 ....153 J3
George Beard Rd, SE8 ...133 J4
George Belt Ho, E2
off Smart St 113 G3
George Comberton Wk, E12
off Gainsborough Av ..98 D5
George Ct, WC2 ....18 B6
George Cres, N10 ....58 A7
George Downing Est, N16 .94 C2
George Eliot Ho, SW1
off Vauxhall Br Rd 33 G2
George Elliston Ho, SE1
off Old Kent Rd 37 H4
George V Av, Pnr. HA5 ....67 G3
George V Cl, Pnr. HA5 ....67 G3
George V Way, Grnf.
(Perivale) UB6 ....105 E1
George Gange Way, Har.
(Wealds.) HA3 ....68 B3
George Gros Rd, SE20 ...188 D1
★ **George Inn**, SE1 ....28 B2
George Inn Yd, SE1 ....28 B2
George La, E18 ....79 G2
SE13 ....154 C6
Bromley BR2 ....205 H1
George La Rbt, E18 ....79 G2
George Lansbury Ho, N22
off Progress Way 75 G1
George Loveless Ho, E2 ...13 G3
George Lowe Ct, W2 ....14 A1
George Mathers Rd,
SE11 ....35 G1
George Ms, NW1 ....9 F4
SW9 *off Brixton Rd* ...151 G2
Enfield EN2
off Church St 44 A3
George Rd, E4 ....62 A6
Kingston upon Thames
KT2 ....164 B7
New Malden KT3 ....183 F4
George Row, SE16 ....29 H4
George Sq, SW19
off Mostyn Rd 184 C3
George's Rd, N7 ....93 F5
Georges Sq, SW6
off North End Rd 128 C6
George St, E16 ....115 F6
W1 ....16 A3
W7 *off The Broadway* ..124 B1
Barking IG11 ....99 F7
Croydon CR0 ....202 A2
Hounslow TW3 ....143 F2
Richmond TW9 ....145 G5
Southall UB2 ....122 E4
George Taylor Ct, N9
off Colthurst Dr 60 E3
Georgetown Cl, SE19
off St. Kitts Ter 170 B5
Georgette Pl, SE10
off King George St ...134 C7
Georgeville Gdns, Ilf. IG6 ..81 E4
George Wyver Cl, SW19
off Beaumont Rd 148 B7
George Yd, EC3 ....20 C4
W1 ....16 C5
Georgiana St, NW1 ....110 C1
Georgian Cl, Brom. BR2 ..191 H7
Stanmore HA7 ....52 D7
Georgian Ct, SW16
off Gleneldon Rd 169 E4
Wembley HA9 ....88 A6
Georgian Way, Har. HA1 ..86 A2
Georgia Rd, N.Mal. KT3 ..182 C4
Thornton Heath CR7 ..187 H1
Georgina Gdns, E2 ....13 G3
Geraint Rd, Brom. BR1 ...173 G4
Geraldine Rd, SW18 ....149 F5
W4 ....126 A6
Geraldine St, SE11 ....27 G6
Gerald Ms, SW1 ....32 C1
Gerald Rd, E16 ....115 F4
SW1 ....32 C1
Dagenham RM8 ....101 F2
Gerard Av, Houns. TW4 ..143 G7
Gerard Pl, E9
off Groombridge Rd ...95 G7
Gerard Rd, SW13 ....147 F1
Harrow HA1 ....68 D6
Gerards Cl, SE16 ....133 F5
Gerda Rd, SE9 ....175 F2
Germander Way, E15 ....115 E3
Gernigan Ho, SW18
off Fitzhugh Gro 149 G6
Gernon Rd, E3 ....113 H2
Geron Way, NW2 ....89 H1
Gerrard Gdns, Pnr. HA5 ...66 A5
Gerrard Ho, SE14
off Briant St 133 G7
Gerrard Pl, W1 ....17 J5
Gerrard Rd, N1 ....11 H1
Gerrards Cl, N14 ....42 C5
Gerrard St, W1 ....17 H5
Gerridge St, SE1 ....27 F4
Gerry Raffles Sq, E15
off Great Eastern Rd ..96 D6
Gertrude Rd, Belv. DA17 .139 G4
Gertrude St, SW10 ....30 D6
Gervase Cl, Wem. HA9 ....88 C3
Gervase Rd, Edg. HA8 ....70 C1
Gervase St, SE15 ....133 E7
Ghent St, SE6 ....172 A2
Ghent Way, E8
off Tyssen St 94 C6
Giant Arches Rd, SE24 ...151 J7
Giant Tree Hill, Bushey
(Bushey Hth) WD23 ....52 A1
Gibbard Ms, SW19 ....166 A5
Gibbfield Cl, Rom. RM6 ...82 E3
Gibbins Rd, E15 ....96 C7
Gibbon Rd, SE15 ....153 F2
W3 ....106 E7
Kingston upon Thames
KT2 ....181 H1
Gibbons Ms, NW11
off Hayes Cres 72 C5
Gibbons Rents, SE1
off Magdalen St 28 D2
Gibbons Rd, NW10 ....88 D6
Gibbon Wk, SW15 ....147 G4
Gibbs Av, SE19 ....170 A5
Gibbs Cl, SE19 ....170 A5
Gibbs Couch, Wat.
WD19 ....50 D3
Gibbs Grn, W14 ....128 C5
Edgware HA8 ....54 C5
Gibbs Rd, N18 ....61 F4
Gibbs Sq, SE19 ....170 A5
Gibney Ter, Brom. BR1
off Durham Hill 173 F4
Gibraltar Wk, E2 ....13 G4
Gibson Business Cen, N17
off High Rd 60 C7
Gibson Cl, E1
off Colebert Av 113 F4
N21 ....43 G6
Chessington KT9 ....195 F6
Isleworth TW7 ....144 A3
Gibson Gdns, N16
off Northwold Rd 94 C2
Gibson Ms, Twick. TW1
off Richmond Rd 145 F7
Gibson Rd, SE11 ....34 D2
Dagenham RM8 ....100 C1
Sutton SM1 ....198 E5
Gibson's Hill, SW16 ....169 G6
Gibson Sq, N1 ....111 G1
Gibson St, SE10 ....134 E5
Gideon Cl, Belv. DA17 ...139 H4
Gideon Ms, W5 ....125 G2
Gideon Rd, SW11 ....150 A3
Giesbach Rd, N19 ....92 C2
Giffard Rd, N18 ....60 B5
Giffin St, SE8 ....134 A7
Gifford Gdns, W7 ....104 A5
Gifford St, N1 ....93 E7
Gift La, E15 ....115 E1
Giggs Hill Gdns, T.Ditt.
KT7 ....194 D1
Giggs Hill Rd, T.Ditt. KT7 ..180 D7
Gilbert Cl, SE18 ....156 C1
Gilbert Gro, Edg. HA8 ....70 D1
Gilbert Ho, EC2
off The Barbican 20 A1
SE8 *off McMillan St* ...134 A6
SW1 ....33 E4
Gilbert Pl, WC1 ....18 A2
Gilbert Rd, SE11 ....35 F2
SW19 ....167 F7
Belvedere DA17 ....139 G3
Bromley BR1 ....173 G7
Pinner HA5 ....66 D4
Gilbert St, E15 ....96 E4
W1 ....16 C4
Hounslow TW3
off High St 143 J3
Gilbert Way, Croy. CR0
*off Beddington
Fm Rd* 201 E1
Gilbert White Cl, Grnf. UB6
off Horsenden La S ..104 D1
Gilbey Rd, SW17 ....167 H4
Gilbeys Yd, NW1 ....92 A7
Gilbourne Rd, SE18 ....137 J6
Gilda Av, Enf. EN3 ....45 H5
Gilda Cres, N16 ....94 D1
Gildea Cl, Pnr. HA5 ....51 G7
Gildea St, W1 ....17 E2
Gilden Cres, NW5 ....92 A5
Gildersome St, SE18
off Nightingale Vale ..136 D6
Gilders Rd, Chess. KT9 ..195 J6
Giles Coppice, SE19 ....170 C4
Gilkes Cres, SE21 ....152 B6
Gilkes Pl, SE21 ....152 B6
Gillan Grn, Bushey
(Bushey Hth) WD23 ....51 J2
Gillards Ms, E17
off Gillards Way 78 A4
Gillards Way, E17 ....78 A4
Gill Av, E16 ....115 G6
Gillender St, E3 ....114 C4
E14 ....114 C4
Gillespie Rd, N5 ....93 G3
Gillett Av, E6 ....116 B2
Gillette Cor, Islw. TW7 ...124 D7
Gillett Pl, N16
off Gillett St 94 B5
Gillett Rd, Th.Hth. CR7 ...188 A4
Gillett St, N16 ....94 B5
Gillfoot, NW1 ....9 F2
Gillham Ter, N17 ....60 D6
Gillian Pk Rd, Sutt. SM3 ..198 C1
Gillian St, SE13 ....154 B5
Gillies St, NW5 ....92 A5
Gilling Ct, NW3 ....91 H6
Gillingham Rd, NW2 ....90 B3
Gillingham Row, SW1 ....33 F1
Gillingham St, SW1 ....33 E1
Gillison Wk, SE16
off Tranton Rd 29 J5
Gillman Dr, E15 ....115 F1
Gill St, E14 ....113 J6
Gillum Cl, Barn. (E.Barn.)
EN4 ....57 J1
Gilmore Rd, SE13 ....154 D4
Gilpin Av, SW14 ....146 D4
Gilpin Cl, W2 ....14 E1
Mitcham CR4 ....185 H2
Gilpin Cres, N18 ....60 C5
Twickenham TW2 ....143 H7
Gilpin Rd, E5 ....95 H4
Gilpin Way, Hayes
(Harling.) UB3 ....121 G7
Gilsland Pl, Th.Hth. CR7
off Gilsland Rd 188 A4
Gilsland Rd, Th.Hth. CR7 .188 A4
Gilstead Ho, Bark. IG11 ...118 B2
Gilstead Rd, SW6 ....149 E2
Gilston Rd, SW10 ....30 D4
Gilton Rd, SE6 ....173 E3

Giltspur St, EC1 .... **19** H3
Gilwell Cl, E4
off Antlers Hill **46** B4
Gilwell La, E4 .... **46** C4
Gilwell Pk, E4 .... **46** C3
Ginsburg Yd, NW3
off Heath St **91** F4
Gippeswyck Cl, Pnr. HA5
off Uxbridge Rd **66** D1
Gipsy Hill, SE19 .... **170** B4
Gipsy La, SW15 .... **147** G3
Gipsy Rd, SE27 .... **169** J4
Welling DA16 .... **158** D1
Gipsy Rd Gdns, SE27 .... **169** J4
Giralda Cl, E16
off Fulmer Rd **116** A5
Giraud St, E14 .... **114** B6
Girdlers Rd, W14 .... **128** A4
Girdlestone Wk, N19 ...... **92** C2
Girdwood Rd, SW18 ..... **148** B7
Girling Way, Felt. TW14 ... **142** A3
Gironde Rd, SW6 .... **128** C7
Girton Av, NW9 .... **70** A3
Girton Cl, Nthlt. UB5 ..... **85** J6
Girton Gdns, Croy. CR0 .. **204** A3
Girton Rd, SE26 .... **171** G5
Northolt UB5 .... **85** J6
Girton Vil, W10 .... **108** A6
Gisbourne Cl, Wall.
SM6 .... **200** D3
Gisburn Rd, N8 .... **75** F4
Gissing Wk, N1
off Lofting Rd **93** G7
Gittens Cl, Brom. BR1 ... **173** F4
Given Wilson Wk, E13 .... **115** F2
Glacier Way, Wem. HA0 .. **105** G2
Gladbeck Way, Enf. EN2 ... **43** H4
Gladding Rd, E12 .... **98** A4
Glade, The, N21 .... **43** F6
SE7 .... **135** J7
Bromley BR1 .... **192** A2
Croydon CR0 .... **189** G5
Enfield EN2 .... **43** G3
Epsom KT17 .... **197** G5
Ilford IG5 .... **80** C1
West Wickham BR4 .... **204** B3
Woodford Green IG8 ... **63** H3
Glade Cl, Surb. (Long Dit.)
KT6 .... **195** G2
Glade Ct, Ilf. IG5 .... **80** C1
Glade Gdns, Croy. CR0 ... **189** H7
Glade La, Sthl. UB2 ..... **123** H2
Gladeside, N21 .... **43** F6
Croydon CR0 .... **189** G6
Gladeside Cl, Chess. KT9 . **195** G7
Gladesmore Rd, N15 ..... **76** C6
Glades Shop Cen, The,
Brom. BR1 .... **191** G2
Gladeswood Rd, Belv.
DA17 .... **139** H4
Gladiator St, SE23 ...... **153** H6
Glading Ter, N16 .... **94** C3
Gladioli Cl, Hmptn. TW12
off Gresham Rd **161** G6
Gladsdale Dr, Pnr. HA5 ... **66** A4
Gladsmuir Rd, N19 .... **92** C1
Barnet EN5 .... **40** B2
Gladstone Av, E12 .... **98** B7
N22 .... **75** G2
Feltham TW14 .... **142** A6
Twickenham TW2 ..... **144** A7
Gladstone Ct, SW1
off Regency St **33** J2
SW8 *off Havelock Ter* .. **150** B1
SW19
off Gladstone Rd **166** D7
Gladstone Gdns,
Houns. TW3
off Palmerston Rd ... **143** J1
Gladstone Ms, N22
off Pelham Rd **75** G2
NW6 *off Cavendish Rd* . **90** C7
SE20 .... **171** F7
Gladstone Par, NW2
off Edgware Rd **89** H1
Gladstone Pk Gdns, NW2 . **89** H3
Gladstone Pl, E3
off Roman Rd **113** J2
Barnet EN5 .... **40** A4
Gladstone Rd, SW19 .... **166** D7
W4 *off Acton La* **126** D3
Buckhurst Hill IG9 ...... **63** H1
Croydon CR0 .... **188** A7
Kingston upon Thames
KT1 .... **182** A3
Orpington BR6 .... **207** F5
Southall UB2 .... **122** E3
Surbiton KT6 .... **195** G2
Gladstone St, SE1 .... **27** G5
Gladstone Ter, SE27
off Bentons La **169** J4
Gladstone Way, Har.
(Wealds.) HA3 .... **68** B3
Gladwell Rd, N8 .... **75** F6
Bromley BR1 .... **173** G6
Gladwyn Rd, SW15 ..... **148** A3
Gladys Rd, NW6 .... **90** D7
Glaisher St, SE8 .... **134** A6
Glamis Cres, Hayes UB3 . **121** F3
Glamis Pl, E1 .... **113** F7
Glamis Rd, E1 .... **113** F7
Glamis Way, Nthlt. UB5 ... **85** J6
Glamorgan Cl, Mitch.
CR4 .... **186** E3
Glamorgan Rd, Kings.T.
KT1 .... **163** F7
Glandford Way, Rom.
(Chad.Hth) RM6 .... **82** B5
Glanfield Rd, Beck. BR3 .. **189** J4
Glanleam Rd, Stan. HA7 .. **53** G4
Glanville Ms, Stan. HA7 ... **52** D5
Glanville Rd, SW2 .... **151** E5
Bromley BR2 .... **191** H3
Glasbrook Av, Twick. TW2 . **161** F1
Glasbrook Rd, SE9 ...... **156** A7
Glaserton Rd, N16 .... **76** B7
Glasford St, SW17 ...... **167** J6
Glasgow Ho, W9 .... **6** B2
Glasgow Rd, E13 .... **115** H2
N18 *off Aberdeen Rd* ... **60** E5
Glasgow Ter, SW1 .... **33** F4
Glasier Ct, E15
off Glenavon Rd **97** E7
Glaskin Ms, E9
off Danesdale Rd **95** H6
Glasse Cl, W13 .... **104** D7
Glasshill St, SE1 .... **27** H3
Glasshouse Flds, E1 ..... **113** G7
Glasshouse St, W1 .... **17** G6
Glasshouse Wk, SE11 ..... **34** B3
Glasshouse Yd, EC1 ...... **11** J6
Glasslyn Rd, N8 .... **74** D5
Glassmill La, Brom. BR2 . **191** F2
Glass St, E2
off Coventry Rd **113** E4
Glass Yd, SE18
off Woolwich High St . **136** D3
Glastonbury Av, Wdf.Grn.
IG8 .... **64** A7
Glastonbury Ho, SW1 .... **32** D3
Glastonbury Pl, E1
off Sutton St **113** F6
Glastonbury Rd, N9 ...... **60** D1
Morden SM4 .... **184** D7
Glastonbury St, NW6 ..... **90** C5
Glaucus St, E3 .... **114** B5
Glazbury Rd, W14 .... **128** B4
Glazebrook Cl, SE21 ..... **170** A2
Glazebrook Rd, Tedd.
TW11 .... **162** C7
Glebe, The, SE3 .... **154** E3
SW16 .... **168** D4
Chislehurst BR7 ...... **193** F1
West Drayton UB7 .... **120** C4
Worcester Park KT4 ... **197** F1
Glebe Av, Enf. EN2 .... **43** H3
Harrow HA3 .... **69** H3
Mitcham CR4 .... **185** H2
Ruislip HA4 .... **84** B6
Woodford Green IG8 ... **63** G6
Glebe Cl, W4
off Prince of
Wales Ter **126** E5
Glebe Cotts, Sutt. SM1
off Vale Rd **198** E4
Glebe Ct, W7 .... **104** A7
Mitcham CR4 .... **185** J3
Stanmore HA7 .... **53** F5
Glebe Cres, NW4 .... **71** J4
Harrow HA3 .... **69** H3
Glebe Gdns, N.Mal. KT3 . **183** E7
Glebe Ho Dr, Brom. BR2 . **205** H1
Glebe Hyrst, SE19 .... **170** B4
Glebelands, W.Mol. KT8 .. **179** H5
Glebelands Av, E18 .... **79** G2
Ilford IG2 .... **81** G7
Glebelands Cl, N12 .... **73** G1
Glebelands Rd, Felt.
TW14 .... **142** A7
Glebe La, Barn. EN5 ...... **39** G5
Harrow HA3 .... **69** H4
Glebe Ms, Sid. DA15 ..... **157** J5
Glebe Path, Mitch. CR4 .. **185** H3
Glebe Pl, SW3 .... **31** G5
Glebe Rd, E8
off Middleton Rd **94** C7
N3 .... **73** F1
N8 .... **75** F4
NW10 .... **89** F6
SW13 .... **147** G2
Bromley BR1 .... **191** G1
Carshalton SM5 ...... **199** J6
Dagenham RM10 ..... **101** H6
Hayes UB3 .... **121** J1
Stanmore HA7 .... **53** F5
Glebe Side, Twick. TW1 ... **144** C6
Glebe Sq, Mitch. CR4 .... **185** J3
Glebe St, W4 .... **126** E5
Glebe Ter, W4
off Glebe St **126** E5
Glebe Way, Felt. (Han.)
TW13 .... **161** G3
West Wickham BR4 .... **204** C2
Glebeway, Wdf.Grn. IG8 .. **63** J5
Gledhow Gdns, SW5 ..... **30** C2
Gledstanes Rd, W14 ..... **128** B5
Gleed Av, Bushey
(Bushey Hth) WD23 .... **52** A2
Gleeson Dr, Orp. BR6 .... **207** J5
Glegg Pl, SW15 .... **148** A4
Glen, The, Brom. BR2 .... **190** E2
Croydon CR0 .... **203** G3
Enfield EN2 .... **43** H4
Orpington BR6 .... **206** C3
Pinner HA5 .... **67** E7
Pinner (Eastcote) HA5 .. **66** B5
Southall UB2 .... **123** F5
Wembley HA9 .... **87** G4
Glenaffric Av, E14 .... **134** D4
Glen Albyn Rd, SW19 .... **166** A2
Glenalmond Rd, Har.
HA3 .... **69** H4
Glenalvon Way, SE18 .... **136** B4
Glena Mt, Sutt. SM1 ..... **199** F4
Glenarm Rd, E5 .... **95** F5
Glenavon Cl, Esher (Clay.)
KT10 .... **194** D7
Glenavon Rd, E15 .... **97** E7
Glenbarr Cl, SE9
off Dumbreck Rd **156** E3
Glenbow Rd, Brom. BR1 . **172** E6
Glenbrook N, Enf. EN2 .... **43** F4
Glenbrook Rd, NW6 ...... **90** D5
Glenbrook S, Enf. EN2 .... **43** F4
Glenbuck Ct, Surb. KT6
off Glenbuck Rd **181** H6
Glenbuck Rd, Surb. KT6 .. **181** G6
Glenburnie Rd, SW17 .... **167** J3
Glencairn Dr, W5 .... **105** E4
Glencairne Cl, E16 .... **116** A5
Glencairn Rd, SW16 ..... **186** E1
Glencoe Av, Ilf. IG2 .... **81** G7
Glencoe Dr, Dag. RM10 .. **101** G4
Glencoe Rd, Hayes UB4 .. **102** E5
Glencorse Grn, Wat.
WD19 .... **50** D4
Glen Cres, Wdf.Grn. IG8 ... **63** H6
Glendale Av, N22 .... **59** G7
Edgware HA8 .... **53** J4
Romford RM6 .... **82** C7
Glendale Cl, SE9
off Dumbreck Rd **156** D3
Glendale Dr, SW19 ...... **166** C5
Glendale Gdns, Wem.
HA9 .... **87** G1
Glendale Ms, Beck. BR3 .. **190** B1
Glendale Rd, Erith DA8 .. **139** J4
Glendale Way, SE28 ..... **118** C7
Glendall St, SW9 .... **151** F4
Glendarvon St, SW15 .... **148** A3
Glendevon Cl, Edg. HA8
off Tayside Dr **54** B3
Glendish Rd, N17 .... **76** D1
Glendor Gdns, NW7 ...... **54** D4
Glendower Gdns, SW14
off Glendower Rd **146** D3
Glendower Pl, SW7 ...... **31** E1
Glendower Rd, E4 .... **62** D1
SW14 .... **146** D3
Glendown Rd, SE2 ...... **138** A5
Glendun Rd, W3 .... **107** E7
Gleneagle Ms, SW16
off Ambleside Av **168** D5
Gleneagle Rd, SW16 ..... **168** D5
Gleneagles, Stan. HA7 .... **52** E6
Gleneagles Cl, SE16
off Ryder Dr **132** E5
Orpington BR6 .... **207** G1
Staines (Stanw.) TW19 . **140** A6
Watford WD19 .... **50** D4
Gleneagles Grn, Orp. BR6
off Tandridge Dr **207** G1
Gleneagles Twr, Sthl.
UB1 .... **103** J6
Gleneldon Ms, SW16 .... **168** E4
Gleneldon Rd, SW16 .... **168** E4
Glenelg Rd, SW2 .... **151** E5
Glenesk Rd, SE9 .... **156** D3
Glenfarg Rd, SE6 .... **172** D1
Glenfield Rd, SW12 ..... **168** C1
W13 .... **125** E2
Glenfield Ter, W13 .... **124** E2
Glenfinlas Way, SE5 ...... **35** H7
Glenforth St, SE10 ...... **135** F5
Glengall Causeway, E14 . **134** A3
Glengall Gro, E14 .... **134** B3
Glengall Rd, NW6 .... **108** C1
SE15 .... **37** G5
Bexleyheath DA7 ..... **159** E3
Glengall Rd, Edgware
HA8 .... **54** B3
Woodford Green IG8 ... **63** G6
Glengall Ter, SE15 .... **37** G5
Glen Gdns, Croy. CR0 .... **201** H3
Glengarnock Av, E14 .... **134** C4
Glengarry Rd, SE22 ..... **152** B5
Glenham Dr, Ilf. IG2 ...... **80** E5
Glenhaven Av, Borwd.
WD6 .... **38** A3
Glenhead Cl, SE9
off Dumbreck Rd **156** E3
Glenhill Cl, N3 .... **72** D2
Glenhouse Rd, SE9 ..... **156** D5
Glenhurst Av, NW5 .... **92** A4
Bexley DA5 .... **177** F1
Glenhurst Ct, SE19 ...... **170** C5
Glenhurst Ri, SE19 ...... **169** J7
Glenhurst Rd, N12 .... **57** G5
Brentford TW8 .... **125** F6
Glenilla Rd, NW3 .... **91** H6
Glenister Ho, Hayes UB3 . **122** B1
Glenister Pk Rd, SW16 ... **168** D7
Glenister Rd, SE10 ...... **135** F5
Glenister St, E16 .... **136** D1
Glenkerry Ho, E14
off Burcham St **114** C6
Glenlea Path, SE9
off Well Hall Rd **156** C5
Glenlea Rd, SE9 .... **156** C5
Glenloch Rd, NW3 .... **91** H6
Enfield EN3 .... **45** F2
Glenluce Rd, SE3 .... **135** G7
Glenlyon Rd, SE9 .... **156** D5
Glenmere Av, NW7 .... **55** G7
Glenmere Row, SE12 .... **155** G6
Glen Ms, E17 *off Glen Rd* .. **77** J5
Glenmill, Hmptn. TW12 .. **161** F5
Glenmore Rd, NW3 ...... **91** H6
Welling DA16 .... **157** J1
Glenmore Way, Bark.
IG11 .... **118** A3
Glenmount Path, SE18
off Raglan Rd **137** F5
Glennie Rd, SE27 .... **169** G3
Glenny Rd, Bark. IG11 .... **99** F6
Glenorchy Cl, Hayes
UB4 .... **103** E5
Glenparke Rd, E7 .... **97** H6
Glen Ri, Wdf.Grn. IG8 ..... **63** H6
Glen Rd, E13 .... **115** J4
E17 .... **77** J5
Chessington KT9 ..... **195** H3
Glenrosa St, SW6 .... **149** F2
Glenrose Ct, Sid. DA14 .. **176** B5
Glenroy St, W12 .... **107** J6
Glensdale Rd, SE4 ...... **153** J3
Glenshiel Rd, SE9 .... **156** D5
Glenside, Chig. IG7 .... **65** E6
Glentanner Way, SW17 .. **167** G3
Glen Ter, E14
off Manchester Rd ... **134** C2
Glentham Gdns, SW13
off Glentham Rd **127** H6
Glentham Rd, SW13 ..... **127** G6
Glenthorne Av, Croy.
CR0 .... **203** E1
Glenthorne Cl, Sutt. SM3 . **198** D1
Glenthorne Gdns, Ilf. IG6 .. **80** D3
Sutton SM3 .... **198** D1
Glenthorne Ms, W6
off Glenthorne Rd ... **127** H4
Glenthorne Rd, E17 ...... **77** H5
N11 .... **57** J5
W6 .... **127** J4
Kingston upon Thames
KT1 .... **181** J4
Glenthorpe Rd, Mord.
SM4 .... **184** A5
Glenton Rd, SE13 .... **154** E4
Glentrammon Av, Orp.
BR6 .... **207** J6
Glentrammon Cl, Orp.
BR6 .... **207** J6
Glentrammon Gdns, Orp.
BR6 .... **207** J6
Glentrammon Rd, Orp.
BR6 .... **207** J6
Glentworth St, NW1 .... **8** A6
Glenure Rd, SE9 .... **156** D5
Glenview, SE2 .... **138** D6
Glenview Rd, Brom. BR1 . **192** A2
Glenville Gro, SE8 ...... **133** J7
Glenville Ms, SW18 ..... **148** E7
Glenville Rd, Kings.T.
KT2 .... **182** A1
Glen Wk, Islw. TW7 ...... **144** A5
Glenwood Av, NW9 .... **88** E1
Glenwood Cl, Har. HA1 ... **68** C5
Glenwood Ct, E18
off Clarendon Rd **79** G3
Glenwood Gdns, Ilf. IG2 ... **80** D5
Glenwood Gro, NW9 ..... **88** C1

Glenwood Rd, N15 .75 H5
NW7 .55 E3
SE6 .171 J1
Epsom KT17 .197 G6
Hounslow TW3 .144 A3
Glenwood Way, Croy.
CR0 .189 G6
Glenworth Av, E14 .134 D4
Gliddon Dr, E5 .94 D4
Gliddon Rd, W14 .128 B4
Glimpsing Grn, Erith
DA18 .139 E3
Global App, E3
off Hancock Rd .114 B2
Globe Pond Rd, SE16 .133 H1
Globe Rd, E1 .113 F3
E2 .113 F3
E15 .97 F5
Woodford Green IG8 .63 J6
Globe Rope Wk, E14 .134 C4
Globe St, SE1 .28 A5
Globe Ter, E2
off Globe Rd .113 F3
Globe Town, E2
off Mace St .113 G2
Globe Wf, SE16
off Rotherhithe St .113 G7
Globe Yd, W1 .16 D4
Gloster Rd, N.Mal. KT3 .182 E4
Gloucester Arc, SW7 .30 C1
Gloucester Av, NW1 .92 A7
Sidcup DA15 .175 H2
Welling DA16 .157 J4
Gloucester Circ, SE10 .134 C7
Gloucester Cl, NW10 .88 D7
Thames Ditton KT7 .194 D1
Gloucester Ct, Rich. TW9 .126 A7
Gloucester Cres, NW1 .110 B1
Gloucester Dr, N4 .93 H2
NW11 .72 D4
Gloucester Gdns, NW11 .72 C7
W2 .14 B3
Barnet (Cockfos.) EN4 .42 A4
Ilford IG1 .80 B7
Sutton SM1 .199 E2
Gloucester Gate, NW1 .8 D1
Gloucester Gate Ms, NW1 .8 D1
Gloucester Gro, Edg. HA8 .70 D1
Gloucester Ho, NW6 .108 D2
Gloucester Ms, E10
off Gloucester Rd .78 A7
W2 .14 D4
Gloucester Ms W, W2 .14 C4
Gloucester Par, Sid.
DA15 .158 A5
Gloucester Pk, SW7 .30 C1
Gloucester Pl, NW1 .7 J5
W1 .16 A1
Gloucester Pl Ms, W1 .16 A2
Gloucester Rd, E10 .78 A7
E11 .79 H5
E12 .98 C3
E17 .77 G2
N17 .76 A2
N18 .60 C5
SW7 .22 C5
W3 .126 C2
W5 .125 F2
Barnet EN5 .41 F5
Belvedere DA17 .139 F5
Croydon CR0 .188 A6
Feltham TW13 .160 C1
Hampton TW12 .161 H7
Harrow HA1 .67 H5
Hounslow TW4 .142 E4
Kingston upon Thames
KT1 .182 B2
Richmond TW9 .126 A7
Teddington TW11 .162 B5
Twickenham TW2 .161 J1
Gloucester Sq, E2
off Whiston Rd .112 D1
W2 .15 F4
Gloucester St, SW1 .33 F4
Gloucester Ter, W2 .14 C3
Gloucester Wk, W8 .128 D2
Gloucester Way, EC1 .11 F4
Glover Cl, SE2 .138 C4
Glover Dr, N18 .61 F6
Glover Rd, Pnr. HA5 .66 D6
Gloxinia Wk, Hmptn.
TW12 .161 G6
Glycena Rd, SW11 .149 J3
Glyn Av, Barn. EN4 .41 G4
Glyn Cl, SE25 .188 B2
Glyn Ct, SW16 .169 G3
Stanmore HA7 .52 E6
Glyndebourne Pk, Orp.
BR6 .207 E2
Glynde Ms, SW3 .23 H6
Glynde Rd, Bexh. DA7 .158 D3
Glynde St, SE4 .153 J6
Glyndon Rd, SE18 .137 F4
Glyn Dr, Sid. DA14 .176 B4
Glynfield Rd, NW10 .89 E7
Glynne Rd, N22 .75 G2
Glyn Rd, E5 .95 G3
Enfield EN3 .45 F4
Worcester Park KT4 .198 A2
Glyn St, SE11 .34 C4
Glynwood Ct, SE23 .171 F2
Goaters All, SW6 .128 C7
Goat La, Surb. KT6 .195 F2
Goat Rd, Mitch. CR4 .186 A7
Goat Wf, Brent. TW8 .125 H6
Godalming Av, Wall.
SM6 .201 E5
Godalming Rd, E14 .114 B5
Godbold Rd, E15 .114 E3
Goddard Pl, N19 .92 C3
Goddard Rd, Beck. BR3 .189 G4
Goddards Way, Ilf. IG1 .99 G1
Godfrey Av, Nthlt. UB5 .102 E1
Twickenham TW2 .144 A7
Godfrey Hill, SE18 .136 B4
Godfrey Ho, EC1 .12 B4
Godfrey Rd, SE18 .136 C4
Godfrey St, E15 .114 C2
SW3 .31 H3
Godfrey Way, Houns.
TW4 .143 E7
Goding St, SE11 .34 B4
Godley Cl, SE14
off Kender St .153 F1
Godley Rd, SW18 .167 G1
Godliman St, EC4 .19 J4
Godman Rd, SE15 .152 E2
Godolphin Cl, N13 .59 H6
Godolphin Pl, W3 .106 D7
Godolphin Rd, W12 .127 H2
Godson Rd, Croy. CR0 .201 G3
Godson St, N1 .11 E1
Godstone Rd, Sutt. SM1 .199 F4
Twickenham TW1 .144 D6
Godstow Rd, SE2 .138 C2
Godwin Cl, N1 .12 A1
Epsom KT19 .196 C6
Godwin Ct, NW1 .9 G1
Godwin Ho, NW6
off Tollgate Gdns .6 A1
Godwin Rd, E7 .97 H4
Bromley BR2 .191 J3
Goffers Rd, SE3 .154 D1
Goidel Cl, Wall. SM6 .200 D4
Golborne Gdns, W10
off Golborne Rd .108 C4
Golborne Ms, W10
off Portobello Rd .108 B5
Golborne Rd, W10 .108 B5
Golda Cl, Barn. EN5 .40 A6
Goldbeaters Gro, Edg.
HA8 .54 E6
Goldcliff Cl, Mord. SM4 .184 D7
Goldcrest Cl, E16
off Sheerwater Rd .116 A5
SE28 .118 C7
Goldcrest Ms, W5 .105 G5
Goldcrest Way, Bushey
WD23 .51 J1
Golden Ct, Islw. TW7
off London Rd .144 A2
Richmond TW9
off George St .145 G5
Golden Cres, Hayes UB3 .121 J1
Golden Cross Ms, W11
off Basing St .108 C6
★ **Golden Hinde**, SE1 .28 B1
Golden Jubilee Br, SE1 .26 C2
WC2 .26 B1
Golden La, EC1 .11 J6
Golden La Est, EC1 .11 J6
Golden Manor, W7 .104 B7
Golden Plover Cl, E16
off Maplin Rd .115 H6
Golden Sq, W1 .17 G5
Golden Yd, NW3
off Heath St .91 F4
Golders Cl, Edg. HA8 .54 B5
Golders Gdns, NW11 .72 B7
GOLDERS GREEN, NW11 .72 D7
Golders Grn Cres, NW11 .72 C7
Golders Grn Rd, NW11 .72 B6
Golders Manor Dr, NW11 .72 A6
Golders Pk Cl, NW11 .90 D1
Golders Ri, NW4 .72 A5
Golders Way, NW11 .72 C7
Goldfinch Rd, SE28 .137 G3
Goldfinch Way, Borwd.
WD6 .38 A4
Goldhawk Ms, W12
off Devonport Rd .127 H2
Goldhawk Rd, W6 .127 F4
W12 .127 G3
Goldhaze Cl, Wdf.Grn. IG8 .64 A7
Gold Hill, Edg. HA8 .54 D6
Goldhurst Ter, NW6 .90 E7
Golding Cl, Chess. KT9
off Coppard Gdns .195 F6
Golding Ct, Ilf. IG1 .98 D3
Goldingham Av, Loug.
IG10 .49 F2
Goldings Hill, Loug. IG10 .48 D1
Goldings Ri, Loug. IG10 .48 D1
Goldings Rd, Loug. IG10 .48 D1
Golding St, E1 .21 J4
Golding Ter, SW11
off Longhedge St .150 A2
Goldington Cres, NW1 .9 H1
Goldington St, NW1 .9 H1
Gold La, Edg. HA8 .54 D6
Goldman Cl, E2 .13 H5
Goldmark Ho, SE3
off Lebrun Sq .155 H3
Goldney Rd, W9 .108 D4
Goldrill Dr, N11 .58 A2
Goldsboro Rd, SW8 .150 D1
Goldsborough Cres, E4 .62 C2
Goldsdown Cl, Enf. EN3 .45 H2
Goldsdown Rd, Enf. EN3 .45 G2
Goldsmid St, SE18
off Sladedale Rd .137 H5
Goldsmith Av, E12 .98 B6
NW9 .71 F6
W3 .106 D7
Romford RM7 .83 G7
Goldsmith Cl, W3 .126 D1
Harrow HA2 .85 H1
Goldsmith Ct, Edg. HA8 .53 J4
Goldsmith La, NW9 .70 B4
Goldsmith Rd, E10 .96 A1
E17 .77 G2
N11 .57 J5
SE15 .152 D1
W3 .126 D1
★ **Goldsmiths' Hall**, EC2 .19 J3
Goldsmith's Pl, NW6
off Springfield La .108 E1
Goldsmith's Row, E2 .13 H2
Goldsmith's Sq, E2 .13 J1
Goldsmith St, EC2 .20 A3
Goldsworthy Gdns, SE16 .133 F4
Goldwell Ho, SE22
off Quorn Rd .152 B3
Goldwell Rd, Th.Hth. CR7 .187 F4
Goldwin Cl, SE14 .153 F1
Goldwing Cl, E16 .115 G6
Golf Cl, Stan. HA7 .53 F7
Thornton Heath CR7
off Kensington Av .187 G1
Golf Club Dr, Kings.T.
KT2 .164 D7
Golfe Rd, Ilf. IG1 .99 G3
Golf Rd, W5
off Boileau Rd .105 J6
Bromley BR1 .192 D3
Golf Side, Twick. TW2 .162 A3
Golfside Cl, N20 .57 H3
New Malden KT3 .183 E2
Gollogly Ter, SE7 .135 J5
Gomer Gdns, Tedd. TW11 .162 D6
Gomer Pl, Tedd. TW11 .162 D6
Gomm Rd, SE16 .133 F3
Gomshall Av, Wall. SM6 .200 E5
Gondar Gdns, NW6 .90 C5
Gonson St, SE8 .134 B6
Gonston Cl, SW19 .166 B2
Gonville Cres, Nthlt. UB5 .85 H6
Gonville Rd, Th.Hth. CR7 .187 F5
Gonville St, SW6
off Putney Br App .148 B3
Gooch Ho, E5 .94 E3
Goodall Rd, E11 .96 C3
Gooden Ct, Har. HA1 .86 B3
Goodenough Rd, SW19 .166 C7
Goodey Rd, Bark. IG11 .99 J7
Goodge Pl, W1 .17 G2
Goodge St, W1 .17 G2
Goodhall Cl, Stan. HA7 .52 D6
Goodhall St, NW10 .107 E3
Goodhart Pl, E14 .113 H7
Goodhart Way, W.Wick.
BR4 .190 E7
Goodhew Rd, Croy. CR0 .188 D6
Gooding Cl, N.Mal. KT3 .182 C4
Goodinge Cl, N7 .92 E6
Goodman Cres, SW2 .168 D2
Goodman Rd, E10 .78 C7
Goodmans Ct, E1 .21 F5
Wembley HA0 .87 G4
Goodman's Stile, E1 .21 H3
Goodmans Yd, E1 .21 F5
GOODMAYES, Ilf. IG3 .100 B2
Goodmayes Av, Ilf. IG3 .100 A1
Goodmayes La, Ilf. IG3 .100 A4
Goodmayes Retail Pk,
Rom. RM6 *off High Rd* .100 B1
Goodmayes Rd, Ilf. IG3 .100 A1
Goodrich Rd, SE22 .152 C6
Goodson Rd, NW10 .89 E7
Goods Way, NW1 .10 A1
Goodway Gdns, E14 .114 D6
Goodwill Dr, Har. HA2 .85 G1
Goodwin Cl, SE16 .29 G6
Mitcham CR4 .185 G3
Goodwin Ct, Barn. EN4 .41 H6
Goodwin Dr, Sid. DA14 .176 D3
Goodwin Gdns, Croy.
CR0 .201 H6
Goodwin Rd, N9 .61 F1
W12 .127 G2
Croydon CR0 .201 H5
Goodwins Ct, WC2 .18 A5
Goodwin St, N4
off Fonthill Rd .93 G2
Goodwood Cl, Mord.
SM4 .184 D4
Stanmore HA7 .53 F5
Goodwood Dr, Nthlt. UB5 .85 G6
Goodwood Path, Borwd.
WD6 *off Stratfield Rd* .38 A2
Goodwood Rd, SE14 .133 H7
Goodwyn Av, NW7 .55 E5
Goodwyns Vale, N10 .74 A1
Goodyers Gdns, NW4 .72 A5
Goosander Way, SE28 .137 G3
Gooseacre La, Har. HA3 .69 G5
Gooseley La, E6 .116 D3
Goosens Cl, Sutt. SM1
off Turnpike La .199 F5
Goose Sq, E6
off Harper Rd .116 C6
Gophir La, EC4 .20 B5
Gopsall St, N1 .112 A1
Goran Ct, N9
off Bedevere Rd .60 D3
Gordon Av, E4 .62 E6
SW14 .146 E4
Stanmore HA7 .52 E6
Twickenham TW1 .144 D5
Gordonbrock Rd, SE4 .154 A5
Gordon Cl, E17 .78 A6
N19
off Highgate Hill .92 C1
Gordon Cres, Croy. CR0 .202 B1
Hayes UB3 .122 A3
Gordondale Rd, SW19 .166 D2
Gordon Gdns, Edg. HA8 .70 B2
Gordon Gro, SE5 .151 H2
Gordon Hill, Enf. EN2 .43 J1
Gordon Ho, E1
off Glamis Rd .113 F7
Gordon Ho Rd, NW5 .92 A4
Gordon Pl, W8 .128 D2
Gordon Rd, E4 .47 E7
E11 .79 G6
E15 .96 C4
E18 .79 H1
N3 .56 C7
N9 .61 E2
N11 .58 D7
SE15 .152 E2
W4 .126 B6
W5 .105 F7
W13 .104 E7
Barking IG11 .117 H1
Beckenham BR3 .189 J3
Belvedere DA17 .139 J4
Carshalton SM5 .199 J6
Enfield EN2 .43 J1
Esher (Clay.) KT10 .194 B6
Harrow HA3 .68 B3
Hounslow TW3 .143 J4
Ilford IG1 .99 G3
Kingston upon Thames
KT2 .181 J1
Richmond TW9 .145 J2
Romford RM6 .83 F6
Sidcup DA15 .157 H5
Southall UB2 .123 E4
Surbiton KT5 .181 J7
Gordon Sq, WC1 .9 J6
Gordon St, E13
off Grange Rd .115 G3
WC1 .9 H5
Gordon Way, Barn. EN5 .40 C4
Bromley BR1 .191 G1
Gore Ct, NW9 .70 A5
Gorefield Pl, NW6 .108 D2
Gore Rd, E9 .113 F1
SW20 .183 J2
Goresbrook Rd, Dag.
RM9 .118 B1
Goresbrook Village,
Dag. RM9
off Goresbrook Rd .118 B1
Gore St, SW7 .22 D5
Gorham Pl, W11
off Mary Pl .108 B7
Goring Cl, Rom. RM5 .83 J1
Goring Gdns, Dag. RM8 .100 C4
Goring Rd, N11 .58 E6
Goring St, EC3 .21 E3

Goring Way, Grnf. UB6 **103** J2
Gorleston Rd, N15 **76** A5
Gorleston St, W14 **128** B4
Gorman Rd, SE18 **136** C4
Gorringe Pk Av, Mitch. CR4 **167** J7
Gorse Cl, E16 **115** G6
Gorse Ri, SW17 **168** A5
Gorse Rd, Croy. CR0 **204** A4
Gorst Rd, NW10 **106** C4
SW11 **149** J6
Gorsuch Pl, E2 **13** F3
Gorsuch St, E2 **13** F3
Gosberton Rd, SW12 **168** A1
Gosbury Hill, Chess. KT9 **195** H4
Gosfield Rd, Dag. RM8 **101** G2
Gosfield St, W1 **17** F1
Gosford Gdns, Ilf. IG4 **80** C5
Gosforth La, Wat. WD19 **50** C3
Gosforth Path, Wat. WD19 **50** A3
Goshawk Way, Felt. TW14 *off Falcon Way* **142** B5
Goslett Yd, WC2 **17** J4
Gosling Cl, Grnf. UB6 **103** G3
Gosling Way, SW9 **151** G1
Gospatrick Rd, N17 **59** J7
GOSPEL OAK, NW5 **92** A4
Gosport Rd, E17 **77** J5
Gosport Wk, N17 *off Yarmouth Cres* **76** E5
Gossage Rd, SE18 **137** G5
Gosset St, E2 **13** G3
Gosshill Rd, Chis. BR7 **192** D2
Gossington Cl, Chis. BR7 *off Beechwood Ri* **175** E4
Gosterwood St, SE8 **133** H6
Gostling Rd, Twick. TW2 **161** G1
Goston Gdns, Th.Hth. CR7 **187** G3
Goswell Rd, EC1 **11** J6
Gothic Ct, Hayes UB3 *off Sipson La* **121** G6
Gothic Rd, Twick. TW2 **162** A2
Gottfried Ms, NW5 *off Fortess Rd* **92** C4
Goudhurst Rd, Brom. BR1 **173** E5
Gough Rd, E15 **97** F4
Enfield EN1 **44** E2
Gough Sq, EC4 **19** F3
Gough St, WC1 **10** D5
Gough Wk, E14 *off Saracen St* **114** A6
Gould Ct, SE19 **170** B5
Goulden Ho App, SW11 **149** H2
Goulding Gdns, Th.Hth. CR7 **187** H2
Gould Rd, Felt. TW14 **141** H7
Twickenham TW2 **162** B1
Gould Ter, E8 *off Kenmure Rd* **95** E5
Goulston St, E1 **21** F3
Goulton Rd, E5 **95** E4
Gourley Pl, N15 *off Gourley St* **76** B5
Gourley St, N15 **76** B5
Gourock Rd, SE9 **156** D5
Govan St, E2 *off Whiston Rd* **112** D1
Govier Cl, E15 **97** E7
Gowan Av, SW6 **148** B1
Gowan Rd, NW10 **89** H6
Gower Cl, SW4 **150** C6
Gower Ct, WC1 **9** H5
Gower Ms, WC1 **17** H2
Gower Pl, WC1 **9** G5
Gower Rd, E7 **97** G6
Isleworth TW7 **124** C6
Gower St, WC1 **9** G5
Gower's Wk, E1 **21** H3
Gowland Pl, Beck. BR3 **189** J2
Gowlett Rd, SE15 **152** D3
Gowlland Cl, Croy. CR0 **188** D7
Gowrie Rd, SW11 **150** A3
Graburn Way, E.Mol. KT8 **180** A3
Grace Av, Bexh. DA7 **159** F2
Grace Business Cen, Mitch. CR4 **185** J6
Gracechurch St, EC3 **20** C5
Grace Cl, SE9 **174** A3
Borehamwood WD6 **38** D1
Edgware HA8 *off Pavilion Way* **54** C7
Ilford IG6 **65** J6
Gracedale Rd, SW16 **168** B5
Gracefield Gdns, SW16 **169** E3
Grace Jones Cl, E8 *off Parkholme Rd* **94** D6
Grace Path, SE26 **171** F4
Grace Pl, E3 *off St. Leonards St* **114** B3
Grace Rd, Croy. CR0 **187** J6
Grace's All, E1 **21** H5
Graces Ms, SE5 **152** B2
Graces Rd, SE5 **152** B2
Grace St, E3 **114** B3
Gradient, The, SE26 **170** D4
Graduate Pl, SE1 *off Long La* **28** D5
Graeme Rd, Enf. EN1 **44** A2
Graemesdyke Av, SW14 **146** B3
Grafton Cl, W13 **104** D6
Hounslow TW4 **161** E1
Worcester Park KT4 **197** E3
Grafton Cres, NW1 **92** B6
Grafton Gdns, N4 **75** J6
Dagenham RM8 **101** E2
Grafton Ho, E3 **114** A3
Grafton Ms, W1 **9** F6
Grafton Pk Rd, Wor.Pk. KT4 **196** E2
Grafton Pl, NW1 **9** H4
Grafton Rd, NW5 **92** A5
W3 **106** C7
Croydon CR0 **201** G1
Dagenham RM8 **101** E2
Enfield EN2 **43** F3
Harrow HA1 **67** J5
New Malden KT3 **182** E3
Worcester Park KT4 **196** D3
Graftons, The, NW2 *off Hermitage La* **90** D3
Grafton Sq, SW4 **150** C3
Grafton St, W1 **17** E6
Grafton Ter, NW5 **91** J5
Grafton Way, W1 **9** F6
WC1 **9** F6
West Molesey KT8 **179** F4
Grafton Yd, NW5 *off Prince of Wales Rd* **92** B6
Graham Av, W13 **124** E2
Mitcham CR4 **186** A1
Graham Cl, Croy. CR0 **204** A2
Grahame Pk Est, NW9 **71** E1
Grahame Pk Way, NW7 **55** F7
NW9 **71** F2
Graham Gdns, Surb. KT6 **195** H1
Graham Rd, E8 **94** C6
E13 **115** G4
N15 **75** H3
NW4 **71** H6
SW19 **166** C7
W4 **126** D3
Bexleyheath DA6 **159** G4
Hampton TW12 **161** G4
Harrow HA3 **68** B3
Mitcham CR4 **186** A1
Graham St, N1 **11** H2
Graham Ter, SW1 **32** B2
Grainger Cl, Nthlt. UB5 *off Lancaster Rd* **85** J5
Grainger Rd, N22 **75** J1
Isleworth TW7 **144** C2
Gramer Cl, E11 *off Norman Rd* **96** D2
Grampian Cl, Hayes (Harling.) UB3 **121** G7
Orpington BR6 *off Clovelly Way* **193** J6
Sutton SM2 **199** F7
Grampian Gdns, NW2 **90** B1
Grampian Ho, N9 *off Edmonton Grn Shop Cen* **60** E2
Gramsci Way, SE6 **172** B3
Granard Av, SW15 **147** H5
Granard Business Cen, NW7 *off Bunns La* **55** E6
Granard Rd, SW12 **149** J7
Granary Cl, N9 **45** F7
Granary Mans, SE28 **137** F2
Granary Rd, E1 **112** E4
Granary Sq, N1 *off Liverpool Rd* **93** G6
Granary St, NW1 **110** D1
Granby Pl, SE1 **26** E4
Granby Rd, SE9 **156** C2
Granby St, E2 **13** G5
Granby Ter, NW1 **9** F2
Grand Arc, N12 *off Ballards La* **57** F5
Grand Av, EC1 **19** H1
N10 **74** A4
Surbiton KT5 **182** B5
Wembley HA9 **88** A5
Grand Av E, Wem. HA9 **88** B5
Grand Dep Rd, SE18 **136** D5
Grand Dr, SW20 **183** J2
Southall UB2 **123** J2
Granden Rd, SW16 **187** E2
Grandison Rd, SW11 **149** J5
Worcester Park KT4 **197** J2
Grand Junct Wf, N1 **11** J2
Grand Par, N4 *off Green Las* **75** H6
Wembley HA9
Grand Par, *off Forty Av* **88** A2
Grand Par Ms, SW15 **148** B5
Grand Union Canal Wk, W7 **124** B3
Grand Union Cl, W9 *off Woodfield Rd* **108** C5
Grand Union Cres, E8 **94** D7
Grand Union Hts, Wem. HA0 **105** G1
Grand Union Ind Est, NW10 **106** B2
Grand Union Wk, NW1 **92** B7
Grand Union Way, Sthl. UB2 *off Bridge Rd* **123** G2
Grand Wk, E1 *off Solebay St* **113** H4
Granfield St, SW11 **149** G1
Grange, The, N20 **57** F1
SE1 **29** F5
SW19 **166** A6
W14 *off Lisgar Ter* **128** C4
Croydon CR0 **203** J2
Wembley HA0 **88** A7
Worcester Park KT4 **196** D3
Grange Av, N12 **57** F5
N20 **40** B7
SE25 **188** B2
Barnet (E.Barn.) EN4 **57** H1
Stanmore HA7 **69** E2
Twickenham TW2 **162** B2
Woodford Green IG8 **63** G6
Grangecliffe Gdns, SE25 **188** B2
Grange Cl, Edg. HA8 **54** C5
Hounslow TW5 **123** F6
Sidcup DA15 **176** A3
West Molesey KT8 **179** H4
Woodford Green IG8 **63** G7
Grange Ct, WC2 **18** D4
Chigwell IG7 **65** F2
Loughton IG10 **48** A5
Northolt UB5 **102** C2
Grangecourt Rd, N16 **94** B1
Grange Cres, SE28 **118** C6
Chigwell IG7 **65** G5
Grange Dr, Chis. BR7 **174** B6
Grange Est, The, N2 **73** G2
Grange Fm Cl, Har. HA2 **85** J2
Grange Gdns, N14 **58** D1
NW3 **91** E3
SE25 **188** B2
Pinner HA5 **67** F4
Grange Gro, N1 **93** H6
GRANGE HILL, Chig. IG7 **65** G6
Grange Hill, SE25 **188** B2
Edgware HA8 **54** C5
Grangehill Pl, SE9 *off Westmount Rd* **156** C3
Grangehill Rd, SE9 **156** C4
Grange Ho, Bark. IG11 *off St. Margarets* **117** G1
Grange La, SE21 **170** C2
Grange Mans, Epsom KT17 **197** F7
Grangemill Rd, SE6 **172** A3
Grangemill Way, SE6 **172** A2
GRANGE PARK, N21 **43** H5
Grange Pk, W5 **125** H1
Grange Pk Av, N21 **43** H6
Grange Pk Pl, SW20 **165** H7
Grange Pk Rd, E10 **96** B1
Thornton Heath CR7 **188** A4
Grange Pl, NW6 **90** D7
Grange Rd, E10 **96** A1
E13 **115** F3
E17 **77** H5
N6 **74** A6
N17 **60** D6
N18 **60** D6
NW10 **89** H6
SE1 **28** E5
SE19 **188** A4
SE25 **188** A4
SW13 **147** G1
W4 **126** B5
W5 **125** G1
Chessington KT9 **195** H4
Edgware HA8 **54** D6
Harrow HA1 **68** D6
Harrow (S.Har.) HA2 **86** A2
Ilford IG1 **99** E4
Kingston upon Thames KT1 **181** H3
Orpington BR6 **207** F2
Southall UB1 **122** E2
Sutton SM2 **198** D7
Thornton Heath CR7 **188** A4
West Molesey KT8 **179** H4
Grange St, N1 **112** A1
Grange Vale, Sutt. SM2 **199** E7
Grange Vw Rd, N20 **57** F1
Grange Wk, SE1 **28** E5
Grange Wk Ms, SE1 **29** E6
Grangeway, N12 **57** E4
NW6 *off Messina Av* **90** D7
Woodford Green IG8 **63** J4
Grangeway, The, N21 **43** H6
Grangeway Gdns, Ilf. IG4 **80** B5
Grangewood, Bex. DA5 *off Hurst Rd* **177** F1
Grangewood Cl, Pnr. HA5 **66** A5
Grangewood La, Beck. BR3 **171** J6
Grangewood St, E6 **115** J1
Grangewood Ter, SE25 *off Grange Rd* **188** A2
Grange Yd, SE1 **29** F6
Granham Gdns, N9 **60** C2
Granite Apts, E15 *off Windmill La* **96** D6
Granite St, SE18 **137** J5
Granleigh Rd, E11 **96** E2
Gransden Av, E8 **95** E7
Gransden Rd, W12 *off Wendell Rd* **127** F2
Grantbridge St, N1 **11** H1
Grantchester Cl, Har. HA1 **86** C3
Grant Cl, N14 **42** C7
N17 **76** B2
Grant Ct, E4 *off The Ridgeway* **62** C1
Grantham Cl, Edg. HA8 **53** H3
Grantham Gdns, Rom. RM6 **83** F6
Grantham Grn, Borwd. WD6 **38** C5
Grantham Pl, W1 **24** D2
Grantham Rd, E12 **98** D4
SW9 **151** E2
W4 **126** E7
Grantley Rd, Houns. TW4 **142** C2
Grantley St, E1 **113** G3
Grantock Rd, E17 **78** D1
Granton Rd, SW16 **186** C1
Ilford IG3 **100** A1
Sidcup DA14 **176** C6
Grant Pl, Croy. CR0 **202** C1
Grant Rd, SW11 **149** G4
Croydon CR0 **202** C1
Harrow HA3 **68** B3
Grants Cl, NW7 **55** J7
Grant's Quay Wf, EC3 **20** C6
Grant St, E13 **115** G3
N1 **11** E1
Grantully Rd, W9 **6** A4
Grant Way, Islw. TW7 **124** D6
Granville Av, N9 **61** F3
Feltham TW13 **160** A2
Hounslow TW3 **143** G5
Granville Cl, Croy. CR0 **202** B2
Granville Ct, N1 **112** A1
Granville Gdns, SW16 **187** F1
W5 **125** J1
Granville Gro, SE13 **154** C3
Granville Ind Est, NW2 **90** C2
Granville Ms, Sid. DA14 **176** A4
Granville Pk, SE13 **154** C3
Granville Pl, N12 (N.Finchley) *off High Rd* **57** F7
SW6 *off Maxwell Rd* **129** E7
W1 **16** B4
Pinner HA5 **66** D3
Granville Pt, NW2 **90** C2
Granville Rd, E17 **78** B6
E18 **79** H2
N4 **75** F6
N12 **57** E7
N13 *off Russell Rd* **59** F6
N22 **75** H1
NW2 **90** C2
NW6 **108** D2
SW18 **148** D7
SW19 *off Russell Rd* **166** D7
Barnet EN5 **39** J4
Hayes UB3 **121** J4
Ilford IG1 **98** E1
Sidcup DA14 **176** A4
Welling DA16 **158** C3
Granville Sq, SE15 **36** E7
WC1 **10** D4
Granville St, WC1 **10** D4
Grape St, WC2 **18** A3
Graphite Sq, SE11 **34** C3
Grapsome Cl, Chess. KT9 *off Nigel Fisher Way* **195** F7
Grasdene Rd, SE18 **138** A7
Grasgarth Cl, W3 **106** C7
Grasmere Av, SW15 **164** D4
SW19 **184** D3
W3 **106** C7
Hounslow TW3 **143** H6
Orpington BR6 **206** E3
Wembley HA9 **69** G7
Grasmere Cl, Loug. IG10 **48** C2
Grasmere Ct, N22 *off Palmerston Rd* **59** F6

Grasmere Gdns, Har. HA3 .68 D2
Ilford IG4 .80 C5
Orpington BR6 .206 E3
Grasmere Pt, SE15 *off Ilderton Rd* .133 F7
Grasmere Rd, E13 .115 G2
N10 .74 B1
N17 .60 D6
SE25 .189 E6
SW16 .169 F5
Bexleyheath DA7 .159 J1
Bromley BR1 .191 F1
Orpington BR6 .206 E3
Grasshaven Way, SE28 .137 J1
Grassington Cl, N11 .58 A5
Grassington Rd, Sid. DA14 .176 A4
Grassmount, SE23 .171 E2
Grass Pk, N3 .72 C1
Grassway, Wall. SM6 .200 C4
Grasvenor Av, Barn. EN5 .40 D6
Gratton Rd, W14 .128 B3
Gratton Ter, NW2 .90 A3
Graveley, Kings.T. KT1 *off Willingham Way* .182 A2
Graveley Av, Borwd. WD6 .38 C4
Gravel Hill, N3 .72 C2
Bexleyheath DA6 .159 H5
Croydon CR0 .203 G6
Gravel Hill Cl, Bexh. DA6 .159 H5
Gravel La, E1 .21 F3
Gravelly Ride, SW19 .165 H4
Gravel Pit La, SE9 .157 F5
Gravel Rd, Brom. BR2 .206 B2
Twickenham TW2 .162 B1
Gravelwood Cl, Chis. BR7 .175 F3
Gravenel Gdns, SW17 *off Nutwell St* .167 H5
Graveney Gro, SE20 .171 F7
Graveney Rd, SW17 .167 H4
Gravesend Rd, W12 .107 G7
Graves Yd Ind Est, Well. DA16 *off Upper Wickham La* .158 B2
Gray Av, Dag. RM8 .101 F1
Grayham Cres, N.Mal. KT3 .182 D4
Grayham Rd, N.Mal. KT3 .182 D4
Grayland Cl, Brom. BR1 .192 A1
Grayling Cl, E16 *off Cranberry La* .115 E4
Grayling Rd, N16 .94 A2
Grayling Sq, E2 .13 J3
Grayscroft Rd, SW16 .168 D7
Grayshott Rd, SW11 .150 A2
★ **Gray's Inn**, WC1 .18 D1
Gray's Inn Pl, WC1 .18 D2
Gray's Inn Rd, WC1 .10 C4
Gray's Inn Sq, WC1 .18 E1
Grayson Ho, EC1 .12 A4
Gray St, SE1 .27 F4
Grayswood Gdns, SW20 *off Farnham Gdns* .183 H2
Grayswood Pt, SW15 *off Norley Vale* .165 G1
Gray's Yd, W1 .16 C4
Graywood Ct, N12 .57 F7
Grazebrook Rd, N16 .94 A2
Grazeley Cl, Bexh. DA6 .159 J5
Grazeley Ct, SE19 *off Gipsy Hill* .170 B5
Great Acre Ct, SW4 *off Clapham Pk Rd* .150 D4
Great Amwell La, N8 .75 F3
Great Arthur Ho, EC1 .11 J6
Great Bell All, EC2 .20 B3
Great Benty, West Dr. UB7 .120 B4
Great Brownings, SE21 .170 C4
Great Bushey Dr, N20 .57 E1
Great Cambridge Ind Est, Enf. EN1 .44 D5
Great Cambridge Junct, N18 .60 A4
Great Cambridge Rd, N9 .60 B1
N17 .60 A5
N18 .60 A5
Enfield EN1 .44 D4
Great Castle St, W1 .17 E3
Great Cen Av, Ruis. HA4 .84 C5
Great Cen St, NW1 .15 J1
Great Cen Way, NW10 .88 E5
Wembley HA9 .88 C4
Great Chapel St, W1 .17 H3
Great Chart St, SW11 .149 G4
Great Chertsey Rd, W4 .146 C2
Feltham TW13 .161 G3
Great Ch La, W6 .128 A5
Great Coll St, SW1 .26 A5
Great Cross Av, SE10 .134 E7
Great Cumberland Ms, W1 .15 J4
Great Cumberland Pl, W1 .15 J3
Great Dover St, SE1 .28 A4
Greatdown Rd, W7 .104 C4
Great Eastern Enterprise Cen, E14 .134 B2
Great Eastern Rd, E15 .96 D7
Great Eastern St, EC2 .12 D4
Great Eastern Wk, EC2 .20 E2
Great Elms Rd, Brom. BR2 .191 J4
Great Fld, NW9 .71 E1
Greatfield Av, E6 .116 C4
Greatfield Cl, N19 *off Warrender Rd* .92 C4
SE4 .154 A4
Greatfields Rd, Bark. IG11 .117 G1
Great Fleete Way, Bark. IG11 *off Choats Rd* .118 C2
Great Galley Cl, Bark. IG11 .118 B3
Great Gatton Cl, Croy. CR0 .189 H7
Great George St, SW1 .25 J4
Great Guildford St, SE1 .27 J1
Great Hall, SW11 *off Battersea Pk Rd* .150 A1
Greatham Wk, SW15 .165 G1
Great Harry Dr, SE9 .174 D3
Great James St, WC1 .10 C6
Great Marlborough St, W1 .17 F4
Great Maze Pond, SE1 .28 C3
Great Newport St, WC2 *off Charing Cross Rd* .17 J5
Great New St, EC4 .19 F3
Great N Leisure Pk, N12 .57 G7
Great N Rd, N2 .73 H4
N6 .73 H4
Barnet (New Barn.) EN5 .40 D5
Great N Way, NW4 .71 J2
Great Oaks, Chig. IG7 .65 F4
Greatorex St, E1 .21 H1
Great Ormond St, WC1 .18 B1
Great Owl Rd, Chig. IG7 .64 D3
Great Percy St, WC1 .10 D3
Great Peter St, SW1 .25 H6
Great Portland St, W1 .17 E1
Great Pulteney St, W1 .17 G5
Great Queen St, WC2 .18 B4
Great Russell St, WC1 .17 J3
Great St. Helens, EC3 .20 D3
Great St. Thomas Apostle, EC4 .20 A5
Great Scotland Yd, SW1 .26 A2
Great Smith St, SW1 .25 J5
Great South-West Rd, Felt. TW14 .141 F7
Hounslow TW4 .141 J4
Great Spilmans, SE22 .152 B5
Great Strand, NW9 .71 F1
Great Suffolk St, SE1 .27 H2
Great Sutton St, EC1 .11 H6
Great Swan All, EC2 .20 B3
Great Thrift, Orp. BR5 .193 F4
Great Titchfield St, W1 .17 F3
Great Twr St, EC3 .20 D5
Great Trade Cen, NW10 *off Hythe Rd* .107 G4
Great Trinity La, EC4 .20 A5
Great Turnstile, WC1 .18 D2
Great Western Rd, W2 .108 C5
W9 .108 C5
W11 .108 C5
Great W Rd, W4 .126 B5
W6 .127 F5
Brentford TW8 .126 B5
Hounslow TW5 .142 D2
Isleworth TW7 .124 B7
Great Winchester St, EC2 .20 C3
Great Windmill St, W1 .17 H5
Greatwood, Chis. BR7 .174 D7
Great Yd, SE1 .28 E3
Greaves Cl, Bark. IG11 .99 G7
Greaves Pl, SW17 .167 H4
Greaves Twr, SW10 .30 D7
Grebe Av, Hayes UB4 *off Cygnet Way* .102 D6
Grebe Cl, E7 *off Cormorant Rd* .97 F5
E17 .61 H7
Barking IG11 .118 A4
Grebe Ct, Sutt. SM1 .198 C5
Grecian Cres, SE19 .169 H6
Gredo Ho, Bark. IG11 .118 B3
Greek Ct, W1 .17 J4
★ **Greek Orthodox Cath of the Divine Wisdom (St. Sophia)**, W2 .14 A5
Greek St, W1 .17 J4
Greek Yd, WC2 .18 A5
Green, The, E4 .62 C1
E11 .79 H6
E15 .97 E6
N9 .60 D2
N14 .58 D3
N21 .43 G7
SW14 .146 C3
SW19 .166 A5
W3 .107 E6
W5 *off High St* .105 G7
Bexleyheath DA7 .159 G1
Bromley BR1 *off Downham Way* .173 G3
Bromley (Hayes) BR2 .191 G7
Carshalton SM5 *off High St* .200 A4
Esher (Clay.) KT10 .194 C6
Feltham TW13 .160 B2
Hounslow TW5 *off Heston Rd* .123 G6
Morden SM4 .184 B4
New Malden KT3 .182 C3
Orpington (St.P.Cray) BR5 *off The Avenue* .176 B7
Richmond TW9 .145 G5
Sidcup DA14 .176 A4
Southall UB2 .123 E3
Sutton SM1 .198 E3
Twickenham TW2 .162 B1
Welling DA16 .157 H4
Wembley HA0 .86 D2
West Drayton UB7 .120 A3
Woodford Green IG8 .63 G5
Greenacre Cl, Nthlt. UB5 .85 F5
Greenacre Gdns, E17 .78 C4
Greenacre Pl, Wall. (Hackbr.) SM6 *off Park Rd* .200 B2
Greenacres, N3 .72 B2
SE9 .156 D6
Barnet EN4 .41 G4
Bushey (Bushey Hth) WD23 .52 A2
Green Acres, Croy. CR0 .202 C3
Greenacres Cl, Orp. BR6 .207 F4
Greenacres Dr, Stan. HA7 .52 E7
Greenacre Sq, SE16 *off Fishermans Dr* .133 G2
Greenacre Wk, N14 .58 D3
Green Arbour Ct, EC1 .19 G3
Green Av, NW7 .54 D4
W13 .125 E3
Greenaway Av, N18 .61 G6
Greenaway Gdns, NW3 .90 E4
Green Bk, E1 .132 E1
N12 .57 E4
Greenbank Av, Wem. HA0 .86 D5
Greenbank Cl, E4 .62 C2
Greenbank Cres, NW4 .72 B4
Greenbay Rd, SE7 .136 A7
Greenberry St, NW8 .7 G2
Greenbrook Av, Barn. EN4 .41 F1
Green Cl, NW9 .70 C6
NW11 .73 F7
Bromley BR2 .190 E3
Carshalton SM5 .199 J2
Feltham TW13 .160 E5
Greencoat Pl, SW1 .33 G1
Greencoat Row, SW1 .25 G6
Greencourt Av, Croy. CR0 .203 E2
Edgware HA8 .70 B1
Greencourt Gdns, Croy. CR0 .203 E1
Greencourt Rd, Orp. BR5 .193 G5
Greencrest Pl, NW2 *off Dollis Hill La* .89 G3
Greencroft, Edg. HA8 .54 C5
Greencroft Av, Ruis. HA4 .84 C2
Greencroft Cl, E6 *off Neatscourt Rd* .116 B5
Greencroft Gdns, NW6 .91 E7
Enfield EN1 .44 B3
Greencroft Rd, Houns. TW5 .143 F1
Green Dale, SE5 .152 A4
SE22 .152 B5
Green Dale Cl, SE22 *off Green Dale* .152 B5
Green Dragon Ct, SE1 .28 B1
Green Dragon La, N21 .43 H6
Brentford TW8 .125 H5
Green Dragon Yd, E1 .21 H2
Green Dr, Sthl. UB1 .123 G1
Green End, N21 .59 H2
Chessington KT9 .195 H4
Greenend Rd, W4 .126 E2
Green Fm Cl, Orp. BR6 .207 J5
Greenfell Mans, SE8 *off Glaisher St* .134 B6
Greenfield Av, Surb. KT5 .182 B7
Watford WD19 .50 D2
Greenfield Dr, N2 .73 J4
Bromley BR1 .191 J2
Greenfield Gdns, NW2 .90 B2
Dagenham RM9 .118 D1
Orpington BR5 .193 G7
Greenfield Rd, E1 .21 J2
N15 .76 B5
Dagenham RM9 .118 C1
Greenfields, Loug. IG10 .48 D4
Greenfields Cl, Loug. IG10 .48 D4
Greenfield Way, Har. HA2 .67 H3
GREENFORD, UB6 .103 H3
Greenford Av, W7 .104 B4
Southall UB1 .103 F7
Greenford Gdns, Grnf. UB6 .103 H3
Greenford Grn Business Pk, Grnf. UB6 *off Green Pk Way* .104 C1
Greenford Rd, Grnf. UB6 .103 J5
Harrow HA1 .86 B5
Southall UB1 .123 J1
Sutton SM1 .198 E4
Greenford Rbt, Grnf. UB6 .104 A2
Green Gdns, Orp. BR6 .207 F5
Greengate, Grnf. UB6 .86 E6
Greengate St, E13 .115 H2
Greenhalgh Wk, N2 .73 F4
Greenham Cl, SE1 .27 E4
Greenham Cres, E4 .61 J6
Greenham Rd, N10 .74 A2
Greenhaven Dr, SE28 .118 B6
Greenheath Business Cen, E2 *off Three Colts La* .113 E4
Greenheys Dr, E18 .79 F3
Greenhill, NW3 *off Prince Arthur Rd* .91 G4
Green Hill, SE18 .136 C5
Buckhurst Hill IG9 .63 J1
Greenhill, Sutt. SM1 .199 F2
Wembley HA9 .88 B2
Greenhill Gdns, Nthlt. UB5 .103 F2
Greenhill Gro, E12 .98 B4
Greenhill Par, Barn. (New Barn.) EN5 *off Great N Rd* .40 E5
Greenhill Pk, NW10 .106 E1
Barnet (New Barn.) EN5 .40 E5
Greenhill Rd, NW10 .106 E1
Harrow HA1 .68 B6
Greenhill's Rents, EC1 .19 G1
Greenhills Ter, N1 *off Baxter Rd* .94 A6
Greenhill Ter, SE18 .136 C5
Northolt UB5 .103 F2
Greenhill Way, Har. HA1 .68 B6
Wembley HA9 .88 B2
Greenhithe Cl, Sid. DA15 .157 H7
Greenholm Rd, SE9 .156 E5
Green Hundred Rd, SE15 .37 J6
Greenhurst Rd, SE27 .169 G5
Greening St, SE2 .138 C4
Green Knight Ct, N9 *off Galahad Rd* .60 D3
Greenland Cres, Sthl. UB2 .122 C3
Greenland Ms, SE8 *off Trundleys Rd* .133 G5
Greenland Pl, NW1 *off Greenland Rd* .110 B1
Greenland Quay, SE16 .133 G4
Greenland Rd, NW1 .110 C1
Barnet EN5 .39 J6
Greenlands La, NW4 .71 H1
Greenland St, NW1 *off Camden High St* .110 B1
Greenland Way, Croy. CR0 .186 D7
Green La, E4 .46 E3
NW4 .72 A5
SE9 .174 D2
SE20 .171 G7
SW16 .169 F7
W7 .124 B2
Chigwell IG7 .65 G2
Chislehurst BR7 .174 E4
Dagenham RM8 .100 A1
Edgware HA8 .54 A5
Feltham TW13 .160 E5
Harrow HA1 .86 B3
Hounslow TW4 .142 B3
Ilford IG1, IG3 .99 F2
Morden SM4 .184 E6
New Malden KT3 .182 C5
Stanmore HA7 .52 E4
Thornton Heath CR7 .187 G1
Watford WD19 .50 C1
West Molesey KT8 .179 H5
Worcester Park KT4 .197 G1
Green La Gdns, Th.Hth. CR7 .187 J2
Green Las, N4 .93 J1
N8 .75 H3

Green Las, N13 ... 59 F6
N15 ... 75 H3
N16 ... 93 J3
N21 ... 59 H1
Greenlaw Ct, W5 ... 105 G6
Greenlaw Gdns, N.Mal. KT3 ... 183 F7
Greenlawn La, Brent. TW8 ... 125 G4
Green Lawns, Ruis. HA4 ... 84 C1
Greenlaw St, SE18 ... 136 D3
Green Leaf Av, Wall. SM6 ... 200 D4
Greenleaf Cl, SW2 *off Tulse Hill* ... 151 G7
Greenleafe Dr, Ilf. IG6 ... 81 E4
Greenleaf Rd, E6 *off Redclyffe Rd* ... 115 J1
E17 ... 77 J3
Greenleaf Way, Har. HA3 ... 68 C3
Greenlea Pk, SW19 ... 167 G7
Greenlink Wk, Rich. TW9 ... 146 B1
Green Man Gdns, W13 ... 104 D7
Green Man La, W13 ... 124 D1
Feltham TW14 ... 142 A4
Green Man Pas, W13 ... 104 D7
Green Man Rbt, E11 ... 79 F7
Greenman St, N1 ... 93 J7
Greenmead Cl, SE25 ... 188 D5
Green Moor Link, N21 ... 43 H7
Greenmoor Rd, Enf. EN3 ... 45 F2
Greenoak Pl, Barn. (Cockfos.) EN4 ... 41 J2
Greenoak Way, SW19 ... 166 A4
Greenock Rd, SW16 ... 186 D1
W3 ... 126 B3
★ **Green Park, The**, SW1 ... 24 E2
Greenpark Ct, Wem. HA0 ... 87 F7
Green Pk Way, Grnf. UB6 ... 104 B1
Green Pl, SE10 *off Millennium Way* ... 134 E2
Green Pt, E15 ... 97 E6
Green Pond Cl, E17 ... 77 J3
Green Pond Rd, E17 ... 77 H3
Green Ride, Loug. IG10 ... 47 G5
Green Rd, N14 ... 42 B6
N20 ... 57 F3
Greenroof Way, SE10 ... 135 F3
Greens Cl, The, Loug. IG10 ... 48 D2
Green's Ct, W1 ... 17 H5
Green's End, SE18 ... 136 E4
Greenshank Cl, E17 *off Banbury Rd* ... 61 H7
Greenshields Ind Est, E16 ... 135 H1
Greenside, Bex. DA5 ... 177 E1
Dagenham RM8 ... 100 C1
Greenside Cl, N20 ... 57 G2
SE6 ... 172 D2
Greenside Rd, W12 ... 127 G3
Croydon CR0 ... 187 G7
Greenslade Rd, Bark. IG11 ... 99 G7
Greenstead Av, Wdf.Grn. IG8 ... 63 J7
Greenstead Cl, Wdf.Grn. IG8 *off Greenstead Gdns* ... 63 J6
Greenstead Gdns, SW15 ... 147 G5
Woodford Green IG8 ... 63 J6
Greensted Rd, Loug. IG10 ... 48 B7
Greenstone Ms, E11 ... 79 G6
Green St, E7 ... 97 H6
E13 ... 115 J1
W1 ... 16 A5
Enfield EN3 ... 45 F2
Sunbury-on-Thames TW16 ... 178 A1
GREEN STREET GREEN, Orp. BR6 ... 207 H6
Green Ter, EC1 ... 11 F4
Green Vale, W5 ... 105 J6
Bexleyheath DA6 ... 158 D5
Greenvale Rd, SE9 ... 156 C4
Green Verges, Stan. HA7 ... 53 G7
Green Vw, Chess. KT9 ... 195 J7
Greenview Av, Beck. BR3 ... 189 H6
Croydon CR0 ... 189 H6
Greenview Cl, W3 ... 126 E1
Green Wk, NW4 ... 72 A5
SE1 ... 28 D6
Buckhurst Hill IG9 ... 48 B7
Hampton TW12 *off Orpwood Cl* ... 161 F6
Southall UB2 ... 123 G5
Woodford Green IG8 ... 64 B6
Green Wk, The, E4 ... 62 C1
Greenway, N14 ... 58 E2
N20 ... 56 D2
Green Way, SE9 ... 156 A5
Greenway, SW20 ... 183 J4
Green Way, Brom. BR2 ... 192 B6
Greenway, Chis. BR7 ... 174 D5
Dagenham RM8 ... 100 C2
Harrow HA3 ... 69 H5
Hayes UB4 ... 102 B4
Greenway, Pinner HA5 ... 66 B2
Green Way, Sun. TW16 ... 178 A4
Greenway, Wall. SM6 ... 200 C4
Woodford Green IG8 ... 63 J5
Greenway, The, NW9 ... 70 D2
Harrow (Har.Wld) HA3 ... 68 B1
Hounslow TW4 ... 143 F4
Pinner HA5 ... 67 F6
Greenway Av, E17 ... 78 D4
Greenway Cl, N4 ... 93 J2
N11 ... 58 A6
N15 *off Copperfield Dr* ... 76 C4
N20 ... 56 D2
NW9 ... 70 D2
Greenway Gdns, NW9 ... 70 D2
Croydon CR0 ... 203 J3
Greenford UB6 ... 103 G3
Harrow HA3 ... 68 B2
Greenways, Beck. BR3 ... 190 A2
Esher KT10 ... 194 B4
Greenways, The, Twick. TW1 *off South Western Rd* ... 144 D6
Greenwell St, W1 ... 9 E6
GREENWICH, SE10 ... 134 D6
Greenwich Cen Business Pk, SE10 *off Norman Rd* ... 134 B7
Greenwich Ch St, SE10 ... 134 C6
Greenwich Cres, E6 *off Swan App* ... 116 B5
Greenwich Foot Tunnel, E14 ... 134 C5
SE10 ... 134 C5
Greenwich Hts, SE18 ... 136 B7
Greenwich High Rd, SE10 ... 154 B1
Greenwich Ho, SE13 *off Hither Grn La* ... 154 D6
Greenwich Ind Est, SE7 ... 135 H4
Greenwich Mkt, SE10 *off King William Wk* ... 134 C6
★ **Greenwich Park**, SE10 ... 134 D7
Greenwich Pk St, SE10 ... 134 D5
Greenwich Quay, SE8 ... 134 B6
Greenwich Shop Pk, SE7 ... 135 H4
Greenwich S St, SE10 ... 154 B1
Greenwich Vw Pl, E14 ... 134 B3
Greenwood Av, Dag. RM10 ... 101 H4
Enfield EN3 ... 45 H2
Greenwood Cl, Mord. SM4 ... 184 B4
Orpington BR5 ... 193 H6
Sidcup DA15 ... 176 A2
Thames Ditton KT7 ... 194 D1
Greenwood Ct, SW1 ... 33 F3
Greenwood Dr, E4 *off Avril Way* ... 62 C5
Greenwood Gdns, N13 ... 59 H3
Ilford IG6 ... 65 F7
Greenwood La, Hmptn. (Hmptn H.) TW12 ... 161 H5
Greenwood Pk, Kings.T. KT2 ... 165 E7
Greenwood Pl, NW5 *off Highgate Rd* ... 92 B5
Greenwood Rd, E8 ... 94 D6
E13 *off Valetta Gro* ... 115 F2
Croydon CR0 ... 187 H7
Isleworth TW7 ... 144 B3
Mitcham CR4 ... 186 D3
Thames Ditton KT7 ... 194 D1
Greenwoods, The, Har. (S.Har.) HA2 ... 85 J3
Greenwood Ter, NW10 ... 106 D1
Green Wrythe Cres, Cars. SM5 ... 199 H1
Green Wrythe La, Cars. SM5 ... 185 G6
Greer Rd, Har. HA3 ... 67 J1
Greet St, SE1 ... 27 F2
Greg Cl, E10 ... 78 C6
Gregor Ms, SE3 ... 135 G7
Gregory Cl, Brom. BR2 ... 191 E4
Gregory Cres, SE9 ... 156 A7
Gregory Pl, W8 ... 22 A3
Gregory Rd, Rom. RM6 ... 82 D4
Southall UB2 ... 123 G3
Gregson Cl, Borwd. WD6 ... 38 C1
Greig Cl, N8 ... 74 E5
Greig Ter, SE17 ... 35 H5
Grenaby Av, Croy. CR0 ... 188 A7
Grenaby Rd, Croy. CR0 ... 188 A7
Grenada Rd, SE7 ... 135 J7
Grenade St, E14 ... 113 J7
Grenadier St, E16 ... 136 D1
Grena Gdns, Rich. TW9 ... 145 J4
Grenard Cl, SE15 ... 132 D7
Grena Rd, Rich. TW9 ... 145 J4
Grendon Gdns, Wem. HA9 ... 88 A2
Grendon Ho, N1 *off Priory Grn Est* ... 10 C2
Grendon St, NW8 ... 7 G5
Grenfell Cl, Borwd. WD6 ... 38 C1
Grenfell Gdns, Har. HA3 ... 69 H7
Grenfell Ho, SE5 *off Comber Gro* ... 131 J7
Grenfell Rd, W11 ... 108 A7
Mitcham CR4 ... 167 J6
Grenfell Twr, W11 ... 108 A7
Grenfell Wk, W11 ... 108 A7
Grennell Cl, Sutt. SM1 ... 199 G2
Grennell Rd, Sutt. SM1 ... 199 F2
Grenoble Gdns, N13 ... 59 G6
Grenville Cl, N3 ... 72 C1
Surbiton KT5 ... 196 C1
Grenville Ct, SE19 *off Lymer Av* ... 170 C5
Grenville Gdns, Wdf.Grn. IG8 ... 79 J1
Grenville Ms, N19 ... 93 E1
Hampton TW12 ... 161 H5
Grenville Pl, NW7 ... 54 D5
SW7 ... 22 C6
Grenville Rd, N19 ... 92 E1
Grenville St, WC1 ... 10 B6
Gresham Av, N20 ... 57 J4
Gresham Cl, Bex. DA5 ... 159 E6
Enfield EN2 ... 43 J3
Gresham Dr, Rom. RM6 ... 82 B5
Gresham Gdns, NW11 ... 90 B1
Gresham Pl, N19 ... 92 D2
Gresham Rd, E6 ... 116 C2
E16 ... 115 H6
NW10 ... 88 D5
SE25 ... 188 D4
SW9 ... 151 G3
Beckenham BR3 ... 189 H2
Edgware HA8 ... 53 J6
Hampton TW12 ... 161 G6
Hounslow TW3 ... 143 J1
Gresham St, EC2 ... 19 J3
Gresham Way, SW19 ... 166 D3
Gresley Cl, E17 ... 77 H6
N15 *off Clinton Rd* ... 76 A4
Gresley Rd, N19 ... 92 C1
Gressenhall Rd, SW18 ... 148 C6
Gresse St, W1 ... 17 H2
Gresswell Cl, Sid. DA14 ... 176 A3
Greswell St, SW6 ... 148 A1
Gretton Rd, N17 ... 60 B7
Greville Cl, Twick. TW1 ... 144 E7
Greville Ct, E5 *off Napoleon Rd* ... 94 E3
Greville Hall, NW6 ... 6 A1
Greville Ms, NW6 *off Greville Rd* ... 108 E2
Greville Pl, NW6 ... 6 B1
Greville Rd, E17 ... 78 C4
NW6 ... 6 A1
Richmond TW10 ... 145 J6
Greville St, EC1 ... 19 F2
Grey Cl, NW11 ... 73 F6
Greycoat Gdns, SW1 *off Greycoat St* ... 25 H6
Greycoat Pl, SW1 ... 25 H6
Greycoat St, SW1 ... 25 H6
Greycot Rd, Beck. BR3 ... 172 A5
Grey Eagle St, E1 ... 21 F1
Greyfell Cl, Stan. HA7 *off Coverdale Cl* ... 53 E5
Greyfriars Pas, EC1 ... 19 H3
Greyhound Hill, NW4 ... 71 G3
Greyhound La, SW16 ... 168 D6
Greyhound Rd, N17 ... 76 B3
NW10 ... 107 H3
W6 ... 128 A6
W14 ... 128 B6
Sutton SM1 ... 199 F5
Greyhound Ter, SW16 ... 186 C1
Greyladies Gdns, SE10 *off Wat Tyler Rd* ... 154 C1
Greys Pk Cl, Kes. BR2 ... 205 J5
Greystead Rd, SE23 ... 153 F7
Greystoke Av, Pnr. HA5 ... 67 G3
Greystoke Gdns, W5 ... 105 H4
Enfield EN2 ... 42 D4
Greystoke Pk Ter, W5 ... 105 G3
Greystoke Pl, EC4 ... 19 E3
Greystone Gdns, Har. HA3 ... 69 F6
Ilford IG6 ... 81 F2
Greystone Path, E11 *off Grove Rd* ... 79 F7
Greyswood Av, N18 ... 61 G6
Greyswood St, SW16 ... 168 B6
Grierson Rd, SE23 ... 153 G7
Griffin Cen, The, Felt. TW14 ... 142 B5
Griffin Cl, NW10 ... 89 H5
Griffin Manor Way, SE28 ... 137 G3
Griffin Rd, N17 ... 76 B2
SE18 ... 137 G5
Griffins Cl, N21 ... 44 A7
Griffin Way, Sun. TW16 ... 178 A2
Griffith Cl, Dag. RM8 *off Gibson Rd* ... 100 C1
Griffiths Cl, Wor.Pk. KT4 ... 197 H2
Griffiths Rd, SW19 ... 166 D7
Griggs App, Ilf. IG1 ... 99 F2
Griggs Pl, SE1 ... 28 E6
Griggs Rd, E10 ... 78 C6
Grilse Cl, N9 ... 61 E4
Grimsby Gro, E16 ... 137 E1
Grimsby St, E2 ... 13 G6
Grimsdyke Cres, Barn. EN5 ... 39 J3
Grimsdyke Rd, Pnr. HA5 ... 51 E7
Grimsel Path, SE5 ... 35 H7
Grimshaw Cl, N6 ... 74 A7
Grimston Rd, SW6 ... 148 C2
Grimthorpe Ho, EC1 ... 11 G5
Grimwade Av, Croy. CR0 ... 202 D3
Grimwade Cl, SE15 ... 153 F3
Grimwood Rd, Twick. TW1 ... 144 C7
Grindall Cl, Croy. CR0 ... 201 H4
Grindal St, SE1 ... 26 E4
Grindleford Av, N11 ... 58 A2
Grindley Gdns, Croy. CR0 ... 188 C6
Grinling Pl, SE8 ... 134 A6
Grinstead Rd, SE8 ... 133 H5
Grittleton Av, Wem. HA9 ... 88 B6
Grittleton Rd, W9 ... 108 D4
Grizedale Ter, SE23 ... 171 E2
Grocer's Hall Ct, EC2 ... 20 B4
Grogan Cl, Hmptn. TW12 ... 161 F6
Groombridge Cl, Well. DA16 ... 158 A5
Groombridge Rd, E9 ... 95 G7
Groom Cl, Brom. BR2 ... 191 H4
Groom Cres, SW18 ... 149 G7
Groomfield Cl, SW17 ... 168 A4
Groom Pl, SW1 ... 24 C5
Grooms Dr, Pnr. HA5 ... 66 A5
Grosmont Rd, SE18 ... 137 J5
Grosse Way, SW15 ... 147 H6
Grosvenor Av, N5 ... 93 J5
SW14 ... 146 E3
Carshalton SM5 ... 199 J6
Harrow HA2 ... 67 H6
Richmond TW10 ... 145 H5
Grosvenor Cl, Loug. IG10 ... 48 E1
Grosvenor Cotts, SW1 ... 32 B1
Grosvenor Ct, N14 ... 42 C7
NW6 ... 108 A1
Grosvenor Cres, NW9 ... 70 A4
SW1 ... 24 C4
Grosvenor Cres Ms, SW1 ... 24 B4
Grosvenor Dr, Loug. IG10 ... 49 E1
Grosvenor Est, SW1 ... 33 J1
Grosvenor Gdns, E6 ... 116 A3
N10 ... 74 C3
N14 ... 42 D5
NW2 ... 89 J5
NW11 ... 72 C6
SW1 ... 24 D5
SW14 ... 146 E3
Kingston upon Thames KT2 ... 163 G6
Wallington SM6 ... 200 C7
Woodford Green IG8 ... 63 G6
Grosvenor Gdns Ms E, SW1 ... 24 E5
Grosvenor Gdns Ms N, SW1 ... 24 D6
Grosvenor Gdns Ms S, SW1 ... 24 E6
Grosvenor Gate, W1 ... 16 A6
Grosvenor Hill, SW19 ... 166 B6
W1 ... 16 D5
Grosvenor Pk, SE5 ... 35 J6
Grosvenor Pk Rd, E17 ... 78 A5
Grosvenor Path, Loug. IG10 ... 49 E1
Grosvenor Pl, SW1 ... 24 C4
Grosvenor Ri E, E17 ... 78 B5
Grosvenor Rd, E6 ... 116 A1
E7 ... 97 H6
E10 ... 96 C1
E11 ... 79 G5
N3 ... 56 C7
N9 ... 60 E1
N10 ... 74 B1
SE25 ... 188 D4
SW1 ... 32 D5
W4 ... 126 B5
W7 ... 124 D1
Belvedere DA17 ... 139 G6
Bexleyheath DA6 ... 158 D5
Borehamwood WD6 ... 38 A3
Brentford TW8 ... 125 G6
Dagenham RM8 ... 101 F1
Hounslow TW3 ... 143 F3
Ilford IG1 ... 99 F3
Orpington BR5 ... 193 H6
Richmond TW10 ... 145 H5

Grosvenor Rd, Southall UB2 123 F3
Twickenham TW1 144 D7
Wallington SM6 200 B6
West Wickham BR4 204 B1
Grosvenor Sq, W1 16 C5
Grosvenor St, W1 16 D5
Grosvenor Ter, SE5 35 H7
Grosvenor Way, E5 95 F2
Grosvenor Wf Rd, E14 134 D4
Grote's Bldgs, SE3 155 E2
Grote's Pl, SE3 154 E2
Groton Rd, SW18 167 E2
Grotto Pas, W1 16 C1
Grotto Rd, Twick. TW1 162 C2
Grove, The, E15 96 E6
N3 72 D1
N4 75 F7
N6 92 A1
N8 74 D5
N13 59 G5
N14 42 C5
NW9 70 D5
NW11 72 B7
SE22 170 D1
W5 125 G1
Bexleyheath DA6 158 D4
Edgware HA8 54 B4
Enfield EN2 43 G2
Greenford UB6 103 J6
Isleworth TW7 144 B1
Sidcup DA14 177 E4
Teddington TW11 162 D4
Twickenham TW1
off Bridge Rd 144 E6
Walton-on-Thames KT12 178 B7
West Wickham BR4 204 B3
Grove Av, N3 56 D7
N10 74 C2
W7 104 B6
Pinner HA5 67 E4
Sutton SM1 198 D6
Twickenham TW1 162 C1
Grove Bk, Wat. WD19 50 D1
Grovebury Rd, SE2 138 B2
Grove Cl, N14 42 C7
SE23 171 G1
Bromley BR2 205 G2
Feltham TW13 160 E4
Kingston upon Thames KT1 181 J4
Grove Cotts, SW3 31 H5
Grove Ct, Barn. EN5
off High St 40 C3
East Molesey KT8
off Walton Rd 180 A5
Grove Cres, E18 79 F2
NW9 70 C4
Feltham TW13 160 E4
Kingston upon Thames KT1 181 H3
Walton-on-Thames KT12 178 B7
Grove Cres Rd, E15 96 D6
Grovedale Rd, N19 92 D2
Grove Dws, E1
off Adelina Gro 113 F5
Grove End, E18
off Grove Hill 79 F2
NW5 *off Chetwynd Rd* 92 B4
Grove End Gdns, NW8
off Grove End Rd 6 E2
Grove End La, Esher KT10 194 A1
Grove End Rd, NW8 6 E2
Grove Fm Ct, Mitch. CR4
off Brookfields Av 185 J4
Grove Fm Retail Pk, Rom. (Chad.Hth) RM6 82 C7
Grove Footpath, Surb. KT5 181 H4
Grove Gdns, NW4 71 G4
NW8 7 H4
Dagenham RM10 101 J3
Enfield EN3 45 G1
Teddington TW11 162 D4
Grove Grn Rd, E11 96 C3
Grove Hall Ct, NW8 6 D3
Grove Hill, E18 79 F2
Harrow HA1 68 B7
Grove Hill Rd, SE5 152 B3
Harrow HA1 68 B7
Grove Ho Rd, N8 74 E4
Groveland Av, SW16 169 F7
Groveland Ct, EC4 20 A4
Groveland Rd, Beck. BR3 189 J3
Grovelands, W.Mol. KT8 179 G4
Grovelands Cl, SE5 152 B2
Harrow HA2 85 H3
Grovelands Ct, N14 42 D7
Grovelands Rd, N13 59 F4
N15 76 D6
Orpington BR5 176 A7
Groveland Way, N.Mal. KT3 182 C5
Grove La, SE5 152 A1
Chigwell IG7 65 J3
Kingston upon Thames KT1 181 H4
Grove La Ter, SE5
off Grove La 152 B3
Grove Mkt Pl, SE9 156 C6
Grove Ms, W6 127 J3
W11
off Portobello Rd 108 C6
Grove Mill, Mitch. CR4 185 H5
Grove Mill Pl, Cars. SM5 200 A3
GROVE PARK, SE12 173 G2
GROVE PARK, W4 126 B7
Grove Pk, E11 79 H6
NW9 70 C4
SE5 152 B2
Grove Pk Av, E4 62 B7
Grove Pk Br, W4 126 C7
Grove Pk Gdns, W4 126 B6
Grove Pk Ms, W4 126 C7
Grove Pk Rd, N15 76 B4
SE9 173 J3
W4 126 B7
Grove Pk Ter, W4 126 B6
Grove Pas, E2 113 E2
Teddington TW11 162 D5
Grove Pl, NW3
off Christchurch Hill 91 G3
SW12 150 B6
W3 126 C1
Barking IG11
off Clockhouse Av 117 F1
Grove Rd, E3 113 G1
E4 62 B4
E11 79 F7
E17 78 B6
E18 79 F2
N11 58 B5
N12 57 G5
N15 76 B5
NW2 89 J6
SW13 147 F2
SW19 167 F7
W3 126 C1
W5 105 G7
Barnet (Cockfos.) EN4 41 H3
Belvedere DA17 139 F6
Bexleyheath DA7 159 J4
Borehamwood WD6 38 A1
Brentford TW8 125 F5
East Molesey KT8 180 A4
Edgware HA8 54 A6
Hounslow TW3 143 H4
Isleworth TW7 144 B1
Mitcham CR4 186 B2
Pinner HA5 67 F5
Richmond TW10 145 J6
Romford RM6 82 B7
Surbiton KT6 181 G5
Sutton SM1 199 E6
Thornton Heath CR7 187 G4
Twickenham TW2 162 A3
Groveside Cl, W3 106 A6
Carshalton SM5 199 H2
Groveside Rd, E4 62 E2
Grovestile Waye, Felt. TW14 141 G7
Grove St, N18 60 C6
SE8 133 J4
Grove Ter, NW5 92 B3
Teddington TW11 162 D4
Grove Ter Ms, NW5
off Grove Ter 92 B3
Grove Vale, SE22 152 B4
Chislehurst BR7 174 D6
Grove Vil, E14 114 B7
Groveway, SW9 151 F1
Dagenham RM8 100 D4
Grove Way, Esher KT10 179 J7
Wembley HA9 88 B5
Grovewood, Rich. TW9
off Sandycombe Rd 146 A1
Grove Wd Cl, Brom. BR1 192 D3
Grovewood Pl, Wdf.Grn. IG8 64 C6
Grummant Rd, SE15 152 C1
Grundy St, E14 114 B6
Gruneisen Rd, N3 56 E7
★ **Guards Mus**, SW1 25 G4
Gubyon Av, SE24 151 H5
Guerin Sq, E3 113 J3
Guernsey Cl, Houns. TW5 143 G1
Guernsey Gro, SE24 151 J7
Guernsey Ho, N1
off Clifton Rd 93 J6
Guernsey Rd, E11 96 D1
Guibal Rd, SE12 155 H7
Guildersfield Rd, SW16 168 E7
Guildford Gro, SE10 154 B1
Guildford Rd, E6 116 B6
E17 78 C1
SW8 151 E1
Croydon CR0 188 A6
Ilford IG3 99 H2
Guildford Way, Wall. SM6 201 E5
★ **Guildhall, The**, EC2 20 B3
★ **Guildhall Art Gall** (Guildhall Lib), EC2 20 A3
Guildhall Bldgs, EC2 20 B3
Guildhall Yd, EC2 20 A3
Guildhouse St, SW1 33 F1
Guildown Av, N12 56 E4
Guild Rd, SE7 136 A5
Guildsway, E17 77 J1
Guilford Av, Surb. KT5 181 J5
Guilford Pl, WC1 10 C6
Guilford St, WC1 10 B6
Guinness Cl, E9 95 H7
Hayes UB3 121 G3
Guinness Ct, E1 21 G4
Guinness Sq, SE1 36 D1
Guinness Trust Bldgs, SE1
off Snowsfields 28 D3
SE11 35 G3
SW3 31 J2
SW9 151 H4
W6
off Fulham Palace Rd 127 J5
Guinness Trust Est, N16
off Holmleigh Rd 94 B1
Guion Rd, SW6 148 C2
Gulland Wk, N1
off Nightingale Rd 93 J6
Gulliver Cl, Nthlt. UB5 103 F1
Gulliver Rd, Sid. DA15 175 H2
Gulliver St, SE16 133 J3
Gulston Wk, SW3 32 A2
Gumleigh Rd, W5 125 F4
Gumley Gdns, Islw. TW7 144 D3
Gumping Rd, Orp. BR5 207 F2
Gundulph Rd, Brom. BR2 191 J3
Gunmakers La, E3 113 H1
Gunnell Cl, SE26 170 D5
Croydon CR0 188 D6
Gunner La, SE18 136 D5
GUNNERSBURY, W4 126 B4
Gunnersbury Av, W3 126 A3
W4 126 A3
W5 125 J1
Gunnersbury Cl, W4
off Grange Rd 126 B5
Gunnersbury Ct, W3 126 B2
Gunnersbury Cres, W3 126 A2
Gunnersbury Dr, W5 125 J2
Gunnersbury Gdns, W3 126 A2
Gunnersbury La, W3 126 A3
Gunnersbury Ms, W4
off Chiswick High Rd 126 B5
★ **Gunnersbury Park**, W3 125 J4
Gunnersbury Pk, W3 125 J4
W5 125 J4
★ **Gunnersbury Park Mus & Art Cen**, W3 126 A3
Gunners Gro, E4 62 C3
Gunners Rd, SW18 167 G2
Gunnery Ter, SE18 137 F4
Gunning St, SE18 137 H4
Gunpowder Sq, EC4 19 F3
Gunstor Rd, N16 94 B4
Gun St, E1 21 F2
Gunter Gro, SW10 30 C6
Edgware HA8 70 D1
Gunterstone Rd, W14 128 B4
Gunthorpe St, E1 21 G2
Gunton Rd, E5 95 E3
SW17 168 A6
Gunwhale Cl, SE16 133 G1
Gurdon Rd, SE7 135 G5
Gurnell Gro, W13 104 C4
Gurney Cl, E15
off Gurney Rd 97 E5
E17 77 G1
Barking IG11 98 E6
Gurney Cres, Croy. CR0 201 F1
Gurney Dr, N2 73 F5
Gurney Rd, E15 96 E5
SW6 149 F3
Carshalton SM5 200 A4
Northolt UB5 102 B3
Guthrie St, SW3 31 G3
Gutter La, EC2 20 A3
Guyatt Gdns, Mitch. CR4
off Ormerod Gdns 186 A2
Guy Barnett Gro, SE3
off Casterbridge Rd 155 G3
Guy Rd, Wall. SM6 200 D3
Guyscliff Rd, SE13 154 C5
Guy St, SE1 28 C3
Gwalior Rd, SW15
off Felsham Rd 148 A3
Gwendolen Av, SW15 148 A5
Gwendolen Cl, SW15 147 J5
Gwendoline Av, E13 115 H1
Gwendwr Rd, W14 128 B5
Gwillim Cl, Sid. DA15 158 A5
Gwydor Rd, Beck. BR3 189 G4
Gwydyr Rd, Brom. BR2 191 F3
Gwyn Cl, SW6 129 F7
Gwynne Av, Croy. CR0 189 G7
Gwynne Cl, W4
off Pumping Sta Rd 127 F6
Gwynne Pk Av, Wdf.Grn. IG8 64 C6
Gwynne Pl, WC1 10 D4
Gwynne Rd, SW11 149 G2
Gylcote Cl, SE5 152 A4
Gyles Pk, Stan. HA7 69 F1
Gyllyngdune Gdns, Ilf. IG3 99 J2
Gypsy Cor, W3 106 C5

H

Haarlem Rd, W14 128 A3
Haberdasher Est, N1
off Haberdasher St 12 C3
Haberdasher Pl, N1 12 C3
Haberdasher St, N1 12 C3
Habgood Rd, Loug. IG10 48 B3
Habitat Cl, SE15
off Gordon Rd 153 E2
Haccombe Rd, SW19
off Haydons Rd 167 F6
HACKBRIDGE, Wall. SM6 200 B2
Hackbridge Grn, Wall. SM6 200 A2
Hackbridge Pk Gdns, Cars. SM5 200 A2
Hackbridge Rd, Wall. SM6 200 A2
Hackford Rd, SW9 151 F1
Hackford Wk, SW9 151 F1
Hackforth Cl, Barn. EN5 39 H5
Hackington Cres, Beck. BR3 172 A6
HACKNEY, E8 94 E6
★ **Hackney City Fm**, E2 13 H2
Hackney Cl, Borwd. WD6 38 D5
Hackney Gro, E8
off Reading La 95 E6
★ **Hackney Marsh**, E9 95 H3
★ **Hackney Mus**, E8 95 E6
Hackney Rd, E2 13 F4
HACKNEY WICK, E9 96 A5
Hackworth Pt, E3
off Rainhill Way 114 B3
Hacon Sq, E8
off Richmond Rd 95 E7
Hadar Cl, N20 56 D1
Hadden Rd, SE28 137 H3
Hadden Way, Grnf. UB6 86 A6
Haddington Rd, Brom. BR1 172 D3
Haddo Ho, SE10
off Haddo St 134 B6
Haddon Cl, Borwd. WD6 38 A2
Enfield EN1 44 D6
New Malden KT3 183 F5
Haddonfield, SE8 133 G4
Haddon Gro, Sid. DA15 158 A7
Haddon Rd, Sutt. SM1 198 E4
Haddo St, SE10 134 B6
Haden Ct, N4
off Lennox Rd 93 G2
Haden La, N11 58 C4
Hadfield Cl, Sthl. UB1
off Adrienne Av 103 F3
Hadfield Rd, Stai. (Stanw.) TW19 140 A6
Hadleigh Cl, E1
off Mantus Rd 113 F4
SW20 184 C2
Hadleigh Rd, N9 44 E7
Hadleigh St, E2 113 F4
Hadleigh Wk, E6 116 B6
HADLEY, Barn. EN5 40 C2
Hadley Cl, N21 43 G6
Hadley Common, Barn. EN5 40 D2
Hadley Gdns, W4 126 D5
Southall UB2 123 F5
Hadley Grn, Barn. EN5 40 C2
Hadley Grn Rd, Barn. EN5 40 C2
Hadley Grn W, Barn. EN5 40 C2
Hadley Gro, Barn. EN5 40 B2
Hadley Hts, Barn. EN5
off Hadley Rd 41 E2
Hadley Highstone, Barn. EN5 40 C1
Hadley Ridge, Barn. EN5 40 C3

Hadley Rd, Barn.
(New Barn.) EN5 . . . . . . .41 E4
Belvedere DA17 . . . . . .139 F4
Mitcham CR4 . . . . .186 D4
Hadley St, NW1 . . . . .92 B6
Hadley Way, N21 . . . . .43 G6
Hadlow Pl, SE19 . . . . .170 D7
Hadlow Rd, Sid. DA14 . . .176 A4
Welling DA16 . . . . .138 C7
Hadrian Cl, E3
off Garrison Rd 114 A1
Staines TW19 . . . . .140 B7
Hadrian Ct, Sutt. SM2
off Stanley Rd 198 E7
Hadrian Est, E2 . . . . .13 J2
Hadrian Ms, N7
off Roman Way 93 F7
Hadrians Ride, Enf. EN1 . . .44 C5
Hadrian St, SE10 . . . . .134 E5
Hadrian Way, Stai. (Stanw.)
TW19 . . . . .140 B7
Hadyn Pk Rd, W12 . . . . . .127 G2
Hafer Rd, SW11 . . . . .149 J4
Hafton Rd, SE6 . . . . .173 E1
Haggard Rd, Twick. TW1 . .144 E7
HAGGERSTON, E2 . . . . . . .13 G1
Haggerston Rd, E8 . . . . .94 C7
Haggerston Studios, E8
off Kingsland Rd 112 C1
Hague St, E2 . . . . .13 J4
Ha-Ha Rd, SE18 . . . . .136 C6
Haig Pl, Mord. SM4
off Green La 184 D6
Haig Rd, Stan. HA7 . . . . . . .53 F5
Haig Rd E, E13 . . . . .115 J3
Haig Rd W, E13 . . . . .115 J3
Haigville Gdns, Ilf. IG6 . . . .81 E4
Hailes Cl, SW19 . . . . .167 F6
Haileybury Av, Enf. EN1 . . .44 C6
Hailey Rd, Erith DA18 . . . .139 G2
Hailsham Av, SW2 . . . . . .169 F2
Hailsham Cl, Surb. KT6 . .181 G7
Hailsham Dr, Har. HA1 . . . .68 A3
Hailsham Rd, SW17 . . . . .168 A6
Hailsham Ter, N18 . . . . .59 J5
Haimo Rd, SE9 . . . . .156 A5
HAINAULT, Ilf. IG6 . . . . . . .65 H7
Hainault Ct, E17 . . . . .78 D4
Hainault Gore, Rom. RM6 .83 E5
Hainault Gro, Chig. IG7 . . .65 F4
Hainault Rd, E11 . . . . .96 C1
Chigwell IG7 . . . . .65 E3
Romford RM5 . . . . .83 J2
Romford (Chad.Hth)
RM6 . . . . .83 F6
Romford (Lt.Hth) RM6 . .82 B3
Hainault St, SE9 . . . . .175 E1
Ilford IG1 . . . . .99 E2
Haines Cl, N1 . . . . .94 B7
Haines Wk, Mord. SM4
off Dorchester Rd 185 E7
Hainford Cl, SE4 . . . . .153 G4
Haining Cl, W4
off Wellesley Rd 126 A5
Hainthorpe Rd, SE27 . . . .169 H3
Hainton Cl, E1 . . . . .113 E6
Halberd Ms, E5
off Knightland Rd 94 E2
Halbutt Gdns, Dag.
RM9 . . . . .101 F3
Halbutt St, Dag. RM9 . . . .101 F4
Halcomb St, N1 . . . . .112 B1
Halcot Av, Bexh. DA6 . . . .159 H5
Halcrow St, E1
off Newark St 113 E5
Haldane Cl, N10 . . . . .58 B7
Haldane Pl, SW18 . . . . . . .166 E1
Haldane Rd, E6 . . . . .116 A3
SE28 . . . . .118 D7
SW6 . . . . .128 C7
Southall UB1 . . . . .103 J6
Haldan Rd, E4 . . . . .62 C6
Haldon Cl, Chig. IG7
off Arrowsmith Rd 65 H5
Haldon Rd, SW18 . . . . . . .148 C5
Hale, The, E4 . . . . .62 D7
N17 . . . . .76 D3
Hale Cl, E4 . . . . .62 C3
Edgware HA8 . . . . .54 C5
Orpington BR6 . . . . . . .207 F4
Hale Dr, NW7 . . . . .54 C6
HALE END, E4 . . . . .62 D6
Hale End Cl, Ruis. HA4 . . . .66 A6
Hale End Rd, E4 . . . . .62 D6
E17 . . . . .78 D1
Woodford Green IG8 . . .62 D7
Halefield Rd, N17 . . . . .76 D1
Hale Gdns, N17 . . . . .76 D3
W3 . . . . .126 A1
Hale Gro Gdns, NW7 . . . . .54 D5
Hale La, NW7 . . . . .54 D5
Edgware HA8 . . . . .54 B5
Hale Path, SE27 . . . . .169 H4
Hale Rd, E6 . . . . .116 B4
N17 . . . . .76 D3
Halesowen Rd, Mord.
SM4 . . . . .184 E7
Hales Prior, N1
off Calshot St 10 C2
Hales St, SE8
off Deptford High St . .134 A7
Hale St, E14 . . . . .114 B7
Halesworth Cl, E5
off Theydon Rd 95 F2
Halesworth Rd, SE13 . . . .154 B3
Hale Wk, W7 . . . . .104 B5
Haley Rd, NW4 . . . . .71 J6
Half Acre, Brent. TW8 . . . .125 G6
Half Acre Rd, W7 . . . . . . .124 B1
Half Moon Ct, EC1 . . . . . . .19 J2
Half Moon Cres, N1 . . . . . .10 D1
Half Moon La, SE24 . . . . .151 J6
Half Moon Pas, E1 . . . . . . .21 G4
Half Moon St, W1 . . . . .24 E1
Halford Cl, Edg. HA8 . . . . . .70 B2
Halford Rd, E10 . . . . .78 D5
SW6 . . . . .128 D6
Richmond TW10 . . . . . .145 H5
Halfway St, Sid. DA15 . . .157 G7
Haliburton Rd, Twick.
TW1 . . . . .144 D5
Haliday Wk, N1
off Balls Pond Rd 94 A6
Halidon Cl, E9
off Urswick Rd 95 F5
Halifax Cl, Tedd. TW11 . . . .162 A6
Halifax Rd, Enf. EN2 . . . . . .43 J2
Greenford UB6 . . . . . . .103 H1
Halifax St, SE26 . . . . .171 E4
Halifield Dr, Belv. DA17 . .138 E3
Haling Gro, S.Croy. CR2 . .201 J7
Haling Pk, S.Croy. CR2 . .201 J6
Haling Pk Gdns, S.Croy.
CR2 . . . . .201 H6
Haling Pk Rd, S.Croy.
CR2 . . . . .201 H5
Haling Rd, S.Croy. CR2 . . .202 A6
Halkin Arc, SW1 . . . . .24 B5
Halkin Ms, SW1 . . . . .24 B5
Halkin Pl, SW1 . . . . .24 B5
Halkin St, SW1 . . . . .24 C4
Hall, The, SE3 . . . . .155 G3
Hallam Cl, Chis. BR7 . . . . .174 C5
Hallam Gdns, Pnr. HA5 . . .51 E7
Hallam Ms, W1 . . . . .16 E1
Hallam Rd, N15 . . . . .75 H4
SW13 . . . . .147 H3
Hallam St, W1 . . . . .8 E6
Hallane Ho, SE27
off Elder Rd 169 J5
Hall Av, N18
off Weir Hall Av 60 A6
Hall Cl, W5 . . . . .105 H5
Hall Ct, Tedd. TW11 . . . . . .162 C5
Hall Dr, SE26 . . . . .171 F5
W7 . . . . .104 B6
Halley Gdns, SE13 . . . . . .154 D4
Halley Rd, E7 . . . . .97 J6
E12 . . . . .98 A6
Halley St, E14 . . . . .113 H5
Hall Fm Cl, Stan. HA7 . . . . .52 E4
Hall Fm Dr, Twick. TW2 . . .144 A7
Hallfield Est, W2 . . . . .14 C3
Hall Gdns, E4 . . . . .61 J4
Hall Gate, NW8 . . . . .6 D3
Halliards, The, Walt. KT12
off Felix Rd 178 A6
Halliday Ho, E1
off Christian St 21 J4
Halliday Sq, Sthl. UB2 . . . .124 A1
Halliford St, N1 . . . . .93 J7
Hallingbury Ct, E17 . . . . . .78 B3
Hallings Wf Studios, E15
off Channelsea Rd . . .114 D1
Halliwell Rd, SW2 . . . . . . .151 F6
Halliwick Rd, N10 . . . . .74 A1
Hall La, E4 . . . . .61 H5
NW4 . . . . .71 G1
Hayes (Harling.) UB3 . .121 G7
Hallmark Trd Cen, Wem.
HA9 . . . . .88 C4
Hallmead Rd, Sutt. SM1 . .198 E3
Hall Oak Wk, NW6
off Barlow Rd 90 C6
Hallowell Av, Croy. CR0 . .200 E4
Hallowell Cl, Mitch. CR4 . .186 A3
Hallowes Cres, Wat. WD19 .50 A3
Hallowfield Way, Mitch.
CR4 . . . . .185 G3
★ **Hall Pl**, Bex. DA5 . . . .159 J6
Hall Pl, W2 . . . . .6 E6
Hall Pl Cres, Bex. DA5 . . .159 J5
Hall Rd, E6 . . . . .116 C1
E15 . . . . .96 D4
NW8 . . . . .6 D4
Isleworth TW7 . . . . .144 A5
Hall Rd, Romford (Chad.Hth)
RM6 . . . . .82 C6
Hall St, EC1 . . . . .11 H3
N12 . . . . .57 F5
Hallsville Rd, E16 . . . . .115 F6
Hallswelle Rd, NW11 . . . . .72 C5
Hall Twr, W2 . . . . .15 F1
Hall Vw, SE9 . . . . .174 A2
Hallywell Cres, E6 . . . . . . .116 C5
Halons Rd, SE9 . . . . .156 D7
Halpin Pl, SE17 . . . . .36 C2
Halsbrook Rd, SE3 . . . . . .156 A3
Halsbury Cl, Stan. HA7 . . . .52 E4
Halsbury Rd, W12 . . . . . . .127 H1
Halsbury Rd E, Nthlt. UB5 .85 J4
Halsbury Rd W, Nthlt. UB5 .85 H5
Halsend, Hayes UB3 . . . . .122 B1
Halsey Ms, SW3 . . . . .31 J1
Halsey St, SW3 . . . . .31 J1
Halsham Cres, Bark. IG11 . .99 J6
Halsmere Rd, SE5 . . . . . . .151 H1
Halstead Cl, Croy. CR0
off Charles St 201 J3
Halstead Ct, N1 . . . . .12 B2
Halstead Gdns, N21 . . . . . .60 A1
Halstead Rd, E11 . . . . .79 G5
N21 . . . . .59 J1
Enfield EN1 . . . . .44 B4
Halston Cl, SW11 . . . . . . .149 J6
Halstow Rd, NW10 . . . . . .108 A3
SE10 . . . . .135 G5
Halsway, Hayes UB3 . . . .122 A1
Halter Cl, Borwd. WD6 . . . .38 D5
Halton Cl, N11 . . . . .57 J6
Halton Cross St, N1 . . . . .111 H1
Halton Pl, N1
off Dibden St 111 J1
Halton Rd, N1 . . . . .93 H7
Halt Robin La, Belv. DA17
off Halt Robin Rd 139 H4
Halt Robin Rd, Belv.
DA17 . . . . .139 G4
HAM, Rich. TW10 . . . . .163 G3
Ham, The, Brent. TW8 . . . .125 F7
Hambalt Rd, SW4 . . . . . . .150 C5
Hamble Ct, Tedd. TW11 . . .163 G7
Hambledon Gdns, SE25 . .188 C3
Hambledon Pl, SE21 . . . . .170 B1
Hambledon Rd, SW18 . . .148 C7
Hambledown Rd, Sid.
DA15 . . . . .157 G7
Hamble St, SW6 . . . . .149 E3
Hambleton Cl, Wor.Pk.
KT4 . . . . .197 J2
Hamble Wk, Nthlt. UB5
off Brabazon Rd 103 G2
Hambley Ho, SE16
off Manor Est 132 E4
Hambridge Way, SW2 . . . .151 G7
Hambro Av, Brom. BR2 . . .205 G1
Hambrook Rd, SE25 . . . . .188 E3
Hambro Rd, SW16 . . . . . .168 D6
Hambrough Rd, Sthl.
UB1 . . . . .122 E1
Ham Cl, Rich. TW10 . . . . . .163 F3
Ham Common, Rich.
TW10 . . . . .163 J4
Ham Cft Cl, Felt. TW13 . . .160 A3
Hamden Cres, Dag.
RM10 . . . . .101 H3
Hamel Cl, Har. HA3 . . . . . . .69 G3
Hamelin St, E14
off St. Leonards Rd . . .114 C6
Hameway, E6 . . . . .116 D4
Ham Fm Rd, Rich. TW10 . .163 G4
Ham Flds, Rich. TW10
off Riverside Dr 162 E3
Hamfrith Rd, E15 . . . . .97 F6
Ham Gate Av, Rich. TW10 .163 G3
★ **Ham Ho**, Rich. TW10 . .163 F1
Hamilton Av, N9 . . . . .44 D7
Ilford IG6 . . . . .81 E4
Surbiton KT6 . . . . .196 B1
Sutton SM3 . . . . .198 B2
Hamilton Cl, N17 . . . . .76 C3
NW8 . . . . .6 E4
SE16
off Somerford Way . . .133 H2
Barnet (Cockfos.) EN4 . .41 H4
Teddington TW11
off Munster Rd 163 F6
Hamilton Ct, W5 . . . . .105 J7
W9 . . . . .6 C3
Hamilton Cres, N13 . . . . . . .59 G4
Harrow HA2 . . . . .85 F3
Hounslow TW3 . . . . . . .143 H5
Hamilton Gdns, NW8 . . . . . .6 D3
Hamilton Ho, SW8
off St. George Wf 34 A5
Hamilton La, N5
off Hamilton Pk 93 H4
Hamilton Ms, SW18
off Merton Rd 166 D1
Hamilton Ms, W1 . . . . .24 D3
Hamilton Pk, N5 . . . . .93 H4
Hamilton Pk W, N5 . . . . . . .93 H4
Hamilton Pl, N19 . . . . .92 D3
W1 . . . . .24 C2
Sunbury-on-Thames
TW16 . . . . .160 B7
Hamilton Rd, E15 . . . . . . .115 E3
E17 . . . . .77 H2
N2 . . . . .73 F3
N9 . . . . .44 D7
NW10 . . . . .89 G5
NW11 . . . . .72 A7
SE27 . . . . .170 A4
SW19 . . . . .167 E7
W4 . . . . .126 E2
W5 . . . . .105 H7
Barnet (Cockfos.) EN4 . .41 H4
Bexleyheath DA7 . . . . .159 E2
Brentford TW8 . . . . .125 G6
Harrow HA1 . . . . .68 B5
Hayes UB3 . . . . .102 B7
Ilford IG1 . . . . .98 E4
Sidcup DA15 . . . . .176 A4
Southall UB1 . . . . .123 F1
Thornton Heath CR7 . . .188 A3
Twickenham TW2 . . . . .162 B1
Watford WD19 . . . . .50 B3
Hamilton Rd Ind Est,
SE27 . . . . .170 A4
Hamilton Rd Ms, SW19
off Hamilton Rd 167 E7
Hamilton Sq, N12
off Sandringham Gdns .57 G6
SE1 . . . . .28 C3
Hamilton St, SE8
off Deptford High St . .134 A6
Hamilton Ter, NW8 . . . . .6 D3
Hamilton Way, N3 . . . . .56 D6
N13 . . . . .59 H4
Hamlea Cl, SE12 . . . . .155 F5
Hamlet, The, SE5 . . . . .152 A3
Hamlet Cl, SE13 . . . . .155 E4
Hamlet Gdns, W6 . . . . . . .127 G4
Hamlet Ms, SE21
off Thurlow Pk Rd 170 A1
Hamleton Ter, Dag. RM9
off Flamstead Rd 100 C7
Hamlet Rd, SE19 . . . . .170 C7
Hamlet Sq, NW2 . . . . .90 B3
Hamlets Way, E3 . . . . .113 J4
Hamlet Way, SE1 . . . . .28 C3
★ **Hamleys**, W1 . . . . .17 F5
Hamlin Cres, Pnr. HA5 . . . .66 C5
Hamlyn Cl, Edg. HA8 . . . . .53 H3
Hamlyn Gdns, SE19 . . . . .170 B7
Hamlyn Ho, Felt. TW13
off High St 160 B1
Hammelton Grn, SW9
off Cromwell Rd 151 H1
Hammelton Rd, Brom.
BR1 . . . . .191 F1
Hammers La, NW7 . . . . . . .55 G5
HAMMERSMITH, W6 . . . .127 J5
Hammersmith Br, SW13 .127 H6
W6 . . . . .127 H6
Hammersmith Br Rd, W6 .127 J5
Hammersmith Bdy, W6 . .127 J4
Hammersmith Flyover,
W6 . . . . .127 J5
Hammersmith Gro, W6 . .127 J3
Hammersmith Rd, W6 . . .128 A4
W14 . . . . .128 A4
Hammersmith Ter, W6 . . .127 G5
Hammet Cl, Hayes UB4 . .102 D5
Hammett St, EC3 . . . . .21 F5
Hammond Av, Mitch.
CR4 . . . . .186 B2
Hammond Cl, Barn. EN5 . .40 B5
Greenford UB6
off Lilian Board Way . . .86 A5
Hampton TW12 . . . . . . .179 G1
Hammond Ho, SE14
off Lubbock St 133 F7
Hammond Rd, Enf. EN1 . . .45 E2
Southall UB2 . . . . .123 E3
Hammonds Cl, Dag. RM8 .100 C3
Hammond St, NW5 . . . . . . .92 C6
Hammond Way, SE28
off Oriole Way 118 B7
Hamonde Cl, Edg. HA8 . . .54 B2
Hamond Sq, N1 . . . . .12 D1
Ham Pk Rd, E7 . . . . .97 F7
E15 . . . . .97 F7
Hampden Av, Beck. BR3 . .189 H2
Hampden Cl, NW1 . . . . .9 J2
Hampden Gurney St, W1 . .15 J4
Hampden La, N17 . . . . .76 C1
Hampden Rd, N8 . . . . .75 G4
N10 . . . . .58 A7
N17 . . . . .76 D1
N19 *off Holloway Rd* . . .92 D2
Beckenham BR3 . . . . . .189 H2

Hampden Rd, Harrow HA3 .....67 J1
Kingston upon Thames KT1 .....182 A3
Hampden Sq, N14 *off Osidge La* 58 B1
Hampden Way, N14 .....58 B2
Hampshire Cl, N18 *off Berkshire Gdns* 60 E5
Hampshire Hog La, W6 *off King St* 127 H4
Hampshire Rd, N22 .....59 F7
Hampshire St, NW5 *off Torriano Av* 92 D6
Hampson Way, SW8 .....151 F1
HAMPSTEAD, NW3 .....91 G4
Hampstead Av, Wdf.Grn. IG8 .....64 D7
Hampstead Cl, SE28 .....138 B1
Hampstead Gdns, NW11 ..72 D6
Romford (Chad.Hth) RM6 .....82 B5
HAMPSTEAD GARDEN SUBURB, N2 .....73 F5
Hampstead Grn, NW3 .....91 H5
Hampstead Gro, NW3 .....91 F3
★ **Hampstead Heath**, NW3 .....91 G2
Hampstead Hts, N2 .....73 F4
Hampstead High St, NW3 .91 F4
Hampstead Hill Gdns, NW3 .....91 G4
Hampstead La, N6 .....73 G7
NW3 .....73 G7
Hampstead Rd, NW1 .....9 F1
Hampstead Sq, NW3 .....91 F3
Hampstead Wk, E3 *off Waterside Cl* 113 J1
Hampstead Way, NW11 ...91 F1
HAMPTON, TW12 .....179 H1
Hampton Cl, N11 .....58 B5
NW6 .....108 D3
SW20 .....165 J7
Borehamwood WD6 .....38 C5
Hampton Ct, N1 *off Upper St* 93 H6
Hampton Ct Av, E.Mol. KT8 .....180 A5
Hampton Ct Cres, E.Mol. KT8 .....180 A3
★ **Hampton Court Palace & Pk**, E.Mol. KT8 .....180 B3
Hampton Ct Par, E.Mol. KT8 *off Creek Rd* 180 B4
Hampton Ct Pk, E.Mol. (Home Pk) KT8 .....180 D4
Kingston upon Thames (Home Pk) KT1 .....180 D4
Hampton Ct Rd, E.Mol. KT8 .....180 C3
Hampton TW12 .....179 J2
Kingston upon Thames KT1 .....180 C3
Hampton Ct Way, E.Mol. KT8 .....180 B6
Esher KT10 .....194 B2
Thames Ditton KT7 .....194 B2
Hampton Fm Ind Est, Felt. TW13 .....161 F3
HAMPTON HILL, Hmptn. TW12 .....161 J6
Hampton Hill Business Pk, Hmptn. TW12 *off Wellington Rd* 161 J5
Hampton La, Felt. TW13 ..161 E4
Hampton Mead, Loug. IG10 .....48 E3
Hampton Ms, NW10 *off Minerva Rd* 106 D3
Hampton Ri, Har. HA3 .....69 H6
Hampton Rd, E4 .....61 J5
E7 .....97 H5
E11 .....96 D1
Croydon CR0 .....187 J6
Hampton (Hmptn H.) TW12 .....162 A5
Ilford IG1 .....99 E4
Teddington TW11 .....162 A5
Twickenham TW2 .....162 A3
Worcester Park KT4 ...197 G2
Hampton Rd E, Felt. (Han.) TW13 .....161 F3
Hampton Rd W, Felt. TW13 .....160 E2
Hampton St, SE1 .....35 H2
SE17 .....35 H2
HAMPTON WICK, Kings.T. KT1 .....181 E1
Ham Ridings, Rich. TW10 .163 J5
Hamshades Cl, Sid. DA15 .....175 J3
Ham St, Rich. TW10 .....163 F2
Ham Vw, Croy. CR0 .....189 H6
Ham Yd, W1 .....17 H5
Hanah Ct, SW19 .....166 A7
Hanameel St, E16 .....135 G1
Hana Ms, E5 *off Goulton Rd* 95 F4
Hanbury Cl, NW4 .....71 J3
Hanbury Dr, E11 *off High Rd Leytonstone* 79 F7
N21 .....43 F5
Hanbury Ms, N1 *off Mary St* 111 J1
Hanbury Rd, N17 .....76 E2
W3 .....126 B2
Hanbury St, E1 .....21 F1
Hancock Ct, Borwd. WD6 ..38 C1
Hancock Rd, E3 .....114 C3
SE19 .....170 A6
Handa Wk, N1 *off Clephane Rd* 93 J6
Hand Ct, WC1 .....18 D2
Handcroft Rd, Croy. CR0 .187 H7
Handel Cl, Edg. HA8 .....53 J6
Handel Pl, NW10 .....88 D6
Handel St, WC1 .....10 A5
Handel Way, Edg. HA8 .....54 A7
Handen Rd, SE12 .....155 E5
Handforth Rd, SW9 .....34 E7
Ilford IG1 *off Winston Way* 99 E3
Handley Gro, NW2 .....90 A3
Handley Page Rd, Wall. SM6 .....201 F7
Handley Rd, E9 .....95 F7
Handowe Cl, NW4 .....71 G4
Handside Cl, Wor.Pk. KT4 .198 A1
Hands Wk, E16 .....115 G6
Handsworth Av, E4 .....62 D6
Handsworth Rd, N17 .....76 A3
Handsworth Way, Wat. WD19 .....50 A3
Handtrough Way, Bark. IG11 *off Fresh Wf Rd* 117 E2
Hanford Cl, SW18 .....166 D1
Hanford Row, SW19 .....165 J6
Hangar Ruding, Wat. WD19 .....51 F3
Hanger Grn, W5 .....106 A4
Hanger La, W5 .....105 J4
Hanger Vale La, W5 .....105 J6
Hanger Vw Way, W3 .....106 A6
Hanging Sword All, EC4 ...19 F4
Hankey Pl, SE1 .....28 C4
Hankins La, NW7 .....54 E3
Hanley Gdns, N4 .....93 E1
Hanley Pl, Beck. BR3 .....172 A7
Hanley Rd, N4 .....93 E1
Hanmer Wk, N7 *off Newington Barrow Way* 93 F3
Hannah Cl, NW10 .....88 C4
Beckenham BR3 .....190 C3
Hannah Ct, N13 .....59 F2
Hannah Mary Way, SE1 ...37 J2
Hannah Ms, Wall. SM6 ...200 C7
Hannay La, N8 .....74 D7
Hannay Wk, SW16 .....168 D2
Hannell Rd, SW6 .....128 B7
Hannen Rd, SE27 *off Norwood High St* .169 H3
Hannibal Rd, E1 .....113 F5
Staines (Stanw.) TW19 .140 A7
Hannibal Way, Croy. CR0 .201 F6
Hannington Rd, SW4 .....150 B3
Hanover Av, E16 .....135 G1
Feltham TW13 .....160 A1
Hanover Cl, Rich. TW9 ...126 A7
Sutton SM3 .....198 C4
Hanover Ct, SE19 *off Anerley Rd* 170 C7
W12 *off Uxbridge Rd* ..127 G1
Hanover Dr, Chis. BR7 ...175 F4
Hanover Gdns, SE11 .....34 E6
Ilford IG6 .....65 F7
Hanover Gate, NW1 .....7 H4
Hanover Gate Mans, NW1 ..7 H5
Hanover Ho, Surb. KT6 *off Lenelby Rd* 196 A1
Hanover Pk, SE15 .....152 D1
Hanover Pl, E3 *off Brokesley St* 113 J3
WC2 .....18 B4
Hanover Rd, N15 .....76 C4
NW10 .....89 J7
SW19 .....167 F7
Hanover Sq, W1 .....17 E4
Hanover Steps, W2 *off St. Georges Flds* ...15 H4
Hanover St, W1 .....17 E4
Croydon CR0 *off Abbey Rd* 201 H3
Hanover Ter, NW1 .....7 H4
Hanover Ter Ms, NW1 .....7 H4
Hanover Way, Bexh. DA6 .158 D3
Hanover W Ind Est, NW10 .....106 D2
Hanover Yd, N1 .....11 H1
Hansard Ms, W14 *off Holland Rd* 128 A2
Hansart Way, Enf. EN2 *off The Ridgeway* 43 G1
Hanscomb Ms, SW4 *off Bromell's Rd* 150 C4
Hans Cres, SW1 .....23 J5
Hanselin Cl, Stan. HA7 .....52 C5
Hansen Dr, N21 .....43 F5
Hanshaw Dr, Edg. HA8 ...70 D1
Hansler Gro, E.Mol. KT8 ..180 A4
Hansler Rd, SE22 .....152 C5
Hansol Rd, Bexh. DA6 ...158 E5
Hanson Cl, SW12 .....150 B7
SW14 .....146 C3
Beckenham BR3 .....172 B6
Loughton IG10 .....49 F2
West Drayton UB7 .....120 C3
Hanson Dr, Loug. IG10 .....49 F2
Hanson Gdns, Sthl. UB1 .123 E2
Hanson Grn, Loug. IG10 ...49 F2
Hanson St, W1 .....17 F1
Hans Pl, SW1 .....24 A5
Hans Rd, SW3 .....23 J5
Hans St, SW1 .....24 A6
Hanway Pl, W1 .....17 H3
Hanway Rd, W7 .....104 A6
Hanway St, W1 .....17 H3
HANWELL, W7 .....124 C1
HANWORTH, Felt. TW13 ..160 D4
Hanworth Rd, Felt. TW13 .160 B1
Hampton TW12 .....161 H6
Hounslow TW3, TW4 ..143 H3
Sunbury-on-Thames TW16 .....160 A7
Hanworth Ter, Houns. TW3 .....143 H4
Hanworth Trd Est, Felt. TW13 .....161 E3
Hapgood Cl, Grnf. UB6 .....86 A5
Harads Pl, E1 .....21 J6
Harben Rd, NW6 .....91 F7
Harberson Rd, E15 .....115 F1
SW12 .....168 B1
Harberton Rd, N19 .....92 C1
Harbet Rd, E4 .....61 G5
N18 .....61 G5
W2 .....15 F2
Harbex Cl, Bex. DA5 .....159 H7
Harbinger Rd, E14 .....134 B4
Harbledown Rd, SW6 .....148 D1
Harbord Cl, SE5 *off De Crespigny Pk* ..152 A2
Harbord St, SW6 .....148 A1
Harborne Cl, Wat. WD19 ...50 C5
Harborough Av, Sid. DA15 .....157 H7
Harborough Rd, SW16 ...169 F4
Harbour Av, SW10 .....149 F1
Harbour Ex Sq, E14 .....134 B2
Harbour Reach, SW6 *off The Boulevard* 149 F1
Harbour Rd, SE5 .....151 J3
Harbour Yd, SW10 *off Harbour Av* 149 F1
Harbridge Av, SW15 .....147 F7
Harbut Rd, SW11 .....149 G4
Harcombe Rd, N16 .....94 B3
Harcourt Av, E12 .....98 C4
Edgware HA8 .....54 C3
Sidcup DA15 .....158 C6
Wallington SM6 .....200 B4
Harcourt Cl, Islw. TW7 ...144 D3
Harcourt Fld, Wall. SM6 ..200 B4
Harcourt Lo, Wall. SM6 *off Croydon Rd* 200 B4
Harcourt Rd, E15 .....115 F2
N22 .....74 D1
SE4 .....153 H4
SW19 *off Russell Rd* ...166 D7
Bexleyheath DA6 .....159 E4
Thornton Heath CR7 ..187 F6
Wallington SM6 .....200 B4
Harcourt St, W1 .....15 H2
Harcourt Ter, SW10 .....30 B4
Hardcastle Cl, Croy. CR0 .188 D6
Hardcourts Cl, W.Wick. BR4 .....204 B3
Hardel Ri, SW2 .....169 H2
Hardel Wk, SW2 *off Papworth Way* 151 G7
Hardens Manorway, SE7 .136 A3
Harders Rd, SE15 .....152 E2
Hardess St, SE24 *off Herne Hill Rd* 151 J3
Hardie Cl, NW10 .....88 D5
Hardie Rd, Dag. RM10 ...101 J3
Harding Cl, SE17 .....35 J5
Croydon CR0 .....202 C3
Hardinge Cres, SE18 .....137 F3
Hardinge Rd, N18 .....60 B5
NW10 .....107 H1
Hardinge St, E1 .....113 F6
Harding Ho, Hayes UB3 ..102 B6
Harding Rd, Bexh. DA7 ..159 F2
Harding's Cl, Kings.T. KT2 .....181 J1
Hardings La, SE20 .....171 G6
Hardman Rd, SE7 .....135 H5
Kingston upon Thames KT2 .....181 H2
Hardwick Cl, Stan. HA7 ...53 F5
Hardwicke Av, Houns. TW5 .....143 G1
Hardwicke Ho, E3 *off Bromley High St* ..114 B3
Hardwicke Ms, WC1 .....10 D4
Hardwicke Rd, N13 .....58 E6
W4 .....126 C4
Richmond TW10 .....163 F4
Hardwicke St, Bark. IG11 .117 F1
Hardwick Grn, W13 .....105 E5
Hardwick St, EC1 .....11 F4
Hardwicks Way, SW18 ...148 D5
Hardwidge St, SE1 .....28 D3
Hardy Av, E16 *off Wesley Av* 135 G1
Ruislip HA4 .....84 B5
Hardy Cl, SE16 *off Middleton Dr* 133 G2
Barnet EN5 .....40 B6
Pinner HA5 .....66 D7
Hardy Pas, N22 *off Berners Rd* 75 G2
Hardy Rd, E4 .....61 J6
SE3 .....135 F7
SW19 .....167 E7
Hardy's Ms, E.Mol. KT8 ..180 B4
Hardy Way, Enf. EN2 .....43 G1
Hare & Billet Rd, SE3 .....154 D1
Harebell Dr, E6 .....116 D5
Harecastle Cl, Hayes UB4 .102 E4
Hare Ct, EC4 .....19 E4
Harecourt Rd, N1 .....93 J6
Haredale Rd, SE24 .....151 J4
Haredon Cl, SE23 .....153 F7
Harefield, Esher KT10 .....194 B4
Harefield Cl, Enf. EN2 .....43 G1
Harefield Ms, SE4 .....153 J3
Harefield Rd, N8 .....74 D5
SE4 .....153 J3
SW16 .....169 F7
Sidcup DA14 .....176 D2
Hare La, Esher (Clay.) KT10 .....194 B6
Hare Marsh, E2 .....13 H5
Hare Pl, EC4 .....19 F4
Hare Row, E2 .....113 E2
Haresfield Rd, Dag. RM10 .101 G6
Hare St, SE18 .....136 D3
Hare Wk, N1 .....12 E2
Harewood Av, NW1 .....7 H6
Northolt UB5 .....85 E7
Harewood Cl, Nthlt. UB5 ..85 F7
Harewood Dr, Ilf. IG5 .....80 C2
Harewood Pl, W1 .....16 E4
Harewood Rd, SW19 .....167 H6
Isleworth TW7 .....124 C7
South Croydon CR2 ...202 B6
Watford WD19 .....50 B3
Harewood Row, NW1 .....15 H1
Harewood Ter, Sthl. UB2 .123 F4
Harfield Gdns, SE5 .....152 B3
Harfield Rd, Sun. TW16 ..178 D2
Harford Cl, E4 .....46 B7
Harford Ms, N19 .....92 D3
Harford Rd, E4 .....46 B7
Harford St, E1 .....113 H4
Harford Wk, N2 .....73 G5
Hargood Cl, Har. HA3 .....69 H6
Hargood Rd, SE3 .....155 J1
Hargrave Pk, N19 .....92 C2
Hargrave Pl, N7 *off Brecknock Rd* 92 D5
Hargrave Rd, N19 .....92 C2
Hargwyne St, SW9 .....151 F3
Haringey Pk, N8 .....74 E6
Haringey Pas, N4 .....75 H6
N8 .....75 G4
Haringey Rd, N8 .....74 E4
Harington Ter, N9 .....60 A3
N18 .....60 A3
Harkett Cl, Har. HA3 *off Byron Rd* 68 C2
Harkett Ct, Har. HA3 .....68 C2
Harkness Ct, Sutt. SM1 *off Cleeve Way* 199 F1
Harkness Ho, E1 *off Christian St* 21 J4
Harland Av, Croy. CR0 ...202 C3
Sidcup DA15 .....175 G3
Harland Cl, SW19 .....184 E3

Harland Rd, SE12 .173 G1
Harlands Gro, Orp. BR6 .207 E4
Harlech Gdns, Houns.
TW5 .122 C6
Pinner HA5 .66 D7
Harlech Rd, N14 .59 E3
Harlech Twr, W3 .126 B2
Harlequin Av, Brent. TW8 .124 D6
Harlequin Cl, Hayes UB4
off Cygnet Way .102 D5
Isleworth TW7 .144 B5
Harlequin Ho, Erith DA18
off Kale Rd .138 E3
Harlequin Rd, Tedd. TW11 .162 E7
★ Harlequins RL, Twick.
TW2 .144 B7
Harlescott Rd, SE15 .153 G4
HARLESDEN, NW10 .106 E2
Harlesden Gdns, NW10 .107 F1
Harlesden La, NW10 .107 G1
Harlesden Rd, NW10 .107 G1
Harleston Cl, E5
off Theydon Rd .95 F2
Harley Cl, Wem. HA0 .87 G6
Harley Ct, E11
off Blake Hall Rd .79 G7
Harley Cres, Har. HA1 .68 A4
Harleyford, Brom. BR1 .191 H1
Harleyford Rd, SE11 .34 C5
Harleyford St, SE11 .34 E6
Harley Gdns, SW10 .30 D4
Orpington BR6 .207 H4
Harley Gro, E3 .113 J3
Harley Pl, W1 .16 D2
Harley Rd, NW3 .91 G7
NW10 .106 E2
Harrow HA1 .68 A4
Harley St, W1 .16 D2
Harling Ct, SW11
off Latchmere Rd .149 J2
Harlinger St, SE18 .136 B3
HARLINGTON, Hayes
UB3 .121 F6
Harlington Cl, Hayes
(Harling.) UB3
off New Rd .121 F7
Harlington Cor, Hayes UB3
off Bath Rd .141 G1
Harlington Rd, Bexh.
DA7 .159 E3
Hounslow (Lon.Hthrw Air.)
TW6 .141 J4
Harlington Rd E, Felt. TW13,
TW14 .142 B7
Harlington Rd W, Felt.
TW14 .142 B6
Harlow Rd, N13 .60 A3
Harlyn Dr, Pnr. HA5 .66 B3
Harman Av, Wdf.Grn. IG8 .63 F7
Harman Cl, E4 .62 D4
NW2 .90 B3
SE1 off Avondale Sq .37 H4
Harman Dr, NW2 .90 B3
Sidcup DA15 .157 J6
Harman Rd, Enf. EN1 .44 C5
HARMONDSWORTH,
West Dr. UB7 .120 A6
Harmondsworth La,
West Dr. UB7 .120 B6
Harmondsworth Rd,
West Dr. UB7 .120 B5
Harmony Cl, NW11 .72 B5
Harmony Pl, SE1 .37 G3
Harmony Ter, Har. HA2
off Goldsmith Cl .85 H1
Harmony Way, NW4
off Victoria Rd .71 J4
Harmood Gro, NW1
off Clarence Way .92 B7
Harmood Pl, NW1
off Harmood St .92 B7
Harmood St, NW1 .92 B7
Harmsworth Ms, SE11 .27 G6
Harmsworth St, SE17 .35 G4
Harmsworth Way, N20 .56 C1
Harold Av, Belv. DA17 .139 F5
Hayes UB3 .121 J3
Harold Est, SE1 .28 E6
Harold Gibbons Ct, SE7 .135 J6
Harold Laski Ho, EC1 .11 G4
Harold Pl, SE11
off Kennington La .34 E4
Harold Rd, E4 .62 C4
E11 .96 E1
E13 .115 H1
N8 .75 F5
N15 .76 C5
NW10 .106 D3
SE19 .170 B6
Sutton SM1 .199 G4
Woodford Green IG8 .79 G1
Haroldstone Rd, E17 .77 G5
Harp All, EC4 .19 G3
Harpenden Rd, E12 .97 J2
SE27 .169 H3
Harpenmead Pt, NW2 .90 C2
Harper Cl, N14
off Alexandra Ct .42 C5
Harper Ms, SW17 .167 F3
Harper Rd, E6 .116 C6
SE1 .27 J5
Harpers Yd, N17
off Ruskin Rd .76 C1
Harp Island Cl, NW10 .88 D2
Harp La, EC3 .20 D6
Harpley Sq, E1 .113 F3
Harpour Rd, Bark. IG11 .99 F6
Harp Rd, W7 .104 C4
Harpsden St, SW11
off Battersea Pk Rd .150 A1
Harpur Ms, WC1 .18 C1
Harpur St, WC1 .18 C1
Harraden Rd, SE3 .155 J1
Harrap St, E14 .114 C7
Harrier Av, E11
off Eastern Av .79 H6
Harrier Ms, SE28 .137 G3
Harrier Rd, NW9 .71 E2
Harriers Cl, W5 .105 H7
Harrier Way, E6 .116 C4
Harries Rd, Hayes UB4 .102 C4
Harriet Cl, E8 .112 D1
Harriet Gdns, Croy. CR0 .202 D2
Harriet St, SW1 .24 A4
Harriet Tubman Cl, SW2 .151 G7
Harriet Wk, SW1 .24 A4
HARRINGAY, N8 .75 G5
Harringay Gdns, N8 .75 H4
Harringay Rd, N15 .75 H5
Harrington Cl, NW10 .88 D3
Croydon CR0 .200 E2
Harrington Ct, W10
off Dart St .108 C3
Croydon CR0
off Altyre Rd .202 A2
Harrington Gdns, SW7 .30 B2
Harrington Hill, E5 .95 E1
Harrington Ho, NW1 .9 F3
Harrington Rd, E11 .97 E1
SE25 .188 D4
SW7 .30 E1
Harrington Sq, NW1 .9 F2
Harrington St, NW1 .9 F3
Harrington Way, SE18 .136 A3
Harriott Cl, SE10 .135 F4
Harris Cl, Enf. EN2 .43 H1
Hounslow TW3 .143 G1
Harrison Cl, N20 .57 H1
Harrison Dr, Brom. BR1 .192 E4
Harrison Rd, Dag. RM10 .101 H6
Harrisons Ri, Croy. CR0 .201 H3
Harrison St, WC1 .10 B4
Harris Rd, Bexh. DA7 .159 E1
Dagenham RM9 .101 F5
Harris St, E17 .77 J7
SE5 .132 A7
★ Harrods, SW1 .23 J5
Harrogate Rd, Wat. WD19 .50 C3
Harrold Rd, Dag. RM8 .100 B5
HARROW, HA1 - HA3 .68 A7
★ Harrow Arts Cen, Pnr.
HA5 .51 H7
Harrow Av, Enf. EN1 .44 C6
Harroway Rd, SW11 .149 G2
Harrowby St, W1 .15 H3
Harrow Cl, Chess. KT9 .195 G7
Harrowdene Cl, Wem.
HA0 .87 G4
Harrowdene Gdns, Tedd.
TW11 .162 D6
Harrowdene Rd, Wem.
HA0 .87 G3
Harrow Dr, N9 .60 C1
Harrowes Meade, Edg.
HA8 .54 A3
Harrow Flds Gdns, Har.
HA1 .86 B3
Harrowgate Rd, E9 .95 H6
Harrow Grn, E11 .96 E3
Harrow La, E14 .114 C7
Harrow Manorway, SE2 .138 C1
★ Harrow Mus, Har.
HA2 .67 J3
HARROW ON THE HILL,
Har. HA1 .86 B2
Harrow Pk, Har. HA1 .86 B2
Harrow Pas, Kings.T. KT1
off Market Pl .181 G2
Harrow Pl, E1 .21 E3
Harrow Rd, E6 .116 B1
E11 .97 E3
NW10 .107 H3
W2 .14 A2
W9 .108 C4
W10 .108 A4
Barking IG11 .117 H1
Harrow Rd, Carshalton
SM5 .199 H5
Ilford IG1 .99 F4
Wembley HA0 .87 F5
Wembley (Tkgtn) HA9 .87 J5
★ Harrow Sch, Har. HA1 .86 B1
Harrow Vw, Har. HA1,
HA2 .68 A4
Hayes UB3 .102 A6
Harrow Vw Rd, W5 .105 E4
Harrow Way, Wat. WD19 .50 E3
HARROW WEALD, Har.
HA3 .68 A1
Harrow Weald Pk, Har.
HA3 .52 A6
Hart Cres, Chig. IG7 .65 J5
Harte Rd, Houns. TW3 .143 F2
Hartfield Av, Borwd. (Els.)
WD6 .38 A5
Northolt UB5 .102 B2
Hartfield Cl, Borwd. (Els.)
WD6 .38 A5
Hartfield Cres, SW19 .166 C7
West Wickham BR4 .205 G3
Hartfield Gro, SE20 .189 E1
Hartfield Rd, SW19 .166 C7
Chessington KT9 .195 G5
West Wickham BR4 .205 G4
Hartfield Ter, E3 .114 A2
Hartford Av, Har. HA3 .68 D3
Hartforde Rd, Borwd.
WD6 .38 A2
Hartford Rd, Bex. DA5 .159 G6
Epsom KT19 .196 A6
Hart Gro, W5 .126 A1
Southall UB1 .103 G5
Hartham Cl, N7 .93 E5
Isleworth TW7 .144 D1
Hartham Rd, N7 .92 E5
N17 .76 C2
Isleworth TW7 .144 C1
Harting Rd, SE9 .174 B4
Hartington Cl, Har. HA1 .86 B4
Orpington (Farnboro.)
BR6 .207 F5
Hartington Ct, W4 .126 B7
Hartington Rd, E16 .115 H6
E17 .77 H6
SW8 .150 E1
W4 .126 B7
W13 .105 E7
Southall UB2 .122 E3
Twickenham TW1 .144 E7
Hartismere Rd, SW6 .128 C7
Hartlake Rd, E9 .95 G6
Hartland Cl, N21
off Elmscott Gdns .43 J6
Edgware HA8 .54 A2
Hartland Dr, Edg. HA8 .54 A2
Ruislip HA4 .84 B3
Hartland Rd, E15 .97 F7
N11 .57 J5
NW1 .92 B7
NW6 .108 C2
Hampton (Hmptn H.)
TW12 .161 H4
Isleworth TW7 .144 D3
Morden SM4 .184 D7
Hartlands Cl, Bex. DA5 .159 F6
Hartland Way, Croy. CR0 .203 H2
Morden SM4 .184 C7
Hartlepool Ct, E16
off Fishguard Way .137 E1
Hartley Av, E6 .116 B1
NW7 .55 F5
Hartley Cl, NW7 .55 F5
Bromley BR1 .192 C2
Hartley Ho, SE1
off Longfield Est .37 G1
Hartley Rd, E11 .97 F1
Croydon CR0 .187 H7
Welling DA16 .138 C7
Hartley St, E2 .113 F3
Hartmann Rd, E16 .136 B1
Hartnoll St, N7
off Eden Gro .93 F5
Harton Cl, Brom. BR1 .192 A1
Harton Rd, N9 .61 E2
Harton St, SE8 .154 A1
Hartopp Pt, SW6
off Pellant Rd .128 B7
Hartsbourne Av, Bushey
(Bushey Hth) WD23 .51 J2
Hartsbourne Cl, Bushey
(Bushey Hth) WD23 .52 A2
Hartsbourne Rd, Bushey
(Bushey Hth) WD23 .52 A2
Harts Gro, Wdf.Grn. IG8 .63 G5
Hartshorn All, EC3 .21 E4
Hartshorn Gdns, E6 .116 D4
Harts La, SE14 .133 H7
Barking IG11 .98 E6
Hartslock Dr, SE2 .138 D2
Hartsmead Rd, SE9 .174 C2
Hart Sq, Mord. SM4 .184 D6
Hart St, EC3 .20 E5
Hartsway, Enf. EN3 .45 F4
Hartswood Gdns, W12 .127 F3
Hartswood Grn, Bushey
(Bushey Hth) WD23 .52 A2
Hartswood Rd, W12 .127 F2
Hartsworth Cl, E13 .115 F2
Hartville Rd, SE18 .137 H4
Hartwell Cl, SW2
off Challice Way .169 F1
Hartwell Dr, E4 .62 C6
Hartwell St, E8
off Dalston La .94 C6
Harvard Hill, W4 .126 B6
Harvard La, W4 .126 B5
Harvard Rd, SE13 .154 C5
W4 .126 B5
Isleworth TW7 .144 B1
Harvel Cres, SE2 .138 D5
Harvest Bk Rd, W.Wick.
BR4 .205 F3
Harvesters Cl, Islw. TW7 .144 A5
Harvest La, Loug. IG10 .48 A7
Thames Ditton KT7 .180 D6
Harvest Rd, Felt. TW13 .160 A4
Harvey Dr, Hmptn. TW12 .179 H1
Harvey Gdns, E11
off Harvey Rd .97 F1
SE7 .135 J5
Loughton IG10 .49 E3
Harvey Ho, Brent. TW8
off Green Dragon La .125 H5
Harvey Rd, E11 .97 E1
N8 .75 F5
SE5 .152 A1
Hounslow TW4 .143 F7
Ilford IG1 .99 E5
Northolt UB5 .84 C7
Walton-on-Thames
KT12 .178 A7
Harvey St, N1 .112 A1
Harvill Rd, Sid. DA14 .176 D5
Harvington Wk, E8
off Wilman Gro .94 D7
Harvist Est, N7 .93 F4
Harvist Rd, NW6 .108 A3
Harwater Dr, Loug. IG10 .48 C2
Harwell Pas, N2 .73 J4
Harwood Av, Brom. BR1 .191 H2
Mitcham CR4 .185 H3
Harwood Cl, N12 .57 H6
Wembley HA0 .87 G3
Harwood Rd, SW6 .128 D7
Harwoods Yd, N21
off Wades Hill .43 G7
Harwood Ter, SW6 .148 E1
Hascombe Ter, SE5
off Love Wk .152 A2
Haselbury Rd, N9 .60 B4
N18 .60 B4
Haseley End, SE23
off Tyson Rd .153 F7
Haselrigge Rd, SW4 .150 D4
Haseltine Rd, SE26 .171 J4
Haselwood Dr, Enf. EN2 .43 H4
Haskard Rd, Dag. RM9 .100 D4
Hasker St, SW3 .31 H1
Haslam Av, Sutt. SM3 .198 B1
Haslam Cl, N1 .93 G7
Haslam Ct, N11
off Waterfall Rd .58 B4
Haslam St, SE15 .132 C7
Haslemere Av, NW4 .72 A6
SW18 .166 E2
W7 .124 D3
W13 .124 D3
Barnet EN4 .57 J1
Hounslow TW5 .142 C2
Mitcham CR4 .185 G2
Haslemere Business Cen,
Enf. EN1 .44 E5
Haslemere Cl, Hmptn.
TW12 .161 F5
Wallington SM6 .201 E5
Haslemere Gdns, N3 .72 C3
Haslemere Heathrow Est,
Houns. TW4 .142 B2
Haslemere Ind Est,
SW18 .167 E2
Haslemere Rd, N8 .74 D7
N21 .59 H2
Bexleyheath DA7 .159 F2
Ilford IG3 .99 J2
Thornton Heath CR7 .187 H5
Hasler Cl, SE28 .118 B7
Hasluck Gdns, Barn.
(New Barn.) EN5 .41 F6
Hassard St, E2 .13 G2
Hassendean Rd, SE3 .135 H6
Hassett Rd, E9 .95 G6
Hassocks Cl, SE26 .171 E3

Hassocks Rd, SW16 **186** D1
Hassock Wd, Kes. BR2 **206** A4
Hassop Rd, NW2 **90** A4
Hassop Wk, SE9 **174** B4
Hasted Rd, SE7 **136** A5
Hastings Av, Ilf. IG6 **81** F4
Hastings Cl, SE15 **132** D7
Barnet EN5 **41** F4
Wembley HA0 **87** F4
Hastings Dr, Surb. KT6 **181** F6
Hastings Ho, SE18 **136** C4
Hastings Pl, Croy. CR0 *off Hastings Rd* **202** C1
Hastings Rd, N11 **58** C5
N17 **76** A3
W13 **104** E7
Bromley BR2 **206** B1
Croydon CR0 **202** C1
Hastings St, SE18 **137** F3
WC1 **10** A4
Hastingwood Trd Est, N18 **61** G6
Hastoe Cl, Hayes UB4 **102** E4
Hasty Cl, Mitch. CR4 *off Slade Way* **186** A1
Hat & Mitre Ct, EC1 **11** H6
Hatch, The, Enf. EN3 **45** G1
Hatcham Ms Business Cen, SE14 *off Hatcham Pk Rd* **153** G1
Hatcham Pk Ms, SE14 *off Hatcham Pk Rd* **153** G1
Hatcham Pk Rd, SE14 **153** G1
Hatcham Rd, SE15 **133** F6
Hatchard Rd, N19 **92** D2
Hatchcroft, NW4 **71** H3
HATCH END, Pnr. HA5 **50** E7
Hatchers Ms, SE1 **28** E4
Hatch Gro, Rom. RM6 **83** E4
Hatch La, E4 **62** D4
West Drayton (Harm.) UB7 **120** A7
Hatch Pl, Kings.T. KT2 **163** J5
Hatch Rd, SW16 **187** E2
Hatch Side, Chig. IG7 **64** D5
Hatchwood Cl, Wdf.Grn. IG8 *off Sunset Av* **63** F4
Hatcliffe Cl, SE3 **155** F3
Hatcliffe St, SE10 **135** F5
Hatfeild Cl, Mitch. CR4 **185** G4
Hatfeild Mead, Mord. SM4 **184** D5
Hatfield Cl, SE14 *off Reaston St* **133** G7
Ilford IG6 **81** E3
Hatfield Ms, Dag. RM9 **101** E7
Hatfield Rd, E15 **97** E5
W4 **126** D2
W13 **124** D1
Dagenham RM9 **101** E6
Hatfields, SE1 **27** F1
Loughton IG10 **48** E3
Hathaway Cl, Brom. BR2 **206** C1
Ilford IG6 **65** E6
Stanmore HA7 **52** D5
Hathaway Cres, E12 **98** C6
Hathaway Gdns, W13 **104** C5
Romford RM6 **82** D5
Hathaway Rd, Croy. CR0 **187** H7
Hatherleigh Cl, NW7 **56** A7
Chessington KT9 **195** G5
Morden SM4 **184** D4
Hatherleigh Rd, Ruis. HA4 **84** A2
Hatherley Cres, Sid. DA14 **176** A2
Hatherley Gdns, E6 **116** A2
N8 **74** E6
Hatherley Gro, W2 **14** A3
Hatherley Ms, E17 **78** A4
Hatherley Rd, E17 **77** J4
Richmond TW9 **145** J1
Sidcup DA14 **176** A4
Hatherley St, SW1 **33** G2
Hathern Gdns, SE9 **174** D4
Hatherop Rd, Hmptn. TW12 **161** F7
Hathersage Ct, N1 *off Newington Grn* **94** A5
Hathorne Cl, SE15 **153** E2
Hathway St, SE15 *off Gibbon Rd* **153** F2
Hathway Ter, SE14 *off Gibbon Rd* **153** G2
Hatley Av, Ilf. IG6 **81** F4
Hatley Cl, N11 **57** J5
Hatley Rd, N4 **93** F2
Hatteraick St, SE16 *off Brunel Rd* **133** F2
Hattersfield Cl, Belv. DA17 **139** F4
HATTON, Felt. TW14 **141** J4
Hatton Cl, SE18 **137** G7
Hatton Cross, Felt. TW14 *off Great South-West Rd* **141** J4
Hatton Cross Rbt, Houns. TW6 *off Southern Perimeter Rd* **141** J3
Hatton Gdn, EC1 **19** F1
Hatton Gdns, Mitch. CR4 **185** J5
Hatton Grn, Felt. TW14 **142** A4
Hatton Gro, West Dr. UB7 **120** A2
Hatton Ho, E1 **21** J5
Hatton Pl, EC1 **11** F6
Hatton Rd, Croy. CR0 **201** G1
Feltham TW14 **141** H5
Hatton Row, NW8 **7** F6
Hatton St, NW8 **7** F6
Hatton Wk, Enf. EN2 *off London Rd* **44** A4
Hatton Wall, EC1 **19** E1
Haul Rd, NW1 **10** A1
Haunch of Venison Yd, W1 **16** D4
Hauteville Ct Gdns, W6 *off Stamford Brook Av* **127** F3
Havana Rd, SW19 **166** D2
Havannah St, E14 **134** A2
Havant Rd, E17 **78** C3
Havelock Cl, W12 *off India Way* **107** H7
Havelock Pl, Har. HA1 **68** B6
Havelock Rd, N17 **76** D2
SW19 **167** F5
Belvedere DA17 **139** F4
Bromley BR2 **191** J4
Croydon CR0 **202** C1
Harrow HA3 **68** B3
Southall UB2 **123** F3
Havelock St, N1 **111** E1
Ilford IG1 **99** E2
Havelock Ter, SW8 **130** B7
Havelock Wk, SE23 **171** F1
Haven, The, SE26 **171** E5
Richmond TW9 **146** A3
Sunbury-on-Thames TW16 **160** A7
Haven Cl, SE9 **174** C3
SW19 **166** A3
Esher KT10 **194** B2
Sidcup DA14 **176** C6
Haven Ct, Esher KT10 *off Portsmouth Rd* **194** B2
Haven Grn, W5 **105** G6
Haven Grn Ct, W5 **105** G6
Havenhurst Ri, Enf. EN2 **43** G2
Haven La, W5 **105** H6
Haven Ms, N1 *off Liverpool Rd* **93** G7
Haven Pl, W5 **105** G7
Esher KT10 **194** B2
Haven St, NW1 *off Castlehaven Rd* **92** B7
Havenwood, Wem. HA9 **88** B3
Haverfield Gdns, Rich. TW9 **126** A7
Haverfield Rd, E3 **113** H3
Haverford Way, Edg. HA8 **69** J1
Haverhill Rd, E4 **62** C1
SW12 **168** C1
Havering Gdns, Rom. RM6 **82** C5
Havering St, E1 *off Devonport St* **113** G6
Havering Way, Bark. IG11 **118** B3
Haversfield Est, Brent. TW8 **125** H5
Haversham Cl, Twick. TW1 **145** G6
Haversham Pl, N6 **91** J2
Haverstock Hill, NW3 **91** H5
Haverstock Pl, N1 *off Haverstock St* **11** H3
Haverstock Rd, NW5 **92** A5
Haverstock St, N1 **11** H2
Haverthwaite Rd, Orp. BR6 **207** G2
Havil St, SE5 **132** B7
Havisham Pl, SE19 **169** H6
Hawarden Gro, SE24 **151** J7
Hawarden Hill, NW2 **89** G3
Hawarden Rd, E17 **77** G4
Hawbridge Rd, E11 **96** D1
Hawes La, W.Wick. BR4 **204** C1
Hawes Rd, N18 **60** E6
Bromley BR1 **191** H1
Hawes St, N1 **93** H7
Haweswater Ho, Islw. TW7 *off Summerwood Rd* **144** C5
Hawgood St, E3 **114** A5
Hawkdene, E4 **46** B6
Hawke Pk Rd, N22 **75** H3
Hawke Pl, SE16 *off Middleton Dr* **133** G2
Hawke Rd, SE19 **170** B6
Hawker Pl, E17 **78** C2
Hawkesbury Rd, SW15 **147** H5
Hawkesfield Rd, SE23 **171** H2
Hawkesley Cl, Twick. TW1 **162** D4
Hawkes Rd, Felt. TW14 **142** A7
Mitcham CR4 **185** H1
Hawke Twr, SE14 *off Nynehead St* **133** H6
Hawkewood Rd, Sun. TW16 **178** A3
Hawkhurst Gdns, Chess. KT9 **195** H4
Hawkhurst Rd, SW16 **186** D1
Hawkhurst Way, N.Mal. KT3 **182** D5
West Wickham BR4 **204** B2
Hawkins Cl, NW7 *off Hale La* **54** D5
Borehamwood WD6 *off Banks Rd* **38** C2
Harrow HA1 **68** A7
Hawkins Rd, NW10 **88** E7
Teddington TW11 **163** E6
Hawkins Ter, SE7 **136** B5
Hawkins Way, SE6 **172** A5
Hawkley Gdns, SE27 **169** H2
Hawkridge, NW5 *off Warden Rd* **92** A6
Hawkridge Cl, Rom. RM6 **82** C7
Hawksbrook La, Beck. BR3 **190** B6
Hawkshaw Cl, SW2 *off Tierney Rd* **150** E7
Hawkshead, NW1 **9** F3
Hawkshead Cl, Brom. BR1 **173** E7
Hawkshead Rd, NW10 **89** F7
W4 **126** E2
Hawkslade Rd, SE15 **153** G5
Hawksley Rd, N16 **94** B3
Hawks Ms, SE10 *off Luton Pl* **134** C7
Hawksmoor Cl, E6 *off Allhallows Rd* **116** B6
SE18 **137** H5
Hawksmoor Ms, E1 *off Cable St* **112** E7
Hawksmoor St, W6 **128** A6
Hawksmouth, E4 **46** B7
Hawks Rd, Kings.T. KT1 **181** J2
Hawkstone Est, SE16 **133** F4
Hawkstone Rd, SE16 **133** F4
Hawk Ter, Ilf. IG5 *off Tiptree Cres* **80** D3
Hawkwell Ct, E4 *off Colvin Gdns* **62** C3
Hawkwell Ho, Dag. RM8 **101** G1
Hawkwell Wk, N1 *off Basire St* **111** J1
Hawkwood Cres, E4 **46** B6
Hawkwood La, Chis. BR7 **193** F1
Hawkwood Mt, E5 **95** E1
Hawlands Dr, Pnr. HA5 **66** E7
Hawley Cl, Hmptn. TW12 **161** F6
Hawley Cres, NW1 **92** B7
Hawley Ms, NW1 *off Hawley St* **92** B7
Hawley Rd, N18 **61** G5
NW1 **92** B7
Hawley St, NW1 **92** B7
Hawstead Rd, SE6 **154** B6
Hawsted, Buck.H. IG9 **47** H7
Hawthorn Av, E3 **113** J1
N13 **59** E5
Richmond (Kew) TW9 **145** H2
Thornton Heath CR7 **187** H1
Hawthorn Cen, The, Har. HA1 **68** C4
Hawthorn Cl, Hmptn. TW12 **161** G5
Hounslow TW5 **122** B7
Orpington BR5 **193** G6
Hawthorn Cres, SW17 **168** A5
Hawthornden Cl, N12 *off Fallowfields Dr* **57** H6
Hawthorndene Cl, Brom. BR2 **205** F2
Hawthorndene Rd, Brom. BR2 **205** F2
Hawthorn Dr, Har. HA2 **67** F6
West Wickham BR4 **205** E4
Hawthorne Av, Cars. SM5 **200** A7
Harrow HA3 **68** D6
Mitcham CR4 **185** G2
Ruislip HA4 **66** B6
Hawthorne Cl, N1 **94** B6
Bromley BR1 **192** C3
Sutton SM1 *off Aultone Way* **199** F2
Hawthorne Ct, Nthwd. HA6 *off Ryefield Cres* **66** A2
Hawthorne Cres, West Dr. UB7 **120** C2
Hawthorne Fm Av, Nthlt. UB5 **103** E1
Hawthorne Gro, NW9 **70** C7
Hawthorne Ms, Grnf. UB6 *off Greenford Rd* **103** J6
Hawthorne Rd, E17 **78** A3
Bromley BR1 **192** B3
Hawthorne Way, N9 **60** B2
Staines (Stanw.) TW19 **140** A7
Hawthorn Gdns, W5 **125** G3
Hawthorn Gro, SE20 **171** E7
Barnet EN5 **39** F6
Hawthorn Hatch, Brent. TW8 **125** E7
Hawthorn Ms, NW7 *off Holders Hill Rd* **72** B1
Hawthorn Pl, Erith DA8 **139** J5
Hawthorn Rd, N8 **74** D3
N18 **60** C6
NW10 **89** G7
Bexleyheath DA6 **159** F4
Brentford TW8 **125** E7
Buckhurst Hill IG9 **64** A4
Feltham TW13 **160** A1
Sutton SM1 **199** H6
Wallington SM6 **200** B7
Hawthorns, Wdf.Grn. IG8 **63** G3
Hawthorns, The, Epsom KT17 *off Kingston Rd* **197** F6
Loughton IG10 **48** D4
Hawthorn Wk, W10 *off Fifth Av* **108** B4
Hawtrey Av, Nthlt. UB5 **102** D2
Hawtrey Dr, Ruis. HA4 **66** A7
Hawtrey Rd, NW3 **91** H7
Haxted Rd, Brom. BR1 *off North Rd* **191** H1
Hay Cl, E15 **97** E7
Borehamwood WD6 **38** C2
Haycroft Gdns, NW10 **107** G1
Haycroft Rd, SW2 **151** E5
Surbiton KT6 **195** H3
Hay Currie St, E14 **114** B6
Hayday Rd, E16 **115** G5
Haydens Pl, W11 *off Portobello Rd* **108** C6
Hayden Way, Rom. RM5 **83** J2
Haydns Ms, W3 **106** C6
Haydock Av, Nthlt. UB5 **85** G6
Haydock Grn, Nthlt. UB5 *off Haydock Av* **85** G6
Haydon Cl, NW9 **70** C4
Enfield EN1 *off Mortimer Dr* **44** B6
Haydon Dr, Pnr. HA5 **66** A4
Haydon Pk Rd, SW19 **166** E5
Haydon Rd, Dag. RM8 **100** C2
Haydons Rd, SW19 **167** E5
Haydon St, EC3 **21** F5
Haydon Wk, E1 **21** G4
Haydon Way, SW11 **149** G4
HAYES, Brom. BR2 **205** G2
Hayes Bypass, Hayes UB3, UB4 **102** D4
Hayes Chase, W.Wick. BR4 **190** E5
Hayes Cl, Brom. BR2 **205** G2
Hayes Ct, SW2 **168** E1
Hayes Cres, NW11 **72** C5
Sutton SM3 **198** A4
Hayesend Ho, SW17 *off Blackshaw Rd* **167** F4
Hayesford Pk Dr, Brom. BR2 **191** F5
Hayes Gdn, Brom. BR2 **205** G2
Hayes Gro, SE22 **152** C4
Hayes Hill, Brom. BR2 **204** E1
Hayes Hill Rd, Brom. BR2 **205** F1
Hayes La, Beck. BR3 **190** C3
Bromley BR2 **191** G5
Hayes Mead Rd, Brom. BR2 **205** E1
Hayes Metro Cen, Hayes UB4 **102** C7
Hayes Pl, NW1 **7** H6
Hayes Rd, Brom. BR2 **191** G4
Southall UB2 **122** B4
Hayes St, Brom. BR2 **205** H1
HAYES TOWN, Hayes UB3 **121** H2
Hayes Way, Beck. BR3 **190** C4
Hayes Wd Av, Brom. BR2 **205** H1
Hayfield Pas, E1 *off Stepney Grn* **113** F4
Hayfield Yd, E1 *off Mile End Rd* **113** F4
Haygarth Pl, SW19 **166** A5
Haygreen Cl, Kings.T. KT2 **164** B6
Hay Hill, W1 **17** E6
Hayland Cl, NW9 **70** D4
Hay La, NW9 **70** D4
Hayles St, SE11 **35** G1

Haylett Gdns, Kings.T. KT1
  off Anglesea Rd 181 G4
Hayling Av, Felt. TW13 ...160 A3
Hayling Cl, N16
  off Boleyn Rd 94 B5
Hayling Rd, Wat. WD19 ...50 B2
Hayman St, N1
  off Hawes St 93 H7
Haymarket, SW1 ....17 H6
Haymarket Arc, SW1 .....17 H6
Haymer Gdns, Wor.Pk.
  KT4 ....197 G3
Haymerle Rd, SE15 ......37 H6
Haymill Cl, Grnf. (Perivale)
  UB6 ....104 C3
Hayne Rd, Beck. BR3 ...189 J2
Haynes Cl, N11 ....58 A3
  N17 ....60 E7
  SE3 ....155 E3
Haynes Dr, N9 ....60 E3
Haynes La, SE19 ......170 B6
Haynes Rd, Wem. HA0 ...87 H7
Hayne St, EC1 ....19 H1
Haynt Wk, SW20 ......184 B3
★ Hay's Galleria, SE1 ....28 D1
Hay's La, SE1 ....28 D2
Haysleigh Gdns, SE20 ..188 D2
Hay's Ms, W1 ....16 D6
Hay St, E2 ....112 D1
Hayter Ct, E11 ....97 H2
Hayter Rd, SW2 ......151 E5
Hayton Cl, E8
  off Buttermere Wk ...94 C6
Hayward Cl, SW19 ....185 E1
★ Hayward Gall, SE1 ....26 D1
Hayward Gdns, SW15 ...147 J6
Hayward Rd, N20 ....57 F2
  Thames Ditton KT7 ..194 D1
Haywards Cl, Rom.
  (Chad.Hth) RM6 ......82 B5
Hayward's Pl, EC1 ......11 G6
Haywood Cl, Pnr. HA5 ...66 D2
Haywood Ri, Orp. BR6 ..207 H4
Haywood Rd, Brom. BR2 192 A4
Hazel Av, West Dr. UB7 ..120 D3
Hazelbank, Surb. KT5 ...196 C1
Hazelbank Rd, SE6 .....172 D2
Hazelbourne Rd, SW12 ..150 B6
Hazelbrouck Gdns, Ilf. IG6 65 G7
Hazelbury Cl, SW19 ....184 D2
Hazelbury Grn, N9 ......60 A3
Hazelbury La, N9 ....60 B3
Hazel Cl, N13 ....60 A3
  N19 off Hargrave Rd ..92 C2
  NW9 ....71 E2
  SE15 ....152 D2
  Brentford TW8 ....125 E7
  Croydon CR0 ....189 G7
  Mitcham CR4 ....186 D4
  Twickenham TW2 ....143 J7
Hazelcroft, Pnr. HA5 ....51 G6
Hazeldean Rd, NW10 ....88 D7
Hazeldene Dr, Pnr. HA5 ..66 C3
Hazeldene Rd, Ilf. IG3 ...100 B2
  Welling DA16 ....158 C2
Hazeldon Rd, SE4 .....153 H5
Hazeleigh Gdns, Wdf.Grn.
  IG8 ....64 B5
Hazel Gdns, Edg. HA8 ...54 B4
Hazelgreen Cl, N21 .....59 H1
Hazel Gro, SE26 ......171 G4
  Enfield EN1
  off Dimsdale Dr 44 D6
  Feltham TW13 ....160 A1
  Orpington BR6 ......206 E2
  Romford RM6 ....82 E3
  Wembley HA0
  off Carlyon Rd 105 H1
Hazel Gro Est, SE26 ...171 G4
Hazel Ho, NW3
  off Maitland Pk Rd ...91 J6
Hazelhurst, Beck. BR3 ..190 D1
Hazelhurst Rd, SW17 ...167 F4
Hazel La, Ilf. IG6 ....64 E7
  Richmond TW10 .....163 H2
Hazell Cres, Rom. RM5 ...83 H1
Hazellville Rd, N19 .....74 D7
Hazel Mead, Barn. EN5 ...39 H5
Hazelmere Cl, Felt. TW14 .141 G6
  Northolt UB5 ....103 F2
Hazelmere Dr, Nthlt. UB5 .103 F2
Hazelmere Rd, NW6 ....108 D1
  Northolt UB5 ....103 F2
  Orpington BR5 ......193 F4
Hazelmere Wk, Nthlt.
  UB5 ....103 F2
Hazelmere Way, Brom.
  BR2 ....191 G6
Hazel Ms, N8
  off Alexandra Rd 75 G3
Hazel Rd, E15
  off Burgess Rd 96 E5
  NW10 ....107 J3

Hazeltree La, Nthlt. UB5 .103 E3
Hazel Wk, Brom. BR2 ...192 D6
Hazel Way, E4 ....61 J6
  SE1 ....37 F1
Hazelwood, Loug. IG10 ...48 A5
Hazelwood Av, Mord.
  SM4 ....185 E4
Hazelwood Cl, W5 .....125 H2
  Harrow HA2 ....67 H4
Hazelwood Ct, NW10
  off Neasden La N 88 E3
Hazelwood Cres, N13 ...59 G4
Hazelwood Cft, Surb.
  KT6 ....181 H6
Hazelwood Dr, Pnr. HA5 ..66 B2
Hazelwood La, N13 .....59 G4
Hazelwood Pk Cl, Chig.
  IG7 ....65 H5
Hazelwood Rd, E17 .....77 H5
  Enfield EN1 ....44 C6
Hazlebury Rd, SW6 ....148 E2
Hazledean Rd, Croy. CR0 .202 A2
Hazledene Rd, W4 .....126 C6
Hazlemere Gdns, Wor.Pk.
  KT4 ....197 H1
Hazlewell Rd, SW15 ...147 H5
Hazlewood Cl, E5 ....95 H3
Hazlewood Cres, W10 ..108 B4
Hazlewood Twr, W10
  off Golborne Rd 108 C4
Hazlitt Cl, Felt. TW13 ...161 E4
Hazlitt Ms, W14
  off Hazlitt Rd 128 B3
Hazlitt Rd, W14 ....128 B3
Headcorn Pl, Th.Hth. CR7
  off Headcorn Rd 187 F4
Headcorn Rd, N17 ......60 C7
  Bromley BR1 ....173 F5
  Thornton Heath CR7 .187 F4
Headfort Pl, SW1 ....24 C4
Headingley Cl, Ilf. IG6 ...65 J6
Headington Rd, SW18 ..167 F1
Headlam Rd, SW4 .....150 D6
Headlam St, E1 ....113 E4
Headley App, Ilf. IG2 ....80 D5
Headley Av, Wall. SM6 ..201 F5
Headley Cl, Epsom KT19 .196 A6
Headley Ct, SE26 ......171 E5
Headley Dr, Croy.
  (New Adgtn) CR0 ....204 B7
  Ilford IG2 ....80 E6
Head's Ms, W11
  off Westbourne Gro .108 D6
HEADSTONE, Har. HA2 ...67 J4
Headstone Dr, Har. HA1,
  HA3 ....68 B3
Headstone Gdns, Har.
  HA2 ....67 J4
Headstone La, Har. HA2,
  HA3 ....67 H4
Headstone Rd, Har. HA1 ..68 B5
Head St, E1 ....113 G6
Headway Cl, Rich. TW10
  off Locksmeade Rd ..163 F4
Heald St, SE14 ....153 J1
Healey St, NW1 ....92 B6
Healy Dr, Orp. BR6 ....207 J4
Heanor Ct, E5
  off Pedro St 95 G4
Hearne Rd, W4 ....126 A6
Hearn Ri, Nthlt. UB5 ...102 D1
Hearn's Bldgs, SE17 ....36 C2
Hearnshaw St, E14 ....113 H5
Hearn St, EC2 ....12 E6
Hearnville Rd, SW12 ..168 A1
Heath, The, W7
  off Lower Boston Rd .124 B1
Heatham Pk, Twick. TW2 .144 C7
Heath Av, Bexh. DA7 ..138 D6
Heathbourne Rd, Bushey
  (Bushey Hth) WD23 ..52 B2
  Stanmore HA7 ....52 B2
Heath Brow, NW3
  off North End Way ...91 F3
Heath Cl, NW11 ....72 E7
  W5 ....105 J4
  Hayes (Harling.) UB3 .121 G7
  South Croydon CR2 .201 H6
Heathcock Ct, WC2
  off Exchange Ct 18 B6
Heathcote Av, Ilf. IG5 ...80 C2
Heathcote Ct, Ilf. IG5
  off Heathcote Av 80 C2
Heathcote Gro, E4 ......62 C3
Heathcote Pt, E9
  off Wick Rd 95 G6
Heathcote St, WC1 .....10 C5
Heathcote Way, West Dr.
  UB7 off Tavistock Rd .120 A1
Heath Ct, SE9 ....175 F1
  Hounslow TW4 ......143 F4

Heathcroft, NW11 ....91 E1
  W5 ....105 J4
Heathcroft Gdns, E17 ...78 D1
Heathdale Av, Houns.
  TW4 ....143 E3
Heathdene Dr, Belv.
  DA17 ....139 H4
Heathedge Rd, SW16 ..169 F7
  Wallington SM6 .....200 B7
Heath Dr, NW3 ....90 E4
  SW20 ....183 J4
Heathedge, SE26 ......170 E2
Heathend Rd, Bex. 156 C2
  Chislehurst BR7 .....192 D2
Heather Cl, E6 ....116 E6
  N7 off Newington
   Barrow Way 93 F3
  SE13 ....154 D6
  SW8 ....150 B3
  Hampton TW12 .....179 F1
  Isleworth TW7
   off Harvesters Cl ...144 A5
Heatherdale Cl, Kings.T.
  KT2 ....164 A6
Heatherdene Cl, N12
  off Bow La 73 F1
  Mitcham CR4 ....185 H4
Heather Dr, Enf. EN2 ...43 H2
Heather Gdns, NW11 ...72 B6
  Sutton SM2 ....198 D6
Heatherlands, Sun. TW16 .160 A6
Heatherley Dr, Ilf. IG5 ...80 B3
Heather Pk Dr, Wem. HA0 .88 A7
Heather Rd, E4 ....61 J6
  NW2 ....89 F2
  SE12 ....173 G2
Heathers, The, Stai.
  TW19 ....140 C7
Heatherset Gdns, SW16 .169 F7
Heatherside Rd, Epsom
  KT19 ....196 D7
  Sidcup DA14
   off Wren Rd 176 C3
Heatherton Ter, N3 ....73 E2
Heather Wk, W10
  off Droop St 108 B4
  Edgware HA8 ....54 B5
  Twickenham TW2
   off Stephenson Rd .143 G7
Heather Way, Stan. HA7 ..52 C6
Heatherwood Cl, E12 ....97 J2
Heathfield, E4 ....62 C3
  Chislehurst BR7 .....175 F6
Heathfield Av, SW18
  off Heathfield Rd ...149 G7
Heathfield Cl, E16 .....116 A5
  Keston BR2 ....205 J5
Heathfield Dr, Mitch.
  CR4 ....185 H1
Heathfield Gdns, NW11 ..72 A6
  SE3 ....154 E2
  SW18 ....149 G6
  W4 ....126 C5
  Croydon CR0
   off Coombe Rd 201 J4
Heathfield La, Chis. BR7 .175 E6
Heathfield N, Twick. TW2 .144 C7
Heathfield Pk, NW2 .....89 J6
Heathfield Pk Dr, Rom.
  (Chad.Hth) RM6 ......82 B5
Heathfield Rd, SW18 ...149 F6
  W3 ....126 B2
  Bexleyheath DA6 ....159 F4
  Bromley BR1 ....173 F7
  Croydon CR0 ....202 A4
  Keston BR2 ....205 J5
Heathfields Ct, Houns. TW4
  off Heathlands Way .143 E5
Heathfield S, Twick. TW2 .144 C7
Heathfield Sq, SW18 ..149 G7
Heathfield St, W11
  off Portland Rd 108 B7
Heathfield Ter, SE18 ...137 J6
  W4 ....126 C5
Heath Gdns, Twick. TW1 .162 C1
Heathgate, NW11 ....72 E6
Heathgate Pl, NW3
  off Agincourt Rd 91 J5
Heath Gro, SE20
  off Maple Rd 171 F7
Heath Hurst Rd, NW3 ...91 H4
Heathland Rd, N16 .....94 B1
Heathlands Cl, Sun.
  TW16 ....178 A2
  Twickenham TW1 ....162 C2
Heathlands Way, Houns.
  TW4 ....143 E5
Heath La, SE3 ....154 D2
Heathlee Rd, SE3 ......155 F4
Heathley End, Chis. BR7 .175 F6
Heathmans Rd, SW6 ..148 C1
Heath Mead, SW19 ....166 A3
Heath Pk Dr, Brom. BR1 .192 B3

Heath Pas, NW3 ....91 E2
Heath Ri, SW15 ....148 A6
  Bromley BR2 ....191 F6
Heath Rd, SW8 ....150 B2
  Bexley DA5 ....177 J1
  Harrow HA1 ....67 J7
  Hounslow TW3 ......143 H4
  Romford RM6 ....82 D7
  Thornton Heath CR7 .187 J3
  Twickenham TW1, TW2 .162 C1
★ Heathrow Airport
   (London), Houns.
  TW6 ....140 E1
Heathrow Ho, Houns. TW5
  off Bath Rd 142 A1
Heathrow Interchange,
  Hayes UB4 ....122 C1
Heathrow Int Trd Est,
  Houns. TW4 ....142 B3
Heathrow Tunnel App,
  Houns. (Lon.Hthrw Air.)
  TW6 ....140 E1
Heathrow Vehicle Tunnel,
  Houns. (Lon.Hthrw Air.)
  TW6 ....140 E1
Heaths Cl, Enf. EN1 .....44 B2
Heath Side, NW3 ....91 G4
Heathside, Esher KT10 ..194 B3
  Hounslow TW4 ......143 F7
Heath Side, Orp. BR5 ..207 F1
Heathside Av, Bexh. DA7 .159 E1
Heathside Cl, Esher KT10 .194 B3
  Ilford IG2 ....81 G5
Heathstan Rd, W12 ....107 G6
Heath St, NW3 ....91 F3
Heath Vw, N2 ....73 F4
Heath Vw Cl, N2 ....73 F4
Heathview Ct, SW19 ...166 A2
Heathview Dr, SE2 ....138 D6
Heathview Gdns, SW15 .147 J7
Heathview Rd, Th.Hth.
  CR7 ....187 G4
Heath Vil, SE18 ....137 J5
  SW18 off Cargill Rd .167 F1
Heathville Rd, N19 .....74 E7
Heathwall St, SW11 ...149 J3
Heathway, SE3 ....135 F7
  Croydon CR0 ....203 J3
  Dagenham RM9,
   RM10 ....101 G7
Heath Way, Erith DA8 ..159 J1
Heathway, Wdf.Grn. IG8 ..63 J6
Heathway Ind Est, Dag.
  RM10 off Manchester
   Way 101 H4
Heathwood Gdns, SE7 ..136 B4
Heathwood Pt, SE23
  off Dacres Rd 171 G3
Heaton Cl, E4 ....62 C3
Heaton Rd, SE15 ......152 D3
  Mitcham CR4 ....168 A7
Heaven Tree Cl, N1 ....93 J5
Heaver Rd, SW11
  off Wye St 149 G3
Heavitree Cl, SE18 ....137 G5
Heavitree Rd, SE18 ...137 G5
Hebden Cl, E2
  off Laburnum St 112 C1
Hebden Ter, N17
  off Queen St 60 B6
Hebdon Rd, SW17 .....167 H3
Heber Rd, NW2 ....90 A5
  SE22 ....152 C6
Hebron Rd, W6 ....127 H3
Hecham Cl, E17 ....77 H2
Heckfield Pl, SW6
  off Fulham Rd 128 D7
Heckford St, E1
  off The Highway 113 G7
Hector Cl, N9 ....60 D2
Hector St, SE18 ....137 H4
Heddington Gro, N7 ....93 F5
Heddon Cl, Islw. TW7 ..144 D4
Heddon Ct Av, Barn. EN4 .41 J5
Heddon Ct Par, Barn. EN4
  off Cockfosters Rd ..42 A5
Heddon Rd, Barn.
  (Cockfos.) EN4 ......41 J5
Heddon St, W1 ....17 F5
Hedge Hill, Enf. EN2 ...43 H1
Hedge La, N13 ....59 H3
Hedgeley, Ilf. IG4 ......80 C4
Hedgemans Rd, Dag.
  RM9 ....100 D7
Hedgemans Way, Dag.
  RM9 ....100 E6
Hedgerley Gdns, Grnf.
  UB6 ....103 J2
Hedgerow La, Barn.
  (Arkley) EN5 ....39 H5
Hedgers Cl, Loug. IG10
  off Newmans La 48 D4
Hedgers Gro, E9 ....95 H6

Hedger St, SE11 ... 35 G1
Hedge Wk, SE6 ... 172 B5
Hedgewood Gdns, Ilf. IG5 ... 80 D4
Hedgley Ms, SE12 *off Hedgley St* ... 155 F5
Hedgley St, SE12 ... 155 F5
Hedingham Cl, N1 *off Popham Rd* ... 93 J7
Hedingham Ho, Kings.T. KT2 *off Kingsgate Rd* ... 181 H1
Hedingham Rd, Dag. RM8 ... 100 B5
Hedley Rd, Twick. TW2 ... 143 G7
Hedley Row, N5 *off Poets Rd* ... 94 A5
Heenan Cl, Bark. IG11 *off Glenny Rd* ... 99 F6
Heene Rd, Enf. EN2 ... 44 A1
Heidegger Cres, SW13 *off Wyatt Dr* ... 127 H7
Heigham Rd, E6 ... 98 A7
Heighton Gdns, Croy. CR0 ... 201 H5
Heights, The, SE7 ... 135 J5
Beckenham BR3 ... 172 C7
Loughton IG10 ... 48 C2
Northolt UB5 ... 85 F5
Heights Cl, SW20 ... 165 H7
Heiron St, SE17 ... 35 H6
Helby Rd, SW4 ... 150 D6
Helder Gro, SE12 ... 155 F7
Helder St, S.Croy. CR2 ... 202 A6
Heldmann Cl, Houns. TW3 ... 144 A4
Helegan Cl, Orp. BR6 ... 207 J4
Helena Pl, E9 *off Fremont St* ... 113 F1
Helena Rd, E13 ... 115 F2
E17 ... 78 A5
NW10 ... 89 H5
W5 ... 105 G5
Helena Sq, SE16 *off Rotherhithe St* ... 113 H7
Helen Av, Felt. TW14 ... 142 B7
Helen Cl, N2 *off Thomas More Way* ... 73 F3
West Molesey KT8 ... 179 H4
Helenslea Av, NW11 ... 90 C1
Helen's Pl, E2 *off Roman Rd* ... 113 F3
Helen St, SE18 *off Wilmount St* ... 137 E4
Helios Rd, Wall. SM6 ... 200 A1
Helix Gdns, SW2 *off Helix Rd* ... 151 F6
Helix Rd, SW2 ... 151 F6
Hellen Way, Wat. WD19 ... 50 C4
Hellings St, E1 ... 29 J2
Helme Cl, SW19 ... 166 C5
Helmet Row, EC1 ... 12 A5
Helmore Rd, Bark. IG11 ... 99 J7
Helmsdale Cl, Hayes UB4 ... 102 E4
Helmsdale Rd, SW16 ... 186 C1
Helmsley Pl, E8 ... 94 E7
Helperby Rd, NW10 ... 88 E7
Helsinki Sq, SE16 ... 133 H3
Helston Cl, Pnr. HA5 ... 51 F7
Helvetia St, SE6 ... 171 J2
Hemans St, SW8 ... 33 J7
Hemberton Rd, SW9 ... 150 E3
Hemery Rd, Grnf. UB6 ... 86 A5
Hemingford Cl, N12 ... 57 G5
Hemingford Rd, N1 ... 111 F1
Sutton SM3 ... 197 J4
Heming Rd, Edg. HA8 ... 54 B7
Hemington Av, N11 ... 57 J5
Hemingway Cl, NW5 ... 92 A4
Hemlock Rd, W12 ... 107 F7
Hemming Cl, Hmptn. TW12 *off Chandler Cl* ... 179 G1
Hemmings Cl, Sid. DA14 ... 176 B2
Hemmings Mead, Epsom KT19 ... 196 B6
Hemming St, E1 ... 13 J6
Hempstead Cl, Buck.H. IG9 ... 63 G2
Hempstead Rd, E17 ... 78 D2
Hemp Wk, SE17 ... 36 C1
Hemsby Rd, Chess. KT9 ... 195 J6
Hemstal Rd, NW6 ... 90 D7
Hemswell Dr, NW9 ... 70 E1
Hemsworth Ct, N1 *off Hemsworth St* ... 112 B2
Hemsworth St, N1 ... 12 D1
Hemus Pl, SW3 ... 31 H4
Hen & Chicken Ct, EC4 ... 19 E4
Henbury Way, Wat. WD19 ... 50 D3
Henchman St, W12 ... 107 F6
Hendale Av, NW4 ... 71 G3
Henderson Cl, NW10 ... 88 C6
Henderson Dr, NW8 ... 7 E5
Henderson Rd, E7 ... 97 J6
N9 ... 60 E1
SW18 ... 149 H7
Croydon CR0 ... 188 A6
Hayes UB4 ... 102 A3
Hendham Rd, SW17 ... 167 H2
HENDON, NW4 ... 71 H4
Hendon Av, N3 ... 72 B1
Hendon Hall Ct, NW4 *off Parson St* ... 72 A3
Hendon La, N3 ... 72 B3
Hendon Pk Row, NW11 ... 72 C6
Hendon Rd, N9 ... 60 D2
Hendon Way, NW2 ... 90 C3
NW4 ... 71 H6
Staines (Stanw.) TW19 ... 140 A6
Hendon Wd La, NW7 ... 39 F6
Hendren Cl, Grnf. UB6 *off Dimmock Dr* ... 86 A5
Hendre Rd, SE1 ... 36 E2
Hendrick Av, SW12 ... 149 J6
Heneage La, EC3 ... 21 E4
Heneage St, E1 ... 21 G1
Henfield Cl, N19 ... 92 C1
Bexley DA5 ... 159 G6
Henfield Rd, SW19 ... 184 C1
Hengelo Gdns, Mitch. CR4 ... 185 G4
Hengist Rd, SE12 ... 155 H7
Erith DA8 ... 139 H7
Hengist Way, Brom. BR2 ... 190 E4
Hengrave Rd, SE23 ... 153 G7
Hengrove Ct, Bex. DA5 *off Hurst Rd* ... 177 E1
Henley Av, Sutt. SM3 ... 198 B3
Henley Cl, SE16 *off St. Marychurch St* ... 133 F2
Greenford UB6 ... 103 J2
Isleworth TW7 ... 144 C1
Henley Ct, N14 ... 42 C7
Henley Cross, SE3 ... 155 H3
Henley Dr, SE1 ... 37 G1
Kingston upon Thames KT2 ... 165 F7
Henley Gdns, Pnr. HA5 ... 66 B3
Romford RM6 ... 82 E5
Henley Prior, N1 *off Collier St* ... 10 C2
Henley Rd, E16 ... 136 C2
N18 ... 60 B4
NW10 ... 107 J1
Ilford IG1 ... 99 F4
Henley St, SW11 ... 150 A2
Henley Way, Felt. TW13 ... 160 D5
Henlow Pl, Rich. TW10 ... 163 G2
Henlys Cor, N3 ... 72 C4
Henlys Rbt, Houns. TW5 *off Bath Rd* ... 142 D2
Hennel Cl, SE23 ... 171 F3
Hennessy Rd, N9 ... 61 F2
Henniker Gdns, E6 ... 116 A3
Henniker Ms, SW3 ... 30 E5
Henniker Pt, E15 ... 96 D5
Henniker Rd, E15 ... 96 D5
Henningham Rd, N17 ... 76 A1
Henning St, SW11 ... 149 H1
Henrietta Cl, SE8 ... 134 A6
Henrietta Ms, WC1 ... 10 B5
Henrietta Pl, W1 ... 16 D4
Henrietta St, E15 ... 96 C5
WC2 ... 18 B5
Henriques St, E1 ... 21 J3
Henry Addlington Cl, E6 ... 116 E5
Henry Cooper Way, SE9 ... 174 A3
Henry Darlot Dr, NW7 ... 56 A5
Henry Dent Cl, SE5 ... 152 A3
Henry Dickens Ct, W11 ... 128 A1
Henry Doulton Dr, SW17 ... 168 B4
Henry Jackson Rd, SW15 ... 148 A3
Henry Macaulay Av, Kings.T. KT2 ... 181 G1
Henry Peters Dr, Tedd. TW11 *off Somerset Gdns* ... 162 B5
Henry Rd, E6 ... 116 B2
N4 ... 93 J1
Barnet EN4 ... 41 G5
Henry's Av, Wdf.Grn. IG8 ... 63 F5
Henryson Rd, SE4 ... 154 A5
Henry St, Brom. BR1 ... 191 H1
Henry's Wk, Ilf. IG6 ... 65 G7
Henry Tate Ms, SW16 ... 169 G5
Henry Wise Ho, SW1 *off Vauxhall Br Rd* ... 33 G2
Hensford Gdns, SE26 *off Wells Pk Rd* ... 171 E4
Henshall Pt, E3 *off Bromley High St* ... 114 B3
Henshall St, N1 ... 94 A6
Henshawe Rd, Dag. RM8 ... 100 D3
Henshaw St, SE17 ... 36 B1
Hensley Pt, E9 *off Wick Rd* ... 95 G6
Henslowe Rd, SE22 ... 152 D5
Henson Av, NW2 ... 89 J5
Henson Cl, Orp. BR6 ... 207 E2
Henson Path, Har. HA3 ... 69 G3
Henson Pl, Nthlt. UB5 ... 102 C1
Henstridge Pl, NW8 ... 7 G1
Henty Cl, SW11 ... 129 H7
Henty Wk, SW15 ... 147 H5
Henville Rd, Brom. BR1 ... 191 H1
Henwick Rd, SE9 ... 156 A3
Henwood Side, Wdf.Grn. IG8 *off Love La* ... 64 C6
Hepburn Gdns, Brom. BR2 ... 205 E1
Hepburn Ms, SW11 *off Webbs Rd* ... 149 J5
Hepple Cl, Islw. TW7 ... 144 E2
Hepplestone Cl, SW15 ... 147 H6
Hepscott Rd, E9 ... 96 A7
Hepworth Ct, SW1 ... 32 C4
Barking IG11 ... 100 A5
Hepworth Gdns, Bark. IG11 ... 100 A5
Hepworth Rd, SW16 ... 169 E7
Hepworth Wk, NW3 *off Haverstock Hill* ... 91 H5
Herald Gdns, Wall. SM6 ... 200 B3
Herald's Pl, SE11 ... 35 G1
Herald St, E2 *off Three Colts La* ... 113 E4
Herbal Hill, EC1 ... 11 F6
Herbert Cres, SW1 ... 24 A5
Herbert Gdns, NW10 ... 107 H2
W4 ... 126 B6
Romford RM6 ... 82 D7
Herbert Ms, SW2 *off Bascombe St* ... 151 G6
Herbert Morrison Ho, SW6 *off Clem Attlee Ct* ... 128 C6
Herbert Pl, SE18 *off Plumstead Common Rd* ... 137 E6
Isleworth TW7 *off Spring Gro Rd* ... 144 A1
Herbert Rd, E12 ... 98 B4
E17 ... 77 J7
N11 ... 58 E7
N15 ... 76 C5
NW9 ... 71 G6
SE18 ... 136 D7
SW19 ... 166 C7
Bexleyheath DA7 ... 159 E2
Bromley BR2 ... 192 A5
Ilford IG3 ... 99 H2
Kingston upon Thames KT1 ... 181 J3
Southall UB1 ... 123 F1
Herbert St, E13 ... 115 G2
NW5 ... 92 A6
Herbert Ter, SE18 ... 136 E7
Herbrand St, WC1 ... 10 A5
Hercules Pl, N7 *off Hercules St* ... 93 E3
Hercules Rd, SE1 ... 26 D6
Hercules St, N7 ... 93 E3
Hereford Av, Barn. EN4 ... 57 J1
Hereford Ct, Sutt. SM2 *off Worcester Rd* ... 198 D7
Hereford Gdns, SE13 *off Longhurst Rd* ... 155 E5
Ilford IG1 ... 80 B7
Pinner HA5 ... 66 E5
Twickenham TW2 ... 161 J1
Hereford Ho, NW6 ... 108 D2
Hereford Ms, W2 *off Hereford Rd* ... 108 D6
Hereford Pl, SE14 *off Royal Naval Pl* ... 133 J7
Hereford Retreat, SE15 ... 37 H6
Hereford Rd, E3 ... 113 J2
E11 ... 79 H5
W2 ... 108 D6
W3 ... 106 B7
W5 ... 125 F3
Feltham TW13 ... 160 C1
Hereford Sq, SW7 ... 30 D2
Hereford St, E2 ... 13 H5
Hereford Way, Chess. KT9 ... 195 F5
Herent Dr, Ilf. IG5 ... 80 B4
Hereward Gdns, N13 ... 59 G5
Hereward Grn, Loug. IG10 ... 49 F1
Hereward Rd, SW17 ... 167 J4
Herga Ct, Har. HA1 ... 86 B3
Herga Rd, Har. HA3 ... 68 C4
Heriot Av, E4 ... 62 A2
Heriot Rd, NW4 ... 71 J5
Heriots Cl, Stan. HA7 ... 52 D4
Heritage Cl, SW9 ... 151 H3
Sunbury-on-Thames TW16 *off Green St* ... 178 A1
Heritage Hill, Kes. BR2 ... 205 J5
Heritage Pl, SW18 *off Earlsfield Rd* ... 167 F1
Heritage Vw, Har. HA1 ... 86 C3
Herlwyn Gdns, SW17 ... 167 J4
Herm Cl, Islw. TW7 *off Jersey Rd* ... 123 J7
Hermes Cl, W9 *off Chippenham Rd* ... 108 D4
Hermes St, N1 ... 10 E2
Hermes Wk, Nthlt. UB5 *off Hotspur Rd* ... 103 G2
Hermes Way, Wall. SM6 ... 200 D7
Hermiston Av, N8 ... 75 E5
Hermitage, The, SE23 ... 171 F1
SW13 ... 147 F1
Richmond TW10 ... 145 G5
Hermitage Cl, E18 ... 79 F4
SE2 *off Felixstowe Rd* ... 138 C3
Enfield EN2 ... 43 H2
Esher (Clay.) KT10 ... 194 D6
Hermitage Ct, E18 ... 79 G4
NW2 *off Hermitage La* ... 90 D3
Hermitage Gdns, NW2 ... 90 D3
SE19 ... 169 J6
Hermitage La, N18 ... 60 A5
NW2 ... 90 D3
SE25 ... 188 D6
SW16 ... 169 F7
Croydon CR0 ... 188 D6
Hermitage Path, SW16 ... 187 E1
Hermitage Rd, N4 ... 75 H7
N15 ... 75 H7
SE19 ... 169 J7
Hermitage Row, E8 ... 94 D5
Hermitage St, W2 ... 15 E2
Hermitage Wk, E18 ... 79 F4
Hermitage Wall, E1 ... 29 J2
Hermitage Waterside, E1 ... 29 H1
Hermitage Way, Stan. HA7 ... 68 D1
Hermit Pl, NW6 *off Belsize Rd* ... 108 E1
Hermit Rd, E16 ... 115 F5
Hermit St, EC1 ... 11 G3
Hermon Gro, Hayes UB3 ... 122 A1
Hermon Hill, E11 ... 79 G5
E18 ... 79 G5
Herndon Rd, SW18 ... 149 F5
Herne Cl, NW10 *off North Circular Rd* ... 88 D5
HERNE HILL, SE24 ... 151 J5
Herne Hill, SE24 ... 151 J6
Herne Hill Ho, SE24 *off Railton Rd* ... 151 H6
Herne Hill Rd, SE24 ... 151 J3
Herne Ms, N18 *off Lyndhurst Rd* ... 60 D4
Herne Pl, SE24 ... 151 H5
Herne Rd, Surb. KT6 ... 195 G2
Heron Cl, E17 ... 77 J2
NW10 ... 89 E6
Buckhurst Hill IG9 ... 63 G1
Sutton SM1 *off Sandpiper Rd* ... 198 C5
Heron Ct, E5 *off Big Hill* ... 95 E1
Bromley BR2 ... 191 J4
Heron Cres, Sid. DA14 ... 175 H3
Herondale Av, SW18 ... 167 G1
Heron Dr, N4 ... 93 J2
Herongate Rd, E12 ... 97 J2
Heron Hill, Belv. DA17 ... 139 F4
Heron Ms, Ilf. IG1 *off Balfour Rd* ... 98 E2
Heron Pl, SE16 ... 133 H1
Heron Quay, E14 ... 134 A1
Heron Rd, SE24 ... 151 J4
Croydon CR0 *off Tunstall Rd* ... 202 B2
Twickenham TW1 ... 144 D4
Herons, The, E11 ... 79 F6
Heronsforde, W13 ... 105 F6
Heronsgate, Edg. HA8 ... 54 A5
Heronslea Dr, Stan. HA7 ... 53 H5
Heron's Pl, Islw. TW7 ... 144 E3
Heron Sq, Rich. TW9 *off Bridge St* ... 145 G5
Herons Ri, Barn. (New Barn.) EN4 ... 41 H4
Heron Trd Est, W3 *off Alliance Rd* ... 106 B4
Heron Way, Felt. TW14 ... 142 A4
Heronway, Wdf.Grn. IG8 ... 63 J4
Herrick Rd, N5 ... 93 J3
Herrick St, SW1 ... 33 J1
Herries St, W10 ... 108 B2
Herringham Rd, SE7 ... 135 J3
Herrongate Cl, Enf. EN1 ... 44 C2
Hersant Cl, NW10 ... 107 G1
Herschell Ms, SE5 *off Bicknell Rd* ... 151 J3
Herschell Rd, SE23 ... 153 G7
Hersham Cl, SW15 ... 147 G7
Hertford Av, SW14 ... 146 D5
Hertford Cl, Barn. EN4 ... 41 G3

Hertford Ct, N13 *off Green Las* 59 G3
Hertford Pl, W1 9 F6
Hertford Rd, N1 112 B1
N2 73 H3
N9 60 E2
Barking IG11 98 E7
Barnet EN4 41 F3
Enfield EN3 45 F3
Ilford IG2 81 H6
Hertford Sq, Mitch. CR4 *off Hertford Way* 186 E4
Hertford St, W1 24 D1
Hertford Wk, Belv. DA17 *off Hoddesdon Rd* 139 G5
Hertford Way, Mitch. CR4 186 E4
Hertslet Rd, N7 93 F3
Hertsmere Ind Pk, Borwd. WD6 38 D3
Hertsmere Rd, E14 114 A7
Hertswood Ct, Barn. EN5 *off Hillside Gdns* 40 B4
Hervey Cl, N3 72 D1
Hervey Pk Rd, E17 77 H4
Hervey Rd, SE3 155 H1
Hesa Rd, Hayes UB3 102 A6
Hesewall Cl, SW4 *off Brayburne Av* 150 C2
Hesketh Pl, W11 108 B7
Hesketh Rd, E7 97 G3
Heslop Rd, SW12 167 J1
Hesper Ms, SW5 30 A3
Hesperus Cres, E14 134 B4
Hessel Rd, W13 124 D2
Hessel St, E1 112 E6
Hestercombe Av, SW6 148 B2
Hesterman Way, Croy. CR0 201 E1
Hester Rd, N18 60 D5
SW11 129 H7
Hester Ter, Rich. TW9 *off Chilton Rd* 146 A3
Hestia Ho, SE1 *off Royal Oak Yd* 28 D4
HESTON, Houns. TW5 123 F7
Heston Av, Houns. TW5 123 E7
Heston Gra, Houns. TW5 *off North Hyde La* 123 F6
Heston Gra La, Houns. TW5 123 F6
Heston Ind Mall, Houns. TW5 123 F7
Heston Rd, Houns. TW5 123 G7
Heston St, SE14 153 J1
Heswell Grn, Wat. WD19 *off Fairhaven Cres* 50 A3
Hetherington Rd, SW4 150 E4
Hetley Gdns, SE19 170 C7
Hetley Rd, W12 127 H1
Heton Gdns, NW4 71 G4
Hevelius Cl, SE10 135 F5
Hever Cft, SE9 174 D4
Hever Gdns, Brom. BR1 192 D2
Heverham Rd, SE18 137 H4
Heversham Rd, Bexh. DA7 159 G2
Hevingham Dr, Rom. (Chad.Hth) RM6 82 C5
Hewer St, W10 108 A5
Hewett Cl, Stan. HA7 53 E4
Hewett Rd, Dag. RM8 100 D5
Hewetts Quay, Bark. IG11 117 E1
Hewett St, EC2 12 E6
Hewish Rd, N18 60 B4
Hewison St, E3 113 J2
Hewitt Av, N22 75 H2
Hewitt Cl, Croy. CR0 204 A3
Hewitt Rd, N8 75 G5
Hewlett Rd, E3 113 H2
Hexagon, The, N6 91 J1
Hexal Rd, SE6 172 E3
Hexham Gdns, Islw. TW7 124 D7
Hexham Rd, SE27 169 J2
Barnet EN5 41 E4
Morden SM4 198 E1
Hexton Ct, N4 *off Brownswood Rd* 93 J2
Heybourne Rd, N17 61 E7
Heybridge Av, SW16 169 E7
Heybridge Dr, Ilf. IG6 81 G2
Heybridge Way, E10 77 H7
Heyford Av, SW8 34 B7
SW20 184 C3
Heyford Rd, Mitch. CR4 185 H2
Heyford Ter, SW8 *off Heyford Av* 34 B7
Heygate St, SE17 35 J2
Heylyn Sq, E3 *off Malmesbury Rd* 113 J3
Heynes Rd, Dag. RM8 100 C4
Heysham Dr, Wat. WD19 50 C5
Heysham La, NW3 91 E3
Heysham Rd, N15 76 A6
Heythorp St, SW18 166 C1
Heywood Av, NW9 70 E1
Heyworth Rd, E5 94 E4
E15 97 F5
Hibbert Rd, E17 77 J7
Harrow HA3 68 C2
Hibbert St, SW11 149 F3
Hibernia Gdns, Houns. TW3 143 G4
Hibernia Pt, SE2 *off Wolvercote Rd* 138 D2
Hibernia Rd, Houns. TW3 143 G4
Hibiscus Cl, Edg. HA8 *off Campion Way* 54 C4
Hibiscus Ho, Felt. TW13 *off High St* 160 B1
Hichisson Rd, SE15 153 F5
Hickeys Almshouses, Rich. TW9 *off St. Mary's Gro* 145 J4
Hickin Cl, SE7 136 A4
Hickin St, E14 *off Plevna St* 134 C3
Hickling Rd, Ilf. IG1 99 E5
Hickman Av, E4 62 C6
Hickman Cl, E16 116 A5
Hickman Rd, Rom. RM6 82 C7
Hickmore Wk, SW4 150 C3
Hickory Cl, N9 44 D7
Hicks Av, Grnf. UB6 104 A2
Hicks Cl, SW11 149 H3
Hicks St, SE8 133 H5
Hidcote Gdns, SW20 183 H3
Hide, E6 *off Downings* 116 D6
Hide Pl, SW1 33 H2
Hide Rd, Har. HA1 68 A4
Hides St, N7 *off Sheringham Rd* 93 F6
Hide Twr, SW1 33 H2
Higgins Wk, Hmptn. TW12 *off Abbott Cl* 161 E6
High Acres, Enf. EN2 *off Old Pk Vw* 43 G3
HIGHAM HILL, E17 77 H2
Higham Hill Rd, E17 77 H2
Higham Ms, Nthlt. UB5 *off Taywood Rd* 103 F4
Higham Pl, E17 77 H3
Higham Rd, N17 76 A3
Woodford Green IG8 63 G6
Highams Ct, E4 *off Friars Cl* 62 D3
Highams Lo Business Cen, E17 77 H3
HIGHAMS PARK, E4 62 D5
Highams Pk Ind Est, E4 62 C6
Higham Sta Av, E4 62 B6
Higham St, E17 77 H3
Highbanks Cl, Well. DA16 138 B7
Highbanks Rd, Pnr. HA5 51 H5
Highbank Way, N8 75 G6
HIGH BARNET, Barn. EN5 40 A2
Highbarrow Rd, Croy. CR0 188 D7
HIGH BEACH, Loug. IG10 47 G1
High Beech, S.Croy. CR2 202 B7
High Beeches, Sid. DA14 176 E5
High Beech Rd, Loug. IG10 48 A4
High Br, SE10 134 D5
Highbridge Rd, Bark. IG11 116 E1
High Br Wf, SE10 134 D5
Highbrook Rd, SE3 156 A3
High Broom Cres, W.Wick. BR4 190 B7
HIGHBURY, N5 93 H5
Highbury Av, Th.Hth. CR7 187 G2
Highbury Cl, N.Mal. KT3 182 C4
West Wickham BR4 204 B2
Highbury Cor, N5 93 G6
Highbury Cres, N5 93 G5
Highbury Est, N5 93 J5
Highbury Gdns, Ilf. IG3 99 H2
Highbury Gra, N5 93 H4
Highbury Gro, N5 93 H6
Highbury Hill, N5 93 G3
Highbury New Pk, N5 93 J5
Highbury Pk, N5 93 H3
Highbury Pl, N5 93 H6
Highbury Quad, N5 93 H3
Highbury Rd, SW19 166 B5
Highbury Sq, N14 *off Burleigh Gdns* 58 C1
Highbury Sta Rd, N1 93 G6
Highbury Ter, N5 93 H5
Highbury Ter Ms, N5 93 H5
High Cedar Dr, SW20 165 H7
Highclere Rd, N.Mal. KT3 182 D3
Highclere St, SE26 171 H4
Highcliffe Dr, SW15 147 F6
Highcliffe Gdns, Ilf. IG4 80 B5
Highcombe, SE7 135 H6
Highcombe Cl, SE9 174 A1
High Coombe Pl, Kings.T. KT2 164 D7
Highcroft, NW9 70 E5
Highcroft Av, Wem. HA0 106 A1
Highcroft Gdns, NW11 72 C6
Highcroft Rd, N19 74 E7
High Cross Cen, The, N15 76 D4
High Cross Rd, N17 76 D3
Highcross Way, SW15 165 G1
Highdaun Dr, SW16 187 F4
Highdown, Wor.Pk. KT4 197 E2
Highdown Rd, SW15 147 H6
High Dr, N.Mal. KT3 182 C1
High Elms, Chig. IG7 65 H4
Woodford Green IG8 63 G5
Highfield, Bushey (Bushey Hth) WD23 52 B2
Watford WD19 51 F3
Highfield Av, NW9 70 C5
NW11 72 A7
Erith DA8 139 H6
Greenford UB6 86 B5
Orpington BR6 207 J5
Pinner HA5 67 F5
Wembley HA9 87 H3
Highfield Cl, N22 75 G1
NW9 70 C5
SE13 154 D6
Surbiton (Long Dit.) KT6 195 F1
Highfield Ct, N14 42 C6
Highfield Dr, Brom. BR2 191 E4
Epsom KT19 197 F7
West Wickham BR4 204 B2
Highfield Gdns, NW11 72 B6
Highfield Hill, SE19 170 A7
Highfield Ms, NW6 *off Compayne Gdns* 90 E7
Highfield Rd, N21 59 H2
NW11 72 B6
W3 106 B5
Bexleyheath DA6 159 F5
Bromley BR1 192 C4
Chislehurst BR7 193 J3
Feltham TW13 160 A2
Isleworth TW7 144 C1
Surbiton KT5 182 C7
Sutton SM1 199 H5
Woodford Green IG8 64 B7
Highfields Gro, N6 91 J1
High Foleys, Esher (Clay.) KT10 194 E7
High Gables, Loug. IG10 48 A5
HIGHGATE, N6 92 A2
Highgate Av, N6 74 B6
★ **Highgate Cem**, N6 92 A1
Highgate Cl, N6 74 A7
Highgate Edge, N2 73 H5
Highgate High St, N6 92 A1
Highgate Hill, N6 92 B1
N19 92 B1
Highgate Ho, SE26 *off Sydenham Hill Est* 170 D3
Highgate Rd, NW5 92 B4
Highgate Spinney, N8 *off Crescent Rd* 74 D6
Highgate Wk, SE23 171 F2
Highgate W Hill, N6 92 A2
High Gro, SE18 137 G7
Bromley BR1 191 J1
Highgrove Cl, N11 *off Balmoral Av* 58 A5
Chislehurst BR7 192 B1
Highgrove Ms, Cars. SM5 199 J3
Highgrove Rd, Dag. RM8 100 C5
Highgrove Way, Ruis. HA4 66 A6
High Hill, E5 *off Mount Pleasant La* 95 E1
High Hill Ferry, E5 *off Big Hill* 95 E1
High Holborn, WC1 18 B3
Highland Av, W7 104 B6
Dagenham RM10 101 J3
Loughton IG10 48 B6
Highland Cotts, Wall. SM6 200 B4
Highland Ct, E18 79 H1
Highland Cft, Beck. BR3 172 B5
Highland Rd, SE19 170 B6
Bexleyheath DA6 159 G5
Bromley BR1, BR2 191 F1
Highlands, Wat. WD19 50 C1
Highlands, The, Barn. EN5 40 E5
Edgware HA8 70 B2
Highlands Av, N21 43 F5
W3 106 C7
Highlands Cl, N4 *off Mount Vw Rd* 75 E7
Hounslow TW3 143 H1
Highlands Gdns, Ilf. IG1 98 C1
Highlands Heath, SW15 147 J7
Highlands Rd, Barn. EN5 40 D5
High La, W7 104 A6
High Lawns, Har. HA1 86 B3
Highlea Cl, NW9 71 E1
High Level Dr, SE26 170 D4
Highlever Rd, W10 107 J5
Highmead, SE18 137 J7
High Mead, Chig. IG7 65 F2
Harrow HA1 68 B5
West Wickham BR4 204 D2
Highmead Cres, Wem. HA0 87 J7
High Meadow Cl, Pnr. HA5 66 C4
Highmeadow Cres, NW9 70 D5
High Meadows, Chig. IG7 65 G5
High Meads Rd, E16 116 A6
Highmore Rd, SE3 135 E7
High Mt, NW4 71 G6
High Pk Av, Rich. TW9 146 A1
High Pk Rd, Rich. TW9 146 A1
High Path, SW19 185 E1
High Pt, N6 74 A7
SE9 175 E3
High Rd, N2 73 H4
N11 58 B5
N12 57 F6
N15 76 C6
N17 76 C1
N20 41 F7
N22 75 G3
NW10 (Willesden) 89 H6
Buckhurst Hill IG9 63 H2
Bushey (Bushey Hth) WD23 52 A1
Chigwell IG7 64 C5
Harrow (Har.Wld) HA3 52 B7
Ilford IG1 98 E3
Ilford (Seven Kings) IG3 99 J1
Loughton IG10 47 J7
Pinner (Eastcote) HA5 66 B4
Romford (Chad.Hth) RM6 100 B1
Wembley HA0, HA9 87 G5
High Rd Leyton, E10 96 B1
E15 96 C3
High Rd Leytonstone, E11 96 E4
E15 96 E4
High Rd Woodford Grn, E18 63 F7
Woodford Green IG8 63 F7
Highshore Rd, SE15 152 C2
High Silver, Loug. IG10 48 A4
Highstone Av, E11 79 G6
High St, E11 79 G5
E13 115 G2
E15 114 C2
E17 77 J5
N8 74 E4
N14 58 D1
NW7 55 H4
NW10 (Harlesden) 107 F2
SE20 171 E6
SE25 (S.Norwood) 188 C4
W3 126 B1
W5 105 G7
Barnet EN5 40 B3
Beckenham BR3 190 A2
Brentford TW8 125 G6
Bromley BR1 191 G2
Carshalton SM5 200 A4
Chislehurst BR7 174 E6
Croydon CR0 201 J2
Edgware HA8 54 A6
Enfield (Pond.End) EN3 45 F5
Esher (Clay.) KT10 194 C6
Feltham TW13 160 A3
Hampton TW12 161 J6
Harrow HA1, HA2 86 B1
Harrow (Wealds.) HA3 68 B3
Hayes (Harling.) UB3 121 H5
Hounslow TW3 143 J3
Hounslow (Cran.) TW5 122 B7
Ilford (Barkingside) IG6 81 F2
Kingston upon Thames KT1 181 G2
Kingston upon Thames (Hmptn W.) KT1 181 F1
New Malden KT3 183 E3
Orpington (Farnboro.) BR6 207 E5
Orpington (Grn St Grn) BR6 207 J7
Pinner HA5 66 E3
Southall UB1 123 F1
Staines (Stanw.) TW19 140 A6
Sutton SM1 198 E4
Sutton (Cheam) SM3 198 B6
Teddington TW11 162 D5
Thames Ditton KT7 180 D7
Thornton Heath CR7 187 J4
Twickenham (Whitton) TW2 143 J7
Wembley HA9 87 J4

High St, West Drayton (Harm.) UB7 **120** A6
West Drayton (Yiew.) UB7 **120** A1
West Molesey KT8 **179** G4
West Wickham BR4 **204** B1
High St Colliers Wd, SW19 **167** G7
High St Ms, SW19 **166** B5
High St N, E6 **116** B1
E12 **98** B5
High St S, E6 **116** C2
High St Wimbledon, SW19 **166** A5
High Timber St, EC4 **19** J5
High Tor Cl, Brom. BR1 **173** H7
High Tor Vw, SE28 **137** H1
High Tree Ct, W7 **104** B7
High Trees, SW2 **169** G1
Barnet EN4 **41** H5
Croydon CR0 **203** H1
Highview, Nthlt. UB5 **103** E3
High Vw, Pnr. HA5 **66** C4
Highview Av, Edg. HA8 **54** C4
Wallington SM6 **201** F5
High Vw Cl, SE19 **188** C2
Loughton IG10 **47** J5
Highview Gdns, N3 **72** B4
N11 **58** C5
Edgware HA8 **54** C4
Highview Ho, Rom. RM6 **83** E4
High Vw Rd, E18 **79** F3
SE19 **170** A6
Highview Rd, W13 **104** D5
Sidcup DA14 **176** B4
Highway, The, E1 **21** J6
E14 **21** J6
Stanmore HA7 **68** C1
Highwood, Brom. BR2 **190** D3
Highwood Av, N12 **57** F4
Highwood Cl, SE22 **170** D1
Orpington BR6 **207** F2
Highwood Dr, Orp. BR6 **207** F2
Highwood Gdns, Ilf. IG5 **80** C5
Highwood Gro, NW7 **54** D5
HIGHWOOD HILL, NW7 **55** G2
Highwood Hill, NW7 **55** F2
Highwood La, Loug. IG10 **48** D5
Highwood Rd, N19 **92** E3
High Worple, Har. HA2 **67** F7
Highworth Rd, N11 **58** D6
Hilary Av, Mitch. CR4 **186** A3
Hilary Cl, SW6 **30** A7
Erith DA8 **159** J1
Hilary Rd, W12 **107** F6
Hilbert Rd, Sutt. SM3 **198** A3
Hilborough Way, Orp. BR6 **207** G5
Hilda Lockert Wk, SW9 *off Fiveways Rd* **151** H2
Hilda Rd, E6 **98** A7
E16 **115** E4
Hilda Ter, SW9 **151** G2
Hilda Vale Cl, Orp. BR6 **206** D4
Hilda Vale Rd, Orp. BR6 **206** D4
Hildenborough Gdns, Brom. BR1 **173** E6
Hildenlea Pl, Brom. BR2 **190** E2
Hildreth St, SW12 **168** B1
Hildreth St Ms, SW12 *off Hildreth St* **168** B1
Hildyard Rd, SW6 **128** D6
Hiley Rd, NW10 **107** J3
Hilgrove Rd, NW6 **91** F7
Hiliary Gdns, Stan. HA7 **69** F2
Hillary Dr, Islw. TW7 **144** C4
Hillary Ri, Barn. EN5 **40** D4
Hillary Rd, Sthl. UB2 **123** G3
Hillbeck Cl, SE15 **133** F7
Hillbeck Way, Grnf. UB6 **104** A1
Hillborne Cl, Hayes UB3 **122** A5
Hillborough Cl, SW19 **167** F7
Hillbrook Rd, SW17 **167** J3
Hill Brow, Brom. BR1 **192** A1
Hillbrow, N.Mal. KT3 **183** F3
Hillbrow Rd, Brom. BR1 **172** E7
Hillbury Av, Har. HA3 **69** E5
Hillbury Rd, SW17 **168** B3
Hill Cl, NW2 **89** H3
NW11 **72** D6
Barnet EN5 **39** J5
Chislehurst BR7 **174** E5
Harrow HA1 **86** B3
Stanmore HA7 **52** E4
Hillcote Av, SW16 **169** G7
Hill Ct, Nthlt. UB5 **85** G5
Hillcourt Av, N12 **56** E6
Hillcourt Est, N16 **94** A1
Hillcourt Rd, SE22 **152** E6
Hill Cres, N20 **56** E2
Bexley DA5 **177** J1
Harrow HA1 **68** D5
Surbiton KT5 **181** J5
Hill Cres, Worcester Park KT4 **197** J2
Hillcrest, N6 **74** A7
N21 **43** H7
SE24 **152** A4
Hill Crest, Sid. DA15 **158** A7
Hillcrest Av, NW11 **72** B5
Edgware HA8 **54** B4
Pinner HA5 **66** D4
Hillcrest Cl, SE26 **170** D4
Beckenham BR3 **189** J5
Hillcrest Ct, Sutt. SM2 *off Eaton Rd* **199** G6
Hillcrest Gdns, N3 **72** B4
NW2 **89** G3
Esher KT10 **194** C3
Hillcrest Rd, E17 **78** D2
E18 **79** F2
W3 **126** A1
W5 **105** H5
Bromley BR1 **173** G5
Loughton IG10 **48** A6
Hillcrest Vw, Beck. BR3 **189** J6
Hillcroft, Loug. IG10 **48** D2
Hillcroft Av, Pnr. HA5 **67** F6
Hillcroft Cres, W5 **105** H6
Ruislip HA4 **84** D3
Watford WD19 **50** B1
Wembley HA9 **87** J4
Hillcroft Rd, E6 **116** E5
Hillcroome Rd, Sutt. SM2 **199** G6
Hillcross Av, Mord. SM4 **184** C5
Hilldale Rd, Sutt. SM1 **198** C4
Hilldown Rd, SW16 **169** E7
Bromley BR2 **205** E1
Hill Dr, NW9 **88** C1
SW16 **187** F3
Hilldrop Cres, N7 **92** D5
Hilldrop Est, N7 **92** D5
Hilldrop La, N7 **92** D5
Hilldrop Rd, N7 **92** D5
Bromley BR1 **173** G6
Hillend, SE18 **156** D1
Hill End, Orp. BR6 *off The Approach* **207** J2
Hillersdon Av, SW13 **147** G2
Edgware HA8 **53** J5
Hillery Cl, SE17 **36** C2
Hill Fm Rd, W10 **107** J5
Hillfield Av, N8 **75** E5
NW9 **71** E5
Morden SM4 **185** H6
Wembley HA0 **87** H7
Hillfield Cl, Har. HA2 **67** J4
Hillfield Ct, NW3 **91** H5
Hillfield Ms, N8 **75** F4
Hillfield Pk, N10 **74** B4
N21 **59** G2
Hillfield Pk Ms, N10 **74** B4
Hillfield Rd, NW6 **90** C5
Hampton TW12 **161** F7
Hillfoot Av, Rom. RM5 **83** J1
Hillfoot Rd, Rom. RM5 **83** J1
Hillgate Pl, SW12 **150** B7
W8 **128** D1
Hillgate St, W8 **128** D1
Hill Gate Wk, N6 **74** C6
Hill Gro, Felt. TW13 *off Watermill Way* **161** F2
Hill Ho, E5 **95** E1
Hill Ho Av, Stan. HA7 **52** C7
Hill Ho Cl, N21 **43** G7
Hill Ho Dr, Hmptn. TW12 **179** G1
Hill Ho Ms, Brom. BR2 **191** F2
Hill Ho Rd, SW16 **169** F5
Hilliards Ct, E1 *off Wapping High St* **133** F1
Hillier Cl, Barn. (New Barn.) EN5 **40** E6
Hillier Gdns, Croy. CR0 **201** G5
Hillier Pl, Chess. KT9 **195** G6
Hillier Rd, SW11 **149** J6
Hilliers La, Croy. CR0 **200** E3
Hillingdon Rd, Bexh. DA7 **159** J2
Hillingdon St, SE17 **35** H6
Hillington Gdns, Wdf.Grn. IG8 **80** A2
Hillman Dr, W10 **107** J4
Hillman St, E8 **95** E6
Hillmarton Rd, N7 **93** E5
Hillmead Dr, SW9 **151** H4
Hillmont Rd, Esher KT10 **194** B3
Hillmore Gro, SE26 **171** G5
Hill Path, SW16 *off Valley Rd* **169** F5
Hillreach, SE18 **136** C5
Hill Ri, N9 **45** E6
NW11 **73** E4
SE23 *off London Rd* **171** E1
Esher KT10 **194** E2
Greenford UB6 **85** J7
Richmond TW10 **145** G5
Hillrise Rd, N19 **74** E7
Hill Rd, N10 **73** J1
NW8 **6** D2
Carshalton SM5 **199** H6
Harrow HA1 **68** D5
Mitcham CR4 **186** B1
Pinner HA5 **66** E5
Sutton SM1 **199** E5
Wembley HA0 **86** E3
Hillsboro Rd, SE22 **152** B5
Hillsborough Grn, Wat. WD19 **50** A3
Hillsgrove, Well. DA16 **138** C7
Hillside, NW9 **70** D4
NW10 **106** C1
SW19 **166** A6
Barnet (New Barn.) EN5 **41** F5
Hillside Av, N11 **57** J6
Borehamwood WD6 **38** B4
Wembley HA9 **87** J4
Woodford Green IG8 **63** J5
Hillside Cl, NW8 **6** B1
Morden SM4 **184** B4
Woodford Green IG8 **63** J5
Hillside Cres, Har. HA2 **85** J1
Northwood HA6 **66** A1
Hillside Dr, Edg. HA8 **54** A6
Hillside Gdns, E17 **78** D3
N6 **74** A6
SW2 **169** G2
Barnet EN5 **40** B4
Edgware HA8 **53** J4
Harrow HA3 **69** H7
Northwood HA6 **50** A7
Wallington SM6 **200** C7
Hillside Gro, N14 **42** D7
NW7 **55** G7
Hillside La, Brom. BR2 **205** G2
Hillside Pas, SW2 **169** F2
Hillside Ri, Nthwd. HA6 **50** A7
Hillside Rd, N15 **76** B7
SW2 **169** G2
W5 **105** H5
Bromley BR2 **191** F3
Croydon CR0 **201** H5
Northwood HA6 **50** A7
Pinner HA5 **50** B7
Southall UB1 **103** G4
Surbiton KT5 **181** J5
Sutton SM2 **198** C7
Hillsleigh Rd, W8 **128** C1
Hills Ms, W5 **105** H7
Hills Pl, W1 **17** F4
Hills Rd, Buck.H. IG9 **63** H1
Hillstowe St, E5 **95** F2
Hill St, W1 **24** C1
Richmond TW9 **145** G5
Hill Top, NW11 **73** E4
Hilltop, Loug. IG10 **48** D2
Hill Top, Mord. SM4 **184** D6
Sutton SM3 **184** C7
Hilltop Av, NW10 **88** C7
Hill Top Cl, Loug. IG10 **48** D3
Hilltop Gdns, NW4 **71** H2
Orpington BR6 **207** H2
Hill Top Pl, Loug. IG10 **48** D3
Hilltop Rd, NW6 **90** D7
Hill Top Vw, Wdf.Grn. IG8 **64** C6
Hilltop Way, Stan. HA7 **52** D3
Hillview, SW20 **165** H7
Mitcham CR4 **186** E4
Hillview Av, Har. HA3 **69** H5
Hillview Cl, Pnr. HA5 **51** F6
Wembley HA9 **87** J2
Hillview Cres, Ilf. IG1 **80** C6
Orpington BR6 **207** H1
Hill Vw Dr, SE28 **137** H1
Welling DA16 **157** H2
Hillview Gdns, NW4 **72** A4
Hill Vw Gdns, NW9 **70** D5
Hillview Gdns, Har. HA2 **67** G3
Hillview Rd, NW7 **56** A4
Chislehurst BR7 **174** D5
Hill Vw Rd, Esher (Clay.) KT10 **194** D7
Hillview Rd, Orp. BR6 **207** J1
Pinner HA5 **51** F7
Sutton SM1 **199** F3
Hill Vw Rd, Twick. TW1 **144** D6
Hillway, N6 **92** A2
NW9 **88** E1
Hillworth Rd, SW2 **151** G7
Hillyard Rd, W7 **104** B5
Hillyard St, SW9 **151** G1
Hillyfield, E17 **77** H2
Hillyfield Cl, E9 *off Mabley St* **95** H5
Hillyfields, Loug. IG10 **48** D2
Hilly Flds Cres, SE4 **154** A3
Hilsea Pt, SW15 *off Wanborough Dr* **165** H1
Hilsea St, E5 **95** F4
Hilton Av, N12 **57** G5
Hilversum Cres, SE22 *off East Dulwich Gro* **152** B5
Himley Rd, SW17 **167** H5
Hinchley Cl, Esher KT10 **194** C3
Hinchley Dr, Esher KT10 **194** C3
Hinchley Manor, Esher KT10 **194** C3
Hinchley Way, Esher KT10 **194** D3
HINCHLEY WOOD, Esher KT10 **194** C3
Hinckley Rd, SE15 **152** D4
Hind Cl, Chig. IG7 **65** J5
Hind Ct, EC4 **19** F4
Hinde Ms, W1 *off Marylebone La* **16** C3
Hindes Rd, Har. HA1 **68** A5
Hinde St, W1 **16** C3
Hind Gro, E14 **114** A6
Hindhead Cl, N16 **94** B1
Hindhead Gdns, Nthlt. UB5 **102** E1
Hindhead Grn, Wat. WD19 **50** C5
Hindhead Pt, SW15 *off Wanborough Dr* **165** H1
Hindhead Way, Wall. SM6 **200** E5
Hind Ho, N7 *off Harvist Est* **93** G4
Hindle Ho, E8 *off Arcola St* **94** C5
Hindmans Rd, SE22 **152** D5
Hindmans Way, Dag. RM9 **119** F4
Hindmarsh Cl, E1 **21** J5
Hindon Ct, SW1 **33** F1
Hindrey Rd, E5 **94** E5
Hindsley's Pl, SE23 **171** F2
Hinkler Rd, Har. HA3 **69** G3
Hinksey Path, SE2 **138** D3
Hinstock Rd, SE18 **137** F6
Hinton Av, Houns. TW4 **142** D4
Hinton Cl, SE9 **174** B1
Hinton Rd, N18 **60** B4
SE24 **151** H3
Wallington SM6 **200** C6
Hippodrome Ms, W11 *off Portland Rd* **108** B7
Hippodrome Pl, W11 **108** B7
Hirst Ct, SW1 **32** D4
Hirst Cres, Wem. HA9 **87** H3
Hitcham Rd, E17 **77** J7
Hitchin Sq, E3 **113** H2
Hithe Gro, SE16 *off Lower Rd* **133** F3
Hitherbroom Rd, Hayes UB3 **122** A1
Hither Fm Rd, SE3 **155** J3
Hitherfield Rd, SW16 **169** F2
Dagenham RM8 **100** E2
HITHER GREEN, SE13 **154** E6
Hither Grn La, SE13 **154** C5
Hitherlands, SW12 **168** B2
Hitherwell Dr, Har. HA3 **68** A1
Hitherwood Dr, SE19 **170** C4
Hive Cl, Bushey (Bushey Hth) WD23 **52** A2
Hive Rd, Bushey (Bushey Hth) WD23 **52** A2
★ **H.M.S. Belfast**, SE1 **28** E1
★ **H.M.S. President**, EC4 **19** F6
★ **H.M. Treasury**, SW1 **26** A3
Hoadly Rd, SW16 **168** D3
Hobart Cl, N20 *off Oakleigh Rd N* **57** H2
Hayes UB4 **102** D4
Hobart Dr, Hayes UB4 **102** D4
Hobart Gdns, Th.Hth. CR7 **188** A3
Hobart La, Hayes UB4 **102** D4
Hobart Pl, SW1 **24** D5
Richmond TW10 *off Chisholm Rd* **145** J6
Hobart Rd, Dag. RM9 **100** D4
Hayes UB4 **102** D4
Ilford IG6 **81** F2
Worcester Park KT4 **197** H3
Hobbayne Rd, W7 **104** A6
Hobbes Wk, SW15 **147** H5
Hobbs Grn, N2 **73** F3
Hobbs Ms, Ilf. IG3 *off Ripley Rd* **99** J2
Hobbs Pl Est, N1 *off Pitfield St* **112** B1
Hobbs Rd, SE27 **169** J4
Hobby St, Enf. EN3 **45** G5
Hobday St, E14 **114** B5
Hobill Wk, Surb. KT5 **181** J6
Hoblands End, Chis. BR7 **175** H6
Hobsons Pl, E1 **21** H1
Hobury St, SW10 **30** D6
Hocker St, E2 **13** F4

Hockett Cl, SE8
off Grove St **133** J4
Hockley Av, E6 . . . . **116** B2
Hockley Ct, E18
off Churchfields **79** G1
Hockley Ms, Bark. IG11 . . . **117** H2
Hocroft Av, NW2 . . . . **90** C3
Hocroft Rd, NW2 . . . . **90** C4
Hocroft Wk, NW2 . . . . **90** C3
Hodder Dr, Grnf. (Perivale) UB6 . . . . **104** C2
Hoddesdon Rd, Belv. DA17 . . . . **139** G5
Hodes Row, NW3
off Estelle Rd **92** A4
Hodford Rd, NW11 . . . . **90** C2
Hodgkin Cl, SE28
off Fleming Way **118** D7
Hodgkins Ms, Stan. HA7 . . **52** E5
Hodister Cl, SE5
off Badsworth Rd **131** J7
Hodnet Gro, SE16 . . . . **133** G4
Hodson Cl, Har. HA2 . . . . . . **85** F3
Hoe, The, Wat. WD19 . . . . . . **50** D2
Hoechst, Houns. TW4 . . . . **142** C3
Hoe St, E17 . . . . **78** A4
Hoffmann Gdns, S.Croy. CR2 . . . . **202** D7
Hoffman Sq, N1
off Chart St **12** C3
Hofland Rd, W14 . . . . **128** A3
Hogan Ms, W2 . . . . **14** E1
Hogan Way, E5
off Geldeston Rd **94** D2
Hogarth Business Pk, W4 . **126** E6
Hogarth Cl, E16 . . . . **116** A5
W5 . . . . **105** H5
Hogarth Ct, EC3 . . . . **20** E5
SE19 *off Fountain Dr* . . **170** C4
Hogarth Cres, SW19 . . . . . **185** G1
Croydon CR0 . . . . **187** J7
Hogarth Gdns, Houns. TW5 . . . . **123** G7
Hogarth Hill, NW11 . . . . **72** C4
Hogarth La, W4 . . . . **126** E6
Hogarth Pl, SW5 . . . . **30** A2
Hogarth Reach, Loug. IG10 . . . . **48** C5
Hogarth Rd, SW5 . . . . **30** A2
Dagenham RM8 . . . . . . **100** B5
Edgware HA8 . . . . **70** A2
Hogarth Rbt, W4 . . . . **127** F6
Hogarth Rbt Flyover, W4
off Burlington La **127** E6
★ **Hogarth's Ho**, W4
off Hogarth La **126** E6
Hogarth Way, Hmptn. TW12 . . . . **179** J1
Hogshead Pas, E1
off Tobacco Dock **113** E7
Hogsmill La, Kings.T. KT1 **181** J3
Hogsmill Way, Epsom KT19 . . . . **196** C5
Holbeach Cl, NW9 . . . . **70** E1
Holbeach Gdns, Sid. DA15 . . . . **157** H6
Holbeach Ms, SW12
off Harberson Rd **168** B1
Holbeach Rd, SE6 . . . . **154** A7
Holbeck Row, SE15 . . . . . **132** D7
Holbein Ms, SW1 . . . . **32** B3
Holbein Pl, SW1 . . . . **32** B2
Holbein Ter, Dag. RM8
off Marlborough Rd . . **100** B4
Holberton Gdns, NW10 . . **107** H3
HOLBORN, WC2 . . . . **18** C3
Holborn, EC1 . . . . **18** E2
Holborn Circ, EC1 . . . . **19** F2
Holborn Pl, WC1 . . . . **18** C2
Holborn Rd, E13 . . . . **115** H4
Holborn Viaduct, EC1 . . . . . **19** F2
Holborn Way, Mitch. CR4 . **185** J2
Holbrook Cl, N19
off Dartmouth Pk Hill . . **92** B1
Enfield EN1 . . . . **44** C1
Holbrooke Ct, N7 . . . . **92** E4
Holbrooke Pl, Rich. TW10 . **145** G5
Holbrook La, Chis. BR7 . . **175** G7
Holbrook Rd, E15 . . . . **115** F2
Holbrook Way, Brom. BR2 . . . . **192** C6
Holburne Cl, SE3 . . . . **155** J1
Holburne Gdns, SE3 . . . . . **156** A1
Holburne Rd, SE3 . . . . **155** J1
Holcombe Hill, NW7 . . . . . . **55** G3
Holcombe Rd, N17 . . . . **76** C3
Ilford IG1 . . . . **80** D7
Holcombe St, W6 . . . . **127** H5
Holcote Cl, Belv. DA17
off Blakemore Way . . . **139** E3
Holcroft Rd, E9 . . . . **95** F7
Holden Av, N12 . . . . **57** E5
NW9 . . . . **88** C1
Holdenby Rd, SE4 . . . . **153** H5
Holden Cl, Dag. RM8 . . . . **100** B3
Holdenhurst Av, N12 . . . . . **57** E7
Holden Pt, E15
off Waddington Rd **96** D6
Holden Rd, N12 . . . . **56** E5
Holden St, SW11 . . . . **150** A2
Holder Cl, N3 . . . . **57** E7
Holdernesse Cl, Islw. TW7 . . . . **144** D1
Holdernesse Rd, SW17 . . . **167** J3
Holderness Way, SE27 . . . **169** H5
HOLDERS HILL, NW4 . . . . . **72** A2
Holders Hill Av, NW4 . . . . . **72** A2
Holders Hill Circ, NW7
off Dollis Rd **56** B7
Holders Hill Cres, NW4 . . . . **72** A2
Holders Hill Dr, NW4 . . . . . **72** A3
Holders Hill Gdns, NW4 . . . **72** B2
Holders Hill Rd, NW4 . . . . . **72** A2
NW7 . . . . **72** A2
Holegate St, SE7
off Westmoor St **136** A3
Holford Ho, SE16
off Manor Est **132** E4
Holford Ms, WC1 . . . . **10** E2
Holford Pl, WC1 . . . . **10** D3
Holford Rd, NW3 . . . . **91** F3
Holford St, WC1 . . . . **10** E3
Holford Yd, WC1 . . . . **10** D2
Holgate Av, SW11 . . . . **149** G3
Holgate Gdns, Dag. RM10 . . . . **101** G5
Holgate Rd, Dag. RM10 . . **101** G5
Holland Av, SW20 . . . . **183** F1
Holland Cl, Barn. (New Barn.) EN5 . . . . **41** G7
Bromley BR2 . . . . **205** F2
Romford RM7 . . . . **83** J5
Stanmore HA7 . . . . **52** E5
Holland Ct, E17
off Evelyn Rd **78** C4
NW7 . . . . **55** G6
Holland Dr, SE23 . . . . **171** H3
Holland Gdns, W14 . . . . . . **128** B3
Brentford TW8 . . . . **125** H6
Holland Gro, SW9 . . . . **131** G7
★ **Holland Pk**, W8 . . . . . . **128** C2
Holland Pk, W11 . . . . **128** B2
Holland Pk Av, W11 . . . . . **128** B2
Ilford IG3 . . . . **81** H6
Holland Pk Gdns, W14 . . . **128** B1
Holland Pk Ms, W11 . . . . . **128** B1
Holland Pk Rd, W14 . . . . . **128** C3
Holland Pk Rbt, W11 . . . . . **128** A2
Holland Pas, N1
off Basire St **111** J1
Holland Pl, W8 . . . . **22** A3
Holland Ri Ho, SW9
off Clapham Rd **131** F7
Holland Rd, E6 . . . . **116** C1
E15 . . . . **115** E3
NW10 . . . . **107** G1
SE25 . . . . **188** D5
W14 . . . . **128** A2
Wembley HA0 . . . . **87** G6
Hollands, The, Felt. TW13 . **160** D4
Worcester Park KT4 . . . **197** F1
Holland St, SE1 . . . . **27** H1
W8 . . . . **128** D2
Holland Town Est, SW9
off Brixton Rd **131** G7
Holland Vil Rd, W14 . . . . . **128** B2
Holland Wk, N19
off Duncombe Rd **92** D1
W8 . . . . **128** C2
Stanmore HA7 . . . . **52** D5
Holland Way, Brom. BR2 . **205** F2
Hollar Rd, N16
off Stoke Newington High St **94** C3
Hollen St, W1 . . . . **17** H3
Holles Cl, Hmptn. TW12 . . **161** G6
Holles St, W1 . . . . **16** E3
Holley Rd, W3 . . . . **127** E2
Hollickwood Av, N12 . . . . . **57** J6
Holliday Sq, SW11
off Fowler Cl **149** G3
Hollidge Way, Dag. RM10 . . . . **101** H6
Hollies, The, E11 . . . . **79** G5
N20
off Oakleigh Pk N **57** G1
Harrow HA3 . . . . **68** D4
Hollies Av, Sid. DA15 . . . . **175** J2
Hollies Cl, SW16 . . . . **169** G6
Twickenham TW1 . . . . . **162** C2
Hollies End, NW7 . . . . **55** H5
Hollies Rd, W5 . . . . **125** F4
Hollies Way, SW12
off Bracken Av **150** A7
Holligrave Rd, Brom. BR1 . . . . **191** G1
Hollingbourne Av, Bexh. DA7 . . . . **139** F7
Hollingbourne Gdns, W13 . . . . **104** E5
Hollingbourne Rd, SE24 . . **151** J5
Hollingsworth Rd, Croy. CR0 . . . . **203** E6
Hollington Cres, N.Mal. KT3 . . . . **183** F6
Hollington Rd, E6 . . . . **116** C3
N17 . . . . **76** D2
Hollingworth Cl, W.Mol. KT8 . . . . **179** F4
Hollingworth Rd, Orp. BR5 . . . . **192** E6
Hollman Gdns, SW16 . . . . **169** H6
Hollow, The, Wdf.Grn. IG8 . **63** F4
HOLLOWAY, N7 . . . . **92** D5
Holloway Cl, West Dr. UB7 . . . . **120** B5
Holloway La, West Dr. UB7 . . . . **120** B6
Holloway Rd, E6 . . . . **116** C3
E11 . . . . **96** E3
N7 . . . . **93** F4
N19 . . . . **92** D2
Holloway St, Houns. TW3 . . . . **143** H3
Hollowfield Wk, Nthlt. UB5 . . . . **84** E6
Hollows, The, Brent. TW8 . **125** J6
Hollow Wk, Rich. (Kew) TW9 *off Royal Botanic Gdns* **125** H7
Holly Av, Stan. HA7 . . . . . . **69** H2
Hollybank Cl, Hmptn. TW12 . . . . **161** G5
Hollyberry La, NW3
off Holly Wk **91** F4
Hollybrake Cl, Chis. BR7 . . **175** G7
Hollybush Cl, E11 . . . . **79** G5
Harrow HA3 . . . . **68** B1
Hollybush Gdns, E2 . . . . . **113** E3
Hollybush Hill, E11 . . . . **79** F6
Holly Bush Hill, NW3 . . . . . **91** F4
Holly Bush La, Hmptn. TW12 . . . . **161** F7
Hollybush Pl, E2
off Bethnal Grn Rd . . . **113** E3
Hollybush Rd, Kings.T. KT2 . . . . **163** H5
Holly Bush Steps, NW3
off Heath St **91** F4
Hollybush St, E13 . . . . **115** H3
Holly Bush Vale, NW3
off Heath St **91** F4
Holly Cl, Beck. BR3 . . . . . . **190** C4
Buckhurst Hill IG9 . . . . . . **64** A3
Feltham TW13 . . . . **160** E5
Wallington SM6 . . . . . . **200** B7
Holly Ct, SE10
off West Parkside **135** F3
Sutton SM2
off Worcester Rd **198** D7
Holly Cres, Beck. BR3 . . . . **189** J5
Woodford Green IG8 . . . **62** D7
Hollycroft Av, NW3 . . . . **90** D3
Wembley HA9 . . . . **87** J2
Hollycroft Cl, S.Croy. CR2 . . . . **202** B5
West Drayton (Sipson) UB7 . . . . **120** D6
Hollycroft Gdns, West Dr. (Sipson) UB7 . . . . **120** D6
Hollydale Cl, Nthlt. UB5
off Dorchester Rd **85** H4
Hollydale Dr, Brom. BR2 . **206** C3
Hollydale Rd, SE15 . . . . . . **153** F1
Hollydene, SE15 . . . . **152** E1
Hollydown Way, E11 . . . . . . **96** D3
Holly Dr, E4 . . . . **46** B7
Brentford TW8 . . . . **124** D6
Holly Fm Rd, Sthl. UB2 . . **122** E5
Hollyfield Av, N11 . . . . **57** J5
Hollyfield Rd, Surb. KT5 . . **181** J7
Holly Gdns, Bexh. DA7 . . . **159** J4
West Drayton UB7 . . . . **120** C2
Holly Gro, NW9 . . . . **70** C7
SE15 . . . . **152** C2
Pinner HA5 . . . . **67** E1
Hollygrove Cl, Houns. TW3
off Staines Rd **143** F4
Holly Hedge Ter, SE13 . . . **154** D5
Holly Hill, N21 . . . . **43** F6
NW3 . . . . **91** F4
Holly Hill Rd, Belv. DA17 . **139** H5
Erith DA8 . . . . **139** H5
Holly Lo Gdns, N6 . . . . **92** A2
Hollymead, Cars. SM5 . . . **199** J3
Holly Ms, SW10 . . . . **30** D4
Holly Mt, NW3
off Holly Bush Hill **91** F4
Hollymount Cl, SE10 . . . . **154** C1
Holly Pk, N3 . . . . **72** C3
N4 . . . . **75** F7
Holly Pk Est, N4
off Blythwood Rd **75** E7
Holly Pk Gdns, N3 . . . . **72** D3
Holly Pk Rd, N11 . . . . **58** A5
W7 . . . . **124** C1
Holly Pl, NW3
off Holly Wk **91** F4
Holly Rd, E11 . . . . **79** F7
W4 *off Dolman Rd* **126** D4
Hampton (Hmptn H.) TW12 . . . . **161** J6
Hounslow TW3 . . . . **143** H4
Twickenham TW1 . . . . . **162** D1
Holly St, E8 . . . . **94** C6
Holly Ter, N6
off Highgate W Hill **92** A1
N20 *off Swan La* **57** F2
Hollytree Cl, SW19 . . . . . . **166** A1
Hollyview Cl, NW4 . . . . **71** G6
Holly Village, N6
off Swains La **92** B2
Holly Wk, NW3 . . . . **91** F4
Enfield EN2 . . . . **43** J3
Richmond TW9 . . . . **145** H2
Holly Way, Mitch. CR4 . . . **186** D4
Hollywood Gdns, Hayes UB4 . . . . **102** B6
Hollywood Ms, SW10 . . . . . **30** C5
Hollywood Rd, E4 . . . . **61** H5
SW10 . . . . **30** C4
Hollywood Way, Wdf.Grn. IG8 . . . . **62** D7
Holman Ho, E2
off Roman Rd **113** G3
Holman Rd, SW11 . . . . **149** G2
Epsom KT19 . . . . **196** C5
Holmbridge Gdns, Enf. EN3 . . . . **45** G4
Holmbrook Dr, NW4 . . . . . . **72** A5
Holmbury Ct, SW17 . . . . . **167** J3
SW19 . . . . **167** H7
Holmbury Gdns, Hayes UB3 *off Church Rd* **121** J1
Holmbury Gro, Croy. CR0 . . . . **203** J7
Holmbury Pk, Brom. BR1 . **174** B7
Holmbury Vw, E5 . . . . **95** E1
Holmbush Rd, SW15 . . . . **148** B6
Holmcote Gdns, N5 . . . . . . **93** J5
Holmcroft Way, Brom. BR2 . . . . **192** C5
Holmdale Gdns, NW4 . . . . . **72** A5
Holmdale Rd, NW6 . . . . **90** D5
Chislehurst BR7 . . . . . . **175** F5
Holmdale Ter, N15 . . . . **76** B7
Holmdene Av, NW7 . . . . . . **55** G6
SE24 . . . . **151** J5
Harrow HA2 . . . . **67** H3
Holmdene Cl, Beck. BR3 . . **190** C2
Holmead Rd, SW6 . . . . . . **129** E7
Holmebury Cl, Bushey (Bushey Hth) WD23 . . . . **52** B2
Holme Ct, Islw. TW7
off Twickenham Rd . . . **144** D3
Holmefield Ct, NW3 . . . . . . **91** H6
Holme Lacey Rd, SE12 . . . **155** F6
Holme Rd, E6 . . . . **116** B1
Holmes Av, E17 . . . . **77** J3
NW7 . . . . **56** B5
Holmes Cl, SE22 . . . . **152** D4
Holmesdale Av, SW14 . . . **146** B3
Holmesdale Cl, SE25 . . . . **188** C3
Holmesdale Rd, N6 . . . . **74** B7
SE25 . . . . **188** A5
Bexleyheath DA7 . . . . . **158** D2
Croydon CR0 . . . . **188** A5
Richmond TW9 . . . . **145** J1
Teddington TW11 . . . . . **163** F6
Holmesley Rd, SE23 . . . . . **153** H6
Holmes Pl, SW10 . . . . **30** D5
Holmes Rd, NW5 . . . . **92** B5
SW19 . . . . **167** F7
Twickenham TW1 . . . . . **162** C2
Holmes Ter, SE1 . . . . **27** E3
Holme Way, Stan. HA7 . . . . **52** C6
Holmewood Gdns, SW2 . **151** F7
Holmewood Rd, SE25 . . . **188** B3
SW2 . . . . **151** E7
Holmfield Av, NW4 . . . . **72** A5
Holmhurst Rd, Belv. DA17 . . . . **139** H5
Holmleigh Rd, N16 . . . . **94** B1
Holmleigh Rd Est, N16
off Holmleigh Rd **94** B1
Holm Oak Cl, SW15 . . . . . **148** C6
Holm Oak Ms, SW4 . . . . . **150** D5
Holmshaw Cl, SE26 . . . . . **171** H4
Holmside Ri, Wat. WD19 . . . **50** B3
Holmside Rd, SW12 . . . . . **150** A6
Holmsley Cl, N.Mal. KT3 . . . . **183** F6

Holmsley Ho, SW15
off Tangley Gro **147** F7
Holms St, E2 . . . . **13** H1
Holmstall Av, Edg. HA8 . . . **70** C3
Holm Wk, SE3
off Blackheath Pk **155** G2
Holmwood Cl, Har. HA2 . . . **67** J3
Northolt UB5 . . . . **85** H6
Holmwood Gdns, N3 . . . . . **72** D2
Wallington SM6 . . . . . . **200** B6
Holmwood Gro, NW7 . . . . . **54** D5
Holmwood Rd, Chess.
KT9 . . . . **195** G5
Ilford IG3 . . . . **99** H2
Holmwood Vil, SE7
off Woolwich Rd **135** G5
Holne Chase, N2 . . . . **73** F6
Morden SM4 . . . . **184** C6
Holness Rd, E15 . . . . **97** F6
Holroyd Rd, SW15 . . . . . . **147** J4
Holstein Way, Erith DA18 . **138** E3
Holstock Rd, Ilf. IG1 . . . . . . **99** F2
Holsworth Cl, Har. HA2 . . . **67** J5
Holsworthy Sq, WC1 . . . . . **10** D6
Holsworthy Way, Chess.
KT9 . . . . **195** F5
Holt, The, Ilf. IG6 . . . . **65** F6
Morden SM4
off London Rd **184** D4
Wallington SM6 . . . . . . **200** C4
Holt Cl, N10 . . . . **74** A4
SE28 . . . . **118** B7
Chigwell IG7 . . . . **65** J5
Holton St, E1 . . . . **113** G4
Holt Rd, E16 . . . . **136** B1
Wembley HA0 . . . . **87** E3
Holt Way, Chig. IG7 . . . . **65** J5
Holtwhite Av, Enf. EN2 . . . . **43** J2
Holtwhites Hill, Enf. EN2 . . **43** H1
Holwell Pl, Pnr. HA5 . . . . . . **66** E4
Holwood Pk Av, Orp.
BR6 . . . . **206** C4
Holwood Pl, SW4 . . . . **150** D4
Holybourne Av, SW15 . . . **147** G7
Holyhead Cl, E3
off Campbell Rd **114** A3
E6 *off Valiant Way* **116** C5
Holyoake Ct, SE16
off Bryan Rd **133** J2
Holyoake Wk, N2 . . . . **73** F3
W5 . . . . **105** F4
Holyoak Rd, SE11 . . . . **35** G1
Holyport Rd, SW6 . . . . **127** J7
Holyrood Av, Har. HA2 . . . . **85** E4
Holyrood Gdns, Edg. HA8 . **70** B3
Holyrood Ms, E16
off Wesley Av **135** G1
Holyrood Rd, Barn.
(New Barn.) EN5 . . . . **41** F6
Holyrood St, SE1 . . . . **28** D2
Holywell Cl, SE3 . . . . **135** G6
SE16 *off Masters Dr* . . . **133** E5
Holywell La, EC2 . . . . **12** E5
Holywell Row, EC2 . . . . **12** D6
Homan Ct, N12 . . . . **57** F4
Home Cl, Cars. SM5 . . . . . **199** J2
Northolt UB5 . . . . **103** F3
Homecroft Gdns, Loug.
IG10 . . . . **48** E4
Homecroft Rd, N22 . . . . **75** H1
SE26 . . . . **171** F5
Home Fm Cl, T.Ditt. KT7 . . **180** C7
Homefarm Rd, W7 . . . . **104** B6
Homefield Av, Ilf. IG2 . . . . . **81** H5
Homefield Cl, NW10 . . . . . . **88** C6
Hayes UB4 . . . . **102** C4
Homefield Gdns, N2 . . . . . . **73** G3
Mitcham CR4 . . . . **185** F2
Homefield Ms, Beck. BR3 . **190** A1
Homefield Pk, Sutt. SM1 . **198** E6
Homefield Rd, SW19 . . . . **166** A6
W4 . . . . **127** F4
Bromley BR1 . . . . **191** J1
Edgware HA8 . . . . **54** D6
Walton-on-Thames
KT12 . . . . **179** E7
Wembley HA0 . . . . **86** D4
Homefield St, N1 . . . . **12** D2
Homefirs Ho, Wem. HA9 . . **87** J3
Home Gdns, Dag. RM10 . . **101** J3
Homelands Dr, SE19 . . . . . **170** B7
Home La, Orp. BR6 . . . . . . **207** J5
Homeleigh Rd, SE15 . . . . . **153** G5
Homemead, SW12 . . . . . . **168** B2
Home Mead, Stan. HA7 . . . **69** F1
Homemead Rd, Brom.
BR2 . . . . **192** C5
Croydon CR0 . . . . **186** C6
★ **Home Office**, SW1 . . . . **25** J6
Home Pk, E.Mol.
(Hampton Ct Pk) KT8 . . **180** E4
Kingston upon Thames
(Hampton Ct Pk) KT1 . **180** E4
Home Pk Par, Kings.T. KT1
off High St **181** G2
Home Pk Rd, SW19 . . . . . **166** D3
Home Pk Wk, Kings.T.
KT1 . . . . **181** G4
Homer Cl, Bexh. DA7 . . . . **159** J1
Homer Dr, E14 . . . . **134** A4
Home Rd, SW11 . . . . **149** H2
Homer Rd, E9 . . . . **95** H6
Croydon CR0 . . . . **189** G6
Homer Row, W1 . . . . **15** H2
Homersham Rd, Kings.T.
KT1 . . . . **182** A2
Homer St, W1 . . . . **15** H2
HOMERTON, E9 . . . . **95** H5
Homerton Gro, E9 . . . . **95** G5
Homerton High St, E9 . . . . **95** F5
Homerton Rd, E9 . . . . **95** H5
Homerton Row, E9 . . . . **95** F5
Homerton Ter, E9
off Morning La **95** F6
Homesdale Cl, E11 . . . . **79** G5
Homesdale Rd, Brom.
BR1, BR2 . . . . **191** J4
Orpington BR5 . . . . **193** H7
Homesfield, NW11 . . . . **72** D5
Homestall Rd, SE22 . . . . . **153** F5
Homestead, The, N11 . . . . . **58** B4
Homestead Gdns, Esher
(Clay.) KT10 . . . . **194** B5
Homestead Paddock, N14 . **42** B5
Homestead Pk, NW2 . . . . . **89** F3
Homestead Rd, SW6 . . . . **128** C7
Dagenham RM8 . . . . . . **101** F2
Homewillow Cl, N21 . . . . . . **43** H6
Homewood Cl, Hmptn. TW12
off Fearnley Cres **161** F6
Homewood Cres, Chis.
BR7 . . . . **175** H6
Homildon Ho, SE26
off Sydenham
Hill Est **170** D3
Honduras St, EC1 . . . . **11** J5
Honeybourne Rd, NW6 . . . **90** E5
Honeybourne Way, Orp.
BR5 . . . . **207** G1
Honeybrook Rd, SW12 . . . **150** C7
Honey Cl, Dag. RM10 . . . . **101** H6
Honeycroft, Loug. IG10 . . . **48** D4
Honeyden Rd, Sid. DA14 . **177** E6
Honey La, EC2 . . . . **20** A4
Honeyman Cl, NW6 . . . . . . **90** A7
Honeypot Business Cen,
Stan. HA7 . . . . **69** H1
Honeypot Cl, NW9 . . . . **69** J4
Honeypot La, NW9 . . . . **69** J3
Stanmore HA7 . . . . **69** J3
Honeysett Rd, N17
off Reform Row **76** C2
Honeysuckle Cl, Sthl.
UB1 . . . . **102** E7
Honeysuckle Gdns, Croy.
CR0 . . . . **189** G7
Honeywell Rd, SW11 . . . . **149** J6
★ **Honeywood Heritage**
Cen, Cars. SM5 . . . . . . **199** J4
Honeywood Rd, NW10 . . . **107** F2
Isleworth TW7 . . . . **144** D4
Honeywood Wk, Cars.
SM5 . . . . **199** J4
Honister Cl, Stan. HA7 . . . . **69** E1
Honister Gdns, Stan. HA7 . **53** E7
Honister Pl, Stan. HA7 . . . . **69** E1
Honiton Gdns, NW7 . . . . . . **56** A7
SE15 *off Gibbon Rd* . . . **153** F2
Honiton Ho, Enf. EN3
off Exeter Rd **45** G3
Honiton Rd, NW6 . . . . **108** C2
Welling DA16 . . . . **157** J2
Honley Rd, SE6 . . . . **154** B7
Honnor Gdns, Islw. TW7 . . **144** A2
HONOR OAK, SE23 . . . . . . **153** F6
HONOR OAK PARK, SE4 . **153** H6
Honor Oak Pk, SE23 . . . . . **153** F6
Honor Oak Ri, SE23 . . . . . **153** F6
Honor Oak Rd, SE23 . . . . . **171** F1
Hood Av, N14 . . . . **42** B6
SW14 . . . . **146** C5
Hood Cl, Croy. CR0 . . . . . . **201** H1
Hoodcote Gdns, N21 . . . . . **43** H7
Hood Ct, EC4 . . . . **19** F4
Hood Rd, SW20 . . . . **165** F7
Hood Wk, Rom. RM7 . . . . . **83** H1
HOOK, Chess. KT9 . . . . . . **195** H4
Hook, The, Barn.
(New Barn.) EN5 . . . . **41** G6
Hookers Rd, E17 . . . . **77** G3
Hook Fm Rd, Brom. BR2 . **192** A5
Hooking Grn, Har. HA2 . . . . **67** H5
Hook Junct, Surb. KT6 . . . **195** G3
Hook La, Well. DA16 . . . . . **157** J5
Hook Ri N, Surb. KT6 . . . . **196** A3
Hook Ri S, Surb. KT6 . . . . **196** B3
Hook Ri S Business Cen,
Surb. KT6 . . . . **196** A3
Hook Ri S Ind Pk, Surb.
KT6 . . . . **195** J3
Hook Rd, Chess. KT9 . . . . **195** G5
Surbiton KT6 . . . . **195** H3
Hooks Cl, SE15
off Woods Rd **152** E1
Hooks Hall Dr, Dag.
RM10 . . . . **101** J3
Hookstone Way, Wdf.Grn.
IG8 . . . . **64** A7
Hook Wk, Edg. HA8 . . . . . . **54** C6
Hool Cl, NW9
off Kingsbury Rd **70** C5
Hooper Rd, E16 . . . . **115** G6
Hooper's Ct, SW3 . . . . **23** J4
Hoopers Ms, W3 . . . . **126** C1
Hooper's Ms, Bushey
WD23 . . . . **51** H1
Hooper St, E1 . . . . **21** H5
Hoop La, NW11 . . . . **72** C7
Hope Cl, N1
off Wallace Rd **93** J6
SE12 . . . . **173** H3
Brentford TW8
off Burford Rd **125** H5
Romford (Chad.Hth)
RM6 . . . . **82** C4
Sutton SM1 . . . . **199** F5
Woodford Green IG8
off West Gro **63** J6
Hopedale Rd, SE7 . . . . **135** H6
Hopefield Av, NW6 . . . . . . **108** B2
Hope Gdns, W3
off Park Rd N **126** B2
Hope La, SE9 . . . . **174** E2
Hope Pk, Brom. BR1 . . . . . **173** F7
Hopes Cl, Houns. TW5
off Old Cote Dr **123** G6
Hope St, SW11 . . . . **149** G3
Hopetown St, E1 . . . . **21** G2
Hopewell St, SE5 . . . . **132** A7
Hopewell Yd, SE5
off Hopewell St **132** A7
Hope Wf, SE16
off St. Marychurch St . **133** F2
Hop Gdns, WC2 . . . . **18** A6
Hopgood St, W12
off Macfarlane Rd **127** J1
Hopkins Cl, N10 . . . . **58** A7
Hopkins Ms, E15
off West Rd **115** F1
Hopkinsons Pl, NW1
off Fitzroy Rd **110** A1
Hopkins Rd, E10 . . . . **78** B7
Hopkins St, W1 . . . . **17** G4
Hoppers Rd, N13 . . . . **59** G2
N21 . . . . **59** G2
Hoppett Rd, E4 . . . . **62** E3
Hopping La, N1
off St. Mary's Gro **93** H6
Hoppingwood Av, N.Mal.
KT3 . . . . **183** E3
Hop St, SE10 . . . . **135** F4
Hopton Gdns, N.Mal.
KT3 . . . . **183** G6
Hopton Rd, SE18 . . . . **137** E3
SW16 . . . . **168** E5
Hopton's Gdns, SE1 . . . . . . **27** H1
Hopton St, SE1 . . . . **27** H1
Hoptree Cl, N12
off Woodside Pk Rd . . . **56** E4
Hopwood Cl, SW17 . . . . . **167** F3
Hopwood Rd, SE17 . . . . **36** C5
Hopwood Wk, E8
off Wilman Gro **94** D7
Horace Av, Rom. RM7 . . . . **101** J1
Horace Bldg, SW8
off Queenstown Rd . . . **32** D7
Horace Rd, E7 . . . . **97** H4
Ilford IG6 . . . . **81** F3
Kingston upon Thames
KT1 . . . . **181** J3
Horatio Ct, SE16
off Rotherhithe St **133** F1
Horatio Pl, E14
off Cold Harbour **134** C2
SW19 *off Kingston Rd* . **184** D1
Horatio St, E2 . . . . **13** H2
Horatius Way, Croy. CR0 . **201** F6
Horbury Cres, W11 . . . . . . **108** D7
Horbury Ms, W11
off Ladbroke Rd **108** C7
Horder Rd, SW6 . . . . **148** B1
Horizon Business Cen, N9
off Goodwin Rd **61** G1
Horizon Way, SE7 . . . . **135** H4
Horle Wk, SE5 . . . . **151** H2
Horley Cl, Bexh. DA6 . . . . **159** G5
Horley Rd, SE9 . . . . **174** B4
Hormead Rd, W9 . . . . **108** C4
Hornbeam Cl, NW7 . . . . **55** F3
SE11 . . . . **34** E1
Barking IG11 . . . . **118** A3
Borehamwood WD6 . . . . **38** A1
Buckhurst Hill IG9
off Hornbeam Rd **64** A3
Ilford IG1 . . . . **99** G5
Hornbeam Cl, Northolt
UB5 . . . . **85** F5
Hornbeam Cres, Brent.
TW8 . . . . **125** E7
Hornbeam Gdns, N.Mal.
KT3 . . . . **183** G6
Hornbeam Gro, E4 . . . . **63** E3
Hornbeam Ho, NW3
off Maitland Pk Vil **91** J6
Hornbeam La, E4 . . . . **47** E5
Bexleyheath DA7 . . . . . **159** J2
Hornbeam Rd, Buck.H.
IG9 . . . . **64** A3
Hayes UB4 . . . . **102** C5
Hornbeam Sq, E3
off Hawthorn Av **113** J1
Hornbeams Ri, N11 . . . . **58** A6
Hornbeam Ter, Cars.
SM5 . . . . **199** H1
Hornbeam Wk, Rich.
TW10 . . . . **163** J3
Hornbeam Way, Brom.
BR2 . . . . **192** D6
Hornblower Cl, SE16
off Greenland Quay . . **133** H4
Hornbuckle Cl, Har. HA2 . . **86** A2
Hornby Cl, NW3 . . . . **91** G7
Horncastle Cl, SE12 . . . . . **155** G7
Horncastle Rd, SE12 . . . . . **155** G7
Hornchurch Cl, Kings.T.
KT2 . . . . **163** G4
Horndean Cl, SW15
off Bessborough Rd . . **165** G1
Horndon Cl, Rom. RM5 . . . **83** J1
Horndon Grn, Rom. RM5 . . **83** J1
Horndon Rd, Rom. RM5 . . . **83** J1
Horner La, Mitch. CR4 . . . **185** G2
Hornet Way, E6
off Armada Way **117** G5
Horne Way, SW15 . . . . **147** J2
Hornfair Rd, SE7 . . . . **135** J6
Horniman Dr, SE23 . . . . . . **171** E1
★ **Horniman Mus**,
SE23 . . . . **170** E1
Horning Cl, SE9 . . . . **174** B4
Horn La, SE10 . . . . **135** G4
W3 . . . . **106** C7
Woodford Green IG8 . . . **63** G6
Horn Link Way, SE10 . . . . **135** G4
Horn Pk Cl, SE12 . . . . **155** H5
Horn Pk La, SE12 . . . . **155** H5
Horns Cft Cl, Bark. IG11
off Thornhill Gdns **99** H7
Horns End Pl, Pnr. HA5 . . . **66** C4
HORNSEY, N8 . . . . **75** F3
Hornsey La, N6 . . . . **92** B1
Hornsey La Est, N19 . . . . . . **74** D7
Hornsey La Gdns, N6 . . . . . **74** C7
Hornsey Pk Rd, N8 . . . . **75** F3
Hornsey Ri, N19 . . . . **74** D7
Hornsey Ri Gdns, N19 . . . . **74** D7
Hornsey Rd, N7 . . . . **93** F2
N19 . . . . **92** E1
Hornsey St, N7 . . . . **93** F5
Hornshay St, SE15 . . . . . . **133** F6
Horns Rd, Ilf. IG2, IG6 . . . . . **81** F5
Hornton Pl, W8 . . . . **128** D2
Hornton St, W8 . . . . **128** D1
Horsa Rd, SE12 . . . . **155** J7
Erith DA8 . . . . **139** J7
Horse & Dolphin Yd, W1 . . . **17** J5
Horsebridge Cl, Dag.
RM9 . . . . **119** E1
Horsecroft Rd, Edg. HA8 . . **54** D7
Horse Fair, Kings.T. KT1 . . **181** G2
Horseferry Pl, SE10 . . . . . . **134** C6
Horseferry Rd, E14 . . . . . . **113** H7
SW1 . . . . **25** H6
Horse Guards Av, SW1 . . . . **26** A2
★ **Horse Guards Par**,
SW1 . . . . **25** J2
Horse Guards Rd, SW1 . . . **25** J2
Horse Leaze, E6 . . . . **116** D6
Horsell Rd, N5 . . . . **93** G5
Horselydown La, SE1 . . . . . **29** F3
Horsemongers Ms, SE1 . . . **28** A4
Horsenden Av, Grnf.
UB6 . . . . **86** B5
Horsenden Cres, Grnf.
UB6 . . . . **86** C5
Horsenden La N, Grnf.
UB6 . . . . **86** C6
Horsenden La S, Grnf.
(Perivale) UB6 . . . . **104** D1
Horse Ride, SW1 . . . . **25** G2
Horse Rd, E7
off Centre Rd **97** H3
Horseshoe Cl, E14 . . . . **134** C5
NW2 . . . . **89** H2
Horse Shoe Ct, EC1
off Brewhouse Yd **11** H5
Horse Shoe Cres, Nthlt.
UB5 . . . . **103** G2
Horse Shoe Grn, Sutt. SM1
off Aultone Way **199** E2

Horseshoe La, N20 ...56 A1
Enfield EN2 off Chase Side ...43 J3
Horseshoe Ms, SW2 off Acre La ...151 E4
Horse Yd, N1 off Essex Rd ...111 H1
Horsfeld Gdns, SE9 ...156 B5
Horsfeld Rd, SE9 ...156 A5
Horsford Rd, SW2 ...151 F5
Horsham Av, N12 ...57 H5
Horsham Rd, Bexh. DA6 .159 G5
Feltham TW14 ...141 F6
Horsleydown Old Stairs, SE1 ...29 F2
Horsley Dr, Croy. (New Adgtn) CR0 ...204 C7
Kingston upon Thames KT2 ...163 G5
Horsley Rd, E4 ...62 C2
Bromley BR1 off Palace Rd ...191 H1
Horsley St, SE17 ...36 B5
Horsmonden Cl, Orp. BR6 ...193 H7
Horsmonden Rd, SE4 ...153 J5
Hortensia Rd, SW10 ...30 C6
Horticultural Pl, W4 off Heathfield Ter ...126 D5
Horton Av, NW2 ...90 B4
Horton Br Rd, West Dr. UB7 ...120 C1
Horton Cl, West Dr. UB7 ..120 C1
Horton Ho, SW8 ...34 C7
Horton Ind Pk, West Dr. UB7 ...120 C1
Horton Rd, E8 ...94 E6
West Drayton UB7 ...120 D1
Horton St, SE13 ...154 B3
Horton Way, Croy. CR0 ...189 G5
Hortus Rd, E4 ...62 C2
Southall UB2 ...123 F2
Hosack Rd, SW17 ...167 J2
Hoser Av, SE12 ...173 G2
Hosier La, EC1 ...19 G2
Hoskins Cl, E16 ...115 J6
Hayes UB3 off Cranford Dr ...121 J5
Hoskins St, SE10 ...134 D5
Hospital Br Rd, Twick. TW2 ...143 H7
Hospital Rd, E9 off Homerton Row ...95 G5
Hounslow TW3 ...143 G3
Hospital Way, SE13 ...154 D7
Hotham Cl, W.Mol. KT8 off Garrick Gdns ...179 G3
Hotham Rd, SW15 ...147 J3
SW19 ...167 F7
Hotham Rd Ms, SW19 off Haydons Rd ...167 F7
Hotham St, E15 ...114 E1
Hothfield Pl, SE16 off Lower Rd ...133 F3
Hotspur Ind Est, N17 ...60 E6
Hotspur Rd, Nthlt. UB5 ..103 G2
Hotspur St, SE11 ...34 E3
Houblon Rd, Rich. TW10 ..145 H5
Houghton Cl, E8 off Buttermere Wk ...94 C6
Hampton TW12 ...161 E6
Houghton Rd, N15 off West Grn Rd ...76 C4
Houghton Sq, SW9 off Clapham Rd ...150 E2
Houghton St, WC2 ...18 D4
Houlder Cres, Croy. CR0 ..201 H6
Houndsden Rd, N21 ...43 F6
Houndsditch, EC3 ...20 E3
Houndsfield Rd, N9 ...44 E7
HOUNSLOW, TW3 - TW6 .143 F4
Hounslow Av, Houns. TW3 ...143 H5
Hounslow Business Pk, Houns. TW3 off Alice Way ...143 H4
Hounslow Gdns, Houns. TW3 ...143 H5
★ **Hounslow Heath**, Houns. TW4 ...142 E6
Hounslow Rd, Felt. TW14 .160 B1
Feltham (Han.) TW13 ..160 D4
Twickenham TW2 ...143 J6
HOUNSLOW WEST, Houns. TW4 ...142 D3
Houseman Way, SE5 off Hopewell St ...132 A7
★ **Houses of Parliament**, SW1 ...26 B4
Houston Pl, Esher KT10 off Lime Tree Av ...194 B1
Houston Rd, SE23 ...171 H2
Surbiton (Long Dit.) KT6 ...181 E6
Hove Av, E17 ...77 J5
Hoveden Rd, NW2 ...90 B5
Hove Gdns, Sutt. SM1 ...199 E1
Hoveton Rd, SE28 ...118 C6
Hoveton Way, Ilf. IG6 ...65 E7
Howard Av, Bex. DA5 ...176 C1
Howard Bldg, SW8 ...32 D6
Howard Cl, N11 ...58 A2
NW2 ...90 B4
W3 ...106 B6
Hampton TW12 ...161 J6
Loughton IG10 ...48 B6
Howard Dr, Borwd. WD6 ...38 D4
Howard Ms, N5 off Hamilton Pk ...93 H4
Howard Rd, E6 ...116 C2
E11 ...97 E3
E17 ...78 A3
N15 ...76 B6
N16 ...94 A4
NW2 ...90 A4
SE20 ...189 F1
SE25 ...188 D5
Barking IG11 ...117 G1
Bromley BR1 ...173 G7
Ilford IG1 ...98 E4
Isleworth TW7 ...144 C3
New Malden KT3 ...183 E3
Southall UB1 ...103 H6
Surbiton KT5 ...181 J6
Howards Cl, Pnr. HA5 ...66 B2
Howards Crest Cl, Beck. BR3 ...190 C2
Howards La, SW15 ...147 H5
Howards Rd, E13 ...115 G3
Howard St, T.Ditt. KT7 ...181 E7
Howard Wk, N2 ...73 F4
Howard Way, Barn. EN5 ...40 A5
Howarth Rd, SE2 ...138 A5
Howberry Cl, Edg. HA8 ...53 G6
Howberry Rd, Edg. HA8 ...53 G6
Stanmore HA7 ...53 G6
Thornton Heath CR7 ..188 A1
Howbury Rd, SE15 ...153 F3
Howcroft Cres, N3 ...56 D7
Howcroft La, Grnf. UB6 off Cowgate Rd ...104 A3
Howden Cl, SE28 ...118 D7
Howden Rd, SE25 ...188 C2
Howden St, SE15 ...152 D3
Howe Cl, Rom. RM7 ...83 G1
Howell Cl, Rom. RM6 ...82 D5
Howell Wk, SE1 ...35 H2
Howerd Way, SE18 ...156 B1
Howes Cl, N3 ...72 D3
Howfield Pl, N17 ...76 C3
Howgate Rd, SW14 ...146 D3
Howick Pl, SW1 ...25 G6
Howie St, SW11 ...129 H7
Howitt Cl, N16 off Allen Rd ...94 B4
NW3 off Howitt Rd ...91 H6
Howitt Rd, NW3 ...91 H6
Howland Est, SE16 ...133 F3
Howland Ms E, W1 ...17 G1
Howland St, W1 ...17 F1
Howland Way, SE16 ...133 H2
Howletts Rd, SE24 ...151 J6
Howley Pl, W2 ...14 D1
Howley Rd, Croy. CR0 ...201 H3
Howsman Rd, SW13 ...127 G6
Howson Rd, SE4 ...153 H4
Howson Ter, Rich. TW10 ..145 H6
Hows St, E2 ...13 F1
Howton Pl, Bushey (Bushey Hth) WD23 ...52 A1
HOXTON, N1 ...12 D2
Hoxton Mkt, N1 ...12 D4
Hoxton Sq, N1 ...12 D4
Hoxton St, N1 ...12 E4
Hoylake Gdns, Mitch. CR4 ...186 C3
Ruislip HA4 ...84 B1
Watford WD19 ...50 D4
Hoylake Rd, W3 ...107 E6
Hoyland Cl, SE15 off Commercial Way ..132 E7
Hoyle Rd, SW17 ...167 H5
Hoy St, E16 ...115 F6
★ **H.Q.S. Wellington, Master Mariners' Hall**, WC2 ...18 E5
Hubbard Dr, Chess. KT9 ..195 F6
Hubbard Rd, SE27 ...169 J4
Hubbard St, E15 ...114 E1
Hubbinet Ind Est, Rom. RM7 ...83 J3
Hubert Gro, SW9 ...151 E3
Hubert Rd, E6 ...116 A3
Huddart St, E3 ...113 J5
Huddleston Cl, E2 ...113 F2
Huddlestone Rd, E7 ...97 F4
NW2 ...89 H6
Huddleston Rd, N7 ...92 D4
Hudson Apts, N8 off Chadwell La ...75 F3
Hudson Cl, E15 off Park Gro ...115 G1
W12 off Canada Way ..107 H7
Hudson Ct, E14 off Maritime Quay ...134 A5
SW19 ...167 E7
Hudson Gdns, Orp. (Grn St Grn) BR6 off Superior Dr ...207 J6
Hudson Pl, SE18 ...137 F5
Hudson Rd, Bexh. DA7 ...159 F2
Hayes (Harling.) UB3 ..121 G6
Hudson's Pl, SW1 ...33 E1
Hudson Way, N9 ...61 F3
NW2 off Gratton Ter ...90 A3
Huggin Ct, EC4 ...20 A5
Huggin Hill, EC4 ...20 A5
Huggins Pl, SW2 off Roupell Rd ...169 F1
Hughan Rd, E15 ...96 D5
Hugh Dalton Av, SW6 ...128 C6
Hughenden Av, Har. HA3 ..69 E5
Hughenden Gdns, Nthlt. UB5 ...102 C3
Hughenden Rd, Wor.Pk. KT4 ...183 G7
Hughendon Ter, E15 off Westdown Rd ...96 C4
Hughes Cl, N12 off Coleridge Rd ...57 F5
Hughes Rd, Hayes UB3 ..102 B7
Hughes Ter, SW9 off Styles Gdns ...151 H3
Hughes Wk, Croy. CR0 off St. Saviours Rd ...187 J7
Hugh Gaitskell Cl, SW6 ..128 C6
Hugh Herland Ho, Kings.T. KT1 ...181 H3
Hugh Ms, SW1 ...32 E2
Hugh St, SW1 ...32 E2
Hugon Rd, SW6 ...148 E3
Hugo Rd, N19 ...92 C4
Huguenot Pl, E1 ...21 G1
SW18 ...149 F5
Huguenot Sq, SE15 off Scylla Rd ...152 E3
Hullbridge Ms, N1 off Sherborne St ...112 A1
Hull Cl, SE16 ...133 G2
Hull Pl, E16 off Fishguard Way ...137 F1
Hull St, EC1 ...11 J4
Hulme Pl, SE1 ...28 A4
Hulse Av, Bark. IG11 ...99 G6
Romford RM7 ...83 H1
Hulse Ter, Ilf. IG1 off Buttsbury Rd ...99 F5
Humber Cl, West Dr. UB7 .120 A1
Humber Dr, W10 ...108 A4
Humber Rd, NW2 ...89 H2
SE3 ...135 F6
Humberstone Rd, E13 ...115 J3
Humberton Cl, E9 off Marsh Hill ...95 H5
Humbolt Rd, W6 ...128 B6
Humes Av, W7 ...124 B3
Hume Ter, E16 off Prince Regent La ..115 J6
Hume Way, Ruis. HA4 ...66 A6
Humphrey Cl, Ilf. IG5 ...80 C1
Humphrey St, SE1 ...37 F3
Humphries Cl, Dag. RM9 .101 F4
Hundred Acre, NW9 ...71 F2
Hungerdown, E4 ...62 C1
Hungerford Br, SE1 ...26 B1
WC2 ...26 B1
Hungerford La, WC2 ...26 A1
Hungerford Rd, N7 ...92 D5
Hungerford St, E1 off Commercial Rd ...113 E6
Hunsdon Cl, Dag. RM9 ...101 E6
Hunsdon Rd, SE14 ...133 G6
Hunslett St, E2 off Royston St ...113 F2
Hunston Rd, Mord. SM4 .198 E1
Hunt Cl, W11 ...128 A1
Hunter Cl, SE1 ...28 C6
SW12 off Balham Pk Rd ...168 A1
Borehamwood WD6 ...38 C5
Wallington SM6 ...201 E7
Huntercrombe Gdns, Wat. WD19 ...50 C5
Hunter Ho, Felt. TW13 ...160 A1
Hunter Rd, SW20 ...183 J1
Ilford IG1 ...99 E5
Thornton Heath CR7 ..188 A3
Hunters, The, Beck. BR3 ..190 C1
Hunters Ct, Rich. TW9 off Friars La ...145 G5
Hunters Gro, Har. HA3 ...69 F4
Hayes UB3 ...122 A1
Orpington BR6 ...207 E4
Hunters Hall Rd, Dag. RM10 ...101 G4
Hunters Hill, Ruis. HA4 ...84 C3
Hunters Meadow, SE19 off Dulwich Wd Av ...170 B4
Hunters Rd, Chess. KT9 ..195 H3
Hunters Sq, Dag. RM10 ..101 G4
Hunter St, WC1 ...10 B5
Hunters Way, Croy. CR0 ..202 B4
Enfield EN2 ...43 G1
Hunter Wk, E13 ...115 G2
Borehamwood WD6 off Hunter Cl ...38 C5
Huntingdon Cl, Mitch. CR4 ...187 E3
Northolt UB5 off Plumpton Cl ...85 G6
Huntingdon Gdns, W4 ...126 C7
Worcester Park KT4 ...197 J3
Huntingdon Rd, N2 ...73 H3
N9 ...61 F1
Huntingdon St, E16 ...115 F6
N1 ...93 F7
Huntingfield, Croy. CR0 ..203 J7
Huntingfield Rd, SW15 ...147 G4
Hunting Gate Cl, Enf. EN2 .43 G3
Hunting Gate Dr, Chess. KT9 ...195 H7
Hunting Gate Ms, Sutt. SM1 ...199 E3
Twickenham TW2 off Colne Rd ...162 B1
Huntings Rd, Dag. RM10 .101 G6
Huntley Cl, Stai. (Stanw.) TW19 off Cambria Gdns ...140 B7
Huntley St, WC1 ...9 G6
Huntley Way, SW20 ...183 G2
Huntly Dr, N3 ...56 D6
Huntly Rd, SE25 ...188 B4
Hunton St, E1 ...13 H6
Hunt Rd, Sthl. UB2 ...123 G3
Hunt's Cl, SE3 ...155 G2
Hunt's Ct, WC2 ...17 J6
Hunts La, E15 ...114 C2
Huntsmans Cl, Felt. TW13 ...160 B4
Huntsman St, SE17 ...36 C2
Hunts Mead, Enf. EN3 ...45 G3
Hunts Mead Cl, Chis. BR7 ...174 C7
Huntsmoor Rd, Epsom KT19 ...196 D5
Huntspill St, SW17 ...167 F3
Hunts Slip Rd, SE21 ...170 B3
Huntsworth Ms, NW1 ...7 J6
Hurdwick Pl, NW1 off Harrington Sq ...9 F1
Hurley Cres, SE16 off Marlow Way ...133 G2
Hurley Ho, SE11 ...35 F2
Hurley Rd, Grnf. UB6 ...103 H6
Hurlingham Business Pk, SW6 ...148 D3
★ **Hurlingham Club**, SW6 ...148 C3
Hurlingham Ct, SW6 ...148 C3
Hurlingham Gdns, SW6 ..148 C3
★ **Hurlingham Park**, SW6 ...148 C2
Hurlingham Retail Pk, SW6 off Carnwath Rd ...149 E3
Hurlingham Rd, SW6 ...148 C2
Bexleyheath DA7 ...139 F7
Hurlingham Sq, SW6 ...148 D3
Hurlock St, N5 ...93 H3
Hurlstone Rd, SE25 ...188 A5
Hurn Ct Rd, Houns. TW4 off Renfrew Rd ...142 D2
Huron Cl, Orp. (Grn St Grn) BR6 off Winnipeg Dr ...207 J6
Huron Rd, SW17 ...168 A2
Hurren Cl, SE3 ...154 E3
Hurricane Rd, Wall. SM6 ..201 E7
Hurricane Trd Cen, NW9 ...71 G1
Hurry Cl, E15 ...97 E7
Hursley Rd, Chig. IG7 ...65 J5
Hurst Av, E4 ...62 A4
N6 ...74 C6
Hurstbourne, Esher (Clay.) KT10 ...194 C6
Hurstbourne Gdns, Bark. IG11 ...99 H6
Hurstbourne Ho, SW15 off Tangley Gro ...147 F6
Hurstbourne Rd, SE23 ...171 H1
Hurst Cl, E4 ...62 A3
NW11 ...72 E6
Bromley BR2 ...205 F1
Chessington KT9 ...196 A5
Northolt UB5 ...85 F6
Hurstcourt Rd, Sutt. SM1 .198 E2
Hurstdene Av, Brom. BR2 ...205 F1
Hurstdene Gdns, N15 ...76 B7
Hurst Est, SE2 ...138 D5

Hurstfield, Brom. BR2 ...191 G5
Hurstfield Rd, W.Mol. KT8 ...179 G3
Hurst La, SE2 ...138 D5
East Molesey KT8 ...179 J4
Hurstleigh Gdns, Ilf. IG5 ...80 C1
Hurstmead Ct, Edg. HA8 ..54 B4
Hurst Ri, Barn. EN5 ...40 D3
Hurst Rd, E17 ...78 B3
N21 ...59 G1
Bexley DA5 ...176 D1
Buckhurst Hill IG9 ...64 A1
Croydon CR0 ...202 A5
East Molesey KT8 ...179 G3
Erith DA8 ...139 J7
Sidcup DA15 ...176 A2
Walton-on-Thames KT12 ...178 C5
West Molesey KT8 ...179 E3
Hurst Springs, Bex. DA5 .177 E1
Hurst St, SE24 ...151 H6
Hurst Vw Rd, S.Croy. CR2 ...202 B7
Hurst Way, S.Croy. CR2 ..202 B6
Hurstway Wk, W11 ...108 A7
Hurstwood Av, E18 ...79 H4
Bexley DA5 ...176 E1
Hurstwood Dr, Brom. BR1 ...192 C3
Hurstwood Rd, NW11 ...72 B4
Hurtwood Rd, Walt. KT12 .179 F7
Huson Cl, NW3 ...91 H7
Hussain Cl, Har. HA1 ...86 C4
Hussars Cl, Houns. TW4 ..142 E3
Husseywell Cres, Brom. BR2 ...205 G1
Hutchings St, E14 ...134 A2
Hutchings Wk, NW11 ...73 E4
Hutchins Cl, E15
off Gibbins Rd ...96 C7
Hutchinson Ter, Wem. HA9 ...87 G3
Hutchins Rd, SE28 ...118 A7
Hutton Cl, Grnf. UB6
off Mary Peters Dr ...86 A5
Woodford Green IG8 ...63 H6
Hutton Gdns, Har. HA3 ...51 J7
Hutton Gro, N12 ...57 E5
Hutton La, Har. HA3 ...51 J7
Hutton Row, Edg. HA8 ...54 C7
Hutton St, EC4 ...19 F4
Hutton Wk, Har. HA3 ...51 J7
Huxbear St, SE4 ...153 J5
Huxley Cl, Nthlt. UB5 ...103 E1
Huxley Dr, Rom. RM6 ...82 B7
Huxley Gdns, NW10 ...105 J3
Huxley Par, N18 ...60 A5
Huxley Pl, N13 ...59 H4
Huxley Rd, E10 ...96 C2
N18 ...60 A4
Welling DA16 ...157 J3
Huxley Sayze, N18 ...60 A5
Huxley St, W10 ...108 B3
Hyacinth Cl, Hmptn. TW12
off Gresham Rd ...161 G6
Ilford IG1 ...98 E6
Hyacinth Ct, Pnr. HA5
off Tulip Ct ...66 C3
Hyacinth Rd, SW15 ...165 G1
Hycliffe Gdns, Chig. IG7 ...65 F4
HYDE, THE, NW9 ...71 F4
Hyde, The, NW9 ...71 E5
Hyde Cl, E13 ...115 G2
Barnet EN5 ...40 C3
Hyde Ct, N20 ...57 G3
Hyde Cres, NW9 ...71 E5
Hyde Est Rd, NW9 ...71 F5
Hyde Fm Ms, SW12
off Telferscot Rd ...168 D1
Hydefield Cl, N21 ...60 A1
Hydefield Ct, N9 ...60 B2
Hyde Ho, NW9 ...71 E5
Hyde La, SW11
off Battersea Br Rd ...149 H1
★ **Hyde Park**, W2 ...23 G1
Hyde Pk, SW7 ...23 G1
W1 ...23 G1
Hyde Pk Av, N21 ...59 J2
Hyde Pk Cor, W1 ...24 C3
Hyde Pk Cres, W2 ...15 G4
Hyde Pk Gdns, N21 ...59 J1
W2 ...15 F5
Hyde Pk Gdns Ms, W2 ...15 F5
Hyde Pk Gate, SW7 ...22 D4
Hyde Pk Gate Ms, SW7 ...22 D4
Hyde Pk Pl, W2 ...15 H5
Hyde Pk Sq, W2 ...15 G4
Hyde Pk Sq Ms, W2 ...15 G4
Hyde Pk St, W2 ...15 G4
Hyderabad Way, E15 ...96 E7
Hyde Rd, N1 ...112 A1
Bexleyheath DA7 ...159 F2
Richmond TW10
off Albert Rd ...145 J5
Hydeside Gdns, N9 ...60 C2
Hydes Pl, N1
off Compton Av ...93 H7
Hyde St, SE8
off Deptford High St ..134 A6
Hydethorpe Av, N9 ...60 C2
Hydethorpe Rd, SW12 ...168 C1
Hyde Vale, SE10 ...134 C7
Hyde Wk, Mord. SM4 ...184 D7
Hyde Way, N9 ...60 C2
Hayes UB3 ...121 J4
Hylands Rd, E17 ...78 D2
Hylton St, SE18 ...137 J4
Hyndewood, SE23 ...171 G3
Hyndman St, SE15 ...132 E6
Hynton Rd, Dag. RM8 ...100 C2
Hyperion Ho, E3
off Arbery Rd ...113 H2
Hyrstdene, S.Croy. CR2 ..201 H4
Hyson Rd, SE16
off Galleywall Rd ...133 E4
Hythe Av, Bexh. DA7 ...139 F7
Hythe Cl, N18 ...60 D4
Hythe Path, Th.Hth. CR7 ..188 A3
Hythe Rd, NW10 ...107 G4
Thornton Heath CR7 ..188 A2
Hythe Rd Ind Est, NW10 ..107 G3
Hyver Hill, NW7 ...38 D6

I

Ian Sq, Enf. EN3
off Lansbury Rd ...45 G1
Ibbetson Path, Loug. IG10 .49 E3
Ibbotson Av, E16 ...115 F6
Ibbott St, E1
off Mantus Rd ...113 F4
Iberian Av, Wall. SM6 ...200 D4
Ibex Ho, E15
off Forest La ...97 E6
Ibis La, W4 ...146 C1
Ibis Way, Hayes UB4
off Cygnet Way ...102 D6
Ibscott Cl, Dag. RM10 ...101 J6
Ibsley Gdns, SW15 ...165 G1
Ibsley Way, Barn. (Cockfos.) EN4 ...41 H5
Iceland Rd, E3 ...114 A1
Iceland Wf, SE16
off Plough Way ...133 H4
Iceni Ct, E3
off Roman Rd ...113 J1
Ice Wf, N1 ...10 B1
Ice Wf Marina, N1
off New Wf Rd ...10 B1
Ickburgh Est, E5
off Ickburgh Rd ...94 E2
Ickburgh Rd, E5 ...94 E3
Ickleton Rd, SE9 ...174 B4
Icknield Dr, Ilf. IG2 ...81 E5
Ickworth Pk Rd, E17 ...77 H4
Idaho Bldg, SE13
off Deals Gateway ...154 B1
Ida Rd, N15 ...76 A5
Ida St, E14 ...114 C6
Iden Cl, Brom. BR2 ...191 E3
Idlecombe Rd, SW17 ...168 A6
Idmiston Rd, E15 ...97 F5
SE27 ...169 J3
Worcester Park KT4 ...183 F7
Idmiston Sq, Wor.Pk. KT4 .183 F7
Idol La, EC3 ...20 D6
Idonia St, SE8 ...133 J7
Idris Ct, N9
off Galahad Rd ...60 D3
Iffley Rd, W6 ...127 H3
Ifield Rd, SW10 ...30 B5
Ifor Evans Pl, E1
off Mile End Rd ...113 G4
Ightham Rd, Erith DA8 ...139 G7
Igraine Ct, N9
off Galahad Rd ...60 D3
Ikea Twr, NW10 ...88 D5
Ilbert St, W10 ...108 A3
Ilchester Gdns, W2 ...14 A5
Ilchester Pl, W14 ...128 C3
Ilchester Rd, Dag. RM8 ...100 B5
Ildersly Gro, SE21 ...170 A2
Ilderton Rd, SE15 ...133 F7
SE16 ...133 E5
Ilex Cl, Sun. TW16
off Oakington Dr ...178 C2
Ilex Ho, N4 ...75 F7
Ilex Rd, NW10 ...89 F6
Ilex Way, SW16 ...169 G5
ILFORD, IG1 - IG6 ...99 F3
Ilford Hill, Ilf. IG1 ...98 D3
Ilford La, Ilf. IG1 ...98 E3
Ilfracombe Gdns, Rom. RM6 ...82 B7
Ilfracombe Rd, Brom. BR1 ...173 F3
Iliffe St, SE17 ...35 H3
Iliffe Yd, SE17 ...35 H3
Ilkeston Ct, E5
off Overbury St ...95 G4
Ilkley Cl, SE19 ...170 A6
Ilkley Rd, E16 ...115 J5
Watford WD19 ...50 D5
Illingworth Cl, Mitch. CR4 ...185 G3
Illingworth Way, Enf. EN1 ...44 B4
Ilmington Rd, Har. HA3 ...69 G6
Ilminster Gdns, SW11 ...149 H4
Imber Cl, N14 ...42 C7
Esher KT10
off Ember La ...194 A1
Imber Ct Trd Est, E.Mol. KT8 ...180 A6
Imber Gro, Esher KT10 ...180 A7
Imber Pk Rd, Esher KT10 .194 A1
Imber St, N1 ...112 A1
Imer Pl, T.Ditt. KT7 ...180 C7
Imperial Av, N16
off Victorian Rd ...94 C3
Imperial Cl, Har. HA2 ...67 G6
★ **Imperial Coll London**, SW7 ...23 E5
Imperial Coll Rd, SW7 ...22 E6
Imperial Ct, NW8 ...7 H1
Imperial Cres, SW6 ...149 F2
Imperial Dr, Har. HA2 ...67 G7
Imperial Gdns, Mitch. CR4 ...186 B3
Imperial Ms, E6
off Central Pk Rd ...115 J2
Imperial Pl, Chis. BR7
off Forest Cl ...192 D1
Imperial Rd, N22 ...74 E1
SW6 ...149 E1
Feltham TW14 ...141 H7
Imperial Sq, SW6 ...149 E1
Imperial St, E3 ...114 C3
★ **Imperial War Mus**, SE1 ...27 F6
Imperial Way, Chis. BR7 ..175 F3
Croydon CR0 ...201 F6
Harrow HA3 ...69 H6
Imperial Wf, SW6 ...149 F2
Imprimo Pk, Loug. IG10 ...49 F4
Imre Cl, W12
off Ellerslie Rd ...127 H1
Inca Dr, SE9 ...156 E7
Inca Ter, N15
off Milton Rd ...75 H3
Inchmery Rd, SE6 ...172 B2
Inchwood, Croy. CR0 ...204 B4
Independence Ho, SW19
off Chapter Way ...185 G1
Independent Pl, E8
off Downs Pk Rd ...94 C5
Independents Rd, SE3
off Blackheath Village .155 F3
Inderwick Rd, N8 ...75 F5
Indescon Ct, E14 ...134 A2
Indiana Bldg, SE13
off Deals Gateway ...154 A1
India Pl, WC2 ...18 C5
India St, EC3 ...21 F4
India Way, W12 ...107 H7
Indigo Ms, E14
off Ashton St ...114 C7
N16 ...94 A3
Indigo Wk, N2 ...73 J4
N6 ...73 J4
Indus Rd, SE7 ...135 J7
Industry Ter, SW9
off Canterbury Cres ..151 G3
Ingal Rd, E13 ...115 G4
Ingate Pl, SW8 ...150 B1
Ingatestone Rd, E12 ...97 J1
SE25 ...188 E4
Woodford Green IG8 ...63 G7
Ingelow Rd, SW8 ...150 B2
Ingersoll Rd, W12 ...127 H1
Ingestre Ct, W1
off Ingestre Pl ...17 G5
Ingestre Pl, W1 ...17 G4
Ingestre Rd, E7 ...97 G4
NW5 ...92 B4
Ingham Rd, NW6 ...90 D4
Inglebert St, EC1 ...11 E3
Ingleborough St, SW9 ...151 G2
Ingleby Dr, Har. HA1 ...86 A3
Ingleby Rd, N7
off Bryett Rd ...93 E3
Dagenham RM10 ...101 H6
Ilford IG1 ...98 E1
Ingleby Way, Chis. BR7 ...174 D5
Ingle Cl, Pnr. HA5 ...67 E3
Ingledew Rd, SE18 ...137 G5
Inglehurst Gdns, Ilf. IG4 ...80 C5
Inglemere Rd, SE23 ...171 G3
Mitcham CR4 ...167 J7
Ingle Ms, EC1 ...11 E3
Inglesham Wk, E9 ...95 J6
Ingleside Cl, Beck. BR3 ...172 A7
Ingleside Gro, SE3 ...135 F6
Inglethorpe St, SW6 ...148 A1
Ingleton Av, Well. DA16 ..158 A5
Ingleton Rd, N18 ...60 D6
Ingleton St, SW9 ...151 G2
Ingleway, N12 ...57 G6
Inglewood Cl, E14 ...134 A4
Ilford IG6 ...65 J6
Inglewood Copse, Brom. BR1 ...192 B2
Inglewood Ms, Surb. KT6 ...196 A1
Inglewood Rd, NW6 ...90 D5
Inglis Barracks, NW7 ...56 A5
Inglis Rd, W5 ...105 J7
Croydon CR0 ...202 C1
Inglis St, SE5 ...151 H1
Ingram Av, NW11 ...73 F7
Ingram Cl, SE11 ...34 D1
Stanmore HA7 ...53 F5
Ingram Ho, E3
off Daling Way ...113 H2
Ingram Rd, N2 ...73 H4
Thornton Heath CR7 ..187 J1
Ingram Way, Grnf. UB6 ...104 A1
Ingrave Ho, Dag. RM9 ...118 B1
Ingrave St, SW11 ...149 G3
Ingress St, W4
off Devonshire Rd ...126 E5
Inigo Jones Rd, SE7 ...136 B7
Inigo Pl, WC2 ...18 A5
Inkerman Rd, NW5 ...92 B6
Inkerman Ter, W8
off Allen St ...128 D3
Inks Grn, E4 ...62 C5
Inkster Ho, SW11
off Ingrave St ...149 H3
Inkwell Cl, N12 ...57 F3
Inman Rd, NW10 ...106 E1
SW18 ...149 F7
Inmans Row, Wdf.Grn. IG8 ...63 G4
Inner Circle, NW1 ...8 B4
Inner Pk Rd, SW19 ...166 A1
Inner Ring E, Houns. (Lon.Hthrw Air.) TW6 ..140 E3
Inner Ring W, Houns. (Lon.Hthrw Air.) TW6 ..140 D3
Inner Temple La, EC4 ...19 E4
Innes Cl, SW20 ...184 B2
Innes Gdns, SW15 ...147 H6
Innes St, SE15 ...37 E7
Innes Yd, Croy. CR0
off Whitgift St ...201 J3
Inniskilling Rd, E13 ...115 J2
Innovation Cl, Wem. HA0 .105 H1
Inskip Cl, E10 ...96 B2
Inskip Rd, Dag. RM8 ...100 D1
Insley Ho, E3 *off Bow Rd* .114 B3
★ **Institute of Contemporary Arts (I.C.A.)**, SW1 ...25 J1
Institute Pl, E8 ...94 E5
Integer Gdns, E11 ...78 D7
Interchange E Ind Est, E5
off Grosvenor Way ...95 F2
International Av, Houns. TW5 ...122 C5
International Trd Est, Sthl. UB2 ...122 B3
Inveraray Pl, SE18
off Old Mill Rd ...137 G6
Inver Cl, E5
off Theydon Rd ...95 F2
Inverclyde Gdns, Rom. RM6 ...82 D4
Inver Ct, W2 ...14 B4
W6 *off Invermead Cl* ..127 G3
Inveresk Gdns, Wor.Pk. KT4 ...197 F3
Inverforth Cl, NW3
off North End Way ...91 F2
Inverforth Rd, N11 ...58 B5
Inverine Rd, SE7 ...135 H5
Invermead Cl, W6 ...127 G4
Invermore Pl, SE18 ...137 F4
Inverness Av, Enf. EN1 ...44 B1
Inverness Dr, Ilf. IG6 ...65 H6
Inverness Gdns, W8 ...22 A2
Inverness Ms, E16 ...137 F1
W2 ...14 B5
Inverness Pl, W2 ...14 B5
Inverness Rd, N18
off Aberdeen Rd ...60 E5
Hounslow TW3 ...143 F4
Southall UB2 ...123 E4
Worcester Park KT4 ...198 A1
Inverness St, NW1 ...110 B1
Inverness Ter, W2 ...14 B5
Inverton Rd, SE15 ...153 G4
Invicta Cl, E3
off Hawgood St ...114 A5
Chislehurst BR7 ...174 D5
Invicta Gro, Nthlt. UB5 ...103 F3
Invicta Plaza, SE1 ...27 G1
Invicta Rd, SE3 ...135 G7
Inville Rd, SE17 ...36 C4
Inwen Ct, SE8 ...133 H5
Inwood Av, Houns. TW3 ..143 J3

Inwood Cl, Croy. CR0 **203** H2
Inwood Ho, SE22 *off Pytchley Rd* **152** B3
Inwood Rd, Houns. TW3 **143** H4
Inworth St, SW11 **149** H2
Inworth Wk, N1 *off Popham St* **111** J1
IO Cen, SE18 *off Armstrong Rd* **137** F3
Iona Cl, SE6 **154** A7
Morden SM4 **184** E7
Ionian Bldg, E14 *off Narrow St* **113** H7
Ion Sq, E2 **13** H2
Ipswich Rd, SW17 **168** A6
Ireland Cl, E6 *off Bradley Stone Rd* **116** C5
Ireland Pl, N22 **59** E7
Ireland Yd, EC4 **19** H4
Irene Rd, SW6 **148** D1
Orpington BR6 **193** J7
Ireton Cl, N10 **58** A7
Ireton St, E3 *off Tidworth Rd* **114** A4
Iris Av, Bex. DA5 **159** E5
Iris Cl, E6 **116** B5
Croydon CR0 **203** G1
Surbiton KT6 **181** J7
Iris Ct, Pnr. HA5 **66** C3
Iris Cres, Bexh. DA7 **139** F6
Iris Rd, Epsom (W.Ewell) KT19 **196** B5
Iris Wk, Edg. HA8 *off Ash Cl* **54** C4
Irkdale Av, Enf. EN1 **44** C1
Iron Br Cl, NW10 **88** E5
Southall UB2 **123** J1
Iron Br Rd, Uxb. UB11 **120** D2
West Drayton UB7 **120** D2
Iron Mill Pl, SW18 *off Garratt La* **149** E6
Iron Mill Rd, SW18 **149** E6
Ironmonger La, EC2 **20** B4
Ironmonger Pas, EC1 **12** A5
Ironmonger Row, EC1 **12** A4
Ironmongers Pl, E14 *off Spindrift Av* **134** A4
Ironside Cl, SE16 *off Kinburn St* **133** G2
Ironside Rd, Brent. TW8 **125** F7
Iron Wks, E3 **114** A1
Irvine Av, Har. HA3 **68** D3
Irvine Cl, E14 *off Uamvar St* **114** C5
N20 **57** H2
Irvine Way, Orp. BR6 **193** J7
Irving Av, Nthlt. UB5 **102** D1
Irving Gro, SW9 **151** F2
Irving Ms, N1 *off Alwyne Rd* **93** J6
Irving Rd, W14 **128** A3
Irving St, WC2 **17** J6
Irving Way, NW9 **71** F5
Irwell Est, SE16 *off Neptune St* **133** F2
Irwin Av, SE18 **137** H7
Irwin Gdns, NW10 **107** H1
Isaac Way, SE1 **28** A3
Isabel Hill Cl, Hmptn. TW12 *off Upper Sunbury Rd* **179** H1
Isabella Cl, N14 **42** C7
Isabella Ct, Rich. TW10 *off Grove Rd* **145** J6
Isabella Dr, Orp. BR6 **207** F4
Isabella Ms, N1 *off Balls Pond Rd* **94** B6
Isabella Pl, Kings.T. KT2 **163** J5
Isabella Rd, E9 **95** F5
Isabella St, SE1 **27** G2
Isabel St, SW9 **151** F1
Isambard Ms, E14 **134** C3
Isambard Pl, SE16 *off Rotherhithe St* **133** F1
Isel Way, SE22 *off East Dulwich Gro* **152** B5
Isham Rd, SW16 **186** E2
Isis Cl, SW15 **147** J4
Isis Reach, Belv. DA17 *off Norman Rd* **139** H1
Isis St, SW18 **167** F2
Island Fm Av, W.Mol. KT8 **179** F5
Island Fm Rd, W.Mol. KT8 **179** F5
Island Rd, SE16 **133** G4
Mitcham CR4 **167** J7
Island Row, E14 **113** J6
Isla Rd, SE18 **137** F6
Islay Gdns, Houns. TW4 **142** D5
Islay Wk, N1 *off Douglas Rd* **93** J6
Isledon Rd, N7 **93** G3
Islehurst Cl, Chis. BR7 **192** D1
ISLEWORTH, TW7 **144** C3
Isleworth Business Complex, Islw. TW7 *off St. John's Rd* **144** C2
Isleworth Prom, Twick. TW1 **144** E4
ISLINGTON, N1 **111** F1
Islington Grn, N1 **111** H1
Islington High St, N1 **11** F2
Islington Pk Ms, N1 *off Islington Pk St* **93** H7
Islington Pk St, N1 **93** G7
Islip Gdns, Edg. HA8 **54** D7
Northolt UB5 **85** E7
Islip Manor Rd, Nthlt. UB5 **85** E7
Islip St, NW5 **92** C5
Ismailia Rd, E7 **97** H7
★ **Ismaili Cen**, SW7 **31** F1
Isom Cl, E13 *off Belgrave Rd* **115** H3
Issa Rd, Houns. TW3 *off Staines Rd* **143** F4
Ivanhoe Dr, Har. HA3 **68** D3
Ivanhoe Rd, SE5 **152** C3
Hounslow TW4 **142** D3
Ivatt Pl, W14 **128** C5
Ivatt Way, N17 **75** H3
Iveagh Av, NW10 **106** A2
Iveagh Cl, E9 **113** G1
NW10 **106** A2
Iveagh Ter, NW10 *off Iveagh Av* **106** A2
Ivedon Rd, Well. DA16 **158** C2
Ive Fm Cl, E10 **96** A2
Ive Fm La, E10 **96** A2
Iveley Rd, SW4 **150** C2
Ivere Dr, Barn. (New Barn.) EN5 **40** E6
Iverhurst Cl, Bexh. DA6 **158** D5
Iverna Ct, W8 **128** D3
Iverna Gdns, W8 **128** D3
Feltham TW14 **141** G5
Iverson Rd, NW6 **90** C6
Ivers Way, Croy. (New Adgtn) CR0 **204** B7
Ives Rd, E16 **114** E5
Ives St, SW3 **31** H1
Ivestor Ter, SE23 **153** F7
Ivimey St, E2 **13** J3
Ivinghoe Cl, Enf. EN1 **44** B2
Ivinghoe Rd, Dag. RM8 **100** B5
Ivor Gro, SE9 **175** E1
Ivor Pl, NW1 **7** J6
Ivor St, NW1 **92** C7
Ivory Ct, Felt. TW13 **160** A1
Ivorydown, Brom. BR1 **173** G4
Ivory Sq, SW11 *off Gartons Way* **149** F3
Ivybridge Cl, Twick. TW1 **144** D6
Ivybridge Est, Islw. TW7 **144** C5
Ivybridge Ho, SE22 *off Pytchley Rd* **152** B3
Ivybridge La, WC2 **18** B6
Ivychurch Cl, SE20 **171** F7
Ivychurch La, SE17 **37** F3
Ivy Cl, Har. HA2 **85** F4
Pinner HA5 **66** C7
Sunbury-on-Thames TW16 **178** C2
Ivy Cotts, E14 *off Grove Vil* **114** B7
Ivy Ct, SE16 **37** J4
Ivy Cres, W4 **126** C4
Ivydale Rd, SE15 **153** G3
Carshalton SM5 **199** J2
Ivyday Gro, SW16 **169** F3
Ivydene, W.Mol. KT8 **179** F5
Ivydene Cl, Sutt. SM1 **199** F4
Ivy Gdns, N8 **74** E6
Mitcham CR4 **186** D3
Ivyhouse Rd, Dag. RM9 **100** D6
Ivy La, Houns. TW4 **143** F4
Ivymount Rd, SE27 **169** G3
Ivy Rd, E16 *off Pacific Rd* **115** G6
E17 **78** A6
N14 **42** C7
NW2 **89** J4
SE4 **153** J4
SW17 *off Tooting High St* **167** H5
Hounslow TW3 **143** H4
Surbiton KT6 **196** A1
Ivy St, N1 **12** D1
Ivy Wk, Dag. RM9 **100** E6
Ixworth Pl, SW3 **31** G3
Izane Rd, Bexh. DA6 **159** F4

J

Jacaranda Cl, N.Mal. KT3 **182** E3
Jacaranda Gro, E8 **94** C7
Jackass La, Kes. BR2 **205** H6
Jack Barnett Way, N22 **75** F2
Jack Clow Rd, E15 **115** E2
Jack Cornwell St, E12 **98** D4
Jack Dash Way, E6 **116** B4
Jack Goodchild Way, Kings.T. KT1 *off Kingston Rd* **182** B3
Jacklin Grn, Wdf.Grn. IG8 **63** G4
Jackman Ms, NW2 **88** E3
Jackman St, E8 **112** E1
Jackson Cl, E9 **95** F7
Jackson Ct, E11 *off Brading Cres* **97** H1
Jackson Rd, N7 **93** F4
Barking IG11 **117** G1
Barnet EN4 **41** H6
Bromley BR2 **206** B2
Jacksons La, N6 **74** A7
Jacksons Pl, Croy. CR0 *off Cross Rd* **202** A1
Jackson St, SE18 **136** D6
Jacksons Way, Croy. CR0 **204** A3
Jackson Way, Sthl. UB2 **123** H2
Jack Walker Ct, N5 **93** H4
Jacob Ho, Erith DA18 *off Kale Rd* **138** D2
Jacob Ms, Stan. HA7 **52** D2
Jacobs Cl, Dag. RM10 **101** H4
Jacobs Ho, E13 **115** J3
Jacob St, SE1 **29** G3
Jacob's Well Ms, W1 **16** C3
Jacqueline Cl, Nthlt. UB5 *off Canford Av* **103** F1
Jade Cl, E16 **116** A6
NW2 **72** A7
Dagenham RM8 **100** C1
Jaffe Rd, Ilf. IG1 **99** F1
Jaffray Pl, SE27 *off Chapel Rd* **169** H4
Jaffray Rd, Brom. BR2 **192** A4
Jaggard Way, SW12 **149** J7
Jago Cl, SE18 **137** F6
Jago Wk, SE5 **132** A7
Jamaica Rd, SE1 **29** G4
SE16 **132** C2
Thornton Heath CR7 **187** H6
Jamaica St, E1 **113** F6
James Av, NW2 **89** J5
Dagenham RM8 **101** F1
James Bedford Cl, Pnr. HA5 **66** C2
James Boswell Cl, SW16 *off Samuel Johnson Cl* **169** G4
James Clavell Sq, SE18 **137** E3
James Cl, E13 *off Richmond St* **115** G2
NW11 *off Woodlands* **72** B6
James Collins Cl, W9 *off Fermoy Rd* **108** C4
James Ct, N1 *off Morton Rd* **93** J7
James Dudson Ct, NW10 **88** C7
James Gdns, N22 **59** H7
James Hammett Ho, E2 **13** G2
James Joyce Wk, SE24 *off Shakespeare Rd* **151** H4
James La, E10 **78** D7
E11 **78** D6
James Newman Ct, SE9 *off Great Harry Dr* **174** D3
Jameson Cl, W3 *off Acton La* **126** C2
Jameson Ct, E2 **113** F2
Jameson Ho, SE11 *off Glasshouse Wk* **34** C3
Jameson St, W8 **128** D1
James Pl, N17 **76** C1
James Riley Pt, E15 *off Carpenters Rd* **114** C1
James's Cotts, Rich. TW9 *off Kew Rd* **126** A7
James Sinclair Pt, E13 **115** J1
James St, W1 **16** C3
WC2 **18** B5
Barking IG11 **99** F7
Enfield EN1 **44** C5
Hounslow TW3 **144** A3
James Ter, SW14 *off Mullins Path* **146** D3
Jamestown Rd, NW1 **110** B1
Jamestown Way, E14 **114** D7
James Way, Wat. WD19 **50** D4
James Yd, E4 **62** D6
Jamieson Ho, Houns. TW4 **143** F7
Jamuna Cl, E14 **113** H5
Jane Seymour Ct, SE9 *off Avery Hill Rd* **157** G7
Jane St, E1 *off Commercial Rd* **112** E6
Janet St, E14 **134** A3
Janeway Pl, SE16 *off Janeway St* **132** E2
Janeway St, SE16 **29** J4
Janice Ms, Ilf. IG1 *off Oakfield Rd* **99** E3
Jansen Wk, SW11 *off Hope St* **149** G4
Janson Cl, E15 *off Janson Rd* **96** E5
NW10 **88** D3
Janson Rd, E15 **96** E5
Jansons Rd, N15 **76** B3
Japan Cres, N4 **93** F1
Japan Rd, Rom. RM6 **82** D6
Jardine Rd, E1 **113** G7
Jarman Ho, E1 *off Jubilee St* **113** F5
Jarrett Cl, SW2 **169** H1
Jarrow Cl, Mord. SM4 **184** E5
Jarrow Rd, N17 **76** E4
SE16 **133** F4
Romford RM6 **82** C6
Jarrow Way, E9 **95** H4
Jarvis Cl, Bark. IG11 *off Westbury Rd* **117** G1
Barnet EN5 **40** A5
Jarvis Rd, SE22 *off Melbourne Gro* **152** B4
South Croydon CR2 **202** A6
Jasmine Cl, Ilf. IG1 **99** E5
Orpington BR6 **206** E2
Southall UB1 **103** E7
Jasmine Gdns, Croy. CR0 **204** B3
Harrow HA2 **85** G2
Jasmine Gro, SE20 **189** E1
Jasmine Sq, E3 *off Birdsfield La* **113** J1
Jasmine Ter, West Dr. UB7 **120** D2
Jasmine Way, E.Mol. KT8 *off Hampton Ct Way* **180** B4
Jasmin Rd, Epsom KT19 **196** B5
Jason Ct, W1 *off Marylebone La* **16** C3
Jason Wk, SE9 **174** D4
Jasper Pas, SE19 **170** C6
Jasper Rd, E16 **116** A6
SE19 **170** C5
Jasper Wk, N1 **12** B3
Javelin Way, Nthlt. UB5 **102** D3
Jaycroft, Enf. EN2 *off The Ridgeway* **43** G1
Jay Gdns, Chis. BR7 **174** C4
Jay Ms, SW7 **22** D4
Jazzfern Ter, Wem. HA0 *off Maybank Av* **86** D5
Jean Batten Cl, Wall. SM6 **201** F7
Jebb Av, SW2 **151** E6
Jebb St, E3 **114** A2
Jedburgh Rd, E13 **115** J3
Jedburgh St, SW11 **150** A4
Jeddo Rd, W12 **127** F2
Jefferson Cl, W13 **125** E3
Ilford IG2 **81** E5
Jefferson Wk, SE18 *off Kempt St* **136** D6
Jeffreys Pl, NW1 *off Jeffreys St* **92** C7
Jeffreys Rd, SW4 **150** E2
Enfield EN3 **45** J3
Jeffreys St, NW1 **92** B7
Jeffreys Wk, SW4 **150** E2
Jeffries Ho, NW10 **106** C1
Jeffs Cl, Hmptn. TW12 *off Uxbridge Rd* **161** H6
Jeffs Rd, Sutt. SM1 **198** C4
Jeger Av, E2 **112** C1
Jeken Rd, SE9 **155** J4
Jelf Rd, SW2 **151** G5
Jellicoe Gdns, Stan. HA7 **52** C6
Jellicoe Ho, SW8 *off St. George Wf* **34** A5
Jellicoe Rd, E13 *off Jutland Rd* **115** G4
N17 **60** A7
Jemma Knowles Cl, SW2 *off Neil Wates Cres* **169** G1
Jemmett Cl, Kings.T. KT2 **182** B1
Jengar Cl, Sutt. SM1 **199** E4
Jenkins La, E6 **116** D2
Barking IG11 **117** E2
Jenkinson Ho, E2 *off Usk St* **113** G3
Jenkins Rd, E13 **115** H4
Jenner Av, W3 **106** D5
Jenner Cl, Sid. DA14 **176** A4
Jenner Pl, SW13 **127** H6
Jenner Rd, N16 **94** C2
Jennett Rd, Croy. CR0 **201** G3
Jennifer Rd, Brom. BR1 **173** F3
Jennings Cl, Surb. (Long Dit.) KT6 **181** F7
Jennings Rd, SE22 **152** C6
Jennings Way, Barn. EN5 **39** J3
Jenningtree Way, Belv. DA17 **139** J2
Jenny Hammond Cl, E11 *off Newcomen Rd* **97** F3

Jenson Way, SE19 .... 170 C7
Jenton Av, Bexh. DA7 .... 158 E1
Jephson Rd, E7 .... 97 J7
Jephson St, SE5
off Grove La 152 A1
Jephtha Rd, SW18 .... 148 D6
Jeppos La, Mitch. CR4 .... 185 J4
Jepson Ho, SW6
off Pearscroft Rd 149 E1
Jerdan Pl, SW6 .... 128 D7
Jeremiah St, E14 .... 114 B6
Jeremys Grn, N18 .... 61 E4
Jermyn St, SW1 .... 25 F1
Jerningham Av, Ilf. IG5 .... 80 E2
Jerningham Rd, SE14 .... 153 H2
Jerome Cres, NW8 .... 7 G5
Jerome Pl, Kings.T. KT1
off Wadbrook St 181 G2
Jerome St, E1 .... 21 F1
Jerome Twr, W3 .... 126 B2
Jerrard St, N1 .... 12 E2
SE13 .... 154 B3
Jersey Av, Stan. HA7 .... 69 E2
Jersey Dr, Orp. BR5 .... 193 G6
Jersey Ho, N1
off Clifton Rd 93 J6
Jersey Par, Houns. TW5 .... 143 H1
Jersey Rd, E11 .... 96 D1
E16
off Prince Regent La 115 J6
SW17 .... 168 B6
W7 .... 124 D2
Hounslow TW3, TW5 .... 143 H1
Ilford IG1 .... 99 E4
Isleworth TW7 .... 124 B6
Jersey St, E2
off Bethnal Grn Rd 113 E3
Jerusalem Pas, EC1 .... 11 G6
Jervis Ct, W1 .... 17 E4
Jervis Rd, SW6
off Lillie Rd 128 C6
Jerviston Gdns, SW16 .... 169 G6
Jesmond Av, Wem. HA9 .... 87 J6
Jesmond Cl, Mitch. CR4 .... 186 B3
Jesmond Rd, Croy. CR0 .... 188 C7
Jesmond Way, Stan.
HA7 .... 53 H5
Jessam Av, E5 .... 94 E1
Jessamine Rd, W7 .... 124 B1
Jessel Dr, Loug. IG10 .... 49 F1
Jessel Ho, SW1
off Page St 33 J1
Jesse Rd, E10 .... 96 C1
Jessica Rd, SW18 .... 149 F6
Jessie Blythe La, N19 .... 74 E7
Jessop Av, Sthl. UB2 .... 123 F4
Jessop Rd, SE24
off Milkwood Rd 151 H4
Jessop Sq, E14
off Heron Quay 134 A1
Jessops Way, Croy. CR0 .... 186 C6
Jessup Cl, SE18 .... 137 F4
Jethou Ho, N1
off Nightingale Rd 93 J6
Jetstar Way, Nthlt. UB5 .... 102 E3
Jevington Way, SE12 .... 173 H2
Jewel Rd, E17 .... 78 A3
★ **Jewel Twr** (Houses of
Parliament), SW1 .... 26 A5
★ **Jewish Mus**, NW1
off Albert St 110 B1
Jewry St, EC3 .... 21 F4
Jew's Row, SW18 .... 149 E4
Jews Wk, SE26 .... 171 E4
Jeymer Av, NW2 .... 89 H5
Jeymer Dr, Grnf. UB6 .... 103 J1
Jeypore Pas, SW18
off Jeypore Rd 149 F6
Jeypore Rd, SW18 .... 149 F7
Jigger Mast Ho, SE18
off Woolwich Ch St 136 C3
Jillian Cl, Hmptn. TW12 .... 161 G7
Jim Bradley Cl, SE18
off John Wilson St 136 D4
Jim Griffiths Ho, SW6
off Clem Attlee Ct 128 C6
Jim O'Neill Wk, Ruis. HA4
off Sidmouth Dr 84 A3
Joan Cres, SE9 .... 156 A7
Joan Gdns, Dag. RM8 .... 100 E2
Joan Rd, Dag. RM8 .... 100 E2
Joan St, SE1 .... 27 G2
Jocelyn Rd, Rich. TW9 .... 145 H3
Jocelyn St, SE15 .... 152 D1
Jockey's Flds, WC1 .... 18 D1
Jodane St, SE8 .... 133 J4
Jodrell Cl, Islw. TW7 .... 144 D1
Jodrell Rd, E3 .... 113 J1
Joel St, Nthwd. HA6 .... 66 A3
Pinner HA5 .... 66 A3
Johanna St, SE1 .... 27 E4
John Adam St, WC2 .... 26 B1
John Aird Ct, W2 .... 14 D1
John Archer Way, SW18 .... 149 G6
John Ashby Cl, SW2 .... 151 E6
John Austin Cl, Kings.T.
KT2 *off Queen*
Elizabeth Rd 181 J1
John Barnes Wk, E15 .... 97 F6
John Bradshaw Rd, N14 .... 58 D1
John Burns Dr, Bark. IG11 .... 99 H7
John Campbell Rd, N16 .... 94 B5
John Carpenter St, EC4 .... 19 G5
John Cornwell VC Ho, E12 .... 98 D4
John Drinkwater Cl, E11
off Browning Rd 79 F7
John Fearon Wk, W10
off Dart St 108 B3
John Felton Rd, SE16 .... 29 H4
John Fisher St, E1 .... 21 H5
John Gooch Dr, Enf. EN2 .... 43 H1
John Harrison Ho, E1
off Philpot St 113 E6
John Harrison Way, SE10 .... 135 F3
John Horner Ms, N1 .... 11 J1
John Islip St, SW1 .... 34 A2
John Keats Ho, N22 .... 59 F7
John Kennedy Ho, SE16
off Rotherhithe
Old Rd 133 G4
John Maurice Cl, SE17 .... 36 B1
John McKenna Wk, SE16 .... 29 J5
John Newton Ct, Well.
DA16 .... 158 B3
John Parker Cl, Dag.
RM10 .... 101 H7
John Parker Sq, SW11
off Thomas
Baines Rd 149 G3
John Penn St, SE13 .... 154 B1
John Perrin Pl, Har. HA3 .... 69 H7
John Princes St, W1 .... 17 E3
John Rennie Wk, E1
off Wine Cl 133 F1
John Roll Way, SE16 .... 29 J5
John Ruskin St, SE5 .... 35 G7
Johns Av, NW4 .... 71 J4
John Silkin La, SE8 .... 133 G5
Johns La, Mord. SM4 .... 185 F5
John's Ms, WC1 .... 10 D6
John Smith Av, SW6 .... 128 C7
John Smith Ms, E14
off Newport Av 114 D7
Johnson Cl, E8 .... 112 D1
Johnson Ho, E2 .... 13 J3
Johnson Rd, NW10 .... 106 D1
Bromley BR2 .... 192 A5
Croydon CR0 .... 188 A7
Hounslow TW5 .... 122 C7
Johnsons Cl, Cars. SM5 .... 199 J3
Johnson's Ct, EC4
off Fleet St 19 F4
Johnsons Dr, Hmptn.
TW12 .... 179 J1
Johnson's Pl, SW1 .... 33 F4
Johnson St, E1
off Cable St 113 F7
Southall UB2 .... 122 C3
Johnsons Way, NW10 .... 106 B4
John Spencer Sq, N1 .... 93 H6
John's Pl, E1
off Damien St 113 E6
John's Ter, Croy. CR0 .... 202 A1
Johnston Cl, SW9
off Hackford Rd 151 F1
Johnston Ct, E10
off Oliver Rd 96 B3
Johnstone Rd, E6 .... 116 C3
Johnston Rd, Wdf.Grn.
IG8 .... 63 G5
Johnston Ter, NW2
off Kara Way 90 A3
John St, E15 .... 115 F1
SE25 .... 188 D4
WC1 .... 10 D6
Enfield EN1 .... 44 C5
Hounslow TW3 .... 143 E2
John Trundle Ct, EC2
off The Barbican 19 J1
John Walsh Twr, E11 .... 97 F2
John Wesley Cl, E6 .... 116 C3
John Williams Cl, SE14 .... 133 G6
Kingston upon Thames
KT2 *off Henry*
Macaulay Av 181 G1
John Wilson St, SE18 .... 136 D3
John Woolley Cl, SE13 .... 154 E4
Joiner's Arms Yd, SE5
off Denmark Hill 152 A1
Joiners Pl, N5
off Leconfield Rd 94 A4
Joiner St, SE1 .... 28 C2
Joiners Yd, N1
off Caledonia St 10 B2
Jolles Ho, E3
off Bromley High St 114 B3
Jollys La, Har. HA2 .... 86 A1
Hayes UB4 .... 102 D5
Jonathan Ct, W4
off Windmill Rd 127 E4
Jonathan St, SE11 .... 34 C3
Jones Rd, E13
off Holborn Rd 115 H4
Jones St, W1 .... 16 D6
Jones Wk, Rich. TW10
off Lower Gro Rd 145 J6
Jonquil Gdns, Hmptn.
TW12 *off Partridge Rd* 161 F6
Jonson Cl, Hayes UB4 .... 102 A5
Mitcham CR4 .... 186 B4
Jordan Cl, Dag. RM10
off Muggeridge Rd 101 H4
Harrow HA2
off Hamilton Cres 85 F3
Jordan Ct, SW15
off Charlwood Rd 148 A4
Jordan Rd, Grnf. (Perivale)
UB6 .... 105 E1
Jordans Cl, Islw. TW7 .... 144 B1
Jordans Ms, Twick. TW2
off Popes Av 162 B2
Joseph Av, W3 .... 106 D6
Joseph Conrad Ho, SW1
off Tachbrook St 33 G2
Joseph Hardcastle Cl,
SE14 .... 133 G7
Josephine Av, SW2 .... 151 F5
Joseph Powell Cl, SW12 .... 150 C6
Joseph Ray Rd, E11 .... 97 E2
Joseph St, E3 .... 113 J4
Joseph Trotter Cl, EC1
off Myddelton St 11 F4
Joshua Cl, N10 .... 58 B7
South Croydon CR2 .... 201 H7
Joshua St, E14
off St. Leonards Rd 114 C6
Joslings Cl, W12 .... 107 H7
Joubert St, SW11 .... 149 J2
Jowett St, SE15 .... 132 C7
Joyce Av, N18 .... 60 C5
Joyce Dawson Way, SE28
off Thamesmere Dr 118 A7
Joyce Dawson Way
Shop Arc, SE28
off Thamesmere Dr 118 A7
Joyce Lattimore Ct, N9
off Colthurst Dr 60 E3
Joyce Page Cl, SE7 .... 136 A6
Joyce Wk, SW2 .... 151 G6
JOYDENS WOOD, Bex.
DA5 .... 177 J5
Joydon Dr, Rom. RM6 .... 82 B6
Joyners Cl, Dag. RM9 .... 101 F4
Jubb Powell Ho, N15 .... 76 B6
Jubilee Av, E4 .... 62 C6
Romford RM7 .... 83 H5
Twickenham TW2 .... 161 J1
Jubilee Cl, NW9 .... 70 D6
NW10 .... 107 E2
Kingston upon Thames
KT1 *off High St* 181 F1
Pinner HA5 .... 66 C2
Romford RM7 .... 83 H5
Jubilee Cres, E14 .... 134 C3
N9 .... 60 D1
Jubilee Dr, Ruis. HA4 .... 84 D4
★ **Jubilee Gdns**, SE1 .... 26 C2
Jubilee Gdns, Sthl. UB1 .... 103 G6
Jubilee La, W5
off Haven La 105 H6
Jubilee Mkt Hall, WC2 .... 18 B5
Jubilee Par, Wdf.Grn. IG8
off Snakes La E 63 J6
Jubilee Pl, SW3 .... 31 H3
Jubilee Rd, Grnf. (Perivale)
UB6 .... 104 E1
Sutton SM3 .... 198 A7
Jubilee St, E1 .... 113 F6
Jubilee Trust, SE10
off Egerton Dr 134 B7
Jubilee Wk, Wat. WD19 .... 50 B4
Jubilee Way, SW19 .... 185 E1
Chessington KT9 .... 196 A4
Sidcup DA14 .... 176 A2
Judd St, WC1 .... 10 A4
Jude St, E16 .... 115 F6
Judge Wk, Esher (Clay.)
KT10 .... 194 B6
Juer St, SW11 .... 129 H7
Jules Thorn Av, Enf. EN1 .... 44 C3
Julia Gdns, Bark. IG11 .... 118 D2
Julia Garfield Ms, E16
off Evelyn Rd 135 H1
Juliana Cl, N2 .... 73 F3
Julian Av, W3 .... 106 B7
Julian Cl, Barn.
(New Barn.) EN5 .... 40 E3
Julian Hill, Har. HA1 .... 86 B2
Julian Ho, SE21
off Kingswood Est 170 B4
Julian Pl, E14 .... 134 B5
Julian Tayler Path, SE23 .... 170 E2
Julia St, NW5
off Oak Village 92 A4
Julien Rd, W5 .... 125 F3
Juliette Rd, E13 .... 115 F2
Julius Caesar Way, Stan.
HA7 .... 53 G4
Julius Nyerere Cl, N1
off Copenhagen St 111 F1
Junction, The, Wem. HA9 .... 88 B4
Junction App, SE13 .... 154 C3
SW11 .... 149 H3
Junction Av, W10
off Harrow Rd 107 J3
Junction Ms, W2 .... 15 G3
Junction Pl, W2 .... 15 F3
Junction Rd, E13 .... 115 H2
N9 .... 60 D1
N17 .... 76 D3
N19 .... 92 C4
W5 .... 125 G4
Brentford TW8 .... 125 G4
Harrow HA1 .... 68 B6
South Croydon CR2 .... 202 A5
Junction Rd E, Rom. RM6
off Kenneth Rd 82 E7
Junction Rd W, Rom. RM6 .... 82 E7
Junction Shop Cen, The,
SW11 *off St. John's*
Hill 149 H4
Juniper Cl, Barn. EN5 .... 40 A5
Chessington KT9 .... 195 J6
Wembley HA9 .... 87 J5
Juniper Cres, NW1 .... 92 A7
Juniper Dr, SW18 .... 149 F4
Juniper Gdns, SW16
off Leonard Rd 186 C1
Juniper La, E6 .... 116 B5
Juniper Rd, Ilf. IG1 .... 98 D4
Juniper St, E1 .... 113 F7
Juno Ho, E3
off Garrison Rd 114 A1
Juno Way, SE14 .... 133 G6
Jupiter Way, N7 .... 93 F6
Jupp Rd, E15 .... 96 D7
Jupp Rd W, E15 .... 114 C1
Justice Wk, SW3 .... 31 G6
Justin Cl, Brent. TW8 .... 125 G7
Justines Pl, E2
off Palmers Rd 113 G3
Justin Rd, E4 .... 61 J6
Jute La, Enf. EN3 .... 45 H2
Jutland Cl, N19
off Sussex Way 92 E1
Jutland Rd, E13 .... 115 G4
SE6 .... 154 C7
Jutsums Av, Rom. RM7 .... 83 H6
Jutsums La, Rom. RM7 .... 83 H6
Juxon Cl, Har. HA3
off Augustine Rd 67 H1
Juxon St, SE11 .... 34 D1

K

Kaduna Cl, Pnr. HA5 .... 66 A5
Kale Rd, Erith DA18 .... 138 E2
Kambala Rd, SW11 .... 149 G2
Kangley Br Rd, SE26 .... 171 J6
Kaplan Dr, N21 .... 43 E5
Kara Way, NW2 .... 90 A4
Karen Ct, SE4
off Wickham Rd 153 J3
Bromley BR1 .... 191 F1
Karen Ter, E11
off Montague Rd 97 F2
Karenza Ct, Wem. HA9
off Lulworth Av 69 F7
Kariba Cl, N9 .... 61 F3
Karina Cl, Chig. IG7 .... 65 H5
Karma Way, Har. HA2 .... 85 G1
Karoline Gdns, Grnf. UB6
off Oldfield La N 104 A2
Kashgar Rd, SE18 .... 137 J5
Kashmir Rd, SE7 .... 136 A7
Kassala Rd, SW11 .... 149 J1
Katella Trd Est, Bark.
IG11 .... 117 H3
Kates Cl, Barn. EN5 .... 39 G5
Katharine St, Croy. CR0 .... 201 J3
Katherine Cl, SE16
off Rotherhithe St 133 G1
Katherine Gdns, SE9 .... 156 A4
Ilford IG6 .... 65 F7
Katherine Rd, E6 .... 98 A7
E7 .... 97 J5
Twickenham TW1
off London Rd 162 D1
Katherine Sq, W11
off Wilsham St 128 B1
Kathleen Av, W3 .... 106 C5
Wembley HA0 .... 87 H7
Kathleen Rd, SW11 .... 149 J3
Kayemoor Rd, Sutt.
SM2 .... 199 H7
Kay Rd, SW9 .... 151 E2
Kays Ter, E18
off Walpole Rd 79 F1
Kay St, E2 .... 13 J1
Welling DA16 .... 158 B1

Kay Way, SE10 *off Greenwich High Rd* **134** B7
Kean St, WC2 **18** C4
Keatley Grn, E4 **61** J6
Keats Av, E16 *off Wesley Av* **135** H1
Keats Cl, E11 *off Nightingale La* **79** H5
NW3 *off Keats Gro* **91** H4
SE1 **37** F2
SW19 **167** G6
Chigwell IG7 **65** F6
Enfield EN3 **45** G5
Hayes UB4 **102** A5
Keats Gro, NW3 **91** G4
★ **Keats Ho**, NW3 **91** H4
Keats Ho, SW1 **33** G5
Beckenham BR3 **172** A6
Keats Pl, EC2 **20** B2
Keats Rd, Belv. DA17 **139** J3
Welling DA16 **157** H1
Keats Way, Croy. CR0 **189** F6
Greenford UB6 **103** H5
West Drayton UB7 **120** C4
Kebbell Ter, E7 **97** H5
Keble Cl, Nthlt. UB5 **85** J5
Worcester Park KT4 **197** F1
Keble Pl, SW13 *off Somerville Av* **127** H6
Keble St, SW17 **167** F4
Kechill Gdns, Brom. BR2 **191** G7
Kedelston Ct, E5 *off Redwald Rd* **95** H4
Kedeston Ct, Sutt. SM1 *off Hurstcourt Rd* **198** E1
Kedleston Dr, Orp. BR5 **193** J6
Kedleston Wk, E2 *off Middleton St* **113** E3
Keedonwood Rd, Brom. BR1 **172** E5
Keel Cl, SE16 **133** G1
Barking IG11 **118** C2
Keel Ct, E14 *off Newport Av* **114** D7
Keeley Rd, Croy. CR0 **201** J2
Keeley St, WC2 **18** C4
Keeling Ho, E2 *off Claredale St* **112** E2
Keeling Rd, SE9 **156** A5
Keely Cl, Barn. EN4 **41** H5
Keemor Cl, SE18 **136** D7
Keens Cl, SW16 **168** D5
Keens Rd, Croy. CR0 **201** J4
Keens Yd, N1 *off St. Paul's Rd* **93** H6
Keep, The, SE3 **155** G2
Kingston upon Thames KT2 **163** J6
Keepers Ms, Tedd. TW11 **163** F6
Keep La, N11 *off Gardeners Cl* **58** A2
Keetons Rd, SE16 **132** E3
Keevil Dr, SW19 **148** A7
Keighley Cl, N7 **93** E4
Keightley Dr, SE9 **175** F1
Keildon Rd, SW11 **149** J4
Keir, The, SW19 **165** J5
Keir Hardie Est, E5 *off Springfield* **94** E1
Keir Hardie Ho, W6 *off Lochaline St* **127** J6
Keir Hardie Way, Bark. IG11 **100** A7
Hayes UB4 **102** A3
Keith Connor Cl, SW8 *off Daley Thompson Way* **150** B3
Keith Gro, W12 **127** G2
Keith Rd, E17 **77** J1
Barking IG11 **117** G2
Hayes UB3 **121** H3
Kelbrook Rd, SE3 **156** B3
Kelby Path, SE9 **175** E3
Kelceda Cl, NW2 **89** G2
Kelfield Gdns, W10 **107** J6
Kelfield Ms, W10 *off Kelfield Gdns* **108** A6
Kelland Cl, N8 *off Palace Rd* **74** D5
Kelland Rd, E13 **115** G4
Kellaway Rd, SE3 **155** J2
Keller Cres, E12 **98** A4
Kellerton Rd, SE13 **154** E5
Kellett Rd, SW2 **151** G4
Kelling Gdns, Croy. CR0 **187** H7
Kellino St, SW17 **167** J4
Kellner Rd, SE28 **137** J3
Kell St, SE1 **27** H5
Kelly Av, SE15 **132** C7
Kelly Cl, NW10 **88** D3
Kelly Ct, Borwd. WD6 **38** C2
Kelly Ms, W9 *off Woodfield Rd* **108** C5
Kelly Rd, NW7 **56** B6
Kelly St, NW1 **92** B6
Kelly Way, Rom. RM6 **82** E5
Kelman Cl, SW4 **150** D2
Kelmore Gro, SE22 **152** D4
Kelmscott Cl, E17 **77** J2
Kelmscott Gdns, W12 **127** G3
Kelmscott Rd, SW11 **149** H5
Kelross Pas, N5 *off Kelross Rd* **93** J4
Kelross Rd, N5 **93** H4
Kelsall Cl, SE3 **155** H2
Kelsall Ms, Rich. TW9 **146** B1
Kelsey Gate, Beck. BR3 **190** B2
Kelsey La, Beck. BR3 **190** A3
Kelsey Pk Av, Beck. BR3 **190** B2
Kelsey Pk Rd, Beck. BR3 **190** A2
Kelsey Sq, Beck. BR3 **190** A2
Kelsey St, E2 **13** J5
Kelsey Way, Beck. BR3 **190** A3
Kelshall Ct, N4 *off Brownswood Rd* **93** J2
Kelsie Way, Ilf. IG6 **65** H7
Kelson Ho, E14 **134** C3
Kelso Pl, W8 **22** B5
Kelso Rd, Cars. SM5 **185** F7
Kelston Rd, Ilf. IG6 **81** E2
Kelvedon Cl, Kings.T. KT2 **163** J6
Kelvedon Ho, SW8 **150** E1
Kelvedon Rd, SW6 **128** C7
Kelvedon Way, Wdf.Grn. IG8 **64** C6
Kelvin Av, N13 **59** F6
Teddington TW11 **162** B6
Kelvinbrook, W.Mol. KT8 **179** H3
Kelvin Cl, Epsom KT19 **196** A6
Kelvin Cres, Har. HA3 **52** B7
Kelvin Dr, Twick. TW1 **145** E6
Kelvin Gdns, Croy. CR0 **187** E7
Southall UB1 **103** G6
Kelvin Gro, SE26 **170** E3
Chessington KT9 **195** G3
Kelvington Cl, Croy. CR0 **189** H7
Kelvington Rd, SE15 **153** G5
Kelvin Ind Est, Grnf. UB6 **85** H7
Kelvin Par, Orp. BR6 **207** H1
Kelvin Rd, N5 **93** H4
Welling DA16 **158** A3
Kember St, N1 *off Carnoustie Dr* **93** F7
Kemble Dr, Brom. BR2 **206** B3
Kemble Rd, N17 **76** D1
SE23 **171** G1
Croydon CR0 **201** G3
Kemble St, WC2 **18** C4
Kemerton Rd, SE5 **151** J3
Beckenham BR3 **190** B2
Croydon CR0 **188** C7
Kemeys St, E9 **95** H5
Kemnal Rd, Chis. BR7 **175** G4
Kemp Ct, SW8 *off Allen Edwards Dr* **130** E7
Kempe Rd, NW6 **108** A2
Kemp Gdns, Croy. CR0 *off St. Saviours Rd* **187** J6
Kemp Ho, W1 *off Berwick St* **17** H5
Kempis Way, SE22 *off East Dulwich Gro* **152** B5
Kemplay Rd, NW3 **91** G4
Kemp Rd, Dag. RM8 **100** D1
Kemp's Ct, W1 **17** G4
Kemps Dr, E14 *off Morant St* **114** A7
Kempsford Gdns, SW5 **128** D5
Kempsford Rd, SE11 **35** F2
Kemps Gdns, SE13 *off Thornford Rd* **154** C5
Kempshott Rd, SW16 **168** D7
Kempson Rd, SW6 **148** D1
Kempthorne Rd, SE8 **133** H4
Kempton Av, Nthlt. UB5 **85** G6
Sunbury-on-Thames TW16 **178** B1
Kempton Cl, Erith DA8 **139** J6
Kempton Ct, E1 *off Durward St* **112** E5
Sunbury-on-Thames TW16 **178** B1
★ **Kempton Park Racecourse**, Sun. TW16 **160** C7
Kempton Rd, E6 **116** C1
Hampton TW12 **179** F2
Kempton Wk, Croy. CR0 **189** H6
Kempt St, SE18 **136** D6
Kemsing Cl, Bex. DA5 **159** E7
Bromley BR2 **205** F2
Thornton Heath CR7 **187** J4
Kemsing Rd, SE10 **135** G5
Kemsley, SE13 **154** C5
Kenbury Gdns, SE5 *off Kenbury St* **151** J2
Kenbury St, SE5 **151** J2
Kenchester Cl, SW8 **131** E7
Kencot Cl, Erith DA18 **139** F2
Kendal Av, N18 **60** A4
W3 **106** A4
Barking IG11 **99** H7
Kendal Cl, N20 **57** H2
SW9 **35** G7
Woodford Green IG8 **63** F2
Kendale Rd, Brom. BR1 **172** E5
Kendal Gdns, N18 **60** A4
Sutton SM1 **199** F2
Kendal Ho, N1 **10** D1
Kendall Av, Beck. BR3 **189** H2
Kendall Ct, SW19 **167** G6
Borehamwood WD6 *off Gregson Cl* **38** C1
Kendall Pl, W1 **16** B2
Kendall Rd, SE18 **156** B1
Beckenham BR3 **189** H2
Isleworth TW7 **144** D2
Kendalmere Cl, N10 **74** B1
Kendal Par, N18 *off Great Cambridge Rd* **60** A4
Kendal Pl, SW15 **148** C5
Kendal Rd, NW10 **89** G4
Kendal Steps, W2 *off St. Georges Flds* **15** H4
Kendal St, W2 **15** H4
Kender St, SE14 **133** F7
Kendoa Rd, SW4 **150** D4
Kendon Cl, E11 **79** H5
Kendra Hall Rd, S.Croy. CR2 **201** H7
Kendrey Gdns, Twick. TW2 **144** B6
Kendrick Ms, SW7 **31** E1
Kendrick Pl, SW7 **31** E2
Kenelm Cl, Har. HA1 **86** D3
Kenerne Dr, Barn. EN5 **40** B5
Kenilford Rd, SW12 **150** B7
Kenilworth Av, E17 **78** A2
SW19 **166** D5
Harrow HA2 **85** F4
Kenilworth Cl, Borwd. WD6 **38** C3
Kenilworth Ct, SW15 *off Lower Richmond Rd* **148** A3
Kenilworth Cres, Enf. EN1 **44** B1
Kenilworth Dr, Borwd. WD6 **38** C3
Kenilworth Gdns, SE18 **156** E2
Ilford IG3 **99** J2
Loughton IG10 **48** C6
Southall UB1 **103** F3
Watford WD19 **50** C5
Kenilworth Rd, E3 **113** H2
NW6 **108** C1
SE20 **189** G1
W5 **125** H1
Edgware HA8 **54** C3
Epsom KT17 **197** G6
Orpington BR5 **193** F6
Kenley, N17 **76** A2
Kenley Av, NW9 **70** E2
Kenley Cl, Barn. EN4 **41** H4
Bexley DA5 **159** G7
Chislehurst BR7 **193** H3
Kenley Gdns, Th.Hth. CR7 **187** H4
Kenley Rd, SW19 **184** C2
Kingston upon Thames KT1 **182** B2
Twickenham TW1 **144** D6
Kenley Wk, W11 **108** B7
Sutton SM3 **198** A4
Kenlor Rd, SW17 **167** G5
Kenmare Dr, N17 **76** C2
Mitcham CR4 **167** J7
Kenmare Gdns, N13 **59** H4
Kenmare Rd, Th.Hth. CR7 **187** G6
Kenmere Gdns, Wem. HA0 **106** A1
Kenmere Rd, Well. DA16 **158** C2
Kenmont Gdns, NW10 **107** H3
Kenmore Av, Har. HA3 **68** D4
Kenmore Cl, Rich. TW9 *off Kent Rd* **126** A7
Kenmore Gdns, Edg. HA8 **70** B2
Kenmore Rd, Har. HA3 **69** G3
Kenmure Rd, E8 **95** E5
Kenmure Yd, E8 *off Kenmure Rd* **95** E5
Kennacraig Cl, E16 *off Hanameel St* **135** G1
Kennard Rd, E15 **96** D7
N11 **57** J5
Kennard St, E16 **136** C1
SW11 **150** A1
Kennedy Av, Enf. EN3 **45** F6
Kennedy Cl, E13 **115** G2
Mitcham CR4 **186** A2
Orpington BR5 **207** G1
Pinner HA5 **51** F6
Kennedy Ho, SE11 *off Vauxhall Wk* **34** C3
Kennedy Path, W7 *off Harp Rd* **104** C4
Kennedy Rd, W7 **104** B5
Barking IG11 **117** H1
Kennedy Wk, SE17 *off Flint St* **36** C2
Kennet Cl, SW11 *off Maysoule Rd* **149** G4
Kenneth Av, Ilf. IG1 **98** E4
Kenneth Cres, NW2 **89** H5
Kenneth Gdns, Stan. HA7 **52** D6
Kenneth More Rd, Ilf. IG1 *off Oakfield Rd* **99** E3
Kennet Ho, NW8 **15** F1
Kenneth Rd, Rom. RM6 **82** D7
Kenneth Robbins Ho, N17 **60** E7
Kennet Rd, W9 **108** C4
Isleworth TW7 **144** C3
Kennet Sq, Mitch. CR4 **185** H1
Kennet St, E1 **29** J1
Kennett Dr, Hayes UB4 **102** E5
Kennet Wf La, EC4 **20** A5
Kenninghall, N18 **60** E5
Kenninghall Rd, E5 **94** D3
N18 **61** F5
Kenning St, SE16 *off Railway Av* **133** F2
Kennings Way, SE11 **35** G3
Kenning Ter, N1 **112** B1
KENNINGTON, SE11 **35** E6
Kennington Grn, SE11 **35** E4
Kennington La, SE11 **35** F3
Kennington Oval, SE11 **34** D5
Kennington Pk, SW9 **35** F7
Kennington Pk Est, SE11 **35** E6
Kennington Pk Gdns, SE11 **35** G5
Kennington Pk Pl, SE11 **35** F4
Kennington Pk Rd, SE11 **35** F5
Kennington Rd, SE1 **27** E5
SE11 **27** E6
Kennoldes, SE21 **170** A2
Kenrick Pl, W1 **16** B1
KENSAL GREEN, NW10 **107** J3
★ **Kensal Green Cem**, W10 **107** J3
KENSAL RISE, NW6 **108** A2
Kensal Rd, W10 **108** B4
KENSAL TOWN, W10 **108** A4
Kensal Wf, W10 *off Ladbroke Gro* **108** A4
KENSINGTON, W8 **128** C2
Kensington Av, E12 **98** B6
Thornton Heath CR7 **187** G1
Kensington Ch Ct, W8 **22** A4
Kensington Ch St, W8 **128** D1
Kensington Ch Wk, W8 **22** A3
Kensington Cl, N11 **58** A5
Kensington Ct, NW7 *off Grenville Pl* **54** D5
W8 **22** B4
Kensington Ct Gdns, W8 *off Kensington Ct Pl* **22** B5
Kensington Ct Ms, W8 **22** B4
Kensington Ct Pl, W8 **22** B5
Kensington Dr, Wdf.Grn. IG8 **80** A1
★ **Kensington Gdns**, W2 **22** D2
Kensington Gdns, Ilf. IG1 **98** C2
Kingston upon Thames KT1 *off Portsmouth Rd* **181** G3
Kensington Gdns Sq, W2 **14** A4
Kensington Gate, W8 **22** C5
Kensington Gore, SW7 **23** E4
Kensington Grn, W8 **22** A6
Kensington Hall Gdns, W14 *off Beaumont Av* **128** C5
Kensington High St, W8 **128** D3
W14 **128** B4
Kensington Mall, W8 **128** D1
★ **Kensington Palace**, W8 **22** B2
Kensington Palace Gdns, W8 **22** A1
Kensington Pk Gdns, W11 **108** C7
Kensington Pk Ms, W11 *off Kensington Pk Rd* **108** C6
Kensington Pk Rd, W11 **108** C7
Kensington Pl, W8 **128** D1
Kensington Rd, SW7 **23** F4
W8 **22** B4
Northolt UB5 **103** G3
Romford RM7 **83** J6
Kensington Sq, W8 **22** A4
Kensington Ter, S.Croy. CR2 **202** A7
Kensington Village, W14 *off Avonmore Rd* **128** C4
Kensington Way, Borwd. WD6 **38** D3
Kent Av, W13 **104** E5
Dagenham RM9 **119** G4
Welling DA16 **157** J5

Kent Cl, Mitch. CR4 ... **187** E4
Orpington BR6 ... **207** H6
Kent Dr, Barn. (Cockfos.) EN4 ... **42** A4
Teddington TW11 ... **162** B5
Kentford Way, Nthlt. UB5 . **102** E1
Kent Gdns, W13 ... **105** E5
Ruislip HA4 ... **66** B6
Kent Gate Way, Croy. CR0 ... **204** A5
Kent Ho La, Beck. BR3 ... **171** H5
Kent Ho Rd, SE26 ... **189** G1
Beckenham BR3 ... **171** H5
Kentish Bldgs, SE1 ... **28** B2
Kentish Rd, Belv. DA17 ... **139** G4
KENTISH TOWN, NW5 ... **92** C6
Kentish Town Rd, NW1 ... **92** B7
NW5 ... **92** B7
Kentish Way, Brom. BR1 . **191** G2
Kentlea Rd, SE28 ... **137** H2
Kentmere Rd, SE18 ... **137** H4
KENTON, Har. HA3 ... **68** E5
Kenton Av, Har. HA1 ... **68** C7
Southall UB1 ... **103** G7
Sunbury-on-Thames TW16 ... **178** E2
Kenton Ct, W14 *off Kensington High St* ... **128** C3
Kenton Gdns, Har. HA3 ... **69** F5
Kenton La, Har. HA3 ... **69** F3
Kenton Pk Av, Har. HA3 ... **69** G4
Kenton Pk Cl, Har. HA3 ... **69** F4
Kenton Pk Cres, Har. HA3 . **69** G4
Kenton Pk Rd, Har. HA3 ... **69** F4
Kenton Rd, E9 ... **95** G6
Harrow HA1, HA3 ... **69** G5
Kenton St, WC1 ... **10** A5
Kent Pas, NW1 ... **7** J5
Kent Rd, N21 ... **60** A1
W4 ... **126** C3
Dagenham RM10 ... **101** H5
East Molesey KT8 ... **179** J4
Kingston upon Thames KT1 *off The Bittoms* ... **181** G3
Richmond TW9 ... **126** A7
West Wickham BR4 ... **204** B1
Kents Pas, Hmptn. TW12 . **179** F1
Kent St, E2 ... **13** G1
E13 ... **115** J3
Kent Ter, NW1 ... **7** H4
Kent Vw Gdns, Ilf. IG3 ... **99** H2
Kent Way, Surb. KT6 ... **195** H3
Kentwell Cl, SE4 ... **153** H4
Kentwode Grn, SW13 ... **127** G7
Kent Yd, SW7 ... **23** H4
Kenver Av, N12 ... **57** G6
Kenward Rd, SE9 ... **155** J5
Kenway, Rom. RM5 ... **83** J2
Ken Way, Wem. HA9 ... **88** C2
Kenway Rd, SW5 ... **30** A2
Kenwood Av, N14 ... **42** D5
SE14 *off Briant St* ... **153** G1
Kenwood Cl, NW3 ... **91** G1
West Drayton (Sipson) UB7 ... **120** D6
Kenwood Dr, Beck. BR3 ... **190** C3
Kenwood Gdns, E18 ... **79** H3
Ilford IG2 ... **80** D4
★ **Kenwood Ho**, NW3 ... **91** H1
Kenwood Rd, N6 ... **73** J6
N9 ... **60** D1
Kenworthy Rd, E9 ... **95** H5
Kenwyn Dr, NW2 ... **89** E3
Kenwyn Rd, SW4 ... **150** D4
SW20 ... **183** J1
Kenya Rd, SE7 ... **136** A7
Kenyngton Dr, Sun. TW16 ... **160** A5
Kenyngton Pl, Har. HA3 ... **69** F5
Kenyon St, SW6 ... **148** A1
Keogh Rd, E15 ... **97** E6
Kepler Rd, SW4 ... **150** E4
Keppel Rd, E6 ... **98** C7
Dagenham RM9 ... **100** E4
Keppel Row, SE1 ... **27** J2
Keppel St, WC1 ... **17** J1
Kerbela St, E2 ... **13** H5
Kerbey St, E14 ... **114** B6
Kerfield Cres, SE5 ... **152** A1
Kerfield Pl, SE5 ... **152** A1
Kerri Cl, Barn. EN5 ... **39** J4
Kerridge Ct, N1 ... **94** B6
Kerrison Pl, W5 ... **125** G1
Kerrison Rd, E15 ... **114** D1
SW11 ... **149** H3
W5 ... **125** G1
Kerrison Vil, W5 *off Kerrison Pl* ... **125** G1
Kerry Av, Stan. HA7 ... **53** G4
Kerry Av N, Stan. HA7 ... **53** G4
Kerry Cl, E16 ... **115** H6
N13 ... **59** F2
Kerry Ct, Stan. HA7 ... **53** G4
Kerry Ho, E1 *off Sidney St* ... **113** F6
Kerry Path, SE14 ... **133** J6
Kerry Rd, SE14 ... **133** J6
Kersey Gdns, SE9 ... **174** B4
Kersfield Rd, SW15 ... **148** A6
Kershaw Cl, SW18 ... **149** F6
Kershaw Rd, Dag. RM10 ... **101** G3
Kersley Ms, SW11 ... **149** J2
Kersley Rd, N16 ... **94** B3
Kersley St, SW11 ... **149** J2
Kerswell Cl, N15 ... **76** B5
Kerwick Cl, N7 *off Sutterton St* ... **93** F7
Keslake Rd, NW6 ... **108** A2
Kessock Cl, N17 ... **76** E5
Kesteven Cl, Ilf. IG6 ... **65** J6
Kestlake Rd, Bex. DA5 *off East Rochester Way* ... **158** C6
KESTON, BR2 ... **205** J5
Keston Av, Kes. BR2 ... **205** J5
Keston Cl, N18 ... **60** A3
Welling DA16 ... **138** C7
Keston Gdns, Kes. BR2 ... **205** J4
Keston Mark, Kes. BR2 ... **206** B3
Keston Pk Cl, Kes. BR2 ... **206** C3
Keston Rd, N17 ... **76** A3
SE15 ... **152** D3
Thornton Heath CR7 ... **187** G6
Kestral Ct, Wall. SM6 *off Carew Rd* ... **200** C5
Kestrel Av, E6 *off Swan App* ... **116** B5
SE24 ... **151** H5
Kestrel Cl, NW9 ... **70** E2
NW10 ... **88** D5
Kingston upon Thames KT2 ... **163** G4
Kestrel Ho, EC1 ... **11** J3
SW8 *off St. George Wf* ... **34** A5
W13 ... **104** C4
Enfield EN3 *off Alma Rd* ... **45** H5
Kestrel Pl, SE14 *off Milton Ct Rd* ... **133** H6
Kestrel Way, Felt. TW14 *off Falcon Way* ... **142** B5
Hayes UB3 ... **121** G2
Keswick Av, SW15 ... **164** E5
SW19 ... **184** D2
Keswick Bdy, SW15 *off Upper Richmond Rd* ... **148** C5
Keswick Cl, Sutt. SM1 ... **199** F4
Keswick Gdns, Ilf. IG4 ... **80** B5
Wembley HA9 ... **87** H4
Keswick Ms, W5 ... **125** H1
Keswick Rd, SW15 ... **148** B5
Bexleyheath DA7 ... **159** G2
Orpington BR6 ... **207** J1
Twickenham TW2 ... **143** J6
West Wickham BR4 ... **204** E2
Kettering St, SW16 ... **168** C6
Kett Gdns, SW2 ... **151** F5
Kettlebaston Rd, E10 ... **95** J1
Kettlewell Cl, N11 ... **58** A6
Kevan Ho, SE5 ... **131** J7
Kevelioc Rd, N17 ... **75** J1
Kevin Cl, Houns. TW4 ... **142** D2
Kevington Cl, Orp. BR5 ... **193** J4
Kevington Dr, Chis. BR7 ... **193** J4
Orpington BR5 ... **193** J4
KEW, Rich. TW9 ... **126** A6
Kew Br, Brent. TW8 ... **125** J6
Richmond TW9 ... **125** J6
Kew Br Arches, Rich. TW9 *off Kew Br* ... **125** J6
Kew Br Ct, W4 ... **126** A5
Kew Br Rd, Brent. TW8 ... **125** J6
★ **Kew Bridge Steam Mus**, Brent. TW8 ... **125** J5
Kew Cres, Sutt. SM3 ... **198** B3
Kew Foot Rd, Rich. TW9 ... **145** H4
Kew Gdns Rd, Rich. TW9 . **125** J7
Kew Grn, Rich. TW9 ... **126** A7
Kew Meadows Path, Rich. TW9 ... **146** B2
★ **Kew Observatory**, Rich. TW9 ... **145** E3
★ **Kew Palace** (Royal Botanic Gdns), Rich. TW9 ... **125** H7
Kew Retail Pk, Rich. TW9 . **146** B1
Kew Rd, Rich. TW9 ... **126** A6
Key Cl, E1 ... **113** E4
Keyes Rd, NW2 ... **90** A5
Keyham Ho, W2 *off Westbourne Pk Rd* . **108** D5
Keymer Rd, SW2 ... **169** F2
Keynes Cl, N2 ... **73** J3
Keynsham Av, Wdf.Grn. IG8 ... **63** E4
Keynsham Gdns, SE9 ... **156** B5
Keynsham Rd, SE9 ... **156** A5
Morden SM4 ... **198** E1
Keynsham Wk, Mord. SM4 ... **198** E1
Keyse Rd, SE1 ... **29** F6
Keysham Av, Houns. TW5 *off The Avenue* ... **142** A1
Keystone Cres, N1 ... **10** B2
Keywood Dr, Sun. TW16 ... **160** A6
Keyworth Cl, E5 ... **95** H4
Keyworth Pl, SE1 ... **27** H5
Keyworth St, SE1 ... **27** H5
Kezia Ms, SE8 *off Trundleys Rd* ... **133** H5
Kezia St, SE8 *off Trundleys Rd* ... **133** H5
Khalsa Ct, N22 *off Acacia Rd* ... **75** H1
Khama Rd, SW17 ... **167** H4
Khartoum Rd, E13 ... **115** H3
SW17 ... **167** G4
Ilford IG1 ... **99** E5
Khyber Rd, SW11 ... **149** H2
Kibworth St, SW8 ... **131** F7
KIDBROOKE, SE3 ... **155** H3
Kidbrooke Gdns, SE3 ... **155** G2
Kidbrooke Gro, SE3 ... **155** G1
Kidbrooke Interchange, SE3 ... **155** J3
Kidbrooke La, SE9 ... **156** B4
Kidbrooke Pk Cl, SE3 ... **155** H1
Kidbrooke Pk Rd, SE3 ... **155** H1
Kidbrooke Way, SE3 ... **155** H2
Kidderminster Pl, Croy. CR0 *off Kidderminster Rd* . **201** H1
Kidderminster Rd, Croy. CR0 ... **201** H1
Kidderpore Av, NW3 ... **90** D4
Kidderpore Gdns, NW3 ... **90** D4
Kidd Pl, SE7 ... **136** B5
Kielder Cl, Ilf. IG6 ... **65** J6
Kiffen St, EC2 ... **12** C5
Kilberry Cl, Islw. TW7 ... **144** A1
KILBURN, NW6 ... **108** C2
Kilburn Br, NW6 *off Kilburn High Rd* ... **108** D1
Kilburn Gate, NW6 ... **6** A1
Kilburn High Rd, NW6 ... **90** C7
Kilburn La, W9 ... **108** A3
W10 ... **108** A3
Kilburn Pk Rd, NW6 ... **108** D3
Kilburn Pl, NW6 ... **108** D1
Kilburn Priory, NW6 ... **108** E1
Kilburn Sq, NW6 ... **108** D1
Kilburn Vale, NW6 *off Belsize Rd* ... **108** E1
Kilby Ct, SE10 *off Child La* ... **135** F3
Kildare Cl, Ruis. HA4 ... **84** C1
Kildare Gdns, W2 ... **108** D6
Kildare Rd, E16 ... **115** G5
Kildare Ter, W2 ... **108** D6
Kildare Wk, E14 *off Farrance St* ... **114** A6
Kildoran Rd, SW2 ... **150** E5
Kildowan Rd, Ilf. IG3 ... **100** A1
Kilgour Rd, SE23 ... **153** H6
Kilkie St, SW6 ... **149** F2
Killarney Rd, SW18 ... **149** F6
Killburns Mill Cl, Wall. SM6 *off London Rd* ... **200** B2
Killearn Rd, SE6 ... **172** D1
Killester Gdns, Wor.Pk. KT4 ... **197** H4
Killick St, N1 ... **10** C1
Killieser Av, SW2 ... **168** E2
Killip Cl, E16 ... **115** F6
Killowen Av, Nthlt. UB5 ... **85** J5
Killowen Rd, E9 ... **95** G6
Killyon Rd, SW8 ... **150** C2
Killyon Ter, SW8 ... **150** C2
Kilmaine Rd, SW6 ... **128** B7
Kilmarnock Gdns, Dag. RM8 *off Lindsey Rd* ... **100** C3
Kilmarnock Rd, Wat. WD19 . **50** D4
Kilmarsh Rd, W6 ... **127** J4
Kilmartin Av, SW16 ... **187** F3
Kilmartin Rd, Ilf. IG3 ... **100** A2
Kilmington Rd, SW13 ... **127** G6
Kilmorey Gdns, Twick. TW1 ... **144** E5
Kilmorey Rd, Twick. TW1 ... **144** E4
Kilmorie Rd, SE23 ... **171** H1
Kiln Cl, Hayes (Harling.) UB3 *off Brickfield La* ... **121** G6
Kilner St, E14 ... **114** A5
Kiln Ms, SW17 ... **167** G5
Kiln Pl, NW5 ... **92** A5
Kilnside, Esher (Clay.) KT10 ... **194** D7
Kilpatrick Way, Hayes UB4 ... **103** E5
Kilravock St, W10 ... **108** B3
Kilsby Wk, Dag. RM9 *off Rugby Rd* ... **100** B6
Kilsha Rd, Walt. KT12 ... **178** B6
Kimbell Gdns, SW6 ... **148** B1
Kimbell Pl, SE3 *off Tudway Rd* ... **155** J4
Kimberley Av, E6 ... **116** B2
SE15 ... **153** E2
Ilford IG2 ... **81** G7
Romford RM7 ... **83** J6
Kimberley Dr, Sid. DA14 ... **176** D2
Kimberley Gdns, N4 ... **75** H5
Enfield EN1 ... **44** C3
Kimberley Ind Est, E17 ... **77** J1
Kimberley Rd, E4 ... **62** E1
E11 ... **96** D2
E16 ... **115** F4
E17 ... **77** J1
N17 ... **76** D2
N18 ... **61** E6
NW6 ... **108** B1
SW9 ... **151** E2
Beckenham BR3 ... **189** G2
Croydon CR0 ... **187** H6
Kimberley Wk, Walt. KT12 *off Cottimore La* ... **178** B7
Kimberley Way, E4 ... **63** E1
Kimber Rd, SW18 ... **148** D7
Kimble Rd, SW19 ... **167** G6
Kimbolton Cl, SE12 ... **155** F6
Kimbolton Grn, Borwd. WD6 ... **38** C4
Kimbolton Row, SW3 ... **31** G2
Kimmeridge Gdns, SE9 ... **174** B4
Kimmeridge Rd, SE9 ... **174** B4
Kimpton Ho, SW15 *off Fontley Way* ... **147** G7
Kimpton Link Business Cen, Sutt. SM3 *off Kimpton Rd* ... **198** C2
Kimpton Pk Way, Sutt. SM3 ... **198** C2
Kimpton Rd, SE5 ... **152** A1
Sutton SM3 ... **198** C2
Kimpton Trade & Business Cen, Sutt. SM3 ... **198** C2
Kinburn St, SE16 ... **133** G2
Kincaid Rd, SE15 ... **132** E7
Kincardine Gdns, W9 *off Harrow Rd* ... **108** D4
Kinch Gro, Wem. HA9 ... **69** J7
Kinder Cl, SE28 ... **118** D7
Kinder St, E1 *off Cannon St Rd* ... **112** E6
Kinderton Cl, N14 ... **58** C1
Kinefold Ho, N7 *off York Way* ... **92** E6
Kinfauns Rd, SW2 ... **169** G2
Ilford IG3 ... **100** A1
King Alfred Av, SE6 ... **172** A3
King & Queen Cl, SE9 *off St. Keverne Rd* ... **174** B4
King & Queen St, SE17 ... **36** A2
King & Queen Wf, SE16 *off Rotherhithe St* ... **133** G1
King Arthur Cl, SE15 ... **133** F7
King Charles Cres, Surb. KT5 ... **181** J7
King Charles Rd, Surb. KT5 ... **181** J5
King Charles St, SW1 ... **25** J3
King Charles Ter, E1 *off Sovereign Cl* ... **113** E7
King Charles Wk, SW19 *off Princes Way* ... **166** B1
Kingcup Cl, Croy. CR0 ... **189** G7
King David La, E1 ... **113** F7
Kingdon Rd, NW6 ... **90** D6
King Edward Dr, Chess. KT9 *off Kelvin Gro* ... **195** H3
King Edward Ms, SW13 ... **147** G1
King Edward Rd, E10 ... **96** C1
E17 ... **77** H3
Barnet EN5 ... **40** D4
King Edward's Gdns, W3 . **126** A1
King Edwards Gro, Tedd. TW11 ... **163** E6
King Edward's Pl, W3 *off King Edward's Gdns* ... **126** A1
King Edwards Rd, E9 ... **113** E1
N9 ... **44** E7
Barking IG11 ... **117** G1
King Edward's Rd, Enf. EN3 ... **45** G4
King Edward St, EC1 ... **19** J3
King Edward III Ms, SE16 *off Paradise St* ... **133** E2
King Edward Wk, SE1 ... **27** F5
Kingfield Rd, W5 ... **105** G4
Kingfield St, E14 ... **134** C4
Kingfisher Av, E11 *off Eastern Av* ... **79** H6
Kingfisher Cl, SE28 ... **118** C7
Harrow (Har.Wld) HA3 ... **52** C7
Kingfisher Ct, SW19 *off Queensmere Rd* ... **166** B2

Kingfisher Ct, Surbiton KT6 *off Ewell Rd* **181** J7
Sutton SM1 *off Sandpiper Rd* **198** C5
Kingfisher Dr, Rich. TW10 **163** E4
Kingfisher Ho, SW18 *off Juniper Dr* **149** F3
Kingfisher Ms, SE13 **154** B4
Kingfisher Pl, N22 *off Clarendon Rd* **75** F2
Kingfisher Sq, SE8 **133** J6
Kingfisher St, E6 **116** B5
Kingfisher Wk, NW9 **71** E2
Kingfisher Way, NW10 **88** D5
Beckenham BR3 **189** G5
King Frederik IX Twr, SE16 **133** J3
King Gdns, Croy. CR0 **201** H5
King George Av, E16 **116** A6
Ilford IG2 **81** G5
King George Cl, Rom. RM7 **83** J3
King George V Dock, E16 **136** C1
King Georges Dr, Sthl. UB1 **103** F5
King George VI Av, Mitch. CR4 **185** J4
King George Sq, Rich. TW10 **145** J6
King George's Trd Est, Chess. KT9 **196** A4
King George St, SE10 **134** C7
Kingham Cl, SW18 **149** F7
W11 **128** B2
King Harolds Way, Bexh. DA7 **138** D7
King Henry Ms, Har. HA2 **86** B1
Orpington BR6 *off Osgood Av* **207** J5
King Henry's Reach, W6 **127** J6
King Henry's Rd, NW3 **91** H7
Kingston upon Thames KT1 **182** B3
King Henry St, N16 **94** B5
King Henry's Wk, N1 **94** B6
King Henry Ter, E1 *off Sovereign Cl* **113** E7
Kinghorn St, EC1 **19** J2
King James Ct, SE1 **27** H4
King James St, SE1 **27** H4
King John Ct, EC2 **12** E5
King John St, E1 **113** G5
King Johns Wk, SE9 **174** A1
Kinglake Est, SE17 **36** E3
Kinglake St, SE17 **36** D4
Kinglet Cl, E7 *off Romford Rd* **97** G6
Kingly Ct, W1 **17** F5
Kingly St, W1 **17** F4
Kingsand Rd, SE12 **173** G2
Kings Arbour, Sthl. UB2 **122** E5
Kings Arms Ct, E1 **21** H2
Kings Arms Yd, EC2 **20** B3
Kingsash Dr, Hayes UB4 **102** E4
Kings Av, N10 **74** A3
N21 **59** H1
King's Av, SW4 **150** D7
SW12 **168** D1
Kings Av, W5 **105** G6
Bromley BR1 **173** F6
Buckhurst Hill IG9 **64** A2
Carshalton SM5 **199** H7
Greenford UB6 **103** H6
Hounslow TW3 **143** H1
New Malden KT3 **183** E4
Romford RM6 **83** F6
Woodford Green IG8 **63** H6
Kings Bench St, SE1 **27** H3
Kings Bench Wk, EC4 **19** F4
Kingsbridge Av, W3 **125** J2
Kingsbridge Ct, E14 *off Dockers Tanner Rd* **134** A3
Kingsbridge Cres, Sthl. UB1 **103** F5
Kingsbridge Dr, NW7 **56** A7
Kingsbridge Rd, W10 **107** J6
Barking IG11 **117** G2
Morden SM4 **184** A7
Southall UB2 **123** F4
Walton-on-Thames KT12 **178** B7
KINGSBURY, NW9 **70** B6
Kingsbury Circle, NW9 **70** A5
Kingsbury Rd, N1 **94** B6
NW9 **70** B5
Kingsbury Ter, N1 **94** B6
Kingsbury Trd Est, NW9 **70** C6
Kings Butts, SE9 *off Strongbow Cres* **156** C5
Kings Chace Vw, Enf. EN2 *off Crofton Way* **43** G2
Kings Chase, E.Mol. KT8 **179** J3
Kingsclere Cl, SW15 **147** G7
Kingsclere Ct, Barn. EN5 *off Gloucester Rd* **41** F5
Kingsclere Pl, Enf. EN2 **43** J2
Kingscliffe Gdns, SW19 **166** C1
Kings Cl, E10 **78** B7
NW4 **72** A4
Thames Ditton KT7 **180** D6
Kings Coll Rd, NW3 **91** H7
Kingscote Rd, W4 **126** D3
Croydon CR0 **188** E7
New Malden KT3 **182** D3
Kingscote St, EC4 **19** G5
Kings Ct, E13 **115** H1
W6 *off Hamlet Gdns* **127** G4
Wembley HA9 **88** B2
Kingscourt Rd, SW16 **168** D3
Kings Ct S, SW3 *off Chelsea Manor Gdns* **31** H4
Kings Cres, N4 **93** J3
Kings Cres Est, N4 **93** J2
Kingscroft Rd, NW2 **90** C6
KING'S CROSS, N1 **110** D1
King's Cross Br, N1 **10** B3
King's Cross Rd, WC1 **10** D3
King's Cross Sta, N1 **10** A2
Kingsdale Gdns, W11 **128** A1
Kingsdale Rd, SE18 **137** J7
SE20 **171** G7
Kingsdown Av, W3 **107** E7
W13 **125** E2
Kingsdown Cl, SE16 *off Masters Dr* **133** E5
W10 **108** A6
Kingsdowne Rd, Surb. KT6 **181** H7
Kingsdown Rd, E11 **97** E3
N19 **92** E2
Sutton SM3 **198** B5
Kingsdown Way, Brom. BR2 **191** G7
Kings Dr, Edg. HA8 **53** J4
Surbiton KT5 **182** A7
Teddington TW11 **162** A5
Thames Ditton KT7 **180** E6
Wembley HA9 **88** B2
Kings Fm Av, Rich. TW10 **146** A4
Kingsfield Av, Har. HA2 **67** H4
Kingsfield Ho, SE9 **174** A3
Kingsfield Rd, Har. HA1 **68** A7
Kingsford St, NW5 **91** J5
Kingsford Way, E6 **116** C5
Kings Gdns, NW6 *off West End La* **90** D7
Ilford IG1 **99** G1
King's Garth Ms, SE23 *off London Rd* **171** F2
Kingsgate, Wem. HA9 **88** C3
Kingsgate Av, N3 **72** D3
Kingsgate Cl, Bexh. DA7 **158** E1
Kingsgate Est, N1 *off Tottenham Rd* **94** B6
Kingsgate Pl, NW6 **90** D7
Kingsgate Rd, NW6 **90** D7
Kingston upon Thames KT2 **181** H1
Kings Grn, Loug. IG10 **48** B3
Kingsground, SE9 **156** B7
Kings Gro, SE15 **133** E7
Kings Hall Ms, SE13 *off Lewisham Rd* **154** C3
Kings Hall Rd, Beck. BR3 **171** H7
Kings Head Hill, E4 **46** B7
Kings Head Yd, SE1 **28** B2
Kings Highway, SE18 **137** H6
Kingshill, SE17 **36** A2
Kings Hill, Loug. IG10 **48** B2
Kingshill Av, Har. HA3 **69** E4
Northolt UB5 **102** A3
Worcester Park KT4 **183** G7
Kingshill Cl, Hayes UB4 **102** A3
Kingshill Dr, Har. HA3 **68** E3
Kingshold Est, E9 *off Victoria Pk Rd* **113** F1
Kingshold Rd, E9 **95** F7
Kingsholm Gdns, SE9 **156** A4
King's Ho, SW8 **34** B7
Kingshurst Rd, SE12 **155** G7
Kingside, SE18 *off Woolwich Ch St* **136** B3
King's Keep, SW15 *off Westleigh Av* **148** A5
Kings Keep, Kings.T. KT1 *off Beaufort Rd* **181** H4
KINGSLAND, N1 **94** B6
Kingsland, NW8 *off Broxwood Way* **109** H1
Kingsland Basin, N1 *off Kingsland Rd* **112** B1
Kingsland Grn, E8 **94** B6
Kingsland High St, E8 **94** C5
Kingsland Pas, E8 *off Kingsland Grn* **94** B6
Kingsland Rd, E2 **13** E3
E8 **112** B2
E13 **115** J3
Kingsland Shop Cen, E8 **94** C6
Kings La, Sutt. SM1 **199** G6
Kingslawn Cl, SW15 **147** H5
Kingsleigh Cl, Brent. TW8 **125** G6
Kingsleigh Pl, Mitch. CR4 **185** J3
Kingsleigh Wk, Brom. BR2 *off Stamford Dr* **191** F4
Kingsley Av, W13 **104** D6
Hounslow TW3 **143** J2
Southall UB1 **103** G7
Sutton SM1 **199** G4
Kingsley Cl, N2 **73** F5
Dagenham RM10 **101** H4
Kingsley Ct, Edg. HA8 **54** B2
Kingsley Dr, Wor.Pk. KT4 *off Badgers Copse* **197** F2
Kingsley Flats, SE1 **36** D1
Kingsley Gdns, E4 **62** A5
Kingsley Ms, E1 *off Wapping La* **113** E7
W8 **22** B6
Chislehurst BR7 **175** E6
Kingsley Pl, N6 **74** A7
Kingsley Rd, E7 **97** G7
E17 **78** C2
N13 **59** G4
NW6 **108** C1
SW19 **167** E5
Croydon CR0 **201** G1
Harrow HA2 **85** J4
Hounslow TW3 **143** J2
Ilford IG6 **81** F1
Loughton IG10 **49** G3
Orpington BR6 **207** J6
Pinner HA5 **67** F4
Kingsley St, SW11 **149** J3
Kingsley Way, N2 **73** F6
Kingsley Wd Dr, SE9 **174** C3
Kingslyn Cres, SE19 **188** B1
Kings Mall, W6 **127** J4
Kingsman Par, SE18 *off Woolwich Ch St* **136** C3
Kingsman St, SE18 **136** C3
Kingsmead, Barn. EN5 **40** D4
Richmond TW10 **145** J6
Kingsmead Av, N9 **60** E1
NW9 **70** D7
Mitcham CR4 **186** C3
Sunbury-on-Thames TW16 **178** C3
Surbiton KT6 **196** A2
Worcester Park KT4 **197** H3
Kingsmead Cl, Epsom KT19 **196** D7
Sidcup DA15 **176** A2
Teddington TW11 **162** E6
Kingsmead Dr, Nthlt. UB5 **85** F7
Kingsmead Est, E9 **95** H5
Kingsmead Ho, E9 *off Kingsmead Way* **95** H4
Kings Mead Pk, Esher (Clay.) KT10 **194** B7
Kingsmead Rd, SW2 **169** G2
Kingsmead Way, E9 **95** H4
Kingsmere Cl, SW15 *off Felsham Rd* **148** A3
Kingsmere Pk, NW9 **88** B1
Kingsmere Pl, N16 **94** A1
Kingsmere Rd, SW19 **166** A2
Kings Ms, SW4 *off King's Av* **150** E5
King's Ms, WC1 **10** D6
Kings Ms, Chig. IG7 **65** F2
Kingsmill Business Pk, Kings.T. KT1 **181** J3
Kingsmill Gdns, Dag. RM9 **101** F5
Kingsmill Rd, Dag. RM9 **101** F5
Kingsmill Ter, NW8 **7** F1
Kingsnympton Pk, Kings.T. KT2 **164** B6
Kings Oak, Rom. RM7 **83** G3
King's Orchard, SE9 **156** B6
Kings Paddock, Hmptn. TW12 **179** J1
Kings Par, Cars. SM5 *off Wrythe La* **199** H3
Kingspark Ct, E18 **79** G3
King's Pas, E11 **78** E7
Kings Pas, Kings.T. KT1 **181** G2
Kings Pl, SE1 **27** J4
W4 **126** C5
Buckhurst Hill IG9 **63** J2
Loughton IG10 **48** A7
King Sq, EC1 **11** J4
King's Quay, SW10 *off Chelsea Harbour* **149** F1
King's Reach Twr, SE1 **27** F1
Kings Ride Gate, Rich. TW10 **146** A4
Kingsridge, SW19 **166** B2
Kings Rd, E4 **62** D1
E6 **115** J1
E11 **78** E7
King's Rd, N17 **76** C1
Kings Rd, N18 **60** D5
N22 **75** F1
NW10 **89** H7
SE25 **188** D3
King's Rd, SW1 **31** H3
SW3 **31** H3
SW6 **148** E1
SW10 **148** E1
Kings Rd, SW14 **146** D3
SW19 **166** D6
W5 **105** G5
Barking IG11 *off North St* **99** F7
Barnet EN5 **39** J3
Feltham TW13 **160** C1
Harrow HA2 **85** F2
Kingston upon Thames KT2 **163** H7
Mitcham CR4 **186** A3
Orpington BR6 **207** J4
Richmond TW10 **145** J5
Surbiton (Long Dit.) KT6 **195** F1
Teddington TW11 **162** A5
Twickenham TW1 **145** E6
West Drayton UB7 **120** C2
Kings Rd Bungalows, Har. HA2 *off Kings Rd* **85** F3
King's Scholars' Pas, SW1 **25** F6
King Stairs Cl, SE16 *off Elephant La* **133** F2
King's Ter, NW1 *off Plender St* **110** C1
Kings Ter, Islw. TW7 *off Worple Rd* **144** D3
Kingsthorpe Rd, SE26 **171** G4
Kingston Av, Felt. TW14 **141** H6
Sutton SM3 **198** B3
Kingston Br, Kings.T. KT1 **181** G2
Kingston Business Cen, Chess. KT9 **195** H3
Kingston Bypass, SW15 **165** E6
SW20 **165** E6
Esher KT10 **194** D3
New Malden KT3 **183** G2
Surbiton KT5, KT6 **195** H3
Kingston Cl, Nthlt. UB5 **85** F7
Romford RM6 **82** E3
Teddington TW11 **162** E6
Kingston Cres, Beck. BR3 **189** J1
Kingston Gdns, Croy. CR0 **201** E3
Kingston Hall Rd, Kings.T. KT1 **181** G3
Kingston Hill, Kings.T. KT2 **164** C6
Kingston Hill Av, Rom. RM6 **82** E2
Kingston Hill Pl, Kings.T. KT2 **164** C4
Kingston Ho Est, Surb. KT6 *off Portsmouth Rd* **181** E6
Kingston La, Tedd. TW11 **162** D5
West Drayton UB7 **120** C2
Kingston Lo, N.Mal. KT3 *off Kingston Rd* **182** E4
★ **Kingston Mus & Heritage Cen**, Kings.T. KT1 **181** H2
Kingston Pk Est, Kings.T. KT2 **164** B6
Kingston Pl, Har. HA3 *off Richmond Gdns* **52** C7
Kingston Rd, N9 **60** D2
SW15 **165** G1
SW19 **184** C1
SW20 **183** J2
Barnet EN4 **41** G5
Epsom KT17, KT19 **196** E5
Ilford IG1 **99** E4
Kingston upon Thames KT1 **182** B3
New Malden KT3 **182** D4
Southall UB2 **123** F2
Surbiton KT5 **196** B2
Teddington TW11 **162** E5
Worcester Park KT4 **196** B2
Kingston Sq, SE19 **170** A5
KINGSTON UPON THAMES, KT1 & KT2 **181** H2
KINGSTON VALE, SW15 **165** E4
Kingston Vale, SW15 **164** D4
Kingstown St, NW1 **110** A1
King St, E13 **115** G4
EC2 **20** A4
N2 **73** G3
N17 **76** C1
SW1 **25** G2
W3 **126** B1
W6 **127** G4
WC2 **18** A5

King St, Richmond TW9 145 G5
Southall UB2 123 E3
Twickenham TW1 162 D1
King St Ms, N2
off King St 73 G3
King's Wk, Kings.T. KT2 181 G1
Kings Wk Shop Mall, SW3
off King's Rd 31 J3
Kingswater Pl, SW11
off Battersea Ch Rd 129 H7
Kingsway, N12 57 F6
SW14 146 B3
WC2 18 C3
Kings Way, Croy. CR0 201 F5
Kingsway, Enf. EN3 45 E5
Kings Way, Har. HA1 68 B4
Kingsway, N.Mal. KT3 183 J4
Orpington BR5 193 H5
Wembley HA9 87 H4
West Wickham BR4 205 E3
Woodford Green IG8 63 J5
Kingsway Business Pk,
Hmptn. TW12 179 F1
Kingsway Cres, Har. HA2 67 J4
Kingsway Pl, EC1 11 F5
Kingsway Rd, Sutt. SM3 198 B7
Kingsway Shop Cen, NW3
off Hampstead High St 91 F4
Kingswear Rd, NW5 92 B3
Ruislip HA4 84 A2
Kings Wf, E8
off Kingsland Rd 112 B1
Kingswood Av, NW6 108 B1
Belvedere DA17 139 F4
Bromley BR2 190 E3
Hampton TW12 161 H6
Hounslow TW3 143 F1
Thornton Heath CR7 187 G5
Kingswood Cl, N20 41 F6
SW8 131 E7
Enfield EN1 44 B5
New Malden KT3 183 F6
Orpington BR6 193 G7
Surbiton KT6 181 H7
Kingswood Ct, SE13
off Hither Grn La 154 D6
Kingswood Dr, SE19 170 B4
Carshalton SM5 199 J1
Kingswood Est, SE21 170 B4
Kingswood Ms, N15
off Harringay Rd 75 H5
Kingswood Pk, N3 72 C2
Kingswood Pl, SE13 155 E4
Kingswood Rd, E11 79 E7
SE20 171 F6
SW2 150 E6
SW19 166 C7
W4 126 C3
Bromley BR2 190 D4
Ilford IG3 100 A1
Wembley HA9 88 A3
Kingswood Ter, W4
off Kingswood Rd 126 C3
Kingswood Way, Wall.
SM6 201 E5
Kingsworth Cl, Beck.
BR3 189 H5
Kingsworthy Cl, Kings.T.
KT1 181 J3
King's Yd, SW15
off Stanbridge Rd 147 J3
Kingthorpe Rd, NW10 88 D7
Kingthorpe Ter, NW10 88 D6
Kingweston Cl, NW2
off Windmill Dr 90 B3
King William IV Gdns, SE20
off St. John's Rd 171 F6
King William La, SE10
off Trafalgar Rd 134 E5
King William St, EC4 20 C6
King William Wk, SE10 134 C6
Kingwood Rd, SW6 148 A1
Kinlet Rd, SE18 157 F1
Kinloch Dr, NW9 70 E7
Kinloch St, N7
off Hornsey Rd 93 F3
Kinloss Ct, N3
off Kinloss Gdns 72 C4
Kinloss Gdns, N3 72 C4
Kinloss Rd, Cars. SM5 185 F7
Kinnaird Av, W4 126 C7
Bromley BR1 173 F6
Kinnaird Cl, Brom.
BR1 173 F6
Kinnaird Ho, N6 74 D7
Kinnaird Way, Wdf.Grn.
IG8 64 C6
Kinnear Rd, W12 127 F2
Kinnerton Pl N, SW1 24 A4
Kinnerton Pl S, SW1 24 A4
Kinnerton St, SW1 24 B4
Kinnerton Yd, SW1 24 A4
Kinnoul Rd, W6 128 B6
Kinross Av, Wor.Pk.
KT4 197 G2
Kinross Cl, Edg. HA8
off Tayside Dr 54 B2
Harrow HA3 69 J5
Kinross Ter, E17 77 J2
Kinsale Rd, SE15 152 D3
Kinsella Gdns, SW19 165 H5
Kinsey Ho, SE21
off Kingswood Est 170 B4
Kintore Way, SE1 37 F1
Kintyre Cl, SW16 187 F2
Kinveachy Gdns, SE7 136 B5
Kinver Rd, SE26 171 F4
Kipling Dr, SW19 167 G6
Kipling Est, SE1 28 C4
Kipling Pl, Stan. HA7 52 C6
Kipling Rd, Bexh. DA7 159 E1
Kipling St, SE1 28 C4
Kipling Ter, N9 60 A3
Kipling Twr, W3 126 C3
Kippington Dr, SE9 174 A1
Kirby Cl, Epsom KT19 197 F5
Ilford IG6 65 H6
Loughton IG10 48 B7
Kirby Est, SE16 132 E3
Kirby Gro, SE1 28 D3
Kirby St, EC1 19 F1
Kirby Way, Walt. KT12 178 C6
Kirchen Rd, W13 104 E7
Kirkby Cl, N11
off Coverdale Rd 58 A6
Kirkcaldy Grn, Wat. WD19
off Trevose Way 50 C3
Kirkdale, SE26 170 E2
Kirkdale Rd, E11 97 E1
Kirkfield Cl, W13
off Broomfield Rd 125 E1
Kirkham Rd, E6 116 B6
Kirkham St, SE18 137 H6
Kirkland Av, Ilf. IG5 80 D2
Kirkland Cl, Sid. DA15 157 H6
Kirkland Dr, Enf. EN2 43 H1
Kirkland Wk, E8 94 C6
Kirk La, SE18 137 F6
Kirkleas Rd, Surb. KT6 195 H1
Kirklees Rd, Dag. RM8 100 C5
Thornton Heath CR7 187 G5
Kirkley Rd, SW19 184 D1
Kirkman Pl, W1 17 H2
Kirkmichael Rd, E14
off Dee St 114 C6
Kirk Ri, Sutt. SM1 199 E3
Kirk Rd, E17 77 J6
Kirkside Rd, SE3 135 G6
Kirkstall Av, N17 76 A4
Kirkstall Gdns, SW2 168 D1
Kirkstall Rd, SW2 168 D1
Kirkstead Ct, E5
off Mandeville St 95 H4
Kirksted Rd, Mord. SM4 198 E1
Kirkstone Lo, Islw. TW7
off Summerwood Rd 144 C5
Kirkstone Way, Brom.
BR1 173 E7
Kirk St, WC1 10 C6
Kirkton Rd, N15 76 B4
Kirkwall Pl, E2 113 F3
Kirkwood Rd, SE15 153 E2
Kirn Rd, W13
off Kirchen Rd 104 E7
Kirrane Cl, N.Mal. KT3 183 F5
Kirtley Rd, SE26 171 H4
Kirtling St, SW8 33 F7
Kirton Cl, W4 126 D4
Kirton Gdns, E2 13 G4
Kirton Rd, E13 115 J2
Kirton Wk, Edg. HA8 54 C7
Kirwyn Way, SE5 35 H7
Kitcat Ter, E3 114 A3
Kitchen Ct, E10
off Brisbane Rd 96 B2
Kitchener Rd, E7 97 H6
E17 78 B1
N2 73 H3
N17 76 A3
Dagenham RM10 101 H6
Thornton Heath CR7 188 A3
Kite Pl, E2 13 J3
Kite Yd, SW11
off Cambridge Rd 149 J1
Kitley Gdns, SE19 188 C1
Kitson Rd, SE5 36 A7
SW13 147 G1
Kittiwake Pl, Sutt. SM1
off Sandpiper Rd 198 C5
Kittiwake Rd, Nthlt. UB5 102 D3
Kittiwake Way, Hayes
UB4 102 D5
Kitto Rd, SE14 153 G2
Kiver Rd, N19 92 D2
Klea Av, SW4 150 C6
Kleine Wf, N1
off Orsman Rd 112 B1
Knapdale Cl, SE23 171 E2
Knapmill Rd, SE6 172 A2
Knapmill Way, SE6 172 B2
Knapp Cl, NW10 89 E6
Knapp Rd, E3 114 A4
Knapton Ms, SW17
off Seely Rd 168 A6
Knaresborough Dr,
SW18 166 E1
Knaresborough Pl, SW5 30 A1
Knatchbull Rd, NW10 106 D1
SE5 151 J1
Knebworth Av, E17 78 A1
Knebworth Cl, Barn. EN5 41 E4
Knebworth Path, Borwd.
WD6 38 D4
Knebworth Rd, N16
off Nevill Rd 94 B4
Knee Hill, SE2 138 C4
Knee Hill Cres, SE2 138 C4
Kneller Gdns, Islw. TW7 144 A5
Kneller Rd, SE4 153 H4
New Malden KT3 182 E7
Twickenham TW2 143 J6
Knevett Ter, Houns. TW3 143 G4
Knight Cl, Dag. RM8 100 C2
Knight Ct, E4
off The Ridgeway 62 C1
Knighten St, E1 132 E1
Knighthead Pt, E14 134 A3
Knightland Rd, E5 94 E2
Knighton Cl, S.Croy. CR2 201 H7
Woodford Green IG8 63 H4
Knighton Dr, Wdf.Grn. IG8 63 G4
Knighton Grn, Buck.H. IG9
off High Rd 63 H2
Knighton La, Buck.H. IG9 63 H2
Knighton Pk Rd, SE26 171 G5
Knighton Rd, E7 97 G3
Romford RM7 83 J6
Knightrider Ct, EC4
off Knightrider St 19 J5
Knightrider St, EC4 19 J5
Knights Arc, SW1 23 J4
Knights Av, W5 125 H2
Knightsbridge, SW1 24 A4
SW7 23 H4
Knightsbridge Apts,
The, SW7
off Knightsbridge 23 J4
Knightsbridge Grn, SW1 23 J4
Knights Cl, E9
off Churchill Wk 95 F5
West Molesey KT8 179 F5
Knights Ct, Kings.T. KT1 181 H3
Romford RM6 83 E6
Knights Hill, SE27 169 H5
Knights Hill Sq, SE27 169 H4
Knights La, N9 60 D3
Knights Ms, Sutt. SM2
off York Rd 198 D7
Knights Pk, Kings.T. KT1 181 H3
Knight's Pl, Twick. TW2
off May Rd 162 B1
Knights Rd, E16 135 G2
Stanmore HA7 53 F4
Knights Wk, SE11 35 G2
Knights Way, Ilf. IG6 65 F6
Knightswood Cl, Edg.
HA8 54 C2
Knightwood Cres, N.Mal.
KT3 182 E6
Knivet Rd, SW6 128 D6
Knobs Hill Rd, E15 114 B1
Knockholt Rd, SE9 156 A5
Knole, The, SE9 174 D4
Knole Cl, Croy. CR0 189 F6
Knole Gate, Sid. DA15
off Woodside Cres 175 H3
Knoll, The, W13 105 F5
Beckenham BR3 190 B1
Bromley BR2 205 G2
Knoll Ct, SE19 170 B5
Knoll Dr, N14 42 A7
Knollmead, Surb. KT5 196 C1
Knoll Ri, Orp. BR6 207 J1
Knoll Rd, SW18 149 F5
Bexley DA5 159 G7
Sidcup DA14 176 B5
Knolls Cl, Wor.Pk. KT4 197 H3
Knollys Cl, SW16 169 G3
Knollys Rd, SW16 169 G3
Knottisford St, E2 113 F3
Knotts Grn Ms, E10 78 B6
Knotts Grn Rd, E10 78 B6
Knowle Av, Bexh. DA7 139 E7
Knowle Cl, SW9 151 G3
Knowle Rd, Brom. BR2 206 B2
Twickenham TW2 162 B1
Knowles Cl, West Dr.
UB7 120 B1
Knowles Hill Cres, SE13 154 D5
Knowles Ho, SW18
off Neville Gill Cl 148 E6
Knowles Wk, SW4 150 C3
Knowlton Grn, Brom. BR2 191 F5
Knowsley Av, Sthl. UB1 123 G1
Knowsley Rd, SW11 149 J2
Knox Rd, E7 97 F6
Knox St, W1 15 J1
Knoyle St, SE14 133 H6
Kohat Rd, SW19 167 E5
Kossuth St, SE10 134 E5
Kotree Way, SE1 37 J2
Kramer Ms, SW5
off Kempsford Gdns 128 D5
Kreedman Wk, E8 94 D5
Kreisel Wk, Rich. TW9 125 J6
Kuala Gdns, SW16 187 F1
Kuhn Way, E7
off Forest La 97 G5
Kydbrook Cl, Orp. BR5 193 F7
Kylemore Cl, E6
off Parr Rd 116 A2
Kylemore Rd, NW6 90 D7
Kymberley Rd, Har. HA1 68 B6
Kynance Gdns, Stan.
HA7 69 F1
Kynance Ms, SW7 22 C6
Kynance Pl, SW7 22 C6
Kynaston Av, N16
off Dynevor Rd 94 C3
Thornton Heath CR7 187 J5
Kynaston Cl, Har. HA3 52 A7
Kynaston Cres, Th.Hth.
CR7 187 J5
Kynaston Rd, N16 94 B3
Bromley BR1 173 G5
Enfield EN2 44 A1
Thornton Heath CR7 187 J5
Kynaston Wd, Har. HA3 52 A7
Kynersley Cl, Cars. SM5
off William St 199 J3
Kynoch Rd, N18 61 F4
Kyrle Rd, SW11 150 A5
Kyverdale Rd, N16 94 C2

L

Laburnum Av, N9 60 B2
N17 60 A7
Sutton SM1 199 H3
Laburnum Cl, E4 61 J6
N11 58 A6
SE15 *off Clifton Way* 133 F7
Wembley HA0 88 A7
Laburnum Ct, E2 112 C1
Stanmore HA7 53 F4
Laburnum Cres, Sun. TW16
off Batavia Rd 178 B1
Laburnum Gdns, N21 59 J2
Croydon CR0 189 G7
Laburnum Gro, N21 59 J2
NW9 70 C7
Hounslow TW3 143 F4
New Malden KT3 182 D2
Southall UB1 103 F4
Laburnum Ho, Dag. RM10
off Bradwell Av 101 G2
Laburnum Rd, SW19 167 F7
Hayes UB3 121 J4
Mitcham CR4 186 A2
Laburnum St, E2 112 C1
Laburnum Way, Brom.
BR2 192 D7
Lacebark Cl, Sid. DA15 157 J7
Lacewing Cl, E13
off Sewell St 115 G3
Lacey Cl, N9 60 D2
Lacey Dr, Dag. RM8 100 B4
Edgware HA8 53 H4
Hampton TW12 179 F1
Lacey Ms, E3 114 A2
Lackington St, EC2 20 C1
Lacock Cl, SW19 167 F6
Lacock Ct, W13
off Singapore Rd 124 D1
Lacon Rd, SE22 152 D4
Lacrosse Way, SW16 186 D1
Lacy Rd, SW15 148 A4
Ladas Rd, SE27 169 J4
Ladbroke Cres, W11
off Ladbroke Gro 108 B6
Ladbroke Gdns, W11 108 C7
Ladbroke Gro, W10 108 A4
W11 108 B6
Ladbroke Ms, W11
off Ladbroke Rd 128 B1
Ladbroke Rd, W11 128 C1
Enfield EN1 44 C6
Ladbroke Sq, W11 108 C7
Ladbroke Ter, W11 108 C7
Ladbroke Wk, W11 128 C1
Ladbrook Cl, Pnr. HA5 67 F5
Ladbrooke Cres, Sid.
DA14 176 D3
Ladbrook Rd, SE25 188 A3
Ladderstile Ride, Kings.T.
KT2 164 B5
Ladderswood Way, N11 58 C5
Ladlands, SE22 152 D7
Lady Aylesford Av, Stan.
HA7 52 E5

Lady Booth Rd, Kings.T. KT1 **181** H2
Ladycroft Gdns, Orp. BR6 **207** F5
Ladycroft Rd, SE13 **154** B3
Ladycroft Wk, Stan. HA7 **69** G1
Ladycroft Way, Orp. BR6 **207** F5
Lady Dock Path, SE16 *off Salter Rd* **133** H2
Ladyfield Cl, Loug. IG10 **49** E4
Ladyfields, Loug. IG10 **49** E4
Lady Hay, Wor.Pk. KT4 **197** F2
Lady Margaret Rd, N19 **92** C4
NW5 **92** C5
Southall UB1 **103** F5
Ladysmith Av, E6 **116** B2
Ilford IG2 **81** G7
Ladysmith Cl, NW7 **55** G7
Ladysmith Rd, E16 **115** F3
N17 **76** D2
N18 **61** E5
SE9 **156** D6
Enfield EN1 **44** B3
Harrow HA3 **68** B2
Lady Somerset Rd, NW5 **92** B4
LADYWELL, SE13 **154** A5
Ladywell Cl, SE4 *off Adelaide Av* **154** A4
Ladywell Hts, SE4 **153** J6
Ladywell Rd, SE13 **154** A5
Ladywell St, E15 *off Plaistow Gro* **115** F1
Ladywood Av, Orp. BR5 **193** H5
Ladywood Rd, Surb. KT6 **196** A2
Lafone Av, Felt. TW13 *off Alfred Rd* **160** C1
Lafone St, SE1 **29** F3
Lagado Ms, SE16 **133** G1
Lagonda Av, Ilf. IG6 **65** J6
Laidlaw Dr, N21 **43** F4
Laing Cl, Ilf. IG6 **65** G6
Laing Dean, Nthlt. UB5 **102** C1
Laing Ho, SE5 *off Comber Gro* **131** J7
Laings Av, Mitch. CR4 **185** J2
Lainlock Pl, Houns. TW3 *off Spring Gro Rd* **143** H1
Lainson St, SW18 **148** D7
Lairdale Cl, SE21 **169** J1
Laird Ho, SE5 **131** J7
Lairs Cl, N7 *off Manger Rd* **93** E6
Lait Ho, Beck. BR3 **190** A1
Laitwood Rd, SW12 **168** B1
Lakanal, SE5 *off Sceaux Gdns* **152** B1
Lake, The, Bushey (Bushey Hth) WD23 **51** J1
Lake Av, Brom. BR1 **173** G6
Lake Business Cen, N17 *off Tariff Rd* **60** D7
Lake Cl, SW19 *off Lake Rd* **166** C5
Dagenham RM8 **100** C3
Lakedale Rd, SE18 **137** H6
Lake Dr, Bushey (Bushey Hth) WD23 **51** J2
Lakefield Cl, SE20 *off Limes Av* **171** E7
Lakefield Rd, N22 **75** H2
Lake Gdns, Dag. RM10 **101** G5
Richmond TW10 **163** E2
Wallington SM6 **200** B3
Lakehall Gdns, Th.Hth. CR7 **187** H5
Lakehall Rd, Th.Hth. CR7 **187** H5
Lake Ho Rd, E11 **97** G3
Lakehurst Rd, Epsom KT19 **196** E5
Lakeland Cl, Har. HA3 **52** A6
Lakenheath, N14 **42** D6
Lake Rd, E10 **78** B7
SW19 **166** C5
Croydon CR0 **203** J2
Romford RM6 **82** D4
Laker Pl, SW15 **148** B6
Lakeside, W13 *off Edgehill Rd* **105** F6
Beckenham BR3 **190** B3
Enfield EN2 **42** D4
Wallington SM6 *off Derek Av* **200** B3
Lakeside Av, SE28 **138** A1
Ilford IG4 **80** A4
Lakeside Cl, SE25 **188** D2
Chigwell IG7 **65** J4
Sidcup DA15 **158** C5
Lakeside Ct, N4 **93** H2
Borehamwood (Els.) WD6 *off Cavendish Cres* **38** A5
Lakeside Cres, Barn. EN4 **41** J5
Lakeside Dr, NW10 **105** J3
Bromley BR2 **206** B3
Lakeside Rd, N13 **59** F4
W14 **128** A3
Lakeside Way, Wem. HA9 **87** J4
Lakes Rd, Kes. BR2 **205** J5
Lakeswood Rd, Orp. BR5 **193** E6
Lake Vw, Edg. HA8 **53** J5
Lakeview Ct, SW19 *off Victoria Dr* **166** B2
Lakeview Est, E3 *off Old Ford Rd* **113** G2
Lakeview Rd, SE27 **169** G5
Welling DA16 **158** B4
Lakis Cl, NW3 *off Flask Wk* **91** F4
Laleham Av, NW7 **54** D3
Laleham Rd, SE6 **154** C6
Lalor St, SW6 **148** B2
Lambarde Av, SE9 **174** D4
Lamb Cl, Nthlt. UB5 **103** E3
Lamberhurst Rd, SE27 **169** G4
Dagenham RM8 **101** F1
Lambert Av, Rich. TW9 **146** B3
Lambert Jones Ms, EC2 *off The Barbican* **19** J1
Lambert Rd, E16 **115** H6
N12 **57** F5
SW2 **151** E5
Lamberts Pl, Croy. CR0 **202** A1
Lamberts Rd, Surb. KT5 **181** H5
Lambert St, N1 **93** G7
Lambert Wk, Wem. HA9 **87** G3
Lambert Way, N12 *off Woodhouse Rd* **57** F5
LAMBETH, SE1 **26** C5
Lambeth Br, SE1 **34** B1
SW1 **34** B1
Lambeth High St, SE1 **34** C2
Lambeth Hill, EC4 **19** J5
★ **Lambeth Palace**, SE1 **26** C6
Lambeth Palace Rd, SE1 **26** C6
Lambeth Pier, SE1 **26** B6
Lambeth Rd, SE1 **26** D6
SE11 **26** D6
Croydon CR0 **187** G7
Lambeth Twrs, SE11 **27** E6
Lambeth Wk, SE1 **34** D1
SE11 **34** D1
Lambfold Ho, N7 *off York Way* **92** E6
Lambkins Ms, E17 **78** C4
Lamb La, E8 **94** E7
Lamble St, NW5 **92** A5
Lambley Rd, Dag. RM9 **100** B6
Lambolle Pl, NW3 **91** H6
Lambolle Rd, NW3 **91** H6
Lambourn Cl, W7 **124** C2
Lambourne Av, SW19 **166** C4
Lambourne Ct, Wdf.Grn. IG8 *off Navestock Cres* **63** J7
Lambourne Gdns, E4 **62** A2
Barking IG11 *off Lambourne Rd* **99** J7
Enfield EN1 **44** C2
Lambourne Gro, SE16 **133** G4
Lambourne Pl, SE3 *off Shooters Hill Rd* **155** H1
Lambourne Rd, E11 **78** C7
Barking IG11 **99** H7
Chigwell IG7 **65** H4
Ilford IG3 **99** H2
Lambourn Gro, Kings.T. KT1 **182** B2
Lambourn Rd, SW4 **150** B3
Lambrook Ter, SW6 **148** B1
Lamb's Bldgs, EC1 **12** B6
Lambs Cl, N9 *off Winchester Rd* **60** D2
Lambs Conduit Pas, WC1 **18** C1
Lamb's Conduit St, WC1 **10** C6
Lambscroft Av, SE9 **173** J3
Lambs Meadow, Wdf.Grn. IG8 **80** A2
Lambs Ms, N1 *off Colebrooke Row* **111** H1
Lamb's Pas, EC1 **20** B1
Lambs Ter, N9 **60** A2
Lamb St, E1 **21** F1
Lambs Wk, Enf. EN2 **43** J2
Lambton Ms, N19 *off Lambton Rd* **92** E1
Lambton Pl, W11 *off Westbourne Gro* **108** C6
Lambton Rd, N19 **92** E1
SW20 **183** J1
Lamb Wk, SE1 **28** D4
Lamerock Rd, Brom. BR1 **173** F4
Lamerton Rd, Ilf. IG6 **81** E2
Lamerton St, SE8 **134** A6
Lamford Cl, N17 **60** A7
Lamington St, W6 **127** H4
Lamlash St, SE11 **35** G1
Lammas Av, Mitch. CR4 **186** A2
Lammas Grn, SE26 **170** E3
Lammas Pk, W5 **125** F2
Lammas Pk Gdns, W5 **125** F2
Lammas Pk Rd, W5 **125** F1
Lammas Rd, E9 **95** G7
E10 **95** H2
Richmond TW10 **163** F4
Lammermoor Rd, SW12 **150** B7
Lamont Rd, SW10 **30** D6
Lamont Rd Pas, SW10 *off Lamont Rd* **30** E6
LAMORBEY, Sid. DA15 **175** J1
Lamorbey Cl, Sid. DA15 **175** J1
Lamorna Cl, E17 **78** C2
Lamorna Gro, Stan. HA7 **69** G1
Lampard Gro, N16 **94** C1
Lampern Sq, E2 **13** J3
Lampeter Cl, NW9 **70** E6
Lampeter Sq, W6 *off Humbolt Rd* **128** B6
Lamplighter Cl, E1 *off Cleveland Way* **113** F4
Lampmead Rd, SE12 **155** E5
Lamp Office Ct, WC1 **10** C6
Lamport Cl, SE18 **136** C4
LAMPTON, Houns. TW3 **143** H1
Lampton Av, Houns. TW3 **143** H1
Lampton Ho Cl, SW19 **166** A4
Lampton Pk Rd, Houns. TW3 **143** H2
Lampton Rd, Houns. TW3 **143** H2
Lanacre Av, NW9 **71** F1
Lanadron Cl, Islw. TW7 *off London Rd* **144** C2
Lanark Cl, W5 **105** F5
Lanark Ms, W9 **6** C4
Lanark Pl, W9 **6** D5
Lanark Rd, W9 **6** C4
Lanark Sq, E14 **134** B3
Lanata Wk, Hayes UB4 *off Ramulis Dr* **102** D4
Lanbury Rd, SE15 **153** G4
Lancashire Ct, W1 **16** E5
Lancaster Av, E18 **79** H4
SE27 **169** H2
SW19 **166** A5
Barking IG11 **99** H7
Mitcham CR4 **186** E5
Lancaster Cl, N1 *off Hertford Rd* **94** B7
N17 *off Park La* **60** D7
NW9 **55** F7
Bromley BR2 **191** F4
Kingston upon Thames KT2 **163** G5
Staines (Stanw.) TW19 **140** B6
Lancaster Cotts, Rich. TW10 *off Lancaster Pk* **145** H6
Lancaster Ct, SE27 **169** H2
SW6 **128** C7
W2 **14** D6
Walton-on-Thames KT12 **178** A7
Lancaster Dr, E14 *off Prestons Rd* **134** C1
NW3 **91** H6
Loughton IG10 **48** B6
Lancaster Gdns, SW19 **166** B5
W13 **125** E2
Bromley BR1 **192** B5
Kingston upon Thames KT2 **163** G5
Lancaster Gate, W2 **14** D6
Lancaster Gro, NW3 **91** G6
★ **Lancaster Ho**, SW1 **25** F3
Lancaster Ms, SW18 *off East Hill* **149** E5
W2 **14** D5
Richmond TW10 *off Richmond Hill* **145** H6
Lancaster Pk, Rich. TW10 **145** H5
Lancaster Pl, SW19 **166** A5
WC2 **18** C5
Hounslow TW4 **142** C2
Ilford IG1 *off Staines Rd* **99** F4
Twickenham TW1 **144** D6
Lancaster Rd, E7 **97** G7
E11 **97** E2
E17 **77** G2
N4 **75** G7
N11 **58** D6
N18 **60** C5
NW10 **89** F5
SE25 **188** C2
SW19 **166** A5
W11 **108** B6
Barnet EN4 **41** G5
Enfield EN2 **44** A1
Harrow HA2 **67** G5
Northolt UB5 **85** J6
Southall UB1 **103** E7
Lancaster St, SE1 **27** H4
Lancaster Ter, W2 **15** E5
Lancaster Wk, W2 **22** E3
Lancaster Way, Wor.Pk. KT4 **183** H7
Lancaster W, W11 *off Grenfell Rd* **108** A7
Lancastrian Rd, Wall. SM6 **201** E7
Lancefield St, W10 **108** C3
Lancell St, N16 *off Stoke Newington Ch St* **94** B2
Lancelot Av, Wem. HA0 **87** G4
Lancelot Cres, Wem. HA0 **87** G4
Lancelot Gdns, Barn. (E.Barn.) EN4 **42** A7
Lancelot Pl, SW7 **23** J4
Lancelot Rd, Ilf. IG6 **65** H6
Welling DA16 **158** A4
Wembley HA0 **87** G5
Lance Rd, Har. HA1 **67** J7
Lancer Sq, W8 **22** A3
Lancey Cl, SE7 *off Cleveley Cl* **136** A4
Lanchester Rd, N6 **73** J5
Lanchester Way, SE14 **153** F1
Lancing Gdns, N9 **60** C1
Lancing Rd, W13 *off Drayton Grn Rd* **104** E7
Croydon CR0 **187** F6
Ilford IG2 **81** G6
Lancing St, NW1 **9** H4
Lancresse Ct, N1 **112** B1
Landcroft Rd, SE22 **152** C6
Landells Rd, SE22 **152** C6
Landford Rd, SW15 **147** J3
Landgrove Rd, SW19 **166** D5
Landmann Ho, SE16 **133** E4
Landmann Way, SE14 **133** G6
Landmark Commercial Cen, N18 **60** B6
Landmark Hts, E5 **95** H4
Landon Pl, SW1 **23** J5
Landons Cl, E14 **134** C1
Landon Wk, E14 *off Cottage St* **114** B7
Landor Rd, SW9 **150** E3
Landor Wk, W12 **127** G2
Landra Gdns, N21 **43** H6
Landridge Rd, SW6 **148** C2
Landrock Rd, N8 **75** E6
Landscape Rd, Wdf.Grn. IG8 **63** H7
Landsdown Cl, Barn. (New Barn.) EN5 **41** F4
Landseer Av, E12 **98** D5
Landseer Cl, SW19 *off Thorburn Way* **185** G1
Edgware HA8 **70** A2
Landseer Rd, N19 **92** E3
Enfield EN1 **44** D5
New Malden KT3 **182** D7
Sutton SM1 **198** D6
Landstead Rd, SE18 **137** G7
Lane, The, NW8 **6** C1
SE3 **155** G3
Lane Cl, NW2 **89** H3
Lane End, Bexh. DA7 **159** H3
Lane Gdns, Esher (Clay.) KT10 **194** C7
Lane Ms, E12 *off Colchester Av* **98** C3
Lanercost Cl, SW2 **169** G2
Lanercost Gdns, N14 **42** E7
Lanercost Rd, SW2 **169** G2
Lanesborough Pl, SW1 **24** C3
Laneside, Chis. BR7 **175** E5
Edgware HA8 **54** C5
Laneside Av, Dag. RM8 **83** F7
Laneway, SW15 **147** H5
Lanfranc Rd, E3 **113** H2
Lanfrey Pl, W14 *off North End Rd* **128** C5
Langbourne Av, N6 **92** A2
Langbourne Pl, E14 **134** B5
Langbourne Way, Esher (Clay.) KT10 **194** D6
Langbrook Rd, SE3 **156** A3
Langcroft Cl, Cars. SM5 **199** J3
Langdale, NW1 **9** F3
Langdale Av, Mitch. CR4 **185** J3
Langdale Cl, SE17 **35** J5
SW14 **146** B4
Dagenham RM8 **100** C1
Orpington BR6 *off Grasmere Rd* **206** E3
Langdale Cres, Bexh. DA7 **139** G7
Langdale Gdns, Grnf. (Perivale) UB6 **105** E3
Langdale Rd, SE10 **134** C7
Thornton Heath CR7 **187** G4
Langdale St, E1 *off Burslem St* **112** E6
Langdon Ct, NW10 **106** E1
Langdon Cres, E6 **116** D2
Langdon Dr, NW9 **88** C1
Langdon Pk, Tedd. TW11 **163** F7
Langdon Pk Rd, N6 **74** C7

Langdon Pl, SW14 **146** C3
Langdon Rd, E6 **116** D1
  Bromley BR2 **191** H3
  Morden SM4 **185** F5
Langdons Ct, Sthl. UB2 **123** G3
Langdon Shaw, Sid. DA14 **175** J5
Langdon Wk, Mord. SM4 **185** F5
Langdon Way, SE1 **37** J2
Langford Cl, E8 **94** D5
  N15 **76** B6
  NW8 **6** D1
  W3 **126** B2
Langford Ct, NW8 **6** C2
Langford Cres, Barn. (Cockfos.) EN4 **41** J4
Langford Grn, SE5 **152** B3
Langford Ms, N1
  off Liverpool Rd **93** G7
Langford Pl, NW8 **6** D2
  Sidcup DA14 **176** A3
Langford Rd, SW6 **149** E2
  Barnet (Cockfos.) EN4 **41** H4
  Woodford Green IG8 **63** J6
Langfords, Buck.H. IG9 **64** A2
Langham Cl, N15
  off Langham Rd **75** H3
Langham Dr, Rom. RM6 **82** B6
Langham Gdns, N21 **43** G5
  W13 **105** E7
  Edgware HA8 **54** C7
  Richmond TW10 **163** F4
  Wembley HA0 **87** F2
Langham Ho Cl, Rich. TW10 **163** G4
Langham Pk Pl, Brom. BR2 **191** F4
Langham Pl, N15 **75** H3
  W1 **16** E2
  W4 *off Hogarth Rbt* **127** E6
Langham Rd, N15 **75** H3
  SW20 **183** J1
  Edgware HA8 **54** C6
  Teddington TW11 **162** E5
Langham St, W1 **17** E2
Langhedge Cl, N18 **60** C6
Langhedge La, N18 **60** C5
Langhedge La Ind Est, N18 **60** C6
Langholm Cl, SW12
  off King's Av **150** D7
Langholme, Bushey WD23 **51** J1
Langhorn Dr, Twick. TW2 **144** B7
Langhorne Ho, SE7
  off Springfield Gro **135** J6
Langhorne Rd, Dag. RM10 **101** G7
Langland Cres, Stan. HA7 **69** H3
Langland Dr, Pnr. HA5 **50** E7
Langland Gdns, NW3 **91** E5
  Croydon CR0 **203** J2
Langler Rd, NW10 **107** J2
Langley Av, Ruis. HA4 **84** B1
  Surbiton KT6 **195** G1
  Worcester Park KT4 **198** A2
Langley Ct, WC2 **18** A5
  Beckenham BR3 **190** B5
Langley Cres, E11 **79** J7
  Dagenham RM9 **100** C7
  Edgware HA8 **54** C3
  Hayes UB3 **121** J7
Langley Dr, E11 **79** H7
  W3 **126** B1
Langley Gdns, Brom. BR2
  off Great Elms Rd **191** J4
  Dagenham RM9 **100** C7
  Orpington BR5 **193** E6
Langley Gro, N.Mal. KT3 **182** E2
Langley La, SW8 **34** B5
Langley Meadow, Loug. IG10 **49** G2
Langley Pk, NW7 **54** E6
Langley Pk Rd, Sutt. SM1, SM2 **199** F5
Langley Rd, SW19 **184** C1
  Beckenham BR3 **189** H4
  Isleworth TW7 **144** C2
  Surbiton KT6 **181** H7
  Welling DA16 **138** C6
Langley Row, Barn. EN5 **40** C1
Langley St, WC2 **18** A4
Langley Way, W.Wick. BR4 **204** D1
Langmead Dr, Bushey (Bushey Hth) WD23 **52** A1
Langmead St, SE27
  off Beadman St **169** H4
Langmore Ct, Bexh. DA6
  off Regency Way **158** D3
Langridge Ms, Hmptn. TW12 *off Oak Av* **161** F6
Langroyd Rd, SW17 **167** J2
Langside Av, SW15 **147** G4
Langside Cres, N14 **58** D3
Langstone Way, NW7 **56** A7
Langston Hughes Cl, SE24
  off Shakespeare Rd **151** H4
Langston Rd, Loug. IG10 **49** F5
Lang St, E1 **113** F4
Langthorn Ct, EC2 **20** B3
Langthorne Rd, E11 **96** D3
Langthorne St, SW6 **128** A7
Langton Av, E6 **116** D3
  N20 **41** F7
Langton Cl, WC1 **10** D4
Langton Ho, SW16
  off Colson Way **168** C4
Langton Pl, SW18
  off Merton Rd **166** D1
Langton Ri, SE23 **152** E7
Langton Rd, NW2 **89** J3
  SW9 **131** H7
  Harrow HA3 **51** J7
  West Molesey KT8 **179** J4
Langton St, SW10 **30** D6
Langton Way, SE3 **155** F1
  Croydon CR0 **202** B4
Langtry Pl, SW6
  off Seagrave Rd **128** D6
Langtry Rd, NW8 **108** E1
  Northolt UB5 **102** D2
Langtry Wk, NW8
  off Alexandra Pl **109** F1
Langwood Chase, Tedd. TW11 **163** F6
Langworth Dr, Hayes UB4 **102** A6
Lanherne Ho, SW20 **166** A7
Lanhill Rd, W9 **108** D4
Lanier Rd, SE13 **154** C6
Lanigan Dr, Houns. TW3 **143** H5
Lankaster Gdns, N2 **73** G1
Lankers Dr, Har. HA2 **67** F6
Lankton Cl, Beck. BR3 **190** C1
Lannock Rd, Hayes UB3 **121** H1
Lannoy Pt, SW6
  off Pellant Rd **128** B7
Lannoy Rd, SE9 **175** F1
Lanrick Rd, E14 **114** D6
Lanridge Rd, SE2 **138** D3
Lansbury Av, N18 **60** A5
  Barking IG11 **100** A7
  Feltham TW14 **142** B6
  Romford RM6 **83** E5
Lansbury Cl, NW10 **88** C5
Lansbury Est, E14 **114** B6
Lansbury Gdns, E14 **114** D6
Lansbury Rd, Enf. EN3 **45** G1
Lansbury Way, N18 **60** B5
Lanscombe Wk, SW8 **150** E1
Lansdell Rd, Mitch. CR4 **186** A2
Lansdowne Av, Bexh. DA7 **138** D7
  Orpington BR6 **207** E1
Lansdowne Cl, SW20 **166** A7
  Surbiton KT5 **196** B2
  Twickenham TW1
  off Lion Rd **162** C1
Lansdowne Copse, Wor.Pk. KT4 **197** G2
Lansdowne Ct, Wor.Pk. KT4 **197** G2
Lansdowne Cres, W11 **108** B7
Lansdowne Dr, E8 **94** D6
Lansdowne Gdns, SW8 **150** E1
Lansdowne Grn, SW8
  off Hartington Rd **150** E1
Lansdowne Gro, NW10 **89** E4
Lansdowne Hill, SE27 **169** H3
Lansdowne La, SE7 **136** A6
Lansdowne Ms, SE7 **136** A5
  W11 *off Lansdowne Rd* **128** C1
Lansdowne Pl, SE1 **28** C5
  SE19 **170** C7
Lansdowne Ri, W11 **108** B7
Lansdowne Rd, E4 **62** A2
  E11 **97** F2
  E17 **78** A5
  E18 **79** G3
  N3 **56** C7
  N10 **74** C2
  N17 **76** C1
  SW20 **165** J7
  W11 **108** B7
  Bromley BR1 **173** G7
  Croydon CR0 **202** A2
  Epsom KT19 **196** C7
  Harrow HA1 **68** B7
  Hounslow TW3 **143** H3
  Ilford IG3 **99** J1
  Stanmore HA7 **53** F6
Lansdowne Row, W1 **24** E1
Lansdowne Ter, WC1 **10** B6
Lansdowne Wk, W11 **128** B1
Lansdowne Way, SW8 **150** D1
Lansdowne Wd Cl, SE27 **169** H3
Lansdown Rd, E7 **97** J7
  Sidcup DA14 **176** B3
Lansfield Av, N18 **60** D4
Lantern Cl, SW15 **147** G4
  Orpington BR6 **206** E4
  Wembley HA0 **87** G5
Lanterns Ct, E14 **134** A2
Lantern Way, West Dr. UB7 **120** B2
Lant St, SE1 **27** J3
Lanvanor Rd, SE15 **153** F2
Lapford Cl, W9 **108** C4
Lapponum Wk, Hayes UB4
  off Lochan Cl **102** D5
Lapse Wd Wk, SE23 **170** E2
Lapstone Gdns, Har. HA3 **69** F6
Lapwing Ct, Surb. KT6
  off Chaffinch Cl **196** A3
Lapwing Ter, E7
  off Hampton Rd **98** A5
Lapwing Twr, SE8
  off Abinger Gro **133** J6
Lapwing Way, Hayes UB4 **102** D6
Lara Cl, SE13 **154** C6
  Chessington KT9 **195** H7
Larbert Rd, SW16 **186** C1
Larch Av, W3 **126** E1
Larch Cl, E13 **115** H4
  N11 **58** A7
  N19 *off Bredgar Rd* **92** C2
  SE8 *off Clyde St* **133** J6
  SW12 **168** B2
Larch Cres, Epsom KT19 **196** B6
  Hayes UB4 **102** C4
Larch Dene, Orp. BR6 **206** D2
Larch Dr, W4
  off Gunnersbury Av **126** A5
Larches, The, N13 **59** J3
Larches Av, SW14 **146** D4
Larch Grn, NW9
  off Clayton Fld **71** E1
Larch Gro, Sid. DA15 **175** J1
Larch Rd, E10
  off Walnut Rd **96** A2
  NW2 **89** J4
Larch Tree Way, Croy. CR0 **204** A3
Larch Way, Brom. BR2 **192** D7
Larchwood Rd, SE9 **175** E2
Larcombe Cl, Croy. CR0 **202** C4
Larcom St, SE17 **36** A2
Larden Rd, W3 **127** E1
Largewood Av, Surb. KT6 **196** A2
Larissa St, SE17 **36** C3
Larkbere Rd, SE26 **171** H4
Larken Cl, Bushey WD23
  off Larken Dr **51** J1
Larken Dr, Bushey WD23 **51** J1
Larkfield Av, Har. HA3 **69** E3
Larkfield Cl, Brom. BR2 **205** F2
Larkfield Rd, Rich. TW9 **145** H4
  Sidcup DA14 **175** J3
Larkhall La, SW4 **150** D2
Larkhall Ri, SW4 **150** C3
Larkhill Ter, SE18
  off Prince Imperial Rd **136** D7
Lark Row, E2 **113** F1
Larksfield Gro, Enf. EN1 **45** E1
Larks Gro, Bark. IG11 **99** H7
Larkshall Ct, Rom. RM7 **83** J2
Larkshall Cres, E4 **62** C4
Larkshall Rd, E4 **62** C5
Larkspur Cl, E6 **116** B5
  N17 *off Fryatt Rd* **60** A7
  NW9 **70** B5
Larkspur Gro, Edg. HA8 **54** C4
Larkspur Way, Epsom KT19 **196** C5
Larkswood Ct, E4 **62** D5
Larkswood Leisure Pk, E4
  off New Rd **62** C4
Larkswood Ri, Pnr. HA5 **66** C4
Larkswood Rd, E4 **62** A4
Lark Way, Cars. SM5 **185** H7
Larkway Cl, NW9 **70** D4
Larnach Rd, W6 **128** A6
Larner Ct, W12
  off Heathstan Rd **107** G6
Larpent Av, SW15 **147** J5
Larwood Cl, Grnf. UB6 **86** A5
Lascelles Av, Har. HA1 **68** A7
Lascelles Cl, E11 **96** D2
Lascotts Rd, N22 **59** F6
Lassa Rd, SE9 **156** B5
Lassell St, SE10 **134** D5
Lasseter Pl, SE3
  off Vanbrugh Hill **135** F6
Latchett Rd, E18 **79** H1
Latchingdon Ct, E17 **77** G4
Latchingdon Gdns, Wdf.Grn. IG8 **64** B6
Latchmere Cl, Rich. TW10 **163** H5
Latchmere La, Kings.T. KT2 **163** J6
Latchmere Pas, SW11
  off Cabul Rd **149** H2
Latchmere Rd, SW11 **149** J2
  Kingston upon Thames KT2 **163** H7
Latchmere St, SW11 **149** J2
Lateward Rd, Brent. TW8 **125** G6
Latham Cl, E6
  off Oliver Gdns **116** B6
  Twickenham TW1 **144** D7
Latham Ho, E1 **113** G6
Latham Rd, Bexh. DA6 **159** G5
  Twickenham TW1 **144** C7
Lathams Way, Croy. CR0 **201** F1
Lathkill Cl, Enf. EN1 **44** D7
Lathom Rd, E6 **98** C7
Latimer, SE17 **36** D4
Latimer Av, E6 **116** C1
Latimer Cl, Pnr. HA5 **66** C1
  Worcester Park KT4 **197** H4
Latimer Gdns, Pnr. HA5 **66** C1
Latimer Pl, W10 **107** J6
Latimer Rd, E7 **97** H4
  N15 **76** B6
  SW19 **166** E6
  W10 **107** J6
  Barnet EN5 **40** E3
  Croydon CR0
  off Abbey Rd **201** H3
  Teddington TW11 **162** C5
Latitude Ct, E16
  off Albert Basin Way **117** F7
Latona Rd, SE15 **37** H6
La Tourne Gdns, Orp. BR6 **207** F3
Lattimer Pl, W4 **127** E6
Latton Cl, Walt. KT12 **179** E7
Latymer Ct, W6 **128** A4
Latymer Rd, N9 **60** C1
Latymer Way, N9 **60** A2
Laubin Cl, Twick. TW1
  off St. Margaret's Dr **144** E4
Lauder Cl, Nthlt. UB5 **102** D2
Lauderdale Dr, Rich. TW10 **163** G3
Lauderdale Pl, EC2
  off The Barbican **19** J1
Lauderdale Rd, W9 **6** A4
Lauderdale Twr, EC2 **19** J1
Laud St, SE11 **34** C3
  Croydon CR0 **201** J3
Laugan Wk, SE17
  off East St **36** A3
Laughton Ct, Borwd. WD6
  off Banks Rd **38** D2
Laughton Rd, Nthlt. UB5 **102** D1
Launcelot Rd, Brom. BR1 **173** G4
Launcelot St, SE1 **26** E4
Launceston Gdns, Grnf. (Perivale) UB6 **105** F1
Launceston Pl, W8 **22** C5
Launceston Rd, Grnf. (Perivale) UB6 **105** F1
Launch St, E14 **134** C3
Launders Gate, W3 **126** B2
Laundress La, N16 **94** D3
Laundry La, N1
  off Greenman St **111** J1
Laundry Ms, SE23 **153** H7
Laundry Rd, W6 **128** B6
Launton Dr, Bexh. DA6 **158** D4
Laura Cl, E11 **79** J5
  Enfield EN1 **44** B5
Lauradale Rd, N2 **73** J4
Laura Pl, E5 **95** F4
Laurel Apts, SE17
  off Townsend St **36** D1
Laurel Av, Twick. TW1 **162** C1
Laurel Bk Gdns, SW6
  off New Kings Rd **148** C2
Laurel Bk Rd, Enf. EN2 **43** J1
Laurel Bk Vil, W7
  off Lower Boston Rd **124** B1
Laurel Cl, N19
  off Hargrave Pk **92** C2
  SW17 **167** H5
  Ilford IG6 **65** F6
  Sidcup DA14 **176** A3
Laurel Cres, Croy. CR0 **204** A3
Laurel Dr, N21 **43** G7
Laurel Gdns, E4 **46** B7
  NW7 **54** D3
  W7 **124** B1
  Bromley BR1 **192** B4
  Hounslow TW4 **142** E4
Laurel Gro, SE20 **171** E7
  SE26 **171** G4
Laurel La, West Dr. UB7 **120** B4
Laurel Manor, Sutt. SM2 **199** F7
Laurel Pk, Har. HA3 **52** C7
Laurel Rd, SW13 **147** G2
  SW20 **183** H1
  Hampton (Hmptn H.) TW12 **162** A5
Laurel St, E8 **94** C6
Laurel Vw, N12 **56** E3

Laurel Way, E18 . . . .79 F4
N20 . . . .56 D3
Laurence Ms, W12
off Askew Rd 127 G2
Laurence Pountney Hill,
EC4 . . . .20 B5
Laurence Pountney La,
EC4 . . . .20 B5
Laurie Gdns, SE14 . . . .153 H1
Laurie Rd, W7 . . . .104 B5
Laurier Rd, NW5 . . . .92 B3
Croydon CR0 . . . .188 C7
Laurinel Cl, Stan. HA7
off September Way 53 E6
Laurino Pl, Bushey
(Bushey Hth) WD23 . . . .51 J2
Lauriston Rd, E9 . . . .113 G1
SW19 . . . .166 A6
Lausanne Rd, N8 . . . .75 G4
SE15 . . . .153 F1
Lavell St, N16 . . . .94 A4
Lavender Av, NW9 . . . .88 C1
Mitcham CR4 . . . .185 H1
Worcester Park KT4 . . . .197 J3
Lavender Cl, SW3 . . . .31 F6
Bromley BR2 . . . .192 B6
Carshalton SM5 . . . .200 A4
Lavender Ct, W.Mol. KT8
off Molesham Way 179 H3
Lavender Gdns, SW11 . . . .149 J4
Enfield EN2 . . . .43 H1
Harrow (Har.Wld) HA3 . . . .52 B6
Lavender Gro, E8 . . . .94 C7
Mitcham CR4 . . . .185 H1
Lavender Hill, SW11 . . . .149 H4
Enfield EN2 . . . .43 G1
Lavender Pl, Ilf. IG1 . . . .98 E5
Lavender Ri, West Dr.
UB7 . . . .120 D2
Lavender Rd, SE16 . . . .133 H1
SW11 . . . .149 G3
Carshalton SM5 . . . .200 A4
Croydon CR0 . . . .187 F6
Enfield EN2 . . . .44 A1
Epsom KT19 . . . .196 B5
Sutton SM1 . . . .199 G4
Lavender St, E15
off Manbey Gro 96 E6
Lavender Sweep, SW11 . . . .149 J4
Lavender Ter, SW11
off Falcon Rd 149 H3
Lavender Vale, Wall. SM6 . . . .200 D6
Lavender Wk, SW11 . . . .149 J4
Mitcham CR4 . . . .186 A3
Lavender Way, Croy. CR0 . . . .189 G6
Lavengro Rd, SE27 . . . .169 J2
Lavenham Rd, SW18 . . . .166 C2
Lavernock Rd, Bexh. DA7 . . . .159 G2
Lavers Rd, N16 . . . .94 B3
Laverstoke Gdns, SW15 . . . .147 G7
Laverton Ms, SW5 . . . .30 A2
Laverton Pl, SW5 . . . .30 B2
Lavidge Rd, SE9 . . . .174 B2
Lavina Gro, N1 . . . .10 C1
Lavington Cl, E9 . . . .95 J6
Lavington Rd, W13 . . . .125 E1
Croydon CR0 . . . .201 F3
Lavington St, SE1 . . . .27 H2
Lawdons Gdns, Croy.
CR0 . . . .201 H4
Lawford Rd, N1 . . . .94 B7
NW5 . . . .92 C6
W4 . . . .126 C7
Law Ho, Bark. IG11 . . . .118 A2
Lawless St, E14 . . . .114 B7
Lawley Rd, N14 . . . .42 B7
Lawley St, E5 . . . .95 F4
Lawn, The, Sthl. UB2 . . . .123 G5
Lawn Cl, N9 . . . .44 C7
Bromley BR1 . . . .173 H6
New Malden KT3 . . . .182 E2
Lawn Cres, Rich. TW9 . . . .145 J2
Lawn Fm Gro, Rom. RM6 . . . .82 E4
Lawn Gdns, W7 . . . .124 B1
Lawn Ho Cl, E14 . . . .134 C2
Lawn La, SW8 . . . .34 B5
Lawn Rd, NW3 . . . .91 J5
Beckenham BR3 . . . .171 J7
Lawns, The, E4 . . . .62 A5
SE3 *off Lee Ter* 155 F3
SE19 . . . .188 A1
Pinner HA5 . . . .51 H1
Sidcup DA14 . . . .176 B4
Sutton SM2 . . . .198 B7
Lawns Ct, Wem. HA9
off The Avenue 87 J2
Lawnside, SE3 . . . .155 F4
Lawn Ter, SE3 . . . .155 E3
Lawn Vale, Pnr. HA5 . . . .66 D2
Lawrence Av, E12 . . . .98 D4
E17 . . . .77 G1
N13 . . . .59 H4
NW7 . . . .55 E4
NW10 . . . .106 D1
New Malden KT3 . . . .182 D6

Lawrence Bldgs, N16 . . . .94 C3
Lawrence Campe Cl, N20
off Friern Barnet La 57 G3
Lawrence Cl, E3 . . . .114 A2
N15 *off Lawrence Rd* 76 B4
W12 *off Australia Rd* 107 H7
Lawrence Ct, NW7 . . . .55 E5
Lawrence Cres, Dag.
RM10 . . . .101 H3
Edgware HA8 . . . .70 A2
Lawrence Gdns, NW7 . . . .55 F3
Lawrence Hall, E13
off Cumberland Rd 115 H4
Lawrence Hill, E4 . . . .62 A2
Lawrence La, EC2 . . . .20 A4
Lawrence Pl, N1
off Outram Pl 111 E1
Lawrence Rd, E6 . . . .116 A1
E13 . . . .115 H1
N15 . . . .76 B4
N18 . . . .60 E4
SE25 . . . .188 C4
Erith DA8 . . . .139 H7
Hampton TW12 . . . .161 F7
Hounslow TW4 . . . .142 C4
Pinner HA5 . . . .66 D5
Richmond TW10 . . . .163 F4
West Wickham BR4 . . . .205 G4
Lawrence St, E16 . . . .115 F5
NW7 . . . .55 F4
SW3 . . . .31 G6
Lawrence Way, NW10 . . . .88 C3
Lawrence Weaver Cl, Mord.
SM4 *off Green La* 184 D6
Lawrie Pk Av, SE26 . . . .171 E4
Lawrie Pk Cres, SE26 . . . .171 E4
Lawrie Pk Gdns, SE26 . . . .171 E4
Lawrie Pk Rd, SE26 . . . .171 E6
Laws Cl, SE25 . . . .188 A4
Lawson Cl, E16 . . . .115 J5
SW19 . . . .166 A3
Ilford IG1 . . . .99 G5
Lawson Ct, N11
off Ringway 58 C6
Lawson Est, SE1 . . . .28 B6
Lawson Gdns, Pnr. HA5 . . . .66 B3
Lawson Rd, Enf. EN3 . . . .45 F1
Southall UB1 . . . .103 F4
Law St, SE1 . . . .28 C5
Laxcon Cl, NW10 . . . .88 C5
Laxey Rd, Orp. BR6 . . . .207 J6
Laxley Cl, SE5 . . . .35 H7
Laxton Pl, NW1 . . . .9 E5
Layard Rd, SE16 . . . .133 E4
Enfield EN1 . . . .44 C1
Thornton Heath CR7 . . . .188 A2
Layard Sq, SE16 . . . .132 E4
Laycock St, N1 . . . .93 G6
Layer Gdns, W3 . . . .106 A7
Layfield Cl, NW4 . . . .71 H7
Layfield Cres, NW4 . . . .71 H7
Layfield Rd, NW4 . . . .71 H7
Layhams Rd, Kes. BR2 . . . .205 F5
West Wickham BR4 . . . .204 D3
Laymarsh Cl, Belv. DA17 . . . .139 F3
Laymead Cl, Nthlt. UB5 . . . .84 E6
Laystall St, EC1 . . . .10 E6
Layton Cres, Croy. CR0 . . . .201 G5
Layton Pl, Rich. (Kew) TW9
off Station Av 146 A1
Layton Rd, Brent. TW8 . . . .125 G5
Hounslow TW3 . . . .143 H4
Laytons Bldgs, SE1 . . . .28 A3
Layzell Wk, SE9
off Mottingham La 174 A1
Lazar Wk, N7
off Briset Way 93 F2
Lazenby Ct, WC2 . . . .18 A5
Leabank Cl, Har. HA1 . . . .86 B3
Leabank Sq, E9 . . . .96 A6
Leabank Vw, N15 . . . .76 D6
Leabourne Rd, N16 . . . .76 D6
LEA BRIDGE, E5 . . . .95 G3
Lea Br Rd, E5 . . . .95 G3
E10 . . . .95 H1
E17 . . . .78 D4
Lea Cl, Twick. TW2 . . . .143 F7
Leacroft Av, SW12 . . . .149 J7
Leacroft Cl, N21 . . . .59 H2
Leadale Av, E4 . . . .62 A2
Leadale Rd, N15 . . . .76 D6
N16 . . . .76 D6
Leadbeaters Cl, N11
off Goldsmith Rd 57 J5
★ Leadenhall Mkt, EC3 . . . .20 D4
Leadenhall Pl, EC3 . . . .20 D4
Leadenhall St, EC3 . . . .20 D4
Leadenham Ct, E3
off Spanby Rd 114 A4
Leader Av, E12 . . . .98 D5

Leadings, The, Wem. HA9 . . . .88 C3
Leaf Cl, T.Ditt. KT7 . . . .180 B5
Leaf Gro, SE27 . . . .169 G5
Leafield Cl, SW16 . . . .169 H6
Leafield La, Sid. DA14 . . . .177 F4
Leafield Rd, SW20 . . . .184 C3
Sutton SM1 . . . .198 D2
Leafy Gro, Kes. BR2 . . . .205 J5
Leafy Oak Rd, SE12 . . . .173 J3
Leafy Way, Croy. CR0 . . . .202 C2
Lea Gdns, Wem. HA9 . . . .87 H4
Leagrave St, E5 . . . .95 F3
Lea Hall Gdns, E10
off Lea Hall Rd 96 A1
Lea Hall Rd, E10 . . . .96 A1
Leahurst Rd, SE13 . . . .154 D5
Lea Interchange, E9 . . . .96 A5
Leake St, SE1 . . . .26 D3
Lealand Rd, N15 . . . .76 C6
Leamington Av, E17 . . . .78 A5
Bromley BR1 . . . .173 J5
Morden SM4 . . . .184 C4
Orpington BR6 . . . .207 H4
Leamington Cl, E12 . . . .98 B5
Bromley BR1 . . . .173 J4
Hounslow TW3 . . . .143 J5
Leamington Cres, Har.
HA2 . . . .85 E3
Leamington Gdns, Ilf. IG3 . . . .99 J2
Leamington Pk, W3 . . . .106 D5
Leamington Rd, Sthl.
UB2 . . . .122 D4
Leamington Rd Vil, W11 . . . .108 C5
Leamore St, W6 . . . .127 H4
Leamouth Rd, E6
off Remington Rd 116 B6
E14 . . . .114 D6
Leander Ct, SE8 . . . .154 A1
Leander Rd, SW2 . . . .151 F6
Northolt UB5 . . . .103 G2
Thornton Heath CR7 . . . .187 F4
Learner Dr, Har. HA2 . . . .85 F2
Lea Rd, Beck. BR3
off Fairfield Rd 190 A2
Enfield EN2 . . . .44 A1
Southall UB2 . . . .122 E4
Learoyd Gdns, E6 . . . .116 D7
Leas Cl, Chess. KT9 . . . .195 J7
Leas Dale, SE9 . . . .174 D3
Leas Grn, Chis. BR7 . . . .175 J6
Leaside Av, N10 . . . .74 A3
Leaside Rd, E5 . . . .95 F1
Leasowes Rd, E10 . . . .96 A1
Lea Sq, E3
off Legion Ter 113 J1
Leatherbottle Grn, Erith
DA18 . . . .139 F3
Leather Bottle La, Belv.
DA17 . . . .139 E4
Leather Cl, Mitch. CR4 . . . .186 A2
Leatherdale St, E1
off Portelet Rd 113 G3
Leather Gdns, E15
off Abbey Rd 115 E1
Leatherhead Cl, N16 . . . .94 C1
Leather La, EC1 . . . .19 F2
Leather Mkt, The, SE1 . . . .28 D4
Leathermarket Ct, SE1 . . . .28 D4
Leathermarket St, SE1 . . . .28 D4
Leather Rd, SE16 . . . .133 G4
Leathersellers Cl, Barn.
EN5 *off The Avenue* 40 B4
Leathsail Rd, Har. HA2 . . . .85 H3
Leathwaite Rd, SW11 . . . .149 J4
Leathwell Rd, SE8 . . . .154 B2
Lea Valley Rd, E4 . . . .45 H5
Enfield EN3 . . . .45 H5
Lea Valley Trd Est, N18 . . . .61 G5
N18 . . . .61 G5
Lea Valley Viaduct, E4 . . . .61 G5
N18 . . . .61 G5
Lea Valley Wk, E3 . . . .114 C4
E5 . . . .95 H3
E9 . . . .95 H3
E10 . . . .95 H3
E14 . . . .114 C3
E15 . . . .114 C3
E17 . . . .77 F1
N9 . . . .61 H1
N15 . . . .76 D6
N16 . . . .76 D6
N17 . . . .77 F1
N18 . . . .77 F1
Enfield EN3 . . . .45 J3
Lea Valley Pathway, E9 . . . .95 J3
E10 . . . .77 F1
E17 . . . .77 F1
Lea Valley Technopark,
N17 . . . .76 D3
Lea Vw Ho, E5
off Springfield 94 E1
Leaway, E10 . . . .95 G1
Lebanon Av, Felt. TW13 . . . .160 D5
Lebanon Cl, Twick. TW1 . . . .144 A7
Lebanon Gdns, SW18 . . . .148 D6
Lebanon Pk, Twick. TW1 . . . .144 E7
Lebanon Rd, SW18 . . . .148 D5
Croydon CR0 . . . .202 B1

Lebrun Sq, SE3 . . . .155 H3
Lechmere App, Wdf.Grn.
IG8 . . . .79 J2
Lechmere Av, Chig. IG7 . . . .65 F4
Woodford Green IG8 . . . .80 A2
Lechmere Rd, NW2 . . . .89 H6
Leckford Rd, SW18 . . . .167 F2
Leckhampton Pl, SW2
off Scotia Rd 151 G7
Leckwith Av, Bexh. DA7 . . . .138 E6
Lecky St, SW7 . . . .31 E3
Leclair Ho, SE3
off Gallus Sq 155 H3
Leconfield Av, SW13 . . . .147 F3
Leconfield Rd, N5 . . . .94 A4
Leda Av, Enf. EN3 . . . .45 G1
Leda Rd, SE18 . . . .136 C3
Ledbury Est, SE15 . . . .132 E7
Ledbury Ho, SE22
off Pytchley Rd 152 B3
Ledbury Ms N, W11
off Ledbury Rd 108 D7
Ledbury Ms W, W11
off Ledbury Rd 108 D7
Ledbury Pl, Croy. CR0 . . . .202 A4
Ledbury Rd, W11 . . . .108 C6
Croydon CR0 . . . .201 J4
Ledbury St, SE15 . . . .37 J7
Ledrington Rd, SE19 . . . .170 D6
Ledway Dr, Wem. HA9 . . . .88 A7
LEE, SE12 . . . .154 E4
Lee Av, Rom. RM6 . . . .82 E6
Lee Br, SE13 . . . .154 C3
Leechcroft Av, Sid. DA15 . . . .157 J5
Leechcroft Rd, Wall. SM6 . . . .200 A3
Lee Ch St, SE13 . . . .155 E4
Lee Cl, E17 . . . .77 G1
Barnet EN5 . . . .41 F4
Lee Conservancy Rd, E9 . . . .95 J5
Leecroft Rd, Barn. EN5 . . . .40 B5
Leeds Pl, N4 . . . .93 F1
Leeds Rd, Ilf. IG1 . . . .99 G1
Leeds St, N18 . . . .60 D5
Leefern Rd, W12 . . . .127 G2
Leegate, SE12 . . . .155 F5
Lee Grn, SE12
off Lee High Rd 155 F5
Lee Gro, Chig. IG7 . . . .64 D2
Lee High Rd, SE12 . . . .154 D3
SE13 . . . .154 D3
Leeke St, WC1 . . . .10 C3
Leeland Rd, W13 . . . .124 D1
Leeland Ter, W13 . . . .124 D1
Leeland Way, NW10 . . . .89 E4
Lee Pk, SE3 . . . .155 F4
Lee Pk Way, N9 . . . .61 G4
Leerdam Dr, E14 . . . .134 C3
Lee Rd, NW7 . . . .56 A7
SE3 . . . .155 F3
SW19 . . . .185 E1
Enfield EN1 . . . .44 D6
Greenford (Perivale)
UB6 . . . .105 F1
Lees, The, Croy. CR0 . . . .203 J2
Leeside, Barn. EN5 . . . .40 B5
Leeside Business Cen,
Enf. EN3 . . . .45 J2
Leeside Ct, SE16
off Rotherhithe St 133 G1
Leeside Cres, NW11 . . . .72 C6
Leeside Ind Est, N17
off Garman Rd 61 F7
Leeside Rd, N17 . . . .61 E6
Leeson Rd, SE24 . . . .151 G4
Leesons Hill, Chis. BR7 . . . .193 H3
Leesons Way, Orp. BR5 . . . .193 J2
Lees Pl, W1 . . . .16 B5
Lee St, E8 . . . .112 C1
Lee Ter, SE3 . . . .154 E3
SE13 . . . .154 E3
Lee Valley Pathway, E9 . . . .95 J3
E10 . . . .77 F1
E17 . . . .77 F1
Lee Valley Technopark,
N17 . . . .76 D3
Lee Vw, Enf. EN2 . . . .43 H1
Leeward Gdns, SW19 . . . .166 C6
Leeway, SE8 . . . .133 J5
Leeway Cl, Pnr.
(Hatch End) HA5 . . . .51 F7
Leewood Cl, SE12
off Upwood Rd 155 F6
Le Fay Ct, N9
off Galahad Rd 60 D3
Lefevre Wk, E3
off Parnell Rd 114 A2
Lefroy Rd, W12 . . . .127 F2
Legard Rd, N5 . . . .93 H4
Legatt Rd, SE9 . . . .156 A5
Leggatt Rd, E15 . . . .114 C2
Legge St, SE13 . . . .154 C5
Leghorn Rd, NW10 . . . .107 F2
SE18 . . . .137 G5
Legion Cl, N1 . . . .93 G6

Legion Ct, Mord. SM4 184 D6
Legion Rd, Grnf. UB6 103 J1
Legion Ter, E3 113 J1
Legion Way, N12 57 H7
Legon Av, Rom. RM7 101 J1
Legrace Av, Houns. TW4 142 D2
Leicester Av, Mitch. CR4 187 E4
Leicester Cl, Wor.Pk. KT4 197 J4
Leicester Ct, WC2 17 J5
Leicester Gdns, Ilf. IG3 81 H7
Leicester Ms, N2 *off Leicester Rd* 73 H3
Leicester Pl, WC2 17 J5
Leicester Rd, E11 79 H5
N2 73 H3
Barnet EN5 40 E5
Croydon CR0 188 B7
Leicester Sq, WC2 17 J6
Leicester St, WC2 17 J5
Leigh, The, Kings.T. KT2 165 E6
Leigham Av, SW16 169 E3
Leigham Cl, SW16 169 F3
Leigham Ct, Wall. SM6 *off Clyde Rd* 200 C6
Leigham Ct Rd, SW16 169 E2
Leigham Dr, Islw. TW7 124 B7
Leigham Vale, SW2 169 F3
SW16 169 F3
Leigh Av, Ilf. IG4 80 A4
Leigh Cl, N.Mal. KT3 182 C4
Leigh Cl Ind Est, N.Mal. KT3 *off Leigh Cl* 182 D4
Leigh Ct, SE4 *off Lewisham Way* 154 A2
Borehamwood WD6 *off Banks Rd* 38 D2
Harrow HA2 86 B1
Leigh Cres, Croy. (New Adgtn) CR0 204 B7
Leigh Gdns, NW10 107 J2
Leigh Hunt Dr, N14 58 D1
Leigh Hunt St, SE1 27 J3
Leigh Orchard Cl, SW16 169 F3
Leigh Pl, EC1 19 E1
Feltham TW13 160 C1
Welling DA16 158 A2
Leigh Rd, E6 98 D6
E10 78 C7
N5 93 H4
Hounslow TW3 144 A4
Leigh Rodd, Wat. WD19 51 F3
Leigh St, WC1 10 A5
Leighton Av, E12 98 D5
Pinner HA5 66 E3
Leighton Cl, Edg. HA8 70 A2
Leighton Cres, NW5 92 C5
Leighton Gdns, NW10 107 H2
Leighton Gro, NW5 92 C5
★ **Leighton Ho Mus**, W14 128 C3
Leighton Pl, NW5 92 C5
Leighton Rd, NW5 92 D5
W13 124 D2
Enfield EN1 44 C5
Harrow (Har.Wld) HA3 68 A2
Leighton St, Croy. CR0 201 H1
Leila Parnell Pl, SE7 135 J6
Leinster Av, SW14 146 C3
Leinster Gdns, W2 14 C4
Leinster Ms, W2 14 C5
Barnet EN5 40 B3
Leinster Pl, W2 14 C4
Leinster Rd, N10 74 B4
Leinster Sq, W2 108 D6
Leinster Ter, W2 14 C5
Leisure Way, N12 57 G7
Leith Cl, NW9 88 D1
Leithcote Gdns, SW16 169 F4
Leithcote Path, SW16 169 F3
Leith Rd, N22 75 H1
Leith Twrs, Sutt. SM2 199 E7
Leith Yd, NW6 *off Quex Rd* 108 D1
Lela Av, Houns. TW4 142 C2
Lelitia Cl, E8 *off Pownall Rd* 112 D1
Leman St, E1 21 G4
Lemark Cl, Stan. HA7 53 F5
Le May Av, SE12 173 H3
Lemmon Rd, SE10 134 E6
Lemna Rd, E11 79 E7
Lemon Gro, Felt. TW13 160 A1
Lemonwell Ct, SE9 *off Lemonwell Dr* 157 F5
Lemonwell Dr, SE9 157 F5
Lemsford Cl, N15 76 D5
Lemsford Ct, N4 *off Brownswood Rd* 93 J2
Borehamwood WD6 38 C4
Lemuel St, SW18 149 E6
Lena Cres, N9 61 F2
Lena Gdns, W6 127 J3
Lena Kennedy Cl, E4 62 B6
Lenanton Steps, E14 *off Manilla St* 134 A2
Lendal Ter, SW4 150 D3
Lenelby Rd, Surb. KT6 196 A1
Len Freeman Pl, SW6 *off John Smith Av* 128 C7
Lenham Rd, SE12 155 F4
Bexleyheath DA7 139 F6
Sutton SM1 199 E4
Thornton Heath CR7 188 A2
Lennard Av, W.Wick. BR4 205 E2
Lennard Cl, W.Wick. BR4 205 E2
Lennard Rd, SE20 171 F6
Beckenham BR3 171 G6
Bromley BR2 206 C1
Croydon CR0 201 J1
Lennon Rd, NW2 89 J5
Lennox Gdns, NW10 89 F4
SW1 23 J6
Croydon CR0 201 H4
Ilford IG1 98 C1
Lennox Gdns Ms, SW1 23 J6
Lennox Rd, E17 77 J6
N4 93 F2
Lenor Cl, Bexh. DA6 159 E4
Lensbury Av, SW6 149 F2
Lensbury Way, SE2 138 C3
Lens Rd, E7 97 J7
Lenthall Ho, SW1 33 G4
Lenthall Rd, E8 94 C7
Loughton IG10 49 G4
Lenthorp Rd, SE10 135 F4
Lentmead Rd, Brom. BR1 173 F3
Lenton Path, SE18 137 G6
Lenton Ri, Rich. TW9 145 H3
Lenton St, SE18 137 G4
Lenton Ter, N4 *off Fonthill Rd* 93 G2
Leof Cres, SE6 172 B5
Leominster Rd, Mord. SM4 185 F6
Leominster Wk, Mord. SM4 185 F6
Leonard Av, Mord. SM4 185 F5
Leonard Pl, N16 *off Allen Rd* 94 B4
Leonard Rd, E4 62 A6
E7 97 G4
N9 60 C3
SW16 186 C1
Southall UB2 122 D3
Leonard Robbins Path, SE28 *off Tawney Rd* 118 B7
Leonard St, E16 136 B1
EC2 12 C5
Leontine Cl, SE15 132 D7
Leopards Ct, EC1 19 E1
Leopold Av, SW19 166 C5
Leopold Ms, E9 *off Fremont St* 113 F1
Leopold Rd, E17 78 A5
N2 73 G3
N18 61 E5
NW10 89 E7
SW19 166 C4
W5 125 J1
Leopold St, E3 113 J5
Leopold Ter, SW19 166 C5
Leo St, SE15 133 E7
Leo Yd, EC1 11 H6
Leppoc Rd, SW4 150 D5
Leroy St, SE1 36 D1
Lerry Cl, W14 *off Thaxton Rd* 128 C6
Lescombe Cl, SE23 171 H3
Lescombe Rd, SE23 171 H3
Lesley Cl, Bex. DA5 159 H7
Leslie Gdns, Sutt. SM2 198 D7
Leslie Gro, Croy. CR0 202 B1
Leslie Gro Pl, Croy. CR0 *off Leslie Gro* 202 B1
Leslie Pk Rd, Croy. CR0 202 B1
Leslie Rd, E11 96 C4
E16 115 H6
N2 73 G3
Leslie Smith Sq, SE18 *off Nightingale Vale* 136 D6
★ **Lesnes Abbey (ruins)**, Erith DA18 138 D4
Lessar Av, SW4 150 C5
Lessingham Av, SW17 167 J4
Ilford IG5 80 D3
Lessing St, SE23 153 H7
Lessington Av, Rom. RM7 83 J6
Lessness Av, Bexh. DA7 138 D7
LESSNESS HEATH, Belv. DA17 139 H5
Lessness Pk, Belv. DA17 139 F5
Lessness Rd, Belv. DA17 *off Stapley Rd* 139 G5
Morden SM4 185 F6
Lester Av, E15 115 E3
Lestock Cl, SE25 188 D3
Leswin Pl, N16 *off Leswin Rd* 94 C3
Leswin Rd, N16 94 C3
Letchford Gdns, NW10 107 G3
Letchford Ms, NW10 *off Letchford Gdns* 107 G3
Letchford Ter, Har. HA3 67 H1
Letchworth Av, Felt. TW14 141 J7
Letchworth Cl, Brom. BR2 191 G5
Watford WD19 50 D5
Letchworth Dr, Brom. BR2 191 G5
Letchworth St, SW17 167 J4
Lethbridge Cl, SE13 154 C1
Letterstone Rd, SW6 *off Varna Rd* 128 C7
Lettice St, SW6 148 C1
Lett Rd, E15 96 D7
Lettsom St, SE5 152 B2
Lettsom Wk, E13 115 G2
Leucha Rd, E17 77 H5
Levana Cl, SW19 166 B1
Levehurst Ho, SE27 *off Elder Rd* 169 J5
Levehurst Way, SW4 150 E2
Leven Cl, Wat. WD19 50 D5
Levendale Rd, SE23 171 H2
Leven Rd, E14 114 C5
Leverett St, SW3 31 H1
Leverholme Gdns, SE9 174 D3
Leverson St, SW16 168 C6
Lever St, EC1 11 H4
Leverton Pl, NW5 *off Leverton St* 92 C5
Leverton St, NW5 92 C5
Levett Gdns, Ilf. IG3 99 J4
Levett Rd, Bark. IG11 99 H6
Levine Gdns, Bark. IG11 118 D2
Levison Way, N19 *off Grovedale Rd* 92 D2
Lewes Cl, Nthlt. UB5 85 G6
Lewesdon Cl, SW19 166 A1
Lewes Rd, N12 57 H5
Bromley BR1 192 A2
Leweston Pl, N16 76 C7
Lewey Ho, E3 113 J4
Lewgars Av, NW9 70 C6
Lewing Cl, Orp. BR6 *off Place Fm Av* 207 H1
Lewin Rd, SW14 146 D3
SW16 168 D6
Bexleyheath DA6 159 E4
Lewin Ter, Felt. TW14 *off Page Rd* 141 G7
Lewis Av, E17 78 A1
Lewis Cl, N14 *off Orchid Rd* 42 C7
Lewis Cres, NW10 88 C5
Lewis Gdns, N2 73 G2
N16 76 C6
Lewis Gro, SE13 154 C3
LEWISHAM, SE13 154 B4
Lewisham Cen, SE13 154 C3
Lewisham High St, SE13 154 C3
Lewisham Hill, SE13 154 C2
Lewisham Pk, SE13 154 B6
Lewisham Rd, SE13 154 B1
Lewisham St, SW1 25 J4
Lewisham Way, SE4 153 J1
SE14 153 J1
Lewis Pl, E8 94 D5
Lewis Rd, Mitch. CR4 185 G2
Richmond TW10 *off Red Lion St* 145 G5
Sidcup DA14 176 C3
Southall UB1 123 E2
Sutton SM1 199 E4
Welling DA16 158 C3
Lewis St, NW1 92 B6
Lewiston Cl, Wor.Pk. KT4 183 H7
Lewis Way, Dag. RM10 101 H6
Lexden Dr, Rom. RM6 82 B6
Lexden Rd, W3 106 B7
Mitcham CR4 186 D4
Lexham Ct, Grnf. UB6 104 A1
Lexham Gdns, W8 30 A1
Lexham Gdns Ms, W8 22 B6
Lexham Ho, Bark. IG11 *off St. Margarets* 117 G1
Lexham Ms, W8 128 D4
Lexham Wk, W8 22 B6
Lexington Apts, EC1 12 B5
Lexington Bldg, E3 *off Fairfield Rd* 114 A2
Lexington Pl, Kings.T. KT1 163 G7
Lexington St, W1 17 G4
Lexington Way, Barn. EN5 40 A4
Lexton Gdns, SW12 168 D1
Leyborne Av, W13 125 E2
Leyborne Pk, Rich. TW9 146 A1
Leybourne Cl, Brom. BR2 191 G6
Leybourne Rd, E11 97 F1
NW1 92 B7
NW9 70 A5
Leybourne St, NW1 *off Hawley St* 92 B7
Leybridge Ct, SE12 155 G5
Leyburn Cl, E17 *off Church La* 78 B4
Leyburn Gdns, Croy. CR0 202 B2
Leyburn Gro, N18 60 D6
Leyburn Rd, N18 60 D6
Leycroft Cl, Loug. IG10 48 D5
Leyden St, E1 21 F2
Leydon Cl, SE16 *off Lagado Ms* 133 G1
Leyfield, Wor.Pk. KT4 197 E1
Leyland Av, Enf. EN3 45 H2
Leyland Gdns, Wdf.Grn. IG8 63 J5
Leyland Rd, SE12 155 G5
Leylang Rd, SE14 133 G7
Leys, The, N2 73 F4
Harrow HA3 69 J6
Leys Av, Dag. RM10 101 J7
Leys Cl, Dag. RM10 101 J7
Harrow HA1 68 A5
Leysdown Av, Bexh. DA7 159 J4
Leysdown Rd, SE9 174 B2
Leysfield Rd, W12 127 G2
Leys Gdns, Barn. EN4 42 A5
Leyspring Rd, E11 97 F1
Leys Rd E, Enf. EN3 45 H1
Leys Rd W, Enf. EN3 45 H1
Ley St, Ilf. IG1, IG2 99 E2
Leyswood Dr, Ilf. IG2 81 H5
Leythe Rd, W3 126 C2
LEYTON, E11 96 B1
Leyton Business Cen, E10 96 A2
Leyton Gra, E10 96 A2
Leyton Gra Est, E10 *off Leyton Gra* 96 A2
Leyton Grn Rd, E10 78 C6
Leyton Ind Village, E10 77 G7
★ **Leyton Orient FC**, E10 96 B3
Leyton Pk Rd, E10 96 C3
Leyton Rd, E15 96 D5
SW19 167 F7
LEYTONSTONE, E11 78 D7
Leytonstone Rd, E15 96 E5
Leywick St, E15 114 E2
Lezayre Rd, Orp. BR6 207 J6
Liardet St, SE14 133 H6
Liberia Rd, N5 93 H6
★ **Liberty**, W1 17 F4
Liberty Av, SW19 185 G1
Liberty Cl, N18 60 C4
Liberty Ms, SW12 150 B6
Liberty St, SW9 151 F1
Libra Rd, E3 113 J1
E13 115 G2
Library Pl, E1 *off Cable St* 113 E7
Library St, SE1 27 G4
Library Way, Twick. TW2 *off Nelson Rd* 143 J7
Lichfield Cl, Barn. EN4 41 J3
Lichfield Ct, Rich. TW9 *off Sheen Rd* 145 H5
Lichfield Gdns, Rich. TW9 145 H4
Lichfield Gro, N3 72 D1
Lichfield Rd, E3 113 H3
E6 116 A3
N9 *off Winchester Rd* 60 D2
NW2 90 B4
Dagenham RM8 100 B4
Hounslow TW4 142 C3
Northwood HA6 66 A3
Richmond TW9 145 J1
Woodford Green IG8 63 E4
Lichlade Cl, Orp. BR6 207 J4
Lickey Ho, W14 *off North End Rd* 128 C6
Lidbury Rd, NW7 56 B6
Lidcote Gdns, SW9 151 G2
Liddall Way, West Dr. UB7 120 C1
Liddell Cl, Har. HA3 69 G3
Liddell Gdns, NW10 107 J2
Liddell Rd, NW6 90 D6
Lidding Rd, Har. HA3 69 G5
Liddington Rd, E15 115 F1
Liddon Rd, E13 115 H3
Bromley BR1 191 J3
Liden Cl, E17 *off Hitcham Rd* 95 J1
Lidfield Rd, N16 94 A4
Lidgate Rd, SE15 *off Chandler Way* 132 C7
Lidiard Rd, SW18 167 F2
Lidlington Pl, NW1 9 F2
Lido Ho, W13 *off Northfield Av* 125 E1
Lido Sq, N17 76 A1

Lidyard Rd, N19 **92** C1
★ **Lifetimes Mus** (Croydon Central Lib), Croy. CR0 **201** J3
Liffler Rd, SE18 **137** H5
Liffords Pl, SW13 **147** F2
Lifford St, SW15 **148** A4
Lightcliffe Rd, N13 **59** G4
Lighter Cl, SE16 **133** H4
Lighterman Ms, E1 **113** G6
Lightermans Rd, E14 **134** A2
Lightfoot Rd, N8 **74** E5
Lightley Cl, Wem. HA0 *off Stanley Av* **87** J7
Ligonier St, E2 **13** F5
Lilac Cl, E4 **61** J6
Lilac Gdns, W5 **125** G3
Croydon CR0 **204** A3
Lilac Ms, N8 *off Courcy Rd* **75** G3
Lilac Pl, SE11 **34** C2
Lilac St, W12 **107** G7
Lilah Ms, Brom. BR2 *off Beckenham La* **191** E2
Lilburne Gdns, SE9 **156** B5
Lilburne Rd, SE9 **156** B5
Lilburne Wk, NW10 **88** C6
Lile Cres, W7 **104** B5
Lilestone St, NW8 **7** G5
Lilford Rd, SE5 **151** H2
Lilian Barker Cl, SE12 **155** G5
Lilian Board Way, Grnf. UB6 **86** A5
Lilian Cl, N16 *off Barbauld Rd* **94** B3
Lilian Gdns, Wdf.Grn. IG8 **79** H1
Lilian Rd, SW16 **186** C1
Lillechurch Rd, Dag. RM8 **100** B6
Lilleshall Rd, Mord. SM4 **185** G6
Lilley Cl, E1 **29** J2
Lilley La, NW7 **54** D5
Lillian Av, W3 **126** A2
Lillian Rd, SW13 **127** G6
Lillie Rd, SW6 **128** B7
Lillieshall Rd, SW4 **150** B3
Lillie Yd, SW6 **128** D6
Lillingston Ho, N7 *off Harvist Est* **93** G4
Lillington Gdns Est, SW1 **33** G2
Lilliput Av, Nthlt. UB5 **103** F1
Lily Cl, W14 **128** B4
Lily Dr, West Dr. UB7 **120** A4
Lily Gdns, Wem. HA0 **105** F2
Lily Pl, EC1 **19** F1
Lily Rd, E17 **78** A6
Lilyville Rd, SW6 **148** C1
Limbourne Av, Dag. RM8 **83** F7
Limburg Rd, SW11 **149** J4
Limeburner La, EC4 **19** G4
Lime Cl, E1 **29** J1
Bromley BR1 **192** B4
Buckhurst Hill IG9 **64** A3
Carshalton SM5 **199** J2
Harrow HA3 **68** C2
Romford RM7 **83** J4
Lime Ct, Mitch. CR4 **185** G2
Lime Cres, Sun. TW16 **178** C2
Limecroft Cl, Epsom KT19 **196** D7
Limedene Cl, Pnr. HA5 **66** D1
Lime Gro, E4 **61** J6
N20 **56** C1
W12 **127** J2
Ilford IG6 **65** J6
New Malden KT3 **182** D3
Orpington BR6 **207** E2
Ruislip HA4 **66** B7
Sidcup DA15 **157** J6
Twickenham TW1 **144** C6
Limeharbour, E14 **134** B3
LIMEHOUSE, E14 **113** H7
Limehouse Causeway, E14 **113** J7
Limehouse Link, E14 **113** H7
Limekiln Dr, SE7 **135** H6
Limekiln Pl, SE19 **170** C7
Limerick Cl, SW12 **150** C7
Limerick Ms, N2 *off Bedford Rd* **73** H3
Lime Rd, Rich. TW9 *off St. Mary's Gro* **145** J4
Lime Row, Erith DA18 *off Northwood Pl* **139** F3
Limerston St, SW10 **30** D5
Limes, The, SW18 **148** D6
W2 *off Linden Gdns* **108** D7
Bromley BR2 **206** B2
Limes Av, E11 **79** H4
N12 **57** F4
NW7 **54** E6
NW11 **72** B7
SE20 **171** E7
SW13 **147** F2
Carshalton SM5 **199** J1
Chigwell IG7 **65** F5
Limes Av, Croydon CR0 **201** G3
Limes Av, The, N11 **58** B5
Limesdale Gdns, Edg. HA8 **70** C2
Limes Fld Rd, SW14 *off White Hart La* **147** E3
Limesford Rd, SE15 **153** G4
Limes Gdns, SW18 **148** D6
Limes Gro, SE13 **154** C4
Limes Pl, Croy. CR0 **188** A7
Limes Rd, Beck. BR3 **190** B2
Croydon CR0 **188** A6
Limes Row, Orp. (Farnboro.) BR6 **207** E5
Limestone Wk, Erith DA18 **138** D3
Lime St, E17 **77** H4
EC3 **20** D5
Lime St Pas, EC3 **20** D4
Limes Wk, SE15 **153** E4
W5 **125** G2
Lime Ter, W7 *off Manor Ct Rd* **104** B7
Lime Tree Av, Esher KT10 **194** A1
Thames Ditton KT7 **194** A1
Lime Tree Cl, E18 **79** J4
Limetree Cl, SW2 **169** F1
Lime Tree Gro, Croy. CR0 **203** J3
Lime Tree Pl, Mitch. CR4 **186** B1
Lime Tree Rd, Houns. TW5 **143** H1
Limetree Wk, SW17 *off Hawthorn Cres* **168** A5
Lime Tree Wk, Bushey (Bushey Hth) WD23 **52** B1
West Wickham BR4 **205** F4
Lime Wk, E15 *off Church St N* **115** E1
Limewood Cl, E17 **77** J4
W13 *off St. Stephens Rd* **105** E6
Beckenham BR3 **190** C5
Limewood Ct, Ilf. IG4 **80** C5
Limewood Rd, Erith DA8 **139** J7
Limpsfield Av, SW19 **166** A2
Thornton Heath CR7 **187** F5
Linacre Cl, SE15 **153** E3
Linacre Ct, W6 **128** A5
Linacre Rd, NW2 **89** H6
Linale Ho, N1 *off Murray Gro* **12** B2
Linberry Wk, SE8 **133** J4
Linchmere Rd, SE12 **155** F7
Lincoln Av, N14 **58** C3
SW19 **166** A3
Twickenham TW2 **161** H2
Lincoln Cl, SE25 *off Woodside Grn* **188** E6
Greenford UB6 **103** J1
Harrow HA2 **67** F5
Lincoln Ct, N16 **76** A7
Borehamwood WD6 **38** D5
Lincoln Cres, Enf. EN1 **44** B5
Lincoln Dr, Wat. WD19 **50** C3
Lincoln Gdns, Ilf. IG1 **80** B7
Lincoln Grn Rd, Orp. BR5 **193** J5
Lincoln Ms, NW6 *off Willesden La* **108** C1
SE21 **170** A1
Lincoln Rd, E7 **98** A6
E13 **115** H4
E18 *off Grove Rd* **79** G1
N2 **73** H3
SE25 **188** E3
Enfield EN1, EN3 **44** D5
Feltham TW13 **161** F3
Harrow HA2 **67** F5
Mitcham CR4 **186** E5
New Malden KT3 **182** C3
Sidcup DA14 **176** B5
Wembley HA0 **87** G6
Worcester Park KT4 **197** H1
Lincolns, The, NW7 **55** F3
★ **Lincoln's Inn**, WC2 **18** D3
Lincoln's Inn Flds, WC2 **18** C3
Lincoln St, E11 **96** E2
SW3 **31** J2
Lincoln Way, Enf. EN1 **44** E5
Lincombe Rd, Brom. BR1 **173** F3
Lindal Cres, Enf. EN2 **43** E4
Lindales, The, N17 *off Brantwood Rd* **60** C6
Lindal Rd, SE4 **153** J5
Lindbergh Rd, Wall. SM6 **200** E7
Linden Av, NW10 **108** A2
Enfield EN1 **44** D1
Hounslow TW3 **143** H5
Ruislip HA4 **84** A1
Thornton Heath CR7 **187** H4
Wembley HA9 **87** J5
Linden Cl, N14 **42** C6
Ruislip HA4 **84** A1
Stanmore HA7 **52** E5
Thames Ditton KT7 **180** C7
Linden Ct, W12 **127** J1
Linden Cres, Grnf. UB6 **86** C6
Kingston upon Thames KT1 **181** J2
Woodford Green IG8 **63** H6
Lindenfield, Chis. BR7 **192** E2
Linden Gdns, W2 **108** D7
W4 **126** D5
Enfield EN1 **44** D1
Linden Gro, SE15 **153** E3
SE26 **171** F6
New Malden KT3 **182** E3
Teddington TW11 *off Waldegrave Rd* **162** C5
Linden Lawns, Wem. HA9 **87** J4
Linden Lea, N2 **73** F5
Linden Leas, W.Wick. BR4 **204** D2
Linden Ms, N1 **94** A5
W2 *off Linden Gdns* **108** D7
Linden Pas, W4 *off Linden Gdns* **126** D5
Linden Pl, Mitch. CR4 **185** H4
Linden Rd, E17 *off High St* **77** J5
N10 **74** B4
N11 **57** J2
N15 **75** J4
Hampton TW12 **161** G7
Lindens, The, N12 **57** G5
W4 **146** C1
Croydon (New Adgtn) CR0 **204** C6
Loughton IG10 **48** C5
Linden Wk, N19 *off Hargrave Pk* **92** C2
Linden Way, N14 **42** C6
Lindeth Cl, Stan. HA7 **53** E6
Lindfield Gdns, NW3 **91** E5
Lindfield Rd, W5 **105** F4
Croydon CR0 **188** C6
Lindfield St, E14 **114** A6
Lindhill Cl, Enf. EN3 **45** G1
Lindisfarne Rd, SW20 **165** G7
Dagenham RM8 **100** C3
Lindisfarne Way, E9 **95** H4
Lindley Est, SE15 **37** H7
Lindley Pl, Rich. (Kew) TW9 **146** A1
Lindley Rd, E10 **96** B2
Lindley St, E1 **113** F5
Lindore Rd, SW11 **149** J4
Lindores Rd, Cars. SM5 **185** F7
Lindo St, SE15 *off Selden Rd* **153** F2
Lind Rd, Sutt. SM1 **199** F5
Lindrop St, SW6 **149** F2
Lindsay Cl, Chess. KT9 **195** H7
Staines (Stanw.) TW19 **140** A5
Lindsay Ct, SW11 *off Battersea High St* **149** G1
Lindsay Dr, Har. HA3 **69** H6
Lindsay Rd, Hmptn. (Hmptn H.) TW12 **161** H4
Worcester Park KT4 **197** H2
Lindsay Sq, SW1 **33** J3
Lindsell St, SE10 **154** C1
Lindsey Cl, Brom. BR1 **192** A3
Mitcham CR4 **187** E4
Lindsey Gdns, Felt. TW14 **141** G7
Lindsey Ms, N1 **93** J7
Lindsey Rd, Dag. RM8 **100** C4
Lindsey St, EC1 **19** H1
Lind St, SE8 **154** B2
Lindum Rd, Tedd. TW11 **163** F7
Lindway, SE27 **169** H5
Lindwood Cl, E6 *off Northumberland Rd* **116** B5
Linfield Cl, NW4 **71** J3
Linford Rd, E17 **78** C3
Linford St, SW8 **150** C1
Lingards Rd, SE13 **154** C4
Lingey Cl, Sid. DA15 **175** J2
Lingfield Av, Kings.T. KT1 **181** H4
Lingfield Cl, Enf. EN1 **44** B6
Lingfield Cres, SE9 **157** G4
Lingfield Gdns, N9 **45** E7
Lingfield Rd, SW19 **166** A5
Worcester Park KT4 **197** J3
Lingham St, SW9 **151** E2
Lingholm Way, Barn. EN5 **40** A5
Lingmere Cl, Chig. IG7 **65** F2
Ling Rd, E16 **115** G5
Erith DA8 **139** J6
Lingrove Gdns, Buck.H. IG9 **63** H3
Lings Coppice, SE21 **170** A2
Lingwell Rd, SW17 **167** H3
Lingwood Gdns, Islw. TW7 **124** B7
Lingwood Rd, E5 **76** D7
Linhope St, NW1 **7** J5
Link, The, SE9 **174** D3
W3 **106** B6
Enfield EN3 **45** H1
Link, The, Northolt UB5 *off Eastcote La* **85** F5
Pinner (Eastcote) HA5 **66** C7
Wembley HA0 *off Nathans Rd* **87** F1
Link Cen, The, Dag. RM10 *off Heathway* **101** G6
Linkfield, Brom. BR2 **191** G6
West Molesey KT8 **179** G3
Linkfield Rd, Islw. TW7 **144** C2
Link La, Wall. SM6 **200** D6
Linklea Cl, NW9 **55** E7
Link Rd, N11 **58** A4
Dagenham RM9 **119** H2
Feltham TW14 **141** J7
Wallington SM6 **200** A1
Links, The, E17 **77** H4
Links Av, Mord. SM4 **184** D4
Links Dr, N20 **56** D1
Links Gdns, SW16 **169** G7
Linkside, N12 **56** C6
Chigwell IG7 **65** F5
New Malden KT3 **183** E2
Linkside Cl, Enf. EN2 **43** F3
Linkside Gdns, Enf. EN2 **43** F3
Links Rd, NW2 **89** F2
SW17 **167** J6
W3 **106** A6
West Wickham BR4 **204** C1
Woodford Green IG8 **63** G5
Links Side, Enf. EN2 **43** G3
Link St, E9 **95** F6
Links Vw, N3 **56** C7
Links Vw Cl, Stan. HA7 **52** D6
Links Vw Rd, Croy. CR0 **204** A3
Hampton (Hmptn H.) TW12 **161** J5
Linksway, NW4 **72** A2
Links Way, Beck. BR3 **190** A6
Links Yd, E1 **21** H1
Linkway, N4 **75** J7
SW20 **183** H3
Link Way, Brom. BR2 **192** B7
Linkway, Dag. RM8 **100** C4
Link Way, Pnr. HA5 **66** D1
Linkway, Rich. TW10 **163** E2
Linkway, The, Barn. EN5 **40** E6
Linkwood Wk, NW1 *off Maiden La* **92** D7
Linley Cres, Rom. RM7 **83** H3
Linley Rd, N17 **76** B2
★ **Linley Sambourne Ho**, W8 **128** D2
Linnell Cl, NW11 **72** E6
Linnell Dr, NW11 **72** E6
Linnell Rd, N18 *off Fairfield Rd* **60** D5
SE5 **152** B2
Linnet Cl, N9 **61** G1
SE28 **118** C7
Linnet Ms, SW12 **150** A7
Linnett Cl, E4 **62** C4
Linnet Ter, Ilf. IG5 *off Tiptree Cres* **80** D3
Linom Rd, SW4 **150** E4
Linscott Rd, E5 **95** F4
Linsdell Rd, Bark. IG11 **117** F1
Linsey St, SE16 **37** H1
Linslade Cl, Houns. TW4 *off Heathlands Way* **143** E5
Pinner HA5 **66** B3
Linstead St, NW6 **90** D7
Linstead Way, SW18 **148** B7
Linsted Ct, SE9 **157** H6
Linster Gro, Borwd. WD6 **38** C5
Lintaine Cl, W6 *off Moylan Rd* **128** B6
Linthorpe Av, Wem. HA0 **87** F6
Linthorpe Rd, N16 **76** B7
Barnet (Cockfos.) EN4 **41** H3
Linton Cl, Mitch. CR4 **185** J7
Welling DA16 *off Anthony Rd* **158** B1
Linton Gdns, E6 **116** B6
Linton Gro, SE27 **169** H5
Linton Rd, Bark. IG11 **99** F7
Lintons, The, Bark. IG11 **99** F7
Linton St, N1 **111** J1
Lintott Ct, Stai. (Stanw.) TW19 **140** A6
Linver Rd, SW6 **148** D2
Linwood Cl, SE5 **152** C2
Linwood Cres, Enf. EN1 **44** D1
Linzee Rd, N8 **74** E4
Lion Av, Twick. TW1 *off Lion Rd* **162** C1
Lion Cl, SE4 **154** A6
Lion Ct, Borwd. WD6 **38** C1
Lionel Gdns, SE9 **156** A5
Lionel Ms, W10 *off Telford Rd* **108** B5
Lionel Rd, SE9 **156** A5
Lionel Rd N, Brent. TW8 **125** H4
Lionel Rd S, Brent. TW8 **125** J5

Liongate Enterprise Pk,
Mitch. CR4 ...**185** G4
Lion Gate Gdns, Rich.
TW9 ...**145** J3
Lion Gate Ms, SW18
off Merton Rd ...**148** D7
Lion Mills, E2 ...**13** J2
Lion Pk Av, Chess. KT9 ...**196** A4
Lion Plaza, EC2
off Lothbury ...**20** B3
Lion Rd, E6 ...**116** C5
N9 ...**60** D2
Bexleyheath DA6 ...**159** F4
Croydon CR0 ...**187** J5
Twickenham TW1 ...**162** C1
Lions Cl, SE9 ...**173** J3
Lion Way, Brent. TW8 ...**125** G7
Lion Wf Rd, Islw. TW7 ...**144** E3
Lion Yd, SW4
off Tremadoc Rd ...**150** D4
Liphook Cres, SE23 ...**153** F7
Liphook Rd, Wat. WD19 ...**50** D4
Lippitts Hill, Loug.
(High Beach) IG10 ...**47** E1
Lipton Cl, SE28
off Aisher Rd ...**118** C7
Lipton Rd, E1
off Bower St ...**113** G6
Lisbon Av, Twick. TW2 ...**161** J2
Lisbon Cl, E17 ...**77** J2
Lisburne Rd, NW3 ...**91** J4
Lisford St, SE15 ...**152** C1
Lisgar Ter, W14 ...**128** C4
Liskeard Cl, Chis. BR7 ...**175** F6
Liskeard Gdns, SE3 ...**155** G1
Lisle Cl, SW17 ...**168** B4
Lisle St, WC2 ...**17** J5
Lismore Circ, NW5 ...**91** J5
Lismore Cl, Islw. TW7 ...**144** D2
Lismore Rd, N17 ...**76** A3
South Croydon CR2 ...**202** B6
Lismore Wk, N1
off Clephane Rd ...**93** J6
Lissant Cl, Surb.
(Long Dit.) KT6 ...**181** G7
Lissenden Gdns, NW5 ...**92** A4
Lisson Grn Est, NW8 ...**7** G4
LISSON GROVE, NW8 ...**7** F5
Lisson Gro, NW1 ...**7** G5
NW8 ...**7** F4
Lisson St, NW1 ...**15** G1
Lister Cl, W3 ...**106** D5
Mitcham CR4 ...**185** H1
Lister Ct, NW9 ...**71** E2
Lister Gdns, N18 ...**59** J5
Lister Rd, E11 ...**97** E1
Lister Wk, SE28
off Haldane Rd ...**118** D7
Liston Rd, N17 ...**76** D1
SW4 ...**150** C3
Liston Way, Wdf.Grn. IG8
off Navestock Cres ...**63** J7
Listowel Cl, SW9 ...**35** F7
Listowel Rd, Dag. RM10 ...**101** G3
Listria Pk, N16 ...**94** B2
Litchfield Av, E15 ...**96** E6
Morden SM4 ...**184** C7
Litchfield Gdns, NW10 ...**89** G6
Litchfield Rd, Sutt. SM1 ...**199** F4
Litchfield St, WC2 ...**17** J5
Litchfield Way, NW11 ...**73** E5
Lithos Rd, NW3 ...**91** E6
Little Acre, Beck. BR3 ...**190** A3
Little Albany St, NW1 ...**8** E5
Little Argyll St, W1 ...**17** F4
Little Benty, West Dr.
UB7 ...**120** A5
Little Birches, Sid. DA15 ...**175** H2
Little Boltons, The, SW5 ...**30** B3
SW10 ...**30** B3
Little Bornes, SE21 ...**170** B4
Little Britain, EC1 ...**19** J3
Littlebrook Cl, Croy. CR0 ...**189** G6
Little Brownings, SE23 ...**170** E2
Littlebury Rd, SW4 ...**150** D3
Little Bury St, N9 ...**60** A1
Little Cedars, N12
off Woodside Av ...**57** F4
Little Chester St, SW1 ...**24** C5
Little Cloisters, SW1
off College Ms ...**26** A5
Little Coll La, EC4
off College St ...**20** B5
Little Coll St, SW1 ...**26** A5
Littlecombe, SE7 ...**135** H6
Littlecombe Cl, SW15 ...**148** A6
Little Common, Stan. HA7 ...**52** D3
Littlecote Cl, SW19 ...**148** A7
Littlecote Pl, Pnr. HA5 ...**67** E1
Little Cottage Pl, SE10
off Tarves Way ...**134** B7
Little Ct, W.Wick. BR4 ...**204** E2
Littlecroft, SE9 ...**156** D3
Littledale, SE2 ...**138** A6
Little Dean's Yd, SW1 ...**26** A5
Little Dimocks, SW12 ...**168** B2
Little Dorrit Ct, SE1 ...**28** A3
Little Dragons, Loug. IG10 ...**48** A4
LITTLE EALING, W5 ...**125** F4
Little Ealing La, W5 ...**125** F4
Little Edward St, NW1 ...**8** E3
Little Elms, Hayes
(Harling.) UB3 ...**121** G7
Little Essex St, WC2 ...**18** E5
Little Ferry Rd, Twick. TW1
off Ferry Rd ...**162** E1
Littlefield Cl, N19
off Tufnell Pk Rd ...**92** C4
Kingston upon Thames
KT1 *off Fairfield W* ...**181** H2
Littlefield Rd, Edg. HA8 ...**54** C7
Little Friday Rd, E4 ...**62** E2
Little Gearies, Ilf. IG6 ...**80** E4
Little George St, SW1 ...**26** A4
Little Gra, Grnf. UB6
off Perivale La ...**104** D3
Little Grn, Rich. TW9 ...**145** G4
Little Grn St, NW5
off College La ...**92** B4
Littlegrove, Barn. (E.Barn.)
EN4 ...**41** H6
Little Halliards, Walt. KT12
off Felix Rd ...**178** A6
Little Heath, SE7 ...**136** B6
Romford (Chad.Hth)
RM6 ...**82** B4
Romford (Junct) RM6 ...**82** B4
Little Heath Rd, Bexh.
DA7 ...**159** F1
Littleheath Rd, S.Croy.
CR2 ...**202** E7
★ **Little Holland Ho**,
Cars. SM5 ...**199** H7
LITTLE ILFORD, E12 ...**98** B5
Little Ilford La, E12 ...**98** C4
Littlejohn Rd, W7 ...**104** C6
Little London, Chig. IG7 ...**49** J4
Little London Ct, SE1
off Mill St ...**29** G4
Little Marlborough St, W1
off Foubert's Pl ...**17** F4
Littlemead, Esher KT10 ...**194** A4
Littlemede, SE9 ...**174** C3
Littlemoor Rd, Ilf. IG1 ...**99** G3
Littlemore Rd, SE2 ...**138** A2
Little Moss La, Pnr. HA5 ...**67** E2
Little Newport St, WC2 ...**17** J5
Little New St, EC4 ...**19** F3
Little Orchard Cl, Pnr. HA5
off Barrow Pt La ...**66** E2
Little Oxhey La, Wat.
WD19 ...**50** D5
Little Pk Dr, Felt. TW13 ...**160** D2
Little Pk Gdns, Enf. EN2 ...**43** J3
Little Pluckets Way,
Buck.H. IG9 ...**63** J1
Little Portland St, W1 ...**17** F3
Little Queens Rd, Tedd.
TW11 ...**162** C6
Little Redlands, Brom.
BR1 ...**192** B2
Little Rd, Croy. CR0
off Lower
Addiscombe Rd ...**202** B1
Hayes UB3 ...**121** J2
Littlers Cl, SW19
off Runnymede ...**185** G1
Little Russell St, WC1 ...**18** A2
Little St. James's St, SW1 ...**25** F2
Little St. Leonards,
SW14 ...**146** C3
Little Sanctuary, SW1 ...**25** J4
Little Smith St, SW1 ...**25** J5
Little Somerset St, E1 ...**21** F4
Littlestone Cl, Beck. BR3 ...**172** A6
Little Strand, NW9 ...**71** F2
Little Thrift, Orp. BR5 ...**193** F4
Little Titchfield St, W1 ...**17** F2
Littleton Av, E4 ...**63** F1
Littleton Cres, Har. HA1 ...**86** C2
Littleton Ho, SW1
off Lupus St ...**33** F4
Littleton Rd, Har. HA1 ...**86** C2
Littleton St, SW18 ...**167** F2
Little Trinity La, EC4 ...**20** A5
Little Turnstile, WC1 ...**18** C3
★ **Little Venice**
(Waterbuses), W2 ...**14** C1
Littlewood, SE13 ...**154** C5
Littlewood Cl, W13 ...**125** E3
Littleworth Av, Esher
KT10 ...**194** A5
Littleworth Common Rd,
Esher KT10 ...**194** A3
Littleworth La, Esher
KT10 ...**194** A4
Littleworth Pl, Esher
KT10 ...**194** A4
Littleworth Rd, Esher
KT10 ...**194** B4
Livermere Rd, E8 ...**112** C1
Liverpool Gro, SE17 ...**36** A4
Liverpool Rd, E10 ...**78** C6
E16 ...**115** E5
N1 ...**111** G2
N7 ...**93** G5
W5 ...**125** G2
Kingston upon Thames
KT2 ...**164** A7
Thornton Heath CR7 ...**187** J3
Liverpool St, EC2 ...**20** D2
Livesey Cl, SE28 ...**137** F3
Kingston upon Thames
KT1 ...**181** J3
★ **Livesey Mus for**
Children, SE15 ...**132** E6
Livesey Pl, SE15 ...**37** J5
Livingstone Ct, E10
off Matlock Rd ...**78** C6
Barnet EN5
off Christchurch La ...**40** B2
Livingstone Pl, E14
off Ferry St ...**134** C5
Livingstone Rd, E15 ...**114** C1
E17 ...**78** B6
N13 ...**59** E6
SW11
off Winstanley Rd ...**149** G3
Hounslow TW3 ...**143** J4
Southall UB1 ...**102** D7
Thornton Heath CR7 ...**187** J2
Livingstone Wk, SW11 ...**149** G3
Livonia St, W1 ...**17** G4
Lizard St, EC1 ...**12** A4
Lizban St, SE3 ...**135** H7
Llanelly Rd, NW2 ...**90** C2
Llanover Rd, SE18 ...**136** D6
Wembley HA9 ...**87** G3
Llanthony Rd, Mord.
SM4 ...**185** G6
Llanvanor Rd, NW2 ...**90** C2
Llewellyn St, SE16 ...**29** J4
Lloyd Av, SW16 ...**187** E1
Lloyd Baker St, WC1 ...**10** D4
Lloyd Ct, Pnr. HA5 ...**66** D5
Lloyd Pk, E17 ...**78** A2
Lloyd Pk Av, Croy. CR0 ...**202** C4
Lloyd Rd, E6 ...**116** C1
E17 ...**77** G4
Dagenham RM9 ...**101** F6
Worcester Park KT4 ...**197** J3
Lloyd's Av, EC3 ...**21** E4
★ **Lloyd's of London**,
EC3 ...**20** D4
Lloyds Pl, SE3 ...**155** E2
Lloyd Sq, WC1 ...**10** E3
Lloyd's Row, EC1 ...**11** F4
Lloyd St, WC1 ...**10** E3
Lloyds Way, Beck. BR3 ...**189** H5
Lloyd Vil, SE4 ...**154** A2
Loampit Hill, SE13 ...**154** A2
Loampit Vale, SE13 ...**154** B3
Loanda Cl, E8
off Clarissa St ...**112** C1
Loats Rd, SW2 ...**150** E6
Lobelia Cl, E6
off Sorrel Gdns ...**116** B5
Locarno Rd, W3 ...**126** C1
Greenford UB6 ...**103** J4
Lochaber Rd, SE13 ...**154** E4
Lochaline St, W6 ...**127** J6
Lochan Cl, Hayes UB4 ...**102** E4
Lochinvar St, SW12 ...**150** B7
Lochmere Cl, Erith DA8 ...**139** H6
Lochnagar St, E14 ...**114** C5
Lock Bldg, The, E15
off High St ...**114** C2
Lock Chase, SE3 ...**155** E3
Lock Cl, Sthl. UB2
off Navigator Dr ...**123** J2
Lockesfield Pl, E14 ...**134** B5
Lockesley Dr, Orp. BR5 ...**193** J6
Lockesley Sq, Surb. KT6
off Lovelace Gdns ...**181** G6
Locket Rd, Har. HA3 ...**68** B3
Locket Rd Ms, Har. HA3
off Locket Rd ...**68** B3
Lockfield Av, Enf. EN3 ...**45** H2
Lockgate Cl, E9
off Lee
Conservancy Rd ...**95** J5
Lockhart Cl, N7 ...**93** F6
Enfield EN3 ...**45** E5
Lockhart St, E3 ...**113** J4
Lockhurst St, E5 ...**95** G4
Lockie Pl, SE25 ...**188** D3
Lockier Wk, Wem. HA9 ...**87** G3
Lockington Rd, SW8 ...**150** B1
Lockmead Rd, N15 ...**76** D6
SE13 ...**154** C3
Lock Ms, NW1
off Northpoint Sq ...**92** D6
Lock Rd, Rich. TW10 ...**163** F4
Locks La, Mitch. CR4 ...**185** J1
Locksley Est, E14 ...**113** J6
Locksley St, E14 ...**113** J5
Locksmeade Rd, Rich.
TW10 ...**163** F4
Locksons Cl, E14
off Broomfield St ...**114** B5
Lockswood Cl, Barn. EN4 ...**41** J4
Lockton St, W10 ...**108** A7
Lockwell Rd, Dag. RM10
off Heathway ...**101** F3
Lockwood Cl, SE26 ...**171** G4
Lockwood Ind Pk, N17 ...**76** E3
Lockwood Pl, E4 ...**62** A6
Lockwood Sq, SE16 ...**132** E3
Lockwood Way, E17 ...**77** G2
Chessington KT9 ...**196** A5
Lockyer Est, SE1 ...**28** C3
Lockyer St, SE1 ...**28** C4
Locomotive Dr, Felt.
TW14 ...**160** A1
Locton Grn, E3
off Ruston St ...**113** J1
Loddiges Rd, E9 ...**95** F7
Loder St, SE15 ...**153** F1
Lodge Av, SW14 ...**146** E3
Croydon CR0 ...**201** G3
Dagenham RM8, RM9 ...**118** A1
Harrow HA3 ...**69** H4
Lodge Av Junct, Bark.
IG11 ...**118** A1
Lodge Cl, N18 ...**59** J5
Edgware HA8 ...**53** J6
Isleworth TW7 ...**144** E1
Wallington SM6 ...**200** A1
Lodge Ct, Wem. HA0 ...**87** H5
Lodge Dr, N13 ...**59** G4
Lodge Gdns, Beck. BR3 ...**189** J5
Lodge Hill, SE2 ...**138** B7
Ilford IG4 ...**80** B4
Welling DA16 ...**138** B7
Lodgehill Pk Cl, Har. HA2 ...**85** H2
Lodge La, N12 ...**57** F5
Bexley DA5 ...**158** D6
Croydon (New Adgtn)
CR0 ...**204** A6
Lodge Pl, Sutt. SM1 ...**199** E5
Lodge Rd, NW4 ...**71** J4
NW8 ...**7** F4
Bromley BR1 ...**173** H7
Croydon CR0 ...**187** H6
Wallington SM6 ...**200** B5
Lodge Vil, Wdf.Grn. IG8 ...**63** F7
Lodore Gdns, NW9 ...**70** E5
Lodore St, E14 ...**114** C6
Lofthouse Pl, Chess. KT9 ...**195** F6
Loftie St, SE16 ...**29** J4
Lofting Rd, N1 ...**93** F7
Loftus Rd, W12 ...**127** H1
Barking IG11 ...**99** F6
Logan Cl, Enf. EN3 ...**45** G1
Hounslow TW4 ...**143** F3
Logan Ms, W8 ...**128** D4
Logan Pl, W8 ...**128** D4
Logan Rd, N9 ...**61** E2
Wembley HA9 ...**87** H2
Loggetts, The, SE21 ...**170** B3
Logs Hill, Brom. BR1 ...**174** B7
Chislehurst BR7 ...**174** B7
Logs Hill Cl, Chis. BR7 ...**192** B1
Lolesworth Cl, E1 ...**21** F2
Lollard St, SE11 ...**34** D1
Loman St, SE1 ...**27** H3
Lomas Cl, Croy. CR0 ...**204** C7
Lomas Dr, E8 ...**94** C7
Lomas St, E1 ...**21** J1
Lombard Av, Enf. EN3 ...**45** F1
Ilford IG3 ...**99** H1
Lombard Business Pk,
SW19 ...**185** E2
Lombard Ct, EC3 ...**20** C5
W3 *off Crown St* ...**126** B1
Lombard La, EC4 ...**19** F4
Lombard Rd, N11 ...**58** B5
SW11 ...**149** G2
SW19 ...**185** E2
Lombard Rbt, Croy.
CR0 ...**187** F7
Lombard St, EC3 ...**20** C4
Lombard Wall, SE7 ...**135** H3
Lombardy Cl, Ilf. IG6
off Hazel La ...**64** E7
Lombardy Pl, W2 ...**14** A6
Lombardy Retail Pk, Hayes
UB3 ...**102** B7
Lomond Cl, N15 ...**76** B4
Wembley HA0 ...**87** J7
Lomond Gdns, S.Croy.
CR2 ...**203** H7
Lomond Gro, SE5 ...**36** B7
Loncroft Rd, SE5 ...**37** E5
Londesborough Rd,
N16 ...**94** B4
Londinium Twr, E1
off Mansell St ...**21** G5
★ **London Aquarium**,
SE1 ...**26** C3

★ **London Brass Rubbing Cen** (St. Martin-in-the-Fields Ch), WC2 18 A6
London Br, EC4 28 C1
SE1 28 C1
London Br St, SE1 28 B2
★ **London Butterfly Ho**, Brent. TW8 145 E1
★ **London Canal Mus, The**, N1 *off New Wf Rd* 10 B1
★ **London Cen Mkts** (Smithfield Mkt), EC1 19 G1
★ **London Cen Mosque**, NW8 7 H3
★ **London City Airport**, E16 136 B1
★ **London Coliseum**, WC2 18 A6
★ **London Dungeon**, SE1 28 C2
★ **London Eye**, SE1 26 C3
London Flds, E8 94 E7
London Flds E Side, E8 94 E7
London Flds W Side, E8 94 D7
★ **London Fire Brigade Mus**, SE1 27 J3
London Fruit Ex, E1 *off Brushfield St* 21 F2
★ **London Heathrow Airport**, Houns. TW6 140 E1
London Ind Est, E6 116 D5
London La, E8 95 E7
Bromley BR1 173 F7
London Master Bakers Almshouses, E10 *off Lea Br Rd* 78 B6
★ **London Met Archives**, EC1 11 F5
London Ms, W2 15 F4
★ **London Palladium**, W1 17 F4
London Pav, The, W1 17 H6
★ **London Peace Pagoda**, SW11 32 A7
★ **London Regatta Cen**, E16 116 A7
London Rd, E13 115 G2
SE1 27 G5
SE23 170 E1
SW16 187 F1
SW17 185 J2
Barking IG11 98 E7
Brentford TW8 125 F7
Bromley BR1 173 F7
Croydon CR0 187 H7
Enfield EN2 44 A3
Harrow HA1 86 B2
Hounslow TW3 143 J3
Isleworth TW7 144 C2
Kingston upon Thames KT2 181 J2
Mitcham CR4 185 J2
Mitcham (Bedd.Cor.) CR4 186 A7
Morden SM4 184 D5
Romford (Abridge) RM4 49 J4
Romford (Chad.Hth) RM6, RM7 83 G6
Stanmore HA7 53 F5
Sutton SM3 198 A3
Thornton Heath CR7 187 G5
Twickenham TW1 144 D5
Wallington SM6 200 B4
Wembley HA9 87 H6
London Rd Rbt, Twick. TW1 *off Chertsey Rd* 144 D6
★ **London Silver Vaults**, WC2 18 E2
London Stile, W4 *off Wellesley Rd* 126 A5
★ **London Stone**, EC4 20 B5
London St, EC3 20 E5
W2 15 E4
★ **London Television Cen**, SE1 27 E1
London Ter, E2 13 H2
★ **London Transport Mus**, WC2 18 B5
★ **London Trocadero, The**, W1 17 H6
London Wall, EC2 20 A2
London Wall Bldgs, EC2 20 C2
★ **London Zoo**, NW1 8 B1
Lonesome Way, SW16 186 B1
Long Acre, WC2 18 A5
Longacre Pl, Cars. SM5 *off Beddington Gdns* 200 A6
Longacre Rd, E17 78 D1
Longbeach Rd, SW11 149 J3
Longberrys, NW2 90 C3
Longboat Row, Sthl. UB1 103 F6
Longbridge Rd, Bark. IG11 99 F7
Dagenham RM8 100 A4
Longbridge Way, SE13 154 C5
Longcliffe Path, Wat. WD19 50 A3
Longcourt Ms, E11 79 J4
Longcroft, SE9 174 C3
Longcrofte Rd, Edg. HA8 53 G7
Longcroft Ri, Loug. IG10 48 D5
Long Deacon Rd, E4 62 E1
LONG DITTON, Surb. KT6 195 F1
Longdon Wd, Kes. BR2 206 B4
Longdown Rd, SE6 172 A4
Long Dr, W3 106 E6
Greenford UB6 103 H1
Ruislip HA4 84 D4
Long Elmes, Har. HA3 67 H1
Longfellow Rd, E17 77 J6
Worcester Park KT4 197 G2
Longfellow Way, SE1 37 G2
Long Fld, NW9 55 E7
Longfield, Brom. BR1 191 F1
Loughton IG10 47 J5
Longfield Av, E17 77 H4
NW7 55 G7
W5 105 F7
Wallington SM6 200 A1
Wembley HA9 87 H1
Longfield Cres, SE26 171 F3
Longfield Dr, SW14 146 B5
Mitcham CR4 167 H7
Longfield Est, SE1 37 G2
Longfield Rd, W5 105 F7
Longfield St, SW18 148 D7
Longfield Wk, W5 105 F6
Longford Av, Felt. TW14 141 H6
Southall UB1 103 G7
Longford Cl, Felt. TW13 *off Swift Rd* 161 E3
Hampton (Hmptn H.) TW12 161 G4
Hayes UB4 *off Longford Gdns* 102 D7
Longford Ct, E5 *off Pedro St* 95 G4
NW4 72 A4
Epsom KT19 196 C4
Longford Gdns, Hayes UB4 102 D7
Sutton SM1 199 F3
Longford Ho, E1 *off Jubilee St* 113 F6
Longford Rd, Twick. TW2 161 G1
Longford St, NW1 8 E5
Longford Wk, SW2 *off Papworth Way* 151 G7
Long Grn, Chig. IG7 65 H4
Longhayes Av, Rom. RM6 82 D4
Longhayes Ct, Rom. RM6 *off Longhayes Av* 82 D4
Longheath Gdns, Croy. CR0 189 F5
Longhedge Ho, SE26 170 C4
Long Hedges, Houns. TW3 143 G1
Longhedge St, SW11 150 A2
Longhill Rd, SE6 172 D2
Longhook Gdns, Nthlt. UB5 102 A2
Longhope Cl, SE15 37 F6
Longhurst Rd, SE13 154 D5
Croydon CR0 189 E6
Longland Ct, SE1 37 H3
Longland Dr, N20 56 E3
LONGLANDS, Chis. BR7 175 F3
Longlands Ct, W11 *off Portobello Rd* 108 C7
Mitcham CR4 *off Summerhill Way* 186 A1
Longlands Pk Cres, Sid. DA15 175 H3
Longlands Rd, Sid. DA15 175 H3
Long La, EC1 19 H1
N2 73 F2
N3 56 E7
SE1 28 B4
Bexleyheath DA7 138 D7
Croydon CR0 189 F5
Staines (Stanw.) TW19 140 C7
Longleat Ho, SW1 *off Rampayne St* 33 H3
Longleat Rd, Enf. EN1 44 B5
Longleat Way, Felt. TW14 141 G7
Longleigh La, SE2 138 C6
Bexleyheath DA7 138 C6
Longlents Ho, NW10 106 D1
Longley Av, Wem. HA0 105 J1
Longley Ct, SW8 *off Lansdowne Way* 150 E1
Longley Rd, SW17 167 H6
Croydon CR0 187 H7
Harrow HA1 67 J5
Long Leys, E4 62 B6
Longley St, SE1 37 H2
Longley Way, NW2 89 J3
Long Mark Rd, E16 *off Fulmer Rd* 116 A5
Longmarsh La, SE28 137 H1
Long Mead, NW9 71 F1
Longmead, Chis. BR7 192 D2
Longmead Dr, Sid. DA14 176 D2
Longmead Ho, SE27 *off Elder Rd* 169 J5
Long Meadow, NW5 *off Torriano Av* 92 D5
Long Meadow Cl, W.Wick. BR4 190 C7
Longmeadow Rd, Sid. DA15 175 H1
Longmead Rd, SW17 167 J5
Thames Ditton KT7 180 B7
Longmoore St, SW1 33 F2
Longmoor Pt, SW15 *off Norley Vale* 165 G1
Longmore Av, Barn. EN4, EN5 41 F6
Longnor Rd, E1 113 G3
Long Pond Rd, SE3 155 E1
Long Reach Ct, Bark. IG11 117 G2
Longreach Rd, Bark. IG11 117 J4
Longridge Ho, SE1 28 A6
Longridge La, Sthl. UB1 103 H7
Longridge Rd, SW5 128 D4
Long Rd, SW4 150 B4
Long's Ct, WC2 17 H5
Longs Ct, Rich. TW9 *off Crown Ter* 145 J4
Longshaw Rd, E4 62 D3
Longshore, SE8 133 J4
Longstaff Cres, SW18 148 D6
Longstaff Rd, SW18 148 D6
Longstone Av, NW10 89 F7
Longstone Ct, SE1 28 A4
Longstone Rd, SW17 168 B5
Long St, E2 13 F3
Longthornton Rd, SW16 186 C2
Longthorpe Ct, W6 *off Invermead Cl* 127 G3
Longton Av, SE26 170 D4
Longton Gro, SE26 170 E4
Longton Ho, SE11 *off Lambeth Wk* 34 D1
Longville Rd, SE11 35 G1
Long Wk, SE1 28 E5
SE18 136 E6
SW13 147 E2
New Malden KT3 182 C3
Longwalk Rd, Uxb. UB11 121 E1
Longwood Dr, SW15 147 G6
Longwood Gdns, Ilf. IG5, IG6 80 C4
Longworth Cl, SE28 118 D6
Long Yd, WC1 10 C6
Loning, The, NW9 71 E4
Lonsdale Av, E6 116 A3
Romford RM7 83 J6
Wembley HA9 87 H5
Lonsdale Cl, E6 *off Lonsdale Av* 116 B4
SE9 174 A3
Edgware HA8 53 J5
Pinner HA5 51 E7
Lonsdale Cres, Ilf. IG2 80 E6
Lonsdale Dr, Enf. EN2 43 E5
Lonsdale Gdns, Th.Hth. CR7 187 F4
Lonsdale Ms, W11 *off Lonsdale Rd* 108 C6
Richmond TW9 *off Elizabeth Cotts* 146 A1
Lonsdale Pl, N1 *off Barnsbury St* 93 G7
Lonsdale Rd, E11 79 F7
NW6 108 C2
SE25 188 E4
SW13 127 G6
W4 127 F4
W11 108 C6
Bexleyheath DA7 159 F2
Southall UB2 122 D3
Lonsdale Sq, N1 93 G7
Loobert Rd, N15 76 B3
Looe Gdns, Ilf. IG6 81 E3
Loop Rd, Chis. BR7 175 F6
Lopen Rd, N18 60 B4
Loraine Cl, Enf. EN3 45 F5
Loraine Rd, N7 93 F4
W4 126 B6
Lord Amory Way, E14 134 C2
Lord Av, Ilf. IG5 80 C4
Lord Chancellor Wk, Kings.T. KT2 182 C1
Lordell Pl, SW19 165 J6
Lorden Wk, E2 13 H4
Lord Gdns, Ilf. IG5 80 B4
Lord Hills Br, W2 14 B2
Lord Hills Rd, W2 14 B1
Lord Holland La, SW9 *off Urlwin Wk* 151 G2
Lord Knyvett Cl, Stai. (Stanw.) TW19 140 A6
Lord Knyvetts Ct, Stai. (Stanw.) TW19 *off De Havilland Way* 140 B6
Lord Napier Pl, W6 *off Oil Mill La* 127 G5
Lord N St, SW1 26 A6
Lord Roberts Ms, SW6 *off Waterford Rd* 128 E7
Lord Roberts Ter, SE18 136 D5
★ **Lord's** (Marylebone CC & Mus, Middlesex CCC), NW8 7 F3
Lord's Cl, SE21 169 J2
Lords Cl, Felt. TW13 161 E2
Lordship Gro, N16 94 A2
Lordship La, N17 75 J1
N22 75 G2
SE22 152 C6
Lordship La Est, SE22 170 D1
Lordship Pk, N16 93 J2
Lordship Pk Ms, N16 93 J2
Lordship Pl, SW3 31 G6
Lordship Rd, N16 94 A2
Northolt UB5 84 E7
Lordship Ter, N16 94 A2
Lordsmead Rd, N17 76 B1
Lord St, E16 136 B1
Lord's Vw, NW8 7 F4
Lordswood Cl, Bexh. DA6 159 E5
Lord Warwick St, SE18 136 C3
Lorenzo St, WC1 10 C3
Loretto Gdns, Har. HA3 69 H4
Lorian Cl, N12 56 E4
Loring Rd, N20 57 H2
SE14 153 H1
Isleworth TW7 144 C2
Loris Rd, W6 127 J3
Lorn Ct, SW9 151 G2
Lorne Av, Croy. CR0 189 G7
Lorne Cl, NW8 7 H4
Lorne Gdns, E11 79 J4
W11 128 A2
Croydon CR0 189 G7
Lorne Rd, E7 97 H4
E17 78 A5
N4 93 F1
Harrow HA3 68 C2
Richmond TW10 *off Albert Rd* 145 J5
Lorn Rd, SW9 151 F2
Lorraine Pk, Har. HA3 52 B7
Lorrimore Rd, SE17 35 H5
Lorrimore Sq, SE17 35 H5
Loseberry Rd, Esher (Clay.) KT10 194 A5
Lothair Rd, W5 125 G2
Lothair Rd N, N4 75 H6
Lothair Rd S, N4 75 G7
Lothair St, SW11 *off Grant Rd* 149 H3
Lothbury, EC2 20 B3
Lothian Av, Hayes UB4 102 B5
Lothian Cl, Wem. HA0 86 D4
Lothian Rd, SW9 151 H1
Lothrop St, W10 108 B3
Lots Rd, SW10 129 F7
Lotus Cl, SE21 169 J3
Loubet St, SW17 167 J6
Loudoun Av, Ilf. IG6 81 E5
Loudoun Rd, NW8 6 D1
Loudwater Cl, Sun. TW16 178 A4
Loudwater Rd, Sun. TW16 178 A4
Loughborough Est, SW9 *off Loughborough Rd* 151 H2
Loughborough Pk, SW9 151 H4
Loughborough Rd, SW9 151 G2
Loughborough St, SE11 34 D3
Lough Rd, N7 93 F6
LOUGHTON, IG10 48 C5
Loughton Seedbed Cen, Loug. IG10 *off Langston Rd* 49 G4
Loughton Way, Buck.H. IG9 64 A1
Louisa Cl, E9 *off Wetherell Rd* 113 G1
Louisa Gdns, E1 *off Louisa St* 113 G4
Louisa Ho, SW15 147 E4
Louisa St, E1 113 G4
Louise Aumonier Wk, N19 *off Hillrise Rd* 74 E7
Louise Bennett Cl, SE24 *off Shakespeare Rd* 151 H4
Louise Ct, E11 *off Grosvenor Rd* 79 H5
Louise Rd, E15 97 E6
Louis Gdns, Chis. BR7 174 C4
Louis Ms, N10 74 B1
Louisville Rd, SW17 168 A3
Louvaine Rd, SW11 149 G4

Lovage App, E6 116 B5
Lovat Cl, NW2 89 F3
Lovat La, EC3 20 D6
Lovatt Cl, Edg. HA8 54 B6
Lovat Wk, Houns. TW5 *off Cranford La* 122 E7
Loveday Rd, W13 125 E1
Lovegrove St, SE1 37 J4
Lovegrove Wk, E14 134 C1
Lovekyn Cl, Kings.T. KT2 *off Queen Elizabeth Rd* 181 J2
Lovelace Av, Brom. BR2 192 D6
Lovelace Gdns, Bark. IG11 100 A4
Surbiton KT6 181 G7
Lovelace Grn, SE9 156 C3
Lovelace Ho, W13 *off Uxbridge Rd* 105 E7
Lovelace Rd, SE21 169 J2
Barnet EN4 41 H7
Surbiton KT6 181 F7
Love La, EC2 20 A3
N17 60 C7
SE18 136 E4
SE25 189 E3
Bexley DA5 159 F6
Mitcham CR4 185 H3
Morden SM4 184 D7
Pinner HA5 66 E3
Surbiton KT6 195 G2
Sutton SM3 198 B6
Woodford Green IG8 64 C6
Lovel Av, Well. DA16 158 A2
Lovelinch Cl, SE15 133 F6
Lovell Ho, E8 112 D1
Lovell Pl, SE16 *off Ropemaker Rd* 133 H3
Lovell Rd, Rich. TW10 163 F3
Southall UB1 103 H6
Loveridge Ms, NW6 *off Loveridge Rd* 90 C6
Loveridge Rd, NW6 90 C6
Lovers Wk, N3 56 D7
NW7 56 C6
SE10 134 E6
Lover's Wk, W1 24 B1
Lovett Dr, Cars. SM5 185 F7
Lovett's Pl, SW18 *off Old York Rd* 149 E4
Lovett Way, NW10 88 C5
Love Wk, SE5 152 A2
Lovibonds Av, Orp. BR6 207 E4
Lowbrook Rd, Ilf. IG1 99 E5
Low Cross Wd La, SE21 170 C3
Lowden Rd, N9 61 E1
SE24 151 H4
Southall UB1 102 E7
Lowe Av, E16 115 G5
Lowell St, E14 113 H6
Lower Addiscombe Rd, Croy. CR0 202 B1
Lower Addison Gdns, W14 128 B2
Lower Alderton Hall La, Loug. IG10 48 D5
Lower Belgrave St, SW1 24 D6
Lower Boston Rd, W7 124 B1
Lower Broad St, Dag. RM10 119 G1
Lower Camden, Chis. BR7 174 C7
Lower Ch St, Croy. CR0 *off Waddon New Rd* 201 H2
LOWER CLAPTON, E5 95 G4
Lower Clapton Rd, E5 95 E5
Lower Clarendon Wk, W11 *off Lancaster Rd* 108 B6
Lower Common S, SW15 147 H3
Lower Coombe St, Croy. CR0 201 J4
Lower Downs Rd, SW20 184 A1
Lower Drayton Pl, Croy. CR0 *off Drayton Rd* 201 H2
LOWER EDMONTON, N9 60 D1
Lower George St, Rich. TW9 145 G5
Lower Gravel Rd, Brom. BR2 206 B1
Lower Grn Gdns, Wor.Pk. KT4 197 G1
Lower Grn W, Mitch. CR4 185 H3
Lower Grosvenor Pl, SW1 24 D5
Lower Gro Rd, Rich. TW10 145 J6
Lower Hall La, E4 61 H5
Lower Hampton Rd, Sun. TW16 178 C3
Lower Ham Rd, Kings.T. KT2 163 G6
LOWER HOLLOWAY, N7 93 F5
Lower James St, W1 17 G5
Lower John St, W1 17 G5
Lower Kenwood Av, Enf. EN2 42 D5
Lower Kings Rd, Kings.T. KT2 181 H1
Lower Lea Crossing, E14 114 E7
E16 114 E7
Lower Maidstone Rd, N11 *off Telford Rd* 58 C6
Lower Mall, W6 127 H5
Lower Mardyke Av, Rain. RM13 119 J2
Lower Marsh, SE1 26 E4
Lower Marsh La, Kings.T. KT1 181 J4
Lower Mast Ho, SE18 *off Woolwich Ch St* 136 C3
Lower Merton Ri, NW3 91 H7
Lower Morden La, Mord. SM4 183 J6
Lower Mortlake Rd, Rich. TW9 145 H4
Lower Pk Rd, N11 58 C5
Belvedere DA17 139 G3
Loughton IG10 48 A5
Lower Queens Rd, Buck.H. IG9 64 A2
Lower Richmond Rd, SW14 146 B3
SW15 147 J3
Richmond TW9 146 A3
Lower Rd, SE1 26 E3
SE8 133 F3
SE16 133 F3
Belvedere DA17 139 G3
Harrow HA2 86 A2
Loughton IG10 48 D2
Sutton SM1 199 F4
Lower Robert St, WC2 *off John Adam St* 18 B6
Lower Sand Hills, T.Ditt. (Long Dit.) KT7 181 F7
Lower Sloane St, SW1 32 B2
Lower Sq, Islw. TW7 144 E3
Lower Strand, NW9 71 F2
Lower Sunbury Rd, Hmptn. TW12 179 F2
LOWER SYDENHAM, SE26 171 G4
Lower Sydenham Ind Est, SE26 *off Kangley Br Rd* 171 J5
Lower Tail, Wat. WD19 51 E3
Lower Talbot Wk, W11 *off Talbot Wk* 108 B6
Lower Teddington Rd, Kings.T. KT1 181 G1
Lower Ter, NW3 91 F3
Lower Thames St, EC3 20 C6
Lower Wd Rd, Esher (Clay.) KT10 194 D6
Lowestoft Cl, E5 *off Theydon Rd* 95 F2
Lowestoft Ms, E16 137 E2
Loweswater Cl, Wem. HA9 87 G2
Lowfield Rd, NW6 90 D7
W3 106 C6
Low Hall Cl, E4 46 A7
Low Hall La, E17 77 H6
Lowick Rd, Har. HA1 68 B4
Lowlands Dr, Stai. (Stanw.) TW19 140 A5
Lowlands Gdns, Rom. RM7 83 H6
Lowlands Rd, Har. HA1 68 B7
Pinner HA5 66 C7
Lowman Rd, N7 93 F4
Lowndes Cl, SW1 24 C6
Lowndes Ct, W1 17 F4
Bromley BR1 *off Queens Rd* 191 G2
Lowndes Pl, SW1 24 B6
Lowndes Sq, SW1 24 A4
Lowndes St, SW1 24 A5
Lowood Ct, SE19 170 C5
Lowood St, E1 *off Dellow St* 113 E7
Lowry Cres, Mitch. CR4 185 H2
Lowry Ho, E14 *off Cassilis Rd* 134 A2
Lowry Rd, Dag. RM8 100 B4
Lowshoe La, Rom. RM5 83 H1
Lowther Dr, Enf. EN2 42 E4
Lowther Gdns, SW7 23 E5
Lowther Hill, SE23 153 H7
Lowther Rd, E17 77 H2
N7 *off Liverpool Rd* 93 G5
SW13 147 F1
Kingston upon Thames KT2 181 J1
Stanmore HA7 69 J3
Lowth Rd, SE5 151 J2
LOXFORD, Ilf. IG1 99 F5
Loxford Av, E6 116 A2
Loxford La, Ilf. IG1, IG3 99 F5
Loxford Rd, Bark. IG11 99 E6
Loxford Ter, Bark. IG11 *off Fanshawe Av* 99 F6
Loxham Rd, E4 62 A7
Loxham St, WC1 10 B4
Loxley Cl, SE26 171 G5
Loxley Rd, SW18 167 G1
Hampton TW12 161 F4
Loxton Rd, SE23 171 G1
Loxwood Rd, N17 76 B3
Lubbock Rd, Chis. BR7 174 C7
Lubbock St, SE14 133 F7
Lucan Pl, SW3 31 G2
Lucan Rd, Barn. EN5 40 B3
Lucas Av, E13 115 H1
Harrow HA2 85 G2
Lucas Cl, NW10 *off Pound La* 89 G7
Lucas Ct, SW11 *off Strasburg Rd* 150 A1
Harrow HA2 85 G1
Lucas Gdns, N2 73 F2
Lucas Rd, SE20 171 F6
Lucas Sq, NW11 *off Hampstead Way* 72 D6
Lucas St, SE8 154 A1
Lucerne Cl, N13 58 E4
Lucerne Ct, Erith DA18 *off Middle Way* 138 E3
Lucerne Gro, E17 78 D4
Lucerne Ms, W8 *off Kensington Mall* 128 D1
Lucerne Rd, N5 93 H4
Orpington BR6 207 J1
Thornton Heath CR7 187 H5
Lucey Rd, SE16 29 H6
Lucey Way, SE16 29 J6
Lucien Rd, SW17 168 A4
SW19 166 E2
Lucknow St, SE18 137 H7
Lucorn Cl, SE12 155 F6
Lucton Ms, Loug. IG10 48 E4
Luctons Av, Buck.H. IG9 63 J1
Lucy Cres, W3 106 C5
Lucy Gdns, Dag. RM8 101 E3
Luddesdon Rd, Erith DA8 139 G7
Ludford Cl, Croy. CR0 *off Warrington Rd* 201 H4
Ludgate Bdy, EC4 19 G4
Ludgate Circ, EC4 19 G4
Ludgate Hill, EC4 19 G4
Ludgate Sq, EC4 19 H4
Ludham Cl, SE28 *off Rollesby Way* 118 C6
Ilford IG6 81 F1
Ludlow Cl, Brom. BR2 *off Aylesbury Rd* 191 G3
Harrow HA2 85 F4
Ludlow Mead, Wat. WD19 50 B3
Ludlow Rd, W5 105 F4
Feltham TW13 160 A4
Ludlow St, EC1 11 J5
Ludlow Way, N2 73 F4
Ludovick Wk, SW15 147 E4
Ludwick Ms, SE14 133 H7
Luffield Rd, SE2 138 B3
Luffman Rd, SE12 173 H3
Lugard Rd, SE15 153 E2
Lugg App, E12 98 D3
Luke Ho, E1 112 E6
Luke St, EC2 12 D5
Lukin Cres, E4 62 D3
Lukin St, E1 113 F6
Lukintone Cl, Loug. IG10 48 B6
Lullingstone Cl, Orp. BR5 *off Lullingstone Cres* 176 B7
Lullingstone Cres, Orp. BR5 176 A7
Lullingstone La, SE13 154 D6
Lullingstone Rd, Belv. DA17 139 F6
Lullington Garth, N12 56 C5
Borehamwood WD6 38 B5
Bromley BR1 173 E7
Lullington Rd, SE20 170 D7
Dagenham RM9 100 E7
Lulot Gdns, N19 92 B2
Lulworth, NW1 *off Agar Pl* 92 D7
SE17 36 B3
Lulworth Av, Houns. TW5 123 H7
Wembley HA9 69 F7
Lulworth Cl, Har. HA2 85 F3
Lulworth Cres, Mitch. CR4 185 H2
Lulworth Dr, Pnr. HA5 66 D7
Lulworth Gdns, Har. HA2 85 E2
Lulworth Ho, SW8 34 C7
Lulworth Rd, SE9 174 B2
SE15 153 E2
Welling DA16 157 J2
Lulworth Waye, Hayes UB4 102 C6
Lumen Rd, Wem. HA9 87 G2
Lumiere Ct, SW17 168 A2
Lumley Cl, Belv. DA17 139 G6
Lumley Ct, WC2 18 B6
Lumley Flats, SW1 *off Holbein Pl* 32 B3
Lumley Gdns, Sutt. SM3 198 B5
Lumley Rd, Sutt. SM3 198 B6
Lumley St, W1 16 C4
Luna Ho, SE16 29 J3
Luna Rd, Th.Hth. CR7 187 J3
Lundin Wk, Wat. WD19 50 D4
Lund Pt, E15 *off Carpenters Rd* 114 C1
Lundy Dr, Hayes UB3 121 H4
Lundy Wk, N1 *off Clifton Rd* 93 J6
Lunham Rd, SE19 170 B6
Lupin Cl, SW2 *off Palace Rd* 169 H2
Croydon CR0 *off Primrose La* 203 G1
West Drayton UB7 *off Magnolia St* 120 A5
Lupin Cres, Ilf. IG1 *off Bluebell Way* 99 E6
Lupino Ct, SE11 34 D2
Lupin Pt, SE1 29 G4
Lupton Cl, SE12 173 H4
Lupton St, NW5 92 C4
Lupus St, SW1 33 G4
Luralda Gdns, E14 *off Saunders Ness Rd* 134 C5
Lurgan Av, W6 128 A6
Lurline Gdns, SW11 150 A1
Luscombe Ct, Brom. BR2 190 E2
Luscombe Way, SW8 34 A7
Lushes Ct, Loug. IG10 *off Lushes Rd* 49 E5
Lushes Rd, Loug. IG10 49 E5
Lushington Rd, NW10 107 H2
SE6 172 B5
Lushington Ter, E8 *off Wayland Av* 94 D5
Luther Cl, Edg. HA8 54 C2
Luther King Cl, E17 77 H6
Luther Ms, Tedd. TW11 *off Luther Rd* 162 C5
Luther Rd, Tedd. TW11 162 C5
Luton Pl, SE10 134 C7
Luton Rd, E13 115 G4
E17 77 J3
Sidcup DA14 176 C3
Luton St, NW8 7 F6
Lutton Ter, NW3 91 F4
Luttrell Av, SW15 147 H5
Lutwyche Rd, SE6 171 J2
Lutyens Ho, SW1 *off Churchill Gdns* 33 F4
Luxborough La, Chig. IG7 64 B3
Luxborough St, W1 16 B1
Luxborough Twr, W1 *off Luxborough St* 16 B1
Luxembourg Ms, E15 *off Leytonstone Rd* 96 E5
Luxemburg Gdns, W6 128 A4
Luxfield Rd, SE9 174 B1
Luxford St, SE16 133 G4
Luxmore St, SE4 153 J1
Luxor St, SE5 151 H2
Lyall Av, SE21 170 B3
Lyall Ms, SW1 24 B6
Lyall Ms W, SW1 24 B6
Lyall St, SW1 24 B6
Lyal Rd, E3 113 H2
Lycée, The, SE11 35 F4
Lycett Pl, W12 *off Becklow Rd* 127 G2
Lyconby Gdns, Croy. CR0 189 H7
Lydd Cl, Sid. DA14 175 H3
Lydden Ct, SE9 157 H6
Lydden Gro, SW18 148 E7
Lydden Rd, SW18 148 E7
Lydd Rd, Bexh. DA7 139 F7
Lydeard Rd, E6 98 C7
Lydford Cl, N16 *off Pellerin Rd* 94 B5
Lydford Rd, N15 76 A5
NW2 90 A6
W9 108 C4
Lydhurst Av, SW2 169 F2
Lydney Cl, SW19 *off Princes Way* 166 B2
Lydon Rd, SW4 150 C3
Lydstep Rd, Chis. BR7 174 D4
Lyford Rd, SW18 149 G7
Lyford St, SE18 136 B4
Lygon Ho, SW6 *off Fulham Palace Rd* 148 B1
Lygon Pl, SW1 24 D6
Lyham Cl, SW2 151 E6
Lyham Rd, SW2 150 E5
Lyle Cl, Mitch. CR4 186 A7
Lyme Fm Rd, SE12 155 G4
Lyme Gro, E9 *off St. Thomas's Sq* 95 F7

Lymer Av, SE19 .....170 C5
Lyme Rd, Well. DA16 .....158 B1
Lymescote Gdns, Sutt. SM1 .....198 D2
Lyme St, NW1 .....92 C7
Lyme Ter, NW1 off Royal Coll St 92 C7
Lyminge Cl, Sid. DA14 .....175 J4
Lyminge Gdns, SW18 .....167 H1
Lymington Av, N22 .....75 G2
Lymington Cl, E6 off Valiant Way 116 C5
SW16 .....186 D2
Lymington Ct, Sutt. SM1 off All Saints Rd 199 F3
Lymington Gdns, Epsom KT19 .....197 F5
Lymington Rd, NW6 .....90 E6
Dagenham RM8 .....100 D1
Lyminster Cl, Hayes UB4 off West Quay Dr 102 E5
Lympstone Gdns, SE15 .....37 J7
Lynbridge Gdns, N13 .....59 H4
Lynbrook Gro, SE15 .....36 E7
Lynch Cl, SE3 off Paragon Pl 155 F2
Lynchen Cl, Houns. TW5 off The Avenue 142 A1
Lynch Wk, SE8 off Prince St 133 J6
Lyncott Cres, SW4 .....150 B4
Lyncroft Av, Pnr. HA5 .....66 E5
Lyncroft Gdns, NW6 .....90 D5
W13 .....125 F2
Hounslow TW3 .....143 J4
Lyndale, NW2 .....90 C4
Lyndale Av, NW2 .....90 C3
Lyndale Cl, SE3 .....135 F6
Lyndhurst Av, N12 .....57 J6
NW7 .....54 E6
SW16 .....186 D2
Pinner HA5 .....66 B1
Southall UB1 .....123 H1
Sunbury-on-Thames TW16 .....178 A3
Surbiton KT5 .....196 B1
Twickenham TW2 .....161 F1
Lyndhurst Cl, NW10 .....88 D3
Bexleyheath DA7 .....159 H3
Croydon CR0 .....202 C3
Orpington BR6 .....207 E4
Lyndhurst Ct, E18 off Churchfields 79 G1
Sutton SM2 off Overton Rd 198 D7
Lyndhurst Dr, E10 .....78 C7
New Malden KT3 .....183 E6
Lyndhurst Gdns, N3 .....72 B1
NW3 .....91 G5
Barking IG11 .....99 H6
Enfield EN1 .....44 B4
Ilford IG2 .....81 G6
Pinner HA5 .....66 B1
Lyndhurst Gro, SE15 .....152 B2
Lyndhurst Ho, SW15 off Ellisfield Dr 147 G7
Lyndhurst Ri, Chig. IG7 .....64 D4
Lyndhurst Rd, E4 .....62 C7
N18 .....60 D4
N22 .....59 F6
NW3 .....91 G5
Bexleyheath DA7 .....159 H3
Greenford UB6 .....103 H4
Thornton Heath CR7 .....187 G4
Lyndhurst Sq, SE15 .....152 C1
Lyndhurst Ter, NW3 .....91 G5
Lyndhurst Way, SE15 .....152 C1
Sutton SM2 .....198 D7
Lyndon Av, Pnr. HA5 .....51 E6
Sidcup DA15 .....157 J5
Wallington SM6 .....200 A3
Lyndon Rd, Belv. DA17 .....139 G4
Lyndon Yd, SW17 .....167 E4
Lyne Cres, E17 .....77 J1
Lyneham Dr, NW9 .....70 E1
Lyneham Wk, E5 off Boscombe Cl 95 H5
Lynette Av, SW4 .....150 B6
Lynett Rd, Dag. RM8 .....100 D2
Lynford Cl, Barn. EN5 off Rowley La 39 F5
Edgware HA8 .....54 C7
Lynford Gdns, Edg. HA8 .....54 B3
Ilford IG3 .....99 J2
Lynmere Rd, Well. DA16 .....158 B2
Lyn Ms, E3 off Tredegar Sq 113 J3
N16 .....94 B4
Lynmouth Av, Enf. EN1 .....44 C6
Morden SM4 .....184 A7
Lynmouth Dr, Ruis. HA4 .....84 B2
Lynmouth Gdns, Grnf. (Perivale) UB6 .....105 E1
Hounslow TW5 .....142 D1
Lynmouth Rd, E17 .....77 H6
N2 .....73 J3
N16 .....94 C1
Greenford (Perivale) UB6 .....105 E1
Lynn Cl, Har. HA3 .....68 A2
Lynne Cl, Orp. (Grn St Grn) BR6 .....207 J6
Lynne Way, Nthlt. UB5 .....102 D2
Lynn Ms, E11 off Lynn Rd 97 E2
Lynn Rd, E11 .....96 E2
SW12 .....150 B7
Ilford IG2 .....81 G7
Lynn St, Enf. EN2 .....44 A1
Lynsted Cl, Bexh. DA6 .....159 H5
Bromley BR1 .....191 J2
Lynsted Ct, Beck. BR3 off Churchfields Rd 189 H2
Lynsted Gdns, SE9 .....156 A3
Lynton Av, N12 .....57 G4
NW9 .....71 F4
W13 .....104 D6
Romford RM7 .....83 G1
Lynton Cl, NW10 .....88 E5
Chessington KT9 .....195 H4
Isleworth TW7 .....144 C4
Lynton Cres, Ilf. IG2 .....80 E6
Lynton Est, SE1 .....37 H2
Lynton Gdns, N11 .....58 D6
Enfield EN1 .....44 B7
Lynton Mead, N20 .....56 D3
Lynton Rd, E4 .....62 B5
N8 .....74 D5
NW6 .....108 C1
SE1 .....37 G2
W3 .....106 A7
Croydon CR0 .....187 G6
Harrow HA2 .....85 E2
New Malden KT3 .....182 D5
Lynton Ter, W3 .....106 B6
Lynwood Cl, E18 .....79 J1
Harrow HA2 .....85 E3
Lynwood Dr, Wor.Pk. KT4 .....197 G2
Lynwood Gdns, Croy. CR0 .....201 F4
Southall UB1 .....103 F6
Lynwood Gro, N21 .....59 G1
Orpington BR6 .....193 H7
Lynwood Rd, SW17 .....167 J3
W5 .....105 H4
Thames Ditton KT7 .....194 C2
Lynx Way, E16 .....116 A7
Lyon Business Pk, Bark. IG11 .....117 H2
Lyon Meade, Stan. HA7 .....69 F1
Lyon Pk Av, Wem. HA0 .....87 H6
Lyon Rd, SW19 .....185 F1
Harrow HA1 .....68 C6
Lyonsdown Av, Barn. (New Barn.) EN5 .....41 F6
Lyonsdown Rd, Barn. (New Barn.) EN5 .....41 F6
Lyons Pl, NW8 .....7 E5
Lyon St, N1 off Caledonian Rd 93 F7
Lyons Wk, W14 .....128 B4
Lyon Way, Grnf. UB6 .....104 B1
Lyoth Rd, Orp. BR5 .....207 F2
Lyric Dr, Grnf. UB6 .....103 H4
★ Lyric Hammersmith, W6 .....127 J4
Lyric Ms, SE26 .....171 F4
Lyric Rd, SW13 .....147 F1
Lyric Sq, W6 off King St 127 J4
Lysander Gdns, Surb. KT6 off Ewell Rd 181 J6
Lysander Gro, N19 .....92 D1
Lysander Ho, E2 off Temple St 112 E2
Lysander Ms, N19 off Lysander Gro 92 D1
Lysander Rd, Croy. CR0 .....201 F6
Lysander Way, Orp. BR6 .....207 F3
Lysias Rd, SW12 .....150 A6
Lysia St, SW6 .....128 A7
Lysons Wk, SW15 .....147 G5
Lytchet Rd, Brom. BR1 .....173 H7
Lytchet Way, Enf. EN3 .....45 F1
Lytchgate Cl, S.Croy. CR2 .....202 B7
Lytcott Dr, W.Mol. KT8 off Freeman Dr 179 F4
Lytcott Gro, SE22 .....152 C5
Lyte St, E2 off Bishops Way 113 F2
Lytham Av, Wat. WD19 .....50 D5
Lytham Cl, SE28 .....118 E6
Lytham Gro, W5 .....105 J3
Lytham St, SE17 .....36 B4
Lyttelton Cl, NW3 .....91 H7
Lyttelton Rd, E10 .....96 B3
N2 .....73 F5
Lyttleton Rd, N8 .....75 G3
Lytton Av, N13 .....59 G2
Lytton Cl, N2 .....73 G5
Loughton IG10 .....49 G3
Northolt UB5 .....85 F7
Lytton Gdns, Wall. SM6 .....200 D4
Lytton Gro, SW15 .....148 A5
Lytton Rd, E11 .....78 E7
Barnet EN5 .....41 F4
Pinner HA5 .....50 E7
Lytton Strachey Path, SE28 off Titmuss Av 118 B7
Lyveden Rd, SE3 .....135 H7
SW17 .....167 H6

M

Maberley Cres, SE19 .....170 D7
Maberley Rd, SE19 .....188 C1
Beckenham BR3 .....189 G3
Mabledon Pl, WC1 .....9 J4
Mablethorpe Rd, SW6 .....128 B7
Mabley St, E9 .....95 H6
McAdam Dr, Enf. EN2 .....43 H2
Macaret Cl, N20 .....41 E7
MacArthur Cl, E7 .....97 G6
Wembley HA9 .....88 B6
MacArthur Ter, SE7 .....136 A6
Macaulay Av, Esher KT10 .....194 B2
Macaulay Ct, SW4 .....150 B3
Macaulay Rd, E6 .....116 A2
SW4 .....150 B3
Macaulay Sq, SW4 .....150 B4
Macaulay Way, SE28 off Booth Cl 118 B7
McAuley Cl, SE1 .....26 E5
SE9 .....156 E5
Macauley Ms, SE13 .....154 C2
Macbean St, SE18 .....136 D3
Macbeth St, W6 .....127 H5
McCall Cl, SW4 off Jeffreys Rd 150 E2
McCall Cres, SE7 .....136 B5
McCarthy Rd, Felt. TW13 .....160 D5
Macclesfield Br, NW1 .....7 H1
Macclesfield Rd, EC1 .....11 J3
SE25 .....189 E5
Macclesfield St, W1 .....17 J5
McCoid Way, SE1 .....27 J4
McCrone Ms, NW3 off Belsize La 91 G6
McCullum Rd, E3 .....113 J1
McDermott Cl, SW11 .....149 H3
McDermott Rd, SE15 .....152 D3
Macdonald Av, Dag. RM10 .....101 H3
Macdonald Rd, E7 .....97 G4
E17 .....78 C2
N11 .....57 J5
N19 .....92 C2
McDonough Cl, Chess. KT9 .....195 H4
McDowall Cl, E16 .....115 F5
McDowall Rd, SE5 .....151 J1
Macduff Rd, SW11 .....150 A1
Mace Cl, E1 off Kennet St 132 E1
McEntee Av, E17 .....77 H1
Mace St, E2 .....113 G2
McEwen Way, E15 .....114 D1
Macey Ho, SW11 off Surrey La 149 H1
Macfarland Gro, SE15 .....36 E7
MacFarlane La, Islw. TW7 .....124 C6
Macfarlane Rd, W12 .....127 J1
Macfarren Pl, NW1 .....8 C6
McGrath Rd, E15 .....97 F5
Macgregor Rd, E16 .....115 J5
McGregor Rd, W11 .....108 C6
Machell Rd, SE15 .....153 F3
McIntosh Cl, Wall. SM6 .....200 E7
Mackay Rd, SW4 .....150 B3
McKay Rd, SW20 .....165 H7
McKellar Cl, Bushey (Bushey Hth) WD23 .....51 J2
Mackennal St, NW8 .....7 H2
Mackenzie Cl, W12 off Australia Rd 107 H7
Mackenzie Rd, N7 .....93 F6
Beckenham BR3 .....189 F2
Mackenzie Wk, E14 .....134 A1
McKerrell Rd, SE15 .....152 D1
Mackeson Rd, NW3 .....91 J4
Mackie Rd, SW2 .....151 G7
Mackintosh La, E9 off Homerton High St 95 G5
Macklin St, WC2 .....18 B3
Mackrow Wk, E14 off Robin Hood La 114 C7
Macks Rd, SE16 .....37 J1
Mackworth St, NW1 .....9 F3
Maclaren Ms, SW15 off Clarendon Dr 147 J4
Maclean Rd, SE23 .....153 H6
Macleod Rd, N21 .....43 E5
McLeod Rd, SE2 .....138 B4
McLeod's Ms, SW7 .....22 B6
Macleod St, SE17 .....36 A4
Maclise Rd, W14 .....128 B3
McMillan St, SE8 .....134 A6
McMillan Student Village, SE8 off Creek Rd 134 A6
Macmillan Way, SW17 .....168 B4
McNair Rd, Sthl. UB2 .....123 H2
McNeil Rd, SE5 .....152 B2
McNicol Dr, NW10 .....106 C2
Macoma Rd, SE18 .....137 G6
Macoma Ter, SE18 .....137 G6
Maconochies Rd, E14 .....134 B5
Macquarie Way, E14 .....134 B4
McRae La, Mitch. CR4 .....185 J7
Macroom Rd, W9 .....108 C3
Mac's Pl, EC4 .....19 F3
★ Madame Tussauds, NW1 .....8 B6
Mada Rd, Orp. BR6 .....206 E3
Maddams St, E3 .....114 B4
Maddison Cl, N2 off Long La 73 F2
Teddington TW11 .....162 C6
Maddocks Cl, Sid. DA14 .....176 E5
Maddock Way, SE17 .....35 H6
Maddox St, W1 .....16 E5
Madeira Av, Brom. BR1 .....172 E7
Madeira Gro, Wdf.Grn. IG8 .....63 J6
Madeira Rd, E11 .....96 D1
N13 .....59 H4
SW16 .....169 E5
Mitcham CR4 .....185 J4
Madeleine Cl, Rom. RM6 .....82 C6
Madeley Rd, W5 .....105 H6
Madeline Gro, Ilf. IG1 .....99 G5
Madeline Rd, SE20 .....188 D1
Madge Gill Way, E6 off Ron Leighton Way 116 B1
Madinah Rd, E8 .....94 D6
Madingley, Kings.T. KT1 off St. Peters Rd 182 A2
Madison Bldg, SE10 off Blackheath Rd 154 B1
Madison Ct, Dag. RM10 off Reede Way 101 H6
Madison Cres, Bexh. DA7 .....138 C7
Madison Gdns, Bexh. DA7 .....138 C7
Bromley BR2 .....191 F3
Madison Hts, Houns. TW3 off High St 143 J3
Madras Pl, N7 .....93 G6
Madras Rd, Ilf. IG1 .....98 E4
Madrid Rd, SW13 .....147 G1
Madrigal La, SE5 .....131 H7
Madron St, SE17 .....36 E3
Mafeking Av, E6 .....116 A2
Brentford TW8 .....125 H6
Ilford IG2 .....81 G7
Mafeking Rd, E16 .....115 F4
N17 .....76 D2
Enfield EN1 .....44 C3
Magdala Av, N19 .....92 B2
Magdala Rd, Islw. TW7 .....144 D3
South Croydon CR2 off Napier Rd 202 A7
Magdalene Cl, SE15 off Pilkington Rd 152 E2
Magdalene Gdns, E6 .....116 D4
N20 .....57 J1
Magdalen Ms, NW3 off Frognal 91 F6
Magdalen Pas, E1 .....21 G5
Magdalen Rd, SW18 .....167 F1
Magdalen St, SE1 .....28 D2
Magee St, SE11 .....35 E5
Magellan Pl, E14 off Maritime Quay 134 A4
Maggie Blakes Causeway, SE1 off Shad Thames 29 F2
Magnet Rd, Wem. HA9 .....87 G2
Magnin Cl, E8 off Wilde Cl 112 D1
Magnolia Cl, E10 .....96 A2
Kingston upon Thames KT2 .....164 B6
Magnolia Ct, Felt. TW13 off Highfield Rd 160 A1
Harrow HA3 .....69 J7
Wallington SM6 off Parkgate Rd 200 B5
Magnolia Gdns, Edg. HA8 .....54 C4
Magnolia Pl, SW4 .....150 D5
W5 .....105 G5
Magnolia Rd, W4 .....126 B6
Magnolia St, West Dr. UB7 .....120 A4
Magnolia Way, Epsom KT19 .....196 C5
Magnum Ho, Kings.T. KT2 off London Rd 182 A1

Magnus Ct, N9
off Bedevere Rd 60 D3
Magpie All, EC4 19 F4
Magpie Cl, E7 97 F5
NW9 *off Eagle Dr* 71 E2
Enfield EN1 44 D1
Magpie Hall Cl, Brom. BR2 192 B6
Magpie Hall La, Brom. BR2 192 C5
Magpie Hall Rd, Bushey (Bushey Hth) WD23 52 B2
Magpie Pl, SE14
off Milton Ct Rd 133 H6
Magri Wk, E1
off Ashfield St 113 F5
Maguire Dr, Rich. TW10 163 F4
Maguire St, SE1 29 G3
Mahatma Gandhi Ind Est, SE24 *off Milkwood Rd* 151 H4
Mahlon Av, Ruis. HA4 84 B5
Mahogany Cl, SE16 133 H1
Mahon Cl, Enf. EN1 44 C1
Maida Av, E4 46 B7
W2 14 D1
MAIDA HILL, W9 108 C4
Maida Rd, Belv. DA17 139 G3
MAIDA VALE, W9 6 B5
Maida Vale, W9 6 C4
Maida Way, E4 46 B7
Maiden Erlegh Av, Bex. DA5 176 E1
Maiden La, NW1 92 D7
SE1 28 A1
WC2 18 B6
Maiden Pl, NW5 92 C3
Maiden Rd, E15 97 E7
Maidenstone Hill, SE10 154 C1
Maids of Honour Row, Rich. TW9
off The Green 145 G5
Maidstone Av, Rom. RM5 83 J2
Maidstone Bldgs Ms, SE1 28 A2
Maidstone Ho, E14
off Carmen St 114 B6
Maidstone Rd, N11 58 C6
Sidcup DA14 176 D6
Main Av, Enf. EN1 44 C5
Main Dr, Wem. HA9 87 G3
Mainridge Rd, Chis. BR7 174 D4
Main Rd, Sid. DA14 175 H3
Main St, Felt. TW13 160 D5
Maismore St, SE15 37 J6
Maisonettes, The, Sutt. SM1 198 C5
Maitland Cl, Houns. TW4 143 F3
Maitland Cl Est, SE10
off Greenwich High Rd 134 B7
Maitland Pk Est, NW3 91 J6
Maitland Pk Rd, NW3 91 J6
Maitland Pk Vil, NW3 91 J6
Maitland Pl, E5
off Lower Clapton Rd 95 F4
Maitland Rd, E15 97 F6
SE26 171 G6
Majendie Rd, SE18 137 G5
Majestic Way, Mitch. CR4 185 J2
Major Cl, SW9 151 H3
Major Rd, E15 96 C5
SE16 29 J5
Makepeace Av, N6 92 A2
Makepeace Rd, E11 79 G4
Northolt UB5 102 E2
Makins St, SW3 31 H2
Malabar St, E14 134 A2
Malam Gdns, E14
off Wades Pl 114 B7
Malbrook Rd, SW15 147 H4
Malcolm Ct, Stan. HA7 53 F5
Malcolm Cres, NW4 71 G6
Malcolm Dr, Surb. KT6 195 H1
Malcolm Pl, E2 113 F4
Malcolm Rd, E1 113 F4
SE20 171 F7
SE25 188 D6
SW19 166 B6
Malcolms Way, N14 42 C5
Malcolm Way, E11 79 G5
Malden Av, SE25 188 E4
Greenford UB6 86 B5
Malden Ct, N.Mal. KT3 183 H3
Malden Cres, NW1 92 A6
Malden Grn Av, Wor.Pk. KT4 197 F1
Malden Grn Ms, Wor.Pk. KT4 *off Malden Rd* 197 G1
Malden Hill, N.Mal. KT3 183 F3
Malden Hill Gdns, N.Mal. KT3 183 F3
Malden Junct, N.Mal. KT3 183 F5
Malden Pk, N.Mal. KT3 183 F6
Malden Pl, NW5
off Grafton Ter 92 A5
Malden Rd, NW5 92 A5
Borehamwood WD6 38 A3
New Malden KT3 183 E5
Sutton SM3 198 A4
Worcester Park KT4 183 F7
Malden Way, N.Mal. KT3 183 F5
Maldon Cl, E15
off Maryland St 96 D5
N1 111 J1
SE5 152 B3
Maldon Ct, Wall. SM6 200 C5
Maldon Rd, N9 60 C3
W3 106 C7
Romford RM7 83 J7
Wallington SM6 200 B5
Maldon Wk, Wdf.Grn. IG8 63 J6
Malet Pl, WC1 9 H6
Malet St, WC1 9 H6
Maley Av, SE27 169 H2
Malford Ct, E18 79 G2
Malford Gro, E18 79 F4
Malfort Rd, SE5 152 B3
Malham Cl, N11
off Catterick Cl 58 A6
Malham Rd, SE23 171 G1
Malham Ter, N18
off Dysons Rd 61 E6
Malins Cl, Barn. EN5 39 H5
Mall, The, N14 58 E3
SW1 25 G3
SW14 146 C5
W5 105 H7
Bromley BR1 191 G3
Croydon CR0 201 J2
Harrow HA3 69 J6
Surbiton KT6 181 G5
Mallams Ms, SW9
off St. James's Cres 151 H3
Mallard Cl, E9
off Berkshire Rd 95 J6
NW6 108 D2
W7 124 B2
Barnet (New Barn.) EN5
off The Hook 41 G6
Twickenham TW2
off Stephenson Rd 143 G7
Mallard Path, SE28
off Goosander Way 137 G3
Mallard Pl, Twick. TW1 162 D3
Mallard Pt, E3
off Rainhill Way 114 B3
Mallards, E11 79 G7
Mallards Rd, Bark. IG11 118 A3
Woodford Green IG8 63 H7
Mallard Wk, Beck. BR3 189 G5
Sidcup DA14 176 C5
Mallard Way, NW9 70 C7
Mall Chambers, W8
off Kensington Mall 128 D1
Mallet Dr, Nthlt. UB5 85 F5
Mallet Rd, SE13 154 D6
Mall Ex, The, Ilf. IG1 98 E2
★ **Mall Galleries**, SW1 25 J1
Malling, SE13 154 C5
Malling Cl, Croy. CR0 189 F6
Malling Gdns, Mord. SM4 185 F6
Malling Way, Brom. BR2 191 F7
Mallinson Rd, SW11 149 H5
Croydon CR0 200 D3
Mallord St, SW3 31 F5
Mallory Cl, E14
off Uamvar St 114 B5
SE4 153 H4
Mallory Gdns, Barn. (E.Barn.) EN4 42 A7
Mallory St, NW8 7 H5
Mallow Cl, Croy. CR0
off Marigold Way 203 G1
Mallow Mead, NW7 56 B7
Mallow St, EC1 12 B5
Mall Rd, W6 127 H5
Mall Shop Cen, The, Dag. RM10 *off Heathway* 101 G6
Mall Walthamstow, The, E17 77 J4
Malmains Cl, Beck. BR3 190 D5
Malmains Way, Beck. BR3 190 C4
Malmesbury, E2
off Cyprus St 113 F2
Malmesbury Rd, E3 113 J3
E16 115 E5
E18 79 F1
Morden SM4 185 F7
Malmesbury Ter, E16 115 F5
Malmsmead Ho, E9
off Kingsmead Way 95 H5
Malory Cl, Beck. BR3 189 H2
Malory Ct, N9
off Galahad Rd 60 D3
Malpas Dr, Pnr. HA5 66 D5
Malpas Rd, E8 94 E6
SE4 153 J2
Dagenham RM9 100 D6
Malta Rd, E10 96 A1
Malta St, EC1 11 H5
Maltby Rd, Chess. KT9 196 A6
Maltby St, SE1 29 F4
Malthouse Dr, W4 127 E6
Feltham TW13 160 D5
Malthouse Pas, SW13
off The Terrace 147 E2
Malthus Path, SE28
off Owen Cl 138 C1
Malting Ho, E14 113 J7
Maltings, The, Orp. BR6 207 J1
Worcester Park KT4
off Sherbrooke Way 183 H7
Maltings Cl, E3 114 C3
SW13
off Cleveland Gdns 147 E2
Maltings Ms, Sid. DA15
off Station Rd 176 A3
Maltings Pl, SE1 29 E4
SW6 149 E1
Malting Way, Islw. TW7 144 C3
Malton Ms, SE18
off Malton St 137 H6
W10
off Cambridge Gdns 108 B6
Malton Rd, W10
off St. Marks Rd 108 B6
Malton St, SE18 137 H6
Maltravers St, WC2 18 D5
Malt St, SE1 37 H5
Malva Cl, SW18
off St. Ann's Hill 149 E5
Malvern Av, E4 62 D7
Bexleyheath DA7 138 E7
Harrow HA2 85 E3
Malvern Cl, SE20
off Derwent Rd 188 D2
W10 108 C5
Mitcham CR4 186 C3
Surbiton KT6 195 H1
Malvern Ct, SE14
off Avonley Rd 133 F7
SW7 31 F2
Sutton SM2
off Overton Rd 198 D7
Malvern Dr, Felt. TW13 160 D5
Ilford IG3 99 J4
Woodford Green IG8 63 J5
Malvern Gdns, NW2 90 B2
NW6 *off Carlton Vale* 108 C2
Harrow HA3 69 H3
Loughton IG10 48 C6
Malvern Ms, NW6
off Malvern Rd 108 D3
Malvern Pl, NW6 108 C3
Malvern Rd, E6 116 B1
E8 94 D7
E11 97 E2
N8 75 F3
N17 76 D3
NW6 108 D3
Hampton TW12 161 G7
Hayes UB3 121 H7
Surbiton KT6 195 H2
Thornton Heath CR7 187 G4
Malvern Ter, N1 111 G1
N9 *off Latymer Rd* 60 C1
Malvern Way, W13
off Templewood 105 E5
Malwood Rd, SW12 150 B6
Malyons Rd, SE13 154 B5
Malyons Ter, SE13 154 B5
Managers St, E14
off Prestons Rd 134 C1
Manatee Pl, Wall. SM6
off Croydon Rd 200 D3
Manaton Cl, SE15 152 E3
Manaton Cres, Sthl. UB1 103 G6
Manbey Gro, E15 96 E6
Manbey Pk Rd, E15 96 E6
Manbey Rd, E15 96 E6
Manbey St, E15 96 E6
Manbre Rd, W6 127 J6
Manbrough Av, E6 116 C3
Manchester Ct, E16 115 H6
Manchester Dr, W10 108 B4
Manchester Gro, E14 134 C5
Manchester Ms, W1 16 B2
Manchester Rd, E14 134 C5
N15 76 A6
Thornton Heath CR7 187 J3
Manchester Sq, W1 16 B3
Manchester St, W1 16 B2
Manchester Way, Dag. RM10 101 H4
Manchuria Rd, SW11 150 A6
Manciple St, SE1 28 B4
Mandalay Rd, SW4 150 C5
Mandarin St, E14
off Salter St 114 A7
Mandarin Way, Hayes UB4 102 D6
Mandela Cl, NW10 88 C7
Mandela Rd, E16 115 G6
Mandela St, NW1 110 C1
SW9 131 G7
Mandela Way, SE1 36 E1
Mandel Ho, SW18
off Eastfields Av 148 D4
Mandeville Cl, SE3
off Vanbrugh Pk 135 F7
SW20 184 B1
Mandeville Ct, E4 61 H4
Mandeville Dr, Surb. KT6 195 G1
Mandeville Ho, SE1 37 G3
Mandeville Ms, SW4
off Clapham Pk Rd 150 E4
Mandeville Pl, W1 16 C3
Mandeville Rd, N14 58 B2
Isleworth TW7 144 D2
Northolt UB5 85 G7
Mandeville St, E5 95 H3
Mandrake Rd, SW17 167 J3
Mandrake Way, E15 96 E7
Mandrell Rd, SW2 150 E5
Manette St, W1 17 J4
Manford Way, Chig. IG7 65 H4
Manfred Rd, SW15 148 C5
Manger Rd, N7 93 E6
Mangold Way, Erith DA18 138 E3
Manhattan Bldg, E3
off Fairfield Rd 114 A2
Manhattan Wf, E16 135 G2
Manilla St, E14 134 A2
Manister Rd, SE2 138 A3
Manitoba Ct, SE16
off Renforth St 133 F2
Manitoba Gdns, Orp. (Grn St Grn) BR6
off Superior Dr 207 J6
Manley Ct, N16
off Stoke Newington High St 94 C3
Manley St, NW1 110 A1
Mann Cl, Croy. CR0
off Scarbrook Rd 201 J3
Manneby Prior, N1
off Cumming St 10 D2
Manningford Cl, EC1 11 G3
Manning Gdns, Har. HA3 69 G7
Manning Pl, Rich. TW10
off Grove Rd 145 J6
Manning Rd, E17
off Southcote Rd 77 H5
Dagenham RM10 101 G6
Manningtree Cl, SW19 166 B1
Manningtree Rd, Ruis. HA4 84 B4
Manningtree St, E1 21 H3
Mannin Rd, Rom. RM6 82 B7
Mannock Dr, Loug. IG10 49 F2
Mannock Ms, E18 79 H1
Mannock Rd, N22 75 H3
Manns Cl, Islw. TW7 144 C5
Manns Rd, Edg. HA8 54 A6
Manoel Rd, Twick. TW2 161 J2
Manor Av, SE4 153 J2
Hounslow TW4 142 D3
Northolt UB5 85 F7
Manorbrook, SE3 155 G4
Manor Circ, Rich. TW9 146 A3
Manor Cl, E17
off Manor Rd 77 H2
NW7 *off Manor Dr* 54 D5
NW9 70 B5
SE28 118 C6
Barnet EN5 40 B4
Worcester Park KT4 197 E1
Manor Cotts App, N2 73 F2
Manor Ct, E10
off Grange Pk Rd 96 B1
N2 73 H5
SW6 *off Bagley's La* 149 E1
Twickenham TW2 161 J2
Wembley HA9 87 H5
Manor Ct Rd, W7 104 B7
Manor Cres, Surb. KT5 182 A6
Manordene Cl, T.Ditt. KT7 194 D1
Manordene Rd, SE28 118 C6
Manor Dr, N14 42 B7
N20 57 H3
NW7 54 D5
Epsom KT19 196 E6
Esher KT10 194 C2
Feltham TW13
off Lebanon Av 160 D5
Sunbury-on-Thames TW16 178 A2
Surbiton KT5 181 J6
Wembley HA9 87 J4
Manor Dr, The, Wor.Pk. KT4 197 E1
Manor Dr N, N.Mal. KT3 182 D7
Worcester Park KT4 196 E1
Manor Est, SE16 132 E4
Manor Fm Cl, Wor.Pk. KT4 196 E1
Manor Fm Dr, E4 63 E3

Manor Fm Rd, Th.Hth. CR7 187 G2
Wembley HA0 105 G2
Manorfield Cl, N19 *off Junction Rd* 92 C4
Manor Flds, SW15 148 A6
Manorfields Cl, Chis. BR7 193 J3
Manor Gdns, N7 92 E3
SW20 184 C2
W3 126 A4
W4 *off Devonshire Rd* 127 E5
Hampton TW12 161 H7
Richmond TW9 145 J4
Ruislip HA4 84 C5
South Croydon CR2 202 C6
Sunbury-on-Thames TW16 178 A2
Manor Gate, Nthlt. UB5 84 E7
Manorgate Rd, Kings.T. KT2 182 A1
Manor Gro, SE15 133 F6
Beckenham BR3 190 B2
Richmond TW9 146 A4
Manor Hall Av, NW4 71 J2
Manor Hall Dr, NW4 72 A2
Manorhall Gdns, E10 96 A1
Manor Ho Dr, NW6 90 A7
Manor Ho Est, Stan. HA7 53 E6
Manor Ho Way, Islw. TW7 144 E3
Manor La, SE12 155 E6
SE13 154 E4
Feltham TW13 160 A2
Hayes (Harling.) UB3 121 G6
Sunbury-on-Thames TW16 178 A2
Sutton SM1 199 F5
Manor La Ter, SE13 154 E4
Manor Ms, NW6 *off Cambridge Av* 108 D2
SE4 153 J2
Manor Mt, SE23 171 F1
Manor Par, NW10 *off Station Rd* 107 F2
MANOR PARK, E12 98 B4
Manor Pk, SE13 154 D4
Chislehurst BR7 193 G2
Richmond TW9 145 J4
Manor Pk Cl, W.Wick. BR4 204 B1
Manor Pk Cres, Edg. HA8 54 A6
Manor Pk Dr, Har. HA2 67 H3
Manor Pk Gdns, Edg. HA8 54 A5
Manor Pk Par, SE13 *off Lee High Rd* 154 D4
Manor Pk Rd, E12 98 A4
N2 73 F3
NW10 107 F1
Chislehurst BR7 193 F1
Sutton SM1 199 F5
West Wickham BR4 204 B1
Manor Pl, SE17 35 H4
Chislehurst BR7 193 G1
Feltham TW14 160 A1
Mitcham CR4 186 C3
Sutton SM1 199 E4
Manor Rd, E10 78 A7
E15 114 E3
E16 114 E3
E17 77 H2
N16 94 A2
N17 76 D1
N22 59 E6
SE25 188 D4
SW20 184 C2
W13 104 D7
Barking IG11 99 J6
Barnet EN5 40 B5
Beckenham BR3 190 B2
Bexley DA5 177 H1
Chigwell IG7 64 E5
Dagenham RM10 101 J6
East Molesey KT8 180 A4
Enfield EN2 44 A2
Harrow HA1 68 D6
Hayes UB3 102 A6
Loughton IG10 47 H6
Mitcham CR4 186 C4
Richmond TW9 145 J3
Romford (Chad.Hth) RM6 82 D6
Sidcup DA15 175 J3
Sutton SM2 198 C7
Teddington TW11 162 E5
Twickenham TW2 161 J2
Wallington SM6 200 B4
West Wickham BR4 204 B2
Woodford Green IG8 64 C6
Manor Rd N, Esher KT10 194 C3
Thames Ditton KT7 194 D2
Wallington SM6 200 B4
Manor Rd S, Esher KT10 194 B4
Manorside, Barn. EN5 40 B4
Manorside Cl, SE2 138 C4
Manor Sq, Dag. RM8 100 D2
Manor Vale, Brent. TW8 125 F5
Manor Vw, N3 72 E2
Manor Way, E4 62 D4
NW9 70 E3
SE3 155 F4
SE23 153 F7
SE28 138 C1
Beckenham BR3 190 A2
Bexley DA5 177 G1
Borehamwood WD6 38 C4
Bromley BR2 192 B6
Manorway, Enf. EN1 44 B7
Manor Way, Har. HA2 67 H4
Mitcham CR4 186 C3
Orpington BR5 193 F4
South Croydon CR2 202 B6
Southall UB2 122 D4
Manorway, Wdf.Grn. IG8 63 J5
Manor Way, Wor.Pk. KT4 197 E1
Manor Way, The, Wall. SM6 200 B4
Manpreet Ct, E12 *off Morris Av* 98 C5
Manresa Rd, SW3 31 G4
Mansard Beeches, SW17 168 A5
Mansard Cl, Pnr. HA5 66 D3
Manse Cl, Hayes (Harling.) UB3 121 G6
Mansel Gro, E17 78 A1
Mansell Rd, W3 126 D2
Greenford UB6 103 H5
Mansell St, E1 21 G6
Mansel Rd, SW19 166 B6
Mansergh Cl, SE18 136 B7
Manse Rd, N16 94 C3
Mansfield Av, N15 76 A4
Barnet EN4 41 J6
Ruislip HA4 84 B1
Mansfield Cl, N9 44 D6
Mansfield Hill, E4 62 B1
Mansfield Ms, W1 16 D2
Mansfield Pl, NW3 *off New End* 91 F4
South Croydon CR2 202 A6
Mansfield Rd, E11 79 H6
E17 77 J4
NW3 91 J5
W3 106 B4
Chessington KT9 195 F5
Ilford IG1 98 D2
South Croydon CR2 202 A6
Mansfield St, W1 16 D2
Mansford St, E2 13 J2
Manship Rd, Mitch. CR4 168 A7
Mansion Cl, SW9 *off Cowley Rd* 151 G1
Mansion Gdns, NW3 91 E3
★ **Mansion Ho**, EC4 20 B4
Mansion Ho Pl, EC4 20 B4
Mansion Ho St, EC4 20 B4
Mansions, The, SW5 *off Earls Ct Rd* 30 A3
Manson Ms, SW7 30 D2
Manson Pl, SW7 30 E2
Mansted Gdns, Rom. RM6 82 C7
Manston Av, Sthl. UB2 123 G4
Manston Cl, SE20 *off Garden Rd* 189 F1
Manstone Rd, NW2 90 B5
Manston Gro, Kings.T. KT2 163 G5
Manthorp Rd, SE18 137 F5
Mantilla Rd, SW17 168 A4
Mantle Rd, SE4 153 H3
Mantlet Cl, SW16 168 C7
Mantle Way, E15 *off Romford Rd* 96 E7
Manton Av, W7 124 C2
Manton Rd, SE2 138 A4
Mantua St, SW11 149 G3
Mantus Cl, E1 *off Mantus Rd* 113 F4
Mantus Rd, E1 113 F4
Manuka Cl, W7 *off Grosvenor Rd* 124 D1
Manus Way, N20 *off Blakeney Cl* 57 F1
Manville Gdns, SW17 168 B3
Manville Rd, SW17 168 A2
Manwood Rd, SE4 153 J5
Manwood St, E16 136 C1
Manygates, SW12 168 B2
Mapesbury Ms, NW4 *off Station Rd* 71 G6
Mapesbury Rd, NW2 90 B7
Mapeshill Pl, NW2 89 J6
Mape St, E2 112 E4
Maple Av, E4 61 J5
W3 127 E1
Harrow HA2 85 H2
Maple Cl, N3 56 D6
N16 76 D6
SW4 150 D6
Maple Cl, Buckhurst Hill IG9 64 A3
Hampton TW12 161 F6
Hayes UB4 102 D3
Ilford IG6 65 H5
Mitcham CR4 186 B1
Orpington BR5 193 G5
Ruislip HA4 66 B6
Maple Ct, N.Mal. KT3 182 D3
Maple Cres, Sid. DA15 158 A6
Maplecroft Cl, E6 *off Allhallows Rd* 116 B6
Mapledale Av, Croy. CR0 202 D2
Mapledene, Chis. BR7 175 F5
Mapledene Est, E8 *off Mapledene Rd* 94 D7
Mapledene Rd, E8 94 C7
Maple Gdns, Edg. HA8 54 E7
Maple Gate, Loug. IG10 48 D2
Maple Gro, NW9 70 C7
W5 125 G3
Brentford TW8 124 E7
Southall UB1 103 F5
Maple Ho, NW3 *off Maitland Pk Vil* 91 J6
Maplehurst Cl, Kings.T. KT1 181 H4
Maple Ind Est, Felt. TW13 *off Maple Way* 160 B3
Maple Leaf Dr, Sid. DA15 175 J1
Mapleleafe Gdns, Ilf. IG6 80 E3
Maple Leaf Sq, SE16 *off Fishermans Dr* 133 G2
Maple Ms, NW6 6 A1
SW16 169 F5
Maple Pl, N17 *off Park La* 60 D7
W1 9 G6
Maple Rd, E11 79 E6
SE20 189 E1
Hayes UB4 102 C3
Surbiton KT6 181 H5
Maples, The, Esher (Clay.) KT10 194 D7
Maples Pl, E1 *off Raven Row* 113 E5
Maplestead Rd, SW2 151 F7
Dagenham RM9 118 B1
Maple St, E2 13 J2
W1 17 F1
Romford RM7 83 J4
Maplethorpe Rd, Th.Hth. CR7 187 G4
Mapleton Cl, Brom. BR2 191 G6
Mapleton Cres, SW18 148 E6
Mapleton Rd, E4 62 C3
SW18 148 E6
Enfield EN1 45 E2
Maple Wk, W10 *off Sixth Av* 108 B4
Maple Way, Felt. TW13 160 A3
Maplin Cl, N21 43 F6
Maplin Ho, SE2 *off Wolvercote Rd* 138 D2
Maplin Rd, E16 115 G6
Maplin St, E3 113 J3
Mapperley Dr, Wdf.Grn. IG8 *off Forest Dr* 62 E7
Marabou Cl, E12 98 B5
Maran Way, Erith DA18 138 D2
Marathon Ho, NW1 15 J1
Marathon Way, SE28 137 J2
Marban Rd, W9 108 C3
★ **Marble Arch**, W1 16 A5
Marble Arch Apts, W1 *off Harrowby St* 15 H3
Marble Cl, W3 126 B1
Marble Dr, NW2 90 A1
Marble Hill Cl, Twick. TW1 144 E7
Marble Hill Gdns, Twick. TW1 144 E7
★ **Marble Hill Ho**, Twick. TW1 145 F7
Marble Ho, SE18 *off Felspar Cl* 137 J5
Marble Quay, E1 29 H1
Marbrook Ct, SE12 173 J3
Marcella Rd, SW9 151 G2
Marcellina Way, Orp. BR6 207 H3
Marchant Rd, E11 96 D2
Marchant St, SE14 133 H6
Marchbank Rd, W14 128 C6
Marchmont Gdns, Rich. TW10 *off Marchmont Rd* 145 J5
Marchmont Rd, Rich. TW10 145 J5
Wallington SM6 200 C7
Marchmont St, WC1 10 A5
March Rd, Twick. TW1 144 D7
Marchside Cl, Houns. TW5 142 D1
Marchwood Cl, SE5 132 B7
Marchwood Cres, W5 105 F6
Marcia Rd, SE1 37 E2
Marcilly Rd, SW18 149 G5
Marco Dr, Pnr. HA5 51 F7
Marconi Pl, N11 58 B4
Marconi Rd, E10 96 A1
Marconi Way, Sthl. UB1 103 H6
Marcon Pl, E8 94 E6
Marco Rd, W6 127 J3
Marcourt Lawns, W5 105 H4
Marcus Ct, E15 115 E1
Marcus Garvey Ms, SE22 *off St. Aidan's Rd* 152 E5
Marcus Garvey Way, SE24 151 G4
Marcus St, E15 115 F1
SW18 149 E6
Marcus Ter, SW18 149 E6
Mardale Dr, NW9 70 D5
Mardell Rd, Croy. CR0 189 G5
Marden Av, Brom. BR2 191 G6
Marden Cres, Bex. DA5 159 J5
Croydon CR0 187 F6
Marden Ho, E8 *off Bodney Rd* 94 E5
Marden Rd, N17 76 B3
Croydon CR0 187 F6
Marden Sq, SE16 132 E3
Marder Rd, W13 124 D2
Mardyke Cl, Rain. RM13 119 J2
Mardyke Ho, SE17 *off Crosslet St* 36 C1
Marechal Niel Av, Sid. DA15 175 G3
Maresfield, Croy. CR0 202 B3
Maresfield Gdns, NW3 91 F5
Mare St, E8 113 E1
Marfleet Cl, Cars. SM5 199 H2
Margaret Av, E4 46 B6
Margaret Bondfield Av, Bark. IG11 100 A7
Margaret Bldgs, N16 *off Margaret Rd* 94 C1
Margaret Ct, W1 17 F3
Margaret Gardner Dr, SE9 174 C2
Margaret Ingram Cl, SW6 *off John Smith Av* 128 C7
Margaret Lockwood Cl, Kings.T. KT1 181 J4
Margaret Rd, N16 94 C1
Barnet EN4 41 G5
Bexley DA5 158 D6
Margaret St, W1 17 E3
Margaretta Ter, SW3 31 G5
Margaretting Rd, E12 97 J2
Margaret Way, Ilf. IG4 80 B6
Margate Rd, SW2 150 E5
Margeholes, Wat. WD19 50 E2
Margery Pk Rd, E7 97 G6
Margery Rd, Dag. RM8 100 D3
Margery St, WC1 10 E4
Margin Dr, SW19 166 A5
Margravine Gdns, W6 128 A5
Margravine Rd, W6 128 A5
Marham Dr, NW9 *off Kenley Av* 70 E1
Marham Gdns, SW18 167 H1
Morden SM4 185 F6
Mar Ho, SE7 *off Springfield Gro* 135 J6
Maria Cl, SE1 37 J1
Marian Cl, Hayes UB4 102 D4
Marian Ct, Sutt. SM1 198 E5
Marian Pl, E2 112 E2
Marian Rd, SW16 186 C1
Marian Sq, E2 13 J1
Marian St, E2 *off Hackney Rd* 112 E2
Marian Way, NW10 89 F7
Maria Ter, E1 113 G5
Maria Theresa Cl, N.Mal. KT3 182 D5
Maricas Av, Har. HA3 68 A1
Marie Curie, SE5 *off Sceaux Gdns* 152 B1
Marie Lloyd Gdns, N19 74 E7
Marie Lloyd Ho, N1 12 B2
Marie Lloyd Wk, E8 *off Forest Rd* 94 D6
Marigold All, SE1 19 G6
Marigold Cl, Sthl. UB1 *off Lancaster Rd* 103 E7
Marigold Rd, N17 61 F7
Marigold St, SE16 132 E2
Marigold Way, E4 *off Silver Birch Av* 61 J6
Croydon CR0 203 G1
Marina App, Hayes UB4 103 E5
Marina Av, N.Mal. KT3 183 H5
Marina Cl, Brom. BR2 191 G3
Marina Dr, Well. DA16 157 H2
Marina Gdns, Rom. RM7 83 J6
Marina Pl, Kings.T. (Hmptn W.) KT1 181 G1

Marina Way, Tedd. TW11
off Fairways ... 163 G7
Marine Dr, SE18 ... 136 C4
Barking IG11 ... 118 B4
Marinefield Rd, SW6 ... 149 E2
Mariner Business Cen, Croy. CR0 ... 201 F5
Mariner Gdns, Rich. TW10 ... 163 F3
Mariner Rd, E12
off Dersingham Av ... 98 D4
Mariners Cl, Barn. EN4 ... 41 G5
Mariners Ms, E14 ... 134 D4
Marine St, SE16 ... 29 H5
Marine Twr, SE8
off Abinger Gro ... 133 J6
Marion Cl, Ilf. IG6 ... 65 G7
Marion Gro, Wdf.Grn. IG8 ... 63 E5
Marion Ms, SE21 ... 170 A3
Marion Rd, NW7 ... 55 G5
Thornton Heath CR7 ... 187 J5
Marischal Rd, SE13 ... 154 D3
Maritime Ho, SE18
off Green's End ... 136 E4
Barking IG11
off Linton Rd ... 99 F7
Maritime Quay, E14 ... 134 A5
Maritime St, E3 ... 113 J4
Marius Pas, SW17
off Marius Rd ... 168 A2
Marius Rd, SW17 ... 168 A2
Marjorams Av, Loug. IG10 . 48 C2
Marjorie Gro, SW11 ... 149 J4
Marjorie Ms, E1
off Arbour Sq ... 113 G6
Mark Av, E4 ... 46 B6
Mark Cl, Bexh. DA7 ... 158 E1
Southall UB1
off Longford Av ... 123 H1
Marke Cl, Kes. BR2 ... 206 B4
Markeston Grn, Wat. WD19 ... 50 D4
Market, The, Cars. SM5
off Wrythe La ... 199 F1
Sutton SM1
off Rose Hill ... 199 F1
Market App, W12
off Lime Gro ... 127 J2
Market Ct, W1 ... 17 F3
Market Dr, W4 ... 126 E7
Market Est, N7 ... 92 E6
Market Hill, SE18 ... 136 D3
Market La, W12
off Goldhawk Rd ... 127 J2
Edgware HA8 ... 70 C1
Market Ms, W1 ... 24 D2
Market Pl, N2 ... 73 H3
NW11 ... 73 F4
SE16 ... 37 J1
W1 ... 17 F3
W3 ... 126 C1
Bexleyheath DA6 ... 159 G4
Brentford TW8 ... 125 F7
Enfield EN2
off The Town ... 44 A3
Kingston upon Thames KT1 ... 181 G2
Market Rd, N7 ... 92 E6
Richmond TW9 ... 146 A3
Market Row, SW9
off Atlantic Rd ... 151 G4
Market Service Rd, The, Sutt. SM1
off Rosehill Av ... 199 F1
Market Sq, E14
off Chrisp St ... 114 B6
N9 *off Edmonton Grn Shop Cen* ... 60 E2
Bromley BR1 ... 191 G2
Market St, E1 ... 21 F1
E6 ... 116 C2
SE18 ... 136 D4
Market Way, E14
off Kerbey St ... 114 B6
Wembley HA0
off Turton Rd ... 87 H5
Market Yd Ms, SE1 ... 28 D5
Markfield Gdns, E4 ... 46 B7
Markfield Rd, N15 ... 76 D4
Markham Pl, SW3 ... 31 J3
Markham Sq, SW3 ... 31 J3
Markham St, SW3 ... 31 H3
Markhole Cl, Hmptn. TW12 *off Priory Rd* ... 161 F7
Markhouse Av, E17 ... 77 H6
Markhouse Rd, E17 ... 77 J5
Markland Ho, W10 ... 108 A7
Mark La, EC3 ... 20 E6
Markmanor Av, E17 ... 77 H7
Mark Rd, N22 ... 75 H2
Marksbury Av, Rich. TW9 . 146 A3
MARK'S GATE, Rom. RM6 . 82 E2
Mark Sq, EC2 ... 12 D5
Marks Rd, Rom. RM7 ... 83 J5
Mark St, E15 ... 96 E7
EC2 ... 12 D5
Mark Wade Cl, E12 ... 98 A1
Markway, Sun. TW16 ... 178 C2
Markwell Cl, SE26 ... 170 E4
Markyate Rd, Dag. RM8 . 100 B5
Marlands Rd, Ilf. IG5 ... 80 B3
Marlborough, SW3 ... 31 H1
Marlborough Av, E8 ... 112 D1
N14 ... 58 C3
Edgware HA8 ... 54 B3
Marlborough Cl, N20
off Marlborough Gdns . 57 J3
SE17 ... 35 H2
SW19 ... 167 H6
Orpington BR6
off Aylesham Rd ... 193 J7
Marlborough Ct, W1 ... 17 F4
W8 ... 128 D4
Wallington SM6
off Cranley Gdns ... 200 C7
Marlborough Cres, W4 ... 126 D3
Hayes (Harling.) UB3 ... 121 G7
Marlborough Dr, Ilf. IG5 ... 80 B3
Marlborough Gdns, N20 . 57 J3
Marlborough Gate Ho, W2 . 14 E5
Marlborough Gro, SE1 ... 37 H4
Marlborough Hill, NW8 . 109 F1
Harrow HA1 ... 68 C4
★ **Marlborough Ho**, SW1 . 25 G2
Marlborough La, SE7 ... 135 J6
Marlborough Ms, SW2
off Acre La ... 151 F4
Marlborough Pk Av, Sid. DA15 ... 158 A7
Marlborough Pl, NW8 ... 6 C2
Marlborough Rd, E4 ... 62 A6
E7 ... 97 J7
E15 *off Borthwick Rd* ... 97 E4
E18 ... 79 G3
N9 ... 60 C1
N19 ... 92 D2
N22 ... 59 E7
SE18 ... 137 E3
SW1 ... 25 G2
SW19 ... 167 H6
W4 ... 126 C5
W5 ... 125 G2
Bexleyheath DA7 ... 158 D3
Bromley BR2 ... 191 J4
Dagenham RM8 ... 100 B4
Feltham TW13 ... 160 D2
Hampton TW12 ... 161 G6
Isleworth TW7 ... 144 E1
Richmond TW10 ... 145 H6
Romford RM7 ... 83 G4
South Croydon CR2 ... 201 J7
Southall UB2 ... 122 C3
Sutton SM1 ... 198 D3
Marlborough St, SW3 ... 31 G2
Marlborough Yd, N19 ... 92 D2
Marler Rd, SE23 ... 171 H1
Marlescroft Way, Loug. IG10 ... 48 E5
Marley Av, Bexh. DA7 ... 138 D6
Marley Cl, N15
off Stanmore Rd ... 75 H4
Greenford UB6 ... 103 G3
Marley St, SE16 ... 133 G4
Marley Wk, NW2
off Lennon Rd ... 89 J5
Marl Fld Cl, Wor.Pk. KT4 . 197 G1
Marlingdene Cl, Hmptn. TW12 ... 161 G6
Marlings Cl, Chis. BR7 ... 193 H4
Marlings Pk Av, Chis. BR7 ... 193 H4
Marlins Cl, Sutt. SM1
off Turnpike La ... 199 F5
Marloes Cl, Wem. HA0 ... 87 G4
Marloes Rd, W8 ... 22 A6
Marlow Cl, SE20 ... 189 E3
Marlow Ct, NW6 ... 90 A7
NW9 ... 71 F3
Marlow Cres, Twick. TW1 . 144 C6
Marlow Dr, Sutt. SM3 ... 198 A2
Marlowe Cl, Chis. BR7 ... 175 G6
Ilford IG6 ... 81 F1
Marlowe Ct, SE19
off Lymer Av ... 170 C5
Marlowe Gdns, SE9 ... 156 D6
Marlowe Path, SE8
off Glaisher St ... 134 B6
Marlowe Rd, E17 ... 78 C4
Marlowes, The, NW8 ... 109 G1
Marlowe Sq, Mitch. CR4 . 186 C4
Marlowe Way, Croy. CR0 ... 201 E2
Marlow Gdns, Hayes UB3 ... 121 G3
Marlow Rd, E6 ... 116 C3
SE20 ... 189 E3
Southall UB2 ... 123 F3
Marlow Way, SE16 ... 133 G2
Marl Rd, SW18 ... 149 E4
Marlton St, SE10
off Woolwich Rd ... 135 F5
Marlwood Cl, Sid. DA15 . 175 H2
Marmadon Rd, SE18 ... 137 J4
Marmara Apts, E16
off Western Gateway . 115 G7
Marmion App, E4 ... 62 A4
Marmion Av, E4 ... 61 J4
Marmion Cl, E4 ... 61 J4
Marmion Ms, SW11
off Taybridge Rd ... 150 A3
Marmion Rd, SW11 ... 150 A4
Marmont Rd, SE15 ... 152 D1
Marmora Rd, SE22 ... 153 F6
Marmot Rd, Houns. TW4 . 142 D3
Marne Av, N11 ... 58 B4
Welling DA16 ... 158 A3
Marnell Way, Houns. TW4 ... 142 D3
Marne St, W10 ... 108 B3
Marney Rd, SW11 ... 150 A4
Marnfield Cres, SW2 ... 169 F1
Marnham Av, NW2 ... 90 B4
Marnham Cres, Grnf. UB6 ... 103 H3
Marnock Rd, SE4 ... 153 H5
Maroon St, E14 ... 113 H5
Maroons Way, SE6 ... 172 A5
Marquess Est, N1 ... 93 J6
Marquess Rd, N1 ... 94 A6
Marquis Cl, Wem. HA0 ... 87 J7
Marquis Rd, N4 ... 93 F1
N22 ... 59 F6
NW1 ... 92 D6
Marrabon Cl, Sid. DA15 . 176 A1
Marrick Cl, SW15 ... 147 G4
Marriott Cl, Felt. TW14 ... 141 G6
Marriott Rd, E15 ... 114 E1
N4 ... 93 F1
N10 ... 73 J1
Barnet EN5 ... 40 A3
Marriotts Cl, NW9 ... 71 F6
Marryat Cl, Houns. TW4 . 143 F4
Marryat Pl, SW19 ... 166 B4
Marryat Rd, SW19 ... 166 A5
Marryat Sq, SW6 ... 148 B1
Marsala Rd, SE13 ... 154 B4
Marsden Rd, N9 ... 60 E2
SE15 ... 152 C3
Marsden St, NW5 ... 92 A6
Marsden Way, Orp. BR6 . 207 J4
Marshall, W2
off Hermitage St ... 14 E2
Marshall Cl, SW18
off Allfarthing La ... 149 F6
Harrow HA1
off Bowen Rd ... 68 A7
Hounslow TW4 ... 143 F5
Marshall Est, NW7 ... 55 G4
Marshall Path, SE28
off Attlee Rd ... 118 B7
Marshall Rd, E10 ... 96 B3
N17 ... 76 A1
Marshalls Cl, N11 ... 58 B4
Marshall's Gro, SE18 ... 136 B4
Marshalls Pl, SE16 ... 29 G6
Marshall's Rd, Sutt. SM1 . 198 E4
Marshall St, NW10 ... 88 D7
W1 ... 17 G4
Marshalsea Rd, SE1 ... 28 A3
Marsham Cl, Chis. BR7 ... 174 E5
Marsham St, SW1 ... 25 J6
Marsh Av, Mitch. CR4 ... 185 J2
Marshbrook Cl, SE3 ... 156 A3
Marsh Cl, NW7 ... 55 F3
Marsh Ct, SW19 ... 185 F1
Marsh Dr, NW9 ... 71 F6
Marsh Fm Rd, Twick. TW2 . 162 C1
Marshfield St, E14 ... 134 C3
Marshgate La, E15 ... 114 B1
Marshgate Path, SE28
off Tom Cribb Rd ... 137 F3
Marshgate Sidings, E15 . 114 B1
Marsh Grn Rd, Dag. RM10 ... 119 G1
Marsh Hill, E9 ... 95 H5
Marsh La, E10 ... 96 A2
N17 ... 61 E7
NW7 ... 54 E4
Stanmore HA7 ... 53 F5
Marsh Rd, Pnr. HA5 ... 66 E4
Wembley HA0 ... 105 G2
Marshside Cl, N9 ... 61 F1
Marsh St, E14
off Harbinger Rd ... 134 B4
Marsh Wall, E14 ... 134 A1
Marsland Cl, SE17 ... 35 H4
Marston, SE17
off Deacon Way ... 36 A1
Marston Av, Chess. KT9 . 195 H6
Dagenham RM10 ... 101 G2
Marston Cl, NW6 ... 91 F7
Dagenham RM10 ... 101 G3
Marston Rd, Ilf. IG5 ... 80 B1
Teddington TW11 ... 162 E5
Marston Way, SE19 ... 169 H7
Marsworth Av, Pnr. HA5 . 66 D1
Marsworth Cl, Hayes UB4 ... 103 E5
Marsworth Ho, E2
off Whiston Rd ... 112 D1
Martaban Rd, N16 ... 94 B2
Martara Ms, SE17 ... 35 J4
Martello St, E8 ... 94 E7
Martello Ter, E8 ... 94 E7
Martell Rd, SE21 ... 170 A3
Martel Pl, E8
off Dalston La ... 94 C6
Marten Rd, E17 ... 78 A2
Martens Av, Bexh. DA7 . 159 J4
Martens Cl, Bexh. DA7 ... 159 J4
Martha Ct, E2 ... 113 E2
Martham Cl, SE28 ... 118 D7
Ilford IG6 ... 81 E1
Martha Rd, E15 ... 97 E6
Martha's Bldgs, EC1 ... 12 B5
Martha St, E1 ... 113 E6
Marthorne Cres, Har. HA3 ... 68 A2
Martina Ter, Chig. IG7
off Manford Way ... 65 H5
Martin Bowes Rd, SE9 ... 156 C3
Martinbridge Trd Est, Enf. EN1 ... 44 D5
Martin Cl, N9 ... 61 G1
Martin Cres, Croy. CR0 ... 201 G1
Martindale, SW14 ... 146 C5
Martindale Av, E16 ... 115 G7
Martindale Rd, SW12 ... 150 B7
Hounslow TW4 ... 142 E3
Martin Dene, Bexh. DA6 . 159 F5
Martin Dr, Nthlt. UB5 ... 85 F5
Martineau Cl, Esher KT10 ... 194 A4
Martineau Dr, Twick. TW1
off St. Margaret's Dr . 145 E4
Martineau Ms, N5
off Martineau Rd ... 93 H4
Martineau Rd, N5 ... 93 H4
Martineau St, E1 ... 113 F7
Martingale Cl, Sun. TW16 . 178 A4
Martingales Cl, Rich. TW10 ... 163 G3
Martin Gdns, Dag. RM8 . 100 C4
Martin Gro, Mord. SM4 ... 184 D3
Martin Ho, SE1 ... 28 A6
Martin La, EC4 ... 20 C5
Martin Ri, Bexh. DA6 ... 159 F5
Martin Rd, Dag. RM8 ... 100 C4
Martins, The, Wem. HA9 ... 87 J3
Martins Cl, W.Wick. BR4 . 204 D1
Martinsfield Cl, Chig. IG7 . 65 H4
Martins Mt, Barn. (New Barn.) EN5 ... 40 D4
Martins Pl, SE28
off Martin St ... 137 H1
Martins Rd, Brom. BR2 . 191 E2
Martin St, SE28 ... 137 H1
Martins Wk, N8
off Alexandra Rd ... 75 G3
N10 ... 74 A1
SE28 ... 137 H1
Borehamwood WD6
off Siskin Cl ... 38 A4
Martin Way, SW20 ... 184 B3
Morden SM4 ... 184 B3
Martlesham Wk, NW9
off Kenley Av ... 70 E2
Martlet Gro, Nthlt. UB5 . 102 D3
Martlett Ct, WC2 ... 18 B4
Martley Dr, Ilf. IG2 ... 80 E5
Martock Cl, Har. HA3 ... 68 D4
Martock Gdns, N11 ... 57 J5
Marton Cl, SE6 ... 172 A3
Marton Rd, N16 ... 94 B2
Martys Yd, NW3
off Hampstead High St . 91 G4
Marvell Av, Hayes UB4 ... 102 A5
Marvels Cl, SE12 ... 173 H2
Marvels La, SE12 ... 173 H2
Marville Rd, SW6 ... 128 C7
Marvin St, E8
off Sylvester Rd ... 95 E6
Marwell Cl, W.Wick. BR4
off Deer Pk Way ... 205 F2
Marwood Cl, Well. DA16 ... 158 B3
Marwood Dr, NW7 ... 56 A7
Mary Adelaide Cl, SW15 . 164 E4
Mary Ann Gdns, SE8 ... 134 A6
Maryatt Av, Har. HA2 ... 85 H2
Marybank, SE18 ... 136 C4
Mary Cl, Stan. HA7 ... 69 J4
Mary Datchelor Cl, SE5 . 152 A1
Mary Grn, NW8 ... 109 E1
Maryland Ind Est, E15
off Maryland Rd ... 96 D5
Maryland Pk, E15 ... 96 E5
Maryland Pt, E15
off The Grove ... 96 E6

Maryland Rd, E15 ....96 D5
N22 ....59 F6
Thornton Heath CR7 ....187 H1
Maryland Sq, E15 ....97 E5
Marylands Rd, W9 ....108 D4
Maryland St, E15 ....96 D5
Maryland Wk, N1
off Popham St 111 J1
Maryland Way, Sun. TW16 ....178 A2
Mary Lawrenson Pl, SE3 ....135 F7
MARYLEBONE, NW1 ....15 J3
Marylebone Flyover, NW1 ....15 F2
W2 ....15 F2
Marylebone Gdns, Rich. TW9 *off Manor Rd* 145 J4
Marylebone High St, W1 ....16 C1
Marylebone La, W1 ....16 D4
Marylebone Ms, W1 ....16 D2
Marylebone Pas, W1 ....17 G3
Marylebone Rd, NW1 ....15 H1
Marylebone St, W1 ....16 C2
Marylee Way, SE11 ....34 D3
Mary Macarthur Ho, E2
off Warley St 113 G3
W6 *off Field Rd* 128 B6
Maryon Gro, SE7 ....136 B4
Maryon Ms, NW3
off South End Rd 91 H4
Maryon Rd, SE7 ....136 B4
SE18 ....136 B4
Mary Peters Dr, Grnf. UB6 ....86 A5
Mary Pl, W11 ....108 B7
Mary Rose Cl, Hmptn. TW12 *off Ashley Rd* 179 G1
Mary Rose Mall, E6
off Frobisher Rd 116 D5
Maryrose Way, N20 ....57 G1
Mary Seacole Cl, E8
off Clarissa St 112 C1
Mary's Ter, Twick. TW1 ....144 D7
Mary St, E16
off Barking Rd 115 F5
N1 ....111 J1
Mary Ter, NW1 ....110 B1
Mary Way, Wat. WD19 ....50 C4
Masbro Rd, W14 ....128 A3
Mascalls Ct, SE7 ....135 J6
Mascalls Rd, SE7 ....135 J6
Mascotte Rd, SW15 ....148 A4
Mascotts Cl, NW2 ....89 H3
Masefield Av, Borwd. WD6 ....38 B5
Southall UB1 ....103 G7
Stanmore HA7 ....52 C5
Masefield Cres, N14 ....42 C6
Masefield Gdns, E6 ....116 D4
Masefield La, Hayes UB4 ....102 B4
Masefield Rd, Hmptn. TW12
off Wordsworth Rd 161 F4
Masefield Vw, Orp. BR6 ....207 F3
Masham Ho, Erith DA18
off Kale Rd 138 D2
Mashie Rd, W3 ....106 E6
Maskall Cl, SW2 ....169 G1
Maskani Wk, SW16
off Bates Cres 168 C7
Maskell Rd, SW17 ....167 F3
Maskelyne Cl, SW11 ....149 H1
Mason Cl, E16 ....115 G7
SE16 ....37 J3
SW20 ....184 A1
Bexleyheath DA7 ....159 H3
Borehamwood WD6 ....38 C2
Hampton TW12 ....179 F1
Mason Ct, Wem. HA9
off The Avenue 88 A2
Mason Rd, Sutt. SM1
off Manor Pl 199 E5
Woodford Green IG8 ....63 E4
Masons Arms Ms, W1 ....17 E4
Masons Av, EC2 ....20 B3
Croydon CR0 ....201 J3
Harrow HA3 ....68 C4
Masons Grn La, W3 ....106 A5
Masons Hill, SE18 ....137 E4
Bromley BR1, BR2 ....191 G3
Masons Pl, EC1 ....11 H3
Mitcham CR4 ....185 J1
Mason St, SE17 ....36 C2
Masons Yd, EC1 ....11 H3
Mason's Yd, SW1 ....25 G1
SW19 *off High St Wimbledon* 166 A5
Massey Cl, N11
off Grove Rd 58 B5
Massey Ct, E6 ....115 J1
Massie Rd, E8
off Graham Rd 94 D6
Massingberd Way, SW17 ....168 B4
Massinger St, SE17 ....36 D2
Massingham St, E1 ....113 G4
Masson Av, Ruis. HA4 ....84 C6
Master Gunner Pl, SE18 ....136 B7
Masterman Ho, SE5 ....36 A7
Masterman Rd, E6 ....116 B3
Masters Cl, SW16 ....168 C6
Masters Dr, SE16 ....132 E5
Masters St, E1 ....113 G5
Mast Ho Ter, E14 ....134 A4
Mast Leisure Pk, SE16 ....133 G3
Mastmaker Rd, E14 ....134 A2
Mast Quay, SE18
off Woolwich Ch St 136 C3
Maswell Pk Cres, Houns. TW3 ....143 J5
Maswell Pk Rd, Houns. TW3 ....143 H5
Matcham Rd, E11 ....97 E3
Matchless Dr, SE18 ....136 D7
Matfield Cl, Brom. BR2 ....191 G5
Matfield Rd, Belv. DA17 ....139 G6
Matham Gro, SE22 ....152 C4
Matham Rd, E.Mol. KT8 ....180 A5
Matheson Rd, W14 ....128 C4
Mathews Av, E6 ....116 D2
Mathews Pk Av, E15 ....97 F6
Matilda Cl, SE19
off Elizabeth Way 170 A7
Matilda Gdns, E3 ....114 A2
Matilda St, N1 ....111 F1
Matisse Rd, Houns. TW3
off Prince Regent Rd 143 H3
Matlock Cl, SE24 ....151 J4
Barnet EN5 ....40 A5
Matlock Ct, SE5
off Denmark Hill Est 152 A4
Matlock Cres, Sutt. SM3 ....198 B4
Watford WD19 ....50 C3
Matlock Gdns, Sutt. SM3 ....198 B4
Matlock Pl, Sutt. SM3 ....198 B4
Matlock Rd, E10 ....78 C6
Matlock St, E14 ....113 H6
Matlock Way, N.Mal. KT3 ....182 D1
Matrimony Pl, SW8 ....150 C2
Matson Ct, Wdf.Grn. IG8
off The Bridle Path 62 E7
Matson Ho, SE16
off Slippers Pl 133 E3
Matthew Cl, W10 ....108 A4
Matthew Ct, Mitch. CR4 ....186 D5
Matthew Parker St, SW1 ....25 J4
Matthews Rd, Grnf. UB6 ....86 A5
Matthews St, SW11 ....149 J2
Matthews Yd, WC2 ....18 A4
Matthias Rd, N16 ....94 A5
Mattingley Way, SE15 ....37 F7
Mattison Rd, N4 ....75 G6
Mattock La, W5 ....125 E1
W13 ....125 E1
Maud Cashmore Way, SE18 ....136 C3
Maud Chadburn Pl, SW4
off Balham Hill 150 B6
Maude Rd, E17 ....77 H5
SE5 ....152 B1
Maudesville Cotts, W7
off The Broadway 124 B1
Maude Ter, E17 ....77 H4
Maud Gdns, E13 ....115 F1
Barking IG11 ....117 J2
Maudlin's Grn, E1 ....29 H1
Maud Rd, E10 ....96 C3
E13 ....115 F2
Maudslay Rd, SE9 ....156 C3
Maudsley Ho, Brent. TW8
off Green Dragon La 125 H5
Maud St, E16 ....115 F5
Maud Wilkes Cl, NW5 ....92 C5
Mauleverer Rd, SW2 ....150 E5
Maundeby Wk, NW10
off Neasden La 89 E6
Maunder Rd, W7 ....124 C1
Maunsel St, SW1 ....33 H1
Maurer Ct, SE10
off John Harrison Way 135 F3
Maurice Av, N22 ....75 H2
Maurice Brown Cl, NW7 ....56 A5
Maurice St, W12 ....107 H6
Maurice Wk, NW11 ....73 F4
Maurier Cl, Nthlt. UB5 ....102 C1
Mauritius Rd, SE10 ....135 E4
Maury Rd, N16 ....94 D2
Mauveine Gdns, Houns. TW3 ....143 G4
Mavelstone Cl, Brom. BR1 ....192 B1
Mavelstone Rd, Brom. BR1 ....192 B1
Maverton Rd, E3 ....114 A1
Mavis Av, Epsom KT19 ....197 E5
Mavis Cl, Epsom KT19 ....197 E5
Mavis Wk, E6 ....116 B5
Mawbey Est, SE1 ....37 H4
Mawbey Ho, SE1
off Old Kent Rd 37 G4
Mawbey Pl, SE1 ....37 G4
Mawbey Rd, SE1 ....37 G4
Mawbey St, SW8 ....130 E7
Mawney Cl, Rom. RM7 ....83 H2
Mawney Rd, Rom. RM7 ....83 J4
Mawson Cl, SW20 ....184 B2
Mawson La, W4
off Great W Rd 127 F6
Maxey Gdns, Dag. RM9 ....101 E4
Maxey Rd, SE18 ....137 F4
Dagenham RM9 ....100 E4
Maxfield Cl, N20 ....41 F7
Maxilla Gdns, W10
off Cambridge Gdns 108 A6
Maxilla Wk, W10
off Kingsdown Cl 108 A6
Maxim Rd, N21 ....43 G6
Maxted Pk, Har. HA1 ....68 B7
Maxted Rd, SE15 ....152 C3
Maxwell Cl, Croy. CR0 ....201 E1
Hayes UB3 ....102 A7
Maxwell Gdns, Orp. BR6 ....207 J3
Maxwell Rd, SW6 ....128 E7
Borehamwood WD6 ....38 B3
Welling DA16 ....158 A4
West Drayton UB7 ....120 C4
Maxwelton Av, NW7 ....54 D5
Maxwelton Cl, NW7 ....54 D5
Maya Angelou Ct, E4
off Bailey Cl 62 C4
Maya Cl, SE15 ....152 E2
Mayall Rd, SE24 ....151 H5
Maya Pl, N11 ....58 D7
Maya Rd, N2 ....73 F4
Maybank Av, E18 ....79 H2
Wembley HA0 ....86 C5
Maybank Gdns, Pnr. HA5 ....66 A5
Maybank Rd, E18 ....79 H1
May Bate Av, Kings.T. KT2 ....181 G1
Maybells Commercial Est, Bark. IG11 ....118 D2
Mayberry Pl, Surb. KT5 ....181 J7
Maybourne Cl, SE26 ....171 E5
Maybrook Meadow Est, Bark. IG11 ....100 A7
Maybury Cl, Loug. IG10 ....48 E4
Orpington BR5 ....193 E5
Maybury Gdns, NW10 ....89 H6
Maybury Ms, N6 ....74 C7
Maybury Rd, E13 ....115 J4
Barking IG11 ....117 J2
Maybury St, SW17 ....167 H5
Maychurch Cl, Stan. HA7 ....53 G7
May Cl, Chess. KT9 ....195 J6
May Ct, SW19 ....185 E1
Maycroft, Pnr. HA5 ....66 B2
Maycross Av, Mord. SM4 ....184 C3
Mayday Gdns, SE3 ....156 B2
Mayday Rd, Th.Hth. CR7 ....187 H6
Maydew Ho, SE16 ....133 F4
Mayerne Rd, SE9 ....156 A5
Mayesbrook Rd, Bark. IG11 ....117 J1
Dagenham RM8 ....100 A3
Ilford IG3 ....100 A3
Mayesford Rd, Rom. RM6 ....82 C7
Mayes Rd, N22 ....75 G2
Mayeswood Rd, SE12 ....173 J3
MAYFAIR, W1 ....16 D6
Mayfair Av, Bexh. DA7 ....158 D1
Ilford IG1 ....98 C2
Romford RM6 ....82 D6
Twickenham TW2 ....143 J7
Worcester Park KT4 ....197 G1
Mayfair Cl, Beck. BR3 ....190 B1
Surbiton KT6 ....195 H1
Mayfair Gdns, N17 ....60 A6
Woodford Green IG8 ....63 G7
Mayfair Ms, NW1
off Regents Pk Rd 91 J7
Mayfair Pl, W1 ....25 E1
Mayfair Ter, N14 ....42 D7
Mayfield, Bexh. DA7 ....159 F3
Mayfield Av, N12 ....57 F4
N14 ....58 C2
W4 ....127 E4
W13 ....124 E3
Harrow HA3 ....68 E5
Orpington BR6 ....207 J1
Woodford Green IG8 ....63 G7
Mayfield Cl, E8
off Forest Rd 94 C6
SW4 ....150 D5
Thames Ditton KT7 ....194 E1
Mayfield Cres, N9 ....44 E6
Thornton Heath CR7 ....187 F4
Mayfield Dr, Pnr. HA5 ....67 F4
Mayfield Gdns, NW4 ....72 A6
W7 ....104 A6
Mayfield Mans, SW15
off West Hill 148 A7
Mayfield Rd, E4 ....62 C2
E8 ....94 C7
E13 ....115 F4
E17 ....77 H2
N8 ....75 F6
SW19 ....184 C1
W3 ....106 B7
Mayfield Rd, W12 ....127 E2
Belvedere DA17 ....139 J4
Bromley BR1 ....192 B5
Dagenham RM8 ....100 C1
Enfield EN3 ....45 G2
Sutton SM2 ....199 G6
Thornton Heath CR7 ....187 F4
Mayfields, Wem. HA9 ....88 A2
Mayfields Cl, Wem. HA9 ....88 A2
Mayflower Cl, SE16
off Greenland Quay 133 G4
Mayflower Ct, SE16
off St. Marychurch St 133 F2
Mayflower Rd, SW9 ....150 E3
Mayflower St, SE16 ....133 F2
Mayfly Cl, Pnr. (Eastcote) HA5 ....66 C7
Mayfly Gdns, Nthlt. UB5
off Ruislip Rd 102 D3
Mayford Cl, SW12 ....149 J7
Beckenham BR3 ....189 G3
Mayford Rd, SW12 ....149 J7
May Gdns, Wem. HA0 ....105 F2
Maygood St, N1 ....10 D1
Maygrove Rd, NW6 ....90 C6
Mayhew Cl, E4 ....62 A3
Mayhill Rd, SE7 ....135 H6
Barnet EN5 ....40 B6
Maylands Dr, Sid. DA14 ....176 D3
Maylands Rd, Wat. WD19 ....50 C4
Maynard Cl, N15
off Brunswick Rd 76 B5
SW6 *off Cambria St* 129 E7
Maynard Path, E17 ....78 C5
Maynard Rd, E17 ....78 C5
Maynards Quay, E1
off Garnet St 113 F7
Maynooth Gdns, Cars. SM5 ....185 J7
Mayola Rd, E5 ....95 F4
Mayo Rd, NW10 ....88 E6
Croydon CR0 ....188 A5
Mayow Rd, SE23 ....171 G3
SE26 ....171 G4
Mayplace Cl, Bexh. DA7 ....159 H3
Mayplace La, SE18 ....137 E7
Mayplace Rd E, Bexh. DA7 ....159 H3
Dartford DA1 ....159 J3
Mayplace Rd W, Bexh. DA7 ....159 G4
Maypole Cres, Ilf. IG6 ....65 G7
May Rd, E4 ....62 A6
E13 ....115 G2
Twickenham TW2 ....162 B1
Mayroyd Av, Surb. KT6 ....196 A2
May's Bldgs Ms, SE10
off Crooms Hill 134 C7
Mays Ct, WC2 ....18 A6
Mays Hill Rd, Brom. BR2 ....191 E2
Mays La, E4 ....62 D2
Barnet EN5 ....40 B5
Maysoule Rd, SW11 ....149 G4
Mays Rd, Tedd. TW11 ....162 A5
Mayston Ms, SE10
off Westcombe Hill 135 G5
May St, W14
off North End Rd 128 C5
Mayswood Gdns, Dag. RM10 ....101 J6
Mayton St, N7 ....93 F3
Maytree Cl, Edg. HA8 ....54 C3
Maytree Gdns, W5
off South Ealing Rd 125 G3
May Tree La, Stan. HA7 ....52 C7
Maytree Wk, SW2 ....169 G2
Mayville Est, N16
off King Henry St 94 B5
Mayville Rd, E11 ....96 E2
Ilford IG1 ....98 E5
May Wk, E13 ....115 H2
Maywood Cl, Beck. BR3 ....172 B7
Maze Hill, SE3 ....134 E6
SE10 ....134 E6
Mazenod Av, NW6 ....90 D7
Maze Rd, Rich. TW9 ....126 A7
Mead, The, N2 ....73 F2
W13 ....104 E5
Beckenham BR3 ....190 C1
Wallington SM6 ....200 D6
Watford WD19 ....50 E3
West Wickham BR4 ....204 D1
Mead Cl, NW1
off Belmont St 92 A7
Harrow HA3 ....68 A1
Loughton IG10 ....48 E2
Mead Ct, NW9 ....70 C5
Mead Cres, E4 ....62 C4
Sutton SM1 ....199 H4
Meadcroft Rd, SE11 ....35 G6
Meade Cl, W4 ....126 A6
Meadfield, Edg. HA8 ....54 B2
Mead Fld, Har. HA2
off Kings Rd 85 F3
Meadfield Grn, Edg. HA8 ....54 B2

Meadfoot Rd, SW16 168 C7
Meadgate Av, Wdf.Grn.
IG8 64 B5
Mead Gro, Rom. RM6 82 D3
Meadlands Dr, Rich.
TW10 163 G2
Meadow, The, Chis. BR7 175 F6
Meadow Av, Croy. CR0 189 G6
Meadow Bk, N21 43 F6
Meadowbank, NW3 91 J7
SE3 155 F3
Surbiton KT5 181 J6
Meadowbank Cl, SW6 127 J7
Meadowbank Gdns,
Houns. TW5 142 A2
Meadowbank Rd, NW9 70 D7
Meadowbanks, Barn.
EN5 39 F5
Meadow Cl, E4 62 B1
E9 95 J5
SE6 172 A5
SW20 183 J4
Barking IG11 117 J1
Barnet EN5 40 C6
Bexleyheath DA6 159 F5
Chislehurst BR7 174 E5
Esher KT10 194 C3
Hounslow TW4 143 G6
Northolt UB5 103 G2
Richmond TW10 163 H1
Sutton SM1
off Aultone Way 199 F2
Meadowcourt Rd, SE3 155 F4
Meadowcroft, Brom. BR1 192 C3
Meadowcroft Rd, N13 59 G2
Meadow Dr, N10 74 B3
NW4 71 J2
Meadowford Cl, SE28 118 A7
Meadow Gdns, Edg. HA8 54 B6
Meadow Garth, NW10 88 C6
Meadowgate Cl, NW7 55 F5
Meadow Hill, N.Mal. KT3 182 E6
Meadow La, SE12 173 H3
Meadowlea Cl, West Dr.
(Harm.) UB7 120 A6
Meadow Ms, SW8 34 C6
Meadow Pl, SW8 34 B7
W4 *off Edensor Rd* 126 E7
Meadow Rd, SW8 34 C7
SW19 167 F7
Barking IG11 99 J7
Borehamwood WD6 38 B2
Bromley BR2 191 E1
Dagenham RM9 101 F6
Esher (Clay.) KT10 194 B6
Feltham TW13 160 E2
Loughton IG10 48 B5
Pinner HA5 66 D5
Romford RM7 101 J1
Southall UB1 103 F7
Sutton SM1 199 H5
Meadow Row, SE1 27 J6
Meadows Cl, E10 96 A2
Meadows End, Sun.
TW16 178 A1
Meadowside, SE9 155 J4
Meadow Stile, Croy. CR0
off High St 201 J3
Meadowsweet Cl, E16
off Monarch Dr 116 A5
SW20 183 J4
Meadow Vw, Har. HA1 86 B1
Sidcup DA15 158 B7
Meadowview Rd, SE6 171 J5
Bexley DA5 159 E6
Meadow Vw Rd, Th.Hth.
CR7 187 H5
Meadow Wk, E18 79 G4
Dagenham RM9 101 F6
Epsom KT17, KT19 197 E6
Wallington SM6 200 B3
Meadow Way, NW9 70 D5
Chessington KT9 195 H5
Chigwell IG7 65 F3
Orpington BR6 206 D3
Ruislip HA4 66 B6
Wembley HA9 87 G4
Meadow Way, The, Har.
HA3 68 B1
Meadow Waye, Houns.
TW5 123 E6
Mead Path, SW17 167 F5
Mead Pl, E9 95 F6
Croydon CR0 201 H1
Mead Plat, NW10 88 C6
Mead Rd, Chis. BR7 175 F6
Edgware HA8 54 A6
Richmond TW10 163 F3
Mead Row, SE1 27 E5
Meads, The, Edg. HA8 54 D6
Sutton SM3 198 B3
Meadside Cl, Beck. BR3 189 H1
Meads La, Ilf. IG3 81 H7
Meads Rd, N22 75 H2
Enfield EN3 45 H1
Mead Ter, Wem. HA9
off Meadow Way 87 G4
Meadvale Rd, W5 105 E4
Croydon CR0 188 C7
Meadway, N14 58 D2
NW11 72 E6
SW20 183 J4
Barnet EN5 40 D4
Beckenham BR3 190 C1
Mead Way, Brom. BR2 191 F6
Croydon CR0 203 H2
Meadway, Ilf. IG3 99 H4
Surbiton KT5 196 C1
Twickenham TW2 162 A1
Woodford Green
IG8 63 J5
Meadway, The, SE3
off Heath La 154 D2
Buckhurst Hill IG9 64 A1
Loughton IG10 48 C6
Meadway Cl, NW11 73 E6
Barnet EN5 40 D4
Pinner HA5
off Highbanks Rd 51 H6
Meadway Ct, NW11 73 E6
Meadway Gate, NW11 72 D6
Meaford Way, SE20 171 E7
Meakin Est, SE1 28 D5
Meanley Rd, E12 98 B4
Meard St, W1 17 H4
Meath Cres, E2 113 G3
Meath Rd, E15 115 F2
Ilford IG1 99 F3
Meath St, SW11 150 B1
Mecklenburgh Pl, WC1 10 C5
Mecklenburgh Sq, WC1 10 C5
Mecklenburgh St, WC1 10 C5
Medburn St, NW1 9 H1
Medcroft Gdns, SW14 146 C4
Medebourne Cl, SE3 155 G3
Medesenge Way, N13 59 H6
Medfield St, SW15 147 H7
Medhurst Cl, E3
off Arbery Rd 113 H2
Median Rd, E5 95 F5
★ **Medici Galleries**, W1 16 E6
Medina Av, Esher KT10 194 B3
Medina Gro, N7
off Medina Rd 93 G3
Medina Rd, N7 93 G3
Medland Cl, Wall. SM6 200 A1
Medland Ho, E14
off Branch Rd 113 H7
Medlar Cl, Nthlt. UB5
off Parkfield Av 102 E2
Medlar St, SE5 151 J1
Medley Rd, NW6 90 D6
Medora Rd, SW2 151 F7
Medusa Rd, SE6 154 B6
Medway Bldgs, E3
off Medway Rd 113 H2
Medway Cl, Croy. CR0 189 F6
Ilford IG1 99 F5
Medway Dr, Grnf.
(Perivale) UB6 104 C2
Medway Gdns, Wem.
HA0 86 D4
Medway Ms, E3
off Medway Rd 113 H2
Medway Par, Grnf.
(Perivale) UB6 104 C2
Medway Rd, E3 113 H2
Medway St, SW1 25 J6
Medwin St, SW4 151 F4
Meecham Ct, SW11
off Shuttleworth Rd 149 G2
Meerbrook Rd, SE3 155 J3
Meeson Rd, E15 115 F1
Meeson St, E5 95 H4
Meeting Fld Path, E9
off Chatham Pl 95 F6
Meeting Ho All, E1
off Watts St 133 E1
Meeting Ho La, SE15 152 E1
Mehetabel Rd, E9 95 F6
Meister Cl, Ilf. IG1 99 G1
Melancholy Wk, Rich.
TW10 163 F2
Melanda Cl, Chis. BR7 174 C5
Melanie Cl, Bexh. DA7 158 E1
Melba Way, SE13 154 B1
Melbourne Av, N13 59 F6
W13 124 D1
Pinner HA5 67 H3
Melbourne Cl, Orp. BR6 193 H7
Wallington SM6
off Melbourne Rd 200 C5
Melbourne Ct, E5
off Daubeney Rd 95 H4
SE20 170 D7
Melbourne Gdns, Rom.
RM6 82 E5
Melbourne Gro, SE22 152 B4
Melbourne Ho, Hayes
UB4 102 C4
Melbourne Ms, SE6 154 C7
SW9 151 G1
Melbourne Pl, WC2 18 D5
Melbourne Rd, E6 116 C1
E10 78 B7
E17 77 H4
SW19 184 D1
Ilford IG1 99 E1
Teddington TW11 163 F6
Wallington SM6 200 B5
Melbourne Sq, SW9
off Melbourne Ms 151 G1
Melbourne Ter, SW6
off Moore Pk Rd 128 E7
Melbourne Way, Enf. EN1 44 C6
Melbray Ms, SW6
off Hurlingham Rd 148 C2
Melbreak Ho, SE22
off Pytchley Rd 152 B3
Melbury Av, Sthl. UB2 123 H3
Melbury Cl, Chis. BR7 174 B6
Esher (Clay.) KT10 194 E6
Melbury Ct, W8 128 C3
Melbury Dr, SE5
off Sedgmoor Pl 132 B7
Melbury Gdns, SW20 183 H1
Melbury Rd, W14 128 C3
Harrow HA3 69 J5
Melcombe Gdns, Har.
HA3 69 J6
Melcombe Ho, SW8
off Dorset Rd 131 F7
Melcombe Pl, NW1 15 J1
Melcombe St, NW1 8 A6
Meldex Cl, NW7 55 J6
Meldon Cl, SW6
off Bagley's La 149 E1
Meldone Cl, Surb. KT5 182 B6
Meldrum Rd, Ilf. IG3 100 A2
Melfield Gdns, SE6 172 B4
Melford Av, Bark. IG11 99 H6
Melford Cl, Chess. KT9 195 J5
Melford Rd, E6 116 C4
E11 96 E2
E17 77 H4
SE22 152 D7
Ilford IG1 99 G2
Melfort Av, Th.Hth. CR7 187 H3
Melfort Rd, Th.Hth. CR7 187 H3
Melgund Rd, N5 93 G5
Melina Pl, NW8 6 E4
Melina Rd, W12 127 H2
Melior Pl, SE1 28 D3
Melior St, SE1 28 C3
Meliot Rd, SE6 172 D2
Meller Cl, Croy. CR0 200 E3
Mellifont Cl, Cars. SM5 185 G7
Melling Dr, Enf. EN1 44 D1
Melling St, SE18 137 H6
Mellish Cl, Bark. IG11 117 J1
Mellish Gdns, Wdf.Grn.
IG8 63 G5
Mellish Ind Est, SE18 136 B3
Mellish St, E14 134 A3
Mellison Rd, SW17 167 H5
Melliss Av, Rich. TW9 146 B1
Mellitus St, W12 107 F6
Mellor Cl, Walt. KT12 179 F7
Mellows Rd, Ilf. IG5 80 C3
Wallington SM6 200 D5
Mells Cres, SE9 174 C4
Mell St, SE10
off Trafalgar Rd 134 E5
Melody La, N5 93 H5
Melody Rd, SW18 149 F5
Melon Pl, W8 22 A3
Melon Rd, E11 96 E3
SE15 152 D1
Melrose Av, N22 75 H1
NW2 89 H5
SW16 187 F3
SW19 166 D2
Borehamwood WD6 38 B5
Greenford UB6 103 H2
Mitcham CR4 168 B7
Twickenham TW2 143 H7
Melrose Cl, SE12 173 G1
Greenford UB6 103 H2
Hayes UB4 102 A5
Melrose Ct, W13
off Williams Rd 124 D1
Melrose Cres, Orp. BR6 207 G4
Melrose Dr, Sthl. UB1 123 G1
Melrose Gdns, W6 127 J3
Edgware HA8 70 B2
New Malden KT3 182 D3
Melrose Rd, SW13 147 F2
SW18 148 C6
SW19 184 D2
W3 *off Stanley Rd* 126 C3
Pinner HA5 67 F4
Melrose Ter, W6 127 J2
Melsa Rd, Mord. SM4 185 F6
Melthorne Dr, Ruis. HA4 84 C3
Melthorpe Gdns, SE3 156 B1
Melton Cl, Ruis. HA4 84 C1
Melton Ct, SW7 31 F2
Sutton SM2 199 F7
Melton St, NW1 9 G4
Melville Av, SW20 165 G7
Greenford UB6 86 C5
South Croydon CR2 202 C5
Melville Gdns, N13 59 H5
Melville Pl, N1
off Essex Rd 93 J7
Melville Rd, E17 77 J3
NW10 88 D7
SW13 147 G1
Sidcup DA14 176 C2
Melville Vil Rd, W3
off High St 126 D1
Melvin Rd, SE20 189 F1
Melwas Ct, N9
off Galahad Rd 60 D3
Melyn Cl, N7
off Anson Rd 92 C4
Memel Ct, EC1 11 J6
Memel St, EC1 11 J6
Memess Path, SE18 136 D6
Memorial Av, E15 114 E3
Memorial Cl, Houns.
TW5 123 F6
Memorial Hts, Ilf. IG2 81 G6
Menai Pl, E3
off Blondin St 114 A2
Mendip Cl, SE26 171 F4
Hayes (Harling.) UB3 121 G7
Worcester Park KT4 197 J1
Mendip Dr, NW2 90 A2
Mendip Ho, N9
off Edmonton Grn
Shop Cen 60 D2
Mendip Hos, E2
off Globe Rd 113 F3
Mendip Rd, SW11 149 F3
Ilford IG2 81 H5
Mendora Rd, SW6 128 B7
Menelik Rd, NW2 90 B4
Menlo Gdns, SE19 170 A7
Menon Dr, N9 60 E3
Menotti St, E2 13 J5
Mentmore Cl, Har. HA3 69 F6
Mentmore Ter, E8 95 E7
Meon Ct, Islw. TW7 144 B2
Meon Rd, W3 126 C2
Meopham Rd, Mitch.
CR4 186 C1
Mepham Cres, Har. HA3 51 J7
Mepham Gdns, Har. HA3 51 J7
Mepham St, SE1 26 D2
Mera Dr, Bexh. DA7 159 G4
Merantun Way, SW19 185 F1
Merbury Cl, SE13 154 C5
SE28 137 G1
Merbury Rd, SE28 137 H2
Mercator Pl, E14
off Napier Av 134 B5
Mercator Rd, SE13 154 D4
Mercer Cl, T.Ditt. KT7 180 C7
Merceron Hos, E2
off Globe Rd 113 F3
Merceron St, E1 112 E4
Mercer Pl, Pnr. HA5 66 C2
Mercers Cl, SE10 135 F4
Mercers Ms, N19
off Mercers Rd 92 D3
Mercers Pl, W6 127 J4
Mercers Rd, N19 92 D3
Mercer St, WC2 18 A4
Merchants Cl, SE25
off Clifford Rd 188 D4
Merchants Ho, SE10
off Hoskins St 134 D5
Merchants Row, SE10
off Hoskins St 134 D5
Merchant St, E3 113 J3
Merchiston Rd, SE6 172 D2
Merchland Rd, SE9 175 F1
Mercia Gro, SE13 154 C4
Mercier Rd, SW15 148 B5
Mercury Cen, Felt. TW14 142 B5
Mercury Ho, E3
off Garrison Rd 114 A1
Mercury Way, SE14 133 G6
Mercy Ter, SE13 154 B4
Merebank La, Croy.
CR0 201 F5
Mere Cl, SW15 148 A7
Orpington BR6 206 E2
Meredith Av, NW2 89 J5
Meredith Cl, Pnr. HA5 50 D7
Meredith Ms, SE4 153 J4
Meredith St, E13 115 G3
EC1 11 G4
Meredyth Rd, SW13 147 G2
Mere End, Croy. CR0 189 G7
Mereside, Orp. BR6 206 D2
Meretone Cl, SE4 153 H4
Mereton Mans, SE8
off Brookmill Rd 154 A1

Merevale Cres, Mord. SM4 . . . . . **185** F6
Mereway Rd, Twick. TW2 . **162** A1
Merewood Cl, Brom. BR1 . . . . . **192** D2
Merewood Gdns, Croy. CR0 . . . . . **189** G7
Merewood Rd, Bexh. DA7 . . . . . **159** J2
Mereworth Cl, Brom. BR2 . . . . . **191** F5
Mereworth Dr, SE18 . . . . . **137** E7
Merganser Gdns, SE28 *off Avocet Ms* **137** G3
Meriden Cl, Brom. BR1 . . . **174** A7
Ilford IG6 . . . . . **81** F1
Meridian Business Pk, Enf. EN3 . . . . . **45** H6
Meridian Cl, NW7 . . . . . **54** D4
Meridian Ct, SE16 *off East La* **29** H3
Meridian Gate, E14 . . . . . **134** C2
Meridian Pl, E14 . . . . . **134** B2
Meridian Rd, SE7 . . . . . **136** A7
Meridian Sq, E15 . . . . . **96** D7
Meridian Trd Est, SE7 . . . . **135** H4
Meridian Wk, N17 *off Commercial Rd* **60** B6
Meridian Way, N9 . . . . . **61** F5
N18 . . . . . **61** F6
Enfield EN3 . . . . . **45** G6
Merifield Rd, SE9 . . . . . **155** J4
Merino Cl, E11 . . . . . **79** J4
Merino Pl, Sid. DA15 *off Blackfen Rd* **158** A6
Merivale Rd, SW15 . . . . . **148** B4
Harrow HA1 . . . . . **67** J7
Merlewood Dr, Chis. BR7 . **192** C1
Merley Ct, NW9 . . . . . **88** C1
Merlin Cl, Croy. CR0 . . . . . **202** B4
Mitcham CR4 . . . . . **185** H3
Northolt UB5 . . . . . **102** C3
Wallington SM6 . . . . . **201** F6
Merlin Ct, Brom. BR2 *off Durham Av* **191** F4
Merlin Cres, Edg. HA8 . . . . **69** J1
Merlin Gdns, Brom. BR1 . **173** G3
Merling Cl, Chess. KT9 *off Coppard Gdns* **195** G5
Merlin Gro, Beck. BR3 . . . **189** J4
Ilford IG6 . . . . . **65** E7
Merlin Ho, Enf. EN3 *off Allington Ct* **45** G5
Merlin Rd, E12 . . . . . **97** J2
Welling DA16 . . . . . **158** A4
Merlin Rd N, Well. DA16 . . **158** A4
Merlins Av, Har. HA2 . . . . . **85** F3
Merlin St, WC1 . . . . . **11** E4
Mermaid Ct, SE1 . . . . . **28** B3
SE16 . . . . . **133** J1
Mermaid Twr, SE8 *off Abinger Gro* **133** J6
Merredene St, SW2 . . . . . **151** F6
Merriam Av, E9 . . . . . **95** J6
Merriam Cl, E4 . . . . . **62** C5
Merrick Rd, Sthl. UB2 . . . . **123** F2
Merrick Sq, SE1 . . . . . **28** A5
Merridale, SE12 . . . . . **155** G5
Merridene, N21 . . . . . **43** H6
Merrielands Cres, Dag. RM9 . . . . . **119** F1
Merrilands Rd, Wor.Pk. KT4 . . . . . **197** J1
Merrilees Rd, Sid. DA15 . . **175** H1
Merrilyn Cl, Esher (Clay.) KT10 . . . . . **194** D6
Merriman Rd, SE3 . . . . . **155** J1
Merrington Rd, SW6 . . . . **128** D6
Merrion Av, Stan. HA7 . . . . **53** G5
Merritt Gdns, Chess. KT9 . . . . . **195** F6
Merritt Rd, SE4 . . . . . **153** J5
Merrivale, N14 . . . . . **42** D6
Merrivale Av, Ilf. IG4 . . . . . **80** A4
Merrow St, SE17 . . . . . **36** B5
Merrow Wk, SE17 . . . . . **36** C3
Merrow Way, Croy. (New Adgtn) CR0 . . . . . **204** C6
Merrydown Way, Chis. BR7 . . . . . **192** B1
Merryfield, SE3 . . . . . **155** F2
Merryfield Gdns, Stan. HA7 . . . . . **53** F5
Merryfield Ho, SE9 *off Grove Pk Rd* **173** J3
Merryfields Way, SE6 . . . . **154** B7
MERRY HILL, Bushey WD23 . . . . . **51** G1
Merryhill Cl, E4 . . . . . **46** B7
Merry Hill Mt, Bushey WD23 . . . . . **51** H1
Merry Hill Rd, Bushey WD23 . . . . . **51** H1
Merryhills Ct, N14 . . . . . **42** C5
Merryhills Dr, Enf. EN2 . . . . **42** D4
Merryweather Ct, N.Mal. KT3 *off Rodney Cl* **182** E5
Mersea Ho, Bark. IG11 . . . . **98** E6
Mersey Rd, E17 . . . . . **77** J3
Mersey Wk, Nthlt. UB5 *off Brabazon Rd* **103** G2
Mersham Dr, NW9 . . . . . **70** A5
Mersham Pl, SE20 . . . . . **189** E1
Mersham Rd, Th.Hth. CR7 . . . . . **188** A3
Merten Rd, Rom. RM6 . . . . **83** E7
Merthyr Ter, SW13 . . . . . **127** H6
MERTON, SW19 . . . . . **184** D1
Merton Abbey Mills, SW19 *off Watermill Way* **185** F1
Merton Av, W4 . . . . . **127** F4
Northolt UB5 . . . . . **85** J5
Merton Ct, Ilf. IG1 *off Castleview Gdns* . . . **80** B6
Merton Gdns, Orp. BR5 . . **193** E5
Merton Hall Gdns, SW20 . **184** B1
Merton Hall Rd, SW19 . . . **184** B1
Merton High St, SW19 . . . **167** E7
Merton Ind Pk, SW19 . . . . **185** F1
Merton La, N6 . . . . . **91** J2
Merton Mans, SW20 . . . . . **184** A2
MERTON PARK, SW19 . . . **184** D2
Merton Pk Par, SW19 *off Kingston Rd* **184** C1
Merton Ri, NW3 . . . . . **91** H7
Merton Rd, E17 . . . . . **78** C5
SE25 . . . . . **188** D5
SW18 . . . . . **148** D5
SW19 . . . . . **166** E7
Barking IG11 . . . . . **99** J7
Harrow HA2 . . . . . **85** J1
Ilford IG3 . . . . . **81** J7
Merton Way, W.Mol. KT8 . . . . . **179** H4
Merttins Rd, SE15 . . . . . **153** G5
Meru Cl, NW5 . . . . . **92** A5
Mervan Rd, SW2 . . . . . **151** G4
Mervyn Av, SE9 . . . . . **175** F3
Mervyn Rd, W13 . . . . . **124** D3
Messaline Av, W3 . . . . . **106** C6
Messent Rd, SE9 . . . . . **155** J5
Messeter Pl, SE9 . . . . . **156** D6
Messina Av, NW6 . . . . . **90** D7
Metcalf Wk, Felt. TW13 *off Cresswell Rd* **160** E4
Meteor St, SW11 . . . . . **150** A4
Meteor Way, Wall. SM6 . . . **200** E7
Methley St, SE11 . . . . . **35** F4
★ **Methodist Cen Hall**, SW1 . . . . . **25** J4
Methuen Cl, Edg. HA8 . . . . **54** A7
Methuen Pk, N10 . . . . . **74** B2
Methuen Rd, Belv. DA17 . **139** H4
Bexleyheath DA6 . . . . . **159** F4
Edgware HA8 . . . . . **54** A7
Methven Ct, N9 *off The Broadway* **60** D3
Methwold Rd, W10 . . . . . **108** A5
Metro Business Cen, SE26 . . . . . **171** J5
Metro Cen Hts, SE1 . . . . . **27** J6
Metro Ind Cen, Islw. TW7 . **144** B2
Metropolis Cen, Borwd. WD6 . . . . . **38** A3
Metropolitan Cen, The, Grnf. UB6 . . . . . **103** H1
Metropolitan Cl, E14 *off Broomfield St* **114** A5
Mews, The, N1 *off St. Paul St* **111** J1
N8 *off Turnpike La* **75** G3
Ilford IG4 . . . . . **80** A5
Twickenham TW1 *off Bridge Rd* **144** E6
Mews Deck, E1 *off Sovereign Cl* **113** E7
Mews Pl, Wdf.Grn. IG8 . . . **63** G4
Mews St, E1 . . . . . **29** H1
Mexfield Rd, SW15 . . . . . **148** C5
Meyer Rd, Erith DA8 . . . . . **139** J6
Meymott St, SE1 . . . . . **27** G2
Meynell Cres, E9 . . . . . **95** G7
Meynell Gdns, E9 . . . . . **95** G7
Meynell Rd, E9 . . . . . **95** G7
Meyrick Rd, NW10 . . . . . **89** G6
SW11 . . . . . **149** G3
★ **MI5 (Security Service) Thames Ho**, SW1 . . . . . **34** A1
Miah Ter, E1 . . . . . **29** J2
Miall Wk, SE26 . . . . . **171** H4
Micawber St, N1 . . . . . **12** A3
Michael Cliffe Ho, EC1 . . . . **11** F4
Michael Faraday Ho, SE17 . . . . . **36** C4
Michael Gaynor Cl, W7 . . . **124** C1
Michaelmas Cl, SW20 . . . **183** J3
Michael Rd, E11 . . . . . **97** E1
SE25 . . . . . **188** B3
SW6 . . . . . **149** E1
Michaels Cl, SE13 . . . . . **154** E4
Michael Stewart Ho, SW6 *off Clem Attlee Ct* **128** C6
Micheldever Rd, SE12 . . . **155** E6
Michelham Gdns, Twick. TW1 . . . . . **162** C3
Michels Row, Rich. TW9 *off Kew Foot Rd* **145** H4
Michel Wk, SE18 . . . . . **137** E5
Michigan Av, E12 . . . . . **98** B4
Michigan Bldg, E14 *off Blackwall Way* **114** C7
Michleham Down, N12 . . . . **56** C4
Mickleham Cl, Orp. BR5 . . **193** J2
Mickleham Gdns, Sutt. SM3 . . . . . **198** B6
Mickleham Rd, Orp. BR5 . **193** J1
Mickleham Way, Croy. (New Adgtn) CR0 . . . . . **204** D7
Micklethwaite Rd, SW6 . . **128** D6
Middle Dartrey Wk, SW10 *off Blantyre St* **30** E7
Middle Dene, NW7 . . . . . **54** D3
Middle Fld, NW8 . . . . . **109** G1
Middlefielde, W13 . . . . . **104** E5
Middlefield Gdns, Ilf. IG2 . . **81** E6
Middle Grn Cl, Surb. KT5 *off Alpha Rd* **181** J6
Middleham Gdns, N18 . . . . **60** D6
Middleham Rd, N18 . . . . . **60** D6
Middle La, N8 . . . . . **74** E5
Teddington TW11 . . . . . **162** C6
Middle La Ms, N8 *off Middle La* **74** E5
Middle Pk Av, SE9 . . . . . **156** A6
Middle Path, Har. HA2 *off Middle Rd* **86** A1
Middle Rd, E13 *off London Rd* **115** G2
SW16 . . . . . **186** D2
Barnet (E.Barn.) EN4 . . . **41** H6
Harrow HA2 . . . . . **86** A2
Middle Row, W10 . . . . . **108** B4
Middlesborough Rd, N18 . . **60** D6
Middlesex Business Cen, Sthl. UB2 . . . . . **123** G2
Middlesex Cl, Sthl. UB1 . . **103** H4
Middlesex Ct, W4 . . . . . **127** F5
Middlesex Ho, Wem. HA0 . . . . . **105** G1
Middlesex Pas, EC1 . . . . . **19** H2
Middlesex Rd, Mitch. CR4 . . . . . **186** E5
Middlesex St, E1 . . . . . **20** E2
Middlesex Wf, E5 . . . . . **95** F2
Middle St, EC1 . . . . . **19** J1
Croydon CR0 *off Surrey St* **201** J2
Middle Temple, EC4 . . . . . **19** E5
Middle Temple La, EC4 . . . . **18** E4
Middleton Av, E4 . . . . . **61** J4
Greenford UB6 . . . . . **104** A2
Sidcup DA14 . . . . . **176** C6
Middleton Cl, E4 . . . . . **61** J3
Middleton Dr, SE16 . . . . . **133** G2
Pinner HA5 . . . . . **66** A3
Middleton Gdns, Ilf. IG2 . . . **80** E6
Middleton Gro, N7 . . . . . **92** E5
Middleton Ms, N7 *off Middleton Gro* **92** E5
Middleton Pl, W1 . . . . . **17** F2
Middleton Rd, E8 . . . . . **94** C7
NW11 . . . . . **72** D7
Carshalton SM5 . . . . . **185** H7
Morden SM4 . . . . . **185** F6
Middleton St, E2 . . . . . **112** E3
Middleton Way, SE13 . . . . **154** D4
Middleway, NW11 . . . . . **73** E5
Middle Way, SW16 . . . . . **186** D2
Erith DA18 . . . . . **138** E3
Hayes UB4 . . . . . **102** C4
Middle Way, The, Har. HA3 . . . . . **68** C2
Middle Yd, SE1 . . . . . **28** D1
Midfield Av, Bexh. DA7 . . **159** J3
Midfield Par, Bexh. DA7 . . **159** J3
Midford Pl, W1 . . . . . **9** G6
Midholm, NW11 . . . . . **72** E4
Wembley HA9 . . . . . **88** A1
Midholm Cl, NW11 . . . . . **72** E4
Midholm Rd, Croy. CR0 . . **203** H2
Midhope St, WC1 . . . . . **10** B4
Midhurst Av, N10 . . . . . **74** A3
Croydon CR0 . . . . . **187** G7
Midhurst Hill, Bexh. DA6 . . . . . **159** G6
Midhurst Rd, W13 . . . . . **124** D2
Midhurst Way, E5 . . . . . **94** D4
Midland Cres, NW3 *off Finchley Rd* **91** F6
Midland Pl, E14 *off Ferry St* **134** C5
Midland Rd, E10 . . . . . **78** C7
NW1 . . . . . **9** J2
Midland Ter, NW2 . . . . . **90** A3
NW10 . . . . . **107** E4
Midleton Rd, N.Mal. KT3 . . . . . **182** C3
Midlothian Rd, E3 *off Burdett Rd* **113** J4
Midmoor Rd, SW12 . . . . . **168** C1
SW19 . . . . . **184** A1
Midship Cl, SE16 *off Surrey Water Rd* . . **133** G1
Midship Pt, E14 . . . . . **134** A2
Midstrath Rd, NW10 . . . . . **89** E4
Midsummer Av, Houns. TW4 . . . . . **143** F4
Midway, Sutt. SM3 . . . . . **184** C7
Midwinter Cl, Well. DA16 *off Hook La* **158** A3
Midwood Cl, NW2 . . . . . **89** H3
Miers Cl, E6 . . . . . **116** D1
Mighell Av, Ilf. IG4 . . . . . **80** A5
Milan Rd, Sthl. UB1 . . . . . **123** F2
Milborne Gro, SW10 . . . . . **30** D4
Milborne St, E9 . . . . . **95** F6
Milborough Cres, SE12 . . . **155** E6
Milcote St, SE1 . . . . . **27** G4
Mildenhall Rd, E5 . . . . . **95** F4
Mildmay Av, N1 . . . . . **94** A6
Mildmay Gro N, N1 . . . . . **94** A5
Mildmay Gro S, N1 . . . . . **94** A5
Mildmay Pk, N1 . . . . . **94** A5
Mildmay Pl, N16 *off Boleyn Rd* **94** B5
Mildmay Rd, N1 . . . . . **94** B5
Ilford IG1 *off Albert Rd* **99** E3
Romford RM7 . . . . . **83** J5
Mildmay St, N1 . . . . . **94** A6
Mildred Av, Borwd. WD6 . . **38** A4
Hayes UB3 . . . . . **121** G4
Northolt UB5 . . . . . **85** H5
MILE END, E1 . . . . . **113** G3
Mile End, The, E17 . . . . . **77** G1
Mile End Pl, E1 . . . . . **113** G4
Mile End Rd, E1 . . . . . **113** F5
E3 . . . . . **113** F5
Mile Rd, Wall. SM6 . . . . . **200** A1
Miles Cl, SE28 . . . . . **137** G1
Miles Dr, SE28 . . . . . **137** G1
Milespit Hill, NW7 . . . . . **55** H5
Miles Pl, NW1 . . . . . **15** F1
Surbiton KT5 *off Villiers Av* **181** J4
Miles Rd, N8 . . . . . **75** E3
Mitcham CR4 . . . . . **185** H3
Miles St, SW8 . . . . . **34** A6
Milestone Cl, N9 *off Chichester Rd* **60** D2
Sutton SM2 . . . . . **199** G6
Milestone Grn, SW14 . . . . **146** C4
Milestone Rd, SE19 . . . . . **170** C6
Miles Way, N20 . . . . . **57** H2
Milfoil St, W12 . . . . . **107** G7
Milford Cl, SE2 . . . . . **139** E6
Milford Gdns, Croy. CR0 *off Tannery Cl* **189** G5
Edgware HA8 . . . . . **54** A7
Wembley HA0 . . . . . **87** G5
Milford Gro, Sutt. SM1 . . . **199** F4
Milford La, WC2 . . . . . **18** D5
Milford Ms, SW16 . . . . . **169** F3
Milford Rd, W13 . . . . . **124** E1
Southall UB1 . . . . . **103** G7
Milford Twrs, SE6 *off Thomas La* **154** B7
Milk St, E16 . . . . . **136** E1
EC2 . . . . . **20** A4
Bromley BR1 . . . . . **173** H6
Milkwell Gdns, Wdf.Grn. IG8 . . . . . **63** H7
Milkwell Yd, SE5 . . . . . **151** J1
Milkwood Rd, SE24 . . . . . **151** H5
Milk Yd, E1 . . . . . **113** F7
Millais Av, E12 . . . . . **98** D5
Millais Cres, Epsom KT19 . . . . . **196** E5
Millais Gdns, Edg. HA8 . . . **70** A2
Millais Rd, E11 . . . . . **96** C4
Enfield EN1 . . . . . **44** C5
New Malden KT3 . . . . . **182** E7
Millais Way, Epsom KT19 . . . . . **196** C4
Milland Ct, Borwd. WD6 . . . **38** D1
Millard Cl, N16 *off Boleyn Rd* **94** B5
Millard Ter, Dag. RM10 *off Church Elm La* **101** G6
Millbank, SW1 . . . . . **26** A6
Millbank Ct, SW1 . . . . . **34** A1
Millbank Twr, SW1 . . . . . **34** A2
Millbank Way, SE12 . . . . . **155** G5
Millbourne Rd, Felt. TW13 . . . . . **161** E4
Mill Br, Barn. EN5 . . . . . **40** C6
Millbrook Av, Well. DA16 . . . . . **157** G4
Millbrook Gdns, Rom. (Chad.Hth) RM6 . . . . . **83** F6

Millbrook Pl, NW1
off Hampstead Rd **9** F1
Millbrook Rd, N9 **60** E1
SW9 **151** H3
Mill Cl, Cars. SM5 **200** A2
West Drayton UB7 **120** A3
Mill Cor, Barn. EN5 **40** C1
Mill Ct, E10 **96** C3
Millcroft Ho, SE6 **172** C4
Millender Wk, SE16 **133** F4
Millennium Br, EC4 **19** J5
SE1 **19** J5
Millennium Cl, E16
off Russell Rd **115** H6
Millennium Dr, E14 **134** D4
Millennium Harbour, E14 **133** J2
Millennium Pl, E2 **113** E2
Millennium Sq, SE1 **29** F3
Millennium Way, SE10 **134** E2
Miller Cl, Brom. BR1 **173** G5
Mitcham CR4 **185** J7
Pinner HA5 **66** C2
Miller Rd, SW19 **167** G6
Croydon CR0 **201** F1
Miller's Av, E8 **94** C5
Millers Cl, NW7 **55** G4
Millers Ct, W4
off Chiswick Mall **127** F5
Millers Grn Cl, Enf. EN2 **43** H3
Millers Meadow Cl, SE3
off Meadowcourt Rd **155** F5
Miller's Ter, E8 **94** C5
Miller St, NW1 **9** F1
Millers Way, W6 **127** J2
Miller Wk, SE1 **27** F2
Millet Rd, Grnf. UB6 **103** H3
Mill Fm Cl, Pnr. HA5 **66** C2
Mill Fm Cres, Houns.
TW4 **161** E1
Millfield, N4
off Six Acres Est **93** G2
Millfield Av, E17 **77** H1
Millfield La, N6 **91** J2
Millfield Pl, N6 **92** A2
Millfield Rd, Edg. HA8 **70** C2
Hounslow TW4 **161** E1
Millfields Est, E5 **95** G3
Millfields Rd, E5 **95** F4
Mill Gdns, SE26 **171** E4
Mill Grn, Mitch. CR4 **186** A7
Mill Grn Business Pk,
Mitch. CR4
off Mill Grn Rd **186** A7
Mill Grn Rd, Mitch. CR4 **185** J7
Millgrove St, SW11 **150** A2
Millharbour, E14 **134** B3
Millhaven Cl, Rom. RM6 **82** B6
MILL HILL, NW7 **55** G5
Mill Hill, SW13
off Mill Hill Rd **147** G2
Mill Hill Circ, NW7 **55** F5
Mill Hill Gro, W3 **126** B1
Mill Hill Ind Est, NW7 **55** F6
Mill Hill Rd, SW13 **147** G2
W3 **126** B2
Mill Hill Ter, W3
off Mill Hill Rd **126** C1
Millhouse Pl, SE27 **169** H4
Millicent Rd, E10 **95** J1
Milligan St, E14 **113** J7
Milliners Ct, Loug. IG10
off The Croft **48** D2
Milliners Ho, SW18
off Eastfields Av **148** D4
Milling Rd, Edg. HA8 **54** D7
Millington Rd, Hayes
UB3 **121** H3
Mill La, E4 **46** B3
NW6 **90** C5
SE18 **136** D5
Carshalton SM5 **199** J4
Croydon CR0 **201** F3
Romford (Chad.Hth)
RM6 **82** E6
Woodford Green IG8 **63** F5
Mill La Trd Est, Croy. CR0 **201** F3
Millman Ms, WC1 **10** C6
Millman Pl, WC1
off Millman St **10** C6
Millman St, WC1 **10** C6
Millmark Gro, SE14 **153** H2
Millmarsh La, Enf. EN3 **45** H2
Mill Mead Rd, N17 **76** E4
Mill Pl, E14
off Commercial Rd **113** H6
Chislehurst BR7
off Old Hill **192** E1
Kingston upon Thames
KT1 **181** J3
Mill Plat, Islw. TW7 **144** D2
Mill Plat Av, Islw. TW7 **144** D2
Mill Pond Cl, SW8
off Thorparch Rd **130** D7
Millpond Est, SE16
off West La **132** E2
Millpond Pl, Cars. SM5 **200** A3
Mill Ridge, Edg. HA8 **53** J5
Mill Rd, E16 **135** H1
SW19 **167** F7
Erith DA8 **139** J7
Ilford IG1 **98** D3
Twickenham TW2 **161** J2
Mill Row, N1 **112** B1
Mills Ct, EC2 **12** E4
Mills Gro, E14
off Dewberry St **114** C5
NW4 **72** A3
Millshott Cl, SW6 **127** J7
Millside, Cars. SM5 **199** J2
Millside Pl, Islw. TW7 **144** E2
Millsmead Way, Loug.
IG10 **48** C2
Millson Cl, N20 **57** G2
Mills Row, W4 **126** D4
Millstream Cl, N13 **59** G5
Millstream Rd, SE1 **29** F4
Mill St, SE1 **29** G4
W1 **17** E5
Kingston upon Thames
KT1 **181** H3
Mill Vale, Brom. BR2 **191** F2
Mill Vw Cl, Epsom (Ewell)
KT17 **197** F7
Mill Vw Gdns, Croy. CR0 **203** G3
MILLWALL, E14 **134** B3
Millwall Dock Rd, E14 **134** A3
★ **Millwall FC**, SE16 **133** F5
Millway, NW7 **54** E5
Mill Way, Felt. TW14 **142** B5
Millway Gdns, Nthlt. UB5 **85** F6
Millwell Cres, Chig. IG7 **65** G5
Millwood Rd, Houns.
TW3 **143** J5
Millwood St, W10
off St. Charles Sq **108** B5
Mill Yd, E1 **21** H5
Mill Yd Indusrial Est, Edg.
HA8 **70** B1
Milman Cl, Pnr. HA5 **66** D3
Milman Rd, NW6 **108** B2
Milman's St, SW10 **31** E6
Milmead Ind Cen, N17 **76** E2
Milne Ct, E18
off Churchfields **79** G1
Milne Feild, Pnr. HA5 **51** G7
Milne Gdns, SE9 **156** B5
Milner Dr, Twick. TW2 **144** A7
Milner Pl, N1 **111** G1
Carshalton SM5
off High St **200** A4
Milner Rd, E15 **114** E3
SW19 **184** E1
Dagenham RM8 **100** C2
Kingston upon Thames
KT1 **181** G3
Morden SM4 **185** G5
Thornton Heath CR7 **188** A3
Milner Sq, N1 **93** H7
Milner St, SW3 **31** J1
Milner Wk, SE9 **175** G2
Milnthorpe Rd, W4 **126** D6
Milo Gdns, SE22
off Milo Rd **152** C6
Milo Rd, SE22 **152** C6
Milroy Wk, SE1 **27** G1
Milson Rd, W14 **128** B3
Milstead Ho, E5
off Pembury Rd **94** E5
Milton Av, E6 **98** A7
N6 **74** C7
NW9 **70** C3
NW10 **106** C1
Barnet EN5 **40** C5
Croydon CR0 **188** A7
Sutton SM1 **199** G3
Milton Cl, N2 **73** F5
SE1 **37** F2
Hayes UB4 **102** A6
Sutton SM1 **199** G3
Milton Ct, EC2 **20** B1
Romford (Chad.Hth)
RM6 *off Cross Rd* **82** C7
Milton Ct Rd, SE14 **133** H6
Milton Cres, Ilf. IG2 **81** F7
Milton Dr, Borwd. WD6 **38** B5
Milton Gdn Est, N16
off Milton Gro **94** B4
Milton Gro, N11 **58** C5
N16 **94** A4
Milton Pk, N6 **74** C7
Milton Pl, N7
off George's Rd **93** G5
Milton Rd, E17 **78** A4
N6 **74** C7
N15 **75** H4
NW7 **55** G5
NW9
off West Hendon Bdy **71** G7
SE24 **151** H6
SW14 **146** D3
Milton Rd, SW19 **167** F6
W3 **126** D1
W7 **104** C7
Belvedere DA17 **139** G4
Croydon CR0 **202** A1
Hampton TW12 **161** G7
Harrow HA1 **68** B4
Mitcham CR4 **168** A7
Sutton SM1 **198** D3
Wallington SM6 **200** C6
Welling DA16 **157** J1
Milton St, EC2 **20** B1
Milton Way, West Dr.
UB7 **120** C4
Milverton Gdns, Ilf. IG3 **99** J2
Milverton Ho, SE23 **171** H3
Milverton Rd, NW6 **89** J7
Milverton St, SE11 **35** F4
Milverton Way, SE9 **174** D4
Milward St, E1
off Stepney Way **113** E5
Milward Wk, SE18
off Spearman St **136** D6
Mimosa Rd, Hayes UB4 **102** C5
Mimosa St, SW6 **148** C1
Minard Rd, SE6 **154** E7
Mina Rd, SE17 **36** E4
SW19 **184** D1
Minchenden Cres, N14 **58** C3
Mincing La, EC3 **20** D5
Minden Rd, SE20 **188** E1
Sutton SM3 **198** C2
Minehead Rd, SW16 **169** F5
Harrow HA2 **85** G3
Mineral Cl, Barn. EN5 **39** J6
Mineral St, SE18 **137** H4
Minera Ms, SW1 **32** C1
Minerva Cl, SW9 **131** G7
Sidcup DA14 **175** H3
Minerva Rd, E4 **62** B7
NW10 **106** C4
Kingston upon Thames
KT1 **181** J2
Minerva St, E2 **112** E2
Minet Av, NW10 **106** E2
Minet Dr, Hayes UB3 **122** A1
Minet Gdns, NW10 **106** E2
Hayes UB3 **122** A1
Minet Rd, SW9 **151** H2
Minford Gdns, W14 **128** A2
Mingard Wk, N7
off Hornsey Rd **93** F3
Ming St, E14 **114** A7
★ **Ministry of Defence**,
SW1 **26** A2
Ministry Way, SE9 **174** C2
Miniver Pl, EC4
off Garlick Hill **20** A5
Mink Ct, Houns. TW4 **142** C3
Minniedale, Surb. KT5 **181** J5
Minnow St, SE17 **36** E2
Minnow Wk, SE17
off Minnow St **36** E2
Minories, EC3 **21** F5
Minshull Pl, Beck. BR3 **172** A7
Minshull St, SW8
off Wandsworth Rd **150** D1
Minson Rd, E9 **113** G1
Minstead Gdns, SW15 **147** F7
Minstead Way, N.Mal.
KT3 **182** E6
Minster Av, Sutt. SM1
off Leafield Rd **198** D2
Minster Ct, EC3 **20** D5
Minster Dr, Croy. CR0 **202** B4
Minster Gdns, W.Mol.
KT8 **179** F4
Minster Pavement, EC3
off Mincing La **20** D5
Minster Rd, NW2 **90** B5
Bromley BR1 **173** H7
Minster Wk, N8
off Lightfoot Rd **74** E4
Minstrel Gdns, Surb.
KT5 **181** J4
Mint Business Pk, E16 **115** G5
Mintern Cl, N13 **59** H3
Minterne Av, Sthl. UB2 **123** G4
Minterne Rd, Har. HA3 **69** J5
Minterne Waye, Hayes
UB4 **102** C6
Mintern St, N1 **12** C1
Minton Ho, SE11
off Walnut Tree Wk **34** E1
Minton Ms, NW6
off Dresden Cl **91** E6
Mint Rd, Wall. SM6 **200** B4
Mint St, SE1 **27** J3
Mint Wk, Croy. CR0
off High St **201** J3
Mirabel Rd, SW6 **128** C7
Miranda Cl, E1
off Sidney St **113** F5
Miranda Ct, W3
off Queens Dr **105** J6
Miranda Rd, N19 **92** C1
Mirfield St, SE7 **136** A4
Miriam Rd, SE18 **137** H5
Mirravale Trd Est, Dag.
RM8 **83** F7
Mirren Cl, Har. HA2 **85** F4
Mirror Path, SE9
off Lambscroft Av **173** J3
Missenden Gdns, Mord.
SM4 **185** F6
Mission Gro, E17 **77** H5
Mission Pl, SE15 **152** D1
Mission Sq, Brent. TW8 **125** H6
Mistletoe Cl, Croy. CR0
off Marigold Way **203** G1
Mistral, SE5
off Sceaux Gdns **152** B1
Mitali Pas, E1 **21** H4
MITCHAM, CR4 **186** A3
Mitcham Gdn Village,
Mitch. CR4 **186** A5
Mitcham Ind Est, Mitch.
CR4 **186** A1
Mitcham La, SW16 **168** C6
Mitcham Pk, Mitch. CR4 **185** J4
Mitcham Rd, E6 **116** B3
SW17 **167** J5
Croydon CR0 **186** E6
Ilford IG3 **81** J7
Mitchellbrook Way, NW10 **88** D6
Mitchell Cl, SE2 **138** C4
Belvedere DA17 **139** J3
Mitchell Rd, N13 **59** H5
Orpington BR6 **207** J4
Mitchell's Pl, SE21
off Dulwich Village **152** B7
Mitchell St, EC1 **11** J5
Mitchell Wk, E6 **116** B5
Mitchell Way, NW10 **88** C6
Bromley BR1 **191** G1
Mitchison Rd, N1 **94** A6
Mitchley Rd, N17 **76** D3
Mitford Cl, Chess. KT9
off Merritt Gdns **195** F6
Mitford Rd, N19 **93** E2
Mitre, The, E14
off Three Colt St **113** J7
Mitre Av, E17
off Greenleaf Rd **77** J3
Mitre Cl, Brom. BR2
off Beckenham La **191** F2
Sutton SM2 **199** F7
Mitre Ct, EC2 **20** A3
Mitre Rd, E15 **114** E2
SE1 **27** F3
Mitre Sq, EC3 **21** E4
Mitre St, EC3 **21** E4
Mitre Way, W10 **107** H4
Mizzen Mast Ho, SE18
off Woolwich Ch St **136** D3
Moat, The, N.Mal. KT3 **182** E1
Moat Cl, Orp. BR6 **207** J6
Moat Cres, N3 **72** E3
Moat Cft, Well. DA16 **158** C3
Moat Dr, E13
off Boundary Rd **115** J2
Harrow HA1 **67** J4
Moat Fm Rd, Nthlt. UB5 **85** F6
Moat Pl, SW9 **151** F3
W3 **106** B6
Moatside, Enf. EN3 **45** G4
Feltham TW13 **160** C4
Moberly Rd, SW4 **150** D7
Moby Dick, Rom. RM6 **83** F4
Modbury Gdns, NW5
off Queen's Cres **92** A6
Modder Pl, SW15 **148** A4
Model Cotts, SW14 **146** C3
Model Fm Cl, SE9 **174** B3
Modling Ho, E2 **113** F2
Moelwyn Hughes Ct, N7
off Hilldrop Cres **92** D5
Moelyn Ms, Har. HA1 **68** D5
Moffat Ho, SE5
off Comber Gro **131** J7
Moffat Rd, N13 **59** E6
SW17 **167** H4
Thornton Heath CR7 **187** J2
Mogden La, Islw. TW7 **144** B5
Mohmmad Khan Rd, E11
off Harvey Rd **97** F1
Moira Cl, N17 **76** B2
Moira Rd, SE9 **156** C4
Molasses Row, SW11
off Cinnamon Row **149** F3
Mole Abbey Gdns, W.Mol.
KT8 *off New Rd* **179** G3
Mole Ct, Epsom KT19 **196** C4
Molember Ct, E.Mol.
KT8 **180** B5
Molember Rd, E.Mol.
KT8 **180** B5
Molescroft, SE9 **175** F3
Molesey Av, W.Mol. KT8 **179** F4
Molesey Dr, Sutt. SM3 **198** B2

Molesey Pk Av, W.Mol. KT8 179 H5
Molesey Pk Cl, E.Mol. KT8 179 J5
Molesey Pk Rd, E.Mol. KT8 180 A5
West Molesey KT8 179 H5
Molesey Rd, W.Mol. KT8 179 E5
Molesford Rd, SW6 148 D1
Molesham Cl, W.Mol. KT8 179 H3
Molesham Way, W.Mol. KT8 179 H3
Molesworth St, SE13 154 C3
Mollison Av, Enf. EN3 45 H5
Mollison Dr, Wall. SM6 201 E6
Mollison Sq, Wall. SM6
off Mollison Dr 200 E7
Mollison Way, Edg. HA8 70 A2
Molly Huggins Cl, SW12 150 C7
Molyneux Dr, SW17 168 B4
Molyneux St, W1 15 H2
Monarch Cl, Felt. TW14 141 H7
West Wickham BR4 205 F4
Monarch Dr, E16 116 A5
Monarch Ms, E17 78 B5
SW16 169 G5
Monarch Par, Mitch. CR4
off London Rd 185 J2
Monarch Pl, Buck.H. IG9 63 J2
Monarch Rd, Belv. DA17 139 G3
Monarchs Ct, NW7
off Grenville Pl 54 D5
Monarch Way, Ilf. IG2 81 G6
Mona Rd, SE15 153 F2
Monastery Gdns, Enf. EN2 44 A2
Mona St, E16 115 F5
Monaveen Gdns, W.Mol. KT8 179 G3
Monck St, SW1 25 J6
Monclar Rd, SE5 152 A4
Moncorvo Cl, SW7 23 G4
Moncrieff Cl, E6
off Linton Gdns 116 B6
Moncrieff Pl, SE15
off Rye La 152 D2
Moncrieff St, SE15 152 D2
Mondial Way, Hayes (Harling.) UB3 121 F7
Monega Rd, E7 97 J6
E12 98 A6
Money La, West Dr. UB7 120 A3
Monier Rd, E3 96 A7
Monivea Rd, Beck. BR3 171 J7
Monkchester Cl, Loug. IG10 48 D1
Monk Dr, E16 115 G6
MONKEN HADLEY, Barn. EN5 40 C1
Monkfrith Av, N14 42 B6
Monkfrith Cl, N14 42 B7
Monkfrith Way, N14 42 A7
Monkhams Av, Wdf.Grn. IG8 63 G5
Monkhams Dr, Wdf.Grn. IG8 63 H4
Monkhams La, Buck.H. IG9 63 H3
Woodford Green IG8 63 G5
Monkleigh Rd, Mord. SM4 184 B3
Monk Pas, E16
off Monk Dr 115 G7
Monks Av, Barn. EN5 41 F6
West Molesey KT8 179 F5
Monks Cl, SE2 138 D4
Enfield EN2 43 J2
Harrow HA2 85 H2
Ruislip HA4 84 D4
Monksdene Gdns, Sutt. SM1 199 E3
Monks Dr, W3 106 A5
Monksgrove, Loug. IG10 48 D5
Monksmead, Borwd. WD6 38 C4
MONKS ORCHARD, Croy. CR0 189 J7
Monks Orchard Rd, Beck. BR3 204 A1
Monks Pk, Wem. HA9 88 C6
Monks Pk Gdns, Wem. HA9 88 B6
Monk's Ridge, N20 55 H1
Monks Rd, Enf. EN2 43 J2
Monk St, SE18 136 D4
Monks Way, NW11
off Hurstwood Rd 72 C4
Beckenham BR3 190 A6
Orpington BR5 207 F1
West Drayton (Harm.) UB7 120 B6
Monkswell Ct, N10 74 A1
Monkswood Gdns, Borwd. WD6 38 D5
Ilford IG5 80 D3
Monkton Ho, E5
off Pembury Rd 94 E5
Monkton Rd, Well. DA16 157 J2
Monkton St, SE11 35 F1
Monkville Av, NW11 72 C4
Monkwell Sq, EC2 20 A2
Monmouth Av, E18 79 H4
Kingston upon Thames KT1 163 F7
Monmouth Cl, W4
off Beaumont Rd 126 D3
Mitcham CR4
off Recreation Way 187 E4
Welling DA16 158 A4
Monmouth Gro, Brent. TW8 *off Sterling Pl* 125 H4
Monmouth Ho, NW5
off Raglan St 92 B6
Monmouth Pl, W2
off Monmouth Rd 108 D6
Monmouth Rd, E6 116 C3
N9 60 E2
W2 108 D6
Dagenham RM9 101 F5
Hayes UB3 121 H4
Monmouth St, WC2 18 A4
Monnery Rd, N19 92 C3
Monnow Rd, SE1 37 H3
Mono La, Felt. TW13 160 B2
Monoux Gro, E17 78 A1
Monroe Cres, Enf. EN1 44 E1
Monroe Dr, SW14 146 B5
Monro Gdns, Har. HA3 52 B7
Monro Way, E5 94 D4
Monsal Ct, E5
off Redwald Rd 95 H4
Monsell Ct, N4
off Monsell Rd 93 H3
Monsell Rd, N4 93 H3
Monson Rd, NW10 107 G2
SE14 133 G7
Mons Way, Brom. BR2 192 B6
Montacute Rd, SE6 153 J7
Morden SM4 185 G6
Montagu Cres, N18 61 E4
Montague Av, SE4 153 J4
W7 124 C1
Montague Cl, SE1 28 B1
Barnet EN5 40 C4
Walton-on-Thames KT12 178 A7
Montague Gdns, W3 106 A7
Montague Pl, WC1 17 J1
Montague Rd, E8 94 D5
E11 97 F2
N8 75 F5
N15 76 D4
SW19 166 E7
W7 124 C1
W13 105 E6
Croydon CR0 201 H1
Hounslow TW3 143 H3
Richmond TW10 145 H6
Southall UB2 122 E4
Montague Sq, SE15
off Clifton Way 133 F7
Montague St, EC1 19 J2
WC1 18 A1
Montague Waye, Sthl. UB2 122 E3
Montagu Gdns, N18 60 E4
Wallington SM6 200 C4
Montagu Mans, W1 16 A1
Montagu Ms N, W1 16 A2
Montagu Ms S, W1 16 A3
Montagu Ms W, W1 16 A3
Montagu Pl, W1 15 J2
Montagu Rd, N9 61 F4
N18 61 E5
NW4 71 G6
Montagu Rd Ind Est, N18 61 F4
Montagu Row, W1 16 A2
Montagu Sq, W1 16 A2
Montagu St, W1 16 A3
Montaigne Cl, SW1 33 J2
Montalt Rd, Wdf.Grn. IG8 63 F5
Montana Bldg, SE13
off Deals Gateway 154 B1
Montana Gdns, SE26 171 J5
Sutton SM1
off Lind Rd 199 F5
Montana Rd, SW17 168 A4
SW20 183 J1
Montbelle Rd, SE9 174 E3
Montcalm Cl, Brom. BR2 191 G6
Hayes UB4
off Ayles Rd 102 B3
Montcalm Rd, SE7 136 A7
Montclare St, E2 13 F4
Monteagle Av, Bark. IG11 99 F6
Monteagle Way, E5 94 D3
SE15 153 E3
Montefiore St, SW8 150 B2
Montego Cl, SE24
off Railton Rd 151 G4
Montem Rd, SE23 153 J7
New Malden KT3 182 E4
Montem St, N4
off Thorpedale Rd 93 F1
Montenotte Rd, N8 74 C5
Monterey Cl, NW7
off The Broadway 55 E5
Bexley DA5 177 J2
Montesole Ct, Pnr. HA5 66 C2
Montevetro, SW11 149 G1
Montford Pl, SE11 34 E4
Montford Rd, Sun. TW16 178 A4
Montfort Gdns, Ilf. IG6 65 F6
Montfort Pl, SW19 166 A1
Montgolfier Wk, Nthlt. UB5
off Wayfarer Rd 102 E3
Montgomerie Ms, SE23 153 F7
Montgomery Av, Esher KT10 194 B3
Montgomery Cl, Mitch. CR4 187 E4
Sidcup DA15 157 J6
Montgomery Ct, W2
off Harrow Rd 14 E2
W4
off St. Thomas' Rd 126 C6
Montgomery Gdns, Sutt. SM2 199 G7
Montgomery Rd, W4 126 C4
Edgware HA8 53 J6
Montgomery St, E14 134 B1
Montholme Rd, SW11 149 J6
Monthope Rd, E1 21 H2
Montolieu Gdns, SW15 147 H5
Montpelier Av, W5 105 F5
Bexley DA5 158 D7
Montpelier Gdns, E6 116 A3
Romford RM6 82 C7
Montpelier Gro, NW5 92 C5
Montpelier Ms, SW7 23 H5
Montpelier Pl, E1 113 F6
SW7 23 H5
Montpelier Ri, NW11 72 B7
Wembley HA9 87 G1
Montpelier Rd, N3 73 F1
SE15 153 E1
W5 105 G5
Sutton SM1 199 F4
Montpelier Row, SE3 155 F2
Twickenham TW1 145 E7
Montpelier Sq, SW7 23 H4
Montpelier St, SW7 23 H4
Montpelier Ter, SW7 23 H4
Montpelier Vale, SE3 155 F2
Montpelier Wk, SW7 23 H5
Montpelier Way, NW11 72 B7
Montrave Rd, SE20 171 F6
Montreal Pl, WC2 18 C5
Montreal Rd, Ilf. IG1 81 F7
Montrell Rd, SW2 169 E1
Montrose Av, NW6 108 B2
Edgware HA8 70 C2
Sidcup DA15 158 A7
Twickenham TW2 143 H7
Welling DA16 157 G3
Montrose Cl, Well. DA16 157 J3
Woodford Green IG8 63 G4
Montrose Ct, SW7 23 F4
Montrose Cres, N12 57 F6
Wembley HA0 87 H6
Montrose Gdns, Mitch. CR4 185 J3
Sutton SM1 199 E2
Montrose Pl, SW1 24 C4
Montrose Rd, Felt. TW14 141 G6
Harrow HA3 68 B2
Montrose Way, SE23 171 G1
Montserrat Av, Wdf.Grn. IG8 62 D7
Montserrat Cl, SE19 170 A5
Montserrat Rd, SW15 148 B4
★ **Monument, The**, EC3 20 C6
Monument Gdns, SE13 154 C5
Monument St, EC3 20 C6
Monument Way, N17 76 C3
Monza St, E1 113 F7
Moodkee St, SE16 133 F3
Moody Rd, SE15 132 C7
Moody St, E1 113 G3
Moon La, Barn. EN5 40 C3
Moon St, N1 111 H1
Moorcroft Gdns, Brom. BR2
off Southborough Rd 192 B5
Moorcroft Rd, SW16 168 E3
Moorcroft Way, Pnr. HA5 66 E5
Moordown, SE18 156 D1
Moore Cl, SW14 146 C3
Mitcham CR4 186 B2
Moore Cres, Dag. RM9 118 B1
Moorefield Rd, N17 76 C2
Moorehead Way, SE3 155 H3
Moore Ho, E14
off Cassilis Rd 134 A2
Mooreland Rd, Brom. BR1 173 F7
Moore Pk Rd, SW6 128 E7
Moore Rd, SE19 169 J6
Moore St, SW3 31 J1
Moore Wk, E7
off Stracey Rd 97 G4
Moorey Cl, E15
off Stephen's Rd 115 F1
Moorfield Av, W5 105 G4
Moorfield Rd, Chess. KT9 195 H5
Enfield EN3 45 F1
Moorfields, EC2 20 B2
Moorfields Highwalk, EC2 20 B2
Moorgate, EC2 20 B3
Moorgate Pl, EC2 20 B3
Moorhouse Rd, W2 108 D6
Harrow HA3 69 G3
Moorings, SE28 118 B7
Moorings, The, E16
off Prince Regent La 115 J5
Moorings Ho, Brent. TW8
off Tallow Rd 125 F7
Moorland Cl, Twick. TW2
off Telford Rd 143 G7
Moorland Rd, SW9 151 H4
Moorlands Av, NW7 55 H6
Moorlands Est, SW9 151 G4
Moor La, EC2 20 B2
Chessington KT9 195 H4
Moormead Dr, Epsom KT19 197 E5
Moor Mead Rd, Twick. TW1 144 D6
Moor Pk Gdns, Kings.T. KT2 165 E7
Moor Pl, EC2 20 B2
Moorside Rd, Brom. BR1 173 E3
Moor St, W1 17 J4
Moortown Rd, Wat. WD19 50 C4
Moot Ct, NW9 70 A5
Morant Pl, N22
off Commerce Rd 75 F1
Morant St, E14 114 A7
Mora Rd, NW2 89 J4
Mora St, EC1 12 A4
Morat St, SW9 151 F1
Moravian Pl, SW10 31 F6
Moravian St, E2 113 F2
Moray Av, Hayes UB3 121 J1
Moray Cl, Edg. HA8
off Pentland Av 54 B2
Moray Ms, N7
off Durham Rd 93 F2
Moray Rd, N4 93 F2
Mordaunt Gdns, Dag. RM9 100 E7
Mordaunt Ho, NW10 106 D1
Mordaunt Rd, NW10 106 D1
Mordaunt St, SW9 151 F3
MORDEN, SM4 184 D3
Morden Ct, Mord. SM4 184 E4
Morden Gdns, Grnf. UB6 86 C5
Mitcham CR4 185 G4
★ **Morden Hall Pk N.T.**, Mord. SM4 185 E3
Morden Hall Rd, Mord. SM4 185 E3
Morden Hill, SE13 154 C2
Morden La, SE13 154 C1
MORDEN PARK, Mord. SM4 184 B5
Morden Rd, SE3 155 G2
SW19 167 E7
Mitcham CR4 185 F4
Romford RM6 83 E7
Morden Rd Ms, SE3 155 G2
Morden St, SE13 154 B1
Morden Way, Sutt. SM3 184 D7
Morden Wf Rd, SE10 134 E3
Mordon Rd, Ilf. IG3 81 J7
Mordred Ct, N9
off Galahad Rd 60 D2
Mordred Rd, SE6 172 E2
Morecambe Cl, E1 113 G5
Morecambe Gdns, Stan. HA7 53 G4
Morecambe St, SE17 36 A2
Morecambe Ter, N18 60 A4
More Cl, E16 115 F6
W14 128 B4
Morecoombe Cl, Kings.T. KT2 164 B7
Moree Way, N18 60 D4
Moreland St, EC1 11 H3
Moreland Way, E4 62 B3
Morella Rd, SW12 149 J7
Morell Cl, Barn. EN5 41 F3
More London Pl, SE1 28 D2
More London Riverside, SE1 28 E2
Moremead Rd, SE6 171 J4
Morena St, SE6 154 B7
Moresby Av, Surb. KT5 182 B7
Moresby Rd, E5 94 E1

Moresby Wk, SW8 **150** B2
Moreton Av, Islw. TW7 **144** B1
Moreton Cl, E5 **95** F2
N15 **76** A6
NW7 **55** J6
SW1 **33** G3
Moreton Gdns, Wdf.Grn. IG8 **64** B5
Moreton Ho, SE16
off Slippers Pl **133** E3
Moreton Pl, SW1 **33** G3
Moreton Rd, N15 **76** A6
South Croydon CR2 **202** A5
Worcester Park KT4 **197** G2
Moreton St, SW1 **33** G3
Moreton Ter, SW1 **33** G3
Moreton Ter Ms N, SW1 **33** G3
Moreton Ter Ms S, SW1 **33** G3
Moreton Twr, W3 **126** B1
Morford Cl, Ruis. HA4 **66** B7
Morford Way, Ruis. HA4 **66** B7
Morgan Av, E17 **78** D4
Morgan Cl, Dag. RM10 **101** G7
Morgan Ct, N9
off Galahad Rd **60** D3
SW11
off Battersea High St **149** G1
Morgan Ho, SW1
off Vauxhall Br Rd **33** G2
Morgan Rd, N7 **93** G5
W10 **108** C5
Bromley BR1 **173** G7
Morgans La, SE1 **28** D2
Morgan St, E3 **113** H3
E16 **115** F5
Morgan Way, Wdf.Grn. IG8 **64** B6
Moriarty Cl, Brom. BR1 **192** E4
Moriatry Cl, N7 **92** E4
Morie St, SW18 **149** E4
Morieux Rd, E10 **95** J1
Moring Rd, SW17 **168** A4
Morkyns Wk, SE21 **170** B3
Morland Av, Croy. CR0 **202** B1
Morland Cl, NW11 **91** E1
Hampton TW12 **161** F5
Mitcham CR4 **185** H3
Morland Est, E8
off Richmond Rd **94** D7
Morland Gdns, NW10 **88** D7
Southall UB1 **123** H1
Morland Ms, N1
off Lofting Rd **93** G7
Morland Rd, E17 **77** G5
SE20 **171** G6
Croydon CR0 **202** B1
Dagenham RM10 **101** G7
Harrow HA3 **69** H5
Ilford IG1 **98** E2
Sutton SM1 **199** F5
Morley Av, E4 **62** D7
N18 **60** D4
N22 **75** G2
Morley Cl, Orp. BR6 **207** E2
Morley Cres, Edg. HA8 **54** C2
Ruislip HA4 **84** C2
Morley Cres E, Stan. HA7 **69** F2
Morley Cres W, Stan. HA7 **69** F2
Morley Rd, E10 **96** C1
E15 **115** F2
SE13 **154** C4
Barking IG11 **117** G1
Chislehurst BR7 **193** F1
Romford RM6 **82** E5
Sutton SM3 **198** C1
Twickenham TW1 **145** G6
Morley St, SE1 **27** F5
Morna Rd, SE5 **151** J2
Morning La, E9 **95** F6
Morningside Rd, Wor.Pk. KT4 **197** H2
Mornington Av, W14 **128** C4
Bromley BR1 **191** J3
Ilford IG1 **80** D7
Mornington Cl, Wdf.Grn. IG8 **63** G4
Mornington Ct, Bex. DA5 **177** J1
Mornington Cres, NW1 **9** F1
Hounslow TW5 **142** B1
Mornington Gro, E3 **114** A3
Mornington Ms, SE5 **151** J1
Mornington Pl, NW1 **9** E1
Mornington Rd, E4 **46** D7
E11 **97** F1
SE8 **133** J7
Greenford UB6 **103** H5
Loughton IG10 **49** F3
Woodford Green IG8 **63** F4
Mornington St, NW1 **8** E1
Mornington Ter, NW1 **110** B1
Mornington Wk, Rich. TW10 **163** F4
Morocco St, SE1 **28** D4
Morpeth Gro, E9 **113** G1
Morpeth Rd, E9 **113** F1
Morpeth St, E2 **113** G3
Morpeth Ter, SW1 **25** F6
Morpeth Wk, N17
off West Rd **60** E7
Morrab Gdns, Ilf. IG3 **99** J3
Morrells Yd, SE11 **35** F3
Morris Av, E12 **98** C5
Morris Cl, Croy. CR0 **189** H6
Orpington BR6 **207** H3
Morris Ct, E4 **62** B3
Morris Gdns, SW18 **148** D7
Morrish Rd, SW2 **151** E7
Morrison Av, E4 **62** A6
N17 **76** B3
Morrison Rd, SW9
off Marcella Rd **151** G2
Barking IG11 **118** E2
Hayes UB4 **102** B3
Morrison St, SW11 **150** A3
Morris Pl, N4 **93** G2
Morris Rd, E14 **114** B5
E15 **96** E4
Dagenham RM8 **101** F2
Isleworth TW7 **144** C3
Morris St, E1 **113** E6
Morriston Cl, Wat. WD19 **50** C5
Morse Cl, E13 **115** G3
Morshead Rd, W9 **108** D3
Morson Rd, Enf. EN3 **45** H6
Morston Gdns, SE9 **174** C4
Morten Cl, SW4 **150** D6
Morteyne Rd, N17 **76** A1
Mortham St, E15 **114** D1
Mortimer Cl, NW2 **90** C3
SW16 **168** D2
Mortimer Cres, NW6 **108** E1
Worcester Park KT4 **196** D3
Mortimer Dr, Enf. EN1 **44** A5
Mortimer Est, NW6 **108** E1
Mortimer Ho, W11
off St. Anns Rd **128** A1
Mortimer Mkt, WC1 **9** G6
Mortimer Pl, NW6 **108** E1
Mortimer Rd, E6 **116** C3
N1 **94** B7
NW10 **107** J3
W13 **105** F6
Mitcham CR4 **185** J1
Mortimer Sq, W11
off St. Anns Rd **108** A7
Mortimer St, W1 **17** F3
Mortimer Ter, NW5
off Gordon Ho Rd **92** B4
MORTLAKE, SW14 **146** C3
Mortlake Cl, Croy. CR0 **201** E3
Mortlake Dr, Mitch. CR4 **185** H1
Mortlake High St, SW14 **146** D3
Mortlake Rd, E16 **115** H6
Ilford IG1 **99** F4
Richmond TW9 **126** A7
Mortlake Sta Pas, SW14
off Sheen La **146** C3
Mortlake Ter, Rich. TW9
off Kew Rd **126** A7
Mortlock Cl, SE15
off Cossall Wk **152** E2
Morton Cl, E1
off Deancross St **113** F6
Wallington SM6 **201** F7
Morton Ct, Nthlt. UB5 **85** J5
Morton Cres, N14 **58** D4
Morton Gdns, Wall. SM6 **200** C5
Morton Ms, SW5 **30** A2
Morton Pl, SE1 **26** E6
Morton Rd, E15 **97** F7
N1 **93** J7
Morden SM4 **185** G5
Morton Way, N14 **58** C3
Morvale Cl, Belv. DA17 **139** F4
Morval Rd, SW2 **151** G5
Morven Rd, SW17 **167** J3
Morville Ho, SW18
off Fitzhugh Gro **149** G6
Morville St, E3 **114** A2
Morwell St, WC1 **17** J2
Moscow Pl, W2 **14** A5
Moscow Rd, W2 **14** A5
Moseley Row, SE10 **135** F4
Moselle Av, N22 **75** G2
Moselle Cl, N8
off Miles Rd **75** E3
Moselle Ho, N17
off William St **60** C7
Moselle Pl, N17
off High Rd **60** C7
Moselle St, N17 **60** C7
Mossborough Cl, N12 **57** E6
Mossbury Rd, SW11 **149** H3
Moss Cl, E1 **21** J1
N9 **60** D1
Pinner HA5 **67** F2
Mossdown Cl, Belv. DA17 **139** G4
Mossford Ct, Ilf. IG6 **81** E3
Mossford Grn, Ilf. IG6 **81** E3
Mossford La, Ilf. IG6 **81** E2
Mossford St, E3 **113** J4
Moss Gdns, Felt. TW13 **160** A2
South Croydon CR2
off Warren Av **203** G7
Moss Hall Ct, N12 **57** E6
Moss Hall Cres, N12 **57** E6
Moss Hall Gro, N12 **56** E6
Mossington Gdns, SE16
off Abbeyfield Rd **133** F4
Moss La, Pnr. HA5 **67** F3
Mosslea Rd, SE20 **171** F7
Bromley BR2 **192** A5
Orpington BR6 **207** F3
Mossop St, SW3 **31** H1
Moss Rd, Dag. RM10 **101** G7
Mossville Gdns, Mord. SM4 **184** C3
Moston Cl, Hayes UB3
off Fuller Way **121** J5
Mostyn Av, Wem. HA9 **87** J5
Mostyn Gdns, NW10 **108** A3
Mostyn Gro, E3 **113** J2
Mostyn Rd, SW9 **151** G1
SW19 **184** C1
Edgware HA8 **54** D7
Mosul Way, Brom. BR2 **192** B6
Motcomb St, SW1 **24** A5
Moth Cl, Wall. SM6 **201** E7
Mothers' Sq, E5 **95** E4
Motley Av, EC2 **12** D5
Motley St, SW8
off St. Rule St **150** C2
MOTSPUR PARK, N.Mal. KT3 **183** H6
Motspur Pk, N.Mal. KT3 **183** F6
MOTTINGHAM, SE9 **173** J2
Mottingham Gdns, SE9 **174** A1
Mottingham La, SE9 **173** J1
SE12 **173** J1
Mottingham Rd, N9 **45** G6
SE9 **174** B2
Mottisfont Rd, SE2 **138** A3
Motts La, Dag. RM8
off Green La **101** F2
Mott St, Loug. (High Beach) IG10 **47** F1
Moulins Rd, E9 **113** F1
Moulsford Ho, N7 **92** D5
Moulton Av, Houns. TW3 **143** E2
Mound, The, SE9 **174** D3
Moundfield Rd, N16 **76** D6
Mount, The, E5 **94** E2
N20 **57** F2
NW3 *off Heath St* **91** F4
W3 **126** B1
New Malden KT3 **183** F3
Wembley HA9 **88** B2
Worcester Park KT4 **197** H4
Mountacre Cl, SE26 **170** C4
Mount Adon Pk, SE22 **152** D7
Mountague Pl, E14 **114** C7
Mountain Ho, SE11 **34** C3
Mount Angelus Rd, SW15 **147** F7
Mount Ararat Rd, Rich. TW10 **145** H5
Mount Ash Rd, SE26 **170** E3
Mount Av, E4 **62** A3
W5 **105** G5
Southall UB1 **103** G6
Mountbatten Cl, SE18 **137** H6
SE19 **170** B5
Mountbatten Ct, SE16
off Rotherhithe St **133** F1
Buckhurst Hill IG9 **64** A2
Mountbatten Gdns, Beck. BR3
off Balmoral Av **189** H4
Mountbatten Ms, SW18
off Inman Rd **167** F1
Mountbel Rd, Stan. HA7 **68** D1
Mount Cl, W5 **105** F5
Barnet (Cockfos.) EN4 **42** A4
Bromley BR1 **192** B1
Mountcombe Cl, Surb. KT6 **181** H7
Mount Cor, Felt. TW13 **160** D2
Mount Ct, SW15
off Weimar St **148** B3
West Wickham BR4 **204** E2
Mount Culver Av, Sid. DA14 **176** D6
Mount Dr, Bexh. DA6 **158** E5
Harrow HA2 **67** F5
Wembley HA9 **88** C2
Mountearl Gdns, SW16 **169** F3
Mount Echo Av, E4 **62** B2
Mount Echo Dr, E4 **62** B1
Mount Ephraim La, SW16 **168** D3
Mount Ephraim Rd, SW16 **168** D3
Mountfield Cl, SE6 **154** D7
Mountfield Rd, E6 **116** D2
N3 **72** D3
W5 **105** G6
Mountfield Ter, SE6
off Mountfield Cl **154** D7
Mountford Mans, SW11
off Battersea Pk Rd **150** A1
Mountfort Cres, N1
off Barnsbury Sq **93** G7
Mountfort Ter, N1
off Barnsbury Sq **93** G7
Mount Gdns, SE26 **170** E3
Mount Gro, Edg. HA8 **54** C3
Mountgrove Rd, N5 **93** H3
Mount Holme, T.Ditt. KT7
off Thorkhill Rd **180** E7
Mounthurst Rd, Brom. BR2 **191** F7
Mountington Pk Cl, Har. HA3 **69** G6
Mountjoy Cl, SE2 **138** B2
Mountjoy Ho, EC2
off The Barbican **20** A2
Mount Ms, Hmptn. TW12 **179** H1
Mount Mills, EC1 **11** H4
Mount Nod Rd, SW16 **169** F3
Mount Pk Av, Har. HA1 **86** A2
Mount Pk Cres, W5 **105** G6
Mount Pk Rd, W5 **105** G5
Harrow HA1 **86** A3
Pinner HA5 **66** A5
Mount Pl, W3 *off High St* **126** B1
Mount Pleasant, SE27 **169** J4
WC1 **10** D6
Barnet EN4 **41** H4
Ruislip HA4 **84** C2
Wembley HA0 **105** H1
Mount Pleasant Cres, N4 **75** F7
Mount Pleasant Est, Ilf. IG1 *off Ilford La* **99** F5
Mount Pleasant Hill, E5 **95** E2
Mount Pleasant La, E5 **94** E2
Mount Pleasant Pl, SE18 **137** G4
Mount Pleasant Rd, E17 **77** H2
N17 **76** B2
NW10 **89** J7
SE13 **154** B6
W5 **105** F4
Chigwell IG7 **65** G4
New Malden KT3 **182** C3
Mount Pleasant Vil, N4 **75** F7
Mount Pleasant Wk, Bex. DA5 **159** J5
Mount Rd, NW2 **89** H3
NW4 **71** G6
SE19 **170** A6
SW19 **166** D2
Barnet EN4 **41** H5
Bexleyheath DA6 **158** D5
Chessington KT9 **195** J5
Dagenham RM8 **101** F1
Feltham TW13 **160** E3
Hayes UB3 **121** J2
Ilford IG1 **98** E5
Mitcham CR4 **185** H2
New Malden KT3 **182** D3
Mount Row, W1 **16** D6
Mountsfield Ct, SE13 **154** D6
Mountside, Felt. TW13 **161** E3
Stanmore HA7 **68** C1
Mounts Pond Rd, SE3 **154** D2
Mount Sq, The, NW3
off Heath St **91** F3
Mount Stewart Av, Har. HA3 **69** G6
Mount St, W1 **16** C6
Mount St Ms, W1 **16** D6
Mount Ter, E1
off New Rd **112** E5
Mount Vernon, NW3 **91** F4
Mount Vw, NW7 **54** D3
W5 **105** G4
Mountview Cl, NW11 **91** E1
Mountview Ct, N8
off Green Las **75** H4
Mount Vw Rd, E4 **46** C7
N4 **75** E7
NW9 **70** D4
Mountview Rd, Esher (Clay.) KT10 **194** E7
Mount Vil, SE27 **169** H3
Mountwood, W.Mol. KT8 **179** G3
Movers La, Bark. IG11 **117** G1
Mowatt Cl, N19 **92** D1
Mowbray Rd, NW6 **90** B7
SE19 **188** C1
Barnet (New Barn.) EN5 **41** F4
Edgware HA8 **54** A4
Richmond TW10 **163** F3
Mowbrays Cl, Rom. RM5 **83** J1
Mowbrays Rd, Rom. RM5 **83** J2
Mowbrey Gdns, Loug. IG10 **49** F2
Mowlem St, E2 **113** E2

Mowlem Trd Est, N17 . . . . .61 F7
Mowll St, SW9 . . . . .131 G7
Moxon Cl, E13
off Whitelegg Rd 115 F2
Moxon St, W1 . . . . .16 B2
Barnet EN5 . . . . .40 C3
Moye Cl, E2 . . . . .13 J1
Moyers Rd, E10 . . . . .78 C7
Moylan Rd, W6 . . . . .128 B6
Moyne Pl, NW10 . . . . .106 A2
Moynihan Dr, N21 . . . . . .43 E5
Moys Cl, Croy. CR0 . . . . . .186 E6
Moyser Rd, SW16 . . . . . . .168 B5
Mozart St, W10 . . . . .108 C3
Mozart Ter, SW1 . . . . .32 C2
Muchelney Rd, Mord. SM4 . . . . .185 F6
Mud La, W5 . . . . .105 G5
Mudlarks Boul, SE10
off John Harrison Way .135 F3
Muggeridge Cl, S.Croy. CR2 . . . . .202 A5
Muggeridge Rd, Dag. RM10 . . . . .101 H4
Muirdown Av, SW14 . . . . .146 C4
Muir Dr, SW18 . . . . .149 H6
Muirfield, W3 . . . . .107 E6
Muirfield Cl, SE16
off Ryder Dr 133 E5
Watford WD19 . . . . .50 C4
Muirfield Cres, E14
off Millharbour 134 B3
Muirfield Grn, Wat. WD19 . .50 C4
Muirfield Rd, Wat. WD19 . .50 D4
Muirkirk Rd, SE6 . . . . .172 C1
Muir Rd, E5 . . . . .94 D3
Muir St, E16
off Newland St 136 C1
Mulberry Business Cen, SE16 *off Quebec Way* . .133 G2
Mulberry Cl, E4 . . . . .62 A2
N8 . . . . .74 E5
NW3
off Hampstead High St .91 G4
NW4 . . . . .71 J3
SE7 . . . . .136 A6
SE22 . . . . .152 D5
SW3 *off Beaufort St* 31 F6
SW16 . . . . .168 C4
Barnet EN4 . . . . .41 G4
Northolt UB5
off Parkfield Av 102 E2
Mulberry Ct, EC1
off Tompion St 11 H4
N2 *off Great N Rd* 73 H3
Barking IG11
off Westrow Dr 99 J6
Surbiton KT6 . . . . .181 G7
Mulberry Cres, Brent. TW8 . . . . .125 E7
West Drayton UB7 . . . .120 D2
Mulberry La, Croy. CR0 . .202 C1
Mulberry Ms, SE14
off Lewisham Way . . .153 J1
Wallington SM6 . . . . . .200 C6
Mulberry Par, West Dr. UB7 . . . . .120 D3
Mulberry Pl, SE9 . . . . .156 A4
W6 *off Chiswick Mall* . .127 G5
Mulberry Rd, E8 . . . . .94 C7
Mulberry St, E1 . . . . .21 H3
Mulberry Tree Ms, W4
off Clovelly Rd 126 C2
Mulberry Wk, SW3 . . . . . . .31 F5
Mulberry Way, E18 . . . . . . .79 H2
Belvedere DA17 . . . . . .139 J2
Ilford IG6 . . . . .81 F4
Mulgrave Rd, NW10 . . . . . .89 F4
SE18 . . . . .136 C4
SW6 . . . . .128 C6
W5 . . . . .105 G3
Croydon CR0 . . . . .202 A3
Harrow HA1 . . . . .86 D2
Sutton SM2 . . . . .198 D6
Mulholland Cl, Mitch. CR4 . . . . .186 B2
Mulkern Rd, N19 . . . . .92 D1
Mullards Cl, Mitch. CR4 . .199 J1
Muller Ho, SE18
off Connaught Rd 136 D5
Muller Rd, SW4 . . . . .150 D6
Mullet Gdns, E2 . . . . .13 J3
Mullins Path, SW14 . . . . .146 D3
Mullion Cl, Har. HA3 . . . . . .67 H1
Mullion Wk, Wat. WD19
off Ormskirk Rd 50 D4
Mull Wk, N1
off Clephane Rd 93 J6
Mulready St, NW8 . . . . .7 G6
Multi-way, W3
off Valetta Rd 127 E2
Multon Rd, SW18 . . . . . . .149 G7
Mulvaney Way, SE1 . . . . . .28 C4
Mumford Mills, SE10
off Greenwich High Rd .154 B1
Mumford Rd, SE24
off Railton Rd 151 H5
Muncaster Rd, SW11 . . . .149 J5
Muncies Ms, SE6 . . . . . . .172 C2
Mundania Rd, SE22 . . . . .153 E6
Munday Rd, E16 . . . . .115 G6
Munden Ho, E3
off Bromley High St . .114 B3
Munden St, W14 . . . . .128 B4
Mundesley Cl, Wat. WD19 .50 C4
Mundford Rd, E5 . . . . .95 F2
Mundon Gdns, Ilf. IG1 . . . .99 G1
Mund St, W14 . . . . .128 C5
Mundy St, N1 . . . . .12 D3
Mungo Pk Cl, Bushey (Bushey Hth) WD23 . . . .51 J2
Munkenbeck, W2
off Hermitage St 15 E2
Munnery Way, Orp. BR6 . .206 D3
Munnings Gdns, Islw. TW7 . . . . .144 A5
Munro Dr, N11 . . . . .58 C6
Munro Ms, W10 . . . . .108 B5
Munro Ter, SW10 . . . . .31 E6
Munslow Gdns, Sutt. SM1 . . . . .199 G4
Munster Av, Houns. TW4 .143 F4
Munster Ct, Tedd. TW11 . .163 F6
Munster Gdns, N13 . . . . . .59 H4
Munster Ms, SW6
off Lillie Rd 128 B7
Munster Rd, SW6 . . . . . . .148 C1
Teddington TW11 . . . . .163 E6
Munster Sq, NW1 . . . . .9 E4
Munton Rd, SE17 . . . . .36 A1
Murchison Av, Bex. DA5 . .176 D1
Murchison Rd, E10 . . . . . . .96 C2
Murdock Cl, E16
off Rogers Rd 115 F6
Murdock St, SE15 . . . . . . .132 E6
Murfett Cl, SW19 . . . . . . .166 B2
Muriel St, N1 . . . . .10 D1
Murillo Rd, SE13 . . . . .154 D4
Murphy St, SE1 . . . . .26 E4
Murray Av, Brom. BR1 . . .191 H2
Hounslow TW3 . . . . . . .143 H5
Murray Cl, SE28 . . . . .137 H1
Murray Ct, W7
off St. Margarets Rd . .124 B2
Murray Cres, Pnr. HA5 . . . .66 D1
Murray Gro, N1 . . . . .12 A2
Murray Ms, NW1 . . . . .92 D7
Murray Rd, SW19 . . . . . . .166 A6
W5 . . . . .125 F4
Richmond TW10 . . . . . .163 E2
Murray Sq, E16 . . . . .115 G6
Murray St, NW1 . . . . .92 D7
Murrays Yd, SE18 . . . . . . .136 E4
Murray Ter, NW3
off Flask Wk 91 G4
W5 *off Murray Rd* 125 G4
Mursell Est, SW8 . . . . . . .151 F1
Murtwell Dr, Chig. IG7 . . . .65 F6
Musard Rd, W6 . . . . .128 B6
W14 . . . . .128 B6
Musbury St, E1 . . . . .113 F6
Muscal, W6 . . . . .128 B6
Muscatel Pl, SE5
off Dalwood St 152 B1
Muschamp Rd, SE15 . . . .152 C3
Carshalton SM5 . . . . . .199 H2
Muscovy Ho, Erith DA18
off Kale Rd 138 E2
Muscovy St, EC3 . . . . .21 E6
★ **Museum in Docklands**, E14 *off Hertsmere Rd* .114 A7
Museum La, SW7 . . . . .23 F6
★ **Museum of Childhood at Bethnal Green**, E2 .113 E3
★ **Museum of Croydon**, Croy. CR0 . . . . .201 J3
★ **Museum of Gdn History**, SE1 . . . . .26 C6
★ **Museum of Instruments** (Royal College of Music), SW7 . . . . .22 E5
★ **Museum of London**, EC2 . . . . .19 J2
★ **Museum of Richmond**, Rich. TW9 . . . . .145 G5
Museum Pas, E2
off Victoria Pk Sq 113 F3
Museum St, WC1 . . . . .18 A2
Museum Way, W3 . . . . . . .126 A2
Musgrave Cl, Barn. EN4 . . .41 F1
Musgrave Cres, SW6 . . . . .148 D1
Musgrave Rd, Islw. TW7 . .144 C1
Musgrove Rd, SE14 . . . . .153 G1
Musjid Rd, SW11
off Kambala Rd 149 G2
Musket Cl, Barn. (E.Barn.) EN4
off East Barnet Rd 41 G5
Musquash Way, Houns. TW4 . . . . .142 C2
Muston Rd, E5 . . . . .94 E2
Mustow Pl, SW6
off Munster Rd 148 C2
Muswell Av, N10 . . . . .74 B2
MUSWELL HILL, N10 . . . . .74 B3
Muswell Hill, N10 . . . . .74 B3
Muswell Hill Bdy, N10 . . . .74 B3
Muswell Hill Pl, N10 . . . . . .74 B4
Muswell Hill Rd, N6 . . . . . .74 A6
N10 . . . . .74 A4
Muswell Ms, N10
off Muswell Rd 74 B3
Muswell Rd, N10 . . . . .74 B3
Mutrix Rd, NW6 . . . . .108 D1
Mutton Pl, NW1
off Harmood St 92 B6
Muybridge Rd, N.Mal. KT3 . . . . .182 C2
Myatt Rd, SW9 . . . . .151 H1
Myatts Flds S, SW9
off St. Lawrence Way .151 G2
Myatts N, SW9
off Fairbairn Grn 151 G1
Mycenae Rd, SE3 . . . . . . .135 G7
Myddelton Cl, Enf. EN1 . . .44 C1
Myddelton Gdns, N21 . . . .43 H7
Myddelton Pk, N20 . . . . . . .57 G3
Myddelton Pas, EC1 . . . . . .11 F3
Myddelton Rd, N8 . . . . . . .75 E4
Myddelton Sq, EC1 . . . . . . .11 F3
Myddelton St, EC1 . . . . . . .11 F4
Myddleton Av, N4 . . . . .93 J2
Myddleton Cl, Stan. HA7 . .52 D2
Myddleton Ms, N22 . . . . . .59 E7
Myddleton Rd, N22 . . . . . .59 E7
Myers La, SE14 . . . . .133 G6
Mylis Cl, SE26 . . . . .171 E4
Mylius Cl, SE14
off Kender St 153 F1
Mylne St, EC1 . . . . .11 E2
Mynterne Ct, SW19
off Swanton Gdns . . .166 A1
Myra St, SE2 . . . . .138 A5
Myrdle St, E1 . . . . .21 J2
Myrna Cl, SW19 . . . . .167 H7
Myron Pl, SE13 . . . . .154 C3
Myrtle Av, Felt. TW14 . . . .141 H4
Ruislip HA4 . . . . .66 A7
Myrtleberry Cl, E8
off Beechwood Rd 94 C6
Myrtle Cl, Barn. (E.Barn.) EN4 . . . . .57 J1
West Drayton UB7 . . . .120 C3
Myrtledene Rd, SE2 . . . . .138 A5
Myrtle Gdns, W7 . . . . .124 B1
Myrtle Gro, N.Mal. KT3 . .182 C2
Myrtle Rd, E6 . . . . .116 B1
E17 . . . . .77 H6
N13 . . . . .59 J3
W3 . . . . .126 C1
Croydon CR0 . . . . .204 A3
Hampton (Hmptn H.) TW12 . . . . .161 J6
Hounslow TW3 . . . . . . .143 J2
Ilford IG1 . . . . .99 E2
Sutton SM1 . . . . .199 F5
Myrtle Wk, N1 . . . . .12 D2
Mysore Rd, SW11 . . . . . . .149 J3
Myton Rd, SE21 . . . . .170 A3

N

N17 Studios, N17 . . . . .60 C7
N1 Shop Cen, N1 . . . . .11 F1
Nadine St, SE7 . . . . .135 J5
Nafferton Ri, Loug. IG10 . . .48 A5
Nagle Cl, E17 . . . . .78 D2
Nags Head, N7 . . . . .93 F4
Nags Head Cen, N7 . . . . . .93 F4
Nag's Head Ct, EC1 . . . . . . .11 J6
Nags Head La, Well. DA16 . . . . .158 B3
Nags Head Rd, Enf. EN3 . .45 F4
Nairne Gro, SE24 . . . . . . .152 A5
Nairn Grn, Wat. WD19 . . . . .50 A3
Nairn Rd, Ruis. HA4 . . . . . .84 C6
Nairn St, E14 . . . . .114 C5
Nallhead Rd, Felt. TW13 . .160 C5
Namba Roy Cl, SW16 . . . .169 F4
Namton Dr, Th.Hth. CR7 . .187 F4
Nan Clark's La, NW7 . . . . . .55 F2
Nankin St, E14 . . . . .114 A6
Nansen Rd, SW11 . . . . . . .150 A4
Nansen Village, N12 . . . . . .57 E4
Nant Ct, NW2
off Granville Rd 90 C2
Nantes Cl, SW18 . . . . .149 F4
Nantes Pas, E1 . . . . .21 F1
Nant Rd, NW2 . . . . .90 C2
Nant St, E2
off Cambridge Heath Rd 113 E3
Naoroji St, WC1 . . . . .11 E4
Napier Av, E14 . . . . .134 A5
SW6 . . . . .148 C3
Napier Cl, SE8
off Amersham Vale . . .133 J7
W14 *off Napier Rd* 128 C3
West Drayton UB7 . . . .120 C3
Napier Ct, SE12 . . . . .173 H3
SW6
off Ranelagh Gdns . . .148 C3
Surbiton KT6 . . . . .181 G6
Napier Gro, N1 . . . . .12 A2
Napier Pl, W14 . . . . .128 C3
Napier Rd, E6 . . . . .116 D1
E11 . . . . .96 E4
E15 . . . . .115 E2
N17 . . . . .76 B3
NW10 . . . . .107 H3
SE25 . . . . .188 E4
W14 . . . . .128 C3
Belvedere DA17 . . . . . .139 F4
Bromley BR2 . . . . .191 H4
Enfield EN3 . . . . .45 G5
Hounslow (Lon.Hthrw Air.) TW6 .140 A1
Isleworth TW7 . . . . .144 D4
South Croydon CR2 . . .202 A7
Wembley HA0 . . . . .87 G5
Napier Ter, N1 . . . . .93 H7
Napoleon Rd, E5 . . . . .94 E3
Twickenham TW1 . . . . .145 E7
Napton Cl, Hayes UB4 . . .102 E4
Narbonne Av, SW4 . . . . . .150 C5
Narborough St, SW6 . . . . .148 E2
Narcissus Rd, NW6 . . . . . . .90 D5
Naresby Fold, Stan. HA7 . .53 F6
Narford Rd, E5 . . . . .94 D3
Narrow Boat Cl, SE28
off Ridge Cl 137 G2
Narrow St, E14 . . . . .113 H7
Narrow Way, Brom. BR2 .192 B6
Nascot St, W12 . . . . .107 J6
Naseberry Ct, E4
off Merriam Cl 62 C5
Naseby Cl, NW6 . . . . .91 F7
Isleworth TW7 . . . . .144 B1
Naseby Rd, SE19 . . . . .170 A6
Dagenham RM10 . . . . .101 G3
Ilford IG5 . . . . .80 C1
Nash Cl, Sutt. SM1 . . . . . .199 G3
Nash Grn, Brom. BR1 . . . .173 G6
Nash Ho, SW1 . . . . .33 E4
Nash La, Kes. BR2 . . . . . .205 G5
Nash Rd, N9 . . . . .61 F2
SE4 . . . . .153 G4
Romford RM6 . . . . .82 D4
Nash St, NW1 . . . . .8 E4
Nash Way, Har. (Kenton) HA3 . . . . .69 E6
Nasmyth St, W6 . . . . .127 H3
Nassau Path, SE28
off Disraeli Cl 138 C1
Nassau Rd, SW13 . . . . . . .147 F1
Nassau St, W1 . . . . .17 F2
Nassington Rd, NW3 . . . . .91 H4
Natalie Cl, Felt. TW14 . . . .141 G7
Natalie Ms, Twick. TW2
off Sixth Cross Rd . . .162 A3
Natal Rd, N11 . . . . .58 E6
SW16 . . . . .168 D6
Ilford IG1 . . . . .98 E4
Thornton Heath CR7 . .188 A3
Nathaniel Cl, E1 . . . . .21 G2
Nathans Rd, Wem. HA0 . . .87 F2
Nathan Way, SE28 . . . . . .137 H4
★ **National Archives, The**, Rich. TW9 . . . . .126 B7
★ **National Army Mus**, SW3 . . . . .32 A5
★ **National Gall**, WC2 . . . .17 J6
★ **National Maritime Mus**, SE10 . . . . .134 D6
★ **National Portrait Gall**, WC2 . . . . .17 J6
National Ter, SE16
off Bermondsey Wall E 132 E2
★ **National Thea**, SE1 . . . .26 D1
Nation Way, E4 . . . . .62 C1
★ **Natural History Mus**, SW7 . . . . .23 E6
Naval Row, E14 . . . . .114 C7
Naval Wk, Brom. BR1
off High St 191 G2
Navarino Gro, E8 . . . . .94 D6
Navarino Rd, E8 . . . . .94 D6
Navarre Rd, E6 . . . . .116 B2
Navarre St, E2 . . . . .13 F5
Navenby Wk, E3
off Burwell Wk 114 A4
Navestock Cl, E4
off Mapleton Rd 62 C3
Navestock Cres, Wdf.Grn. IG8 . . . . .79 J1
Navestock Ho, Bark. IG11 .118 B2
Navigation Ct, E16
off Gallions Rd 117 F7
Navigator Dr, Sthl. UB2 . .123 J2

Navigator Pk, Sthl. UB2 122 C4
Navy St, SW4 150 D3
Naxos Bldg, E14 *off Hutchings St* 134 A2
Nayim Pl, E8 *off Amhurst Rd* 94 E5
Naylor Gro, Enf. EN3 *off South St* 45 G5
Naylor Rd, N20 57 F2
SE15 132 E7
Nazareth Gdns, SE15 152 E2
Nazrul St, E2 13 F3
Neagle Cl, Borwd. WD6 *off Balcon Way* 38 C1
Neal Av, Sthl. UB1 103 F4
Neal Cl, Nthwd. HA6 66 A1
Nealden St, SW9 151 F3
Neale Cl, N2 73 F3
Neal St, WC2 18 A4
Neal's Yd, WC2 18 A4
Near Acre, NW9 71 F1
NEASDEN, NW2 89 E3
Neasden Cl, NW10 89 E5
Neasden Junct, NW10 *off North Circular Rd* 88 E4
Neasden La, NW10 89 E4
Neasden La N, NW10 88 D3
Neasham Rd, Dag. RM8 100 B5
Neate St, SE5 37 F5
Neath Gdns, Mord. SM4 185 F6
Neathouse Pl, SW1 33 F1
Neatscourt Rd, E6 116 A5
Nebraska Bldg, SE13 *off Deals Gateway* 154 B1
Nebraska St, SE1 28 B4
★ **NEC Harlequins RFC**, Twick. TW2 144 B7
Neckinger, SE16 29 G5
Neckinger Est, SE16 29 G5
Neckinger St, SE1 29 G4
Nectarine Way, SE13 154 B2
Needham Rd, W11 *off Westbourne Gro* 108 D6
Needham Ter, NW2 *off Kara Way* 90 A3
Needleman St, SE16 133 G2
Neeld Cres, NW4 71 H5
Wembley HA9 88 A5
Neeld Par, Wem. HA9 *off Harrow Rd* 88 A5
Neil Wates Cres, SW2 169 G1
Nelgarde Rd, SE6 154 A7
Nella Rd, W6 128 A6
Nelldale Rd, SE16 133 F4
Nello James Gdns, SE27 170 A4
Nelson Cl, NW6 108 D3
Croydon CR0 201 H1
Romford RM7 83 H1
Nelson Ct, SE16 *off Brunel Rd* 133 F1
Nelson Gdns, E2 13 J3
Hounslow TW3 143 G6
Nelson Gro Rd, SW19 185 E1
Nelson Mandela Cl, N10 74 A2
Nelson Mandela Rd, SE3 155 J3
Nelson Pas, EC1 12 A4
Nelson Pl, N1 11 H2
Sidcup DA14 *off Sidcup High St* 176 A4
Nelson Rd, E4 62 B6
E11 79 G4
N8 75 F5
N9 61 E2
N15 76 B4
SE10 134 C6
SW19 167 E7
Belvedere DA17 139 F5
Bromley BR2 191 J4
Enfield EN3 45 G6
Harrow HA1 86 A1
Hounslow TW3, TW4 143 G6
Hounslow (Lon.Hthrw Air.) TW6 140 C1
New Malden KT3 182 D5
Sidcup DA14 *off Sidcup High St* 176 A4
Stanmore HA7 53 F6
Twickenham TW2 143 J6
★ **Nelson's Column**, WC2 26 A1
Nelson Sq, SE1 27 G3
Nelson's Row, SW4 150 D4
Nelson St, E1 112 E6
E6 116 C2
E16 *off Huntingdon St* 115 F6
Nelsons Yd, NW1 9 F1
Nelson Ter, N1 11 H2
Nelson Trd Est, SW19 184 E1
Nelson Wk, SE16 *off Salter Rd* 133 H1
Nemoure Rd, W3 106 C7
Nene Gdns, Felt. TW13 161 F2
Nene Rd, Houns. (Lon.Hthrw Air.) TW6 141 E1
Nepaul Rd, SW11 149 H2
Nepean St, SW15 147 G6
Neptune Ct, Borwd. WD6 *off Clarendon Rd* 38 A3
Neptune Ho, E3 *off Garrison Rd* 114 A1
Neptune Rd, Har. HA1 68 A6
Hounslow (Lon.Hthrw Air.) TW6 141 G1
Neptune St, SE16 133 F3
Nero Ct, Brent. TW8 *off Justin Cl* 125 G7
Nesbit Rd, SE9 156 A4
Nesbitt Cl, SE3 *off Hurren Cl* 154 E3
Nesbitts All, Barn. EN5 *off Bath Pl* 40 C3
Nesbitt Sq, SE19 *off Coxwell Rd* 170 B7
Nesham St, E1 29 H1
Ness St, SE16 29 H5
Nesta Rd, Wdf.Grn. IG8 63 E6
Nestles Av, Hayes UB3 121 J3
Nestor Av, N21 43 H6
Netheravon Rd, W4 127 F4
W7 124 C1
Netheravon Rd S, W4 127 F5
Netherbury Rd, W5 125 G3
Netherby Gdns, Enf. EN2 42 E4
Netherby Rd, SE23 153 F7
Nether Cl, N3 56 D7
Nethercourt Av, N3 56 D6
Netherfield Gdns, Bark. IG11 99 G6
Netherfield Rd, N12 57 E5
SW17 168 A3
Netherford Rd, SW4 150 C2
Netherhall Gdns, NW3 91 F6
Netherhall Way, NW3 *off Netherhall Gdns* 91 F5
Netherlands Rd, Barn. (New Barn.) EN5 41 G6
Netherleigh Cl, N6 92 B1
Nether St, N3 72 D1
N12 56 D7
Netherton Gro, SW10 30 D6
Netherton Rd, N15 76 A6
Twickenham TW1 144 D5
Netherwood, N2 73 G2
Netherwood Pl, W14 *off Netherwood Rd* 128 A3
Netherwood Rd, W14 128 A3
Netherwood St, NW6 90 C7
Netley Cl, Croy. (New Adgtn) CR0 204 C7
Sutton SM3 198 A5
Netley Dr, Walt. KT12 179 F7
Netley Gdns, Mord. SM4 185 F7
Netley Rd, E17 77 J5
Brentford TW8 125 H6
Hounslow (Lon.Hthrw Air.) TW6 141 G1
Ilford IG2 81 G5
Morden SM4 185 F7
Netley St, NW1 9 F4
Nettleden Av, Wem. HA9 88 A6
Nettlefold Pl, SE27 169 H3
Nettlestead Cl, Beck. BR3 189 J1
Nettleton Rd, SE14 153 G1
Hounslow (Lon.Hthrw Air.) TW6 141 E1
Nettlewood Rd, SW16 168 D7
Neuchatel Rd, SE6 171 J2
Nevada Bldg, SE10 *off Blackheath Rd* 154 B1
Nevada Cl, N.Mal. KT3 182 C4
Nevada St, SE10 134 C6
Nevern Pl, SW5 128 D4
Nevern Rd, SW5 128 D4
Nevern Sq, SW5 128 D4
Neville Av, N.Mal. KT3 182 D1
Neville Cl, E11 97 F3
NW1 9 J2
NW6 108 C2
SE15 132 D7
W3 *off Acton La* 126 C2
Hounslow TW3 143 H2
Sidcup DA15 175 J4
Neville Dr, N2 73 F6
Neville Gdns, Dag. RM8 100 D3
Neville Gill Cl, SW18 148 D6
Neville Pl, N22 75 F1
Neville Rd, E7 97 G7
NW6 108 C2
W5 105 G4
Croydon CR0 188 A7
Dagenham RM8 100 D2
Ilford IG6 81 F1
Kingston upon Thames KT1 182 A2
Richmond TW10 163 F3
Nevilles Ct, NW2 89 G3
Neville St, SW7 31 E3
Neville Ter, SW7 31 E3
Neville Wk, Cars. SM5 185 H7
Nevill Rd, N16 94 B4
Nevill Way, Loug. IG10 *off Valley Hill* 48 B7
Nevin Dr, E4 62 B1
Nevinson Cl, SW18 149 G6
Nevis Rd, SW17 168 A2
New Acres Rd, SE28 137 H2
Newall Ct, W12 *off Heathstan Rd* 107 G6
Newall Ho, SE1 28 A5
Newall Rd, Houns. (Lon.Hthrw Air.) TW6 141 F1
Newark Cres, NW10 106 D3
Newark Grn, Borwd. WD6 38 D3
Newark Knok, E6 116 D6
Newark Rd, S.Croy. CR2 202 A6
Newark St, E1 112 E5
Newark Way, NW4 71 G4
New Ash Cl, N2 73 G3
New Atlas Wf, E14 *off Arnhem Pl* 134 A3
New Barn Cl, Wall. SM6 201 F6
NEW BARNET, Barn. EN5 41 E4
New Barns Av, Mitch. CR4 186 D4
New Barn St, E13 115 G4
New Barns Way, Chig. IG7 64 E3
NEW BECKENHAM, Beck. BR3 171 J6
Newbiggin Path, Wat. WD19 50 C4
Newbolt Av, Sutt. SM3 197 J5
Newbolt Rd, Stan. HA7 52 C6
New Bond St, W1 16 D4
Newborough Grn, N.Mal. KT3 182 D4
New Brent St, NW4 71 J5
Newbridge Pt, SE23 *off Windrush La* 171 G3
New Br St, EC4 19 G4
New Broad St, EC2 20 D2
New Bdy, W5 105 F7
Hampton (Hmptn H.) TW12 *off Hampton Rd* 162 A5
New Bdy Bldgs, W5 *off New Bdy* 105 G7
Newburgh Rd, W3 126 C1
Newburgh St, W1 17 F4
New Burlington Ms, W1 17 F5
New Burlington Pl, W1 17 F5
New Burlington St, W1 17 F5
Newburn St, SE11 34 D4
Newbury Cl, Nthlt. UB5 85 F6
Newbury Gdns, Epsom KT19 197 F4
Newbury Ho, N22 75 E1
Newbury Ms, NW5 *off Malden Rd* 92 A6
NEWBURY PARK, Ilf. IG2 81 G5
Newbury Rd, E4 62 C6
Bromley BR2 191 G3
Hounslow (Lon.Hthrw Air.) TW6 140 C1
Ilford IG2 81 G6
Newbury St, EC1 19 J2
Newbury Way, Nthlt. UB5 85 E6
New Butt La, SE8 134 A7
New Butt La N, SE8 *off Reginald Rd* 134 A7
Newby Cl, Enf. EN1 44 B2
Newby Pl, E14 114 C7
Newby St, SW8 150 B3
New Caledonian Wf, SE16 133 J3
Newcastle Cl, EC4 19 G3
Newcastle Pl, W2 15 F2
Newcastle Row, EC1 11 F5
New Cavendish St, W1 17 E1
New Change, EC4 19 J4
New Chapel Rd, Felt. TW13 *off High St* 160 B1
New Chapel Sq, Felt. TW13 160 B1
New Charles St, EC1 11 H3
NEW CHARLTON, SE7 135 J4
New Ch Ct, SE19 *off Waldegrave Rd* 170 D7
New Ch Rd, SE5 36 A7
New City Rd, E13 115 J3
New Cl, SW19 185 F3
Feltham TW13 160 E5
New Coll Ct, NW3 *off Finchley Rd* 91 F6
New Coll Ms, N1 *off Islington Pk St* 93 G7
New Coll Par, NW3 *off Finchley Rd* 91 G6
Newcombe Gdns, SW16 169 E4
Hounslow TW4 143 F4
Newcombe Pk, NW7 55 E5
Wembley HA0 105 J1
Newcombe St, W8 *off Kensington Pl* 128 D1
Newcomen Rd, E11 97 F3
SW11 149 G3
Newcomen St, SE1 28 B3
New Compton St, WC2 17 J4
New Concordia Wf, SE1 29 G3
New Ct, EC4 18 E5
Newcourt St, NW8 7 G2
★ **New Covent Garden Flower Mkt**, SW8 33 J6
★ **New Covent Garden Mkt**, SW8 130 D7
New Crane Pl, E1 *off Garnet St* 133 F1
NEW CROSS, SE14 153 H1
New Cross, SE14 133 J7
NEW CROSS GATE, SE14 153 G1
New Cross Rd, SE14 133 F7
Newdales Cl, N9 60 D2
Newdene Av, Nthlt. UB5 102 D2
New Ealing Bdy, W5 *off Haven Grn* 105 G7
Newell St, E14 113 J6
NEW ELTHAM, SE9 174 D2
New End, NW3 91 F4
New End Sq, NW3 91 G4
Newent Cl, SE15 36 D7
Carshalton SM5 199 J1
New Fm Av, Brom. BR2 191 G4
New Ferry App, SE18 136 D3
New Fetter La, EC4 19 F3
Newfield Cl, Hmptn. TW12 *off Percy Rd* 179 G1
Newfield Ri, NW2 89 H3
New Forest La, Chig. IG7 64 D6
Newgale Gdns, Edg. HA8 69 J1
New Gdn Dr, West Dr. UB7 *off Drayton Gdns* 120 B2
Newgate, Croy. CR0 201 J1
Newgate Cl, Felt. TW13 161 E2
Newgate St, E4 63 F3
EC1 19 H3
New Globe Wk, SE1 27 J1
New Goulston St, E1 21 F3
New Grn Pl, SE19 170 B6
Newhams Row, SE1 28 E4
Newham Way, E6 115 J5
E16 115 F5
Newhaven Cl, Hayes UB3 121 J4
Newhaven Gdns, SE9 156 A4
Newhaven La, E16 115 F4
Newhaven Rd, SE25 188 A5
New Heston Rd, Houns. TW5 123 F7
New Horizons Ct, Brent. TW8 *off Shield Dr* 124 D6
Newhouse Av, Rom. RM6 82 D3
Newhouse Cl, N.Mal. KT3 183 E7
Newhouse Wk, Mord. SM4 185 F7
Newick Cl, Bex. DA5 159 H6
Newick Rd, E5 95 E3
Newing Grn, Brom. BR1 174 A7
NEWINGTON, SE1 35 J1
Newington Barrow Way, N7 93 F3
Newington Butts, SE1 35 H2
SE11 35 H2
Newington Causeway, SE1 27 H6
Newington Grn, N1 94 A5
N16 94 A5
Newington Grn Rd, N1 94 A6
New Inn Bdy, EC2 12 E5
New Inn Pas, WC2 18 D4
New Inn Sq, EC2 12 E5
New Inn St, EC2 12 E5
New Inn Yd, EC2 12 E5
New James Ct, SE15 *off Nunhead La* 153 E3
New Jersey Ter, SE15 *off Nunhead La* 152 E3
New Jubilee Ct, Wdf.Grn. IG8 *off Grange Av* 63 G7
New Kent Rd, SE1 27 J6
New Kings Rd, SW6 148 C2
New King St, SE8 134 A6
Newland Cl, Pnr. HA5 51 E6
Newland Ct, EC1 *off St. Luke's Est* 12 B5
Wembley HA9 *off Barn Ri* 88 A2
Newland Dr, Enf. EN1 44 E1
Newland Gdns, W13 124 D2
Newland Rd, N8 74 E3
Newlands, The, Wall. SM6 200 C7
Newlands Av, T.Ditt. KT7 194 B1
Newlands Cl, Edg. HA8 53 H3
Southall UB2 122 E5
Wembley HA0 87 F6
Newlands Ct, SE9 156 D6

Newlands Pk, SE26 **171** G5
Newlands Pl, Barn. EN5 **40** A5
Newlands Quay, E1 **113** F7
Newlands Rd, SW16 **187** E2
Woodford Green IG8 **63** F2
Newlands Ter, SW8
off Queenstown Rd **150** B2
Newland St, E16 **136** B1
Newlands Way, Chess. KT9 **195** F5
Newling Cl, E6
off Porter Rd **116** C6
New London St, EC3 **21** E5
New Lydenburg Commercial Est, SE7
off New Lydenburg St **135** J3
New Lydenburg St, SE7 **135** J3
Newlyn Cl, Orp. BR6 **207** J4
Newlyn Gdns, Har. HA2 **67** F7
Newlyn Rd, N17 **76** C1
Barnet EN5 **40** C4
Welling DA16 **157** J2
NEW MALDEN, KT3 **182** D3
Newman Pas, W1 **17** G2
Newman Rd, E13 **115** H3
E17 *off Southcote Rd* **77** G5
Bromley BR1 **191** G1
Croydon CR0 **201** F1
Hayes UB3 **102** B7
Newmans Cl, Loug. IG10 **48** E3
Newman's Ct, EC3 **20** C4
Newmans La, Loug. IG10 **48** D3
Surbiton KT6 **181** G6
Newman's Row, WC2 **18** D2
Newman St, W1 **17** G2
Newmans Way, Barn. EN4 **41** F1
Newman Yd, W1 **17** G3
Newmarket Av, Nthlt. UB5 **85** G5
Newmarket Grn, SE9
off Middle Pk Av **156** A7
Newmarsh Rd, SE28 **137** J1
Newminster Rd, Mord. SM4 **185** F6
New Mt St, E15 **96** D7
Newnes Path, SW15
off Putney Pk La **147** H4
Newnham Av, Ruis. HA4 **84** C1
Newnham Cl, Loug. IG10 **48** A6
Northolt UB5 **85** J5
Thornton Heath CR7 **187** J2
Newnham Gdns, Nthlt. UB5 **85** J5
Newnham Ms, N22
off Newnham Rd **75** F1
Newnham Rd, N22 **75** F1
Newnhams Cl, Brom. BR1 **192** C3
Newnham Ter, SE1 **26** E5
Newnham Way, Har. HA3 **69** H5
New N Pl, EC2 **12** D6
New N Rd, N1 **12** C2
Ilford IG6 **65** G7
New N St, WC1 **18** C1
Newnton Cl, N4 **76** A7
New Oak Rd, N2 **73** F2
New Orleans Wk, N19 **74** D7
New Oxford St, WC1 **17** J3
New Pk Av, N13 **59** J3
New Pk Cl, Nthlt. UB5 **84** E6
New Pk Ct, SW2 **151** E7
New Pk Ind Est, N18 **61** F5
New Pk Par, SW2
off New Pk Rd **151** E7
New Pk Rd, SW2 **168** D1
Newpiece, Loug. IG10 **48** E3
New Pl Sq, SE16 **132** E3
New Plaistow Rd, E15 **115** E1
Newport Av, E13 **115** H4
E14 **114** D7
Newport Ct, WC2 **17** J5
Newport Mead, Wat. WD19
off Kilmarnock Rd **50** D4
Newport Pl, WC2 **17** J5
Newport Rd, E10 **96** C2
E17 **77** H4
SW13 **147** G1
W3 **126** C2
Hounslow (Lon.Hthrw Air.) TW6 **140** D1
Newport St, SE11 **34** C2
New Priory Ct, NW6
off Mazenod Av **90** D7
New Providence Wf, E14 **134** D1
Newquay Cres, Har. HA2 **85** E2
Newquay Gdns, Wat. WD19 *off Fulford Gro* **50** B2
Newquay Rd, SE6 **172** B2
New Quebec St, W1 **16** A4
New Ride, SW7 **23** J3
New River Av, N8 **75** F3
New River Ct, N5 **94** A4
New River Cres, N13 **59** H4
New River Head, EC1 **11** F3
New River Wk, N1 **93** J6
New River Way, N4 **76** A7
New Rd, E1 **112** E5
E4 **62** B4
N8 **74** E5
N9 **60** E2
N17 **76** C1
N22 **75** J1
NW7 **56** B7
NW7 (Barnet Gate) **39** F7
SE2 **138** D4
Brentford TW8 **125** G6
Dagenham RM9, RM10 **119** G1
Feltham TW14 **160** B1
Feltham (E.Bed.) TW14 **141** G6
Feltham (Han.) TW13 **160** E5
Harrow HA1 **86** C4
Hayes (Harling.) UB3 **121** F7
Hounslow TW3 **143** H4
Ilford IG3 **99** H2
Kingston upon Thames KT2 **164** A7
Mitcham CR4 **199** J1
Richmond TW10 **163** F4
Welling DA16 **158** B2
West Molesey KT8 **179** G3
New Row, WC2 **18** A5
Newry Rd, Twick. TW1 **144** D4
Newsam Av, N15 **76** A5
★ **New Scotland Yd**, SW1 **25** H5
Newsholme Dr, N21 **43** F5
NEW SOUTHGATE, N11 **58** D4
New Southgate Ind Est, N11 **58** C5
New Spitalfields Mkt, E10 **96** A3
New Spring Gdns Wk, SE11 **34** B4
New Sq, WC2 **18** D3
Newstead Av, Orp. BR6 **207** G3
Newstead Rd, SE12 **155** E7
Newstead Wk, Cars. SM5 **185** F7
Newstead Way, SW19 **166** A4
New St, EC2 **20** E2
New St Hill, Brom. BR1 **173** H5
New St Sq, EC4 **19** F3
Newton Av, N10 **74** A1
W3 **126** C2
Newton Cl, E17 **77** H6
Harrow HA2 **85** G2
Newton Cres, Borwd. WD6 **38** C4
Newton Gro, W4 **126** E4
Newton Ho, Enf. EN3
off Exeter Rd **45** G3
Newton Pl, E14 **134** A4
Newton Rd, E15 **96** D5
N15 **76** C5
NW2 **89** J3
SW19 **166** B7
W2 **108** D6
Harrow HA3 **68** B2
Isleworth TW7 **144** C2
Welling DA16 **158** A3
Wembley HA0 **87** J7
Newton St, WC2 **18** B3
Newtons Yd, SW18
off Wandsworth High St **148** D5
Newton Wk, Edg. HA8
off Roscoff Cl **70** C1
Newton Way, N18 **59** J5
Newtown St, SW11
off Strasburg Rd **150** B1
New Trinity Rd, N2 **73** G3
New Turnstile, WC1 **18** C2
New Union Cl, E14 **134** C3
New Union St, EC2 **20** B2
New Wanstead, E11 **79** F6
New Way Rd, NW9 **71** E4
New Wf Rd, N1 **10** B1
New Zealand Way, W12 **107** H7
Niagara Av, W5 **125** F4
Niagara Cl, N1
off Cropley St **12** A1
Nibthwaite Rd, Har. HA1 **68** B5
Nicholas Cl, Grnf. UB6 **103** H2
Nicholas Ct, E13
off Tunmarsh La **115** H3
Nicholas Gdns, W5 **125** G2
Nicholas La, EC4 **20** C5
Nicholas Ms, W4
off Short Rd **126** E6
Nicholas Pas, EC4 **20** C5
Nicholas Rd, E1 **113** F4
Croydon CR0 **201** E4
Dagenham RM8 **101** F2
Nicholay Rd, N19 **92** D2
Nichol Cl, N14 **58** D1
Nicholes Rd, Houns. TW3 **143** G4
Nichol La, Brom. BR1 **173** G7
Nichollsfield Wk, N7
off Hillmarton Rd **93** F5
Nicholls Pt, E15 **115** G1
Nicholl St, E2 **112** D1
Nichols Cl, N4
off Osborne Rd **93** G1
Chessington KT9
off Merritt Gdns **195** F6
Nichols Ct, E2 **13** F2
Nichols Grn, W5 **105** H5
Nicholson Rd, Croy. CR0 **202** C1
Nicholson St, SE1 **27** G2
Nickelby Cl, SE28 **118** C6
Nickols Wk, SW18
off Jew's Row **149** E4
Nicola Cl, Har. HA3 **68** A2
South Croydon CR2 **201** J6
Nicola Ms, Ilf. IG6 **65** E7
Nicol Cl, Twick. TW1
off Cassilis Rd **145** E6
Nicoll Pl, NW4 **71** H6
Nicoll Rd, NW10 **107** E1
Nicoll Way, Borwd. WD6 **38** D5
Nicolson Dr, Bushey (Bushey Hth) WD23 **51** J1
Nicosia Rd, SW18 **149** H7
Niederwald Rd, SE26 **171** H4
Nield Rd, Hayes UB3 **121** J2
Nigel Cl, Nthlt. UB5
off Church Rd **102** E1
Nigel Fisher Way, Chess. KT9 **195** F7
Nigel Ms, Ilf. IG1 **98** E4
Nigel Playfair Av, W6
off King St **127** H4
Nigel Rd, E7 **97** J5
SE15 **152** D3
Nigeria Rd, SE7 **135** J7
Nightingale Av, E4 **62** E5
Harrow HA1 **68** E7
Nightingale Cl, E4 **62** E4
W4 *off Grove Pk Ter* **126** C6
Carshalton SM5 **200** A2
Pinner HA5 **66** C5
Nightingale Ct, E11
off Nightingale La **79** H5
Sutton SM1
off Lind Rd **199** F5
Nightingale Dr, Epsom KT19 **196** B6
Nightingale Est, E5 **94** D3
Nightingale Gro, SE13 **154** D5
Nightingale Hts, SE18
off Nightingale Vale **136** E6
Nightingale Ho, E1
off Thomas More St **29** H1
Nightingale La, E11 **79** G5
N6 **91** H1
N8 **74** E4
SW4 **149** J7
SW12 **149** J7
Bromley BR1 **191** J2
Richmond TW10 **145** H7
Nightingale Ms, E3
off Chisenhale Rd **113** H2
E11 **79** G5
SE11 **35** F1
Kingston upon Thames KT1 *off South La* **181** G3
Nightingale Pl, SE18 **136** D6
SW10 **30** D5
Nightingale Rd, E5 **94** E3
N1 **93** J6
N9 **45** F6
N22 **75** E1
NW10 **107** F2
W7 **124** C1
Carshalton SM5 **199** J3
Hampton TW12 **161** G5
Orpington BR5 **193** F6
Walton-on-Thames KT12 **178** B7
West Molesey KT8 **179** H5
Nightingales, The, Stai. TW19 **140** C7
Nightingale Sq, SW12 **150** A7
Nightingale Vale, SE18 **136** D6
Nightingale Wk, SW4 **150** B6
Nightingale Way, E6 **116** B5
Nile Cl, N16
off Evering Rd **94** C3
Nile Dr, N9 **61** F2
Nile Path, SE18
off Jackson St **136** D6
Nile Rd, E13 **115** J2
Nile St, N1 **12** A3
Nile Ter, SE15 **37** F4
Nimegen Way, SE22 **152** B5
Nimrod Cl, Nthlt. UB5 **102** D3
Nimrod Pas, N1
off Tottenham Rd **94** B6
Nimrod Rd, SW16 **168** B6
Nina Mackay Cl, E15
off Arthingworth St **114** E1
Nine Acres Cl, E12 **98** B5
Hayes UB3
off Bourne Av **121** F3
NINE ELMS, SW8 **33** G7
Nine Elms La, SW8 **33** G6
Nineteenth Rd, Mitch. CR4 **186** E4
Ninhams Wd, Orp. BR6 **206** D4
Ninth Av, Hayes UB3 **102** A7
Nisbet Ho, E9
off Homerton High St **95** G5
Nisbett Wk, Sid. DA14
off Sidcup High St **176** A4
Nithdale Rd, SE18 **137** E7
Niton Cl, Barn. EN5 **40** A6
Niton Rd, Rich. TW9 **146** A3
Niton St, SW6 **128** A7
Niven Cl, Borwd. WD6 **38** C1
N.L.A. Twr, Croy. CR0 **202** A2
No. 1 St, SE18 **137** E3
Nobel Dr, Hayes (Harling.) UB3 **121** G7
Nobel Rd, N18 **61** F5
Noble Ct, Mitch. CR4 **185** G2
Noble St, EC2 **19** J3
Noel Coward Ho, SW1
off Vauxhall Br Rd **33** G2
NOEL PARK, N22 **75** G2
Noel Pk Rd, N22 **75** G2
Noel Rd, E6 **116** B4
N1 **11** G1
W3 **106** B6
Noel Sq, Dag. RM8 **100** C4
Noel St, W1 **17** G4
Noel Ter, SE23
off Dartmouth Rd **171** F2
Noko, W10 **108** A3
Nolan Way, E5 **94** D4
Nolton Pl, Edg. HA8 **69** J1
Nonsuch Cl, Ilf. IG6 **65** E6
Nonsuch Ho, SW19
off Chapter Way **185** G1
★ **Nonsuch Mansion**, Sutt. SM3 **197** J6
Nora Gdns, NW4 **72** A4
NORBITON, Kings.T. KT2 **182** B2
Norbiton Av, Kings.T. KT1 **182** A2
Norbiton Common Rd, Kings.T. KT1 **182** B3
Norbiton Rd, E14 **113** J6
Norbreck Gdns, NW10
off Lytham Gro **105** J3
Norbreck Par, NW10
off Lytham Gro **105** J3
Norbroke St, W12 **107** F7
Norburn St, W10
off Chesterton Rd **108** B5
NORBURY, SW16 **187** G1
Norbury Av, SW16 **187** F1
Hounslow TW3 **144** A5
Thornton Heath CR7 **187** G2
Norbury Cl, SW16 **187** G1
Norbury Ct Rd, SW16 **186** E3
Norbury Cres, SW16 **187** F1
Norbury Cross, SW16 **186** E3
Norbury Gdns, Rom. RM6 **82** D5
Norbury Gro, NW7 **54** E3
Norbury Hill, SW16 **169** G7
Norbury Ri, SW16 **186** E3
Norbury Rd, E4 **62** A5
Thornton Heath CR7 **187** J2
Norcombe Gdns, Har. HA3 **69** F6
Norcott Cl, Hayes UB4 **102** C4
Norcott Rd, N16 **94** D2
Norcroft Gdns, SE22 **152** D7
Norcutt Rd, Twick. TW2 **162** B1
Norfield Rd, Dart. DA2 **177** J4
Norfolk Av, N13 **59** H6
N15 **76** C6
Norfolk Cl, N2 **73** H3
N13 **59** H6
Barnet EN4 **42** A4
Twickenham TW1
off Cassilis Rd **145** E6
Norfolk Cres, W2 **15** H3
Sidcup DA15 **157** H7
Norfolk Gdns, Bexh. DA7 **159** F1
Borehamwood WD6 **38** D4
Norfolk Ho, SE3 **135** E6
SW1 *off Regency St* **33** J1
Norfolk Ho Rd, SW16 **168** D3
Norfolk Ms, W10
off Blagrove Rd **108** C5
Norfolk Pl, W2 **15** F3
Welling DA16 **158** A2
Norfolk Rd, E6 **116** C1
E17 **77** G2
NW8 **109** G1
NW10 **88** E7
SW19 **167** H7
Barking IG11 **99** H7
Barnet EN5 **40** D3
Dagenham RM10 **101** H5
Enfield EN3 **45** E6
Esher (Clay.) KT10 **194** B5
Feltham TW13 **160** C1

Norfolk Rd, Harrow HA1 . . **67** H5
Ilford IG3 . . **99** H1
Romford RM7 . . **83** J6
Thornton Heath CR7 . . **187** J3
Norfolk Row, SE1 . . **34** C1
Norfolk Sq, W2 . . **15** F4
Norfolk Sq Ms, W2 . . **15** F4
Norfolk St, E7 . . **97** G4
Norfolk Ter, W6
off Field Rd . . **128** B5
Norgrove St, SW12 . . **150** A7
Norhyrst Av, SE25 . . **188** C3
Norland Ho, W11 . . **128** A1
Norland Pl, W11 . . **128** B1
Norland Rd, W11 . . **128** A1
Norlands Cres, Chis. BR7 . . **192** E1
Norlands Gate, Chis. BR7 . . **193** E1
Norland Sq, W11 . . **128** B1
Norley Vale, SW15 . . **165** G1
Norlington Rd, E10 . . **96** C1
E11 . . **96** C1
Norman Av, N22 . . **75** H1
Feltham TW13 . . **161** E2
Southall UB1 . . **103** E7
Twickenham TW1 . . **145** E7
Normanby Cl, SW15 . . **148** C5
Normanby Rd, NW10 . . **89** F4
Norman Cl, Orp. BR6 . . **207** F3
Romford RM5 . . **83** H2
Norman Ct, Ilf. IG2 . . **81** G7
Woodford Green IG8
off Monkhams Av . . **63** H5
Norman Cres, Houns. TW5 . . **142** D1
Pinner HA5 . . **66** C1
Normand Gdns, W14
off Greyhound Rd . . **128** B6
Normand Ms, W14
off Normand Rd . . **128** C6
Normand Rd, W14 . . **128** C6
Normandy Av, Barn. EN5 . . **40** C5
Normandy Cl, SE26 . . **171** H3
Normandy Rd, SW9 . . **151** G1
Normandy Ter, E16 . . **115** H6
Norman Gro, E3 . . **113** H2
Normanhurst Av, Bexh. DA7 . . **158** D1
Normanhurst Dr, Twick. TW1
off St. Margarets Rd . . **144** E5
Normanhurst Rd, SW2 . . **169** F2
Norman Rd, E6 . . **116** C4
E11 . . **96** D2
N15 . . **76** C5
SE10 . . **134** B7
SW19 . . **167** F7
Belvedere DA17 . . **139** H3
Ilford IG1 . . **99** E5
Sutton SM1 . . **198** D5
Thornton Heath CR7 . . **187** H5
Normans Cl, NW10 . . **88** D6
Normansfield Av, Tedd. TW11 . . **163** F7
Normanshire Av, E4 . . **62** C4
Normanshire Dr, E4 . . **62** A4
Normans Mead, NW10 . . **88** D6
Norman St, EC1 . . **11** J4
Normanton Av, SW19 . . **166** D2
Normanton Pk, E4 . . **62** E3
Normanton Rd, S.Croy. CR2 . . **202** B6
Normanton St, SE23 . . **171** G2
Norman Way, N14 . . **58** E2
W3 . . **106** B5
Normington Cl, SW16 . . **169** G5
Norrice Lea, N2 . . **73** G5
Norris St, SW1 . . **17** H6
Norroy Rd, SW15 . . **148** A4
Norrys Cl, Barn. (Cockfos.) EN4 . . **41** J5
Norrys Rd, Barn. (Cockfos.) EN4 . . **41** J4
Norseman Cl, Ilf. IG3 . . **100** B1
Norseman Way, Grnf. UB6
off Olympic Way . . **103** H1
Norstead Pl, SW15 . . **165** G2
North Access Rd, E17 . . **77** G6
North Acre, NW9 . . **71** E1
NORTH ACTON, W3 . . **106** D4
North Acton Rd, NW10 . . **106** D3
Northall Rd, Bexh. DA7 . . **159** J2
Northampton Gro, N1 . . **94** A5
Northampton Pk, N1 . . **93** J6
Northampton Rd, EC1 . . **11** F5
Croydon CR0 . . **202** D2
Enfield EN3 . . **45** H4
Northampton Row, EC1 . . **11** F4
Northampton Sq, EC1 . . **11** G4
Northampton St, N1 . . **93** J7
Northanger Rd, SW16 . . **168** E6
North Arc, Croy. CR0
off North End . . **201** J2
North Audley St, W1 . . **16** B4
North Av, N18 . . **60** D4
W13 . . **104** E6
Carshalton SM5 . . **200** A7
Harrow HA2 . . **67** H6
Hayes UB3 . . **102** A7
Richmond TW9
off Sandycombe Rd . . **146** A1
Southall UB1 . . **103** F7
North Bk, NW8 . . **7** F4
Northbank Rd, E17 . . **78** C2
NORTH BECKTON, E6 . . **116** B4
North Birkbeck Rd, E11 . . **96** D3
Northborough Rd, SW16 . . **186** D3
Northbourne, Brom. BR2 . . **191** G7
Northbourne Ho, E5
off Pembury Rd . . **94** E5
Northbourne Rd, SW4 . . **150** D4
North Branch Av, W10
off Harrow Rd . . **107** J3
Northbrook Rd, N22 . . **59** E7
SE13 . . **154** D5
Barnet EN5 . . **40** B6
Croydon CR0 . . **188** A5
Ilford IG1 . . **98** D2
Northburgh St, EC1 . . **11** H5
North Carriage Dr, W2 . . **15** G5
NORTH CHEAM, Sutt. SM3 . . **197** J4
Northchurch, SE17 . . **36** C3
Northchurch Rd, N1 . . **94** A7
Wembley HA9 . . **87** J6
Northchurch Ter, N1 . . **94** B7
North Circular Rd,
E4 (A406) . . **61** J7
E6 (A406) . . **117** E2
E11 (A406) . . **79** J2
E12 (A406) . . **98** E5
E17 (A406) . . **61** J7
E18 (A406) . . **79** J2
N3 (A406) . . **72** E3
N11 (A406) . . **73** G1
N12 (A406) . . **73** G1
N13 (A406) . . **59** G5
N18 (A406) . . **60** B5
NW2 (A406) . . **88** E3
NW10 (A406) . . **88** B7
NW11 (A406) . . **72** B4
W3 (A406) . . **125** J2
W4 (A406) . . **125** J2
W5 (A406) . . **125** J2
Barking (A406) IG11 . . **117** E2
Ilford (A406) IG1, IG4 . . **98** B1
Northcliffe Cl, Wor.Pk. KT4 . . **197** E3
Northcliffe Dr, N20 . . **56** C1
North Cl, Barn. EN5 . . **39** J5
Bexleyheath DA6 . . **158** D4
Dagenham RM10 . . **119** G1
Feltham TW14
off North Rd . . **141** G6
Morden SM4 . . **184** B4
North Colonnade, The, E14 . . **134** A1
North Common Rd, W5 . . **105** H7
Northcote, Pnr. HA5 . . **66** C2
Northcote Av, W5 . . **105** H7
Isleworth TW7 . . **144** D5
Southall UB1 . . **103** E7
Surbiton KT5 . . **182** A7
Northcote Ms, SW11
off Northcote Rd . . **149** H4
Northcote Rd, E17 . . **77** H4
NW10 . . **89** E7
SW11 . . **149** H4
Croydon CR0 . . **188** A6
New Malden KT3 . . **182** C3
Sidcup DA14 . . **175** H4
Twickenham TW1 . . **144** D5
Northcott Av, N22 . . **75** E1
North Countess Rd, E17 . . **77** J2
NORTH CRAY, Sid. DA14 . . **177** G3
North Cray Rd, Bex. DA5 . . **177** F3
Sidcup DA14 . . **176** E6
North Cres, E16 . . **114** D4
N3 . . **72** C2
WC1 . . **17** H1
Northcroft Rd, W13 . . **124** E2
Epsom KT19 . . **196** D7
Northcroft Ter, W13
off Northcroft Rd . . **125** E2
North Cross Rd, SE22 . . **152** C5
Ilford IG6 . . **81** F4
North Dene, NW7 . . **54** D3
Northdene, Chig. IG7 . . **65** G5
North Dene, Houns. TW3 . . **143** H1
Northdene Gdns, N15 . . **76** C6
Northdown Gdns, Ilf. IG2 . . **81** H5
Northdown Rd, Well. DA16 . . **158** B2
Northdown St, N1 . . **10** B1
North Dr, SW16 . . **168** C4
Beckenham BR3 . . **190** B4
Hounslow TW3 . . **143** J2
Orpington BR6 . . **207** H4
North End, NW3 . . **91** F2
North End, Buckhurst Hill IG9 . . **47** J7
Croydon CR0 . . **201** J2
North End Av, NW3 . . **91** F2
North End Cres, W14 . . **128** C4
North End Ho, W14 . . **128** B4
North End Par, W14
off North End Rd . . **128** B4
North End Rd, NW11 . . **90** D1
SW6 . . **128** C6
W14 . . **128** B4
Wembley HA9 . . **88** A3
North End Way, NW3 . . **91** F2
Northern Av, N9 . . **60** C2
Northernhay Wk, Mord. SM4 . . **184** B4
Northern Perimeter Rd, Houns. (Lon.Hthrw Air.) TW6 . . **141** F1
Northern Perimeter Rd W, Houns. (Lon.Hthrw Air.) TW6 . . **140** A1
Northern Relief Rd, Bark. IG11 . . **99** E7
Northern Rd, E13 . . **115** H1
Northern Service Rd, Barn. EN5 . . **40** B3
North Eyot Gdns, W6 . . **127** G5
Northey St, E14 . . **113** H7
Northfield, Loug. IG10 . . **48** A4
Northfield Av, W5 . . **125** E2
W13 . . **125** E2
Pinner HA5 . . **66** D4
Northfield Cl, Brom. BR1 . . **192** B1
Hayes UB3 . . **121** H3
Northfield Cres, Sutt. SM3 . . **198** B4
Northfield Gdns, Dag. RM9 *off Northfield Rd* . . **101** F4
Northfield Pk, Hayes UB3 . . **121** J3
Northfield Path, Dag. RM9 . . **101** F3
Northfield Rd, E6 . . **98** C7
N16 . . **76** B7
W13 . . **124** E2
Barnet EN4 . . **41** H3
Borehamwood WD6 . . **38** B1
Dagenham RM9 . . **101** F4
Enfield EN3 . . **44** E5
Hounslow TW5 . . **122** D6
Northfields, SW18 . . **148** D4
Northfields Ind Est, Wem. HA0 . . **106** A1
Northfields Rd, W3 . . **106** B5
NORTH FINCHLEY, N12 . . **57** G5
North Flockton St, SE16 . . **29** H3
North Gdn, E14
off Westferry Circ . . **133** J1
North Gdns, SW19 . . **167** G7
North Gate, NW8 . . **7** G2
Northgate Ct, SW9
off Canterbury Cres . . **151** G3
Northgate Dr, NW9 . . **70** E6
Northgate Ind Pk, Rom. RM5 . . **83** F2
North Glade, The, Bex. DA5 . . **159** F7
North Gower St, NW1 . . **9** G4
North Grn, NW9
off Clayton Fld . . **55** E7
North Gro, N6 . . **74** A7
N15 . . **76** A5
NORTH HARROW, Har. HA2 . . **67** G6
North Hatton Rd, Houns. (Lon.Hthrw Air.) TW6 . . **141** G1
North Hill, N6 . . **73** J6
North Hill Av, N6 . . **74** A6
NORTH HYDE, Sthl. UB2 . . **123** E4
North Hyde Gdns, Hayes UB3 . . **122** A4
North Hyde La, Houns. TW5 . . **123** E5
Southall UB2 . . **123** E5
North Hyde Rd, Hayes UB3 . . **121** J3
Northiam, N12 . . **56** D3
Northiam St, E9 . . **113** E1
Northington St, WC1 . . **10** C6
NORTH KENSINGTON, W10 . . **107** J6
Northlands Av, Orp. BR6 . . **207** H4
Northlands St, SE5 . . **151** J2
North La, Tedd. TW11 . . **162** C6
North Lo Cl, SW15 . . **148** A5
North London Business Pk, N11 . . **57** J2
North Mall, N9
off Edmonton Grn Shop Cen . . **60** E2
North Ms, WC1 . . **10** D6
Northolm, Edg. HA8 . . **54** D4
Northolme Gdns, Edg. HA8 . . **70** A1
Northolme Ri, Orp. BR6 . . **207** H2
Northolme Rd, N5 . . **93** J4
NORTHOLT, UB5 . . **85** F7
Northolt, N17 . . **76** A2
Northolt Av, Ruis. HA4 . . **84** B5
Northolt Gdns, Grnf. UB6 . . **86** C5
Northolt Rd, Har. HA2 . . **85** H4
Hounslow (Lon.Hthrw Air.) TW6 . . **140** A1
Northover, Brom. BR1 . . **173** F3
North Par, Chess. KT9 . . **195** H5
Edgware HA8
off Mollison Way . . **70** A2
North Pk, SE9 . . **156** C6
North Pas, SW18 . . **148** D4
North Pl, Mitch. CR4 . . **167** J7
Teddington TW11 . . **162** C6
Northpoint, Brom. BR1
off Sherman Rd . . **191** G1
Northpoint Cl, Sutt. SM1 . . **199** F3
Northpoint Sq, NW1 . . **92** D6
North Pole La, Kes. BR2 . . **205** F6
North Pole Rd, W10 . . **107** J5
Northport St, N1 . . **112** A1
North Ride, W2 . . **15** G6
North Ri, W2
off St. Georges Flds . . **15** H4
North Rd, N6 . . **74** A7
N7 . . **92** E6
N9 . . **60** E1
SE18 . . **137** H4
SW19 . . **167** F6
W5 . . **125** G3
Belvedere DA17 . . **139** H3
Brentford TW8 . . **125** H6
Bromley BR1 . . **191** H1
Edgware HA8 . . **70** B1
Feltham TW14 . . **141** G6
Ilford IG3 . . **99** H2
Richmond TW9 . . **146** A3
Romford (Chad.Hth) RM6 . . **82** E5
Southall UB1 . . **103** G7
Surbiton KT6 . . **181** G6
West Drayton UB7 . . **120** C3
West Wickham BR4 . . **204** B1
Northrop Rd, Houns. (Lon.Hthrw Air.) TW6 . . **141** H1
North Row, W1 . . **16** A5
North Several, SE3
off Orchard Rd . . **154** D2
NORTH SHEEN, Rich. TW9 . . **146** A2
Northside Rd, Brom. BR1
off Mitchell Way . . **191** G1
North Side Wandsworth Common, SW18 . . **149** F5
Northspur Rd, Sutt. SM1 . . **198** D3
North Sq, N9
off Edmonton Grn Shop Cen . . **60** E2
NW11 . . **72** D5
Northstead Rd, SW2 . . **169** G2
North St, E13 . . **115** G2
NW4 . . **71** J5
SW4 . . **150** C3
Barking IG11 . . **99** E6
Bexleyheath DA7 . . **159** G4
Bromley BR1 . . **191** G1
Carshalton SM5 . . **199** J3
Isleworth TW7 . . **144** D3
North St Pas, E13 . . **115** H2
North Tenter St, E1 . . **21** G4
North Ter, SW3 . . **23** G6
Northumberland All, EC3 . . **21** E4
Northumberland Av, E12 . . **97** J1
WC2 . . **26** A1
Enfield EN1 . . **45** E1
Isleworth TW7 . . **144** C1
Welling DA16 . . **157** G4
Northumberland Cl, Erith DA8 . . **139** J7
Staines (Stanw.) TW19 . . **140** B6
Northumberland Cres, Felt. TW14 . . **141** H6
Northumberland Gdns, N9 . . **60** C3
Bromley BR1 . . **192** D4
Isleworth TW7 . . **124** D7
Mitcham CR4 . . **186** D5
Northumberland Gro, N17 . . **60** E7
NORTHUMBERLAND HEATH, Erith DA8 . . **139** J7
Northumberland Pk, N17 . . **60** C7
Erith DA8 . . **139** J7
Northumberland Pk Ind Est, N17
off Willoughby La . . **61** E7
Northumberland Pl, W2 . . **108** D6
Richmond TW10 . . **145** G5
Northumberland Rd, E6 . . **116** B6
E17 . . **78** A7
Barnet (New Barn.) EN5 . . **41** F6
Harrow HA2 . . **67** F5

Northumberland Row, Twick. TW2 *off Colne Rd* ... **162** B1
Northumberland St, WC2 ... **26** A1
Northumberland Way, Erith DA8 ... **159** J1
Northumbria St, E14 ... **114** A6
North Verbena Gdns, W6 *off St. Peter's Sq* ... **127** G5
Northview, N7 ... **93** E3
North Vw, SW19 ... **165** H5
W5 ... **105** F4
Pinner HA5 ... **66** C7
Northview Cres, NW10 ... **89** F4
North Vw Dr, Wdf.Grn. IG8 ... **80** A2
North Vw Rd, N8 ... **74** D3
North Vil, NW1 ... **92** D6
North Wk, W2 ... **14** C6
Croydon (New Adgtn) CR0 ... **204** B5
North Way, N9 ... **61** F2
N11 ... **58** C6
NW9 ... **70** B3
Northway, NW11 ... **72** E5
Morden SM4 ... **184** B3
North Way, Pnr. HA5 ... **66** C3
Northway, Wall. SM6 ... **200** C4
Northway Circ, NW7 ... **54** D4
Northway Cres, NW7 ... **54** D4
Northway Ho, N20 ... **57** F1
Northway Rd, SE5 ... **151** J3
Croydon CR0 ... **188** C6
Northways Par, NW3 *off Finchley Rd* ... **91** G7
Northweald La, Kings.T. KT2 ... **163** G5
NORTH WEMBLEY, Wem. HA0 ... **87** E2
Northwest Pl, N1 ... **11** F1
North Wf Rd, W2 ... **14** E2
Northwick Av, Har. HA3 ... **68** D6
Northwick Circle, Har. HA3 ... **69** F6
Northwick Cl, NW8 ... **6** E5
Harrow HA1 ... **86** E1
Northwick Pk Rd, Har. HA1 ... **68** C6
Northwick Rd, Wat. WD19 ... **50** C4
Wembley HA0 ... **105** G1
Northwick Ter, NW8 ... **6** E5
Northwick Wk, Har. HA1 ... **68** C7
Northwold Dr, Pnr. HA5 *off Cuckoo Hill* ... **66** C3
Northwold Est, E5 ... **94** D2
Northwold Rd, E5 ... **94** C2
N16 ... **94** C2
North Wd Ct, SE25 *off Regina Rd* ... **188** D3
Northwood Gdns, N12 ... **57** G5
Greenford UB6 ... **86** C5
Ilford IG5 ... **80** D4
Northwood Hall, N6 ... **74** C7
Northwood Ho, SE27 ... **170** A4
Northwood Pl, Erith DA18 ... **139** F3
Northwood Rd, N6 ... **74** B7
SE23 ... **171** J1
Carshalton SM5 ... **200** A6
Hounslow (Lon.Hthrw Air.) TW6 ... **140** A1
Thornton Heath CR7 ... **187** H2
Northwood Twr, E17 ... **78** C4
Northwood Way, SE19 *off Roman Ri* ... **170** A6
Northwood HA6 ... **50** A7
NORTH WOOLWICH, E16 ... **136** B2
★ **North Woolwich Old Sta Mus**, E16 ... **136** D2
North Woolwich Rd, E16 ... **135** G1
North Woolwich Rbt, E16 ... **135** J1
North Worple Way, SW14 ... **146** D3
Norton Av, Surb. KT5 ... **182** B7
Norton Cl, E4 ... **62** A5
Borehamwood WD6 ... **38** A1
Enfield EN1 *off Brick La* ... **44** E2
Norton Folgate, E1 ... **21** E1
Norton Gdns, SW16 ... **186** E2
Norton Rd, E10 ... **95** J1
Wembley HA0 ... **87** G6
Norval Rd, Wem. HA0 ... **86** E2
Norway Gate, SE16 ... **133** H3
Norway Pl, E14 *off Commercial Rd* ... **113** J6
Norway St, SE10 ... **134** B6
Norwich Cres, Rom. (Chad.Hth) RM6 ... **82** B5
Norwich Ho, E14 *off Cordelia St* ... **114** B6
Norwich Ms, Ilf. IG3 *off Ashgrove Rd* ... **100** A1
Norwich Pl, Bexh. DA6 ... **159** G4
Norwich Rd, E7 ... **97** G5
Dagenham RM9 ... **119** G2
Norwich Rd, Greenford UB6 ... **103** H1
Thornton Heath CR7 ... **187** J3
Norwich St, EC4 ... **19** E3
Norwich Wk, Edg. HA8 ... **54** C7
NORWOOD, SE19 ... **170** A6
Norwood Av, Wem. HA0 ... **105** J1
Norwood Cl, NW2 ... **90** B3
Southall UB2 ... **123** G4
Twickenham TW2 *off Fourth Cross Rd* ... **162** A2
Norwood Cres, Houns. (Lon.Hthrw Air.) TW6 ... **141** F1
Norwood Dr, Har. HA2 ... **67** F6
Norwood Gdns, Hayes UB4 ... **102** C4
Southall UB2 ... **123** F4
NORWOOD GREEN, Sthl. UB2 ... **123** G4
Norwood Grn Rd, Sthl. UB2 ... **123** G4
Norwood High St, SE27 ... **169** H3
NORWOOD NEW TOWN, SE19 ... **169** J6
Norwood Pk Rd, SE27 ... **169** J5
Norwood Rd, SE24 ... **169** H1
SE27 ... **169** H2
Southall UB2 ... **123** F4
Norwood Ter, Sthl. UB2 *off Tentelow La* ... **123** H4
Notley St, SE5 ... **36** B7
Notre Dame Est, SW4 ... **150** C4
Notson Rd, SE25 ... **188** E4
Notting Barn Rd, W10 ... **108** A4
Nottingdale Sq, W11 *off Wilsham St* ... **128** B1
Nottingham Av, E16 ... **115** J5
Nottingham Ct, WC2 ... **18** A4
Nottingham Pl, W1 ... **8** B6
Nottingham Rd, E10 ... **78** C6
SW17 ... **167** J1
Isleworth TW7 ... **144** C2
South Croydon CR2 ... **201** J4
Nottingham St, W1 ... **16** B1
Nottingham Ter, NW1 ... **8** B6
NOTTING HILL, W11 ... **108** B7
Notting Hill Gate, W11 ... **128** D1
Nova, E14 *off Newton Pl* ... **134** A4
Nova Ms, Sutt. SM3 ... **198** B1
Novar Cl, Orp. BR6 ... **193** J7
Nova Rd, Croy. CR0 ... **201** H1
Novar Rd, SE9 ... **175** F1
Novello St, SW6 ... **148** D1
Novello Way, Borwd. WD6 ... **38** D1
Nowell Rd, SW13 ... **127** G6
Nower Hill, Pnr. HA5 ... **67** F4
Noyna Rd, SW17 ... **167** J3
Nubia Way, Brom. BR1 ... **173** E3
Nuding Cl, SE13 ... **154** A3
Nugent Rd, N19 ... **93** E1
SE25 ... **188** C3
Nugents Ct, Pnr. HA5 *off St. Thomas' Dr* ... **67** E1
Nugents Pk, Pnr. HA5 ... **67** E1
Nugent Ter, NW8 ... **6** D2
Numa Ct, Brent. TW8 *off Justin Cl* ... **125** G7
Nun Ct, EC2 ... **20** B3
Nuneaton Rd, Dag. RM9 ... **100** D7
Nuneham Est, SW16 *off Prentis Rd* ... **168** D4
NUNHEAD, SE15 ... **153** F3
Nunhead Cres, SE15 ... **152** E3
Nunhead Est, SE15 ... **152** E4
Nunhead Grn, SE15 ... **153** E3
Nunhead Gro, SE15 ... **153** E3
Nunhead La, SE15 ... **152** E3
Nunhead Pas, SE15 *off Peckham Rye* ... **152** D3
Nunnington Cl, SE9 ... **174** B3
Nunns Rd, Enf. EN2 ... **43** J2
Nupton Dr, Barn. EN5 ... **39** J6
Nurse Cl, Edg. HA8 *off Gervase Rd* ... **70** C1
Nursery Av, N3 ... **73** F2
Bexleyheath DA7 ... **159** F3
Croydon CR0 ... **203** G2
Nursery Cl, SE4 ... **153** J2
SW15 ... **148** A4
Croydon CR0 ... **203** G2
Enfield EN3 ... **45** G1
Feltham TW14 ... **142** B7
Orpington BR6 ... **193** J7
Romford RM6 ... **82** D6
Watford WD19 ... **50** B1
Woodford Green IG8 ... **63** H5
Nursery Ct, N17 *off Nursery St* ... **60** C7
Nursery Gdns, Chis. BR7 ... **174** E6
Enfield EN3 ... **45** G1
Hampton TW12 *off Hanworth Rd* ... **161** F4
Hounslow TW4 ... **143** F5
Nursery La, E2 ... **112** C1
E7 ... **97** G6
W10 ... **107** J5
Nurserymans Rd, N11 ... **58** A2
Nursery Rd, E9 *off Morning La* ... **95** F6
N2 ... **73** G1
N14 ... **42** C7
SW9 ... **151** F4
Loughton IG10 ... **47** J5
Pinner HA5 ... **66** C3
Sutton SM1 ... **199** F4
Thornton Heath CR7 ... **188** A4
Nursery Rd Merton, SW19 ... **184** E2
Nursery Rd Mitcham, Mitch. CR4 ... **185** H3
Nursery Rd Wimbledon, SW19 *off Worple Rd* ... **166** B7
Nursery Row, SE17 ... **36** B2
Barnet EN5 *off St. Albans Rd* ... **40** B3
Nursery St, N17 ... **60** C7
Nursery Wk, NW4 ... **71** H3
Nurstead Rd, Erith DA8 ... **139** G7
Nutbourne St, W10 ... **108** B3
Nutbrook St, SE15 ... **152** D3
Nutbrowne Rd, Dag. RM9 ... **119** F1
Nutcroft Rd, SE15 ... **132** E7
Nutfield Cl, N18 ... **60** D6
Carshalton SM5 ... **199** H3
Nutfield Gdns, Ilf. IG3 ... **99** J2
Northolt UB5 ... **102** C2
Nutfield Rd, E15 ... **96** C4
NW2 ... **89** G2
SE22 ... **152** C5
Thornton Heath CR7 ... **187** H4
Nutfield Way, Orp. BR6 ... **206** D2
Nutford Pl, W1 ... **15** H3
Nuthatch Gdns, SE28 ... **137** G2
Nuthurst Av, SW2 ... **169** F2
Nutley Ter, NW3 ... **91** F6
Nutmead Cl, Bex. DA5 ... **177** J1
Nutmeg Cl, E16 *off Cranberry La* ... **115** E4
Nutmeg La, E14 ... **114** D6
Nuttall St, N1 ... **12** E1
Nutter La, E11 ... **79** J6
Nutt Gro, Edg. HA8 ... **53** G2
Nutt St, SE15 ... **37** G7
Nutwell St, SW17 ... **167** H5
Nuxley Rd, Belv. DA17 ... **139** F6
Nyanza St, SE18 ... **137** G6
Nye Bevan Est, E5 ... **95** G3
Nylands Av, Rich. TW9 ... **146** A1
Nymans Gdns, SW20 *off Hidcote Gdns* ... **183** H3
Nynehead St, SE14 ... **133** H7
Nyon Gro, SE6 ... **171** J2
Nyssa Cl, Wdf.Grn. IG8 *off Gwynne Pk Av* ... **64** C6
Nyton Cl, N19 *off Courtauld Rd* ... **92** E1

O

★ **O2, The**, SE10 ... **134** E1
O2 Shop Cen, NW3 *off Finchley Rd* ... **91** F6
Oak Apple Ct, SE12 ... **173** G2
Oak Av, N8 ... **74** E4
N10 ... **58** B7
N17 ... **60** A7
Croydon CR0 ... **204** A2
Hampton TW12 ... **161** E5
Hounslow TW5 ... **122** D7
West Drayton UB7 ... **120** D3
Oak Bk, Croy. (New Adgtn) CR0 ... **204** C6
Oakbank Av, Walt. KT12 ... **179** F7
Oakbank Gro, SE24 ... **151** J4
Oakbark Ho, Brent. TW8 *off High St* ... **125** F7
Oakbrook Cl, Brom. BR1 ... **173** H4
Oakbury Rd, SW6 ... **149** E2
Oak Cl, N14 ... **42** B7
Sutton SM1 ... **199** F2
Oakcombe Cl, N.Mal. KT3 ... **182** E1
Oak Cottage Cl, SE6 ... **173** F1
Oak Cres, E16 ... **115** E5
Oakcroft Cl, Pnr. HA5 ... **66** B2
Oakcroft Rd, SE13 ... **154** D2
Chessington KT9 ... **195** J4
Oakcroft Vil, Chess. KT9 ... **195** J4
Oakdale, N14 ... **58** B1
Oakdale Av, Har. HA3 ... **69** H5
Northwood HA6 ... **66** A2
Oakdale Cl, Wat. WD19 ... **50** C4
Oakdale Gdns, E4 ... **62** C5
Oakdale Rd, E7 ... **97** H7
E11 ... **96** D2
E18 ... **79** H2
N4 ... **75** J6
Oakdale Rd, SE15 ... **153** F3
SW16 ... **169** E5
Watford WD19 ... **50** C3
Oakdale Way, Mitch. CR4 ... **186** A7
Oakdene, SE15 *off Carlton Gro* ... **152** E1
Oak Dene, W13 *off The Dene* ... **104** E5
Oakdene Av, Chis. BR7 ... **174** D5
Erith DA8 ... **139** J6
Thames Ditton KT7 ... **194** D1
Oakdene Cl, Pnr. HA5 ... **51** F7
Oakdene Dr, Surb. KT5 ... **182** C7
Oakdene Ms, Sutt. SM3 ... **198** C1
Oakdene Pk, N3 ... **56** C7
Oakdene Rd, Orp. BR5 ... **193** J5
Oakden St, SE11 ... **35** F1
Oake Ct, SW15 *off Portinscale Rd* ... **148** B5
Oaken Dr, Esher (Clay.) KT10 ... **194** C6
Oakenholt Ho, SE2 *off Hartslock Dr* ... **138** D2
Oaken La, Esher (Clay.) KT10 ... **194** B5
Oakenshaw Cl, Surb. KT6 ... **181** H7
Oakes Cl, E6 *off Savage Gdns* ... **116** C6
Oakeshott Av, N6 ... **92** A2
Oakey La, SE1 ... **27** E5
Oak Fm, Borwd. WD6 ... **38** C5
Oakfield, E4 ... **62** B5
Oakfield Av, Har. HA3 ... **69** E3
Oakfield Cl, N.Mal. KT3 *off Blakes La* ... **183** F5
Oakfield Ct, N8 ... **74** E7
NW2 *off Hendon Way* ... **72** A7
Borehamwood WD6 ... **38** B3
Oakfield Gdns, N18 ... **60** B4
SE19 ... **170** B5
Beckenham BR3 ... **190** A5
Carshalton SM5 ... **199** H1
Greenford UB6 ... **104** A4
Oakfield La, Kes. BR2 ... **205** J4
Oakfield Lo, Ilf. IG1 *off Albert Rd* ... **99** E3
Oakfield Rd, E6 ... **116** B1
E17 ... **77** H2
N3 ... **72** E1
N4 ... **75** G6
N14 ... **58** E3
SE20 ... **171** E7
SW19 ... **166** A3
Croydon CR0 ... **201** J1
Ilford IG1 ... **99** E2
Oakfield Rd Ind Est, SE20 *off Oakfield Rd* ... **171** E7
Oakfields Rd, NW11 ... **72** B6
Oakfield St, SW10 ... **30** C5
Oakford Rd, NW5 ... **92** C4
Oak Gdns, Croy. CR0 ... **204** A2
Edgware HA8 ... **70** C2
Oak Gro, NW2 ... **90** B4
Ruislip HA4 ... **66** B7
Sunbury-on-Thames TW16 ... **160** B7
West Wickham BR4 ... **204** C2
Oak Gro Rd, SE20 ... **189** F1
Oakhall Ct, E11 ... **79** H6
Oak Hall Rd, E11 ... **79** H6
Oakham Cl, SE6 *off Rutland Wk* ... **171** J2
Barnet EN4 ... **41** J3
Oakham Dr, Brom. BR2 ... **191** F4
Oakhampton Rd, NW7 ... **56** A7
Oakhill, Esher (Clay.) KT10 ... **194** D6
Oak Hill, Surb. KT6 ... **181** H7
Woodford Green IG8 ... **62** D7
Oakhill Av, NW3 ... **90** E4
Pinner HA5 ... **66** E2
Oak Hill Cl, Wdf.Grn. IG8 ... **62** D7
Oakhill Ct, SW19 ... **166** A7
Oak Hill Cres, Surb. KT6 ... **181** H7
Woodford Green IG8 ... **62** D7
Oakhill Dr, Surb. KT6 ... **181** H7
Oak Hill Gdns, Wdf.Grn. IG8 ... **79** E1
Oak Hill Gro, Surb. KT6 ... **181** H6
Oak Hill Pk, NW3 ... **91** E4
Oak Hill Pk Ms, NW3 ... **91** F4
Oakhill Path, Surb. KT6 ... **181** H6
Oakhill Pl, SW15 *off Oakhill Rd* ... **148** D5
Oakhill Rd, SW15 ... **148** C5
SW16 ... **187** E1
Beckenham BR3 ... **190** C2
Orpington BR6 ... **207** J1
Oak Hill Rd, Surb. KT6 ... **181** H6
Oakhill Rd, Sutt. SM1 ... **199** E3
Oak Hill Way, NW3 ... **91** F4

Oak Ho, NW3
 off Maitland Pk Vil 91 J6
Oakhouse Rd, Bexh. DA6 .159 G5
Oakhurst Av, Barn.
 (E.Barn.) EN4 ....41 H7
Bexleyheath DA7 .....138 E7
Oakhurst Cl, E17 ....78 E4
Chislehurst BR7 ....192 C1
Ilford IG6 ....81 F1
Teddington TW11 .....162 B5
Oakhurst Gdns, E4 ......63 F1
E17 ....78 E4
Bexleyheath DA7 .....139 E7
Oakhurst Gro, SE22 ...152 D4
Oakhurst Rd, Epsom
KT19 ....196 C6
Oakington Av, Har. HA2 ..67 G7
Hayes UB3 ....121 G4
Wembley HA9 ....87 J3
Oakington Cl, Sun. TW16 .178 C2
Oakington Dr, Sun. TW16 .178 C2
Oakington Manor Dr,
 Wem. HA9 ....88 A5
Oakington Rd, W9 .....108 D4
Oakington Way, N8 .....75 E6
Oakland Pl, Buck.H. IG9 ..63 G2
Oakland Rd, E15 ....96 D4
Oaklands, N21 ....59 F2
Twickenham TW2 .....143 J7
Oaklands Av, N9 ....44 E6
Esher KT10 ....194 A1
Isleworth TW7 ....124 C6
Sidcup DA15 ....157 J7
Thornton Heath CR7 ..187 G4
Watford WD19 ....50 B1
West Wickham BR4 ...204 B3
Oaklands Cl, Bexh. DA6 .159 F5
Chessington KT9 .....195 F4
Orpington BR5 ....193 H6
Oaklands Ct, W12
 off Uxbridge Rd 127 H1
Wembley HA0 ....87 G5
Oaklands Est, SW4 ...150 C6
Oaklands Gro, W12 ...127 G1
Oaklands La, Barn. EN5 ..39 H4
Oaklands Ms, NW2
 off Oaklands Rd 90 A4
Oaklands Pk Av, Ilf. IG1
 off High Rd 99 G2
Oaklands Pl, SW4
 off St. Alphonsus Rd .150 C4
Oaklands Rd, N20 ......40 C7
NW2 ....90 A4
SW14 ....146 D3
W7 ....124 C2
Bexleyheath DA6 .....159 F4
Bromley BR1 ....173 E7
Oaklands Way, Wall.
SM6 ....200 D7
Oakland Way, Epsom
KT19 ....196 D6
Oak La, E14 ....113 J7
N2 ....73 G2
N11 ....58 D6
Isleworth TW7 ....144 B4
Twickenham TW1 .....144 D7
Woodford Green IG8 ...63 F4
Oakleafe Gdns, Ilf. IG6 ...80 E3
Oaklea Pas, Kings.T.
KT1 ....181 G3
Oakleigh Av, N20 ....57 G2
Edgware HA8 ....70 B2
Surbiton KT6 ....196 A1
Oakleigh Cl, N20 ....57 J3
Edgware HA8 ....70 C2
Oakleigh Cres, N20 ....57 H2
Oakleigh Gdns, N20 ....57 F1
Edgware HA8 ....53 J5
Orpington BR6 ....207 H4
Oakleigh Ms, N20
 off Oakleigh Rd N 57 F2
OAKLEIGH PARK, N20 ...57 G1
Oakleigh Pk N, Chis.
BR7 ....192 D1
Oakleigh Pk N, N20 ....57 G1
Oakleigh Pk S, N20 ....57 H2
Oakleigh Rd, Pnr. HA5 ...51 F6
Oakleigh Rd N, N20 ....57 G2
Oakleigh Rd S, N11 .....58 A3
Oakleigh Way, Mitch.
CR4 ....186 B1
Surbiton KT6 ....196 A1
Oakley Av, W5 ....106 A7
Barking IG11 ....99 J7
Croydon CR0 ....201 E4
Oakley Cl, E4 ....62 C3
E6 off Northumberland
 Rd 116 B6
W7 ....104 B7
Isleworth TW7 ....144 A1
Oakley Ct, Loug. IG10
 off Hillyfields 48 D2
Mitcham CR4 ....186 A7
Oakley Cres, EC1 ......11 H2

Oakley Dr, SE9 ....175 G1
SE13 ....154 D6
Bromley BR2 ....206 B3
Oakley Gdns, N8 ....75 F5
SW3 ....31 H5
Oakley Pk, Bex. DA5 ..158 C7
Oakley Pl, SE1 ....37 F4
Oakley Rd, N1 ....94 A7
SE25 ....188 E5
Bromley BR2 ....206 B3
Harrow HA1 ....68 B6
Oakley Sq, NW1 ....9 G2
Oakley St, SW3 ....31 G5
Oakley Wk, W6 ....128 A6
Oakley Yd, E2 ....13 G5
Oak Lo Av, Chig. IG7 ....65 G5
Oak Lo Cl, Stan. HA7
 off Dennis La 53 F5
Oak Lo Dr, W.Wick. BR4 .190 B7
Oaklodge Way, NW7 ....55 F5
Oak Manor Dr, Wem.
HA9 off Oakington
 Manor Dr 87 J5
Oakmead Av, Brom. BR2 .191 G6
Oakmeade, Pnr. HA5 ....51 G6
Oakmead Gdns, Edg. HA8 .54 D4
Oakmead Pl, Mitch. CR4 .185 H1
Oakmead Rd, SW12 ....168 A1
Croydon CR0 ....186 D6
Oakmere Rd, SE2 .....138 A6
Oakmont Pl, Orp. BR6 .207 G1
Oakmoor Way, Chig. IG7 ..65 H5
Oak Pk Gdns, SW19 ...148 A7
Oak Pk Ms, N16
 off Brooke Rd 94 C3
Oak Pl, SW18
 off East Hill 149 E5
Oakridge Dr, N2 ....73 G3
Oakridge La, Brom. BR1 .172 D5
Oakridge Rd, Brom. BR1 .172 D4
Oak Ri, Buck.H. IG9 ....64 A3
Oak Rd, W5
 off The Broadway 105 G7
Erith (Northumb.Hth)
 DA8 ....139 J7
New Malden KT3 .....182 D2
Oak Row, SW16 ....186 C2
Oaks, The, N12 ....57 E4
SE18 ....137 F5
Morden SM4 ....184 B4
Watford WD19 ....50 C1
Woodford Green IG8 ...63 E6
Oaks Av, SE19 ....170 B5
Feltham TW13 ....160 E2
Romford RM5 ....83 J2
Worcester Park KT4 ..197 H3
Oaksford Av, SE26 ....170 E3
Oaks Gro, E4 ....62 E2
Oakshade Rd, Brom. BR1 .172 D4
Oakshaw Rd, SW18 ...149 E7
Oakside Ct, Ilf. IG6 .....81 G1
Oaks La, Croy. CR0 ...203 F3
Ilford IG2 ....81 H5
Oaks Rd, Croy. CR0 ...201 J5
Staines (Stanw.) TW19 .140 A6
Oaks Shop Cen, W3
 off High St 126 C1
Oak St, Rom. RM7 ......83 J5
Oaks Way, Cars. SM5 ..199 J7
Surbiton (Long Dit.)
KT6 ....195 G2
Oaktree Av, N13 ....59 G5
Oak Tree Cl, W5
 off Pinewood Gro 105 F6
Loughton IG10 ....49 F4
Stanmore HA7 ....53 F7
Oak Tree Dell, NW9 ....70 C5
Oak Tree Gdns, Brom.
BR1 ....173 H5
Oaktree Gro, Ilf. IG1 ...99 G5
Oak Tree Rd, NW8 ....7 F4
Oakview Gdns, N2 .....73 G4
Oakview Gro, Croy. CR0 .203 H1
Oakview Rd, SE6 .....172 B5
Oak Village, NW5 ....92 A4
Oak Wk, Wall. SM6
 off Helios Rd 200 A1
Oak Way, N14 ....42 B7
Oakway, SW20 ....183 J4
Oak Way, W3 ....126 E1
Oakway, Brom. BR2 ...190 D2
Oak Way, Croy. CR0 ...189 G6
Oakway Cl, Bex. DA5 ..159 E6
Oakways, SE9 ....156 E6
OAKWOOD, N14 ....42 D6
Oakwood Av, N14 ......42 D7
Beckenham BR3 ......190 C2
Borehamwood WD6 ....38 B4
Bromley BR2 ....191 H3
Mitcham CR4 ....185 G2
Southall UB1 ....103 G7
Oakwood Cl, N14 ......42 C6
SE13 ....154 D7

Oakwood Cl, Chislehurst
BR7 ....174 C6
Woodford Green IG8
 off Green Wk 64 B6
Oakwood Ct, W14 .....128 C3
Oakwood Cres, N21 ....43 E6
Greenford UB6 ....86 D6
Oakwood Dr, SE19 ....170 A6
Edgware HA8 ....54 C6
Oakwood Gdns, Ilf. IG3 ..99 J2
Orpington BR6 ....207 F2
Sutton SM1 ....198 D2
Oakwood Hill, Loug. IG10 .48 C6
Oakwood Hill Ind Est,
 Loug. IG10 ....49 E5
Oakwood La, W14 .....128 C3
Oakwood Pk Rd, N14 ...42 D7
Oakwood Pl, Croy. CR0 .187 G6
Oakwood Rd, NW11 ....72 E5
SW20 ....183 G1
Croydon CR0 ....187 G6
Orpington BR6 ....207 F2
Pinner HA5 ....66 B2
Oakwood Vw, N14 ......42 D6
Oakworth Rd, W10 ....107 J5
Oarsman Pl, E.Mol. KT8 .180 B4
Oates Cl, Brom. BR2 ...190 D3
Oatfield Ho, N15 ....76 B6
Oatfield Rd, Orp. BR6 .207 J1
Oatland Ri, E17 ....77 H2
Oatlands Rd, Enf. EN3 ...45 F1
Oat La, EC2 ....19 J3
Oban Cl, E13 ....115 J4
Oban Ho, E14
 off Oban St 114 D6
Barking IG11
 off Wheelers Cross ...117 G2
Oban Rd, E13 ....115 J3
SE25 ....188 A4
Oban St, E14 ....114 D6
Oberon Cl, Borwd. WD6 ..38 C1
Oberstein Rd, SW11 ...149 G4
Oborne Cl, SE24 .....151 H5
O'Brien Ho, E2
 off Smart St 113 G3
Observatory Gdns, W8 .128 D2
Observatory Ms, E14
 off Storers Quay 134 D4
Observatory Rd, SW14 .146 C4
Occupation La, SE18 ..156 E1
SE5 ....125 G4
Occupation Rd, SE17 ...35 J3
W13 ....124 E2
Ocean Est, E1 ....113 G4
Ocean St, E1 ....113 G5
Ocean Wf, E14 ....133 J2
Ockendon Ms, N1
 off Ockendon Rd 94 A6
Ockendon Rd, N1 ......94 A6
Ockham Dr, Orp. BR5 ..176 A7
Ockley Ct, Sutt. SM1
 off Oakhill Rd 199 F4
Ockley Rd, SW16 .....168 E3
Croydon CR0 ....187 F7
Octagon Arc, EC2 ....20 D2
Octavia Cl, Mitch. CR4 .185 H5
Octavia Ms, W9
 off Bravington Rd 108 C4
Octavia Rd, Islw. TW7 .144 C2
Octavia St, SW11 .....149 H1
Octavia Way, SE28
 off Booth Cl 118 B7
Octavius St, SE8 .....134 A7
Odard Rd, W.Mol. KT8
 off Down St 179 G4
Oddesey Rd, Borwd.
WD6 ....38 B1
Odell Cl, Bark. IG11 ....99 J7
Odell Wk, SE13
 off Bankside Av 154 B3
Odeon, The, Bark. IG11
 off Longbridge Rd 99 G2
Odessa Rd, E7 ....97 F3
NW10 ....107 G2
Odessa St, SE16 .....133 J2
Odger St, SW11 .....149 J2
Odhams Wk, WC2 ......18 B4
Odyssey Business Pk,
 Ruis. HA4 ....84 B5
Offa's Mead, E9
 off Lindisfarne Way ...95 H4
Offenbach Ho, E2 .....113 G2
Offenham Rd, SE9 ....174 C4
Offers Ct, Kings.T. KT1
 off Winery La 181 J3
Offerton Rd, SW4 ....150 C3
Offham Slope, N12 .....56 C5
Offley Pl, Islw. TW7 ...144 A2
Offley Rd, SW9 ....35 E7
Offord Cl, N17 ....60 D6
Offord Rd, N1 ....93 F7
Offord St, N1 ....93 F7
Ogilby St, SE18 ......136 C4
Oglander Rd, SE15 ...152 C4
Ogle St, W1 ....17 F1

Oglethorpe Rd, Dag.
RM10 ....101 F3
Ohio Bldg, SE13
 off Deals Gateway ...154 B1
Ohio Rd, E13 ....115 F4
Oil Mill La, W6 ....127 G5
Okeburn Rd, SW17 ...168 A5
Okehampton Cl, N12 ...57 G5
Okehampton Cres, Well.
 DA16 ....158 B1
Okehampton Rd, NW10 .107 J1
Olaf St, W11 ....108 A7
Oldacre Ms, SW12
 off Balham Gro 150 B7
★ Old Admiralty Bldg
 (M.o.D.), SW1 ....25 J2
Old Bailey, EC4 ....19 H4
Old Barge Ho All, SE1
 off Upper Grd 27 F1
Old Barn Cl, Sutt. SM2 .198 B7
Old Barrack Yd, SW1 ...24 B3
Old Barrowfield, E15
 off Stephen's Rd 115 F1
Old Bellgate Pl, E14 ...134 A3
Oldberry Rd, Edg. HA8 ..54 D6
Old Bethnal Grn Rd, E2 ..13 H3
OLD BEXLEY, Bex. DA5 .159 H7
Old Billingsgate Mkt, EC3
 off Lower Thames St ..20 D6
Old Bond St, W1 ....17 F6
Oldborough Rd, Wem.
HA0 ....87 F2
Old Brewers Yd, WC2 ...18 A4
Old Brewery Ms, NW3
 off Hampstead High St .91 G4
Old Br Cl, Nthlt. UB5 ...103 G2
Old Br St, Kings.T.
 (Hmptn W.) KT1 ......181 G2
Old Broad St, EC2 ......20 C4
Old Bromley Rd, Brom.
BR1 ....172 D5
Old Brompton Rd, SW5 .128 D5
SW7 ....128 D5
Old Bldgs, WC2 ....18 E3
Old Burlington St, W1 ...17 F5
Oldbury Pl, W1 ....16 C1
Oldbury Rd, Enf. EN1 ...44 D2
Old Canal Ms, SE15 ....37 G4
Old Castle St, E1 ......21 F2
Old Cavendish St, W1 ...16 D3
Old Change Ct, EC4
 off Carter La 19 J4
Old Chelsea Ms, SW3 ...31 F5
Old Ch La, NW9 ....88 C2
Greenford (Perivale)
 UB6 off Perivale La ...104 D3
Stanmore HA7 ....53 F7
Old Ch Rd, E1 ....113 G6
E4 ....62 A4
Old Ch St, SW3 ....31 F4
Old Claygate La, Esher
 (Clay.) KT10 ....194 D6
Old Clem Sq, SE18
 off Kempt St 136 D6
Old Coal Yd, SE28
 off Pettman Cres 137 G4
Old Compton St, W1 ...17 H5
Old Cote Dr, Houns. TW5 .123 G6
Old Ct Pl, W8 ....22 A3
★ Old Curiosity Shop,
 WC2 ....18 C3
Old Dairy Ms, SW12 ...168 A1
Old Dairy Sq, N21
 off Wades Hill 43 G7
Old Deer Pk Gdns, Rich.
TW9 ....145 H3
Old Devonshire Rd,
 SW12 ....150 B7
Old Dock Cl, Rich. TW9
 off Watcombe Cotts ..126 A6
Old Dover Rd, SE3 ....135 G7
Old Fm Av, N14 ....42 C7
Sidcup DA15 ....175 G1
Old Fm Cl, Houns. TW4 .143 F4
Old Fm Pas, Hmptn.
TW12 ....179 J1
Old Fm Rd, N2 ....73 G1
Hampton TW12 ......161 F6
West Drayton UB7 ...120 A2
Old Fm Rd E, Sid. DA15 .176 A2
Old Fm Rd W, Sid. DA15 .175 J2
Oldfield Cl, Brom. BR1 .192 C4
Greenford UB6 ....86 B5
Stanmore HA7 ....52 D5
Oldfield Fm Gdns, Grnf.
UB6 ....104 A1
Oldfield Gro, SE16 ...133 G4
Oldfield La N, Grnf. UB6 ..86 B6
Oldfield La S, Grnf. UB6 .103 J4
Oldfield Ms, N6 ....74 C7
Oldfield Rd, N16 ....94 B3
NW10 ....89 F7
SW19 ....166 B6
W3 off Valetta Rd 127 F2
Bexleyheath DA7 .....159 E2

Oldfield Rd, Bromley BR1 **192** C4
Hampton TW12 **179** F1
Oldfields Circ, Nthlt. UB5 **85** J6
Oldfields Rd, Sutt. SM1 **198** C3
Oldfields Trd Est, Sutt. SM1 **198** D3
Old Fish St Hill, EC4 **19** J5
Old Fleet La, EC4 **19** G3
Old Fold Cl, Barn. EN5 *off Old Fold La* **40** C1
Old Fold La, Barn. EN5 **40** C1
Old Fold Vw, Barn. EN5 **39** J3
OLD FORD, E3 **95** J7
Old Ford Rd, E2 **113** F2
E3 **113** H2
Old Forge Cl, Stan. HA7 **52** D4
Old Forge Ms, W12 *off Goodwin Rd* **127** H2
Old Forge Rd, N19 *off Elthorne Rd* **92** D2
Old Forge Way, Sid. DA14 **176** B4
Old Fox Footpath, S.Croy. CR2 *off Essenden Rd* **202** B7
Old Gloucester St, WC1 **18** B1
Old Hall Cl, Pnr. HA5 **67** E1
Old Hall Dr, Pnr. HA5 **66** E1
Oldham Ter, W3 **126** C1
Old Hill, Chis. BR7 **192** D1
Orpington BR6 **207** G6
Oldhill St, N16 **94** D1
Old Homesdale Rd, Brom. BR2 **191** J4
Old Hosp Cl, SW12 **167** J1
Old Ho Cl, SW19 **166** B5
Old Ho Gdns, Twick. TW1 **145** F5
Old Jamaica Rd, SE16 **29** H5
Old James St, SE15 **152** E3
Old Jewry, EC2 **20** B4
Old Kenton La, NW9 **70** B5
Old Kent Rd, SE1 **28** C6
SE15 **37** J5
Old Kingston Rd, Wor.Pk. KT4 **196** C3
Old Lo Pl, Twick. TW1 *off St. Margarets Rd* **145** E6
Old Lo Way, Stan. HA7 **52** D5
Old London Rd, Kings.T. KT2 **181** H2
Old Maidstone Rd, Sid. DA14 **177** F7
OLD MALDEN, Wor.Pk. KT4 **196** D1
Old Malden La, Wor.Pk. KT4 **196** D2
Old Manor Dr, Islw. TW7 **143** J6
Old Manor Rd, Sthl. UB2 **122** D4
Old Manor Way, Chis. BR7 **174** C5
Old Manor Yd, SW5 *off Earls Ct Rd* **128** E4
Old Mkt Sq, E2 **13** F3
Old Marylebone Rd, NW1 **15** H2
Old Ms, Har. HA1 *off Hindes Rd* **68** B5
Old Mill Ct, E18 **79** J3
Old Mill Rd, SE18 **137** G6
Old Mitre Ct, EC4 **19** F4
Old Montague St, E1 **21** H2
Old Nichol St, E2 **13** F5
Old N St, WC1 **18** C1
Old Oak Cl, Chess. KT9 **195** J4
OLD OAK COMMON, NW10 **107** F5
Old Oak Common La, NW10 **107** E5
W3 **107** E5
Old Oak La, NW10 **107** E3
Old Oak Rd, W3 **107** F7
★ **Old Operating Thea Mus & Herb Garret**, SE1 **28** C2
Old Orchard, Sun. TW16 **178** C2
Old Orchard, The, NW3 *off Nassington Rd* **91** J4
Old Palace La, Rich. TW9 **145** F5
Old Palace Rd, Croy. CR0 **201** H3
Old Palace Ter, Rich. TW9 *off King St* **145** G5
Old Palace Yd, SW1 **26** A5
Richmond TW9 **145** F5
Old Paradise St, SE11 **34** C1
Old Pk Av, SW12 **150** A6
Enfield EN2 **43** J4
Old Pk Gro, Enf. EN2 **43** J4
Old Pk La, W1 **24** C2
Old Pk Ms, Houns. TW5 **123** F7
Old Pk Ridings, N21 **43** H6
Old Pk Rd, N13 **59** F4
SE2 **138** A5
Enfield EN2 **43** H3
Old Pk Rd S, Enf. EN2 **43** H4
Old Pk Vw, Enf. EN2 **43** G3
Old Pearson St, SE10 **134** B7
Old Perry St, Chis. BR7 **175** H7
Old PO La, SE3 **155** H3
Old Pound Cl, Islw. TW7 **144** D1
Old Pye St, SW1 **25** H5
Old Quebec St, W1 **16** A4
Old Queen St, SW1 **25** J4
Old Rectory Gdns, Edg. HA8 **54** A6
Old Redding, Har. HA3 **51** J4
Oldridge Rd, SW12 **150** A7
Old River Lea Towpath, E15 *off City Mill River Towpath* **96** B7
Old Rd, SE13 **155** E4
Enfield EN3 **45** F1
Old Rope Wk, Sun. TW16 *off The Avenue* **178** B3
Old Royal Free Pl, N1 *off Liverpool Rd* **111** G1
Old Royal Free Sq, N1 **111** G1
Old Ruislip Rd, Nthlt. UB5 **102** D2
Old Savill's Cotts, Chig. IG7 *off The Chase* **65** F4
Old Sch Cl, SE10 **135** E3
SW19 **184** D2
Beckenham BR3 **189** G2
Old Sch Cres, E7 **97** G6
Old Sch Pl, Croy. CR0 **201** G4
Old Sch Sq, E14 *off Pelling St* **114** A6
Thames Ditton KT7 **180** C6
Old Seacoal La, EC4 **19** G3
Old S Cl, Pnr. (Hatch End) HA5 **66** D1
Old S Lambeth Rd, SW8 **34** B7
★ **Old Spitalfields Mkt**, E1 **21** F1
Old Sq, WC2 **18** D3
Old Sta Rd, Hayes UB3 **121** J3
Loughton IG10 **48** B5
Old Sta Way, SW4 *off Voltaire Rd* **150** D3
Old Sta Yd, Brom. BR2 *off Bourne Way* **205** F1
Oldstead Rd, Brom. BR1 **172** D4
Old Stockley Rd, West Dr. UB7 **120** E2
Old St, E13 **115** H2
EC1 **11** J5
Old Studio Cl, Croy. CR0 **188** A7
Old Swan Yd, Cars. SM5 **199** J4
Old Thea Ct, SE1 *off Porter St* **28** A1
Old Town, SW4 **150** C3
Croydon CR0 **201** H3
Old Tram Yd, SE18 *off Lakedale Rd* **137** H4
Old Twelve Cl, W7 *off Greenford Av* **104** B4
Old Woolwich Rd, SE10 **134** D6
Old York Rd, SW18 **149** E5
Oleander Cl, Orp. BR6 **207** G5
O'Leary Sq, E1 **113** F5
Olga St, E3 **113** H2
Olinda Rd, N16 **76** C6
Oliphant St, W10 **108** A3
Olive Gro, N15 **75** J4
Oliver Av, SE25 **188** C3
Oliver Cl, W4 **126** B6
Oliver Gdns, E6 **116** B6
Oliver-Goldsmith Est, SE15 **152** D1
Oliver Gro, SE25 **188** C4
Oliver Ms, SE15 **152** D2
Olive Rd, E13 **115** J3
NW2 **89** J4
SW19 *off Norman Rd* **167** F7
W5 **125** G3
Oliver Rd, E10 **96** B2
E17 **78** C5
NW10 **106** C2
New Malden KT3 **182** C2
Sutton SM1 **199** G4
Olivers Yd, EC1 **12** C5
Olivette St, SW15 **148** A3
Ollards Gro, Loug. IG10 **48** A4
Ollerton Grn, E3 **113** J1
Ollerton Rd, N11 **58** D5
Olley Cl, Wall. SM6 **200** E7
Ollgar Cl, W12 **127** F1
Olliffe St, E14 **134** C3
Olmar St, SE1 **37** H5
Olney Rd, SE17 **35** J5
Olron Cres, Bexh. DA6 **158** D5
Olven Rd, SE18 **137** F7
Olveston Wk, Cars. SM5 **185** G6
Olwen Ms, Pnr. HA5 **66** D2
Olyffe Av, Well. DA16 **158** A2
Olyffe Dr, Beck. BR3 **190** C1
★ **Olympia**, W14 **128** B3
Olympia Ms, W2 **14** B6
Olympia Way, W14 **128** B3
Olympic Way, Grnf. UB6 **103** H1
Wembley HA9 **88** A4
Olympus Gro, N22 **75** G1
Olympus Sq, E5 *off Nolan Way* **94** D3
Oman Av, NW2 **89** J4
O'Meara St, SE1 **28** A2
Omega Bldg, SW18 *off Smugglers Way* **149** E4
Omega Cl, E14 *off Tiller Rd* **134** B3
Omega Ct, Rom. RM7 **83** J6
Omega Pl, N1 **10** B2
Omega St, SE14 **154** A1
Omega Wks, E3 **96** A7
Ommaney Rd, SE14 **153** G1
Omnibus Way, E17 **78** A2
Ondine Rd, SE15 **152** C4
Onega Gate, SE16 **133** H3
O'Neill Path, SE18 *off Kempt St* **136** D6
One Tree Cl, SE23 **153** F6
Ongar Cl, Rom. RM6 **82** C5
Ongar Rd, SW6 **128** D6
Onra Rd, E17 **78** A7
Onslow Av, Rich. TW10 **145** H5
Onslow Cl, E4 **62** C2
W10 *off Dowland St* **108** C3
Thames Ditton KT7 **194** B1
Onslow Cres, SW7 **31** F2
Chislehurst BR7 **192** E1
Onslow Dr, Sid. DA14 **176** D2
Onslow Gdns, E18 **79** H3
N10 **74** B5
N21 **43** G5
SW7 **30** E2
Thames Ditton KT7 **194** B1
Wallington SM6 **200** C6
Onslow Ms E, SW7 **31** E2
Onslow Ms W, SW7 **30** E2
Onslow Par, N14 *off Osidge La* **58** B1
Onslow Rd, Croy. CR0 **187** F7
New Malden KT3 **183** G4
Richmond TW10 **145** H5
Onslow Sq, SW7 **31** F1
Onslow St, EC1 **11** F6
Onslow Way, T.Ditt. KT7 **194** B1
Ontario St, SE1 **27** H6
Ontario Twr, E14 **114** D7
Ontario Way, E14 **114** A7
On The Hill, Wat. WD19 **50** E2
Onyx Ms, E15 *off Vicarage La* **97** E6
Opal Cl, E16 **116** A6
Opal Ms, NW6 *off Priory Pk Rd* **108** D1
Ilford IG1 **99** E2
Opal St, SE11 **35** G2
Openshaw Rd, SE2 **138** B4
Openview, SW18 **167** F1
Ophelia Gdns, NW2 *off Hamlet Sq* **90** B3
Ophir Ter, SE15 **152** D1
Opossum Way, Houns. TW4 **142** C2
Oppenheim Rd, SE13 **154** C2
Oppidans Ms, NW3 *off Meadowbank* **91** J7
Oppidans Rd, NW3 **91** J7
Orange Ct, E1 *off Hermitage Wall* **29** J2
Orange Gro, E11 **96** D3
Chigwell IG7 **65** F6
Orange Hill Rd, Edg. HA8 **54** C7
Orange Pl, SE16 *off Lower Rd* **133** F3
Orangery, The, Rich. TW10 **163** F2
Orangery La, SE9 **156** C5
Orange Sq, SW1 **32** C2
Orange St, WC2 **17** H6
Orange Yd, W1 **17** J4
Oransay Rd, N1 **93** J6
Oransay Wk, N1 *off Oransay Rd* **93** J6
Oratory La, SW3 **31** F3
Orbain Rd, SW6 **128** B7
Orbel St, SW11 **149** H1
Orb St, SE17 **36** B2
Orchard, The, N14 **42** B5
N20 **57** E1
N21 **44** A6
NW11 **72** D5
SE3 **154** D2
W4 **126** D4
W5 *off Montpelier Rd* **105** G5
Epsom KT17 **197** F7
Hounslow TW3 **143** J2
Orchard Av, N3 **72** D3
N14 **42** C6
N20 **57** G2
Belvedere DA17 **139** E6
Croydon CR0 **189** H7
Feltham TW14 **141** G5
Hounslow TW5 **123** E7
Mitcham CR4 **200** A1
Orchard Av, New Malden KT3 **183** E2
Southall UB1 **123** E1
Thames Ditton KT7 **194** D1
Orchard Cl, E4 *off Chingford Mt Rd* **62** A4
E11 **79** H4
N1 **93** J7
NW2 **89** G3
SE23 *off Brenchley Gdns* **153** F6
SW20 *off Grand Dr* **183** J4
W10 **108** B5
Bexleyheath DA7 **158** E1
Bushey (Bushey Hth) WD23 **52** A1
Edgware HA8 **53** H6
Epsom (W.Ewell) KT19 **196** B6
Northolt UB5 **85** J5
Surbiton (Long Dit.) KT6 **181** E7
Walton-on-Thames KT12 **178** B7
Wembley HA0 **105** H1
Orchard Ct, Islw. TW7 *off Thornbury Av* **124** A7
Twickenham TW2 **162** A2
Wallington SM6 *off Parkgate Rd* **200** B5
Worcester Park KT4 **197** G1
Orchard Cres, Edg. HA8 **54** C5
Enfield EN1 **44** C1
Orchard Dr, SE3 *off Orchard Rd* **154** E2
Edgware HA8 **53** J5
Orchard Est, Wdf.Grn. IG8 **63** J7
Orchard Gdns, Chess. KT9 **195** H4
Sutton SM1 **198** D5
Orchard Gate, NW9 **70** E4
Esher KT10 **194** A1
Greenford UB6 **86** E6
Orchard Grn, Orp. BR6 **207** H2
Orchard Gro, SE20 **170** D7
Croydon CR0 **189** H7
Edgware HA8 **70** A1
Harrow HA3 **69** J5
Orpington BR6 **207** J2
Orchard Hill, SE13 *off Coldbath St* **154** B2
Carshalton SM5 **199** J5
Orchard La, SW20 **183** H1
East Molesey KT8 **180** A6
Woodford Green IG8 **63** J4
Orchardleigh Av, Enf. EN3 **45** F2
Orchardmede, N21 **44** A6
Orchard Ms, N1 *off Southgate Gro* **94** A7
N6 *off Orchard Rd* **74** B7
SW17 *off Franche Ct Rd* **167** F3
Orchard Pl, E5 **95** E5
E14 **114** E7
N17 **60** C7
Orchard Ri, Croy. CR0 **203** H1
Kingston upon Thames KT2 **182** C1
Richmond TW10 **146** B4
Orchard Ri E, Sid. DA15 **157** J5
Orchard Ri W, Sid. DA15 **157** H5
Orchard Rd, N6 **74** B7
SE3 **154** E2
SE18 **137** G4
Barnet EN5 **40** C4
Belvedere DA17 **139** G4
Brentford TW8 **125** F6
Bromley BR1 **191** J1
Chessington KT9 **195** H4
Dagenham RM10 **119** G1
Enfield EN3 **45** F5
Feltham TW13 **160** A1
Hampton TW12 **161** F7
Hounslow TW4 **143** F5
Kingston upon Thames KT1 **181** H2
Mitcham CR4 **200** A1
Orpington (Farnboro.) BR6 **207** E5
Richmond TW9 **146** A3
Romford RM7 **83** H1
Sidcup DA14 **175** H4
Sunbury-on-Thames TW16 *off Hanworth Rd* **160** B7
Sutton SM1 **198** D5
Twickenham TW1 **144** D5
Welling DA16 **158** B3
Orchardson Ho, NW8 *off Orchardson St* **7** F5
Orchardson St, NW8 **7** E6
Orchard Sq, W14 *off Sun Rd* **128** C5
Orchard St, E17 **77** H4
W1 **16** B4

Orchard Ter, Enf. EN1 .....44 D6
Orchard Vil, Sid. DA14 ...176 B6
Orchard Wk, Kings.T. KT2
off Clifton Rd 182 A1
Orchard Way, Beck. BR3 ..189 H5
Croydon CR0 ....203 H1
Enfield EN1 ....44 B3
Sutton SM1 ....199 G4
Orchestra Cl, Edg. HA8
off Symphony Cl 54 B7
Orchid Cl, E6 ....116 B5
SE13 ....154 D5
Chessington KT9 .....195 F7
Southall UB1 ....103 E6
Orchid Gdns, Houns. TW3
off Staines Rd 143 F4
Orchid Rd, N14 ....42 C7
Orchid St, W12 ....107 G7
Orde Hall St, WC1 ....10 C6
Ordell Rd, E3 ....113 J2
Ordnance Cl, Felt. TW13 ..160 A3
Ordnance Cres, SE10 ....134 D2
Ordnance Hill, NW8 .....109 G1
Ordnance Ms, NW8 ....7 F1
Ordnance Rd, E16 ....115 F5
SE18 ....136 D6
Oregano Dr, E14 ....114 D6
Oregon Av, E12 ....98 C4
Oregon Bldg, SE13
off Deals Gateway ...154 B1
Oregon Cl, N.Mal. KT3
off Georgia Rd 182 C4
Oregon Sq, Orp. BR6 ....207 G1
Orestes Ms, NW6
off Aldred Rd 90 D5
Orford Ct, SE27 ....169 H2
Orford Gdns, Twick. TW1 .162 C2
Orford Rd, E17 ....78 A5
E18 ....79 H3
SE6 ....172 B3
Organ Crossroads, Epsom
KT17 ....197 G7
Organ La, E4 ....62 C2
Oriel Cl, Mitch. CR4 ......186 D4
Oriel Ct, NW3
off Heath St 91 F4
Oriel Dr, SW13 ....127 H6
Oriel Gdns, Ilf. IG5 ....80 C3
Oriel Pl, NW3
off Heath St 91 F4
Oriel Rd, E9 ....95 G6
Oriel Way, Nthlt. UB5 .....85 H7
Oriental City, NW9 ....70 D3
Oriental Rd, E16 ....136 A1
Oriental St, E14
off Morant St 114 A7
Orient Ind Pk, E10 ....96 A2
Orient St, SE11 ....35 G1
Orient Way, E5 ....95 G3
E10 ....95 H2
Oriole Way, SE28 ....118 B7
Orion Cen, The, Croy.
CR0 ....200 E2
Orion Ho, E1
off Coventry Rd 113 E4
Orion Pt, E14
off Crews St 134 A4
Orion Rd, N11 ....58 B6
Orissa Rd, SE18 ....137 H5
Orkney St, SW11 ....150 A2
Orlando Rd, SW4 ....150 C3
Orleans Cl, Esher KT10 ...194 A2
★ Orleans Ho Gall, Twick.
TW1 ....163 E1
Orleans Rd, SE19 ....170 A6
Twickenham TW1 .....145 E7
Orleston Ms, N7 ....93 G6
Orleston Rd, N7 ....93 G6
Orley Fm Rd, Har. HA1 ....86 B3
Orlop St, SE10 ....134 E5
Ormanton Rd, SE26 .....170 D4
Orme Ct, W2 ....14 A6
Orme Ct Ms, W2 ....14 B6
Orme La, W2 ....14 A6
Ormeley Rd, SW12 ......168 B1
Orme Rd, Kings.T. KT1 ...182 B2
Sutton SM1
off Grove Rd 199 E6
Ormerod Gdns, Mitch.
CR4 ....186 A2
Ormesby Cl, SE28
off Wroxham Rd 118 D7
Ormesby Way, Har. HA3 ...69 J6
Orme Sq, W2 ....14 A6
Ormiston Gro, W12 ......127 H1
Ormiston Rd, SE10 ......135 G5
Ormond Av, Hmptn.
TW12 ....179 H1
Richmond TW10
off Ormond Rd 145 G5
Ormond Cl, WC1 ....18 B1
Ormond Cres, Hmptn.
TW12 ....179 H1
Ormond Dr, Hmptn.
TW12 ....161 H7
Ormonde Av, Orp. BR6 ...207 F2
Ormonde Gate, SW3 .....32 A4
Ormonde Pl, SW1 ....32 B2
Ormonde Ri, Buck.H. IG9 ..63 J1
Ormonde Rd, SW14 ......146 B3
Ormonde Ter, NW8 ......109 J1
Ormond Ms, WC1 ....10 B6
Ormond Rd, N19 ....93 E1
Richmond TW10 ....145 G5
Ormond Yd, SW1 ....25 G1
Ormsby, Sutt. SM2
off Grange Rd 198 E7
Ormsby Gdns, Grnf. UB6 .103 J2
Ormsby Pl, N16
off Victorian Gro 94 C3
Ormsby Pt, SE18
off Vincent Rd 137 E4
Ormsby St, E2 ....13 F1
Ormside St, SE15 ....133 F6
Ormskirk Rd, Wat. WD19 ..50 D4
Ornan Rd, NW3 ....91 H5
Orpen Wk, N16 ....94 B3
Orpheus St, SE5 ....152 A1
ORPINGTON, BR5 & BR6 .207 H1
Orpington Gdns, N18 .....60 B3
Orpington Rd, N21 ....59 H1
Chislehurst BR7 ......193 H3
Orpwood Cl, Hmptn.
TW12 ....161 F5
Orsett St, SE11 ....34 D3
Orsett Ter, W2 ....14 B3
Woodford Green IG8 ...79 J1
Orsman Rd, N1 ....112 B1
Orton Gro, Enf. EN1 ......44 D1
Orton Pl, SW19 ....167 E7
Orton St, E1 ....29 H2
Orville Rd, SW11 ....149 G2
Orwell Ct, N5 ....93 J4
Orwell Rd, E13 ....115 J2
Osbaldeston Rd, N16 .....94 D2
Osberton Rd, SE12 ......155 G5
Osbert St, SW1 ....33 H2
Osborn Cl, E8 ....112 D1
Osborne Cl, Barn. EN4 ....41 J3
Beckenham BR3 ......189 H4
Feltham TW13 ....160 D5
Osborne Gdns, Th.Hth.
CR7 ....187 J2
Osborne Gro, E17 ....77 J4
N4 ....93 G1
Osborne Ms, E17
off Osborne Gro 77 J4
Osborne Pl, Sutt. SM1 ...199 G5
Osborne Rd, E7 ....97 H5
E9 ....95 J6
E10 ....96 B3
N4 ....93 F1
N13 ....59 G3
NW2 ....89 H6
W3 ....126 B3
Belvedere DA17 ......139 F5
Buckhurst Hill IG9 ......63 H1
Dagenham RM9 ......101 F5
Enfield EN3 ....45 H2
Hounslow TW3 ....143 F3
Kingston upon Thames
KT2 ....163 H7
Southall UB1 ....103 J6
Thornton Heath CR7 ..187 J2
Osborne Sq, Dag. RM9 ...101 F4
Osborne Ter, SW17
off Church La 168 A5
Osborne Way, Chess. KT9
off Bridge Rd 195 J5
Osborn Gdns, NW7 ....56 A7
Osborn La, SE23 ....153 H7
Osborn St, E1 ....21 G2
Osborn Ter, SE3
off Lee Rd 155 F4
Osbourne Ct, W5 ....105 H5
Oscar Faber Pl, N1
off St. Peter's Way 94 B7
Oscar St, SE8 ....154 A1
Oseney Cres, NW5 ....92 C6
Osgood Av, Orp. BR6 ....207 J5
Osgood Gdns, Orp. BR6 ..207 J5
OSIDGE, N14 ....58 B1
Osidge La, N14 ....58 A1
Osier Cres, N10 ....73 J1
Osier La, SE10 ....135 F3
Osier Ms, W4 ....127 F6
Osiers Rd, SW18 ....148 D4
Osier St, E1 ....113 F4
Osier Way, E10 ....96 B3
Mitcham CR4 ....185 H5
Oslac Rd, SE6 ....172 B5
Oslo Ct, NW8 ....7 G2
Oslo Sq, SE16 ....133 H3
Osman Cl, N15
off Tewkesbury Rd 76 A6
Osman Rd, N9 ....60 D3
W6 off Batoum Gdns .127 J3
Osmington Ho, SW8
off Dorset Rd 131 F7
Osmond Cl, Har. HA2 .....85 J2
Osmond Gdns, Wall.
SM6 ....200 C5
Osmund St, W12
off Braybrook St 107 F5
Osnaburgh St, NW1 ....9 E6
NW1 (north section) 9 E4
Osnaburgh Ter, NW1 ......8 E5
Osney Ho, SE2
off Hartslock Dr 138 D2
Osney Wk, Cars. SM5 ....185 G6
Osprey Cl, E6
off Dove App 116 B5
E11 ....79 G4
E17 ....61 H7
Bromley BR2 ....206 B1
Sutton SM1
off Sandpiper Rd 198 C5
West Drayton UB7 ....120 A2
Osprey Hts, SW11
off Bramlands Cl 149 H3
Osprey Ms, Enf. EN3 .....45 E5
Ospringe Cl, SE20 ....171 F7
Ospringe Ct, SE9 ....157 G6
Ospringe Rd, NW5 ....92 C4
Osram Ct, W6
off Lena Gdns 127 J3
Osram Rd, Wem. HA9 .....87 G3
Osric Path, N1 ....12 D2
Ossian Ms, N4 ....75 F7
Ossian Rd, N4 ....75 F7
Ossie Garvin Rbt, Hayes
UB4 off The Parkway ..102 C7
Ossington Bldgs, W1 .....16 B1
Ossington Cl, W2
off Ossington St 108 D7
Ossington St, W2 ....108 D7
Ossory Rd, SE1 ....37 H4
Ossulston St, NW1 ....9 H2
Ossulton Pl, N2
off East End Rd 73 F3
Ossulton Way, N2 ....73 F4
Ostade Rd, SW2 ....151 F7
Osten Ms, SW7 ....22 B6
OSTERLEY, Islw. TW7 ....123 J7
Osterley Av, Islw. TW7 ...124 A7
Osterley Ct, Islw. TW7 ...144 A1
Osterley Cres, Islw. TW7 .144 B1
Osterley Gdns, Sthl. UB2
off Chevy Rd 124 A2
Thornton Heath CR7 ..187 J2
Osterley Ho, E14
off Giraud St 114 B6
Osterley La, Islw. TW7 ...124 B5
Southall UB2 ....123 G5
Osterley Pk, Islw. TW7 ...124 A5
★ Osterley Park Ho, Islw.
TW7 ....123 J5
Osterley Pk Rd, Sthl.
UB2 ....123 F3
Osterley Pk Vw Rd, W7 ...124 B2
Osterley Rd, N16 ....94 B4
Isleworth TW7 ....124 B7
Osterley Views, Sthl.
UB2 off West Pk Rd ...124 A1
Oster Ter, E17
off Southcote Rd 77 G5
Ostliffe Rd, N13 ....59 J5
Oswald Bldg, SW8 ....32 D6
Oswald Rd, Sthl. UB1 ....123 E1
Oswald's Mead, E9
off Lindisfarne Way ...95 H4
Oswald St, E5 ....95 G3
Oswald Ter, NW2
off Temple Rd 89 J3
Osward Pl, N9 ....60 E2
Osward Rd, SW17 ....167 J2
Oswell Ho, E1 ....133 E1
Oswin St, SE11 ....35 H1
Oswyth Rd, SE5 ....152 B2
Otford Cl, SE20 ....189 F1
Bexley DA5
off Southwold Rd 159 H6
Bromley BR1 ....192 D3
Otford Cres, SE4 ....153 J6
Othello Cl, SE11 ....35 G3
Otho Ct, Brent. TW8 .....125 G7
Otis St, E3 ....114 C3
Otley App, Ilf. IG2 ....81 E6
Otley Dr, Ilf. IG2 ....80 E5
Otley Rd, E16 ....115 J6
Otley Ter, E5 ....95 G2
Otley Way, Wat. WD19 ....50 C3
Ottaway St, E5 ....94 D3
Ottenden Cl, Orp. BR6
off Southfleet Rd 207 H4
Otterbourne Rd, E4 ....62 D3
Croydon CR0 ....201 J2
Otterburn Gdns, Islw.
TW7 ....124 D7
Otterburn Ho, SE5 ....35 J7
Otterburn St, SW17 .....167 J6
Otter Cl, E15 ....114 C1
Otterden St, SE6 ....172 A4
Otter Rd, Grnf. UB6 .....103 J4
Otto Cl, SE26 ....170 E3
Otto St, SE17 ....35 G6
Oulton Cl, E5
off Mundford Rd 95 F2
SE28
off Rollesby Way 118 C6
Oulton Cres, Bark. IG11 ...99 J6
Oulton Rd, N15 ....76 A5
Oulton Way, Wat. WD19 ...51 E4
Ouseley Rd, SW12 ......167 J1
Outer Circle, NW1 ....8 B6
Outgate Rd, NW10 ....89 F7
Outram Pl, N1 ....111 E1
Outram Rd, E6 ....116 B1
N22 ....74 D1
Croydon CR0 ....202 C1
Outwich St, EC3 ....20 E3
★ Oval, The (Surrey CCC),
SE11 ....34 D5
Oval, The, E2 ....112 E2
Sidcup DA15 ....158 A7
Oval Pl, SW8 ....34 C7
Oval Rd, NW1 ....110 B1
Croydon CR0 ....202 B1
Oval Rd N, Dag. RM10 ...119 H1
Oval Rd S, Dag. RM10 ...119 H2
Oval Way, SE11 ....34 D4
Overbrae, Beck. BR3 ....172 A6
Overbrook Wk, Edg. HA8 ..54 A7
Overbury Av, Beck. BR3 ..190 B3
Overbury Rd, N15 ....76 A6
Overbury St, E5 ....95 G4
Overcliff Rd, SE13 ......154 A3
Overcourt Cl, Sid. DA15 ..158 B6
Overdale Av, N.Mal. KT3 .182 C2
Overdale Rd, W5 ....125 F3
Overdown Rd, SE6 ......172 A4
Overhill Rd, SE22 ....152 D7
Overhill Way, Beck. BR3 ..190 D5
Overlea Rd, E5 ....76 D7
Overmead, Sid. DA15 ....157 G7
Oversley Ho, W2 ....108 D5
Overstand Cl, Beck. BR3 .190 A5
Overstone Gdns, Croy.
CR0 ....189 J7
Overstone Rd, W6 ....127 J3
Overton Cl, NW10 ....88 C6
Isleworth TW7
off Avenue Rd 144 C1
Overton Ct, E11 ....79 G7
Overton Dr, E11 ....79 H7
Romford RM6 ....82 C7
Overton Ho, SW15
off Tangley Gro 147 F7
Overton Rd, E10 ....95 H1
N14 ....42 E5
SE2 ....138 C3
SW9 ....151 G2
Sutton SM2 ....198 D6
Overton Rd E, SE2 ......138 D3
Overtons Yd, Croy. CR0 ..201 J3
Ovesdon Av, Har. HA2 ....85 F1
Ovett Cl, SE19 ....170 B6
Ovex Cl, E14 ....134 C2
Ovington Gdns, SW3 .....23 H6
Ovington Ms, SW3 ....23 H6
Ovington Sq, SW3 ....23 H6
Ovington St, SW3 ....23 H6
Owen Cl, SE28 ....138 C1
Croydon CR0 ....188 A6
Hayes UB4 ....102 B3
Northolt UB5 ....85 E6
Owen Gdns, Wdf.Grn. IG8 .64 B6
Owenite St, SE2 ....138 B4
Owen Rd, N13 ....59 J5
Hayes UB4 ....102 B3
Owens Ms, E11
off Short Rd 96 E2
Owen's Row, EC1 ....11 G3
Owen St, EC1 ....11 G2
Owens Way, SE23 ....153 H7
Owen Wk, SE20
off Sycamore Gro 188 D1
Owen Waters Ho, Ilf. IG5 ..80 C1
Owen Way, NW10 ....88 C6
Owgan Cl, SE5
off Benhill Rd 132 A7
Owl, The, Loug.
(High Beach) IG10 ......47 F2
Oxberry Av, SW6 ....148 B2
Oxendon St, SW1 ....17 H6
Oxenford St, SE15 ......152 C3
Oxenholme, NW1 ....9 G2
Oxenpark Av, Wem.
HA9 ....69 H7
Oxestalls Rd, SE8 ....133 H5
Oxford Av, N14 ....58 C1
SW20 ....184 B2
Hayes UB3 ....121 J7
Hounslow TW5 ....123 G5
★ Oxford Circ, W1 ....17 F3
Oxford Circ Av, W1 ....17 F4
Oxford Cl, N9 ....60 E2
Mitcham CR4 ....186 C3
Oxford Ct, EC4 ....20 B5
W3 ....106 A6

Oxford Ct, Feltham TW13 *off Oxford Way* 160 D4
Oxford Cres, N.Mal. KT3 182 D6
Oxford Dr, SE1 28 D2
Ruislip HA4 84 C2
Oxford Gdns, N20 57 G1
N21 43 J7
W4 126 A5
W10 108 B6
Oxford Gate, W6 128 A4
Oxford Ms, Bex. DA5 177 G1
Oxford Pl, NW10 *off Press Rd* 88 D3
Oxford Rd, E15 96 D6
N4 93 G1
N9 61 E2
NW6 108 D2
SE19 170 A6
SW15 148 B4
W5 105 G7
Carshalton SM5 199 H6
Enfield EN3 45 E5
Harrow HA1 67 J6
Harrow (Wealds.) HA3 68 C3
Ilford IG1 99 F4
Sidcup DA14 176 B5
Teddington TW11 162 A5
Wallington SM6 200 C5
Woodford Green IG8 63 J5
Oxford Rd N, W4 126 B5
Oxford Rd S, W4 126 A5
Oxford Sq, W2 15 H4
Oxford St, W1 17 G3
Oxford Wk, Sthl. UB1 123 F1
Oxford Way, Felt. TW13 160 D4
Oxgate Cen Ind Est, The, NW2 89 H1
Oxgate Gdns, NW2 89 H3
Oxgate La, NW2 89 H2
Oxhawth Cres, Brom. BR2 192 D5
Oxhey Dr, Nthwd. HA6 50 B5
Watford WD19 50 C3
Oxhey Dr S, Nthwd. HA6 50 B5
Oxhey La, Har. HA3 51 G5
Pinner HA5 51 G5
Watford WD19 51 F2
Oxhey Ridge Cl, Nthwd. HA6 50 A5
Oxleas, E6 116 E6
Oxleas Cl, Well. DA16 157 G2
Oxleay Ct, Har. HA2 85 G1
Oxleay Rd, Har. HA2 85 G1
Oxleigh Cl, N.Mal. KT3 183 E5
Oxley Cl, SE1 37 G3
Oxleys Rd, NW2 89 H3
Oxlip Cl, Croy. CR0 *off Marigold Way* 203 G1
Oxlow La, Dag. RM9, RM10 101 G4
Oxonian St, SE22 152 C4
Oxo Twr Wf, SE1 19 F6
Oxted Cl, Mitch. CR4 185 G3
Oxtoby Way, SW16 186 D2
Oyster Catchers Cl, E16 *off Freemasons Rd* 115 H6
Oyster Catcher Ter, Ilf. IG5 *off Tiptree Cres* 80 D3
Oystergate Wk, EC4 *off Swan La* 20 B6
Oyster Row, E1 *off Lukin St* 113 F6
Oyster Wf, SW11 149 G2
Ozolins Way, E16 115 G6

P

Pablo Neruda Cl, SE24 *off Shakespeare Rd* 151 H4
Pace Pl, E1 *off Bigland St* 113 E6
Pacific Ms, SW9 *off Saltoun Rd* 151 G4
Pacific Rd, E16 115 G6
Pacific Wf, SE16 *off Rotherhithe St* 133 G1
Packham Ct, Wor.Pk. KT4 *off Lavender Av* 197 J3
Packington Rd, W3 126 C3
Packington Sq, N1 111 J1
Packington St, N1 111 H1
Packmores Rd, SE9 157 G5
Padbury, SE17 36 D4
Padbury Ct, E2 13 G4
Padcroft Rd, West Dr. UB7 120 A1
Paddenswick Rd, W6 127 G3
PADDINGTON, W2 14 C2
Paddington Cl, Hayes UB4 102 D4
Paddington Grn, W2 15 F1
Paddington Sta, W2 14 E3
Paddington St, W1 16 B1
Paddington Underground Sta, W2 14 E3
Paddock Cl, SE3 155 G2
SE26 171 G4
Northolt UB5 103 G2
Orpington (Farnboro.) BR6 *off State Fm Av* 207 E4
Worcester Park KT4 196 E1
Paddock Gdns, SE19 *off Westow St* 170 B6
Paddock Rd, NW2 89 G3
Bexleyheath DA6 159 E4
Ruislip HA4 84 D3
Paddocks, The, NW7 56 B6
Barnet (Cockfos.) EN4 41 J3
Wembley HA9 88 B2
Paddocks Cl, Har. HA2 85 H4
Paddock Way, SW15 147 J7
Chislehurst BR7 175 G7
Padfield Ct, Wem. HA9 *off Forty Av* 87 J3
Padfield Rd, SE5 151 J3
SW9 151 J3
Padley Cl, Chess. KT9 195 J5
Padnall Ct, Rom. RM6 *off Padnall Rd* 82 D3
Padnall Rd, Rom. RM6 82 D4
Padstow Cl, Orp. BR6 207 J4
Padstow Rd, Enf. EN2 43 H2
Padua Rd, SE20 189 F1
Pagden St, SW8 150 B1
Pageant Av, NW9 70 D1
Pageant Cres, SE16 *off Rotherhithe St* 133 H1
Pageantmaster Ct, EC4 19 G4
Pageant Wk, Croy. CR0 202 B3
Page Av, Wem. HA9 88 C3
Page Cl, Dag. RM9 101 E5
Hampton TW12 161 E6
Harrow HA3 69 J6
Page Cres, Croy. CR0 201 G5
Page Grn Rd, N15 76 D5
Page Grn Ter, N15 76 C5
Page Heath La, Brom. BR1 192 A3
Page Heath Vil, Brom. BR1 192 A3
Pagehurst Rd, Croy. CR0 188 E7
Page Meadow, NW7 55 G7
Page Rd, Felt. TW14 141 G6
Pages Hill, N10 74 A2
Pages La, N10 74 A2
Page St, NW7 71 G1
SW1 33 J1
Pages Wk, SE1 36 D1
Pages Yd, W4 *off Church St* 127 E6
Paget Av, Sutt. SM1 199 G3
Paget Cl, Hmptn. TW12 162 A4
Paget Gdns, Chis. BR7 192 E1
Paget La, Islw. TW7 144 A3
Paget Pl, Kings.T. KT2 164 C6
Thames Ditton KT7 *off Brooklands Rd* 194 D1
Paget Ri, SE18 136 D7
Paget Rd, N16 94 A1
Ilford IG1 98 E4
Paget St, EC1 11 G3
Paget Ter, SE18 136 D6
Pagitts Gro, Barn. EN4 40 E1
Pagnell St, SE14 133 J7
Pagoda Av, Rich. TW9 145 J3
Pagoda Gdns, SE3 154 D2
Pagoda Gro, SE27 169 J2
Pagoda Vista, Rich. TW9 145 J2
Paignton Rd, N15 76 B6
Ruislip HA4 84 A3
Paines Cl, Pnr. HA5 67 E3
Paines La, Pnr. HA5 66 E1
Pains Cl, Mitch. CR4 186 B2
Painsthorpe Rd, N16 *off Oldfield Rd* 94 B3
Painters Ms, SE16 *off Macks Rd* 37 J1
Painters Rd, Ilf. IG2 81 J3
Paisley Rd, N22 75 H1
Carshalton SM5 199 G1
Paisley Ter, Cars. SM5 185 G7
Pakeman St, N7 93 F3
Pakenham Cl, SW12 *off Balham Pk Rd* 168 A1
Pakenham St, WC1 10 D4
Palace Av, W8 22 B2
Palace Ct, NW3 91 E5
W2 14 A5
Harrow HA3 69 H6
Palace Ct Gdns, N10 74 C3
Palace Ex, Enf. EN2 44 A4
Palace Gdns, Buck.H. IG9 64 A1
Enfield EN2 44 A4
Palace Gdns Ms, W8 128 D1
Palace Gdns Ter, W8 128 D1
Palace Gate, W8 22 C4
Palace Gates Rd, N22 74 D1
Palace Grn, W8 22 B3
Croydon CR0 203 J7
Palace Gro, SE19 170 C7
Bromley BR1 191 H1
Palace Ms, E17 77 J4
SW1 32 C2
SW6 *off Hartismere Rd* 128 C7
Palace of Industry, Wem. HA9 *off Fulton Rd* 88 A4
Palace Par, E17 78 A4
Palace Pl, SW1 25 F5
Palace Rd, N8 74 D5
N11 58 E7
SE19 170 C7
SW2 169 F1
Bromley BR1 191 H1
East Molesey KT8 180 A3
Kingston upon Thames KT1 181 G4
Ruislip HA4 84 E4
Palace Rd Est, SW2 169 F1
Palace Sq, SE19 170 C7
Palace St, SW1 25 F5
Palace Vw, SE12 173 G2
Bromley BR1 191 G3
Croydon CR0 203 J4
Palace Vw Rd, E4 62 B5
Palamos Rd, E10 96 A1
Palatine Av, N16 *off Stoke Newington Rd* 94 C4
Palatine Rd, N16 94 B4
Palemead Cl, SW6 147 J1
Palermo Rd, NW10 107 G2
Palestine Gro, SW19 185 G1
Palewell Common Dr, SW14 146 D5
Palewell Pk, SW14 146 D5
Paley Gdns, Loug. IG10 49 E3
Palfrey Pl, SW8 34 D7
Palgrave Av, Sthl. UB1 103 G7
Palgrave Gdns, NW1 7 H5
Palgrave Ho, NW3 91 J5
Palgrave Rd, W12 127 F3
Palissy St, E2 13 F4
Palladino Ho, SW17 *off Laurel Cl* 167 H5
Pallant Way, Orp. BR6 206 D3
Pallet Way, SE18 156 B1
Palliser Rd, W14 128 B5
Pallister Ter, SW15 *off Roehampton Vale* 165 F3
Pall Mall, SW1 25 G2
Pall Mall E, SW1 25 J1
Palmar Cres, Bexh. DA7 159 G3
Palmar Rd, Bexh. DA7 159 G2
Palm Av, Sid. DA14 176 D6
Palm Cl, E10 96 B3
Palmeira Rd, Bexh. DA7 158 D3
Palmer Av, Sutt. SM3 197 J4
Palmer Cl, Houns. TW5 143 G1
Northolt UB5 85 E6
West Wickham BR4 204 D3
Palmer Cres, Kings.T. KT1 181 H3
Palmer Dr, Brom. BR1 192 E4
Palmer Gdns, Barn. EN5 40 A5
Palmer Ho, SE14 *off Lubbock St* 133 G7
Palmer Pl, N7 93 G5
Palmer Rd, E13 115 H4
Dagenham RM8 100 D1
PALMERS GREEN, N13 59 G3
Palmers Gro, W.Mol. KT8 179 G4
Palmers La, Enf. EN1, EN3 45 E1
Palmers Pas, SW14 *off Palmers Rd* 146 C3
Palmers Rd, E2 113 G2
N11 58 C5
SW14 146 C3
SW16 187 F2
Borehamwood WD6 38 B1
Palmerston Cres, N13 59 F5
SE18 137 F6
Palmerston Gro, SW19 166 D7
Palmerston Ho, SW11 *off Strasburg Rd* 150 A1
W8 *off Kensington Pl* 128 D1
Palmerston Rd, E7 97 H5
E17 77 J4
N22 59 F7
NW6 90 D7
SW14 146 C4
SW19 166 D7
W3 126 C3
Buckhurst Hill IG9 63 H2
Carshalton SM5 199 J4
Croydon CR0 188 A5
Harrow HA3 68 C3
Hounslow TW3 143 J1
Orpington BR6 207 F4
Sutton SM1 *off Vernon Rd* 199 F5
Twickenham TW2 144 C6
Palmerston Way, SW8 *off Bradmead* 130 B7
Palmer St, SW1 25 H4
Palm Gro, W5 125 H3
Palm Rd, Rom. RM7 83 J5
Pamela Gdns, Pnr. HA5 66 B5
Pamela Wk, E8 *off Marlborough Av* 112 D1
Pampisford Rd, S.Croy. CR2 201 H7
Pams Way, Epsom KT19 196 D5
Pancras La, EC4 20 A4
Pancras Rd, NW1 9 H1
Pancras Way, E3 114 A2
Pandian Way, NW1 *off Busby Pl* 92 D6
Pandora Rd, NW6 90 D6
Panfield Ms, Ilf. IG2 *off Cranbrook Rd* 80 D6
Panfield Rd, SE2 138 A3
Pangbourne Av, W10 107 J5
Pangbourne Dr, Stan. HA7 53 G5
Pangbourne Ho, N7 92 E5
Panhard Pl, Sthl. UB1 103 H7
Pank Av, Barn. EN5 41 F5
Pankhurst Av, E16 *off Wesley Av* 135 H1
Pankhurst Cl, SE14 *off Briant St* 133 G7
Isleworth TW7 144 C3
Pankhurst Rd, Walt. KT12 178 C7
Panmuir Rd, SW20 183 H1
Panmure Cl, N5 93 H4
Panmure Rd, SE26 170 E3
Pannells Ct, Houns. TW5 *off Heston Rd* 123 G6
Panoramic, The, NW3 *off Pond St* 91 H5
Pansy Gdns, W12 107 G7
Panther Dr, NW10 88 D5
Pantiles, The, NW11 *off Willifield Way* 72 C4
Bexleyheath DA7 139 F7
Bromley BR1 192 B3
Pantiles Cl, N13 59 H5
Panton Cl, Croy. CR0 201 H1
Panton St, SW1 17 H6
Panyer All, EC4 19 J4
Papermill Cl, Cars. SM5 200 A4
Papillons Wk, SE3 155 G2
Papworth Gdns, N7 *off Chillingworth Rd* 93 F5
Papworth Way, SW2 151 G7
Parade, The, SW11 32 A7
Carshalton SM5 *off Beynon Rd* 199 J5
Esher (Clay.) KT10 194 B6
Hampton TW12 *off Hampton Rd* 162 A5
Watford (Carp.Pk) WD19 50 E3
Watford (S.Oxhey) WD19 *off Prestwick Rd* 50 D3
Parade Ms, SE27 *off Norwood Rd* 169 H2
Paradise Pas, N7 93 G5
Paradise Path, SE28 *off Birchdene Dr* 138 A1
Paradise Pl, SE18 *off Godfrey Hill* 136 B4
Paradise Rd, SW4 150 E2
Richmond TW9 145 G5
Paradise Row, E2 *off Bethnal Grn Rd* 113 E3
Paradise St, SE16 132 E2
Paradise Wk, SW3 31 J5
Paragon, The, SE3 155 F2
Paragon Cl, E16 115 G6
Paragon Gro, Surb. KT5 181 J6
Paragon Ms, SE1 36 C1
Paragon Pl, SE3 155 F2
Surbiton KT5 *off Berrylands Rd* 181 J6
Paragon Rd, E9 95 F6
Parbury Ri, Chess. KT9 195 H6
Parbury Rd, SE23 153 H6
Parchmore Rd, Th.Hth. CR7 187 H2
Parchmore Way, Th.Hth. CR7 187 H2
Pardoe Rd, E10 78 B7
Pardoner St, SE1 28 C5
Pardon St, EC1 11 H5
Parfett St, E1 21 J2
Parfitt Cl, NW3 *off North End* 91 F2
Parfrey St, W6 127 J6
Parham Dr, Ilf. IG2 80 E6
Parham Way, N10 74 C2
Paris Gdn, SE1 27 G1
Parish Gate Dr, Sid. DA15 157 H6
Parish La, SE20 171 G6

Parish Ms, SE20 171 G7
Parish Wf, SE18
off Woodhill 136 B4
Park, The, N6 74 A6
NW11 90 E1
SE19 170 B7
SE23 *off Park Hill* 171 F1
W5 125 G1
Carshalton SM5 199 J5
Sidcup DA14 176 A5
Park App, Well. DA16 158 B4
Park Av, E6 116 D1
E15 96 E6
N3 73 E1
N13 59 G3
N18 60 D4
N22 75 E2
NW2 89 H6
NW10 105 J3
NW11 90 E1
SW14 146 D4
Barking IG11 99 F6
Bromley BR1 173 F6
Carshalton SM5 200 A6
Enfield EN1 44 B6
Hounslow TW3 143 H6
Ilford IG1 98 D2
Mitcham CR4 168 B7
Orpington (Farnboro.)
BR6 206 C3
Southall UB1 123 G1
West Wickham BR4 204 C2
Woodford Green IG8 63 H5
Park Av E, Epsom KT17 197 G6
Park Av Ms, Mitch. CR4
off Park Av 168 B7
Park Av N, N8 74 D3
NW10 89 H5
Park Av Rd, N17 61 E7
Park Av S, N8 74 D4
Park Av W, Epsom KT17 197 G6
Park Cen Bldg, E3
off Fairfield Rd 114 A2
Park Chase, Wem. HA9 87 J4
Park Cl, E9 113 F1
NW2 89 H3
NW10 105 J3
SW1 23 J4
W4 126 D5
W14 128 C3
Carshalton SM5 199 J6
Hampton TW12 179 J1
Harrow HA3 68 B1
Hounslow TW3 143 J5
Kingston upon Thames
KT2 182 A1
Park Ct, SE21 169 J3
SE26 171 E6
SW11
off Battersea Pk Rd 150 B1
Kingston upon Thames
(Hmptn W.) KT1 181 F1
New Malden KT3 182 D4
Wembley HA9 87 H5
Park Cres, N3 57 E7
W1 8 D6
Enfield EN2 44 A4
Erith DA8 139 J6
Harrow HA3 68 B1
Twickenham TW2 162 A1
Park Cres Ms E, W1 8 E6
Park Cres Ms W, W1 16 D1
Park Cft, Edg. HA8 70 C1
Parkcroft Rd, SE12 155 F7
Park Dale, N11 58 D6
Parkdale Cres, Wor.Pk.
KT4 196 D3
Parkdale Rd, SE18 137 H5
Park Dr, N21 43 J6
NW11 90 E1
SE7 136 B6
SW14 146 D4
W3 126 A3
Dagenham RM10 101 J3
Harrow (Har.Wld) HA3 52 B6
Harrow (N.Har.) HA2 67 G7
Park Dr Cl, SE7 136 B5
Park E Bldg, E3
off Fairfield Rd 114 A2
Park End, NW3
off South Hill Pk 91 H4
Bromley BR1 191 F1
Parker Cl, E16 136 B1
Carshalton SM5 199 J6
Parker Ms, WC2 18 B3
Parke Rd, SW13 147 G1
Sunbury-on-Thames
TW16 178 A4
Parker Rd, Croy. CR0 201 J4
Parkers Row, SE1 29 G4
Parker St, E16 136 B1
WC2 18 B3
Parkes Rd, Chig. IG7 65 H5
Park Fm Cl, N2 73 F3
Pinner HA5 66 B5
Park Fm Rd, Brom. BR1 192 A1
Kingston upon Thames
KT2 163 H7
Parkfield Av, SW14 146 E4
Feltham TW13 160 A3
Harrow HA2 67 J2
Northolt UB5 102 D2
Parkfield Cl, Edg. HA8 54 B6
Northolt UB5 102 E2
Parkfield Cres, Felt.
TW13 160 A3
Harrow HA2 67 J2
Ruislip HA4 84 E3
Parkfield Dr, Nthlt. UB5 102 D2
Parkfield Gdns, Har. HA2 67 H3
Parkfield Rd, NW10 89 G7
SE14 153 J1
Feltham TW13 160 A3
Harrow HA2 85 J3
Northolt UB5 102 E2
Parkfields, SW15 147 J4
Croydon CR0 203 J1
Parkfields Av, NW9 88 D1
SW20 183 H1
Parkfields Cl, Cars. SM5 200 A4
Parkfields Rd, Kings.T.
KT2 163 J5
Parkfield St, N1 11 F1
Parkfield Way, Brom.
BR2 192 C6
Park Gdns, NW9 70 B3
Kingston upon Thames
KT2 163 J5
Park Gate, N2 73 G3
N21 43 F7
Parkgate, SE3 155 F3
Park Gate, W5 105 G5
Parkgate Av, Barn. EN4 41 F1
Parkgate Cl, Kings.T. KT2
off Warboys App 164 B6
Parkgate Cres, Barn.
EN4 41 F2
Parkgate Gdns, SW14 146 D5
Parkgate Ms, N6 74 C7
Parkgate Rd, SW11 129 H7
Wallington SM6 200 A5
Park Gates, Har. HA2 85 G4
Park Gro, E15 115 G1
N11 58 D7
Bexleyheath DA7 159 J4
Bromley BR1 191 H1
Edgware HA8 53 J5
Park Gro Rd, E11 96 E2
Park Hall Rd, N2 73 H4
SE21 169 J3
Park Hall Trd Est, SE21 169 J3
Parkham Ct, Brom. BR2 191 E2
Parkham St, SW11 149 H1
Park Hill, SE23 171 E2
SW4 150 D5
W5 105 G5
Bromley BR1 192 B4
Carshalton SM5 199 H6
Loughton IG10 48 A5
Richmond TW10 145 J6
Park Hill Cl, Cars. SM5 199 H5
Park Hill Ct, SW17
off Beeches Rd 167 J3
Park Hill Ri, Croy. CR0 202 B2
Parkhill Rd, E4 62 C1
NW3 91 J5
Bexley DA5 159 F7
Park Hill Rd, Brom. BR2 190 E2
Croydon CR0 202 B2
Parkhill Rd, Sid. DA15 175 G3
Park Hill Rd, Wall. SM6 200 B7
Parkhill Wk, NW3 91 J5
Parkholme Rd, E8 94 C6
Park Ho, N21 43 F7
Park Ho Gdns, Twick.
TW1 145 F6
Parkhouse St, SE5 36 C7
Parkhurst Gdns, Bex.
DA5 159 G7
Parkhurst Rd, E12 98 D4
E17 77 H4
N7 92 E4
N11 58 A4
N17 76 D2
N22 59 F7
Bexley DA5 159 G7
Sutton SM1 199 G4
Parkinson Ho, SW1
off Tachbrook St 33 H3
Parkland Cl, Chig. IG7 65 F3
Parkland Gdns, SW19 166 A1
Parkland Mead, Brom.
BR1 *off Gardenia Rd* 192 E3
Parkland Rd, N22 75 F2
Woodford Green IG8 63 G7
Parklands, N6 74 B7
Chigwell IG7 65 F3
Surbiton KT5 181 J5
Parklands Cl, SW14 146 C5
Ilford IG2 81 F7
Parklands Ct, Houns.
TW5 142 D2
Parklands Dr, N3 72 B3
Parklands Gro, Islw. TW7
off College Rd 144 C1
Parklands Rd, SW16 168 B5
Parklands Way, Wor.Pk.
KT4 197 E3
Parkland Wk, N4 75 F7
N6 74 D7
N10 74 B4
Park La, E15 *off High St* 114 D1
N9 60 C3
N17 60 D7
W1 24 C2
Carshalton SM5 200 A4
Croydon CR0 202 A3
Harrow HA2 85 H3
Hounslow (Cran.) TW5 122 A7
Richmond TW9 145 G4
Romford (Chad.Hth)
RM6 82 D6
Stanmore HA7 52 D3
Sutton SM3 198 B6
Teddington TW11 162 C6
Wallington SM6 200 A4
Wembley HA9 87 H5
Park La Cl, N17 60 D7
PARK LANGLEY, Beck.
BR3 190 C5
Park Lawns, Wem. HA9 87 J4
Parklea Cl, NW9 71 E1
Parkleigh Rd, SW19 184 E2
Parkleys, Rich. TW10 163 G4
Park Lo Av, West Dr. UB7
off Porters Way 120 C2
Park Mans, SW1
off Knightsbridge 23 J4
SW8 34 B5
Parkmead, SW15 147 H6
Park Mead, Har. HA2 85 H3
Parkmead, Loug. IG10 48 D5
Park Mead, Sid. DA15 158 B5
Parkmead Gdns, NW7 55 F6
Park Ms, SE10
off Calvert Rd 135 F5
SE24 *off Croxted Rd* 151 J6
Chislehurst BR7 175 E6
East Molesey KT8 179 J4
Hampton (Hmptn H.)
TW12 *off Park Rd* 161 J5
Parkmore Cl, Wdf.Grn.
IG8 63 G4
Park Par, NW10 107 F2
Park Pl, E14 134 A1
N1 112 A1
SW1 25 F2
W3 126 A4
W5 125 G1
Hampton (Hmptn H.)
TW12 161 J6
Wembley HA9 87 J4
Park Pl Vil, W2 14 D1
Park Ridings, N8 75 G3
Park Ri, SE23 171 H1
Harrow HA3 68 B1
Park Ri Rd, SE23 171 H1
Park Rd, E6 115 J1
E10 96 A1
E12 97 H1
E15 115 G1
E17 77 J5
N2 73 G3
N8 74 C4
N11 58 D7
N14 42 D7
N15 75 H4
N18 60 C4
NW1 7 G3
NW4 71 G7
NW8 7 G3
NW9 70 D7
NW10 106 E1
SE25 188 B4
SW19 167 G6
W4 126 C7
W7 104 C7
Barnet (High Barn.)
EN5 40 C4
Barnet (New Barn.)
EN4 41 H4
Beckenham BR3 171 J7
Bromley BR1 191 H1
Chislehurst BR7 175 E6
East Molesey KT8 179 J4
Feltham TW13 160 D4
Hampton (Hmptn H.)
TW12 161 H4
Hounslow TW3 143 J4
Ilford IG1 99 G3
Isleworth TW7 144 E1
Kingston upon Thames
KT2 163 J5
Kingston upon Thames
(Hmptn W.) KT1 181 F1
Park Rd, New Malden
KT3 182 D4
Richmond TW10 145 J6
Sunbury-on-Thames
TW16 160 B7
Surbiton KT5 181 J5
Sutton SM3 198 B6
Teddington TW11 162 C6
Twickenham TW1 145 F6
Wallington SM6 200 B5
Wallington (Hackbr.)
SM6 200 B2
Wembley HA0 87 H6
Park Rd E, W3 126 B2
Park Rd N, W3 126 B2
W4 126 D5
Park Row, SE10 134 D6
PARK ROYAL, NW10 106 A3
Park Royal Metro Cen,
NW10 106 B4
Park Royal Rd, NW10 106 C3
W3 106 C3
Parkshot, Rich. TW9 145 H4
Parkside, N3 72 E1
NW2 89 G3
NW7 55 G6
SE3 135 F7
SW19 166 A4
Buckhurst Hill IG9 63 H2
Hampton (Hmptn H.)
TW12 162 A5
Sidcup DA14 176 B2
Sutton SM3 198 B6
Parkside Av, SW19 166 A5
Bromley BR1 192 B4
Parkside Business Est,
SE8 *off Rolt St* 133 H6
Parkside Cl, SE20 171 F7
Parkside Cres, N7 93 G3
Surbiton KT5 182 C6
Parkside Dr, Edg. HA8 54 A3
Parkside Est, E9
off Rutland Rd 113 G1
Parkside Gdns, SW19 166 A4
Barnet (E.Barn.) EN4 57 J1
Parkside Ho, Dag. RM10 101 J3
Parkside Rd, SW11 150 A1
Belvedere DA17 139 J4
Hounslow TW3 143 H5
Parkside Ter, N18
*off Great
Cambridge Rd* 60 A4
Orpington BR6
off Willow Wk 206 E3
Parkside Wk, SE10 134 E5
Parkside Way, Har. HA2 67 H4
Park S, SW11
off Austin Rd 150 A1
Park Sq E, NW1 8 D5
Park Sq Ms, NW1 8 D6
Park Sq W, NW1 8 D5
Parkstead Rd, SW15 147 G5
Park Steps, W2
off St. Georges Flds 15 H5
Parkstone Av, N18 60 C5
Parkstone Rd, E17 78 C3
SE15 *off Rye La* 152 D2
Park St, SE1 27 J1
W1 16 B5
Croydon CR0 201 J2
Teddington TW11 162 B6
Park Ter, Wor.Pk. KT4 197 G1
Parkthorne Cl, Har. HA2 67 H6
Parkthorne Dr, Har. HA2 67 G6
Parkthorne Rd, SW12 150 D7
Park Twrs, W1
off Brick St 24 D2
Park Vw, N21 43 F7
W3 106 C5
New Malden KT3 183 F3
Pinner HA5 67 F1
Wembley HA9 88 B5
Parkview Cl, Cars. SM5 199 J7
Parkview Ct, SW18
off Broomhill Rd 148 D6
Park Vw Ct, Ilf. IG2
off Brancaster Rd 81 H6
Park Vw Cres, N11 58 B4
Parkview Dr, Mitch. CR4 185 G2
Park Vw Est, E2 113 F2
N5 93 J4
Park Vw Gdns, NW4 71 J5
Ilford IG4 80 C4
Park Vw Ho, SE24
off Hurst St 151 H6
Park Vw Ms, SW9 151 F2
Park Vw Rd, N3 73 E1
N17 76 D3
NW10 89 F4
Parkview Rd, SE9 174 E1
Park Vw Rd, W5 105 H5
Parkview Rd, Croy. CR0 202 D1
Park Vw Rd, Pnr. HA5 50 B7
Southall UB1 123 G1
Welling DA16 158 C3

Park Vw Rd Est, N17 76 E2
Park Village E, NW1 110 B2
Park Village W, NW1 8 D1
Park Vil, Rom. RM6 82 D6
Parkville Rd, SW6 128 C7
Park Vista, SE10 134 D6
Park Wk, N6 *off North Rd* 74 A7
SE10 *off Crooms Hill* 134 D7
SW10 30 D5
Parkway, N14 58 E2
Park Way, N20 57 J4
Parkway, NW1 110 B1
Park Way, NW11 72 B5
Parkway, SW20 184 A4
Park Way, Edg. HA8 70 B1
Enfield EN2 43 G2
Parkway, Erith DA18 139 E3
Park Way, Felt. TW14 142 B7
Parkway, Ilf. IG3 99 J3
Park Way, Ruis. HA4 84 A1
West Molesey KT8 179 H3
Parkway, Wdf.Grn. IG8 63 J5
Parkway, The, Hayes UB3, UB4 102 C6
Hounslow (Cran.) TW4, TW5 142 B2
Northolt UB5 102 D3
Southall UB2 122 A5
Parkway Trd Est, Houns. TW5 122 C6
Park W, W2 15 H4
Park W Bldg, E3 *off Fairfield Rd* 114 A2
Park W Pl, W2 15 H3
Parkwood, N20 57 J3
Beckenham BR3 190 A1
Parkwood Gro, Sun. TW16 178 A3
Parkwood Ms, N6 74 B6
Parkwood Rd, SW19 166 C5
Bexley DA5 159 F7
Isleworth TW7 144 C1
Parliament Ct, E1 21 E2
Parliament Hill, NW3 91 H4
Parliament Ms, SW14 *off Thames Bk* 146 C2
Parliament Sq, SW1 26 A4
Parliament St, SW1 26 A4
Parliament Vw Apts, SE1 34 C1
Parma Cres, SW11 149 J4
Parmiter St, E2 113 E2
Parmoor Ct, EC1 11 J5
Parnell Cl, W12 127 H3
Edgware HA8 54 B4
Parnell Rd, E3 113 J1
Parnham Cl, Brom. BR1 *off Stoneleigh Rd* 192 E3
Parnham St, E14 *off Blount St* 113 H6
Parolles Rd, N19 92 C1
Paroma Rd, Belv. DA17 139 G3
Parr Cl, N9 60 E4
N18 60 E4
Parr Ct, N1 12 B1
Feltham TW13 160 C4
Parr Pl, W4 *off Chiswick High Rd* 127 F4
Parr Rd, E6 116 A1
Stanmore HA7 69 G1
Parrs Pl, Hmptn. TW12 161 G7
Parr St, N1 12 B1
Parry Av, E6 116 C6
Parry Cl, Epsom KT17 197 G7
Parry Pl, SE18 137 E4
Parry Rd, SE25 188 B3
W10 108 B3
Parry St, SW8 34 A5
Parsifal Rd, NW6 90 D5
Parsley Gdns, Croy. CR0 *off Primrose La* 203 G1
Parsloes Av, Dag. RM9 100 D4
Parsonage Gdns, Enf. EN2 43 J2
Parsonage La, Enf. EN1, EN2 44 A2
Sidcup DA14 177 F4
Parsonage Manorway, Belv. DA17 139 G6
Parsonage St, E14 134 C4
Parsons Cl, Sutt. SM1 199 E3
Parsons Cres, Edg. HA8 54 A3
PARSONS GREEN, SW6 148 D1
Parsons Grn, SW6 148 D1
Parsons Grn La, SW6 148 D1
Parsons Gro, Edg. HA8 54 A3
Parsons Ho, SW2 *off New Pk Rd* 150 E7
Parson's Ho, W2 7 E6
Parson's Mead, Croy. CR0 201 H1
Parsons Mead, E.Mol. KT8 179 J3
Parsons Rd, E13 *off Old St* 115 J2
Parson St, NW4 71 J4
Parthenia Rd, SW6 148 D1
Partingdale La, NW7 56 A5
Partington Cl, N19 92 D1
Partridge Cl, E16 *off Fulmer Rd* 116 A5
Barnet EN5 39 J6
Bushey WD23 51 H1
Stanmore HA7 53 H4
Partridge Dr, Orp. BR6 207 F3
Partridge Grn, SE9 174 D3
Partridge Rd, Hmptn. TW12 161 F6
Sidcup DA14 175 H3
Partridge Sq, E6 *off Nightingale Way* 116 B5
Partridge Way, N22 75 E1
Parvin St, SW8 150 D1
Pasadena Cl, Hayes UB3 122 B2
Pasadena Cl Trd Est, Hayes UB3 *off Pasadena Cl* 122 B2
Pasadena Trd Est, Hayes UB3 *off Pasadena Cl* 122 B2
Pascal Ms, SE19 *off Anerley Hill* 170 D7
Pascal St, SW8 33 J7
Pascoe Rd, SE13 154 D5
Pasgen Ct, N9 *off Galahad Rd* 60 D2
Pasley Cl, SE17 35 J4
Pasquier Rd, E17 77 H3
Passey Pl, SE9 156 C6
Passfield Dr, E14 *off Uamvar St* 114 B5
Passfield Path, SE28 *off Booth Cl* 118 B7
Passing All, EC1 11 H6
Passmore Gdns, N11 58 D6
Passmore St, SW1 32 B2
★ **Passport Office**, SW1 33 E1
Pasteur Cl, NW9 71 E2
Pasteur Gdns, N18 59 H5
Paston Cl, E5 *off Caldecott Way* 95 G3
Wallington SM6 200 C3
Paston Cres, SE12 155 H7
Pastor St, SE11 35 H1
Pasture Cl, Wem. HA0 86 E3
Pasture Rd, SE6 173 F1
Dagenham RM9 101 F4
Wembley HA0 86 E2
Pastures, The, N20 56 C1
Patcham Ter, SW8 150 B1
Patching Way, Hayes UB4 102 E5
Paternoster La, EC4 *off Warwick La* 19 H4
Paternoster Row, EC4 19 J4
Paternoster Sq, EC4 19 H4
Paterson Ct, EC1 *off St. Luke's Est* 12 B4
Pater St, W8 128 D3
Pates Manor Dr, Felt. TW14 141 G7
Path, The, SW19 184 E1
Pathfield Rd, SW16 168 D6
Pathway, The, Wat. WD19 *off Anthony Cl* 50 D1
Patience Rd, SW11 149 H2
Patio Cl, SW4 150 D6
Patmore Est, SW8 150 C1
Patmore St, SW8 150 C1
Patmos Rd, SW9 131 H7
Paton Cl, E3 114 A3
Paton St, EC1 11 J4
Patricia Ct, Chis. BR7 *off Manor Pk Rd* 193 G1
Welling DA16 138 B7
Patrick Connolly Gdns, E3 *off Talwin St* 114 B3
Patrick Rd, E13 115 J3
Patriot Sq, E2 113 E2
Patrol Pl, SE6 154 B6
Patshull Pl, NW5 *off Patshull Rd* 92 C6
Patshull Rd, NW5 92 C6
Patten All, Rich. TW10 *off The Hermitage* 145 G5
Pattenden Rd, SE6 171 J1
Patten Rd, SW18 149 H7
Patterdale Cl, Brom. BR1 173 F6
Patterdale Rd, SE15 133 F7
Patterson Ct, SE19 170 C7
Patterson Rd, SE19 170 C6
Pattina Wk, SE16 133 J1
Pattison Rd, NW2 90 D3
Pattison Wk, SE18 137 F5
Paul Cl, E15 96 E7
Paulet Rd, SE5 151 H2
Paulet Way, NW10 88 E7
Paul Gdns, Croy. CR0 202 C2
Paulhan Rd, Har. HA3 69 G4
Paulin Dr, N21 43 G7
Pauline Cres, Twick. TW2 161 J1
Pauline Ho, E1 21 J1
Paul Julius Cl, E14 114 D7
Paul Robeson Cl, E6 116 D3
Paul's Nurs Rd, Loug. (High Beach) IG10 47 H1
Paul St, E15 114 D1
EC2 12 C6
Paul's Wk, EC4 19 H5
Paultons Sq, SW3 31 F5
Paultons St, SW3 31 F6
Pauntley St, N19 92 C1
Paved Ct, Rich. TW9 145 G5
Paveley Ct, NW7 56 A7
Paveley Dr, SW11 129 H7
Paveley Ho, N1 *off Priory Grn Est* 10 C2
Paveley St, NW8 7 H5
Pavement, The, SW4 150 C4
W5 *off Popes La* 125 H3
Isleworth TW7 *off South St* 144 D3
Pavement Ms, Rom. RM6 *off Clarissa Rd* 82 D7
Pavement Sq, Croy. CR0 202 D1
Pavet Cl, Dag. RM10 101 H6
Pavilion La, Beck. BR3 171 J6
Pavilion Ms, N3 *off Windermere Av* 72 D2
Pavilion Par, W12 *off Wood La* 107 J6
Pavilion Rd, SW1 24 A6
Ilford IG1 80 C7
Pavilion Sq, SW17 167 H3
Pavilion St, SW1 24 A6
Pavilion Ter, W12 *off Wood La* 107 J6
East Molesey KT8 180 C4
Ilford IG2 *off Southdown Cres* 81 H5
Pavilion Way, Edg. HA8 54 B7
Ruislip HA4 84 C2
Pavillion Ms, N4 93 F2
Pawleyne Cl, SE20 171 F7
Pawsey Cl, E13 *off Plashet Rd* 115 G1
Pawson's Rd, Croy. CR0 187 J6
Paxford Rd, Wem. HA0 86 E2
Paxton Cl, Rich. TW9 145 J2
Walton-on-Thames KT12 178 C7
Paxton Ct, Borwd. WD6 *off Manor Way* 38 C4
Paxton Pl, SE27 170 B4
Paxton Rd, N17 60 C7
SE23 171 H3
W4 126 E6
Bromley BR1 173 G7
Paxton Ter, SW1 33 E5
Payne Cl, Bark. IG11 99 H7
Paynell Ct, SE3 *off Lawn Ter* 155 E3
Payne Rd, E3 114 B2
Paynesfield Av, SW14 146 D3
Payne St, SE8 133 J6
Paynes Wk, W6 128 B6
Payzes Gdns, Wdf.Grn. IG8 *off Chingford La* 63 F5
Peabody Av, SW1 32 D3
Peabody Cl, SE10 *off Devonshire Dr* 154 B1
SW1 32 E5
Croydon CR0 203 F1
Peabody Cotts, SE24 *off Rosendale Rd* 151 J7
Peabody Dws, WC1 10 A5
Peabody Est, EC1 (Clerkenwell) *off Farringdon La* 11 F6
EC1 (St. Luke's) 12 A6
N1 (Islington) *off Greenman St* 111 J1
N17 76 B1
SE1 27 F2
SE17 36 B2
SE24 151 H7
SW1 33 F1
SW3 31 H5
SW6 *off Lillie Rd* 128 D6
W6 *off The Square* 127 J5
W10 107 J5
Peabody Hill, SE21 169 H1
Peabody Hill Est, SE21 151 H7
Peabody Sq, SE1 27 G4
Peabody Twr, EC1 *off Golden La* 12 A6
Peabody Trust, SE1 27 J2
Peabody Trust Camberwell Grn Est, SE5 *off Camberwell Grn* 152 A1
Peabody Trust Old Pye St Est, SW1 *off Old Pye St* 25 H6
Peabody Yd, N1 *off Greenman St* 111 J1
Peace Cl, N14 42 B5
SE25 188 B4
Greenford UB6 *off Oldfield La N* 104 A1
Peace Gro, Wem. HA9 88 B3
Peace St, SE18 *off Nightingale Vale* 136 E6
Peaches Cl, Sutt. SM2 198 B7
Peach Gro, E11 96 D3
Peach Rd, W10 108 A3
Feltham TW13 160 A1
Peachum Rd, SE3 135 F6
Peachwalk Ms, E3 *off Grove Rd* 113 G2
Peachy Cl, Edg. HA8 *off Manor Pk Cres* 54 A6
Peacock Cl, E4 61 J7
Dagenham RM8 100 C1
Peacock Ind Est, N17 60 C7
Peacock St, SE17 35 H2
Peacock Wk, E16 115 H6
Peacock Yd, SE17 35 H2
Peak, The, SE26 171 F3
Peaketon Av, Ilf. IG4 80 A4
Peak Hill, SE26 171 F4
Peak Hill Av, SE26 171 F4
Peak Hill Gdns, SE26 171 F4
Peal Gdns, W13 *off Ruislip Rd E* 104 D4
Peall Rd, Croy. CR0 187 F6
Pearce Cl, Mitch. CR4 186 A2
Pearcefield Av, SE23 171 F1
Pear Cl, NW9 70 D4
SE14 *off Southerngate Way* 133 H7
Pearcroft Rd, E11 96 D2
Peardon St, SW8 150 B3
Peareswood Gdns, Stan. HA7 69 G1
Pearfield Rd, SE23 171 H3
Pearl Cl, E6 116 D6
NW2 72 A7
Pearl Rd, E17 78 A3
Pearl St, E1 *off Penang St* 133 E1
Pearman St, SE1 27 F5
Pear Pl, SE1 27 E3
Pear Rd, E11 96 D3
Pearscroft Ct, SW6 149 E1
Pearscroft Rd, SW6 148 E1
Pearse St, SE15 36 E6
Pearson Cl, SE5 *off Medlar St* 151 J1
Barnet EN5 40 E4
Pearson Ms, SW4 150 D3
Pearsons Av, SE14 *off Tanners Hill* 154 A1
Pearson St, E2 13 E1
Pearson Way, Mitch. CR4 186 A1
Pears Rd, Houns. TW3 143 J3
Peartree Av, SW17 167 F3
Pear Tree Cl, E2 112 C1
Bromley BR2 192 A5
Chessington KT9 196 A5
Mitcham CR4 185 H2
Peartree Ct, E18 *off Churchfields* 79 H1
Pear Tree Ct, EC1 11 F6
Peartree Gdns, Dag. RM8 100 B4
Romford RM7 83 H2
Peartree La, E1 *off Glamis Rd* 113 F7
Peartree Rd, Enf. EN1 44 B3
Pear Tree St, EC1 11 H5
Peartree Way, SE10 135 G4
Peary Pl, E2 *off Kirkwall Pl* 113 F3
Peatfield Cl, Sid. DA15 *off Woodside Rd* 175 H3
Pebble Way, W3 126 B1
Pebworth Rd, Har. HA1 86 D2
Peckarmans Wd, SE26 170 D3
Peckett Sq, N5 *off Highbury Gra* 93 H4
Peckford Pl, SW9 151 G2
PECKHAM, SE15 152 D1
Peckham Gro, SE15 36 E7
Peckham High St, SE15 152 D1
Peckham Hill St, SE15 37 H7
Peckham Pk Rd, SE15 37 H7
Peckham Rd, SE5 152 B1
SE15 152 B1
Peckham Rye, SE15 152 D3
SE22 152 D4
Pecks Yd, E1 21 F1
Peckwater St, NW5 92 C5
Pedlars Wk, N7 93 E6
Pedley Rd, Dag. RM8 100 C1
Pedley St, E1 13 G6
Pedro St, E5 95 G3
Pedworth Gdns, SE16 *off Rotherhithe New Rd* 133 F4
Peek Cres, SW19 166 A5
Peel Cl, E4 62 B2
N9 *off Plevna Rd* 60 D3
Peel Dr, NW9 71 F3
Ilford IG5 80 B3
Peel Gro, E2 113 F2

Peel Pas, W8 *off Peel St* 128 D1
Peel Pl, Ilf. IG5 80 B2
Peel Prec, NW6 108 D2
Peel Rd, E18 79 F1
NW6 108 C3
Harrow (Wealds.) HA3 68 C3
Orpington BR6 207 F5
Wembley HA9 87 G3
Peel St, W8 128 D1
Peerglow Est, Enf. EN3 45 F4
Peerless St, EC1 12 B4
Pegamoid Rd, N18 61 F3
Pegasus Cl, N16 *off Green Las* 94 A4
Pegasus Ct, W3 *off Horn La* 106 C6
Harrow HA3 69 G5
Pegasus Pl, SE11 35 E5
SW6 *off Ackmar Rd* 148 D1
Pegasus Rd, Croy. CR0 201 G6
Pegasus Way, N11 58 B6
Pegg Rd, Houns. TW5 122 D7
Pegley Gdns, SE12 173 G2
Pegwell St, SE18 137 H7
Pekin Cl, E14 *off Pekin St* 114 A6
Pekin St, E14 114 A6
Peldon Ct, Rich. TW9 145 J4
Peldon Pas, Rich. TW10 *off Worple Way* 145 J4
Peldon Wk, N1 *off Britannia Row* 111 H1
Pelham Av, Bark. IG11 117 J1
Pelham Cl, SE5 152 B2
Pelham Cres, SW7 31 G2
Pelham Ho, W14 *off Mornington Av* 128 C4
Pelham Pl, SW7 31 G2
W13 *off Ruislip Rd E* 104 C4
Pelham Rd, E18 79 H3
N15 76 C4
N22 75 G2
SW19 166 D7
Beckenham BR3 189 F2
Bexleyheath DA7 159 G3
Ilford IG1 99 G2
Pelham St, SW7 31 F1
Pelican Est, SE15 152 C1
Pelican Ho, SE5 *off Peckham Rd* 152 C1
Pelican Pas, E1 *off Cambridge Heath Rd* 113 F4
Pelier St, SE17 36 A5
Pelinore Rd, SE6 172 E2
Pellant Rd, SW6 128 B7
Pellatt Gro, N22 75 G1
Pellatt Rd, SE22 152 C5
Wembley HA9 87 H2
Pellerin Rd, N16 94 B5
Pellings Cl, Brom. BR2 190 E3
Pelling St, E14 114 A6
Pellipar Cl, N13 59 G3
Pellipar Gdns, SE18 136 C5
Pelly Rd, E13 115 G2
Pelter St, E2 13 F3
Pelton Rd, SE10 134 E5
Pembar Av, E17 77 H3
Pemberley Chase, Epsom (W.Ewell) KT19 196 B5
Pemberley Cl, Epsom (W.Ewell) KT19 196 B5
Pember Rd, NW10 108 A3
Pemberton Gdns, N19 92 C3
Romford RM6 82 E5
Pemberton Ho, SE26 *off High Level Dr* 170 D4
Pemberton Pl, E8 *off Mare St* 95 E7
Pemberton Rd, N4 75 G5
East Molesey KT8 179 J4
Pemberton Row, EC4 19 F3
Pemberton Ter, N19 92 C3
Pembridge Av, Twick. TW2 161 F1
Pembridge Cres, W11 108 D7
Pembridge Gdns, W2 108 D7
Pembridge Ms, W11 108 D7
Pembridge Pl, SW15 148 D5
W2 108 D7
Pembridge Rd, W11 108 D7
Pembridge Sq, W2 108 D7
Pembridge Vil, W2 108 D7
W11 108 D7
Pembroke Av, N1 111 E1
Harrow HA3 68 D3
Pinner HA5 84 D1
Surbiton KT5 182 B5
Pembroke Cl, SW1 24 C4
Pembroke Cotts, W8 *off Pembroke Sq* 128 D3
Pembroke Gdns, W8 128 C4
Dagenham RM10 101 H3
Pembroke Gdns Cl, W8 128 D3
Pembroke Ms, E3 *off Morgan St* 113 H3
N10 74 A1
W8 *off Earls Wk* 128 D3
Pembroke Pl, W8 128 D3
Edgware HA8 54 A7
Isleworth TW7 *off Thornbury Rd* 144 B2
Pembroke Rd, E6 116 C5
E17 78 B5
N8 74 E4
N10 74 A1
N13 59 J3
N15 76 C5
SE25 188 B4
W8 128 D4
Bromley BR1 191 J2
Erith DA8 139 J5
Greenford UB6 103 H4
Ilford IG3 99 J1
Mitcham CR4 186 A2
Wembley HA9 87 G3
Pembroke Sq, W8 128 D3
Pembroke St, N1 93 E7
Pembroke Studios, W8 128 C3
Pembroke Vil, W8 128 D4
Richmond TW9 145 G4
Pembroke Wk, W8 128 D4
Pembroke Way, Hayes UB3 121 F3
Pembry Cl, SW9 151 G1
Pembury Av, Wor.Pk. KT4 183 G7
Pembury Cl, E5 *off Shellness Rd* 95 E5
Bromley BR2 191 F7
Pembury Ct, Hayes (Harling.) UB3 121 G6
Pembury Cres, Sid. DA14 176 E2
Pembury Pl, E5 94 E5
Pembury Rd, E5 94 E5
N17 76 C2
SE25 188 D4
Bexleyheath DA7 139 E7
Pemdevon Rd, Croy. CR0 187 G7
Pemell Cl, E1 *off Colebert Av* 113 F4
Pemerich Cl, Hayes UB3 121 J5
Pempath Pl, Wem. HA9 87 G2
Penally Pl, N1 *off Shepperton Rd* 112 A1
Penang St, E1 133 E1
Penard Rd, Sthl. UB2 123 G3
Penarth St, SE15 133 F6
Penates, Esher KT10 194 A4
Penberth Rd, SE6 172 C2
Penbury Rd, Sthl. UB2 123 F4
Pencombe Ms, W11 *off Denbigh Rd* 108 C7
Pencraig Way, SE15 132 E6
Pendall Cl, Barn. EN4 41 H4
Penda Rd, Erith DA8 139 H7
Pendarves Rd, SW20 183 J1
Penda's Mead, E9 *off Lindisfarne Way* 95 H4
Pendell Av, Hayes UB3 121 J7
Pendennis Rd, N17 76 A3
SW16 168 E4
Penderel Rd, Houns. TW3 143 G5
Penderry Ri, SE6 172 D2
Penderyn Way, N7 92 D4
Pendle Rd, SW16 168 B6
Pendlestone Rd, E17 78 A5
Pendlewood Cl, W5 *off Queens Wk* 105 F5
Pendolino Way, NW10 88 A7
Pendragon Rd, Brom. BR1 173 F3
Pendragon Wk, NW9 70 E6
Pendrell Rd, SE4 153 H2
Pendrell St, SE18 137 G7
Pendula Dr, Hayes UB4 102 D4
Pendulum Ms, E8 *off Birkbeck Rd* 94 C5
Penerley Rd, SE6 172 B1
Penfields Ho, N7 *off York Way* 92 E6
Penfold Cl, Croy. CR0 201 G3
Penfold La, Bex. DA5 176 D2
Penfold Pl, NW1 15 F1
Penfold Rd, N9 61 G1
Penfold St, NW1 7 F6
NW8 7 F6
Penford Gdns, SE9 156 A3
Penford St, SE5 151 H2
Pengarth Rd, Bex. DA5 158 D5
PENGE, SE20 171 F7
Penge Ho, SW11 *off Wye St* 149 G3
Penge La, SE20 171 F7
Penge Rd, E13 97 J7
SE20 188 D3
SE25 188 D3
Penhall Rd, SE7 136 A4
Penhill Rd, Bex. DA5 158 C7
Penhurst Pl, SE1 26 D6
Penhurst Rd, Ilf. IG6 65 E7
Penifather La, Grnf. UB6 104 A3
Peninsula Apts, W2 *off Praed St* 15 G2
Peninsula Hts, SE1 34 B3
Peninsular Cl, Felt. TW14 141 G6
Peninsular Pk Rd, SE7 135 G4
Penistone Rd, SW16 168 E7
Penketh Dr, Har. HA1 86 A3
Penmon Rd, SE2 138 A3
Pennack Rd, SE15 37 G6
Pennant Ms, W8 30 A1
Pennant Ter, E17 77 J2
Pennard Rd, W12 127 J2
Pennards, The, Sun. TW16 178 C2
Penn Cl, Grnf. UB6 103 H2
Harrow HA3 69 F4
Penner Cl, SW19 166 B2
Penners Gdns, Surb. KT6 181 H7
Pennethorne Cl, E9 *off Victoria Pk Rd* 113 F1
Pennethorne Ho, SW11 *off Wye St* 149 G3
Pennethorne Rd, SE15 132 E7
Penn Gdns, Chis. BR7 192 E2
Pennine Dr, NW2 90 B2
Pennine Ho, N9 *off Edmonton Grn Shop Cen* 60 D3
Pennine La, NW2 *off Pennine Dr* 90 B2
Pennine Way, Hayes (Harling.) UB3 121 G7
Pennington Cl, SE27 *off Hamilton Rd* 170 A4
Pennington Dr, N21 43 E5
Pennington St, E1 21 J6
Pennington Way, SE12 173 H2
Penniston Cl, N17 75 J2
Penn La, Bex. DA5 158 D5
Penn Rd, N7 93 E5
Penn St, N1 112 A1
Pennyfather La, Enf. EN2 43 J2
Pennyfields, E14 114 A7
Penny Ms, SW12 150 B7
Pennymoor Wk, W9 *off Riverton Cl* 108 C3
Penny Rd, NW10 106 B3
Pennyroyal Av, E6 116 D6
Penpoll Rd, E8 94 E6
Penpool La, Well. DA16 158 B3
Penrhyn Av, E17 77 J1
Penrhyn Cres, E17 78 A1
SW14 146 C4
Penrhyn Gdns, Kings.T. KT1 *off Surbiton Rd* 181 G4
Penrhyn Gro, E17 78 A1
Penrhyn Rd, Kings.T. KT1 181 H3
Penrith Cl, SW15 148 B5
Beckenham BR3 190 B1
Penrith Pl, SE27 169 H2
Penrith Rd, N15 76 A5
Ilford IG6 65 J6
New Malden KT3 182 D4
Thornton Heath CR7 187 J2
Penrith St, SW16 168 C6
Penrose Av, Wat. WD19 50 D2
Penrose Gro, SE17 35 J4
Penrose Ho, SE17 35 J4
Penrose St, SE17 35 J4
Penryn St, NW1 9 H1
Penry St, SE1 37 E2
Pensbury Pl, SW8 150 C2
Pensbury St, SW8 150 C2
Penscroft Gdns, Borwd. WD6 38 D4
Pensford Av, Rich. TW9 146 A2
Penshurst Av, Sid. DA15 158 A6
Penshurst Gdns, Edg. HA8 54 B5
Penshurst Grn, Brom. BR2 191 F5
Penshurst Rd, E9 95 G7
N17 60 C7
Bexleyheath DA7 159 F1
Thornton Heath CR7 187 H5
Penshurst Wk, Brom. BR2 *off Penshurst Grn* 191 F5
Penshurst Way, Sutt. SM2 198 D7
Pensilver Cl, Barn. EN4 41 H4
Penstemon Cl, N3 56 D7
Penstock Footpath, N22 75 E3
Pentavia Retail Pk, NW7 55 F7
Pentelow Gdns, Felt. TW14 142 A6
Pentire Rd, E17 78 D1
Pentland Av, Edg. HA8 54 B2
Pentland Cl, N9 61 F2
NW11 90 B2
Pentland Gdns, SW18 *off St. Ann's Hill* 149 F6
Pentland Pl, Nthlt. UB5 102 E1
Pentland Rd, NW6 108 D3
Pentlands Cl, Mitch. CR4 186 B3
Pentland St, SW18 149 F6
Pentlow St, SW15 147 J3
Pentlow Way, Buck.H. IG9 48 B7
Pentney Rd, E4 62 D1
SW12 168 C1
SW19 *off Midmoor Rd* 184 B1
Penton Gro, N1 11 E2
Penton Ho, SE2 *off Hartslock Dr* 138 D2
Penton Pl, SE17 35 H3
Penton Ri, WC1 10 D3
Penton St, N1 10 E1
PENTONVILLE, N1 10 E2
Pentonville Rd, N1 10 C2
Pentridge St, SE15 37 F7
Pentyre Av, N18 60 A5
Penwerris Av, Islw. TW7 123 J7
Penwith Rd, SW18 166 E2
Penwood Ho, SW15 *off Tunworth Cres* 147 F6
Penwortham Rd, SW16 168 B6
Penylan Pl, Edg. HA8 54 A7
Penywern Rd, SW5 128 D5
Penzance Pl, W11 128 B1
Penzance St, W11 128 B1
Peony Ct, Wdf.Grn. IG8 *off The Bridle Path* 63 E7
Peony Gdns, W12 107 G7
Pepler Ms, SE5 37 F5
Peploe Rd, NW6 108 A2
Peplow Cl, West Dr. UB7 *off Tavistock Rd* 120 A1
Pepper All, Loug. (High Beach) IG10 47 G1
Pepper Cl, E6 116 C5
Peppercorn Cl, Th.Hth. CR7 188 A2
Peppermead Sq, SE13 154 A5
Peppermint Cl, Croy. CR0 186 E7
Peppermint Pl, E11 *off Birch Gro* 96 E3
Pepper St, E14 134 B3
SE1 27 J3
Peppie Cl, N16 94 B2
Pepys Cres, E16 *off Britannia Gate* 135 G1
Barnet EN5 39 J5
Pepys Ri, Orp. BR6 207 J1
Pepys Rd, SE14 153 G1
SW20 183 J1
Pepys St, EC3 21 E5
Perceval Av, NW3 91 H5
Percheron Cl, Islw. TW7 144 D3
Percheron Rd, Borwd. WD6 38 D6
Perch St, E8 94 C4
Percival Ct, N17 *off High Rd* 60 C7
Northolt UB5 85 G5
★ **Percival David Foundation of Chinese Art**, WC1 9 J5
Percival Gdns, Rom. RM6 82 C6
Percival Rd, SW14 146 C4
Enfield EN1 44 C4
Orpington BR6 207 E2
Percival St, EC1 11 G5
Percival Way, Epsom KT19 196 C4
Percy Bush Rd, West Dr. UB7 120 C3
Percy Circ, WC1 10 D3
Percy Gdns, Enf. EN3 45 G5
Isleworth TW7 144 D2
Worcester Park KT4 196 D1
Percy Ho, SW16 *off Pringle Gdns* 168 C4
Percy Ms, W1 17 H2
Percy Pas, W1 17 G2
Percy Rd, E11 78 E7
E16 115 E5
N12 57 F5
N21 43 J7
SE20 189 G1
SE25 188 D5
W12 127 G2
Bexleyheath DA7 159 E2
Hampton TW12 161 G7
Ilford IG3 82 A7
Isleworth TW7 144 D4
Mitcham CR4 186 A7
Romford RM7 83 H3
Twickenham TW2 161 H1
Percy St, W1 17 H2
Percy Ter, Brom. BR1 192 E3
Percy Way, Twick. TW2 161 J1
Percy Yd, WC1 10 D3
Peregrine Cl, NW10 88 D5
Peregrine Ct, SW16 169 F4
Welling DA16 157 J1
Peregrine Gdns, Croy. CR0 203 H2
Peregrine Ho, EC1 11 H3
Peregrine Rd, N17 59 J7

Peregrine Way, SW19 ....165 J7
Perham Rd, W14 ....128 B5
Peridot St, E6 ....116 B5
Perifield, SE21 ....169 J1
Perimeade Rd, Grnf. UB6 .105 F2
Periton Rd, SE9 ....156 A4
PERIVALE, Grnf. UB6 ....105 F1
Perivale, Grnf. UB6 ......104 C3
Perivale Gdns, W13
off Bellevue Rd 104 E4
Perivale Gra, Grnf.
(Perivale) UB6 ....104 D3
Perivale Ind Pk, Grnf.
(Perivale) UB6 ....104 D2
Perivale La, Grnf.
(Perivale) UB6 ....104 D3
Perivale New Business Cen,
Grnf. (Perivale) UB6 ...105 E2
Periwood Cres, Grnf. UB6
off Horsenden La S ..104 D1
Perkin Cl, Houns. TW3 ...143 H4
Wembley HA0 ....86 E5
Perkin's Rents, SW1 ......25 H5
Perkins Rd, Ilf. IG2 ....81 G5
Perkins Sq, SE1 ....28 A1
Perks Cl, SE3
off Hurren Cl 154 E3
Perpins Rd, SE9 ....157 H6
Perran Rd, SW2
off Christchurch Rd ..169 H2
Perran Wk, Brent. TW8 ...125 H5
Perren St, NW5
off Ryland Rd 92 B6
Perrers Rd, W6 ....127 H4
Perrin Rd, Wem. HA0 .....86 D4
Perrins Ct, NW3
off Hampstead High St .91 F4
Perrins La, NW3 ....91 F4
Perrin's Wk, NW3 ....91 F4
Perrott St, SE18 ....137 F4
Perry Av, W3 ....106 D6
Perry Ct, E14
off Maritime Quay ...134 A5
N15 ....76 B6
Perryfield Way, NW9 ......71 F6
Richmond TW10 ......163 E2
Perry Gdns, N9
off Deansway 60 B3
Perry Garth, Nthlt. UB5 ..102 C1
Perry Hall Rd, Orp. BR6 ..193 J6
Perry Hill, SE6 ....171 J3
Perry Ho, SW2
off Tierney Rd 150 E7
Perry How, Wor.Pk. KT4 ..197 F1
Perryman Ho, Bark. IG11 ..117 F1
Perrymans Fm Rd, Ilf. IG2 .81 G6
Perry Mead, Enf. EN2 .....43 H2
Perrymead St, SW6 .....148 D1
Perryn Rd, SE16
off Drummond Rd ...132 E3
W3 ....106 D7
Perry Ri, SE23 ....171 H3
Perry Rd, Dag. RM9 ......119 F4
Perrys Pl, W1 ....17 H3
Perry St, Chis. BR7 ......175 G6
Perry St Gdns, Chis. BR7
off Old Perry St 175 H6
Perry Vale, SE23 ....171 F2
Perrywood Ho, E5
off Pembury Rd 94 E5
Persant Rd, SE6 ....172 E2
Perseverance Pl, SW9 ...131 G7
Richmond TW9
off Shaftesbury Rd ...145 H3
Pershore Cl, Ilf. IG2 ....81 E5
Pershore Gro, Cars.
SM5 ....185 G6
Pert Cl, N10 ....58 B7
Perth Av, NW9 ....70 D7
Hayes UB4 ....102 C4
Perth Cl, SW20
off Huntley Way 183 G2
Northolt UB5
off Ascot Cl 85 G5
Perth Rd, E10 ....95 H1
E13 ....115 H2
N4 ....93 G1
N22 ....75 H1
Barking IG11 ....117 G2
Beckenham BR3 ......190 C2
Ilford IG2 ....80 D6
Perth Ter, Ilf. IG2 ....81 F7
Perwell Av, Har. HA2 ......85 F1
Perwell Ct, Har. HA2 ......85 F1
Peter Av, NW10 ....89 H7
Peterboat Cl, SE10
off Tunnel Av 135 E4
Peterborough Gdns, Ilf.
IG1 ....80 B7
Peterborough Ms, SW6 ..148 D2
Peterborough Rd, E10 ....78 C5
SW6 ....148 D2
Carshalton SM5 ......185 H6
Harrow HA1 ....86 B1
Peterborough Vil, SW6 ...148 E1
Peterchurch Ho, SE15
off Commercial Way ..132 E6
Petergate, SW11 ....149 F4
Peter Heathfield Ho, E15
off High St 114 D1
Peterhouse Gdns, SW6
off Bagley's La 149 E1
Peter James Business Cen,
Hayes UB3 ....122 A2
Peterley Business Cen, E2
off Hackney Rd 113 E2
Peter Moore Ct, N9
off Menon Dr 60 E3
★ **Peter Pan Statue**, W2 ..23 E1
Peters Cl, Dag. RM8 .....100 D1
Stanmore HA7 ....53 G6
Welling DA16 ....157 H2
Petersfield Cl, N18 ....59 J5
Petersfield Ri, SW15 .....165 H1
Petersfield Rd, W3 ......126 C2
PETERSHAM, Rich. TW10 .163 H1
Petersham Cl, Rich.
TW10 ....163 G2
Sutton SM1 ....198 D5
Petersham Dr, Orp. BR5 ..193 J2
Petersham Gdns, Orp.
BR5 ....193 J2
Petersham La, SW7 ......22 C5
Petersham Ms, SW7 ......22 C6
Petersham Pl, SW7 ....22 C5
Petersham Rd, Rich.
TW10 ....145 H6
Peters Hill, EC4 ....19 J5
Peter's La, EC1 ....19 H1
Peters Path, SE26 ....170 E4
Peterstone Rd, SE2 ......138 B3
Peterstow Cl, SW19 .....166 B2
Peter St, W1 ....17 G5
Peterwood Way, Croy.
CR0 ....201 F2
Petherton Rd, N5 ....93 J5
Petiver Cl, E9
off Frampton Pk Rd ...95 F7
Petley Rd, W6 ....127 J6
Peto Pl, NW1 ....8 E5
Peto St N, E16
off Victoria Dock Rd ..115 F7
Petrie Cl, NW2 ....90 B6
★ **Petrie Mus of Egyptian
Archaeology**, WC1
off Malet Pl 9 H6
Petros Gdns, NW3
off Lithos Rd 91 F5
Pettacre Cl, SE28 ....137 F3
★ **Petticoat Lane Mkt**,
E1 ....21 E2
Petticoat Sq, E1 ....21 F3
Petticoat Twr, E1 ....21 F3
Pettits Pl, Dag. RM10 ....101 G5
Pettits Rd, Dag. RM10 ....101 G5
Pettiward Cl, SW15 ......147 J4
Pettman Cres, SE28 .....137 G3
Pettsgrove Av, Wem. HA0 .87 F5
Petts Hill, Nthlt. UB5 .....85 H5
Pett St, SE18 ....136 B4
PETTS WOOD, Orp. BR5 ..193 G5
Petts Wd Rd, Orp. BR5 ...193 F5
Petty France, SW1 ....25 G5
Petty Wales, EC3 ....21 E6
Petworth Cl, Nthlt. UB5 ...85 F7
Petworth Gdns, SW20
off Hidcote Gdns 183 H3
Petworth Ho, SE22
off Pytchley Rd 152 B3
Petworth Rd, N12 ....57 H5
Bexleyheath DA6 .....159 G5
Petworth St, SW11 ....149 H1
Petyt Pl, SW3 ....31 G6
Petyward, SW3 ....31 H2
Pevensey Av, N11 ....58 D5
Enfield EN1 ....44 A2
Pevensey Cl, Islw. TW7 ...123 J7
Pevensey Rd, E7 ....97 F4
SW17 ....167 G4
Feltham TW13 ....160 E1
Peverel, E6 *off Downings* .116 D6
Peverel Ho, Dag. RM10 ...101 G2
Peveret Cl, N11
off Woodland Rd 58 B5
Peveril Dr, Tedd. TW11 ....162 A5
Pewsey Cl, E4 ....62 A5
Peyton Pl, SE10 ....134 C7
Pharaoh Cl, Mitch. CR4 ...185 J7
Pheasant Cl, E16
off Maplin Rd 115 G6
Phelp St, SE17 ....36 B5
Phelps Way, Hayes UB3 ..121 J4
Phene St, SW3 ....31 H5
Pheonix Cl, W12 ....107 H7
Philbeach Gdns, SW5 ....128 D5
Phil Brown Pl, SW8
*off Daley
Thompson Way* 150 B3
Philchurch Pl, E1 ....21 J4
Philimore Cl, SE18 ....137 H5
Philip Gdns, Croy. CR0 ...203 J2
Philip La, N15 ....76 A4
Philipot Path, SE9 ....156 C6
Philippa Gdns, SE9 ......156 A5
Philips Cl, Cars. SM5 ....200 A1
Philip St, E13 ....115 G4
Philip Wk, SE15 ....152 D3
Phillimore Gdns, NW10 ..107 J1
W8 ....128 D2
Phillimore Gdns Cl, W8
off Phillimore Gdns ..128 D3
Phillimore Pl, W8 ....128 D2
Phillimore Wk, W8 ....128 D3
Phillipp St, N1 ....112 B1
Philpot La, EC3 ....20 D5
Philpot Path, Ilf. IG1
off Richmond Rd 99 F3
Philpot Sq, SW6
off Peterborough Rd .148 E3
Philpot St, E1 ....113 E6
Phineas Pett Rd, SE9 ....156 B3
Phipps Br Rd, SW19 .....185 F2
Mitcham CR4 ....185 F2
Phipp's Ms, SW1 ....24 E6
Phipp St, EC2 ....12 D5
Phoebeth Rd, SE4 ....154 A5
Phoenix Cl, E8
off Stean St 112 C1
E17 ....77 J2
West Wickham BR4 ....204 E2
Phoenix Ct, N.Mal. KT3 ..183 F3
Phoenix Dr, Kes. BR2 ....206 A3
Phoenix Pk, Brent. TW8 ..125 G5
Phoenix Pl, WC1 ....10 D5
Phoenix Rd, NW1 ....9 H3
SE20 ....171 F6
Phoenix St, WC2 ....17 J4
Phoenix Way, SW18
*off North Side
Wandsworth Common* .149 F5
Hounslow TW5 ....122 C6
Phoenix Wf, SE10 ....135 F2
Phoenix Wf Rd, SE1 ......29 G4
Phoenix Yd, WC1 ....10 D4
★ **Photographers' Gall**,
WC2 ....17 J5
Phyllis Av, N.Mal. KT3 ...183 H5
★ **Physical Energy Statue**,
W2 ....22 D2
Physic Pl, SW3 ....31 J5
Picardy Manorway, Belv.
DA17 ....139 H3
Picardy Rd, Belv. DA17 ...139 G4
Picardy St, Belv. DA17 ...139 G3
Piccadilly, W1 ....24 E2
Piccadilly Arc, SW1 ....25 F1
Piccadilly Circ, W1 ....17 H6
Piccadilly Ct, N7
off Caledonian Rd 93 F6
Piccadilly Pl, W1 ....17 G6
Pickard Cl, N14 ....58 D1
Pickard St, EC1 ....11 H3
Pickering Av, E6 ....116 D2
Pickering Cl, E9
off Cassland Rd 95 G7
Pickering Gdns, N11 ......58 A6
Croydon CR0 ....188 C6
Pickering Ms, W2 ....14 B3
Pickering Pl, SW1 ....25 G2
Pickering Rd, Bark. IG11 ...99 F6
Pickering St, N1
off Essex Rd 111 H1
Pickets Cl, Bushey
(Bushey Hth) WD23 ....52 A1
Pickets St, SW12 ....150 B7
Pickett Cft, Stan. HA7 .....69 G1
Picketts Lock La, N9 ......61 F2
Pickford Cl, Bexh. DA7 ...158 E2
Pickford La, Bexh. DA7 ...159 E2
Pickford Rd, Bexh. DA7 ..158 E3
Pickfords Wf, N1 ....11 J2
Pickhurst Grn, Brom.
BR2 ....191 F7
Pickhurst La, Brom. BR2 .205 F1
West Wickham BR4 ....191 E6
Pickhurst Mead, Brom.
BR2 ....191 F7
Pickhurst Pk, Brom. BR2 .191 E5
Pickhurst Ri, W.Wick.
BR4 ....190 C7
Pickwick Cl, Houns. TW4
off Dorney Way 143 E5
Pickwick Ct, SE9 ....174 B1
Pickwick Ms, N18 ....60 B5
Pickwick Pl, Har. HA1 .....68 B7
Pickwick Rd, SE21 ....152 A7
Pickwick St, SE1 ....27 J4
Pickwick Way, Chis. BR7 .175 F6
Pickworth Cl, SW8
off Kenchester Cl 131 E7
Picton Pl, W1 ....16 C4
Surbiton KT6 ....196 A1
Picton St, SE5 ....132 A7
Picture Ho, SW16
off Streatham High Rd .168 E2
Pied Bull Yd, N1
off Theberton St 111 H1
Piedmont Rd, SE18 ......137 G5
Pier Head, E1
off Wapping High St ..132 E1
Pieris Ho, Felt. TW13
off High St 160 A2
Piermont Grn, SE22 .....152 E5
Piermont Pl, Brom. BR1 ..192 B2
Piermont Rd, SE22 ......152 E5
Pier Par, E16
off Pier Rd 136 D1
Pierrepoint Arc, N1 ....11 G1
Pierrepoint Rd, W3 ......106 B7
Pierrepoint Row, N1 ......11 G1
Pier Rd, E16 ....136 D2
Feltham TW14 ....142 B5
Pier St, E14 ....134 C4
Pier Ter, SW18
off Jew's Row 149 E4
Pier Way, SE28 ....137 G3
Pigeon La, Hmptn. TW12 .161 G4
Pigott St, E14 ....114 A6
Pike Cl, Brom. BR1 ......173 H5
Pike Rd, NW7
off Ellesmere Av 54 D4
Pikes End, Pnr. HA5 ......66 B4
Pikestone Cl, Hayes UB4
off Berrydale Rd 102 E4
Pilgrimage St, SE1 ....28 B4
Pilgrim Cl, Mord. SM4 ...185 E7
Pilgrim Hill, SE27 ....169 J4
Pilgrims Cl, N13 ....59 F4
Northolt UB5 ....85 J5
Pilgrims Ct, SE3 ....155 G1
Pilgrim's La, NW3 ....91 G4
Pilgrims Ms, E14
off Newport Av 114 D7
Pilgrims Pl, NW3
off Hampstead High St ..91 G4
Pilgrims Ri, Barn. EN4 ....41 H5
Pilgrim St, EC4 ....19 G4
Pilgrims Way, E6
off High St N 116 B1
N19 ....92 D1
South Croydon CR2 ...202 C5
Pilgrim's Way, Wem. HA9 ..88 B1
Pilkington Rd, SE15 .....152 E2
Orpington BR6 ....207 F2
Pilot Busway, SE10 ......135 E2
Pilot Cl, SE8 ....133 J6
Pilsdon Cl, SW19
off Inner Pk Rd 166 A1
Piltdown Rd, Wat. WD19 ..50 D4
Pilton Ind Est, Croy. CR0 .201 H2
Pilton Pl, SE17 ....36 A3
Pimento Ct, W5
off Olive Rd 125 G3
PIMLICO, SW1 ....33 F3
Pimlico Rd, SW1 ....32 B3
Pimlico Wk, N1 ....12 D3
Pinchbeck Rd, Orp. BR6 ..207 J6
Pinchin St, E1 ....21 J5
Pincott Pl, SE4 ....153 G4
Pincott Rd, SW19 ....167 F7
Bexleyheath DA6 .....159 G5
Pindar St, EC2 ....20 D1
Pindock Ms, W9 ....6 B6
Pineapple Ct, SW1 ....25 F5
Pine Av, E15 ....96 D5
West Wickham BR4 ....204 B1
Pine Cl, E10
off Walnut Rd 96 B2
N14 ....42 C7
N19 *off Hargrave Pk* 92 C2
SE20 ....189 F1
Stanmore HA7 ....52 E4
Pine Coombe, Croy. CR0 .203 G4
Pinecrest Gdns, Orp.
BR6 ....207 E4
Pinecroft Cres, Barn. EN5
off Hillside Gdns 40 B4
Pinedene, SE15
off Meeting Ho La ...152 E1
Pinefield Cl, E14 ....114 A7
Pine Gdns, Ruis. HA4 .....84 B1
Surbiton KT5 ....182 A6
Pine Glade, Orp. BR6 ....206 C4
Pine Gro, N4 ....93 E2
N20 ....56 C1
SW19 ....166 C5
Pinehurst Wk, Orp. BR6 ..207 H1
Pinelands Cl, SE3
off St. John's Pk 135 F7
Pinemartin Cl, NW2 ......89 J3
Pine Ms, NW10
off Clifford Gdns 108 A2
Pine Rd, N11 ....58 A2
NW2 ....89 J4
Pines, The, N14 ....42 C5
Sunbury-on-Thames
TW16 ....178 A3
Woodford Green IG8 ...63 G3
Pines Rd, Brom. BR1 ....192 B2
Pine St, EC1 ....11 E5

Pine Tree Cl, Houns. TW5 142 B1
Pine Tree Way, SE13 *off Elmira St* 154 B3
Pine Wk, Brom. BR1 191 J1
Surbiton KT5 182 A6
Pine Wd, Sun. TW16 178 A1
Pinewood Av, Pnr. HA5 51 H6
Sidcup DA15 175 H1
Pinewood Cl, Borwd. WD6 38 D1
Croydon CR0 203 H3
Northwood HA6 50 B5
Orpington BR6 207 G2
Pinner HA5 51 H6
Pinewood Dr, Orp. BR6 207 H5
Pinewood Gro, W5 105 F6
Pinewood Ms, Stai. (Stanw.) TW19 140 A6
Pinewood Pl, Epsom KT19 196 D4
Pinewood Rd, SE2 138 D6
Bromley BR2 191 G4
Feltham TW13 160 B3
Pinfold Rd, SW16 168 E4
Pinglestone Cl, West Dr. (Harm.) UB7 120 B7
Pinkcoat Cl, Felt. TW13 *off Tanglewood Way* 160 B3
Pinkerton Pl, SW16 168 D4
Pinkham Way, N11 58 A7
Pinkwell Av, Hayes UB3 121 G4
Pinkwell La, Hayes UB3 121 F4
Pinley Gdns, Dag. RM9 *off Stamford Rd* 118 B1
Pinnacle Hill, Bexh. DA7 159 H4
Pinnacle Hill N, Bexh. DA7 159 H3
Pinnell Rd, SE9 156 A4
PINNER, HA5 67 E4
Pinner Ct, Pnr. HA5 67 G4
PINNER GREEN, Pnr. HA5 66 D2
Pinner Grn, Pnr. HA5 66 C2
Pinner Gro, Pnr. HA5 67 E4
Pinner Hill, Pnr. HA5 66 C1
Pinner Hill Rd, Pnr. HA5 66 C2
Pinner Pk, Pnr. HA5 67 G1
Pinner Pk Av, Har. HA2 67 H3
Pinner Pk Gdns, Har. HA2 67 J2
Pinner Rd, Har. HA1, HA2 67 H5
Pinner HA5 67 F4
Pinner Vw, Har. HA1, HA2 67 J6
PINNERWOOD PARK, Pnr. HA5 50 C7
Pintail Cl, E6 *off Swan App* 116 B5
Pintail Rd, Wdf.Grn. IG8 63 H7
Pintail Way, Hayes UB4 102 D5
Pinter Ho, SW9 *off Grantham Rd* 151 E2
Pinto Cl, Borwd. WD6 *off Percheron Rd* 38 D6
Pinto Way, SE3 155 H4
Pioneer Cl, E14 *off Broomfield St* 114 B5
Pioneers Ind Pk, Croy. CR0 200 E1
Pioneer St, SE15 152 D1
Pioneer Way, W12 *off Du Cane Rd* 107 H6
Piper Cl, N7 93 F6
Piper Rd, Kings.T. KT1 182 A3
Piper's Gdns, Croy. CR0 189 H7
Pipers Grn, NW9 70 C5
Pipers Grn La, Edg. HA8 53 H3
Piper Way, Ilf. IG1 99 G1
Pipewell Rd, Cars. SM5 185 H6
Pippin Cl, NW2 89 H3
Croydon CR0 203 J1
Pippins Cl, West Dr. UB7 120 A3
Piquet Rd, SE20 189 F2
Pirbright Cres, Croy. (New Adgtn) CR0 204 C6
Pirbright Rd, SW18 166 C1
Pirie Cl, SE5 *off Denmark Hill* 152 A3
Pirie St, E16 135 H1
Pitcairn Cl, Rom. RM7 83 G4
Pitcairn Rd, Mitch. CR4 167 J7
Pitcairn's Path, Har. HA2 *off Eastcote Rd* 85 J3
Pitchford St, E15 96 D7
Pitfield Cres, SE28 138 A1
Pitfield Est, N1 12 C3
Pitfield St, N1 12 D4
Pitfield Way, NW10 88 C6
Enfield EN3 45 F1
Pitfold Cl, SE12 155 G6
Pitfold Rd, SE12 155 G6
Pitlake, Croy. CR0 201 H2
Pitman Ho, SE8 *off Tanners Hill* 154 A1
Pitman St, SE5 35 J7
Pitmaston Ho, SE13 *off Lewisham Rd* 154 C2
Pitmaston Rd, SE13 *off Morden Hill* 154 C2
Pitsea Pl, E1 *off Pitsea St* 113 G6
Pitsea St, E1 113 G6
Pitshanger La, W5 105 E4
★ **Pitshanger Manor Ho & Gall**, W5 125 F1
Pitshanger Pk, W13 105 F3
Pitt Cres, SW19 166 E4
Pitt Ho, SW11 *off Maysoule Rd* 149 G4
Pittman Gdns, Ilf. IG1 99 F5
Pitt Rd, Croy. CR0 187 J5
Orpington BR6 207 F4
Thornton Heath CR7 187 J5
Pitt's Head Ms, W1 24 C2
Pittsmead Av, Brom. BR2 191 G7
Pitt St, W8 128 D2
Pittville Gdns, SE25 188 D3
Pixfield Ct, Brom. BR2 *off Beckenham La* 191 F2
Pixley St, E14 113 J6
Place Fm Av, Orp. BR6 207 G1
PLAISTOW, E13 115 F3
PLAISTOW, Brom. BR1 173 F6
Plaistow Gro, E15 115 F1
Bromley BR1 173 H7
Plaistow La, Brom. BR1 173 G7
Plaistow Pk Rd, E13 115 H2
Plaistow Rd, E13 115 F1
E15 115 F1
Plane St, SE26 170 E3
Plane Tree Cres, Felt. TW13 160 B3
Plane Tree Wk, N2 73 G3
SE19 *off Lunham Rd* 170 B6
Plantagenet Cl, Wor.Pk. KT4 196 D4
Plantagenet Gdns, Rom. RM6 82 D7
Plantagenet Pl, Rom. RM6 82 D7
Plantagenet Rd, Barn. EN5 41 F4
Plantain Gdns, E11 *off Hollydown Way* 96 D3
Plantain Pl, SE1 28 B3
Plantation, The, SE3 155 G2
Plantation Cl, SW4 *off King's Av* 150 E5
Plantation La, EC3 *off Rood La* 20 D5
Plantation Wf, SW11 149 F3
Plashet Gro, E6 115 J1
Plashet Rd, E13 115 G1
Plassy Rd, SE6 154 B7
Platina St, EC2 12 C5
Platinum Ho, Har. HA1 68 C6
Plato Rd, SW2 151 E4
Platt, The, SW15 148 A3
Platt's Eyot, Hmptn. TW12 179 G2
Platt's La, NW3 90 D4
Platts Rd, Enf. EN3 45 F1
Platt St, NW1 9 H1
Plawsfield Rd, Beck. BR3 189 G1
Plaxtol Cl, Brom. BR1 191 J1
Plaxtol Rd, Erith DA8 139 G7
Plaxton Ct, E11 *off Woodhouse Rd* 97 F3
Playfair St, W6 *off Winslow Rd* 127 J5
Playfield Av, Rom. RM5 83 J1
Playfield Cres, SE22 152 C5
Playfield Rd, Edg. HA8 70 C2
Playford Rd, N4 93 F2
Playgreen Way, SE6 172 A4
Playground Cl, Beck. BR3 *off Churchfields Rd* 189 G2
Playhouse Ct, SE1 *off Southwark Br Rd* 27 J3
Playhouse Yd, EC4 19 G4
Plaza Business Cen, Enf. EN3 *off Stockingswater La* 45 J2
Plaza Par, NW6 *off Kilburn High Rd* 6 A1
Plaza Shop Cen, The, W1 17 G3
Plaza W, Houns. TW3 143 H1
Pleasance, The, SW15 147 H4
Pleasance Rd, SW15 147 H5
Pleasant Gro, Croy. CR0 203 J3
Pleasant Pl, N1 93 H7
Pleasant Row, NW1 110 B1
Pleasant Vw Pl, Orp. BR6 *off High St* 207 E5
Pleasant Way, Wem. HA0 105 F2
Plender St, NW1 110 C1
Pleshey Rd, N7 92 D4
Plevna Cres, N15 76 B6
Plevna Rd, N9 60 D3
Hampton TW12 179 H1
Plevna St, E14 134 C3
Pleydell Av, SE19 170 C7
W6 127 F4
Pleydell Ct, EC4 19 F4
Pleydell Est, EC1 *off Radnor St* 12 A4
Pleydell St, EC4 19 F4
Plimley Pl, W12 *off Sterne St* 128 A2
Plimsoll Cl, E14 *off Grundy St* 114 B6
Plimsoll Rd, N4 93 G3
Plough Ct, EC3 20 C5
Plough La, SE22 152 C6
SW17 167 E5
SW19 167 E5
Teddington TW11 162 D5
Wallington SM6 200 E4
Plough La Cl, Wall. SM6 200 E5
Ploughmans Cl, NW1 *off Crofters Way* 110 D1
Ploughmans End, Islw. TW7 144 A5
Ploughmans Wk, N2 *off Long La* 73 F2
Plough Ms, SW11 *off Plough Ter* 149 G4
Plough Pl, EC4 19 F3
Plough Rd, SW11 149 G3
Plough St, E1 21 H3
Plough Ter, SW11 149 G4
Plough Way, SE16 133 G4
Plough Yd, EC2 12 E6
Plover Way, SE16 133 H3
Hayes UB4 102 D6
Plowden Bldgs, EC4 *off Middle Temple La* 19 E5
Plowman Cl, N18 60 A5
Plowman Way, Dag. RM8 100 C1
Plumbers Row, E1 21 H2
Plumbridge St, SE10 *off Blackheath Hill* 154 C1
Plum Cl, Felt. TW13 160 A1
Plum Garth, Brent. TW8 125 G4
Plum La, SE18 137 E7
Plummer La, Mitch. CR4 185 J2
Plummer Rd, SW4 150 D7
Plumpton Cl, Nthlt. UB5 85 G6
Plumpton Way, Cars. SM5 199 H3
PLUMSTEAD, SE18 137 H5
Plumstead Common Rd, SE18 136 E6
Plumstead High St, SE18 137 H4
Plumstead Rd, SE18 137 E4
Plumtree Cl, Dag. RM10 101 H6
Wallington SM6 200 D7
Plumtree Ct, EC4 19 F3
Plumtree Mead, Loug. IG10 48 D3
Plymouth Rd, E16 115 G5
Bromley BR1 191 H1
Plymouth Wf, E14 134 D4
Plympton Av, NW6 90 C7
Plympton Cl, Belv. DA17 *off Halifield Dr* 139 E3
Plympton Pl, NW8 7 G6
Plympton Rd, NW6 90 C7
Plympton St, NW8 7 G6
Plymstock Rd, Well. DA16 138 C7
Pocklington Cl, NW9 70 E2
Pocock Av, West Dr. UB7 120 C3
Pocock St, SE1 27 G3
Podium, The, E2 *off Roman Rd* 113 F3
Podmore Rd, SW18 149 F4
Poets Rd, N5 94 A5
Poets Way, Har. HA1 *off Blawith Rd* 68 B4
Point, The, E17 *off Tower Ms* 78 A4
Pointalls Cl, N3 73 F2
Point Cl, SE10 *off Point Hill* 154 C1
Pointer Cl, SE28 118 D6
Pointers Cl, E14 134 B5
Point Hill, SE10 134 C7
Point of Thomas Path, E1 *off Glamis Rd* 113 F7
Point Pl, Wem. HA9 88 B7
Point Pleasant, SW18 148 D4
Point W, SW7 30 B1
Point Wf La, Brent. TW8 *off Town Meadow* 125 H7
Poland Ho, E15 114 D1
Poland St, W1 17 G4
Polar Pk, West Dr. UB7 120 C7
Polebrook Rd, SE3 155 J3
Pole Cat All, Brom. BR2 205 F2
Polecroft La, SE6 171 J2
Polehamptons, The, Hmptn. TW12 *off High St* 161 J7
Pole Hill Rd, E4 46 C7
Polesden Gdns, SW20 183 H2
Polesworth Ho, W2 108 D5
Polesworth Rd, Dag. RM9 100 D7
★ **Polish Inst & Sikorski Mus**, SW7 *off Princes Gate* 23 F4
Polish War Mem, Ruis. HA4 84 B7
Pollard Cl, E16 115 G7
N7 93 F5
Pollard Rd, N20 57 H2
Morden SM4 185 G5
Pollard Row, E2 13 J3
Pollards Cl, Loug. IG10 47 J5
Pollards Cres, SW16 187 E3
Pollards Hill E, SW16 187 F3
Pollards Hill N, SW16 187 E3
Pollards Hill S, SW16 187 E3
Pollards Hill W, SW16 187 E3
Pollard St, E2 13 J3
Pollards Wd Rd, SW16 187 E2
Pollard Wk, Sid. DA14 176 C6
Pollen St, W1 17 E4
Pollitt Dr, NW8 7 E5
★ **Pollock's Toy Mus**, W1 17 G1
Polperro Cl, Orp. BR6 *off Cotswold Ri* 193 J6
Polperro Ms, SE11 35 F1
Polsted Rd, SE6 153 J7
Polthorne Est, SE18 137 F4
Polthorne Gro, SE18 137 F4
Polworth Rd, SW16 168 E5
Polygon, The, SW4 *off Old Town* 150 C4
Polygon Rd, NW1 9 H2
Polytechnic St, SE18 136 D4
Pomell Way, E1 21 G3
Pomeroy Cl, Twick. TW1 *off St. Margaret's Dr* 145 E4
Pomeroy St, SE14 153 F1
Pomfret Rd, SE5 *off Flaxman Rd* 151 H3
Pomoja La, N19 92 D2
Pond Cl, N12 57 H6
SE3 155 F2
Pond Cottage La, W.Wick. BR4 204 A1
Pond Cotts, SE21 170 B1
PONDERS END, Enf. EN3 45 F5
Ponders End Ind Est, Enf. EN3 45 J4
Ponder St, N7 93 F7
Pond Fm Est, E5 *off Millfields Rd* 95 F3
Pond Fld End, Loug. IG10 47 J7
Pondfield Ho, SE27 *off Elder Rd* 169 J5
Pondfield Rd, Brom. BR2 205 E1
Dagenham RM10 101 H5
Orpington BR6 207 E3
Pond Hill Gdns, Sutt. SM3 198 B6
Pond Mead, SE21 152 A6
Pond Path, Chis. BR7 *off Heathfield La* 175 F6
Pond Pl, SW3 31 G2
Pond Rd, E15 114 E2
SE3 155 F2
Pondside Cl, Hayes (Harling.) UB3 *off Providence La* 121 G7
Pond Sq, N6 *off South Gro* 92 A1
Pond St, NW3 91 H5
Pond Way, Tedd. TW11 *off Holmesdale Rd* 163 F6
Pondwood Ri, Orp. BR6 193 H7
Ponler St, E1 112 E6
Ponsard Rd, NW10 107 H3
Ponsford St, E9 95 F6
Ponsonby Pl, SW1 33 J3
Ponsonby Rd, SW15 147 H7
Ponsonby Ter, SW1 33 J3
Pontefract Rd, Brom. BR1 173 F5
Ponton Rd, SW8 33 J6
Pont St, SW1 23 J6
Pont St Ms, SW1 23 J6
Pontypool Pl, SE1 27 G3
Pool Cl, Beck. BR3 172 A5
West Molesey KT8 179 F5
Pool Ct, SE6 172 A2
Poole Ct Rd, Houns. TW4 *off Vicarage Fm Rd* 142 E2
Poole Ho, SE11 *off Lambeth Wk* 26 D6
Poole Rd, E9 95 G6
Epsom KT19 196 D6
Pooles Bldgs, EC1 10 E6
Pooles La, SW10 *off Lots Rd* 129 F7
Dagenham RM9 119 E2
Pooles Pk, N4 93 G2
Poole St, N1 112 A1
Pooley Dr, SW14 *off Moore Cl* 146 C3

Poolmans St, SE16 ... **133** G2
Pool Rd, Har. HA1 ... **68** A7
West Molesey KT8 ... **179** F6
Poolsford Rd, NW9 ... **71** E4
Poonah St, E1
off Hardinge St ... **113** F6
Pope Cl, SW19 ... **167** G6
Pope Ho, SE16
off Manor Est ... **132** E4
Pope Rd, Brom. BR2 ... **192** A5
Popes Av, Twick. TW2 ... **162** B2
Popes Dr, N3 ... **72** D1
Popes Gro, Croy. CR0 ... **203** J3
Twickenham TW1, TW2 ... **162** C2
Pope's Head All, EC3
off Cornhill ... **20** C4
Popes La, W5 ... **125** G3
Popes Rd, SW9 ... **151** G3
Pope St, SE1 ... **29** E4
Popham Cl, Felt. (Han.) TW13 ... **161** F3
Popham Gdns, Rich. TW9 *off Lower Richmond Rd* ... **146** A3
Popham Rd, N1 ... **111** J1
Popham St, N1 ... **111** H1
Popin Business Cen, Wem. HA9 ... **88** B5
POPLAR, E14 ... **114** B7
Poplar Av, Mitch. CR4 ... **185** J1
Orpington BR6 ... **207** E2
Southall UB2 ... **123** H3
Poplar Bath St, E14
off Lawless St ... **114** B7
Poplar Business Pk, E14 ... **114** C7
Poplar Cl, E9 *off Lee Conservancy Rd* ... **95** J5
Pinner HA5 ... **66** D1
Poplar Ct, SW19 ... **166** D5
Poplar Cres, Epsom KT19 ... **196** C6
Poplar Fm Cl, Epsom KT19 ... **196** C6
Poplar Gdns, N.Mal. KT3 ... **182** D2
Poplar Gro, N11 ... **58** A6
W6 ... **127** J2
New Malden KT3 ... **182** D3
Wembley HA9 ... **88** C3
Poplar High St, E14 ... **114** A7
Poplar Mt, Belv. DA17 ... **139** H4
Poplar Pl, SE28 ... **118** C7
W2 ... **14** A5
Hayes UB3
off Central Av ... **102** A7
Poplar Rd, SE24 ... **151** J4
SW19 ... **184** D2
Sutton SM3 ... **198** C1
Poplar Rd S, SW19 ... **184** D3
Poplars, The, N14 ... **42** B5
Borehamwood WD6
off Grove Rd ... **38** A1
Poplars Av, NW10 ... **89** J6
Poplars Rd, E17 ... **78** B6
Poplar St, Rom. RM7 ... **83** J4
Poplar Vw, Wem. HA9
off Magnet Rd ... **87** G2
Poplar Wk, SE24 ... **151** J4
Croydon CR0 ... **201** J2
Poplar Way, Felt. TW13 ... **160** A3
Ilford IG6 ... **81** F4
Poppins Ct, EC4 ... **19** G4
Poppleton Rd, E11 ... **79** E6
Poppy Cl, Barn. EN5 ... **41** F6
Belvedere DA17 ... **139** H3
Northolt UB5 ... **85** F6
Wallington SM6 ... **200** A1
★ **Poppy Factory Mus, The**, Rich. TW10 ... **145** G6
Poppy La, Croy. CR0 ... **189** F7
Porchester Cl, SE5 ... **151** J4
Porchester Gdns, W2 ... **14** A5
Porchester Gdns Ms, W2 ... **14** B4
Porchester Gate, W2
off Bayswater Rd ... **14** C6
Porchester Mead, Beck. BR3 ... **172** A6
Porchester Ms, W2 ... **14** B3
Porchester Pl, W2 ... **15** H4
Porchester Rd, W2 ... **14** A3
Kingston upon Thames KT1 ... **182** B2
Porchester Sq, W2 ... **14** B3
Porchester Sq Ms, W2 ... **14** B3
Porchester Ter, W2 ... **14** C4
Porchester Ter N, W2 ... **14** B3
Porch Way, N20 ... **57** J3
Porcupine Cl, SE9 ... **174** B2
Porden Rd, SW2 ... **151** F4
Porlock Av, Har. HA2 ... **85** J1
Porlock Rd, Enf. EN1 ... **44** C7
Porlock St, SE1 ... **28** B3
Porrington Cl, Chis. BR7 ... **192** C1
Portal Cl, SE27 ... **169** G3
Ruislip HA4 ... **84** A4
Portal Way, W3 ... **106** D5
Portbury Cl, SE15
off Clayton Rd ... **152** D1
Port Cres, E13
off Jenkins Rd ... **115** H4
★ **Portcullis Ho**, SW1
off Bridge St ... **26** A4
Portcullis Lo Rd, Enf. EN2 ... **44** A3
Portelet Ct, N1
off De Beauvoir Est ... **112** B1
Portelet Rd, E1 ... **113** G3
Porten Rd, W14 ... **128** B3
Porter Rd, E6 ... **116** C6
Porters Av, Dag. RM8, RM9 ... **100** B6
Portersfield Rd, Enf. EN1 ... **44** B4
Porter Sq, N19 ... **92** E1
Porter St, SE1 ... **28** A1
W1 ... **16** A1
Porters Wk, E1
off Tobacco Dock ... **113** E7
Porters Way, N12 ... **57** H7
West Drayton UB7 ... **120** C3
Porteus Rd, W2 ... **14** D2
Portgate Cl, W9 ... **108** C4
Porthallow Cl, Orp. BR6 ... **207** J4
Porthcawe Rd, SE26 ... **171** H4
Porthkerry Av, Well. DA16 ... **158** A4
Portia Way, E3 ... **113** J4
Portinscale Rd, SW15 ... **148** B5
Portland Av, N16 ... **76** C7
New Malden KT3 ... **183** F7
Sidcup DA15 ... **158** A6
Portland Cl, Rom. RM6 ... **82** E5
Worcester Park KT4 ... **183** H7
Portland Ct, SE1
off Falmouth Rd ... **28** B5
Portland Cres, SE9 ... **174** B2
Greenford UB6 ... **103** H4
Stanmore HA7 ... **69** G2
Portland Gdns, N4 ... **75** H6
Romford RM6 ... **82** D5
Portland Gro, SW8 ... **151** F1
Portland Ms, W1 ... **17** G4
Portland Pl, W1 ... **16** E2
Portland Ri, N4 ... **93** H1
Portland Ri Est, N4 ... **93** H1
Portland Rd, N15 ... **76** C4
SE9 ... **174** B2
SE25 ... **188** D4
W11 ... **108** B7
Bromley BR1 ... **173** J4
Kingston upon Thames KT1 ... **181** H3
Mitcham CR4 ... **185** H2
Southall UB2 ... **123** F3
Portland Sq, E1
off Reardon St ... **132** E1
Portland St, SE17 ... **36** B3
Portland Ter, Rich. TW9 ... **145** G4
Portland Wk, SE17 ... **36** C5
Portman Av, SW14 ... **146** D3
Portman Cl, W1 ... **16** A3
Bexleyheath DA7
off Queen Anne's Gate ... **158** D3
Portman Dr, Wdf.Grn. IG8 ... **80** A2
Portman Gdns, NW9 ... **70** D2
Portman Gate, NW1 ... **7** H6
Portman Hall, Har. HA3 ... **52** A5
Portman Ms S, W1 ... **16** B4
Portman Pl, E2 ... **113** F3
Portman Rd, Kings.T. KT1 ... **181** J2
Portman Sq, W1 ... **16** A3
Portman St, W1 ... **16** B4
Portmeadow Wk, SE2 ... **138** D2
Portmeers Cl, E17
off Lennox Rd ... **78** A6
Portnall Rd, W9 ... **108** C2
Portobello Ct, W11
off Westbourne Gro ... **108** C6
Portobello Ms, W11
off Portobello Rd ... **108** D7
Portobello Rd, W10 ... **108** C6
W11 ... **108** C6
Porton Ct, Surb. KT6 ... **181** F6
Portpool La, EC1 ... **18** E1
Portree Cl, N22 ... **59** F7
Portree St, E14 ... **114** D6
Portsdown, Edg. HA8
off Rectory La ... **54** A5
Portsdown Av, NW11 ... **72** C6
Portsdown Ms, NW11 ... **72** C6
Portsea Ms, W2 ... **15** H4
Portsea Pl, W2 ... **15** H4
Portslade Rd, SW8 ... **150** C2
Portsmouth Av, T.Ditt. KT7 ... **180** D7
Portsmouth Ms, E16
off Wesley Av ... **135** H1
Portsmouth Rd, SW15 ... **147** H7
Esher KT10 ... **194** B2
Kingston upon Thames KT1 ... **181** F5
Portsmouth Rd, Surbiton KT6 ... **181** F5
Thames Ditton KT7 ... **194** B2
Portsmouth St, WC2 ... **18** C4
Portsoken St, E1 ... **21** F5
Portugal Gdns, Twick. TW2
off Fulwell Pk Av ... **161** J2
Portugal St, WC2 ... **18** C4
Portway, E15 ... **115** F1
Portway Gdns, SE18
off Shooters Hill Rd ... **156** A1
Postern Grn, Enf. EN2 ... **43** G2
Post La, Twick. TW2 ... **162** A1
Postmill Cl, Croy. CR0 ... **203** G3
Post Office App, E7 ... **97** H5
Post Office Ct, EC3 ... **20** C4
Post Office Way, SW8 ... **33** H7
Post Rd, Sthl. UB2 ... **123** H3
Postway Ms, Ilf. IG1
off Clements Rd ... **98** E3
Potier St, SE1 ... **28** C6
Potter Cl, Mitch. CR4 ... **186** B2
Potteries, The, Barn. EN5 ... **40** D5
Potterne Cl, SW19 ... **148** A7
Potters Cl, SE15 ... **37** E7
Croydon CR0 ... **203** H1
Loughton IG10 ... **48** B2
Potters Flds, SE1 ... **29** E2
Potters Gro, N.Mal. KT3 ... **182** C4
Potters Hts Cl, Pnr. HA5 ... **50** B7
Potters La, SW16 ... **168** D6
Barnet EN5 ... **40** D4
Borehamwood WD6 ... **38** C1
Potters Rd, SW6 ... **149** F2
Barnet EN5 ... **40** E4
Potter St, Nthwd. HA6 ... **66** A1
Pinner HA5 ... **66** B1
Potter St Hill, Pnr. HA5 ... **50** B6
Pottery La, W11
off Penzance Pl ... **128** B1
Pottery Rd, Bex. DA5 ... **177** J2
Brentford TW8 ... **125** H6
Pottery St, SE16 ... **132** E2
Pott St, E2 ... **113** E3
Poulett Gdns, Twick. TW1 ... **162** D1
Poulett Rd, E6 ... **116** C2
Poulters Wd, Kes. BR2 ... **206** A5
Poulton Av, Sutt. SM1 ... **199** G3
Poulton Cl, E8
off Marcon Pl ... **94** E5
Poultry, EC2 ... **20** B4
Pound Cl, Orp. BR6 ... **207** G2
Surbiton (Long Dit.) KT6 ... **195** F1
Pound Ct Dr, Orp. BR6 ... **207** G2
Pound Fm Cl, Esher KT10 ... **194** A1
Poundfield Rd, Loug. IG10 ... **48** D5
Pound La, NW10 ... **89** G6
Pound Pk Rd, SE7 ... **136** A4
Pound Pl, SE9 ... **156** D6
Pound St, Cars. SM5 ... **199** J5
Pountney Rd, SW11 ... **150** A3
POVEREST, Orp. BR5 ... **193** J5
Poverest Rd, Orp. BR5 ... **193** J5
Powder Mill La, Twick. TW2 ... **161** F1
Powell Cl, Chess. KT9
off Coppard Gdns ... **195** G5
Edgware HA8 ... **53** J6
Wallington SM6 ... **200** D7
Powell Gdns, Dag. RM10 ... **101** G4
Powell Rd, E5 ... **95** E3
Buckhurst Hill IG9 ... **47** J7
Powell's Wk, W4 ... **127** E6
Powergate Business Pk, NW10 ... **106** D3
Power Rd, W4 ... **126** A4
Powers Ct, Twick. TW1 ... **145** G7
Powerscroft Rd, E5 ... **95** F4
Sidcup DA14 ... **176** C6
Powis Gdns, NW11 ... **72** C7
W11 ... **108** C6
Powis Ms, W11
off Westbourne Pk Rd ... **108** C6
Powis Pl, WC1 ... **10** B6
Powis Rd, E3 ... **114** B3
Powis Sq, W11 ... **108** C6
Powis St, SE18 ... **136** D3
Powis Ter, W11 ... **108** C6
Powle Ter, Ilf. IG1
off Oaktree Gro ... **99** G5
Powlett Pl, NW1
off Harmood St ... **92** B6
Pownall Gdns, Houns. TW3 ... **143** H4
Pownall Rd, E8 ... **112** C1
Hounslow TW3 ... **143** H4
Pownsett Ter, Ilf. IG1
off Buttsbury Rd ... **99** F5
Powster Rd, Brom. BR1 ... **173** H5
Powys Cl, Bexh. DA7 ... **138** D6
Powys Ct, Borwd. WD6 ... **38** D3
Powys La, N13 ... **58** E5
N14 ... **58** E4
Poynders Ct, SW4
off Poynders Rd ... **150** C6
Poynders Gdns, SW4 ... **150** C7
Poynders Rd, SW4 ... **150** C6
Poynings Rd, N19 ... **92** C3
Poynings Way, N12 ... **56** D5
Poyntell Cres, Chis. BR7 ... **193** G1
Poynter Ho, W11 ... **128** A1
Poynter Rd, Enf. EN1 ... **44** D5
Poynton Rd, N17 ... **76** D2
Poyntz Rd, SW11 ... **149** J2
Poyser St, E2 ... **113** E2
Praed Ms, W2 ... **15** F3
Praed St, W2 ... **15** G2
Pragel St, E13 ... **115** H2
Pragnell Rd, SE12 ... **173** H2
Prague Pl, SW2 ... **150** E5
Prah Rd, N4 ... **93** G2
Prairie St, SW8 ... **150** A2
Pratt Ms, NW1
off Pratt St ... **110** C1
Pratts Pas, Kings.T. KT1
off Clarence St ... **181** H2
Pratt St, NW1 ... **110** C1
Pratt Wk, SE11 ... **34** D1
Prayle Gro, NW2 ... **90** A1
Prebend Gdns, W4 ... **127** F3
W6 ... **127** F3
Prebend St, N1 ... **111** J1
Precinct, The, W.Mol. KT8 *off Victoria Av* ... **179** H3
Precinct Rd, Hayes UB3 ... **102** A7
Precincts, The, Mord. SM4 *off Green La* ... **184** D6
Premier Cor, W9
off Kilburn La ... **108** C2
Premiere Pl, E14
off Garford St ... **114** A7
Premier Pk, NW10 ... **106** B1
Premier Pk Rd, NW10 ... **106** B2
Prendergast Rd, SE3 ... **155** E3
Prentis Rd, SW16 ... **168** D4
Prentiss Ct, SE7 ... **136** A4
Presburg Rd, N.Mal. KT3 ... **183** E5
Prescelly Pl, Edg. HA8 ... **69** J1
Prescot St, E1 ... **21** G5
Prescott Av, Orp. BR5 ... **192** E6
Prescott Cl, SW16 ... **168** E7
Prescott Grn, Loug. IG10 ... **49** F3
Prescott Ho, SE17 ... **35** H6
Prescott Pl, SW4 ... **150** D3
Presentation Ms, SW2
off Palace Rd ... **169** F1
Preshaw Cres, Mitch. CR4 *off Lower Grn W* ... **185** H3
President Dr, E1
off Waterman Way ... **132** E1
President St, EC1 ... **11** J3
Prespa Cl, N9
off Hudson Way ... **61** F2
Press Ct, SE1 ... **37** H3
Press Rd, NW10 ... **88** D3
Prestage Way, E14 ... **114** C7
Prestbury Rd, E7 ... **97** J7
Prestbury Sq, SE9 ... **174** C4
Prested Rd, SW11
off St. John's Hill ... **149** H4
Prestige Way, NW4
off Heriot Rd ... **71** J5
PRESTON, Wem. HA9 ... **69** G7
Preston Av, E4 ... **62** D6
Preston Cl, SE1 ... **36** D1
Twickenham TW2 ... **162** B3
Preston Dr, E11 ... **79** J5
Bexleyheath DA7 ... **158** D1
Epsom KT19 ... **197** E6
Preston Gdns, NW10
off Church Rd ... **89** E6
Ilford IG1 ... **80** B6
Preston Hill, Har. HA3 ... **69** J6
Preston Pl, NW2 ... **89** G6
Richmond TW10 ... **145** H5
Preston Rd, E11 ... **79** E6
SE19 ... **169** H6
SW20 ... **165** F7
Harrow HA3 ... **69** H7
Wembley HA9 ... **87** H2
Prestons Rd, E14 ... **134** C2
Bromley BR2 ... **205** G3
Preston Waye, Har. HA3 ... **87** H1
Prestwick Cl, Sthl. UB2
off Ringway ... **122** E5
Prestwick Rd, Wat. WD19 ... **50** D5
Prestwood Av, Har. HA3 ... **69** E4
Prestwood Cl, SE18 ... **138** A7
Harrow HA3 ... **69** E4
Prestwood Gdns, Croy. CR0 ... **187** J7
Prestwood St, N1 ... **12** A2
Pretoria Av, E17 ... **77** H4
Pretoria Cl, N17 ... **60** C7
Pretoria Cres, E4 ... **62** C1

Pretoria Rd, E4 62 C1
E11 96 D1
E16 115 F3
N17 60 C7
SW16 168 B6
Ilford IG1 98 E5
Romford RM7 83 J4
Pretoria Rd N, N18 60 C6
Prevost Rd, N11 58 A2
Price Cl, NW7 56 B6
SW17 167 J3
Price Rd, Croy. CR0 201 H5
Price's Ct, SW11 149 G3
Prices Ms, N1 111 F1
Price's St, SE1 27 H2
Price Way, Hmptn. TW12 off Victors Dr 161 E6
Pricklers Hill, Barn. EN5 41 E6
Prickley Wd, Brom. BR2 205 F1
Priddy's Yd, Croy. CR0 off Church St 201 J2
Prideaux Pl, W3 106 D7
WC1 10 D3
Prideaux Rd, SW9 151 E3
Pridham Rd, Th.Hth. CR7 188 A4
Priest Ct, EC2 19 J3
Priestfield Rd, SE23 171 H3
Priestlands Pk Rd, Sid. DA15 175 J3
Priestley Cl, N16 off Ravensdale Rd 76 C7
Priestley Gdns, Rom. RM6 82 B6
Priestley Rd, Mitch. CR4 186 A2
Priestley Way, E17 77 G3
NW2 89 G1
Priestman Pt, E3 off Rainhill Way 114 B3
Priest Pk Av, Har. HA2 85 G2
Priests Br, SW14 147 E4
SW15 147 E4
Prima Rd, SW9 35 E7
Primrose Av, Enf. EN2 44 A1
Romford RM6 82 B7
Primrose Cl, E3 114 A2
N3 73 E2
SE6 172 C5
Harrow HA2 85 F4
Wallington SM6 200 B1
Primrose Dr, West Dr. UB7 120 A4
Primrose Gdns, NW3 91 H6
Ruislip HA4 84 C5
PRIMROSE HILL, NW8 109 J1
Primrose Hill, EC4 19 F4
Primrose Hill Ct, NW3 91 J7
Primrose Hill Rd, NW3 91 H7
Primrose Hill Studios, NW1 off Fitzroy Rd 110 A1
Primrose La, Croy. CR0 203 G1
Primrose Ms, NW1 off Sharpleshall St 91 J7
SE3 135 H7
W5 off St. Mary's Rd 125 G2
Primrose Pl, Islw. TW7 144 C2
Primrose Rd, E10 96 B1
E18 79 H2
Primrose Sq, E9 95 F7
Primrose St, EC2 20 D1
Primrose Wk, SE14 off Alexandra St 133 H7
Epsom (Ewell) KT17 197 F7
Primrose Way, Wem. HA0 105 G2
Primula St, W12 107 G6
Prince Albert Rd, NW1 7 H2
NW8 7 H2
Prince Arthur Ms, NW3 off Perrins La 91 F4
Prince Arthur Rd, NW3 91 F5
Prince Charles Dr, NW4 71 J7
Prince Charles Rd, SE3 155 F1
Prince Charles Way, Wall. SM6 200 B3
Prince Consort Dr, Chis. BR7 193 G1
Prince Consort Rd, SW7 22 D5
Princedale Rd, W11 128 B1
Prince Edward Rd, E9 95 J6
Prince George Av, N14 42 C4
Prince George Duke of Kent Ct, Chis. BR7 off Holbrook La 175 G7
Prince George Rd, N16 94 B4
Prince George's Av, SW20 183 J2
Prince George's Rd, SW19 185 G1
Prince Henry Rd, SE7 136 A7
★ Prince Henry's Room, EC4 19 E4
Prince Imperial Rd, SE18 156 C1
Chislehurst BR7 175 E7
Prince John Rd, SE9 156 B5
Princelet St, E1 21 G1
Prince of Orange La, SE10 off Greenwich High Rd 134 C7
Prince of Wales Cl, NW4 off Church Ter 71 H4
Prince of Wales Dr, SW8 130 B7
SW11 149 J1
Prince of Wales Gate, SW7 23 G3
Prince of Wales Pas, NW1 9 F4
Prince of Wales Rd, NW5 92 A6
SE3 155 F1
Sutton SM1 199 G2
Prince of Wales Ter, W4 126 E5
W8 22 B4
Prince Regent La, E13 115 H3
E16 115 J5
Prince Regent Ms, NW1 9 F4
Prince Regent Rd, Houns. TW3 143 J3
Prince Rd, SE25 188 B5
Prince Rupert Rd, SE9 156 C4
Prince's Arc, SW1 25 G1
Princes Av, N3 72 D1
N10 74 A3
N13 59 G5
N22 74 D1
NW9 70 B4
W3 126 A3
Carshalton SM5 199 J7
Greenford UB6 103 H6
Orpington BR5 193 H5
Surbiton KT6 196 A1
Woodford Green IG8 63 H4
Princes Cl, N4 93 H1
NW9 70 A4
SW4 off Old Town 150 C3
Edgware HA8 54 A5
Sidcup DA14 176 D3
Teddington TW11 162 A4
Princes Ct, SE16 133 J3
SW3 off Brompton Rd 23 J5
Wembley HA9 87 H5
Princes Ct Business Cen, E1 113 E7
Princes Dr, Har. HA1 68 B3
Princes Gdns, SW7 23 F5
W3 106 A5
W5 105 F4
Princes Gate, SW7 23 G4
Princes Gate Ct, SW7 23 F4
Princes Gate Ms, SW7 23 F5
Princes La, N10 74 B3
Princes Ms, W2 14 A5
Hounslow TW3 off Albert Rd 143 G4
Princes Pk Av, NW11 72 B6
Princes Pl, SW1 25 G1
W11 128 B1
Princes Plain, Brom. BR2 192 B7
Princes Ri, SE13 154 C2
Princes Riverside Rd, SE16 133 G1
Princes Rd, N18 61 F4
SE20 171 G6
SW14 146 D3
SW19 166 D6
W13 off Broomfield Rd 125 E1
Buckhurst Hill IG9 63 J2
Ilford IG6 81 G4
Kingston upon Thames KT2 164 A7
Richmond TW10 145 J5
Richmond (Kew) TW9 145 J1
Teddington TW11 162 A4
Princess Alice Way, SE28 137 G2
Princess Av, Wem. HA9 87 H2
Princess Cl, SE28 118 D6
Princess Cres, N4 93 H2
Princesses Wk, Rich. (Kew) TW9 off Royal Botanic Gdns 125 H7
Princess Louise Cl, W2 15 F1
Princess May Rd, N16 94 B4
Princess Ms, NW3 off Belsize Cres 91 G6
Kingston upon Thames KT1 181 J3
Princess Par, Orp. BR6 off Crofton Rd 206 D3
Princess Pk Manor, N11 58 A5
Princes Sq, W2 14 A5
Princess Rd, NW1 110 A1
NW6 108 D2
Croydon CR0 187 J6
Princess St, SE1 27 H6
Princes St, EC2 20 B3
N17 off Queen St 60 B6
W1 17 E4
Bexleyheath DA7 159 F4
Richmond TW9 off Sheen Rd 145 H5
Sutton SM1 199 G4
Princes Ter, E13 115 H1
Prince St, SE8 133 J6
Princes Way, SW19 148 A7
Buckhurst Hill IG9 63 J2
Princes Way, Croydon CR0 201 F5
Ruislip HA4 84 E4
West Wickham BR4 205 F4
Princes Yd, W11 off Princedale Rd 128 B1
Princethorpe Ho, W2 108 D5
Princethorpe Rd, SE26 171 G4
Princeton Ct, SW15 off Felsham Rd 148 A3
Princeton St, WC1 18 C1
Principal Cl, N14 58 C1
Principal Sq, E9 off Chelmer Rd 95 G5
Pringle Gdns, SW16 168 C4
Printers Inn Ct, EC4 19 E3
Printers Ms, E3 113 H1
Printer St, EC4 19 F3
Printing Ho La, Hayes UB3 121 H2
Printing Ho Yd, E2 13 E3
Print Village, SE15 off Chadwick Rd 152 C2
Priolo Rd, SE7 135 J5
Prior Av, Sutt. SM2 199 H7
Prior Bolton St, N1 93 H6
Prioress Ho, E3 off Bromley High St 114 B3
Prioress Rd, SE27 169 H3
Prioress St, SE1 28 C6
Prior Rd, Ilf. IG1 98 D3
Priors Cft, E17 77 H2
Priors Fm La, Nthlt. UB5 85 F6
Priors Fld, Nthlt. UB5 off Arnold Rd 85 E6
Priors Gdns, Ruis. HA4 84 C5
Priors Mead, Enf. EN1 44 B1
Prior St, SE10 134 C7
Priory, The, SE3 155 F4
Croydon CR0 off Epsom Rd 201 G4
Priory Av, E4 61 J3
E17 78 A5
N8 74 D4
W4 127 E4
Orpington BR5 193 G6
Sutton SM3 198 A4
Wembley HA0 86 C4
Priory Cl, E4 61 J3
E18 79 G1
N3 off Church Cres 72 C1
N14 42 B5
N20 40 C7
SW19 off High Path 185 E1
Beckenham BR3 189 H3
Chislehurst BR7 192 C1
Hampton TW12 off Priory Gdns 179 F1
Hayes UB3 102 B7
Stanmore HA7 52 C3
Sunbury-on-Thames TW16 off Staines Rd E 160 A7
Wembley (Sudbury) HA0 86 C4
Priory Ct, E17 77 J3
EC4 off Carter La 19 H4
SW8 150 D1
Priory Ct Est, E17 off Priory Ct 77 J2
Priory Cres, SE19 169 J7
Sutton SM3 198 A4
Wembley HA0 86 D3
Priory Dr, SE2 138 D5
Stanmore HA7 52 C3
Priory Fld Dr, Edg. HA8 54 B4
Priory Gdns, N6 74 B6
SE25 188 C4
SW13 147 F3
W4 127 E4
W5 off Hanger La 105 J3
Hampton TW12 161 F7
Wembley HA0 86 D4
Priory Grn Est, N1 10 C1
Priory Gro, SW8 150 E1
Barnet EN5 40 D5
Priory Hts, N1 10 C1
Priory Hill, Wem. HA0 86 D4
Priory Ho, SE7 off Springfield Gro 135 J6
Priory La, SW15 147 E6
Richmond TW9 off Forest Rd 126 A7
West Molesey KT8 179 G4
Priory Ms, SW8 150 D1
Priory Pk, SE3 155 F3
Priory Pk Rd, NW6 108 C1
Wembley HA0 86 D4
Priory Rd, E6 116 A1
N8 74 D4
NW6 108 E1
SW19 167 G7
W4 126 D3
Barking IG11 99 G7
Chessington KT9 195 H3
Priory Rd, Croydon CR0 187 G7
Hampton TW12 161 F7
Hounslow TW3 143 J5
Loughton IG10 48 B4
Richmond TW9 126 A6
Sutton SM3 198 A4
Priory St, E3 114 B3
Priory Ter, NW6 108 E1
Sunbury-on-Thames TW16 off Staines Rd E 160 A7
Priory Wk, SW10 30 D4
Priory Way, Har. HA2 67 H4
Southall UB2 122 D3
West Drayton (Harm.) UB7 120 B6
Priscilla Cl, N15 off Conway Rd 75 J5
Pritchard's Rd, E2 112 D1
Priter Rd, SE16 29 J6
Private Rd, Enf. EN1 44 B5
Probert Rd, SW2 151 G5
Probyn Ho, SW1 off Page St 33 J1
Probyn Rd, SW2 169 H2
Procter Ho, SE1 37 H3
Procter St, WC1 18 C2
Proctor Cl, Mitch. CR4 186 A1
Proctors Cl, Felt. TW14 160 A1
Progress Business Pk, Croy. CR0 201 F2
Progress Way, N22 75 G1
Croydon CR0 201 F2
Enfield EN1 44 D5
Promenade, Edg. HA8 54 A5
Promenade, The, W4 147 E1
Promenade App Rd, W4 126 E7
Promenade Mans, Edg. HA8 off Hale La 54 A5
Prospect Business Pk, Loug. IG10 49 G4
Prospect Cl, SE26 170 E4
Belvedere DA17 139 G4
Hounslow TW3 143 F1
Ruislip HA4 66 D7
Prospect Cotts, SW18 off Point Pleasant 148 D4
Prospect Cres, Twick. TW2 143 J6
Prospect Hill, E17 78 B4
Prospect Ho, SW19 off Chapter Way 185 G1
Prospect Pl, E1 133 F1
N2 73 G4
N7 off Parkhurst Rd 93 E4
N17 60 B7
NW2 off Ridge Rd 90 C3
NW3 off Holly Wk 91 F4
SW20 165 H7
W4 off Chiswick High Rd 126 D5
Bromley BR2 191 H3
Romford RM5 83 J2
Prospect Quay, SW18 148 D4
Prospect Ring, N2 73 G3
Prospect Rd, NW2 90 C3
Barnet EN5 40 D5
Surbiton (Long Dit.) KT6 181 F6
Woodford Green IG8 63 J5
Prospect St, SE16 off Jamaica Rd 133 E2
Prospect Vale, SE18 136 B4
Prospero Rd, N19 92 C1
Protea Cl, E16 off Hermit Rd 115 F4
Prothero Gdns, NW4 71 H5
Prothero Ho, NW10 88 D7
Prothero Rd, SW6 128 B7
Prout Gro, NW10 89 E4
Prout Rd, E5 95 E3
Provence St, N1 11 J1
Providence Av, Har. HA2 off Goodwill Dr 85 G1
Providence Cl, E9 off Wetherell Rd 113 G1
Providence Ct, W1 16 C5
Providence La, Hayes (Harling.) UB3 121 G7
Providence Pl, N1 off Upper St 111 H1
Romford RM5 83 F2
Providence Rd, West Dr. UB7 120 B1
Providence Row, N1 off Pentonville Rd 10 C2
Providence Row Cl, E2 off Ainsley St 113 E3
Providence Sq, SE1 off Jacob St 29 H3
Providence Yd, E2 13 H3
Provident Ind Est, Hayes UB3 122 A2
Provost Est, N1 12 B3
Provost Rd, NW3 91 J7
Provost St, N1 12 B4

Prowse Av, Bushey (Bushey Hth) WD23 ....**51** J2
Prowse Pl, NW1 *off Bonny St* **92** B7
Prudence La, Orp. BR6 ...**206** D4
Pruden Cl, N14 ....**58** C2
Prudent Pas, EC2 ....**20** A3
Prusom St, E1 ....**133** E1
Pryors, The, NW3 ....**91** G3
★ **P.S. Tattershall Castle**, SW1 ....**26** B2
Pudding La, EC3 ....**20** C6
Chigwell IG7 ....**65** J1
Pudding Mill La, E15 .....**114** B1
Puddle Dock, EC4 ....**19** H5
Puffin Cl, Bark. IG11 .....**118** B3
Beckenham BR3 ......**189** G5
Puffin Ter, Ilf. IG5 *off Tiptree Cres* **80** D3
Pulborough Rd, SW18 ...**148** C7
Pulborough Way, Houns. TW4 ....**142** C4
Pulford Rd, N15 ....**76** A6
Pulham Av, N2 ....**73** F4
Pulham Ho, SW8 *off Dorset Rd* **131** F7
Puller Rd, Barn. EN5 ......**40** B2
Pulleyns Av, E6 ....**116** B3
Pullman Ct, SW2 ....**169** E1
Pullman Gdns, SW15 ....**147** J6
Pullman Ms, SE12 ....**173** H3
Pullman Pl, SE9 ....**156** B5
Pulross Rd, SW9 ....**151** F3
Pulse Apts, NW6 *off Lymington Rd* **91** E5
Pulteney Cl, E3 ....**113** J1
Isleworth TW7 *off Gumley Gdns* **144** D3
Pulteney Gdns, E18 *off Pulteney Rd* **79** H3
Pulteney Rd, E18 ....**79** H3
Pulteney Ter, N1 ....**111** F1
Pulton Pl, SW6 ....**128** D7
Puma Ct, E1 ....**21** F1
Pump All, Brent. TW8 ....**125** G7
Pump Cl, Nthlt. UB5 *off Union Rd* **103** G2
Pump Ct, EC4 ....**19** E4
Pumphandle Path, N2 *off Tarling Rd* **73** F2
Pump Hill, Loug. IG10 ....**48** C2
Pump Ho Cl, SE16 *off Renforth St* **133** F2
Bromley BR2 ....**191** F2
★ **Pumphouse Ed Mus, Rotherhithe**, SE16 ...**133** H1
Pump Ho Ms, E1 ....**21** H5
Pumping Sta Rd, W4 ....**127** E7
Pump La, SE14 ....**133** F7
Hayes UB3 ....**122** B2
Pump Pail N, Croy. CR0 *off Old Town* **201** J3
Pump Pail S, Croy. CR0 *off Southbridge Rd* ...**201** J3
Pundersons Gdns, E2 ....**113** E3
Punjab La, Sthl. UB1 *off Herbert Rd* **123** F1
Purbeck Av, N.Mal. KT3 ..**183** F6
Purbeck Dr, NW2 ....**90** B2
Purbeck Ho, SW8 *off Bolney St* **131** F7
Purbrook Est, SE1 ....**29** E4
Purbrook St, SE1 ....**29** E5
Purcell Cres, SW6 ....**128** B7
Purcell Rd, Grnf. UB6 ....**103** H5
Purcells Av, Edg. HA8 .....**54** A5
Purcell St, N1 ....**12** D1
Purchese St, NW1 ....**9** J1
Purdy St, E3 ....**114** B4
Purelake Ms, SE13 ....**154** D3
Purland Cl, Dag. RM8 ....**101** F1
Purland Rd, SE28 ....**137** J2
Purleigh Av, Wdf.Grn. IG8 ....**64** B6
Purley Av, NW2 ....**90** B3
Purley Cl, Ilf. IG5 ....**80** D2
Purley Pl, N1 *off Islington Pk St* **93** H7
Purley Rd, N9 ....**60** A3
South Croydon CR2 ...**202** A7
Purley Way, Croy. CR0 ...**187** F7
Purley CR8 ....**201** G7
Purley Way Cres, Croy. CR0 *off Purley Way* **187** F7
Purneys Rd, SE9 ....**156** A4
Purrett Rd, SE18 ....**137** J5
Purser's Cross Rd, SW6 ..**148** C1
Pursewardens Cl, W13 ...**125** F1
Pursley Rd, NW7 ....**55** H7
Purves Rd, NW10 ....**107** J2
Puteaux Ho, E2 ....**113** G2
PUTNEY, SW15 ....**148** B4
Putney Br, SW6 ....**148** B3
SW15 ....**148** B3
Putney Br App, SW6 .....**148** B3
Putney Br Rd, SW15 .....**148** B4
SW18 ....**148** B4
Putney Common, SW15 ..**147** J3
Putney Ex Shop Cen, SW15 ....**148** A4
Putney Gdns, Rom. (Chad.Hth) RM6 *off Heathfield Pk Dr* ...**82** B5
PUTNEY HEATH, SW15 ...**147** J6
Putney Heath, SW15 ....**147** J6
Putney Heath La, SW15 ..**148** A6
Putney High St, SW15 ...**148** A4
Putney Hill, SW15 ....**148** A6
Putney Pk Av, SW15 .....**147** G4
Putney Pk La, SW15 .....**147** H4
PUTNEY VALE, SW15 ....**165** F3
Putney Wf Twr, SW15 ....**148** B3
Puttenham Cl, Wat. WD19 .**50** C3
Pycroft Way, N9 ....**60** D4
Pyecombe Cor, N12 ......**56** C4
Pylbrook Rd, Sutt. SM1 ..**198** D3
Pylon Way, Croy. CR0 ....**201** E1
Pym Cl, Barn. (E.Barn.) EN4 ....**41** G5
Pymers Mead, SE21 .....**169** J1
Pymmes Brook Dr, Barn. EN4 ....**41** H4
Pymmes Cl, N13 ....**59** F5
N17 ....**76** E1
Pymmes Gdns N, N9 .....**60** C3
Pymmes Gdns S, N9 .....**60** C3
Pymmes Grn Rd, N11 .....**58** B4
Pymmes Rd, N13 ....**59** E6
Pyne Rd, Surb. KT6 .....**196** A1
Pynfolds, SE16 *off Paradise St* **133** E2
Pynham Cl, SE2 ....**138** A3
Pynnacles Cl, Stan. HA7 ...**52** E5
Pyrland Rd, N5 ....**94** A5
Richmond TW10 ......**145** J6
Pyrles Grn, Loug. IG10 ....**48** E1
Pyrles La, Loug. IG10 .....**48** E2
Pyrmont Gro, SE27 ......**169** H3
Pyrmont Rd, W4 ....**126** A6
Pytchley Cres, SE19 .....**169** J6
Pytchley Rd, SE22 ....**152** B3

Q

Quadrangle, The, SE24 ...**151** J5
SW10 *off Chelsea Harbour* ..**149** F1
W2 ....**15** G3
Quadrangle Cl, SE1 ......**36** D1
Quadrangle Ho, E15 *off Romford Rd* **97** E6
Quadrangle Ms, Stan. HA7 ....**53** F7
Quadrant, The, SW20 ....**184** B1
Bexleyheath DA7 .....**138** D7
Richmond TW9 ....**145** H4
Sutton SM2 ....**199** F6
Quadrant Arc, W1 ....**17** G6
Quadrant Cl, NW4 *off The Burroughs* **71** H5
Quadrant Gro, NW5 ......**91** J5
Quadrant Ho, Sutt. SM2 ..**199** F6
Quadrant Rd, Rich. TW9 ..**145** G4
Thornton Heath CR7 ..**187** H4
Quad Rd, Wem. HA9 ......**87** G3
Quaggy Wk, SE3 ....**155** G4
Quainton St, NW10 ......**88** D3
Quaker Ct, E1 ....**13** F6
EC1 ....**12** B5
Quaker La, Sthl. UB2 ....**123** G3
Quakers Course, NW9 ....**71** F1
Quakers La, Islw. TW7 ....**144** D1
Quaker's Pl, E7 ....**98** A5
Quaker St, E1 ....**13** F6
Quakers Wk, N21 ....**44** A6
Quality Ct, WC2 ....**18** E3
Quantock Cl, Hayes (Harling.) UB3 ....**121** G7
Quantock Dr, Wor.Pk. KT4 ....**197** J2
Quantock Gdns, NW2 ....**90** A2
Quantock Ms, SE15 *off Choumert Gro* **152** D2
Quarles Pk Rd, Rom. RM6 ....**82** B6
Quarrendon St, SW6 .....**148** D2
Quarr Rd, Cars. SM5 .....**185** G6
Quarry Pk Rd, Sutt. SM1 ....**198** C6
Quarry Ri, Sutt. SM1 .....**198** C6
Quarry Rd, SW18 ....**149** F6
Quarterdeck, The, E14 ....**134** A2
Quarter Mile La, E10 ......**96** B4
Quayside Wk, Kings.T. KT1 *off Bishop's Hall* ..**181** G2
Quay W, Tedd. TW11 .....**162** E5
Quebec Ms, W1 ....**16** A4
Quebec Rd, Hayes UB4 ..**102** C7
Ilford IG1, IG2 ....**81** E7
Quebec Way, SE16 ......**133** G2
Queen Adelaide Rd, SE20 ....**171** F6
Queen Alexandra's Ct, SW19 ....**166** C5
Queen Anne Av, N15 *off Suffield Rd* **76** C5
Bromley BR2 ....**191** F3
Queen Anne Dr, Esher (Clay.) KT10 ....**194** B7
Queen Anne Ms, W1 ......**16** E2
Queen Anne Rd, E9 ....**95** G6
Queen Anne's Cl, Twick. TW2 ....**162** A3
Queen Anne's Gdns, W4 ..**127** E3
Queen Annes Gdns, W5 ..**125** H2
Enfield EN1 ....**44** B6
Queen Anne's Gdns, Mitch. CR4 ....**185** J3
Queen Anne's Gate, SW1 ..**25** H4
Bexleyheath DA7 .....**158** D3
Queen Anne's Gro, W4 ...**126** E3
Queen Annes Gro, W5 ....**125** H2
Enfield EN1 ....**44** A7
Queen Annes Pl, Enf. EN1 .**44** B6
Queen Anne St, W1 ......**16** D3
Queen Anne's Wk, WC1 *off Queen Sq* **10** B6
Queen Anne Ter, E1 *off Sovereign Cl* **113** E7
Queenborough Gdns, Chis. BR7 ....**175** G6
Ilford IG2 ....**80** D4
Queen Caroline Est, W6 ..**127** J5
Queen Caroline St, W6 ...**127** J4
Queen Elizabeth Gdns, Mord. SM4 ....**184** D4
★ **Queen Elizabeth Hall & Purcell Room**, SE1 ....**26** C1
Queen Elizabeth Rd, E17 ..**77** H3
Kingston upon Thames KT2 ....**181** J1
Queen Elizabeths Cl, N16 .**94** A2
Queen Elizabeth's Coll, SE10 *off Greenwich High Rd* **134** C7
Queen Elizabeths Dr, N14 .**58** E1
★ **Queen Elizabeth II Conf Cen**, SW1 ....**25** J4
★ **Queen Elizabeth's Hunting Lo**, E4 ....**47** F7
Queen Elizabeth St, SE1 ..**29** E3
Queen Elizabeths Wk, N16 .**94** A2
Queen Elizabeth's Wk, Wall. SM6 ....**200** D4
Queen Elizabeth Wk, SW13 ....**147** H1
Queenhithe, EC4 ....**20** A5
Queen Margaret's Gro, N1 .**94** B5
Queen Mary Av, Mord. SM4 ....**184** A5
Queen Mary Cl, Surb. KT6 ....**196** A3
Queen Mary Rd, SE19 ...**169** H6
Queen Mary's Av, Cars. SM5 ....**199** J7
Queen Marys Bldgs, SW1 *off Stillington St* **33** G1
★ **Queen Mary's Gdns**, NW1 ....**8** B4
Queen of Denmark Ct, SE16 ....**133** J3
Queens Acre, Sutt. SM3 ..**198** A7
Queens Av, N3 ....**57** F7
N10 ....**74** A3
N20 ....**57** G2
Queen's Av, N21 ....**59** H1
Queens Av, Felt. TW13 ...**160** C4
Greenford UB6 ....**103** H6
Stanmore HA7 ....**69** F3
Woodford Green IG8 ...**63** H5
Queensberry Ms W, SW7 ..**30** E1
Queensberry Pl, E12 ......**98** A5
SW7 ....**30** E1
Richmond TW9 *off Friars La* **145** G5
Queensberry Way, SW7 ...**31** E1
Queensborough Ms, W2 ..**14** C5
Queensborough Pas, W2 ..**14** C5
Queensborough Studios, W2 ....**14** C5
Queensborough Ter, W2 ...**14** B5
Queensbridge Pk, Islw. TW7 ....**144** B5
Queensbridge Rd, E2 ....**112** C1
E8 ....**94** C7
QUEENSBURY, Har. HA3 ..**69** G3
Queensbury Circle Par, Har. HA3 *off Streatfield Rd* **69** H3
Stanmore HA7 *off Streatfield Rd* **69** H3
Queensbury Rd, NW9 .....**70** D7
Wembley HA0 ....**105** J2
Queensbury Sta Par, Edg. HA8 ....**69** J3
Queensbury St, N1 ....**93** J7
Queen's Circ, SW8 *off Queenstown Rd* ..**130** B7
SW11 *off Queenstown Rd* ..**130** B7
Queens Cl, Edg. HA8 .....**54** A5
Wallington SM6 *off Queens Rd* **200** B5
★ **Queens Club (Tennis Cen)**, W14 ....**128** B5
Queens Club Gdns, W14 .**128** B6
Queens Ct, SE23 ....**171** F1
Richmond TW10 ....**145** J6
Queenscourt, Wem. HA9 ..**87** H4
Queen's Cres, NW5 ....**92** A6
Queens Cres, Rich. TW10 .**145** J5
Queenscroft Rd, SE9 ....**156** A5
Queensdale Cres, W11 ...**128** A1
Queensdale Pl, W11 .....**128** B1
Queensdale Rd, W11 .....**128** A1
Queensdale Wk, W11 ....**128** B1
Queensdown Rd, E5 ......**94** E4
Queens Dr, E10 ....**78** A7
N4 ....**93** H2
W3 ....**105** J6
W5 ....**105** J6
Surbiton KT5 ....**182** A7
Thames Ditton KT7 ....**180** D7
Queens Elm Par, SW3 *off Old Ch St* **31** F3
Queen's Elm Sq, SW3 ....**31** F4
Queensferry Wk, N17 *off Jarrow Rd* **76** E4
★ **Queen's Gall, The**, SW1 ....**24** E4
Queens Gdns, NW4 ......**71** J5
W2 ....**14** C5
W5 ....**105** F4
Queen's Gdns, Houns. TW5 ....**142** E1
Queen's Gate, SW7 ......**22** D4
Queen's Gate Gdns, SW7 ....**22** D6
Queens Gate Gdns, SW15 *off Upper Richmond Rd* **147** H4
Queensgate Gdns, Chis. BR7 ....**193** G1
Queensgate Ho, E3 *off Hereford Rd* **113** J2
Queen's Gate Ms, SW7 ...**22** D4
Queensgate Ms, Beck. BR3 *off Queens Rd* **189** H1
Queensgate Pl, NW6 .....**90** D7
Queen's Gate Pl, SW7 ....**22** D6
Queen's Gate Pl Ms, SW7 ....**22** D6
Queen's Gate Ter, SW7 ....**22** C5
Queen's Gro, NW8 ......**109** G1
Queen's Gro Ms, NW8 ...**109** G1
Queens Gro Rd, E4 ....**62** D1
Queen's Head Pas, EC4 ...**19** J3
Queen's Head St, N1 .....**111** H1
Queens Head Yd, SE1 .....**28** B2
Queens Ho, Tedd. TW11 ...**162** C6
★ **Queen's Ice & Bowl**, W2 ....**14** B6
Queensland Av, N18 ......**59** J6
SW19 ....**184** E1
Queensland Cl, E17 ......**77** J2
Queensland Ho, E16 *off Rymill St* **136** D1
Queensland Rd, N7 ....**93** G4
Queens La, N10 ....**74** B3
Queens Mkt, E13 *off Green St* **115** J1
Queensmead, NW8 ......**109** G1
Queens Mead, Edg. HA8 ..**53** J6
Queensmead Rd, Brom. BR2 ....**191** F2
Queensmere Cl, SW19 ...**166** A2
Queensmere Rd, SW19 ..**166** A2
Queens Ms, W2 ....**14** B5
Queensmill Rd, SW6 ....**128** A7
Queens Par, N11 *off St. Johns Av* **57** J5
W5 ....**105** J6
Queens Par Cl, N11 *off Colney Hatch La* ...**57** J5
Queens Pk Ct, W10 ......**108** A3
★ **Queens Park Rangers FC**, W12 ....**127** H1
Queens Pas, Chis. BR7 *off High St* **175** E6
Queens Pl, Mord. SM4 ...**184** D4
Queen's Prom, Kings.T. KT1 *off Portsmouth Rd* ...**181** G3
Queen Sq, WC1 ....**10** B6
Queen Sq Pl, WC1 ....**10** B6
Queens Reach, E.Mol. KT8 ....**180** B4
Queens Ride, SW13 .....**147** G3
SW15 ....**147** G3
Queen's Ride, Rich. TW10 ....**164** B1

Queens Ri, Rich. TW10 **145** J6
Queens Rd, E11 **78** D7
E13 **115** H1
Queen's Rd, E17 **77** J6
Queens Rd, N3 **73** F1
N9 **60** E3
Queen's Rd, N11 **58** E7
Queens Rd, NW4 **71** J5
SE14 **152** E1
SE15 **152** E1
SW14 **146** D3
SW19 **166** C6
W5 **105** H6
Barking IG11 **99** F7
Barnet EN5 **40** A3
Beckenham BR3 **189** H2
Bromley BR1 **191** G2
Buckhurst Hill IG9 **63** H2
Chislehurst BR7 **175** E6
Queen's Rd, Croy. CR0 **187** H6
Queens Rd, Enf. EN1 **44** B4
Feltham TW13 **160** B1
Hampton (Hmptn H.) TW12 **161** H4
Queen's Rd, Houns. TW3 **143** H3
Queens Rd, Kings.T. KT2 **164** A7
Loughton IG10 **48** B3
Morden SM4 **184** D4
New Malden KT3 **183** F4
Richmond TW10 **145** J5
Southall UB2 **122** D2
Queen's Rd, Tedd. TW11 **162** B6
Thames Ditton KT7 **180** C5
Queens Rd, Twick. TW1 **162** C1
Wallington SM6 **200** B5
Queen's Rd, Well. DA16 **158** B2
Queens Rd, West Dr. UB7 **120** C2
Queens Rd W, E13 **115** G2
Queen's Row, SE17 **36** B5
Queens Ter, E13 **115** H1
Queen's Ter, NW8 **7** E1
Queens Ter, Islw. TW7 **144** D4
Queens Ter Cotts, W7
off Boston Rd **124** B2
Queensthorpe Rd, SE26 **171** G4
★ **Queen's Twr**, SW7 **23** E5
Queenstown Ms, SW8
off Queenstown Rd **150** B1
Queenstown Rd, SW8 **32** D6
Queen St, EC4 **20** A5
N17 **60** B6
W1 **24** D1
Bexleyheath DA7 **159** F3
Croydon CR0 **201** J4
Queen St Pl, EC4 **20** A6
Queensville Rd, SW12 **150** D7
Queens Wk, E4 **62** D1
NW9 **88** C2
Queen's Wk, SW1 **25** F2
Queens Wk, W5 **105** F4
Queen's Wk, Har. HA1 **68** B4
Queens Wk, Ruis. HA4 **84** D3
Queen's Wk, The, SE1 **26** C2
Queens Way, NW4 **71** J5
Queensway, W2 **14** B4
Queensway, Croy. CR0 **201** F6
Queensway, Enf. EN3 **45** E4
Queens Way, Felt. TW13 **160** C4
Queensway, Orp. BR5 **193** F5
Sunbury-on-Thames TW16 **178** B2
West Wickham BR4 **205** E3
Queensway Business Cen, Enf. EN3
off Queensway **45** F4
Queenswell Av, N20 **57** H4
Queenswood Av, E17 **78** C1
Hampton TW12 **161** H6
Hounslow TW3 **143** F2
Thornton Heath CR7 **187** G5
Wallington SM6 **200** D4
Queenswood Gdns, E11 **97** G1
Queenswood Pk, N3 **72** B2
Queen's Wd Rd, N10 **74** B6
Queenswood Rd, SE23 **171** G3
Sidcup DA15 **157** J5
Queens Yd, WC1 **9** G6
Queen Victoria, Sutt. SM3 **197** J4
Queen Victoria Av, Wem. HA0 **87** G7
★ **Queen Victoria Mem**, SW1 **25** F3
Queen Victoria St, EC4 **19** H5
Queen Victoria Ter, E1
off Sovereign Cl **113** E7
Quemerford Rd, N7 **93** F5
Quentin Pl, SE13 **155** E3
Quentin Rd, SE13 **155** E3
Quernmore Cl, Brom. BR1 **173** G6
Quernmore Rd, N4 **75** G6
Bromley BR1 **173** G6
Querrin St, SW6 **149** F2
Quex Ms, NW6
off Quex Rd **108** D1
Quex Rd, NW6 **108** D1
Quick Rd, W4 **126** E5
Quicks Rd, SW19 **167** E7
Quick St, N1 **11** H2
Quick St Ms, N1 **11** G2
Quickswood, NW3
off King Henry's Rd **91** H7
Quiet Nook, Brom. BR2
off Croydon Rd **206** A3
Quill La, SW15 **148** A4
Quill St, N4 **93** G3
W5 **105** H3
Quilp St, SE1 **27** J3
Quilter St, E2 **13** H3
SE18 **137** J5
Quilting Ct, SE16
off Poolmans St **133** G2
Quince Ho, Felt. TW13
off High St **160** B1
Quince Rd, SE13 **154** B2
Quinnell Cl, SE18
off Rippolson Rd **137** J5
Quinta Dr, Barn. EN5 **39** H5
Quintin Av, SW20 **184** C1
Quintin Cl, Pnr. HA5
off High Rd **66** B5
Quinton Cl, Beck. BR3 **190** C3
Hounslow TW5 **122** B7
Wallington SM6 **200** B4
Quinton Rd, T.Ditt. KT7 **194** D1
Quinton St, SW18 **167** F2
Quixley St, E14 **114** D7
Quorn Rd, SE22 **152** B4

R

Rabbit Row, W8
off Kensington Mall **128** D1
Rabbits Rd, E12 **98** B4
Rabournmead Dr, Nthlt. UB5 **84** E5
Raby Rd, N.Mal. KT3 **182** D4
Raby St, E14
off Salmon La **113** H6
Raccoon Way, Houns. TW4 **142** C2
Rachel Cl, Ilf. IG6 **81** G3
Rackham Cl, Well. DA16 **158** B2
Rackham Ms, SW16 **168** C6
Racton Rd, SW6 **128** D6
Radbourne Av, W5 **125** F4
Radbourne Cl, E5
off Overbury St **95** G4
Radbourne Cres, E17 **78** D2
Radbourne Rd, SW12 **168** D1
Radcliffe Av, NW10 **107** G2
Enfield EN2 **43** J1
Radcliffe Gdns, Cars. SM5 **199** H7
Radcliffe Ms, Hmptn. (Hmptn H.) TW12
off Taylor Cl **161** J5
Radcliffe Path, SW8
off Robertson St **150** B2
Radcliffe Rd, N21 **59** H1
SE1 **29** E5
Croydon CR0 **202** C2
Harrow HA3 **68** D2
Radcliffe Sq, SW15 **148** A6
Radcliffe Way, Nthlt. UB5 **102** D3
Radcot Pt, SE23 **171** G3
Radcot St, SE11 **35** F4
Raddington Rd, W10 **108** B5
Radfield Way, Sid. DA15 **157** G7
Radford Rd, SE13 **154** C6
Radford Way, Bark. IG11 **117** J3
Radipole Rd, SW6 **148** C1
Radius Pk, Felt. TW14 **141** J4
Radland Rd, E16 **115** F6
Radlet Av, SE26 **171** E3
Radlett Cl, E7 **97** F6
Radlett Pl, NW8 **109** H1
Radley Av, Ilf. IG3 **99** J4
Radley Ct, SE16
off Marlow Way **133** G2
Radley Gdns, Har. HA3 **69** H4
Radley Ho, SE2
off Wolvercote Rd **138** D2
Radley Ms, W8 **128** D3
Radley Rd, N17 **76** B2
Radley's La, E18 **79** G2
Radleys Mead, Dag. RM10 **101** H6
Radley Sq, E5
off Dudlington Rd **95** F2
Radlix Rd, E10 **96** A1
Radnor Av, Har. HA1 **68** B5
Welling DA16 **158** B5
Radnor Cl, Chis. BR7 **175** H6
Mitcham CR4 **187** E4
Radnor Cres, SE18 **138** A6
Ilford IG4 **80** C5
Radnor Gdns, Enf. EN1 **44** B1
Twickenham TW1 **162** C2
Radnor Ho, SW16 **187** F2
Radnor Ms, W2 **15** F4
Radnor Pl, W2 **15** G4
Radnor Rd, NW6 **108** B1
SE15 **37** H7
Harrow HA1 **68** A5
Twickenham TW1 **162** C2
Radnor St, EC1 **12** A4
Radnor Ter, W14 **128** C4
Radnor Wk, E14
off Copeland Dr **134** A4
SW3 **31** H4
Croydon CR0 **189** J6
Radnor Way, NW10 **106** B4
Radstock Av, Har. HA3 **68** D3
Radstock Cl, N11 **58** A5
Radstock St, SW11 **129** H7
Raebarn Gdns, Barn. EN5 **39** H5
Raeburn Av, Surb. KT5 **182** B6
Raeburn Cl, NW11 **73** F6
Kingston upon Thames KT1 **163** G7
Raeburn Rd, Edg. HA8 **70** A2
Sidcup DA15 **157** H6
Raeburn St, SW2 **151** E4
Raffles Ct, Edg. HA8 **53** J4
Rafford Way, Brom. BR1 **191** H2
Raft Rd, SW18
off North Pas **148** D4
★ **Ragged Sch Mus**, E3
off Copperfield Rd **113** H5
Raggleswood, Chis. BR7 **192** D1
Raglan Cl, Houns. TW4 **143** F5
Raglan Ct, SE12 **155** G5
South Croydon CR2 **201** H5
Wembley HA9 **87** J4
Raglan Gdns, Wat. WD19 **50** B1
Raglan Rd, E17 **78** C5
SE18 **137** F5
Belvedere DA17 **139** F4
Bromley BR2 **191** J4
Enfield EN1 **44** B7
Raglan St, NW5 **92** B6
Raglan Ter, Har. HA2 **85** H4
Raglan Way, Nthlt. UB5 **85** J6
Ragley Cl, W3
off Church Rd **126** C2
Ragwort Ct, SE26 **170** E5
Rahere Ho, EC1 **11** J3
Raider Cl, Rom. RM7 **83** G1
Railey Ms, NW5 **92** C5
Railshead Rd, Islw. TW7 **144** E4
Railton Rd, SE24 **151** G4
Railway App, N4
off Wightman Rd **75** G6
SE1 **28** C1
Harrow HA1, HA3 **68** C4
Twickenham TW1 **144** D7
Wallington SM6 **200** B6
Railway Arches, W12
off Shepherds Bush Mkt **127** J2
Railway Av, SE16 **133** F2
Railway Children Wk, SE12 **173** G2
Bromley BR1 **173** G2
Railway Ms, E3
off Wellington Way **114** A3
W10 *off Ladbroke Gro* **108** B6
Railway Pas, Tedd. TW11
off Victoria Rd **162** D6
Railway Pl, SW19
off Hartfield Rd **166** C6
Belvedere DA17 **139** G3
Railway Ri, SE22
off Grove Vale **152** B4
Railway Rd, Tedd. TW11 **162** C4
Railway Side, SW13 **147** E3
Railway St, N1 **10** B2
Romford RM6 **100** C1
Railway Ter, E17 **78** C1
SE13 *off Ladywell Rd* **154** B5
Rainborough Cl, NW10 **88** C6
Rainbow Av, E14 **134** B5
Rainbow Ind Pk, SW20 **183** H2
Rainbow Quay, SE16 **133** H3
Rainbow St, SE5 **132** B7
Raines Ct, N16
off Northwold Rd **94** C2
Raine St, E1 **133** E1
Rainham Cl, SE9 **157** G6
SW11 **149** H6
Rainham Rd, NW10 **107** J3
Rainham Rd N, Dag. RM10 **101** H2
Rainham Rd S, Dag. RM10 **101** H4
Rainhill Way, E3 **114** A3
Rainsborough Av, SE8 **133** H4
Rainsford Cl, Stan. HA7 **53** F4
Rainsford Rd, NW10 **106** B3
Rainsford St, W2 **15** G3
Rainton Rd, SE7 **135** G5
Rainville Rd, W6 **127** J6
Raisins Hill, Pnr. HA5 **66** C3
Raith Av, N14 **58** D3
Raleana Rd, E14 **134** C1
Raleigh Av, Hayes UB4 **102** B5
Wallington SM6 **200** D4
Raleigh Cl, NW4 **71** J5
Pinner HA5 **66** D7
Raleigh Ct, SE19
off Lymer Av **170** C5
Beckenham BR3 **190** B1
Wallington SM6 **200** B6
Raleigh Dr, N20 **57** H3
Esher (Clay.) KT10 **194** A5
Surbiton KT5 **196** C1
Raleigh Gdns, SW2
off Brixton Hill **151** F6
Mitcham CR4 **185** J2
Raleigh Ms, N1
off Queen's Head St **111** H1
Orpington BR6
off Osgood Av **207** J5
Raleigh Rd, N8 **75** G4
SE20 **171** G7
Enfield EN2 **44** A4
Richmond TW9 **145** J3
Southall UB2 **122** E5
Raleigh St, N1 **111** H1
Raleigh Way, N14 **58** D1
Feltham TW13 **160** C5
Ralph Ct, W2 **14** B3
Ralph Perring Ct, Beck. BR3 **190** A4
Ralston St, SW3 **31** J4
Ralston Way, Wat. WD19 **50** D2
Rama Cl, SW16 **168** D7
Rama Ct, Har. HA1 **86** B2
Ramac Way, SE7 **135** H4
Rama La, SE19 **170** C7
Rambler Cl, SW16 **168** C4
Rame Cl, SW17 **168** A5
Ramilles Cl, SW2 **151** E6
Ramillies Pl, W1 **17** F4
Ramillies Rd, NW7 **54** E2
W4 **126** D4
Sidcup DA15 **158** B6
Ramillies St, W1 **17** F4
Rampart St, E1
off Commercial Rd **112** E6
Ram Pas, Kings.T. KT1
off High St **181** G2
Rampayne St, SW1 **33** H3
Ram Pl, E9
off Chatham Pl **95** F6
Rampton Cl, E4 **62** A3
Ramsay Ms, SW3 **31** G5
Ramsay Pl, Har. HA1 **86** B1
Ramsay Rd, E7 **97** E4
W3 **126** C3
Ramscroft Cl, N9 **44** B7
Ramsdale Rd, SW17 **168** A5
Ramsden Rd, N11 **57** J5
SW12 **150** A6
Ramsey Cl, NW9 **71** F6
Greenford UB6 **85** J5
Ramsey Ho, SW11
off Maysoule Rd **149** G4
Wembley HA9 **87** H6
Ramsey Rd, Th.Hth. CR7 **187** F6
Ramsey St, E2 **13** J5
Ramsey Wk, N1 **94** A6
Ramsey Way, N14 **42** C7
Ramsfort Ho, SE16
off Manor Est **132** E4
Ramsgate Cl, E16
off Hanameel St **135** H1
Ramsgate St, E8
off Dalston La **94** C6
Ramsgill App, Ilf. IG2 **81** J4
Ramsgill Dr, Ilf. IG2 **81** J5
Rams Gro, Rom. RM6 **83** E4
Ram St, SW18 **148** E5
Ramulis Dr, Hayes UB4 **102** D4
Ramus Wd Av, Orp. BR6 **207** H5
Rancliffe Gdns, SE9 **156** B4
Rancliffe Rd, E6 **116** B2
Randall Av, NW2 **89** F3
Randall Cl, SW11 **149** H1
Erith DA8 **139** J6
Randall Ct, NW7 **55** G7
Randall Pl, SE10 **134** C7
Randall Rd, SE11 **34** C3
Randall Row, SE11 **34** C2
Randell's Rd, N1 **111** E1
Randisbourne Gdns, SE6 **172** B3
Randle Rd, Rich. TW10 **163** F4
Randlesdown Rd, SE6 **172** A4
Randolph App, E16 **116** A6
Randolph Av, W9 **6** D5
Randolph Cl, Bexh. DA7 **159** J3
Kingston upon Thames KT2 **164** C5
Randolph Cres, W9 **6** C6
Randolph Gdns, NW6 **6** A2
Randolph Gro, Rom. RM6
off Donald Dr **82** C5
Randolph Ho, Croy. CR0 **201** J1
Randolph Ms, W9 **6** D6

Randolph Rd, E17 … 78 B5
W9 … 6 C6
Bromley BR2 … 206 C1
Southall UB1 … 123 F2
Randolph St, NW1 … 92 C7
Randon Cl, Har. HA2 … 67 H2
Ranelagh Av, SW6 … 148 C3
SW13 … 147 G2
Ranelagh Br, W2 *off Gloucester Ter* … 14 B2
Ranelagh Cl, Edg. HA8 … 54 A4
Ranelagh Dr, Edg. HA8 … 54 A4
Twickenham TW1 … 145 E5
★ Ranelagh Gdns, SW3 … 32 B4
Ranelagh Gdns, E11 … 79 J5
SW6 … 148 C3
W4 … 126 C7
W6 … 127 F3
Ilford IG1 … 98 D1
Ranelagh Gdns Mans, SW6 *off Ranelagh Gdns* … 148 B3
Ranelagh Gro, SW1 … 32 C3
Ranelagh Ms, W5 … 125 G2
Ranelagh Pl, N.Mal. KT3 … 182 E5
Ranelagh Rd, E6 … 116 D1
E11 … 96 E4
E15 … 115 E1
N17 … 76 B3
N22 … 75 F1
NW10 … 107 F2
SW1 … 33 G4
W5 … 125 G2
Southall UB1 … 122 D1
Wembley HA0 … 87 G5
Ranfurly Rd, Sutt. SM1 … 198 D2
Rangefield Rd, Brom. BR1 … 172 E5
Rangemoor Rd, N15 … 76 C5
Rangers Rd, E4 … 47 E7
Loughton IG10 … 47 E7
Rangers Sq, SE10 … 154 D1
Rangeworth Pl, Sid. DA15 *off Priestlands Pk Rd* … 175 J3
Rangoon St, EC3 … 21 F4
Rankin Cl, NW9 … 71 E3
Rankine Ho, SE1 *off Bath Ter* … 27 J6
Ranleigh Gdns, Bexh. DA7 … 139 F7
Ranmere St, SW12 *off Ormeley Rd* … 168 B1
Ranmoor Cl, Har. HA1 … 68 A4
Ranmoor Gdns, Har. HA1 … 68 A4
Ranmore Av, Croy. CR0 … 202 C3
Rannoch Cl, Edg. HA8 … 54 B2
Rannoch Rd, W6 … 127 J6
Rannock Av, NW9 … 70 E7
Ranskill Rd, Borwd. WD6 … 38 A1
Ransome's Dock Business Cen, SW11 *off Parkgate Rd* … 129 H7
Ransom Rd, SE7 *off Floyd Rd* … 135 J5
Ransom Wk, SE7 *off Woolwich Rd* … 135 J4
Ranston St, NW1 … 15 G1
Ranulf Rd, NW2 … 90 C4
Ranwell Cl, E3 *off Beale Rd* … 113 J1
Ranwell St, E3 … 113 J1
Ranworth Rd, N9 … 61 F2
Ranyard Cl, Chess. KT9 … 195 J3
Raphael Dr, T.Ditt. KT7 … 180 C7
Raphael St, SW7 … 23 J4
Rashleigh St, SW8 *off Peardon St* … 150 B2
Rasper Rd, N20 … 57 F2
Rastell Av, SW2 … 168 D2
Ratcliffe Cl, SE12 … 155 G7
Ratcliffe Cross St, E1 … 113 G6
Ratcliffe La, E14 … 113 H6
Ratcliffe Orchard, E1 *off Cranford St* … 113 G7
Ratcliff Rd, E7 … 97 J5
Rathbone Mkt, E16 *off Barking Rd* … 115 F5
Rathbone Pl, W1 … 17 H3
Rathbone St, E16 … 115 F5
W1 … 17 G2
Rathcoole Av, N8 … 75 F4
Rathcoole Gdns, N8 … 75 F5
Rathfern Rd, SE6 … 171 J1
Rathgar Av, W13 … 125 E1
Rathgar Cl, N3 … 72 C2
Rathgar Rd, SW9 *off Coldharbour La* … 151 H3
Rathmell Dr, SW4 … 150 D6
Rathmore Rd, SE7 … 135 H5
Rattray Rd, SW2 … 151 G4
Raul Rd, SE15 … 152 D2
Raveley St, NW5 … 92 C4
Raven Cl, NW9 … 71 E2
Raven Ct, E5 *off Stellman Cl* … 94 D3
Ravenet St, SW11 *off Strasburg Rd* … 150 B1
Ravenfield Rd, SW17 … 167 J3
Ravenhill Rd, E13 … 115 J2
Ravenna Rd, SW15 … 148 A5
Ravenoak Way, Chig. IG7 … 65 H5
Ravenor Pk Rd, Grnf. UB6 … 103 H3
Raven Rd, E18 … 79 J2
Raven Row, E1 … 113 E5
Ravensbourne Av, Beck. BR3 … 172 D7
Bromley BR2 … 172 D7
Ravensbourne Business Cen, Kes. BR2 … 206 A4
Ravensbourne Gdns, W13 … 104 E5
Ilford IG5 … 80 D1
Ravensbourne Pk, SE6 … 154 A7
Ravensbourne Pk Cres, SE6 … 153 J7
Ravensbourne Pl, SE13 … 154 B2
Ravensbourne Rd, SE6 … 153 J7
Bromley BR1 … 191 G3
Twickenham TW1 … 145 F6
Ravensbury Av, Mord. SM4 … 185 F5
Ravensbury Ct, Mitch. CR4 *off Ravensbury Gro* … 185 G4
Ravensbury Gro, Mitch. CR4 … 185 G4
Ravensbury La, Mitch. CR4 … 185 G4
Ravensbury Path, Mitch. CR4 … 185 G4
Ravensbury Rd, SW18 … 166 D2
Orpington BR5 … 193 J4
Ravensbury Ter, SW18 … 166 E2
Ravenscar Rd, Brom. BR1 … 172 E4
Surbiton KT6 … 195 J2
Ravens Cl, Brom. BR2 … 191 F2
Enfield EN1 … 44 B2
Surbiton KT6 … 181 G6
Ravenscourt Av, W6 … 127 G4
Ravenscourt Gdns, W6 … 127 G4
Ravenscourt Pk, W6 … 127 G3
Ravenscourt Pl, W6 … 127 H4
Ravenscourt Rd, W6 … 127 H4
Ravenscourt Sq, W6 … 127 G3
Ravenscraig Rd, N11 … 58 B4
Ravenscroft Av, NW11 … 72 C7
Wembley HA9 … 87 J1
Ravenscroft Cl, E16 … 115 G5
Ravenscroft Cres, SE9 … 174 C3
Ravenscroft Pk, Barn. EN5 … 40 A4
Ravenscroft Pt, E9 *off Kenton Rd* … 95 G6
Ravenscroft Rd, E16 … 115 G5
W4 … 126 C4
Beckenham BR3 … 189 F2
Ravenscroft St, E2 … 13 G2
Ravensdale Av, N12 … 57 F4
Ravensdale Gdns, SE19 … 170 A7
Hounslow TW4 … 142 E3
Ravensdale Rd, N16 … 76 C7
Hounslow TW4 … 142 E3
Ravensdon St, SE11 … 35 F4
Ravensfield Cl, Dag. RM9 … 100 D4
Ravensfield Gdns, Epsom KT19 … 197 E5
Ravens Gate Ms, Brom. BR2 *off Meadow Rd* … 191 E2
Ravenshaw St, NW6 … 90 C5
Ravenshill, Chis. BR7 … 192 E1
Ravenshurst Av, NW4 … 71 J4
Ravenside Cl, N18 … 61 G6
Ravenside Retail Pk, N18 … 61 G5
Ravenslea Rd, SW12 … 149 J7
Ravensleigh Gdns, Brom. BR1 *off Pike Cl* … 173 H5
Ravensmead Rd, Brom. BR2 … 172 D7
Ravensmede Way, W4 … 127 F4
Ravens Ms, SE12 *off Ravens Way* … 155 G5
Ravenstone, SE17 … 36 E4
Ravenstone Rd, N8 … 75 F3
NW9 *off West Hendon Bdy* … 71 F6
Ravenstone St, SW12 … 168 A1
Ravens Way, SE12 … 155 G5
Ravenswood, Bex. DA5 … 177 E1
Ravenswood Av, Surb. KT6 … 195 J2
West Wickham BR4 … 204 C1
Ravenswood Ct, Kings.T. KT2 … 164 B6
Ravenswood Cres, Har. HA2 … 85 F2
West Wickham BR4 … 204 C1
Ravenswood Gdns, Islw. TW7 … 144 B1
Ravenswood Pk, Nthwd. HA6 … 50 A6
Ravenswood Rd, E17 … 78 B4
SW12 … 150 B7
Croydon CR0 … 201 H3
Ravensworth Rd, NW10 … 107 H3
SE9 … 174 C4
Ravey St, EC2 … 12 D5
Ravine Gro, SE18 … 137 H6
Rav Pinter Cl, N16 … 76 B7
Rawlings Cl, Beck. BR3 … 190 C5
Orpington BR6 … 207 J5
Rawlings Cres, Wem. HA9 … 88 B3
Rawlings St, SW3 … 31 J1
Rawlins Cl, N3 … 72 B3
South Croydon CR2 … 203 H7
Rawlinson Ho, SE13 *off Mercator Rd* … 154 D4
Rawnsley Av, Mitch. CR4 … 185 G5
Rawreth Wk, N1 *off Basire St* … 111 J1
Rawson Ct, SW11 *off Strasburg Rd* … 150 B1
Rawson St, SW11 *off Alfreda St* … 150 B1
Rawsthorne Cl, E16 *off Kennard St* … 136 C1
Rawstone Wk, E13 … 115 G2
Rawstorne Pl, EC1 … 11 G3
Rawstorne St, EC1 … 11 G3
Ray Cl, Chess. KT9 *off Merritt Gdns* … 195 F6
Raydean Rd, Barn. (New Barn.) EN5 … 40 E5
Raydons Gdns, Dag. RM9 … 101 E5
Raydons Rd, Dag. RM9 … 100 E5
Raydon St, N19 … 92 B2
Rayfield Cl, Brom. BR2 … 192 B6
Rayford Av, SE12 … 155 F7
Ray Gdns, Bark. IG11 … 118 A2
Stanmore HA7 … 53 E5
Rayleas Cl, SE18 … 156 E1
Rayleigh Av, Tedd. TW11 … 162 B6
Rayleigh Cl, N13 *off Rayleigh Rd* … 60 A3
Rayleigh Ct, Kings.T. KT1 … 181 J2
Rayleigh Ri, S.Croy. CR2 … 202 B6
Rayleigh Rd, E16 … 135 H1
N13 … 59 J3
SW19 … 184 C1
Woodford Green IG8 … 63 J6
Ray Lo Rd, Wdf.Grn. IG8 … 63 J6
Ray Massey Way, E6 *off Ron Leighton Way* … 116 B1
Raymead, NW4 *off Tenterden Gro* … 71 J4
Raymead Av, Th.Hth. CR7 … 187 G5
Raymead Pas, Th.Hth. CR7 *off Raymead Av* … 187 G5
Raymere Gdns, SE18 … 137 G7
Raymond Av, E18 … 79 F3
W13 … 124 D3
Raymond Bldgs, WC1 … 18 D1
Raymond Cl, SE26 … 171 F5
Raymond Ct, N10 *off Pembroke Rd* … 58 A7
Raymond Rd, E13 … 97 J7
SW19 … 166 B6
Beckenham BR3 … 189 H4
Ilford IG2 … 81 G7
Raymond Way, Esher (Clay.) KT10 … 194 D6
Raymouth Rd, SE16 … 133 E4
Rayne Ct, E18 … 79 F4
Rayners Cl, Wem. HA0 … 87 G5
Rayners Ct, Har. HA2 … 85 G1
Rayners Cres, Nthlt. UB5 … 102 B3
Rayners Gdns, Nthlt. UB5 … 102 B2
RAYNERS LANE, Har. HA2 … 85 F1
Rayners La, Har. HA2 … 85 H2
Pinner HA5 … 67 F6
Rayners Rd, SW15 … 148 B5
Rayner Twr, E10 … 78 A7
Raynes Av, E11 … 79 J7
RAYNES PARK, SW20 … 183 H3
Raynham, W2 … 15 G4
Raynham Av, N18 … 60 D6
Raynham Rd, N18 … 60 D5
W6 … 127 H4
Raynham Ter, N18 … 60 D5
Raynor Cl, Sthl. UB1 … 123 F1
Raynor Pl, N1 *off Elizabeth Av* … 111 J1
Raynton Cl, Har. HA2 … 85 E1
Ray Rd, W.Mol. KT8 … 179 H5
Rays Av, N18 … 61 F4
Rays Rd, N18 … 61 F4
West Wickham BR4 … 190 C7
Ray St, EC1 … 11 F6
Ray St Br, EC1 … 11 F6
Ray Wk, N7 *off Andover Rd* … 93 F2
Raywood Cl, Hayes (Harling.) UB3 … 121 F7
Reach, The, SE28 … 137 H2
Reachview Cl, NW1 *off Baynes St* … 92 C7
Read Cl, T.Ditt. KT7 … 180 D7
Reading La, E8 … 94 E6
Reading Rd, Nthlt. UB5 … 85 H5
Sutton SM1 … 199 F5
Reading Way, NW7 … 56 A5
Reads Cl, Ilf. IG1 *off Chapel Rd* … 98 E3
Reapers Cl, NW1 *off Crofters Way* … 110 D1
Reapers Way, Islw. TW7 *off Hall Rd* … 144 A5
Reardon Ct, N21 *off Cosgrove Cl* … 59 J2
Reardon Path, E1 … 133 E1
Reardon St, E1 … 132 E1
Reaston St, SE14 … 133 F7
Reckitt Rd, W4 … 126 E5
Record St, SE15 … 133 F6
Recovery St, SW17 … 167 H5
Recreation Av, Rom. RM7 … 83 J5
Recreation Rd, SE26 … 171 G4
Bromley BR2 … 191 F2
Sidcup DA15 *off Woodside Rd* … 175 H3
Southall UB2 … 122 E4
Recreation Way, Mitch. CR4 … 186 D3
Rector St, N1 … 111 J1
Rectory Cl, E4 … 62 A3
N3 … 72 C1
SW20 … 183 J3
Sidcup DA14 … 176 B4
Stanmore HA7 … 53 E6
Surbiton (Long Dit.) KT6 … 195 F1
Rectory Cres, E11 … 79 J6
Rectory Fld Cres, SE7 … 135 J7
Rectory Gdns, N8 … 74 E4
SW4 *off Fitzwilliam Rd* … 150 C3
Northolt UB5 … 103 F1
Rectory Grn, Beck. BR3 … 189 J1
Rectory Gro, SW4 … 150 C3
Croydon CR0 … 201 H2
Hampton TW12 … 161 F4
Rectory La, SW17 … 168 A6
Edgware HA8 … 54 A6
Loughton IG10 … 48 D2
Sidcup DA14 … 176 B4
Stanmore HA7 … 52 E5
Surbiton (Long Dit.) KT6 … 195 E1
Wallington SM6 … 200 C4
Rectory Orchard, SW19 … 166 B4
Rectory Pk Av, Nthlt. UB5 … 103 F3
Rectory Pl, SE18 … 136 D4
Rectory Rd, E12 … 98 C5
E17 … 78 B3
N16 … 94 C3
SW13 … 147 G2
W3 … 126 B1
Beckenham BR3 … 190 A1
Dagenham RM10 … 101 G7
Hayes UB3 … 102 A6
Hounslow TW4 … 142 B1
Keston BR2 … 206 A7
Southall UB2 … 123 F3
Sutton SM1 … 198 D3
Rectory Sq, E1 … 113 G5
Reculver Ms, N18 *off Lyndhurst Rd* … 60 D4
Reculver Rd, SE16 … 133 G5
Red Anchor Cl, SW3 … 31 G6
Redan Pl, W2 … 14 A4
Redan St, W14 … 128 A3
Redan Ter, SE5 *off Flaxman Rd* … 151 J2
Red Barracks Rd, SE18 … 136 C4
Redberry Gro, SE26 … 171 F3
Redbourne Av, N3 … 72 D1
Redbourne Dr, SE28 … 118 D6
REDBRIDGE, Ilf. IG1 … 80 C6
Redbridge Enterprise Cen, Ilf. IG1 … 99 F2
Redbridge Gdns, SE5 … 132 B7
Redbridge La E, Ilf. IG4 … 80 A6
Redbridge La W, E11 … 79 H6
Redbridge Rbt, Ilf. IG4 … 79 J6
Redburn St, SW3 … 31 J5
Redcar Cl, Nthlt. UB5 … 85 H5
Redcar St, SE5 … 131 J7
Redcastle Cl, E1 … 113 F7
Red Cedars Rd, Orp. BR6 … 193 H7
Redchurch St, E2 … 13 F5
Redcliffe Cl, SW5 *off Old Brompton Rd* … 30 A4
Redcliffe Ct, E5 *off Napoleon Rd* … 94 E3
Redcliffe Gdns, SW5 … 30 B4
SW10 … 30 B4
W4 … 126 B7

Redcliffe Gdns, Ilford IG1 98 D1
Redcliffe Ms, SW10 30 B4
Redcliffe Pl, SW10 30 C6
Redcliffe Rd, SW10 30 C4
Redcliffe Sq, SW10 30 B4
Redcliffe St, SW10 30 B5
Redclose Av, Mord. SM4 184 D5
Redclyffe Rd, E6 115 J1
Redcroft Rd, Sthl. UB1 103 J7
Redcross Way, SE1 28 A3
Reddings, The, NW7 55 F3
Reddings Cl, NW7 55 F4
Reddington Ho, N1 10 D1
Reddins Rd, SE15 37 H6
Reddons Rd, Beck. BR3 171 H7
Redenham Ho, SW15
off Tangley Gro 147 F7
Rede Pl, W2
off Chepstow Pl 108 D6
Redesdale Gdns, Islw.
TW7 124 D7
Redesdale St, SW3 31 H5
Redfern Av, Houns. TW4 143 G7
Redfern Rd, NW10 89 E7
SE6 154 C7
Redfield La, SW5 128 D4
Redfield Ms, SW5
off Redfield La 128 D4
Redford Av, Th.Hth. CR7 187 F4
Wallington SM6 200 E6
Redford Wk, N1
off Britannia Row 111 H1
Redgate Dr, Brom. BR2 205 H2
Redgate Ter, SW15 148 B6
Redgrave Cl, Croy. CR0 188 C6
Redgrave Rd, SW15 148 A3
Red Hill, Chis. BR7 174 D5
Redhill Dr, Edg. HA8 70 C2
Redhill St, NW1 8 E3
★ **Red Ho, The**
(William Morris Ho),
Bexh. DA6 158 E4
Red Ho La, Bexh. DA6 158 D4
Red Ho Rd, Croy. CR0 186 D6
Red Ho Sq, N1
off Ashby Gro 93 J7
Redington Gdns, NW3 90 E4
Redington Rd, NW3 90 E4
Redland Gdns, W.Mol.
KT8 *off Dunstable Rd* 179 F4
Redlands Ct, Brom. BR1 173 F7
Redlands Rd, Enf. EN3 45 H1
Redlands Way, SW2 151 F7
Red La, Esher (Clay.)
KT10 194 D6
Redleaf Cl, Belv. DA17 139 G6
Redlees Cl, Islw. TW7 144 D4
Red Lion Business Pk,
Surb. KT6 195 J2
Red Lion Cl, SE17 36 A5
Red Lion Ct, EC4 19 F3
Red Lion Hill, N2 73 G2
Red Lion La, SE18 136 D7
Red Lion Pl, SE18
off Shooters Hill Rd 156 D1
Red Lion Rd, Surb. KT6 195 J2
Red Lion Row, SE17 36 A5
Red Lion Sq, SW18
off Wandsworth
High St 148 D5
WC1 18 C2
Red Lion St, WC1 18 C1
Richmond TW9 145 G5
Red Lion Yd, W1 24 C1
Red Lo Rd, Beck. BR3 190 D6
West Wickham BR4 204 C1
Redman Cl, Nthlt. UB5 102 C2
Redman's Rd, E1 113 F5
Redmead La, E1 29 H2
Redmead Rd, Hayes UB3 121 H4
Redmore Rd, W6 127 H4
Red Oak Cl, Orp. BR6 207 E3
Red Path, E9 95 J6
Red Pl, W1 16 B5
Redpoll Way, Erith DA18 138 D3
Red Post Hill, SE21 152 A5
SE24 152 A4
Redriffe Rd, E13 115 F1
Redriff Est, SE16 133 J3
Redriff Rd, SE16 133 G4
Romford RM7 83 H2
Redroofs Cl, Beck. BR3 190 B1
Red Rover, SW15 147 F3
Redruth Cl, N22 59 F7
Redruth Gdns, Esher
KT10 *off Common Rd* 194 D7
Redruth Rd, E9 113 G1
Red Sq, N16 94 A3
Redstart Cl, E6
off Columbine Av 116 B5
SE14
off Southerngate Way 133 H7
Redstart Mans, Ilf. IG1
off Mill Rd 98 D3
Redston Rd, N8 74 D4
Redvers Rd, N22 75 G2
Redvers St, N1 13 E3
Redwald Rd, E5 95 G4
Redway Dr, Twick. TW2 143 J7
Redwing Ms, SE5
off Vaughan Rd 151 J2
Redwing Path, SE28 137 G2
Redwing Rd, Wall. SM6 201 E7
Redwood Cl, E3 114 A2
N14 *off The Vale* 42 D7
SE16 133 H1
Sidcup DA15 158 A7
Watford WD19 50 C4
Redwood Ct, NW6
off The Avenue 90 B7
Redwood Est, Houns.
TW5 122 B6
Redwood Gdns, E4 46 B6
Redwood Gro, W5
off Northfield Av 125 F3
Redwood Ms, SW4
off Hannington Rd 150 B3
Redwoods, SW15 165 G1
Redwoods Cl, Buck.H. IG9 63 H2
Redwood Wk, Surb. KT6 195 G1
Redwood Way, Barn. EN5 40 A5
Reece Ms, SW7 30 E1
Reed Av, Orp. BR6 207 H3
Reed Cl, E16 115 G5
SE12 155 G5
Reede Gdns, Dag. RM10 101 H5
Reede Rd, Dag. RM10 101 G6
Reede Way, Dag. RM10 101 H6
Reedham Cl, N17 76 E4
Reedham St, SE15 152 D2
Reedholm Vil, N16
off Winston Rd 94 A4
Reed Pl, SW4 150 D4
Reed Rd, N17 76 C2
Reeds Pl, NW1
off Royal Coll St 92 C7
Reedworth St, SE11 35 F2
Ree La Cotts, Loug. IG10
off Englands La 48 D1
Reenglass Rd, Stan. HA7 53 G4
Rees Dr, Stan. HA7 53 H4
Rees Gdns, Croy. CR0 188 C6
Reesland Cl, E12 98 D6
Rees St, N1 111 J1
Reets Fm Cl, NW9 71 E6
Reeves Av, NW9 70 D7
Reeves Cor, Croy. CR0
off Roman Way 201 H2
Reeves Ms, W1 16 B6
Reeves Rd, E3 114 B4
SE18 136 E6
Reflection, The, E16
off Woolwich
Manor Way 136 E2
Reform Row, N17 76 C2
Reform St, SW11 149 J2
Regal Cl, E1 21 J1
W5 105 G5
Regal Ct, N18
off College Cl 60 C5
Regal Cres, Wall. SM6 200 B3
Regal Dr, N11 58 B5
Regal Ho, SW6
off Lensbury Av 149 F2
Ilford IG2
off Royal Cres 81 G6
Regal La, NW1
off Regents Pk Rd 110 A1
Regal Pl, E3
off Coborn St 113 J3
SW6 *off Maxwell Rd* 129 E7
Regal Row, SE15
off Astbury Rd 153 F1
Regal Way, Har. HA3 69 H6
Regan Way, N1 12 D2
Regatta Ho, Tedd. TW11
off Twickenham Rd 162 D4
Regency Cl, W5 105 H6
Chigwell IG7 65 F5
Hampton TW12 161 F5
Regency Ct, E18 79 G2
Sutton SM1
off Brunswick Rd 199 E4
Regency Cres, NW4 72 A2
Regency Ho, SW6
off The Boulevard 149 F1
Regency Lo, Buck.H. IG9 64 A2
Regency Ms, NW10
off High Rd 89 G6
SW9 *off Lothian Rd* 131 H7
Beckenham BR3 190 C1
Isleworth TW7
off Queensbridge Pk 144 B5
Regency Pl, SW1 33 J1
Regency St, NW10 106 E4
SW1 33 H1
Regency Ter, SW7
off Fulham Rd 31 E3
Regency Wk, Croy. CR0 189 H6
Richmond TW10
off Grosvenor Rd 145 H5
Regency Way, Bexh. DA6 158 D3
Regeneration Rd, SE16 133 G4
Regent Cl, N12
off Nether St 57 F5
Harrow HA3 69 H6
Hounslow TW4 142 B1
Regent Gdns, Ilf. IG3 82 A6
Regent Pk, Barn. EN4 40 E1
Regent Pl, SW19
off Haydons Rd 167 E5
W1 17 G5
Croydon CR0
off Grant Rd 202 C1
Regent Rd, SE24 151 H6
Surbiton KT5 181 J5
Regents Av, N13 59 F5
Regents Br Gdns, SW8 34 B7
Regents Cl, S.Croy. CR2 202 B6
Regents Dr, Kes. BR2 206 A5
Woodford Green IG8 64 D6
Regents Ms, NW8 6 D1
REGENT'S PARK, NW1 8 C2
★ **Regent's Park, The**,
NW1 8 A2
Regent's Pk Est, NW1 9 E4
Regents Pk Rd, N3 72 C3
NW1 109 J1
Regents Pk Ter, NW1
off Oval Rd 110 B1
Regent's Pl, SE3 155 G2
Regents Pl, Loug. IG10 48 A7
Regent Sq, E3 114 B3
WC1 10 B4
Belvedere DA17 139 H4
Regents Row, E8 112 D1
Regent St, NW10
off Wellington Rd 108 A3
SW1 17 H6
W1 17 E3
W4 126 A5
Regents Wf, N1 10 C1
Regina Cl, Barn. EN5 40 A3
Reginald Rd, E7 97 G7
SE8 134 A7
Reginald Sq, SE8 134 A7
Regina Pt, SE16
off Renforth St 133 F3
Regina Rd, N4 93 F1
SE25 188 D3
W13 124 D1
Southall UB2 122 E4
Regina Ter, W13 124 D1
Regis Pl, SW2 151 F4
Regis Rd, NW5 92 B5
Regnart Bldgs, NW1 9 G5
Reid Cl, Pnr. HA5 66 A4
Reidhaven Rd, SE18 137 H4
Reigate Av, Sutt. SM1 198 D1
Reigate Rd, Brom. BR1 173 F3
Ilford IG3 99 J2
Reigate Way, Wall. SM6 201 E5
Reighton Rd, E5 94 D3
Reindeer Cl, E13
off Stratford Rd 115 G1
Reinickendorf Av, SE9 157 F5
Reizel Cl, N16 94 C1
Relay Rd, W12 107 J7
Relf Rd, SE15 152 D3
Reliance Sq, EC2 13 E5
Relko Gdns, Sutt. SM1 199 G5
Relton Ms, SW7 23 H5
Rembrandt Cl, E14 134 D3
SW1 32 B2
Rembrandt Ct, Epsom
KT19 197 F6
Rembrandt Rd, SE13 154 E4
Edgware HA8 70 A2
Remington Rd, E6 116 B6
N15 76 A6
Remington St, N1 11 H2
Remnant St, WC2 18 C3
Remus Rd, E3
off Monier Rd 96 A7
Renaissance Ct, Houns.
TW3 *off Prince*
Regent Rd 143 J3
Renaissance Wk, SE10 135 F3
Rendle Cl, Croy. CR0 188 C5
Rendlesham Rd, E5 94 D4
Enfield EN2 43 H1
Renforth St, SE16 133 F2
Renfrew Cl, E6 116 D7
Renfrew Ho, E17
off Sherwood Cl 77 J2
Renfrew Rd, SE11 35 G1
Hounslow TW4 142 D2
Kingston upon Thames
KT2 164 B7
Renmuir St, SW17 167 J6
Rennell St, SE13 154 C3
Rennels Way, Islw. TW7 144 B2
Renness Rd, E17 77 H3
Rennets Cl, SE9 157 H5
Rennets Wd Rd, SE9 157 G5
Rennie Ct, SE1
off Upper Grd 27 G1
Rennie Est, SE16 133 E4
Rennie Ho, SE1
off Bath Ter 27 J6
Rennie St, SE1 27 G1
Renovation, The, E16
off Woolwich
Manor Way 136 E2
Renown Cl, Croy. CR0 201 H1
Romford RM7 83 G1
Rensburg Rd, E17 77 G5
Renshaw Cl, Belv. DA17
off Grove Rd 139 F6
Renters Av, NW4 71 J6
Renwick Ind Est, Bark.
IG11 118 B1
Renwick Rd, Bark. IG11 118 B4
Repens Way, Hayes UB4
off Stipularis Dr 102 D4
Rephidim St, SE1 28 D6
Replingham Rd, SW18 166 C1
Reporton Rd, SW6 148 B1
Repository Rd, SE18 136 C6
Repton Av, Hayes UB3 121 G4
Wembley HA0 87 F4
Repton Cl, Cars. SM5 199 H5
Repton Ct, Beck. BR3 190 B1
Ilford IG5
off Repton Gro 80 C1
Repton Gro, Ilf. IG5 80 C1
Repton Rd, Har. HA3 69 J4
Repton St, E14 113 H6
Repulse Cl, Rom. RM5 83 G1
Reservoir Cl, Th.Hth. CR7 188 A4
Reservoir Rd, N14 42 C5
SE4 153 H2
Resham Cl, Sthl. UB2 122 C3
Resolution Wk, SE18 136 C3
Resolution Way, SE8
off Deptford High St 134 A7
Restell Cl, SE3 135 E6
Restmor Way, Wall. SM6 200 A2
Reston Pl, SW7 22 C4
Restons Cres, SE9 157 G6
Restoration Sq, SW11
off Battersea High St 149 G1
Restormel Cl, Houns.
TW3 143 G5
Retcar Cl, N19
off Dartmouth Pk Hill 92 B2
Retcar Pl, N19 92 B2
Retford St, N1 13 E2
Retingham Way, E4 62 B2
Retreat, The, NW9 70 D5
SW14
off South Worple Way 147 E3
Harrow HA2 67 G7
Surbiton KT5 181 J6
Thornton Heath CR7 188 A4
Worcester Park KT4 197 H3
Retreat Cl, Har. HA3 69 F5
Retreat Pl, E9 95 F6
Retreat Rd, Rich. TW9 145 G5
Reunion Row, E1
off Tobacco Dock 113 E7
Reuters Plaza, E14
off The South
Colonnade 134 B1
Reveley Sq, SE16
off Howland Way 133 H2
Revell Ri, SE18 137 J6
Revell Rd, Kings.T. KT1 182 B1
Sutton SM1 198 C6
Revelon Rd, SE4 153 H4
Revelstoke Rd, SW18 166 C2
Reventlow Rd, SE9 175 F1
Reverdy Rd, SE1 37 H2
Reverend Cl, Har. HA2 85 H3
Revesby Rd, Cars. SM5 185 G6
Review Rd, NW2 89 F2
Dagenham RM10 119 H1
Rewell St, SW6
off King's Rd 129 F7
Rewley Rd, Cars. SM5 185 G6
Rex Pl, W1 16 C6
Reydon Av, E11 79 J6
Reynard Cl, SE4
off Foxwell St 153 H3
Bromley BR1 192 C3
Reynard Dr, SE19 170 C7
Reynard Pl, SE14
off Milton Ct Rd 133 H6
Reynardson Rd, N17 59 J7
Reynolah Gdns, SE7
off Rathmore Rd 135 H5
Reynolds Av, E12 98 D5
Chessington KT9 195 H7
Romford RM6 82 C7
Reynolds Cl, NW11 72 E7
SW19 185 G1
Carshalton SM5 199 J1
Reynolds Ct, E11
off Cobbold Rd 97 F3
Romford RM6 82 D3
Reynolds Dr, Edg. HA8 69 J3
Reynolds Pl, SE3 135 H7
Richmond TW10
off Cambrian Rd 145 J6

Reynolds Rd, SE15 ... 153 F5
W4 ... 126 C3
Hayes UB4 ... 102 C4
New Malden KT3 ... 182 D7
Reynolds Way, Croy. CR0 . 202 B4
Rheidol Ms, N1 ... 11 J1
Rheidol Ter, N1 ... 11 H1
Rheola Cl, N17 ... 76 C1
Rhoda St, E2 ... 13 G5
Rhodes Av, N22 ... 74 C1
Rhodesia Rd, E11 ... 96 D2
SW9 ... 151 E2
Rhodes Moorhouse Ct, Mord. SM4 ... 184 D6
Rhodes St, N7
off Mackenzie Rd ... 93 F5
Rhodeswell Rd, E14 ... 113 H5
Rhodrons Av, Chess. KT9 . 195 H5
Rhondda Gro, E3 ... 113 H3
Rhyl Rd, Grnf. (Perivale) UB6 ... 104 C2
Rhyl St, NW5 ... 92 A6
Rhys Av, N11 ... 58 D7
Rialto Rd, Mitch. CR4 ... 186 A2
Ribble Cl, Wdf.Grn. IG8
off Prospect Rd ... 63 J6
Ribblesdale Av, N11 ... 58 A6
Northolt UB5 ... 85 H6
Ribblesdale Rd, N8 ... 75 F4
SW16 ... 168 B6
Ribbon Dance Ms, SE5
off Camberwell Gro .. 152 A1
Ribchester Av, Grnf. (Perivale) UB6 ... 104 C3
Ribston Cl, Brom. BR2 ... 206 C1
Ricardo Path, SE28
off Byron Cl ... 138 C1
Ricardo St, E14 ... 114 B6
Ricards Rd, SW19 ... 166 C5
Richard Cl, SE18 ... 136 B4
Richard Fell Ho, E12
off Walton Rd ... 98 D4
Richard Foster Cl, E17 ... 77 J7
Richard Ho Dr, E16 ... 116 A6
Richard Robert Res, The, E15 *off Broadway* ... 96 D6
Richards Av, Rom. RM7 ... 83 J5
Richards Cl, Har. HA1 ... 68 D5
Hayes (Harling.) UB3 .. 121 G6
Richardson Cl, E8
off Clarissa St ... 112 C1
Richardson Rd, E15 ... 114 E2
Richardson's Ms, W1 ... 9 F6
Richards Pl, E17 ... 78 A3
SW3 ... 31 H1
Richard St, E1
off Commercial Rd ... 112 E6
Richbell Pl, WC1 ... 18 C1
Richborne Ter, SW8 ... 34 D7
Richborough Ho, E5
off Pembury Rd ... 94 E5
Richborough Rd, NW2 ... 90 A4
Richbourne Ct, W1
off Harrowby St ... 15 H3
Richens Cl, Houns. TW3 .. 144 A2
Riches Rd, Ilf. IG1 ... 99 F2
Richford Gate, W6
off Richford St ... 127 J3
Richford Rd, E15 ... 115 F1
Richford St, W6 ... 127 J2
Rich Ind Est, SE1 ... 29 E6
Richlands Av, Epsom KT17 ... 197 G4
Rich La, SW5 ... 30 A4
RICHMOND, TW9 & TW10 ... 145 H6
Richmond Av, E4 ... 62 D5
N1 ... 111 F1
NW10 ... 89 J6
SW20 ... 184 B1
Feltham TW14 ... 141 H6
Richmond Br, Rich. TW9 .. 145 G6
Twickenham TW1 ... 145 G6
Richmond Bldgs, W1 ... 17 H4
Richmond Circ, Rich. TW9 ... 145 H4
Richmond Cl, E17 ... 77 J6
Borehamwood WD6 ... 38 D5
Richmond Ct, Mitch. CR4
off Phipps Br Rd ... 185 G3
Richmond Cres, E4 ... 62 D5
N1 ... 111 F1
N9 ... 60 D1
Richmond Dr, Wdf.Grn. IG8 ... 64 D7
Richmond Gdns, NW4 ... 71 G5
Harrow HA3 ... 52 C6
Richmond Grn, Croy. CR0 ... 201 E3
Richmond Gro, N1 ... 93 H7
Surbiton KT5
off Ewell Rd ... 181 J6
Richmond Hill, Rich. TW10 ... 145 H6
Richmond Hill Ct, Rich. TW10 ... 145 H6
Richmond Ho, NW1
off Park Village E ... 9 E2
Richmond Ms, W1 ... 17 H4
Teddington TW11
off Broad St ... 162 C6
★ **Richmond Park**, Rich. TW10 ... 164 A1
Richmond Pk, Kings.T. KT2 ... 164 A1
Loughton IG10
off Fallow Flds ... 48 A7
Richmond TW10 ... 164 A1
Richmond Pk Rd, SW14 .. 146 C5
Kingston upon Thames KT2 ... 163 H7
Richmond Pl, SE18 ... 137 F4
Richmond Rd, E4 ... 62 D1
E7 ... 97 H5
E8 ... 94 C7
E11 ... 96 D2
N2 ... 73 F2
N11 ... 58 E6
N15 ... 76 B6
SW20 ... 183 H1
W5 ... 125 H2
Barnet (New Barn.) EN5 ... 41 E5
Croydon CR0 ... 200 E3
Ilford IG1 ... 99 F3
Isleworth TW7 ... 144 D3
Kingston upon Thames KT2 ... 163 G5
Thornton Heath CR7 .. 187 H3
Twickenham TW1 ... 145 F6
Richmond St, E13 ... 115 G2
Richmond Ter, SW1 ... 26 A3
Richmond Way, E11 ... 97 G2
W12 ... 128 A2
W14 ... 128 A3
Richmount Gdns, SE3 ... 155 G3
Rich St, E14 ... 113 J7
Rickard Cl, NW4 ... 71 H4
SW2 ... 169 F1
West Drayton UB7 ... 120 A3
Rickards Cl, Surb. KT6 ... 195 H1
Rickett St, SW6 ... 128 D6
Rickman St, E1
off Mantus Rd ... 113 F3
Rickmansworth Rd, Pnr. HA5 ... 66 B2
Rick Roberts Way, E15 ... 114 C1
Rickthorne Rd, N19 ... 92 E2
Rickyard Path, SE9 ... 156 B4
Ridding La, Grnf. UB6 ... 86 C5
Riddons Rd, SE12 ... 173 J3
Ride, The, Brent. TW8 ... 125 E5
Enfield EN3 ... 45 F3
Rideout St, SE18 ... 136 C4
Rider Cl, Sid. DA15 ... 157 H6
Ridgdale St, E3 ... 114 B2
Ridge, The, Barn. EN5 ... 40 C5
Bexley DA5 ... 159 F7
Orpington BR6 ... 207 G2
Surbiton KT5 ... 182 A5
Twickenham TW2 ... 144 A7
Ridge Av, N21 ... 43 J7
Ridgebrook Rd, SE3 ... 155 J4
Ridge Cl, NW4 ... 72 A2
NW9 ... 70 D4
SE28 ... 137 G2
Ridge Crest, Enf. EN2 ... 43 F1
Ridgecroft Cl, Bex. DA5 .. 177 J1
Ridge Hill, NW11 ... 90 B1
Ridgemead Cl, N14 ... 59 E2
Ridgemont Gdns, Edg. HA8 ... 54 C4
Ridgemount Av, Croy. CR0 ... 203 G1
Ridgemount Cl, SE20 ... 170 E7
Ridgemount Gdns, Enf. EN2 ... 43 H2
Ridge Rd, N8 ... 75 F6
N21 ... 59 J1
NW2 ... 90 C3
Mitcham CR4 ... 168 B7
Sutton SM3 ... 198 B1
Ridgeview Cl, Barn. EN5 .. 40 A6
Ridgeview Rd, N20 ... 57 E3
Ridge Way, SE19
off Vicars Oak Rd ... 170 B6
Ridgeway, SE28
off Pettman Cres ... 137 G4
Bromley BR2 ... 205 G2
Ridge Way, Felt. TW13 ... 160 E3
Ridgeway, Wdf.Grn. IG8 ... 63 J4
Ridgeway, The, E4 ... 62 B2
N3 ... 56 E7
N11 ... 57 J4
N14 ... 59 E2
NW7 ... 55 G4
NW9 ... 70 E4
NW11 ... 90 C1
W3 ... 126 A2
Croydon CR0 ... 201 F3
Enfield EN2 ... 43 G1
Harrow (Kenton) HA3 .. 69 F6
Ridgeway, The, Harrow (N.Har.) HA2 ... 67 G6
Ruislip HA4 ... 66 A7
Stanmore HA7 ... 53 F6
Ridgeway Av, Barn. EN4 .. 41 J6
Ridgeway Cres, Orp. BR6 . 207 H3
Ridgeway Cres Gdns, Orp. BR6 ... 207 H2
Ridgeway Dr, Brom. BR1 . 173 H4
Ridgeway E, Sid. DA15 ... 157 J5
Ridgeway Gdns, N6 ... 74 C7
Ilford IG4 ... 80 B5
Ridgeway Rd, SW9 ... 151 H3
Isleworth TW7 ... 124 B7
Ridgeway Rd N, Islw. TW7 ... 124 B6
Ridgeway Wk, Nthlt. UB5
off Arnold Rd ... 85 E6
Ridgeway W, Sid. DA15 .. 157 H5
Ridgewell Cl, N1
off Basire St ... 111 J1
SE26 ... 171 J4
Dagenham RM10 ... 119 H1
Ridgmount Gdns, WC1 ... 9 H6
Ridgmount Pl, WC1 ... 17 H1
Ridgmount Rd, SW18 ... 149 E5
Ridgmount St, WC1 ... 17 H1
Ridgway, SW19 ... 166 A6
Ridgway, The, Sutt. SM2 . 199 G7
Ridgway Gdns, SW19 ... 166 A6
Ridgway Pl, SW19 ... 166 B6
Ridgwell Rd, E16 ... 115 J5
Riding, The, NW11
off Golders Grn Rd ... 72 C7
Riding Ho St, W1 ... 17 F2
Ridings, The, E11
off Malcolm Way ... 79 G5
W5 ... 105 J4
Sunbury-on-Thames TW16 ... 178 A1
Surbiton KT5 ... 182 A5
Ridings Av, N21 ... 43 H4
Ridings Cl, N6
off Hornsey La Gdns .. 74 C7
Ridley Av, W13 ... 124 E3
Ridley Cl, Bark. IG11 ... 99 J7
Ridley Rd, E7 ... 97 J4
E8 ... 94 C5
NW10 ... 107 G2
SW19 ... 166 E7
Bromley BR2 ... 191 F3
Welling DA16 ... 158 B1
Ridsdale Rd, SE20 ... 188 E1
Riefield Rd, SE9 ... 157 F4
Riesco Dr, Croy. CR0 ... 203 F6
Riffel Rd, NW2 ... 89 J5
Rifle Ct, SE11 ... 35 F5
Rifle St, E14 ... 114 B5
Riga Ms, E1
off Commercial Rd ... 21 H3
Rigault Rd, SW6 ... 148 B2
Rigby Cl, Croy. CR0 ... 201 G3
Rigby La, Hayes UB3 ... 121 G2
Rigby Ms, Ilf. IG1 ... 98 D2
Rigden St, E14 ... 114 B6
Rigeley Rd, NW10 ... 107 G3
Rigg App, E10 ... 95 G1
Rigge Pl, SW4 ... 150 D4
Riggindale Rd, SW16 ... 168 D5
Riley Rd, SE1 ... 29 E5
Riley St, SW10 ... 31 E7
Rinaldo Rd, SW12 ... 150 B7
Ring, The, W2 ... 15 G5
Ring Cl, Brom. BR1 ... 173 H7
Ringcroft St, N7 ... 93 G5
Ringers Rd, Brom. BR1 ... 191 G3
Ringford Rd, SW18 ... 148 C5
Ringlet Cl, E16 ... 115 H5
Ringlewell Cl, Enf. EN1
off Central Av ... 44 E2
Ringmer Av, SW6 ... 148 B1
Ringmer Gdns, N19 ... 93 E2
Ringmer Ho, SE22
off Pytchley Rd ... 152 B3
Ringmer Pl, N21 ... 44 A5
Ringmer Way, Brom. BR1 . 192 C5
Ringmore Ri, SE23 ... 153 E7
Ringmore Vw, SE23
off Ringmore Ri ... 153 E7
Ring Rd, W12 ... 107 J7
Ringslade Rd, N22 ... 75 F2
Ringstead Rd, SE6 ... 154 B7
Sutton SM1 ... 199 G4
Ringway, N11 ... 58 C6
Southall UB2 ... 123 E5
Ringwold Cl, Beck. BR3 .. 171 H7
Ringwood Av, N2 ... 73 J2
Croydon CR0 ... 187 E7
Ringwood Cl, Pnr. HA5 ... 66 C3
Ringwood Gdns, E14
off Inglewood Cl ... 134 A4
SW15 ... 165 G2
Ringwood Rd, E17 ... 77 J6
Ringwood Way, N21 ... 59 H1
Hampton (Hmptn H.) TW12 ... 161 G4
Ripley Cl, Brom. BR1 ... 192 C5
Croydon (New Adgtn) CR0 ... 204 C6
Ripley Gdns, SW14 ... 146 D3
Sutton SM1 ... 199 F4
Ripley Ms, E11 ... 78 E6
Ripley Rd, E16 ... 115 J6
Belvedere DA17 ... 139 G4
Enfield EN2 ... 43 J1
Hampton TW12 ... 161 G7
Ilford IG3 ... 99 J2
Ripley Vil, W5
off Castlebar Rd ... 105 F6
Riplington Ct, SW15 ... 147 G7
Ripon Cl, Nthlt. UB5 ... 85 G5
Ripon Gdns, Chess. KT9 . 195 G5
Ilford IG1 ... 80 B6
Ripon Rd, N9 ... 44 E7
N17 ... 76 A3
SE18 ... 136 E6
Ripon Way, Borwd. WD6 .. 38 C5
Rippersley Rd, Well. DA16 ... 158 A1
Ripple Rd, Bark. IG11 ... 99 F7
Dagenham RM9 ... 118 B1
Rippleside Commercial Est, Bark. IG11 ... 118 C2
Ripplevale Gro, N1 ... 93 F7
Rippolson Rd, SE18 ... 137 J5
Risborough, SE17
off Deacon Way ... 35 J1
Risborough Dr, Wor.Pk. KT4 ... 183 G7
Risborough St, SE1 ... 27 H3
Risdon St, SE16 ... 133 F2
Rise, The, E11 ... 79 G5
N13 ... 59 G4
NW7 ... 55 F6
NW10 ... 88 D4
Bexley DA5 ... 158 C7
Buckhurst Hill IG9 ... 48 A7
Edgware HA8 ... 54 B5
Greenford UB6 ... 86 D5
Risedale Rd, Bexh. DA7 .. 159 H3
Riseholme Ho, SE22
off Albrighton Rd ... 152 B3
Riseldine Rd, SE23 ... 153 H6
Risinghill St, N1 ... 10 D1
Risingholme Cl, Har. HA3 . 68 B1
Risingholme Rd, Har. HA3 . 68 B2
Risings, The, E17 ... 78 D4
Rising Sun Ct, EC1 ... 19 H2
Risley Av, N17 ... 75 J1
Rita Rd, SW8 ... 34 B6
Ritches Rd, N15 ... 75 J5
Ritchie Rd, Croy. CR0 ... 189 E6
Ritchie St, N1 ... 11 F1
Ritchings Av, E17 ... 77 H4
Ritherdon Rd, SW17 ... 168 A2
Ritson Rd, E8 ... 94 D6
Ritter St, SE18 ... 136 D6
Ritz Par, W5
off Connell Cres ... 105 J4
Rivaz Pl, E9 ... 95 F6
Rivenhall Gdns, E18 ... 79 F4
River App, Edg. HA8 ... 70 C1
River Av, N13 ... 59 H3
Thames Ditton KT7 ... 180 D7
River Bk, N21 ... 43 J7
East Molesey KT8 ... 180 B3
Thames Ditton KT7 ... 180 C5
West Molesey KT8 ... 179 F3
Riverbank Rd, Brom. BR1 ... 173 G3
Riverbank Way, Brent. TW8 ... 125 F6
River Barge Cl, E14
off Stewart St ... 134 C2
River Brent Business Pk, W7 ... 124 B3
River Cl, E11 ... 79 J6
Southall UB2 ... 123 J2
Surbiton KT6
off Catherine Rd ... 181 G5
River Ct, SE1 ... 19 G6
Rivercourt Rd, W6 ... 127 H4
River Crane Wk, Felt. TW13 ... 160 D1
Hounslow TW4 ... 160 D1
River Crane Way, Felt. TW13
off Watermill Way ... 161 F2
Riverdale, SE13
off Lewisham High St . 154 C3
Riverdale Cl, Bark. IG11 .. 118 B4
Riverdale Dr, SW18
off Knaresborough Dr . 166 E1
Riverdale Gdns, Twick. TW1 ... 145 F6
Riverdale Rd, SE18 ... 137 J5
Bexley DA5 ... 159 F7
Erith DA8 ... 139 H5
Feltham TW13 ... 161 E4
Twickenham TW1 ... 145 F6
Riverdene, Edg. HA8 ... 54 C3
Riverdene Rd, Ilf. IG1 ... 98 D3

River Front, Enf. EN1 .... 44 A3
River Gdns, Cars. SM5 .... 200 A2
Feltham TW14 .... 142 B5
River Gro Pk, Beck. BR3 .... 189 J1
Riverhead Cl, E17 .... 77 G2
Riverhill, Wor.Pk. KT4 .... 196 D2
Riverhill Ms, Wor.Pk. KT4 .... 196 D3
River La, Rich. TW10 .... 163 G1
Rivermead, E.Mol. KT8 .... 179 J3
Kingston upon Thames KT1 .... 181 G5
Rivermead Cl, Tedd. TW11 .... 163 E5
Rivermead Ct, SW6 .... 148 C3
Rivermead Ho, E9 *off Kingsmead Way* 95 H5
Rivermead Rd, N18 .... 61 G6
Rivermeads Av, Twick. TW2 .... 161 G3
Rivermill, SW1 .... 33 J4
Rivernook Cl, Walt. KT12 .... 178 C5
River Pk Gdns, Brom. BR2 .... 172 D7
River Pk Rd, N22 .... 75 F2
River Pl, N1 .... 93 J7
River Reach, Tedd. TW11 .... 163 F5
River Rd, Bark. IG11 .... 117 H2
Buckhurst Hill IG9 .... 64 B1
River Rd Business Pk, Bark. IG11 .... 117 J3
Riversdale Rd, N5 .... 93 H3
Thames Ditton KT7 .... 180 D5
Riversfield Rd, Enf. EN1 .... 44 B3
Rivers Ho, Brent. TW8 *off Chiswick High Rd* 126 A5
Riverside, NW4 .... 71 H7
SE7 .... 135 H3
Richmond TW9, TW10 *off Water La* 145 G5
Twickenham TW1 .... 162 E1
Riverside, The, E.Mol. KT8 .... 180 A3
Riverside Av, E.Mol. KT8 .... 180 A5
Riverside Business Cen, SW18 .... 166 E1
Riverside Cl, E5 .... 95 F1
W7 .... 104 B4
Kingston upon Thames KT1 .... 181 G4
Wallington SM6 .... 200 B3
Riverside Ct, E4 *off Chelwood Cl* 46 B6
SW8 .... 33 J5
Riverside Dr, NW11 .... 72 B6
W4 .... 126 E7
Mitcham CR4 .... 185 H5
Richmond TW10 .... 162 E2
Riverside Gdns, N3 .... 72 B3
W6 .... 127 H5
Enfield EN2 .... 43 J2
Wembley HA0 .... 105 H2
Riverside Ind Est, Bark. IG11 .... 118 A3
Enfield EN3 .... 45 H6
Riverside Mans, E1 *off Milk Yd* 113 F7
Riverside Pl, Stai. (Stanw.) TW19 .... 140 A6
Riverside Rd, E15 .... 114 C2
N15 .... 76 D6
SW17 .... 167 E4
Sidcup DA14 .... 177 E3
Staines (Stanw.) TW19 .... 140 A5
Riverside Twr, SW6 .... 149 F2
Riverside Wk, E14 *off Ferry St* 134 C5
Bexley DA5 .... 158 C7
Isleworth TW7 .... 144 B3
Kingston upon Thames KT1 *off High St* 181 G3
Loughton IG10 .... 48 E6
West Wickham BR4 *off The Alders* 204 B1
Riverside Yd, SW17 .... 167 F4
Riverstone Cl, Har. HA2 .... 86 A1
Riverstone Ct, Kings.T. KT2 *off Queen Elizabeth Rd* 181 J1
River St, EC1 .... 11 E3
River Ter, W6 *off Crisp Rd* 127 J5
Riverton Cl, W9 .... 108 C3
River Vw, Enf. EN2 *off Chase Side* 43 J3
Riverview Gdns, SW13 .... 127 H6
Twickenham TW1 .... 162 C2
Riverview Gro, W4 .... 126 B6
River Vw Hts, SE16 .... 29 H3
Riverview Pk, SE6 .... 172 A2
Riverview Rd, W4 .... 126 B7
Epsom KT19 .... 196 C4
River Wk, E4 *off Winchester Rd* 62 C7
Walton-on-Thames KT12 .... 178 A6
Riverwalk Business Pk, Enf. EN3 .... 45 J3
Riverwalk Rd, Enf. EN3 .... 45 J4
Riverway, N13 .... 59 G5
River Way, SE10 .... 135 F3
Epsom KT19 .... 196 D5
Loughton IG10 .... 48 D6
Twickenham TW2 .... 161 H2
Riverwood La, Chis. BR7 .... 193 G1
Rivet Ho, SE1 .... 37 G3
Rivington Av, Wdf.Grn. IG8 .... 80 A2
Rivington Ct, NW10 .... 107 G1
Dagenham RM10 *off Reede Way* 101 H6
Rivington Cres, NW7 .... 55 F7
Rivington Pl, EC2 .... 12 E4
Rivington St, EC2 .... 12 D4
Rivington Wk, E8 *off Wilde Cl* 112 D1
Rivulet Rd, N17 .... 59 J7
Rixon Ho, SE18 .... 137 E6
Rixon St, N7 .... 93 G3
Rixsen Rd, E12 .... 98 B5
Roach Rd, E3 .... 96 A7
Roads Pl, N19 .... 93 E2
Roan St, SE10 .... 134 C6
Robarts Cl, Pnr. HA5 .... 66 B5
Robb Rd, Stan. HA7 .... 52 D6
Robert Adam St, W1 .... 16 B3
Roberta St, E2 .... 13 H3
Robert Burns Ms, SE24 *off Mayall Rd* 151 H5
Robert Cl, W9 .... 6 D6
Chigwell IG7 .... 65 J5
Robert Dashwood Way, SE17 .... 35 J2
Robert Keen Cl, SE15 *off Cicely Rd* 152 D1
Robert Lowe Cl, SE14 .... 133 G7
Roberton Dr, Brom. BR1 .... 191 J1
Robert Owen Ho, SW6 .... 148 A1
Robertsbridge Rd, Cars. SM5 .... 199 F1
Roberts Cl, SE9 .... 175 G1
SE16 .... 133 G2
Barking IG11 *off Tanner St* 99 F6
Sutton SM3 .... 198 A7
Thornton Heath CR7 *off Kitchener Rd* 188 A3
West Drayton UB7 .... 120 B1
Roberts Ms, SW1 .... 24 B6
Robertson Rd, E15 .... 114 C1
Robertson St, SW8 .... 150 B3
Robert's Pl, EC1 .... 11 F5
Roberts Pl, Dag. RM10 .... 101 G6
Robert Sq, SE13 .... 154 C4
Roberts Rd, E17 .... 78 B1
NW7 .... 56 B6
Belvedere DA17 .... 139 G5
Robert St, E16 .... 136 E1
NW1 .... 8 E4
SE18 .... 137 G4
WC2 .... 18 B6
Croydon CR0 *off High St* 201 J3
Robert Sutton Ho, E1 *off Tarling St* 113 F6
Robeson St, E3 *off Ackroyd Dr* 113 J5
Robeson Way, Borwd. WD6 .... 38 C1
Robina Cl, Bexh. DA6 .... 158 D4
Robin Cl, NW7 .... 54 E3
Hampton TW12 .... 161 E5
Robin Ct, SE16 .... 37 H1
Wallington SM6 *off Carew Rd* 200 C6
Robin Cres, E6 .... 116 A5
Robin Gro, N6 .... 92 A2
Brentford TW8 .... 125 F6
Harrow HA3 .... 69 J6
Robin Hill Dr, Chis. BR7 .... 174 B6
Robin Hood, SW15 .... 165 E3
Robinhood Cl, Mitch. CR4 .... 186 C3
Robin Hood Dr, Har. HA3 .... 52 C7
Robin Hood Gdns, E14 *off Woolmore St* 114 C7
Robin Hood La, E14 .... 114 C7
SW15 .... 164 E4
Bexleyheath DA6 .... 159 E5
Robinhood La, Mitch. CR4 .... 186 C3
Robin Hood La, Sutt. SM1 .... 198 D5
Robin Hood Rd, SW19 .... 165 H5
Robin Hood Way, SW15 .... 165 E4
SW20 .... 165 E4
Greenford UB6 .... 86 C6
Robin Ho, NW8 *off Newcourt St* 7 G2
Robinia Cl, SE20 *off Sycamore Gro* 188 D1
Ilford IG6 .... 65 H6
Robinia Cres, E10 .... 96 B2
Robin La, NW4 .... 72 A3
Robins Ct, SE12 .... 173 J3
Robinscroft Ms, SE10 *off Sparta St* 154 B1
Robins Gro, W.Wick. BR4 .... 205 G3
Robinson Cl, E11 .... 97 E3
Enfield EN2 .... 43 J3
Robinson Cres, Bushey (Bushey Hth) WD23 .... 51 J1
Robinson Ho, W10 *off Bramley Rd* 108 A6
Robinson Rd, E2 .... 113 F2
SW17 .... 167 H6
Dagenham RM10 .... 101 G4
Robinsons Cl, W13 .... 104 D5
Robinson St, SW3 .... 31 J5
Robinwood Pl, SW15 .... 164 D4
Robsart St, SW9 .... 151 F2
Robson Av, NW10 .... 107 G1
Robson Cl, E6 *off Linton Gdns* 116 B6
Enfield EN2 .... 43 H2
Robson Rd, SE27 .... 169 H3
Rocastle Rd, SE4 .... 153 H5
Roch Av, Edg. HA8 .... 69 J2
Rochdale Rd, E17 .... 78 A7
SE2 .... 138 B5
Rochdale Way, SE8 *off Octavius St* 134 A7
Rochelle Cl, SW11 .... 149 G4
Rochelle St, E2 .... 13 F4
Rochemont Wk, E8 *off Pownall Rd* 112 C1
Roche Rd, SW16 .... 187 F1
Rochester Av, E13 .... 115 J1
Bromley BR1 .... 191 H2
Rochester Cl, SW16 .... 169 E7
Enfield EN1 .... 44 B1
Sidcup DA15 .... 158 B6
Rochester Dr, Bex. DA5 .... 159 F6
Pinner HA5 .... 66 D5
Rochester Gdns, Croy. CR0 .... 202 B3
Ilford IG1 .... 80 C7
Rochester Ms, NW1 .... 92 C7
Rochester Pl, NW1 .... 92 C6
Rochester Rd, NW1 .... 92 C6
Carshalton SM5 .... 199 J4
Rochester Row, SW1 .... 33 G1
Rochester Sq, NW1 .... 92 C7
Rochester St, SW1 .... 25 H6
Rochester Ter, NW1 .... 92 C6
Rochester Wk, SE1 .... 28 B1
Rochester Way, SE3 .... 155 H1
SE9 .... 156 C3
Rochester Way Relief Rd, SE3 .... 155 H1
SE9 .... 156 B4
Roche Wk, Cars. SM5 .... 185 G6
Rochford Av, Loug. IG10 .... 49 F3
Romford RM6 .... 82 C5
Rochford Cl, E6 *off Boleyn Rd* 116 A2
Rochford Grn, Loug. IG10 .... 49 F3
Rochford St, NW5 .... 91 J5
Rochford Wk, E8 *off Wilman Gro* 94 D7
Rochford Way, Croy. CR0 .... 186 E6
Rock Av, SW14 *off South Worple Way* 146 D3
Rockbourne Rd, SE23 .... 171 G1
Rock Cl, Mitch. CR4 .... 185 G2
Rockells Pl, SE22 .... 153 E6
Rockford Av, Grnf. (Perivale) UB6 .... 104 D2
Rock Gdns, Dag. RM10 .... 101 H5
Rock Gro Way, SE16 .... 37 J1
Rockhall Rd, NW2 .... 90 A4
Rockhall Way, NW2 *off Midland Ter* 90 A3
Rockhampton Cl, SE27 .... 169 G4
Rockhampton Rd, SE27 .... 169 G4
South Croydon CR2 .... 202 B6
Rock Hill, SE26 .... 170 C4
Rockingham Cl, SW15 .... 147 F4
Rockingham Est, SE1 .... 27 J6
Rockingham St, SE1 .... 27 J6
Rockland Rd, SW15 .... 148 B4
Rocklands Dr, Stan. HA7 .... 69 E2
Rockley Rd, W14 .... 128 A2
Rockmount Rd, SE18 .... 137 J5
SE19 .... 170 A6
Rocks La, SW13 .... 147 G1
Rock St, N4 .... 93 G2
Rockware Av, Grnf. UB6 .... 104 A1
Rockways, Barn. EN5 .... 39 F6
Rockwell Gdns, SE19 .... 170 B5
Rockwell Rd, Dag. RM10 .... 101 H5
Rockwood Pl, W12 .... 127 J2
Rocliffe St, N1 .... 11 H2
Rocombe Cres, SE23 .... 153 F7
Rocque La, SE3 .... 155 F3
Rodborough Rd, NW11 .... 90 D1
Roden Ct, N6 .... 74 D7
Roden Gdns, Croy. CR0 .... 188 B6
Rodenhurst Rd, SW4 .... 150 C6
Roden St, N7 .... 93 F3
Ilford IG1 .... 98 D3
Roderick Rd, NW3 .... 91 J4
Roding Av, Wdf.Grn. IG8 .... 64 B6
Roding Gdns, Loug. IG10 .... 48 B6
Roding La, Buck.H. IG9 .... 64 B1
Chigwell IG7 .... 64 D1
Roding La N, Wdf.Grn. IG8 .... 80 A2
Roding La S, Ilf. IG4 .... 80 A4
Woodford Green IG8 .... 80 A4
Roding Ms, E1 .... 29 J1
Roding Rd, E5 .... 95 G4
E6 .... 116 E5
Loughton IG10 .... 48 B5
Rodings, The, Wdf.Grn. IG8 .... 63 J6
Rodings Row, Barn. EN5 *off Leecroft Rd* 40 B5
Roding Trd Est, Bark. IG11 .... 98 E7
Roding Vw, Buck.H. IG9 .... 64 A1
Rodmarton St, W1 .... 16 A2
Rodmell Cl, Hayes UB4 .... 102 E4
Rodmell Slope, N12 .... 56 C5
Rodmere St, SE10 *off Trafalgar Rd* 135 E5
Rodmill La, SW2 .... 151 E7
Rodney Cl, Croy. CR0 .... 201 H1
New Malden KT3 .... 182 E5
Pinner HA5 .... 66 E7
Rodney Ct, W9 .... 6 D5
Rodney Gdns, Pnr. HA5 .... 66 B5
West Wickham BR4 .... 205 G4
Rodney Pl, E17 .... 77 H2
SE17 .... 36 A1
SW19 .... 185 F1
Rodney Rd, E11 .... 79 H4
SE17 .... 36 A1
Mitcham CR4 .... 185 H2
New Malden KT3 .... 182 E5
Twickenham TW2 .... 143 G6
Rodney St, N1 .... 10 D1
Rodney Way, Rom. RM7 .... 83 G1
Rodway Rd, SW15 .... 147 G7
Bromley BR1 .... 191 H1
Rodwell Cl, Ruis. HA4 .... 84 C1
Rodwell Pl, Edg. HA8 *off Whitchurch La* 54 A6
Rodwell Rd, SE22 .... 152 C6
Roebourne Way, E16 .... 136 D2
Roebuck Cl, Felt. TW13 .... 160 B4
Roebuck La, N17 *off High Rd* 60 C6
Buckhurst Hill IG9 .... 47 J7
Roebuck Rd, Chess. KT9 .... 196 A5
Roedean Av, Enf. EN3 .... 45 F1
Roedean Cl, Enf. EN3 .... 45 F1
Roedean Cres, SW15 .... 146 E6
Roe End, NW9 .... 70 C4
Roe Grn, NW9 .... 70 C5
ROEHAMPTON, SW15 .... 147 G5
Roehampton Cl, SW15 .... 147 G4
Roehampton Dr, Chis. BR7 .... 175 F6
Roehampton Gate, SW15 .... 146 E6
Roehampton High St, SW15 .... 147 H7
Roehampton La, SW15 .... 147 G4
Roehampton Vale, SW15 .... 165 E3
Roe La, NW9 .... 70 B4
Roe Way, Wall. SM6 .... 201 E6
Roffey St, E14 .... 134 C2
Rogate Ho, E5 *off Muir Rd* 94 E3
Roger Dowley Ct, E2 .... 113 F2
Rogers Est, E2 *off Globe Rd* 113 F3
Rogers Gdns, Dag. RM10 .... 101 G5
Rogers Ho, SW1 *off Page St* 33 J1
Rogers Rd, E16 .... 115 F6
SW17 .... 167 G4
Dagenham RM10 .... 101 G5
Roger St, WC1 .... 10 D6
Rogers Wk, N12 *off Holden Rd* 57 E3
Rojack Rd, SE23 .... 171 G1
Rokeby Gdns, Wdf.Grn. IG8 .... 79 G1
Rokeby Pl, SW20 .... 165 H7
Rokeby Rd, SE4 .... 153 J2
Rokeby St, E15 .... 114 E1
Rokesby Cl, Well. DA16 .... 157 G2
Rokesby Pl, Wem. HA0 .... 87 G5
Rokesly Av, N8 .... 74 E5
Roland Gdns, SW7 .... 30 D3
Feltham TW13 .... 161 E3
Roland Ms, E1 *off Stepney Grn* 113 G5
Roland Rd, E17 .... 78 D4
Roland Way, SE17 .... 36 C4
SW7 .... 30 D3
Worcester Park KT4 .... 197 F2
Roles Gro, Rom. RM6 .... 82 D4

Rolfe Cl, Barn. EN4 41 H4
Rolinsden Way, Kes. BR2 206 A4
Rollesby Rd, Chess. KT9 196 A6
Rollesby Way, SE28 118 C7
Rolleston Av, Orp. BR5 192 E6
Rolleston Cl, Orp. BR5 193 E7
Rolleston Rd, S.Croy. CR2 202 A7
Roll Gdns, Ilf. IG2 80 D5
Rollins St, SE15 133 F6
Rollit Cres, Houns. TW3 143 G5
Rollit St, N7 *off Hornsey Rd* 93 G5
Rolls Bldgs, EC4 19 E3
Rollscourt Av, SE24 151 J5
Rolls Pk Av, E4 62 A6
Rolls Pk Rd, E4 62 B5
Rolls Pk Rbt, Chig. IG7 49 G7
Rolls Pas, EC4 18 E3
Rolls Rd, SE1 37 G3
Rolls Royce Cl, Wall. SM6 200 E7
Rolt St, SE8 133 H6
Rolvenden Gdns, Brom. BR1 174 A7
Rolvenden Pl, N17 60 D7
Roman Cl, W3 *off Avenue Gdns* 126 B2
Feltham TW14 142 C5
Romanfield Rd, SW2 151 F7
Romanhurst Av, Brom. BR2 191 E4
Romanhurst Gdns, Brom. BR2 190 E4
Roman Ind Est, Croy. CR0 188 B7
Roman Ri, SE19 170 A6
Roman Rd, E2 113 F3
E3 113 H2
E6 116 B4
N10 58 B7
NW2 89 J3
W4 127 E4
Ilford IG1 99 E6
Roman Sq, SE28 138 A1
Roman Way, N7 93 F6
SE15 *off Clifton Way* 133 F7
Croydon CR0 201 H2
Enfield EN1 44 C5
Roman Way Ind Est, N1 *off Offord St* 93 F7
Romany Gdns, E17 *off McEntee Av* 77 H1
Sutton SM3 184 D7
Romany Ri, Orp. BR5 207 F1
Roma Read Cl, SW15 147 H7
Roma Rd, E17 77 H3
Romberg Rd, SW17 168 A3
Romborough Gdns, SE13 154 C5
Romborough Way, SE13 154 C5
Romero Cl, SW9 *off Stockwell Rd* 151 F3
Romero Sq, SE3 155 J4
Romeyn Rd, SW16 169 F3
Romford Rd, E7 97 H5
E12 98 B4
E15 96 E7
Romford St, E1 21 J2
Romilly Dr, Wat. WD19 51 E4
Romilly Rd, N4 93 H2
Romilly St, W1 17 H5
Rommany Rd, SE27 170 A4
Romney Cl, N17 76 E1
NW11 91 F1
SE14 *off Kender St* 133 F7
Chessington KT9 195 H4
Harrow HA2 67 G7
Romney Dr, Brom. BR1 174 A7
Harrow HA2 67 G7
Romney Gdns, Bexh. DA7 159 F1
Romney Ms, W1 16 B1
Romney Rd, SE10 134 C6
New Malden KT3 182 D6
Romney Row, NW2 *off Brent Ter* 90 A2
Romney St, SW1 25 J6
Romola Rd, SE24 169 H1
Romsey Cl, Orp. BR6 207 E4
Romsey Gdns, Dag. RM9 118 D1
Romsey Rd, W13 104 D7
Dagenham RM9 118 D1
Romulus Ct, Brent. TW8 *off Justin Cl* 125 G7
Ronald Av, E15 115 E3
Ronald Cl, Beck. BR3 189 J4
Ronald Ho, SE3 *off Cambert Way* 155 J4
Ronalds Rd, N5 93 G5
Bromley BR1 191 G1
Ronaldstone Rd, Sid. DA15 157 H6
Ronald St, E1 *off Devonport St* 113 F6
Rona Rd, NW3 92 A4
Ronart St, Har. (Wealds.) HA3 68 C3
Rona Wk, N1 *off Ramsey Wk* 94 A6
Rondu Rd, NW2 90 B5
Ronelean Rd, Surb. KT6 195 J3
Ron Leighton Way, E6 116 B1
Ronnie La, E12 98 D4
Ron Todd Cl, Dag. RM10 *off Heathway* 119 G1
Ronver Rd, SE12 155 F7
Rood La, EC3 20 D5
Rookby Ct, N21 59 H2
Rook Cl, Wem. HA9 88 B3
Rookeries Cl, Felt. TW13 160 B3
Rookery Cl, NW9 71 F5
Rookery Cres, Dag. RM10 101 H7
Rookery Dr, Chis. BR7 192 D1
Rookery La, Brom. BR2 192 A6
Rookery Rd, SW4 150 C4
Rookery Way, NW9 71 F5
Rooke Way, SE10 135 F5
Rookfield Av, N10 74 C4
Rookfield Cl, N10 74 C4
Rookstone Rd, SW17 167 J5
Rook Wk, E6 *off Allhallows Rd* 116 B6
Rookwood Av, Loug. IG10 49 F3
New Malden KT3 183 G4
Wallington SM6 200 D4
Rookwood Gdns, E4 63 F2
Loughton IG10 49 F3
Rookwood Ho, Bark. IG11 *off St. Marys* 117 G2
Rookwood Rd, N16 76 C7
★ **Roosevelt Mem**, W1 16 C5
Rootes Dr, W10 108 A4
Ropemaker Rd, SE16 133 H3
Ropemakers Flds, E14 *off Narrow St* 113 J7
Ropemaker St, EC2 20 B1
Roper La, SE1 29 E3
Ropers Av, E4 62 C5
Ropers Orchard, SW3 31 F6
Roper St, SE9 156 C6
Ropers Wk, SW2 *off Brockwell Pk Gdns* 151 G7
Roper Way, Mitch. CR4 186 A2
Ropery St, E3 113 J4
Rope St, SE16 133 H4
Rope Wk, Sun. TW16 178 C3
Ropewalk Gdns, E1 21 J4
Ropewalk Ms, E8 *off Middleton Rd* 94 D7
Rope Yd Rails, SE18 136 E3
Ropley St, E2 13 H2
Rosa Alba Ms, N5 *off Kelross Rd* 93 J4
Rosaline Rd, SW6 128 B7
Rosamond St, SE26 170 E3
Rosamund Cl, S.Croy. CR2 202 A4
Rosamun St, Sthl. UB2 123 E4
Rosary Cl, Houns. TW3 142 E2
Rosary Gdns, SW7 30 C2
Rosaville Rd, SW6 128 C7
Roscoe St, EC1 12 A6
Roscoff Cl, Edg. HA8 70 C1
Roseacre Cl, W13 *off Middlefielde* 104 E5
Sutton SM1 199 F2
Roseacre Rd, Well. DA16 158 B3
Rose All, EC2 *off New St* 20 E2
SE1 28 A1
Rose & Crown Ct, EC2 19 J3
Rose & Crown Yd, SW1 25 G1
Roseary Cl, West Dr. UB7 120 A4
Rose Av, E18 79 H2
Mitcham CR4 185 J1
Morden SM4 185 F5
Rosebank, SE20 170 E7
Rosebank Av, Wem. HA0 86 C4
Rosebank Cl, N12 57 H5
Teddington TW11 162 D6
Rosebank Gdns, E3 113 J2
Rosebank Gro, E17 77 J3
Rosebank Rd, E17 78 B6
W7 124 B2
Rosebank Vil, E17 78 A4
Rosebank Wk, NW1 *off Maiden La* 92 D7
SE18 *off Woodhill* 136 B4
Rosebank Way, W3 106 D6
Rose Bates Dr, NW9 70 A4
Roseberry Gdns, N4 75 H6
Orpington BR6 207 H3
Roseberry Pl, E8 94 C6
Roseberry St, SE16 132 E4
Rosebery Av, E12 98 B6
EC1 10 E6
N17 76 D2
Harrow HA2 85 F4
New Malden KT3 183 F2
Sidcup DA15 157 H7
Thornton Heath CR7 187 J2
Rosebery Cl, Mord. SM4 184 A6
Rosebery Ct, EC1 *off Rosebery Av* 11 E5
Rosebery Gdns, N8 74 E5
W13 104 D6
Sutton SM1 199 E4
Rosebery Ind Pk, N17 76 E2
Rosebery Ms, N10 74 C2
SW2 *off Rosebery Rd* 150 E6
Rosebery Rd, N10 74 C2
SW2 150 E6
Hounslow TW3 143 J5
Kingston upon Thames KT1 182 B2
Sutton SM1 198 C6
Rosebery Sq, EC1 10 E6
Kingston upon Thames KT1 182 A2
Rosebine Av, Twick. TW2 144 A7
Rosebury Rd, SW6 149 E2
Rosebury Sq, Wdf.Grn. IG8 64 D7
Rose Ct, E1 21 F2
Pinner HA5 *off Nursery Rd* 66 C3
Rosecourt Rd, Croy. CR0 187 F6
Rosecroft Av, NW3 90 D3
Rosecroft Gdns, NW2 89 G3
Twickenham TW2 162 A1
Rosecroft Rd, Sthl. UB1 103 G4
Rosecroft Wk, Pnr. HA5 66 D5
Wembley HA0 87 G5
Rose Dale, Orp. BR6 207 E2
Rosedale Cl, SE2 *off Finchale Rd* 138 B3
W7 *off Boston Rd* 124 C2
Stanmore HA7 53 E6
Rosedale Ct, N5 93 H4
Rosedale Dr, Dag. RM9 118 B1
Rosedale Gdns, Dag. RM9 100 B7
Rosedale Pl, Croy. CR0 189 G7
Rosedale Rd, E7 97 J5
Dagenham RM9 100 B7
Epsom KT17 197 G5
Richmond TW9 145 H4
Romford RM1 83 J2
Rosedale Ter, W6 *off Dalling Rd* 127 H3
Rosedene, NW6 108 A1
Rosedene Av, SW16 169 F3
Croydon CR0 187 F7
Greenford UB6 103 G3
Morden SM4 184 D5
Rosedene Gdns, Ilf. IG2 80 D4
Rosedene Ter, E10 96 B2
Rosedew Rd, W6 128 A6
Rose End, Wor.Pk. KT4 198 A1
Rosefield Cl, Cars. SM5 199 H5
Rosefield Gdns, E14 114 A7
Roseford Ct, W12 128 A2
Rose Gdn Cl, Edg. HA8 53 H6
Rose Gdns, W5 125 G3
Feltham TW13 160 A2
Southall UB1 103 G4
Staines (Stanw.) TW19 *off Diamedes Av* 140 A7
Rosegate Ho, E3 *off Hereford Rd* 113 J2
Rose Glen, NW9 70 D4
Rosehart Ms, W11 *off Westbourne Gro* 108 D6
Rose Hatch Av, Rom. RM6 82 D3
Roseheath Rd, Houns. TW4 143 F5
ROSEHILL, Sutt. SM1 198 E1
Rosehill, Esher (Clay.) KT10 194 D6
Hampton TW12 179 G1
Rose Hill, Sutt. SM1 199 E2
Rosehill Av, Sutt. SM1 199 F1
Rosehill Gdns, Grnf. UB6 86 C5
Sutton SM1 199 E2
Rose Hill Pk W, Sutt. SM1 199 F1
Rosehill Rd, SW18 149 F6
Rose Joan Ms, NW6 90 D4
Roseland Cl, N17 *off Cavell Rd* 60 A7
Rose La, Rom. RM6 82 D3
Rose Lawn, Bushey (Bushey Hth) WD23 51 J1
Roseleigh Av, N5 93 H4
Roseleigh Cl, Twick. TW1 145 G6
Rosemary Av, N3 73 E2
N9 60 E1
Enfield EN2 44 A1
Hounslow TW4 142 D2
West Molesey KT8 179 G3
Rosemary Cl, Croy. CR0 186 E6
Rosemary Dr, E14 114 D6
Ilford IG4 80 A5
Rosemary Gdns, SW14 *off Rosemary La* 146 C3
Chessington KT9 195 H4
Dagenham RM8 101 F1
Rosemary La, SW14 146 C3
Rosemary Rd, SE15 37 G7
SW17 167 F3
Welling DA16 157 J1
Rosemary St, N1 *off Shepperton Rd* 112 A1
Rosemead, NW9 71 F7
Rosemead Av, Mitch. CR4 186 C2
Wembley HA9 87 H5
Rose Ms, N18 60 E4
Rosemont Av, N12 57 F6
Rosemont Rd, NW3 91 F6
W3 106 B7
New Malden KT3 182 C3
Richmond TW10 145 H6
Wembley HA0 105 H1
Rosemoor St, SW3 31 J2
Rosemount, Wall. SM6 200 C6
Rosemount Cl, Wdf.Grn. IG8 *off Chapelmount Rd* 64 C6
Rosemount Dr, Brom. BR1 192 C4
Rosemount Pt, SE23 *off Dacres Rd* 171 G3
Rosemount Rd, W13 104 D6
Rosenau Cres, SW11 149 H1
Rosenau Rd, SW11 149 H1
Rosendale Rd, SE21 151 J7
SE24 151 J7
Roseneath Av, N21 59 H1
Roseneath Pl, SW16 *off Curtis Fld Rd* 169 F4
Roseneath Rd, SW11 150 A6
Roseneath Wk, Enf. EN1 44 A4
Rosens Wk, Edg. HA8 54 B3
Rosenthal Rd, SE6 154 B6
Rosenthorpe Rd, SE15 153 G5
Rose Pk Cl, Hayes UB4 102 C4
Rosepark Ct, Ilf. IG5 80 C2
Roserton St, E14 134 C2
Rosery, The, Croy. CR0 189 G6
Roses, The, Wdf.Grn. IG8 63 F7
Rose Sq, SW3 31 F3
Rose St, EC4 19 H3
WC2 18 A5
Rosethorn Cl, SW12 150 C7
Rose Tree Ms, Wdf.Grn. IG8 *off Chigwell Rd* 64 B6
Rosetree Pl, Hmptn. TW12 *off Broad La* 161 G6
Rosetta Cl, SW8 131 E7
Rosetti Ter, Dag. RM8 *off Marlborough Rd* 100 B4
Roseveare Rd, SE12 173 J4
Roseville Av, Houns. TW3 143 G5
Roseville Rd, Hayes UB3 122 A5
Rosevine Rd, SW20 183 J1
Rose Wk, Surb. KT5 182 B5
West Wickham BR4 204 D2
Rose Way, SE12 155 G5
Roseway, SE21 152 A6
Rose Way, Edg. HA8 54 C4
Rosewell Cl, SE20 170 E7
Rosewood, Esher KT10 194 D2
Rosewood Av, Grnf. UB6 86 D5
Rosewood Cl, Sid. DA14 176 C3
Rosewood Ct, Brom. BR1 191 J1
Romford RM6 82 C5
Rosewood Gdns, SE13 *off Morden Hill* 154 C2
Rosewood Gro, Sutt. SM1 199 F2
Rosewood Sq, W12 *off Primula St* 107 G6
Rosewood Ter, SE20 *off Laurel Gro* 171 F7
Rosher Cl, E15 96 D7
Rosina St, E9 95 G5
Roskell Rd, SW15 148 A3
Roslin Rd, W3 126 B3
Roslin Sq, W3 126 B3
Roslin Way, Brom. BR1 173 G5
Roslyn Cl, Mitch. CR4 185 G2
Roslyn Rd, N15 76 A5
Rosmead Rd, W11 108 B7
Rosoman Pl, EC1 11 F5
Rosoman St, EC1 11 F4
Rossall Cres, NW10 105 J3
Ross Av, Dag. RM8 101 F2
Ross Cl, Har. HA3 51 J7
Hayes UB3 121 G4
Northolt UB5 86 A4
Ross Ct, E5 *off Napoleon Rd* 94 E4
SW15 148 A7
Rossdale, Sutt. SM1 199 H5
Rossdale Dr, N9 45 F6
NW9 88 C1
Rossdale Rd, SW15 147 J4
Rosse Gdns, SE13 *off Desvignes Dr* 154 D6
Rosse Ms, SE3 155 H1
Rossendale St, E5 94 E2
Rossendale Way, NW1 92 C7

Rossetti Ms, NW8 *off Ordnance Hill* 109 G1
Rossetti Rd, SE16 . . . . . . .132 E5
Rossignol Gdns, Cars. SM5 . . . . .200 A2
Rossindel Rd, Houns. TW3 . . . . .143 G5
Rossington St, E5 . . . . .94 D2
Rossiter Flds, Barn. EN5 . .40 B6
Rossiter Rd, SW12 . . . . . .168 B1
Rossland Cl, Bexh. DA6 . .159 H5
Rosslyn Av, E4 . . . . .63 F2
SW13 . . . . .147 E3
Barnet (E.Barn.) EN4 . . .41 H6
Dagenham RM8 . . . . . . .83 F7
Feltham TW14 . . . . .142 A6
Rosslyn Cl, W.Wick. BR4 . .205 F3
Rosslyn Cres, Har. HA1 . . .68 C5
Wembley HA9 . . . . .87 H4
Rosslyn Gdns, Wem. HA9 *off Rosslyn Cres* 87 H3
Rosslyn Hill, NW3 . . . . .91 G4
Rosslyn Ms, NW3 *off Rosslyn Hill* 91 G4
Rosslyn Pk Ms, NW3 *off Lyndhurst Rd* 91 G5
Rosslyn Rd, E17 . . . . .78 C4
Barking IG11 . . . . .99 G7
Twickenham TW1 . . . . .145 F6
Rossmore Cl, Enf. EN3 . . . .45 G4
Rossmore Ct, NW1 . . . . .7 J5
Rossmore Rd, NW1 . . . . . . .7 H6
Ross Par, Wall. SM6 . . . . .200 B6
Ross Rd, SE25 . . . . .188 A3
Twickenham TW2 . . . . .161 H1
Wallington SM6 . . . . . .200 C5
Ross Way, SE9 . . . . .156 B3
Rosswood Gdns, Wall. SM6 . . . . .200 C6
Rostella Rd, SW17 . . . . . .167 G4
Rostrevor Av, N15 . . . . .76 C6
Rostrevor Gdns, Hayes UB3 . . . . .121 H1
Southall UB2 . . . . .122 E5
Rostrevor Ms, SW6 . . . . .148 C1
Rostrevor Rd, SW6 . . . . . .148 C1
SW19 . . . . .166 D5
Rotary St, SE1 . . . . .27 G5
Rothbury Gdns, Islw. TW7 . . . . .124 D7
Rothbury Rd, E9 . . . . .95 J7
Rothbury Wk, N17 . . . . . . .60 D7
Rotherfield Rd, Cars. SM5 . . . . .200 A4
Rotherfield St, N1 . . . . .93 J7
Rotherham Wk, SE1 . . . . . .27 G2
Rotherhill Av, SW16 . . . . .168 D6
ROTHERHITHE, SE16 . . . .133 G3
Rotherhithe New Rd, SE16 . . . . .37 J4
Rotherhithe Old Rd, SE16 . . . . .133 G4
Rotherhithe St, SE16 . . . .133 F2
Rotherhithe Tunnel, E1 . . .133 F1
Rotherhithe Tunnel App, E14 . . . . .113 H7
SE16 . . . . .133 F2
Rotherwick Hill, W5 . . . . .105 J4
Rotherwick Rd, NW11 . . . .72 D7
Rotherwood Cl, SW20 . . .184 B1
Rotherwood Rd, SW15 . .148 A3
Rothery St, N1 *off Gaskin St* 111 H1
Rothery Ter, SW9 . . . . . . .131 H7
Rothesay Av, SW20 . . . . . .184 B2
Greenford UB6 . . . . .86 A6
Richmond TW10 . . . . . .146 B4
Rothesay Rd, SE25 . . . . . .188 A4
Rothsay Rd, E7 . . . . .97 J7
Rothsay St, SE1 . . . . .28 D5
Rothsay Wk, E14 *off Charnwood Gdns* .134 A4
Rothschild Rd, W4 . . . . . .126 C4
Rothschild St, SE27 . . . . .169 H4
Roth Wk, N7 *off Durham Rd* 93 G2
Rothwell Gdns, Dag. RM9 . . . . .118 C1
Rothwell Ho, Houns. TW5 *off Biscoe Cl* 123 G6
Rothwell Rd, Dag. RM9 . .118 C1
Rothwell St, NW1 . . . . . . .109 J1
Rotten Row, SW1 . . . . .24 B3
SW7 . . . . .23 G3
Rotterdam Dr, E14 . . . . . .134 C3
Rouel Rd, SE16 . . . . .29 H6
Rougemont Av, Mord. SM4 . . . . .184 D6
Roundacre, SW19 . . . . . . .166 A2
Roundaway Rd, Ilf. IG5 . . . .80 C2
Roundel Cl, SE4 *off Adelaide Av* 153 J4
Round Gro, Croy. CR0 . . .189 G7
Roundhay Cl, SE23 . . . . . .171 G2
Round Hill, SE26 . . . . .171 F2
Roundhill Dr, Enf. EN2 . . . .43 F4
Roundmead Av, Loug. IG10 . . . . .48 D3
Roundmead Cl, Loug. IG10 . . . . .48 D3
Roundtable Rd, Brom. BR1 . . . . .173 F3
Roundtree Rd, Wem. HA0 . . . . .86 E5
Roundway, The, N17 . . . . . .75 J1
Esher (Clay.) KT10 . . . .194 C5
Roundwood, Chis. BR7 . .192 E2
Roundwood Av, Uxb. UB11 . . . . .121 F1
Roundwood Pk, NW10 . . . .89 G7
Roundwood Rd, NW10 . . . .89 F6
Rounton Rd, E3 . . . . .114 A4
Roupell Rd, SW2 . . . . .169 F1
Roupell St, SE1 . . . . .27 F2
Rousden St, NW1 . . . . .92 C7
Rouse Gdns, SE21 . . . . . .170 B4
Rous Rd, Buck.H. IG9 . . . . .64 B1
Routemaster Cl, E13 . . . . .115 H3
Routh Rd, SW18 . . . . .149 H7
Routh St, E6 . . . . .116 C5
Rover Av, Ilf. IG6 . . . . .65 J6
Rover Ho, N1 *off Phillipp St* 112 B1
Rowallan Rd, SW6 . . . . . .128 B7
Rowan Av, E4 . . . . .61 J6
Rowan Cl, SW16 . . . . .186 C1
W5 . . . . .125 H2
Ilford IG1 . . . . .99 G5
New Malden KT3 . . . . .182 E2
Stanmore HA7 . . . . .52 C6
Wembley HA0 . . . . .86 D3
Rowan Cres, SW16 . . . . . .186 C1
Rowan Dr, NW9 . . . . .71 G4
Rowan Gdns, Croy. CR0 . .202 C3
Rowan Ho, NW3 *off Maitland Pk Rd* 91 J6
Rowan Rd, SW16 . . . . . . .186 C2
W6 . . . . .128 A4
Bexleyheath DA7 . . . . .159 E3
Brentford TW8 . . . . .125 E7
West Drayton UB7 . . . .120 A4
Rowans, The, N13 . . . . .59 H3
Rowans Way, Loug. IG10 . .48 C4
Rowan Ter, SE20 *off Sycamore Gro* 188 D1
W6 *off Bute Gdns* 128 A4
Rowantree Cl, N21 . . . . . . .60 A1
Rowantree Rd, N21 . . . . . .60 A1
Enfield EN2 . . . . .43 H2
Rowan Wk, N2 . . . . .73 F6
N19 *off Bredgar Rd* 92 C2
W10 *off Sixth Av* 108 B4
Barnet EN5 . . . . .40 E5
Bromley BR2 . . . . .206 C3
Rowan Way, Rom. RM6 . . .82 C3
Rowanwood Av, Sid. DA15 . . . . .176 A1
Rowanwood Ms, Enf. EN2 .43 H2
Rowben Cl, N20 . . . . .56 E1
Rowberry Cl, SW6 . . . . . .127 J7
Rowcross St, SE1 . . . . .37 F3
Rowdell Rd, Nthlt. UB5 . .103 G1
Rowden Pk Gdns, E4 *off Rowden Rd* 62 A6
Rowden Rd, E4 . . . . .62 A6
Beckenham BR3 . . . . . .189 H1
Epsom KT19 . . . . .196 B4
Rowditch La, SW11 . . . . . .150 A2
Rowdon Av, NW10 . . . . . . .89 H7
Rowdowns Rd, Dag. RM9 . . . . .119 F1
Rowe Gdns, Bark. IG11 . . .117 J2
Rowe La, E9 . . . . .95 F5
Rowena Cres, SW11 . . . . .149 H2
Rowe Wk, Har. HA2 . . . . . .85 G3
Rowfant Rd, SW17 . . . . . .168 A1
Rowhill Rd, E5 . . . . .95 E4
Rowington Cl, W2 . . . . .14 A1
Rowland Av, Har. HA3 . . . . .69 F3
Rowland Ct, E16 . . . . .115 F4
Rowland Cres, Chig. IG7 . .65 H4
Rowland Gro, SE26 *off Dallas Rd* 171 E3
Rowland Hill Av, N17 . . . . .59 J7
Rowland Hill St, NW3 . . . .91 H5
Rowlands Av, Pnr. HA5 . . .51 G6
Rowlands Cl, N6 *off North Hill* 74 A6
NW7 . . . . .55 G7
Rowlands Rd, Dag. RM8 .101 F2
Rowland Way, SW19 *off Hayward Cl* 185 E1
Rowley Av, Sid. DA15 . . . .158 B7
Rowley Cl, Wem. HA0 . . . . .87 J7
Rowley Gdns, N4 . . . . .75 J7
ROWLEY GREEN, Barn. EN5 . . . . .39 F4
Rowley Grn Rd, Barn. EN5 . . . . .39 F5
Rowley Ind Pk, W3 . . . . . .126 B3
Rowley La, Barn. EN5 . . . . .39 F5
Borehamwood WD6 . . . .38 D1
Rowley Rd, N15 . . . . .75 J5
Rowley Way, NW8 . . . . . . .109 E1
Rowlheys Pl, West Dr. UB7 . . . . .120 B3
Rowlls Rd, Kings.T. KT1 . .181 J3
Rowney Gdns, Dag. RM9 .100 C6
Rowney Rd, Dag. RM9 . . .100 B6
Rowntree Clifford Cl, E13 *off Liddon Rd* 115 H3
Rowntree Cl, NW6 *off Iverson Rd* 90 D6
Rowntree Path, SE28 *off Booth Cl* 118 B7
Rowntree Rd, Twick. TW2 .162 B1
Rowse Cl, E15 . . . . .114 C1
Rowsley Av, NW4 . . . . .71 J3
Rowstock Gdns, N7 . . . . . .92 D5
Rowton Rd, SE18 . . . . . . .137 F7
Roxborough Av, Har. HA1 .68 A7
Isleworth TW7 . . . . .124 C7
Roxborough Pk, Har. HA1 .68 B7
Roxborough Rd, Har. HA1 .68 A5
Roxbourne Cl, Nthlt. UB5 . .84 D6
Roxburgh Rd, SE27 . . . . . .169 H5
Roxby Pl, SW6 . . . . .128 D6
ROXETH, Har. HA2 . . . . . . .86 A2
Roxeth Grn Av, Har. HA2 . .85 H3
Roxeth Gro, Har. HA2 . . . . .85 H4
Roxeth Hill, Har. HA2 . . . . .86 A2
Roxley Rd, SE13 . . . . .154 B6
Roxton Gdns, Croy. CR0 .204 A5
Roxwell Rd, W12 . . . . .127 G2
Barking IG11 . . . . .118 A2
Roxwell Trd Pk, E10 . . . . . .77 G7
Roxwell Way, Wdf.Grn. IG8 . . . . .63 J7
Roxy Av, Rom. RM6 . . . . . .82 C7
★ **Royal Acad of Arts**, W1 . . . . .17 F6
★ **Royal Acad of Dramatic Art (R.A.D.A.)**, WC1 . . .17 J1
★ **Royal Acad of Music**, NW1 . . . . .8 C6
★ **Royal Air Force Mus**, NW9 . . . . .71 G2
Royal Albert Dock, E16 . . .116 B7
★ **Royal Albert Hall**, SW7 . . . . .22 E4
Royal Albert Rbt, E16 . . . .116 A7
Royal Albert Way, E16 . . . .116 A7
Royal Arc, W1 . . . . .17 F6
Royal Artillery Barracks, SE18 *off Repository Rd* 136 D5
Royal Av, SW3 . . . . .31 J3
Worcester Park KT4 . . .197 E2
★ **Royal Botanic Gdns, Kew**, Rich. TW9 . . . . . .125 H7
Royal Circ, SE27 . . . . .169 G3
Royal Cl, N16 *off Manor Rd* 94 B1
SE8 . . . . .133 J6
SW19 . . . . .166 A3
Ilford IG3 . . . . .82 A7
Orpington BR6 . . . . . . .206 E4
Worcester Park KT4 . . .196 E2
★ **Royal Coll of Art**, SW7 .22 D4
★ **Royal Coll of Music**, SW7 . . . . .22 E5
★ **Royal College of Surgeons of England**, WC2 . . . . .18 D3
Royal Coll St, NW1 . . . . . . .92 C7
Royal Ct, EC3 *off Royal Ex Bldgs* 20 C4
SE16 . . . . .133 J3
★ **Royal Courts of Justice**, WC2 . . . . .18 D4
Royal Cres, W11 . . . . .128 A1
Ilford IG2 . . . . .81 G6
Ruislip HA4 . . . . .84 E4
Royal Cres Ms, W11 *off Queensdale Rd* . . .128 A1
Royal Docks Rd, E6 . . . . . .117 E6
★ **Royal Dress Collection** (Kensington Palace), W8 . . . . .22 B2
Royal Dr, N11 . . . . .58 A5
Royal Duchess Ms, SW12 *off Dinsmore Rd* 150 B7
Royale Leisure Pk, W3 . . .106 A4
★ **Royal Exchange**, EC3 . . . . .20 C4
Royal Ex Av, EC3 . . . . .20 C4
Royal Ex Bldgs, EC3 . . . . . .20 C4
★ **Royal Festival Hall**, SE1 . . . . .26 D2
Royal Gdns, W7 . . . . .124 D3
★ **Royal Geographical Society**, SW7 . . . . .23 E4
Royal Herbert Pavilions, SE18 . . . . .156 C1
Royal Hill, SE10 . . . . .134 C7
★ **Royal Horticultural Society (Lawrence Hall)**, SW1 . . . . .25 H6
★ **Royal Horticultural Society (Lindley Hall)**, SW1 . . . . .33 H1
★ **Royal Hosp Chelsea & Mus**, SW3 . . . . .32 B4
Royal Hosp Rd, SW3 . . . . .31 J5
★ **Royal Mews, The**, SW1 . . . . .24 E5
Royal Mint Ct, EC3 . . . . . . .21 G6
Royal Mint Pl, E1 . . . . .21 G5
Royal Mint St, E1 . . . . .21 G5
Royal Mt Ct, Twick. TW2 . .162 B3
Royal Naval Pl, SE14 . . . .133 J7
Royal Oak Ct, N1 . . . . .12 D3
Royal Oak Ms, Tedd. TW11 *off High St* 162 D5
Royal Oak Pl, SE22 . . . . . .153 E6
Royal Oak Rd, E8 . . . . .94 E6
Bexleyheath DA6 . . . . .159 F5
Royal Oak Yd, SE1 . . . . . . .28 D4
★ **Royal Observatory Greenwich** (Flamsteed Ho), SE10 .134 D7
Royal Opera Arc, SW1 . . . .25 H1
★ **Royal Opera Ho**, WC2 . .18 B4
Royal Orchard Cl, SW18 . .148 B7
Royal Par, SE3 . . . . .155 E2
SW6 *off Dawes Rd* 128 B7
W5 *off Western Av* 105 H3
Chislehurst BR7 . . . . . .175 F7
Richmond TW9 *off Station App* 146 A1
Royal Par Ms, SE3 *off Royal Par* 155 F2
Chislehurst BR7 . . . . . .175 F7
Royal Pl, SE10 . . . . .134 C7
Royal Quarter, Kings.T. KT2 . . . . .181 H1
Royal Rd, E16 . . . . .116 A6
SE17 . . . . .35 G5
Sidcup DA14 . . . . .176 D3
Teddington TW11 . . . . .162 A5
Royal Route, Wem. HA9 . . .87 J4
Royals Business Pk, The, E16 . . . . .116 B7
Royal St, SE1 . . . . .26 D5
Royalty Ms, W1 . . . . .17 H4
Royal Victoria Dock, E16 . . .115 G7
Royal Victoria Patriotic Bldg, SW18 . . . . .149 G6
Royal Victoria Pl, E16 *off Wesley Av* 135 H1
Royal Victoria Sq, E16 *off Western Gateway* .115 H7
Royal Victor Pl, E3 . . . . . . .113 G2
Royal Wk, Wall. SM6 *off Prince Charles Way* 200 B3
Roycraft Av, Bark. IG11 . . .117 J2
Roycroft Cl, Bark. IG11 . . .117 J2
Roycroft Cl, E18 . . . . .79 H1
SW2 . . . . .169 G1
Roydene Rd, SE18 . . . . . .137 H6
Roydon Cl, SW11 *off Reform St* 149 J2
Loughton IG10 . . . . .48 B7
Roydon St, SW11 *off Southolm St* 150 B1
Roy Gdns, Ilf. IG2 . . . . .81 H4
Roy Gro, Hmptn. TW12 . . .161 H6
Royle Bldg, N1 . . . . .11 J1
Royle Cres, W13 . . . . .104 D4
Roy Sq, E14 *off Narrow St* 113 H7
Royston Av, E4 . . . . .62 A5
Sutton SM1 . . . . .199 G3
Wallington SM6 . . . . . .200 D4
Royston Cl, Houns. TW5 . .142 B1
Royston Ct, SE24 *off Burbage Rd* 151 J6
Richmond TW9 . . . . . . .145 J1
Surbiton KT6 . . . . .196 A3
Royston Gdns, Ilf. IG1 . . . .80 A6
Royston Gro, Pnr. HA5 . . . .51 F6
Royston Par, Ilf. IG1 . . . . . .80 A6
Royston Pk Rd, Pnr. HA5 . .51 F6
Royston Rd, SE20 . . . . . . .189 G1
Richmond TW10 . . . . . .145 H5
Roystons, The, Surb. KT5 .182 B5
Royston St, E2 . . . . .113 F2
Rozel Ct, N1 . . . . .112 B1
Rozel Rd, SW4 . . . . .150 C2
Rubastic Rd, Sthl. UB2 . . .122 C3
Rubens Pl, SW4 *off Dolman St* 151 F4
Rubens Rd, Nthlt. UB5 . . .102 C2
Rubens St, SE6 . . . . .171 J2
Ruby Ms, E17 *off Ruby Rd* 78 A3
Ruby Rd, E17 . . . . .78 A3
Ruby St, NW10 . . . . .88 C7
SE15 . . . . .132 E6
Ruby Triangle, SE15 *off Sandgate St* 132 E6
Ruby Way, NW9 . . . . .71 F1
Ruckholt Cl, E10 . . . . .96 B3

Ruckholt Rd, E10 . . . . .96 A4
Rucklidge Av, NW10 . . . .107 F2
Rudall Cres, NW3
  off Willoughby Rd 91 G4
Ruddington Cl, E5 . . . . . . .95 H4
Ruddock Cl, Edg. HA8 . . . .54 C7
Ruddstreet Cl, SE18 . . . .137 E4
Rudgwick Ter, NW8
  off Avenue Rd 109 H1
Rudland Rd, Bexh.
  DA7 . . . . .159 H3
Rudloe Rd, SW12 . . . . . .150 C7
Rudolf Pl, SW8 . . . . .34 B6
Rudolph Rd, E13 . . . . . . .115 F2
  NW6 . . . . .108 D2
Rudstone Ho, E3
  off Bromley High St . .114 B3
Rudyard Gro, NW7 . . . . . .54 C6
Ruffetts, The, S.Croy.
  CR2 . . . . .203 E7
Ruffetts Cl, S.Croy. CR2 . .202 E7
Ruffle Cl, West Dr. UB7 . .120 B2
Rufford Cl, Har. HA3 . . . . .68 D6
Rufford St, N1 . . . . .111 E1
Rufford Twr, W3 . . . . . . .126 B1
Rufus Business Cen,
  SW18 . . . . .167 E2
Rufus Cl, Ruis. HA4 . . . . . .84 E3
Rufus St, N1 . . . . .12 D4
Rugby Av, N9 . . . . .60 C1
  Greenford UB6 . . . . . . .86 A6
  Wembley HA0 . . . . .87 E5
Rugby Cl, Har. HA1 . . . . . .68 B5
★ Rugby Football Union
  Twickenham, Twick.
  TW1 . . . . .144 B6
Rugby Gdns, Dag. RM9 . .100 C6
Rugby Rd, NW9 . . . . .70 B4
  W4 . . . . .126 D2
  Dagenham RM9 . . . . .100 B7
  Twickenham TW1 . . . .144 B6
Rugby St, WC1 . . . . .10 C6
Rugg St, E14 . . . . .114 A7
Ruislip Cl, Grnf. UB6 . . . .103 H4
RUISLIP MANOR, Ruis.
  HA4 . . . . .84 A2
Ruislip Retail Pk, Ruis.
  HA4 off Victoria Rd 85 E4
Ruislip Rd, Grnf. UB6 . . . .103 G3
  Northolt UB5 . . . . .102 D2
  Southall UB1 . . . . .103 G3
Ruislip Rd E, W7 . . . . . . .104 A4
  W13 . . . . .104 A4
  Greenford UB6 . . . . . .104 A4
Ruislip St, SW17 . . . . . . .167 J4
Rumbold Rd, SW6 . . . . . .129 E7
Rum Cl, E1 . . . . .113 F7
Rumford Ho, SE1
  off Bath Ter 27 J5
Rumsey Cl, Hmptn.
  TW12 . . . . .161 F6
Rumsey Ms, N4
  off Monsell Rd 93 H3
Rumsey Rd, SW9 . . . . . . .151 F3
Runbury Circle, NW9 . . . . .88 D2
Runcorn Cl, N17 . . . . .76 E4
Runcorn Pl, W11 . . . . . . .108 B7
Rundell Cres, NW4 . . . . . .71 H5
Rundell Twr, SW8
  off Portland Gro 151 F1
Runes Cl, Mitch. CR4 . . . .185 G4
Runnel Fld, Har. HA1 . . . . .86 B3
Running Horse Yd, Brent.
  TW8 off Pottery Rd . . .125 H6
Runnymede, SW19 . . . . . .185 G1
Runnymede Cl, Twick.
  TW2 . . . . .143 H6
Runnymede Ct, Croy.
  CR0 . . . . .202 C2
Runnymede Cres, SW16 . .186 D1
Runnymede Gdns, Grnf.
  UB6 . . . . .104 A2
  Twickenham TW2 . . . .143 H6
Runnymede Ho, E9
  off Kingsmead Way . . .95 H4
Runnymede Rd, Twick.
  TW2 . . . . .143 H6
Runway, The, Ruis. HA4 . . .84 B5
Runway Cl, NW9
  off Great Strand 71 F2
Rupack St, SE16
  off St. Marychurch St .133 F2
Rupert Av, Wem. HA9 . . . .87 H5
Rupert Ct, W1 . . . . .17 H5
  West Molesey KT8
  off St. Peter's Rd 179 G4
Rupert Gdns, SW9 . . . . . .151 H2
Rupert Rd, N19
  off Holloway Rd 92 D2
  NW6 . . . . .108 C2
  W4 . . . . .127 E3
Rupert St, W1 . . . . .17 H5
Rural Way, SW16 . . . . . . .168 B7
Rusbridge Cl, E8
  off Amhurst Rd 94 D5
Ruscoe Rd, E16 . . . . .115 F6

Ruscombe Way, Felt.
  TW14 . . . . .141 J7
Rush, The, SW19
  off Kingston Rd 184 C1
Rusham Rd, SW12 . . . . . .149 A6
Rushbrook Cres, E17 . . . . .77 J1
Rushbrook Rd, SE9 . . . . .175 F2
Rush Common Ms, SW12 .151 F7
Rushcroft Rd, E4 . . . . .62 A7
  SW2 . . . . .151 G4
Rushden Cl, SE19 . . . . . .170 A7
Rushdene, SE2 . . . . .138 D3
Rushdene Av, Barn. EN4 . .41 H7
Rushdene Cl, Nthlt. UB5 .102 C3
Rushdene Cres, Nthlt.
  UB5 . . . . .102 C2
Rushdene Rd, Pnr. HA5 . . .66 D6
Rushden Gdns, NW7 . . . . .55 J6
  Ilford IG5 . . . . .80 D3
Rushen Wk, Cars. SM5
  off Paisley Rd 199 G1
Rushett Cl, T.Ditt. KT7 . . .194 E1
Rushett Rd, T.Ditt. KT7 . .180 E7
Rushey Cl, N.Mal. KT3 . . .182 D4
Rushey Grn, SE6 . . . . . . .154 B7
Rushey Hill, Enf. EN2 . . . . .43 F4
Rushey Mead, SE4 . . . . . .154 A5
Rushford Rd, SE4 . . . . . . .153 J6
RUSH GREEN, Rom. RM7 .83 J7
Rush Grn Gdns, Rom.
  RM7 . . . . .101 J1
Rush Grn Rd, Rom. RM7 .101 J1
Rushgrove Av, NW9 . . . . . .71 F5
Rushgrove St, SE18 . . . . .136 C4
Rush Hill Ms, SW11
  off Rush Hill Rd 150 A3
Rush Hill Rd, SW11 . . . . .150 A3
Rushley Cl, Kes. BR2 . . . .206 A4
Rushmead, E2 . . . . .112 E3
  off Florida St
  Richmond TW10 . . . . .163 E3
Rushmead Cl, Croy. CR0 .202 C4
Rushmere Ct, Wor.Pk.
  KT4 off The Avenue . . .197 G2
Rushmere Ho, SW15
  off Fontley Way 165 G1
Rushmere Pl, SW19 . . . . .166 A5
Rushmoor Cl, Pnr. HA5 . . .66 B4
Rushmore Cl, Brom. BR1 .192 B3
Rushmore Cres, E5
  off Rushmore Rd 95 G4
Rushmore Rd, E5 . . . . .95 F4
Rusholme Av, Dag. RM10 .101 G3
Rusholme Gro, SE19 . . . .170 B5
Rusholme Rd, SW15 . . . .148 A6
Rushout Av, Har. HA3 . . . . .68 E6
Rushton St, N1 . . . . .12 C1
Rushworth St, SE1 . . . . . .27 H3
Rushy Meadow La, Cars.
  SM5 . . . . .199 H2
Ruskin Av, E12 . . . . .98 B6
  Feltham TW14 . . . . . .141 J6
  Richmond TW9 . . . . . .126 A7
  Welling DA16 . . . . . . .158 A3
Ruskin Cl, NW11 . . . . .72 E6
Ruskin Dr, Orp. BR6 . . . . .207 H3
  Welling DA16 . . . . . . .158 A3
  Worcester Park KT4 . . .197 H2
Ruskin Gdns, W5 . . . . . . .105 G4
  Harrow HA3 . . . . .69 J4
Ruskin Gro, Well. DA16 . .158 A2
Ruskin Pk Ho, SE5 . . . . . .152 A3
Ruskin Rd, N17 . . . . .76 C1
  Belvedere DA17 . . . . .139 G4
  Carshalton SM5 . . . . .199 J5
  Croydon CR0 . . . . .201 H2
  Isleworth TW7 . . . . . . .144 C3
  Southall UB1 . . . . .102 E7
Ruskin Wk, N9 . . . . .60 D2
  SE24 . . . . .151 J5
  Bromley BR2 . . . . .192 C6
Ruskin Way, SW19 . . . . . .185 G1
Rusland Av, Orp. BR6 . . . .207 G3
Rusland Hts, Har. HA1
  off Rusland Pk Rd 68 B4
Rusland Pk Rd, Har.
  HA1 . . . . .68 B4
Rusper Cl, NW2 . . . . .89 J3
  Stanmore HA7 . . . . . . .53 F4
Rusper Rd, N22 . . . . .75 J2
  Dagenham RM9 . . . . .100 C6
Russell Av, N22 . . . . .75 H2
Russell Cl, NW10 . . . . .88 C7
  SE7 . . . . .135 J7
  W4 . . . . .127 F6
  Beckenham BR3 . . . . .190 B3
  Bexleyheath DA7 . . . . .159 G4
  Ruislip HA4 . . . . .84 C2
Russell Ct, SW1 . . . . .25 G2
  Surbiton KT6 . . . . .181 H7
Russell Dr, Stai. (Stanw.)
  TW19 . . . . .140 A6
Russell Gdns, N20 . . . . . . .57 H2
  NW11 . . . . .72 B6
  W14 . . . . .128 B3
  Richmond TW10 . . . . .163 F2

Russell Gdns, West Drayton
  (Sipson) UB7 . . . . . . .120 D5
Russell Gdns Ms, W14 . .128 B3
Russell Gro, NW7 . . . . . . .54 E5
  SW9 . . . . .131 G7
Russell Kerr Cl, W4
  off Burlington La 126 C7
Russell La, N20 . . . . .57 H2
Russell Lo, SE1
  off Spurgeon St 28 B5
Russell Mead, Har.
  (Har.Wld) HA3 . . . . . . .68 C1
Russell Par, NW11
  off Golders Grn Rd 72 B6
Russell Pl, NW3
  off Aspern Gro 91 H5
  SE16 off Onega Gate . .133 H3
Russell Rd, E4 . . . . .61 J4
  E10 . . . . .78 B6
  E16 . . . . .115 G6
  E17 . . . . .77 J3
  N8 . . . . .74 D6
  N13 . . . . .59 F6
  N15 . . . . .76 B5
  N20 . . . . .57 H2
  NW9 . . . . .71 F5
  SW19 . . . . .166 D7
  W14 . . . . .128 B3
  Buckhurst Hill IG9 . . . . .63 H1
  Mitcham CR4 . . . . . . .185 H3
  Northolt UB5 . . . . .85 J5
  Twickenham TW2 . . . .144 C6
  Walton-on-Thames
  KT12 . . . . .178 A6
Russell's Footpath,
  SW16 . . . . .169 E5
Russell Sq, WC1 . . . . .10 A6
Russell St, WC2 . . . . .18 B5
Russell's Wf Flats, W10
  off Harrow Rd 108 C4
Russell Wk, Rich. TW10
  off Park Hill 145 J6
Russet Cres, N7
  off Stock Orchard Cres .93 F5
Russet Dr, Croy. CR0 . . . .203 H1
Russets Cl, E4
  off Larkshall Rd 62 D4
Russett Way, SE13
  off Conington Rd 154 B2
Russia Dock Rd, SE16 . . .133 H1
Russia La, E2 . . . . .113 F2
Russia Row, EC2 . . . . .20 A4
Russia Wk, SE16 . . . . . . .133 H2
Rusthall Av, W4 . . . . .126 D4
Rusthall Cl, Croy. CR0 . . .189 F6
Rustic Av, SW16 . . . . . . .168 B7
Rustic Pl, Wem. HA0 . . . . .87 G4
Rustic Wk, E16
  off Lambert Rd 115 H6
Rustington Wk, Mord.
  SM4 . . . . .184 C7
Ruston Av, Surb. KT5 . . . .182 B7
Ruston Gdns, N14
  off Byre Rd 42 A6
Ruston Ms, W11
  off St. Marks Rd 108 B6
Ruston Rd, SE18 . . . . . . .136 B3
Ruston St, E3 . . . . .113 J1
Rust Sq, SE5 . . . . .36 B7
Rutford Rd, SW16 . . . . . .168 E5
Ruth Cl, Stan. HA7 . . . . . . .69 J4
Rutherford Cl, Borwd.
  WD6 . . . . .38 C2
  Sutton SM2 . . . . .199 G6
Rutherford St, SW1 . . . . . .33 H1
Rutherford Twr, Sthl.
  UB1 . . . . .103 H6
Rutherford Way, Bushey
  (Bushey Hth) WD23 . . . .52 A1
  Wembley HA9 . . . . .88 A4
Rutherglen Rd, SE2 . . . . .138 A6
Rutherwyke Cl, Epsom
  KT17 . . . . .197 G6
Ruthin Cl, NW9 . . . . .70 E6
Ruthin Rd, SE3 . . . . .135 G6
Ruthven St, E9
  off Lauriston Rd 95 G1
Rutland Av, Sid. DA15 . . .158 A7
Rutland Cl, SW14 . . . . . . .146 B3
  SW19 off Rutland Rd . .167 H7
  Bexley DA5 . . . . .176 D1
  Chessington KT9 . . . . .195 J6
Rutland Ct, SW7 . . . . .23 H4
  Enfield EN3 . . . . .45 F5
Rutland Dr, Mord. SM4 . .184 C6
  Richmond TW10 . . . . .163 G1
Rutland Gdns, N4 . . . . . . .75 H6
  SW7 . . . . .23 H4
  W13 . . . . .104 D5
  Croydon CR0 . . . . .202 B4
  Dagenham RM8 . . . . .100 C5
Rutland Gdns Ms, SW7 . . .23 H4
  Belvedere DA17 . . . . .139 H5
  Bromley BR2 . . . . .191 F4
Rutland Gate Ms, SW7 . . .23 G4

Rutland Gro, W6 . . . . . . .127 H5
Rutland Ms, NW8
  off Boundary Rd 109 E1
Rutland Ms E, SW7 . . . . . .23 G5
Rutland Ms S, SW7 . . . . . .23 G5
Rutland Ms W, SW7
  off Ennismore St 23 G5
Rutland Pk, NW2 . . . . .89 J6
  SE6 . . . . .171 J2
Rutland Pk Gdns, NW2
  off Rutland Pk 89 J6
Rutland Pk Mans, NW2
  off Rutland Pk 89 J6
Rutland Pl, EC1 . . . . .11 J6
  Bushey (Bushey Hth)
  WD23 off The Rutts . . .52 A1
Rutland Rd, E7 . . . . .98 A7
  E9 . . . . .113 F1
  E11 . . . . .79 H5
  E17 . . . . .78 A6
  SW19 . . . . .167 H7
  Harrow HA1 . . . . .67 J6
  Hayes UB3 . . . . .121 G4
  Ilford IG1 . . . . .99 E4
  Southall UB1 . . . . .103 G5
  Twickenham TW2 . . . .162 A2
Rutland St, SW7 . . . . .23 H5
Rutland Wk, SE6 . . . . . . .171 J2
Rutley Cl, SE17 . . . . .35 G5
Rutlish Rd, SW19 . . . . . . .184 D1
Rutter Gdns, Mitch. CR4 .185 F4
Rutters Cl, West Dr. UB7 .120 D2
Rutts, The, Bushey
  (Bushey Hth) WD23 . . . .52 A1
Rutts Ter, SE14 . . . . .153 G1
Ruvigny Gdns, SW15 . . . .148 A3
Ruxley Cl, Epsom KT19 . .196 B5
  Sidcup DA14 . . . . .176 D6
Ruxley Cor, Sid. DA14 . . .176 E6
Ruxley Cor Ind Est, Sid.
  DA14 . . . . .176 D6
Ruxley Cres, Esher (Clay.)
  KT10 . . . . .194 E6
Ruxley La, Epsom KT19 . .196 D5
Ruxley Ms, Epsom KT19 .196 B5
Ruxley Ridge, Esher
  (Clay.) KT10 . . . . .194 D7
Ryalls Ct, N20 . . . . .57 J3
Ryan Cl, SE3 . . . . .155 J4
  Ruislip HA4 . . . . .84 B1
Ryan Dr, Brent. TW8 . . . .124 D6
Ryarsh Cres, Orp. BR6 . . .207 H4
Rycott Path, SE22
  off Lordship La 152 D7
Rycroft Way, N17 . . . . .76 C3
Rycullf Sq, SE3 . . . . .155 F2
Rydal Cl, NW4 . . . . .72 B1
Rydal Cres, Grnf.
  (Perivale) UB6 . . . . . .105 E3
Rydal Dr, Bexh. DA7 . . . .159 G1
  West Wickham BR4 . . .205 E2
Rydal Gdns, NW9 . . . . . . .71 E5
  SW15 . . . . .164 E5
  Hounslow TW3 . . . . . .143 H6
  Wembley HA9 . . . . .87 F1
Rydal Rd, SW16 . . . . .168 D4
Rydal Way, Enf. EN3 . . . . .45 F6
  Ruislip HA4 . . . . .84 C4
Ryde Pl, Twick. TW1 . . . . .145 F6
Ryder Cl, Brom. BR1 . . . .173 H5
Ryder Ct, SW1 . . . . .25 G1
Ryder Dr, SE16 . . . . .132 E5
Ryder Ms, E9
  off Homerton High St . .95 F5
Ryders Ter, NW8 . . . . .6 C1
Ryder St, SW1 . . . . .25 G1
Ryder Yd, SW1 . . . . .25 G1
Ryde Vale Rd, SW12 . . . .168 B2
Rydon Ms, SW19 . . . . . . .165 J7
Rydons Cl, SE9 . . . . .156 B3
Rydon St, N1
  off St. Paul St 111 J1
Rydston Cl, N7 . . . . .93 F7
Rye, The, N14 . . . . .42 C7
Rye Cl, Bex. DA5 . . . . . . .159 H6
Ryecotes Mead, SE21 . . .170 B1
Ryecroft Av, Ilf. IG5 . . . . . .80 E2
  Twickenham TW2 . . . .143 H7
Ryecroft Cres, Barn. EN5 . .39 H5
Ryecroft Rd, SE13 . . . . . .154 C5
  SW16 . . . . .169 G6
  Orpington BR5 . . . . . .193 G6
Ryecroft St, SW6 . . . . . . .148 E1
Ryedale, SE22 . . . . .152 E6
Ryefield Ct, Nthwd. HA6
  off Ryefield Cres 66 A2
Ryefield Cres, Nthwd.
  HA6 . . . . .66 A2
Ryefield Par, Nthwd. HA6
  off Ryefield Cres 66 A2
Ryefield Path, SW15 . . . .165 G1
Ryefield Rd, SE19 . . . . . .169 J6
Ryegates, SE15
  off Caulfield Rd 153 E2
Rye Hill Pk, SE15 . . . . . . .153 F4

Ryelands Cres, SE12 ....155 J6
Rye La, SE15 ....152 D1
Rye Pas, SE15 ....152 D3
Rye Rd, SE15 ....153 G4
Rye Wk, SW15 ....148 A5
Rye Way, Edg. HA8
off Canons Dr 53 J6
Ryfold Rd, SW19 ....166 D3
Ryhope Rd, N11 ....58 B4
Rylandes Rd, NW2 ....89 G3
Ryland Ho, Croy. CR0 ....201 J3
Ryland Rd, NW5 ....92 B6
Rylett Cres, W12 ....127 F3
Rylett Rd, W12 ....127 F2
Rylston Rd, N13 ....60 A3
SW6 ....128 C6
Rymer Rd, Croy. CR0 ....188 B7
Rymer St, SE24 ....151 H6
Rymill St, E16 ....136 D1
Rysbrack St, SW3 ....23 J5
Rythe Cl, Chess. KT9
off Nigel Fisher Way ..195 F7
Esher KT10
off Rythe Rd 194 B5
Rythe Ct, T.Ditt. KT7 ....180 D7
Rythe Rd, Esher (Clay.)
KT10 ....194 A5

S

★ Saatchi Gall, The,
SW3 ....32 A3
Sabbarton St, E16
off Silvertown Way ...115 F6
Sabella Ct, E3
off Mostyn Gro 113 J2
Sabine Rd, SW11 ....149 J3
Sable Cl, Houns. TW4 ....142 C3
Sable St, N1 ....93 H7
Sach Rd, E5 ....95 E2
Sackville Av, Brom. BR2 ..205 G1
Sackville Cl, Har. HA2 ....86 A3
Sackville Est, SW16 ....169 E3
Sackville Gdns, Ilf. IG1 ....98 C1
Sackville Rd, Sutt. SM2 ..198 D7
Sackville St, W1 ....17 G6
Saddlers Cl, Barn.
(Arkley) EN5 ....39 H5
Borehamwood WD6
off Farriers Way 38 D6
Pinner HA5 ....51 G6
Saddlers Ms, SW8
off Portland Gro 151 E1
Kingston upon Thames
(Hmptn W.) KT1 ....181 F1
Wembley HA0
off The Boltons 86 C4
Saddlers Path, Borwd.
WD6 ....38 D5
Saddlescombe Way, N12 ..56 D5
Saddle Yd, W1 ....24 D1
Sadler Cl, Mitch. CR4 ....185 J2
Sadler Ho, E3
off Bromley High St ..114 B3
Sadlers Gate Ms, SW15
off Commondale 147 J3
Sadlers Ride, W.Mol.
KT8 ....179 J2
★ Sadler's Wells Thea,
EC1 ....11 G3
Saffron Av, E14 ....114 D7
Saffron Cl, NW11 ....72 C5
Croydon CR0 ....186 E6
Saffron Ct, Felt. TW14
off Staines Rd 141 F7
Saffron Hill, EC1 ....11 F6
Saffron Rd, Rom. RM5 ....83 J2
Saffron St, EC1 ....19 F1
Saffron Way, Surb. KT6 ..195 G1
Sage Cl, E6
off Bradley Stone Rd .116 C5
Sage Ms, SE22
off Lordship La 152 C5
Sage St, E1 off Cable St ..113 F7
Sage Way, WC1 ....10 C4
Saigasso Cl, E16
off Royal Rd 116 A6
Sailacre Ho, SE10
off Calvert Rd 135 F5
Sail Ct, E14
off Newport Av 114 D7
Sailmakers Ct, SW6
off William
Morris Way 149 F3
Sail St, SE11 ....34 D1
Sainfoin Rd, SW17 ....168 A2
Sainsbury Rd, SE19 ....170 B5
St. Agatha's Dr, Kings.T.
KT2 ....163 J6
St. Agathas Gro, Cars.
SM5 ....199 J1
St. Agnes Cl, E9
off Gore Rd 113 F1
St. Agnes Pl, SE11 ....35 G6
St. Agnes Well, EC1
off Old St 12 C5
St. Aidans Ct, W13
off St. Aidans Rd 125 F2
Barking IG11
off Choats Rd 118 B3
St. Aidan's Rd, SE22 ....152 E6
St. Aidans Rd, W13 ....125 E2
St. Albans Av, E6 ....116 C3
St. Alban's Av, W4 ....126 D4
St. Albans Av, Felt. TW13 .160 D5
St. Albans Cl, NW11 ....90 D1
St. Albans Ct, EC2 ....20 A3
St. Albans Cres, N22 ....75 G1
St. Alban's Cres, Wdf.Grn.
IG8 ....63 G7
St. Alban's Gdns, Tedd.
TW11 ....162 D5
St. Albans Gro, W8 ....22 B5
St. Alban's Gro, Cars.
SM5 ....185 H7
St. Albans La, NW11 ....90 D1
St. Alban's Pl, N1 ....111 H1
St. Albans Rd, NW5 ....92 A3
NW10 ....106 E1
Barnet EN5 ....40 A1
Ilford IG3 ....99 J1
St. Alban's Rd, Kings.T.
KT2 ....163 H6
Sutton SM1 ....198 C4
Woodford Green IG8 ...63 G7
St. Albans St, SW1 ....17 H6
St. Albans Ter, W6
off Margravine Rd ...128 B6
St. Alban's Vil, NW5
off Highgate Rd 92 A3
St. Alfege Pas, SE10 ....134 C6
St. Alfege Rd, SE7 ....136 A6
St. Alphage Gdns, EC2 ....20 A2
St. Alphage Highwalk,
EC2 ....20 B2
St. Alphage Wk, Edg. HA8 .70 C2
St. Alphege Rd, N9 ....45 F7
St. Alphonsus Rd, SW4 ..150 C4
St. Amunds Cl, SE6 ....172 A4
St. Andrews Av, Wem.
HA0 ....86 D4
St. Andrew's Cl, N12
off Woodside Av 57 F4
St. Andrews Cl, NW2 ....89 H3
SE16 off Ryder Dr 133 E5
SE28 ....118 D6
SW19 ....166 E6
St. Andrew's Cl, Islw.
TW7 ....144 A1
St. Andrews Cl, Ruis. HA4 .84 D2
Stanmore HA7 ....69 F2
Thames Ditton KT7 ....194 E1
St. Andrew's Ct, SW18 ...167 F2
St. Andrews Dr, Stan.
HA7 ....69 F1
St. Andrew's Gro, N16 ....94 A1
St. Andrew's Hill, EC4 ....19 H5
St. Andrew's Ms, N16 ....94 B1
St. Andrews Ms, SE3
off Mycenae Rd 135 G7
SW12
off Emmanuel Rd 168 D1
St. Andrews Pl, NW1 ....8 E5
St. Andrews Rd, E11 ....78 E6
E13 ....115 H3
E17 ....77 G2
N9 ....45 F7
NW9 ....88 D1
NW10 ....89 H6
NW11 ....72 C6
W3 ....107 E7
W7
off Churchfield Rd ...124 B2
W14 ....128 B6
Carshalton SM5 ....199 H3
Croydon CR0
off Lower Coombe St .201 J4
Enfield EN1 ....44 A3
Ilford IG1 ....80 C7
Sidcup DA14 ....176 D3
St. Andrew's Rd, Surb.
KT6 ....181 G6
St. Andrews Rd, Wat.
WD19 ....50 D3
St. Andrews Sq, W11
off Bartle Rd 108 B6
St. Andrew's Sq, Surb.
KT6 ....181 G6
St. Andrews Twr, Sthl.
UB1 ....103 J7
St. Andrew St, EC4 ....19 F2
St. Andrews Way, E3 ....114 B4
St. Anna Rd, Barn. EN5
off Sampson Av 40 A5
St. Annes Av, Stai.
(Stanw.) TW19 ....140 A7
St. Anne's Cl, N6 ....92 A3
Watford WD19 ....50 C4
St. Anne's Ct, W1 ....17 H4
St. Annes Gdns, NW10 ...105 J3
St. Annes Pas, E14
off Newell St 113 J6
St. Annes Rd, E11 ....96 D2
St. Anne's Rd, Wem. HA0 ..87 G5
St. Anne's Row, E14
off Commercial Rd ...113 J6
St. Anne St, E14
off Commercial Rd ...113 J6
St. Ann's, Bark. IG11 ....117 F1
St. Ann's Cres, SW18 ....149 F6
St. Ann's Gdns, NW5
off Queen's Cres 92 A6
St. Ann's Hill, SW18 ....149 E5
St. Ann's La, SW1 ....25 J5
St. Ann's Pk Rd, SW18 ...149 F6
St. Ann's Pas, SW13 ....147 E3
St. Anns Rd, N9 ....60 C2
St. Ann's Rd, N15 ....75 H5
SW13 ....147 F2
St. Anns Rd, W11 ....108 A7
St. Ann's Rd, Bark. IG11
off Axe St 117 F1
Harrow HA1 ....68 B6
St. Ann's Shop Cen, Har.
HA1 ....68 B6
St. Ann's St, SW1 ....25 J5
St. Ann's Ter, NW8 ....7 F1
St. Anns Vil, W11 ....128 A1
St. Anns Way, S.Croy.
CR2 ....201 H6
St. Anselm's Pl, W1 ....16 D4
St. Anselms Rd, Hayes
UB3 ....121 J2
St. Anthonys Av, Wdf.Grn.
IG8 ....63 J6
St. Anthonys Cl, E1 ....29 H1
SW17
off College Gdns 167 H2
St. Anthony's Way, Felt.
TW14 ....141 J4
St. Antony's Rd, E7 ....97 H7
St. Arvans Cl, Croy. CR0 ..202 B3
St. Asaph Rd, SE4 ....153 G3
St. Aubins Ct, N1
off De Beauvoir Est ..112 A1
St. Aubyn's Av, SW19 ....166 C5
St. Aubyns Av, Houns.
TW3 ....143 G5
St. Aubyns Cl, Orp. BR6 ..207 J3
St. Aubyns Gdns, Orp.
BR6 ....207 J2
St. Aubyn's Rd, SE19 ....170 C6
St. Audrey Av, Bexh. DA7 .159 G2
St. Augustine's Av, W5 ...105 H2
St. Augustines Av, Brom.
BR2 ....192 B5
St. Augustine's Av, S.Croy.
CR2 ....201 J6
St. Augustines Av, Wem.
HA9 ....87 H3
St. Augustines Ct, SE1
off Lynton Rd 132 E5
St. Augustine's Path, N5
off Highbury New Pk ..93 J4
St. Augustines Rd, NW1 ...92 D7
St. Augustine's Rd, Belv.
DA17 ....139 F4
St. Austell Cl, Edg. HA8 ...69 J2
St. Austell Rd, SE13 ....154 C2
St. Awdry's Rd, Bark. IG11 .99 G7
St. Awdry's Wk, Bark. IG11
off Station Par 99 F7
St. Barnabas Cl, SE22
off East Dulwich Gro .152 B5
Beckenham BR3 ....190 C2
St. Barnabas Ct, Har. HA3 .67 J1
St. Barnabas Gdns, W.Mol.
KT8 ....179 G5
St. Barnabas Rd, E17 ....78 A6
Mitcham CR4 ....168 A7
Sutton SM1 ....199 G5
Woodford Green IG8 ...79 H1
St. Barnabas St, SW1 ....32 C3
St. Barnabas Ter, E9 ....95 G5
St. Barnabas Vil, SW8 ....151 E1
St. Bartholomews Cl,
SE26 ....171 F4
St. Bartholomew's Rd,
E6 ....116 B1
★ St. Bartholomew-
the-Great Ch, EC1 ....19 H2
St. Benedict's Cl, SW17
off Church La 168 A5
St. Benet's Cl, SW17
off College Gdns 167 H2
St. Benet's Gro, Cars.
SM5 ....185 F7
St. Benet's Pl, EC3 ....20 C5
St. Bernards, Croy. CR0 ..202 B3
St. Bernard's Cl, SE27 ....170 A4
St. Bernard's Rd, E6 ....116 A1
St. Blaise Av, Brom. BR1 .191 H2
St. Botolph Row, EC3 ....21 F4
St. Botolph St, EC3 ....21 F4
St. Brelades Ct, N1
off Balmes Rd 112 A1
St. Brides Av, EC4 ....19 G4
Edgware HA8 ....69 J1
★ St. Bride's Ch, EC4 ....19 G4
St. Brides Cl, Erith DA18
off St. Katherines Rd .138 D2
St. Bride's Pas, EC4
off Salisbury Ct 19 G4
St. Bride St, EC4 ....19 G3
St. Catherines Cl, SW17 ..167 H2
Chessington KT9 ....195 G6
St. Catherines Ct, Felt.
TW13 ....160 A1
St. Catherines Dr, SE14
off Kitto Rd 153 G2
St. Catherine's Ms, SW3 ....31 J1
St. Catherines Rd, E4 ....62 A2
St. Cecelia's Pl, SE3
off Humber Rd 135 G5
St. Cecilia's Cl, Sutt. SM3 .198 B1
St. Chads Cl, Surb.
(Long Dit.) KT6 ....181 F7
St. Chad's Gdns, Rom.
RM6 ....82 E7
St. Chad's Pl, WC1 ....10 B3
St. Chad's Rd, Rom.
RM6 ....82 E6
St. Chad's St, WC1 ....10 B3
St. Charles Pl, W10
off Chesterton Rd 108 B5
St. Charles Sq, W10 ....108 B5
St. Christopher's Cl, Islw.
TW7 ....144 B1
St. Christopher's Dr,
Hayes UB3 ....102 B7
St. Christophers Gdns,
Th.Hth. CR7 ....187 G3
St. Christophers Ms,
Wall. SM6 ....200 C5
St. Christopher's Pl, W1 ...16 C3
St. Clair Cl, Ilf. IG5 ....80 C2
St. Clair Dr, Wor.Pk. KT4 ..197 H3
St. Clair Rd, E13 ....115 H2
St. Clair's Rd, Croy. CR0 ..202 B2
St. Clare Business Pk,
Hmptn. TW12 ....161 J6
St. Clare St, EC3 ....21 F4
★ St. Clement Danes Ch,
WC2 ....18 D4
St. Clements Ct, EC4
off Clements La 20 C5
N7 off Arundel Sq 93 F6
St. Clements Hts, SE26 ..170 D3
St. Clement's La, WC2 ....18 D4
St. Clements St, N7 ....93 G6
St. Clements Yd, SE22
off Archdale Rd 152 C5
St. Cloud Rd, SE27 ....169 J4
St. Crispins Cl, NW3 ....91 H4
Southall UB1 ....103 F6
St. Cross St, EC1 ....19 F1
St. Cuthberts Gdns, Pnr.
HA5 off Westfield Pk 51 F7
St. Cuthberts Rd, N13 ....59 G6
NW2 ....90 C6
St. Cyprian's St, SW17 ...167 J4
St. Davids Cl, SE16
off Masters Dr 133 E5
Wembley HA9 ....88 C3
St. David's Cl, W.Wick.
BR4 ....190 B7
St. David's Ct, E17 ....78 C3
St. Davids Dr, Edg. HA8 ...69 J1
St. Davids Ms, E3
off Morgan St 113 H3
St. Davids Pl, NW4 ....71 H7
St. Davids Sq, E14 ....134 B5
St. Denis Rd, SE27 ....170 A4
St. Dionis Rd, SW6 ....148 C2
St. Donatts Rd, SE14 ....153 J1
St. Dunstans, Sutt. SM1
off Cheam Rd 198 C6
St. Dunstan's All, EC3 ....20 D5
St. Dunstans Av, W3 ....106 D7
St. Dunstans Cl, Hayes
UB3 ....121 J4
St. Dunstan's Ct, EC4
off Fleet St 19 F4
St. Dunstans Gdns, W3
off St. Dunstans Av ...106 D7
St. Dunstan's Hill, EC3 ....20 D6
Sutton SM1 ....198 B5
St. Dunstan's La, EC3 ....20 D6
Beckenham BR3 ....190 C6
St. Dunstan's Rd, E7 ....97 J6
St. Dunstans Rd, SE25 ...188 C4
W6 ....128 A5
W7 ....124 B2
Hounslow TW4 ....142 C2
St. Edmunds Cl, NW8
off St. Edmunds Ter ..109 J1
SW17
off College Gdns 167 H2
Erith DA18
off St. Katherines Rd .138 D2
St. Edmunds Dr, Stan.
HA7 ....68 D1
St. Edmund's La, Twick.
TW2 ....143 H7

St. Edmunds Rd, N9 .....44 D7
Ilford IG1 .....80 C6
St. Edmunds Sq, SW13 ..127 J6
St. Edmunds Ter, NW8 .....7 H1
St. Edwards Cl, NW11 ....72 D6
St. Egberts Way, E4 .....62 C1
St. Elmo Rd, W12 .....127 F1
St. Elmos Rd, SE16 .....133 G2
St. Erkenwald Ms,
Bark. IG11
off St. Erkenwald Rd ..117 G1
St. Erkenwald Rd, Bark.
IG11 .....117 G1
St. Ermin's Hill, SW1 .....25 H5
St. Ervans Rd, W10 .....108 B5
St. Faiths Cl, Enf. EN2 .....43 J1
St. Faith's Rd, SE21 .....169 H1
St. Fillans Rd, SE6 .....172 C1
St. Francis Cl, Orp. BR5 ..193 H6
Watford WD19 .....50 B1
St. Francis Pl, SW12
off Malwood Rd 150 B6
St. Francis Rd, SE22 .....152 B4
St. Francis Way, Ilf. IG1 ....99 H4
St. Frideswides Ms, E14
off Lodore St 114 C6
St. Gabriel's Cl, E11 .....97 H2
E14 *off Morris Rd* 114 B5
St. Gabriels Rd, NW2 .....90 A5
St. George's, Har. HA1 ....68 B6
St. Georges Av, E7 .....97 H7
N7 .....92 D4
NW9 .....70 C4
St. George's Av, W5 .....125 G2
St. Georges Av, Sthl.
UB1 .....103 F7
St. Georges Circ, SE1 .....27 G5
St. Georges Cl, NW11 .....72 C6
SE28
off Redbourne Dr 118 D6
St. George's Cl, SW8
off Patmore St 150 C1
St. Georges Cl, Wem. HA0 .86 D3
St. Georges Ct, E6 .....116 C4
EC4 .....19 G3
SW7 .....22 C5
St. George's Dr, SW1 .....32 E2
St. Georges Dr, Wat.
WD19 .....50 E3
St. Georges Flds, W2 .....15 H4
St. George's Gdns, Surb.
KT6 .....196 B2
St. Georges Gro, SW17 ..167 G3
St. George's Ind Est, N22 ..59 H7
St. Georges Ind Est,
Kings.T. KT2 .....163 G5
St. Georges La, EC3
off Pudding La 20 C5
St. Georges Ms, NW1
off Regents Pk Rd 91 J7
SE1 .....27 F5
SE8 *off Grove St* 133 J4
St. Georges Pl, Twick.
TW1 *off Church St* 162 D1
St. Georges Rd, E7 .....97 H6
E10 .....96 C3
N9 .....60 D3
N13 .....59 F3
NW11 .....72 C6
SE1 .....27 F5
St. George's Rd, SW19 ...166 C6
St. Georges Rd, W4 .....126 E2
W7 .....124 C1
St. George's Rd, Beck.
BR3 .....190 B1
St. Georges Rd, Brom.
BR1 .....192 C2
Dagenham RM9 .....100 E5
St. George's Rd, Felt.
TW13 .....160 D4
St. Georges Rd, Ilf. IG1 ....80 C7
St. George's Rd, Kings.T.
KT2 .....164 A7
Mitcham CR4 .....186 B3
Orpington BR5 .....193 G6
St. Georges Rd, Rich.
TW9 .....145 J3
St. George's Rd, Sid.
DA14 .....176 D6
St. Georges Rd, Twick.
TW1 .....145 E5
Wallington SM6 .....200 B5
St. Georges Rd W, Brom.
BR1 .....192 B1
St. Georges Sq, E7 .....97 H7
E14 *off Narrow St* 113 H7
SE8 .....133 J4
St. George's Sq, SW1 .....33 H3
New Malden KT3
off High St 183 E3
St. George's Sq Ms, SW1 ..33 H4
St. Georges Ter, NW1
off Regents Pk Rd 91 J7
St. George St, W1 .....17 E4
St. Georges Wk, Croy.
CR0 .....201 J3
St. Georges Way, SE15 ....36 D6
St. George Wf, SW8 .....34 A4
St. Gerards Cl, SW4 .....150 C5
St. German's Pl, SE3 .....155 G1
St. Germans Rd, SE23 ...171 H1
St. Giles Av, Dag. RM10 ..101 H7
St. Giles Cl, Dag. RM10
off St. Giles Av 101 H7
Hounslow TW5 .....123 E7
Orpington BR6 .....207 G5
St. Giles Ct, WC2
off St. Giles High St ...18 A3
St. Giles High St, WC2 ....17 J3
St. Giles Pas, WC2 .....17 J4
St. Giles Rd, SE5 .....132 B7
St. Gilles Ho, E2 .....113 G2
St. Gothard Rd, SE27 ....170 A4
St. Gregory Cl, Ruis. HA4 ..84 C4
St. Helena Rd, SE16 .....133 G4
St. Helena St, WC1 .....10 E4
St. Helens Cres, SW16
off St. Helens Rd 187 F1
St. Helens Gdns, W10 ....108 A6
St. Helens Pl, EC3 .....20 D3
St. Helens Rd, SW16 ....187 F1
St. Helen's Rd, W13
off Dane Rd 125 F1
St. Helens Rd, Erith
DA18 .....138 D2
Ilford IG1 .....80 C6
ST. HELIER, Cars. SM5 ...185 G7
St. Helier Av, Mord. SM4 .185 F7
St. Heliers Av, Houns.
TW3 .....143 G5
St. Heliers Rd, E10 .....78 C6
St. Hildas Cl, NW6 .....90 A7
SW17 .....167 H2
St. Hilda's Rd, SW13 .....127 H6
St. Hughe's Cl, SW17 ....167 H2
St. Hughs Rd, SE20
off Ridsdale Rd 188 E1
St. James Av, N20 .....57 H3
W13 .....124 D1
Sutton SM1 .....198 D5
St. James Cl, N20 .....57 H3
NW8
off Prince Albert Rd ..109 J1
SE18
off Congleton Gro ...137 F5
Barnet EN4 .....41 G4
New Malden KT3 .....183 F5
Ruislip HA4 .....84 C2
St. James Gdns, Rom.
(Lt.Hth) RM6 .....82 B4
Wembley HA0 .....87 G7
St. James Gate, NW1
off St. Paul's Cres 92 D7
St. James Gro, SW11
off Reform St 149 J2
St. James Ms, E14 .....134 C3
E17
off St. James's St 77 H5
St. James Rd, E15 .....97 F5
N9 *off Queens Rd* 60 E2
Carshalton SM5 .....199 H3
Kingston upon Thames
KT1 .....181 H2
Mitcham CR4 .....168 A7
Surbiton KT6 .....181 G6
Sutton SM1 .....198 D5
ST. JAMES'S, SW1 .....25 G2
St. James's, SE14 .....153 H1
St. James's Av, E2 .....113 F2
Beckenham BR3 .....189 H3
Hampton (Hmptn H.)
TW12 .....161 J5
St. James's Cl, SW17 ....167 J2
St. James's Cotts, Rich.
TW9 *off Paradise Rd* ..145 H5
St. James's Ct, SW1 .....25 G5
St. James's Cres, SW9 ...151 G3
St. James's Dr, SW12 ....167 J1
SW17 .....167 J1
St. James's Gdns, W11 ...128 B1
St. James's La, N10 .....74 B4
St. James's Mkt, SW1 ....17 H6
★ **St. James's Palace**,
SW1 .....25 G3
★ **St. James's Park**,
SW1 .....25 H3
St. James's Pk, Croy.
CR0 .....187 J7
St. James's Pas, EC3 .....21 E4
St. James's Pl, SW1 .....25 F2
St. James's Rd, SE1 .....37 J3
SE16 .....29 J5
Croydon CR0 .....187 H7
Hampton (Hmptn H.)
TW12 .....161 H5
St. James's Sq, SW1 .....25 G1
St. James's St, E17 .....77 H5
SW1 .....25 F1
St. James's Ter, NW8 .....7 J1
St. James's Ter Ms, NW8 .109 J1
St. James St, W6 .....127 J5
St. James's Wk, EC1 .....11 G5
St. James Ter, SW12 .....168 A1
St. James Way, Sid.
DA14 .....177 E5
St. Joans Rd, N9 .....60 C1
St. John Fisher Rd, Erith
DA18 .....138 D3
ST. JOHN'S, SE8 .....154 A2
St. Johns Av, N11 .....57 J5
St. John's Av, NW10 .....107 F1
SW15 .....148 A5
St. John's Ch Rd, E9 .....95 F5
St. Johns Cl, N14 .....42 C6
St. John's Cl, SW6
off Dawes Rd 128 D7
Wembley HA9 .....87 H5
St. John's Cotts, SE20
off Maple Rd 171 F7
St. Johns Cotts, Rich. TW9
off Kew Foot Rd 145 H3
St. Johns Ct, Buck.H. IG9 ..63 H1
St. John's Ct, Islw. TW7 ..144 C2
St. John's Cres, SW9 ....151 G3
St. Johns Dr, SW18 .....166 E1
St. John's Est, N1 .....12 C2
SE1 .....29 F4
St. John's Gdns, W11 ....108 C7
★ **St. John's Gate & Mus of the Order of St. John**,
EC1 .....11 G6
St. Johns Gro, N19 .....92 C2
SW13
off Terrace Gdns 147 F2
Richmond TW9
off Kew Foot Rd 145 H4
St. John's Hill, SW11 ....149 G4
St. John's Hill Gro, SW11 .149 G4
St. John's La, EC1 .....11 G6
St. John's Ms, W11
off Ledbury Rd 108 D6
St. Johns Par, Sid. DA14 .176 A4
St. John's Pk, SE3 .....135 F7
St. John's Pas, SW19
off Ridgway Pl 166 B6
St. John's Path, EC1 .....11 G6
St. Johns Pathway, SE23
off Devonshire Rd ...171 F1
St. John's Pl, EC1 .....11 G6
St. John's Rd, E4 .....62 B3
E6
off Ron Leighton Way .116 B1
St. Johns Rd, E16 .....115 G6
St. John's Rd, E17 .....78 B2
N15 .....76 B6
St. Johns Rd, NW11 .....72 C6
St. John's Rd, SE20 .....171 F7
SW11 .....149 H4
SW19 .....166 B7
Barking IG11 .....117 H1
Carshalton SM5 .....199 H3
St. Johns Rd, Croy. CR0
off Waddon Rd 201 H3
East Molesey KT8 .....180 A4
St. John's Rd, Felt. TW13 .161 E4
Harrow HA1 .....68 C6
St. Johns Rd, Ilf. IG2 .....81 G7
St. John's Rd, Islw. TW7 ..144 B2
Kingston upon Thames
(Hmptn W.) KT1 .....181 F2
St. Johns Rd, Loug. IG10 ..48 C2
New Malden KT3 .....182 C3
St. John's Rd, Orp. BR5 ..193 G6
Richmond TW9 .....145 H4
St. Johns Rd, Sid. DA14 ..176 B4
Southall UB2 .....122 E3
Sutton SM1 .....198 D2
St. John's Rd, Well. DA16 .158 B3
Wembley HA9 .....87 G4
St. John's Sq, EC1 .....11 G6
St. Johns Ter, E7 .....97 H6
SE18 .....137 F6
SW15
off Kingston Vale 164 E3
W10 *off Harrow Rd* 108 A4
St. John St, EC1 .....11 H6
St. Johns Vale, SE8 .....154 A2
St. Johns Vil, N19 .....92 D2
St. John's Vil, W8 .....22 B6
St. Johns Way, N19 .....92 D1
ST. JOHN'S WOOD, NW8 ...6 E3
St. John's Wd Ct, NW8 .....7 F4
St. John's Wd High St,
NW8 .....7 F2
St. John's Wd Pk, NW8 ..109 G1
St. John's Wd Rd, NW8 ....6 E5
St. John's Wd Ter, NW8 ....7 G1
St. Josephs Cl, W10
off Bevington Rd 108 B5
St. Joseph's Cl, Orp. BR6 .207 J4
St. Joseph's Ct, SE7 .....135 H6
St. Josephs Dr, Sthl. UB1 123 E1
St. Joseph's Gro, NW4 ....71 H4
St. Josephs Rd, N9 .....45 E7
St. Josephs St, SW8
off Battersea Pk Rd ...150 B1
St. Joseph's Vale, SE3 ....154 D2
St. Jude's Rd, E2 .....113 E2
St. Jude St, N16 .....94 B5
St. Julian's Cl, SW16 ....169 G4
St. Julian's Fm Rd, SE27 .169 G4
St. Julian's Rd, NW6 .....90 C7
★ **St. Katharine Docks**,
E1 .....21 G6
St. Katharines Prec, NW1 ...8 D1
St. Katharine's Way, E1 ....29 G1
St. Katherines Rd, Erith
DA18 .....138 D2
St. Katherine's Row, EC3
off Fenchurch St 21 E4
St. Katherine's Wk, W11
off Freston Rd 108 A7
St. Keverne Rd, SE9 .....174 B4
St. Kilda Rd, W13 .....124 D1
Orpington BR6 .....207 J1
St. Kilda's Rd, N16 .....94 A1
Harrow HA1 .....68 B6
St. Kitts Ter, SE19 .....170 B5
St. Laurence Cl, NW6 ....108 A1
St. Lawrence Cl, Edg. HA8 .53 J7
St. Lawrence Dr, Pnr. HA5 .66 B6
★ **St. Lawrence Jewry Ch**,
EC2 .....20 A3
St. Lawrence St, E14 .....134 C1
St. Lawrence Ter, W10 ....108 B5
St. Lawrence Way, SW9 ..151 G1
St. Leonards Av, E4 .....62 D6
Harrow HA3 .....69 F4
St. Leonard's Cl, Well.
DA16 *off Hook La* 158 A3
St. Leonards Ct, N1 .....12 C3
St. Leonard's Gdns,
Houns. TW5 .....122 E7
St. Leonards Gdns, Ilf. IG1 .99 F5
St. Leonards Ri, Orp.
BR6 .....207 H4
St. Leonards Rd, E14 ....114 B5
NW10 .....106 D4
St. Leonard's Rd, SW14 ..146 B3
St. Leonards Rd, W13 ....105 F7
Croydon CR0 .....201 H3
Esher (Clay.) KT10 ....194 C6
St. Leonard's Rd, Surb.
KT6 .....181 G5
St. Leonards Rd, T.Ditt.
KT7 .....180 D6
St. Leonards Sq, NW5 ....92 A6
St. Leonard's Sq, Surb.
KT6 .....181 G5
St. Leonards St, E3 .....114 B3
St. Leonard's Ter, SW3 ....31 J4
St. Leonards Wk, SW16 ..169 F7
St. Loo Av, SW3 .....31 H5
St. Louis Rd, SE27 .....169 J4
St. Loy's Rd, N17 .....76 B2
St. Lucia Dr, E15 .....115 F1
ST. LUKE'S, EC1 .....12 A5
St. Luke's Av, SW4 .....150 D4
Ilford IG1 .....99 E5
St. Luke's Cl, EC1 .....12 A5
SE25 .....189 E6
St. Luke's Est, EC1 .....12 B4
St. Lukes Ms, W11
off Basing St 108 C6
St. Lukes Rd, W11 .....108 C5
St. Lukes Sq, E16 .....115 F6
St. Luke's St, SW3 .....31 G3
St. Luke's Yd, W9 .....108 C2
St. Malo Av, N9 .....61 F3
ST. MARGARETS, Twick.
TW1 .....144 D5
St. Margarets, Bark. IG11 .117 G1
St. Margarets Av, N15 ....75 H4
N20 .....57 F2
Harrow HA2 .....85 J3
Sidcup DA15 .....175 G3
St. Margaret's Av, Sutt.
SM3 .....198 B3
St. Margarets Cl, EC2
off Lothbury 20 B3
St. Margaret's Ct, SE1 ....28 A2
St. Margaret's Cres,
SW15 .....147 H5
St. Margaret's Dr, Twick.
TW1 .....144 E5
St. Margaret's Gro, E11 ...97 F3
SE18 .....137 F6
St. Margarets Gro, Twick.
TW1 .....144 D6
St. Margarets La, W8 .....22 A6
St. Margarets Pas, SE13
off Church Ter 154 E3
St. Margarets Path,
SE18 .....137 F5
St. Margarets Rd, E12 ....97 J2
St. Margaret's Rd, N17 ....76 B3
NW10 .....107 J3
St. Margarets Rd, SE4 ...153 J4
W7 .....124 B2
Edgware HA8 .....54 B5
Isleworth TW7 .....144 E4
Twickenham TW1 .....144 E4
St. Margarets Rbt, Twick.
TW1 *off Chertsey Rd* ..144 E6

St. Margarets Sq, SE4
off Adelaide Av 153 J4
St. Margaret's St, SW1 ....26 A4
St. Margaret's Ter, SE18 ..137 F5
St. Marks Cl, SE10
off Ashburnham Gro .134 C7
SW6 off Ackmar Rd ...148 D1
W11 off St. Marks Rd ..108 B6
St. Mark's Cl, Barn. EN5 ...40 E3
St. Marks Cl, Har. HA1
off Nightingale Av 68 E7
St. Marks Cres, NW1 .....110 A1
St. Mark's Gate, E9
off Cadogan Ter 95 J7
St. Mark's Gro, SW10 .....30 B6
St. Mark's Hill, Surb. KT6 .181 H6
St. Mark's Pl, SW19
off Wimbledon Hill Rd .166 C6
St. Marks Pl, W11 ....108 B6
St. Mark's Pl, Dag. RM10
off Reede Way 101 H6
St. Marks Ri, E8 ....94 C5
St. Marks Rd, SE25
off Coventry Rd 188 D4
St. Mark's Rd, W5 ....125 H1
St. Marks Rd, W7 ....124 B2
W10 ....108 A6
W11 ....108 B6
Bromley BR2 ....191 H3
Enfield EN1 ....44 C6
Mitcham CR4 ....185 J2
St. Mark's Rd, Tedd.
TW11 ....163 E7
St. Marks Sq, NW1 ......110 A1
St. Mark St, E1 ....21 G4
★ St. Martin-in-the-Fields
Ch, WC2 ....18 A6
St. Martins Av, E6 ....116 A2
St. Martins Cl, NW1 .....110 C1
Enfield EN1 ....44 E1
Erith DA18
off St. Helens Rd 138 D2
St. Martin's Cl, Wat. WD19 .50 C4
West Drayton UB7
off St. Martin's Rd 120 A3
St. Martin's Ct, WC2
off St. Martin's La 18 A5
St. Martins Est, SW2 .....169 G1
St. Martin's La, WC2 ......18 A5
St. Martins La, Beck. BR3 .190 B5
St. Martin's-le-Grand, EC1 .19 J3
St. Martin's Ms, WC2 .....18 A6
St. Martin's Pl, WC2 ......18 A6
St. Martins Rd, N9 ....60 E2
St. Martin's Rd, SW9 ....151 F2
West Drayton UB7 ....120 A3
St. Martin's St, WC2 ......17 J6
St. Martins Ter, N10
off Pages La 74 A2
St. Martins Way, SW17 ...167 F3
St. Mary Abbots Pl, W8 ..128 C3
St. Mary Abbots Ter, W14 .128 C3
St. Mary at Hill, EC3 ......20 D6
★ St. Mary at Hill Ch,
EC3 ....20 D6
St. Mary Av, Wall. SM6 ...200 A3
St. Mary Axe, EC3 ....20 D4
St. Marychurch St, SE16 .133 F2
St. Mary Graces Ct, E1 ....21 G5
St. Marylebone Cl, NW10
off Craven Pk 106 E1
★ St. Mary-le-Bow Ch,
EC2 ....20 A4
St. Mary Newington Cl,
SE17
off Surrey Sq 36 E3
St. Mary Rd, E17 ....78 A4
St. Marys, Bark. IG11 ....117 G1
St. Marys App, E12 ....98 C5
St. Marys Av, E11 ....79 H6
St. Mary's Av, N3 ....72 B2
Bromley BR2 ....191 E3
Staines (Stanw.) TW19 .140 A7
Teddington TW11 .....162 C6
St. Mary's Av Cen, Sthl.
UB2 ....123 H4
St. Mary's Av N, Sthl.
UB2 ....123 H4
St. Mary's Av S, Sthl.
UB2 ....123 H4
St. Mary's Cl, N17
off Kemble Rd 76 C1
St. Marys Cl, Chess. KT9 .195 J7
Epsom KT17 ....197 G7
St. Mary's Cl, Stai.
(Stanw.) TW19 ....140 A7
Sunbury-on-Thames
TW16 off Green Way .178 A4
St. Mary's Copse, Wor.Pk.
KT4 ....197 E2
St. Marys Ct, E6 ....116 C4
St. Mary's Ct, SE7 ....136 A7
W5 off St. Mary's Rd ..125 G2
St. Mary's Cres, NW4 .....71 H3
St. Marys Cres, Islw.
TW7 ....124 A7
St. Mary's Cres, Stai.
(Stanw.) TW19 ....140 A7
St. Marys Dr, Felt. TW14 ..141 F7
St. Marys Est, SE16
off St. Marychurch St .133 F2
St. Mary's Gdns, SE11 ....35 F1
St. Mary's Gate, W8 ......22 A6
St. Marys Grn, N2
off Thomas More Way .73 F3
St. Mary's Gro, N1 ....93 H6
SW13 ....147 H3
W4 ....126 B6
Richmond TW9 ....145 J4
St. Marys Mans, W2 ......14 E1
St. Mary's Ms, NW6
off Priory Rd 90 E7
Richmond TW10 ......163 F2
St. Marys Path, N1 ......111 H1
St. Mary's Pl, SE9
off Eltham High St ...156 D6
W5 off St. Mary's Rd ..125 G2
W8 ....22 A6
St. Marys Rd, E10 ....96 C3
E13 ....115 H2
N8 off High St 75 E4
N9 ....61 F1
St. Mary's Rd, NW10 ....107 E1
St. Marys Rd, NW11 ......72 B7
St. Mary's Rd, SE15 .....153 F1
SE25 ....188 B3
SW19 (Wimbledon) ...166 B5
W5 ....125 G2
Barnet EN4 ....41 J7
Bexley DA5 ....177 J1
St. Marys Rd, E.Mol. KT8 .180 A5
Ilford IG1 ....99 F2
Surbiton KT6 ....181 G6
Surbiton (Long Dit.)
KT6 ....181 F7
St. Mary's Rd, Wor.Pk.
KT4 ....197 E2
St. Marys Sq, W2 ....14 E1
St. Mary's Sq, W5
off St. Mary's Rd 125 G2
St. Marys Ter, W2 ....14 E1
St. Mary's Twr, EC1
off Fortune St 12 A6
St. Mary St, SE18 ....136 C4
St. Marys Vw, Har. HA3 ...69 F5
St. Mary's Wk, SE11 ......35 F1
St. Mary's Way, Chig. IG7 .64 D5
St. Matthew's Av, Surb.
KT6 ....195 H1
St. Matthew's Dr, Brom.
BR1 ....192 C3
St. Matthew's Rd, SW2 ..151 F4
St. Matthews Rd, W5
off The Common 125 H1
St. Matthew's Row, E2 ....13 H4
St. Matthew St, SW1 .....25 H6
St. Matthias Cl, NW9 .....71 F5
St. Maur Rd, SW6 ....148 C1
St. Mellion Cl, SE28 .....118 D6
St. Merryn Cl, SE18 .....137 G7
St. Michael's All, EC3 .....20 C4
St. Michaels Av, N9 ......45 F7
St. Michael's Av, Wem.
HA9 ....88 A6
St. Michaels Cl, E16
off Fulmer Rd 116 A5
St. Michael's Cl, N3 ......72 C2
St. Michaels Cl, N12 ......57 H5
Bromley BR1 ....192 B3
Erith DA18
off St. Helens Rd 138 D2
Worcester Park KT4 ...197 F2
St. Michaels Cres, Pnr.
HA5 ....67 E6
St. Michaels Gdns, W10
off St. Lawrence Ter ..108 B5
St. Michael's Ms, SW1 ....32 B2
St. Michaels Rd, NW2 ....89 J4
St. Michael's Rd, SW9 ...151 F2
St. Michaels Rd, Croy.
CR0 ....201 J1
Wallington SM6 ......200 C6
Welling DA16 ....158 B3
St. Michaels St, W2 ......15 F3
St. Michaels Ter, N22 .....75 E2
St. Mildred's Ct, EC2
off Poultry 20 B4
St. Mildreds Rd, SE12 ...155 E7
St. Nicholas Cen,
Sutt. SM1
off St. Nicholas Way ..199 E5
St. Nicholas Glebe,
SW17 ....168 A6
St. Nicholas Pl, Loug.
IG10 ....48 D4
St. Nicholas Rd, SE18 ....137 J5
Sutton SM1 ....199 E5
Thames Ditton KT7 ....180 C6
St. Nicholas St, SE8
off Lucas St 154 A1
St. Nicholas Way, Sutt.
SM1 ....198 E4
St. Nicolas La, Chis. BR7 .192 B1
St. Ninian's Ct, N20 ......57 J3
St. Norbert Grn, SE4 .....153 H4
St. Norbert Rd, SE4 .....153 H4
St. Olaf's Rd, SW6 ......128 B7
St. Olaves Ct, EC2 ....20 B4
St. Olave's Est, SE1 ......29 E3
St. Olaves Gdns, SE11 ....34 E1
St. Olaves Rd, E6 ....116 D1
St. Olave's Wk, SW16 ....186 C2
St. Olav's Sq, SE16 ......133 F2
St. Oswald's Pl, SE11 .....34 C4
St. Oswald's Rd, SW16 ...187 H1
St. Oswulf St, SW1 ....33 J2
ST. PANCRAS, WC1 ....10 A4
St. Pancras Way, NW1 ....92 C7
St. Patrick's Ct, Wdf.Grn.
IG8 ....63 E7
St. Paul's All, EC4
off St. Paul's Chyd 19 H4
St. Paul's Av, NW2 ....89 H6
SE16 ....133 G1
St. Pauls Av, Har. HA3 ....69 J5
★ St. Paul's Cath, EC4 ...19 J4
St. Paul's Chyd, EC4 ......19 H4
St. Paul's Cl, SE7 ....136 A5
W5 ....125 J2
St. Pauls Cl, Borwd. WD6 ..38 C5
St. Paul's Cl, Cars. SM5 ..199 H1
St. Pauls Cl, Chess. KT9 .195 G4
Hayes (Harling.) UB3 ..121 G5
St. Paul's Cl, Houns.
TW3 ....143 E2
St. Paul's Ct, W14
off Colet Gdns 128 A4
St. Pauls Ctyd, SE8
off Deptford High St ..134 A6
St. Pauls Cray Rd, Chis.
BR7 ....193 G1
St. Paul's Cres, NW1 ......92 D7
St. Pauls Dr, E15 ....96 D5
St. Paul's Ms, NW1 ....92 D7
St. Paul's Pl, N1 ....94 A6
St. Pauls Ri, N13 ....59 H6
St. Paul's Rd, N1 ....93 H6
N17 ....60 D7
Barking IG11 ....117 F1
Brentford TW8 ....125 G6
Erith DA8 ....139 J7
Richmond TW9 ....145 J3
Thornton Heath CR7 ..187 J3
St. Paul's Shrubbery, N1 ..94 A6
St. Pauls Sq, Brom. BR2 ..191 G2
St. Paul's Ter, SE17 ....35 H5
St. Paul St, N1 ....111 J1
St. Pauls Wk, Kings.T. KT2
off Alexandra Rd 164 A7
St. Pauls Way, E3 ....113 J5
E14 ....113 J5
St. Paul's Way, N3 ....56 E7
St. Pauls Wd Hill, Orp.
BR5 ....193 H2
St. Peter's All, EC3 ....20 C4
St. Peter's Av, E2 ....13 J2
E17 ....78 E4
St. Peters Av, N18 ....60 D4
St. Petersburgh Ms, W2 ...14 A5
St. Petersburgh Pl, W2 ....14 A5
St. Peter's Cl, E2 ....13 J2
St. Peters Cl, SW17 ......167 H2
St. Peter's Cl, Barn. EN5 ...39 H5
St. Peters Cl, Bushey
(Bushey Hth) WD23 ....52 A1
Chislehurst BR7 ......175 G7
Ilford IG2 ....81 H4
St. Peter's Cl, Ruis. HA4 ...84 D2
St. Peter's Ct, NW4 ....71 J5
St. Peters Ct, SE3
off Eltham Rd 155 F5
SE4 off Wickham Rd ...153 J2
West Molesey KT8 ....179 G4
St. Peter's Gdns, SE27 ...169 G3
St. Peter's Gro, W6 ......127 G4
St. Peters Ms, N4
off Warham Rd 75 H5
St. Peter's Pl, W9 ....6 A6
St. Peters Rd, N9 ....61 F1
St. Peter's Rd, W6 ....127 G5
Croydon CR0 ....202 A4
St. Peters Rd, Kings.T.
KT1 ....182 A2
Southall UB1 ....103 G5
Twickenham TW1 .....145 E5
St. Peter's Rd, W.Mol.
KT8 ....179 G4
St. Peter's Sq, E2 ....13 J2
W6 ....127 G5
St. Peters St, N1 ....111 H1
St. Peter's St, S.Croy.
CR2 ....202 A5
St. Peter's St Ms, N1 ......11 H1
St. Peters Ter, SW6 ......128 B7
St. Peter's Vil, W6 ....127 F4
St. Peter's Way, N1 ....94 B7
St. Peters Way, W5 ......105 G5
Hayes (Harling.) UB3 ..121 G5
St. Philip's Av, Wor.Pk.
KT4 ....197 H2
St. Philips Gate, Wor.Pk.
KT4 ....197 H2
St. Philip Sq, SW8 ......150 B2
St. Philip's Rd, E8 ....94 D6
St. Philips Rd, Surb. KT6 .181 G6
St. Philip St, SW8 ....150 B2
St. Philip's Way, N1
off Linton St 111 J1
St. Quentin Ho, SW18
off Fitzhugh Gro 149 G6
St. Quentin Rd, Well.
DA16 ....157 J3
St. Quintin Av, W10 .....107 J5
St. Quintin Gdns, W10 ...107 J5
St. Quintin Rd, E13 .....115 H2
St. Raphael's Way, NW10 ..88 C5
St. Regis Cl, N10 ....74 B2
St. Ronans Cres, Wdf.Grn.
IG8 ....63 G7
St. Rule St, SW8 ....150 C2
St. Saviour's Est, SE1 .....29 F5
St. Saviour's Rd, SW2 ...151 F5
St. Saviours Rd, Croy.
CR0 ....187 J6
Saints Cl, SE27
off Wolfington Rd 169 H4
Saints Dr, E7 ....98 A5
St. Silas Pl, NW5 ....92 A6
St. Silas St Est, NW5 .....92 A6
St. Simon's Av, SW15 ....147 J5
St. Stephens Av, E17 .....78 C5
W12 ....127 H2
W13 ....104 E6
St. Stephens Cl, E17 ......78 B5
NW8 off Avenue Cl 109 H1
Southall UB1 ....103 G5
St. Stephens Cres, W2 ...108 D6
Thornton Heath CR7 ..187 G3
St. Stephens Gdn Est, W2
off Shrewsbury Rd ...108 D6
St. Stephens Gdns, SW15
off Manfred Rd 148 C5
W2 ....108 D6
Twickenham TW1 .....145 F6
St. Stephens Gro, SE13 ..154 C3
St. Stephens Ms, W2
off Chepstow Rd 108 D5
St. Stephen's Par, E7
off Green St 97 J7
St. Stephen's Pas, Twick.
TW1 off Richmond Rd .145 F6
St. Stephen's Rd, E3 .....113 J2
St. Stephens Rd, E6 ......97 J7
St. Stephen's Rd, E17
off Grove Rd 78 B5
St. Stephens Rd, W13 ....105 E6
St. Stephen's Rd, Barn.
EN5 ....40 A5
St. Stephens Rd, Houns.
TW3 ....143 G6
St. Stephen's Rd, West Dr.
UB7 ....120 A1
St. Stephens Row, EC4 ...20 B4
St. Stephens Ter, SW8 ...131 F7
St. Stephen's Wk, SW7 ...30 C1
St. Swithin's La, EC4 .....20 B5
St. Swithun's Rd, SE13 ..154 D5
St. Theresa's Rd, Felt.
TW14 ....141 J4
St. Thomas' Cl, Surb.
KT6 ....195 J1
St. Thomas Ct, Bex. DA5 .159 G7
St. Thomas Dr, Orp. BR5 .207 F1
St. Thomas' Dr, Pnr. HA5 ..67 E1
St. Thomas Gdns, Ilf. IG1 ..99 F6
St. Thomas Rd, E16 ......115 G6
N14 ....42 D7
St. Thomas' Rd, W4 .....126 C6
St. Thomas Rd, Belv.
DA17 ....139 J2
St. Thomas's Gdns, NW5
off Queen's Cres 92 A6
St. Thomas's Pl, E9 ....95 F7
St. Thomas's Rd, N4 ......93 G2
NW10 ....107 E1
St. Thomas's Sq, E9 ......95 E7
St. Thomas St, SE1 ....28 B2
St. Thomas's Way, SW6 ..128 C7
St. Timothy's Ms, Brom.
BR1 off Wharton Rd ...191 H1
St. Ursula Gro, Pnr. HA5 ..66 D5
St. Ursula Rd, Sthl. UB1 ..103 G6
St. Vincent Cl, SE27 .....169 H5
St. Vincent Rd, Twick.
TW2 ....143 J6
St. Vincents La, NW7 .....55 J5
St. Vincent St, W1 ....16 C2
St. Wilfrids Cl, Barn. EN4 .41 H5
St. Wilfrids Rd, Barn. EN4 .41 G5
St. Winefride's Av, E12 ....98 C5
St. Winifreds Cl, Chig. IG7 .65 F5
St. Winifred's Rd, Tedd.
TW11 ....163 E6
Sakura Dr, N22 ....74 D1

Sala Ho, SE3
off Pinto Way 155 H4
Salamanca Pl, SE1 ....34 C2
Salamanca St, SE1 ....34 B2
Salamander Cl, Kings.T.
KT2 ....163 F5
Salcombe Dr, Mord.
SM4 ....198 A1
Romford RM6 ....83 F6
Salcombe Gdns, NW7 ....55 J6
Salcombe Pk, Loug. IG10 ..48 A5
Salcombe Rd, E17 ....77 J7
N16 ....94 B5
Salcombe Vil, Rich. TW10
off The Vineyard 145 H5
Salcombe Way, Ruis. HA4 .84 A2
Salcott Rd, SW11 ....149 H5
Croydon CR0 ....201 E3
Salehurst Cl, Har. HA3 ....69 H5
Salehurst Rd, SE4 ....153 J6
Salem Pl, Croy. CR0 .....201 J3
Salem Rd, W2 ....14 B5
Sale Pl, W2 ....15 G2
Sale St, E2 ....13 H5
Salford Rd, SW2 ....168 D1
Salhouse Cl, SE28
off Rollesby Way 118 C6
Salisbury Av, N3 ....72 C3
Barking IG11 ....99 G7
Sutton SM1 ....198 C6
Salisbury Cl, SE17 ....36 B1
Worcester Park KT4 ...197 F3
Salisbury Ct, EC4 ....19 G4
Edgware HA8 ....53 J4
Salisbury Gdns, SW19 ..166 B7
Buckhurst Hill IG9 ......64 A2
Salisbury Hall Gdns, E4 ...62 A6
Salisbury Ho, E14
off Hobday St 114 B6
Salisbury Ms, SW6
off Dawes Rd 128 C7
Bromley BR2 ....192 B5
Salisbury Pl, SW9 ....131 H7
W1 ....15 J1
Salisbury Rd, E4 ....62 A3
E7 ....97 G6
E10 ....96 C2
E12 ....98 A5
E17 ....78 C5
N4 ....75 H5
N22 ....75 H1
SE25 ....188 D6
SW19 ....166 B7
W13 ....124 D2
Barnet EN5 ....40 B3
Bexley DA5 ....177 G1
Bromley BR2 ....192 B5
Carshalton SM5 ......199 J6
Dagenham RM10 .....101 H6
Feltham TW13 ....160 C1
Harrow HA1 ....68 A5
Hounslow TW4 ....142 C3
Hounslow
(Lon.Hthrw Air.) TW6 .141 F5
Ilford IG3 ....99 H2
New Malden KT3 .....182 D3
Pinner HA5 ....66 A4
Richmond TW9 ....145 H4
Southall UB2 ....123 E4
Worcester Park KT4 ...197 F3
Salisbury Sq, EC4 ....19 F4
Salisbury St, NW8 ....7 F6
W3 ....126 C2
Salisbury Ter, SE15 ......153 F3
Salisbury Wk, N19 ....92 C2
Salix Cl, Sun. TW16
off Oak Gro 160 B7
Salliesfield, Twick. TW2 ...144 A6
Sally Murray Cl, E12 ......98 D4
Salmen Rd, E13 ....115 F2
Salmond Cl, Stan. HA7 ...52 D6
Salmon La, E14 ....113 H6
Salmon Rd, Belv.
DA17 ....139 G5
Salmons Rd, N9 ....60 D1
Chessington KT9 .....195 G6
Salmon St, E14
off Salmon La 113 J6
NW9 ....88 B1
Salomons Rd, E13
off Chalk Rd 115 J5
Salop Rd, E17 ....77 G6
Saltash Cl, Sutt. SM1 ....198 C4
Saltash Rd, Ilf. IG6 ....65 G7
Welling DA16 ....158 C1
Saltcoats Rd, W4 ....126 E2
Saltcroft Cl, Wem. HA9 ....88 B1
Salter Cl, Har. HA2 ....85 F3
Salterford Rd, SW17 .....168 A6
Saltern Ct, Bark. IG11
off Puffin Cl 118 B3
Salter Rd, SE16 ....133 G1
Salters Hall Ct, EC4 ....20 B5
Salters Hill, SE19 ....170 A5
Salters Rd, E17 ....78 D4
W10 ....108 A4
Salter St, E14 ....114 A7
NW10 ....107 G3
Salter St Alleyway, NW10
off Hythe Rd 107 G4
Salterton Rd, N7 ....93 E3
Saltley Cl, E6
off Dunnock Rd 116 B6
Saltoun Rd, SW2 ....151 G4
Saltram Cl, N15 ....76 C4
Saltram Cres, W9 ....108 C3
Saltwell St, E14 ....114 A7
Saltwood Gro, SE17 ......36 B4
Salusbury Rd, NW6 ......108 B1
Salutation Rd, SE10 .....135 E4
Salvia Gdns, Grnf.
(Perivale) UB6
off Selborne Gdns ...104 D2
Salvin Rd, SW15 ....148 A3
Salway Cl, Wdf.Grn.
IG8 ....63 F7
Salway Pl, E15
off Broadway 96 E6
Salway Rd, E15
off Great Eastern Rd ..96 D6
Samantha Cl, E17 ....77 J7
Sam Bartram Cl, SE7 ....135 J5
Sambruck Ms, SE6 ......172 B1
Samels Ct, W6 *off South*
Black Lion La 127 G5
Samford Ho, N1
off Barnsbury Rd 111 G1
Samford St, NW8 ....7 F6
Samira Cl, E17
off Colchester Rd 77 J6
Samos Rd, SE20 ....189 E2
Sampson Av, Barn. EN5 ...40 A5
Sampson Cl, Belv. DA17
off Carrill Way 138 D3
Sampson St, E1 ....29 J2
Samson St, E13 ....115 J2
Samuel Cl, E8
off Pownall Rd 112 C1
SE14 ....133 G6
SE18 ....136 B4
Stanmore HA7 ....52 D2
Samuel Gray Gdns,
Kings.T. KT2 ....181 G1
Samuel Johnson Cl,
SW16 ....169 F4
Samuel Lewis Trust Dws,
N1 *off Liverpool Rd* 93 G6
SW3 ....31 G2
SW6 ....128 D7
W14 *off Lisgar Ter* 128 C4
Samuel Lewis Trust Est,
SE5 *off Warner Rd* ...151 J1
Samuels Ct, W6 *off South*
Black Lion La 127 G5
Samuel St, SE15 ....37 F7
SE18 ....136 C4
Sancroft Cl, NW2 ....89 H3
Sancroft Rd, Har. HA3 ....68 C2
Sancroft St, SE11 ....34 D3
Sanctuary, The, SW1 .....25 J4
Bexley DA5 ....158 D6
Morden SM4 ....184 D6
Sanctuary Ms, E8
off Queensbridge Rd ..94 C6
Sanctuary Rd, Houns.
(Lon.Hthrw Air.) TW6 ..140 D6
Sanctuary St, SE1 ....28 A4
Sandale Cl, N16
off Stoke Newington
Ch St 94 A3
Sandall Cl, W5 ....105 H4
Sandall Ho, E3
off Daling Way 113 H2
Sandall Rd, NW5 ....92 C6
W5 ....105 H4
Sandal Rd, N18 ....60 D5
New Malden KT3 .....182 D5
Sandal St, E15 ....114 E1
Sandalwood Cl, E1
off Solebay St 113 H4
Sandalwood Rd, Felt.
TW13 ....160 B3
Sandbach Pl, SE18 ......137 F4
Sandbourne Av, SW19 ...184 E3
Sandbourne Rd, SE4 .....153 H2
Sandbrook Cl, NW7 ......54 D6
Sandbrook Rd, N16 ......94 B3
Sandby Grn, SE9 ....156 B3
Sandcroft Cl, N13 ....59 H6
Sandell St, SE1 ....27 E3
Sanders Cl, Hmptn.
(Hmptn H.) TW12 .....161 J5
Sanders La, NW7 ....56 A7
Sanderson Cl, NW5 ....92 B4
Sanderson Sq, Brom.
BR1 ....192 D3
Sanderstead Av, NW2 ....90 B2
Sanderstead Cl, SW12 ...150 C7
Sanderstead Rd, E10 ....95 H1
South Croydon CR2 ...202 A7
Sanders Way, N19
off Sussex Way 92 D1
Sandfield Gdns, Th.Hth.
CR7 ....187 H3
Sandfield Pas, Th.Hth.
CR7 ....187 J3
Sandfield Rd, Th.Hth.
CR7 ....187 H3
Sandford Av, N22 ....59 J7
Loughton IG10 ....49 F3
Sandford Cl, E6 ....116 C4
Sandford Ct, N16 ....94 B1
Sandford Rd, E6 ....116 B4
Bexleyheath DA7 .....159 E4
Bromley BR2 ....191 G4
Sandford St, SW6
off King's Rd 129 E7
Sandgate Ho, E5
off Downs Pk Rd 95 E4
W5 *off Queens Wk* 105 F5
Sandgate La, SW18 .....167 H1
Sandgate Rd, Well. DA16 .138 C7
Sandgate St, SE15 ......132 E6
Sandham Pt, SE18
off Vincent Rd 137 E4
Sandhills, Wall. SM6 .....200 D4
Sandhills, The, SW10
off Limerston St 30 D5
Sandhurst Av, Har. HA2 ...67 H6
Surbiton KT5 ....182 B7
Sandhurst Cl, NW9 ....70 A3
Sandhurst Dr, Ilf. IG3 .....99 J4
Sandhurst Rd, N9 ....45 F6
NW9 ....70 A3
SE6 ....172 D1
Bexley DA5 ....158 D5
Sidcup DA15 ....175 J3
Sandhurst Way, S.Croy.
CR2 ....202 B7
Sandifer Dr, NW2 ....90 A3
Sandiford Rd, Sutt. SM3 .198 C2
Sandiland Cres, Brom.
BR2 ....205 F2
Sandilands, Croy. CR0 ...202 D2
Sandilands Rd, SW6 .....148 E1
Sandison St, SE15 ......152 C3
Sandland St, WC1 ....18 D2
Sandlewood Cl, Barn.
EN5 ....39 F5
Sandling Ri, SE9 ....174 D3
Sandlings, The, N22 ......75 G2
Sandlings Cl, SE15
off Pilkington Rd 152 E2
Sandmartin Way, Wall.
SM6 ....186 A7
Sandmere Rd, SW4 .....150 E4
Sandon Cl, Esher KT10 ...180 A7
Sandow Cres, Hayes
UB3 ....121 J3
Sandown Av, Dag. RM10 .101 J6
Sandown Cl, Houns.
TW5 ....142 A1
Sandown Ct, Sutt. SM2
off Grange Rd 198 E7
Sandown Rd, SE25 ......188 E5
Sandown Way, Nthlt. UB5 .85 E6
Sandpiper Cl, E17 ....77 G1
SE16 ....133 J2
Sandpiper Rd, Sutt. SM1 .198 C5
Sandpit Pl, SE7 ....136 B5
Sandpit Rd, Brom. BR1 ..172 E5
Sandpits Rd, Croy. CR0 ..203 G4
Richmond TW10 ......163 G2
Sandra Cl, N22
off New Rd 75 J1
Hounslow TW3 ....143 H5
Sandridge Cl, Har. HA1 ...68 B4
Sandridge St, N19 ....92 C2
Sandringham Av, SW20 ..184 B1
Sandringham Cl, SW19 ..166 A1
Enfield EN1 ....44 B2
Ilford IG6 ....81 F3
Sandringham Ct, W9 ......6 D4
Kingston upon Thames
KT2 *off Skerne Wk* ...181 G1
Sandringham Cres, Har.
HA2 ....85 G2
Sandringham Dr, Well.
DA16 ....157 H2
Sandringham Flats, WC2
off Charing Cross Rd ..17 J5
Sandringham Gdns, N8 ...75 E6
N12 ....57 F6
Hounslow TW5 ....142 A1
Ilford IG6 ....81 F3
West Molesey KT8
off Rosemary Av 179 G4
Sandringham Ms, W5
off High St 105 G7
Hampton TW12
off Oldfield Rd 179 F1
Sandringham Rd, E7 .....97 J5
E8 ....94 C5
E10 ....78 D6
N22 ....75 J3
NW2 ....89 H6
NW11 ....72 B7
Barking IG11 ....99 J6
Sandringham Rd, Bromley
BR1 ....173 G5
Hounslow
(Lon.Hthrw Air.) TW6 .140 B5
Northolt UB5 ....85 G7
Thornton Heath CR7 ..187 J5
Worcester Park KT4 ..197 G3
Sandrock Pl, Croy. CR0 ..203 G4
Sandrock Rd, SE13 ......154 A3
SANDS END, SW6 ......149 F1
Sand's End La, SW6 .....149 E1
Sandstone La, E16 ......115 H7
Sandstone Pl, N19 ....92 B2
Sandstone Rd, SE12 .....173 H2
Sands Way, Wdf.Grn. IG8 .64 B6
Sandtoft Rd, SE7 ....135 H6
Sandwell Cres, NW6 ......90 D6
Sandwich St, WC1 ....10 A4
Sandwick Cl, NW7 ....55 G7
Sandy Bury, Orp. BR6 ...207 G3
Sandycombe Rd, Felt.
TW14 ....160 A1
Richmond TW9 ....146 A3
Sandycoombe Rd, Twick.
TW1 ....145 F6
Sandycroft, SE2 ....138 A6
Sandy Hill Av, SE18 .....136 E5
Sandy Hill Rd, SE18 .....136 E5
Sandyhill Rd, Ilf. IG1 ......98 E4
Sandy La, Har. HA3 ....69 J6
Kingston upon Thames
KT1 ....162 D7
Mitcham CR4 ....186 A1
Northwood HA6 ....50 A5
Richmond TW10 ......163 F2
Sidcup DA14 ....176 D7
Sutton SM2 ....198 B7
Teddington TW11 .....162 D7
Walton-on-Thames
KT12 ....178 B6
Sandy La Est, Rich. TW10 .163 G2
Sandy La N, Wall. SM6 ...200 D6
Sandy La S, Wall. SM6 ...200 D6
Sandymount Av, Stan.
HA7 ....53 F5
Sandy Ridge, Chis. BR7 ..174 D6
Sandy Rd, NW3 ....90 E3
Sandy's Row, E1 ....21 E2
Sandy Way, Croy. CR0 ...203 J3
Sanford La, N16
off Lawrence Bldgs ...94 C2
Sanford St, SE14 ....133 H6
Sanford Ter, N16 ....94 C3
Sanford Wk, N16
off Sanford Ter 94 C2
SE14
off Cold Blow La 133 H6
Sangam Cl, Sthl. UB2
off Dudley Rd 122 E3
Sanger Av, Chess. KT9 ...195 H5
Sangley Rd, SE6 ....154 B7
SE25 ....188 B4
Sangora Rd, SW11 ......149 G4
San Ho, E9
off Bradstock Rd 95 G6
Sansom Rd, E11 ....97 E2
Sansom St, SE5 ....132 A7
Sans Wk, EC1 ....11 F5
Santley St, SW4 ....151 F4
Santos Rd, SW18 ....148 D5
Santway, The, Stan. HA7 ..52 B5
Sapcote Trd Cen, NW10 ...89 F5
Saperton Wk, SE11 ....34 D1
Saphora Cl, Orp. BR6 ....207 G5
Sapperton Ct, EC1 ....11 J5
Sapphire Cl, E6 ....116 D6
Dagenham RM8 ......100 C1
Sapphire Rd, NW10 ......88 C7
SE8 ....133 H4
Saracen Cl, Croy. CR0 ...188 A6
Saracen's Head Yd, EC3 ...21 E4
Saracen St, E14 ....114 A6
Sara Ct, Beck. BR3 ......190 B1
Sarah Ho, SW15 ....147 F4
Saratoga Rd, E5 ....95 F4
Sardinia St, WC2 ....18 C4
Sarita Cl, Har. HA3 ....68 A2
Sarjant Path, SW19
off Queensmere Rd ..166 A2
Sark Cl, Houns. TW5 .....123 G7
Sark Ho, N1
off Clifton Rd 93 J6
Sark Twr, SE28 ....137 F2
Sark Wk, E16 ....115 H6
Sarnesfield Ho, SE15
off Pencraig Way 132 E6
Sarnesfield Rd, Enf. EN2
off Church St 44 A3
Sarre Rd, NW2 ....90 C5
Sarsen Av, Houns. TW3 ..143 F2
Sarsfeld Rd, SW12 ......167 J1
Sarsfield Rd, Grnf.
(Perivale) UB6 ....105 E2
Sartor Rd, SE15 ....153 G4
Sarum Ter, E3
off Bow Common La .113 J4

Satanita Cl, E16
off High Meads Rd 116 A6
Satchell Mead, NW9 71 F1
Satchwell Rd, E2 13 H4
Sattar Ms, N16
off Clissold Rd 94 A3
Saturn Ho, E3
off Garrison Rd 114 A1
Sauls Grn, E11
off Napier Rd 97 E3
Saunders Cl, E14
off Limehouse Causeway 113 J7
Ilford IG1 99 G1
Saunders Ness Rd, E14 134 C5
Saunders Rd, SE18 137 J5
Saunders St, SE11 34 E2
Saunders Way, SE28
off Oriole Way 118 B7
Saunderton Rd, Wem. HA0 86 E5
Saunton Av, Hayes UB3 121 J7
Savage Gdns, E6 116 C6
EC3 21 E5
Savannah Cl, SE15
off Chandler Way 132 C7
Savera Cl, Sthl. UB2
off Scotts Rd 122 C3
Savernake Rd, N9 44 D6
NW3 91 J4
Savery Dr, Surb. (Long Dit.) KT6 181 F7
Savile Cl, N.Mal. KT3 183 E5
Thames Ditton KT7 194 C1
Savile Gdns, Croy. CR0 202 C2
Savile Row, W1 17 F5
Saville Rd, E16 136 B1
W4 126 D3
Romford RM6 83 F6
Twickenham TW1 162 C1
Saville Row, Brom. BR2 205 F1
Enfield EN3 45 G2
Savill Gdns, SW20
off Bodnant Gdns 183 G3
Savill Row, Wdf.Grn. IG8 63 F6
Savona Cl, SW19 166 B7
Savona Est, SW8 130 C7
Savona St, SW8 130 C7
Savoy Av, Hayes UB3 121 H5
Savoy Bldgs, WC2 18 C6
Savoy Circ, W3 107 F7
Savoy Cl, E15
off Arthingworth St 114 E1
Edgware HA8 54 A5
Savoy Ct, WC2 18 B6
Savoy Hill, WC2 18 C6
Savoy Ms, SW9 150 E3
Savoy Pl, WC2 18 B6
Savoy Row, WC2 18 C5
Savoy Steps, WC2
off Savoy Row 18 C6
Savoy St, WC2 18 C5
Savoy Way, WC2 18 C6
Sawbill Cl, Hayes UB4 102 D5
Sawkins Cl, SW19 166 B2
Sawley Rd, W12 127 G1
Sawmill Yd, E3 113 H1
Sawtry Cl, Cars. SM5 185 G7
Sawyer Cl, N9 60 D2
Sawyers Cl, Dag. RM10 101 J6
Sawyer's Hill, Rich. TW10 146 B7
Sawyers Lawn, W13 104 C6
Sawyer St, SE1 27 J3
Saxby Rd, SW2 150 E7
Saxham Rd, Bark. IG11 117 H2
Saxlingham Rd, E4 62 D3
Saxon Av, Felt. TW13 161 F2
Saxonbury Av, Sun. TW16 178 B3
Saxonbury Cl, Mitch. CR4 185 G3
Saxonbury Gdns, Surb. (Long Dit.) KT6 195 F1
Saxon Cl, E17 78 A7
Surbiton KT6 181 G6
Saxon Dr, W3 106 B6
Saxonfield Cl, SW2 151 F7
Saxon Gdns, Sthl. UB1
off Saxon Rd 103 E7
Saxon Rd, E3 113 J2
E6 116 C4
N22 75 H1
SE25 188 A5
Bromley BR1 173 F7
Ilford IG1 99 E6
Kingston upon Thames KT2 181 H1
Southall UB1 123 E1
Wembley HA9 88 C3
Saxon Ter, SE6
off Neuchatel Rd 171 J2
Saxon Wk, Sid. DA14 176 C6
Saxon Way, N14 42 D6
Saxton Cl, SE13 154 D3
Sayers Wk, Rich. TW10
off Stafford Pl 145 J7
Sayesbury La, N18 60 D5
Sayes Ct, SE8
off Sayes Ct St 133 J6
Sayes Ct St, SE8 133 J6
Scadbury Pk, Chis. BR7 175 J6
Scads Hill Cl, Orp. BR6 193 J6
Scala St, W1 17 G1
Scales Rd, N17 76 C3
Scampston Ms, W10 108 A6
Scampton Rd, Houns. (Lon.Hthrw Air.) TW6
off Southampton Rd E 140 C6
Scandrett St, E1 132 E1
Scarba Wk, N1
off Marquess Rd 94 A6
Scarborough Rd, E11 96 D1
N4 75 G7
N9 45 F7
Hounslow (Lon.Hthrw Air.) TW6 off Southern Perimeter Rd 141 F6
Scarborough St, E1 21 G4
Scarbrook Rd, Croy. CR0 201 J3
Scarle Rd, Wem. HA0 87 G6
Scarlet Rd, SE6 172 E3
Scarlette Manor Way, SW2
off Papworth Way 151 G7
Scarsbrook Rd, SE3 156 A3
Scarsdale Pl, W8 22 A5
Scarsdale Rd, Har. HA2 85 J3
Scarsdale Vil, W8 128 D3
Scarth Rd, SW13 147 F3
Scawen Cl, Cars. SM5 200 A4
Scawen Rd, SE8 133 H5
Scawfell St, E2 13 G2
Scaynes Link, N12 56 D5
Sceaux Gdns, SE5 152 B1
Sceptre Rd, E2 113 F3
Schofield Wk, SE3
off Dornberg Cl 135 H7
Scholars Cl, Barn. EN5 40 B4
Scholars Pl, N16
off Oldfield Rd 94 B3
Scholars Rd, E4 62 C1
SW12 168 C1
Scholefield Rd, N19 92 D1
Schomberg Ho, SW1
off Page St 33 J1
Schonfeld Sq, N16 94 A2
Schoolbank Rd, SE10 135 F4
Schoolbell Ms, E3
off Arbery Rd 113 H2
Schoolhouse Gdns, Loug. IG10 48 E4
Schoolhouse La, E1 113 G7
School Ho La, Tedd. TW11 163 E7
Schoolhouse Yd, SE18
off Bloomfield Rd 137 E5
School La, Chig. IG7 65 J4
Kingston upon Thames KT1 off School Rd 181 F1
Pinner HA5 66 E4
Surbiton KT6 196 A1
Welling DA16 158 B3
School Pas, Kings.T. KT1 181 J2
Southall UB1 123 F1
School Rd, E12
off Sixth Av 98 C4
NW10 106 D4
Chislehurst BR7 193 F1
Dagenham RM10 119 G1
East Molesey KT8 180 A4
Hampton (Hmptn H.) TW12 161 J6
Hounslow TW3 143 J3
Kingston upon Thames KT1 181 F1
West Drayton (Harm.) UB7 120 A6
School Rd Av, Hmptn. (Hmptn H.) TW12 161 J6
School Sq, SE10
off Greenroof Way 135 F3
School Way, N12
off High Rd 57 F4
Schoolway, N12 (Woodhouse Rd) 57 G6
School Way, Dag. RM8 100 C3
Schooner Cl, E14 134 D3
SE16 off Kinburn St 133 G2
Barking IG11 118 B3
Schubert Rd, SW15 148 C5
★ **Science Mus**, SW7 23 F6
Scilly Isles, Esher KT10 194 B2
Sclater St, E1 13 F5
Scoble Pl, N16
off Shacklewell La 94 C4
Scoles Cres, SW2 169 G1
Scope Way, Kings.T. KT1 181 H4
Scoresby St, SE1 27 G2
Scorton Av, Grnf. (Perivale) UB6 104 D2
Scotch Common, W13 104 D5
Scoter Cl, Wdf.Grn. IG8
off Mallards Rd 63 H7
Scot Gro, Pnr. HA5 50 D7
Scotia Rd, SW2 151 G7
Scotland Grn, N17 76 C2
Scotland Grn Rd, Enf. EN3 45 G5
Scotland Grn Rd N, Enf. EN3 45 G4
Scotland Pl, SW1 26 A1
Scotland Rd, Buck.H. IG9 63 J1
Scotney Cl, Orp. BR6 206 D4
Scotsdale Cl, Orp. BR5 193 H4
Sutton SM3 198 B7
Scotsdale Rd, SE12 155 H5
Scotswood St, EC1 11 F5
Scotswood Wk, N17 60 D7
Scott Av, SW15 148 B6
Scott Cl, SW16 187 F1
Epsom KT19 196 C5
West Drayton UB7 120 C4
Scott Ct, SW8
off Silverthorne Rd 150 B2
W3
off Petersfield Rd 126 D2
Scott Cres, Har. HA2 85 H1
Scott Ellis Gdns, NW8 6 E4
Scottes La, Dag. RM8
off Valence Av 100 D1
Scott Fm Cl, T.Ditt. KT7 194 E1
Scott Gdns, Houns. TW5 122 D7
Scott Ho, E13
off Queens Rd W 115 G2
N18 60 D5
Scott Lidgett Cres, SE16 29 H4
Scott Rd, Edg. HA8 70 B2
Scott Russell Pl, E14
off Westferry Rd 134 B5
Scotts Av, Brom. BR2 190 D2
Scotts Dr, Hmptn. TW12 161 H7
Scotts Fm Rd, Epsom KT19 196 C6
Scotts La, Brom. BR2 190 D3
Scotts Pas, SE18
off Spray St 137 E4
Scotts Rd, E10 96 C1
W12 127 H2
Bromley BR1 173 G7
Southall UB2 122 C3
Scott St, E1 112 E4
Scott Trimmer Way, Houns. TW3 143 E2
Scottwell Dr, NW9 71 F5
Scoulding Rd, E16 115 F6
Scouler St, E14
off Quixley St 114 D7
Scout App, NW10 88 E4
Scout La, SW4
off Old Town 150 C3
Scout Way, NW7 54 D4
Scovell Cres, SE1 27 J4
Scovell Rd, SE1 27 J4
Scrattons Ter, Bark. IG11 118 D2
Scriven St, E8 112 C1
Scrooby St, SE6 154 B6
Scrubs La, NW10 107 G3
W10 107 G3
Scrutton Cl, SW12 150 D7
Scrutton St, EC2 12 D6
Scudamore La, NW9 70 C3
Scutari Rd, SE22 153 F5
Scylla Cres, Houns. (Lon.Hthrw Air.) TW6 141 E7
Scylla Rd, SE15 152 E3
Hounslow (Lon.Hthrw Air.) TW6 141 E6
Seabright St, E2
off Bethnal Grn Rd 112 E3
Seabrook Dr, W.Wick. BR4 204 E2
Seabrook Gdns, Rom. RM7 83 G7
Seabrook Rd, Dag. RM8 100 D3
Seacole Cl, W3 106 D5
Seacon Twr, E14 133 J2
Seacourt Rd, SE2 138 D2
Seacroft Gdns, Wat. WD19 50 D3
Seafield Rd, N11 58 D4
Seaford Rd, E17 78 B3
N15 76 A5
W13 124 E1
Enfield EN1 44 B4
Hounslow (Lon.Hthrw Air.) TW6 140 A5
Seaford St, WC1 10 B4
Seaforth Av, N.Mal. KT3 183 H5
Seaforth Cres, N5 93 J5
Seaforth Gdns, N21 43 F7
Epsom KT19 197 F4
Woodford Green IG8 63 J5
Seaforth Pl, SW1
off Buckingham Gate 25 G5
Seagrave Cl, E1
off Wellesley St 113 G5
Seagrave Rd, SW6 128 D6
Seagry Rd, E11 79 G6
Seagull Cl, Bark. IG11 118 A3
Seagull La, E16 115 G7
Sealand Rd, Houns. (Lon.Hthrw Air.) TW6 140 D6
Sealand Wk, Nthlt. UB5
off Wayfarer Rd 102 E3
Seal St, E8 94 C4
Searle Pl, N4 93 F1
Searles Cl, SW11 129 H7
Searles Dr, E6 116 E5
Searles Rd, SE1 36 C1
Sears St, SE5 36 B7
Seasons Cl, W7
off Boston Rd 124 B1
Seasprite Cl, Nthlt. UB5 102 D3
Seaton Av, Ilf. IG3 99 H5
Seaton Cl, E13
off New Barn St 115 H4
SE11 35 F3
SW15 165 H1
Twickenham TW2 144 A6
Seaton Gdns, Ruis. HA4 84 A3
Seaton Pt, E5 94 D4
Seaton Rd, Hayes UB3 121 G4
Mitcham CR4 185 H2
Twickenham TW2 143 J6
Welling DA16 138 C7
Wembley HA0 105 H2
Seaton Sq, NW7
off Tavistock Av 56 A7
Seaton St, N18 60 D5
Sebastian Ct, Bark. IG11
off Meadow Rd 99 J7
Sebastian St, EC1 11 H4
Sebastopol Rd, N9 60 D4
Sebbon St, N1 93 H7
Sebergham Gro, NW7 55 G7
Sebert Rd, E7 97 H5
Sebright Pas, E2 13 J2
Sebright Rd, Barn. EN5 40 A2
Secker Cres, Har. HA3 67 J1
Secker St, SE1 27 E2
Second Av, E12 98 B4
E13 115 G3
E17 78 A5
N18 61 F4
NW4 72 A4
SW14 146 E3
W3 127 F1
W10 108 B4
Dagenham RM10 119 H1
Enfield EN1 44 C5
Hayes UB3 121 J1
Romford RM6 82 C5
Walton-on-Thames KT12 178 B6
Wembley HA9 87 G2
Second Cl, W.Mol. KT8 179 J4
Second Cross Rd, Twick. TW2 162 B2
Second Way, Wem. HA9 88 B4
Sedan Way, SE17 36 D3
Sedcombe Cl, Sid. DA14
off Knoll Rd 176 B4
Sedcote Rd, Enf. EN3 45 F5
Sedding St, SW1 32 B1
Seddon Highwalk, EC2
off The Barbican 19 J1
Seddon Ho, EC2
off The Barbican 19 J1
Seddon Rd, Mord. SM4 185 G5
Seddon St, WC1 10 D4
Sedgebrook Rd, SE3 156 A2
Sedgecombe Av, Har. HA3 69 F5
Sedgeford Rd, W12 127 F1
Sedgehill Rd, SE6 172 A4
Sedgemere Av, N2 73 F3
Sedgemere Rd, SE2 138 C3
Sedgemoor Dr, Dag. RM10 101 G4
Sedge Rd, N17 61 F7
Sedgeway, SE6 173 F1
Sedgewood Cl, Brom. BR2 191 F7
Sedgmoor Pl, SE5 132 B7
Sedgwick Rd, E10 96 C2
Sedgwick St, E9 95 G5
Sedleigh Rd, SW18 148 C6
Sedlescombe Rd, SW6 128 C6
Sedley Pl, W1 16 D4
Sedley Ri, Loug. IG10 48 C2
Sedum Cl, NW9 70 B5
Seeley Dr, SE21 170 B4
Seelig Av, NW9 71 G7
Seely Rd, SW17 168 A6
Seething La, EC3 21 E6
Seething Wells La, Surb. KT6 181 F6
Sefton Av, NW7 54 D5
Harrow HA3 68 A1
Sefton Cl, Orp. BR5 193 J4
Sefton Rd, Croy. CR0 202 D1
Orpington BR5 193 J4
Sefton St, SW15 147 J2
Segal Cl, SE23 153 H7
Sekforde St, EC1 11 G6
Sekhon Ter, Felt. TW13 161 G3

Selan Gdns, Hayes UB4 **102** B5
Selbie Av, NW10 **89** F5
Selborne Av, E12
off Walton Rd **98** D4
Bexley DA5 **176** E1
Selborne Gdns, NW4 **71** G4
Greenford (Perivale)
UB6 **104** D1
Selborne Rd, E17 **77** J5
N14 **58** E3
N22 **75** F1
SE5 *off Denmark Hill* **152** A2
Croydon CR0 **202** B3
Ilford IG1 **98** D2
New Malden KT3 **182** E2
Sidcup DA14 **176** B4
Selborne Wk, E17
off The Mall
Walthamstow **77** J4
Selbourne Av, E17 **77** J4
Surbiton KT6 **195** J2
Selby Chase, Ruis. HA4 **84** B2
Selby Cl, E6
off Linton Gdns **116** B5
Chessington KT9 **195** H7
Chislehurst BR7 **174** D6
Selby Gdns, Sthl. UB1 **103** G4
Selby Grn, Cars. SM5 **185** H7
Selby Rd, E11 **96** E3
E13 **115** H5
N17 **60** B6
SE20 **188** D2
W5 **105** E4
Carshalton SM5 **185** H7
Selby Sq, W10 **108** B3
Selby St, E1 **13** J6
Selden Rd, SE15 **153** F2
Selden Wk, N7
off Durham Rd **93** F2
★ **Selfridges**, W1 **16** C4
SELHURST, SE25 **188** B6
Selhurst Cl, SW19 **166** A1
Selhurst New Rd, SE25 **188** B6
Selhurst Pl, SE25 **188** B6
Selhurst Rd, N9 **60** A3
SE25 **188** B5
Selinas La, Dag. RM8 **83** E7
Selkirk Rd, SW17 **167** H4
Twickenham TW2 **161** J2
Sellers Cl, Borwd. WD6 **38** C1
Sellers Hall Cl, N3 **56** D7
Sellincourt Rd, SW17 **167** H5
Sellindge Cl, Beck. BR3 **171** J7
Sellons Av, NW10 **107** F1
Sellwood Dr, Barn. EN5 **40** A5
Sellwood St, SW2
off Brockwell Pk Row **151** G7
Selsdon Av, S.Croy. CR2 **202** A6
Selsdon Cl, Rom. RM5 **83** J1
Surbiton KT6 **181** H5
Selsdon Rd, E11 **79** G7
E13 **115** J1
NW2 **89** F2
SE27 **169** H3
South Croydon CR2 **202** A5
Selsdon Rd Ind Est,
S.Croy. CR2
off Selsdon Rd **202** A7
Selsdon Way, E14 **134** B3
Selsea Pl, N16
off Crossway **94** B5
Selsey Cres, Well. DA16 **158** D1
Selsey St, E14 **114** A5
Selvage La, NW7 **54** D5
Selway Cl, Pnr. HA5 **66** B4
Selway Ho, SW8
off South Lambeth Rd **151** E1
Selwood Pl, SW7 **30** E3
Selwood Rd, Chess. KT9 **195** G4
Croydon CR0 **202** E2
Sutton SM3 **198** C1
Selwood Ter, SW7 **31** E3
Selworthy Cl, E11 **79** G5
Selworthy Ho, SW11 **149** G1
Selworthy Rd, SE6 **171** J3
Selwyn Av, E4 **62** C6
Ilford IG3 **81** H6
Richmond TW9 **145** H3
Selwyn Cl, Houns. TW4 **143** E4
Selwyn Ct, SE3 **155** E3
Edgware HA8 **54** B7
Selwyn Cres, Well. DA16 **158** B4
Selwyn Rd, E3 **113** J2
E13 **115** H1
NW10 **88** D7
New Malden KT3 **182** D5
Semley Pl, SW1 **32** C2
Semley Rd, SW16 **187** E2
Senate St, SE15 **153** F2
Senator Wk, SE28
off Broadwater Rd **137** G3
Sendall Ct, SW11 **149** G3
Seneca Rd, Th.Hth. CR7 **187** J4
Senga Rd, Wall. SM6 **200** A1
Senhouse Rd, Sutt. SM3 **198** A3
Senior St, W2 **14** A1
Senlac Rd, SE12 **173** H1
Sennen Rd, Enf. EN1 **44** C7
Sennen Wk, SE9 **174** B3
Senrab St, E1 **113** G6
Sentamu Cl, SE24 **169** H1
Sentinel Cl, Nthlt. UB5 **103** E4
Sentinel Pt, SW8
off St. George Wf **34** A5
Sentinel Sq, NW4 **71** J4
September Way, Stan.
HA7 **53** E6
Sequoia Cl, Bushey
(Bushey Hth) WD23
off Giant Tree Hill **52** A1
Sequoia Gdns, Orp. BR6 **193** J7
Sequoia Pk, Pnr. HA5 **51** H6
Serbin Cl, E10 **78** C7
Serenaders Rd, SW9 **151** G2
Serjeants Inn, EC4 **19** F4
Serle St, WC2 **18** D3
Sermon La, EC4 **19** J4
★ **Serpentine, The**, W2 **23** G2
★ **Serpentine Gall**, W2 **23** F2
Serpentine Rd, W2 **23** J2
Serviden Dr, Brom. BR1 **192** A1
Setchell Rd, SE1 **37** F1
Setchell Way, SE1 **37** F1
Seth St, SE16
off Swan Rd **133** F2
Seton Gdns, Dag. RM9 **100** C7
Settle Pt, E13
off London Rd **115** G2
Settle Rd, E13
off London Rd **115** G2
Settlers Ct, E14
off Newport Av **114** D7
Settles St, E1 **21** J2
Settrington Rd, SW6 **148** E2
Seven Acres, Cars. SM5 **199** H2
Northwood HA6 **50** A6
SEVEN KINGS, Ilf. IG3 **81** H7
Seven Kings Rd, Ilf. IG3 **99** J2
Seven Kings Way, Kings.T.
KT2 **181** H1
Sevenoaks Cl, Bexh. DA7 **159** J4
Sevenoaks Ho, SE25 **188** D3
Sevenoaks Rd, SE4 **153** H6
Orpington BR6 **207** J5
Orpington (Pr.Bot.)
BR6 **207** J7
Sevenoaks Way, Orp.
BR5 **176** C7
Sidcup DA14 **176** C7
Sevenseas Rd, Houns.
TW6 *off Stratford Rd* **141** F6
Seven Sisters Rd, N4 **93** F3
N7 **93** F3
N15 **75** J7
Seven Stars Cor, W12
off Goldhawk Rd **127** G3
Seven Stars Yd, E1 **21** G1
Seventh Av, E12 **98** C4
Hayes UB3 **122** A1
Severnake Cl, E14 **134** A4
Severn Av, W10
off Selby Sq **108** B3
Severn Dr, Esher KT10 **194** D2
Severn Way, NW10 **89** F5
Severus Rd, SW11 **149** H4
Seville Ms, N1 **94** B7
Seville St, SW1 **24** A4
Sevington Rd, NW4 **71** H6
Sevington St, W9 **6** A6
Seward Rd, W7 **124** D2
Beckenham BR3 **189** G2
SEWARDSTONE, E4 **46** C1
SEWARDSTONEBURY, E4 **46** E4
Sewardstone Gdns, E4 **46** B5
Sewardstone Grn, E4 **46** E4
Sewardstone Rd, E2 **113** F2
E4 **46** B7
Seward St, EC1 **11** H5
Sewdley St, E5 **95** G3
Sewell Rd, SE2 **138** A3
Sewell St, E13 **115** G3
Sextant Av, E14 **134** D4
Sexton Ct, E14
off Newport Av **114** D7
Seymour Av, N17 **76** D2
Morden SM4 **184** A7
Seymour Cl, E.Mol.
KT8 **179** J5
Loughton IG10 **48** B6
Pinner HA5 **67** F1
Seymour Ct, E4 **63** F2
Seymour Dr, Brom.
BR2 **206** C1
Seymour Gdns, SE4 **153** H3
Feltham TW13 **160** C4
Ilford IG1 **98** C1
Ruislip HA4 **84** D1
Surbiton KT5 **181** J5
Twickenham TW1 **144** E7
Seymour Ms, W1 **16** B3
Seymour Pl, SE25 **188** E4
W1 **15** J2
Seymour Rd, E4 **62** B1
E6 **116** A2
E10 **95** J1
N3 **57** E7
N8 **75** G5
N9 **61** E2
SW18 **148** C7
SW19 **166** A2
W4 **126** C4
Carshalton SM5 **200** A5
East Molesey KT8 **179** J5
Hampton (Hmptn H.)
TW12 **161** J5
Kingston upon Thames
KT1 **181** G1
Mitcham CR4 **186** A7
Seymours, The, Loug.
IG10 **48** D1
Seymour St, SE18 **137** F3
W1 **15** J4
W2 **15** J4
Seymour Ter, SE20 **188** E1
Seymour Vil, SE20 **188** E1
Seymour Wk, SW10 **30** C5
Seyssel St, E14 **134** C4
Shaa Rd, W3 **106** D7
Shacklegate La, Tedd.
TW11 **162** B4
Shackleton Cl, SE23
off Featherstone Av **171** E2
Shackleton Ct, E14
off Maritime Quay **134** A5
W12 **127** H2
Shackleton Rd, Sthl.
UB1 **103** F7
SHACKLEWELL, N16 **94** C4
Shacklewell Grn, E8 **94** C4
Shacklewell La, E8 **94** C5
Shacklewell Rd, N16 **94** C4
Shacklewell Row, E8 **94** C4
Shacklewell St, E2 **13** G5
Shadbolt Av, E4 **61** H5
Shadbolt Cl, Wor.Pk.
KT4 **197** F2
Shad Thames, SE1 **29** F2
SHADWELL, E1 **113** F7
Shadwell Ct, Nthlt. UB5
off Shadwell Dr **103** F2
Shadwell Dr, Nthlt. UB5 **103** F3
Shadwell Gdns Est, E1
off Martha St **113** F7
Shadwell Pierhead, E1
off Glamis Rd **113** F7
Shadwell Pl, E1
off Sutton St **113** F7
Shaef Way, Tedd. TW11 **162** D7
Shafter Rd, Dag. RM10 **101** J6
Shaftesbury, Loug. IG10 **48** A3
Shaftesbury Av, W1 **17** H5
WC2 **17** H5
Barnet (New Barn.)
EN5 **41** F4
Enfield EN3 **45** G2
Feltham TW14 **142** A6
Harrow (Kenton) HA3 **69** G6
Harrow (S.Har.) HA2 **85** H1
Southall UB2 **123** G4
Shaftesbury Circle, Har.
(S.Har.) HA2
off Shaftesbury Av **85** J1
Shaftesbury Ct, N1 **12** B2
SE1 *off Alderney Ms* **28** B5
Shaftesbury Gdns, NW10 **107** E4
Shaftesbury Ms, SW4
off Clapham
Common S Side **150** C5
W8 *off Stratford Rd* **128** D3
Shaftesbury Pl, W14
off Warwick Rd **128** C4
Shaftesbury Pt, E13
off High St **115** H2
Shaftesbury Rd, E4 **62** D1
E7 **97** J7
E10 **96** A1
E17 **78** B6
N18 **60** B6
N19 **92** E1
Beckenham BR3 **189** J2
Carshalton SM5 **185** G7
Richmond TW9 **145** H3
Shaftesburys, The, Bark.
IG11 **117** F1
Shaftesbury St, N1 **12** A2
Shaftesbury Way, Twick.
TW2 **162** A3
Shaftesbury Waye, Hayes
UB4 **102** B5
Shafto Ms, SW1 **23** J6
Shafton Rd, E9 **113** G1
Shakespeare Av, N11 **58** C5
NW10 **106** D1
Feltham TW14 **142** A6
Hayes UB4 **102** B4
Shakespeare Cres, E12 **98** C6
Shakespeare Dr, Har. HA3 **69** J6
Shakespeare Gdns, N2 **73** J4
Shakespeare Rd, E17 **77** G2
N3 *off Popes Dr* **72** D1
NW7 **55** F4
NW10 **106** D1
SE24 **151** H5
W3 **126** C1
W7 **104** C7
Bexleyheath DA7 **158** E1
★ **Shakespeare's Globe**
Thea, SE1 **19** J6
Shakespeare Sq, Ilf. IG6 **65** F6
Shakespeare Twr, EC2 **20** A1
Shakespeare Way, Felt.
TW13 **160** C4
Shakspeare Ms, N16
off Shakspeare Wk **94** B4
Shakspeare Wk, N16 **94** B4
Shalbourne Sq, E9 **95** J5
Shalcomb St, SW10 **30** D6
Shalden Ho, SW15
off Tunworth Cres **147** F6
Shaldon Dr, Mord. SM4 **184** B5
Ruislip HA4 **84** C3
Shaldon Rd, Edg. HA8 **69** J1
Shalfleet Dr, W10 **108** A7
Shalford Cl, Orp. BR6 **207** F4
Shalimar Gdns, W3 **106** C7
Shalimar Rd, W3 **106** C7
Shallons Rd, SE9 **174** E4
Shalstone Rd, SW14 **146** B3
Shalston Vil, Surb. KT6 **181** J6
Shamrock Ho, SE26
off Talisman Sq **170** D4
Shamrock Rd, Croy. CR0 **187** F6
Shamrock St, SW4 **150** D3
Shamrock Way, N14 **58** B1
Shandon Rd, SW4 **150** C6
Shand St, SE1 **28** D3
Shandy St, E1 **113** G5
Shanklin Gdns, Wat.
WD19 **50** C4
Shanklin Ho, E17
off Sherwood Cl **77** J2
Shanklin Rd, N8 **74** D5
N15 **76** D4
Shannon Cl, NW2 **90** A3
Southall UB2 **122** D5
Shannon Commercial Cen,
N.Mal. KT3
off Beverley Way **183** G4
Shannon Cor, N.Mal.
KT3 **183** G4
Shannon Cor Retail Pk,
N.Mal. KT3 **183** G4
Shannon Gro, SW9 **151** F4
Shannon Pl, NW8 **7** H1
Shannon Way, Beck. BR3 **172** B6
Shap Cres, Cars. SM5 **199** J1
Shapland Way, N13 **59** F5
Shapwick Cl, N11 **57** J5
Shardcroft Av, SE24 **151** H5
Shardeloes Rd, SE4 **153** J3
SE14 **153** J3
Sharland Cl, Th.Hth. CR7
off Dunheved Rd N **187** G6
Sharman Ct, Sid. DA14 **176** A4
Sharnbrooke Cl, Well.
DA16 **158** C3
Sharnbrook Ho, W14
off Marchbank Rd **128** D6
Sharon Cl, Surb.
(Long Dit.) KT6 **195** F1
Sharon Gdns, E9 **113** F1
Sharon Rd, W4 **126** D5
Enfield EN3 **45** H2
Sharpe Cl, W7
off Templeman Rd **104** C5
Sharpleshall St, NW1 **91** J7
Sharpness Cl, Hayes
UB4 **102** E5
Sharratt St, SE15 **133** F6
Sharsted St, SE17 **35** G4
Sharvel La, Nthlt. UB5 **102** A1
Shavers Pl, SW1 **17** H6
Shaw Av, Bark. IG11 **118** E2
Shawbrooke Rd, SE9 **155** J5
Shawbury Cl, NW9 **71** E2
Shawbury Rd, SE22 **152** C5
Shaw Cl, SE28 **138** B1
Bushey (Bushey Hth)
WD23 **52** B2
Shaw Ct, SW11 **149** G3
Morden SM4 **185** F7
Shaw Cres, E14 **113** H5
Shaw Dr, Walt. KT12 **178** C7
Shawfield Ct, West Dr.
UB7 **120** B3
Shawfield Pk, Brom.
BR1 **192** A2
Shawfield St, SW3 **31** H4
Shawford Ct, SW15 **147** G7
Shawford Rd, Epsom
KT19 **196** D6
Shaw Gdns, Bark. IG11 **118** E2
Shaw Ho, N17
off Queen St **60** B6

Shaw Path, Brom. BR1
off Shroffold Rd 173 F3
Shaw Rd, SE22 152 B4
Bromley BR1 173 F3
Enfield EN3 45 G1
Shaws Cotts, SE23 171 H3
Shaw Sq, E17 77 H1
Shaw Way, Wall. SM6 200 E7
Shearing Dr, Cars. SM5
off Stavordale Rd 185 F7
Shearling Way, N7 93 E6
Shearman Rd, SE3 155 F4
Shearsmith Ho, E1 21 J5
Shearwater Cl, Bark. IG11 118 A3
Shearwater Rd, Sutt. SM1 198 C5
Shearwater Way, Hayes UB4 102 D6
Sheaveshill Av, NW9 71 E4
Sheba Pl, E1 13 G6
Sheen Common, SW14 146 B5
Sheen Common Dr, Rich. TW10 146 A4
Sheen Ct, Rich. TW10 146 A4
Sheen Ct Rd, Rich. TW10 146 A4
Sheendale Rd, Rich. TW9 145 J4
Sheenewood, SE26 171 E5
Sheen Gate Gdns, SW14 146 C4
Sheen Gate Mans Pas, SW14
off East Sheen Av 146 D4
Sheen Gro, N1
off Richmond Av 111 G1
Sheen La, SW14 146 C3
Sheen Pk, Rich. TW9 145 J4
Sheen Rd, Orp. BR5 193 J4
Richmond TW9, TW10 145 H5
Sheen Way, Wall. SM6 201 F5
Sheen Wd, SW14 146 C5
Sheepcote Cl, Houns. TW5 122 A7
Sheepcote La, SW11 149 J2
Sheepcote Rd, Har. HA1 68 C6
Sheepcotes Rd, Rom. RM6 82 D4
Sheephouse Way, N.Mal. KT3 182 E7
Sheep La, E8 112 E1
Sheep Wk Ms, SW19 166 A6
Sheerness Ms, E16 137 E2
Sheerwater Rd, E16 116 A5
Sheffield Rd, Houns. (Lon.Hthrw Air.) TW6
off Southern Perimeter Rd 141 G5
Sheffield Sq, E3
off Malmesbury Rd 113 J3
Sheffield St, WC2 18 C4
Sheffield Ter, W8 128 D1
Shefton Ri, Nthwd. HA6 50 A7
Shelbourne Cl, Pnr. HA5 67 F3
Shelbourne Pl, Beck. BR3 171 J7
Shelbourne Rd, N17 76 E2
Shelburne Dr, Houns. TW4
off Hanworth Rd 143 G6
Shelburne Rd, N7 93 F4
Shelbury Cl, Sid. DA14 176 A3
Shelbury Rd, SE22 153 E5
Sheldon Av, N6 73 H7
Ilford IG5 80 E2
Sheldon Cl, SE12 155 H5
SE20 189 E1
Sheldon Ct, SW8
off Thorncroft St 130 E7
Sheldon Pl, E2 13 J2
Sheldon Rd, N18 60 B4
NW2 90 A4
Bexleyheath DA7 159 F1
Dagenham RM9 100 E7
Sheldon Sq, W2 14 D2
Sheldon St, Croy. CR0 201 J3
Sheldrake Cl, E16 136 C1
Sheldrake Pl, W8 128 C2
Sheldrick Cl, SW19 185 G2
Shelduck Cl, E15 97 F5
Sheldwich Ter, Brom. BR2 192 B6
Shelford Pl, N16
off Stoke Newington Ch St 94 A3
Shelford Ri, SE19 170 C7
Shelford Rd, Barn. EN5 39 J6
Shelgate Rd, SW11 149 H5
★ **Shell Cen**, SE1 26 D2
Shell Cl, Brom. BR2 192 C6
Shellduck Cl, NW9
off Swan Dr 70 E2
Shelley Av, E12 98 B6
Greenford UB6 104 A3
Shelley Cl, SE15 153 E2
Borehamwood WD6 38 A4
Edgware HA8 54 A4
Greenford UB6 104 A3
Hayes UB4 102 A5
Orpington BR6 207 H3
Shelley Ct, N4 93 F1
Shelley Cres, Houns. TW5 142 D2
Southall UB1 103 F6
Shelley Dr, Well. DA16 157 H1
Shelley Gdns, Wem. HA0 87 F2
Shelley Gro, Loug. IG10 48 C4
Shelley Ho, SW1 33 G5
Shelley Rd, NW10 106 D1
Shelley Way, SW19 167 G6
Shellgrove Est, N16 94 B5
Shellness Rd, E5 95 E5
Shell Rd, SE13 154 B3
Shellwood Rd, SW11 149 J2
Shelmerdine Cl, E3 114 A5
Shelton Rd, SW19 184 D1
Shelton St, WC2 18 A4
Shenfield Ho, SE18
off Shooters Hill Rd 136 A7
Shenfield Rd, Wdf.Grn. IG8 63 H7
Shenfield St, N1 12 E2
Shenley Rd, SE5 152 B1
Borehamwood WD6 38 A4
Hounslow TW5 142 E1
Shepcot Ho, N14 42 C6
Shepherd Cl, Felt. (Han.) TW13 161 E4
Shepherdess Pl, N1 12 A3
Shepherdess Wk, N1 12 A1
Shepherd Mkt, W1 24 D1
SHEPHERD'S BUSH, W12 127 J1
Shepherds Bush Grn, W12 127 J2
Shepherds Bush Mkt, W12 127 J2
Shepherds Bush Pl, W12 128 A2
Shepherds Bush Rd, W6 127 J4
Shepherds Cl, N6 74 B6
W1 *off Lees Pl* 16 B5
Orpington BR6
off Stapleton Rd 207 J3
Romford RM6 82 D5
Stanmore HA7 52 D5
Shepherds Ct, W12
off Shepherds Bush Grn 128 A2
Shepherds Grn, Chis. BR7 175 G7
Shepherds Hill, N6 74 B6
Shepherds Ho, N7
off York Way 92 E6
Shepherds La, E9 95 G5
SE28 137 H1
Shepherds Path, Nthlt. UB5 *off Cowings Mead* 85 E6
Shepherd's Pl, W1 16 B5
Shepherd St, W1 24 D2
Shepherds Wk, NW2 89 G2
NW3 91 G5
Bushey (Bushey Hth) WD23 52 A2
Shepherds Way, S.Croy. CR2 203 G7
Shepiston La, Hayes UB3 121 G4
West Drayton UB7 121 F4
Shepley Cl, Cars. SM5 200 A3
Sheppard Cl, Kings.T. KT1
off Beaufort Rd 181 H4
Sheppard Dr, SE16 132 E5
Sheppard St, E16 115 F4
Shepperton Cl, Borwd. WD6 38 D1
Shepperton Rd, N1 111 J1
Orpington BR5 193 F6
Sheppey Gdns, Dag. RM9
off Sheppey Rd 100 C7
Sheppey Rd, Dag. RM9 100 B7
Sheppey Wk, N1
off Ashby Gro 93 J7
Shepton Hos, E2
off Globe Rd 113 F3
Sherard Ct, N7
off Manor Gdns 92 E3
Sherard Rd, SE9 156 B5
Sheraton Business Cen, Grnf. (Perivale) UB6 105 E2
Sheraton St, W1 17 H4
Sherborne Av, Enf. EN3 45 F2
Southall UB2 123 G4
Sherborne Cl, Hayes UB4 102 C6
Sherborne Cres, Cars. SM5 185 H7
Sherborne Gdns, NW9 70 A3
W13 105 E6
Sherborne Ho, SW8
off Bolney St 131 F7
Sherborne La, EC4 20 B5
Sherborne Rd, Chess. KT9 195 H5
Feltham TW14 141 G7
Orpington BR5 193 J4
Sutton SM3 198 D2
Sherborne St, N1 112 A1
Sherboro Rd, N15
off Ermine Rd 76 C6
Sherbourne Pl, Stan. HA7 52 D6
Sherbrooke Cl, Bexh. DA6 159 G4
Sherbrooke Rd, SW6 128 C7
Sherbrooke Way, Wor.Pk. KT4 183 H7
Sherbrook Gdns, N21 43 H7
Shere Cl, Chess. KT9 195 G5
Sheredan Rd, E4 62 D5
Shere Rd, Ilf. IG2 80 D5
Sherfield Cl, N.Mal. KT3 182 B4
Sherfield Gdns, SW15 147 F6
Sheridan Ct, Houns. TW4
off Vickers Way 143 E5
Northolt UB5 85 H5
Sheridan Cres, Chis. BR7 192 E2
Sheridan Gdns, Har. HA3 69 G6
Sheridan Ms, E11
off Woodbine Pl 79 H6
Sheridan Pl, SW13
off Brookwood Av 147 F2
Bromley BR1 192 A2
Hampton TW12 179 H1
Sheridan Rd, E7 97 F3
E12 98 B5
SW19 184 C1
Belvedere DA17 139 G4
Bexleyheath DA7 158 E3
Richmond TW10 163 F3
Sheridan Ter, Nthlt. UB5
off Whitton Av W 85 H5
Sheridan Wk, NW11 72 D6
Carshalton SM5
off Carshalton Pk Rd 199 J5
Sheridan Way, Beck. BR3
off Turners Meadow Way 189 J1
Sheringham Av, E12 98 C4
N14 42 D5
Feltham TW13 160 A3
Romford RM7 83 J6
Twickenham TW2 161 F1
Sheringham Ct, Hayes UB3 *off Clayton Rd* 121 J2
Sheringham Dr, Bark. IG11 99 J5
Sheringham Rd, N7 93 F6
SE20 189 E3
Sheringham Twr, Sthl. UB1 103 H7
Sherington Av, Pnr. HA5 51 G7
Sherington Rd, SE7 135 H6
Sherland Rd, Twick. TW1 162 C1
Sherlies Av, Orp. BR6 207 H2
★ **Sherlock Holmes Mus**, NW1 8 A6
Sherlock Ms, W1 16 B1
Sherman Gdns, Rom. (Chad.Hth) RM6 82 C6
Sherman Rd, Brom. BR1 191 G1
Shernhall St, E17 78 C5
Sherrard Rd, E7 97 J6
E12 98 A6
Sherrards Way, Barn. EN5 40 D5
Sherrick Grn Rd, NW10 89 H5
Sherriff Rd, NW6 90 D6
Sherringham Av, N17 76 D2
Sherrin Rd, E10 96 A4
Sherrock Gdns, NW4 71 G4
Sherry Ms, Bark. IG11 99 G7
Sherwin Rd, SE14 153 G1
Sherwood Av, E18 79 H3
SW16 168 D7
Greenford UB6 86 B6
Hayes UB4 102 B4
Sherwood Cl, E17 77 J2
SW13
off Lower Common S 147 H3
W13 124 E1
Bexley DA5 158 C6
Sherwood Gdns, E14 134 A4
SE16 37 J4
Barking IG11 99 G7
Sherwood Pk Av, Sid. DA15 158 A7
Sherwood Pk Rd, Mitch. CR4 186 C4
Sutton SM1 198 D5
Sherwood Rd, NW4 71 J3
SW19 166 C7
Croydon CR0 188 E7
Hampton (Hmptn H.) TW12 161 J5
Harrow HA2 85 J2
Ilford IG6 81 G4
Welling DA16 157 H2
Sherwood St, N20 57 G3
W1 17 G5
Sherwood Ter, N20
off Green Rd 57 G3
Sherwood Way, W.Wick. BR4 204 B2
Shetland Cl, Borwd. WD6 38 D6
Shetland Rd, E3 113 J2
Shield Dr, Brent. TW8 124 D6
Shieldhall St, SE2 138 C4
Shifford Path, SE23 171 G3
Shillibeer Pl, W1 15 H1
Shillibeer Wk, Chig. IG7 65 J3
Shillingford Cl, NW7 56 A7
Shillingford St, N1
off Hawes St 93 H7
Shinfield St, W12 107 J6
Shinglewell Rd, Erith DA8 139 G7
Shinners Cl, SE25 188 D5
Ship All, W4
off Thames Rd 126 A6
Ship & Half Moon Pas, SE18 *off Warren La* 136 E3
Ship & Mermaid Row, SE1 28 C3
Shipka Rd, SW12 168 B1
Ship La, SW14 146 C2
Shipman Rd, E16 115 H6
SE23 171 G2
Ship St, SE8 154 A1
Ship Tavern Pas, EC3 20 D5
Shipton Cl, Dag. RM8 100 D3
Shipton St, E2 13 G3
Shipwright Rd, SE16 133 H2
Shipwright Yd, SE1 28 D2
Ship Yd, E14
off Napier Av 134 B5
Shirburn Cl, SE23
off Tyson Rd 153 F7
Shirbutt St, E14 114 B7
Shirebrook Rd, SE3 156 A2
Shire Ct, Epsom KT17 197 F7
Erith DA18 *off St. John Fisher Rd* 138 D3
Shirehall Cl, NW4 72 A6
Shirehall Gdns, NW4 72 A6
Shirehall La, NW4 72 A6
Shirehall Pk, NW4 72 A6
Shire Horse Way, Islw. TW7 144 C3
Shire La, Kes. BR2 206 C7
Orpington BR6 207 G6
Shire Ms, Twick. TW2
off Prospect Cres 143 J6
Shire Pl, SW18
off Swaffield Rd 149 E7
Shires, The, Rich. (Ham) TW10 163 H4
Shirland Ms, W9 108 C3
Shirland Rd, W9 108 D3
SHIRLEY, Croy. CR0 203 G3
Shirley Av, Bex. DA5 158 D7
Croydon CR0 203 F1
Sutton SM1 199 H4
Shirley Ch Rd, Croy. CR0 203 G3
Shirley Cl, E17
off Addison Rd 78 B5
Hounslow TW3 143 J5
Shirley Ct, Croy. CR0 203 G3
Shirley Cres, Beck. BR3 189 H4
Shirley Dr, Houns. TW3 143 J5
Shirley Gdns, W7 124 C1
Barking IG11 99 H6
Shirley Gro, N9 45 F7
SW11 150 A3
Shirley Hills Rd, Croy. CR0 203 G5
Shirley Ho Dr, SE7 135 J7
Shirley Oaks Rd, Croy. CR0 203 G1
Shirley Pk Rd, Croy. CR0 203 E1
Shirley Rd, E15 97 E7
W4 126 D2
Croydon CR0 189 E7
Enfield EN2 43 J3
Sidcup DA15 175 H3
Shirley St, E16 115 F6
Shirley Way, Croy. CR0 203 H3
Shirlock Rd, NW3 91 J4
Shirwell Cl, NW7 56 A7
Shobden Rd, N17 76 A1
Shobroke Cl, NW2 89 J3
Shoebury Rd, E6 98 C7
Shoe La, EC4 19 F3
Sholto Rd, Houns. (Lon.Hthrw Air.) TW6 140 C5
Shona Ho, E13
off Prince Regent La 115 J5
Shooters Av, Har. HA3 69 F4
SHOOTER'S HILL, SE18 157 F1
Shooters Hill, SE18 156 D1
Welling DA16 156 D1
Shooters Hill Rd, SE3 155 F1
SE10 154 D1
SE18 135 H7
Shooters Rd, Enf. EN2 43 H1
Shoot Up Hill, NW2 90 B5
Shore Cl, Felt. TW14 142 A7
Hampton TW12
off Stewart Cl 161 E5
SHOREDITCH, E1 13 F6
Shoreditch High St, E1 13 E6

Shoreditch Ho, N1 ....12 C4
Shore Gro, Felt. TW13 ....161 G2
Shoreham Cl, SW18
off Ram St 148 E5
Bexley DA5 ....176 D1
Croydon CR0 ....189 F6
Shoreham Rd E, Houns.
(Lon.Hthrw Air.) TW6 ..140 B5
Shoreham Rd W, Houns.
(Lon.Hthrw Air.) TW6 ..140 B5
Shoreham Way, Brom.
BR2 ....191 G6
Shore Pl, E9 ....95 F7
Shore Pt, Buck.H. IG9 .....63 H2
Shore Rd, E9 ....95 F7
Shore Way, SW9 ....151 G2
Shorncliffe Rd, SE1 ....37 F3
Shorndean St, SE6 ....172 C1
Shorne Cl, Sid. DA15 ....158 B6
Shornefield Cl, Brom.
BR1 ....192 D3
Shornells Way, SE2
off Willrose Cres 138 C5
Shorrolds Rd, SW6 ......128 C7
Shortcroft Rd, Epsom
KT17 ....197 F7
Shortcrofts Rd, Dag.
RM9 ....101 F6
Shorter St, E1 ....21 G5
Shortgate, N12 ....56 C4
Short Hedges, Houns.
TW3, TW5 ....143 H1
Short Hill, Har. HA1
off High St 86 B1
SHORTLANDS, Brom.
BR1 ....190 E3
Shortlands, W6 ....128 A4
Hayes (Harling.) UB3 ..121 G6
Shortlands Cl, N18 ....60 A3
Belvedere DA17 ....139 F3
Shortlands Gdns, Brom.
BR2 ....191 E2
Shortlands Gro, Brom.
BR2 ....190 D3
Shortlands Rd, E10 ....78 B7
Bromley BR2 ....190 D3
Kingston upon Thames
KT2 ....163 J7
Short Path, SE18
off Long Wk 136 E6
Short Rd, E11 ....96 E2
W4 ....126 E6
Hounslow
(Lon.Hthrw Air.) TW6 .140 B6
Shorts Cft, NW9 ....70 B4
Shorts Gdns, WC2 ....18 A4
Shorts Rd, Cars. SM5 ....199 H4
Short St, NW4
off New Brent St 71 J4
SE1 ....27 F3
Short Wall, E15 ....114 C3
Shortway, N12 ....57 H6
Short Way, SE9 ....156 B3
Twickenham TW2 .....143 J7
Shotfield, Wall. SM6 .....200 B6
Shott Cl, Sutt. SM1
off Turnpike La 199 F5
Shottendane Rd, SW6 ...148 D1
Shottery Cl, SE9 ....174 B3
Shottfield Av, SW14 .....146 E4
Shoulder of Mutton All,
E14 *off Narrow St* 113 H7
Shouldham St, W1 ....15 H2
Showers Way, Hayes
UB3 ....122 A1
Shrapnel Cl, SE18 ....136 B7
Shrapnel Rd, SE9 ....156 C3
Shrewsbury Av, SW14 ...146 C4
Harrow HA3 ....69 H4
Shrewsbury Cl, Surb.
KT6 ....195 H2
Shrewsbury Ct, EC1
off Whitecross St 12 A6
Shrewsbury Cres, NW10 .106 D1
Shrewsbury La, SE18 ....156 E1
Shrewsbury Ms, W2
off Chepstow Rd 108 D5
Shrewsbury Rd, E7 ....98 A5
N11 ....58 C6
NW10
off Shakespeare Rd ..106 D1
W2 ....108 D6
Beckenham BR3 ......189 H3
Carshalton SM5 ......185 H6
Hounslow
(Lon.Hthrw Air.) TW6 .141 F6
Shrewsbury St, W10 .....107 J4
Shrewsbury Wk, Islw. TW7
off South St 144 D3
Shrewton Rd, SW17 .....167 J7
Shroffold Rd, Brom. BR1 .173 E4
Shropshire Cl, Mitch.
CR4 ....187 E4
Shropshire Ho, N18 ......61 E5
Shropshire Pl, WC1 ....9 G6
Shropshire Rd, N22 ......59 F7
Shroton St, NW1 ....15 G1
Shrubberies, The, E18 .....79 G2
Chigwell IG7 ....65 F5
Shrubbery, The, E11 ......79 H5
Shrubbery Cl, N1
off St. Paul St 111 J1
Shrubbery Gdns, N21 .....43 H7
Shrubbery Rd, N9 ....60 D3
SW16 ....168 E4
Southall UB1 ....123 F1
Shrubland Gro, Wor.Pk.
KT4 ....197 J3
Shrubland Rd, E8 ....112 D1
E10 ....78 A7
E17 ....78 A5
Shrublands Av, Croy.
CR0 ....204 A4
Shrublands Cl, N20 ....57 G1
SE26 ....171 F3
Chigwell IG7 ....65 F6
Shrubsall Cl, SE9 ....174 B1
Shuna Wk, N1
off St. Paul's Rd 94 A6
Shurland Av, Barn. EN4 ...41 G6
Shurland Gdns, SE15 .....37 G7
Shurlock Dr, Orp. BR6 ...207 F4
Shuters Sq, W14
off Sun Rd 128 C5
Shuttle Cl, Sid. DA15 ....157 J7
Shuttlemead, Bex. DA5 ..159 F7
Shuttle St, E1 ....13 H6
Shuttleworth Rd, SW11 ..149 H2
Siamese Ms, N3
off Station Rd 72 D1
Siani Ms, N8 ....75 H4
Sibella Rd, SW4 ....150 D2
Sibford Ct, Mitch. CR4
off Lower Grn W 185 J3
Sibley Cl, Bexh. DA6 .....158 E5
Bromley BR1 ....192 B5
Sibley Gro, E12 ....98 B7
Sibthorpe Rd, SE12 .....155 H6
Sibthorp Rd, Mitch. CR4
off Holborn Way 185 J2
Sibton Rd, Cars. SM5 ....185 H7
Sicilian Av, WC1 ....18 B2
Sidbury St, SW6 ....148 B1
SIDCUP, DA14 & DA15 ...175 J4
Sidcup Bypass, Chis.
BR7 ....175 H4
Orpington BR5 ....176 D7
Sidcup DA14 ....175 H4
Sidcup High St, Sid.
DA14 ....176 A4
Sidcup Hill, Sid. DA14 ...176 B4
Sidcup Hill Gdns, Sid.
DA14 *off Sidcup Hill* ...176 C5
Sidcup Pl, Sid. DA14 .....176 A5
Sidcup Rd, SE9 ....156 A7
SE12 ....155 H5
Sidcup Tech Cen, Sid.
DA14 ....176 D5
Siddeley Dr, Houns.
TW4 ....142 E3
Siddons La, NW1 ....8 A6
Siddons Rd, N17 ....76 D1
SE23 ....171 H2
Croydon CR0 ....201 G3
Side Rd, E17 ....77 J5
Sidewood Rd, SE9 ......175 G1
Sidford Ho, SE1
off Briant Est 26 D6
Sidford Pl, SE1 ....26 D6
Sidi Ct, N15 ....75 H3
Sidings, The, E11 ....96 C1
Loughton IG10 ....48 B6
Sidings Ms, N7 ....93 G3
Sidmouth Av, Islw. TW7 ..144 B2
Sidmouth Cl, Wat. WD19 ..50 B2
Sidmouth Dr, Ruis. HA4 ...84 A3
Sidmouth Par, NW2
off Sidmouth Rd 89 J7
Sidmouth Rd, E10 ....96 C3
NW2 ....89 J7
Welling DA16 ....138 C7
Sidmouth St, WC1 ....10 B4
Sidney Av, N13 ....59 F5
Sidney Elson Way, E6
off Edwin Av 116 D2
Sidney Gdns, Brent. TW8 .125 F6
Sidney Gro, EC1 ....11 G2
Sidney Rd, E7 ....97 G3
N22 ....59 F7
SE25 ....188 D5
SW9 ....151 F2
Beckenham BR3 ......189 H2
Harrow HA2 ....67 J3
Twickenham TW1 .....144 D6
Walton-on-Thames
KT12 ....178 A7
Sidney Sq, E1 ....113 F6
Sidney St, E1 ....113 E5
Sidney Webb Ho, SE1 .....28 C5
Sidworth St, E8 ....95 E7
Siebert Rd, SE3 ....135 G6
Siemens Rd, SE18 ....136 A3
Sienna Cl, Chess. KT9 ...195 G6
Sigdon Pas, E8
off Sigdon Rd 94 D5
Sigdon Rd, E8 ....94 D5
Sigers, The, Pnr. HA5 .....66 B6
Signmakers Yd, NW1
off Delancey St 110 B1
Sigrist Sq, Kings.T. KT2 ..181 H1
Silbury Av, Mitch. CR4 ...185 H1
Silbury Ho, SE26
off Sydenham Hill Est .170 D3
Silbury St, N1 ....12 B3
Silchester Rd, W10 ......108 A6
Silecroft Rd, Bexh. DA7 ..159 G1
Silesia Bldgs, E8
off London La 95 E7
Silex St, SE1 ....27 H4
Silk Br Retail Pk, NW9 ....71 F6
Silk Cl, SE12 ....155 G5
Silkfield Rd, NW9 ....71 E5
Silkin Ms, SE15
off Fenham Rd 132 D7
Silk Mills Pas, SE13
off Egeremont Rd 154 B2
Silk Mills Path, SE13
off Lewisham Rd 154 C3
Silk Mills Sq, E9 ....95 J6
Silkstream Rd, Edg. HA8 ..70 C1
Silk St, EC2 ....20 A1
Silsoe Ho, NW1
off Park Village E 8 E2
Silsoe Rd, N22 ....75 F2
Silver Birch Av, E4 ....61 J6
Silver Birch Cl, N11 ....58 A6
SE6 ....171 J3
SE28 ....138 A1
Silver Birch Gdns, E6 ....116 C4
Silver Birch Ms, Ilf. IG6
off Fencepiece Rd 65 F6
Silverbirch Wk, NW3
off Queen's Cres 92 A6
Silvercliffe Gdns, Barn.
EN4 ....41 H4
Silver Cl, SE14
off Southerngate Way .133 H7
Harrow HA3 ....52 A7
Silver Cres, W4 ....126 B4
Silverdale, NW1 ....9 F3
SE26 ....171 F4
Enfield EN2 ....43 E4
Silverdale Av, Ilf. IG3 .....81 H5
Silverdale Cl, W7 ....124 B1
Northolt UB5 ....85 F5
Sutton SM1 ....198 C4
Silverdale Dr, SE9 ....174 B2
Sunbury-on-Thames
TW16 ....178 B2
Silverdale Gdns, Hayes
UB3 ....122 A2
Silverdale Rd, E4 ....62 D6
Bexleyheath DA7 .....159 H2
Hayes UB3 ....122 A2
Orpington (Petts Wd)
BR5 ....193 F4
Silvergate, Epsom KT19 ..196 C5
Silverhall St, Islw. TW7 ...144 D3
Silverholme Cl, Har. HA3 ..69 G7
Silver Jubilee Way, Houns.
TW4 ....142 B2
Silverland St, E16 ....136 C1
Silver La, W.Wick. BR4 ...204 D2
Silverleigh Rd, Th.Hth.
CR7 ....187 F4
Silvermead, E18
off Churchfields 79 G1
Silvermere Dr, N18 ....61 G6
Silvermere Rd, SE6 ......154 B6
Silver Pl, W1 ....17 G5
Silver Rd, SE13 ....154 B3
W12 ....108 A7
Silver Spring Cl, Erith
DA8 ....139 H6
Silverston Way, Stan.
HA7 ....53 F6
Silver St, N18 ....60 B4
Enfield EN1 ....44 A3
Silverthorne Rd, SW8 ....150 B2
Silverthorn Gdns, E4 .....62 A2
Silverton Rd, W6 ....128 A6
SILVERTOWN, E16 ....135 J2
Silvertown Way, E16 .....115 F6
Silvertree La, Grnf. UB6
off Cowgate Rd 104 A3
Silver Wk, SE16 ....133 J1
Silver Way, Rom. RM7 ....83 H3
Silverwing Ind Est, Croy.
CR0 ....201 F5
Silverwood Cl, Beck.
BR3 ....172 A7
Silvester Rd, SE22 ......152 C5
Silvester St, SE1 ....28 A4
Silvocea Way, E14 ......114 D6
Silwood Est, SE16
off Concorde Way 133 G4
Silwood St, SE16 ....133 F4
Simla Ho, SE1 ....28 C4
Simmil Rd, Esher (Clay.)
KT10 ....194 B5
Simmons Cl, N20 ....57 H1
Chessington KT9 .....195 F6
Simmons Dr, Dag. RM8 ..101 E3
Simmons La, E4 ....62 D2
Simmons Rd, SE18 ......136 E5
Simmons Way, N20 ....57 H2
Simms Cl, Cars. SM5 ....199 H2
Simms Gdns, N2 ....73 F2
Simms Rd, SE1 ....37 H2
Simnel Rd, SE12 ....155 H7
Simon Cl, W11
off Portobello Rd 108 C7
Simon Ct, N11
off Ringway 58 C6
Simonds Rd, E10 ....96 A2
Simone Cl, Brom. BR1 ...192 A1
Simons Wk, E15
off Waddington Rd 96 D5
Simpson Cl, N21
off Macleod Rd 43 E5
Simpson Dr, W3 ....106 D6
Simpson Rd, Houns.
TW4 ....143 F6
Richmond TW10 ......163 F4
Simpsons Rd, E14 ....114 B7
Bromley BR2 ....191 G3
Simpson St, SW11 ......149 H2
Simpson Way, Surb. KT6
off Portsmouth Rd ...181 F6
Simrose Ct, SW18
*off Wandsworth
High St* 148 D5
Sims Wk, SE3 ....155 F4
Sinclair Ct, Beck. BR3 ....172 A7
Sinclair Gdns, W14 ......128 A2
Sinclair Gro, NW11 ....72 A6
Sinclair Pl, SE4 ....154 A6
Sinclair Rd, E4 ....61 J5
W14 ....128 A2
Sinclare Cl, Enf. EN1 ......44 C1
Singapore Rd, W13 ......124 D1
Singer St, EC2 ....12 C4
Singleton Cl, SW17 .....167 J7
Croydon CR0
off St. Saviours Rd ...187 J7
Singleton Rd, Dag. RM9 ..101 F5
Singleton Scarp, N12 .....56 D5
Sinnott Rd, E17 ....77 G1
Sion Rd, Twick. TW1 .....162 E1
SIPSON, West Dr. UB7 ...120 D6
Sipson Cl, West Dr.
(Sipson) UB7 ....120 D6
Sipson La, Hayes
(Harling.) UB3 ....120 D6
West Drayton
(Sipson) UB7 ....120 D6
Sipson Rd, West Dr. UB7 .120 D5
Sipson Way, West Dr.
(Sipson) UB7 ....120 D7
Sir Alexander Cl, W3 .....127 F1
Sir Alexander Rd, W3 ....127 F1
Sir Cyril Black Way,
SW19 ....166 D7
Sirdar Rd, N22 ....75 H3
W11 ....108 A7
Mitcham CR4
off Grenfell Rd 168 A6
**Sir Giles Gilbert Scott
Bldg, The**, SW15 ......148 B6
Sirinham Pt, SW8 ....34 C6
Sirius Rd, Nthwd. HA6 ....50 A5
Sir James Black Ho, SE5
off Coldharbour La ...152 A2
Sir John Kirk Cl, SE5 .....35 J7
★ **Sir John Soane's Mus**,
WC2 *off Lincoln's
Inn Flds* 18 C3
Sir Martin Bowles Ho, SE18
off Calderwood St ...136 D4
Sir Thomas More Est,
SW3 ....31 F6
Sise La, EC4 ....20 B4
Siskin Cl, Borwd. WD6 ....38 A4
Sisley Rd, Bark. IG11 .....117 H1
Sispara Gdns, SW18 .....148 C6
Sissinghurst Cl, Brom.
BR1 ....173 E5
Sissinghurst Rd, Croy.
CR0 ....188 D7
Sissulu Ct, E6 ....115 J1
Sister Mabel's Way, SE15 ..37 H7
Sisters Av, SW11 ....149 J4
Sistova Rd, SW12 ....168 B1
Sisulu Pl, SW9 ....151 G3
Sittingbourne Av, Enf.
EN1 ....44 A6
Sitwell Gro, Stan. HA7 ....52 C5
Siverst Cl, Nthlt. UB5 .....85 H6
Sivill Ho, E2 ....13 G3
Siviter Way, Dag. RM10 ..101 H7
Siward Rd, N17 ....76 A1
SW17 ....167 F3
Bromley BR2 ....191 H3
Six Acres Est, N4 ....93 G2

Six Bridges Trd Est, SE1 ... 37 J4
Sixth Av, E12 ... 98 C4
W10 ... 108 B3
Hayes UB3 ... 121 J1
Sixth Cross Rd, Twick.
TW2 ... 161 J3
Skardu Rd, NW2 ... 90 B5
Skeena Hill, SW18 ... 148 B7
Skeffington Rd, E6 ... 116 B1
Skeffington St, SE18 ... 137 F3
Skelbrook St, SW18 ... 167 E2
Skelgill Rd, SW15 ... 148 C4
Skelley Rd, E15 ... 97 F7
Skelton Cl, E8
off Buttermere Wk ... 94 C6
Skelton Rd, E7 ... 97 G6
Skeltons La, E10 ... 78 B7
Skelwith Rd, W6 ... 127 J6
Skenfrith Ho, SE15
off Commercial Way ... 132 E6
Skerne Rd, Kings.T. KT2 ... 181 G1
Skerne Wk, Kings.T. KT2 ... 181 G1
Sketchley Gdns, SE16 ... 133 G5
Sketty Rd, Enf. EN1 ... 44 B3
Skiers St, E15 ... 114 E1
Skiffington Cl, SW2 ... 169 G1
Skinner Ct, E2
off Parmiter St ... 113 E2
Skinner Pl, SW1 ... 32 B2
★ **Skinners' Hall**, EC4
off Dowgate Hill ... 20 B5
Skinners La, EC4 ... 20 A5
Hounslow TW5 ... 143 H1
Skinner St, EC1 ... 11 F4
Skipsea Ho, SW18
off Fitzhugh Gro ... 149 G6
Skipsey Av, E6 ... 116 C3
Skipton Cl, N11 ... 58 A6
Skipton Dr, Hayes UB3 ... 121 F3
Skipworth Rd, E9 ... 113 F1
Skomer Wk, N1
off Ashby Gro ... 93 J7
Skylines Village, E14 ... 134 C2
Sky Peals Rd, Wdf.Grn.
IG8 ... 78 D1
Skyport Dr, West Dr.
(Harm.) UB7 ... 120 A7
Skyvan Cl, Houns. TW6
off Southern Perimeter Rd ... 141 F5
Slade, The, SE18 ... 137 H6
Sladebrook Rd, SE3 ... 156 A3
Sladedale Rd, SE18 ... 137 H5
Slade Ho, Houns. TW4 ... 143 F6
Slades Cl, Enf. EN2 ... 43 G3
Slades Dr, Chis. BR7 ... 175 F3
Slades Gdns, Enf. EN2 ... 43 G2
Slades Hill, Enf. EN2 ... 43 G3
Slades Ri, Enf. EN2 ... 43 G3
Slade Twr, E10 ... 96 A2
Slade Wk, SE17 ... 35 H6
Slade Way, Mitch. CR4 ... 186 A1
Slagrove Pl, SE13 ... 154 A5
Slaidburn St, SW10 ... 30 D6
Slaithwaite Rd, SE13 ... 154 C4
Slaney Pl, N7
off Hornsey Rd ... 93 G5
Slater Cl, SE18
off Woolwich New Rd ... 136 D5
Slater Ms, SW4
off Old Town ... 150 C3
Slattery Rd, Felt. TW13 ... 160 C1
Sleaford Grn, Wat.
WD19 ... 50 D3
Sleaford Ho, E3 ... 114 A4
Sleaford St, SW8 ... 33 F7
Slievemore Cl, SW4
off Voltaire Rd ... 150 D3
Slingsby Pl, WC2 ... 18 A5
Slippers Pl, SE16 ... 133 E3
Slippers Pl Est, SE16
off Slippers Pl ... 133 E3
Sloane Av, SW3 ... 31 H2
Sloane Ct E, SW3 ... 32 B3
Sloane Ct W, SW3 ... 32 B3
Sloane Gdns, SW1 ... 32 B2
Orpington BR6 ... 207 F3
Sloane Ms, N8 ... 75 E5
Sloane Sq, SW1 ... 32 B2
Sloane St, SW1 ... 24 A5
Sloane Ter, SW1 ... 32 A1
Sloane Wk, Croy. CR0 ... 189 J6
Slocum Cl, SE28 ... 118 C7
Slough La, NW9 ... 70 C6
Sly St, E1
off Cannon St Rd ... 112 E6
Smaldon Cl, West Dr. UB7
off Walnut Av ... 120 D3
Smallberry Av, Islw. TW7 ... 144 C2
Smallbrook Ms, W2 ... 14 E4
Smalley Cl, N16 ... 94 C3
Smalley Rd Est, N16
off Smalley Cl ... 94 C2
Smallwood Rd, SW17 ... 167 G4
Smardale Rd, SW18
off Alma Rd ... 149 F5
Smarden Cl, Belv. DA17
off Essenden Rd ... 139 G5
Smarden Gro, SE9 ... 174 C4
Smarts La, Loug. IG10 ... 48 A4
Smarts Pl, N18
off Fore St ... 60 D5
Smart's Pl, WC2 ... 18 B3
Smart St, E2 ... 113 G3
Smead Way, SE13 ... 154 B3
Smeaton Cl, Chess. KT9 ... 195 G6
Smeaton Ct, SE1 ... 27 J6
Smeaton Rd, SW18 ... 148 D7
Woodford Green IG8 ... 64 C5
Smeaton St, E1 ... 132 E1
Smedley St, SW4 ... 150 D2
SW8 ... 150 D2
Smeed Rd, E3 ... 96 A7
Smiles Pl, SE13 ... 154 C2
Smith Cl, SE16 ... 133 G1
Smithfield St, EC1 ... 19 G2
Smithies Rd, SE2 ... 138 B4
Smith's Ct, W1 ... 17 G5
Smiths Fm Est, Nthlt.
UB5 ... 103 G2
Smithson Rd, N17 ... 76 A1
Smiths Pt, E13 ... 115 G1
Smith Sq, SW1 ... 26 A6
Smith St, SW3 ... 31 J3
Surbiton KT5 ... 181 J6
Smiths Yd, SW18
off Summerley St ... 167 F2
Smith's Yd, Croy. CR0
off St. Georges Wk ... 201 J3
Smith Ter, SW3 ... 31 J4
Smithwood Cl, SW19 ... 166 B1
Smithy St, E1 ... 113 F5
Smock Wk, Croy. CR0 ... 187 J6
Smokehouse Yd, EC1 ... 19 H1
Smugglers Way, SW18 ... 149 E4
Smyrks Rd, SE17 ... 36 E4
Smyrna Rd, NW6 ... 90 D7
Smythe Cl, N9 ... 60 D3
Smythe St, E14 ... 114 B7
Snakes La, Barn. EN4 ... 42 B3
Snakes La E, Wdf.Grn.
IG8 ... 63 J6
Snakes La W, Wdf.Grn.
IG8 ... 63 G6
Snakey La, Felt. TW13 ... 160 A4
SNARESBROOK, E11 ... 79 E5
Snaresbrook Dr, Stan.
HA7 ... 53 G4
Snaresbrook Rd, E11 ... 78 E4
Snarsgate St, W10 ... 107 J5
Sneath Av, NW11 ... 72 C7
Snells Pk, N18 ... 60 C6
Sneyd Rd, NW2 ... 89 J4
Snowberry Cl, E15 ... 96 D4
Snowbury Rd, SW6 ... 149 E2
Snowden St, EC2 ... 12 D6
Snowdon Cres, Hayes
UB3 ... 121 F3
Snowdon Dr, NW9 ... 70 E6
Snowdon Rd, Houns.
(Lon.Hthrw Air.) TW6
off Southern Perimeter Rd ... 141 F5
Snowdown Cl, SE20 ... 189 G1
Snowdrop Cl, Hmptn.
TW12 *off Gresham Rd* ... 161 G6
Snow Hill, EC1 ... 19 G2
Snow Hill Ct, EC1 ... 19 H3
Snowman Ho, NW6 ... 109 E1
Snowsfields, SE1 ... 28 C3
Snowshill Rd, E12 ... 98 B5
Snowy Fielder Waye, Islw.
TW7 ... 144 E2
Soames Pl, Barn. EN4 ... 41 E2
Soames St, SE15 ... 152 C3
Soames Wk, N.Mal. KT3 ... 182 E1
Soane Cl, W5 ... 125 G2
Soap Ho La, Brent. TW8
off Ferry La ... 125 H6
Socket La, Brom. BR2 ... 191 H6
SOHO, W1 ... 17 H5
Soho Sq, W1 ... 17 H3
Soho St, W1 ... 17 H3
Sojourner Truth Cl, E8
off Richmond Rd ... 95 E6
Solander Gdns, E1
off Dellow St ... 113 E7
Solebay St, E1 ... 113 H4
Solent Ri, E13 ... 115 G3
Solent Rd, NW6 ... 90 D5
Soley Ms, WC1 ... 10 E3
Solna Av, SW15 ... 147 J5
Solna Rd, N21 ... 60 A1
Solomon Av, N9 ... 60 D4
Solomon's Pas, SE15 ... 152 E4
Solon New Rd, SW4 ... 150 E4
Solon Rd, SW2 ... 151 E4
Solway Cl, E8
off Buttermere Wk ... 94 C6
Hounslow TW4 ... 143 E3
Solway Rd, N22 ... 75 H1
SE22 ... 152 D4
Somaford Gro, Barn. EN4 ... 41 G6
Somali Rd, NW2 ... 90 C4
Somborne Ho, SW15
off Fontley Way ... 147 G7
Somerby Rd, Bark. IG11 ... 99 G7
Somercoates Cl, Barn.
EN4 ... 41 H3
Somerfield Rd, N4 ... 93 H2
Somerfield St, SE16 ... 133 G5
Somerford Cl, Pnr.
(Eastcote) HA5 ... 66 A4
Somerford Gro, N16 ... 94 C4
N17 ... 60 D7
Somerford Gro Est, N16
off Somerford Gro ... 94 C4
Somerford St, E1 ... 112 E4
Somerford Way, SE16 ... 133 H2
Somerhill Av, Sid. DA15 ... 158 B7
Somerhill Rd, Well. DA16 ... 158 B2
Somerleyton Pas, SW9 ... 151 H4
Somerleyton Rd, SW9 ... 151 G4
Somersby Gdns, Ilf. IG4 ... 80 C5
Somers Cl, NW1 ... 9 H1
Somers Cres, W2 ... 15 G4
Somerset Av, SW20 ... 183 H2
Chessington KT9 ... 195 G4
Welling DA16 ... 157 J5
Somerset Cl, N17 ... 76 A2
New Malden KT3 ... 183 E6
Woodford Green IG8 ... 79 G1
Somerset Est, SW11 ... 149 G1
Somerset Gdns, N6 ... 74 A7
N17 ... 60 B7
SE13 ... 154 B2
SW16 ... 187 F3
Teddington TW11 ... 162 B5
Somerset Hall, N17 ... 60 B7
★ **Somerset Ho**, WC2 ... 18 C5
Somerset Ho, SW19 ... 166 A3
Somerset Rd, E17 ... 78 A5
N17 ... 76 C3
N18 ... 60 C5
NW4 ... 71 J4
SW19 ... 166 B4
W4 ... 126 D3
W13 ... 125 E1
Barnet (New Barn.)
EN5 ... 41 E5
Brentford TW8 ... 125 F6
Harrow HA1 ... 67 J6
Kingston upon Thames
KT1 ... 181 J2
Southall UB1 ... 103 F5
Teddington TW11 ... 162 B5
Somerset Sq, W14 ... 128 B2
Somerset Waye, Houns.
TW5 ... 122 E6
Somersham Rd, Bexh.
DA7 ... 159 E2
Somers Ms, W2 ... 15 G4
Somers Pl, SW2 ... 151 F7
Somers Rd, E17 ... 77 J4
SW2 ... 151 F6
SOMERS TOWN, NW1 ... 9 J3
Somerton Av, Rich. TW9 ... 146 B3
Somerton Rd, NW2 ... 90 B3
SE15 ... 153 E4
Somertrees Av, SE12 ... 173 H2
Somervell Rd, Har. HA2 ... 85 F5
Somerville Av, SW13 ... 127 H6
Somerville Cl, SW9
off Stockwell Pk Cres ... 151 F2
Somerville Rd, SE20 ... 171 G7
Romford RM6 ... 82 C6
Sonderburg Rd, N7 ... 93 F2
Sondes St, SE17 ... 36 B5
Songhurst Cl, Croy. CR0 ... 187 F6
Sonia Ct, Har. HA1 ... 68 C6
Sonia Gdns, N12
off Woodside Av ... 57 F4
NW10 ... 89 F4
Hounslow TW5 ... 123 G7
Sonning Gdns, Hmptn.
TW12 ... 161 E6
Sonning Rd, SE25 ... 188 D6
Soper Cl, E4 ... 61 J5
SE23 ... 171 G1
Sophia Cl, N7
off Mackenzie Rd ... 93 F6
Sophia Rd, E10 ... 96 B1
E16 ... 115 H6
Sophia Sq, SE16
off Rotherhithe St ... 113 H7
Sopwith Av, Chess. KT9 ... 195 H5
Sopwith Cl, Kings.T. KT2 ... 163 J5
Sopwith Rd, Houns. TW5 ... 122 C7
Sopwith Way, SW8 ... 32 D7
Kingston upon Thames
KT2 ... 181 H1
Sorrel Cl, SE28 ... 138 A1
Sorrel Gdns, E6 ... 116 B5
Sorrel La, E14 ... 114 D6
Sorrell Cl, SE14
off Southerngate Way ... 133 H7
Sorrento Rd, Sutt. SM1 ... 198 E3
Sotheby Rd, N5 ... 93 H3
Sotheran Cl, E8 ... 112 D1
Sotheron Rd, SW6 ... 129 E7
Soudan Rd, SW11 ... 149 J1
Souldern Rd, W14 ... 128 A3
South Access Rd, E17 ... 77 H7
Southacre Way, Pnr. HA5 ... 66 C1
SOUTH ACTON, W3 ... 126 A3
South Acton Est, W3 ... 126 B2
South Africa Rd, W12 ... 127 H1
SOUTHALL, UB1 & UB2 ... 122 D1
Southall La, Houns. TW5 ... 122 B6
Southall UB2 ... 122 B6
Southall Pl, SE1 ... 28 B4
Southampton Bldgs, WC2 ... 18 E3
Southampton Gdns, Mitch.
CR4 ... 186 E5
Southampton Ms, E16
off Wesley Av ... 135 H1
Southampton Pl, WC1 ... 18 B2
Southampton Rd, NW5 ... 91 J5
Southampton Rd E, Houns.
(Lon.Hthrw Air.) TW6 ... 140 D6
Southampton Rd W, Houns.
(Lon.Hthrw Air.) TW6 ... 140 B6
Southampton Row, WC1 ... 18 B1
Southampton St, WC2 ... 18 B5
Southampton Way, SE5 ... 36 C7
Southam St, W10 ... 108 B4
South Audley St, W1 ... 16 C6
South Av, E4 ... 46 B7
Carshalton SM5 ... 200 A7
Richmond TW9
off Sandycombe Rd ... 146 A2
Southall UB1 ... 103 F7
South Av Gdns, Sthl.
UB1 ... 103 F7
South Bk, Chis. BR7 ... 175 F3
Surbiton KT6 ... 181 H6
Southbank, T.Ditt. KT7 ... 180 E7
Southbank Business Cen,
SW8 ... 33 J6
South Bk Ter, Surb. KT6 ... 181 H6
SOUTH BEDDINGTON,
Wall. SM6 ... 200 D6
South Birkbeck Rd, E11 ... 96 D3
South Black Lion La, W6 ... 127 G5
South Bolton Gdns, SW5 ... 30 B3
SOUTHBOROUGH, Brom.
BR2 ... 192 C6
Southborough Cl, Surb.
KT6 ... 195 G1
Southborough La, Brom.
BR2 ... 192 B5
Southborough Rd, E9 ... 113 F1
Bromley BR1 ... 192 B3
Surbiton KT6 ... 195 H1
Southbourne, Brom. BR2 ... 191 G7
Southbourne Av, NW9 ... 70 C2
Southbourne Cl, Pnr. HA5 ... 67 E7
Southbourne Cres, NW4 ... 72 B4
Southbourne Gdns,
SE12 ... 155 H5
Ilford IG1 ... 99 F5
Ruislip HA4 ... 84 B1
Southbridge Pl, Croy.
CR0 ... 201 J4
Southbridge Rd, Croy.
CR0 ... 201 J4
Southbridge Way, Sthl.
UB2 ... 123 E2
Southbrook Ms, SE12 ... 155 F6
Southbrook Rd, SE12 ... 155 F6
SW16 ... 187 E1
Southbury Av, Enf. EN1 ... 44 D5
Southbury Rd, Enf.
EN1, EN3 ... 44 A3
South Carriage Dr, SW1 ... 23 J3
SW7 ... 23 F4
SOUTH CHINGFORD, E4 ... 61 J5
Southchurch Rd, E6 ... 116 C2
South Circular Rd,
SE6 (A205) ... 154 D7
SE9 (A205) ... 156 C3
SE12 (A205) ... 155 H6
SE18 (A205) ... 136 D6
SE21 (A205) ... 170 B1
SE22 (A205) ... 171 E1
SE23 (A205) ... 171 J1
SW2 (A205) ... 169 G1
SW4 (A205) ... 150 A5
SW11 (A3) ... 149 H5
SW12 (A205) ... 169 G1
SW14 (A205) ... 147 E4
SW15 (A205) ... 147 J4
SW18 (A3) ... 149 H5
W4 (A205) ... 126 A5
Brentford (A205) TW8 ... 126 A5
Richmond (A205) TW9 ... 146 B2
South City Ct, SE15 ... 36 E7
South Cl, N6 ... 74 B6
Barnet EN5 ... 40 C3
Bexleyheath DA6 ... 158 D4
Dagenham RM10 ... 119 G1
Morden SM4 ... 184 D6
Pinner HA5 ... 67 F7
Twickenham TW2 ... 161 G3

South Cl, West Drayton UB7 120 C3
South Colonnade, The, E14 134 A1
Southcombe St, W14 128 B4
Southcote Av, Surb. KT5 182 B7
Southcote Rd, E17 77 G5
N19 92 C4
SE25 189 E6
Southcott Ms, NW8 7 G2
South Countess Rd, E17 77 J3
South Cres, E16 114 D4
WC1 17 H2
Southcroft Av, Well. DA16 157 H3
West Wickham BR4 204 C2
Southcroft Rd, SW16 168 A6
SW17 168 A6
Orpington BR6 207 H3
South Cross Rd, Ilf. IG6 81 F5
South Croxted Rd, SE21 170 A3
SOUTH CROYDON, CR2 201 J6
Southdale, Chig. IG7 65 G6
Southdean Gdns, SW19 166 C2
South Dene, NW7 54 D3
Southdown Av, W7 124 D3
Southdown Cres, Har. HA2 85 H1
Ilford IG2 81 H5
Southdown Dr, SW20 166 A7
Southdown Rd, SW20 184 A1
South Dr, Orp. BR6 207 H5
South Ealing Rd, W5 125 G2
South Eastern Av, N9 60 C3
South Eaton Pl, SW1 32 C1
South Eden Pk Rd, Beck. BR3 190 B6
South Edwardes Sq, W8 128 C3
SOUTHEND, SE6 172 B4
South End, W8 22 B5
Croydon CR0 201 J4
South End Cl, NW3 91 H4
Southend Cl, SE9 156 E6
Southend Cres, SE9 156 D6
South End Grn, NW3 *off South End Rd* 91 H4
Southend La, SE6 171 J4
SE26 171 J4
Southend Rd, E4 61 H5
E6 98 C7
E17 78 B1
E18 79 G1
South End Rd, NW3 91 H4
Southend Rd, Beck. BR3 172 A7
Woodford Green IG8 79 J2
South End Row, W8 22 B5
Southern Av, SE25 188 C3
Feltham TW14 160 A1
Southern Dr, Loug. IG10 48 C6
Southerngate Way, SE14 133 H7
Southern Gro, E3 113 J3
Southernhay, Loug. IG10 48 A5
Southern Perimeter Rd, Houns. (Lon.Hthrw Air.) TW6 141 G5
Southern Pl, Har. HA1 86 C4
Southern Rd, E13 115 H2
N2 73 J4
Southern Row, W10 108 B4
Southern St, N1 10 C1
Southern Way, SE10 135 F4
Romford RM7 83 G6
Southerton Rd, W6 127 J3
South Esk Rd, E7 97 J6
Southey Ms, E16 *off Wesley Av* 135 G1
Southey Rd, N15 76 B5
SW9 151 G1
SW19 166 D7
Southey St, SE20 171 G7
Southfield, Barn. EN5 40 A6
Southfield Cotts, W7 *off Oaklands Rd* 124 C2
Southfield Gdns, Twick. TW1 162 C4
Southfield Pk, Har. HA2 67 H4
Southfield Rd, N17 *off The Avenue* 76 B2
W4 126 E3
Chislehurst BR7 193 J3
Enfield EN3 45 E6
SOUTHFIELDS, SW18 166 D1
Southfields, NW4 71 G3
East Molesey KT8 180 B6
Southfields Ct, SW19 166 B1
Sutton SM1 *off Sutton Common Rd* 198 D2
Southfields Ms, SW18 *off Southfields Rd* 148 D6
Southfields Pas, SW18 148 D6
Southfields Rd, SW18 148 D6
Southfleet Rd, Orp. BR6 207 H3
South Gdns, SW19 167 G7
Wembley HA9 *off The Avenue* 87 J2
SOUTHGATE, N14 58 C2
Southgate Circ, N14 *off The Bourne* 58 D1
Southgate Gro, N1 94 A7
Southgate Rd, N1 112 A1
South Gipsy Rd, Well. DA16 158 D3
South Glade, The, Bex. DA5 177 F1
South Grn, NW9 *off Clayton Fld* 71 E1
South Gro, E17 77 J5
N6 92 A1
N15 76 A5
South Gro Ho, N6 92 A1
SOUTH HACKNEY, E9 95 F7
SOUTH HAMPSTEAD, NW6 91 E7
SOUTH HARROW, Har. HA2 85 H3
South Hill, Chis. BR7 174 C6
South Hill Av, Har. HA1, HA2 85 J3
South Hill Gro, Har. HA1 86 B4
South Hill Pk, NW3 91 H4
South Hill Pk Gdns, NW3 91 H4
South Hill Rd, Brom. BR2 190 E3
Southholme Cl, SE19 188 B1
South Huxley, N18 60 A5
Southill La, Pnr. HA5 66 A4
Southill Rd, Chis. BR7 174 B7
Southill St, E14 *off Chrisp St* 114 B6
South Island Pl, SW9 131 F7
SOUTH KENSINGTON, SW7 30 C2
South Kensington Sta Arc, SW7 *off Pelham St* 31 F1
South Kensington Underground Sta, SW7 31 F1
SOUTH LAMBETH, SW8 151 E1
South Lambeth Est, SW8 *off Dorset Rd* 131 F7
South Lambeth Pl, SW8 34 B5
South Lambeth Rd, SW8 34 B6
Southland Rd, SE18 137 J7
Southlands Av, Orp. BR6 207 G4
Southlands Dr, SW19 166 A2
Southlands Gro, Brom. BR1 192 B3
Southlands Rd, Brom. BR1, BR2 191 J5
Southland Way, Houns. TW3 144 A5
South La, Kings.T. KT1 181 G3
New Malden KT3 182 D4
South La W, N.Mal. KT3 182 D4
South Lo, NW8 6 E3
SW7 *off Knightsbridge* 23 H4
South Lo Av, Mitch. CR4 186 E4
South Lo Cres, Enf. EN2 42 D4
South Lo Dr, N14 42 E5
★ South London Art Gall, SE5 152 B1
Southly Cl, Sutt. SM1 198 D3
South Mall, N9 *off Edmonton Grn Shop Cen* 60 D3
South Mead, NW9 71 F1
Epsom KT19 197 E7
Southmead Gdns, Tedd. TW11 *off Cromwell Rd* 162 D6
South Meadows, Wem. HA9 87 H5
Southmead Rd, SW19 166 B1
South Molton La, W1 16 D4
South Molton Rd, E16 115 G6
South Molton St, W1 16 D4
Southmont Rd, Esher KT10 194 B2
Southmoor Way, E9 95 J6
SOUTH NORWOOD, SE25 188 C3
South Norwood Hill, SE25 188 B2
South Oak Rd, SW16 169 F4
Southold Ri, SE9 174 C3
Southolm St, SW11 150 B1
Southover, N12 56 D4
Bromley BR1 173 G5
SOUTH OXHEY, Wat. WD19 50 C3
South Par, SW3 31 F3
W4 126 D4
Edgware HA8 *off Mollison Way* 70 A2
South Pk, SW6 148 D2
South Pk Cres, SE6 173 F1
Ilford IG1 99 G3
South Pk Dr, Bark. IG11 99 H4
Ilford IG3 99 H4
South Pk Gro, N.Mal. KT3 182 C4
South Pk Hill Rd, S.Croy. CR2 202 A5
South Pk Ms, SW6 148 E3
South Pk Rd, SW19 166 D6
Ilford IG1 99 G3
South Pk Ter, Ilf. IG1 99 G3
South Pk Way, Ruis. HA4 84 C6
South Penge Pk Est, SE20 188 E2
South Pl, EC2 20 C1
Enfield EN3 45 F5
Surbiton KT5 181 J7
South Pl Ms, EC2 20 C2
South Pt, Sutt. SM1 199 F6
Southport Rd, SE18 137 G4
South Quay Plaza, E14 134 B2
South Quay Sq, E14 *off Marsh Wall* 134 B2
Southridge Pl, SW20 166 A7
South Ri Way, SE18 137 G5
South Rd, N9 60 D1
SE23 171 G2
SW19 167 F6
W5 125 G4
Edgware HA8 70 B1
Feltham TW13 160 D5
Hampton TW12 161 E6
Romford (Chad.Hth) RM6 82 E6
Romford (Lt.Hth) RM6 82 C5
Southall UB1 123 F2
Twickenham TW2 162 A3
West Drayton UB7 120 C3
South Row, SE3 155 F2
SOUTH RUISLIP, Ruis. HA4 84 C4
Southsea Rd, Kings.T. KT1 181 H4
South Sea St, SE16 133 J3
South Side, W6 127 F3
Southside Common, SW19 165 J6
Southside Shop Cen, SW18 148 E6
Southspring, Sid. DA15 157 G7
South Sq, NW11 72 E6
WC1 18 E2
South St, W1 24 C1
Bromley BR1 191 G2
Enfield EN3 45 G5
Isleworth TW7 144 D3
Rainham RM13 119 J2
South Tenter St, E1 21 G5
South Ter, SW7 31 G1
Surbiton KT6 181 H6
SOUTH TOTTENHAM, N15 76 B5
South Vale, SE19 170 B6
Harrow HA1 86 B4
Southvale Rd, SE3 155 E2
South Vw, Brom. BR1 191 H2
Southview Av, NW10 89 F5
Southview Cl, SW17 168 A5
Bexley DA5 159 F6
Southview Cres, Ilf. IG2 80 E6
South Vw Dr, E18 79 H3
Southview Gdns, Wall. SM6 200 C7
South Vw Rd, N8 74 D3
Southview Rd, Brom. BR1 172 D4
South Vw Rd, Loug. IG10 48 C6
Pinner HA5 50 B6
South Vil, NW1 92 D6
Southville, SW8 150 D1
Southville Rd, T.Ditt. KT7 180 E7
South Wk, W.Wick. BR4 204 E3
SOUTHWARK, SE1 27 H2
Southwark Br, EC4 28 A1
SE1 28 A1
Southwark Br Rd, SE1 27 H5
★ Southwark Cath, SE1 28 B1
Southwark Pk, SE16 133 F4
Southwark Pk Est, SE16 133 E4
Southwark Pk Rd, SE16 37 G1
Southwark Pl, Brom. BR1 192 C3
Southwark St, SE1 27 H1
Southwater Cl, E14 113 J6
Beckenham BR3 172 B7
South Way, N9 61 F2
N11 *off Ringway* 58 C6
Southway, N20 56 D2
NW11 72 E6
SW20 183 J4
South Way, Brom. (Hayes) BR2 191 G7
Croydon CR0 203 H3
Harrow HA2 67 G4
Southway, Wall. SM6 200 C4
South Way, Wem. HA9 88 A5
Southway Cl, W12 127 H2
Southwell Av, Nthlt. UB5 85 G6
Southwell Gdns, SW7 30 C1
Southwell Gro Rd, E11 96 E2
Southwell Rd, SE5 151 J3
Croydon CR0 187 G6
Harrow HA3 69 G6
South Western Rd, Twick. TW1 144 D6
Southwest Rd, E11 96 D1
South Wf Rd, W2 15 E3
Southwick Ms, W2 15 F3
Southwick Pl, W2 15 G4
Southwick St, W2 15 G3
SOUTH WIMBLEDON, SW19 166 E7
Southwold Dr, Bark. IG11 100 A5
Southwold Rd, E5 95 E2
Bexley DA5 159 H6
Southwood Av, N6 74 B7
Kingston upon Thames KT2 182 C1
Southwood Cl, Brom. BR1 192 C4
Worcester Park KT4 198 A1
Southwood Dr, Surb. KT5 182 C7
SOUTH WOODFORD, E18 79 F2
Southwood Gdns, Esher KT10 194 D3
Ilford IG2 80 E4
Southwood La, N6 74 A7
Southwood Lawn Rd, N6 74 A7
Southwood Pk, N6 74 A7
Southwood Rd, SE9 174 E2
SE28 138 B1
Southwood Smith St, N1 *off Old Royal Free Sq* 111 G1
South Worple Av, SW14 146 E3
South Worple Way, SW14 146 D3
Sovereign Business Cen, Enf. EN3 45 J2
Sovereign Cl, E1 113 E7
W5 105 F5
Sovereign Ct, W.Mol. KT8 179 F4
Sovereign Cres, SE16 *off Rotherhithe St* 133 H1
Sovereign Gro, Wem. HA0 87 G3
Sovereign Ms, E2 13 F1
Barnet EN4 41 J3
Sovereign Pk, NW10 106 B4
Sovereign Pl, Har. HA1 68 C5
Sovereign Rd, Bark. IG11 118 C3
Sowerby Cl, SE9 156 B5
Space Waye, Felt. TW14 142 A5
Spa Cl, SE25 188 B1
Spafield St, EC1 11 E5
Spa Grn Est, EC1 11 F3
Spa Hill, SE19 188 A1
Spalding Cl, Edg. HA8 55 E7
Spalding Rd, NW4 71 J6
SW17 168 B5
Spanby Rd, E3 114 A4
Spaniards Cl, NW11 91 G1
Spaniards End, NW3 91 F1
Spaniards Rd, NW3 91 F2
Spanish Pl, W1 16 C3
Spanish Rd, SW18 149 F5
Spareleaze Hill, Loug. IG10 48 C5
Sparkbridge Rd, Har. HA1 68 B4
Sparkes Cl, Brom. BR2 191 H4
Sparke Ter, E16 *off Clarkson Rd* 115 F6
Sparkford Gdns, N11 58 A5
Sparkford Ho, SW11 149 G1
Sparks Cl, W3 106 D6
Dagenham RM8 100 D2
Hampton TW12 *off Victors Dr* 161 E6
Spa Rd, SE16 29 F6
Sparrow Cl, Hmptn. TW12 160 E6
Sparrow Dr, Orp. BR5 207 F1
Sparrow Fm Dr, Felt. TW14 142 D7
Sparrow Fm Rd, Epsom KT17 197 G4
Sparrow Grn, Dag. RM10 101 H3
Sparrows La, SE9 157 F7
Sparsholt Rd, N19 93 E1
Barking IG11 117 H1
Spartan Cl, Wall. SM6 200 E7
Sparta St, SE10 154 B1
★ Speaker's Cor, W2 16 A5
Speaker's Ct, Croy. CR0 *off St. James's Rd* 202 A1
Spearman St, SE18 136 D6
Spear Ms, SW5 128 D4
Spearpoint Gdns, Ilf. IG2 81 J4
Spears Rd, N19 92 E1
Speart La, Houns. TW5 122 E7
Spedan Cl, NW3 91 E3
Speechly Ms, E8 *off Alvington Cres* 94 C5
Speed Highwalk, EC2 *off Silk St* 20 A1
Speed Ho, EC2 20 B1

Speedwell St, SE8
off Comet St **134** A7
Speedy Pl, WC1 **10** A4
Speer Rd, T.Ditt. KT7 **180** C5
Speirs Cl, N.Mal. KT3 **183** F6
Spekehill, SE9 **174** C3
Speke Rd, Th.Hth. CR7 **188** A2
Speldhurst Cl, Brom. BR2 **191** F5
Speldhurst Rd, E9 **95** G7
W4 **126** D3
Spellbrook Wk, N1
off Basire St **111** J1
Spelman St, E1 **21** H1
Spence Cl, SE16
off Vaughan St **133** J2
Spencer Av, N13 **59** F6
Hayes UB4 **102** A5
Spencer Cl, N3 **72** C2
NW10 **105** J3
Orpington BR6 **207** H2
Woodford Green IG8 **63** J5
Spencer Ctyd, N3
off Regents Pk Rd **72** C2
Spencer Dr, N2 **73** F6
Spencer Gdns, SE9 **156** C5
SW14 **146** C5
Spencer Hill, SW19 **166** B6
Spencer Hill Rd, SW19 **166** B7
★ **Spencer Ho**, SW1 **25** F2
Spencer Ms, SW8
off Lansdowne Way **151** F1
W6 *off Greyhound Rd* **128** B6
Spencer Pk, SW18 **149** G5
Spencer Pas, E2
off Pritchard's Rd **112** E2
Spencer Pl, N1
off Canonbury La **93** H7
Croydon CR0 **188** A7
Spencer Ri, NW5 **92** B4
Spencer Rd, E6 **116** A1
E17 **78** C2
N8 **75** F5
N11 **58** B4
N17 **76** D1
SW18 **149** G4
SW20 **183** H1
W3 **126** C1
W4 **126** C7
Bromley BR1 **173** E7
East Molesey KT8 **179** J5
Harrow HA3 **68** B2
Ilford IG3 **99** J1
Isleworth TW7 **144** A1
Mitcham CR4 **186** A3
Mitcham (Bedd.Cor.) CR4 **186** A7
South Croydon CR2 **202** B5
Twickenham TW2 **162** B3
Wembley HA0 **87** F2
Spencer St, EC1 **11** G4
Southall UB2 **122** D2
Spencer Wk, NW3 **91** G4
SW15 **148** A4
Spencer Yd, SE3
off Blackheath Village **155** F2
Spenser Gro, N16 **94** B4
Spenser Ms, SE21 **170** A1
Spenser Rd, SE24 **151** G5
Spenser St, SW1 **25** G5
Spensley Wk, N16
off Clissold Rd **94** A3
Speranza St, SE18 **137** J5
Sperling Rd, N17 **76** B2
Spert St, E14 **113** H7
Speyside, N14 **42** C6
Spey St, E14 **114** C5
Spezia Rd, NW10 **107** G2
Sphere, The, E16
off Hallsville Rd **115** F6
Spice Quay Hts, SE1 **29** G2
Spicer Cl, SW9 **151** H2
Walton-on-Thames KT12 **178** C6
Spice's Yd, Croy. CR0 **201** J4
Spigurnell Rd, N17 **76** A1
Spikes Br Moorings, Hayes UB4 **102** E7
Spikes Br Rd, Sthl. UB1 **103** E6
Spindle Cl, SE18 **136** B3
Spindlewood Gdns, Croy. CR0 **202** B4
Spindrift Av, E14 **134** B4
Spinel Cl, SE18 **137** J5
Spinnaker Cl, Bark. IG11 **118** B3
Spinnells Rd, Har. HA2 **85** F1
Spinney, The, N21 **43** G7
SW16 **168** D3
Barnet EN5 **41** E2
Loughton IG10 **48** E4
Sidcup DA14 **176** E5
Stanmore HA7 **53** H4
Sunbury-on-Thames TW16 **178** A1
Sutton SM3 **197** J4
Wembley HA0 **86** D3
Spinney Cl, Beck. BR3 **190** B4
New Malden KT3 **182** E5
Worcester Park KT4 **197** F3
Spinney Dr, Felt. TW14 **141** F7
Spinney Gdns, SE19 **170** C5
Dagenham RM9 **101** E5
Spinney Oak, Brom. BR1 **192** B2
Spinneys, The, Brom. BR1 **192** C2
Spire Ho, W2 **14** D5
Spires Shop Cen, The, Barn. EN5 **40** B3
Spirit Quay, E1 **29** J1
★ **Spitalfields City Fm**, E1 **13** H6
Spital Sq, E1 **21** E1
Spital St, E1 **21** H1
Spital Yd, E1 **21** E1
Spitfire Business Pk, Croy. CR0 **201** G6
Spitfire Est, Houns. TW5 **122** C5
Spitfire Rd, Wall. SM6 **201** E7
Spitfire Way, Houns. TW5 **122** C5
Spode Ho, SE11
off Lambeth Wk **26** E6
Spode Wk, NW6
off Dresden Cl **91** E5
Spondon Rd, N15 **76** D4
Spoonbill Way, Hayes UB4
off Cygnet Way **102** D5
Spooners Ms, W3
off Churchfield Rd **126** D1
Spooner Wk, Wall. SM6 **200** D5
Sporle Ct, SW11 **149** G3
Sportsbank St, SE6 **154** C7
Sportsman Ms, E2
off Whiston Rd **112** D1
Spotted Dog Path, E7
off Upton La **97** G6
Spottons Gro, N17
off Gospatrick Rd **75** J1
Spout Hill, Croy. CR0 **204** A5
Spratt Hall Rd, E11 **79** G6
Spray La, Twick. TW2 **144** B6
Spray St, SE18 **137** E4
Spreighton Rd, W.Mol. KT8 **179** H4
Sprimont Pl, SW3 **31** J3
Springall St, SE15 **133** E7
Springbank, N21 **43** F6
Springbank Rd, SE13 **154** D6
Springbank Wk, NW1
off St. Paul's Cres **92** D7
Springbourne Ct, Beck. BR3 **190** C1
Spring Br Ms, W5
off Spring Br Rd **105** G7
Spring Br Rd, W5 **105** G7
Spring Cl, Barn. EN5 **40** A5
Borehamwood WD6 **38** A1
Dagenham RM8 **100** D1
Springclose La, Sutt. SM3 **198** B6
Spring Cotts, Surb. KT6 **181** G5
Spring Ct, Sid. DA15
off Station Rd **176** A3
Springcroft Av, N2 **73** J4
Springdale Ms, N16
off Springdale Rd **94** A4
Springdale Rd, N16 **94** A4
Spring Dr, Pnr. HA5 **66** A6
Springfield, E5 **94** E1
Bushey (Bushey Hth) WD23 **52** A1
Springfield Av, N10 **74** C3
SW20 **184** C3
Hampton TW12 **161** H6
Springfield Cl, N12 **56** E5
Stanmore HA7 **52** D3
Springfield Ct, Wall. SM6
off Springfield Rd **200** B5
Springfield Dr, Ilf. IG2 **81** F6
Springfield Gdns, E5 **95** E1
NW9 **70** D5
Bromley BR1 **192** C4
Ruislip HA4 **84** B1
West Wickham BR4 **204** B2
Woodford Green IG8 **63** J7
Springfield Gro, SE7 **135** J6
Springfield Gro Est, SE7 **135** J6
Springfield La, NW6 **108** E1
Springfield Mt, NW9 **70** E5
Springfield Pl, N.Mal. KT3 **182** C4
Springfield Ri, SE26 **170** E3
Springfield Rd, E4 **62** E1
E6 **98** C7
E15 **115** E3
E17 **77** J6
N11 **58** B5
N15 **76** D4
NW8 **109** F1
SE26 **171** E5
SW19 **166** C5
W7 **124** B1
Bexleyheath DA7 **159** H3
Springfield Rd, Bromley BR1 **192** C4
Harrow HA1 **68** B6
Hayes UB4 **122** C1
Kingston upon Thames KT1 **181** H3
Teddington TW11 **162** D5
Thornton Heath CR7 **187** J1
Twickenham TW2 **161** G1
Wallington SM6 **200** B5
Welling DA16 **158** B3
Springfield Wk, NW6 **108** E1
Orpington BR6
off Place Fm Av **207** G1
Spring Gdns, N5
off Grosvenor Av **93** J5
SW1 **25** J1
Romford RM7 **83** J5
Wallington SM6 **200** C5
West Molesey KT8 **179** J5
Woodford Green IG8 **63** J7
Spring Gdns Business Pk, Rom. RM7 **83** J5
SPRING GROVE, Islw. TW7 **144** C1
Spring Gro, SE19
off Alma Pl **170** C7
W4 **126** A5
Hampton TW12
off Plevna Rd **179** H1
Loughton IG10 **48** A6
Mitcham CR4 **186** A1
Spring Gro Cres, Houns. TW3 **143** J1
Spring Gro Rd, Houns. TW3 **143** H1
Isleworth TW7 **143** H1
Richmond TW10 **145** J5
Spring Hill, E5 **76** D7
SE26 **171** F4
Springhill Cl, SE5 **152** A3
Springhurst Cl, Croy. CR0 **203** J4
Spring Lake, Stan. HA7 **52** E4
Spring La, E5 **95** E1
N10 **74** A3
SE25 **188** E6
Spring Ms, W1 **16** A1
Richmond TW9
off Rosedale Rd **145** H4
Spring Pk Av, Croy. CR0 **203** G2
Spring Pk Dr, N4 **93** J1
Springpark Dr, Beck. BR3 **190** C3
Spring Pk Rd, Croy. CR0 **203** G2
Spring Pas, SW15
off Embankment **148** A3
Spring Path, NW3 **91** G5
Spring Pl, N3
off Windermere Av **72** D2
NW5 **92** B5
Springpond Rd, Dag. RM9 **101** E5
Springrice Rd, SE13 **154** C6
Spring St, W2 **15** E4
Spring Ter, Rich. TW9 **145** H5
Spring Tide Cl, SE15
off Staffordshire St **152** D1
Spring Vale, Bexh. DA7 **159** H4
Springvale Av, Brent. TW8 **125** G5
Springvale Est, W14
off Blythe Rd **128** B3
Springvale Ter, W14 **128** A3
Spring Vil Rd, Edg. HA8 **54** A7
Spring Wk, E1 **21** J1
Springwater Cl, SE18 **156** D1
Springway, Har. HA1 **68** A7
Springwell Av, NW10 **107** F1
Springwell Cl, SW16
off Etherstone Rd **169** G4
Springwell Ct, Houns. TW4 **142** D2
Springwell Rd, SW16 **169** G4
Hounslow TW4, TW5 **142** D1
Springwood Cl, E3 **114** A2
Springwood Cres, Edg. HA8 **54** B2
Sprowston Ms, E7 **97** G6
Sprowston Rd, E7 **97** G5
Spruce Ct, W5
off Elderberry Rd **125** H3
Sprucedale Gdns, Croy. CR0 **203** G4
Spruce Hills Rd, E17 **78** C2
Spruce Pk, Brom. BR2
off Cumberland Rd **191** F4
Sprules Rd, SE4 **153** H2
Spurfield, W.Mol. KT8 **179** H3
Spurgeon Av, SE19 **188** A1
Spurgeon Rd, SE19 **188** A1
Spurgeon St, SE1 **28** B6
Spurling Rd, SE22 **152** C4
Dagenham RM9 **101** F6
Spur Rd, N15
off Philip La **76** A4
SE1 **26** E3
Spur Rd, SW1 **25** F4
Barking IG11 **117** F2
Edgware HA8 **53** H4
Feltham TW14 **142** B5
Isleworth TW7 **124** E7
Spur Rd Est, Edg. HA8
off Green La **53** J4
Spurstowe Rd, E8
off Marcon Pl **94** E5
Spurstowe Ter, E8 **94** E5
Square, The, E10 **96** C3
W6 **127** J5
Carshalton SM5 **200** A5
Ilford IG1 **80** D7
Richmond TW9 **145** G5
Uxbridge UB11 **121** G1
Woodford Green IG8 **63** G5
Square Rigger Row, SW11
off York Pl **149** F3
Squarey St, SW17 **167** F3
Squire Gdns, NW8 **7** E4
Squires, The, Rom. RM7 **83** J6
Squires Ct, SW19 **166** D4
Squires La, N3 **73** E2
Squires Mt, NW3
off East Heath Rd **91** G3
Squires Wd Dr, Chis. BR7 **174** B7
Squirrel Cl, Houns. TW4 **142** C2
Squirrel Ms, W13 **104** D7
Squirrels, The, SE13 **154** D3
Pinner HA5 **67** F3
Squirrels Cl, N12
off Woodside Av **57** F4
Orpington BR6 **207** H1
Squirrels Grn, Wor.Pk. KT4 **197** F1
Squirrels La, Buck.H. IG9 **64** A3
Squirrels Trd Est, The, Hayes UB3 **121** J3
Squirries St, E2 **13** J3
Stable Cl, Kings.T. KT2 **163** J6
Northolt UB5 **103** G2
Stable Ms, NW5
off Grafton Rd **92** B6
Twickenham TW1 **162** C1
Stables, The, Buck.H. IG9 **47** J7
Stables End, Orp. BR6 **207** F3
Stables Ms, SE27 **169** J5
Stables Way, SE11 **35** E3
Stable Wk, N1
off Wharfdale Rd **111** E2
N2 *off Old Fm Rd* **73** G1
Stable Way, W10
off Latimer Rd **107** J6
Stable Yd, SW1 **25** F3
SW9
off Broomgrove Rd **151** F2
SW15 *off Danemere St* **147** J3
Stable Yd Rd, SW1 **25** F2
Stacey Av, N18 **61** F4
Stacey Cl, E10
off Halford Rd **78** D5
Stacey St, N7 **93** G3
WC2 **17** J4
Stackhouse St, SW3 **23** J5
Stacy Path, SE5
off Harris St **132** B7
Staddon Cl, Beck. BR3 **189** H4
Stadium Business Cen, Wem. HA9 **88** B3
Stadium Retail Pk, Wem. HA9
off Wembley Pk Dr **88** A3
Stadium Rd, NW2 **71** H7
SE18 **136** B7
Stadium Rd E, NW2 **71** J7
Stadium St, SW10 **129** F7
Stadium Way, Wem. HA9 **87** J4
Staffa Rd, E10 **95** H1
Stafford Cl, E17 **77** J6
N14 **42** C5
NW6 **108** D3
Sutton SM3 **198** B6
Stafford Ct, SW8
off Allen Edwards Dr **130** E7
W8 **128** D3
Stafford Cripps Ho, E2
off Globe Rd **113** F3
SW6
off Clem Attlee Ct **128** C6
Stafford Cross Business Pk, Croy. CR0 **201** F5
Stafford Gdns, Croy. CR0 **201** F5
Stafford Pl, SW1 **25** F5
Richmond TW10 **145** J7
Stafford Rd, E3 **113** J2
E7 **97** J7
NW6 **108** D3
Croydon CR0 **201** G4
Harrow HA3 **51** J7
New Malden KT3 **182** C3
Sidcup DA14 **175** H4
Wallington SM6 **200** C6
Staffordshire St, SE15 **152** D1
Stafford St, W1 **25** F1
Stafford Ter, W8 **128** D3

Staff St, EC1 ....12 C4
Stag Cl, Edg. HA8 ....70 B2
Staggart Grn, Chig. IG7 ..65 J6
Stag La, NW9 ....70 C3
  SW15 ....165 F2
  Buckhurst Hill IG9 ...63 H2
  Edgware HA8 ....70 B2
Stag Ride, SW19 ....165 F3
Stagshaw Ho, SE22
  off Pytchley Rd 152 B3
Stags Way, Islw. TW7 ....124 C6
Stainbank Rd, Mitch.
  CR4 ....186 B3
Stainby Cl, West Dr. UB7 .120 B3
Stainby Rd, N15 ....76 C4
Stainer Ho, SE3
  off Ryan Cl 155 J4
Stainer St, SE1 ....28 C2
Staines Av, Sutt. SM3 ...198 A2
Staines Rd, Felt. TW14 ..141 G7
  Hounslow TW3, TW4 ..143 H3
  Ilford IG1 ....99 F4
  Twickenham TW2 ......161 G3
Staines Rd E, Sun. TW16 .160 A7
Staines Wk, Sid. DA14
  off Evry Rd 176 C6
Stainforth Rd, E17 ....78 A4
  Ilford IG2 ....81 G7
Staining La, EC2 ....20 A3
Stainmore Cl, Chis. BR7 ..193 G1
Stainsbury St, E2
  off Royston St 113 F2
Stainsby Rd, E14 ....114 A6
Stainton Rd, SE6 ....154 D6
  Enfield EN3 ....45 F1
Stalbridge St, NW1 ....15 H1
Stalham St, SE16 ....133 E3
Stalham Way, Ilf. IG6 ....81 E1
Stambourne Way, SE19 ..170 B7
  West Wickham BR4 ...204 C3
Stamford Brook Av, W6 ..127 F3
Stamford Brook Gdns,
  W6 off Stamford
  Brook Rd 127 F3
Stamford Brook Rd, W6 .127 F3
Stamford Cl, N15 ....76 D4
  Harrow HA3 ....52 B7
  Southall UB1 ....103 G7
Stamford Cotts, SW10 ...30 B7
Stamford Ct, W6 ....127 F4
  Edgware HA8 ....53 J4
Stamford Dr, Brom. BR2 .191 F4
Stamford Gdns, Dag.
  RM9 ....100 C7
Stamford Gro E, N16
  off Oldhill St 94 D1
Stamford Gro W, N16
  off Oldhill St 94 D1
STAMFORD HILL, N16 ...94 B1
Stamford Hill, N16 ....94 C2
Stamford Hill Est, N16 ...94 C1
Stamford Rd, E6 ....116 B1
  N1 ....94 B7
  N15 ....76 D5
  Dagenham RM9 ......118 B1
Stamford St, SE1 ....27 E2
Stamp Pl, E2 ....13 F3
Stanard Cl, N16 ....76 B7
Stanborough Cl, Hmptn.
  TW12 ....161 F6
Stanborough Pas, E8
  off Kingsland Rd 94 C6
Stanborough Rd, Houns.
  TW3 ....144 A3
Stanbridge Pl, N21 ......59 H2
Stanbridge Rd, SW15 ...147 J3
Stanbrook Rd, SE2 ....138 B2
Stanbury Rd, SE15 ......153 E1
Stancroft, NW9 ....70 E4
Standard Ind Est, E16 ...136 C2
Standard Pl, EC2 ....12 E4
Standard Rd, NW10 .....106 C4
  Belvedere DA17 ......139 G5
  Bexleyheath DA6 .....159 E4
  Hounslow TW4 ....143 E3
Standen Rd, SW18 ......148 C7
Standfield Gdns,
  Dag. RM10
  off Standfield Rd 101 G6
Standfield Rd, Dag.
  RM10 ....101 G5
Standish Ho, SE3
  off Elford Cl 155 J4
Standish Rd, W6 ....127 G4
Standlake Pt, SE23 ......171 G3
Stane Cl, SW19
  off Hayward Cl 167 E7
Stane Gro, SW9 ....150 E2
Stane Way, SE18 ....136 A7
Stanfield Ho, NW8
  off Frampton St 7 F5
Stanfield Rd, E3 ....113 H2
Stanford Cl, Hmptn.
  TW12 ....161 F6
  Romford RM7 ....83 H6
  Woodford Green IG8 ..64 B5

Stanford Ct, SW6
  off Bagley's La 149 E1
Stanford Ho, Bark. IG11 .118 B2
Stanford Ms, E8
  off Dalston La 94 D5
Stanford Pl, SE17 ....36 D2
Stanford Rd, N11 ....57 J5
  SW16 ....186 D2
  W8 ....22 B5
Stanford St, SW1 ....33 H2
Stanford Way, SW16 ....186 D2
Stangate, SE1 ....26 C5
Stangate Cres, Borwd.
  WD6 ....38 E5
Stangate Gdns, Stan.
  HA7 ....53 E4
Stanger Rd, SE25 ....188 D4
Stanhope Av, N3 ....72 C3
  Bromley BR2 ....205 F1
  Harrow HA3 ....68 A1
Stanhope Cl, SE16
  off Middleton Dr 133 G2
Stanhope Gdns, N4 .....75 H6
  N6 ....74 B6
  NW7 ....55 F5
  SW7 ....30 D1
  Dagenham RM8 ......101 F3
  Ilford IG1 ....98 C1
Stanhope Gate, W1 ......24 C1
Stanhope Gro, Beck. BR3 .189 J5
Stanhope Ms E, SW7 ...30 D1
Stanhope Ms S, SW7 ....30 D2
Stanhope Ms W, SW7 ...30 D1
Stanhope Par, NW1
  off Stanhope St 9 F3
Stanhope Pk Rd, Grnf.
  UB6 ....103 J4
Stanhope Pl, W2 ....15 J4
Stanhope Rd, E17 ....78 B5
  N6 ....74 C6
  N12 ....57 F5
  Barnet EN5 ....39 J6
  Bexleyheath DA7 .....159 E2
  Carshalton SM5 .....200 A7
  Croydon CR0 ....202 B3
  Dagenham RM8 ......101 F2
  Greenford UB6 ....103 J5
  Sidcup DA15 ....176 A4
Stanhope Row, W1 ......24 D2
Stanhope St, NW1 ....9 F4
Stanhope Ter, W2 ....15 F5
Stanier Cl, W14
  off Aisgill Av 128 C5
Stanlake Ms, W12 ......127 J1
Stanlake Rd, W12 ......127 H1
Stanlake Vil, W12 ......127 H1
Stanley Av, Bark. IG11 ...117 J2
  Beckenham BR3 ......190 C2
  Dagenham RM8 ......101 F1
  Greenford UB6 ....103 J1
  New Malden KT3 .....183 G5
  Wembley HA0 ....87 H7
Stanley Cl, SE9 ....175 F1
  SW8 ....34 C6
  Wembley HA0 ....87 H7
Stanley Cl, Cars. SM5
  off Stanley Pk Rd ...200 A7
Stanley Cres, W11 ......108 C7
Stanleycroft Cl, Islw.
  TW7 ....144 B1
Stanley Gdns, NW2 ......89 J5
  W3 ....126 E1
  W11 ....108 C7
  Mitcham CR4
  off Ashbourne Rd 168 A6
  Wallington SM6 .....200 C6
Stanley Gdns Ms, W11
  off Kensington Pk Rd .108 C7
Stanley Gdns Rd, Tedd.
  TW11 ....162 B5
Stanley Gro, SW8 ......150 A2
  Croydon CR0 ....187 G6
Stanley Pk Dr, Wem. HA0 .87 J7
Stanley Pk Rd, Cars.
  SM5 ....199 J7
  Wallington SM6 .....200 B6
Stanley Rd, E4 ....62 D1
  E10 ....78 B6
  E12 ....98 B5
  E15 ....114 D1
  E18 ....79 F1
  N2 ....73 G3
  N9 ....60 C1
  N10 ....58 B7
  N11 ....58 D6
  N15 ....75 H4
  NW9
  off West Hendon Bdy ..71 G7
  SW14 ....146 B4
  SW19 ....166 D7
  W3 ....126 C3
  Bromley BR2 ....191 H4
  Carshalton SM5 .....200 A7
  Croydon CR0 ....187 G6
  Enfield EN1 ....44 B3
  Harrow HA2 ....85 J2

Stanley Rd, Hounslow
  TW3 ....143 J4
  Ilford IG1 ....99 G2
  Mitcham CR4 ....168 A7
  Morden SM4 ....184 D4
  Northwood HA6 ....66 A1
  Sidcup DA14 ....176 A3
  Southall UB1 ....102 E7
  Sutton SM2 ....198 E6
  Teddington TW11 .....162 B4
  Twickenham TW2 .....162 A3
  Wembley HA9 ....87 J6
Stanley St, SE8 ....133 J7
Stanley Ter, N19 ....92 E2
Stanliff Ho, E14
  off Lightermans Rd ..134 A3
Stanmer St, SW11 ......149 H1
STANMORE, HA7 ....52 D5
Stanmore Gdns, Rich.
  TW9 ....145 J3
  Sutton SM1 ....199 F3
Stanmore Hall, Stan. HA7 .52 D3
Stanmore Hill, Stan. HA7 .52 D3
Stanmore Rd, E11 ....97 F1
  N15 ....75 H4
  Belvedere DA17 ......139 J4
  Richmond TW9 ....145 J3
Stanmore St, N1
  off Caledonian Rd ...111 F1
Stanmore Ter, Beck. BR3 .190 A2
Stanmore Way, Loug.
  IG10 ....48 D1
Stannard Ms, E8 ....94 D6
Stannard Rd, E8 ....94 D6
Stannary St, SE11 ....35 F5
Stannet Way, Wall. SM6 ..200 C4
Stannington Path, Borwd.
  WD6 ....38 A1
Stansbury Sq, W10
  off Beethoven St 108 B3
Stansfeld Rd, E6 ....116 A6
  E16 ....116 A5
Stansfield Rd, SW9 ......151 F3
  Hounslow TW4 ....142 B2
Stansgate Rd, Dag.
  RM10 ....101 G2
Stanstead Cl, Brom. BR2 .191 F5
Stanstead Gro, SE6
  off Stanstead Rd 171 J1
Stanstead Manor, Sutt.
  SM1 ....198 D6
Stanstead Rd, E11 ....79 H5
  SE6 ....171 G1
  SE23 ....171 G1
  Hounslow
  (Lon.Hthrw Air.) TW6 .140 C6
Stansted Cres, Bex. DA5 .176 D1
Stanswood Gdns, SE5 ..132 B7
Stanthorpe Cl, SW16 ...168 E5
Stanthorpe Rd, SW16 ...168 E5
Stanton Av, Tedd. TW11 .162 B5
Stanton Cl, Epsom KT19 .196 B5
  Worcester Park KT4 ..198 A1
Stanton Ho, SE16
  off Rotherhithe St ...133 J2
Stanton Rd, SE26
  off Stanton Way 171 J4
  SW13 ....147 F2
  SW20 ....184 A2
  Croydon CR0 ....187 J7
Stanton Sq, SE26
  off Stanton Way 171 J4
Stanton Way, SE26 ......171 J4
  SE26 (Sydenham)
  off Sydenham Rd 171 J5
Stanway Cl, Chig. IG7 ...65 H5
Stanway Ct, N1 ....13 E2
Stanway Gdns, W3 ......126 A1
  Edgware HA8 ....54 C5
Stanway St, N1 ....12 E1
STANWELL, Stai. TW19 .140 B7
Stanwell Cl, Stai.
  (Stanw.) TW19 ....140 A6
Stanwell Gdns, Stai.
  (Stanw.) TW19 ....140 A6
Stanwell Rd, Felt. TW14 .141 F7
Stanwick Rd, W14 ......128 C4
Stanworth St, SE1 ....29 F4
Stanwyck Dr, Chig. IG7 ...65 F5
Stapenhill Rd, Wem. HA0 .86 E3
Staplefield Cl, SW2 .....169 E1
  Pinner HA5 ....50 E7
Stapleford Av, Ilf. IG2 ...81 H5
Stapleford Cl, E4 ....62 C3
  SW19 ....148 B7
  Kingston upon Thames
  KT1 ....182 A3
Stapleford Rd, Wem.
  HA0 ....87 G7
Stapleford Way, Bark.
  IG11 ....118 B3
Staplehurst Rd, SE13 ...154 E5
  Carshalton SM5 .....199 H7
Staple Inn, WC1 ....19 E2
Staple Inn Bldgs, WC1 ...18 E2
Staples Cl, SE16 ....133 H1
Staples Cor, NW2 ....89 H1

Staples Cor Retail Pk, NW2
  off Geron Way 89 H2
Staples Rd, Loug. IG10 ...48 B3
Staple St, SE1 ....28 C4
Stapleton Gdns, Croy.
  CR0 ....201 G5
Stapleton Hall Rd, N4 ...75 F7
Stapleton Rd, SW17 ....168 A3
  Bexleyheath DA7 .....139 F7
  Orpington BR6 ......207 J3
Stapley Rd, Belv. DA17 ..139 G5
Stapylton Rd, Barn. EN5 ..40 B3
Star All, EC3 ....20 E5
Star & Garter Hill, Rich.
  TW10 ....163 H1
Starboard Way, E14 ....134 A3
Starbuck Cl, SE9 ....156 D7
Starch Ho La, Ilf. IG6 ....81 G2
Star Cl, Enf. EN3 ....45 F6
Starcross St, NW1 ....9 G4
Starfield Rd, W12 ......127 G2
Star La, E16 ....115 E4
Starlight Way, Houns.
  TW6 off Southern
  Perimeter Rd 141 F5
Starling Cl, Buck.H. IG9 ..63 G1
  Croydon CR0 ....189 H6
  Pinner HA5 ....66 C3
Starling Wk, Hmptn. TW12
  off Oak Av 161 E5
Starmans Cl, Dag. RM9 .119 E1
Star Path, Nthlt. UB5
  off Brabazon Rd 103 G2
Star Pl, E1 ....21 G6
Star Rd, W14 ....128 C6
  Isleworth TW7 ....144 A2
Star St, E16 ....115 F5
  W2 ....15 F3
Starts Cl, Orp. BR6 .....206 D3
Starts Hill Av, Orp.
  (Farnboro.) BR6 .....207 E5
Starts Hill Rd, Orp.
  BR6 ....206 D3
Starveall Cl, West Dr.
  UB7 ....120 C3
Star Yd, WC2 ....18 E3
State Fm Av, Orp. BR6 ..207 E4
Staten Bldg, E3
  off Fairfield Rd 114 A2
Staten Gdns, Twick. TW1 .162 C1
Statham Ct, N7 ....92 E3
Statham Gro, N16
  off Green Las 94 A4
  N18 ....60 B5
Station App, E4 (Chingford)
  off Station Rd 46 E7
  E4 (Highams Pk)
  off The Avenue 62 D6
  E7 off Woodford Rd ...97 H4
  E11 (Snaresbrook)
  off High St 79 G5
  N11
  off Friern Barnet Rd ..58 B5
  N12 (Woodside Pk) ...56 E4
  N16 (Stoke Newington)
  off Stamford Hill 94 C2
  NW10 off Station Rd .107 F3
  SE1 ....26 D2
  SE3
  off Kidbrooke Pk Rd ..155 H3
  SE9 (Mottingham) ...174 C1
  SE26 (Lwr Sydenham)
  off Worsley Br Rd ...171 J5
  SE26 (Sydenham)
  off Sydenham Rd 171 F4
  SW6 ....148 B3
  SW16 ....168 D5
  SW20 ....183 J2
  W7 ....124 B1
  Barnet (High Barn.) EN5
  off Barnet Hill 40 D4
  Barnet (New Barn.)
  EN5 ....41 F4
  Beckenham BR3
  off Rectory Rd 190 A1
  Bexley DA5
  off Bexley High St ..159 G7
  Bexleyheath DA7
  off Avenue Rd 159 E2
  Bexleyheath (Barne.)
  DA7 ....159 J2
  Bromley (Hayes) BR2 .205 G1
  Buckhurst Hill IG9
  off Cherry Tree Ri ...64 A3
  Chislehurst BR7 .....192 D1
  Chislehurst (Elm.Wds)
  BR7 ....174 B6
  Epsom (Stoneleigh)
  KT19 ....197 G5
  Esher (Hinch.Wd)
  KT10 ....194 C3
  Greenford UB6 ....86 A7
  Hampton TW12
  off Milton Rd 179 G1
  Harrow HA1 ....68 B7
  Hayes UB3 ....121 J4

Station App, Kingston upon Thames KT1 ....182 A1
Loughton IG10 ....48 B5
Loughton (Debden) IG10 ....49 F4
Orpington BR6 ....207 J2
Pinner HA5 ....66 E3
Pinner (Hatch End) HA5 *off Uxbridge Rd* 51 G7
Richmond TW9 ....146 A1
Ruislip (S.Ruis.) HA4 ....84 B5
Sunbury-on-Thames TW16 ....178 A1
Sutton (Cheam) SM2 ....198 B7
Watford (Carp.Pk) WD19 *off Prestwick Rd* 50 D3
Wembley HA0 ....87 E6
West Drayton UB7 ....120 B1
West Wickham BR4 ....204 C1
Woodford Green IG8 *off The Broadway* 63 H6
Worcester Park KT4 ....197 G1
Station App N, Sid. DA15 ....176 A2
Station App Path, SE9 *off Glenlea Rd* 156 C5
Station App Rd, W4 ....126 C7
Station Av, SW9 *off Coldharbour La* 151 H3
New Malden KT3 ....183 E3
Richmond (Kew) TW9 ....146 A1
Station Cl, N3 ....72 D1
N12 (Woodside Pk) 56 E4
Hampton TW12 ....179 H1
Station Ct, SW6 ....149 F1
Station Cres, N15 ....76 A4
SE3 ....135 G5
Wembley HA0 ....87 E6
Stationers Hall Ct, EC4 *off Ludgate Hill* 19 H4
Station Est, Beck. BR3 *off Elmers End Rd* 189 G4
Station Est Rd, Felt. TW14 ....160 B1
Station Gar Ms, SW16 *off Estreham Rd* 168 D6
Station Gdns, W4 ....126 C7
Station Gro, Wem. HA0 ....87 H6
Station Hill, Brom. BR2 ....205 G2
Station Ho Ms, N9 *off Fore St* 60 D4
Station Ms Ter, SE3 *off Halstow Rd* 135 G5
Station Par, E11 ....79 G5
N14 *off High St* 58 D1
NW2 ....89 J6
SW12 *off Balham High Rd* 168 A1
W3 ....106 A6
W5 *off Uxbridge Rd* 125 J1
Barking IG11 ....99 F7
Barnet EN4 *off Cockfosters Rd* 42 A4
Edgware HA8 ....53 H7
Feltham TW14 ....142 B7
Richmond TW9 ....146 A1
Station Pas, E18 *off Maybank Rd* 79 H2
SE15 ....153 F1
Station Path, E8 *off Amhurst Rd* 95 E6
Station Pl, N4 *off Seven Sisters Rd* 93 G2
Station Ri, SE27 *off Norwood Rd* 169 H2
Station Rd, E4 (Chingford) 62 D1
E7 ....97 G4
E12 ....98 A4
E17 ....77 H6
N3 ....72 D1
N11 ....58 B5
N17 ....76 D3
N19 ....92 C3
N21 ....59 H1
N22 ....75 F2
NW4 ....71 G6
NW7 ....55 E5
NW10 ....107 F2
SE13 ....154 C3
SE20 ....171 F6
SE25 (Norwood Junct.) 188 C4
SW13 ....147 G3
SW19 ....185 F1
W5 ....105 J6
W7 (Hanwell) 124 B1
Barnet (New Barn.) EN5 ....40 E5
Belvedere DA17 ....139 G3
Bexleyheath DA7 ....159 E3
Borehamwood WD6 ....38 A4
Brentford TW8 ....125 F6
Bromley BR1 ....191 G1
Bromley (Short.) BR2 ....191 E2
Carshalton SM5 ....199 J4
Chessington KT9 ....195 H5
Chigwell IG7 ....64 E3
Station Rd, Croydon CR0 ....201 J1
Edgware HA8 ....54 A6
Esher KT10 ....194 A2
Esher (Clay.) KT10 ....194 A5
Hampton TW12 ....179 G1
Harrow HA1 ....68 C7
Harrow (N.Har.) HA2 ....67 H5
Hayes UB3 ....121 J3
Hounslow TW3 ....143 H4
Ilford IG1 ....98 E3
Ilford (Barkingside) IG6 ....81 G3
Kingston upon Thames KT2 ....182 A1
Kingston upon Thames (Hmptn W.) KT1 ....181 F1
Loughton IG10 ....48 B4
New Malden (Mots.Pk) KT3 ....183 H5
Orpington BR6 ....207 J2
Romford (Chad.Hth) RM6 ....82 D7
Sidcup DA15 ....176 A4
Sunbury-on-Thames TW16 ....160 A7
Teddington TW11 ....162 C5
Thames Ditton KT7 ....180 C7
Twickenham TW1 ....162 C1
West Drayton UB7 ....120 A1
West Wickham BR4 ....204 C1
Station Rd N, Belv. DA17 ....139 H3
Station Sq, Orp. (Petts Wd) BR5 ....193 F5
Station St, E15 ....96 D7
E16 ....136 E1
Station Ter, NW10 ....108 A2
SE5 ....151 J1
Station Vw, Grnf. UB6 ....104 A1
Station Way, Buck.H. (Rod.Val.) IG9 ....63 J4
Esher (Clay.) KT10 ....194 B6
Sutton (Cheam) SM3 ....198 B6
Station Yd, Twick. TW1 ....144 D7
Staunton Rd, Kings.T. KT2 ....163 H6
Staunton St, SE8 ....133 J6
★ **Stave Hill Ecological Pk**, SE16 ....133 H2
Staveley Cl, E9 *off Churchill Wk* 95 F5
N7 ....93 E4
SE15 *off Asylum Rd* 153 E1
Staveley Gdns, W4 ....146 D1
Staveley Rd, W4 ....126 D7
Staverton Rd, NW2 ....89 J7
Stave Yd Rd, SE16 ....133 H1
Stavordale Rd, N5 ....93 H4
Carshalton SM5 ....185 F7
Stayner's Rd, E1 ....113 G4
Stayton Rd, Sutt. SM1 ....198 D3
Steadfast Rd, Kings.T. KT1 ....181 G1
Stead St, SE17 ....36 B2
Steam Fm La, Felt. TW14 ....141 J4
Stean St, E8 ....112 C1
Stebbing Ho, W11 ....128 A1
Stebbing Way, Bark. IG11 ....118 A2
Stebondale St, E14 ....134 C5
Stedham Pl, WC1 ....18 A3
Steedman St, SE17 ....35 J2
Steeds Rd, N10 ....73 J1
Steeds Way, Loug. IG10 ....48 B3
Steele Rd, E11 ....96 E4
N17 ....76 B3
NW10 ....106 C2
W4 ....126 C3
Isleworth TW7 ....144 D4
Steeles Ms N, NW3 *off Steeles Rd* 91 J6
Steeles Ms S, NW3 *off Steeles Rd* 91 J6
Steeles Rd, NW3 ....91 J6
Steele Wk, Erith DA8 ....139 H6
Steel's La, E1 *off Devonport St* 113 F6
Steelyard Pas, EC4 ....20 B6
Steen Way, SE22 *off East Dulwich Gro* 152 B5
Steep Cl, Orp. BR6 ....207 J6
Steep Hill, SW16 ....168 D3
Croydon CR0 ....202 B4
Steeple Cl, SW6 ....148 B2
SW19 ....166 B5
Steeple Ct, E1 *off Coventry Rd* 113 E4
Steeplestone Cl, N18 ....59 J5
Steeple Wk, N1 *off Basire St* 111 J1
Steerforth St, SW18 ....167 E2
Steering Cl, N9 ....61 F1
Steers Mead, Mitch. CR4 ....185 J1
Steers Way, SE16 ....133 H2
Stellar Ho, N17 ....60 C6
Stella Rd, SW17 ....167 J6
Stellman Cl, E5 ....94 D3
Stembridge Rd, SE20 ....188 E2
Stephan Cl, E8 ....112 D1
Stephen Cl, Orp. BR6 ....207 J3
Stephendale Rd, SW6 ....149 E2
Stephen Ms, W1 ....17 H2
Stephen Pl, SW4 *off Rectory Gro* 150 C3
Stephen Rd, Bexh. DA7 ....159 J3
Stephenson Cl, Well. DA16 ....158 A2
Stephenson Ho, SE1 *off Bath Ter* 27 J5
Stephenson Rd, E17 ....77 H5
W7 ....104 C6
Twickenham TW2 ....143 G7
Stephenson St, E16 ....114 E4
NW10 ....107 E3
Stephenson Way, NW1 ....9 G5
Stephen's Rd, E15 ....115 E1
Stephen St, W1 ....17 H2
STEPNEY, E1 ....113 F5
Stepney Causeway, E1 ....113 G6
Stepney Cl, Mitch. CR4 ....186 A1
Stepney Grn, E1 ....113 F5
Stepney High St, E1 ....113 G5
Stepney Way, E1 ....112 E5
Sterling Av, Edg. HA8 ....53 J4
Sterling Cl, NW10 ....89 G6
Sterling Gdns, SE14 ....133 H6
Sterling Ho, SE3 *off Cambert Way* 155 H4
Sterling Ind Est, Dag. RM10 ....101 H4
Sterling Pl, W5 ....125 H4
Sterling Rd, Enf. EN2 ....44 A1
Sterling St, SW7 ....23 H5
Sterling Way, N18 ....60 A5
★ **Sternberg Cen**, N3 ....72 E2
Stern Cl, Bark. IG11 ....118 C2
Sterndale Rd, W14 ....128 A3
Sterne St, W12 ....128 A2
Sternhall La, SE15 ....152 D3
Sternhold Av, SW2 ....168 D2
Sterry Cres, Dag. RM10 *off Alibon Rd* 101 G5
Sterry Dr, Epsom KT19 ....196 E4
Thames Ditton KT7 ....180 B6
Sterry Gdns, Dag. RM10 ....101 G6
Sterry Rd, Bark. IG11 ....117 J1
Dagenham RM10 ....101 G4
Sterry St, SE1 ....28 B4
Steucers La, SE23 ....153 H7
Steve Biko La, SE6 ....172 A4
Steve Biko Rd, N7 ....93 G3
Steve Biko Way, Houns. TW3 ....143 G3
Stevedale Rd, Well. DA16 ....158 C2
Stevedore St, E1 *off Waterman Way* 132 E1
Stevenage Rd, E6 ....98 D6
SW6 ....128 A7
Stevens Av, E9 ....95 F6
Stevens Cl, Beck. BR3 ....172 A6
Hampton TW12 ....161 E6
Pinner HA5 ....66 C5
Stevens Grn, Bushey (Bushey Hth) WD23 ....51 J1
Stevens La, Esher (Clay.) KT10 ....194 D7
Stevenson Cl, Barn. EN5 ....41 G6
Stevenson Cres, SE16 ....37 J3
Stevens Rd, Dag. RM8 ....100 B3
Stevens St, SE1 ....29 E5
Stevens Way, Chig. IG7 ....65 H4
Steventon Rd, W12 ....107 F7
Stewards Holte Wk, N11 *off Coppies Gro* 58 B4
Steward St, E1 ....21 E2
Stewart Cl, NW9 ....70 C6
Chislehurst BR7 ....175 E5
Hampton TW12 ....161 E5
Stewart Rainbird Ho, E12 ....98 D5
Stewart Rd, E15 ....96 C4
Stewartsby Cl, N18 ....59 J5
Stewart's Gro, SW3 ....31 F3
Stewart's Rd, SW8 ....130 C7
Stewart St, E14 ....134 C2
Stew La, EC4 ....19 J5
Steyne Rd, W3 ....126 C1
Steyning Gro, SE9 ....174 C4
Steynings Way, N12 ....56 D5
Steyning Way, Houns. TW4 ....142 C4
Steynton Av, Bex. DA5 ....176 D2
Stickland Rd, Belv. DA17 *off Picardy Rd* 139 G4
Stickleton Cl, Grnf. UB6 ....103 H3
Stilecroft Gdns, Wem. HA0 ....86 E3
Stile Hall Gdns, W4 ....126 A5
Stile Hall Par, W4 *off Chiswick High Rd* 126 A5
Stile Path, Sun. TW16 ....178 A4
Stiles Cl, Brom. BR2 ....192 C6
Erith DA8 *off Riverdale Rd* 139 H5
Stillingfleet Rd, SW13 ....127 G6
Stillington St, SW1 ....33 G1
Stillness Rd, SE23 ....153 H6
Stipularis Dr, Hayes UB4 ....102 D4
Stirling Av, Pnr. HA5 ....66 E7
Wallington SM6 ....201 E7
Stirling Cl, SW16 ....186 C1
Sidcup DA14 ....175 H4
Stirling Cor, Barn. EN5 ....38 D6
Borehamwood WD6 ....38 D6
Stirling Gro, Houns. TW3 ....143 J2
Stirling Ind Cen, Borwd. WD6 ....38 D5
Stirling Retail Pk, Borwd. WD6 ....38 D6
Stirling Rd, E13 ....115 H2
E17 ....77 H3
N17 ....76 D1
N22 ....75 H1
SW9 ....150 E2
W3 ....126 B3
Harrow HA3 ....68 C3
Hayes UB3 ....102 B7
Hounslow (Lon.Hthrw Air.) TW6 ....140 C6
Twickenham TW2 ....143 G7
Stirling Rd Path, E17 ....77 H3
Stirling Wk, N.Mal. KT3 ....182 C5
Surbiton KT5 ....182 B6
Stirling Way, Borwd. WD6 ....38 D6
Croydon CR0 ....186 E7
Stiven Cres, Har. HA2 ....85 F3
Stockbury Rd, Croy. CR0 ....189 F6
Stockdale Rd, Dag. RM8 ....101 F2
Stockdove Way, Grnf. (Perivale) UB6 ....104 C3
Stocker Gdns, Dag. RM9 ....100 C7
★ **Stock Exchange**, EC4 ....19 H3
Stockfield Rd, SW16 ....169 F3
Esher (Clay.) KT10 ....194 B5
Stockford Av, NW7 ....56 A7
Stockholm Ho, E1 ....112 D7
Stockholm Rd, SE16 ....133 F5
Stockholm Way, E1 ....29 H1
Stockhurst Cl, SW15 ....147 J2
Stockingswater La, Enf. EN3 ....45 H3
Stockleigh Hall, NW8 *off Prince Albert Rd* 7 J1
Stockley Cl, West Dr. UB7 ....120 E2
Stockley Fm Rd, West Dr. UB7 *off Stockley Rd* 120 E3
Stockley Pk, Uxb. UB11 ....121 E1
Stockley Pk Rbt, Uxb. UB11 ....120 E1
Stockley Rd, West Dr. UB7 ....120 E4
Stock Orchard Cres, N7 ....93 F5
Stock Orchard St, N7 ....93 F5
Stockport Rd, SW16 ....186 D1
Stocksfield Rd, E17 ....78 C3
Stocks Pl, E14 *off Grenade St* 113 J7
Stock St, E13 ....115 G2
Stockton Cl, Barn. (New Barn.) EN5 ....41 F4
Stockton Gdns, N17 *off Stockton Rd* 59 J7
NW7 ....54 D3
Stockton Ho, E2 *off Ellsworth St* 112 E3
Stockton Rd, N17 ....59 J7
N18 ....60 D6
STOCKWELL, SW9 ....151 F1
Stockwell Av, SW9 ....151 F3
Stockwell Cl, Brom. BR1 ....191 H2
Edgware HA8 ....70 C2
Stockwell Gdns, SW9 ....151 F2
Stockwell Gdns Est, SW9 ....151 E2
Stockwell Grn, SW9 ....151 F2
Stockwell La, SW9 ....151 F2
Stockwell Ms, SW9 *off Stockwell Rd* 151 F2
Stockwell Pk Cres, SW9 ....151 F2
Stockwell Pk Est, SW9 ....151 F2
Stockwell Pk Rd, SW9 ....151 F1
Stockwell Pk Wk, SW9 ....151 F3
Stockwell Rd, SW9 ....151 F2
Stockwell St, SE10 ....134 C6
Stockwell Ter, SW9 ....151 F1
Stodart Rd, SE20 ....189 F1
Stofield Gdns, SE9 *off Aldersgrove Av* 174 A3
Stoford Cl, SW19 ....148 B7
Stokenchurch St, SW6 ....148 E1
STOKE NEWINGTON, N16 ....94 B2
Stoke Newington Ch St, N16 ....94 A3
Stoke Newington Common, N16 ....94 C3
Stoke Newington High St, N16 ....94 C3
Stoke Newington Rd, N16 ....94 C5

Stoke Pl, NW10 ....107 F3
Stoke Rd, Kings.T. KT2 ...164 C7
Stokesby Rd, Chess. KT9 .195 J6
Stokesley St, W12 ....107 F6
Stokes Rd, E6 ....116 B4
Croydon CR0 ....189 G6
Stoll Cl, NW2 ....89 J3
Stonard Rd, N13 ....59 G3
Dagenham RM8 ......100 B5
Stonards Hill, Loug. IG10 ..48 C6
Stondon Pk, SE23 ....153 H7
Stondon Wk, E6 ....116 A2
Stonebanks, Walt. KT12 ..178 A7
STONEBRIDGE, NW10 ...106 B1
Stonebridge Common, E8
off Mayfield Rd 94 C7
Stonebridge Pk, NW10 ....88 D7
Stonebridge Rd, N15 .....76 B5
Stonebridge Way, Wem.
HA9 ....88 B6
Stone Bldgs, WC2 ....18 D2
Stonechat Sq, E6
off Peridot St 116 B5
Stone Cl, SW4
off Larkhall Ri 150 C2
Dagenham RM8 ......101 F2
West Drayton UB7 ....120 C1
Stonecot Cl, Sutt. SM3 ...198 B1
Stonecot Hill, Sutt. SM3 .198 B1
Stone Cres, Felt. TW14 ...141 J7
Stonecroft Cl, Barn. EN5 ..39 H4
Stonecroft Rd, Erith DA8 .139 J7
Stonecroft Way, Croy.
CR0 ....187 E7
Stonecrop Cl, NW9 ....70 D3
Stonecutter St, EC4 ......19 G3
Stonefield, N4 ....93 F2
Stonefield Cl, Bexh. DA7 .159 G3
Ruislip HA4 ....84 E5
Stonefield St, N1 ....111 G1
Stonefield Way, SE7
off Greenbay Rd 136 A7
Ruislip HA4 ....84 E4
Stonegrove, Edg. HA8 .....53 H4
Stonegrove Est, Edg. HA8
off Lacey Dr 53 J4
Stonegrove Gdns, Edg.
HA8 ....53 J5
Stonehall Av, Ilf. IG1 ......80 B6
Stone Hall Gdns, W8 .....22 A6
Stone Hall Pl, W8 ....22 A6
Stone Hall Rd, N21 ....43 F7
Stoneham Rd, N11 ....58 C6
Stonehill Business Pk, N18
off Silvermere Dr 61 G6
Stonehill Cl, SW14 ......146 D5
Stonehill Grn, Dart. DA2 .177 J7
Stonehill Rd, SW14 ......146 C5
W4 *off Wellesley Rd* ...126 A5
Stonehills Ct, SE21 ......170 B3
Stonehill Wds Pk, Sid.
DA14 ....177 H6
Stonehorse Rd, Enf. EN3 ..45 F5
Stone Ho Ct, EC3 ....20 D3
Stone Lake Retail Pk,
SE7 ....135 H4
Stone Lake Rbt, SE7 .....135 J4
STONELEIGH, Epsom
KT17 ....197 G5
Stoneleigh Av, Enf. EN1 ...45 E1
Worcester Park KT4 ...197 G4
Stoneleigh Bdy, Epsom
KT17 ....197 G5
Stoneleigh Cres, Epsom
KT19 ....197 F5
Stoneleigh Ms, E3
off Stanfield Rd 113 H2
Stoneleigh Pk Av, Croy.
CR0 ....189 G6
Stoneleigh Pk Rd, Epsom
KT19 ....197 F6
Stoneleigh Pl, W11 ......108 A7
Stoneleigh Rd, N17 ....76 C3
Bromley BR1 ....192 E3
Carshalton SM5 ......185 H7
Ilford IG5 ....80 B3
Stoneleigh St, W11 ......108 A7
Stoneleigh Ter, N19 ....92 B2
Stonells Rd, SW11
off Chatham Rd 149 J5
Stonemasons Cl, N15 .....76 A4
Stonenest St, N4 ....93 F1
Stone Pk Av, Beck. BR3 ..190 A4
Stone Pl, Wor.Pk. KT4 ....197 G2
Stone Rd, Brom. BR2 .....191 F5
Stones End St, SE1 ......27 J4
Stonewall, E6 ....116 D5
Stoney All, SE18 ....156 D2
Stoneyard La, E14
off Poplar High St 114 B7
Stoneycroft Cl, SE12 .....155 F7
Stoneycroft Rd, Wdf.Grn.
IG8 ....64 B6
Stoneydeep, Tedd. TW11
off Twickenham Rd ...162 D4
Stoneydown, E17 ....77 H4
Stoneydown Av, E17 .....77 H4
Stoneyfields Gdns, Edg.
HA8 ....54 C4
Stoneyfields La, Edg.
HA8 ....54 C5
Stoney La, E1 ....21 E3
SE19 *off Church Rd* ...170 C6
Stoney St, SE1 ....28 B1
Stonhouse St, SW4 .....150 D3
Stonor Rd, W14 ....128 C4
Stonycroft Cl, Enf. EN3
off Brimsdown Av 45 H2
Stony Path, Loug. IG10 ...48 C2
Stopes St, SE15 ....132 C7
Stopford Rd, E13 ....115 G1
SE17 ....35 H4
Store Rd, E16 ....136 D2
Storers Quay, E14 ....134 D4
Store St, E15 ....96 D5
WC1 ....17 H2
Storey Ct, NW8
off St. John's Wd Rd 7 E4
Storey Rd, E17 ....77 J4
N6 ....73 J6
Storey's Gate, SW1 ......25 J4
Storey St, E16 ....136 D1
Stories Ms, SE5 ....152 B2
Stories Rd, SE5 ....152 B3
Stork Rd, E7 ....97 F6
Storksmead Rd, Edg. HA8 .54 E7
Storks Rd, SE16 ....29 J6
Stormont Rd, N6 ....73 J7
SW11 ....150 A3
Stormont Way, Chess.
KT9 ....195 F5
Stormount Dr, Hayes
UB3 ....121 F2
Storrington Rd, Croy.
CR0 ....202 C1
Story St, N1
off Carnoustie Dr 93 F7
Stothard Pl, E1
off Bishopsgate 21 E1
Stothard St, E1
off Colebert Av 113 F4
Stott Cl, SW18 ....149 G6
Stoughton Av, Sutt. SM3 .198 A5
Stoughton Cl, SE11 ....34 D2
SW15
off Bessborough Rd ..165 G1
Stour Av, Sthl. UB2 ......123 G3
Stourcliffe St, W1 ....15 J4
Stour Cl, Kes. BR2 ......205 J4
Stourhead Cl, SW19
off Castlecombe Dr ..148 A7
Stourhead Gdns, SW20 ..183 G3
Stourhead Ho, SW1
off Tachbrook St 33 H3
Stour Rd, E3 ....96 A7
Dagenham RM10 .....101 G2
Stourton Av, Felt. TW13 ..161 F4
Stowage, SE8 ....134 A6
Stow Cres, E17 ....61 H7
Stowe Gdns, N9 ....60 C1
Stowe Pl, N15 ....76 B3
Stowe Rd, W12 ....127 H2
Stowting Rd, Orp. BR6 ...207 H4
Stox Mead, Har. HA3 .....68 A1
Stracey Rd, E7 ....97 G4
NW10 ....106 D1
Strachan Pl, SW19 ......165 J6
Stradbroke Dr, Chig. IG7 ..64 D6
Stradbroke Gro, Buck.H.
IG9 ....64 A1
Ilford IG5 ....80 B3
Stradbroke Pk, Chig. IG7 ..64 E6
Stradbroke Rd, N5 ....93 J4
Stradbrook Cl, Har. HA2
off Stiven Cres 85 F3
Stradella Rd, SE24 ......151 J6
Strafford Av, Ilf. IG5 ......80 D2
Strafford Rd, W3 ....126 C2
Barnet EN5 ....40 B3
Hounslow TW3 ....143 F3
Twickenham TW1 .....144 D7
Strafford St, E14 ....134 A2
Strahan Rd, E3 ....113 H3
Straight, The, Sthl. UB1 ..122 D2
Straightsmouth, SE10 ...134 C7
Strait Rd, E6 ....116 B7
Straker's Rd, SE15 ......152 E4
STRAND, WC2 ....18 A5
Strand, WC2 ....18 A6
Strand Ct, SE18
off Strandfield Cl 137 H5
Strand Dr, Rich. TW9 ....126 B7
Strandfield Cl, SE18 .....137 H5
Strand Ho, SE28
off Merbury Cl 137 G1
Strand La, WC2 ....18 D5
Strand on the Grn, W4 ...126 A6
Strand Pl, N18 ....60 A4
Strand Sch App, W4
off Thames Rd 126 A6
Strangways Ter, W14
off Holland Pk Rd 128 C3
Stranraer Rd, Houns.
(Lon.Hthrw Air.) TW6 ..140 B6
Stranraer Way, N1 ....93 E7
Strasburg Rd, SW11 .....150 B1
Stratfield Pk Cl, N21 ......43 H7
Stratfield Rd, Borwd. WD6 .38 A3
STRATFORD, E15 ....96 C6
Stratford Av, W8
off Stratford Rd 128 E3
Stratford Cen, The, E15 ...96 D7
Stratford Cl, Bark. IG11 ...100 A7
Dagenham RM10 .....101 J7
Stratford Ct, N.Mal. KT3 .182 D4
Stratford Gro, SW15 .....148 A4
Stratford Ho Av, Brom.
BR1 ....192 B3
Stratford Pl, W1 ....16 D4
Stratford Rd, E13 ....115 F1
NW4 ....72 A4
W8 ....128 D3
Hayes UB4 ....102 B4
Hounslow
(Lon.Hthrw Air.) TW6 .141 E6
Southall UB2 ....122 E4
Thornton Heath CR7 ..187 G4
Stratford Vil, NW1 ....92 C7
Strathan Cl, SW18 ......148 B6
Strathaven Rd, SE12 .....155 H6
Strathblaine Rd, SW11 ...149 G4
Strathbrook Rd, SW16 ...169 F7
Strathcona Rd, Wem. HA9 .87 G2
Strathdale, SW16 ....169 F5
Strathdon Dr, SW17 .....167 G3
Strathearn Av, Hayes
UB3 ....121 J7
Twickenham TW2 .....161 H1
Strathearn Pl, W2 ....15 F5
Strathearn Rd, SW19 .....166 D5
Sutton SM1 ....198 D5
Stratheden Par, SE3
off Stratheden Rd 135 G7
Stratheden Rd, SE3 .....155 G1
Strathfield Gdns, Bark.
IG11 ....99 G6
Strathleven Rd, SW2 ....151 E5
Strathmore Gdns, N3 .....72 E1
W8
off Palace Gdns Ter ...128 D1
Edgware HA8 ....70 B2
Strathmore Rd, SW19 ....166 D3
Croydon CR0 ....187 J7
Teddington TW11 .....162 B4
Strathnairn St, SE1 ....37 J2
Strathray Gdns, NW3 .....91 H6
Strath Ter, SW11 ....149 H4
Strathville Rd, SW18 .....166 E2
Strathyre Av, SW16 ......187 G3
Stratton Cl, SW19 ....184 D2
Bexleyheath DA7 .....159 E3
Edgware HA8 ....53 J7
Hounslow TW3 ....143 F1
Stratton Ct, Surb. KT6
off Adelaide Rd 181 H5
Strattondale St, E14 .....134 C3
Stratton Dr, Bark. IG11 ....99 J5
Stratton Gdns, Sthl. UB1 .103 F6
Stratton Rd, SW19 ....184 D2
Bexleyheath DA7 .....159 E3
Stratton St, W1 ....25 E1
Strauss Rd, W4 ....126 D2
Strawberry Flds, Orp.
(Farnboro.) BR6 ......207 E5
STRAWBERRY HILL, Twick.
TW1 ....162 B3
Strawberry Hill, Twick.
TW1 ....162 C3
Strawberry Hill Cl, Twick.
TW1 ....162 C3
Strawberry Hill Rd, Twick.
TW1 ....162 C3
Strawberry La, Cars.
SM5 ....199 J3
Strawberry Vale, N2 ......73 G1
Twickenham TW1 .....162 D3
Streakes Fld Rd, NW2 ....89 G2
Streamdale, SE2 ....138 A6
Stream La, Edg. HA8 .....54 B5
Streamline Ms, SE22 ....170 D1
Streamside Cl, N9 ....60 C1
Bromley BR2 ....191 G4
Streamway, Belv. DA17 ..139 G6
Streatfeild Av, E6 ....116 C1
Streatfield Rd, Har. HA3 ...69 G3
STREATHAM, SW16 ......169 E4
Streatham Cl, SW16 .....169 E2
Streatham Common N,
SW16 ....168 E5
Streatham Common S,
SW16 ....169 E6
Streatham Ct, SW16 .....168 E3
Streatham High Rd,
SW16 ....168 E5
STREATHAM HILL, SW2 ..151 F7
Streatham Hill, SW2 ......169 E2
STREATHAM PARK,
SW16 ....168 C4
Streatham Pl, SW2 ......150 E7
Streatham Rd, SW16 ....186 A1
Mitcham CR4 ....186 A1
Streatham St, WC1 ....17 J3
STREATHAM VALE,
SW16 ....168 D7
Streatham Vale, SW16 ...168 C7
Streathbourne Rd, SW17 .168 A2
Streatley Pl, NW3
off New End 91 F4
Streatley Rd, NW6 ....90 C7
Streeters La, Wall. SM6 ..200 D3
Streetfield Ms, SE3 ......155 G3
Streimer Rd, E15 ....114 C2
Strelley Way, W3 ....106 E7
Stretton Mans, SE8
off Glaisher St 134 A6
Stretton Rd, Croy. CR0 ...188 B7
Richmond TW10 ......163 F2
Strickland Row, SW18 ...149 G7
Strickland St, SE8 ....154 A2
Strickland Way, Orp. BR6 .207 J4
Stride Rd, E13 ....115 F2
Strimon Cl, N9 ....61 F2
Strode Cl, N10 ....58 A7
Strode Rd, E7 ....97 G4
N17 ....76 B2
NW10 ....89 G6
SW6 ....128 A7
Strone Rd, E7 ....97 J6
E12 ....98 A6
Strone Way, Hayes UB4 ..102 E4
Strongbow Cres, SE9 ....156 C5
Strongbow Rd, SE9 .....156 C5
Strongbridge Cl, Har. HA2 .85 G1
Stronsa Rd, W12 ....127 F2
Stroud Cres, SW15 ......165 G3
Stroudes Cl, Wor.Pk. KT4 .183 E7
Stroud Fld, Nthlt. UB5 ....84 E6
Stroud Gate, Har. HA2 ....85 H4
STROUD GREEN, N4 .....75 F6
Stroud Grn Gdns, Croy.
CR0 ....189 F7
Stroud Grn Rd, N4 ....93 F1
Stroud Grn Way, Croy.
CR0 ....189 E7
Stroudley Wk, E3 ....114 B3
Stroud Rd, SE25 ....188 D6
SW19 ....166 D3
Strouds Cl, Rom.
(Chad.Hth) RM6 ....82 B5
Strouts Pl, E2 ....13 F3
Strutton Grd, SW1 ....25 H5
Strype St, E1 ....21 F2
Stuart Av, NW9 ....71 G7
W5 ....125 J1
Bromley BR2 ....205 G1
Harrow HA2 ....85 F3
Stuart Cres, N22 ....75 F1
Croydon CR0 ....203 J3
Stuart Evans Cl, Well.
DA16 ....158 C3
Stuart Gro, Tedd. TW11 ...162 B5
Stuart Pl, Mitch. CR4 ....185 J1
Stuart Rd, NW6 ....108 D3
SE15 ....153 F4
SW19 ....166 D3
W3 ....126 C1
Barking IG11 ....99 J7
Barnet (E.Barn.) EN4 ...41 H7
Harrow HA3 ....68 C2
Richmond TW10 ......163 E2
Thornton Heath CR7 ..187 J4
Welling DA16 ....158 B1
Stuart Twr, W9 ....6 D4
Stubbs Cl, NW9 ....70 C5
Stubbs Dr, SE16 ....132 E5
Stubbs Ms, Dag. RM8
off Marlborough Rd ..100 B4
Stubbs Pt, E13 ....115 H4
Stubbs Way, SW19
off Ruskin Way 185 G1
Stucley Pl, NW1
off Hawley Cres 92 B7
Stucley Rd, Houns.
TW5 ....123 J7
Studdridge St, SW6 .....148 D2
Studd St, N1 ....111 H1
Studholme Ct, NW3 ......90 D4
Studholme St, SE15 .....132 E7
Studio Ms, NW4
off Glebe Cres 71 J4
Studio Pl, SW1 ....24 A4
Studio Way, Borwd.
WD6 ....38 C2
Studland, SE17 ....36 B3
Studland Cl, Sid. DA15 ...175 J3
Studland Ho, E14
off Aston St 113 H6
Studland Rd, SE26 ......171 G5
W7 ....104 A6
Kingston upon Thames
KT2 ....163 H6
Studland St, W6 ....127 H4
Studley Av, E4 ....62 D7
Studley Cl, E5 ....95 H5

Studley Ct, E14
off Jamestown Way . . **114** D7
Sidcup DA14 . . . . **176** B5
Studley Dr, Ilf. IG4 . . . . . . **80** A6
Studley Est, SW4 . . . . . . **150** E1
Studley Gra Rd, W7 . . . . . **124** B2
Studley Rd, E7 . . . . **97** H6
SW4 . . . . **150** E1
Dagenham RM9 . . . . . . **100** D7
Stukeley Rd, E7 . . . . **97** H7
Stukeley St, WC1 . . . . **18** B3
WC2 . . . . **18** B3
Stumps Hill La, Beck.
BR3 . . . . **172** A6
Sturdy Rd, SE15 . . . . **152** E2
Sturge Av, E17 . . . . **78** B2
Sturgeon Rd, SE17 . . . . **35** J4
Sturges Fld, Chis. BR7 . . . **175** G6
Sturgess Av, NW4 . . . . **71** H7
Sturge St, SE1 . . . . **27** J3
Sturmer Way, N7 . . . . **93** F5
Sturminster Cl, Hayes
UB4 . . . . **102** C6
Sturrock Cl, N15 . . . . **76** A4
Sturry St, E14 . . . . **114** B6
Sturt St, N1 . . . . **12** A2
Stutfield St, E1 . . . . **21** J4
Styles Gdns, SW9 . . . . **151** H3
Styles Way, Beck. BR3 . . . **190** C4
Stylus Ho, E1
off Devonport St **113** F6
Sudbourne Rd, SW2 . . . . . **151** E5
Sudbrooke Rd, SW12 . . . . **149** J6
Sudbrook Gdns, Rich.
TW10 . . . . **163** G3
Sudbrook La, Rich.
TW10 . . . . **163** H1
SUDBURY, Wem. HA0 . . . . **86** D5
Sudbury, E6
off Newark Knok **116** D6
Sudbury Av, Wem. HA0 . . . **87** G3
Sudbury Ct, SW8
off Allen Edwards Dr . **150** E1
Sudbury Ct Dr, Har. HA1 . . **86** C3
Sudbury Ct Rd, Har. HA1 . . **86** C3
Sudbury Cres, Brom.
BR1 . . . . **173** G6
Wembley HA0 . . . . **87** E5
Sudbury Cft, Wem. HA0 . . . **86** C4
Sudbury Gdns, Croy.
CR0 . . . . **202** B4
Sudbury Hts Av, Grnf.
UB6 . . . . **86** C5
Sudbury Hill, Har. HA1 . . . . **86** B2
Sudbury Hill Cl, Wem.
HA0 . . . . **86** C4
Sudbury Ho, SW18
off Wandsworth High St **148** E5
Sudbury Rd, Bark. IG11 . . . **99** J5
Sudeley St, N1 . . . . **11** H2
Sudlow Rd, SW18 . . . . **148** D4
Sudrey St, SE1 . . . . **27** J4
Suez Av, Grnf. UB6 . . . . . . **104** C2
Suez Rd, Enf. EN3 . . . . **45** H4
Suffield Rd, E4 . . . . **62** B3
N15 . . . . **76** C5
SE20 . . . . **189** F2
Suffolk Cl, Borwd. WD6 . . . **38** D5
Suffolk Ct, E10 . . . . **78** A7
Ilford IG3 . . . . **81** H6
Suffolk La, EC4 . . . . **20** B5
Suffolk Pk Rd, E17 . . . . **77** H4
Suffolk Pl, SW1 . . . . **25** J1
Suffolk Rd, E13 . . . . **115** F3
N15 . . . . **76** A6
NW10 . . . . **89** E7
SE25 . . . . **188** C4
SW13 . . . . **127** F7
Barking IG11 . . . . **99** G7
Dagenham RM10 . . . . . **101** J5
Enfield EN3 . . . . **45** E5
Harrow HA2 . . . . **67** F6
Ilford IG3 . . . . **81** H6
Sidcup DA14 . . . . **176** C6
Worcester Park KT4 . . . **197** F2
Suffolk St, E7 . . . . **97** G5
SW1 . . . . **25** J1
Sugar Bakers Ct, EC3
off Creechurch La **21** E4
Sugar Ho La, E15 . . . . **114** C2
Sugar Loaf Wk, E2
off Victoria Pk Sq **113** F3
Sugar Quay Wk, EC3 . . . . . **20** E6
Sugden Rd, SW11 . . . . **150** A3
Thames Ditton KT7 . . . . **194** E1
Sugden Way, Bark. IG11 . . **117** J2
Sulgrave Gdns, W6
off Sulgrave Rd **127** J2
Sulgrave Rd, W6 . . . . **127** J2
Sulina Rd, SW2 . . . . **150** E7
Sulivan Ct, SW6 . . . . **148** D3
Sulivan Rd, SW6 . . . . **148** D3
Sulkin Ho, E2
off Knottisford St **113** G3
Sullivan Av, E16 . . . . **116** A5
Sullivan Cl, SW11 . . . . **149** H3
Hayes UB4 . . . . **102** C5
West Molesey KT8
off Victoria Av **179** G3
Sullivan Ho, SW1
off Churchill Gdns **33** E4
Sullivan Rd, SE11 . . . . **35** F1
Sultan Rd, E11 . . . . **79** H4
Sultan St, SE5 . . . . **35** J7
Beckenham BR3 . . . . . . **189** G2
Sultan Ter, N22
off Vincent Rd **75** G2
Sumatra Rd, NW6 . . . . **90** D5
Sumburgh Rd, SW12 . . . . . **150** A6
Summer Av, E.Mol. KT8 . . **180** B5
Summercourt Rd, E1 . . . . **113** F6
Summer Crossing, T.Ditt.
KT7 . . . . **180** B4
Summerene Cl, SW16 . . . **168** C7
Summerfield Av, NW6 . . . **108** B2
Summerfield La, Surb.
(Long Dit.) KT6 . . . . . . **195** G2
Summerfield Rd, W5 . . . . **105** E4
Loughton IG10 . . . . **48** A6
Summerfields Av, N12 . . . . **57** H6
Summerfield St, SE12 . . . **155** F7
Summer Gdns, E.Mol.
KT8 . . . . **180** B5
Summer Gro, W.Wick.
BR4 . . . . **205** E2
Summer Hill, Borwd.
(Els.) WD6 . . . . **38** A5
Chislehurst BR7 . . . . . . **192** D2
Summerhill Cl, Orp. BR6 . **207** H3
Summerhill Gro, Enf. EN1 . **44** B6
Summerhill Rd, N15 . . . . . . **76** A4
Summer Hill Vil, Chis.
BR7 . . . . **192** D1
Summerhill Way, Mitch.
CR4 . . . . **186** A1
Summerhouse Av, Houns.
TW5 . . . . **142** E1
Summerhouse La, West Dr.
(Harm.) UB7 . . . . **120** A6
Summerhouse Rd, N16 . . . **94** B2
Summerland Gdns, N10 . . . **74** B3
Summerlands Av, W3 . . . . **106** C7
Summerlee Av, N2 . . . . **73** J4
Summerlee Gdns, N2 . . . . . **73** J4
Summerley St, SW18 . . . . **167** E2
Summer Rd, E.Mol. KT8 . **180** B5
Thames Ditton KT7 . . . . **180** C5
Summersby Rd, N6 . . . . . . **74** B6
Summers Cl, Sutt. SM2
off Overton Rd **198** D7
Wembley HA9 . . . . **88** B1
Summerskill Cl, SE15
off Philip Wk **152** E3
Summerskille Cl, N9
off Plevna Rd **60** E2
Summers La, N12 . . . . **57** G7
Summers Row, N12 . . . . . . **57** H6
Summers St, EC1 . . . . **11** E6
SUMMERSTOWN, SW17 . **166** E3
Summerstown, SW17 . . . **167** F3
Summerton Way, SE28 . . . **118** D6
Summer Trees, Sun. TW16
off The Avenue **178** B1
Summerville Gdns, Sutt.
SM1 . . . . **198** C6
Summerwood Rd, Islw.
TW7 . . . . **144** C5
Summit, The, Loug. IG10 . . **48** C1
Summit Av, NW9 . . . . **70** D5
Summit Cl, N14 . . . . **58** C2
NW9 . . . . **70** D4
Edgware HA8 . . . . **54** A7
Summit Ct, NW2 . . . . **90** B5
Summit Dr, Wdf.Grn. IG8 . . **80** A2
Summit Est, N16 . . . . **76** D7
Summit Rd, E17 . . . . **78** B4
Northolt UB5 . . . . **85** G7
Summit Way, N14 . . . . **58** B2
SE19 . . . . **170** B7
Sumner Av, SE15
off Peckham Rd **152** C1
Sumner Cl, Orp. BR6 . . . . **207** F4
Sumner Ct, SW8
off Darsley Dr **150** E1
Sumner Gdns, Croy. CR0 . **201** G1
Sumner Pl, SW7 . . . . **31** F2
Sumner Pl Ms, SW7 . . . . . . **31** F2
Sumner Rd, SE15 . . . . **37** G6
Croydon CR0 . . . . **201** G1
Harrow HA1 . . . . **67** J7
Sumner Rd S, Croy. CR0 . **201** G1
Sumner St, SE1 . . . . **27** H1
Sumpter Cl, NW3 . . . . **91** F6
Sun All, Rich. TW9
off Kew Rd **145** H4
Sunbeam Cres, W10 . . . . . **107** J4
Sunbeam Rd, NW10 . . . . . **106** C4
SUNBURY, Sun. TW16 . . . **178** B3
Sunbury Av, NW7 . . . . **54** D5
SW14 . . . . **146** D4
Sunbury Cl, Walt. KT12 . . . **178** A6
Sunbury Ct, Sun. TW16 . . **178** D2
Sunbury Ct Island, Sun.
TW16 . . . . **178** D3
Sunbury Ct Ms, Sun.
TW16 *off Lower Hampton Rd* **178** D2
Sunbury Ct Rd, Sun.
TW16 . . . . **178** C2
Sunbury Cross, Sun. TW16
off Staines Rd E **160** A7
Sunbury Gdns, NW7 . . . . . **54** D5
Sunbury La, SW11 . . . . . . **149** G1
Walton-on-Thames
KT12 . . . . **178** A6
Sunbury Lock Ait, Walt.
KT12 . . . . **178** B4
Sunbury Rd, Sutt. SM3 . . **198** A3
Sunbury St, SE18 . . . . **136** C3
Sunbury Way, Felt. (Han.)
TW13 . . . . **160** C5
Sunbury Workshops, E2
off Swanfield St **13** F4
Sun Ct, EC3 . . . . **20** C4
Suncroft Pl, SE26 . . . . **171** F3
Sunderland Ct, SE22 . . . . **152** D7
Sunderland Mt, SE23 . . . . **171** G2
Sunderland Rd, SE23 . . . . **171** G1
W5 . . . . **125** G3
Sunderland Ter, W2 . . . . **14** A3
Sunderland Way, E12 . . . . . **98** A2
Sundew Av, W12 . . . . **107** G7
Sundew Cl, W12 . . . . **107** G7
Sundial Av, SE25 . . . . **188** C3
Sundorne Rd, SE7 . . . . . . **135** H5
Sundra Wk, E1
off Beaumont Gro **113** G4
SUNDRIDGE, Brom. BR1 . **173** J6
Sundridge Av, Brom. BR1 **192** A1
Chislehurst BR7 . . . . . . **174** A7
Welling DA16 . . . . **157** G2
Sundridge Ho, Brom. BR1
off Burnt Ash La **173** H5
Sundridge Pl, Croy. CR0
off Inglis Rd **202** D1
Sundridge Rd, Croy. CR0 . **188** C7
Sunfields Pl, SE3 . . . . **135** H7
Sun-In-The-Sands, SE3 . . **135** H7
Sunken Rd, Croy. CR0 . . . **203** F5
Sunland Av, Bexh. DA6 . . **159** E4
Sun La, SE3 . . . . **135** H7
Sunleigh Rd, Wem. HA0 . . **105** H1
Sunley Gdns, Grnf.
(Perivale) UB6 . . . . **104** D1
Sunlight Cl, SW19 . . . . . . **167** F6
Sunlight Sq, E2 . . . . **113** E3
Sunmead Rd, Sun. TW16 . **178** A3
Sunna Gdns, Sun. TW16 . **178** B2
Sunningdale, N14
off Wilmer Way **58** D5
Sunningdale Av, W3 . . . . . **107** E7
Barking IG11 . . . . **117** G1
Feltham TW13 . . . . **160** E2
Ruislip HA4 . . . . **84** C1
Sunningdale Cl, E6 . . . . . . **116** C3
SE16 *off Ryder Dr* **132** E5
SE28 . . . . **118** E6
Stanmore HA7 . . . . **52** D7
Surbiton KT6
off Culsac Rd **195** H2
Sunningdale Gdns, NW9 . . **70** C5
W8 *off Lexham Ms* **128** D3
Sunningdale Rd, Brom.
BR1 . . . . **192** B4
Sutton SM1 . . . . **198** C4
Sunningfields Cres, NW4 . . **71** H2
Sunningfields Rd, NW4 . . . **71** H2
Sunninghill Ct, W3
off Bollo Br Rd **126** C2
Sunninghill Rd, SE13 . . . . **154** B2
Sunny Bk, SE25 . . . . **188** D3
Sunny Cres, NW10 . . . . **88** C7
Sunnycroft Rd, SE25 . . . . . **188** D3
Hounslow TW3 . . . . **143** H2
Southall UB1 . . . . **103** G5
Sunnydale, Orp. BR6 . . . . **206** D2
Sunnydale Gdns, NW7 . . . . **54** D6
Sunnydale Rd, SE12 . . . . . **155** H5
Sunnydene Av, E4 . . . . **62** D5
Ruislip HA4 . . . . **84** A1
Sunnydene Gdns, Wem.
HA0 . . . . **87** F6
Sunnydene St, SE26 . . . . . **171** H4
Sunnyfield, NW7 . . . . **55** F4
Sunny Gdns Par, NW4
off Great N Way **71** J2
Sunny Gdns Rd, NW4 . . . . . **71** H2
Sunny Hill, NW4 . . . . **71** H3
Sunnyhill Cl, E5 . . . . **95** H4
Sunnyhill Rd, SW16 . . . . . **168** E4
Sunnyhurst Cl, Sutt.
SM1 . . . . **198** D3
Sunnymead Av, Mitch.
CR4 . . . . **186** C3
Sunnymead Rd, NW9 . . . . . **70** D7
SW15 . . . . **147** H5
Sunnymede Dr, Ilf. IG6 . . . . **80** E4
Sunny Nook Gdns, S.Croy.
CR2 . . . . **202** A6
Sunny Pl, NW4
off Sunny Gdns Rd **71** J4
Sunny Rd, The, Enf. EN3 . . **45** G1
Sunnyside, NW2 . . . . **90** C3
SW19 . . . . **166** B6
Walton-on-Thames
KT12 . . . . **178** C5
Sunnyside Dr, E4 . . . . **46** C7
Sunnyside Pas, SW19 . . . . **166** B6
Sunnyside Pl, SW19
off Sunnyside **166** B6
Sunnyside Rd, E10 . . . . **96** A1
N19 . . . . **74** D7
W5 . . . . **125** G1
Ilford IG1 . . . . **99** F3
Teddington TW11 . . . . . **162** A4
Sunnyside Rd E, N9 . . . . . . **60** D3
Sunnyside Rd N, N9 . . . . . . **60** C3
Sunnyside Rd S, N9 . . . . . . **60** C3
Sunnyside Ter, NW9
off Edgware Rd **70** D3
Sunny Vw, NW9 . . . . **70** D4
Sunny Way, N12 . . . . **57** H7
Sun Pas, SE16 . . . . **29** H5
Sunray Av, SE24 . . . . **152** A4
Bromley BR2 . . . . **192** B6
Surbiton KT5 . . . . **196** B2
West Drayton UB7 . . . . **120** A2
Sunrise Cl, Felt. TW13
off Exeter Rd **161** F3
Sun Rd, W14 . . . . **128** C5
Sunset Av, E4 . . . . **62** B1
Woodford Green IG8 . . . **63** F4
Sunset Ct, Wdf.Grn. IG8
off Navestock Cres **63** J7
Sunset Gdns, SE25 . . . . . . **188** C2
Sunset Rd, SE5 . . . . **151** J4
SE28 . . . . **138** A2
Sunset Vw, Barn. EN5 . . . . **40** B2
Sunshine Way, Mitch.
CR4 . . . . **185** J2
Sun St, EC2 . . . . **20** D2
Sun Wk, E1 . . . . **21** H6
Sunwell Cl, SE15
off Cossall Wk **152** E2
Superior Dr, Orp.
(Grn St Grn) BR6 . . . . . **207** J6
SURBITON, KT5 & KT6 . . . **181** J7
Surbiton Ct, Surb. KT6 . . . **181** F6
Surbiton Cres, Kings.T.
KT1 . . . . **181** H4
Surbiton Hall Cl, Kings.T.
KT1 . . . . **181** H4
Surbiton Hill Pk, Surb.
KT5 . . . . **182** A5
Surbiton Hill Rd, Surb.
KT6 . . . . **181** H4
Surbiton Par, Surb. KT6
off St. Mark's Hill **181** H6
Surbiton Rd, Kings.T.
KT1 . . . . **181** H4
Surlingham Cl, SE28 . . . . . **118** D7
Surma Cl, E1 . . . . **112** E4
Surmans Cl, Dag. RM9 . . . **118** C1
Surrendale Pl, W9 . . . . **108** D4
Surrey Canal Rd, SE14 . . . **133** F6
SE15 . . . . **133** F6
Surrey Cl, N3 . . . . **72** B3
Surrey Cres, W4 . . . . **126** A5
★ **Surrey Docks Fm**,
SE16 . . . . **133** J2
Surrey Gdns, N4 . . . . **75** J6
Surrey Gro, SE17 . . . . **36** D4
Sutton SM1 . . . . **199** G3
Surrey La, SW11 . . . . **149** H1
Surrey La Est, SW11 . . . . . **149** H1
Surrey Ms, SE27
off Hamilton Rd **170** B4
Surrey Mt, SE23 . . . . **171** E1
Surrey Quays Rd, SE16 . . **133** F3
Surrey Quays Shop Cen,
SE16 . . . . **133** G3
Surrey Rd, SE15 . . . . **153** G5
Barking IG11 . . . . **117** H1
Dagenham RM10 . . . . . **101** H5
Harrow HA1 . . . . **67** J5
West Wickham BR4 . . . . **204** B1
Surrey Row, SE1 . . . . **27** G3
Surrey Sq, SE17 . . . . **36** D3
Surrey St, E13 . . . . **115** H3
WC2 . . . . **18** D5
Croydon CR0 . . . . **201** J3
Surrey Ter, SE17 . . . . **36** E2
Surrey Water Rd, SE16 . . . **133** G1
Surridge Gdns, SE19
off Hancock Rd **170** A6
Surr St, N7 . . . . **92** E5
Sury Basin, Kings.T. KT2 . **181** H1
Susan Cl, Rom. RM7 . . . . . **83** J3
Susan Constant Ct, E14
off Newport Av **114** D7
Susan Lawrence Ho, E12
off Walton Rd **98** D4
Susannah St, E14 . . . . **114** B6

Susan Rd, SE3 155 H2
Susan Wd, Chis. BR7 192 D1
Sussex Av, Islw. TW7 144 B3
Sussex Cl, N19 92 E2
Ilford IG4 80 C6
New Malden KT3 183 E4
Twickenham TW1
off Westmorland Cl 145 E6
Sussex Cres, Nthlt. UB5 85 G6
Sussex Gdns, N4 75 J5
N6 73 J5
W2 15 E5
Chessington KT9 195 G6
Sussex Ms, SE6
off Ravensbourne Pk 154 A7
Sussex Ms E, W2 15 F4
Sussex Ms W, W2 15 F5
Sussex Pl, NW1 7 J4
W2 15 F4
W6 127 J5
Erith DA8 139 H7
New Malden KT3 183 E4
Sussex Ring, N12 56 D5
Sussex Rd, E6 116 D1
Carshalton SM5 199 J6
Erith DA8 139 H7
Harrow HA1 67 J5
Mitcham CR4
off Lincoln Rd 186 E5
New Malden KT3 183 E4
Sidcup DA14 176 B5
South Croydon CR2 202 A6
Southall UB2 122 D3
West Wickham BR4 204 B1
Sussex Sq, W2 15 F5
Sussex St, E13 115 H3
SW1 32 E4
Sussex Way, N7 93 E2
N19 92 E1
Barnet (Cockfos.) EN4 42 A5
Sutcliffe Cl, NW11 73 E5
Sutcliffe Ho, Hayes UB3 102 A6
Sutcliffe Rd, SE18 137 H6
Welling DA16 158 C2
Sutherland Av, W9 6 C4
W13 104 E6
Hayes UB3 122 A4
Orpington BR5 193 J6
Welling DA16 157 H4
Sutherland Cl, Barn. EN5 40 B4
Sutherland Ct, NW9 70 B5
Sutherland Dr, SW19 185 G1
Sutherland Gdns, SW14 147 E3
Worcester Park KT4 197 H1
Sutherland Gro, SW18 148 B6
Teddington TW11 162 B5
Sutherland Pl, W2 108 D6
Sutherland Rd, E17 77 G2
N9 60 D1
N17 60 D7
W4 126 E6
W13 104 D6
Belvedere DA17 139 G3
Croydon CR0 187 G7
Enfield EN3 45 G5
Southall UB1 103 F6
Sutherland Rd Path, E17 77 G3
Sutherland Row, SW1 32 E3
Sutherland Sq, SE17 35 J4
Sutherland St, SW1 32 D3
Sutherland Wk, SE17 36 A4
Sutlej Rd, SE7 135 J7
Sutterton St, N7 93 F6
SUTTON, SM1 - SM3 198 E6
Sutton Cl, Beck. BR3 190 B1
Loughton IG10 48 B7
Pinner HA5 66 A5
Sutton Common Rd, Sutt.
SM1, SM3 184 C7
Sutton Ct, W4 126 C6
Sutton SM2 199 F6
Sutton Ct Rd, E13 115 J3
W4 126 C7
Sutton SM1 199 F6
Sutton Cres, Barn. EN5 40 A5
Sutton Dene, Houns.
TW3 143 H1
Sutton Est, SW3 31 H3
W10 107 J5
Sutton Est, The, N1 93 H7
Sutton Gdns, Bark. IG11
off Sutton Rd 117 H1
Croydon CR0 188 C5
Sutton Grn, Bark. IG11
off Sutton Rd 117 H1
Sutton Gro, Sutt. SM1 199 G4
Sutton Hall Rd, Houns.
TW5 123 G7
Sutton Hts, Sutt. SM2 199 G7
★ **Sutton Ho**, E9 95 F5
Sutton La, EC1 11 H6
Hounslow TW3 143 F3
Sutton La N, W4 126 C5
Sutton La S, W4 126 C6
Sutton Par, NW4
off Church Rd 71 J4
Sutton Pk Rd, Sutt. SM1 198 E6
Sutton Path, Borwd. WD6
off Stratfield Rd 38 A2
Sutton Pl, E9 95 F5
Sutton Rd, E13 115 F4
E17 77 G1
N10 74 A2
Barking IG11 117 H2
Hounslow TW5 143 G1
Sutton Row, W1 17 J3
Sutton Sq, E9
off Urswick Rd 95 F5
Hounslow TW5 143 F1
Sutton St, E1 113 F6
Sutton's Way, EC1 12 A6
Sutton Wk, SE1 26 D2
Sutton Way, W10 107 J5
Hounslow TW5 143 F1
Swaby Rd, SW18 167 F1
Swaffham Way, N22 59 H7
Swaffield Rd, SW18 149 E7
Swain Cl, SW16 168 B6
Swain Rd, Th.Hth. CR7 187 J5
Swains Cl, West Dr. UB7 120 B2
Swains La, N6 92 A3
Swainson Rd, W3 127 F2
Swains Rd, SW17 167 J7
Swain St, NW8 7 G5
Swaledale Cl, N11
off Ribblesdale Av 58 A6
Swallands Rd, SE6 172 A3
Swallow Cl, SE14 153 F1
Bushey WD23 51 J1
Swallow Dr, NW10
off Kingfisher Way 88 D6
Northolt UB5 103 G2
Swallowfield, NW1
off Munster Sq 9 E4
Swallowfield Rd, SE7 135 H5
Swallowfield Way, Hayes
UB3 121 G2
Swallow Gdns, SW16 168 D5
Swallow Ho, NW8
off Allitsen Rd 7 G1
Swallow Pas, W1
off Swallow Pl 17 E4
Swallow Pl, W1 17 E4
Swallow St, E6 116 B5
W1 17 G6
Swanage Ho, SW8
off Dorset Rd 131 F7
Swanage Rd, E4 62 C7
SW18 149 F6
Swanage Waye, Hayes
UB4 102 C6
Swan App, E6 116 B5
Swanbourne, SE17 35 J2
Swanbridge Rd, Bexh.
DA7 159 G1
Swan Cen, The, SW17
off Rosemary Rd 167 F3
Swan Cl, E17 77 H1
Croydon CR0 188 B7
Feltham TW13 161 E4
Swan Ct, SW3 31 H4
Swandon Way, SW18 149 E5
Swan Dr, NW9 70 E2
Swanfield St, E2 13 F4
Swan Junct, The, W.Wick.
BR4 204 C2
Swan La, EC4 20 B6
N20 57 F3
Loughton IG10 47 J7
Swanley Rd, Well. DA16 158 C1
Swan Mead, SE1 28 D6
Swan Ms, SW6
off Purser's Cross Rd 148 D1
Romford RM7 83 H4
Swan Pas, E1
off Cartwright St 21 G6
Swan Path, E10
off Jesse Rd 96 C1
Swan Pl, SW13 147 F2
Swan Rd, SE16 133 F2
SE18 136 A3
Feltham TW13 160 E5
Southall UB1 103 H6
West Drayton UB7 120 A2
Swanscombe Ho, W11
off St. Anns Rd 128 A1
Swanscombe Rd, W4 127 E5
W11 128 A1
Swansea Ct, E16
off Fishguard Way 137 E1
Swansea Rd, Enf. EN3 45 F4
Hounslow
(Lon.Hthrw Air.) TW6
off Southern
Perimeter Rd 141 F6
Swanshope, Loug. IG10 49 E2
Swansland Gdns, E17
off McEntee Av 77 H1
Swanston Path, Wat.
WD19 50 C3
Swan St, SE1 28 A5
Isleworth TW7 144 E3
Swanton Gdns, SW19 166 A1
Swanton Rd, Erith
DA8 139 H7
Swan Wk, SW3 31 J5
Swan Way, Enf. EN3 45 G2
Swanwick Cl, SW15 147 F7
Swan Yd, N1
off Highbury Sta Rd 93 H6
Swaton Rd, E3 114 A4
Swaylands Rd, Belv.
DA17 139 G6
Swaythling Cl, N18 61 E4
Swaythling Ho, SW15
off Tunworth Cres 147 F6
Swedenborg Gdns, E1 21 J5
Sweden Gate, SE16 133 H3
Sweeney Cres, SE1 29 G4
Sweet Briar Grn, N9 60 C3
Sweet Briar Gro, N9 60 C3
Sweet Briar Wk, N18 60 C4
Sweetmans Av, Pnr.
HA5 66 D3
Sweets Way, N20 57 G2
Swetenham Wk, SE18
off Sandbach Pl 137 F5
Swete St, E13 115 G2
Sweyn Pl, SE3 155 G2
Swift Cl, E17 61 H7
SE28
off Greenhaven Dr 118 B6
Harrow HA2 85 H2
Swift Rd, Felt. TW13 161 E3
Southall UB2 123 F3
Swiftsden Way, Brom.
BR1 173 E6
Swift St, SW6 148 C1
Swinbrook Rd, W10 108 B5
Swinburne Ct, SE5
off Basingdon Way 152 A4
Swinburne Cres, Croy.
CR0 189 F6
Swinburne Rd, SW15 147 G4
Swinderby Rd, Wem. HA0 87 H6
Swindon Cl, Ilf. IG3
off Salisbury Rd 99 H2
Swindon Rd, Houns.
(Lon.Hthrw Air.) TW6 141 F5
Swindon St, W12 127 H1
Swinfield Cl, Felt. TW13 160 E4
Swinford Gdns, SW9 151 H3
Swingate La, SE18 137 H6
Swinnerton St, E9 95 H5
Swinton Cl, Wem. HA9 88 B1
Swinton Pl, WC1 10 C3
Swinton St, WC1 10 C3
Swires Shaw, Kes. BR2 206 A4
Swiss Ct, W1 17 J6
Swiss Ter, NW6 91 G7
Switch Ho, E14
off Blackwall Way 114 D7
Swithland Gdns, SE9 174 D4
Swyncombe Av, W5 125 E4
Swynford Gdns, NW4 71 G4
Sybil Ms, N4
off Lothair Rd N 75 H6
Sybil Phoenix Cl, SE8 133 G5
Sybourn St, E17 77 J7
Sycamore Av, E3 113 J1
W5 125 G3
Sidcup DA15 157 J6
Sycamore Cl, E16
off Clarence Rd 115 E4
N9 *off Pycroft Way* 60 D4
SE9 174 B2
W3 *off Bromyard Av* 126 E1
Barnet EN4 41 G6
Carshalton SM5 199 J4
Edgware HA8
off Ash Cl 54 C4
Feltham TW13 160 A3
Loughton IG10 49 E2
Northolt UB5 103 E1
South Croydon CR2 202 B5
Sycamore Ct, Surb. KT6
off Penners Gdns 181 H7
Sycamore Gdns, W6 127 H2
Mitcham CR4 185 G2
Sycamore Gro, NW9 70 C7
SE6 154 C6
SE20 170 D7
New Malden KT3 182 D3
Sycamore Hill, N11 58 A6
Sycamore Ho, NW3
off Maitland Pk Vil 91 J6
Sycamore Ms, SW4 150 C3
Sycamore Pl, Brom. BR1 192 D3
Sycamore Rd, SW19 165 J6
Sycamore St, EC1 11 J6
Sycamore Wk, W10
off Fifth Av 108 B4
Ilford IG6
off Civic Way 81 F4
Sycamore Way, Tedd.
TW11 163 F6
Thornton Heath CR7 187 G5
SYDENHAM, SE26 171 F5
Sydenham Av, N21
off Fleming Dr 43 F5
SE26 171 E5
Sydenham Cotts, SE12 173 J2
Sydenham Hill, SE23 170 E1
SE26 170 D3
Sydenham Hill Est, SE26 170 D3
Sydenham Pk, SE26 171 F3
Sydenham Pk Rd, SE26 171 F3
Sydenham Pl, SE27
off Lansdowne Hill 169 H3
Sydenham Ri, SE23 170 E2
Sydenham Rd, SE26 171 F4
Croydon CR0 188 A7
Sydmons Ct, SE23 153 F7
Sydner Ms, N16
off Sydner Rd 94 C4
Sydner Rd, N16 94 C4
Sydney Chapman Way,
Barn. EN5 40 C2
Sydney Cl, SW3 31 F2
Sydney Gro, NW4 71 J5
Sydney Ms, SW3 31 F2
Sydney Pl, SW7 31 F2
Sydney Rd, E11
off Mansfield Rd 79 H6
N8 75 G4
N10 74 A1
SE2 138 C3
SW20 184 A2
W13 124 D1
Bexleyheath DA6 158 D4
Enfield EN2 44 A4
Feltham TW14 160 A1
Ilford IG6 81 F2
Richmond TW9 145 H4
Sidcup DA14 175 H4
Sutton SM1 198 D4
Teddington TW11 162 C5
Woodford Green IG8 63 G4
Sydney St, SW3 31 G3
Sylvan Av, N3 72 D2
N22 59 F7
NW7 55 F6
Romford RM6 83 F6
Sylvan Ct, N12 56 E4
Sylvan Est, SE19 188 C1
Sylvan Gdns, Surb. KT6 181 G7
Sylvan Gro, NW2 90 A4
SE15 133 E7
Sylvan Hill, SE19 188 B1
Sylvan Rd, E7 97 G6
E11 79 G5
E17 78 A5
SE19 188 C1
Ilford IG1 99 F2
Sylvan Wk, Brom. BR1 192 C3
Sylvan Way, Dag. RM8 100 B3
West Wickham BR4 204 E4
Sylverdale Rd, Croy. CR0 201 H3
Sylvester Av, Chis. BR7 174 C6
Sylvester Path, E8
off Sylvester Rd 95 E6
Sylvester Rd, E8 95 E6
E17 77 J7
N2 73 F2
Wembley HA0 87 F5
Sylvestrus Cl, Kings.T.
KT1 182 A1
Sylvia Av, Pnr. HA5 51 F6
Sylvia Ct, Wem. HA9
off Harrow Rd 88 B7
Sylvia Gdns, Wem. HA9 88 B7
Symes Ms, NW1 9 F1
Symington Ho, SE1 28 B6
Symington Ms, E9
off Coopersale Rd 95 G5
Symister Ms, N1 12 D4
Symons Cl, SE15 153 F2
Symons St, SW3 32 A2
Symphony Cl, Edg. HA8 54 B7
Symphony Ms, W10
off Third Av 108 B3
Syon Gate Way, Brent.
TW8 124 D7
★ **Syon Ho & Pk**, Brent.
TW8 145 F1
Syon La, Islw. TW7 124 E7
Syon Pk Gdns, Islw. TW7 124 C7
Syon Vista, Rich. TW9 145 G1

T

Tabard Cen, SE1
off Prioress St 28 C6
Tabard Gdns Est, SE1 28 C4
Tabard St, SE1 28 B4
Tabernacle Av, E13
off Barking Rd 115 G4
Tabernacle St, EC2 12 C6
Tableer Av, SW4 150 C5
Tabley Rd, N7 92 E4
Tabor Gdns, Sutt. SM3 198 C6
Tabor Gro, SW19 166 B7
Tabor Rd, W6 127 H3
Tachbrook Est, SW1 33 J4

Tachbrook Ms, SW1 **33** F1
Tachbrook Rd, Felt. TW14 **141** J7
Southall UB2 **122** D4
Tachbrook St, SW1 **33** G2
Tack Ms, SE4 **154** A3
Tadema Ho, NW8 **7** F6
Tadema Rd, SW10 **30** D7
Tadmor St, W12 **128** A1
Tadworth Av, N.Mal. KT3 **183** F5
Tadworth Rd, NW2 **89** G2
Taeping St, E14 **134** B4
Taffy's How, Mitch. CR4 **185** H3
Taft Way, E3 *off Franklin St* **114** B3
Tagg's Island, Hmptn. TW12 **180** A2
Tailworth St, E1 **21** H2
Tait Ct, SW8 *off Darsley Dr* **150** D1
Tait Rd, Croy. CR0 **188** B7
Tait Rd Ind Est, Croy. CR0 **188** B7
Tait St, E1 **112** E6
Takhar Ms, SW11 *off Cabul Rd* **149** H2
Talacre Rd, NW5 **92** A6
Talbot Av, N2 **73** G3
Talbot Cl, N15 **76** C4
Talbot Ct, EC3 **20** C5
Talbot Cres, NW4 **71** G5
Talbot Gdns, Ilf. IG3 **100** A2
Talbot Ho, E14 *off Giraud St* **114** B6
N7 *off Harvist Est* **93** G3
Talbot Pl, SE3 **154** E2
Talbot Rd, E6 **116** D2
E7 **97** G4
N6 **74** A6
N15 **76** C4
N22 **74** C2
SE22 **152** B4
W2 **108** D6
W11 **108** C6
W13 **104** D7
Carshalton SM5 **200** A5
Dagenham RM9 **101** F6
Harrow HA3 **68** C2
Isleworth TW7 **144** D4
Southall UB2 **123** E4
Thornton Heath CR7 **188** A4
Twickenham TW2 **162** B1
Wembley HA0 **87** G5
Talbot Sq, W2 **15** F4
Talbot Wk, NW10 *off Garnet Rd* **89** E6
W11 **108** B6
Talbot Yd, SE1 **28** B2
Talfourd Pl, SE15 **152** C1
Talfourd Rd, SE15 **152** C1
Talgarth Rd, W6 **128** B5
W14 **128** B5
Talgarth Wk, NW9 **70** E5
Talisman Cl, Ilf. IG3 **100** B1
Talisman Sq, SE26 **170** D4
Talisman Way, Wem. HA9 **87** J3
Tallack Cl, Har. HA3 **52** B7
Tallack Rd, E10 **95** J1
Tall Elms Cl, Brom. BR2 **191** F5
Tallis Cl, E16 **115** H6
Tallis Gro, SE7 **135** H6
Tallis St, EC4 **19** F5
Tallis Vw, NW10 **88** D6
Tallow Cl, Dag. RM9 *off Hedgemans Rd* **100** D7
Tallow Rd, Brent. TW8 **125** F6
Tall Trees, SW16 **187** F3
Tally Ho Cor, N12 **57** F5
Talma Gdns, Twick. TW2 **144** B6
Talmage Cl, SE23 *off Tyson Rd* **153** F7
Talman Gro, Stan. HA7 **53** G6
Talma Rd, SW2 **151** G4
Talwin St, E3 **114** B3
Tamar Cl, E3 *off Legion Ter* **113** J1
Tamarind Yd, E1 **29** J1
Tamarisk Sq, W12 **107** F7
Tamar Sq, Wdf.Grn. IG8 **63** H6
Tamar St, SE7 *off Woolwich Rd* **136** B4
Tamar Way, N17 **76** D3
Tamesis Gdns, Wor.Pk. KT4 **196** E1
Tamian Way, Houns. TW4 **142** C4
Tamworth Av, Wdf.Grn. IG8 **63** E6
Tamworth La, Mitch. CR4 **186** B2
Tamworth Pk, Mitch. CR4 **186** B4
Tamworth Pl, Croy. CR0 **201** J2
Tamworth Rd, Croy. CR0 **201** H2
Tamworth St, SW6 **128** D6
Tancred Rd, N4 **75** H6
Tandem Cen, SW19 **185** G1
Tandem Way, SW19 **185** G1
Tandridge Dr, Orp. BR6 **207** G1
Tandridge Pl, Orp. BR6 **207** G1
Tanfield Av, NW2 **89** F4
Tanfield Rd, Croy. CR0 **201** J4
Tangier Rd, Rich. TW10 **146** B3
Tangleberry Cl, Brom. BR1 **192** B4
Tangle Tree Cl, N3 **73** E2
Tanglewood Cl, Croy. CR0 **203** F3
Stanmore HA7 **52** B2
Tanglewood Way, Felt. TW13 **160** B3
Tangley Gro, SW15 **147** F7
Tangley Pk Rd, Hmptn. TW12 **161** F6
Tangmere Gdns, Nthlt. UB5 **102** C2
Tangmere Gro, Kings.T. KT2 **163** G5
Tangmere Way, NW9 **71** E2
Tanhurst Wk, SE2 *off Alsike Rd* **138** D3
Tankerton Rd, Surb. KT6 **195** J2
Tankerton St, WC1 **10** B4
Tankerton Ter, Croy. CR0 *off Mitcham Rd* **187** F7
Tankerville Rd, SW16 **168** D6
Tankridge Rd, NW2 **89** H2
Tanner Pt, E13 **115** G1
Tanners Cl, Walt. KT12 **178** B6
Tanners End La, N18 **60** B4
Tanners Hill, SE8 **153** J1
Tanners La, Ilf. IG6 **81** F3
Tanners Ms, SE8 *off Tanners Hill* **153** J1
Tanner St, SE1 **28** E4
Barking IG11 **99** F6
Tanners Yd, E2 *off Treadway St* **112** E2
Tannery Cl, Beck. BR3 **189** G5
Dagenham RM10 **101** H3
Tannington Ter, N5 **93** G3
Tannsfeld Rd, SE26 **171** G5
Tansley Cl, N7 *off Hilldrop La* **92** D5
Tanswell Est, SE1 **27** E4
Tanswell St, SE1 **27** E4
Tansy Cl, E6 **116** D6
Tantallon Rd, SW12 **168** A1
Tant Av, E16 **115** F6
Tantony Gro, Rom. RM6 **82** D3
Tanworth Gdns, Pnr. HA5 **66** B2
Tanyard Ho, Brent. TW8 *off High St* **125** F7
Tanyard La, Bex. DA5 **177** G1
Tanza Rd, NW3 **91** J4
Tapestry Cl, Sutt. SM2 **198** E7
Taplow, NW3 **91** G7
SE17 **36** C3
Taplow Rd, N13 **59** J4
Taplow St, N1 **12** A2
Tappesfield Rd, SE15 **153** F3
Tapp St, E1 **113** E4
Tapster St, Barn. EN5 **40** C4
Tara Ms, N8 *off Edison Rd* **74** D6
Taransay Wk, N1 *off Essex Rd* **94** A6
Tarbert Ms, N15 *off Roslyn Rd* **76** B5
Tarbert Rd, SE22 **152** B5
Tarbert Wk, E1 *off Juniper St* **113** F7
Target Cl, Felt. TW14 **141** H6
Target Rbt, Nthlt. UB5 *off Western Av* **103** F1
Tariff Cres, SE8 **133** J4
Tariff Rd, N17 **60** D6
Tarleton Gdns, SE23 **171** E1
Tarling Cl, Sid. DA14 **176** B3
Tarling Rd, E16 **115** F6
N2 **73** F2
Tarling St, E1 **113** E6
Tarling St Est, E1 **113** F6
Tarnbank, Enf. EN2 **43** E5
Tarn St, SE1 **27** J6
Tarnwood Pk, SE9 **174** C1
Tarquin Ho, SE26 **170** D4
Tarragon Cl, SE14 **133** H7
Tarragon Gro, SE26 **171** G6
Tarrant Pl, W1 **15** J2
Tarrington Cl, SW16 **168** D3
Tarver Rd, SE17 **35** H4
Tarves Way, SE10 **134** B7
Tash Pl, N11 *off Woodland Rd* **58** B5
Tasker Cl, Hayes (Harling.) UB3 **121** F7
Tasker Ho, Bark. IG11 *off Dovehouse Mead* **117** G2
Tasker Rd, NW3 **91** J5
Tasman Ct, E14 *off Westferry Rd* **134** B4
Tasmania Ter, N18 **59** J6
Tasman Rd, SW9 **151** E3
Tasman Wk, E16 *off Royal Rd* **116** A6
Tasso Rd, W6 **128** B6
Tatam Rd, NW10 **88** C7
Tatchbury Ho, SW15 *off Tunworth Cres* **147** F6
Tate & Lyle Jetty, E16 **136** B2
★ **Tate Britain**, SW1 **34** A2
★ **Tate Modern**, SE1 **27** H1
Tate Rd, E16 *off Newland St* **136** C1
Sutton SM1 **198** D5
Tatham Pl, NW8 **7** F1
Tatnell Rd, SE23 **153** H6
Tattersall Cl, SE9 **156** B5
Tatton Cres, N16 *off Clapton Common* **76** C7
Tatum St, SE17 **36** C2
Tauheed Cl, N4 **93** J2
Taunton Av, SW20 **183** H2
Hounslow TW3 **143** J2
Taunton Cl, Ilf. IG6 **65** J6
Sutton SM3 **198** D1
Taunton Dr, N2 **73** F2
Enfield EN2 **43** G3
Taunton Ms, NW1 **7** J6
Taunton Pl, NW1 **7** J5
Taunton Rd, SE12 **155** E5
Greenford UB6 **103** H1
Taunton Way, Stan. HA7 **69** H3
Tavern Cl, Cars. SM5 **185** H7
Taverners Cl, W11 *off Addison Av* **128** B1
Taverner Sq, N5 *off Highbury Gra* **93** J4
Taverners Way, E4 **62** E1
Tavern La, SW9 **151** G2
Tavistock Av, E17 **77** H3
NW7 **56** A7
Greenford (Perivale) UB6 **104** D2
Tavistock Cl, N16 *off Crossway* **94** B5
Tavistock Ct, WC2 *off Tavistock St* **18** B5
Tavistock Cres, W11 **108** C5
Mitcham CR4 **186** E4
Tavistock Gdns, Ilf. IG3 **99** H4
Tavistock Gate, Croy. CR0 **202** A1
Tavistock Gro, Croy. CR0 **188** A7
Tavistock Ms, E18 *off Avon Way* **79** G4
Tavistock Pl, E18 *off Avon Way* **79** G3
N14 **42** B6
WC1 **9** J5
Tavistock Rd, E7 **97** F4
E15 **97** F6
E18 **79** G3
N4 **76** A6
NW10 **107** F2
W11 **108** C6
Bromley BR2 **191** F4
Carshalton SM5 **199** G1
Croydon CR0 **202** A1
Edgware HA8 **70** A1
Welling DA16 **158** C1
West Drayton UB7 **120** A1
Tavistock Sq, WC1 **9** J5
Tavistock St, WC2 **18** B5
Tavistock Ter, N19 **92** D3
Tavistock Twr, SE16 *off Finland St* **133** H3
Tavistock Wk, Cars. SM5 *off Tavistock Rd* **199** G1
Taviton St, WC1 **9** H5
Tavy Cl, SE11 **35** F3
Tawney Rd, SE28 **118** B7
Tawny Cl, W13 **124** E1
Feltham TW13 *off Chervil Cl* **160** A3
Tawny Way, SE16 **133** G4
Tayben Av, Twick. TW2 **144** B6
Taybridge Rd, SW11 **150** A3
Tayburn Cl, E14 **114** C6
Taylor Av, Rich. TW9 **146** B2
Taylor Cl, N17 **60** D7
SE8 **133** J6
Hampton (Hmptn H.) TW12 **161** J5
Hounslow TW3 **143** J1
Orpington BR6 **207** J4
Taylor Rd, Mitch. CR4 **167** H7
Wallington SM6 **200** B5
Taylors Bldgs, SE18 *off Spray St* **137** E4
Taylors Cl, Sid. DA14 **175** J4
Taylors Ct, Felt. TW13 **160** A2
Taylors Grn, W3 **107** E6
Taylors La, SE26 **170** E4
Barnet EN5 **40** C1
Taymount Ri, SE23 **171** F2
Tayport Cl, N1 **93** E7
Tayside Dr, Edg. HA8 **54** B3
Taywood Rd, Nthlt. UB5 **103** F3
Teak Cl, SE16 **133** H1
Teal Cl, E16 *off Fulmer Rd* **116** A5
Teal Ct, Wall. SM6 *off Carew Rd* **200** C6
Teale St, E2 **13** J1
Tealing Dr, Epsom KT19 **196** D4
Teal Pl, Sutt. SM1 *off Sandpiper Rd* **198** C5
Teal St, SE10 **135** F3
Teasel Cl, Croy. CR0 **203** G1
Teasel Cres, SE28 **137** H1
Teasel Way, E15 **114** E3
Tebworth Rd, N17 **60** C7
Teck Cl, Islw. TW7 **144** D2
Tedder Cl, Chess. KT9 **195** F6
Ruislip HA4 *off West End Rd* **84** B5
Tedder Rd, S.Croy. CR2 **203** F7
TEDDINGTON, TW11 **162** D6
Teddington Lock, Tedd. TW11 **162** E4
Teddington Pk, Tedd. TW11 **162** C5
Teddington Pk Rd, Tedd. TW11 **162** C4
Tedworth Gdns, SW3 **31** J4
Tedworth Sq, SW3 **31** J4
Tee, The, W3 **106** E6
Tees Av, Grnf. (Perivale) UB6 **104** B2
Teesdale Av, Islw. TW7 **144** D1
Teesdale Cl, E2 **13** J2
Teesdale Gdns, SE25 **188** B2
Isleworth TW7 **144** D1
Teesdale Rd, E11 **79** F6
Teesdale St, E2 **112** E2
Teesdale Yd, E2 **13** J1
Teeswater Ct, Erith DA18 *off Middle Way* **138** D3
Teevan Cl, Croy. CR0 **188** D7
Teevan Rd, Croy. CR0 **188** D7
Teign Ms, SE9 **174** B2
Teignmouth Cl, SW4 **150** D4
Edgware HA8 **69** J2
Teignmouth Gdns, Grnf. (Perivale) UB6 **104** C2
Teignmouth Par, Grnf. UB6 *off Teignmouth Gdns* **104** E2
Teignmouth Rd, NW2 **90** A5
Welling DA16 **158** C2
Telcote Way, Ruis. HA4 *off Woodlands Av* **66** C7
★ **Telecom Twr**, W1 **17** F1
Telegraph Hill, NW3 **90** E3
Telegraph La, Esher (Clay.) KT10 **194** C6
Telegraph Ms, Ilf. IG3 **100** A1
Telegraph Path, Chis. BR7 **174** E5
Telegraph Pl, E14 **134** B4
Telegraph Rd, SW15 **147** H7
Telegraph St, EC2 **20** B3
Telemann Sq, SE3 **155** H3
Telephone Pl, SW6 *off Lillie Rd* **128** C6
Telfer Cl, W3 *off Church Rd* **126** C2
Telferscot Rd, SW12 **168** D1
Telford Av, SW2 **168** E1
Telford Cl, E17 **77** H7
SE19 *off St. Aubyn's Rd* **170** C6
Telford Dr, Walt. KT12 **178** C7
Telford Ho, SE1 **27** J6
Telford Rd, N11 **58** C6
NW9 *off West Hendon Bdy* **71** G6
SE9 **175** G2
W10 **108** B5
Southall UB1 **103** H7
Twickenham TW2 **143** G7
Telfords Yd, E1 **21** J6
Telford Ter, SW1 **33** F5
Telford Way, W3 **106** E5
Hayes UB4 **102** E5
Telham Rd, E6 **116** D2
Tell Gro, SE22 **152** C4
Tellson Av, SE18 **156** B1
Telscombe Cl, Orp. BR6 **207** H2
Temair Ho, SE10 *off Tarves Way* **134** B7
Temeraire Pl, Brent. TW8 **125** J5
Temeraire St, SE16 *off Albion St* **133** F2
Temperley Rd, SW12 **150** A7
Templar Ct, NW8 *off St. John's Wd Rd* **7** E4
Templar Dr, SE28 **118** D6
Templar Ho, NW2 *off Shoot Up Hill* **90** C6
Harrow HA2 *off Northolt Rd* **86** A2
Templar Pl, Hmptn. TW12 **161** G7
Templars Av, NW11 **72** C6

Templars Cres, N3 . . . . .72 D2
Templars Dr, Har. HA3 . . . .52 A6
Templar St, SE5 . . . . .151 H2
★ **Temple, The**, EC4 . . . . .19 E5
Temple Av, EC4 . . . . .19 F5
N20 . . . . .41 G7
Croydon CR0 . . . . .203 J2
Dagenham RM8 . . . . . .101 G1
★ **Temple Bar**, EC4 . . . . . .19 H4
★ **Temple Bar Mem**, EC4 .18 E4
Temple Cl, E11 . . . . .78 E7
N3 *off Cyprus Rd* 72 C2
SE28 . . . . .137 F3
Templecombe Rd, E9 . . . . .113 F1
Templecombe Way, Mord. SM4 . . . . .184 B5
Temple Ct, E1 *off Rectory Sq* 113 G5
SW8 *off Thorncroft St* 130 E7
Temple Dws, E2 *off Temple St* 112 E2
Temple Fortune Hill, NW11 . . . . .72 D5
Temple Fortune La, NW11 . . . . .72 D6
Temple Fortune Par, NW11 *off Finchley Rd* 72 C5
Temple Gdns, N21 *off Barrowell Grn* 59 H2
NW11 . . . . .72 C6
Dagenham RM8 . . . . . .100 D3
Temple Gro, NW11 . . . . . . .72 D6
Enfield EN2 . . . . .43 H3
Templehof Av, NW2 . . . . . .71 J7
Temple La, EC4 . . . . .19 F4
Templeman Rd, W7 . . . . . .104 C5
Templemead Cl, W3 . . . . . .106 E6
Temple Mead Cl, Stan. HA7 . . . . .52 E6
Templemead Ho, E9 *off Kingsmead Way* . . .95 H4
Temple Mill La, E15 . . . . . .96 B4
★ **Temple of Mithras**, EC4 *off Queen Victoria St* . .20 B4
Temple Pl, WC2 . . . . .18 D5
Temple Rd, E6 . . . . .116 B1
N8 . . . . .75 F4
NW2 . . . . .89 J4
W4 . . . . .126 C3
W5 . . . . .125 G3
Croydon CR0 . . . . .202 A4
Hounslow TW3 . . . . . . .143 H4
Richmond TW9 . . . . . . .145 J3
Temple Sheen, SW14 . . . .146 C5
Temple Sheen Rd, SW14 .146 B4
Temple St, E2 . . . . .112 E2
Templeton Av, E4 . . . . .62 A4
Templeton Cl, N16 *off Boleyn Rd* 94 B5
SE19 . . . . .188 A1
Templeton Ct, NW7 *off Kingsbridge Dr* 56 A7
Templeton Pl, SW5 . . . . . .128 D4
Templeton Rd, N15 . . . . . . .76 A6
Temple Way, Sutt. SM1 . .199 G3
Temple W Ms, SE11 . . . . . .27 G6
Templewood, W13 . . . . . .105 E5
Templewood Av, NW3 . . . . .90 E3
Templewood Gdns, NW3 . .91 E3
Templewood Pt, NW2 . . . .90 C2
Temple Yd, E2 *off Temple St* 112 E2
Tempsford Av, Borwd. WD6 . . . . .38 D4
Tempsford Cl, Enf. EN2 *off Gladbeck Way* 43 J3
Tempus Ct, E18 . . . . .79 G1
Temsford Cl, Har. HA2 . . . .67 J2
Tenbury Cl, E7 *off Romford Rd* 98 A5
Tenbury Ct, SW2 . . . . .168 D1
Tenby Av, Har. HA3 . . . . . . .68 E2
Tenby Cl, N15 . . . . .76 C4
Romford RM6 . . . . .82 E6
Tenby Gdns, Nthlt. UB5 . . .85 G6
Tenby Rd, E17 . . . . .77 H5
Edgware HA8 . . . . .69 J1
Enfield EN3 . . . . .45 F3
Romford RM6 . . . . .83 E6
Welling DA16 . . . . .158 D1
Tench St, E1 . . . . .132 E1
Tenda Rd, SE16 *off Roseberry St* 132 E4
Tendring Way, Rom. RM6 . .82 C5
Tenham Av, SW2 . . . . .168 D1
Tenison Ct, W1 . . . . .17 F5
Tenison Way, SE1 . . . . .26 E2
Tenniel Cl, W2 . . . . .14 C4
Tennis Ct La, E.Mol. KT8 *off Hampton Ct Way* . .180 B3
Tennison Av, Borwd. WD6 .38 B5
Tennison Rd, SE25 . . . . . .188 C4
Tennis St, SE1 . . . . .28 B3
Tenniswood Rd, Enf. EN1 . . . . .44 C1
Tennyson Av, E11 . . . . .79 G7
E12 . . . . .98 B7
NW9 . . . . .70 C3
New Malden KT3 . . . . .183 H5
Twickenham TW1 . . . . .162 C1
Tennyson Cl, Enf. EN3 . . . .45 G5
Feltham TW14 . . . . .141 J6
Welling DA16 . . . . .157 H1
Tennyson Rd, E10 . . . . .96 B2
E15 . . . . .96 E7
E17 . . . . .77 J6
NW6 . . . . .108 C1
NW7 . . . . .55 G5
SE20 . . . . .171 G7
SW19 . . . . .167 F6
W7 . . . . .104 C7
Hounslow TW3 . . . . . . .143 J2
Tennyson St, SW8 . . . . . .150 B2
Tensing Rd, Sthl. UB2 . . . .123 G3
Tentelow La, Sthl. UB2 . . .123 G5
Tenterden Cl, NW4 . . . . . . .72 A3
SE9 . . . . .174 C4
Tenterden Dr, NW4 . . . . . . .72 A3
Tenterden Gdns, NW4 . . . .72 A3
Croydon CR0 . . . . .188 D7
Tenterden Gro, NW4 . . . . . .71 J4
Tenterden Rd, N17 . . . . . . .60 C7
Croydon CR0 . . . . .188 D7
Dagenham RM8 . . . . . .101 F2
Tenterden St, W1 . . . . .16 E4
Tenter Grd, E1 . . . . .21 F2
Tenter Pas, E1 . . . . .21 G4
Tent Peg La, Orp. BR5 . . . .193 F5
Tent St, E1 . . . . .112 E4
Tequila Wf, E14 *off Commercial Rd* . . .113 H6
Terborch Way, SE22 *off East Dulwich Gro* .152 B5
Teredo St, SE16 . . . . .133 G3
Terence Ct, Belv. DA17 *off Nuxley Rd* 139 F6
Teresa Ms, E17 . . . . .78 A4
Teresa Wk, N10 *off Connaught Gdns* . . .74 B5
Terling Cl, E11 . . . . .97 F3
Terling Rd, Dag. RM8 . . . .101 G2
Terling Wk, N1 *off Britannia Row* 111 J1
Terminal Four Rbt, Houns. TW6 *off Shrewsbury Rd* . . .141 F6
Terminus Pl, SW1 . . . . .25 E6
Terrace, The, E4 *off Chingdale Rd* 62 E3
N3 *off Hendon La* 72 C2
NW6 . . . . .108 D1
SW13 . . . . .147 E2
Woodford Green IG8 *off Broadmead Rd* 63 G6
Terrace Apts, N5 *off Drayton Pk* 93 G5
Terrace Gdns, SW13 . . . . .147 F2
Terrace La, Rich. TW10 . . .145 H6
Terrace Rd, E9 . . . . .95 F7
E13 . . . . .115 G1
Walton-on-Thames KT12 . . . . .178 A7
Terrace Wk, Dag. RM9 . . . .101 E5
Terrapin Rd, SW17 . . . . . .168 B3
Terretts Pl, N1 *off Upper St* 93 H7
Terrick Rd, N22 . . . . .75 E1
Terrick St, W12 . . . . .107 H6
Terrilands, Pnr. HA5 . . . . . .67 F3
Terront Rd, N15 . . . . .75 J5
Tersha St, Rich. TW9 . . . . .145 J4
Tessa Sanderson Pl, SW8 . . . . .150 B3
Tessa Sanderson Way, Grnf. UB6 *off Lilian Board Way* . . .86 A5
Testerton Wk, W11 . . . . . .108 A7
Tetbury Pl, N1 *off Upper St* 111 H1
Tetcott Rd, SW10 . . . . .30 C7
Tetherdown, N10 . . . . .74 A3
Tetty Way, Brom. BR2 . . . .191 G2
Teversham La, SW8 . . . . . .151 E1
Teviot Cl, Well. DA16 . . . . .158 B1
Teviot St, E14 . . . . .114 C5
Tewkesbury Av, SE23 . . . .171 E1
Pinner HA5 . . . . .67 E5
Tewkesbury Cl, N15 *off Tewkesbury Rd* 76 A6
Barnet EN4 *off Approach Rd* 41 G4
Loughton IG10 . . . . .48 B6
Tewkesbury Gdns, NW9 . . .70 B3
Tewkesbury Rd, N15 . . . . . .76 A6
W13 . . . . .104 D7
Carshalton SM5 . . . . . .199 G1
Tewkesbury Ter, N11 . . . . .58 C6
Tewson Rd, SE18 . . . . . . .137 H5
Teynham Av, Enf. EN1 . . . .44 A6
Teynham Grn, Brom. BR2 . . . . .191 G5
Teynton Ter, N17 . . . . .75 J1
Thackeray Av, N17 . . . . . . .76 D2
Thackeray Cl, SW19 . . . . .166 A7
Isleworth TW7 . . . . .144 D2
Thackeray Dr, Rom. RM6 . .82 A7
Thackeray Rd, E6 . . . . .116 A2
SW8 . . . . .150 B2
Thackeray St, W8 . . . . .22 B4
Thakeham Cl, SE26 . . . . . .170 E5
Thalia Cl, SE10 . . . . .134 D6
Thame Rd, SE16 . . . . .133 G2
Thames Av, SW10 . . . . . . .149 F1
Dagenham RM9 . . . . . .119 H4
Greenford (Perivale) UB6 . . . . .104 C2
Thames Bk, SW14 . . . . . .146 C2
Thamesbank Pl, SE28 . . . .118 C6
★ **Thames Barrier Information & Learning Cen**, SE18 . .136 A3
Thames Circle, E14 *off Westferry Rd* 134 A4
Thames Cl, Hmptn. TW12 .179 H2
Thames Ct, W.Mol. KT8 . .179 H2
Thames Cres, W4 *off Corney Rd* 127 E7
THAMES DITTON, KT7 . . .180 C6
Thames Ditton Island, T.Ditt. KT7 . . . . .180 D5
Thamesgate Cl, Rich. TW10 *off Locksmeade Rd* . . .163 F4
Thames Gateway, Dag. RM9 . . . . .119 F2
Thames Gateway Pk, Dag. RM9 . . . . .119 F3
Thameshill Av, Rom. RM5 .83 J2
Thameside, Tedd. TW11 . .163 G7
Thameside Ind Est, E16 . .136 B2
Thameside Wk, SE28 . . . .117 J6
Thames Link, SE16 *off Salter Rd* 133 G1
THAMESMEAD, SE28 . . . .137 J1
Thamesmead, Walt. KT12 . . . . .178 A7
THAMESMEAD NORTH, SE28 . . . . .118 D6
Thames Meadow, W.Mol. KT8 . . . . .179 G2
Thamesmead Spine Rd, Belv. DA17 . . . . .139 H2
THAMESMEAD WEST, SE18 . . . . .136 E3
Thamesmere Dr, SE28 . . .118 A7
Thames Pl, SW15 . . . . . . .148 A3
Thames Pt, SW6 *off The Boulevard* 149 F2
Thamespoint, Tedd. TW11 .163 G7
Thames Quay, SW10 *off Harbour Av* 149 F1
Thames Rd, E16 . . . . .136 A1
W4 . . . . .126 A6
Barking IG11 . . . . .117 J3
Thames Side, Kings.T. KT1 . . . . .181 G1
Thames St, SE10 . . . . .134 B6
Hampton TW12 . . . . . . .179 H1
Kingston upon Thames KT1 . . . . .181 G2
Sunbury-on-Thames TW16 . . . . .178 B4
Thames Tunnel Mills, SE16 *off Rotherhithe St* 133 F2
Thamesvale Cl, Houns. TW3 . . . . .143 G3
Thames Vw, Ilf. IG1 *off Axon Pl* 99 F2
Thames Village, W4 . . . . .146 C1
Thames Wf, E16 . . . . .135 F1
Thanescroft Gdns, Croy. CR0 . . . . .202 B3
Thanet Dr, Kes. BR2 *off Phoenix Dr* 206 A3
Thanet Pl, Croy. CR0 . . . . .201 J4
Thanet Rd, Bex. DA5 . . . .159 G7
Thanet St, WC1 . . . . .10 A4
Thane Vil, N7 . . . . .93 F3
Thane Wks, N7 . . . . .93 F3
Thanington Ct, SE9 . . . . .157 H6
Thant Cl, E10 . . . . .96 B3
Tharp Rd, Wall. SM6 . . . . .200 D5
Thatcham Gdns, N20 . . . . .41 F7
Thatcher Cl, West Dr. UB7 *off Classon Cl* 120 B2
Thatchers Cl, Loug. IG10 . .49 F2
Thatchers Way, Islw. TW7 .144 A5
Thatches Gro, Rom. RM6 . .82 E4
Thavies Inn, EC1 . . . . .19 F3
Thaxted Ct, N1 . . . . .12 B2
Thaxted Ho, Dag. RM10 . .101 H7
Thaxted Pl, SW20 . . . . . . .166 A7
Thaxted Rd, SE9 . . . . .175 F2
Buckhurst Hill IG9 . . . . . .48 B7
Thaxton Rd, W14 . . . . . . .128 C6
Thayers Fm Rd, Beck. BR3 . . . . .189 H1
Thayer St, W1 . . . . .16 C2
★ **Theatre Royal**, WC2 . . .18 B4
Theatre Sq, E15 *off Great Eastern Rd* . .96 D6
Theatre St, SW11 . . . . . . .149 J3
Theberton St, N1 . . . . .111 G1
Theed St, SE1 . . . . .27 E2
Thelma Gdns, SE3 . . . . . .156 A1
Feltham TW13 . . . . .161 E3
Thelma Gro, Tedd. TW11 . .162 D6
Theobald Cres, Har. HA3 . .67 H1
Theobald Rd, E17 . . . . .77 J7
Croydon CR0 . . . . .201 H2
Theobalds Av, N12 . . . . . . .57 F4
Theobalds Ct, N4 *off Queens Dr* 93 J3
Theobald's Rd, WC1 . . . . . .18 C1
Theobald St, SE1 . . . . .28 B6
Theodore Rd, SE13 . . . . . .154 C6
Therapia La, Croy. CR0 . . .187 E6
Therapia Rd, SE22 . . . . . .153 F6
Theresa Rd, W6 . . . . .127 G4
Therfield Ct, N4 *off Brownswood Rd* . . .93 J2
Thermopylae Gate, E14 . .134 B4
Theseus Wk, N1 . . . . .11 H2
Thesiger Rd, SE20 . . . . . .171 G7
Thessaly Rd, SW8 . . . . . . .130 C7
Thetford Cl, N13 . . . . .59 H7
Thetford Gdns, Dag. RM9 . . . . .100 D7
Thetford Rd, Dag. RM9 . . .118 D1
New Malden KT3 . . . . .182 D6
Thetis Ter, Rich. TW9 *off Kew Grn* 126 A6
Theydon Gro, Wdf.Grn. IG8 . . . . .63 J6
Theydon Pk Rd, Epp. (They.B.) CM16 . . . . .49 H1
Theydon Rd, E5 . . . . .95 F2
Theydon St, E17 . . . . .77 J7
Thicket Cres, Sutt. SM1 . .199 F4
Thicket Gro, SE20 *off Anerley Rd* 170 D7
Dagenham RM9 . . . . . .100 C6
Thicket Rd, SE20 . . . . .170 D7
Sutton SM1 . . . . .199 F4
Third Av, E12 . . . . .98 B4
E13 . . . . .115 G3
E17 . . . . .78 A5
W3 . . . . .127 F1
W10 . . . . .108 B3
Dagenham RM10 . . . . .119 H1
Enfield EN1 . . . . .44 C5
Hayes UB3 . . . . .121 J1
Romford RM6 . . . . .82 C5
Wembley HA9 . . . . .87 G2
Third Cl, W.Mol. KT8 . . . . .179 H4
Third Cross Rd, Twick. TW2 . . . . .162 A2
Third Way, Wem. HA9 . . . . .88 B4
Thirleby Rd, SW1 . . . . .25 G6
Edgware HA8 . . . . .70 D1
Thirlmere Av, Grnf. (Perivale) UB6 . . . . .105 F3
Thirlmere Gdns, Wem. HA9 . . . . .87 F1
Thirlmere Ho, Islw. TW7 *off Summerwood Rd* .144 C5
Thirlmere Ri, Brom. BR1 . .173 F6
Thirlmere Rd, N10 . . . . . . .74 B1
SW16 . . . . .168 D4
Bexleyheath DA7 . . . . .159 J2
Thirsk Cl, Nthlt. UB5 . . . . . .85 G6
Thirsk Rd, SE25 . . . . .188 A4
SW11 . . . . .150 A3
Mitcham CR4 . . . . .168 A7
Thirston Path, Borwd. WD6 . . . . .38 A2
Thistlebrook, SE2 . . . . . . .138 C3
Thistlebrook Ind Est, SE2 .138 C2
Thistlecroft Gdns, Stan. HA7 . . . . .69 G1
Thistledene, T.Ditt. KT7 . . .180 B6
Thistledene Av, Har. HA2 . .85 E3
Thistlefield Cl, Bex. DA5 .176 D1
Thistle Gro, SW10 . . . . .30 D3
Thistlemead, Chis. BR7 . .192 E2
Thistle Mead, Loug. IG10 . .48 D3
Thistlewaite Rd, E5 . . . . . . .95 E3
Thistlewood Cl, N7 . . . . . . .93 F2
Thistleworth Cl, Islw. TW7 . . . . .124 A7
Thistley Cl, N12 *off Summerfields Av* . .57 H6
Thistley Ct, SE8 *off Glaisher St* 134 B6
Thomas a'Beckett Cl, Wem. HA0 . . . . .86 C4
Thomas Baines Rd, SW11 . . . . .149 G3
Thomas Cribb Ms, E6 . . . .116 C6
Thomas Darby Ct, W11 . . .108 B6
Thomas Dean Rd, SE26 *off Kangley Br Rd* 171 J4
Thomas Dinwiddy Rd, SE12 . . . . .173 H2

Thomas Doyle St, SE1 27 G5
Thomas Hardy Ho, N22 59 F7
Thomas Hollywood Ho, E2
off Approach Rd 113 F2
Thomas La, SE6 154 A7
Thomas More Ho, EC2
off The Barbican 19 J2
Thomas More St, E1 21 H6
Thomas More Way, N2 73 F3
Thomas N Ter, E16
off Barking Rd 115 F5
Thomas Pl, W8 22 A6
Thomas Rd, E14 113 J6
Thomas St, SE18 136 D4
Thomas Wall Cl, Sutt. SM1
off Clarence Rd 198 E5
Thompson Av, Rich. TW9 146 A3
Thompson Cl, Ilf. IG1
off High Rd 99 F2
Sutton SM3
off Barrington Rd 198 D1
Thompson Rd, SE22 152 C6
Dagenham RM9 101 F3
Hounslow TW3 143 H4
Thompsons Av, SE5 35 J7
Thompson's La, Loug. (High Beach) IG10 47 F1
Thomson Cres, Croy. CR0 201 G1
Thomson Rd, Har. HA3 68 B3
Thorburn Sq, SE1 37 H2
Thorburn Way, SW19 185 F1
Thoresby St, N1 12 A3
Thorkhill Gdns, T.Ditt. KT7 194 D1
Thorkhill Rd, T.Ditt. KT7 180 E7
Thornaby Gdns, N18 60 D6
Thorn Av, Bushey (Bushey Hth) WD23 51 J1
Thornbury Av, Islw. TW7 124 A7
Thornbury Cl, N16
off Boleyn Rd 94 B5
NW7
off Kingsbridge Dr 56 A7
Thornbury Gdns, Borwd. WD6 38 C4
Thornbury Rd, SW2 150 E6
Isleworth TW7 144 A1
Thornbury Sq, N6 92 C1
Thornby Rd, E5 95 F3
Thorncliffe Rd, SW2 150 E6
Southall UB2 123 F5
Thorn Cl, Brom. BR2 192 D6
Northolt UB5 103 F3
Thorncombe Rd, SE22 152 B5
Thorncroft Rd, Sutt. SM1 198 E4
Thorncroft St, SW8 130 E7
Thorndean St, SW18 167 F2
Thorndene Av, N11 58 A1
Thorndike Av, Nthlt. UB5 102 D1
Thorndike Cl, SW10 30 C7
Thorndike Ho, SW1
off Vauxhall Br Rd 33 H3
Thorndike Rd, N1 93 J6
Thorndike St, SW1 33 H2
Thorndon Cl, Orp. BR5 193 J2
Thorndon Gdns, Epsom KT19 196 E4
Thorndon Rd, Orp. BR5 193 J2
Thorndyke Ct, Pnr. HA5
off Westfield Pk 51 F7
Thorne Cl, E11 96 E4
E16 115 G6
Erith DA8 139 J6
Esher (Clay.) KT10 194 D7
Thorneloe Gdns, Croy. CR0 201 G5
Thorne Pas, SW13 147 E2
Thorne Rd, SW8 130 E7
Thornes Cl, Beck. BR3 190 C3
Thorne St, E16 115 F6
SW13 147 E3
Thornet Wd Rd, Brom. BR1 192 D3
Thorney Cres, SW11 129 G7
Thorneycroft Cl, Walt. KT12 178 C6
Thorney Hedge Rd, W4 126 B4
Thorney St, SW1 34 A1
Thornfield Av, NW7 72 B1
Thornfield Rd, W12 127 H2
Thornford Rd, SE13 154 C5
Thorngate Rd, W9 108 D4
Thorngrove Rd, E13 115 H1
Thornham Gro, E15 96 D5
Thornham St, SE10 134 B6
Thornhaugh Ms, WC1 9 J6
Thornhaugh St, WC1 17 J1
Thornhill Av, SE18 137 H7
Surbiton KT6 195 H2
Thornhill Br Wf, N1
off Caledonian Rd 111 F1
Thornhill Cres, N1 93 F7
Thornhill Gdns, E10 96 B2
Barking IG11 99 H7
Thornhill Gro, N1
off Lofting Rd 93 F7
Thornhill Rd, E10 96 B2
N1 93 G7
Croydon CR0 187 J7
Surbiton KT6 195 H2
Thornhill Sq, N1 93 F7
Thorn Ho, Beck. BR3 189 H1
Thornlaw Rd, SE27 169 G4
Thornley Cl, N17 60 D7
Thornley Dr, Har. HA2 85 H2
Thornley Pl, SE10
off Caradoc St 134 E5
Thornsbeach Rd, SE6 172 C1
Thornsett Pl, SE20 188 E2
Thornsett Rd, SE20 188 E2
SW18 167 E2
Thornside, Edg. HA8
off High St 54 A6
Thorn Ter, SE15
off Nunhead Gro 153 F3
Thornton Av, SW2 168 D1
W4 127 E4
Croydon CR0 187 F6
West Drayton UB7 120 C3
Thornton Cl, West Dr. UB7 120 C3
Thornton Ct, SW20 184 A5
Thornton Dene, Beck. BR3 190 A2
Thornton Gdns, SW12 168 D1
Thornton Gro, Pnr. HA5 51 G6
THORNTON HEATH, CR7 187 H4
Thornton Heath Pond, Th.Hth. CR7 187 G5
Thornton Hill, SW19 166 B7
Thornton Ho, SE17 36 C2
Thornton Pl, W1 16 A1
Thornton Rd, E11 96 D2
N18 61 F3
SW12 150 D7
SW14 146 D3
SW19 166 A6
Barnet EN5 40 B3
Belvedere DA17 139 H4
Bromley BR1 173 G5
Carshalton SM5 199 G1
Croydon CR0 187 F7
Ilford IG1 98 E4
Thornton Heath CR7 187 F7
Thornton Rd E, SW19
off Thornton Rd 166 A6
Thornton Rd Ind Est, Croy. CR0 187 E6
Thornton Row, Th.Hth. CR7
off London Rd 187 G5
Thornton St, SW9 151 G2
Thornton Way, NW11 73 E5
Thorntree Rd, SE7 136 A5
Thornville Gro, Mitch. CR4 185 F2
Thornville St, SE8 154 A1
Thornwood Cl, E18 79 H2
Thornwood Gdns, W8
off Campden Hill 128 D2
Thornwood Rd, SE13 154 E5
Thorogood Gdns, E15 97 E5
Thorold Rd, N22 59 E7
Ilford IG1 98 E2
Thorparch Rd, SW8 150 D1
Thorpebank Rd, W12 127 G1
Thorpe Cl, W10
off Cambridge Gdns 108 B6
Orpington BR6 207 H2
Thorpe Cres, E17 77 J2
Thorpedale Gdns, Ilf. IG2, IG6 80 D4
Thorpedale Rd, N4 93 E1
Thorpe Hall Rd, E17 78 C1
Thorpe Rd, E6 116 C1
E7 97 F4
E17 78 C2
N15 76 B6
Barking IG11 99 G7
Kingston upon Thames KT2 163 H7
Thorpe Wk, Grnf. UB6 104 B2
Thorpewood Av, SE26 171 E2
Thorsden Way, SE19
off Oaks Av 170 B5
Thorverton Rd, NW2 90 B3
Thoydon Rd, E3 113 H2
Thrale Rd, SW16 168 C5
Thrale St, SE1 28 A2
Thrasher Cl, E8
off Dunston Rd 112 C1
Thrawl St, E1 21 G2
Threadneedle St, EC2 20 C4
Three Barrels Wk, EC4 20 A6
Three Colts Cor, E2 13 H5
Three Colts La, E2 113 E4
Three Colt St, E14 113 J7
Three Cors, Bexh. DA7 159 H2
Three Cranes Wk, EC4
off Bell Wf La 20 A6
Three Cups Yd, WC1 18 D2
Three Kings Rd, Mitch. CR4 186 A3
Three Kings Yd, W1 16 D5
Three Meadows Ms, Har. HA3 68 C1
Three Mill La, E3 114 C3
Three Oak La, SE1 29 F3
Three Quays Wk, EC3 20 E6
Threshers Pl, W11 108 B7
Thriffwood, SE26 171 F3
Thrift Fm La, Borwd. WD6 38 B2
Thrigby Rd, Chess. KT9 195 J6
Throckmorton Rd, E16 115 H6
Throgmorton Av, EC2 20 C3
Throgmorton St, EC2 20 C3
Throwley Cl, SE2 138 C3
Throwley Rd, Sutt. SM1 199 E5
Throwley Way, Sutt. SM1 199 E4
Thrupp Cl, Mitch. CR4 186 B2
Thrush Grn, Har. HA2 67 G4
Thrush St, SE17 35 J3
Thunderer Rd, Dag. RM9 118 E4
Thurbarn Rd, SE6 172 B5
Thurland Ho, SE16
off Manor Est 132 E4
Thurland Rd, SE16 29 H5
Thurlby Cl, Har. HA1
off Gayton Rd 68 D6
Woodford Green IG8 64 C5
Thurlby Rd, SE27 169 G4
Wembley HA0 87 G6
Thurleigh Av, SW12 150 A6
Thurleigh Rd, SW12 150 A6
Thurleston Av, Mord. SM4 184 B5
Thurlestone Av, N12 57 J6
Ilford IG3 99 J4
Thurlestone Rd, SE27 169 G3
Thurloe Cl, SW7 31 G1
Thurloe Pl, SW7 31 F1
Thurloe Pl Ms, SW7 31 F1
Thurloe Sq, SW7 31 G1
Thurloe St, SW7 31 F1
Thurlow Cl, E4
off Higham Sta Av 62 B6
Thurlow Gdns, Ilf. IG6 65 G6
Wembley HA0 87 G5
Thurlow Hill, SE21 169 J1
Thurlow Pk Rd, SE21 169 H1
Thurlow Rd, NW3 91 G5
W7 124 D2
Thurlow St, SE17 36 C3
Thurlow Ter, NW5 92 A5
Thurlstone Rd, Ruis. HA4 84 A3
Thurnby Ct, Twick. TW2 162 B3
Thursland Rd, Sid. DA14 176 E5
Thursley Cres, Croy. (New Adgtn) CR0 204 D7
Thursley Gdns, SW19 166 A2
Thursley Rd, SE9 174 C3
Thurso Ho, NW6 6 A2
Thurso St, SW17 167 G4
Thurstan Rd, SW20 165 H7
Thurston Rd, SE13 154 B2
Southall UB1 103 F6
Thurston Rd Ind Est, SE13
off Jerrard St 154 B3
Thurtle Rd, E2 112 C1
Thwaite Cl, Erith DA8 139 J6
Thyer Cl, Orp. BR6
off Isabella Dr 207 F4
Thyme Cl, SE3 155 J3
Thyra Gro, N12 57 E6
Tibbatts Rd, E3 114 B4
Tibbenham Pl, SE6 172 A2
Tibbenham Wk, E13 115 F2
Tibberton Sq, N1
off Popham Rd 93 J7
Tibbets Cl, SW19 166 A1
Tibbet's Cor, SW15 148 A7
Tibbet's Cor Underpass, SW15 *off West Hill* 148 A7
Tibbet's Ride, SW15 148 A7
Tiber Cl, E3
off Garrison Rd 114 A1
Tiber Gdns, N1
off Copenhagen St 111 E1
Ticehurst Cl, Orp. BR5 176 A7
Ticehurst Rd, SE23 171 H2
Tickford Cl, SE2
off Ampleforth Rd 138 C2
Tidal Basin Rd, E16 115 F7
Tideham Ho, SE28
off Merbury Cl 137 G1
Tidenham Gdns, Croy. CR0 202 B3
Tideslea Path, SE28 137 G1
Tideslea Twr, SE28 137 G2
Tideswell Rd, SW15 147 J5
Croydon CR0 204 A3
Tideway Cl, Rich. TW10
off Locksmeade Rd 163 F4
Tideway Ind Est, SW8 33 G6
Tideway Wk, SW8 33 F6
Tidey St, E3 114 A5
Tidford Rd, Well. DA16 157 J2
Tidlock Ho, SE28 137 G2
Tidworth Ho, SE22
off Albrighton Rd 152 B3
Tidworth Rd, E3 114 A4
Tiepigs La, Brom. BR2 205 E2
West Wickham BR4 205 E2
Tierney Rd, SW2 168 E1
Tiger Way, E5 94 E4
Tigris Cl, N9 61 F2
Tilbrook Rd, SE3 155 J3
Tilbury Cl, SE15 37 G7
Pinner HA5 51 F7
Tilbury Rd, E6 116 C2
E10 78 C7
Tildesley Rd, SW15 147 J6
Tile Fm Rd, Orp. BR6 207 G3
Tilehurst Pt, SE2
off Yarnton Way 138 C2
Tilehurst Rd, SW18 167 G1
Sutton SM3 198 B5
Tile Kiln La, N6 92 C1
N13 59 J5
Bexley DA5 177 J2
Tile Yd, E14
off Commercial Rd 113 J6
Tileyard Rd, N7 92 E7
Tilford Gdns, SW19 166 A2
Tilia Cl, Sutt. SM1 198 C5
Tilia Rd, E5
off Clarence Rd 95 E4
Tilia Wk, SW9 151 H4
Tiller Rd, E14 134 A3
Tillett Cl, NW10 88 C6
Tillett Sq, SE16
off Howland Way 133 H2
Tillett Way, E2 13 H3
Tilley Rd, Felt. TW13 160 A1
Tillingbourne Gdns, N3 72 C3
Tillingbourne Way, N3
off Tillingbourne Gdns 72 C4
Tillingham Way, N12 56 D4
Tilling Rd, NW2 89 J1
Tillings Cl, SE5 151 J1
Tilling Way, Wem. HA9 87 G2
Tillman St, E1
off Bigland St 113 E6
Tilloch St, N1
off Carnoustie Dr 93 F7
Tillotson Ct, SW8
off Wandsworth Rd 130 E7
Tillotson Rd, N9 60 C2
Harrow HA3 51 H7
Ilford IG1 80 D7
Tilney Ct, EC1 12 A5
Tilney Dr, Buck.H. IG9 63 G2
Tilney Gdns, N1 94 A6
Tilney Rd, Dag. RM9 101 F6
Southall UB2 122 C4
Tilney St, W1 24 C1
Tilson Cl, SE5 36 D7
Tilson Gdns, SW2 150 E7
Tilson Ho, SW2 150 E7
Tilson Rd, N17 76 D1
Tilston Cl, E11
off Matcham Rd 97 F3
Tilton St, SW6 128 B6
Tiltwood, The, W3 106 C7
Tilt Yd App, SE9 156 C6
Timber Cl, Chis. BR7 192 D2
Timbercroft, Epsom KT19 196 E4
Timbercroft La, SE18 137 H6
Timberdene, NW4 72 A2
Timberdene Av, Ilf. IG6 81 E1
Timberland Cl, SE15
off Peckham Hill St 132 D7
Timberland Rd, E1 113 E6
Timber Mill Way, SW4 150 D3
Timber Pond Rd, SE16 133 G2
Timber St, EC1 11 J5
Timber Wf, E2
off Kingsland Rd 112 C1
Timberwharf Rd, N16 76 D6
Timbrell Pl, SE16
off Silver Wk 133 J1
Time Sq, E8 94 C5
Times Sq, Sutt. SM1 199 E5
Times Sq Shop Cen, Sutt. SM1 *off High St* 199 E5
Timms Cl, Brom. BR1 192 C4
Timothy Cl, SW4 150 C5
Bexleyheath DA6 158 E5
Timothy Ho, Erith DA18
off Kale Rd 138 E2
Timsbury Wk, SW15 165 G1
Tindal St, SW9 151 H1
Tinderbox All, SW14 146 D3
Tine Rd, Chig. IG7 65 H5
Tinniswood Cl, N5
off Drayton Pk 93 G5
Tinsley Cl, SE25 188 E3
Tinsley Rd, E1 113 F5
Tintagel Cres, SE22 152 C4
Tintagel Dr, Stan. HA7 53 G4
Tintagel Gdns, SE22
off Oxonian St 152 C4
Tintern Av, NW9 70 B3
Tintern Cl, SW15 148 B5
SW19 167 F7
Tintern Ct, W13
off Green Man La 104 D7
Tintern Gdns, N14 43 E7
Tintern Path, NW9
off Ruthin Cl 71 E6
Tintern Rd, N22 75 J1
Carshalton SM5 199 G1
Tintern St, SW4 151 E4
Tintern Way, Har. HA2 85 H1
Tinto Rd, E16 115 G4
Tinwell Ms, Borwd. WD6
off Cranes Way 38 C5
Tinworth St, SE11 34 B3
Tippetts Cl, Enf. EN2 43 J1
Tipthorpe Rd, SW11 150 A3
Tipton Dr, Croy. CR0 202 B4
Tiptree Cl, E4
off Mapleton Rd 62 C3
Tiptree Cres, Ilf. IG5 80 D3
Tiptree Dr, Enf. EN2 44 A4
Tiptree Est, Ilf. IG5 80 D3
Tiptree Rd, Ruis. HA4 84 B4
Tirlemont Rd, S.Croy. CR2 201 J7
Tirrell Rd, Croy. CR0 187 J6
Tisbury Ct, W1
off Rupert St 17 H5
Tisbury Rd, SW16 186 E2

Tisdall Pl, SE17 .36 C2
Tissington Ct, SE16 off Rotherhithe New Rd .133 G4
Titchborne Row, W2 .15 H4
Titchfield Rd, NW8 .109 J1
Carshalton SM5 .199 G1
Titchfield Wk, Cars. SM5 off Titchfield Rd .185 G7
Titchwell Rd, SW18 .149 G7
Tite St, SW3 .31 J4
Tithe Barn Cl, Kings.T. KT2 .181 J1
Tithe Barn Way, Nthlt. UB5 .102 B3
Tithe Cl, NW7 .71 G1
Walton-on-Thames KT12 .178 B6
Tithe Fm Av, Har. HA2 .85 G3
Tithe Fm Cl, Har. HA2 .85 G3
Tithe Wk, NW7 .71 G1
Titley Cl, E4 .62 A5
Titmuss Av, SE28 .118 B7
Titmuss St, W12 off Goldhawk Rd .127 J2
Tiverton Av, Ilf. IG5 .80 D3
Tiverton Cl, Croy. CR0 off Exeter Rd .188 C7
Tiverton Dr, SE9 .175 F1
Tiverton Ho, Enf. EN3 .45 G3
Tiverton Rd, N15 .76 A6
N18 .60 B5
NW10 .108 A1
Edgware HA8 .69 J2
Hounslow TW3 .143 J2
Ruislip HA4 .84 A3
Thornton Heath CR7 off Willett Rd .187 G5
Wembley HA0 .105 H2
Tiverton St, SE1 .27 J6
Tiverton Way, NW7 .56 A7
Chessington KT9 .195 F5
Tivoli Ct, SE16 .133 J2
Tivoli Gdns, SE18 .136 B4
Tivoli Rd, N8 .74 D5
SE27 .169 J5
Hounslow TW4 .142 E4
Toad La, Houns. TW4 .143 F4
Tobacco Dock, E1 .112 E7
Tobacco Quay, E1 off Wapping La .113 E7
Tobago St, E14 off Manilla St .134 A2
Tobin Cl, NW3 .91 H7
Toby La, E1 .113 H4
Toby Way, Surb. KT5 .196 B2
Todds Wk, N7 off Andover Rd .93 F2
Todhunter Ter, Barn. EN5 off Prospect Rd .40 D4
Tokenhouse Yd, EC2 .20 B3
Token Yd, SW15 off Montserrat Rd .148 B4
TOKYNGTON, Wem. HA9 .88 B6
Tokyngton Av, Wem. HA9 .88 A6
Toland Sq, SW15 .147 G5
Tolcarne Dr, Pnr. HA5 .66 B3
Toley Av, Wem. HA9 .69 H7
Tolhurst Dr, W10 off Beethoven St .108 B3
Tollbridge Cl, W10 off Kensal Rd .108 B4
Tollesbury Gdns, Ilf. IG6 .81 G3
Tollet St, E1 .113 G4
Tollgate Dr, SE21 .170 B2
Hayes UB4 .102 D7
Tollgate Gdns, NW6 .6 A1
Tollgate Ho, NW6 .6 A1
Tollgate Rd, E6 .116 A5
E16 .115 J5
Tollhouse Way, N19 .92 C2
Tollington Pk, N4 .93 F2
Tollington Pl, N4 .93 F2
Tollington Rd, N7 .93 F4
Tollington Way, N7 .92 E3
Tolmers Sq, NW1 .9 G5
Tolpuddle Av, E13 off Rochester Av .115 J1
Tolpuddle St, N1 .10 E1
Tolsford Rd, E5 .95 E5
Tolson Rd, Islw. TW7 .144 D3
Tolverne Rd, SW20 .183 J1
TOLWORTH, Surb. KT6 .196 A2
Tolworth Bdy, Surb. KT6 .196 B1
Tolworth Cl, Surb. KT6 .196 B1
Tolworth Gdns, Rom. RM6 .82 D5
Tolworth Junct, Surb. KT5 .196 B2
Tolworth Pk Rd, Surb. KT6 .195 J2
Tolworth Ri N, Surb. KT5 off Elmbridge Av .182 C7
Tolworth Ri S, Surb. KT5 off Warren Dr S .196 C1
Tolworth Rd, Surb. KT6 .195 H2
Tolworth Twr, Surb. KT6 .196 B2
Tomahawk Gdns, Nthlt. UB5 off Javelin Way .102 D3
Tom Coombs Cl, SE9 .156 B4
Tom Cribb Business Cen, SE28 off Tom Cribb Rd .137 G3
Tom Cribb Rd, SE28 .137 F3
Tom Gros Cl, E15 off Maryland St .96 D5
Tom Hood Cl, E15 off Maryland St .96 D5
Tom Jenkinson Rd, E16 .135 G1
Tomlins Gro, E3 .114 A3
Tomlinson Cl, E2 .13 G4
W4 .126 B5
Tomlins Orchard, Bark. IG11 .117 F1
Tomlins Ter, E14 off Rhodeswell Rd .113 J5
Tomlins Wk, N7 off Briset Way .93 F2
Tom Mann Cl, Bark. IG11 .117 H1
Tom Nolan Cl, E15 .114 E2
Tompion Ho, EC1 off Percival St .11 H5
Tompion St, EC1 .11 G4
Tom Smith Cl, SE10 off Maze Hill .134 E6
Tomswood Ct, Ilf. IG6 .81 F1
Tomswood Hill, Ilf. IG6 .65 E7
Tomswood Rd, Chig. IG7 .64 D6
Tom Thumbs Arch, E3 off Malmesbury Rd .114 A2
Tom Williams Ho, SW6 off Clem Attlee Ct .128 C6
Tonbridge Cres, Har. HA3 .69 H4
Tonbridge Ho, SE25 .188 D3
Tonbridge Rd, W.Mol. KT8 .179 E4
Tonbridge St, WC1 .10 A3
Tonbridge Wk, WC1 off Bidborough St .10 A3
Tonfield Rd, Sutt. SM3 .198 C1
Tonge Cl, Beck. BR3 .190 A5
Tonsley Hill, SW18 .149 E5
Tonsley Pl, SW18 .149 E5
Tonsley Rd, SW18 .149 E5
Tonsley St, SW18 .149 E5
Tonstall Rd, Mitch. CR4 .186 A2
Tony Cannell Ms, E3 off Maplin St .113 J3
Tooke Cl, Pnr. HA5 .66 E1
Tookey Cl, Har. HA3 .69 J7
Took's Ct, EC4 .19 E3
Tooley St, SE1 .28 C1
Toorack Rd, Har. HA3 .68 A2
Tooting Bec, SW17 .167 J3
Tooting Bec Gdns, SW16 .168 D4
Tooting Bec Rd, SW16 .168 A3
SW17 .168 A3
Tooting Bdy, SW17 .167 H4
TOOTING GRAVENEY, SW17 .167 H6
Tooting Gro, SW17 .167 H5
Tooting High St, SW17 .167 H6
Tooting Mkt, SW17 off Tooting High St .167 J4
Tootswood Rd, Brom. BR2 .190 E5
Topaz Ct, E11 off High Rd Leytonstone .97 E1
Topaz Ho, E15 off Romford Rd .97 F6
Topaz Wk, NW2 off Marble Dr .72 A7
Topcliffe Dr, Orp. BR6 .207 G4
Topham Sq, N17 .75 J1
Topham St, EC1 .11 E5
Top Ho Ri, E4 off Parkhill Rd .46 C7
Topiary Sq, Rich. TW9 .145 J3
Topley St, SE9 .156 A4
Topmast Pt, E14 .134 A2
Top Pk, Beck. BR3 .190 E5
Topp Wk, NW2 .89 J2
Topsfield Cl, N8 off Wolseley Rd .74 D5
Topsfield Par, N8 off Tottenham La .75 E5
Topsfield Rd, N8 .74 E5
Topsham Rd, SW17 .167 J3
Torbay Rd, NW6 .90 C7
Harrow HA2 .84 E2
Torbay St, NW1 off Hawley Rd .92 B7
Torbitt Way, Ilf. IG2 .81 J5
Torbridge Cl, Edg. HA8 .53 H7
Torbrook Cl, Bex. DA5 .159 E6
Torcross Dr, SE23 .171 F2
Torcross Rd, Ruis. HA4 .84 B3
Tor Gdns, W8 .128 D2
Tor Gro, SE28 .137 H1
Tormead Cl, Sutt. SM1 .198 D6
Tormount Rd, SE18 .137 H6
Tornay Ho, N1 off Priory Grn Est .10 C1
Toronto Av, E12 .98 C4
Toronto Rd, Ilf. IG1 .99 E1
Torquay Gdns, Ilf. IG4 .80 A4
Torquay St, W2 .14 A2
Torrance Cl, SE7 .136 A6
Torrens Rd, E15 .97 F6
SW2 .151 F5
Torrens Sq, E15 .97 E6
Torrens St, EC1 .11 F2
Torres Sq, E14 off Maritime Quay .134 A5
Torre Wk, Cars. SM5 .199 H1
Torrey Dr, SW9 off Overton Rd .151 G2
Torriano Av, NW5 .92 D5
Torriano Cotts, NW5 off Torriano Av .92 D5
Torriano Ms, NW5 .92 C5
Torridge Gdns, SE15 .153 F4
Torridge Rd, Th.Hth. CR7 .187 H5
Torridon Ho, NW6 .6 A2
Torridon Rd, SE6 .172 D1
SE13 .154 D7
Torrington Av, N12 .57 G5
Torrington Cl, N12 .57 G4
Esher (Clay.) KT10 .194 B6
Torrington Dr, Har. HA2 .85 H4
Loughton IG10 .49 F4
Torrington Gdns, N11 .58 C6
Greenford (Perivale) UB6 .87 F7
Loughton IG10 .49 F4
Torrington Gro, N12 .57 H5
Torrington Pk, N12 .57 F5
Torrington Pl, E1 .29 J1
WC1 .17 G1
Torrington Rd, E18 .79 G3
Dagenham RM8 .101 F1
Esher (Clay.) KT10 .194 B6
Greenford (Perivale) UB6 .105 F1
Torrington Sq, WC1 .9 J6
Croydon CR0 off Tavistock Gro .188 A7
Torrington Way, Mord. SM4 .184 D6
Tor Rd, Well. DA16 .158 C1
Torr Rd, SE20 .171 G7
Torver Rd, Har. HA1 .68 B4
Torver Way, Orp. BR6 .207 G3
Torwood Rd, SW15 .147 G5
Tothill Ho, SW1 off Page St .33 J1
Tothill St, SW1 .25 H4
Totnes Rd, Well. DA16 .138 B7
Totnes Wk, N2 .73 G4
Tottan Ter, E1 .113 G6
Tottenhall Rd, N13 .59 G6
TOTTENHAM, N17 .76 B1
Tottenham Ct Rd, W1 .9 G6
Tottenham Grn E, N15 .76 C4
TOTTENHAM HALE, N17 .76 E3
Tottenham Hale, N17 .76 C4
Tottenham Hale Retail Pk, N15 .76 D4
★ Tottenham Hotspur FC, N17 .60 C7
Tottenham La, N8 .74 E5
Tottenham Ms, W1 .17 G1
Tottenham Rd, N1 .94 B6
Tottenham St, W1 .17 G2
Totterdown St, SW17 .167 J4
TOTTERIDGE, N20 .56 B1
Totteridge Common, N20 .55 G2
Totteridge Grn, N20 .56 D2
Totteridge Ho, SW11 .149 G2
Totteridge La, N20 .56 D2
Totteridge Village, N20 .56 B1
Totternhoe Cl, Har. HA3 .69 F5
Totton Rd, Th.Hth. CR7 .187 G3
Toucan Cl, NW10 .106 A3
Toulmin St, SE1 .27 J4
Toulon St, SE5 .35 J7
Tournay Rd, SW6 .128 C7
Tours Pas, SW11 .149 G4
Toussaint Wk, SE16 .29 J5
Tovil Cl, SE20 .188 D2
Tovy Ho, SE1 .37 H4
Towcester Rd, E3 .114 B4
Tower 42, EC2 .20 D3
Tower Br, E1 .29 F2
SE1 .29 F2
Tower Br App, E1 .29 F1
★ Tower Br Exhib, SE1 .29 F2
Tower Br Ms, Har. HA1 off Greenford Rd .86 C4
Tower Br Piazza, SE1 .29 F2
Tower Br Rd, SE1 .28 D6
Tower Br Wf, E1 .29 H2
Tower Bldgs, E1 off Brewhouse La .133 E1
Tower Cl, NW3 off Lyndhurst Rd .91 G5
SE20 .170 E7
Ilford IG6 .65 E6
Orpington BR6 .207 J2
Tower Ct, WC2 .18 A4
Tower Gdns, Esher (Clay.) KT10 .194 D7
Tower Gdns Rd, N17 .75 J1
Tower Hamlets Rd, E7 .97 F4
E17 .78 A3
Tower Hill, EC3 .21 F6
Tower Hill Ter, EC3 off Byward St .21 E6
Tower La, Wem. HA9 off Main Dr .87 G3
Tower Ms, E17 .78 A4
★ Tower Millennium Pier, EC3 .29 E1
Tower Mill Rd, SE15 .36 D6
★ Tower of London, EC3 .21 F6
Tower Pl E, EC3 .20 E6
Tower Pl W, EC3 .20 E6
Tower Pt, Enf. EN2 .44 A4
Tower Ri, Rich. TW9 off Jocelyn Rd .145 H3
Tower Rd, NW10 .89 G7
Belvedere DA17 .139 J4
Bexleyheath DA7 .159 H4
Orpington BR6 .207 J2
Twickenham TW1 .162 C3
Tower Royal, EC4 .20 A5
Towers Pl, Rich. TW9 .145 H5
Towers Rd, Pnr. HA5 .66 E1
Southall UB1 .103 G4
Tower St, WC2 .17 J4
Tower Ter, N22 off Mayes Rd .75 F2
SE4 off Foxberry Rd .153 H4
Tower Vw, Croy. CR0 .189 G7
Towfield Rd, Felt. TW13 .161 F2
Towing Path Wk, N1 .10 A1
Town, The, Enf. EN2 .44 A3
Towncourt Cres, Orp. BR5 .193 F5
Towncourt La, Orp. BR5 .193 G6
Town Ct Path, N4 .93 J1
Towney Mead, Nthlt. UB5 .103 F2
Towney Mead Ct, Nthlt. UB5 off Towney Mead .103 F2
Town Fm Way, Stai. (Stanw.) TW19 off Town La .140 A7
Townfield Rd, Hayes UB3 .121 J1
Townfield Sq, Hayes UB3 .121 J1
Townfield Way, Islw. TW7 .144 D2
Town Hall App, N16 off Milton Gro .94 B4
Town Hall App Rd, N15 .76 C4
Town Hall Av, W4 .126 D5
Town Hall Rd, SW11 .149 J3
Townholm Cres, W7 .124 C3
Town La, Stai. (Stanw.) TW19 .140 A6
Townley Ct, E15 .97 F6
Townley Rd, SE22 .152 B5
Bexleyheath DA6 .159 F5
Townley St, SE17 .36 B3
Townmead Business Cen, SW6 off William Morris Way .149 F3
Town Meadow, Brent. TW8 .125 G6
Townmead Rd, SW6 .149 F2
Richmond TW9 .146 B2
Town Quay, Bark. IG11 .117 E1
Town Rd, N9 .60 E2
Townsend Av, N14 .58 D4
Townsend Ind Est, NW10 .106 D2
Townsend La, NW9 .70 D7
Townsend Ms, SW18 off Waynflete St .167 F2
Townsend Rd, N15 .76 C5
Southall UB1 .122 E1
Townsend St, SE17 .36 C2
Townsend Yd, N6 .92 B1
Townshend Cl, Sid. DA14 .176 B6
Townshend Est, NW8 .7 G1
Townshend Rd, NW8 .109 H1
Chislehurst BR7 .174 E5
Richmond TW9 .145 J4
Townshend Ter, Rich. TW9 .145 J4
Townson Av, Nthlt. UB5 .102 A3
Townson Way, Nthlt. UB5 off Townson Av .102 A2
Town Sq, Bark. IG11 off Clockhouse Av .117 F1
Towpath Rd, N18 .61 G6
Towpath Wk, E9 .95 J5
Towpath Way, Croy. CR0 .188 C6
Towton Rd, SE27 .169 J2
Toynbec Cl, Chis. BR7 off Beechwood Ri .175 E4
Toynbee Rd, SW20 .184 B1
Toynbee St, E1 .21 F2
Toyne Way, N6 off Gaskell Rd .73 J6
Tracey Av, NW2 .89 J5
Tracy Ct, Stan. HA7 .53 F7
Trade Cl, N13 .59 G4
Trader Rd, E6 .116 E6
Tradescant Rd, SW8 .131 E7
Trading Est Rd, NW10 .106 C4
Trafalgar Av, N17 .60 B6
SE15 .37 G4
Worcester Park KT4 .198 A1
Trafalgar Business Cen, Bark. IG11 .117 J4
Trafalgar Cl, SE16 off Greenland Quay .133 H4
Trafalgar Ct, E1 off Glamis Rd .113 F7
Trafalgar Gdns, E1 .113 G5
W8 .22 A5
Trafalgar Gro, SE10 .134 D6
Trafalgar Ms, E9 .95 J6
Trafalgar Pl, E11 .79 G4
N18 .60 D5
Trafalgar Rd, SE10 .134 D6
SW19 .167 E7
Twickenham TW2 .162 A2
Trafalgar Sq, SW1 .25 J1
WC2 .25 J1
Trafalgar St, SE17 .36 B3

Trafalgar Ter, Har. HA1
off Nelson Rd 86 B1
Trafalgar Trd Est, Enf. EN3 45 H4
Trafalgar Way, E14 134 C1
Croydon CR0 201 F2
Trafford Cl, Ilf. IG6 65 J6
Trafford Rd, Th.Hth. CR7 187 F5
Trahorn Cl, E1 112 D4
Tralee Ct, SE16
off Masters Dr 133 E5
Tram Cl, SE24
off Hinton Rd 151 H3
Tramsheds Ind Est, Croy.
CR0 186 D7
Tramway Av, E15 96 E7
N9 45 E7
Tramway Cl, SE20 189 F1
Tramway Path, Mitch.
CR4 185 J5
Tranby Pl, E9
off Homerton High St 95 G5
Tranley Ms, NW3
off Fleet Rd 91 H5
Tranmere Rd, N9 44 C7
SW18 167 F2
Twickenham TW2 143 H7
Tranquil Pas, SE3
off Tranquil Vale 155 F2
Tranquil Vale, SE3 155 E2
Transept St, NW1 15 G2
Transmere Cl, Orp. BR5 193 F6
Transmere Rd, Orp. BR5 193 F6
Transom Cl, SE16
off Plough Way 133 H4
Transom Sq, E14 134 B4
Transport Av, Brent. TW8 124 D5
Tranton Rd, SE16 29 J5
Trappes Ho, SE16
off Manor Est 132 E4
Traps Hill, Loug. IG10 48 C3
Traps La, N.Mal. KT3 182 E1
Travellers Way, Houns.
TW4 142 C2
Travers Cl, E17 77 G1
Travers Rd, N7 93 G3
Treacy Cl, Bushey
(Bushey Hth) WD23 51 J2
Treadgold St, W11 108 A7
Treadway St, E2 112 E2
Treasury Cl, Wall. SM6 200 D5
Treaty Cen, Houns. TW3 143 H3
Treaty Rd, Houns. TW3
off Hanworth Rd 143 H3
Treaty St, N1 111 F1
Trebeck St, W1 24 D1
Trebovir Rd, SW5 128 D5
Treby St, E3 113 J4
Trecastle Way, N7
off Carleton Rd 92 D4
Tredegar Ms, E3
off Tredegar Ter 113 J3
Tredegar Rd, E3 113 J2
N11 58 D7
Tredegar Sq, E3 113 J3
Tredegar Ter, E3 113 J3
Trederwen Rd, E8 112 D1
Tredown Rd, SE26 171 F5
Tredwell Cl, SW2
off Hillside Rd 169 F2
Bromley BR2 192 B4
Tredwell Rd, SE27 169 H4
Tree Cl, Rich. TW10 163 G1
Treen Av, SW13 147 F3
Tree Rd, E16 115 J6
Treeside Cl, West Dr. UB7 120 A4
Treetops Cl, SE2 139 E5
Treetops Vw, Loug. IG10 48 A7
Treeview Cl, SE19 188 B1
Treewall Gdns, Brom.
BR1 173 H4
Trefgarne Rd, Dag. RM10 101 G2
Trefil Wk, N7 93 E4
Trefoil Ho, Erith DA18
off Kale Rd 138 E2
Trefoil Rd, SW18 149 F5
Tregaron Av, N8 74 E6
Tregaron Gdns, N.Mal. KT3
off Avenue Rd 183 E4
Tregarvon Rd, SW11 150 A4
Tregenna Av, Har. HA2 85 F4
Tregenna Cl, N14 42 C5
Tregenna Ct, Har. HA2 85 G4
Tregony Rd, Orp. BR6 207 J4
Trego Rd, E9 96 A7
Tregothnan Rd, SW9 151 E3
Tregunter Rd, SW10 30 C5
Trehearn Rd, Ilf. IG6 65 G7
Treherne Ct, SW9
off Eythorne Rd 151 H1
SW17 168 A4
Trehern Rd, SW14 146 D3
Trehurst St, E5 95 H5
Trelawney Cl, E17
off Orford Rd 78 B4
Trelawney Est, E9 95 F6
Trelawney Rd, Ilf. IG6 65 G7
Trelawn Rd, E10 96 C3
SW2 151 G5
Trellick Twr, W10 108 C4
Trellis Sq, E3
off Malmesbury Rd 113 J3
Treloar Gdns, SE19
off Hancock Rd 170 A6
Tremadoc Rd, SW4 150 D4
Tremaine Cl, SE4 154 A2
Tremaine Rd, SE20 189 E2
Trematon Pl, Tedd. TW11 163 F7
Tremlett Gro, N19 92 C3
Tremlett Ms, N19 92 C3
Trenance Gdns, Ilf. IG3 100 A3
Trenchard Av, Ruis. HA4 84 B4
Trenchard Cl, NW9
off Fulbeck Dr 70 E1
Stanmore HA7 52 D6
Trenchard Ct, Mord. SM4
off Green La 184 D6
Trenchard St, SE10 134 D5
Trenchold St, SW8 34 A6
Trenholme Cl, SE20 171 E7
Trenholme Rd, SE20 170 E7
Trenholme Ter, SE20 170 E7
Trenmar Gdns, NW10 107 H3
Trent Av, W5 125 F3
Trentbridge Cl, Ilf. IG6 65 J6
Trent Gdns, N14 42 B6
Trentham St, SW18 166 D1
★ **Trent Park Country Pk**,
Barn. EN4 42 A2
Trent Rd, SW2 151 F5
Buckhurst Hill IG9 63 H1
Trent Way, Wor.Pk. KT4 197 J3
Trentwood Side, Enf. EN2 43 F3
Treport St, SW18 149 E7
Tresco Cl, Brom. BR1 172 E6
Trescoe Gdns, Har. HA2 67 E7
Tresco Gdns, Ilf. IG3 100 A2
Tresco Rd, SE15 153 E4
Tresham Cres, NW8 7 G5
Tresham Rd, Bark. IG11 99 J7
Tresham Wk, E9
off Churchill Wk 95 F5
Tresilian Av, N21 43 F5
Tressell Cl, N1
off Sebbon St 93 H7
Tressillian Cres, SE4 154 A3
Tressillian Rd, SE4 153 J4
Trestis Cl, Hayes UB4
off Jollys La 102 E5
Treswell Rd, Dag. RM9 119 E1
Tretawn Gdns, NW7 55 E4
Tretawn Pk, NW7 55 E4
Trevanion Rd, W14 128 B5
Treve Av, Har. HA1 67 J7
Trevelyan Av, E12 98 C4
Trevelyan Cres, Har. HA3 69 G7
Trevelyan Gdns, NW10 107 J1
Trevelyan Ho, E2
off Morpeth St 113 G3
Trevelyan Rd, E15 97 E4
SW17 167 H5
Treveris St, SE1 27 G2
Treverton St, W10 108 A4
Treves Cl, N21 43 F5
Treville St, SW15 147 H7
Treviso Rd, SE23
off Farren Rd 171 H2
Trevithick Ho, SE16 133 E4
Trevithick St, SE8 134 A5
Trevone Gdns, Pnr. HA5 67 E6
Trevor Cl, Barn. (E.Barn.)
EN4 41 G5
Bromley BR2 191 F7
Harrow HA3
off Kenton La 52 C7
Isleworth TW7 144 C5
Northolt UB5 102 C2
Trevor Gdns, Edg. HA8 70 D1
Northolt UB5 102 C2
Trevor Pl, SW7 23 H4
Trevor Rd, SW19 166 B7
Edgware HA8 70 D1
Hayes UB3 121 H2
Woodford Green IG8 63 G7
Trevor Sq, SW7 23 J4
Trevor St, SW7 23 H4
Trevor Wk, SW7
off Trevor Sq 23 J4
Trevose Rd, E17 78 D1
Trevose Way, Wat. WD19 50 C3
Trewenna Dr, Chess. KT9 195 G5
Trewince Rd, SW20 183 J1
Trewint St, SW18 167 F2
Trewsbury Ho, SE2
off Hartslock Dr 138 D2
Trewsbury Rd, SE26 171 G5
Triandra Way, Hayes UB4 102 D5
Triangle, The, EC1 11 H5
N13 *off Green Las* 59 F4
Barking IG11
off Tanner St 99 F6
Hampton TW12
off High St 179 J1
Kingston upon Thames
KT1 *off Kenley Rd* 182 C2
Triangle Business Cen,
NW10
off Enterprise Way 107 G3
Triangle Ct, E16
off Tollgate Rd 116 A5
Triangle Est, SE11 35 E4
Triangle Pas, Barn. EN4
off Station App 41 F4
Triangle Pl, SW4 150 D4
Triangle Rd, E8 112 E1
Triangle Wks, N9
off Centre Way 61 F2
Tricorn Ho, SE28
off Miles Dr 137 G1
Trident Gdns, Nthlt. UB5
off Jetstar Way 102 D3
Trident Ho, SE28
off Merbury Rd 137 G1
Trident St, SE16 133 G4
Trident Way, Sthl. UB2 122 B3
Trig La, EC4 19 J5
Trigon Rd, SW8 34 D7
Trilby Rd, SE23 171 G2
Trimmer Wk, Brent. TW8 125 H6
Trim St, SE14 133 J6
Trinder Gdns, N19 93 E1
Trinder Ms, Tedd. TW11 162 D5
Trinder Rd, N19 93 E1
Barnet EN5 39 J5
Tring Av, W5 125 J1
Southall UB1 103 F6
Wembley HA9 88 A6
Tring Cl, Ilf. IG2 81 F5
Trinidad St, E14 113 J7
Trinity Av, N2 73 G3
Enfield EN1 44 C6
Trinity Buoy Wf, E14 115 F7
Trinity Business Pk, E4
off Trinity Way 61 J6
Trinity Ch Pas, SW13 127 H6
Trinity Ch Rd, SW13 127 H6
Trinity Ch Sq, SE1 28 A5
Trinity Cl, E8 94 C6
E11 97 E2
NW3
off Willoughby Rd 91 G4
SE13 154 D4
SW4 *off The Pavement* 150 C4
Bromley BR2 206 B1
Hounslow TW4 143 E4
Trinity Cotts, Rich. TW9
off Trinity Rd 145 J3
Trinity Ct, N1
off Downham Rd 94 B7
NW2 *off Anson Rd* 89 J5
SE7 *off Charlton La* 136 A4
Trinity Cres, SW17 167 J2
Trinity Gdns, E16
off Cliff Wk 115 F5
SW9 151 F4
Trinity Gro, SE10 154 C1
★ **Trinity Ho**, EC3 21 E5
Trinity Ho, SE1
off Bath Ter 28 A5
Trinity Ms, SE20 189 E1
W10
off Cambridge Gdns 108 A6
Trinity Path, SE26 171 F3
Trinity Pl, EC3 21 F6
Bexleyheath DA6 159 F4
Trinity Ri, SW2 169 G1
Trinity Rd, N2 73 G3
N22 75 E1
SW17 167 J2
SW18 149 G5
SW19 166 D6
Ilford IG6 81 F3
Richmond TW9 145 J3
Southall UB1 122 E1
Trinity Sq, EC3 21 E6
Trinity St, E16
off Vincent St 115 G5
SE1 28 A4
Enfield EN2 43 J2
Trinity Wk, NW3 91 F6
Trinity Way, E4 61 J6
W3 107 E7
Trio Pl, SE1 28 A4
Tristan Sq, SE3 155 E3
Tristram Cl, E17 78 D3
Tristram Dr, N9 60 D3
Tristram Rd, Brom. BR1 173 F4
Triton Sq, NW1 9 F5
Tritton Av, Croy. CR0 200 E4
Tritton Rd, SE21 170 A3
Triumph Cl, Hayes
(Harling.) UB3 121 F7
Triumph Ho, Bark. IG11 118 A3
Triumph Rd, E6 116 C6
Triumph Trd Est, N17 60 D6
Trojan Way, Croy. CR0 201 F3
Troon Cl, SE16
off Masters Dr 133 E5
SE28 *off Fairway Dr* 118 D6
Troon St, E1
off White Horse Rd 113 H6
Trosley Rd, Belv. DA17 139 G6
Trossachs Rd, SE22 152 B5
Trothy Rd, SE1 37 J1
Trott Rd, N10 57 J7
Trott St, SW11 149 H1
Trotwood, Chig. IG7 65 G6
Troughton Rd, SE7 135 H5
Troutbeck Rd, SE14 153 H1
Trout Rd, West Dr. UB7 120 A1
Trouville Rd, SW4 150 C6
Trowbridge Est, E9
off Osborne Rd 95 J6
Trowbridge Rd, E9 95 J6
Trowlock Av, Tedd. TW11 163 F6
Trowlock Island, Tedd.
TW11 163 G5
Trowlock Way, Tedd.
TW11 163 G6
Troy Ct, SE18
off Wilmount St 137 E4
W8 *off Kensington*
High St 128 D3
Troy Rd, SE19 170 A6
Troy Town, SE15 152 D3
Trubshaw Rd, Sthl. UB2
off Havelock Rd 123 H3
Trueman Cl, Edg. HA8 54 C7
Truesdale Rd, E6 116 C6
Trulock Ct, N17 60 D7
Trulock Rd, N17 60 D7
Truman's Rd, N16 94 B5
Trumpers Way, W7 124 B3
Trumpington Rd, E7 97 F4
Trump St, EC2 20 A4
Trundlers Way, Bushey
(Bushey Hth) WD23 52 B1
Trundle St, SE1 27 J3
Trundleys Rd, SE8 133 G5
Trundleys Ter, SE8 133 G4
Truro Gdns, Ilf. IG1 80 B7
Truro Rd, E17 77 J4
N22 59 E7
Truro St, NW5 92 A6
Truslove Rd, SE27 169 G5
Trussley Rd, W6 127 J3
Trust Wk, SE21
off Peabody Hill 169 H1
Tryfan Cl, Ilf. IG4 80 A5
Tryon Cres, E9 113 F1
Tryon St, SW3 31 J3
Trystings Cl, Esher (Clay.)
KT10 194 D6
Tuam Rd, SE18 137 G6
Tubbenden Cl, Orp. BR6 207 H2
Tubbenden Dr, Orp. BR6 207 G4
Tubbenden La, Orp. BR6 207 H3
Tubbenden La S, Orp.
BR6 207 G5
Tubbs Rd, NW10 107 F2
Tudor Av, Hmptn. TW12 161 G6
Worcester Park KT4 197 H3
Tudor Cl, N6 74 C7
NW3 91 H5
NW7 55 G6
NW9 88 C2
SW2 151 F6
Chessington KT9 195 H5
Chigwell IG7 64 D4
Chislehurst BR7 192 C1
Pinner HA5 66 A5
Sutton SM3 198 A5
Wallington SM6 200 C7
Woodford Green IG8 63 H5
Tudor Ct, E17 77 H7
Feltham TW13 160 C4
Tudor Ct N, Wem. HA9 88 A5
Tudor Ct S, Wem. HA9 88 A5
Tudor Cres, Enf. EN2 43 H1
Ilford IG6 65 E6
Tudor Dr, Kings.T. KT2 163 H5
Morden SM4 184 A6
Tudor Est, NW10 106 B2
Tudor Gdns, NW9 88 C2
SW13 *off Treen Av* 147 E3
W3 106 A6
Harrow HA3
off Tudor Rd 68 A2
Twickenham TW1 162 C1
West Wickham BR4 204 C3
Tudor Gro, E9 95 F7
N20 *off Church Cres* 57 H3
Tudor Ho, Surb. KT6
off Lenelby Rd 196 A1
Tudor Pl, Mitch. CR4 167 H7
Tudor Rd, E4 62 B6
E6 115 J1
E9 113 E1
N9 45 E7
SE19 170 C7
SE25 189 E5
Barking IG11 117 J1
Barnet EN5 40 D3
Tudor Rd, Beckenham
BR3 190 B3
Hampton TW12 161 G7
Harrow HA3 68 A2
Hounslow TW3 144 A4
Kingston upon Thames
KT2 164 A7
Pinner HA5 66 C2
Southall UB1 102 E7
Tudor St, EC4 19 F5
Tudor Wk, Bex. DA5 159 E6
Tudor Way, N14 58 D1
W3 126 A2
Orpington BR5 193 G6
Tudor Well Cl, Stan. HA7 53 E5
Tudway Rd, SE3 155 H3
TUFNELL PARK, N7 92 D4
Tufnell Pk Rd, N7 92 C4
N19 92 C4
Tufter Rd, Chig. IG7 65 J5
Tufton Gdns, W.Mol.
KT8 179 H2
Tufton Rd, E4 62 A4
Tufton St, SW1 25 J5
Tugboat St, SE28 137 H2
Tugela Rd, Croy. CR0 188 A6
Tugela St, SE6 171 J2
Tugmutton Cl, Orp. BR6 207 E4
Tuilerie St, E2 13 H1
Tulip Cl, E6
off Bradley Stone Rd 116 C5
Croydon CR0 203 G1
Hampton TW12
off Partridge Rd 161 F6

Tulip Cl, Southall UB2
off Chevy Rd **123** J2
Tulip Ct, Pnr. HA5 ....**66** C3
Tulip Gdns, Ilf. IG1 ....**98** E6
Tulip Way, West Dr. UB7 ..**120** A4
Tull St, Mitch. CR4 ......**185** J7
Tulse Cl, Beck. BR3 ......**190** C3
TULSE HILL, SE21 ....**169** J1
Tulse Hill, SW2 ....**151** G6
Tulse Hill Est, SW2 ......**151** G6
Tulsemere Rd, SE27 .....**169** J2
Tumbling Bay, Walt.
KT12 ....**178** A6
Tummons Gdns, SE25 ...**188** B2
Tump Ho, SE28 ....**137** H1
Tuncombe Rd, N18 ....**60** B4
Tunis Rd, W12 ....**127** H1
Tunley Grn, E14
off Burdett Rd **113** J5
Tunley Rd, NW10 ....**106** E1
SW17 ....**168** A1
Tunmarsh La, E13 ....**115** J3
Tunnan Leys, E6 ....**116** D6
Tunnel Av, SE10 ....**134** D2
Tunnel Gdns, N11 ....**58** C7
Tunnel Rd, SE16
off St. Marychurch St .**133** F2
Tunstall Cl, Orp. BR5 ....**207** H4
Tunstall Rd, SW9 ....**151** F4
Croydon CR0 ....**202** B1
Tunstall Wk, Brent. TW8 ..**125** H6
Tunstock Way, Belv.
DA17 ....**139** E3
Tunworth Cl, NW9 ....**70** C6
Tunworth Cres, SW15 ....**147** F6
Tun Yd, SW8
off Peardon St **150** B2
Tupelo Rd, E10 ....**96** B2
Tuppy St, SE28 ....**137** F3
Turenne Cl, SW18 ....**149** F4
Turin Rd, N9 ....**45** F7
Turin St, E2 ....**13** H4
Turkey Oak Cl, SE19 .....**188** B1
Turk's Head Yd, EC1 ......**19** G1
Turks Row, SW3 ....**32** A3
Turle Rd, N4 ....**93** F1
SW16 ....**186** E2
Turlewray Cl, N4 ....**93** F1
Turley Cl, E15 ....**115** E1
Turnagain La, EC4 ....**19** G3
Turnage Rd, Dag. RM8 ....**100** E1
Turnberry Cl, NW4 ....**72** A2
SE16 *off Ryder Dr* **133** E5
Turnberry Ct, Wat. WD19 ..**50** C3
Turnberry Quay, E14
off Pepper St **134** B3
Turnberry Way, Orp.
BR6 ....**207** G1
Turnbury Cl, SE28 ....**118** D6
Turnchapel Ms, SW4
off Cedars Rd **150** B3
Turner Av, N15 ....**76** B4
Mitcham CR4 ....**185** J1
Twickenham TW2 ......**161** J3
Turner Cl, NW11 ....**72** E6
SW9 ....**151** H1
Wembley HA0 ....**87** G5
Turner Ct, N15
off St. Ann's Rd **76** A5
Turner Dr, NW11 ....**72** E6
Turner Ho, E14
off Cassilis Rd **134** A2
Turner Ms, Sutt. SM2 ....**198** E7
Turner Pl, SW11
off Cairns Rd **149** H5
Turner Rd, E17 ....**78** C3
Edgware HA8 ....**69** J3
New Malden KT3 .....**182** D7
Turners Cl, N20
off Oakleigh Rd N **57** J3
Turners Meadow Way,
Beck. BR3 ....**189** J1
Turners Rd, E3 ....**113** J5
Turner St, E1 ....**112** E5
E16 ....**115** F6
Turners Way, Croy. CR0 ..**201** G2
Turners Wd, NW11 ....**91** F1
Turneville Rd, W14 ....**128** C6
Turney Rd, SE21 ....**152** A7
Turnham Grn Ter, W4 ....**126** E4
Turnham Grn Ter Ms, W4
off Turnham Grn Ter ..**126** E4
Turnham Rd, SE4 ....**153** H5
Turnmill St, EC1 ....**11** F6
Turnpike Cl, SE8
off Amersham Vale ...**133** J7
Turnpike Ho, EC1 ....**11** H4
Turnpike La, N8 ....**75** F4
Sutton SM1 ....**199** F5
Turnpike Link, Croy. CR0 .**202** B2
Turnpike Ms, N8 ....**75** G4
Turnpike Way, Islw. TW7 ..**144** D1
Turnpin La, SE10 ....**134** C6
Turnstone Cl, E13 ....**115** G3
NW9 *off Kestrel Cl* **71** E2
Turpentine La, SW1 ......**32** E3
Turpington Cl, Brom.
BR2 ....**192** B6
Turpington La, Brom.
BR2 ....**192** B7
Turpin Ho, SW11
off Strasburg Rd **150** B1
Turpin Rd, Felt. TW14
off Staines Rd **141** J6
Turpins La, Wdf.Grn. IG8 ..**64** C5
Turpin Way, N19 ....**92** D2
Wallington SM6 ......**200** B7
Turquand St, SE17 ....**36** A2
Turret Gro, SW4 ....**150** C3
Turton Rd, Wem. HA0 .....**87** H5
Turville St, E2 ....**13** F5
Tuscan Ho, E2 ....**113** F3
Tuscan Rd, SE18 ....**137** G5
Tuscany Ho, E17
off Sherwood Cl **77** J2
Tuskar St, SE10 ....**134** E5
Tustin Est, SE15 ....**133** F6
Tuttlebee La, Buck.H. IG9 ..**63** G2
Tweeddale Rd, Cars.
SM5 ....**199** G1
Tweedmouth Rd, E13 ....**115** H2
Tweedy Cl, Enf. EN1 ......**44** C5
Tweedy Rd, Brom. BR1 ..**191** F1
Tweezer's All, WC2 ....**18** E5
Twelve Acre Ho, E12
off Grantham Rd **98** D3
Twelvetrees Business Pk, E3
off Twelvetrees Cres ..**114** D4
Twelvetrees Cres, E3 .....**114** C4
Twentyman Cl, Wdf.Grn.
IG8 ....**63** G5
TWICKENHAM,
TW1 & TW2 ....**162** D2
Twickenham Br, Rich.
TW9 ....**145** F5
Twickenham TW1 .....**145** F5
Twickenham Cl, Croy.
CR0 ....**201** F3
Twickenham Gdns, Grnf.
UB6 ....**86** D5
Harrow HA3 ....**52** B7
Twickenham Rd, E11 ......**96** D2
Feltham TW13 ....**161** F3
Isleworth TW7 ....**144** D3
Richmond TW9 ....**145** F4
Teddington TW11 .....**162** D5
Twickenham Trd Est, Twick.
TW1 ....**144** C6
Twig Folly Cl, E2
off Roman Rd **113** G2
Twilley St, SW18 ....**148** E7
Twine Cl, Bark. IG11
off Thames Rd **118** B3
Twine Ct, E1 ....**113** F7
Twineham Grn, N12 ......**56** D4
Twine Ter, E3
off Ropery St **113** J4
Twining Av, Twick. TW2 ...**161** J3
Twinn Rd, NW7 ....**56** B6
Twin Tumps Way, SE28 ...**118** A7
Twisden Rd, NW5 ....**92** B4
Twybridge Way, NW10 ....**88** C7
Twycross Ms, SE10
off Blackwall La **135** E4
Twyford Abbey Rd,
NW10 ....**105** J3
Twyford Av, N2 ....**73** J3
W3 ....**106** A7
Twyford Cres, W3 ....**126** A1
Twyford Ho, N15 ....**76** B6
Twyford Pl, WC2 ....**18** C3
Twyford Rd, Cars. SM5 ...**199** G1
Harrow HA2 ....**85** H1
Ilford IG1 ....**99** F5
Twyford St, N1 ....**111** F1
Tyas Rd, E16 ....**115** F4
Tybenham Rd, SW19 .....**184** D3
Tyberry Rd, Enf. EN3 ......**45** E3
Tyburn La, Har. HA1 ......**68** B7
Tyburn Way, W1 ....**16** A5
Tycehurst Hill, Loug.
IG10 ....**48** C4
Tye La, Orp. BR6 ....**207** F5
Tyers Est, SE1 ....**28** D3
Tyers Gate, SE1 ....**28** D3
Tyers St, SE11 ....**34** C3
Tyers Ter, SE11 ....**34** C4
Tyeshurst Cl, SE2 ....**139** E5
Tylecroft Rd, SW16 ......**186** E2
Tylehurst Gdns, Ilf. IG1 ....**99** F5
Tyler Cl, E2 ....**13** F1
Erith DA8 ....**139** H7
Tyler Rd, Sthl. UB2
off McNair Rd **123** H3
Tylers Cl, Loug. IG10 ......**48** B7
Tyler's Ct, W1 ....**17** H4
Tylers Gate, Har. HA3 .....**69** H6
Tylers Path, Cars. SM5
off Rochester Rd **199** J4
Tyler St, SE10 ....**135** E5
Tylney Av, SE19 ....**170** C5
Tylney Cl, Chig. IG7 ......**65** J4
Tylney Rd, E7 ....**97** J4
Bromley BR1 ....**192** A2
Tymperley Ct, SW19
off Windlesham Gro ..**166** B1
Tynan Cl, Felt. TW14
off Sandycombe Rd ..**160** A1
Tyndale Ct, E14 ....**134** B5
Tyndale La, N1
off Upper St **93** H7
Tyndale Ter, N1
off Canonbury La **93** H7
Tyndall Rd, E10 ....**96** C2
Welling DA16 ....**157** J3
Tyneham Cl, SW11
off Shirley Gro **150** A3
Tyneham Rd, SW11 ......**150** A2
Tynemouth Cl, E6
off Covelees Wall **116** E6
Tynemouth Rd, N15 ......**76** C4
SE18 ....**137** J5
Mitcham CR4 ....**168** A7
Tynemouth St, SW6 .....**149** F2
Tyne St, E1
off Old Castle St **21** G3
Tynsdale Rd, NW10 ....**88** E7
Tynwald Ho, SE26
off Sydenham Hill Est .**170** D3
Type St, E2 ....**113** G2
Typhoon Way, Wall. SM6 .**200** E7
Tyrawley Rd, SW6 ....**148** E1
Tyre La, NW9 ....**70** E4
Tyrell Cl, Har. HA1 ....**86** B4
Tyrell Ct, Cars. SM5 .....**199** J4
Tyrols Rd, SE23
off Wastdale Rd **171** G1
Tyrone Rd, E6 ....**116** C2
Tyron Way, Sid. DA14 ....**175** H4
Tyrrell Av, Well. DA16 ....**158** A5
Tyrrell Rd, SE22 ....**152** D4
Tyrrell Sq, Mitch. CR4 ....**185** H1
Tyrrel Way, NW9 ....**71** F7
Tyrwhitt Rd, SE4 ....**154** A3
Tysoe St, EC1 ....**11** E4
Tyson Rd, SE23 ....**153** F7
Tyssen Pas, E8 ....**94** C6
Tyssen Rd, N16 ....**94** C3
Tyssen St, E8 ....**94** C6
N1 ....**12** E1
Tytherton Rd, N19 ....**92** D3

U

Uamvar St, E14 ....**114** B5
Uckfield Gro, Mitch. CR4 .**186** A1
Udall St, SW1 ....**33** G2
Udney Pk Rd, Tedd. TW11 .**162** D5
Uffington Rd, NW10 .....**107** G1
SE27 ....**169** G4
Ufford Cl, Har. HA3 ....**51** H7
Ufford Rd, Har. HA3 ....**51** H7
Ufford St, SE1 ....**27** F3
Ufton Gro, N1 ....**94** A7
Ufton Rd, N1 ....**94** A7
Uhura Sq, N16 ....**94** B3
Ujima Ct, SW16 ....**169** E4
Ullathorne Rd, SW16 ....**168** C4
Ulleswater Rd, N14 ....**59** E4
Ullin St, E14
off St. Leonards Rd ...**114** C5
Ullswater Cl, SW15 ....**164** D4
Bromley BR1 ....**173** E6
Ullswater Ct, Har. HA2 ....**67** G7
Ullswater Cres, SW15 ...**164** D4
Ullswater Rd, SE27 ......**169** H2
SW13 ....**127** G7
Ulster Gdns, N13 ....**59** J4
Ulster Pl, NW1 ....**8** D6
Ulster Ter, NW1 ....**8** D6
Ulundi Rd, SE3 ....**135** E6
Ulva Rd, SW15 ....**148** A5
Ulverscroft Rd, SE22 .....**152** C5
Ulverstone Rd, SE27 ....**169** H2
Ulverston Rd, E17 ....**78** D2
Ulysses Rd, NW6 ....**90** C5
Umberston St, E1
off Hessel St **112** E6
Umbria St, SW15 ....**147** G6
Umfreville Rd, N4 ....**75** H6
Undercliff Rd, SE13 ......**154** A3
UNDERHILL, Barn. EN5 ...**40** D5
Underhill, Barn. EN5 ......**40** D5
Underhill Pas, NW1
off Camden High St ..**110** B1
Underhill Rd, SE22 ......**152** E6
Underhill St, NW1
off Arlington Rd **110** B1
Underne Av, N14 ....**58** B2
Undershaft, EC3 ....**20** D4
Undershaw Rd, Brom.
BR1 ....**173** E3
Underwood, Croy.
(New Adgtn) CR0 .....**204** C5
Underwood, The, SE9 ....**174** C2
Underwood Rd, E1 ....**13** H6
E4 ....**62** B5
Woodford Green IG8 ...**64** A7
Underwood Row, N1 .....**12** A3
Underwood St, N1 ....**12** A3
Undine Rd, E14 ....**134** B4
Undine St, SW17 ....**167** J5
Uneeda Dr, Grnf. UB6 ....**104** A1
Unicorn Pas, SE1
off Tooley St **28** E2
Union Cl, E11 ....**96** D4
Union Cotts, E15
off Welfare Rd **97** E7
Union Ct, EC2 ....**20** D3
Richmond TW9
off Eton St **145** H5
Union Dr, E1
off Canal Cl **113** H4
Union Gro, SW8 ....**150** D2
Union Jack Club, SE1 .....**27** E3
Union Pk, SE10 ....**135** F5
Union Rd, N11 ....**58** D6
SW4 ....**150** D2
SW8 ....**150** D2
Bromley BR2 ....**192** A5
Croydon CR0 ....**187** J7
Northolt UB5 ....**103** G2
Union Rd, Wembley HA0 ..**87** H6
Union Sq, N1 ....**111** J1
Union St, E15 ....**114** C1
SE1 ....**27** H2
Barnet EN5 ....**40** B4
Kingston upon Thames
KT1 ....**181** G2
Union Wk, E2 ....**13** E3
Union Wf, N1 ....**11** J2
West Drayton UB7
off Bentinck Rd **120** B1
Unity Cl, NW10 ....**89** G6
SE19 *off Crown Dale* ..**169** J5
Unity Ct, SE1
off Mawbey Pl **37** G3
Unity Ter, Har. HA2
off Scott Cres **85** H1
Unity Trd Est, Wdf.Grn.
IG8 ....**80** A3
Unity Way, SE18 ....**136** A3
Unity Wf, SE1 ....**29** G3
University Cl, NW7 ....**55** F7
★ **University Coll London**,
WC1 ....**9** H5
University Gdns, Bex.
DA5 ....**159** F7
★ **University of London**,
WC1 ....**17** J1
University Pl, Erith DA8
off Belmont Rd **139** J7
University Rd, SW19 ....**167** G6
University St, WC1 ....**9** G6
University Way, E16 .....**116** D7
Unwin Av, Felt. TW14 ....**141** H5
Unwin Cl, SE15 ....**37** H6
Unwin Rd, SW7 ....**23** F5
Isleworth TW7 ....**144** B3
Upbrook Ms, W2 ....**14** D4
Upcerne Rd, SW10 ......**129** F7
Upchurch Cl, SE20 ......**171** E7
Upcroft Av, Edg. HA8 .....**54** C5
Updale Rd, Sid. DA14 ....**175** J4
Upfield, Croy. CR0 ......**203** E2
Upfield Rd, W7 ....**104** C4
Upgrove Manor Way, SW2
off Trinity Ri **151** G7
Uphall Rd, Ilf. IG1 ....**99** E5
Upham Pk Rd, W4 ....**127** E4
Uphill Dr, NW7 ....**55** E5
NW9 ....**70** C5
Uphill Gro, NW7 ....**55** E4
Uphill Rd, NW7 ....**54** E4
Upland Ms, SE22
off Upland Rd **152** D5
Upland Rd, E13
off Sutton Rd **115** F4
SE22 ....**152** D5
Bexleyheath DA7 .....**159** F3
South Croydon CR2 ...**202** A5
Sutton SM2 ....**199** G7
Uplands, Beck. BR3 ......**190** A2
Uplands, The, Loug. IG10 ..**48** C3
Ruislip HA4 ....**84** A1
Uplands Av, E17
off Blackhorse La **77** G2
Uplands Business Pk, E17 .**77** G2
Uplands Cl, SW14
off Monroe Dr **146** B5
Uplands End, Wdf.Grn.
IG8 ....**64** B7
Uplands Pk Rd, Enf. EN2 ..**43** G3
Uplands Rd, N8 ....**75** F5
Barnet (E.Barn.) EN4 ...**58** A1
Romford RM6 ....**82** D3
Woodford Green IG8 ...**64** B7
Uplands Way, N21 ....**43** G5
Upney La, Bark. IG11 .....**99** H6
Upnor Way, SE17 ....**37** E3
Uppark Dr, Ilf. IG2 ....**81** F6
Upper Abbey Rd, Belv.
DA17 ....**139** F4
Upper Addison Gdns,
W14 ....**128** B2
Upper Bk St, E14 ....**134** B1
Upper Bardsey Wk, N1
off Clephane Rd **93** J6
Upper Belgrave St, SW1 ..**24** C5
Upper Berenger Wk, SW10
off Blantyre St **30** E7
Upper Berkeley St, W1 ....**15** J4
Upper Beulah Hill, SE19 ..**188** B1
Upper Blantyre Wk, SW10
off Blantyre St **30** E7
Upper Brighton Rd, Surb.
KT6 ....**181** G6
Upper Brockley Rd, SE4 ..**153** J2
Upper Brook St, W1 ......**16** B6
Upper Butts, Brent. TW8 .**125** F6
Upper Caldy Wk, N1
off Clifton Rd **93** J6
Upper Camelford Wk, W11
off St. Marks Rd **108** B6
Upper Cavendish Av, N3 ..**72** D3
Upper Cheyne Row, SW3 .**31** G6
UPPER CLAPTON, E5 .....**94** E1
Upper Clapton Rd, E5 ....**94** E1
Upper Clarendon Wk, W11
off Clarendon Wk **108** B6
Upper Dartrey Wk, SW10
off Blantyre St **30** E7
Upper Dengie Wk, N1
off Popham Rd **111** J1
UPPER EDMONTON,
N18 ....**60** D6

UPPER ELMERS END, Beck. BR3 **189** J6
Upper Elmers End Rd, Beck. BR3 **189** H4
Upper Fm Rd, W.Mol. KT8 **179** F4
Upper Fosters, NW4 *off New Brent St* **71** J5
Upper Grn E, Mitch. CR4 **185** J3
Upper Grn W, Mitch. CR4 *off London Rd* **185** J3
Upper Grosvenor St, W1 **16** B6
Upper Grotto Rd, Twick. TW1 **162** C2
Upper Grd, SE1 **26** E1
Upper Gro, SE25 **188** B4
Upper Gro Rd, Belv. DA17 **139** F6
Upper Gulland Wk, N1 *off Nightingale Rd* **93** J6
Upper Hampstead Wk, NW3 *off New End* **91** F4
Upper Ham Rd, Kings.T. KT2 **163** G4
Richmond TW10 **163** G4
Upper Handa Wk, N1 *off Clephane Rd* **93** J6
Upper Hawkwell Wk, N1 *off Popham Rd* **111** J1
Upper Hitch, Wat. WD19 **51** E1
UPPER HOLLOWAY, N19 **92** C3
Upper Holly Hill Rd, Belv. DA17 **139** H5
Upper James St, W1 **17** G5
Upper John St, W1 **17** G5
Upper Lismore Wk, N1 *off Clephane Rd* **93** J6
Upper Mall, W6 **127** G5
Upper Marsh, SE1 **26** D5
Upper Montagu St, W1 **15** J1
Upper Mulgrave Rd, Sutt. SM2 **198** B7
Upper N St, E14 **114** A5
UPPER NORWOOD, SE19 **170** A7
Upper Palace Rd, E.Mol. KT8 **179** J3
Upper Pk, Loug. IG10 **48** A4
Upper Pk Rd, N11 **58** B5
NW3 **91** J5
Belvedere DA17 **139** H4
Bromley BR1 **191** H1
Kingston upon Thames KT2 **164** A6
Upper Phillimore Gdns, W8 **128** D2
Upper Ramsey Wk, N1 *off Ramsey Wk* **94** A6
Upper Rawreth Wk, N1 *off Popham Rd* **111** J1
Upper Richmond Rd, SW15 **148** B4
Upper Richmond Rd W, SW14 **146** B4
Richmond TW10 **146** A4
Upper Rd, E13 **115** G3
Wallington SM6 **200** D5
Upper St. Martin's La, WC2 **18** A5
Upper Selsdon Rd, S.Croy. CR2 **202** C7
Upper Sheridan Rd, Belv. DA17 *off Coleman Rd* **139** G4
Upper Shirley Rd, Croy. CR0 **203** F2
Upper Sq, Islw. TW7 **144** D3
Upper St, N1 **11** F1
Upper Sunbury Rd, Hmptn. TW12 **179** E1
Upper Sutton La, Houns. TW5 **123** G7
UPPER SYDENHAM, SE26 **170** D4
Upper Tachbrook St, SW1 **33** F1
Upper Tail, Wat. WD19 **51** E3
Upper Talbot Wk, W11 *off Talbot Wk* **108** B6
Upper Teddington Rd, Kings.T. KT1 **181** F1
Upper Ter, NW3 **91** F3
Upper Thames St, EC4 **19** H5
Upper Tollington Pk, N4 **93** G1
Upperton Rd, Sid. DA14 **175** J5
Upperton Rd E, E13 *off Inniskilling Rd* **115** J3
Upperton Rd W, E13 **115** J3
UPPER TOOTING, SW17 **167** H3
Upper Tooting Pk, SW17 **167** J2
Upper Tooting Rd, SW17 **167** J4
Upper Town Rd, Grnf. UB6 **103** H4
Upper Tulse Hill, SW2 **151** F7
Upper Vernon Rd, Sutt. SM1 **199** G5
UPPER WALTHAMSTOW, E17 **78** B4
Upper Walthamstow Rd, E17 **78** D4
Upper Whistler Wk, SW10 *off Blantyre St* **30** D7
Upper Wickham La, Well. DA16 **138** B7
Upper Wimpole St, W1 **16** D1
Upper Woburn Pl, WC1 **9** J4
Uppingham Av, Stan. HA7 **69** E1
Upsdell Av, N13 **59** G6
Upstall St, SE5 **151** H1
UPTON, E7 **97** H7
Upton Av, E7 **97** G7
Upton Cl, NW2 *off Somerton Rd* **90** B3
Bexley DA5 **159** F6
Upton Ct, SE20 *off Blean Gro* **171** F7
Upton Dene, Sutt. SM2 **198** E7
Upton Gdns, Har. HA3 **69** E5
Upton La, E7 **97** G7
UPTON PARK, E6 **115** J1
Upton Pk Rd, E7 **97** H7
Upton Rd, N18 **60** D5
SE18 **137** F6
Bexley DA5 **159** F6
Bexleyheath DA6 **158** E4
Hounslow TW3 **143** G3
Thornton Heath CR7 **188** A2
Upton Rd S, Bex. DA5 **159** F6
Upway, N12 **57** H7
Upwood Rd, SE12 **155** F6
SW16 **187** E1
Urban Ms, N4 **75** H7
Urlwin St, SE5 **35** J6
Urlwin Wk, SW9 **151** G2
Urmston Dr, SW19 **166** B1
Ursula Ms, N4 **93** H1
Ursula St, SW11 **149** H1
Urswick Gdns, Dag. RM9 *off Urswick Rd* **100** E7
Urswick Rd, E9 **95** F5
Dagenham RM9 **100** D7
Usborne Ms, SW8 **34** C7
Usher Rd, E3 **113** J2
Usk Rd, SW11 **149** F4
Usk St, E2 **113** G3
Utah Bldg, SE13 *off Deals Gateway* **154** B1
Utopia Village, NW1 *off Chalcot Rd* **110** A1
Uvedale Rd, Dag. RM10 **101** G3
Enfield EN2 **44** A5
Uverdale Rd, SW10 **129** F7
Uxbridge Gdns, Felt. TW13 *off Marlborough Rd* **160** D2
Uxbridge Rd, W3 **105** H7
W5 **105** F7
W5 (Ealing Com.) **105** H7
W7 **124** B1
W12 **127** G1
W13 **124** E1
Feltham TW13 **160** C2
Hampton TW12 **161** G4
Harrow HA3 **51** J7
Hayes UB4 **102** C7
Kingston upon Thames KT1 **181** G4
Pinner HA5 **51** H7
Southall UB1 **123** G1
Stanmore HA7 **52** C6
Uxbridge St, W8 **128** D1
Uxendon Cres, Wem. HA9 **87** H1
Uxendon Hill, Wem. HA9 **87** J1

V

Valance Av, E4 **63** F1
Valan Leas, Brom. BR2 **191** E3
Vale, The, N10 **74** A1
N14 **42** D7
NW11 **90** A3
SW3 **31** E5
W3 **126** D1
Croydon CR0 **203** G2
Feltham TW14 **142** B6
Hounslow TW5 **122** E6
Ruislip HA4 **84** C4
Sunbury-on-Thames TW16 *off Ashridge Way* **160** A6
Woodford Green IG8 **63** G7
Vale Av, Borwd. WD6 **38** B5
Vale Cl, N2 **73** J3
W9 **6** C4
Orpington BR6 **206** D4
Vale Cotts, SW15 **164** E3
Vale Ct, W3 *off The Vale* **127** F1
W9 **6** C4
Vale Cres, SW15 **165** E3
Vale Cft, Pnr. HA5 **66** E5
Vale Dr, Barn. EN5 **40** C4
Vale End, SE22 *off Grove Vale* **152** B4
Vale Gro, N4 **75** J7
W3 *off The Vale* **126** D1
Vale La, W3 **106** A5
Valence Av, Dag. RM8 **100** D3
Valence Circ, Dag. RM8 **100** D3
★ **Valence Ho Mus**, Dag. RM8 **100** D3
Valence Wd Rd, Dag. RM8 **100** D3
Valencia Rd, Stan. HA7 **53** F4
Valentia Pl, SW9 *off Brixton Sta Rd* **151** G4
Valentine Av, Bex. DA5 **176** E2
Valentine Ct, SE23 **171** G2
Valentine Ho, E3 *off Garrison Rd* **113** J1
Valentine Pl, SE1 **27** G3
Valentine Rd, E9 **95** G6
Harrow HA2 **85** J3
Valentine Row, SE1 **27** G4
Valentines Rd, Ilf. IG1 **98** E1
Vale of Health, NW3 *off East Heath Rd* **91** G3
Vale Par, SW15 *off Kingston Vale* **164** E3
Valerian Wk, N11 *off Nurserymans Rd* **58** A2
Valerian Way, E15 **115** E3
Valerie Ct, Sutt. SM2 *off Stanley Rd* **198** E7
Vale Ri, NW11 **90** C1
Vale Rd, E7 **97** H6
N4 **75** J7
Bromley BR1 **192** D2
Epsom KT19 **197** F4
Mitcham CR4 **186** D3
Sutton SM1 **198** E4
Worcester Park KT4 **197** F4
Vale Rd N, Surb. KT6 **195** H2
Vale Rd S, Surb. KT6 **195** H2
Vale Row, N5 *off Gillespie Rd* **93** H3
Vale Royal, N7 **92** E7
Valery Pl, Hmptn. TW12 **161** G7
Vale St, SE27 **170** A3
Valeswood Rd, Brom. BR1 **173** F5
Vale Ter, N4 **75** J6
Valetta Gro, E13 **115** G2
Valetta Rd, W3 **126** E2
Valette St, E9 **95** E6
Valiant Cl, Nthlt. UB5 *off Ruislip Rd* **102** D3
Romford RM7 **83** G2
Valiant Ho, SE7 **135** J5
Valiant Path, NW9 **71** E1
Valiant Way, E6 **116** C5
Vallance Rd, E1 **13** J4
E2 **13** J4
N22 **74** C2
Vallentin Rd, E17 **78** C4
Valley Av, N12 **57** G4
Valley Cl, Loug. IG10 **48** C6
Pinner HA5 **66** B2
Valley Dr, NW9 **70** A6
Valleyfield Rd, SW16 **169** F5
Valley Flds Cres, Enf. EN2 **43** G2
Valley Gdns, SW19 **167** G7
Wembley HA0 **87** J7
Valley Gro, SE7 **135** J5
Valley Hill, Loug. IG10 **48** B7
Valleylink Est, Enf. EN3 *off Meridian Way* **45** H6
Valley Ms, Twick. TW1 *off Cross Deep* **162** D2
Valley Pt Ind Est, Croy. CR0 **186** E7
Valley Rd, SW16 **169** F4
Belvedere DA17 **139** H4
Bromley BR2 **191** E2
Valley Side, E4 **62** A2
Valley Side Par, E4 *off Valley Side* **62** A2
Valley Vw, Barn. EN5 **40** B6
Valley Wk, Croy. CR0 **203** F2
Valliere Rd, NW10 **107** H3
Valliers Wd Rd, Sid. DA15 **175** G1
Vallis Way, W13 **104** D5
Chessington KT9 **195** G4
Valmar Rd, SE5 **151** J1
Val McKenzie Av, N7 *off Parkside Cres* **93** G3
Valnay St, SW17 **167** J5
Valognes Av, E17 **77** H1
Valonia Gdns, SW18 **148** C6
Vambery Rd, SE18 **137** F6
Vanbrough Cres, Nthlt. UB5 **102** C1
Vanbrugh Cl, E16 *off Fulmer Rd* **116** A5
Vanbrugh Dr, Walt. KT12 **178** C7
Vanbrugh Flds, SE3 **135** F7
Vanbrugh Hill, SE3 **135** F5
SE10 **135** F5
Vanbrugh Pk, SE3 **135** F7
Vanbrugh Pk Rd, SE3 **135** F7
Vanbrugh Pk Rd W, SE3 **135** F7
Vanbrugh Rd, W4 **126** D3
Vanbrugh Ter, SE3 **155** F1
Vanburgh Cl, Orp. BR6 **207** H1
Vancouver Rd, SE23 **171** H2
Edgware HA8 **70** B1
Hayes UB4 **102** B4
Richmond TW10 **163** F4
Vanderbilt Rd, SW18 **167** E1
Vanderville Gdns, N2 **73** F2
Vandome Cl, E16 **115** H6
Vandon Pas, SW1 **25** G5
Vandon St, SW1 **25** G5
Van Dyck Av, N.Mal. KT3 **182** D7
Vandyke Cl, SW15 **148** A7
Vandyke Cross, SE9 **156** B5
Vandy St, EC2 **12** D6
Vane Cl, NW3 **91** G4
Harrow HA3 **69** J6
Vanessa Cl, Belv. DA17 **139** G5
Vane St, SW1 **33** G1
Van Gogh Cl, Islw. TW7 *off Twickenham Rd* **144** D3
Vanguard Cl, E16 **115** G5
Croydon CR0 **201** H1
Romford RM7 **83** H2
Vanguard Ho, E8 *off Martello St* **95** E7
Vanguard St, SE8 **154** A1
Vanguard Way, Wall. SM6 **200** E7
Vanneck Sq, SW15 **147** G5
Vanner Pt, E9 *off Wick Rd* **95** G6
Vanoc Gdns, Brom. BR1 **173** G4
Vansittart Rd, E7 **97** F4
Vansittart St, SE14 **133** H7
Vanston Pl, SW6 **128** D7
Vantage Ms, E14 *off Prestons Rd* **134** C1
Vantage Pl, W8 *off Abingdon Rd* **128** D3
Feltham TW14 *off Staines Rd* **142** A6
Vant Rd, SW17 **167** J5
Varcoe Rd, SE16 **133** E5
Vardens Rd, SW11 **149** G4
Varden St, E1 **112** E6
Vardon Cl, W3 **106** D6
Varley Par, NW9 **70** E4
Varley Rd, E16 **115** H6
Varley Way, Mitch. CR4 **185** G2
Varna Rd, SW6 **128** B7
Hampton TW12 **179** H1
Varndell St, NW1 **9** F3
Varnishers Yd, N1 *off Caledonian Rd* **111** E2
Varsity Dr, Twick. TW1 **144** B5
Varsity Row, SW14 **146** C2
Vartry Rd, N15 **76** A6
Vassall Rd, SW9 **131** G7
Vauban Est, SE16 **29** G6
Vauban St, SE16 **29** G6
Vaughan Av, NW4 **71** G5
W6 **127** F4
Vaughan Cl, Hmptn. TW12 *off Oak Av* **161** E6
Vaughan Gdns, Ilf. IG1 **80** C7
Vaughan Rd, E15 **97** F6
SE5 **151** J2
Harrow HA1 **67** J7
Thames Ditton KT7 **180** E7
Welling DA16 **157** J2
Vaughan St, SE16 **133** J2
Vaughan Way, E1 **21** H6
Vaughan Williams Cl, SE8 *off Watson's St* **134** A7
VAUXHALL, SE11 **34** B4
Vauxhall Br, SE1 **34** A4
SW1 **34** A4
Vauxhall Br Rd, SW1 **33** G1
Vauxhall Gdns, S.Croy. CR2 **201** J6
Vauxhall Gdns Est, SE11 **34** C4
Vauxhall Gro, SW8 **34** C5
Vauxhall St, SE11 **34** D3
Vauxhall Wk, SE11 **34** C3
Vawdrey Cl, E1 **113** F4
Veals Mead, Mitch. CR4 **185** H1
Vectis Gdns, SW17 *off Vectis Rd* **168** B6
Vectis Rd, SW17 **168** B6
Veda Rd, SE13 **154** A4
Veldene Way, Har. HA2 **85** F3
Velde Way, SE22 *off East Dulwich Gro* **152** B5
Velletri Ho, E2 **113** G2
Vellum Dr, Cars. SM5 **200** A3
Venables Cl, Dag. RM10 **101** H4
Venables St, NW8 **7** F6
Vencourt Pl, W6 **127** G5
Venetian Rd, SE5 **151** J2
Venetia Rd, N4 **75** H6
W5 **125** G2
Venner Rd, SE26 **171** F6
Venn St, SW4 **150** C4
Ventnor Av, Stan. HA7 **69** E1
Ventnor Dr, N20 **56** E3
Ventnor Gdns, Bark. IG11 **99** H6
Ventnor Rd, SE14 **133** G7
Sutton SM2 **199** E7
Venture Cl, Bex. DA5 **158** E7
Venue St, E14 **114** C5
Venus Ho, E3 *off Garrison Rd* **114** A1
E14 *off Crews St* **134** A4
Venus Ms, Mitch. CR4 **185** H3
Venus Rd, SE18 **136** C3
Vera Av, N21 **43** G5
Vera Lynn Cl, E7 *off Dames Rd* **97** G4
Vera Rd, SW6 **148** B1
Verbena Cl, E16 *off Pretoria Rd* **115** F4
West Drayton UB7 *off Magnolia St* **120** A5
Verbena Gdns, W6 **127** G5
Verdant La, SE6 **173** E1
Verdayne Av, Croy. CR0 **203** G1
Verdi Cres, W10 *off Herries St* **108** B2
Verdun Rd, SE18 **138** A6
SW13 **127** G6
Vereker Dr, Sun. TW16 **178** A3
Vereker Rd, W14 **128** B5
Vere Rd, Loug. IG10 **49** F4
Vere St, W1 **16** D4

Veridion Way, Erith DA18
off Waldrist Way 139 F2
Verity Cl, W11 108 B6
Vermeer Gdns, SE15
off Elland Rd 153 F4
Vermont Cl, Enf. EN2 43 H4
Vermont Rd, SE19 170 A6
SW18 149 E6
Sutton SM1 198 E3
Verney Gdns, Dag. RM9 100 E4
Verney Rd, SE16 37 J5
Dagenham RM9 100 E5
Verney St, NW10 88 D3
Verney Way, SE16 132 E5
Vernham Rd, SE18 137 F6
Vernon Av, E12 98 C4
SW20 184 A2
Woodford Green IG8 63 H7
Vernon Cl, Epsom KT19 196 C6
Vernon Ct, Stan. HA7
off Vernon Dr 68 E1
Vernon Cres, Barn. EN4 42 A6
Vernon Dr, Stan. HA7 68 D1
Vernon Ms, E17
off Vernon Rd 77 J4
W14 *off Vernon St* 128 B4
Vernon Pl, WC1 18 B2
Vernon Ri, WC1 10 D3
Greenford UB6 86 A5
Vernon Rd, E3 113 J2
E11 97 E1
E15 97 E7
E17 77 J5
N8 75 G3
SW14 146 D3
Ilford IG3 99 J1
Sutton SM1 199 F5
Vernon Sq, WC1 10 D3
Vernon St, W14 128 B4
Vernon Yd, W11
off Portobello Rd 108 C7
Veroan Rd, Bexh. DA7 158 E2
Verona Ct, W4
off Chiswick La 127 E5
Verona Dr, Surb. KT6 195 H2
Verona Rd, E7
off Upton La 97 G7
Veronica Gdns, SW16 186 C1
Veronica Rd, SW17 168 B3
Veronique Gdns, Ilf. IG6 81 E5
Verran Rd, SW12 150 B7
Versailles Rd, SE20 170 D7
Verulam Av, E17 77 J6
Verulam Bldgs, WC1 18 D1
Verulam Ct, NW9 71 G7
Verulam Ho, W6
off Hammersmith Gro 127 J2
Verulam Rd, Grnf. UB6 103 G4
Verulam St, WC1 18 E1
Verwood Dr, Barn. EN4 41 J3
Verwood Rd, Har. HA2 67 J2
Vesage Ct, EC1 19 F2
Vesey Path, E14
off East India Dock Rd 114 B6
Vespan Rd, W12 127 G2
Vesta Ct, SE1
off Morocco St 28 D4
Vesta Ho, E3
off Garrison Rd 114 A1
Vesta Rd, SE4 153 H2
Vestris Rd, SE23 171 G2
Vestry Ms, SE5 152 B1
Vestry Rd, E17 78 B4
SE5 152 B1
Vestry St, N1 12 B3
Vevey St, SE6 171 J2
Veysey Gdns, Dag. RM10 101 G3
Viaduct Pl, E2
off Viaduct St 112 E3
Viaduct St, E2 112 E3
Vian St, SE13 154 B3
Vibart Gdns, SW2 151 F7
Vibart Wk, N1
off Outram Pl 111 E1
Vibia Cl, Stai. TW19
off Hadrian Way 140 A7
Vicarage Av, SE3 155 G1
Vicarage Cl, Erith DA8 139 J6
Northolt UB5 85 F7
Worcester Park KT4 196 E1
Vicarage Ct, W8
off Vicarage Gate 22 A3
Feltham TW14 141 F7
Vicarage Cres, SW11 149 G1
Vicarage Dr, SW14 146 D5
Barking IG11 99 F7
Beckenham BR3 190 A1
Vicarage Fm Rd, Houns.
TW3, TW5 142 E2
Vicarage Flds, Walt. KT12 178 C6
Vicarage Fld Shop Cen,
Bark. IG11 99 F7
Vicarage Gdns, SW14
off Vicarage Rd 146 C5
W8 128 D1
Mitcham CR4 185 H3
Vicarage Gate, W8 22 A3
Vicarage Gro, SE5 152 A1
Vicarage La, E6 116 C3
E15 97 E7
Chigwell IG7 65 F2
Ilford IG1 99 G1
Vicarage Par, N15
off West Grn Rd 75 J4
Vicarage Pk, SE18 137 F5
Vicarage Path, N8 74 E7
Vicarage Rd, E10 96 B1
E15 97 F7
N17 60 D7
NW4 71 G6
SE18 137 F5
SW14 146 C5
Bexley DA5 177 H1
Croydon CR0 201 G3
Dagenham RM10 101 H6
Kingston upon Thames
KT1 181 G2
Kingston upon Thames
(Hmptn W.) KT1 181 F1
Sutton SM1 198 E4
Teddington TW11 162 D5
Twickenham TW2 162 B2
Twickenham (Whitton)
TW2 143 J6
Woodford Green IG8 64 B7
Vicarage Wk, SW11
off Battersea Ch Rd 149 G1
Vicarage Way, NW10 88 D3
Harrow HA2 67 G7
Vicars Br Cl, Wem. HA0 105 H2
Vicars Cl, E9
off Northiam St 113 F1
E15 115 G1
Enfield EN1 44 B2
Vicars Hill, SE13 154 B4
Vicars Moor La, N21 43 G7
Vicars Oak Rd, SE19 170 B6
Vicars Rd, NW5 92 A5
Vicars Wk, Dag. RM8 100 B3
Viceroy Cl, N2
off Market Pl 73 H4
Viceroy Ct, NW8 7 H1
Viceroy Par, N2
off High Rd 73 H4
Viceroy Rd, SW8 150 E1
Vickers Cl, Wall. SM6 201 F7
Vickers Way, Houns.
TW4 143 E5
Victor Gro, Wem. HA0 87 H7
★ **Victoria & Albert Mus**,
SW7 23 F6
Victoria Arc, SW1
off Terminus Pl 25 E6
Victoria Av, E6 116 A1
EC2 20 E2
N3 72 C1
Barnet EN4 41 G4
Hounslow TW3 143 F5
Surbiton KT6 181 G7
Wallington SM6 200 A3
Victoria Av, Wembley
HA9 88 B6
West Molesey KT8 179 G3
Victoria Cl, SE22
off Underhill Rd 152 D5
Barnet EN4 41 G4
West Molesey KT8
off Victoria Av 179 G3
★ **Victoria Coach Sta**,
SW1 32 D2
Victoria Cotts, Rich.
TW9 145 J1
Victoria Ct, Wem. HA9 88 A6
Victoria Cres, N15 76 B5
SE19 170 B6
SW19 166 C7
Victoria Dock Rd, E16 115 F6
Victoria Dr, SW19 148 A7
Victoria Embk, EC4 18 C6
SW1 26 B3
WC2 18 C6
★ **Victoria Embankment
Gdns**, WC2 18 B6
Victoria Gdns, W11 128 D1
Hounslow TW5 142 E1
Victoria Gro, N12 57 F5
W8 22 C5
Victoria Gro Ms, W2
off Ossington St 108 E7
Victoria Ho, SW8
off South Lambeth Rd 34 B7
Victoria Ind Est, NW10 106 E3
Victoria La, Barn. EN5 40 C4
Hayes (Harling.) UB3 121 F5
Victoria Mans, SW8
off South Lambeth Rd 34 B7
Victoria Ms, E8
off Dalston La 94 D6
NW6 108 D1
SW4 *off Victoria Ri* 150 B4
SW18 167 F1
Victoria Mills Studios, E15
off Burford Rd 114 D1
Victorian Gro, N16 94 B3
Victorian Hts, SW8
off Thackeray Rd 150 B2
Victorian Rd, N16 94 B3
★ **Victoria Park**, E9 95 H7
Victoria Pk Rd, E9 113 F1
Victoria Pk Sq, E2 113 F3
Victoria Pas, NW8 7 E5
Victoria Pl, SW1 32 E1
Richmond TW9 145 G5
Victoria Pt, E13
off Victoria Rd 115 G2
Victoria Retail Pk, Ruis.
HA4 84 D5
Victoria Ri, SW4 150 B3
Victoria Rd, E4 63 E1
E11 96 E4
E13 115 G2
E17 78 C2
E18 79 H2
N4 75 F7
N9 60 C4
N15 76 D4
N18 60 C4
N22 74 C1
NW4 71 J4
NW6 108 C1
NW7 55 F5
NW10 106 D5
SW14 146 D3
W3 106 D5
W5 105 E5
W8 22 C6
Barking IG11 99 E6
Barnet EN4 41 G4
Bexleyheath DA6 159 G4
Bromley BR2 192 A5
Buckhurst Hill IG9 64 A2
Bushey WD23 51 H1
Chislehurst BR7 174 D5
Dagenham RM10 101 H5
Feltham TW13 160 B1
Kingston upon Thames
KT1 181 J2
Mitcham CR4 167 H7
Ruislip HA4 84 C5
Sidcup DA15 175 J3
Southall UB2 123 F3
Surbiton KT6 181 G6
Sutton SM1 199 G5
Teddington TW11 162 D6
Twickenham TW1 144 D7
Victoria Sq, SW1 24 E5
Victoria Sta, SW1 32 E1
Victoria Steps, Brent. TW8
off Kew Br Rd 125 J6
Victoria St, E15 96 E7
SW1 25 F6
Belvedere DA17 139 F5
Victoria Ter, N4 93 G1
NW10 *off Old Oak La* 107 E4
Harrow HA1 86 B1
Victoria Vil, Rich. TW9 145 J3
Victoria Way, SE7 135 H5
Ruislip HA4
off Civic Way 84 D5
Victoria Wf, E14 113 H7
Victoria Yd, E1 21 J4
Victor Rd, NW10 107 H3
SE20 171 G7
Harrow HA2 67 J3
Teddington TW11 162 B4
Victors Dr, Hmptn.
TW12 161 E6
Victors Way, Barn. EN5 40 C3
Victor Vil, N9 60 A3
Victor Wk, NW9 71 E2
Victory Av, Mord. SM4 185 F5
Victory Business Cen, Islw.
TW7 144 C3
Victory Pl, E14
off Northey St 113 H7
SE17 36 B1
SE19 *off Westow St* 170 B6
Victory Rd, E11 79 H4
SW19 167 F7
Victory Rd Ms, SW19
off Victory Rd 167 F7
Victory Wk, SE8
off Ship St 154 A1
Victory Way, SE16 133 H2
Hounslow TW5 122 C5
Romford RM7 83 H2
Vidler Cl, Chess. KT9
off Merritt Gdns 195 F6
Vienna Cl, Ilf. IG5 80 A3
View, The, SE2 139 E5
View Cl, N6 73 J7
Chigwell IG7 65 G5
Harrow HA1 68 A4
Viewfield Cl, Har. HA3 69 H7
Viewfield Rd, SW18 148 C6
Bexley DA5 176 C1
Viewland Rd, SE18 137 J5
View Rd, N6 73 J7
Viga Rd, N21 43 G6
Vigilant Cl, SE26 170 D4
Vignoles Rd, Rom. RM7 83 G7
Vigo St, W1 17 F6
Viking Cl, E3
off Selwyn Rd 113 J2
Viking Ct, SW6 128 D6
Viking Gdns, E6
off Jack Dash Way 116 B4
Viking Pl, E10 95 J1
Viking Rd, Sthl. UB1 103 E7
Viking Way, Erith DA8 139 J3
Villacourt Rd, SE18 138 A7
Village, The, SE7 135 J6
Village Arc, E4
off Station Rd 62 D1
Village Cl, E4 62 C5
NW3 *off Belsize La* 91 G5
Village Ct, E17
off Eden Rd 78 B5
Village Hts, Wdf.Grn.
IG8 63 F5
Village Ms, NW9 88 D2
Village Pk Cl, Enf. EN1 44 B6
Village Rd, N3 72 B1
Enfield EN1 44 B6
Village Row, Sutt. SM2 198 D7
Village Way, NW10 88 D4
SE21 152 A6
Beckenham BR3 190 A2
Ilford IG6 81 F3
Pinner HA5 67 E7
Village Way E, Har. HA2 67 F7
Villa Rd, SW9 151 G3
Villas Rd, SE18 137 F4
Villa St, SE17 36 C4
Villiers Av, Surb. KT5 181 J5
Twickenham TW2 161 F1
Villiers Cl, E10 96 A2
Surbiton KT5 181 J4
Villiers Ct, N20
off Buckingham Av 41 F7
Villiers Path, Surb. KT5 181 H5
Villiers Rd, NW2 89 G6
Beckenham BR3 189 G2
Isleworth TW7 144 B2
Kingston upon Thames
KT1 181 J3
Southall UB1 123 F1
Villiers St, WC2 18 A6
Vimy Cl, Houns. TW4
off Vickers Way 143 F5
Vincam Cl, Twick. TW2 143 G7
Vince Ct, N1
off Charles Sq 12 C4
Vincent Av, Surb. KT5 196 B1
Vincent Cl, SE16 133 H2
Barnet EN5 40 D3
Bromley BR2 191 H4
Ilford IG6 65 F6
Sidcup DA15 175 H1
West Drayton (Sipson)
UB7 120 D6
Vincent Gdns, NW2 89 F3
Vincent Ms, E3
off Fairfield Rd 114 A2
Vincent Rd, E4 62 D6
N15 75 J4
N22 75 G2
SE18 137 E4
W3 126 C3
Croydon CR0 188 B7
Dagenham RM9 100 E7
Hounslow TW4 142 D2
Isleworth TW7 144 A1
Vincent Rd, Kingston upon
Thames KT1 182 A3
Wembley HA0 87 J7
Vincent Row, Hmptn.
(Hmptn H.) TW12 161 J6
Vincents Path, Nthlt. UB5
off Arnold Rd 84 E6
Vincent Sq, N22 75 G2
SW1 33 G1
Vincent St, E16 115 F5
SW1 33 H1
Vincent Ter, N1 11 G1
Vince St, EC1 12 C4
Vine Cl, Surb. KT5 181 J6
Sutton SM1 199 F3
West Drayton UB7 120 D4
Vine Ct, E1 21 J2
Harrow HA3 69 H6
Vinegar All, E17 78 B4
Vine Gdns, Ilf. IG1 99 F5
Vinegar St, E1
off Reardon St 132 E1
Vinegar Yd, SE1 28 D3
Vine Hill, EC1 10 E6
Vine La, SE1 28 E2
Vine Pl, W5
off St. Mark's Rd 125 H1
Hounslow TW3 143 H4
Viner Cl, Walt. KT12 178 C6
Vineries, The, N14 42 C6
SE6 172 A1
Enfield EN1 44 B3
Vineries Bk, NW7 55 H5
Vineries Cl, Dag. RM9
off Heathway 101 G6
West Drayton (Sipson)
UB7 120 D6
Vine Rd, E15 97 F7
SW13 147 F3
East Molesey KT8 179 J4
Orpington BR6 207 J6
Vines Av, N3 72 E1
Vine Sq, W14 128 C5
Vine St, EC3 21 F5
W1 17 G6
Romford RM7 83 J5
Vine St Br, EC1 11 F6
Vine Yd, SE1 28 A3
Vineyard, The, Rich.
TW10 145 H5
Vineyard Av, NW7 56 B7
Vineyard Cl, SE6 172 A1
Kingston upon Thames
KT1 181 J3
Vineyard Gro, N3 73 E1
Vineyard Hill Rd, SW19 166 D4
Vineyard Pas, Rich. TW9
off Paradise Rd 145 H5
Vineyard Path, SW14 146 D3
Vineyard Rd, Felt. TW13 160 A3
Vineyard Row, Kings.T.
(Hmptn W.) KT1 181 F1
Vineyard Wk, EC1 11 E5

Viney Rd, SE13 154 B3
Vining St, SW9 151 G4
★ Vinopolis, SE1 28 A1
Vintners Ct, EC4 20 A5
Vintners Pl, EC4 off Vintners Ct 20 A5
Vintry Ms, E17 off Cleveland Pk Cres 78 A4
Viola Av, SE2 138 B4
Feltham TW14 142 C6
Viola Sq, W12 107 F7
Violet Cl, E16 115 E4
SE8 off Dorking Cl 133 J6
Sutton SM3 198 B1
Wallington SM6 200 A1
Violet Gdns, Croy. CR0 201 H5
Violet Hill, NW8 6 C2
Violet La, Croy. CR0 201 H5
Violet Rd, E3 114 B4
E17 78 A6
E18 79 H2
Violet St, E2 off Three Colts La 113 E4
Virgil Pl, W1 15 J2
Virgil St, SE1 26 D5
Virginia Cl, N.Mal. KT3 off Willow Rd 182 C4
Virginia Gdns, Ilf. IG6 81 F2
Virginia Rd, E2 13 F4
Thornton Heath CR7 187 H1
Virginia St, E1 21 J6
Virginia Wk, SW2 151 F6
Visage Apts, NW3 off Winchester Rd 91 G7
Viscount Cl, N11 58 B5
Viscount Dr, E6 116 C5
Viscount Gro, Nthlt. UB5 102 D3
Viscount St, EC1 11 J6
Viscount Way, Houns. (Lon.Hthrw Air.) TW6 141 H4
Vista, The, E4 46 D7
SE9 156 A6
Sidcup DA14 175 J5
Vista Av, Enf. EN3 45 G2
Vista Bldg, The, SE18 off Calderwood St 136 D4
Vista Dr, Ilf. IG4 80 A5
Vista Ho, SW19 off Chapter Way 185 G1
Vista Way, Har. HA3 69 H6
Viveash Cl, Hayes UB3 121 J3
Vivian Av, NW4 71 H5
Wembley HA9 88 A5
Vivian Cl, Wat. WD19 50 A1
Vivian Comma Cl, N4 off Blackstock Rd 93 H3
Vivian Ct, W9 6 A1
Vivian Gdns, Wat. WD19 50 A1
Wembley HA9 88 A5
Vivian Rd, E3 113 H2
Vivian Sq, SE15 off Scylla Rd 152 E3
Vivian Way, N2 73 G5
Vivien Cl, Chess. KT9 195 H7
Vivien Ct, N9 off Galahad Rd 60 D2
Vivienne Cl, Twick. TW1 145 F6
Voce Rd, SE18 137 G7
Voewood Cl, N.Mal. KT3 183 F6
Vogans Mill, SE1 29 G3
Volta Cl, N9 off Hudson Way 61 F3
Voltaire Bldgs, SW18 off Garratt La 167 E1
Voltaire Rd, SW4 150 D3
Volt Av, NW10 106 D3
Volta Way, Croy. CR0 201 F1
Voluntary Pl, E11 79 G6
Vorley Rd, N19 92 C2
Voss Ct, SW16 169 E6
Voss St, E2 13 J4
Voyagers Cl, SE28 118 C6
Voysey Cl, N3 72 B3
Vulcan Cl, E6 116 D6
Vulcan Gate, Enf. EN2 43 G2
Vulcan Rd, SE4 153 J2
Vulcan Sq, E14 off Britannia Rd 134 A4
Vulcan Ter, SE4 153 J2
Vulcan Way, N7 93 F6
Vyne, The, Bexh. DA7 159 H3
Vyner Rd, W3 106 D7
Vyner St, E2 113 E1
Vyse Cl, Barn. EN5 39 J4

W

Wadbrook St, Kings.T. KT1 181 G2
Wadding St, SE17 36 B2
Waddington Cl, Enf. EN1 44 B4
Waddington Rd, E15 96 D5
Waddington St, E15 96 D6
Waddington Way, SE19 169 J7
WADDON, Croy. CR0 201 G2
Waddon Cl, Croy. CR0 201 G3
Waddon Ct Rd, Croy. CR0 201 G4
Waddon Marsh Way, Croy. CR0 201 F1
Waddon New Rd, Croy. CR0 201 H3
Waddon Pk Av, Croy. CR0 201 G4
Waddon Rd, Croy. CR0 201 G3
Waddon Way, Croy. CR0 201 H6
Wades Gro, N21 43 G7
Wades Hill, N21 43 G6
Wades La, Tedd. TW11 off High St 162 D5
Wadeson St, E2 113 E2
Wades Pl, E14 114 B7
Wadeville Av, Rom. RM6 83 F7
Wadeville Cl, Belv. DA17 139 G6
Wadham Av, E17 62 B7
Wadham Gdns, NW3 109 H1
Greenford UB6 86 A6
Wadham Rd, E17 78 B1
SW15 148 B4
Wadhurst Cl, SE20 188 E2
Wadhurst Rd, SW8 150 C1
W4 126 D3
Wadley Rd, E11 78 E7
Wadsworth Business Cen, Grnf. UB6 105 F2
Wadsworth Cl, Enf. EN3 45 G5
Greenford (Perivale) UB6 105 F2
Wadsworth Rd, Grnf. (Perivale) UB6 105 E2
Wager St, E3 113 J4
Waggoners Rbt, Houns. TW5 off Bath Rd 142 B1
Waggon Ms, N14 off Chase Side 58 C1
Waghorn Rd, E13 115 J1
Harrow HA3 69 G3
Waghorn St, SE15 152 D3
Wagner St, SE15 133 F7
Wagstaff Gdns, Dag. RM9 100 C7
Wagtail Cl, NW9 70 E2
Enfield EN1 45 E1
Wagtail Wk, Beck. BR3 190 C5
Waights Ct, Kings.T. KT2 181 H1
Wainfleet Av, Rom. RM5 83 J2
Wainford Cl, SW19 off Windlesham Gro 166 A1
Wainwright Gro, Islw. TW7 144 A4
Waite Davies Rd, SE12 155 F7
Waite St, SE15 37 F5
Waithman St, EC4 19 G4
Wakefield Gdns, SE19 170 B7
Ilford IG1 80 B6
Wakefield Ms, WC1 10 B4
Wakefield Rd, N11 58 D5
N15 76 C5
Richmond TW10 145 G5
Wakefield St, E6 116 A1
N18 60 D5
WC1 10 B5
Wakeford Cl, SW4 150 C5
Wakehams Hill, Pnr. HA5 67 F3
Wakeham St, N1 94 A6
Wakehurst Rd, SW11 149 H5
Wakeling La, Wem. HA0 86 E3
Wakeling Rd, W7 104 C5
Wakeling St, E14 113 H6
Wakelin Rd, E15 114 E2
Wakeman Rd, NW10 107 J3
Wakemans Hill Av, NW9 70 D5
Wakering Rd, Bark. IG11 99 F7
Wakerley Cl, E6 off Truesdale Rd 116 C6
Wakley St, EC1 11 G3
Walberswick St, SW8 131 E7
Walbrook, EC4 20 B5
Walbrook Ho, N9 61 F2
Walbrook Wf, EC4 off Bell Wf La 20 A6
Walburgh St, E1 off Bigland St 112 E6
Walcorde Av, SE17 36 A2
Walcot Ho, SE22 off Albrighton Rd 152 B3
Walcot Rd, Enf. EN3 45 J2
Walcot Sq, SE11 35 F1
Walcott St, SW1 33 G1
Waldair Ct, E16 off Barge Ho Rd 137 E2
Waldair Wf, E16 136 E2
Waldeck Gro, SE27 169 H3
Waldeck Rd, N15 75 H4
SW14 off Lower Richmond Rd 146 C3
W4 126 A6
W13 104 E6
Waldeck Ter, SW14 off Lower Richmond Rd 146 C3
Waldegrave Av, Tedd. TW11 off Waldegrave Rd 162 C5
Waldegrave Gdns, Twick. TW1 162 C2
Waldegrave Pk, Twick. TW1 162 C4
Waldegrave Rd, N8 75 G3
SE19 170 C7
W5 105 J6
Bromley BR1 192 B4
Dagenham RM8 100 C2
Teddington TW11 162 C4
Twickenham TW1 162 C4
Waldegrove, Croy. CR0 202 C3
Waldemar Av, SW6 148 B1
W13 125 F1
Waldemar Rd, SW19 166 D5
Walden Av, N13 59 J4
Chislehurst BR7 174 C4
Walden Cl, Belv. DA17 139 F5
Walden Ct, SW8 off Wandsworth Rd 150 D1
Walden Gdns, Th.Hth. CR7 187 F3
Walden Par, Chis. BR7 off Walden Rd 174 C6
Walden Rd, N17 76 A1
Chislehurst BR7 174 C6
Waldenshaw Rd, SE23 171 F1
Walden St, E1 112 E6
Walden Way, NW7 56 A6
Ilford IG6 65 H7
Waldo Cl, SW4 150 C5
Waldo Pl, Mitch. CR4 167 H7
Waldo Rd, NW10 107 G3
Bromley BR1 192 A3
Waldram Cres, SE23 171 F1
Waldram Pk Rd, SE23 171 G1
Waldram Pl, SE23 off Waldram Cres 171 F1
Waldrist Way, Erith DA18 139 F2
Waldron Gdns, Brom. BR2 190 D3
Waldronhyrst, S.Croy. CR2 201 H4
Waldron Ms, SW3 31 F5
Waldron Rd, SW18 167 F3
Harrow HA1, HA2 86 B1
Waldrons, The, Croy. CR0 201 H4
Waldrons Path, S.Croy. CR2 201 J4
Waldrons Yd, Har. HA2 off Northolt Rd 86 A2
Waldstock Rd, SE28 118 A7
Waleran Cl, Stan. HA7 52 C6
Walerand Rd, SE13 154 C2
Waleran Flats, SE1 36 D1
Wales Av, Cars. SM5 199 J5
Wales Cl, SE15 132 E7
Wales Fm Rd, W3 106 D5
Waleton Acres, Wall. SM6 200 C6
Waley St, E1 113 G5
Walfield Av, N20 41 E7
Walford Rd, N16 94 B4
Walfrey Gdns, Dag. RM9 101 E7
WALHAM GREEN, SW6 128 E7
Walham Grn Ct, SW6 off Waterford Rd 128 E7
Walham Gro, SW6 128 D7
Walham Ri, SW19 166 B6
Walham Yd, SW6 off Eustace Rd 128 D7
Walkden Rd, Chis. BR7 174 D5
Walker Cl, N11 58 C4
SE18 137 F4
W7 124 B1
Feltham TW14 141 J7
Hampton TW12 off Fearnley Cres 161 F6
Walker Ms, SW2 off Effra Rd 151 G5
Walkers Ct, E8 off Wilton Way 94 D6
W1 17 H5
Walkerscroft Mead, SE21 169 J1
Walkers Pl, SW15 off Felsham Rd 148 B4
Walks, The, N2 73 G3
Walkynscroft, SE15 off Firbank Rd 153 E2
Wallace Cl, SE28 off Haldane Rd 118 D7
★ Wallace Collection, W1 16 B3
Wallace Cres, Cars. SM5 199 J5
Wallace Rd, N1 93 J6
Wallace Way, N19 off Giesbach Rd 92 D2
Wallbutton Rd, SE4 153 H2
Wallcote Av, NW2 90 A1
Walled Gdn Cl, Beck. BR3 190 B4
Wall End Rd, E6 98 C7
Waller Dr, Nthwd. HA6 66 A2
Waller Rd, SE14 153 G1
Wallers Cl, Dag. RM9 119 E1
Woodford Green IG8 64 C6
Waller's Hoppet, Loug. IG10 48 B2
Waller Way, SE10 off Greenwich High Rd 134 B7
Wallflower St, W12 107 F7
Wallgrave Rd, SW5 30 A1
Wallingford Av, W10 108 A5
WALLINGTON, SM6 200 C5
Wallington Cor, Wall. SM6 off Manor Rd N 200 B4
Wallington Grn, Wall. SM6 off Croydon Rd 200 B4
Wallington Rd, Ilf. IG3 81 J7
Wallington Sq, Wall. SM6 off Woodcote Rd 200 B6
Wallis All, SE1 28 A3
Wallis Cl, SW11 149 G3
Wallis Ms, N8 off Courcy Rd 75 G3
Wallis Rd, E9 95 J6
Southall UB1 103 H6
Wallis's Cotts, SW2 150 E7
Wallman Pl, N22 off Bounds Grn Rd 75 F1
Wallorton Gdns, SW14 146 D4
Wallside, EC2 20 A2
Wall St, N1 94 A6
Wallwood Rd, E11 96 D1
Wallwood St, E14 113 J5
Walmar Cl, Barn. EN4 41 G1
Walmer Cl, E4 62 B2
Orpington (Farnboro.) BR6 off Tubbenden La S 207 G4
Romford RM7 83 H2
Walmer Gdns, W13 124 D2
Walmer Ho, N9 44 C7
Walmer Pl, W1 15 J1
Walmer Rd, W10 off Latimer Rd 107 J6
W11 108 B7
Walmer St, W1 15 J1
Walmer Ter, SE18 137 F4
Walmgate Rd, Grnf. (Perivale) UB6 104 E1
Walmington Fold, N12 56 D6
Walm La, NW2 90 A5
Walmsley Ho, SW16 off Colson Way 168 C4
Walney Wk, N1 off St. Paul's Rd 93 J6
Walnut Av, West Dr. UB7 120 D3
Walnut Cl, SE8 off Clyde St 133 J6
Carshalton SM5 199 J5
Ilford IG6 off Civic Way 81 F4
Walnut Ct, W5 125 H2
Walnut Gdns, E15 off Burgess Rd 96 E5
Walnut Gro, Enf. EN1 44 A5
Walnut Ms, Sutt. SM2 199 F7
Walnut Rd, E10 96 A2
Walnut Tree Av, Mitch. CR4 off De'Arn Gdns 185 H3
Walnut Tree Cl, SW13 147 F1
Chislehurst BR7 193 F1
Walnut Tree Cotts, SW19 off Church Rd 166 B5
Walnut Tree Rd, SE10 135 E5
Brentford TW8 125 H6
Dagenham RM8 100 D2
Hounslow TW5 123 F6
Walnut Tree Wk, SE11 34 E1
Walnut Way, Buck.H. IG9 64 A3
Ruislip HA4 84 C6
Walpole Av, Rich. TW9 145 J2
Walpole Cl, W13 125 F2
Pinner HA5 51 G6
Walpole Cres, Tedd. TW11 162 C5
Walpole Gdns, W4 126 C5
Twickenham TW2 162 B2
Walpole Ms, NW8 off Queen's Gro 109 G1
SW19 off Walpole Rd 167 G6
Walpole Pk, W5 125 F1
Walpole Pl, SE18 off Brookhill Rd 136 E4
Teddington TW11 162 C5
Walpole Rd, E6 97 J7
E17 77 H4
E18 79 F1
N17 (Downhills Way) 75 J3
N17 (Lordship La) 75 J2
SW19 167 G6
Bromley BR2 192 A5
Croydon CR0 202 A2
Surbiton KT6 181 H7
Teddington TW11 162 C5
Twickenham TW2 162 B2
Walpole St, SW3 31 J3
Walrond Av, Wem. HA9 87 H5
Walsham Cl, N16 off Clarke Path 94 D1
SE28 118 D7
Walsham Rd, SE14 153 G2
Feltham TW14 142 B7
Walsingham Gdns, Epsom KT19 197 E4
Walsingham Pk, Chis. BR7 193 G2
Walsingham Pl, SW4 off Clapham Common W Side 149 J4
SW11 150 A6
Walsingham Rd, E5 94 D3
W13 124 D1
Enfield EN2 44 A4
Mitcham CR4 185 J5
Walsingham Wk, Belv. DA17 139 G6
Walter Hurford Par, E12 off Walton Rd 98 D4
Walter Rodney Cl, E6 off Stevenage Rd 98 C6
Walters Cl, SE17 36 A2
Hayes UB3 121 J2
Walters Ho, SE17 35 G6
Walters Rd, SE25 188 B4
Enfield EN3 45 F5
Walter St, E2 113 G3
Kingston upon Thames KT2 off Sopwith Way 181 H1

Walters Way, SE23 153 G6
Walters Yd, Brom. BR1 191 G2
Walter Ter, E1 113 G6
Walterton Rd, W9 108 C4
Walter Wk, Edg. HA8 54 C6
Waltham Av, NW9 70 A6
Hayes UB3 121 F3
Waltham Dr, Edg. HA8 70 A2
Waltham Pk Way, E17 78 A1
Waltham Rd, Cars. SM5 185 G7
Southall UB2 122 E3
Woodford Green IG8 64 B6
WALTHAMSTOW, E17 78 B2
Walthamstow Av, E4 61 J7
Walthamstow Business Cen, E17 78 C2
Waltham Way, E4 61 J4
Waltheof Av, N17 76 A1
Waltheof Gdns, N17 76 A1
Walton Av, Har. HA2 85 F5
New Malden KT3 183 F4
Sutton SM3 198 C3
Wembley HA9 88 B3
Walton Cl, E5 off Orient Way 95 G3
NW2 89 H2
SW8 34 B7
Harrow HA1 68 A4
Walton Cres, Har. HA2 85 F4
Walton Dr, NW10 88 D6
Harrow HA1 68 A4
Walton Gdns, W3 106 B5
Wembley HA9 87 H2
Walton Grn, Croy. (New Adgtn) CR0 204 C7
Walton Pl, SW3 23 J5
Walton Rd, E12 98 D4
E13 115 J2
Walton Rd, N15 76 C4
East Molesey KT8 179 G4
Harrow HA1 68 A4
Sidcup DA14 176 C2
Walton-on-Thames KT12 178 C5
West Molesey KT8 179 E5
Walton St, SW3 31 H1
Enfield EN2 44 A1
Walton Way, W3 106 B5
Mitcham CR4 186 C4
Walt Whitman Cl, SE24 off Shakespeare Rd 151 H4
WALWORTH, SE17 35 J3
★ **Walworth Garden Fm - Horticultural Training Cen**, SE17 35 H4
Walworth Pl, SE17 36 A4
Walworth Rd, SE1 35 J1
SE17 35 J1
Walwyn Av, Brom. BR1 192 A3
Wanborough Dr, SW15 165 H1
Wanderer Dr, Bark. IG11 118 B3
Wandle Bk, SW19 167 G6
Croydon CR0 200 E3
Wandle Ct, Epsom KT19 196 C4
Wandle Ct Gdns, Croy. CR0 200 E3
Wandle Rd, SW17 167 H2
Croydon CR0 201 J3
Croydon (Bedd.) CR0 201 E3
Morden SM4 185 F4
Wallington SM6 200 B2
Wandle Side, Croy. CR0 201 F3
Wallington SM6 200 B3
Wandle Tech Pk, Mitch. CR4 185 J7
Wandle Trd Est, Mitch. CR4 off Budge La 185 J7
Wandle Way, SW18 166 E1
Mitcham CR4 185 J5
Wandon Rd, SW6 129 E7
WANDSWORTH, SW18 148 C5
Wandsworth Br, SW6 149 E3
SW18 149 E3
Wandsworth Br Rd, SW6 148 E1
Wandsworth Common, SW12 149 H6
Wandsworth Common W Side, SW18 149 F5
Wandsworth High St, SW18 148 D5
★ **Wandsworth Mus**, SW18 off Garratt La 148 E5
Wandsworth Plain, SW18 148 E5
Wandsworth Rd, SW8 34 A5
Wandsworth Town, SW18 148 D5
Wangey Rd, Rom. RM6 82 D7
Wanless Rd, SE24 151 J3
Wanley Rd, SE5 152 A4
Wanlip Rd, E13 115 H4
Wannock Gdns, Ilf. IG6 65 E7
Wansbeck Rd, E3 95 J7
E9 95 J7
Wansdown Pl, SW6 30 A7
Wansey St, SE17 36 A2
Wansford Pk, Borwd. WD6 38 E4
Wansford Rd, Wdf.Grn. IG8 79 J1
WANSTEAD, E11 79 H7
Wanstead Cl, Brom. BR1 191 J2
Wanstead La, Ilf. IG1 80 A6
Wanstead Pk, E11 80 A7
Wanstead Pk Av, E12 98 A2
Wanstead Pk Rd, Ilf. IG1 98 C1
Wanstead Pl, E11 79 G6
Wanstead Rd, Brom. BR1 191 J2
Wansunt Rd, Bex. DA5 177 J1
Wantage Rd, SE12 155 F5
Wantz Rd, Dag. RM10 101 H4
WAPPING, E1 29 J1
Wapping Dock St, E1 off Cinnamon St 133 E1
Wapping High St, E1 29 H2
Wapping La, E1 113 E7
Wapping Wall, E1 133 F1
Warbank La, Kings.T. KT2 165 F7
Warbeck Rd, W12 127 H1
Warberry Rd, N22 75 F2
Warboys App, Kings.T. KT2 164 B6
Warboys Cres, E4 62 C5
Warboys Rd, Kings.T. KT2 164 B6
Warburton Cl, N1 off Culford Rd 94 B6
Harrow HA3 52 A6
Warburton Ho, E8 off Warburton Rd 112 E1
Warburton Rd, E8 113 E1
Twickenham TW2 161 H1
Warburton St, E8 off Warburton Rd 112 E1
Warburton Ter, E17 78 B2
Wardalls Gro, SE14 133 F7
Ward Cl, S.Croy. CR2 202 B5
Wardell Cl, NW7 55 E7
Wardell Fld, NW9 71 E1
Warden Av, Har. HA2 85 F1
Warden Rd, NW5 92 A6
Wardens Fld Cl, Orp. (Grn St Grn) BR6 207 H6
Wardens Gro, SE1 27 J2
Wardle St, E9 95 G5
Wardley St, SW18 off Garratt La 149 E7
Wardo Av, SW6 148 B1
Wardour Ms, W1 17 G4
Wardour St, W1 17 H5
Ward Pt, SE11 35 E2
Ward Rd, E15 114 D1
N19 92 C3
Wardrobe Pl, EC4 off St. Andrew's Hill 19 H4
Wardrobe Ter, EC4 19 H4
Wards Rd, Ilf. IG2 81 G7
Wards Wf App, E16 136 A2
Wareham Cl, Houns. TW3 143 H4
Wareham Ho, SW8 34 C7
Waremead Rd, Ilf. IG2 80 E5
Warenford Way, Borwd. WD6 38 A1
Ware Pt Dr, SE28 137 G2
Warfield Rd, NW10 108 A3
Feltham TW14 141 H7
Hampton TW12 179 H1
Warfield Yd, NW10 off Warfield Rd 108 A3
Wargrave Av, N15 76 C6
Wargrave Rd, Har. HA2 85 J3
Warham Rd, N4 75 G5
Harrow HA3 68 C2
South Croydon CR2 201 H5
Warham St, SE5 35 H7
Waring Cl, Orp. BR6 207 J6
Waring Dr, Orp. BR6 207 J6
Waring Rd, Sid. DA14 176 C6
Waring St, SE27 169 J4
Warkworth Gdns, Islw. TW7 124 D7
Warkworth Rd, N17 60 A7
Warland Rd, SE18 137 G7
Warley Av, Dag. RM8 83 F7
Hayes UB4 102 A5
Warley Cl, E10 off Millicent Rd 95 J1
Warley Rd, N9 61 F2
Hayes UB4 102 A6
Ilford IG5 80 D1
Woodford Green IG8 63 H7
Warley St, E2 113 G3
Warlingham Rd, Th.Hth. CR7 187 H4
Warlock Rd, W9 108 D4
Warlters Cl, N7 off Warlters Rd 93 E4
Warlters Rd, N7 93 E4
Warltersville Rd, N19 74 E7
Warmington Cl, E5 off Denton Way 95 G3
Warmington Rd, SE24 151 J6
Warmington St, E13 off Barking Rd 115 G4
Warminster Gdns, SE25 188 D2
Warminster Rd, SE25 188 C2
Warminster Sq, SE25 188 D2
Warminster Way, Mitch. CR4 186 B1
Warmwell Av, NW9 70 E1
Warndon St, SE16 133 G4
Warneford Rd, Har. HA3 69 G3
Warneford St, E9 113 E1
Warne Pl, Sid. DA15 off Westerham Dr 158 B6
Warner Av, Sutt. SM3 198 B2
Warner Cl, E15 97 E5
NW9 71 F7
Hampton TW12 off Tangley Pk Rd 161 F5
Hayes (Harling.) UB3 121 G7
Warner Ho, SE13 off Conington Rd 154 B2
Warner Par, Hayes UB3 121 G7
Warner Pl, E2 13 J2
Warner Rd, E17 77 H4
N8 74 D4
SE5 151 J1
Bromley BR1 173 F7
Warners Cl, Wdf.Grn. IG8 63 G5
Warners La, Kings.T. KT2 163 G4
Warners Path, Wdf.Grn. IG8 63 G5
Warner St, EC1 11 E6
Warner Ter, E14 off Broomfield St 114 A5
Warner Yd, EC1 10 E6
Warnford Ho, SW15 off Tunworth Cres 147 F6
Warnford Ind Est, Hayes UB3 121 H2
Warnford Rd, Orp. BR6 207 J5
Warnham Ct Rd, Cars. SM5 199 J7
Warnham Rd, N12 57 H5
Warple Ms, W3 off Warple Way 126 E2
Warple Way, W3 126 E1
Warren, The, E12 98 B4
Hayes UB4 102 A6
Hounslow TW5 123 F7
Worcester Park KT4 196 D4
Warren Av, E10 96 C3
Bromley BR1 172 E7
Orpington BR6 207 J5
Richmond TW10 146 B4
South Croydon CR2 203 G7
Warren Cl, N9 45 G7
SE21 151 J7
Bexleyheath DA6 159 G5
Hayes UB4 102 C5
Wembley HA9 87 G2
Warren Ct, N17 off High Cross Rd 76 D3
SE7 135 J5
Chigwell IG7 65 G4
Warren Cres, N9 44 C7
Warren Cutting, Kings.T. KT2 164 D7
Warrender Rd, N19 92 C3
Warrender Way, Ruis. HA4 66 A7
Warren Dr, Grnf. UB6 103 H4
Ruislip HA4 66 D7
Warren Dr, The, E11 79 J7
Warren Dr N, Surb. KT5 196 B1
Warren Dr S, Surb. KT5 196 C1
Warren Flds, Stan. HA7 off Valencia Rd 53 F4
Warren Footpath, Twick. TW1 145 G7
Warren Gdns, E15 off Ashton Rd 96 D5
Warren Gro, Borwd. WD6 38 D4
Warren Hts, Loug. IG10 47 J5
Warren Hill, Loug. IG10 47 J6
Warren Ho, E3 off Bromley High St 114 B3
Warren La, SE18 136 E3
Stanmore HA7 52 C3
Warren La Gate, SE18 136 E3
Warren Ms, W1 9 F6
Warren Pk, Kings.T. KT2 164 C6
Warren Pk Rd, Sutt. SM1 199 G6
Warren Pond Rd, E4 63 F1
Warren Ri, N.Mal. KT3 182 D1
Warren Rd, E4 62 C2
E10 96 C3
E11 97 J1
NW2 89 F2
SW19 167 H6
Bexleyheath DA6 159 G5
Bromley BR2 205 G2
Bushey (Bushey Hth) WD23 51 J1
Croydon CR0 202 B1
Ilford IG6 81 G5
Kingston upon Thames KT2 164 C6
Orpington BR6 207 J5
Sidcup DA14 176 C3
Twickenham TW2 143 J6
Warrens Shawe La, Edg. HA8 54 B1
Warren St, W1 9 E6
Warren Ter, Rom. RM6 82 D4
Warren Wk, SE7 135 J6
Warren Way, Edg. HA8 70 B2
Warren Wd Cl, Brom. BR2 205 F2
Warriner Dr, N9 60 D3
Warriner Gdns, SW11 149 J1
Warrington Cres, W9 6 C6
Warrington Gdns, W9 6 C6
Warrington Rd, Croy. CR0 201 H3
Dagenham RM8 100 D2
Harrow HA1 68 B5
Richmond TW10 145 G5
Warrington Sq, Dag. RM8 100 D2
Warrior Cl, SE28 137 G1
Warrior Sq, E12 98 D4
Warsaw Cl, Ruis. HA4 off Glebe Av 84 B6
Warsdale Dr, NW9 off Mardale Dr 70 D5
Warspite Rd, SE18 136 B3
Warton Rd, E15 96 C7
Warwall, E6 116 E6
Warwick Av, W2 6 C6
W9 6 C6
Edgware HA8 54 B3
Harrow HA2 85 F4
Warwick Bldg, SW8 32 D7
Warwick Chambers, W8 off Pater St 128 D3
Warwick Cl, Barn. EN4 41 G5
Bexley DA5 159 F7
Hampton TW12 161 J7
Warwick Ct, SE15 152 D2
WC1 18 D2
Surbiton KT6 195 H2
Warwick Cres, W2 14 C1
Warwick Dene, W5 125 H1
Warwick Dr, SW15 147 H3
Warwick Est, W2 14 A2
Warwick Gdns, N4 75 J5
W14 128 C3
Ilford IG1 99 E1
Warwick Gdns, Thames Ditton KT7 180 C5
Thornton Heath CR7 off London Rd 187 G3
Warwick Gro, E5 94 E1
Surbiton KT5 181 J7
Warwick Ho St, SW1 25 J1
Warwick La, EC4 19 H4
Warwick Pas, EC4 19 H3
Warwick Pl, W5 off Warwick Rd 125 G2
W9 14 C1
Warwick Pl N, SW1 33 F2
Warwick Rd, E4 62 A5
E11 79 H5
E12 98 B5
E15 97 F6
E17 77 J1
N11 58 D6
N18 60 B4
SE20 189 E3
SW5 128 C4
W5 125 G2
W14 128 C4
Barnet EN5 40 E4
Borehamwood WD6 38 D3
Hounslow TW4 142 B3
Kingston upon Thames KT1 181 F1
New Malden KT3 182 C3
Sidcup DA14 176 B5
Southall UB2 123 F3
Sutton SM1 199 F4
Thames Ditton KT7 180 C5
Thornton Heath CR7 187 G3
Twickenham TW2 162 B1
Welling DA16 158 C3
West Drayton UB7 120 B2
Warwick Row, SW1 25 E5
Warwickshire Path, SE8 133 J7
Warwick Sq, EC4 19 H3
SW1 33 F3
Warwick Sq Ms, SW1 33 F2
Warwick St, W1 17 G5
Warwick Ter, SE18 137 G6
Warwick Way, SW1 33 F2
Warwick Yd, EC1 12 A6
Washington Av, E12 98 B4
Washington Bldg, SE13 off Deals Gateway 154 B1
Washington Cl, E3 114 B3
Washington Rd, E6 off St. Stephens Rd 97 J7
E18 79 F2
SW13 127 G7
Kingston upon Thames KT1 182 A2
Worcester Park KT4 197 H2
Wastdale Rd, SE23 171 G1
Watchfield Ct, W4 126 C5
Watcombe Cotts, Rich. TW9 126 A6
Watcombe Pl, SE25 off Albert Rd 189 E4
Watcombe Rd, SE25 188 E5
Waterbank Rd, SE6 172 C4
Waterbeach Rd, Dag. RM9 100 C6
Water Brook La, NW4 71 J5
Watercress Pl, N1 off Hertford Rd 94 B7
Waterdale Rd, SE2 138 A6
Waterden Cres, E15 96 A5
Waterden Rd, E15 96 A5
Waterer Ri, Wall. SM6 200 D6
Waterfall Cl, N14 58 C3
Waterfall Cotts, SW19 167 G6
Waterfall Rd, N11 58 B4
N14 58 C3
SW19 167 G6
Waterfall Ter, SW17 167 H6
Waterfield Cl, SE28 138 B1
Belvedere DA17 139 G3

Waterfield Gdns, SE25 . . . 188 A4
Waterford Rd, SW6 . . . 149 E1
Waterford Way, NW10 . . . 89 H5
Waterfront Studios Business Cen, E16
 off Silvertown Way . . . 135 G1
Water Gdns, Stan. HA7 . . . 53 E6
Water Gdns, The, W2 . . . 15 H3
Watergardens, The, Kings.T. KT2 . . . 164 C6
Watergate, EC4 . . . 19 G5
Watergate, The, Wat. WD19 . . . 50 D2
Watergate St, SE8 . . . 134 A6
Watergate Wk, WC2 . . . 26 B1
Waterhall Av, E4 . . . 62 E4
Waterhall Cl, E17 . . . 77 G1
Waterhouse Cl, E16 . . . 116 A5
 NW3 off Lyndhurst Rd . . . 91 G5
 W6 off Great Ch La . . . 128 A5
Waterhouse Sq, EC1 . . . 19 E2
Wateridge Cl, E14
 off Westferry Rd . . . 134 A3
Water La, E15 . . . 97 E6
 EC3 . . . 20 D6
 N9 . . . 60 E1
 NW1
 off Kentish Town Rd . . . 92 B7
Water La, SE14 . . . 133 F7
 Ilford IG3 . . . 99 H3
 Kingston upon Thames KT1 . . . 181 G1
 Richmond TW9 . . . 145 G5
 Sidcup DA14 . . . 177 F2
 Twickenham TW1
 off The Embankment . . . 162 D1
Water Lily Cl, Sthl. UB2
 off Navigator Dr . . . 123 J2
Waterloo Br, SE1 . . . 18 C6
 WC2 . . . 18 C6
Waterloo Cl, E9
 off Churchill Wk . . . 95 F5
Waterloo Est, E2 . . . 113 F2
Waterloo Gdns, E2 . . . 113 F2
 N1 off Barnsbury St . . . 93 G7
Waterloo Pas, NW6 . . . 90 C7
Waterloo Pl, SW1 . . . 25 H1
 Richmond TW9
 off The Quadrant . . . 145 H4
 Richmond (Kew) TW9 . . . 126 A6
Waterloo Rd, E6 . . . 97 J7
 E7 off Wellington Rd . . . 97 F5
 E10 . . . 78 A7
 NW2 . . . 89 G1
 SE1 . . . 27 E3
 Ilford IG6 . . . 81 F2
 Sutton SM1 . . . 199 G5
Waterloo Sta, SE1 . . . 26 E3
Waterloo Ter, N1 . . . 93 H7
Waterlow Ct, NW11
 off Heath Cl . . . 72 E7
Waterlow Rd, N19 . . . 92 C1
★ Watermans Art Cen, Brent. TW8 . . . 125 H6
Waterman's Cl, Kings.T.
 KT2 off Woodside Rd . . . 163 H7
Waterman St, SW15 . . . 148 A3
Waterman's Wk, EC4
 off Allhallows La . . . 20 B6
Watermans Wk, SE16 . . . 133 H3
Waterman Way, E1 . . . 132 E1
Watermead Ho, E9
 off Kingsmead Way . . . 95 H5
Watermead La, Cars. SM5
 off Middleton Rd . . . 185 J7
Watermeadow La, SW6 . . . 149 F2
Watermead Rd, SE6 . . . 172 C4
Watermead Way, N17 . . . 76 E3
Watermen's Sq, SE20 . . . 171 F7
Water Ms, SE15 . . . 153 F4
Watermill Business Cen, Enf. EN3 . . . 45 J2
Watermill Cl, Rich. TW10 . . . 163 F3
Watermill La, N18 . . . 60 B5
Watermill Way, SW19 . . . 185 F1
 Feltham TW13 . . . 161 F2
Watermint Quay, N16 . . . 76 D7
Water Rd, Wem. HA0 . . . 105 J1
Watersedge, Epsom KT19 . . . 196 C4
Watersfield Way, Edg. HA8 . . . 53 G7
Waters Gdns, Dag. RM10 . . . 101 G5
Waterside, Beck. BR3
 off Rectory Rd . . . 190 A1
Waterside Av, Beck. BR3
 off Brockwell Av . . . 190 B5
Waterside Cl, E3 . . . 113 J1
 SE16 . . . 29 J4
 SE28 . . . 137 J1
 Barking IG11 . . . 100 A4
 Northolt UB5 . . . 103 F3
 Surbiton KT6
 off Culsac Rd . . . 195 H2
Waterside Ct, SE13
 off Weardale Rd . . . 154 D4
Waterside Dr, Walt. KT12 . . . 178 A5
Waterside Path, SW18
 off Smugglers Way . . . 149 E4
Waterside Pl, NW1
 off Princess Rd . . . 110 A1
Waterside Pt, SW11 . . . 31 H7
Waterside Rd, Sthl. UB2 . . . 123 G3
Waterside Twr, SW6 . . . 149 F1
Waterside Trd Cen, W7 . . . 124 B3
Waterside Way, SW17 . . . 167 F4
Watersmeet Way, SE28 . . . 118 C6
Waterson St, E2 . . . 13 E3
Waters Pl, SW15
 off Danemere St . . . 147 J2
Watersplash Cl, Kings.T. KT1 . . . 181 H3
Watersplash La, Hayes UB3 . . . 122 A4
 Hounslow TW5 . . . 122 B5
Waters Rd, SE6 . . . 172 E3
 Kingston upon Thames KT1 . . . 182 B2
Waters Sq, Kings.T. KT1 . . . 182 B3
Water St, WC2 . . . 18 D5
Water Twr Hill, Croy. CR0 . . . 202 A4
Water Twr Pl, N1
 off Old Royal Free Sq . . . 111 G1
Waterview Cl, Bexh. DA6
 off Danson Rd . . . 158 D5
Waterview Ho, E14 . . . 113 H5
Waterway Av, SE13 . . . 154 B3
Waterworks Cor, E18 . . . 79 E2
Waterworks La, E5 . . . 95 G2
Waterworks Rd, SW2 . . . 151 E6
Waterworks Yd, Croy. CR0
 off Surrey St . . . 201 J3
Watery La, SW20 . . . 184 C2
 Northolt UB5 . . . 102 C2
 Sidcup DA14 . . . 176 B6
Wates Way, Mitch. CR4 . . . 185 J6
Wates Way Ind Est, Mitch. CR4 . . . 185 J6
Wateville Rd, N17 . . . 75 J1
Watford Cl, SW11
 off Petworth St . . . 149 H1
WATFORD HEATH, Wat. WD19 . . . 50 E1
Watford Rd, E16 . . . 115 G5
 Harrow HA1 . . . 86 D2
 Wembley HA0 . . . 86 D2
Watford Way, NW4 . . . 71 G4
 NW7 . . . 55 F6
Watkin Rd, Wem. HA9 . . . 88 B3
Watkinson Rd, N7 . . . 93 F6
Watling Av, Edg. HA8 . . . 54 D7
Watling Ct, EC4 . . . 20 A4
Watling Fm Cl, Stan. HA7 . . . 53 F1
Watling Gdns, NW2 . . . 90 B6
Watlings Cl, Croy. CR0 . . . 189 H6
Watling St, EC4 . . . 19 J4
 SE15 . . . 36 E6
 Bexleyheath DA6 . . . 159 H4
Watlington Gro, SE26 . . . 171 H5
Watney Cotts, SW14
 off Lower Richmond Rd . . . 146 C3
Watney Mkt, E1
 off Commercial Rd . . . 113 E6
Watney Rd, SW14 . . . 146 C3
Watneys Rd, Mitch. CR4 . . . 186 D5
Watney St, E1 . . . 113 E6
Watson Av, E6 . . . 98 D7
 Sutton SM3 . . . 198 B2
Watson Cl, N16
 off Matthias Rd . . . 94 A5
 SW19 . . . 167 H6
Watsons Ms, W1 . . . 15 H2
Watsons Rd, N22 . . . 75 F1
Watson's St, SE8 . . . 134 A7
Watson St, E13 . . . 115 H2
Watsons Yd, NW2
 off North Circular Rd . . . 89 F2
Wattisfield Rd, E5 . . . 95 F3
Watts Cl, N15
 off Seaford Rd . . . 76 B5
Wattsdown Cl, E13 . . . 115 G1
Watts Gro, E3 . . . 114 B5
Watts La, Chis. BR7 . . . 193 E1
 Teddington TW11 . . . 162 D5
Watts Rd, T.Ditt. KT7 . . . 180 D7
Watts St, E1 . . . 133 E1
 SE15 . . . 152 C1
Watts Way, SW7 . . . 23 F5
Wat Tyler Rd, SE3 . . . 154 C2
 SE10 . . . 154 C2
Wauthier Cl, N13 . . . 59 H5
Wavell Dr, Sid. DA15 . . . 157 H6
Wavel Ms, N8 . . . 74 D4
 NW6 off Acol Rd . . . 90 E7
Wavel Pl, SE26
 off Sydenham Hill . . . 170 C4
Wavendon Av, W4 . . . 126 D5
Waveney Av, SE15 . . . 153 E4
Waveney Cl, E1 . . . 29 J1
Waverley Av, E4 . . . 61 J4
 E17 . . . 78 D3
 Surbiton KT5 . . . 182 B6
 Sutton SM1 . . . 199 E2
 Twickenham TW2 . . . 161 F1
 Wembley HA9 . . . 87 J5
Waverley Cl, E18 . . . 79 J1
 Bromley BR2 . . . 192 A5
 Hayes UB3 . . . 121 G4
 West Molesey KT8 . . . 179 G5
Waverley Cres, SE18 . . . 137 G5
Waverley Gdns, E6
 off Oliver Gdns . . . 116 B5
 NW10 . . . 105 J3
 Barking IG11 . . . 117 H2
 Ilford IG6 . . . 81 F2
 Northwood HA6 . . . 66 A1
Waverley Gro, N3 . . . 72 A3
Waverley Ind Est, Har. HA1 . . . 68 A3
Waverley Pl, N4 . . . 93 H1
 NW8 . . . 6 E1
Waverley Rd, E17 . . . 78 C3
 E18 . . . 79 J1
 N8 . . . 74 D6
 N17 . . . 60 E7
 SE18 . . . 137 F5
 SE25 . . . 188 E4
 Enfield EN2 . . . 43 H4
 Epsom KT17 . . . 197 H5
 Harrow HA2 . . . 85 F1
 Southall UB1 . . . 103 G7
Waverley Vil, N17 . . . 76 C2
Waverley Wk, W2 . . . 108 D5
Waverley Way, Cars. SM5 . . . 199 H6
Waverton Ho, E3 . . . 113 J1
Waverton Rd, SW18 . . . 149 F7
Waverton St, W1 . . . 24 C1
Wavertree Ct, SW2
 off Streatham Hill . . . 169 E1
Wavertree Rd, E18 . . . 79 G2
 SW2 . . . 169 E1
Waxham, NW3 . . . 91 J5
Waxlow Cres, Sthl. UB1 . . . 103 G6
Waxlow Rd, NW10 . . . 106 C2
Waxlow Way, Nthlt. UB5 . . . 103 F4
Waxwell Cl, Pnr. HA5 . . . 66 D2
Waxwell La, Pnr. HA5 . . . 66 D2
Waye Av, Houns. TW5 . . . 142 A1
Wayfarer Rd, Nthlt. UB5 . . . 102 D4
Wayfield Link, SE9 . . . 157 G6
Wayford St, SW11 . . . 149 H2
Wayland Av, E8 . . . 94 D5
Wayland Ho, SW9 . . . 151 G2
Waylands Mead, Beck. BR3 . . . 190 B1
Wayleave, The, SE28 . . . 118 B7
Waylett Ho, SE11 . . . 34 E4
Waylett Pl, SE27 . . . 169 H3
 Wembley HA0 . . . 87 G4
Wayman Ct, E8 . . . 94 E6
Wayne Cl, Orp. BR6 . . . 207 J3
Waynflete Av, Croy. CR0 . . . 201 H3
Waynflete Sq, W10 . . . 108 A7
Waynflete St, SW18 . . . 167 F2
Wayside, NW11 . . . 90 B1
 SW14 . . . 146 C5
 Croydon (New Adgtn) CR0 . . . 204 B6
Wayside Cl, N14 . . . 42 C6
Wayside Commercial Est, Bark. IG11 . . . 118 A1
Wayside Ct, Twick. TW1 . . . 145 F6
 Wembley HA9
 off Oakington Av . . . 88 A3
Wayside Gdns, SE9
 off Wayside Gro . . . 174 C4
 Dagenham RM10 . . . 101 G5
Wayside Gro, SE9 . . . 174 C4
Wayside Ms, Ilf. IG2
 off Gaysham Av . . . 80 D5
Weald, The, Chis. BR7 . . . 174 C6
Weald Cl, SE16
 off Stevenson Cres . . . 132 E5
 Bromley BR2 . . . 206 B2
Weald La, Har. HA3 . . . 68 A2
Weald Ri, Har. HA3 . . . 52 C7
Weald Sq, E5 . . . 94 D2
WEALDSTONE, Har. HA3 . . . 68 C3
Wealdstone Rd, Sutt. SM3 . . . 198 C2
Weald Way, Rom. RM7 . . . 83 H6
Wealdwood Gdns, Pnr. HA5
 off Highbanks Rd . . . 51 H6
Weale Rd, E4 . . . 62 D3
Weardale Gdns, Enf. EN2 . . . 44 A1
Weardale Rd, SE13 . . . 154 D4
Wear Pl, E2 . . . 112 E3
Wearside Rd, SE13 . . . 154 B4
Weatherley Cl, E3 . . . 113 J5
Weaver Cl, E6
 off Trader Rd . . . 116 E7
 Croydon CR0 . . . 202 C4
Weavers Almshouses, E11
 off New Wanstead . . . 79 G6
Weavers Cl, Islw. TW7 . . . 144 B4
Weavers Ter, SW6 . . . 128 D6
Weaver St, E1 . . . 13 H6
Weavers Way, NW1 . . . 110 D1
Weaver Wk, SE27 . . . 169 H4
Webb Cl, W10 . . . 107 J4
Webber Row, SE1 . . . 27 F5
Webber St, SE1 . . . 27 F3
Webb Est, E5 . . . 76 D7
Webb Gdns, E13
 off Kelland Rd . . . 115 G4
Webb Pl, NW10 . . . 107 F3
Webb Rd, SE3 . . . 135 F6
Webbscroft Rd, Dag. RM10 . . . 101 H4
Webbs Rd, SW11 . . . 149 J5
 Hayes UB4 . . . 102 B3
Webb St, SE1 . . . 28 D6
Webheath Est, NW6 . . . 90 C7
Webster Gdns, W5 . . . 125 G1
Webster Rd, E11 . . . 96 C3
 SE16 . . . 29 J6
Wedderburn Rd, NW3 . . . 91 G5
 Barking IG11 . . . 117 G1
Wedgwood Ho, SE11 . . . 27 E6
Wedgwood Ms, W1 . . . 17 J4
Wedgwood Wk, NW6
 off Dresden Cl . . . 91 E5
Wedgwood Way, SE19 . . . 169 J7
Wedlake St, W10
 off Kensal Rd . . . 108 B4
Wedmore Av, Ilf. IG5 . . . 80 D1
Wedmore Gdns, N19 . . . 92 D2
Wedmore Ms, N19 . . . 92 D3
Wedmore Rd, Grnf. UB6 . . . 104 A3
Wedmore St, N19 . . . 92 D3
Weech Rd, NW6 . . . 90 D4
Weedington Rd, NW5 . . . 92 A5
Weekley Sq, SW11
 off Thomas Baines Rd . . . 149 G3
Weigall Rd, SE12 . . . 155 G4
Weighhouse St, W1 . . . 16 C4
Weighton Rd, SE20 . . . 188 E2
 Harrow HA3 . . . 68 A1
Weihurst Gdns, Sutt. SM1 . . . 199 G5
Weimar St, SW15 . . . 148 B3
Weirdale Av, N20 . . . 57 J2
Weir Est, SW12 . . . 150 C7
Weir Hall Av, N18 . . . 60 A6
Weir Hall Gdns, N18 . . . 60 A5
Weir Hall Rd, N17 . . . 60 A5
 N18 . . . 60 A5
Weir Rd, SW12 . . . 150 C7
 SW19 . . . 167 E3
 Bexley DA5 . . . 159 H7
 Walton-on-Thames KT12 . . . 178 A6
Weirside Gdns, West Dr. UB7 . . . 120 A1
Weir's Pas, NW1 . . . 9 J3
Weiss Rd, SW15 . . . 148 A3
Welbeck Av, Brom. BR1 . . . 173 G4
 Hayes UB4 . . . 102 B4
 Sidcup DA15 . . . 176 A1
Welbeck Cl, N12
 off Torrington Pk . . . 57 G5
 Borehamwood WD6 . . . 38 A3
 Epsom KT17 . . . 197 G7
 New Malden KT3 . . . 183 F5
Welbeck Rd, E6 . . . 116 A3
 Barnet EN4 . . . 41 G6
 Carshalton SM5 . . . 199 H1
 Harrow HA2 . . . 85 H1
 Sutton SM1 . . . 199 G2
Welbeck St, W1 . . . 16 D3
Welbeck Wk, Cars. SM5
 off Welbeck Rd . . . 199 H1
Welbeck Way, W1 . . . 16 D3
Welby St, SE5 . . . 151 H1
Welch Pl, Pnr. HA5 . . . 66 C1
Weldon Cl, Ruis. HA4 . . . 84 B6
Weldon Dr, W.Mol. KT8 . . . 179 F4
Weld Pl, N11 . . . 58 B5
Welfare Rd, E15 . . . 97 E7
Welford Cl, E5
 off Denton Way . . . 95 G3
Welford Pl, SW19 . . . 166 B4
Welham Rd, SW16 . . . 168 A5
 SW17 . . . 168 A5
Welhouse Rd, Cars. SM5 . . . 199 H1
Wellacre Rd, Har. HA3 . . . 69 E6
Wellan Cl, Sid. DA15 . . . 158 B5
Welland Gdns, Grnf. (Perivale) UB6 . . . 104 C2
Welland Ms, E1 . . . 29 J1
Wellands Cl, Brom. BR1 . . . 192 C2
Welland St, SE10 . . . 134 C6
Well App, Barn. EN5 . . . 39 J5
Wellbrook Rd, Orp. BR6 . . . 206 D4
Wellby Cl, N9 . . . 60 D1
Well Cl, SW16 . . . 169 F4
 Ruislip HA4
 off Parkfield Cres . . . 84 E3
Wellclose Sq, E1 . . . 21 J5
Wellclose St, E1 . . . 21 J6
★ Wellcome Trust, NW1 . . . 9 G5
Well Cottage Cl, E11 . . . 79 J7
Well Ct, EC4 . . . 20 A4
 SW16 . . . 169 F4
Welldon Cres, Har. HA1 . . . 68 B6
Weller Ms, Brom. BR2 . . . 191 H4
Weller St, SE1 . . . 27 J3
Wellesley Av, W6 . . . 127 H3
Wellesley Cl, SE7
 off Wellington Gdns . . . 135 J5
Wellesley Ct, W9 . . . 6 C3
 Sutton SM3
 off Stonecot Hill . . . 198 B1
Wellesley Ct Rd, Croy. CR0 . . . 202 A2
Wellesley Cres, Twick. TW2 . . . 162 B2
Wellesley Gro, Croy. CR0 . . . 202 A2
Wellesley Pk Ms, Enf. EN2 . . . 43 H2
Wellesley Pas, Croy. CR0
 off Wellesley Rd . . . 201 J2
Wellesley Pl, NW1 . . . 9 H4
Wellesley Rd, E11 . . . 79 G5
 E17 . . . 78 A6
 N22 . . . 75 G2
 NW5 . . . 92 A5
 W4 . . . 126 A5
 Croydon CR0 . . . 201 J1
 Harrow HA1 . . . 68 B5
 Ilford IG1 . . . 98 E2
 Sutton SM2 . . . 199 F6
 Twickenham TW2 . . . 162 A3

Wellesley St, E1 113 G5
Wellesley Ter, N1 12 A3
Wellfield Av, N10 74 B3
Wellfield Rd, SW16 169 E4
Wellfields, Loug. IG10 48 D3
Wellfield Wk, SW16 169 F5
Wellfit St, SE24
off Hinton Rd 151 H3
Wellgarth, Grnf. UB6 86 E6
Wellgarth Rd, NW11 91 E1
Well Gro, N20 41 F7
Well Hall Par, SE9
off Well Hall Rd 156 C4
Well Hall Rd, SE9 156 C3
Well Hall Rbt, SE9 156 B3
Wellhouse La, Barn. EN5 39 J4
Wellhouse Rd, Beck. BR3 189 J4
Wellhurst Cl, Orp. BR6 207 J7
WELLING, DA16 158 A3
Welling High St, Well.
DA16 158 B3
Wellings Ho, Hayes UB3 122 B1
★ **Wellington Arch**, W1 24 C3
Wellington Av, E4 62 A2
N9 61 E3
N15 76 C6
Hounslow TW3 143 G5
Pinner HA5 67 F1
Sidcup DA15 158 A6
Worcester Park KT4 197 J3
Wellington Bldgs, SW1 32 C4
Wellington Cl, SE14
off Rutts Ter 153 G1
W11 *off Ledbury Rd* 108 D6
Dagenham RM10 101 J7
Watford WD19 51 F3
Wellington Ct, NW8 7 E2
Staines TW19
off Clare Rd 140 B7
Wellington Cres, N.Mal.
KT3 182 C3
Wellington Dr, Dag.
RM10 101 J7
Wellington Gdns, SE7 135 J6
Twickenham TW2 162 A4
Wellington Gro, SE10
off Crooms Hill 134 D7
Wellington Ms, SE7 135 J6
SE22 *off Peckham Rye* 152 D4
SW16
off Woodbourne Av 168 D3
Wellington Par, Sid.
DA15 158 A5
Wellington Pk Est, NW2 89 G2
Wellington Pas, E11
off Wellington Rd 79 G5
Wellington Pl, N2
off Great N Rd 73 H5
NW8 7 F3
Wellington Rd, E6 116 C2
E7 97 F4
E10 95 H1
E11 79 G5
E17 77 H3
NW8 7 E1
NW10 108 A3
SW19 166 D2
W5 125 F3
Belvedere DA17 139 F5
Bexley DA5 158 D6
Bromley BR2 191 J4
Croydon CR0 187 H7
Enfield EN1 44 B4
Feltham TW14 141 H5
Hampton TW12 162 A5
Harrow HA3 68 B3
Pinner HA5 67 F1
Twickenham TW2 162 A5
Wellington Rd N, Houns.
TW4 143 F3
Wellington Rd S, Houns.
TW4 143 F4
Wellington Row, E2 13 G3
Wellington Sq, N1
off Pembroke Av 111 F1
SW3 31 J3
Wellington St, SE18 136 D4
WC2 18 B5
Barking IG11
off Axe St 117 F1
Wellington Ter, E1 132 E1
W2
off Notting Hill Gate 14 A6
Harrow HA1
off West St 86 A1
Wellington Way, E3 114 A3
Welling Way, SE9 157 G3
Welling DA16 157 G3
Well La, SW14 146 C5
Wellmeadow Rd, SE6 155 E7
SE13 154 E6
W7 124 D4
Wellow Wk, Cars. SM5 199 G1
Well Pas, NW3 91 G3
Well Rd, NW3 91 G3
Barnet EN5 39 J5
Wells, The, N14 42 D7
Wells Cl, Nthlt. UB5
off Yeading La 102 C3
South Croydon CR2 202 B5
Wells Dr, NW9 88 D1
Wells Gdns, Dag. RM10 101 H5
Ilford IG1 80 B7
Wells Ho Rd, NW10 106 E5
Wellside Cl, Barn. EN5 39 J4
Wellside Gdns, SW14
off Well La 146 C5
Wells Ms, W1 17 G2
Wellsmoor Gdns, Brom.
BR1 192 D3
Wells Pk Rd, SE26 170 D3
Wells Pl, SW18 149 F7
Wellspring Cres, Wem.
HA9 88 B3
Wellspring Ms, SE26
off Wells Pk Rd 171 E4
Wells Ri, NW8 109 J1
Wells Rd, W12 127 J2
Bromley BR1 192 C2
Wells Sq, WC1 10 C4
Wells St, W1 17 F2
Wellstead Av, N9 45 F7
Wellstead Rd, E6 116 D2
Wells Ter, N4 93 G2
Well St, E9 95 E7
E15 96 E6
Wells Way, SE5 36 C5
SW7 22 E5
Wells Yd S, N7
off George's Rd 93 G5
Well Wk, NW3 91 G4
Wellwood Rd, Ilf. IG3 100 A1
Welmar Ms, SW4 150 D4
Welsford St, SE1 37 H3
Welsh Cl, E13 115 G3
Welshpool Ho, E8
off Benjamin Cl 112 D1
Welshpool St, E8
off Broadway Mkt 112 E1
Welshside Wk, NW9
off Fryent Gro 71 E6
Welstead Way, W4 127 F4
Weltje Rd, W6 127 G5
Welton Rd, SE18 137 H7
Welwyn Av, Felt. TW14 141 J6
Welwyn St, E2
off Globe Rd 113 F3
WEMBLEY, HA0 & HA9 87 H5
Wembley Commercial Cen,
Wem. HA9 87 G2
Wembley Hill Rd, Wem.
HA9 87 J5
WEMBLEY PARK, Wem.
HA9 87 J2
Wembley Pk Business Cen,
Wem. HA9 88 B3
Wembley Pk Dr, Wem.
HA9 87 J3
Wembley Pt, Wem. HA9 88 B7
Wembley Rd, Hmptn.
TW12 161 G7
★ **Wembley Stadium**,
Wem. HA9 88 A4
Wembley Way, Wem. HA9 88 B6
Wemborough Rd, Stan.
HA7 53 F7
Wembury Ms, N6
off Wembury Rd 74 B7
Wembury Rd, N6 74 B7
Wemyss Rd, SE3 155 F2
Wendela Ct, Har. HA1 86 B3
Wendell Rd, W12 127 F2
Wendle Ct, SW8 34 A6
Wendle Sq, SW11
off Petworth St 149 H1
Wendling, NW5 91 J5
Wendling Rd, Sutt. SM1 199 G1
Wendon St, E3 113 J1
Wendover, SE17 36 D3
Wendover Cl, Hayes UB4 102 D4
Wendover Ct, W3 106 B4
Wendover Dr, N.Mal.
KT3 183 F6
Wendover Rd, NW10 107 F2
SE9 156 A3
Bromley BR2 191 H3
Wendover Way, Well.
DA16 158 A5
Wendy Cl, Enf. EN1 44 C6
Wendy Way, Wem. HA0 105 H1
Wenlock Ct, N1 12 C2
Wenlock Gdns, NW4 71 G4
Wenlock Rd, N1 11 J1
Edgware HA8 54 B7
Wenlock St, N1 12 A2
Wennington Rd, E3 113 G2
Wensley Av, Wdf.Grn. IG8 63 F7
Wensley Cl, N11 58 A6
SE9 156 C6
Wensleydale Av, Ilf. IG5 80 B2
Wensleydale Gdns, Hmptn.
TW12 161 H7
Wensleydale Pas, Hmptn.
TW12 179 G1
Wensleydale Rd, Hmptn.
TW12 161 G6
Wensley Rd, N18 60 E6
Wentland Cl, SE6 172 D2
Wentland Rd, SE6 172 D2
Wentworth Av, N3 56 D7
Wentworth Cl, N3 56 E7
SE28 118 D6
Bromley (Hayes) BR2
off Hillside La 205 G2
Morden SM4 184 D7
Orpington BR6 207 H5
Surbiton (Long Dit.)
KT6 195 G2
Wentworth Ct, Surb. KT6
off Culsac Rd 195 H2
Wentworth Cres, SE15 132 D7
Hayes UB3 121 G3
Wentworth Dr, Pnr. HA5 66 A5
Watford WD19 50 D5
Wentworth Gdns, N13 59 H4
Wentworth Hill, Wem.
HA9 87 J1
Wentworth Ms, E3
off Eric St 113 J4
W3 107 E6
Wentworth Pk, N3 56 D7
Wentworth Pl, Stan. HA7
off Greenacres Dr 52 E6
Wentworth Rd, E12 98 A4
NW11 72 C6
Barnet EN5 40 A3
Croydon CR0 187 G7
Southall UB2 122 C4
Wentworth St, E1 21 F3
Wentworth Way, Pnr. HA5 66 D4
Wenvoe Av, Bexh. DA7 159 H2
Wepham Cl, Hayes UB4 102 D5
Wernbrook St, SE18 137 F6
Werndee Rd, SE25 188 D4
Werneth Hall Rd, Ilf. IG5 80 C3
Werrington St, NW1 9 G2
Werter Rd, SW15 148 B4
Wesleyan Pl, NW5
off Gordon Ho Rd 92 B4
Wesley Av, E16 135 G1
NW10 106 D3
Hounslow TW3 143 E2
Wesley Cl, N7 93 F2
SE17 35 H2
Harrow HA2 85 J2
Wesley Rd, E10 78 C7
NW10 106 C1
Hayes UB3 102 A7
★ **Wesley's Ho**, EC1 12 B6
Wesley Sq, W11
off Bartle Rd 108 B6
Wesley St, W1 16 C2
Wessex Av, SW19 184 D2
Wessex Cl, Ilf. IG3 81 H6
Kingston upon Thames
KT1 182 B1
Thames Ditton KT7 194 C2
Wessex Ct, Wem. HA9 87 J2
Wessex Dr, Pnr. HA5 51 E7
Wessex Gdns, NW11 90 B1
Wessex Ho, SE1 37 G3
Wessex La, Grnf. UB6 104 A2
Wessex St, E2 113 F3
Wessex Way, NW11 72 B7
Wessonmead, SE5
off Camberwell Rd 131 J7
West 12 Shop Cen, W12 128 A2
Westacott Cl, N19 92 D1
WEST ACTON, W3 106 A6
Westall Rd, Loug. IG10 49 E3
West App, Orp. BR5 193 F5
West Arbour St, E1 113 G6
West Av, E17 78 B4
N3 56 D6
NW4 72 A5
Pinner HA5 67 F6
Southall UB1 103 F7
Wallington SM6 201 E5
West Av Rd, E17 78 A4
West Bk, N16 76 B7
Barking IG11
off Highbridge Rd 117 E1
Enfield EN2 43 J2
Westbank Rd, Hmptn.
(Hmptn H.) TW12 161 J6
WEST BARNES, N.Mal.
KT3 183 G5
West Barnes La, SW20 183 H2
New Malden KT3 183 H3
Westbeech Rd, N22 75 G3
Westbere Dr, Stan. HA7 53 G4
Westbere Rd, NW2 90 B4
Westbourne Av, W3 106 D6
Sutton SM3 198 B2
Westbourne Br, W2 14 C2
Westbourne Cl, Hayes
UB4 102 B4
Westbourne Cres, W2 14 E5
Westbourne Cres Ms,
W2 14 E5
Westbourne Dr, SE23 171 G2
Westbourne Gdns, W2 14 A3
WESTBOURNE GREEN,
W2 108 D5
Westbourne Gro, W2 108 D6
W11 108 D6
Westbourne Gro Ms, W11
off Westbourne Gro 108 D6
Westbourne Gro Ter, W2 14 A3
Westbourne Ho, Houns.
TW5 *off Wheatlands* 123 G6
Westbourne Pk Ms, W2 14 A3
Westbourne Pk Pas, W2
off Westbourne Pk Vil 108 D5
Westbourne Pk Rd, W2 108 D5
W11 108 B6
Westbourne Pk Vil, W2 108 D5
Westbourne Pl, N9 61 E3
Westbourne Rd, N7 93 G6
SE26 171 G6
Bexleyheath DA7 138 E7
Croydon CR0 188 C6
Westbourne St, W2 15 E5
Westbourne Ter, SE23
off Westbourne Dr 171 G2
W2 14 D3
Westbourne Ter Ms, W2 14 C3
Westbourne Ter Rd, W2 14 C2
West Br Cl, W12
off Percy Rd 127 G1
Westbridge Rd, SW11 149 G1
WEST BROMPTON, SW10 30 A5
Westbrook Av, Hmptn.
TW12 161 F7
Westbrook Cl, Barn. EN4 41 G3
Westbrook Cres, Barn.
(Cockfos.) EN4 41 G3
Westbrooke Cres, Well.
DA16 158 C3
Westbrooke Rd, Sid.
DA15 175 G2
Welling DA16 158 B3
Westbrook Rd, SE3 155 H1
Hounslow TW5 123 F7
Thornton Heath CR7 188 A1
Westbrook Sq, Barn. EN4
off Westbrook Cres 41 G3
Westbury Av, N22 75 H3
Esher (Clay.) KT10 194 C6
Southall UB1 103 G4
Wembley HA0 87 H7
Westbury Cl, Ruis. HA4 66 A7
Westbury Gro, N12 56 D6
Westbury La, Buck.H. IG9 63 J2
Westbury Lo Cl, Pnr. HA5 66 D3
Westbury Par, SW12
off Balham Hill 150 B6
Westbury Pl, Brent. TW8 125 G6
Westbury Rd, E7 97 H5
E17 78 A4
N11 58 E6
N12 56 D6
SE20 189 G1
W5 105 H6
Barking IG11 117 G1
Beckenham BR3 189 H3
Bromley BR1 192 A1
Buckhurst Hill IG9 63 J2
Croydon CR0 188 A6
Feltham TW13 160 D1
Ilford IG1 98 C2
New Malden KT3 182 D4
Wembley HA0 87 H7
Westbury St, SW8 150 C2
Westbury Ter, E7 97 H6
West Carriage Dr, W2 23 F2
West Cen St, WC1 18 A3
West Cen Av, W10
off Harrow Rd 107 H3
West Chantry, Har. HA3
off Chantry Rd 67 H1
Westchester Dr, NW4 72 A3
Westcliffe Apts, W2 15 F2
West Cl, N9 60 C3
Barnet EN5 39 H5
Barnet (Cockfos.) EN4 42 A4
Greenford UB6 103 J2
Hampton TW12
off Oak Av 161 E6
Wembley HA9 87 J1
Westcombe Av, Croy.
CR0 187 E6
Westcombe Ct, SE3
off Westcombe Pk Rd 135 F7
Westcombe Dr, Barn. EN5 40 D5
Westcombe Hill, SE3 135 G5
SE10 135 G5
Westcombe Pk Rd, SE3 135 E6
West Common Rd, Brom.
BR2 205 G2
Keston BR2 205 H4
Westcoombe Av, SW20 183 F1
Westcote Rd, SW16 168 C5
West Cotts, NW6 90 D5
Westcott Cl, N15
off Ermine Rd 76 C6
Bromley BR1 192 B5
Westcott Cres, W7 104 B6
Westcott Ho, E14
off East India Dock Rd 114 A7
Westcott Rd, SE17 35 G5
West Ct, SE18
*off Prince
Imperial Rd* 156 C1
Westcourt, Sun. TW16 178 B2
West Ct, Wem. HA0 87 F2
Westcroft Cl, NW2 90 B4
Westcroft Gdns, Mord.
SM4 184 C3
Westcroft Rd, Cars. SM5 200 A4
Wallington SM6 200 A4
Westcroft Sq, W6 127 G4
Westcroft Way, NW2 90 B4
West Cromwell Rd,
SW5 128 C4
W14 128 C4
West Cross Cen, Brent.
TW8 124 D6
West Cross Route, W10 108 A7
W11 108 A7
West Cross Way, Brent.
TW8 124 E6
Westdale Pas, SE18 136 E6
Westdale Rd, SE18 137 E6
Westdean Av, SE12 173 H1
Westdean Cl, SW18 149 E5

West Dene, Sutt. SM3
off Park La 198 B6
Westdown Rd, E15 96 C4
SE6 154 A7
WEST DRAYTON, UB7 120 A3
West Drayton Pk Av,
West Dr. UB7 120 B3
West Dr, SW16 168 C4
Harrow HA3 52 A6
West Dr Gdns, Har. HA3 52 A6
WEST DULWICH, SE21 170 A3
West Eaton Pl, SW1 32 B1
West Eaton Pl Ms, SW1 32 B1
West Ella Rd, NW10 88 E7
West End Av, E10 78 C5
Pinner HA5 66 D4
West End Cl, NW10 88 C7
West End Ct, Pnr. HA5 66 D4
West End Gdns, Nthlt. UB5
off Edward Cl 102 C2
West End La, NW6 90 D7
Barnet EN5 40 A4
Hayes (Harling.) UB3 121 F7
Pinner HA5 66 D3
West End Rd, Nthlt. UB5 84 C7
Ruislip HA4 84 B5
Southall UB1 122 E1
Westerdale Rd, SE10 135 G5
Westerfield Rd, N15 76 C5
Westergate Rd, SE2 138 E6
Westerham Av, N9 60 A3
Westerham Dr, Sid.
DA15 158 B6
Westerham Rd, E10 78 B6
Keston BR2 206 A6
Westerley Cres, SE26 171 J5
Westerley Ware, Rich. TW9
off Kew Grn 126 A6
Western Av, NW11 72 A6
W3 106 D5
W5 105 J3
Dagenham RM10 101 J6
Greenford UB6 104 C3
Northolt UB5 103 F1
Western Av Business Pk,
W3 off Mansfield Rd 106 B4
Western Av Underpass, W5
off Western Av 105 J3
Western Beach Apts, E16
off Hanover Av 135 G1
Western Ct, N3
off Huntly Dr 56 D6
Western Gdns, W5 106 A7
Western Gateway, E16 115 G7
Western Int Mkt, Sthl.
UB2 122 B4
Western La, SW12 150 A7
Western Ms, W9
off Great Western Rd 108 C4
Western Par, Barn.
(New Barn.) EN5
off Great N Rd 40 D5
Western Pl, SE16
off Canon Beck Rd 133 F2
Western Rd, E13 115 J1
E17 78 C5
N2 73 J4
N22 75 F2
NW10 106 C4
SW9 151 G3
SW19 185 G1
W5 105 G7
Mitcham CR4 185 G1
Southall UB2 122 D3
Sutton SM1 198 D5
Western Ter, W6
off Chiswick Mall 127 G5
Western Trd Est, NW10 106 C4
Western Vw, Hayes UB3 121 J2
Westernville Gdns, Ilf. IG2 81 F7
Western Way, SE28 137 G3
Barnet EN5 40 D6
WEST EWELL, Epsom
KT19 196 E7
Westferry Circ, E14 133 J1
Westferry Rd, E14 134 A1
Westfield, Loug. IG10 47 J5
Westfield Cl, NW9 70 C3
SW10 129 F7
Enfield EN3 45 H3
Sutton SM1 198 C4
Westfield Dr, Har. HA3 69 G5
Westfield Gdns, Har. HA3 69 G4
Romford RM6 82 C6
Westfield La, Har. HA3 69 G4
Westfield London, W12 127 J1
Westfield Pk, Pnr. HA5 51 F7
Westfield Pk Dr, Wdf.Grn.
IG8 64 B6
Westfield Rd, NW7 54 D3
W13 124 D1
Beckenham BR3 189 J2
Bexleyheath DA7 159 J2
Croydon CR0 201 H2
Dagenham RM9 101 E4
Mitcham CR4 185 J2
Surbiton KT6 181 G5
Sutton SM1 198 C4
Walton-on-Thames
KT12 179 E7
Westfields, SW13 147 F3
Westfields Av, SW13 147 E3
Westfields Rd, W3 106 B5
Westfield St, SE18 136 A3
Westfield Way, E1 113 H3
West Gdn Pl, W2 15 H4
West Gdns, E1 113 E7
SW17 167 H6
West Gate, W5 105 H3
Westgate Ct, SW9
off Canterbury Cres 151 G3
Westgate Rd, SE25 188 E4
Beckenham BR3 190 B2
Westgate St, E8 112 E1
Westgate Ter, SW10 30 B4
Westglade Ct, Har. HA3 69 G5
WEST GREEN, N15 75 J3
West Grn Pl, Grnf. UB6
off Uneeda Dr 104 A1
West Grn Rd, N15 75 H4
West Gro, SE10 154 C1
Woodford Green IG8 63 J6
Westgrove La, SE10 154 C1
West Halkin St, SW1 24 B5
West Hallowes, SE9 174 A1
West Hall Rd, Rich. TW9 146 B1
WEST HAM, E15 97 F7
West Ham La, E15 96 E7
West Ham Pk, E7 97 F7
WEST HAMPSTEAD, NW6 90 E5
West Hampstead Ms,
NW6 90 E6
★ **West Ham United FC**,
E13 115 J2
West Harding St, EC4 19 F3
WEST HARROW, Har. HA1 67 J7
Westhay Gdns, SW14 146 B5
WEST HEATH, SE2 138 D6
West Heath Av, NW11 90 D1
West Heath Cl, NW3 90 D3
West Heath Dr, NW11 90 D1
West Heath Gdns, NW3 90 D2
West Heath Rd, NW3 90 D2
SE2 138 C6
WEST HENDON, NW9 71 E7
West Hendon Bdy, NW9 71 F6
West Herts Business Cen,
Borwd. WD6
off Brook Rd 38 B3
West Hill, SW15 148 A7
SW18 148 D5
Harrow HA2 86 B2
Wembley HA9 87 J1
West Hill Ct, N6 92 A3
West Hill Pk, N6
off Merton La 91 J2
West Hill Rd, SW18 148 D6
West Hill Way, N20 56 E1
Westholm, NW11 72 E4
West Holme, Erith DA8 159 J1
Westholme, Orp. BR6 193 H7
Westholme Gdns, Ruis.
HA4 84 A1
Westhorne Av, SE9 155 J6
SE12 155 G7
Westhorpe Gdns, NW4 71 J3
Westhorpe Rd, SW15 147 J3
West Ho Cl, SW19 166 B1
Westhurst Dr, Chis. BR7 175 E5
West India Av, E14 134 A1
West India Dock Rd, E14 113 J6
West Kensington Ct, W14
off Edith Vil 128 C5
WEST KILBURN, W9 108 C3
Westlake Cl, N13 59 G3
Hayes UB4
off Lochan Cl 102 E4
Westlake Rd, Wem. HA9 87 G2
Westland Cl, Stai.
(Stanw.) TW19 140 B6
Westland Dr, Brom. BR2 205 F2
Westland Ho, E16
off Rymill St 136 D1
Westland Pl, N1 12 B3
Westlands Cl, Hayes UB3
off Granville Rd 122 A4
Westlands Ter, SW12
off Gaskarth Rd 150 C6
West La, SE16 132 E2
Westlea Rd, W7 124 D3
Westleigh Av, SW15 147 H5
Westleigh Dr, Brom. BR1 192 B1
Westleigh Gdns, Edg.
HA8 70 A1
Westlinks, Wem. HA0
off Alperton La 105 G2
Westlinton Cl, NW7 56 B6
West Lo Av, W3 126 A1
West Mall, W8
off Palace Gdns Ter 128 D1
Westmark Pt, SW15
off Norley Vale 165 H1
Westmead, SW15 147 H6
West Mead, Epsom KT19 197 E6
Ruislip HA4 84 C4
Westmead Cor, Cars. SM5
off Colston Av 199 H4
Westmead Rd, Sutt.
SM1 199 G4
Westmede, Chig. IG7 65 F6
Westmere Dr, NW7 54 D3
West Mersea Cl, E16
off Hanameel St 135 H1
West Ms, N17 60 E6
SW1 33 E2
WESTMINSTER, SW1 25 F5
★ **Westminster Abbey**,
SW1 26 A5
★ **Westminster Abbey**
Mus, SW1 26 A5
Westminster Av, Th.Hth.
CR7 187 H2
Westminster Br, SE1 26 B4
SW1 26 B4
Westminster Br Rd, SE1 26 D4
Westminster Business Sq,
SE11 off Durham St 34 C4
★ **Westminster Cath**,
SW1 25 F6
★ **Westminster City Hall**,
SW1 25 G5
Westminster Cl, Felt.
TW14 160 A1
Ilford IG6 81 G2
Teddington TW11 162 D5
Westminster Dr, N13 58 E5
Westminster Gdns, E4 63 E1
SW1 34 A1
Barking IG11 117 H2
Ilford IG6 81 F2
★ **Westminster Millennium**
Pier, SW1 26 B3
Westminster Palace Gdns,
SW1 off Artillery Row 25 H6
Westminster Rd, N9 61 E1
W7 124 B1
Sutton SM1 199 G2
Westmoat Cl, Beck. BR3 172 C7
WEST MOLESEY, KT8 179 F5
Westmont Rd, Esher
KT10 194 B2
Westmoor Gdns, Enf. EN3 45 G2
Westmoor Rd, Enf. EN3 45 G2
Westmoor St, SE7 135 J3
Westmoreland Av, Well.
DA16 157 H3
Westmoreland Pl, SW1 33 E4
W5 105 G5
Bromley BR1 191 G3
Westmoreland Rd, NW9 70 A4
SE17 36 A5
SW13 147 F1
Bromley BR1, BR2 191 E5
Westmoreland St, W1 16 C2
Westmoreland Ter, SE20 171 E7
SW1 32 E4
Westmoreland Wk, SE17 36 C5
Westmorland Cl, E12 98 A2
Twickenham TW1 144 E6
Westmorland Rd, E17 78 A6
Harrow HA1 67 H5
Westmorland Sq, Mitch.
CR4
off Westmorland Way 186 E5
Westmorland Way, Mitch.
CR4 186 D4
Westmount Rd, SE9 156 C2
WEST NORWOOD, SE27 169 J3
West Oak, Beck. BR3 190 D1
Westoe Rd, N9 61 E2
Weston Av, T.Ditt. KT7 180 B7
West Molesey KT8 179 E3
Weston Ct, N4
off Queens Dr 93 J3
N20 off Farnham Cl 41 F7
Weston Dr, Stan. HA7 68 E1
West One Shop Cen, W1 16 C4
Weston Gdns, Islw. TW7 144 A1
WESTON GREEN, T.Ditt.
KT7 194 C1
Weston Grn, Dag. RM9 101 F4
Thames Ditton KT7 194 B1
Weston Grn Rd, Esher
KT10 194 A1
Thames Ditton KT7 194 B1
Weston Gro, Brom. BR1 191 F1
Weston Pk, N8 75 E6
Kingston upon Thames
KT1 off Clarence St 181 H2
Thames Ditton KT7 194 B1
Weston Pk Cl, T.Ditt. KT7
off Weston Pk 194 B1
Weston Ri, WC1 10 D2
Weston Rd, W4 126 C3
Bromley BR1 173 F7
Dagenham RM9 101 E4
Enfield EN2 44 A1
Thames Ditton KT7 194 B1
Weston St, SE1 28 C4
Weston Wk, E8
off Mare St 95 E7
Westover Hill, NW3 90 D2
Westover Rd, SW18 149 F6
Westow Hill, SE19 170 B6
Westow St, SE19 170 B6
West Pk, SE9 174 B2
West Pk Av, Rich. TW9 146 A1
West Pk Cl, Houns. TW5
off Heston Gra La 123 F6
Romford RM6 82 D5
West Pk Rd, Rich. TW9 146 A1
Southall UB2 123 J1
West Parkside, SE10 135 E2
West Pier, E1
off Wapping High St 132 E1
West Pl, SW19 165 J5
West Pt, SE1 37 H3
Westpoint Apts, N8
off Turnpike La 75 F4
West Pt Cl, Houns. TW4
off Ede Cl 143 F3
Westpoint Trd Est, W3 106 B5
Westpole Av, Barn.
(Cockfos.) EN4 42 A4
Westport Rd, E13 115 H4
Westport St, E1 113 G6
West Poultry Av, EC1 19 G2
West Quarters, W12 107 G6
West Quay Dr, Hayes
UB4 102 E5
West Ramp, Houns.
(Lon.Hthrw Air.) TW6 140 D1
West Ridge Gdns, Grnf.
UB6 103 J2
West Rd, E15 115 F1
N17 60 E6
SW3 32 A4
SW4 150 D5
W5 105 H5
Barnet EN4 58 A1
Feltham TW14 141 G6
Kingston upon Thames
KT2 182 C1
Romford (Chad.Hth)
RM6 82 D6
West Drayton UB7 120 C3
Westrow, SW15 147 J5
West Row, W10 108 B4
Westrow Dr, Bark. IG11 99 J6
Westrow Gdns, Ilf. IG3 99 J2
West Sheen Vale, Rich.
TW9 145 J4
Westside, NW4 71 H2
Westside Apts, Ilf. IG1
off Roden St 98 D3
West Side Common,
SW19 165 J5
West Smithfield, EC1 19 G2
West Sq, SE11 27 G6
West St, E2 113 E2
E11 96 E3
E17 off Grove Rd 78 B5
WC2 17 J4
Bexleyheath DA7 159 F4
Brentford TW8 125 F6
Bromley BR1 191 G1
Carshalton SM5 199 J3
Croydon CR0 201 J4
Harrow HA1 86 A1
Sutton SM1 198 E5
West St La, Cars. SM5 199 J4
West Temple Sheen,
SW14 146 B4
West Tenter St, E1 21 G4
West Thamesmead
Business Pk, SE28 137 J3
West Twrs, Pnr. HA5 66 D6
Westvale Ms, W3 127 E1
West Vw, NW4 71 J4
Feltham TW14 141 F7
Loughton IG10 48 C3
Westview Cl, NW10 89 F5
W7 104 B6
W10 107 J6
Westview Cres, N9 44 B7
Westview Dr, Wdf.Grn.
IG8 80 A2
Westville Rd, W12 127 G2
Thames Ditton KT7 194 D1
West Wk, W5 105 H5
Barnet (E.Barn.) EN4 42 A7
Hayes UB3 122 A1
West Walkway, The, Sutt.
SM1 off Cheam Rd 198 E5
Westward Rd, E4 61 J5
Westward Way, Har. HA3 69 H6
West Warwick Pl, SW1 33 F2
West Way, N18 60 A4
NW10 88 D3
Westway, SW20 183 H3
W2 108 D5
W9 108 D5
W10 108 B6
W12 107 G7
West Way, Croy. CR0 203 H2
Edgware HA8 54 B6
Hounslow TW5 143 F1
Orpington (Petts Wd)
BR5 193 G5
Pinner HA5 66 D4
West Wickham BR4 190 D6
Westway Cl, SW20 183 H3
Westway Cross Shop Pk,
Grnf. UB6 104 B1
West Way Gdns, Croy.
CR0 203 G2
Westways, Epsom KT19 197 F4
Westwell Rd, SW16 168 E6
Westwell Rd App, SW16
off Westwell Rd 168 E6
Westwick Gdns, W14 128 A2
Hounslow TW4 142 B2
WEST WICKHAM, BR4 204 C2
Westwood Av, SE19 187 J1
Harrow HA2 85 H4
Westwood Cl, Brom.
BR1 192 A3
Westwood Gdns, SW13 147 F3
Westwood Hill, SE26 170 D5
Westwood La, Sid. DA15 158 A5
Welling DA16 157 J3
Westwood Pk, SE23 153 E7
Westwood Pl, SE26 170 D4
Westwood Rd, E16 135 H1
SW13 147 F3
Ilford IG3 99 J1

West Woodside, Bex. DA5 **159** E7
West World, W5 **105** H3
Wetheral Dr, Stan. HA7 **69** E1
Wetherby Cl, Nthlt. UB5 **85** H6
Wetherby Gdns, SW5 **30** C2
Wetherby Ms, SW5 **30** A3
Wetherby Pl, SW7 **30** C2
Wetherby Rd, Enf. EN2 **43** J1
Wetherby Way, Chess. KT9 **195** H7
Wetherden St, E17 **77** J7
Wetherell Rd, E9 **113** G1
Wetherill Rd, N10 **74** A1
★ **Wetland Cen, The**, SW13 **127** H7
Wexford Rd, SW12 **149** J7
Weybourne St, SW18 **167** F2
Weybridge Ct, SE16 **37** J4
Weybridge Pt, SW11 **150** A2
Weybridge Rd, Th.Hth. CR7 **187** G4
Wey Ct, Epsom KT19 **196** C4
Weydown Cl, SW19 **166** B1
Weyhill Rd, E1 **21** J3
Weylond Rd, Dag. RM8 **101** F3
Weyman Rd, SE3 **155** J1
Weymouth Av, NW7 **54** E5
W5 **125** F3
Weymouth Cl, E6 *off Covelees Wall* **116** E6
Weymouth Ct, Sutt. SM2 **198** D7
Weymouth Ho, SW8 *off Bolney St* **131** F7
Weymouth Ms, W1 **16** D1
Weymouth St, W1 **16** C2
Weymouth Ter, E2 **13** G1
Weymouth Wk, Stan. HA7 **52** D6
Whadcote St, N4 **93** G2
Whaddon Ho, SE22 *off Albrighton Rd* **152** B3
Whalebone Av, Rom. RM6 **83** F6
Whalebone Ct, EC2 **20** C3
Whalebone Gro, Rom. RM6 **83** F6
Whalebone La, E15 *off West Ham La* **96** E7
Whalebone La N, Rom. RM6 **83** E5
Whalebone La S, Dag. RM8 **83** F7
Romford RM6 **83** F7
Whales Yd, E15 *off West Ham La* **96** E7
Wharfdale Cl, N11 **58** A6
Wharfdale Ct, E5 *off Pedro St* **95** G4
Wharfdale Rd, N1 **10** B1
Wharfedale Gdns, Th.Hth. CR7 **187** F4
Wharfedale St, SW10 **30** A4
Wharf La, E14 *off Commercial Rd* **113** J6
Twickenham TW1 **162** D1
Wharf Pl, E2 **112** D1
Wharf Rd, N1 **11** J1
N1 (King's Cross) **10** A1
Enfield EN3 **45** H6
Wharfside Rd, E16 **114** E5
Wharf St, E16 **114** E5
Wharncliffe Dr, Sthl. UB1 **124** A1
Wharncliffe Gdns, SE25 **188** B2
Wharncliffe Rd, SE25 **188** B2
Wharton Cl, NW10 **89** E6
Wharton Cotts, WC1 *off Wharton St* **10** D4
Wharton Rd, Brom. BR1 **191** H1
Wharton St, WC1 **10** D4
Whateley Rd, SE20 **171** G7
SE22 **152** C5
Whatley Av, SW20 **184** B3
Whatman Rd, SE23 **153** G7
Wheatcroft Ct, Sutt. SM1 *off Cleeve Way* **199** E1
Wheatfields, E6 *off Oxleas* **116** E6
Enfield EN3 **45** H2
Wheatfield Way, Kings.T. KT1 **181** H2
Wheathill Rd, SE20 **188** E3
Wheatland Ho, SE22 *off Albrighton Rd* **152** B3
Wheatlands, Houns. TW5 **123** G6
Wheatlands Rd, SW17 *off Stapleton Rd* **168** A3
Wheatley Cl, NW4 **71** G2
Wheatley Cres, Hayes UB3 **102** A7
Wheatley Gdns, N9 **60** B2
Wheatley Ho, SW15 *off Tangley Gro* **147** G7
Wheatley Rd, Islw. TW7 **144** C3
Wheatley's Ait, Sun. TW16 **178** A5
Wheatley St, W1 **16** C2
Wheat Sheaf Cl, E14 **134** B4
Wheatsheaf Cl, Nthlt. UB5 **84** E5
Wheatsheaf La, SW6 **127** J7
SW8 **34** B7
Wheatsheaf Ter, SW6 **128** C7
Wheatstone Cl, Mitch. CR4 **185** H1
Wheatstone Rd, W10 **108** B5
Wheeler Cl, Wdf.Grn. IG8 *off Chigwell Rd* **64** C5
Wheeler Gdns, N1 *off Outram Pl* **111** E1
Wheeler Pl, Brom. BR2 **191** H4
Wheelers Cross, Bark. IG11 **117** G2
Wheel Fm Dr, Dag. RM10 **101** J3
Wheelock Cl, Erith DA8 **139** H7
Wheelwright St, N7 **93** F7
Whelan Way, Wall. SM6 **200** D3
Wheler St, E1 **13** F6
Whellock Rd, W4 **126** E3
Whenman Av, Bex. DA5 **177** J2
Whernside Cl, SE28 **118** C7
WHETSTONE, N20 **57** E2
Whetstone Cl, N20 *off Oakleigh Rd N* **57** G2
Whetstone Pk, WC2 **18** C3
Whetstone Rd, SE3 **155** J2
Whewell Rd, N19 **93** E2
Whichcote St, SE1 **26** E2
Whidborne Cl, SE8 *off Cliff Ter* **154** A2
Whidborne St, WC1 **10** B4
Whimbrel Cl, SE28 **118** C7
Whimbrel Way, Hayes UB4 **102** D6
Whinchat Rd, SE28 **137** G3
Whinfell Cl, SW16 **168** D5
Whinyates Rd, SE9 **156** B3
Whipps Cross, E17 **78** D5
Whipps Cross Rd, E11 **78** D5
Whiskin St, EC1 **11** G4
Whisperwood Cl, Har. HA3 **52** B7
Whistler Gdns, Edg. HA8 **69** J2
Whistler Ms, SE15 *off Kelly Av* **132** C7
Dagenham RM8 *off Fitzstephen Rd* **100** B5
Whistlers Av, SW11 **129** G7
Whistler St, N5 **93** H4
Whistler Twr, SW10 **30** D7
Whistler Wk, SW10 *off Blantyre St* **30** D7
Whiston Rd, E2 **13** F1
Whitacre Ms, SE11 **35** F4
Whitakers Way, Loug. IG10 **48** C1
Whitbread Cl, N17 **76** D1
Whitbread Rd, SE4 **153** H4
Whitburn Rd, SE13 **154** B4
Whitby Av, NW10 **106** B3
Whitby Ct, N7 *off Camden Rd* **93** E4
Whitby Gdns, NW9 **70** A3
Sutton SM1 **199** G2
Whitby Rd, SE18 **136** C4
Harrow HA2 **85** J3
Ruislip HA4 **84** B3
Sutton SM1 **199** G2
Whitby St, E1 **13** F5
Whitcher Cl, SE14 **133** H6
Whitcher Pl, NW1 *off Rochester Rd* **92** C7
Whitchurch Av, Edg. HA8 **53** J7
Whitchurch Cl, Edg. HA8 **53** J6
Whitchurch Gdns, Edg. HA8 **53** J6
Whitchurch La, Edg. HA8 **53** G7
Whitchurch Rd, W11 **108** A7
Whitcomb Ct, WC2 *off Whitcomb St* **17** J6
Whitcomb St, WC2 **17** J6
Whitcome Ms, Rich. TW9 **146** B1
Whiteadder Way, E14 **134** B4
Whitear Wk, E15 **96** D6
Whitebarn La, Dag. RM10 **119** G1
Whitebeam Av, Brom. BR2 **192** D6
Whitebeam Cl, SW9 *off Clapham Rd* **131** F7
Whitebeam Ho, NW3 *off Maitland Pk Rd* **91** J6
White Bear Pl, NW3 *off New End Sq* **91** G4
White Br Av, Mitch. CR4 **185** G4
Whitebridge Cl, Felt. TW14 **141** J6
White Butts Rd, Ruis. HA4 **84** D3
WHITECHAPEL, E1 **21** H4
★ **Whitechapel Art Gall**, E1 **21** G3
Whitechapel High St, E1 **21** G3
Whitechapel Rd, E1 **21** H3
White Ch La, E1 **21** H3
White Ch Pas, E1 **21** H3
White City Cl, W12 **107** J7
White City Est, W12 **107** H7
White City Rd, W12 **107** H7
White Conduit St, N1 **11** F1
Whitecote Rd, Sthl. UB1 **103** H6
White Craig Cl, Pnr. HA5 **51** G5
Whitecroft Cl, Beck. BR3 **190** D4
Whitecroft Way, Beck. BR3 **190** C5
Whitecross Pl, EC2 **20** C1
Whitecross St, EC1 **12** A5
★ **White Cube**, N1 *off Hoxton Sq* **12** D4
★ **White Cube**, SW1 **25** G1
Whitefield Av, NW2 **71** J7
Whitefield Cl, SW15 **148** B6
Whitefoot La, Brom. BR1 **172** C4
Whitefoot Ter, Brom. BR1 **173** E3
Whitefriars Av, Har. HA3 **68** B2
Whitefriars Dr, Har. HA3 **68** A2
Whitefriars St, EC4 **19** F4
White Gdns, Dag. RM10 **101** G6
Whitegate Gdns, Har. HA3 **52** C7
Whitehall, SW1 **26** A1
Whitehall Cl, Borwd. WD6 **38** A4
Whitehall Ct, SW1 **26** A2
Whitehall Cres, Chess. KT9 **195** G5
Whitehall Gdns, E4 **62** E1
SW1 **26** A2
W3 **126** A1
W4 **126** B6
Whitehall La, Buck.H. IG9 **63** G2
Whitehall Pk, N19 **92** C1
Whitehall Pk Rd, W4 **126** B6
Whitehall Pl, E7 *off Brooking Rd* **97** G5
SW1 **26** A2
Wallington SM6 *off Bernard Rd* **200** B4
Whitehall Rd, E4 **62** E2
W7 **124** D2
Bromley BR2 **192** A5
Harrow HA1 **68** B7
Thornton Heath CR7 **187** G5
Woodford Green IG8 **62** E2
Whitehall St, N17 **60** C7
White Hart Av, SE18 **137** J3
SE28 **137** J3
White Hart Ct, EC2 **20** D2
White Hart La, N17 **60** A7
N22 **75** G1
NW10 *off Church Rd* **89** F6
SW13 **147** E3
Romford RM7 **83** G1
White Hart Rd, SE18 **137** H4
White Hart Rbt, Nthlt. UB5 *off The Parkway* **102** D2
White Hart Slip, Brom. BR1 *off Market Sq* **191** G2
White Hart St, EC4 **19** H3
SE11 **35** F3
White Hart Yd, SE1 **28** B2
Whitehaven Cl, Brom. BR2 **191** G4
Whitehaven St, NW8 **7** G6
Whitehead Cl, N18 **60** A5
SW18 **149** F7
Whitehead's Gro, SW3 **31** H3
White Heron Ms, Tedd. TW11 **162** C6
Whitehills Rd, Loug. IG10 **48** D3
White Horse All, EC1 **19** G1
White Horse Hill, Chis. BR7 **174** D4
White Horse La, E1 **113** G4
Whitehorse La, SE25 **188** A4
White Horse Ms, SE1 **27** F5
White Horse Rd, E1 **113** H6
E6 **116** C3
Whitehorse Rd, Croy. CR0 **188** A6
Thornton Heath CR7 **188** A6
White Horse St, W1 **24** D2
White Horse Yd, EC2 **20** B3
Whitehouse Apts, SE1 *off Belvedere Rd* **26** D2
Whitehouse Av, Borwd. WD6 **38** B3
White Ho Dr, Stan. HA7 **53** F4
Whitehouse Way, N14 **58** B2
Whitehurst Dr, N18 **61** G6
White Kennett St, E1 **21** E3
Whitelands Cres, SW18 **148** B7
Whiteledges, W13 **105** F6
Whitelegg Rd, E13 **115** F2
Whiteley Rd, SE19 **170** A5
Whiteleys Shop Cen, W2 **14** A4
Whiteleys Way, Felt. (Han.) TW13 **161** G3
White Lion Ct, EC3 **20** D4
White Lion Hill, EC4 **19** H5
White Lion St, N1 **11** E2
White Lo, SE19 **169** H7
White Lo Cl, N2 **73** G6
Isleworth TW7 **144** D2
Sutton SM2 **199** F7
White Lyon Ct, EC2 **19** J1
White Oak Dr, Beck. BR3 **190** C2
White Oak Gdns, Sid. DA15 **157** J7
Whiteoaks La, Grnf. UB6 **104** A2
White Orchards, N20 **40** C7
Stanmore HA7 **52** D5
White Post La, E9 **96** A6
SE13 **154** A3
White Post St, SE15 **133** F7
White Rd, E15 **97** E7
Whites Av, Ilf. IG2 **81** H6
Whites Grds, SE1 **28** E4
Whites Grds Est, SE1 *off Whites Grds* **28** E3
Whites Meadow, Brom. BR1 *off Blackbrook La* **192** D4
White's Row, E1 **21** F2
White's Sq, SW4 *off Nelson's Row* **150** D4
Whitestile Rd, Brent. TW8 **125** F5
Whitestone La, NW3 *off Heath St* **91** F3
Whitestone Wk, NW3 *off North End Way* **91** F3
White St, Sthl. UB1 **122** D2
White Swan Ms, W4 *off Bennett St* **126** E6
Whitethorn Gdns, Croy. CR0 **203** E2
Enfield EN2 **44** A5
Whitethorn St, E3 **114** A4
Whitewebbs Way, Orp. BR5 **193** J1
Whitfield Pl, W1 **9** F6
Whitfield Rd, E6 **97** J7
SE3 **154** D1
Bexleyheath DA7 **139** F7
Whitfield St, W1 **17** H2
Whitford Gdns, Mitch. CR4 **185** J3
Whitgift Av, S.Croy. CR2 **201** H5
Whitgift Cen, Croy. CR0 **201** J2
Whitgift Ho, SW11 *off Westbridge Rd* **149** H1
Whitgift St, SE11 **34** C1
Croydon CR0 **201** J3
Whiting Av, Bark. IG11 **99** E7
Whitings, Ilf. IG2 **81** G5
Whitings Rd, Barn. EN5 **39** J5
Whitings Way, E6 **116** D5
Whitland Rd, Cars. SM5 **199** G1
Whitley Cl, Stai. (Stanw.) TW19 **140** B6
Whitley Ho, SW1 **33** G4
Whitley Rd, N17 **76** B2
Whitlock Dr, SW19 **148** B7
Whitman Rd, E3 *off Mile End Rd* **113** H4
Whitmead Cl, S.Croy. CR2 **202** B6
Whitmore Cl, N11 **58** B5
Whitmore Est, N1 **112** B1
Whitmore Gdns, NW10 **107** J2
Whitmore Rd, N1 **112** B1
Beckenham BR3 **189** J3
Harrow HA1 **67** J7
Whitnell Way, SW15 **148** A5
Whitney Av, Ilf. IG4 **80** A4
Whitney Ho, SE22 *off Albrighton Rd* **152** B3
Whitney Rd, E10 **78** B7
Whitney Wk, Sid. DA14 **176** E6
Whitstable Cl, Beck. BR3 **189** J1
Whitstable Ho, W10 **108** A6
Whitstable Pl, Croy. CR0 **201** J4
Whitstone La, Beck. BR3 **190** B5
Whittaker Av, Rich. TW9 *off Hill St* **145** G5
Whittaker Rd, E6 **97** J7
Sutton SM3 **198** C3
Whittaker St, SW1 **32** B2
Whittaker Way, SE1 **37** J2
Whitta Rd, E12 **98** A4
Whittell Gdns, SE26 **171** F3
Whittingstall Rd, SW6 **148** C1
Whittington Av, EC3 **20** D4
Whittington Ct, N2 **73** J5
Whittington Ms, N12 **57** F4
Whittington Rd, N22 **58** E7
Whittington Way, Pnr. HA5 **67** E5
Whittlebury Cl, Cars. SM5 **199** J7
Whittle Cl, E17 **77** H6
Southall UB1 **103** H6
Whittle Rd, Houns. TW5 **122** C7
Southall UB2 *off Post Rd* **123** H2
Whittlesea Cl, Har. HA3 **51** J7
Whittlesea Path, Har. HA3 **67** J1
Whittlesea Rd, Har. HA3 **67** J1
Whittlesey St, SE1 **27** E2
WHITTON, Twick. TW2 **143** H7
Whitton Av E, Grnf. UB6 **86** B5
Whitton Av W, Grnf. UB6 **85** J5
Northolt UB5 **85** J5
Whitton Cl, Grnf. UB6 **87** E6
Whitton Dene, Houns. TW3 **143** H5
Isleworth TW7 **144** A5
Whitton Dr, Grnf. UB6 **86** D6
Whitton Manor Rd, Islw. TW7 **143** J5
Whitton Rd, Houns. TW3 **143** H4
Twickenham TW1, TW2 **144** C6
Whitton Rd Rbt, Twick. TW1 *off Chertsey Rd* **144** C6
Whitton Wk, E3 **114** A2
Whitton Waye, Houns. TW3 **143** G6
Whitwell Rd, E13 **115** G3
Whitworth Ho, SE1 **28** A6
Whitworth Rd, SE18 **136** D7
SE25 **188** B3
Whitworth St, SE10 **135** E5
Whorlton Rd, SE15 **152** E3
Whychcote Pt, NW2 *off Claremont Rd* **71** J7
Whymark Av, N22 **75** G3
Whytecroft, Houns. TW5 **122** D7
Whyteville Rd, E7 **97** H6
Wickersley Rd, SW11 **150** A2
Wickers Oake, SE19 **170** C4

Wicker St, E1
off Burslem St 112 E6
Wicket, The, Croy. CR0 204 A5
Wicket Rd, Grnf. (Perivale) UB6 104 D3
Wickets Way, Ilf. IG6 65 J6
Wickford St, E1 113 F4
Wickford Way, E17 77 G4
Wickham Av, Croy. CR0 203 H2
Sutton SM3 197 J5
Wickham Chase, W.Wick. BR4 190 D7
Wickham Cl, E1 113 F5
Enfield EN3 45 E3
New Malden KT3 183 F5
Wickham Ct Rd, W.Wick. BR4 204 C2
Wickham Cres, W.Wick. BR4 204 C2
Wickham Gdns, SE4 153 J3
Wickham La, SE2 138 A5
Welling DA16 138 A5
Wickham Ms, SE4 153 J2
Wickham Rd, E4 62 C7
SE4 153 J4
Beckenham BR3 190 B2
Croydon CR0 203 G2
Harrow HA3 68 A2
Wickham St, SE11 34 C3
Welling DA16 157 H2
Wickham Way, Beck. BR3 190 C4
Wick La, E3 114 A2
Wickliffe Av, N3 72 B2
Wickliffe Gdns, Wem. HA9 88 B2
Wicklow St, WC1 10 C3
Wick Rd, E9 95 G6
Teddington TW11 163 E7
Wicks Cl, SE9 174 A4
Wicksteed Ho, SE1 28 A6
Brentford TW8 *off Green Dragon La* 125 J5
Wickway Ct, SE15 37 F6
Wickwood St, SE5 151 H2
Widdecombe Av, Har. HA2 84 E2
Widdenham Rd, N7 93 F4
Widdin St, E15 96 D7
Widecombe Gdns, Ilf. IG4 80 B4
Widecombe Rd, SE9 174 B3
Widecombe Way, N2 73 G5
Widegate St, E1 21 E2
Widenham Cl, Pnr. HA5 66 C5
Wide Way, Mitch. CR4 186 D3
Widewing Cl, Tedd. TW11 163 E7
Widgeon Cl, E16 *off Maplin Rd* 115 H6
Widley Rd, W9 108 D3
WIDMORE, Brom. BR1 191 H3
WIDMORE GREEN, Brom. BR1 191 J1
Widmore Lo Rd, Brom. BR1 192 A2
Widmore Rd, Brom. BR1 191 G2
Wieland Rd, Nthwd. HA6 50 A7
Wigan Ho, E5 94 E1
Wigeon Path, SE28 137 G3
Wigeon Way, Hayes UB4 102 D6
Wiggins La, Rich. TW10 163 F2
Wiggins Mead, NW9 55 F7
Wigginton Av, Wem. HA9 88 B6
Wigham Ho, Bark. IG11 99 F7
Wightman Rd, N4 75 G5
N8 75 G4
Wighton Ms, Islw. TW7 *off London Rd* 144 B2
Wigley Rd, Felt. TW13 160 D1
Wigmore Ct, W13 *off Singapore Rd* 124 D1
Wigmore Pl, W1 16 D3
Wigmore Rd, Cars. SM5 199 G2
Wigmore St, W1 16 B4
Wigmore Wk, Cars. SM5 199 G2
Wigram Rd, E11 79 J6
Wigram Sq, E17 78 C2
Wigston Cl, N18 60 B5
Wigston Rd, E13 115 H4
Wigton Gdns, Stan. HA7 69 H1
Wigton Pl, SE11 35 F4
Wigton Rd, E17 77 J1
Wilberforce Ct, Edg. HA8 53 J4
Keston BR2 206 A6
Wilberforce Ms, SW4 *off Stonhouse St* 150 D4
Wilberforce Rd, N4 93 H2
NW9 71 G6
Wilberforce Way, SW19 166 A6
Wilbraham Pl, SW1 32 A1
Wilbury Way, N18 60 A5
Wilby Ms, W11 128 C1
Wilcox Cl, SW8 34 B7
Borehamwood WD6 38 C1
Wilcox Pl, SW1 25 G6
Wilcox Rd, SW8 34 A7
Sutton SM1 198 E4
Teddington TW11 162 A4
Wild Ct, WC2 18 C3
Wildcroft Gdns, Edg. HA8 53 G6
Wildcroft Rd, SW15 147 J7
Wilde Cl, E8 112 D1
Wilde Pl, N13 *off Medesenge Way* 59 H6
SW18 149 G7
Wilder Cl, Ruis. HA4 84 B1
Wilderness, The, E.Mol. KT8 179 J5
Hampton (Hmptn H.) TW12 *off Park Rd* 161 H4
Wilderness Ms, SW4 *off The Chase* 150 B4
Wilderness Rd, Chis. BR7 175 E7
Wilde Rd, Erith DA8 139 H7
Wilderton Rd, N16 76 B7
Wildfell Rd, SE6 154 B7
Wild Goose Dr, SE14 153 F1
Wild Hatch, NW11 72 D6
Wild's Rents, SE1 28 D5
Wild St, WC2 18 B4
Wildwood Cl, SE12 155 F7
Wildwood Gro, NW3 *off North End Way* 91 F1
Wildwood Ri, NW11 91 F1
Wildwood Rd, NW11 73 F7
Wildwood Ter, NW3 91 F1
Wilford Cl, Enf. EN2 44 A3
Wilfred Owen Cl, SW19 167 F6
Wilfred St, SW1 25 F5
Wilfred Turney Est, W6 *off Hammersmith Gro* 127 J2
Wilfrid Gdns, W3 106 C5
Wilkes Rd, Brent. TW8 125 H6
Wilkes St, E1 21 G1
Wilkins Cl, Hayes UB3 121 J5
Mitcham CR4 185 H1
Wilkins Ho, SW1 *off Churchill Gdns* 33 F5
Wilkinson Gdns, SE25 188 B1
Wilkinson Rd, E16 115 J6
Wilkinson St, SW8 131 F7
Wilkinson Way, W4 126 D2
Wilkin St, NW5 92 B6
Wilkin St Ms, NW5 *off Wilkin St* 92 B6
Wilks Gdns, Croy. CR0 203 H1
Wilks Pl, N1 12 E2
Willan Rd, N17 76 A2
Willan Wall, E16 *off Victoria Dock Rd* 115 F7
Willard St, SW8 150 B3
Willcocks Cl, Chess. KT9 195 H3
Willcott Rd, W3 126 B1
Will Crooks Gdns, SE9 155 J4
Willen Fld Rd, NW10 106 C2
Willenhall Av, Barn. (New Barn.) EN5 41 F6
Willenhall Rd, SE18 136 E5
Willersley Av, Orp. BR6 207 G3
Sidcup DA15 175 J1
Willersley Cl, Sid. DA15 175 J1
WILLESDEN, NW10 89 F6
WILLESDEN GREEN, NW10 89 H7
Willesden La, NW2 90 A6
NW6 90 A6
Willes Rd, NW5 92 B6
Willett Cl, Nthlt. UB5 *off Broomcroft Av* 102 C3
Orpington BR5 193 H6
Willett Ho, E13 *off Queens Rd W* 115 G2
Willett Pl, Th.Hth. CR7 *off Willett Rd* 187 G5
Willett Rd, Th.Hth. CR7 187 G5
Willett Way, Orp. BR5 193 G5
William Ash Cl, Dag. RM9 *off Rugby Rd* 100 B6
William Barefoot Dr, SE9 174 D4
William Bonney Est, SW4 150 D4
William Booth Rd, SE20 188 D1
William Carey Way, Har. HA1 68 B7
William Cl, N2 73 G2
SE13 154 C2
SW6 *off Pellant Rd* 128 B7
Romford RM5 83 J1
Southall UB2 *off Windmill Av* 123 J2
William Dr, Stan. HA7 52 D6
William Dunbar Ho, NW6 108 C2
William Dyce Ms, SW16 *off Babington Rd* 168 D4
William Ellis Way, SE16 29 J6
William Foster La, Well. DA16 158 A2
William IV St, WC2 18 A6
William Gdns, SW15 147 H5
William Guy Gdns, E3 *off Talwin St* 114 B3
William Harvey Ho, SW19 *off Whitlock Dr* 166 B1
William Henry Wk, SW8 33 H6
William Margrie Cl, SE15 *off Moncrieff St* 152 D2
William Ms, SW1 24 A4
William Morley Cl, E6 116 A1
William Morris Cl, E17 77 J3
★ **William Morris Gall**, E17 *off Lloyd Pk* 78 A3
William Morris Way, SW6 149 F3
William Perkin Ct, Grnf. UB6 *off Greenford Rd* 86 B6
William Pl, E3 *off Roman Rd* 113 J2
William Rd, NW1 9 F4
SW19 166 B7
Sutton SM1 199 F5
William Rushbrooke Ho, SE16 *off Eveline Lowe Est* 37 H1
Williams Av, E17 77 J1
William Saville Ho, NW6 108 C2
Williams Bldgs, E2 113 F4
Williams Cl, N8 *off Coolhurst Rd* 74 D6
Williams Dr, Houns. TW3 143 G4
Williams Gro, N22 75 G1
Surbiton (Long Dit.) KT6 181 F6
William's La, SW14 146 C3
Williams La, Mord. SM4 185 F5
Williamson Cl, SE10 *off Lenthorp Rd* 135 F4
Williamson St, N7 93 E4
William Sq, SE16 *off Rotherhithe St* 113 H7
Williams Rd, W13 104 D7
Southall UB2 122 E4
Williams Ter, Croy. CR0 201 G6
William St, E10 78 B6
N17 60 C7
SW1 24 A4
Barking IG11 99 F7
Carshalton SM5 199 H3
Willifield Way, NW11 72 C4
Willingale Cl, Loug. IG10 *off Willingale Rd* 49 F2
Woodford Green IG8 63 J6
Willingale Rd, Loug. IG10 49 F3
Willingdon Rd, N22 75 H2
Willingham Cl, NW5 92 C5
Willingham Ter, NW5 92 C5
Willingham Way, Kings.T. KT1 182 A3
Willington Ct, E5 *off Mandeville St* 95 H3
Willington Rd, SW9 150 E3
Willis Av, Sutt. SM2 199 H6
Willis Ho, E12 *off Grantham Rd* 98 D3
Willis Rd, E15 115 F1
Croydon CR0 187 J7
Erith DA8 139 J4
Willis St, E14 114 B6
Willmore End, SW19 184 E1
Willoughby Av, Croy. CR0 201 F4
Willoughby Gro, N17 60 E7
Willoughby Ho, EC2 *off The Barbican* 20 B2
Willoughby La, N17 61 E7
Willoughby Ms, SW4 *off Wixs La* 150 B4
Willoughby Pk Rd, N17 60 E7
Willoughby Pas, E14 134 A1
Willoughby Rd, N8 75 G3
NW3 91 G4
Kingston upon Thames KT2 181 J1
Twickenham TW1 145 G6
Willoughbys, The, SW14 *off Upper Richmond Rd W* 147 E3
Willoughby St, WC1 18 A2
Willoughby Way, SE7 135 H4
Willow Av, SW13 147 F2
Sidcup DA15 158 A6
Willow Bk, SW6 148 B3
Richmond TW10 163 E3
Willowbay Cl, Barn. EN5 40 A6
Willow Br Rd, N1 93 J6
Willowbrook Est, SE15 *off Shurland Gdns* 37 G7
Willowbrook Rd, SE15 37 G6
Southall UB2 123 G3
Willow Cen, Mitch. CR4 185 J5
Willow Cl, SE6 *off Verdant La* 173 F1
Bexley DA5 159 F6
Brentford TW8 125 F6
Bromley BR2 192 C5
Buckhurst Hill IG9 64 A3
Thornton Heath CR7 187 H6
Willow Cotts, Mitch. CR4 186 C3
Richmond TW9 *off Kew Grn* 126 A6
Willow Ct, EC2 12 D5
Edgware HA8 53 H4
Willowcourt Av, Har. HA3 69 E5
Willowdene, N6 *off Denewood Rd* 73 J7
Willow Dene, Pnr. HA5 66 D2
Willowdene Cl, Twick. TW2 143 J7
Willow Dr, Barn. EN5 40 B4
Willow End, N20 56 D2
Northwood HA6 50 A6
Surbiton KT6 195 H1
Willow Fm La, SW15 *off Queens Ride* 147 H3
Willowfields Cl, SE18 137 H5
Willow Gdns, Houns. TW3 143 G1
Willow Grn, NW9 *off Clayton Fld* 71 E1
Borehamwood WD6 38 D5
Willow Gro, E13 *off Libra Rd* 115 G2
Chislehurst BR7 174 D6
Willowhayne Dr, Walt. KT12 178 B7
Willowhayne Gdns, Wor.Pk. KT4 197 J3
Willow Ho, NW3 *off Maitland Pk Vil* 91 J6
Willow La, SE18 136 C4
Mitcham CR4 185 J5
Willow La Ind Est, Mitch. CR4 185 J5
Willowmead Cl, W5 105 G5
Willow Mt, Croy. CR0 *off Langton Way* 202 B3
Willow Pl, SW1 33 G1
Willow Rd, NW3 91 G4
W5 125 H2
Enfield EN1 44 B3
New Malden KT3 182 C4
Romford RM6 83 E6
Wallington SM6 200 B7
Willows, The, Buck.H. IG9 64 A3
Esher (Clay.) KT10 194 B6
Willows Av, Mord. SM4 185 E5
Willows Cl, Pnr. HA5 66 C2
Willow St, E4 46 D7
EC2 12 D5
Romford RM7 83 J4
Willow Tree Cl, E3 *off Birdsfield La* 113 J1
SW18 *off Cargill Rd* 167 E1
Hayes UB4 102 C4
Willowtree Cl, Nthlt. UB5 85 E6
Willow Tree La, Hayes UB4 102 C4
Willowtree Marina, Hayes UB4 103 E6
Willow Tree Rbt, Hayes UB4 *off The Parkway* 102 D5
Willow Tree Wk, Brom. BR1 191 H1
Willowtree Way, Th.Hth. CR7 *off Kensington Av* 187 G1
Willow Vale, W12 127 G1
Chislehurst BR7 174 E6
Willow Vw, SW19 185 G1
Willow Wk, E17 77 J5
N2 73 G2
N15 75 H4
N21 43 F6
SE1 37 E1
Orpington BR6 206 E3
Sutton SM3 198 C3
Willow Way, N3 56 E7
SE26 171 E3
W11 *off Freston Rd* 108 A7
Epsom KT19 196 D6
Sunbury-on-Thames TW16 178 A4
Twickenham TW2 161 H2
Wembley HA0 86 D3
Willow Wd Cres, SE25 188 B6
Willrose Cres, SE2 138 C5
Wills Cres, Houns. TW3 143 H6
Wills Gro, NW7 55 G5
Wilman Gro, E8 94 D7
Wilmar Gdns, W.Wick. BR4 204 B1
Wilmcote Ho, W2 108 D5
Wilmer Cl, Kings.T. KT2 163 J5
Wilmer Cres, Kings.T. KT2 163 J5
Wilmer Gdns, N1 112 B1
Wilmer Ho, E3 *off Daling Way* 113 H2
Wilmer Lea Cl, E15 96 C7
Wilmer Pl, N16 *off Stoke Newington Ch St* 94 C2
Wilmer Way, N14 58 D5
Wilmington Av, W4 126 D7
Wilmington Gdns, Bark. IG11 99 G6
Wilmington Sq, WC1 11 E4
Wilmington St, WC1 11 E4
Wilmot Cl, N2 73 F2
SE15 132 D7
Wilmot Pl, NW1 92 C7
W7 *off Boston Rd* 124 B1
Wilmot Rd, E10 96 B2
N17 76 A3
Carshalton SM5 199 J5
Wilmot St, E2 112 E4
Wilmount St, SE18 136 E4
Wilna Rd, SW18 149 F7
Wilsham St, W11 128 A1
Wilshaw Cl, NW4 71 G3
Wilshaw St, SE14 154 A1
Wilsmere Dr, Har. (Har.Wld) HA3 52 B7
Northolt UB5 85 E6
Wilson Av, Mitch. CR4 167 H7
Wilson Cl, S.Croy. CR2 *off Bartlett St* 202 A5
Wembley HA9 69 J7
Wilson Dr, Wem. HA9 69 J7
Wilson Gdns, Har. HA1 67 J7
Wilson Gro, SE16 132 E2
Wilson Ho, SE7 *off Springfield Gro* 135 J6
Wilson Rd, E6 116 A3
SE5 152 B1
Chessington KT9 195 J6
Ilford IG1 80 C7
Wilsons Pl, E14 *off Salmon La* 113 J6

Wilsons Rd, W6 **128** A5
Wilson St, E17 **78** C5
EC2 **20** C1
N21 **43** G7
Wilstone Cl, Hayes UB4 **102** E4
Wilthorne Gdns, Dag. RM10 *off Acre Rd* **101** H7
Wilton Av, W4 **127** E5
Wilton Cl, West Dr. (Harm.) UB7 **120** A6
Wilton Cres, SW1 **24** B4
SW19 **184** C1
Wilton Est, E8 *off Greenwood Rd* **94** D6
Wilton Gdns, W.Mol. KT8 **179** G3
Wilton Gro, SW19 **166** C7
New Malden KT3 **183** F6
Wilton Ho, SE22 *off Albrighton Rd* **152** B3
Wilton Ms, SW1 **24** C5
Wilton Par, Felt. TW13 *off High St* **160** A2
Wilton Pk Ct, SE18 *off Prince Imperial Rd* **156** D1
Wilton Pl, SW1 **24** B4
Wilton Rd, N10 **74** A2
SE2 **138** C3
SW1 **25** E6
SW19 **167** H7
Barnet (Cockfos.) EN4 **41** J4
Hounslow TW4 **142** D3
Ilford IG1 **98** E4
Wilton Row, SW1 **24** B4
Wilton Sq, N1 **112** A1
Wilton St, SW1 **24** D5
Wilton Ter, SW1 **24** B5
Wilton Vil, N1 **112** A1
Wilton Way, E8 **94** D6
Wiltshire Cl, NW7 **55** F5
SW3 **31** J1
Wiltshire Gdns, N4 **75** J6
Twickenham TW2 **161** J1
Wiltshire Rd, SW9 **151** G3
Thornton Heath CR7 **187** G3
Wiltshire Row, N1 **112** A1
Wilverley Cres, N.Mal. KT3 **183** E6
Wimbart Rd, SW2 **151** F7
WIMBLEDON, SW19 **166** B6
★ **Wimbledon (All England Tenn & Croquet Club)**, SW19 **166** B4
Wimbledon Br, SW19 **166** C6
★ **Wimbledon Common**, SW19 **165** F4
Wimbledon Hill Rd, SW19 **166** B6
WIMBLEDON PARK, SW19 **166** C3
Wimbledon Pk, SW19 **166** C2
Wimbledon Pk Est, SW19 **166** B1
Wimbledon Pk Rd, SW18 **148** C7
SW19 **166** C1
Wimbledon Pk Side, SW19 **166** A2
Wimbledon Rd, SW17 **167** F4
Wimbledon Stadium Business Cen, SW17 **167** E3
Wimbledon Sta, SW19 **166** C6
★ **Wimbledon Windmill Mus**, SW19 **165** H2
Wimbolt St, E2 **13** H3
Wimborne Av, Chis. BR7 **193** J4
Hayes UB4 **102** B6
Orpington BR5 **193** J4
Southall UB2 **123** G4
Wimborne Cl, SE12 **155** F5
Buckhurst Hill IG9 **63** H2
Worcester Park KT4 **197** J1
Wimborne Dr, NW9 **70** A3
Pinner HA5 **66** D7
Wimborne Gdns, W13 **105** E6
Wimborne Ho, SW8 *off Dorset Rd* **131** F7
Wimborne Rd, N9 **60** D2
N17 **76** B2
Wimborne Way, Beck. BR3 **189** G3
Wimbourne Ct, N1 **12** B1
Wimbourne St, N1 **12** B1
Wimpole Cl, Brom. BR2 **191** J4
Kingston upon Thames KT1 **181** J2
Wimpole Ms, W1 **16** D1
Wimpole Rd, West Dr. UB7 **120** A1
Wimpole St, W1 **16** D3
Wimshurst Cl, Croy. CR0 **201** E1
Winans Wk, SW9 **151** G2
Wincanton Cres, Nthlt. UB5 **85** G5
Wincanton Gdns, Ilf. IG6 **80** E3
Wincanton Rd, SW18 **148** C7
Winchcombe Rd, Cars. SM5 **185** G7
Winchcomb Gdns, SE9 **156** A3
Winchelsea Av, Bexh. DA7 **139** F7
Winchelsea Cl, SW15 **148** A5
Winchelsea Rd, E7 **97** G3
N17 **76** B3
NW10 **106** D1
Winchelsey Ri, S.Croy. CR2 **202** C6
Winchendon Rd, SW6 **128** C7
Teddington TW11 **162** A4
Winchester Av, NW6 **108** B1
NW9 **70** A3
Hounslow TW5 **123** F6
Winchester Cl, E6 *off Boultwood Rd* **116** C6
SE17 **35** H2
Bromley BR2 **191** F3
Enfield EN1 **44** B5
Kingston upon Thames KT2 **164** B7
Winchester Ct, E17 *off Billet Rd* **77** H1
Winchester Dr, Pnr. HA5 **66** D5
Winchester Ho, SE18 *off Shooters Hill Rd* **136** A7
Winchester Ms, NW3 *off Winchester Rd* **91** G7
Worcester Park KT4 **198** A2
Winchester Pk, Brom. BR2 **191** F3
Winchester Pl, E8 *off Kingsland High St* **94** C5
N6 **92** B1
Winchester Rd, E4 **62** C7
N6 **92** B1
N9 **60** D1
NW3 **91** G7
Bexleyheath DA7 **158** D2
Bromley BR2 **191** F3
Feltham TW13 **161** F3
Harrow HA3 **69** H4
Hayes UB3 **121** H7
Ilford IG1 **99** G3
Twickenham TW1 **144** E6
Winchester Sq, SE1 **28** B1
Winchester St, SW1 **32** E3
W3 **126** C1
Winchester Wk, SE1 **28** B1
Winchet Wk, Croy. CR0 **189** F6
Winchfield Cl, Har. HA3 **69** F6
Winchfield Ho, SW15 *off Highcliffe Dr* **147** F6
Winchfield Rd, SE26 **171** H5
Winchilsea Cres, W.Mol. KT8 **179** J2
WINCHMORE HILL, N21 **43** F7
Winchmore Hill Rd, N14 **58** D1
N21 **58** D1
Winckley Cl, Har. HA3 **69** J5
Wincott St, SE11 **35** F1
Wincrofts Dr, SE9 **157** G4
Windall Cl, SE19 **188** D1
Windborough Rd, Cars. SM5 **200** A7
Windermere Av, N3 **72** D3
NW6 **108** B1
SW19 **184** E3
Harrow HA3 **69** F7
Ruislip HA4 **66** C7
Wembley HA9 **69** F7
Windermere Cl, Orp. BR6 **206** E3
Windermere Ct, SW13 **127** F6
Wembley HA9 *off Windermere Av* **69** F7
Windermere Gdns, Ilf. IG4 **80** B5
Windermere Gro, Wem. HA9 *off Windermere Av* **87** F1
Windermere Ho, Islw. TW7 *off Summerwood Rd* **144** C5
Windermere Pt, SE15 *off Ilderton Rd* **133** F7
Windermere Rd, N10 **74** B1
N19 *off Holloway Rd* **92** C2
SW15 **164** E4
SW16 **186** C1
W5 **125** F3
Bexleyheath DA7 **159** J2
Croydon CR0 **202** C1
Southall UB1 **103** F5
West Wickham BR4 **204** E2
Windermere Way, West Dr. UB7 *off Providence Rd* **120** B1
Winders Rd, SW11 **149** H2
Windfield Cl, SE26 **171** G4
Windham Rd, Rich. TW9 **145** J3
Winding Way, Dag. RM8 **100** C3
Harrow HA1 **86** B4
Windlass Pl, SE8 **133** H4
Windlesham Gro, SW19 **166** A1
Windley Cl, SE23 **171** F2
Windmill All, W4 *off Windmill Rd* **127** E4
Windmill Av, Sthl. UB2 **123** J2
Windmill Br Ho, Croy. CR0 **202** A1
Windmill Cl, SE1 **37** J1
SE13 **154** C2
Surbiton (Long Dit.) KT6 **195** E1
Windmill Ct, NW2 **90** B6
Windmill Dr, NW2 **90** B3
SW4 **150** C5
Keston BR2 **205** J4
Windmill Gdns, Enf. EN2 **43** G3
Windmill Gro, Croy. CR0 **187** J7
Windmill Hill, NW3 **91** F3
Enfield EN2 **43** H3
Windmill Ho, E14 *off Westferry Rd* **134** A4
Windmill La, E15 **96** D6
Barnet EN5 **39** F6
Bushey (Bushey Hth) WD23 **52** B1
Greenford UB6 **103** J5
Isleworth TW7 **124** B4
Southall UB2 **123** J3
Surbiton (Long Dit.) KT6 **181** E6
Windmill Ms, W4 *off Windmill Rd* **126** E4
Windmill Pas, W4 **126** E4
Windmill Ri, Kings.T. KT2 **164** B7
Windmill Rd, N18 **60** A4
SW18 **149** G6
SW19 **165** H1
W4 **126** E4
W5 **125** F4
Brentford TW8 **125** G5
Croydon CR0 **187** J7
Hampton (Hmptn H.) TW12 **161** H5
Mitcham CR4 **186** C5
Windmill Row, SE11 **35** E4
Windmill St, W1 **17** H2
Bushey (Bushey Hth) WD23 **52** B1
Windmill Trd Est, Mitch. CR4 **186** C4
Windmill Wk, SE1 **27** F2
Windmore Cl, Wem. HA0 **86** D5
Windover Av, NW9 **70** D4
Windrose Cl, SE16 **133** G2
Windrush, N.Mal. KT3 **182** B4
Windrush Cl, N17 **76** B1
SW11 *off Maysoule Rd* **149** G4
W4 **146** C1
Windrush La, SE23 **171** G3
Windrush Rd, NW10 **106** D1
Windrush Sq, SW2 *off Rushcroft Rd* **151** G4
Windsock Cl, SE16 **133** J4
Windsor Av, E17 **77** H2
SW19 **185** F1
Edgware HA8 **54** B4
New Malden KT3 **182** C5
Sutton SM3 **198** B3
West Molesey KT8 **179** G3
Windsor Cen, The, SE27 **169** J4
Windsor Cl, N3 **72** B2
SE27 **169** J4
Borehamwood WD6 **38** A1
Brentford TW8 **124** E6
Chislehurst BR7 **175** E5
Harrow HA2 **85** G3
Northwood HA6 **66** A2
Windsor Ct, N14 **42** C7
Sunbury-on-Thames TW16 *off Windsor Rd* **160** A6
Windsor Cres, Har. HA2 **85** G4
Wembley HA9 **88** B3
Windsor Dr, Barn. EN4 **41** J6
Windsor Gdns, W9 **108** D5
Croydon CR0 *off Richmond Rd* **201** E3
Hayes UB3 **121** G3
Windsor Gro, SE27 **169** J4
Windsor Ho, N1 **11** J1
Windsor Ms, SE6 **172** C1
SE23 **171** H1
Windsor Pk Rd, Hayes UB3 **121** J7
Windsor Pl, SW1 **25** G6
Windsor Rd, E4 *off Chivers Rd* **62** B4
E7 **97** H5
E10 **96** B2
E11 **97** G1
N3 **72** B2
N7 **93** E3
N13 **59** G3
N17 **76** D2
NW2 **89** H6
W5 **105** H7
Barnet EN5 **40** A6
Bexleyheath DA6 **158** E4
Dagenham RM8 **101** E3
Harrow HA3 **68** A1
Hounslow TW4 **142** B2
Ilford IG1 **99** E4
Kingston upon Thames KT2 **163** H7
Richmond TW9 **145** J2
Southall UB2 **123** F3
Sunbury-on-Thames TW16 **160** A6
Teddington TW11 **162** A5
Thornton Heath CR7 **187** H2
Worcester Park KT4 **197** G2
Windsors, The, Buck.H. IG9 **64** B2
Windsor St, N1 **111** H1
Windsor Ter, N1 **12** A3
Windsor Wk, SE5 **152** A2
Windsor Way, W14 **128** A4
Windsor Wf, E9 **95** J5
Windspoint Dr, SE15 *off Ethnard Rd* **132** E6
Windus Rd, N16 **94** C1
Windus Wk, N16 **94** C1
Windy Ridge, Brom. BR1 **192** B1
Windy Ridge Cl, SW19 **166** A5
Wine Cl, E1 **113** F7
Wine Office Ct, EC4 **19** F3
Winery La, Kings.T. KT1 **181** J3
Winey Cl, Chess. KT9 *off Nigel Fisher Way* **195** F7
Winford Ho, E3 **95** J7
Winford Par, Sthl. UB1 *off Telford Rd* **103** H6
Winforton St, SE10 **154** C1
Winfrith Rd, SW18 **149** F7
Wingate Cres, Croy. CR0 **186** D6
Wingate Rd, W6 **127** H3
Ilford IG1 **99** E5
Sidcup DA14 **176** C5
Wingfield Ct, E14 *off Newport Av* **114** D7
Wingfield Ho, NW6 *off Tollgate Gdns* **6** A1
Wingfield Ms, SE15 *off Wingfield St* **152** D3
Wingfield Rd, E15 **96** E5
E17 **78** B5
Kingston upon Thames KT2 **164** A6
Wingfield St, SE15 **152** D3
Wingfield Way, Ruis. HA4 **84** B6
Wingford Rd, SW2 **150** E6
Wingmore Rd, SE24 **151** J3
Wingrave Rd, W6 **127** J6
Wingrove Rd, SE6 **173** E2
Wings Cl, Sutt. SM1 **198** D4
Winifred Cl, Barn. EN5 **39** F6
Winifred Gro, SW11 **149** J4
Winifred Pl, N12 *off High Rd* **57** F5
Winifred Rd, SW19 **184** D1
Dagenham RM8 **101** E2
Hampton (Hmptn H.) TW12 **161** G4
Winifred St, E16 **136** C1
Winifred Ter, E13 *off Victoria Rd* **115** G2
Enfield EN1 **44** C7
Winkfield Rd, E13 **115** H2
N22 **75** G1
Winkley St, E2 **112** E2
Winlaton Rd, Brom. BR1 **172** D4
Winmill Rd, Dag. RM8 **101** F3
Winn Common Rd, SE18 **137** H6
Winnett St, W1 **17** H5
Winningales Ct, Ilf. IG5 *off Vienna Cl* **80** B3
Winnings Wk, Nthlt. UB5 *off Arnold Rd* **85** E6
Winnington Cl, N2 **73** G6
Winnington Rd, N2 **73** G7
Winnipeg Dr, Orp. (Grn St Grn) BR6 **207** J6
Winnock Rd, West Dr. UB7 **120** A1
Winn Rd, SE12 **173** G1
Winns Av, E17 **77** H3
Winns Ms, N15 **76** B4
Winns Ter, E17 **78** A2
Winsbeach, E17 **78** D3
Winscombe Cres, W5 **105** G4
Winscombe St, N19 **92** B2
Winscombe Way, Stan. HA7 **52** D5
Winsford Rd, SE6 **171** J3
Winsford Ter, N18 **60** A5
Winsham Gro, SW11 **150** A5
Winslade Rd, SW2 **151** E5
Winslade Way, SE6 *off Rushey Grn* **154** B7
Winsland Ms, W2 **15** E3
Winsland St, W2 **15** E3
Winsley St, W1 **17** F3
Winslow, SE17 **36** D4
Winslow Cl, NW10 *off Neasden La N* **88** E3
Pinner HA5 **66** B6
Winslow Gro, E4 **62** E2
Winslow Rd, W6 **127** J6
Winslow Way, Felt. TW13 **160** D3
Winsor Ter, E6 **116** D5
Winstanley Est, SW11 **149** G3
Winstanley Rd, SW11 **149** G3
Winstead Gdns, Dag. RM10 **101** J5
Winston Av, NW9 **70** E7
Winston Cl, Har. HA3 **52** C6
Romford RM7 **83** H4
Winston Ct, Har. HA3 **51** H7
Winston Rd, N16 **94** A4
Winston Wk, W4 *off Beaconsfield Rd* **126** D4
Winston Way, Ilf. IG1 **99** E3
Winstre Rd, Borwd. WD6 **38** A1
Winter Av, E6 **116** B1
Winterborne Av, Orp. BR6 **207** G3
Winterbourne Rd, SE6 **171** J1
Dagenham RM8 **100** C2
Thornton Heath CR7 **187** G4
Winter Box Wk, Rich. TW10 **145** J4
Winterbrook Rd, SE24 **151** J6
Winterburn Cl, N11 **58** A6
Winterfold Cl, SW19 **166** B2

Winter Gdn Ho, WC2
off Macklin St 18 B3
Wintergreen Cl, E6
off Yarrow Cres 116 B5
Winters Rd, T.Ditt. KT7 . . .180 E7
Winterstoke Gdns, NW7 . .55 G5
Winterstoke Rd, SE6 . . . .171 J1
Winterton Ho, E1 . . . . . . .113 F6
Winterton Pl, SW10 . . . . . .30 D5
Winterwell Rd, SW2 . . . . .151 E5
Winthorpe Rd, SW15 . . . .148 B4
Winthrop St, E1 . . . . .112 E5
Winthrop Wk, Wem. HA9
off Everard Way 87 H3
Winton Av, N11 . . . . .58 C7
Winton Cl, N9 . . . . .45 G7
Winton Gdns, Edg. HA8 . . .53 J7
Winton Rd, Orp. BR6 . . . .206 E4
Winton Way, SW16 . . . . . .169 G5
Wirrall Ho, SE26
off Sydenham Hill Est .170 D3
Wirral Wd Cl, Chis. BR7 . .174 D6
Wisbeach Rd, Croy. CR0 . .188 A5
Wisdons Cl, Dag. RM10 . . .101 H1
Wise La, NW7 . . . . .55 H6
West Drayton UB7 . . . .120 A4
Wiseman Ct, SE19 . . . . . .170 B5
Wiseman Rd, E10 . . . . .96 A2
Wise Rd, E15 . . . . .114 D1
Wiseton Rd, SW17 . . . . . .167 H1
Wishart Rd, SE3 . . . . .156 A1
Wishaw Wk, N13
off Elvendon Rd 59 E6
Wisley Rd, SW11 . . . . .150 A5
Orpington BR5 . . . . . . .176 A7
Wistaria Cl, Orp. BR6 . . . .207 E2
Wisteria Cl, NW7 . . . . .55 F6
Ilford IG1 . . . . .98 E5
Wisteria Rd, SE13 . . . . . . .154 D4
Witanhurst La, N6 . . . . . . .92 A1
Witan St, E2 . . . . .113 E3
Witcombe Pt, SE15 . . . . . .152 D1
Witham Cl, Loug. IG10 . . . .48 B6
Witham Rd, SE20 . . . . . . .189 F3
W13 . . . . .124 D1
Dagenham RM10 . . . . .101 G5
Isleworth TW7 . . . . .144 A1
Witherby Cl, Croy. CR0 . .202 B5
Witherington Rd, N5 . . . . .93 G5
Withers Cl, Chess. KT9
off Coppard Gdns 195 F6
Withers Mead, NW9 . . . . . .71 F1
Witherston Way, SE9 . . . .174 D2
Withycombe Rd, SW19 . . .148 A7
Withy Mead, E4 . . . . .62 D3
Witley Cres, Croy.
(New Adgtn) CR0 . . . . .204 C6
Witley Gdns, Sthl. UB2 . .123 F4
Witley Pt, SW15
off Wanborough Dr . .165 H1
Witley Rd, N19
off Holloway Rd 92 C2
Witney Cl, Pnr. HA5 . . . . . .51 F6
Witney Path, SE23 . . . . . .171 G3
Wittenham Way, E4 . . . . . .62 D3
Wittering Cl, Kings.T.
KT2 . . . . .163 G5
Wittersham Rd, Brom.
BR1 . . . . .173 F5
Wivenhoe Cl, SE15 . . . . . .152 E3
Wivenhoe Ct, Houns.
TW3 . . . . .143 F4
Wivenhoe Rd, Bark. IG11 .118 A2
Wiverton Rd, SE26 . . . . . .171 F6
Wixom Ho, SE3
off Romero Sq 155 J4
Wix Rd, Dag. RM9 . . . . . . .118 D1
Wixs La, SW4 . . . . .150 B4
Woburn Cl, SE28
off Summerton Way . .118 D6
SW19 . . . . .167 F6
Woburn Ct, SE16
off Masters Dr 133 E5
Woburn Pl, WC1 . . . . .9 J5
Woburn Rd, Cars. SM5 . . .199 H1
Croydon CR0 . . . . .201 J1
Woburn Sq, WC1 . . . . .9 J6
Woburn Wk, WC1 . . . . .9 J4
Wodeham Gdns, E1 . . . . . .21 J1
Wodehouse Av, SE5 . . . . .152 C1
Woffington Cl, Kings.T.
KT1 . . . . .181 F1
Woking Cl, SW15 . . . . . . .147 F4
Woldham Pl, Brom. BR2 .191 J4
Woldham Rd, Brom. BR2 .191 J4
Wolds Dr, Orp. BR6 . . . . .206 D4
Wolfe Cl, Brom. BR2 . . . . .191 G6
Hayes UB4
off Ayles Rd 102 B3
Wolfe Cres, SE7 . . . . .136 A5
SE16 . . . . .133 G2
Wolferton Rd, E12 . . . . .98 C4
Wolffe Gdns, E15 . . . . .97 F6
Wolffram Cl, SE13 . . . . . . .154 E5
Wolfington Rd, SE27 . . . .169 H4
Wolftencroft Cl, SW11 . . .149 G3
Wollaston Cl, SE1 . . . . .35 J1
Wolmer Cl, Edg. HA8 . . . . .54 B4
Wolmer Gdns, Edg. HA8 . .54 A3
Wolseley Av, SW19 . . . . . .166 D2
Wolseley Gdns, W4 . . . . . .126 B6
Wolseley Rd, E7 . . . . .97 H7
N8 . . . . .74 D6
N22 . . . . .75 F1
Wolseley Rd, W4 . . . . .126 C4
Harrow HA3 . . . . .68 B3
Mitcham CR4 . . . . .186 A7
Wolseley St, SE1 . . . . .29 G4
Wolsey Av, E6 . . . . .116 D3
E17 . . . . .77 J3
Thames Ditton KT7 . . . .180 C5
Wolsey Cl, SW20 . . . . .165 H7
Hounslow TW3 . . . . . . .143 J4
Kingston upon Thames
KT2 . . . . .182 B1
Southall UB2 . . . . .123 J3
Worcester Park KT4 . . .197 G4
Wolsey Cres, Mord. SM4 .184 B7
Wolsey Dr, Kings.T. KT2 . .163 H5
Wolsey Gdns, Ilf. IG6 . . . . .65 F6
Wolsey Gro, Edg. HA8 . . . .54 D7
Wolsey Ms, NW5 . . . . .92 C6
Orpington BR6 . . . . . . .207 J5
Wolsey Rd, N1 . . . . .94 A5
East Molesey KT8 . . . . .180 A4
Enfield EN1 . . . . .45 E2
Hampton (Hmptn H.)
TW12 . . . . .161 H6
Wolsey St, E1
off Sidney St 113 F5
Wolsey Way, Chess. KT9 .196 A5
Wolstonbury, N12 . . . . .56 D5
Wolvercote Rd, SE2 . . . . .138 D2
Wolverley St, E2
off Bethnal Grn Rd . . .112 E3
Wolverton, SE17 . . . . .36 C3
Wolverton Av, Kings.T.
KT2 . . . . .182 A1
Wolverton Gdns, W5 . . . . .105 J7
W6 . . . . .128 A4
Wolverton Rd, Stan. HA7 . .53 E6
Wolverton Way, N14 . . . . . .42 C5
Wolves La, N13 . . . . .59 G7
N22 . . . . .59 G7
Womersley Rd, N8 . . . . . . .75 F6
Wonford Cl, Kings.T. KT2 .183 E1
Wontner Cl, N1
off Greenman St 93 J7
Wontner Rd, SW17 . . . . . .167 J2
Woodall Cl, E14
off Lawless St 114 B7
Chessington KT9 . . . . .195 G7
Woodall Rd, Enf. EN3 . . . . .45 G6
Woodbank Rd, Brom.
BR1 . . . . .173 F3
Woodbastwick Rd, SE26 .171 G5
Woodberry Av, N21 . . . . . .59 G2
Harrow HA2 . . . . .67 H4
Woodberry Cl, NW7 . . . . . .56 A7
Sunbury-on-Thames
TW16
off Ashridge Way 160 A6
Woodberry Cres, N10 . . . . .74 B3
Woodberry Down, N4 . . . .75 J7
Woodberry Down Est, N4 .75 J7
Woodberry Gdns, N12 . . . .57 F6
Woodberry Gro, N4 . . . . . .75 J7
N12 . . . . .57 F6
Woodberry Way, E4 . . . . . .62 C1
N12 . . . . .57 F6
Woodbine Cl, Twick. TW2 .162 A2
Woodbine Gro, SE20 . . . .171 E7
Woodbine La, Wor.Pk.
KT4 . . . . .197 H3
Woodbine Pl, E11 . . . . .79 G6
Woodbine Rd, Sid. DA15 .175 H1
Woodbines Av, Kings.T.
KT1 . . . . .181 G3
Woodbine Ter, E9
off Morning La 95 F6
Woodborough Rd, SW15 .147 H4
Woodbourne Av, SW16 . .168 D3
Woodbourne Cl, SW16
off Woodbourne Av . .168 E3
Woodbourne Dr, Esher
(Clay.) KT10 . . . . .194 C6
Woodbourne Gdns, Wall.
SM6 . . . . .200 B7
Woodbridge Cl, N7 . . . . . . .93 F2
NW2 . . . . .89 G3
Woodbridge Ct, Wdf.Grn.
IG8 . . . . .64 B7
Woodbridge Rd, Bark.
IG11 . . . . .99 J5
Woodbridge St, EC1 . . . . . .11 G5
Woodbrook Rd, SE2 . . . . .138 A6
Woodburn Cl, NW4 . . . . . . .72 A5
Woodbury Cl, E11 . . . . .79 H4
Croydon CR0 . . . . .202 C2
Woodbury Gdns, SE12 . . .173 H3
Woodbury Hill, Loug. IG10 .48 B3
Woodbury Hollow, Loug.
IG10 . . . . .48 B2
Woodbury Pk Rd, W13 . . .104 E4
Woodbury Rd, E17 . . . . . . .78 B4
Woodbury St, SW17 . . . . .167 H5
Woodchester Sq, W2 . . . . .14 A1
Woodchurch Cl, Sid.
DA14 . . . . .175 G3
Woodchurch Dr, Brom.
BR1 . . . . .174 A7
Woodchurch Rd, NW6 . . . .90 D7
Wood Cl, E2 . . . . .13 H5
NW9 . . . . .70 D7
Harrow HA1 . . . . .68 A7
Woodclyffe Dr, Chis.
BR7 . . . . .192 D2
Woodcock Ct, Har. HA3 . . .69 H7
Woodcock Dell Av, Har.
HA3 . . . . .69 G7
Woodcock Hill, Har. HA3 . .69 G7
Woodcocks, E16 . . . . .115 J5
Woodcombe Cres, SE23 . .171 F1
Woodcote Av, NW7 . . . . . .55 J6
Thornton Heath CR7 . .187 H4
Wallington SM6 . . . . . .200 B7
Woodcote Cl, Enf. EN3 . . . .45 F6
Kingston upon Thames
KT2 . . . . .163 J5
Woodcote Dr, Orp. BR6 . .207 G1
Woodcote Ms, Loug. IG10 .48 A7
Wallington SM6 . . . . . .200 B6
Woodcote Pl, SE27 . . . . . .169 H5
Woodcote Rd, E11 . . . . .79 G7
Wallington SM6 . . . . . .200 B6
Woodcott Ho, SW15
off Ellisfield Dr 147 G7
Wood Ct, W12
off Heathstan Rd 107 G6
Woodcroft, N21 . . . . .59 F1
SE9 . . . . .174 C3
Greenford UB6 . . . . .86 D6
Woodcroft Av, NW7 . . . . . .55 E7
Stanmore HA7 . . . . .68 C1
Woodcroft Ms, SE8
off Croft St 133 H4
Woodcroft Rd, Th.Hth.
CR7 . . . . .187 H5
Wood Dr, Chis. BR7 . . . . .174 B6
Woodedge Cl, E4 . . . . .63 F1
Woodend, SE19 . . . . .169 J6
Sutton SM1 . . . . .199 F2
Wood End Av, Har. HA2 . . .85 H4
Wood End Cl, Nthlt. UB5 . .86 A5
Woodend Gdns, Enf. EN2 .42 E4
Wood End Gdns, Nthlt.
UB5 . . . . .85 J5
Wood End La, Nthlt. UB5 . .85 H6
Woodend Rd, E17 . . . . .78 C2
Wood End Rd, Har. HA1 . . .86 A4
Wood End Way, Nthlt.
UB5 . . . . .85 J5
Wooder Gdns, E7 . . . . .97 F4
Wooderson Cl, SE25 . . . . .188 B4
Woodfall Av, Barn. EN5 . . .40 C5
Woodfall Rd, N4 . . . . .93 G1
Woodfall St, SW3 . . . . .31 J4
Woodfarrs, SE5 . . . . .152 A4
Wood Fld, NW3
off Parkhill Rd 91 J5
Woodfield Av, NW9 . . . . . .71 E4
SW16 . . . . .168 D3
W5 . . . . .105 F4
Carshalton SM5 . . . . . .200 A6
Wembley HA0 . . . . .87 F3
Woodfield Cl, SE19 . . . . . .169 J7
Enfield EN1 . . . . .44 B4
Woodfield Cres, W5 . . . . .105 F4
Woodfield Dr, Barn.
(E.Barn.) EN4 . . . . .58 A1
Woodfield Gdns, W9
off Woodfield Rd 108 C5
New Malden KT3 . . . . .183 F5
Woodfield Gro, SW16 . . . .168 D3
Woodfield La, SW16 . . . . .168 D3
Woodfield Pl, W9 . . . . .108 C4
Woodfield Rd, W5 . . . . . . .105 F4
W9 . . . . .108 C5
Hounslow TW4 . . . . . . .142 B2
Thames Ditton KT7 . . . .194 C2
Woodfield Way, N11 . . . . . .58 D7
WOODFORD, Wdf.Grn.
IG8 . . . . .63 H6
Woodford Av, Ilf. IG2, IG4 .80 C5
Woodford Green IG8 . . .80 A3
WOODFORD BRIDGE,
Wdf.Grn. IG8 . . . . .64 C7
Woodford Br Rd, Ilf. IG4 . . .80 A3
Woodford Ct, W12
off Shepherds
Bush Grn 128 A2
Woodford Cres, Pnr. HA5 . .66 B2
WOODFORD GREEN, IG8 . .63 F4
Woodford New Rd, E17 . . .78 E4
E18 . . . . .79 E1
Woodford Green IG8 . . .79 E1
Woodford Pl, Wem. HA9 . .87 H1
Woodford Rd, E7 . . . . .97 H4
E18 . . . . .79 G4
WOODFORD WELLS,
Wdf.Grn. IG8 . . . . .63 H4
Woodgate Av, Chess.
KT9 . . . . .195 G5
Woodgate Cres, Nthwd.
HA6 . . . . .50 A6
Woodgate Dr, SW16 . . . . .168 D7
Woodger Rd, W12
off Goldhawk Rd 127 J2
Woodget Cl, E6
off Remington Rd 116 B6
Woodgrange Av, N12 . . . . .57 G6
W5 . . . . .126 A1
Enfield EN1 . . . . .44 D6
Harrow HA3 . . . . .69 F5
Woodgrange Cl, Har. HA3 .69 G5
Woodgrange Gdns, Enf.
EN1 . . . . .44 D6
Woodgrange Rd, E7 . . . . . .97 H4
Woodgrange Ter, Enf. EN1 .44 D6
WOOD GREEN, N22 . . . . . .74 E1
Wood Grn Shop City, N22 .75 G2
Woodhall, NW1 . . . . .9 F4
Woodhall Av, SE21 . . . . . .170 C3
Pinner HA5 . . . . .66 E2
Woodhall Dr, SE21 . . . . . .170 C3
Pinner HA5 . . . . .66 D1
Woodhall Gate, Pnr. HA5 . .50 D7
Woodhall Ho, SW18
off Fitzhugh Gro 149 G6
Woodhall La, Wat. WD19 . .50 D4
Woodhall Rd, Pnr. HA5 . . . .50 D7
Woodham Ct, E18 . . . . .79 F4
Woodham Rd, SE6 . . . . . .172 C3
Woodhatch Cl, E6
off Remington Rd 116 B6
Woodhaven Gdns, Ilf. IG6
off Brandville Gdns . . .81 F4
Woodhayes Rd, SW19 . . .165 J7
Woodhead Dr, Orp. BR6
off Sherlies Av 207 H2
Woodheyes Rd, NW10 . . . .88 D5
Woodhill, SE18 . . . . .136 B4
Woodhill Cres, Har. HA3 . .69 G6
Wood Ho, SW17
off Laurel Cl 167 H5
Woodhouse Av, Grnf.
(Perivale) UB6 . . . . .104 C2
Woodhouse Cl, SE22 . . . .152 D4
Greenford (Perivale)
UB6 . . . . .104 C2
Hayes UB3 . . . . .121 H3
Woodhouse Eaves, Nthwd.
HA6 . . . . .50 A5
Woodhouse Gro, E12 . . . . .98 B6
Woodhouse Rd, E11 . . . . . .97 F3
N12 . . . . .57 G6
Woodhurst Av, Orp. BR5 .193 F6
Woodhurst Rd, SE2 . . . . .138 A5
W3 . . . . .106 C7
Woodington Cl, SE9 . . . . .156 D6
Woodknoll Dr, Chis.
BR7 . . . . .192 C1
Woodland App, Grnf.
UB6 . . . . .86 D6
Woodland Cl, NW9 . . . . . . .70 C6
SE19 . . . . .170 B6
Epsom KT19 . . . . .197 E6
Woodford Green IG8 . . .63 H3
Woodland Cres, SE10 . . . .134 E6
SE16 . . . . .133 G2
Woodland Gdns, N10 . . . . .74 B5
Isleworth TW7 . . . . .144 B2
Woodland Gro, SE10 . . . . .134 E5
Woodland Hts, SE3
off Vanbrugh Hill 135 F6
Woodland Hill, SE19 . . . . .170 B6
Woodland Ms, SW16 . . . . .169 E2
Woodland Ri, N10 . . . . .74 B4
Greenford UB6 . . . . .86 D6
Woodland Rd, E4 . . . . .62 C1
N11 . . . . .58 B5
SE19 . . . . .170 B5
Loughton IG10 . . . . .48 B3
Thornton Heath CR7 . .187 G4
WOODLANDS, Islw.
TW7 . . . . .144 B2
Woodlands, NW11 . . . . . . .72 B6
SW20 . . . . .183 J4
Harrow HA2 . . . . .67 G4
Woodlands, The, N14 . . . . .58 B1
SE13 . . . . .154 D7
SE19 . . . . .169 J7
Beckenham BR3 . . . . . .190 C1
Isleworth TW7 . . . . .144 C2
Woodlands Av, E11 . . . . . . .97 H1
N3 . . . . .57 F7
W3 . . . . .126 B1
New Malden KT3 . . . . .182 C1
Romford RM6 . . . . .82 E6
Ruislip HA4 . . . . .84 C1
Sidcup DA15 . . . . .175 H1
Worcester Park KT4 . . .197 F2
Woodlands Cl, NW11 . . . . .72 B5
Borehamwood WD6 . . . .38 B4
Bromley BR1 . . . . .192 C2
Esher (Clay.) KT10 . . . .194 C7
Woodlands Dr, Stan. HA7 .52 C6
Sunbury-on-Thames
TW16 . . . . .178 C2
Woodlands Gro, Islw.
TW7 . . . . .144 B2
Woodlands Pk, Bex. DA5 .177 J4
Woodlands Pk Rd, N15 . . .75 H5
SE10 . . . . .134 E6
Woodlands Rd, E11 . . . . . . .96 E2
E17 . . . . .78 C3
N9 . . . . .61 F1
SW13 . . . . .147 F3
Bexleyheath DA7 . . . . .159 E3
Bromley BR1 . . . . .192 B2
Enfield EN2 . . . . .44 A1
Harrow HA1 . . . . .68 C5
Ilford IG1 . . . . .99 F3
Isleworth TW7 . . . . .144 B2
Southall UB1 . . . . .122 D1
Surbiton KT6 . . . . .181 G7
Woodlands St, SE13 . . . . .154 D7
Woodland St, E8
off Dalston La 94 C6
Woodlands Way, SW15 . . .148 C5
Woodland Ter, SE7 . . . . . .136 B4
Woodland Wk, NW3 . . . . . .91 H5
SE10
off Woodland Gro 135 E5
Bromley BR1 . . . . .172 E4
Epsom KT19 . . . . .196 A6

Woodland Way, N21 59 G2
NW7 55 E6
SE2 138 D4
Croydon CR0 203 H1
Mitcham CR4 168 A7
Morden SM4 184 C4
Orpington BR5 193 F4
Surbiton KT5 196 B2
West Wickham BR4 204 B4
Woodford Green IG8 63 H3
Wood La, N6 74 B6
NW9 70 E7
W12 107 J6
Dagenham
RM8, RM9, RM10 100 C4
Isleworth TW7 124 C7
Stanmore HA7 52 D3
Woodford Green IG8 63 F5
Woodlawn Cl, SW15 148 C5
Woodlawn Cres, Twick.
TW2 161 H2
Woodlawn Dr, Felt. TW13 160 D2
Woodlawn Rd, SW6 128 A7
Woodlea Dr, Brom. BR2 191 E5
Woodlea Rd, N16 94 B3
Woodleigh, E18
off Churchfields 79 G1
Woodleigh Av, N12 57 H6
Woodleigh Gdns, SW16 169 E3
Woodley Cl, SW17
off Arnold Rd 167 J7
Woodley La, Cars. SM5 199 G3
Wood Lo Gdns, Brom.
BR1 174 B7
Wood Lo La, W.Wick.
BR4 204 C3
Woodman La, E4 46 E5
Woodman Ms, Rich. TW9 146 B1
Woodman Path, Ilf. IG6 65 H6
Woodmans Gro, NW10 89 F5
Woodmans Ms, W12 107 H5
Woodmansterne Rd,
SW16 186 D1
Woodman St, E16 136 D1
Woodmere, SE9 174 C1
Woodmere Av, Croy.
CR0 189 G7
Woodmere Cl, SW11
off Lavender Hill 150 A3
Croydon CR0 189 G7
Woodmere Gdns, Croy.
CR0 189 G7
Woodmere Way, Beck.
BR3 190 D5
Woodmill Rd, E5
off Mount
Pleasant Hill 95 F2
Woodnook Rd, SW16 168 B5
Woodpecker Cl, N9 44 E6
Bushey WD23 51 J1
Harrow HA3 68 C1
Woodpecker Ms, SE13
off Mercator Rd 154 D4
Woodpecker Rd, SE14 133 H6
SE28 118 C7
Woodquest Av, SE24 151 J5
Wood Retreat, SE18 137 G7
Wood Ride, Barn. EN4 41 G1
Orpington BR5 193 G4
Woodridge Cl, Enf. EN2 43 G1
Woodridings Av, Pnr. HA5 67 F1
Woodridings Cl, Pnr. HA5 51 E7
Woodriffe Rd, E11 78 D7
Wood Ri, Pnr. HA5 66 A5
Wood Rd, NW10 88 C7
Woodrow, SE18 136 C4
Woodrow Cl, Grnf.
(Perivale) UB6 87 E7
Woodrow Ct, N17 61 E7
Woodrush Cl, SE14
off Southerngate Way 133 H7
Woodrush Way, Rom.
RM6 82 D4
Woods, The, Nthwd. HA6 50 A5
Wood's Bldgs, E1
off Whitechapel Rd 112 E5
Woodseer St, E1 21 G1
Woodsford, SE17 36 B4
Woodsford Sq, W14 128 B2
Woodshire Rd, Dag.
RM10 101 H3
WOODSIDE, SE25 188 D6
Woodside, NW11 72 D5
SW19 166 C6
Buckhurst Hill IG9 63 J2
Woodside Av, N6 73 J5
N10 73 J5
N12 57 F4
SE25 188 E6
Chislehurst BR7 175 F5
Esher KT10 180 B7
Wembley HA0 105 H1
Woodside Cl, Stan. HA7 52 E5
Surbiton KT5 182 C7
Wembley HA0 105 H1
Woodside Ct, N12 57 E4
Woodside Ct Rd, Croy.
CR0 188 D7
Woodside Cres, Sid.
DA15 175 H3
Woodside End, Wem.
HA0 105 H1
Woodside Gdns, E4 62 B5
N17 76 B2
Woodside Gra Rd, N12 57 E4
Woodside Grn, SE25 188 E6
Woodside Gro, N12 57 F3
Woodside La, N12 57 E3
Bexley DA5 158 D6
Woodside Ms, SE22
off Heber Rd 152 C6
Woodside Pk, SE25 188 D5
Woodside Pk Av, E17 78 D4
Woodside Pk Rd, N12 57 E4
Woodside Pl, Wem. HA0 105 H1
Woodside Rd, E13 115 J4
N22 59 F7
SE25 188 E6
Bromley BR1 192 B5
Kingston upon Thames
KT2 163 H7
New Malden KT3 182 D2
Sidcup DA15 175 H3
Sutton SM1 199 F3
Woodford Green IG8 63 G4
Woodside Way, Croy.
CR0 189 E6
Mitcham CR4 186 B1
Woods Ms, W1 16 A5
Woodsome Rd, NW5 92 A3
Woods Pl, SE1 28 E6
Woodspring Rd, SW19 166 B2
Woods Rd, SE15 152 E1
Woodstead Gro, Edg.
HA8 53 H6
Woodstock, The, Sutt.
SM3 184 B7
Woodstock Av, NW11 72 B7
W13 124 D3
Isleworth TW7 144 D5
Southall UB1 103 F3
Sutton SM3 184 C7
Woodstock Cl, Bex. DA5 177 F1
Stanmore HA7 69 H2
Woodstock Ct, SE12 155 G6
Woodstock Cres, N9 44 E6
Woodstock Gdns, Beck.
BR3 190 B1
Ilford IG3 100 A2
Woodstock Gro, W12 128 A2
Woodstock La N, Surb.
(Long Dit.) KT6 195 F2
Woodstock La S, Chess.
KT9 195 F4
Esher (Clay.) KT10 194 E5
Woodstock Ms, W1 16 C2
Woodstock Ri, Sutt. SM3 184 C7
Woodstock Rd, E7 97 J7
E17 78 D2
N4 93 G1
NW11 72 C7
W4 127 E3
Woodstock Rd, Carshalton
SM5 200 A5
Croydon CR0 202 A3
Wembley HA0 87 J7
Woodstock St, W1 16 D4
Woodstock Ter, E14 114 B7
Woodstock Way, Mitch.
CR4 186 B2
Woodstone Av, Epsom
KT17 197 G5
Wood St, E17 78 C3
EC2 20 A4
W4 126 E5
Barnet EN5 39 J4
Kingston upon Thames
KT1 181 G1
Mitcham CR4 186 A7
Woodsyre, SE26 170 C4
Woodthorpe Rd, SW15 147 H4
Woodtree Cl, NW4
off Ashley La 71 J2
Wood Vale, N10 74 C5
SE23 170 E1
Woodvale Av, SE25 188 C3
Wood Vale Est, SE23 153 F6
Woodvale Est, SE27 169 J5
Woodvale Wk, SE27 169 J5
Woodvale Way, NW11
off The Vale 90 A3
Woodview Av, E4 62 C4
Woodview Cl, N4 75 H7
SW15 164 D4
Orpington BR6 207 F2
Woodville, SE3 155 H1
Woodville Cl, SE12 155 G5
Teddington TW11 162 D4
Woodville Gdns, NW11 72 A7
W5 105 H6
Ilford IG6 80 E3
Woodville Gro, Well.
DA16 158 A3
Woodville Rd, E11 97 F1
E17 77 H4
E18 79 H2
N16 94 B5
NW6 108 C2
NW11 72 A7
W5 105 G6
Barnet EN5 40 E3
Morden SM4 184 D4
Richmond TW10 163 E3
Thornton Heath CR7 187 J4
Woodville St, SE18 136 B4
Woodward Av, NW4 71 G5
Woodward Cl, Esher
(Clay.) KT10 194 C6
Woodwarde Rd, SE22 152 B6
Woodward Gdns, Dag. RM9
off Woodward Rd 100 C7
Stanmore HA7 52 C7
Woodward Rd, Dag.
RM9 100 B7
Wood Way, Orp. BR6 206 D2
Woodway Cres, Har.
HA1 68 D6
Woodwell St, SW18
off Huguenot Pl 149 F5
Wood Wf, SE10 134 B6
Wood Wf Apts, SE10
off Horseferry Pl 134 C6
Woodyard Cl, NW5
off Gillies St 92 A5
Woodyard La, SE21 152 B7
Woodyates Rd, SE12 155 G6
Woolacombe Rd, SE3 155 J1
Woolacombe Way, Hayes
UB3 121 H4
Wooler St, SE17 36 B4
Woolf Cl, SE28 138 B1
Woolf Ms, WC1 9 J5
Woollaston Rd, N4 75 H6
Woolmead Av, NW9 71 G7
Woolmer Gdns, N18 60 D6
Woolmer Rd, N18 60 D5
Woolmore St, E14 114 C7
Woolneigh St, SW6 148 E3
Woolridge Way, E9
off Loddiges Rd 95 F7
Wool Rd, SW20 165 H6
Woolstaplers Way, SE16 29 H6
Woolston Cl, E17
off Riverhead Cl 77 G2
Woolstone Rd, SE23 171 H2
WOOLWICH, SE18 136 D5
Woolwich Ch St, SE18 136 B3
★ **Woolwich Common**,
SE18 136 C7
Woolwich Common,
SE18 136 D6
Woolwich Dockyard
Ind Est, SE18
off Woolwich Ch St 136 B3
Woolwich Ferry Pier, E16 136 D2
Woolwich Foot Tunnel,
E16 136 D2
SE18 136 D2
Woolwich Garrison,
SE18 136 B6
Woolwich High St, SE18 136 D3
Woolwich Manor Way,
E6 116 C4
E16 117 E7
Woolwich Mkt, SE18 136 E4
Woolwich New Rd, SE18 136 D5
Woolwich Rd, SE2 138 D6
SE7 135 G5
SE10 135 F5
Belvedere DA17 138 D6
Bexleyheath DA6, DA7 159 G4
Woolwich Trade Pk, SE28 137 G3
Wooster Gdns, E14 114 D6
Wooster Ms, Har. HA2
off Fairfield Dr 67 J3
Wooster Pl, SE1 36 C1
Wootton Gro, N3 72 D1
Wootton St, SE1 27 F3
Worbeck Rd, SE20 189 E2
Worcester Av, N17 60 D7
Worcester Cl, NW2
off Newfield Ri 89 H3
Croydon CR0 203 J2
Mitcham CR4 186 A2
Worcester Cres, NW7 54 E3
Woodford Green IG8 63 H5
Worcester Dr, W4 127 E2
Worcester Gdns, SW11
off Grandison Rd 149 J5
Greenford UB6 85 J6
Ilford IG1 80 B7
Worcester Park KT4 197 E3
Worcester Ho, SE11
off Kennington Rd 27 E6
Worcester Ms, NW6
off Dresden Cl 91 E6
WORCESTER PARK, KT4 197 F2
Worcester Pk Rd, Wor.Pk.
KT4 196 C3
Worcester Rd, E12 98 C4
E17 77 G2
SW19 166 C5
Sutton SM2 199 E6
Wordsworth Av, E12 98 B7
E18 79 F3
Greenford UB6 104 A2
Wordsworth Dr, Sutt.
SM3 197 J4
Wordsworth Gdns, Borwd.
WD6 38 A5
Wordsworth Pl, NW5
off Southampton Rd 91 J5
Wordsworth Rd, N16 94 B4
SE1 37 F2
SE20 171 G7
Hampton TW12 161 F4
Wallington SM6 200 C6
Welling DA16 157 H1
Wordsworth Wk, NW11 72 C4
Wordsworth Way, West Dr.
UB7 120 B4
Worfield St, SW11 129 H7
Worgan St, SE11 34 C3
SE16 133 G3
Worland Rd, E15 97 E7
WORLD'S END, Enf. EN2 43 G3
Worlds End La, N21 43 F5
Enfield EN2 43 F5
Orpington BR6 207 J6
World's End Pas, SW10 30 E7
World's End Pl, SW10
off King's Rd 30 D7
Worleys Dr, Orp. BR6 207 G4
Worlidge St, W6 127 J5
Worlingham Rd, SE22 152 C4
Wormholt Rd, W12 107 G7
Wormwood St, EC2 20 D3
Wornington Rd, W10 108 B5
Woronzow Rd, NW8 109 G1
Worple Av, SW19 166 A7
Isleworth TW7 144 D5
Worple Cl, Har. HA2 85 F1
Worple Rd, SW19 166 B7
SW20 183 J2
Isleworth TW7 144 D4
Worple Rd Ms, SW19 166 C6
Worple St, SW14 146 D3
Worple Way, Har. HA2 85 F1
Richmond TW10 145 H5
Worship St, EC2 12 C6
Worslade Rd, SW17 167 G4
Worsley Br Rd, SE26 171 J4
Beckenham BR3 171 J5
Worsley Gra, Chis. BR7 175 F6
Worsley Gro, E5 94 D4
Worsley Rd, E11 96 E4
Worsopp Dr, SW4 150 C5
Worth Cl, Orp. BR6 207 H4
Worthfield Cl, Epsom
KT19 196 D7
Worth Gro, SE17 36 B4
Worthing Cl, E15
off Mitre Rd 115 E1
Worthing Rd, Houns.
TW5 123 F6
Worthington Cl, Mitch.
CR4 186 B3
Worthington Rd, Surb.
KT6 195 J1
Worthy Down Ct, SE18
off Prince Imperial Rd 156 D1
Wortley Rd, E6 98 A7
Croydon CR0 187 G7
Worton Gdns, Islw.
TW7 144 A2
Worton Hall Ind Est, Islw.
TW7 144 B4
Worton Rd, Islw. TW7 144 B3
Worton Way, Houns.
TW3 144 A2
Isleworth TW7 143 J1
Wotton Rd, NW2 89 J4
SE8 133 J6
Wouldham Rd, E16 115 F6
Wragby Rd, E11 97 E3
Wrampling Pl, N9 60 D1
Wrangthorn Wk, Croy. CR0
off Fernleigh Cl 201 G4
Wray Av, Ilf. IG5 80 D3
Wray Cres, N4 93 E2
Wrayfield Rd, Sutt. SM3 198 A3
Wraysbury Cl, Houns.
TW4 143 E5
Wrekin Rd, SE18 137 F7
Wren Av, NW2 89 J5
Southall UB2 123 F4
Wren Cl, E16
off Ibbotson Av 115 F6
N9 *off Chaffinch Cl* 61 G1
Wren Cres, Bushey WD23 51 J1
Wren Dr, West Dr. UB7 120 A3
Wren Gdns, Dag. RM9 100 D5
Wren Landing, E14
off Cabot Sq 134 A1
Wren Ms, SE13
off Lee High Rd 154 E4
Wren Path, SE28 137 G3
Wren Rd, SE5 152 A1
Dagenham RM9 100 D5
Sidcup DA14 176 C4
Wren St, WC1 10 D5
Wren Ter, Ilf. IG5
off Tiptree Cres 80 D3
Wrentham Av, NW10 108 A2
Wrenthorpe Rd, Brom.
BR1 172 E4
Wrenwood Way, Pnr.
HA5 66 B4
Wrestlers Ct, EC3
off Camomile St 20 D3
Wrexham Rd, E3 114 A2
Wricklemarsh Rd, SE3 155 H1
Wrigglesworth St, SE14 133 G7
Wright Rd, N1
off Burder Cl 94 B6
Hounslow TW5 122 C7
Wrights All, SW19 165 J6
Wrights Cl, SE13 154 D4
Dagenham RM10 101 H3
Wrights Grn, SW4
off Nelson's Row 150 D4
Wrights La, W8 22 A5
Wrights Pl, NW10
off Mitchell Way 88 C6
Wrights Rd, E3 113 J2
SE25 188 B3

Wrights Row, Wall.
  SM6 ....200 B4
Wrights Wk, SW14 ...146 D3
Wrigley Cl, E4 ....62 D5
Wrotham Rd, NW1
  off Agar Pl 92 C7
  W13 off Mattock La ..125 F1
  Barnet EN5 ....40 B2
  Welling DA16 ....158 C1
Wroths Path, Loug. IG10 ..48 C1
Wrottesley Rd, NW10 ...107 G2
  SE18 ....137 F6
Wroughton Rd, SW11 ..149 J6
Wroughton Ter, NW4 ...71 J4
Wroxall Rd, Dag. RM9 ..100 C6
Wroxham Gdns, N11 ...58 C7
Wroxham Rd, SE28 ....118 D7
Wroxham Way, Ilf. IG6 ..81 E1
Wroxton Rd, SE15 .....153 E2
WRYTHE, THE, Cars.
  SM5 ....199 J2
Wrythe Grn, Cars. SM5
  off Wrythe Grn Rd ...199 J3
Wrythe Grn Rd, Cars.
  SM5 ....199 J3
Wrythe La, Cars. SM5 ..199 F1
Wulfstan St, W12 .....107 F6
Wyatt Cl, SE16 ....133 J2
  Feltham TW13 ....160 C1
  Hayes UB4 ....102 A5
Wyatt Dr, SW13 ......127 J7
Wyatt Pk Rd, SW2 ....169 E2
Wyatt Pt, SE28
  off Erebus Dr 137 F2
Wyatt Rd, E7 ....97 G6
  N5 ....93 J3
Wyatts La, E17 ....78 C3
Wybert St, NW1 ......9 E5
Wyborne Way, NW10 ..88 C7
Wyburn Av, Barn. EN5 ..40 C3
Wyche Gro, S.Croy.
  CR2 ....201 J7
Wych Elm Pas, Kings.T.
  KT2 ....163 J7
Wycherley Cl, SE3 ....135 F7
Wycherley Cres, Barn.
  (New Barn.) EN5 .....40 E6
Wychwood Av, Edg.
  HA8 ....53 G6
  Thornton Heath CR7 ..187 J3
Wychwood Cl, Edg. HA8 ..53 G6
  Sunbury-on-Thames
  TW16 ....160 A6
Wychwood End, N6 ....74 C7
Wychwood Gdns, Ilf. IG5 ..80 C4
Wychwood Way, SE19
  off Roman Ri 170 A6
Wyclif Ct, EC1
  off Wyclif St 11 G4
Wycliffe Rd, Well. DA16 ..157 J1
Wycliffe Rd, SW11 ....150 A2
  SW19 ....167 E6
Wyclif St, EC1 ....11 G4
Wycombe Gdns, NW11 ..90 D2
Wycombe Pl, SW18 ...149 F6
Wycombe Rd, N17 ....76 D1
  Ilford IG2 ....80 C5
  Wembley HA0 ....106 A1
Wycombe Sq, W8 .....128 C1
Wydehurst Rd, Croy.
  CR0 ....188 D7
Wydell Cl, Mord. SM4 ..183 J6
Wydeville Manor Rd,
  SE12 ....173 H4
Wye Cl, Orp. BR6 .....193 J7
Wyemead Cres, E4 ....62 E2
Wye St, SW11 ....149 G2
Wyevale Cl, Pnr. HA5 ..66 A3
Wyfields, Ilf. IG5
  off Ravensbourne
  Gdns 81 E1
Wyfold Ho, SE2
  off Wolvercote Rd ...138 D2
Wyfold Rd, SW6 ......128 B7
Wyhill Wk, Dag. RM10 ..101 J6
Wyke Cl, Islw. TW7 ...124 C4
Wyke Gdns, W7 ......124 D3
Wykeham Av, Dag. RM9 ..100 C6
Wykeham Cl, West Dr.
  (Sipson) UB7 ....120 D5
Wykeham Grn, Dag.
  RM9 ....100 C6
Wykeham Hill, Wem.
  HA9 ....87 J1
Wykeham Ri, N20 .....56 B1
Wykeham Rd, NW4 ...71 J5
  Harrow HA3 ....68 D4
Wyke Rd, E3 ....96 A7
  SW20 ....183 J2
Wyldes Cl, NW11
  off Hampstead Way ..91 F1
Wyldfield Gdns, N9 ...60 C2
Wyld Way, Wem. HA9 ..88 B6
Wyleu St, SE23 ....153 H7
Wylie Rd, Sthl. UB2 ...123 G3
Wyllen Cl, E1 ....113 F4
Wylo Dr, Barn. EN5 ...39 G6
Wymering Rd, W9 ....108 D3
Wymond St, SW15 ....147 J3
Wynan Rd, E14 ....134 B5
Wynash Gdns, Cars.
  SM5 ....199 H5
Wynaud Ct, N22
  off Palmerston Rd ...59 F6

Wyncham Av, Sid. DA15 ..175 H1
Wynchgate, N14 ......58 D1
  N21 ....58 E1
  Harrow HA3 ....52 B7
Wyncroft Cl, Brom. BR1 ..192 C3
Wyndale Av, NW9 .....70 A6
Wyndcliff Rd, SE7 ....135 H6
Wyndcroft Cl, Enf. EN2 ..43 H3
Wyndham Cl, Orp. BR6 ..207 F1
  Sutton SM2 ....198 D7
Wyndham Cres, N19 ..92 C3
  Hounslow TW4 ......143 G6
Wyndham Est, SE5 ....35 J7
Wyndham Ms, W1 ....15 J2
Wyndham Pl, W1 .....15 J2
Wyndham Rd, E6 .....98 A7
  SE5 ....131 H7
  W13 ....124 E3
  Barnet EN4 ....41 H6
  Kingston upon Thames
  KT2 ....163 J7
Wyndham St, W1 .....15 J1
Wyndham Yd, W1 .....15 J2
Wyndhurst Cl, S.Croy.
  CR2 ....201 H7
Wyneham Rd, SE24 ...152 A5
Wynell Rd, SE23 .....171 G3
Wynford Pl, Belv. DA17 ..139 G6
Wynford Rd, N1 ......10 C1
Wynford Way, SE9 ....174 C3
Wynlie Gdns, Pnr. HA5 ..66 B2
Wynn Br Cl, Wdf.Grn. IG8
  off Chigwell Rd 79 J1
Wynndale Rd, E18 ....79 H1
Wynne Rd, SW9 ......151 G2
Wynns Av, Sid. DA15 ..158 A5
Wynnstay Gdns, W8 ..128 D3
Wynter St, SW11 .....149 F4
Wynton Gdns, SE25 ..188 C5
Wynton Pl, W3 ....106 B6
Wynyard Ter, SE11 ...34 D3
Wynyatt St, EC1 ......11 G4
Wyre Gro, Edg. HA8 ..54 B3
  Hayes UB3 ....122 A4
Wyresdale Cres, Grnf.
  (Perivale) UB6 ......104 C3
Wythburn Pl, W1 .....15 J4
Wythenshawe Rd, Dag.
  RM10 ....101 G3
Wythens Wk, SE9 ....156 E6
Wythes Cl, Brom. BR1 ..192 C2
Wythes Rd, E16 ......136 B1
Wythfield Rd, SE9 ....156 C6
Wyvenhoe Rd, Har. HA2 ..85 J3
Wyvern Est, N.Mal. KT3 ..183 G4
Wyvern Gro, Hayes UB3 ..121 E7
Wyvil Est, SW8 ......34 A7
Wyvil Rd, SW8 ....34 A6
Wyvis St, E14 ....114 B5

Y

Yabsley St, E14 ......134 C1
Yalding Rd, SE16 .....29 H6
Yale Cl, Houns. TW4 ..143 F5
Yarborough Rd, SW19 ..185 G1
Yardley Cl, E4 ....46 B5
Yardley Ct, Sutt. SM3
  off Hemingford Rd ...197 J4
Yardley La, E4 ....46 B5
Yardley St, WC1 ......10 E4
Yarmouth Cres, N17 ..76 E5
Yarmouth Pl, W1 .....24 D2
Yarnfield Sq, SE15
  off Clayton Rd 152 D1
Yarnton Way, SE2 ....138 D2
  Erith DA18 ....139 F3
Yarrow Cres, E6 ......116 B5
Yateley St, SE18 .....136 A3
Yates Ct, NW2 ....90 A6
Yates Ho, E2
  off Roberta St 13 J3
YEADING, Hayes UB4 ..102 B3
Yeading Av, Har. HA2 ..84 E2
Yeading Fork, Hayes UB4 ..102 C5
Yeading Gdns, Hayes
  UB4 ....102 B5
Yeading La, Hayes UB4 ..102 B6
  Northolt UB5 ....102 C3
Yeames Cl, W13 ......104 D6
Yeate St, N1 ....94 A7
Yeatman Rd, N6 ......73 J6
Yeats Cl, NW10 ......88 E6
Yeats Ct, N15
  off Tynemouth Rd ...76 C4
Yeend Cl, W.Mol. KT8 ..179 G4
Yeldham Rd, W6 .....128 A5
Yellow Hammer Ct, NW9
  off Eagle Dr 71 E2
Yelverton Rd, SW11 ..149 G2
Yenston Cl, Mord. SM4 ..184 D6
Yeoman Cl, E6
  off Ferndale Rd 116 E7
  SE27 ....169 H3
Yeoman Rd, Nthlt. UB5 ..85 E7
Yeomans Acre, Ruis. HA4 ..66 A6
Yeoman's Ms, Islw. TW7
  off Queensbridge Pk ..144 B5
Yeoman's Row, SW3 ..23 H6
Yeoman St, SE8 ......133 H4
Yeomans Way, Enf. EN3 ..45 F2
Yeomans Yd, E1 ......21 G5
Yeomen Way, Ilf. IG6 ..65 F6

Yeo St, E3 ....114 B5
Yeovil Cl, Orp. BR6 ...207 H2
Yeovilton Pl, Kings.T.
  KT2 ....163 F5
Yerbury Rd, N19 ......92 D3
Yester Dr, Chis. BR7 ..174 B7
Yester Pk, Chis. BR7 ..174 C7
Yester Rd, Chis. BR7 ..174 C7
Yew Cl, Buck.H. IG9 ..64 A2
Yewdale Cl, Brom. BR1 ..173 E6
Yewfield Rd, NW10 ...89 F7
Yew Gro, NW2 ....90 A4
Yew Tree Cl, N21 .....43 G7
Yewtree Cl, N22 ......74 C1
Yew Tree Cl, SE13
  off Bankside Av 154 C3
Yewtree Cl, Har. HA2 ..67 H4
Yew Tree Cl, Well. DA16 ..158 A1
  Worcester Park KT4 ..197 E1
Yew Tree Gdns, Rom.
  (Chad.Hth) RM6 .....83 E5
Yew Tree Lo, SW16 ..168 C4
Yew Tree Rd, W12 ...107 F7
  Beckenham BR3 ....189 J3
Yew Tree Wk, Houns.
  TW4 ....143 F5
Yew Wk, Har. HA1 ....86 B1
YIEWSLEY, West Dr. UB7 ..120 B1
Yoakley Rd, N16 .....94 B2
Yoga Way, Wor.Pk. KT4 ..197 G2
Yoke Cl, N7 off Ewe Cl ..93 E6
Yolande Gdns, SE9 ...156 B5
Yonge Pk, N4 ....93 G3
York Av, SW14 ......146 C5
  W7 ....124 B1
  Sidcup DA15 ....175 H2
  Stanmore HA7 ....68 E1
York Br, NW1 ....8 B5
York Bldgs, WC2 .....18 B6
York Cl, E6
  off Boultwood Rd ...116 C6
  W7 off York Av 124 B1
  Morden SM4 ....184 E4
York Cres, Borwd WD6 ..38 D2
  Loughton IG10 ......48 B3
York Gate, N14 ......42 E7
  NW1 ....8 B6
York Gro, SE15 ......153 F1
York Hill, SE27 ......169 H3
  Loughton IG10 ......48 B3
York Hill Est, SE27 ...169 H3
York Ho, Wem. HA9 ..87 J4
York Ho Pl, W8 ......22 A3
Yorkland Av, Well. DA16 ..157 J3
York Ms, NW5
  off Kentish Town Rd ..92 B5
  Ilford IG1 ....98 D3
York Par, Brent. TW8 ..125 G5
York Pl, SW11 ....149 G3
  WC2 ....18 B6
  Dagenham RM10 ....101 J6
  Ilford IG1
  off York Rd 98 D3
  Orpington BR6 ......207 H1
York Ri, NW5 ....92 B3
York Rd, E4 ....62 A5
  E7 ....97 G6
  E10 ....96 C3
  E17 ....77 G5
  N11 ....58 D6
  N18 ....60 E6
  N21 ....44 A7
  SE1 ....26 D3
  SW11 ....149 F4
  SW18 ....149 F4
  SW19 ....167 F6
  W3 ....106 C6
  W5 ....125 F3
  Barnet (New Barn.)
  EN5 ....41 G5
  Brentford TW8 ......125 G5
  Croydon CR0 ....187 G7
  Hounslow TW3 .....143 H3
  Ilford IG1 ....98 D3
  Kingston upon Thames
  KT2 ....163 J7
  Northwood HA6 .....66 A2
  Richmond TW10
  off Albert Rd 145 J5
  Sutton SM2 ....198 D6
  Teddington TW11 ...162 B4
Yorkshire Cl, N16 ....94 B3
Yorkshire Gdns, N18 ..60 E5
Yorkshire Grey, SE9 ..156 A5
Yorkshire Grey Pl, NW3
  off Heath St 91 F4
Yorkshire Grey Yd, WC1 ..18 C2
Yorkshire Rd, E14 ...113 H6
  Mitcham CR4 ....186 E5
York Sq, E14 ....113 H6
York St, W1 ....16 A1
  Mitcham CR4 ....186 A7
  Twickenham TW1 ...162 D1
York Ter, Erith DA8 ...159 J1
York Ter E, NW1 .....8 C6
York Ter W, NW1 ....8 B6
Yorkton St, E2 ....13 H2
York Way, N1 ....111 E1
  N7 ....92 D6
  N20 ....57 J3
  Borehamwood WD6 ..38 D2
  Chessington KT9 ...195 H7
  Feltham TW13 .....161 F3
York Way Ct, N1 .....111 E1

York Way Est, N7
  off York Way 92 E6
Youngmans Cl, Enf. EN2 ..43 J1
Young Rd, E16 ....115 J6
Young's Bldgs, EC1 ...12 A5
Youngs Ct, SW11
  off Charlotte
  Despard Av 150 A1
Youngs Rd, Ilf. IG2 ...81 G5
Young St, W8 ....22 A4
Yoxley App, Ilf. IG2 ..81 F6
Yoxley Dr, Ilf. IG2 ....81 F6
Yukon Rd, SW12 .....150 B7
Yunus Khan Cl, E17 ..78 A5

Z

Zambezie Dr, N9 .....61 F3
Zampa Rd, SE16 .....133 F5
Zander Ct, E2 ....13 J2
Zangwill Rd, SE3 .....156 A1
Zealand Av, West Dr.
  (Harm.) UB7 ....120 A7
Zealand Rd, E3 ......113 H2
Zennor Rd, SW12 ....168 C1
Zennor Rd Ind Est, SW12
  off Zennor Rd 168 C1
Zenoria St, SE22 ....152 C4
Zermatt Rd, Th.Hth. CR7 ..187 J4
Zetland St, E14 ......114 B5
Zion Ho, E1
  off Jubilee St 113 F6
Zion Pl, Th.Hth. CR7 ..188 A4
Zion Rd, Th.Hth. CR7 ..188 A4
Zoar St, SE1 ....27 J1
Zodiac Ct, Croy. CR0
  off London Rd 201 H1
Zoffany St, N19 ......92 D2